Collins

# COMPLETE BRITISH HIT ALBUMS

## GRAHAM BETTS

THE OFFICIAL UKCHARTS COMPANY

First published in 2004 by Collins
an imprint of
HarperCollins*Publishers*
77–85 Fulham Palace Road
Hammersmith
London, W6 8JB

The Collins website address is www.colllins.co.uk

Collins is a registered trademark of
HarperCollins*Publishers* Ltd.

04
10 9 8 7 6 5 4 3 2 1

## The Author – Graham Betts

UK writer (born 28/6/1957, London); he began his working career training to be an architect before switching to the music industry in 1978 as a Press Officer with Pye Records. He subsequently went on to work for CBS Records (where he was Head of Press) and a number of budget labels, including Tring, before becoming Artist & Repertoire Manager for the Hallmark label. He is currently A&R Manager for the Pickwick Group. He has written for numerous magazines and publications over the last twenty five years, including *Blues & Soul*, *Record Buyer* and *The History Of Rock*. A contributor to numerous books on music and football, he has also had nine published under his own name, including *Read Without Prejudice* (a biography of George Michael) and *Spurs Day By Day* (a history of Tottenham Hotspur). He also won the 1978 *Melody Maker* essay contest. He currently lives in Aston Clinton with his wife and two children.

**PRODUCED BY**
Essential Works
168a Camden Street, London NW1 9PT

**PROJECT EDITOR** Mani Ramaswamy
**EDITORS** Mike Evans, Karen Fitzpatrick, Jo Lethaby and Nina Sharman
**EDITORIAL ASSISTANT** Lisa Thiel
**DESIGNERS** Barbara Saulini, Mark Stevens and Kate Ward

If you have any additonal, verifiable information about any of the artists or their hits, please feel free to email the author at: hit.albums@harpercollins.co.uk

# INTRODUCTION

Because of the popularity of the compact disc, the 50th anniversary in 1998 of the long player, or LP as it was more commonly known, largely passed unnoticed. Like most great inventions (and there is little doubt that the long playing album was a great invention), it had its roots in simplicity; Dr Peter Goldmark of the CBS (Columbia Broadcasting Systems) company expressed himself fed up with having to keep getting up to change several 78 RPM (revolutions per minute) discs whilst listening to his favourite classical pieces. By changing the speed of the disc to 33 1/3 RPM an entire opera could be fitted onto just two sides of a disc instead of filling several of the old discs.

There were a couple of other changes made to the discs too, which went from the old 10-inch shellac to the new 12-inch vinyl format, which were cheaper to produce and much more durable than the old 78s. America and eventually the rest of the world took to the new format almost immediately and whilst Dr Peter Goldmark may have come up with the format specifically for classical music, it soon proved its worth for film soundtracks, stage recordings and popular music.

As was noted in the introduction to Complete UK Hit Singles, something of a sister publication to this book, Britain's first singles chart was launched by the New Musical Express in 1952. For many years it was believed that the album chart was not launched by Melody Maker until 1958, ten years after LPs first found their way onto the market, but recent research has uncovered an additional two years worth of chart data, giving us a starting point of 1956.

Britain's first album chart was therefore launched in July 1956 by Record Mirror (another music paper that, like Melody Maker, is now sadly defunct). It was not as sophisticated as the Top 75 and Top 20 compilations chart that we see today, for it only contained five titles, increasing to six whenever there was a tie in the chart. That is something else that has fallen by the wayside as the compilation of the chart has got more sophisticated; when was the last time you saw two titles tied in the chart?

The size of the chart would not have mattered to artists such as Tommy Steele, Frank Sinatra, Bill Haley, Louis Armstrong and Nat King Cole, all of whom topped the charts with releases between July 1956 and November 1958, when the expanded Melody Maker chart came into being. Tommy Steele and Mel Torme have not come close to the charts since Melody Maker and Record Retailer data has been used, so they would have had special reason to cheer this recent discovery!

There is one other important development that has come to light as a result of the extra two years chart data; whilst *South Pacific* is still unrivalled as the album that has topped the charts for longer than anything else, it was overshadowed in the chart's early days by *The King And I*, which enjoyed 48 weeks on top of the charts, and *Pal Joey*, with eleven weeks. Indeed, *South Pacific* didn't top the charts until Melody Maker introduced their chart on 8th November 1958!

Once it had hit the summit however, *South Pacific* made the slot its own, topping the charts for 70 straight weeks. After a brief seven-day sojourn at number two, during which time Freddy Cannon took over at the top (with his only chart album!), *South Pacific* resumed its domination, going on to rack up 115 weeks at number one. Only *The Sound Of Music*, another film soundtrack, comes anywhere near to challenging, having registered 70 weeks on top of the charts.

Indeed, both Record Mirror and Melody Maker show film soundtracks and stage recordings dominating the early years of the charts (much like multi-artist compilations were to do in the 1980s), and it was not until the arrival of performers such as Elvis Presley and The Beatles that popular music as we would know it began to take hold.

As with the single, changing fads and fashion have had an impact on the charts, but whereas the chart career of the Bay City Rollers might be over as far as singles are concerned, a greatest hits package with TV advertising will usually ensure they make the occasional appearance on the album chart.

TV advertising began to make a major impact during the 1970s when K-Tel and Ronco and other marketing companies like them put together compilation albums, featuring hits of the day from a wide variety of artists and invariably saw them top the charts. Indeed, by 1988 the charts were virtually awash with multi-artist compilation albums; only two of the long-running series *Now That's What I Call Music* failed to top the charts, but only just since they peaked at number two.

In January 1989 the chart was effectively split into two – the main chart gives details of single artist albums and features the best-selling 75 titles each week, and a compilation chart of twenty titles. There have been other amendments made to the chart over the years: budget albums (which were usually sound-alike compilations such as the hugely successful *Top Of The Pops* series) were admitted into the main chart on 7th August 1971 only to be excluded again on 8th January 1972, although not before two of the *Top Of The Pops* and one of the *Hot Hits* albums had topped the charts.

Perhaps the biggest innovation to have made an impact was the introduction of the compact disc in the mid-1980s. Dire Straits' *Brothers In Arms* holds the honour of being the first CD to register more than 1 million sales and it has since gone on to be joined by many more. The introduction of the CD has also been responsible for a variety of albums enjoying something of a renaissance as people looked to replace their old, worn out and scratched vinyl copies with brand new shiny CDs – look at the chart performance of virtually the entire Beatles' catalogue for an indication of how successful the format has been.

Whilst single sales continue to show a downward turn, sales of albums have held steady, creating two distinctive markets for pre-recorded music. Norah Jones and Eva Cassidy have hardly set the singles chart alight with their respective single releases but both can boast albums that have sold more than one million copies. Indeed, in March 2004 the upper echelons of the album charts were filled with artists who were struggling to make the singles chart as Daniel O'Donnell, Jamie Cullum, Lionel Richie, Harry Connick Jr and Engelbert Humperdinck joined Norah Jones and Katie Melua to give the top ten something of an easy listening feel. Whilst the traditional rock press was aghast, it was proof that those sectors of the market with the largest disposable income could be persuaded to buy albums and in large quantities.

It should also be noted the effect supermarket chains have had on the music market. Many of those who bought Daniel O'Donnell, Jamie Cullum et al invariably did so from their local Tesco, Sainsbury or Asda and probably haven't been inside an HMV or Virgin Megastore for years. Price may well have been an issue, but surely more important was being able to see and pick up Jamie Cullum's CD from a general rack and not having to work out for yourself which musical category he fits into before you can begin looking. Add to this the number of CDs that are being bought over the internet and there is a whole subculture blissfully ignorant of battling its way around a 21st-century record store before you can get your musical fix!

This is the first album chart book (as far as I am aware) that has been published mid-year and therefore includes an extra six months of chart data from 2004. Whilst there is a flurry of excitement and activity surrounding the singles chart come each December as artists and record labels vie for the honour of having the Christmas number one, there is nowhere near the same kind of importance attached to the album chart. Most of the big blockbuster albums will be released in time to capitalise on the Christmas market, around October and November, with volume of sales being more important than topping the last chart of the year. The extra six months of data enables you to see how well these blockbusters did over a longer period of time. It also enables the BRIT and Grammy Awards from earlier this year, together with the Birthday Honours List awards and various other accolades to be included, thus updating some of the biographies from the singles book.

As will be seen from the various chart peaks, the size of the chart has fluctuated over the years, from Record Mirror's top five, Melody Maker's top ten and an ever-expanding chart in Record Retailer/Music Week that by August 1981 was a Top 100. Since the chart split into two in January 1989, the main chart lists the top 75 artists albums and the top twenty compilation albums have their own chart.

There is one other anomaly that should be explained. A postal strike between early February and late March 1971 meant there was no new Record Retailer chart compiled, with the chart positions of 30 January repeated throughout the period. This is unfortunate for the likes of Grand Funk Railroad, Grateful Dead and Jefferson Airplane, all of whom released albums during this period (and which charted on the unaffected Melody Maker listings), together with artists such as Judy Collins, whose Whales And Nightingales peaked at 37 on the Record Retailer but took its expected place in the Top Ten in Melody Maker and George Harrison, who topped the Melody Maker charts for six weeks with All Things Must Pass but found his album stalling at number four in Record Retailer.

# How to use this book

This book provides detailed information on each artist and their rise to chart success since the first chart was compiled in the UK in 1956 (by Record Mirror) through to the present day. The book is organised alphabetically according to the surname of the artist/group.

**COLUMNS** The date the album made its chart debut, the highest chart position it attained and the number of weeks it was in the chart

**BPI AWARDS** BPI certified awards were introduced into the UK in April 1973, with qualification based on the revenue received by the manufacturers. A silver disc was awarded for revenue of £250,000, a gold disc for £500,000 and a platinum disc for £1,000,000. In January 1978, this was changed, so now a silver disc is awarded for sales in excess of 60,000 units, a gold disc for over 100,000 and a platinum disc for more than 300,000.

**LABEL & NUMBER** Record label and catalogue number. This number is that of the most popular format at the time of the hit

| R | DATE | POS | WKS | BPI | ALBUM TITLE | LABEL & NUMBER |
|---|------|-----|-----|-----|-------------|----------------|

**KEITH RICHARDS** UK male singer and guitarist (born 18/12/1943, Dartford, Kent) who was a founding member of The Rolling Stones in 1963 with Mick Jagger, Brian Jones, Bill Wyman, Ian Stewart and Charlie Watts. He and Jagger soon became the chief songwriters within the group.

| | | | | | |
|---|---|---|---|---|---|
| 15/10/1988 | 37 | 3 | | TALK IS CHEAP | Virgin V 2554 |
| 31/10/1992 | 45 | 1 | | MAIN OFFENDER | Virgin America CDVUS 59 |

**LIONEL RICHIE** US singer (born 20/6/1949, Tuskegee, AL) who was a founding member of The Commodores in 1967 and quickly emerged as an accomplished songwriter, penning their biggest hits (usually ballads). He began writing for other artists in 1980, penning Kenny Rogers' hit *Lady* and left the group in 1982. He also co-wrote (with Michael Jackson) the USA for Africa single *We Are The World*. He has won four Grammy Awards including: Best Pop Vocal Performance in 1982 for *Truly*, Producer of the Year in 1984 with James Anthony Carmichael and Song of the Year in 1985 with Michael Jackson for *We Are The World*. He also won an Oscar for Best Original Song for *Say You Say Me* in 1985 and was given a Lifetime Achievement Award at the 1996 MOBO Awards. He has a star on the Hollywood Walk of Fame.

**TOP 500 ARTISTS** have an album sleeve beside their entry where possible

**UK No.1 HITS** with weeks at number one

**TOP 10 HITS** in bold

| | | | | | |
|---|---|---|---|---|---|
| 27/11/1982 | 9 | 86 | ○ | LIONEL RICHIE | Motown STMA 8037 |
| 29/10/1983 | ❶³ | 154 | ○³ | CAN'T SLOW DOWN ▲² ◆¹⁰ 1984 Grammy Award for Album of the Year | Motown STMA 8041 |
| 23/08/1986 | 2 | 53 | ○² | DANCING ON THE CEILING ▲² | Motown ZL 72412 |
| 06/06/1992 | ❶⁶ | 81 | ○⁴ | BACK TO FRONT | Motown 5300182 |
| 20/04/1996 | 11 | 5 | ○ | LOUDER THAN WORDS | Mercury 5322412 |
| 31/01/1998 | 5 | 21 | ○ | TRULY – THE LOVE SONGS ◇ | Motown 5308432 |
| 11/07/1998 | 31 | 3 | | TIME | Mercury 5585182 |
| 28/10/2000 | 6 | 24 | ○ | RENAISSANCE ◇ | Mercury 5482222 |
| 07/12/2002 | 8 | 10 | ● | ENCORE | Mercury 0633482 |
| 22/11/2003 | 10 | 20 | ○ | THE DEFINITIVE COLLECTION LIONEL RICHIE/THE COMMODORES | Universal TV 9861394 |
| 20/03/2004 | 5 | 7 | ● | JUST FOR YOU | Mercury 9861710 |

**RIAA DIAMOND AWARDS** Given to albums that have sold more than 10 million copies in the USA, with copies sold indicated

**US No.1 HITS** with weeks at number one

**IFPI PLATINUM EUROPE AWARDS** Given to albums since 1996 that sell in excess of 1 million units in Europe

**JONATHAN RICHMAN AND THE MODERN LOVERS** US singer (born 16/5/1951, Boston, MA) who formed The Modern Lovers with Jerry Harrison (born 21/2/1949, Milwaukee, WI, guitar) and David Robinson (drums). By 1977 the Modern Lovers consisted of Leroy Radcliffe (guitar), Greg 'Curly' Kerenen (bass) and D Sharpe (drums).

| | | | | | |
|---|---|---|---|---|---|
| 27/08/1977 | 50 | 3 | | ROCK 'N' ROLL WITH THE MODERN LOVERS | Beserkeley BSERK 9 |

**RICHMOND STRINGS WITH THE MIKE SAMMES SINGERS** UK orchestra and vocal choir.

| | | | | | |
|---|---|---|---|---|---|
| 17/01/1976 | 18 | 7 | | MUSIC OF AMERICA | Ronco TRD 2016 |

**ADAM RICKITT** UK singer (born 29/5/1978, Crewe) who first came to prominence as an actor, playing the role of Nicky Tilsley in the TV soap *Coronation Street*.

| | | | | | |
|---|---|---|---|---|---|
| 30/10/1999 | 41 | 1 | | GOOD TIMES | Polydor 5431422 |

**FRANK RICOTTI ALL STARS** UK percussionist/vibe player (born 31/1/1949, London) who spent most of the 1970s as an accomplished session musician. The following decade he moved into film and TV soundtrack work as well as forming Paragonine.

| | | | | | |
|---|---|---|---|---|---|
| 24/12/1988 | 89 | 2 | | THE BEIDERBECKE COLLECTION | Dormouse DM 20CD |
| 14/01/1989 | 14 | 5 | ○ | THE BEIDERBECKE COLLECTION This was the album's placing in the compilation chart, where it was incorrectly listed | Dormouse DM 20CD |
| 26/06/1993 | 73 | 1 | | THE BEIDERBECKE COLLECTION | Dormouse DM 20CD |

**ADDITIONAL INFO**

**NELSON RIDDLE ORCHESTRA** US orchestra leader (born 1/6/1921, Oradell, NJ) who learned to play the trombone whilst a teenager and worked with many big bands during the late 1930s, including those of Charlie Spivak, Tommy Dorsey and Bob Crosby. He served in the army and then moved to California. By the end of the 1940s, after a spell at NBC, he joined Capitol Records as an in-house arranger. He worked on recordings by artists such as Nat King Cole and Frank Sinatra and then on various TV series and films. Later he worked with artists outside Capitol, including Ella Fitzgerald, Sammy Davis Jr, Peggy Lee, Jack Jones, Eddie Fisher, Shirley Bassey and Dinah Shore, among others. After a brief retirement spell in the 1970s he returned to work in the early 1980s, although he suffered ill health in his later years and died on 6/10/1985. He won three Grammy Awards: Best Composition in 1958 for *Cross Country Suite*, Best Instrumental Arrangement Accompanying Vocal in 1983 for Linda Ronstadt's *What's New* and Best Instrumental Arrangement Accompanying Vocal in 1985 for Linda Ronstadt's *Lush Life*. He also won an Academy Award (Oscar) in 1974 for his music to the film *The Great Gatsby*.

**COLLABORATIONS** The hit is credited to more than one artist

| | | | | | |
|---|---|---|---|---|---|
| 15/12/1962 | 12 | 7 | | LET'S FACE THE MUSIC SHIRLEY BASSEY WITH THE NELSON RIDDLE ORCHESTRA | Columbia 33SX 1454 |
| 26/10/1985 | 40 | 29 | ● | BLUE SKIES KIRI TE KAWANA WITH NELSON RIDDLE AND HIS ORCHESTRA | London KTKT 1 |
| 28/01/1984 | 31 | 5 | | WHAT'S NEW | Asylum 9602601 |
| 19/01/1985 | 100 | 1 | | LUSH LIFE This and the above hit credited to **LINDA RONSTADT WITH THE NELSON RIDDLE ORCHESTRA** | Asylum 9603871 |

**RIDE** UK rock group formed in Oxford by Mark Gardner (born 6/12/1969, Oxford, guitar/vocals), Andy Bell (born 11/8/1970, Cardiff, guitar/vocals), Stephan Queralt (born 4/2/1968, Oxford, bass) and Laurence Colbert (born 27/6/1970, Kingston, drums). All four had met whilst at art school. The group disbanded in 1996, with Bell forming Hurricane #1 and later joining Oasis, and Gardner and Colbert forming Animalhouse.

| | | | | | |
|---|---|---|---|---|---|
| 27/10/1990 | 11 | 5 | ○ | NOWHERE | Creation CRELP 074 |

332   ○ Silver disc  ● Gold disc  ○ Platinum disc (additional platinum units are indicated by a figure following the symbol)  ❶⁹ Number of weeks album topped the UK chart

**SYMBOLS** Certified sales awards

**BIOGRAPHY** A brief background of the artist together with any awards and honours received, such as BRIT, Grammy and MTV Europe Awards, and details of OBEs, MBEs, etc. The year given for BRIT Awards is the year the award actually took place. With Grammy Awards, the year refers to the qualifying year, thus Evanescence's awards for the 2003 Best New Artist and Best Hard Rock Performance were presented in 2004.

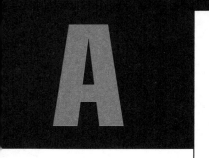

**A** UK rock group with Jason Perry (vocals), Mark Chapman (guitar), Giles Perry (keyboards), Daniel Carter (bass) and Adam Perry (drums).

| | | | |
|---|---|---|---|
| 28/08/1999 | 62 | 1 | |
| 16/03/2002 | 18 | 9 | ○ |

MONKEY KONG . . . . . . . . . . . . . . . . . . . . . . . . . . . . . . . . . . . . . . . . . . . . . . . . . . . . . . . . . . . . . . . . . . . . . . . . . . . Tycoon 3984276952
HI-FI SERIOUS . . . . . . . . . . . . . . . . . . . . . . . . . . . . . . . . . . . . . . . . . . . . . . . . . . . . . . . . . . . . . . . . . . . . . . . . . . London 0927447762

**AALIYAH** US R&B singer (born Aaliyah Haughton, 16/1/1979, Brooklyn, NYC) whose name is Swahili for 'highest, most exulted one'. She appeared in the films *Romeo Must Die* (2000), *Sparkle* (2000), *Queen Of The Damned* (2002), and *The Matrix Reloaded* (2003). She is rumoured to have married fellow singer R Kelly in August 1994, though it may have been a publicity hoax. She was killed on 25/8/2001 when her plane crashed on take-off in the Bahamas. It was revealed that there were eight people on a plane designed for only five; excess weight was the most likely cause of the crash.

| | | | |
|---|---|---|---|
| 23/07/1994 | 23 | 6 | ○ |
| 07/09/1996 | 33 | 3 | |
| 28/07/2001 | 5 | 31 | ✪ |
| 15/02/2003 | 4 | 16 | ● |

AGE AIN'T NOTHING BUT A NUMBER . . . . . . . . . . . . . . . . . . . . . . . . . . . . . . . . . . . . . . . . . . . . . . . . . . . . . . . . Jive CHIP 149
ONE IN A MILLION . . . . . . . . . . . . . . . . . . . . . . . . . . . . . . . . . . . . . . . . . . . . . . . . . . . . . . . . . . . . . Atlantic 7567927152
**AALIYAH ▲¹** . . . . . . . . . . . . . . . . . . . . . . . . . . . . . . . . . . . . . . . . . . . . . . . . . . . . . . . . . . . . . . . . . Virgin CDVUSX 199
**I CARE 4 U** . . . . . . . . . . . . . . . . . . . . . . . . . . . . . . . . . . . . . . . . . . . . Independiente/Blackground/Unique ISOM 37CDL

**AARONSON** — see **SAMMY HAGAR**

**ABBA** Swedish/Norwegian group formed by Anna-Frid (Frida) Lyngstad-Ruess (born 15/11/1945, Bjorkasen, Norway), Benny Andersson (born Goran Bror Benny Andersson, 16/12/1946, Stockholm), Bjorn Ulvaeus (born 25/4/1945, Gothenburg, Sweden) and Agnetha Ase Faltskog (born 5/4/1950, Jonkoping, Sweden), their name being their initials. After winning the 1974 Eurovision Song Contest they became one of the most popular groups of the decade. Bjorn and Agnetha married in 1971 and divorced in 1979; Benny and Frida married in 1978 and divorced in 1979. When the band split in the early 1980s, both female members went solo while Benny and Bjorn concentrated on songwriting, linking with Tim Rice to pen the stage musical *Chess*. At the height of their popularity in 1977, the Royal Albert Hall reported 3.5 million applications for 11,212 available tickets.

| | | | |
|---|---|---|---|
| 08/06/1974 | 28 | 2 | ○ |
| 31/01/1976 | 13 | 10 | ● |
| 10/04/1976 | ❶¹¹ | 130 | ✪ |
| 27/11/1976 | ❶¹⁰ | 92 | ✪ |
| 04/02/1978 | ❶⁷ | 61 | ✪ |
| 19/05/1979 | ❶⁴ | 43 | ✪ |
| 10/11/1979 | ❶⁴ | 63 | ✪ |
| 22/11/1980 | ❶⁹ | 43 | ✪ |
| 19/12/1981 | ❶³ | 21 | ✪ |
| 20/11/1982 | ❶¹ | 22 | ✪ |
| 19/11/1983 | 17 | 12 | ● |
| 19/11/1988 | 70 | 7 | ● |
| 03/10/1992 | ❶⁶ | 338 | ✪¹² |
| 05/06/1993 | 13 | 23 | ✪ |
| 07/11/1998 | 51 | 2 | |
| 10/11/2001 | 17 | 8 | |

WATERLOO . . . . . . . . . . . . . . . . . . . . . . . . . . . . . . . . . . . . . . . . . . . . . . . . . . . . . . . . . . . . . . . . . . . . . . Epic EPC 80179
ABBA . . . . . . . . . . . . . . . . . . . . . . . . . . . . . . . . . . . . . . . . . . . . . . . . . . . . . . . . . . . . . . . . . . . . . . . . Epic EPC 80835
**GREATEST HITS** . . . . . . . . . . . . . . . . . . . . . . . . . . . . . . . . . . . . . . . . . . . . . . . . . . . . . . . . . . . . . . . Epic EPC 69218
**ARRIVAL** . . . . . . . . . . . . . . . . . . . . . . . . . . . . . . . . . . . . . . . . . . . . . . . . . . . . . . . . . . . . . . . . . . Epic EPC 86018
**THE ALBUM** . . . . . . . . . . . . . . . . . . . . . . . . . . . . . . . . . . . . . . . . . . . . . . . . . . . . . . . . . . . . . . . . Epic EPC 86052
**VOULEZ-VOUS** . . . . . . . . . . . . . . . . . . . . . . . . . . . . . . . . . . . . . . . . . . . . . . . . . . . . . . . . . . . . . . . Epic EPC 86086
**GREATEST HITS VOLUME 2** . . . . . . . . . . . . . . . . . . . . . . . . . . . . . . . . . . . . . . . . . . . . . . . . . . . . . . Epic EPC 10017
**SUPER TROUPER** . . . . . . . . . . . . . . . . . . . . . . . . . . . . . . . . . . . . . . . . . . . . . . . . . . . . . . . . . . . . . Epic EPC 10022
**THE VISITORS** . . . . . . . . . . . . . . . . . . . . . . . . . . . . . . . . . . . . . . . . . . . . . . . . . . . . . . . . . . . . . . . Epic EPC 10032
**THE SINGLES – THE FIRST TEN YEARS** . . . . . . . . . . . . . . . . . . . . . . . . . . . . . . . . . . . . . . . . . . . . . Epic ABBA 10
THANK YOU FOR THE MUSIC . . . . . . . . . . . . . . . . . . . . . . . . . . . . . . . . . . . . . . . . . . . . . . . . . . . . . . Epic EPC 10043
ABSOLUTE ABBA . . . . . . . . . . . . . . . . . . . . . . . . . . . . . . . . . . . . . . . . . . . . . . . . . . . . . . . . . . Telstar STAR 2329
**GOLD – GREATEST HITS** . . . . . . . . . . . . . . . . . . . . . . . . . . . . . . . . . . . . . . . . . . . . . . . . . . . . . . Polydor 5170072
MORE ABBA GOLD – MORE ABBA HITS . . . . . . . . . . . . . . . . . . . . . . . . . . . . . . . . . . . . . . . . . . . Polydor 5193532
LOVE SONGS . . . . . . . . . . . . . . . . . . . . . . . . . . . . . . . . . . . . . . . . . . . . . . . . . . . . . . . . . . . . . Polydor 5592212
THE DEFINITIVE COLLECTION . . . . . . . . . . . . . . . . . . . . . . . . . . . . . . . . . . . . . . . . . . . . . . . . . . . Polar 5499742

**RUSS ABBOT** UK singer/comedian/actor (born Russell Roberts, 16/9/1947, Chester) who was a former member of the Black Abbotts and had his own network TV show.

| | | | |
|---|---|---|---|
| 05/11/1983 | 41 | 7 | ○ |
| 23/11/1985 | 12 | 9 | ● |

RUSS ABBOT'S MADHOUSE . . . . . . . . . . . . . . . . . . . . . . . . . . . . . . . . . . . . . . . . . . . . . . . . . . . . . . . Ronco RTL 2096
I LOVE A PARTY . . . . . . . . . . . . . . . . . . . . . . . . . . . . . . . . . . . . . . . . . . . . . . . . . . . . . . . . . . . . K-Tel ONE 1313

**GREGORY ABBOTT** US R&B singer (born 2/4/1954, New York) of Antiguan and Venezuelan ancestry who was previously an English teacher at the University of Berkeley and married to fellow singer Freda Payne.

| | | | |
|---|---|---|---|
| 10/01/1987 | 53 | 5 | |

SHAKE YOU DOWN . . . . . . . . . . . . . . . . . . . . . . . . . . . . . . . . . . . . . . . . . . . . . . . . . . . . . . . . . . . . . CBS 4500611

○ Silver disc  ● Gold disc  ✪ Platinum disc (additional platinum units are indicated by a figure following the symbol)  ❶⁹ Number of weeks album topped the UK chart

**ABC** UK group formed in Sheffield in 1980 by Martin Fry (born 9/3/1959, Manchester, vocals) and Mark White (born 1/4/1961, Sheffield, guitar), with Stephen Singleton (born 17/4/1959, Sheffield), Mark Lickley, David Robinson and David Palmer also contributing over the years. They launched the Neutron label to release their material in the UK. By 1997 the group was effectively just Martin Fry, who chose the name because 'the first three letters of the alphabet are known the world over'.

| DATE | POS | WKS | BPI | ALBUM TITLE | LABEL & NUMBER |
|------|-----|-----|-----|-----------|----------------|
| 03/07/1982 | ❶⁴ | 50 | ✪ | **THE LEXICON OF LOVE** | Neutron NTRS 1 |
| 26/11/1983 | 12 | 13 | ● | BEAUTY STAB | Neutron NTRL 2 |
| 26/10/1985 | 28 | 3 | ● | HOW TO BE A ZILLIONAIRE | Neutron NTRH 3 |
| 24/10/1987 | 7 | 10 | | **ALPHABET CITY** | Neutron NTRH 4 |
| 28/10/1989 | 58 | 1 | | UP | Neutron 8386461 |
| 21/04/1990 | 7 | 12 | ● | **ABSOLUTELY** | Neutron 8429671 |
| 24/08/1991 | 50 | 1 | | ABRACADABRA | Parlophone PCS 7355 |
| 04/08/2001 | 69 | 1 | | LOOK OF LOVE — THE VERY BEST OF ABC | Mercury 5862372 |

**PAULA ABDUL** US singer (born 19/6/1963, Los Angeles, CA) and former cheerleader for the Los Angeles Lakers who began her career as a choreographer, notably for Janet Jackson. She married and later divorced actor Emilio Estevez. A marriage to record company executive Brad Beckerman also ended in divorce. She has a star on the Hollywood Walk of Fame.

| DATE | POS | WKS | BPI | ALBUM TITLE | LABEL & NUMBER |
|------|-----|-----|-----|-----------|----------------|
| 15/04/1989 | 3 | 39 | ✪ | **FOREVER YOUR GIRL** ▲¹⁰ | Siren SRNLP 19 |
| 10/11/1990 | 40 | 2 | | SHUT UP AND DANCE | Virgin America VUSLP 28 |
| 27/07/1991 | 4 | 9 | ● | **SPELLBOUND** ▲² | Virgin America VUSLP 33 |
| 01/07/1995 | 61 | 1 | | HEAD OVER HEELS | Virgin America CDVUS 90 |

**A.B.'S** Japanese instrumental funk group formed by Fujimal Yoshino, Makoto Matsushita, Yoshihiko Ando, Naoki Watanabe and Atsuo Okamoto. Their debut hit was actually a 12-inch single that was too long for the singles chart.

| DATE | POS | WKS | BPI | ALBUM TITLE | LABEL & NUMBER |
|------|-----|-----|-----|-----------|----------------|
| 14/04/1984 | 80 | 2 | | DEJA VU | Street Sounds XKHAN 503 |

**ABS** UK singer (born Richard Abidin Breen, 29/6/1979, Enfield) who was a founder member of Five, going solo when they disbanded in September 2001.

| DATE | POS | WKS | BPI | ALBUM TITLE | LABEL & NUMBER |
|------|-----|-----|-----|-----------|----------------|
| 13/09/2003 | 29 | 3 | | ABSTRACT THEORY | BMG 82876538802 |

**AC/DC** Australian hard-rock group formed in 1974 by brothers Angus (born 31/3/1959, Glasgow, Scotland, guitar) and Malcolm Young (born 6/1/1953, Glasgow, guitar), Bon Scott (born Ron Belford, 9/7/1946, Kirriemuir, Scotland, vocals), Phil Rudd (born 19/5/1954, Melbourne, drums) and Mark Evans (born 2/3/1956, bass). Scott died of alcohol poisoning on 19/2/1980, with former Geordie lead singer Brian Johnson (born 5/10/1947, Newcastle-upon-Tyne) his replacement. Simon Wright replaced Rudd in 1985, and when he left to join Dio in 1989 Chris Slade took his place. They were inducted into the Rock & Roll Hall of Fame in 2003.

| DATE | POS | WKS | BPI | ALBUM TITLE | LABEL & NUMBER |
|------|-----|-----|-----|-----------|----------------|
| 05/11/1977 | 17 | 5 | ○ | LET THERE BE ROCK | Atlantic K 50366 |
| 20/05/1978 | 26 | 9 | ○ | POWERAGE | Atlantic K 50483 |
| 28/10/1978 | 13 | 58 | ● | IF YOU WANT BLOOD YOU'VE GOT IT | Atlantic K 50532 |
| 18/08/1979 | 8 | 32 | ● | **HIGHWAY TO HELL** | Atlantic K 50628 |
| 09/08/1980 | ❶² | 40 | ● | **BACK IN BLACK** ◆¹⁹ | Atlantic K 50735 |
| 05/12/1981 | 3 | 29 | ● | **FOR THOSE ABOUT TO ROCK WE SALUTE YOU** ▲³ | Atlantic K 50851 |
| 03/09/1983 | 4 | 9 | ● | **FLICK OF THE SWITCH** | Atlantic 7801001 |
| 13/07/1985 | 7 | 10 | ○ | **FLY ON THE WALL** | Atlantic 7812631 |
| 07/06/1986 | 11 | 12 | | WHO MADE WHO | Atlantic WX 57 |
| 13/02/1988 | 2 | 14 | ● | **BLOW UP YOUR VIDEO** | Atlantic WX 144 |
| 06/10/1990 | 4 | 18 | ● | **THE RAZOR'S EDGE** | Atco WX 364 |
| 07/11/1992 | 5 | 7 | ● | **AC/DC LIVE** | Atco 7567922152 |
| 07/10/1995 | 6 | 8 | | **BALLBREAKER** ◇ | East West 7559617802 |
| 11/03/2000 | 12 | 4 | | **STIFF UPPER LIP** ◇ | EMI 5256672 |

### ACADEMY OF ANCIENT MUSIC (CONDUCTED BY CHRISTOPHER HOGWOOD) UK vocal group formed in 1973, named after an 18th-century London concert-giving organisation. Performers on the hit album include Alison Bury (violin), Christopher Hirons (violin), John Holloway (violin) and Catherine Mackintosh (violin).

| DATE | POS | WKS | BPI | ALBUM TITLE | LABEL & NUMBER |
|------|-----|-----|-----|-----------|----------------|
| 16/03/1985 | 85 | 2 | | VIVALDI'S THE FOUR SEASONS | L'oiseau Lyre 4101261 |

**ACCEPT** German heavy rock group formed in 1977 by Udo Dirkschneider (vocals), Jan Kommet (guitar), Wolf Hoffman (guitar), Peter Baltes (bass) and Frank Friedrich (drums). Friedrich left after one album, replaced by Stefan Kaufmann. Dirkschneider left in 1985

to form Udo, replaced by Rob Armitage, David Reese and then Jim Stacey. Kaufmann then left due to a muscular disease, replaced by Ken Mary but the group disbanded in 1989. The group reassembled in the 1990s, with Dirkschneider, Hoffman, Baltes and Kaufmann.

| | | | | |
|---|---|---|---|---|
| 07/05/1983 | 98 | 2 | | RESTLESS AND WILD ................................................ Heavy Metal International HMILP 6 |
| 30/03/1985 | 50 | 1 | | METAL HEART ................................................ Portrait PRT 26358 |
| 15/02/1986 | 91 | 1 | | KAIZOKU-BAN ................................................ Portrait PRT 54916 |
| 03/05/1986 | 80 | 1 | | RUSSIAN ROULETTE ................................................ Portrait PRT 26893 |

## ACE OF BASE
Swedish group formed by sisters Jenny (born 19/5/1972, Gothenburg) and Malin Bergren (born 31/10/1970, Gothenburg) with brother Jonas (born 21/3/1967, Gothenburg) and family friend and programmer Ulf Ekberg (born 6/12/1970, Gothenburg) as Tech Noir, later changing their name to Ace Of Base. Initially signed to Danish record company Mega Records, their debut album *Happy Nation* sold over 21 million copies worldwide, making them the most successful debut act of all time.

| | | | | |
|---|---|---|---|---|
| 19/06/1993 | ❶² | 38 | ✪² | **HAPPY NATION** ▲² The album changed its catalogue number to 5214722 during its chart run .. London 5177492/London 5214722 |
| 02/12/1995 | 66 | 1 | | THE BRIDGE ◇ ................................................ London 5296552 |
| 22/08/1998 | 15 | 5 | ○ | FLOWERS ................................................ London 5576912 |
| 27/11/1999 | 62 | 1 | | SINGLES OF THE 90S ................................................ Polydor 5432272 |

## ADAM AND THE ANTS/ADAM ANT
UK group formed in 1976 by Adam Ant (born Stuart Leslie Goddard, 3/11/1954, London, vocals). The original line-up was poached by Malcolm McLaren to form Bow Wow Wow. Adam replaced them with Marco Pirroni (born 27/4/1959, London), Kevin Mooney, Terry Lee Miall (born 8/11/1958, London) and Merrick (born Chris Hughes, 3/3/1954). He dissolved the group in 1982, retaining Pirroni as co-writer for his solo career. In 1985 Adam moved to the US to pursue acting, returning to the UK in 1990 to revive his musical career. Hughes became a successful producer with Tears For Fears.

| | | | | |
|---|---|---|---|---|
| 15/11/1980 | ❶¹² | 66 | ✪ | **KINGS OF THE WILD FRONTIER** 1982 BRIT Award for Best Album ................................................ CBS 84549 |
| 17/01/1981 | 16 | 29 | ● | DIRK WEARS WHITE SOX ................................................ Do It RIDE 3 |
| 14/11/1981 | 2 | 21 | ✪ | **PRINCE CHARMING** This and the above two hits credited to **ADAM AND THE ANTS** ................................................ CBS 85268 |
| 23/10/1982 | 5 | 12 | ● | **FRIEND OR FOE** ................................................ CBS 25040 |
| 19/11/1983 | 20 | 8 | ○ | STRIP ................................................ CBS 25705 |
| 14/09/1985 | 42 | 3 | | VIVE LE ROCK ................................................ CBS 26583 |
| 24/03/1990 | 19 | 3 | | MANNERS AND PHYSIQUE ................................................ MCA MCG 6068 |
| 28/08/1993 | 6 | 11 | | **ANTMUSIC – THE VERY BEST OF ADAM ANT** ................................................ Arcade ARC 3100052 |
| 15/04/1995 | 24 | 2 | | WONDERFUL ................................................ EMI CDEMC 3687 |
| 03/04/1999 | 33 | 5 | | THE VERY BEST OF ADAM AND THE ANTS **ADAM AND THE ANTS** ................................................ Columbia 4942292 |

## BRYAN ADAMS
Canadian singer (born 5/11/1959, Kingston, Ontario) who was lead singer with local band Sweeney Todd in 1976 before forming a songwriting partnership with Jim Vallence in 1977 (for Bachman-Turner Overdrive, Loverboy, Bonnie Tyler and Joe Cocker, among others). He later worked with songwriter/producer Robert John 'Mutt' Lange. Adams won the 1994 MTV Europe Music Award for Best Male.

| | | | | |
|---|---|---|---|---|
| 02/03/1985 | 7 | 115 | ✪³ | **RECKLESS** ▲² ................................................ A&M AMA 5013 |
| 24/08/1985 | 78 | 5 | | YOU WANT IT, YOU GOT IT ................................................ A&M AMLH 64864 |
| 15/03/1986 | 21 | 6 | ○ | CUTS LIKE A KNIFE ................................................ A&M AMLH 64919 |
| 11/04/1987 | 10 | 21 | ● | **INTO THE FIRE** ................................................ A&M AMA 3907 |
| 05/10/1991 | ❶¹ | 54 | ✪³ | **WAKING UP THE NEIGHBOURS** ................................................ A&M 3971641 |
| 20/11/1993 | ❶¹ | 55 | ✪³ | **SO FAR SO GOOD** ................................................ A&M 5401572 |
| 06/08/1994 | 17 | 4 | | LIVE! LIVE! LIVE! ................................................ A&M 3970942 |
| 22/06/1996 | ❶¹ | 40 | ✪² | **18 TIL I DIE** ◇ ................................................ A&M 5405372 |
| 13/12/1997 | 19 | 19 | ● | UNPLUGGED ................................................ A&M 5408312 |
| 31/10/1998 | 11 | 35 | ● | ON A DAY LIKE TODAY ◇ ................................................ A&M 5410512 |
| 27/11/1999 | 12 | 39 | ● | THE BEST OF ME ◇² ................................................ A&M 4905222 |
| 27/07/2002 | 8 | 5 | ○ | **SPIRIT – STALLION OF THE CIMARRON** Original soundtrack to the film ................................................ A&M 4933622 |

## CLIFF ADAMS SINGERS
UK orchestra leader (born 21/8/1923, London), previously a member of the Stargazers. He devised the radio programme *Sing Something Simple* in 1959, which remains one of the longest-running in the country. He died on 22/10/2001.

| | | | | |
|---|---|---|---|---|
| 16/04/1960 | 15 | 4 | | SING SOMETHING SIMPLE ................................................ Pye MPL 28013 |
| 24/11/1962 | 15 | 2 | | SING SOMETHING SIMPLE ................................................ Pye Golden Guinea GGL 0150 |
| 20/11/1976 | 23 | 8 | | SING SOMETHING SIMPLE '76 ................................................ Warwick WW 5016/17 |
| 25/12/1982 | 39 | 6 | | SING SOMETHING SIMPLE ................................................ Ronco RTD 2087 |

**OLETA ADAMS** US singer (born 4/5/1962, Yakima, WA) who was discovered singing in Kansas City by Tears For Fears. She subsequently became their backing singer for the *Seeds Of Love* album and tou. Roland Orzabal produced her debut album. She later recorded gospel material for Harmony Records.

| 26/05/1990 | ❶¹ | 26 | ● | CIRCLE OF ONE | Fontana 8427441 |
| 07/08/1993 | 10 | 7 | | EVOLUTION | Fontana 5149652 |
| 04/11/1995 | 59 | 1 | | MOVING ON | Fontana 5285302 |

**RYAN ADAMS** US singer/songwriter (born 5/11/1974) who was lead singer with Whiskeytown before going solo in 2000.

| 06/10/2001 | 20 | 9 | ● | GOLD | Lost Highway 1702522 |
| 05/10/2002 | 22 | 2 | | DEMOLITION | Lost Highway 1703332 |
| 15/11/2003 | 41 | 1 | | ROCK N ROLL | Lost Highway 9861324 |
| 15/11/2003 | 62 | 1 | | LOVE IS HELL PART 1 | Lost Highway 9813666 |
| 15/05/2004 | 68 | 1 | | LOVE IS HELL | Lost Highway 9862325 |

**ADAMSKI** UK singer (born Adam Tinley, 1966) who made his first record at the age of eleven as The Stupid Babies with *The Babysitters*. He signed with MCA in 1989 and initially recorded instrumentals before linking with the then-unknown Seal, later recording for ZTT.

| 09/12/1989 | 47 | 11 | ○ | LIVEANDIRECT | MCA MCL 1900 |
| 13/10/1990 | 8 | 5 | ○ | DOCTOR ADAMSKI'S MUSICAL PHARMACY | MCA MCG 6107 |

**BARRY ADAMSON** UK bass player, the original bassist for Magazine and later in Visage and Nick Cave's Bad Seeds before going solo. His albums *Soul Murder* (1992) and *The Negro Inside Me* (1994) both earned nominations for the Mercury Music Prize.

| 10/08/1996 | 51 | 1 | | OEDIPUS SCHMOEDIPUS | Mute CDSTUMM 134 |

**KING SUNNY ADE & HIS AFRICAN BEATS** Nigerian singer/guitarist (born Sunday Adeniyi, 1/9/1946, Oshogbo); his parents were from the royal family of Ondo. He dropped out of school in 1963, and by the following year was lead guitarist with The Rhythm Dandies. He formed the Green Spots in 1966, changing their name in the 1970s. Reported dead after he collapsed on stage in Lagos in 1991. However, this turned out to be unfounded and he later spent some time in London recuperating.

| 09/07/1983 | 93 | 1 | | SYNCHRO SYSTEM | Island ILPS 9737 |

**ADEVA** US R&B singer (born Patricia Daniels, Patterson, NJ), the youngest of six children, who started singing in her local church choir. She was a schoolteacher before becoming a professional singer against her parents' wishes.

| 09/09/1989 | 6 | 24 | ✪ | ADEVA | Cooltempo ICTLP 13 |

**ADICTS** UK punk group formed in Ipswich in 1980 by Monkey (born Keith Warren, vocals), Pete Davidson (guitar), Mel Ellis (bass) and Kid Dee (born Michael Davidson, drums), adopting bowler hats and face make-up from Stanley Kubrick's *A Clockwork Orange*.

| 04/12/1982 | 99 | 1 | | SOUND OF MUSIC | Razor RAZ 2 |

**ADIEMUS** UK instrumental duo Karl Jenkins and Mike Ratledge.

| 01/07/1995 | 35 | 12 | ● | SONGS OF SANCTUARY | Venture CDVE 925 |
| 01/03/1997 | 15 | 9 | ● | ADIEMUS II – CANTATA MUNDI | Venture CDVE 932 |
| 24/10/1998 | 58 | 1 | | ADIEMUS III – DANCES OF TIME | Venture CDVE 940 |

**LARRY ADLER** US mouth-organist (born 10/2/1914, Baltimore, MD) who won the Maryland Harmonica Championship in 1927 before running away to New York. Best known for his interpretations of Gershwin's music, it was his version of *Summertime* that accompanied Torville and Dean's ice dance routine in 1984. He also composed the music to the film *Genevieve*, which earned him an Academy Award nomination, although because of the McCarthy communist witch-hunt his name was removed from the film's credits and he did not receive his Oscar nomination certificate until many years later. His hit album also featured performances by Sting, Kate Bush, Meat Loaf, Elvis Costello and Cher. After battling against cancer and two heart attacks he died from pneumonia on 7/8/2001.

| 06/08/1994 | 2 | 18 | ● | THE GLORY OF GERSHWIN | Mercury 5227272 |

**ADORABLE** UK group formed by Piotr Fijalkowski (guitar/vocals), Robert Dillam (guitar), Wil (bass) and Kevin Gritton (drums).

| 13/03/1993 | 70 | 1 | | AGAINST PERFECTION | Creation CRECD 138 |

**ADVENTURES** UK group formed in Belfast in 1984 by Terry Sharpe (vocals), Pat Gribben (guitar), Pat's wife Eileen (vocals), Gerard 'Spud' Murphy (guitar), Tony Ayre (bass) and Paul Crowder (drums), originally recording for Chrysalis. Eileen Gribben and Murphy left in 1989.

| 21/05/1988 | 30 | 10 | ○ | THE SEA OF LOVE | Elektra EKT 45 |
| 17/03/1990 | 64 | 1 | | TRADING SECRETS WITH THE MOON | Elektra EKT 63 |

**ADVERTS** UK punk group formed in 1977 by Tim 'TV' Smith (guitar/vocals), Gaye Advert (bass), Howard Pickup (guitar) and Laurie Driver (drums). They later included John Towe, Rod Latter and Tim Cross. After disbanding in 1979, Smith formed TV Smith's Explorers. Pickup died from a brain tumour in July 1997.

| 11/03/1978 | 38 | 1 | | CROSSING THE RED SEA WITH THE ADVERTS | Bright BRL 201 |

### AEROSMITH
US hard-rock band formed in 1970 by Steven Tyler (born Steven Tallarico, 26/3/1948, Yonkers, NY, vocals), Joe Perry (born 10/9/1950, Boston, MA, guitar), Brad Whitford (born 23/2/1952, Winchester, MA, guitar), Tom Hamilton (born 31/12/1951, Colorado Springs, CO, bass) and Joey Kramer (born 21/6/1950, The Bronx, NYC; drums). Their debut album was released in 1973. Perry left in 1979 to form the Joe Perry Project and was replaced by Jimmy Crespo. Whitford left in 1981 and was replaced by Rick Dulay. The original line-up re-formed in 1984. They have won four Grammy Awards: the non-charting Best Rock Performance by a Group with Vocal in 1990 for *Jane's Got A Gun,* Best Rock Performance by a Group with Vocal in 1993 for *Livin' On The Edge*, the same category in 1994 for *Crazy* and Best Rock Group Performance in 1998 for *Pink*. They were named Best Rock Act at the 1994 and 1998 MTV Europe Music Awards and were inducted into the Rock & Roll Hall of Fame in 2001.

| | | | | |
|---|---|---|---|---|
| 05/09/1987 | 37 | 14 | ● | PERMANENT VACATION .................................................. Geffen WX 126 |
| 23/09/1989 | 3 | 26 | ● | PUMP The album changed its catalogue number to GEF 24245 during its chart run ........ Geffen WX 304/GEF 24245 |
| 01/05/1993 | 2 | 38 | ✪ | GET A GRIP ▲¹ ................................................. Geffen GED 24444 |
| 12/11/1994 | 7 | 16 | ● | BIG ONES ...................................................... Geffen GED 24546 |
| 22/03/1997 | 4 | 11 | ○ | NINE LIVES ◇ ▲¹ ............................................... Columbia 4850206 |
| 31/10/1998 | 36 | 2 | | A LITTLE SOUTH OF SANITY ...................................... Geffen GED 25221 |
| 24/03/2001 | 7 | 5 | | JUST PUSH PLAY ................................................ Columbia 5015352 |
| 08/12/2001 | 32 | 14 | ● | YOUNG LUST – THE ANTHOLOGY ................................... Universal TV 4931192 |
| 03/08/2002 | 6 | 8 | ● | O YEAH – ULTIMATE HITS ........................................ Sony TV 5084679 |
| 10/04/2004 | 28 | 3 | | HONKIN' ON BOBO .............................................. Columbia CK92079 |

### AFGHAN WHIGS
US rock group formed in Cincinnati by Greg Dulli (born 11/3/1965, Ohio, guitar/vocals), Rick McCollum (born 14/7/1965, Kentucky), Steve Earle (born 28/3/1966, Cincinnati) and John Curley (born 15/3/1965, Trenton, NJ). Dulli, who began his career studying film, later took part in the Stuart Sutcliffe biopic *Backbeat*, singing the John Lennon part on the soundtrack.

| | | | |
|---|---|---|---|
| 16/10/1993 | 58 | 1 | GENTLEMEN ..................................................... Blast First BFFP 90CD |
| 23/03/1996 | 41 | 2 | BLACK LOVE .................................................... Mute CDSTUMM 143 |

### A.F.I.
US rock group formed in Ukiah, CA in 1991 by college students Davey Havok (vocals), Markus Stopholese (guitar), Vick (bass) and Adam Carson (drums). Vick left after a few months and was replaced by Geoff Kresge. By 1997 the line-up was Havok, Jade Puger (guitar), Hunter (bass) and Carson. Their name is short for A Fire Inside.

| | | | |
|---|---|---|---|
| 22/03/2003 | 52 | 1 | SING THE SORROW .............................................. DreamWorks 04504482 |

### AFRICAN BEATS — see KING SUNNY ADE & HIS AFRICAN BEATS

### AFRO CELT SOUND SYSTEM
UK/Irish/African group with Iarla O'Lionard (vocals), Davy Spillane (uillean pipes), Ronan Browne (uillean pipes), Jo Bruce (keyboards), James McNally (whistle), Ayub Ogada (nyatiti), Kauwding Cissakho and Massamba Diop.

| | | | | |
|---|---|---|---|---|
| 27/07/1996 | 59 | 2 | ○ | VOLUME 1: SOUND MAGIC ........................................ Realworld CDRW 61 |
| 08/05/1999 | 38 | 3 | | VOLUME 2: RELEASE ............................................. Realworld CDRW 76 |

### AFTER DARK
UK studio group assembled by producer Mark Smith and featuring Mornington Lockett on saxophone.

| | | | |
|---|---|---|---|
| 03/02/1996 | 18 | 5 | LATE NIGHT SAX ................................................ EMI TV CDEMTV 108 |

### AFTER THE FIRE
UK rock group formed in 1974 by Andy Piercy (vocals/bass), Peter Banks (keyboards), John Russell (guitar) and Pete King (drums) who later formed the Rapid label and recorded gospel music.

| | | | |
|---|---|---|---|
| 13/10/1979 | 57 | 1 | LASER LOVE .................................................... CBS 83795 |
| 01/11/1980 | 69 | 1 | 80 F .......................................................... Epic 84545 |
| 03/04/1982 | 82 | 2 | BATTERIES NOT INCLUDED ....................................... CBS 85566 |

### CHRISTINA AGUILERA
US singer (born 18/12/1980, Staten Island, NYC) who, at the age of twelve, landed a role on *The New Mickey Mouse Club* for Disney, the TV show that also gave a start to Britney Spears and Justin Timberlake. Awards include a Grammy for Best New Artist in 1999, the 2001 award for Best Pop Collaboration with Vocals with Lil' Kim, Mya and Pink for *Lady Marmalade*, Best Female Pop Vocal Performance for *Beautiful* in 2003, and the MTV Europe Music Award for Best Female Artist in 2003.

| | | | | |
|---|---|---|---|---|
| 30/10/1999 | 14 | 26 | ● | CHRISTINA AGUILERA ◇ ▲¹ ...................................... RCA 74321780542 |
| 09/11/2002 | 2 | 82 | ✪³ | STRIPPED ◇² ................................................... RCA 74321961252 |

○ Silver disc  ● Gold disc  ✪ Platinum disc (additional platinum units are indicated by a figure following the symbol)  ❶⁹ Number of weeks album topped the UK chart

**A-HA** Norwegian trio formed by Morten Harket (born 14/9/1959, Konigsberg, vocals), Pal Waaktaar (born 6/9/1961, Oslo, guitar) and Magne 'Mags' Furuholmen (born 1/11/1962, Oslo, keyboards). They moved to London in January 1983 and signed with Warners in late 1983. Furuholmen chose their name, a simple exclamation known the world over. The group went into semi-retirement in 1995 in order to undertake individual projects. Harket recorded a solo album and Waaktaar formed Savoy, before they re-formed in 1999.

| 09/11/1985 | 2 | 78 | ⊙³ | HUNTING HIGH AND LOW | Warner Brothers WX 30 |
| 18/10/1986 | 2 | 29 | ⊙ | SCOUNDREL DAYS | Warner Brothers WX 62 |
| 14/05/1988 | 2 | 19 | ● | STAY ON THESE ROADS | Warner Brothers WX 166 |
| 03/11/1990 | 12 | 4 | ○ | EAST OF THE SUN, WEST OF THE MOON | Warner Brothers WX 378 |
| 16/11/1991 | 12 | 12 | ○ | HEADLINES AND DEADLINES – THE HITS OF A-HA | Warner Brothers WX 450 |
| 26/06/1993 | 17 | 3 | | MEMORIAL BEACH | Warner Brothers 9362452292 |
| 17/06/2000 | 27 | 2 | | MINOR EARTH MAJOR SKY | WEA 8573821832 |
| 22/06/2002 | 67 | 1 | | LIFELINES | WEA 0927448492CD |

**AIM** UK producer Andy Turner who began his career as a rap DJ and signed with Grand Central in 1995, releasing his debut album in 1999.

| 09/03/2002 | 47 | 1 | | HINTERLAND | Grand Central GCCD 112 |

**AIR** French instrumental production duo formed in Paris in 1996 by Jean-Benoit Dunckel and Nicolas Godin. The pair first met whilst at school in Versailles.

| 31/01/1998 | 6 | 61 | ⊙ | MOON SAFARI | Virgin CDV 2848 |
| 18/09/1999 | 12 | 7 | ○ | PREMIERS SYMPTOMES | Virgin CDVX 2895 |
| 11/03/2000 | 14 | 4 | | THE VIRGIN SUICIDES Original soundtrack to the film | Virgin CDV 2910 |
| 09/06/2001 | 7 | 5 | ● | 10,000 HZ LEGEND | Virgin CDV 2945 |
| 02/03/2002 | 67 | 1 | | EVERYBODY HERTZ | Virgin CDV 2956 |
| 07/02/2004 | 2 | 6 | ● | TALKIE WALKIE | Virgin CDVX 2980 |

**AIRHEAD** UK group formed by Michael Wallis (vocals), Steve Marshall (keyboards), Ben Kesteven (bass) and Sam Kesteven (drums). They briefly changed their name to Jefferson Airhead, inspired by Jefferson Airplane, but after objections from Airplane's record company reverted back to Airhead.

| 01/02/1992 | 29 | 7 | | BOING! | Korova 9031746792 |

**ROBERTO ALAGNA/ANGELA GHEORGIU** Italian male and Romanian female singers: Alagna was born in France to Sicilian parents and studied music in Paris, Gheorgiu was born in Adjud and graduated from the Bucharest Music Academy in 1990.

| 18/05/1996 | 42 | 5 | | DUETS & ARIAS | EMI Classics CDC 5561172 |

**ALARM** UK group formed in Rhyl, North Wales in 1977 as The Toilets, comprising Mike Peters (born 25/2/1959, Prestatyn, guitar/vocals), Dave Sharp (born 28/1/1959, Salford, guitar), Eddie MacDonald (born 1/11/1959, St Asaph, bass) and Nigel Twist (born 18/7/1958, Manchester, drums). They changed their name to Alarm in 1981. They disbanded in 1991, with Peters going solo and Twist forming Fringe. The group re-formed in 2003 and initially recorded as The Poppyfields.

| 25/02/1984 | 6 | 11 | ○ | DECLARATION | I.R.S. IRSA 7044 |
| 26/10/1985 | 18 | 6 | ○ | STRENGTH | I.R.S. MIRF 1004 |
| 14/11/1987 | 23 | 4 | ○ | EYE OF THE HURRICANE | I.R.S. MIRG 1023 |
| 05/11/1988 | 62 | 2 | | ELECTRIC FOLKLORE LIVE | I.R.S. MIRMC 5001 |
| 30/09/1989 | 13 | 3 | ○ | CHANGE | I.R.S. EIRSAX 1020 |
| 24/11/1990 | 47 | 1 | ○ | STANDARDS | I.R.S. EIRSA 1043 |
| 04/05/1991 | 33 | 2 | | RAW | I.R.S. EIRSA 1055 |

**ALEXANDER BROTHERS** UK vocal duo formed in 1960 by Tom and Jack Alexander, both born in Cambusnethan.

| 10/12/1966 | 29 | 1 | | THESE ARE MY MOUNTAINS | Pye Golden Guinea GGL 0375 |

**ALFIE** UK group formed in Manchester by Lee Gorton (vocals), Ian Smith (guitar), Matt McGeever (cello), Sam Morris (bass) and Sean Kelly (drums).

| 07/04/2001 | 62 | 1 | | IF YOU HAPPY WITH YOU NEED DO NOTHING | Twisted Nerve TN 026CD |

**TATYANA ALI** US singer (born Tatyana Marisol Ali, 24/1/1979, Brooklyn, NYC) who relocated to Los Angeles, CA with her family at the age of four. She appeared as an actress in TV's *Sesame Street* and (as Ashley Banks) with Will Smith in *The Fresh Prince Of Bel Air*, before launching a singing career.

| | | | |
|---|---|---|---|
| 20/02/1999 | 41 | 4 | |

KISS THE SKY . . . . . . . . . . . . . . . . . . . . . . . . . . . . . . . . . . . . . . . . . . . . . . . . . . . . . . . . . . . . . . . . . . . . . . MJJ 4916512

**ALICE BAND** UK/Irish/US group with Amy (born in Glasgow), Audrey (born in Dublin) and Charity (born in Plant City, FL).

| | | | |
|---|---|---|---|
| 25/05/2002 | 55 | 1 | |

THE LOVE JUNK STORE . . . . . . . . . . . . . . . . . . . . . . . . . . . . . . . . . . . . . . . . . . . . . . . . . . . . . . . Instant Karma KARMACD 4

**ALICE DEEJAY** Dutch dance group formed by producers Pronti (born Eelke Kalberg), Kalmani (born Sebastiaan Molijn) and DJ Jurgen, fronted by 23-year-old singer Judy with Gaby and Jane.

| | | | |
|---|---|---|---|
| 29/07/2000 | 8 | 11 | ● |

WHO NEEDS GUITARS ANYWAY . . . . . . . . . . . . . . . . . . . . . . . . . . . . . . . . . . . . . . . . . . . . . . . . . . . . . Positiva 5270010

**ALICE IN CHAINS** US group formed in Seattle, WA in 1987 by Jerry Cantrell (born 18/3/1966, Tacoma, WA, guitar), Layne Stanley (born 22/8/1967, Kirkland, WA, vocals), Mike Inez (born 14/5/1966, San Fernando, CA, bass) and Sean Kinney (born 27/6/1966, Seattle, drums). Signed by Columbia in 1989, their debut album appeared in 1990. Cantrell went solo in 1997. Stanley was found dead in his apartment on 19/4/2002, cause of death unknown, but the body may have lain undiscovered for up to two weeks.

| | | | |
|---|---|---|---|
| 24/10/1992 | 42 | 13 | ● |
| 05/02/1994 | 4 | 5 | ○ |
| 18/11/1995 | 37 | 2 | |
| 10/08/1996 | 20 | 2 | |

DIRT . . . . . . . . . . . . . . . . . . . . . . . . . . . . . . . . . . . . . . . . . . . . . . . . . . . . . . . . . . . . . . . . . . . . . . . . . . . Columbia 4723302
JAR OF FLIES/SAP ▲[1] . . . . . . . . . . . . . . . . . . . . . . . . . . . . . . . . . . . . . . . . . . . . . . . . . . . . . . . . . . . . Columbia 4757132
ALICE IN CHAINS ▲[1] . . . . . . . . . . . . . . . . . . . . . . . . . . . . . . . . . . . . . . . . . . . . . . . . . . . . . . . . . . . . . Columbia 4811149
MTV UNPLUGGED . . . . . . . . . . . . . . . . . . . . . . . . . . . . . . . . . . . . . . . . . . . . . . . . . . . . . . . . . . . . . . . . . Columbia 4843002

**ALIEN ANT FARM** US rock group formed in Los Angeles, CA in 1995 by Dryden Mitchell (vocals), Terry Corso (guitar), Tye Zamora (bass) and Mike Cosgrove (drums). They signed with Dreamworks imprint New Noize in 2000.

| | | | |
|---|---|---|---|
| 18/08/2001 | 11 | 23 | ● |
| 30/08/2003 | 68 | 1 | |

ANTHOLOGY . . . . . . . . . . . . . . . . . . . . . . . . . . . . . . . . . . . . . . . . . . . . . . . . . . . . . . . . . . . . . . . . DreamWorks 4502932
TRUANT . . . . . . . . . . . . . . . . . . . . . . . . . . . . . . . . . . . . . . . . . . . . . . . . . . . . . . . . . . . . . . . . . . . DreamWorks 4505014

**ALIEN SEX FIEND** UK rock group formed in 1982 by Nick Wade (vocals), David James (guitar), Christine Wade (synthesizer) and Johnny 'Ha Ha' Freshwater (drums). Nick Wade's previous groups included The Earwigs, Mr & Mrs Demeanour and Demon Preacher. Freshwater left the group in 1985 and they continued as a trio.

| | | | |
|---|---|---|---|
| 12/10/1985 | 100 | 1 | |

MAXIMUM SECURITY . . . . . . . . . . . . . . . . . . . . . . . . . . . . . . . . . . . . . . . . . . . . . . . . . . . . . . . . . . Anagram GRAM 24

**ALISHA'S ATTIC** UK duo from Essex, sisters Karen (born 8/1/1971) and Shelley Poole (born 20/3/1972); daughters of ex-Tremeloes frontman Brian Poole who were discovered after sending a demo to Dave Stewart who produced their debut album.

| | | | |
|---|---|---|---|
| 23/11/1996 | 14 | 43 | ✪ |
| 17/10/1998 | 15 | 3 | ○ |
| 04/08/2001 | 55 | 1 | |

ALISHA RULES THE WORLD . . . . . . . . . . . . . . . . . . . . . . . . . . . . . . . . . . . . . . . . . . . . . . . . . . . . . . Mercury 5340272
ILLUMINA . . . . . . . . . . . . . . . . . . . . . . . . . . . . . . . . . . . . . . . . . . . . . . . . . . . . . . . . . . . . . . . . . . . Mercury 5589912
THE HOUSE WE BUILT . . . . . . . . . . . . . . . . . . . . . . . . . . . . . . . . . . . . . . . . . . . . . . . . . . . . . . . . . . Mercury 5428542

**ALKALINE TRIO** UK rock group formed in 1997 by Matt Skiba (guitar/vocals), Rob Doran (bass/vocals) and Glenn Porter (drums/vocals). Doran left the same year and was replaced by Dan Andriano. Porter left in 2000 and was replaced by Mike Felumlee.

| | | | |
|---|---|---|---|
| 24/05/2003 | 32 | 1 | |

GOOD MOURNING . . . . . . . . . . . . . . . . . . . . . . . . . . . . . . . . . . . . . . . . . . . . . . . . . . . . . . . . . . . . Vagrant 9801238

**ALL ABOUT EVE** UK gothic-style group formed in 1985 as The Swarm by Julianne Regan (vocals), Manuella Zwingman, James Jackson (bass) and Tim Bricheno (guitar). By the time they re-formed as All About Eve they comprised Regan, Bricheno, Andy Cousin (bass) and Mark Price (drums). They also set up the Eden label. Regan had previously been a journalist for *Zig Zag* magazine and then a member of Gene Loves Jezebel. The group disbanded in 1992 with Cousin joining The Mission and Regan eventually launched a solo career in 1995. The group re-formed in 2004.

| | | | |
|---|---|---|---|
| 27/02/1988 | 7 | 29 | ● |
| 28/10/1989 | 9 | 4 | ● |
| 07/09/1991 | 17 | 3 | |
| 07/11/1992 | 46 | 1 | |

ALL ABOUT EVE . . . . . . . . . . . . . . . . . . . . . . . . . . . . . . . . . . . . . . . . . . . . . . . . . . . . . . . . . . . . . . Mercury MERH 119
SCARLET AND OTHER STORIES . . . . . . . . . . . . . . . . . . . . . . . . . . . . . . . . . . . . . . . . . . . . . . . . . . . Mercury 8389651
TOUCHED BY JESUS . . . . . . . . . . . . . . . . . . . . . . . . . . . . . . . . . . . . . . . . . . . . . . . . . . . . . . . . . . . Vertigo 5104611
ULTRAVIOLET . . . . . . . . . . . . . . . . . . . . . . . . . . . . . . . . . . . . . . . . . . . . . . . . . . . . . . . . . . . . . . . . MCA MCD 10712

**ALL AMERICAN REJECTS** US rock group formed in Stillwater, OK in 2000 by Tyson Ritter (bass/vocals), Nick Wheeler (guitar/programming), Mike Kennerty (guitar) and Chris Gaylor (drums).

| | | | |
|---|---|---|---|
| 09/08/2003 | 50 | 5 | |

ALL-AMERICAN REJECTS . . . . . . . . . . . . . . . . . . . . . . . . . . . . . . . . . . . . . . . . . . . . . . . . . . . . . DreamWorks 4504606

**ALL-4-ONE** US R&B vocal group formed in California by Jamie Jones, Tony Borowiak, Delious Kennedy and Alfred Nevarez. The group won the 1994 Grammy Award for Best Pop Performance by a Group for their single *I Swear*.

| | | | |
|---|---|---|---|
| 23/07/1994 | 25 | 5 | |

ALL-4-ONE . . . . . . . . . . . . . . . . . . . . . . . . . . . . . . . . . . . . . . . . . . . . . . . . . . . . . . . . . . . . . . Atlantic 7567825882

○ Silver disc ● Gold disc ✪ Platinum disc (additional platinum units are indicated by a figure following the symbol) ❶[9] Number of weeks album topped the UK chart

**ALL SAINTS** UK/Canadian vocal group formed by Melanie Blatt (born 25/3/1975, London), Shaznay Tricia Lewis (born 14/10/1975, London) and sisters Nicole (born 7/12/1974, Canada) and Natalie Appleton (born 14/5/1973, Canada). Originally formed as a trio in 1993 with Melanie, Shaznay and Simone Rainford, they recorded three singles for ZTT as All Saints 1.9.7.5. They won two MTV Europe Music Awards: Breakthrough Act in 1998 and Best Pop Act in 2000. Natalie, Nicole and Melanie appeared in the 2000 film *Honest*, directed by Dave Stewart. They disbanded in 2001.

| | | | | | |
|---|---|---|---|---|---|
| 06/12/1997 | 2 | 71 | ○5 | **ALL SAINTS** ◇2 | London 5560172 |
| 28/10/2000 | ❶1 | 21 | ○2 | **SAINTS & SINNERS** ◇ | London 8573852955 |
| 17/11/2001 | 18 | 4 | ● | ALL HITS | London 0927421522 |

**ALL SEEING I** UK production trio from Sheffield with Parrot, 'Rubber' Johnny Buckel and Dean Honer, and vocal contributions from Jarvis Cocker, Phil Oakey and Tony Christie. The group has its own studio, The Fractal Cabbage, and has launched its own website with a dedicated channel for net radio broadcasts. Honer later recorded with Jarrod Gosling of Add N To X as I Monster.

| | | | | |
|---|---|---|---|---|
| 02/10/1999 | 45 | 1 | PICKLED EGGS & SHERBET | ffrr 3984292412 |

**ED ALLEYNE-JOHNSON** UK violinist born in Liverpool; he studied Fine Art at Oxford University and after graduating busked through Europe with a home-made electric violin. He became a member of New Model Army in 1989 and made five albums with the group before going solo.

| | | | | |
|---|---|---|---|---|
| 18/06/1994 | 68 | 1 | ULTRAVIOLET | Equation EQCD 002 |

**MOSE ALLISON** US pianist (born 11/11/1927, Tippo, MS) who began taking piano lessons at the age of five and played trumpet whilst at high school. Although most of his career has seen him active in jazz circles, he is acknowledged as having had a major influence on the R&B scene, and his works have been recorded by acts as diverse as The Who and John Martyn.

| | | | | |
|---|---|---|---|---|
| 04/06/1966 | 30 | 1 | MOSE ALIVE | Atlantic 587007 |

**ALLMAN BROTHERS BAND** US rock group formed in Macon, GA in 1969 by Greg Allman (born 8/12/1947, Nashville, TN, keyboards/vocals), his brother Duane (born 20/11/1946, Nashville, guitar), Richard 'Dickey' Betts (born 12/12/1943, Palm Beach, FL, guitar), Berry Oakley (born 4/4/1948, Chicago, IL, bass), Butch Trucks (born in Jacksonville, FL, drums) and Jai Johnny Johanson (born 8/7/1944, Ocean Springs, MS, drums). Duane Allman was killed in a motorcycle accident on 29/10/1971. Berry Oakley was killed in a motorcycle accident on 11/11/1972, less than a mile from the spot where Allman had been killed. Oakley was replaced by Lamar Williams (born 14/1/1949, Gulfport, MS). They disbanded in 1976, and re-formed in the 1990s with Greg Allman, Dickey Betts, Warren Hayes (guitars/vocals), Allen Woody (bass), Butch Trucks (drums), Jaimoe (drums) and Mark Quinones (percussion). Williams died from cancer on 25/1/1983, Allen from a heart attack on 26/8/2000. Greg Allman was briefly married to Cher twice. They were inducted into the Rock & Roll Hall of Fame in 1995, the same year they won the Grammy Award for Best Rock Instrumental Performance for *Jessica*.

| | | | | |
|---|---|---|---|---|
| 06/10/1973 | 42 | 3 | BROTHERS AND SISTERS ▲5 | Warner Brothers K 47507 |
| 06/03/1976 | 54 | 1 | THE ROAD GOES ON FOREVER | Capricorn 2637 101 |

**ALLSTARS** UK vocal group formed by Sandi Lee Hughes, Thaila Zucchi, Ashley Dawson, Rebecca Hunter and Sam Bloom, first seen in the TV series *Starstreet*.

| | | | | |
|---|---|---|---|---|
| 25/05/2002 | 43 | 2 | ALLSTARS | Island CIDD 8116 |

**ALMIGHTY** UK heavy metal group formed in Scotland by Ricky Warwick (vocals), Tantrum (guitar), Floyd London (bass) and Stumpt Munroe (drums). They made their first album for Polydor in 1989. Tantrum left in 1991 and was replaced by Peter Friesen.

| | | | | |
|---|---|---|---|---|
| 20/10/1990 | 62 | 1 | BLOOD, FIRE AND LIVE | Polydor 8471071 |
| 30/03/1991 | 22 | 4 | SOUL DESTRUCTION | Polydor 8479611 |
| 17/04/1993 | 5 | 4 | **POWERTRIPPIN'** | Polydor 5191042 |
| 08/10/1994 | 15 | 2 | CRANK | Chrysalis CDCHRZ 6086 |
| 30/03/1996 | 34 | 2 | JUST ADD LIFE | Chrysalis CDCHR 6112 |

**MARC ALMOND** UK male singer (born 9/7/1957, Southport) who first came to prominence as member of Soft Cell with David Ball, before going solo in 1984. He also records as Marc And The Mambas and Marc Almond And The Willing Sinners.

| | | | | |
|---|---|---|---|---|
| 16/10/1982 | 42 | 4 | UNTITLED | Some Bizzare BZA 13 |
| 20/08/1983 | 28 | 5 | TORMENT AND TOREROS This and the above hit credited to **MARC & THE MAMBAS** | Some Bizzare BIZL 4 |
| 10/11/1984 | 36 | 2 | VERMIN IN ERMINE **MARC ALMOND & THE WILLING SINNERS** | Some Bizzare BIZL 8 |
| 05/10/1985 | 22 | 3 | STORIES OF JOHNNY | Some Bizzare FAITH 1 |
| 18/04/1987 | 41 | 2 | MOTHER FIST AND HER FIVE DAUGHTERS **MARC ALMOND & THE WILLING SINNERS** | Some Bizzare FAITH 2 |
| 08/10/1988 | 41 | 5 | ○ THE STARS WE ARE | Parlophone PCS 7324 |
| 16/06/1990 | 52 | 1 | ENCHANTED | Parlophone PCS 7344 |
| 01/06/1991 | 8 | 13 | **MEMORABILIA – THE SINGLES SOFT CELL & MARC ALMOND** | Mercury 8485121 |
| 26/10/1991 | 39 | 3 | TENEMENT SYMPHONY | Some Bizzare WX 442 |
| 09/03/1996 | 54 | 1 | FANTASTIC STAR | Some Bizzare 5286592 |

The Very Best Of Herb Alpert

## HERB ALPERT AND THE TIJUANA BRASS
US trumpeter (born 31/3/1935, Los Angeles, CA) who began playing at the age of eight. He was a staff writer for Keen Records in 1958, penning four consecutive hits for Sam Cooke before cutting his own records for Dore Records. He teamed up with Jerry Moss in 1962 and founded Carnival Records, which later became A&M (based on their initials) and was subsequently sold to Seagram for $500 million in 1989. He has won six Grammy Awards: Record of the Year, Best Instrumental Performance and Best Instrumental Arrangement in 1965 for *A Taste Of Honey*, Best Instrumental Performance and Best Instrumental Arrangement in 1965 for *What Now My Love* , and Best Pop Instrumental Performance in 1979 for *Rise*. Tijuana Brass was a studio band until 1965 when a proper group was assembled. Along with Jerry Moss he has a star on the Hollywood Walk of Fame. Alpert and Moss later formed Almo Records.

| DATE | POS | WKS | BPI | ALBUM TITLE | LABEL & NUMBER |
|---|---|---|---|---|---|
| 29/01/1966 | 4 | 138 | | **GOING PLACES** ▲[6] The album changed its label and catalogue number to A&M AMLS 965 during its chart run .................. | |
| | | | | | Pye NPL 28065/A&M AMLS 965 |
| 23/04/1966 | 2 | 42 | | **WHIPPED CREAM AND OTHER DELIGHTS** ▲[8] | Pye NPL 28058 |
| 28/05/1966 | 18 | 17 | | WHAT NOW MY LOVE ▲[9] The album changed its label and catalogue number to A&M AMLS 977 during its chart run ........... | |
| | | | | | Pye NPL 28077/A&M AMLS 977 |
| 11/02/1967 | 5 | 26 | | **S.R.O.** | Pye NSPL 28088 |
| 15/07/1967 | 21 | 10 | | SOUNDS LIKE | A&M AMLS 900 |
| 03/02/1968 | 26 | 19 | | NINTH | A&M AMLS 905 |
| 29/06/1968 | 4 | 21 | | **BEAT OF THE BRASS** ▲[2] | A&M AMLS 916 |
| 09/08/1969 | 30 | 4 | | WARM | A&M AMLS 937 |
| 14/03/1970 | 40 | 1 | | THE BRASS ARE COMIN' | A&M AMLS 962 |
| 30/05/1970 | 8 | 27 | | **GREATEST HITS** | A&M AMLS 980 |
| 27/06/1970 | 64 | 1 | | DOWN MEXICO WAY | A&M AMLS 974 |
| 13/11/1971 | 45 | 1 | | AMERICA | A&M AMLB 1000 |
| 12/11/1977 | 45 | 2 | | 40 GREATEST | K-Tel NE 1005 |
| 17/11/1979 | 37 | 7 | ○ | RISE | A&M AMLH 64790 |
| 04/04/1987 | 79 | 3 | | KEEP YOUR EYE ON ME | Breakout AMA 5125 |
| 28/09/1991 | 34 | 3 | ○ | THE VERY BEST OF HERB ALPERT | A&M 3971651 |

## ALT
Irish/ New Zealand group formed in Dublin in 1993 by Liam O'Maonlai (born 7/11/1964, Dublin) formerly of Hothouse Flowers, Andy White and Tim Finn (born 25/6/1952, Te Awamuta), formerly with Split Enz.

| | | | | | |
|---|---|---|---|---|---|
| 24/06/1995 | 67 | 1 | | ALTITUDE | Parlophone CDPCS 7377 |

## ALTERED IMAGES
UK group formed in Scotland by Claire Grogan (born 17/3/1962, vocals), Tony McDaid (guitar), Jim McKinven (guitar/keyboards), Michael 'Tich' Anderson (drums) and John McElhone (bass). Grogan later became an actress (having made her debut in the 1981 film *Gregory's Girl* and later appearing in *Eastenders* as Ros Thorne) and formed Universal Love School in 1989 whilst McElhone joined Hipsway and then Texas.

| | | | | | |
|---|---|---|---|---|---|
| 19/09/1981 | 26 | 21 | ○ | HAPPY BIRTHDAY | Epic EPC 84893 |
| 15/05/1982 | 12 | 10 | ○ | PINKY BLUE | Epic EPC 85665 |
| 25/06/1983 | 16 | 9 | | BITE | Epic EPC 25413 |

## ALTERN 8
UK keyboard duo Chris Peat and Mark Archer, who claimed to have been deckchair attendants and met while working as studio engineers at Blue Chip Studios. Archer later joined Slo-Moshun.

| | | | | | |
|---|---|---|---|---|---|
| 25/07/1992 | 11 | 4 | | FULL ON... MASK HYSTERIA | Network TOPCD 1 |

## SHOLA AMA
UK singer (born Mathurin Campbell) who was discovered at the age of fifteen by D'Influence, making her recording debut for Freak Street in 1995. She was named Best R&B Act and Best Newcomer at the 1997 MOBO Awards and Best UK Female Artist at the 1998 BRIT Awards.

| | | | | | |
|---|---|---|---|---|---|
| 13/09/1997 | 6 | 32 | ● | **MUCH LOVE** | WEA 3984200202 |

## AMAZULU
UK group formed by Annie Ruddock (born 2/7/1961, vocals), Rose Minor (vocals), Sharon Bailey (born 22/11/1957, percussion), Lesley Beach (born 30/9/1954, saxophone), Margo Sagov (guitar), Claire Kenny (bass) and Debbie Evans (drums).

| | | | | | |
|---|---|---|---|---|---|
| 06/12/1986 | 97 | 1 | | AMAZULU | Island ILPS 9851 |

## AMEN CORNER
UK group formed in Cardiff in 1966 by Andy Fairweather-Low (born 2/8/1950, Ystrad Mynach, Wales, guitar/vocals), Blue Weaver (born Derek Weaver, 3/3/1949, Cardiff, organ), Neil Jones (born 25/3/1949, Llanbradach, Wales, guitar), Clive Taylor (born 27/4/1949, Cardiff, bass), Mike Smith (born 4/11/1947, Neath, tenor sax), Alan Jones (born 6/2/1947, Swansea, baritone sax) and Dennis Bryon (born 14/4/1949, Cardiff, drums). Following their split in 1970, Fairweather-Low went solo. The group appeared in the 1969 horror film *Scream And Scream Again*.

| | | | | | |
|---|---|---|---|---|---|
| 30/03/1968 | 26 | 7 | | ROUND AMEN CORNER | Deram SML 1021 |
| 01/11/1969 | 19 | 1 | | EXPLOSIVE COMPANY | Immediate IMSP 023 |

## AMERICA
US trio formed in the UK in 1969 by Dewey Bunnell (born 19/1/1951, Harrogate), Gerry Beckley (born 12/9/1952, Forth Worth, TX) and Dan Peek (born 1/11/1950, Panama City, FL); the sons of US Air Force servicemen stationed in the UK. They re-located to the US after the success of their debut single. Peek left in 1976 to become a contemporary Christian artist. The group was named Best New Artist at the 1972 Grammy Awards.

| | | | | | |
|---|---|---|---|---|---|
| 22/01/1972 | 14 | 13 | | AMERICA ▲[1] | Warner Brothers K 46093 |
| 09/12/1972 | 21 | 5 | | HOMECOMING | Warner Brothers K 46180 |

| 10/11/1973 | 41 | 3 | ○ | HAT TRICK | Warner Brothers K 56016 |
| 07/02/1976 | 60 | 1 | ○ | HISTORY – AMERICA'S GREATEST HITS | Warner Brothers K 56169 |

**AMERICAN MUSIC CLUB** US group formed in San Francisco, CA by Mark Eitzel (born 1959, Walnut Creek, San Francisco, CA, guitar/vocals), Danny Pearson (bass), Vudi (guitar), Bruce Kaphan (steel guitar) and Tim Mooney (drums). Eitzel went solo in 1995.

| 27/03/1993 | 41 | 2 | | MERCURY | Virgin CDV 2708 |
| 24/09/1994 | 72 | 1 | | SAN FRANCISCO | Virgin CDV 2752 |

**AMICI FOREVER** UK/New Zealand/South African vocal operatic group formed by Jo Appleby (born Blackpool, soprano), Tsakane Valentine (born Pretoria, South Africa, soprano), Geoff Sewell (born Hawkes Bay, New Zealand, tenor), Nick Habbin (born Bournemouth, tenor) and David Garrett (born London, bass).

| 27/09/2003 | 39 | 9 | ● | THE OPERA BAND | Victor 82876558822 |

**AMORPHOUS ANDROGYNOUS** UK instrumental/production duo, formed by Garry Cobain and Brian Dougan, who also record as The Future Sound Of London. Their debut album under Amorphous Androgynous features Gary Lucas (formerly of Captain Beefheart) and Baluji Shrivastav.

| 17/08/2002 | 68 | 1 | | FSOL PRESENTS AMORPHOUS ANDROGYNOUS: THE ISNESS | Artful FSOLCD 101 |

**TORI AMOS** US singer (born Myra Ellen Amos, 22/8/1963, Newton, NC) who first made demos with Narada Michael Walden in 1983, without success. She signed with US Atlantic in 1987 and fronted Y Kant Tori Read before going solo in 1991.

| 18/01/1992 | 14 | 23 | ● | LITTLE EARTHQUAKES | East West 7567823582 |
| 12/02/1994 | ❶¹ | 13 | ● | UNDER THE PINK | East West 7567825672 |
| 03/02/1996 | 2 | 6 | ● | BOYS FOR PELE | East West 7567828622 |
| 16/05/1998 | 6 | 5 | ○ | FROM THE CHOIRGIRL HOTEL | Atlantic 7567830952 |
| 02/10/1999 | 22 | 2 | | TO VENUS AND BACK | Atlantic 7567832422 |
| 29/09/2001 | 16 | 2 | | STRANGE LITTLE GIRLS | Atlantic 7567834862 |
| 09/11/2002 | 26 | 1 | | SCARLET'S WALK | Epic 5087829 |
| 29/11/2003 | 74 | 1 | | TALES OF A LIBRARIAN | Atlantic 7567932232 |

**AMPS** US rock group formed in 1994 by Kim Deal (guitar/vocals), Nathan Farley (guitar), Luis Lerma (bass) and Jim MacPherson (drums) as Tammy & The Amps, shortening their name soon after. Deal and MacPherson had previously been members of The Breeders.

| 11/11/1995 | 60 | 1 | | PACER | 4AD CAD 5016CD |

**ANASTACIA** US singer (born Anastacia Newkirk, 17/9/1973, New York, raised in Chicago, IL) who, following her parents' divorce, graduated from the Professional Children's School in Manhattan. Diagnosed as suffering from Crohn's Disease at the age of thirteen, she overcame the symptoms to become a dancer, appearing on *Club MTV* and in the Salt-N-Pepa videos for *Everybody Get Up* and *Twist And Shout* (although in January 2003 she was diagnosed with breast cancer). After winning through to the final of the *Star Search* contest, she was signed by Daylight Records in March 1999. Named Best Pop Act at the 2001 MTV Europe Music Awards, she also performed at the 2002 FIFA World Cup draw in Japan.

| 14/10/2000 | 2 | 65 | ✪² | NOT THAT KIND ◇³ | Epic 4974122 |
| 08/12/2001 | 4 | 42 | ✪² | FREAK OF NATURE ◇³ | Epic 5047572 |
| 10/04/2004 | ❶² | 12+ | ✪ | ANASTACIA ◇ | Epic 5134717 |

**AND WHY NOT?** UK group formed by Wayne Gidden (guitar/vocals), Hylton Hayles (bass) and Michael Steer (drums).

| 10/03/1990 | 24 | 3 | | MOVE YOUR SKIN | Island ILPS 9935 |

**... AND YOU WILL KNOW US BY THE TRAIL OF DEAD** US band formed in Austin, TX in 1994 by Jason Reece (guitar/drums/vocals), Conrad Keely (guitar/drums/vocals), Kevin Allen (guitar) and Neil Busch (bass/samples). Their debut album was for Trance Syndicate in 1998; following the label's collapse, the group joined Merge in 1999.

| 16/03/2002 | 73 | 1 | | SOURCE TAGS AND CODES | Interscope 4932492 |

**CARLEEN ANDERSON** US R&B singer (born 1957, Houston, TX) who is the daughter of former James Brown backing singer Vicki Anderson (her stepfather is Bobby Byrd, a member of Brown's Famous Flames). She trained as a music teacher in Los Angeles, CA before coming to London and guesting on The Young Disciples' hit *Apparently Nothing*. She became the Brand New Heavies' lead singer from 1999; their first hit was a cover version of *Apparently Nothing*.

| 13/11/1993 | 38 | 1 | | DUSKY SAPPHO EP | Circa YRCDG 108 |
| 18/06/1994 | 12 | 4 | ○ | TRUE SPIRIT | Circa CIRCDX 30 |
| 02/05/1998 | 51 | 2 | | BLESSED BURDEN | Circa CIRCD 35 |

**IAN ANDERSON** UK singer (born 10/8/1947, Edinburgh) who had been a member of Blades until helping form Jethro Tull in 1967. In 1983 he launched a parallel solo career.

| 26/11/1983 | 78 | 1 | | WALK INTO LIGHT | Chrysalis CDL 1443 |

▲⁹ Number of weeks album topped the US chart  ◆¹² RIAA Diamond Awards  ◇³ IFPI Platinum Europe Awards

### JON ANDERSON
UK singer (born 25/10/1944, Accrington, Lancashire) who began his career with The Warriors before launching a solo career in 1967 as Hans Christian Anderson. He then joined Mabel Greer's Toyshop, which evolved into Yes. After a brief collaboration with Vangelis he went solo again in 1980 but found greater success with subsequent recordings with Vangelis. He returned to Yes in 1983, only to leave once again to tour with ex-members of the group as Anderson Wakeman Bruford Howe.

| | | | | |
|---|---|---|---|---|
| 24/07/1976 . . . . . 8 . . . . . . 10 . . . . . . O | **OLIAS OF SUNHILLOW** . . . . . . . . . . . . . . . . . . . . . . . . . . . . . . . . . . . . . . . . . . . . . . . . . . . . . . Atlantic K 50261 |
| 15/11/1980 . . . . . 38 . . . . . 3 . . . . . | SONG OF SEVEN . . . . . . . . . . . . . . . . . . . . . . . . . . . . . . . . . . . . . . . . . . . . . . . . . . . . . . . . Atlantic K 50756 |
| 05/06/1982 . . . . . 43 . . . . . 6 . . . . . | ANIMATION . . . . . . . . . . . . . . . . . . . . . . . . . . . . . . . . . . . . . . . . . . . . . . . . . . . . . . . . . . . Polydor POLD 5044 |

### LAURIE ANDERSON
US singer/composer/violinist/sculptor/filmmaker (born 5/6/1947, Chicago, IL) who has made and scored films/multimedia productions including *United States I–IV* (1983; the soundtrack was originally released as a five-album box set), *Mister Heartbreak* (1984) and *Home Of The Brave* (1986).

| | | | | |
|---|---|
| 01/05/1982 . . . . . 29 . . . . . 6 . . . . . | BIG SCIENCE . . . . . . . . . . . . . . . . . . . . . . . . . . . . . . . . . . . . . . . . . . . . . . . . . . . . Warner Brothers K 57002 |
| 10/03/1984 . . . . . 93 . . . . . 2 . . . . . | MISTER HEARTBREAK . . . . . . . . . . . . . . . . . . . . . . . . . . . . . . . . . . . . . . . . . . . . . . Warner Brothers 9250771 |

### LYNN ANDERSON
US country singer (born 26/9/1947, Grand Forks, ND, raised in Sacramento, CA) who won the California Horse Show Queen title in 1966.

| | |
|---|---|
| 17/04/1971 . . . . . 45 . . . . . . 1 . . . . . | ROSE GARDEN 1970 Grammy Award for Best Country and Western Vocal Performance . . . . . . . . . . . . . . . . . . . . . . . . . CBS 64333 |

### MOIRA ANDERSON
UK singer (born 1938, Kirkintilloch, East Dunbartonshire) educated at Ayr Academy.

| | |
|---|---|
| 20/06/1970 . . . . . 50 . . . . . . 1 . . . . . | THESE ARE MY SONGS **HARRY SECOMBE AND MOIRA ANDERSON** . . . . . . . . . . . . . . . . . . . . . . . . . . . . . . . . . . . . Decca SKL 5016 |
| 05/12/1981 . . . . . 46 . . . . . 5 . . . . . | GOLDEN MEMORIES . . . . . . . . . . . . . . . . . . . . . . . . . . . . . . . . . . . . . . . . . . . . . . . . . . . Warwick WW 5107 |

### SUNSHINE ANDERSON
US singer (born 26/10/1975, Charlotte, NC) who was discovered while queuing at a cafe at North Carolina Central University (where she earned a Bachelor of Science degree in criminal justice). She moved to Washington DC to work for the government, then relocated to Los Angeles and is managed by Macy Gray.

| | |
|---|---|
| 26/05/2001 . . . . . 39 . . . . . 6 . . . . . | YOUR WOMAN . . . . . . . . . . . . . . . . . . . . . . . . . . . . . . . . . . . . . . . . . . . . . . . . . . . . . . Atlantic 7567930112 |

### ANDERSON BRUFORD WAKEMAN HOWE
UK group formed by Jon Anderson (born 25/10/1944, Accrington, vocals), Bill Bruford (born 17/5/1948, London, drums), Rick Wakeman (born 18/5/1949, London, keyboards) and Steve Howe (born 8/4/1947, London, guitar), all four ex-members of Yes.

| | |
|---|---|
| 08/07/1989 . . . . . 14 . . . . . . 6 . . . . . O | ANDERSON BRUFORD WAKEMAN HOWE . . . . . . . . . . . . . . . . . . . . . . . . . . . . . . . . . . . . . . . . . . . . . . Arista 209970 |

### JOHN ANDERSON ORCHESTRA
Irish orchestra leader.

| | |
|---|---|
| 25/11/1995 . . . . . 56 . . . . . 5 . . . . . . O | PAN PIPES – ROMANCE OF IRELAND . . . . . . . . . . . . . . . . . . . . . . . . . . . . . . . . . . . . . . . . . . MCA MCD 60004 |

### PETER ANDRE
UK singer (born Peter James Andrea, 27/2/1973, London, raised in Australia) who began his career as a model. He went into semi-retirement in 1998 but returned in 2004 after appearing in the TV series *I'm A Celebrity... Get Me Out Of Here.*

| | |
|---|---|
| 12/10/1996 . . . . ❶¹ . . . . . 23 . . . . . . ✪ | **NATURAL** . . . . . . . . . . . . . . . . . . . . . . . . . . . . . . . . . . . . . . . . . . . . . . . . . . . . . . . . . Mushroom DX 2005 |
| 29/11/1997 . . . . . 28 . . . . . 4 . . . . . ● | TIME . . . . . . . . . . . . . . . . . . . . . . . . . . . . . . . . . . . . . . . . . . . . . . . . . . . . . . . . . . Mushroom MUSH 18CD |
| 19/06/2004 . . . . . 44 . . . . . . 1 . . . . . | THE LONG ROAD BACK . . . . . . . . . . . . . . . . . . . . . . . . . . . . . . . . . . . . . . . . . . . . . . East West 5046738102 |

### JULIE ANDREWS
UK singer (born Julia Wells, 1/10/1935, Walton-On-Thames, Surrey) who debuted at the age of ten in a her parent's variety act, appearing at the London Hippodrome in *Starlight Roof* two years later. After stage shows including *The Boy Friend* and *My Fair Lady*, her big break came in the title role of *Mary Poppins* and then in *The Sound Of Music*. She has since delved into other areas of film, and had her own comedy series on US TV, *Julie*. She won the 1964 Grammy Award for Best Recording For Children with Dick Van Dyke, David Tomlinson, Glynis Johns and Ed Wynn for *Mary Poppins*.

| | |
|---|---|
| 16/07/1983 . . . . . 63 . . . . . 5 . . . . . | LOVE ME TENDER . . . . . . . . . . . . . . . . . . . . . . . . . . . . . . . . . . . . . . . . . . . . . . . . . . . . . Peach River JULIE 1 |

### ANGEL – see BALAAM AND THE ANGEL

### ANGELIC UPSTARTS
UK punk group formed in South Shields in 1977 by Mensi (born Thomas Mensforth, vocals), Mond (guitar), Ronnie Wooden (bass) and Decca (drums). They signed to Small Wonder indie label before joining Warner Brothers. They disbanded in 1986, re-forming in 1988 and 1992.

| | |
|---|---|
| 18/08/1979 . . . . . 29 . . . . . . 7 . . . . . | TEENAGE WARNING . . . . . . . . . . . . . . . . . . . . . . . . . . . . . . . . . . . . . . . . . . . . . . . Warner Brothers K 50634 |
| 12/04/1980 . . . . . 54 . . . . . 3 . . . . . | WE'VE GOTTA GET OUT OF THIS PLACE . . . . . . . . . . . . . . . . . . . . . . . . . . . . . . . . . . . . Warner Brothers K 56806 |
| 07/06/1981 . . . . . 32 . . . . . 3 . . . . . | 2,000,000 VOICES . . . . . . . . . . . . . . . . . . . . . . . . . . . . . . . . . . . . . . . . . . . . . . . . . Zonophone ZONO 104 |
| 26/09/1981 . . . . . 27 . . . . . . 7 . . . . . | ANGELIC UPSTARTS . . . . . . . . . . . . . . . . . . . . . . . . . . . . . . . . . . . . . . . . . . . . . . . . . Zonophone ZEM 102 |

### ANIMAL NIGHTLIFE
UK group formed by Andy Polaris (vocals), Billy Chapman (saxophone), Steve Shawley (bass), John Crichison (piano), Len Chignoli (percussion), Steve 'Flid' Brown (guitar), Declan John Barclay (trumpet) and Paul Waller (drums).

| | |
|---|---|
| 24/08/1985 . . . . . 36 . . . . . 6 . . . . . | SHANGRI-LA . . . . . . . . . . . . . . . . . . . . . . . . . . . . . . . . . . . . . . . . . . . . . . . . . . . . . . . . . . Island ILPS 9830 |

## ANIMALS
**ANIMALS** UK rock group formed in 1962 by Eric Burdon (born 11/5/1941, Newcastle-upon-Tyne, vocals), Alan Price (born 19/4/1941, Fatfield, keyboards), Hilton Valentine (born 21/5/1943, North Shields, guitar), Chas Chandler (born Bryan Chandler, 18/12/1938, Heaton, bass) and John Steel (born 4/2/1941, Gateshead, drums) who made their first recordings in 1964. Following early success they split in 1966 (mainly through internal divisions centred around Burdon), with Burdon re-forming the group and taking top billing, then recording with War. The Animals re-formed in 1983. Chandler died after a lengthy illness on 17/7/1996. The group was inducted into the Rock & Roll Hall of Fame in 1994.

| DATE | POS | WKS | | ALBUM TITLE | LABEL & NUMBER |
|---|---|---|---|---|---|
| 14/11/1964 | 6 | 20 | | THE ANIMALS | Columbia 33SX 1669 |
| 22/05/1965 | 6 | 26 | | ANIMAL TRACKS | Columbia 33SX 1708 |
| 16/04/1966 | 4 | 20 | | MOST OF THE ANIMALS | Columbia 33SX 6035 |
| 28/05/1966 | 4 | 17 | | ANIMALISMS | Decca LK 4797 |
| 25/09/1971 | 18 | 3 | | MOST OF THE ANIMALS | MFP MFP 5218 |

**ANNIHILATOR** Canadian rock group formed by Jeff Waters (guitar), Randy Rampage (vocals) and Ray Hartmann (drums), with contributions from Anthony Greenham (guitar) and Wayne Darley (bass) when the group performed live. Greenham was later replaced by Dave Scott Davis, and Rampage was replaced by Coburn Pharr. Later members included Neil Goldberg (guitar) and Aaron Randall (vocals) and the group left Roadrunner for the Music Of Nations label.

| | | | | | |
|---|---|---|---|---|---|
| 11/08/1990 | 48 | 1 | | NEVER NEVERLAND | Roadrunner RR 93741 |

**ANOTHER LEVEL** UK vocal group formed in London by Bobak Kianoush (born 1/11/1978), Mark Baron (born 17/8/1974), Dane Bowers (born 28/11/1979) and Wayne Williams (born 20/1/1977). Williams quit in November 1999, Kianoush in December. Bowers later recorded with True Steppers. In June 2000 the remaining pair disbanded. Despite their nationality, they were named Best International Act at the 1997 MOBO Awards.

| DATE | POS | WKS | BPI | ALBUM TITLE | LABEL & NUMBER |
|---|---|---|---|---|---|
| 21/11/1998 | 13 | 25 | ✪ | ANOTHER LEVEL | Northwestside 74321582412 |
| 25/09/1999 | 7 | 15 | ● | NEXUS | Northwestside 74321700532 |

**ANT AND DEC** UK duo Anthony McPartlin (born 18/11/1975, Newcastle-Upon-Tyne) and Declan Donnelly (born 25/9/1975, Newcastle-upon-Tyne) who both began as actors. They first recorded as PJ And Duncan (the names of their characters in the children's TV programme *Byker Grove*). Later they found greater acclaim presenting the TV shows *CD:UK* and *Pop Idol*. In 2002 they appeared in a remake of the TV comedy *The Likely Lads*.

| DATE | POS | WKS | BPI | ALBUM TITLE | LABEL & NUMBER |
|---|---|---|---|---|---|
| 19/11/1994 | 5 | 20 | ✪ | PSYCHE – THE ALBUM | Xsrhythm TCD 2746 |
| 18/11/1995 | 46 | 8 | ● | TOP KATZ – THE ALBUM This and the above album credited to **PJ AND DUNCAN** | Telstar TCD 2793 |
| 24/05/1997 | 15 | 3 | | THE CULT OF ANT & DEC | Telstar TCD 2887 |

**ANTHRAX** US thrash group formed in New York by Scott 'Not' Ian (born 31/12/1963, New York, guitar), Neil Turbin (vocals), Dan Spitz (born 28/1/1963, Queens, NYC, guitar), Dan Lilker (born 18/10/1964, Queens, NYC, bass) and Charlie Benante (born 27/11/1962, New York, drums). Their first release was on their Megaforce label. Turbin and Lilker were replaced later by Frank Bello (born 9/7/1965, New York) and Joey Belladonna (born 30/10/1960, Oswego, NY) respectively, with John Bush (born 24/8/1963, Los Angeles, CA) in turn replacing Belladonna in 1992. Lilker went on to form Nuclear Assault.

| DATE | POS | WKS | BPI | ALBUM TITLE | LABEL & NUMBER |
|---|---|---|---|---|---|
| 18/04/1987 | 18 | 5 | ○ | AMONG THE LIVING | Island ILPS 9865 |
| 24/09/1988 | 12 | 4 | ○ | STATE OF EUPHORIA | Island ILPS 9916 |
| 08/09/1990 | 13 | 5 | | PERSISTENCE OF TIME | Island ILPS 9967 |
| 20/07/1991 | 13 | 5 | | ATTACK OF THE KILLER B'S | Island ILPS 9980 |
| 29/05/1993 | 14 | 3 | | SOUND OF THE WHITE NOISE | Elektra 7559614302 |
| 01/08/1998 | 73 | 1 | | VOLUME 8 – THE THREAT IS REAL! | Ignition IGN 740303 |

**ANTI-NOWHERE LEAGUE** UK punk group formed in Tunbridge Wells and led by Animal (born Nick Karmer, vocals) and Magoo (guitar). The single *Streets Of London* (a thrash version of the Ralph McTell folk classic) was banned and copies seized by the police after the B-side *So What* was considered to be obscene. They disbanded in 1988 and briefly re-formed in 1989 for a one-off album.

| DATE | POS | WKS | | ALBUM TITLE | LABEL & NUMBER |
|---|---|---|---|---|---|
| 22/05/1982 | 24 | 11 | | WE ARE… THE LEAGUE | WXYZ LMNOP 1 |
| 05/11/1983 | 88 | 1 | | LIVE IN YUGOSLAVIA | I.D. NOSE 3s |

**ANTI-PASTI** UK punk group formed in Derby in 1978 by Dugi Bell (guitar), Russell Maw (bass) and Eddie Barke (drums), adding Martin Roper (vocals). Barke left soon after their formation (he objected to a song entitled *Nailed To The Cross* because of his religious beliefs), as did Maw, replaced by Stu Winfield and Stan Smith respectively. By 1981 the line-up was Roper, Bell, Will Hoon (bass) and Kevin Nixon (drums), with Ollie Hoon (Will's brother) joining on guitar soon after. They disbanded in 1984.

| | | | | | |
|---|---|---|---|---|---|
| 15/08/1981 | 31 | 7 | | THE LAST CALL | Rondelet ABOUT 5 |

**A1** UK/Norwegian vocal group formed by Ben Adams (born 22/11/1981, Middlesex), Christian Ingebrigtsen (born 25/1/1977, Oslo), Paul Marrazi (born 24/1/1975, London) and Mark Read (born 7/11/1978, Kingston). Best UK Newcomer at the 2001 BRIT Awards.

| DATE | POS | WKS | BPI | ALBUM TITLE | LABEL & NUMBER |
|---|---|---|---|---|---|
| 04/12/1999 | 20 | 8 | ● | HERE WE COME | Columbia 4961362 |
| 02/12/2000 | 14 | 9 | ● | THE A LIST | Columbia 5011952 |
| 08/06/2002 | 15 | 2 | | MAKE IT GOOD | Columbia 5082212 |

## APACHE INDIAN
UK reggae singer (born Steve Kapur, 11/5/1967, Birmingham) of Asian descent. He first recorded in 1990 (*Movie Over India* on white label, which was subsequently distributed by Jet Star) and signed with Island in 1992.

06/02/1993 . . . . . 36 . . . . . . 2 . . . . . . NO RESERVATIONS . . . . . . . . . . . . . . . . . . . . . . . . . . . . . . . . . . . . . . . . . . . . . . . . . . . . . . . . . . . . . . . . . . . . . Island CID 8001

## APHEX TWIN
UK producer born in Limerick in Ireland on 18/8/1971 (real name Richard James). He allegedly used his royalties to buy an armoured tank! He also records as Powerpill and Polygon Window.

| | | | | |
|---|---|---|---|---|
| 19/03/1994 . . . . . 11 . . . . . . 3 . . . . . . | SELECTED AMBIENT WORKS VOLUME II | . . . . . . . . . . . . . . . | Warp WARPCD 21 |
| 11/02/1995 . . . . . 24 . . . . . . 2 . . . . . . | CLASSICS | . . . . . . . . . . . . . | R&S RS 94035CD |
| 06/05/1995 . . . . . 24 . . . . . . 2 . . . . . . | . . . I CARE BECAUSE YOU DO | . . . . . . . . . . . . . | Warp WARPCD 30 |
| 16/11/1996 . . . . . 62 . . . . . . 1 . . . . . . | RICHARD D JAMES ALBUM | . . . . . . . . . . . . . | Warp WARPCD 43 |
| 03/11/2001 . . . . . 22 . . . . . . 2 . . . . . . | DRUKQS | . . . . . . . . . . . . . | Warp WARPCD 92 |
| 05/04/2003 . . . . . 63 . . . . . . 1 . . . . . . | 26 MIXES FOR CASH | . . . . . . . . . . . . . | Warp WARPCD 102 |

## APOLLO 440
UK production/instrumental group formed by Trevor Gray (keyboards/vocals), Howard Gray (backing vocals) and Noko (vocals/guitar/keyboards), who amended their name to Apollo Four Forty. They also remix as Stealthsonic.

15/03/1997 . . . . . 62 . . . . . . 1 . . . . . . ELECTRO GLIDE IN BLUE . . . . . . . . . . . . . . . . . . . . . . . . . . . . . . . . . . . . . . . . . . . . . . . . . . . . . . . . Stealth Sonic SSX 2440CDR
18/09/1999 . . . . . 20 . . . . . . 3 . . . . . . GETTING' HIGH ON YOUR OWN SUPPLY . . . . . . . . . . . . . . . . . . . . . . . . . . . . . . . . . . . . . . . . . . . . . . . . . . . Epic SSX 3440CD

## APOLLO 2000
UK instrumental group assembled to record themes from various science fiction films and TV programmes.

27/04/1996 . . . . . 43 . . . . . . 2 . . . . . . OUT OF THIS WORLD . . . . . . . . . . . . . . . . . . . . . . . . . . . . . . . . . . . . . . . . . . . . . . . . . . . . . . . . . . . . . . . . . Telstar TCD 2816

## CARMEN APPICE — see JEFF BECK

## FIONA APPLE
US singer/songwriter (born Fiona Apple Maggart, 13/9/1977, New York City) signed by Clean Slate Records in 1994. She won the 1997 Grammy Award for Best Female Rock Vocal Performance for *Criminal*.

11/03/2000 . . . . . 46 . . . . . . 1 . . . . . . WHEN THE PAWN HITS THE CONFLICTS HE THINKS LIKE A KING WHAT HE KNOWS THROWS THE BLOWS WHEN HE GOES TO THE FIGHT AND HE'LL WIN THE WHOLE THING 'FORE HE ENTERS THE RING THERE'S NOBODY TO BATTER WHEN YOUR MIND IS YOUR MIGHT SO WHEN YOU GO SOLO YOU HOLD YOUR OWN HAND AND REMEMBER THAT DEPTH IS THE GREATEST OF HEIGHTS AND IF YOU KNOW WHERE YOU STAND THEN YOU KNOW WHERE TO LAND AND IF YOU FALL IT WON'T MATTER CUZ YOU'LL KNOW THAT YOU'RE RIGHT . . . . . . . . . . . . . . . . . . . . . . . . . . . . . . . . . . . . . . . . . . . . . . . . . . . . . . . . . . . . . . . . . . . . . . . Columbia 4964282

## KIM APPLEBY
UK singer (born 28/8/1961, London) who formed half of Mel And Kim with her sister until Mel's death in 1990.

08/12/1990 . . . . . 23 . . . . . 13 . . . . . . ● KIM APPLEBY . . . . . . . . . . . . . . . . . . . . . . . . . . . . . . . . . . . . . . . . . . . . . . . . . . . . . . . . . . . . . . . . Parlophone PCS 7348

## APPLETON
Canadian vocal duo formed by ex-All Saints sisters Nicole (born 7/12/1974, Canada) and Natalie (born 14/5/1973, Canada) Appleton. Natalie married Prodigy's Liam Howlett in June 2002.

08/03/2003 . . . . . 9 . . . . . 6 . . . . . . ○ EVERYTHING'S EVENTUAL . . . . . . . . . . . . . . . . . . . . . . . . . . . . . . . . . . . . . . . . . . . . . . . . . . . . . . . . . . Polydor 0651992

## APRIL WINE
Canadian group formed in Montreal, Quebec in 1969 by Myles Goodwyn (born 23/6/1948, Halifax, Nova Scotia, vocals), David Henman (guitar), Jim Clench (bass) and Richie Henman (drums). The best-known line-up featured Goodwyn, Brian Greenway (born 1/10/1951, guitar), Gary Moffet (born 22/6/1949, guitar), Steve Lang (born 24/3/1949, bass) and Jerry Mercer (born 27/4/1939, drums). They disbanded in 1985 and re-formed in 2000.

15/03/1980 . . . . . 34 . . . . . . 5 . . . . . . HARDER... FASTER . . . . . . . . . . . . . . . . . . . . . . . . . . . . . . . . . . . . . . . . . . . . . . . . . . . . . . . . . . . . . . . . . Capitol EST 12013
24/01/1981 . . . . . 48 . . . . . . 3 . . . . . . THE NATURE OF THE BEAST . . . . . . . . . . . . . . . . . . . . . . . . . . . . . . . . . . . . . . . . . . . . . . . . . . . . . . . . Capitol EST 12125

## AQUA
Danish pop group formed by Rene Dif (born 17/10/1967, Fredriksberg), Lene Nystrom (born 2/10/1973, Tonsberg, Norway), Soren Rasted (born 13/6/1969, Blovstod) and Claus Norreen (born 5/6/1970, Charlottenlund).

15/11/1997 . . . . . 6 . . . . . 47 . . . . . . ✪ AQUARIUM ◇⁴ . . . . . . . . . . . . . . . . . . . . . . . . . . . . . . . . . . . . . . . . . . . . . . . . . . . . . . . . . . Universal UMD 85020
11/03/2000 . . . . . 24 . . . . . . 2 . . . . . . AQUARIUS ◇ . . . . . . . . . . . . . . . . . . . . . . . . . . . . . . . . . . . . . . . . . . . . . . . . . . . . . . . . . . . . . . . . . Universal 1538102

## AQUALUNG
UK singer Matt Hayes.

12/10/2002 . . . . . 15 . . . . . . 6 . . . . . . ○ AQUALUNG . . . . . . . . . . . . . . . . . . . . . . . . . . . . . . . . . . . . . . . . . . . . . . . . . . . . . . . . . . . . . . . . . . B Unique 5046606982

## ARAB STRAP
UK group formed in 1995 by long-time friends Aidan Moffett (vocals) and Malcolm Middleton (multi-instrumentalist). They released their debut record in 1996.

02/05/1998 . . . . . 37 . . . . . . 2 . . . . . . PHILOPHOBIA. . . . . . . . . . . . . . . . . . . . . . . . . . . . . . . . . . . . . . . . . . . . . . . . . . . . . . . Chemikal Underground CHEM 021CD

## ARCADIA
UK group formed by Simon Le Bon (born 27/10/1958, Bushey), Nick Rhodes (born Nicholas Bates, 8/6/1962, Birmingham) and Roger Taylor (born 26/4/1960, Castle Bromwich). They were all previously in Duran Duran.

07/12/1985 . . . . . 30 . . . . . 10 . . . . . . SO RED THE ROSE. . . . . . . . . . . . . . . . . . . . . . . . . . . . . . . . . . . . . . . . . . . . . . . . . . . . . . . . . . . Parlophone Odeon PCSD 101

## TASMIN ARCHER
UK singer (born 1964, Bradford) who was a backing singer at Flexible Response studios when she formed a songwriting partnership with John Hughes and John Beck. She was named Best UK Newcomer at the 1993 BRIT Awards.

31/10/1992 . . . . . 8 . . . . . 42 . . . . . . ● GREAT EXPECTATIONS. . . . . . . . . . . . . . . . . . . . . . . . . . . . . . . . . . . . . . . . . . . . . . . . . . . . . . . . . EMI CDEMC 3624

## TINA ARENA
Australian singer/songwriter (born Phillipa Arena, 1/11/1967, Melbourne) who began performing at eight and made her record debut in 1985. She married her manager Ralph Carr.

20/05/1995 . . . . . 11 . . . . . 15 . . . . . . ○ DON'T ASK . . . . . . . . . . . . . . . . . . . . . . . . . . . . . . . . . . . . . . . . . . . . . . . . . . . . . . . . . . . . . . . . . . Columbia 4778862

## ARGENT
UK group formed in Hertfordshire in 1969 by Rod Argent (born 14/6/1945, St Albans, vocals/keyboards) with Jim Rodford (born 7/7/1941, St Albans, bass), Robert Henrit (born 2/5/1944, Broxbourne, drums) and Russ Ballard (born 31/10/1947, Waltham Cross, guitar). They disbanded in 1976, Argent later recording as Rodriguez Argentina and Ballard becoming a successful songwriter. Rodford and Henrit later joined The Kinks.

| 29/04/1972 | 13 | 8 | | ALL TOGETHER NOW | Epic EPC 64962 |
| 31/03/1973 | 49 | 1 | | IN DEEP | Epic EPC 65475 |

## INDIA.ARIE
US singer (born India Arie Simpson, 1976, Denver, CO) who moved to Atlanta, GA when she was thirteen. She initially worked with Groovement and the EarthShare label. Groovement covered her songs on the EarthShare label and this led to a deal with Motown in 1998. She received the 2002 Grammy Award for the Best R&B Album for *Voyage To India*.

| 07/07/2001 | 55 | 3 | ○ | ACOUSTIC SOUL | Motown 137702 |

## JOAN ARMATRADING
UK singer/guitarist/pianist (born 9/12/1950, Basseterre, St Kitts, West Indies) whose family relocated to Birmingham in 1958. Linking with lyricist Pam Nestor in 1972, she made her first recordings for Cube Records in 1973. She also took part in the *Perfect Day* project for the BBC's Children In Need charity. She was awarded an MBE in the 2001 Queen's Birthday Honours List.

| 04/09/1976 | 12 | 27 | ● | JOAN ARMATRADING | A&M AMLH 64588 |
| 01/10/1977 | 6 | 11 | ● | SHOW SOME EMOTION | A&M AMLH 68433 |
| 14/10/1978 | 13 | 10 | | TO THE LIMIT | A&M AMLH 64732 |
| 24/05/1980 | 5 | 23 | ● | ME MYSELF I | A&M AMLH 64809 |
| 12/09/1981 | 6 | 29 | ● | WALK UNDER LADDERS | A&M AMLH 64876 |
| 12/03/1983 | 10 | 14 | ● | THE KEY | A&M AMLX 64912 |
| 26/11/1983 | 18 | 32 | | TRACK RECORD | A&M JA 2001 |
| 16/02/1985 | 14 | 12 | ○ | SECRET SECRETS | A&M AMA 5040 |
| 24/05/1986 | 34 | 6 | ○ | SLEIGHT OF HAND | A&M AMA 5130 |
| 16/07/1988 | 28 | 10 | ○ | THE SHOUTING STAGE | A&M AMA 5211 |
| 16/06/1990 | 29 | 4 | | HEARTS AND FLOWERS | A&M 3952981 |
| 16/03/1991 | 9 | 11 | ● | THE VERY BEST OF JOAN ARMATRADING | A&M 3971221 |
| 20/06/1992 | 34 | 2 | | SQUARE THE CIRCLE | A&M 3953882 |
| 10/06/1995 | 48 | 2 | | WHAT'S INSIDE | RCA 74321272692 |

## ARMOURY SHOW
UK group formed in 1984 by Richard Jobson (born 6/10/1960, Dunfermline, guitar/vocals), Russell Webb (bass/vocals), John McGeoch (born 28/5/1955, Greenock, guitar) and John Doyle (drums). Jobson was previously in The Skids. Armoury Show disbanded in 1987.

| 21/09/1985 | 57 | 1 | | WAITING FOR THE FLOODS | Parlophone ARM 1 |

## CRAIG ARMSTRONG
UK composer/arranger who studied at the Royal Academy of Music and the Scottish Arts Council, winning various awards for his compositions. As well as writing a number of hits for the likes of Texas, Big Dish and Massive Attack, he conducted the strings on albums by Madonna, U2 and Passengers.

| 27/04/2002 | 61 | 1 | | AS IF TO NOTHING | Melankolic CDSAD 13 |

## LOUIS ARMSTRONG
US trumpeter/vocalist (born 4/8/1901, New Orleans, LA, although Armstrong claimed his birthday was 4/7/1900) who joined his first band in 1922. By 1930 he was the most successful black musician in the world, influencing just about every trumpeter around. Universally known as 'Satchmo', he made numerous appearances in films and on TV. He died on 6/7/1971 in New York and was inducted into the Rock & Roll Hall of Fame in 1990. His 1928 recording *West End Blues* was awarded a special Grammy in 1974. He has a star on the Hollywood Walk of Fame.

| 28/07/1956 | 4 | 1 | | AT THE CRESCENDO | Brunswick LAT 8084 |
| 22/10/1960 | 20 | 1 | | SATCHMO PLAYS KING OLIVER | Audio Fidelity AFLP 1930 |
| 28/10/1961 | 20 | 1 | | JAZZ CLASSICS | Ace Of Hearts AH 7 |
| 27/06/1964 | 11 | 6 | | HELLO DOLLY ▲[6] | London HAR 8190 |
| 16/11/1968 | 37 | 3 | | WHAT A WONDERFUL WORLD | Stateside SSL 10247 |
| 20/02/1982 | 30 | 3 | | THE VERY BEST OF LOUIS ARMSTRONG | Warwick WW 5112 |
| 21/05/1994 | 48 | 3 | | THE ULTIMATE COLLECTION | Bluebird 74321197062 |
| 17/12/1994 | 10 | 12 | ● | WE HAVE ALL THE TIME IN THE WORLD – THE VERY BEST OF LOUIS ARMSTRONG | EMI CDEMTV 89 |
| 25/10/2003 | 75 | 1 | | AT HIS VERY BEST | UCJ 9812425 |

## DAVID ARNOLD
UK pianist/composer (born 1962, Luton); after failing auditions for The Waterboys and The Clash, he scored numerous low-budget films before bigger commissions such as *Stargate* (1994) and *Independence Day* (1996). In 1997 he put together *Shaken Not Stirred*, a collection of James Bond themes, featuring The Propellerheads, Chrissie Hynde, Pulp, David McAlmont and Iggy Pop among others.

| 17/08/1996 | 71 | 1 | | INDEPENDENCE DAY Original soundtrack to the film and 1996 Grammy Award for Best Instrumental for a Movie | RCA Victor 09026685642 |

01/11/1997 . . . . . 11 . . . . . 9 . . . . . . O | SHAKEN AND STIRRED . . . . . . . . . . . . . . . . . . . . . . . . . . . . . . . . . . . . . . . . . . . . . . . East West 3984207382

**ARRESTED DEVELOPMENT** US hip hop group formed in Atlanta, GA in 1988 by Speech (born Todd Thomas, 25/10/1968, Milwaukee, WI), Aerie Taree (born 10/1/1973, Milwaukee), Monto Eshe (born 23/12/1974, Georgia), Nadriah, Rasa Don (born Donald Jones, 22/11/1968, New Jersey), DJ Headliner (born Tim Barnwell, 26/7/1967, New Jersey) and Baba Oje (born 15/5/1932, Laurie, MS). They disbanded in 1994, Speech going solo in 1996. They won two Grammy Awards: Best New Artist and Best Rap Performance by a Group for *Tennessee*, both in 1992.

31/10/1992 . . . . . 3 . . . . . 34 . . . . . . ✪ | **3 YEARS, 5 MONTHS AND 2 DAYS IN THE LIFE OF…** The title refers to the length of time spent negotiating with Chrysalis before signing with the label . . . . . . . . . . . . . . . . . . . . . . . . . . . . . . . . . . . . . . . . . . . . . . . . . . . . . . . . . Cooltempo CCD 1929
10/04/1993 . . . . . 40 . . . . . 3 . . . . . . O | UNPLUGGED . . . . . . . . . . . . . . . . . . . . . . . . . . . . . . . . . . . . . . . . . . . . . . . . . . . . . . . . . . . . . Cooltempo CTCD 33
18/06/1994 . . . . . 16 . . . . . 3 . . . . . | ZINGALAMDUNI . . . . . . . . . . . . . . . . . . . . . . . . . . . . . . . . . . . . . . . . . . . . . . . . . . . . . . . . . Cooltempo CTCD 42

**STEVE ARRINGTON** US singer (born in Dayton, OH) who was lead singer with funk group Slave before going solo in 1982.
13/04/1985 . . . . . 41 . . . . . 11 . . . . . | DANCIN' IN THE KEY OF LIFE . . . . . . . . . . . . . . . . . . . . . . . . . . . . . . . . . . . . . . . . . . . . . . . . . . . Atlantic 7812451

**ART OF NOISE** UK studio group formed by Anne Dudley (born 7/5/1960, Chatham), Jonathan 'JJ' Jeczalik (born 11/5/1955) and Gary Langan, with Trevor Horn and Paul Morley of ZTT Records also contributing. They disbanded in 1990. Dudley was later a songwriter, winning an Oscar for her work on the 1997 film *The Full Monty*. The group was named by ZTT Records' Paul Morley after the 1909 avant garde Futurist Manifesto in Italy. Max Headroom is a TV animated character with Matt Frewer providing the voice. They won the 1986 Grammy Award for Best Rock Instrumental Performance with Duane Eddy for *Peter Gunn*.

03/11/1984 . . . . . 27 . . . . . 17 . . . . . . O | (WHO'S AFRAID OF) THE ART OF NOISE . . . . . . . . . . . . . . . . . . . . . . . . . . . . . . . . . . . . . . . . . . ZTT ZTTIQ 2
26/04/1986 . . . . . 18 . . . . . 15 . . . . . | IN VISIBLE SILENCE . . . . . . . . . . . . . . . . . . . . . . . . . . . . . . . . . . . . . . . . . . . . . . . . . . . . . . . Chrysalis WOL 2
10/10/1987 . . . . . 55 . . . . . 2 . . . . . | IN NO SENSE/NONSENSE . . . . . . . . . . . . . . . . . . . . . . . . . . . . . . . . . . . . . . . . . . . . . . . . . . . China WOL 4
03/12/1988 . . . . . 55 . . . . . 3 . . . . . | THE BEST OF ART OF NOISE . . . . . . . . . . . . . . . . . . . . . . . . . . . . . . . . . . . . . . . . . . . . . . . . China 8373671

**ARTFUL DODGER** UK production duo Mark Hill and Pete Devereux from Southampton. They split in July 2001, Devereux later joining Dave Low. The group also launched the Centric label.
02/12/2000 . . . . . 18 . . . . . 27 . . . . . . ● | IT'S ALL ABOUT THE STRAGGLERS . . . . . . . . . . . . . . . . . . . . . . . . . . . . . . . . . . . . . . . . . . . ffrr 8573859092

**DAVEY ARTHUR —** see **FUREYS WITH DAVEY ARTHUR**

**A.S.A.P.** UK group that includes Adrian Smith (guitar/vocals), Andy Barnett (guitar/vocals), Dave Colwell (guitar/vocals), Richard Young (keyboards), Robin Clayton (bass) and Zak Starkey (drums). Smith had previously been with Iron Maiden; Starkey is the son of Beatles drummer Ringo Starr. Their name stands for Adrian Smith And Project.
04/11/1989 . . . . . 70 . . . . . 1 . . . . . | SILVER AND GOLD . . . . . . . . . . . . . . . . . . . . . . . . . . . . . . . . . . . . . . . . . . . . . . . . . . . . . . EMI EMC 3566

**ASH** UK group formed in Ulster by Tim Wheeler (born 4/1/1977, Downpatrick, vocals/guitar), Mark Hamilton (born 21/3/1977, Lisburn, bass) and Rick McMurray (born 11/7/1975, Larne, drums). They were still at school when they formed and signed with Infectious, adding Charlotte Hatherley (born 20/6/1979, London) for the single *A Life Less Ordinary*.

18/05/1996 . . . ❶¹ . . . . 27 . . . . . . ✪ | **1977** . . . . . . . . . . . . . . . . . . . . . . . . . . . . . . . . . . . . . . . . . . . . . . . . . . . . . . . . . . . . Infectious INFECT 40CD
17/10/1998 . . . . . 7 . . . . . 4 . . . . . ● | **NU-CLEAR SOUNDS** . . . . . . . . . . . . . . . . . . . . . . . . . . . . . . . . . . . . . . . . . . . . . . . . . . . Infectious INFECT 060CD
05/05/2001 . . . ❶¹ . . . . 28 . . . . . . ✪ | **FREE ALL ANGELS** . . . . . . . . . . . . . . . . . . . . . . . . . . . . . . . . . . . . . . . . . . . . . . . . . . . Infectious INFECT 100CD
21/09/2002 . . . . . 3 . . . . . 6 . . . . . ● | **INTERGALACTIC SONIC 7'S** . . . . . . . . . . . . . . . . . . . . . . . . . . . . . . . . . . . . . . . . . . . . Infectious INFECT 120CD
29/05/2004 . . . . . 5 . . . . . 5+ . . . . . . O | **MELTDOWN** . . . . . . . . . . . . . . . . . . . . . . . . . . . . . . . . . . . . . . . . . . . . . . . . . . . . . . . . Infectious 5046732462

**ASHANTI** US singer (born Ashanti Douglas, 13/10/1980, Glen Cove, NY) first known as an actress. She appeared in *Malcolm X* (1992) and *Who's Da Man* and was guest singer on hits by Ja Rule and Fat Joe before going solo. On 20th April 2002 her debut album *Ashanti* entered the US charts at #1 (with a female debut record for first week sales of 503,000, the same week her first solo single *Foolish* topped the singles chart. Also, her single with Fat Joe (*What's Luv*) was at #2, making her the first female to hold the top two positions on the *Billboard* Hot 100. She won the 2002 MOBO Award for Best R&B Act.

20/04/2002 . . . . . 3 . . . . . 36 . . . . . . ✪ | **ASHANTI** ▲³ 2002 Grammy Award for Best Contemporary R&B Album . . . . . . . . . . . . . . . . . Mercury 5868302
12/07/2003 . . . . . 5 . . . . . 8 . . . . . ● | **CHAPTER II** ▲² . . . . . . . . . . . . . . . . . . . . . . . . . . . . . . . . . . . . . . . . . . . . . . . . . . . . . . . . Murder Inc 9808434

**RICHARD ASHCROFT** UK singer (born 11/9/1971, Wigan) who was lead vocalist with The Verve from their formation in 1989. He went solo when they disbanded in April 1999.
08/07/2000 . . . ❶¹ . . . . 20 . . . . . . ✪ | **ALONE WITH EVERYBODY** . . . . . . . . . . . . . . . . . . . . . . . . . . . . . . . . . . . . . . . . . . . . . . Hut CDHUTX 63
02/11/2002 . . . . . 3 . . . . . 10 . . . . . ● | **HUMAN CONDITIONS** . . . . . . . . . . . . . . . . . . . . . . . . . . . . . . . . . . . . . . . . . . . . . . . . . . Hut CDHUT 77

**ASHFORD AND SIMPSON** US husband and wife vocal duo Nicholas Ashford (born 4/5/1942, Fairfield, SC) and Valerie Simpson (born 26/8/1946, New York) who first recorded as Valerie & Nick in 1964. They became more successful as songwriters and producers at Motown Records. They resumed recording in 1973. Valerie made a number of singles with Marvin Gaye, uncredited, standing in for the ill Tammi Terrell. Ashford appeared in the 1991 film *New Jack City*.
16/02/1985 . . . . . 42 . . . . . 6 . . . . . | SOLID . . . . . . . . . . . . . . . . . . . . . . . . . . . . . . . . . . . . . . . . . . . . . . . . . . . . . . . . . . . . . Capitol SASH 1

**ASIA** UK art rock group with John Wetton (born 12/7/1949, Derby, vocals, ex-King Crimson, Uriah Heep and Roxy Music), Steve Howe (born 8/4/1947, London, guitar, ex-Yes), Carl Palmer (born 20/3/1947, Birmingham, drums/percussion, ex-Emerson, Lake And Palmer) and Geoff Downes (keyboards, ex-Buggles and Yes). Later members included Mandy Meyer and Pat Thrall. Wetton was replaced by Greg Lake (born 10/11/1948, Bournemouth, ex-Emerson, Lake And Palmer) between 1983 and 1985.
10/04/1982 . . . . . 11 . . . . . 38 . . . . . . ● | ASIA ▲⁹ . . . . . . . . . . . . . . . . . . . . . . . . . . . . . . . . . . . . . . . . . . . . . . . . . . . . . . . . . . . Geffen GEF 85577

O Silver disc  ● Gold disc  ✪ Platinum disc (additional platinum units are indicated by a figure following the symbol)  ❶⁹ Number of weeks album topped the UK chart

| DATE | POS | WKS | BPI | | |
|------|-----|-----|-----|---|---|
| 20/08/1983 | 5 | 11 | ○ | ALPHA | Geffen GEF 25508 |
| 14/12/1985 | 68 | 1 | | ASTRA | Geffen GEF 26413 |

**ASIAN DUB FOUNDATION** UK rock group formed in London in 1993 by Aniruddha Das (aka Doctor Das, bass), Deeder Zaman (aka Master D, raps), DJ John Pandit (aka Panfit G), Steve Chandra Savale (aka Chandrasonic, guitar) and Sanjay Tailor (aka Sun J).

| | | | | | |
|------|-----|-----|-----|---|---|
| 23/05/1998 | 20 | 3 | | RAFI'S REVENGE | ffrr 5560062 |
| 01/04/2000 | 20 | 3 | | COMMUNITY MUSIC | ffrr 8573820422 |

**ASSOCIATES** UK new wave group formed in Dundee by Billy MacKenzie (born 27/3/1957, Dundee) and Alan Rankine who first met in 1976. Rankine later left and MacKenzie re-formed the group. MacKenzie was found dead in a garden shed on 22/1/1997, believed to have commited suicide following his mother's death, just after signing a six-album solo artist deal with Nude.

| | | | | | |
|------|-----|-----|-----|---|---|
| 22/05/1982 | 10 | 20 | | **SULK** | Associates ASCL 1 |
| 16/02/1985 | 23 | 7 | | PERHAPS | WEA WX 9 |
| 31/03/1990 | 71 | 1 | | WILD AND LONELY | Circa 11 |

**RICK ASTLEY** UK singer (born 6/2/1966, Newton-le-Willows) who played drums with FBI before becoming their lead singer and subsequently being discovered by Stock, Aitken And Waterman. Won 1998 Best Single BRIT Award for *Never Gonna Give You Up*.

| | | | | | |
|------|-----|-----|-----|---|---|
| 28/11/1987 | ❶[1] | 34 | ○[4] | **WHENEVER YOU NEED SOMEBODY** | RCA PL 71529 |
| 10/12/1988 | 8 | 19 | ○ | HOLD ME IN YOUR ARMS | RCA PL 71932 |
| 02/03/1991 | 9 | 9 | ● | FREE | RCA PL 74896 |
| 14/09/2002 | 16 | 4 | ● | GREATEST HITS | BMG 74321955122 |

**ASWAD** UK reggae group formed in 1975 by Brinsley Forde (born 1952, Guyana, guitar/vocals), Donald Benjamin (guitar), Courtney Hemmings (keyboards), Ras George (bass) and Angus 'Drummie' Zeb (drums), named from the Arabic word for 'black'. By 1986 they were the trio of Forde, Zeb and Tony Gad (guitar). Forde was previously a child actor in the TV series *Here Come The Double Deckers*. They received the Outstanding Contribution Award at the 2000 MOBO Awards.

| | | | | | |
|------|-----|-----|-----|---|---|
| 24/07/1982 | 50 | 6 | | NOT SATISFIED | CBS 85666 |
| 10/12/1983 | 57 | 16 | | LIVE AND DIRECT | Island IMA 6 |
| 03/11/1984 | 48 | 2 | | REBEL SOULS | Island ILPS 9780 |
| 28/06/1986 | 71 | 3 | | TO THE TOP | Simba SIMBALP 2 |
| 09/04/1988 | 10 | 15 | ● | **DISTANT THUNDER** | Mango ILPS 9895 |
| 03/12/1988 | 52 | 8 | | RENAISSANCE | Stylus SMR 866 |
| 22/09/1990 | 51 | 2 | | TOO WICKED | Mango MLPS 1054 |
| 09/07/1994 | 38 | 5 | | RISE AND SHINE | Bubblin' BUBBCD 1 |
| 24/08/2002 | 54 | 1 | | COOL SUMMER REGGAE | Universal Music TV 0643762 |

**AT THE DRIVE IN** US rock group from El Paso, TX with Cedric Bixler (vocals), Omar Rodriguez (guitar), Jim Ward (guitar), Paul Hinojos (bass) and Tony Hajjar (drums).

| | | | | | |
|------|-----|-----|-----|---|---|
| 30/09/2000 | 33 | 2 | | RELATIONSHIP OF COMMAND | Grand Royal CDVUS 184 |

**ATB** German DJ/producer Andre Tanneburger.

| | | | | | |
|------|-----|-----|-----|---|---|
| 08/04/2000 | 32 | 3 | ○ | MOVIN MELODIES | Sound Of Ministry ATB CDZ1 |

**ATHLETE** UK group formed in London in 2000 by Joel Pott (guitar/vocals), Carey Willetts (bass/vocals), Tim Wanstall (keyboards/vocals) and Steve Roberts (drums/vocals).

| | | | | | |
|------|-----|-----|-----|---|---|
| 19/04/2003 | 19 | 21 | ● | VEHICLES & ANIMALS | Parlophone 5842112 |

**ATHLETICO SPIZZ 80** UK group formed in Birmingham in 1977 by Spizz and Pete O'Dowd as Spizz 77. They changed name to Spizz Oil in 1978 but disbanded after two EPs. Spizz then linked with Jim Solar and Mark Coalfield as Spizzenergi, with O'Dowd returning soon after (although he had by now changed name to Pete Petrol). Dave Scott and Hiro Shima joined in 1979, Shima later replaced by CP Snare. They changed name again to Athletico Spizz 80 on New Year's Day 1980, a year later changing to The Spizzles. They have since recorded as Spizzenergi 2, Spizzorwell, Spizz's Big Business, Spizzsexual, Spizzvision, Spizz Oil and Spizzmas.

| | | | | | |
|------|-----|-----|-----|---|---|
| 26/07/1980 | 27 | 5 | | DO A RUNNER | A&M AMLE 68514 |

**CHET ATKINS** US guitarist (born Chester Burton Atkins, 20/6/1924 Luttrell, TN) who began as a fiddler with the Dixieland Swingers in Knoxville, TN in the 1940s. First recording in 1946, he joined RCA the following year, staying until the early 1980s. As well as being an artist in his own right (with over 100 albums to his name), Atkins worked with numerous RCA stars (as either a producer or session guitarist) including Elvis Presley, Jim Reeves and Don Gibson. He moved to Columbia in the early 1980s. He won thirteen Grammy Awards: Best Instrumental Performance (other than Jazz) in 1967 for *Chet Atkins Picks The Best*; Best Country Instrumental Performance in 1970 with Jerry Reed for *Me And Jerry*; Best Country Instrumental Performance in 1971 for *Snowbird*; Best Country Instrumental Performance in 1974 with Merle Travis for *The Atkins-Travis Traveling Show*; Best Country Instrumental Performance in 1975 for *The Entertainer*; Best Country Instrumental Performance in 1976 with Les Paul for *Chester And Lester*; Best Country Instrumental Performance in 1981 for *Country, After All These Years*; Best Country Instrumental Performance in 1985 with Mark Knoffler for *Cosmic Square Dance*; Best Country Vocal Collaboration in 1990 with Mark Knoffler for *Poor Boy Blues*; Best Country Instrumental Performance in 1990 with Mark Knoffler for *So Soft Your Goodbye*; Best Country Instrumental Performance in 1992 with Jerry Reed for *Sneakin' Around;* Best Country Instrumental Performance in 1994 for *Young Thing;* and Best Country Instrumental in 1996 for *Jam Man*. He died from cancer on 30/6/2001 and was inducted into the Rock and Roll Hall of Fame in 2002.

| | | | | | |
|------|-----|-----|-----|---|---|
| 18/03/1961 | 20 | 1 | | THE OTHER CHET ATKINS | RCA RD 27194 |

| | | | | |
|---|---|---|---|---|
| 17/06/1961.....19......1..... | CHET ATKINS WORKSHOP............................................................RCA RD 27214 |
| 23/02/1963.....17......3..... | CARIBBEAN GUITAR ..............................................................RCA RD 7519 |
| 24/11/1990.....41.....11..... | NECK AND NECK **CHET ATKINS AND MARK KNOPFLER** .....................................CBS 4674351 |

**ROWAN ATKINSON** UK comedian (born 6/1/1955, Newcastle-Upon-Tyne) who was first known as part of the *Not The Nine O'clock News* team before going solo as a stand-up comedian. His later comic creations include Mr Bean and Edmund Blackadder.

| | |
|---|---|
| 07/02/1981.....44......9......O | LIVE IN BELFAST ..............................................................Arista SPART 1150 |

**ATLANTIC STARR** US soul group formed in White Plains, NY in 1976 by Sharon Bryant (vocals), David Lewis (vocals/keyboards/guitar), Jonathan Lewis (keyboards/trombone), Wayne Lewis (keyboards/vocals), Koran Daniels (saxophone), William Suddeeth (trumpet), Clifford Archer (bass), Joseph Phillips (percussion) and Porter Caroll Jr (drums). Bryant left in 1984 and was replaced by Barbara Weathers; Weathers left in 1989 and was replaced by Porscha Martin. Martin left in 1991 and was replaced by Rachel Oliver, who in turn left in 1993 and was replaced by Aisha Tanner.

| | |
|---|---|
| 15/06/1985.....64......3..... | AS THE BAND TURNS ..............................................................A&M AMA 5019 |
| 13/07/1985.....45......4..... | THE ARTISTS VOLUME 2 **LUTHER VANDROSS/TEDDY PENDERGRASS/CHANGE/ATLANTIC STARR** .............Street Sounds ARTIS 2 |
| 11/07/1987.....48.....12..... | ALL IN THE NAME OF LOVE .......................................................WEA WX 115 |

**ATOMIC KITTEN** UK vocal group formed in Liverpool by Natasha Hamilton (born 17/7/1982), Kerry Katona (born 6/9/1980) and Liz McClarnon (born 10/4/1981). Katona left the group in January 2001 and was replaced by Precious member Jenny Frost (born 22/2/1978). Early member Heidi Range later became a member of Sugababes. Katona presented the TV show *Elimidate*. Frost and McClarnon appeared in the 2001 film *Mike Bassett England Manager*.

| | |
|---|---|
| 04/11/2000 ....❶¹.....37......✪ | RIGHT NOW ..............................................................Innocent CDSIN 6 |
| 21/09/2002 ....❶¹.....27......✪² | FEELS SO GOOD ◇ ..............................................................Innocent CDSIN 10 |
| 22/11/2003 ....5.....11......✪ | LADIES NIGHT ..............................................................Innocent CDSIN 14 |
| 17/04/2004 ....5......8......● | THE GREATEST HITS ..............................................................Innocent CDSIN 16 |

**ATOMIC ROOSTER** UK rock band formed in 1969 by Vincent Crane (born Vincent Rodney Chessman, 21/5/1943, Reading, formerly organist with The Crazy World Of Arthur Brown), Nick Graham (bass) and Carl Palmer (born 20/3/1951, Birmingham, drums). The latter pair quit not long after the debut album (Palmer going on to Emerson, Lake And Palmer) and new recruits Paul Hammond (drums) and John Cann (guitar/vocals) were drafted in. The group disbanded in 1974, despite a change to blue-eyed soul with singer Chris Farlowe. Crane commited suicide by overdosing on sleeping pills on 4/2/1989. Cann later recorded solo as John Du Cann.

| | |
|---|---|
| 13/06/1970.....49......1..... | ATOMIC ROOSTER ..............................................................B&C CAS 1010 |
| 16/01/1971.....12......8..... | DEATH WALKS BEHIND YOU..............................................................Charisma CAS 1026 |
| 21/08/1971.....18......4..... | IN HEARING OF ATOMIC ROOSTER..............................................................Pegasus PEG 1 |

**AU PAIRS** UK punk rock group formed in Birmingham in 1979 by Lesley Woods (guitar/vocals), Paul Ford (guitar/vocals), Jane Munro (bass) and Pete Hammond (drums). The group formed their own 021 label (021 being the telephone code for Birmingham at the time), their second single and debut album being snapped up by Human Records. A further single, *Come Again*, was banned by the BBC because of the lyrical content. They added Tina Wawrzynowicz (keyboards) in 1982 and disbanded in 1983.

| | |
|---|---|
| 06/06/1981.....33......7..... | PLAYING WITH A DIFFERENT SEX..............................................................Human 1 |
| 04/09/1982.....79......3..... | SENSE AND SENSUALITY ..............................................................Kamera KAM 010 |

**AUDIO BULLYS** UK production duo formed in London by Tom Dinsdale and Simon Franks.

| | |
|---|---|
| 14/06/2003.....19......3......O | EGO WAR..............................................................Source CDSOUR073 |

**AUDIOSLAVE** US group formed by Chris Cornell (born 20/7/1964, Seattle, WA, vocals), Tom Morello (guitar), Tim Commerford (bass) and Brad Wilk (drums). Cornell was previously in Soundgarden, Commerford in Rage Against The Machine.

| | |
|---|---|
| 30/11/2002.....19.....20......● | AUDIOSLAVE ..............................................................Epic/Interscope 5101302 |

**AUDIOWEB** UK group formed in Manchester by Martin 'Sugar' Merchant (vocals), Robin File (guitar), Sean McCann (bass) and Maxi (drums), evolving from Sugar Merchant.

| | |
|---|---|
| 09/11/1996.....70......1..... | AUDIOWEB ..............................................................Mother MUMCD 9604 |

**BRIAN AUGER** — see **JULIE DRISCOLL, BRIAN AUGER AND THE TRINITY**

**AUF DER MAUR** Canadian singer/guitarist (born Melissa Auf Der Maur, 17/3/1972, Montreal); he was in Hole before going solo.

| | |
|---|---|
| 13/03/2004.....31......1..... | AUF DER MAUR..............................................................EMI 5943082CD |

**PATTI AUSTIN** US singer (born 10/8/1948, New York City) who is the goddaughter of Quincy Jones. She made her Apollo Theatre debut aged four and signed with RCA Records at five. She won the 1981 Grammy Award, with Quincy Jones, for Best Rhythm & Blues Vocal Performance by a Duo for *The Dude*.

| | |
|---|---|
| 26/09/1981.....99......1..... | EVERY HOME SHOULD HAVE ONE ..............................................................Qwest K 56931 |

O Silver disc  ● Gold disc  ✪ Platinum disc (additional platinum units are indicated by a figure following the symbol)  ❶⁹ Number of weeks album topped the UK chart

### AUTEURS
UK rock group formed in 1991 by Luke Haines (born 7/10/1967, Walton-on-Thames, guitar/vocals), Alice Readman (born 1967, Harrow, bass) and Glenn Collins (born 7/2/1968, Cheltenham, drums). Haines and Readman were previously in The Servants. James Banbury (cello) joined the line-up in 1993.

| | | | | |
|---|---|---|---|---|
| 06/03/1993 | 35 | 2 | | NEW WAVE .......... Hut CDHUT 7 |
| 21/05/1994 | 27 | 1 | | NOW I'M A COWBOY .......... Hut CDHUT 16 |
| 16/03/1996 | 53 | 1 | | AFTER MURDER PARK .......... Hut DGHUT 33 |

### AVALANCHES
Australian group of Robbie Chater, Darren Seltmann, Gordon McQuilten, Tony Diblasi, Dexter Fabay and James De La Cruz. The video for the single *Since I Met You* was named Best Video at the 2001 MTV Europe Music Awards.

| | | | | |
|---|---|---|---|---|
| 28/04/2001 | 8 | 25 | ● | **SINCE I LEFT YOU** .......... XL Recordings XLCD 138 |

### AVERAGE WHITE BAND
UK soul group formed by Hamish Stuart (born 8/10/1949, Glasgow, guitar/vocals), Alan Gorrie (born 19/7/1946, Perth, bass/vocals), Onnie McIntyre (born 25/9/1945, Lennoxtown, guitar/vocals), Malcolm 'Molly' Duncan (born 25/8/1945, Montrose, saxophone), Roger Ball (born 4/6/1944, Dundee, keyboards/saxophone) and Robbie McIntosh (born 6/5/1950, Dundee, drums). McIntosh died from drug poisoning on 23/9/1974 during the recording of their debut album and was replaced by Steve Ferrone (born 25/4/1950, Brighton) who was the only black member of the Average White Band. They later recorded with Ben E King. They were apparently named after a saying of a friend: any problem that was 'too much for the average white man to understand'; it's also been claimed that they were named by Bonnie Bramlett, who was surprised to see white soul musicians in Scotland.

| | | | | |
|---|---|---|---|---|
| 01/03/1975 | 6 | 14 | ○ | AVERAGE WHITE BAND ▲[1] .......... Atlantic K 50058 |
| 05/07/1975 | 28 | 4 | | CUT THE CAKE .......... Atlantic K 50146 |
| 31/07/1976 | 60 | 1 | | SOUL SEARCHING TIME .......... Atlantic K 50272 |
| 10/03/1979 | 15 | 15 | ○ | I FEEL NO FRET .......... RCA XL 13063 |
| 31/05/1980 | 14 | 13 | | SHINE .......... RCA XL 13123 |
| 02/04/1994 | 38 | 3 | ○ | LET'S GO ROUND AGAIN – THE BEST OF AWB .......... The Hit Label AHLCD 15 |

### ROY AYERS
US vibraphonist/singer (born 10/9/1940, Los Angeles, CA) who played piano as a child, becoming interested in the vibes after meeting Lionel Hampton. His professional career began with Curtis Edward Amy, before recording for United Artists under his own name in 1964. Later with Atlantic, Polydor and CBS, he formed Ubiquity and recorded with former Crusader Wayne Henderson.

| | | | | |
|---|---|---|---|---|
| 26/10/1985 | 91 | 2 | | YOU MIGHT BE SURPRISED .......... CBS 26653 |

### PAM AYRES
UK singer/songwriter (born1947, Stanford-In-The-Vale, Berkshire), first known after winning TV talent contest *Opportunity Knocks* with poetry set to music. Said to have worked as an intelligence officer for the Royal Air Force for four years.

| | | | | |
|---|---|---|---|---|
| 27/03/1976 | 13 | 23 | ○ | SOME OF ME POEMS AND SONGS .......... Galaxy GAL 6003 |
| 11/12/1976 | 23 | 6 | | SOME MORE OF ME POEMS AND SONGS .......... Galaxy GAL 6010 |

### CHARLES AZNAVOUR
French singer (born Shahnour Varenagh Aznavurjan, 22/5/1924, Paris) who was one of France's top performers of the 1950s, making his UK breakthrough when in his 50s. A prolific songwriter, his many film parts include *Candy* (1968), *The Blockhouse* (1973) and *The Heist* (1979).

| | | | | |
|---|---|---|---|---|
| 29/06/1974 | 23 | 7 | ○ | AZNAVOUR SINGS AZNAVOUR VOLUME 3 .......... Barclay 80472 |
| 07/09/1974 | 9 | 13 | ● | **A TAPESTRY OF DREAMS** .......... Barclay 90003 |
| 02/08/1980 | 73 | 1 | | HIS GREATEST LOVE SONGS .......... K-Tel NE 1078 |

### AZTEC CAMERA
UK group with a fluctuating line-up from 1980 to 1986, a vehicle for singer/guitarist/songwriter Roddy Frame (born 29/1/1964, East Kilbride).

| | | | | |
|---|---|---|---|---|
| 23/04/1983 | 22 | 18 | | HIGH LAND HARD RAIN .......... Rough Trade 47 |
| 29/09/1984 | 14 | 6 | ○ | KNIFE .......... WEA WX 8 |
| 21/11/1987 | 10 | 43 | ✪ | **LOVE** .......... WEA WX 128 |
| 16/06/1990 | 22 | 7 | ○ | STRAY .......... WEA WX 350 |
| 29/05/1993 | 21 | 2 | | DREAMLAND .......... WEA 4509924922 |
| 07/08/1999 | 36 | 4 | | THE BEST OF AZTEC CAMERA .......... warner.esp 3984289842 |

# B

**DEREK B** UK rapper (born Derek Bowland, 1966, East London) who began as a pirate radio DJ, later forming the Tuff Audio label.

| | | |
|---|---|---|
| 28/05/1988 . . . . . 11 . . . . . . 9 . . . . . . | BULLET FROM A GUN . . . . . . . . . . . . . . . . . . . . . . . . . . . . . . . . . . . . . . . . . . . . . . . . . . . . . . . . . . . . . . Tuff Audio DRKLP 1 | |

**ERIC B AND RAKIM** US hip hop duo Eric B (born Eric Barrier, Elmhurst, NY) and Rakim (born William Griffin, 28/1/1968, Long Island, NY) who later produced MCA acts including Jody Watley, and appeared in the 1994 film *Gunmen*. Rakim later went solo.

| | |
|---|---|
| 12/09/1987 . . . . . 85 . . . . . . 4 . . . . . . | PAID IN FULL . . . . . . . . . . . . . . . . . . . . . . . . . . . . . . . . . . . . . . . . . . . . . . . . . . . . . . . . . . . . . Fourth & Broadway BRLP 514 |
| 06/08/1988 . . . . . 25 . . . . . . 4 . . . . . . | FOLLOW THE LEADER . . . . . . . . . . . . . . . . . . . . . . . . . . . . . . . . . . . . . . . . . . . . . . . . . . . . . . . . . . . . MCA MCG 6031 |
| 07/07/1990 . . . . . 58 . . . . . . 1 . . . . . . | LET THE RHYTHM HIT 'EM . . . . . . . . . . . . . . . . . . . . . . . . . . . . . . . . . . . . . . . . . . . . . . . . . . . . . . . MCA MCG 6097 |
| 11/07/1992 . . . . . 73 . . . . . . 1 . . . . . . | DON'T SWEAT THE TECHNIQUE . . . . . . . . . . . . . . . . . . . . . . . . . . . . . . . . . . . . . . . . . . . . . . . . . . MCA MCAD 10594 |

**HOWIE B** UK singer/musician/DJ (born Howard Bernstein, Glasgow) who was the producer for Everything But The Girl, U2's *Pop* album and engineer for Skylab before going solo. He later launched the Pussyfoot label.

| | |
|---|---|
| 09/08/1997 . . . . . 58 . . . . . . 1 . . . . . . | TURN THE DARK OFF . . . . . . . . . . . . . . . . . . . . . . . . . . . . . . . . . . . . . . . . . . . . . . . . . . . . . . . . . . . Polydor 5379342 |

**MELANIE B** UK singer (born Melanie Brown, 29/5/1973, Leeds) who was also a member of the Spice Girls (known as Mel B and/or Scary Spice). After marrying dancer Jimmy Gulzar she recorded as Melanie G, but reverted to Melanie B following their divorce in October 2000. She had an acting role in the TV series *Burn It*.

| | |
|---|---|
| 21/10/2000 . . . . . 28 . . . . . . 2 . . . . . . ○ | HOT . . . . . . . . . . . . . . . . . . . . . . . . . . . . . . . . . . . . . . . . . . . . . . . . . . . . . . . . . . . . . . . . . . . . Virgin CDVX 2918 |

**B BOYS** US hip hop group with MC Donald D, Brother B and DJ Mixmaster T. Donald D later became a member of Rhyme Syndicate

| | |
|---|---|
| 28/01/1984 . . . . . 90 . . . . . . 1 . . . . . . | CUTTIN' HERBIE . . . . . . . . . . . . . . . . . . . . . . . . . . . . . . . . . . . . . . . . . . . . . . . . . . . . . . . . . . . . Streetwave XKHAN 501 |

**B*WITCHED** Irish vocal group formed in Dublin by Sinead O'Carroll (born 14/5/1973, Dublin, although she has sometimes claimed the year was 1978), Lindsay Armaou (born 18/12/1980, Athens, Greece) and twin sisters Edele and Keavy Lynch (born 15/12/1979, Dublin), who are also sisters of Shane Lynch of Boyzone. The first group to have their first four singles enter the chart at #1, they took part in the BRITS Trust *Thank Abba For The Music* project.

| | |
|---|---|
| 24/10/1998 . . . . . 3 . . . . . 36 . . . . . ✪² | **B*WITCHED** ◇ . . . . . . . . . . . . . . . . . . . . . . . . . . . . . . . . . . . . . . . . . . . . . . . . . . . . . . . . . . Glow Worm 4917042 |
| 30/10/1999 . . . . . 5 . . . . . 12 . . . . . ✪ | **AWAKE AND BREATHE** . . . . . . . . . . . . . . . . . . . . . . . . . . . . . . . . . . . . . . . . . . . . . . . . . . . Glow Worm 4960792 |

**BABES IN TOYLAND** US rock group formed by Kat Bjelland (born in Woodburn, OR, guitar/vocals), Michelle Leon (bass) and Lori Barbero (drums/vocals). Bjelland had previously been in Sugar Baby Doll with Courtney Love (who went on to form Hole) and Jennifer Finch (who later joined L7). Leon left in 1992, replaced by Maureen Herman (born in Chicago, IL). They then took a sabbatical with Bjelland and her husband Stuart Grey setting up Crunt and KatSu.

| | |
|---|---|
| 05/09/1992 . . . . . 24 . . . . . . 2 . . . . . . | FONTANELLE . . . . . . . . . . . . . . . . . . . . . . . . . . . . . . . . . . . . . . . . . . . . . . . . . . . . . . . . . . . . . Southern 185012 |
| 03/07/1993 . . . . . 53 . . . . . . 1 . . . . . . | PAINKILLER . . . . . . . . . . . . . . . . . . . . . . . . . . . . . . . . . . . . . . . . . . . . . . . . . . . . . . . . . . . . . Southern 185122 |

**BABY ANIMALS** Australian rock group formed in 1990 by Suzi Demarchi (vocals), Dave Leslie (guitar), Eddie Parise (bass) and Frank Delenza (drums).

| | |
|---|---|
| 14/03/1992 . . . . . 70 . . . . . . 1 . . . . . . | BABY ANIMALS . . . . . . . . . . . . . . . . . . . . . . . . . . . . . . . . . . . . . . . . . . . . . . . . . . . . . . . . . . . Imago PD 90580 |

**BABY D** Maltese singer Dee Galdes who began as backing vocalist for a number of chart acts. Her first recording was with Jazz And The Brothers Grimm in 1989. The rest of her group comprises MC Nino, Claudio Galdez and Dice. They won Best Dance Act at the 1996 MOBO Awards.

| | |
|---|---|
| 10/02/1996 . . . . . 5 . . . . . . 5 . . . . . . ○ | **DELIVERANCE** . . . . . . . . . . . . . . . . . . . . . . . . . . . . . . . . . . . . . . . . . . . . . . . . . . . . . . . . . . Systematic 8286832 |

**BABYBIRD** UK group formed in Telford in 1995 by Stephen Jones (vocals), Luke Scott (guitar), John Pedder (bass), Huw Chadbourn (keyboards) and Robert Gregory (drums), originally on Babybird Recordings before signing with Echo.

| | |
|---|---|
| 02/11/1996 . . . . . 9 . . . . . 12 . . . . . ● | **UGLY BEAUTIFUL** . . . . . . . . . . . . . . . . . . . . . . . . . . . . . . . . . . . . . . . . . . . . . . . . . . . . . . . . Echo ECHCD 11 |
| 05/09/1998 . . . . . 28 . . . . . . 2 . . . . . . | THERE'S SOMETHING GOING ON . . . . . . . . . . . . . . . . . . . . . . . . . . . . . . . . . . . . . . . . . . . . . . . Echo ECHCD 024 |

**BABYFACE** US singer (born Kenneth Edmonds, 10/4/1959, Indianapolis, IN) who was a guitarist and backing singer for Manchild before meeting Antonio 'LA' Reid via the group Deele. The pair made their names as songwriters (usually with fellow Manchild member Daryl Simmons), forming the LaFace record label. Bootsy Collins coined Edmonds' nickname Babyface because of his youthful looks. He has won eight Grammy Awards: Best Rhythm & Blues Song in 1992 with LA Reid and Daryl Simmons for *The End Of The Road*; Best Rhythm & Blues Song for *I'll Make Love To You* and Best Rhythm & Blues Vocal Performance for *When Can I See You*, both in 1994; Best Rhythm & Blues Song in 1996 for *Exhale (Shoop Shoop)*; and Producer of the Year in 1992, 1995, 1996 and 1997.

| | |
|---|---|
| 16/11/1996 . . . . . 34 . . . . . . 5 . . . . . . ○ | THE DAY . . . . . . . . . . . . . . . . . . . . . . . . . . . . . . . . . . . . . . . . . . . . . . . . . . . . . . . . . . . . . . . Epic 4853682 |

○ Silver disc   ● Gold disc   ✪ Platinum disc (additional platinum units are indicated by a figure following the symbol)   ❶⁹ Number of weeks album topped the UK chart

### BABYLON ZOO
UK group formed by Asian/native US Jas Mann (born Jaswinder Mann, 24/4/1971, Dudley). Signed by EMI's Parlophone in 1993 on the strength of a demo, they later followed their A&R director to WEA, and then back to EMI.

17/02/1996 ..... 6 ...... 5 ...... ●  THE BOY WITH THE X-RAY EYES ............................................................ EMI CDEMC 3742

### BACCARA
Spanish duo of Maria Mendiola and Mayte Mateus.

04/03/1978 ..... 26 ...... 6 ......  BACCARA ............................................................ RCA PL 28316

### BURT BACHARACH
US orchestra leader (born 12/5/1928, Kansas City, MO) and a hugely prolific and successful songwriter, often in conjunction with Hal David. He married singer Paula Stewart in 1953 (divorced 1958), actress Angie Dickinson in 1966 (divorced 1980) and fellow songwriter Carole Bayer Sager in 1982 (divorced 1992). Songwriting credits include *Magic Moments* (a hit for Perry Como), *Walk On By, Don't Make Me Over* and *Do You Know The Way To San Jose* (all Dionne Warwick) and *Arthur's Theme* (Christopher Cross). He has won five Grammy Awards: Best Instrumental Arrangement in 1967 for *Alfie*; Best Original Cast Show Album in 1969 for *Promises Promises*; Best Original Score in 1969 for *Butch Cassidy & The Sundance Kid*; Song of the Year in 1986 with Carole Bayer Sager for *That's What Friends Are For*; and Best Pop Collaboration with Vocals in 1998 with Elvis Costello for *I Still Have That Other Girl*.

22/05/1965 ..... 3 ...... 18 ......  **HIT MAKER – BURT BACHARACH** ............................................... London HAR 8233
22/07/1967 ..... 35 ...... 1 ......  CASINO ROYALE Original soundtrack to the film ...................................... RCA Victor SF 7874
28/11/1970 ..... 52 ...... 3 ......  REACH OUT ............................................................ A&M AMLS 908
03/04/1971 ..... 5 ...... 22 ......  **PORTRAIT IN MUSIC** ............................................................ A&M AMLS 2010
10/10/1998 ..... 32 ...... 2 ......  PAINTED FROM MEMORY **ELVIS COSTELLO WITH BURT BACHARACH** ........................... Mercury 5380022

### BACHELORS
Irish vocal group formed in Dublin in 1953 by brothers Declan (born 12/12/1942, Dublin) and Conleth Clusky (born 18/3/1941, Dublin) and John Stokes (born 13/8/1940, Dublin), originally known as The Harmonichords. They changed their name to The Bachelors despite the fact all were married. Stokes left in 1984 and was replaced by Peter Phipps.

27/06/1964 ..... 2 ...... 44 ......  **THE BACHELORS AND 16 GREAT SONGS** ............................................ Decca LK 4614
09/10/1965 ..... 15 ...... 6 ......  MORE GREAT SONG HITS FROM THE BACHELORS ......................................... Decca LK 4721
09/07/1966 ..... 12 ...... 9 ......  HITS OF THE SIXTIES ............................................................ Decca TXL 102
05/11/1966 ..... 24 ...... 8 ......  BACHELORS' GIRLS ............................................................ Decca LK 4827
01/07/1967 ..... 19 ...... 7 ......  GOLDEN ALL TIME HITS ............................................................ Decca SKL 4849
14/06/1969 ..... 8 ...... 18 ......  **WORLD OF THE BACHELORS** ...................................................... Decca SPA 2
23/08/1969 ..... 11 ...... 7 ......  WORLD OF THE BACHELORS VOLUME 2 .................................................. Decca SPA 22
22/12/1979 ..... 38 ...... 4 ...... ●  25 GOLDEN GREATS ............................................................ Warwick WW 5068

### BACHMAN-TURNER OVERDRIVE
Canadian rock group formed in Winnipeg in 1972 by brothers Randy (born 27/9/1943, Winnipeg, guitar/vocals) and Robbie Bachman (born 18/2/1953, Winnipeg, drums) and C Fred Turner (born 16/10/1943, Winnipeg, bass/vocals). Chad Allen was a member briefly and was replaced by Tim Bachman (born 18/2/1953, Winnipeg). Tim left in 1973 and was replaced by Blair Thornton. Randy went solo in 1977.

14/12/1974 ..... 12 ...... 13 ...... ○  NOT FRAGILE ▲¹ ............................................................ Mercury 9100 007

### BACK TO THE PLANET
UK group formed in London in 1989 by Fil 'The Girl' Walters (vocals), Fraggle (born David Fletcher, guitar), Guy McAffer (keyboards) and Henry Nicholas Cullen (drums). Cullen left in 1993 and was replaced by Amire Mojarad.

18/09/1993 ..... 32 ...... 2 ......  MIND AND SOUL COLLABORATORS ................................................... Parallel ALLCD 2

### BACKBEAT BAND
US studio group assembled by producer Don Was for the soundtrack to the 1994 Beatles biopic film *Backbeat*, with Greg Dulli (of The Afghan Whigs), Dave Grohl (Nirvana), Mike Mills (R.E.M.), Thurston Moore (Sonic Youth) and Dave Pirner (Soul Asylum).

16/04/1994 ..... 39 ...... 2 ......  BACKBEAT Original soundtrack to the film ........................................... Virgin CDV 2729

### BACKSTREET BOYS
US vocal group formed in Orlando, FL in 1993 by Kevin Richardson (born 3/10/1972, Lexington, KY), Brian 'B-Rok' Littrell (born 20/2/1975, Lexington), Alexander James 'AJ' McLean (born 9/1/1978, Boynton Beach, FL), Nick Carter (born 28/1/1980, NYC) and Howard 'Howie D' Dorough (born 22/8/1973, Orlando). Carter's younger brother Aaron is a successful solo artist. They have won four MTV Europe Music Awards: Best Video in 1996 for *Get Down (You're The One For Me)*, Best Video in 1997 for *As Long As You Love Me*, and Best Group in 1999 and 2000.

21/09/1996 ..... 12 ...... 19 ...... ●  BACKSTREET BOYS ◇³ ◆¹⁴ .......................................................... Jive CHIPR 169
23/08/1997 ..... 2 ...... 44 ...... ●²  **BACKSTREET'S BACK** ◇⁵ ........................................................ Jive CHIP 186

▲⁹ Number of weeks album topped the US chart  ◆¹² RIAA Diamond Awards  ◇³ IFPI Platinum Europe Awards

| | | | | | |
|---|---|---|---|---|---|
| 29/05/1999 | 2 | 56 | ✪ | **MILLENNIUM** ◇² ▲¹⁰ ◆¹³ | Jive 0523222 |
| 02/12/2000 | 13 | 9 | ● | BLACK AND BLUE ▲² | Jive 9221172 |
| 10/11/2001 | 5 | 18 | ✪ | **GREATEST HITS – CHAPTER ONE** ◇ | Jive 9222672 |

**BAD BOYS INC** UK vocal group formed by Matthew Pateman, David Ross, Tony Dowding and Ally Begg.

| | | | | | |
|---|---|---|---|---|---|
| 16/04/1994 | 13 | 6 | | BAD BOYS INC | A&M 5402002 |

**BAD COMPANY** UK rock group formed in 1973 by Paul Rodgers (born 17/12/1949, Middlesbrough, vocals), Simon Kirke (born 28/7/1949, London, drums), Mick Ralphs (born 31/3/1948, Hereford, guitar) and Raymond 'Boz' Burrell (born 1/8/1946, Lincoln, bass). Rodgers and Kirke had previously been in Free, Ralphs in Mott The Hoople and Burrell in King Crimson. They disbanded in 1983 and re-formed in 1986. Burrell left in 1987 and by 1996 the line-up was Kirke, Ralphs, singer Robert Hart, guitarist Dave Colwell and bassist Rick Wills. Rodgers was later with Firm and The Law.

| | | | | | |
|---|---|---|---|---|---|
| 15/06/1974 | 3 | 25 | ● | **BAD COMPANY** ▲¹ | Island ILPS 9279 |
| 12/04/1975 | 3 | 27 | ● | **STRAIGHT SHOOTER** | Island ILPS 9304 |
| 21/02/1976 | 4 | 12 | ● | **RUN WITH THE PACK** | Island ILPS 9346 |
| 19/03/1977 | 17 | 8 | | BURNIN' SKY | Island ILPS 9441 |
| 17/03/1979 | 10 | 9 | | **DESOLATION ANGELS** | Swan Song SSK 59408 |
| 28/08/1982 | 15 | 6 | | ROUGH DIAMONDS | Swan Song SSK 59419 |

**BAD ENGLISH** UK/US rock group formed in 1988 by John Waite (born 4/7/1955, London, vocals), Neal Schon (guitar), Jonathan Cain (keyboards), Ricky Phillips (bass) and Dene Castronovo (drums). Waite, Cain and Phillips were all previously in The Babys, Schon with Santana and Journey (that also included Cain), and Castronovo with Wild Dogs. They disbanded in 1991. Waite went solo, Phillips and Castronovo linked up with Jimmy Page and David Coverdale, and Schon and Cain re-formed Journey.

| | | | | | |
|---|---|---|---|---|---|
| 16/09/1989 | 74 | 1 | | BAD ENGLISH | Epic 4634471 |
| 19/10/1991 | 64 | 1 | | BACKLASH | Epic 4685691 |

**BAD MANNERS** UK ska group formed in London in 1980 by Buster Bloodvessel (born Doug Trendle, 6/9/1958, London, vocals), Louis 'Alphonso' Cook (guitar), Winston Bazoomies (born Alan Sayag, harmonica), Brian 'Chew-It' Tuit (drums), David Farren (bass), Paul Hyman (trumpet), Gus 'Hot Lips' Herman (trumpet), Chris Kane (saxophone), Andrew 'Marcus Absent' Marson (saxophone) and Martin Stewart (keyboards).

| | | | | | |
|---|---|---|---|---|---|
| 26/04/1980 | 34 | 13 | ○ | SKA 'N' B | Magnet MAG 5033 |
| 29/11/1980 | 36 | 12 | ○ | LOONEE TUNES | Magnet MAG 5038 |
| 24/10/1981 | 18 | 12 | ○ | GOSH IT'S BAD MANNERS | Magnet MAGL 5043 |
| 27/11/1982 | 78 | 1 | | FORGING AHEAD | Magnet MAGL 5050 |
| 07/05/1983 | 23 | 6 | | THE HEIGHT OF BAD MANNERS | Telstar STAR 2229 |

**BAD NEWS** UK group formed by Vim Fuego (guitar/vocals, played by Adrian Edmondson), Colin Grigson (bass, played by Rik Mayall), Den Dennis (guitar, played by Nigel Planer) and Spider Webb (drums, played by Peter Richardson) for *The Comic Strip Presents* TV show, a one-off parody of a London heavy metal band travelling to Grantham for a show. Its success prompted a second appearance, the group being required to play live at the Donington Festival.

| | | | | | |
|---|---|---|---|---|---|
| 24/10/1987 | 69 | 1 | | BAD NEWS | EMI EMC 3535 |

**ANGELO BADALAMENTI** US composer born in Italy, composer of many film and TV themes, including *Twin Peaks*. Booth is UK singer Tim Booth, lead singer with James. Badalamenti won the 1990 Grammy Award for Best Pop Instrumental Performance for *Twin Peaks Theme*.

| | | | | | |
|---|---|---|---|---|---|
| 17/11/1990 | 27 | 25 | ● | MUSIC FROM 'TWIN PEAKS' | Warner Brothers 7599263161 |
| 13/07/1996 | 35 | 2 | | BOOTH AND THE BAD ANGEL **BOOTH AND THE BAD ANGEL** | Fontana 5268522 |

**BADLANDS** UK group formed in 1988 by Ray Gillen (vocals), Jake E Lee (guitar), Greg Chaisson (bass) and Eric Singer (drums), signing with Atlantic the following year. Singer left the group in 1991 and was replaced by Jeff Martin.

| | | | | | |
|---|---|---|---|---|---|
| 24/06/1989 | 39 | 2 | | BADLANDS | WEA 7819661 |
| 22/06/1991 | 74 | 1 | | VOODOO HIGHWAY | Atlantic 7567822511 |

○ Silver disc  ● Gold disc  ✪ Platinum disc (additional platinum units are indicated by a figure following the symbol)  ❶⁹ Number of weeks album topped the UK chart

**BADLY DRAWN BOY** UK singer/songwriter (born Damon Gough, Manchester) named after a character in the adult cartoon magazine *Viz*.

| | | | | | |
|---|---|---|---|---|---|
| 08/07/2000 | 13 | 47 | ✪ | THE HOUR OF BEWILDERBEAST 2000 Mercury Music Prize . . . . . . . . . . . . . . . . . . . . . . . . . . . . . . . . . . . . . . . | XL Recordings TNXLCD 133 |
| 20/04/2002 | 6 | 18 | ● | **ABOUT A BOY** Original soundtrack to the film . . . . . . . . . . . . . . . . . . . . . . . . . . . . . . . . . . . . . . . . . . . . . | Twisted Nerve TNXLCD 152 |
| 16/11/2002 | 10 | 20 | ● | **HAVE YOU FED THE FISH?** . . . . . . . . . . . . . . . . . . . . . . . . . . . . . . . . . . . . . . . . . . . . . . . . . . . . . . . . . . | XL Recordings TNXLCD 156 |

**ERYKAH BADU** US singer (born Erica Wright, 26/2/1972, Dallas, TX) who began as rapper MC Apples and later relocated to New York. She appeared in the films *Blues Brothers 2000* (1998) and *The Cider House Rules* (1999). She has won three Grammy Awards including Best Female Rhythm & Blues Vocal Performance in 1997 for *On &On* and Best Rap Group Performance with The Roots for *You Got Me* in 1999.

| | | | | | |
|---|---|---|---|---|---|
| 01/03/1997 | 17 | 25 | ● | BADUIZM 1997 Grammy Award for Best Rhythm & Blues Album . . . . . . . . . . . . . . . . . . . . . . . . . . . . . . . . . . | MCA UND 53027 |

**JOAN BAEZ** US singer (born 9/1/1941, Staten Island, NYC) who first attracted attention at the 1959 Newport Folk Festival, later touring with Bob Dylan. Recording her debut in 1958, she signed with Vanguard in 1960. Initially with a broad-based repertoire, she became associated with the US civil rights movement, *We Shall Overcome*, becoming an anthem of the movement. Twice jailed for her part in anti-war protests, she is still involved in humanitarian work, founding Humanitas International in 1979.

| | | | | |
|---|---|---|---|---|
| 18/07/1964 | 8 | 19 | **JOAN BAEZ IN CONCERT VOLUME 2** . . . . . . . . . . . . . . . . . . . . . . . . . . . . . . . . . . . . . . . . | Fontana TFL 6033 |
| 15/05/1965 | 3 | 27 | **JOAN BAEZ NO. 5** . . . . . . . . . . . . . . . . . . . . . . . . . . . . . . . . . . . . . . . . . . . . . . . . . . . . . . | Fontana TFL 6043 |
| 19/06/1965 | 9 | 13 | **JOAN BAEZ** . . . . . . . . . . . . . . . . . . . . . . . . . . . . . . . . . . . . . . . . . . . . . . . . . . . . . . . . . . | Fontana TFL 6002 |
| 27/11/1965 | 5 | 23 | **FAREWELL ANGELINA** . . . . . . . . . . . . . . . . . . . . . . . . . . . . . . . . . . . . . . . . . . . . . . . . . . . | Fontana TFL 6058 |
| 19/07/1969 | 15 | 5 | JOAN BAEZ ON VANGUARD . . . . . . . . . . . . . . . . . . . . . . . . . . . . . . . . . . . . . . . . . . . . . . . . | Vanguard SVXL 100 |
| 03/04/1971 | 41 | 1 | FIRST TEN YEARS . . . . . . . . . . . . . . . . . . . . . . . . . . . . . . . . . . . . . . . . . . . . . . . . . . . . . . . | Vanguard 6635 003 |

**PHILIP BAILEY** US singer (born 8/5/1951, Denver, CO) who joined Earth Wind & Fire as lead singer in 1971, going solo in 1983. He later recorded a number of gospel albums, winning the 1986 Grammy Award for Best Gospel Performance for *Triumph*.

| | | | |
|---|---|---|---|
| 30/03/1985 | 29 | 17 | CHINESE WALL . . . . . . . . . . . . . . . . . . . . . . . . . . . . . . . . . . . . . . . . . . . . . . . . . . . . . . . . . . . . . . . . CBS 26161 |

**ANITA BAKER** US singer (born 20/12/1957, Toledo, OH, raised in Detroit, MI) who was lead singer with soul group Chapter 8 from 1976–80. She then worked in an office prior to a solo deal with Beverly Glen. She has won eight Grammy Awards including: Best Rhythm & Blues Song in 1986 with Louis Johnson and Gary Bias for *Sweet Love*; Best Soul Gospel Performance by a Group in 1987 with The Winans for *Ain't No Need To Worry*; Best Rhythm & Blues Song with Skip Scarborough and Randy Holland, and Best Rhythm & Blues Vocal Performance for *Giving You The Best That I Got* both in 1988; Best Rhythm & Blues Vocal Performance in 1989 again for *Giving You The Best That I Got*; and Best Rhythm & Blues Singer in 1995 for *I Apologize*. She has a star on the Hollywood Walk of Fame.

| | | | | | |
|---|---|---|---|---|---|
| 03/05/1986 | 13 | 47 | ✪ | RAPTURE 1986 Grammy Award for Best Rhythm and Blues Performance . . . . . . . . . . . . . . . . . . . . . . . . . . . . . | Elektra EKT 37 |
| 29/10/1988 | 9 | 20 | ● | **GIVING YOU THE BEST THAT I GOT** ▲[4] . . . . . . . . . . . . . . . . . . . . . . . . . . . . . . . . . . . . . . . . . . . . . | Elektra EKT 49 |
| 14/07/1990 | 7 | 9 | ● | **COMPOSITIONS** 1990 Grammy Award for Best Rhythm and Blues Performance . . . . . . . . . . . . . . . . . . . . . | Elektra EKT 72 |
| 24/09/1994 | 14 | 5 | | RHYTHM OF LOVE . . . . . . . . . . . . . . . . . . . . . . . . . . . . . . . . . . . . . . . . . . . . . . . . . . . . . . . . . . . . | Elektra 7559615552 |
| 01/06/2002 | 49 | 2 | | SWEET LOVE — THE VERY BEST OF ANITA BAKER . . . . . . . . . . . . . . . . . . . . . . . . . . . . . . . . . . . . . . . | Atlantic 8122736032 |

**GINGER BAKER'S AIRFORCE** UK rock group formed in 1969 Ginger Baker (born Peter Baker, 19/8/1939, London, drums), Steve Winwood (born 12/5/1948, Birmingham, keyboards), Ric Grech (born 1/11/1945, Bordeaux, France, bass), Graham Bond (born 28/10/1937, Romford, saxophone/keyboards/vocals), Denny Laine (born Brian Hines, 29/10/1944, Jersey, guitar/vocals), Phil Seaman (born 28/8/1928, Burton-On-Trent, drums), Bud Beadle (horns), Remi Kabaka (percussion), Harold McNair (flute), Chris Wood (saxophone) and Diane Stewart (backing vocals). Winwood, Wood, Seaman, Kabaka and McNair all left after the first album and were replaced by eight new members, although this second line-up also disintegrated and Ginger Baker went off to study African drumming in Lagos. Seaman died from drug addiction on 13/10/1972. Bon died after falling in front of a train at Finsbury Park Underground Station (although it has not been established whether this was an accident or suicide) on 8/5/1974. Grech died from kidney and liver failure on 17/3/1990.

| 13/06/1970.....37......1...... | GINGER BAKER'S AIR FORCE ............................................................. Polydor 2662 001 |

### BAKER GURVITZ ARMY
UK rock group formed by Ginger Baker (born Peter Baker, 19/8/1939, London, drums), Adrian Gurvitz (born 26/6/1949, London, guitar) and his brother Paul (born 6/7/1947, bass).

| 22/02/1975.....22......5...... | BAKER-GURVITZ ARMY ............................................................. Vertigo 9103 201 |

### BALAAM AND THE ANGEL
UK rock group formed in Motherwell, Scotland by brothers Mark Morris (born 15/1/1963, Motherwell, bass/vocals), Jim Morris (born 25/11/1960, Motherwell, guitar) and Des Morris (born 27/6/1964, Motherwell, drums). They set up Chapter 22 Records, later shortening their name to Balaam.

| 16/08/1986.....67......2...... | THE GREATEST STORY EVER TOLD ............................................................. Virgin V 2377 |

### KENNY BALL AND HIS JAZZMEN
UK trumpeter (born 22/5/1931, Ilford) originally with Charlie Galbraith's All Star Jazz Band from 1951. He formed the Jazzmen in 1958 and they made their TV debut on *New Faces*. Lonnie Donegan recommended him to Pye.

| 25/08/1962 ....❶²......24...... | BEST OF BALL, BARBER AND BILK KENNY BALL, CHRIS BARBER & ACKER BILK.................... Pye Golden Guinea GGL 0131 |
| 07/09/1963.....4......26...... | KENNY BALL'S GOLDEN HITS ............................................................. Pye Golden Guinea GGL 0209 |

### MICHAEL BALL
UK singer/actor (born 27/7/1962, Stratford-upon-Avon) who first made his mark in the Andrew Lloyd Webber musical *Aspects Of Love*.

| 30/05/1992 ....❶¹.....10......● | MICHAEL BALL ............................................................. Polydor 5113302 |
| 17/07/1993 .....3.....11......● | ALWAYS............................................................. Polydor 5196662 |
| 13/08/1994 .....7......6......● | ONE CAREFUL OWNER ............................................................. Columbia 4772802 |
| 19/11/1994 ....25......7......● | THE BEST OF MICHAEL BALL ............................................................. Polygram TV 5238912 |
| 27/01/1996 .....4......6......○ | FIRST LOVE ............................................................. Columbia 4835992 |
| 16/11/1996 ....20.....10......● | THE MUSICALS ............................................................. Polygram TV 5338922 |
| 07/11/1998 ....13.....17......✪ | THE MOVIES ............................................................. Polygram TV 5592412 |
| 20/11/1999 ....18......7......● | THE VERY BEST OF MICHAEL BALL IN CONCERT AT THE ROYAL ALBERT HALL .................... Universal Music TV 5238912 |
| 11/11/2000 ....20......8......○ | THIS TIME IT'S PERSONAL ............................................................. Universal TV 1597282 |
| 29/09/2001 ....11......7......○ | CENTRE STAGE ............................................................. Universal TV 160712 |
| 01/11/2003 ....41......1...... | A LOVE STORY ............................................................. Liberty 5919492 |

### BANANARAMA
UK vocal group formed by flatmates Sarah Dallin (born 17/12/1961, Bristol) and Keren Woodward (born 2/4/1961, Bristol) with Siobhan Fahey (born 10/9/1957, London). At one point they were the most successful girl group in the UK. Fahey left in 1988 to enjoy married life to Eurythmic Dave Stewart before forming Shakespears Sister, and was replaced by Jacqui Sullivan (born 7/8/1960, London). Sullivan left in 1991 and the group continued as a duo.

| 19/03/1983 .....7......16......○ | DEEP SEA SKIVING............................................................. London RAMA 1 |
| 28/04/1984 ....16.....11......○ | BANANARAMA............................................................. London RAMA 2 |
| 19/07/1986 ....46......5...... | TRUE CONFESSIONS............................................................. London RAMA 3 |
| 19/09/1987 ....26.....26......● | WOW! ............................................................. London RAMA 4 |
| 22/10/1988 .....3.....37......✪³ | THE GREATEST HITS COLLECTION ............................................................. London RAMA 5 |
| 25/05/1991.....42......1...... | POP LIFE ............................................................. London 8282461 |
| 10/04/1993 ....46......1...... | PLEASE YOURSELF ............................................................. London 8283572 |
| 10/11/2001 ....43......2...... | THE VERY BEST OF............................................................. London 0927414992 |

### BANCO DE GAIA
UK multi-instrumentalist Toby Marks. The 'group' was originally formed as a duo in Leamington Spa in 1989, although the other member quit before they released any records.

| 12/03/1994 ....34......2...... | MAYA ............................................................. Planet Dog BARKCD 3 |
| 13/05/1995 ....31......2...... | LAST TRAIN TO LHASA ............................................................. Planet Dog BARKCD 0115 |

### BAND
Canadian group formed by Robbie Robertson (born 5/7/1944, Toronto, guitar/vocals), Richard Manuel (born 3/4/1945, Stratford, Ontario, piano/vocals), Garth Hudson (born 2/8/1937 London, Ontario, organ), Rick Danko (born 9/12/1943, Simcoe, bass/vocals) and Levon Helm (born 26/5/1942, Marvell, AR, drums/vocals). They recorded and toured extensively with Bob Dylan.

Manuel committed suicide by hanging himself after a concert on 6/3/1986. Danko died in his sleep on 10/12/1999. They were inducted into the Rock & Roll Hall of Fame in 1994.

| | | | | | |
|---|---|---|---|---|---|
| 31/01/1970 | 25 | 11 | | THE BAND | Capitol EST 132 |
| 03/10/1970 | 15 | 6 | | STAGE FRIGHT | Capitol EA SW 425 |
| 27/11/1971 | 41 | 1 | | CAHOOTS | Capitol EAST 651 |
| 30/08/1997 | 41 | 1 | | THE BAND Re-charted after being featured on a 'classic albums' TV series | Capitol 5253892 |

### BANDERAS UK duo Caroline Buckley (vocals) and Sally Herbert (keyboards/violin).

| | | | | | |
|---|---|---|---|---|---|
| 13/04/1991 | 40 | 3 | | RIPE | London 8282471 |

### BANGLES US rock group formed in Los Angeles, CA in 1981 and known as Supersonic Bangs, comprising Susanna Hoffs (born 17/1/1957, Los Angeles, guitar/vocals), Debbi Peterson (born 22/8/1961, Los Angeles, drums/vocals), Vicki Peterson (born 11/1/1958, Los Angeles, guitar/vocals) and Annette Zilinskas (born 6/11/1964, Van Nuys, CA, bass). Michael Steele (born 2/6/1954, Los Angeles) replaced Zilinskas in 1983 shortly after the group signed with CBS. They changed their name to Bangs but were forced to amend it to Bangles in 1982 as there was another group with the same name. They disbanded in 1989, with Hoffs, who had starred in films, going solo, although they re-formed in 2002. They won the Best International Group category of the 1987 BRIT Awards.

| | | | | | |
|---|---|---|---|---|---|
| 16/03/1985 | 86 | 1 | | ALL OVER THE PLACE | CBS 26015 |
| 15/03/1986 | 3 | 47 | ✪ | **DIFFERENT LIGHT** | CBS 26659 |
| 10/12/1988 | 5 | 26 | ✪ | **EVERYTHING** | CBS 4629791 |
| 09/06/1990 | 4 | 23 | ✪ | **GREATEST HITS** | CBS 4667691 |
| 04/08/2001 | 17 | 7 | ◯ | ETERNAL FLAME – THE BEST OF THE BANGLES | Columbia STVCD 121 |
| 29/03/2003 | 62 | 1 | | DOLL REVOLUTION | Liberty 5815102 |

### TONY BANKS UK keyboard player (born 27/3/1950, East Heathley, Sussex) who was also a member of Genesis.

| | | | | | |
|---|---|---|---|---|---|
| 20/10/1979 | 21 | 5 | | A CURIOUS FEELING | Charisma CAS 1148 |
| 25/06/1983 | 50 | 2 | | THE FUGITIVE | Charisma TBLP 1 |

### CHRIS BARBER'S JAZZ BAND UK trombonist (born 17/4/1930, Welwyn Garden City) who played with Cy Laurie's band after World War II before forming his own band in 1949, which included Lonnie Donegan and clarinettist Monty Sunshine (born 8/4/1928, London).

| | | | | | |
|---|---|---|---|---|---|
| 24/09/1960 | 17 | 1 | | CHRIS BARBER BAND BOX NO. 2 | Columbia 33SCX 3277 |
| 05/11/1960 | 18 | 1 | | ELITE SYNCOPATIONS | Columbia 33SX 1245 |
| 12/11/1960 | 17 | 1 | | BEST OF CHRIS BARBER | Ace Of Clubs ACL 1037 |
| 27/05/1961 | 4 | 43 | | **BEST OF BARBER AND BILK VOLUME 1** | Pye Golden Guinea GGL 0075 |
| 11/11/1961 | 8 | 18 | | **BEST OF BARBER AND BILK VOLUME 2** This and the above hit credited to **CHRIS BARBER AND ACKER BILK** | |
| | | | | | Pye Golden Guinea GGL 0096 |
| 25/08/1962 | ❶² | 24 | | **BEST OF BALL, BARBER AND BILK** KENNY BALL, CHRIS BARBER AND ACKER BILK | Pye Golden Guinea GGL 0131 |
| 29/01/2000 | 14 | 3 | | THE SKIFFLE SESSIONS – LIVE IN BELFAST **VAN MORRISON/LONNIE DONEGAN/CHRIS BARBER** | Venture CDVE 945 |

### BARCLAY JAMES HARVEST UK group formed in Oldham by Stewart 'Wooly' Wolstenholme (born 15/4/1947, Oldham, keyboards/vocals), John Lees (born 13/1/1947, Oldham, guitar/vocals), Les Holroyd (born 12/3/1948, Bolton, bass/vocals) and Mel Pritchard (born 20/1/1948, Oldham, drums). Wolstenholme and Lees were previously with Heart And Soul; Holroyd and Pritchard were with The Wickeds. Pritchard died from a heart attack on 28/1/2004.

| | | | | | |
|---|---|---|---|---|---|
| 14/12/1974 | 40 | 2 | ◯ | BARCLAY JAMES HARVEST LIVE | Polydor 2683 052 |
| 18/10/1975 | 32 | 3 | ◯ | TIME HONOURED GHOST | Polydor 2383 361 |
| 23/10/1976 | 19 | 4 | ◯ | OCTOBERON | Polydor 2442 144 |
| 01/10/1977 | 30 | 7 | ◯ | GONE TO EARTH | Polydor 2442 148 |
| 21/10/1978 | 31 | 2 | | BARCLAY JAMES HARVEST XII | Polydor POLD 5006 |
| 23/05/1981 | 55 | 1 | | TURN OF THE TIDE | Polydor POLD 5040 |
| 24/07/1982 | 15 | 11 | | A CONCERT FOR THE PEOPLE (BERLIN) | Polydor POLD 5052 |
| 28/05/1983 | 36 | 4 | | RING OF CHANGES | Polydor POLH 3 |
| 14/04/1984 | 33 | 6 | | VICTIMS OF CIRCUMSTANCES | Polydor POLD 5135 |
| 14/02/1987 | 65 | 1 | | FACE TO FACE | Polydor POLD 5209 |

### BARENAKED LADIES Canadian rock group formed in Scarborough, Toronto in 1988 by Steven Page (born 22/6/1970, Scarborough, guitar/vocals) and Ed Robertson (born 25/10/1970, Scarborough, guitar) with brothers Jim (born 12/2/1970, double

bass) and Andrew Creegan (born 4/7/1971, keyboards) and Tyler Stewart (born 21/9/1967, drums). They signed with Warners subsidiary Sire in 1992. Keyboardist Kevin Hearn joined the live line-up in 1994, but was forced to take an eighteen-month sabbatical when leukaemia was diagnosed (Chris Brown was his temporary replacement); later he was given a clean bill of health.

| 27/08/1994 | 57 | 1 | | MAYBE YOU SHOULD DRIVE | Reprise 9362457092 |
| 06/03/1999 | 20 | 16 | ● | STUNT | Reprise 9362469632 |
| 30/09/2000 | 64 | 1 | | MAROON | Reprise 9362478912 |

### DANIEL BARENBOIM — see ENGLISH CHAMBER ORCHESTRA

### GARY BARLOW UK singer (born 20/1/1971, Frodsham) and founding member of Take That in 1990 who quickly emerged as their chief songwriter. He went solo when the group disbanded in 1996.

| 07/06/1997 | ❶¹ | 26 | ✪ | OPEN ROAD | RCA 74321417202 |
| 23/10/1999 | 35 | 1 | | TWELVE MONTHS, ELEVEN DAYS | RCA 74321707662 |

### SYD BARRETT UK guitarist/singer (born Roger Barrett, 6/1/1946, Cambridge) who was a member of and chief songwriter for Pink Floyd before launching a solo career in April 1969.

| 07/02/1970 | 40 | 1 | | MADCAP LAUGHS | Harvest SHVL 765 |

### BARRON KNIGHTS UK comedy/vocal group formed in Leighton Buzzard in 1960 by Barron Anthony Osmond (bass/vocals), Butch Baker (guitar/banjo/vocals), Dave Ballinger (drums), Duke D'Mond (born Richard Palmer, guitar/vocals) and Peter 'Peanuts' Langford (guitar/vocals).

| 02/12/1978 | 15 | 13 | ● | NIGHT GALLERY | Epic EPC 83221 |
| 01/12/1979 | 51 | 4 | | TEACH THE WORLD TO LAUGH | Epic EPC 83891 |
| 13/12/1980 | 45 | 5 | ○ | JUST A GIGGLE | Epic EPC 84550 |

### JOHN BARRY UK bandleader (born John Barry Prendergast, 3/11/1933, York) who arranged Adam Faith's early hits and later became synonymous with film and TV scores, in particular for James Bond films. He won Oscars for *Born Free* (1966), *The Lion In Winter* (1968), *Out Of Africa* (1985) and *Dances With Wolves* (1990). Awarded the OBE in 1999, his three Grammy Awards include Best Instrumental Theme for *Midnight Cowboy* in 1969 and Best Jazz Performance by a Big Band with Bob Wilber for *The Cotton Club Soundtrack* in 1985.

| 31/10/1964 | 14 | 5 | | JAMES BOND 007 – GOLDFINGER Original soundtrack to the film | United Artists ULP 1076 |
| 29/01/1972 | 18 | 9 | | THE PERSUADERS Music from the TV series | CBS 64816 |
| 22/06/1985 | 81 | 1 | | JAMES BOND 007 – A VIEW TO A KILL Original soundtrack to the film | Parlophone BOND 1 |
| 26/04/1986 | 81 | 2 | | OUT OF AFRICA 1986 Grammy Award for Best Instrumental Composition, and Original soundtrack to the film | MCA MCF 3310 |
| 01/08/1987 | 57 | 6 | | JAMES BOND 007 – THE LIVING DAYLIGHTS Original soundtrack to the film | Warner Brothers WX 111 |
| 20/04/1991 | 45 | 8 | | DANCES WITH WOLVES Original soundtrack to the film | Epic 4675911 |
| 08/05/1999 | 67 | 1 | | THE BEYONDNESS OF THINGS ENGLISH CHAMBER ORCHESTRA CONDUCTED BY JOHN BARRY | Decca 4600092 |

### BASEMENT JAXX UK dance/production duo formed in London by DJ's Felix Buxton and Simon Ratcliffe who also ran the Atlantic Jaxx label. Previously recording as Summer Daze, they won Best Dance Act at the 2002 and 2004 BRIT Awards.

| 22/05/1999 | 4 | 45 | ● | REMEDY | XL Recordings XLCD 129 |
| 07/07/2001 | 5 | 26 | ● | ROOTY | XL Recordings XLCD 143 |
| 01/11/2003 | 17 | 14 | ● | KISH KASH | XL Recordings XLCD 174 |

### BASIA Polish singer (born Basha Trzetrzelewska, 30/9/1954, Jaworzno, Poland) who was a member of Matt Bianco before going solo.

| 13/02/1988 | 61 | 3 | | TIME AND TIDE | Portrait 4502631 |
| 03/03/1990 | 68 | 1 | | LONDON WARSAW NEW YORK | Portrait 4632821 |

### COUNT BASIE US band leader/pianist (born William Basie, 21/8/1904, Red Bank, NJ) who was taught piano by his mother. He worked as a cinema pianist before joining Walter Page's Blue Devil's. After a brief spell with Bennie Moten, he launched his own band in 1935. He appeared in films including *Sex And The Single Girl* and *Made In Paris* and was a regular on TV shows in the 1950s. He died on 26/4/1984. He has won eight Grammy Awards: Best Performance by a Dance Band and Best Jazz Performance in 1958 for *Basie*; Best Performance by a Dance Band for Dancing in 1960 for *Dance With Basie*; Best Performance by an Orchestra For Dancing in 1963 for *This Time By Basie! Hits of the '50s and '60s*; Best Jazz Performance by a Soloist in 1976 for *Basie And Zoot*; Best Jazz Performance by a Big Band in 1980 for *On The Road*; Best Jazz Performance by a Big Band in 1982 for *Warm Breeze*; and Best Jazz Performance by a Big Band in 1984 for *88 Basie Street*. Since his death his orchestra has gone on to win a further five Grammy's: Best Jazz Vocal Performance, Female in 1987 for *Diane Schuur and the Count Basie Orchestra*, Best Jazz Performance by a Big Band in 1990 for *Basie's Bag*, Best Large Jazz Ensemble in 1996 for *Live at Manchester Craftsmen's Guild*, and Best Large Jazz Ensemble in 1998 for *Count Plays Duke* (plus the same award the following year). He has a star on the Hollywood Walk of Fame.

| 16/04/1960 | 17 | 1 | | CHAIRMAN OF THE BOARD | Columbia 33SX 1209 |

○ Silver disc ● Gold disc ✪ Platinum disc (additional platinum units are indicated by a figure following the symbol) ❶⁹ Number of weeks album topped the UK chart

| 23/02/1963 . . . . . 2 . . . . . . 23 . . . . . . | SINATRA-BASIE **FRANK SINATRA AND COUNT BASIE** . . . . . . . . . . . . . . . . . . . . . . . . . . . . . . . . . . . . . . . . . . . . . Reprise R 1008 |
| 19/09/1964 . . . . . 17 . . . . . . 4 . . . . . | IT MIGHT AS WELL BE SWING **FRANK SINATRA AND COUNT BASIE AND HIS ORCHESTRA** . . . . . . . . . . . . . . . . . . . . . Reprise R 1012 |

### TONI BASIL
US singer (born Antonia Basilotta, 22/9/1948, Philadelphia, PA) who was originally an actress, then a dancer, choreographer (working on the 1973 film *American Graffiti*) and video producer before recording her debut album in 1981.

| 06/02/1982 . . . . . 15 . . . . . 16 . . . . . . | WORD OF MOUTH . . . . . . . . . . . . . . . . . . . . . . . . . . . . . . . . . . . . . . . . . . . . . . . . . . . . . . . . . . . . . . . . . . . Radialchoice BASIL 1 |

### BASS-O-MATIC
UK multi-instrumentalist William Orbit (real name William Wainwright).

| 13/10/1990 . . . . . 57 . . . . . . 2 . . . . . | SET THE CONTROLS FOR THE HEART OF THE BASS . . . . . . . . . . . . . . . . . . . . . . . . . . . . . . . . . . . . . . . . . . . . . . Virgin V 2641 |

### SHIRLEY BASSEY
UK singer (born 8/1/1937, Cardiff) who turned professional at sixteen touring with the revue *Memories Of Al Jolson*. Discovered by Jack Hylton she became the most successful female performer in the UK for over a quarter of a century until eclipsed in the 1990s by Diana Ross and Madonna. She was named Best British Female Solo Artist at the 1977 BRIT Awards, awarded a CBE in 1993, named Show Business Personality of the Year in 1995 by the Variety Club, and was made a Dame in the 2000 New Year's Honours List.

| 28/01/1961 . . . . 12 . . . . . 2 . . . . . | FABULOUS SHIRLEY BASSEY . . . . . . . . . . . . . . . . . . . . . . . . . . . . . . . . . . . . . . . . . . . . . . . . . . . Columbia 33SX 1178 |
| 25/02/1961 . . . . . 9 . . . . . 10 . . . . . | **SHIRLEY** . . . . . . . . . . . . . . . . . . . . . . . . . . . . . . . . . . . . . . . . . . . . . . . . . . . . . . . . . . . . . . . . . . Columbia 33SX 1286 |
| 17/02/1962 . . . . 14 . . . . . 11 . . . . . | SHIRLEY BASSEY . . . . . . . . . . . . . . . . . . . . . . . . . . . . . . . . . . . . . . . . . . . . . . . . . . . . . . . . . . Columbia 33SX 1382 |
| 15/12/1962 . . . . 12 . . . . . 7 . . . . . | LET'S FACE THE MUSIC **SHIRLEY BASSEY WITH THE NELSON RIDDLE ORCHESTRA** . . . . . . . . . . . . . . . . Columbia 33SX 1454 |
| 04/12/1965 . . . . 15 . . . . . 7 . . . . . | SHIRLEY BASSEY AT THE PIGALLE . . . . . . . . . . . . . . . . . . . . . . . . . . . . . . . . . . . . . . . . . . . . . . . Columbia 33SX 1787 |
| 27/08/1966 . . . . 26 . . . . . 1 . . . . . | I'VE GOT A SONG FOR YOU . . . . . . . . . . . . . . . . . . . . . . . . . . . . . . . . . . . . . . . . . . . . . . . . . . . United Artists ULP 1142 |
| 17/02/1968 . . . . 38 . . . . . 3 . . . . . | TWELVE OF THOSE SONGS . . . . . . . . . . . . . . . . . . . . . . . . . . . . . . . . . . . . . . . . . . . . . . . . . . . . Columbia SCX 6204 |
| 07/12/1968 . . . . 28 . . . . 40 . . . . . | GOLDEN HITS OF SHIRLEY BASSEY . . . . . . . . . . . . . . . . . . . . . . . . . . . . . . . . . . . . . . . . . . . . . . Columbia SCX 6294 |
| 11/07/1970 . . . . 38 . . . . . 6 . . . . . | LIVE AT THE TALK OF THE TOWN . . . . . . . . . . . . . . . . . . . . . . . . . . . . . . . . . . . . . . . . . . . United Artists UAS 29095 |
| 29/08/1970 . . . . . 5 . . . . 28 . . . . . | **SOMETHING** . . . . . . . . . . . . . . . . . . . . . . . . . . . . . . . . . . . . . . . . . . . . . . . . . . . . . . . . . United Artists UAS 29100 |
| 15/05/1971 . . . . . 7 . . . . . 9 . . . . . | SOMETHING ELSE . . . . . . . . . . . . . . . . . . . . . . . . . . . . . . . . . . . . . . . . . . . . . . . . . . . . . . United Artists UAG 29149 |
| 02/10/1971 . . . . 27 . . . . . 8 . . . . . | BIG SPENDER . . . . . . . . . . . . . . . . . . . . . . . . . . . . . . . . . . . . . . . . . . . . . . . . . . . . . . . . . . . . . . Sunset SLS 50262 |
| 30/10/1971 . . . . 32 . . . . . 1 . . . . . | IT'S MAGIC . . . . . . . . . . . . . . . . . . . . . . . . . . . . . . . . . . . . . . . . . . . . . . . . . . . . . . . . . . . . . . . Starline SRS 5082 |
| 06/11/1971 . . . . 48 . . . . . 1 . . . . . | THE FABULOUS SHIRLEY BASSEY . . . . . . . . . . . . . . . . . . . . . . . . . . . . . . . . . . . . . . . . . . . . . . . . . . . . . MFP 1398 |
| 04/12/1971 . . . . 17 . . . . . 5 . . . . . | WHAT NOW MY LOVE . . . . . . . . . . . . . . . . . . . . . . . . . . . . . . . . . . . . . . . . . . . . . . . . . . . . . . . . . . . . MFP 5230 |
| 08/01/1972 . . . . 37 . . . . . 1 . . . . . | THE SHIRLEY BASSEY COLLECTION . . . . . . . . . . . . . . . . . . . . . . . . . . . . . . . . . . . . . . . United Artists UAD 60013/4 |
| 19/02/1972 . . . . 13 . . . . . 11 . . . . . | I CAPRICORN . . . . . . . . . . . . . . . . . . . . . . . . . . . . . . . . . . . . . . . . . . . . . . . . . . . . . . . United Artists UAS 29246 |
| 25/11/1972 . . . . 24 . . . . . 9 . . . . . | AND I LOVE YOU SO . . . . . . . . . . . . . . . . . . . . . . . . . . . . . . . . . . . . . . . . . . . . . . . . . . . United Artists UAS 29385 |
| 02/06/1973 . . . . 10 . . . . 10 . . . . . ○ | **NEVER NEVER NEVER** . . . . . . . . . . . . . . . . . . . . . . . . . . . . . . . . . . . . . . . . . . . . . . . . . United Artists UAG 29471 |
| 15/03/1975 . . . . . 2 . . . . . 23 . . . . . ● | **THE SHIRLEY BASSEY SINGLES ALBUM** . . . . . . . . . . . . . . . . . . . . . . . . . . . . . . . . . . . . . United Artists UAS 29728 |
| 01/11/1975 . . . . 13 . . . . . 7 . . . . . ○ | GOOD, BAD BUT BEAUTIFUL . . . . . . . . . . . . . . . . . . . . . . . . . . . . . . . . . . . . . . . . . . . . . United Artists UAS 29881 |
| 15/05/1976 . . . . 13 . . . . . 5 . . . . . ○ | LOVE, LIFE AND FEELINGS . . . . . . . . . . . . . . . . . . . . . . . . . . . . . . . . . . . . . . . . . . . . . . United Artists UAS 29944 |
| 04/12/1976 . . . . 15 . . . . . 9 . . . . . ● | THOUGHTS OF LOVE . . . . . . . . . . . . . . . . . . . . . . . . . . . . . . . . . . . . . . . . . . . . . . . . . United Artists UAS 30011 |
| 25/06/1977 . . . . 34 . . . . . 5 . . . . . | YOU TAKE MY HEART AWAY . . . . . . . . . . . . . . . . . . . . . . . . . . . . . . . . . . . . . . . . . . . . . United Artists UAS 30037 |
| 04/11/1978 . . . . . 3 . . . . . 12 . . . . . ✪ | **25TH ANNIVERSARY ALBUM** . . . . . . . . . . . . . . . . . . . . . . . . . . . . . . . . . . . United Artists SBTV 601 4748 |
| 12/05/1979 . . . . 40 . . . . . 5 . . . . . | THE MAGIC IS YOU . . . . . . . . . . . . . . . . . . . . . . . . . . . . . . . . . . . . . . . . . . . . . . . . United Artists UATV 30230 |
| 17/07/1982 . . . . 48 . . . . . 5 . . . . . | LOVE SONGS . . . . . . . . . . . . . . . . . . . . . . . . . . . . . . . . . . . . . . . . . . . . . . . . . . . . . . . . . Applause APKL 1163 |
| 20/10/1984 . . . . 25 . . . . 18 . . . . . ● | I AM WHAT I AM . . . . . . . . . . . . . . . . . . . . . . . . . . . . . . . . . . . . . . . . . . . . . . . . . . . . . . Towerball TOWLP 7 |
| 18/05/1991 . . . . 25 . . . . . 7 . . . . . | KEEP THE MUSIC PLAYING . . . . . . . . . . . . . . . . . . . . . . . . . . . . . . . . . . . . . . . . . . . . . . . . . . . . Dino DINTV 21 |
| 05/12/1992 . . . . 27 . . . . . 5 . . . . . | THE BEST OF SHIRLEY BASSEY . . . . . . . . . . . . . . . . . . . . . . . . . . . . . . . . . . . . . . . . . . . . . . . . Dino DINCD 49 |
| 04/12/1993 . . . . 34 . . . . . 5 . . . . . ● | SHIRLEY BASSEY SINGS ANDREW LLOYD WEBBER . . . . . . . . . . . . . . . . . . . . . . . . . . . . . . . . Premier CDDPR 114 |
| 11/11/1995 . . . . 24 . . . . . 9 . . . . . ● | SHIRLEY BASSEY SINGS THE MOVIES . . . . . . . . . . . . . . . . . . . . . . . . . . . . . . . . . . . . . . . Polygram TV 5293992 |
| 09/11/1996 . . . . 47 . . . . . 8 . . . . . ○ | THE SHOW MUST GO ON . . . . . . . . . . . . . . . . . . . . . . . . . . . . . . . . . . . . . . . . . . . . . . . Polygram TV 5337122 |
| 09/09/2000 . . . . 62 . . . . . 1 . . . . . | THE REMIX ALBUM – DIAMONDS ARE FOREVER . . . . . . . . . . . . . . . . . . . . . . . . . . . . . . . . . . . EMI 5258732 |
| 25/11/2000 . . . . 54 . . . . . 4 . . . . . ● | THIS IS MY LIFE – THE GREATEST HITS . . . . . . . . . . . . . . . . . . . . . . . . . . . . . . . . . . . . . . . . . Liberty 5258742 |
| 07/06/2003 . . . . 19 . . . . . 4 . . . . . ○ | THANK YOU FOR THE YEARS . . . . . . . . . . . . . . . . . . . . . . . . . . . . . . . . . . . . . . . . . . . . . . . . . . Citrus 5122722 |

### MIKE BATT – see JUSTIN HAYWARD

### BAUHAUS
UK group formed in Northampton in 1978 by Peter Murphy (born 11/7/1957, Northampton, vocals), Daniel Ash (born 31/7/1957, Northampton, guitar/vocals), David Jay (born David Haskinsin, 24/4/1957, Northampton, bass/vocals) and Kevin Haskins (born 19/7/1960, Northampton, drums), originally known as Bauhaus 1919 (after the German art/design movement launched in 1919). They disbanded in 1983. Murphy linked up with Mick Karn (of Japan) to record one album as Dali's Car before going solo.

| 15/11/1980 . . . . . 72 . . . . . . 1 . . . . . | IN THE FLAT FIELD . . . . . . . . . . . . . . . . . . . . . . . . . . . . . . . . . . . . . . . . . . . . . . . . . . . . . . . . . . . 4AD CAD 13 |
| 24/10/1981 . . . . . 30 . . . . . . 5 . . . . . ○ | MASK . . . . . . . . . . . . . . . . . . . . . . . . . . . . . . . . . . . . . . . . . . . . . . . . . . . . . . . . . . . . . . Beggars Banquet BEGA 29 |
| 30/10/1982 . . . . . 4 . . . . . . 6 . . . . . ○ | **THE SKY'S GONE OUT** . . . . . . . . . . . . . . . . . . . . . . . . . . . . . . . . . . . . . . . . . . . . . . . . . Beggars Banquet BEGA 42 |
| 23/07/1983 . . . . . 13 . . . . . 10 . . . . . | BURNING FROM THE INSIDE . . . . . . . . . . . . . . . . . . . . . . . . . . . . . . . . . . . . . . . . . . Beggars Banquet BEGA 45 |
| 30/11/1985 . . . . . 36 . . . . . . 2 . . . . . ○ | 1979–1983 . . . . . . . . . . . . . . . . . . . . . . . . . . . . . . . . . . . . . . . . . . . . . . . . . . . . . . . . . Beggars Banquet BEGA 64 |

## BAY CITY ROLLERS
UK group formed in Edinburgh in 1967 by Leslie McKeown (born 12/11/1955, Edinburgh, vocals), Eric Faulkner (born 21/10/1955, Edinburgh, guitar), Stuart 'Woody' Wood (born 25/2/1957, Edinburgh, guitar), Alan Longmuir (born 20/6/1953, Edinburgh, bass) and his brother Derek (born 19/5/1955, Edinburgh, drums) as The Saxons. Bandleader Tom Paton discovered them, quit his job to become their manager and chose their name by sticking a pin in a map of the US. Although a group bearing their name still tours the nostalgia circuit to this day, the original line-up effectively dispersed in 1978.

| | | | | | |
|---|---|---|---|---|---|
| 12/10/1974 | ❶⁴ | 62 | ✪ | ROLLIN' | Bell BELLS 244 |
| 03/05/1975 | ❶³ | 37 | ✪ | ONCE UPON A STAR | Bell SYBEL 8001 |
| 13/12/1975 | 3 | 12 | ● | WOULDN'T YOU LIKE IT | Bell SYBEL 8002 |
| 25/09/1976 | 4 | 12 | ○ | DEDICATION | Bell SYBEL 8005 |
| 13/08/1977 | 18 | 4 | | IT'S A GAME | Arista SPARTY 1009 |
| 17/04/2004 | 11 | 9+ | | THE VERY BEST OF | Bell/Arista 82876608192 |

## BBC SYMPHONY ORCHESTRA
UK orchestra and chorus.

| | | | | | |
|---|---|---|---|---|---|
| 04/10/1969 | 36 | 1 | | LAST NIGHT AT THE PROMS **COLIN DAVIS CONDUCTING THE BBC SYMPHONY ORCHESTRA, SINGERS & CHORUS** | Philips SFM 23033 |
| 11/12/1982 | 69 | 5 | ● | HIGHLIGHTS FROM LAST NIGHT AT THE PROMS '82 **BBC SYMPHONY ORCHESTRA, SINGERS AND SYMPHONY CHORUS CONDUCTED BY JAMES LOUGHRAN** | K-Tel NE 1198 |
| 28/02/1998 | 44 | 1 | | ELGAR/PAYNE SYMPHONY NO. 3 **BBC SYMPHONY ORCHESTRA CONDUCTED BY ANDREW DAVIS** | NMC NMCD 053 |

## BBE
Italian/French dance group formed by Bruno Sanchioni, Bruno Quartier and Emmanuel Top. Sanchioni is also responsible for Age Of Love.

| | | | | | |
|---|---|---|---|---|---|
| 28/02/1998 | 60 | 2 | | GAMES | Positiva 4934932 |

## BBM
UK rock group formed by Jack Bruce (born John Bruce, 14/5/1943, Lanarkshire, vocals/bass), Ginger Baker (born Peter Baker, 19/8/1939, London, drums) and Gary Moore (born 4/4/1952, Belfast, guitar). Bruce and Baker had previously been in Cream, Moore in Thin Lizzy.

| | | | | | |
|---|---|---|---|---|---|
| 18/06/1994 | 9 | 4 | | **AROUND THE NEXT DREAM** | Virgin CDV 2745 |

## BBMAK
UK vocal group formed in 1996 by Christian Burns (born 18/1/1974), Mark Barry (born 26/10/1978) and Stephen McNalty (born 4/7/1978).

| | | | | | |
|---|---|---|---|---|---|
| 09/06/2001 | 16 | 3 | | SOONER OR LATER | Telstar TCD 3179 |

## BE BOP DELUXE
UK band formed in 1971 by Bill Nelson (born 18/12/1948, Wakefield, guitar/vocals), Nick Chatterton-Dew (drums), Robert Bryan (bass), Ian Parkin (guitar) and Richard Brown (keyboards). Re-formed by Nelson in 1974 with Charlie Tummahai (bass), Simon Fox (drums) and Andrew Clarke (keyboards). They disbanded in 1978 and Nelson formed Red Noise.

| | | | | | |
|---|---|---|---|---|---|
| 31/01/1976 | 17 | 12 | ○ | SUNBURST FINISH | Harvest SHSP 4053 |
| 25/09/1976 | 12 | 6 | ○ | MODERN MUSIC | Harvest SHSP 4058 |
| 06/08/1977 | 10 | 5 | | **LIVE! IN THE AIR AGE** | Harvest SHVL 816 |
| 25/02/1978 | 22 | 5 | | DRASTIC PLASTIC | Harvest SHSP 4091 |

## BEACH BOYS
US group formed in 1961 in Hawthorne, CA by brothers Brian (born 20/6/1942, Hawthorne, keyboards/bass), Carl (born 21/12/1946, Hawthorne, guitar) and Dennis Wilson (born 4/12/1944, Hawthorne, drums), cousin Mike Love (born 15/3/1941, Los Angeles, CA, lead vocals/saxophone) and Al Jardine (born 3/9/1942, Lima, OH, guitar). Originally called Carl And The Passions (later an album title), then The Pendeltones, they were eventually named The Beach Boys to reflect the Californian 'surfing' subject matter of their early singles. They quickly became one of the biggest US bands of the era, scoring worldwide hits. Dennis Wilson drowned on 28/12/1983 (his family's request that he should be buried at sea was only granted after personal intervention of President Ronald Reagan), while chief songwriter Brian Wilson stopped touring in 1964 (Glen Campbell was his replacement). His daughters, Carnie and Wendy Wilson, are members of Wilson Phillips. Carl Wilson, listed as a 'conscientious objector' during the Vietnam War (he was briefly jailed for refusing to undertake bedpan changing duties at the Los Angeles' Veterans Hospital in lieu of military service), died from cancer on 6/2/1998. The group was inducted into the Rock & Roll Hall of Fame in 1988 and has a star on the Hollywood Walk of Fame.

| | | | | | |
|---|---|---|---|---|---|
| 25/09/1965 | 17 | 7 | | SURFIN' USA | Capitol T 1890 |
| 19/02/1966 | 3 | 14 | | **BEACH BOYS PARTY** | Capitol T 2398 |
| 16/04/1966 | 6 | 25 | | **BEACH BOYS TODAY** | Capitol T 2269 |
| 09/07/1966 | 2 | 39 | | **PET SOUNDS** | Capitol T 2458 |
| 16/07/1966 | 4 | 22 | | **SUMMER DAYS (AND SUMMER NIGHTS)** | Capitol T 2354 |
| 12/11/1966 | 2 | 142 | | **BEST OF THE BEACH BOYS** | Capitol T 20865 |
| 11/03/1967 | 13 | 14 | | SURFER GIRL | Capitol T 1981 |
| 21/10/1967 | 3 | 39 | | **BEST OF THE BEACH BOYS VOLUME 2** | Capitol ST 20956 |
| 18/11/1967 | 9 | 8 | | SMILEY SMILE | Capitol ST 9001 |
| 16/03/1968 | 7 | 15 | | **WILD HONEY** | Capitol ST 2859 |
| 21/09/1968 | 13 | 8 | | FRIENDS | Capitol ST 2895 |
| 23/11/1968 | 8 | 12 | | **BEST OF THE BEACH BOYS VOLUME 3** | Capitol ST 21142 |
| 29/03/1969 | 3 | 10 | | **20/20** | Capitol EST 133 |

○ Silver disc  ● Gold disc  ✪ Platinum disc (additional platinum units are indicated by a figure following the symbol)  ❶⁹ Number of weeks album topped the UK chart

| Date | POS | WKS | BPI | Album Title | Label & Number |
|------|-----|-----|-----|-------------|----------------|
| 19/09/1970 | 5 | 30 | | GREATEST HITS | Capitol T 21628 |
| 05/12/1970 | 29 | 6 | | SUNFLOWER | Stateside SSL 8251 |
| 27/11/1971 | 15 | 7 | | SURF'S UP | Stateside SLS 10313 |
| 24/06/1972 | 25 | 1 | | CARL AND THE PASSIONS/SO TOUGH | Reprise K 44184 |
| 17/02/1973 | 20 | 7 | ○ | HOLLAND | Reprise K 54008 |
| 10/07/1976 | ❶¹⁰ | 86 | ✪ | 20 GOLDEN GREATS | Capitol EMTV 1 |
| 24/07/1976 | 31 | 3 | ○ | 15 BIG ONES | Reprise K 54079 |
| 07/05/1977 | 28 | 1 | | THE BEACH BOYS LOVE YOU | Reprise K 54087 |
| 21/04/1979 | 32 | 6 | | LA (LIGHT ALBUM) | Caribou CRB 86081 |
| 12/04/1980 | 54 | 3 | | KEEPING THE SUMMER ALIVE | Caribou CRB 86109 |
| 30/07/1983 | ❶³ | 17 | ✪ | THE VERY BEST OF THE BEACH BOYS | Capitol BBTV 1867193 |
| 22/06/1985 | 60 | 2 | | THE BEACH BOYS | Caribou CRB 26378 |
| 23/06/1990 | 2 | 27 | ✪ | SUMMER DREAMS – 28 CLASSIC TRACKS | Capitol EMTVD 51 |
| 01/07/1995 | 25 | 6 | ○ | THE BEST OF THE BEACH BOYS | Capitol CDESTVD 3 |
| 16/09/1995 | 59 | 4 | | PET SOUNDS | Fame CDFA 3298 |
| 11/07/1998 | 28 | 4 | | GREATEST HITS | EMI 4956962 |
| 19/09/1998 | 56 | 1 | | ENDLESS HARMONY SOUNDTRACK | Capitol 4963912 |
| 21/07/2001 | 31 | 5 | ○ | THE VERY BEST OF THE BEACH BOYS | Capitol 5326152 |

**BEASTIE BOYS** US rap trio formed in New York by King Ad-Rock (born Adam Horovitz, 31/10/1966, New York, son of playwright and screenwriter Israel Horovitz), MCA Adam (born Adam Yauch, 15/8/1967, New York, MCA stands for Master of Ceremonies) and Mike D (born Michael Diamond, 20/11/1965, New York). Their first DJ was DJ Double RR (record executive Rick Rubin) and later Dr Dre who went on to host MTV's *Yo! MTV Raps*. They started a craze for wearing logos from VW cars, which led to Volkswagen supplying them directly to fans to prevent them from stealing them. They have won two Grammies including Best Rap Group Performance in 1998 for the single *Intergalactic*, and they were named Best Rap Act at the 1998 MTV Europe Music Awards. They launched the Grand Royal Records label in 1993 (acts included Bran Van 3000) that ceased business in August 2001.

| Date | POS | WKS | BPI | Album Title | Label & Number |
|------|-----|-----|-----|-------------|----------------|
| 31/01/1987 | 7 | 40 | ● | LICENSE TO ILL ▲⁷ | Def Jam 450062 |
| 05/08/1989 | 44 | 2 | | PAUL'S BOUTIQUE | Capitol EST 2102 |
| 04/06/1994 | 10 | 15 | ● | ILL COMMUNICATION ▲¹ | Grand Royal CDEST 2229 |
| 10/06/1995 | 23 | 2 | | ROOT DOWN (EP) | Grand Royal CDEST 2262 |
| 06/04/1996 | 45 | 1 | | THE IN SOUND FROM WAY OUT! | Grand Royal CDEST 2281 |
| 18/07/1998 | ❶¹ | 21 | ● | HELLO NASTY ▲³ 1998 Grammy for Best Alternative Music Performance | Grand Royal 4957232 |
| 04/12/1999 | 36 | 7 | | ANTHOLOGY – THE SOUNDS OF SCIENCE | Grand Royal 5236642 |
| 26/06/04 | 2 | 1+ | ● | TO THE 5 BOROUGHS | Capitol 4733390 |

**BEAT** UK ska group formed in Birmingham in 1978 by Dave Wakeling (born 19/2/1956, Birmingham, guitar/vocals), Andy Cox (born 25/1/1956, Birmingham, guitar), David Steele (born 8/9/1960, Isle of Wight, bass) and Everett Morton (born 5/4/1951, St Kitts, drums), with 'toaster' Ranking Roger and saxophonist Saxa (who was 50 when they signed their record deal). The reggae/ska revival helped their debut single on 2 Tone to hit the top ten, before they launched the Go Feet label. They split in 1983, Cox and Steele forming Fine Young Cannibals with Roland Gift. They were named The English Beat in the US as there was already a US group called The Beat.

| Date | POS | WKS | BPI | Album Title | Label & Number |
|------|-----|-----|-----|-------------|----------------|
| 31/05/1980 | 3 | 32 | ● | JUST CAN'T STOP IT | Go-Feet BEAT 001 |
| 16/05/1981 | 3 | 18 | ○ | WHA'PPEN | Go-Feet BEAT 3 |
| 09/10/1982 | 21 | 6 | | SPECIAL BEAT SERVICE | Go-Feet BEAT 5 |
| 11/06/1983 | 10 | 13 | ○ | WHAT IS BEAT? (THE BEST OF THE BEAT) | Go-Feet BEAT 6 |
| 10/02/1996 | 13 | 4 | | BPM... THE VERY BEST OF THE BEAT | Go-Feet 74321231952 |

**BEATLES** UK group formed in Liverpool in 1957 as the Quarrymen, then Johnny & The Moondogs, The Silver Beetles and The Beatals, before settling on The Beatles in 1960 (in honour of The Crickets). The original line-up consisted of Paul McCartney (born 18/6/1942, Liverpool, guitar/vocals), John Lennon (born 9/10/1940, Liverpool, guitar/vocals), George Harrison (born 24/2/1943, Liverpool, guitar/vocals) and Stuart Sutcliffe (born 23/6/1940, Edinburgh, bass), with drummer Pete Best (born 24/11/1941, Madras, India) passing an audition in time for their first visit to Germany. Sutcliffe (who died from a brain haemorrhage on 10/4/1962) stayed in Hamburg with his fiancee Astrid Kirchher and McCartney switched to bass. An enquiry by Raymond Jones at Brian Epstein's NEMS record shop in Liverpool for a German recording of *My Bonnie* by Tony Sheridan & The Beat Brothers (the name Beatles was considered too risque by the German record company) led to Epstein managing the band in place of bar owner Alan Williams. They signed with Parlophone after being turned down by other companies including, most notably, Decca, for whom they auditioned. Two months later Ringo Starr (born Richard Starkey, 7/7/1940, Liverpool) replaced Best, although the original choice had been Johnny Hutchinson of The Big Three who turned it down. Parlophone's A&R manager George Martin produced all their singles. On 7/12/1963 all four members made up the panel for *Juke Box Jury* and successfully predicted the success (or not) for seven of the ten titles. They starred in the films *A Hard Day's Night* (1964), *Help!* (1965), *Let It Be* (1965; it won an Oscar for Best Original Song Score) and the TV special *Magical*

*Mystery Tour*. They formed the Apple label in 1968 (signing Mary Hopkin and Badfinger among others) but split in 1970, each going solo. They have won eight Grammy Awards: Best New Artist and Best Performance by a Vocal Group for *A Hard Day's Night*, both in 1964; Album of the Year and Best Contemporary Album in 1967 for *Sgt Pepper's Lonely Hearts Club Band*; Best Original Score Written for a Motion Picture or TV Show in 1970 for *Let It Be*; Best Pop Duo or Group and Best Music Video Short Form in 1996 for *Free As A Bird*; and Best Music Video Long Form in 1996 for *The Beatles Anthology*. Both *Revolver* and *Sgt Pepper's Lonely Hearts Club Band* won Grammy Awards for Best Album Cover, whilst *Michelle* was named Song of the Year in 1966 (despite the fact it has not been released as a single, although this has not stopped it receiving over four million radio plays in the USA alone). Paul McCartney was given the Best Contemporary Rock & Roll Vocal Performance Grammy Award in 1966 for *Eleanor Rigby*, even though it was a group effort. The murder of John Lennon, shot in New York by fan Mark David Chapman on 8/12/1980, brought any reunion hopes to an end, although the remaining members have linked together. Having survived an attack by another crazed fan in December 1999, George Harrison died from cancer on 29/11/2001. The group was presented with the Outstanding Contribution Award at the 1983 BRIT Awards (in 1977 they were presented with the same award, named Best Group and saw *Sgt Pepper's Lonely Hearts Club Band* named Best Album). Total worldwide sales by 1999 were estimated at 1 billion records: the 1996 double album *Anthology* sold 10 million copies worldwide in just four weeks, while the 2000 album *1* was the fastest selling album in the world, with 13.5 million copies sold in its first month. They were inducted into the Rock & Roll Hall of Fame in 1988. The group has a star on the Hollywood Walk of Fame.

| DATE | POS | WKS | BPI | ALBUM TITLE | LABEL & NUMBER |
|------|-----|-----|-----|-------------|----------------|
| 06/04/1963 | ❶[30] | 70 | | **PLEASE PLEASE ME** | Parlophone PMC 1202 |
| 30/11/1963 | ❶[21] | 51 | | **WITH THE BEATLES** | Parlophone PMC 1206 |
| 18/07/1964 | ❶[21] | 38 | | **A HARD DAY'S NIGHT** ▲[14] | Parlophone PMC 1230 |
| 12/12/1964 | ❶[11] | 46 | | **BEATLES FOR SALE** | Parlophone PMC 1240 |
| 14/08/1965 | ❶[9] | 37 | | **HELP!** ▲[9] | Parlophone PMC 1255 |
| 11/12/1965 | ❶[9] | 42 | | **RUBBER SOUL** ▲[1] | Parlophone PMC 1267 |
| 13/08/1966 | ❶[7] | 34 | | **REVOLVER** ▲[6] 1966 Grammy Award for Best Album Cover | Parlophone PMC 7009 |
| 10/12/1966 | 7 | 34 | | **A COLLECTION OF BEATLES OLDIES** | Parlophone PMC 7016 |
| 03/06/1967 | ❶[27] | 149 | | **SGT PEPPER'S LONELY HEARTS CLUB BAND** ▲[15] ◆[11] 1967 Grammy Awards for Album of the Year, Best Contemporary Album and Best Album Cover (designer Peter Blake was knighted in the 2002 Queen's Birthday Honours List). 1977 BRIT Award for Best Album. The cover depicts the following celebrities: Unknown US Legionnaire, Aleister Crowley, Mae West, Lenny Bruce, Karl-Heinz Stockhausen, W.C. Fields, Carl Gustav Jung, Edgar Allan Poe, Fred Astaire, Merkin, Unknown, Huntz Hall, Simon Rodia, Bob Dylan, Aubrey Beardsley, Sir Robert Peel, Aldous Huxley, Terry Southern, Tony Curtis, Wallace Berman, Tommy Handley, Marilyn Monroe, William Burroughs, Unknown, Richard Lindner, Oliver Hardy, Karl Marx, H.G. Wells, Unknown, Unknown, Stuart Sutcliffe, Unknown, Dylan Thomas, Dion, Dr David Livingstone (waxwork), Stan Laurel, George Bernard Shaw (waxwork), Unknown, Max Miller, Unknown, Marlon Brando, Tom Mix, Oscar Wilde, Tyrone Power, Larry Bell, Johnny Weissmuller, Stephen Crane, Issy Bonn, Albert Stubbins, Unknown, Albert Einstein, Lewis Carroll, T.E. Lawrence (waxwork), Sonny Liston (waxwork), George Harrison (waxwork), John Lennon (waxwork), Ringo Starr (waxwork), Paul McCartney (waxwork), Unknown, John Lennon, Ringo Starr, Paul McCartney, George Harrison, Bobby Breen, Marlene Dietrich, Unknown, Diana Dors (waxwork) and Shirley Temple. This is the best selling album in the UK with sales in excess of 4.5 million copies. .......... .......... Parlophone PCS 7027 |
| 13/01/1968 | 31 | 2 | | MAGICAL MYSTERY TOUR (IMPORT) ▲[8] | Capitol SMAL 2835 |
| 07/12/1968 | ❶[8] | 22 | | **THE BEATLES (WHITE ALBUM)** ▲[9] ◆[19] | Apple PCS 7067/8 |
| 01/02/1969 | 3 | 10 | | **YELLOW SUBMARINE** | Apple PCS 7070 |
| 04/10/1969 | ❶[17] | 81 | | **ABBEY ROAD** ▲[11] ◆[12] | Apple PCS 7088 |
| 23/05/1970 | ❶[3] | 59 | | **LET IT BE** ▲[4] 1970 Grammy Award for Best Original Score for a Motion Picture or TV Show | Apple PXS 1 |
| 16/01/1971 | 30 | 1 | | A HARD DAY'S NIGHT | Parlophone PCS 3058 |
| 24/07/1971 | 33 | 2 | | HELP! | Parlophone PCS 3071 |
| 05/05/1973 | 3 | 114 | ✪ | **THE BEATLES 1962–1966** ◆[15] | Apple PCSP 718 |
| 05/05/1973 | 2 | 148 | ✪ | **THE BEATLES 1967–1970** ▲[1] ◆[16] | Apple PCSP 717 |
| 26/06/1976 | 11 | 15 | ● | ROCK 'N' ROLL MUSIC | Parlophone PCSP 719 |
| 21/08/1976 | 45 | 1 | | THE BEATLES TAPES | Polydor 2683 068 |
| 21/05/1977 | ❶[1] | 17 | ● | **THE BEATLES AT THE HOLLYWOOD BOWL** | Parlophone EMTV 4 |
| 17/12/1977 | 7 | 17 | ● | LOVE SONGS | Parlophone PCSP 721 |
| 03/11/1979 | 71 | 1 | ○ | RARITIES | Parlophone PCM 1001 |
| 15/11/1980 | 17 | 16 | ● | BEATLES BALLADS | Parlophone PCS 7214 |
| 30/10/1982 | 10 | 30 | ✪ | **20 GREATEST HITS** | Parlophone PCTC 260 |
| 07/03/1987 | 30 | 4 | | A HARD DAY'S NIGHT | Parlophone CDP 7464372 |
| 07/03/1987 | 32 | 4 | | PLEASE PLEASE ME | Parlophone CDP 7464352 |
| 07/03/1987 | 40 | 3 | | WITH THE BEATLES | Parlophone CDP 7464362 |
| 07/03/1987 | 45 | 2 | | BEATLES FOR SALE | Parlophone CDP 7464382 |
| 09/05/1987 | 46 | 12 | | REVOLVER | Parlophone CDP 7464412 |
| 09/05/1987 | 60 | 5 | | RUBBER SOUL | Parlophone CDP 7464402 |
| 09/05/1987 | 61 | 2 | | HELP! | Parlophone CDP 7464392 |
| 06/06/1987 | 3 | 49 | | **SGT PEPPER'S LONELY HEARTS CLUB BAND** | Parlophone CDP 7464422 |
| 05/09/1987 | 18 | 2 | | THE BEATLES (WHITE ALBUM) | Apple CDS 7464439 |
| 05/09/1987 | 60 | 1 | | YELLOW SUBMARINE | Parlophone CDP 7464452 |
| 03/10/1987 | 52 | 1 | | MAGICAL MYSTERY TOUR | Parlophone PCTC 255 |
| 31/10/1987 | 30 | 11 | | ABBEY ROAD | Apple CDP 7464462 |
| 31/10/1987 | 50 | 1 | | LET IT BE This and the above twelve albums are CD re-issues. | Parlophone CDP 7464472 |
| 19/03/1988 | 46 | 1 | | PAST MASTERS VOLUME 1 | Parlophone CDBPM 1 |
| 19/03/1988 | 49 | 1 | | PAST MASTERS VOLUME 2. | Parlophone CDBPM 2 |
| 02/10/1993 | 3 | 24 | | **THE BEATLES 1962–1966** | Parlophone BEACD 2511 |
| 02/10/1993 | 4 | 24 | | **THE BEATLES 1967–1970** | Parlophone BEACD 2512 |
| 10/12/1994 | ❶[1] | 20 | ✪[2] | **LIVE AT THE BBC** ◇ | Apple CDS 8317962 |

○ Silver disc  ● Gold disc  ✪ Platinum disc (additional platinum units are indicated by a figure following the symbol)  ❶[9] Number of weeks album topped the UK chart

| | | | | | |
|---|---|---|---|---|---|
| 02/12/1995 | 2 | 10 | ✪² | **ANTHOLOGY 1** ◇² ▲³ | Apple CDPCSP 727 |
| 30/03/1996 | ❶¹ | 12 | ✪ | **ANTHOLOGY 2** ▲¹ | Apple CDPCSP 728 |
| 09/11/1996 | 4 | 11 | ● | **ANTHOLOGY 3** ▲¹ 1996 Grammy Award for Best Music Video Long Form | Apple CDPCSP 729 |
| 25/09/1999 | 8 | 5 | ● | **YELLOW SUBMARINE SONGTRACK** Original soundtrack to the film | Parlophone 5214812 |
| 25/11/2000 | ❶⁹ | 46 | ✪⁸ | **1** ◇⁸ ▲⁸ | Apple 5299702 |
| 29/11/2003 | 7 | 7 | ● | **LET IT BE – NAKED** | Apple 5957132 |

**BEATMASTERS** UK group formed by Paul Carter, Amanda Glanfield and Richard Walmsley (born 28/9/1962) who had begun as jingle writers. They were also responsible for Yazz's hit *Stand Up For Your Love Rights*. Walmsley was later in Goldbug.

| | | | | | |
|---|---|---|---|---|---|
| 01/07/1989 | 30 | 10 | ○ | **ANYWAYYAWANNA** | Rhythm King LEFTLP 10 |

**BEATS INTERNATIONAL** UK group formed by ex-Housemartin Norman Cook (born Quentin Cook, 31/7/1963, Brighton) after a stint as a record remixer, fronting the Urban All Stars and as a solo artist. The line-up comprised Andy Boucher (keyboards), Luke Cresswell (drums), Lester Noel (born 3/9/1962, London, vocals) and Lindy Layton (born Belinda Kimberley Layton, 7/12/1970 Chiswick, London, vocals). Layton was previously an actress, appearing in the children's TV series *Grange Hill*. She later recorded solo. The group disbanded in 1993 and Cook went on to launch Freak Power.

| | | | | | |
|---|---|---|---|---|---|
| 14/04/1990 | 17 | 15 | ● | **LET THEM EAT BINGO** | Go Beat 8421961 |

**BEAUTIFUL SOUTH** UK group formed by Paul Heaton (born 9/5/1962, Birkenhead, vocals), Dave Hemingway (born 20/9/1960, Hull, vocals), Jacqueline Abbott (born 10/11/1973, Merseyside, vocals), Dave Rotheray (born 9/2/1963, Hull, guitar), Sean Welch (born 12/4/1965, Enfield, bass) and Dave Stead (born 15/10/1966, Huddersfield, drums). Heaton and Hemingway were previously in The Housemartins. Abbott left in 2000 and was replaced by Briana Corrigan.

| | | | | | |
|---|---|---|---|---|---|
| 04/11/1989 | 2 | 26 | ✪ | **WELCOME TO THE BEAUTIFUL SOUTH** | Go Discs AGOLP 16 |
| 10/11/1990 | 2 | 22 | ✪ | **CHOKE** | Go Discs 8282331 |
| 11/04/1992 | 4 | 17 | ✪ | **0898: BEAUTIFUL SOUTH** | Go Discs 8283102 |
| 09/04/1994 | 6 | 24 | ● | **MIAOW** | Go Discs 8285072 |
| 19/11/1994 | ❶⁷ | 89 | ✪⁶ | **CARRY ON UP THE CHARTS – THE BEST OF THE BEAUTIFUL SOUTH** ◇² | Go Discs 8285722 |
| 02/11/1996 | ❶¹ | 46 | ✪⁵ | **BLUE IS THE COLOUR** ◇ | Go Discs 8288452 |
| 24/10/1998 | ❶² | 37 | ✪³ | **QUENCH** ◇ | Go Discs 5381662 |
| 21/10/2000 | 2 | 11 | ● | **PAINTING IT RED** | Go Discs 5483352 |
| 24/11/2001 | 10 | 13 | ✪ | **SOLID BRONZE – GREAT HITS** | Go Discs 5864442 |
| 08/11/2003 | 14 | 3 | ○ | **GAZE** | Go Discs 9865694 |

**BECK** US singer (born Beck David Campbell, 8/7/1970, Los Angeles, CA) who adopted the name Beck Hansen when his parents separated. He first recorded for the independent labels Bong Load, Sonic Enemy and Fingerpaint, before being snapped up by Geffen. He was named Best International Male at the BRIT Awards in 1997, 1999 and 2000. He has won three Grammy Awards including Best Male Rock Vocal Performance for the single *Where It's At* in 1996.

| | | | | | |
|---|---|---|---|---|---|
| 02/04/1994 | 41 | 4 | | **MELLOW GOLD** | Geffen GED 24634 |
| 06/07/1996 | 17 | 51 | ✪ | **O-DE-LAY** 1996 Grammy Award for Best Alternative Music Performance | Geffen GED 24926 |
| 14/11/1998 | 24 | 6 | | **MUTATIONS** 1999 Grammy Award for Best Alternative Music Performance | Geffen GED 25184 |
| 04/12/1999 | 19 | 14 | ● | **MIDNITE VULTURES** | Geffen 4905272 |
| 05/10/2002 | 20 | 3 | | **SEA CHANGE** | Geffen 4933932 |

**JEFF BECK** UK singer/guitarist (born 24/6/1944, Wallington) who played with Screaming Lord Sutch And The Nightshifts before replacing Eric Clapton in The Yardbirds. He formed the Jeff Beck Group in 1966 with Rod Stewart, Ron Wood and Aynsley Dunbar. He has won four Grammy Awards: Best Rock Instrumental Performance in 1985 for *Escape,* Best Rock Instrumental Performance in 1989 with Terry Bozzio and Tony Hyman for *Jeff Beck's Guitar Shop With Terry Bozzio And Tony Hyman*, Best Rock Instrumental Performance in 2001 for *Dirty Mind* and Best Rock Instrumental Peformance in 2003 for *Plan B*.

| | | | | | |
|---|---|---|---|---|---|
| 13/09/1969 | 39 | 1 | | **COSA NOSTRA BECK – OLA** | Columbia SCX 6351 |
| 28/04/1973 | 28 | 3 | | JEFF BECK, TIM BOGERT & CARMINE APPICE **JEFF BECK, TIM BOGERT AND CARMINE APPICE** | Epic EPC 65455 |
| 24/07/1976 | 38 | 5 | | **WIRED** | CBS 86012 |
| 19/07/1980 | 38 | 4 | | **THERE AND BACK** | Epic EPC 83288 |
| 17/08/1985 | 83 | 1 | | **FLASH** | Epic EPC 26112 |
| 27/03/1999 | 74 | 1 | | **WHO ELSE?** | Epic 4930412 |

▲⁹ Number of weeks album topped the US chart   ◆¹² RIAA Diamond Awards   ◇³ IFPI Platinum Europe Awards

### VICTORIA BECKHAM

UK singer (born Victoria Adams, 7/4/1974, Essex), a founding member of the Spice Girls, who launched a parallel solo career in 2000. Married to football star David Beckham, she was dropped by Virgin in June 2002 and subsequently signed to Telstar.

13/10/2001 . . . . . 10 . . . . . . 3 . . . . . . VICTORIA BECKHAM . . . . . . . . . . . . . . . . . . . . . . . . . . . . . . . . . . . . . . . . . . . . . . . . . . . . . Virgin CDV 2942

### DANIEL BEDINGFIELD

UK singer/producer (born 1980, New Zealand, raised in London) whose debut hit was one of five songs he recorded at home for £1,000 on a Making Waves computer audio programme. He later wrote with Mariah Carey.and was named best male at the 2004 BRITS. His sister Natasha later launched a singing career. He was involved in a serious road accident on New Year's Day 2004 in New Zealand when his car crashed, leaving him with a fractured skull.

07/09/2002 . . . . . 2 . . . . . . 79 . . . . . ✪⁵ GOTTA GET THRU THIS ◇ . . . . . . . . . . . . . . . . . . . . . . . . . . . . . . . . . . . . . . . . . . . . . . . . . Polydor 651252

### BEE GEES

UK group formed in Manchester in 1955 by brothers Barry (born 1/9/1947, Douglas, Isle of Man) and twins Robin and Maurice Gibb (born 22/12/1949, Douglas). The family emigrated to Australia soon after the birth of a fourth son Andy in 1958. At their first professional performance in 1955 they had intended miming to a Tommy Steele record that broke on the way to the concert so they had to sing live. Originally called The Gibbs and then The BG's (it's often thought this stands for 'Brothers Gibb' but they were named by early mentors Bill Good and Bill Gates), they finally settled on the Bee Gees. First successful as songwriters, penning Col Joye's Australian chart topper *Starlight Of Love,* they signed to Festival Records' Leedon subsidiary. A return to England in February 1967 saw two years of huge success before Barry and Maurice went solo in August 1969. The brothers reunited eight months later. The mid-1970s saw them embracing the disco scene, scoring the films *Saturday Night Fever* (1978), the soundtrack sold over 30 million copies worldwide, and *Staying Alive* (1983). They also appeared in the film *Sgt Pepper's Lonely Hearts Club Band* (1978). Younger brother Andy also embarked on a solo career. They have won five Grammy Awards: Best Pop Vocal Performance by a Group in 1977 for *How Deep Is Your Love*, Best Arrangement for Vocals in 1978 for *Stayin' Alive*, Best Pop Vocal Performance by a Group in 1978 for *Night Fever*, Album of the Year in 1978 for *Saturday Night Fever* Soundtrack, and Producer of the Year in 1978. Barry Gibb also won the 1980 Grammy Award for Best Pop Vocal Performance by a Duo with Barbra Streisand for *Guilty*. They received an Outstanding Achievement Award at the 1997 BRIT Awards and were inducted into the Rock & Roll Hall of Fame in 1997. Barry, Robin and Maurice were awarded CBEs in the 2002 New Year's Honours List. Maurice died from a heart attack on 12/1/2003.

| | | | | | |
|---|---|---|---|---|---|
| 12/08/1967 . . . . . 8 . . . . . . 26 . . . . . . | BEE GEE FIRST | Polydor 583012 |
| 24/02/1968 . . . . . 16 . . . . . 15 . . . . . . | HORIZONTAL | Polydor 582020 |
| 28/09/1968 . . . . . 4 . . . . . . 18 . . . . . . | IDEA | Polydor 583036 |
| 05/04/1969 . . . . . 10 . . . . . . 1 . . . . . . | ODESSA | Polydor 583049/50 |
| 08/11/1969 . . . . . 7 . . . . . . 22 . . . . . . | BEST OF THE BEE GEES | Polydor 583063 |
| 09/05/1970 . . . . . 57 . . . . . . 2 . . . . . . | CUCUMBER CASTLE | Polydor 2383 010 |
| 17/02/1979 . . . . ❶² . . . . 33 . . . . . . ✪ | SPIRITS HAVING FLOWN ▲⁶ | RSO RSBG 001 |
| 10/11/1979 . . . . 6 . . . . . . 25 . . . . . . ✪ | BEE GEES GREATEST ▲¹ | RSO RSDX 001 |
| 07/11/1981 . . . . 73 . . . . . . 8 . . . . . . | LIVING EYES | RSO RSBG 002 |
| 03/10/1987 . . . . 5 . . . . . . 24 . . . . . . ✪ | E.S.P | Warner Brothers WX 83 |
| 29/04/1989 . . . . 29 . . . . . . 3 . . . . . . | ONE | Warner Brothers WX 252 |
| 17/11/1990 . . . . 6 . . . . . . 108 . . . . . ✪³ | THE VERY BEST OF THE BEE GEES | Polydor 8473391 |
| 06/04/1991 . . . . 24 . . . . . . 5 . . . . . . | HIGH CIVILIZATION | Warner Brothers WX 417 |
| 25/09/1993 . . . . 23 . . . 13 . . . . . . ● | SIZE ISN'T EVERYTHING | Polydor 5199452 |
| 22/03/1997 . . . . 2 . . . . . . 19 . . . . . . ● | STILL WATERS ◇ | Polydor 5373022 |
| 19/09/1998 . . . . 4 . . . . . . 44 . . . . . . ✪³ | LIVE ONE NIGHT ONLY ◇² Recorded live at the MGM Grand in Las Vegas, NV during November 1997 | Polydor 5592202 |
| 14/04/2001 . . . . 6 . . . . . . 6 . . . . . . ● | THIS IS WHERE I CAME IN | Polydor 5494582 |
| 24/11/2001 . . . . 5 . . . . . . 33 . . . . . . ✪² | THEIR GREATEST HITS – THE RECORD ◇ | Polydor 5894492 |

### LOU BEGA

German singer (born David Lubega, 13/4/1975, Munich) .

18/09/1999 . . . . . 50 . . . . . . 2 . . . . . . A LITTLE BIT OF MAMBO ◇ . . . . . . . . . . . . . . . . . . . . . . . . . . . . . . . . . . . . . . . . . . . . . . . . . RCA 74321688612

### BELL BIV DEVOE

US vocal group formed in Boston, MA in 1989 by Ricky Bell (born 18/9/1967, Boston), Michael Bivins (born 10/8/1968, Boston) and Ronnie DeVoe (born 17/11/1967, Boston), all ex-members of teen sensation group New Edition.

01/09/1990 . . . . . 35 . . . . . . 5 . . . . . . POISON . . . . . . . . . . . . . . . . . . . . . . . . . . . . . . . . . . . . . . . . . . . . . . . . . . . . . . . . . . . . . MCA MCG 6094

### BELLAMY BROTHERS

US brothers Howard (born 2/2/1946, Darby, FL, guitar) and David Bellamy (born 16/9/1950, Darby, guitar/keyboards) who made their professional debut in 1958.

19/06/1976 . . . . . 21 . . . . . . 6 . . . . . O BELLAMY BROTHERS . . . . . . . . . . . . . . . . . . . . . . . . . . . . . . . . . . . . . . . . . . . . . . . . Warner Brothers K 56242

### REGINA BELLE

US singer (born 17/7/1963, Engelwood, NJ) who sang with The Manhattans for a year prior to signing a solo deal with CBS and releasing her debut album in 1987. She has won one Grammy Award: Best Pop Performance by a Duo or Group with Vocal in 1993 with Peabo Bryson for *A Whole New World (Aladdin's Theme)*.

01/08/1987 . . . . . 53 . . . . . . 4 . . . . . . ALL BY MYSELF . . . . . . . . . . . . . . . . . . . . . . . . . . . . . . . . . . . . . . . . . . . . . . . . . . . . . . CBS 4509981
16/09/1989 . . . . . 62 . . . . . . 1 . . . . . . STAY WITH ME . . . . . . . . . . . . . . . . . . . . . . . . . . . . . . . . . . . . . . . . . . . . . . . . . . . . . . CBS 4651321

## BELLE AND SEBASTIAN
UK group formed in Glasgow in 1996 by Chris Geddes (keyboards), Richard Colburn (drums), Mick Cooke (trumpet), Stuart Murdoch (guitar/vocals), Sarah Martin (violin), Stuart David (bass), Isobel Campbell (cello/vocals) and Stevie Jackson (guitar). They won the Best UK Newcomer award at the 1999 BRIT Awards.

| 19/09/1998 | 12 | 6 | ● | THE BOY WITH THE ARAB STRAP | Jeepster JPRCD 003 |
| 24/07/1999 | 13 | 4 | | TIGERMILK | Jeepster JPRCD 007 |
| 17/06/2000 | 10 | 3 | | **FOLD YOUR HANDS CHILD YOU WALK LIKE A PEASANT** | Jeepster JPRCD 010 |
| 15/06/2002 | 26 | 2 | | STORYTELLING | Jeepster JRPCD 014 |
| 18/10/2003 | 21 | 3 | ○ | DEAR CATASTROPHE WAITRESS | Rough Trade RTRADECD 080 |

## BELLE STARS
UK group formed by Jane Hirst (keyboards/saxophone), Jenni McKeown (vocals), Judy Parsons (drums), Lesley Shone (bass), Miranda Joyce (saxophone), Sarah Jane Owen (guitar) and Stella Barker (guitar). They all adopted the surname Belle Star. Judy, Miranda, Sarah Jane and Stella were previously in the Bodysnatchers, at the forefront of the ska revival. Sarah Jane later went solo.

| 05/02/1983 | 15 | 12 | ○ | THE BELLE STARS | Stiff SEEZ 45 |

## BELLRAYS
US R&B group formed in Los Angeles, CA in 1995 by Lisa Kekaula (vocals), Tony Fate (guitar), Bob Vennum (bass) and Todd Westover (drums). Kekaula later recorded with Basement Jaxx.

| 18/05/2002 | 73 | 1 | | MEET THE BELLRAYS | Poptones MC5069CD |

## BELLY
US rock group formed in Newport, RI in 1991 by Tanya Donelly (born 14/7/1966, Newport, guitar/vocals), Thomas Gorman (born 20/5/1966, Buffalo, NY, guitar), Chris Gorman (born 29/7/1967, Buffalo, drums) and Fred Abong (bass). Abong left in 1993 and was replaced by Gail Greenwood (born 10/3/1960, Providence, RI). Donelly had been in Throwing Muses and The Breeders, and also recorded solo. They disbanded in 1997.

| 13/02/1993 | 2 | 10 | ○ | **STAR** | 4AD 3002CD |
| 25/02/1995 | 6 | 3 | | KING | 4AD CADD 5004CD |

## PIERRE BELMONDE
French panpipe player.

| 07/06/1980 | 13 | 10 | ○ | THEMES FOR DREAMS | K-Tel ONE 1077 |

## BELMONTS — see DION AND THE BELMONTS

## BELOVED
UK rock group formed in London in 1983 by Jon Marsh (guitar/vocals), Guy Gousden (drums) and Tim Harvard (bass) as the Journey Through. Steve Waddington (guitar/keyboards) joined in 1984, although by 1993 it was a duo of Marsh and his wife Helena. Marsh once reached the semi-final as a contestant on Channel 4's *Countdown*.

| 03/03/1990 | 14 | 14 | ● | HAPPINESS | East West WX 299 |
| 01/12/1990 | 38 | 2 | | BLISSED OUT | East West WX 383 |
| 20/02/1993 | 2 | 12 | ● | **CONSCIENCE** | East West 4509914832 |
| 20/04/1996 | 25 | 3 | | X | East West 0630133162 |

## PAT BENATAR
US singer (born Patricia Andrzejewski, 10/1/1953, Long Island, NY) who trained as an opera singer before turning to rock music. She married her guitarist/producer Neil Giraldo in 1982 and later acted in the 1980 film *Union City*. She has won four Grammy Awards: Best Rock Vocal Performance in 1980 for *Crimes Of Passion,* Best Rock Vocal Performance in 1981 for *Fire And Ice,* Best Rock Vocal Performance in 1982 for *Shadows Of The Night,* and Best Rock Vocal Performance in 1983 for *Love Is A Battlefield.*

| 25/07/1981 | 30 | 7 | | PRECIOUS TIME ▲[1] | Chrysalis CHR 1346 |
| 13/11/1982 | 73 | 6 | | GET NERVOUS | Chrysalis CHR 1396 |
| 15/10/1983 | 60 | 5 | | LIVE FROM EARTH | Chrysalis CHR 1451 |
| 17/11/1984 | 31 | 25 | ○ | TROPICO | Chrysalis CHR 1471 |
| 24/08/1985 | 98 | 1 | | IN THE HEAT OF THE NIGHT | Chrysalis CHR 1236 |
| 07/12/1985 | 69 | 4 | | SEVEN THE HARD WAY | Chrysalis CHR 1507 |
| 07/11/1987 | 6 | 19 | ✪ | **BEST SHOTS** | Chrysalis PATV 1 |
| 16/07/1988 | 11 | 14 | ● | WIDE AWAKE IN DREAMLAND | Chrysalis CDL 1628 |
| 04/05/1991 | 40 | 3 | | TRUE LOVE | Chrysalis CHR 1805 |

## ERIC BENET
US singer (born Eric Benet Jordan, 5/10/1969, Milwaukee, WI) who` was previously in a group called Benet with his sister Lisa.

| 15/05/1999 | 67 | 1 | | A DAY IN THE LIFE | Warner Brothers 9362473702 |

## CLIFF BENNETT AND THE REBEL ROUSERS
UK singer (born 4/6/1940, Slough) who formed the Rebel Rousers in 1959 with Mick King (guitar), Frank Allen (born Francis McNeice, 14/12/1943, Hayes, bass), Ricky Winters (drums) and Sid Phillips (saxophone/piano) covering US soul hits for the UK market. They split in 1969. Bennett attempted to move into the progressive rock market without success and Frank Allen joined The Searchers.

| 22/10/1966 | 25 | 3 | | DRIVIN' ME WILD | MFP 1121 |

**TONY BENNETT** US jazz-influenced singer (born Anthony Dominick Benedetto, 13/8/1925, Queens, NYC); popular on both sides of the Atlantic, he enjoyed a renaissance in the 1990s. He has won eleven Grammy Awards including: Record of the Year and Best Male Solo Performance for *I Left My Heart in San Francisco*; Best Traditional Pop Performance in 1992 for *Perfectly Frank;* Best Traditional Pop Performance in 1993 for *Steppin' Out;* Album of the Year and Best Traditional Pop Vocal Performance in 1994 for *MTV Unplugged;* Best Traditional Pop Vocal in 1996 for *Here's To The Ladies;* Best Traditional Pop Vocal Performance in 1997 for *Tony Bennett On Holiday;* Best Traditional Pop Vocal in 1999 for *Bennett Sings Ellington – Hot And Cool;* and Best Traditional Pop Vocal Album in 2002 for *Playin' With My Friends: Bennett Sings The Blues*. He appeared as himself in the films *Analyze This* (1999) and *Bruce Almighty* (2003), and has a star on the Hollywood Walk of Fame.

| 29/05/1965 | 13 | 14 | | I LEFT MY HEART IN SAN FRANCISCO | CBS BGP 62201 |
| 19/02/1966 | 9 | 13 | | **A STRING OF TONY'S HITS** | CBS DP 66010 |
| 10/06/1967 | 14 | 24 | | TONY'S GREATEST HITS | CBS SBPG 62821 |
| 23/09/1967 | 31 | 3 | | TONY MAKES IT HAPPEN | CBS SBPG 63055 |
| 23/03/1968 | 29 | 5 | | FOR ONCE IN MY LIFE | CBS SBPG 63166 |
| 26/02/1977 | 23 | 4 | | THE VERY BEST OF TONY BENNETT – 20 GREATEST HITS | Warwick PA 5021 |
| 28/11/1998 | 49 | 4 | ○ | THE ESSENTIAL TONY BENNETT | Columbia 4928222 |
| 05/07/2003 | 33 | 3 | | A WONDERFUL WORLD **TONY BENNETT AND k.d.lang** 2003 Grammy Award for Best Traditional Pop Vocal Album | Columbia 5098702 |

**GEORGE BENSON** US singer/guitarist (born 22/3/1943, Pittsburgh, PA) who played guitar from the age of eight and joined Brother Jack McDuff's trio in 1963. House guitarist for Creed Taylor's CTI label in the early 1970s, ambitions as a vocalist led him to Warners. There, with producers including Tommy Lipuma and Quincy Jones, he became the biggest-selling jazz artist of the era, his style greatly influenced by Wes Montgomery. He has won ten Grammy Awards: Record of the Year in 1976 for *This Masquerade;* Best Pop Instrumental Performance in 1976 for *Breezin';* Best Rhythm & Blues Instrumental Performance in 1976 for *Theme From 'Good King Bad';* Best Rhythm & Blues Vocal Performance in 1978 for *On Broadway;* Best Rhythm & Blues Instrumental Performance in 1980 for *Off Broadway;* Best Rhythm & Blues Vocal Performance in 1980 for *Give Me The Night;* Best Jazz Vocal Performance in 1980 for *Moody's Mood;* Best Recording for Children in 1980 with various others for *In Harmony;* Best Pop Instrumental Performance in 1983 for *Being With You;* and Best Jazz Performance by a Big Band in 1990 with the Count Basie Orchestra for *Basie's Bag*. He also won the 2003 MOBO Award for Lifetime Achievement. He has a star on the Hollywood Walk of Fame.

| 19/03/1977 | 19 | 23 | ○ | IN FLIGHT | Warner Brothers K 56237 |
| 18/02/1978 | 47 | 1 | ○ | WEEKEND IN L.A | Warner Brothers K 66074 |
| 24/03/1979 | 24 | 14 | | LIVING INSIDE YOUR LOVE | Warner Brothers K 66085 |
| 26/07/1980 | 3 | 40 | ✪ | **GIVE ME THE NIGHT** | Warner Brothers K 56823 |
| 14/11/1981 | 19 | 35 | ✪ | THE GEORGE BENSON COLLECTION | Warner Brothers K 66107 |
| 11/06/1983 | 3 | 53 | ✪ | IN YOUR EYES | Warner Brothers 9237441 |
| 26/01/1985 | 9 | 19 | ● | 20/20 | Warner Brothers 9251781 |
| 19/10/1985 | ❶² | 26 | ✪² | **THE LOVE SONGS** | K-Tel NE 1308 |
| 06/09/1986 | 13 | 27 | ● | WHILE THE CITY SLEEPS | Warner Brothers WX 55 |
| 11/07/1987 | 47 | 6 | | COLLABORATION **GEORGE BENSON AND EARL KLUGH** | Warner Brothers WX 91 |
| 10/09/1988 | 16 | 10 | ○ | TWICE THE LOVE | Warner Brothers WX 160 |
| 08/07/1989 | 52 | 3 | | TENDERLY | Warner Brothers WX 263 |
| 26/10/1991 | 25 | 12 | ● | MIDNIGHT MOODS – THE LOVE COLLECTION | Telstar STAR 2450 |
| 29/06/1996 | 61 | 1 | | THAT'S RIGHT | GRP 98242 |
| 25/04/1998 | 8 | 10 | ● | **ESSENTIALS – THE VERY BEST OF GEORGE BENSON** | warner.esp/Jive 9548362292 |
| 05/07/2003 | 4 | 18 | ✪ | **GREATEST HITS OF ALL** | WSM 8122736932 |
| 27/03/2004 | 58 | 1 | | IRREPLACEABLE | GRP 9861996 |

**BENTLEY RHYTHM ACE** UK dance group formed by Richard March (aka Barry Island), Mike Stokes (aka Michael Barrywoosh), James and Fuzz, taking their name from a drum machine. March previously played bass for Pop Will Eat Itself.

| 24/05/1997 | 13 | 5 | ● | BENTLEY RHYTHM ACE | Skint BRASSIC 5CD |
| 10/06/2000 | 48 | 1 | | FOR YOUR EARS ONLY | Parlophone 5257322 |

**BERLIN** US electro-pop group formed in Los Angeles, CA in 1979 by John Crawford (born 17/1/1957, bass/keyboards), Terri Nunn (born 26/6/1961, vocals), Virginia McCalino (vocals), Jo Julian (keyboards), Chris Velasco (guitar) and Dan Van Patten (drums). They made one single before disbanding in 1981. Crawford and Nunn then recruited David Diamond (guitar), Rick Olsen (guitar), Matt Reid (keyboards) and Rod Learned (bass). By 1984 the group consisted of Crawford, Nunn and Rob Brill (born 21/1/1956, drums), Nunn left in 1987.

| 17/01/1987 | 32 | 11 | ○ | COUNT THREE AND PRAY | Mercury MER 101 |

**SHELLEY BERMAN** US comedian who began his career as a straight actor, training at the Goodman Theater in Chicago. He turned to comedy in 1957 and was still recording into the 1990s.

| 19/11/1960 | 12 | 4 | | INSIDE SHELLEY BERMAN 1959 Grammy Award for Best Comedy Performance, Spoken Word | Capitol CLP 1300 |

**LEONARD BERNSTEIN** US conductor/composer/pianist (born 25/8/1918, Lawrence, MA) who studied at Harvard and the Curtis Institute, by 1944 having a reputation as a conductor. He was associated with the Israel Philharmonic Orchestra, the Boston Symphony Orchestra and the New York Philharmonic Orchestra, musical director with the latter from 1958–69. He won fifteen Grammy

○ Silver disc  ● Gold disc  ✪ Platinum disc (additional platinum units are indicated by a figure following the symbol)  ❶⁹ Number of weeks album topped the UK chart

Awards: Best Documentary or Spoken Word Recording for *Humor In Music* and Best Recording for Children for *Prokofiev: Peter And The Wolf* in 1961; Best Recording for Children in 1962 for *Saint-Saens: Carnival Of The Animals*; Best Recording for Children in 1963 conducting the New York Philharmonic with *Britten: Young Person's Guide To The Orchestra*; Album of the Year, Classical in 1964 conducting the New York Philharmonic for *Symphony No. 3 (Kaddish)*; Best Classical Performance, Choral (other than opera) in 1967 conducting the London Symphony Chorus and Orchestra for *Mahler: Symphony No. 8 In E Flat Major*; Best Opera Recording in 1973 conducting the Metropolitan Opera Orchestra and Manhattan Opera Chorus for *Bizet: Carmen*; Album of the Year, Classical in 1977 with Vladimir Horowitz, Isaac Stern, Mstislav Rostropovich, Dietrich Fischer-Dieskau, Yehudi Menuhin and Lyndon Woodside for *Concert Of The Century*; Best Classical Orchestral Recording (conductors award) in 1989 conducting the New York Philharmonic Orchestra for *Mahler: Symphony No. 3 In D Minor*; Best Classical Album in 1990 conducting the New York Philharmonic Orchestra for *Ives: Symphony No. 2: The Gong On The Hook And Ladder: Central Park In The Dark: The Unanswered Question*; Best Classical Orchestral Performance (conductors award) in 1990 conducting the Chicago Symphony Orchestra for *Shostakovich: Symphonies No. 1, Op. 10 And No. 7, Op. 60*; Best Contemporary Composition in 1990 for *Arias And Barcarolles*; Best Classical Album in 1991 conducting the London Symphony Orchestra for *Candide*; and Best Classical Album and Best Orchestral Performance in 1992 conducting the Berlin Philharmonic Orchestra for *Mahler: Symphonie No. 9*. He died in New York on 14/10/1990.

| | | | | | |
|---|---|---|---|---|---|
| 10/02/1990 | 54 | 2 | | BERNSTEIN IN BERLIN – BEETHOVEN SYMPHONY NO. 9 | Deutsche Grammophon 42986 |

**CHUCK BERRY** US singer/guitarist (born Charles Edward Anderson Berry, 18/10/1926, San Jose, CA) who learned the guitar after leaving reform school in 1947. In 1952 he joined The Johnnie Johnson Trio, which became the Chuck Berry Trio. Introduced to Chess Records by Muddy Waters in 1955, he became a major force in music, winning Best New R&B Artist in *Billboard* in 1955. In 1959, after a show in El Paso, he was introduced to Janice Norine Escalanti, an Apache Indian, who was, unknown to Berry, only fourteen years old and working as a waitress and prostitute. Berry offered her a hat-check girl job at his club in St Louis, then fired her, suspecting she was working as a prostitute. She complained to the police and Berry was charged with violating the Mann Act for transporting a girl across state lines for immoral purposes. He was fined $2,000 and jailed for five years, the maximum punishment. When transcripts of the trial were made public, they revealed that judge George H Moore Jr had made racist remarks against Berry, who was freed pending a retrial. In 1962 he was convicted again and sentenced to three years, of which he served two. He also served time on armed robbery charges and income tax evasion, (the latter one month after performing at the White House for President Jimmy Carter in 1979). He appeared in the 1956 film *Rock Rock Rock*, was inducted into the Rock & Roll Hall of Fame in 1986 and has a star on the Hollywood Walk of Fame.

| | | | | | |
|---|---|---|---|---|---|
| 25/05/1963 | 12 | 16 | | CHUCK BERRY | Pye International NPL 28024 |
| 05/10/1963 | 6 | 11 | | **CHUCK BERRY ON STAGE** | Pye International NPL 28027 |
| 07/12/1963 | 9 | 8 | | **MORE CHUCK BERRY** | Pye International NPL 28028 |
| 30/05/1964 | 8 | 7 | | **HIS LATEST AND GREATEST** | Pye International NPL 28037 |
| 03/10/1964 | 18 | 2 | | YOU NEVER CAN TELL | Pye International NPL 29039 |
| 12/02/1977 | 7 | 9 | | **MOTORVATIN'** | Chess 9288 690 |

**MIKE BERRY** UK singer (born Michael Bourne, 24/9/1942, London) whose debut record was a cover of the Shirelles' *Will You Love Me Tomorrow*. The Outlaws, a group that included Ritchie Blackmore and Chas Hodges, backed his early hits. Hodges produced his comeback hit in 1980. After his recording career he turned to acting; regular TV appearances included *Are You Being Served*.

| | | | | | |
|---|---|---|---|---|---|
| 24/01/1981 | 63 | 3 | | THE SUNSHINE OF YOUR SMILE | Polydor 2383 592 |

**NICK BERRY** UK actor (born 16/5/1963, Woodford) who played Simon Wicks in TV's *Eastenders* and later PC Nick Rowan in *Heartbeat*. His 1981 record debut was *Diana*, which failed to chart. Despite similar titles, his two hits are different albums.

| | | | | | |
|---|---|---|---|---|---|
| 20/12/1986 | 99 | 1 | | NICK BERRY | BBC REB 618 |
| 21/11/1992 | 28 | 7 | ● | NICK BERRY | Columbia 4727182 |

**BETA BAND** UK rock group formed by Stephen Mason (guitar/vocals), Richard Greentree (bass), Robin Jones (drums) and John McLean (decks/samples).

| | | | | | |
|---|---|---|---|---|---|
| 10/10/1998 | 35 | 1 | | THE THREE E.P.'s | Regal REG 023CD |
| 03/07/1999 | 18 | 2 | | THE BETA BAND | Regal REG 030CD |
| 28/07/2001 | 13 | 3 | | HOT SHOTS II | Regal REG 59CDX |
| 08/05/2004 | 18 | 3 | | HEROES TO ZEROS | Regal REG101CD |

**MARTIN BETTINGHAUS** – see TIMO MAAS/MARTIN BETTINGHAUS

**BEVERLEY/PHILLIPS ORCHESTRA** UK orchestra that despite the title of their hit album attained no sales awards.

| | | | | | |
|---|---|---|---|---|---|
| 09/10/1976 | 22 | 9 | | GOLD ON SILVER | Warwick WW 5018 |

**B-52'S** US rock group formed in Athens, GA in 1977 by Cindy Wilson (born 28/2/1957, Athens, guitar/vocals), Kate Pierson (born 27/4/1948, New Jersey, organ/vocals), Ricky Wilson (born 19/3/1953, Athens, guitar), Fred Schneider (born 1/7/1951, New Jersey, keyboards/vocals) and Keith Strickland (born 26/10/1953, Athens, drums). They took their name from the hairstyles of the two female members (B-52 being slang for the bouffant style). Ricky Wilson died from AIDS on 12/10/1985. They appeared in the 1994 film *The Flintstones* and also an episode of *The Simpsons*, performing *Glove Slap* (a song based on their own *Love Shack* hit).

| | | | | | |
|---|---|---|---|---|---|
| 04/08/1979 | 22 | 12 | | THE B-52'S | Island ILPS 9580 |

| | | | | | |
|---|---|---|---|---|---|
| 13/09/1980 | 18 | 4 | | WILD PLANET | Island ILPS 9622 |
| 11/07/1981 | 36 | 5 | | THE PARTY MIX ALBUM | Island IPM 1001 |
| 27/02/1982 | 18 | 6 | | MESOPOTAMIA | EMI ISSP 4006 |
| 21/05/1983 | 33 | 4 | | WHAMMY! | Island ILPS 9759 |
| 08/08/1987 | 74 | 2 | | BOUNCING OFF THE SATELLITES | Island ILPS 9871 |
| 29/07/1989 | 8 | 27 | ✪ | **COSMIC THING** | Reprise WX 283 |
| 14/07/1990 | 36 | 3 | ○ | THE BEST OF THE B-52'S – DANCE THIS MESS AROUND | Island ILPS 9959 |
| 11/07/1992 | 8 | 6 | ○ | **GOOD STUFF** | Reprise 7599269432 |

**BIBLE** UK rock group formed in Cambridge by Boo Hewerdine (guitar/vocals), Tony Shepherd (keyboards), Leroy Lendor (bass) and Dave Larcombe (drums) who released their debut single in 1986. Hewerdine later worked with US singer/songwriter Darden Smith.

| | | | | | |
|---|---|---|---|---|---|
| 04/06/1988 | 71 | 1 | | EUREKA | Chrysalis CHR 1646 |
| 07/10/1989 | 67 | 1 | | THE BIBLE | Ensign CHEN 12 |

**BIFFY CLYRO** UK group formed in Kilmarnock by Simon Neil (guitar/vocals), James Johnston (bass) and Ben Johnston (drums).

| | | | | | |
|---|---|---|---|---|---|
| 28/06/2003 | 48 | 1 | | THE VERTIGO OF BLISS | Beggars Banquet BBQCD233 |

**BIG AUDIO DYNAMITE** UK rock group formed by Mick Jones (born 26/6/1955, Brixton, guitar/vocals) after he left The Clash, featuring Don Letts (effects/vocals), Dan Donovan (keyboards), Leo Williams (bass) and Greg Roberts (drums). Jones reassembled the group in 1990 (as BAD II) with Nick Hawkins (born 3/2/1965, Luton, guitar), Gary Stonedage (born 24/11/1962, Southampton, bass) and Chris Kavanagh (born 4/6/1964, Woolwich, drums), later adding DJ Zonka (born Michael Custance, 4/7/1962, London).

| | | | | | |
|---|---|---|---|---|---|
| 16/11/1985 | 27 | 27 | ● | THIS IS BIG AUDIO DYNAMITE | CBS 26714 |
| 08/11/1986 | 11 | 8 | ○ | NO. 10 UPPING STREET | CBS 4501371 |
| 09/07/1988 | 33 | 3 | | TIGHTEN UP VOLUME 88 | CBS 4611991 |
| 16/09/1989 | 26 | 3 | | MEGATOP PHOENIX | CBS 4657901 |
| 03/11/1990 | 55 | 1 | | KOOL-AID | CBS 4674661 |
| 17/08/1991 | 63 | 1 | | THE GLOBE This and the above hit credited to **BAD II** | Columbia 4677061 |

**BIG BAND** UK big band featuring Derek Watkins, Ralph Salmins, Jamie Talbo, Simon Gardner, Paul Morgan and Steve Sidwell.

| | | | | | |
|---|---|---|---|---|---|
| 16/11/2002 | 62 | 1 | | SWINGIN' WITH THE BIG BAND | Columbia STVCD 157 |

**BIG BEN BANJO BAND** UK instrumental group whose style borrowed heavily from that of Winifred Atwell: a collection of popular oldies put together in a medley, with the banjo substituting for Atwell's piano

| | | | | | |
|---|---|---|---|---|---|
| 17/12/1960 | 20 | 1 | | MORE MINSTREL MELODIES | Columbia 33SX 1254 |

**BIG BROVAZ** UK vocal group formed in London by Cherise Roberts (born 29/12/1982, London), Dion Howell (21 at the time of their debut hit) and Nadia (born 28/1/1980, Reading) with members Flawless (born Tayo Aisida, 23/5/1981, Nigeria), J-Rock (born John Paul Horsley, 21/8/1979, Washington DC) and Skillz (born Abdul Bello, 23/11/1978, Kingston, Jamaica). They won the 2003 MOBO Awards for Best Newcomer and Best UK Act (won jointly with Lisa Maffia). Flawless was sacked in March 2004 after being caught carrying cannabis through customs at an US airport.

| | | | | | |
|---|---|---|---|---|---|
| 16/11/2002 | 6 | 35 | ✪ | **NU FLOW** | Epic 5099402 |

**BIG COUNTRY** UK group formed in Dunfermline by ex-Skids Stuart Adamson (born 11/4/1958, Manchester, guitar/synthesizer/ vocals), Bruce Watson (born 11/3/1961, Ontario, Canada, guitar), Tony Butler (born 3/2/1957, London, bass) and Mark Brzezicki (born 21/6/1957, Slough, drums). Brzezicki left in 1991, rejoining two years later. They disbanded in 2000 amd Adamson became a country singer/songwriter, but on 17/12/2001 he was found hanged in a hotel room in Honolulu, Hawaii, having been dead for a couple of days. Depressed after his second marriage collapsed, he had been declared missing from Nashville by his wife on 26/11/2001, failing to turn up after arranging to meet her.

| | | | | | |
|---|---|---|---|---|---|
| 06/08/1983 | 3 | 80 | ✪ | **THE CROSSING** | Mercury MERH 27 |
| 27/10/1984 | ❶[1] | 21 | ● | **STEELTOWN** | Mercury MERH 49 |
| 12/07/1986 | 2 | 16 | ● | **THE SEER** | Mercury MERH 87 |
| 08/10/1988 | 9 | 6 | ○ | **PEACE IN OUR TIME** | Mercury MERH 130 |
| 26/05/1990 | 2 | 17 | ● | **THROUGH A BIG COUNTRY – GREATEST HITS** | Mercury 8460221 |
| 28/09/1991 | 28 | 2 | | NO PLACE LIKE HOME | Vertigo 5102301 |
| 03/04/1993 | 25 | 2 | | THE BUFFALO SKINNERS | Compulsion CDNOIS 2 |
| 18/06/1994 | 35 | 1 | | WITHOUT THE AID OF A SAFETY NET (LIVE) | Compulsion CDNOIS 5 |
| 24/06/1995 | 48 | 2 | | WHY THE LONG FACE | Transatlantic TRACD 109 |
| 24/08/1996 | 41 | 1 | | ECLECTIC | Transatlantic TRACD 234 |
| 08/06/2002 | 71 | 1 | | THE GREATEST HITS OF BIG COUNTRY AND THE SKIDS – THE BEST OF STUART ADAMSON **BIG COUNTRY AND THE SKIDS** | Universal TV 5869892 |

**BIG DADDY** US rock group who claimed to be the last great-unsigned 1950s rock band and who finally emerged in the 1980s. According to members Mark Kaniger (guitar/vocals), Tom Lee (guitar/vocals), Bob Wayne (keyboards/vocals), Don Raymond

(guitar/vocals), John Hatton (bass), Norman A Norman (keyboards),Bob Sandman (reeds) and Damon DeGrignon (drums), their absence for over 24 years was due to having been kidnapped in Southeast Asia by Laolian guerrillas.

| 30/09/1989 | 37 | 3 | | IT'S A BIG DADDY THING | Cold Chillin' WX 305 |

**BIG DISH** UK group formed in Airdrie in 1983 by Stephen Lindsay (vocals/guitar/keyboards), Brian McFie (guitar), Raymond Docherty (bass) and Ian Ritchie (saxophone), by 1991 the group being a duo of Lindsay and McFie.

| 11/10/1986 | 85 | 1 | | SWIMMER | Virgin V 2374 |
| 23/02/1991 | 43 | 2 | | SATELLITES | East West WX 400 |

**BIG FUN** UK vocal group formed by Phil Cheswick (born 12/10/1965, Charlwood), Jason John (born 18/3/1967, Coventry) and Mark Gillespie (born 28/11/1966, Elgin, Scotland).

| 12/05/1990 | 7 | 11 | ● | A POCKETFUL OF DREAMS | Jive FUN 1 |

**BIG SOUND** — see **SIMON DUPREE AND THE BIG SOUND**

**MR ACKER BILK AND HIS PARAMOUNT JAZZ BAND** UK clarinettist/singer (born Bernard Stanley Bilk, 28/1/1929, Somerset) who took up the clarinet while jailed in an army guardhouse in Egypt in 1947. His band, formed in 1958, was one of the most popular of the traditional jazz boom era. He received an MBE in the 2001 New Year's Honours List.

| 19/03/1960 | 6 | 6 | | SEVEN AGES OF ACKER | Columbia 33SX 1205 |
| 09/04/1960 | 14 | 3 | | ACKER BILK'S OMNIBUS | Pye NJL 22 |
| 04/03/1961 | 17 | 1 | | ACKER | Columbia 33SX 1248 |
| 01/04/1961 | 11 | 6 | | GOLDEN TREASURY OF BILK | Columbia 33SX 1304 |
| 27/05/1961 | 4 | 43 | | BEST OF BARBER AND BILK VOLUME 1 | Pye Golden Guinea GGL 0075 |
| 11/11/1961 | 8 | 18 | | BEST OF BARBER AND BILK VOLUME 2 This and the above hit credited to **CHRIS BARBER AND ACKER BILK** | Pye Golden Guinea GGL 0096 |
| 26/05/1962 | 6 | 28 | | STRANGER ON THE SHORE | Columbia 33SX 1407 |
| 25/08/1962 | ❶² | 24 | | BEST OF BALL, BARBER AND BILK KENNY BALL, CHRIS BARBER AND ACKER BILK | Pye Golden Guinea GGL 0131 |
| 04/05/1963 | 17 | 4 | | A TASTE OF HONEY | Columbia 33SX 1493 |
| 09/10/1976 | 38 | 6 | ○ | THE ONE FOR ME | Pye NSPX 41052 |
| 04/06/1977 | 5 | 8 | | SHEER MAGIC | Warwick WW 5028 |
| 11/11/1978 | 17 | 14 | | EVERGREEN | Warwick PW 5045 |

**BIOHAZARD** US rock group formed in Brooklyn, NYC in 1988 by Evan Seinfeld (bass/vocals), Billy Graziedi (guitar/vocals), Bobby Hambel (guitar) and Danny Swchuler (drums). Hambel was sacked in 1995 and replaced by Rob Echeverria.

| 14/05/1994 | 72 | 1 | | STATE OF THE WORLD ADDRESS | Warner Brothers 9362455952 |
| 08/06/1996 | 72 | 1 | | MATA LEAO | Warner Brothers 9362462082 |

**BIOSPHERE** Norwegian keyboard player Geir Jenssen who was previously in Bel Canto.

| 05/03/1994 | 50 | 1 | | PATASHNIK | Apollo AMB 3927CDX |

**BIRDLAND** UK rock group formed by Robert Vincent (vocals), his brother Lee (guitar), Simon Rogers (bass) and Neil Hughes (drums).

| 02/03/1991 | 44 | 1 | | BIRDLAND | Lazy 25 |

**BIRTHDAY PARTY** Australian rock group formed by Nick Cave (born 22/9/1957, Wangarrata, vocals), Roland Howard (guitar), Mick Harvey (guitar/keyboards), Tracy Pew (bass) and Phil Calvert (drums). Pew spent three months in prison on drink-driving charges, briefly replaced by Barry Adamson, with Harry Howard and Chris Walsh also assisting. Cave went solo and also founded The Bad Seeds.

| 24/07/1982 | 73 | 3 | | JUNKYARD | 4AD CAD 207 |

**BIS** UK rock group formed in Glasgow in 1994 by Manda Rin (keyboards/vocals) and brothers Stephen (aka Sci-Fi Steve, guitar/vocals) and John Disko (guitar/vocals). In 1996 they were the first unsigned band to perform on *Top Of The Pops*.

| 19/04/1997 | 55 | 1 | | THE NEW TRANSISTOR HEROES | Wiiija WIJCD 1064 |

**STEPHEN BISHOP** US pianist (born Stephen Bishop-Kovacevich, 17/10/1940, Los Angeles, CA) who debuted in 1951.

| 01/04/1972 | 34 | 3 | | GREIG AND SCHUMANN PIANO CONCERTOS | Philips 6500 166 |

**BIZARRE INC** UK production/instrumental group formed in Stafford by Andrew Meecham (born 1968), Dean Meredith (born 1969) and Carl Turner (born 1969), with Angie Brown and Yvonne Yanni providing the vocals. Altern 8's Mark Archer was also briefly a member.

| 07/11/1992 | 41 | 2 | | ENERGIQUE | Vinyl Solution STEAM 47CD |

### BJORK
Icelandic singer (born Bjork Gudmundsdottir, 21/10/1965, Reykjavik) who fronted the Sugarcubes before going solo in 1993, though she'd recorded her first solo album in 1977 aged eleven. Bjork has won four BRIT Awards: Best International Newcomer in 1994 and and Best International Female in 1994, 1996 and 1998. Also named Best Female at the 1995 MTV Europe Music Awards, she later acted in the film *The Dancer In The Dark* that won the Palme d'Or award at the 2000 Cannes Film Festival and collected a nomination for the Best Soundtrack at the 2001 BRIT Awards.

| DATE | POS | WKS | BPI | ALBUM TITLE | LABEL & NUMBER |
|---|---|---|---|---|---|
| 17/07/1993 | 3 | 69 | ✪² | DEBUT | One Little Indian TPLP 31CD |
| 24/06/1995 | 2 | 38 | ✪ | POST/TELEGRAM ◇ *Telegram* is a remix album that was added to *Post* from 7/12/1996 | One Little Indian TPLP 51CD |
| 04/10/1997 | 4 | 13 | ● | HOMOGENIC ◇ | One Little Indian TPLP 71CD |
| 30/09/2000 | 34 | 1 | | SELMA SONGS Original soundtrack to the film. | One Little Indian TPLP 151CD |
| 08/09/2001 | 8 | 4 | ○ | VESPERTINE | One Little Indian TPLP 101CD |
| 16/11/2002 | 53 | 2 | | GREATEST HITS | One Little Indian TPLP 359CD |

### BLACK
UK group that began as a trio of Dave Dickie (keyboards), Jimmy Sangster (bass) and Colin Vearncombe (vocals), but soon trimmed down to a one-man band; Vearncombe recording on his own under the group name.

| DATE | POS | WKS | BPI | ALBUM TITLE | LABEL & NUMBER |
|---|---|---|---|---|---|
| 26/09/1987 | 3 | 23 | ✪ | WONDERFUL LIFE | A&M AMA 5165 |
| 29/10/1988 | 32 | 4 | ○ | COMEDY | A&M AMA 5222 |
| 01/06/1991 | 42 | 2 | | BLACK | A&M 3971261 |

### CILLA BLACK
UK singer (born Priscilla Marie Veronica White, 27/5/1943, Liverpool) who worked as a hat-check girl at The Cavern when discovered by Brian Epstein, who decided that as her voice sounded 'black' she should adopt that as her surname. Signed by Parlophone in 1963 and produced by George Martin, she became the most successful female singer of the Merseybeat boom. Later she became a leading TV presenter, hosting shows such as *Blind Date* and *Surprise Surprise*. She was awarded an OBE in the 1996 New Year's Honours List.

| DATE | POS | WKS | BPI | ALBUM TITLE | LABEL & NUMBER |
|---|---|---|---|---|---|
| 13/02/1965 | 5 | 11 | | CILLA | Parlophone PMC 1243 |
| 14/05/1966 | 4 | 15 | | CILLA SINGS A RAINBOW | Parlophone PMC 7004 |
| 13/04/1968 | 7 | 11 | | SHER-OO | Parlophone PCS 7041 |
| 30/11/1968 | 21 | 11 | | THE BEST OF CILLA BLACK | Parlophone PCS 7065 |
| 25/07/1970 | 42 | 4 | | SWEET INSPIRATION | Parlophone PCS 7103 |
| 29/01/1983 | 20 | 9 | ○ | THE VERY BEST OF CILLA BLACK | Parlophone EMTV 38 |
| 02/10/1993 | 41 | 2 | | THROUGH THE YEARS | Columbia 4746502 |
| 04/10/2003 | 68 | 1 | | BEGINNINGS — GREATEST HITS AND NEW SONGS | EMI 5931812 |

### FRANK BLACK
US singer (born Charles Francis Kitteridge III, 1965, Boston, MA) who was originally a singer/guitarist with The Pixies under the name Black Francis. He reverted to Frank Black for his solo career when The Pixies disbanded in 1993.

| DATE | POS | WKS | BPI | ALBUM TITLE | LABEL & NUMBER |
|---|---|---|---|---|---|
| 20/03/1993 | 9 | 3 | | FRANK BLACK | 4AD CAD 3004CD |
| 04/06/1994 | 21 | 2 | | TEENAGER OF THE YEAR | 4AD DAD 4009CD |
| 03/02/1996 | 39 | 2 | | THE CULT OF RAY | Dragnet 4816472 |
| 16/05/1998 | 61 | 1 | | FRANK BLACK AND THE CATHOLICS | Play It BIAS 370CD |

### MARY BLACK
Irish singer (born 22/5/1955) from a musical family; she began her career touring folk clubs in Ireland and recorded her debut album in 1983. She later had a brief spell with De Dannan.

| DATE | POS | WKS | BPI | ALBUM TITLE | LABEL & NUMBER |
|---|---|---|---|---|---|
| 03/07/1993 | 58 | 2 | | THE HOLY GROUND | Grapevine GRACD 11 |
| 16/09/1995 | 16 | 4 | | CIRCUS | Grapevine GRACD 014 |
| 29/03/1997 | 33 | 3 | | SHINE | Grapevine GRACD 15 |
| 28/08/1999 | 61 | 1 | | SPEAKING WITH THE ANGEL | Grapevine GRACD 264 |

### BLACK BOX
Italian group who began life as a studio production, the creation of producer Daniel 'DJ Lelewel' Davoli, keyboard player Mirko Limoni and engineer Valerio Semplici, with the Loleatta Holloway song *Love Sensation*. For TV and video performances, model Katrine Quinol performed the role of lead singer, but an inability to mime the lyrics (she couldn't speak English) gave the game away and legal action was threatened. A session singer then re-recorded *Ride On Time* note for note and later releases invariably featured ex-Weather Girl Martha Wash.

| DATE | POS | WKS | BPI | ALBUM TITLE | LABEL & NUMBER |
|---|---|---|---|---|---|
| 05/05/1990 | 14 | 30 | ● | DREAMLAND | Deconstruction PL 74572 |

### BLACK BOX RECORDER
UK group formed by Luke Haines (born 7/10/1967, Walton-on-Thames), Sarah Nixey and John Moore. Haines was earlier in The Servants and The Auteurs, his spell in The Auteurs temporarily halted due to his breaking both ankles after a fall in Spain.

| DATE | POS | WKS | BPI | ALBUM TITLE | LABEL & NUMBER |
|---|---|---|---|---|---|
| 13/05/2000 | 37 | 1 | | THE FACTS OF LIFE | Nude 16CD |

### BLACK CROWES
US metal band formed in Atlanta, GA in 1984 by Chris Robinson (born 20/12/1966, Atlanta, vocals), Rich Robinson (born 24/5/1969, Atlanta, guitar), Jeff Cease (born 24/6/1967, Nashville, TN, guitar), Johnny Colt (born 1/5/1966, Cherry Point, NC, bass) and Steve Gorman (born 17/8/1965, Hopkinsville, KY, drums), and signed to the Def American label in 1989. Cease left in 1991 and was replaced by Marc Ford (born 13/4/1966, Los Angeles, CA). In 1995 they added Eddie Harsch (keyboards) and Chris Trujillo (percussion) to the line-up.

| DATE | POS | WKS | BPI | ALBUM TITLE | LABEL & NUMBER |
|------|-----|-----|-----|-------------|----------------|
| 24/08/1991 | 36 | 11 | ○ | SHAKE YOUR MONEY MAKER | Def American 8425151 |
| 23/05/1992 | 2 | 7 | | **THE SOUTHERN HARMONY AND MUSICAL COMPANION** ▲[1] | Def American 5122632 |
| 12/11/1994 | 8 | 4 | ○ | **AMORICA** | American Recordings 74321241942 |
| 03/08/1996 | 17 | 3 | | THREE SNAKES AND ONE CHARM | American Recordings 74321384842 |
| 23/01/1999 | 34 | 2 | | BY YOUR SIDE | Columbia 4916692 |
| 22/07/2000 | 39 | 4 | | LIVE AT THE GREEK **JIMMY PAGE AND THE BLACK CROWES** | SPV Recordings SPV 09172022 |
| 19/05/2001 | 37 | 2 | | LIONS | V2 VVR 1015672 |

**BLACK DOG** UK multi-instramentalist/producer Ken Downie who has also recorded with Ofra Haza.

| | | | | | |
|------|-----|-----|-----|-------------|----------------|
| 28/01/1995 | 30 | 2 | | SPANNERS | Warp PUPCD 1 |

**BLACK EYED PEAS** US hip hop trio formed in Los Angeles, CA by Will I Am (born William Adams, 15/3/1975), Apl de Ap (born Alan Ap Pineda, 28/11/1974) and Taboo (born Jamie Gomez, 14/7/1975). They later added female singer Fergie (born Stacey Ferguson) to the line-up.

| | | | | | |
|------|-----|-----|-----|-------------|----------------|
| 30/08/2003 | 3 | 43+ | ○[4] | **ELEPHUNK** ◇[2] | A&M 9860365 |

**BLACK GRAPE** UK group formed by ex-Happy Mondays Shaun Ryder (born 23/8/1962, Little Hulton, vocals), Mark 'Bez' Berry (born 18/4/1964, Manchester, vibes), Paul 'Kermit' Leveridge (born 10/11/1969, Manchester, vocals), Ged Lynch (born 19/7/1968, Oswaldtwistle, drums), Danny Saber (born 22/12/1966, New York, bass) and Paul 'Wags' Wagstaff (born 28/12/1964, Stockport, guitar). By the end of 1997, the group comprised Ryder and Saber.

| | | | | | |
|------|-----|-----|-----|-------------|----------------|
| 19/08/1995 | ❶[2] | 39 | ○ | **IT'S GREAT WHEN YOU'RE STRAIGHT… YEAH** | Radioactive RAD 11224 |
| 22/11/1997 | 11 | 7 | ● | STUPID STUPID STUPID | Radioactive RARD 11716 |

**BLACK LACE** UK pop group formed in 1979 by Alan Barton (born 16/9/1953, Barnsley) and Colin Routh to represent the UK in the Eurovision Song Contest (their record *Mary Ann* finished seventh). They re-formed in 1983 with Dean Michael replacing Routh. Barton later joined Smokie and was killed in a car crash on 23/3/1995.

| | | | | | |
|------|-----|-----|-----|-------------|----------------|
| 08/12/1984 | 4 | 14 | ○ | **PARTY PARTY – 16 GREAT PARTY ICEBREAKERS** | Telstar STAR 2250 |
| 07/12/1985 | 18 | 6 | ○ | PARTY PARTY 2 | Telstar STAR 2266 |
| 06/12/1986 | 58 | 6 | | PARTY CRAZY | Telstar STAR 2288 |

**BLACK REBEL MOTORCYCLE CLUB** US rock group formed in San Francisco, CA in 1998 by Robert Turner (guitar/bass/vocals), Peter Hayes (guitar/bass/vocals) and Nick Jago (drums) as The Elements, changing their name soon after.

| | | | | | |
|------|-----|-----|-----|-------------|----------------|
| 26/01/2002 | 25 | 17 | ● | BLACK REBEL MOTORCYCLE CLUB | Virgin CDVUS 207 |
| 06/09/2003 | 3 | 4 | ● | **TAKE THEM ON ON YOUR OWN** | Virgin CDVUS 245 |

**BLACK ROCK AND RON** US male rap group.

| | | | | | |
|------|-----|-----|-----|-------------|----------------|
| 22/04/1989 | 72 | 1 | | STOP THE WORLD | Supreme SU 5 |

**BLACK SABBATH** UK rock group formed in Birmingham in 1967 as Polka Tulk, soon changing their name to Earth. They were re-named Black Sabbath after an early Polka Tulk song in 1969. The group comprised John 'Ozzy' Osbourne (born 3/12/1948, Birmingham, vocals), Tony Iommi (born 19/2/1948, Birmingham, guitar), Terry 'Geezer' Butler (born 17/7/1949, Birmingham, bass) and Bill Ward (born 5/5/1948, Birmingham, drums). They were early pioneers of metal music, especially in the US where they were extremely popular. Osbourne left in 1979 and was replaced by Ronnie James Dio (born 10/7/1949, New Hampshire); Ward left the following year and was replaced by Vincent Appice. The group disbanded in 1983. The original line-up re-formed in 1985 for Live Aid, and the group won the 1999 Grammy Award for Best Metal Performance for *Iron Man*.

| | | | | | |
|------|-----|-----|-----|-------------|----------------|
| 07/03/1970 | 8 | 42 | | **BLACK SABBATH** | Vertigo VO 6 |
| 26/09/1970 | ❶[1] | 27 | | **PARANOID** | Vertigo 6360 011 |
| 21/08/1971 | 5 | 13 | | **MASTER OF REALITY** | Vertigo 6360 050 |
| 30/09/1972 | 8 | 10 | | **BLACK SABBATH VOLUME 4** | Vertigo 6360 071 |
| 08/12/1973 | 4 | 11 | ○ | **SABBATH BLOODY SABBATH** | WWA WWA 005 |
| 27/09/1975 | 7 | 7 | ○ | **SABOTAGE** | NEMS 9119 001 |
| 07/02/1976 | 35 | 5 | ○ | WE SOLD OUR SOUL FOR ROCK 'N' ROLL | NEMS 6641 335 |
| 06/11/1976 | 13 | 6 | | TECHNICAL ECSTASY | Vertigo 9102 750 |
| 14/10/1978 | 12 | 6 | | NEVER SAY DIE | Vertigo 9102 751 |
| 26/04/1980 | 9 | 22 | ● | **HEAVEN AND HELL** | Vertigo 9102 752 |
| 05/07/1980 | 5 | 15 | | **BLACK SABBATH LIVE AT LAST** | NEMS BS 001 |
| 27/09/1980 | 54 | 2 | | PARANOID | NEMS NEL 6003 |
| 14/11/1981 | 12 | 14 | ○ | MOB RULES | Mercury 6V02119 |
| 22/01/1983 | 13 | 11 | | LIVE EVIL | Vertigo SAB 10 |
| 24/09/1983 | 4 | 7 | | **BORN AGAIN** | Vertigo VERL 8 |
| 01/03/1986 | 27 | 5 | | SEVENTH STAR **BLACK SABBATH FEATURING TONY IOMMI** | Vertigo VERH 29 |
| 28/11/1987 | 66 | 1 | | THE ETERNAL IDOL | Vertigo VERH 51 |
| 29/04/1989 | 31 | 2 | | HEADLESS CROSS | I.R.S. EIRSA 1002 |
| 01/09/1990 | 24 | 3 | | TYR | I.R.S. EIRSA 1038 |
| 04/07/1992 | 28 | 2 | | DEHUMANIZER | I.R.S. EIRSCD 1064 |

▲[9] Number of weeks album topped the US chart ◆[12] RIAA Diamond Awards ◇[3] IFPI Platinum Europe Awards

| DATE | POS | WKS | BPI | ALBUM TITLE | LABEL & NUMBER |
|---|---|---|---|---|---|
| 12/02/1994 | 41 | 1 | | CROSS PURPOSES | I.R.S. EIRSCD 1067 |
| 17/06/1995 | 71 | 1 | | FORBIDDEN | I.R.S. EIRSCD 1072 |
| 31/10/1998 | 41 | 1 | | REUNION | Epic 4919542 |
| 17/06/2000 | 24 | 6 | ● | THE BEST OF BLACK SABBATH | Metal IS RAWDD145 |
| 06/07/2002 | 63 | 1 | | PARANOID | Castle Music ESMCD 302 |

**BLACK SCIENCE ORCHESTRA** UK group formed by Ashley Beedle (born 1962, Hemel Hempstead), Rob Mello and John Howard. They later added Marc Woolford and Uschi Classen. In 1994 Beedle also formed The Ballistic Brothers and later X-Press 2 and Black Jazz Chronicles. Beedle also operates three labels: Soundboy Entertainment, Afroart and III Sun.

| DATE | POS | WKS | BPI | ALBUM TITLE | LABEL & NUMBER |
|---|---|---|---|---|---|
| 03/08/1996 | 68 | 1 | | WALTERS ROOM | Junior Boy's Own JBOCD 5 |

**BLACK STAR LINER** UK group formed by Choque Hosein, Chris Harrop and Tom Salmon.

| DATE | POS | WKS | BPI | ALBUM TITLE | LABEL & NUMBER |
|---|---|---|---|---|---|
| 07/09/1996 | 66 | 1 | | YEMEN CUTTA CONNECTION | EXP EXPCD 006 |

**BLACK UHURU** Jamaican reggae group formed in 1974 by Garth Dennis, Derrick 'Ducky' Simpson and Don McCarlos. Dennis and McCarlos left after soon after and were replaced by Michael Rose and Errol Nelson. Puma Jones replaced Nelson in 1977 and Michael Rose left in the mid-1980s to be replaced by Junior Reid. By the early 1990s the original line-up of Dennis, Simpson and Carlos (Don having dropped the Mc part of his name) had re-formed. Jones died from cancer on 28/1/1990.

| DATE | POS | WKS | BPI | ALBUM TITLE | LABEL & NUMBER |
|---|---|---|---|---|---|
| 13/06/1981 | 28 | 13 | | RED | Island ILPS 9625 |
| 22/08/1981 | 81 | 2 | | BLACK UHURU | Virgin VX 1004 |
| 19/06/1982 | 38 | 6 | | CHILL OUT | Island ILPS 9701 |
| 25/08/1984 | 90 | 1 | | ANTHEM 1984 Grammy Award for Best Reggae Recording | Island ILPS 9773 |

**BAND OF THE BLACK WATCH** UK bagpipe band produced by John Carter who also worked on more mainstream pop material by First Class and the Flowerpot Men. The band, officially formed in 1739 and consisting of 80 bagpipers, played at the funeral of US President John F Kennedy.

| DATE | POS | WKS | BPI | ALBUM TITLE | LABEL & NUMBER |
|---|---|---|---|---|---|
| 07/02/1976 | 11 | 13 | | SCOTCH ON THE ROCKS | Spark SRLM 503 |

**BLACK WIDOW** UK rock group formed in Leicester in 1966 by Jim Gannon (guitar/vibes/vocals), Kay Garrett (vocals), Kip Trevor (guitar/harmonica/vocals), Zoot Taylor (keyboards), Clive Jones (woodwind), Bob Bond (bass) and Clive Box (drums) as Pesky Gee. They made one album for Pye before re-forming, without Garrett, as Black Widow. Box and Bond left after the group's debut album (for CBS), replaced by Romeo Challenger and Geoff Griffiths. Gannon left after their second album, replaced by John Culley.

| DATE | POS | WKS | BPI | ALBUM TITLE | LABEL & NUMBER |
|---|---|---|---|---|---|
| 04/04/1970 | 32 | 2 | | SACRIFICE | CBS 63948 |

**BLACKFOOT** US rock group formed in Jacksonville, FL in 1971 by ex-Lynyrd Skynyrd Rick Medlocke (guitar/vocals), Charlie Hargrett (guitar), Greg Walker (bass) and Jackson Spires (drums). They disbanded in 1984 following the release of *Vertical Smiles* but re-formed in 1989 with Medlocke, Neal Casal (guitar), Rikki Mayer (bass) and Gunner Ross (drums). By 1994 the line-up consisted of Medlocke, Mark Woerpel (guitar/vocals), Tim Stunson (bass) and Benny Rappa (drums); Rappa was replaced by Stet Howland during tours.

| DATE | POS | WKS | BPI | ALBUM TITLE | LABEL & NUMBER |
|---|---|---|---|---|---|
| 18/07/1981 | 38 | 12 | | MARAUDER | Atco K 50799 |
| 11/09/1982 | 14 | 6 | | HIGHWAY SONG – BLACKFOOT LIVE | Atco K 50910 |
| 21/05/1983 | 28 | 3 | | SIOGO | Atlantic 7900801 |
| 29/09/1984 | 82 | 1 | | VERTICAL SMILES | Atco 790218 |

**BLACKHEARTS** – see JOAN JETT AND THE BLACKHEARTS

**BLACKSTREET** US hip hop group formed by Teddy 'Street' Riley (born 8/10/1966, Harlem, NYC), Chauncey 'Black' Hannibal, Levi Little and David Hollister. By 1996, the group comprised Riley, Hannibal, Mark L Middleton and Eric 'E' Williams. In August 1999 they split following bad publicity from Chauncey's revelation that he was bisexual, although they re-formed in 2001. Named Best R&B Group at the 1997 MTV Europe Music Awards, Riley had earlier won the 1992 Grammy Award for Best Engineered Album with Bruce Swedien for Michael Jackson's *Dangerous*. Riley also won the 1996 MOBO Award for Best Producer.

| DATE | POS | WKS | BPI | ALBUM TITLE | LABEL & NUMBER |
|---|---|---|---|---|---|
| 09/07/1994 | 35 | 6 | ○ | BLACKstreet | Interscope 6544923512 |
| 21/09/1996 | 26 | 26 | ● | ANOTHER LEVEL | Interscope INTD 90071 |
| 03/04/1999 | 27 | 4 | | FINALLY | Interscope IND 90323 |

**RICHARD BLACKWOOD** UK singer/MTV presenter/comedian who is the nephew of fellow singer Junior.

| DATE | POS | WKS | BPI | ALBUM TITLE | LABEL & NUMBER |
|---|---|---|---|---|---|
| 30/09/2000 | 35 | 2 | | YOU'LL LOVE TO HATE THIS | Hopefield 8573844882 |

**HOWARD BLAKE CONDUCTING THE SINFONIA OF LONDON** UK conductor with the Sinfonia Of London. His debut hit album features the uncredited narration of Bernard Cribbins.

| DATE | POS | WKS | BPI | ALBUM TITLE | LABEL & NUMBER |
|---|---|---|---|---|---|
| 22/12/1984 | 54 | 12 | ● | THE SNOWMAN | CBS 71116 |

**BLANCMANGE** UK synthesizer duo Neil Arthur (born 15/6/1958, Darwen) and Steven Luscombe (born 29/10/1954) who released their first record in 1980 and signed with London in 1981, disbanding in 1986 with Arthur going solo.

| DATE | POS | WKS | BPI | ALBUM TITLE | LABEL & NUMBER |
|---|---|---|---|---|---|
| 09/10/1982 | 30 | 38 | ● | HAPPY FAMILIES | London SH 8552 |
| 26/05/1984 | 8 | 17 | ● | MANGE TOUT | London SH 8554 |
| 26/10/1985 | 54 | 2 | | BELIEVE YOU ME | London LONLP 10 |

**BLAZIN' SQUAD** UK vocal group formed in London by MC Freek, Melo-D, Strider, Reepa, Krazy, Spike-E, Flava, Rockie B, Kenzie and DJ Tommy B. The ten members, most of whom were sixteen years of age at the time of their debut hit, met at Highams Park School.

| 07/12/2002 | 33 | 6 | ● | IN THE BEGINNING | East West 5046610792 |
| 29/11/2003 | 37 | 2 | | NOW OR NEVER | East West 5046703662 |

**MARY J. BLIGE** US R&B singer (born 11/1/1971, Atlanta, GA, raised in The Bronx, NYC) who signed with Uptown in 1991 on the strength of a demo of the Anita Baker song *Caught Up In The Rapture* made in a shopping mall karaoke studio. She took part in the *It's Only Rock 'N' Roll* project for the Children's Promise charity. She has won two Grammy awards: Best Female R&B Vocal Performance for *He Think I Don't Know* in 2002, and Best Pop Collaboration with Vocals with Sting for *Whenever I Say Your Name* in 2003.

| 20/03/1993 | 53 | 1 | | WHAT'S THE 411? | Uptown UPTD 10681 |
| 17/12/1994 | 59 | 3 | | MY LIFE | Uptown UPTD 11156 |
| 26/04/1997 | 8 | 32 | ● | **SHARE MY WORLD** ▲¹ | MCA MCD 11619 |
| 28/08/1999 | 5 | 6 | ○ | **MARY** | MCA MCD 11976 |
| 08/09/2001 | 4 | 58 | ✪ | **NO MORE DRAMA** ◇ | MCA 1126322 |
| 06/09/2003 | 8 | 5 | | **LOVE & LIFE** ▲¹ | Geffen 9860700 |

**BLIND FAITH** UK rock group formed in 1969 by Eric Clapton (born Eric Clapp, 30/3/1945, Ripley, guitar), Ginger Baker (born Peter Baker, 19/8/1939, London, drums), Steve Winwood (born 12/5/1948, Birmingham, keyboards/vocals) and Ric Grech (born 1/11/1945, Bordeaux, France, bass). They disbanded after one album. Grech died from kidney and liver failure on 17/3/1990.

| 13/09/1969 | ❶² | 10 | | **BLIND FAITH** ▲² | Polydor 583059 |

**BLIND MELON** US pop-rock group formed in Los Angeles, CA in 1990 by Glen Graham (born Columbus, MS, drums), Shannon Hoon (born 26/9/1967, Lafayette, IN, vocals), Roger Stevens (born West Point, MS, guitar), Christopher Thorn (born Dover, PA, guitar) and Brad Smith (born West Point, bass). Hoon died from a drug overdose on 21/10/1995.

| 22/01/1994 | 53 | 3 | | BLIND MELON | Capitol CDEST 2188 |
| 19/08/1995 | 48 | 1 | | SOUP | Capitol CDEST 2261 |

**BLINK 182** US group formed in San Diego, CA in 1993 by Tom Delonge (born 13/12/1975, guitar), Markus Hoppus (born 15/3/1972, bass/vocals) and Travis Barker (born 14/11/1975, drums) as Blink, then Blink 182 in 1995 after a similarly titled group threatened legal action. They were named Best New Act at the 2000 MTV Europe Music Awards and Best Rock Act in 2001. Delonge and Barker later formed Box Car Racer.

| 11/03/2000 | 15 | 32 | ● | ENEMA OF THE STATE ◇ | MCA MCD 11950 |
| 18/11/2000 | 69 | 1 | | THE MARK TOM & TRAVIS SHOW | MCA 1123792 |
| 23/06/2001 | 4 | 24 | ● | **TAKE OFF YOUR PANTS AND JACKET** ▲¹ | MCA 1126712 |
| 29/11/2003 | 22 | 21+ | ● | BLINK 182 | Geffen 9861408 |

**BLITZ** UK punk rock group formed in New Mills, Cheshire by Carl (vocals), Mackie (bass), Charlie (drums) and Nidge Miller (guitar). By 1983 the group was effectively a duo of Nidge and Tim Harris.

| 06/11/1982 | 27 | 3 | | VOICE OF A GENERATION | No Future PUNK 1 |

**BLOCKHEADS** UK group formed by Ian Dury (born 12/5/1942, Upminster) with Chaz Jankel, Davey Payne, John Turnball, Norman Watt-Roy, Mickey Gallagher and Charley Charles (born 1945, died from cancer on 5/9/1990). Dury died from cancer on 27/3/2000. Their hit album is a remake of Ian Dury's 1977 album *New Boots And Panties* with various guest artists including Sinead O'Connor, Robbie Williams, Paul McCartney, Madness, Billy Bragg And The Blokes, Wreckless Eric, Cerys Matthews, Grant Nicholas, Shane MacGowan and Keith Allen.

| 21/04/2001 | 44 | 3 | | BRAND NEW BOOTS AND PANTIES | East Central One NEWBOOTS 2CD |

**BLODWYN PIG** UK rock group formed in 1969 by Mick Abrahams (born 7/4/1943 Luton, guitar), Jack Lancaster (saxophone), Andy Pyle (bass) and Ron Berg (drums). Abrahams had previously been a member of Jethro Tull. He left Blodwyn Pig after their second album and was replaced by Pete Banks and Larry Wallis. The group subsequently changed their name to Lancaster's Bomber before disbanding. Abrahams and Lancaster re-formed the group with Pyle and Clive Bunker (another ex-Jethro Tull member), although this was shortlived. Abrahams re-formed the group a second time in the 1990s with Dick Hestall-Smith, Bunker and Pyle, whilst a later line-up featured Abrahams, David Lennox, Mike Summerland, Jackie Challoner and Graham Walker.

| 16/04/1969 | 9 | 4 | | **AHEAD RINGS OUT** | Island ILPS 9101 |
| 25/04/1970 | 8 | 7 | | **GETTING TO THIS** | Chrysalis ILPS 9122 |

**BLONDIE** US new wave group formed in New York in 1975 by Debbie Harry (born 1/7/1945, Miami, FL, lead vocals), Chris Stein (born 5/1/1950, New York, guitar), Jimmy Destri (born 13/4/1954, New York, keyboards), Gary Valentine (bass) and Clem Burke (born 24/11/1955, New York, drums). Valentine left in 1977 and was replaced by New Yorker Frank Infante. Originally signed to Private Stock, Chrysalis bought their contract in 1977. They disbanded in 1983, Harry went solo, and they later re-formed in 1998.

| 04/03/1978 | 10 | 54 | ✪ | PLASTIC LETTERS | Chrysalis CHR 1166 |
| 23/09/1978 | ❶⁴ | 106 | ✪ | PARALLEL LINES | Chrysalis CDL 1192 |
| 10/03/1979 | 75 | 1 | ● | BLONDIE | Chrysalis CHR 1165 |
| 13/10/1979 | ❶¹ | 38 | ✪ | EAT TO THE BEAT | Chrysalis CDL 1225 |
| 29/11/1980 | 3 | 16 | ✪ | AUTOAMERICAN | Chrysalis CDL 1290 |
| 31/10/1981 | 4 | 40 | ✪² | THE BEST OF BLONDIE | Chrysalis CDLTV 1 |
| 05/06/1982 | 9 | 12 | | THE HUNTER | Chrysalis CDL 1384 |
| 17/12/1988 | 50 | 4 | | ONCE MORE INTO THE BLEACH DEBBIE HARRY AND BLONDIE | Chrysalis CJB 2 |
| 16/03/1991 | 3 | 22 | | THE COMPLETE PICTURE – THE VERY BEST OF DEBORAH HARRY AND BLONDIE DEBORAH HARRY AND BLONDIE | Chrysalis CHR 1817 |
| 29/07/1995 | 25 | 2 | | BEAUTIFUL – THE REMIX ALBUM | Chrysalis CDCHR 6105 |
| 25/07/1998 | 12 | 34 | ✪ | ATOMIC/ATOMIX – THE VERY BEST OF BLONDIE | EMI 4992882 |
| 27/02/1999 | 3 | 15 | ● | NO EXIT | Beyond 74321641142 |
| 02/11/2002 | 38 | 4 | ○ | GREATEST HITS | Chrysalis 5431052 |
| 25/10/2003 | 36 | 1 | | THE CURSE OF BLONDIE | Epic 5119219 |
| 10/04/2004 | 60 | 2 | | PARALLEL LINES | Fame CD 25CR01 |

**BLOOD SWEAT AND TEARS** US rock group formed by Al Kooper (born 5/2/1944, NYC) as a jazz-rock group in 1968 with David Clayton-Thomas (born David Thompsett, 13/9/1941, Walton-on-Thames, lead vocals), Steve Katz (born 9/5/1945, NYC, guitar/harmonica/vocals), Jim Fielder (born 4/10/1947, Denton, TX, bass), Bobby Colomby (born 20/12/1944, NYC, drums/vocals), Fred Lipsius (born 19/11/1943, NYC, saxophone), Dick Halligan (born 29/8/1943, NYC, trombone), Chuck Wingfield (born 5/2/1943, Monessen, PA, trumpet/flugelhorn), Lew Soloff (born 20/2/1944, NYC, trumpet/flugelhorn) and Jerry Hyman (born 19/5/1947, NYC, trombone/recorder). They won two Grammy Awards including Best Contemporary Instrumental Performance in 1969 for *Variations On A Theme By Erik Satie*.

| 13/07/1968 | 40 | 1 | | CHILD IS THE FATHER TO THE MAN | CBS 63296 |
| 12/04/1969 | 15 | 8 | | BLOOD SWEAT AND TEARS ▲⁷ 1969 Grammy Award for Album of the Year | CBS 63504 |
| 08/08/1970 | 14 | 12 | | BLOOD SWEAT AND TEARS 3 ▲² | CBS 64024 |

**BLOODHOUND GANG** US rock group formed by Jimmy Pop Ali (vocals), Lupus Thunder (guitar), Evil Jared Hasselhoff (bass), DJ Q-Ball (DJ) and Spanky G (drums), although he was subsequently replaced by Willie The New Guy.

| 06/05/2000 | 37 | 7 | | HOORAY FOR BOOBIES ◇ | Geffen 4904572 |

**BLOW MONKEYS** UK group formed by Dr Robert (born Bruce Robert Howard, 2/5/1961, Norfolk, guitar/vocals), Mick Anker (born 2/7/1957, bass), Neville Henry (saxophone) and Tony Kiley (born 16/2/1962, drums), taking their name from jazz slang for saxophone players. They first signed with RCA in 1984. Robert Howard later recorded solo, worked with Kym Mazelle and also became a successful songwriter.

| 19/04/1986 | 21 | 8 | ○ | ANIMAL MAGIC | RCA PL 70910 |
| 25/04/1987 | 20 | 8 | ○ | SHE WAS ONLY A GROCER'S DAUGHTER | RCA PL 71245 |
| 11/02/1989 | 46 | 2 | | WHOOPS! THERE GOES THE NEIGHBOURHOOD | RCA PL 71858 |
| 26/08/1989 | 5 | 9 | ● | CHOICES – THE SINGLES COLLECTION | RCA PL 74191 |

**BLOWING FREE** UK instrumental duo formed by Stewart James and Bradley James.

| 29/07/1995 | 6 | 13 | | SAX MOODS | Dino DINCD 106 |
| 30/11/1996 | 70 | 1 | | SAX MOODS – VOLUME 2 | Dino DINCD 118 |

**BLUE** UK vocal group formed in London by Antony 'Ant' Costa (born 23/6/1981, Edgeware), Lee Ryan (born 17/6/1983, Chatham), Simon 'Shaft' Webbe (born 30/3/1978, Manchester) and Duncan 'Dunk' James (born 7/4/1979, Salisbury). They were named Best UK Newcomer at the 2002 BRIT Awards, and Best Pop Act the following year.

| 08/12/2001 | ❶¹ | 63 | ✪⁴ | ALL RISE ◇ | Innocent CDSIN 8 |
| 16/11/2002 | ❶¹ | 29 | ✪⁴ | ONE LOVE ◇ | Innocent CDSIN 11 |
| 15/11/2003 | ❶¹ | 16 | ✪² | GUILTY ◇ | Innocent CDSIN 13 |

○ Silver disc ● Gold disc ✪ Platinum disc (additional platinum units are indicated by a figure following the symbol) ❶⁹ Number of weeks album topped the UK chart

## BLUE AEROPLANES
UK rock group formed in Bristol by Gerard Langley (vocals), Nick Jacobs (guitar), Dave Chapman (various instruments), Wojtek Dmochowski (dancer) and John Langley (drums). Other members of the group at various times have included Angelo Bruschini, John Steapleton, Ruth Coltrane, Caroline Halcrow, Ian Kearey, Simon Heathfield and Rodney Allen.

| Date | POS | WKS | Title | Label & Number |
|---|---|---|---|---|
| 24/02/1990 | 54 | 1 | SWAGGER | Ensign CHEN 13 |
| 17/08/1991 | 33 | 3 | BEATSONGS | Ensign CHEN 21 |
| 12/03/1994 | 59 | 1 | LIFE MODEL | Beggars Banquet BBQCD 143 |

## BLUE MURDER
US group formed by John Sykes (formerly of Whitesnake, guitar), Tony Franklin (formerly of The Firm, bass) and Carmine Appice (of various groups, drums).

| Date | POS | WKS | Title | Label & Number |
|---|---|---|---|---|
| 06/05/1989 | 45 | 3 | BLUE MURDER | Geffen WX 245 |

## BLUE NILE
UK rock group formed in Glasgow in 1981 by Paul Buchanan (vocals/guitar/synthesizer), Robert Bell (keyboards) and Paul Joseph Moore (keyboards). Originally signed by RSO, the label folded after the group's first single. They added Nigel Thomas to the line-up in 1996.

| Date | POS | WKS | Title | Label & Number |
|---|---|---|---|---|
| 19/05/1984 | 80 | 2 | A WALK ACROSS THE ROOFTOPS | Linn LKH 1 |
| 21/10/1989 | 12 | 4 | HATS | Linn LKH 2 |
| 22/06/1996 | 13 | 4 | PEACE AT LAST | Warner Brothers 9362458482 |

## BLUE OYSTER CULT
US heavy rock group formed in New York in 1969 by Eric Bloom (born 1/12/1944, vocals/guitar/keyboards), Donald 'Buck Dharma' Roeser (born 12/11/1947, guitar/vocals), Albert Bouchard (born 24/5/1947, Watertown, NY, drums/vocals), Allen Lanier (born 25/6/1946, rhythm guitar/keyboards) and Joe Bouchard (born 9/11/1948, Watertown, bass/vocals) as Soft White Underbelly (a name they retain for low-key concerts). They became Blue Oyster Cult the following year.

| Date | POS | WKS | Title | Label & Number |
|---|---|---|---|---|
| 03/07/1976 | 26 | 10 | AGENTS OF FORTUNE | CBS 81385 |
| 04/02/1978 | 60 | 1 | SPECTRES | CBS 86050 |
| 28/10/1978 | 18 | 4 | SOME ENCHANTED EVENING | CBS 86074 |
| 18/08/1979 | 46 | 5 | MIRRORS | CBS 86087 |
| 19/07/1980 | 12 | 7 | CULTOSAURUS ERECTUS | CBS 86120 |
| 25/07/1981 | 29 | 7 | FIRE OF UNKNOWN ORIGIN | CBS 85137 |
| 22/05/1982 | 39 | 5 | EXTRATERRESTRIAL LIVE | CBS 22203 |
| 19/11/1983 | 95 | 1 | THE REVOLUTION TONIGHT | CBS 25686 |

## BLUE PEARL
UK/US group formed by Pig Youth (Martin 'Pig Youth' Glover, born 27/12/1960, Africa) and Brilliant, with vocals by Pamela Carol 'Durga' McBroom.

| Date | POS | WKS | Title | Label & Number |
|---|---|---|---|---|
| 01/12/1990 | 58 | 2 | NAKED | Big Life BLR LP4 |

## BLUE RONDO A LA TURK
UK group formed in London in 1981 by Moses Mount Bassie, Lloyd Bynoe, Art Collins, Geraldo D'Arbilly, Kito Poccioni, Mark Reilly (born 20/2/1960, High Wycombe), Chris Sullivan, Chris Tolera, Tholo Peter Tsegona and Daniel White (born 26/8/1959, High Wycombe), named after composition by jazz musician Dave Brubeck. Reilly and White later formed Matt Bianco.

| Date | POS | WKS | Title | Label & Number |
|---|---|---|---|---|
| 06/11/1982 | 80 | 2 | CHEWING THE FAT | Diable Noir V 2240 |

## BLUEBELLS
UK rock group formed in 1982 by Ken McCluskey (born 8/2/1962, vocals), David McCluskey (born 13/1/1964, drums), Robert 'Bobby Bluebell' Hodgens (born 6/6/1959, guitar) and Craig Gannon (born 30/7/1966, guitar). They were sued, unsuccessfully, in 1982 by a French dance troupe called the Blubells who felt the Scottish group's scruffy image tarnished their own.

| Date | POS | WKS | Title | Label & Number |
|---|---|---|---|---|
| 11/08/1984 | 22 | 10 | SISTERS | London LONLP 1 |
| 17/04/1993 | 27 | 5 | THE BLUEBELLS – THE SINGLES COLLECTION | London 8284052 |

## BLUES BAND
UK group formed in 1979 by ex-Manfred Mann vocalist Paul Jones (born Paul Pond, 24/2/1942, Portsmouth).

| Date | POS | WKS | Title | Label & Number |
|---|---|---|---|---|
| 08/03/1980 | 40 | 9 | OFFICIAL BOOTLEG ALBUM | Arista BBBP 101 |
| 18/10/1980 | 36 | 6 | READY | Arista BB 2 |
| 17/10/1981 | 60 | 3 | ITCHY FEET | Arista BB 3 |

## BLUETONES
UK rock group formed in London in 1990 by Adam Devlin (born 17/9/1969, Hounslow, Middlesex, lead guitar), Mark Morriss (born 18/10/1971, Hounslow, lead vocals), Ed Chesters (born 24/10/1971, Darlington, drums) and Scott Morriss (born 10/10/1973, Hounslow, drums). They spent the first year rehearsing their act before performing live.

| Date | POS | WKS | BPI | Title | Label & Number |
|---|---|---|---|---|---|
| 24/02/1996 | ❶[1] | 25 | ✪ | EXPECTING TO FLY | Superior Quality BLUE 004CD |
| 21/03/1998 | 10 | 16 | ● | RETURN TO THE LAST CHANCE SALOON | Superior Quality BLUED 008 |
| 27/05/2000 | 7 | 4 | | SCIENCE & NATURE | Superior Quality BLUECD 014 |
| 20/04/2002 | 14 | 4 | | THE SINGLES | Superior Quality BLUEDD 017 |
| 24/05/2003 | 49 | 1 | | LUXEMBOURG | Superior Quality BLUE019CD |

**BLUR** UK rock group formed in London in 1988 by Damon Albarn (born 23/3/1968, London, guitar/keyboards/vocals), Alex James (born 21/11/1968, Boscombe, bass) and Graham Coxon (born 12/3/1969, Rintein, Germany, guitar), later adding Dave Rowntree (born 8/5/1964, Colchester, drums) to the line-up. Originally named Seymour, they changed to Blur upon signing with Food in 1991. They were the major winners at the 1995 BRIT Awards, heading four categories including Best UK Group, Best Single and Best Video for *Parklife* (the most won by a group or artist in a single year). In 1999, they won the MTV Europe Music Award for Best Video for the single *Coffee + TV*. Albarn later formed Gorillaz with Jamie Elliott, and Coxon recorded solo.

| | | | | | |
|---|---|---|---|---|---|
| 07/09/1991 | 7 | 12 | ● | LEISURE | Food FOODLP 6 |
| 22/05/1993 | 15 | 14 | ● | MODERN LIFE IS RUBBISH | Food FOODCD 9 |
| 07/05/1994 | ❶¹ | 106 | ✪⁴ | PARKLIFE ◇ 1995 BRIT Award for Best Album | Food FOODCD 10 |
| 23/09/1995 | ❶² | 47 | ✪³ | THE GREAT ESCAPE ◇ | Food FOODCD 14 |
| 22/02/1997 | ❶¹ | 65 | ✪ | BLUR ◇ | Food FOODCD 19 |
| 27/03/1999 | ❶² | 27 | ✪ | 13 | Food FOODCD 29 |
| 11/11/2000 | 3 | 28 | ✪² | BLUR: BEST OF ◇ | Food FOODCD 33 |
| 17/05/2003 | ❶¹ | 8 | ● | THINK TANK | Parlophone 5829972 |

**B M EX** UK instrumental/production group fronted by Tom Frederikse.

| | | | |
|---|---|---|---|
| 30/01/1993 | 17 | 2 | APPOLONIA/FEEL THE DROP This was a 12-inch double pack single containing four mixes of *Appolonia* on one disc and two mixes of *Feel The Drop* on the other ... Union City UCRCD 14 |

**BOARDS OF CANADA** UK electronic duo Mike Sandison (born 14/7/1971) and Marcus Eoin (born 27/5/1973); they originally recorded for Skam Records in 1996 and later recorded for Mask and Ampoule before linking with Warp.

| | | | |
|---|---|---|---|
| 02/03/2002 | 21 | 2 | GEOGADDI ... Warp WARPCD 101 |

**BOB THE BUILDER** UK animated TV character whose voice is supplied by actor Neil Morrissey. As the name implies, Bob The Builder is a building contractor.

| | | | | |
|---|---|---|---|---|
| 13/10/2001 | 4 | 12 | ● | THE ALBUM ... BBC Music WMSF 60472 |

**ANDREA BOCELLI** Italian singer (born 22/9/1958, Laiatico, near Pisa); he studied law at the University of Pisa before launching his singing career. Visually impaired from birth, he lost his eyesight completely at the age of twelve following an accident playing football.

| | | | | | |
|---|---|---|---|---|---|
| 31/05/1997 | 6 | 25 | ✪ | ROMANZA ◇⁶ | Philips Classics 4564562 |
| 09/05/1998 | 33 | 5 | | ARIA – THE OPERA ALBUM | Philips 4620332 |
| 13/02/1999 | 24 | 10 | ✪ | VIAGGIO ITALIANO ◇ | Philips 4621962 |
| 10/04/1999 | 4 | 42 | ✪ | SOGNO ◇² | Sugar 5472212 |
| 20/11/1999 | 20 | 12 | | SACRED ARIAS ◇ | Philips 4626002 |
| 23/09/2000 | 17 | 10 | ○ | VERDI | Philips 4646002 |
| 27/10/2001 | 3 | 16 | ✪ | CIELI DE TOSCANA ◇ | Polydor 5892452 |
| 16/11/2002 | 7 | 15 | ✪ | SENTIMENTO ◇ 2003 Classical BRIT Awards for Album of the Year and Best Selling Album | Philips 4734102 |

**BODINES** UK rock group formed by Mike Ryan (vocals), Paul Brotherton (guitar), Tim Burtonwood (bass) and John Rowland (drums). The group first recorded for Creation.

| | | | |
|---|---|---|---|
| 29/08/1987 | 94 | 1 | PLAYED ... Pop BODL 2001 |

**BODY COUNT** US rap/heavy metal group assembled by Ice-T (born Tracy Morrow, 16/2/1958, Los Angeles, CA) and featuring Ernie-C (guitar), D-Roc (guitar), Mooseman (bass) and Beatmaster V (drums). Their *Cop Killer* got them thrown off Sire Records after protests led by actor Charlton Heston (a major shareholder in Time Warner, owners of Sire), Oliver North and President George Bush, with death threats being made to record company employees.

| | | | |
|---|---|---|---|
| 17/09/1994 | 15 | 2 | BORN DEAD ... Rhyme Syndicate RSYND 2 |

**TIM BOGERT** – see **JEFF BECK**

**SUZY BOGGUS** US country singer (born 30/12/1956 Aledo, IL); she toured across the USA in a van for five years before securing a residency at a restaurant in Nashville.

| | | | |
|---|---|---|---|
| 25/09/1993 | 69 | 1 | SOMETHING UP MY SLEEVE ... Liberty CDEST 221 |

○ Silver disc ● Gold disc ✪ Platinum disc (additional platinum units are indicated by a figure following the symbol) ❶⁹ Number of weeks album topped the UK chart

**C J BOLLAND** UK producer (born Christian Jay Bolland, 18/6/1971, Stockton-on-Tees, raised in Antwerp, Belgium) who has also recorded as Sonic Solution, Ravesignal III, Pulse, The Project and Space Opera.

26/10/1996 . . . . . 43 . . . . . 2 . . . . . .    THE ANALOGUE THEATRE . . . . . . . . . . . . . . . . . . . . . . . . . . . . . . . . . . . . . . . . . . . . . . . . . . . . . . . . . . Internal TRUCD 13

**BOLSHOI** UK rock group formed by Trevor Tanner (guitar/vocals), Nick Chown (bass) and Jan Kalicki (drums), adding Paul Clark (keyboards) before their debut album for Beggar's Banquet in 1984. They disbanded after their third album.

03/10/1987 . . . . 100 . . . . . 1 . . . . . .    LINDY'S PARTY . . . . . . . . . . . . . . . . . . . . . . . . . . . . . . . . . . . . . . . . . . . . . . . . . . . . . . . . . . . . . . . . . Beggars Banquet BEGA 86

**MICHAEL BOLTON** US singer (born Michael Bolotin, 26/2/1953, New Haven, CT) who was lead singer with Blackjack in the late 1970s. He went solo as Michael Bolton in 1983. He released an album of operatic pieces in 1998 as *Secret Passion – The Arias*. He has won two Grammy Awards: Best Pop Vocal Performance in 1989 for *How Am I Supposed To Live Without You* and Best Pop Vocal Performance in 1991 for *When A Man Loves A Woman*. He has a star on the Hollywood Walk of Fame.

| DATE | POS | WKS | BPI | ALBUM TITLE | LABEL & NUMBER |
|---|---|---|---|---|---|
| 17/03/1990 | 4 | 72 | ●[4] | SOUL PROVIDER | CBS 4653431 |
| 11/08/1990 | 44 | 5 | | THE HUNGER | CBS 4601631 |
| 18/05/1991 | 2 | 57 | ●[4] | TIME, LOVE AND TENDERNESS ▲[1] | Columbia 4678121 |
| 10/10/1992 | 3 | 24 | ● | TIMELESS (THE CLASSICS) ▲[1] | Columbia 4723022 |
| 27/11/1993 | 4 | 24 | ● | THE ONE THING | Columbia 4743552 |
| 30/09/1995 | 2 | 30 | ● | GREATEST HITS 1985–1995 ◇ | Columbia 4810022 |
| 22/11/1997 | 20 | 7 | ● | ALL THAT MATTERS | Columbia 4885312 |
| 02/05/1998 | 25 | 5 | | MY SECRET PASSION – THE ARIAS | Sony Classical SK 63077 |
| 04/12/1999 | 50 | 2 | | TIMELESS – THE CLASSICS VOLUME 2 | Columbia 4723022 |
| 06/04/2002 | 19 | 2 | | ONLY A WOMAN LIKE YOU | Jive 9223522 |
| 27/03/2004 | 23 | 2 | | VINTAGE | Universal TV 9817973 |

**BOMB THE BASS** UK studio group, the brainchild of writer and producer Tim Simenon (born in London in 1968). He recorded under his own name (owing to the Gulf War making the group name insensitive) before returning as Bomb The Bass in 1994 with his own Stoned Heights label.

| | | | | | |
|---|---|---|---|---|---|
| 22/10/1988 | 18 | 10 | ● | INTO THE DRAGON | Rhythm King DOOD 1 |
| 31/08/1991 | 19 | 4 | | UNKNOWN TERRITORY | Rhythm King 4687740 |
| 15/04/1995 | 22 | 2 | | CLEAR | Fourth & Broadway BRCD 611 |

**BOMBALURINA FEATURING TIMMY MALLETT** UK studio group assembled by Andrew Lloyd-Webber and produced by Nigel Wright. The record and name of the group (after a character in Lloyd-Webber's musical *Cats*) were selected before the actual performers. Timmy Mallett is a children's TV presenter.

15/12/1990 . . . . . 55 . . . . . 5 . . . . . . ○    HUGGIN' AN' A KISSIN' . . . . . . . . . . . . . . . . . . . . . . . . . . . . . . . . . . . . . . . . . . . . . . . . . . . . . . . . . . . . . Polydor 8476481

**BOMFUNK MC'S** UK/Finnish dance group formed by Raymond Ebanks and Jaakko Salovaara, aka B.O.W. and DJ Gismo. Salovaara also produces as JS 16. They were named Best Nordic Act at the 2000 MTV Europe Music Awards.

26/08/2000 . . . . . 33 . . . . . 2 . . . . . .    IN STEREO . . . . . . . . . . . . . . . . . . . . . . . . . . . . . . . . . . . . . . . . . . . . . . . . . . . . . . . . . . . . . . . . . . . . . Epidrome 4943096

**BON JOVI** US hard rock quintet formed in New Jersey in 1982 by Jon Bon Jovi (born Jon Bongiovi, 2/3/1962, Perth Amboy, NJ, lead vocals), Richie Sambora (born 11/7/1959, Perth Amboy, guitar), Dave Bryan (born David Rashbaum, 7/2/1962, Edison, NJ, keyboards), Alec John Such (born 14/11/1956, Yonkers, NY, bass) and Tico Torres (born 7/10/1953, Colonia, NJ, drums). Sambora is married to actress Heather Locklear, who was previously married to ex-Motley Crue drummer Tommy Lee, Torres is married to supermodel Eva Herzigova. They were named Best International Group at the 1996 BRIT Awards and Best Rock Act at the 1995 MTV Europe Music Awards.

| | | | | | |
|---|---|---|---|---|---|
| 28/04/1984 | 71 | 3 | | BON JOVI | Vertigo VERL 14 |
| 11/05/1985 | 28 | 12 | | 7800° FAHRENHEIT | Vertigo VERL 24 |
| 20/09/1986 | 6 | 123 | ●[3] | SLIPPERY WHEN WET ▲[8] ◆[12] | Vertigo VERH 38 |
| 01/10/1988 | ●[2] | 47 | ●[2] | NEW JERSEY ▲[4] | Vertigo VERH 62 |
| 14/11/1992 | ●[1] | 70 | ● | KEEP THE FAITH | Jambco 5141972 |
| 22/10/1994 | ●[5] | 68 | ●[5] | CROSS ROAD – THE BEST OF BON JOVI ◇[7] | Jambco 5229362 |
| 01/07/1995 | ●[4] | 50 | ●[2] | THESE DAYS ◇[3] | Vertigo 5282482 |
| 10/06/2000 | ●[1] | 29 | ● | CRUSH ◇[2] | Mercury 5425622 |
| 26/05/2001 | 2 | 9 | ● | ONE WILD NIGHT – LIVE 1985–2001 ◇ | Mercury 5488652 |
| 05/10/2002 | 2 | 9 | ● | BOUNCE ◇ | Mercury 0633952 |
| 15/11/2003 | 4 | 8 | ● | THIS LEFT FEELS RIGHT | Mercury 9861391 |

## JON BON JOVI
US singer (born John Bongiovi, 2/3/1962, Perth Amboy, NJ) who is lead singer with Bon Jovi. He wrote the soundtrack to the 1990 film *Young Guns II*, making a cameo appearance in the film. He also appeared in the films *The Leading Man* (1997) and *U-571* (2000). Named Best International Male Artist at the 1998 BRIT Awards and Best Male Artist at the 1995 and 1997 MTV Europe Music Awards, he took part in the *It's Only Rock 'N' Roll* project for the Children's Promise charity.

| | | | | | |
|---|---|---|---|---|---|
| 25/08/1990 | 2 | 23 | ● | **BLAZE OF GLORY/YOUNG GUNS II** Original soundtrack to the film | Vertigo 8464731 |
| 28/06/1997 | 2 | 18 | ● | **DESTINATION ANYWHERE** ◇ | Mercury 5360112 |

## BOND
UK classical group formed by Eos (violin), Haylie Ecker (violin), Gay-Yee Westerhoff (cello) and Tania Davis (viola). Prior to forming Bond, the four girls had appeared on albums by acts as diverse as Embrace, Divine Comedy, Primal Scream and Mark Knopfler. They appeared in the 2003 film *Johnny English*.

| | | | | |
|---|---|---|---|---|
| 14/10/2000 | 16 | 18 | ● | BORN | Decca 4670912 |
| 16/11/2002 | 26 | 3 | | SHINE | Decca 4734602 |

## GRAHAM BOND
UK keyboard player/singer (born 28/10/1937, Romford) who began his professional career as a saxophone player with The Don Rendell Quintet and subsequently joined Alexis Korner's Blues Incorporated in 1962. He formed his own group in 1963 with Ginger Baker and Jack Bruce, later adding John McLaughlin, although the group disbanded in 1965. After a brief solo spell, he joined Ginger Baker's Airforce and then formed Magick with his wife-to-be Diane Stewart. After their divorce, Bond formed Magus but with little success. He died on 8/5/1974 after falling in front of a train at Finsbury Park Underground station, although it has not been established whether this was an accident or suicide.

| | | | | |
|---|---|---|---|---|
| 20/06/1970 | 40 | 2 | | SOLID BOND | Warner Brothers WS 3001 |

## GARY U.S. BONDS
US singer (born Gary Anderson, 6/6/1939, Jacksonville, FL) christened US Bonds by record boss Frank Guida, with 'buy US Bonds' the marketing slogan. He made modest chart entries twenty years later with titles produced by Bruce Springsteen and Miami Steve Van Zandt.

| | | | | |
|---|---|---|---|---|
| 22/08/1981 | 43 | 3 | | DEDICATION | EMI America AML 3017 |
| 10/07/1982 | 55 | 5 | | ON THE LINE | EMI America AML 3022 |

## BONE THUGS-N-HARMONY
US rap group from Cleveland, OH formed by Krayzie Bone (born Anthony Henderson), Layzie Bone (Steven Howse), Bizzy Bone (Byron McCane), Wish Bone (Curtis Scruggs) and Flesh-N-Bone (Stanley Howse), discovered by Eazy-E of NWA. They won the 1996 Grammy Award for Best Rap Group Performance foir their single *Tha Crossroads*.

| | | | | |
|---|---|---|---|---|
| 31/08/1996 | 39 | 3 | | E.1999 ETERNAL ▲² | Epic 4810386 |
| 09/08/1997 | 42 | 1 | | THE ART OF WAR ▲¹ | Epic 4880802 |

## BONEY M
Jamaican/Antilles/Montserrat brainchild of German record producer Frank Farian who recorded the first single (*Baby Do You Wanna Bump*) and then advertised for four singers to become Boney M. Marcia Barrett (born 14/10/1948, St Catherines, Jamaica), Bobby Farrell (born 6/6/1949, Aruba, West Indies), Liz Mitchell (born 12/7/1952, Clarendon, Jamaica) and Masie Williams (born 25/3/1951, Montserrat, West Indies) became one of Eurodisco's most successful acts, Farian repeating the formula with Milli Vanilli and Far Corporation.

| | | | | | |
|---|---|---|---|---|---|
| 23/04/1977 | 40 | 15 | ○ | TAKE THE HEAT OFF ME | Atlantic K 50314 |
| 06/08/1977 | 60 | 1 | ● | LOVE FOR SALE | Atlantic K 50385 |
| 29/07/1978 | ●⁴ | 65 | ✪ | **NIGHT FLIGHT TO VENUS** | Atlantic/Hansa K 50498 |
| 29/09/1979 | ●¹ | 18 | ✪ | **OCEANS OF FANTASY** | Atlantic/Hansa K 50610 |
| 12/04/1980 | ●² | 26 | ● | **THE MAGIC OF BONEY M** | Atlantic/Hansa BMTV 1 |
| 06/09/1986 | 35 | 5 | | THE BEST OF 10 YEARS – 32 SUPERHITS | Stylus SMR 621 |
| 27/03/1993 | 14 | 10 | | THE GREATEST HITS | Telstar TCD 2656 |
| 15/12/2001 | 66 | 3 | | THE GREATEST HITS | BMG 74321896142 |

## BONFIRE
German rock group formed in Ingolstadt in 1985 by Claus Lessmann (vocals), Hans Ziller (guitar), Horst Makr Thorn (guitar) and a nameless drummer who was soon sacked. By 1990 the line-up comprised Lessmann, Angel Schaeffer (guitar), Michael Voss (guitar), Jorg Deisinger (bass) and Edgar Patrik (drums). They disbanded in 1993, Lessman and Ziller forming a folk rock group.

| | | | | |
|---|---|---|---|---|
| 21/10/1989 | 74 | 1 | | POINT BLANK | MSA ZL 74249 |

## GRAHAM BONNET
UK singer (born 12/12/1947, Skegness) who was formerly a member of Marbles before joining heavy rock group Rainbow in 1979 as lead singer, leaving after eighteen months to go solo.

| | | | | |
|---|---|---|---|---|
| 07/11/1981 | 62 | 3 | | LINE UP | Vertigo 6302 151 |

## BONNIE PRINCE BILLY
US singer Will Oldham. He also records as the Palace Brothers and Palace Music.

| | | | | |
|---|---|---|---|---|
| 08/02/2003 | 48 | 1 | | MASTER AND EVERYONE | Domino Recordings WIGCD121 |
| 03/04/2004 | 63 | 1 | | SINGS GREATEST PALACE MUSIC | Domino Recordings WIGCD140 |

## BONZO DOG DOO-DAH BAND
UK group formed in 1966 by London art students Vivian Stanshall (born 21/3/1943, Shillingford, vocals), Neil Innes (born 9/12/1944, Danbury, guitar), 'Legs' Larry Smith (born 18/1/1944, Oxford, drums), Dennis Cowan (born 6/5/1947, London, bass), Roger Ruskin Spear (born 29/6/1943, London, saxophone/robots), Rodney Slater (born 8/11/1941,

○ Silver disc   ● Gold disc   ✪ Platinum disc (additional platinum units are indicated by a figure following the symbol)   ●⁹ Number of weeks album topped the UK chart

Crowland, saxophone) and Sam Spoons (born Martin Stafford Ashon, 8/2/1942, Bridgewater, percussion). Their act, a mix of traditional jazz and comedy, included mechanical robots. They appeared in The Beatles TV film *Magical Mystery Tour* (1967) and Monty Python's TV series *Do Not Adjust Your Set*. They disbanded in 1969, Innes forming The Beatles parody The Rutles with Eric Idle. Stanshall died in a house fire on 5/3/1995.

| | | | | | |
|---|---|---|---|---|---|
| 18/01/1969 | 40 | 1 | | DOUGHNUT IN GRANNY'S GREENHOUSE | Liberty LBS 83158 |
| 30/08/1969 | 36 | 1 | | TADPOLES | Liberty LBS 83257 |
| 22/06/1974 | 41 | 2 | | THE HISTORY OF THE BONZOS | United Artists UAD 60071 |

**BETTY BOO** UK singer (born Alison Moira Clarkson, 6/3/1970, Kensington, London) who began her career with She-Rockers, an all-girl rap trio based in London. She then became Betty Boo (basing her name on the 1930s cartoon character Betty Boop, the first name she adopted until forced to amend it by lawyers representing the cartoon character) and signed with Rhythm King Records, guesting with label mates The Beatmasters on a top ten record. She launched a solo career in 1990 and in 1991 was named Best UK Newcomer at the BRIT Awards. She was forced to cancel a 1991 Australian tour after it was discovered she was miming to backing tracks.

| | | | | | |
|---|---|---|---|---|---|
| 22/09/1990 | 4 | 24 | ✪ | **BOOMANIA** | Rhythm King LEFTLP 12 |
| 24/10/1992 | 62 | 1 | | GRRR! IT'S BETTY BOO | WEA 4509909082 |

**BOO RADLEYS** UK rock group formed in Liverpool in 1988 by Sice (born Simon Rowbottom, 18/6/1969, Wallasey, guitar/vocals), Martin Carr (born 29/11/1968, Turso, Highlands, guitar), Timothy Brown (born 26/2/1969, Wallasey, bass) and Steve Drewitt (drums), named after a character in the novel *To Kill A Mockingbird*. Drewitt left in 1990, replaced by Robert Cieka (born 4/8/1968, Birmingham).

| | | | | | |
|---|---|---|---|---|---|
| 04/04/1992 | 55 | 1 | | EVERYTHING'S ALRIGHT FOREVER | Creation CRECD 120 |
| 28/08/1993 | 17 | 4 | | GIANT STEPS | Creation CRECD 149 |
| 08/04/1995 | ❶[1] | 21 | ● | **WAKE UP!** | Creation CRECD 179 |
| 21/09/1996 | 20 | 2 | | C'MON KIDS | Creation CRECD 194 |
| 31/10/1998 | 62 | 1 | | KINGSIZE | Creation CRECD 228 |

**BOO-YAA T.R.I.B.E.** US rap group formed in Los Angeles by Samoan brothers Ted, Donald, Danny, Paul and Roscoe Devoux. Having been in various gangs in and around Los Angeles, the group took to music after a further brother, Robert, was shot to death. The group derived their name from the slang for a shotgun being fired.

| | | | | | |
|---|---|---|---|---|---|
| 14/04/1990 | 74 | 1 | | NEW FUNKY NATION | Fourth & Broadway BRLP 544 |

**BOOGIE DOWN PRODUCTIONS** US rap duo formed in The Bronx, NYC by DJ Scott LaRock (born 2/3/1962) and KRS-One (born Lawrence 'Kris' Parker, 1966), having first met at a homeless person's shelter. LaRock was shot to death sitting in his pick-up truck on 27/8/1987 and KRS-One (Knowledge Reigns Supreme Over Nearly Everyone) went solo.

| | | | | | |
|---|---|---|---|---|---|
| 18/06/1988 | 38 | 3 | | BY ALL MEANS NECESSARY | Jive HIP 63 |
| 22/07/1989 | 32 | 4 | | GHETTO MUSIC: THE BLUEPRINT OF HIP HOP | Jive HIP 80 |
| 25/08/1990 | 52 | 2 | | EDUTAINMENT | Jive HIP 100 |

**BOOKER T AND THE M.G.'S** US group formed in 1962 by Booker T Jones (born 12/11/1944, Memphis, TN, keyboards), Steve Cropper (born 21/10/1941, Ozark Mountains, MO, guitar), Lewis Steinberg (born 13/9/1933, Memphis, bass) and Al Jackson Jr (born 27/11/1935, Memphis, drums). Steinberg was replaced in 1964 by Donald 'Duck' Dunn (born 24/11/1941, Memphis). Al Jackson was murdered by two intruders at his Memphis home on 1/10/1975; his wife, who was tied up and unable to warn him as he entered the house, was first suspected as she had shot him the previous July. No one has ever been charged with the crime. Cropper and Dunn later appeared in the 1980 film *The Blues Brothers*. MG stands for Memphis Group. They were inducted into the Rock & Roll Hall of Fame in 1992, and won the 1994 Grammy Award for Best Pop Instrumental Performance for *Cruisin'*.

| | | | | | |
|---|---|---|---|---|---|
| 25/07/1964 | 11 | 4 | | GREEN ONIONS | London HAK 8182 |
| 11/07/1970 | 70 | 1 | | McLEMORE AVENUE | Stax SKATS 1031 |

**BOOMTOWN RATS** Irish group formed in Dublin in 1975 by former music journalist Bob Geldof (born 5/10/1954, Dublin), Johnnie Fingers (born John Moylett, 10/9/1956, keyboards), Pete Briquette (born Patrick Cusack, 2/7/1954, bass), Gerry Roberts (born 16/6/1954, guitar) and Simon Crowe (drums). Originally The Nightlife Thugs, they signed to Ensign in 1976 as The Boomtown Rats. Their chart career ended in 1984 (with one re-issue entry in 1994). Geldof founded Band Aid and Live Aid, devoting much of his time to famine relief, and later also to single fathers' rights.

| | | | | | |
|---|---|---|---|---|---|
| 17/09/1977 | 18 | 11 | ○ | BOOMTOWN RATS | Ensign ENVY 1 |
| 08/07/1978 | 8 | 44 | ✪ | **TONIC FOR THE TROOPS** | Ensign ENVY 3 |
| 03/11/1979 | 7 | 26 | ● | **THE FINE ART OF SURFACING** | Ensign ENROX 11 |
| 24/01/1981 | 6 | 7 | ● | **MONDO BONGO** | Mercury 6359 042 |
| 03/04/1982 | 64 | 5 | | V DEEP | Mercury 6359 082 |
| 09/07/1994 | 10 | 3 | | **LOUDMOUTH – THE BEST OF THE BOOMTOWN RATS & BOB GELDOF** BOOMTOWN RATS AND BOB GELDOF | Vertigo 5222852 |
| 08/05/2004 | 44 | 2 | | BEST OF BOOMTOWN RATS | Universal TV 9819145 |

**PAT BOONE** US singer (born Charles Eugene Boone, 1/6/1934, Jacksonville, FL) who was a direct descendant of US pioneer Daniel Boone. Two talent contest wins led to a contract with Republic Records in 1954, Boone continuing studies alongside recording, graduating from Columbia University, NY in 1958. His third daughter Debby later launched a singing career. After his chart career

finished, he recorded sporadically for ABC, MCA, Hitsville, Motown and Lamb & Lion. He hosts a weekly TV show *Gospel America*. He has two stars on the Hollywood Walk of Fame, one for his contribution to the recording arts and one for TV.

| | | | | | |
|---|---|---|---|---|---|
| 22/11/1958 | 10 | 1 | | **STARDUST** | London HAD 2127 |
| 28/05/1960 | 12 | 2 | | HYMNS WE HAVE LOVED | London HAD 2228 |
| 25/06/1960 | 14 | 1 | | HYMNS WE LOVE | London HAD 2092 |
| 24/04/1976 | 16 | 8 | ○ | PAT BOONE ORIGINALS | ABC ABSD 301 |

### BOOTH AND THE BAD ANGEL
UK/US duo formed by Tim Booth (lead singer with James) and Angelo Badalamenti, the Italian composer of film and TV themes, including *Twin Peaks* for which he won the 1990 Grammy Award for Best Pop Instrumental Performance.

| | | | | | |
|---|---|---|---|---|---|
| 13/07/1996 | 35 | 2 | | BOOTH AND THE BAD ANGEL | Fontana 5268522 |

### BOSTON
US rock group featuring songwriter Tom Scholz (born 10/3/1947, Toledo, OH) with Brad Delp (born 12/6/1951, Boston, MA, guitar), Fran Sheehan (born 26/3/1949, Boston, bass), Barry Goudreau (born 29/11/1951, Boston, guitar) and Sib Hashian (born 17/8/1949, Boston, drums). Scholz's apparent perfectionism did not please his record labels, the band being absent from the US charts for eight years after their peak.

| | | | | | |
|---|---|---|---|---|---|
| 05/02/1977 | 11 | 20 | ● | BOSTON ▲² ◆¹⁷ | Epic EPC 81611 |
| 09/09/1978 | 9 | 10 | ○ | **DON'T LOOK BACK** | Epic EPC 86057 |
| 04/04/1981 | 58 | 2 | | BOSTON | Epic EPC 32038 |
| 18/10/1986 | 37 | 11 | | THIRD STAGE ▲⁴ | MCA MCG 6017 |
| 25/06/1994 | 56 | 1 | | WALK ON | MCA MCD 10973 |

### JUDY BOUCHER
UK reggae singer born in St Vincent but who moved to the UK at the age of fifteen.

| | | | | | |
|---|---|---|---|---|---|
| 25/04/1987 | 95 | 1 | | CAN'T BE WITH YOU TONIGHT | Orbitone OLP 024 |

### BOW WOW WOW
UK group formed by Malcolm McLaren who lured Dave Barbarossa (born 1961, Mauritius, drums), Matthew Ashman (born 1962, London, guitar) and Leigh Gorman (born 1961, London, bass) away from Adam and the Ants, teaming them with fourteen-year-old Burmese-born Annabella Lwin (born Myant Myant Aye, 1966, Rangoon, vocals). McLaren created extensive news exposure, including having Lwin controversially pose naked for an album sleeve, her mother claiming to have not been consulted. They split after recording with producer Mike Chapman in 1983; a new line-up played US live dates in 1997. Barbarossa was later in Republica. Ashman died from diabetes on 21/11/1995.

| | | | | | |
|---|---|---|---|---|---|
| 24/10/1981 | 26 | 32 | | SEE JUNGLE! SEE JUNGLE! GO JOIN YOUR GANG YEAH CITY ALL OVER! GO APE CRAZY | RCA RCALP 00273000 |
| 07/08/1982 | 26 | 6 | | I WANT CANDY | EMI EMC 3416 |

### DAVID BOWIE
UK singer (born David Robert Jones, 8/1/1947, Brixton) who debuted in 1964 as Davy Jones With The King Bees with *Liza Jane* on the Vocation Pop label. Contracts with Parlophone and Pye (with three singles produced by Tony Hatch) followed without success. To avoid confusion with The Monkees' Davy Jones, he chose the name David Bowie 'after the knife, to cut through the bullshit'. He signed with Deram in 1966 (his second single there, a novelty item *The Laughing Gnome,* finally charted in 1973), was rejected by Apple and finally appeared on Philips in 1969. His debut hit was originally released in July 1969, making the top ten after use on a BBC astronomy programme. Signed by RCA on the strength of demos for *Hunky Dory* and his songwriting (he penned *Oh You Pretty Thing*, a hit for Peter Noone) in 1971, he was successful throughout the decade. He switched to EMI in 1983 and also made a mark as an actor in *The Elephant Man* (1980) and *Merry Christmas, Mr Lawrence* (1983). He won the 1984 award for Best UK Male, and Outstanding Contribution at the 1996 BRIT Awards. In 1997 he raised £33 million ($55 million) by issuing bonds against his catalogue and publishing royalties that were bought by Prudential Insurance. Inducted into the Rock & Roll Hall of Fame in 1996, he also took part in the *Perfect Day* project for the BBC's Children In Need charity. He won the 1984 Grammy Award for Best Video Short Form for *David Bowie* and has a star on the Hollywood Walk of Fame.

| | | | | | |
|---|---|---|---|---|---|
| 01/07/1972 | 5 | 106 | | THE RISE AND FALL OF ZIGGY STARDUST AND THE SPIDERS FROM MARS | RCA Victor SF 8287 |
| 23/09/1972 | 3 | 69 | ✪ | **HUNKY DORY** | RCA Victor SF 8244 |
| 25/11/1972 | 26 | 22 | | THE MAN WHO SOLD THE WORLD | RCA Victor LSP 4816 |
| 25/11/1972 | 17 | 37 | | SPACE ODDITY | RCA Victor LSP 4813 |
| 05/05/1973 | ❶⁵ | 47 | | **ALADDIN SANE** | RCA Victor RS 1001 |
| 03/11/1973 | ❶⁵ | 21 | ● | **PIN-UPS** | RCA Victor RS 1003 |
| 08/06/1974 | ❶⁴ | 17 | | **DIAMOND DOGS** | RCA Victor APLI 0576 |
| 16/11/1974 | 2 | 12 | | **DAVID LIVE** | RCA Victor APL 2 0771 |
| 05/04/1975 | 2 | 12 | ○ | **YOUNG AMERICANS** | RCA Victor RS 1006 |
| 07/02/1976 | 5 | 16 | | **STATION TO STATION** | RCA Victor APLI 1327 |
| 12/06/1976 | 2 | 28 | | **CHANGESONEBOWIE** | RCA Victor RS 1055 |
| 29/01/1977 | 2 | 18 | ○ | **LOW** | RCA Victor PL 12030 |
| 29/10/1977 | 3 | 18 | | **HEROES** | RCA Victor PL 12522 |
| 14/10/1978 | 5 | 10 | ● | **STAGE** | RCA Victor PL 02913 |
| 09/06/1979 | 4 | 17 | | **LODGER** | RCA Victor BOW LP 1 |
| 27/09/1980 | ❶² | 32 | ✪ | **SCARY MONSTERS AND SUPER CREEPS** | RCA BOW LP 2 |
| 10/01/1981 | 3 | 20 | ✪ | **THE VERY BEST OF DAVID BOWIE** | K-Tel NE 1111 |
| 17/01/1981 | 32 | 51 | | HUNKY DORY | RCA International INTS 5064 |
| 31/01/1981 | 33 | 62 | | THE RISE AND FALL OF ZIGGY STARDUST AND THE SPIDERS FROM MARS | RCA International INTS 5063 |
| 28/11/1981 | 24 | 17 | ● | CHANGESTWOBOWIE | RCA BOW LP 3 |
| 06/03/1982 | 49 | 24 | | ALADDIN SANE Re-issue | RCA International INTS 5067 |
| 15/01/1983 | 34 | 11 | | RARE | RCA PL 45406 |
| 23/04/1983 | ❶³ | 56 | ✪ | **LET'S DANCE** ▲ | EMI America AML 3029 |

| DATE | POS | WKS | BPI | ALBUM TITLE | LABEL & NUMBER |
|---|---|---|---|---|---|
| 30/04/1983 | 57 | 15 | | PIN-UPS | RCA International INTS 5236 |
| 30/04/1983 | 64 | 8 | | THE MAN WHO SOLD THE WORLD | RCA International INTS 5237 |
| 14/05/1983 | 60 | 14 | | DIAMOND DOGS | RCA International INTS 5068 |
| 11/06/1983 | 75 | 8 | | HEROES | RCA International INTS 5066 |
| 11/06/1983 | 85 | 5 | | LOW This and the above four albums are all re-issues | RCA International INTS 5065 |
| 20/08/1983 | 33 | 5 | | GOLDEN YEARS | RCA BOWLP 4 |
| 05/11/1983 | 17 | 6 | ✪ | ZIGGY STARDUST – THE MOTION PICTURE | RCA PL 84862 |
| 28/04/1984 | 40 | 6 | | FAME AND FASHION (BOWIE'S ALL TIME GREATEST HITS) | RCA PL 84919 |
| 19/05/1984 | 53 | 4 | | LOVE YOU TILL TUESDAY | Deram BOWIE 1 |
| 06/10/1984 | ❶¹ | 19 | ● | TONIGHT | EMI America DB 1 |
| 02/05/1987 | 6 | 16 | ● | NEVER LET ME DOWN | EMI America AMLS 3117 |
| 24/03/1990 | ❶¹ | 29 | ✪ | CHANGESBOWIE | EMI DBTV 1 |
| 14/04/1990 | 39 | 6 | | HUNKY DORY | EMI EMC 3572 |
| 14/04/1990 | 64 | 1 | | SPACE ODDITY | EMI EMC 3571 |
| 14/04/1990 | 66 | 1 | | THE MAN WHO SOLD THE WORLD | EMI EMC 3573 |
| 23/06/1990 | 25 | 4 | | THE RISE AND FALL OF ZIGGY STARDUST AND THE SPIDERS FROM MARS | EMI EMC 3577 |
| 28/07/1990 | 43 | 1 | | ALADDIN SANE | EMI EMC 3579 |
| 28/07/1990 | 52 | 1 | | PIN-UPS | EMI EMC 3580 |
| 27/10/1990 | 67 | 3 | | DIAMOND DOGS | EMI EMC 3584 |
| 04/05/1991 | 54 | 1 | | YOUNG AMERICANS | EMI EMD 1021 |
| 04/05/1991 | 57 | 1 | | STATION TO STATION | EMI EMD 1020 |
| 07/09/1991 | 64 | 1 | | LOW This and the above four albums are all re-issues | EMI EMD 1027 |
| 17/04/1993 | ❶¹ | 11 | ● | BLACK TIE WHITE NOISE | Arista 74321136972 |
| 20/11/1993 | 9 | 15 | ✪ | THE SINGLES COLLECTION | EMI CDEM 1512 |
| 07/05/1994 | 74 | 1 | | SANTA MONICA '72 | Trident GY 002 |
| 07/10/1995 | 8 | 4 | ○ | OUTSIDE | RCA 74321310662 |
| 15/02/1997 | 6 | 4 | ○ | EARTHLING | RCA 74321449442 |
| 08/11/1998 | 13 | 17 | ● | THE BEST OF 1969/1974 | EMI 8218492 |
| 02/05/1998 | 39 | 2 | ○ | THE BEST OF 1974/1979 | EMI 4943002 |
| 16/10/1999 | 5 | 5 | ○ | HOURS... | Virgin CDV 2900 |
| 07/10/2000 | 7 | 4 | ○ | BOWIE AT THE BEEB | EMI 5289582 |
| 22/06/2002 | 5 | 18 | ● | HEATHEN | Columbia 5082222 |
| 20/07/2002 | 36 | 2 | | THE RISE AND FALL OF ZIGGY STARDUST AND THE SPIDERS FROM MARS Re-issue | EMI 5398262 |
| 16/11/2002 | 11 | 29 | ✪ | BEST OF BOWIE ◇ | EMI 5398212 |
| 07/06/2003 | 53 | 1 | | ALADDIN SANE 30th anniversary re-issue | EMI 58030122 |
| 27/09/2003 | 3 | 4 | ● | REALITY | Columbia 5125552 |

**BOWLING FOR SOUP** US rock group formed in Wichita Falls, TX in 1994 by Jaret Reddick (guitar/vocals), Chris Burney (guitar/vocals), Erik Chandler (bass) and Gary Wiseman (drums).

| DATE | POS | WKS | BPI | ALBUM TITLE | LABEL & NUMBER |
|---|---|---|---|---|---|
| 07/09/2002 | 14 | 4 | ○ | DRUNK ENOUGH TO DANCE | Music For Nations JIV 418192 |

**BOX CAR RACER** US group formed by ex-Blink 182 Tom Delonge (guitar) and Travis Landon Barker (drums), plus David Kennedy (guitar) and Anthony Celestino (bass).

| DATE | POS | WKS | BPI | ALBUM TITLE | LABEL & NUMBER |
|---|---|---|---|---|---|
| 08/06/2002 | 27 | 3 | | BOX CAR RACER | MCA 1129472 |

**BOXCAR WILLIE** US country singer (born Lecil Travis Martin, 1/9/1931, Sterratt near Dallas, TX) who took his name in honour of the first song he ever wrote, *Boxcar Willie*, although he did not adopt this name until 1975. Since then he has become one of the best-selling country acts of all time and has composed hundreds of songs.

| DATE | POS | WKS | BPI | ALBUM TITLE | LABEL & NUMBER |
|---|---|---|---|---|---|
| 31/05/1980 | 5 | 12 | | KING OF THE ROAD | Warwick WW 5084 |

**BOY GEORGE** UK singer (born George O'Dowd, 14/6/1961, Eltham), formerly lead singer with Culture Club, who began his career as Lieutenant Lush, a backing singer for Bow Wow Wow – Malcolm McLaren planned that he would replace Annabella Lwin as lead singer. He went solo in 1987 after receiving treatment for drug abuse and later recorded as Jesus Loves You.

| DATE | POS | WKS | BPI | ALBUM TITLE | LABEL & NUMBER |
|---|---|---|---|---|---|
| 27/06/1987 | 29 | 6 | ○ | SOLD | Virgin V 2430 |
| 13/04/1991 | 60 | 1 | | THE MARTYR MANTRAS **JESUS LOVES YOU** | More Protein CUMLP 1 |
| 02/10/1993 | 24 | 5 | ○ | AT WORST... THE BEST OF BOY GEORGE & CULTURE CLUB **BOY GEORGE/CULTURE CLUB** | Virgin VTCD 19 |
| 12/03/1994 | 26 | 2 | | THE DEVIL IN SISTER GEORGE **BOY GEORGE/JESUS LOVES YOU/CULTURE CLUB** | Virgin VSCDG 1490 |
| 03/06/1995 | 44 | 1 | | CHEAPNESS AND BEAUTY | Virgin CDV 2780 |

**BOY MEETS GIRL** US husband and wife (they married in 1988) songwriting and recording duo of Shannon Rubicam and George Merrill.

| DATE | POS | WKS | BPI | ALBUM TITLE | LABEL & NUMBER |
|---|---|---|---|---|---|
| 04/02/1989 | 74 | 1 | | REEL LIFE | RCA PL 88414 |

## MAX BOYCE
UK male comedian and singer (born 27/9/1943, Glynneath, South Wales) who has also appeared in numerous TV shows.

| | | | | |
|---|---|---|---|---|
| 05/07/1975 | 21 | 32 | ● | LIVE AT TREORCHY . . . . . . . . . . . . . . . . . . . . . . . . . . . . . . . . . . . . . . . . . . . . . . . . . . . . . . . . . . . . . . . . . . . One Up OU 2033 |
| 01/11/1975 | ❶¹ | 17 | ● | **WE ALL HAD DOCTOR'S PAPERS** . . . . . . . . . . . . . . . . . . . . . . . . . . . . . . . . . . . . . . . . . . . . . . . . . . . . . . . . . EMI MB 101 |
| 20/11/1976 | 9 | 12 | ● | **THE INCREDIBLE PLAN** . . . . . . . . . . . . . . . . . . . . . . . . . . . . . . . . . . . . . . . . . . . . . . . . . . . . . . . . . . . . . . . EMI MB 102 |
| 07/01/1978 | 50 | 3 | ○ | THE ROAD AND THE MILES . . . . . . . . . . . . . . . . . . . . . . . . . . . . . . . . . . . . . . . . . . . . . . . . . . . . . . . . . . . . . EMI MB 103 |
| 11/03/1978 | 42 | 6 | | LIVE AT TREORCHY . . . . . . . . . . . . . . . . . . . . . . . . . . . . . . . . . . . . . . . . . . . . . . . . . . . . . . . . . . . . . . . One Up OU 54043 |
| 27/05/1978 | 6 | 14 | ● | **I KNOW COS I WAS THERE** . . . . . . . . . . . . . . . . . . . . . . . . . . . . . . . . . . . . . . . . . . . . . . . . . . . . . . . . . . . EMI MAX 1001 |
| 13/10/1979 | 27 | 13 | ○ | NOT THAT I'M BIASED . . . . . . . . . . . . . . . . . . . . . . . . . . . . . . . . . . . . . . . . . . . . . . . . . . . . . . . . . . . . . . . EMI MAX 1002 |
| 15/11/1980 | 37 | 8 | ○ | ME AND BILLY WILLIAMS . . . . . . . . . . . . . . . . . . . . . . . . . . . . . . . . . . . . . . . . . . . . . . . . . . . . . . . . . . . . . EMI MAX 1003 |

## BOYS
UK punk group formed by John Plain (guitar), Duncan Reid (bass/vocals) and Jack Black (drums), all three having met whilst working at the same factory. They subsequently added Matt Dangerfield (guitar) and Casino Steel (keyboards) in 1976. Initially signed by NEMS they later recorded for Safari (Dangerfield would later produce labelmate Toyah). The Boys disbanded in 1981.

| | | | | |
|---|---|---|---|---|
| 01/10/1977 | 50 | 1 | | THE BOYS . . . . . . . . . . . . . . . . . . . . . . . . . . . . . . . . . . . . . . . . . . . . . . . . . . . . . . . . . . . . . . . . . . . . . . NEMS NEL 6001 |

## BOYZ II MEN
US R&B quartet formed by Wanya 'Squirt' Morris (born 29/7/1973, Philadelphia, PA), Michael 'Bass' McCrary (born 16/12/1972, Philadelphia), Shawn 'Slim' Stockman (born 26/9/1972, Philadelphia) and Nathan 'Alex Vanderpool' Morris (born 18/6/1971, Philadelphia) at Philadelphia's High School of Creative and Performing Arts. Michael Bivins (of Bell Biv DeVoe) helped get them a contract with Motown. They appeared in the 1992 TV mini-series *The Jacksons: An American Dream*. Their debut hit single (*End Of The Road*) spent the most consecutive weeks at #1 in the US, racking up thirteen weeks, surpassing Elvis Presley's record, then beating their own record with first *I'll Make Love To You* (fourteen weeks) and then *One Sweet Day* (sixteen weeks) with Mariah Carey. Four Grammy Awards include Best Rhythm & Blues Performance by a Group with Vocal in 1992 for *The End Of The Road* (which also won the Best Rhythm & Blues Song award for writers LA Reid, Babyface and Daryl Simmons), and Best Rhythm & Blues Performance by a Group with Vocal in 1994 for *I'll Make Love To You*. Wanya Morris later wrote and produced Uncle Sam.

| | | | | |
|---|---|---|---|---|
| 31/10/1992 | 7 | 18 | ● | **COOLEYHIGHHARMONY** 1991 Grammy Award for Best Rhythm & Blues Performance by a Group with Vocal . . . . . . Motown 5300892 |
| 24/09/1994 | 17 | 5 | | **BOYS II MEN II** ◇ ▲¹ ◆¹² 1994 Grammy Award for Best Rhythm & Blues Album . . . . . . . . . . . . . . . . . . . . . . . . . Motown 5304312 |
| 04/10/1997 | 12 | 5 | | EVOLUTION ▲¹ . . . . . . . . . . . . . . . . . . . . . . . . . . . . . . . . . . . . . . . . . . . . . . . . . . . . . . . . . . . . . . . . . . . Motown 5308222 |
| 23/09/2000 | 54 | 1 | | NATHAN MICHAEL SHAWN WANYA . . . . . . . . . . . . . . . . . . . . . . . . . . . . . . . . . . . . . . . . . . . . . . . . . . . . . Universal 1592812 |
| 16/02/2002 | 2 | 15 | ● | **LEGACY – THE GREATEST HITS COLLECTION** . . . . . . . . . . . . . . . . . . . . . . . . . . . . . . . . . . . . . . . . . . . . . . Universal 0165622 |
| 03/08/2002 | 56 | 2 | | FULL CIRCLE . . . . . . . . . . . . . . . . . . . . . . . . . . . . . . . . . . . . . . . . . . . . . . . . . . . . . . . . . . . . . . . . . . . Arista 07822147412 |

## BOYZONE
Irish vocal group comprising Ronan Keating (born 3/3/1977, Dublin), Stephen Gately (born 17/3/1976, Dublin), Keith Duffy (born 1/10/1974, Dublin), Shane Lynch (born 3/7/1976, Dublin) and Mikey Graham (born 15/8/1972, Dublin), put together by manager Louis Walsh. Mark Walton, whose idea it was to form the band, left before they made their breakthrough. Shane Lynch married Eternal singer Easther Bennett in March 1998, and his two sisters, Edele and Keavy, are members of B*Witched. Thus the Lynch family offshoots have enjoyed eleven #1 hit singles (six for Boyzone, four for B*Witched and one for Eternal). Part of the *Perfect Day* project for the BBC's Children In Need charity, they won the Select UK & Ireland Award at the 1999 MTV Europe Music Awards. They disbanded in 2000, Keating, Graham and Gately going solo and Duffy and Lynch recording as a duo. Duffy then became an actor, appearing in the TV series *Coronation Street* as Ciaran McCarthy.

| | | | | |
|---|---|---|---|---|
| 02/09/1995 | ❶¹ | 58 | ✪³ | **SAID AND DONE** ◇ . . . . . . . . . . . . . . . . . . . . . . . . . . . . . . . . . . . . . . . . . . . . . . . . . . . . . . . . . . . . . . . . Polydor 5278012 |
| 09/11/1996 | ❶¹ | 24 | ✪³ | **A DIFFERENT BEAT** ◇ . . . . . . . . . . . . . . . . . . . . . . . . . . . . . . . . . . . . . . . . . . . . . . . . . . . . . . . . . . . . . . . Polydor 5337422 |
| 06/06/1998 | ❶³ | 55 | ✪⁵ | **WHERE WE BELONG** ◇² . . . . . . . . . . . . . . . . . . . . . . . . . . . . . . . . . . . . . . . . . . . . . . . . . . . . . . . . . . . . . . Polydor 5592002 |
| 12/06/1999 | ❶⁹ | 57 | ✪⁶ | **BY REQUEST** ◇³ 1999 MTV Europe Music Award for Best Album . . . . . . . . . . . . . . . . . . . . . . . . . . . . . . . . . Polydor 5475992 |
| 29/03/2003 | 6 | 9 | ● | **BALLADS – THE LOVE SONG COLLECTION** . . . . . . . . . . . . . . . . . . . . . . . . . . . . . . . . . . . . . . . . . . . . . Universal TV 0760742 |

## BRAD
US rock group formed by Stone Gossard of Pearl Jam as a one-off project, also featuring Shawn Smith (keyboards/vocals), Jeremy Toback (bass) and Regan Hagar (drums). They were originally to be called Shame, but Los Angeles musician Brad Wilson held the copyright to that name so they became known as Brad, something of a tongue-in-cheek retort. The album was called *Shame*, however!

| | | | | |
|---|---|---|---|---|
| 15/05/1993 | 72 | 1 | | SHAME . . . . . . . . . . . . . . . . . . . . . . . . . . . . . . . . . . . . . . . . . . . . . . . . . . . . . . . . . . . . . . . . . . . . . . . . . . . Epic 4735962 |

## PAUL BRADY
Irish singer/guitarist (born 19/5/1947, Strabane, County Tyrone) who was briefly in R&B outfit Kult while studying in Dublin, then the folk group The Johnstons. After a spell with Planxty and as a duo with Andy Irvine, he went solo in 1978. His songs have been covered by Santana, Dave Edmunds and Roger Chapman, and he has worked with Mark Knopfler (they shared the same management for a time).

| | | | | |
|---|---|---|---|---|
| 06/04/1991 | 62 | 1 | | TRICK OR TREAT . . . . . . . . . . . . . . . . . . . . . . . . . . . . . . . . . . . . . . . . . . . . . . . . . . . . . . . . . . . . . . . . . Fontana 8484541 |

### BILLY BRAGG
UK singer (born Steven William Bragg, 20/12/1957, Barking) who formed Riff Raff in 1977, which recorded for Chiswick and Geezer before disbanding. He then spent 90 days in the army before going solo in 1982.

| DATE | POS | WKS | BPI | ALBUM TITLE | LABEL & NUMBER |
|---|---|---|---|---|---|
| 21/01/1984 | 30 | 30 | ● | LIFE'S A RIOT WITH SPY VS SPY | Utility UTIL 1 |
| 20/10/1984 | 16 | 21 | ○ | BREWING UP WITH BILLY BRAGG | Go Discs AGOLP 4 |
| 04/10/1986 | 8 | 8 | ○ | **TALKING WITH THE TAXMAN ABOUT POETRY** | Go Discs AGOLP 6 |
| 13/06/1987 | 37 | 4 | | BACK TO BASICS | Go Discs AGOLP 8 |
| 01/10/1988 | 17 | 4 | | WORKERS PLAYTIME | Go Discs AGOLP 15 |
| 12/05/1990 | 34 | 4 | | THE INTERNATIONALE | Utility UTIL 11 |
| 28/09/1991 | 8 | 6 | ● | **DON'T TRY THIS AT HOME** | Go Discs 8282791 |
| 21/09/1996 | 16 | 3 | | WILLIAM BLOKE | Cooking Vinyl COOKCD 100 |
| 28/06/1997 | 72 | 1 | | BLOKE ON BLOKE | Cooking Vinyl COOKCD 127 |
| 11/07/1998 | 34 | 2 | | MERMAID AVENUE **BILLY BRAGG AND WILCO** | Elektra 7559622042 |
| 11/09/1999 | 41 | 2 | | REACHING TO THE CONVERTED | Cooking Vinyl COOKCD 186 |
| 10/06/2000 | 61 | 1 | | MERMAID AVENUE – VOLUME 2 **BILLY BRAGG AND WILCO** | Elektra 7559625222 |
| 16/03/2002 | 51 | 2 | | ENGLAND HALF ENGLISH **BILLY BRAGG AND THE BLOKES** | Cooking Vinyl COOKCD 222 |
| 18/10/2003 | 49 | 1 | | MUST I PAINT YOU A PICTURE | Cooking Vinyl COOKCD 266X |

### WILFRID BRAMBELL AND HARRY H CORBETT
UK actors from the TV comedy series *Steptoe And Son*. Wilfred Brambell (born 22/3/1912, Dublin) died on 18/1/1985, Harry H Corbett (born 28/2/1925, Rangoon, Burma) died on 21/3/1982.

| DATE | POS | WKS | ALBUM TITLE | LABEL & NUMBER |
|---|---|---|---|---|
| 23/03/1963 | 4 | 28 | **STEPTOE AND SON** | Pye NPL 18081 |
| 11/01/1964 | 14 | 5 | STEPTOE AND SON | Pye Golden Guinea GGL 0217 |
| 14/03/1964 | 19 | 1 | MORE JUNK | Pye NPL 18090 |

### MICHELLE BRANCH
US singer (born 2/7/1983, Sedona, AZ) who learned to play guitar at fourteen, signing with Maverick Records three years later and later appearing in the TV series *Buffy The Vampire Slayer*. She won the 2002 Grammy Award for Best Pop Collaboration With Vocals with Santana for *The Game Of Love*.

| DATE | POS | WKS | ALBUM TITLE | LABEL & NUMBER |
|---|---|---|---|---|
| 27/04/2002 | 54 | 2 | THE SPIRIT ROOM | Maverick WB479852 |
| 19/07/2003 | 35 | 3 | HOTEL PAPER | Maverick MAV 484262 |

### BRAND NEW HEAVIES
UK/US jazz-funk group comprising Simon Bartholomew (born 16/10/1965, London, guitar), Andy Levy (born 20/7/1966, London, bass), Jan Kincaid (born 17/5/1966, London, drums) and Ceri Evans (keyboards). They first recorded for Acid Jazz and their breakthrough came via former George Clinton backing singer N'Dea Davenport. Evans left in 1992, and Davenport left in 1996, being replaced by Seidah Garrett. Garrett left in 1999 and was replaced by Carleen Anderson who covered *Apparently Nothing* with The Brand New Heavies, having been the singer on the original by The Young Disciples.

| DATE | POS | WKS | BPI | ALBUM TITLE | LABEL & NUMBER |
|---|---|---|---|---|---|
| 14/03/1992 | 25 | 16 | ○ | BRAND NEW HEAVIES | ffrr 8283002 |
| 05/09/1992 | 38 | 2 | | HEAVY RHYME EXPERIENCE VOLUME 1 | ffrr 8283352 |
| 16/04/1994 | 4 | 48 | ✪ | **BROTHER SISTER** | ffrr 8284902 |
| 12/11/1994 | 64 | 1 | | ORIGINAL FLAVA | Acid Jazz JAZIDCD 114 |
| 03/05/1997 | 5 | 33 | ✪ | **SHELTER** | ffrr 8288872 |
| 25/09/1999 | 13 | 3 | ○ | TRUNK FUNK – THE BEST OF THE BRAND NEW HEAVIES | ffrr 3984291642 |

### BRAND X
UK jazz-rock group formed by John Goodsall (guitar), Robin Lumley (keyboards), Percy Jones (bass), Phil Collins (drums) and Maurice Pert (percussion). Collins was a member of Genesis and subsequently left Brand X in order to concentrate on his own solo career, being replaced by first Chuck Burgi and then Mike Clarke. Jones was later replaced by John Gilbin.

| DATE | POS | WKS | ALBUM TITLE | LABEL & NUMBER |
|---|---|---|---|---|
| 21/05/1977 | 37 | 5 | MOROCCAN ROLL | Charisma CAS 1126 |
| 11/09/1982 | 93 | 1 | IS THERE ANYTHING ABOUT | CBS 85967 |

### BRANDY
US singer (born Brandy Norwood, 11/2/1979, McComb, MS, raised in California) who appeared on the TV show *Thea*. Signed by Atlantic at thirteen years of age, she appeared in the 1997 film *I Know What You Did Last Summer* and the 1999 film *Double Platinum* (alongside Diana Ross). Her brother Ray J is also a professional singer. Brandy and Monica won the 1998 Grammy Award for Best Rhythm & Blues Performance by a Duo for *The Boy Is Mine*.

| DATE | POS | WKS | BPI | ALBUM TITLE | LABEL & NUMBER |
|---|---|---|---|---|---|
| 20/06/1998 | 19 | 31 | ● | NEVER S-A-Y NEVER | Atlantic 7567830392 |
| 09/03/2002 | 9 | 15 | ● | **FULL MOON** | Atlantic 7567931102 |

### LAURA BRANIGAN
US singer (born 3/7/1957, Brewster, NY) who was a former backing singer with Leonard Cohen and also appeared in the TV show *CHIPS* and the 1984 film *Mugsy's Girl*.

| | | | | | |
|---|---|---|---|---|---|
| 18/08/1984 | 16 | 14 | ○ | SELF CONTROL | Atlantic 7801471 |
| 24/08/1985 | 64 | 4 | | HOLD ME | Atlantic 7812651 |

### BRASS CONSTRUCTION
Multinational funk outfit formed in 1968 by Randy Muller (keyboards/flute/percussion), US Larry Payton (drums), Jamaican Wayne Parris (trumpet), Trinidadian Joseph Arthur Wong (guitar), US Sandy Billups (congas), Jamaican Michael 'Mickey' Grudge (saxophone), US Morris Price (trumpet/percussion), US Jesse Ward (saxophone) and Wade Williamston (bass) as Dynamic Soul. They disbanded in 1986, Muller producing the likes of New York Skyy and Tamiko Jones

| | | | | | |
|---|---|---|---|---|---|
| 20/03/1976 | 9 | 11 | ○ | **BRASS CONSTRUCTION** | United Artists UAS 29923 |
| 30/06/1984 | 94 | 1 | | RENEGADES | Capitol EJ 24 01601 |

### TONI BRAXTON
US singer (born 7/10/1968, Severn, MD) who originally recorded with her sisters as The Braxtons for Arista. She went solo in 1992 with LaFace Records. A 1997 lawsuit against Arista and LaFace was an attempt to dissolve her contract with the companies, though she did record a third album for them in 2000. In January 1998 she filed for Chapter 7 bankruptcy protection for her companies Madame Ashlee, Princess Ashlee and Lady Ashlee. She married keyboard player Keri Lewis (of Mint Condition) in April 2001 Toni has won six Grammy Awards: Best New Artist in 1993, Best Female Rhythm & Blues Vocal Performance in 1993 for *Another Sad Love Song*, Best Female Rhythm & Blues Vocal Performance in 1994 for *Breathe Again*, Best Female Pop Vocal Performance in 1996 for *Un-break My Heart*, Best Female Rhythm & Blues Vocal Performance in 1996 for *You're Makin' Me High* and Best Female Rhythm & Blues Vocal Performance in 2000 for *He Wasn't Man Enough*.

| | | | | | |
|---|---|---|---|---|---|
| 29/01/1994 | 4 | 33 | ● | **TONI BRAXTON** ▲² | LaFace 74321162682 |
| 29/06/1996 | 10 | 81 | ✪² | **SECRETS** ◇³ | LaFace 73008260202 |
| 06/05/2000 | 3 | 19 | ● | **THE HEAT** | LaFace 73008260692 |
| 15/11/2003 | 23 | 3 | | ULTIMATE | Arista 82876574852 |

### BREAD
US singer/guitarist/keyboard player/songwriter David Gates (born 11/12/1940, Tulsa, OK) who was a successful session musician (with Chuck Berry, Duane Eddy, Glen Campbell and Merle Haggard among others) before forming Bread in 1969 with James Griffin (born 10/8/1943, Cincinnati, guitar), Robb Royer (guitar) and Jim Gordon (drums). Larry Knetchtel (born 4/8/1940, Bell, CA) and Mike Botts (born 8/12/1944, Sacramento, CA) later replaced Griffin, Royer and Gordon. They disbanded in 1973 but briefly reunited in 1976. Gates enjoyed a brief solo career before going into retirement.

| | | | | | |
|---|---|---|---|---|---|
| 26/09/1970 | 34 | 5 | | ON THE WATERS | Elektra 2469 005 |
| 18/03/1972 | 9 | 19 | | **BABY I'M A-WANT YOU** | Elektra K 42100 |
| 28/10/1972 | 7 | 100 | | **THE BEST OF BREAD** | Elektra K 42115 |
| 27/07/1974 | 48 | 1 | | THE BEST OF BREAD VOLUME 2 | Elektra K 42161 |
| 29/01/1977 | 17 | 6 | | LOST WITHOUT YOUR LOVE | Elektra K 52044 |
| 05/11/1977 | ❶³ | 46 | ✪ | **THE SOUND OF BREAD** | Elektra K 52062 |
| 28/11/1987 | 84 | 2 | | THE COLLECTION – THE VERY BEST OF BREAD AND DAVID GATES **BREAD AND DAVID GATES** | Telstar STAR 2303 |
| 05/07/1997 | 9 | 19 | ● | **DAVID GATES AND BREAD: ESSENTIALS DAVID GATES AND BREAD** | warner.esp/Jive 9548354082 |

### BREAK MACHINE
US dance trio formed in New York by brothers Lindsay and Lindell Blake and Cortez Jordan.

| | | | | | |
|---|---|---|---|---|---|
| 09/06/1984 | 17 | 16 | | BREAK MACHINE | Record Shack SOHOLP 3 |

### BREAKBEAT ERA
UK drum and bass trio Roni Size, DJ Die and singer/songwriter Leonie Laws.

| | | | | | |
|---|---|---|---|---|---|
| 11/09/1999 | 31 | 2 | | ULTRA OBSCENE | XL Recordings XLCD 130 |

### JULIAN BREAM
UK guitarist (born 1933, London) who studied at the Royal College of Music and made his public debut in 1950. He founded the Julian Bream Consort in 1960, reviving Elizabethan music. He was made an Officer of the OBE in 1964 and later collected a CBE. He has won four Grammy Awards: Best Chamber Music Performance in 1963 with the Julian Bream Consort for *An Evening of Elizabethan Music*, Best Classical Performance, Instrumental Soloist with orchestral accompaniment in 1966 for *Baroque Guitar*, Best Classical Performance, Instrumental Soloist (with orchestra) in 1971 for *Villa-Lobos: Concerto for Guitar* and Best Chamber Music Performance in 1972 with John Williams for *Julian And John*.

| | | | | | |
|---|---|---|---|---|---|
| 27/04/1996 | 66 | 2 | | THE ULTIMATE GUITAR COLLECTION | RCA Victor 74321337052 |

### BREATHE
UK group formed in London by David Glasper (born 4/1/1965, vocals), Ian 'Spike' Spice (born 18/9/1966, drums), Marcus Lillington (guitar) and Michael Delahunty (bass) who left in 1988.

| | | | | | |
|---|---|---|---|---|---|
| 08/10/1988 | 22 | 5 | ○ | ALL THAT JAZZ | Siren SRNLP 12 |

### BREED 77
Gibraltarian group formed by Paul Isola (vocals), Danny Felice (guitar), Pedro Caparros (guitar), Stuart Cavilla (bass) and Pete Chichone (drums); they relocated to London in 1997.

| | | | | | |
|---|---|---|---|---|---|
| 15/05/2004 | 61 | 1 | | CULTURA | Albert Productions JASCDUK 008 |

**BREEDERS** US/UK rock group formed by Kim Deal (guitar/synthesizer/vocals), previously with The Puxies and Amps, and Tayna Donelly (guitar), with Josephine Wiggs (bass) and Britt Walford (drums) joining later. By the time of their hit the group consisted of Deal, her sister Kelley (guitar), Wiggs and Jim MacPherson (drums), Donelly later joined Belly.

| 09/06/1990 | 22 | 3 | | POD | 4AD CAD 0006 |
| 11/09/1993 | 5 | 5 | O | LAST SPLASH | 4AD CAD 3014CD |
| 01/06/2002 | 51 | 1 | | TITLE TK. | 4AD CAD 2205CD |

**MAIRE BRENNAN** Irish singer (born Maire Ni Bhraonain, 4/8/1952, Dublin) and lead singer with family group Clannad. She is sister to vocalist Enya.

| 13/06/1992 | 53 | 2 | | MAIRE | RCA PD 75358 |

**ADRIAN BRETT** UK flautist.

| 10/11/1979 | 19 | 11 | ● | ECHOES OF GOLD | Warwick WW 5062 |

**PAUL BRETT** UK guitarist, previously a member of Sage. He also formed the Phoenix Future label and later became a journalist, writing for a number of music magazines.

| 19/07/1980 | 24 | 7 | | ROMANTIC GUITAR | K-Tel ONE 1079 |

**EDIE BRICKELL AND THE NEW BOHEMIANS** US singer Brickell (born 10/3/1966 Oak Cliff, TX) who joined the Dallas-based band as lead singer in 1985. The rest of the group comprised Brad Hauser (bass), Kenny Withrow (guitar), John Bush (percussion) and Brandon Ally (drums). Ally left and was replaced by Matt Chamberlain, with Wes Martin (guitar) joining at the same time. The New Bohemians disbanded in 1991. Brickell married singer Paul Simon in May 1992.

| 04/02/1989 | 25 | 17 | ● | SHOOTING RUBBERBANDS AT THE STARS | Geffen WX 215 |
| 10/11/1990 | 63 | 1 | | GHOST OF A DOG | Geffen WX 386 |
| 03/09/1994 | 59 | 1 | | PICTURE PERFECT MORNING EDIE BRICKELL | Geffen GED 24715 |

**BRIGHOUSE AND RASTRICK BRASS BAND** UK brass band from the West Yorkshire towns of Brighouse and Rastrick (situated between Bradford and Huddersfield). They appeared in the 2000 film Brassed Off.

| 28/01/1978 | 10 | 11 | O | FLORAL DANCE | Logo 1001 |

**SARAH BRIGHTMAN** UK singer (born 14/8/1961) and a member of the dance troupe Hot Gossip. She fronted their first single, a top ten hit, and its less successful follow-up (the rest of the group comprised Debbie Ash, Floyd, Roy Gayle, Virginia Hartley, Alison Hierlehy, Richard Lloyd King, Kim Leeson, Perry Lister, Jane Newman, Julia Redburn and Chrissie Wickham). She re-emerged in 1981 in the hit musical Phantom Of The Opera, since becoming highly successful in the MOR market. She was married to songwriter Andrew Lloyd-Webber from 1984–90.

| 23/03/1985 | 4 | 18 | | ANDREW LLOYD WEBBER: REQUIEM PLACIDO DOMINGO, SARAH BRIGHTMAN, PAUL MILES-KINGSTON, WINCHESTER CATHEDRAL CHOIR AND THE ENGLISH CHAMBER ORCHESTRA CONDUCTED BY LORIN MAAZEL | HMV ALW 1 |
| 17/06/1989 | 48 | 2 | | THE SONGS THAT GOT AWAY | Really Useful 8391161 |
| 08/08/1992 | 53 | 4 | | AMIGOS PARA SIEMPRE (FRIENDS FOR LIFE) JOSE CARRERAS AND SARAH BRIGHTMAN | East West 4509902562 |
| 11/11/1995 | 45 | 2 | | THE UNEXPECTED SONGS – SURRENDER | Really Useful 5277022 |
| 14/06/1997 | 2 | 21 | ● | TIMELESS ◇ | Coalition 630191812 |
| 20/01/2001 | 37 | 2 | | LA LUNA | East West 8573859152 |

**BRILLIANT** UK group formed by Jimmy Cauty of KLF and Youth of Killing Joke and also featuring June Montana (vocals). Their debut album was produced by Stock Atiken Waterman.

| 20/09/1986 | 83 | 1 | | KISS THE LIPS OF LIFE | Food BRILL 1 |

**JOHNNY BRISTOL** US singer (born 3/2/1939, Morgantown, NC) who began his career with Jackie Beaver, billed as Johnny & Jackie and signed by Tri-Phi. He was a successful songwriter and producer at Motown Records, usually with his mentor Harvey Fuqua. When Motown relocated to California he started producing for Columbia, although the label rejected him as a singer and he signed with MGM. Writing credits include Someday We'll Be Together (Diana Ross & The Supremes) and Love Me For A Reason (Osmonds and Boyzone). He died on 21/3/2004.

| 05/10/1974 | 12 | 7 | | HANG ON IN THERE BABY | MGM 2315 303 |

**BRITISH SEA POWER** UK rock group formed in Brighton in 2000 by Yan (vocals), Noble (guitar), Hamilton (bass) and Wood (drums), with the group wearing militaristic uniforms on stage.

| 14/06/2003 | 54 | 1 | | THE DECLINE OF BRITISH SEA POWER | Rough Trade RTRADECD090 |

**JUNE BRONHILL AND THOMAS ROUND** Australian/UK vocal duo: Bronhill (born June Gough, 26/6/1929, Broken Hill, New South Wales) and Round (born 18/10/1915, Barrow-In-Furness). Round was a war-time pilot who joined the D'Oyly Carte Opera Company in 1946.

| 18/06/1960 | 17 | 1 | | LILAC TIME | HMV CLP 1248 |

**BRONSKI BEAT** UK trio formed by Jimmy Somerville (born 22/6/1961, Glasgow), Larry Steinbachek (born 6/5/1960, London) and Steve Bronski (born 7/2/1960, Glasgow) with a strong gay following reflecting their musical stance on gay issues. Despite quitting through 'pop star pressure', Somerville later successfully fronted The Communards before going solo.

| | | | | |
|---|---|---|---|---|
| 20/10/1984 ..... 4..... 53..... ✪ | THE AGE OF CONSENT .................................................. Forbidden Fruit BITLP 1 |
| 21/09/1985..... 24...... 6..... ○ | HUNDREDS AND THOUSANDS................................................ Forbidden Fruit BITLP 2 |
| 10/05/1986..... 18...... 6 ..... | TRUTHDARE DOUBLEDARE ................................................ Forbidden Fruit BITLP 3 |
| 22/09/2001..... 29...... 4 ..... | THE VERY BEST OF JIMMY SOMERVILLE BRONSKI BEAT AND THE COMMUNARDS **JIMMY SOMERVILLE** |
| | **BRONSKI BEAT AND THE COMMUNARDS** ................................ London 0927412582 |

**MICHAEL BROOK —** see **NUSRAT FATEH ALI KHAN/MICHAEL BROOK**

**ELKIE BROOKS** UK singer (born Elaine Bookbinder, 25/2/1945, Manchester) whose career began in the 1960s with a dance band, touring with jazz musician Humphrey Lyttelton and session work. She was in Vinegar Joe with Robert Palmer, both of them going solo when the group folded in 1973.

| | | |
|---|---|---|
| 18/06/1977..... 16 ..... 20 ..... ● | TWO DAYS AWAY ................................................... A&M AMLH 68409 |
| 13/05/1978..... 20 ..... 13 ..... ○ | SHOOTING STAR ................................................... A&M AMLH 64695 |
| 13/10/1979..... 34 ..... 6 ..... | LIVE AND LEARN ................................................... A&M AMLH 68509 |
| 14/11/1981 ..... 2 ..... 79 ..... ✪ | **PEARLS**.................................................... A&M ELK 1981 |
| 13/11/1982..... 5 ..... 25 ..... ✪ | **PEARLS II** ................................................... A&M ELK 1982 |
| 14/07/1984..... 35 ..... 7 ..... | MINUTES ...................................................... A&M AML 68565 |
| 08/12/1984..... 35 ..... 11 ..... ● | SCREEN GEMS ................................................... EMI SCREEN 1 |
| 06/12/1986..... 5 ..... 23 ..... ● | **NO MORE THE FOOL** ............................................ Legend LMA 1 |
| 27/12/1986..... 10 ..... 18 ..... ● | **THE VERY BEST OF ELKIE BROOKS** ................................ Telstar STAR 2284 |
| 11/06/1988..... 57 ..... 3 ..... | BOOKBINDER'S KID ............................................... Legend LMA 3 |
| 18/11/1989..... 58 ..... 3 ..... | INSPIRATIONS ................................................... Telstar STAR 2354 |
| 13/03/1993..... 27 ..... 4 ..... | ROUND MIDNIGHT ....................................... Castle Communications CTVCD 113 |
| 16/04/1994..... 58 ..... 2 ..... | NOTHIN' BUT THE BLUE .................................. Castle Communications CTVCD 127 |
| 13/04/1996..... 49 ..... 2 ..... | AMAZING **ELKIE BROOKS WITH THE ROYAL PHILHARMONIC ORCHESTRA** ...... Carlton Premiere 3036000282 |
| 15/03/1997..... 23 ..... 7 ..... | THE VERY BEST OF ELKIE BROOKS ........................................ Polygram TV 5407122 |

**GARTH BROOKS** US male singer (born Troyal Garth Brooks, Yukon, OK) who spent four years working as a performer in Nashville before landing a contract with Capitol on the strength of his performance at the Bluebird Cafe when he filled in for a no-show artist. He has since become the biggest selling country artist and also appeared in the film *The Lamb* as Chris Gaines. He has won two Grammy Awards: Best Male Country Vocal Performance in 1991 for *Ropin' The Wind* and Best Country Collaboration with Vocals in 1997 with Trisha Yearwood for *In Another's Eyes*. He has a star on the Hollywood Walk of Fame.

| | | |
|---|---|---|
| 15/02/1992..... 41 ..... 2 ..... | ROPIN' THE WIND ▲[18] ◆[14] ........................................... Capitol CDESTU 2162 |
| 12/02/1994..... 2 ..... 11 ..... ● | **IN PIECES** ▲[5] ................................................. Capitol/Liberty CDEST 2212 |
| 24/12/1994..... 11 ..... 21 ..... ● | THE HITS ▲[8] ◆[10] .............................................. Liberty CDP 8320812 |
| 02/12/1995..... 22 ..... 6 ..... ● | FRESH HORSES ................................................... Capitol CDGB 1 |
| 13/12/1997..... 34 ..... 7 ..... ○ | SEVENS ▲[5] .................................................... Capitol 8565992 |
| 28/11/1998..... 57 ..... 1 ..... | DOUBLE LIVE ▲[5] ◆[15] ........................................... Capitol 4974242 |

**MEREDITH BROOKS** US singer (born 12/6 – she refuses to reveal year, probably 1958 – Oregon City, OR) who was a member of Lips and The Graces before going solo.

| | | |
|---|---|---|
| 23/08/1997 ..... 5 ..... 10 ..... ● | **BLURRING THE EDGES** ............................................. Capitol CDEST 2298 |

**NIGEL BROOKS SINGERS** UK choir formed by Nigel Brooks who had originally formed the group for the BBC and had also been a composer for the Cuddington Players.

| | | |
|---|---|---|
| 29/11/1975..... 5 ..... 16 ..... ● | **SONGS OF JOY** ................................................. K-Tel NE 706 |
| 05/06/1976..... 44 ..... 1 ..... | 20 ALL TIME EUROVISION FAVOURITES.................................... K-Tel NE 712 |

**BROS** UK group who were originally the trio Caviar, and then Gloss with twin brothers Matt and Luke Goss (born 29/9/1968, London) and Craig Logan (born 22/4/1969, Fife, Scotland). Songwriter/producer Nicky Graham spotted them, changed the name to Bros and signed them to CBS. Logan was sacked in 1989, winning a court settlement of £1 million. The two brothers continued as a duo. Financial and management problems – and declining popularity – heralded their splitting in 1991, both brothers trying solo and group projects. Logan later worked in the record business and band management. Named Best British Newcomers at the 1989 BRIT Awards.

| | | | | | |
|---|---|---|---|---|---|
| 09/04/1988 | 2 | 54 | ✪4 | PUSH | CBS 4606291 |
| 28/10/1989 | 4 | 13 | ● | THE TIME | CBS 4659181 |
| 12/10/1991 | 18 | 2 | | CHANGING FACES | Columbia 4688171 |

**BROTHER BEYOND** UK pop group formed by Nathan Moore (vocals), David White (guitar), Carl Fysh (keyboards) and Steve Alexander (drums).

| | | | | | |
|---|---|---|---|---|---|
| 26/11/1988 | 9 | 23 | ✪ | GET EVEN | Parlophone PCS 7327 |
| 25/11/1989 | 60 | 1 | ● | TRUST | Parlophone PCS 7337 |

**BROTHERHOOD** UK hip hop group formed in London by Spice, Dexter and Shylock, evolving out of Jewish Public Enemy.

| | | | | | |
|---|---|---|---|---|---|
| 17/02/1996 | 50 | 1 | | ELEMENTALZ | Bite-It CDBHOOD 1 |

**BROTHERHOOD OF MAN** UK group with two incarnations. The first was in 1970 when ex- Edison Lighthouse and Pipkins session singer Tony Burrows (born 14/4/1942, Exeter) was asked to sing *United We Stand*. A group was formed to promote the record, with Johnny Goodison, singers Sue and Sunny and UK songwriter Roger Greenaway. The group was re-formed in 1976 when songwriter/producer Tony Hiller (responsible for *United We Stand*) penned *Save All Your Kisses For Me*, the UK's entry for the Eurovision Song Contest, this time with Nicky Stevens, Sandra Stevens, Lee Sheridan and Martin Lee. Success in the competition and a UK #1 heralded more hit singles.

| | | | | | |
|---|---|---|---|---|---|
| 24/04/1976 | 20 | 8 | ○ | LOVE AND KISSES FROM | Pye NSPL 18490 |
| 12/08/1978 | 18 | 9 | ○ | B FOR BROTHERHOOD | Pye NSPL 18567 |
| 07/10/1978 | 6 | 15 | | BROTHERHOOD OF MAN | K-Tel BML 7980 |
| 29/11/1980 | 14 | 8 | ● | BROTHERHOOD OF MAN SING 20 NUMBER ONE HITS | Warwick WW 5087 |

**BROTHERS JOHNSON** US duo George (born 17/5/1953, Los Angeles, CA) and Louis Johnson (born 13/4/1955, Los Angeles), originally in Billy Preston's band before being discovered by producer Quincy Jones who took guitarist George (aka Lightning Licks) and bass player Louis (Thunder Thumbs) on tour to Japan. Recording a number of their songs for his *Mellow Madness* album, Jones fixed a contract with A&M and the duo became mainstays of the jazz-funk circuit. They won the 1977 Grammy Award for Best Rhythm & Blues Instrumental Performance for *Q*. Louis Johnson also won the 1986 Grammy Award for Best Rhythm & Blues Song with Anita Baker and Gary Bias for *Sweet Love*.

| | | | | | |
|---|---|---|---|---|---|
| 19/08/1978 | 48 | 8 | | BLAM! | A&M AMLH 64714 |
| 23/02/1980 | 22 | 12 | | LIGHT UP THE NIGHT | A&M AMLK 63716 |
| 18/07/1981 | 42 | 2 | | WINNERS | A&M AMLK 63724 |

**EDGAR BROUGHTON BAND** UK rock band formed in 1969 by Edgar Broughton (guitar/vocals), Steve Broughton (drums), Arthur Grant (bass) and Victor Unitt (guitar).

| | | | | | |
|---|---|---|---|---|---|
| 20/06/1970 | 18 | 4 | | SING BROTHER SING | Harvest SHVL 772 |
| 05/06/1971 | 28 | 2 | | THE EDGAR BROUGHTON BAND | Harvest SHVL 791 |

**BOBBY BROWN** US singer (born 5/2/1969, Roxbury, MA) who was a member of teen group New Edition, formed in 1983. He left in 1986 to go solo (replaced by Johnny Gill), becoming the most successful of the ex-members. He married Whitney Houston in 1992 and their first child was born the following year. Imprisoned in January 1998 for driving under the influence of alcohol and drugs, in May 2000 (having tested positive for cocaine), he was refused bail and incarcerated while waiting sentence the following month.

| | | | | | |
|---|---|---|---|---|---|
| 28/01/1989 | 3 | 41 | ✪2 | DON'T BE CRUEL ▲6 | MCA MCF 3425 |
| 05/08/1989 | 40 | 6 | | KING OF STAGE | MCA MCL 1886 |
| 02/12/1989 | 26 | 10 | ● | DANCE… YA KNOW IT! | MCA MCG 6074 |
| 05/09/1992 | 11 | 5 | | BOBBY | MCA MCAD 10695 |
| 05/08/1995 | 24 | 3 | | TWO CAN PLAY THAT GAME | MCA MCD 11334 |

**CRAZY WORLD OF ARTHUR BROWN** UK singer (born Arthur Wilton, 24/6/1944, Whitby) and former philosophy student who was in R&B bands before forming The Crazy World Of Arthur Brown with Vincent Crane (born Vincent Rodney Chessman, 21/5/1943, Reading, keyboards) and Drachen Theaker (drums) who was replaced by Carl Palmer (born 20/3/1947, Birmingham). Crane and Palmer later formed Atomic Rooster, before Palmer became one third of Emerson Lake & Palmer. Crane committed suicide on 14/2/1989.

| | | | | | |
|---|---|---|---|---|---|
| 06/07/1968 | 2 | 16 | | THE CRAZY WORLD OF ARTHUR BROWN | Track 612005 |

**DENNIS BROWN** Jamaican singer (born Clarence Brown, 1/2/1956, Kingston) who took up professional music as a child and later joined the Falcons. He was admitted to hospital with respiratory problems and died from pneumonia on 1/7/1999, leaving a wife and thirteen children.

26/06/1982 . . . . . 72 . . . . . . 6 . . . . . .    LOVE HAS FOUND ITS WAY . . . . . . . . . . . . . . . . . . . . . . . . . . . . . . . . . . . . . . . . . . . . . . A&M AMLH 64886

**ERROL BROWN** UK singer (born 12/11/1948, Kingston, Jamaica) who formed Hot Chocolate in 1970. The group disbanded in 1987 and Brown went solo, with production by Tony Swain and Steve Jolley. He was awarded an MBE in the Queen's 2003 Birthday Honours List.

09/06/2001 . . . . . 44 . . . . . . 2 . . . . . .    STILL SEXY – THE ALBUM . . . . . . . . . . . . . . . . . . . . . . . . . . . . . . . . . . . . . . . . . . . . Universal TV 138162

**FOXY BROWN** US singer (born Inga Marchand, 6/9/1979, Brooklyn, NYC) who first appeared guesting on other artists' records before going solo with Def Jam.

06/02/1999 . . . . . 51 . . . . . . 1 . . . . . .    CHYNA DOLL ▲¹ . . . . . . . . . . . . . . . . . . . . . . . . . . . . . . . . . . . . . . . . . . . . . . . . . . Def Jam 5589332

**HORACE BROWN** US R&B singer (born in Charlotte, NC) who also recorded with Case and Faith Evans, and previously supplied backing vocals for the likes of Father MC and Christopher Williams.

06/07/1996 . . . . . 48 . . . . . . 1 . . . . . .    HORACE BROWN . . . . . . . . . . . . . . . . . . . . . . . . . . . . . . . . . . . . . . . . . . . . . . . . . Motown 5306942

**IAN BROWN** UK singer (born Ian George Brown, 20/2/1963, Ancoats) who formed The Stone Roses in 1984. He went solo in 1997. In 1998 he was jailed after being found guilty of air rage.

14/02/1998 . . . . . 4 . . . . . . 24 . . . . . . ●    **UNFINISHED MONKEY BUSINESS** . . . . . . . . . . . . . . . . . . . . . . . . . . . . . . . . . . . Polydor 5395652
20/11/1999 . . . . . 14 . . . . . . 6 . . . . . . ●    GOLDEN GREATS . . . . . . . . . . . . . . . . . . . . . . . . . . . . . . . . . . . . . . . . . . . . . . Polydor 5431412
13/10/2001 . . . . . 3 . . . . . . 5 . . . . . . ●    **MUSIC OF THE SPHERES** . . . . . . . . . . . . . . . . . . . . . . . . . . . . . . . . . . . . . . . Polydor 5891262

**JAMES BROWN** US singer (born 3/5/1928 – often given as 3/5/1933 due to Brown's frequent use of fake ID – Macon, GA) who was abandoned by his mother at the age of four and raised by his aunt Handsome 'Honey' Washington in Augusta, GA. Frequently in trouble as a teenager and once sentenced to serve eight to sixteen years hard labour for petty theft, then released on parole after three years and one day, he recorded a demo version of *Please Please Please* with pianist Bobby Byrd. Radio plays led to a contract with King's Federal subsidiary and a re-recorded version of the single, under the name James Brown And The Famous Flames, hit #6 on the R&B charts, selling over 1 million copies but never making the pop top 100. His US top 40 debut with *Think* in 1960 heralded fourteen years as a chart regular. As well as the Famous Flames, his groups have included the JB's (spotlighting Bootsy Collins, Maceo Parker and Fred Wesley for the first time), and he has been known as 'The Godfather of Soul', 'Soul Brother #1' and 'The New Minister of Super Heavy Heavy Funk', all self-bestowed. He made a cameo appearance in the 1980 film *The Blues Brothers*. In 1988 he was sentenced to six years for possession of firearms and evading arrest charges, serving three. He has won three Grammy Awards: Best Rhythm & Blues Recording in 1965 for the single *Papa's Got A Brand New Bag*, Best Rhythm & Blues Vocal Performance in 1986 for the single *Living In America*, and Best Album Notes in 1991 for *Star Time*. Inducted into the Rock & Roll Hall of Fame in 1986, he also took part in the *It's Only Rock 'N' Roll* project for the Children's Promise charity. In 1991 Brown collected the NARAS' Lifetime Achievement Award. He has a star on the Hollywood Walk of Fame.

18/10/1986 . . . . . 85 . . . . . . 3 . . . . . .    GRAVITY . . . . . . . . . . . . . . . . . . . . . . . . . . . . . . . . . . . . . . . . . . . Scotti Brothers SCT 57108
10/10/1987 . . . . . 17 . . . . . . 21 . . . . . . ●    THE BEST OF JAMES BROWN – THE GODFATHER OF SOUL . . . . . . . . . . . . . . . . . . . Scotti Brothers POLD 5230
25/06/1988 . . . . . 27 . . . . . . 5 . . . . . .    I'M REAL . . . . . . . . . . . . . . . . . . . . . . . . . . . . . . . . . . . . . . . . . . . . . . . . K-Tel NE 1376
16/11/1991 . . . . . 19 . . . . . . 22 . . . . . . ●    SEX MACHINE – THE VERY BEST OF JAMES BROWN . . . . . . . . . . . . . . . . . . . . . . . Polydor 8458281
11/05/2002 . . . . . 30 . . . . . . 3 . . . . . .    THE GODFATHER – THE VERY BEST OF . . . . . . . . . . . . . . . . . . . . . . . . . . . . Universal Music TV 5898412

**JOE BROWN AND THE BRUVVERS** UK singer (born 13/5/1941, Lincolnshire) who began as guitarist with Clay Nicholls & The Blue Flames, then was discovered by Larry Parnes when appearing on ITV's *Boy Meets Girl*. He graduated from solo guitar spots to singing and enjoyed a string of hit singles, then went into films and West End musicals. His wife, the late Vicki Brown, appeared (uncredited) on the #1 hit by JJ Barrie, and daughter Sam has also hit the charts. Bruvvers' member and songwriter Peter Oakman (he penned *A Picture Of* You) later fronted Harley Quinne.

01/09/1962 . . . . . 3 . . . . . . 39 . . . . . .    **A PICTURE OF YOU** . . . . . . . . . . . . . . . . . . . . . . . . . . . . . . . . . . . . Pye Golden Guinea GGL 0146
25/05/1963 . . . . . 14 . . . . . . 8 . . . . . .    JOE BROWN – LIVE **JOE BROWN** . . . . . . . . . . . . . . . . . . . . . . . . . . . . . . . . . . Piccadilly NPL 38006

**ROY CHUBBY BROWN** UK comedian (born Royston Vasey, 5/2/1945, Middlesbrough) whose real name was adopted for the fictional village in the TV comedy series *League Of Gentlemen*.

25/11/1995 . . . . . 29 . . . . . . 7 . . . . . . ○    TAKE FAT AND PARTY . . . . . . . . . . . . . . . . . . . . . . . . . . . . . . . . . . . . . . . . Polystar 5297842
07/12/1996 . . . . . 67 . . . . . . 1 . . . . . .    FAT OUT OF HELL . . . . . . . . . . . . . . . . . . . . . . . . . . . . . . . . . . . . . . . . . . Polystar 5370602

**SAM BROWN** UK singer (born 7/10/1964, London) who is the daughter of singer Joe Brown and his late wife Vicki. With a recording debut at the age of twelve, she appeared in numerous TV shows including Jack Good's *Let's Rock* as well as performing with Adam & The Ants and Spandau Ballet.

11/03/1989 . . . . . 4 . . . . . . 18 . . . . . . ●    **STOP!** . . . . . . . . . . . . . . . . . . . . . . . . . . . . . . . . . . . . . . . . . . . . . . . A&M AMA 5195
14/04/1990 . . . . . 38 . . . . . . 12 . . . . . . ○    APRIL MOON . . . . . . . . . . . . . . . . . . . . . . . . . . . . . . . . . . . . . . . . . . . . A&M AMA 9014

**JACKSON BROWNE** US singer (born 9/10/1948, Heidelberg, West Germany) whose family settled in Los Angeles, CA in 1951. He was a successful songwriter for Linda Ronstadt, Joe Cocker, The Byrds, Bonnie Raitt and others before launching his own career in 1972. His US top ten hit *Doctor My Eyes* was a UK hit for the Jackson Five. His wife Phyllis committed suicide on 25/03/76. He took part in the *It's Only Rock 'N' Roll* project for the Children's Promise charity and was inducted into the Rock & Roll Hall of Fame in 2004.

04/12/1976 . . . . . 26 . . . . . . 5 . . . . . . ○    THE PRETENDER . . . . . . . . . . . . . . . . . . . . . . . . . . . . . . . . . . . . . . . . . . Asylum K 53048

| DATE | POS | WKS | BPI | ALBUM TITLE | LABEL & NUMBER |
|------|-----|-----|-----|-------------|----------------|
| 21/01/1978 | 28 | 7 | ● | RUNNING ON EMPTY | Asylum K 53070 |
| 12/07/1980 | 44 | 5 | | HOLD OUT ▲¹ | Asylum K 52226 |
| 13/08/1983 | 37 | 7 | | LAWYERS IN LOVE | Asylum 9602681 |
| 08/03/1986 | 36 | 7 | | LIVES IN THE BALANCE | Asylum EKT 31 |
| 17/06/1989 | 39 | 2 | | WORLD IN MOTION | Elektra EKT 50 |
| 06/11/1993 | 35 | 3 | | I'M ALIVE | Elektra 7559615242 |
| 09/03/1996 | 47 | 1 | | LOOKING EAST | Elektra 7559618672 |
| 26/10/2002 | 53 | 1 | | THE NAKED RIDE HOME | Elektra EA627932 |

**BROWNSTONE** US R&B vocal group based in Los Angeles, CA and featuring Monica 'Mimi' Dolby, Nichole 'Nicci' Gilbert and Charmayne 'Maxee' Maxwell. Doby left in 1995 due to ill health and was replaced by Kina Cosper.

| DATE | POS | WKS | BPI | ALBUM TITLE | LABEL & NUMBER |
|------|-----|-----|-----|-------------|----------------|
| 29/04/1995 | 18 | 13 | O | FROM THE BOTTOM UP | MJJ 4773622 |
| 31/05/1997 | 19 | 3 | | STILL CLIMBING | Epic 4853882 |

**DAVE BRUBECK QUARTET** US pianist (born David Warren, 6/12/1920, Concord, CA) with Paul Desmond (alto saxophone), Joe Morello (drums) and Eugene Wright (bass). They were initially popular on the US college circuit. Brubeck founded Fantasy Records in 1949 with Sol and Max Weiss. He has a star on the Hollywood Walk of Fame. Desmond died on 30/5/1977.

| DATE | POS | WKS | BPI | ALBUM TITLE | LABEL & NUMBER |
|------|-----|-----|-----|-------------|----------------|
| 25/06/1960 | 11 | 1 | | TIME OUT | Fontana TFL 5085 |
| 07/04/1962 | 12 | 16 | | TIME FURTHER OUT **DAVE BRUBECK** | Fontana TFL 5161 |

**JACK BRUCE** UK bass player (born John Symon Archer, 4/5/1943, Glasgow) who was first known as a member of Alexis Korner's group, then Graham Bond's Organisation, John Mayall's Bluesbreakers and Manfred Mann. He linked with Ginger Baker and Eric Clapton to form Cream, one of the first 'supergroups', albeit shortlived. After going solo, over the next few years he assembled various groups including Jack Bruce And Friends with Larry Coryell and Mitch Mitchell, and a line-up with Dave 'Clem' Clempson and David Sancious that was popular in Germany. BLT with Robin Trower and Bill Lordan in 1981 did not fare so well and disbanded after two albums, after which Bruce maintained a low profile as he struggled with drug and alcohol problems. He returned towards the end of the decade with a low profile album and then the critically acclaimed *A Question Of Time* in 1990.

| DATE | POS | WKS | BPI | ALBUM TITLE | LABEL & NUMBER |
|------|-----|-----|-----|-------------|----------------|
| 27/09/1969 | 6 | 9 | | **SONGS FOR A TAILOR** | Polydor 583058 |

**BRUFORD** — see **ANDERSON BRUFORD WAKEMAN HOWE**

**BRUVVERS** — see **JOE BROWN AND THE BRUVVERS**

**PEABO BRYSON AND ROBERTA FLACK** US vocal duo with Peabo Bryson (born 13/4/1951, Greenville, SC) and Roberta Flack (born 10/2/1937, Black Mountain, near Asheville, NC). Despite a debut single for Bang Records in 1975 Peabo has proved more successful singing duets. He has won two Grammy Awards: Best Pop Performance by a Duo in 1992 with Celine Dion for *Beauty And The Beast* and Best Pop Performance by a Duo in 1993 with Regina Belle for *A Whole New World (Aladdin's Theme)*.

| DATE | POS | WKS | BPI | ALBUM TITLE | LABEL & NUMBER |
|------|-----|-----|-----|-------------|----------------|
| 17/09/1983 | 15 | 10 | O | BORN TO LOVE | Capitol EST 7122841 |

**BT** US producer (born Brian Transeau, 1973, Maryland) and a major name on the UK dance scene who also worked with Echobelly singer Sonya Madden and Tori Amos.

| DATE | POS | WKS | BPI | ALBUM TITLE | LABEL & NUMBER |
|------|-----|-----|-----|-------------|----------------|
| 21/10/1995 | 45 | 4 | | IMA | Perfecto 0630123452 |
| 04/10/1997 | 35 | 1 | | ESCM | Perfecto 3984200652 |

**B2K** US vocal group formed in Los Angeles, CA by Omarion (born Omarion Grandberry, 12/11/1985), Raz-B (born De-Maio Thornton, 13/6/1985), Lil Fizz (born Druex Fredericks, 26/11/1985) and J-Boog (born Jarrell Houston, 11/8/1985). The group disbanded in 2004 to pursue solo careers.

| DATE | POS | WKS | BPI | ALBUM TITLE | LABEL & NUMBER |
|------|-----|-----|-----|-------------|----------------|
| 05/04/2003 | 35 | 12 | O | PANDEMONIUM | Epic 5105342 |

**MICHAEL BUBLE** Canadian singer (born 9/9/1975, Burnaby, British Columbia) and raised in Vancouver; he was discovered by David Foster after singing at the wedding of the daughter of the Canadian Prime Minister.

| DATE | POS | WKS | BPI | ALBUM TITLE | LABEL & NUMBER |
|------|-----|-----|-----|-------------|----------------|
| 18/10/2003 | 6 | 24 | ✪ | **MICHAEL BUBLE** | Reprise 9362485352 |
| 29/05/2004 | 52 | 2 | | COME FLY WITH ME | Reprise 9362486832 |

**BUCKETHEADS** US producer/guitarist Kenny 'Dope' Gonzalez who was also a member of Masters At Work and the mastermind behind Nuyorican Soul.

| DATE | POS | WKS | BPI | ALBUM TITLE | LABEL & NUMBER |
|------|-----|-----|-----|-------------|----------------|
| 27/01/1996 | 74 | 1 | | ALL IN THE MIND | Positiva CDTIVA 1010 |

**LINDSEY BUCKINGHAM** US singer (born 3/10/1947, Palo Alto, CA) who was a member of Fritz before joining Fleetwood Mac in 1975 with girlfriend Stevie Nicks. He made his first solo album during a lull in group activities and left the band in 1987.

| DATE | POS | WKS | BPI | ALBUM TITLE | LABEL & NUMBER |
|------|-----|-----|-----|-------------|----------------|
| 08/08/1992 | 51 | 1 | | OUT OF THE CRADLE | Mercury 5126582 |

### JEFF BUCKLEY

**JEFF BUCKLEY** US singer/guitarist (born 1/8/1966, Orange County, CA) and the son of musician Tim Buckley, whom he met only once at the age of eight, some two months before his father died from a heroin overdose. Raised by his mother and stepfather, after training at the Los Angeles Musicians' Institute he moved to Manhattan where after a brief spell with Gods & Monsters he went solo. On the night of 29/5/1997 he jumped fully clothed into the Mississippi River at Memphis Harbour after saying he fancied a late night swim. Drowned when the waves from two passing boats swept him under, his body was not washed ashore for several days.

| | | | | |
|---|---|---|---|---|
| 27/08/1994 | 50 | 7 | | GRACE ◇ ........................................................ Columbia 4759282 |
| 23/05/1998 | 7 | 4 | | **SKETCHES FOR MY SWEETHEART THE DRUNK** ............... Columbia 4886612 |
| 20/05/2000 | 8 | 2 | | **MYSTERY WHITE BOY – LIVE 95–96** ....................... Columbia 4979729 |

**BUCKS FIZZ** UK vocal group formed by Cheryl Baker (born Rita Crudgington, 8/3/1954, London), Jay Aston (born 4/5/1961, London), Mike Nolan (born 7/12/1954, Dublin) and Bobby G (born Robert Gubby, 23/8/1953, Epsom) to represent the UK in the 1981 Eurovision Song Contest. Baker was previously in Co-Co, the 1978 entrants. The win in Dublin – with *Making Your Mind Up* – owed as much to the dance routine (in which the girls' skirts were ripped off) as to the song. Aston left in 1985 after an alleged affair with songwriter Andy Hill (who was married to the group's manager) and was replaced by Shelley Preston (born 14/5/1960, Salisbury). They dissolved in 1989, regrouping for occasional live projects. Baker became a TV presenter.

| | | | | |
|---|---|---|---|---|
| 08/08/1981 | 14 | 28 | ● | BUCKS FIZZ ........................................................ RCA RCALP 5050 |
| 08/05/1982 | 10 | 23 | ● | **ARE YOU READY?** ................................................ RCA RCALP 8000 |
| 19/03/1983 | 17 | 13 | ○ | HAND CUT ......................................................... RCA RCALP 6100 |
| 03/12/1983 | 25 | 13 | | GREATEST HITS .................................................... RCA PL 70022 |
| 24/11/1984 | 66 | 2 | | I HEAR TALK ...................................................... RCA PL 70397 |
| 13/12/1986 | 89 | 1 | | THE WRITING ON THE WALL ................................... Polydor POHL 30 |

### HAROLD BUDD/ELIZABETH FRASER/ROBIN GUTHRIE/SIMON RAYMONDE

**HAROLD BUDD/ELIZABETH FRASER/ROBIN GUTHRIE/SIMON RAYMONDE** US pianist (born 24/5/1936, Los Angeles) who gained a master degree in music and attended the California Institute of the Arts before signing with the Obscure label in 1978. Elizabeth Fraser, Robin Guthrie and Simon Raymonde, also on his debut hit album, are The Cocteau Twins.

| | | | | |
|---|---|---|---|---|
| 22/11/1986 | 46 | 2 | | THE MOON AND THE MELODIES ................................. 4AD CAD 611 |

**ROY BUDD** UK composer/jazz pianist (born 14/3/1947, London) who made his name writing various movie themes including the films *Soldier Blue* (1970), *Pulp* (1972), *Paper Tiger* (1975), *Sinbad And The Eye Of The Tiger* (1977) and *The Wild Geese* (1978). *Get Carter*, his first chart album, was originally released in 1971. Married to French singer Caterina Valente from 1972–79, he died from a brain haemorrhage on 7/8/1993.

| | | | | |
|---|---|---|---|---|
| 19/09/1998 | 68 | 1 | | GET CARTER Original soundtrack to the film ................. Cinephile CINCD 001 |

**JOE BUDDEN** US rapper (born 1981, Harlem, NYC, raised in Queens, NYC and Jersey City, NJ).

| | | | | |
|---|---|---|---|---|
| 28/06/2003 | 55 | 1 | | JOE BUDDEN ...................................................... Def Jam 9807936 |

**BUDGIE** UK hard rock group formed in Cardiff in 1968 by John Shelley (born 10/4/1947, Cardiff, bass/guitar/vocals), Tony Bourge (born 23/11/1948, Cardiff, guitar/vocals) and Ray Phillips (drums). Phillips left in 1974 and was replaced by Pete Boot (born 30/9/1950, West Bromwich), who left later the same year and was replaced by Steve Williams. Bourge left in 1978 (to join Phillips in a venture called Tredegar) and was replaced by John Thomas. Shelley disbanded the group in 1987.

| | | | | |
|---|---|---|---|---|
| 08/06/1974 | 29 | 3 | | IN FOR THE KILL .................................................. MCA MCF 2546 |
| 27/09/1975 | 36 | 4 | | BANDOLIER ....................................................... MCA MCF 2723 |
| 31/10/1981 | 68 | 2 | | NIGHT FLIGHT ..................................................... RCA RCALP 6003 |
| 23/10/1982 | 62 | 1 | | DELIVER US FROM EVIL ........................................... RCA RCALP 6054 |

**BUFFALO TOM** US rock group formed in Boston in 1986 by Chris Colbourn (vocals/bass), Bill Janovitz (guitar/vocals) and Tom Maginnis (drums).

| | | | | |
|---|---|---|---|---|
| 14/03/1992 | 49 | 1 | | LET ME COME OVER ............................................... Situation Two SITU 36CD |
| 09/10/1993 | 17 | 3 | | (BIG RED LETTER DAY) ............................................ Beggars Banquet BBQCD 142 |
| 22/07/1995 | 31 | 1 | | SLEEPY EYED ...................................................... Beggars Banquet BBQCD 177 |

**BUGGLES** UK duo Geoff Downes and Trevor Horn who were previously together in Tina Charles' backing group. They began writing songs with friend Bruce Woolley in 1978, releasing *Video Killed The Radio Star* a year later. Both went on to join Yes, with Downes later joining Asia and Horn becoming a major producer.

| | | | | |
|---|---|---|---|---|
| 16/02/1980 | 27 | 6 | | THE AGE OF PLASTIC ............................................. Island ILPS 9585 |

**LTJ BUKEM** UK drum and bass producer (born Danny Williamson, 1967, London) and the founder of Good Looking Records.

| | | | | |
|---|---|---|---|---|
| 08/04/2000 | 40 | 3 | | JOURNEY INWARDS ............................................... Good Looking GLRAA 001 |

### BUNNYMEN – see ECHO AND THE BUNNYMEN

### EMMA BUNTON
UK singer (born 21/1/1976, London) who was also a member of the Spice Girls and known as Baby Spice. She began her career acting in the TV soap *Eastenders*.

| | | | | | |
|---|---|---|---|---|---|
| 28/04/2001 | 4 | 12 | ● | A GIRL LIKE ME | Virgin CDV 2935 |
| 21/02/2004 | 7 | 11+ | ○ | FREE ME | 19 9866158 |

### ERIC BURDON AND WAR
UK singer (born 11/5/1941, Newcastle-upon-Tyne) who was a founding member of The Animals in 1962; the group split acrimoniously in 1966. Burdon then linked with US group War.

| | | | | | |
|---|---|---|---|---|---|
| 03/10/1970 | 50 | 2 | | ERIC BURDON DECLARES WAR | Polydor 2310 041 |

### TIM BURGESS
UK singer (born 30/5/1968, Salford) who was a founder member of The Charlatans.

| | | | | | |
|---|---|---|---|---|---|
| 20/09/2003 | 38 | 1 | | I BELIEVE | PIAS PIASB 099CD |

### JEAN-JACQUES BURNEL
UK singer/bassist (born 21/2/1952, London) who was a founding member of The Stranglers. He launched a parallel solo career in 1979 with the release of *Euroman Cometh*, an album that featured guest appearances from Brian James (guitar), Lew Lewis (harmonica), Carey Fortune (drums) and Pete Howells (drums). Following its success, a touring group was assembled, featuring John Ellis, Lew Lewis, Pete Howells and Penny Tobin, but this proved shortlived. Burnel later recorded with fellow Stranglers member Dave Greenfield (born 29/3/1949, Brighton, keyboards) with *Fire And Water* being their joint collaboration.

| | | | | | |
|---|---|---|---|---|---|
| 21/04/1979 | 40 | 5 | | EUROMAN COMETH | United Artists UAG 30214 |
| 03/12/1983 | 94 | 1 | | FIRE AND WATER **DAVE GREENFIELD AND JEAN-JACQUES BURNEL** | Epic EPC 25707 |

### BUSH
UK rock group from London formed by Gavin Rossdale (born 30/10/1967, London, guitar/vocals), Nigel Pulsford (born 11/4/1965, Newport, guitar), ex-Transvision Vamp Dave Parsons (born 2/7/1966, Uxbridge, bass) and Robin Goodridge (born 10/9/1966, Crawley, drums), taking their name from Shepherd's Bush, the London area where they grew up. The group made their initial breakthrough in the USA where their debut album sold over 8 million copies.

| | | | | | |
|---|---|---|---|---|---|
| 15/06/1996 | 42 | 3 | | SIXTEEN STONE | Atlantic 6544925312 |
| 01/02/1997 | 4 | 12 | ● | RAZORBLADE SUITCASE ▲[2] | Interscope IND 90091 |
| 06/11/1999 | 28 | 2 | | THE SCIENCE OF THINGS | Polydor 4904832 |
| 10/11/2001 | 53 | 1 | | GOLDEN STATE | Atlantic 7567834882 |

### KATE BUSH
UK singer (born 30/7/1958, Bexleyheath) who signed with EMI while still at convent school and spent the next two years writing material for her first album. The lyrics of her first single, *Wuthering Heights*, were inspired by Emily Bronte's novel (Bronte and Bush shared the same birthday); it was a UK smash with subsequent albums selling well. She won the Best UK Female Award at the 1987 BRIT Awards

| | | | | | |
|---|---|---|---|---|---|
| 11/03/1978 | 3 | 70 | ✪ | THE KICK INSIDE | EMI EMC 3223 |
| 25/11/1978 | 6 | 36 | ✪ | LIONHEART | EMI EMA 787 |
| 20/09/1980 | ❶[1] | 23 | ● | NEVER FOR EVER | EMI EMA 7964 |
| 25/09/1982 | 3 | 10 | ○ | THE DREAMING | EMI EMC 3419 |
| 28/09/1985 | ❶[3] | 52 | ✪[2] | HOUNDS OF LOVE | EMI KAB 1 |
| 22/11/1986 | ❶[2] | 55 | ✪[4] | THE WHOLE STORY | EMI KBTV 1 |
| 28/01/1989 | 2 | 20 | ✪ | THE SENSUAL WORLD | EMI EMD 1010 |
| 13/11/1993 | 2 | 15 | ✪ | THE RED SHOES | EMI CDEMD 1047 |

### BUSTED
UK group formed by James Bourne (born 13/9/1983, Southend-on-Sea, guitar/piano), Charlie Simpson (born 7/6/1985, Ipswich, guitar/bass/drums/piano) and Mattie Jay (born 8/5/1983, Kingston, bass/guitar/drums). They were named British Breakthrough Act and Best Pop Act at the 2004 BRIT Awards.

| | | | | | |
|---|---|---|---|---|---|
| 12/10/2002 | 2 | 73 | ✪[3] | BUSTED ◇ | Universal MCD 60084 |
| 29/11/2003 | 2 | 29 | ✪[3] | A PRESENT FOR EVERYONE | Universal MCD 60090 |

### BERNARD BUTLER
UK guitarist (born 1/5/1970) who joined Suede in 1990, later recording with David McAlmont before going solo.

| | | | | | |
|---|---|---|---|---|---|
| 09/12/1995 | 33 | 8 | | THE SOUND OF McALMONT AND BUTLER **McALMONT AND BUTLER** | Hut CDHUT 32 |
| 18/04/1998 | 11 | 8 | ○ | PEOPLE MOVE ON | Creation CRECD 221 |
| 06/11/1999 | 43 | 1 | | FRIENDS AND LOVERS | Creation CRECD 248 |
| 24/08/2002 | 18 | 2 | | BRING IT BACK **McALMONT AND BUTLER** | Chrysalis 5399772 |

▲[9] Number of weeks album topped the US chart  ◆[12] RIAA Diamond Awards  ◇[3] IFPI Platinum Europe Awards

### JONATHAN BUTLER

South African singer born in Athlone, Cape Town and the youngest of seventeen children. He began singing professionally as a child and was an established artist by the age of thirteen. He emigrated to London in 1985, following his disillusionment with the apartheid regime in South Africa, at the invitation of Jive Records' founders Clive Calder and Ralph Simon.

| | | | | |
|---|---|---|---|---|
| 12/09/1987 | 12 | 11 | ● | JONATHAN BUTLER .................................................................. Jive HIP 46 |
| 04/02/1989 | 29 | 3 | | MORE THAN FRIENDS ............................................................... Jive HIP 70 |

### BUTTHOLE SURFERS

US rock group originally known as Ashtray Baby Heads, formed in Austin, TX by Gibson 'Gibby' Haynes (vocals), Paul Leary (guitar) and King Koffey (drums), with Jeff Pinker later joining on bass. Leary subsequently recorded solo and Haynes became a DJ at KROX Radio in Austin.

| | | | |
|---|---|---|---|
| 16/03/1991 | 68 | 1 | PIOUHGD ....................................................... Rough Trade R 20812601 |
| 03/04/1993 | 73 | 1 | INDEPENDENT WORM SALOON ................................................. Capitol CDEST 2192 |

### BUZZCOCKS

UK rock group formed in Manchester by philosophy student Howard Devoto (born Howard Trafford, vocals), Pete Shelley (born Peter McNeish, 17/4/1955, guitar/vocals), Steve Garvey (bass), Steve Diggle (guitar) and John Maher (drums). Devoto left after their debut release to form Magazine, Shelley taking over as lead singer and chief songwriter. They launched the New Hormones label in 1979.

| | | | | |
|---|---|---|---|---|
| 25/03/1978 | 15 | 11 | O | ANOTHER MUSIC IN A DIFFERENT KITCHEN ................................ United Artists UAG 30159 |
| 07/10/1978 | 13 | 9 | O | LOVE BITES ................................................ United Artists UAG 30184 |
| 06/10/1979 | 26 | 3 | | A DIFFERENT KIND OF TENSION .......................... United Artists UAG 30260 |

### BY ALL MEANS

US group formed in Los Angeles, CA by Lynn Roderick (vocals), James Varner (vocals) and Billy Sheppard (guitar), with various session musicians also helping out.

| | | | |
|---|---|---|---|
| 16/07/1988 | 80 | 1 | BY ALL MEANS ............................................. Fourth & Broadway BRLP 520 |

### MAX BYGRAVES

UK singer (born Walter Bygraves, 16/10/1922, London) who named himself after comic Max Miller. After successful singles in the 1950s he became an all-round entertainer, but scored biggest with a series of 'sing-a-long' albums, medleys of well-known numbers appealing to a middle-of-the-road market. An astute businessman, he set up Lakeview Music, which paid £350 for the rights to Lionel Bart's *Oliver!* show and later sold them to Essex Music for £250,000. He was awarded an OBE in 1982 and later hosted the TV show *Family Fortunes*.

| | | | | |
|---|---|---|---|---|
| 23/09/1972 | 4 | 44 | | SING ALONG WITH MAX ........................................... Pye NSPL 18361 |
| 02/12/1972 | 11 | 23 | O | SING ALONG WITH MAX VOLUME 2 ............................... Pye NSPL 18383 |
| 05/05/1973 | 5 | 30 | O | SINGALONGAMAX VOLUME 3 ..................................... Pye NSPL 18401 |
| 29/09/1973 | 7 | 12 | O | SINGALONGAMAX VOLUME 4 ..................................... Pye NSPL 18410 |
| 15/12/1973 | 15 | 6 | O | SINGALONGPARTY SONG ......................................... Pye NSPL 18419 |
| 12/10/1974 | 39 | 3 | | YOU MAKE ME FEEL LIKE SINGING A SONG ..................... Pye NSPL 18436 |
| 07/12/1974 | 21 | 6 | O | SINGALONGXMAS ................................................ Pye NSPL 18439 |
| 13/11/1976 | 3 | 21 | ✪ | 100 GOLDEN GREATS ............................................ Ronco RTDX 2019 |
| 28/10/1978 | 39 | 5 | | LINGALONGAMAX ............................................... Ronco RPL 2033 |
| 16/12/1978 | 67 | 1 | | THE SONG AND DANCE MEN ..................................... Pye NSPL 18574 |
| 19/08/1989 | 5 | 19 | ● | SINGALONGAWARYEARS .......................................... Parkfield Music PMLP 5001 |
| 25/11/1989 | 33 | 6 | ● | SINGALONGAWARYEARS VOLUME 2 .............................. Parkfield PMLP 5006 |

### CHARLIE BYRD — see STAN GETZ

### DONALD BYRD

US trumpeter (born 9/12/1932, Detroit, MI) who began his jazz career performing with the likes of John Coltrane, Art Blakey, Sonny Rollins and Jackie McLean before linking with Pepper Adams. At the turn of the 1960s he began tutoring at Rutgers and Howard Universities, encountering the Mizell brothers, Fonce and Larry, who made him one of the pioneers of jazz-funk, or fusion music. He in turn assembled The Blackbyrds from students of his at university.

| | | | |
|---|---|---|---|
| 10/10/1981 | 70 | 3 | LOVE BYRD ....................................................... Elektra K 52301 |

### BYRDS

US folk-pop group formed in 1964 by Roger McGuinn (born 13/7/1942, Chicago, IL, guitar/vocals), Gene Clark (born 17/11/1944, Tipton, OH, percussion), David Crosby (born David Van Cortland, 14/8/1941, Los Angeles, CA, guitar/vocals), Chris Hillman (born 4/12/1942, Los Angeles, bass/vocals) and Michael Clarke (born 3/6/1944, Spokane, WA, drums). Gene Clark left in 1966, Crosby the following year, with McGuinn, Hillman, Kevin Kelly (drums) and Gram Parsons re-forming. Parsons and Hillman left the same year, McGuinn then recruited Clarence White (guitar), John York (bass) and Gene Parsons (drums). The original members reunited in 1973 and 1979. White was killed by a drunk driver while loading equipment on 14/7/1973, Gram Parsons died from a heroin overdose on 19/9/1973 (his body was stolen by manager Phil Kaufmann and burned), Gene Clark died on 24/5/1991 of natural causes (although a heavy drug and alcohol user) and Michael Clarke died from liver failure caused by alcohol abuse on 19/12/1993. The group was inducted into the Rock & Roll Hall of Fame in 1991.

| | | | |
|---|---|---|---|
| 28/08/1965 | 7 | 12 | MR. TAMBOURINE MAN ........................................... CBS BPG 62571 |
| 09/04/1966 | 11 | 5 | TURN, TURN, TURN ............................................... CBS BPG 62652 |
| 01/10/1966 | 27 | 2 | 5TH DIMENSION ................................................. CBS BPG 62783 |
| 22/04/1967 | 37 | 4 | YOUNGER THAN YESTERDAY ..................................... CBS SBPG 62988 |

O Silver disc  ● Gold disc  ✪ Platinum disc (additional platinum units are indicated by a figure following the symbol)  ●⁹ Number of weeks album topped the UK chart

| | | | | | |
|---|---|---|---|---|---|
| 04/05/1968 | 12 | 11 | | THE NOTORIOUS BYRD BROTHERS | CBS 63169 |
| 24/05/1969 | 15 | 1 | | DR. BYRD AND MR HYDE | CBS 63545 |
| 14/02/1970 | 41 | 1 | | BALLAD OF EASY RIDER | CBS 63795 |
| 28/11/1970 | 11 | 4 | | UNTITLED | CBS 66253 |
| 14/04/1973 | 31 | 1 | | BYRDS | Asylum SYLA 8754 |
| 19/05/1973 | 47 | 1 | | HISTORY OF THE BYRDS | CBS 68242 |

**DAVID BYRNE** UK singer (born 14/5/1952, Dumbarton, Scotland) who was raised in Baltimore, MD, USA. After graduating from the Rhode Island School of Design he formed Talking Heads in 1974 with Tina Weymouth and Chris Frantz, expanding the group in 1977. Talking Heads disbanded in 1991, although David Byrne had already begun a solo career.

| | | | | | |
|---|---|---|---|---|---|
| 21/02/1981 | 29 | 8 | | MY LIFE IN THE BUSH OF GHOSTS **BRIAN ENO AND DAVID BYRNE** | E.G. EGLP 48 |
| 21/10/1989 | 52 | 2 | | REI MOMO | Warner Brothers WX 319 |
| 14/03/1992 | 26 | 5 | | UH-OH | Luaka Bop 7599267992 |
| 04/06/1994 | 44 | 2 | | DAVID BYRNE | Luaka Bop 9362455582 |
| 19/05/2001 | 58 | 1 | | LOOK INTO THE EYEBALL | Luaka Bop CDVUS 189 |

## MELANIE C
UK singer (born 12/1/1974, Liverpool), aka Mel C and Sporty Spice, who was a founder member of The Spice Girls and launched a solo career in 1998.

| 30/10/1999 | 4 | 69 | ✪³ | **NORTHERN STAR** ◇ ........................................................................... Virgin CDVX 2893 |
| 22/03/2003 | 5 | 4 | ● | **REASON** ........................................................................... Virgin CDV 2969 |

## C & C MUSIC FACTORY/CLIVILLES & COLE
US production duo David Cole (born 3/6/1962, Johnson City, TN) and Robert Clivilles (born 30/8/1964, New York City) who began by remixing other people's work. Their first own production was as Adonis Featuring Two Puerto Ricans, A Black Man And A Dominican, with a minor hit before the first C & C Music Factory record in 1990. Thereafter releases were as C & C Music Factory or Clivilles & Cole. They also recorded as S.O.U.L. System. David Cole died from meningitis on 24/1/1995.

| 09/02/1991 | 8 | 13 | ● | **GONNA MAKE YOU SWEAT** ........................................................................... Columbia 4678141 |
| 28/03/1992 | 45 | 1 | | GREATEST REMIXES VOLUME I ........................................................................... Columbia 4694462 |

## MONTSERRAT CABALLE
Spanish operatic singer (born 12/4/1933, Barcelona) who studied at the Barcelona Liceo, making her concert debut in 1954. Famous as a Verdi and Donizetti soprano, she debuted at Covent Garden in 1972. She won the 1968 Grammy Award for Best Classical Solo Vocal Performance for *Rossini Rarities*.

| 22/10/1988 | 15 | 8 | ○ | BARCELONA **FREDDIE MERCURY AND MONTSERRAT CABALLE** ........................................... Polydor POLH 44 |
| 08/08/1992 | 41 | 3 | | FROM THE OFFICIAL BARCELONA GAMES CEREMONY **PLACIDO DOMINGO, JOSE CARRERAS & MONTSERRAT CABALLE** ...........  ........................................................................... RCA Red Seal 9026612042 |

## CABARET VOLTAIRE
UK group formed in Sheffield in 1974 by Stephen Mallinder (bass/vocals), Richard Kirk (guitar) and Chris Watson (electronics/tapes). Watson left in 1981 and was eventually replaced by Eric Random (guitar); until such time Mallinder and Kirk continued as a duo.

| 26/06/1982 | 98 | 1 | | 2 X 45. ........................................................................... Rough Trade 42 |
| 13/08/1983 | 31 | 5 | | THE CRACKDOWN. ........................................................................... Some Bizzare CV 1 |
| 10/11/1984 | 69 | 1 | | MICRO-PHONIES ........................................................................... Some Bizzare CV 2 |
| 03/08/1985 | 71 | 2 | | DRINKING GASOLINE. ........................................................................... Some Bizzare CVM 1 |
| 26/10/1985 | 57 | 2 | | THE COVENANT, THE SWORD AND THE ARM OF THE LAW ........................................... Some Bizzare CV 3 |

## CACTUS WORLD NEWS
Irish group formed in Dublin in 1985 by Eoin Moody (vocals), Frank Kearns (guitar), Fergal MacAindris (bass) and Wayne Sheehy (drums). A demo tape sent to Bono of U2 led to his recording their debut album. They were signed by MCA in 1986, who deleted their second album, *No Shelter*, in 1989 before it was distributed. They disbanded in 1990.

| 24/05/1986 | 56 | 2 | | URBAN BEACHES ........................................................................... MCA MCG 6005 |

## CAKE
US rock group formed in Sacramento, CA in 1991 by John McCrea (guitar/vocals), Vince di Fiore (trumpet), Victor Damien (bass), Todd Roper (drums) and Greg Brown (guitar). Their debut album was with Capricorn in 1994.

| 05/04/1997 | 53 | 2 | | FASHION NUGGET ........................................................................... Capricorn 5328672 |

## J.J. CALE
US guitarist/singer, Jean-Jacques Cale (born 5/12/1938, Tulsa, OK) who began his professional career with a western swing group before switching styles with the launch of the rock 'n' roll group Johnny Cale And The Valentines. A further switch to country music after moving to Nashville proved unsuccessful and he moved onto Los Angeles to perform in various bars around the city. He returned home to Tulsa in 1967 and might have remained undiscovered but for Eric Clapton covering one of his songs (*After Midnight*), which led to an invitation for Cale to record the album *Naturally* and ultimately made his reputation.

| 02/10/1976 | 53 | 1 | ○ | TROUBADOUR ........................................................................... Island ISA 50141 |
| 25/08/1979 | 40 | 6 | | 5 ........................................................................... Shelter ISA 5018 |
| 21/02/1981 | 44 | 7 | | SHADES ........................................................................... Shelter ISA 5021 |
| 20/03/1982 | 36 | 5 | | GRASSHOPPER ........................................................................... Shelter IFA 5022 |
| 24/09/1983 | 47 | 3 | | NUMBER 8 ........................................................................... Mercury MERL 22 |
| 26/09/1992 | 58 | 2 | | NUMBER 10 ........................................................................... Silvertone ORECD 523 |

## CALEXICO
US group formed in Tucson, AZ by Joey Burns and John Conventino. They first met in 1990 and did much session work together. Their first release was issued by Haus Musik Records in 1996. Later members of the group included Martin Wenck, Volker Zander and Jacob Valenzuela.

| 20/05/2000 | 57 | 1 | | HOT RAIL. ........................................................................... City Slang 201532 |
| 22/02/2003 | 71 | 1 | | FEAST OF WIRE. ........................................................................... City Slang 5816932 |

○ Silver disc  ● Gold disc  ✪ Platinum disc (additional platinum units are indicated by a figure following the symbol)  ●⁹ Number of weeks album topped the UK chart

**MARIA CALLAS** Greek soprano singer (born Maria Cecilia Sophia Anna Kalogeropoulou, 2/12/1923, New York) who left the USA in 1937 to study at the Athens Conservatory. She made her debut in *Tosca* in Athens in 1941, in London in 1952 and in New York four years later. She retired from the stage in 1965 and died in Paris on 16/9/1977. She has a star on the Hollywood Walk of Fame.

| | | | | | |
|---|---|---|---|---|---|
| 20/06/1987 | 50 | 7 | | THE MARIA CALLAS COLLECTION | Stylus SMR 732 |
| 24/02/1996 | 61 | 1 | | DIVA – THE ULTIMATE COLLECTION | EMI CDEMTV 113 |
| 11/11/2000 | 45 | 8 | ● | POPULAR MUSIC FROM TV FILM & OPERA | EMI Classics CDC 5570622 |
| 27/10/2001 | 32 | 3 | ○ | ROMANTIC CALLAS – THE BEST OF | EMI Classics CDC 5572112 |

**CALLING** US rock group formed in Los Angeles, CA by Alex Band (vocals), Aaron Kamin (guitar), Sean Woolstenhulme (guitar), Billy Mohler (bass) and Nate Wood (drums). They debuted for RCA in 2001 and were named Best New Act at the 2002 MTV Europe Music Awards.

| | | | | | |
|---|---|---|---|---|---|
| 29/06/2002 | 12 | 25 | ● | CAMINO PALMERO | RCA 74321916102 |
| 12/06/2004 | 9 | 3+ | | TWO | RCA 82876622622 |

**CAMEL** UK rock group formed in 1972 by Andy Latimer (born 17/5/1947, Guildford, guitar/flute/vocals), Peter Bardens (born 19/6/194, London, keyboards), Doug Ferguson (born 4/4/1947, Carlisle, bass) and Andy Ward (born 28/9/1952, Epsom, drums). Changes in the line-up meant that by 1993 only Latimer from the original group remained, having been joined by Christopher Rainbow (vocals), Tom Scherpenzeel (keyboards), Paul Bass (bass) and Paul Burgess (drums). Bardens died from lung cancer on 22/1/2002.

| | | | | | |
|---|---|---|---|---|---|
| 24/05/1975 | 22 | 13 | ○ | THE SNOW GOOSE | Decca SKL 5207 |
| 17/04/1976 | 15 | 6 | ○ | MOON MADNESS | Decca TXS 115 |
| 17/09/1977 | 20 | 8 | | RAIN DANCES | Decca TXS 124 |
| 14/10/1978 | 26 | 1 | | BREATHLESS | Decca TXS 132 |
| 27/10/1979 | 45 | 3 | | I CAN SEE YOUR HOUSE FROM HERE | Decca TXS 137 |
| 31/01/1981 | 34 | 7 | | NUDE | Decca SKL 5323 |
| 15/05/1982 | 57 | 5 | | THE SINGLE FACTOR | Decca SKL 5328 |
| 21/04/1984 | 57 | 4 | | STATIONARY TRAVELLER | Decca SKL 5334 |

**CAMEO** US R&B group formed in 1976 as a thirteen-piece band, the New York City Players, becoming Cameo a year later. By the 1980s they were a three-piece under leader Larry Blackmon (born 29/5/1956, New York, vocals/drums), Tomi Jenkins (vocals) and Nathan Leftenant (trumpet). Blackmon moved the group to Atlanta, GA, founding the Atlanta Artists label with acts including Cashflow. In 1992 he was made R&B A&R Vice President for Warner Brothers Records, a position he held for three years.

| | | | | | |
|---|---|---|---|---|---|
| 10/08/1985 | 66 | 12 | | SINGLE LIFE | Club JABH 11 |
| 18/10/1986 | 7 | 34 | ● | **WORD UP** | Club JABH 19 |
| 26/11/1988 | 86 | 1 | | MACHISMO | Club 836002 |

**ALI CAMPBELL** UK singer (born 15/2/1959, Birmingham), son of Scottish folk singer Ian Campbell and lead singer with UB40. He set up the Kuff label through Virgin Records. Kibibi is his daughter.

| | | | | | |
|---|---|---|---|---|---|
| 17/06/1995 | 6 | 11 | ● | **BIG LOVE** | Kuff CDV 2783 |

**GLEN CAMPBELL** US singer (born 22/4/1936, Billstown, AR) who joined his uncle Dick Bills' band in 1954. After four years he moved to Los Angeles, CA and recorded with The Champs. An in-demand studio guitarist for the next five years, he briefly replaced Brian Wilson in The Beach Boys in 1965. After going solo he appeared in films including *True Grit* (1969) and *Strange Homecoming* (1974) and hosted his own TV show. He has won six Grammy Awards: Best Male Solo Vocal Performance and Best Contemporary Solo Vocal Performance in 1967 for *By The Time I Get To Phoenix*, Best Country & Western Recording and Best Country & Western Vocal Performance in 1967 for *Gentle On My Mind*, Album of the Year in 1968 for *By The Time I Get To Phoenix*, and Best Recording for Children in 1981 with Crystal Gayle, Loretta Lynn, Tanya Tucker and the Muppets for *Sesame Country*. He has a star on the Hollywood Walk of Fame.

| | | | | | |
|---|---|---|---|---|---|
| 31/01/1970 | 16 | 14 | | GLEN CAMPBELL LIVE | Capitol SB 21444 |
| 28/02/1970 | 50 | 1 | | BOBBIE GENTRY AND GLEN CAMPBELL **BOBBIE GENTRY AND GLEN CAMPBELL** | Capitol ST 2928 |
| 30/05/1970 | 37 | 10 | | TRY A LITTLE KINDNESS | Capitol ESW 389 |
| 12/12/1970 | 16 | 5 | | THE GLEN CAMPBELL ALBUM | Capitol ST 22493 |
| 27/11/1971 | 8 | 113 | | **GLEN CAMPBELL'S GREATEST HITS** | Capitol ST 21885 |
| 25/10/1975 | 38 | 9 | ○ | RHINESTONE COWBOY | Capitol ESW 11430 |
| 20/11/1976 | ❶[6] | 27 | ✪ | **20 GOLDEN GREATS** | Capitol EMTV 2 |
| 23/04/1977 | 51 | 1 | | SOUTHERN NIGHTS | Capitol EST 11601 |
| 22/07/1989 | 47 | 4 | | THE COMPLETE GLEN CAMPBELL | Stylus SMR 979 |
| 02/10/1999 | 50 | 1 | | MY HITS AND LOVE SONGS | Capitol 5223002 |

**CANIBUS** US rapper (born Germaine Williams, 1975, Jamaica, raised in UK and US) who was discovered and managed by Wyclef Jean of The Fugees.

| | | | | | |
|---|---|---|---|---|---|
| 19/09/1998 | 43 | 1 | | CAN-I-BUS | Universal UND 53222 |

**CANNED HEAT** US blues-rock band formed in Los Angeles, CA in 1966 by Bob 'The Bear' Hite (born 26/2/1945, Torrance, CA, vocals/harmonica), Alan 'Blind Owl' Wilson (born 4/7/1943, Boston, MA, guitar/harmonica/vocals), Henry Vestine (born 25/12/1944, Washington DC, guitar), Larry Taylor (born 26/6/1942, New York, bass) and Frank Cook (drums). Cook was replaced by Fito De La Parra (born 8/2/1946, Mexico City) in 1968, Vestine by Harvey Mandel in 1969. Wilson died from a drug overdose on 3/9/1970, Hite died on

5/4/1981 from a drug-related heart attack and Vestine died from respiratory failure on 21/10/1997. They took their name from a song by Tommy Johnson.

| 29/06/1968 ..... 5 ...... 21 ...... | **BOOGIE WITH CANNED HEAT** ................................................. | Liberty LBL 83103 |
|---|---|---|
| 14/02/1970 ..... 8 ...... 12 ...... | **CANNED HEAT COOKBOOK** ................................................. | Liberty LBS 83303 |
| 04/07/1970 ..... 15 ...... 3 ...... | CANNED HEAT '70 CONCERT ................................................. | Liberty LBS 83333 |
| 10/10/1970 ..... 27 ...... 4 ...... | FUTURE BLUES ................................................. | Liberty LBS 83364 |

### FREDDY CANNON
US singer (born Frederick Picariello, 4/12/1939, Lynn, MA) whose first band was Freddy Kamon & The Hurricanes. He changed his name to Freddy Cannon, the surname being a derivative of Kamon and reflecting his nickname 'Boom Boom' (after the big bass drum sound on his records).

| 27/02/1960 .... ❶[1] ..... 11 ...... | **THE EXPLOSIVE FREDDY CANNON** ................................................. | Top Rank 25/108 |
|---|---|---|

### BLU CANTRELL
US R&B singer (born Tiffany Cantrell, 13/12/1976, Providence, RI) who began as a backing singer for Gerald Levert, Faith Evans and Puff Daddy before going solo. It was later revealed that she had previously been a nude model.

| 09/08/2003 ..... 20 ...... 11 ...... O | BITTERSWEET ................................................. | Arista 82876534042 |
|---|---|---|

### CAPERCAILLIE
UK/Canadian/Irish group formed in Oban in 1984 by Karen Matheson (born 11/2/1963, Oban, vocals), Marc Duff (born 8/9/1963, Ontario, Canada, bodhran/whistles), Manus Lunny (born 8/2/1962, Dublin, bouzouki/vocals), Charlie McKerron (born 14/6/1960, London, fiddle), John Saich (born 22/5/1960, Irvine, bass/vocals) and Donald Shaw (born 6/5/1967, Ketton, keyboards/accordion/vocals).

| 25/09/1993 ..... 40 ...... 3 ...... O | SECRET PEOPLE ................................................. | Arista 74321162742 |
|---|---|---|
| 17/09/1994 ..... 61 ...... 1 ...... | CAPERCAILLIE ................................................. | Survival 74321229112 |
| 04/11/1995 ..... 41 ...... 2 ...... | TO THE MOON ................................................. | Survival SURCD 019 |
| 20/09/1997 ..... 55 ...... 2 ...... | BEAUTIFUL WASTELAND ................................................. | Survival SURCD 021 |

### CAPPADONNA
US rapper (born Darryl Hill, 1969, Brooklyn, NY) who joined the Wu-Tang Clan in 1995 having previously worked on Raekwon's *Only Built 4 Cuban Linx* album. He launched his own solo career in 1998.

| 04/04/1998 ..... 43 ...... 1 ...... | THE PILLAGE ................................................. | Epic 4888502 |
|---|---|---|

### CAPPELLA
Italian producer Gianfranco Bortolotti who also produced The 49ers. In 1993 he assembled a vocal duo comprising Rodney Bishop (who later became a member of Perpetual Motion) and Kelly Overett. Bortolotti later formed Anticappella.

| 26/03/1994 ..... 10 ...... 9 ...... ● | **U GOT 2 KNOW** ................................................. | Internal Dance CAPPC 1 |
|---|---|---|

### CAPTAIN BEEFHEART
US rock singer (born Don Van Vliet, 15/1/1941, Glendale, CA) who formed the Magic Band in 1964. Two years later they landed a recording contract. The group consisted of Beefheart (vocals), Alex St Clair Snouffer (guitar), Doug Moon (guitar), Paul Blakely (drums) and Jerry Handley (bass). Although the line-up changed many times over the years, the two constants were Captain Beefheart and Frank Zappa, the latter in the capacity of mentor and/or producer. After 1982 Captain Beefheart effectively stopped recording and concentrated on a career as an artist and painter under his real name.

| 06/12/1969 ..... 21 ...... 1 ...... | TROUT MASK REPLICA ................................................. | Straight STS 1053 |
|---|---|---|
| 23/01/1971 ..... 20 ...... 10 ...... | LICK MY DECALS OFF BABY ................................................. | Straight STS 1063 |
| 29/05/1971 ..... 49 ...... 1 ...... | MIRROR MAN ................................................. | Buddah 2365 002 |
| 19/02/1971 ..... 44 ...... 2 ...... | THE SPOTLIGHT KID ................................................. | Reprise K 44162 |
| 18/09/1982 ..... 90 ...... 2 ...... | ICE CREAM FOR CROW ................................................. | Virgin V 2337 |

### CAPTAIN AND TENNILLE
US husband and wife duo Captain (born Daryl Dragon, 27/8/1942, Los Angeles, CA) and Toni Tennille (born 27/8/1942, Montgomery, AL). Dragon, the son of noted conductor Carmen Dragon, met Toni when both were performing in a musical in San Francisco. They toured with The Beach Boys; Dragon as keyboard player and Tennille a backing singer. Toni eventually went solo.

| 22/03/1980 ..... 33 ...... 6 ...... | MAKE YOUR MOVE ................................................. | Casablanca CAL 2060 |
|---|---|---|

### CAPTAIN SENSIBLE
UK singer (born Raymond Burns, 23/4/1955, London) who was bass player in the early punk band The Damned. Going solo in 1982, he didn't actually leave The Damned until 1984.

| 11/09/1982 ..... 64 ...... 3 ...... | WOMEN AND CAPTAIN FIRST ................................................. | A&M AMLH 68548 |
|---|---|---|

### CARAVAN
UK rock group formed in 1968 by Pye Hastings (born 21/1/1947, Canterbury, guitar/vocals), David Sinclair (born 24/11/1947, Herne Bay, keyboards), Richard Sinclair (born 6/6/1948, Canterbury, bass/vocals) and Richard Coughlan (born 2/9/1947, Herne Bay, drums). By the mid-1970s the group comprised Coughlan, Hastings, Sinclair, John Perry (born 19/1/1947, Auburn, NY, guitar) and Geoff Richardson (born 15/7/1950, Hinckley, strings). By the mid-1990s the line-up featured Sinclair, Coughlan, Richardson, Pye Hastings, Jimmy Hastings and Jim Levington.

| 30/08/1975 ..... 50 ...... 1 ...... | CUNNING STUNTS ................................................. | Decca SKL 5210 |
|---|---|---|
| 15/05/1976 ..... 53 ...... 1 ...... | BLIND DOG AT ST. DUNSTAN'S ................................................. | BTM 1007 |

### CARCASS
UK metal group formed in Liverpool in 1987 by Bill Steer (guitar/vocals), Jeff Walker (bass/vocals) and Ken Owen (drums). Michael Amott (guitar) and Carlo Regedas (guitar) joined later.

| 06/11/1993 ..... 67 ...... 1 ...... | HEARTWORK ................................................. | Earache MOSH 097CD |
|---|---|---|
| 06/07/1996 ..... 68 ...... 1 ...... | SWANSONG ................................................. | Earache MOSH 160CDL |

○ Silver disc  ● Gold disc  ✪ Platinum disc (additional platinum units are indicated by a figure following the symbol)  ❶[9] Number of weeks album topped the UK chart

**CARDIGANS** Swedish rock group formed in Jonkoping in 1992 by Peter Svensson (born 1974, guitar), Magnus Sveningsson (born 1972, bass), Nina Persson (born 1975, vocals), Bengt Lagerberg (born 1973, drums) and Olaf-Lasse Johansson (born 1973, guitar/keyboards). Persson later formed A Camp.

| Date | Pos | Wks | BPI | Title | Label & Number |
|---|---|---|---|---|---|
| 08/07/1995 | 51 | 9 | | LIFE | Stockholm 5235562 |
| 12/10/1996 | 18 | 10 | ○ | FIRST BAND ON THE MOON | Stockholm 5331172 |
| 31/10/1998 | 8 | 49 | ✪ | **GRAN TURISMO** ◇ | Stockholm 5590812 |
| 05/04/2003 | 47 | 2 | | LONG GONE BEFORE DAYLIGHT | Stockholm 0381092 |

**MARIAH CAREY** US singer (born 22/3/1970, New York City) with Irish and black/Venezuelan parents, who began as a backing singer for Brenda K Starr while songwriting with Ben Margulies. In 1990 she was signed by Columbia president Tommy Mottola after he heard her demo tape. Mariah and Tommy were married on 5/6/1993, separated in 1997 and divorced on 4/3/1998. She launched Crave in 1997; Allure was the first act signed and the label later closed down. Her acting debut was in the 1999 film *The Bachelor*. She has won two Grammy Awards: Best New Artist and Best Pop Vocal Performance for *Visions of Love* both in 1990. She also won the 1994 MTV Europe Music Award for Best Female. Her deal with Virgin is the largest in recording history, netting $25 million per album; she left after just one album with a $30 million 'golden handshake' and subsequently signed with Island. She also formed another label, Monarc.

| Date | Pos | Wks | BPI | Title | Label & Number |
|---|---|---|---|---|---|
| 15/09/1990 | 6 | 40 | ✪ | **MARIAH CAREY** ▲[11] | CBS 4668151 |
| 26/10/1991 | 4 | 40 | ✪ | **EMOTIONS** | Columbia 4688511 |
| 18/07/1992 | 3 | 10 | ● | **MTV UNPLUGGED (EP)** | Columbia 4718692 |
| 11/09/1993 | ❶[6] | 77 | ✪[5] | **MUSIC BOX** ▲[8] ◆[10] | Columbia 4742702 |
| 19/11/1994 | 32 | 7 | ● | **MERRY CHRISTMAS** ◇ | Columbia 4773422 |
| 07/10/1995 | ❶[1] | 46 | ✪[2] | **DAYDREAM** ◇[3] ▲[6] ◆[10] | Columbia 4813672 |
| 20/09/1997 | 2 | 27 | ● | **BUTTERFLY** ◇ ▲[1] | Columbia 4885372 |
| 28/11/1998 | 10 | 32 | ✪ | **#1S** ◇[2] | Columbia 4926042 |
| 13/11/1999 | 8 | 15 | ● | **RAINBOW** ◇ | Columbia 4950652 |
| 22/09/2001 | 10 | 3 | | **GLITTER** Soundtrack for the 2001 film *Glitter* in which Carey starred | Virgin CDVUS 201 |
| 15/12/2001 | 46 | 4 | | GREATEST HITS | Columbia 5054612 |
| 14/12/2002 | 52 | 3 | ● | CHARMBRACELET | Island 0633842 |
| 18/10/2003 | 35 | 2 | | THE REMIXES | Columbia 5107542 |

**BELINDA CARLISLE** US singer (born 17/8/1958, Hollywood, CA) named after her mother's favourite film, *Johnny Belinda* (1948). Lead singer with the all-girl group The Go-Go's from 1978 until their split in 1985, she went solo while still signed to the Go-Go's label (IRS), before signing with MCA for the US, and Virgin for the UK, in 1987.

| Date | Pos | Wks | BPI | Title | Label & Number |
|---|---|---|---|---|---|
| 02/01/1988 | 4 | 54 | ✪[3] | **HEAVEN ON EARTH** | Virgin V 2496 |
| 04/11/1989 | 4 | 39 | ✪ | **RUNAWAY HORSES** | Virgin V 2599 |
| 26/10/1991 | 7 | 16 | ● | **LIVE YOUR LIFE BE FREE** | Virgin V 2680 |
| 19/09/1992 | ❶[1] | 35 | ✪[2] | **THE BEST OF BELINDA VOLUME 1** | Virgin BELCD 1 |
| 23/10/1993 | 9 | 5 | | **REAL** | Virgin CDV 2725 |
| 05/10/1996 | 12 | 5 | ● | A WOMAN AND A MAN | Chrysalis CDCHR 6115 |
| 13/11/1999 | 15 | 6 | ● | A PLACE ON EARTH – THE GREATEST HITS | Virgin CDVX 2901 |

**VANESSA CARLTON** US singer/keyboardist/songwriter (born 16/8/1980, Milford, PA) who first signed with Universal in 1999.

| Date | Pos | Wks | BPI | Title | Label & Number |
|---|---|---|---|---|---|
| 27/07/2002 | 7 | 15 | ● | **BE NOT NOBODY** | A&M 4933672 |

**CARMEL** UK group formed by Carmel McCourt (born 24/11/1958, Scunthorpe, vocals), Jim Paris (born 13/1/1957, London, bass) and Gerry Darby (born 13/10/1959, London, drums). Carmel left in 1991 for a solo deal with Warner Brothers.

| Date | Pos | Wks | BPI | Title | Label & Number |
|---|---|---|---|---|---|
| 01/10/1983 | 94 | 2 | | CARMEL 6-TRACK (EP) | Red Flame RFM 9 |
| 24/03/1984 | 19 | 8 | | THE DRUM IS EVERYTHING | London SH 8555 |
| 27/09/1986 | 88 | 1 | | THE FALLING | London LONLP 17 |

### ERIC CARMEN
**ERIC CARMEN** US classically trained singer (born 11/8/1949, Cleveland, OH) who sang lead with the Raspberries from 1970–74, before going solo in 1975.

| | | | |
|---|---|---|---|
| 15/05/1976 . . . . . 58 . . . . . . 1 . . . . . . | ERIC CARMEN . . . . . . . . . . . . . . . . . . . . . . . . . . . . . . . . . . . . . . . . . . . . . . . . . . . . . . . . . . . . . . . . . . . . . . . . . . Arista ARTY 120 |

### JEAN CARN
**JEAN CARN** – see **EARTH WIND AND FIRE: ROSE ROYCE**

### KIM CARNES
**KIM CARNES** US singer (born 20/7/1946, Los Angeles, CA) who was a member of the New Christy Minstrels with her husband/co-writer Dave Ellington and Kenny Rogers. She also wrote and performed in commercials, making her US chart debut as one of the Sugar Bears. After a debut solo album in 1976, she later recorded with Kenny Rogers, Gene Cotton and James Ingram.

| | |
|---|---|
| 20/06/1981 . . . . . 26 . . . . . 16 . . . . . . | MISTAKEN IDENTITY ▲4 . . . . . . . . . . . . . . . . . . . . . . . . . . . . . . . . . . . . . . . . . . . . . . . . . . . . . . . . . EMI America AML 3018 |

### MARY CHAPIN CARPENTER
**MARY CHAPIN CARPENTER** US singer (born 21/2/1958, Princeton, NJ) who began as a folk singer in clubs and bars around Washington. Five local music awards led to her debut album for Columbia in 1987. Scoring in both the pop and country charts, her five Grammy Awards include Best Female Country Vocal Performance in 1991 for *Down At The Twist And Shout,* Best Female Country Vocal Performance in 1992 for *I Feel Lucky,* Best Female Country Vocal Performance in 1993 for *Passionate Kisses* and Best Female Country Vocal Performance in 1994 for *Shut Up And Kiss Me.*

| | |
|---|---|
| 29/10/1994 . . . . . 26 . . . . . . 5 . . . . . . O | STONES IN THE ROAD 1994 Grammy Award for Best Country Album . . . . . . . . . . . . . . . . . . . . . . . . . . . . . . . . . . . Columbia CK 64327 |
| 02/11/1996 . . . . . 36 . . . . . . 2 . . . . . . | A PLACE IN THE WORLD . . . . . . . . . . . . . . . . . . . . . . . . . . . . . . . . . . . . . . . . . . . . . . . . . . . . . . . . . . . . . Columbia 4851822 |
| 05/06/1999 . . . . . 65 . . . . . . 1 . . . . . . | PARTY DOLL AND OTHER FAVOURITES . . . . . . . . . . . . . . . . . . . . . . . . . . . . . . . . . . . . . . . . . . . . . . . . . . . . Columbia 4886592 |
| 26/05/2001 . . . . . 57 . . . . . . 1 . . . . . . | TIME SEX LOVE . . . . . . . . . . . . . . . . . . . . . . . . . . . . . . . . . . . . . . . . . . . . . . . . . . . . . . . . . . . . . . . . . . . . Columbia 5023542 |

### CARPENTERS
**CARPENTERS** US brother and sister duo Richard (born 15/10/1946, New Haven, CT) and Karen Carpenter (born 2/3/1950, New Haven) whose family relocated to Downey, CA in 1963. Richard played piano from nine, while Karen began learning bass from thirteen. By 1965 both were in the same group, along with Wes Jacobs. After their 1966 debut single *Looking For Love* for the Magic Lamp label, they signed as the Richard Carpenter Trio to RCA in 1966, but were dropped before releasing anything. Signed by A&M in 1969 (minus Jacobs, but using other outside musicians), they later hosted their own TV show. Karen died on 4/2/1983 from heart failure due to the slimming disease anorexia. Three Grammy Awards include Best New Artist in 1970 and Best Contemporary Pop Vocal Performance in 1970 for *Close To You.* They have a star on the Hollywood Walk of Fame.

| | |
|---|---|
| 23/01/1971 . . . . . 23 . . . . 82 . . . . . . | CLOSE TO YOU . . . . . . . . . . . . . . . . . . . . . . . . . . . . . . . . . . . . . . . . . . . . . . . . . . . . . . . . . . . . . . . . . . . A&M AMLS 998 |
| 30/10/1971 . . . . . 12 . . . . 36 . . . . . . | THE CARPENTERS 1971 Grammy Award for Best Pop Vocal Performance . . . . . . . . . . . . . . . . . . . . . . . . . . . A&M AMLS 63502 |
| 15/04/1972 . . . . . 20 . . . . . 3 . . . . . . | TICKET TO RIDE . . . . . . . . . . . . . . . . . . . . . . . . . . . . . . . . . . . . . . . . . . . . . . . . . . . . . . . . . . . . . . . . A&M AMLS 64342 |
| 23/09/1972 . . . . . 13 . . . . 37 . . . . . . | A SONG FOR YOU . . . . . . . . . . . . . . . . . . . . . . . . . . . . . . . . . . . . . . . . . . . . . . . . . . . . . . . . . . . . . . . A&M AMLS 63511 |
| 07/07/1973 . . . . . 2 . . . . 65 . . . . . . ● | **NOW AND THEN** . . . . . . . . . . . . . . . . . . . . . . . . . . . . . . . . . . . . . . . . . . . . . . . . . . . . . . . . . . . . . . . A&M AMLH 63519 |
| 26/01/1974 . . . . ❶17 . . . 125 . . . . . ✪ | **THE SINGLES 1969–1973** ▲1 . . . . . . . . . . . . . . . . . . . . . . . . . . . . . . . . . . . . . . . . . . . . . . . . . . . . A&M AMLH 63601 |
| 28/06/1975 . . . . ❶5 . . . . 27 . . . . . . ● | **HORIZON** . . . . . . . . . . . . . . . . . . . . . . . . . . . . . . . . . . . . . . . . . . . . . . . . . . . . . . . . . . . . . . . . . . A&M AMLK 64530 |
| 23/08/1975 . . . . . 35 . . . . . 2 . . . . . . | TICKET TO RIDE . . . . . . . . . . . . . . . . . . . . . . . . . . . . . . . . . . . . . . . . . . . . . . . . . . . . . . . . . . . . . . . Hamlet AMLP 8001 |
| 03/07/1976 . . . . . 3 . . . . 15 . . . . . . ● | **A KIND OF HUSH** . . . . . . . . . . . . . . . . . . . . . . . . . . . . . . . . . . . . . . . . . . . . . . . . . . . . . . . . . . . . A&M AMLK 64581 |
| 08/01/1977 . . . . . 28 . . . . . 3 . . . . . . ● | LIVE AT THE PALLADIUM . . . . . . . . . . . . . . . . . . . . . . . . . . . . . . . . . . . . . . . . . . . . . . . . . . . . . . . . A&M AMLS 68403 |
| 08/10/1977 . . . . . 12 . . . . 12 . . . . . . ● | PASSAGE . . . . . . . . . . . . . . . . . . . . . . . . . . . . . . . . . . . . . . . . . . . . . . . . . . . . . . . . . . . . . . . . . . . A&M AMLK 64703 |
| 02/12/1978 . . . . . 2 . . . . 27 . . . . . . ✪ | **THE SINGLES 1974–1978** . . . . . . . . . . . . . . . . . . . . . . . . . . . . . . . . . . . . . . . . . . . . . . . . . . . . . A&M AMLT 19748 |
| 27/06/1981 . . . . . 12 . . . . 10 . . . . . . O | MADE IN AMERICA . . . . . . . . . . . . . . . . . . . . . . . . . . . . . . . . . . . . . . . . . . . . . . . . . . . . . . . . . . . . A&M AMLK 63723 |
| 15/10/1983 . . . . . 6 . . . . 19 . . . . . . ● | **VOICE OF THE HEART** . . . . . . . . . . . . . . . . . . . . . . . . . . . . . . . . . . . . . . . . . . . . . . . . . . . . . . . A&M AMLX 64954 |
| 20/10/1984 . . . . . 10 . . . . 26 . . . . . . ✪ | **YESTERDAY ONCE MORE** . . . . . . . . . . . . . . . . . . . . . . . . . . . . . . . . . . . . . . . . . . . . . . . . . . . . EMI/A&M SING 1 |
| 13/01/1990 . . . . . 73 . . . . . 1 . . . . . . | LOVELINES . . . . . . . . . . . . . . . . . . . . . . . . . . . . . . . . . . . . . . . . . . . . . . . . . . . . . . . . . . . . . . . . . . A&M AMA 3931 |
| 31/03/1990 . . . . ❶7 . . . . 82 . . . . . ✪5 | **ONLY YESTERDAY – RICHARD & KAREN CARPENTER'S GREATEST HITS** . . . . . . . . . . . . . . . . . . . . . . A&M AMA 1990 |
| 15/10/1994 . . . . . 29 . . . . 10 . . . . . . ● | INTERPRETATIONS . . . . . . . . . . . . . . . . . . . . . . . . . . . . . . . . . . . . . . . . . . . . . . . . . . . . . . . . . . . . A&M 5402512 |
| 22/11/1997 . . . . . 47 . . . . . 8 . . . . . . ● | LOVE SONGS . . . . . . . . . . . . . . . . . . . . . . . . . . . . . . . . . . . . . . . . . . . . . . . . . . . . . . . . . . . . . . . . A&M 5408382 |
| 09/12/2000 . . . . . 21 . . . . 20 . . . . . . ✪ | GOLD – GREATEST HITS . . . . . . . . . . . . . . . . . . . . . . . . . . . . . . . . . . . . . . . . . . . . . . . . . . . . . . . . A&M 4908652 |

### VIKKI CARR
**VIKKI CARR** US singer (born Florencia Bisenta de Casillas Martinez Cardona, 19/7/1941, El Paso, TX). After successful English versions of her Spanish hits she performed many hospital benefits, set up a scholarship foundation for Chicano children and resumed her Spanish singing career in Mexico. She has won three Grammy Awards: Best Mexican-American Performance in 1985 for *Simplemente Mujer,* Best Latin Pop Album in 1991 for *Cosas Del Amor* and Best Mexican-American Album in 1994 for *Recuerdo A Javier Solis.* She has a star on the Hollywood Walk of Fame.

| | |
|---|---|
| 22/07/1967 . . . . . 31 . . . . . 2 . . . . . . | WAY OF TODAY . . . . . . . . . . . . . . . . . . . . . . . . . . . . . . . . . . . . . . . . . . . . . . . . . . . . . . . . . . . . . . Liberty SLBY 1331 |
| 12/08/1967 . . . . . 12 . . . . 10 . . . . . . | IT MUST BE HIM . . . . . . . . . . . . . . . . . . . . . . . . . . . . . . . . . . . . . . . . . . . . . . . . . . . . . . . . . . . . . . Liberty LBS 83037 |

### PAUL CARRACK
**PAUL CARRACK** UK singer (born 22/4/1951, Sheffield) who was lead vocalist with Ace 1973–76 and later played with Squeeze, Roxy Music and Mike + The Mechanics. He launched a solo career in 1982.

| | |
|---|---|
| 03/02/1996 . . . . . 55 . . . . . 7 . . . . . . | BLUE VIEWS . . . . . . . . . . . . . . . . . . . . . . . . . . . . . . . . . . . . . . . . . . . . . . . . . . . . . . . . . . . . . . . I.R.S. EIRSCD 1075 |
| 24/06/2000 . . . . . 63 . . . . . 1 . . . . . . | SATISFY MY SOUL . . . . . . . . . . . . . . . . . . . . . . . . . . . . . . . . . . . . . . . . . . . . . . . . . . . . . . . . . Carrack-UK PCARCD 1 |

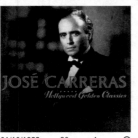

**JOSE CARRERAS** Spanish singer (born 5/12/1946, Barcelona) who is considered, alongside Luciano Pavarotti and Placido Domingo, one of the finest operatic tenors in the world. Like Pavarotti he survived leukaemia in the late 1980s and set up the Jose Carreras International Leukaemia Foundation. He was the musical director for both the opening and closing ceremonies at the 1992 Olympic Games in Barcelona. Mehta is Indian conductor Zubin Mehta (born 29/4/1936, Bombay).

| 01/10/1988 | 90 | 4 | ○ | JOSE CARRERAS COLLECTION | Stylus SMR 860 |
| 23/12/1989 | 42 | 6 | ○ | JOSE CARRERAS SINGS ANDREW LLOYD WEBBER | WEA WX 325 |
| 01/09/1990 | ❶⁵ | 78 | ✪⁵ | **IN CONCERT** LUCIANO PAVAROTTI, PLACIDO DOMINGO AND JOSE CARRERAS 1990 Grammy Award for Best Classical Performance Vocal Soloist | Decca 4304331 |
| 23/02/1991 | 24 | 9 | ● | THE ESSENTIAL JOSE CARRERAS | Philips 4326921 |
| 06/04/1991 | 47 | 3 | | HOLLYWOOD GOLDEN CLASSICS | East West WX 416 |
| 08/08/1992 | 53 | 4 | | AMIGOS PARA SIEMPRE (FRIENDS FOR LIFE) **JOSE CARRERAS AND SARAH BRIGHTMAN** | East West 4509902562 |
| 08/08/1992 | 41 | 3 | | FROM THE OFFICIAL BARCELONA GAMES CEREMONY **PLACIDO DOMINGO, JOSE CARRERAS & MONTSERRAT CABALLE** | RCA Red Seal 9026612042 |
| 16/10/1993 | 73 | 1 | | WITH A SONG IN MY HEART | Teldec 4509923692 |
| 25/12/1993 | 71 | 2 | | CHRISTMAS IN VIENNA **PLACIDO DOMINGO, DIANA ROSS & JOSE CARRERAS** | Sony Classical SK 53358 |
| 10/09/1994 | ❶¹ | 26 | ✪² | **THE THREE TENORS IN CONCERT 1994** ◇³ JOSE CARRERAS, PLACIDO DOMINGO AND LUCIANO PAVAROTTI WITH MEHTA | Teldec 4509962002 |
| 03/02/1996 | 21 | 8 | ○ | PASSION | Erato 0630125962 |
| 23/12/2000 | 57 | 2 | | THE THREE TENORS CHRISTMAS **CARRERAS/DOMINGO/PAVAROTTI FEATURING MEHTA** | Sony Classical SK 89131 |

**DINA CARROLL** UK singer (born 21/8/1968, Newmarket) with a British mother and US serviceman father. Dina spent a few years in Philadelphia, PA but was mainly brought up in England. She began doing session work for Streetsounds, and as a member of Masquerade, releasing her first record for Jive in 1989 (as Deana Carroll). Named Best British Female at the 1994 BRIT Awards, she also took part in the *It's Only Rock 'N' Roll* project for the Children's Promise charity.

| 30/01/1993 | 2 | 63 | ✪⁴ | **SO CLOSE** | A&M 5400342 |
| 26/10/1996 | 2 | 13 | ✪ | **ONLY HUMAN** | Mercury 5340962 |
| 23/06/2001 | 15 | 4 | ○ | THE VERY BEST OF | Mercury 5489182 |

**JASPER CARROTT** UK singer/comedian (born Bob Davies, 14/3/1945, Birmingham) and a popular figure on UK TV with his own show and numerous spin-offs, including *The Detectives* and *Carrott Commercial*. He was awarded an MBE in the 2003 New Year's Honours List.

| 18/10/1975 | 10 | 7 | ○ | **RABBITS ON AND ON** | DJM DJLPS 462 |
| 06/11/1976 | 56 | 1 | ○ | CARROTT IN NOTTS | DJM DJF 20482 |
| 25/11/1978 | 38 | 13 | ● | THE BEST OF JASPER CARROTT | DJM DJF 20549 |
| 20/10/1979 | 19 | 15 | ● | THE UNRECORDED JASPER CARROTT | DJM DJF 20560 |
| 19/09/1981 | 13 | 16 | ● | BEAT THE CARROTT | DJM DJF 20575 |
| 25/12/1982 | 80 | 3 | | CARROTT'S LIB | DJM DJF 20580 |
| 19/11/1983 | 57 | 8 | ○ | THE STUN (CARROTT TELLS ALL) | DJM DJF 20582 |
| 07/02/1987 | 66 | 3 | | COSMIC CARROTT | Portrait LAUGH 1 |

**CARS** US rock group formed in Boston, MA in 1976 by Ric Ocasek (born Richard Otcasek, 23/3/1949, Baltimore, MD, lead guitar/vocals), Benjamin Orr (born Benjamin Orzechowski, 9/8/1955, Cleveland, OH, bass/vocals), Elliot Easton (born Elliot Shapiro, 18/12/1953, Brooklyn, NYC, guitar), Greg Hawkes (born in Baltimore, keyboards) and David Robinson (born 2/1/1953, Boston, drums). Robinson chose the name Cars, Ocasek wrote all of the songs. Although they didn't appear, The Cars produced one of the most memorable moments of 1985's Live Aid, a video of Ethiopian famine footage, accompanied by *Drive*. Ocasek donated all royalties from the single to the Band Aid Trust. The group disbanded in 1988, and Benjamin Orr died from pancreatic cancer on 3/10/2000.

| 02/12/1978 | 29 | 15 | ○ | CARS | Elektra K 52088 |
| 07/07/1979 | 30 | 6 | | CANDY-O | Elektra K 52148 |
| 06/10/1984 | 25 | 30 | ● | HEARTBEAT CITY | Elektra 960296 |
| 09/11/1985 | 27 | 19 | ● | THE CARS GREATEST HITS | Elektra EKT 25 |

| | | | | | |
|---|---|---|---|---|---|
| 05/09/1987 | 72 | 2 | | DOOR TO DOOR | Elektra EKT 42 |

**AARON CARTER** US singer (born 7/12/1987, Tampa, FL), younger brother of Nick Carter of The Backstreet Boys. The fourth youngest UK chart entrant under the age of ten at the time of his debut hit.

| | | | | | |
|---|---|---|---|---|---|
| 28/02/1998 | 12 | 8 | | AARON CARTER | Ultra Pop 0099572 |

**CARTER – THE UNSTOPPABLE SEX MACHINE** UK rock group formed in London in 1986 by Fruitbat (born Leslie Carter, 12/12/1958, London, guitar/programming) and Jimbob (born Jim Morrison, 22/11/1960, London, vocals). In 1995 they recruited full-time drummer Wez, and split in January 1998.

| | | | | | |
|---|---|---|---|---|---|
| 02/03/1991 | 8 | 9 | ● | **30 SOMETHING** | Rough Trade R2011 2702 |
| 21/09/1991 | 29 | 6 | | 101 DAMNATIONS | Big Cat ABB 101 |
| 01/02/1992 | 21 | 4 | | 30 SOMETHING | Chrysalis CHR 1897 |
| 16/05/1992 | ❶[1] | 9 | ● | **1992 – THE LOVE ALBUM** | Chrysalis CCD 1946 |
| 18/09/1993 | 5 | 4 | | **POST HISTORIC MONSTERS** | Chrysalis CDCHR 7090 |
| 26/03/1994 | 22 | 2 | | STARRY EYED AND BOLLOCK NAKED | Chrysalis CDCHR 6069 |
| 18/02/1995 | 9 | 3 | | **WORRY BOMB** | Chrysalis CDCHRX 6096 |
| 14/10/1995 | 37 | 2 | | STRAW DONKEY... THE SINGLES | Chrysalis CDCHR 6110 |
| 05/04/1997 | 73 | 1 | | A WORLD WITHOUT DAVE | Cooking Vinyl COOKCD 120 |

**CARTOONS** Danish pop group formed by Toonie, Sponge, Shooter, Buzz, Puddy and Boop.

| | | | | | |
|---|---|---|---|---|---|
| 17/04/1999 | 17 | 14 | ● | TOONAGE | Flex 4966922 |

**JOHNNY CASH** US country singer (born 26/2/1932, Kingsland, AR) who moved with his family to Dyees, AR aged three. After serving in the US Air Force (1950–54) he formed a trio with Luther Perkins and Marshall Grant in 1955, later the same year making debut recordings for Sun. He worked with June Carter from 1961 and married her in 1968. His daughter Rosanne Cash and stepdaughter Carlene Carter are also successful vocalists. Famous for his concerts recorded in prisons, the album *Johnny Cash At San Quentin* topped the US charts in 1969. He announced in 1997 that he had Parkinson's Disease after falling on stage while picking up a guitar pick. Perkins died after falling asleep smoking and setting fire to his house on 5/8/1968. Cash has suffered similar tragedies and mishaps: a brother died when he fell on an electric saw, a drunken doctor removed a cyst from Cash's cheek and left a visible scar, and a German girl stuck a pencil down his ear, leaving him partially deaf. He was inducted into the Rock & Roll Hall of Fame in 1992. His thirteen Grammy Awards include: Best Country & Western Performance by a Duo in 1967 with June Carter for *Jackson;* Best Country & Western Vocal Performance in 1969 for *A Boy Names Sue;* Best Album Notes in 1969 for Bob Dylan's *Nashville Skyline;* Best Country & Western Performance by a Duo in 1970 with June Carter for *If I Were A Carpenter;* Best Spoken Word Documentary in 1986 with various others for *Interviews From The Class of '55;* Best Contemporary Folk Album in 1994 for *American Recordings;* Best Country Album in 1997 for *Unchained;* Best Male Country Vocal Performance in 2000 for *Solitary Man;* and Best Male Country Vocal Performance in 2002 for *Give My Love To Rose* and Best Short Form Music Video in 2003 for *Hurt*. He has a star on the Hollywood Walk of Fame. Johnny died on 12/9/2003.

| | | | | | |
|---|---|---|---|---|---|
| 23/07/1966 | 28 | 1 | | EVERYBODY LOVES A NUT | CBS BPG 62717 |
| 04/05/1968 | 40 | 1 | | FROM SEA TO SHINING SEA | CBS 62972 |
| 06/07/1968 | 37 | 2 | | OLD GOLDEN THROAT | CBS 63316 |
| 24/08/1968 | 8 | 53 | | **JOHNNY CASH AT FOLSOM PRISON** 1968 Grammy Awards for Best Country & Western Performance and Best Album Notes (under its US title *Folsom Prison Blues*) | CBS 63308 |
| 23/08/1969 | 2 | 114 | | **JOHNNY CASH AT SAN QUENTIN** ▲[4] | CBS 63629 |
| 04/10/1969 | 23 | 25 | | GREATEST HITS VOLUME 1 | CBS 63062 |
| 07/03/1970 | 6 | 16 | | **HELLO I'M JOHNNY CASH** | CBS 63796 |
| 15/08/1970 | 5 | 31 | | **THE WORLD OF JOHNNY CASH** | CBS 66237 |
| 12/12/1970 | 18 | 6 | | THE JOHNNY CASH SHOW | CBS 64089 |
| 18/09/1971 | 18 | 7 | | MAN IN BLACK | CBS 64331 |
| 13/11/1971 | 43 | 2 | | JOHNNY CASH | Hallmark SHM 739 |
| 20/05/1972 | 8 | 11 | | **A THING CALLED LOVE** | CBS 64898 |
| 14/10/1972 | 16 | 7 | | STAR PORTRAIT | CBS 67201 |
| 10/07/1976 | 49 | 3 | | ONE PIECE AT A TIME | CBS 81416 |
| 09/10/1976 | 48 | 2 | | THE BEST OF JOHNNY CASH | CBS 10000 |
| 02/09/1978 | 36 | 4 | | ITCHY FEET | CBS 10009 |
| 27/08/1994 | 15 | 5 | | THE MAN IN BLACK – DEFINITIVE COLLECTION | Columbia MOODCD 35 |
| 09/03/2002 | 39 | 4 | | MAN IN BLACK – THE VERY BEST OF | Columbia 5063452 |
| 06/03/2004 | 40 | 3 | ● | AMERICAN RECORDINGS TV – THE MAN COMES AROUND | Lost Highway 0633392 |

**CA$HFLOW** US soul group formed in Atlanta, GA by Gaylord Parsons (drums/vocals/raps), Kary Hubbert (lead vocals), James Duffie (keyboards/vocals) and Regis Ferguson (keyboards). They were discovered by Cameo leader Larry Blackmon, who signed them to his Atlanta Artists label.

| | | | | | |
|---|---|---|---|---|---|
| 28/06/1986 | 33 | 3 | | CA$HFLOW | Club JABH 17 |

**CASHMERE** US group formed in 1982 by two top session musicians, Daryl Burgess and Dwight Ronnell Dukes. They later added pianist/songwriter McKinley Horton (co-writer of Eugene Wilde's *Got To Get You Home Tonight*) to the line-up in 1984.

| | | | | | |
|---|---|---|---|---|---|
| 02/03/1985 | 63 | 5 | | CASHMERE | Fourth & Broadway BRLP 503 |

**DAVID CASSIDY** US singer/actor (born 12/4/1950, New York), son of actor Jack Cassidy and Evelyn Ward, who appeared in various TV shows before being cast as Keith Partridge in *The Partridge Family* in 1970 (with his stepmother Shirley Jones playing his mother Shirley). The 'Family' were subsequently signed by Bell Records. After considerable success with the group, Cassidy concentrated on his solo career from 1973, especially in the UK where his fan base was strongest.

| 20/05/1972 | 2 | 43 | | CHERISH | Bell BELLS 210 |
| 24/02/1973 | 2 | 20 | | ROCK ME BABY | Bell BELLS 218 |
| 24/11/1973 | ❶¹ | 13 | ● | DREAMS ARE NUTHIN' MORE THAN WISHES | Bell BELLS 231 |
| 03/08/1974 | 9 | 7 | ● | CASSIDY LIVE | Bell BELLS 243 |
| 09/08/1975 | 22 | 5 | | THE HIGHER THEY CLIMB | RCA Victor RS 1012 |
| 08/06/1985 | 20 | 6 | ○ | ROMANCE | Arista 206 983 |
| 13/10/2001 | 5 | 15 | ● | THEN AND NOW | Universal TV 0160822 |
| 15/11/2003 | 61 | 1 | | A TOUCH OF BLUE | Universal TV 9812859 |

**EVA CASSIDY** US singer (born 2/2/1963, Oxon Hill, MD) who began her career as a backing singer before teaming up with soul singer Chuck Brown. She first recorded in her own right in 1994 for Blue Note Records, touring with Pieces Of A Dream, but was experiencing increasing pain owing to a hip problem. Tests revealed she had advanced melanoma, and she died on 2/11/1996. Five years later Radio 2 began playing two albums that she had recorded for Blix Street and this led to a resurgence of interest in her career.

| 03/06/2000 | 25 | 14 | | TIME AFTER TIME | Blix Street G210073 |
| 10/02/2001 | ❶² | 110 | ✪⁴ | SONGBIRD ◇ | Blix Street G210045 |
| 31/08/2002 | ❶¹ | 20 | ✪ | IMAGINE | Blix Street G210075 |
| 23/08/2003 | ❶² | 11 | ● | AMERICAN TUNE Eva became the first solo artist to have had as many as three posthumous #1 albums | Blix Street G210079 |

**CASSIUS** French production duo of Phillipe Zdar and Hubert Blanc-Francart (also known as Boombass) who also record as Motorbass and La Funk Mob.

| 06/02/1999 | 28 | 2 | | 1999 | Virgin CDVIR 76 |

**CAST** UK rock group formed in Liverpool in 1994 by John Power (born 14/9/1967, Liverpool, guitar/vocals), Skin (born Liam Tyson, 7/9/1969, Liverpool, guitar), Peter Wilkinson (born 9/5/1969, Liverpool, bass) and Keith O'Neill (born 18/2/1969, Liverpool, drums). Power had previously been in The La's, naming Cast after a line from The La's *Looking Glass*. They disbanded in August 2001 after Power walked out following disagreements with the others.

| 28/10/1995 | 7 | 67 | ✪ | ALL CHANGE | Polydor 5293122 |
| 26/04/1997 | 3 | 42 | ✪ | MOTHER NATURE CALLS | Polydor 5375672 |
| 29/05/1999 | 6 | 7 | | MAGIC HOUR | Polydor 5471762 |

**CATATONIA** UK rock group formed in Cardiff in 1992 by Cerys Matthews (born 11/4/1969, Cardiff, vocals), Mark Roberts (born 3/11/1969, Colwyn Bay, guitar), Owen Powell (born 9/7/1969, Cambridge, guitar), Paul Jones (born 5/2/1960, Colwyn Bay, bass) and Aled Richards (born 5/7/1969, Carmarthen, drums). Former member Dafydd Leuan went on to join Super Furry Animals. In September 2001 Cerys returned from a rehabilitation unit and announced to the rest of the group her intention of leaving for a solo career.

| 12/10/1996 | 32 | 3 | | WAY BEYOND BLUE | Blanco Y Negro 0630163052 |
| 14/02/1998 | ❶¹ | 93 | ✪³ | INTERNATIONAL VELVET ◇ | Blanco Y Negro 3984208342 |
| 24/04/1999 | ❶¹ | 23 | ✪ | EQUALLY CURSED AND BLESSED | Blanco Y Negro 3984270942 |

| | DATE | POS | WKS | BPI | ALBUM TITLE | LABEL & NUMBER |
|---|---|---|---|---|---|---|
| | 18/08/2001 | 6 | 4 | ○ | **PAPER SCISSORS STONE** | Blanco Y Negro 8573888482 |
| | 14/09/2002 | 24 | 2 | | GREATEST HITS | Blanco Y Negro 0927491942 |

**CATHERINE WHEEL** UK rock group formed in Great Yarmouth in 1990 by Rob Dickinson (guitar/vocals), Brian Futter (guitar), Neil Sims (drums) and David Hawes (bass). They recorded for local Norwich label Wilde Club before signing with Fontana.

| | DATE | POS | WKS | BPI | ALBUM TITLE | LABEL & NUMBER |
|---|---|---|---|---|---|---|
| | 29/02/1992 | 36 | 1 | | FERMENT | Fontana 5109032 |
| | 31/07/1993 | 58 | 1 | | CHROME | Fontana 5180392 |
| | 16/05/1998 | 53 | 1 | | ADAM AND EVE | Chrysalis 4930992 |

**NICK CAVE** Australian singer (born 22/9/1957, Wangarrata) who was a member of Birthday Party until 1983 when he went solo. He appeared in the film *Wings Of Desire* in 1987. The Bad Seeds comprised Mick Harvey (born 29/9/1958, Rochester, Australia, multi-instrumentalist), Blixa Bargeld (born 12/1/1959, Berlin, Germany, guitar/vocals), Conway Savage (born 27/7/1960, Foster, Australia, bass), Thomas Wydler (born 9/10/1959, Zurich, Switzerland, drums) and Martyn Casey (born 10/7/1960, Chesterfield, keyboards).

| | DATE | POS | WKS | BPI | ALBUM TITLE | LABEL & NUMBER |
|---|---|---|---|---|---|---|
| | 02/06/1984 | 40 | 3 | | FROM HER TO ETERNITY | Mute STUMM 17 |
| | 15/06/1985 | 53 | 1 | | THE FIRST BORN IS DEAD | Mute STUMM 21 |
| | 30/08/1986 | 89 | 1 | | KICKING AGAINST THE PRICKS | Mute STUMM 28 |
| | 01/10/1988 | 67 | 1 | | TENDER PREY | Mute STUMM 52 |
| | 28/04/1990 | 47 | 1 | | THE GOOD SON | Mute STUMM 76 |
| | 09/05/1992 | 29 | 2 | | HENRY'S DREAM | Mute CDSTUMM 92 |
| | 18/09/1993 | 67 | 1 | | LIVE SEEDS | Mute CDSTUMM 122 |
| | 30/04/1994 | 12 | 2 | | LET LOVE IN | Mute LCDSTUMM 123 |
| | 17/02/1996 | 8 | 5 | ○ | **MURDER BALLADS** | Mute LCDSTUMM 138 |
| | 15/03/1997 | 22 | 3 | | THE BOATMAN'S CALL | Mute CDSTUMM 142 |
| | 23/05/1998 | 11 | 4 | | THE BEST OF NICK CAVE & THE BAD SEEDS | Mute CDMUTEL 004 |
| | 14/04/2001 | 15 | 3 | | NO MORE SHALL WE PART | Mute LCDSTUMM 164 |
| | 15/02/2003 | 20 | 2 | | NOCTURAMA | Mute LCDSTUMM 207 |

**CAVE IN** US alternative metal group formed in Methuen, MA in 1995 by Jay Frechette (vocals), Stephen Brodsky (guitar), Adam McGrath (guitar), Justin Matthes (bass) and John-Robert Conners (drums). Matthes left after their debut release and was replaced by Andy Kyte; Frechette was replaced by Dave Scrod in 1997. Scrod left in 1998 and was replaced by Caleb Scofield.

| | DATE | POS | WKS | BPI | ALBUM TITLE | LABEL & NUMBER |
|---|---|---|---|---|---|---|
| | 29/03/2003 | 67 | 1 | | ANTENNA | RCA 82876515552 |

**CAVEMAN** UK male rap duo formed by MCM and Diamond J.

| | DATE | POS | WKS | BPI | ALBUM TITLE | LABEL & NUMBER |
|---|---|---|---|---|---|---|
| | 13/04/1991 | 43 | 2 | | POSITIVE REACTION | Profile FILER 406 |

**C.C.S.** UK blues/pop group assembled by guitarist/singer Alexis Korner (born 19/4/1928, Paris), Peter Thorup and arranger John Cameron, featuring a flexible line-up. The name stood for Collective Consciousness Society. Korner died from cancer on 1/1/1984.

| | DATE | POS | WKS | BPI | ALBUM TITLE | LABEL & NUMBER |
|---|---|---|---|---|---|---|
| | 08/04/1972 | 23 | 5 | | C.C.S | RAK SRAK 503 |

**CELTIC SPIRIT** UK studio group.

| | DATE | POS | WKS | BPI | ALBUM TITLE | LABEL & NUMBER |
|---|---|---|---|---|---|---|
| | 31/01/1998 | 62 | 1 | | CELTIC DREAMS | Polygram TV 5399992 |

**CENTRAL LINE** UK funk group formed in London by Linton Breckles (vocals/percussion), Camelle Hinds (bass/vocals), Lipson Francis (keyboards) and Henry Defoe (guitar).

| | DATE | POS | WKS | BPI | ALBUM TITLE | LABEL & NUMBER |
|---|---|---|---|---|---|---|
| | 13/02/1982 | 64 | 5 | | BREAKING POINT | Mercury MERA 001 |

**CERRONE** French producer/multi-instrumentalist (born Jean-Marc Cerrone, 1952, Paris) who recorded in the US and returned to France in 1983, becoming a best-selling author. He composed the music for the 1990 film *Dancing Machine*.

| | DATE | POS | WKS | BPI | ALBUM TITLE | LABEL & NUMBER |
|---|---|---|---|---|---|---|
| | 30/09/1978 | 60 | 1 | | SUPERNATURE | Atlantic K 50431 |

**A CERTAIN RATIO** UK punk group formed in Manchester by Simon Topping (vocals/trumpet), Martin Moscrop (guitar/trumpet), Martha Tilson (vocals), Jeremy Kerr (bass), Peter Terrell (electronics) and Donald Johnson (drums). Tilson left in 1982; Topping and Terrell left in 1983 and were replaced by Andy Connell. The group signed with Factory in 1979, then A&M in 1987, though with no new material until 1989. They left the label soon after.

| | DATE | POS | WKS | BPI | ALBUM TITLE | LABEL & NUMBER |
|---|---|---|---|---|---|---|
| | 30/01/1982 | 53 | 3 | | SEXTET | Factory FACT 55 |

**PETER CETERA** US singer (born 13/9/1944, Chicago, IL) who was the lead singer and bass guitarist with The Exceptions before joining Chicago in 1967, with whom he stayed until 1985. He recorded his debut solo album in 1981.

| | DATE | POS | WKS | BPI | ALBUM TITLE | LABEL & NUMBER |
|---|---|---|---|---|---|---|
| | 13/09/1986 | 56 | 4 | | SOLITUDE/SOLITAIRE | Full Moon 9254741 |

**RICHARD CHAMBERLAIN** US singer/actor (born 31/3/1935, Los Angeles, CA) who played the lead in *Dr Kildare* 1961–66 and later starred in *The Thorn Birds*. He has a star on the Hollywood Walk of Fame.

| | DATE | POS | WKS | BPI | ALBUM TITLE | LABEL & NUMBER |
|---|---|---|---|---|---|---|
| | 16/03/1963 | 8 | 8 | | **RICHARD CHAMBERLAIN SINGS** | MGM C 923 |

**CHAMELEONS** UK group formed in Manchester in 1981 by Mark Burgess (bass/vocals), Reg Smithies (guitar), Dave Fielding (guitar) and Brian Schofield (drums).

| | DATE | POS | WKS | BPI | ALBUM TITLE | LABEL & NUMBER |
|---|---|---|---|---|---|---|
| | 25/05/1985 | 60 | 2 | | WHAT DOES ANYTHING MEAN? BASICALLY | Statik STAT LP 22 |
| | 20/09/1986 | 44 | 2 | | STRANGE TIMES | Geffen 9241191 |

○ Silver disc ● Gold disc ✪ Platinum disc (additional platinum units are indicated by a figure following the symbol) ❶⁹ Number of weeks album topped the UK chart

**CHAMPAIGN** US soul group formed in Champaign, IL by Michael Day (lead vocals), Pauli Carmen (lead vocals), Rena Jones (lead vocals), Howard Reeder (guitar), Dana Walden (keyboards), Michael Reed (bass) and Rocky Maffitt (percussion), with Marshall Titus joining later.

27/06/1981 . . . . . 38 . . . . . . 4 . . . . . . HOW 'BOUT US . . . . . . . . . . . . . . . . . . . . . . . . . . . . . . . . . . . . . . . . . . . . . . . . . . . . . . . . . . . . . . . CBS 84927

**CHANGE** US group originally conceived as a studio group by French producers Jacques Fred Petrus and Mauro Malavasi, featuring Paolo Granolio (guitar) and David Romani (bass). After their first two hit singles, a group was formed with James Robinson on lead vocals. When Robinson went solo, a new group was assembled, featuring Debra Cooper (vocals), Rick Brenna (vocals), Timmy Allen (bass), Vince Henry (saxophone) and Michael Campbell (guitar). Jam and Lewis handled later production work.

| 19/05/1984 . . . . . 34 . . . . . 17 . . . . . . | CHANGE OF HEART . . . . . . . . . . . . . . . . . . . . . . . . . . . . . . . . . . . . . . . . . . . . . . . . . . . . . . . . . . . . . WEA WX 5 |
| 27/04/1985 . . . . . 39 . . . . . 6 . . . . . . | TURN ON THE RADIO . . . . . . . . . . . . . . . . . . . . . . . . . . . . . . . . . . . . . . . . . . . . . . . . . . Cooltempo CHR 1504 |
| 13/07/1985 . . . . . 45 . . . . . 4 . . . . . . | THE ARTISTS VOLUME 2 **LUTHER VANDROSS/TEDDY PENDERGRASS/CHANGE/ATLANTIC STARR** . . . . . . . . . . . Street Sounds ARTIS 2 |

**BETH NIELSEN CHAPMAN** US female singer and songwriter (born in 1956, Harlington, TX) who first came to prominence penning country hits for a number of artists before launching her own solo career in 1990.

12/06/2004 . . . . . 63 . . . . . . 1 . . . . . . LOOK . . . . . . . . . . . . . . . . . . . . . . . . . . . . . . . . . . . . . . . . . . . . . . . . . . . . . . . . . . . . . . . . . . . . Sanctuary SANCD269

**MICHAEL CHAPMAN** UK singer and guitarist (born 24/1/1941, Leeds) who made his debut album in 1968. He worked with Rick Kemp until he joined Steeleye Span. As well as Harvest, Chapman also recorded for Deram, Criminal and Coda Records.

21/03/1970 . . . . . 45 . . . . . . 1 . . . . . . FULLY QUALIFIED SURVIVOR . . . . . . . . . . . . . . . . . . . . . . . . . . . . . . . . . . . . . . . . . . . . . . . . . . . . . . . Harvest SHVL 764

**TRACY CHAPMAN** US singer (born 30/3/1964, Cleveland, OH) who graduated from Tufts University with degrees in anthropology and African studies. Her UK break came at the 1988 Nelson Mandela Birthday Show at Wembley when her set was extended owing to Stevie Wonder's enforced curtailment after his synthesizer programmes were stolen. She was named Best International Female and Best International Newcomer at the 1989 BRIT Awards. Her four Grammy Awards include Best New Artist in 1988, Best Pop Vocal Performance in 1988 for *Fast Car* and Best Rock Song in 1996 for *Give Me One Reason*.

| 21/05/1988 . . . . ❶³ . . . . 188 . . . . . ✪⁴ | **TRACY CHAPMAN** ▲¹ 1988 Grammy Award for Best Contemporary Folk Recording . . . . . . . . . . . . . . . . . . . . . . . . . Elektra EKT 44 |
| 14/10/1989 . . . . ❶¹ . . . . . 16 . . . . . . ✪ | **CROSSROADS** . . . . . . . . . . . . . . . . . . . . . . . . . . . . . . . . . . . . . . . . . . . . . . . . . . . . . . . . . . . . . . . . Elektra EKT 61 |
| 09/05/1992 . . . . . 19 . . . . . 3 . . . . . . | MATTERS OF THE HEART . . . . . . . . . . . . . . . . . . . . . . . . . . . . . . . . . . . . . . . . . . . . . . . Elektra 7559612152 |
| 06/10/2001 . . . . . 3 . . . . . 18 . . . . . . ✪ | **COLLECTION** ◇ . . . . . . . . . . . . . . . . . . . . . . . . . . . . . . . . . . . . . . . . . . . . . . . . . . . . . . . . Elektra 7559627002 |
| 02/11/2002 . . . . . 36 . . . . . . 2 . . . . . . | LET IT RAIN . . . . . . . . . . . . . . . . . . . . . . . . . . . . . . . . . . . . . . . . . . . . . . . . . . . . . . . . . . . Elektra 7559628362 |

**CHAPTERHOUSE** UK rock group formed in Reading in 1987 by Andrew Sherriff (born 5/5/1969, Wokingham, guitar/vocals), Stephen Patman (born 8/11/1968, Windsor, guitar), Simon Rowe (born 23/6/1969, Reading, guitar), Jon Curtis (bass) and Ashley Bates (born 2/11/1971, Reading, drums). Curtis left soon after, replaced by Russell Barrett (born 7/11/1968, Vermont, US).

11/05/1991 . . . . . 23 . . . . . . 3 . . . . . . WHIRLPOOL . . . . . . . . . . . . . . . . . . . . . . . . . . . . . . . . . . . . . . . . . . . . . . . . . . . . . . . . . . . Dedicated DEDLP 001

**CHAQUITO ORCHESTRA** UK orchestra arranged and produced by Johnny Gregory.

| 24/02/1968 . . . . . 36 . . . . . . 1 . . . . . | THIS IS CHAQUITO **CHAQUITO AND QUEDO BRASS** . . . . . . . . . . . . . . . . . . . . . . . . . . . . . . . . . . . . . . . Fontana SFXL 50 |
| 04/03/1972 . . . . . 48 . . . . . . 1 . . . . . | THRILLER THEMES . . . . . . . . . . . . . . . . . . . . . . . . . . . . . . . . . . . . . . . . . . . . . . . . . . . . . . . Philips 6308 087 |

**CHARGED GBH** UK group formed in 1980 by Colin Abrahall (vocals), Jock Blyth (guitar), Ross (bass) and Wilf (drums) as Charged GBH (the 'gbh' standing for grievous bodily harm). They became GBH in 1986. Kai replaced Wilf on drums in 1989 and Anthony Morgan later took over on bass.

14/08/1982 . . . . . 17 . . . . . . 6 . . . . . . CITY BABY ATTACKED BY RATS . . . . . . . . . . . . . . . . . . . . . . . . . . . . . . . . . . . . . . . . . . . . . . . . . . . . Clay CLAYLP 4

**CHARLATANS** UK rock group formed in Manchester, Lancashire by Tim Burgess (born in Salford, Lancashire on 30/5/1968, vocals), Martin Blunt (born on 21/5/1964, bass), Jon Baker (born in 1969, guitar), Jon Brookes (born on 21/9/1968, drums) and Rob Collins (born in Sedgeley, Warwickshire on 23/2/1963, keyboards). Blunt suffered a nervous breakdown in 1991, whilst Baker left the group and was replaced by Mark Collins (born on 14/8/1965, guitar) the same year. Rob Collins was then involved in an armed robbery and subsequently jailed for eight months in 1993. He was killed in a road accident, with his blood-alcohol content at more than twice the legal limit on 22/7/1996. Tony Rodgers subsequently replaced him in the group.

THE CHARLATANS
TELLIN' STORIES

| 20/10/1990 . . . . ❶¹ . . . . 17 . . . . . . ● | **SOME FRIENDLY** . . . . . . . . . . . . . . . . . . . . . . . . . . . . . . . . . . . . . . . . . . . . . . . . . . . . . . . Situation Two SITU 30 |
| 04/04/1992 . . . . . 21 . . . . . 4 . . . . . . | BETWEEN 10TH AND 11TH . . . . . . . . . . . . . . . . . . . . . . . . . . . . . . . . . . . . . . . . . . . . . . Situation Two SITU 37CD |
| 02/04/1994 . . . . . 8 . . . . . 3 . . . . . . | UP TO OUR HIPS . . . . . . . . . . . . . . . . . . . . . . . . . . . . . . . . . . . . . . . . . . . . . . . . Beggars Banquet BBQCD 147 |
| 09/09/1995 . . . . ❶¹ . . . . 13 . . . . . . ● | **THE CHARLATANS** . . . . . . . . . . . . . . . . . . . . . . . . . . . . . . . . . . . . . . . . . . . . . . . . Beggars Banquet BBQCD 174 |
| 03/05/1997 . . . . ❶² . . . . 28 . . . . . . ✪ | **TELLIN' STORIES** . . . . . . . . . . . . . . . . . . . . . . . . . . . . . . . . . . . . . . . . . . . . . . . . Beggars Banquet BBQCD 190 |
| 07/03/1998 . . . . . 4 . . . . . 25 . . . . . | **MELTING POT** . . . . . . . . . . . . . . . . . . . . . . . . . . . . . . . . . . . . . . . . . . . . . . . . . . . Beggars Banquet BBQCD 198 |

▲⁹ Number of weeks album topped the US chart   ◆¹² RIAA Diamond Awards   ◇³ IFPI Platinum Europe Awards

| | | | | ALBUM TITLE | LABEL & NUMBER |
|---|---|---|---|---|---|
| 30/10/1999 | 2 | 10 | ● | US AND US ONLY | Universal MCD 60069 |
| 22/09/2001 | 2 | 5 | ● | WONDERLAND | Universal MCD 60076 |
| 01/06/2002 | 55 | 1 | | SONGS FROM THE OTHER SIDE | Beggars Banquet 2032CD |
| 03/08/2002 | 40 | 2 | | LIVE IT LIKE YOU LOVE IT | Universal MCD 60080 |
| 29/05/2004 | 13 | 4 | ○ | UP AT THE LAKE | Universal MCD 60093 |

**CHARLENE** US singer (born Charlene D'Angelo, later Duncan, 1/6/1950, Hollywood, CA) whose debut hit had originally been released in 1977 on the Motown subsidiary Prodigal and was revived in the US following extensive plays on a Tampa, FL radio station. She later recorded with Stevie Wonder.

| 17/07/1982 | 43 | 4 | | I'VE NEVER BEEN TO ME | Motown STML 12171 |

**RAY CHARLES** US singer (born Ray Charles Robinson, 23/9/1930, Albany, GA) who moved to Greenville, FL while still a child. He was partially blinded at five and totally blind at seven due to glaucoma. After the death of both parents in 1948 he became a full-time musician and moved to Seattle, WA and then on to Los Angeles, CA. After debut records in 1949 for Swingtime, he switched to Atlantic in 1952 and had many US soul and pop hits over the next eight years. He signed for ABC in 1960, founding the Tangerine label (through ABC) in 1968 and changing its name to Crossover in 1973. He toured relentlessly with his own band and backing singers The Raelettes. Thirteen Grammy Awards include: Best Male Vocal Performance Album in 1960 for *The Genius Of Ray Charles*; Best Rhythm & Blues Performance in 1960 for *Let The Good Times Roll*; Best Male Vocal Performance Single or Track and Best Performance by a Pop Single Artist in 1960 for *Georgia On My Mind*; Best Vocal Performance Album in 1961 for *The Genius Of Ray Charles*; Best Rhythm & Blues Recording in 1961 for *Hit The Road Jack*; Best Rhythm & Blues Recording in 1962 for *I Can't Stop Loving You*; Best Rhythm & Blues Recording in 1963 for *Busted*; Best Rhythm & Blues Recording and Best Rhythm & Blues Solo Vocal Performance in 1966 for *Cryin' Time* ; and, with Chaka Khan, Best Rhythm & Blues Vocal Performance by a Duo for *I'll Be Good To You*; Best Rhythm & Blues Vocal Performance in 1975 for *Living For The City*; and Best Rhythm & Blues Male Vocal Performance in 1993 for *A Song For You*. He was inducted into the Rock & Roll Hall of Fame in 1986. Ray is the only artist to appear in advertisements for both Coca-Cola and Pepsi Cola, in 1969 and 1992 respectively. He has a star on the Hollywood Walk of Fame. Ray died from liver disease on 9/6/2004.

| 28/07/1962 | 6 | 16 | | MODERN SOUNDS IN COUNTRY AND WESTERN MUSIC ▲[14] | HMV CLP 1580 |
| 23/02/1963 | 15 | 5 | | MODERN SOUNDS IN COUNTRY AND WESTERN MUSIC VOLUME 2 | HMV CLP 1613 |
| 20/07/1963 | 16 | 5 | | GREATEST HITS | HMV CLP 1626 |
| 05/10/1968 | 24 | 8 | | GREATEST HITS VOLUME 2 | Stateside SSL 10241 |
| 19/07/1980 | 29 | 5 | | HEART TO HEART – 20 HOT HITS | London RAY TV 1 |
| 24/03/1990 | 36 | 3 | | COLLECTION | Arcade RCLP 101 |
| 13/03/1993 | 48 | 3 | | RAY CHARLES – LIVING LEGEND | Arcade ARC 946422 |
| 25/08/2001 | 13 | 5 | ○ | THE DEFINITIVE | warner.esp 8122735562 |

**TINA CHARLES** UK singer (born Tina Hoskins, 10/3/1954, London) who was working as a session musician in 1975 when she sang lead on a track called *I'm On Fire*, later released under the group name 5000 Volts. A different person was chosen for their TV performances, so Tina went solo, with production handled by Biddu. Her touring band included Trevor Horn and Geoff Downes, who later formed Buggles.

| 03/12/1977 | 35 | 7 | ○ | HEART 'N' SOUL | CBS 82180 |

**CHARLES AND EDDIE** US duo Charles Pettigrew (from Philadelphia, PA) and Eddie Chacon (from Oakland, CA) who discovered a mutual interest in soul music after meeting on the New York subway. Chacon had been with The Dust Brothers and Daddy-O, Pettigrew with Down Avenue. Pettigrew died from cancer on 6/4/2001 at the age of 37.

| 12/12/1992 | 19 | 15 | ● | DUOPHONIC | Capitol CDESTU 2186 |

**CHAS AND DAVE** UK duo formed by Chas Hodges (born Charles Hodges, 28/12/1943, London, piano) and Dave Peacock (born 25/5/1945, London, guitar); their mix of rock and Cockney humour was dubbed Rockney (also the nickname of their drummer Mickey Burt). First known through TV commercials, they also made the Tottenham Hotspur hit singles.

| 05/12/1981 | 25 | 15 | ● | CHAS AND DAVE'S CHRISTMAS JAMBOREE BAG | Warwick WW 5166 |
| 17/04/1982 | 35 | 11 | ○ | MUSTN'T GRUMBLE | Rockney 909 |
| 08/01/1983 | 59 | 15 | ○ | JOB LOT | Rockney ROC 910 |
| 15/10/1983 | 7 | 17 | ✪ | CHAS AND DAVE'S KNEES UP – JAMBOREE BAG NUMBER 2 | Rockney WW 5166 |
| 11/08/1984 | 27 | 10 | | WELL PLEASED | Rockney ROC 912 |
| 17/11/1984 | 16 | 10 | ✪ | CHAS AND DAVE'S GREATEST HITS | Rockney ROC 913 |
| 15/12/1984 | 87 | 1 | | CHAS AND DAVE'S CHRISTMAS JAMBOREE BAG | Rockney ROCM 001 |
| 09/11/1985 | 15 | 13 | ● | JAMBOREE BAG NUMBER 3 | Rockney ROC 914 |
| 13/12/1986 | 37 | 4 | | CHAS AND DAVE'S CHRISTMAS CAROL ALBUM | Telstar STAR 2293 |
| 29/04/1995 | 3 | 5 | ○ | STREET PARTY | Telstar TCD 2765 |

**JC CHASEZ** US male singer (born Joshua Scott Chasez, 8/8/1976, Washington DC); he was a founder member of N Sync and launched a solo career in 2004.

| | | | | |
|---|---|---|---|---|
| 08/05/2004 | 46 | 2 | | SCHIZOPHRENIC ........................................................ Jive JIV537242 |

**CHEAP TRICK** US rock group formed in Rockford, IL by Bun E Carlos (born Brad Carlson, 12/6/1951, Rockford, drums), Rick Nielsen (born 22/12/1946, Rockford, guitar), Tom Petersson (born 9/5/1950, Rockford, bass) and Robin Zender (born 23/1/1953, Loves Park, IL, vocals). Petersson was replaced by Jon Brant in 1980 but returned in 1988.

| | | | | |
|---|---|---|---|---|
| 24/02/1979 | 29 | 9 | | CHEAP TRICK AT BUDOKAN ........................................... Epic EPC 86083 |
| 06/10/1979 | 41 | 5 | | DREAM POLICE ......................................................... Epic EPC 83522 |
| 05/06/1982 | 95 | 1 | | ONE ON ONE ........................................................... Epic EPC 85740 |

**CHUBBY CHECKER** US singer (born Ernest Evans, 3/10/1941, Andrews, SC) raised in Philadelphia, PA where he was working at a chicken market when he signed with the Cameo Parkway label. His debut single *The Class* featured impersonations of Fats Domino, the Coasters, Elvis Presley, Cozy Cole and the Chipmunks. Dick Clark, host of top TV show *American Bandstand*, then suggested he cover Hank Ballard's *The Twist*. Checker's version swept to # 1 in the US, while his most popular UK hit, *Let's Twist Again*, was originally released in the US on the first anniversary of *The Twist*. He won the 1961 Grammy Award for Best Rock & Roll Recording for *Let's Twist Again*.

| | | | | |
|---|---|---|---|---|
| 27/01/1962 | 13 | 4 | | TWIST WITH CHUBBY CHECKER ...................................... Columbia 33SX 1315 |
| 03/03/1962 | 17 | 3 | | FOR TWISTERS ONLY .................................................. Columbia 33SX 1341 |

**CHEEKY GIRLS** Romanian duo, twin sisters Monica and Gabriela Irimia (born 31/10/1982, Transylvania), Gabriela being older by ten minutes. They attracted attention after auditioning for *Popstars* where Pete Waterman rated them the worst act ever.

| | | | | |
|---|---|---|---|---|
| 23/08/2003 | 14 | 6 | ○ | PARTY TIME ........................................................... Multiply MULTYCD 13 |

**CHEMICAL BROTHERS** UK acid house and hip hop duo Ed Simons (born 9/6/1970, Oxford) and Tom Rowlands (born 11/1/1971, Kingston) who formed as The Dust Brothers in 1994, becoming the Chemical Brothers in 1995. Named Best UK Dance Act at the 2000 BRIT Awards.

| | | | | |
|---|---|---|---|---|
| 08/07/1995 | 9 | 41 | ✪ | **EXIT PLANET DUST** ................................................. Junior Boy's Own XDUSTCD 1 |
| 19/04/1997 | ❶¹ | 27 | ✪ | **DIG YOUR OWN HOLE** ............................................... Virgin XDUSTCD 2 |
| 03/07/1999 | ❶¹ | 47 | ✪ | **SURRENDER** ◇ ...................................................... Virgin XDUSTCD 4 |
| 09/02/2002 | ❶¹ | 11 | ● | **COME WITH US** .................................................... Virgin XDUSTCDX 5 |
| 04/10/2003 | 9 | 6 | ● | **SINGLES 93–03** .................................................... Virgin XDUSTCDX 6 |

**CHER** US singer (born Cherilyn Sarkasian LaPierre, 20/5/1946, El Centro, CA) who began her career as a backing singer for Phil Spector. She later recorded solo as Bonnie Jo Mason (her first single was *Ringo I Love You*, a Beatlemania cash-in) and Cherilyn, teaming up with Sonny Bono in 1963 as Caesar & Cleo. The duo (who later married) recorded as Sonny And Cher from 1963 to 1974, both also pursuing solo projects from 1965 onwards, Cher with considerably more success. She divorced Sonny in 1974 and married Greg Allman in 1975, a marriage that lasted ten days. They were divorced in 1979. She later became an actress, appearing in *Mask* (1974), *The Witches Of Eastwick* (1987) and *Moonstruck* (1987), for which she won an Oscar as Best Actress. She won the 1999 Grammy Award for Best Pop Dance Performance for *Believe*.

| | | | | |
|---|---|---|---|---|
| 02/10/1965 | 7 | 9 | | **ALL I REALLY WANT TO DO** .......................................... Liberty LBY 3058 |
| 07/05/1966 | 11 | 11 | | SONNY SIDE OF CHER .................................................. Liberty LBY 3072 |
| 16/01/1988 | 26 | 22 | ● | **CHER** ............................................................... Geffen WX 132 |
| 22/07/1989 | 7 | 82 | ✪ | **HEART OF STONE** The album changed its catalogue number from WX 262 during its chart run ......... Geffen WX 262/GEF 24239 |
| 29/06/1991 | ❶¹ | 51 | ✪³ | **LOVE HURTS** ........................................................ Geffen GEF 24427 |
| 21/11/1992 | ❶⁷ | 33 | ✪³ | **CHER'S GREATEST HITS: 1965-1992** ................................ Geffen GED 24439 |
| 18/11/1995 | 10 | 18 | ● | **IT'S A MAN'S WORLD** ............................................... WEA 0630126702 |
| 07/11/1998 | 7 | 44 | ✪² | **BELIEVE** ◇⁴ ........................................................ WEA 3984253192 |
| 20/11/1999 | 7 | 24 | ✪² | **THE GREATEST HITS** ◇² .............................................. WEA/Universal Music TV 8573804202 |
| 01/12/2001 | 46 | 2 | ● | LIVING PROOF ........................................................ WEA 0927424632 |
| 06/12/2003 | 17 | 14 | ● | THE VERY BEST OF ..................................................... UMTV/WSM 5046685862 |

**CHERRELLE** US singer (born Cheryl Norton, 1958, Los Angeles, CA) who, after moving to Detroit, MI with her family, was invited by next-door neighbour Michael Henderson to sing on his *Night Time* album and spent the next four years touring. Back in Los Angeles she was signed by Tabu and was teamed with the Jam and Lewis hit production team. Also a capable drummer, she is the cousin of singer Pebbles.

| | | | | |
|---|---|---|---|---|
| 25/01/1986 | 17 | 9 | | HIGH PRIORITY ....................................................... Tabu TBU 26699 |

▲⁹ Number of weeks album topped the US chart   ◆¹² RIAA Diamond Awards   ◇³ IFPI Platinum Europe Awards

**EAGLE-EYE CHERRY** US singer (born 7/5/1969, Stockholm, Sweden), son of jazz musician Don Cherry and stepbrother of Neneh Cherry. After auditioning with MTV as a DJ, he made his debut album in 1997 for Swedish label Superstudio/Diesel, winning the Select North award at the 1998 MTV Europe Music Awards.

| | | | | | | |
|---|---|---|---|---|---|---|
| 01/08/1998 | 3 | 29 | ● | **DESIRELESS** ◇ | Polydor 5372262 |
| 20/05/2000 | 12 | 3 | | LIVING IN THE PRESENT FUTURE | Polydor 5437442 |

**NENEH CHERRY** US singer (born 10/8/1964, Stockholm, Sweden) of Swedish and West African parents, raised in New York City. The stepdaughter of jazz trumpeter Don Cherry, she was previously in the jazz trio Rip Rig And Panic. She was named Best International Female and Best International Newcomer at the 1990 BRIT Awards and is married to producer Cameron McVey. They won, along with Youssou N'Dour, the MTV Europe Music Award for Best Song in 1994 for *7 Seconds*.

| | | | | | | |
|---|---|---|---|---|---|---|
| 17/06/1989 | 2 | 43 | ✪ | **RAW LIKE SUSHI** | Circa 8 |
| 07/11/1992 | 27 | 2 | | HOMEBREW | Circa CIRCD 25 |
| 14/09/1996 | 16 | 4 | ○ | MAN | Hut CDHUT 38 |

**CHIC** US R&B group formed by Bernard Edwards (born 31/10/1952, Greensville, NC) and Nile Rodgers (born 19/9/1952, New York), who teamed with Tony Thompson (born 15/11/1954) in 1972 and formed The Big Apple Band, a rock-fusion group that backed the likes of New York City and Carol Douglas. Singer Norma Jean Wright joined in 1976 but was soon replaced by Luci Martin (born 10/1/1955). Known as Allah And The Knife-Wielding Punks, they then added another singer, Alfa Anderson (born 7/9/1946), to the line-up and became Chic. As top production team of the era, Rodgers and Edwards produced albums for Diana Ross, Sister Sledge, Norma Jean Wright, Sheila B Devotion and later David Bowie and Madonna. The group disbanded in 1983, re-forming in 1992 with singers Sylvester Logan Sharp and Jenn Thomas. Bernard Edwards was found dead in a hotel room on 18/4/1996, during a Japanese tour, the cause of death given as pneumonia. Tony Thompson died from renal cell cancer 12/11/2003.

| | | | | | | |
|---|---|---|---|---|---|---|
| 03/02/1979 | 2 | 24 | ● | **C'EST CHIC** | Atlantic K 50565 |
| 18/08/1979 | 29 | 12 | ○ | RISQUE | Atlantic K 50634 |
| 15/12/1979 | 30 | 8 | | BEST OF CHIC | Atlantic K 50686 |
| 05/12/1987 | 72 | 3 | | FREAK OUT **CHIC AND SISTER SLEDGE** | Telstar STAR 2319 |

**CHICAGO** US rock group formed in Chicago, IL in 1966 by Peter Cetera (born 13/9/1944, Chicago, bass/vocals), Robert Lamm (born 13/10/1944, Brooklyn, NY, keyboards), Terry Kath (born 31/1/1946, Chicago, guitar), Danny Seraphine (born 28/8/1948, Chicago, drums), James Pankow (born 20/8/1947, Chicago, trombone), Lee Loughnane (born 21/10/1946, Chicago, trumpet), Walter Parazaider (born 14/3/1945, Chicago, reeds) and Laudir de Oliveira (percussion) as Big Thing. After legal threats from the Chicago transport department, their 1967 name-change to Chicago Transit Authority was amended to Chicago a few months later. The group won a Grammy Award in 1976 for Best Pop Vocal Performance by a Group for *If You Leave Me Now*. Kath shot himself to death on 23/1/1978, cleaning a gun he thought was unloaded, he was replaced by Donnie Dacus. Bill Champlin (keyboards) joined in 1982. Cetera went solo in 1985 and was replaced by Jason Scheff; DaWayne Bailey joined in 1989 as a replacement for Seraphine. Chicago have a star on the Hollywood Walk of Fame.

| | | | | | | |
|---|---|---|---|---|---|---|
| 27/09/1969 | 9 | 14 | | **CHICAGO TRANSIT AUTHORITY** | CBS 66221 |
| 04/04/1970 | 6 | 27 | | **CHICAGO** | CBS 66233 |
| 03/04/1971 | 31 | 1 | | CHICAGO 3 | CBS 66260 |
| 30/09/1972 | 24 | 2 | | CHICAGO 5 ▲[9] | CBS 69708 |
| 23/10/1976 | 21 | 11 | ○ | CHICAGO X | CBS 86010 |
| 02/10/1982 | 44 | 9 | | CHICAGO 16 | Full Moon K 99235 |
| 04/12/1982 | 42 | 8 | | LOVE SONGS | TV Records TVA 6 |
| 01/12/1984 | 24 | 20 | ● | CHICAGO 17 | Full Moon 925060 |
| 25/11/1989 | 6 | 25 | ✪ | **THE HEART OF CHICAGO** | Reprise WX 328 |
| 13/02/1999 | 21 | 4 | | THE HEART OF CHICAGO – 1967–1997 | Reprise 9362465542 |
| 14/09/2002 | 11 | 7 | ● | THE CHICAGO STORY – COMPLETE GREATEST | Rhino 8122736302 |

**CHICANE** UK production artist Nick Bracegirdle who also records as the Disco Citizens and later launched the Modena Records and Cyanide Music labels.

| | | | | | | |
|---|---|---|---|---|---|---|
| 01/11/1997 | 49 | 1 | | FAR FROM THE MADDENING CROWDS | Xtravaganza 0091372EXT |
| 08/04/2000 | 10 | 8 | ● | **BEHIND THE SUN** | Xtravaganza XTRAV 10CD |

**CHICKEN SHACK** UK group formed in Birmingham in 1965 by Stan Webb (guitar/vocals) and Andy Sylvester (bass). Christine Perfect (born 12/7/1943, Birmingham, piano/vocals) and Dave Bidwell (drums) joined later. After their brief success Perfect left to join her husband John McVie in Fleetwood Mac. Chicken Shack, who later recruited Tony Ashton (piano), Bob Daisley (bass), John Glascock (bass), Paul Hancox (drums/percussion), Chris Mercer (saxophone) and Paul Raymond (guitar/keyboards/vocals), continued until 1974.

| | | | | | | |
|---|---|---|---|---|---|---|
| 22/06/1968 | 12 | 8 | | FORTY FINGERS FRESHLY PACKED | Blue Horizon 763203 |
| 15/02/1969 | 9 | 1 | | **OK KEN?** | Blue Horizon 763209 |

**CHIEFTAINS** Irish folk group originally formed by Paddy Moloney (uillean pipes/tin whistle), Michael Tubridy (flute/concertina/tin whistle), Sean Potts (tin whistle), Martin Fay (fiddle) and David Fallon (bodhran). By 1973 the line-up was Moloney, Fay, Potts, Tubridy, Pendar Mercier (bodhran/bones) and Derek Bell (harp/oboe/tiompan). Over the years collaborating with artists as diverse as The Corrs, James Galway, Art Garfunkel, Gary Moore, Van Morrison and Nanci Griffith, they have won six Grammy Awards including: Best Traditional Folk Album in 1992 for *An Irish Evening Live At The Grand Opera House, Belfast, With Roger Daltry And Nanci Griffith*; Best Contemporary Folk Album in 1992 for *Another Country*; Best Traditional Folk Album in 1993 for *The Celtic Harp*; Best Pop Collaboration

with Vocal in 1995 for *Have I Told You Lately That I Love You;* Best World Music Album in 1996 for *Santiago;* and Best Traditional Folk Album in 1998 for *Long Journey Home.*

| DATE | POS | WKS | BPI | ALBUM TITLE | LABEL & NUMBER |
|------|-----|-----|-----|-----------|----------------|
| 28/03/1987 | 32 | 5 | | JAMES GALWAY AND THE CHIEFTAINS IN IRELAND **JAMES GALWAY AND THE CHIEFTAINS** | RCA Red Seal RL 85798 |
| 02/07/1988 | 18 | 7 | | IRISH HEARTBEAT **VAN MORRISON AND THE CHIEFTAINS** | Mercury MERH 124 |
| 04/02/1995 | 17 | 9 | ○ | THE LONG BLACK VEIL | RCA 74321251672 |
| 06/03/1999 | 36 | 4 | ○ | TEARS OF STONE | RCA Victor 09026689682 |
| 23/03/2002 | 37 | 2 | | THE WIDE WORLD OVER | RCA Victor 09026639172 |

**TONI CHILDS** US singer (born 1958, Orange County, CA) who grew up in various parts of the USA and Europe, spending four years in the UK. After a first contract with Island Records in London, she enjoyed greater success with Warner Brothers USA.

| | | | | | |
|------|-----|-----|-----|-----------|----------------|
| 22/04/1989 | 73 | 1 | | UNION | A&M AMA 5175 |

**CHIMES** UK group formed in the late 1980s by Edinburgh-born musicians Mike Peden (keyboards/bass) and James Locke (keyboards/drums), with singer Pauline Henry from London who later recorded solo.

| | | | | | |
|------|-----|-----|-----|-----------|----------------|
| 23/06/1990 | 17 | 19 | ○ | THE CHIMES | CBS 4664811 |

**CHINA BLACK** UK vocal/instrumental duo Errol Reid and Simon Fung. They later worked with Ladysmith Black Mambazo.

| | | | | | |
|------|-----|-----|-----|-----------|----------------|
| 11/03/1995 | 27 | 4 | | BORN | Wild Card 5237552 |

**CHINA CRISIS** UK group formed in Kirkby, Merseyside in 1979 by Gary Daly (born 5/5/1962, Kirkby, vocals), Eddie Lundon (born 9/6/1962, Kirkby, guitar), Brian McNeil (keyboards), Gazza Johnson (bass) and Kevin Wilkinson (drums). Kevin Wilkinson committed suicide in July 1999.

| | | | | | |
|------|-----|-----|-----|-----------|----------------|
| 20/11/1982 | 21 | 18 | ○ | DIFFICULT SHAPES AND PASSIVE RHYTHMS SOME PEOPLE THINK IT'S FUN TO ENTERTAIN | Virgin V 2243 |
| 12/11/1983 | 20 | 16 | ● | WORKING WITH FIRE AND STEEL – POSSIBLE POP SONGS VOLUME 2 | Virgin V 2286 |
| 11/05/1985 | 9 | 22 | ● | **FLAUNT THE IMPERFECTION** | Virgin V 2342 |
| 06/12/1986 | 63 | 6 | | WHAT PRICE PARADISE? | Virgin V 2410 |
| 13/05/1989 | 58 | 2 | | DIARY OF A HOLLOW HORSE | Virgin V 2567 |
| 15/09/1990 | 32 | 4 | | CHINA CRISIS COLLECTION – THE VERY BEST OF CHINA CRISIS | Virgin V 2613 |

**CHINA DRUM** UK group formed in 1989 by Bill McQueen (guitar/vocals), Dave McQueen (bass/vocals) and Adam Lee (drums/vocals). They later added Jan Alkema to the line-up and shortened their name to The Drum.

| | | | | | |
|------|-----|-----|-----|-----------|----------------|
| 11/05/1996 | 53 | 1 | | GOOSEFAIR | Mantra MNTCD 1002 |

**CHINGY** US rapper (born Howard Bailey Jr, 1980, St Louis, MO) discovered by Ludacris.

| | | | | | |
|------|-----|-----|-----|-----------|----------------|
| 29/05/2004 | 73 | 1 | | JACKPOT | Capitol 5818270 |

**CHOIR OF NEW COLLEGE OXFORD/EDWARD HIGGINBOTTOM** UK choir conducted by Edward Higginbottom.

| | | | | | |
|------|-----|-----|-----|-----------|----------------|
| 12/10/1996 | 49 | 5 | ● | AGNUS DEI | Erato 0630146342 |
| 18/04/1998 | 57 | 2 | | AGNUS DEI II | Erato 3984216592 |

**CHORDS** UK group formed during the late-1970s Mod-revival by Brett 'Buddy' Ascott (drums), Billy Hassett (guitar), Chris Pope (guitar/vocals) and Mick Talbot (born 11/9/1958, London, keyboards) who was later in Style Council.

| | | | | | |
|------|-----|-----|-----|-----------|----------------|
| 24/05/1980 | 30 | 3 | | SO FAR AWAY | Polydor POLS 1019 |

**CHRISTIANS** UK group formed in 1984 by ex-It's Immaterial Henry Priestman (born 21/6/1955, Hull) after meeting three of the eleven Christian brothers – Garry (born Garrison Christian, 27/2/1955, Liverpool), Russell (born 8/7/1956, Liverpool) and Roger (born 13/2/1950. Liverpool). Previously called Equal Temperament, The Gems and Natural High, the latter name was used when they appeared on *Opportunity Knocks* in 1974. The group took part in the *Ferry Across the Mersey* charity record to raise funds for the victims of the Hillsborough stadium football disaster in 1989.

| | | | | | |
|------|-----|-----|-----|-----------|----------------|
| 31/10/1987 | 2 | 68 | ◇3 | **THE CHRISTIANS** | Island ILPS 9876 |
| 27/01/1990 | ❶1 | 17 | ◇ | **COLOUR** | Island ILPS 9948 |
| 10/10/1992 | 18 | 3 | | HAPPY IN HELL | Island CID 9996 |
| 20/11/1993 | 22 | 8 | ● | THE BEST OF THE CHRISTIANS | Island CIDTV 6 |

**TONY CHRISTIE** UK singer (born Anthony Fitzgerald, 25/4/1944, Conisborough), professional from the age of twenty, produced by Mitch Murray and Pete Callander.

| DATE | POS | WKS | BPI | ALBUM TITLE | LABEL & NUMBER |
|---|---|---|---|---|---|
| 24/07/1971 | 37 | 1 | | I DID WHAT I DID FOR MARIA | MCA MKPS 2016 |
| 17/02/1973 | 19 | 2 | | WITH LOVING FEELING | MCA MUPS 468 |
| 31/05/1975 | 33 | 3 | | TONY CHRISTIE – LIVE | MCA MCF 2703 |
| 06/11/1976 | 28 | 4 | | BEST OF TONY CHRISTIE | MCA MCF 2769 |

**CHRON GEN** UK group formed in 1978 by Glynn Barber (guitar/vocals), Pete Dimmock (bass), John Thurlow (guitar) and John Johnson (drums).

| DATE | POS | WKS | BPI | ALBUM TITLE | LABEL & NUMBER |
|---|---|---|---|---|---|
| 03/04/1982 | 53 | 3 | | CHRONIC GENERATION | Secret SEC 3 |

**CHUMBAWAMBA** UK rock group formed in Leeds in 1983 by Alice Nutter (vocals), Harry Hamer, Boff (guitar), Mavis Dillon (horns), Louise Mary Watts (keyboards), Danbert Nobacon, Paul Greco and Dunstan Bruce. They had previously recorded for Agit Prop and One Little Indian, where they recorded with Credit To The Nation.

| DATE | POS | WKS | BPI | ALBUM TITLE | LABEL & NUMBER |
|---|---|---|---|---|---|
| 07/05/1994 | 29 | 2 | | ANARCHY | One Little Indian TPLP 46CD |
| 04/11/1995 | 70 | 1 | | SWINGIN' WITH RAYMOND | One Little Indian TPLP 66CDS |
| 13/09/1997 | 19 | 7 | ○ | TUBTHUMPER | EMI 4952382 |

**CHARLOTTE CHURCH** UK singer (born 21/2/1986, Cardiff) who, with her debut album *Voice Of An Angel*, is the youngest female to appear in the US top 30, while her *Dream A Dream* Christmas album made her the youngest female to make the top ten. In January 2000 she sacked her manager Jonathan Shalit who received a £2.3 million out-of-court settlement in November 2000. She appeared in the 2003 film *I'll Be There*.

| DATE | POS | WKS | BPI | ALBUM TITLE | LABEL & NUMBER |
|---|---|---|---|---|---|
| 21/11/1998 | 4 | 20 | ✪2 | **VOICE OF AN ANGEL** | Sony Classical SK 60957 |
| 27/11/1999 | 8 | 10 | ✪ | **CHARLOTTE CHURCH** | Sony Classical SK 89003 |
| 02/12/2000 | 30 | 6 | ● | DREAM A DREAM | Sony Classical SK 89459 |
| 03/11/2001 | 24 | 9 | ● | ENCHANTMENT | Sony Classical SK 89710 |

**SIR WINSTON CHURCHILL** UK statesman (born Winston Leonard Spencer Churchill, 30/11/1874, Blenheim Palace) who served as an officer in the 4th Hussars during the Boer War and first ran for parliament in 1900. He served as Prime Minister from 1940–45 and again from 1951–55, remaining a Member of Parliament until 1964. He was knighted in 1953 and awarded the Nobel Prize for Literature (he published many books, both historical and on English Literature, and was also an accomplished painter). He died on 24/1/1965 and was given a State Funeral by a grateful nation, the first commoner to be so honoured since the Duke of Wellington, and the last thus far.

| DATE | POS | WKS | BPI | ALBUM TITLE | LABEL & NUMBER |
|---|---|---|---|---|---|
| 13/02/1965 | 6 | 8 | | **THE VOICE OF CHURCHILL** | Decca LXT 6200 |

**CINDERELLA** US rock group formed in Philadelphia, PA in 1983 by Tom Keifer (guitar/vocals), Eric Brittingham (bass), Michael Kelly Smith (guitar) and Tony Destra (drums). Smith and Destra left soon after and were replaced by Jeff LaBar and Jody Cortez. Cortez left in 1986, replaced by Fred Coury. Coury also left a few years later and was initially replaced by Kevin Valentine before Keifer's health problems put the group on hold. They returned in 1994 with the album *Still Climbing* and with Kevin Conway as the new drummer.

| DATE | POS | WKS | BPI | ALBUM TITLE | LABEL & NUMBER |
|---|---|---|---|---|---|
| 23/07/1988 | 30 | 6 | | LONG COLD WINTER | Vertigo VERH 59 |
| 01/12/1990 | 36 | 2 | | HEARTBREAK STATION | Vertigo 8480181 |

**CINEMATIC ORCHESTRA** UK group formed by Jason Swinscoe (multi-instrumentalist), Tom Chant (saxophone and keyboards), Phil France (bass) and Daniel Howard (drums).

| DATE | POS | WKS | BPI | ALBUM TITLE | LABEL & NUMBER |
|---|---|---|---|---|---|
| 25/05/2002 | 54 | 2 | | EVERY DAY | Ninja Tune ZENCD 59 |

**GARY CLAIL ON-U SOUND SYSTEM** UK singer/producer with musical backing provided by musicians from Tackhead, Roots Radics, Akabu and Dub Syndicate. Clail, of Irish descent, grew up in Bristol.

| DATE | POS | WKS | BPI | ALBUM TITLE | LABEL & NUMBER |
|---|---|---|---|---|---|
| 04/05/1991 | 35 | 2 | | THE EMOTIONAL HOOLIGAN | Perfecto PL 74965 |

**CLANCY BROTHERS AND TOMMY MAKEM** Irish group formed in the 1950s by brothers Tom (born 1923, Carrick-on-Suir), Paddy (born 1923, Carrick-on-Suir) and Liam Clancy (born 1936, Carrick-on-Suir). Tom and Paddy emigrated to the USA during the late 1940s and were subsequently joined in 1956 by Liam and then Tommy Maken (born 1932, Keady, County Armagh) in a folk quartet that was immensely popular on both sides of the Atlantic. Makem left for a solo career in 1969. The original group reunited for an album and tour in 1984. Tom Clancy died from cancer on 7/11/1990, Paddy died from cancer on 11/11/1998.

| DATE | POS | WKS | BPI | ALBUM TITLE | LABEL & NUMBER |
|---|---|---|---|---|---|
| 16/04/1966 | 22 | 5 | | ISN'T IT GRAND BOYS | CBS BPG 62674 |

**CLANNAD** Irish folk band formed in Dublin in 1970 by Maire Ni Bhraonain (born 4/8/1952, Dublin), Pol O'Bhraonain, Calran O'Bhraonain and their uncles Noel O'Dugain and Padraig O'Dugain: *Clannad* is Gaelic for 'family'. They were joined by sister Enya Ni Bhraonain (born 17/5/1961) in 1980 who left in 1982 and emerged in 1988 as Enya. They won the 1998 Grammy Award for Best New Age Recording for *Landmarks*.

| DATE | POS | WKS | BPI | ALBUM TITLE | LABEL & NUMBER |
|---|---|---|---|---|---|
| 02/04/1983 | 26 | 21 | | MAGICAL RING | RCA RCALP 6072 |

○ Silver disc ● Gold disc ✪ Platinum disc (additional platinum units are indicated by a figure following the symbol) ❶⁹ Number of weeks album topped the UK chart

| 12/05/1984 | 15 | 40 | ● | LEGEND (MUSIC FROM ROBIN OF SHERWOOD) | RCA PL 70188 |
| 02/06/1984 | 91 | 1 | | MAGICAL RING | RCA PL 70003 |
| 26/10/1985 | 33 | 24 | ● | MACALLA | RCA PL 70894 |
| 07/11/1987 | 34 | 4 | | SIRIUS | RCA PL 71513 |
| 04/02/1989 | 41 | 3 | | ATLANTIC REALM Original TV soundtrack | BBC REB 727 |
| 06/05/1989 | 5 | 26 | ✪ | **PASTPRESENT** The album changed its catalogue number to 74321289812 during its chart run | RCA PL 74074/RCA 74321289812 |
| 20/10/1990 | 14 | 7 | O | ANAM | RCA PL 74762 |
| 15/05/1993 | 5 | 11 | | **BANBA** | RCA 74321139612 |
| 06/04/1996 | 14 | 7 | O | LORE | RCA 74321300802 |
| 31/05/1997 | 46 | 4 | | THE ULTIMATE COLLECTION | RCA 74321486742 |
| 11/04/1998 | 34 | 2 | | LANDMARKS 1998 Grammy Award for Best New Age Recording | RCA 74321560072 |
| 18/10/2003 | 23 | 4 | | THE BEST OF – IN A LIFETIME | RCA 82876564022 |

## ERIC CLAPTON

UK singer/guitarist (born Eric Clapp, 30/3/1945, Ripley) who joined the Yardbirds in 1963 and left in 1965 for John Mayall's Bluesbreakers. He then formed Cream with Ginger Baker and Jack Bruce. Blind Faith and tours with Delaney and Bonnie preceded his first solo record in 1970. One of the best guitarists of his era, he has had to overcome personal tragedies and drug addiction. He received the Outstanding Contribution to British Music Award at the 1987 BRIT Awards and was awarded an OBE in the 1995 New Year's Honours List. He also recorded as Derek And The Dominos. Eric has won fifteen Grammy Awards including: Best Rock Vocal Performance in 1990 for *Bad Love;* Record of the Year, Song of the Year (with Will Jennings) and Best Male Pop Vocal Performance in 1992 for *Tears In Heaven;* Best Rock Song in 1992 for *Layla* (even though it was originally written in 1972); Record of the Year and Best Male Pop Vocal Performance in 1996 for *Change The World;* Best Rock Instrumental Performance in 1996 with Jimmie Vaughan, Bonnie Raitt, Robert Cray, BB King, Buddy Guy, Dr John and Art Neville for *SRV Shuffle;* Best Male Pop Vocal Performance in 1998 for *My Father's Eyes;* Best Rock Instrumental in 1999 with Santana for *The Calling;* and Best Pop Instrumental Performance in 2001 for *Reptile*. He was inducted in to the Rock & Roll Hall of Fame in 2000 and was awarded a CBE in the 2004 New Year's Honours List.

| 30/07/1966 | 6 | 17 | | **BLUES BREAKERS** JOHN MAYALL WITH ERIC CLAPTON | Decca LK 4804 |
| 06/06/1970 | 39 | 3 | | ON TOUR WITH ERIC CLAPTON **DELANEY AND BONNIE AND FRIENDS FEATURING ERIC CLAPTON** | Atlantic 2400 013 |
| 05/09/1970 | 17 | 8 | | ERIC CLAPTON | Polydor 2383 021 |
| 26/08/1972 | 20 | 6 | | HISTORY OF ERIC CLAPTON | Polydor 2671 107 |
| 24/03/1973 | 36 | 1 | | DEREK AND THE DOMINOS IN CONCERT **DEREK AND THE DOMINOS** | RSO 2659 020 |
| 24/08/1974 | 3 | 19 | ● | **461 OCEAN BOULEVARD ▲⁴** | RSO 2479 118 |
| 12/04/1975 | 15 | 8 | O | THERE'S ONE IN EVERY CROWD | RSO 2479 132 |
| 13/09/1975 | 14 | 6 | O | E.C. WAS HERE | RSO 2394 160 |
| 11/09/1976 | 8 | 7 | O | **NO REASON TO CRY** | RSO 2479 179 |
| 26/11/1977 | 23 | 13 | ● | SLOWHAND | RSO 2479 201 |
| 09/12/1978 | 18 | 12 | O | BACKLESS | RSO RSD 5001 |
| 10/05/1980 | 3 | 12 | O | **JUST ONE NIGHT** | RSO RSDX 2 |
| 07/03/1981 | 3 | 8 | | ANOTHER TICKET | RSO RSD 5008 |
| 24/04/1982 | 20 | 16 | ● | TIME PIECES – THE BEST OF ERIC CLAPTON | RSO RSD 5010 |
| 19/02/1983 | 13 | 17 | | MONEY & CIGARETTES | Duck W 3773 |
| 09/06/1984 | 29 | 16 | | BACKTRACKIN' | Starblend ERIC 1 |
| 23/03/1985 | 8 | 14 | | BEHIND THE SUN | Duck 9251661 |
| 06/12/1986 | 3 | 46 | ✪ | **AUGUST** | Duck WX 71 |
| 26/09/1987 | 3 | 109 | ✪³ | **THE CREAM OF ERIC CLAPTON** ERIC CLAPTON AND CREAM | Polydor ECTV 1 |
| 18/11/1989 | 2 | 34 | ✪ | **JOURNEYMAN** | Duck WX 322 |
| 26/10/1991 | 17 | 7 | ● | 24 NIGHTS | Duck WX 373 |
| 12/09/1992 | 2 | 90 | ✪³ | **UNPLUGGED ▲³ ◆¹⁰** 1992 Grammy Awards for Album of the Year and Best Male Rock Vocal Performance | Duck 9362450242 |
| 24/09/1994 | ❶¹ | 18 | ✪ | **FROM THE CRADLE** ◇ ▲¹ 1994 Grammy Award for Best Traditional Blues Album | Duck 9362457352 |
| 21/03/1998 | 6 | 15 | ● | **PILGRIM** ◇ | Duck 9362465774 |
| 26/06/1999 | 52 | 2 | | BLUES | Polydor 5471782 |
| 30/10/1999 | 6 | 21 | ✪ | **CLAPTON CHRONICLES – THE BEST OF ERIC CLAPTON** ◇ | Duck 9362475642 |
| 24/06/2000 | 15 | 15 | ● | RIDING WITH THE KING ◇ **B.B. KING AND ERIC CLAPTON** 2000 Grammy Award for Best Traditional Blues Album ..... Reprise 9362476122 |
| 15/07/2000 | 73 | 2 | | TIME PIECES – THE BEST OF ERIC CLAPTON | Polydor 8000142 |
| 17/03/2001 | 7 | 7 | ● | **REPTILE** 2001 Grammy Award for Best Pop Instrumental Performance | Reprise 9362479662 |
| 16/11/2002 | 69 | 1 | | ONE MORE CAR ONE MORE RIDER | Reprise 9362483972 |
| 03/04/2004 | 10 | 8 | O | **ME AND MR JOHNSON** Tribute to blues guitarist Robert Johnson | Reprise 9362487302 |

## DAVE CLARK FIVE

UK group formed in London in 1958 by film stuntman Dave Clark (born 15/12/1942, Tottenham, London, drums) and Chris Walls (bass), who advertised for musicians, enrolling Rick Huxley (born 5/8/1942, Dartford, guitar), Stan Saxon (saxophone/vocals) and Mick Ryan (guitar). By 1961 they had a long-term residency on the Mecca ballroom circuit with a line-up of Clark, Huxley, Lenny Davidson (born 30/5/1944, Enfield, guitar/vocals), Denis Payton (born 11/8/1943, Walthamstow, saxophone) and Mike Smith (born 12/12/1943, Edmonton, keyboards/vocals). According to one US source, they were formed to raise funds for 'Tottenham Hotspurs' (sic). After two singles on Piccadilly they signed with Columbia in 1963, turning professional the following year. They made their first film (*Catch Us If You Can*) in 1965 and disbanded in 1970. Clark later wrote the musical *Time*.

| 18/04/1964 | 3 | 8 | | **A SESSION WITH THE DAVE CLARK FIVE** | Columbia 33SX 1598 |
| 14/08/1965 | 8 | 8 | | **CATCH US IF YOU CAN** | Columbia 33SX 1756 |
| 04/03/1978 | 7 | 10 | ● | **25 THUMPING GREAT HITS** | Polydor POLTV 7 |
| 17/04/1993 | 28 | 5 | | GLAD ALL OVER AGAIN | EMI CDEMTV 75 |

▲⁹ Number of weeks album topped the US chart   ◆¹² RIAA Diamond Awards   ◇³ IFPI Platinum Europe Awards

### GARY CLARK
UK singer/drummer/guitarist/keyboard player, previously with Danny Wilson and King L.90. His backing group featured his brother Kit, Karlos Edwards, Ged Grimes and Gary Thompson.

| 08/05/1993 | 25 | 2 | | TEN SHORT SONGS ABOUT LOVE | Circa CIRCD 23 |

### PETULA CLARK
UK singer (born 15/11/1932, Epsom) who was a child performer on radio during World War II and in over 150 shows between 1942–44. She made her first film, *Murder In Reverse*, in 1943, making more than twenty films over the next decade, including *Vice Versa* (1948), *The Happiness Of Three Women* (1954) and *The Runaway Bus* (1954). Her record debut was in 1949 for EMI's Columbia label (*Put Your Shoes On Lucy*), switching to Polygon in 1950 and remaining with them through label name changes of Nixa and Pye until 1971. Numerous US hits include two #1s (*Downtown* and *My Love*). She was popular in Europe (frequently singing in French) and was still recording in the 1990s. She was awarded a CBE in the 1998 New Year's Honours List.

| 30/07/1966 | 11 | 10 | | I COULDN'T LIVE WITHOUT YOUR LOVE | Pye NPL 18148 |
| 04/02/1967 | 18 | 13 | | HIT PARADE | Pye NPL 18159 |
| 18/02/1967 | 16 | 9 | | COLOUR MY WORLD | Pye NSPL 18171 |
| 07/10/1967 | 38 | 3 | | THESE ARE MY SONGS | Pye NSPL 18197 |
| 06/04/1968 | 37 | 1 | | THE OTHER MAN'S GRASS IS ALWAYS GREENER | Pye NSPL 18211 |
| 05/02/1977 | 18 | 7 | | 20 ALL TIME GREATEST | K-Tel NE 945 |
| 27/04/2002 | 18 | 4 | | THE ULTIMATE COLLECTION | Sanctuary SANDD 111 |

### DAVE CLARKE
UK DJ/producer who had previously recorded for XL and also set up the Magnetic North label.

| 17/02/1996 | 36 | 2 | | ARCHIVE ONE | Bush 74321320672 |

### GILBY CLARKE
US rock singer/guitarist, originally a member of Kill For Thrills, who recorded their debut album in 1990. He then replaced Izzy Staddlin' in Guns N Roses in 1991 and subsequently launched a parallel solo career in 1994. He was later a member of Snakepit with fellow Guns N Roses members Slash and Matt Sorum and subsequently became a member of Colonel Parker with Slim Jim Phantom (formerly of The Stray Cats), Muddy Stardust (formerly of L.A. Guns) and Teddy Andreadis (formerly of Slash's Snakepit), the first contemporary act signed to actor Mel Gibson's Icon Records label.

| 06/08/1994 | 39 | 1 | | PAWNSHOP GUITARS | Virgin CDVUS 76 |

### JOHN COOPER CLARKE
UK singer (born 25/1/1949, Manchester), known as the UK's only punk poet, who reads his poems to music invariably produced by Martin Hannett and featuring the Invisible Girls. For many years he provided the voice for the Sugar Puff's Honey Monster.

| 19/04/1980 | 26 | 7 | | SNAP CRACKLE AND BOP | Epic EPC 84083 |
| 05/06/1982 | 97 | 2 | | ZIP STYLE METHOD | Epic EPC 85667 |

### STANLEY CLARKE
US jazz bass guitarist (born 21/7/1951, Philadelphia, PA) who learned to play the violin, cello and double bass before switching to bass guitar. He studied at the Philadelphia Musical Academy before becoming a professional musician, playing with a number of R&B outfits before linking with jazz musician Horace Silver in 1970. He then went on to play with the likes of Joe Henderson and Pharoah Sanders before joining Chick Corea. He later formed a partnership with George Duke and formed Rite Of Strings in 1995 with Al DiMeola (guitar) and Jean Luc Ponty (violin).

| 12/07/1980 | 42 | 2 | | ROCK PEBBLES AND SAND | Epic EPC 84342 |

### KELLY CLARKSON
US singer (born 24/4/1982, Burleson, TX) who won *American Idol* in September 2002, with her debut single *A Moment Like This* rising from #52 to #1, the biggest ever leap to #1 in US chart history.

| 06/09/2003 | 52 | 4 | | THANKFUL | S 82876540882 |

### CLASH
UK rock group formed in London in 1976 by Mick Jones (born 26/6/1955, London, guitar), Paul Simonon (born 15/12/1955, London, bass), Keith Levene (guitar) and Terry Chimes (later calling himself Tory Crimes, drums), with Joe Strummer (born John Mellors, 21/8/1952, Ankara, Turkey, singer/guitarist) being persuaded to leave the 101ers to join them. Chimes left in 1977 as the group recorded their debut album and was replaced by Nicky 'Topper' Headon (born 30/5/1955, Bromley). With four top ten albums they were a massive draw live. Debut album *The Clash* was deemed unsuitable for US release, but still sold over 100,000 import copies. Headon left in 1983 and was replaced by Pete Howard; Strummer and Simonon announced Mick Jones' departure in September 1983. Jones formed Big Audio Dynamite, while after one more album (*Cut The Crap*) The Clash disbanded in 1986. In November 1987 Headon was jailed for fifteen months for supplying heroin to an addict who subsequently died. Strummer died from a heart attack on 22/12/2002. The group's *Westway To The World* video, directed by Don Letts, won the 2002 Grammy Award for Best Long Form Music Video. The group was inducted into the Rock & Roll Hall of Fame in 2003.

| 30/04/1977 | 12 | 16 | ● | THE CLASH | CBS 82000 |
| 25/11/1978 | 2 | 14 | ● | GIVE 'EM ENOUGH ROPE | CBS 82431 |
| 22/12/1979 | 9 | 20 | ● | LONDON CALLING | CBS CLASH 3 |
| 20/12/1980 | 19 | 9 | | SANDINISTA | CBS FSLN 1 |
| 22/05/1982 | 2 | 23 | ○ | COMBAT ROCK | CBS FMLN 2 |
| 16/11/1985 | 16 | 3 | ○ | CUT THE CRAP | CBS 26601 |
| 02/04/1988 | 7 | 21 | ● | THE STORY OF THE CLASH – VOLUME 1 | CBS 4602441 |
| 16/11/1991 | 68 | 2 | | THE SINGLES COLLECTION | Columbia 4689461 |
| 16/10/1999 | 13 | 3 | | FROM HERE TO ETERNITY | Columbia 4981832 |
| 16/10/1999 | 63 | 1 | | LONDON CALLING | Columbia 4953472 |
| 22/03/2003 | 18 | 3 | | THE ESSENTIAL CLASH | Columbia 05109982 |

### CLASSIX NOUVEAUX
UK group formed in London in 1979 by singer/songwriter Sal Solo (born 5/9/1954, Hatfield) with Gary Steadman (guitar), Mik Sweeney (bass/vocals) and BP Hurding (drums). Steadman left in 1982 to be replaced by Jimi Sumen. BP Hurding and Sumen left in 1984, replaced by Rick Driscoll and Paul Turley. They disbanded in 1985; Solo (living up to his name) went solo.

| | | | | | |
|---|---|---|---|---|---|
| 30/05/1981 | 66 | 2 | | NIGHT PEOPLE | Liberty LBG 30325 |
| 24/04/1982 | 44 | 4 | | LA VERITE | Liberty LBG 30346 |

### RICHARD CLAYDERMAN
French pianist (born Philippe Pages, 28/12/1953, Paris) who enrolled at the Conservatoire in Paris at the age of twelve. Although he studied classical piano his heart lay with rock and he performed on pop hits by the likes of Michel Sardou and Johnny Halliday. After a spell as a bank clerk he launched a solo career, offering interpretations of film themes and classical music. He has sold in excess of 60 million albums worldwide.

| | | | | | |
|---|---|---|---|---|---|
| 13/11/1982 | 2 | 64 | ✪ | INTRODUCING RICHARD CLAYDERMAN | Decca SKL 5329 |
| 08/10/1983 | 21 | 28 | ✪ | THE MUSIC OF RICHARD CLAYDERMAN | Decca SKL 5333 |
| 24/11/1984 | 28 | 21 | ● | THE MUSIC OF LOVE | Decca SKL 5340 |
| 01/12/1984 | 53 | 5 | | RICHARD CLAYDERMAN – CHRISTMAS | Decca SKL 5337 |
| 23/11/1985 | 17 | 18 | ● | THE CLASSIC TOUCH RICHARD CLAYDERMAN WITH THE ROYAL PHILHARMONIC ORCHESTRA | Decca SKL 5343 |
| 22/11/1986 | 28 | 9 | | HOLLYWOOD AND BROADWAY | Decca SKL 5344 |
| 28/11/1987 | 19 | 13 | ● | SONGS OF LOVE | Decca SKL 5345 |
| 03/12/1988 | 52 | 5 | | A LITTLE NIGHT MUSIC | Decca Delpine 8281251 |
| 25/11/1989 | 18 | 10 | | THE LOVE SONGS OF ANDREW LLOYD WEBBER | Decca Delpine 8281751 |
| 24/11/1990 | 29 | 7 | | MY CLASSIC COLLECTION RICHARD CLAYDERMAN WITH THE ROYAL PHILHARMONIC ORCHESTRA | Decca 8282281 |
| 09/11/1991 | 14 | 15 | ✪ | TOGETHER AT LAST RICHARD CLAYDERMAN AND JAMES LAST | Decca Delpine 5115251 |
| 14/11/1992 | 47 | 5 | ○ | THE VERY BEST OF RICHARD CLAYDERMAN RICHARD CLAYDERMAN WITH THE ROYAL PHILHARMONIC ORCHESTRA | Decca Delpine 8283362 |
| 19/11/1994 | 28 | 7 | ● | IN HARMONY RICHARD CLAYDERMAN AND JAMES LAST | Polydor 5238242 |
| 25/11/1995 | 65 | 2 | | THE CARPENTERS COLLECTION | Polygram TV 8286882 |
| 20/12/1997 | 73 | 1 | | THE BEST OF RICHARD CLAYDERMAN | Decca Delpine DTVCD 700 |
| 18/09/1999 | 62 | 1 | | WITH LOVE | Music Collection MCITV 002 |

### CLAYTOWN TROUPE
UK group formed by Christian Riou (vocals), Adrian Bennett (guitar), Paul Waterson (bass), Rick Williams (keyboards) and Andy Holt (drums).

| | | | | | |
|---|---|---|---|---|---|
| 21/10/1989 | 72 | 1 | | THROUGH THE EVIL | Island ILPS 9933 |

### CLEOPATRA
UK vocal trio of sisters Yonah (born 27/4/1984, Birmingham), Cleopatra (born 29/4/1982, Birmingham) and Zainam Higgins (born 5/12/1980, Birmingham). The girls were signed by Madonna's Maverick label for America. They also took part in the BRITS Trust Thank Abba For The Music project.

| | | | | | |
|---|---|---|---|---|---|
| 06/06/1998 | 20 | 4 | ○ | COMIN' ATCHA! | WEA 3984233562 |

### CLIMAX BLUES BAND
UK group formed in Stafford in 1968 by Colin Cooper (born 7/10/1939, Stafford, saxophone/vocals), Peter Haycock (born 4/4/1952, Stafford, guitar/vocals), Derek Holt (born 26/1/1949, Stafford, bass) and George Newsome (born 14/8/1947, Stafford, drums) as Climax Chicago Blues Band, with Richard Jones (bass) also a member at the time of their hit.

| | | | | | |
|---|---|---|---|---|---|
| 13/11/1976 | 56 | 1 | | GOLD PLATED | BTM BTM 1009 |

### CLIMIE FISHER
UK duo Simon Climie (born 7/4/1960, vocals/keyboards) and ex-Naked Eyes' Rob Fisher (born 5/11/1959, keyboards). Climie is also a songwriter – I Knew You Were Waiting (For Me) for George Michael and Aretha Franklin – and producer (Eric Clapton's The Pilgrim album). Fisher died after stomach surgery on 25/8/1999.

| | | | | | |
|---|---|---|---|---|---|
| 13/02/1988 | 14 | 36 | ● | EVERYTHING | EMI EMC 3538 |
| 21/10/1989 | 35 | 2 | | COMING IN FOR THE KILL | EMI EMC 3565 |

### PATSY CLINE
US singer (born Virginia Patterson Hensley, 8/9/1932, Gore, VA) who made her first record in 1955 and debuted at the Grand Old Opry the same year. She was killed in a plane crash, with Cowboy Copas and Hawkshaw Hawkins, on 5/3/1963 near Camden, TN. A film of her life, Sweet Dreams starring Jessica Lange, was made in 1985. She has a star on the Hollywood Walk of Fame.

| | | | | | |
|---|---|---|---|---|---|
| 19/01/1991 | 18 | 10 | ○ | SWEET DREAMS | MCA MCG 6003 |
| 19/01/1991 | 55 | 4 | | DREAMING | Platinum Musix PLAT 303 |
| 05/09/1992 | 11 | 8 | | THE DEFINITIVE PATSY CLINE 1932–1963 | Arcade ARC 94992 |
| 06/07/1996 | 21 | 6 | | THE VERY BEST OF PATSY CLINE | MCA MCD 11483 |

### CLIVILLES AND COLES – see C & C MUSIC FACTORY

### CLOCK
UK dance group formed by DJ and songwriter Stu Allen and Pete Pritchard. They later added O.D.C., M.C. and Tinka before Lorna Saunders and Che-Gun Peters became permanent members.

| | | | | | |
|---|---|---|---|---|---|
| 23/09/1995 | 27 | 2 | | IT'S TIME | Media MCD 11355 |

05/04/1997 . . . . . 56 . . . . . 2 . . . . . .     ABOUT TIME 2 . . . . . . . . . . . . . . . . . . . . . . . . . . . . . . . . . . . . . . Media MCD 60032

**COAL CHAMBER** US group formed in Los Angeles, CA in 1994 by Brad 'B Dez' Fafara (vocals), Miguel 'Meegs' Rascon (guitar), Rayna Foss (bass) and Mike 'Mikee' Cox (drums). They were initially due to sign with Roadrunner in 1994 but Fafara suddenly quit the band after disagreements with his wife! He changed his mind the following year and returned and the group signed with Roadrunner at the end of 1995, although the Fafara's marriage ended at around the same time!

18/09/1999 . . . . . 21 . . . . . . 2 . . . . . .     CHAMBER MUSIC . . . . . . . . . . . . . . . . . . . . . . . . . . . . . . . . . . . . . Roadrunner RR 86592
18/05/2002 . . . . . 43 . . . . . . 2 . . . . . .     DARK DAYS . . . . . . . . . . . . . . . . . . . . . . . . . . . . . . . . . . . . . . . . Roadrunner RR 84849

**LUIS COBOS** Spanish orchestra leader whose debut hit album featured the Royal Philharmonic Orchestra, Chorus Royal Opera House and the London Symphony Orchestra.

21/04/1990 . . . . . 72 . . . . . . 1 . . . . . .     OPERA EXTRAVAGANZA . . . . . . . . . . . . . . . . . . . . . . . . . . . . . . . . . . Epic MOOD 12

**EDDIE COCHRAN** US singer (born Edward Ray Cochrane, 3/10/1938, Oklahoma City, OK, raised in Minnesota). After moving to Bell Gardens in California in 1953 he teamed up with Hank Cochran (no relation) as the Cochran Brothers, who recorded for Ekko Records in 1954 as a country act. They parted in 1956, Eddie making a single for Crest before landing roles in a number of films. A popular live act, he was on a UK tour in 1960 when the car carrying him and Gene Vincent (on the London-bound A4) skidded into a lamppost. Vincent suffered numerous fractures but Cochran was thrown head first through the windscreen, dying sixteen hours later on 17/4/1960 without regaining consciousness. He was inducted into the Rock & Roll Hall of Fame in 1987.

30/07/1960 . . . . . 19 . . . . . 1 . . . . . .     SINGING TO MY BABY . . . . . . . . . . . . . . . . . . . . . . . . . . . . . . . . . . London HAU 2093
01/10/1960 . . . . . 9 . . . . . 12 . . . . . .     **THE EDDIE COCHRAN MEMORIAL ALBUM** . . . . . . . . . . . . . . . . . . . . London HAG 2267
12/01/1963 . . . . . 15 . . . . . 3 . . . . . .     CHERISHED MEMORIES . . . . . . . . . . . . . . . . . . . . . . . . . . . . . . . . Liberty LBY 1109
20/04/1963 . . . . . 11 . . . . . 18 . . . . . .     THE EDDIE COCHRAN MEMORIAL ALBUM . . . . . . . . . . . . . . . . . . . . . Liberty LBY 1127
19/10/1963 . . . . . 20 . . . . . 1 . . . . . .     SINGING TO MY BABY . . . . . . . . . . . . . . . . . . . . . . . . . . . . . . . . . Liberty LBY 1158
09/05/1970 . . . . . 34 . . . . . 3 . . . . . .     VERY BEST OF EDDIE COCHRAN . . . . . . . . . . . . . . . . . . . . . . . . . . Liberty LBS 83337
18/08/1979 . . . . . 39 . . . . . 6 . . . . . O     THE EDDIE COCHRAN SINGLES ALBUM . . . . . . . . . . . . . . . . . . . United Artists UAK 30244
16/04/1988 . . . . . 53 . . . . . 3 . . . . . .     C'MON EVERYBODY . . . . . . . . . . . . . . . . . . . . . . . . . . . . . . . . . . . Liberty ECR 1

**BRENDA COCHRANE** Irish singer who first came to prominence winning the televison talent series *Opportunity Knocks*.

14/04/1990 . . . . . 14 . . . . . 11 . . . . . . ●     THE VOICE . . . . . . . . . . . . . . . . . . . . . . . . . . . . . . . . . . . . . . . . Polydor 8431411
06/04/1991 . . . . . 55 . . . . . 3 . . . . . .     IN DREAMS . . . . . . . . . . . . . . . . . . . . . . . . . . . . . . . . . . . . . . . Polydor 8490341

JOE COCKER
GREATEST HITS

**JOE COCKER** UK singer (born John Robert Cocker, 20/5/1944, Sheffield) who formed his own skiffle group the Cavaliers in 1960 and signed his first contract with Decca in 1964 while working for the Gas Board. After little success he returned to the Gas Board, forming the Grease Band in 1965, and two years later signed with Regal Zonophone in 1968. He hit #1 in the UK with a cover of The Beatles' *With A Little Help From My Friends* (who were so impressed they sent him a telegram of congratulations). Subsequent appearances at Woodstock, Filmore and the Isle of Wight broadened his appeal. He took part in the *It's Only Rock 'N' Roll* project for the Children's Promise charity. He won the 1982 Grammy Award for Best Vocal Performance by a Duo with Jennifer Warnes for *Up Where We Belong*.

26/09/1970 . . . . . 16 . . . . . 8 . . . . . .     MAD DOGS AND ENGLISHMEN . . . . . . . . . . . . . . . . . . . . . . . . . . . A&M AMLS 6002
06/05/1972 . . . . . 29 . . . . . 4 . . . . . .     JOE COCKER/WITH A LITTLE HELP FROM MY FRIENDS . . . . . . . . . . . Double Back TOOFA 1/2
30/06/1984 . . . . 100 . . . . . 1 . . . . . .     A CIVILISED MAN . . . . . . . . . . . . . . . . . . . . . . . . . . . . . . . . . . . Capitol EJ 2401391
11/04/1992 . . . . . 25 . . . . . 14 . . . . . O     NIGHT CALLS . . . . . . . . . . . . . . . . . . . . . . . . . . . . . . . . . . . . Capitol CDESTU 2167
27/06/1992 . . . . . 4 . . . . . 20 . . . . . .     **THE LEGEND – THE ESSENTIAL COLLECTION** . . . . . . . . . . . . . . . Polygram TV 5154112
17/09/1994 . . . . . 9 . . . . . 15 . . . . . ✪     HAVE A LITTLE FAITH ◇ . . . . . . . . . . . . . . . . . . . . . . . . . . . . . . . Capitol CDEST 2233
26/10/1996 . . . . . 49 . . . . . 1 . . . . . .     ORGANIC . . . . . . . . . . . . . . . . . . . . . . . . . . . . . . . . . . . . . Parlophone CDESTD 6
20/02/1999 . . . . . 24 . . . . . 2 . . . . . .     GREATEST HITS ◇ . . . . . . . . . . . . . . . . . . . . . . . . . . . . . . . . . . . EMI 4977192
23/10/1999 . . . . . 63 . . . . . 1 . . . . . .     NO ORDINARY WORLD . . . . . . . . . . . . . . . . . . . . . . . . . . . . . . Parlophone 5230912
15/06/2002 . . . . . 51 . . . . . 2 . . . . . .     RESPECT YOURSELF . . . . . . . . . . . . . . . . . . . . . . . . . . . . . . . . . . . Parlophone

**COCKNEY REBEL** — see STEVE HARLEY

**COCKNEY REJECTS** UK punk group formed in London in 1978 by Jefferson 'Stinky' Turner (vocals), Vince Riordan (bass), Micky Geggus (guitar) and Keith Warrington (drums). They disbanded in 1985, re-forming in 1990.

15/03/1980 . . . . . 22 . . . . . 11 . . . . .     GREATEST HITS VOLUME 1 . . . . . . . . . . . . . . . . . . . . . . . . . . . . Zonophone ZONO 101
25/10/1980 . . . . . 23 . . . . . 3 . . . . .     GREATEST HITS VOLUME 2 . . . . . . . . . . . . . . . . . . . . . . . . . . . . Zonophone ZONO 102
18/04/1981 . . . . . 27 . . . . . 3 . . . . .     GREATEST HITS VOLUME 3 (LIVE AND LOUD) . . . . . . . . . . . . . . . . . Zonophone ZEM 101

**COCTEAU TWINS** UK group formed in Grangemouth in 1981 by Elizabeth Fraser (born 29/8/1958, Grangemouth, vocals), Robin Guthrie (born 4/1/1962, Grangemouth, bass/drum programming/keyboards) and Will Heggie. Heggie left in 1984 and was replaced by Simon Raymonde (born 3/4/1962, London, bass/piano/keyboards). Guthrie and Raymonde launched the Bella Union label in 1997. Fraser has also recorded with the Future Sound Of London, Massive Attack and Ian McCulloch.

29/10/1983 . . . . . 51 . . . . . 15 . . . . . O     HEAD OVER HEELS . . . . . . . . . . . . . . . . . . . . . . . . . . . . . . . . . . 4AD CAD 313
24/11/1984 . . . . . 29 . . . . . 8 . . . . . O     TREASURE . . . . . . . . . . . . . . . . . . . . . . . . . . . . . . . . . . . . . . . 4AD CAD 412
26/04/1986 . . . . . 10 . . . . . 7 . . . . . .     **VICTORIALAND** . . . . . . . . . . . . . . . . . . . . . . . . . . . . . . . . . . . 4AD CAD 602

| 22/11/1986 | 46 | 2 | | THE MOON AND THE MELODIES **HAROLD BUDD, ELIZABETH FRASER, ROBIN GUTHRIE & SIMON RAYMONDE** | 4AD CAD 611 |
| 01/10/1988 | 15 | 4 | | BLUE BELL KNOLL | 4AD CAD 807 |
| 29/09/1990 | 7 | 5 | O | **HEAVEN OR LAS VEGAS** | 4AD CAD 0012 |
| 30/10/1993 | 13 | 3 | | FOUR-CALENDAR CAFE | Fontana 5182592 |
| 27/04/1996 | 17 | 3 | | MILK & KISSES | Fontana 5045012 |
| 28/10/2000 | 63 | 1 | | STARS AND TOPSOIL – A COLLECTION 1982–1990 | 4AD CAD2K 019CD |

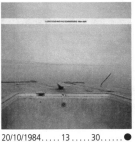

## LEONARD COHEN

Canadian singer (born 21/9/1934, Montreal) who first came to prominence as a novelist, penning *The Favourite Game* and *Beautiful Losers* during the 1960s, before he turned to writing songs. Some of his earliest songs were covered by Judy Collins and Tim Hardin, and prompted the launch of a solo career in 1968. His appeal fluctuated thereafter, although former Cohen backing singer Jennifer Warnes' 1987 album *Famous Blue Raincoat*, which comprised solely of songs written by Cohen, revived interest in his work. He later became a Buddhist monk, adopting the name Jikan (meaning 'ordinary silence').

| 31/08/1968 | 13 | 71 | | SONGS OF LEONARD COHEN | CBS 63241 |
| 03/05/1969 | 2 | 26 | | **SONGS FROM A ROOM** | CBS 63587 |
| 24/04/1971 | 4 | 18 | | **SONGS OF LOVE AND HATE** | CBS 69004 |
| 28/09/1974 | 24 | 3 | O | NEW SKIN FOR THE OLD CEREMONY | CBS 69087 |
| 10/12/1977 | 35 | 5 | | DEATH OF A LADIES MAN | CBS 86042 |
| 16/02/1985 | 52 | 6 | | VARIOUS POSITIONS | CBS 26222 |
| 27/02/1988 | 48 | 13 | O | I'M YOUR MAN | CBS 4606421 |
| 06/08/1988 | 99 | 1 | O | GREATEST HITS | CBS 32644 |
| 05/12/1992 | 36 | 3 | O | THE FUTURE | Columbia 4724982 |
| 06/08/1994 | 35 | 4 | | COHEN LIVE | Columbia 4771712 |
| 20/10/2001 | 26 | 3 | | TEN NEW SONGS | Columbia 5012022 |
| 01/02/2003 | 70 | 1 | | THE ESSENTIAL | Columbia 4979952 |

## MARC COHN

US singer/pianist/songwriter (born 5/7/1959, Cleveland, OH); he formed a fourteen-piece band called the Supreme Court and was discovered by Carly Simon. He performed at the wedding of Caroline Kennedy and won the 1991 Grammy Award for Best New Artist.

| 29/06/1991 | 27 | 20 | ● | MARC COHN | Atlantic 7567821781 |
| 12/06/1993 | 24 | 3 | | THE RAINY SEASON | Atlantic 7567824912 |

## COLDCUT

UK duo Matt Black and Jonathan Moore who also remix other people's hits. They launched their own Ahead Of Our Time and Ninjas Tune labels.

| 29/04/1989 | 20 | 4 | O | WHAT'S THAT NOISE | Ahead Of Our Time CCUTLP 1 |
| 20/09/1997 | 33 | 1 | | LET US PLAY! | Ninja Tune ZENCD 30 |

## COLDPLAY

UK rock group formed in London in January 1998 by Chris Martin (born 2/3/1977, Exeter, guitar/keyboards/vocals), Jonny Buckland (born 11/9/1977, Mold, guitar), Guy Berryman (born 12/4/1978, Kirkcaldy, bass) and Will Champion (born 31/7/1978, Southampton, drums) as Starfish, then changing their name to Coldplay. Financing their first release, they also recorded for Fierce Panda before linking with Parlophone in 1999. They won two BRIT Awards in 2001 including Best UK Group, and two BRITS in 2003, including Best UK Group once again. They have also won four Grammy Awards including Best Rock Performance By A Duo Or Group With Vocal for *In My Place* the same year and Record of the Year in 2003 for *Clocks*. They also won the 2002 MTV Europe Music Award for Select UK & Ireland Act and the 2003 award for Best Group. Martin married actress Gwyneth Paltrow in December 2003 and the couple had a daughter, Apple, in May 2004.

| 22/07/2000 | ●[1] | 111 | ✪[7] | **PARACHUTES** ◇[2] 2001 BRIT Award for Best Album and 2001 Grammy Award for Best Alternative Music Album Parlophone 5277832 |
| 07/09/2002 | ●[3] | 86 | ✪[7] | **A RUSH OF BLOOD TO THE HEAD** ◇[3] 2003 BRIT Award for Best Album and 2002 Grammy Award for Best Alternative Music Album ... Parlophone 5405042 |

## LLOYD COLE AND THE COMMOTIONS

UK singer (born 31/1/1961, Buxton, guitar/vocals) who formed the Commotions in 1983 with Blair Cowan (keyboards), Neil Clark (born 3/7/1955, guitar), Steven Irvine (born 16/12/1959, drums) and Lawrence Donegan (born 13/7/1961, bass). They signed with Polydor on the strength of demo tapes and local gigs. The group disbanded in 1989 and Cole went solo.

| 20/10/1984 | 13 | 30 | ● | RATTLESNAKES | Polydor LCLP 1 |

| | DATE | POS | WKS | BPI | ALBUM TITLE | LABEL & NUMBER |
|---|---|---|---|---|---|---|
| | 30/11/1985 | 5 | 18 | ● | EASY PIECES | Polydor LCLP 2 |
| | 07/11/1987 | 9 | 20 | ● | MAINSTREAM | Polydor LCLP 3 |
| | 08/04/1989 | 14 | 7 | ● | 1984–1989 LLOYD COLE: | Polydor 8377361 |
| | 03/03/1990 | 11 | 6 | ○ | LLOYD COLE | Polydor 8419071 |
| | 28/09/1991 | 21 | 3 | | DON'T GET WEIRD ON ME BABE | Polydor 5110931 |
| | 23/10/1993 | 38 | 2 | | BAD VIBES | Fontana 5183182 |
| | 07/10/1995 | 27 | 2 | | LOVE STORY | Fontana 5285292 |
| | 23/01/1999 | 24 | 4 | | THE COLLECTION | Mercury 5381042 |

**MJ COLE** UK producer Matt Coleman who won the 2000 MOBO Award for Best Producer.

| | DATE | POS | WKS | BPI | ALBUM TITLE | LABEL & NUMBER |
|---|---|---|---|---|---|---|
| | 19/08/2000 | 14 | 4 | ○ | SINCERE | Talkin Loud 5425792 |

**NAT 'KING' COLE** US singer/pianist (born Nathaniel Adams Coles, 17/3/1917, Montgomery, AL, raised in Chicago, IL) who formed the Royal Dukes in 1934 and recorded two years later with his brother Eddie. In 1939 he formed a trio with Oscar Moore (guitar) and Wesley Prince (bass), who was later replaced by Johnny Miller. The trio's success led to his going solo in 1950. He later moved into films, which included *St Louis Blues* (1958), an inaccurate biopic of WC Handy, and *Cat Ballou* (1965). He won one Grammy Award during his career: Best Performance by a Top 40 Artist in 1959 for *Midnight Flyer*. However, his 1946 recording *The Christmas Song* was honoured with a Grammy Hall of Fame award in 1974 (and daughter Natalie won three awards in 1991 for her use of his vocal on *Unforgettable* and a further award in 1996 for *When I Fall In Love*). He stopped performing in 1964 due to ill health and died from lung cancer on 15/2/1965. Inducted into the Rock & Roll Hall of Fame in 2000, he has a star on the Hollywood Walk of Fame for his contribution to recording, and a second star for TV.

| | DATE | POS | WKS | BPI | ALBUM TITLE | LABEL & NUMBER |
|---|---|---|---|---|---|---|
| | 18/05/1957 | ●[1] | 14 | | LOVE IS THE THING | Capitol LCT 6129 |
| | 19/08/1961 | 12 | 9 | | STRING ALONG WITH NAT 'KING' COLE | Encore ENC 102 |
| | 20/10/1962 | 8 | 7 | | NAT 'KING' COLE SINGS AND THE GEORGE SHEARING QUARTET PLAYS NAT 'KING COLE/GEORGE SHEARING QUARTET | Capitol W 1675 |
| | 27/03/1965 | 11 | 8 | | UNFORGETTABLE NAT 'KING' COLE | Capitol W 20664 |
| | 07/12/1968 | 5 | 18 | | THE BEST OF NAT 'KING' COLE | Capitol ST 21139 |
| | 05/12/1970 | 39 | 2 | | THE BEST OF NAT 'KING' COLE VOLUME 2 | Capitol ST 21687 |
| | 27/11/1971 | 45 | 1 | | WHITE CHRISTMAS NAT 'KING' COLE AND DEAN MARTIN | MFP 5224 |
| | 08/04/1978 | ●[3] | 37 | ✪ | 20 GOLDEN GREATS | Capitol EMTV 9 |
| | 20/11/1982 | 7 | 26 | ✪ | 20 GREATEST LOVE SONGS | Capitol EMTV 35 |
| | 26/11/1988 | 25 | 9 | ● | CHRISTMAS WITH NAT 'KING' COLE | Stylus SMR 868 |
| | 23/11/1991 | 23 | 9 | | THE UNFORGETTABLE NAT 'KING' COLE | EMI EMTV 61 |
| | 20/11/1999 | 26 | 7 | ● | THE ULTIMATE COLLECTION | EMI 4995752 |
| | 15/02/2003 | 20 | 3 | ○ | LOVE SONGS | Capitol 05815132 |

**NATALIE COLE** US singer (born 6/2/1950, Los Angeles, CA) and daughter of Nat 'King' Cole. She made her debut aged eleven, and was working as a club singer when she met producers Charles Jackson and Marvin Yancy in 1973 and landed a deal with Capitol in 1975. She married Yancy, later divorced him and married ex-Rufus drummer Andre Fischer. She has won eight Grammy Awards: Best New Artist in 1975; Best Rhythm & Blues Vocal Performance in 1975 for *This Will Be;* Best Rhythm & Blues Vocal Performance in 1976 for *Sophisticated Lady;* Record of the Year, Album of the Year and Best Traditional Pop Vocal Performance in 1991 for *Unforgettable* (which won the Song of the Year award for writer Irving Gordon); Best Jazz Vocal Performance in 1993 for *Take A Look;* and Best Pop Collaboration with Vocals in 1996 for *When I Fall In Love*. She has a star on the Hollywood Walk of Fame.

| | DATE | POS | WKS | BPI | ALBUM TITLE | LABEL & NUMBER |
|---|---|---|---|---|---|---|
| | 17/09/1983 | 5 | 16 | | UNFORGETTABLE: A MUSICAL TRIBUTE TO NAT KING COLE JOHNNY MATHIS AND NATALIE COLE | CBS 10042 |
| | 07/05/1988 | 62 | 4 | ○ | EVERLASTING | Manhattan MTL 1012 |
| | 20/05/1989 | 10 | 12 | ● | GOOD TO BE BACK | EMI-USA MTL 1042 |
| | 27/07/1991 | 11 | 29 | ● | UNFORGETTABLE – WITH LOVE ▲[5] 1991 Grammy Award for Album of the Year | Elektra EKT 91 |
| | 26/06/1993 | 16 | 4 | | TAKE A LOOK | Elektra 7559614962 |
| | 30/11/2002 | 63 | 1 | | ASK A WOMAN WHO KNOWS | Verve AA3145897742 |

**PAULA COLE** US singer/songwriter/producer (born 5/4/1968, Rockport, MA) who was previously in Peter Gabriel's backing band. She won the Best New Artist award at the 1997 Grammy Awards and appeared in the 1998 film *Don't Explain*.

| | DATE | POS | WKS | BPI | ALBUM TITLE | LABEL & NUMBER |
|---|---|---|---|---|---|---|
| | 26/07/1997 | 60 | 1 | | THIS FIRE | Warner Brothers 9362464242 |

**DAVE AND ANSIL COLLINS** Jamaican duo of session singer Dave Barker and keyboard player Ansell Collins who linked in 1971. Ansell's forename has caused confusion ever since – he was billed Ansil on the hit single but records as Ansell solo.

| | DATE | POS | WKS | BPI | ALBUM TITLE | LABEL & NUMBER |
|---|---|---|---|---|---|---|
| | 07/08/1971 | 41 | 2 | | DOUBLE BARREL | Trojan TBL 162 |

**EDWYN COLLINS** UK singer (born 23/8/1959, Edinburgh) and a member of the Nu-Sonics before singing lead with Orange Juice in 1979.

| | DATE | POS | WKS | BPI | ALBUM TITLE | LABEL & NUMBER |
|---|---|---|---|---|---|---|
| | 22/07/1995 | 8 | 8 | ○ | GORGEOUS GEORGE | Setanta AHOAON 058 |
| | 13/09/1997 | 55 | 1 | | I'M NOT FOLLOWING YOU | Setanta SETCD 039 |

**JUDY COLLINS** US singer (born 1/5/1939, Seattle, WA, raised in Denver) who originally trained as a classical pianist but became involved in folk music from the mid-1950s. She turned professional in 1959 and signed with Elektra in 1961, initially recording traditional folk before more contemporary material. She was awarded the 1968 Best Folk Recording Grammy for *Both Sides Now*. By the 1990s she was still recording and had also become an author.

| | DATE | POS | WKS | BPI | ALBUM TITLE | LABEL & NUMBER |
|---|---|---|---|---|---|---|
| | 10/04/1971 | 37 | 2 | | WHALES AND NIGHTINGALES | Elektra EKS 75010 |

○ Silver disc ● Gold disc ✪ Platinum disc (additional platinum units are indicated by a figure following the symbol) ●[9] Number of weeks album topped the UK chart

31/05/1975 ..... 7 ...... 12 ...... JUDITH ........................................................................ Elektra K 52019
14/12/1985 ..... 34 ...... 4 ...... AMAZING GRACE ................................................................ Elektra STAR 2265

**PHIL COLLINS** UK singer/drummer (born 31/1/1951, London), a former child actor, he joined Genesis as drummer in 1970, assuming the dual role of lead singer when Peter Gabriel left in 1975. In 1981 he went solo, was in demand as a producer (Adam Ant and Philip Bailey) and played with the progressive jazz-rock outfit Brand X. He appeared in the 1988 film *Buster* (Best Soundtrack at the 1989 BRIT Awards) and later *Frauds,* and was named Best British Male at the 1986, 1989 and 1990 BRIT Awards, and in 1990 he won Best Single Award for *Another Day In Paradise*. He has also won six Grammy Awards including: Best Pop Vocal Performance in 1984 for *Against All Odds;* Producer of the Year in 1985 with Hugh Padgham; Best Song Written Specifically for a Motion Picture in 1988 with Lamont Dozier for *Two Hearts;* and Record of the Year in 1990 for *Another Day In Paradise*. In 2000 he won an Oscar for Best Film Song with *You'll Be In My Heart* from the Walt Disney film *Tarzan* (1999). He has a star on the Hollywood Walk of Fame.

21/02/1981 .... ❶³ .... 274 .... ✪⁵ **FACE VALUE** ................................................................. Virgin V 2185
13/11/1982 ..... 2 ..... 163 ..... ✪³ **HELLO, I MUST BE GOING** ................................................... Virgin V 2252
02/03/1985 .... ❶⁵ .... 176 .... ✪⁶ **NO JACKET REQUIRED** ▲⁷ ◆¹² 1986 BRIT Award for Best Album and 1985 Grammy Awards for Album of the Year and Best Pop Vocal Performance ................................................................................ Virgin V 2345
02/12/1989 ... ❶¹⁵ .... 72 ..... ✪⁸ **... BUT SERIOUSLY** ▲³ ................................................... Virgin V 2620
17/11/1990 ..... 2 ..... 50 ..... ✪⁴ **SERIOUS HITS... LIVE!** ................................................... Virgin PCLP 1
20/11/1993 ... ❶¹ .... 21 ..... ✪² **BOTH SIDES OF THE STORY** ................................................ Virgin CDV 2800
02/11/1996 ..... 4 ..... 13 ..... ● **DANCE INTO THE LIGHT** ◇ ........................................... Face Value 0630160002
17/10/1998 ... ❶¹ .... 27 ..... ✪⁴ **HITS** ◇³ ....................................................... Virgin CDV 2870
23/11/2002 ..... 15 ..... 7 ..... ● **TESTIFY** ◇ ................................................... Face Value 5046614842
12/06/2004 ..... 4 ..... 3+ ..... ○ **THE PLATINUM COLLECTION** This is a triple album containing *Face Value, No Jacket Required* and *... But Seriously* Virgin PHILCD1

**WILLIE COLLINS** US singer (born in New York) who was working as a postman before being discovered as a singer and signing with Capitol Records.
14/06/1986 ..... 97 ...... 1 ...... WHERE ARE YOU GONNA BE TONIGHT? .................................. Capitol EST 2012

**COLOR ME BADD** US vocal group formed in high school in Oklahoma City, OK by Bryan Abrams (born 16/11/1969), Sam Watters (born 23/7/1970), Mark Calderon (born 27/9/1970) and Kevin Thomton (born 17/6/1969). Spotted by Robert Bell (of Kool & The Gang), the dance-orientated group relocated to New York.
24/08/1991 ..... 3 ..... 22 ..... ● **C.M.B** ................................................................... Giant WX 425

**COLOSSEUM** UK jazz rock group formed in 1968 by Jon Hiseman (born 21/6/1944, London, drums), Dick Hestall-Smith (born 26/9/1934, Ludlow, saxophone), Dave Greenslade (born 18/1/1943, Woking, keyboards), Tony Reeves (born 18/4/1943, London, bass) and James Litherland (born 6/9/1949, Manchester, guitar/vocals). Litherland left the group in 1969 and was replaced by Clem Clempson (born on 5/9/1949). Chris Farlowe joined in 1970, the same year Reeves left to be replaced by Mark Clarke. Colosseum disbanded in 1971, with Hiseman and Clarke going on to form Tempest. They re-formed in 1975 as Colosseum II, with Hiseman, Gary Moore (guitar), Neil Murray (bass), Don Airey (keyboards) and Mike Starrs (vocals). This outfit lasted for three albums before disbanding.
17/05/1969 ..... 15 ...... 1 ...... COLOSSEUM ................................................................. Fontana S 5510
22/11/1969 ..... 15 ...... 2 ...... VALENTYNE SUITE ............................................................ Vertigo VO 1
05/12/1970 ..... 23 ...... 5 ...... DAUGHTER OF TIME ....................................................... Vertigo 6360 017
26/06/1971 ..... 17 ...... 6 ...... COLOSSEUM LIVE ............................................................ Bronze ICD 1

**COLOUR FIELD** UK group formed in Coventry in 1983 by former Specials and Fun Boy Three member Terry Hall (born 19/3/1959, Coventry, vocals) with Karl Sharle (bass), Paul Burgess (drums) and Toby Lyons (guitar/keyboards). Burgess left in 1985 and was replaced by Gary Dwyer. The group dissolved in 1987 with Hall subsequently recording solo.
04/05/1985 ..... 12 ...... 7 ...... VIRGINS AND PHILISTINES ............................................... Chrysalis CHR 1480
04/04/1987 ..... 95 ...... 1 ...... DECEPTION ................................................................ Chrysalis CDL 1546

**COLOURBOX** UK group formed in 1981 by Martyn Young, his brother Steven and Debian Curry. They released their debut on 4AD in 1982. Curry left soon after and was replaced by Lorita Grahame. The Young brothers teamed up with Alex and Rudi Kane, of fellow 4AD group AR Kane, to record as M/A/R/R/S.
24/08/1985 ..... 67 ...... 2 ...... COLOURBOX ................................................................. 4AD CAD 508

**SHAWN COLVIN** US female singer/guitarist (born 10/1/1958, Vermillion, SD) who taught herself to play guitar at the age of ten. Formerly a member of Suzanne Vega's backing group, she has won three Grammy Awards: Best Contemporary Folk Recording in 1990 for *Steady On* and Record of the Year and Song of the Year in 1997 for *Sunny Came Home*.
17/09/1994 ..... 67 ...... 1 ...... COVER GIRL ................................................................. Columbia 4772402

**COMIC RELIEF** UK charity ensemble of comedians organised to raise funds for Comic Relief.
10/05/1986 ..... 10 ...... 8 ...... **COMIC RELIEF PRESENTS UTTERLY UTTERLY LIVE!** ....................................... WEA WX 51

---

▲⁹ Number of weeks album topped the US chart ◆¹² RIAA Diamond Awards ◇³ IFPI Platinum Europe Awards

**COMMITMENTS** Irish group assembled by film director Alan Parker for the film *The Commitments*. The story line concerned a soul tribute group assembled in Dublin and featured Andrew Strong on lead vocals with Robert Arkins, Michael Aherne, Angeline Ball, Maria Doyle, Dave Finnegan, Bronagh Gallagher, Felim Gormley, Glen Hansard, Dick Massey, Johnny Murphy and Kenneth McCluskey also appearing in the film.

| | | | | | |
|---|---|---|---|---|---|
| 26/10/1991 | 4 | 136 | ✪³ | **THE COMMITMENTS** Original soundtrack to the film. 1992 BRIT Award for Best Soundtrack Album | MCA 10286 |
| 25/04/1992 | 13 | 11 | ● | THE COMMITMENTS VOLUME 2 | MCA MCAD 10506 |

**COMMODORES** US R&B group formed in Tuskegee, AL in 1967 by Lionel Richie (born 20/6/1949, Tuskegee, vocals/piano/saxophone), William King (born 30/1/1949, Alabama, trumpet), Thomas McClary (born 6/10/1950, guitar) and Milan Williams (born 28/3/1948, Mississippi, keyboards) as the Mighty Mystics, with Ronald LaPread (born 4/9/1946, Alabama, bass) and Walter 'Clyde' Orange (born 10/12/1947, Florida, drums) joining in 1969, by which time they were the Commodores, having picked the name at random from a dictionary. After one single for Atlantic they were signed by Motown in 1972. They formed their own backing band the Mean Machine and appeared in the 1978 film *Thank God It's Friday*. Richie left to go solo in 1982. McClary also recorded solo in 1983. By 1993 the group was down to a trio of Orange, King and ex-Heatwave singer J D Nicholas (born 12/4/1952, Watford). The group won the 1985 Grammy Award for Best Rhythm & Blues Vocal Performance by a Group for *Nightshift*.

| | | | | | |
|---|---|---|---|---|---|
| 13/05/1978 | 60 | 1 | | COMMODORES LIVE! | Motown TMSP 6007 |
| 10/06/1978 | 8 | 23 | ● | **NATURAL HIGH** | Motown STML 12087 |
| 02/12/1978 | 19 | 16 | ● | GREATEST HITS | Motown STML 12100 |
| 18/08/1979 | 15 | 25 | ● | MIDNIGHT MAGIC | Motown STMA 8032 |
| 28/06/1980 | 50 | 5 | | HEROES | Motown STMA 8034 |
| 18/07/1981 | 69 | 5 | | IN THE POCKET | Motown STML 12156 |
| 14/08/1982 | 5 | 28 | ● | **LOVE SONGS** | K-Tel NE 1171 |
| 23/02/1985 | 13 | 10 | | NIGHTSHIFT | Motown ZL 72343 |
| 09/11/1985 | 25 | 13 | ● | THE VERY BEST OF THE COMMODORES – 16 CLASSIC TRACKS | Telstar STAR 2249 |
| 06/05/1995 | 26 | 3 | | THE VERY BEST OF THE COMMODORES | Motown 5305472 |
| 22/11/2003 | 10 | 20 | ✪ | **THE DEFINITIVE COLLECTION** LIONEL RICHIE/THE COMMODORES | Universal TV 9861394 |

**COMMUNARDS** UK duo formed in 1985 by ex-Bronski Beat singer Jimmy Somerville (born 22/6/1961, Glasgow) and keyboard player Richard Coles (born 23/6/1962, Northampton). They were going to be called The Committee but the name was already in use. They disbanded in 1988 and Somerville went solo the following year.

| | | | | | |
|---|---|---|---|---|---|
| 02/08/1986 | 7 | 45 | ✪ | **COMMUNARDS** | London LONLP 18 |
| 17/10/1987 | 4 | 29 | ✪ | **RED** | London LONLP 39 |
| 22/09/2001 | 29 | 4 | | THE VERY BEST OF JIMMY SOMERVILLE BRONSKI BEAT AND THE COMMUNARDS **JIMMY SOMERVILLE BRONSKI BEAT AND THE COMMUNARDS** | London 0927412582 |

**PERRY COMO** US singer (born Pierino Como, 18/5/1912, Canonsburg, PA) initially dubbed the 'singing barber' (he owned a barbershop in his hometown). He began singing in 1933 with the Freddy Carlone band, moving to Ted Weems in 1936. After six years with Weems he went solo and became one of the most popular singers of the era, scoring hits in the UK up until the 1970s. Como also made a number of films, including *Something For The Boys* (1944), *Doll Face* (1945) and *Words And Music* (1948). He launched his own TV show that ran from 1948 until 1963. He won the 1958 Grammy Award for Best Male Vocal Performance for *Catch A Falling Star*, and he also received the very first US gold disc for the same record, presented on 14/3/1958. He died in his sleep on 12/5/2001. He has a star on the Hollywood Walk of Fame for his contribution to radio, and another for TV.

| | | | | | |
|---|---|---|---|---|---|
| 28/06/1958 | 4 | 7 | | **WE GET LETTERS (VOL.2)** | RCA RD 27070 |
| 08/11/1958 | 6 | 5 | | **DEAR PERRY** | RCA RD 27078 |
| 31/01/1959 | 4 | 5 | | **COMO'S GOLDEN RECORDS** | RCA RD 27100 |
| 10/04/1971 | 13 | 13 | | IT'S IMPOSSIBLE | RCA Victor SF 8175 |
| 07/07/1973 | ❶¹ | 109 | ✪ | **AND I LOVE YOU SO** | RCA Victor SF 8360 |

○ Silver disc  ● Gold disc  ✪ Platinum disc (additional platinum units are indicated by a figure following the symbol)  ❶⁹ Number of weeks album topped the UK chart

| 24/08/1974 | 26 | 3 | ● | PERRY | RCA Victor APLI 0585 |
| 19/04/1975 | 14 | 16 | ○ | MEMORIES ARE MADE OF HITS | RCA Victor RS 1005 |
| 25/10/1975 | ❶⁶ | 34 | ✪ | **40 GREATEST HITS** | K-Tel NE 700 |
| 03/12/1983 | 41 | 6 | | FOR THE GOOD TIMES | Telstar STAR 2235 |
| 17/11/2001 | 55 | 2 | | GOLD – GREATEST HITS | RCA 74321865542 |
| 04/10/2003 | 54 | 2 | | THE ESSENTIAL PERRY COMO | RCA 82876560172 |
| 05/06/2004 | 63 | 1 | | PAPA LOVES MAMBO – THE VERY BEST OF | RCA 82876616572 |

**COMPULSION** Irish and Dutch group based in London and formed by Josephmary Barry (vocals), Sid Rainey (bass), Garrett Lee (guitar/vocals) and Jan-Willem Alkema (drums).

| 09/04/1994 | 59 | 1 | | COMFORTER | One Little Indian TPLP 59CDL |

**COMSAT ANGELS** UK rock group formed in Sheffield by Stephen Fellows (guitar/vocals), Kevin Bacon (bass), Andy Peake (keyboards) and Mik Gaisher (drums) as Radio Earth, changing their name to Comsat Angels soon after (although in the USA they were forced to change their name again to CS Angels after the Comsat communications company threatened legal action). They have recorded for Polydor, CBS, Island and RPM Records and also briefly changed name a third time to Headhunters.

| 05/09/1981 | 51 | 5 | | SLEEP NO MORE | Polydor POLS 1038 |
| 18/09/1982 | 94 | 2 | | FICTION | Polydor POLS 1075 |
| 08/10/1983 | 91 | 2 | | LAND | Jive HIP 8 |

**CONNELLS** US rock group formed in Raleigh, NC in 1984 by David Connell (bass), Mike Connell (guitar), John Schultz (drums) and Doug MacMillan (vocals). Peele Wimberley replaced Schultz on drums, and Steve Potak (keyboards) joined in 1990.

| 09/09/1995 | 36 | 2 | | RING | London 8286602 |

**HARRY CONNICK JR.** US singer (born 11/9/1967, New Orleans, LA) who later became an actor, appearing in the films *Memphis Belle* (1990), *Copycat* (1995) and *Independence Day* (1996). He has won three Grammy Awards: Best Male Jazz Vocal Performance in 1989 for *When Harry Met Sally,* Best Male Jazz Vocal Performance in 1990 for *We Are In Love* and Best Traditional Pop Vocal Album in 2001 for *Songs I Heard*.

| 22/09/1990 | 7 | 46 | ● | **WE ARE IN LOVE** | CBS 4667361 |
| 26/10/1991 | 16 | 11 | ● | BLUE LIGHT, RED LIGHT | Columbia 4690871 |
| 30/01/1993 | 35 | 2 | | 25 | Columbia 4728092 |
| 12/06/1993 | 32 | 5 | | FOREVER FOR NOW | Columbia 4738732 |
| 27/08/1994 | 21 | 3 | | SHE | Columbia 4768162 |
| 20/03/2004 | 6 | 6 | ● | **ONLY YOU** | Columbia 5150462 |

**RAY CONNIFF** US orchestra leader (born 6/11/1916, Attelboro, MA) who was taught to play the trombone as a child and who sent off for a mail order course in musical arranging. After graduating from college he joined Bunny Berigan as a trombonist and arranger and later worked with Bob Crosby and Artie Shaw. After the Second World War he joined Columbia Records, where he worked with artists of the calibre of Guy Mitchell, Rosemary Clooney and Johnnie Ray before launching a new sound of his own in 1956. Taking familiar songs and giving them an arrangement that mixed a full orchestra with a chorus proved immensely popular worldwide, and in a little over ten years he registered nearly thirty Top 40 hit albums in the US. In 1974 he became the first popular US musician to record in Russia. He won the 1966 Grammy Award for Best Performance by a Chorus for *Somewhere My Love (Lara's Theme From Dr. Zhivago)*. He died on 12/10/2002.

| 28/05/1960 | 15 | 1 | | IT'S THE TALK OF THE TOWN | Philips BBL 7354 |
| 25/06/1960 | 13 | 1 | | S AWFUL NICE | Philips BBL 7281 |
| 26/11/1960 | 3 | 44 | | **HI-FI COMPANION ALBUM** | Philips BET 101 |
| 20/05/1961 | 14 | 4 | | MEMORIES ARE MADE OF THIS | Philips BBL 7439 |
| 29/12/1962 | 18 | 3 | | S WONDERFUL 'S MARVELLOUS | CBS DPG 66001 |
| 29/12/1962 | 12 | 1 | | WE WISH YOU A MERRY CHRISTMAS | CBS BPG 62092 |
| 16/04/1966 | 24 | 4 | ● | HI-FI COMPANION ALBUM | CBS DP 66011 |
| 09/09/1967 | 34 | 3 | | SOMEWHERE MY LOVE | CBS SBPG 62740 |
| 21/06/1969 | ❶³ | 16 | | **HIS ORCHESTRA, HIS CHORUS, HIS SINGERS, HIS SOUND** | CBS SPR 27 |
| 23/05/1970 | 30 | 14 | ○ | BRIDGE OVER TROUBLED WATER | CBS 64020 |
| 12/06/1971 | 34 | 4 | | LOVE STORY | CBS 64294 |
| 19/02/1972 | 17 | 4 | | I'D LIKE TO TEACH THE WORLD TO SING | CBS 64449 |

## BILLY CONNOLLY
Scottish singer/comedian (born 24/11/1942, Glasgow) whose career began with the Humblebums (which included Gerry Rafferty), before going solo. Eventually as the stories and jokes between the songs got longer and longer he moved from music to comedy, becoming a big hit with ex-patriate audiences in the USA and Australia. Known as The Big Yin, he moved to the south of England in 1971 and by the mid-1970s had broadened his appeal to include the UK. His hit singles were usually parodies of other well-known songs. He later appeared in the film *Still Crazy* and was awarded a CBE in the Queen's 2003 Birthday Honours List.

| 20/07/1974 | 8 | 33 | ● | SOLO CONCERT | Transatlantic TRA 279 |
| 18/01/1975 | 10 | 29 | ● | COP YER WHACK OF THIS | Polydor 2383 310 |
| 20/09/1975 | 34 | 10 | | WORDS AND MUSIC | Transatlantic TRA SAM 32 |
| 06/12/1975 | 6 | 14 | ● | GET RIGHT INTAE HIM | Polydor 2383 368 |
| 11/12/1976 | 20 | 9 | ○ | ATLANTIC BRIDGE | Polydor 2383 419 |
| 28/01/1978 | 57 | 3 | ○ | RAW MEAT FOR THE BALCONY | Polydor 2383 463 |
| 05/12/1981 | 23 | 8 | ● | THE PICK OF BILLY CONNOLLY | Polydor POLTV 15 |
| 05/12/1987 | 81 | 2 | | BILLY AND ALBERT | 10 Records DIX 65 |

## CONSOLIDATED
US rock group formed in San Francisco, CA by Adam Sherbourne (guitar/vocals), Mark Pistel (samples and tapes) and Philip Steir (drums). Sherbourne also recorded solo under the name Childman.

| 30/07/1994 | 53 | 1 | | BUSINESS OF PUNISHMENT | London 8285142 |

## RUSS CONWAY
UK pianist (born Trevor Stanford, 2/9/1927, Bristol) who left the Royal Navy in 1955 to become a pianist (despite having lost part of a finger in an accident with a bread slicer), accompanying the likes of Gracie Fields, Lita Rosa and Dorothy Squires. Signed by EMI in 1957, his run of hits was curtailed by the early 1960s' beat boom, but he continued to perform live until ill-health forced retirement. He died from cancer on 16/11/2000.

| 22/11/1958 | 9 | 5 | | PACK UP YOUR TROUBLES | Columbia 33SX 1120 |
| 02/05/1959 | 8 | 10 | | SONGS TO SING IN YOUR BATH | Columbia 33SX 1149 |
| 19/09/1959 | 3 | 16 | | FAMILY FAVOURITES | Columbia 33SX 1169 |
| 19/12/1959 | 3 | 7 | | TIME TO CELEBRATE | Columbia 33SX 1197 |
| 26/03/1960 | 5 | 17 | | MY CONCERTO FOR YOU | Columbia 33SX 1214 |
| 17/12/1960 | 7 | 11 | | PARTY TIME | Columbia 33SX 1279 |
| 23/04/1977 | 25 | 3 | | RUSS CONWAY PRESENTS 24 PIANO GREATS | Ronco RTL 2022 |

## RY COODER
US guitarist/singer (born Ryland Peter Cooder, 15/3/1947, Los Angeles, CA) who learned to play the guitar as a child and at the age of seventeen was playing with Jackie DeShannon. He formed the Rising Sons with Taj Mahal and Ed Cassidy, although this was shortlived and he turned to studio work for producer Terry Melcher. After guesting on Captain Beefheart's debut album (and declining an invitation to join the band) he continued as a studio musician, appearing on tracks by Randy Newman and Little Feat. He contributed to the Rolling Stones *Let It Bleed* album and was heralded as a likely replacement for Brian Jones until he got into a clash with Keith Richards. Ry Cooder's debut album appeared in 1970 and he has maintained a solo career in conjunction with regular studio work. In 1992 he linked with John Hiatt, Jim Keltner and Nick Lowe in Little Village. He has won five Grammy Awards including Best Recording for Children in 1988 with Robin Williams for *Pecos Bill* and Best World Music Album in 1993 with Vishwa Mohan Bhatt for *A Meeting By The River*.

| 11/08/1979 | 36 | 9 | ○ | BOP TILL YOU DROP | Warner Brothers K 56691 |
| 18/10/1980 | 35 | 6 | | BORDER LINE | Warner Brothers K 56864 |
| 24/04/1982 | 18 | 12 | | THE SLIDE AREA | Warner Brothers K 56976 |
| 14/11/1987 | 75 | 3 | ○ | GET RHYTHM | Warner Brothers WX 121 |
| 09/04/1994 | 44 | 3 | | TALKING TIMBUKTU **ALI FARKA TOURE AND RY COODER** 1994 Grammy Award for Best World Music Album | World Circuit WCD 040 |
| 05/07/1997 | 44 | 15 | ● | BUENA VISTA SOCIAL CLUB ◇³ 1997 Grammy Award for Best Tropical Latin Performance | World Circuit WCD 050 |
| 08/02/2003 | 40 | 1 | | MAMBO SINUENDO **RY COODER AND MANUEL GALBAM** 2003 Grammy Award for Best Pop Instrumental Album | |
| | | | | | Nonesuch 7559796912 |

## PETER COOK AND DUDLEY MOORE
UK comedy duo formed by Peter Cook (born 17/11/1937, Torquay) and Dudley Moore (born 19/4/1935, Dagenham). They first came to prominence on their own TV series *Not Only … But Also*. After the pair split Cook became a successful writer, performer and entrepreneur, whilst Moore eventually went to live and work in Hollywood, starring in the films *10* and *Arthur*. The pair revived their partnership for the *Derek And Clive* albums that were immensely successful despite no radio play. Cook died from cancer in January 1995. They won the 1974 Grammy Award for Best Spoken Word Recording for *Good Evening*. Dudley Moore was awarded a CBE in the 2001 Queen's Birthday Honours List and died from brain disease on 27/3/2002.

| 21/05/1966 | 25 | 1 | | ONCE MOORE WITH COOK | Decca LK 4785 |
| 18/09/1976 | 12 | 25 | ○ | DEREK AND CLIVE LIVE | Island ILPS 9434 |

24/12/1977 . . . . . 18 . . . . . 8 . . . . . ○  COME AGAIN This and the above hit credited to *Derek And Clive* . . . . . . . . . . . . . . . . . . . . . . . . . . . . . . . . . . . . . . . Virgin V 2094

**SAM COOKE** US singer (born 22/1/1931, Clarksdale, MS, raised in Chicago, IL) who sang with the gospel group the Highway QC's before joining the Soul Stirrers as lead singer in 1950, leaving in 1956 to go solo. He was replaced by Johnnie Taylor. His first official release *You Send Me* was a US #1 and began a string of hits over the next seven years. His son Vincent drowned in the family's swimming pool in 1963. Sam was shot to death in a Los Angeles, CA motel on 11/12/1964 by the owner Bertha Franklin amid rumours of rape and assault on 22-year-old Elisa Boyer (who had accompanied Cooke to the motel), although Franklin was later cleared on the grounds of justifiable homicide. It was later claimed that Boyer, a known prostitute, had been robbing Cooke as she ran out of his room carrying his clothes, although this was not followed up by the police, who did not make public the details surrounding his death for almost two years in order to protect his family. Over 200,000 people tried to attend his funeral (the bronze marker at Forest Lawn in Los Angeles, under which lies his body, has the year of Sam's birth wrongly engraved as 1930). He was inducted into the Rock & Roll Hall of Fame in 1986. He has a star on the Hollywood Walk of Fame. Elisa Boyer (aka Crystal Chan Young, Jasmine Jay and Elsie Nakama) was convicted of the second-degree murder of her lover Louis Reynolds in 1979.

26/04/1986 . . . . . 8 . . . . . . 27 . . . . . ●  THE MAN AND HIS MUSIC . . . . . . . . . . . . . . . . . . . . . . . . . . . . . . . . . . . . . . . . . . . . . . . . . . . . . . . . . . . . . . . RCA PL 87127
25/10/2003 . . . . . 30 . . . . . 5 . . . . . . ○  PORTRAIT OF A LEGEND . . . . . . . . . . . . . . . . . . . . . . . . . . . . . . . . . . . . . . . . . . . . . . . . . . . . . . . . . . . . Universal TV 9807446

**COOKIE CREW** UK rap group with Susie Q (Susie Banfield, sister of The Pasadenas' Andrew Banfield), MC Remedee (Debbie Prince) and DJ Max (Maxine).

06/05/1989 . . . . . 24 . . . . . . 4 . . . . . .  BORN THIS WAY! . . . . . . . . . . . . . . . . . . . . . . . . . . . . . . . . . . . . . . . . . . . . . . . . . . . . . . . . . . . . . . . London 8281341

**COOL NOTES** UK group formed in London by Steve McIntosh (keyboards/vocals), Lorraine McIntosh (lead vocals), Heather Austin (lead vocals), Joseph 'JC' Charles (guitar), Ian Dunstan (bass), Peter 'Lee' Gordon (guitar) and Peter 'Rattie' Rolands (drums). By 1988 they were the trio of Steve and Lorraine McIntosh and JC.

09/11/1985 . . . . . 66 . . . . . . 2 . . . . . .  HAVE A GOOD FOREVER . . . . . . . . . . . . . . . . . . . . . . . . . . . . . . . . . . . . . . . . . . . . . . . . . . . . . . . . . . Abstract Dance ADLP 1

**RITA COOLIDGE** US singer (born 1/5/1944, Nashville, TN) who toured with Delaney & Bonnie, Joe Cocker and Leon Russell before going solo. Married to Kris Kristofferson from 1973 to 1980, she was known as the Delta Lady; the title of a US hit for Leon Russell written in her honour. She recorded *All Time High* – the theme to the James Bond film *Octopussy* and has two Grammy Awards with Kris Kristofferson for Best Country & Western Performance by a Duo in 1973 for *From The Bottle To The Bottom,* and Best Country Performance by a Duo in 1975 for *Lover Please*.

06/08/1977 . . . . . 6 . . . . . . 28 . . . . . ●  ANYTIME ANYWHERE . . . . . . . . . . . . . . . . . . . . . . . . . . . . . . . . . . . . . . . . . . . . . . . . . . . . . . . . . A&M AMLH 64616
06/05/1978 . . . . . 35 . . . . . 4 . . . . . .  NATURAL ACT **KRIS KRISTOFFERSON AND RITA COOLIDGE** . . . . . . . . . . . . . . . . . . . . . . . . . . . A&M AMLH 64690
08/07/1978 . . . . . 51 . . . . . 1 . . . . . . ○  LOVE ME AGAIN . . . . . . . . . . . . . . . . . . . . . . . . . . . . . . . . . . . . . . . . . . . . . . . . . . . . . . . . . . . . . . . A&M AMLH 64699
14/03/1981 . . . . . 6 . . . . . . 11 . . . . . ●  THE VERY BEST OF RITA COOLIDGE . . . . . . . . . . . . . . . . . . . . . . . . . . . . . . . . . . . . . . . . . . . . . . A&M AMLH 68520

**COOLIO** US rapper (born Artis Ivey Jr, 1/8/1963, Compton, CA) and a member of WC and the MAAD Circle. His DJ partner is Bryan 'Wino' Dobbs. His first US hit was in June 1994 with *Fantastic Voyage*. He won the 1995 Grammy Award for Best Rap Solo Performance for *Gangsta's Paradise* and the 1997 MOBO Award for Best International Hip Hop Act. In 1999 he was jailed for ten days for illegal possession of a firearm, his second such conviction. He has also recorded with LV, B Real, Busta Rhymes, LL Cool J and Method Man.

29/10/1994 . . . . . 67 . . . . . . 1 . . . . . .  IT TAKES A THIEF . . . . . . . . . . . . . . . . . . . . . . . . . . . . . . . . . . . . . . . . . . . . . . . . . . . . . . . . . . Tommy Boy TBCD 1083
18/11/1995 . . . . 18 . . . . . 24 . . . . . . ●  GANGSTA'S PARADISE . . . . . . . . . . . . . . . . . . . . . . . . . . . . . . . . . . . . . . . . . . . . . . . . . . . . . . Tommy Boy TBCD 1141
13/09/1997 . . . . . 28 . . . . . . 2 . . . . . .  MY SOUL . . . . . . . . . . . . . . . . . . . . . . . . . . . . . . . . . . . . . . . . . . . . . . . . . . . . . . . . . . . . . . . . . . Tommy Boy TBV 1180

**ALICE COOPER** US singer (born Vincent Furnier, 4/2/1948, Detroit, MI) who formed his first band in 1965 and moved to Los Angeles, CA in 1968. The band became known as Alice Cooper (after a ouija board had spelled out the name) and so did Furnier. They debuted on Frank Zappa's Straight label in 1969, before signing with Warner Brothers in 1971. The line-up for these hits featured Cooper (vocals), Glen Buxton (guitar), Michael Bruce (guitar/keyboards), Dennis Dunaway (bass) and Neal Smith (drums). Cooper re-emerged in the late 1980s as a solo artist, also making film appearances, including the role of Freddy Krueger's father in *A Nightmare On Elm Street* (1984), *Prince Of Darkness* (1987) and *Wayne's World* (1992). In April 1988 he nearly strangled himself when a safety rope snapped during a concert, leaving him dangling off the ground before a roadie saved him. Buxton died from drug and alcohol abuse on 19/10/1997. Alice Cooper was awarded a star on the Hollywood Walk of Fame at 7000 Hollywood Boulevard.

05/02/1972 . . . . . 27 . . . . . 18 . . . . . .  KILLER . . . . . . . . . . . . . . . . . . . . . . . . . . . . . . . . . . . . . . . . . . . . . . . . . . . . . . . . . . . . . . . Warner Brothers K 56005
22/07/1972 . . . . . 4 . . . . . . 20 . . . . . .  SCHOOL'S OUT . . . . . . . . . . . . . . . . . . . . . . . . . . . . . . . . . . . . . . . . . . . . . . . . . . . . . . . . . Warner Brothers K 56007
09/09/1972 . . . . . 28 . . . . . 7 . . . . . .  LOVE IT TO DEATH . . . . . . . . . . . . . . . . . . . . . . . . . . . . . . . . . . . . . . . . . . . . . . . . . . . . . . . Warner Brothers K 46177
24/03/1973 . . . . ●[1] . . . 23 . . . . . .  BILLION DOLLAR BABIES ▲[1] . . . . . . . . . . . . . . . . . . . . . . . . . . . . . . . . . . . . . . . . . . Warner Brothers K 56013
12/01/1974 . . . . . 34 . . . . . 4 . . . . . .  MUSCLE OF LOVE . . . . . . . . . . . . . . . . . . . . . . . . . . . . . . . . . . . . . . . . . . . . . . . . . . . . . . . . Warner Brothers K 56018
15/03/1975 . . . . . 19 . . . . . 8 . . . . . . ○  WELCOME TO MY NIGHTMARE . . . . . . . . . . . . . . . . . . . . . . . . . . . . . . . . . . . . . . . . . . . . . . . Anchor ANCL 2011
24/07/1976 . . . . . 23 . . . . . 7 . . . . . .  ALICE COOPER GOES TO HELL . . . . . . . . . . . . . . . . . . . . . . . . . . . . . . . . . . . . . . . . . . . Warner Brothers K 56171
28/05/1977 . . . . . 33 . . . . . 3 . . . . . .  LACE AND WHISKY . . . . . . . . . . . . . . . . . . . . . . . . . . . . . . . . . . . . . . . . . . . . . . . . . . . . Warner Brothers K 56365
23/12/1978 . . . . . 68 . . . . . 3 . . . . . .  FROM THE INSIDE . . . . . . . . . . . . . . . . . . . . . . . . . . . . . . . . . . . . . . . . . . . . . . . . . . . . . Warner Brothers K 56577
17/05/1980 . . . . . 56 . . . . . 3 . . . . . .  FLUSH THE FASHION . . . . . . . . . . . . . . . . . . . . . . . . . . . . . . . . . . . . . . . . . . . . . . . . . . Warner Brothers K 56805
12/09/1981 . . . . . 96 . . . . . 1 . . . . . .  SPECIAL FORCES . . . . . . . . . . . . . . . . . . . . . . . . . . . . . . . . . . . . . . . . . . . . . . . . . . . . . . Warner Brothers K 56927
12/11/1983 . . . . . 93 . . . . . 1 . . . . . .  DADA . . . . . . . . . . . . . . . . . . . . . . . . . . . . . . . . . . . . . . . . . . . . . . . . . . . . . . . . . . . . . . Warner Brothers 9239691
01/11/1986 . . . . . 41 . . . . . 2 . . . . . .  CONSTRICTOR . . . . . . . . . . . . . . . . . . . . . . . . . . . . . . . . . . . . . . . . . . . . . . . . . . . . . . . . . . . . MCA MCF 3341
07/11/1987 . . . . . 48 . . . . . 3 . . . . . .  RAISE YOUR FIST AND YELL . . . . . . . . . . . . . . . . . . . . . . . . . . . . . . . . . . . . . . . . . . . . . . . . MCA MCF 3392
26/08/1989 . . . . 2 . . . . . 12 . . . . . .  TRASH . . . . . . . . . . . . . . . . . . . . . . . . . . . . . . . . . . . . . . . . . . . . . . . . . . . . . . . . . . . . . . . . . . Epic 4651301

| | DATE | POS | WKS | BPI | ALBUM TITLE | LABEL & NUMBER |
|---|---|---|---|---|---|---|
| | 13/07/1991 | 4 | 7 | ○ | HEY STOOPID | Epic 4684161 |
| | 18/06/1994 | 6 | 5 | | THE LAST TEMPTATION | Epic 4765949 |
| | 24/06/2000 | 38 | 1 | | BRUTAL PLANET | Eagle EAGCD 115 |
| | 10/03/2001 | 33 | 5 | ○ | THE DEFINITIVE ALICE COOPER | Rhino 8122735342 |

### COOPER TEMPLE CLAUSE
UK rock group formed in Reading by Ben Gautrey (vocals), Tom Bellamy (guitar), Dan Fisher (bass), Didz (bass), Kieran Mayhem (keyboards) and Jon Harpener (drums).

| | DATE | POS | WKS | BPI | ALBUM TITLE | LABEL & NUMBER |
|---|---|---|---|---|---|---|
| | 23/02/2002 | 27 | 3 | | SEE THIS THROUGH AND LEAVE | Morning 19 |
| | 20/09/2003 | 5 | 2 | | KICK UP THE FIRE AND LET THE FLAMES BREAK LOOSE | Morning 36 |

### JULIAN COPE
UK singer (born 21/10/1957, Bargoed, Wales) and a member of The Crucial Three with Ian McCulloch and Pete Wylie, before forming Teardrop Explodes in 1978. He went solo in 1984.

| | DATE | POS | WKS | BPI | ALBUM TITLE | LABEL & NUMBER |
|---|---|---|---|---|---|---|
| | 03/03/1984 | 40 | 4 | | WORLD SHUT YOUR MOUTH | Mercury MERL 37 |
| | 24/11/1984 | 87 | 1 | | FRIED' | Mercury MERL 48 |
| | 14/03/1987 | 11 | 10 | ○ | SAINT JULIAN | Island ILPS 9861 |
| | 29/10/1988 | 42 | 2 | | MY NATION UNDERGROUND | Island ILPS 9918 |
| | 16/03/1991 | 23 | 7 | | PEGGY SUICIDE | Island ILPSD 9977 |
| | 15/08/1992 | 22 | 3 | | FLOORED GENIUS – THE BEST OF JULIAN COPE AND THE TEARDROP EXPLODES JULIAN COPE AND THE TEARDROP EXPLODES | Island CID 8000 |
| | 31/10/1992 | 20 | 2 | | JEHOVAHKILL | Island 5140522 |
| | 16/07/1994 | 16 | 3 | | AUTOGEDDON | Echo ECHCD 1 |
| | 09/09/1995 | 20 | 2 | | JULIAN COPE PRESENTS 20 MOTHERS | Echo ECHCD 5 |
| | 26/10/1996 | 39 | 1 | | INTERPRETER | Echo ECHCD 012 |

### CORAL
UK group formed in Liverpool in 1996 by James Skelly (lead vocals), Lee Southall (guitar/vocals), Paul Duffy (bass/saxophone), Nick Power (keyboards/vocals), Bill Ryder-Jones (guitar/trumpet) and Ian Skelly (drums).

| | DATE | POS | WKS | BPI | ALBUM TITLE | LABEL & NUMBER |
|---|---|---|---|---|---|---|
| | 10/08/2002 | 5 | 34 | ● | THE CORAL | Deltasonic DLTCD 006 |
| | 09/08/2003 | ❶¹ | 9 | ● | MAGIC AND MEDICINE | Deltasonic DLTCDPS014 |
| | 07/02/2004 | 5 | 3 | | NIGHTFREAK AND THE SONS OF BECKER | Deltasonic DLTCD018 |

### HARRY H CORBETT – see WILFRID BRAMBELL AND HARRY H CORBETT

### CORDUROY
UK group formed by Wade Driver Jr (guitar/vocals), Maximum Gross Weight (bass), Gary Gutfeld (drums) and Designated Hitter (drums).

| | DATE | POS | WKS | BPI | ALBUM TITLE | LABEL & NUMBER |
|---|---|---|---|---|---|---|
| | 08/10/1994 | 73 | 1 | | OUT OF HERE | Acid Jazz JAZIDCD 107 |

### CHRIS CORNELL
US singer (born 20/7/1964, Seattle, WA), guitarist and lead singer with Soundgarden from their formation in 1984. He remained with the group until they disbanded in 1997 and then launched a solo career.

| | DATE | POS | WKS | BPI | ALBUM TITLE | LABEL & NUMBER |
|---|---|---|---|---|---|---|
| | 02/10/1999 | 31 | 1 | | EUPHORIA MORNING | A&M 4904222 |

### CORNERSHOP
UK group formed in Leicester in 1991 by Tjinder Singh (guitar/vocals), Avtar Singh (bass), Ben Ayres (guitar/vocals), Anthony Saffrey (sitar) and David Chambers (drums). By the time of their debut hit, they were a duo of Singh and Ayres.

| | DATE | POS | WKS | BPI | ALBUM TITLE | LABEL & NUMBER |
|---|---|---|---|---|---|---|
| | 20/09/1997 | 17 | 15 | ● | WHEN I WAS BORN FOR THE 7TH TIME | Wiiija WIJCD 1065 |
| | 13/04/2002 | 30 | 3 | | HANDCREAM FOR A GENERATION | Wiiija WIJCD 1115 |

### HUGH CORNWELL
UK guitarist/singer (born 28/8/1949, London) who was a founder of The Stranglers in 1974 until he left in 1990, having already begun a parallel solo career. In 1980 he was sentenced to three months imprisonment on drugs charges.

| | DATE | POS | WKS | BPI | ALBUM TITLE | LABEL & NUMBER |
|---|---|---|---|---|---|---|
| | 18/06/1988 | 98 | 1 | | WOLF | Virgin V 2420 |

### CORO DE MUNJES DEL MONASTERIO BENEDICTINO DE SANTO DOMINGO DE SILOS
Spanish monastic choir whose debut hit album led to a host of copycat Gregorian Chant albums.

| | DATE | POS | WKS | BPI | ALBUM TITLE | LABEL & NUMBER |
|---|---|---|---|---|---|---|
| | 05/03/1994 | 7 | 25 | ● | CANTO GREGORIANO ◇ | EMI Classics CMS 5652172 |
| | 17/12/1994 | 53 | 3 | | CANTO NOEL | EMI Classics CDC 5552172 |

### CORONA
Italian studio creation of producers Checco and Soul Train with vocals by Ice MC and Brazilian singer Olga DeSouza. The name is Spanish for 'crown'.

| | DATE | POS | WKS | BPI | ALBUM TITLE | LABEL & NUMBER |
|---|---|---|---|---|---|---|
| | 20/05/1995 | 18 | 7 | | THE RHYTHM OF THE NIGHT | Eternal 0630103312 |

### CORRIES
UK group formed in Edinburgh in 1962 by Roy Williamson, Ronnie Browne and Bill Smith. They added Paddie Bell to the line-up the following year, although she left in order to have a child in 1965. Smith left in 1966, after which Williamson and Browne continued as a duo. Williamson died from a brain tumour in 1990 and Browne has since worked as a soloist.

| | DATE | POS | WKS | BPI | ALBUM TITLE | LABEL & NUMBER |
|---|---|---|---|---|---|---|
| | 09/05/1970 | 46 | 4 | | SCOTTISH LOVE SONGS | Fontana 6306 004 |
| | 16/09/1972 | 39 | 1 | | SOUND OF PIBROCH | Columbia SCX 6511 |

### CORROSION OF CONFORMITY
US rock group formed in Raleigh, NC in 1982 by Mike Dean (bass/vocals), Woody Weatherman (guitar) and Reed Mullin (drums) as No Labels. They later added Eric Eyke (vocals) to the line-up, who was replaced by Simon Bob. Bob and Dean left the group and Mullin and Weatherman regrouped with Karl Agell (vocals), Pepper Keenan (guitar/vocals) and Phil Swisher (bass). By 1994 Agell and Swisher were replaced by the returning Mike Dean, and Keenan took over on lead vocals.

| | DATE | POS | WKS | BPI | ALBUM TITLE | LABEL & NUMBER |
|---|---|---|---|---|---|---|
| | 14/09/1996 | 43 | 1 | | WISEBLOOD | Columbia 4843282 |

○ Silver disc ● Gold disc ✪ Platinum disc (additional platinum units are indicated by a figure following the symbol) ❶⁹ Number of weeks album topped the UK chart

**CORRS** Irish family group formed in Dundalk (where they were all born) in 1990 by Andrea (born 17/5/1974, whistle/lead vocals), Caroline (born 17/3/1973, drums), Sharon (born 24/3/1970, violin) and Jim Corr (born 31/7/1968, guitar/keyboards). They were named Best International Group at the 1999 BRIT Awards. The group also took part in the *It's Only Rock 'N' Roll* project for the Children's Promise charity.

| Date | Pos | Wks | BPI | Title | Label & Number |
|---|---|---|---|---|---|
| 02/03/1996 | 2 | 113 | ✪ | **FORGIVEN, NOT FORGOTTEN** ◇² | Atlantic 7567926122 |
| 01/11/1997 | ❶¹⁰ | 142 | ✪⁹ | **TALK ON CORNERS** ◇⁶ | Atlantic 7567831062 |
| 27/11/1999 | 7 | 25 | ✪ | **UNPLUGGED** ◇² | Atlantic 7567809862 |
| 29/07/2000 | ❶² | 45 | ✪³ | **IN BLUE** ◇³ | Atlantic 7567833522 |
| 17/11/2001 | 6 | 21 | ✪ | **THE BEST OF** ◇ | Atlantic 7567930752 |
| 12/06/2004 | 2 | 3+ | ○ | **BORROWED HEAVEN** | Atlantic 7567932432 |

**COSMIC BABY** German producer (born 1966) who studied at the Nuremberg Conservatory at the age of seven, first coming to the attention of UK audiences with his collaboration with Paul Van Dyk as Visions of Shiva.

| Date | Pos | Wks | BPI | Title | Label & Number |
|---|---|---|---|---|---|
| 23/04/1994 | 60 | 1 | | THINKING ABOUT MYSELF | Logic 74321196052 |

**ELVIS COSTELLO** UK singer (born Declan McManus, 25/8/1954, Liverpool), son of bandleader Ross McManus. Renamed himself Elvis Costello (Costello is his grandmother's maiden name) in 1976 and formed the Attractions in 1977, shortly after signing with Radar Records. He also recorded infrequently as the Imposter for his Imp label. He married Pogues bass player Cait O'Riordan in 1986 and has made a number of film appearances. He won the 1998 Grammy Award for Best Pop Collaboration with Vocals with Burt Bacharach for *I Still Have That Other Girl*. He was inducted into the Rock & Roll Hall of Fame in 2003.

| Date | Pos | Wks | BPI | Title | Label & Number |
|---|---|---|---|---|---|
| 06/08/1977 | 14 | 12 | ○ | MY AIM IS TRUE | Stiff SEEZ 3 |
| 01/04/1978 | 4 | 14 | ● | **THIS YEAR'S MODEL** | Radar RAD 3 |
| 20/01/1979 | 2 | 28 | ✪ | **ARMED FORCES** | Radar RAD 14 |
| 23/02/1980 | 2 | 14 | ● | **GET HAPPY!** | F-Beat XXLP 1 |
| 31/01/1981 | 9 | 7 | | **TRUST** | F-Beat XXLP 11 |
| 31/10/1981 | 7 | 18 | ● | **ALMOST BLUE** | F-Beat XXLP 13 |
| 10/07/1982 | 6 | 12 | | **IMPERIAL BEDROOM** | F-Beat XXLP 17 |
| 06/08/1983 | 3 | 13 | | **PUNCH THE CLOCK** | F-Beat XXLP 19 |
| 07/07/1984 | 10 | 10 | ○ | **GOODBYE CRUEL WORLD** | F-Beat ZL 70317 |
| 20/04/1985 | 8 | 25 | ● | **THE BEST OF ELVIS COSTELLO – THE MAN** This and the above seven hits credited to **ELVIS COSTELLO & THE ATTRACTIONS** | Telstar STAR 2247 |
| 01/03/1986 | 11 | 9 | ○ | KING OF AMERICA **COSTELLO SHOW** | F-Beat ZL 70496 |
| 27/09/1986 | 16 | 5 | ● | BLOOD AND CHOCOLATE **ELVIS COSTELLO & THE ATTRACTIONS** | Imp XFIEND 80 |
| 18/02/1989 | 5 | 16 | ● | **SPIKE** | Warner Brothers WX 238 |
| 28/10/1989 | 67 | 1 | | GIRLS GIRLS GIRLS | Demon DFIEND 160 |
| 25/05/1991 | 5 | 6 | ○ | **MIGHTY LIKE A ROSE** | Warner Brothers WX 419 |
| 30/01/1993 | 18 | 3 | | THE JULIET LETTERS **ELVIS COSTELLO & THE BRODSKY QUARTET** | Warner Brothers 9362451802 |
| 19/03/1994 | 2 | 5 | ○ | **BRUTAL YOUTH** | Warner Brothers 9362455352 |
| 12/11/1994 | 57 | 2 | | THE VERY BEST OF ELVIS COSTELLO AND THE ATTRACTIONS This and the above hit credited to **ELVIS COSTELLO & THE ATTRACTIONS** | Demon DPAM 13 |
| 27/05/1995 | 21 | 2 | | KOJAK VARIETY | Warner Brothers 9362459032 |
| 12/08/1995 | 71 | 1 | | KING OF AMERICA **COSTELLO SHOW** | Demon DPAM 11 |
| 25/05/1996 | 28 | 3 | | ALL THIS USELESS BEAUTY **ELVIS COSTELLO & THE ATTRACTIONS** | Warner Brothers 9362461982 |
| 10/10/1998 | 32 | 2 | ○ | PAINTED FROM MEMORY **ELVIS COSTELLO WITH BURT BACHARACH** | Mercury 5380022 |
| 14/08/1999 | 4 | 10 | ● | **THE VERY BEST OF ELVIS COSTELLO** | Universal Music TV 5464902 |
| 31/03/2001 | 67 | 1 | | FOR THE STARS **VON OTTER MEETS COSTELLO** | Deutsche Grammophon 4695302 |
| 27/04/2002 | 17 | 4 | ○ | WHEN I WAS CRUEL | Mercury 5868292 |
| 27/09/2003 | 44 | 1 | | NORTH | Deutsche Grammophon 9809656 |

**PHIL COULTER** Irish orchestra leader/pianist/producer/songwriter (born February 1942, Derry, Northern Ireland) who began songwriting whilst studying at Queen's University, Dublin and went on to compose Ireland's 1965 Eurovision Song Contest entry. He then linked with Philip Solomon, working with his acts, including Twinkle, before teaming up with Bill Martin in 1967. They were responsible for hits by Sandie Shaw, Dana, Cliff Richard (as well as Eurovision Song Contest winners *Puppet On A String* by Sandie Shaw and *All Kinds Of Everything* by Dana), the England World Cup Squad, the Bay City Rollers and Slik. Phil Coulter ended his partnership with Bill Martin at the end of the 1970s and recorded a number of orchestral albums, especially popular in Ireland.

| Date | Pos | Wks | BPI | Title | Label & Number |
|---|---|---|---|---|---|
| 13/10/1984 | 46 | 14 | | SEA OF TRANQUILLITY | K-Tel Ireland KLP 185 |

| | DATE | POS | WKS | BPI | ALBUM TITLE | LABEL & NUMBER |
|---|------|-----|-----|-----|-------------|----------------|
| | 18/05/1985 | 86 | 1 | | PHIL COULTER'S IRELAND | K-Tel ONE 1296 |

**COUNTING CROWS** US folk-rock group formed in San Francisco, CA by Adam Duritz (born 1/8/1964, Baltimore, MD, vocals), David Byron (born 5/10/1961, San Francisco, guitar), Matt Malley (born 4/7/1963, bass), Steve Bowman (born 14/1/1967, drums), Charlie Gillingham (born 12/1/1960, Torrance, CA, keyboards) and Dan Vickrey (born 26/8/1966, Walnut Creek, CA, guitar). Bowman joined Third Eye Blind in 1994 and was replaced by Ben Mize (born 2/2/1971).

| | DATE | POS | WKS | BPI | ALBUM TITLE | LABEL & NUMBER |
|---|------|-----|-----|-----|-------------|----------------|
| | 12/03/1994 | 16 | 38 | ● | AUGUST AND EVERYTHING AFTER | Geffen GED 24528 |
| | 26/10/1996 | 4 | 4 | ● | RECOVERING THE SATELLITES ▲[1] | Geffen GED 24975 |
| | 25/07/1998 | 27 | 4 | | ACROSS THE WIRE – LIVE IN NEW YORK | Geffen GED 25226 |
| | 13/11/1999 | 19 | 3 | ○ | THIS DESERT LIFE | Geffen 4904152 |
| | 20/07/2002 | 9 | 11 | ● | HARD CANDY | Geffen 4933662 |
| | 07/02/2004 | 15 | 5 | | FILMS ABOUT GHOSTS – THE BEST OF | Geffen 9861505 |

**TINA COUSINS** UK singer who began as a model, appearing in a Rolling Stones video before going solo. She also took part in the BRITS Trust *Thank Abba For The Music* project.

| | DATE | POS | WKS | BPI | ALBUM TITLE | LABEL & NUMBER |
|---|------|-----|-----|-----|-------------|----------------|
| | 24/07/1999 | 50 | 1 | | KILLING TIME | Jive 0519342 |

**DAVID COVERDALE** UK singer (born 22/9/1949, Saltburn-By-The-Sea, Cleveland) who was formerly a member of Deep Purple and Whitesnake. Page is former Led Zeppelin member Jimmy Page.

| | DATE | POS | WKS | BPI | ALBUM TITLE | LABEL & NUMBER |
|---|------|-----|-----|-----|-------------|----------------|
| | 27/02/1982 | 78 | 1 | | NORTHWINDS | Purple TTS 3513 |
| | 27/03/1993 | 4 | 8 | ○ | COVERDALE PAGE COVERDALE PAGE | EMI CDEMD 1041 |
| | 07/10/2000 | 75 | 1 | | INTO THE LIGHT | EMI 5281242 |

**COWBOY JUNKIES** Canadian rock group formed in Toronto, Montreal by Margo Timmins (born 27/6/1961, Montreal, vocals), her brothers Michael (born 21/4/1959, Montreal, guitar) and Peter (born 29/10/1965, Montreal, drums) and Alan Anton (born Alan Alizojvodic, 22/6/1959, Montreal, bass).

| | DATE | POS | WKS | BPI | ALBUM TITLE | LABEL & NUMBER |
|---|------|-----|-----|-----|-------------|----------------|
| | 24/03/1990 | 33 | 4 | | THE CAUTION HORSES | RCA PL 90450 |
| | 15/02/1992 | 21 | 3 | | BLACK EYED MAN | RCA PD 90620 |

**CARL COX** UK producer (born 29/7/1962, Oldham) who worked as a painter and decorator, hod carrier, plasterer and scaffolder before turning to music.

| | DATE | POS | WKS | BPI | ALBUM TITLE | LABEL & NUMBER |
|---|------|-----|-----|-----|-------------|----------------|
| | 15/06/1996 | 23 | 4 | | AT THE END OF THE CLICHÉ | Edel 00990752C0X |

**PETER COX** UK singer (born 17/11/1955) who was previously a songwriter and member of Go West before going solo.

| | DATE | POS | WKS | BPI | ALBUM TITLE | LABEL & NUMBER |
|---|------|-----|-----|-----|-------------|----------------|
| | 29/11/1997 | 64 | 1 | | PETER COX | Chrysalis 4949692 |

**GRAHAM COXON** UK guitarist (born 12/3/1969, Rintein, Germany) and a founder member of Seymour in 1988. The group subsequently changed its name to Blur in 1991 when they signed with Food Records. Coxon then launched the Transcopic label in 1997, with a debut release of his own album. He issued a follow-up, *The Golden D* in 2000.

| | DATE | POS | WKS | BPI | ALBUM TITLE | LABEL & NUMBER |
|---|------|-----|-----|-----|-------------|----------------|
| | 22/08/1998 | 31 | 2 | | THE SKY IS TOO HIGH | Transcopic TRANCD 005 |
| | 29/05/2004 | 19 | 3 | | HAPPINESS IN MAGAZINES | Transcopic 5775192 |

**CRACKER** US rock group formed in 1991 by David Lowery (guitar/vocals) and Johnny Hickman (guitar) with an ever-changing rhythm section. Lowery had previously been with Camper Van Beethoven.

| | DATE | POS | WKS | BPI | ALBUM TITLE | LABEL & NUMBER |
|---|------|-----|-----|-----|-------------|----------------|
| | 25/06/1994 | 44 | 2 | | KEROSENE HAT | Virgin CDVUS 67 |

**CRADLE OF FILTH** UK group formed in 1991 by Dani Davey (vocals), Paul Ryan (guitar), his brother Benjamin (keyboards), John Richard (bass) and Darren (drums). Robin Eaglestone (guitar) was added to the line-up the following year, switching to bass on the departure of Richard. Paul Allender (guitar) joined at the same time and Nicholas Barker (drums) shortly after. The Ryan brothers and Allender left in 1995 and were replaced by Stuart Antsis (guitar), Jared Demeter (guitar) and Damien Gregori (keyboards). Demeter and Gregori left later the same year and were replaced by Gian Pyres and Les Smith. By 2000 Adrian Erlandson had joined on drums, Allender had returned and Martin Powell was on keyboards in place of Smith.

| | DATE | POS | WKS | BPI | ALBUM TITLE | LABEL & NUMBER |
|---|------|-----|-----|-----|-------------|----------------|
| | 16/05/1998 | 48 | 1 | | CRUELTY AND THE BEAST | Music For Nations CDMFN 242 |
| | 11/11/2000 | 63 | 1 | | MIDIAN | Music For Nations CDMFN 666 |
| | 30/06/2001 | 63 | 1 | | BITTER SUITES TO SUCCUBI | Snapper Music COF 001CD |
| | 22/03/2003 | 44 | 1 | | DAMNATION AND A DAY | Epic 5109632 |

**CRAMPS** US group formed in New York by Lux Interior (Erick Lee Purkhiser, vocals), Poison Ivy Rorschach (Kirsty Marlana Wallace, guitar), Bryan Gregory (guitar) and Mariam Linna (drums). Linna left in 1977 and was replaced by Nick Knox; Gregory left in 1980 and was replaced by Kid Congo Powers. By 1991 the group were Interior, Rorschach, Slim Chance (bass) and Jim Sclavunos (drums). Gregory died on 7/1/2001 at 46 from unknown causes, although he had recently suffered a heart attack.

| | DATE | POS | WKS | BPI | ALBUM TITLE | LABEL & NUMBER |
|---|------|-----|-----|-----|-------------|----------------|
| | 25/06/1983 | 44 | 4 | ○ | OFF THE BONE | Illegal ILP 012 |
| | 26/11/1983 | 74 | 2 | | SMELL OF FEMALE | Ace NED 6 |
| | 01/03/1986 | 34 | 6 | | A DATE WITH ELVIS | Big Beat WIKA 46 |
| | 24/02/1990 | 62 | 1 | | STAY STICK! | Ensign ENVLP 1001 |

○ Silver disc  ● Gold disc  ✪ Platinum disc (additional platinum units are indicated by a figure following the symbol)  ❶[9] Number of weeks album topped the UK chart

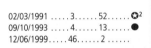

### CRANBERRIES
Irish rock group formed in Limerick in 1990 by Noel Hogan (born 25/12/1971, Woycross, guitar), Mike Hogan (born 29/4/1973, Woycross, bass) and Fergal Lawler (born 4/3/1971, Limerick, drums) as The Cranberry Saw Us. Joined by Delores O'Riordan (born 6/9/1971, Limerick, lead vocals) in 1991, they shortened their name to The Cranberries. The group won the 1995 MTV Europe Music Award for Best Song for *Zombie*.

| 13/03/1993 | ❶¹ | 86 | ✪² | EVERYBODY ELSE IS DOING IT, SO WHY CAN'T WE? | Island CID 8003 |
| 15/10/1994 | 2 | 78 | ✪³ | NO NEED TO ARGUE ◇⁵ | Island CID 8029 |
| 11/05/1996 | 2 | 19 | ● | TO THE FAITHFUL DEPARTED ◇ | Island CID 8048 |
| 01/05/1999 | 7 | 5 | ○ | BURY THE HATCHET ◇ | Island US 5246442 |
| 03/11/2001 | 61 | 1 | | WAKE UP AND SMELL THE COFFEE | MCA 1127062 |
| 28/09/2002 | 20 | 4 | | STARS – THE BEST OF 1992–2002 | Universal TV 0633862 |

### CRANES
UK rock group formed in Portsmouth in 1988 by Alison Shaw (bass/vocals), Jim Shaw (drums), Mark Francombe (guitar) and Matt Cope (bass).

| 28/09/1991 | 52 | 1 | | WINGS OF JOY | Dedicated DEDLP 003 |
| 08/05/1993 | 40 | 1 | | FOREVER | Dedicated DEDCD 009 |

### CRASH TEST DUMMIES
Canadian rock group formed by Brad Roberts (born 10/1/1964, Winnipeg, vocals), Dan Roberts (born 22/5/1967, Winnipeg, bass), Ellen Reid (born 14/7/1966, Selkirk, keyboards) and Benjamin Darvill (born 4/1/1967, Winnipeg, harmonica), adding drummer Mitch Dorge (born 15/9/1960, Winnipeg) after their first album. They won the 1994 MTV Europe Music Award for Breakthrough Artist.

| 14/05/1994 | 2 | 23 | ● | GOD SHUFFLED HIS FEET ◇² | RCA 74321201522 |

### CRASS
UK group formed in 1978 by Steve Ignorant (vocals) and Penny Rimbaud (drums), later adding Eve Libertine (vocals), Joy de Vivra (vocals), Phil Free (guitar), Andy Palmer (guitar), Pete Wright (bass) and Mick G Duffield (backing vocals) to the line-up.

| 28/08/1982 | 26 | 2 | | CHRIST THE ALBUM | Crass BOLLOX 2U2 |

### BEVERLEY CRAVEN
UK singer/pianist (born 28/6/1963, Sri Lanka) who grew up in England and moved to London at the age of nineteen. Named Best British Newcomer at the 1992 BRIT Awards.

| 02/03/1991 | 3 | 52 | ✪² | BEVERLEY CRAVEN | Epic 4670531 |
| 09/10/1993 | 4 | 13 | ● | LOVE SCENES | Epic 4745172 |
| 12/06/1999 | 46 | 2 | | MIXED EMOTIONS | Epic 4941502 |

### MICHAEL CRAWFORD
UK actor (born Michael Patrick Dumble-Smith, 19/1/1942, Salisbury) best known as Frank Spencer, the unlikely hero in the TV comedy *Some Mothers Do 'Ave 'Em*. Also a noted musical actor, having appeared in *Barnum* and *Phantom Of The Opera*. He was awarded an OBE in 1987.

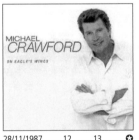

| 28/11/1987 | 12 | 13 | ✪ | SONGS FROM STAGE AND SCREEN **MICHAEL CRAWFORD & THE LONDON SYMPHONY ORCHESTRA** | Telstar STAR 2308 |
| 02/12/1989 | 31 | 7 | ● | WITH LOVE | Telstar STAR 2340 |
| 09/11/1991 | 3 | 36 | ✪² | **MICHAEL CRAWFORD PERFORMS ANDREW LLOYD WEBBER MICHAEL CRAWFORD & THE LONDON SYMPHONY ORCHESTRA** | Telstar STAR 2544 |
| 13/11/1993 | 12 | 11 | ✪ | A TOUCH OF MUSIC IN THE NIGHT | Telstar TCD 2676 |
| 19/11/1994 | 64 | 3 | | THE LOVE SONGS ALBUM | Telstar TCD 2748 |
| 21/11/1998 | 65 | 2 | | ON EAGLE'S WINGS | Atlantic 7567830762 |
| 25/12/1999 | 69 | 1 | | THE MOST WONDERFUL TIME OF THE YEAR | Telstar TV TTVCD 3111 |

## RANDY CRAWFORD
US singer (born 18/2/1952, Macon, GA) who began singing professionally in 1967 but did not release a debut album until 1976. The success of the Crusaders' *Street Life* in 1979, on which she was lead vocalist, led to the group producing *Now We May Begin*, her solo chart breakthrough. She won the 1982 BRIT Award for Best Female (even though the award was actually for the Best *British* Female).

| Date | POS | WKS | BPI | Album Title | Label & Number |
|---|---|---|---|---|---|
| 28/06/1980 | 10 | 16 | ○ | **NOW WE MAY BEGIN** | Warner Brothers K 56791 |
| 16/05/1981 | 2 | 60 | ✪ | **SECRET COMBINATION** | Warner Brothers K 56904 |
| 12/06/1982 | 7 | 17 | ○ | **WINDSONG** | Warner Brothers K 57011 |
| 22/10/1983 | 37 | 4 | | NIGHTLINE | Warner Brothers 9239761 |
| 13/10/1984 | 10 | 17 | ● | **MISS RANDY CRAWFORD – THE GREATEST HITS** | K-Tel NE 1281 |
| 28/06/1986 | 14 | 10 | ○ | ABSTRACT EMOTIONS | Warner Brothers WX 46 |
| 10/10/1987 | 27 | 13 | ● | THE LOVE SONGS | Telstar STAR 2299 |
| 21/10/1989 | 63 | 1 | | RICH AND POOR | Warner Brothers WX 308 |
| 27/03/1993 | 8 | 13 | | **THE VERY BEST OF RANDY CRAWFORD** | Dino DINCD 58 |
| 12/02/2000 | 22 | 4 | | LOVES SONGS – THE VERY BEST OF RANDY CRAWFORD | warner.esp WMMCD 002 |

## ROBERT CRAY BAND
US blues guitarist (born 1/8/1953, Columbus, GA) who formed his first band in 1974 with the best-known line-up of Jim Pugh (keyboards), Karl Sevareid (bass) and Kevin Haves (drums). He also recorded with Eric Clapton. He has won five Grammy Awards including Best Traditional Blues Recording in 1986 with Albert Collins and Johnny Copeland for *Showdown*, Best Contemporary Blues Recording in 1988 for *Don't Be Afraid Of The Dark*, Best Rock instrumental in 1996 with Jimmie Vaughan, Eric Clapton, Bonnie Raitt, B.B. King, Buddy Guy, Dr. John and Art Neville for *SRV Shuffle* and Best Contemporary Blues Recording in 1999 for *Take Your Shoes Off*. The Memphis Horns are led by Wayne Jackson (trumpet) and Andrew Love (tenor saxophone).

| Date | POS | WKS | BPI | Album Title | Label & Number |
|---|---|---|---|---|---|
| 12/10/1985 | 68 | 1 | ○ | FALSE ACCUSATIONS | Demon FIEND 43 |
| 15/11/1986 | 34 | 28 | ○ | STRONG PERSUADER 1987 Grammy Award for Best Contemporary Blues Recording | Mercury MERH 97 |
| 03/09/1988 | 13 | 12 | ● | DON'T BE AFRAID OF THE DARK | Mercury MERH 129 |
| 29/09/1990 | 19 | 7 | ○ | MIDNIGHT STROLL **ROBERT CRAY BAND WITH THE MEMPHIS HORNS** | Mercury 8466521 |
| 12/09/1992 | 29 | 3 | | I WAS WARNED **ROBERT CRAY** | Mercury 5127212 |
| 16/01/1993 | 48 | 1 | | SHAME AND SIN | Mercury 5185172 |
| 20/05/1995 | 63 | 1 | | SOME RAINY MORNING **ROBERT CRAY** | Mercury 5269282 |

## CRAZY TOWN
US rock/rap group formed in Los Angeles, CA by lyricists/singers/producers Seth 'Shifty Shellshock' Binzer and Bret 'Epic' Mazur, Doug 'Faydoedeelay' Miller (bass), Kraig 'Squirrel' Tyler (guitar), Rust Epique (guitar), Anthony 'Trouble' Valli (guitar), DJ AM (turntables) and James 'JBJ' Bradley Junior (drums). Epique died from a heart attack on 9/3/2004.

| Date | POS | WKS | BPI | Album Title | Label & Number |
|---|---|---|---|---|---|
| 21/04/2001 | 15 | 9 | ○ | THE GIFT OF GAME | Columbia 4952972 |

## CREAM
UK group formed in 1966 by Eric Clapton (born Eric Clapp, 30/3/1945, Ripley, guitar/vocals), Jack Bruce (born John Bruce, 14/5/1943, Lanarkshire, vocals/bass) and Ginger Baker (born Peter Baker, 19/8/1939, London, drums). All three members had achieved considerable success with other outfits: Clapton with the Yardbirds, Bruce with Manfred Mann, and Baker with Alexis Korner and Graham Bond. They announced their intention to split in 1968, finally disbanding in August 1969. The group was inducted into the Rock & Roll Hall of Fame in 1993.

| Date | POS | WKS | BPI | Album Title | Label & Number |
|---|---|---|---|---|---|
| 24/12/1966 | 6 | 17 | | **FRESH CREAM** | Reaction 593001 |
| 18/11/1967 | 5 | 42 | | **DISRAELI GEARS** | Reaction 594003 |
| 17/08/1968 | 7 | 13 | | **WHEELS OF FIRE (SINGLE: IN THE STUDIO)** ▲[4] | Polydor 583033 |
| 17/08/1968 | 3 | 26 | | **WHEELS OF FIRE (DOUBLE: LIVE AND STUDIO)** | Polydor 583031/2 |
| 08/02/1969 | 7 | 2 | | **FRESH CREAM** Re-issue of Reaction 593001 | Reaction 594001 |
| 15/03/1969 | ❶[4] | 28 | | **GOODBYE** | Polydor 583053 |
| 08/11/1969 | 6 | 34 | | **THE BEST OF CREAM** | Polydor 583060 |
| 04/07/1970 | 4 | 15 | | **LIVE CREAM** | Polydor 2383 016 |
| 24/06/1972 | 15 | 5 | | LIVE CREAM VOLUME 2 | Polydor 2383 119 |
| 26/09/1987 | 3 | 109 | ✪[3] | **THE CREAM OF ERIC CLAPTON ERIC CLAPTON AND CREAM** | Polydor ECTV 1 |

## CREATURES
UK spin-off group formed by ex-Siouxsie And The Banshees Siouxsie (born Susan Dillon, 27/5/1957) and her husband drummer Budgie (born Peter Clark, 21/8/1957).

| Date | POS | WKS | BPI | Album Title | Label & Number |
|---|---|---|---|---|---|
| 28/05/1983 | 17 | 9 | | FEAST | Wonderland SHELP 1 |

## CREDIT TO THE NATION
UK rap group comprising of Matty Hanson (also known as MC Fusion) and dancers Tyrone (also known as T-Swing) and Kelvin (also known as Mista G). The group also recorded with Chumbawamba.

○ Silver disc ● Gold disc ✪ Platinum disc (additional platinum units are indicated by a figure following the symbol) ❶[9] Number of weeks album topped the UK chart

| | | | | | |
|---|---|---|---|---|---|
| 09/04/1994 | 20 | 3 | | TAKE DIS | One Little Indian TPLP 44CDH |

## CREED
US rock group formed in Tallahassee, FL in 1995 by Scott Stapp (vocals), Mark Tremonti (guitar), Brian Marshall (bass) and Scott Phillips (drums). Marshall left in 2000 and was replaced by Brett Hestla. Scott Stapp and Mark Tremonti won the 2000 Grammy Award for Best Rock Song for *With Arms Wide Open*.

| | | | | | |
|---|---|---|---|---|---|
| 03/02/2001 | 29 | 4 | | HUMAN CLAY ▲² ◆¹⁰ | Epic 4950272 |
| 01/12/2001 | 44 | 17 | ● | WEATHERED ▲⁸ | Epic 5049792 |

## CREEDENCE CLEARWATER REVIVAL
US rock group formed at high school at El Cerrito, CA by John Fogerty (born 28/5/1945, Berkeley, CA, guitar/vocals), Tom Fogerty (born 9/11/1941, Berkeley, guitar), Stuart Cook (born 25/4/1945, Oakland, CA, keyboards/bass) and Doug 'Cosmo' Clifford (born 24/4/1945, Palo Alto, CA, drums). Their first dates were as Tommy Fogerty And The Blue Velvets, and they first recorded as the Golliwogs For Fantasy in 1964. The name changed again in 1967; 'Creedence' was the name of a friend, 'Clearwater' was from a beer commercial and 'Revival' reflected their music. Tom Fogerty went solo in 1971 and the group disbanded in 1972. Tom Fogerty died from tuberculosis on 6/9/1990. They were inducted into the Rock & Roll Hall of Fame in 1993. John Fogerty won the 1997 Grammy Award for Best Rock Album for *Blue Moon Swamp;* he has a star on the Hollywood Walk of Fame.

| | | | | | |
|---|---|---|---|---|---|
| 24/01/1970 | 20 | 6 | | GREEN RIVER ▲⁴ | Liberty LBS 83273 |
| 28/03/1970 | 10 | 24 | | WILLY AND THE POOR BOYS | Liberty LBS 83338 |
| 02/05/1970 | 62 | 1 | | BAYOU COUNTRY | Liberty LBS 83261 |
| 12/09/1970 | ❶¹ | 15 | | COSMO'S FACTORY ▲⁹ | Liberty LBS 83388 |
| 23/01/1971 | 23 | 12 | | PENDULUM | Liberty LBG 83400 |
| 30/06/1979 | 35 | 5 | | GREATEST HITS | Fantasy FT 558 |
| 19/10/1985 | 68 | 2 | | THE CREEDENCE COLLECTION | Impression IMDP 3 |

## KID CREOLE AND THE COCONUTS
US singer Kid Creole (born Thomas Darnell August Browder in 1951 in Haiti) moved to New York with his family and took a songwriting job with Chappell before linking with his brother Stony to form Dr Buzzard's Original Savannah Band that achieved some success in the UK during the swing revival of the mid 1970s. Litigation ended Dr Buzzard and Darnell then joined up with Coati Mundi (real name Andy Hernandez) to form the Coconuts, with Fonda Rae, Lordes Cotto, Brooksi Wells, Franz Krauns, Andrew Lloyd, Winston Grennan and Peter Schott, signing with the Ze label. Both the Coconuts and Coati Mundi subsequently recorded on their own. Kid Creole appeared in the film *Against All Odds*.

| | | | | | |
|---|---|---|---|---|---|
| 22/05/1982 | 3 | 40 | ✪ | TROPICAL GANGSTERS | Ze ILPS 7016 |
| 26/06/1982 | 99 | 1 | | FRESH FRUIT IN FOREIGN PLACES | Ze ILPS 7014 |
| 17/09/1983 | 21 | 6 | | DOPPELGANGER | Island ILPS 9743 |
| 15/09/1984 | 21 | 7 | | CRE-OLE (BEST OF KID CREOLE AND COCONUTS) | Island IMA 13 |

## CRICKETS
US group formed by Buddy Holly who had signed with Decca Records in 1956. The Crickets included long-term drummer Jerry Allison (born 31/8/1939, Hillsboro, TX), Niki Sullivan (rhythm guitar) and Joe Maudlin (bass). They re-recorded *That'll Be The Day*, which was released by Brunswick in the US. Its success enabled Holly to operate as a soloist with Coral and as a member of The Crickets for Brunswick, although both labels were from the same stable. Holly split with The Crickets in 1958 and the group underwent numerous personnel changes based around the nucleus of Allison and singer/guitarist Sonny Curtis (born 9/5/1937, Meadow, TX). The Crickets also provided backing on Holly's early hits. Sullivan died on 6/4/2004.

| | | | | | |
|---|---|---|---|---|---|
| 19/04/1958 | 5 | 1 | | CHIRPING CRICKETS | Coral LVA 9081 |
| 25/03/1961 | 13 | 7 | | IN STYLE WITH THE CRICKETS | Coral LVA 9142 |
| 27/10/1962 | 2 | 27 | | BOBBY VEE MEETS THE CRICKETS | Liberty LBY 1086 |
| 11/03/1978 | ❶³ | 20 | ✪ | 20 GOLDEN GREATS | EMI EMTV 8 |
| 20/02/1993 | ❶¹ | 9 | ● | WORDS OF LOVE | Polygram TV 5144872 |
| 28/09/1999 | 25 | 3 | | THE VERY BEST OF BUDDY HOLLY AND THE CRICKETS This and the above two hits credited to **BUDDY HOLLY & THE CRICKETS** | Universal Music TV 1120462 |

## BING CROSBY
US singer/actor (born Harry Lills Crosby, 2/5/1901, Tacoma, WA, though his year of birth is sometimes given as 1904); he first teamed with Al Rinker in 1926 in Paul Whiteman's band. They later added Harry Barris to the line-up and became the Rhythm Boys. The trio split with Whiteman in 1930; the following year Crosby won a CBS radio contract and went solo. He sold more than 300 million records and starred in more than 50 films, earning an Oscar for *Going My Way* in 1944. His 1942 recording of *White Christmas* was honoured with a Grammy Hall of Fame Award in 1974. He died from a heart attack while playing golf near Madrid on 14/10/1977. He has a star on the Hollywood Walk of Fame for his contribution to recording, a second for motion pictures and a third star for radio.

| | | | | | |
|---|---|---|---|---|---|
| 08/10/1960 | 7 | 11 | | JOIN BING AND SING ALONG | Warner Brothers WM 4021 |
| 21/12/1974 | 45 | 3 | ○ | WHITE CHRISTMAS | MCA MCF 2568 |
| 20/09/1975 | 28 | 6 | ○ | THAT'S WHAT LIFE IS ALL ABOUT | United Artists UAG 29730 |
| 05/11/1977 | 9 | 2 | | LIVE AT THE LONDON PALLADIUM | K-Tel NE 951 |
| 05/11/1977 | 41 | 7 | | THE BEST OF BING | MCA MCF 2540 |
| 17/12/1977 | 25 | 7 | ○ | SEASONS | Polydor 2442 151 |
| 05/05/1979 | 29 | 3 | | SONGS OF A LIFETIME | Philips 6641 923 |
| 14/12/1991 | 66 | 3 | | CHRISTMAS WITH BING CROSBY | Telstar STAR 2468 |
| 23/11/1996 | 59 | 3 | | THE BEST OF BING CROSBY | MCA MCD 11561 |

---

▲⁹ Number of weeks album topped the US chart   ◆¹² RIAA Diamond Awards   ◇³ IFPI Platinum Europe Awards

**CROSBY STILLS NASH AND YOUNG** US/UK rock trio formed in 1968 by David Crosby (born David Van Cortland, 14/8/1941, Los Angeles, CA, guitar), Stephen Stills (born 3/1/1945, Dallas, TX, guitar/keyboards/bass) and Graham Nash (born 2/2/1942, Blackpool, guitar), all of whom had achieved success with other groups: Crosby with Byrds, Stills with Buffalo Springfield and Nash with the Hollies. Canadian guitarist Neil Young (born 12/11/1945, Toronto) joined in 1969 and left in 1974; the group reunited in 1988. David Crosby spent periods in prison for drug-related offences but was allowed out to join with Stills and Nash at Live Aid in 1984. The group was named Best New Artist at the 1969 Grammy Awards and was inducted into the Rock & Roll Hall of Fame in 1997. They have a star on the Hollywood Walk of Fame.

| | | | | | |
|---|---|---|---|---|---|
| 24/04/1971 | 12 | 7 | | IF ONLY I COULD REMEMBER MY NAME **DAVID CROSBY** | Atlantic 2401 005 |
| 13/05/1972 | 13 | 5 | | GRAHAM NASH AND DAVID CROSBY **GRAHAM NASH AND DAVID CROSBY** | Atlantic K 50011 |
| 23/08/1969 | 25 | 5 | | CROSBY, STILLS AND NASH **DAVID CROSBY, STEPHEN STILLS AND GRAHAM NASH** | Atlantic 588189 |
| 30/05/1970 | 5 | 61 | | DÉJÀ VU ▲[1] | Atlantic 2401 001 |
| 22/05/1971 | 5 | 12 | | FOUR-WAY STREET ▲[1] | Atlantic 2956 004 |
| 21/09/1974 | 25 | 6 | | SO FAR ▲[1] | Atlantic K 50023 |
| 09/07/1977 | 23 | 9 | | CSN **DAVID CROSBY, STEPHEN STILLS AND GRAHAM NASH** | Atlantic K 50369 |
| 06/11/1999 | 54 | 1 | | LOOKING FORWARD | Atlantic 9362474362 |

**CROSS** UK group formed in 1987 by Roger Taylor (born Roger Meddows-Taylor, 26/1/1949, King's Lynn, Norfolk, guitar/vocals), Clayton Moss (guitar), Spike Edney (keyboards), Peter Noone (bass) and Josh Macrae (drums). Taylor was also in Queen and had made two solo albums prior to forming Cross.

| | | | | | |
|---|---|---|---|---|---|
| 06/02/1988 | 58 | 2 | | SHOVE IT | Virgin V 2477 |

**CHRISTOPHER CROSS** US singer (born Christopher Geppert, 3/5/1951, San Antonio, TX) who formed his own group in 1973 with Rob Meurer, Andy Salmon and Tommy Taylor. He went solo in 1980 and won four Grammy Awards that year including: Record of the Year and Song of the Year for *Sailing* and Best New Artist. He also won the 1982 Oscar for Best Film Song for *Arthur's Theme (Best That You Can Do)* from the 1981 film *Arthur* with Burt Bacharach, Carole Bayer Sager and Peter Allen.

| | | | | | |
|---|---|---|---|---|---|
| 21/02/1981 | 14 | 77 | ○ | CHRISTOPHER CROSS 1980 Grammy Award for Album of the Year | Warner Brothers K 56789 |
| 19/02/1983 | 4 | 16 | ● | ANOTHER PAGE | Warner Brothers W 3757 |

**SHERYL CROW** US singer (born 11/2/1963, Kennett, MO) who began as a backing singer for Michael Jackson, Don Henley and George Harrison among others, before signing with A&M in 1991. She was named Best International Female at the 1997 BRIT Awards. She has also won nine Grammy Awards including: Record of the Year and Best Female Pop Vocal Performance in 1994 for *All I Wanna Do*; Best New Artist in 1994; Best Female Rock Vocal Performance in 1996 for *If It Makes You Happy*; Best Female Rock Vocal Performance in 1999 for *Sweet Child O' Mine*; Best Female Rock Vocal Performance in 2000 for *There Goes The Neighborhood*; and Best Female Rock Vocal Performance in 2002 for *Steve McQueen*.

| | | | | | |
|---|---|---|---|---|---|
| 12/02/1994 | 8 | 55 | ○[2] | TUESDAY NIGHT MUSIC CLUB ◇ | A&M 5401262 |
| 12/10/1996 | 5 | 70 | ○[3] | SHERYL CROW ◇ 1996 Grammy Award for Best Rock Album | A&M 5405902 |
| 03/10/1998 | 2 | 32 | ○ | THE GLOBE SESSIONS 1998 Grammy Award for Best Rock Album | A&M 5409742 |
| 20/04/2002 | 2 | 8 | ● | C'MON C'MON | A&M 4932622 |
| 25/10/2003 | 2 | 16 | ○ | THE VERY BEST OF | A&M 9861092 |

**CROWDED HOUSE** Australian/New Zealand group formed in 1985 by Neil Finn (born 27/5/1958, Te Awamutu, New Zealand, guitar/vocals), Paul Hester (born 8/1/1959, Melbourne, Australia, drums) and Nick Seymour (born 9/12/1958, Benalla, Australia, bass) following the demise of Split Enz. Neil's brother and another former Split Enz member Tim (born 25/6/1952, Te Awamutu) briefly joined the group in 1991 before going solo. Named Best International Group at the 1994 BRIT Awards, they disbanded in 1996.

| | | | | | |
|---|---|---|---|---|---|
| 13/07/1991 | 6 | 86 | ○[2] | WOODFACE | Capitol EST 2144 |
| 23/10/1993 | 4 | 32 | ○ | TOGETHER ALONE | Capitol CDESTU 2215 |

○ Silver disc ● Gold disc ○ Platinum disc (additional platinum units are indicated by a figure following the symbol) ❶[9] Number of weeks album topped the UK chart

| | | | | | |
|---|---|---|---|---|---|
| 06/07/1996 .... **❶**² ..... 66 ...... ✪⁴ | | | | RECURRING DREAM – THE VERY BEST OF CROWDED HOUSE ◇² ........................ | Capitol CDESTX 2283 |
| 19/02/2000 ..... 18 ...... 2 ...... | | | | AFTERGLOW ................................................................ | Capitol 5248042 |

**CROWN HEIGHTS AFFAIR** US R&B group formed in New York by Philip Thomas (vocals), Bert Reid (saxophone), Raymond Reid (guitar), William Anderson (guitar), James 'Ajax' Baynard (trumpet), Raymond Rock (drums/percussion), Howie Young (keyboards) and Muki Wilson (bass) in the early 1970s as Neu Day Express. They made one album for RCA before switching to De-Lite in 1975.

| 23/09/1978 ..... 40 ...... 3 ...... | | | | DREAM WORLD ............................................................. | Philips 6372 754 |

**CRUSADERS** US group formed in Houston, TX by Joe Sample (born 1/2/1939, Houston, keyboards), Wilton Felder (born 31/8/1940, Houston, saxophone), Nesbert 'Stix' Hooper (born 15/8/1938, Houston, drums), Wayne Henderson (born 24/9/1938, Houston, trombone) and Robert 'Pops' Popwell (bass) as the Swingsters in the early 1950s. Relocating to Los Angeles, CA in the 1960s, they became session regulars and made their own jazz recordings for Pacific. They switched to Blue Thumb/ABC and scored numerous club hits as pioneers of jazz-funk, then in 1979 made the pop charts with *Street Life*. By then they were a trio of Sample, Felder and Hooper. The group split in the 1990s, all the members undertaking solo projects, before Sample, Hooper and Felder reunited in 2002.

| 21/07/1979 ..... 10 ..... 16 ...... | | | | STREET LIFE ............................................................... | MCA MCF 3008 |
| 19/07/1980 ..... 40 ...... 5 ...... | | | | RHAPSODY AND BLUE ....................................................... | MCA MCG 4010 |
| 12/09/1981 ..... 47 ...... 5 ...... | | | | STANDING TALL ............................................................ | MCA MCF 3122 |
| 07/04/1984 ..... 46 ...... 4 ...... | | | | GHETTO BLASTER ........................................................... | MCA MCF 3176 |

**BOBBY CRUSH** UK pianist who charted briefly when he won TV's *Opportunity Knocks* in 1972. In the 1980s he wrote the music for the hit single *Orville's Song* by Keith Harris.

| 25/11/1972 ..... 15 ...... 7 ...... | | | | BOBBY CRUSH ............................................................. | Philips 6308 135 |
| 18/12/1982 ..... 53 ...... 5 ...... | | | | THE BOBBY CRUSH INCREDIBLE DOUBLE DECKER PARTY 101 GREAT SONGS .......... | Warwick WW 5126/7 |

**CUD** UK rock group formed in Leeds by Carl Puttnam (born 1967, Ilford, vocals), Mike Dunphy (born 1967, Northumberland, guitar), William Porter (born 1968, Derby, bass) and Steve 'The Drummer From Cud' Goodwin (born 1967, Croydon, drums). They first recorded for Reception.

| 11/07/1992 ..... 30 ...... 1 ...... | | | | ASQUARIUS ................................................................ | A&M 3953902 |
| 23/04/1994 ..... 46 ...... 1 ...... | | | | SHOWBIZ .................................................................. | A&M 5402112 |

**CUDDLES –** see KEITH HARRIS

**JAMIE CULLUM** UK singer/pianist born in 1981 in Wiltshire, he formed the Jamie Cullum Trio with Geoff Gascoyne and Sebastian De Krom.

| 01/11/2003 ..... 3 ..... 35+ .... ✪² | | | | TWENTYSOMETHING ......................................................... | UCJ 9865574 |
| 13/03/2004 ..... 55 ...... 2 ...... ○ | | | | POINTLESS NOSTALGIC Originally released in 2002 without success ............... | Candid CCD79782 |

**CULT** UK rock group formed in Bradford in 1982 by singer Ian Astbury (born Ian Lindsey, 14/5/1962, Heswell) as Southern Death Cult. The group lasted one year before disbanding. Astbury joined guitarist Billy Duffy (born 12/5/1962, Manchester), the two remaining the nucleus ever since, and shortened the name to Cult in 1984. They achieved a US breakthrough with Def Jam label chief Rick Rubin in 1987 and moved to Los Angeles, CA in 1988.

| 18/06/1983 ..... 43 ...... 3 ...... | | | | THE SOUTHERN DEATH CULT **SOUTHERN DEATH CULT** ............................ | Beggars Banquet BEGA 46 |
| 08/09/1984 ..... 21 ...... 8 ...... ○ | | | | DREAMTIME ............................................................... | Beggars Banquet BEGA 57 |
| 26/10/1985 ..... 4 ..... 22 ...... ● | | | | **LOVE SCENES** ............................................................. | Beggars Banquet BEGA 65 |
| 18/04/1987 ..... 4 ..... 27 ...... ● | | | | **ELECTRIC** ................................................................. | Beggars Banquet BEGA 80 |
| 22/04/1989 ..... 3 ..... 11 ...... ● | | | | **SONIC TEMPLE** ............................................................ | Beggars Banquet BEGA 98 |
| 05/10/1991 ..... 9 ...... 4 ...... | | | | CEREMONY ................................................................ | Beggars Banquet BEGA 122 |
| 13/02/1993 ..... **❶**¹ .... 8 ...... ● | | | | PURE CULT ................................................................ | Beggars Banquet BEGACD 130 |
| 22/10/1994 ..... 21 ...... 2 ...... | | | | THE CULT ................................................................. | Beggars Banquet BBQCD 164 |
| 23/06/2001 ..... 69 ...... 1 ...... | | | | BEYOND GOOD AND EVIL .................................................... | Atlantic 7567834402 |

**CULTURE** Jamaican reggae group formed by Joseph Hill, Albert Walker and Kenneth Paley (also known as Kenneth Dayes). Hill, chief songwriter and lead singer, split with the other singers in 1982 but continued to work under the Culture moniker.

| 01/04/1978 ..... 60 ...... 1 ...... | | | | TWO SEVENS CLASH ........................................................ | Lightning LIP 1 |

**CULTURE BEAT** Multinational dance group formed by German producer Torsten Fenslau, Juergen Katzmann and Peter Zweier with stage performances handled by Tania Evans and rapper Jay Supreme. Fenslau was killed in a car crash on 6/11/1993 aged 29.

| 25/09/1993 ..... 13 ..... 10 ...... ● | | | | SERENITY ................................................................. | Dance Pool 4741012 |

## CULTURE CLUB

UK group formed in London in 1981 by Boy George (born George O'Dowd, 14/6/1961, Bexley, vocals), Roy Hay (born 12/8/1961, Southend-on-Sea, guitar/keyboards), Michael Craig (born 15/2/1960, London, bass) and Jon Moss (born 11/9/1957, London, drums). Signed to Virgin six months after their debut gig, they were one of the top groups of the early 1980s, the media focusing on the gender of the lead singer. They disbanded in 1987, Boy George having already gone solo, although they re-formed in 1997. They were named Best UK Group at the 1984 BRIT Awards, the same year as winning the Best Single category with *Karma Chameleon*. They also won the 1983 Grammy Award for Best New Artist.

| | | | | |
|---|---|---|---|---|
| 16/10/1982 | 5 | 59 | ✪ | KISSING TO BE CLEVER ............................................................. Virgin V 2232 |
| 22/10/1983 | ❶⁵ | 56 | ✪³ | COLOUR BY NUMBERS ............................................................. Virgin V 2285 |
| 03/11/1984 | 2 | 13 | ✪ | WAKING UP WITH THE HOUSE ON FIRE ................................. Virgin V 2330 |
| 12/04/1986 | 10 | 6 | ○ | FROM LUXURY TO HEARTACHE ................................................ Virgin V 2380 |
| 18/04/1987 | 8 | 10 | ● | THIS TIME THE FIRST FOUR YEARS ........................................ Virgin VTV 1 |
| 02/10/1993 | 24 | 5 | | AT WORST… THE BEST OF BOY GEORGE & CULTURE CLUB **BOY GEORGE/CULTURE CLUB** ........ Virgin VTCD 19 |
| 21/11/1998 | 15 | 13 | ✪ | GREATEST MOMENTS ............................................................. Virgin CDV 2865 |
| 04/12/1999 | 64 | 1 | | DON'T MIND IF I DO ............................................................. Virgin CDV 2887 |

## CURE

UK rock group initially formed in 1977 in response to an advertisement by a record company offering a contract. Known as Easy Cure, they were dropped before releasing anything because they wanted to record their own material. They subsequently signed with Fiction in 1978. With various changes over the years, the chief line-up was Robert Smith (born 21/4/1959, Blackpool, guitar/vocals), Lol Tolhurst (born 3/2/1959, keyboards), Simon Gallup (born 1/6/1960, Duxhurst, bass), Porl Thompson (born 8/11/1957, London, guitar) and Boris Williams (born 24/4/1958, Versailles, France, drums). Smith later joined Siouxsie & The Banshees member Steve Severin in the one-off project The Glove. The Cure won the 1990 BRIT Award for Best Video for *Lovesong* and Best British Group at the 1991 BRIT Awards.

| | | | | |
|---|---|---|---|---|
| 02/06/1979 | 44 | 3 | | THREE IMAGINARY BOYS .......................................................... Fiction FIX 001 |
| 03/05/1980 | 20 | 10 | | 17 SECONDS .......................................................................... Fiction FIX 004 |
| 25/04/1981 | 14 | 8 | ○ | FAITH ................................................................................... Fiction FIX 6 |
| 15/05/1982 | 8 | 9 | | **PORNOGRAPHY** ..................................................................... Fiction FIX D7 |
| 03/09/1983 | 71 | 7 | ✪ | BOYS DON'T CRY .................................................................... Fiction SPELP 26 |
| 24/12/1983 | 26 | 14 | ○ | JAPANESE WHISPERS: SINGLES NOV 82–NOV 83 ...................... Fiction FIXM 8 |
| 12/05/1984 | 10 | 10 | ○ | THE TOP .............................................................................. Fiction FIXS 9 |
| 03/11/1984 | 26 | 4 | | CONCERT – THE CURE LIVE ...................................................... Fiction FIXH 10 |
| 07/09/1985 | 7 | 13 | ● | **THE HEAD ON THE DOOR** ....................................................... Fiction FIXH 11 |
| 31/05/1986 | 4 | 35 | ● | **STANDING ON A BEACH – THE SINGLES** ................................. Fiction FIXH 12 |
| 06/06/1987 | 6 | 15 | ● | KISS ME KISS ME KISS ME ....................................................... Fiction FIXH 13 |
| 13/05/1989 | 3 | 26 | ● | **DISINTEGRATION** ................................................................. Fiction FIXH 14 |
| 17/11/1990 | 8 | 17 | ● | MIXED UP ............................................................................ Fiction 8470991 |
| 06/04/1991 | 10 | 5 | | **ENTREAT** ............................................................................ Fiction FIXH 17 |
| 02/05/1992 | ❶¹ | 13 | ● | WISH .................................................................................. Fiction FIXCD 20 |
| 25/09/1993 | 29 | 2 | | SHOWBIZ ............................................................................. Fiction FIXCD 25 |
| 06/11/1993 | 56 | 1 | | PARIS .................................................................................. Fiction FIXCD 26 |
| 18/05/1996 | 9 | 6 | | **WILD MOOD SWINGS** ........................................................... Fiction FIXCD 28 |
| 15/11/1997 | 37 | 2 | | GALORE – THE SINGLES 1987–1997 .......................................... Fiction FIXCD 30 |
| 26/02/2000 | 14 | 2 | | BLOODFLOWERS ..................................................................... Fiction FIXCD 31 |
| 24/11/2001 | 33 | 5 | | GREATEST HITS ...................................................................... Fiction 5894352 |

## CURIOSITY KILLED THE CAT

UK four-piece group formed by Ben Volpeliere-Pierrot (born 19/5/1964, London, vocals), Julian Godfrey Brookhouse (born 13/5/1963, London, guitar), Nicholas Bernard Throp (born 25/10/1964, London, bass) and Michael Drummond (born 27/1/1964, Middlesex, drums) as The Twilight Children. Adding keyboard player Toby Anderson in 1984, they changed their name to Curiosity Killed The Cat, later shortening it to Curiosity.

| | | | | |
|---|---|---|---|---|
| 09/05/1987 | ❶² | 24 | ✪ | KEEP YOUR DISTANCE ............................................................. Mercury CATLP 1 |
| 04/11/1989 | 29 | 3 | ○ | GETAHEAD ............................................................................ Mercury 8420101 |

## CURVE

UK rock group formed by Toni Halliday (vocals), Dean Garcia (guitar), Debbie Smith (guitar), Alex Mitchell (guitar) and Monti (drums). They disbanded in 1994 but re-formed in 1997.

| | | | | |
|---|---|---|---|---|
| 21/03/1992 | 11 | 3 | | DOPPELGANGER ..................................................................... AnXious ANXCD 77 |
| 19/06/1993 | 72 | 1 | | RADIO SESSIONS .................................................................... AnXious ANXCD 80 |
| 25/09/1993 | 23 | 2 | | CUCKOO ............................................................................... AnXious ANXCD 81 |

## CURVED AIR

UK rock group formed by Ian Eyre (born 11/9/1949, Knaresborough, bass), Sonia Kristina (born 14/4/1949, Brentwood, vocals), Francis Monkman (born 9/6/1949, London, guitar/keyboards), Florian Pilkington-Miska (born 3/6/1950, London, drums) and Darryl Way (born 17/12/1948, Taunton, violin). After a 1970 debut album they were college circuit regulars for the rest of

the decade. When Pilkington-Miska left, he was replaced by Stewart Copeland (born 16/7/1952, Alexandria, Egypt), later in Police. Monkman later became a founding member of Sky.

| | | | | | |
|---|---|---|---|---|---|
| 05/12/1970 | 8 | 21 | | AIR CONDITIONING | Warner Brothers WSX 3012 |
| 09/10/1971 | 11 | 6 | | CURVED AIR | Warner Brothers K 46092 |
| 13/05/1972 | 20 | 5 | | PHANTASMAGORIA | Reprise K 46158 |

### MALACHI CUSH
Irish singer (born 1980, Donaghmore, County Tyrone) first known as one of the competitors on *Fame Academy*. He worked as a gas fitter before turning to singing.

| | | | | | |
|---|---|---|---|---|---|
| 05/04/2003 | 17 | 4 | | MALACHI | Mercury/Universal TV 0772802 |

### CUTTING CREW
UK rock group formed by Nick Van Eede (born 14/6/1958, East Grinstead, vocals), Kevin Scott MacMichael (born 7/11/1951, Halifax, Canada, guitar), Colin Farley (born 24/2/1959, bass) and Martin Beedle (born 18/9/1961, Hull, drums). MacMichael died from cancer on 31/12/2002.

| | | | | | |
|---|---|---|---|---|---|
| 29/11/1986 | 41 | 6 | ○ | BROADCAST | Siren SIRENLP 7 |

### CYPRESS HILL
US rap group formed in Los Angeles, CA by Sennen 'Sen Dog' Reyes (born 20/11/1965, Cuba), Louis 'B Real' Freeze (born 2/6/1970, Los Angeles, CA) and Lawrence 'Mixmaster Muggs' Muggerud (born 28/1/1968, New York). B Real later recorded solo. They appeared in the 1993 film *The Meteor Man*.

| | | | | | |
|---|---|---|---|---|---|
| 07/08/1993 | 13 | 49 | ● | BLACK SUNDAY ▲2 | Columbia 4740752 |
| 11/11/1995 | 11 | 5 | ○ | CYPRESS HILL III (TEMPLES OF BOOM) | Columbia 4781279 |
| 24/08/1996 | 29 | 4 | | UNRELEASED AND REVAMPED | Columbia 4852302 |
| 17/10/1998 | 25 | 3 | | IV | Columbia 4916046 |
| 06/05/2000 | 6 | 5 | | SKULL & BONES | Columbia 4951839 |
| 15/12/2001 | 71 | 1 | | STONED RAIDERS | Columbia 5041712 |
| 03/04/2004 | 53 | 1 | | TILL DEATH DO US PART | Columbia 5150292 |

### BILLY RAY CYRUS
US singer (born 25/8/1961, Flatwood, KY) who initially made his name backing country star Reba McEntire. Signed by Mercury as a solo artist in 1992, he scored a US #1 with his debut single and album. He later recorded a parody of his debut with The Chipmunks and became an actor, appearing on the TV series *Doc*.

| | | | | | |
|---|---|---|---|---|---|
| 29/08/1992 | 9 | 10 | ● | SOME GAVE ALL ▲17 | Mercury 5106352 |

### HOLGAR CZUKAY
German bass player (born 24/3/1938 , Danzig) and a founding member of Can in 1968; he left towards the end of the 1970s. He recorded with Brian Eno and later worked with Jah Wobble as well as David Sylvian. He rejoined Can in 1989.

| | | | | | |
|---|---|---|---|---|---|
| 02/04/1988 | 71 | 1 | | PLIGHT AND PREMONITION DAVID SYLVAN AND HOLGAR CZUKAY | Virgin VE 11 |

# D

### D-INFLUENCE
UK vocal/instrumental/production group formed by Kwame Amankwa Kwaten, Edward James Baden-Powell, Steven Marston and Sarah-Ann Webb.

25/10/1997 . . . . . 56 . . . . . . 1 . . . . . . LONDON . . . . . . . . . . . . . . . . . . . . . . . . . . . . . . . . . . . . . . . . . . . . . . . . . . . . . . . . . . . . . . . . . . . . . . . . . . . . . . . . . . . . . . . . . . . . . . . . . . Echo ECHDD 27

### D MOB
UK dance/disco aggregation led by producer/writer Dancin' Danny D (born Daniel Kojo Poku) who first recorded as The Taurus Boys before adopting the D Mob moniker.

11/11/1989 . . . . . 46 . . . . . 11 . . . . . . A LITTLE BIT OF THIS, A LITTLE BIT OF THAT . . . . . . . . . . . . . . . . . . . . . . . . . . . . . . . . . . . . . . . . . . . . . . . . . . . . . . . . . . . . . . . . ffrr 8281591

### D:REAM
UK duo Peter Cunnah (born 30/8/1966, Derry, Northern Ireland, vocals) and Al McKenzie (born 31/10/1968, Edinburgh, keyboards). Cunnah began his career with Ciderboy before moving to London where he met McKenzie, a successful DJ, at the Gardening Club, and the two formed D:Ream. Cunnah was later a successful songwriter.

30/10/1993 . . . . . 5 . . . . . . 37 . . . . . . ✪ **DREAM ON VOLUME 1** . . . . . . . . . . . . . . . . . . . . . . . . . . . . . . . . . . . . . . . . . . . . . . . . . . . . . . . . . . . . . Magnet 4509933712
30/09/1995 . . . . . 5 . . . . . . 4 . . . . . . ○ **WORLD** . . . . . . . . . . . . . . . . . . . . . . . . . . . . . . . . . . . . . . . . . . . . . . . . . . . . . . . . . . . . . . . . . . . . . . . . . . . . . . Magnet 0630117962

### D-SIDE
Irish vocal group formed in Dublin by Derek Moran (born 15/12/1983, Dublin), Dane Guiden (born in Dublin), Damien Bowe (born 5/5/1981, Laois), Shane Creevey (born 13/12/1982, Dublin) and Derek Ryan (born in Carlow).

17/01/2004 . . . . . 62 . . . . . . 1 . . . . . . STRONGER TOGETHER . . . . . . . . . . . . . . . . . . . . . . . . . . . . . . . . . . . . . . . . . . . . . . . . . . . . . . . . . . . . . . . . . . . Blacklist/Edel 9866006

### D TRAIN
US singer/songwriter James Williams (born in Brooklyn, NYC) with Hubert Eaves III (keyboards). They split in 1985 and Williams went solo. He also recorded with Bob Sinclair.

08/05/1982 . . . . . 72 . . . . . . 4 . . . . . . D-TRAIN . . . . . . . . . . . . . . . . . . . . . . . . . . . . . . . . . . . . . . . . . . . . . . . . . . . . . . . . . . . . . . . . . . . . . . . . . . . . . . . . . . . . . . . . Epic EPC 85683

### DAFT PUNK
French production duo Thomas Bangalter (born 1/1/1975) and Guy Manuel De Homem Christo (born 8/2/1974). Bangalter also produces Stardust and recorded with DJ Falcon.

01/02/1997 . . . . . 8 . . . . . . 17 . . . . . . ● **HOMEWORK** . . . . . . . . . . . . . . . . . . . . . . . . . . . . . . . . . . . . . . . . . . . . . . . . . . . . . . . . . . . . . . . . . . . . . . . . . . Virgin CDV 2821
24/03/2001 . . . . . 2 . . . . . . 37 . . . . . . ✪ **DISCOVERY** ◇ . . . . . . . . . . . . . . . . . . . . . . . . . . . . . . . . . . . . . . . . . . . . . . . . . . . . . . . . . . . . . . . . . . . . . . . Virgin CDVX 2940

### DAISY CHAINSAW
UK group with Katie Jane Garside (vocals), Richard Adams (drums), Vince Johnson (drums) and Crispin Grey (guitar). Garside left after their album debut in 1992.

10/10/1992 . . . . . 62 . . . . . . 1 . . . . . . ELEVENTEEN . . . . . . . . . . . . . . . . . . . . . . . . . . . . . . . . . . . . . . . . . . . . . . . . . . . . . . . . . . . . . . . . . . . . . . . . . . Deva TPLP 100CD

### DAKOTAS – see BILLY J. KRAMER AND THE DAKOTAS

### DALEK I
UK group formed in Liverpool in 1977 by Alan Gill (guitar), David Balfe (bass), Dave Hughes (keyboards), Chris 'Teepee' Shaw (keyboards) and a drum machine. Balfe left in 1979, Hughes left in 1980 and the group finally split in 1985. The group was originally known as Dalek I Love You.

09/08/1980 . . . . . 54 . . . . . . 2 . . . . . . ⟩ COMPASS KUMPAS . . . . . . . . . . . . . . . . . . . . . . . . . . . . . . . . . . . . . . . . . . . . . . . . . . . . . . . . . . . . . . . . . . . Backdoor OPEN 1

### DALI'S CAR
UK group formed in 1984 by Peter Murphy (born 11/7/195, Northampton, vocals) and Mick Karn (born Anthony Michaelides, 24/7/1958, London, bass). They recorded one album before both members concentrated on solo careers.

01/12/1984 . . . . . 84 . . . . . . 1 . . . . . . THE WAKING HOUR . . . . . . . . . . . . . . . . . . . . . . . . . . . . . . . . . . . . . . . . . . . . . . . . . . . . . . . . . . . . . . . . . . Paradox DOXLP 1

### ROGER DALTREY
UK singer (born 1/3/1944, Hammersmith, London) and lead singer with The Who. By 1972 the members of the band were involved in various solo projects, Daltrey opening his own barn studio to work on an album with songwriters Dave Courtney and Leo Sayer. He later appeared in films, including the lead in *McVicar* (1980). Also a fish breeder, he got a settlement of £155,000 from Home Farm after 500,000 fish were found dead at his Iwerne Springs trout farm in Dorset. He featured on The Chieftains' *An Irish Evening Live*, which won the 1992 Grammy Award for Best Traditional Folk Album.

26/07/1975 . . . . . 14 . . . . . 10 . . . . . . ○ RIDE A ROCK HORSE . . . . . . . . . . . . . . . . . . . . . . . . . . . . . . . . . . . . . . . . . . . . . . . . . . . . . . . . . . . . . Polydor 2442 135
04/06/1977 . . . . . 45 . . . . . . 1 . . . . . . ONE OF THE BOYS . . . . . . . . . . . . . . . . . . . . . . . . . . . . . . . . . . . . . . . . . . . . . . . . . . . . . . . . . . . . . . Polydor 2442 146
23/08/1980 . . . . . 39 . . . . . 11 . . . . . . McVICAR Original soundtrack to the film . . . . . . . . . . . . . . . . . . . . . . . . . . . . . . . . . . . . . . . . . . . . . . . . . Polydor POLD 5034
02/11/1985 . . . . . 52 . . . . . . 2 . . . . . . UNDER A RAGING MOON . . . . . . . . . . . . . . . . . . . . . . . . . . . . . . . . . . . . . . . . . . . . . . . . . . . . . . . . . . 10 Records DIX 17

### GLEN DALY
UK singer born in Glasgow who later recorded a number of tribute songs to Celtic FC.

20/11/1971 . . . . . 28 . . . . . . 2 . . . . . . GLASGOW NIGHT OUT . . . . . . . . . . . . . . . . . . . . . . . . . . . . . . . . . . . . . . . . . . . . . . . . . . . . . . . . . Pye Golden Guinea GGL 0479

### DAMAGE
UK R&B vocal group formed in London by Andrez Harriott (born 11/8/1978), Coree Richards (born 29/3/1978), Jayde Jones (born 12/2/1979), Noel Simpson (born 1/1/1976) and Rahsaan 'Ras' Bromfield (born 3/11/1976).

○ Silver disc   ● Gold disc   ✪ Platinum disc (additional platinum units are indicated by a figure following the symbol)   ❶⁹ Number of weeks album topped the UK chart

| 19/04/1997 | 13 | 12 | ○ | FOREVER | Big Life BLRCD 31X |
| 14/04/2001 | 16 | 10 | ● | SINCE YOU'VE BEEN GONE | Cooltempo 5289592 |

**DAMNED** UK punk group formed in 1976 by Captain Sensible (born Raymond Burns, 23/4/1955, London, bass), Brian James (born Brian Robertson, 18/2/1955, Brighton, guitar) and Rat Scabies (born Chris Miller, 30/7/1957, Kingston-upon-Thames, drums), with Dave Vanian (born David Letts, 12/10/1956, Hemel Hempstead, lead vocals) joining later. Debuting as support to the Sex Pistols, two months later they signed with Stiff Records, releasing *New Rose* the following month. It failed to chart, but is regarded as the first UK punk record (and was also Stiff's first release). The first UK punk group to tour the US, they also released the first UK punk album, *Damned Damned Damned*. They split in 1978, later re-forming (after a legal wrangle over the name the Damned) with Alistair Ward replacing James. Ward left in 1980 and was replaced by ex-Eddie & The Hot Rods Paul Gray. Sensible had a simultaneous solo career in 1982, before leaving the group in 1984. The others split in 1989, re-forming in 1991.

| 12/03/1977 | 36 | 10 | | DAMNED DAMNED DAMNED | Stiff SEEZ 1 |
| 17/11/1979 | 31 | 5 | ○ | MACHINE GUN ETIQUETTE | Chiswick CWK 3011 |
| 29/11/1980 | 29 | 3 | | THE BLACK ALBUM | Chiswick CWK 3015 |
| 28/11/1981 | 43 | 12 | | THE BEST OF THE DAMNED | Big Beat DAM 1 |
| 23/10/1982 | 15 | 4 | | STRAWBERRIES | Bronze BRON 542 |
| 27/07/1985 | 11 | 17 | ○ | PHANTASMAGORIA | MCA MCF 542 |
| 13/12/1986 | 40 | 2 | ○ | ANYTHING | MCA MCG 6015 |
| 12/12/1987 | 87 | 1 | | LIGHT AT THE END OF THE TUNNEL | MCA MCSP 312 |

**VIC DAMONE** US singer (born Vito Farinola, 12/6/1928, Brooklyn, NYC) who was a popular ballad singer in the 1950s. He also appeared in films including *Rich Young And Pretty* (1951), *Deep In My Heart* (1954) and *Kismet* (1955), and had his own TV series for two years. He has a star on the Hollywood Walk of Fame, as does his wife Diahann Carroll, whom he married in 1987.

| 25/04/1981 | 28 | 7 | | NOW? | RCA International INTS 5080 |
| 02/04/1983 | 87 | 1 | | VIC DAMONE SINGS THE GREAT SONGS | Cameo 32261 |

**DANA** UK singer (born Rosemary Brown, 30/8/1951, Belfast) whose family moved to the Irish Republic when she was two. She began singing professionally at sixteen and won the Eurovision Song Contest, with *All Kinds Of Everything*, while still at school. She was the first Irish winner and the first Eurovision entry from a foreign country to make the UK top ten. A regular TV performer, in 1997 she came third in the election for President of Eire.

| 27/12/1980 | 43 | 3 | | EVERYTHING IS BEAUTIFUL | Warwick WW 5099 |

**EVAN DANDO** US guitarist/singer (born 4/3/1967, Boston) and ex-leader of The Lemonheads.

| 29/03/2003 | 30 | 1 | | BABY I'M BORED | Setanta SETCD 114 |

**SUZANNE DANDO** UK gymnast (born 3/7/1961) who represented Great Britain at the Olympics and Commonweatlh Games. She also appeared in the 1983 James Bond film *Octopussy* and later became a TV presenter for Sky.

| 17/03/1984 | 87 | 1 | | SHAPE UP AND DANCE WITH SUZANNE DANDO | Lifestyle LEG 21 |

**DANDY WARHOLS** US group formed in Portland, OR in 1994 by Courtney Taylor (vocals/guitar/keyboards), Peter Holmstrom (guitar), Zia McCabe (keyboards/bass) and Eric Hedford (drums). Hedford left in 1998 and was replaced by Brent De Boer.

| 16/05/1998 | 16 | 8 | | COME DOWN | Capitol 8365052 |
| 24/06/2000 | 32 | 9 | ● | THIRTEEN TALES FROM URBAN BOHEMIA | Capitol 8577872 |
| 31/05/2003 | 20 | 3 | | WELCOME TO THE MONKEYHOUSE | Parlophone 5901232 |

**D'ANGELO** US singer (born Michael D'Angelo Archer, 11/2/1974, Richmond, VA), the son of a preacher, who began singing in church and with the Boys Choir of Harlem before signing with EMI in 1993. His partner Angie Stone is also a successful singer. He won two 2000 Grammy Awards including Best Male R&B Vocal Performance for *How Does It Feel*.

| 28/10/1995 | 57 | 2 | ● | BROWN SUGAR | Cooltempo CTCD 46 |
| 26/02/2000 | 21 | 3 | | VOODOO ▲² 2000 Grammy Award for Best R&B Album | Cooltempo 5233732 |

**CHARLIE DANIELS BAND** US singer/guitarist/fiddle player (born 28/10/1937, Wilmington, NC) whose band, formed in 1971, included Tom Crain (guitar), Joe 'Taz' DiGregorio (keyboards), Charles Hayward (bass) and James W Marshall (drums). Later playing sessions in Nashville, he appeared in the 1980 film *Urban Cowboy*. The group won the 1979 Grammy Award for Best Country Performance by a Group for *The Devil Went Down To Georgia*.

| 10/11/1979 | 74 | 1 | | MILLION MILE REFLECTIONS | Epic EPC 83446 |

**DANNY WILSON** UK group formed by Gary Clark (lead guitar/vocals), his brother Kit (keyboards/percussion) and Ged Grimes (bass). Originally called Spencer Tracy, their name came from the 1952 Frank Sinatra film *Meet Danny Wilson*. They disbanded in 1990, with Clark pursuing a solo career and releasing a debut album in 1993.

| 30/04/1988 | 65 | 5 | | MEET DANNY WILSON | Virgin V 2419 |
| 29/07/1989 | 24 | 5 | | BEEBOP MOPTOP | Virgin V 2594 |
| 31/08/1991 | 54 | 1 | | SWEET DANNY WILSON | Virgin V 2669 |

**DANSE SOCIETY** UK group formed in Sheffield by Steve Rawlings (vocals), Dave Patrick (guitar), Bubble (bass), Paul Hampshire (keyboards) and Paul Gilmartin (drums) and known as Y?. Paul Nash (guitar) and Lyndon Scarfe (guitar) were added to the line-up and the name changed to Danse Crazy. Hampshire and Patrick left at the end of 1980 and the name changed again to Danse Society. Tim Wright (bass) joined in 1981. After early releases on IKF and Pax, they signed with Arista in 1983.

| 11/02/1984 | 39 | 4 | | HEAVEN IS WAITING | Society 205 972 |

▲⁹ Number of weeks album topped the US chart ◆¹² RIAA Diamond Awards ◇³ IFPI Platinum Europe Awards

**STEVEN DANTE** UK R&B singer (born Steven Dennis, London) who was taken to the US in search of a recording contract. While there he worked with Marcus Miller and Ray Bardini (Luther Vandross' producers) and sang with Jellybean.

03/09/1988 . . . . . 87 . . . . . . 1 FIND OUT . . . . . . . . . . . . . . . . . . . . . . . . . . . . . . . . . . . . . . . . . . . . . . . . . . . . . . . . . . . . . . . . . . . . Cooltempo CTLP 6

**TERENCE TRENT D'ARBY** US singer (born 15/3/1962, New York) who enlisted in the US Army in 1980 and was discharged in 1983. He moved to London in 1984, making demos for two years before signing with CBS/Columbia. A former regional Golden Gloves boxing champion, he was named Best International Newcomer at the 1988 BRIT Awards. He also won the 1988 Grammy Award for Best Rhythm & Blues Vocal Performance for *Introducing The Hardline According To Terence Trent D'Arby*.

25/07/1987 . . . . ❶⁹ . . . . . 67 . . . . . . ✪⁵ **INTRODUCING THE HARDLINE ACCORDING TO TERENCE TRENT D'ARBY** 1988 Grammy Award for Best Rhythm & Blues Vocal Performance . . . . . . . . . . . . . . . . . . . . . . . . . . . . . . . . . . . . . . . . . . . . . . . . . . . . . . . . . . . . . . . . . . . . . . . . . . CBS 4509111
04/11/1989 . . . . . 12 . . . . . . 5 . . . . . . ● NEITHER FISH NOR FLESH . . . . . . . . . . . . . . . . . . . . . . . . . . . . . . . . . . . . . . . . . . . . . . . . . . . . . . . . . . CBS 4658091
15/05/1993 . . . . . 4 . . . . . . 19 . . . . . . ● **SYMPHONY OR DAMN** . . . . . . . . . . . . . . . . . . . . . . . . . . . . . . . . . . . . . . . . . . . . . . . . . . . . . . . Columbia 4735612
29/04/1995 . . . . . 11 . . . . . . 5 TERENCE TRENT D'ARBY'S VIBRATOR . . . . . . . . . . . . . . . . . . . . . . . . . . . . . . . . . . . . . . . . . Columbia 4785052

**DARE** UK rock group formed in 1978 by Darren Wharton (keyboards/vocals), Vinny Burns (guitar), Shelley (bass), Brian Cox (keyboards) and James Ross (drums).

14/09/1991 . . . . . 48 . . . . . . 1 BLOOD FROM STONE . . . . . . . . . . . . . . . . . . . . . . . . . . . . . . . . . . . . . . . . . . . . . . . . . . . . . . . . . . . A&M 3953601

**BOBBY DARIN** US singer/pianist/guitarist/drummer (born Walden Robert Cassotto, 14/5/1936, The Bronx, NYC) who first recorded with the Jaybirds in 1956, also having US success under the pseudonym the Rinky Dinks. Two Grammy Awards include a Special Trustees Awards for Artists & Repertoire Contribution with Ahmet Ertegun for *Mack The Knife,* and he was nominated for an Oscar for Best Supporting Actor for his performance in the 1963 film *Captain Newman, MD.* He formed the Direction record company and later signed for Motown. He died following surgery to repair a heart valve on 20/12/1973. He was inducted into the Rock & Roll Hall of Fame in 1990 and has a star on the Hollywood Walk of Fame.

19/03/1960 . . . . . 4 . . . . . . 8 **THIS IS DARIN** . . . . . . . . . . . . . . . . . . . . . . . . . . . . . . . . . . . . . . . . . . . . . . . . . . . . . . . . . . . . London HA 2235
09/04/1960 . . . . . 15 . . . . . . 1 THAT'S ALL . . . . . . . . . . . . . . . . . . . . . . . . . . . . . . . . . . . . . . . . . . . . . . . . . . . . . . . . . . . . . London HAE 2172
05/10/1985 . . . . . 39 . . . . . . 6 THE LEGEND OF BOBBY DARIN – HIS GREATEST HITS . . . . . . . . . . . . . . . . . . . . . . . . . . . . . . . . . Stylus SMR 8504

**DARIO G** UK dance trio formed in Crewe by Scott Rosser, Paul Spencer and Stephen Spencer and named after Crewe Alexandra's manager Dario Gradi. Their debut single was personally selected by Nelson Mandela as the anthem of the South African Red Cross.

11/07/1998 . . . . . 26 . . . . . . 4 SUNMACHINE . . . . . . . . . . . . . . . . . . . . . . . . . . . . . . . . . . . . . . . . . . . . . . . . . . . . . . . . . . Eternal 3984233782

**DARIUS** UK singer (born Darius Danesh, 19/8/1980, Glasgow) who first became known as a contestant on *Popstars*. He then competed in *Pop Idol* and made the final 50, although he was later eliminated. When illness struck Rik Waller, Darius was reinstated and finished third behind Will Young and Gareth Gates.

14/12/2002 . . . . . 6 . . . . . . 19 . . . . . . ✪ **DIVE IN** . . . . . . . . . . . . . . . . . . . . . . . . . . . . . . . . . . . . . . . . . . . . . . . . . . . . . . . . . . . . Mercury 0635922

**DARKNESS** UK rock group formed in London by Justin Hawkins (guitar/vocals), Dan Hawkins (guitar), Frankie Poullain (bass) and Ed Graham (drums). They won Best UK and Ireland Act at the MTV Europe Music Awards and three awards at the 2004 BRITS, including Best British Group and Best Rock Act.

19/07/2003 . . . . ❶⁴ . . . . . 45 . . . . . . ✪⁴ **PERMISSION TO LAND** ◇ 2004 BRIT Award for Best British Album . . . . . . . . . . . . . . . . . . . . . . . . . . . Must Destroy 5046674522

**DARLING BUDS** UK rock group formed in Wales in 1987 by Andrea Lewis (born 25/3/1967, Newport, vocals), Harley Farr (born 4/7/1964, Singapore, guitar), Bloss (drums) and Chris McDonagh (born 6/3/1962, Newport, bass). The group was named after the novel *The Darling Buds of May* by HE Bates. They first recorded for the Native label before signing with CBS in 1988. Bloss was later replaced by Liverpool-born Jimmy Hughes.

18/02/1989 . . . . . 23 . . . . . . 3 POP SAID . . . . . . . . . . . . . . . . . . . . . . . . . . . . . . . . . . . . . . . . . . . . . . . . . . . . . . . . . . . . . . . Epic 4628941

**DARTS** UK doo wop revival group formed in the mid-1970s by George Currie (vocals), John Drummer (drums), Griff Fender (born Ian Collier, vocals), Bob Fish (vocals), Den Hegarty (vocals), Horatio Hornblower (born Nigel Trubridge, saxophone), Hammy Howell (keyboards), Ian 'Thump' Thompson (bass) and Rita Ray (vocals). Hegarty left in 1979 to form Rocky Sharpe And The Replays and was replaced by Kenny Andrews. Howell left in 1980 and was replaced by Mike Deacon; Howell returned later.

03/12/1977 . . . . . 9 . . . . . . 22 . . . . . . ● **DARTS** . . . . . . . . . . . . . . . . . . . . . . . . . . . . . . . . . . . . . . . . . . . . . . . . . . . . . . . . . . . . Magnet MAG 5020
03/06/1978 . . . . . 12 . . . . . . 18 . . . . . . ● EVERYONE PLAY DARTS . . . . . . . . . . . . . . . . . . . . . . . . . . . . . . . . . . . . . . . . . . . . . . . . Magnet MAG 5022
18/11/1978 . . . . . 8 . . . . . . 13 . . . . . . ● **AMAZING DARTS** . . . . . . . . . . . . . . . . . . . . . . . . . . . . . . . . . . . . . . . . . . . . . . . . . . . . . . Magnet DLP 7981
06/10/1979 . . . . . 38 . . . . . . 4 . . . . . . ○ DART ATTACK . . . . . . . . . . . . . . . . . . . . . . . . . . . . . . . . . . . . . . . . . . . . . . . . . . . . . . Magnet MAG 5030

**DATSUNS** New Zealand rock group formed in Cambridge by Wolf De Datsun (bass/vocals), Christian Livingstone Datsun (guitar), Phil Buscke Datsun (guitar) and Matt Osment Datsun (drums), all four adopting the surname Datsun.

19/10/2002 . . . . . 17 . . . . . . 3 . . . . . . ○ THE DATSUNS . . . . . . . . . . . . . . . . . . . . . . . . . . . . . . . . . . . . . . . . . . . . . . . . . . . . . . V2 VVR 1020962
19/06/2004 . . . . . 58 . . . . . . 1 OUTTA SIGHT OUTTA MIND . . . . . . . . . . . . . . . . . . . . . . . . . . . . . . . . . . . . . . . . . . . . . V2 VVR 1026942

## CRAIG DAVID
UK singer (born 5/5/1981, Southampton) discovered by production duo Artful Dodger. He has won four MOBO Awards: Best UK Act, Best Newcomer and Best UK Single for *Fill Me In* in 2000, and Best UK Act again in 2001, although it was the outcome of the 2001 BRIT Awards that attracted widespread publicity: nominated in six categories, he won nothing. Compensation of sorts was received when he made a major US breakthrough and then he won two MTV Europe Music Awards: Best R&B Act and Select UK & Ireland Act.

| 26/08/2000 | ❶² | 50 | ✪⁶ | BORN TO DO IT ◇³ | Wildstar CDWILD 32 |
| 23/11/2002 | 4 | 35 | ✪² | SLICKER THAN YOUR AVERAGE ◇ | Wildstar CDWILD 42 |

## F.R. DAVID
French singer (born Elli Robert Fitoussi, 1/1/1947, Tunis) who moved to Paris in 1964. He also recorded with Vangelis' group Les Variations.

| 07/05/1983 | 46 | 6 | | WORDS | Carrere CAK 145 |

## DAVID DEVANT AND HIS SPIRIT WIFE
UK group formed by Vessel (vocals/various instruments), Colonel (bass), Professor G Rimschott (drums), Pope (guitar), Bryn (keyboards), Foz (guitar), Iceman, Cocky Young 'Un, Lantern, Jet Boy and The Spectrettes.

| 05/07/1997 | 70 | 1 | | WORK, LOVELIFE, MISCELLANEOUS | Kindness KINDCD 1 |

## WINDSOR DAVIES – see DON ESTELLE AND WINDSOR DAVIES

## ANDREW DAVIS – see BBC SYMPHONY ORCHESTRA

## CARL DAVIS
US composer/orchestra leader (born in 1936) who later relocated to the UK and made his reputation providing new scores to classic silent films. He also composed the music for numerous films and TV series, including *The French Lieutenant's Woman* and *The World At War*.

| 19/10/1991 | 36 | 4 | | PAUL McCARTNEY'S LIVERPOOL ORATORIO | EMI Classics PAUL 1 |

## COLIN DAVIS – see BBC SYMPHONY ORCHESTRA

## MILES DAVIS
US trumpeter (born 25/5/1926, Alton, IL) whose father gave him a trumpet at the age of thirteen. He played in his school band and joined Eddie Randall's band in 1941, as well as performing with other groups. Davis entered Julliard School of Music in 1945 but soon began playing with the likes of Charlie Parker and Coleman Hawkins, Dizzy Gillespie and Benny Carter. His performances in the bands of Billy Eckstine and Benny Carter earned him *Esquire* magazine's 1947 critics poll for best new star. He also made a series of influential recordings with Gil Evans that were finally released in 1957. Heroin addiction halted his career temporarily in the early 1950s, but he re-emerged in 1954 with his own band, featuring Paul Chambers, John Coltrane, Bill Evans, Red Garland, Philly Joe Jones, Charles Mingus and Sonny Rollins at various times. He made his reputation at the 1955 Newport Jazz Festival, but his recordings for Columbia (at Prestige his albums were under-promoted) confirmed his status as the leading jazz exponent. Davis recorded a series of innovative orchestral albums with Gil Evans and then assembled a sextet that produced classic jazz albums such as *Milestones* and *Kind Of Blue* (the latter charted in the UK nearly forty years after its original release). Davis' audience grew during the 1960s as he moved into fusion with *Bitches Brew* – one of the first jazz-rock albums, and a regular on the album charts. He retired in 1975 after further drug problems, a car crash and various other ailments had left him seriously ill, but he returned in 1981 with *The Man With The Horn* and even toured again. Later he recorded pop tunes on *You're Under Arrest* and even made a move towards disco on *Tutu*, but his health was deteriorating. He died from a combination of a stroke, pneumonia and respiratory failure on 18/9/1991. He won ten Grammy Awards including: Best Jazz Composition, More Than 5 Minutes in 1960 for *Sketches Of Spain;* Best Jazz Instrumental by a Soloist in 1982 for *We Want Miles*; Best Jazz Instrumental Performance by a Soloist and Best Jazz Performance by a Big Band in 1989 for *Aura*, Best Rhythm and Blues Instrumental Performance in 1992 for *Doo-Bop,* Best Large Jazz Ensemble Performance in 1993 with Quincy Jones for *Miles And Quincy Live At Montreaux*, Best R&B Instrumental Performance in 1995 for *Doo-Bop* and Best Historical Album in 1996 with Gil Evans for *The Complete Columbia Studio Recordings*. He has a star on the Hollywood Walk of Fame.

| 11/07/1970 | 71 | 1 | | BITCHES BREW 1970 Grammy Award for Best Instrumental Jazz Performance, Solo or Soloist, Large Group | CBS 66236 |
| 15/06/1985 | 88 | 1 | | YOU'RE UNDER ARREST | CBS 26447 |
| 18/10/1986 | 74 | 2 | | TUTU 1986 Grammy Award for Best Jazz Instrumental Performance by a Soloist | Warner Brothers 9254901 |
| 03/06/1989 | 49 | 2 | | AMANDLA | Warner Brothers WX 250 |
| 05/10/1996 | 64 | 1 | | THE VERY BEST OF MILES DAVIS | Columbia SONYTV 17CD |
| 28/04/2001 | 63 | 2 | ● | KIND OF BLUE ◇ Originally released in 1962 | Columbia CK 64935 |

## SAMMY DAVIS JR
US singer/actor/dancer (born 8/12/1925, Harlem, NYC) who debuted at the age of three as 'Silent Sam, The Dancing Midget'. After World War II army service he appeared in countless Broadway, film and TV shows. A member of the infamous Rat Pack with Frank Sinatra and Dean Martin, he lost his left eye and broke his nose in a car crash in 1954 but was performing two months later. His films include *Anna Lucasta* (1949), *Porgy And Bess* (1959) and *Sweet Charity* (1969). He died from cancer of the throat on 16/5/1990. He has a star on the Hollywood Walk of Fame.

| 13/04/1963 | 19 | 1 | | SAMMY DAVIS JR AT THE COCONUT GROVE | Reprise R 6063/2 |

## SPENCER DAVIS GROUP
UK rock group formed in 1963 by Spencer Davis (born 14/7/1941, Swansea, guitar), Steve Winwood (born 12/5/1948, Birmingham, guitar/keyboards/vocals), his brother Mervin (known as 'Muff', after TV puppet Muffin The

Mule, born 15/6/1943, Birmingham, bass) and Pete York (born 15/8/1942, Redcar, Cleveland, drums). Initially called The Muff-Woody Jazz Band, then Rhythm & Blues Quartet, they were signed by Island Records' Chris Blackwell, although the label was still developing and licensing its product to Fontana. Covers of US hits preceded their #1 charter *Keep On Running*, written by Blackwell protege, Jamaican Jackie Edwards. The group appeared in the 1966 film *The Ghost Goes Gear*. Winwood left in 1967 to form Traffic, before going solo. Muff left the same year for band management, went on to produce (including Dire Straits' first album) and then became an A&R director with Island and CBS/Columbia. They disbanded in 1969; Davis re-formed a Spencer Davis Group in 1990.

| | | | | |
|---|---|---|---|---|
| 01/01/1966 | 6 | 9 | | THEIR FIRST LP ..... Fontana TL 5242 |
| 22/01/1966 | 3 | 18 | | THE SECOND ALBUM ..... Fontana TL 5295 |
| 10/09/1966 | 4 | 20 | | AUTUMN '66 ..... Fontana TL 5359 |

**DAWN** US vocal trio formed in New York City by Tony Orlando (born 3/4/1944, NYC). A solo singer from 1961–63, Orlando was working at music publishers April-Blackwood when he formed Dawn with backing singers Telma Hopkins and Joyce Vincent. The group had their own TV show from 1974 to 1976, after which Orlando played the cabaret circuit while Hopkins appeared in various TV series.
04/05/1974 ..... 46 ...... 2 ...... GOLDEN RIBBONS ..... Bell BELLS 236

**DAWN OF THE REPLICANTS** UK group with Paul Vickers (vocals), Roger Simian (guitar), Donald Kyle (bass), Grant Pringle (drums) and Mike Small (various instruments).
28/02/1998 ..... 62 ...... 1 ...... ONE HEAD, TWO ARMS, TWO LEGS ..... East West 0630196002

**DAY ONE** UK electronic duo formed in Bristol, Avon by Phelim Byrne (vocals) and Donni Hardwidge (all instruments). They were signed by Massive Attack's Melankolic label via a three-song demo sent to 3D.
25/03/2000 ..... 70 ...... 1 ...... ORDINARY MAN ..... Melankolic CDSAD 8

**DARREN DAY** UK singer (born 17/7/1968, Colchester) who came to prominence as a TV presenter, most notably with *You Bet* and also appeared in the revival of the musical *Summer Holiday*.
18/04/1998 ..... 62 ...... 1 ...... DARREN DAY ..... East Coast DAYCD 01

**DORIS DAY** US singer (born Doris Kappelhoff, 3/4/1922, Cincinnati, OH) who was initially a dancer but turned to singing after she broke her leg in a car crash aged fourteen. First working with Bob Crosby, she became a star with the Les Brown band before going solo. Movies followed pop success, with her debut in the 1948 film *Romance On The High Sea* being the first of many, making her the #1 box office star of the 1950s and early 1960s. Her son Terry Melcher was a musician, producing The Beach Boys and The Byrds, and Day's last UK hit *Move Over Darling*. She has a star on the Hollywood Walk of Fame for her contribution to recording, and a second one for motion pictures.

| | | | | |
|---|---|---|---|---|
| 06/01/1979 | 12 | 11 | | 20 GOLDEN GREATS ..... Warwick PR 5053 |
| 11/11/1989 | 32 | 9 | ● | A PORTRAIT OF DORIS DAY ..... Stylus SMR 984 |
| 06/11/1993 | 14 | 12 | ● | GREATEST HITS ..... Telstar TCD 2659 |
| 10/12/1994 | 64 | 3 | | THE LOVE ALBUM ..... Vision VIS CD2 |
| 20/11/1999 | 63 | 1 | | THE MAGIC OF THE MOVIES ..... Columbia SONYTV 79CD |
| 20/04/2002 | 73 | 1 | | 41 HOLLYWOOD GREATS – THE BEST OF ..... Columbia 5079632 |

**TAYLOR DAYNE** US singer (born Leslie Wunderman, 7/3/1963, Baldwin, NY). Debuting at the age of six, she was in rock groups Felony and Next before signing solo with Arista in 1987.
05/03/1988 ..... 24 ...... 17 ...... TELL IT TO MY HEART ..... Arista 208898

**CHRIS DE BURGH** UK singer (born Christopher Davidson, 15/10/1948, Buenos Aires, Argentina) who graduated from Trinity College in Dublin and toured Eire with Horslips, before developing as a singer/songwriter while helping run his family's 12th-century hotel in Ireland. Signing with A&M in 1974, he released his debut album the following year. His daughter, Rosanna Davison, was named Miss World in 2003.

| | | | | |
|---|---|---|---|---|
| 12/09/1981 | 65 | 4 | | BEST MOVES ..... A&M AMLH 68532 |
| 09/10/1982 | 30 | 16 | | THE GETAWAY ..... A&M AMLH 58549 |
| 19/05/1984 | 11 | 24 | O | MAN ON THE LINE ..... A&M AMLX 65002 |
| 29/12/1984 | 6 | 70 | ● | THE VERY BEST OF CHRIS DE BURGH ..... Telstar STAR 2248 |
| 24/08/1985 | 78 | 3 | | SPANISH TRAIN AND OTHER STORIES ..... A&M AMLH 68343 |
| 07/06/1986 | 2 | 59 | ✪² | INTO THE LIGHT ..... A&M AM 5121 |
| 04/10/1986 | 72 | 1 | | CRUSADER ..... A&M AMLH 64746 |
| 15/10/1988 | ❶¹ | 30 | ✪ | FLYING COLOURS ..... A&M AMA 5224 |
| 04/11/1989 | 4 | 29 | ✪² | FROM A SPARK TO A FLAME – THE VERY BEST OF CHRIS DE BURGH ..... A&M CDBLP 100 |
| 22/09/1990 | 15 | 6 | ● | HIGH ON EMOTION – LIVE FROM DUBLIN ..... A&M 3970861 |
| 09/05/1992 | 3 | 10 | ● | POWER OF TEN ..... A&M 3971882 |
| 28/05/1994 | 5 | 6 | O | THIS WAY UP ..... A&M 5402332 |
| 18/11/1995 | 33 | 8 | ● | BEAUTIFUL DREAMS ..... A&M 5404322 |
| 11/10/1997 | 8 | 7 | ● | THE LOVE SONGS ..... A&M 5407942 |

O Silver disc  ● Gold disc  ✪ Platinum disc (additional platinum units are indicated by a figure following the symbol)  ❶⁹ Number of weeks album topped the UK chart

| | | | | |
|---|---|---|---|---|
| 02/10/1999 | 23 | 3 | | QUIET REVOLUTION . . . . . . . . . . . . . . . . . . . . . . . . . . . . . . . . . . . . . . . . . . . . . . . . . . . . . . . A&M 4904462 |
| 31/03/2001 | 19 | 4 | | THE ULTIMATE COLLECTION . . . . . . . . . . . . . . . . . . . . . . . . . . . . . . . . . . . . . . . . . . . . . . . . Mercury 4908992 |
| 28/09/2002 | 41 | 1 | | TIMING IS EVERYTHING . . . . . . . . . . . . . . . . . . . . . . . . . . . . . . . . . . . . . . . . . . . . . . . . . . Mercury 4934292 |
| 27/03/2004 | 75 | 1 | | THE ROAD TO FREEDOM . . . . . . . . . . . . . . . . . . . . . . . . . . . . . . . . . . . . . . . . . . . . . . . . . . Ferryman FERRY888 |

**DE LA SOUL** US rap trio from Amityville, Long Island, NY formed by Kelvin Mercer (born 17/8/1969, Brooklyn, NYC), Vincent Mason Jr (born 24/3/1970, Brooklyn) and David Jolicoeur (born 21/9/1968, Brooklyn) as The Monkeys Of Hip Hop. They adopted stage names Posdnous (Mercer), PA Pacemaker Mase (Mason) and Trugoy The Dove (Jolicoeur).

| | | | | |
|---|---|---|---|---|
| 25/03/1989 | 13 | 56 | ✪ | 3 FEET HIGH AND RISING . . . . . . . . . . . . . . . . . . . . . . . . . . . . . . . . . . . . . . . . . . . . . . . . . . Big Life DLSLP 1 |
| 25/05/1991 | 7 | 11 | | **DE LA SOUL IS DEAD** . . . . . . . . . . . . . . . . . . . . . . . . . . . . . . . . . . . . . . . . . . . . . . . . . . Big Life BLRLP 8 |
| 09/10/1993 | 37 | 2 | | BUHLOONE MINDSTATE . . . . . . . . . . . . . . . . . . . . . . . . . . . . . . . . . . . . . . . . . . . . . . . . . . Big Life BLRCD 25 |
| 13/07/1996 | 42 | 1 | | STAKES IS HIGH . . . . . . . . . . . . . . . . . . . . . . . . . . . . . . . . . . . . . . . . . . . . . . . . . . . . . Tommy Boy TBCD 1149 |
| 09/10/1999 | 17 | 2 | | 3 FEET HIGH AND RISING . . . . . . . . . . . . . . . . . . . . . . . . . . . . . . . . . . . . . . . . . . . . . . . . Tommy Boy TBCD 1019 |
| 19/08/2000 | 22 | 4 | | ART OFFICIAL INTELLIGENCE: MOSIAC THUMP . . . . . . . . . . . . . . . . . . . . . . . . . . . . . . . . . . Tommy Boy TBCD 1348 |
| 14/06/2003 | 17 | 10 | ● | THE BEST OF . . . . . . . . . . . . . . . . . . . . . . . . . . . . . . . . . . . . . . . . . . . . . . . . . . . . . . . Tommy Boy 8122736652 |

**WALDO DE LOS RIOS** Argentinian orchestra leader (born Osvaldo Ferraro Guiterrez) who composed *South American Suite* and the music to many films, including *Murders In The Rue Morgue* (1971), *Bad Man's River* (1972) and *La Espada Negra* (1976). He committed suicide on 28/3/1977.

| | | | | |
|---|---|---|---|---|
| 01/05/1971 | 6 | 26 | | **SYMPHONIES FOR THE SEVENTIES** . . . . . . . . . . . . . . . . . . . . . . . . . . . . . . . . . . . . . . . . . . A&M AMLS 2014 |

**MANITAS DE PLATA** Spanish flamenco guitarist (born Ricardo Baliardo in 1921, Sete) who invariably worked with singers Jose Reyes (his cousin) and Manero Baliardo. His name means 'man with the silver hands'.

| | | | | |
|---|---|---|---|---|
| 29/07/1967 | 40 | 1 | | FLAMENCO GUITAR . . . . . . . . . . . . . . . . . . . . . . . . . . . . . . . . . . . . . . . . . . . . . . . . . . . . Philips SBL 7786 |

**DEACON BLUE** UK rock group formed in Scotland in 1985 by Ricky Ross (born 22/12/1957, Dundee, vocals), James Prime (born 3/11/1960, Kilmarnock, keyboards), Douglas Vipond (born 15/10/1966, Johnstone, drums/percussion), Graeme Kelling (born 4/4/1957, Paisley, guitar) and Ewan Vernal (born 27/2/1964, Glasgow, bass/keyboards), with Ross' girlfriend and future wife Lorraine McIntosh (born 13/5/1964, Glasgow) joining in 1987. The group took their name from a song by Steely Dan. Ricky Ross later recorded solo. Kelling died after a lengthy illness on 10/6/2004.

| | | | | |
|---|---|---|---|---|
| 06/06/1987 | 14 | 77 | ✪ | RAINTOWN . . . . . . . . . . . . . . . . . . . . . . . . . . . . . . . . . . . . . . . . . . . . . . . . . . . . . . . . . CBS 4505491 |
| 15/04/1989 | ❶² | 54 | ✪² | **WHEN THE WORLD KNOWS YOUR NAME** . . . . . . . . . . . . . . . . . . . . . . . . . . . . . . . . . . . . . . . . CBS 4633211 |
| 22/09/1990 | 3 | 8 | ● | **OOH LAS VEGAS** . . . . . . . . . . . . . . . . . . . . . . . . . . . . . . . . . . . . . . . . . . . . . . . . . . . . . CBS 4672421 |
| 15/06/1991 | 2 | 27 | ✪ | **FELLOW HOODLUMS** . . . . . . . . . . . . . . . . . . . . . . . . . . . . . . . . . . . . . . . . . . . . . . . . . . Columbia 4685501 |
| 13/03/1993 | 4 | 10 | ● | **WHATEVER YOU SAY, SAY NOTHING** . . . . . . . . . . . . . . . . . . . . . . . . . . . . . . . . . . . . . . . . Columbia 4735272 |
| 16/04/1994 | ❶² | 38 | ✪² | **OUR TOWN – THE GREATEST HITS OF DEACON BLUE** . . . . . . . . . . . . . . . . . . . . . . . . . . . . . Columbia 4766422 |
| 23/10/1999 | 39 | 2 | | WALKING BACK HOME . . . . . . . . . . . . . . . . . . . . . . . . . . . . . . . . . . . . . . . . . . . . . . . . . . Columbia 4963802 |
| 12/05/2001 | 59 | 1 | | HOMESICK . . . . . . . . . . . . . . . . . . . . . . . . . . . . . . . . . . . . . . . . . . . . . . . . . . . . . . . . Papillion BTFLYCD 0014 |

**DEAD CAN DANCE** Australian duo formed by Brendan Perry (guitar/percussion/vocals) and Lisa Gerrard (percussion/vocals), with assorted studio/guest musicians. Perry started working on a solo album in 1995 and Gerrard later fronted an orchestral recording.

| | | | | |
|---|---|---|---|---|
| 25/09/1993 | 47 | 1 | | INTO THE LABYRINTH . . . . . . . . . . . . . . . . . . . . . . . . . . . . . . . . . . . . . . . . . . . . . . . . . . 4AD CAD 3013CD |
| 29/06/1996 | 43 | 2 | | SPIRITCHASER . . . . . . . . . . . . . . . . . . . . . . . . . . . . . . . . . . . . . . . . . . . . . . . . . . . . . . 4AD CAD 6008CD |

**DEAD KENNEDYS** US punk group formed in San Francisco, CA in 1977 by Jello Biafra (born Eric Boujet, 17/6/1958, Boulder, CO, vocals), East Bay Ray (born Ray Glasser, Castro Valley, CA, guitar), Klaus Flurodie (born in Detroit, MI, bass) and Bruce 'Ted' Slesinger (drums). Darren Peligro (born in East St Louis, IL) replaced Slesinger in 1982. Their debut single *California Uber Alles*, an attack on California Governor Jerry Brown, was banned by many stores, equally offended by the group's name. Many US and UK shops refused to stock their *Frankenchrist* album because of the cover. Biafra, who was charged under obscenity laws, stood for election as San Francisco mayor, finishing fourth out of ten. Later recording solo, in 1994 he had both legs broken by members of the audience, who accused him of 'selling out'.

| | | | | |
|---|---|---|---|---|
| 13/09/1980 | 33 | 6 | ● | FRESH FRUIT FOR ROTTING VEGETABLES . . . . . . . . . . . . . . . . . . . . . . . . . . . . . . . . . . . . . Cherry Red BRED 10 |
| 04/07/1987 | 84 | 2 | | GIVE ME CONVENIENCE OR GIVE ME DEATH . . . . . . . . . . . . . . . . . . . . . . . . . . . . . . . . . Alternative Tentacles VIRUS 5 |

**DEAD OR ALIVE** UK group formed in Liverpool in 1979 by Pete Burns (born 5/8/1959, Liverpool, lead singer) as Nightmares In Wax, the name changing to Dead Or Alive in 1980. When they charted the remaining three members comprised Timothy Lever (born 21/5/1960, keyboards), Michael Percy (born 11/3/1961, bass) and Stephen McCoy (born 15/3/1962, drums), Burns having gone through over 30 musicians, including Wayne Hussey, later of Sisters Of Mercy and Mission.

| | | | | |
|---|---|---|---|---|
| 28/04/1984 | 29 | 3 | | SOPHISTICATED BOOM BOOM ............................................................................ Epic EPC 25835 |
| 25/05/1985 | 9 | 15 | ● | YOUTHQUAKE ............................................................................................. Epic EPC 26420 |
| 14/02/1987 | 27 | 4 | | MAD, BAD AND DANGEROUS TO KNOW ........................................................... Epic 4502571 |

**HAZELL DEAN** UK singer (born 27/10/1958, Chelmsford, Essex) who began her career by fronting various groups. In the early 1980s she attempted to represent the UK in the Eurovision Song Contest and first recorded for Proto in 1983.

22/10/1988 ..... 38 ..... 3 ...... ALWAYS .................................................................................................... EMI EMC 3546

**DEATH IN VEGAS** UK production duo formed in 1995 by Richard Fearless and Steve Hellier as Dead Elvis. Hellier left in 1997 and was replaced by Tim Holmes.

| | | | | |
|---|---|---|---|---|
| 29/03/1997 | 52 | 1 | | DEAD ELVIS ..................................................................................... Concrete HARD 22LPCD |
| 25/09/1999 | 19 | 12 | ○ | THE CONTINO SESSIONS ..................................................................... Concrete HARD 41CDU |
| 28/09/2002 | 19 | 3 | | SCORPIO RISING .................................................................................. Concrete HARD 53CD |

**DeBARGE** US family group formed in Los Angeles, CA by brothers Eldra (born 4/6/1961, Grand Rapids, MI, keyboards/vocals), James (keyboards/vocals), Randy (bass/vocals), Mark (trumpet/saxophone/vocals) and sister Bunny DeBarge (vocals). They formed as Switch with elder brothers Bobby and Tommy as members, signing with Motown as DeBarge in 1982. Eldra (El) and Bunny and a further brother Chico (born Jonathan DeBarge, 1966, Grand Rapids) later recorded solo albums for Motown, while James eloped with the youngest member of the family which DeBarge were hoping to emulate: Janet Jackson. Bobby died from AIDS on 16/8/1995.

25/05/1985 ..... 94 ..... 2 ...... RHYTHM OF THE NIGHT ............................................................................ Gordy ZL 72340

**DECLAN** UK singer Declan Galbraith who was ten years of age at the time of his debut hit.

05/10/2002 ..... 44 ..... 3 ...... DECLAN .................................................................................................... Liberty 5416012

**DAVE DEE, DOZY, BEAKY, MICK AND TICH** UK group formed in Salisbury in 1961 by Dave Dee (born David Harman, 17/12/1943, Salisbury, lead vocals), Dozy (born Trevor Davies, 27/11/1944, Enford, bass), Beaky (born John Dymond, 10/7/1944, Salisbury, guitar) and Tich (born Ian Amey, 15/5/1944, Salisbury, lead guitar) as Dave Dee And The Bostons, with Mick (born Michael Wilson, 4/3/1944, Amesbury) joining at the end of the year. The name change in 1964 was suggested by managers Ken Howard and Alan Blaikley (who also managed the Honeycombs). Their debut single was released in 1965. Dee went solo 1969 and was later A&R director at WEA. After one hit single as D,B,M & T, the remaining group disbanded in 1970. Briefly reunited in 1974 and 1982, D,B,M & T still play the nostalgia circuit.

| | | | | |
|---|---|---|---|---|
| 02/07/1966 | 11 | 10 | | DAVE DEE, DOZY, BEAKY, MICK AND TICH ...................................................... Fontana STL 5350 |
| 07/01/1967 | 27 | 5 | | IF MUSIC BE THE FOOD OF LOVE... PREPARE FOR INDIGESTION ......................... Fontana STL 5388 |

**KIKI DEE** UK singer (born Pauline Matthews, 6/3/1947, Yorkshire) who recorded soul covers from 1963 and was the first white UK artist to sign for the Motown label. She signed with Elton John's Rocket Records in 1973, where Anne Orson and Carte Blanche provided most of her material (pseudonyms of John and co-writer Bernie Taupin). Originally intended for a cover version of the Four Tops' *Loving You Is Sweeter Than Ever,* her collaboration with Elton John on a John/Taupin original became a UK and US #1. She later appeared in stage in musicals, such as *Pump Boys And Dinettes,* and was nominated for a Laurence Olivier Award for her role in the stage musical *Blood Brothers.*

| | | | | |
|---|---|---|---|---|
| 26/03/1977 | 24 | 5 | | KIKI DEE ................................................................................................... Rocket ROLA 3 |
| 18/07/1981 | 47 | 4 | | PERFECT TIMING ....................................................................................... Ariola ARL 5050 |
| 09/04/1994 | 62 | 2 | | THE VERY BEST OF KIKI DEE ...................................................................... Rocket 5167282 |

**DEEE-LITE** Multinational New York-based dance trio formed in 1982 by Super DJ Dmitry (born Dmitry Brill, Kiev, Russia), Jungle DJ Towa Towa (born Doug Wa-Chung, Tokyo, Japan) and lead singer Lady Miss Kirby (born Kierin Kirby, Youngstown, OH). Towa left in 1994, renaming himself Towa Tei; he was replaced by Ani. Brill and Kirby were later married.

| | | | | |
|---|---|---|---|---|
| 08/09/1990 | 14 | 18 | ● | WORLD CLIQUE .......................................................................................... Elektra EKT 77 |
| 04/07/1992 | 37 | 1 | | INFINITY WITHIN .................................................................................. Elektra 7559613132 |

**DEEJAY PUNK-ROC** US DJ (born 1971, Brooklyn, NYC) who was in the US Army from the age of sixteen. He was stationed in Japan, Germany and England, where he first recorded *My Beatbox* for the Airdog Recordings label.

30/05/1998 ..... 47 ..... 1 ...... CHICKENEYE ..................................................................................... Independiente ISOM 5CD

**DEEP BLUE SOMETHING** US rock group formed in Denton, Dallas in 1992 by Todd Pipes (born 9/11/1967, bass/vocals), Toby Pipes (born 28/6/1971, guitar), Kirk Tatom (guitar) and John Kirkland (born 16/7/1969, drums) as Leper Messiah, changing their name the following year. Tatom was later replaced by Clay Bergus (born 29/4/1971).

05/10/1996 ..... 24 ..... 5 ...... HOMEWORK ........................................................................................ Interscope IND 90002

**DEEP DISH** US production/instrumental duo formed in 1992 by Ali 'Dubfire' Shirizania and Sharam Tayebi, both originally from Iran. They won the 2001 Grammy Award for Best Remix for Dido's *Thank You.*

18/07/1998 ..... 37 ..... 2 ...... JUNK SCIENCE ............................................................................ Deconstruction 74321580342

**DEEP FOREST** French instrumental duo formed in Paris in 1993 by Eric Mouquet and film music composer Michael Sanchez.

26/02/1994 ..... 15 ..... 11 ...... ● DEEP FOREST ........................................................................................ Columbia 4741782

| | | | | | |
|---|---|---|---|---|---|
| 03/06/1995 | 12 | 5 | | BOHEME 1995 Grammy Award for Best World Music Album | Columbia 4786232 |
| 31/01/1998 | 60 | 1 | | COMPARSA | Columbia 4887252 |

**DEEP PURPLE** UK heavy rock group formed by Ritchie Blackmore (born 14/4/1945, Weston-super-Mare, guitar), Jon Lord (born 9/6/1941, Leicester, keyboards), Chris Curtis (born 26/8/1941, Oldham, vocals), Dave Curtis (bass) and Bobby Woodman (drums) as Roundabout in 1968. After a month of rehearsals, both Curtises and Woodman left and were replaced by Ian Paice (born 29/6/1948, Nottingham, drums), Rod Evans (born 19/1/1945, Edinburgh, vocals) and Nick Simper (born 3/11/1946, Southall, bass). Debuting in Denmark, they changed their name to Deep Purple in April 1968, signing to EMI the following month. Evans and Simper left in 1969, with Roger Glover (born 30/11/1945, Brecon, bass) and Ian Gillan (born 19/8/1945, Hounslow, vocals) replacing them. Gillan and Glover left in 1973 and were replaced by David Coverdale (born 22/9/1949, Saltburn-by-the-Sea) and Glenn Hughes (born 21/8/1952, Penkridge). Blackmore quit after two further albums to form Rainbow; Tommy Bolin (born 1/8/1951, Sioux City, IN) was recruited, but they disbanded in 1976. They re-formed in 1984 with Blackmore, Gillan, Lord and Paice, with Gillan leaving in 1989. Bolin died from a drug overdose on 4/12/1976, reportedly wearing the same ring Jimi Hendrix had been wearing when he died.

| | | | | | |
|---|---|---|---|---|---|
| 24/01/1970 | 26 | 4 | | CONCERTO FOR GROUP AND ORCHESTRA | Harvest SHVL 767 |
| 20/06/1970 | 4 | 68 | | **DEEP PURPLE IN ROCK** | Harvest SHVL 777 |
| 18/09/1971 | ❶[1] | 25 | | **FIREBALL** | Harvest SHVL 793 |
| 15/04/1972 | ❶[3] | 24 | ● | **MACHINE HEAD** | Purple TPSA 7504 |
| 06/01/1973 | 16 | 14 | ● | MADE IN JAPAN | Purple TPSP 351 |
| 17/02/1973 | 4 | 11 | | **WHO DO WE THINK WE ARE** | Purple TPSA 7508 |
| 02/03/1974 | 3 | 21 | ● | **BURN** | Purple TPA 3505 |
| 23/11/1974 | 6 | 12 | ○ | **STORM BRINGER** | Purple TPS 3508 |
| 05/07/1975 | 14 | 17 | ○ | 24 CARAT PURPLE | Purple TPSM 2002 |
| 22/11/1975 | 19 | 4 | ○ | COME TASTE THE BAND | Purple TPSA 7515 |
| 27/11/1976 | 12 | 6 | | DEEP PURPLE LIVE | Purple TPSA 7517 |
| 21/04/1979 | 24 | 6 | | THE MARK II PURPLE SINGLES | Purple TPS 3514 |
| 19/07/1980 | ❶[1] | 15 | ● | **DEEPEST PURPLE** | Harvest EMTV 25 |
| 13/12/1980 | 30 | 8 | | IN CONCERT | Harvest SHDW 4121/4122 |
| 04/09/1982 | 23 | 5 | | DEEP PURPLE LIVE IN LONDON | Harvest SHSP 4124 |
| 10/11/1984 | 5 | 15 | ● | **PERFECT STRANGERS** | Polydor POLH 16 |
| 29/06/1985 | 50 | 3 | | THE ANTHOLOGY | Harvest PUR 1 |
| 24/01/1987 | 10 | 9 | ○ | **THE HOUSE OF BLUE LIGHT** | Polydor POLH 32 |
| 16/07/1988 | 38 | 2 | | NOBODY'S PERFECT | Polydor PODV 10 |
| 03/11/1990 | 45 | 2 | | SLAVES AND MASTERS | RCA PL 90535 |
| 07/08/1993 | 21 | 3 | | THE BATTLE RAGES ON... | RCA 74321154202 |
| 17/02/1996 | 58 | 1 | | PURPENDICULAR | RCA 74321338022 |
| 31/01/1998 | 73 | 1 | | MADE IN JAPAN | EMI 8578642 |
| 24/10/1998 | 39 | 2 | | VERY BEST OF DEEP PURPLE | EMI 4968072 |

**DEEPEST BLUE** Israeli producer Matti Schwartz with vocals by Joel Edwards. Schwartz is also in 4 Tune 500.

| | | | | | |
|---|---|---|---|---|---|
| 19/06/2004 | 22 | 2+ | | LATE SEPTEMBER | Open OPENCD3 |

**DEF LEPPARD** UK heavy rock group formed in Sheffield in 1977 by Joe Elliott (born 1/8/1959, Sheffield, vocals), Rick Savage (born 2/12/1960, Sheffield, bass), Steve Clark (born 23/4/1960, Sheffield, guitar), Frank Noon (drums) and Pete Willis (guitar). Drummer Rick Allen (born 1/11/1963, Sheffield) was recruited in 1978 shortly after they recorded their first EP, *Getcha Rocks Off*, Noon having left to rejoin the Next Band. Local sales and national radio plays led to a deal with Phonogram (although all releases are on their own Bludgeon Riffola label). In 1982 Willis was fired and replaced by Phil Collen (born 8/12/1957, London). Allen lost an arm in a road crash midway through recording a new album in 1984, but with the aid of modern technology has remained the group's drummer (and managed to play 'acoustic' drums on the 1996 album *Slang*). Clark died on 8/1/1991 from excessive alcohol mixed with anti-depressants and painkillers, and was replaced the following year by Vivian Campbell (born 25/8/1962, Belfast).

| | | | | | |
|---|---|---|---|---|---|
| 22/03/1980 | 15 | 8 | | ON THROUGH THE NIGHT | Vertigo 9102 040 |
| 25/07/1981 | 26 | 8 | | HIGH 'N' DRY | Vertigo 6359 045 |
| 12/03/1983 | 18 | 8 | ○ | PYROMANIA | Vertigo VERS 2 |
| 29/08/1987 | ❶[1] | 101 | ✪[2] | **HYSTERIA** ▲[6] ◆[12] | Bludgeon Riffola HYSLP 1 |
| 11/04/1992 | ❶[1] | 30 | ● | **ADRENALIZE** ▲[5] | Bludgeon Riffola 5109782 |
| 16/10/1993 | 6 | 5 | | **RETRO ACTIVE** | Bludgeon Riffola 5183052 |
| 04/11/1995 | 3 | 14 | ✪[2] | **VAULT – THE GREATEST HITS 1980–1995** | Bludgeon Riffola 5286572 |
| 25/05/1996 | 5 | 8 | ● | SLANG | Bludgeon Riffola 5324862 |
| 26/06/1999 | 11 | 5 | | EUPHORIA | Bludgeon Riffola 5462442 |
| 24/08/2002 | 14 | 3 | | X | Bludgeon Riffola 0631202 |

**DEFINITION OF SOUND** UK rap duo Kevvon (born Kevin Anthony Clark, 1971) and The Don (born Desmond Raymond Weekes, 1969). Kevvon first became known guesting on Krush's *House Arrest* before teaming with The Don in 1988 as Top Billin'. They changed their name after their record label Dance Yard closed.

| | | | | | |
|---|---|---|---|---|---|
| 29/06/1991 | 38 | 3 | | LOVE AND LIFE | Circa 14 |

**DEFTONES** US rock group formed in Los Angeles, CA in 1988 by Chino Moreno (vocals), Stephen Carpenter (guitar), Chi Cheng (bass/vocals) and Abe Cunningham (drums). They recorded their debut album for Maverick in 1995 and won the 2000 Grammy Award for Best Metal Performance for *Elite*.

| | | | | | |
|---|---|---|---|---|---|
| 08/11/1997 | 56 | 1 | ○ | AROUND THE FUR | Maverick 9362468102 |
| 01/07/2000 | 13 | 2 | | WHITE PONY | Maverick 9362477992 |
| 24/03/2001 | 35 | 1 | | BACK TO SCHOOL (MINI MAGGIT) | WEA 9362480822 |
| 31/05/2003 | 7 | 3 | | **DEFTONES** | Maverick 9362483912 |

**DEICIDE** US rock group formed in Florida in 1987 by Glen Benton (bass/vocals), Eric Hoffman (guitar), his brother Brian (guitar) and Steve Asheim (drums). Benton's views concerning small animals attracted bomb threats from the Animal Militia during their European tour and there was an explosion during a 1992 date in Stockholm. The group allegedly made a pact to commit suicide when they reached the age of 33! Their debut hit album was released with two covers: one was 'clean' and the other was explicit.

| | | | | | |
|---|---|---|---|---|---|
| 13/05/1995 | 66 | 1 | | ONCE UPON THE CROSS | Roadrunner RR 89492 |

**DESMOND DEKKER AND THE ACES** Jamaican singer (born Desmond Dacres, 16/7/1941, Kingston) who made his first single in 1963. He formed the Aces and teamed up with hit producer Leslie Kong in 1966 (with whom he worked until Kong's death in 1971). With over twenty domestic #1s, he was the first Jamaican to top the UK charts and also hit the US top ten with the single *Israelites*.

| | | | | | |
|---|---|---|---|---|---|
| 05/07/1969 | 27 | 4 | | THIS IS DESMOND DEKKER | Trojan TTL 4 |

**DEL AMITRI** UK rock group formed in Glasgow in 1982 by Justin Currie (born 11/12/1964, Glasgow, vocals/bass), Bryan Tolland (guitar), Iain Harvie (born 19/5/1962, Glasgow, guitar) and Paul Tyagi (drums). Brian McDermott (drums) and David Cummings (guitar) replaced Tolland and Tyagi. McDermott left in 1995, and later members included Mark Price (drums) and Kris Dollimore (guitar). They first recorded for the No Strings label before being snapped up by Chrysalis for their Big Star imprint. After one album they left the label and subsequently signed with A&M in 1987.

| | | | | | |
|---|---|---|---|---|---|
| 24/02/1990 | 6 | 44 | ✪² | **WAKING HOURS** | A&M AMA 9006 |
| 13/06/1992 | 2 | 20 | ● | **CHANGE EVERYTHING** | A&M 3953852 |
| 11/03/1995 | 3 | 25 | ● | **TWISTED** | A&M 5403112 |
| 12/07/1997 | 6 | 5 | | **SOME OTHER SUCKER'S PARADE** | A&M 5407052 |
| 19/09/1998 | 5 | 11 | ● | **THE BEST OF DEL AMITRI – HATFUL OF RAIN** | Mercury 5410312 |
| 20/04/2002 | 30 | 3 | | CAN YOU DO ME GOOD | Mercury 4932162 |

**DE'LACY** US R&B group formed by De Lacy Davis (percussion), Glen Branch (drums/vocals), Gary Griffin (bass/keyboards) and Raine Lassiter, all ex-members of Spectrum.

| | | | | | |
|---|---|---|---|---|---|
| 01/07/1995 | 53 | 1 | | HIDEAWAY | Slip 'N' Slide SLIP 023 |

**DELAKOTA** UK vocal/instrumental duo formed in 1997 by Des Murphy and ex-Smashing Things Cass Browne.

| | | | | | |
|---|---|---|---|---|---|
| 03/10/1998 | 58 | 1 | | ONE LOVE | Go Beat 5578612 |

**DELANEY AND BONNIE AND FRIENDS FEATURING ERIC CLAPTON** US husband and wife duo Delaney Bramlett (born 1/7/1939, Pontotoc County, MS) and Bonnie Lynn Bramlett (born 8/11/1944, Acton, IL) whose friends included, at various times, Leon Russell, Rita Coolidge, Dave Mason, Duane Allman and Eric Clapton, who toured with them following his departure from Blind Faith. They split in 1973, both recording solo – Delaney for MGM and Prodigal, Bonnie (who later recorded gospel material) for Capricorn.

| | | | | | |
|---|---|---|---|---|---|
| 06/06/1970 | 39 | 3 | | ON TOUR WITH ERIC CLAPTON | Atlantic 2400 013 |

**DELAYS** UK rock group formed in Southampton by Greg Gilbert (guitar/vocals), Aaron Gilbert (keyboards), Colin Fox (bass) and Rowdy (drums).

| | | | | | |
|---|---|---|---|---|---|
| 17/04/2004 | 17 | 4 | ○ | FADED SEASIDE GLAMOUR | Rough Trade RTRADDVCD114 |

**DELGADOS** UK group formed by Emma Pollock (guitar/vocals), Alun Woodward (guitar/vocals), Stewart Henderson (bass) and Paul Savage (drums). Woodward, Henderson and Savage were all ex-Bubblegum. They also formed the Chemikal Underground label.

| | | | | | |
|---|---|---|---|---|---|
| 20/06/1998 | 56 | 1 | | PELOTON | Chemikal Underground CHEM 024CD |
| 29/04/2000 | 72 | 1 | | THE GREAT EASTERN | Chemikal Underground CHEM 040CD |
| 26/10/2002 | 57 | 1 | | HATE | Mantra MNTCD 1031 |

**DELIRIOUS?** UK gospel/rock group formed in Littlehampton by Martin Smith (guitar/vocals), Stewart Smith (drums), Tim Jupp (keyboards), Stuart Garrad (guitar) and Jon Thatcher (bass).

| | | | | | |
|---|---|---|---|---|---|
| 28/06/1997 | 13 | 3 | | KING OF FOOLS | Furious? FURYCD 1 |
| 24/04/1999 | 25 | 2 | | MEZZAMORPHIS | Furious? FURYCD 002 |
| 18/08/2001 | 58 | 1 | | AUDIO LESSNOVER | Furious? FURYCD 3 |

## DEMON
**DEMON** UK group formed in 1980 by Dave Hill (vocals), Mal Spooner (guitar), Paul Riley (bass), Clive Cook (guitar) and John Wright (drums). Riley and Cook left in 1981 and were replaced by Chris Ellis and Les Hunt. They added Andy Richards (keyboards) in 1982. By 2001 the group consisted of John Cotterill, Ray Walmersley, Dave Hill, Andy Dale, Duncan Hanssel and Steve Brookes.

| | | | | | |
|---|---|---|---|---|---|
| 14/08/1982 | 47 | 3 | | THE UNEXPECTED GUEST | Carrere CAL 139 |
| 02/07/1983 | 73 | 2 | | THE PLAGUE | Clay CLAYLP 6 |

## CHAKA DEMUS AND PLIERS
**CHAKA DEMUS AND PLIERS** Jamaican singer (born John Taylor, 1964) who was a DJ when he teamed up with reggae singer Pliers (born Everton Bonner, 1963, Jamaica) and producer Sly Dunbar.

| | | | | | |
|---|---|---|---|---|---|
| 10/07/1993 | ❶² | 30 | ✪ | TEASE ME | Mango CIDM 1102 |

## CATHY DENNIS
**CATHY DENNIS** UK singer (born 25/3/1970, Norwich) who debuted with her father's Alan Dennis Band at holiday camps, before singing lead with D Mob in 1989. She went solo, with success on both sides of the Atlantic, working with Shep Pettibone and later Mark Saunders. She is also a successful songwriter, penning #1 hits for S Club 7 (*Never Had A Dream Come True*) and Kylie Minogue (*Can't Get You Out Of My Head*).

| | | | | | |
|---|---|---|---|---|---|
| 10/08/1991 | 3 | 31 | ● | MOVE TO THIS | Polydor 8495031 |
| 23/01/1993 | 8 | 4 | | INTO THE SKYLINE | Polydor 5139352 |

## SANDY DENNY
**SANDY DENNY** UK singer (born 6/1/1947, London) who joined Fairport Convention in 1968 and remained with the group for three albums. She left to form Fotheringay but they folded after one album. Sandy then went solo in 1971 with limited success and married Trevor Lucas (ex-Fotheringay) and joined him in a revived Fairport Convention in 1974. They both left the following year with Sandy recording one further solo album. She died from a brain haemorrhage on 21/4/1978 after falling down a friend's stairs.

| | | | | | |
|---|---|---|---|---|---|
| 02/10/1971 | 31 | 3 | | THE NORTH STAR GRASSMAN AND THE RAVENS | Island ILPS 9765 |

## JOHN DENVER

**JOHN DENVER** US singer (born John Henry Deutschendorf, 31/12/1943, Roswell, NM) who moved to Los Angeles, CA in 1964 and was a member of the Chad Mitchell Trio from 1965 until 1968. His 1969 debut album included his composition *Leaving On A Jet Plane*, successfully covered by Peter, Paul & Mary. He appeared in the 1977 film *Oh, God!* and numerous TV specials. He had a life-long love of flying and in 1988 he asked the Russians if he could go to the Mir Space Station, a request the Russians were considering for a fee of $10 million. He was killed in a plane crash at Monterey Bay, CA on 12/10/1997. It was later revealed that he was flying illegally as the Federal Aviation Authority had suspended his medical certificate. He won the 1997 Grammy Award for Best Musical Album for Children for *All Aboard!* He was awarded a star on the Hollywood Walk of Fame in 1982 but at the time of his death it had not been installed as Denver had been unable to schedule the investiture.

| | | | | | |
|---|---|---|---|---|---|
| 17/03/1973 | 11 | 15 | | ROCKY MOUNTAIN HIGH | RCA Victor SF 2308 |
| 02/06/1973 | 19 | 5 | | POEMS, PRAYERS AND PROMISES | RCA Victor SF 8219 |
| 23/06/1973 | 21 | 5 | ○ | RHYMES AND REASONS | RCA Victor SF 8348 |
| 30/03/1974 | 7 | 69 | ● | **THE BEST OF JOHN DENVER** ▲³ | RCA Victor APLI 0374 |
| 07/09/1974 | 3 | 29 | ● | **BACK HOME AGAIN** ▲¹ | RCA Victor APLI 0548 |
| 22/03/1975 | 31 | 4 | | AN EVENING WITH JOHN DENVER | RCA Victor LSA 3211/12 |
| 11/10/1975 | 14 | 21 | | WIND SONG ▲² | RCA Victor APLI 1183 |
| 15/05/1976 | 2 | 29 | | **LIVE IN LONDON** | RCA Victor RS 1050 |
| 04/09/1976 | 9 | 11 | | **SPIRIT** | RCA Victor APLI 1694 |
| 19/03/1977 | 9 | 9 | ● | **BEST OF JOHN DENVER VOLUME 2** | RCA Victor PL 42120 |
| 11/02/1978 | 25 | 5 | | I WANT TO LIVE | RCA Victor PL 12561 |
| 21/04/1979 | 68 | 1 | | JOHN DENVER | RCA Victor PL 13075 |
| 28/11/1981 | 17 | 21 | | PERHAPS LOVE | CBS 73592 |
| 22/10/1983 | 90 | 2 | | IT'S ABOUT TIME | RCA RCALP 6087 |
| 01/12/1984 | 20 | 11 | ● | JOHN DENVER – COLLECTION | Telstar STAR 2253 |
| 23/08/1986 | 91 | 3 | | ONE WORLD | RCA PL 85811 |
| 22/03/1997 | 19 | 9 | ● | THE ROCKY MOUNTAIN COLLECTION | RCA 07863668372 |

## KARL DENVER
**KARL DENVER** UK singer/guitarist (born Angus McKenzie, 16/12/1934, Glasgow) with a trio featuring Kevin Neill and Gerry Cottrell. He died from a brain tumour on 21/12/1998.

| | | | | | |
|---|---|---|---|---|---|
| 23/12/1961 | 7 | 27 | | **WIMOWEH** | Ace Of Clubs ACL 1098 |

## DEPECHE MODE
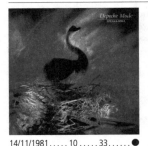

**DEPECHE MODE** UK synthesizer group formed in Basildon, Essex in 1980 by Vince Clarke (born 3/7/1960, South Woodford), Martin Gore (born 23/7/1961, Dagenham), Andy Fletcher (born 9/7/1960, Nottingham) and David Gahan (born 9/5/1962, Epping, lead vocals), taking their name from a French fashion magazine (the name means 'fast fashion'). Clarke left in 1981 and was replaced by Alan Wilder (born 1/6/1959, London); Gahan has provided much of the group's material since. The group won the 1991 BRIT Award for Best Single for *Enjoy The Silence*.

| | | | | | |
|---|---|---|---|---|---|
| 14/11/1981 | 10 | 33 | ● | **SPEAK AND SPELL** | Mute STUMM 5 |
| 09/10/1982 | 8 | 11 | ● | **A BROKEN FRAME** | Mute STUMM 9 |

▲⁹ Number of weeks album topped the US chart ◆¹² RIAA Diamond Awards ◇³ IFPI Platinum Europe Awards

| DATE | POS | WKS | BPI | ALBUM TITLE | LABEL & NUMBER |
|---|---|---|---|---|---|
| 03/09/1983 | 6 | 12 | ● | CONSTRUCTION TIME AGAIN | Mute STUMM 13 |
| 06/10/1984 | 5 | 12 | ○ | SOME GREAT REWARD | Mute STUMM 19 |
| 26/10/1985 | 6 | 22 | ● | THE SINGLES 81–85 | Mute MUTEL 1 |
| 29/03/1986 | 4 | 11 | ○ | BLACK CELEBRATION | Mute STUMM 26 |
| 10/10/1987 | 10 | 4 | ○ | MUSIC FOR THE MASSES | Mute STUMM 47 |
| 25/03/1989 | 5 | 8 | ○ | 101 | Mute STUMM 101 |
| 31/03/1990 | 2 | 30 | ● | VIOLATOR | Mute STUMM 64 |
| 03/04/1993 | ❶[1] | 16 | ● | SONGS OF FAITH AND DEVOTION ▲[1] | Mute CDSTUMM 106 |
| 26/04/1997 | ❶[1] | 11 | ● | ULTRA ◇ | Mute CDSTUMM 148 |
| 10/10/1998 | 5 | 6 | ● | THE SINGLES 86–98 ◇ | Mute CDMUTEL 005 |
| 07/11/1998 | 57 | 1 | | THE SINGLES 81–85 | Mute LCDMUTEL 1 |
| 26/05/2001 | 9 | 4 | | EXCITER ◇ | Mute CDSTUMM 190 |

## DEREK AND CLIVE – see PETER COOK AND DUDLEY MOORE

## DEREK AND THE DOMINOS
UK group formed in 1970 by Eric Clapton (born 30/3/1945, Ripley, guitar/vocals) after he left Blind Faith and Delaney and Bonnie, and featuring Carl Radle (bass), Bobby Whitlock (keyboards/vocals) and Jim Gordon (drums). Duane Allman (born 20/11/1946, Nashville, TN) appeared on the album but was killed in a motorcycle accident on 29/10/1971. The group disbanded after two albums. Radle died on 30/5/1980.

| DATE | POS | WKS | BPI | ALBUM TITLE | LABEL & NUMBER |
|---|---|---|---|---|---|
| 24/03/1973 | 36 | 1 | | DEREK AND THE DOMINOS IN CONCERT | RSO 2659 020 |

## DES'REE
UK singer (born Des'ree Weeks, 30/11/1968, London) with West Indian parents; she spent three years in Barbados before returning to London. Writing her first song at thirteen, she signed with Dusted Sound in 1991. She was named Best British Female Artist at the 1999 BRIT Awards.

| DATE | POS | WKS | BPI | ALBUM TITLE | LABEL & NUMBER |
|---|---|---|---|---|---|
| 29/02/1992 | 26 | 5 | ○ | MIND ADVENTURES | Dusted Sound 4712632 |
| 21/05/1994 | 13 | 6 | | I AIN'T MOVIN' | Dusted Sound 4758432 |
| 11/07/1998 | 16 | 16 | | SUPERNATURAL | Dusted Sound 4897192 |

## DESTINY'S CHILD

US vocal group formed in Houston, TX by Beyonce Knowles (born 18/9/1981, Houston), Kelendria 'Kelly' Rowland (born 11/2/1981, Houston), LaTavia Roberson (born 1/11/1981, Houston) and LeToya Luckett (born 11/3/1981, Houston). Roberson and Luckett left early in 2000 and were replaced by Farrah Franklin and Michelle Williams (born 23/7/1980). Franklin left soon after and the group continued as a trio of Knowles, Rowland and Williams. They won the 2000 Grammy Award for Best R&B Performance by a Duo or Group with Vocal for *Say My Name*, and the song won the award for Best R&B Song for writers LaShawn Daniels, Fred Jerkins III, Rodney Jerkins, Beyonce Knowles, LeToya Luckett, LaTavia Roberson and Kelendria Rowland. They repeated their success in 2001, winning the Best R&B Performance by a Duo or Group with Vocal for *Survivor*. In 1999 they received a MOBO Award for Best International Act and the 2001 Award for Best Single for *Independent Women Part 1*, and were named Best International Group at the 2002 BRIT Awards. When *Survivor* reached #1 in April 2001, they were the first US female group to have two UK #1 hits. Beyonce began acting, appearing in *Carmen, A Hip Hopera* (2001) and *Austin Powers, Goldmember* (2002), for which she recorded the theme song. She also wrote a number of hits with her father, Matthew, who launched the Music World Music label that released the *Carmen, A Hip Hopera* soundtrack. Rowland later recorded with Nelly and solo, Beyonce also recorded solo, while Williams recorded gospel material.

| DATE | POS | WKS | BPI | ALBUM TITLE | LABEL & NUMBER |
|---|---|---|---|---|---|
| 14/03/1998 | 45 | 4 | | DESTINY'S CHILD | Columbia 4885352 |
| 07/08/1999 | 10 | 87 | ✪[3] | THE WRITING'S ON THE WALL ◇[2] | Columbia 4943942 |
| 12/05/2001 | ❶[4] | 44 | ✪[3] | SURVIVOR ◇[2] ▲[2] | Columbia 5017832 |
| 30/03/2002 | 25 | 3 | | THIS IS THE REMIX | Columbia 5076272 |

## MARCELLA DETROIT
US singer (born Marcella Levy, 21/6/1959, Detroit, MI) who was first known as a songwriter, co-writing Eric Clapton's hit *Lay Down Sally*, before joining ex-Bananarama Siobhan Fahey in Shakespears Sister in 1989. The duo had a two-year break (both having babies), resuming in 1991. They disbanded in 1993, Marcella going solo.

| DATE | POS | WKS | BPI | ALBUM TITLE | LABEL & NUMBER |
|---|---|---|---|---|---|
| 09/04/1994 | 15 | 5 | ○ | JEWEL | London 8284912 |

## DETROIT SPINNERS
US R&B vocal group formed in Detroit, MI in 1955 by Henry Famborough (born 10/5/1935, Detroit), Billy Henderson (born 9/8/1939, Detroit), Pervis Jackson, CP Spencer and Bobby Smith (born 10/4/1937, Detroit) as the Domingos. They changed their name in 1957 to avoid confusion with the Flamingos and the Dominoes. Spinners are the hubcaps on Cadillacs. They signed with ex-Moonglows Harvey Fuqua's Tri-Phi label, which was acquired by Motown in 1964. Leaving Motown for Atlantic and producer Thom Bell in 1972, they became a major R&B group of the era. Line-up changes have included the departure of CP Spencer; a later addition GC Cameron leaving to go solo with Motown and being replaced by Philippe Wynne (born Philip Walker, 3/4/1941, Detroit), who also recorded solo and toured with Parliament/Funkadelic; and John Edwards, who joined in 1977. Wynne died from a heart attack on 14/7/1984, performing in San Francisco, CA. The group has a star on the Hollywood Walk of Fame.

| DATE | POS | WKS | BPI | ALBUM TITLE | LABEL & NUMBER |
|---|---|---|---|---|---|
| 14/05/1977 | 37 | 3 | | DETROIT SPINNERS' SMASH HITS | Atlantic K 50363 |

## DEUCE
UK vocal group formed in 1994 by Kelly O-Keefe, Lisa Armstrong, Paul Holmes and Craig Young. Kelly left in 1995 and was replaced by Mandy Perkins.

| DATE | POS | WKS | BPI | ALBUM TITLE | LABEL & NUMBER |
|---|---|---|---|---|---|
| 09/09/1995 | 18 | 2 | | ON THE LOOSE | London 8286642 |

## dEUS
Belgian rock group formed in Antwerp by Tom Barman (guitar/vocals), Rudy Toruve (guitar), Steff Kamil Carlens (bass), Klaas Janzoons (violin) and Julle De Borgher (drums).

| DATE | POS | WKS | BPI | ALBUM TITLE | LABEL & NUMBER |
|---|---|---|---|---|---|
| 03/04/1999 | 64 | 1 | | THE IDEAL CRASH | Island CID 8082 |

○ Silver disc  ● Gold disc  ✪ Platinum disc (additional platinum units are indicated by a figure following the symbol)  ❶[9] Number of weeks album topped the UK chart

### SYDNEY DEVINE
UK singer who began his career in 1957, still touring with his band The Legend at the turn of the century.

| 10/04/1976 | 14 | 10 | ○ | DOUBLE DEVINE | Philips 6625 019 |
| 11/12/1976 | 49 | 1 | ○ | DEVINE TIME | Philips 6308 283 |

### DEVO
US rock group formed in Akron, OH in 1972 by Mark Mothersbaugh (keyboards/guitar/vocals), his brother Bob (guitar/vocals), Bob Casle (guitar/vocals), his brother Gerald (bass/vocals) and Alan Myers (drums). Myers was later replaced by David Kendrick.

| 16/09/1978 | 12 | 7 | ○ | Q: ARE WE NOT MEN? A: NO WE ARE DEVO | Virgin V 2106 |
| 23/06/1979 | 49 | 6 | | DUTY NOW FOR THE FUTURE | Virgin V 2125 |
| 24/05/1980 | 47 | 5 | | FREEDOM OF CHOICE | Virgin V 2162 |
| 05/09/1981 | 50 | 4 | | NEW TRADITIONALISTS | Virgin V 2191 |

### HOWARD DEVOTO
UK singer (Howard Trafford) who was an original member of The Buzzcocks before leaving to form Magazine. They split in the early 1980s and Devoto had a brief solo career before launching a series of monikers for subsequent releases.

| 06/08/1983 | 57 | 2 | | JERKY VERSIONS OF THE DREAM | Virgin V 2272 |

### DEXY'S MIDNIGHT RUNNERS
UK group formed in 1978 by Kevin Rowland (born 17/8/1953, Wolverhampton, guitar/vocals), Al Archer (guitar), Pete Saunders (organ), Steve 'Babyface' Spooner (alto saxophone), 'Big' Jimmy Patterson (trombone), Pete Williams (bass), Jeff 'J.B.' Blythe (tenor saxophone) and Bobby Junior (drums). Their name is taken from the drug Dexedrine (despite their strict 'no drink and no drugs' policy). Signing with EMI in 1979, their brief success was followed by the group splitting up after Rowland insisted on releasing *Keep It* against the instinct of both the record company and the rest of the band. Most of them re-formed as Bureau, while Rowland moved to Phonogram with the remaining members. By 1986 it was basically a vehicle for Rowland as a soloist, despite a 1991 comeback with Creation Records. Ex-member Nick Gatfield became an A&R manager (responsible for signing Radiohead) and later MD of Polydor. The group won the 1983 BRIT Award for Best Single for *Come On Eileen*.

| 26/07/1980 | 6 | 10 | ○ | SEARCHING FOR THE YOUNG SOUL REBELS | Parlophone PCS 7213 |
| 07/08/1982 | 2 | 46 | ✪³ | **TOO-RYE-AY** KEVIN ROWLAND & DEXY'S MIDNIGHT RUNNERS | Mercury MERS 5 |
| 26/03/1983 | 79 | 2 | | GENO | EMI EMS 1007 |
| 21/09/1985 | 22 | 6 | | DON'T STAND ME DOWN | Mercury MERH 56 |
| 08/06/1991 | 12 | 15 | ● | THE VERY BEST OF DEXY'S MIDNIGHT RUNNERS | Mercury 8464601 |
| 04/10/2003 | 75 | 1 | | LET'S MAKE THIS PRECIOUS – THE BEST OF | EMI 5926802 |

### JIM DIAMOND
UK singer (born 28/9/1953, Scotland) who was a member of PhD before going solo.

| 22/05/1993 | 16 | 5 | | JIM DIAMOND | Polygram TV 8438472 |

### NEIL DIAMOND
US singer (born Noah Kaminsky, 24/1/1941, Brooklyn, NYC), initially a songwriter, who made the big time in 1966 with several top twenty hits in both the UK and US (although his first royalty cheque was for just 73 cents). Simultaneously performing, he made his debut single in 1965. Initially signed to Bang, he linked with MCA (through its Uni imprint) in 1968, then CBS/Columbia in 1973. His films included a 1980 remake of *The Jazz Singer*. He won the 1973 Grammy Award for Best Album of Original Score Written for a Motion Picture for *Jonathan Livingston Seagull*.

| 03/04/1971 | 19 | 12 | | TAP ROOT MANUSCRIPT | Uni UNLS 117 |
| 03/04/1971 | 23 | 11 | | GOLD | Uni UNLS 116 |
| 11/12/1971 | 18 | 14 | | STONES | Uni UNLS 121 |
| 05/08/1972 | 7 | 19 | | **MOODS** | Uni UNLS 128 |
| 12/01/1974 | 32 | 2 | | HOT AUGUST NIGHT | Uni ULD 1 |
| 16/02/1974 | 35 | 1 | ● | JONATHAN LIVINGSTONE SEAGULL Original soundtrack to the film. 1973 Grammy Award for Best Album of Original Score Written for a Motion Picture | CBS 69047 |
| 09/03/1974 | 39 | 5 | ● | RAINBOW | MCA MCF 2529 |
| 29/06/1974 | 13 | 78 | ● | HIS 12 GREATEST HITS | MCA MCF 2550 |
| 09/11/1974 | 11 | 14 | ● | SERENADE | CBS 69067 |
| 10/07/1976 | 10 | 26 | ● | **BEAUTIFUL NOISE** | CBS 86004 |
| 12/03/1977 | 3 | 32 | ✪ | **LOVE AT THE GREEK** | CBS 95001 |
| 06/08/1977 | 60 | 1 | ● | HOT AUGUST NIGHT | MCA MCSP 255 |
| 17/12/1977 | 16 | 12 | ● | I'M GLAD YOU'RE HERE WITH ME TONIGHT | CBS 86044 |
| 25/11/1978 | 2 | 29 | ✪ | **20 GOLDEN GREATS** | MCA EMTV 14 |
| 06/01/1979 | 15 | 23 | ● | YOU DON'T BRING ME FLOWERS | CBS 86077 |
| 19/01/1980 | 14 | 11 | ● | SEPTEMBER MORN | CBS 86096 |
| 22/11/1980 | 3 | 110 | ✪ | **THE JAZZ SINGER** Original soundtrack to the film | Capitol EAST 12120 |
| 28/02/1981 | 43 | 6 | | LOVE SONGS | MCA MCF 3092 |
| 05/12/1981 | 39 | 13 | ○ | THE WAY TO THE SKY | CBS 85343 |
| 19/06/1982 | 32 | 8 | ○ | 12 GREATEST HITS VOLUME 2 | CBS 85844 |
| 13/11/1982 | 43 | 10 | ○ | HEARTLIGHT | CBS 25073 |

| DATE | POS | WKS | BPI | ALBUM TITLE | LABEL & NUMBER |
|---|---|---|---|---|---|
| 10/12/1983 | 33 | 11 | ● | THE VERY BEST OF NEIL DIAMOND | K-Tel NE 1265 |
| 28/07/1984 | 7 | 10 | ○ | **PRIMITIVE** | CBS 86306 |
| 24/05/1986 | 36 | 8 | | HEADED FOR THE FUTURE | CBS 26952 |
| 28/11/1987 | 74 | 4 | | HOT AUGUST NIGHT II | CBS 4604081 |
| 25/02/1989 | 42 | 6 | | THE BEST YEARS OF OUR LIVES | CBS 4632011 |
| 09/11/1991 | 36 | 13 | ● | LOVESCAPE | Columbia 4688901 |
| 04/07/1992 | ❶[3] | 30 | ✪ | **THE GREATEST HITS 1966–1992** | Columbia 4715022 |
| 28/11/1992 | 50 | 6 | ○ | THE CHRISTMAS ALBUM | Columbia 4724102 |
| 09/11/1993 | 28 | 10 | ○ | UP ON THE ROOF – SONGS FROM THE BRILL BUILDING | Columbia 4743562 |
| 17/02/1996 | 12 | 13 | ○ | TENNESSEE MOON (THE NASHVILLE COLLECTION) | Columbia 4813782 |
| 25/05/1996 | 68 | 1 | | THE BEST OF NEIL DIAMOND | MCA MCD 11452 |
| 31/08/1996 | 5 | 20 | ● | **THE ULTIMATE COLLECTION** | Sony TV/MCA MOODCD 45 |
| 14/11/1998 | 68 | 2 | | THE MOVIE ALBUM – AS TIME GOES BY | Columbia 4916552 |
| 15/09/2001 | 49 | 1 | | THREE CHORD OPERA | Columbia 5024932 |
| 16/03/2002 | 11 | 12 | ● | THE ESSENTIAL COLLECTION | Columbia 5010662 |

**DIAMOND HEAD** UK group formed in Stourbridge in 1979 by Sean Harris (vocals), Brian Tatler (guitar), Colin Kimberley (bass) and Duncan Scott (drums). Kimberley and Scott left in 1983 and were replaced by Merv Goldsworthy and Robbie France. They disbanded in 1985, re-forming in 1991 with Sean Harris, Brian Tatler, Eddie Nooham (bass) and Karl Wilcox (drums).

| DATE | POS | WKS | BPI | ALBUM TITLE | LABEL & NUMBER |
|---|---|---|---|---|---|
| 23/10/1982 | 24 | 5 | | BORROWED TIME | MCA DH 1001 |
| 24/09/1983 | 32 | 4 | | CANTERBURY | MCA DH 1002 |

**DICKIES** US punk group formed in Los Angeles, CA in 1977 by Chuck Wagon (keyboards), Stan Lee (guitar), Billy Club (bass), Leonard Graves Phillips (vocals) and Karlos Kaballero (drums). Wagon committed suicide in 1981.

| DATE | POS | WKS | BPI | ALBUM TITLE | LABEL & NUMBER |
|---|---|---|---|---|---|
| 17/02/1979 | 18 | 17 | | THE INCREDIBLE SHRINKING DICKIES | A&M AMLE 64742 |
| 24/11/1979 | 60 | 2 | | DAWN OF THE DICKIES | A&M AMLE 68510 |

**BRUCE DICKINSON** UK singer (born Paul Bruce Dickinson, 7/8/1958, Worksop, raised in Sheffield) who was a member of Samson before replacing Paul Di'anno as lead singer with Iron Maiden in 1981. In 1990 he launched a parallel solo career. He represented Great Britain in fencing, at one stage being ranked seventh in the country.

| DATE | POS | WKS | BPI | ALBUM TITLE | LABEL & NUMBER |
|---|---|---|---|---|---|
| 19/05/1990 | 14 | 9 | ○ | TATTOOED MILLIONAIRE | EMI EMC 3574 |
| 18/06/1994 | 21 | 3 | | BALLS TO PICASSO | EMI CDEMX 1057 |
| 09/03/1996 | 41 | 1 | | SKUNKWORTHS | Raw Power RAWCD 106 |
| 24/05/1997 | 53 | 1 | | ACCIDENT OF BIRTH | Raw Power ESMCD 767 |
| 26/09/1998 | 55 | 1 | | THE CHEMICAL WEDDING | Air Raid AIRCD 1 |

**BARBARA DICKSON** UK singer (born 27/9/1947, Dunfermline) who began her career singing folk music, making her first albums in the early 1970s. She appeared in the show *John Paul George Ringo And Bert* and signed with RSO in 1975. She later became a popular TV presenter and also appeared on stage, winning a Laurence Olivier Award for her role in the stage musical *Blood Brothers*. She was awarded an OBE in the 2002 New Year's Honours List.

| DATE | POS | WKS | BPI | ALBUM TITLE | LABEL & NUMBER |
|---|---|---|---|---|---|
| 18/06/1977 | 58 | 1 | | MORNING COMES QUICKLY | RSO 2394 188 |
| 12/04/1980 | 7 | 12 | ● | **THE BARBARA DICKSON ALBUM** | Epic EPC 84088 |
| 16/05/1981 | 39 | 6 | | YOU KNOW IT'S ME | Epic EPC 84551 |
| 06/02/1982 | 3 | 38 | ✪ | **ALL FOR A SONG** | Epic 10030 |
| 24/09/1983 | 100 | 1 | | TELL ME IT'S NOT TRUE 'FROM THE MUSICAL BLOOD BROTHERS' | Legacy LLM 101 |
| 23/06/1984 | 21 | 8 | | HEARTBEATS | Epic EPC 25706 |
| 12/01/1985 | 5 | 19 | ● | **THE BARBARA DICKSON SONGBOOK** | K-Tel NE 1287 |
| 23/11/1985 | 11 | 18 | ✪ | GOLD | K-Tel ONE 1312 |
| 15/11/1986 | 78 | 8 | | THE VERY BEST OF BARBARA DICKSON | Telstar STAR 2276 |
| 29/11/1986 | 39 | 8 | ● | THE RIGHT MOMENT | K-Tel ONE 1335 |
| 06/05/1989 | 30 | 7 | | COMING ALIVE AGAIN | Telstar STAR 2349 |
| 15/08/1992 | 32 | 5 | | DON'T THINK TWICE IT'S ALL RIGHT | Columbia MOODCD 25 |
| 28/11/1992 | 22 | 9 | | THE BEST OF ELAINE PAIGE AND BARBARA DICKSON **ELAINE PAIGE AND BARBARA DICKSON** | Telstar TCD 2632 |
| 05/03/1994 | 30 | 3 | | PARCEL OF ROGUES | Castle Communications CTVCD 126 |
| 20/03/2004 | 35 | 2 | | THE PLATINUM COLLECTION | Sony Music TV 5161092 |

**BO DIDDLEY** US singer/guitarist (born Otha Elias Bates McDaniel, 30/12/1928, McComb, MS) who debuted with Checker/Chess in 1955. Named after a one-stringed African guitar, he was first called the name as a youth when he trained as a boxer. He appeared in the 1984 film *Trading Places* and was inducted into the Rock & Roll Hall of Fame in 1987. He was also a successful songwriter.

| DATE | POS | WKS | BPI | ALBUM TITLE | LABEL & NUMBER |
|---|---|---|---|---|---|
| 05/10/1963 | 11 | 8 | | BO DIDDLEY | Pye International NPL 28026 |
| 09/11/1963 | 20 | 1 | | BO DIDDLEY IS A GUNSLINGER | Pye NJL 33 |
| 30/11/1963 | 19 | 1 | | BO DIDDLEY RIDES AGAINS | Pye International NPL 28029 |

15/02/1964 . . . . . 13 . . . . . . 6 . . . . . .          BO DIDDLEY'S BEACH PARTY . . . . . . . . . . . . . . . . . . . . . . . . . . . . . . . . . . . . . . . . . . . . . . . . . . . . . . . . . . . . . . . . . . . Pye NPL 28032

**DIDO** UK singer (born Dido Florian Cloud de Bounevialle Armstrong, 25/12/1971, London) and sister of Rollo Armstrong of Faithless. Initially she was more successful in the USA and achieved her UK breakthrough after a sample of *Thank You* was included on Eminem's #1 hit single *Stan*. She was named Best New Act at the 2001 MTV Europe Music Awards and then won two BRIT Awards in 2002 including Best UK Female. Dido collected a further two awards in 2004: Best British Female and Best British Single for *White Flag*.

28/10/2000 . . . . ❶[7] . . . . 130 . . . . . ⓪[9]    **NO ANGEL** ◇[5] 2002 BRIT Award for Best Album. Total worldwide sales exceed 12 million, making this the most successful debut album by a UK female singer . . . . . . . . . . . . . . . . . . . . . . . . . . . . . . . . . . . . . . . . . . . . . . . . . . . . . . . . . . . . . . . Cheeky 74321832742

11/10/2003 . . . . ❶[9] . . . . 34+ . . . . . ⓪[7]    **LIFE FOR RENT** ◇[5] . . . . . . . . . . . . . . . . . . . . . . . . . . . . . . . . . . . . . . . . . . . . . . . . . . . . . . . . . . . . . . . . . . . . . . . . . Cheeky 82876545982

**DIESEL PARK WEST** UK group formed by Richie Barton (guitar/vocals), Geoff Beavan (bass/vocals), John Butler (guitar/vocals), Rick Willson (guitar/vocals) and Dave Anderson (drums).

11/02/1989 . . . . . 55 . . . . . . 2 . . . . . .    SHAKESPEARE ALABAMA . . . . . . . . . . . . . . . . . . . . . . . . . . . . . . . . . . . . . . . . . . . . . . . . . . . . . . . . . . . . . . . . . . . . . . . . Food FOODLP 2

15/02/1992 . . . . . 57 . . . . . . 1 . . . . . .    DECENCY . . . . . . . . . . . . . . . . . . . . . . . . . . . . . . . . . . . . . . . . . . . . . . . . . . . . . . . . . . . . . . . . . . . . . . . . . . . . . . . . Food FOODCD 7

**DIFFORD AND TILBROOK** UK duo Chris Difford (born 4/11/1954, London, guitar/vocals) and Glenn Tilbrook (born 31/8/1957, London, guitar/vocals), both ex-Squeeze, who disbanded in 1982. The eponymous group also featured Keith Wilkinson (bass), Guy Fletcher (keyboards) and Andy Duncan (drums). Difford and Tilbrook rejoined a revived Squeeze in 1985.

14/07/1984 . . . . . 47 . . . . . . 3 . . . . . .    DIFFORD AND TILBROOK . . . . . . . . . . . . . . . . . . . . . . . . . . . . . . . . . . . . . . . . . . . . . . . . . . . . . . . . . . . . . . . . . A&M AMLX 64985

**DIGITAL UNDERGROUND** US rap group formed in Oakland, CA by Shock-G (born Gregory Jacobs, keyboards/vocals), Chopmaster J (samples/percussion) and DJ Fuze (born David Elliott) with various floating members including Tupac Shakur, DJ Jay-Z and Saafir The Saucy Nomad.

07/04/1990 . . . . . 59 . . . . . . 1 . . . . . .    SEX PACKETS . . . . . . . . . . . . . . . . . . . . . . . . . . . . . . . . . . . . . . . . . . . . . . . . . . . . . . . . . . . . . . . . . . . . . . . . . . . . BCM 377LP

30/06/1990 . . . . . 59 . . . . . . 1 . . . . . .    DOOWUTCHYALIKE/PACKET MAN . . . . . . . . . . . . . . . . . . . . . . . . . . . . . . . . . . . . . . . . . . . . . . . . . . . . . . . . . . . . BCM 463X

**DILATED PEOPLES** US rap group formed in Los Angeles, CA by Evidence, Iriscience and DJ Babu.

02/03/2002 . . . . . 55 . . . . . . 1 . . . . . .    EXPANSION TEAM . . . . . . . . . . . . . . . . . . . . . . . . . . . . . . . . . . . . . . . . . . . . . . . . . . . . . . . . . . . . . . . . . . . . . . Capitol 5314772

**RICHARD DIMBLEBY** UK broadcaster (born 25/5/1913) who made his name as the presenter of *Panorama*, which began on BBC TV in 1953. His excellent broadcasting reputation led to a number of film offers, and he appeared in such films as *Rockets Galore* and *Libel*. The father of fellow broadcasters, David and Jonathan Dimbleby, he died from cancer on 22/12/1965.

04/06/1966 . . . . . 14 . . . . . . 5 . . . . . .    THE VOICE OF RICHARD DIMBLEBY . . . . . . . . . . . . . . . . . . . . . . . . . . . . . . . . . . . . . . . . . . . . . . . . . . . . . . . . . . . . . . MFP 1087

**DINOSAUR JR.** US rock group formed in Amherst, MA in 1984 by Joseph Mascis (born 10/12/1965, Amherst, guitar/vocals), Lou Barlow (born 17/7/1966, Northampton, MA, bass), both ex-Deep Wound, and ex-All White Jury member, Emmett Murphy (born 21/12/1964, drums). Later members included Mike Johnson, Don Fleming, Jay Spiegel and Van Connor. Mascis went solo in 1995 and the group split in 1997.

02/03/1991 . . . . . 36 . . . . . . 2 . . . . . .    GREEN MIND . . . . . . . . . . . . . . . . . . . . . . . . . . . . . . . . . . . . . . . . . . . . . . . . . . . . . . . . . . . . . . . . . . . Blanco Y Negro BYN 24

20/02/1993 . . . . . 10 . . . . . . 3 . . . . . .    **WHERE YOU BEEN** . . . . . . . . . . . . . . . . . . . . . . . . . . . . . . . . . . . . . . . . . . . . . . . . . . . . . . . . . . . . . Blanco Y Negro 4509916272

10/09/1994 . . . . . 24 . . . . . . 2 . . . . . .    WITHOUT A SOUND . . . . . . . . . . . . . . . . . . . . . . . . . . . . . . . . . . . . . . . . . . . . . . . . . . . . . . . . . . . . Blanco Y Negro 4509969332

**DIO** US heavy rock group named after lead singer Ronnie James Dio (born Ronald Padavona, 10/7/1949, New Hampshire). Dio had previously been with Rainbow and Black Sabbath (replacing Ozzy Osbourne). The group also included Vinny Appice (drums), Jimmy Bain (bass), Vivian Campbell (guitar) and Claude Schnell (keyboards). Campbell left in 1987 and was replaced by Craig Goldie.

11/06/1983 . . . . . 13 . . . . . 15 . . . . . . O    HOLY DIVER . . . . . . . . . . . . . . . . . . . . . . . . . . . . . . . . . . . . . . . . . . . . . . . . . . . . . . . . . . . . . . . . . . . . . . . . . Vertigo VERS 5

21/07/1984 . . . . . . 4 . . . . . 14 . . . . . . O    **THE LAST IN LINE** . . . . . . . . . . . . . . . . . . . . . . . . . . . . . . . . . . . . . . . . . . . . . . . . . . . . . . . . . . . . . . . . . . Vertigo VERL 16

07/09/1985 . . . . . . 4 . . . . . . 6 . . . . . .    **SACRED HEART** . . . . . . . . . . . . . . . . . . . . . . . . . . . . . . . . . . . . . . . . . . . . . . . . . . . . . . . . . . . . . . . . . . . . . Vertigo VERH 30

05/07/1986 . . . . . 22 . . . . . . 5 . . . . . .    INTERMISSION . . . . . . . . . . . . . . . . . . . . . . . . . . . . . . . . . . . . . . . . . . . . . . . . . . . . . . . . . . . . . . . . . . . . . Vertigo VERB 40

22/08/1987 . . . . . . 8 . . . . . . 5 . . . . . .    **DREAM EVIL** . . . . . . . . . . . . . . . . . . . . . . . . . . . . . . . . . . . . . . . . . . . . . . . . . . . . . . . . . . . . . . . . . . . . . . . Vertigo VERH 46

26/05/1990 . . . . . 28 . . . . . . 3 . . . . . .    LOCK UP THE WOLVES . . . . . . . . . . . . . . . . . . . . . . . . . . . . . . . . . . . . . . . . . . . . . . . . . . . . . . . . . . . . . . . Vertigo 8460331

**DION AND THE BELMONTS** US singer (born Dion DiMucci, 18/7/1939, The Bronx, NYC) who debuted in 1957. The following year he formed the Belmonts (named after Belmont Avenue in The Bronx) with Angelo D'Aleo (born 3/2/1940), Fred Milano (born 22/8/1939) and Carlo Mastrangelo (born 5/10/1938), all from The Bronx. Dion went solo in 1960, occasionally reviving the Belmonts since, and has also recorded contemporary Christian material. He was inducted into the Rock & Roll Hall of Fame in 1989.

12/04/1980 . . . . . 31 . . . . . . 5 . . . . . .    20 GOLDEN GREATS . . . . . . . . . . . . . . . . . . . . . . . . . . . . . . . . . . . . . . . . . . . . . . . . . . . . . . . . . . . . . . . . . . . K-Tel NE 1057

### CELINE DION
Canadian singer (born 30/3/1968, Charlemagne, Quebec) who won the Eurovision Song Contest for Switzerland in 1988 singing *Ne Partez Sans Moi*. Since switching from singing in French to English she has become one of the most popular singers on both sides of the Atlantic. She is married to Rene Angelil, her manager since 1981. She has won five Grammy Awards including: Best Pop Performance by a Duo in 1992 with Peabo Bryson for *Beauty And The Beast,* and Record of the Year and Best Female Pop Vocal Performance in 1998 for *My Heart Will Go On* (which also won the Grammy Awards for Song of the Year and Best Song for a Motion Picture and the Oscar for Best Film Song for writers James Horner and Will Jennings). She had a son in January 2001. She has a star on the Hollywood Walk of Fame at 6801 Hollywood Boulevard.

| DATE | POS | WKS | BPI | ALBUM TITLE | LABEL & NUMBER |
|---|---|---|---|---|---|
| 05/03/1994 | ❶⁷ | 109 | ✪⁵ | **THE COLOUR OF MY LOVE** ◇⁴ | Epic 4747432 |
| 16/09/1995 | 55 | 3 | | UNISON | Epic 4672032 |
| 07/10/1995 | 7 | 9 | ● | **D'EUX – THE FRENCH ALBUM** ◇⁵ | Epic 4802862 |
| 23/03/1996 | ❶¹ | 113 | ✪⁷ | **FALLING INTO YOU** ◇⁶ ▲³ ◆¹¹ 1996 Grammy Awards for Album of the Year and Best Pop Album | Epic 4837922 |
| 09/11/1996 | 53 | 1 | | LIVE A PARIS ◇ | Epic 4866062 |
| 15/03/1997 | 49 | 3 | | C'EST POUR VIVRE | Nectar Masters EURCD 405 |
| 29/11/1997 | ❶⁵ | 73 | ✪⁶ | **LET'S TALK ABOUT LOVE** ◇⁹ ▲¹ ◆¹⁰ | Epic 4891592 |
| 19/09/1998 | 17 | 4 | ● | S'IL SUFFISAIT D'AIMER ◇² | Epic 4918592 |
| 26/09/1998 | 70 | 2 | | CELINE DION | Epic 4715089 |
| 14/11/1998 | 20 | 10 | ● | THESE ARE SPECIAL TIMES ◇ | Epic 4927302 |
| 27/11/1999 | ❶¹ | 40 | ✪² | **ALL THE WAY… A DECADE OF SONGS** ◇⁵ ▲³ | Epic 4960942 |
| 11/11/2000 | 30 | 3 | | THE COLLECTOR'S SERIES VOLUME 1 | Epic 5009952 |
| 06/04/2002 | ❶⁴ | 23 | ✪ | **A NEW DAY HAS COME** ◇³ ▲¹ | Epic 5062262 |
| 05/04/2003 | 4 | 9 | ● | **ONE HEART** ◇ | Epic 5108772 |
| 26/06/2004 | 22 | 1+ | | A NEW DAY – LIVE IN LAS VEGAS | Columbia 5152253 |

### DIRE STRAITS
UK rock group formed in 1977 by Mark Knopfler (born 12/8/1949, Glasgow, guitar/vocals), his brother David (born 27/12/1952, Glasgow, guitar), John Illsley (born 24/6/1949, Leicester, bass) and Pick Withers (born 4/4/1948, Leicester, drums). After radio plays of their self-funded debut record they signed with Phonogram's Vertigo label. David left in 1980 and was replaced by Hal Lindes (born 30/6/1953, Monterey, CA), who left in 1985. Withers left in 1983; Terry Williams was his replacement. Alan Clark (born 5/3/1955, Durham, keyboards) joined in 1980 and Guy Fletcher in 1984. Their name reflects the financial state they were in at the time of their formation. Knopfler has recorded solo and with Fletcher was in The Notting Hillbillies. Dire Straits were named Best UK Group at the 1983 and 1986 BRIT Awards and they have won two Grammy Awards including: Best Rock Vocal Performance by a Group in 1985 for *Money for Nothing* and Best Video Short Form for *Brothers In Arms*. Mark Knopfler was awarded an OBE in the 2000 New Year's Honours List.

| DATE | POS | WKS | BPI | ALBUM TITLE | LABEL & NUMBER |
|---|---|---|---|---|---|
| 22/07/1978 | 5 | 132 | ✪² | **DIRE STRAITS** | Vertigo 9102 021 |
| 23/06/1979 | 5 | 32 | ✪ | **COMMUNIQUE** | Vertigo 9102 031 |
| 25/10/1980 | 4 | 251 | ✪² | **MAKING MOVIES** | Vertigo 6359 034 |
| 02/10/1982 | ❶⁴ | 200 | ✪² | **LOVE OVER GOLD** | Vertigo 6359 109 |
| 24/03/1984 | 3 | 163 | ✪ | **ALCHEMY – DIRE STRAITS LIVE** | Vertigo VERY 11 |
| 25/05/1985 | ❶¹⁴ | 228 | ✪¹³ | **BROTHERS IN ARMS** 1987 BRIT Award for Best Album. The first CD to sell in excess of 1 million copies in the UK | Vertigo VERH 25 |
| 29/10/1988 | ❶³ | 64 | ✪⁴ | **MONEY FOR NOTHING** | Vertigo VERH 64 |
| 21/09/1991 | ❶¹ | 35 | ✪² | **ON EVERY STREET** | Vertigo 5101601 |
| 22/05/1993 | 4 | 7 | | **ON THE NIGHT** | Vertigo 5147662 |
| 08/07/1995 | 71 | 1 | | LIVE AT THE BBC | Windsong WINCD 072X |
| 31/10/1998 | 6 | 21+ | ● | **SULTANS OF SWING – THE VERY BEST OF DIRE STRAITS** ◇³ | Vertigo 5586582 |

### DIRTY VEGAS
UK production group formed by Paul Harris, Steve Smith and Ben Harris. They won the 2002 Grammy Award for Best Dance Recording for *Days Go By*.

| DATE | POS | WKS | BPI | ALBUM TITLE | LABEL & NUMBER |
|---|---|---|---|---|---|
| 17/08/2002 | 40 | 3 | ○ | DIRTY VEGAS | Credence 5399852 |

### DISCHARGE
UK rock group formed in 1977 by Terry 'Tezz' Roberts (vocals), his brother Tony 'Bones' (guitar), Roy 'Rainy' Wainwright (bass) and Hacko (drums). Hacko left in 1979, at which point Terry Roberts switched to drums, with Cal joining as lead singer. Terry Roberts left in 1981; Bambi was the temporary drummer until Garry Maloney joined. Tony Roberts left in 1982 and was replaced by Peter 'Pooch' Pyrtle, who left after a year along with Maloney. Their replacements were Les 'The Mole' Hunt (guitar) and Nick Haymaker (drums). These two proved short-lived too, Maloney returning in 1986 and Stephen Brooks joining on guitar. By 1997 the early line-up of Cal, Bones, Rainy and Tezz had re-formed.

| DATE | POS | WKS | BPI | ALBUM TITLE | LABEL & NUMBER |
|---|---|---|---|---|---|
| 15/05/1982 | 40 | 5 | | HEAR NOTHING, SEE NOTHING, SAY NOTHING | Clay CLAYLP 3 |

### DISPOSABLE HEROES OF HIPHOPRISY
US hip hop duo formed in San Francisco, CA by Michael Franti (vocals) and Rono Tse (percussion), both previously in The Beatnigs.

| DATE | POS | WKS | BPI | ALBUM TITLE | LABEL & NUMBER |
|---|---|---|---|---|---|
| 16/05/1992 | 40 | 3 | | HYPOCRISY IS THE GREATEST LUXURY | Fourth & Broadway BRCD 584 |

### SACHA DISTEL
French singer/guitarist (born 29/1/1933, Paris) who was especially popular during the 1970s. He has also appeared in films, his first being the 1953 film *Femmes De Paris*. He died on 21/7/2004.

| DATE | POS | WKS | BPI | ALBUM TITLE | LABEL & NUMBER |
|---|---|---|---|---|---|
| 02/05/1970 | 21 | 14 | | SACHA DISTEL | Warner Brothers WS 3003 |

○ Silver disc ● Gold disc ✪ Platinum disc (additional platinum units are indicated by a figure following the symbol) ❶⁹ Number of weeks album topped the UK chart

**DISTILLERS** US and Australian rock group formed in 1998 by Brody Armstrong (guitar and vocals), Rose Casper (guitar), Kim Chi (bass) and Matt (drums). By 2002 the group consisted of Brody, Tony (guitar), Ryan (bass) and Andy (drums).

25/10/2003 . . . . . 46 . . . . . . 1 . . . . . . CORAL FANG . . . . . . . . . . . . . . . . . . . . . . . . . . . . . . . . . . . . . . . . . . . . . . . . . . . . . . . . . . . . . . . . . . . Sire 9362484202

**DISTURBED** US rock group formed in Chicago, IL by David Craiman (vocals), Dan Donegan (guitar), Fuzz Kmak (bass) and Mike Wengren (drums).

05/10/2002 . . . . . 41 . . . . . . 1 . . . . . . BELIEVE ▲¹ . . . . . . . . . . . . . . . . . . . . . . . . . . . . . . . . . . . . . . . . . . . . . . . . . . . . . . . . . . . . . . . . . . . . . . Reprise WB 483202

**DIVINE COMEDY** UK group formed in Enniskillen, Northern Ireland in 1989 as a five-piece band, reducing to just Neil Hannon (born 7/11/1970, Londonderry) after one album.

| | | | | | |
|---|---|---|---|---|---|
| 11/05/1996 | 48 | 9 | ● | CASANOVA | Setanta SETCD 025 |
| 22/02/1997 | 13 | 6 | | A SHORT ALBUM ABOUT LOVE | Setanta SETCD 036 |
| 12/09/1998 | 9 | 14 | ● | FIN DE SIECLE | Setanta SETCD 057 |
| 11/09/1999 | 3 | 11 | | A SECRET HISTORY – THE BEST OF DIVINE COMEDY | Setanta SETCDL 100 |
| 24/03/2001 | 14 | 3 | ○ | REGENERATION | Parlophone 5317612 |
| 10/04/2004 | 23 | 3 | | ABSENT FRIENDS | Parlophone 5962802 |

**DIVINE WORKS** German male producer Claus Zundel who also records as Sacred Spirit.

16/08/1997 . . . . . 43 . . . . . . 2 . . . . . . DIVINE WORKS . . . . . . . . . . . . . . . . . . . . . . . . . . . . . . . . . . . . . . . . . . . . . . . . . . . . . . . . . . . . . . . . . . . . . Virgin VTCD 119

**DIVINYLS** Australian rock group formed in Sydney in 1981 by Christina Amphlett (vocals), Mark McEntee (guitar), Bjorn Olin (keyboards), JJ Harris (drums) and Rick Grossman (bass). By 1991 the group was a duo of Amphlett and McEntee.

20/07/1991 . . . . . 59 . . . . . . 1 . . . . . . DIVINYLS . . . . . . . . . . . . . . . . . . . . . . . . . . . . . . . . . . . . . . . . . . . . . . . . . . . . . . . . . . . . . . . . . . . Virgin America VUSLP 30

**DIXIE CHICKS** US country group formed by Martha Seide (born 12/10/1969, fiddle/mandolin), her sister Emily Robinson (born 16/8/1972, guitar/banjo) and Natalie Maines (born 14/10/1974, lead vocals). The group has won seven Grammy Awards including: Best Country Group Performance in 1998 for *There's Your Trouble*; Best Country Group Performance in 1999 for *Ready To Run*; Best Country Performance By a Duo Or Group With Vocal in 2002 for *Long Time Gone*; and Best Country Instrumental Performance in 2002 for *Lil' Jack Slade*. In July 2001 they filed a suit against Sony Music seeking to break their recording contract, even though they were still required to deliver a further five albums (their first two for the label had sold over 20 million copies in the US alone). Sony claimed non-delivery of the five albums could cost them as much as $100 million. A compromise was reached a year later when the group were given their own label, Open Wide Records, via Sony.

| | | | | | |
|---|---|---|---|---|---|
| 03/07/1999 | 26 | 6 | ○ | WIDE OPEN SPACES ◆¹² 1998 Grammy Award for Best Country Album | Epic 4898422 |
| 11/09/1999 | 38 | 2 | | FLY ▲² ◆¹⁰ 1999 Grammy Award for Best Country Album | Epic 4951512 |
| 22/03/2003 | 33 | 12 | ● | HOME 2002 Grammy Award for Best Country Album | Epic 5096032 |

**DJ HYPE PRESENTS GANJA KRU** UK DJ Kevin Ford began producing in 1990 and later launched Ganja Records. He was named Best Male DJ 1994 and Best Radio DJ 1995 at the UK Hardcore Awards.

30/08/1997 . . . . . 56 . . . . . . 1 . . . . . . NEW FRONTIERS (EP) . . . . . . . . . . . . . . . . . . . . . . . . . . . . . . . . . . . . . . . . . . . . . . . . . . . . . . . . . . . . . . Parousia 74321501072

**DJ JAZZY JEFF AND FRESH PRINCE** – see JAZZY JEFF AND FRESH PRINCE

**DJ KRUSH** US producer/DJ Hideaki Ishii from New York who first recorded in 1990. He set up the Power Music Records, Power Music Trax, Sex Mania and DJ Exclusive labels and also records as Club People, Inner Soul, The Music Choir, The Pleasure Dome and Tribal Liberation.

| | | | | | |
|---|---|---|---|---|---|
| 03/09/1994 | 58 | 1 | | BAD BROTHERS RONNY JORDAN MEETS DJ KRUSH | Island IMCD 8024 |
| 11/11/1995 | 64 | 1 | | MEISO | Mo Wax MW 039CD |

**DJ QUICKSILVER** Belgian/Turkish production duo Tomasso De Donatis and Ohran Terzi who also record as Watergate.

07/03/1998 . . . . . 26 . . . . . . 3 . . . . . . QUICKSILVER . . . . . . . . . . . . . . . . . . . . . . . . . . . . . . . . . . . . . . . . . . . . . . . . . . . . . . . . . . . . . . . . . . . . . . Positiva 4934942

**DJ SAMMY** Spanish DJ/producer Samuel Bouriah (born 29/10/1969, Majorca) who also recorded as DJ Porno.

22/03/2003 . . . . . 14 . . . . . . 9 . . . . . . ● HEAVEN . . . . . . . . . . . . . . . . . . . . . . . . . . . . . . . . . . . . . . . . . . . . . . . . . . . . . . . . . . . Data/Ministry Of Sound DATACD 01X

**DJ SHADOW** US producer (born Josh Davis, 1973, Los Angeles, CA) who worked with Depeche Mode and Massive Attack.

| | | | | | |
|---|---|---|---|---|---|
| 28/09/1996 | 17 | 3 | ● | ENTRODUCING... | Mo Wax MW 059CD |
| 15/06/2002 | 8 | 3 | | THE PRIVATE PRESS | Island CIDD 8118 |

**DMX** US male rapper/producer (born Earl Simmons, 18/12/1973, Yonkers, NY) whose name stands for Dark Man X. He is also known as Divine Master of the Unknown. He later launched Bloodline Records through Def Jam and became an actor, appearing in *Never Die Alone*.

| | | | | | |
|---|---|---|---|---|---|
| 03/11/2001 | 20 | 3 | ○ | THE GREAT DEPRESSION ▲¹ | Def Jam 5864502 |
| 27/09/2003 | 6 | 8 | | GRAND CHAMP ▲¹ | Def Jam 9861021 |

**DOCTOR AND THE MEDICS** UK group with Clive Jackson (Doctor), sisters Collette and Wendi (aka the Anadin Brothers), Steve (guitar), Steve 'Vom' Ritchie (drums) and Richard Searle (bass; he was later a TV presenter).

21/06/1986 . . . . . 25 . . . . . . 3 . . . . . . LAUGHING AT THE PIECES . . . . . . . . . . . . . . . . . . . . . . . . . . . . . . . . . . . . . . . . . . . . . . . . . . . . . . . . . I.R.S. MIRG 1010

## DR. DRE
US rapper (born Andre Young, 18/2/1965 Compton, CA) and founder member of NWA (Niggaz With Attitude) and World Class Wreckin' Cru. He also founded Death Row Records, although he sold his stake in 1996. Dr. Dre is Warren G's half-brother. He won the 1993 Grammy Award for Best Rap Solo Performance for *Let Me Ride* and the 2000 Grammy Award for Best Rap Performance by a Duo with Eminem for *Forget About Dre* as well as the 2000 Best Producer Award. In addition he was named Best Producer at the 2001 MOBO Awards, and has also worked with 2Pac, BLACKstreet, LL Cool J, Eminem and Snoop Doggy Dogg.

| | | | | | |
|---|---|---|---|---|---|
| 27/11/1999 | 4 | 76 | ● | 2001 ◇ | Interscope 4904862 |
| 09/09/2000 | 52 | 2 | ○ | THE CHRONIC | Interscope 7567922332 |

## DR. FEELGOOD
UK group formed on Canvey Island in 1971 by Lee Brilleaux (born Lee Collinson, 10/5/1952, Durban, South Africa, guitar/vocals), Wilko Johnson (born John Wilkinson, 12/7/1947, guitar), John B Sparks (born 22/2/1953, bass) and The Big Figure (born Johnny Martin, 8/11/1946, drums). They backed 1960s star Heinz for three years before signing with United Artists, and took their name from a record by US bluesman Piano Red. Brilleaux died from throat cancer on 7/4/1994.

| | | | | | |
|---|---|---|---|---|---|
| 18/10/1975 | 17 | 6 | ○ | MALPRACTICE | United Artists UAS 29880 |
| 02/10/1976 | ❶¹ | 9 | ○ | STUPIDITY | United Artists UAS 29990 |
| 04/06/1977 | 10 | 6 | | SNEAKIN' SUSPICION | United Artists UAS 30075 |
| 08/10/1977 | 55 | 3 | | BE SEEING YOU | United Artists UAS 30123 |
| 07/10/1978 | 41 | 5 | | PRIVATE PRACTICE | United Artists UAG 30184 |
| 02/06/1979 | 42 | 4 | | AS IT HAPPENS | United Artists UAK 30239 |

## DR. HOOK
US group formed in Union City, NJ in 1968 by Dennis Locorriere (born 13/6/1949, Union City, NJ, guitar), Ray Sawyer (born 1/2/1937, Chicksaw, AL, lead guitar/vocals), who became known as Dr. Hook because of his eye patch, George Cummings (born 1938, steel and lead guitar), Jance Garfat (born 3/3/1944, California, bass), Rik Elswit (born 6/7/1945, New York, guitar) and John Wolters (born 28/4/1945, drums), calling themselves Dr. Hook & The Medicine Show the following year. They shortened their name in 1974. They disbanded in 1982; Sawyer formed a new group in 1988. Wolters died from liver cancer on 16/6/1997.

| | | | | | |
|---|---|---|---|---|---|
| 26/06/1976 | 5 | 42 | ● | A LITTLE BIT MORE | Capitol EST 23795 |
| 29/10/1977 | 39 | 4 | | MAKING LOVE AND MUSIC | Capitol EST 11632 |
| 27/10/1979 | 47 | 6 | | PLEASURE AND PAIN | Capitol EAST 11859 |
| 17/11/1979 | 14 | 44 | ● | SOMETIMES YOU WIN | Capitol EST 12018 |
| 29/11/1980 | 44 | 5 | ○ | RISING | Mercury 6302 076 |
| 06/12/1980 | 2 | 28 | ✪ | DR. HOOK'S GREATEST HITS | Capitol EST 26037 |
| 14/11/1981 | 90 | 1 | | DR. HOOK LIVE IN THE UK | Capitol EST 26706 |
| 13/06/1992 | 3 | 19 | ✪ | COMPLETELY HOOKED – THE BEST OF DR. HOOK | Capitol CDESTV 2 |
| 13/02/1999 | 8 | 8 | ● | LOVE SONGS | EMI 4979432 |

## DR. JOHN
US singer/pianist/guitarist (born Malcolm John Rebennack, 20/11/1940, New Orleans, LA); he wrote his first songs at the age of fourteen and was a studio musician at seventeen. He made his own recordings that same year (1957) and released his first album, for Rex Records, in 1958. He first recorded as Dr. John (aka Dr John Creux, The Night Tripper) in the mid-1960s, recording 'swamp-rock' material and later used The Meters as backing musicians. He has won six Grammy Awards: Best Recording for Children in 1980 with Doobie Brothers, James Taylor, Carly Simon, Bette Midler, Muppets, Al Jarreau, Linda Ronstadt, Wendy Waldman, Libby Titus, Livingston Taylor, George Benson, Pauline Wilson, Lucy Simon, Kate Taylor and the Simon/Taylor Family In Harmony for *A Sesame Street Record*; Best Recording for Children in 1982 with Billy Joel, Bruce Springsteen, James Taylor, Kenny Loggins, Carly and Lucy Simon, Teddy Pendergrass, Crystal Gayle, Lou Rawls, Deniece Williams and Janis Ian for *In Harmony 2*; Best Jazz Vocal Performance by a duo or group in 1989 with Rickie Lee Jones for *Makin' Whoopee;* Best Traditional Blues Album in 1992 for *Goin' Back To New Orleans*; Best Rock instrumental in 1996 with Jimmie Vaughan, Eric Clapton, Bonnie Raitt, Robert Cray, B.B. King, Buddy Guy and Art Neville for *SRV Shuffle;* and Best Pop Collaboration with vocals in 2000 with BB King for *Is You Is, Or Is You Ain't (My Baby)*.

| | | | | | |
|---|---|---|---|---|---|
| 27/06/1998 | 33 | 3 | | ANUTHA ZONE | Parlophone 4954902 |

## DOCTOR WHO
UK TV character created by Sydney Newman in 1963. The Doctor ( he is not actually called Doctor Who in the series) was played by William Hartnell (1963–66), Patrick Troughton (1966–69), Jon Pertwee (1970–74), Tom Baker (1974–81), Peter Davison (1982–84), Colin Baker (1984–86) and Sylvester McCoy (1987–89).

| | | | | | |
|---|---|---|---|---|---|
| 18/07/1992 | 72 | 1 | | DOCTOR WHO – THE EVIL OF THE DALEKS | BBC ZBBC 1303 |
| 14/08/1993 | 71 | 1 | | DOCTOR WHO – THE POWER OF THE DALEKS | BBC ZBBC 1433 |
| 18/09/1993 | 48 | 1 | | DOCTOR WHO – THE PARADISE OF DEATH | BBC ZBBC 1494 |

## KEN DODD
UK singer/comedian (born 8/11/1927, Liverpool) who began his professional career in 1954. In the 1960s and 1970s he became a household name thanks to numerous TV appearances and the creation of the Diddymen, characters who were based in Knotty Ash, Liverpool. Despite his comedy background, his hits were almost all romantic ballads. He was awarded the OBE in 1982.

| DATE | POS | WKS | BPI | ALBUM TITLE | LABEL & NUMBER |
|------|-----|-----|-----|-------------|----------------|
| 25/12/1965 | 6 | 12 | | TEARS OF HAPPINESS | Columbia 33SX 1793 |
| 23/07/1966 | 14 | 11 | | HITS FOR NOW AND ALWAYS | Columbia SX 6060 |
| 14/01/1967 | 40 | 1 | | FOR SOMEONE SPECIAL | Columbia SCX 6224 |
| 29/11/1980 | 8 | 12 | ● | **20 GOLDEN GREATS OF KEN DODD** | Warwick WW 5098 |

**DODGY** UK group formed in Birmingham in 1986 by Nigel Clarke (born 18/9/1966, Redditch, vocals/bass), Andy Miller (born 18/12/1968, London, guitar) and Matthew Priest (born 2/4/1970, Birmingham, drums). They disbanded in 1998, re-forming soon after with Miller, Priest, David Bassey (vocals), Nick Abnett (bass) and Chris Hallam (keyboards).

| DATE | POS | WKS | BPI | ALBUM TITLE | LABEL & NUMBER |
|------|-----|-----|-----|-------------|----------------|
| 05/06/1993 | 75 | 1 | | THE DODGY ALBUM | A&M 5400822 |
| 05/11/1994 | 28 | 14 | ○ | HOMEGROWN | A&M 5402822 |
| 29/06/1996 | 7 | 38 | ✪ | **FREE PEACE SWEET** | A&M 5405732 |
| 17/10/1998 | 55 | 1 | | ACE A'S + KILLER B'S | A&M 5410182 |

**DOG EAT DOG** US rock/rap six-piece group formed in New York by John Connor (vocals), Dan Nastasi (guitar/vocals), Marc DeBacker (guitar), Dave Neabore (bass), Sean Kilkenny (guitar), Brandon Finley (drums) and Scott Mueller (saxophone/keyboards). They recorded their debut album in 1994, having issued an EP the year before. They were named Breakthrough Act at the 1995 MTV Europe Music Awards.

| DATE | POS | WKS | BPI | ALBUM TITLE | LABEL & NUMBER |
|------|-----|-----|-----|-------------|----------------|
| 27/07/1996 | 40 | 2 | | PLAY GAMES | Roadrunner RR 88762 |

**DOGS D'AMOUR** UK heavy rock group formed in Birmingham in 1983 by Tyla (guitar), Ned Christie (vocals), Nick Halls (guitar), Carl (bass) and Bam Bam (drums). Halls, Bam Bam and Christie soon left and were replaced by Dave Kusworth (guitar) and Paul Hornby (drums). They were based in Finland in 1983–85, where they became popular. Later members included Mark Duncan and Steve James. The group disbanded in 1991 and a 1993 reunion was short-lived, Tyla going solo and James and Bam Bam forming Mary Jane.

| DATE | POS | WKS | BPI | ALBUM TITLE | LABEL & NUMBER |
|------|-----|-----|-----|-------------|----------------|
| 22/10/1988 | 97 | 1 | | IN THE DYNAMITE JET SALOON | China WOL 8 |
| 25/03/1989 | 16 | 4 | | A GRAVEYARD OF EMPTY BOTTLES | China 8390741 |
| 30/09/1989 | 22 | 3 | | ERROL FLYNN | China 8397001 |
| 06/10/1990 | 32 | 2 | | STRAIGHT | China 8437961 |
| 07/09/1991 | 58 | 1 | | DOG'S HITS AND THE BOOTLEG ALBUM | China WOL 1020 |
| 15/05/1993 | 30 | 1 | | MORE UNCHARTED HEIGHTS OF DISGRACE | China WOLCD 1032 |

**DOKKEN** US rock group formed in 1982 by Don Dokken (vocals), George Lynch (guitar), Juan Croucier (bass) and Mick Brown (drums). Croucier left and was replaced by Jeff Pilson. They disbanded in 1988 with Don Dokken going solo with Geffen Records.

| DATE | POS | WKS | BPI | ALBUM TITLE | LABEL & NUMBER |
|------|-----|-----|-----|-------------|----------------|
| 21/11/1987 | 96 | 1 | | BACK FOR THE ATTACK | Elektra EKT 43 |

**THOMAS DOLBY** UK singer (born Thomas Morgan Robertson, 14/10/1958, Cairo, Egypt) who was a session musician for the likes of Foreigner, Joan Armatrading and Lene Lovich before going solo. He named himself after the sound engineer (Dolby Laboratories sued him for copyright infringement and he had to license the name). He later worked with George Clinton and Joni Mitchell.

| DATE | POS | WKS | BPI | ALBUM TITLE | LABEL & NUMBER |
|------|-----|-----|-----|-------------|----------------|
| 22/05/1982 | 65 | 10 | | THE GOLDEN AGE OF WIRELESS | Venice In Peril VIP 1001 |
| 18/02/1984 | 14 | 14 | ○ | THE FLAT EARTH | Parlophone Odeon PCS 2400341 |
| 07/05/1988 | 30 | 3 | | ALIENS ATE MY BUICK | Manhattan MTL 1020 |
| 08/08/1992 | 35 | 2 | | ASTRONAUTS AND HERETICS | Virgin CDV 2701 |

**DOLLAR** UK duo David Van Day (born 28/11/1957) and Thereze Bazar, both ex-Guys And Dolls. Produced by Trevor Horn, they both later went solo, although by 2000 Van Day was operating a burger van in Brighton.

| DATE | POS | WKS | BPI | ALBUM TITLE | LABEL & NUMBER |
|------|-----|-----|-----|-------------|----------------|
| 15/09/1979 | 36 | 8 | | SHOOTING STARS | Carrere CAL 111 |
| 24/04/1982 | 31 | 9 | ○ | THE VERY BEST OF DOLLAR | Carrere CAL 3001 |
| 30/10/1982 | 18 | 11 | ○ | THE DOLLAR ALBUM | WEA DTV 1 |

**PLACIDO DOMINGO** Spanish opera singer (born 21/1/1941, Madrid) whose first venture into pop territory was an album with John Denver. He has won three Grammy Awards: Best Latin Pop Recording in 1984 for *Always In My Heart (Siempre En Mi Corazon)*, Best Classical Performance Vocal Soloist in 1990 with Jose Carreras and Luciano Pavarotti for *Carreras, Domingo, Pavarotti In Concert* and Best Mexican-US Performance in 1999 for *100 Anos De Mariachi*.

| DATE | POS | WKS | BPI | ALBUM TITLE | LABEL & NUMBER |
|------|-----|-----|-----|-------------|----------------|
| 28/11/1981 | 17 | 21 | ● | PERHAPS LOVE **PLACIDO DOMINGO AND JOHN DENVER** | CBS 73592 |
| 21/05/1983 | 31 | 8 | | MY LIFE FOR A SONG | CBS 73683 |
| 27/12/1986 | 30 | 14 | | PLACIDO DOMINGO COLLECTION | Stylus SMR 625 |
| 23/04/1988 | 63 | 2 | | GREATEST LOVE SONGS | CBS 44701 |
| 17/06/1989 | 20 | 8 | ● | THE ESSENTIAL DOMINGO | Deutsche Grammophon PDTV 1 |
| 17/06/1989 | 36 | 4 | | GOYA … A LIFE IN A SONG | CBS 4632941 |
| 01/09/1990 | ❶⁵ | 78 | ✪⁵ | **IN CONCERT** 1990 Grammy Award for Best Classical Performance Vocal Soloist | Decca 4304331 |
| 24/11/1990 | 14 | 12 | | BE MY LOVE... AN ALBUM OF LOVE | EMI EMTV 54 |
| 07/12/1991 | 45 | 6 | ○ | THE BROADWAY I LOVE | East West 9031755901 |
| 13/06/1992 | 47 | 3 | ○ | DOMINGO: ARIAS AND SPANISH SONGS | Deutsche Grammophon 4371122 |

▲⁹ Number of weeks album topped the US chart   ◆¹² RIAA Diamond Awards   ◇³ IFPI Platinum Europe Awards

| | | | | | |
|---|---|---|---|---|---|
| 08/08/1992 | 41 | 3 | | FROM THE OFFICIAL BARCELONA GAMES CEREMONY | RCA Red Seal 09026612042 |
| 25/12/1993 | 71 | 2 | | CHRISTMAS IN VIENNA | Sony Classical SK 53358 |
| 10/09/1994 | ❶[1] | 26 | ✪[2] | **THE THREE TENORS IN CONCERT 1994** ◇[3] | Teldec 4509962002 |
| 10/12/1994 | 60 | 2 | | CHRISTMAS IN VIENNA II | Sony Classical SK 64304 |
| 29/08/1998 | 14 | 6 | | THE THREE TENORS PARIS 1998 **CARRERAS DOMINGO PAVAROTTI WITH JAMES LEVINE** | Decca 4605002 |
| 28/10/2000 | 53 | 2 | | SONGS OF LOVE | EMI CDC 5571042 |
| 23/12/2000 | 57 | 2 | | THE THREE TENORS CHRISTMAS | Sony Classical SK 89131 |

**FATS DOMINO** US singer (born Antoine Domino, 26/2/1928, New Orleans, LA) who joined the Dave Bartholomew Band in the 1940s, signing solo with Imperial Records in 1949. His 1949 debut single *The Fat Man* had sold over 1 million by 1953. Through the 1950s and early 1960s he had over 60 pop hits. A pioneer of rock 'n' roll, he was inducted into the Rock & Roll Hall of Fame in 1986. He has a star on the Hollywood Walk of Fame.

| | | | | | |
|---|---|---|---|---|---|
| 16/05/1970 | 56 | 1 | | VERY BEST OF FATS DOMINO | Liberty LBS 83331 |
| 06/03/2004 | 58 | 2 | | THE BEST OF | EMI 5964972 |

**LONNIE DONEGAN** UK singer (born Anthony Donegan, 29/4/1931, Glasgow) who named himself after US blues singer Lonnie Johnson. He joined Ken Colyer's Jazzmen on guitar and banjo in 1952, leaving for Chris Barber's Jazz Band in 1954, newly signed to Decca. His debut hit single *Rock Island Line* was originally a track on a Barber album credited to Lonnie Donegan's Skiffle Group. It made the US top ten and sold over 1 million copies, but Donegan received no royalties, having been paid a flat £50 session fee. He was hugely successful in his own right with Pye Nixa through the mid- to late 1950s. He appeared as a panellist on the TV talent show *New Faces* in the 1970s and still played the cabaret circuit until 1976, when a heart attack forced him into semi-retirement. After various come-back tours, he was awarded an MBE in the 2000 Queen's Birthday Honours List. He collapsed and died on 4/11/2002.

| | | | | | |
|---|---|---|---|---|---|
| 17/11/1956 | 2 | 22 | | **LONNIE DONEGAN SHOWCASE** | Pye Nixa NPT 19012 |
| 12/07/1958 | 3 | 13 | | **LONNIE** | Pye Nixa NPT 19027 |
| 01/09/1962 | 3 | 23 | | **GOLDEN AGE OF DONEGAN** | Pye Golden Guinea GGL 0135 |
| 09/02/1963 | 15 | 3 | | GOLDEN AGE OF DONEGAN VOLUME 2 | Pye Golden Guinea GGL 0170 |
| 25/02/1978 | 51 | 3 | | PUTTING ON THE STYLE | Chrysalis CHR 1158 |
| 29/01/2000 | 14 | 3 | | THE SKIFFLE SESSIONS – LIVE IN BELFAST **VAN MORRISON/LONNIE DONEGAN/CHRIS BARBER** | Venture CDVE 945 |
| 08/03/2003 | 45 | 2 | | PUTTIN' ON THE STYLE – THE GREATEST HITS | Castle Music TVSAN002 |

**TANYA DONELLY** US guitarist/singer (born 14/7/1966, Newport, RI), founder member of Throwing Muses, and sister of Kristine Hersh, also ex-Throwing Muses. She was later with The Breeders and Belly before going solo when Belly disbanded in 1999.

| | | | | | |
|---|---|---|---|---|---|
| 20/09/1997 | 36 | 1 | | LOVESONGS FOR UNDERDOGS | 4AD CAD 7008CD |

**DONOVAN** UK singer (born Donovan Leitch, 10/5/1946, Maryhill, Glasgow) who was a part-time waiter and performer at folk clubs when discovered in 1964. Initial demos got him a three-week spot on TV's *Ready Steady Go* and subsequently a contract with Pye Records. Likened to Bob Dylan (they met in 1965, and both their chart debuts were in the same week), Donovan moved from folk material in 1965, with production handled by Mickie Most. He later scored and appeared in films, including *Brother Sun, Sister Moon* (1973), and was still touring in the 1990s.

| | | | | | |
|---|---|---|---|---|---|
| 05/06/1965 | 3 | 16 | | **WHAT'S BIN DID AND WHAT'S BIN HID** | Pye NPL 18117 |
| 06/11/1965 | 20 | 2 | | FAIRY TALE | Pye NPL 18128 |
| 08/07/1967 | 25 | 7 | | SUNSHINE SUPERMAN | Pye NPL 18181 |
| 14/10/1967 | 5 | 18 | | **UNIVERSAL SOLDIER** | Marble Arch MAL 718 |
| 11/05/1968 | 13 | 14 | | A GIFT FROM A FLOWER TO A GARDEN | Pye NSPL 20000 |
| 12/09/1970 | 30 | 4 | | OPEN ROAD | Dawn DNLS 3009 |
| 24/03/1973 | 15 | 12 | | COSMIC WHEELS | Epic EPC 65450 |

**JASON DONOVAN** Australian singer (born 1/6/1968, Malvern, Melbourne), son of TV actor Terry and presenter Sue McIntosh, who began as an actor. He appeared in the TV series *Skyways* (opposite actress Kylie Minogue), *Home* and *Marshland*, and then took the role of Scott Robinson in *Neighbours* (also with Minogue) in 1986. Travelling to London in 1986 to record two numbers for Mushroom Records written by Noiseworks, he met Pete Waterman, who had guided Minogue's early recording career, and agreed to record a Stock Aitken Waterman song. Record success prompted him to leave *Neighbours* in 1989, although he later appeared in films and the stage musical *Joseph And The Amazing Technicolour Dreamcoat*.

| | | | | | |
|---|---|---|---|---|---|
| 13/05/1989 | ❶[4] | 54 | ✪[5] | **TEN GOOD REASONS** | PWL HF 7 |
| 09/06/1990 | 2 | 26 | ✪ | **BETWEEN THE LINES** | PWL HF 14 |
| 31/08/1991 | ❶[2] | 38 | ✪ | **JOSEPH AND THE AMAZING TECHNICOLOUR DREAMCOAT** JASON DONOVAN/ORIGINAL LONDON STAGE CAST SOUNDTRACK | |
| | | | | | Really Useful/Polydor 5111301 |
| 28/09/1991 | 9 | 17 | | **GREATEST HITS** | PWL HF 20 |

○ Silver disc ● Gold disc ✪ Platinum disc (additional platinum units are indicated by a figure following the symbol) ❶[9] Number of weeks album topped the UK chart

11/09/1993 . . . . . 27 . . . . . . 2 . . . . . . ALL AROUND THE WORLD. . . . . . . . . . . . . . . . . . . . . . . . . . . . . . . . . . . . . . . . . . . . . . . . . . . . . . . . . . . . . . . . Polydor 8477452

**DOOBIE BROTHERS** US rock group formed in San Jose, CA by Tom Johnston (born in Visalia, CA, guitar/vocals), John Hartman (born 18/3/1950, Falls Church, VA, drums) and Greg Murph (bass) and known as Pud In March. Patrick Simmons (born 23/1/1950, Aberdeen, WA, guitar/vocals) joined in September 1970, and they changed their name to Doobie Brothers ('doobie' is California slang for a marijuana joint), signing with Warner's on the strength of their demo. Numerous changes have included Michael McDonald (2/12/1952, St Louis, MO, keyboards/vocals), Jeff 'Skunk' Baxter (born 13/12/1948, Washington DC, guitars), Tiran Porter (born in Los Angeles, CA, bass), Mike Hossack (born 17/10/1946, Paterson, NJ, drums), Keith Knudsen (born 18/2/1948, LeMars, IN, drums/vocals), Cornelius Bumpus (born 13/1/1952, saxophone) and Dave Shogren (bass). Both Baxter and McDonald were ex-Steely Dan. They disbanded in 1982 and re-formed in 1988. One-time percussionist Bobby LaKind died from cancer on 24/12/1992. The group has won three Grammy Awards: Record of the Year in 1979 for *What A Fool Believes*, Best Pop Vocal Performance by a Group in 1979 for *Minute By Minute* and Best Record for Children in 1980 with various others for *In Harmony*. Group member Michael McDonald also won Grammy Awards for Song of the Year in 1979 with Kenny Loggins for *What A Fool Believes* and Best Arrangement Accompanying Singer in 1979 for *What A Fool Believes* from his time with the group.

30/03/1974 . . . . . 19 . . . . . 10 . . . . . . ○ WHAT WERE ONCE VICES ARE NOW HABITS . . . . . . . . . . . . . . . . . . . . . . . . . . . . . . . . . . . . . . . . . . . Warner Brothers K 56206
17/05/1975 . . . . . 14 . . . . . 11 . . . . . . ○ STAMPEDE . . . . . . . . . . . . . . . . . . . . . . . . . . . . . . . . . . . . . . . . . . . . . . . . . . . . . . . . . . . . . . . Warner Brothers K 56094
10/04/1976 . . . . . 42 . . . . . . 2 . . . . . . ○ TAKIN' IT TO THE STREETS . . . . . . . . . . . . . . . . . . . . . . . . . . . . . . . . . . . . . . . . . . . . . . . . . . . . Warner Brothers K 56196
17/09/1977 . . . . . 25 . . . . . . 5 . . . . . . LIVING ON THE FAULT LINE . . . . . . . . . . . . . . . . . . . . . . . . . . . . . . . . . . . . . . . . . . . . . . . . . . . . Warner Brothers K 56383
11/10/1980 . . . . . 53 . . . . . . 2 . . . . . . ONE STEP CLOSER . . . . . . . . . . . . . . . . . . . . . . . . . . . . . . . . . . . . . . . . . . . . . . . . . . . . . . . . Warner Brothers K 56824

**DOOLEYS** UK family vocal group comprising Jim, John, Frank, Kathy, Anne and Helen Dooley, together with Bob Walsh (Anne's husband) and Alan Bogan.

30/06/1979 . . . . . 6 . . . . . 21 . . . . . . ● **BEST OF THE DOOLEYS** . . . . . . . . . . . . . . . . . . . . . . . . . . . . . . . . . . . . . . . . . . . . . . . . . . . . . . . . GTO GTTV 038
03/11/1979 . . . . . 56 . . . . . . 4 . . . . . . THE CHOSEN FEW . . . . . . . . . . . . . . . . . . . . . . . . . . . . . . . . . . . . . . . . . . . . . . . . . . . . . . . . . . . . GTO GTLP 040
25/10/1980 . . . . . 54 . . . . . . 2 . . . . . . FULL HOUSE . . . . . . . . . . . . . . . . . . . . . . . . . . . . . . . . . . . . . . . . . . . . . . . . . . . . . . . . . . . . . . GTO GTTV 050

**VAL DOONICAN** Irish singer (born Michael Valentine Doonican, 3/2/1928, Waterford) who played mandolin and guitar as a young boy and toured Ireland with various bands. He came to England in 1951, joining Irish vocal quartet the Four Ramblers, who had a BBC radio show. Going solo in the late 1950s, he was the first Irish act to top the UK albums chart with *Val Doonican Rocks But Gently* in 1967 (a reference to the trademark rocking chair ever-present in his act). With his own TV series in the late 1970s and early 1980s, he was voted Television Personality of the Year on three occasions.

12/12/1964 . . . . . 2 . . . . . 27 . . . . . . **LUCKY 13 SHADES OF VAL DOONICAN** . . . . . . . . . . . . . . . . . . . . . . . . . . . . . . . . . . . . . . . . . . . . . . . . . Decca LK 4648
03/12/1966 . . . . . 5 . . . . . 52 . . . . . . **GENTLE SHADES OF VAL DOONICAN** . . . . . . . . . . . . . . . . . . . . . . . . . . . . . . . . . . . . . . . . . . . . . . . . Decca LK 4831
02/12/1967 . . . ❶³ . . . 23 . . . . . . **VAL DOONICAN ROCKS BUT GENTLY** . . . . . . . . . . . . . . . . . . . . . . . . . . . . . . . . . . . . . . . . . . . . . . . . Pye NSPL 18204
30/11/1968 . . . . . 6 . . . . . 11 . . . . . . **VAL** . . . . . . . . . . . . . . . . . . . . . . . . . . . . . . . . . . . . . . . . . . . . . . . . . . . . . . . . . . . . . . . . . . . Pye NSPL 18236
14/06/1969 . . . . . 2 . . . . . 31 . . . . . . **THE WORLD OF VAL DOONICAN** . . . . . . . . . . . . . . . . . . . . . . . . . . . . . . . . . . . . . . . . . . . . . . . . . . . Decca SPA 3
13/12/1969 . . . . . 22 . . . . . . 9 . . . . . . SOUNDS GENTLE . . . . . . . . . . . . . . . . . . . . . . . . . . . . . . . . . . . . . . . . . . . . . . . . . . . . . . . . . . . Pye NSPL 18321
19/12/1970 . . . . . 34 . . . . . . 3 . . . . . . THE MAGIC OF VAL DOONICAN . . . . . . . . . . . . . . . . . . . . . . . . . . . . . . . . . . . . . . . . . . . . . . . . . Philips 6642 003
27/11/1971 . . . . . 40 . . . . . . 1 . . . . . . THIS IS VAL DOONICAN . . . . . . . . . . . . . . . . . . . . . . . . . . . . . . . . . . . . . . . . . . . . . . . . . . . . . . Philips 6382 017
22/02/1975 . . . . . 37 . . . . . . 2 . . . . . . I LOVE COUNTRY MUSIC . . . . . . . . . . . . . . . . . . . . . . . . . . . . . . . . . . . . . . . . . . . . . . . . . . . . . Philips 9299 261
21/05/1977 . . . . . 29 . . . . . . 5 . . . . . . ● SOME OF MY BEST FRIENDS ARE SONGS . . . . . . . . . . . . . . . . . . . . . . . . . . . . . . . . . . . . . . . . . . Philips 6641 607
24/03/1990 . . . . . 33 . . . . . . 6 . . . . . . ○ SONGS FROM MY SKETCHBOOK . . . . . . . . . . . . . . . . . . . . . . . . . . . . . . . . . . . . . . . . . . . . . . . Parkfield PMLP 5014

**DOORS** US rock group formed in Los Angeles, CA in 1965 by Jim Morrison (born on 9/12/1943, Melbourne, FL, lead singer), Ray Manzarek (born 12/2/1935, Chicago, IL, keyboards), John Densmore (born 1/12/1944, Los Angeles, drums) and Robbie Krieger (born 8/1/1946, Los Angeles, guitar). Initially signed by CBS/Columbia in 1965, they were released without producing any records and promptly signed with Elektra. Morrison's controversial stage shows involved several brushes with the law: he was arrested in New Haven, CT in December 1967 for breach of the peace and resisting arrest; in Las Vegas in 1968 for public drunkenness; in Miami in March 1969 for lewd and lascivious behaviour, indecent exposure, open profanity and public drunkenness; in Phoenix in November 1969 for drunk and disorderly conduct and interfering with airline staff while on board the plane; and finally in Los Angeles in August 1970 for public drunkenness. After being given eight months hard labour and a $500 fine for the Miami offences, he appealed, announced he was leaving The Doors and moved to Paris to write poetry, with the rest of the group staying in the US, hoping he might change his mind. On 3/7/1971 he was found dead in his bath in his Paris apartment. Despite rumours of a drug overdose, the cause of death was given as heart failure caused by acute respiratory distress; he had twice called doctors out to treat his asthma, but not on the night he died. With the only witnesses his wife Pam and the doctor who signed the death certificate, there has been speculation that he is still alive and that his pet Alsatian dog is buried in his grave. His grave in Paris has been an attraction for many years since. In 1991 a film of their career, *The Doors* starring Val Kilmer as Morrison, was released. The group took their name from a section of text by Aldous Huxley: 'all the other Doors in the Wall are labelled Dope.' They were inducted into the Rock & Roll Hall of Fame in 1993.

28/09/1968 . . . . . 16 . . . . . 10 . . . . . . ● WAITING FOR THE SUN ▲⁴ . . . . . . . . . . . . . . . . . . . . . . . . . . . . . . . . . . . . . . . . . . . . . . . . . Elektra EKS7 4024
11/04/1970 . . . . . 12 . . . . . . 8 . . . . . . MORRISON HOTEL . . . . . . . . . . . . . . . . . . . . . . . . . . . . . . . . . . . . . . . . . . . . . . . . . . . . . . . Elektra EKS 75007
26/09/1970 . . . . . 69 . . . . . . 1 . . . . . . ABSOLUTELY LIVE . . . . . . . . . . . . . . . . . . . . . . . . . . . . . . . . . . . . . . . . . . . . . . . . . . . . . . . . . Elektra 2665 002
31/07/1971 . . . . . 28 . . . . . . 4 . . . . . . ● L.A. WOMAN . . . . . . . . . . . . . . . . . . . . . . . . . . . . . . . . . . . . . . . . . . . . . . . . . . . . . . . . . . . . Elektra K 42090
01/04/1972 . . . . . 50 . . . . . . 1 . . . . . . WEIRD SCENES INSIDE THE GOLD MINE . . . . . . . . . . . . . . . . . . . . . . . . . . . . . . . . . . . . . . . . . . . Elektra K 62009

| DATE | POS | WKS | BPI | ALBUM TITLE | LABEL & NUMBER |
|------|-----|-----|-----|-------------|----------------|
| 29/10/1983 | 36 | 5 | | ALIVE, SHE CRIED | Elektra 9602691 |
| 04/07/1987 | 51 | 3 | | LIVE AT THE HOLLYWOOD BOWL | Elektra EKT 40 |
| 06/04/1991 | 11 | 17 | ● | THE DOORS Original soundtrack to the film | Elektra EKT 85 |
| 20/04/1991 | 17 | 18 | ○ | THE BEST OF THE DOORS | Elektra EKT 21 |
| 20/04/1991 | 43 | 13 | | THE DOORS | Elektra K 42012 |
| 01/06/1991 | 24 | 5 | ○ | IN CONCERT | Elektra EKT 88 |
| 21/03/1998 | 37 | 8 | | THE BEST OF THE DOORS | Elektra K9803452 |
| 23/09/2000 | 9 | 15 | ○ | **THE BEST OF THE DOORS** | Elektra 1592812 |

**LEE DORSEY** US singer (born Irving Lee Dorsey, 24/12/1924, New Orleans, LA) who was a boxer (Kid Chocolate) in the early 1950s before launching a singing career, guided by Allen Toussaint and Marshall Sehorn. He went into semi-retirement, concentrating on his panel-beating workshop, before returning and supporting The Clash on their 1980 US tour. He died from emphysema on 1/12/1986.

| DATE | POS | WKS | BPI | ALBUM TITLE | LABEL & NUMBER |
|------|-----|-----|-----|-------------|----------------|
| 17/12/1966 | 34 | 4 | | NEW LEE DORSEY | Stateside SSL 10192 |

**DOUBLE** Swiss vocal/instrumental duo Kurt Maloo and Felix Haug who previously recorded with jazz trio Ping Pong.

| DATE | POS | WKS | BPI | ALBUM TITLE | LABEL & NUMBER |
|------|-----|-----|-----|-------------|----------------|
| 08/03/1986 | 69 | 4 | | BLUE | Polydor POLD 5187 |

**DOUBLE TROUBLE AND THE REBEL MC** UK instrumental/production duo Leigh Guest and Michael Menson who paired with Rebel MC (born Mike West, 27/8/1965, London) for their initial hits. Rebel MC went his own way in 1990 and Guest joined Airheadz. Menson died in January 1997 after being soaked in petrol and set alight, surviving long enough to tell the police that it wasn't a suicide attempt as they first believed.

| DATE | POS | WKS | BPI | ALBUM TITLE | LABEL & NUMBER |
|------|-----|-----|-----|-------------|----------------|
| 04/08/1990 | 73 | 1 | | AS ONE | Desire LULP 6 |

**CRAIG DOUGLAS** UK singer (born Terence Perkins, 13/8/1941, Isle of Wight) who was was working as a milkman when he won a local talent contest, subsequently appearing on the 6.5 Special TV show. He appeared in the film It's Trad Dad (1961), later playing the international cabaret circuit.

| DATE | POS | WKS | BPI | ALBUM TITLE | LABEL & NUMBER |
|------|-----|-----|-----|-------------|----------------|
| 06/08/1960 | 17 | 2 | | CRAIG DOUGLAS | Top Rank BUY 049 |

**DOVES** UK group formed in Manchester by Jez and Andy Williams and Jimi Goodwin, who previously recorded as Sub Sub.

| DATE | POS | WKS | BPI | ALBUM TITLE | LABEL & NUMBER |
|------|-----|-----|-----|-------------|----------------|
| 15/04/2000 | 16 | 16 | ● | LOST SOULS | Heavenly HVNLP 26CD |
| 11/05/2002 | ❶² | 23 | ● | **THE LAST BROADCAST** | Heavenly HVNLP 35CD |
| 11/10/2003 | 50 | 1 | | LOST SIDES | Heavenly HVNLP 46CDX |

**DOWN** US rock super group formed by Philip Anselmo (born 30/6/196, New Orleans, vocals, and lead singer with Pantera), Pepper Keenan (guitarist/singer with Corrosion Of Conformity), Kirk Windstine (guitarist/singer with Crowbar), Todd Strange (bassist with Crowbar) and Jimmy Bower (drummer with Eye Hate God). Their debut album also featured contributions from Lil' Daddy (percussion) and Ross Karpelman (keyboards).

| DATE | POS | WKS | BPI | ALBUM TITLE | LABEL & NUMBER |
|------|-----|-----|-----|-------------|----------------|
| 30/09/1995 | 68 | 1 | | NOLA | Atlantic 7559618302 |

**WILL DOWNING** US singer (born in New York) who was a session vocalist before joining producer Arthur Baker's group Wally Jump Jr. He went solo in 1988, his biggest success so far being in the UK.

| DATE | POS | WKS | BPI | ALBUM TITLE | LABEL & NUMBER |
|------|-----|-----|-----|-------------|----------------|
| 26/03/1988 | 20 | 23 | ● | WILL DOWNING | Fourth & Broadway BRLP 518 |
| 18/11/1989 | 36 | 2 | | COME TOGETHER AS ONE | Fourth & Broadway BRLP 538 |
| 06/04/1991 | 43 | 3 | | A DREAM FULFILLED | Fourth & Broadway BRLP 565 |

**JASON DOWNS** US singer (born in Arkansas) and New York University drama graduate, whose musical style is a mixture of country and hip hop.

| DATE | POS | WKS | BPI | ALBUM TITLE | LABEL & NUMBER |
|------|-----|-----|-----|-------------|----------------|
| 28/07/2001 | 64 | 1 | | WHITE BOY WITH A FEATHER | Pepper 9230452 |

**DOWNSIDE ABBEY MONKS AND CHOIRBOYS** UK male vocal choir. The abbey was established in 1814 and the monastry completed in 1876.

| DATE | POS | WKS | BPI | ALBUM TITLE | LABEL & NUMBER |
|------|-----|-----|-----|-------------|----------------|
| 02/11/1996 | 54 | 5 | ○ | THE ABBEY | Virgin VTCD 99 |
| 03/01/1998 | 59 | 1 | | GREGORIAN MOODS | Virgin VTCD 171 |

**NICK DRAKE** UK male singer (born19/6/1948, Rangoon, Burma) who made his debut album in 1969 and made two further albums before his death from an overdose of antidepressant tablets on 25/11/1974, although this was not believed to have been a suicide.

| DATE | POS | WKS | BPI | ALBUM TITLE | LABEL & NUMBER |
|------|-----|-----|-----|-------------|----------------|
| 05/06/2004 | 27 | 2 | | MADE TO LOVE MAGIC | Island CID 8141 |

**DREAD ZEPPELIN** US rock group formed in 1989 by Greg 'Tortelvis' Tortell (vocals), Carl 'Jah' Hassis (guitar), Joe 'Jah Paul Jo' Ramsey (guitar), Gary 'Put-Mon' Putman (bass), Bryant 'Ed Zeppelin' Fernandez (percussion) and Paul 'Fresh Cheese' Masselli (drums). Tortelvis left the group in 1992.

| DATE | POS | WKS | BPI | ALBUM TITLE | LABEL & NUMBER |
|------|-----|-----|-----|-------------|----------------|
| 11/08/1990 | 71 | 2 | | UN-LED-ED | I.R.S. EIRSA 1042 |

**DREADZONE** UK group formed by Greg Roberts ('Dread creator and sample scanner'), Tim Bran ('Computer roots and sound navigator') and Leo Williams ('Earth to bass transmitter'). Roberts and Williams had previously been with Big Audio Dynamite before forming Screaming Target with Don Letts.

| DATE | POS | WKS | BPI | ALBUM TITLE | LABEL & NUMBER |
|------|-----|-----|-----|-------------|----------------|
| 10/06/1995 | 37 | 4 | | SECOND LIGHT | Virgin CDV 2778 |
| 09/08/1997 | 45 | 1 | | BIOLOGICAL RADIO | Virgin CDV 2808 |

### DREAM ACADEMY
UK trio formed by Nick Laird-Clowes (guitar/vocals), Gilbert Gabriel (keyboards) and Kate St John (vocals).

12/10/1985.....58......2......  THE DREAM ACADEMY ................................................................ Blanco Y Negro BYN 6

### DREAM THEATER
US rock group formed by John Petrucci (guitar), John Myung (bass) and Mike Portnoy (drums). The three were all students at the Berklee College of Music. Subsequently Kevin Moore (keyboards) and Charlie Dominici (vocals) joined the line-up. Dominici left after their debut album and was replaced by James LaBrie. Moore left in 1994 and was replaced by Derek Sherinian, although Sherinian left in 1999 and was replaced by Jordan Rudess.

15/10/1994.....65......1......  AWAKE ................................................................ East West 7567901262

### DREAM WARRIORS
Canadian rap group formed by King Lou (born Louis Robinson, Jamaica) and Capital Q (born Frank Lennon Alert, 10/8/1969, Port of Spain, Trinidad).

16/02/1991.....18......7......○  AND NOW THE LEGACY BEGINS ................................................ Fourth & Broadway BRLP 560

### DREAMKEEPER
UK studio group.

09/08/1997.....71......1......  SPIRIT OF RELAXATION ................................................................ Flute SPIRICD 1

### DRIFTERS
US R&B group formed by ex-Domino Clyde McPhatter (born 15/11/1931, Durham, NC) and his manager George Treadwell, and comprising Gerhard Thrasher, David Baughan, Andrew Thrasher and Willie Ferbee. The original line-up signed with Atlantic in 1953. McPhatter went solo in 1955; the group continued with various lead singers until Treadwell disbanded them in 1958. He brought in the Five Crowns and re-christened them The Drifters. The lead singers were Ben E King (born 23/9/1938, Henderson, NC) 1959–60, Rudy Lewis (born 27/5/1935, Chicago, IL) 1961–63 and Johnny Moore (born 1934, Selina, AL) 1955–57 and again in 1964–66. Their later success in the 1970s (all their Bell and Arista hits were UK-made and didn't chart in the US) featured Bill Fredericks and then Johnny Moore on lead. Their 1959 US hit *There Goes My Baby* was the first song of the rock era to use a string section. There have been countless line-up changes with departing members laying claim to the name hence several groups, all with the Drifters name, have appeared at more than one venue at the same time. Lewis died from a heart attack on 20/5/1964, Baughan died in 1970, McPhatter died from heart, kidney and liver disease on 13/6/1972 and Moore died from respiratory failure on 30/12/1998. McPhatter was inducted into the Rock & Roll Hall of Fame in 1987 while the group were inducted in 1988.

18/05/1968.....27......7......  GOLDEN HITS ................................................................ Atlantic 588103
10/06/1972.....26......8......  GOLDEN HITS ................................................................ Atlantic K 40018
08/11/1975.....2......34......✪  **24 ORIGINAL HITS** ................................................................ Atlantic K 60106
13/12/1975.....51......1......○  LOVE GAMES ................................................................ Bell BELLS 246
18/10/1986.....24......15......●  THE VERY BEST OF THE DRIFTERS ................................................ Telstar STAR 2280
14/03/1987.....14......8......●  STAND BY ME (THE ULTIMATE COLLECTION) ...................................... Atlantic WX 90
20/10/1990.....15......16......●  THE VERY BEST OF BEN E. KING & THE DRIFTERS ................................ Telstar STAR 2373
07/11/1998.....41......3......  THE VERY BEST OF BEN E. KING & THE DRIFTERS This and the above two hits credited to **BEN E KING & THE DRIFTERS** ............
................................................................ warner.esp/Global TV RADCD 108
17/05/2003.....8......17......●  **THE DEFINITIVE** ................................................................ Atlantic WSMCD137

### JULIE DRISCOLL, BRIAN AUGER AND THE TRINITY
UK singer (born 8/6/1947, London) who first starred in the R&B group Steampacket, then briefly went solo when they folded in 1968. She joined Steampacket's backing band Brian Auger (born 18/7/1939, London, keyboards) and The Trinity, which also featured Rick Laird (bass), John McLaughlin (guitar), Glen Hughes (saxophone) and Phil Kinnora (drums). Driscoll quit in 1968 following their hit and married jazz pianist/composer Ken Tippett.

08/06/1968.....12......13......  OPEN ROAD ................................................................ Marmalade 608002

### DRIZABONE
UK production/instrumental group with Vincent Garcia, Billy Jones and singer Sophie Jones, who left after one single and was replaced by Dee Heron. She too left after one single and was replaced by Kymberly Peer. They later shortened their name to Driza.

19/11/1994.....72......1......  CONSPIRACY ................................................................ Fourth & Broadway BRCD 593

### DROWNING POOL
US rock group formed in Dallas, TX by Dave Williams (vocals), CJ Pierce (guitar), Stevie Benton (bass) and Mike Luce (drums), taking their name from the 1975 film of the same name. Williams was found dead on 19/8/2002 with the cause of death later being given as cardiomyopathy, a disease of the heart muscle.

16/02/2002.....70......1......  SINNER ................................................................ Epic 5040912
01/05/2004.....66......1......  DESENSITIZED ................................................................ Epic 5154112

### DRU HILL
US R&B vocal group formed by Sisqo (born Mark Andrews, 9/11/1977, Baltimore, MD), Woody (born James Green), Nokio (born Tamir Ruffin, 21/1/1979) and Jazz (born Larry Anthony Jr). They were named after their Baltimore neighbourhood Druid Hill Park. Woody left in 1999 for a gospel career as Woody Rock. Sisqo started a parallel solo career in 2000.

07/11/1998.....42......7......○  ENTER THE DRU ................................................................ Island Black Music 5245422

### DRUGSTORE
UK/US/Brazilian rock group formed by Brazilian Isabel Monteiro (bass/vocals), US Mike Chylinski (drums) and Briton Daron Robinson (guitar). Their debut hit single *El Presidente* also featured Radiohead's Thom Yorke.

08/04/1995.....31......2......  DRUGSTORE ................................................................ Honey 8286170
16/05/1998.....45......1......  WHITE MAGIC FOR LOVERS ................................................ Roadrunner RR 87112

### DRUM CLUB
UK duo formed by Lol Hammond (born 7/1/1960, London) and Charlie Hall (born 25/10/1959, Whitstable) they were named after a club in Sunderland and made their debut single in 1992.

20/08/1994.....53......1......  DRUMS ARE DANGEROUS ................................................ Butterfly BFLCD 10

**D12** US rap group formed in Detroit, MI in 1990 by Bizarre (Rufus Johnson aka Peter S Bizarre) and Proof (DeShaun Holton aka Dirty Harry), later adding Eminem (born Marshall Bruce Mathers III, 17/10/1972, Kansas City, MO), Kon Artis (Denine Porter), Bugz and Kuniva (aka Von Carlisle and Hannz G) to the line-up. Eminem later went solo and Bugz was shot dead at a picnic party in 1998; he was replaced by Swift (aka O'Moore and Swifty McVay). Their name stands for Dirty Dozen.

| 30/06/2001 | 2 | 17 | ● | **DEVIL'S NIGHT** ▲² | Shady 4930792 |
| 08/05/2004 | ❶¹ | 8+ | ● | **D12 WORLD** | Interscope 9862431 |

**DUBLINERS** Irish folk group formed in Dublin in 1962 by Ciaran Bourke (born 18/2/1936, Dublin), Ronnie Drew (born 18/9/1935, Dun Laoghaire, Dublin), Luke Kelly (born 16/11/1940, Dublin) and Barny McKenna (born 16/12/1939, Dublin). Kelly left in 1964 and two new members were recruited, Bob Lynch and John Shehan (born 19/5/1939, Dublin). Lynch left in 1965 and was replaced by a returning Kelly. Bourke was forced into retirement following a brain haemorrhage in 1974 and was replaced by Jim McCann (born 26/10/1944, Dublin).

| 13/05/1967 | 5 | 41 | | **A DROP OF THE HARD STUFF** | Major Minor MMLP 3 |
| 09/09/1967 | 25 | 11 | | BEST OF THE DUBLINERS | Transatlantic TRA 158 |
| 07/10/1967 | 8 | 23 | | **MORE OF THE HARD STUFF** | Major Minor MMLP 5 |
| 02/03/1968 | 31 | 3 | | DRINKIN' AND COURTIN' | Major Minor SMLP 14 |
| 25/04/1987 | 43 | 10 | | THE DUBLINERS 25 YEARS CELEBRATION | Stylus SMR 731 |
| 22/03/2003 | 19 | 3 | ○ | SPIRIT OF THE IRISH | Sanctuary TVSAN 003 |

**DUBSTAR** UK group formed in Gateshead in 1994 by Sarah Blackwood (born 6/5/1971, Halifax, vocals), Steve Hillier (born 14/5/1969, Kent, keyboards) and Chris Wilkie (born 25/1/1973, Gateshead, guitar). The group disbanded in 2000 and Blackwood later linked up with Kate Holmes (of Frazier Chorus) to form Client.

| 21/10/1995 | 30 | 18 | ● | DISGRACEFUL | Food FOODCDX 13 |
| 04/10/1997 | 18 | 2 | | GOODBYE | Food FOODCD 23 |

**DUEL** UK violin duo formed in Manchester by Greg Scott and Craig Owen, both graduates from the Royal Northern College of Music. They were discovered busking in Manchester by producer Pete Waterman.

| 28/02/2004 | 47 | 2 | | DUEL | Decca 4739992 |

**HILARY DUFF** US singer (born 28/9/1987, Houston, TX) who was first known as an actress in the TV shows *True Women* and *Caspar Meets Wendy* before playing the lead in *Lizzie McGuire*, a role that required her to sing and prompted a recording career.

| 15/11/2003 | 69 | 1 | | METAMORPHOSIS | Hollywood 5046692682 |

**STEPHEN 'TIN TIN' DUFFY** UK singer (born 30/5/1960, Birmingham) and an original member of Duran Duran. He appeared as lead singer at many of their early dates. He left in 1979 to go solo.

| 20/04/1985 | 35 | 7 | | THE UPS AND DOWNS | 10 Records DIX 5 |

**GEORGE DUKE** US singer/keyboard player (born 12/1/1946, San Raphael, CA) who began as a jazz pianist, backing Al Jarreau and working with Jean Luc-Ponty. Later a member of Frank Zappa's Mothers Of Invention, he also formed the Cobham/Duke Band (with drummer Billy Cobham), the Clarke-Duke Project (with bass player Stanley Clarke) and recorded solo. As a producer he has worked with Sister Sledge, The Blackbyrds, Deniece Williams and Smokey Robinson.

| 26/07/1980 | 33 | 4 | | BRAZILIAN LOVE AFFAIR | Epic EPC 84311 |

**DUKES** – see STEVE EARLE

**CANDY DULFER** Dutch saxophonist (born 19/9/1970, Amsterdam) who first became known via Prince and then David A Stewart. She later recorded with Dave Gilmour and Van Morrison as well as maintaining a solo career.

| 18/08/1990 | 27 | 9 | ● | SAXUALITY | RCA PL 74661 |
| 13/03/1993 | 56 | 2 | | SAX-A-GO-GO | Ariola 74321111812 |

**DUM DUMS** UK group formed by Josh Doyle (guitar/vocals), Steve Clark (bass/vocals) and Stuart 'Baxter' Wilkinson (drums/vocals).

| 30/09/2000 | 27 | 2 | | IT GOES WITHOUT SAYING | Good Behaviour CDGOOD 4 |

**SIMON DUPREE AND THE BIG SOUND** UK group formed by Derek Shulman (born 11/2/1947, Glasgow, vocals), Ray Shulman (born 3/12/1949, Portsmouth, guitar), Phil Shulman (born 27/8/1937, Glasgow, saxophone/trumpet), Eric Hine (keyboards), Pete O'Flaherty (bass) and Tony Ransley (drums). They became Gentle Giant in the 1970s.

| 19/08/1967 | 39 | 1 | | WITHOUT RESERVATIONS | Parlophone PCS 7029 |

○ Silver disc ● Gold disc ✪ Platinum disc (additional platinum units are indicated by a figure following the symbol) ❶⁹ Number of weeks album topped the UK chart

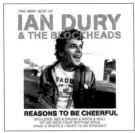

## DURAN DURAN
UK pop group formed in Birmingham in 1978 by Nick Rhodes (born Nicholas Bates, 8/6/1962, Birmingham, keyboards), John Taylor (born Nigel John Taylor, 20/6/1960, Birmingham, guitar, later bass), Simon Colley (bass/clarinet), Stephen Duffy (born on 30/5/1960, Birmingham, vocals) and a drum machine. Colley and Duffy left in 1979 and were replaced by Andy Wickett (vocals) and Roger Taylor (born 26/4/1960, Birmingham, drums), with Andy Taylor (born 16/2/1961, Wolverhampton, guitar) joining later in the year after responding to an ad. Eventually Simon Le Bon (born 27/10/1958, Bushey) joined as singer after finishing university. Andy and Roger left in 1984; Andy and John later joined Power Station. Simon, Nick and Roger recorded as Arcadia. In 1986 Duran Duran was the trio of Simon, Nick and John, with Warren Cuccurullo and Sterling Campbell joining later. They were named after Milo O'Shea's character in the Jane Fonda film *Barbarella*, which was also the name of the club where they first played. None of the Taylors are related. The group have won two Grammy Awards: Best Video Album for *Duran Duran* and Best Video Short Form for *Girls on Film/Hungry Like the Wolf*, both in 1983. They have a star on the Hollywood Walk of Fame and were presented with the Outstanding Achievement Award at the 2004 BRIT Awards.

| 27/06/1981 | 3 | 118 | ✪ | DURAN DURAN | EMI EMC 3372 |
| 22/05/1982 | 2 | 109 | ✪ | RIO | EMI EMC 3411 |
| 03/12/1983 | ❶[1] | 47 | ✪ | SEVEN AND THE RAGGED TIGER | EMI DD 1 |
| 24/11/1984 | 6 | 31 | ✪ | ARENA | Parlophone DD 2 |
| 06/12/1986 | 16 | 16 | ● | NOTORIOUS | EMI DDN 331 |
| 29/10/1988 | 15 | 5 | ○ | BIG THING | EMI DDB 33 |
| 25/11/1989 | 5 | 16 | ✪ | DECADE | EMI DDX 10 |
| 01/09/1990 | 8 | 4 | ○ | LIBERTY | Parlophone PCSD 112 |
| 27/02/1993 | 4 | 23 | ● | DURAN DURAN (THE WEDDING ALBUM) | Parlophone CDDB 34 |
| 08/04/1995 | 12 | 3 | | THANK YOU | Parlophone CDDDB 36 |
| 21/11/1998 | 4 | 39 | ✪[2] | GREATEST ◇ | EMI 4962392 |
| 27/03/1999 | 70 | 1 | | STRANGE BEHAVIOUR | EMI 4939722 |
| 01/07/2000 | 53 | 1 | | POP TRASH | Hollywood 0107512HWR |

## DEANNA DURBIN
Canadian singer (born 4/12/1921, Winnipeg) who moved to Los Angeles with her family. She was spotted by an MGM agent at the age of fourteen. After starring with Judy Garland in *Every Sunday* she was released by MGM and snapped up by Universal, putting in a sterling performance in *Three Smart Girls* (it is believed that the film's receipts of over $2 million saved Universal from bankruptcy). Deanna, with her fine soprano voice, proved popular on the Eddie Cantor Radio Hour, and her abilities as a singer and actress made her a top box office draw of the 1930s and 1940s. Awarded a special Oscar in 1938, she retired in 1948 to the French village of Neauphle-le-Château with her third husband, refusing requests from producer Joe Pasternak to return to Hollywood.

| 30/01/1982 | 84 | 4 | ○ | THE BEST OF DEANNA DURBIN | MCA International MCL 1634 |

## JUDITH DURHAM
Australian singer (born 3/7/1943, Melbourne) and lead singer with The Seekers. She went solo shortly before the group disbanded.

| 23/04/1994 | 7 | 14 | ● | CARNIVAL OF HITS JUDITH DURHAM AND THE SEEKERS | EMI CDEMTV 83 |
| 30/03/1996 | 46 | 2 | | MONA LISA | EMI Premier CDJDTV 112 |

## IAN DURY AND THE BLOCKHEADS
UK singer (born 12/5/1942, Upminster, Essex) who contracted polio at the age of seven, leaving him partially disabled. He formed Kilburn & The High Roads in 1970, signing with Raft (who closed down before releasing anything), then Dawn. The High Roads disbanded in 1975 and Dury formed a new group with Chaz Jankel, signing with Stiff in 1977. At their peak the Blockheads comprised Dury, Jankel, Davey Payne, John Turnball, Norman Watt-Roy, Mickey Gallagher and Charley Charles (born 1945). Charles died from cancer on 5/9/1990. Dury died from cancer on 27/3/2000.

| 22/10/1977 | 5 | 90 | ✪ | NEW BOOTS AND PANTIES | Stiff SEEZ 4 |
| 02/06/1979 | 2 | 18 | ● | DO IT YOURSELF | Stiff SEEZ 14 |
| 06/12/1980 | 48 | 4 | ○ | LAUGHTER | Stiff SEEZ 30 |
| 10/10/1981 | 53 | 4 | | LORD UPMINSTER | Polydor POLD 5042 |
| 04/02/1984 | 54 | 2 | | 4,000 WEEKS HOLIDAY IAN DRURY AND THE MUSIC STUDENTS | Polydor POLD 5112 |
| 11/07/1998 | 57 | 2 | | MR. LOVE PANTS | Ronnie Harris DUR 1 |
| 09/10/1999 | 40 | 2 | ○ | REASONS TO BE CHEERFUL – THE VERY BEST OF IAN DURY AND THE BLOCKHEADS | EMI 5228882 |
| 30/03/2002 | 60 | 1 | | TEN MORE TURNIPS FROM THE TIP | Ronnie Harris DUR 2 |

## DUST JUNKYS
UK group with Nicky Lockett (vocals), Steve Oliver Jones (bass), Mykey Wilson (drums), Sam Brox (guitar) and Ganiyu Pierre Gasper (DJ). Lockett previously recorded as MC Tunes.

| 21/03/1998 | 35 | 2 | | DONE AND DUSTED | Polydor 5570432 |

**BOB DYLAN** US singer/guitarist (born Robert Allen Zimmerman, 24/5/1941, Duluth, MN) who was named after the poet Dylan Thomas. He moved to New York in 1960 and worked in Greenwich Village folk clubs. He signed with CBS/Columbia in 1961 after appearing on a Carolyn Hester recording session. A folk-rock pioneer, he briefly retired after a 1966 motorcycle accident before returning to the studio (with The Band) in 1967. He later appeared in films including *Don't Look Back* (1967) and *Pat Garrett And Billy The Kid* (1973). He formed Accomplice Records in 1979, and was in the Traveling Wilburys supergroup in 1988. He was the only musical artist (apart from The Beatles) on the cover of *Sgt Pepper's Lonely Hearts Club Band*. He was inducted into the Rock & Roll Hall of Fame in 1988. He has won six Grammy Awards including Best Rock Vocal Performance in 1979 for *Gotta Serve Somebody* and Best Male Rock Vocal Performance in 1997 for *Cold Irons Bound*. He also collected the 1989 Grammy Award for Best Rock Performance by a Group with Vocals as a member of the Traveling Wilburys for *Traveling Wilburys Volume One* (the album was known as *Handle With Care* in the UK). He won the 2000 Oscar for Best Original Song for *Things Have Changed* from the film *Wonder Boys*. His son Jakob is lead singer with rock group The Wallflowers.

| DATE | POS | WKS | BPI | ALBUM TITLE | LABEL & NUMBER |
|---|---|---|---|---|---|
| 23/05/1964 | ❶² | 49 | | THE FREEWHEELIN' BOB DYLAN | CBS BPG 62193 |
| 11/07/1964 | 4 | 20 | | THE TIMES THEY ARE A-CHANGIN' | CBS BPG 62251 |
| 21/11/1964 | 8 | 19 | | ANOTHER SIDE OF BOB DYLAN | CBS BPG 62429 |
| 08/05/1965 | 13 | 6 | | BOB DYLAN | CBS BPG 62022 |
| 15/05/1965 | ❶¹ | 29 | | BRINGING IT ALL BACK HOME | CBS BPG 62515 |
| 09/10/1965 | 4 | 15 | | HIGHWAY 61 REVISITED | CBS BPG 62572 |
| 20/08/1966 | 3 | 15 | | BLONDE ON BLONDE | CBS DDP 66012 |
| 14/01/1967 | 6 | 82 | | GREATEST HITS | CBS SBPG 62847 |
| 02/03/1968 | ❶¹³ | 29 | | JOHN WESLEY HARDING | CBS SBPG 63252 |
| 17/05/1969 | ❶⁴ | 42 | | NASHVILLE SKYLINE | CBS 63601 |
| 11/07/1970 | ❶¹ | 15 | | SELF PORTRAIT | CBS 66250 |
| 28/11/1970 | ❶¹ | 18 | | NEW MORNING | CBS 69001 |
| 25/12/1971 | 12 | 15 | | MORE BOB DYLAN GREATEST HITS | CBS 67238/9 |
| 29/09/1973 | 29 | 11 | | PAT GARRETT & BILLY THE KID Original soundtrack to the film | CBS 69042 |
| 23/02/1974 | 7 | 8 | O | PLANET WAVES ▲⁴ | Island ILPS 9261 |
| 13/07/1974 | 8 | 7 | O | BEFORE THE FLOOD | Asylum IDBD 1 |
| 15/02/1975 | 4 | 16 | ● | BLOOD ON THE TRACKS ▲² | CBS 69097 |
| 26/07/1975 | 8 | 10 | ● | THE BASEMENT TAPES | CBS 88147 |
| 31/01/1976 | 3 | 35 | ● | DESIRE ▲⁵ | CBS 86003 |
| 09/10/1976 | 3 | 7 | ● | HARD RAIN | CBS 86016 |
| 01/07/1978 | 2 | 20 | ✪ | STREET LEGAL | CBS 86067 |
| 26/05/1979 | 4 | 19 | ● | BOB DYLAN AT BUDOKAN | CBS 96004 |
| 08/09/1979 | 2 | 13 | ● | SLOW TRAIN COMING | CBS 86095 |
| 28/06/1980 | 3 | 8 | O | SAVED | CBS 86113 |
| 29/08/1981 | 6 | 8 | O | SHOT OF LOVE | CBS 85178 |
| 12/11/1983 | 9 | 12 | O | INFIDELS | CBS 25539 |
| 15/12/1984 | 54 | 2 | | REAL LIVE | CBS 26334 |
| 22/06/1985 | 11 | 6 | | EMPIRE BURLESQUE | CBS 86313 |
| 02/08/1986 | 35 | 5 | | KNOCKED OUT LOADED | CBS 86326 |
| 23/04/1988 | 47 | 3 | | GREATEST HITS VOLUME 3 | CBS 4602671 |
| 25/06/1988 | 32 | 3 | | DOWN IN THE GROOVE | CBS 4602671 |
| 18/02/1989 | 38 | 3 | | DYLAN AND THE DEAD | CBS 4633811 |
| 14/10/1989 | 6 | 7 | ● | OH MERCY | CBS 4658001 |
| 29/09/1990 | 13 | 3 | O | UNDER THE RED SKY | CBS 4671881 |
| 13/04/1991 | 32 | 5 | | THE BOOTLEG SERIES VOLUMES 1–3 | Columbia 4680861 |
| 14/11/1992 | 18 | 3 | | GOOD AS I BEEN TO YOU | Columbia 4727102 |
| 20/11/1993 | 35 | 2 | | WORLD GONE WRONG 1994 Grammy Award for Best Traditional Folk Album | Columbia 4748572 |
| 29/04/1995 | 10 | 5 | | UNPLUGGED | Columbia 4783742 |
| 14/06/1997 | 6 | 18 | ● | THE BEST OF BOB DYLAN ◇ | Columbia SONYTV 28CD |
| 11/10/1997 | 10 | 6 | ● | TIME OUT OF MIND 1997 Grammy Awards for Album of the Year and Best Contemporary Folk Album | Columbia 4869362 |
| 24/10/1998 | 19 | 2 | | LIVE AT THE ROYAL ALBERT HALL | Legacy 4914852 |
| 20/05/2000 | 22 | 2 | | BEST OF – VOLUME 2 | Columbia 4983619 |
| 02/06/2001 | 9 | 14+ | ● | THE ESSENTIAL | Columbia STVCD 116 |
| 22/09/2001 | 3 | 5 | | LOVE AND THEFT 2001 Grammy Award for Best Contemporary Folk Album | Columbia 5043642 |
| 07/12/2002 | 69 | 1 | | LIVE 1975 – THE ROLLING THUNDER REVUE | Columbia 5101403 |
| 10/04/2004 | 33 | 1 | | BOOTLEG SERIES VOLUME 6 | Columbia 5123582 |

**E-17** – see EAST 17

**EAGLES** US rock group formed in Los Angeles, CA in 1971 by Glenn Frey (born 6/11/1948, Detroit, MI, guitar/vocals), Bernie Leadon (born 19/7/1947, Minneapolis, MN, guitar), Randy Meisner (born 8/3/1946, Scottsbluff, NE, bass) and Don Henley (born 22/7/1947, Gilmer, TX, drums). Signed by David Geffen to Asylum, they recorded their 1972 debut LP in England with Glyn Johns. Don Felder (born 21/9/1947, Topanga, CA, guitars) was added in 1975. Leadon left in the same year and was replaced by Joe Walsh (born 20/11/1947, Wichita, KS). Meisner was replaced by Timothy Schmidt (born 30/10/1947, Sacramento, CA) in 1977. The group has won four Grammy Awards: Best Pop Vocal Performance by a Group in 1975 for *Lyin' Eyes,* Record of the Year in 1977 for the single *Hotel California,* Best Arrangement for Vocals in 1977 for *New Kid In Town,* and Best Rock Performance by a Group in 1979 for *Heartache Tonight*. They disbanded in 1982, all launching solo ventures, Frey and Henley with greatest success. Walsh tried for the nomination of Vice President of the USA in two presidential campaigns. They were inducted into the Rock & Roll Hall of Fame in 1998.

| | | | |
|---|---|---|---|
| 27/04/1974 | 28 | 9 | ○ |
| 12/07/1975 | 39 | 9 | |
| 12/07/1975 | 8 | 41 | |
| 06/03/1976 | 2 | 77 | ✪ |
| 25/12/1976 | 2 | 70 | ✪ |
| 13/10/1979 | 4 | 16 | ● |
| 22/11/1980 | 24 | 13 | ● |
| 18/05/1985 | 8 | 74 | ✪⁴ |
| 23/07/1994 | 4 | 54 | ✪ |
| 19/11/1994 | 18 | 21 | ● |
| 09/06/2001 | 3 | 47 | ✪ |
| 01/11/2003 | 27 | 4 | ● |

ON THE BORDER . . . . . . . . . . . . . . . . . . . . . . . . . . . . . . . . . . . . . . . . . . . . . . . . . . . . . . . . . . . . . Asylum SYL 9016
DESPERADO . . . . . . . . . . . . . . . . . . . . . . . . . . . . . . . . . . . . . . . . . . . . . . . . . . . . . . . . . . . . . . Asylum SYLA 8759
**ONE OF THESE NIGHTS** ▲⁵ . . . . . . . . . . . . . . . . . . . . . . . . . . . . . . . . . . . . . . . . . . . . . . . . . . . . . Asylum SYLL 9011
**THEIR GREATEST HITS 1971–1975** ▲⁵ ◆²⁸ . . . . . . . . . . . . . . . . . . . . . . . . . . . . . . . . . . . . . . . . Asylum K 53017
**HOTEL CALIFORNIA** ▲⁸ ◆¹⁶ . . . . . . . . . . . . . . . . . . . . . . . . . . . . . . . . . . . . . . . . . . . . . . . . . . . . Asylum K 53051
**THE LONG RUN** ▲⁹ . . . . . . . . . . . . . . . . . . . . . . . . . . . . . . . . . . . . . . . . . . . . . . . . . . . . . . . . . Asylum K 52181
LIVE . . . . . . . . . . . . . . . . . . . . . . . . . . . . . . . . . . . . . . . . . . . . . . . . . . . . . . . . . . . . . . . . . . . . Asylum K 62032
**THE BEST OF THE EAGLES** . . . . . . . . . . . . . . . . . . . . . . . . . . . . . . . . . . . . . . . . . . . . . . . . . . . . . . Asylum EKT 5
**THE VERY BEST OF THE EAGLES** ◇² . . . . . . . . . . . . . . . . . . . . . . . . . . . . . . . . . . . . . . . . . Elektra 9548323752
HELL FREEZES OVER ▲² . . . . . . . . . . . . . . . . . . . . . . . . . . . . . . . . . . . . . . . . . . . . . . . . . . Geffen GED 24725
**THE VERY BEST OF THE EAGLES** . . . . . . . . . . . . . . . . . . . . . . . . . . . . . . . . . . . . . . . . . . . . Elektra 7559626802
THE COMPLETE GREATEST HITS . . . . . . . . . . . . . . . . . . . . . . . . . . . . . . . . . . . . . . . . . . . . WSM 8122737312

**EAMON** US singer (born Eamon Doyle, 1984, Staten Island, NYC).

| | | | |
|---|---|---|---|
| 17/04/2004 | 6 | 9 | ● |

**I DON'T WANT YOU BACK (IMPORT)** . . . . . . . . . . . . . . . . . . . . . . . . . . . . . . . . . . . . . . . . . . Jive JIV583702

**STEVE EARLE** US guitarist/singer (born 17/1/1955, Fort Monroe, VA) who formed the Dukes in Texas, signing with Columbia then MCA. Married six times (to five women), he served time in prison for offences including assaulting a police officer. A heroin user at thirteen, he kicked the habit in the mid-1990s, claiming his 1997 album *El Corazon* 'the first I've ever done 100 per cent clean'.

| | | | |
|---|---|---|---|
| 04/07/1987 | 77 | 2 | |
| 19/11/1988 | 42 | 8 | ○ |
| 07/07/1990 | 22 | 4 | |
| 19/10/1991 | 62 | 1 | |
| 23/03/1996 | 44 | 3 | |
| 18/10/1997 | 59 | 1 | |
| 06/03/1999 | 51 | 1 | |
| 17/06/2000 | 32 | 1 | |

EXIT 0 . . . . . . . . . . . . . . . . . . . . . . . . . . . . . . . . . . . . . . . . . . . . . . . . . . . . . . . . . . . . . . . . MCA MCF 3379
COPPERHEAD ROAD . . . . . . . . . . . . . . . . . . . . . . . . . . . . . . . . . . . . . . . . . . . . . . . . . . . . . MCA MCF 3426
THE HARD WAY . . . . . . . . . . . . . . . . . . . . . . . . . . . . . . . . . . . . . . . . . . . . . . . . . . . . . . . . MCA MCG 6095
SHUT UP AND DIE LIKE AN AVIATOR This and the above hit credited to **STEVE EARLE AND THE DUKES** . . . . . . . . . . . . . . . . MCA 10315
I FEEL ALRIGHT . . . . . . . . . . . . . . . . . . . . . . . . . . . . . . . . . . . . . . . . . . . . . . . . . . . . Transatlantic TRACD 227
EL CORAZON . . . . . . . . . . . . . . . . . . . . . . . . . . . . . . . . . . . . . . . . . . . . . . . . . . . Warner Brothers 9362467892
THE MOUNTAIN **STEVE EARLE AND THE DEL McCOURY BAND** . . . . . . . . . . . . . . . . . . . . . . . . . . . . . . . . . . Grapevine GRACD 252
TRANSCENDENTAL BLUES . . . . . . . . . . . . . . . . . . . . . . . . . . . . . . . . . . . . . . . . . . . . . . . . . . . Epic 4989749

**EARTH, WIND AND FIRE** US soul group formed by Maurice White (born 19/12/194, Chicago, IL) who was a session musician and drummer with Ramsey Lewis. The ten-strong band signed with Warner's, releasing two albums before White dismantled the group, and then re-assembled it with his brother Verdine (born 25/7/1951, vocals/bass), Philip Bailey (born 8/5/1951, Denver, CO, vocals), Larry Dunn (born 19/6/1953, Colorado, keyboards), Al McKay (guitars), Fred White (drums), Ralph Johnson (born 4/7/1951, drums), Johnny Graham (guitar) and Andrew Woolfolk (saxophone). White produced after the death of Charles Stepney, later founding the American Record Company (ARC) with acts like Deniece Williams and the Emotions. Dunn and Verdine also produced the Pockets and Level 42. The group appeared in the films *That's The Way Of The World* (1975) and *Sgt Pepper's Lonely Hearts Club Band* (1978). They have won five Grammy Awards including: Best Rhythm & Blues Vocal Performance by a Group in 1975 for *Shining Star;* Best Rhythm & Blues Instrumental Performance in 1978 for *Runnin';* Best Rhythm & Blues Instrumental Performance in 1979 for *Boogie Wonderland;* and Best Rhythm & Blues Vocal Performance by a Group in 1979 for *After The Love Has Gone*. Saxophonist Donald Myrick, in the band from 1975–82, was shot dead by police searching his home for drugs on 30/7/1993 after they mistook a butane lighter he was holding for a gun. In 2000 it was announced that Maurice White was suffering from Parkinson's Disease, which was first diagnosed in 1992. Inducted into the Rock & Roll Hall of Fame in 2000, they also have a star on the Hollywood Walk of Fame.

| | | | |
|---|---|---|---|
| 21/01/1978 | 13 | 23 | ○ |
| 16/12/1978 | 6 | 42 | ✪ |
| 23/06/1979 | 5 | 41 | ✪ |

ALL 'N' ALL 1978 Grammy Award for Best Rhythm & Blues Vocal Performance by a Group . . . . . . . . . . . . . . . . . . . . . . . CBS 86051
**THE BEST OF EARTH WIND & FIRE VOLUME 1** . . . . . . . . . . . . . . . . . . . . . . . . . . . . . . . . . . . . . . . . . . . . . CBS 83284
**I AM** . . . . . . . . . . . . . . . . . . . . . . . . . . . . . . . . . . . . . . . . . . . . . . . . . . . . . . . . . . . . . . . . . . . CBS 86084

▲⁹ Number of weeks album topped the US chart   ◆¹² RIAA Diamond Awards   ◇³ IFPI Platinum Europe Awards

| | | | | |
|---|---|---|---|---|
| 01/11/1980 | 10 | 6 | | FACES .................................................................. CBS 88498 |
| 14/11/1981 | 14 | 22 | ● | RAISE ................................................................... CBS 85272 |
| 19/02/1983 | 22 | 7 | | POWERLIGHT ......................................................... CBS 25120 |
| 09/03/1985 | 65 | 4 | | THE ARTISTS VOLUME 1 **EARTH WIND & FIRE/JEAN CARN/ROSE ROYCE** ......... Street Sounds ARTIS 1 |
| 10/05/1986 | 5 | 13 | ● | **THE COLLECTION – 24 ESSENTIAL HITS** ......................... K-Tel NE 1322 |
| 28/11/1992 | 40 | 6 | | THE VERY BEST OF EARTH WIND & FIRE .......................... Telstar TCD 2631 |
| 28/09/1996 | 29 | 4 | | BOOGIE WONDERLAND – THE VERY BEST OF EARTH WIND & FIRE ......... Telstar TCD 2879 |
| 07/08/1999 | 34 | 3 | | THE ULTIMATE COLLECTION ..................................... Columbia SONYTV 66CD |

**EARTHLING** UK production duo formed in Bristol by Andy Edison and Tim Saul with vocals by Mau.

| | | | | |
|---|---|---|---|---|
| 03/06/1995 | 66 | 1 | | RADAR .............................................................. Cooltempo CTCD 44 |

**EAST OF EDEN** UK group formed in 1968 by Dave Arbus (violin), Ron Gaines (saxophone), Geoff Nicholson (guitar), Andy Sneddon (bass) and Geoff Britton (drums). By 1972 the group comprised Joe O'Donnell (violin), Garth Watt-Roy (guitar), Martin Fisher (bass) and Jeff Allen (drums).

| | | | | |
|---|---|---|---|---|
| 14/03/1970 | 29 | 2 | | SNAFU ............................................................ Deram SML 1050 |

**EAST 17** UK group formed by Tony Mortimer (born 21/10/1970, London), John Hendy (born 26/3/1971, Barking), Brian Harvey (born 8/8/1974, London) and Terry Coldwell (born 21/7/1974, London), named after the local postcode for Walthamstow. They were named Best Dance Act at the 1995 MTV Europe Music Awards. Harvey was sacked in January 1997 but later reinstated. When Mortimer left to pursue songwriting, the group re-formed as E-17, disbanding at the end of 1999. Brian Harvey later went solo on Edel Records.

| | | | | |
|---|---|---|---|---|
| 27/02/1993 | ❶[1] | 33 | ✪ | WALTHAMSTOW The album changed its catalogue number to 8284262 during its chart run. .............. London 8283732 |
| 29/10/1994 | 3 | 36 | ✪[2] | STEAM ◇ ......................................................... London 8285422 |
| 25/11/1995 | 7 | 15 | ✪ | UP ALL NIGHT ................................................... London 8286992 |
| 16/11/1996 | 3 | 16 | ✪[2] | AROUND THE WORLD – THE JOURNEY SO FAR ◇ .................... London 8288522 |
| 28/11/1998 | 43 | 2 | ○ | RESURRECTION E-17 .............................................. Telstar TCD 3015 |

**EASTERHOUSE** UK rock group formed in Manchester by Andy Perry (vocals), his brother Ivor (guitar), Mike Murray (guitar), Peter Vanden (bass) and Gary Rostock (drums). The two brothers fell out prior to the release of their debut album with Ivor Perry going on to form Cradle and Andy retaining the name Easterhouse (which had been adopted from an area of Glasgow). Andy re-formed the group with Neil Taylor (guitar), Steve Lovell (guitar), Lance Sabin (guitar) and David Verner (drums).

| | | | | |
|---|---|---|---|---|
| 28/06/1986 | 91 | 1 | | CONTENDERS ................................................... Rough Trade ROUGH 94 |

**SHEENA EASTON** UK singer (born Sheena Orr, 27/4/1959, Glasgow) whose debut EMI single *Modern Girl* was a minor hit. When she was the subject of the TV documentary *Big Time* as an up-and-coming singer, however, her second single exploded onto the charts, followed by a re-entry for her debut record. After moving to the US, she became an actress (appearing in the TV show *Miami Vice* as Sonny Crockett's wife) and property speculator. She also worked extensively with Prince. She has won two Grammy Awards: Best New Artist in 1981 and Best Mexican-American Performance in 1984 with Luis Miguel for *Me Gustas Tal Como Eres*.

| | | | | |
|---|---|---|---|---|
| 31/01/1981 | 17 | 9 | ● | TAKE MY TIME .................................................. EMI EMC 3354 |
| 03/10/1981 | 33 | 6 | ○ | YOU COULD HAVE BEEN WITH ME ................................ EMI EMC 3378 |
| 25/09/1982 | 44 | 4 | | MADNESS, MONEY AND MUSIC .................................. EMI EMC 3414 |
| 15/10/1983 | 99 | 1 | | BEST KEPT SECRET ............................................. EMI EMC 1077951 |
| 04/03/1989 | 30 | 7 | | THE LOVER IN ME .............................................. MCA MCG 6036 |

**CLINT EASTWOOD AND GENERAL SAINT** UK vocal duo formed in the early 1980s. Clint Eastwood (Robert Brammer) was already known in reggae circles for earlier Jamaican hits, General Saint (Winston Hislop) being known as a dancehall DJ. Eastwood's brother Trinity has also enjoyed a successful recording career.

| | | | | |
|---|---|---|---|---|
| 06/02/1982 | 99 | 2 | | TWO BAD DJ ..................................................... Greensleeves GREL 24 |
| 28/05/1983 | 98 | 1 | | STOP THAT TRAIN ............................................... Greensleeves GREL 53 |

**EAT STATIC** UK instrumental duo formed in Somerset by Merv Peopler (drums) and Joe Hinton (keyboards), both previously in Ozric Tentacles. Eat Static are primarily concerned with UFOs, the inspiration for all their hit albums.

| | | | | |
|---|---|---|---|---|
| 15/05/1993 | 62 | 1 | | ABDUCTION ...................................................... Planet Dog BARKCD 1 |
| 25/06/1994 | 13 | 3 | | IMPLANT ......................................................... Planet Dog BARKCD 005 |
| 25/10/1997 | 60 | 1 | | SCIENCE OF THE GODS ......................................... Planet Dog BARKCD 029 |

**EAZY-E** US rapper (born Eric Wright, 7/9/1964, Compton, CA) who was also a member of NWA (Niggaz With Attitude) and founded Ruthless Records (supposedly using money that was raised from drug dealing). He died from AIDS on 26/3/1995.

| | | | | |
|---|---|---|---|---|
| 10/02/1996 | 66 | 1 | | STR8 OFF THA STREETZ OF MUTHAPHUKKIN COMPTON ............... Epic 4835762 |

## ECHO AND THE BUNNYMEN
UK rock group formed in Liverpool in 1978 by Ian McCulloch (born 5/5/1959, Liverpool, vocals, formerly of the Crucial Three with Pete Wylie and Julian Cope), Will Sergeant (born 12/4/1958, Liverpool, guitar) and Les Pattinson (born 18/4/1958, Liverpool, bass), plus a drum machine called 'Echo'. They signed with Korova in 1979, adding Pete De Freitas (born 2/8/1961, Port of Spain, Trinidad, drums) and making Echo redundant. They split in 1988, McCulloch going solo before forming Electrafixion, then re-formed in 1996. De Freitas was killed in a motorcycle crash on 15/6/1989. They were in the England United recording for the 1998 World Cup finals.

| | | | | | |
|---|---|---|---|---|---|
| 26/07/1980 | 17 | 6 | ● | CROCODILES | Korova KODE 1 |
| 06/01/1981 | 10 | 16 | | HEAVEN UP HERE | Korova KODE 3 |
| 12/02/1983 | 2 | 17 | ● | PORCUPINE | Korova KODE 6 |
| 12/05/1984 | 4 | 26 | ● | OCEAN RAIN | Korova KODE 8 |
| 23/11/1985 | 6 | 15 | ● | SONGS TO LEARN AND SING | Korova KODE 13 |
| 18/07/1987 | 4 | 9 | ○ | ECHO AND THE BUNNYMEN | WEA WX 108 |
| 21/06/1997 | 59 | 1 | | BALLYHOO – THE BEST OF ECHO AND THE BUNNYMEN | Korova 0630191032 |
| 26/07/1997 | 8 | 7 | | EVERGREEN | London 8289052 |
| 17/04/1999 | 21 | 2 | | WHAT ARE YOU GOING TO DO WITH YOUR LIFE? | London 5560802 |
| 26/05/2001 | 56 | 1 | | FLOWERS | Cooking Vinyl COOKCD 208 |

## ECHOBELLY
UK rock group formed in London in 1993 by Sonya Aurora Madan (vocals), Glenn Johannson (guitar), Debbie Smith (guitar), Andy Henderson (drums) and Alex Keyser (bass). Madan later recorded with Victor Imbres as Lithium, and Smith left in 1997.

| | | | | | |
|---|---|---|---|---|---|
| 03/09/1994 | 8 | 3 | ○ | EVERYONE'S GOT ONE | Fauve FAUV 3CD |
| 30/09/1995 | 4 | 24 | ● | ON | Fauve FAUV 6CD |
| 22/11/1997 | 47 | 1 | | LUSTRA | Epic 4889672 |

## EDDIE AND THE HOTRODS
UK rock group formed in Southend in 1975 by Barrie Masters (vocals), Dave Higgs (guitar), Paul Gray (bass) and Steve Nicol (drums). Graeme Douglas (guitar) was added to the line-up in 1977. They disbanded in 1978, Masters forming a new Eddie And The Hot Rods for one album in 1985.

| | | | | | |
|---|---|---|---|---|---|
| 18/12/1976 | 43 | 1 | | TEENAGE DEPRESSION | Island ILPS 9457 |
| 03/12/1977 | 27 | 3 | | LIFE ON THE LINE | Island ILPS 9509 |
| 24/03/1979 | 50 | 1 | | THRILLER | Island ILPS 9563 |

## DUANE EDDY AND THE REBELS
US singer/guitarist (born 26/4/1938, New York) who played guitar from the age of five. In his teens he formed the Rebels, recording a debut single in 1958 with producer Lee Hazlewood. They included top session players Larry Knechtel (piano, later in Bread), Jim Horn and Steve Douglas (saxophone). Eddy appeared in films, including *The Savage Seven* (1968) and *Because They're Young* (1960). Douglas died from heart failure on 19/4/1993. Eddy was inducted into the Rock & Roll Hall of Fame in 1994.

| | | | | | |
|---|---|---|---|---|---|
| 06/06/1959 | 6 | 3 | | HAVE TWANGY GUITAR WILL TRAVEL | London HAW 2160 |
| 31/10/1959 | 6 | 8 | | SPECIALLY FOR YOU | London HAW 2191 |
| 19/03/1960 | 2 | 25 | | THE TWANG'S THE THANG | London HAW 2236 |
| 26/11/1960 | 13 | 5 | | SONGS OF OUR HERITAGE | London HAW 2285 |
| 01/04/1961 | 5 | 19 | | A MILLION DOLLARS' WORTH OF TWANG | London HAW 2325 |
| 09/06/1962 | 18 | 1 | | A MILLION DOLLARS' WORTH OF TWANG VOLUME 2 | London HAW 2435 |
| 21/07/1962 | 8 | 12 | | TWISTIN' AND TWANGIN' | RCA RD 27264 |
| 08/12/1962 | 13 | 11 | | TWANGY GUITAR – SILKY STRINGS | RCA Victor RD 7510 |
| 16/03/1963 | 14 | 4 | | DANCE WITH THE GUITAR MAN | RCA Victor RD 7545 |

## DAVE EDMUNDS
UK singer/guitarist (born 15/4/1944, Cardiff) who learnt to play guitar while at school. He was in the Raiders in the mid-1960s before joining Love Sculpture. They split in 1969; Edmunds set up Rockfield Recording Studios in Wales and embarked on a solo career. As a producer, he worked with Shakin' Stevens, Brinsley Schwarz and the Stray Cats.

| | | | | | |
|---|---|---|---|---|---|
| 23/06/1979 | 39 | 12 | ○ | REPEAT WHEN NECESSARY | Swan Song SSK 59409 |
| 18/04/1981 | 37 | 4 | | TWANGIN' | Swan Song SSK 59411 |
| 03/04/1982 | 60 | 3 | | DE 7 | Arista SPART 1184 |
| 30/04/1983 | 92 | 2 | | INFORMATION | Arista 205 348 |

## DENNIS EDWARDS
US singer (born 3/2/1943, Birmingham, AL) who was in The Fireworks before joining The Contours, signing to Motown Records in 1965. When the Contours disbanded in 1967 he joined The Temptations, replacing David Ruffin as lead singer in 1968. He stayed with Motown as a solo act when the group moved to Atlantic, rejoining them when they returned two albums later. He went solo again in 1984, with more success, returning to the group a third time in 1987, leaving for good a few years later. He later toured as Dennis Edwards' Temptations, until blocked by The Temptations.

14/04/1984 . . . . . 91 . . . . . . 1 . . . . . .    DON'T LOOK ANY FURTHER . . . . . . . . . . . . . . . . . . . . . . . . . . . . . . . . . . . . . . . . . . . . . . . . . Gordy ZL 72148

**TODD EDWARDS** US DJ born in New Jersey, who produced for the Nervous label in the early 1990s. He first recorded as The Messenger in 1993, later as The Sample Choir and under his own name. His debut hit was a 12-inch single too long for the singles chart.

24/08/1996 . . . . . 69 . . . . . . 1 . . . . . .    SAVED MY LIFE . . . . . . . . . . . . . . . . . . . . . . . . . . . . . . . . . . . . . . . . . . . . . . . . . . . . . . . . . . ffrr FX 279

**EEK-A-MOUSE** Jamaican singer (born Ripton Joseph Hilton, 1957, Kingston in 1957), named after a racehorse he regularly backed and lost money on. After recording under his real name during the 1970s, he made his debut album as Eek-A-Mouse in 1981.

14/08/1982 . . . . . 61 . . . . . . 3 . . . . . .    SKIDIP . . . . . . . . . . . . . . . . . . . . . . . . . . . . . . . . . . . . . . . . . . . . . . . . . . . . . . . . . Greensleeves GREL 41

**EELS** US rock group formed in Los Angeles, CA in 1995 by E (born Mark Everett, guitar/vocals), Butch Norton (drums) and Tommy Walter (bass). They were named Best International Newcomer at the 1998 BRIT Awards.

| | | | | | |
|---|---|---|---|---|---|
| 08/02/1997 | 5 | 27 | ● | **BEAUTIFUL FREAK** . . . . . . . . . . . . . . . . . . . . . . . . . . . . . . . . . . . . . . | DreamWorks DRD 50001 |
| 03/10/1998 | 12 | 4 | | ELECTRO-SHOCK BLUES . . . . . . . . . . . . . . . . . . . . . . . . . . . . . . . . . . | DreamWorks DRD 50052 |
| 11/03/2000 | 8 | 5 | ○ | **DAISIES OF THE GALAXY** . . . . . . . . . . . . . . . . . . . . . . . . . . . . . . . . . . | DreamWorks 4502182 |
| 06/10/2001 | 12 | 2 | | SOULJACKER . . . . . . . . . . . . . . . . . . . . . . . . . . . . . . . . . . . . . . . . . | DreamWorks 4503462 |
| 14/06/2003 | 35 | 2 | | SHOOTENANNY . . . . . . . . . . . . . . . . . . . . . . . . . . . . . . . . . . . . . . . | DreamWorks 4504588 |

**EIFFEL 65** Italian dance group formed by Maurizio Lobina, Gianfranco Radone and Gabrielle Ponte. Randone is also a member of Minimal Funk 2.

04/03/2000 . . . . . 12 . . . . . . 4 . . . . . .    EUROPOP . . . . . . . . . . . . . . . . . . . . . . . . . . . . . . . . . . . . . . . . . . . . . . . . . . . . Eternal 8573814552

**808 STATE** UK group formed in Manchester in 1988 by Graham Massey (born 4/8/1960, Manchester), Martin Price (born 26/3/1955, Manchester) and DJ Gerald Simpson, naming themselves after a drum machine. Simpson left and recorded as A Guy Called Gerald, with DJs Andrew Barker (born 9/3/1968, Manchester) and Darren Partington (born 1/11/1969, Manchester) joining 808 State. Price left in 1990.

| | | | | | |
|---|---|---|---|---|---|
| 16/12/1989 | 57 | 5 | ● | NINETY . . . . . . . . . . . . . . . . . . . . . . . . . . . . . . . . . . . . . . . . . . . . . . | ZTT 2 |
| 16/03/1991 | 4 | 10 | ● | **EX-EL** . . . . . . . . . . . . . . . . . . . . . . . . . . . . . . . . . . . . . . . . . . . . . . . | ZTT 6 |
| 13/02/1993 | 17 | 3 | | GORGEOUS . . . . . . . . . . . . . . . . . . . . . . . . . . . . . . . . . . . . . . . . . | ZTT 4509911002 |
| 30/05/1998 | 40 | 2 | | 808:88:98 . . . . . . . . . . . . . . . . . . . . . . . . . . . . . . . . . . . . . . . . . . | ZTT 100CD |

**801** UK rock group formed in 1975 by Phil Manzanera (born Philip Targett Adams, 31/1/1951, London, guitar), Lloyd Watson (guitar/vocals), Francis Monkman (keyboards), Bill MacCormick (bass) and Simon Phillips (drums) during a lull in Roxy Music's activities. Their debut hit album was recorded at the Queen Elizabeth Hall in London on 3/9/1976. Manzanera disbanded the group in 1978 after Roxy Music went back into action. Monkman later became a member of Sky.

20/11/1976 . . . . . 52 . . . . . . 2 . . . . . .    801 LIVE . . . . . . . . . . . . . . . . . . . . . . . . . . . . . . . . . . . . . . . . . . . . . . . . . . . . Island ILPS 9444

**EIGHTH WONDER** UK group originally formed as Spice by Jamie Kensit (guitar), later featuring his sister Patsy (born 4/3/1968, London, lead singer), Geoff Beauchamp (guitar) and Alex Godson (keyboards). Patsy began as a child actress, appearing as the 'pea pod' girl for Birds Eye. She subsequently resumed acting (appearing in the 1989 film *Lethal Weapon 2*) and has been married to Dan Donovan (Big Audio Dynamite), Jim Kerr (Simple Minds) and Liam Gallagher (Oasis), all three marriages ending in divorce.

23/07/1988 . . . . . 47 . . . . . . 4 . . . . . .    FEARLESS . . . . . . . . . . . . . . . . . . . . . . . . . . . . . . . . . . . . . . . . . . . . . . . . . . . . CBS 4606281

**LUDOVICO EINAUDI** Italian composer (born 1955, Turin); he studied at the Conservatorio in Milan and received a scholarship from the Tanglewood Festival.

13/09/2003 . . . . . 40 . . . . . . 4 . . . . . . ○    ECHOES – THE COLLECTION . . . . . . . . . . . . . . . . . . . . . . . . . . . . . . . . . . . . . . . . BMG 82876550892

**ELASTICA** UK rock group formed in London in 1993 by Justine Frischmann (born 16/9/1969, Twickenham, guitar/vocals), Donna Matthews (born 2/12/1971, Newport, Wales, guitar), Justin Welch (born 4/12/1972, Nuneaton, drums) and Annie Holland (born 26/8/1965, Brighton, bass). They added Dave Bush (keyboards) in 1995. Holland left in 1995 and was replaced by Abby Travis. Travis later left and was replaced by Sheila Chipperfield (born 17/6/1976). Frischmann had been rhythm guitarist with Suede. They split in 2001

| | | | | | |
|---|---|---|---|---|---|
| 25/03/1995 | ❶[1] | 25 | ● | **ELASTICA** . . . . . . . . . . . . . . . . . . . . . . . . . . . . . . . . . . . . . . . . . . . . | Deceptive BLUFF 014CD |
| 15/04/2000 | 24 | 2 | | THE MENACE . . . . . . . . . . . . . . . . . . . . . . . . . . . . . . . . . . . . . . . . . | Deceptive BLUFF 075CD |

**ELBOW** UK group formed by Guy Garvey (vocals), Craig Potter (keyboards), brother Mark (guitar), Pete Turner (bass) and Richard Jupp (drums), known as General Public, RPM and Miscellaneous Sales before Elbow. Signed by Island, they were dropped after a year.

| | | | | | |
|---|---|---|---|---|---|
| 19/05/2001 | 14 | 5 | ● | ASLEEP IN THE BACK . . . . . . . . . . . . . . . . . . . . . . . . . . . . . . . . . . . . | V2 VVR 1015882 |
| 30/08/2003 | 7 | 4 | | **CAST OF THOUSANDS** . . . . . . . . . . . . . . . . . . . . . . . . . . . . . . . . . . . | V2 VVR 1021812 |

**ELECTRAFIXION** UK group formed in 1994 by Ian McCulloch (born 5/5/195, Liverpool, vocals) and Will Sergeant (born 12/4/1958, Liverpool, guitar), both ex-Echo & The Bunnymen, with Leon De Sylva (bass) and Tony McGuigan (drums). McCulloch and Sergeant re-formed Echo & The Bunnymen at the end of 1996..

07/10/1995 . . . . . 38 . . . . . . 2 . . . . . .    BURNED . . . . . . . . . . . . . . . . . . . . . . . . . . . . . . . . . . . . . . . . . . . . . . . Space Junk 00630112482

**ELECTRASY** UK vocal/instrumental group featuring Nigel Nisbet (bass), Ali McKinnel (vocals), Steve, Paul and Jim. According to the *Guinness Book Of Records* the video for *Best Friend's Girl* features the group and members of the Laurel And Hardy Fan Club throwing 4,400 custard pies in three minutes.

26/09/1998 . . . . . 48 . . . . . . 1 . . . . . .    BEAUTIFUL INSANE . . . . . . . . . . . . . . . . . . . . . . . . . . . . . . . . . . . . . . . . . . . . MCA MCD 60051

### ELECTRIBE 101
UK group formed in 1987 by Joe Stevens, Les Fleming, Rob Cimarosti, Brian Nordhoff and singer Billie Ray Martin. They split in 1990, with Martin going solo and Stevens, Fleming, Cimarosti and Nordhoff forming Groove Corporation.

| 20/10/1990 | 26 | 3 | | ELECTRIBAL MEMORIES | Mercury 8429651 |

### ELECTRIC BOYS
Swedish rock group formed in 1988 by Conny Blomquist (guitar/vocals), Andy Christell (bass), Franco Santunione (guitar) and Niclas Sigevall (drums). Santunione and Sigevall left after a US tour to promote *Groovus Maximus*, and were replaced by Martin Thomander and Thomas Brogman respectively. The group disbanded after one more album.

| 06/06/1992 | 61 | 1 | | GROOVUS MAXIMUS | Vertigo 5122552 |

### ELECTRIC LIGHT ORCHESTRA
UK rock group formed in Birmingham in 1971 by Jeff Lynne (born 20/12/1947, Birmingham, guitar/vocals), Roy Wood (born Ulysses Wood, 8/11/1946, Birmingham, guitar/vocals), Bev Bevan (born Beverley Bevan, 24/11/1946, Birmingham, drums), Hugh McDowell (born 31/7/1953, London, cello), Richard Tandy (born 26/3/1948, Birmingham, keyboards/vocals) and Andy Craig, Wilf Gibson and Bill Hunt. Wood, Lynne and Bevan had previously been in The Move. Wood left after one album to form Wizzard, Lynne taking over as leader. By 1986 ELO were the trio of Lynne, Bevan and Tandy. Lynne later became a member of The Traveling Wilburys.

| 12/08/1972 | 32 | 4 | | ELECTRIC LIGHT ORCHESTRA | Harvest SHVL 797 |
| 31/03/1973 | 35 | 1 | | ELECTRIC LIGHT ORCHESTRA II | Harvest SHVL 806 |
| 11/12/1976 | 6 | 100 | ✪ | **A NEW WORLD RECORD** The album changed its catalogue number to Jet LP 200 during its chart run | Jet UAG 30017 |
| 12/11/1977 | 4 | 108 | ✪ | **OUT OF THE BLUE** The album changed its catalogue number to Jet DP 400 during its chart run | Jet UAR 100 |
| 06/01/1979 | 38 | 9 | ● | THREE LIGHT YEARS | Jet BX 1 |
| 16/06/1979 | ❶⁵ | 46 | ✪ | **DISCOVERY** | Jet LX 500 |
| 01/12/1979 | 7 | 18 | ✪ | **ELO'S GREATEST HITS** | Jet LX 525 |
| 19/07/1980 | 2 | 17 | ✪ | **XANADU (SOUNDTRACK) ELECTRIC LIGHT ORCHESTRA AND OLIVIA NEWTON-JOHN** | Jet LX 526 |
| 08/08/1981 | ❶² | 32 | ✪ | **TIME** | Jet JETLP 236 |
| 02/07/1983 | 4 | 15 | ● | **SECRET MESSAGES** | Jet LX 527 |
| 15/03/1986 | 9 | 12 | ○ | **BALANCE OF POWER** | Epic EPC 26467 |
| 16/12/1989 | 23 | 21 | ● | THE GREATEST HITS | Telstar STAR 2370 |
| 01/06/1991 | 34 | 4 | | ELECTRIC LIGHT ORCHESTRA PART TWO **ELECTRIC LIGHT ORCHESTRA PART TWO** | Telstar STAR 2503 |
| 02/07/1994 | 4 | 11 | | **THE VERY BEST OF THE ELECTRIC LIGHT ORCHESTRA** | Dino DINCD 90 |
| 08/11/1997 | 60 | 4 | ○ | LIGHT YEARS – THE VERY BEST OF ELECTRIC LIGHT ORCHESTRA | Epic 4890392 |
| 23/06/2001 | 34 | 2 | | ZOOM | Epic 5025002 |
| 03/11/2001 | 18 | 6 | ● | THE ULTIMATE COLLECTION | Columbia STVCD 126 |

### ELECTRIC SIX
US rock group formed in Detroit, MI in 1997 by Dick Valentine (vocals), Surge Joebot (guitar), Rock 'N' Roll Indian (guitar), Disco (bass), Tait Nucleus (keyboards) and M (drums) as The Wildbunch. Rock 'N' Roll Indian, Surge Joebot and Disco left in June 2003 and were replaced by Johnny Nashinal, The Colonel and Frank Lloyd Bonaventure.

| 12/07/2003 | 7 | 10 | ● | **FIRE** | XL Recordings XLCD 169 |

### ELECTRIC SOFT PARADE
UK rock group formed by brothers Alex (guitar/vocals) and Tom White (drums) who were nineteen and seventeen respectively at the time of their debut hit. Originally called Feltro Media, they changed their name in 2001 to Soft Parade, a Doors tribute band of the same name prompting a further change to Electric Soft Parade. They were later augmented by Matt (bass) and Steve (keyboards).

| 16/02/2002 | 35 | 2 | | HOLES IN THE WALL | DB DB002 CDLP |
| 25/10/2003 | 45 | 1 | | THE AMERICAN ADVENTURE | BMG 82876563692 |

### ELECTRIC WIND ENSEMBLE
UK studio group.

| 18/02/1984 | 28 | 9 | | HAUNTING MELODIES | Nouveau Music NML 1007 |

### ELECTRONIC
UK group originally formed as an ad hoc combination of Johnny Marr (born John Maher, 31/10/1963, Ardwick, Manchester) of The Smiths, Pet Shop Boys singer Neil Tennant (born 19/7/1954, Gosforth, Tyne & Wear) and New Order's Barney Sumner, (born Bernard Dicken, 4/1/1956, Salford). By the 1990s they were down to a duo of Marr and Sumner, both having left their respective groups. Marr had been a much-in-demand session guitarist since the demise of The Smiths.

| 08/06/1991 | 2 | 16 | ● | **ELECTRONIC** | Factory FACT 290 |
| 20/07/1996 | 8 | 5 | ○ | **RAISED THE PRESSURE** | Parlophone CDPCS 7382 |
| 08/05/1999 | 9 | 3 | | **TWISTED TENDERNESS** | Parlophone S201462 |

### DANNY ELFMAN
US singer/guitarist/orchestra leader, first known as leader of Oingo Boingo, an eight-piece band based in Los Angeles, CA. He later launched a solo career and enjoyed considerable success with film scores, including *Batman, Dick Tracy, Scrooged* and *The Simpsons*. He won the 1989 Grammy Award for Best Instrumental Composition for *The Batman Theme*.

| 19/08/1989 | 45 | 6 | | BATMAN Soundtrack of the 1989 film *Batman* | Warner Brothers WX 287 |

### DUKE ELLINGTON
US orchestra leader (born Edward Kennedy Ellington, 29/4/1899, Washington DC) who led a number of bands in Washington before moving to New York and establishing his band, the core of which remained unchanged for the next 30 years, making frequent concert tours in Europe. He won eleven Grammy Awards: Best Performance by a Dance Band, Best Musical Composition

and Best Soundtrack Album of Background Score in 1959 for *Anatomy Of A Murder*; Best Jazz Performance, Large Group in 1965 for *Ellington 66*; Best Original Jazz Composition in 1966 for *In The Beginning*; Best Instrumental Jazz Performance in 1967 for *Far East Suite*; Best Instrumental Jazz Performance in 1968 for *And His Mother Called Him Bill*; Best Jazz Performance by a Big Band in 1971 for *New Orleans Suite*; Best Jazz Performance by a Big Band in 1972 for *Togo Brava Suite*; Best Jazz Performance by a Big Band in 1976 for *The Ellington Suites*; and Best Jazz Performance by a Big Band in 1979 for *At Fargo, 1940 Live* (the Duke Ellington Orchestra also won the Best Jazz Performance by a Big Band in 1987 for *Digital Duke*). Three of his recordings have gained Grammy Hall of Fame Awards: 1928's *Black and Tan Fantasy*, 1931's *Mood Indigo* and 1941's *Take The A Train*. He died on 24/5/1974. He has a star on the Hollywood Walk of Fame.

| 08/04/1961 | 11 | 2 | | NUTCRACKER SUITE | Philips BBL 7418 |

### MISSY 'MISDEMEANOR' ELLIOTT

US rapper(born Melissa Elliott, 1972, Portsmouth, VA) who was originally a member of Sista where she was known as Misdemeanor of Sista. After the group dissolved she concentrated on songwriting, penning hits for SWV, Aaliyah, MC Lyte and Jodeci before going solo. She has won three Grammy Awards: the Award for Best Rap Solo Performance for *Get Ur Freak On* in 2001, Best Female Rap Solo Performance in 2002 for *Scream A.K.A. Itchin'* and Best Female Rap Solo Performance in 2003 for *Work It*. She also won the 2001 MOBO Award for Best Hip Hop Act.

| 10/07/1999 | 40 | 2 | ○ | DA REAL WORLD | Elektra 7559624362 |
| 26/05/2001 | 10 | 26 | ● | **MISS E... SO ADDICTIVE** | Elektra 7559626432 |
| 23/11/2002 | 23 | 22 | ● | UNDER CONSTRUCTION | Elektra 7559628132 |
| 06/12/2003 | 47 | 4 | ● | THIS IS NOT A TEST | Elektra 7559629052 |

### SOPHIE ELLIS BEXTOR

UK singer (born 10/4/1979, London) and daughter of former *Blue Peter* presenter Janet Ellis). She was lead singer with Theaudience and then fronted Spiller's hit Groovejet before signing as solo with Polydor in October 2000.

| 15/09/2001 | 2 | 44 | ✪² | **READ MY LIPS** ◇ | Polydor 5891742 |
| 08/11/2003 | 19 | 2 | | SHOOT FROM THE HIP | Polydor 9865834 |

### BEN ELTON

UK comedian/novelist/playwright (born 3/5/1959, London), first known as a scriptwriter for the series *The Young Ones* and later *Blackadder*. As a performer in his own right he performed on the Channel 4 TV series *Friday Night Live*.

| 14/11/1987 | 86 | 2 | | MOTORMOUTH | Mercury BENLP 1 |

### EMBRACE

UK rock group formed in Huddersfield in 1991 by Danny McNamara (guitar/vocals), Richard McNamara (guitar/vocals), Steven Firth (bass) and Mike Heaton (drums). They previously recorded for Dischord Records, releasing their debut in 1992.

| 20/06/1998 | ●¹ | 21 | ✪ | **THE GOOD WILL OUT** | Hut CDHUT 46 |
| 08/04/2000 | 8 | 13 | ● | **DRAWN FROM MEMORY** | Hut CDHUT 60 |
| 15/09/2001 | 9 | 3 | | **IF YOU'VE NEVER BEEN** | Hut CDHUT 68 |
| 06/04/2002 | 36 | 2 | | FIREWORKS (SINGLES 1997–2002) | Hut CDHUT 74 |

### EMERSON, LAKE AND PALMER

UK rock group formed in 1970 by Keith Emerson (born 2/11/1944, Todmorden, keyboards), Greg Lake (born 10/11/1948, Bournemouth, bass/vocals) and Carl Palmer (born 20/3/1947, Birmingham, drums). Lake had previously been with King Crimson, Palmer with Crazy World Of Arthur Brown, Atomic Rooster and Chris Farlowe. They split in 1979, Emerson and Lake reunited (with Cozy Powell, born 29/12/1947) in 1986, Palmer himself returned the following year and Powell joined Black Sabbath in 1990. Powell was killed in a road crash on 5/4/1998.

| 05/12/1970 | 4 | 28 | | **EMERSON, LAKE AND PALMER** | Island ILPS 9132 |
| 19/06/1971 | ●¹ | 17 | | **TARKUS** | Island ILPS 9155 |
| 04/12/1971 | 3 | 5 | ○ | **PICTURES AT AN EXHIBITION** | Island HELP 1 |
| 08/07/1972 | 2 | 29 | | **TRILOGY** | Island ILPS 9186 |
| 22/12/1973 | 2 | 17 | ● | **BRAIN SALAD SURGERY** | Manticore K 53501 |
| 24/08/1974 | 5 | 5 | | **WELCOME BACK MY FRIENDS TO THE SHOW THAT NEVER ENDS – LADIES AND GENTLEMEN: EMERSON, LAKE AND PALMER** | |
| | | | | | Manticore K 63500 |
| 09/04/1977 | 9 | 25 | ● | WORKS | Atlantic K 80009 |
| 10/12/1977 | 20 | 5 | | WORKS VOLUME 2 | Atlantic K 50422 |
| 09/12/1978 | 48 | 4 | ○ | LOVE BEACH | Atlantic K 50552 |
| 14/06/1986 | 35 | 5 | | EMERSON, LAKE AND POWELL **EMERSON, LAKE AND POWELL** | Polydor POLD 5191 |
| 26/06/2004 | 43 | 1+ | | THE ULTIMATE COLLECTION | Sanctuary TDSAN009X |

### EMF

UK rock group formed in a sports shop in Cinderford, Forest of Dean in 1989 by Zak Foley (born 9/12/1970, Gloucester, bass), Ian Dench (born 7/8/1964, Cheltenham, guitar), Derry Brownson (born Derry Brownstone, 10/11/1970, Gloucester, keyboards/percussion), James Atkin (born 28/3/1969, Cinderford, vocals) and Mark Decloedt (born 26/6/1969, Gloucester, drums) as a dance-punk outfit. Their name stands for either Ecstasy Mother Fuckers or Epsom Mad Funkers depending on sources. They disbanded in 1996. Foley collapsed and died on 3/1/2002.

| 18/05/1991 | 3 | 19 | ● | **SCHUBERT DIP** | Parlophone PCS 7353 |
| 10/10/1992 | 19 | 2 | | STIGMA | Parlophone CDPCSD 122 |
| 18/03/1995 | 30 | 1 | | CHA CHA CHA | Parlophone CDPCSD 165 |

○ Silver disc  ● Gold disc  ✪ Platinum disc (additional platinum units are indicated by a figure following the symbol)  ●⁹ Number of weeks album topped the UK chart

**EMINEM** US rapper (born Marshall Bruce Mathers III, 17/10/1972, Kansas City, MO) who began performing at fourteen and made his debut album in 1996. He is also known as Slim Shady, the title of his 1999 album. He has won nine Grammy Awards including Best Rap Solo Performance in 1999 for *My Name Is*; Best Rap Solo Performance for *The Real Slim Shady*; Best Rap Performance by a Duo in 2000 with Dr Dre for *Forget About Dre*; Best Short Form Music Video in 2002 for *Without Me*, and Best Male Rap Solo Performance and Best Rap Song in 2003, both for *Lose Yourself*, with the song going on to win the Oscar for Best Film Song for writers Eminem, Jeff Bass and Luis Resto in 2003. Named Best International Male at the 2001 and 2003 BRIT Awards, he has also won eight MTV Europe Music Awards including Best Male in 2002 and Best Hip Hop Act in 1999, 2000, 2001 2002 and 2003 (each of the five years it has been awarded). Eminem has also collected two MOBO Awards: Best International Single in 1999 for *My Name Is* and Best Hip Hop Act in 2000. He made his film debut on 2002 in *8 Mile*. In July 2001 the following message appeared on the internet: 'Eminem's tour of Australia is to go ahead despite a sickening attitude to women, appallingly obscene language, an irresponsible attitude to sex and violence and, of course, the dungarees. But Eminem said despite these shocking traits he was willing to judge Australians for himself.'

| | | | | |
|---|---|---|---|---|
| 24/04/1999 . . . . . 10 . . . . 114 . . . . ✪² | **SLIM SHADY** ◇ 1999 Grammy Award for Best Rap Album . . . . . . . . . . . . . . . . . . . . . . . . . . . . . . . . . . . . . . . . . . . . Interscope IND 90321 |
| 03/06/2000 . . . . ❶² . . . . . 74 . . . . . . ✪⁶ | **THE MARSHALL MATHERS LP** ◇⁵ ▲⁸ 2000 Grammy Award for Best Rap Album and the 2000 MTV Europe Music Award for Best Album. . . . . . . . . . . . . . . . . . . . . . . . . . . . . . . . . . . . . . . . . . . . . . . . . . . . . . . . . . . . . . . . . . . . . . . . . . . . . Interscope 4906292 |
| 08/06/2002 . . . . ❶⁵ . . . . . 69 . . . . . . ✪⁴ | **THE EMINEM SHOW** ◇⁴ ▲⁶ 2002 Grammy Award for Best Rap Album, 2002 MTV Europe Award for Best Album and 2003 BRIT Award for Best International Album . . . . . . . . . . . . . . . . . . . . . . . . . . . . . . . . . . . . . . . . . . . . . . . . . . Interscope 4932922 |

**AN EMOTIONAL FISH** Irish group formed in Dublin by Gerard Whelan (vocals), Dave Frew (guitar), Enda Wyatt (bass) and Martin Murphy (drums), first signed by U2's Mother label. They had domestic success with *Celebrate*, subsequently issued in the UK.

25/08/1990 . . . . . 40 . . . . . . 3 . . . . . .   AN EMOTIONAL FISH . . . . . . . . . . . . . . . . . . . . . . . . . . . . . . . . . . . . . . . . . . . . . . . . . . . . . . . . . . . . . . . East West WX 359

**ALEC EMPIRE** German producer who is also a member of Atari Teenage Riot and formed the Digital Hardcore label.

04/05/2002 . . . . . 71 . . . . . . 1 . . . . . .   INTELLIGENCE AND SACRIFICE . . . . . . . . . . . . . . . . . . . . . . . . . . . . . . . . . . . . . . . . . . . . . . . . . . . . . . Digital Hardcore DHRCD 29

**EN VOGUE** US vocal group formed in San Francisco, CA in 1988 by Terry Ellis (born 5/9/1966, Houston, TX), Cindy Herron (born 26/9/1965, San Francisco, CA), Dawn Robinson (born 28/11/1968, New London, CT) and Maxine Jones (born 16/1/1965, Paterson, NJ), and produced by Thomas McElroy and Denzil Foster. Robinson went solo in 1996 and Ellis recorded solo in 1995. Robinson later became a member of Lucy Pearl with Raphael Saadiq (of Tony Toni Tone) and Ali Shaheed Muhammad (of A Tribe Called Quest) before going solo again in 2001.

| | |
|---|---|
| 02/06/1990 . . . . . 23 . . . . . . 13 . . . . . . ○ | BORN TO SING. . . . . . . . . . . . . . . . . . . . . . . . . . . . . . . . . . . . . . . . . . . . . . . . . . . . . . . . . . . . . . . . . Atlantic 7567820841 |
| 23/05/1992 . . . . . 4 . . . . . 29 . . . . . . ● | **FUNKY DIVAS** . . . . . . . . . . . . . . . . . . . . . . . . . . . . . . . . . . . . . . . . . . . . . . . . . . . . . . . . . . . East West America 7567921212 |
| 28/06/1997 . . . . . 9 . . . . . . 8 . . . . . . ○ | EV3 . . . . . . . . . . . . . . . . . . . . . . . . . . . . . . . . . . . . . . . . . . . . . . . . . . . . . . . . . . . . . . . East West America 7559620972 |
| 31/10/1998 . . . . . 39 . . . . . . 2 . . . . . . | BEST OF EN VOGUE . . . . . . . . . . . . . . . . . . . . . . . . . . . . . . . . . . . . . . . . . . . . . . . . . . . . . . . East West America 7559623222 |

**ENERGY ORCHARD** Irish group formed in Belfast by Martin 'Bap' Kennedy (born 17/6/1962, vocals) and Paul Toner (guitar).

12/05/1990 . . . . . 53 . . . . . . 2 . . . . . .   ENERGY ORCHARD . . . . . . . . . . . . . . . . . . . . . . . . . . . . . . . . . . . . . . . . . . . . . . . . . . . . . . . . . . . . . . . MCA MCG 6083

**ENGLAND WORLD CUP SQUAD** The England football team (the Football Association was formed in 1863 and the team played their first match in 1872). Needless to say, the 'group' line-up differs on each hit.

| | |
|---|---|
| 16/05/1970 . . . . . 4 . . . . . . 8 . . . . . . | **THE WORLD BEATERS SING THE WORLD BEATERS** ENGLAND FOOTBALL WORLD CUP SQUAD 1970 . . . . . . . . . . . . . . . Pye NSPL 18337 |
| 15/05/1982 . . . . . 37 . . . . . 10 . . . . . . ○ | THIS TIME. . . . . . . . . . . . . . . . . . . . . . . . . . . . . . . . . . . . . . . . . . . . . . . . . . . . . . . . . . . . . . . . . . K-Tel NE 1169 |

**ENGLISH CHAMBER ORCHESTRA** UK orchestra formed in 1948 by Arnold Goldsborough and Lawrence Leonard as the Goldsborough Orchestra it mainly covered 18th-century works up until 1960 when it was renamed. It became resident orchestra at the Aldeburgh Festival in 1961 and made its first world tour in 1969.

| | |
|---|---|
| 07/02/1976 . . . . . 20 . . . . . 9 . . . . . . ● | RODRIGO: CONCERTO DE ARANJUEZ **JOHN WILLIAMS WITH THE ENGLISH CHAMBER ORCHESTRA CONDUCTED BY DANIEL BARENBOIM** . . . . . . . . . . . . . . . . . . . . . . . . . . . . . . . . . . . . . . . . . . . . . . . . . . . . . . . . . . . . . . . . . . . CBS 79369 |
| 02/04/1983 . . . . . 57 . . . . . . 1 . . . . . . | CHANTS D'AUVERGNE VOLUME 1 **KIRI TE KANAWA WITH THE ENGLISH CHAMBER ORCHESTRA** . . . . . . . . . . . . . . Decca SXDL 7604 |
| 07/10/1989 . . . . . 3 . . . . . . 81 . . . . . . ✪² | **VIVALDI: THE FOUR SEASONS** NIGEL KENNEDY WITH THE ENGLISH CHAMBER ORCHESTRA . . . . . . . . . . . . . . . . . . . . . . . EMI NIGE 2 |
| 05/05/1990 . . . . . 28 . . . . . 15 . . . . . . ● | MENDELSSOHN/BRUCH/SCHUBERT **NIGEL KENNEDY WITH JEFFREY TATE CONDUCTING THE ENGLISH CHAMBER ORCHESTRA** . . . . . . . . . . . . . . . . . . . . . . . . . . . . . . . . . . . . . . . . . . . . . . . . . . . . . . . . . . . . . . . . . . . . . . . . . HMV 7496631 |
| 27/03/1999 . . . . . 34 . . . . . . 2 . . . . . . | RETURN TO THE CENTRE OF THE EARTH **RICK WAKEMAN: LONDON SYMPHONY ORCHESTRA: ENGLISH CHAMBER CHOIR: NARRATED BY PATRICK STEWART** . . . . . . . . . . . . . . . . . . . . . . . . . . . . . . . . . . . . . . . . . . . . . . . EMI Classics CDC 5567632 |
| 08/05/1999 . . . . . 67 . . . . . . 1 . . . . . . | THE BEYONDNESS OF THINGS **ENGLISH CHAMBER ORCHESTRA CONDUCTED BY JOHN BARRY**. . . . . . . . . . . . . . . . Decca 4600092 |
| 06/11/1999 . . . . . 51 . . . . . . 6 . . . . . . | CLASSIC KENNEDY **NIGEL KENNEDY WITH THE ENGLISH CHAMBER ORCHESTRA** . . . . . . . . . . . . . . . . . . . EMI Classics CDC 5568902 |

**ENIGMA** UK studio group put together to record cover versions of hits made famous by others in a similar style to Star Sound.

05/09/1981 . . . . . 80 . . . . . . 3 . . . . . .   AIN'T NO STOPPIN' . . . . . . . . . . . . . . . . . . . . . . . . . . . . . . . . . . . . . . . . . . . . . . . . . . . . . . . . . . . . . . . . . Creole CRX 1

## ENIGMA
Romanian/German group of husband and wife duo Michael and Sandra Cretu. Michael (born 18/5/1957, Bucharest, Romania) moved to Germany in 1975, working as a studio musician with the likes of Vangelis before recording his own material. His German-born wife provided the vocals, which were released under the group name Enigma. In 1999 EMI Records settled out of court a claim by Kuo Ying-nan, a Taiwanese tribesman, that he sang on the chorus of the hit single *Return To Innocence*. Accordingly, Kuo and his wife Kuo Hsiu-chu were presented with platinum discs for worldwide sales in excess of 1 million copies.

| 22/12/1990 | ❶¹ | 83 | ✪³ | MCMXC A.D | Virgin International VIR 11 |
| 19/02/1994 | ❶¹ | 35 | ✪² | THE CROSS OF CHANGES ◇ | Virgin CDVIR 20 |
| 07/12/1996 | 12 | 12 | ● | LE ROI EST MORT, VIVE LE ROI! | Virgin CDVIR 60 |
| 29/01/2000 | 7 | 6 | ○ | THE SCREEN BEHIND THE MIRROR | Virgin DGVIR 100 |
| 17/11/2001 | 29 | 4 | ● | LOVE SENSUALITY DEVOTION – GREATEST HITS | Virgin DGVIR 150 |
| 20/09/2003 | 46 | 2 | | VOYAGEUR | Virgin CDVIRX 211 |

## BRIAN ENO
UK keyboard player (born Brian Peter George St John le Baptiste de la Salle Eno, 15/5/1948, Woodbridge) self-taught as a musician, he joined Roxy Music in 1971. He remained with the group for two years before leaving to form a brief partnership with Robert Fripp, but later made his reputation as a producer, winning the BRIT Award for Best Producer in 1994 and 1996. David Byrne is the lead singer with Talking Heads.

| 09/03/1974 | 26 | 2 | | HERE COME THE WARM JETS | Island ILPS 9268 |
| 21/10/1978 | 55 | 1 | | MUSIC FOR FILMS | Polydor 2310 623 |
| 21/02/1981 | 29 | 8 | | MY LIFE IN THE BUSH OF GHOSTS **BRIAN ENO AND DAVID BYRNE** | E.G. EGLP 48 |
| 08/05/1982 | 93 | 1 | | AMBIENT 4 ON LAND | E.G. EGED 20 |
| 12/09/1992 | 70 | 1 | | NERVE NET | Opal 9362450332 |
| 24/09/1994 | 11 | 2 | | WAH WAH | Fontana 5228272 |
| 14/10/1995 | 71 | 1 | | SPINNER **BRIAN ENO AND JAH WOBBLE** | All Saints ASCD 023 |

## ENTOMBED
Swedish rock group formed in Stockholm in 1987 by Lars Goren-Petrov (vocals), Ulf Cederlund (guitar), Alex Hellid (guitar), Lars Rosenburg (bass) and Nicke Andersson (drums). Goren-Petrov left after the first album and was replaced by Orvar Safstrom and then Johnny Dordevic.

| 15/03/1997 | 75 | 1 | | TO RIDE, SHOOT STRAIGHT AND SPEAK THE TRUTH | Threeman Recordings CDMFNX 216 |

## ENUFF Z'NUFF
US rock group formed in Chicago, IL by Chip Z'Nuff (bass), Donny Vie (vocals), Derek Frigo (guitar) and Vikki Fox (drums). Fox left after three albums and was replaced by Ricky Parent.

| 13/04/1991 | 56 | 1 | | STRENGTH | Atco 7567916381 |

## ENYA
Irish singer (born Eithne Ni Bhraonain, 17/5/1961, Gweedore, County Donegal) who joined the family group Clannad in 1979 as singer/keyboard player before going solo after two albums. After a 1987 debut album for the BBC her career took off with *Watermark*. Plays on Radio 1 for *Orinoco Flow* ensured its chart success. She has won three Grammy Awards.

| 06/06/1987 | 69 | 4 | | ENYA Soundtrack from the TV series *The Celts* | BBC REB 605 |
| 15/10/1988 | 5 | 92 | ✪⁴ | WATERMARK | WEA WX 199 |
| 16/11/1991 | ❶¹ | 90 | ✪⁴ | SHEPHERD MOONS 1992 Grammy Award for Best New Age Album | WEA WX 431 |
| 28/11/1992 | 10 | 19 | ✪ | THE CELTS | WEA 4509911672 |
| 02/12/1995 | 24 | ✪² | | THE MEMORY OF TREES ◇² 1996 Grammy Award for Best New Age Album | WEA 0630128792 |
| 15/11/1997 | 4 | 28 | ✪ | PAINT THE SKY WITH STARS – THE BEST OF ENYA ◇³ | WEA 3984208952 |
| 02/12/2000 | 6 | 17 | ✪ | A DAY WITHOUT RAIN ◇³ 2001 Grammy Award for Best New Age Album | WEA 8573859862 |

## EPMD
US rap duo Erick 'E' Sermon (born 25/11/1968, Brentwood) and Parrish 'P' Smith (born 13/5/1968, Brentwood) whose name stands for Erick and Parrish Making Dollars. They split in 1993, Sermon recording solo and Smith as PMD.

| 16/02/1991 | 69 | 1 | | BUSINESS AS USUAL | Def Jam 4676971 |

## EQUALS
Multinational pop group formed in England in 1965 by Derv Gordon (born 29/6/1948, Jamaica, vocals), his twin brother Lincoln (guitar), Eddie Grant (born 5/3/1948, Guyana, guitar), John Hall (born 25/10/1947, London, drums) and Pat Lloyd (born 17/3/1948, London, guitar). Legal problems with the record company stopped them recording, but Grant later emerged as a solo artist.

| 18/11/1967 | 10 | 9 | | UNEQUALLED EQUALS | President PTL 1006 |
| 09/03/1968 | 32 | 1 | | EQUALS EXPLOSION | President PTLS 1015 |

○ Silver disc  ● Gold disc  ✪ Platinum disc (additional platinum units are indicated by a figure following the symbol)  ❶⁹ Number of weeks album topped the UK chart

### ERASURE
UK group formed in London in 1985 by ex-Depeche Mode, Yazoo and Assembly keyboard wizard Vince Clarke (born 3/7/1960, South Woodford) who advertised for a singer in *Melody Maker* and picked Andy Bell (born 25/4/1964, Peterborough) from the 42 he auditioned. They were named Best UK Group at the 1989 BRIT Awards.

| DATE | POS | WKS | BPI | ALBUM TITLE | LABEL & NUMBER |
|---|---|---|---|---|---|
| 14/06/1986 | 71 | 7 | | WONDERLAND | Mute STUMM 25 |
| 11/04/1987 | 6 | 107 | ✪ | **THE CIRCUS** | Mute STUMM 35 |
| 30/04/1988 | ❶[1] | 78 | ✪[2] | **THE INNOCENTS** | Mute STUMM 55 |
| 28/10/1989 | ❶[2] | 48 | ✪[2] | **WILD!** | Mute STUMM 75 |
| 26/10/1991 | ❶[1] | 25 | ✪ | **CHORUS** | Mute STUMM 95 |
| 28/11/1992 | ❶[2] | 26 | ✪[3] | **POP! – THE FIRST 20 HITS** | Mute CDMUTEL 2 |
| 28/05/1994 | ❶[1] | 15 | ● | **I SAY I SAY I SAY** | Mute LCDSTUMM 115 |
| 04/11/1995 | 14 | 5 | | ERASURE | Mute CDSTUMM 145 |
| 12/04/1997 | 10 | 4 | | **COWBOY** | Mute CDSTUMM 155 |
| 04/11/2000 | 45 | 1 | | LOVEBOAT | Mute CDSTUMM 175 |
| 08/02/2003 | 17 | 2 | | OTHER PEOPLE'S SONGS | Mute CDSTUMM 215 |
| 01/11/2003 | 15 | 5 | ● | HITS! THE VERY BEST OF ERASURE | Mute LCDMUTEL 10 |

### DAVID ESSEX
UK singer (born David Albert Cook, 23/7/1947, Plaistow, London) who began his career as drummer with the Everons before going solo in 1964. Singles with Fontana, Uni, Pye and Decca led to the role of Jesus in the West End musical *Godspell* and the lead role in the 1973 film *That'll Be The Day*. He was awarded an OBE in the 1999 New Year's Honours List.

| DATE | POS | WKS | BPI | ALBUM TITLE | LABEL & NUMBER |
|---|---|---|---|---|---|
| 24/11/1973 | 7 | 22 | ○ | **ROCK ON** | CBS 65823 |
| 19/10/1974 | 2 | 24 | ● | **DAVID ESSEX** | CBS 69088 |
| 27/09/1975 | 3 | 20 | ● | **ALL THE FUN OF THE FAIR** | CBS 69160 |
| 05/06/1976 | 51 | 1 | ○ | ON TOUR | CBS 95000 |
| 30/10/1976 | 31 | 9 | ● | OUT ON THE STREET | CBS 86017 |
| 08/10/1977 | 29 | 4 | ○ | GOLD AND IVORY | CBS 86038 |
| 06/01/1979 | 29 | 7 | ○ | THE DAVID ESSEX ALBUM | CBS 10011 |
| 31/03/1979 | 12 | 9 | | IMPERIAL WIZARD | Mercury 6359 616 |
| 12/07/1980 | 75 | 1 | | HOT LOVE | Mercury 6359 017 |
| 19/06/1982 | 31 | 15 | | STAGE-STRUCK | Mercury MERS 4 |
| 27/11/1982 | 37 | 11 | | THE VERY BEST OF DAVID ESSEX | TV Records TVA 4 |
| 15/10/1983 | 39 | 4 | | MUTINY (STUDIO CAST RECORDING) **DAVID ESSEX, FRANK FINLAY & VARIOUS ARTISTS** | Mercury MERH 30 |
| 17/12/1983 | 67 | 6 | | THE WHISPER | Mercury MERH 34 |
| 06/12/1986 | 82 | 4 | | CENTRE STAGE | K-Tel ONE 1333 |
| 19/10/1991 | 13 | 13 | ● | HIS GREATEST HITS | Mercury 5103081 |
| 10/04/1993 | 3 | 8 | ● | **COVER SHOT** | Polygram TV 5145632 |
| 22/10/1994 | 33 | 2 | | BACK TO BACK | Polygram TV 5237902 |
| 09/12/1995 | 26 | 9 | ○ | MISSING YOU | Polygram TV 5295822 |
| 17/05/1997 | 14 | 5 | | A NIGHT AT THE MOVIES | Polygram TV 5376082 |
| 13/06/1998 | 31 | 4 | | GREATEST HITS | Polygram TV 5584842 |

### GLORIA ESTEFAN
US singer (born Gloria Maria Fajardo, 1/9/1957, Havana, Cuba) whose family moved to Miami when she was two (her father had been President Batista's bodyguard). She joined future husband Emilio Estefan's Miami Latin Boys in 1974, suggesting a name change to Miami Sound Machine. They recorded in English for the first time in 1984 and by 1987 Gloria was getting top billing. In 1989 the name was shortened further. Both were injured (Gloria seriously) in a crash in their tour bus in 1990. She has won three Grammy Awards including Best Tropical Latin Performance in 1993 for the single *Abriendo Puertas* and Best Traditional Tropical Latin Album in 2000 for *Alma Caribe*. She has a star on the Hollywood Walk of Fame.

| DATE | POS | WKS | BPI | ALBUM TITLE | LABEL & NUMBER |
|---|---|---|---|---|---|
| 19/11/1988 | ❶[1] | 54 | ✪[4] | **ANYTHING FOR YOU** GLORIA ESTEFAN AND MIAMI SOUND MACHINE | Epic 4631251 |
| 05/08/1989 | ❶[6] | 64 | ✪[3] | **CUTS BOTH WAYS** | Epic 4651451 |

▲[9] Number of weeks album topped the US chart　◆[12] RIAA Diamond Awards　◇[3] IFPI Platinum Europe Awards

| DATE | POS | WKS | BPI | ALBUM TITLE | LABEL & NUMBER |
|------|-----|-----|-----|-------------|----------------|
| 16/02/1991 | 2 | 36 | ✪ | **INTO THE LIGHT** | Epic 4677821 |
| 14/11/1992 | 2 | 47 | ✪3 | **GREATEST HITS** | Epic 4723322 |
| 10/07/1993 | 11 | 11 | | MI TIERRA 1993 Grammy Award for Best Tropical Latin Album | Epic 4737992 |
| 29/10/1994 | 5 | 19 | ✪ | **HOLD ME, THRILL ME, KISS ME** | Epic 4774162 |
| 21/10/1995 | 70 | 1 | | ABRIENDO PUERTAS ◇ | Epic 4809922 |
| 15/06/1996 | 12 | 9 | | DESTINY | Epic 4839322 |
| 13/06/1998 | 16 | 4 | | GLORIA! | Epic 4898502 |
| 24/02/2001 | 60 | 1 | | GREATEST HITS VOLUME 2 | Epic 5016372 |

## DON ESTELLE AND WINDSOR DAVIES

UK actors, paired in the TV comedy *It Ain't Half Hot Mum*, the story of a concert party operating in the Far East at the end of the Second World War. Davies (born 28/8/1930, London) played the role of Battery Sgt Major Williams, Estelle (born 1933, Manchester) played Gunner 'Lofty' Sugden. Estelle died on 2/8/2003.

| DATE | POS | WKS | BPI | ALBUM TITLE | LABEL & NUMBER |
|------|-----|-----|-----|-------------|----------------|
| 10/01/1976 | 10 | 8 | ◯ | **SING LOFTY** | EMI EMC 3102 |

## ETERNAL

UK R&B vocal group formed by Kelle Bryan (born 12/3/1975, London), sisters Easther (born 11/12/1972, Croydon) and Vernie Bennett (born 17/5/1971, Croydon) and Louise Nurding (born 4/11/1974, Lewisham, London). Nurding went solo in 1995. Easther married Boyzone singer Shane Lynch in 1998. Kelle went solo in 1999 and was replaced by TJ, but Easther and Vernie later decided to continue as a duo. They won the 1997 MOBO Award for Best Single with BeBe Winans for *I Wanna Be The Only One*.

| DATE | POS | WKS | BPI | ALBUM TITLE | LABEL & NUMBER |
|------|-----|-----|-----|-------------|----------------|
| 11/12/1993 | 2 | 76 | ✪4 | **ALWAYS & FOREVER** | EMI CDEMD 1053 |
| 11/11/1995 | 6 | 31 | ✪2 | **POWER OF A WOMAN** | EMI CDEMD 1090 |
| 29/03/1997 | 3 | 29 | ✪ | **BEFORE THE RAIN** | EMI CDEMD 1103 |
| 01/11/1997 | 2 | 27 | ✪3 | **GREATEST HITS** ◇ | EMI 8217982 |

## MELISSA ETHERIDGE

US singer/guitarist (born 29/5/1961, Leavenworth, KS) who studied at Berklee College of Music and began her career in clubs in Boston, MA. She then relocated to Los Angeles and was discovered by Island Records' Chris Blackwell, signing with them in 1986. She has won two Grammy Awards: Best Rock Vocal Performance, Female in 1992 for *Ain't It Heavy* and Best Rock Vocal Performance, Female in 1994 for *Come To My Window*.

| DATE | POS | WKS | BPI | ALBUM TITLE | LABEL & NUMBER |
|------|-----|-----|-----|-------------|----------------|
| 30/09/1989 | 63 | 1 | | BRAVE AND CRAZY | Island ILPS 9939 |
| 09/05/1992 | 56 | 1 | | NEVER ENOUGH | Island CID 9990 |

## EUROPE

Swedish rock group formed in 1983 by Joey Tempest (born 19/8/1963, Stockholm, vocals), John Norum (guitar), John Leven (bass), Mic Michael (keyboards) and Ian Haugland (drums) as Force. The group won a national talent contest and recorded two albums before signing with Epic in 1986. The line-up comprised Tempest, Haughland, Michael and Kee Marcello (who replaced Norum).

| DATE | POS | WKS | BPI | ALBUM TITLE | LABEL & NUMBER |
|------|-----|-----|-----|-------------|----------------|
| 22/11/1986 | 9 | 37 | ● | **THE FINAL COUNTDOWN** | Epic EPC 26808 |
| 17/09/1988 | 12 | 5 | | OUT OF THIS WORLD | Epic 4624491 |
| 19/10/1991 | 61 | 1 | | PRISONERS IN PARADISE | Epic 4687551 |

## EUROPEANS

UK group formed by Geoff Dugmore, Fergus Harper, Steve Hogarth and Colin Woore.

| DATE | POS | WKS | BPI | ALBUM TITLE | LABEL & NUMBER |
|------|-----|-----|-----|-------------|----------------|
| 11/02/1984 | 100 | 1 | | LIVE | A&M SCOT 1 |

## EURYTHMICS

UK group formed in 1980 by ex-Tourists Annie Lennox (born 25/12/1954, Aberdeen, vocals) and Dave Stewart (born 9/9/1952, Sunderland, keyboards/guitar). Their album debut was released in Germany with former members of Can and DAF. They were signed to RCA Records (after legal wrangles with the Tourists' former label, Logo) and named after the 1900s' music-through-movement dance mime of Emile Jacques-Dalcrose. Stewart married ex-Bananarama and Shakespear's Sister member Siobhan Fahey in 1987 (she appeared in the video to *Who's That Girl*). Lennox left in 1990 but the pair reunited in 1999. Although the Eurythmics (as a group) have not been named on a single BRIT award, the pair have been among the biggest winners, with Lennox having walked away with the Best UK Female award in 1984, 1986, 1989, 1990 (all of which relate to her time with the group), 1993 and 1996 and the Best Album Award (for *Diva*) in 1993. Stewart has won the Best Producer category on three occasions: 1986, 1987 and 1990. The Eurythmics finally received the Outstanding Contribution to UK Music Award at the 1999 BRIT Awards. They won the 1986 Grammy Award for Best Rock Vocal Performance by a Duo for *Missionary Man*.

| DATE | POS | WKS | BPI | ALBUM TITLE | LABEL & NUMBER |
|------|-----|-----|-----|-------------|----------------|
| 12/02/1983 | 3 | 60 | ✪ | **SWEET DREAMS (ARE MADE OF THIS)** | RCA RCALP 6063 |
| 26/11/1983 | ●2 | 48 | ✪ | **TOUCH** | RCA PL 70109 |
| 09/06/1984 | 31 | 5 | | TOUCH DANCE | RCA PG 70354 |
| 24/11/1984 | 23 | 17 | ● | 1984 (FOR THE LOVE OF BIG BROTHER) Original soundtrack to the film | Virgin V 1984 |
| 11/05/1985 | 3 | 80 | ✪2 | **BE YOURSELF TONIGHT** | RCA PL 70711 |
| 12/07/1986 | 3 | 52 | ✪2 | **REVENGE** | RCA PL 71050 |
| 21/11/1987 | 7 | 33 | ✪ | **SAVAGE** | RCA PL 71555 |
| 23/09/1989 | ●1 | 32 | ✪2 | **WE TOO ARE ONE** | RCA PL 74251 |
| 30/03/1991 | ●10 | 122 | ✪6 | **GREATEST HITS** | RCA PL 74856 |
| 27/11/1993 | 22 | 7 | ● | EURYTHMICS LIVE 1983–1989 | RCA 74321171452 |
| 30/10/1999 | 4 | 20 | ● | **PEACE** ◇ | RCA 74321695622 |

◯ Silver disc  ● Gold disc  ✪ Platinum disc (additional platinum units are indicated by a figure following the symbol)  ●9 Number of weeks album topped the UK chart

### EVANESCENCE US rock group formed in Little Rock, AR by Amy Lee (vocals), Ben Moody (guitar), John LeCompt (guitar) and Rocky Gray (drums). They won two Grammy Awards in 2003; Best New Artist and Best Hard Rock Performance for *Bring Me To Life*.

| | | | | |
|---|---|---|---|---|
| 10/05/2003 .... ❶¹ .... 60+ ..... ✪³ | | | | FALLEN ◇³ ................................................. Epic 5108792 |

### FAITH EVANS US rapper (born 10/6/1973, New York City) married to fellow rapper The Notorious B.I.G. She began her career providing backing vocals for the likes of Usher, Mary J Blige and Hi-Five. She won the 1997 Grammy Award for Best Rap Performance by a Group with Puff Daddy and 112 for *I'll Be Missing You*.

07/11/1998 ..... 69 ...... 1 ...... KEEP THE FAITH ................................................. Puff Daddy 74321614672

### EVE US rapper (born Eve Jeffers, 10/11/1978, Philadelphia, PA) who is also a member of Ruff Ryders. She won the 2001 Grammy Award for Best Rap/Sung Performance with Gwen Stefani for *Let Me Blow Ya Mind*.

11/08/2001 ..... 22 ...... 8 ...... SCORPION ................................................. Interscope 4930212
07/09/2002 ..... 47 ...... 5 ...... EVE-OLUTION ................................................. Interscope 4934722

### EVERCLEAR US rock group formed in Portland, OR in 1993 by Art Alexakis (guitar/vocals), Craig Montoya (bass/vocals) and Greg Eklund (drums). They originally recorded for Fire Records.

14/03/1998 ..... 63 ...... 1 ...... SO MUCH FOR THE AFTERGLOW ................................................. Capitol 8365032
19/08/2000 ..... 51 ...... 1 ...... SONGS FROM AN AMERICAN MOVIE VOLUME 1 ................................................. Capitol 5278642
28/04/2001 ..... 69 ...... 1 ...... SONGS FROM AN AMERICAN MOVIE VOLUME 2 ................................................. Capitol 5304192

### EVERLAST US rapper (born Erik Schrody, 18/8/1969, New York) who was previously a member of House Of Pain.

13/03/1999 ..... 65 ...... 1 ...... WHITEY FORD SINGS THE BLUES ................................................. Tommy Boy TBCD 1236

### PHIL EVERLY US singer (born 19/1/1939, Chicago, IL) and one of The Everly Brothers until 1973. The brothers reunited in 1983, although Phil has also recorded with Cliff Richard.

07/05/1983 ..... 61 ...... 1 ...... PHIL EVERLY ................................................. Capitol EST 27670

### EVERLY BROTHERS US family duo formed by Donald (born Isaac Donald, 1/2/1937, Brownie, KY) and Philip Everly (born 19/1/1939, Chicago, IL) who debuted at the age of eight and six as Little Donnie & Baby Boy Phil on their parents' radio show. Their first recordings with Chet Atkins in 1957 were unsuccessful. They subsequently signed to Cadence in the same year. In 1973 they split but reunited in 1983. They were inducted into the Rock & Roll Hall of Fame in 1986 and also have a star on the Hollywood Walk of Fame.

02/07/1960 ..... 2 ...... 23 ...... **IT'S EVERLY TIME** ................................................. Warner Brothers WM 4006
15/10/1960 ..... 4 ...... 11 ...... **FABULOUS STYLE OF THE EVERLY BROTHERS** ................................................. London HAA 2266
04/03/1961 ..... 3 ...... 14 ...... **A DATE WITH THE EVERLY BROTHERS** ................................................. Warner Brothers WM 4028
21/07/1962 ..... 20 ...... 1 ...... INSTANT PARTY ................................................. Warner Brothers WM 4061
12/09/1970 ..... 7 ...... 16 ...... **ORIGINAL GREATEST HITS** ................................................. CBS 66255
08/06/1974 ..... 43 ...... 1 ...... THE VERY BEST OF THE EVERLY BROTHERS ................................................. Warner Brothers K 46008
29/11/1975 ..... 10 ...... 10 ...... ✪ **WALK RIGHT BACK WITH THE EVERLYS** ................................................. Warner Brothers K 56118
09/04/1977 ..... 12 ...... 10 ...... LIVING LEGENDS ................................................. Warwick WW 5027
18/12/1982 ..... 22 ...... 22 ...... ● LOVE HURTS ................................................. K-Tel NE 1197
07/01/1984 ..... 47 ...... 6 ...... ○ EVERLY BROTHERS REUNION CONCERT – LIVE AT THE ROYAL ALBERT HALL ................................................. Impression IMDP 1
03/11/1984 ..... 36 ...... 4 ...... THE EVERLY BROTHERS ................................................. Mercury MERH 44
29/05/1993 ..... 26 ...... 5 ...... ○ THE GOLDEN YEARS OF THE EVERLY BROTHERS – THEIR 24 GREATEST HITS ................................................. Warner Brothers 9548319922
01/06/2002 ..... 10 ...... 7 ...... ○ **THE DEFINITIVE** ................................................. WSM 0927473042

### EVERYTHING BUT THE GIRL UK duo Tracey Thorn (born 26/9/1962, Brookman's Park, vocals) and Ben Watt (born 6/12/1962, London, guitars/keyboards/vocals) who were introduced in 1982 and debuted in 1983. Their name came from a second-hand furniture store in Hull (where both attended university). Thorn was also in Marine Girls.

16/06/1984 ..... 14 ...... 22 ...... ● EDEN ................................................. Blanco Y Negro BYN 2
27/04/1985 ..... 10 ...... 9 ...... ● **LOVE NOT MONEY** ................................................. Blanco Y Negro BYN 3
06/09/1986 ..... 22 ...... 9 ...... ● BABY THE STARS SHINE BRIGHT ................................................. Blanco Y Negro BYN 9
12/03/1988 ..... 13 ...... 9 ...... ● IDLEWILD ................................................. Blanco Y Negro BYN 14
06/08/1988 ..... 21 ...... 6 ...... IDLEWILD ................................................. Blanco Y Negro BYN 16
17/02/1990 ..... 10 ...... 6 ...... ● **THE LANGUAGE OF LOVE** ................................................. Blanco Y Negro BYN 21

▲⁹ Number of weeks album topped the US chart   ◆¹² RIAA Diamond Awards   ◇³ IFPI Platinum Europe Awards

| DATE | POS | WKS | BPI | ALBUM TITLE | LABEL & NUMBER |
|------|-----|-----|-----|-------------|----------------|
| 05/10/1991 | 29 | 5 | | WORLD WIDE | Blanco Y Negro BYN 25 |
| 22/05/1993 | 5 | 8 | ● | **HOME MOVIES – THE BEST OF EVERYTHING BUT THE GIRL** | Blanco Y Negro 4509923192 |
| 25/06/1994 | 20 | 15 | ● | AMPLIFIED HEART | Blanco Y Negro 4509964822 |
| 18/05/1996 | 4 | 27 | ✪ | **WALKING WOUNDED** | Blanco Y Negro CDV 2803 |
| 09/11/1996 | 23 | 12 | ✪ | THE BEST OF EVERYTHING BUT THE GIRL | Blanco Y Negro 0630166372 |
| 09/10/1999 | 16 | 3 | | TEMPERAMENTAL | Blanco Y Negro CDV 2892 |
| 02/11/2002 | 58 | 1 | | LIKE THE DESERTS MISS THE RAIN | Virgin CDV 2966 |

**EXODUS** US rock group formed in San Francisco, CA in 1982 by Paul Baloff (vocals), Gary Holt (guitar), Kirk Hammett (guitar), Rick Hunolt (guitar), Rob McKillop (bass) and Tom Hunting (drums), although Hammett left before they recorded their debut album. Baloff left after the album, was replaced by Steve Sousa, and then Hunting left to be replaced by John Tempesta. They disbanded in 1992.

| DATE | POS | WKS | BPI | ALBUM TITLE | LABEL & NUMBER |
|------|-----|-----|-----|-------------|----------------|
| 11/02/1989 | 67 | 1 | | FABULOUS DISASTER | Music For Nations MFN 90 |

**EXPLOITED** UK punk-rock group formed in East Kilbride in 1979 by Wattie Buchan (vocals), Gary McCormick (bass), Big John Duncan (guitar) and Dru Stix Campbell (drums).

| DATE | POS | WKS | BPI | ALBUM TITLE | LABEL & NUMBER |
|------|-----|-----|-----|-------------|----------------|
| 16/05/1981 | 20 | 11 | | PUNK'S NOT DEAD | Secret SEC 1 |
| 14/11/1981 | 52 | 3 | | EXPLOITED LIVE | Superville EXPLP 2001 |
| 19/06/1982 | 17 | 12 | | TROOPS OF TOMORROW | Secret SEC 8 |

**EXTREME** US metal/funk quartet formed in Boston, MA in 1985 by Gary Cherone (born 24/7/1961, Malden, MA, vocals) and Paul Geary (born 2/7/1961, Medford, MA, drums), both ex-Dream, and Sinful member Nuno Bettencourt (born 20/9/1966, Azores, Portugal). Pat Badger (born 22/7/1967, Boston, bass) joined in 1986. They were signed to A&M on the strength of winning an MTV video contest. Cherone later joined Van Halen as lead singer.

| DATE | POS | WKS | BPI | ALBUM TITLE | LABEL & NUMBER |
|------|-----|-----|-----|-------------|----------------|
| 01/06/1991 | 12 | 61 | ✪ | EXTREME II PORNAGRAFFITTI | A&M 3953131 |
| 26/09/1992 | 2 | 11 | ● | **III SIDES TO EVERY STORY** | A&M 5400062 |
| 11/02/1995 | 10 | 3 | | **WAITING FOR THE PUNCHLINE** | A&M 5403052 |

**E.Y.C.** US vocal group formed by Damon Butler, David Loeffler, Trey Parker, Marlen Landin and rapper Gangsta Ridd. The name stands for Express Yourself Clearly.

| DATE | POS | WKS | BPI | ALBUM TITLE | LABEL & NUMBER |
|------|-----|-----|-----|-------------|----------------|
| 16/04/1994 | 14 | 5 | | EXPRESS YOURSELF CLEARLY | MCA MCD 11061 |

# F

**ADAM F** UK drum and bass producer (born Adam Fenton, 8/2/1972, Liverpool), son of singer Shane Fenton (aka Alvin Stardust), who launched the F-Jam label.

| | | | |
|---|---|---|---|
| 15/11/1997 | 47 | 1 | COLOURS 1998 MOBO Award for Best Album . . . . . . . . . . . . . . . . . . . . . . . . . . . . . . . . . . . . . . . . . . . . . . . Positiva 8217252 |
| 22/09/2001 | 44 | 2 | KAOS – THE ANTI ACOUSTIC WARFARE . . . . . . . . . . . . . . . . . . . . . . . . . . . . . . . . . . . . . . . . . . . . . . . Chrysalis 5342502 |

**F.A.B.** UK production group formed by Rod Anderson and Jason Mayo.

| | | | | |
|---|---|---|---|---|
| 10/11/1990 | 53 | 3 | O | POWER THEMES 90 . . . . . . . . . . . . . . . . . . . . . . . . . . . . . . . . . . . . . . . . . . . . . . . . . . . . . . . . . . . . . . . Telstar STAR 2430 |

**FABOLOUS** US rapper (born John Jackson, 18/11/1979, Brooklyn, NYC).

| | | | |
|---|---|---|---|
| 02/08/2003 | 51 | 10 | STREET DREAMS . . . . . . . . . . . . . . . . . . . . . . . . . . . . . . . . . . . . . . . . . . . . . . . . . . . . . . . . . . . . . Elektra 7559627912 |

**FACES** UK rock group formed in 1969 by members of the Small Faces and Jeff Beck Group, comprising Rod Stewart (born 10/1/1945, London, lead vocals), Ronnie Lane (born 1/4/1946, London, guitar), Kenny Jones (born 16/9/1948, London, drums), Ron Wood (born 1/6/1947, Hillingdon, guitar) and Ian McLagan (born 12/5/1945, Hounslow, keyboards), with Art Wood (Ron's elder brother), Long John Baldry and Jimmy Horowitz augmenting the line-up. Initially known as Quiet Melon, they changed their name in 1971. Lane left in 1973 and was replaced by Tetsu Yamauchi (ex-Free bass player). Jones joined The Who in 1978. Stewart signed a solo contract at the time the Faces were formed, consequently the billing was often Rod Stewart & The Faces. The group eventually disbanded in 1975. Wood joined The Rolling Stones in 1976. Lane died from multiple sclerosis on 4/6/1997.

| | | | | |
|---|---|---|---|---|
| 04/04/1970 | 45 | 1 | | FIRST STEP . . . . . . . . . . . . . . . . . . . . . . . . . . . . . . . . . . . . . . . . . . . . . . . . . . . . . . . . . . . . . . . . . Warner Brothers WS 3000 |
| 08/05/1971 | 31 | 7 | | LONG PLAYER . . . . . . . . . . . . . . . . . . . . . . . . . . . . . . . . . . . . . . . . . . . . . . . . . . . . . . . . . . . . . . . . Warner Brothers W 3011 |
| 25/12/1971 | 2 | 22 | | **A NOD'S AS GOOD AS A WINK... TO A BLIND HORSE** . . . . . . . . . . . . . . . . . . . . . . . . . . . . . . . . . . . . . . Warner Brothers K 56006 |
| 21/04/1973 | ❶[1] | 13 | | OOH-LA-LA . . . . . . . . . . . . . . . . . . . . . . . . . . . . . . . . . . . . . . . . . . . . . . . . . . . . . . . . . . . . . . . . . Warner Brothers K 56011 |
| 26/01/1974 | 3 | 7 | | OVERTURE AND BEGINNERS **ROD STEWART AND THE FACES** . . . . . . . . . . . . . . . . . . . . . . . . . . . . . . . . Mercury 9100 001 |
| 21/05/1977 | 24 | 6 | | THE BEST OF THE FACES . . . . . . . . . . . . . . . . . . . . . . . . . . . . . . . . . . . . . . . . . . . . . . . . . . . . . . . . . . . . . Riva RVLP 3 |
| 07/11/1992 | 58 | 1 | | THE BEST OF ROD STEWART AND THE FACES 1971–1975 . . . . . . . . . . . . . . . . . . . . . . . . . . . . . . . . . . . Mercury 5141802 |
| 01/11/2003 | 13 | 5 | ● | CHANGING FACES – THE VERY BEST OF This and the above hit credited to **ROD STEWART AND THE FACES** . . . . Universal TV 9812604 |

**DONALD FAGEN** US singer/keyboard player (born 10/1/1948, Passiac, NJ) who first teamed up with long-time musical partner Walker Becker while they were still students, both backing Jay & The Americans before launching Steely Dan in the early 1970s, basically a vehicle for the songwriting and production of Becker and Fagen. They split in 1981, and Fagen went solo. Steely Dan was revived in the late 1980s and went on to win three Grammy Awards in 2000.

| | | | | |
|---|---|---|---|---|
| 30/10/1982 | 44 | 16 | O | THE NIGHTFLY . . . . . . . . . . . . . . . . . . . . . . . . . . . . . . . . . . . . . . . . . . . . . . . . . . . . . . . . . . . . . . Warner Brothers 9236961 |
| 05/06/1993 | 3 | 9 | ● | **KAMAKIRIAD** . . . . . . . . . . . . . . . . . . . . . . . . . . . . . . . . . . . . . . . . . . . . . . . . . . . . . . . . . . . . . . . . . Reprise 9362452302 |

**FAIRGROUND ATTRACTION** UK skiffle-style group formed in Scotland by Eddi Reader (born 28/8/1959, Glasgow, vocals), Mark Nevin (guitar), Simon Edwards (bass) and Roy Dodds (drums). They won two BRIT Awards in 1989 including Best Single for *Perfect*. Reader later recorded solo.

| | | | | |
|---|---|---|---|---|
| 28/05/1988 | 2 | 52 | ✪[2] | **THE FIRST OF A MILLION KISSES** 1989 BRIT Award for Best Album . . . . . . . . . . . . . . . . . . . . . . . . . . . . . . . . . . RCA PL 71696 |
| 30/06/1990 | 55 | 2 | | AY FOND KISS . . . . . . . . . . . . . . . . . . . . . . . . . . . . . . . . . . . . . . . . . . . . . . . . . . . . . . . . . . . . . . . . . . . RCA PL 74596 |

**FAIRPORT CONVENTION** UK group formed in London in 1966 by Ashley Hutchings (born 26/1/1945, London, bass), Simon Nicol (born 13/10/1950, London, guitar), Richard Thompson (born 3/4/1949, London, bass), Judy Dyble (born 13/2/1949, London, vocals), Ian Matthews (born 16/6/1946, Scunthorpe, vocals) and Shaun Frater (drums) as the Ethnic Shuffle Orchestra. Frater left after one concert and was replaced by Martin Lamble (born 28/8/1949, London). Dyble left in 1968 and was replaced by Sandy Denny (born 6/1/1947, London). Lamble was killed on 14/5/1969 in a group van accident; Dave Mattacks (born March 1948, London) was his replacement. Numerous additional changes before they split in 1979 have been followed by many reunions since. Denny died of a brain haemorrhage on 21/4/1978.

| | | | |
|---|---|---|---|
| 02/08/1969 | 12 | 8 | UNHALFBRICKING. . . . . . . . . . . . . . . . . . . . . . . . . . . . . . . . . . . . . . . . . . . . . . . . . . . . . . . . . . . . . . . Island ILPS 9102 |
| 17/01/1970 | 17 | 15 | LIEGE AND LIEF . . . . . . . . . . . . . . . . . . . . . . . . . . . . . . . . . . . . . . . . . . . . . . . . . . . . . . . . . . . . . . . Island ILPS 9115 |
| 18/07/1970 | 13 | 11 | FULL HOUSE. . . . . . . . . . . . . . . . . . . . . . . . . . . . . . . . . . . . . . . . . . . . . . . . . . . . . . . . . . . . . . . . . . Island ILPS 9130 |
| 03/07/1971 | 8 | 5 | **ANGEL DELIGHT** . . . . . . . . . . . . . . . . . . . . . . . . . . . . . . . . . . . . . . . . . . . . . . . . . . . . . . . . . . . . . . . Island ILPS 9162 |
| 12/07/1975 | 52 | 1 | RISING FOR THE MOON . . . . . . . . . . . . . . . . . . . . . . . . . . . . . . . . . . . . . . . . . . . . . . . . . . . . . . . . . . Island ILPS 9313 |
| 28/01/1989 | 74 | 1 | RED AND GOLD . . . . . . . . . . . . . . . . . . . . . . . . . . . . . . . . . . . . . . . . . . . . . . . . . . . . . . . . . . . . . . New Routes RUE 002 |

**ADAM FAITH** UK singer (born Terence Nelhams, 23/6/1940, Acton, London) who first worked as assistant film editor for Rank Screen Service. His skiffle group made up of fellow workmates appeared on TV's *6.5 Special*; Faith went solo and signed with EMI in

1957. He acted in films (including *Beat Girl*, 1961) and TV shows (including *Budgie* and *Love Hurts*), produced Roger Daltrey's first solo album and managed Leo Sayer. He died from a heart attack on 8/3/2003.

| | | | | | |
|---|---|---|---|---|---|
| 19/11/1960 | 6 | 36 | | **ADAM** | Parlophone PMC 1128 |
| 11/02/1961 | 11 | 3 | | BEAT GIRL Original soundtrack to the film | Columbia 33SX 1225 |
| 24/03/1962 | 20 | 1 | | ADAM FAITH | Parlophone PMC 1162 |
| 25/09/1965 | 19 | 1 | | FAITH ALIVE | Parlophone PMC 1249 |
| 19/12/1981 | 61 | 3 | | 20 GOLDEN GREATS | Warwick WW 5113 |
| 27/11/1993 | 43 | 2 | | MIDNIGHT POSTCARDS | Polygram TV 8213982 |

**FAITH BROTHERS** UK group formed by Billy Franks (guitar/vocals), Lee Hirons (bass), Mark Hirons (guitar), Steve Howlett (drums), Will Tipper (trumpet), Henry Trezise (keyboards) and Mark Waterman (saxophone).

| | | | | | |
|---|---|---|---|---|---|
| 09/11/1985 | 66 | 1 | | EVENTIDE | Siren SIRENLP 1 |

**FAITH NO MORE** US rock group formed in San Francisco, CA in 1980 by Billy Gould (born 24/4/1963, Los Angeles, CA, bass), Roddy Bottum (born 1/7/1963, Los Angeles, keyboards), Mike 'Puffy' Bordin (born 27/11/1962, San Francisco, drums) and Jim Martin (born 21/7/1961, Oakland, CA, guitar), and named after a greyhound on which they had placed a bet. Singer Chuck Mosely joined in 1983 but was replaced by Mike Patton (born 27/1/1968, Eureka, CA) in 1988. Signed to Mordam in 1984, then Warners' subsidiary Slash in 1986, they split in 1998.

| | | | | | |
|---|---|---|---|---|---|
| 17/02/1990 | 30 | 35 | ○ | THE REAL THING | Slash 8281541 |
| 16/02/1991 | 20 | 4 | | LIVE AT THE BRIXTON ACADEMY | Slash 8282381 |
| 20/06/1992 | 2 | 25 | ○ | ANGEL DUST | Slash 8283212 |
| 25/03/1995 | 5 | 6 | ● | **KING FOR A DAY, FOOL FOR A LIFETIME** | Slash 8285602 |
| 21/06/1997 | 7 | 3 | | **ALBUM OF THE YEAR** | Slash 8288022 |
| 21/11/1998 | 37 | 1 | ○ | WHO CARES A LOT? – THE GREATEST HITS | Slash 5560522 |

**MARIANNE FAITHFULL** UK singer (born 29/12/1946, London) discovered by Rolling Stones manager Andrew Loog Oldham. Her debut hit was a Jagger/Richards song. She married artist John Dunbar in 1965, then later Vibrators' bass player Ben Brierly and writer Giorgio Della Terza, and also had a long relationship with Mick Jagger. She appeared in a number of films.

| | | | | | |
|---|---|---|---|---|---|
| 05/06/1965 | 12 | 7 | | COME MY WAY | Decca LK 4688 |
| 05/06/1965 | 15 | 2 | | MARIANNE FAITHFULL | Decca LK 4689 |
| 24/11/1979 | 57 | 3 | | BROKEN ENGLISH | Island M1 |
| 17/10/1981 | 45 | 4 | | DANGEROUS ACQUAINTANCES | Island ILPS 9648 |
| 26/03/1983 | 99 | 1 | | A CHILD'S ADVENTURE | Island ILPS 9734 |
| 08/08/1987 | 78 | 2 | | STRANGE WEATHER | Island ILPS 9874 |

**FAITHLESS** UK group formed in 1995 by producer Rollo (born Roland Armstrong), DJ Sister Bliss (born Ayalah Ben-Tovim), singer Jamie Catto and rapper Maxi Jazz (born Max Fraser). Ex-Dusted Rollo had previously recorded as Rollo Goes Mystic and Rollo Goes Camping, and written with his sister Dido.

| | | | | | |
|---|---|---|---|---|---|
| 23/11/1996 | 26 | 14 | ● | REVERENCE | Cheeky CHEKLP 500 |
| 03/10/1998 | 10 | 7 | ● | **SUNDAY 8PM** | Cheeky CHEKCD 503 |
| 30/06/2001 | 4 | 22 | ● | **OUTROSPECTIVE** | Cheeky 74321862802 |
| 19/06/2004 | ❶[1] | 2+ | | **NO ROOTS** | Cheeky 82876618702 |

**FALCO** Austrian singer (born Johann Holzel, 19/2/1957, Vienna) was killed in a car crash in the Dominican Republic on 6/2/1998.

| | | | | | |
|---|---|---|---|---|---|
| 26/04/1986 | 32 | 15 | | FALCO 3 | A&M AMA 5105 |

**FALL** UK group formed in Manchester in 1977 by Mark E Smith (born 5/3/1957, Manchester, vocals), Martin Bramah (guitar), Una Baines (keyboards), Tony Friel (bass) and Karl Burns (drums). Smith's wife Brix joined in 1983 and left in 1989. Smith is the only original member left in the group.

| | | | | | |
|---|---|---|---|---|---|
| 20/03/1982 | 71 | 3 | | THE EDUCATION HOUR | Kamera KAM 005 |
| 20/10/1984 | 62 | 2 | | THE WONDERFUL AND FRIGHTENING WORLD OF | Beggars Banquet BEGA 58 |
| 05/10/1985 | 54 | 2 | | THIS NATION'S SAVING GRACE | Beggars Banquet BEGA 67 |
| 11/10/1986 | 36 | 3 | | BEND SINISTER | Beggars Banquet BEGA 75 |
| 12/03/1988 | 19 | 4 | | THE FRENZ EXPERIMENT | Beggars Banquet BEGA 91 |
| 12/11/1988 | 54 | 2 | | I AM KURIOUS, ORANJ | Beggars Banquet BEGA 96 |
| 08/07/1989 | 40 | 2 | | SEMINAL LIVE | Beggars Banquet BBL 102 |
| 03/03/1990 | 31 | 3 | | EXTRICATE | Cog Sinister 8422041 |
| 15/09/1990 | 44 | 2 | | 458489 A-SIDES | Beggars Banquet BEGA 111 |
| 04/05/1991 | 17 | 2 | | SHIFT-WORK | Cog Sinister 8485941 |
| 28/03/1992 | 21 | 1 | | CODE-SELFISH | Cog Sinister 5121622 |
| 08/05/1993 | 9 | 3 | | **INFOTAINMENT SCAN** | Permanent PERMCD 12 |
| 14/05/1994 | 48 | 1 | | MIDDLE CLASS REVOLT | Permanent PERMCD 16 |
| 11/03/1995 | 67 | 1 | | CEREBRAL CAUSTIC | Permanent PERMCD 30 |

22/06/1996 . . . . . 54 . . . . . . 1 . . . . . .     THE LIGHT USER SYNDROME . . . . . . . . . . . . . . . . . . . . . . . . . . . . . . . . . . . . . . . . . . . . . . . . . . . . . . . . . . . . . . . Jet JETLP 1012

### AGNETHA FALTSKOG
Swedish singer (born 5/4/1950, Jonkoping) who signed with CBS at seventeen and had a Swedish #1 with *I Was So In Love*. She appeared in the Swedish production of *Jesus Christ Superstar* before meeting Bjorn Ulvaeus in 1969 and marrying him in 1971. They formed ABBA in 1972 with Benny Andersson and Frida Lyngstad. They disbanded in 1982 and Agnetha went solo. She divorced Bjorn in 1979, married surgeon Tomas Sonnenfield in 1990 and retired from the record industry, although she returned in 2004.

| | | | | | |
|---|---|---|---|---|---|
| 11/06/1983 | 18 | 13 | | WRAP YOUR ARMS AROUND ME | Epic EPC 25505 |
| 04/05/1985 | 38 | 3 | | EYES OF A WOMAN | Epic EPC 26446 |
| 12/03/1988 | 72 | 1 | | I STAND ALONE | WEA WX 150 |
| 01/05/2004 | 12 | 4 | ○ | MY COLOURING BOOK | WEA 5046731222 |

### GEORGIE FAME
UK singer/pianist (born Clive Powell, 26/9/1943, Leigh) who was signed and given his stage name by manager Larry Parnes after doing holiday camp gigs in 1959. His first recording was backing Gene Vincent on *Pistol Packin' Mama* in 1960. In 1961 he joined Billy Fury's group the Blue Flames. He went on to lead the Blue Flames until 1966, thereafter fronting various ensembles. By 2001 he was a member of Bill Wyman's Rhythm Kings.

*The two faces of Fame*

| | | | | | |
|---|---|---|---|---|---|
| 17/10/1964 | 15 | 8 | | FAME AT LAST | Columbia 33SX 1638 |
| 14/05/1966 | 6 | 22 | | **SWEET THINGS** | Columbia SX 6043 |
| 15/10/1966 | 9 | 9 | | **SOUND VENTURE** | Columbia SX 6076 |
| 11/03/1967 | 12 | 18 | | HALL OF FAME | Columbia SX 6120 |
| 01/07/1967 | 22 | 15 | | TWO FACES OF FAME | CBS DBPG 63018 |

### FAMILY
UK rock group formed in Leicester as the Farinas in 1966, evolving into Family in 1967 with Roger Chapman (born 8/4/1942, Leicester, vocals), Charlie Whitney (born 24/6/1944, Skipton, guitar), Ron Townsend (born 7/7/1947, Leicester, drums), Rick Grech (born 1/11/1946, Bordeaux, France, violin/bass) and John 'Poli' Palmer (born 25/5/1942, keyboards). Grech left in 1969 and was replaced by John Weider (born 21/4/1947). Weider left in 1971 and was replaced by John Wetton. Palmer and Wetton left in 1972 and were replaced by Tony Ashton (born 1/3/1946, Blackburn) and Jim Cregan. They disbanded in 1973. Grech died from kidney and liver failure on 16/3/1990 and Ashton died from cancer on 28/5/2001.

| | | | | | |
|---|---|---|---|---|---|
| 10/08/1968 | 35 | 3 | | MUSIC IN THE DOLLS HOUSE | Reprise RLP 6312 |
| 22/03/1969 | 6 | 3 | | **FAMILY ENTERTAINMENT** | Reprise RLP 6340 |
| 07/02/1970 | 4 | 13 | | **A SONG FOR ME** | Reprise RSLP 9001 |
| 28/11/1970 | 7 | 7 | | **ANYWAY** | Reprise RSX 9005 |
| 20/11/1971 | 14 | 2 | | FEARLESS | Reprise K 54003 |
| 30/09/1972 | 15 | 10 | | BANDSTAND | Reprise K 54006 |
| 29/09/1973 | 30 | 3 | | IT'S ONLY A MOVIE | Raft RA 58501 |

### FAMILY CAT
UK group formed in Yeovil in 1988 by Paul Frederick (guitar/vocals), Steven Jelbert (guitar), Tim McVey (guitar), John Graves (bass) and Kevin Downing (drums).

| | | | | | |
|---|---|---|---|---|---|
| 04/07/1992 | 55 | 1 | | FURTHEST FROM THE SUN | Dedicated DEDCD 007 |

### FAMILY STAND
US group formed in 1986 by Peter Lord (vocals/keyboards), V Jeffrey Smith (guitar/ bass/flute/saxophone/ vocals/drum programmes) and Sandra St Victor (vocals) as The Stand. Lord and Smith later produced Goodfellaz, among others.

| | | | | | |
|---|---|---|---|---|---|
| 19/05/1990 | 52 | 3 | | CHAIN | Atlantic WX 349 |

### CHRIS FARLOWE
UK singer (born John Henry Deighton, 13/10/1940, London) and talent contest winner in 1957 with the John Henry Skiffle Group. Fronting the Thunderbirds from 1962, he later signed solo with Andrew Loog Oldham's Immediate label. Also ex-lead singer with Colosseum and Atomic Rooster, when not singing he runs a shop in Islington, London.

| | | | | | |
|---|---|---|---|---|---|
| 02/04/1966 | 19 | 1 | | 14 THINGS TO THINK ABOUT | Immediate IMLP 005 |
| 10/12/1966 | 37 | 2 | | THE ART OF CHRIS FARLOWE | Immediate IMLP 006 |

### FARM
UK group formed in Liverpool in 1983 by Peter Hooton (born 28/9/1962, Liverpool, lead vocals) and Steve Grimes (born 4/6/1962, Liverpool, guitar) as the Excitements, with Roy Boulter (born 2/7/1964, Liverpool, drums), Carl Hunter (born 14/4/1965, Bootle, bass), Ben Leach (born 2/5/1969, Liverpool, keyboards) and Keith Mullen (guitar). Renamed The Farm in 1984, they founded the Produce label in 1989 with £20,000 from Littlewoods pools heir Barney Moore.

| | | | | | |
|---|---|---|---|---|---|
| 16/03/1991 | ❶[1] | 17 | ● | **SPARTACUS** | Produce MILKLP 1 |

### FARMERS BOYS
UK group formed in Norwich by Baz, Frog, Mark and Stan (only using their forenames). They debuted in 1983 and disbanded in 1985.

| | | | | | |
|---|---|---|---|---|---|
| 29/10/1983 | 49 | 1 | | GET OUT AND WALK | EMI EMC 1077991 |

### JOHN FARNHAM
UK singer/actor (born 1/7/1949, Dagenham) who emigrated to Australia, having a hit there in 1968 with *Sadie The Cleaning Lady* and later joining the Little River Band.

| | | | | | |
|---|---|---|---|---|---|
| 11/07/1987 | 35 | 9 | | WHISPERING JACK | RCA PL 71224 |

**FASHION** UK group formed in Birmingham by John Mulligan (bass), Luke (guitar) and Dix (drums), later adding Tony (vocals), De Harris (vocals) and Martin Stoker (drums) to the line-up.

| | | | | | |
|---|---|---|---|---|---|
| 03/07/1982 | 10 | 16 | | FABRIQUE | Arista SPART 1185 |
| 16/06/1984 | 69 | 1 | | TWILIGHT OF IDOLS | De Stijl EPC 25909 |

**FASTER PUSSYCAT** US rock group formed in Los Angeles, CA in 1986 by Taime Downe (vocals), Greg Steele (guitar), Brent Muscat (guitar), Eric Stacy (bass) and Mark Michaels (drums), named after the Russ Meyer film *Faster Pussycat Kill! Kill!* Mick Cripps (guitar) and Kelly Nickels (bass) were both briefly members before going on to join L.A. Guns. Faster Pussycat disbanded in 1993.

| | | | | | |
|---|---|---|---|---|---|
| 16/09/1989 | 35 | 2 | | WAKE ME WHEN IT'S OVER | Elektra EKT 64 |
| 22/08/1992 | 58 | 1 | | WHIPPED! | Elektra 7559611242 |

**FASTWAY** UK rock group formed in 1982 by ex-Motorhead 'Fast' Eddie Clarke (guitar) and Pete Way (bass), with Dave King (vocals) and Jerry Shirley (drums). Way left and was replaced by Charlie McCracken. Shirley and McCracken left after their second album, Clarke re-forming in 1988 with Paul Gray (bass), Lea Hart (guitar/vocals) and Steve Clarke (drums). After one album this line-up was replaced by Eddie Clarke, Lea Hart, KB Bren (bass) and Riff Raff (drums), who disbanded after a further LP, Clarke going solo.

| | | | | | |
|---|---|---|---|---|---|
| 30/04/1983 | 43 | 2 | | FASTWAY | CBS 25359 |

**FAT BOYS** US rap group formed in Brooklyn, NYC by Darren 'The Human Beat Box' Robinson (born 10/6/1967, New York), Mark 'Prince Markie Dee' Morales and Damon 'Kolo Rock-ski' Wimbley and named after their combined weight of over 750 pounds. They appeared in the 1987 film *Disorderlies*. Robinson died from a heart attack on 10/12/1995.

| | | | | | |
|---|---|---|---|---|---|
| 03/10/1987 | 49 | 4 | | CRUSHIN' | Urban URBLP 3 |
| 30/07/1988 | 98 | 1 | | COMING BACK HARD AGAIN | Urban URBLP 13 |

**FAT JOE** US rapper (born Joseph Cartagena, The Bronx, NYC) with Puerto Rican and Cuban parents.

| | | | | | |
|---|---|---|---|---|---|
| 27/04/2002 | 19 | 10 | ○ | JEALOUS ONES STILL ENVY (J.O.S.E.) | Atlantic 7567834722 |

**FAT LADY SINGS** Irish vocal/instrumental group formed in Dublin in 1986 by Robert Hamilton (vocals), Nick Kelly (guitar/ vocals), Tim Bradhsaw (keyboards), Dermot Lynch (bass) and Nic France (drums). Hamilton left in 1991.

| | | | | | |
|---|---|---|---|---|---|
| 18/05/1991 | 50 | 1 | | TWIST | East West WX 418 |

**FAT LARRY'S BAND** US group formed in Philadelphia, PA in 1977 by drummer/singer/producer Larry James (born 2/8/1949, Philadelphia) with Theodore Cohen (guitar), Larry La Bes (bass/percussion), Terry Price (keyboards/vocals), Frederick Campbell (vocals), Alfonzo Smith (percussion/vocals) and Douglas Jones (saxophone/vocals). James died from a heart attack on 5/12/1987.

| | | | | | |
|---|---|---|---|---|---|
| 09/10/1982 | 58 | 4 | | BREAKIN' OUT | WMOT V 2229 |

**FATBACK BAND** US funk group formed in the late 1960s by Bill Curtis (born 1932, Fayetteville, NC, drums/percussion) as a house band for his Fatback Records. Closing the label in 1972, he signed the group to New York-based Perception Records, then to Event (via Spring) in 1973. Initially they featured Curtis, Johnny King (guitar), Johnny Flippin (bass), George Adams (trumpet), Earl Shelton (saxophone), Wayne Woolford (congas), Artie Simmons (trombone), Gerry Thomas (keyboards) and two backing singers. Shortening their name to Fatback in 1982, they added Michael Walker (vocals) and also recorded with Evelyn Thomas. Fatback is a style of drumming.

| | | | | | |
|---|---|---|---|---|---|
| 06/03/1976 | 19 | 6 | | RAISING HELL | Polydor 2391 203 |
| 04/07/1987 | 80 | 1 | | FATBACK LIVE | Start STL 12 |

**FATBOY SLIM** UK singer Norman Cook (born Quentin Cook, 31/7/1963, Brighton) and former member of the Housemartins; he recorded solo and formed Beats International and Freakpower. He also records as Pizzaman and The Mighty Dub Katz. He married DJ Zoe Ball in August 1999. Named Best Dance Act at the 1999 and 2001 BRIT Awards, he was also cited as the Best Dance Act at the 1999 MTV Europe Music Awards, and won the 2001 Grammy for Best Short Form Music Video with Bootsy Collins for *Weapon Of Choice*.

| | | | | | |
|---|---|---|---|---|---|
| 28/09/1996 | 69 | 3 | | BETTER LIVING THROUGH CHEMISTRY | Skint BRASSIC 2CD |
| 31/10/1998 | ●⁴ | 86 | ✪³ | YOU'VE COME A LONG WAY, BABY ◇² | Skint BRASSIC 11CD |
| 18/11/2000 | 8 | 22 | ✪ | HALFWAY BETWEEN THE GUTTER AND THE STARS | Skint BRASSIC 20CD |

○ Silver disc ● Gold disc ✪ Platinum disc (additional platinum units are indicated by a figure following the symbol) ●⁹ Number of weeks album topped the UK chart

### FATHER ABRAHAM AND THE SMURFS
Dutch novelty act assembled by Pierre Kartner that became extremely popular in Holland in the early 1970s and broke into the UK charts when the Smurfs cartoon characters achieved popularity. They were revived in 1996.

| | | | | | |
|---|---|---|---|---|---|
| 25/11/1978 | 19 | 11 | ● | FATHER ABRAHAM IN SMURFLAND | Decca SMURF 1 |
| 06/07/1996 | 2 | 33 | ✪² | **THE SMURFS GO POP!** | EMI TV CDEMTV 121 |
| 16/11/1996 | 8 | 9 | ✪ | **SMURF'S CHRISTMAS PARTY** | EMI TV CDEMTV 140 |
| 22/02/1997 | 2 | 11 | ● | **THE SMURFS HITS '97 – VOLUME 1** | EMI TV CDEMTV 150 |
| 06/09/1997 | 15 | 7 | | GO POP! AGAIN | EMI CDEMTV 155 |
| 18/04/1998 | 28 | 6 | | GREATEST HITS This and the above four hits credited to **THE SMURFS** | EMI 4941952 |

### FATIMA MANSIONS
Irish rock group formed by ex-Microdisney member Cathal Coughlan (vocals) with Andreas O'Gruama (guitar), first recording for Kitchenware and named after a housing estate in Dublin.

| | | | | | |
|---|---|---|---|---|---|
| 06/06/1992 | 52 | 1 | | VALHALLA AVENUE | Radioactive KWCD 18 |

### FAWLTY TOWERS
UK TV comedy written by John Cleese (born 27/10/1939, Weston-super-Mare) and his then wife Connie Booth (born 1944, Indianapolis, IN), who played Basil Fawlty and Polly respectively, Prunella Scales (born 22/6/1932, Sutton Abinger, Surrey) as Sybil Fawlty and Andrew Sachs (born 7/4/1930, Berlin, Germany) as Manuel. Cleese had previously been a member of Monty Python's Flying Circus.

| | | | | | |
|---|---|---|---|---|---|
| 15/12/1979 | 25 | 10 | ○ | FAWLTY TOWERS Features the episodes *Mrs Richards* and *Hotel Inspectors* | BBC REB 377 |
| 07/02/1981 | 26 | 7 | | FAWLTY TOWERS SECOND SITTING (TV ORIGINAL CAST) Features the episodes *The Rat* and *The Builders* | BBC REB 405 |

### FEAR FACTORY
US rock group formed in Los Angeles, CA in 1991 by Burton Bell (vocals), Dino Cazares (guitar), Andrew Shives (bass) and Raymond Herrera (drums).

| | | | | | |
|---|---|---|---|---|---|
| 01/07/1995 | 27 | 1 | | DEMANUFACTURE | Roadrunner RR 89565 |
| 14/06/1997 | 22 | 1 | | REMANUFACTURE – CLONING TECHNOLOGY | Roadrunner RR 88342 |
| 08/08/1998 | 20 | 2 | | OBSOLETE | Roadrunner RR 87525 |
| 05/05/2001 | 24 | 2 | | DIGIMORTAL | Roadrunner RR 85615 |
| 01/05/2004 | 41 | 1 | | ARCHETYPE | Roadrunner RR 83115 |

### PHIL FEARON AND GALAXY
UK singer (born 30/7/1950, Jamaica) who was lead vocalist with Kandidate before launching Galaxy in the early 1980s, then going solo in 1986.

| | | | | | |
|---|---|---|---|---|---|
| 25/08/1984 | 8 | 8 | | **PHIL FEARON AND GALAXY** | Ensign ENCL 2 |
| 14/09/1985 | 98 | 1 | | THIS KIND OF LOVE | Ensign ENCL 4 |

### FEEDER
UK group formed in Newport, Wales in 1992 by Grant Nicholas (guitar/vocals) and Jon Lee (drums), with Japanese bassist Taka Hirose joining later. Lee committed suicide on 7/1/2002, hanging himself in Miami, allegedly taking revenge on his wife after she refused to move to Wales.

| | | | | | |
|---|---|---|---|---|---|
| 31/05/1997 | 65 | 1 | ○ | POLYTHENE | Echo ECHCD 015 |
| 11/09/1999 | 8 | 3 | ● | **YESTERDAY WENT TOO SOON** | Echo ECHCD 28 |
| 05/05/2001 | 5 | 9 | ✪ | **ECHO PARK** | Echo ECHCD 34 |
| 02/11/2002 | 6 | 31 | ✪ | **COMFORT IN SOUND** | Echo ECHCD 43 |

### WILTON FELDER FEATURING BOBBY WOMACK
US saxophonist/bass player (born 31/8/1940, Houston, TX) and a member of The Crusaders from their inception in 1953. Womack is a US singer (born 4/3/1944, Cleveland, OH).

| | | | | | |
|---|---|---|---|---|---|
| 23/02/1985 | 77 | 3 | | SECRETS | MCA MCF 3237 |

### JOSE FELICIANO
US singer/guitarist (born 10/9/1945, Lares, Puerto Rico, raised in New York), blind from birth, he left home at eighteen for a musical career, making his debut album in 1964. Many TV appearances included *Kung Fu* and *McMillan & Wife*. He has won six Grammy Awards: Best New Artist in 1968, Best Solo Vocal Performance in 1968 for *Light My Fire*, Best Latin Pop Recording in 1983 for *Me Enamore*, Best Latin Pop Recording in 1986 for *Lelolai*, Best Latin Pop Recording in 1989 for *Cielito Lindo* and Best Latin Pop Recording in 1990 for *Por Que Te Tengo Que Olvidar?* He has a star on the Hollywood Walk of Fame.

| | | | | | |
|---|---|---|---|---|---|
| 02/11/1968 | 6 | 36 | | **FELICIANO** | RCA Victor SF 7946 |
| 29/11/1969 | 29 | 2 | | JOSE FELICIANO | RCA Victor LSP 4421 |
| 14/02/1970 | 38 | 1 | | 10 TO 23 | RCA Victor SF 7946 |
| 22/08/1970 | 65 | 1 | | FIREWORKS | RCA Victor SF 8124 |

### FELIX
UK producer/house artist (born Francis Wright, 1972, Essex). Maintaining complete anonymity, at one awards ceremony he turned up in a lion's outfit.

| | | | | | |
|---|---|---|---|---|---|
| 10/04/1993 | 26 | 4 | | FELIX #1 | Deconstruction 74321137002 |

**JULIE FELIX** US folk singer/guitarist (born 14/6/1938, Santa Barbara, CA) who moved to the UK in the mid-1960s, getting her break on TV's *The Frost Report*. She appeared in the 1980 film *Fabian*.

10/09/1966 . . . . . 27 . . . . . . 4 . . . . . . CHANGES . . . . . . . . . . . . . . . . . . . . . . . . . . . . . . . . . . . . . . . . . . . . . . . . . . . . . . . Fontana TL 5368

**IBRAHIM FERRER** Cuban singer (born 1927, Santiago) who began performing publicly at fourteen and went on to front Pacha Alonso's orchestra. After over twenty years with the band he retired in the 1980s, living on a meagre state pension and supplementing his income by shining shoes. He was lured out of retirement in 1997, going on to win the Best New Artist Award at the inaugural Latin Grammy Awards in 2000. He also won the 2003 MOBO Award for Best World Music Act and the 2003 Grammy Award for Best Traditional Tropical Latin Album *Buenos Hermanos*.

05/06/1999 . . . . . 42 . . . . . . 3 . . . . . . BUENA VISTA SOCIAL CLUB PRESENTS IBRAHIM FERRER . . . . . . . . . . . . . . . . . . . . . . . . . . . . . . . . . . . . . World Circuit WCD 055

**BRYAN FERRY** UK singer (born 26/9/1945, Washington, Tyne & Wear) who formed the Banshees in 1964 but by 1970 was a full-time teacher. Sacked for making his lessons musical ones, he formed Roxy Music in 1971 and went solo in parallel in 1973.

| 03/11/1973 | 5 | 42 | ● | THESE FOOLISH THINGS . . . . . . . . . . . . . . . . . . . . . . . . . . . . . . . . . . . . . . . . . . . . . . Island ILPS 9249 |
| 20/07/1974 | 4 | 25 | ● | ANOTHER TIME, ANOTHER PLACE . . . . . . . . . . . . . . . . . . . . . . . . . . . . . . . . . . . . . . . Island ILPS 9284 |
| 02/10/1976 | 19 | 5 | | LET'S STICK TOGETHER . . . . . . . . . . . . . . . . . . . . . . . . . . . . . . . . . . . . . . . . . . . . Island ILPSX 1 |
| 05/03/1977 | 5 | 17 | ● | IN YOUR MIND . . . . . . . . . . . . . . . . . . . . . . . . . . . . . . . . . . . . . . . . . . . . . . . . Polydor 2302 055 |
| 30/09/1978 | 13 | 5 | ○ | THE BRIDE STRIPPED BARE . . . . . . . . . . . . . . . . . . . . . . . . . . . . . . . . . . . . . . . . . Polydor POLD 5003 |
| 15/06/1985 | ❶² | 44 | ✪³ | BOYS AND GIRLS . . . . . . . . . . . . . . . . . . . . . . . . . . . . . . . . . . . . . . . . . . . . . . . E.G. EGLP 62 |
| 26/04/1986 | ❶⁵ | 77 | ✪ | STREET LIFE – 20 GREAT HITS BRYAN FERRY AND ROXY MUSIC . . . . . . . . . . . . . . . . . . . . . . . . . . E.G. EGTV 1 |
| 14/11/1987 | 9 | 16 | ● | BETE NOIRE . . . . . . . . . . . . . . . . . . . . . . . . . . . . . . . . . . . . . . . . . . . . . . . . Virgin V 2474 |
| 19/11/1988 | 6 | 35 | ✪³ | THE ULTIMATE COLLECTION BRYAN FERRY AND ROXY MUSIC . . . . . . . . . . . . . . . . . . . . . . . . . . . E.G. EGTV 2 |
| 03/04/1993 | 2 | 14 | ● | TAXI . . . . . . . . . . . . . . . . . . . . . . . . . . . . . . . . . . . . . . . . . . . . . . . . . . . Virgin CDV 2700 |
| 17/09/1994 | 11 | 4 | | MAMOUNA . . . . . . . . . . . . . . . . . . . . . . . . . . . . . . . . . . . . . . . . . . . . . . . . . Virgin CDV 2751 |
| 04/11/1995 | 15 | 15 | ✪ | MORE THAN THIS – THE BEST OF BRYAN FERRY AND ROXY MUSIC BRYAN FERRY AND ROXY MUSIC . . . . . . . . . . . Virgin CDV 2791 |
| 06/11/1999 | 16 | 10 | ● | AS TIME GOES BY . . . . . . . . . . . . . . . . . . . . . . . . . . . . . . . . . . . . . . . . . . . . . Virgin CDVIR 89 |
| 22/07/2000 | 11 | 11 | ● | SLAVE TO LOVE . . . . . . . . . . . . . . . . . . . . . . . . . . . . . . . . . . . . . . . . . . . . . . Virgin CDV 2921 |
| 11/05/2002 | 6 | 5 | ○ | FRANTIC . . . . . . . . . . . . . . . . . . . . . . . . . . . . . . . . . . . . . . . . . . . . . . . . . Virgin CDVIR 167 |
| 19/06/2004 | 17 | 2+ | ○ | PLATINUM COLLECTION BRYAN FERRY AND ROXY MUSIC . . . . . . . . . . . . . . . . . . . . . . . . . . . . . Virgin BFRM1 |

**FFWD** UK/Swiss group formed by Thomas Fehlmann, Robert Fripp (born 16/5/1946, Wimbourne), Kris Weston and Dr Alex Paterson. Paterson, Weston and Fehlmann were also members of The Orb whilst Fripp is a guitarist, composer and in-demand producer.

13/08/1994 . . . . . 48 . . . . . . 1 . . . . . . FFWD . . . . . . . . . . . . . . . . . . . . . . . . . . . . . . . . . . . . . . . . . . . . . . . . . . . . . . . . Inter INTA 001CD

**BRAD FIDEL** German arranger whose hit album was the soundtrack to the film starring Arnold Schwarzanegger. He later became a snowboard teacher and worked part time at the Anchorage Science Centre.

31/08/1991 . . . . . 26 . . . . . . 7 . . . . . . TERMINATOR 2 Original soundtrack to the film . . . . . . . . . . . . . . . . . . . . . . . . . . . . . . . . . . . Varese Sarabande VS 5335

**GRACIE FIELDS** UK singer (born Grace Stansfield, 9/1/1898, Rochdale) who first recorded in 1928, making her film debut in 1931. By 1939 she was the most popular and highest paid performer in the UK, but her marriage to Italian Monty Banks in 1940 (having divorced comedian Archie Pitt) and move to the US (Banks being threatened with World War II internment in the UK) meant a brief slump in her popularity. She returned in triumph to the Palladium theatre in 1946. Semi-retiring to Capri in 1960 with third husband Boris Alperovic, she made her last London appearance in 1978. Awarded a CBE in 1938, she was made a Dame shortly before her death on 27/9/1979. She has a star on the Hollywood Walk of Fame.

20/12/1975 . . . . . 48 . . . . . 3 . . . . . . THE GOLDEN YEARS . . . . . . . . . . . . . . . . . . . . . . . . . . . . . . . . . . . . . . . . . . . . . . . . Warwick WW 5007

**FIELDS OF THE NEPHILIM** UK rock group formed in Stevenage in 1983 by Carl McCoy (vocals), Tony Pettitt (bass), Peter Yates (guitar) and brothers Alexander 'Nod' (drums) and Paul Wright (guitar). McCoy left in 1991, retaining rights to the name. The other members regrouping with singer Alan Delaney as Rubicon.

| 30/05/1987 | 62 | 2 | | DAWNRAZOR . . . . . . . . . . . . . . . . . . . . . . . . . . . . . . . . . . . . . . . . . . . . . . . . Situation Two SITU 18 |
| 17/09/1988 | 14 | 3 | | THE NEPHILIM . . . . . . . . . . . . . . . . . . . . . . . . . . . . . . . . . . . . . . . . . . . . . . . Situation Two SITU 22 |
| 06/10/1990 | 22 | 2 | | ELIZIUM . . . . . . . . . . . . . . . . . . . . . . . . . . . . . . . . . . . . . . . . . . . . . . . . Beggars Banquet BEGA 115 |
| 06/04/1991 | 39 | 2 | | EARTH INFERNO . . . . . . . . . . . . . . . . . . . . . . . . . . . . . . . . . . . . . . . . . . . . . Beggars Banquet BEGA 120 |

**FIERCE** US R&B vocal group formed by Aisha, Chantal and Sabrina, masterminded by ex-Boogie Box High leader Andreas Georgiou.

28/08/1999 . . . . . 27 . . . . . 2 . . . . . . RIGHT HERE RIGHT NOW . . . . . . . . . . . . . . . . . . . . . . . . . . . . . . . . . . . . . . . . . . . . . . Wildstar CXWILD 14

**50 CENT** US rapper (born Curtis Jackson, 6/7/1976 Queens, NYC) whose debut album on Columbia, *Power Of The Dollar*, was planned for 2000 but, after he was shot nine times on 24/5/2000, the label dropped him. Signed with Eminem and Dr Dre's

Shady/Aftermath labels, he won three MOBO Awards in 2003 including Best Hip Hop Act and Best Single for *In Da Club*. He was then named Best International Breakthrough Act at the 2004 BRIT Awards.

01/02/2003 . . . . . 2 . . . . . . 60 . . . . . . ⊘² **GET RICH OR DIE TRYIN'** ◇ ▲⁶ 2003 MOBO Award for Best Album . . . . . . . . . . . . . . . . . . . . . . . . . . . . . . . . . . . Interscope ISC 4935442

**FILTER** US rock group formed in Chicago, IL by Richard Patrick (born 10/5/1968, Chicago, guitar), Brian Liesegang (programming), Frank Cavanagh (bass), Geno Lenardo (guitar) and Matt Walker (drums), who was later replaced by Steven Gillis.

19/04/1986 . . . . . 71 . . . . . . 1 . . . . . CHILDREN OF THE NIGHT . . . . . . . . . . . . . . . . . . . . . . . . . . . . . . . . . . . . . . . . . . . . . . . . . . . . . . . . . . 10 Records DIX 25
04/09/1999 . . . . . 75 . . . . . . 1 . . . . . TITLE OF RECORD . . . . . . . . . . . . . . . . . . . . . . . . . . . . . . . . . . . . . . . . . . . . . . . . . . . . . . . . . . . . . Reprise 9362475192
10/08/2002 . . . . . 68 . . . . . . 1 . . . . . AMALGAMUT . . . . . . . . . . . . . . . . . . . . . . . . . . . . . . . . . . . . . . . . . . . . . . . . . . . . . . . . . . . . . . . . . Reprise 9362479632

**FINE YOUNG CANNIBALS** UK group formed in 1984 by ex-Beat members Andy Cox (born 25/1/1960, Birmingham, guitar) and David Steele (born 8/9/1960, Isle of Wight, keyboards/bass) with singer Roland Gift (born 28/5/1962, Birmingham). Named after a 1960 Natalie Wood and Robert Wagner film (*All The Fine Young Cannibals*), they signed with London Records after a home video appeared on the TV music show *The Tube*. They won two BRIT awards including Best British Group at the 1990 BRIT Awards. They returned both trophies stating 'it is wrong and inappropriate for us to be associated with what amounts to a photo opportunity for Margaret Thatcher and the Conservative Party'. Gift signed solo with MCA in 2001.

21/12/1985 . . . . . 11 . . . . . 27 . . . . . . ● FINE YOUNG CANNIBALS . . . . . . . . . . . . . . . . . . . . . . . . . . . . . . . . . . . . . . . . . . . . . . . . . . . . . . London LONLP 16
18/02/1989 . . . . ❶¹ . . . . . 66 . . . . . . ⊘³ **THE RAW AND THE COOKED** ▲⁷ 1990 BRIT Award for Best Album . . . . . . . . . . . . . . . . . . . . . . . . . . . . . . . . London 8280691
15/12/1990 . . . . . 61 . . . . . . 1 . . . . . FYC . . . . . . . . . . . . . . . . . . . . . . . . . . . . . . . . . . . . . . . . . . . . . . . . . . . . . . . . . . . . . . . . . . . . . . . London 8282211
23/11/1996 . . . . . 10 . . . . . 13 . . . . . . ⊘ THE FINEST . . . . . . . . . . . . . . . . . . . . . . . . . . . . . . . . . . . . . . . . . . . . . . . . . . . . . . . . . . . . . . . . . ffrr 8288552

**FRANK FINLAY** – see **DAVID ESSEX**

**FINN** New Zealand vocal/instrumental duo of brothers Tim (born 25/6/1952, Te Awamutu) and Neil Finn (born 27/5/1958, Te Awamutu), both ex-Split Enz and Crowded House.

28/10/1995 . . . . . 15 . . . . . . 3 . . . . . FINN . . . . . . . . . . . . . . . . . . . . . . . . . . . . . . . . . . . . . . . . . . . . . . . . . . . . . . . . . . . . . . . . . . Parlophone CDFINN 1

**NEIL FINN** New Zealand guitarist/singer (born 27/5/1958, Te Awamutu) previously with Split Enz, Finn and Crowded House (all with brother Tim) before going solo.

27/06/1998 . . . . . 5 . . . . . . 11 . . . . . . ● **TRY WHISTLING THIS** . . . . . . . . . . . . . . . . . . . . . . . . . . . . . . . . . . . . . . . . . . . . . . . . . . . . . . Parlophone 4951392
21/04/2001 . . . . . 14 . . . . . . 4 . . . . . O ONE NIL . . . . . . . . . . . . . . . . . . . . . . . . . . . . . . . . . . . . . . . . . . . . . . . . . . . . . . . . . . . . . . Parlophone 5326962

**TIM FINN** New Zealand singer (born 25/6/1952, Te Awamutu) previously with Split Enz, Crowded House and Finn (all with brother Neil) before going solo.

10/07/1993 . . . . . 29 . . . . . . 2 . . . . . BEFORE AND AFTER . . . . . . . . . . . . . . . . . . . . . . . . . . . . . . . . . . . . . . . . . . . . . . . . . . . . . . . Capitol CDEST 2202

**FIRM** UK group formed in 1984 by Jimmy Page (born 9/1/1944, Heston, guitar), Paul Rodgers (born 12/12/1949, Middlesbrough, vocals), Tony Franklin (bass) and Chris Slade (born 30/10/1946, drums). Page had previously been with Led Zeppelin and worked solo, Rodgers with Free, Bad Company and worked solo, and Slade with Uriah Heep and Manfred Mann. Franklin was relatively unknown at the time of his recruitment. They disbanded after two albums, Page and Rodgers returning to their solo careers.

02/03/1985 . . . . . 15 . . . . . . 5 . . . . . THE FIRM ▲¹ . . . . . . . . . . . . . . . . . . . . . . . . . . . . . . . . . . . . . . . . . . . . . . . . . . . . . . . . . . . . Atlantic 7812391
05/04/1986 . . . . . 46 . . . . . . 3 . . . . . MEAN BUSINESS . . . . . . . . . . . . . . . . . . . . . . . . . . . . . . . . . . . . . . . . . . . . . . . . . . . . . . . . . . Atlantic WX 35

**FIRST CIRCLE** US soul group formed in New York by Albert Lee (vocals), Larry Marsden (guitar/vocals), Anthony McEwan (bass), Glenn 'Chango' Everett (drums/vocals) and Richard Sinclair (percussion) as Full Circle, changing to First Circle as the name was already taken by another group. Initial copies of the hit album were credited to Full Circle before being re-pressed as First Circle.

02/05/1987 . . . . . 70 . . . . . . 2 . . . . . BOY'S NIGHT OUT . . . . . . . . . . . . . . . . . . . . . . . . . . . . . . . . . . . . . . . . . . . . . . . . . . . . . . . EMI America AML 3118

**FISCHER-Z** UK group formed by multi-instrumentalist/songwriter John Watts. By 1982 Watts recorded solo under his own name.

23/06/1979 . . . . . 66 . . . . . . 1 . . . . . WORD SALAD . . . . . . . . . . . . . . . . . . . . . . . . . . . . . . . . . . . . . . . . . . . . . . . . . . . . . . . . . United Artists UAG 30232

**FISH** UK singer (born Derek William Dick, 25/5/1958, Dalkeith, Edinburgh) who was with Nottingham band the Stone Dome before successfully auditioning with Marillion in 1981. Fish left to go solo in September 1989.

10/02/1990 . . . . . 5 . . . . . . 6 . . . . . . O **VIGIL IN A WILDERNESS OF MIRRORS** . . . . . . . . . . . . . . . . . . . . . . . . . . . . . . . . . . . . . . . . . . EMI EMD 1015
09/11/1991 . . . . . 21 . . . . . . 3 . . . . . INTERNAL EXILE . . . . . . . . . . . . . . . . . . . . . . . . . . . . . . . . . . . . . . . . . . . . . . . . . . . . . . . . . Polydor 5110491
30/01/1993 . . . . . 46 . . . . . . 2 . . . . . SONGS FROM THE MIRROR . . . . . . . . . . . . . . . . . . . . . . . . . . . . . . . . . . . . . . . . . . . . . . . . . . . Polydor 5174992
11/06/1994 . . . . . 18 . . . . . . 2 . . . . . SUITS . . . . . . . . . . . . . . . . . . . . . . . . . . . . . . . . . . . . . . . . . . . . . . . . . . . . . . . . The Dick Brothers DDICK 004CD
16/09/1995 . . . . . 52 . . . . . . 1 . . . . . YANG . . . . . . . . . . . . . . . . . . . . . . . . . . . . . . . . . . . . . . . . . . . . . . . . . . . . . . . . . The Dick Brothers DDICK 012CD
16/09/1995 . . . . . 58 . . . . . . 1 . . . . . YIN . . . . . . . . . . . . . . . . . . . . . . . . . . . . . . . . . . . . . . . . . . . . . . . . . . . . . . . . . . The Dick Brothers DDICK 011CD
31/05/1997 . . . . . 42 . . . . . . 1 . . . . . SUNSETS ON EMPIRE . . . . . . . . . . . . . . . . . . . . . . . . . . . . . . . . . . . . . . . . . . . . . . . . . The Dick Brothers DDICK 25CD
01/05/1999 . . . . . 57 . . . . . . 1 . . . . . RAINGODS WITH ZIPPOS . . . . . . . . . . . . . . . . . . . . . . . . . . . . . . . . . . . . . . . . . . . . . . . . . . . Roadrunner RR 86772

**FISHBONE** US group formed in Los Angeles, CA by 'Big' John Bigham (born 3/3/1969, Lidsville), Chris 'Maverick Meat' Dowd (born 20/9/1965, Las Vegas, NV), John Fisher (born 9/12/1965, El Camino, CA), Philip 'Fish' Fisher (born 16/7/1967, El Camino), Kendall

Jones, 'Dirty' Walter Kibby (born 13/11/1964, Columbus, OH) and Angelo Moore (born 5/11/1965). Jones left in 1993 to join a religious sect, the rest being accused of kidnap when they tried to 'rescue' him.

| | | | | |
|---|---|---|---|---|
| 13/07/1991 | 75 | 1 | | THE REALITY OF MY SURROUNDINGS ............................................................. Columbia 4676151 |

### ELLA FITZGERALD

**ELLA FITZGERALD** US singer (born 25/4/1917, Newport News, VA) who was discovered after winning the Harlem Amateur Hour in 1934 and hired by Chick Webb. After his death in 1939 she fronted Webb's band for the next three years. Known as 'The First Lady Of Jazz', her films include *St Louis Blues* (1939) and *Pete Kelly's Blues* (1955). She won thirteen Grammy Awards including Best Individual Jazz Performance for *Ella Swings Lightly* and Best Female Vocal Performance for *But Not For Me*, both in 1959; Best Female Vocal Performance in 1960 for *Mack The Knife* (one award for the Album and one for the Single or Track); Best Female Solo Vocal Performance in 1962 for *Ella Swings Brightly With Nelson Riddle*; Best Jazz Vocal Performance in 1976 for *Fitzgerald And Pass … Again*; Best Jazz Vocal Performance in 1979 for *Fine And Mellow*; Best Female Jazz Vocal Performance in 1980 for *A Perfect Match*; Best Female Jazz Vocal Performance in 1981 for *Digital III At Montreaux*; Best Female Jazz Vocal Performance in 1983 for *The Best Is Yet To Come*; and Best Female Jazz Vocal Performance in 1990 for *All That Jazz*. She was awarded a Lifetime Achievement Grammy in 1967. After complications from diabetes she had both legs amputated below the knee in 1993, and died from a stroke on 15/6/1996. She has a star on the Hollywood Walk of Fame.

| | | | | |
|---|---|---|---|---|
| 19/07/1958 | 5 | 1 | | **ELLA FITZGERALD SINGS THE IRVING BERLIN SONG BOOK** 1958 Grammy Awards for Best Female Vocal Performance and Best Individual Jazz Performance ..................................................... HMV CLP 1183 |
| 11/06/1960 | 13 | 3 | | ELLA SINGS GERSHWIN ................................................ Brunswick LA 8648 |
| 18/06/1960 | 16 | 1 | | ELLA AT THE OPERA HOUSE ............................................. Columbia 3SX 10126 |
| 23/05/1960 | 18 | 2 | | ELLA SINGS GERSHWIN VOLUME 5 ......................................... HMV CLP 1353 |
| 10/05/1980 | 40 | 7 | | THE INCOMPARABLE ELLA .............................................. Polydor POLTV 9 |
| 27/02/1988 | 42 | 10 | ○ | A PORTRAIT OF ELLA FITZGERALD ....................................... Stylus SMR 847 |
| 19/11/1994 | 35 | 14 | ● | ESSENTIAL ELLA ................................................... Polygram TV 5239902 |
| 23/03/1996 | 19 | 6 | | FOREVER ELLA .............................................. Verve/Polygram TV 5293872 |
| 15/02/2003 | 15 | 13 | ● | GOLD ............................................................. Verve 654842 |

### FIVE

**FIVE** UK vocal group formed by James 'J' Brown (born 13/6/1976, Aldershot), Scott Robinson (born 22/11/1979, Basildon), Sean Conlon (born 20/5/1981, Leeds), Abs (born Richard Abidin Breen, 29/6/1979, Enfield) and Richard Neville (born Richard Dobson, 23/8/1979, Birmingham). They began as 5IVE, changing to Five after three singles. Named Best Pop Act at the 2000 BRIT Awards, they had previously won the Select UK & Ireland Award at the 1998 MTV Europe Music Awards. They disbanded in September 2001.

| | | | | |
|---|---|---|---|---|
| 04/07/1998 | ❶[1] | 36 | ✪ | **FIVE** ◇ ............................................................. RCA 74321589762 |
| 20/11/1999 | 4 | 39 | ✪[2] | **INVINCIBLE** ◇ ....................................................... RCA 74321713922 |
| 08/09/2001 | 3 | 11 | ● | **KINGSIZE** .......................................................... RCA 74321875972 |
| 01/12/2001 | 9 | 10 | ✪ | **GREATEST HITS** ..................................................... RCA 74321913432 |

### FIVE STAR

**FIVE STAR** UK family group formed as a trio in Romford in 1983 by Doris (born 8/6/1966, Romford), Lorraine (born 10/8/1967, Romford) and Deniece Pearson (born 13/6/1968, Romford). A successful demo prompted father Buster to launch the Tent label, adding his two sons Stedman (born 29/6/1964, Romford) and Delroy (born 11/4/1970, Romford) to the line-up, although they were still studying. Appearing as Five Star on BBC's *Pebble Mill At One* they attracted RCA, Buster informed the company that the group was already signed but that Tent as a label was available. They were named Best British Group at the 1987 BRIT Awards.

| | | | | |
|---|---|---|---|---|
| 03/08/1985 | 12 | 70 | ✪ | LUXURY OF LIFE ...................................................... Tent PL 70735 |
| 30/08/1986 | ❶[1] | 58 | ✪[4] | **SILK AND STEEL** ..................................................... Tent PL 71100 |
| 26/09/1987 | 7 | 17 | ✪ | **BETWEEN THE LINES** .................................................. Tent PL 71505 |
| 27/08/1988 | 17 | 5 | ○ | ROCK THE WORLD ...................................................... Tent PL 71747 |
| 21/10/1989 | 53 | 3 | | GREATEST HITS ....................................................... Tent PL 74080 |

### FIVE THIRTY

**FIVE THIRTY** UK group formed in London by Tara Milton (bass/vocals), Paul Bassett (guitar/vocals) and Phil Hooper (drums).

| | | | | |
|---|---|---|---|---|
| 31/08/1991 | 57 | 1 | | BED ............................................................ East West WX 530 |

### FIVEPENNY PIECE

**FIVEPENNY PIECE** UK group formed in Stalybridge, Cheshire in 1967 by Lynda Meeks (vocals), her brother John (guitar), Eddie Crotty (guitar/vocals), George Radcliffe (bass/vocals) and his brother Colin (guitar/vocals).

| | | | | |
|---|---|---|---|---|
| 24/03/1973 | 37 | 1 | | MAKING TRACKS. ..................................................... Columbia SCX 6536 |
| 03/07/1976 | 9 | 5 | | **KING COTTON** ....................................................... EMI EMC 3129 |

### FIXX

**FIXX** UK group formed in London by Cy Curnin (guitar/vocals), Jamie West-Oram (guitar), Rupert Greenall (keyboards), Charlie Barrett (bass) and Adam Woods (drums). Barrett left in 1983, was replaced by Alfred Agies who left in 1985 to be replaced by Dan K Brown.

| | | | | |
|---|---|---|---|---|
| 22/05/1982 . . . . . 54 . . . . . . 6 . . . . . . | | | | SHUTTERED ROOM . . . . . . . . . . . . . . . . . . . . . . . . . . . . . . . . . . . . . . . . . . . . . . . . . . . . . . . . . . MCA FX 1001 |
| 21/05/1983 . . . . . 91 . . . . . . 1 . . . . . . | | | | REACH THE BEACH . . . . . . . . . . . . . . . . . . . . . . . . . . . . . . . . . . . . . . . . . . . . . . . . . . . . . . . . . MCA FX 1002 |

**ROBERTA FLACK** US singer (born 10/2/1937, Black Mountain, NC) who was a university classmate of Donny Hathaway. After graduating in music, she taught at high school, singing in clubs in her spare time. She was spotted by Atlantic artist Les McCann and released her first album in 1970. She has won four Grammy Awards: Record of the Year in 1972 for *The First Time Ever I Saw Your Face*, Best Pop Vocal Performance by a Duo in 1972 with Donny Hathaway for *Where Is The Love*, and Record of the Year and Best Pop Vocal Performance in 1973 for *Killing Me Softly With His Song* .

| | | | | |
|---|---|---|---|---|
| 15/07/1972 . . . . . 47 . . . . . . 2 . . . . . . | FIRST TAKE ▲⁵ . . . . . . . . . . . . . . . . . . . . . . . . . . . . . . . . . . . . . . . . . . . . . . . . . . . . . . . . . . . Atlantic K 40040 |
| 13/10/1973 . . . . . 40 . . . . . . 2 . . . . . . | KILLING ME SOFTLY . . . . . . . . . . . . . . . . . . . . . . . . . . . . . . . . . . . . . . . . . . . . . . . . . . . . . . . Atlantic K 50021 |
| 07/06/1980 . . . . . 31 . . . . . . 7 . . . . . . | ROBERTA FLACK AND DONNY HATHAWAY **ROBERTA FLACK AND DONNY HATHAWAY** . . . . . . . . . . . . . . . . Atlantic K 50696 |
| 17/09/1983 . . . . . 15 . . . . . . 10 . . . . . . ○ | BORN TO LOVE **PEABO BRYSON AND ROBERTA FLACK** . . . . . . . . . . . . . . . . . . . . . . . . . . . . . . . . . Capitol EST 7122841 |
| 31/03/1984 . . . . . 35 . . . . . . 14 . . . . . . | ROBERTA FLACK'S GREATEST HITS . . . . . . . . . . . . . . . . . . . . . . . . . . . . . . . . . . . . . . . . . . . . . K-Tel NE 1269 |
| 19/02/1994 . . . . . 7 . . . . . . 15 . . . . . . ✪ | **SOFTLY WITH THESE SONGS – THE BEST OF ROBERTA FLACK** . . . . . . . . . . . . . . . . . . . . . . Atlantic 7567824982 |

**FLAMING LIPS** US rock group formed in Oklahoma City in 1983 by Michael Ivins (born 17/3/1965, Omaha, NE, bass/vocals), Ron Jones (born 26/11/1970, Angeles, Philippines, guitar), Mark Coyne and Wayne Coyne (born 17/3/1965, Pittsburgh, PA, guitar/ vocals). By 1999 the group comprised Ivins, Wayne Coyne and Steven Drozd (born 6/12/1969, Houston, TX, drums). They won the 2002 Grammy Award for Best Rock Instrumental Performance for *Approaching Pavonis Mons By Balloon (Utopia Planitia)*.

| | | | | |
|---|---|---|---|---|
| 29/05/1999 . . . . . 39 . . . . . . 2 . . . . . . ○ | THE SOFT BULLETIN . . . . . . . . . . . . . . . . . . . . . . . . . . . . . . . . . . . . . . . . . . . . . . . . . . . . . . . Warner Brothers 9362473932 |
| 27/07/2002 . . . . . 13 . . . . . 15 . . . . . . ● | YOSHIMI BATTLES THE PINK ROBOTS . . . . . . . . . . . . . . . . . . . . . . . . . . . . . . . . . . . . . . . . . Warner Brothers 9362481412 |

**FLASH AND THE PAN** Australian group built around George Young (born 6/11/1947, Glasgow), elder brother of AC/DC's Angus and Malcolm, and Harry Vanda (born Harold Wandon, 22/3/1947, The Hague, Holland), both of whom were ex-Easybeats and later responsible for John Paul Young's hit *Love Is In The Air*.

| | | | | |
|---|---|---|---|---|
| 16/07/1983 . . . . . 69 . . . . . . 2 . . . . . . | PAN-ORAMA . . . . . . . . . . . . . . . . . . . . . . . . . . . . . . . . . . . . . . . . . . . . . . . . . . . . . . . . . . . . Easy Beat EASLP 100 |

**FLEETWOOD MAC** UK/US rock group formed in 1967 by Mick Fleetwood (born 24/6/1942, Redruth, Cornwall, drums), Peter Green (born Peter Greenbaum, 29/10/1946, London, guitar), Jeremy Spencer (born 4/7/1948, West Hartlepool, guitar) and Bob Brunning (bass). John McVie (born 26/11/1945, London), who had been in John Mayall's Bluesbreakers with Fleetwood and Green, replaced Brunning a month later. Among numerous changes, Danny Kirwan (guitar) was added in 1968, Green and Spencer left in 1970, McVie's wife Christine (born Christine Perfect, 12/7/1943, Birmingham, keyboards) joined in 1970, Bob Welch (guitar) joined in 1971 and left in 1974 when they moved to California. There they recuited Lindsey Buckingham (born 3/10/1947, Palo Alto, CA) and his girlfriend Stevie Nicks (born 26/5/1948, Pheonix, AZ) in December 1974. Buckingham went solo in 1987. Christine McVie and Nicks stopped touring in 1990, both going solo. The group was presented with the Outstanding Contribution to British Music at the 1998 BRIT Awards and were inducted into the Rock & Roll Hall of Fame in 1998, and have a star on the Hollywood Walk of Fame.

| | | | | |
|---|---|---|---|---|
| 02/03/1968 . . . . . 4 . . . . . . 37 . . . . . . | FLEETWOOD MAC . . . . . . . . . . . . . . . . . . . . . . . . . . . . . . . . . . . . . . . . . . . . . . . . . . . . . . . . Blue Horizon BPG 763200 |
| 07/09/1968 . . . . . 10 . . . . . . 11 . . . . . . | MR. WONDERFUL . . . . . . . . . . . . . . . . . . . . . . . . . . . . . . . . . . . . . . . . . . . . . . . . . . . . . . . . . Blue Horizon 763205 |
| 30/08/1969 . . . . . 18 . . . . . . 4 . . . . . . | THE PIOUS BIRD OF GOOD OMEN . . . . . . . . . . . . . . . . . . . . . . . . . . . . . . . . . . . . . . . . . . . . . . Blue Horizon 763215 |
| 04/10/1969 . . . . . 6 . . . . . . 11 . . . . . . | **THEN PLAY ON** . . . . . . . . . . . . . . . . . . . . . . . . . . . . . . . . . . . . . . . . . . . . . . . . . . . . . . . . . Reprise RSLP 9000 |
| 10/10/1970 . . . . . 39 . . . . . . 2 . . . . . . | KILN HOUSE . . . . . . . . . . . . . . . . . . . . . . . . . . . . . . . . . . . . . . . . . . . . . . . . . . . . . . . . . . . . Reprise RSLP 9004 |
| 19/02/1972 . . . . . 36 . . . . . . 14 . . . . . . | GREATEST HITS The album changed its catalogue number to 4607041 during its chart run . . . . . . . . . . . . . . . . . . CBS 69011 |
| 06/11/1976 . . . . . 23 . . . . . . 19 . . . . . . ● | FLEETWOOD MAC ▲¹ . . . . . . . . . . . . . . . . . . . . . . . . . . . . . . . . . . . . . . . . . . . . . . . . . . . . . Reprise K 54043 |
| 26/02/1977 . . . . ❶¹ . . . 477 . . . . . ✪¹⁰ | **RUMOURS** ▲³¹ ◆¹⁹ 1977 Grammy Award for Album of the Year. The tally of 477 weeks is the highest number of weeks any album has spent on the album charts . . . . . . . . . . . . . . . . . . . . . . . . . . . . . . . . . . . . . . . . . . . . Warner Brothers K 56344 |
| 27/10/1979 . . . . ❶¹ . . . . . 26 . . . . . . ✪ | **TUSK** . . . . . . . . . . . . . . . . . . . . . . . . . . . . . . . . . . . . . . . . . . . . . . . . . . . . . . . . . . . Warner Brothers K 66088 |
| 13/12/1980 . . . . . 31 . . . . . . 9 . . . . . . ● | FLEETWOOD MAC LIVE . . . . . . . . . . . . . . . . . . . . . . . . . . . . . . . . . . . . . . . . . . . . . . . . . . . Warner Brothers K 66097 |
| 10/07/1982 . . . . . 5 . . . . . . 39 . . . . . . ✪ | **MIRAGE** ▲⁵ . . . . . . . . . . . . . . . . . . . . . . . . . . . . . . . . . . . . . . . . . . . . . . . . . . . . . . . Warner Brothers K 56592 |
| 25/04/1987 . . . . ❶⁵ . . . . 115 . . . . . . ✪⁷ | **TANGO IN THE NIGHT** . . . . . . . . . . . . . . . . . . . . . . . . . . . . . . . . . . . . . . . . . . . . . . . . . Warner Brothers WX 65 |
| 14/05/1988 . . . . . 3 . . . . . . 52 . . . . . . ✪³ | **GREATEST HITS** . . . . . . . . . . . . . . . . . . . . . . . . . . . . . . . . . . . . . . . . . . . . . . . . . . . . Warner Brothers WX 221 |
| 21/04/1990 . . . . ❶¹ . . . . . 21 . . . . . . ✪ | **BEHIND THE MASK** . . . . . . . . . . . . . . . . . . . . . . . . . . . . . . . . . . . . . . . . . . . . . . . . . . Warner Brothers WX 335 |
| 23/09/1995 . . . . . 48 . . . . . . 2 . . . . . . | LIVE AT THE BBC . . . . . . . . . . . . . . . . . . . . . . . . . . . . . . . . . . . . . . . . . . . . . . . . . . . . . Essential EDFCD 297 |
| 21/10/1995 . . . . . 47 . . . . . . 1 . . . . . . | TIME . . . . . . . . . . . . . . . . . . . . . . . . . . . . . . . . . . . . . . . . . . . . . . . . . . . . . . . . . . . . . . . Warner Brothers 9362459202 |
| 06/09/1997 . . . . . 15 . . . . . . 10 . . . . . . ○ | THE DANCE ▲¹ . . . . . . . . . . . . . . . . . . . . . . . . . . . . . . . . . . . . . . . . . . . . . . . . . . . . . . . . Reprise 9362467022 |
| 26/10/2002 . . . . . 7 . . . . . . 22 . . . . . . ○ | **THE VERY BEST OF** . . . . . . . . . . . . . . . . . . . . . . . . . . . . . . . . . . . . . . . . . . . Warner Special Markets 8122736352 |
| 10/05/2003 . . . . . 6 . . . . . . 8 . . . . . . ● | **SAY YOU WILL** . . . . . . . . . . . . . . . . . . . . . . . . . . . . . . . . . . . . . . . . . . . . . . . . . . . . . . . Reprise 9362484792 |

**FLIP AND FILL** UK production duo Graham Turner and Mark Hall. They also record as Bus Stop.

| | | | | |
|---|---|---|---|---|
| 19/07/2003 . . . . . 29 . . . . . . 7 . . . . . . | FLOOR FILLAS . . . . . . . . . . . . . . . . . . . . . . . . . . . . . . . . . . . . . . . . . . . . . . . . . . . . . All Around The World 0392192 |

**BERNIE FLINT** UK singer (born 1952, Southport) who won various TV talent contests, including *Opportunity Knocks* twelve times. When the album charted he was working as a delivery man for a laundry company.

| | | | | |
|---|---|---|---|---|
| 02/07/1977 . . . . . 37 . . . . . . 6 . . . . . . | I DON'T WANT TO PUT A HOLD ON YOU . . . . . . . . . . . . . . . . . . . . . . . . . . . . . . . . . . . . . . . . . . . . EMI EMC 3184 |

**FLOATERS** US R&B vocal group assembled in Detroit, MI by ex-Detroit Emeralds James Mitchell and Marvin Willis, with Charles Clark (Libra), Larry Cunningham (Cancer), Paul Mitchell (Leo) and Ralph Mitchell (Aquarius).

| | | | | |
|---|---|---|---|---|
| 20/08/1977 . . . . . 17 . . . . . . 8 . . . . . . | FLOATERS . . . . . . . . . . . . . . . . . . . . . . . . . . . . . . . . . . . . . . . . . . . . . . . . . . . . . . . . . . . . ABC ABCL 5229 |

▲⁹ Number of weeks album topped the US chart   ◆¹² RIAA Diamond Awards   ◇³ IFPI Platinum Europe Awards

### FLOCK
US group formed in Chicago, IL in 1966 by Jerry Goodman (violin), Fred Glickstein (guitar/vocals), Tom Webb (saxophone), Rick Canoff (saxophone), Jerry Smith (bass), Frank Posa (trumpet) and Ron Karpman (drums). Goodman left the group in 1971 in order to join the Mahavishnu Orchestra.

| 02/05/1970 | 59 | 2 | | FLOCK | CBS 63733 |

### A FLOCK OF SEAGULLS
UK techno-rock group formed in Liverpool in 1979 by Mike Score (born 5/11/1957, keyboards/vocals), Frank Maudsley (born 10/11/1959, bass), Paul Reynolds (born 4/8/1962, guitar) and Ali Score (drums). They won the 1982 Grammy Award for Best Rock Instrumental Performance for *D.N.A.*, disbanding in 1986.

| 17/04/1982 | 32 | 44 | O | A FLOCK OF SEAGULLS | Jive HOP 201 |
| 07/05/1983 | 16 | 10 | | LISTEN | Arista HIP 4 |
| 01/09/1984 | 30 | 5 | | THE STORY OF A YOUNG HEART | Jive HIP 14 |

### FLOWERED UP
UK group formed in London in 1989 by Liam Maher (vocals), Joe Maher (guitar), Andy Jackson (bass), Tim Dorney (keyboards) and John Tovey (drums), their act often 'supplemented' by Barry Mooncult dancing on stage wearing a giant flower.

| 07/09/1991 | 23 | 3 | | A LIFE WITH BRIAN | London 8282441 |

### EDDIE FLOYD
US singer (born 25/6/1935, Montgomery, AL, raised in Detroit, MI) who was a founder member of the Falcons. He recorded solo for Lupine and Safice before moving to Memphis in 1965 and signing with Stax.

| 29/04/1967 | 36 | 5 | | KNOCK ON WOOD | Stax 589006 |

### FLUKE
UK instrumental/production group formed in 1989 by Mike Bryant (born 1/5/1960, High Wycombe), Michael Tournier (born 24/5/1963, High Wycombe) and Jonathan Fugler (born 13/10/1962, St Austell, Cornwall). They also record as Lucky Monkeys. Tournier and Fugler were both previously in Skin and Tournier later recorded as Syntax.

| 23/10/1993 | 41 | 1 | | SIX WHEELS ON MY WAGON | Circa CIRCDX 27 |
| 19/08/1995 | 44 | 1 | | OTO | Circa CIRCD 31 |
| 11/10/1997 | 45 | 1 | | RISOTTO | Circa CIRCD 33 |

### A FLUX OF PINK INDIANS
UK group formed in 1980 by Colin Latter (vocals), Kevin Hunter (guitar), Derek Birkett (bass) and Martin Wilson (drums). It was claimed that the group's anarchic punk leanings led to them being placed under surveillance by MI5. Birkett later formed the One Little Indian label.

| 05/02/1983 | 79 | 2 | | STRIVE TO SURVIVE CAUSING LEAST SUFFERING POSSIBLE | Spiderleg SDL 8 |

### FLYING LIZARDS
UK group formed by David Cunningham and featuring the half-sung, half-spoken vocals of Deborah Evans. Later members included Patti Paladin, Peter Gordan, Steve Beresford and David Toop.

| 16/02/1980 | 60 | 3 | | FLYING LIZARDS | Virgin V 2150 |

### FLYING PICKETS
UK a cappella group formed in 1980 by Rick Lloyd, Ken Gregson, Gareth Williams, David Brett, Brian Hibbard (born 25/11/1946, Wales) and Red Stripe. Hibbard was later an actor, playing garage mechanic Doug Murray in *Coronation Street*.

| 17/12/1983 | 48 | 11 | O | LIVE AT THE ALBANY EMPIRE | Vam AVMLP 0001 |
| 09/06/1984 | 11 | 11 | O | LOST BOYS | 10 Records DIX 4 |

### FM
UK rock group formed in 1985 by Steve Overland (guitar/vocals), Chris Overland (guitar), Didge Digital (keyboards), Merv Goldsworthy (bass) and Pete Jupp (drums). They disbanded in 1990, re-forming in 1991 with Andy Barnett replacing Chris Overland, and Digital leaving after one more album.

| 20/09/1986 | 76 | 1 | | INDISCREET | Portrait PRT 26827 |
| 14/10/1989 | 34 | 2 | | TOUGH IT OUT | Epic 4655891 |

### FOCUS
Dutch rock group formed in Amsterdam in 1969 by Jan Akkerman (born 24/12/1946, Amsterdam, guitar), Thijs Van Leer (born 31/3/1948, Amsterdam, flute/keyboards), Martin Dresden (bass) and Hans Cleuver (drums). They disbanded in 1978.

| 11/11/1972 | 2 | 34 | | MOVING WAVES | Polydor 2931 002 |
| 02/12/1972 | 6 | 15 | | FOCUS 3 | Polydor 2383 016 |
| 20/10/1973 | 23 | 5 | O | FOCUS AT THE RAINBOW | Polydor 2442 118 |
| 25/05/1974 | 20 | 5 | O | HAMBURGER CONCERTO | Polydor 2442 124 |
| 09/08/1975 | 23 | 6 | | FOCUS | Polydor 2384 070 |

### DAN FOGELBERG
US guitarist/songwriter (born 13/8/1951, Peoria, IL) who began as a folk singer in Los Angeles. He toured with Van Morrison before relocating to Nashville and signing solo with Columbia. He later switched to Full Moon.

| 29/03/1980 | 42 | 3 | | PHOENIX | Full Moon EPC 83317 |

### JOHN FOGERTY
US singer/guitarist (born 28/5/1945 Berkeley, CA) who was a founding member of Creedence Clearwater Revival with his brother Tom and wrote most of their material. He went solo in 1972 after the group disbanded, but after problems with his record label Fantasy he released his product in the US on Asylum and for the rest of the world on Fantasy . In 1985 his album contained two tracks, *Mr Greed* and *Zanz Kan't Danz*, which Fantasy owner Saul Zaentz assumed were aimed at him and so he launched a $142 million suit alleging slander. The same year Fogerty was also sued for infringing the copyright of *Run Through The Jungle*, written by Fogerty! It had been a hit for Creedence Clearwater Revival in 1970 (it was the B-side to *Up Around The Bend*, which made #3, and then when promoted in its own right in the US reached #48) on the Fantasy label. He scored his biggest hit with *The Old Man Down The Road*, a top ten US hit in 1985. The seeming similarities between *Run* and *Old Man* were pointed out to Fantasy by former Revivalist Doug 'Cosmo' Clifford and a copyright infringement suit was launched. Although John Fogerty was eventually cleared

(he sang the two songs in the courtroom to prove his case!) it cost him more than $400,000 in legal fees and when Creedence were inducted into the Rock & Roll Hall of Fame in 1993 Fogerty refused to share the stage with his former band.

16/02/1985 . . . . . 48 . . . . . 11 . . . . . . CENTERFIELD ▲¹ . . . . . . . . . . . . . . . . . . . . . . . . . . . . . . . . . . . . . . . . . . . . . . . . . . . . . . . . . Warner Brothers 9252031

### BEN FOLDS FIVE
US rock group formed in North Carolina in 1993 by Ben Folds (born 12/9/1966, Winston-Salem, NC, keyboards/vocals), Darren Jessee (born 8/4/1971, drums) and Robert Sledge (born 9/3/1968, bass). They disbanded in 2001, Folds went solo.

| | | | | | |
|---|---|---|---|---|---|
| 15/03/1997 | 30 | 3 | | WHATEVER AND EVER AMEN . . . . . . . . . . . . . . . . . . . . . . . . . . . . . . . . . . . . . . . . . . . . . . . . . . . . . . . . . | Epic 4866982 |
| 24/01/1998 | 65 | 1 | | NAKED BABY PHOTOS . . . . . . . . . . . . . . . . . . . . . . . . . . . . . . . . . . . . . . . . . . . . . . . . . . . . . . . . . . . . | Virgin CAR 7554 |
| 08/05/1999 | 22 | 2 | | THE UNAUTHORIZED BIOGRAPHY OF REINHOLD MESSNER . . . . . . . . . . . . . . . . . . . . . . . . . . . . . . . . . . . . . | Epic 4933122 |
| 06/10/2001 | 73 | 1 | | ROCKIN' THE SUBURBS **BEN FOLDS** . . . . . . . . . . . . . . . . . . . . . . . . . . . . . . . . . . . . . . . . . . . . . . . . . . . | Epic 5040632 |

### ELLEN FOLEY
US singer (born 5/6/1951, St Louis, MO), first prominent as the female singer on Meat Loaf's album, she subsequently signed a solo deal with Epic Records. She is also an actress, having appeared in the films *Tootsie* and *Hair* and numerous TV shows.

| | | | | | |
|---|---|---|---|---|---|
| 17/11/1979 | 68 | 1 | | NIGHT OUT . . . . . . . . . . . . . . . . . . . . . . . . . . . . . . . . . . . . . . . . . . . . . . . . . . . . . . . . . . . . . . . . . . . | Epic EPC 83718 |
| 04/04/1981 | 57 | 2 | | SPIRIT OF ST LOUIS . . . . . . . . . . . . . . . . . . . . . . . . . . . . . . . . . . . . . . . . . . . . . . . . . . . . . . . . . . . . . . | Epic EPC 84809 |

### JANE FONDA
US actress (born 21/12/1937, NYC) and daughter of actor Henry Fonda and Frances Seymour Brokaw, the second marriage for both parents. Her mother later committed suicide by slitting her throat (for many years Jane was convinced she had died from a heart attack, learning the truth via a film magazine) and Jane was brought up by her father. She began her career modelling and then went into the theatre before appearing in her first film, *Tall Story*, in 1960. Her best-known films include *Barefoot In The Park*, *Barbarella*, *They Shoot Horses Don't They*, *Klute*, *The China Syndrome*, *9 To 5* and *On Golden Pond*, the latter also being the last made by her father. An active opponent against US involvement in the Vietnam War, she later became a highly successful businesswoman, with fitness videos, albums and books. She was married to film director Roger Vadim, politician Tom Hayden and then media mogul Ted Turner, all three marriages ending in divorce. She won an Emmy Award for the TV film *The Dollmaker* in 1984 and has won two Oscars: Best Actress for *Klute* in 1971 and *Coming Home* in 1978.

| | | | | | |
|---|---|---|---|---|---|
| 29/01/1983 | 7 | 47 | ● | **JANE FONDA'S WORKOUT RECORD** . . . . . . . . . . . . . . . . . . . . . . . . . . . . . . . . . . . . . . . . . . . . . . . . . . . | CBS 88581 |
| 22/09/1984 | 60 | 4 | | JANE FONDA'S WORKOUT RECORD: NEW AND IMPROVED. . . . . . . . . . . . . . . . . . . . . . . . . . . . . . . . . . . . . . | CBS 88640 |

### WAYNE FONTANA AND THE MINDBENDERS
UK group formed in Manchester in 1963 by Wayne Fontana (born Glyn Geoffrey Ellis, 28/10/1945, Manchester). The Mindbenders comprised Eric Stewart (born 20/1/1946, Manchester, lead guitar/vocals), Bob Lang (born 10/1/1946, Manchester, bass) and Ric Rothwell (born Eric Rothwell, 11/3/1944, Stockport, drums). Fontana left acrimoniously in 1965 for a solo career, the group enjoying a few more hits. He named the group after a film thriller starring Dirk Bogarde.

20/02/1965 . . . . . 18 . . . . . . 1 . . . . . . WAYNE FONTANA AND THE MINDBENDERS . . . . . . . . . . . . . . . . . . . . . . . . . . . . . . . . . . . . . . . . . . Fontana TL 5230

### FOO FIGHTERS
US rock group formed in 1994 by Dave Grohl (born 14/1/1969, Warren, OH, guitar/vocals), Nate Mendel (bass), William Goldsmith (drums), Pat Smear (guitar) and Greg Dulli (drums). Grohl had been drummer with Nirvana and considered joining Tom Petty And The Heartbreakers when Nirvana disbanded following Kurt Cobain's death. Smear left in 1997 and by 1999 the group consisted of Grohl, Mendel, Franz Stahl (guitar, left in 1999), Taylor Hawkins (drums) and Chris Shiflett (guitar, only plays on tour). The group took their name from a term used by World War II pilots for UFOs. They have won four Grammy Awards including Best Short Form Video for *Learn To Fly* in 2000 and Best Hard Rock Performance in 2002 for *All My Life*.

| | | | | | |
|---|---|---|---|---|---|
| 08/07/1995 | 3 | 17 | ● | **FOO FIGHTERS** . . . . . . . . . . . . . . . . . . . . . . . . . . . . . . . . . . . . . . . . . . . . . . . . . . . . . . . . . . . . . . . | Roswell CDSET 2266 |
| 24/05/1997 | 3 | 12 | ● | **THE COLOUR AND THE SHAPE**. . . . . . . . . . . . . . . . . . . . . . . . . . . . . . . . . . . . . . . . . . . . . . . . . . . . . . . | Roswell CDEST 2295 |
| 13/11/1999 | 10 | 16 | ● | **THERE IS NOTHING LEFT TO LOSE** 2000 Grammy Award for Best Rock Album . . . . . . . . . . . . . . . . . . . . . . . | RCA 74321716992 |
| 02/11/2002 | ❶¹ | 41 | ◌ | **ONE BY ONE** 2003 Grammy Award for Best Rock Album . . . . . . . . . . . . . . . . . . . . . . . . . . . . . . . . . . . . . . | RCA 74321973482 |

### STEVE FORBET
US singer/guitarist/harmonica player (born 1955, Meridien, MS), after playing in local bands he moved to New York in 1976. Signed by Nemperor Records after being spotted busking at Grand Central Station, he released his debut album in 1977.

| | | | | | |
|---|---|---|---|---|---|
| 09/06/1979 | 56 | 1 | | ALIVE ON ARRIVAL. . . . . . . . . . . . . . . . . . . . . . . . . . . . . . . . . . . . . . . . . . . . . . . . . . . . . . . . . . . . . . . | Epic EPC 83308 |
| 24/11/1979 | 54 | 2 | | JACK RABBIT SLIM . . . . . . . . . . . . . . . . . . . . . . . . . . . . . . . . . . . . . . . . . . . . . . . . . . . . . . . . . . . . . . . | Epic EPC 83879 |

### CLINTON FORD
UK singer (born Ian George Stopford-Harrison) who also recorded for Pye, Channel, Columbia and Warwick.

26/05/1962 . . . . . 16 . . . . . . 4 . . . . . . CLINTON FORD . . . . . . . . . . . . . . . . . . . . . . . . . . . . . . . . . . . . . . . . . . . . . . . . . . . . . . . . . . . . . . . . . Oriole PS 40021

### LITA FORD
UK singer/guitarist (born 23/9/1959, London) who was a member of The Runaways (which also included Joan Jett and future Bangles member Micki Steele), joining the group in 1975 at the age of fifteen. She left in 1979, initially combining her solo career with working as a beautician. She was briefly married to W.A.S.P. guitarist Chris Holmes.

| | | | | | |
|---|---|---|---|---|---|
| 26/05/1984 | 96 | 1 | | DANCIN' ON THE EDGE . . . . . . . . . . . . . . . . . . . . . . . . . . . . . . . . . . . . . . . . . . . . . . . . . . . . . . . . . . . | Vertigo VERL 13 |
| 23/06/1990 | 66 | 1 | | STILETTO . . . . . . . . . . . . . . . . . . . . . . . . . . . . . . . . . . . . . . . . . . . . . . . . . . . . . . . . . . . . . . . . . . . . . | RCA PL 82090 |
| 25/01/1992 | 51 | 2 | | DANGEROUS CURVES . . . . . . . . . . . . . . . . . . . . . . . . . . . . . . . . . . . . . . . . . . . . . . . . . . . . . . . . . . . . . | RCA PD 90592 |

## JULIA FORDHAM

UK singer (born 10/8/1962, Portsmouth) who was in Mari Wilson's backing group The Wilsations before going solo in 1986

| | | | | |
|---|---|---|---|---|
| 18/06/1988 | 20 | 22 | ● | JULIA FORDHAM .............................................................. Circa 4 |
| 21/10/1989 | 13 | 5 | ○ | PORCELAIN .................................................................. Circa 10 |
| 02/11/1991 | 33 | 6 | | SWEPT ..................................................................... Circa 18 |
| 21/05/1994 | 21 | 3 | | FALLING FORWARD ..................................................... Circa CIRCD 28 |

## FOREIGNER

UK/US rock group formed by Londoners Mick Jones (born 27/12/1944, guitar), Dennis Elliott (born 18/8/1950, drums), Ian McDonald (born 25/6/1946, guitar/keyboards) and Americans Ed Gagliardi (born 13/2/1952, New York, bass), Al Greenwood (born 20/10/1951, New York, keyboards) and Lou Gramm (born Lou Grammatico, 2/5/1950, Rochester, NY, vocals). Gagliardi left in 1979 and was replaced by Rick Wills. Greenwood and McDonald left in 1980. Gramm left in 1991 and was replaced by Johnny Edwards. They were so named because of the multi-national line-up.

| | | | | |
|---|---|---|---|---|
| 26/08/1978 | 32 | 5 | | DOUBLE VISION .................................................. Atlantic K 50476 |
| 25/07/1981 | 5 | 62 | ● | 4 ▲10 ......................................................... Atlantic K 50796 |
| 18/12/1982 | 58 | 11 | ○ | RECORDS: THE BEST OF FOREIGNER ................................. Atlantic A 0999 |
| 22/12/1984 | ❶3 | 32 | ✪ | AGENT PROVOCATEUR ......................................... Atlantic 7819991 |
| 19/12/1987 | 64 | 7 | | INSIDE INFORMATION ............................................ Atlantic WX 143 |
| 06/07/1991 | 56 | 1 | | UNUSUAL HEAT .................................................. Atlantic WX 424 |
| 02/05/1992 | 19 | 7 | ○ | THE VERY BEST OF FOREIGNER ................................ Atlantic 7567805112 |
| 12/11/1994 | 59 | 1 | | MR. MOONLIGHT ............................................... Arista 74321232852 |

## 49ERS

Italian studio project assembled by producers Gianfranco Bortolotti and Paolo Rossini with singer Dawn Mitchell (later replaced by Ann-Marie Smith), the 49th person they auditioned. Bortolotti also produces Cappella.

| | | | | |
|---|---|---|---|---|
| 10/03/1990 | 51 | 5 | | THE 49ERS .............................................. Fourth & Broadway BRLP 547 |

## FOSTER AND ALLEN

Irish duo formed in 1975 by Mick Foster (born in County Kildare) and Tony Allen (born in Mount Temple).

| | | | | |
|---|---|---|---|---|
| 14/05/1983 | 72 | 6 | ○ | MAGGIE ...................................................... Ritz RITZLP 0012 |
| 05/11/1983 | 71 | 6 | | I WILL LOVE YOU ALL OF MY LIFE ................................ Ritz RITZLP 0015 |
| 17/11/1984 | 18 | 18 | | THE VERY BEST OF FOSTER AND ALLEN ............................... Ritz LPTV 1 |
| 29/03/1986 | 82 | 2 | | AFTER ALL THESE YEARS ......................................... Ritz RITZLP 0032 |
| 25/10/1986 | 11 | 15 | ✪ | REMINISCING .................................................. Stylus SMR 623 |
| 27/06/1987 | 92 | 1 | | LOVE SONGS – THE VERY BEST OF FOSTER AND ALLEN VOLUME 2 ........... Ritz RITZLP 0036 |
| 10/10/1987 | 16 | 16 | ✪ | REFLECTIONS .................................................. Stylus SMR 739 |
| 30/04/1988 | 16 | 15 | ● | REMEMBER YOU'RE MINE ......................................... Stylus SMR 853 |
| 01/10/1988 | 16 | 18 | ● | THE WORLDS OF FOSTER AND ALLEN ............................... Stylus SMR 861 |
| 28/10/1989 | 29 | 12 | ● | THE MAGIC OF FOSTER AND ALLEN (THEIR GREATEST HITS) ............. Stylus SMR 989 |
| 09/12/1989 | 40 | 4 | ● | FOSTERS AND ALLEN'S CHRISTMAS COLLECTION ..................... Stylus SMR 995 |
| 10/11/1990 | 15 | 12 | ● | SOUVENIRS ................................................. Telstar STAR 2457 |
| 08/12/1990 | 44 | 4 | | THE CHRISTMAS COLLECTION ................................... Telstar STAR 2459 |
| 02/11/1991 | 18 | 11 | ● | MEMORIES .................................................. Telstar STAR 2527 |
| 31/10/1992 | 37 | 10 | | HEART STRINGS .............................................. Telstar TCD 2608 |
| 23/10/1993 | 14 | 12 | ● | BY REQUEST ................................................. Telstar TCD 2670 |
| 05/11/1994 | 41 | 9 | | SONGS WE LOVE TO SING ....................................... Telstar TCD 2741 |
| 04/11/1995 | 30 | 12 | ● | 100 GOLDEN GREATS .......................................... Telstar TCD 2791 |
| 02/11/1996 | 46 | 10 | | SOMETHING SPECIAL – 100 GOLDEN LOVE SONGS ................... Telstar TCD 2791 |
| 26/04/1997 | 55 | 2 | | SHADES OF GREEN ............................................ Telstar TCD 2899 |
| 15/11/1997 | 36 | 8 | ● | BEST FRIENDS ............................................ Telstar TV TTVCD 2935 |
| 12/12/1998 | 52 | 4 | | GREATEST HITS ........................................... Telstar TV TTVCD 3000 |
| 25/12/1999 | 61 | 1 | | ONE DAY AT A TIME ....................................... Telstar TV TTVCD 3090 |
| 15/11/2003 | 30 | 8 | | BY SPECIAL REQUEST – THE VERY BEST OF ...................... DMG TV DMGTV003 |

○ Silver disc   ● Gold disc   ✪ Platinum disc (additional platinum units are indicated by a figure following the symbol)   ❶9 Number of weeks album topped the UK chart

**FOTHERINGAY** UK folk rock group formed in 1970 by former Fairport Convention singer Sandy Denny (born 6/1/1947, London), with Trevor Lucas (guitar/vocals), Jerry Donahue (guitar), Pat Donaldson (bass) and Gerry Conway (drums), taking their name from a song Denny had written for Fairport Convention. The group disbanded midway through the sessions for their second album.

11/07/1970 . . . . . 18 . . . . . . 6 . . . . . .    FOTHERINGAY . . . . . . . . . . . . . . . . . . . . . . . . . . . . . . . . . . . . . . . . . . . . . . . . . . . . . . . . . . . . . . . . Island ILPS 9125

**FOUNTAINS OF WAYNE** US duo formed by Chris Collingwood and Adam Schlesinger, both hailing from New York. Schlesinger wrote The Wonders' hit in the 1996 Tom Hanks film *That Thing You Do!*.

07/06/1997 . . . . . 67 . . . . . . 1 . . . . . .    FOUNTAINS OF WAYNE . . . . . . . . . . . . . . . . . . . . . . . . . . . . . . . . . . . . . . . . . . . . . . . . . . . . . . . . . Atlantic 7567927252

**4 HERO** UK group formed in 1986 by Dego McFarlane, Mark 'Mac' Clair, Iain Bardouille and Gus Lawrence. By 1989 Dego and Mark Mac were performing as a duo, while Bardouille and Lawrence ran the quartet's label Reinforced Records. Dego later recorded as Tek9, Mark Mac as Nu Era. Both also linked up as Jacob's Optical Stairway. They signed with Talkin Loud in 1998. Mark Mac and Bardouille also recorded as Manix. They won the 1998 MOBO Award for Best Drum & Bass Act.

25/07/1998 . . . . . 38 . . . . . . 6 . . . . . .    TWO PAGES . . . . . . . . . . . . . . . . . . . . . . . . . . . . . . . . . . . . . . . . . . . . . . . . . . . . . . . . . . . . . . . . Talkin Loud 5584652
10/11/2001 . . . . . 65 . . . . . . 1 . . . . . .    CREATING PATTERNS . . . . . . . . . . . . . . . . . . . . . . . . . . . . . . . . . . . . . . . . . . . . . . . . . . . . . . . . . Talkin Loud 5860572

**4 NON BLONDES** US rock group formed in San Francisco, CA in 1989 by Linda Perry (guitar/vocals), Christa Hillhouse (bass), Roger Rocha (guitar) and Dawn Richardson (drums). They disbanded in 1996, Perry becoming a successful songwriter.

17/07/1993 . . . . . 4 . . . . . . 18 . . . . . . ●    **BIGGER, BETTER, FASTER, MORE!** . . . . . . . . . . . . . . . . . . . . . . . . . . . . . . . . . . . . . . . . . . . . . . Interscope 7567921122

**4 OF US** Irish group formed in Newry, County Down by Brendan Murphy (vocals), Declan Murphy (guitar), Paul Murphy (piano), Peter McKinney (drums) and John McCandless (bass).

20/03/1993 . . . . . 64 . . . . . . 1 . . . . . .    MAN ALIVE . . . . . . . . . . . . . . . . . . . . . . . . . . . . . . . . . . . . . . . . . . . . . . . . . . . . . . . . . . . . . . . Columbia 4723262

**FOUR PENNIES** UK pop group formed in Blackburn by Lionel Morton (born 14/8/1942, Blackburn, lead vocals/rhythm guitar), Fritz Fryer (born 6/12/1944, Oldham, guitar), Mike Wilsh (born 21/7/1945, Stoke-on-Trent, piano) and Alan Buck (born 7/4/1943, Brierfield, drums) as the Lionel Morton Four before name-changing to the Four Pennies.

07/11/1964 . . . . . 13 . . . . . . 5 . . . . . .    TWO SIDES OF THE FOUR PENNIES . . . . . . . . . . . . . . . . . . . . . . . . . . . . . . . . . . . . . . . . . . . . . . . . . . Philips BL 7642

**FOUR SEASONS** US vocal group formed in 1954 by Frankie Valli (born Francis Castelluccio, 3/5/1937, Newark, NJ), Tommy DeVito (born 19/6/1936, Montclair, NJ), Nick DeVito and Hank Majewski as the Variatones. Signing to RCA in 1956 as the Four Lovers, in 1959 they became Frank Valle & the Romans on Cindy. Nick Massi (born Nicholas Macioco, 19/9/1935, Newark) replaced Majewski in 1960. Nick DeVito quit in 1961 and was replaced by Bob Gaudio (born 17/11/1942, The Bronx, NYC). They became the Four Seasons in 1962, named after a New Jersey bowling alley. Producer Bob Crewe leased *Sherry* (written by Gaudio) to Vee-Jay, and it became the US #1 in four weeks. Massi left in 1965 and was replaced by their arranger Charlie Callelo, and later Joe Long (born 5/9/1941). Tommy DeVito retired in 1971, Gaudio left in 1972 and along with other changes Valli has recorded solo. They also recorded as the Wonder Who? The group was inducted into the Rock & Roll Hall of Fame in 1990. Nick Massi died of cancer on 24/12/2000

06/07/1963 . . . . . 20 . . . . . . 1 . . . . . .    SHERRY . . . . . . . . . . . . . . . . . . . . . . . . . . . . . . . . . . . . . . . . . . . . . . . . . . . . . . . . . . . . Stateside SL 10033
10/04/1971 . . . . . 11 . . . . . . 7 . . . . . .    EDIZIOBE D'ORO . . . . . . . . . . . . . . . . . . . . . . . . . . . . . . . . . . . . . . . . . . . . . . . . . . . . . . . . . Philips 6640 002
20/11/1971 . . . . . 37 . . . . . . 1 . . . . . .    THE BIG ONES . . . . . . . . . . . . . . . . . . . . . . . . . . . . . . . . . . . . . . . . . . . . . . . . . . . . . . . . . . Philips 6336 208
06/03/1976 . . . . . 20 . . . . . . 8 . . . . . . ○    THE FOUR SEASONS STORY . . . . . . . . . . . . . . . . . . . . . . . . . . . . . . . . . . . . . . . . . . . . . Private Stock DAPS 1001
06/03/1976 . . . . . 12 . . . . . . 17 . . . . . . ●    WHO LOVES YOU . . . . . . . . . . . . . . . . . . . . . . . . . . . . . . . . . . . . . . . . . . . . . . . . . . Warner Brothers K 56179
20/03/1976 . . . . . 4 . . . . . . 6 . . . . . . ✪    **GREATEST HITS** . . . . . . . . . . . . . . . . . . . . . . . . . . . . . . . . . . . . . . . . . . . . . . . . . . . . . . . . . . . K-Tel NE 942
21/05/1988 . . . . . 38 . . . . . . 9 . . . . . .    THE COLLECTION – THE 20 GREATEST HITS . . . . . . . . . . . . . . . . . . . . . . . . . . . . . . . . . . . . . . . . Telstar STAR 2320
07/03/1992 . . . . . 7 . . . . . . 15 . . . . . . ●    **THE VERY BEST OF FRANKIE VALLI AND THE FOUR SEASONS** . . . . . . . . . . . . . . . . . . . . . . . . . . . . Polygram TV 5131192
13/10/2001 . . . . . 26 . . . . . . 4 . . . . . . ○    THE DEFINITIVE FRANKIE VALLI & THE FOUR SEASONS This and the above hit credited to **FRANKIE VALLI AND THE FOUR SEASONS** . . . . . . . . . . . . . . . . . . . . . . . . . . . . . . . . . . . . . . . . . . . . . . . . . . . . . . . . . . . . . . . . . . . . . . . . . . . . . . WSM 812273552

**FOUR TET** UK guitarist/singer Kieran Hebdan who is also a member of Fridge.

17/05/2003 . . . . . 60 . . . . . . 1 . . . . . .    ROUND . . . . . . . . . . . . . . . . . . . . . . . . . . . . . . . . . . . . . . . . . . . . . . . . . . . . . . . . Domino Recordings WIGCD126

**FOUR TOPS** US vocal group formed in Detroit, MI in 1953 by Levi Stubbs (born Levi Stubbles, 6/6/1936, Detroit), Renaldo 'Obie' Benson (born 1937, Detroit), Lawrence Payton (born 2/3/1938, Detroit) and Abdul 'Duke' Fakir (born 26/12/1935, Detroit) as the Four Aims, changing their name in 1956 to avoid confusion with the Ames Brothers. Debuting for Chess, they also recorded for Red Top and Columbia before signing with Tamla Motown in 1963. They were initially jazz-orientated until they worked with the songwriting/production team Holland/Dozier/Holland. They stayed in Detroit when Motown switched to LA, signing with Dunhill. The first personnel change came with the death of Payton from liver cancer on 20/6/1997; ex-Temptation Theo Peoples his replacement. Levi Stubbs provided the voice of Audrey II (the voracious vegetation) in the 1986 film *The Little Shop Of Horrors*. They were inducted into the Rock & Roll Hall of Fame in 1990 and have a star on the Hollywood Walk of Fame.

19/11/1966 . . . . . 9 . . . . . . 23 . . . . . .    **FOUR TOPS ON TOP** . . . . . . . . . . . . . . . . . . . . . . . . . . . . . . . . . . . . . . . . . . . . . . . . Tamla Motown STML 11037
11/02/1967 . . . . . 4 . . . . . . 72 . . . . . .    **FOUR TOPS LIVE!** . . . . . . . . . . . . . . . . . . . . . . . . . . . . . . . . . . . . . . . . . . . . . . . . . . Tamla Motown STML 11041
25/11/1967 . . . . . 4 . . . . . . 34 . . . . . .    **REACH OUT** . . . . . . . . . . . . . . . . . . . . . . . . . . . . . . . . . . . . . . . . . . . . . . . . . . . . . . Tamla Motown STML 11056
20/01/1968 . . . . . ●1 . . . . . . 67 . . . . . .    **FOUR TOPS GREATEST HITS** . . . . . . . . . . . . . . . . . . . . . . . . . . . . . . . . . . . . . . . . . . . . . Tamla Motown STML 11061

| DATE | POS | WKS | BPI | ALBUM TITLE | LABEL & NUMBER |
|---|---|---|---|---|---|
| 08/02/1969 | 37 | 1 | | YESTERDAY'S DREAMS | Tamla Motown STML 11087 |
| 27/06/1970 | 29 | 8 | | STILL WATERS RUN DEEP | Tamla Motown STML 11149 |
| 29/05/1971 | 6 | 11 | | **THE MAGNIFICENT SEVEN** THE SUPREMES AND THE FOUR TOPS | Tamla Motown STML 11179 |
| 27/11/1971 | 25 | 10 | | FOUR TOPS GREATEST HITS VOLUME 2 | Tamla Motown STML 11195 |
| 10/11/1973 | 35 | 5 | | THE FOUR TOPS STORY 1964–1972 | Tamla Motown TMSP 11241/2 |
| 13/02/1982 | 13 | 13 | ● | THE BEST OF THE FOUR TOPS | K-Tel NE 1160 |
| 08/12/1990 | 47 | 6 | | THEIR GREATEST HITS | Telstar STAR 2437 |
| 19/09/1992 | 11 | 5 | ○ | THE SINGLES COLLECTION | Polygram TV 5157102 |

**4-SKINS** UK rock group that originally featured Panther on lead vocals and Hoxton Tom on bass and went through four lead singers in three years, including one spell when their manager had to take over! Only Hoxton Tom remained from the original line-up when they disbanded in 1984. Their racial undertones were largely believed to have been responsible for the Southall riots of July 1981 when skinhead followers of the group clashed with local Asian youths. In the aftermath the Hambrough Tavern was left in flames.

| DATE | POS | WKS | BPI | ALBUM TITLE | LABEL & NUMBER |
|---|---|---|---|---|---|
| 17/04/1982 | 80 | 4 | | THE GOOD, THE BAD AND THE 4-SKINS | Secret SEC 4 |

**FOX** UK group formed by Noosha Fox (vocals), Herbie Armstrong (guitar/vocals), Kenny Young (guitar/vocals) and Jim Gannon (guitar/vocals), with session musicians Pete Solley (keyboards), Jim Frank (drums) and Gary Taylor (bass) in the line-up. Fox later went solo, Young and Armstrong forming Yellow Dog.

| DATE | POS | WKS | BPI | ALBUM TITLE | LABEL & NUMBER |
|---|---|---|---|---|---|
| 17/05/1975 | 7 | 8 | ○ | FOX | GTO GTLP 001 |

**SAMANTHA FOX** UK singer/model (born 15/4/1966, London) best known as a topless Page 3 model with *The Sun*. Later a successful actress in Bollywood films, she also appeared in the 1999 film *The Match*.

| DATE | POS | WKS | BPI | ALBUM TITLE | LABEL & NUMBER |
|---|---|---|---|---|---|
| 26/07/1986 | 17 | 10 | ○ | TOUCH ME | Jive HIP 39 |
| 01/08/1987 | 22 | 6 | | SAMANTHA FOX | Jive HIP 48 |
| 18/02/1989 | 46 | 2 | | I WANNA HAVE SOME FUN | Jive HIP 72 |

**BRUCE FOXTON** UK singer/bass player (born 1/9/1955, Woking) who was a founder member of The Jam in 1976 and with them until their disbandment in 1982.

| DATE | POS | WKS | BPI | ALBUM TITLE | LABEL & NUMBER |
|---|---|---|---|---|---|
| 12/05/1984 | 68 | 4 | | TOUCH SENSITIVE | Arista 206 251 |

**JOHN FOXX** UK singer (born Dennis Leigh, Chorley) who was a founder member of Tiger Lily in 1973. Tiger Lily became Ultravox in 1976. Foxx went solo in 1979.

| DATE | POS | WKS | BPI | ALBUM TITLE | LABEL & NUMBER |
|---|---|---|---|---|---|
| 02/02/1980 | 18 | 7 | | METAMATIC | Metal Beat V 2146 |
| 03/10/1981 | 24 | 6 | | THE GARDEN | Metal Beat V 2194 |
| 08/10/1983 | 27 | 3 | | THE GOLDEN SECTION | Virgin V 2233 |
| 05/10/1985 | 85 | 1 | | IN MYSTERIOUS WAYS | Virgin V 2355 |

**FRAGGLES** UK/US puppet group created by Jim Henson (best known for *The Muppets* and *Sesame Street*) with Gobo, Red, Travelling Matt, Mokey, Boober and Wembley.

| DATE | POS | WKS | BPI | ALBUM TITLE | LABEL & NUMBER |
|---|---|---|---|---|---|
| 21/04/1984 | 38 | 4 | | FRAGGLE ROCK | RCA PL 70221 |

**FRAGMA** German production team formed by DJs Dirk and Murko Duderstadt and Ramon Zenker, with singer Eva Martinez. Zenker had also produced Ariel and Hardfloor. By 2001 they were joined by singer Damae.

| DATE | POS | WKS | BPI | ALBUM TITLE | LABEL & NUMBER |
|---|---|---|---|---|---|
| 27/01/2001 | 19 | 12 | ● | TOCA | Positiva 8506770 |

**RODDY FRAME** UK singer/guitarist (born 29/1/1964, East Kilbride), a founder member of Aztec Camera, who later went solo.

| DATE | POS | WKS | BPI | ALBUM TITLE | LABEL & NUMBER |
|---|---|---|---|---|---|
| 03/10/1998 | 55 | 1 | | THE NORTH STAR | Independiente ISOM 7CD |

**PETER FRAMPTON** UK singer/guitarist (born 22/4/1950, Beckenham) who learned guitar as a child, joining the Herd in 1966. He formed Humble Pie in 1969, leaving in 1971 to form Frampton's Camel, then went solo in 1974. He has a star on the Hollywood Walk of Fame.

| DATE | POS | WKS | BPI | ALBUM TITLE | LABEL & NUMBER |
|---|---|---|---|---|---|
| 22/05/1976 | 6 | 39 | ● | FRAMPTON COMES ALIVE ▲[10] | A&M AMLM 63703 |
| 18/06/1977 | 19 | 10 | ○ | I'M IN YOU | A&M AMLK 64039 |

**CONNIE FRANCIS** US singer (born Concetta Rosa Maria Franconero, 12/12/1938, Newark, NJ) who debuted for MGM at the age of sixteen, hitting the US charts for the first time in 1957. She made her first film *Where The Boys Are* in 1961, but stopped performing after being raped following a show at Howard Johnson's Motel on 8/11/1974 (for which she was awarded $3 million). She made a showbiz comeback in 1981.

| DATE | POS | WKS | BPI | ALBUM TITLE | LABEL & NUMBER |
|---|---|---|---|---|---|
| 26/03/1960 | 12 | 1 | | ROCK 'N' ROLL MILLION SELLERS | MGM C 804 |
| 11/02/1961 | 16 | 3 | | CONNIE'S GREATEST HITS | MGM C 831 |
| 18/06/1977 | ❶[2] | 22 | ● | **20 ALL TIME GREATS** First solo female album to top the UK charts | Polydor 2391 290 |
| 24/04/1993 | 12 | 5 | | THE SINGLES COLLECTION | Polygram TV 5191312 |

**FRANK AND WALTERS** Irish trio formed in Cork by Paul Linehan (vocals/bass), Niall Linehan (guitar) and Ashley Keating (drums), naming themselves after two tramps from a nearby village.

| DATE | POS | WKS | BPI | ALBUM TITLE | LABEL & NUMBER |
|---|---|---|---|---|---|
| 07/11/1992 | 36 | 1 | | TRAINS, BOATS AND PLANES | Setanta 8283692 |

**FRANKEE** US female singer (born 9/6/1983, Staten Island, NY).

| DATE | POS | WKS | BPI | ALBUM TITLE | LABEL & NUMBER |
|---|---|---|---|---|---|
| 19/06/2004 | 51 | 2+ | | THE GOOD THE BAD THE UGLY | Universal TV 9867000 |

## FRANKIE GOES TO HOLLYWOOD
**FRANKIE GOES TO HOLLYWOOD** UK group formed in Liverpool in 1980 by William 'Holly' Johnson (born 19/2/1960, Khartoum, Sudan, vocals), Paul Rutherford (born 8/12/1959, Liverpool, vocals), Brian 'Nasher' Nash (born 20/5/1963, Liverpool, guitar), Mark O'Toole (born 6/1/1964, Liverpool, bass) and Peter 'Ged' Gill (born 8/3/1964, Liverpool, drums). Signed by ZTT (Zang Tumb Tumm) in 1982, their 1983 debut reached #1 after a ban by the BBC, orchestrated by DJ Mike Read. Johnson went solo in 1987, Rutherford in 1988. Cited Best British Newcomers at the 1985 BRIT Awards, their name has been alternatively explained as being from an old newspaper headline covering either Frank Sinatra's or Frankie Vaughan's move to Hollywood.

| DATE | POS | WKS | BPI | ALBUM TITLE | LABEL & NUMBER |
|---|---|---|---|---|---|
| 10/11/1984 | ❶¹ | 66 | ◆³ | WELCOME TO THE PLEASUREDOME | ZTT ZTTIQ 1 |
| 01/11/1986 | 5 | 13 | ● | LIVERPOOL | ZTT ZTTIQ 8 |
| 30/10/1993 | 4 | 15 | ● | BANG! – GREATEST HITS OF FRANKIE GOES TO HOLLYWOOD | ZTT 4509939122 |
| 07/10/2000 | 54 | 1 | | MAXIMUM JOY | ZTT 165CD |

## ARETHA FRANKLIN
**ARETHA FRANKLIN** US singer (born 25/3/1942, Memphis, TN) who recorded religious material for Wand from 1956. She switched to secular music at the suggestion of Sam Cooke in 1960, signing to Columbia. Hits on Atlantic from 1966 earned her the nickname First Lady Of Soul. She appeared in the 1980 film *The Blues Brothers,* performing *Think*. In 1984 she was sued for failing to appear in the Broadway musical *Mahalia,* due to a fear of flying. She has won sixteen Grammy Awards including Best Rhythm & Blues Recording and Best Rhythm & Blues Vocal Performance in 1967 for *Respect;* Best Rhythm & Blues Vocal Performance in 1968 for *Chain Of Fools;* Best Rhythm & Blues Vocal Performance in 1969 for *Share Your Love With Me;* Best Rhythm & Blues Vocal Performance in 1970 for *Don't Play That Song;* Best Rhythm & Blues Vocal Performance in 1971 for *Bridge Over Troubled Water;* Best Rhythm & Blues Vocal Performance in 1972 for *Young Gifted And Black;* Best Soul Gospel Performance in 1972 for *Amazing Grace;* Best Rhythm & Blues Vocal Performance in 1973 for *Master Of Eyes;* Best Rhythm & Blues Vocal Performance in 1974 for *Ain't Nothing Like The Real Thing;* Best Rhythm & Blues Vocal Performance in 1981 for *Hold On I'm Comin';* Best Rhythm & Blues Vocal Performance in 1985 for *Freeway Of Love;* Best Rhythm & Blues Vocal Performance by a Duo in 1987 with George Michael for *I Knew You Were Waiting (For Me);* Best Soul Gospel Performance in 1988 for *One Lord, One Faith, One Baptism;* and Best Traditional R&B Vocal Performance in 2003 for *Wonderful*. She was inducted into the Rock & Roll Hall of Fame in 1987 and has a star on the Hollywood Walk of Fame.

| DATE | POS | WKS | BPI | ALBUM TITLE | LABEL & NUMBER |
|---|---|---|---|---|---|
| 12/08/1967 | 36 | 2 | | I NEVER LOVED A MAN THE WAY I LOVE YOU | Atlantic 587066 |
| 13/04/1968 | 25 | 18 | | LADY SOUL | Atlantic 588099 |
| 14/09/1968 | 6 | 11 | | ARETHA NOW | Atlantic 588114 |
| 18/01/1986 | 49 | 12 | ○ | WHO'S ZOOMIN' WHO? | Arista 207 202 |
| 24/05/1986 | 89 | 1 | ○ | THE FIRST LADY OF SOUL | Stylus SMR 8506 |
| 08/11/1986 | 51 | 13 | | ARETHA 1987 Grammy Award for Best Rhythm & Blues Vocal Performance | Arista 208 020 |
| 03/06/1989 | 46 | 1 | | THROUGH THE STORM | Arista 209842 |
| 19/03/1994 | 27 | 3 | | GREATEST HITS 1980–1994 | Arista 74321162022 |
| 29/10/1994 | 20 | 5 | ○ | QUEEN OF SOUL – THE VERY BEST OF ARETHA FRANKLIN | Atlantic 8122713962 |
| 21/11/1998 | 38 | 10 | ● | GREATEST HITS | Global Television RADCD 110 |
| 15/06/2002 | 15 | 9 | ● | RESPECT – THE VERY BEST OF | WSM/BMG 0927470542 |

## RODNEY FRANKLIN
**RODNEY FRANKLIN** US pianist (born 16/9/1958, Berkeley, CA) who learnt jazz piano aged six, signing with CBS in 1978.

| DATE | POS | WKS | BPI | ALBUM TITLE | LABEL & NUMBER |
|---|---|---|---|---|---|
| 24/05/1980 | 64 | 2 | | YOU'LL NEVER KNOW | CBS 83812 |

**ELIZABETH FRASER** – see HAROLD BUDD/ELIZABETH FRASER/ROBIN GUTHRIE/SIMON RAYMONDE

## FRANZ FERDINAND
**FRANZ FERDINAND** UK rock group formed in Glasgow by Alexander Kapranos (guitar/vocals), Nicholas McCarthy (guitar). Robert Hardy (bass) and Paul Thomson (drums).

| DATE | POS | WKS | BPI | ALBUM TITLE | LABEL & NUMBER |
|---|---|---|---|---|---|
| 21/02/2004 | 3 | 19+ | ◆ | FRANZ FERDINAND | Domino WIGCD136X |

## FRAZIER CHORUS
**FRAZIER CHORUS** UK group formed in Brighton by Tim Freeman (keyboards/vocals), Kate Holmes (flute), Chris Taplin (clarinet) and Michele Allardyce (percussion) as Plop! (the name a parody of Wham!), becoming Frazier Chorus (seen on the back of a 1950s baseball jacket) upon signing with 4AD in 1987. Holmes later formed Client with Sarah Blackwood (formerly of Dubstar).

| DATE | POS | WKS | BPI | ALBUM TITLE | LABEL & NUMBER |
|---|---|---|---|---|---|
| 20/05/1989 | 56 | 1 | | SUE | Virgin V 2578 |
| 16/03/1991 | 66 | 1 | | RAY | Virgin VFC 2654 |

## FREAK OF NATURE
**FREAK OF NATURE** US/Danish group formed by Mike Tramp (vocals), Kenny Korade (guitar), Dennis Chick (guitar), Jerry Best (bass) and Johnny Haro (drums).

| DATE | POS | WKS | BPI | ALBUM TITLE | LABEL & NUMBER |
|---|---|---|---|---|---|
| 01/10/1994 | 66 | 1 | | GATHERING OF FREAKS | Music For Nations CDMFN 169 |

## FREAKPOWER
**FREAKPOWER** UK group formed by ex-Housemartin and Beats International Norman Cook (born Quentin Cook, 31/7/1963, Brighton) who also records as Pizzaman and The Mighty Dub Katz.

| DATE | POS | WKS | BPI | ALBUM TITLE | LABEL & NUMBER |
|---|---|---|---|---|---|
| 15/04/1995 | 11 | 5 | | DRIVE-THRU BOOTY | Fourth & Broadway BRCDX 606 |

## FREDDIE AND THE DREAMERS
**FREDDIE AND THE DREAMERS** UK group formed in Manchester in 1961 by Freddie Garrity (born 14/11/1936, Manchester, vocals), Roy Crewdson (born 29/5/1941, rhythm guitar), Derek Quinn (born 24/5/1942, lead guitar), Pete Birrell (born 9/5/1941, bass) and Bernie Dwyer (born 11/9/1940, drums). They disbanded in 1968, Garrity continuing on the cabaret circuit with a new line-up. They appeared in the 1965 film *Cuckoo Patrol* and Garrity was in the TV series *Heartbeat* in the 1990s.

| DATE | POS | WKS | BPI | ALBUM TITLE | LABEL & NUMBER |
|---|---|---|---|---|---|
| 09/11/1963 | 5 | 26 | | FREDDIE AND THE DREAMERS | Columbia 33SX 1577 |

**FREE** UK rock group formed in London in 1968 by Paul Kossoff (born 14/9/1950, London, guitar), Simon Kirke (born 28/7/1949, London, drums), Paul Rodgers (born 12/12/1949, Middlesbrough, lead vocals) and Andy Fraser (born 7/8/1952, London, bass). Disbanding in 1971, Kossoff and Kirke joined bass player Tetsu Yamauchi (born 21/10/1947, Japan) and keyboard player John 'Rabbit' Bundrick for *Kossoff, Kirke, Tetsu And Rabbit*. This four re-formed Free with Rodgers in 1972 but Kossoff was often too ill to tour or record. Splitting again in 1973, Rodgers and Kirke formed Bad Company. Kossoff died from a heart attack on 19/3/1976 on a Los Angeles to New York flight. Rodgers was later in The Firm and The Law.

| | | | | | |
|---|---|---|---|---|---|
| 11/07/1970 | 2 | 18 | | FIRE AND WATER | Island ILPS 9120 |
| 23/01/1971 | 41 | 10 | | HIGHWAY | Island ILPS 9138 |
| 26/06/1971 | 4 | 12 | | FREE LIVE! | Island ILPS 9160 |
| 17/06/1972 | 9 | 9 | | FREE AT LAST | Island ILPS 9192 |
| 03/02/1973 | 9 | 7 | | HEARTBREAKER | Island ILPS 9217 |
| 16/03/1974 | 2 | 6 | | THE FREE STORY | Island ISLD 4 |
| 02/03/1991 | 9 | 9 | ○ | THE BEST OF FREE – ALL RIGHT NOW | Island ILPTV 2 |

**FREE THE SPIRIT** UK instrumental duo Rod Edwards and Nick Magnus.

| | | | | | |
|---|---|---|---|---|---|
| 04/02/1995 | 2 | 26 | ✪ | PAN PIPE MOODS | Polygram TV 5271972 |
| 04/11/1995 | 18 | 11 | ● | PAN PIPE MOODS TWO | Polygram TV 5293952 |
| 25/05/1996 | 26 | 5 | | PAN PIPE MOODS IN PARADISE | Polygram TV 5319612 |

**FREEEZ** UK funk group formed by John Rocca (born 23/9/1960, London, vocals), Peter Maas (bass), Andy Stenner (keyboards) and Paul Morgan (drums). Their self-funded debut *Keep In Touch* for their own Pink I label was subsequently picked up by Pye's Calibre Records. Rocca went solo in 1984.

| | | | | | |
|---|---|---|---|---|---|
| 07/02/1981 | 17 | 15 | | SOUTHERN FREEZ | Beggars Banquet BEGA 22 |
| 22/10/1983 | 46 | 3 | | GONNA GET YOU | Beggars Banquet BEGA 48 |

**FREESTYLERS** UK group formed by Matt Cantor, Aston Harvey and Andrew Galea. Galea was later in Giresse.

| | | | | | |
|---|---|---|---|---|---|
| 15/08/1998 | 33 | 3 | | WE ROCK HARD | Freskanova FNTCD 004 |

**FREHLEY'S COMET** US group formed in 1987 by Ace Frehley (born Paul Frehley, 22/4/1951, The Bronx, NYC, guitar), Tod Howarth (guitar/vocals), John Regan (bass) and Anton Fig (drums). Frehley had been a member of Kiss up until 1981, when drug and alcohol problems forced him to leave the group and spend four years recuperating. By the time of the third album Howarth left to be replaced by Richie Scarlet, with Kiss drummer Peter Criss joining as guest singer (Fig had been his replacement in Kiss in 1980). The rest of the group quit midway through a tour in support of the third album; Frehley retired, but joined a revived Kiss in 1996.

| | | | | | |
|---|---|---|---|---|---|
| 18/06/1988 | 79 | 1 | | SECOND SIGHTING | Atlantic 7818621 |

**FRESH PRINCE** – see DJ JAZZY JEFF AND THE FRESH PRINCE

**GLENN FREY** US singer (born 6/11/1948, Detroit, MI) who was a founder member of the Eagles, going solo when they disbanded in 1981.

| | | | | | |
|---|---|---|---|---|---|
| 06/07/1985 | 31 | 9 | | THE ALLNIGHTER | MCA MCF 3277 |

**FRIDA** Norwegian singer (born Anna-Frid Lyngstad-Ruess, 15/11/1945, Bjorkasen) who was a founder member of Abba. When they disbanded in 1981, she was the first to make a solo album, with Phil Collins producing. Married to Abba's Benny Andersson in 1978, they divorced in 1979.

| | | | | | |
|---|---|---|---|---|---|
| 18/09/1982 | 18 | 7 | ○ | SOMETHING'S GOING ON | Epic EPC 85966 |
| 20/10/1984 | 67 | 1 | | SHINE | Epic EPC 26178 |

**DEAN FRIEDMAN** US singer/songwriter/guitarist/keyboard player (born 1955, New Jersey) who was prevented from recording for two years due to legal problems.

| | | | | | |
|---|---|---|---|---|---|
| 21/10/1978 | 21 | 14 | ● | WELL, WELL SAID THE ROCKING CHAIR | Lifesong LSLP 6019 |

**ROBERT FRIPP** UK guitarist/composer/producer (born 16/5/1946, Wimbourne); he began his professional career with League Of Gentlemen before forming Giles, Giles & Fripp with Pete and Mike Giles in 1968. They evolved into King Crimson with Fripp as its leader, a position he retained from 1969–74. He then effectively retired from the music business, only to return in 1977 as producer of Peter Gabriel and later Daryl Hall. King Crimson was revived in 1981, whilst he also resurrected League Of Gentlemen, disbanding both units towards the end of the 1980s. He later recorded with ex-Japan David Sylvian, and is married to singer Toyah Wilcox.

| | | | | | |
|---|---|---|---|---|---|
| 12/05/1979 | 71 | 1 | | EXPOSURE | Polydor EGLP 101 |
| 17/07/1993 | 21 | 2 | | THE FIRST DAY | Virgin CDVX 2712 |

**FRONT 242** Belgian duo Patrick Codenys (born 16/11/1958, Brussels) and Daniel Bressanutti (born 27/8/1954, Brussels). They also formed a trio with Jean-Luc De Meyer and a quartet with Geoff Bellingham (later replaced by ex-Revolting Cocks Richard 23).

| | | | | | |
|---|---|---|---|---|---|
| 02/02/1991 | 49 | 1 | | TYRANNY FOR YOU | RRE 011 |
| 22/05/1993 | 44 | 1 | | 06:21:03:11 UP EVIL | RRE 021CD |
| 04/09/1993 | 46 | 1 | | 05:22:09:12 OFF | RRE 022CD |

### JOHN FRUSCIANTE
US guitarist/singer (born 5/3/1970, NYC) who joined Red Hot Chili Peppers in 1988 and remained with the group until 1992. He rejoined the group in 1998 before going solo.

13/03/2004.....53......1...... SHADOWS COLLIDE WITH PEOPLE . . . . . . . . . . . . . . . . . . . . . . . . . . . . . . . . . . . . . . . . . . Warner Brothers 9362486602

### FUGAZI
US rock group formed by ex-Minor Threat Ian Mackaye (guitar/vocals), ex-Rites Of Spring Guy Picciotto (guitar/vocals), Joe Lally (bass) and Brendan Canty (drums).

| 21/09/1991.....63......1...... | STEADY DIET OF NOTHIMG . . . . . . . . . . . . . . . . . . . . . . . . . . . . . . . . . . . . . . . . . . . . . . . Dischord 60 |
| 19/06/1993.....24......2...... | IN ON THE KILLTAKER . . . . . . . . . . . . . . . . . . . . . . . . . . . . . . . . . . . . . . . . . . Dischord DIS 70CD |
| 13/05/1995.....18......2...... | RED MEDICINE. . . . . . . . . . . . . . . . . . . . . . . . . . . . . . . . . . . . . . . . . . . . . Dischord DIS 90CD |
| 25/04/1998.....47......1...... | END HITS . . . . . . . . . . . . . . . . . . . . . . . . . . . . . . . . . . . . . . . . . . . Dischord DIS 100CD |
| 20/10/2001.....63......1...... | THE ARGUMENT . . . . . . . . . . . . . . . . . . . . . . . . . . . . . . . . . . . . . . . . . . Dischord DIS 130CD |

### FUGEES
US rap band formed in New York in 1994 by Wyclef 'Clef' Jean (born 17/10/1972, Haiti), Lauryn 'L-Boogie' Hill (born 25/5/1975, East Orange, NJ) and Prakazrel 'Pras' Michel (born 19/10/1972, Haiti). Their name, short for 'refugees', was chosen because their parents were refugees from Haiti. They later recorded as The Refugee Allstars. The band have won two Grammy Awards including Best Rhythm & Blues Performance by a Group in 1996 for *Killing Me Softly*. They also won the MTV (Europe) Amour Award and MOBO Award for Best International Act and Best International Single for *Killing Me Softly*, all in 1996. In 1997 they were named Best International Group at the BRIT Awards.

| 30/03/1996 .....2....70...... ✪4 | THE SCORE ◇6 ▲4 1996 Grammy Award for Best Rap Album. . . . . . . . . . . . . . . . . . . . . . . . . . . . . . . Columbia 4935242 |
| 07/12/1996.....55......2...... | THE BOOTLEG VERSIONS . . . . . . . . . . . . . . . . . . . . . . . . . . . . . . . . . . . . . . . . . Columbia 4868242 |

### FUN BOY THREE
UK group formed in 1981 by three ex-Specials, Terry Hall (born 19/3/1959, Coventry), Lynval Golding (born 7/7/1952, St Catherine's, Jamaica) and Neville Staples (born 11/4/1956, Christiana, Jamaica). They split after two years, Hall forming Colour Field.

| 20/03/1982 .....7......20...... ● | THE FUN BOY THREE . . . . . . . . . . . . . . . . . . . . . . . . . . . . . . . . . . . . . . . . Chrysalis CHR 1383 |
| 19/02/1983.....14.....20...... ○ | WAITING . . . . . . . . . . . . . . . . . . . . . . . . . . . . . . . . . . . . . . . . . . . . Chrysalis CHR 1417 |

### FUN-DA-MENTAL
UK group formed in Bradford in 1991 by Propa-Ghandi (born Aki Nawaz), DJ Obeyo, Bad-Shaq Lalliman and Man Tharoo Goldfinger (born Inder Matharu). They split in 1995, one half forming Detri-Mental and the other half continuing as Fun-Da-Mental and comprising Propa-Ghandi, Impi D, MC Mushtaq, Hot Dog, Neil Sparkes, Nick Page, Tim Whelan, Dave Watts, Satin 'Indio' Singh and Phil Pickering.

25/06/1994.....74......1...... SEIZE THE TIME . . . . . . . . . . . . . . . . . . . . . . . . . . . . . . . . . . . . . . . . . . . Nation NATCD 33

### FUN LOVIN' CRIMINALS
US rock group formed in Syracuse, NY in 1993 by New Yorkers Hugh 'Huey' Morgan (guitar/vocals), Steve Borovini (drums) and Brian 'Fast' Leiser (bass/trumpet). Huey was in the *Perfect Day* project for the BBC's Children In Need charity, and the group was in *It's Only Rock 'N' Roll* for the Children's Promise charity.

| 13/07/1996 .....7......72...... ✪ | COME FIND YOURSELF. . . . . . . . . . . . . . . . . . . . . . . . . . . . . . . . . . . . . . . Chrysalis CDCHR 6114 |
| 05/09/1998 .....3......26...... ✪ | 100% COLOMBIAN . . . . . . . . . . . . . . . . . . . . . . . . . . . . . . . . . . . . . . . . . Chrysalis 4970562 |
| 11/12/1999.....37......9...... ● | MIMOSA. . . . . . . . . . . . . . . . . . . . . . . . . . . . . . . . . . . . . . . . . . . . . Chrysalis 5234592 |
| 10/03/2001 .....5......6...... ● | LOCO . . . . . . . . . . . . . . . . . . . . . . . . . . . . . . . . . . . . . . . . . . . . . . Chrysalis 5314712 |
| 03/08/2002.....11......6...... ● | BAG OF HITS. . . . . . . . . . . . . . . . . . . . . . . . . . . . . . . . . . . . . . . . . . . Chrysalis 5399542 |
| 20/09/2003.....20......2...... | WELCOME TO POPPY'S . . . . . . . . . . . . . . . . . . . . . . . . . . . . . . . . . . . . . Sanctuary SANCD 187 |

### FUNERAL FOR A FRIEND
UK group formed in Wales by Matt Davies (vocals), Kris Roberts (guitar), Darren Smith (guitar), Gareth Davies (bass) and Ryan Richards (drums/vocals).

25/10/2003.....12......3...... CASUALLY DRESSED AND DEEP IN CONVERSATION . . . . . . . . . . . . . . . . . . . . . . . . . . . . . . Infectious 2564609472

### FUNKADELIC
US funk group formed by George Clinton (born 22/7/1941, Kannapolis, NC), Gary Shider, Mike 'Kidd Funkadelic' Hampton, Bobby Lewis, Bernie Worrell (born 19/4/1944, New Jersey), Junie Morrison, Tyrone Lampkin, Jerome Brailey, Eddie Hazel (born 10/4/1950, New York), Larry Fratangelo, Cordell 'Boogie' Mosson, Rodney 'Skeet' Curtis, Glen Goins and William 'Bootsy' Collins (born 26/10/1951, Cincinnati, OH) and seven more singers. They also recorded as Parliament. Goins died from Parkinson's Disease on 30/7/1978, Hazel from stomach cancer on 23/12/1992. As Parliament/Funkadelic they were inducted into the Rock & Roll Hall of Fame in 1997.

23/12/1978.....56......5...... ONE NATION UNDER A GROOVE . . . . . . . . . . . . . . . . . . . . . . . . . . . . . . . . . . . . . Warner Brothers K 56539

### FUNKDOOBIEST
US rap group with Jason 'Son Doobie' Vasquez, Ralph 'DJ Ralph M The Mexican' Medrano and Tyrone 'Tomahawk Funk (T-Bone)' Pachenco.

---

▲9 Number of weeks album topped the US chart   ◆12 RIAA Diamond Awards   ◇3 IFPI Platinum Europe Awards

15/07/1995 . . . . . 62 . . . . . . 1 . . . . . .      BROTHAS DOOBIE . . . . . . . . . . . . . . . . . . . . . . . . . . . . . . . . . . . . . . . . . . . . . . . . . . . . . . . . . . . . . . Epic 4783812

### FUNKSTAR DE LUXE Danish producer/remixer Martin Ottesen (born 1973, Odense).

04/09/1999 . . . . . 40 . . . . . . 3 . . . . . .      THE SUN IS SHINING **BOB MARLEY VS FUNKSTAR DELUXE** This was an import single that was ineligible for the singles chart . . . . . . . .
. . . . . . . . . . . . . . . . . . . . . . . . . . . . . . . . . . . . . . . . . . . . . . . . . . . . . . . . . . . . . . . Club Tools 0066735 CLU

### FUREYS Irish family group from Ballyfermont formed by brothers Eddie (born 23/12/1944, Dublin, guitar/mandola/mandolin/harmonica/fiddle/bodhran/vocals), Finbar (born 28/9/1946, Dublin, pipes/banjo/whistles/flute/vocals), George (born 11/6/1951, Dublin, guitar/accordion/mandola/autoharp/whistles/vocals) and Paul Furey (born 6/5/1948, Dublin, accordion/melodeon/concertina/whistles/bones/spoons/vocals), and their friend Davey Arthur (born 24/9/1954, Edinburgh, assorted instruments) who left in 1993 to form Davey Arthur And Co.

08/05/1982 . . . . . 99 . . . . . . 1 . . . . . . ○      WHEN YOU WERE SWEET SIXTEEN . . . . . . . . . . . . . . . . . . . . . . . . . . . . . . . . . . . . . . . . . . . . . . . . . . . Ritz RITZLP 0004
10/11/1984 . . . . . 17 . . . . 19 . . . . . . ●      GOLDEN DAYS . . . . . . . . . . . . . . . . . . . . . . . . . . . . . . . . . . . . . . . . . . . . . . . . . . . . . . . . . K-Tel ONE 1283
26/10/1985 . . . . . 35 . . . . 11 . . . . . . ●      AT THE END OF THE DAY . . . . . . . . . . . . . . . . . . . . . . . . . . . . . . . . . . . . . . . . . . . . . . . . . . . . K-Tel ONE 1310
21/11/1987 . . . . . 65 . . . . . . 7 . . . . . .      FUREYS FINEST . . . . . . . . . . . . . . . . . . . . . . . . . . . . . . . . . . . . . . . . . . . . . . . . . . . . . . . . Telstar HSTAR 2311

### FURIOUS FIVE – see GRANDMASTER FLASH AND THE FURIOUS FIVE

### NELLY FURTADO Canadian singer (born 2/12/1978, Victoria, British Columbia) with Portuguese parents who plays guitar, ukulele and trombone, and sings in English, Portuguese and Hindi. She won four Juno Awards (Canadian equivalent of Grammies and BRITs) at the 2001 ceremony, and one Grammy in 2002 for Best Female Pop Vocal Performance, for the single *I'm Like A Bird*.

24/03/2001 . . . . . 2 . . . . . . 47 . . . . . ✪²      **WHOA NELLY** ◇ . . . . . . . . . . . . . . . . . . . . . . . . . . . . . . . . . . . . . . . . . . . . . . . . . . . DreamWorks 4502852
06/12/2003 . . . . . 11 . . . . 14 . . . . . . ●      FOLKLORE . . . . . . . . . . . . . . . . . . . . . . . . . . . . . . . . . . . . . . . . . . . . . . . . . . . . . . . DreamWorks 4505089

### BILLY FURY UK singer (born Ronald Wycherley, 17/4/1941, Liverpool) who had rheumatic fever as a child, leaving him with a weak heart. Talking his way into Marty Wilde's dressing room in 1958, manager Larry Parnes signed him, changing his name. Health problems plagued his later career and he was attempting a comeback when he died from heart failure on 28/1/1983.

04/06/1960 . . . . . 18 . . . . . . 2 . . . . .      THE SOUND OF FURY . . . . . . . . . . . . . . . . . . . . . . . . . . . . . . . . . . . . . . . . . . . . . . . . . . . . . Decca LF 1329
23/09/1961 . . . . . 5 . . . . . . 9 . . . . .      **HALFWAY TO PARADISE** . . . . . . . . . . . . . . . . . . . . . . . . . . . . . . . . . . . . . . . . . . . . . . . Ace Of Clubs ACL 1083
11/05/1963 . . . . . 6 . . . . . . 21 . . . . .      **BILLY** . . . . . . . . . . . . . . . . . . . . . . . . . . . . . . . . . . . . . . . . . . . . . . . . . . . . . . . . . . . Decca LK 4533
26/10/1963 . . . . . 14 . . . . . . 2 . . . . .      WE WANT BILLY . . . . . . . . . . . . . . . . . . . . . . . . . . . . . . . . . . . . . . . . . . . . . . . . . . . . . . Decca LK 4548
19/02/1983 . . . . . 44 . . . . 15 . . . . .      THE BILLY FURY HIT PARADE . . . . . . . . . . . . . . . . . . . . . . . . . . . . . . . . . . . . . . . . . . . . . . . Decca TAB 37
26/03/1983 . . . . . 56 . . . . . . 2 . . . . .      THE ONE AND ONLY BILLY FURY . . . . . . . . . . . . . . . . . . . . . . . . . . . . . . . . . . . . . . . . . . . . Polydor POLD 5069

### FUSE Canadian keyboard player Richie Hawtin who also records as Plastik Man.

19/06/1993 . . . . . 63 . . . . . . 1 . . . . .      DIMENSION INTRUSION . . . . . . . . . . . . . . . . . . . . . . . . . . . . . . . . . . . . . . . . . . . . . . Warp WARPCD 12

### FUTURE SOUND OF LONDON UK instrumental/production duo Garry Cobain and Brian Dougan who later launched the Electronic Brain Violence label, recording as Amorphous Androgynous. Cobain had mercury poisoning (from teeth fillings) in 1998, halting their career. They resumed in late 2000 when Cobain had recovered.

18/07/1992 . . . . . 75 . . . . . . 1 . . . . .      ACCELERATOR . . . . . . . . . . . . . . . . . . . . . . . . . . . . . . . . . . . . . . . . . . . . . . . Jumpin' & Pumpin' CDTOT 2
04/06/1994 . . . . . 6 . . . . . . 5 . . . . . ○      **LIFEFORMS** . . . . . . . . . . . . . . . . . . . . . . . . . . . . . . . . . . . . . . . . . . . . . . . . . . . . . . . . Virgin CDV 2722
17/12/1994 . . . . . 62 . . . . . . 1 . . . . .      ISDN . . . . . . . . . . . . . . . . . . . . . . . . . . . . . . . . . . . . . . . . . . . . . . . . . . . . . . . . . . Virgin CDV 2755
17/06/1995 . . . . . 44 . . . . . . 1 . . . . .      ISDN (REMIX) . . . . . . . . . . . . . . . . . . . . . . . . . . . . . . . . . . . . . . . . . . . . . . . . . . . . . Virgin CDVX 2755
09/11/1996 . . . . . 26 . . . . . . 2 . . . . .      DEAD CITIES . . . . . . . . . . . . . . . . . . . . . . . . . . . . . . . . . . . . . . . . . . . . . . . . . . . . . . . . Virgin CDV 2184

# G

**GINA G** Australian singer (born Gina Gardiner, 3/8/1970, Queensland) who began as a DJ and singer before emigrating to the UK in 1994. She recorded her debut *Ooh Aah… Just A Little Bit* after hearing it in a studio and was offered a contract by Warner's on its strength. It was heard by Jonathan King who suggested entering it into Song For Europe. Gina G was the first overseas singer to represent the UK in the Eurovision competition. The song failed to win but became a worldwide smash. Reaching the US top 20, it was the most successful UK Eurovision entry on the US charts. Her career was delayed for two years in 1998 with the collapse of record company FX Music, boss Steve Rodway (who previously recorded as Motiv8) being made bankrupt for 'having acted improperly and dishonestly in knowingly swearing false evidence'.

05/04/1997 . . . . . 12 . . . . . . 4 . . . . . . ○    FRESH! . . . . . . . . . . . . . . . . . . . . . . . . . . . . . . . . . . . . . . . . . . . . . . . . . . . . . . . . . . . . . . . . . . . . . Eternal 0630178402

**KENNY G** US saxophonist (born Kenny Gorelick, 6/7/1956, Seattle, WA) who was in the Love Unlimited Orchestra at seventeen, later auditioning for Jeff Lorber who got him a contract with Arista. He recorded his debut album in 1982 and won the 1993 Grammy Award for Best Instrumental Composition for *Forever In Love*. He has a star on the Hollywood Walk of Fame.

| | | | |
|---|---|---|---|
| 17/03/1984 . . . . . 56 . . . . . 5 . . . . . | G FORCE . . . . . . . . . . . . . . . . . . . . . . . . . . . . . . . . . . . . . . . . . . . . . . . . . . . . . . . . . . . . . . . . Arista 206 168 |
| 08/08/1987 . . . . . 28 . . . . . 5 . . . . . | DUOTONES . . . . . . . . . . . . . . . . . . . . . . . . . . . . . . . . . . . . . . . . . . . . . . . . . . . . . . . . . . . . . . Arista 207 792 |
| 14/04/1990 . . . . . 32 . . . . . 7 . . . . . | MONTAGE . . . . . . . . . . . . . . . . . . . . . . . . . . . . . . . . . . . . . . . . . . . . . . . . . . . . . . . . . . . . . . . Arista 210621 |
| 15/05/1993 . . . . . 4 . . . . . 27 . . . . . ● | **BREATHLESS** ◆[12] . . . . . . . . . . . . . . . . . . . . . . . . . . . . . . . . . . . . . . . . . . . . . . . . . . . Arista 07822186462 |
| 19/10/1996 . . . . . 19 . . . . . 9 . . . . . ● | THE MOMENT . . . . . . . . . . . . . . . . . . . . . . . . . . . . . . . . . . . . . . . . . . . . . . . . . . . . . . . . Arista 07822189352 |
| 13/12/1997 . . . . . 38 . . . . . 5 . . . . . ○ | GREATEST HITS . . . . . . . . . . . . . . . . . . . . . . . . . . . . . . . . . . . . . . . . . . . . . . . . . . . . . . . Arista 07822189912 |

**WARREN G** US rapper (born Warren Griffin III, 1971, Long Beach, CA) who had been part of Dr Dre's Dogg Pound Collective and who later set up the G-Funk label. He is Dr Dre's half-brother, and later formed rap supergroup 213 with Nate Dogg and Snoop Dogg.

| | | |
|---|---|---|
| 06/08/1994 . . . . . 25 . . . . . . 6 . . . . . . ○ | REGULATE…G FUNK ERA . . . . . . . . . . . . . . . . . . . . . . . . . . . . . . . . . . . . . . . . . . . . . . . . RAL 5233352 |
| 08/03/1997 . . . . . 20 . . . . . 4 . . . . . | TAKE A LOOK OVER YOUR SHOULDER (REALITY) . . . . . . . . . . . . . . . . . . . . . . . . . . . . . . . . . . . Def Jam 5334842 |

**G-UNIT** US rap group formed by 50 Cent (born Curtis Jackson in Queens, NY on 6/7/1976), Lloyd Banks (born Christopher Lloyd in Jamaica, NY on 30/4/1982) and Tony Yayo with DJ's Whookid and Cutmaster C. Yayo left the group after being sent to prison for gun possession and was replaced by Young Buck (born David Brown on 15/3/1981).

29/11/2003 . . . . . 13 . . . . . 10 . . . . . . ●    BEG FOR MERCY . . . . . . . . . . . . . . . . . . . . . . . . . . . . . . . . . . . . . . . . . . . . . . . . . . . . . . . Interscope 9861498

**PETER GABRIEL** UK singer (born 13/2/1950, London) who was lead singer with Genesis from 1966 to 1975 when he went solo. His debut album took two years to materialise. He won Best British Male at the 1987 BRIT Awards and Best Producer at the 1993 awards. His four Grammy Awards included Best New Age Recording in 1989 for *Passion – Music For 'The Last Temptation Of Christ'*, Best Video Short Form in 1992 for *Digging In The Dirt*, Best Music Video Short Form in 1993 for *Steam* and Best Music Video Long Form in 1995 for *Secret World Live*.

| | | |
|---|---|---|
| 12/03/1977 . . . . . 7 . . . . . . 19 . . . . . . ● | **PETER GABRIEL** . . . . . . . . . . . . . . . . . . . . . . . . . . . . . . . . . . . . . . . . . . . . . . . . . . . . . Charisma CDS 4006 |
| 17/06/1978 . . . . . 10 . . . . . 8 . . . . . | **PETER GABRIEL** . . . . . . . . . . . . . . . . . . . . . . . . . . . . . . . . . . . . . . . . . . . . . . . . . . . . . Charisma CDS 4013 |
| 07/06/1980 . . . . . ❶[2] . . . . 18 . . . . . . ● | **PETER GABRIEL** . . . . . . . . . . . . . . . . . . . . . . . . . . . . . . . . . . . . . . . . . . . . . . . . . . . . . Charisma CDC 4019 |
| 18/09/1982 . . . . . 6 . . . . . 16 . . . . . . ● | **PETER GABRIEL** . . . . . . . . . . . . . . . . . . . . . . . . . . . . . . . . . . . . . . . . . . . . . . . . . . . . . . . Charisma PG 4 |
| 18/06/1983 . . . 8 . . . . . 9 . . . . . | **PETER GABRIEL PLAYS LIVE** . . . . . . . . . . . . . . . . . . . . . . . . . . . . . . . . . . . . . . . . . . . . . Charisma PGDL 1 |
| 30/03/1985 . . . . . 51 . . . . . 3 . . . . . | BIRDY Soundtrack from the 1984 film *Birdy* . . . . . . . . . . . . . . . . . . . . . . . . . . . . . . . . . . . . Charisma CAS 1167 |
| 31/05/1986 . . . . . ❶[2] . . . . 76 . . . . . ✪[3] | **SO** . . . . . . . . . . . . . . . . . . . . . . . . . . . . . . . . . . . . . . . . . . . . . . . . . . . . . . . . . . . . . . . . . . . Virgin PG 5 |
| 17/06/1989 . . . . . 29 . . . . . 5 . . . . . | PASSION . . . . . . . . . . . . . . . . . . . . . . . . . . . . . . . . . . . . . . . . . . . . . . . . . . . . . . . . . . . . . . Virgin RWLP 1 |
| 01/12/1990 . . . . . 11 . . . . . 18 . . . . . . ✪[2] | SHAKING THE TREE – GOLDEN GREATS . . . . . . . . . . . . . . . . . . . . . . . . . . . . . . . . . . . . . . . . Virgin PGTV 6 |
| 10/10/1992 . . . . . 2 . . . . . 29 . . . . . . ✪ | **US** . . . . . . . . . . . . . . . . . . . . . . . . . . . . . . . . . . . . . . . . . . . . . . . . . . . . . . . . . . . . . . . Virgin PGCD 7 |
| 10/09/1994 . . . . . 10 . . . . . 4 . . . . . . ○ | **SECRET WORLD LIVE** . . . . . . . . . . . . . . . . . . . . . . . . . . . . . . . . . . . . . . . . . . . . . . . . . Virgin PGDCD 8 |
| 24/06/2000 . . . . . 24 . . . . . 2 . . . . . | OVO . . . . . . . . . . . . . . . . . . . . . . . . . . . . . . . . . . . . . . . . . . . . . . . . . . . . . . . . . . . Realworld RWPG 01 |
| 05/10/2002 . . . . . 11 . . . . . 4 . . . . . . ○ | UP . . . . . . . . . . . . . . . . . . . . . . . . . . . . . . . . . . . . . . . . . . . . . . . . . . . . . . . . . . . . Realworld PGCD 11 |
| 15/11/2003 . . . . . 29 . . . . . 4 . . . . . . ● | HIT . . . . . . . . . . . . . . . . . . . . . . . . . . . . . . . . . . . . . . . . . . . . . . . . . . . . . . . . . . . . . Realworld 5952372 |

---

▲[9] Number of weeks album topped the US chart    ◆[12] RIAA Diamond Awards    ◇[3] IFPI Platinum Europe Awards

**GABRIELLE** UK singer (born Louise Gabrielle Bobb, 16/4/1970, London) whose debut hit was initially a white-label release on the Victim label before being picked up by Jetstar. It was deleted after objections by Tracy Chapman to the sample of *Fast Car*. Signed by Go Beat, the song was re-recorded without the sample. She was named Best British Newcomer at the 1994 BRIT Awards and Best British Female at the 1997 Awards and also took part in the *Perfect Day* project for the BBC's Children In Need charity. In December 1995 former boyfriend Tony Antoniou, with whom she had a son, was charged with the murder of his father after beheading him with a samurai sword. Gabrielle was taken in for questioning and had to give evidence at his trial.

| DATE | POS | WKS | BPI | ALBUM TITLE | LABEL & NUMBER |
|---|---|---|---|---|---|
| 30/10/1993 | 9 | 22 | ● | FIND YOUR WAY | Go Beat 8284412 |
| 08/06/1996 | 11 | 30 | ✪ | GABRIELLE | Go Beat 8287242 |
| 30/10/1999 | ❶³ | 87 | ✪⁴ | RISE ◇ 2000 MOBO Award for Best Album | Go Beat 5477682 |
| 24/11/2001 | 2 | 26 | ✪⁴ | DREAMS CAN COME TRUE – GREATEST HITS VOLUME 1 ◇ | Go Beat 5893742 |
| 29/05/2004 | 10 | 5+ | ● | PLAY TO WIN | Go Beat 9866530 |

**DAVE GAHAN** UK singer (born 9/5/1962, Epping, Essex) who is also lead singer with Depeche Mode.

| DATE | POS | WKS | BPI | ALBUM TITLE | LABEL & NUMBER |
|---|---|---|---|---|---|
| 14/06/2003 | 36 | 2 | | PAPER MONSTERS | Mute CDSTUMM216 |

**RORY GALLAGHER** Irish singer/ guitarist (born 2/3/1949, Ballyshannon, County Donegal); he formed Taste in 1965, a group that enjoyed a five year career before disbanding in 1970. Gallagher then linked with Gerry McAvoy and Wilgar Campbell as he embarked on a solo career with greater success. Campbell left the touring group and was replaced by Rod De'Ath and also added Lou Marrin on keyboards in 1972, these two remaining with the group until 1978. Gallagher died from complications brought on by a liver transplant on 14/6/1995.

| DATE | POS | WKS | BPI | ALBUM TITLE | LABEL & NUMBER |
|---|---|---|---|---|---|
| 29/05/1971 | 32 | 2 | | RORY GALLAGHER | Polydor 2383 044 |
| 04/12/1971 | 39 | 1 | | DEUCE | Polydor 2383 076 |
| 20/05/1972 | 9 | 15 | | LIVE! IN EUROPE | Polydor 2383 112 |
| 24/02/1973 | 12 | 7 | | BLUE PRINT | Polydor 2383 189 |
| 17/11/1973 | 32 | 3 | | TATTOO | Polydor 2383 230 |
| 27/07/1974 | 36 | 2 | ○ | IRISH TOUR '74 | Polydor 2659 031 |
| 30/10/1976 | 32 | 1 | | CALLING CARD | Chrysalis CHR 1124 |
| 22/09/1979 | 56 | 4 | | TOP PRIORITY | Chrysalis CHR 1235 |
| 08/11/1980 | 40 | 3 | | STAGE STRUCK | Chrysalis CHR 1280 |
| 08/05/1982 | 68 | 5 | | JINX | Chrysalis CHR 1359 |

**GALLAGHER AND LYLE** UK duo Benny Gallagher and Graham Lyle (both born in Largs, Scotland) originally teamed up in Scotland before moving to London to join McGuinness Flint and then Slim Chance. Debuting together in 1974, their final album was in 1979. Lyle's songwriting included Grammy Award winner *What's Love Got To Do With It*, a smash for Tina Turner and Warren G.

| DATE | POS | WKS | BPI | ALBUM TITLE | LABEL & NUMBER |
|---|---|---|---|---|---|
| 28/02/1976 | 6 | 35 | ● | BREAKAWAY | A&M AMLH 68348 |
| 29/01/1977 | 19 | 9 | ○ | LOVE ON THE AIRWAYS | A&M AMLH 64620 |

**GALLIANO** UK jazz funk group with Rob Gallagher, Constantine Weir, Crispin Robinson and Michael Snaith. Gallagher also adopted the name Galliano.

| DATE | POS | WKS | BPI | ALBUM TITLE | LABEL & NUMBER |
|---|---|---|---|---|---|
| 20/06/1992 | 28 | 3 | | A JOYFUL NOISE UNTO THE CREATOR | Talkin Loud 8480802 |
| 11/06/1994 | 7 | 12 | | THE PLOT THICKENS | Talkin Loud 5224522 |

**GALLON DRUNK** UK group formed in London in 1990 by James Johnston (guitar/keyboards/vocals), Mike Delanian (bass), Joe Byfield (percussion) and Nick Combe (drums), although Combe soon left and was replaced by Max Decharne. After releasing records on their own Massive label they signed with Clawfist in 1993. They later added Terry Edwards on horns. James Johnston made his acting debut in *The Fall Of The Louse Of Usher* in 2001.

| DATE | POS | WKS | BPI | ALBUM TITLE | LABEL & NUMBER |
|---|---|---|---|---|---|
| 13/03/1993 | 67 | 1 | | FROM THE HEART OF TOWN | Clawfist HUNKACDL 005 |

**JAMES GALWAY** UK flautist (born 8/12/1939, Belfast) who is considered one of the world's top flautists. His interpretation of Elton John's song *Basque* was named Best Instrumental Composition at the 1991 Grammy Awards.

| DATE | POS | WKS | BPI | ALBUM TITLE | LABEL & NUMBER |
|---|---|---|---|---|---|
| 27/05/1978 | 43 | 6 | | THE MAGIC FLUTE OF JAMES GALWAY | RCA Red Seal LRLI 5131 |
| 01/07/1978 | 52 | 3 | | THE MAN WITH THE GOLDEN FLUTE | RCA Red Seal LRLI 5127 |
| 09/09/1978 | 7 | 40 | ✪ | JAMES GALWAY PLAYS SONGS FOR ANNIE | RCA Red Seal RL 25163 |
| 15/12/1979 | 39 | 6 | ● | SONGS OF THE SEASHORE | Solar RL 25253 |
| 31/05/1980 | 15 | 14 | ● | SOMETIMES WHEN WE TOUCH **CLEO LAINE AND JAMES GALWAY** | RCA PL 25296 |

| | | | | |
|---|---|---|---|---|
| 18/12/1982 | 41 | 8 | | THE JAMES GALWAY COLLECTION | Telstar STAR 2224 |
| 08/12/1984 | 62 | 6 | | IN THE PINK **JAMES GALWAY AND HENRY MANCINI** | RCA Red Seal RL 85315 |
| 28/03/1987 | 32 | 5 | | JAMES GALWAY AND THE CHIEFTAINS IN IRELAND **JAMES GALWAY AND THE CHIEFTAINS** | RCA Red Seal RL 85798 |
| 17/04/1993 | 30 | 5 | | MASTERPIECES – THE ESSENTIAL FLUTE OF JAMES GALWAY | RCA Victor 74321133852 |
| 18/02/1995 | 59 | 2 | | I WILL ALWAYS LOVE YOU | RCA Victor 74321262212 |
| 20/07/1996 | 45 | 5 | | CLASSICAL MEDITATIONS | RCA Victor 74321377312 |

**GANG OF FOUR** UK rock group formed in Leeds in 1977 by Jon King (melodica/vocals), Andy Gill (guitar), Dave Allen (drums) and Hugo Barnham (drums). Allen left in 1981 and was replaced by bassist Sara Lee. Barnham was sacked in 1983, the group using session drummers before disbanding soon after. They were revived in 1990 by Jon King and Andy Gill, adding drummer Steve Monti to the line-up the following year.

| | | | | |
|---|---|---|---|---|
| 13/10/1979 | 45 | 3 | | ENTERTAINMENT | EMI EMC 3313 |
| 21/03/1981 | 52 | 2 | | SOLID GOLD | EMI EMC 3364 |
| 29/05/1982 | 61 | 4 | | SONGS OF THE FREE | EMI EMC 3412 |

**GANG STARR** US hip hop duo Guru Keith (born Keith Elam, 18/7/1966, Boston, MA) and DJ Premier (born Christopher Martin, Brooklyn, NYC). Guru later recorded solo.

| | | | | |
|---|---|---|---|---|
| 26/01/1991 | 36 | 3 | | STEP IN THE ARENA | Cooltempo ZCTLP 21 |
| 12/03/1994 | 29 | 3 | | HARD TO EARN | Cooltempo CTCD 38 |
| 11/04/1998 | 43 | 1 | | MOMENT OF TRUTH | Cooltempo 8455852 |
| 07/08/1999 | 47 | 2 | | FULL CLIP: A DECADE OF GANG STARR | Cooltempo 5211892 |
| 05/07/2003 | 74 | 1 | | THE OWNERZ | Virgin CDVUS235 |

**GANJA KRU** – see **DJ HYPE PRESENTS GANJA KRU**

**GAP BAND** US R&B group with brothers Charles, Ronnie and Robert Wilson. They took their name from three streets in their hometown of Tulsa in Oklahoma: Greenwood, Archer and Pine. They are cousins of William 'Bootsy' Collins.

| | | | | |
|---|---|---|---|---|
| 07/02/1987 | 47 | 3 | | GAP BAND 8 | Total Experience FL 89992 |

**GARBAGE** US/UK group formed by Butch Vig (born Brian Vig, Viroqua, US), Steve Markes, Duke Erikson and lead singer Shirley Manson (born in Edinburgh). Manson had been singer with Goodbye Mr McKenzie. Vig is also an independent producer, having produced albums by The Smashing Pumpkins, U2 and Nirvana. Named Breakthrough Act at the 1996 MTV Europe Music Awards.

| | | | | |
|---|---|---|---|---|
| 14/10/1995 | 6 | 100 | ✪² | GARBAGE | Mushroom D 31450 |
| 23/05/1998 | ❶¹ | 65 | ✪² | VERSION 2.0 ◇ | Mushroom MUSH 29CD |
| 13/10/2001 | 6 | 4 | ● | BEAUTIFUL GARBAGE | Mushroom MUSH 95CDX |

**JAN GARBAREK** Norwegian saxophonist (born 4/3/1947), inspired to play saxophone by hearing John Coltrane on the radio.

| | | | | |
|---|---|---|---|---|
| 04/05/1996 | 69 | 1 | | VISIBLE WORLD | ECM 5290862 |

**ART GARFUNKEL** US singer (born 13/10/1942, Forest Hills, NYC) who teamed up with Queens schoolmate Paul Simon when aged eleven, becoming the most successful duo since the Everly Brothers. They split in 1970 after completing *Bridge Over Troubled Water*, Garfunkel appearing in the film *Catch 22* the same year. He returned to music in 1973 and has since reunited with Simon on numerous occasions. He was inducted into the Rock & Roll Hall of Fame in 1990 (as part of Simon & Garfunkel).

| | | | | |
|---|---|---|---|---|
| 13/10/1973 | 14 | 7 | ○ | ANGEL CLARE | CBS 69021 |
| 01/11/1975 | 7 | 10 | ● | **BREAKAWAY** | CBS 86002 |
| 18/03/1978 | 25 | 5 | ○ | WATER MARK | CBS 86054 |
| 21/04/1979 | 2 | 20 | ● | **FATE FOR BREAKFAST** | CBS 86082 |
| 19/09/1981 | 51 | 3 | | SCISSORS CUT | CBS 85259 |
| 17/11/1984 | 12 | 13 | ● | THE ART GARFUNKEL ALBUM | CBS 10046 |
| 14/12/1996 | 35 | 6 | ○ | THE VERY BEST OF ART GARFUNKEL – ACROSS AMERICA | Virgin VTCD 113 |

**JUDY GARLAND** US singer/actress (born Frances Ethel Gumm, 10/6/1922, Grand Rapids, MN) who made her stage debut at three and then worked with her siblings as The Gumm Sisters. Signed by Louis B Mayer to MGM Pictures at twelve, she made her first film in 1936 (a short, *Every Sunday*, followed by her debut feature film *Pigskin Parade*), her most famous role being Dorothy in *The Wizard Of Oz* in 1939 (gaining a Special Academy Award 'for her outstanding performance as a screen juvenile'). She died from an accidental drug overdose in London on 22/6/1969. She has a star on the Hollywood Walk of Fame. Liza Minnelli is her daughter by film director Vincent Minnelli.

| | | | | |
|---|---|---|---|---|
| 03/03/1962 | 13 | 3 | | JUDY AT CARNEGIE HALL ▲¹³ 1961 Grammy Awards: Album of the Year and Best Female Solo Vocal Performance | Capitol W 1569 |

**ERROLL GARNER** US pianist/songwriter (born 15/6/1921, Pittsburgh, PA), self-taught, he was appearing on radio by the age of ten. After playing with various bands around Pittsburgh he moved to New York in 1944. A resident musician at the Rendezvous

and Melody Bar nightclubs, he had formed his own trio by the end of the '40s. He toured for the next three decades, proving as popular in the UK and Europe as he was in his homeland. He was also an accomplished songwriter, despite never learning to read music, and is perhaps best known for the composition *Misty* which, with lyrics added by Johnny Burke has become a jazz standard (and even inspired a film title in Clint Eastwood's directorial debut *Play Misty For Me*). Known throughout his career as 'The Elf' in reference to his size, he died on 2/1/1977. He has a star on the Hollywood Walk of Fame.

| | | | | | | |
|---|---|---|---|---|---|---|
| 14/07/1962 | 20 | 1 | | CLOSE UP IN SWING | Philips BBL 7579 |

## LESLEY GARRETT
UK operatic singer (born 10/4/1955) she also took part in the *Perfect Day* project for the BBC's Children In Need charity and was awarded a CBE in the 2002 New Year's Honours List.

| | | | | | | |
|---|---|---|---|---|---|---|
| 12/02/1994 | 25 | 7 | | AVE MARIA – THE ALBUM | Telstar TCD 2709 |
| 18/11/1995 | 59 | 8 | ○ | SOPRANO IN RED | Silva Classics SILKTVCD 1 |
| 19/10/1996 | 53 | 4 | | SOPRANO IN HOLLYWOOD | Silva Classics SILKTVCD 2 |
| 18/10/1997 | 53 | 2 | ○ | THE SOPRANO'S GREATEST HITS | Silva Classics SILKTVCD 3 |
| 22/11/1997 | 48 | 7 | ○ | A SOPRANO INSPIRED | Conifer Classics 75605513292 |
| 14/11/1998 | 34 | 8 | | LESLEY GARRETT | BBC 75605513382 |
| 27/05/2000 | 28 | 7 | | I WILL WAIT FOR YOU | BBC/BMG Conifer 75605513542 |
| 24/11/2001 | 75 | 1 | | TRAVELLING LIGHT | EMI Classics CDC 5572512 |

## STEPHEN GATELY
Irish singer (born 17/3/1976, Dublin) who was with Boyzone from 1993 to 2000.

| | | | | | | |
|---|---|---|---|---|---|---|
| 01/07/2000 | 9 | 4 | | NEW BEGINNING | A&M 5439102 |

## DAVID GATES
US singer/guitarist/producer/songwriter (born 11/12/1940, Tulsa, OK) who began as a session musician for Chuck Berry, Duane Eddy, Glen Campbell, Merle Haggard and others. He formed Bread in 1969 with James Griffin (guitar), Robb Rover (guitar) and Jim Gordon (drums), Larry Knetchtel and Mike Botts later replacing the latter two. They disbanded in 1973, briefly reuniting in 1976, with Gates enjoying a brief solo career before going into retirement.

| | | | | | | |
|---|---|---|---|---|---|---|
| 31/05/1975 | 32 | 1 | | NEVER LET HER GO | Elektra K 52012 |
| 29/07/1978 | 28 | 3 | ○ | GOODBYE GIRL | Elektra K 52091 |
| 28/11/1987 | 94 | 2 | | THE COLLECTION – THE VERY BEST OF BREAD AND DAVID GATES **BREAD AND DAVID GATES** | Telstar STAR 2303 |
| 05/07/1997 | 9 | 19 | ● | **DAVID GATES AND BREAD: ESSENTIALS DAVID GATES AND BREAD** | warner.esp/Jive 9548354082 |
| 12/10/2002 | 11 | 7 | ● | SONGBOOK – A LIFETIME OF MUSIC | Jive 0927491402 |

## GARETH GATES
UK singer (born 12/7/1984, Bradford) who became famous in the TV series *Pop Idol*, overcoming a chronic stammer during the course of the competition and finishing second to Will Young. He was seventeen at the time of his debut hit and duly became the youngest British male to top the UK singles chart.

| | | | | | | |
|---|---|---|---|---|---|---|
| 09/11/2002 | 2 | 17 | ✪² | **WHAT MY HEART WANTS TO SAY** | S 74321975172 |
| 04/10/2003 | 11 | 4 | | GO YOUR OWN WAY | S 82876557452 |

## GAY DAD
UK rock group formed in 1996 by ex-*Mojo* and *The Face* journalist Cliff Jones (guitar/vocals), Nigel Hoyle (bass/guitar), Nicholas 'Baz' Crowe (drums) and James Risebero (keyboards). They are augmented by singer/guitarist Charley Stone for live dates.

| | | | | | | |
|---|---|---|---|---|---|---|
| 19/06/1999 | 14 | 3 | | LEISURE NOISE | London 5561032 |

## MARVIN GAYE
US singer (born Marvin Pentz Gay Jr, 2/4/1939, Washington DC) who sang in his father's church before joining local groups the Rainbows and Marquees. Invited by Harvey Fuqua to join the re-formed Moonglows for two singles for Chess, he followed Fuqua to Detroit, MI and joined Motown as a session drummer. First recording for the label in 1961, he established himself as a solo performer, also recording highly successful duets. The death of Tammi Terrell in 1970 sent him into seclusion, but his brother Frankie's accounts of the horrors of Vietnam prompted him to record *What's Going On*. He also appeared in the 1971 film *Chrome And Hot Leather*. After various problems he left Motown and lived in Europe for three years. He returned to the US following the success of *(Sexual) Healing*. He married Berry Gordy's sister Anna in 1961; they divorced in 1975 (part of the alimony settlement called for Anna to receive all royalties from a forthcoming album: he recorded *Here My Dear* detailing almost every aspect of their relationship together). His second marriage to Jan also ended in divorce. He was inducted into the Rock & Roll Hall of Fame in 1987 and has a star on the Hollywood Walk of Fame. He won the 1982 Grammy for Best Rhythm and Blues Vocal Performance and Best Rhythm & Blues Instrumental Performance for *Sexual Healing*. He was shot to death by his father the day before his birthday on 1/4/1984.

| | | | | | | |
|---|---|---|---|---|---|---|
| 16/03/1968 | 40 | 1 | | GREATEST HITS | Tamla Motown STML 11065 |
| 22/08/1970 | 60 | 4 | | GREATEST HITS **MARVIN GAYE AND TAMMI TERRELL** | Tamla Motown STML 11153 |
| 10/11/1973 | 39 | 1 | | LET'S GET IT ON | Tamla Motown STMA 8013 |
| 19/01/1974 | 6 | 43 | ● | **DIANA AND MARVIN DIANA ROSS AND MARVIN GAYE** | Tamla Motown STMA 8015 |
| 15/05/1976 | 22 | 5 | | I WANT YOU | Tamla Motown STML 12025 |
| 30/10/1976 | 56 | 1 | | THE BEST OF MARVIN GAYE | Tamla Motown STML 12042 |
| 28/02/1981 | 48 | 4 | | IN OUR LIFETIME | Motown STML 12149 |
| 29/08/1981 | 78 | 2 | | DIANA AND MARVIN **DIANA ROSS AND MARVIN GAYE** Re-issue of Tamla Motown STMA 8015 | Motown STMS 5001 |
| 20/11/1982 | 10 | 16 | ● | **MIDNIGHT LOVE** | CBS 85977 |
| 12/11/1983 | 13 | 61 | ● | GREATEST HITS | Telstar STAR 2234 |
| 15/06/1985 | 46 | 4 | | DREAM OF A LIFETIME | CBS 26239 |
| 12/11/1988 | 69 | 9 | ● | LOVE SONGS **MARVIN GAYE AND SMOKEY ROBINSON** | Telstar STAR 2331 |
| 03/11/1990 | 39 | 5 | | LOVE SONGS | Telstar STAR 2427 |
| 09/04/1994 | 3 | 19 | ● | **THE VERY BEST OF MARVIN GAYE** | Motown 5302922 |
| 24/07/1999 | 56 | 4 | | WHAT'S GOING ON? First released in the US in 1971, it made UK chart after being on a 'classic albums' TV series. | Motown 5300222 |
| 19/02/2000 | 8 | 7 | ● | **THE LOVE SONGS** | Motown 5454702 |
| 01/09/2001 | 15 | 4 | | THE VERY BEST OF MARVIN GAYE ◇ | Motown 0143672 |

○ Silver disc   ● Gold disc   ✪ Platinum disc (additional platinum units are indicated by a figure following the symbol)   ❶⁹ Number of weeks album topped the UK chart

### GAYE BYKERS ON ACID
UK group formed by Mary Millington (aka Mary Mary, born Ian Hoxley, vocals), Robber (born Ian Reynolds, bass), Tony (born Richard Anthony Horsfall, guitar) and Kevin Hyde (drums). The group set up their own Naked Brain label.

| 14/11/1987 | 95 | 1 | | DRILL YOUR OWN HOLE | Virgin V 2478 |

### CRYSTAL GAYLE
US country singer (born Brenda Gail Web, 9/1/1951, Paintsville, KY, raised in Wabash, IN) who began in sister Loretta Lynn's road show at sixteen, scoring her first country hit in 1970. Three Grammy Awards include: Best Comedy Vocal Performance in 1977 for *Don't It Make My Brown Eyes Blue*; Best Recording for Children in 1981 with The Muppets, Glen Campbell, Loretta Lynn and Tanya Tucker for *Sesame Country*; and Best Recording for Children in 1982 with various others for *In Harmony 2*.

| 21/01/1978 | 15 | 7 | ○ | WE MUST BELIEVE IN MAGIC | United Artists UAG 30108 |
| 23/09/1978 | 25 | 8 | ○ | WHEN I DREAM | United Artists UAG 30169 |
| 22/03/1980 | 7 | 10 | ● | **THE CRYSTAL GAYLE SINGLES ALBUM** | United Artists UAG 30287 |

### MICHELLE GAYLE
UK singer (born 2/2/1971, London) who was first known as an actress in the TV series *Grange Hill* and as Hattie Tavernier in *Eastenders* before launching a singing career. She married footballer Mark Bright in 1997.

| 22/10/1994 | 30 | 10 | ● | MICHELLE GAYLE | RCA 74321234122 |
| 10/05/1997 | 17 | 3 | | SENSATIONAL | RCA 74321419322 |

### GLORIA GAYNOR
US singer (born 7/9/1949, Newark, NJ) who began with the Soul Satisfiers before signing solo with CBS in the early 1970s. She switched to MGM in 1974 and quickly became established as one of the top disco singers of the era.

| 08/03/1975 | 32 | 8 | ○ | NEVER CAN SAY GOODBYE | MGM 2315 321 |
| 24/03/1979 | 31 | 7 | | LOVE TRACKS | Polydor 2391 385 |
| 16/08/1986 | 81 | 2 | | THE POWER OF GLORIA GAYNOR | Stylus SMR 618 |

### J. GEILS BAND
US group formed in Boston, MA in 1967 by Jerome Geils (born 20/2/1946, New York, guitar), Danny Klein (born 13/5/1946, New York, bass), Magic Dick (born Richard Salwitz, 13/5/1945, New London, CT, harmonica), Peter Wolf (born Peter Blankfield, 7/3/1946, The Bronx, NYC, vocals) and Stephen Jo Bladd (born 13/7/1942, Boston, drums/vocals) as the J. Geils Blues Band. Seth Justman (born 27/1/1951, Washington DC, keyboards) joined in 1969 and 'Blues' was dropped from their name. Wolf went solo in 1983; the group split in 1987.

| 27/02/1982 | 12 | 15 | | FREEZE-FRAME ▲⁴ | EMI America AML 3020 |

### BOB GELDOF
Irish singer (born 5/10/1954, Dublin), formerly a journalist with the *NME*, who formed the Boomtown Rats in 1975. In 1984, moved by TV coverage of the famine in Ethiopia, he organised Band Aid with Midge Ure. The single's success prompted the 1985 'global concert' Live Aid, taking up much of Geldof's time over the next five years. He appeared in the 1982 film *The Wall* and went solo in 1986. With Band Aid raising over $100 million, he was awarded an honorary knighthood in 1986 and nominated for a Nobel Peace Prize.

| 06/12/1986 | 79 | 1 | ● | DEEP IN THE HEART OF NOWHERE | Mercury BOBLP 1 |
| 04/08/1990 | 21 | 6 | | THE VEGETARIANS OF LOVE | Mercury 8462501 |
| 09/07/1994 | 10 | 3 | | LOUDMOUTH – THE BEST OF THE BOOMTOWN RATS AND BOB GELDOF **BOOMTOWN RATS AND BOB GELDOF** | Vertigo 5222832 |

### GENE
UK group formed in 1993 by Steve Mason (born 1971, guitar), Martin Rossiter (born 1971, vocals), Kevin Miles (born 1967, bass) and Matt James (born 1966, drums). The Costermonger label was formed for Gene.

| 01/04/1995 | 8 | 6 | ○ | **OLYMPIAN** | Costermonger 5274462 |
| 03/02/1996 | 11 | 3 | | TO SEE THE LIGHTS | Costermonger GENE 002CD |
| 01/03/1997 | 8 | 3 | | **DRAWN TO THE DEEP END** | Polydor GENEC 3 |
| 13/03/1999 | 25 | 2 | | REVELATIONS | Polydor GENEC 4 |

### GENE LOVES JEZEBEL
UK group formed in 1981 by twin brothers Jay (vocals) and Mike Aston (vocals) with Ian Hudson (guitar), Julianne Regan (bass) and Dick Hawkins (drums). Hawkins left soon after their debut and was replaced by John Murphy and then Steve Goulding. Regan left to join All About Eve. Subsequent changes included Pete Rizzo (bass), Chris Bell (drums) and James Stevenson (guitar) joining in 1984. Mike Aston left in 1989. By 1993 they were Jay Aston, Rizzo, Stevenson and Robert Adam (drums).

| 19/07/1986 | 32 | 4 | | DISCOVER | Beggars Banquet BEGA 73 |
| 24/10/1987 | 81 | 1 | | HOUSE OF DOLLS | Beggars Banquet BEGA 87 |

### GENERATION X
UK punk group comprising Billy Idol (born William Broad, 30/11/1955, Stanmore, vocals), Tony James (bass), John Trowe (drums), Bob Andrews (guitar) in 1976. Idol later went solo while James was a founding member of Sigue Sigue Sputnik.

| 08/04/1978 | 29 | 4 | | GENERATION X | Chrysalis CHR 1169 |
| 17/02/1979 | 51 | 5 | | VALLEY OF THE DOLLS | Chrysalis CHR 1193 |

### GENESIS
UK rock group formed at Charterhouse School in Godalming by Peter Gabriel (born 13/5/1950, Cobham, vocals), Tony Banks (born 27/3/1950, East Heathley, keyboards), Chas Stewart (drums), Mike Rutherford (born 2/10/1950, Guildford, guitars) and Anthony Phillips (guitar) from the remnants of Garden Wall and Anon. They adopted the name (New) Anon, sending a demo to Jonathan King at Decca, who renamed them Genesis. Stewart left in 1968 after their debut single and was replaced by John Silver. Their first album, *From Genesis To Revelation,* sold 650 copies, the group temporarily going under the name Revelation (there was a US group Genesis: when they disbanded, the English group reverted back). Silver left in 1969 and was replaced by John Mayhew. They signed with Charisma in 1970, and shortly after their first album there Phillips and Mayhew left. Steve Hackett (born 12/2/1950, London) joined from 1971 to 1977. Phil Collins (born 31/1/1951, Chiswick, London) was brought in on drums. Gabriel went solo in 1975, Collins becoming lead singer. Banks, Collins and Rutherford all launched parallel careers: Banks and Collins solo, Rutherford with Mike + The Mechanics. By 1997 the group comprised Banks, Rutherford and new singer Ray Wilson (formerly of Stiltskin). They won the 1987 Grammy Award for Best Concept Music Video for *Land Of Confusion*.

▲⁹ Number of weeks album topped the US chart ◆¹² RIAA Diamond Awards ◇³ IFPI Platinum Europe Awards

| DATE | POS | WKS | BPI | ALBUM TITLE | LABEL & NUMBER |
|---|---|---|---|---|---|
| 14/10/1972 | 12 | 7 | | FOXTROT | Charisma CAS 1058 |
| 11/08/1973 | 9 | 10 | | GENESIS LIVE | Charisma CLASS 1 |
| 20/10/1973 | 3 | 21 | ○ | SELLING ENGLAND BY THE POUND | Charisma CAS 1074 |
| 11/05/1974 | 39 | 1 | | NURSERY CRYME | Charisma CAS 1052 |
| 07/12/1974 | 10 | 6 | ● | THE LAMB LIES DOWN ON BROADWAY | Charisma CGS 101 |
| 28/02/1976 | 3 | 39 | ● | A TRICK OF THE TRAIL | Charisma CDS 4001 |
| 15/01/1977 | 7 | 22 | ● | WIND AND WUTHERING | Charisma CDS 4005 |
| 29/10/1977 | 4 | 17 | ● | SECONDS OUT | Charisma GE 2001 |
| 15/04/1978 | 3 | 32 | ● | ... AND THEN THERE WERE THREE... | Charisma CDS 4010 |
| 05/04/1980 | ❶² | 30 | ✪² | DUKE | Charisma CBR 101 |
| 26/09/1981 | ❶² | 27 | ● | ABACAB | Charisma CBR 102 |
| 12/06/1982 | 2 | 19 | ● | THREE SIDES LIVE | Charisma GE 2002 |
| 15/10/1983 | ❶¹ | 51 | ✪² | GENESIS | Charisma GENLP 1 |
| 31/03/1984 | 68 | 1 | | NURSERY CRYME Re-issue of Charisma CAS 1052 | Charisma CHC 22 |
| 21/04/1984 | 98 | 1 | | TRESPASS | Charisma CHC 12 |
| 21/06/1986 | ❶³ | 96 | ✪⁴ | INVISIBLE TOUCH | Charisma GENLP 2 |
| 23/11/1991 | ❶² | 61 | ✪⁵ | WE CAN'T DANCE | Virgin GENLP 3 |
| 28/11/1992 | 3 | 18 | ✪² | LIVE – THE WAY WE WALK VOLUME 1: THE SHORTS | Virgin GENCD 4 |
| 23/01/1993 | ❶² | 9 | ● | LIVE – THE WAY WE WALK VOLUME 2: THE LONGS | Virgin GENCD 5 |
| 13/09/1997 | 2 | 7 | ● | CALLING ALL STATIONS | Virgin GENCD 6 |
| 04/07/1998 | 35 | 1 | | ARCHIVE 1967–1975 | Virgin CDBOX 6 |
| 06/11/1999 | 4 | 15 | ✪ | TURN IT ON AGAIN – THE HITS ◇ | Virgin GENCD 8 |

**GENEVA** UK rock group formed in Aberdeen in 1992 by Andrew Montgomery (vocals), Steven Dara (guitar), Stuart Evans (guitar), Keith Graham (bass) and Douglas Caskie (drums) as Sunfish, changing their name upon signing with Nude.

| DATE | POS | WKS | ALBUM TITLE | LABEL & NUMBER |
|---|---|---|---|---|
| 21/06/1997 | 20 | 2 | FURTHER | Nude 7CD |

**GENIUS/GZA** US rapper (born Gary Grice, 22/8/1966, Brooklyn, NYC) whose debut album in 1989 was for Cold Chillin' Records. Genius/GZA is also in the rap supergroup Wu-Tang Clan.

| DATE | POS | WKS | ALBUM TITLE | LABEL & NUMBER |
|---|---|---|---|---|
| 02/12/1995 | 73 | 1 | LIQUID SWORDS | Geffen GED 24813 |
| 10/07/1999 | 56 | 1 | BENEATH THE SURFACE | MCA MCD 11969 |

**JACKIE GENOVA** UK fitness instructor.

| DATE | POS | WKS | ALBUM TITLE | LABEL & NUMBER |
|---|---|---|---|---|
| 21/05/1983 | 74 | 2 | WORK THAT BODY | Island ILPS 9732 |

**BOBBIE GENTRY** US singer (born Roberta Lee Streeter, 27/7/1944, Chickasaw County, MS, raised in Greenwood) who launched her solo career in 1967. She has won three Grammy Awards: Best Contemporary Solo Vocal Performance and Best Female Vocal Performance in 1967 for *Ode To Billy Joe* and Best New Artist for that year. She married singer Jim Stafford in 1978.

| DATE | POS | WKS | ALBUM TITLE | LABEL & NUMBER |
|---|---|---|---|---|
| 25/10/1969 | 21 | 1 | TOUCH 'EM WITH LOVE | Capitol EST 155 |
| 28/02/1970 | 50 | 1 | BOBBIE GENTRY AND GLEN CAMPBELL **BOBBIE GENTRY AND GLEN CAMPBELL** | Capitol ST 2928 |

**LOWELL GEORGE** US singer/guitarist (born 13/4/1945, Los Angeles, CA) he played with the Standells and then Frank Zappa's Mothers of Invention before setting up Little Feat in 1969. Although signed by Warner Brothers and immediately critically acclaimed, sales of their first three albums were disappointing. Their fourth album made the charts and their reputation, but by this time Lowell George was over-indulging on drugs and alcohol. Although an accomplished guitarist and songwriter, his debut album concentrated on his singing, bringing a critical rebuke. George was on a solo tour when he suffered a heart attack and died on 29/6/1979.

| DATE | POS | WKS | ALBUM TITLE | LABEL & NUMBER |
|---|---|---|---|---|
| 21/04/1979 | 71 | 1 | THANKS BUT I'LL EAT IT HERE | Warner Brothers K 56487 |

**ROBIN GEORGE** UK guitarist/producer (born in Wolverhampton) who began in the Byron Band, including playing on their debut album in 1981. A year later he went solo, signed with Arista in 1983, was dropped in 1984 and then signed with Bronze. He was more successful as a producer.

| DATE | POS | WKS | ALBUM TITLE | LABEL & NUMBER |
|---|---|---|---|---|
| 02/03/1985 | 65 | 3 | DANGEROUS MUSIC | Bronze BRON 554 |

**GEORGIA SATELLITES** US rock group formed in Atlanta, GA in 1980 by Dan Baird (vocals), Rick Richards (guitar), Rick Price (bass) and Mauro Magellan (drums). They disbanded in 1991 with Richards going on to join Izzy Staddlin & The Ju Ju Hounds.

| DATE | POS | WKS | ALBUM TITLE | LABEL & NUMBER |
|---|---|---|---|---|
| 07/02/1987 | 52 | 7 | GEORGIA SATELLITES | Elektra 9804961 |
| 02/07/1988 | 39 | 2 | OPEN ALL NIGHT | Elektra EKT 47 |

**GERRY AND THE PACEMAKERS** UK group formed in Liverpool in 1959 by Gerry Marsden (born 24/9/1942, Liverpool, vocals/lead guitar), brother Freddie (born 23/11/1940, Liverpool, drums), Les Chadwick (born John Leslie Chadwick, 11/5/1943, Liverpool, bass) and Anthony McMahon (piano) as the Mars Bars. The name was intended to get sponsorship from the confectionery company, who instead insisted that they change it: they settled on the Pacemakers. McMahon left in 1961 and was replaced by Les Maguire (born 27/12/1941, Wallasey, piano/saxophone). They signed with Brian Epstein in 1962, securing a contract with Parlophone. They split in 1967. They were the first act to get their first three singles at #1, a record broken by the Spice Girls in 1997. Marsden was awarded an MBE in the Queen's 2003 Birthday Honours List.

| DATE | POS | WKS | ALBUM TITLE | LABEL & NUMBER |
|---|---|---|---|---|
| 26/10/1963 | 2 | 28 | HOW DO YOU LIKE IT? | Columbia 33SX 1546 |
| 06/02/1965 | 19 | 1 | FERRY ACROSS THE MERSEY | Columbia 33SX 1676 |

**STAN GETZ AND CHARLIE BIRD** US saxophonist (born Stan Gayetzsky, 2/2/1927, Philadelphia, PA) who played with Stan Kenton, Jimmy Dorsey, Benny Goodman and Woody Herman's bands, one of the the top tenor saxophonists in the world. Getz died from liver cancer on 6/6/1991. Charlie Byrd is a US guitarist (born 16/9/1925, Chuckatuck, VA). Getz won five Grammy Awards: Best Jazz Performance in 1962 with Charlie Byrd for *Desafinado*, Record of the Year 1964 with Astrud Gilberto (born in Bahia, Brazil in 1940) for *The Girl From Ipanema* (even though the UK release of the single credited Joao Gilberto rather than singer Astrud) and Album of the Year and Best Jazz Performance in 1964 with Astrud Gilberto for *Getz/Gilberto* and Best Jazz Instrumental Solo in 1991 for *I Remember You*. Byrd's only Grammy Award came with the afore-mentioned *Desafinado*.

23/02/1963 . . . . . 15 . . . . . 7 . . . . . . JAZZ SAMBA . . . . . . . . . . . . . . . . . . . . . . . . . . . . . . . . . . . . . . . . . . . . . . . Verve SULP 9013

**ANGELA GHEORGIU** – see ROBERTO ALAGNA/ANGELA GHEORGIU

**GHOSTFACE KILLAH** US rapper (born Dennis Coles, 9/5/1970, Staten Island, NYC) who also records under the names Tony Starks and Ironman. He is also a member of the rap supergroup Wu-Tang Clan.

09/11/1996 . . . . . 38 . . . . . . 2 . . . . . . IRONMAN . . . . . . . . . . . . . . . . . . . . . . . . . . . . . . . . . . . . . . . . . . . . . . . . . . . . Epic 4853892

**ANDY GIBB** UK singer (born 5/3/1958, Manchester) whose family emigrated to Australia when he was six months old, returning nine years later. Encouraged by his brothers (Barry, Robin and Maurice – the Bee Gees) to pursue a musical career, his debut single penned by Barry hit #1 in the US. He later hosted the TV programme *Solid Gold* in the US. He died from a heart virus on 10/3/1988.

19/08/1978 . . . . . 15 . . . . . 9 . . . . . . O SHADOW DANCING . . . . . . . . . . . . . . . . . . . . . . . . . . . . . . . . . . . . . . . . . . . RSO RSS 0001

**BARRY GIBB** UK singer (born 1/9/1946, Douglas, Isle of Man), the eldest of four sons he first came to prominence as a member of The Bee Gees with twin brothers Robin and Maurice. When the brothers fell out towards the end of the 1960s and Robin opted for a solo career, Barry preferred to retain the Bee Gees name with Maurice and also undertook a series of outside writing and production assignments. He finally released a solo album in 1984, by which time The Bee Gees had re-formed and established themselves as one of the most successful groups of all time. Barry Gibb also recorded as The Bunburys.

20/10/1984 . . . . . 85 . . . . . . 2 . . . . . . NOW VOYAGER . . . . . . . . . . . . . . . . . . . . . . . . . . . . . . . . . . . . . . . . . . . . . Polydor POLH 14

**ROBIN GIBB** UK singer (born 22/12/1949, Douglas, Isle of Man), one third of the Bee Gees with brothers Barry and Maurice (Robin is Maurice's twin brother). He left to go solo in 1969, prompting manager Robert Stigwood to issue legal proceedings against him. The Bee Gees reunited in 1970.

15/02/2003 . . . . . 43 . . . . . . 1 . . . . . . MAGNET . . . . . . . . . . . . . . . . . . . . . . . . . . . . . . . . . . . . . SPV Recordings SPV 08571472

**BETH GIBBONS AND RUSTIN MAN** UK vocal duo Beth Gibbons (born 4/1/1965, Devon) and Rustin Man (born Paul Webb). Gibbons was previously lead singer with Portishead.

09/11/2002 . . . . . 28 . . . . . . 2 . . . . . . OUT OF SEASON . . . . . . . . . . . . . . . . . . . . . . . . . . . . . . . . . . . . . . . . . . . . Go Beat 665742

**STEVE GIBBONS BAND** UK group formed in Birmingham by Steve Gibbons (guitar/vocals), Bob Wilson (guitar), Trevor Burton (bass) and Bob Lamb (drums).

22/10/1977 . . . . . 22 . . . . . . 3 . . . . . . CAUGHT IN THE ACT . . . . . . . . . . . . . . . . . . . . . . . . . . . . . . . . . . . . . . . Polydor 2478 112

**DEBBIE GIBSON** US singer (born 31/8/1970, Long Island, NY) who learned piano from five, wrote her first song at six and signed with Atlantic while still at school. In 1993 she took on the role of Sandy in the 20th anniversary production of *Grease,* having previously been Eponine in the Broadway version of *Les Miserables*.

30/01/1988 . . . . . 26 . . . . . 35 . . . . . ● OUT OF THE BLUE . . . . . . . . . . . . . . . . . . . . . . . . . . . . . . . . . . . . . . . . . Atlantic WX 139
11/02/1989 . . . . . 8 . . . . 16 . . . . . ● ELECTRIC YOUTH ▲5 . . . . . . . . . . . . . . . . . . . . . . . . . . . . . . . . . . . . . Atlantic WX 231
30/03/1991 . . . . . 69 . . . . . . 1 . . . . . . ANYTHING IS POSSIBLE . . . . . . . . . . . . . . . . . . . . . . . . . . . . . . . . . . . . Atlantic WX 399

**DON GIBSON** US singer (born 3/4/1928, Shelby, NC) who began singing professionally in 1942 and joined the Grand Ole Opry in 1958. He died from natural causes on 17/11/2003.

22/03/1980 . . . . . 13 . . . . . 10 . . . . . COUNTRY NUMBER ONE . . . . . . . . . . . . . . . . . . . . . . . . . . . . . . . . . . Warwick WW 5079

**GIBSON BROTHERS** Martinique family group formed by Chris (percussion/vocals), Patrick (drum/vocals) and Alex Gibson (piano/vocals). The family relocated to Paris while the brothers were still children.

30/08/1980 . . . . . 50 . . . . . . 3 . . . . . . ON THE RIVIERA . . . . . . . . . . . . . . . . . . . . . . . . . . . . . . . . . . . . . . . . . Island ILPS 9620

**BEBEL GILBERTO** Brazilian singer born in New York, the daughter of Joao Gilberto and Miucha Gilberto.

31/08/2002 . . . . . 49 . . . . . 5 . . . . . . O TANTO TEMPO . . . . . . . . . . . . . . . . . . . . . . . . . . . . . . . . . . . . . . . . East West 0927474072
19/06/2004 . . . . . 49 . . . . 2+ . . . . . . BEBEL GILBERTO . . . . . . . . . . . . . . . . . . . . . . . . . . . . . . . . . . . East West 5046732665

**JOHNNY GILL** US singer (born 22/5/1966, Washington DC) who sang with family gospel group Wings Of Faith with his three brothers before recording with Stacy Lattishaw, who passed on his demo tape to Atlantic Records. He signed with them in 1983, though with little initial success. He replaced Bobby Brown in New Edition and when they disbanded relaunched his solo career, with Jimmy Jam, Terry Lewis, LA Reid and Babyface handling production, and with greater success second time around.

19/06/1993 . . . . . 41 . . . . . . 3 . . . . . . PROVOCATIVE . . . . . . . . . . . . . . . . . . . . . . . . . . . . . . . . . . . . . . . . . . Motown 5302062

**GILLAN** UK singer (born Ian Gillan, 19/8/1945, Hounslow) who was in Episode Six when invited to join Deep Purple as lead singer in 1969, leaving to go solo in 1973. In 1983 he joined Black Sabbath as lead, then left the following year to rejoin Deep Purple, whom he left again in 1989. He played the role of Jesus on the album version of *Jesus Christ Superstar*.

17/07/1976 . . . . . 55 . . . . . . 1 . . . . . . CHILD IN TIME **IAN GILLAN BAND** . . . . . . . . . . . . . . . . . . . . . . . . . . . . . . . . . Polydor 2490 136

| DATE | POS | WKS | BPI | ALBUM TITLE | LABEL & NUMBER |
|------|-----|-----|-----|-------------|----------------|
| 20/10/1979 | 11 | 6 | | MR. UNIVERSE | Acrobat ACRO 3 |
| 16/08/1980 | 3 | 12 | ○ | **GLORY ROAD** | Virgin V 2171 |
| 25/04/1981 | 2 | 13 | ○ | **FUTURE SHOCK** | Virgin VK 2196 |
| 07/11/1981 | 12 | 15 | | DOUBLE TROUBLE | Virgin VGD 3506 |
| 02/10/1982 | 17 | 6 | | MAGIC | Virgin V 2238 |
| 28/07/1990 | 63 | 1 | | NAKED THUNDER **IAN GILLAN** | Teldec 9031718991 |

### THEA GILMORE UK singer (born 1979, Oxfordshire).

| | | | | | |
|------|-----|-----|-----|-------------|----------------|
| 23/08/2003 | 63 | 1 | | AVALANCHE | Hungry Dog YRGNUHA 1 |

### DAVID GILMOUR UK singer/guitarist (born 6/3/1947, Cambridge), he joined Pink Floyd in 1968 in place of the erratic Syd Barrett, eventually becoming lead singer. He began a solo career in 1978 whilst Pink Floyd were between projects and returned to his solo career in 1984 after the group disbanded. In 1987 he linked up with Nick Mason and Rick Wright to revive Pink Floyd, effectively bringing his solo career to a second halt. He was awarded a CBE in the Queen's 2003 Birthday Honours List.

| | | | | | |
|------|-----|-----|-----|-------------|----------------|
| 10/06/1978 | 17 | 9 | | DAVID GILMOUR | Harvest SHVL 817 |
| 17/03/1984 | 21 | 9 | | ABOUT FACE | Harvest SHSP 2400791 |

### GORDON GILTRAP UK guitarist/session musician (born 6/4/1948, Tonbridge) who began his solo career in 1971.

| | | | | | |
|------|-----|-----|-----|-------------|----------------|
| 18/02/1978 | 29 | 7 | | PERILOUS JOURNEY | Electric TRIX 4 |

### GIN BLOSSOMS US rock group formed in Tempe, AZ in 1989 by Robin Wilson (guitar/vocals), Jesse Valenzuela (guitar/vocals), Scott Johnson (guitar), Bill Leen (bass) and Philip Rhodes (drums). They financed their own debut release, attracting interest from A&M, who signed them in 1992. Original member and songwriter Doug Hopkins was sacked in 1992 and committed suicide by shooting himself on 4/12/1993, two weeks after an earlier suicide attempt from a drugs overdose. They split in 1997, re-forming in 2001.

| | | | | | |
|------|-----|-----|-----|-------------|----------------|
| 26/02/1994 | 53 | 4 | | NEW MISERABLE EXPERIENCE | Fontana 3954032 |
| 24/02/1996 | 42 | 2 | | CONGRATULATIONS, I'M SORRY | A&M 5404702 |

### GINUWINE US singer (Elgin Baylor Lumpkin, named after a basketball player, 15/10/1975, Washington DC).

| | | | | | |
|------|-----|-----|-----|-------------|----------------|
| 28/03/1998 | 74 | 1 | | GINUWINE… THE BACHELOR | Epic 4895892 |
| 27/03/1999 | 42 | 1 | | 100% GINUWINE | Epic 4919922 |

### GIPSY KINGS French flamenco group formed from the family group Los Reyes and led by Jose Reyes. They changed their name to the Gipsy Kings in 1983. The many musicians who have been members of the Gipsy Kings include Nicolas Reyes, Andre Reyes, Canut Reyes, Paul Reyes, Patchai Reyes, Francois Reyes, Chico Bouchiki, Tonino Baliardo, Diego Baliardo, Paco Baliardo, Claude Maissoneuve, Walter De Auraujo, Guillermo Fellove, Christian Martinez, Philippe Slominiski, Dominique Perrier, Dominique Droin, Jean Musy, Gerard Prevost, Claude Salmieri, Negrito Trasante-Crocco, Marc Chantereau and Charles Benarroch.

| | | | | | |
|------|-----|-----|-----|-------------|----------------|
| 15/04/1989 | 16 | 29 | ● | GIPSY KINGS | Telstar STAR 2355 |
| 25/11/1989 | 27 | 13 | ● | MOSAIQUE | Telstar STAR 2398 |
| 13/07/1991 | 19 | 7 | ○ | ESTE MUNDO | Columbia 4686481 |
| 06/08/1994 | 11 | 11 | ○ | GREATEST HITS ◇² | Columbia 4772422 |
| 24/07/1999 | 20 | 5 | | VOLARE – THE VERY BEST OF THE GIPSY KINGS | Columbia SONYTV 69CD |

### GIRL UK rock group formed in London in 1979 by Philip Lewis (vocals), Phil Collen (guitar), Gerry Laffy (guitar), his brother Simon (bass) and Dave Gaynor (drums). Gaynor left after their debut album and was replaced by Pete Barnacle. The group disbanded after their second album. Collen later joined Def Leppard, while Lewis joined LA Guns.

| | | | | | |
|------|-----|-----|-----|-------------|----------------|
| 09/02/1980 | 33 | 5 | | SHEER GREED | Jet JETLP 224 |
| 23/01/1982 | 92 | 1 | | WASTED YOUTH | Jet JETLP 238 |

### GIRLS ALOUD UK vocal group formed by Cheryl Tweedy (born 30/6/1983, Newcastle-upon-Tyne), Nadine Coyle (born 15/6/1985, Derry, Ireland), Sarah Harding (born 17/11/1981, Ascot), Nicola Roberts (born 5/10/1985, Stanford) and Kimberly Walsh (born 20/11/1981, Bradford). They were the winners of the TV programme Popstars: The Rivals.

| | | | | | |
|------|-----|-----|-----|-------------|----------------|
| 07/06/2003 | 2 | 18 | ✪ | **SOUND OF THE UNDERGROUND** | Polydor 9865315 |

### GIRLS AT OUR BEST UK group formed in Leeds, Yorkshire in 1979 by Judy Evans (vocals), James Alan (guitar) and Gerald Swift (bass) as The Butterflies. They added drummer Chris Oldroyd for their recording debut as Girls At Our Best, used session drummer Paul Simon for their second and added Carl Harper as permanent drummer thereafter.

| | | | | | |
|------|-----|-----|-----|-------------|----------------|
| 07/11/1981 | 60 | 3 | | PLEASURE | Happy Birthday RVLP 1 |

### GIRLSCHOOL UK heavy metal group formed in 1978 by Kim McAuliffe (born 13/4/1959, rhythm guitar/vocals), Kelly Johnson (lead guitar), Enid Williams (bass) and Denise Dufort (drums) as Painted Lady. They changed their name the same year and signed with Bronze in 1980. They disbanded in 1988 but re-formed in 1992.

| | | | | | |
|------|-----|-----|-----|-------------|----------------|
| 05/07/1980 | 28 | 10 | | DEMOLITION | Bronze BRON 525 |
| 25/04/1981 | 5 | 6 | | **HIT 'N' RUN** | Bronze BRON 534 |
| 12/06/1982 | 27 | 6 | | SCREAMING BLUE MURDER | Bronze BRON 541 |
| 12/11/1983 | 66 | 1 | | PLAY DIRTY | Bronze BRON 548 |

### GLAMMA KID UK singer/rapper (born Iyael Iyasus Tafari Constable) who won the 1998 MOBO Award for Best Reggae Act.

| | | | | | |
|------|-----|-----|-----|-------------|----------------|
| 16/09/2000 | 66 | 1 | | KIDOLOGY | WEA 3984298572 |

## GARY GLITTER
UK singer (born Paul Gadd, 8/5/1940, Banbury, Oxon) who adopted his stepfather's surname to front Paul Russell & His Rebels in 1958 and made his first record with Decca as Paul Raven. Unsuccessful, he dropped out of recording in 1961 and linked with the Mike Leander Orchestra, before forming Paul Raven & Boston International, a popular live draw in West Germany. After one single as Rubber Bucket in 1969, he adopted the name Gary Glitter in 1971. The early hits were all written by Glitter and Leander (born 30/6/1941, died 18/4/1996). In November 1999 Glitter was jailed for four months after admitting 54 offences of downloading child pornography. He served two months before being released and was then believed to be going to Cuba to live.

| 21/10/1972 | 8 | 40 | ○ | GLITTER | Bell BELLS 216 |
| 16/06/1973 | 2 | 33 | ○ | TOUCH ME | Bell BELLS 222 |
| 29/06/1974 | 5 | 14 | | REMEMBER ME THIS WAY | Bell BELLS 237 |
| 27/03/1976 | 33 | 5 | | GARY GLITTER'S GREATEST HITS | Bell BELLS 262 |
| 14/11/1992 | 35 | 8 | | MANY HAPPY RETURNS – THE HITS | EMI CDEMTV 68 |

## GLITTER BAND
UK backing band for Gary Glitter on tour (producer Mike Leander reportedly played all instruments in the studio), given a parallel recording career while their frontman was at the peak of his popularity. The band featured John Springate, Tony Leonard, Pete Phipps, Harvey Ellison and Gerry Shephard. Shephard died from cancer in May 2003.

| 14/09/1974 | 13 | 12 | ○ | HEY | Bell BELLS 241 |
| 03/05/1975 | 17 | 4 | ○ | ROCK 'N' ROLL DUDES | Bell BELLS 253 |
| 19/06/1976 | 52 | 1 | | GREATEST HITS | Bell BELLS 264 |

## GLOVE
UK group formed by The Cure's Robert Smith (born 21/4/1959, Blackpool, guitar/vocals), The Banshees' Steve 'Havoc' Severin (born Steven Bailey, 25/9/1955, London, bass) and Jeanette Landray (vocals/dancing), a one-off project for Smith and Severin.

| 17/09/1983 | 35 | 3 | | BLUE SUNSHINE | Wonderland SHELP 2 |

## DANA GLOVER
US singer (born in Rocky Mount, NC, raised in Nashville, Los Angeles and New York) who was a model before launching a singing career.

| 17/05/2003 | 43 | 2 | | TESTIMONY | DreamWorks 4504522 |

## GO-BETWEENS
Australian group formed in Brisbane, Queensland by Robert Forster (born 29/6/1957, Brisbane, vocals/ guitar), Grant McLennan (born 12/2/1958, Rock Hampton, Queensland) and Dennis Cantwell (drums). Although they later expanded with the addition of Malcolm Kelly (keyboards), Tim Mustafa (drums) and Candice and Jaqueline on tambourine/vocals respectively, they trimmed back down to a trio of Forster, McLennan and Lindy Morrison (born 2/11/1951, drums). In 1983 they added bass player Robert Vickers (born 25/11/1959) and three years later multi-instrumentalist Amanda Brown (born 17/11/1965). Vickers left in 1987, replaced by John Willsteed (born 13/2/1957), the group disbanding two years later. Forster and McLennan, always the group leaders, both went solo.

| 13/06/1987 | 91 | 1 | | TALLULAH | Beggars Banquet BEGA 81 |
| 10/09/1988 | 81 | 1 | | 16 LOVER'S LANE | Beggars Banquet BEGA 95 |

## GO-GO'S
US rock group formed in Los Angeles, CA in 1978 by Belinda Carlisle (born 17/8/1958, Hollywood, vocals), Jane Wiedlin (born 20/5/1958, Oconomowoc, WI, guitar), Charlotte Caffey (born 21/10/1953, Santa Monica, CA, guitar), Kathy Valentine (born 7/1/1959, Austin, TX, bass) and Gina Schock (born 31/8/1957, Baltimore, MD, drums). They disbanded in 1984 (Carlisle and Wiedlin pursued successful solo careers) and held a reunion tour in 1990.

| 21/08/1982 | 75 | 3 | | VACATION | I.R.S. SP 70031 |
| 18/03/1995 | 52 | 1 | | RETURN TO THE VALLEY OF THE GO-GO'S | I.R.S. EIRSCD 1071 |

## GO WEST
UK duo Peter Cox (born 17/11/1955, vocals) and Richard Drummie (guitar/vocals). They wrote songs for Peter Frampton and David Grant among others before launching Go West in 1982. They were named Best British Newcomer at the 1986 BRIT Awards. Cox later went solo.

| 13/04/1985 | 8 | 83 | ◇² | GO WEST/BANGS AND CRASHES | Chrysalis CHR 1495 |
| 06/06/1987 | 19 | 5 | | DANCING ON THE COUCH | Chrysalis CDL 1550 |
| 14/11/1992 | 13 | 16 | ● | INDIAN SUMMER | Chrysalis CDCHR 1964 |
| 16/10/1993 | 5 | 15 | ● | ACES AND KINGS – THE BEST OF GO WEST | Chrysalis CDCHR 6050 |

## GOATS
US rap trio formed in Philadelphia, PA by Oatie Kato, Madd and Swayzack. Oatie left in 1993 and Madd and Swayzack continued as a duo.

| 27/08/1994 | 58 | 1 | | NO GOATS, NO GLORY | Columbia 4769372 |

**GOD MACHINE** US group of San Diego, CA school friends Robyn Proper-Sheppard (guitar/vocals), Jimmy Fernandez (bass) and Ronald Austin (drums), forming the group in London in 1990. They disbanded after Fernandez died from a brain tumour on 23/5/1994.

20/02/1993.....55......1...... SCENES FROM THE SECOND STORY............................................................. Fiction 5171562

**GODFATHERS** UK group formed in London in 1985 by Peter Coyne (vocals), his brother Chris (bass), Mike Gibson (guitar), Kris Dollimore (guitar) and George Mazur (drums), with their debut release being issued on their own Corporate Image label. Dollimore left in 1989 and was replaced the following year by Chris Burrows.

13/02/1988.....80......2...... BIRTH, SCHOOL, WORK, DEATH............................................................. Epic 4602631
20/05/1989.....49......1...... MORE SONGS ABOUT LOVE AND HATE............................................................. Epic 4633941

**GODLEY AND CREME** UK duo Kevin Godley (born 7/10/1945, Manchester) and Lol Creme (born 19/9/1947, Manchester). Both had been in Hotlegs, which became 10CC. They left 10CC in 1976 to work as a duo, later moving into video production.

19/11/1977.....52......1...... CONSEQUENCES............................................................. Mercury CONS 017
09/09/1978.....47......2...... L............................................................. Mercury 9109 611
17/10/1981.....29.....13..... ISMISM............................................................. Polydor POLD 5043
29/08/1987.....4.....18..... **CHANGING FACES – THE VERY BEST OF 10CC AND GODLEY AND CRÈME** 10CC AND GODLEY AND CRÈME............ ProTV TGCLP 1

**GODSPEED YOU BLACK EMPEROR!** Canadian group formed in Montreal who shun publicity, keeping in touch with the media via e-mail. The nine-piece features Efrim, Dave ( guitars), Mauro (bass), Sophie (violin), Norsola (cello), Bruce and Aidan (both on percussion) among their members, with at least one further guitarist (possibly Bryant) and a bassist completing the line-up.

21/10/2000.....66......1...... LIFT YOUR SKINNY FISTS LIKE ANTENNAS TO HEAVEN............................................................. Kranky KRANK 043

**ANDREW GOLD** US singer/pianist (born 2/8/1951 Burbank, CA), session singer and Linda Ronstadt arranger from the early 1970s. He later formed Wax with former 10CC member Graham Gouldman.

15/04/1978.....31......7......O ALL THIS AND HEAVEN TOO............................................................. Asylum K 53072

**GOLDEN EARRING** Dutch group formed in 1964 by Barry Hay (born 16/8/1948, Faizabad, India, vocals), George Kooymans (born 11/3/1948, The Hague, guitar/vocals), Cesar Zuiderwijk (born 18/7/1950, The Hague, drums) and Rinus Gerritsen (born Marinus Gerritsen, 9/8/1946, The Hague, bass/keyboards). An early member was Jaap Eggermont, successful in the 1980s as Starsound.

02/02/1974.....24......4...... MOONTAN.............................................................Track 2406 112

**GOLDFRAPP** UK duo Allison Goldfrapp (born in Bath, keyboards/vocals) and Will Gregory. Allison began as a solo artist and backing singer, appearing on Tricky's album *Maxinquaye* and Orbital's *Snivilisation*. She linked with Gregory in 1999.

25/08/2001.....57......5......● FELT MOUNTAIN............................................................. Mute CDSTUMM 188
10/05/2003.....19.....19......● BLACK CHERRY............................................................. Mute CDSTUMM 196

**GOLDIE** UK dance artist (born Clifford Price, 1966, Walsall) who was earlier a graffiti artist, working with Afrika Bambaata and appearing with him in the 1986 film *Bombing*. Goldie later worked with Soul II Soul before launching Metalheads. Also an actor, he had roles in the TV series *Eastenders* and the 1999 James Bond film *The World Is Not Enough*. Two MOBO Awards in 1996 included Best Jungle Artist.

19/08/1995.....7.....12......● **TIMELESS** 1996 MOBO Award for Best Album............................................................. ffrr 8286142
14/02/1998.....15......4...... SATURNZ RETURN............................................................. ffrr 8289902

**GLEN GOLDSMITH** UK pop/soul singer (born Glenford Norman Goldsmith, Slough) who later did sessions, providing backing vocals for the likes of Juliet Rogers.

23/07/1988.....14......9......O WHAT YOU SEE IS WHAT YOU GET............................................................. RCA PL 71750

**GOMEZ** UK group formed in Liverpool in 1996 by Tom Gray (vocal/guitar/keyboards), Ian Ball (guitar/vocals), Ben Ottewell (guitar), Paul Blackburn (bass) and Olly Peacock (drums).

25/04/1998.....11.....60......✪ BRING IT ON 1998 Mercury Music Prize............................................................. Hut CDHUTX 49
25/09/1999.....2.....28......✪ **LIQUID SKIN**............................................................. Hut CDHUT 54
07/10/2000.....10......4......O **ABANDONED SHOPPING TROLLEY HOTLINE**............................................................. Hut CDHUTX 62
30/03/2002.....8......7......O **IN OUR GUN**............................................................. Hut CDHUT 72
29/05/2004.....35......2...... SPLIT THE DIFFERENCE............................................................. Hut CDHUTX 84

**GOO GOO DOLLS** US group formed in New York in 1985 by Johnny Rzenzik (born 5/12/1965, Buffalo, NY, guitar/vocals), Robby Takac (born 30/9/1964, Buffalo, bass/vocals) and George Tutuska (drums) as the Sex Maggots, changing their name soon after. Mike Mallini (born 10/10/1967, Washington DC) replaced George Tutuska in 1995.

31/07/1999.....47......1...... DIZZY UP THE GIRL............................................................. Hollywood 0102042HWR
04/05/2002.....56......1...... GUTTERFLOWER............................................................. Warner Brothers 9362483112

O Silver disc  ● Gold disc  ✪ Platinum disc (additional platinum units are indicated by a figure following the symbol)  ❶9 Number of weeks album topped the UK chart

### GOOD CHARLOTTE
US rock group formed in Waldorf, MD in 1996 by Joel Madden (born 3/11/1979, Waldorf, vocals), his twin brother Benji (guitar), Billy Martin (born 15/6/1981, Naptown, MD, guitar), Paul Thomas (born 5/10/1980, Waldorf, bass) and Aaron (drums). Aaron left in 2002 and was replaced by Chris Wilson.

25/01/2003 . . . . . 15 . . . . . 38 . . . . . . ✪  THE YOUNG AND THE HOPELESS . . . . . . . . . . . . . . . . . . . . . . . . . . . . . . . . . . . . . . . . . . . . . . Epic 5094889

### GOODBYE MR MACKENZIE
UK group formed in 1981 by Martin Metcalfe (guitar/vocals), Rona Scobie (keyboards/vocals), Shirley Manson (keyboards/vocals), Chuck Parker (bass) and Derek Kelly (drums). They made their first record for Wet Wet Wet's Precious Organisation. They disbanded in 1995, with Manson later fronting Garbage.

22/04/1989 . . . . . 26 . . . . . 3 . . . . .  GOOD DEEDS AND DIRTY RAGS . . . . . . . . . . . . . . . . . . . . . . . . . . . . . . . . . . . . . . . . . . . . Capitol EST 2089
16/03/1991 . . . . . 61 . . . . . 1 . . . . .  HAMMER AND TONGS . . . . . . . . . . . . . . . . . . . . . . . . . . . . . . . . . . . . . . . . . . . . . . Radioactive RAR 10227

### GOODIES
UK TV comedy trio formed by Tim Brooke-Taylor (born 17/7/1940, Buxton), Graeme Garden (born 18/2/1943, Aberdeen) and Bill Oddie (born 7/7/1941, Rochdale). Oddie was awarded an OBE in the Queen's 2003 Birthday Honours List.

08/11/1975 . . . . . 25 . . . . . 11 . . . . .  THE NEW GOODIES LP . . . . . . . . . . . . . . . . . . . . . . . . . . . . . . . . . . . . . . . . . . . . . . . . Bradley's BRADL 1010

### BENNY GOODMAN
US clarinettist/bandleader (born 30/5/1909, Chicago, IL ), he learned clarinet as a child, joining the American Federation of Musicians at only fourteen years of age. He joined Ben Pollack's band in 1925, remaining with them until 1929 when he left for a career as a session musician, his fellow musicians rating him the best clarinet player in the country. He formed his own dance band in 1934, and the band's performance at the Los Angeles Palomar Ballroom in 1935 is widely regarded as the start of the swing era. Goodman and his band remained an integral part of the jazz scene for the next 40 years or so, with the autobiographical film *The Benny Goodman Story* appearing in 1955. He toured regularly and in 1962 was one of the first artists to tour the USSR, a visit sponsored by the US State Department. Ever the perfectionist, Goodman practiced every single day and it is generally accepted that he had practiced on the day of his death, which occurred on 20/6/1986. He has a star on the Hollywood Walk of Fame.

03/04/1971 . . . . . 49 . . . . . 1 . . . . .  BENNY GOODMAN TODAY . . . . . . . . . . . . . . . . . . . . . . . . . . . . . . . . . . . . . . . . . . . . . . . . . Decca DDS 3

### DELTA GOODREM
Australian singer (born 9/11/1984, Sydney,) who first became famous as an actress, playing Nina Tucker on the TV series *Neighbours*. She was diagnosed as having Hodgkin's disease in July 2003.

12/07/2003 . . . . . 2 . . . . . 33 . . . . . ✪²  INNOCENT EYES ◇ . . . . . . . . . . . . . . . . . . . . . . . . . . . . . . . . . . . . . . . . . . . . . . . . . . . Epic 5109512

### RON GOODWIN
UK orchestra leader (born 17/2/1925, Plymouth) who began as an arranger and bandleader, later becoming a conductor and composer. He scored his first film in 1958 (*Whirlpool*) and wrote the music to over 60 others. He died on 8/1/2003.

02/05/1970 . . . . . 49 . . . . . 1 . . . . .  LEGEND OF THE GLASS MOUNTAIN . . . . . . . . . . . . . . . . . . . . . . . . . . . . . . . . . . . . . . . . . Studio Two 220

### GOOMBAY DANCE BAND
Multinational dance band comprising Oliver Bendt, his wife Alicia, Dorothy Hellings, Wendy Dorseen and Mario Slijngaard. The Bendt's two children, Danny and Yasmin, also appeared as backing singers.

10/04/1982 . . . . . 16 . . . . . 9 . . . . .  SEVEN TEARS . . . . . . . . . . . . . . . . . . . . . . . . . . . . . . . . . . . . . . . . . . . . . . . . . . . . . Epic EPC 85702

### GOONS
UK radio comedy trio formed by Spike Milligan (born Terence Alan Milligan, 16/4/1918, Ahmed Nagar, India), Peter Sellers (born 8/9/1925, Southsea) and Harry Secombe (born 8/9/1921, Swansea). Michael Bentine (born 26/1/1922, Watford) was also an early member. Peter Sellers died from a heart attack on 24/7/1980, Michael Bentine died from prostate cancer on 26/11/1996 and Harry Secombe died from cancer on 11/4/2001. Spike Milligan was knighted in the 2001 New Year's Honours List and died on 27/2/2002.

28/11/1959 . . . . . 8 . . . . . 14 . . . . .  BEST OF THE GOONS SHOWS . . . . . . . . . . . . . . . . . . . . . . . . . . . . . . . . . . . . . . . . . Parlophone PMC 1108
17/12/1960 . . . . . 11 . . . . . 6 . . . . .  BEST OF THE GOONS SHOWS VOLUME 2 . . . . . . . . . . . . . . . . . . . . . . . . . . . . . . . . . Parlophone PMC 1129
04/11/1972 . . . . . 8 . . . . . 11 . . . . .  LAST GOON SHOW OF ALL . . . . . . . . . . . . . . . . . . . . . . . . . . . . . . . . . . . . . . . . . . . . . . . BBC REB 142

### MARTIN L GORE
UK multi-instrumentalist/producer (born 23/7/1961, Dagenham, Essex) who was a founding member of Depeche Mode. He launched a parallel solo career in 1989.

24/06/1989 . . . . . 51 . . . . . 1 . . . . .  COUNTERFEIT (EP) . . . . . . . . . . . . . . . . . . . . . . . . . . . . . . . . . . . . . . . . . . . . . . . . Mute STUMM 67

### GORILLAZ
UK animated group formed by Murdoc, 2-D, Noodle and Russel. The ad hoc group was assembled by Damon Albarn of Blur (born 23/3/1968, London) and Jamie Hewlett, the illustrator of *Tank Girl*. Their self-titled debut album was nominated for a Mercury Music Prize, although the group refused to accept the nomination. They did, however, accept two awards at the 2001 MTV Europe Music Awards, for Best Song for *Clint Eastwood* and Best Dance Act.

07/04/2001 . . . . . 3 . . . . . 52 . . . . . ✪²  GORILLAZ ◇ . . . . . . . . . . . . . . . . . . . . . . . . . . . . . . . . . . . . . . . . . . . . . . . . Parlophone 5320930
23/03/2002 . . . . . 65 . . . . . 1 . . . . .  THE G SIDES . . . . . . . . . . . . . . . . . . . . . . . . . . . . . . . . . . . . . . . . . . . . . . . . . . . Parlophone 536942

### GORKY'S ZYGOTIC MYNCI
UK group formed in Carmarthen, Wales in 1990 by Euros Childs (keyboards/vocals), John Lawrence (guitar), Richard James (bass), Megan Childs (violin) and Euros Rowlands (drums). They were signed with Ankst before joining Mercury Records in 1996.

19/04/1997 . . . . . 46 . . . . . 1 . . . . .  BARAFUNDLE . . . . . . . . . . . . . . . . . . . . . . . . . . . . . . . . . . . . . . . . . . . . . . . . . . . . Fontana 5347692
12/09/1998 . . . . . 67 . . . . . 1 . . . . .  GORKY 5 . . . . . . . . . . . . . . . . . . . . . . . . . . . . . . . . . . . . . . . . . . . . . . . . . . . . . . . . . Fontana 5588222

### IRV GOTTI PRESENTS THE INC
US producer/record company executive (born Irving Lorenzo, 1971, New York) who first became prominent producing the likes of Ja Rule, Ashanti and Jennifer Lopez. He launched the Murder Inc label in 1997.

20/07/2002 . . . . . 68 . . . . . 3 . . . . .  IRV GOTTI PRESENTS THE INC . . . . . . . . . . . . . . . . . . . . . . . . . . . . . . . . . . . . . . . . . Murder Inc 0630332

### JAKI GRAHAM
UK singer (born 15/9/1956, Birmingham) who sang with the Medium Wave Band before linking with Derek Bramble and signing with EMI as a solo artist, recording her debut in 1984. She later formed Kiss The Sky with Paul Hardcastle.

| | | | | |
|---|---|---|---|---|
| 14/09/1985 | 48 | 5 | | HEAVEN KNOWS | EMI JK 1 |
| 20/09/1986 | 25 | 5 | O | BREAKING AWAY | EMI EMC 3514 |

### GRAND PRIX
UK rock group formed by Bernard Shaw (vocals), Michael O'Donahue (guitar/vocals), Ralph Hood (bass), Phil Lanzon (keyboards/vocals) and Andy Beirne (drums). Shaw was later replaced by Robin McAuley.

| | | | | |
|---|---|---|---|---|
| 18/06/1983 | 65 | 2 | | SAMURAI | Chrysalis CHR 1430 |

### GRANDADDY
US rock group formed in Modesto, CA in 1992 by Jason Lytle (guitar/vocals), Kevin Garcia (bass) and Aaron Burtch (drums). They added Jim Fairchild (guitar) and Tim Dryden (keyboards) in 1995.

| | | | | |
|---|---|---|---|---|
| 20/05/2000 | 36 | 4 | O | SOPHTWARE SLUMP | V2 VVR 1012252 |
| 21/06/2003 | 22 | 2 | | SUMDAY | V2 VVR 1022238 |

### GRANDMASTER FLASH AND THE FURIOUS FIVE
US rapper (born Joseph Saddler, 1/1/1958, Barbados) who was a mobile DJ when he formed the Furious Five, adding rappers Cowboy (born Keith Wiggins, 20/9/1960), Kidd Creole (Nathaniel Glover), Melle Mel (Melvin Glover), Duke Bootee (Ed Fletcher) and Kurtis Blow. Blow was later replaced by Raheim (Guy Todd Williams). They made their record debut for Enjoy in 1979. Melle Mel won the 1990 Grammy Award for Best Rap Performance by a Group with Ice-T, Daddy Kane and Kool Moe Dee for *Back On The Block* by Quincy Jones.

| | | | | |
|---|---|---|---|---|
| 23/10/1982 | 77 | 3 | | THE MESSAGE | Sugar Hill SHLP 1007 |
| 23/06/1984 | 41 | 16 | | GREATEST MESSAGES | Sugar Hill SHLP 5552 |
| 23/02/1985 | 95 | 1 | | THEY SAID IT COULDN'T BE DONE **GRANDMASTER FLASH** | Elektra 9603891 |

### GRANDMASTER MELLE MEL
US rapper (born Melvin Glover), also in The Furious Five before going solo. Won the 1990 Grammy Award for Best Rap Performance by a Group with Ice-T, Daddy Kane and Kool Moe Dee for *Back On The Block* by Quincy Jones.

| | | | | |
|---|---|---|---|---|
| 20/10/1984 | 45 | 5 | | WORK PARTY | Sugar Hill SHLP 5553 |

### AMY GRANT
US singer (born 25/11/1960, Augusta, GA) who made her debut album in 1976 and is regarded as the first lady of contemporary Christian music, selling more than 15 million albums in her career. She has won five Grammies: Best Contemporary Gospel Performance in 1982 for *Age To Age*, Best Gospel Performance in 1983 for *Ageless Melody*, Best Gospel Performance in 1984 for *Angels*, Best Gospel Performance in 1985 for *Unguarded* and Best Gospel Performance in 1988 for *Lead Me On*.

| | | | | |
|---|---|---|---|---|
| 22/06/1991 | 25 | 15 | ● | HEART IN MOTION | A&M 3953211 |

### DAVID GRANT
UK singer (born 8/8/1956, Hackney, London) who was a founding member of Linx in the early 1980s before launching a solo career masterminded by Derek Bramble. He won the 1998 MOBO Award for Best Gospel Act with Carrie.

| | | | | |
|---|---|---|---|---|
| 05/11/1983 | 32 | 6 | | DAVID GRANT | Chrysalis CHR 1448 |
| 18/05/1985 | 96 | 1 | | HOPES AND DREAMS | Chrysalis CHR 1483 |

### EDDY GRANT
Guyanan singer/multi-instrumentalist (born Edmond Montague Grant, 5/3/1948, Plaisance) who moved to London in 1960 and formed The Equals in 1967. When legal problems prevented the group from recording in the early 1970s, Grant concentrated on production, in 1977 going solo. A shrewd businessman, his earnings set up Ice Records in Guyana and then in the UK.

| | | | | |
|---|---|---|---|---|
| 30/05/1981 | 39 | 6 | | CAN'T GET ENOUGH | Ice ICELP 21 |
| 27/11/1982 | 7 | 23 | O | **KILLER ON THE RAMPAGE** | Ice ICELP 3023 |
| 17/11/1984 | 23 | 10 | ● | ALL THE HITS | K-Tel NE 1284 |
| 01/07/1989 | 20 | 8 | O | WALKING ON SUNSHINE (THE VERY BEST OF EDDY GRANT) | Parlophone PCSD 108 |
| 19/05/2001 | 3 | 15 | ✪ | **THE GREATEST HITS** | East West 8573885972 |

### GRANT LEE BUFFALO
US rock group formed in Los Angeles, CA in 1989 by Grant Lee Phillips (guitar/vocals), Paul Kimble (bass and keyboards) and Joey Peters (drums). After a brief deal with SOL (Singles Only Label) they signed with Slash Records in 1991.

| | | | | |
|---|---|---|---|---|
| 10/07/1993 | 74 | 1 | | FUZZY | Slash 8283892 |
| 01/10/1994 | 24 | 2 | | MIGHTY JOE MOON | Slash 8285412 |
| 15/06/1996 | 34 | 2 | | COPPEROPOLIS | Slash 8287602 |

### GRATEFUL DEAD
US rock group formed in San Francisco, CA in 1965 by Jerry Garcia (born 1/8/1942, San Francisco, guitar), Bob Weir (born Robert Hall 16/10/1947, San Francisco, guitar), Phil Lesh (born Philip Chapman 15/3/1940, Berkeley, CA, bass), Ron 'Pigpen' McKernan (born 8/9/1945, San Bruno, CA, keyboards) and Bill Kreutzmann (born in Palo Alto, CA, drums) as The Warlocks. They were first known as the house band for Ken Kesey's Acid Tests in which they were supplied with large amounts of LSD (then legal) and the results monitored over a six month period. By 1967, as Grateful Dead, they had recorded their eponymous debut album (reportedly recorded in just three days). In 1968 they added Mickey Hart (drums) and Tom Constanten (keyboards). McKernan died from alcohol abuse on 8/3/1973 and was replaced by Keith Godcheaux, whose wife Donnas also joined as singer. They remained with the band until 1979 (Keith was killed in a car crash on 21/7/1980) with Brent Mydland joining on keyboards. Garcia collapsed into a diabetic coma in 1986 but recovered to continue to lead the band. Mydland died from a drugs overdose on 26/7/1990, temporarily replaced by Bruce Hornsby (born 23/11/1954, Williamsburg, VA) and then Vince Welnick. Garcia died from a heart attack on 9/8/1995, and at the end of the year the rest of the group announced that the name of the group would be buried with him. They were inducted into the Rock & Roll Hall of Fame in 1994.

| | | | | |
|---|---|---|---|---|
| 19/09/1970 | 69 | 2 | | WORKINGMAN'S DEAD | Warner Brothers WS 1869 |
| 03/08/1974 | 47 | 1 | | GRATEFUL DEAD FROM THE MARS HOTEL | Warner Brothers K 59302 |
| 01/11/1975 | 45 | 1 | | BLUES FOR ALLAH | United Artists UAS 29895 |
| 04/09/1976 | 42 | 1 | | STEAL YOUR FACE | United Artists UAS 60131/2 |
| 20/08/1977 | 30 | 1 | | TERRAPIN STATION | Arista SPARTY 1016 |

| | | | | | |
|---|---|---|---|---|---|
| 19/09/1987 | 57 | 3 | | IN THE DARK | Arista 208 564 |
| 18/02/1989 | 38 | 3 | | DYLAN AND THE DEAD **BOB DYLAN AND THE GRATEFUL DEAD** | CBS 4633811 |

**GRAVEDIGGAZ** US rap group formed by Prince Paul (born Paul Huston, also a member of Stetsasonic), RZA (born Robert Diggs, member of Wu-Tang Clan) and Fruitkwan (born Arnold Hamilton). Prince Paul and Fruitkwan also adopted additional stage names in the Undertaker and the Gatekeeper respectively. The group also featured Poetic The Grym Reaper and re-christened RZA the Ressurector. Poetic The Grym Reaper died from colon cancer in July 2001.

| | | | | | |
|---|---|---|---|---|---|
| 04/10/1997 | 24 | 1 | | THE PICK, THE SICKLE AND THE SHOVEL | Gee Street GEE 1000562 |

**DAVID GRAY AND TOMMY TYCHO** UK arrangers. Tommy Tycho has also worked with Mary Schneider and Anthony Warlow and was the arranger for the soundtrack to the film *Young Einstein*.

| | | | | | |
|---|---|---|---|---|---|
| 16/10/1976 | 21 | 6 | | ARMCHAIR MELODIES | K-Tel NE 927 |

**DAVID GRAY** UK singer (born 1968, some sources give 1970, Manchester) who made his debut album in 1993 for Hut Records, later recording for EMI and forming the IHT label. His *White Ladder* album finally hit the #1 spot two years and five months after it was released, the second longest run to #1 by any album (only Tyrannosaurus Rex's *My People Were Fair And Had Sky In Their Hair* took longer, at nearly four years).

| | | | | | |
|---|---|---|---|---|---|
| 13/05/2000 | ❶² | 144 | ✪⁸ | **WHITE LADDER** ◇² | IHT/East West 8573829832 |
| 12/08/2000 | 55 | 1 | | LOST SONGS 95–98 | IHT IHTCD 002 |
| 24/02/2001 | 7 | 10 | ● | **LOST SONGS 95–98** | East West 8573869532 |
| 14/07/2001 | 68 | 1 | | THE EP'S 1992–1994 | Hut CDHUT 67 |
| 09/11/2002 | ❶¹ | 47 | ✪² | **A NEW DAY AT MIDNIGHT** | East West 5046616582 |

**MACY GRAY** US singer (born Natalie McIntyre,1969, Canton, OH) who moved to Los Angeles, CA to enrol in a screenwriting programme before beginning a singing career. Her backing group comprises Dawn Beckman (vocals), Musiic Galloway (vocals), DJ Kiilu (DJ), Dion Murdock (drums), Jeremy Ruzumna (keyboards), Dave Wilder (bass), Arik Marshall (guitar), Matt DeMerritt, Tracy Wannomae and Todd Simon (all horns). Best International Newcomer and Best International Female Artist at the 2000 BRIT Awards.

| | | | | | |
|---|---|---|---|---|---|
| 17/07/1999 | 3 | 67 | ✪⁴ | **ON HOW LIFE IS** ◇² | Epic 4944232 |
| 29/09/2001 | ❶¹ | 8 | ● | **THE ID** | Epic 5040899 |
| 10/05/2003 | 17 | 5 | | THE TROUBLE WITH BEING MYSELF | Epic 5108102 |

**GREAT WHITE** US rock group formed in Los Angeles, CA in 1981 by Jack Russell (vocals), Mark Kendall (guitar), Lorne Black (bass) and Gary Holland (drums). Holland left in 1986 and was replaced by Audie Desbrow; Black left in 1987 and was replaced by Tony Montana. Michael Lardie was added on keyboards in 1987. Montana left in 1993 and was replaced by Teddy Cook. On 21/2/2003 a fire in a Rhode Island club, sparked by the group's pyrotechnics, left 97 people dead, including the group's bass player Ty Longley.

| | | | | | |
|---|---|---|---|---|---|
| 09/03/1991 | 43 | 1 | | HOOKED | Capitol EST 2138 |

**MARTIN GRECH** UK guitarist/singer (born 1982, Aylesbury) whose band features Peter Miles (keyboards/guitar), Tim Elsenburg (guitar), Bish (bass) and Al Hamer (drums).

| | | | | | |
|---|---|---|---|---|---|
| 03/08/2002 | 54 | 2 | | OPEN HEART ZOO | Island CID 8119 |

**AL GREEN** US singer (born Al Greene, 13/4/1946, Forrest City, AR) who joined the family gospel group and was fired by his father for listening to Jackie Wilson records. He formed the Creations in 1964, going solo when they disbanded in 1968. He returned to gospel music in 1980, although apparently his spiritual rebirth occurred in 1973 (as Green claims) or 1974 when ex-girlfriend Mary Woodson attacked him with boiling hot grits and shot herself with Green's own gun. He was inducted into the Rock & Roll Hall of Fame in 1995. He has won nine Grammy Awards: Best Traditional Soul Gospel Performance in 1981 for *The Lord Will Make A Way*; Best Traditional Soul Gospel Performance in 1982 for *Precious Lord*; Best Contemporary Soul Gospel Performance in 1982 for *Higher Plane*; Best Soul Gospel Performance in 1983 for *I'll Rise Again*; Best Soul Gospel Performance by a Duo in 1984 with Shirley Caesar for *Sailin' On The Sea Of Your Love*; Best Soul Gospel Performance in 1986 for *Going Away*; Best Soul Gospel Performance in 1987 for *Everything's Gonna Be Alright*; Best Soul Gospel Performance in 1989 for *As Long As We're Together*; and Best Pop Vocal Collaboration in 1994 with Lyle Lovett for *Funny How Time Slips Away*.

| | | | | | |
|---|---|---|---|---|---|
| 26/04/1975 | 18 | 16 | ○ | AL GREEN'S GREATEST HITS | London SHU 8481 |
| 01/10/1988 | 34 | 7 | ○ | HI LIFE – THE BEST OF AL GREEN | K-Tel NE 1420 |
| 24/10/1992 | 41 | 2 | | AL | Beechwood AGREECD 1 |
| 16/02/2002 | 18 | 6 | | LOVE – THE ESSENTIAL | Hi ALTV 2002 |

▲⁹ Number of weeks album topped the US chart ◆¹² RIAA Diamond Awards ◇³ IFPI Platinum Europe Awards

**PETER GREEN** UK singer/guitarist (born Peter Greenbaum, 29/10/1946, Bethnal Green, London), he played with semi-professional groups such as The Muskrats and The Tridents before joining John Mayall's Bluesbreakers in 1965. He then formed The Peter B's with Peter Bardens, Dave Ambrose and Mick Fleetwood, this band soon becoming Shotgun Express that backed Rod Stewart among others. Green rejoined the Bluesbreakers in 1966 and remained with them for a year before linking again with Mick Fleetwood, this time in Fleetwood Mac with Jeremy Spencer and John McVie. As they became more successful, Green became more detached, and in 1970 he announced his departure. His appearances since then have been sporadic, either solo or fronting a group called Kolors.

| | | | | |
|---|---|---|---|---|
| 09/06/1979 | 32 | 13 | | IN THE SKIES . . . . . . . . . . . . . . . . . . . . . . . . . . . . . . . . . . . . . . . . . . . . . Creole PULS 101 |
| 24/05/1980 | 34 | 4 | | LITTLE DREAMER . . . . . . . . . . . . . . . . . . . . . . . . . . . . . . . . . . . . . . . . . . . . Puk PULS 102 |
| 24/05/1997 | 71 | 1 | | SPLINTER GROUP . . . . . . . . . . . . . . . . . . . . . . . . . . . . . . . . . . . . . . . . . Artisan SARCD 101 |
| 30/05/1998 | 57 | 1 | | THE ROBERT JOHNSON SONGBOOK **PETER GREEN WITH NIGEL WATSON AND THE SPLINTER GROUP** . . . . . . . . Artisan SARCD 002 |

**ROBSON GREEN AND JEROME FLYNN** UK vocal duo Robson Golightly Green (born 18/12/1964, Hexham, Northumberland) and Jerome Flynn (born 16/3/1963), first known as Paddy and Dave in the TV series *Soldier Soldier*.

| | | | | |
|---|---|---|---|---|
| 25/11/1995 | ❶[7] | 31 | ✪[6] | **ROBSON & JEROME** ◇[2] . . . . . . . . . . . . . . . . . . . . . . . . . . . . . . . . . . . . . RCA 74321323902 |
| 23/11/1996 | ❶[2] | 16 | ✪[4] | **TAKE TWO** ◇ . . . . . . . . . . . . . . . . . . . . . . . . . . . . . . . . . . . . . . . . . . RCA 74321426252 |
| 29/11/1997 | 20 | 6 | | HAPPY DAYS – THE BEST OF ROBSON AND JEROME . . . . . . . . . . . . . . . . . . . RCA 74321542602 |
| 14/12/2002 | 49 | 4 | | MOMENT IN TIME **ROBSON GREEN**. . . . . . . . . . . . . . . . . . . . . . . . . . . . . . . . . T2 TCD3300 |

**GREEN DAY** US rock group formed in Berkeley, CA in 1989 by Billy Joe Armstrong (born 17/2/1972, San Pablo, CA, guitar/vocals), Mike Dirnt (born Michael Pritchard, 4/5/1972, Berkeley, bass/vocals) and Tre Cool (born Frank Edwin Wright III, 9/12/1972, Willis, CA, drums). Successful touring led to a bidding war that was finally won by Reprise in 1993. They have won one Grammy Award.

| | | | | |
|---|---|---|---|---|
| 05/11/1994 | 13 | 55 | ✪ | DOOKIE ◇ ◆[10] 1994 Grammy Award for Best Alternative Music Performance . . . . . . . . . . . . Reprise 9362457952 |
| 21/10/1995 | 8 | 5 | ○ | **INSOMNIAC** . . . . . . . . . . . . . . . . . . . . . . . . . . . . . . . . . . . . . . . . . . Reprise 9362460462 |
| 25/10/1997 | 11 | 11 | ○ | NIMROD . . . . . . . . . . . . . . . . . . . . . . . . . . . . . . . . . . . . . . . . . . . . . Reprise 9362467942 |
| 14/10/2000 | 4 | 14 | ● | **WARNING**. . . . . . . . . . . . . . . . . . . . . . . . . . . . . . . . . . . . . . . . . . . . Reprise 9362480302 |
| 24/11/2001 | 15 | 10 | ● | INTERNATIONAL SUPERHITS . . . . . . . . . . . . . . . . . . . . . . . . . . . . . . . . . Reprise 9362481452 |
| 13/07/2002 | 32 | 3 | | SHENANIGANS . . . . . . . . . . . . . . . . . . . . . . . . . . . . . . . . . . . . . . . . . Reprise 9362482082 |

**GREEN JELLY** US comedy act with twelve members led by Bill Manspeaker (aka Marshall 'Duh' Staxx and Moronic Dicktator). The group formed in 1981 as Green Jello and has since got through 74 members. Up until 1993, their US releases were only available on video.

| | | | | |
|---|---|---|---|---|
| 03/07/1993 | 18 | 10 | | CEREAL KILLER SOUNDTRACK. . . . . . . . . . . . . . . . . . . . . . . . . . . . . . . . . . Zoo 72445110382 |

**GREEN ON RED** US rock group formed in Tucson, AZ in 1981 by Dan Stuart (guitar/vocals), Jack Waterson (drums) and Van Christian (drums) as The Serfers. By the time the group came to record their debut album, Christian had been replaced by Alex MacNicol and Chris Cacavas added on keyboards. Guitarist Chuck Prophet joined in 1984. Waterson and Cacavas left on 1987, leaving Prophet and Stuart to continue as a duo using session musicians. Prophet launched a parallel solo career in 1993.

| | | | | |
|---|---|---|---|---|
| 26/10/1985 | 99 | 1 | | NO FREE LUNCH . . . . . . . . . . . . . . . . . . . . . . . . . . . . . . . . . . . . . . . . Mercury MERM 78 |

**DAVE GREENFIELD** – see **JEAN-JACQUES BURNEL**

**GREENSLADE** UK rock group formed in 1972 by Dave Greenslade (born 18/1/1943, Woking, Surrey, keyboards), Tony Reeves (born 18/4/1943, London, bass), Dave Lawson (keyboards/vocals) and Andrew McCulloch (drums). Greenslade and Reeves had previously been members of Colosseum, and a further former member of the band in Dave Clempson joined Greenslade later at the same time as Graham Smith (violin). Reeves left in 1975, shortly before they disbanded. Dave Greenslade re-assembled the group in 1977 with Jon Hiseman (another ex-Colosseum, drums), Tony Reeves and Mick Rodgers, this line-up lasting for one tour before disbanding.

| | | | | |
|---|---|---|---|---|
| 14/09/1974 | 34 | 3 | | SPYGLASS GUEST . . . . . . . . . . . . . . . . . . . . . . . . . . . . . . . . . . . . . . Warner Brothers K 56055 |

**CHRISTINA GREGG** UK fitness instructor.

| | | | | |
|---|---|---|---|---|
| 27/05/1978 | 51 | 1 | | MUSIC 'N' MOTION . . . . . . . . . . . . . . . . . . . . . . . . . . . . . . . . . . . . . . . Warwick WW 5041 |

**GRID** UK duo of ex-Soft Cell David Ball (born 3/5/1959, Blackpool) and Richard Norris (born 23/6/1965, London), who teamed up in 1990 for East-West Records. Norris had been with East Of Eden, Innocent Vicars and The Fruitbats, and later set up Candy Records.

| | | | | |
|---|---|---|---|---|
| 01/10/1994 | 14 | 3 | | EVOLVER . . . . . . . . . . . . . . . . . . . . . . . . . . . . . . . . . . . . . . . . Deconstruction 74321227182 |
| 14/10/1995 | 67 | 1 | | MUSIC FOR DANCING . . . . . . . . . . . . . . . . . . . . . . . . . . . . . . . . . Deconstruction 74321276702 |

**ALISTAIR GRIFFIN** UK singer (born 1/11/1977, Castleton), first known as one of the contestants on *Fame Academy*.

| | | | | |
|---|---|---|---|---|
| 24/01/2004 | 12 | 3 | | BRING IT ON . . . . . . . . . . . . . . . . . . . . . . . . . . . . . . . . . . . . . . . . Universal TV 9816116 |

**NANCI GRIFFITH** US singer/guitarist (born 6/7/1953, Seguin, TX), she began performing in public in 1967 and made her first album in 1978. Having initially found success within the country music market, her later releases touched on soft rock. She has won two

Grammy Awards including Best Traditional Folk Album in 1992 with the Chieftains for *An Irish Evening Live at the Grand Opera House, Belfast, with Roger Daltry and Nanci Griffith.*

| | | | | | |
|---|---|---|---|---|---|
| 26/03/1988 | 78 | 1 | | LITTLE LOVE AFFAIRS | MCA MCF 3413 |
| 23/09/1989 | 38 | 3 | | STORMS | MCA MCG 6066 |
| 28/09/1991 | 40 | 5 | | LATE NIGHT GRANDE HOTEL | MCA 10306 |
| 20/03/1993 | 18 | 6 | | OTHER VOICES/OTHER ROOMS 1993 Grammy Award for Best Contemporary Folk Album | MCA 10796 |
| 13/11/1993 | 27 | 4 | ○ | THE BEST OF NANCI GRIFFITH | MCA MCD 10966 |
| 01/10/1994 | 20 | 4 | | FLYER | MCA MCD 11155 |
| 05/04/1997 | 64 | 3 | | BLUE ROSES FROM THE MOONS | Elektra 7559620152 |

### GRIMTHORPE COLLIERY BAND
UK brass band formed in the Yorkshire town of Grimthorpe.

| | | | | | |
|---|---|---|---|---|---|
| 06/06/1998 | 36 | 4 | | BRASSED OFF Soundtrack from the 1998 film *Brassed Off* | RCA Victor 09026687572 |

### JOSH GROBAN
US singer born in Los Angeles, CA he was discovered by producer David Foster. Prior to launching his solo career he appeared on the soundtrack to *A.I: Artificial Intelligence* and in the TV series *Ally McBeal.*

| | | | | | |
|---|---|---|---|---|---|
| 15/02/2003 | 32 | 8 | | JOSH GROBAN | Reprise 9362481542 |

### GROOVE ARMADA
UK production/instrumental duo Tom Findlay and Andy Cato.

| | | | | | |
|---|---|---|---|---|---|
| 05/06/1999 | 23 | 18 | ● | VERTIGO | Pepper 0530332 |
| 06/05/2000 | 68 | 1 | | THE REMIXES | Pepper 9230102 |
| 22/09/2001 | 5 | 8 | ● | GOODBYE COUNTRY (HELLO NIGHTCLUB) | Pepper 9230492 |
| 16/11/2002 | 41 | 2 | ○ | LOVEBOX | Pepper 9230682 |

### GROOVERIDER
UK singer/DJ (born 16/4/1967, London) who doesn't reveal his real name, but admits to being also known as Ray B. He made his name as a radio presenter with Fabio, first with Kiss FM and then later Radio 1. He previously recorded as Codename John and won the 1999 MOBO Award for Best Drum & Bass Act.

| | | | | | |
|---|---|---|---|---|---|
| 10/10/1998 | 50 | 1 | | MYSTERIES OF FUNK | Higher Ground HIGH 6CD |

### GROUNDHOGS
UK rock group formed in 1963 by Tony McPhee (born 22/3/1944, Humberstone, Lincolnshire, guitar), John Cruickshank (harp/vocals), Bob Hall (piano), Pete Cruickshank (born 2/7/1945, Calcutta, India, bass) and Dave Boorman (drums), the group having first been known as The Dollarbills. They re-formed in 1968 with McPhee, Pete Cruickshank, Steve Rye (vocals/ harmonica) and Ken Pustelnik (drums), although Rye left after one album. Pustelnik left in 1972, replaced by Clive Brooks (born 28/12/1949, London), with the group effectively disbanding in 1975. Although McPhee toured using the name Groundhogs sporadically thereafter, it was not until 1984 that the group re-formed with McPhee, Dave Anderson (bass) and Mike Jones (drums).

| | | | | | |
|---|---|---|---|---|---|
| 06/06/1970 | 9 | 13 | | THANK CHRIST FOR THE BOMB | Liberty LBS 83295 |
| 03/04/1971 | 5 | 27 | | SPLIT | Liberty LBG 83401 |
| 18/03/1972 | 8 | 9 | | WHO WILL SAVE THE WORLD | United Artists UAG 29237 |
| 13/07/1974 | 31 | 1 | | SOLID | WWA 004 |

### GTR
UK rock group formed in 1985 by Steve Hackett (born 12/2/1950, London, guitar), Steve Howe (born 8/4/1947, London, guitar), Max Bacon (vocals), Phil Spalding (bass) and Jonathon Mover (drums). They enjoyed two minor US hits before disbanding with Hackett going on to pursue a solo career.

| | | | | | |
|---|---|---|---|---|---|
| 19/07/1986 | 41 | 4 | | GTR | Arista 207 716 |

### GUILDFORD CATHEDRAL CHOIR
UK choir formed in Guildford and conducted by Barry Rose.

| | | | | | |
|---|---|---|---|---|---|
| 10/12/1966 | 24 | 4 | | CHRISTMAS CAROLS FROM GUILDFORD CATHEDRAL | MFP 1104 |

### GUITAR CORPORATION
UK instrumental group.

| | | | | | |
|---|---|---|---|---|---|
| 15/02/1992 | 41 | 5 | | IMAGES | Quality Television QTVCD 002 |

### GUN
UK heavy rock group formed in Glasgow in 1986 by Mark Rankin (vocals), Baby Stafford (guitar), Giuliano 'Joolz' Gizzi (guitar), Dante Gizzi and Scott Shields (drums). By 1995 the group was a four-piece comprising Rankin, both Gizzi's and drummer Mark Kerr. They won the 1994 MTV Europe Music Award for Best Cover for *Word Up*.

| | | | | | |
|---|---|---|---|---|---|
| 22/07/1989 | 44 | 10 | ○ | TAKING ON THE WORLD | A&M AMA 7007 |
| 18/04/1992 | 14 | 4 | | GALLUS | A&M 3953832 |
| 13/08/1994 | 5 | 7 | ○ | SWAGGER | A&M 5402542 |
| 24/05/1997 | 32 | 2 | | 0141 632 6326 The album took its title from the information number for the group | A&M 5407232 |

### GUNS N' ROSES
US heavy rock group formed in Los Angeles, CA in 1985 by Axl Rose (born William Bailey, 6/2/1962, Lafayette, lead vocals) who allegedly adopted the name because it is an anagram of oral sex, Izzy Stradlin (born Jeffrey Isbell, 8/4/1962, Lafayette, guitar), Steven Adler (born 22/1/1965, Cleveland, drums), Michael 'Duff' McKagan (born 5/2/1964, Seattle, bass) and Slash (born Saul Hudson, 23/7/1965, Stoke-on-Trent, guitar). Adler left in 1990 and was replaced by ex-Cult drummer Matt Sorum (born 19/11/1960), with keyboard player Dizzy Reed supplementing the group the same year. Stradlin left in 1991 and was replaced by Gilby Clarke. Clarke later became a member of Colonel Parker with ex-Stray Cats Slim Jim Phantom, ex-LA Guns Muddy Stardust and Teddy Andreadis (formerly of Slash's Snakepit), the first contemporary act signed to actor Mel Gibson's Icon Records label.

| | | | | | |
|---|---|---|---|---|---|
| 01/08/1987 | 5 | 161 | ✪² | **APPETITE FOR DESTRUCTION** ▲⁵ ◆¹⁵ | Geffen WX 125 |
| 17/12/1988 | 22 | 41 | ● | G N' R THE LIES, THE SEX, THE DRUGS, THE VIOLENCE, THE SHOCKING TRUTH | Geffen WX 218 |
| 28/09/1991 | 2 | 84 | ✪ | **USE YOUR ILLUSION I** | Geffen GEF 24415 |
| 28/09/1991 | ❶¹ | 84 | ✪ | **USE YOUR ILLUSION II** ▲² Above two albums were released on the same day and entered the charts in the top two positions | Geffen GEF 24420 |
| 04/12/1993 | 2 | 10 | ● | **THE SPAGHETTI INCIDENT?** | Geffen GED 24617 |
| 11/12/1999 | 45 | 2 | | LIVE – ERA '87–'93 | Geffen 4905142 |
| 27/03/2004 | ❶³ | 14+ | ✪² | **GREATEST HITS** ◇ | Geffen 9862108 |

**GUNSHOT** UK rap group formed in London in 1990 by former school friends MC Mercury, Akaline and DJ White-Child Rix.

| | | | | | |
|---|---|---|---|---|---|
| 19/06/1993 | 60 | 1 | | PATRIOT GAMES | Vinyl Solution STEAM 43CD |

**DAVID GUNSON** UK after-dinner speaker born in Yorkshire, he was an air traffic controller at Birmingham airport for 23 years before becoming an after dinner speaker.

| | | | | | |
|---|---|---|---|---|---|
| 25/12/1982 | 92 | 2 | | WHAT GOES UP MIGHT COME DOWN | Big Ben BB 0012 |

**GURU** US instrumentalist/rapper (born Keith Elam, 18/7/1966, Boston, MA) who is also a member of Gang Starr with Chris Martin and has recorded as Guru's Jazzamatazz. His debut solo album featured Donald Byrd and Roy Ayers.

| | | | | | |
|---|---|---|---|---|---|
| 29/05/1993 | 58 | 2 | ○ | JAZZMATAZZ | Cooltempo CTCD 34 |
| 15/07/1995 | 12 | 9 | ○ | JAZZMATAZZ VOLUME II – THE NEW REALITY | Cooltempo CTCD 47 |
| 14/10/2000 | 74 | 1 | | STREETSOUL **GURU'S JAZZMATAZZ** | Virgin CDVUS 178 |

**GURU JOSH** UK producer Paul Walden (born 1964) who had previously been with Joshua Cries Wolf.

| | | | | | |
|---|---|---|---|---|---|
| 14/07/1990 | 41 | 2 | | INFINITY | Deconstruction PL 74701 |

**G.U.S. (FOOTWEAR) BAND AND THE MORRISTON ORPHEUS CHOIR** UK instrumental group with a vocal choir.

| | | | | | |
|---|---|---|---|---|---|
| 03/10/1970 | 54 | 1 | | LAND OF HOPE AND GLORY | Columbia SCX 6406 |

**ARLO GUTHRIE** US guitarist/singer (born 10/7/1947, Coney Island, NY), the son of legendary folk singer Woody Guthrie. Arlo made his reputation with his appearance at the 1967 Newport Folk Festival and his composition *Alice's Restaurant Massacre*, which was later made into a film with Guthrie starring as himself. He later worked extensively with fellow singer Pete Seeger.

| | | | | | |
|---|---|---|---|---|---|
| 07/03/1970 | 44 | 1 | | ALICE'S RESTAURANT | Reprise RSLP 6267 |

**GWEN GUTHRIE** US singer (born 9/7/1950, Newark, NJ) who began as a backing singer for the likes of Billy Preston and Aretha Franklin as well as songwriting before going solo in 1982. She also provided the lead vocals to the Limit hit single. She died from cancer on 4/2/1999.

| | | | | | |
|---|---|---|---|---|---|
| 23/08/1986 | 42 | 14 | | GOOD TO GO LOVER | Boiling Point POLD 5201 |

**ROBIN GUTHRIE** – see **HAROLD BUDD/ELIZABETH FRASER/ROBIN GUTHRIE/SIMON RAYMONDE**

**GUY** US R&B group formed in New York in 1988 by Teddy Riley (born 8/10/1966, Harlem, NYC) and brothers Damion (born 6/6/1968, Brooklyn, NYC) and Aaron Hall (born 10/8/1964, Brooklyn). They disbanded in 1991, with Riley forming BLACKstreet and working extensively as a producer, while Aaron Hall recorded solo. Guy re-formed in 1999 after Riley had dissolved BLACKstreet.

| | | | | | |
|---|---|---|---|---|---|
| 05/02/2000 | 55 | 1 | | III | MCA 1121702 |

**BUDDY GUY** US singer/guitarist (born George Guy, 30/7/1936, Lettsworth, LA) he moved to Chicago, IL in 1957 and worked with the Rufus Foreman Band before becoming an artist in his own right. He then worked as part of the Chess Records houseband and made a number of recordings under his own name as well as a series of influential albums for Vanguard. He was exposed to a wider audience after supporting The Rolling Stones on their 1970 world tour and repeated this twenty years later when he appeared as one of the guests on Eric Clapton's blues night. Clapton, along with Jeff Beck and Mark Knopfler, subsequently appeared on Guy's *Damn Right I've Got The Blues* album the following year. He won the 2003 Grammy Award for Best Traditional Blues Album for *Blues Singer*.

| | | | | | |
|---|---|---|---|---|---|
| 22/06/1991 | 43 | 5 | | DAMN RIGHT, I'VE GOT THE BLUES | Silvertone ORELP 516 |
| 13/03/1993 | 36 | 4 | | FEELS LIKE RAIN | Silvertone ORECD 525 |

**A GUY CALLED GERALD** UK producer Gerald Simpson who had previously been a member of 808 State.

| | | | | | |
|---|---|---|---|---|---|
| 14/04/1990 | 68 | 1 | | AUTOMANIKK | Subscape 4664821 |
| 01/04/1995 | 64 | 1 | | BLACK SECRET TECHNOLOGY | Juice Box JBCD 25 |

**GUYS AND DOLLS** UK vocal group formed in 1969 by Vicky Marcelle and two other singers. The group was re-formed in 1973 with Paul Griggs, Dominic Grant, David Van Day, Thereze Bazar, Martine Howard and Julie Forsythe. Van Day and Bazar left to form Dollar, with the remaining members continuing as a quartet until the early 1980s.

| | | | | | |
|---|---|---|---|---|---|
| 31/05/1975 | 43 | 1 | | GUYS 'N' DOLLS | Magnet MAG 5005 |

○ Silver disc ● Gold disc ✪ Platinum disc (additional platinum units are indicated by a figure following the symbol) ❶⁹ Number of weeks album topped the UK chart

# H

**H AND CLAIRE** UK vocal duo formed by ex-Steps members Ian Watkins (born 8/5/1976) and Claire Richards (born 17/8/1977).

30/11/2002 . . . . . 58 . . . . . 1 . . . . . . ○    ANOTHER YOU ANOTHER ME . . . . . . . . . . . . . . . . . . . . . . . . . . . . . . . . . . . . . . . . . . . . . . . . . . . . . . . . WEA 0927494622

**STEVE HACKETT** UK singer/guitarist (born 12/2/1950, London) who played with numerous groups, including Canterbury Glass, Heel Pier, Quiet World and Sarabande, before joining Genesis in 1971. Hackett remained with them until 1977 when he went solo, his debut album having been released in 1975. In 1985 he was a founding member of GTR with Steve Howe and Max Bacon; they enjoyed two minor US hits before disbanding. Hackett then resumed his solo career.

| | | | |
|---|---|---|---|
| 01/11/1975 . . . . . 26 . . . . . . 4 . . . . . . | VOYAGE OF THE ACOLYTE . . . . . . . . . . . . . . . . . . . . . . . . . . . . . . . . . . . . . . . . . . . . . . . . . . . . . . . . . . Charisma CAS 1111 |
| 06/05/1978 . . . . . 38 . . . . . . 5 . . . . . . | PLEASE DON'T TOUCH . . . . . . . . . . . . . . . . . . . . . . . . . . . . . . . . . . . . . . . . . . . . . . . . . . . . . . . . . . Charisma CDS 4012 |
| 26/05/1979 . . . . . 22 . . . . . 11 . . . . . . | SPECTRAL MORNINGS . . . . . . . . . . . . . . . . . . . . . . . . . . . . . . . . . . . . . . . . . . . . . . . . . . . . . . . . . . Charisma CDS 4017 |
| 21/06/1980 . . . . . 9 . . . . . . 7 . . . . . . | DEFECTOR . . . . . . . . . . . . . . . . . . . . . . . . . . . . . . . . . . . . . . . . . . . . . . . . . . . . . . . . . . . . . . . . . Charisma CDS 4018 |
| 29/08/1981 . . . . . 15 . . . . . . 5 . . . . . . | CURED . . . . . . . . . . . . . . . . . . . . . . . . . . . . . . . . . . . . . . . . . . . . . . . . . . . . . . . . . . . . . . . . . . . . Charisma CDS 4021 |
| 30/04/1983 . . . . . 16 . . . . . . 3 . . . . . . | HIGHLY STRUNG . . . . . . . . . . . . . . . . . . . . . . . . . . . . . . . . . . . . . . . . . . . . . . . . . . . . . . . . . . . . . Charisma HACK 1 |
| 19/11/1983 . . . . . 70 . . . . . . 1 . . . . . . | BAY OF KINGS . . . . . . . . . . . . . . . . . . . . . . . . . . . . . . . . . . . . . . . . . . . . . . . . . . . . . . . . . . Lamborghini LMGLP 3000 |
| 22/09/1984 . . . . . 54 . . . . . . 2 . . . . . . | TILL WE HAVE FACES . . . . . . . . . . . . . . . . . . . . . . . . . . . . . . . . . . . . . . . . . . . . . . . . . . . . . . Lamborghini LMGLP 4000 |

**HADDAWAY** Trinidadian singer/dancer (born Nestor Alexander Haddaway, 1966) who moved with his family to Chicago, IL at the age of nine. He was a professional US footballer with the Cologne Crocodiles before launching a singing career.

23/10/1993 . . . . . 9 . . . . . 16 . . . . . . ●    **HADDAWAY – THE ALBUM** . . . . . . . . . . . . . . . . . . . . . . . . . . . . . . . . . . . . . . . . . . . . . . . . . . . . Logic 74321169222

**TONY HADLEY** UK singer (born 2/6/1960, London) and founding member of New Romantic group Spandau Ballet in 1979; he later went solo. In 2003 he won ITV's *Reborn In The USA* competition.

| | | |
|---|---|---|
| 20/09/1997 . . . . . 45 . . . . . 3 . . . . . . | TONY HADLEY . . . . . . . . . . . . . . . . . . . . . . . . . . . . . . . . . . . . . . . . . . . . . . . . . . . . . . . . . . . . Polygram TV 5393012 |
| 10/05/2003 . . . . . 31 . . . . . 3 . . . . . . | TRUE BALLADS . . . . . . . . . . . . . . . . . . . . . . . . . . . . . . . . . . . . . . . . . . . . . . . . . . . . . . . . . . . Universal TV 0382882 |

**SAMMY HAGAR** US singer/guitarist (born 13/10/1947, Monterey, CA) who played with the Fabulous Castillas, Skinny, Justice Brothers and Dust Cloud before becoming lead singer of Montrose in 1973. He went solo in 1975, his own band comprising Bill Church (bass), Alan Fitzgerald (keyboards) and Denny Carmassi (drums). He replaced David Lee Roth as lead singer with Van Halen in 1986.

| | | |
|---|---|---|
| 29/09/1979 . . . . . 38 . . . . . . 4 . . . . . . | STREET MACHINE . . . . . . . . . . . . . . . . . . . . . . . . . . . . . . . . . . . . . . . . . . . . . . . . . . . . . . . . . . . Capitol EST 11983 |
| 22/03/1980 . . . . . 12 . . . . . . 8 . . . . . . | LOUD AND CLEAR . . . . . . . . . . . . . . . . . . . . . . . . . . . . . . . . . . . . . . . . . . . . . . . . . . . . . . . . . . . Capitol EST 25330 |
| 07/06/1980 . . . . . 25 . . . . . . 3 . . . . . . | DANGER ZONE . . . . . . . . . . . . . . . . . . . . . . . . . . . . . . . . . . . . . . . . . . . . . . . . . . . . . . . . . . . . . Capitol EST 12069 |
| 13/02/1982 . . . . . 84 . . . . . . 2 . . . . . . | STANDING HAMPTON . . . . . . . . . . . . . . . . . . . . . . . . . . . . . . . . . . . . . . . . . . . . . . . . . . . . . . . . Geffen GEF 85456 |
| 04/07/1987 . . . . . 86 . . . . . . 2 . . . . . . | SAMMY HAGAR . . . . . . . . . . . . . . . . . . . . . . . . . . . . . . . . . . . . . . . . . . . . . . . . . . . . . . . . . . . . . Geffen WX 114 |
| 19/05/1984 . . . . . 92 . . . . . . 1 . . . . . . | THROUGH THE FIRE **HAGAR, SCHON, AARONSON, SHRIEVE** . . . . . . . . . . . . . . . . . . . . . . . . . . . . . Geffen GEF 25893 |

**PAUL HAIG** UK lead singer with Josef K until they disbanded in the early 1980s; he then went solo. His debut hit album featured contributions from Bernie Worrell (of Parliament/Funkadelic), Tom Bailey (The Thompson Twins) and Anton Fier (Pere Ubu). He then recorded with Cabaret Voltaire and Bernard Sumner before linking with Alan Rankine. He recorded for Crepuscule and Circa Haig and launched his own Rhythm Of Life label.

22/10/1983 . . . . . 82 . . . . . . 2 . . . . . .    RHYTHM OF LIFE . . . . . . . . . . . . . . . . . . . . . . . . . . . . . . . . . . . . . . . . . . . . . . . . . . . . . . Crepuscule ILPS 9742

**HAIRCUT 100** UK pop group formed in Beckenham in 1980 by Nick Heyward (born 20/5/1961, Beckenham, guitar/vocals), Les Nemes (born 5/12/1960, Croydon, bass) and Graham Jones (born 8/7/1961, Bridlington, Humberside, guitar), with Phil Smith (born 1/5/1959, Redbridge, saxophone), Mark Fox (born 13/2/1958, percussion/congas) and Blair Cunningham (born 11/10/1957, Harlem, NYC, drums) joining the following year. Heyward went solo in 1982, with Fox taking over as lead singer when the group switched to Polydor. They disbanded in 1984 and Cunningham later resurfaced as drummer with The Pretenders.

06/03/1982 . . . . . 2 . . . 34 . . . . . . ✪    **PELICAN WEST** . . . . . . . . . . . . . . . . . . . . . . . . . . . . . . . . . . . . . . . . . . . . . . . . . . . . . . . . . . . . . . . Arista HCC 100

**BILL HALEY AND HIS COMETS** US singer/guitarist (born William John Clifton Haley Jr, 6/7/1925, Highland Park, Detroit, MI) who joined the Downhomers in 1944 replacing Kenny Roberts (who had been drafted: Haley was exempt as he was blind in one eye). He formed the Four Aces Of Western Swing in 1948, disbanded them in 1950, formed the Saddlemen and recorded for a number of labels before discarding the cowboy image and becoming Bill Haley & His Comets in 1953. The line-up at this time comprised Danny Cedrone (lead guitar), Joey D'Ambrose (saxophone), Billy Williamson (steel guitar), Johnny Grande (piano), Marshall Lytle (bass) and Dick Richards (drums). They introduced *Shake Rattle And Roll* to their stage act in 1953 (the song had first been recorded in 1952 by Sunny Dae & His Knights) and made their first recordings for Decca in 1954. Cedrone died after falling down a flight of stairs on 18/6/1954. Haley died of a heart attack on 9/2/1981. He was inducted into the Rock & Roll Hall of Fame in 1987 and has a star on the Hollywood Walk of Fame.

---

▲⁹ Number of weeks album topped the US chart    ◆¹² RIAA Diamond Awards    ◇³ IFPI Platinum Europe Awards

| | | | | |
|---|---|---|---|---|
| 04/08/1956 . . . . . 2 . . . . . . 18 . . . . . | | ROCK AROUND THE CLOCK . . . . . . . . . . . . . . . . . . . . . . . . . . . . . . . . . . . . . . . . . . . . . . . . . . . . . . . . . . . . . | Brunswick LAT 8177 |
| 20/10/1956 . . . ❶¹ . . . . . 8 . . . . . | | ROCK 'N ROLL STAGE SHOWS . . . . . . . . . . . . . . . . . . . . . . . . . . . . . . . . . . . . . . . . . . . . . . . . . . . . . | Brunswick LAT 8139 |
| 16/07/1957 . . . . . 5 . . . . . . 1 . . . . . | | ROCK THE JOINT . . . . . . . . . . . . . . . . . . . . . . . . . . . . . . . . . . . . . . . . . . . . . . . . . . . . . . . . . . . . . . . . . . | London HAF 2037 |
| 18/05/1968 . . . . . 34 . . . . . . 5 . . . . . | | ROCK AROUND THE CLOCK . . . . . . . . . . . . . . . . . . . . . . . . . . . . . . . . . . . . . . . . . . . . . . . . . . . . . . . . . | Ace Of Clubs AH 13 |

**HALF MAN HALF BISCUIT** UK group formed in Birkenhead, Merseyside by Nigel Crossley (bass/vocals), Simon Blackwell (guitar), Nigel Blackwell (guitar/vocals), David Lloyd (keyboards) and Paul Wright (drums) their debut album cost just £40 to record. They signed with Probe Records in 1985, disbanded towards the end of the decade and re-formed during the mid-1990s.

| | | |
|---|---|---|
| 08/02/1986 . . . . . 60 . . . . . . 9 . . . . . | BACK IN THE D.H.S.S . . . . . . . . . . . . . . . . . . . . . . . . . . . . . . . . . . . . . . . . . . . . . . . . . . . . . . . . . . . . . . . . | Probe Plus 4 |
| 21/02/1987 . . . . . 59 . . . . . . 5 . . . . . | BACK AGAIN IN THE D.H.S.S . . . . . . . . . . . . . . . . . . . . . . . . . . . . . . . . . . . . . . . . . . . . . . . . . . . . . . . | Probe Plus 8 |

**DARYL HALL** US singer (born Daryl Franklin Hohl, 11/10/1948, Philadelphia, PA) who began his career as a backing singer for the likes of The Delfonics and The Stylistics before he teamed with John Oates in 1969 and launched a parallel solo career in 1986. He also recorded one single as part of Kenny Gamble & The Romeos with Kenny Gamble and Leon Huff.

| | | |
|---|---|---|
| 23/08/1986 . . . . . 26 . . . . . . 5 . . . . . | THREE HEARTS IN THE HAPPY ENDING MACHINE . . . . . . . . . . . . . . . . . . . . . . . . . . . . . . . . . . . . . . | RCA PL 87196 |
| 23/10/1993 . . . . . 55 . . . . . . 4 . . . . . | SOUL ALONE . . . . . . . . . . . . . . . . . . . . . . . . . . . . . . . . . . . . . . . . . . . . . . . . . . . . . . . . . . . . . . . . . . . . . . . | Epic 4732912 |

**LYNDEN DAVID HALL** UK singer/multi-instrumentalist (born 1974, London) who played guitar, bass guitar, keyboards and drums on every track of his debut album. He won the 1998 MOBO Award for Best Newcomer.

| | | |
|---|---|---|
| 14/11/1998 . . . . . 43 . . . . . . 2 . . . . . ● | MEDICINE 4 MY PAIN . . . . . . . . . . . . . . . . . . . . . . . . . . . . . . . . . . . . . . . . . . . . . . . . . . . . . . . . . . . . . | Cooltempo 4959952 |
| 10/06/2000 . . . . . 36 . . . . . . 2 . . . . . | THE OTHER SIDE . . . . . . . . . . . . . . . . . . . . . . . . . . . . . . . . . . . . . . . . . . . . . . . . . . . . . . . . . . . . . . . . . | Cooltempo 5261492 |

**TERRY HALL** UK singer (born 19/3/1959, Coventry) who sang with The Specials, Fun Boy Three, Colour Field, Terry Blair & Anouchka and Vegas, as well as launching a solo career in 1994.

| | | |
|---|---|---|
| 18/10/1997 . . . . . 50 . . . . . . 1 . . . . . | LAUGH . . . . . . . . . . . . . . . . . . . . . . . . . . . . . . . . . . . . . . . . . . . . . . . . . . . . . . . . . . . . . | Southsea Bubble Co CDBUBBLE 3 |

**DARYL HALL AND JOHN OATES** US duo formed by Daryl Hall (born Daryl Franklin Hohl, 11/10/1948, Philadelphia, PA) and John Oates (born 7/4/1949, New York). They first met in 1967 and recorded a number of demos in 1969. Their official pairing came in 1972 when they signed with Atlantic. They made their US chart breakthrough in 1974. Daryl Hall later went solo.

| | | |
|---|---|---|
| 03/07/1976 . . . . . 56 . . . . . . 1 . . . . . | HALL AND OATES . . . . . . . . . . . . . . . . . . . . . . . . . . . . . . . . . . . . . . . . . . . . . . . . . . . . . . . . . . . . . . . | RCA Victor APL1 1144 |
| 18/09/1976 . . . . . 25 . . . . . . 7 . . . . . | BIGGER THAN BOTH OF US . . . . . . . . . . . . . . . . . . . . . . . . . . . . . . . . . . . . . . . . . . . . . . . . . . . . . . . | RCA Victor APL1 1467 |
| 15/10/1977 . . . . . 40 . . . . . . 2 . . . . . | BEAUTY ON A BACK STREET . . . . . . . . . . . . . . . . . . . . . . . . . . . . . . . . . . . . . . . . . . . . . . . . . . . . . . | RCA Victor PL 12300 |
| 06/02/1982 . . . . . 8 . . . . . . 21 . . . . . ○ | PRIVATE EYES . . . . . . . . . . . . . . . . . . . . . . . . . . . . . . . . . . . . . . . . . . . . . . . . . . . . . . . . . . . . . . . . . . . | RCA RCALP 6001 |
| 23/10/1982 . . . . . 24 . . . . . . 35 . . . . . ● | H2O . . . . . . . . . . . . . . . . . . . . . . . . . . . . . . . . . . . . . . . . . . . . . . . . . . . . . . . . . . . . . . . . . . . . . . . . . . . | RCA RCALP 6056 |
| 29/10/1983 . . . . . 16 . . . . . . 45 . . . . . | ROCK 'N' SOUL (PART ONE) . . . . . . . . . . . . . . . . . . . . . . . . . . . . . . . . . . . . . . . . . . . . . . . . . . . . . . | RCA PL 84858 |
| 27/10/1984 . . . . . 28 . . . . . . 13 . . . . . ○ | BIG BAM BOOM . . . . . . . . . . . . . . . . . . . . . . . . . . . . . . . . . . . . . . . . . . . . . . . . . . . . . . . . . . . . . . . . . | RCA PL 85309 |
| 28/09/1985 . . . . . 32 . . . . . . 5 . . . . . | HALL AND OATES LIVE AT THE APOLLO WITH DAVID RUFFIN AND EDDIE KENDRICK . . . . . . . . . . . . . . . . . . | RCA PL 87035 |
| 18/06/1988 . . . . . 52 . . . . . . 3 . . . . . | OOH YEAH! . . . . . . . . . . . . . . . . . . . . . . . . . . . . . . . . . . . . . . . . . . . . . . . . . . . . . . . . . . . . . . . . . . . . . | RCA 208895 |
| 27/10/1990 . . . . . 44 . . . . . . 2 . . . . . | CHANGE OF SEASON . . . . . . . . . . . . . . . . . . . . . . . . . . . . . . . . . . . . . . . . . . . . . . . . . . . . . . . . . . . . | Arista 210548 |
| 19/10/1991 . . . . . 9 . . . . . . 16 . . . . . ● | THE BEST OF DARYL HALL AND JOHN OATES – LOOKING BACK . . . . . . . . . . . . . . . . . . . . . . . . . . . | Arista PL 90388 |
| 06/10/2001 . . . . . 26 . . . . . . 2 . . . . . | THE ESSENTIAL COLLECTION . . . . . . . . . . . . . . . . . . . . . . . . . . . . . . . . . . . . . . . . . . . . . . . . . . . . | RCA 74321886972 |
| 12/04/2003 . . . . . 37 . . . . . . 2 . . . . . | DO IT FOR LOVE . . . . . . . . . . . . . . . . . . . . . . . . . . . . . . . . . . . . . . . . . . . . . . . . . . . . . . . . . . . . . . . | Sanctuary SANCD 166 |

**GERI HALLIWELL** UK singer (born 6/8/1972: year of birth variously listed as 1970, 1972 and 1975, Watford) who was a founding member of all-girl group The Spice Girls (as Ginger Spice) before leaving for a solo career. The Union Jack dress she wore at the 1997 BRIT Awards was auctioned in 1998 for £41,320. She also served the United Nations as a Goodwill Ambassador.

| | | |
|---|---|---|
| 19/06/1999 . . . . . 4 . . . . . . 43 . . . . . ✪² | SCHIZOPHONIC . . . . . . . . . . . . . . . . . . . . . . . . . . . . . . . . . . . . . . . . . . . . . . . . . . . . . . . . . . . . . . . . . | EMI 5210092 |
| 26/05/2001 . . . . . 5 . . . . . . 15 . . . . . ● | SCREAM IF YOU WANT TO GO FASTER . . . . . . . . . . . . . . . . . . . . . . . . . . . . . . . . . . . . . . . . . . . . . . | EMI 5333692 |

**HALO JAMES** UK group formed by Christian James (vocals), Ray St John (guitar) and Neil Palmer (keyboards).

| | | |
|---|---|---|
| 14/04/1990 . . . . . 18 . . . . . . 4 . . . . . ● | WITNESS . . . . . . . . . . . . . . . . . . . . . . . . . . . . . . . . . . . . . . . . . . . . . . . . . . . . . . . . . . . . . . . . . . . . . . . | Epic 4667611 |

**HAMBURG STUDENTS' CHOIR** German vocal group.

| | | |
|---|---|---|
| 17/12/1960 . . . . . 11 . . . . . . 6 . . . . . | HARK THE HERALD ANGELS SING . . . . . . . . . . . . . . . . . . . . . . . . . . . . . . . . . . . . . . . . . . . . . . . . . | Pye Golden Guinea GGL 0023 |

**GEORGE HAMILTON IV** US singer (born 19/7/1937, Winston-Salem, NC), he toured with Buddy Holly, Gene Vincent and the Everly Brothers, before moving to Nashville and joining the Grand Ole Opry. He later had his own TV series.

| | | |
|---|---|---|
| 10/04/1971 . . . . . 45 . . . . . . 1 . . . . . | CANADIAN PACIFIC . . . . . . . . . . . . . . . . . . . . . . . . . . . . . . . . . . . . . . . . . . . . . . . . . . . . . . . . . . . . . . | RCA Victor SF 8062 |
| 10/02/1979 . . . . . 25 . . . . . . 9 . . . . . ○ | REFLECTIONS . . . . . . . . . . . . . . . . . . . . . . . . . . . . . . . . . . . . . . . . . . . . . . . . . . . . . . . . . . . . . . . . . . | Lotus WH 5008 |
| 13/11/1982 . . . . . 94 . . . . . . 1 . . . . . | SONGS FOR A WINTER'S NIGHT . . . . . . . . . . . . . . . . . . . . . . . . . . . . . . . . . . . . . . . . . . . . . . . . . . . | Ronco RTL 2082 |

### MARVIN HAMLISCH
US pianist (born 2/6/1944, New York City) who became one of the top composers of film scores, including *The Way We Were*, which won him an Oscar and a Grammy. He also collaborated with Carole Bayer Sager. He won four Grammy Awards in 1974: Song of the Year with Marilyn and Alan Bergman for *The Way We Were*, Best Pop Instrumental Performance for *The Entertainer*, Best Album of Original Score Written for a Motion Picture for *The Way We Were* and Best New Artist.

23/03/1974 . . . . . 7 . . . . . . 35 . . . . . . O    **THE STING** Soundtrack from the 1973 film *The Sting* . . . . . . . . . . . . . . . . . . . . . . . . . . . . . . . . . . . . . . . . . . MCA MCF 2537

### HAMMER
US rapper (born Stanley Burrell, 30/3/1962, Oakland, CA) who began his musical career after baseball players Mike Davis and Dwayne Murphy invested $40,000 for him to make his first record in 1987, copies of which he sold from the boot of his car. He was named Best International Newcomer at the 1991 BRIT Awards. He has also won three Grammy Awards: Best Rhythm & Blues Song with Rick James and Alonzo Miller and Best Rap Solo Performance in 1990, both for *U Can't Touch This* and Best Music Video Long Form for *Please Hammer Don't Hurt 'Em The Movie*.

28/07/1990 . . . . . 8 . . . . . . 59 . . . . . . ✪²    **PLEASE HAMMER DON'T HURT 'EM** ▲²¹ ◆¹⁰ . . . . . . . . . . . . . . . . . . . . . . . . . . . . . . . . . . . . . . . . Capitol EST 2120
06/04/1991 . . . . . 46 . . . . . . 2 . . . . . .    LET'S GET IT STARTED This and the above hit credited to **MC HAMMER** . . . . . . . . . . . . . . . . . . . . . . . . . . . Capitol EST 2140
02/11/1991 . . . . . 41 . . . . . . 6 . . . . . . O    TOO LEGIT TO QUIT . . . . . . . . . . . . . . . . . . . . . . . . . . . . . . . . . . . . . . . . . . . . . . . . . . . . . . . . . . Capitol ESTP 26

### JAN HAMMER
Czechoslovakian keyboard player (born 17/4/1948, Prague) who won a scholarship to Berkley in Boston, MA and subsequently played with jazz-rock artists Billy Cobham, Stanley Clarke and the Mahavishnu Orchestra. He has won two Grammy Awards: Best Pop Instrumntal Performance and Best Instrumental Composition in 1985 for *Miami Vice Theme*.

14/11/1987 . . . . . 34 . . . . . 12 . . . . . . ●    ESCAPE FROM TV . . . . . . . . . . . . . . . . . . . . . . . . . . . . . . . . . . . . . . . . . . . . . . . . . . . . . . . . . . MCA MCF 3407

### HERBIE HANCOCK
US pianist/keyboard player (born 12/4/1940, Chicago, IL) who joined Donald Byrd's band in 1960 and recorded solo for Blue Note in 1963. He joined Miles Davis in 1963 and left in 1968 to form his own sextet. In 1978 he began recording with a vocoder and introduced 'scratching' to the UK. He won an Oscar in 1986 for the music to the film *Round Midnight* (in which he appeared) and also took part in the *It's Only Rock 'N' Roll* project for the Children's Promise charity. He has won nine Grammy Awards: Best Rhythm & Blues Instrumental Performance in 1983 for *Rockit*; Best Rhythm & Blues Instrumental Performance in 1984 for *Sound System*; Best Instrumental Composition in 1987 with Dexter Gordon, Wayne Shorter, Ron Carter and Billy Higgins for *Call Street Blues*; Best Jazz Instrumental Performance in 1994 with Ron Carter, Wallace Ronay, Wayne Shorter and Tony Williams for *A Tribute To Miles*; Best Instrumental Composition in 1996 with Jean Hancock for *Manhattan*; Best Jazz Instrumental Performance in 1998 for *Gershwin's World*; Best Instrumental Arrangement with Vocals in 1998 with Stevie Wonder and Robert Sadin for *St Louis Blues*; Best Jazz Instrumental Solo in 2002 for *My Ship*; and Best Jazz Instrumental Album, Individual or Group in 2002 with Michael Brecker and Roy Hargrove for *Directions In Music*. He has a star on the Hollywood Walk of Fame.

09/09/1978 . . . . . 27 . . . . . . 6 . . . . . .    SUNLIGHT . . . . . . . . . . . . . . . . . . . . . . . . . . . . . . . . . . . . . . . . . . . . . . . . . . . . . . . . . . . . . . CBS 82240
24/02/1979 . . . . . 28 . . . . . . 8 . . . . . .    FEETS DON'T FAIL ME NOW . . . . . . . . . . . . . . . . . . . . . . . . . . . . . . . . . . . . . . . . . . . . . . . . . . . CBS 83491
27/08/1983 . . . . . 27 . . . . . 10 . . . . . .    FUTURE SHOCK . . . . . . . . . . . . . . . . . . . . . . . . . . . . . . . . . . . . . . . . . . . . . . . . . . . . . . . . . . . CBS 25540

### TONY HANCOCK
UK comedian (born 12/5/1924, Birmingham), he served in the Royal Air Force ground crew during World War II and also appeared in the RAF Gang Show in 1942. After being de-mobbed in 1946 he toured the theatre and landed his own radio show, *Hancock's Half Hour* in 1951. The show, written by Ray Galton and Alan Simpson and also starring Hattie Jacques, Kenneth Williams and Sid James, ran for two years and was later revived for TV with the same writers and co-stars, with the 'Blood Donor' episode perhaps the best known. Hancock committed suicide in Sydney, Australia by taking a drug overdose on 25/6/1968.

09/04/1960 . . . . . 2 . . . . . . 22 . . . . . .    **THIS IS HANCOCK** . . . . . . . . . . . . . . . . . . . . . . . . . . . . . . . . . . . . . . . . . . . . . . . . . . . . . Pye NPL 10845
12/11/1960 . . . . . 17 . . . . . . 2 . . . . . .    PIECES OF HANCOCK . . . . . . . . . . . . . . . . . . . . . . . . . . . . . . . . . . . . . . . . . . . . . . . . . . . . Pye NPL 18054
03/03/1962 . . . . . 12 . . . . . 23 . . . . . .    HANCOCK . . . . . . . . . . . . . . . . . . . . . . . . . . . . . . . . . . . . . . . . . . . . . . . . . . . . . . . . . . . Pye NPL 18068
14/09/1963 . . . . . 16 . . . . . . 4 . . . . . .    THIS IS HANCOCK Re-issue of Pye NPL 10845 . . . . . . . . . . . . . . . . . . . . . . . . . . Pye Golden Guinea GGL 0206

### BO HANNSON
Swedish multi-instrumentalist, he recorded with Jimi Hendrix early in his career., effectively retiring in the 1980s.

18/11/1972 . . . . . 34 . . . . . . 2 . . . . .    LORD OF THE RINGS . . . . . . . . . . . . . . . . . . . . . . . . . . . . . . . . . . . . . . . . . . . . . . . . . . . Charisma CAS 1059

### HANOI ROCKS
Finnish rock group formed in 1980 by Michael Monroe (born Matti Fagerholm, vocals), Nasty Suicide (born Jan Stenfors, guitar), Andy McCoy (born Antti Hulkko, guitar), Sam Yaffa (born Sami Takamaki, bass) and Gyp Casino (born Jesper Sporre, drums). Casino was sacked after two albums and replaced by Razzle (born Nicholas Dingley) as the group relocated to London. Signed by CBS in 1983, they released their major label debut in 1984. Razzle was killed on 7/12/1984 when a car driven by Motley Crue's Vince Neil was involved in a head-on crash (Neil was charged with drunken driving and vehicular manslaughter and sentenced to five years probation, 30 days in jail, 200 hours of community service and ordered to pay $2.6 million in damages, although only $200,000 went to the family of the only dead victim, Razzle). Razzle was replaced by Terry Chimes (ex-The Clash), Yaffa left to be replaced by Rene Berg; group leader Monroe never fully accepted the loss of Razzle and announced his departure soon after. They disbanded in 1985.

11/06/1983 . . . . . 87 . . . . . . 1 . . . . . .    BACK TO THE MYSTERY CITY . . . . . . . . . . . . . . . . . . . . . . . . . . . . . . . . . . . . . . . . . . . . . . . . Lick LICLP 1
20/10/1984 . . . . . 28 . . . . . . 3 . . . . . .    TWO STEPS FROM THE MOVE . . . . . . . . . . . . . . . . . . . . . . . . . . . . . . . . . . . . . . . . . . . . . . . . CBS 26066

### HANSON
US family group from Tulsa, OK formed by brothers Isaac (born Clark Isaac Hanson, 17/11/1980), Taylor (born Jordan Taylor Hanson, 14/3/1983) and Zachary (born Zachary Taylor Hanson, 22/10/1985). In 1997 they won two MTV Europe Music Awards: Breakthrough Act and Best Song for *Mmm-Bop*.

21/06/1997 . . . . ❶¹ . . . 29 . . . . . . ●    **MIDDLE OF NOWHERE** ◇ . . . . . . . . . . . . . . . . . . . . . . . . . . . . . . . . . . . . . . . . . . . . . Mercury 5346152
13/06/1998 . . . . . 39 . . . . . . 1 . . . . . .    3 CAR GARAGE – INDIE RECORDINGS 95–96 . . . . . . . . . . . . . . . . . . . . . . . . . . . . . . . . . . Mercury 5583992
13/05/2000 . . . . . 33 . . . . . . 1 . . . . . .    THIS TIME AROUND . . . . . . . . . . . . . . . . . . . . . . . . . . . . . . . . . . . . . . . . . . . . . . . . . . . . Mercury 5427212

### JOHN HANSON
UK singer; he also recorded for Embassy and with Doreen Hume.

23/04/1960 . . . . . 17 . . . . . . 1 . . . . . .    THE STUDENT PRINCE . . . . . . . . . . . . . . . . . . . . . . . . . . . . . . . . . . . . . . . . . . . . . . . . . . . Pye NPL 18046
02/09/1961 . . . . . 9 . . . . . . 7 . . . . . .    **THE STUDENT PRINCE/THE VAGABOND KING** . . . . . . . . . . . . . . . . . . . . . . . . . . Pye Golden Guinea GGL 0086

▲⁹ Number of weeks album topped the US chart   ◆¹² RIAA Diamond Awards   ◇³ IFPI Platinum Europe Awards

10/12/1977 . . . . . 16 . . . . . . 4 . . . . . .    JOHN HANSON SINGS 20 SHOWTIME GREATS . . . . . . . . . . . . . . . . . . . . . . . . . . . . . . . . . . . . . . . . . K-Tel NE 1002

**HAPPY MONDAYS** UK group formed in Manchester in 1984 by Shaun Ryder (born 23/8/1962, Little Hulton, vocals), brother Paul Ryder (born 24/4/1964, Manchester, bass), Mark 'Cow' Day (born 29/12/1961, Manchester, guitar), Gary 'Gaz' Whelan (born 12/2/1966, Manchester, drums) and Paul Davis (born 7/3/1966, Manchester, keyboards), adding Mark 'Bez' Berry (born 18/4/1964, Manchester, percussion) in 1985. First record for Factory in 1985 but after Factory's demise in 1992 the group split. Ryder went on to form Black Grape and re-formed the Happy Mondays in 1998. Their name was inspired by the New Order hit *Blue Monday*.

27/01/1990 . . . . . 59 . . . . . 14 . . . . . .    BUMMED . . . . . . . . . . . . . . . . . . . . . . . . . . . . . . . . . . . . . . . . . . . . . . . . . . . . . . . . . . . . . . . Factory FACT 220
17/11/1990 . . . . . . 4 . . . . . 29 . . . . . ✪   **PILLS 'N' THRILLS AND BELLYACHES** . . . . . . . . . . . . . . . . . . . . . . . . . . . . . . . . . . . . . . . . . . . . . . Factory FACT 320
12/10/1991 . . . . . 21 . . . . . 3 . . . . . .     HAPPY MONDAYS – LIVE . . . . . . . . . . . . . . . . . . . . . . . . . . . . . . . . . . . . . . . . . . . . . . . . . . . . . . . Factory FACT 322
10/10/1992 . . . . . 14 . . . . . 3 . . . . . .     . . . YES PLEASE! . . . . . . . . . . . . . . . . . . . . . . . . . . . . . . . . . . . . . . . . . . . . . . . . . . . . . . . . . Factory FACD 420
18/11/1995 . . . . . 41 . . . . . 2 . . . . . .     LOADS – THE BEST OF THE HAPPY MONDAYS . . . . . . . . . . . . . . . . . . . . . . . . . . . . . . . . . Factory Once 5203432
05/06/1999 . . . . . 11 . . . . . 4 . . . . . .     GREATEST HITS . . . . . . . . . . . . . . . . . . . . . . . . . . . . . . . . . . . . . . . . . . . . . . . . . . . . . . . . . London 5561052
06/07/2002 . . . . . 47 . . . . . 2 . . . . . .     PILLS 'N' THRILLS AND BELLYACHES Re-issue of Factory FACT 320 . . . . . . . . . . . . . . . . . . . . London 3984282512

**ED HARCOURT** UK multi-instrumentalist and singer (born 14/8/1977), with Snug before going solo.

01/03/2003 . . . . . 39 . . . . . . 1 . . . . . .    FROM EVERY SPHERE . . . . . . . . . . . . . . . . . . . . . . . . . . . . . . . . . . . . . . . . . . . . . . . . . . . . Heavenly HVNLP 39CD

**PAUL HARDCASTLE** UK producer (born 10/12/1957, London) who played with Direct Drive and First Light, and formed the Total Control record company in 1984. Also recorded as Silent Underdog, the Def Boys, Beeps International, Jazzmasters and Kiss The Sky, the latter with singer Jaki Graham.

30/11/1985 . . . . . 53 . . . . . . 5 . . . . . . ○   PAUL HARDCASTLE . . . . . . . . . . . . . . . . . . . . . . . . . . . . . . . . . . . . . . . . . . . . . . . . . . . . . . Chrysalis CHR 1517

**HARDFLOOR** German group formed by Oliver Bandzio and Ramon Zenker; record debut in 1992 for the Harthouse label. Zenker was later responsible for Ariel and Fragma.

29/06/1996 . . . . . 68 . . . . . . 1 . . . . . .    HOME RUN . . . . . . . . . . . . . . . . . . . . . . . . . . . . . . . . . . . . . . . . . . . . . . . . . . . . . . . . . . Harthouse HHCD 19

**RONAN HARDIMAN** Irish orchestra leader/composer who is considered the most prolific and successful man in either field in contemporary Irish film and TV. Among his many credits are the score to the film *My Friend Joe* that won the Crystal Bear for Best Children's Film at the Berlin Film Festival.

02/11/1996 . . . . . 37 . . . . . . 8 . . . . . . ●   MICHAEL FLATLEY'S LORD OF THE DANCE . . . . . . . . . . . . . . . . . . . . . . . . . . . . . . . . . . . . . Polygram TV 5337572

**MIKE HARDING** UK singer/comedian (born Rochdale) who charted one hit single with his theme tune and scored considerable success on the album charts with his brand of comedy.

30/08/1975 . . . . . 24 . . . . . . 6 . . . . . .    MRS 'ARDIN'S KID . . . . . . . . . . . . . . . . . . . . . . . . . . . . . . . . . . . . . . . . . . . . . . . . . . . . . . Rubber RUB 011
10/07/1976 . . . . . 19 . . . . . 10 . . . . . . ○   ONE MAN SHOW . . . . . . . . . . . . . . . . . . . . . . . . . . . . . . . . . . . . . . . . . . . . . . . . . . . . . . Philips 6625 022
11/06/1977 . . . . . 31 . . . . . . 6 . . . . . .    OLD FOUR EYES IS BACK . . . . . . . . . . . . . . . . . . . . . . . . . . . . . . . . . . . . . . . . . . . . . . . . Philips 6308 290
24/06/1978 . . . . . 60 . . . . . . 2 . . . . . .    CAPTAIN PARALYTIC AND THE BROWN ALE COWBOY Title inspired by the Elton John album *Captain Fantastic And The Brown Dirt Cowboy* . . . . . . . . . . . . . . . . . . . . . . . . . . . . . . . . . . . . . . . . . . . . . . . . . . . . . . . . . . . . . Philips 6641 798

**STEVE HARLEY** UK singer (born Steven Nice, 27/2/1951, London); he was a local journalist before forming his first band Cockney Rebel in 1973; the band comprised Milton Reame (keyboards), Jean Paul Crocker (violin/guitars), Paul Jeffreys (born 13/2/1952, bass) and Stuart Elliott (drums). The original line-up survived one album before disbanding. They re-formed with Harley and Elliott being joined by Jim Cregan (born 9/3/1946, guitar), Duncan Mackay (born 2/7/1950, keyboards) and George Ford (bass) as the new Cockney Rebel. Harley disbanded the group for good in 1977, by which time he was already recording solo. Paul Jeffreys was killed in the Lockerbie air disaster on 21/12/1988 whilst flying out for his honeymoon with his wife Rachel.

22/06/1974 . . . . . . 8 . . . . . 20 . . . . . . ●   **THE PSYCHOMODO** COCKNEY REBEL . . . . . . . . . . . . . . . . . . . . . . . . . . . . . . . . . . . . . . . . . . EMI EMC 3033
22/03/1975 . . . . . . 4 . . . . . 19 . . . . . . ●   **THE BEST YEARS OF OUR LIVES** . . . . . . . . . . . . . . . . . . . . . . . . . . . . . . . . . . . . . . . . . . . . . . . EMI EMC 3068
14/02/1976 . . . . . 18 . . . . . . 6 . . . . . . ○   TIMELESS FLIGHT . . . . . . . . . . . . . . . . . . . . . . . . . . . . . . . . . . . . . . . . . . . . . . . . . . . . . . . EMI EMA 775
27/11/1976 . . . . . 28 . . . . . . 3 . . . . . . ○   LOVE'S A PRIMA DONNA . . . . . . . . . . . . . . . . . . . . . . . . . . . . . . . . . . . . . . . . . . . . . . . . . EMI EMC 3156
30/07/1977 . . . . . 40 . . . . . . 4 . . . . . .    FACE TO FACE – A LIVE RECORDING . . . . . . . . . . . . . . . . . . . . . . . . . . . . . . . . . . . . . . . . . . EMI EMSP 320

**HARMONIUM** UK studio group formed by Stewart and Bradley James.

21/03/1998 . . . . . 25 . . . . . . 4 . . . . . .    SPIRIT OF TRANQUILLITY . . . . . . . . . . . . . . . . . . . . . . . . . . . . . . . . . . . . . . . . . . . . Global Television RADCD 79

**ROY HARPER** UK singer/guitarist (born 12/6/1941, Manchester) he spent time in the RAF (he feigned mental illness in order to get a discharge!) before becoming a street busker in London and throughout Europe. He recorded his debut album in 1966 and has since gone on to work with many of the leading names of UK music, including Paul and Linda McCartney, Chris Spedding, Pink Floyd, Jimmy Page and Ian Anderson. During the 1990s he performed regularly with his son Nigel.

09/03/1974 . . . . . 27 . . . . . . 1 . . . . . .    VALENTINE . . . . . . . . . . . . . . . . . . . . . . . . . . . . . . . . . . . . . . . . . . . . . . . . . . . . . . . . Harvest SHSP 4027
21/06/1975 . . . . . 31 . . . . . . 2 . . . . . .    H.Q. . . . . . . . . . . . . . . . . . . . . . . . . . . . . . . . . . . . . . . . . . . . . . . . . . . . . . . . . . . . . Harvest SHSP 4046
12/03/1977 . . . . . 25 . . . . . . 2 . . . . . .    BULLINAMINGVASE . . . . . . . . . . . . . . . . . . . . . . . . . . . . . . . . . . . . . . . . . . . . . . . . . . Harvest SHSP 4060
16/03/1985 . . . . . 44 . . . . . . 4 . . . . . .    WHATEVER HAPPENED TO JUGULA? **ROY HARPER AND JIMMY PAGE** . . . . . . . . . . . . . . . . . . . . . . . . . Beggars Banquet BEGA 60

**ANITA HARRIS** UK singer/actress (born 8/6/1944, Midsomer Norton, Somerset) who began her career as a cabaret singer at the age of 17. She later joined the Cliff Adams Singers and made her first solo record in 1961 for Parlophone. She also appeared in two of the *Carry On* films and is married to writer-director Mike Margolis.

27/01/1968 . . . . . 29 . . . . . . 5 . . . . . .    JUST LOVING YOU . . . . . . . . . . . . . . . . . . . . . . . . . . . . . . . . . . . . . . . . . . . . . . . . . . . . . . CBS SBPG 63182

### EMMYLOU HARRIS
US singer (born 2/4/1947, Birmingham, AL) who released her debut album in 1970 before linking up with Gram Parsons. Following his death in 1973 she resumed her solo career. She also took part in the *Perfect Day* project for the BBC's Children In Need charity. Ten Grammy Awards include: Best Country Vocal Performance in 1979 for *Blue Kentucky Girl*; Best Country Vocal Performance by a Duo in 1980 with Roy Orbison for *That Lovin' You Feelin' Again*; Best Country Vocal Performance in 1984 for *In My Dreams*; Best Country Performance by a Group in 1992 with the Nash Ramblers for *Emmylou Harris And The Nash Ramblers At The Ryman*; Best Country Vocal Collaboration in 1998 with various others for *Same Old Train*; and Best Country Vocal Collaboration in 1999 with Dolly Parton and Linda Ronstadt for *After The Gold Rush*.

| 14/02/1976 | 17 | 11 | O | ELITE HOTEL 1976 Grammy Award for Best Country Vocal Performance | Reprise K 54060 |
| 29/01/1977 | 17 | 6 | O | LUXURY LINER | Warner Brothers K 56344 |
| 04/02/1978 | 40 | 5 | | QUARTER MOONS IN A TEN CENT TOWN | Warner Brothers K 56433 |
| 29/03/1980 | 36 | 3 | | HER BEST SONGS | K-Tel NE 1058 |
| 14/02/1981 | 53 | 4 | | EVANGELINE | Warner Brothers K 56880 |
| 14/03/1987 | 60 | 4 | | TRIO **DOLLY PARTON, LINDA RONSTADT AND EMMYLOU HARRIS** 1987 Grammy Award for Best Country Performance by a Group.... Warner Brothers 9254911 |
| 07/10/1995 | 46 | 1 | | WRECKING BALL 1995 Grammy Award for Best Contemporary Folk Album | Grapevine GRACD 102 |
| 29/08/1998 | 57 | 1 | | SPYBOY | Grapevine GRACD 241 |
| 30/09/2000 | 45 | 1 | | RED DIRT GIRL 2000 Grammy Award for Best Contemporary Folk Album | Grapevine GRACD 103 |
| 04/10/2003 | 52 | 1 | | STUMBLE INTO GRACE | Nonesuch 7559798052 |

### KEITH HARRIS, ORVILLE AND CUDDLES
UK singer/ventriloquist (born 21/9/1947, Lyndhurst) with dummy duck (Orville) and ape (Cuddles) whose act was extremely popular on TV. Pianist Bobby Crush supplied the music.

| 04/06/1983 | 92 | 1 | | AT THE END OF THE RAINBOW | BBC REH 465 |

### ROLF HARRIS
Australian singer/TV personality/painter (born 30/3/1930, Perth, Australia); he moved to the UK in the mid-1950s, eventually becoming a kids' TV presenter with his own series from 1970 and later presenting *Animal Hospital*.

| 01/11/1997 | 70 | 1 | | CAN YOU TELL WHAT IT IS YET? | EMI 8218802 |

### GEORGE HARRISON
UK singer/guitarist (born 24/2/1943, Liverpool, although George believed it to be the 25th until learning in his 40s that he had been born at 11.42pm on the 24th); he formed his first group, The Rebels, when he was thirteen and linked with Paul McCartney and John Lennon in the Quarrymen in 1958; the group subsequently became The Beatles. After The Beatles split he achieved his first #1 with his debut solo single, although legal wrangles with the estate of Ronnie Mack and the song *He's So Fine* blighted its success. He launched the Dark Horse record label and in 1988 became a member of the Traveling Wilburys (as Nelson). He was attacked by a crazed fan in December 1999 and received multiple stab wounds but survived the attempted murder. Having won eight Grammy Awards whilst a member of The Beatles, George won the 1972 Album of the Year award for *The Concert For Bangla Desh* and the 2003 Award for Best Pop Instrumental Performance for *Marwa Blues*. He also collected the 1989 Grammy Award for Best Rock Performance by a Group with Vocals as a member of the Traveling Wilburys for *Traveling Wilburys Volume One* (the album was known as *Handle With Care* in the UK). He 'appeared' in an episode of *The Simpsons* chatting to Homer Simpson backstage at the Grammy Awards ceremony. In 1999 it was reported that he was battling throat cancer, and despite frequent announcements that the treatment he was receiving was working, he died in Los Angeles on 29/11/2001. A family statement issued after his death said, "He left this world as he lived in it, conscious of God, fearless of death, and at peace, surrounded by family and friends. He often said, `Everything else can wait but the search for God cannot wait, and love one another.'" He was inducted into the Rock & Roll Hall of Fame in 2004.

| 26/12/1970 | 4 | 24 | | **ALL THINGS MUST PASS** ▲7 | Apple STCH 639 |
| 07/07/1973 | 2 | 12 | | **LIVING IN THE MATERIAL WORLD** ▲5 | Apple PAS 10006 |
| 18/10/1975 | 16 | 4 | | EXTRA TEXTURE (READ ALL ABOUT IT) | Apple PAS 10009 |
| 18/12/1976 | 35 | 4 | O | THIRTY THREE AND A THIRD | Dark Horse K 56319 |
| 17/03/1979 | 39 | 5 | | GEORGE HARRISON | Dark Horse K 56562 |
| 13/06/1981 | 13 | 4 | | SOMEWHERE IN ENGLAND | Dark Horse K 56870 |
| 14/11/1987 | 10 | 23 | ● | **CLOUD NINE** | Dark Horse WX 123 |
| 03/02/2001 | 68 | 2 | | ALL THINGS MUST PASS | Parlophone CDS 7466888 |
| 30/11/2002 | 29 | 4 | ● | BRAINWASHED | Parlophone 5803450 |

### JANE HARRISON
UK operatic singer.

| 04/02/1989 | 70 | 1 | | NEW DAY | Stylus SMR 869 |

### DEBORAH HARRY
US singer (born 1/7/1945, Miami, FL) who was a Playboy bunny waitress before launching Wind In The Willows, the Stilettos and finally Blondie in 1974. When Blondie dissolved in 1982 she concentrated on a film career and then went solo. Blondie re-formed in 1998 with Harry once again lead singer.

| 08/08/1981 | 6 | 7 | O | KOO KOO | Chrysalis CHR 1347 |
| 29/11/1986 | 31 | 11 | ● | ROCKBIRD | Chrysalis CHR 1540 |
| 17/12/1988 | 50 | 4 | | ONCE MORE INTO THE BLEACH **DEBBIE HARRY AND BLONDIE** | Chrysalis CJB 2 |
| 28/10/1989 | 12 | 7 | O | DEF DUMB AND BLONDE | Chrysalis CHR 1650 |
| 16/03/1991 | 3 | 22 | ● | THE COMPLETE PICTURE – THE VERY BEST OF DEBORAH HARRY AND BLONDIE **DEBORAH HARRY AND BLONDIE** | Chrysalis CHR 1817 |
| 31/07/1993 | 24 | 2 | | DEBRAVATION | Chrysalis CDCHR 6033 |

### KEEF HARTLEY BAND
UK rock group formed by Keef Hartley (born 8/3/1944, Preston, drums), Miller Anderson (guitar/vocals), Gary Thain (bass), Peter Dines (keyboards) and Spit James (guitar). Later members included Johnny Almond, Harry Beckett, Jon Hiseman, Jimmy Jewell, Henry Lowther and Mick Weaver, with ex-Rory Storm & The Hurricanes Hartley the focal point.

| 05/09/1970 | 41 | 3 | | THE TIME IS NEAR | Deram SML 1071 |

---

▲9 Number of weeks album topped the US chart ◆12 RIAA Diamond Awards ◇3 IFPI Platinum Europe Awards

## SENSATIONAL ALEX HARVEY BAND
UK rock group formed in 1972 by Alex Harvey (born 5/2/1935, Glasgow, vocals), Hugh McKenna (keyboards), Chris Glen (bass), Zal Cleminson (guitar) and Ted McKenna (drums). Harvey died from a heart attack on 4/2/1982.

| DATE | POS | WKS | BPI | ALBUM TITLE | LABEL & NUMBER |
|------|-----|-----|-----|-------------|----------------|
| 26/10/1974 | 16 | 4 | ○ | THE IMPOSSIBLE DREAM | Vertigo 6360 112 |
| 10/05/1975 | 9 | 10 | ○ | **TOMORROW BELONGS TO ME** | Vertigo 9102 003 |
| 23/08/1975 | 37 | 5 | ○ | NEXT | Vertigo 6360 103 |
| 27/09/1975 | 14 | 7 | ○ | SENSATIONAL ALEX HARVEY BAND LIVE | Vertigo 6360 122 |
| 10/04/1976 | 14 | 7 | ○ | PENTHOUSE TAPES | Vertigo 9102 007 |
| 31/07/1976 | 11 | 9 | ○ | SAHB STORIES | Mountain TOPS 112 |

## PJ HARVEY
UK band formed in Yeovil, Somerset in 1991 by Polly Jean Harvey (born 9/10/1969, Yeovil, Somerset), Ian Olliver (bass) and Rob Ellis (born 13/2/1962, Bristol, drums). Olliver left in 1991 and was replaced by Stephen Vaughan (born 22/6/1962, Wolverhampton), although by 1995 the group consisted of Harvey, John Parish (guitar), Jean-Marc Butty (drums), Nick Bagnoll (bass), Joe Gore (guitar) and Eric Drew Feldman (keyboards).

| DATE | POS | WKS | BPI | ALBUM TITLE | LABEL & NUMBER |
|------|-----|-----|-----|-------------|----------------|
| 11/04/1992 | 11 | 5 | ○ | DRY | Too Pure PURECD 10 |
| 08/05/1993 | 3 | 4 | ○ | **RID OF ME** | Island CID 8002 |
| 30/10/1993 | 19 | 2 | | 4-TRACK DEMOS | Island IMCD 170 |
| 11/03/1995 | 12 | 6 | ○ | TO BRING YOU MY LOVE | Island CID 8035 |
| 05/10/1996 | 46 | 1 | | DANCE HALL AT LOUSE POINT **JOHN PARISH AND POLLY JEAN HARVEY** | Island CIDX 8051 |
| 10/10/1998 | 17 | 2 | | IS THIS DESIRE? | Island CID 8076 |
| 04/11/2000 | 23 | 13 | ● | STORIES FROM THE CITY STORIES FROM THE SEA 2001 Mercury Music Prize | Island CIDX 8099 |
| 12/06/2004 | 12 | 3+ | ○ | UH HUH HER | Island CIDX 8143 |

## RICHARD HARVEY AND FRIENDS
UK multi-instrumentalist (born 25/9/1953, Enfield, Middlesex), he first came to prominence as a member of Gryphon, who were formed in 1971. Royal College of Music student Harvey had turned down a chance to join the London Philharmonia Orchestra in order to form Gryphon, who stayed together throughout the 1970s. Harvey then wrote commercial jingles and TV themes as well as recording a number of orchestral albums.

| DATE | POS | WKS | BPI | ALBUM TITLE | LABEL & NUMBER |
|------|-----|-----|-----|-------------|----------------|
| 06/05/1989 | 72 | 1 | | EVENING FALLS | Telstar STAR 2350 |

## GORDON HASKELL
UK singer/guitarist who was a member of King Crimson before going solo. After missing out with the single *Boat Trip* in 1969 he did not release another single until 2001.

| DATE | POS | WKS | BPI | ALBUM TITLE | LABEL & NUMBER |
|------|-----|-----|-----|-------------|----------------|
| 19/01/2002 | 2 | 10 | ● | **HARRY'S BAR** | East West 0927439762 |
| 26/10/2002 | 44 | 1 | | SHADOWS ON THE WALL | Flying Sparks TDBCD 068 |

## HATFIELD AND THE NORTH
UK group formed in 1972 by Richard Sinclair (born 6/6/1948, Canterbury, bass/vocals), Phil Miller (born 22/1/1949, Barnet, Hertfordshire, guitar), David Sinclair (born 24/11/1947, Herne Bay, Kent, keyboards) and Pip Pyle (born 4/4/1950, Sawbridgeworth, Hertfordshire, drums). David Sinclair left soon after their formation, replaced by Dave Stewart (born 30/12/1950, London), the group disbanding in 1975.

| DATE | POS | WKS | BPI | ALBUM TITLE | LABEL & NUMBER |
|------|-----|-----|-----|-------------|----------------|
| 29/03/1975 | 43 | 1 | | ROTTERS CLUB | Virgin V 2030 |

## JULIANA HATFIELD
US singer/guitarist (born 2/7/1967, Wiscasset, ME) who attended the Berklee College of Music and became a member of Blake Babies before going solo. She formed the Juliana Hatfield Three with Dean Fisher (bass) and Todd Phillips (drums) and has also played with the Lemonheads (she has had an on-off relationship with Evan Dando of that group).

| DATE | POS | WKS | BPI | ALBUM TITLE | LABEL & NUMBER |
|------|-----|-----|-----|-------------|----------------|
| 14/08/1993 | 44 | 2 | | BECOME WHAT YOU ARE | Mammoth 4509935292 |
| 08/04/1995 | 59 | 1 | | ONLY EVERYTHING | East West 4509998862 |

## HAVEN
UK rock group formed in Cornwall by Gary Briggs (guitar/vocals), Nat Wason (guitar), Iwan Gronow (bass) and Jack Mitchell (drums). The four relocated to Manchester in 1999.

| DATE | POS | WKS | BPI | ALBUM TITLE | LABEL & NUMBER |
|------|-----|-----|-----|-------------|----------------|
| 16/02/2002 | 26 | 3 | | BETWEEN THE SENSES | Radiate RDTCD 1 |

## CHESNEY HAWKES
UK singer (born 12/9/1971) who is the son of the Tremeloes' lead singer Chip Hawkes. He starred in the film *Buddy's Song* as Roger Daltrey's son Buddy.

| DATE | POS | WKS | BPI | ALBUM TITLE | LABEL & NUMBER |
|------|-----|-----|-----|-------------|----------------|
| 13/04/1991 | 18 | 8 | ○ | BUDDY'S SONG Original soundtrack to the film | Chrysalis CHR 1812 |

## SOPHIE B HAWKINS
US singer (born Sophie Ballantine Hawkins, 1967, Manhattan, NYC), percussionist with Bryan Ferry's backing group in the early 1980s before going solo. She launched Trumpet Swan Records in 2000 as a joint venture with Rykodisc.

| DATE | POS | WKS | BPI | ALBUM TITLE | LABEL & NUMBER |
|------|-----|-----|-----|-------------|----------------|
| 01/08/1992 | 46 | 2 | | TONGUES AND TAILS | Columbia 4688232 |
| 03/09/1994 | 46 | 4 | | WHALER | Columbia 4765122 |

## TED HAWKINS
US singer/guitarist (born 28/10/1937, Biloxi, MS), after learning to play the guitar at the age of twelve he spent much of his career singing and busking on the street. He first recorded for the Money label in 1966 and died on 1/1/1995.

| DATE | POS | WKS | BPI | ALBUM TITLE | LABEL & NUMBER |
|------|-----|-----|-----|-------------|----------------|
| 18/04/1987 | 82 | 1 | | HAPPY HOUR | Windows WOLP 2 |

## HAWKLORDS – see HAWKWIND

○ Silver disc ● Gold disc ✪ Platinum disc (additional platinum units are indicated by a figure following the symbol) ●⁹ Number of weeks album topped the UK chart

### HAWKWIND
UK rock group formed in London in 1969 by Dave Brock (born 20/8/1941, Isleworth, guitar/vocals), Mick Slattery (guitar) and Nick Turner (born 26/8/1940, Oxford, saxophone/flute/vocals) as Group X, changing the name shortly after to Hawkwind Zoo and subsequently Hawkwind. Numerous personnel changes have included Lemmy (born Ian Kilmister, 24/12/1945, Stoke-on-Trent, who later formed Motorhead), Dik Mik and Robert Calvert (born 9/3/1945, Pretoria, South Africa, died from a heart attack 14/8/1988). Legal problems in 1978 prevented them from using the name Hawkwind and they recorded one album as Hawklords.

| Date | Pos | Wks | BPI | Album Title | Label & Number |
|------|-----|-----|-----|-------------|----------------|
| 06/11/1971 | 18 | 19 | ● | IN SEARCH OF SPACE | United Artists UAS 29202 |
| 23/12/1972 | 14 | 5 | | DOREMI FASOL LATIDO | United Artists UAS 29364 |
| 02/06/1973 | 9 | 5 | O | **SPACE RITUAL ALIVE** | United Artists UAD 60037/8 |
| 21/09/1974 | 16 | 5 | O | HALL OF THE MOUNTAIN GRILL | United Artists UAG 29672 |
| 31/05/1975 | 13 | 7 | O | WARRIOR ON THE EDGE OF TIME | United Artists UAG 29766 |
| 24/04/1976 | 34 | 4 | O | ROAD HAWKS | United Artists UAK 29919 |
| 18/09/1976 | 33 | 5 | | ASTONISHING SOUNDS, AMAZING MUSIC | Charisma CDS 4004 |
| 09/07/1977 | 30 | 6 | | QUARK STRANGENESS AND CHARM | Charisma CDS 4008 |
| 21/10/1978 | 48 | 3 | | 25 YEARS ON **HAWKLORDS** | Charisma CD 4014 |
| 30/06/1979 | 59 | 5 | | PXR 5 | Charisma CDS 4016 |
| 09/08/1980 | 15 | 7 | | LIVE 1979 | Bronze BRON 527 |
| 08/11/1980 | 21 | 4 | | LEVITATION | Bronze BRON 530 |
| 24/10/1981 | 19 | 5 | | SONIC ATTACK | RCA RCALP 5004 |
| 22/05/1982 | 26 | 6 | | THE CHURCH OF HAWKWIND | RCA RCALP 9004 |
| 23/10/1982 | 29 | 5 | | CHOOSE YOUR MASQUES | RCA RCALP 6055 |
| 05/11/1983 | 57 | 2 | | ZONES | Flicknife SHARP 014 |
| 25/02/1984 | 75 | 1 | | HAWKWIND | Liberty SLS 1972921 |
| 16/11/1985 | 65 | 2 | | CHRONICLE OF THE BLACK SWORD | Flicknife SHARP 033 |
| 14/05/1988 | 79 | 2 | | THE XENON CODEX | GWR GWLP 26 |
| 06/10/1990 | 70 | 1 | | SPACE BANDITS | GWR GWLP 103 |
| 23/05/1992 | 53 | 1 | | ELECTRIC TEPEE | Essential ESSCD 181 |
| 06/11/1993 | 75 | 1 | | IT IS THE BUSINESS OF THE FUTURE TO BE DANGEROUS | Essential ESCDCD 196 |

### DARREN HAYES
Australian singer (born 1973, Brisbane) who was lead singer with Savage Garden before going solo.

| Date | Pos | Wks | BPI | Album Title | Label & Number |
|------|-----|-----|-----|-------------|----------------|
| 13/04/2002 | 2 | 28 | ✪ | **SPIN** | Columbia 5053192 |

### GEMMA HAYES
Irish singer (born 1978, County Tipperary) signed by French label Source after submitting a demo in 2001.

| Date | Pos | Wks | BPI | Album Title | Label & Number |
|------|-----|-----|-----|-------------|----------------|
| 08/06/2002 | 52 | 1 | | NIGHT ON MY SIDE | Source CDSOUR 049 |

### ISAAC HAYES
US singer (born 20/8/1942, Covington, TN) who formed numerous groups in Memphis before being taken on by Stax as an in-house musician and producer. He scored the films *Shaft* and *Truck Turner,* appeared in the film *Escape From New York* and launched the Hot Buttered Soul label. He was jailed in 1989 for owing over $346,000 in child support and alimony. In 1994 he was crowned a King in Ghana and given the title Nene Katey Ocansey in return for having brought investors into the country. He also recorded as Chef, a character from the cartoon series *South Park* in 1998. He has won three Grammy Awards including Best Instrumental Arrangement (with Johnny Allen) and Best Original Score Written for a Motion Picture in 1971 for *Theme From Shaft* (which also won the Oscar for Best Film Song). *Theme From Shaft* was re-issued on LaFace Records in 2000 after the film had been remade with Samuel L Jackson in the lead role and made #53. Isaac was inducted into the Rock and Roll Hall of Fame in 2002.

| Date | Pos | Wks | BPI | Album Title | Label & Number |
|------|-----|-----|-----|-------------|----------------|
| 18/12/1971 | 17 | 13 | | SHAFT ▲[1] | Polydor 2659 007 |
| 12/02/1972 | 38 | 1 | | BLACK MOSES 1972 Grammy Award for Best Pop Instrumental Performance with Vocal Coloring | Stax 2628 004 |

### HAYSI FANTAYZEE
UK trio formed by Kate Garner (born 9/7/1953, Wigan), Paul Caplin and Jeremiah Healy (born 18/1/1962), with both male members recording solo after their group success. Healy is also a much in-demand remixer.

| Date | Pos | Wks | BPI | Album Title | Label & Number |
|------|-----|-----|-----|-------------|----------------|
| 26/02/1983 | 53 | 5 | | BATTLE HYMNS FOR CHILDREN SINGING | Regard RGLP 6000 |

### JUSTIN HAYWARD
UK singer/guitarist (born David Justin Hayward, 14/10/1946, Swindon); he worked briefly with Marty Wilde before launching an unsuccessful solo career and then joined the Moody Blues as guitarist in 1966. The group took a break in 1974, with Hayward linking with fellow Moody Blue John Lodge (born 20/7/1945, Birmingham) for his initial hit.

| Date | Pos | Wks | BPI | Album Title | Label & Number |
|------|-----|-----|-----|-------------|----------------|
| 29/03/1975 | 4 | 18 | ● | **BLUE JAYS JUSTIN HAYWARD AND JOHN LODGE** | Threshold THS 12 |
| 05/03/1977 | 28 | 5 | | SONGWRITER | Deram SDL 15 |
| 19/07/1980 | 41 | 4 | | NIGHT FLIGHT | Decca TXS 138 |
| 19/10/1985 | 78 | 1 | | MOVING MOUNTAINS | Towerbell TOWLP 15 |
| 28/10/1989 | 47 | 7 | | CLASSIC BLUE **JUSTIN HAYWARD WITH MIKE BATT AND THE LONDON PHILHARMONIC ORCHESTRA** | Trax MODEM 1040 |

### LEE HAZLEWOOD
US singer/songwriter/producer (born Barton Lee Hazlewood, 9/7/1929, Mannford, OK) who produced Sanford Clark before devising the distinctive 'twangy' guitar sound for Duane Eddy. He formed the Dot and LHI labels, then joined Reprise as staff producer in 1965 and worked with Dean Martin, Dino Desi and Billy before enjoying major success with Nancy Sinatra.

| Date | Pos | Wks | BPI | Album Title | Label & Number |
|------|-----|-----|-----|-------------|----------------|
| 29/06/1968 | 17 | 12 | | NANCY AND LEE | Reprise RSLP 6273 |
| 25/09/1971 | 42 | 1 | | NANCY AND LEE Despite the similar titles this and the above album are different | Reprise K 44126 |

| | | | | |
|---|---|---|---|---|
| 29/01/1972.....31......4...... | DID YOU EVER All three albums credited to **NANCY SINATRA AND LEE HAZLEWOOD** ........................ RCA Victor SF 8240 |

**HEADSWIM** UK rock group formed by Dan Glendining (vocals), Tom Glendining (drums), Nick Watts (keyboards) and Clovis Taylor (bass).

30/05/1998.....24......2...... DESPITE YOURSELF ........................................................................... Epic 4877262

**JEFF HEALEY BAND** Canadian guitarist/singer (born 25/3/1966, Toronto), he developed eye cancer at the age of one and was left blind thereafter. He learned to play the guitar at the age of three and formed his first band in 1981. He formed the Jeff Healey Band in 1985 with Joe Rockman (born 1/1/1957, Toronto, bass/vocals) and Tom Stephen (born 2/2/1955, St John, New Brunswick, drums). He appeared in the 1989 film *Roadhouse*.

14/01/1989.....58......7......O SEE THE LIGHT ........................................................................... Arista 209441
09/06/1990.....18......6......O HELL TO PAY ........................................................................... Arista 210815
28/11/1992.....72......1...... FEEL THIS ........................................................................... Arista 74321120872
18/03/1995.....50......2...... COVER TO COVER ........................................................................... Arista 74321238882

**HEAR'SAY** UK group comprising Myleene Klass (born 6/4/1978, Norfolk), Kym Marsh (born 13/6/1976, Wiston), Suzanne Shaw (born 29/9/1981, Bury), Noel Sullivan (born 28/7/1980, Cardiff) and Danny Foster (born 3/5/1979, London). They were the winners of the TV series *Popstars*, which had auditioned over 2,000 hopefuls. Their debut single *Pure And Simple* was the biggest selling UK chart debut ever, shifting more than 500,000 copies in its first week. They became only the fourth act (after The Monkees in 1967, Tubeway Army in 1979 and Hanson in 1997) to simultaneously top the single and album charts with their debut releases. In January 2002 Kym Marsh left to go solo. After auditioning some 5,000 entrants, Johnny Shentall was announced as her replacement. It was later claimed to have been a 'fix' as he had performed with the group as a dancer at the Top of the Pops Awards. They disbanded in September 2002.

07/04/2001 .... ❶² .....27......❸³ **POPSTARS** ◇ ........................................................................... Polydor 5498212
15/12/2001.....24......5...... EVERYBODY ........................................................................... Polydor 5895412

**HEART** US rock group formed in 1970 by Ann Wilson (born 19/6/1951, San Diego, CA, lead vocals), Steve Fossen (born 15/11/1949, bass) and brothers Mike and Roger Fisher (born 14/2/1950, guitar) as the Army. Renamed White Heart in 1972, they shortened it to Heart in 1974. Ann's sister Nancy (born 16/3/1954, San Francisco, CA) joined in 1974 with Mike Fisher becoming manager. The group relocated to Vancouver, Canada in 1975 so Mike Fisher could avoid being drafted. Roger Fisher left in 1980, being replaced by Howard Leese (born 13/6/1951, Los Angeles, CA, keyboards/guitar). Since 1982 the line-up has consisted of the Wilson sisters, Leese, bass player Mark Andes (born 19/2/1948) and drummer Denny Carmassi.

22/01/1977.....36......8...... DREAMBOAT ANNIE ........................................................................... Arista ARTY 139
23/07/1977.....34......4...... LITTLE QUEEN ........................................................................... Portrait PRT 82075
19/06/1982.....77......2...... PRIVATE AUDITION ........................................................................... Epic EPC 85792
26/10/1985.....19......43......● HEART ▲¹ The album changed its catalogue number to Capitol LOVE 1 during its chart run ................ Capitol EJ 2403721
06/06/1987.....7......56......❸ **BAD ANIMALS** ........................................................................... Capitol ESTU 2032
14/04/1990 .....3......20......● **BRIGADE** ........................................................................... Capitol ESTU 2121
28/09/1991.....45......2...... ROCK THE HOUSE 'LIVE' ........................................................................... Capitol ESTU 2154
11/12/1993.....32......2...... DESIRE WALKS ON ........................................................................... Capitol CDEST 2216
19/04/1997.....33......6......O THESE DREAMS – GREATEST HITS ........................................................................... Capitol CDEMC 3765

**HEARTBREAKERS** US rock group formed in New York in 1975 by Richard Hell (born Richard Myers, 2/10/1949, Lexington, KY, bass), Johnny Thunders (born John Anthony Genzale, 15/7/1952, guitar/vocals) and Jerry Nolan (drums). Hell had previously been a member of Television while Thunders and Nolan were with New York Dolls. They disbanded in 1977, re-forming in 1978 with Hell, Thunders and Ty Styx. Thunders died on 23/4/1991 from a suspected heroin overdose, Nolan died on 14/1/1992 from a stroke.

05/11/1977.....55......1...... L.A.M.F ........................................................................... Track 2409 218

**TED HEATH AND HIS MUSIC** UK orchestra leader/trombonist (born 30/3/1900, Wandsworth, London) who formed his own band in 1944 and led it until ill-health forced him to leave in 1964, although the band carried on with the same name for a further five years. In 1957 he was awarded the Ivor Novello Oustanding Personal Services to Popular Music Award. Heath died on 18/11/1969.

21/04/1962.....17......5...... BIG BAND PERCUSSION ........................................................................... Decca PFM 24004

**HEATWAVE** US/UK soul group formed in Germany by American GI Johnnie Wilder (born 3/7/1949, Dayton, OH, vocals) and his brother Keith (born Dayton, OH, vocals). The best-known line-up featured Rod Temperton (who retired from live work to concentrate on writing), Eric Johns, Mario Mantese and Ernest 'Bilbo' Berger. Other group members included Jessie Whitten (stabbed to death in 1977), his replacement Roy Carter and Derek Bramble. Mantese was paralysed in a car crash in July 1978 and forced to retire, whilst Johnnie Wilder was left paralysed from a car accident on 24/2/1979 but returned to the group. Rod Temperton went on to win the 1990 Grammy Award for Best Arrangement on an Instrumental with Quincy Jones and Jerry Hey for *Birdland* by Quincy Jones.

11/06/1977.....46......2......O TOO HOT TO HANDLE ........................................................................... GTO GTLP 013
06/05/1978.....26......15......O CENTRAL HEATING ........................................................................... GTO GTLP 027
14/02/1981.....29......9...... CANDLES ........................................................................... GTO GTLP 047
23/02/1991.....56......1...... GANGSTERS OF THE GROOVE – THE 90'S MIX ........................................................................... Telstar STAR 2434

**HEAVEN 17** UK electronic dance group formed in Sheffield by ex-Human League members Ian Craig Marsh (born 11/11/1956, Sheffield) and Martyn Ware (born 19/5/1956, Sheffield) with Glenn Gregory (born 16/5/1958, Sheffield). Also responsible for BEF (British Electric Foundation). They were named after the group in Anthony Burgess' novel and Stanley Kubrick's film *A Clockwork Orange*.

| | | | | | |
|---|---|---|---|---|---|
| 26/09/1981 | 14 | 76 | ● | PENTHOUSE AND PAVEMENT | Virgin V 2208 |
| 07/05/1983 | 4 | 36 | ✪ | **THE LUXURY GAP** | Virgin V 2253 |
| 06/10/1984 | 12 | 11 | ○ | HOW MEN ARE | B.E.F. V 2326 |
| 12/07/1986 | 70 | 2 | | ENDLESS | Virgin TCVB/CDV 2383 |
| 29/11/1986 | 78 | 1 | | PLEASURE ONE | Virgin V 2400 |
| 20/03/1993 | 31 | 2 | | HIGHER AND HIGHER – THE BEST OF HEAVEN 17 | Virgin CVD 2717 |

**HEAVY D AND THE BOYZ** US rap group formed in Mount Vernon, NY by Heavy D (born Dwight Meyers, 24/5/1957), G Whiz (born Glen Parrish), Trouble T-Roy (born Troy Dixon) and DJ Eddie F (born Edward Ferrell). Dixon was killed after falling off a balcony on 15/7/1990. Heavy D made his film debut in the 1993 film *Who's The Man?*

| | | | | | |
|---|---|---|---|---|---|
| 10/08/1991 | 40 | 3 | | PEACEFUL JOURNEY | MCA 10289 |

**HEAVY PETTIN'** UK group formed in Glasgow by Steve Hayman (vocals), Gordon Bonnar (guitar), Punky Mendoza (guitar), Brian Waugh (bass) and Gary Moat (drums).

| | | | | | |
|---|---|---|---|---|---|
| 29/10/1983 | 55 | 2 | | LETTIN' LOOSE | Polydor HEPLP 1 |
| 13/07/1985 | 81 | 2 | | ROCK AIN'T DEAD | Polydor HEPLP 2 |

**HED PLANET EARTH** US group formed in Orange County, CA by M.C.U.D. (vocals), Wesstyle (guitar), Chizad (guitar), Mawk (bass), B.C. (drums) and DJ Product (turntables). The group financed their initial release before signing with Silvertone in 1995.

| | | | | | |
|---|---|---|---|---|---|
| 02/09/2000 | 73 | 1 | | BROKE | Music For Nations CDFMN 262 |

**HELL IS FOR HEROES** UK rock group formed in London in 2000 by Justin Schlossberg (vocals), Will McGonagle (guitar), Tom O'Donoghue (guitar), James 'Fin' Findlay (bass) and Joe Birch (drums).

| | | | | | |
|---|---|---|---|---|---|
| 15/02/2003 | 16 | 2 | | THE NEON HANDSHAKE | EMI 5409232 |

**HELLOWEEN** German rock group formed in Hamburg in 1984 by Kai Hansen (guitar/vocals), Michael Weikath (guitar), Markus Grosskopf (bass) and Ingo Schwichenburg (drums), later adding Michael Kiske (vocals). Hansen left in 1989 and was briefly replaced by Roland Grapow. Kiske and Schwichenburg were sacked in 1990 and replaced by Andri Deris and Ulli Kusch respectively.

| | | | | | |
|---|---|---|---|---|---|
| 17/09/1988 | 24 | 5 | | KEEPER OF THE SEVEN KEYS PART 2 | Noise International NUK 117 |
| 15/04/1989 | 26 | 2 | | LIVE IN THE UK | EMI EMC 3558 |
| 23/03/1991 | 41 | 2 | | PINK BUBBLES GO APE | EMI EMC 3588 |

**HELMET** US group formed by Page Hamilton (guitar/vocals), Peter Mengede (guitar), Henry Bogdan (bass) and John Stanier (drums). Mengede left in 1993, replaced by Rob Echeverria.

| | | | | | |
|---|---|---|---|---|---|
| 02/07/1994 | 38 | 1 | | BETTY | Interscope 6544924042 |

**JIMI HENDRIX** US singer/guitarist (born Johnny Allen Hendrix 27/11/1942, Seattle, WA and renamed James Marshall Hendrix four years later by his father) who taught himself to play the guitar at the age of twelve. After serving a year in the army (he was discharged after breaking his ankle in a parachute jump) he toured with Curtis Mayfield, The Marvelettes, Sam Cooke, Jackie Wilson and a host of others as well as appearing on numerous sessions. Briefly a member of the Isley Brothers, he formed his own group in 1966, Jimmy James & the Blue Flames, and was spotted by Chas Chandler of The Animals. Chandler brought him to London and formed a new group with Mitch Mitchell (born John Mitchell, 9/6/1947, Ealing, London) and Noel Redding (born David Redding, 25/12/1945, Folkestone), the Jimi Hendrix Experience. Hendrix formed the Band of Gypsies in 1969 with Buddy Miles (drums) and Billy Cox (bass). He died from a drug overdose in London on 18/9/1970. One of the most influential guitarists of all time, his back catalogue sells an estimated 3 million units a year. He was inducted into the Rock & Roll Hall of Fame in 1992 and won the 1999 Grammy Award for Best Video Long Form for *Jimi Hendrix's Band Of Gypsys – Live At Fillmore East*. He has a star on the Hollywood Walk of Fame. Redding died on 12/5/2003.

| | | | | | |
|---|---|---|---|---|---|
| 27/05/1967 | 2 | 33 | | **ARE YOU EXPERIENCED** | Track 612001 |
| 16/12/1967 | 5 | 16 | | **AXIS: BOLD AS LOVE** | Track 613003 |
| 27/04/1968 | 4 | 25 | | **SMASH HITS** This and the above two hits credited to **JIMI HENDRIX EXPERIENCE** | Track 613004 |
| 18/05/1968 | 39 | 2 | | GET THAT FEELING **JIMI HENDRIX AND CURTIS KNIGHT** | London HA 8349 |
| 16/11/1968 | 6 | 12 | | **ELECTRIC LADYLAND** ▲² **JIMI HENDRIX EXPERIENCE** | Track 613008/9 |
| 04/07/1970 | 6 | 30 | | **BAND OF GYPSIES** | Track 2406 001 |
| 03/04/1971 | 2 | 14 | | **CRY OF LOVE** | Track 2408 101 |
| 28/08/1971 | 9 | 6 | | **EXPERIENCE** | Ember NR 5057 |
| 20/11/1971 | 17 | 2 | | JIMI HENDRIX AT THE ISLE OF WIGHT | Track 2302 016 |
| 04/12/1971 | 16 | 8 | | RAINBOW BRIDGE Soundtrack from the 1970 film *Rainbow Bridge* | Reprise K 44159 |
| 05/02/1972 | 7 | 14 | | **HENDRIX IN THE WEST** | Polydor 2302 018 |

| DATE | POS | WKS | BPI | ALBUM TITLE | LABEL & NUMBER |
|---|---|---|---|---|---|
| 11/11/1972 | 23 | 3 | | WAR HEROES | Polydor 2302 020 |
| 21/07/1973 | 37 | 1 | | SOUNDTRACK RECORDINGS FROM THE FILM 'JIMI HENDRIX' | Warner Brothers K 64017 |
| 29/03/1975 | 35 | 4 | | JIMI HENDRIX | Polydor 2343 080 |
| 30/08/1975 | 35 | 3 | | CRASH LANDING | Polydor 2310 398 |
| 29/11/1975 | 46 | 1 | | MIDNIGHT LIGHTNING | Polydor 2310 415 |
| 14/08/1982 | 16 | 11 | | THE JIMI HENDRIX CONCERTS | CBS 88592 |
| 19/02/1983 | 77 | 4 | | THE SINGLES ALBUM | Polydor PODV 6 |
| 11/03/1989 | 30 | 6 | ● | RADIO ONE | Castle Collectors CCSLP 212 |
| 03/11/1990 | 5 | 16 | ● | **CORNERSTONES – JIMI HENDRIX 1967–1970** | Polydor 8472311 |
| 14/11/1992 | 25 | 26 | ● | JIMI HENDRIX – THE ULTIMATE EXPERIENCE | Polygram TV 5172352 |
| 30/04/1994 | 10 | 3 | | **BLUES** | Polydor 5210372 |
| 13/08/1994 | 32 | 3 | | WOODSTOCK | Polydor 5233842 |
| 10/05/1997 | 37 | 2 | | FIRST RAYS OF THE NEW RISING SUN | MCA MCD 11599 |
| 02/08/1997 | 47 | 1 | | ELECTRIC LADYLAND | MCA MCD 11600 |
| 13/09/1997 | 18 | 15 | ○ | EXPERIENCE HENDRIX – THE BEST OF JIMI HENDRIX | Telstar TV TTVCD 2930 |
| 13/06/1998 | 42 | 2 | | BBC SESSIONS **JIMI HENDRIX EXPERIENCE** | MCA MCD 11742 |
| 23/09/2000 | 10 | 7 | ○ | **EXPERIENCE HENDRIX – THE BEST** | Universal TV 1123832 |
| 20/07/2002 | 10 | 13 | ● | **VOODOO CHILD – THE COLLECTION** | Universal TV 1703222 |

**DON HENLEY** US singer (born 22/7/1947, Gilmer, TX); he was a member of the Four Speeds in the mid-1960s, moving to Los Angeles, CA in 1970 to record an album with Shiloh. He formed the Eagles with Glenn Frey in 1971 and when they ceased recording in 1980 he went solo. Having won four Grammy Awards with The Eagles, Don has collected a further two awards as a solo artist including Best Rock Vocal Performance in 1985 for *The Boys Of Summer*.

| DATE | POS | WKS | BPI | ALBUM TITLE | LABEL & NUMBER |
|---|---|---|---|---|---|
| 09/03/1985 | 14 | 11 | ○ | BUILDING THE PERFECT BEAST | Geffen GEF 25939 |
| 08/07/1989 | 17 | 16 | ● | THE END OF THE INNOCENCE 1989 Grammy for Best Rock Vocal Performance | Geffen WX 253 |
| 03/06/2000 | 25 | 3 | | INSIDE JOB | Warner Brothers 9362470832 |

**PAULINE HENRY** UK singer (born London) who was lead singer with The Chimes before going solo.

| DATE | POS | WKS | BPI | ALBUM TITLE | LABEL & NUMBER |
|---|---|---|---|---|---|
| 19/02/1994 | 45 | 1 | | PAULINE | Sony S2 4747442 |

**HEPBURN** UK female group formed by Jamie Benson (vocals), Lisa Lister (guitar), Sara Davies (bass) and Beverley Fullen (drums).

| DATE | POS | WKS | BPI | ALBUM TITLE | LABEL & NUMBER |
|---|---|---|---|---|---|
| 11/09/1999 | 28 | 2 | | HEPBURN | Columbia 4948352 |

**BAND AND CHORUS OF HER MAJESTY'S GUARDS DIVISION** UK military band.

| DATE | POS | WKS | BPI | ALBUM TITLE | LABEL & NUMBER |
|---|---|---|---|---|---|
| 22/11/1975 | 38 | 4 | | 30 SMASH HITS OF THE WAR YEARS | Warwick WW 5006 |

**HERBALISER** UK band formed by Ollie Teeba and Jake Wherry in the early 1990s; they released their first records on Ninja in 1994. Wherry also worked solo under the moniker The Meateaters.

| DATE | POS | WKS | BPI | ALBUM TITLE | LABEL & NUMBER |
|---|---|---|---|---|---|
| 30/03/2002 | 71 | 1 | | SOMETHING WICKED THIS WAY COMES | Ninja Tune ZENCD 64 |

**HERD** UK group formed in 1965 by Andy Bown (bass, keyboards/vocals), Peter Frampton (born 22/4/1950, Beckenham, guitar), Andrew Steele (drums) and Gary Taylor (guitar). Frampton quit in 1969 to form Humble Pie and subsequently went solo.

| DATE | POS | WKS | BPI | ALBUM TITLE | LABEL & NUMBER |
|---|---|---|---|---|---|
| 24/02/1968 | 38 | 1 | | PARADISE LOST | Fontana STL 5458 |

**HERMAN'S HERMITS** UK pop group formed in Manchester in 1963 by Peter Noone (born 5/11/1947, Davyhulme, Manchester, vocals), Karl Green (born 31/7/1947, Salford, bass), Keith Hopwood (born 26/10/1946, Manchester, rhythm guitar), Derek 'Lek' Leckenby (born 14/5/1946, Leeds, lead guitar) and Barry 'Bean' Whitwam (born 21/7/1946, Manchester, drums) as the Heartbeats. They changed their name in 1963 to Herman's Hermits, which was derived from the character Sherman in *The Rocky And Bullwinkle Show* cartoon series. Noone left for a solo career in 1972. The Hermits didn't actually play on their hits, producer Mickie Most used session musicians. Leckenby died from non-Hodgkin's lymphoma on 4/6/1996.

| DATE | POS | WKS | BPI | ALBUM TITLE | LABEL & NUMBER |
|---|---|---|---|---|---|
| 18/09/1965 | 16 | 2 | | HERMAN'S HERMITS | Columbia 33SX 1727 |
| 25/09/1971 | 14 | 5 | | THE MOST OF HERMAN'S HERMITS | MFP 5216 |
| 08/10/1977 | 37 | 4 | | GREATEST HITS | Columbia NE 1001 |

**KRISTIN HERSH** US guitarist/singer (born 1966, Atlanta, GA); she was a founding member of Throwing Muses with her step-sister Tanya Donelly. The group effectively disbanded in 1993, and Hersh went solo the following year, although she re-formed Throwing Muses after the success of *Hips And Makers*.

| DATE | POS | WKS | BPI | ALBUM TITLE | LABEL & NUMBER |
|---|---|---|---|---|---|
| 05/02/1994 | 7 | 4 | | **HIPS AND MAKERS** | 4AD CAD 4002CD |
| 14/02/1998 | 64 | 1 | | STRANGE ANGELS | 4AD CAD 8003CD |

**NICK HEYWARD** UK singer (born 20/5/1961, Beckenham) who formed Haircut 100 in 1980 and was responsible for penning all their hits. Following a series of personality clashes with other members, in 1982 he left the group and went solo.

| DATE | POS | WKS | BPI | ALBUM TITLE | LABEL & NUMBER |
|---|---|---|---|---|---|
| 29/10/1983 | 10 | 13 | ● | **NORTH OF A MIRACLE** | Arista NORTH 1 |

**HI JACK** UK rap group formed by Kamanchi Sly, DJ Supreme, DJ Undercover, Agent Cleuso, Agent Fritz and Ulysses.

| DATE | POS | WKS | BPI | ALBUM TITLE | LABEL & NUMBER |
|---|---|---|---|---|---|
| 19/10/1991 | 54 | 1 | | THE HORNS OF JERICO | Warner Brothers 7599263861 |

**HI TENSION** UK funk group formed as Hot Waxx by David Joseph (keyboards/vocals), Ken Joseph (bass/vocals), Paul Phillips (guitar/vocals), Leroy Williams (percussion), Jeff Guishard (percussion/lead vocals), Paul McLean (saxophone), David Reid (drums), Paapa

Mensah (drums), Guy Barker (trumpet), Peter Thomas (trombone), Bob Sydor (saxophone) and Ray Alan Eko (saxophone). They changed their name to Hi Tension in 1977.

06/01/1979 . . . . . 74 . . . . . . 4 . . . . . .
HI TENSION . . . . . . . . . . . . . . . . . . . . . . . . . . . . . . . . . . . . . . . . . . . . . . . . . . . . . . . . . . . . . . . . . . . . . . . . . Island ILPS 9564

### JOHN HIATT
US guitarist/singer (born 1952, Indianapolis, IN), he was a member of the White Ducks before going solo in 1970. He formed the 'supergroup' Little Village in 1992 with Nick Lowe, Ry Cooder and Jim Keltner.

07/07/1990 . . . . . 72 . . . . . . 1 . . . . . .
STOLEN MOMENTS . . . . . . . . . . . . . . . . . . . . . . . . . . . . . . . . . . . . . . . . . . . . . . . . . . . . . . . . . . . . . . . . . . . . . . . A&M 3953101

11/09/1993 . . . . . 67 . . . . . . 1 . . . . . .
PERFECTLY GOOD GUITAR . . . . . . . . . . . . . . . . . . . . . . . . . . . . . . . . . . . . . . . . . . . . . . . . . . . . . . . . . . . . . . . . . . A&M 5401302

11/11/1995 . . . . . 74 . . . . . . 1 . . . . . .
WALK ON . . . . . . . . . . . . . . . . . . . . . . . . . . . . . . . . . . . . . . . . . . . . . . . . . . . . . . . . . . . . . . . . . . . . . . . . Capitol CDP 8334162

### HINDA HICKS
UK singer (born Tunisia, raised West Sussex) discovered by producer Jazz Black who became her manager.

29/08/1998 . . . . . 20 . . . . . . 4 . . . . . .
HINDA . . . . . . . . . . . . . . . . . . . . . . . . . . . . . . . . . . . . . . . . . . . . . . . . . . . . . . . . . . . . . . . . . . . . . . . . . . . . . Island CID 8068

### EDWARD HIGGINBOTTOM – see CHOIR OF NEW COLLEGE OXFORD/ EDWARD HIGGINBOTTOM

### HIGH
UK group formed in Manchester in 1987 by Andy Couzens (guitar), John Matthews (vocals), Simon Davies (bass) and Chris Goodwin (drums).

17/11/1990 . . . . . 59 . . . . . . 2 . . . . . .
SOMEWHERE SOON . . . . . . . . . . . . . . . . . . . . . . . . . . . . . . . . . . . . . . . . . . . . . . . . . . . . . . . . . . . . . . . . . . . London 8282241

### HIGH LLAMAS
UK group formed by Sean O'Hagan (guitar/keyboards/vocals), Marcus Holdaway (cello/harpsichord), John Fell (bass), Anne Woods (violin), Jocelyn Pook (viola), Marcel Corientes (flute) and Rob Allum (drums).

06/04/1996 . . . . . 62 . . . . . . 1 . . . . . .
HAWAII . . . . . . . . . . . . . . . . . . . . . . . . . . . . . . . . . . . . . . . . . . . . . . . . . . . . . . . . . . . . . . . . . . . . . . . Alpaca Park CDWOOL 2

### BENNY HILL
UK singer/comedian (born Alfred Hawthorne Hill, 25/1/1924, Southampton); he made his name after World War II and had his own TV comedy show in the 1960s for the BBC but switched to ITV in 1969. He died from a heart attack on 18/4/1992.

11/12/1971 . . . . . 9 . . . . . 8 . . . . . .
**WORDS AND MUSIC** . . . . . . . . . . . . . . . . . . . . . . . . . . . . . . . . . . . . . . . . . . . . . . . . . . . . . . . . . . . . . . . . Columbia SCX 6479

### FAITH HILL
US country singer (born Audrey Faith Perry Hill, 21/9/1967, Jackson, MS) who made her debut album in 1993, the same year she made her debut at the Grand Ol' Opry. She later launched the Faith Hill Family Literacy Project. Her touring group features Steve Hornbeak (keyboards), Anthony Joyner (bass), Tom Rutledge (guitar and fiddle), Karen Staley (guitar/vocals), Lou Toomey (guitar), Gary Carter (guitar) and Trey Grey (drums). She has won four Grammy Awards including Best Country Collaboration with Vocals with Tim McGraw for *Let's Make Love* in 2000.

03/06/2000 . . . . . 19 . . . . . 16 . . . . . . ●
BREATHE ▲¹ 2000 Grammy Awards for Best Country Album and Best Female Country Vocal Performance  Warner Brothers 2473732

27/10/2001 . . . . . 6 . . . . . 11 . . . . . . ●
**THERE YOU'LL BE** . . . . . . . . . . . . . . . . . . . . . . . . . . . . . . . . . . . . . . . . . . . . . . . . . . . . . . . Warner Brothers 9362482402

09/11/2002 . . . . . 29 . . . . . . 2 . . . . . .
CRY ▲¹ 2002 Grammy Award for Best Female Country Performance . . . . . . . . . . . . . . . . . . . . . . . . . . . Warner Brothers 9362483682

### LAURYN HILL
US rapper (born 25/5/1975, East Orange, NJ) who was a member of both The Fugees and the Refugee All Stars before going solo. Having won two Grammy Awards as a member of The Fugees, Lauryn has collected a further five awards as a solo artist including Best Female Rhythm & Blues Vocal Performance and Best Rhythm & Blues Song for *Doo Wop (That Thing)* and Best New Artist in 1998. She also won the 1999 MOBO Award for Best International Act. She is married to Bob Marley's son Ziggy.

10/10/1998 . . . . . 2 . . . . 72 . . . . . . ✪²
THE MISEDUCATION OF LAURYN HILL ◇² ▲⁴ 1998 Grammy Awards for Album of the Year and Best Rhythm & Blues Album . . . . . . . .
. . . . . . . . . . . . . . . . . . . . . . . . . . . . . . . . . . . . . . . . . . . . . . . . . . . . . . . . . . . . . . . . . . . . . . . Ruffhouse 4898432

18/05/2002 . . . . . 40 . . . . . . 2 . . . . . .
MTV UNPLUGGED 2.0 . . . . . . . . . . . . . . . . . . . . . . . . . . . . . . . . . . . . . . . . . . . . . . . . . . . . . . . . . . . . . . . . Columbia 5080032

### VINCE HILL
UK singer (born 16/4/1937, Coventry) who trained as a baker and then became a soft drinks salesman whilst singing part time. Formed The Raindrops in 1958 before going solo in 1962.

20/05/1967 . . . . . 23 . . . . . . 9 . . . . . .
EDELWEISS . . . . . . . . . . . . . . . . . . . . . . . . . . . . . . . . . . . . . . . . . . . . . . . . . . . . . . . . . . . . . . . . . . . . Columbia SCX 6141

29/04/1978 . . . . . 51 . . . . . . 1 . . . . . .
THAT LOVING FEELING . . . . . . . . . . . . . . . . . . . . . . . . . . . . . . . . . . . . . . . . . . . . . . . . . . . . . . . . . . . . . . K-Tel NE 1017

### STEVE HILLAGE
UK guitarist( born 2/8/1951), he joined Uriel in 1967 and then formed Khan in 1971 with Nick Greenwood, Dick Henningham and Eric Peachey. After a spell with Decadence he went solo in 1975, subsequently becoming a noted producer. In 1991 he became a member of System 7.

03/05/1975 . . . . . 33 . . . . . . 3 . . . . . .
FISH RISING . . . . . . . . . . . . . . . . . . . . . . . . . . . . . . . . . . . . . . . . . . . . . . . . . . . . . . . . . . . . . . . . . . . . . . Virgin V 2031

16/10/1976 . . . . . 10 . . . . 12 . . . . . . ○
L . . . . . . . . . . . . . . . . . . . . . . . . . . . . . . . . . . . . . . . . . . . . . . . . . . . . . . . . . . . . . . . . . . . . . . . . . . . Virgin V 2066

22/10/1977 . . . . . 28 . . . . . . 5 . . . . . .
MOTIVATION RADIO . . . . . . . . . . . . . . . . . . . . . . . . . . . . . . . . . . . . . . . . . . . . . . . . . . . . . . . . . . . . . . . . . Virgin V 2777

29/04/1978 . . . . . 30 . . . . . . 8 . . . . . .
GREEN VIRGIN . . . . . . . . . . . . . . . . . . . . . . . . . . . . . . . . . . . . . . . . . . . . . . . . . . . . . . . . . . . . . . . . . . . . Virgin 2098

17/02/1979 . . . . . 54 . . . . . . 5 . . . . . .
LIVE HERALD . . . . . . . . . . . . . . . . . . . . . . . . . . . . . . . . . . . . . . . . . . . . . . . . . . . . . . . . . . . . . . . . . . Virgin VGD 3502

05/05/1979 . . . . . 52 . . . . . . 5 . . . . . .
RAINBOW DOME MUSIC . . . . . . . . . . . . . . . . . . . . . . . . . . . . . . . . . . . . . . . . . . . . . . . . . . . . . . . . . . . . . . Virgin VR 1

27/10/1979 . . . . . 71 . . . . . . 1 . . . . . .
OPEN . . . . . . . . . . . . . . . . . . . . . . . . . . . . . . . . . . . . . . . . . . . . . . . . . . . . . . . . . . . . . . . . . . . . . . . . . Virgin V 2135

05/03/1983 . . . . . 48 . . . . . . 2 . . . . . .
FOR TO NEXT . . . . . . . . . . . . . . . . . . . . . . . . . . . . . . . . . . . . . . . . . . . . . . . . . . . . . . . . . . . . . . . . . . . . Virgin V 2244

▲⁹ Number of weeks album topped the US chart  ◆¹² RIAA Diamond Awards  ◇³ IFPI Platinum Europe Awards

**H.I.M.** Finnish rock group formed in 1995 by Ville Valo (born Ville Hermanni Valo, 22/11/1976, vocals), Linde Lazer (born Mikko Lindstrom, 12/8/1976, guitar), Mige Amour (born Mikko Pannanen, 19/12/1974, bass), Zoltan Pluto (born Juska Salminen, 26/9/1976, keyboards) and Gas Lipstick (born Mikko Karppinen, 8/2/1971, drums). Pluto left in 2000 and was replaced by Emerson Burton (born Jani Purttinen, 17/10/1974). Their name stands for His Infernal Majesty.

| 26/04/2003.....55......3...... | LOVE METAL............................................................ RCA 82876505042 |
| 27/03/2004.....30......2...... | AND LOVE SAID NO – 1997–2004............................................ RCA 82876606102 |

**HIPSWAY** UK group formed by Graham Skinner (vocals), John McElhone (bass), Pim Jones (guitar) and Harry Travers (drums). McElhone was an ex-member of Altered Images and later joined Texas.

| 19/04/1986.....42.....23...... | HIPSWAY.............................................................. Mercury MERH 85 |

**DAVID HIRSCHFELDER** Australian singer, ex-Little River Band, who performed most of the soundtrack to *Strictly Ballroom*.

| 02/08/1997.....46......9......O | SHINE Soundtrack from the 1996 film *Shine*..................................... Philips 4547102 |

**HIVES** Swedish rock group formed in Fagersta in 1993 by Vigilante Carlstroem, Dr Matt Destruction, Howlin' Pelle Almqvist, Chris Dangerous and Nicholaus Arson, originally signing with Burning Heart in 1995.

| 12/01/2002 .....7......30......✪ | **YOUR NEW FAVOURITE BAND**................................................ Poptones MC5055CD |

**ROGER HODGSON** UK male singer/guitarist (born 21/3/1950, Portsmouth), a founder member of Supertramp in 1969 after answering an advertisement in *Melody Maker*. He left the group in 1980 to pursue a solo career.

| 20/10/1984.....70......4...... | IN THE EYE OF THE STORM................................................. A&M AMA 5004 |

**GERARD HOFFNUNG** UK humourist and after dinner speaker (born 1925, Berlin), he came to London as a refugee in 1939. He was an artist, teacher, cartoonist, musician, broadcaster and speaker as well as finding time to be a prison visitor. He died in 1959.

| 03/09/1960 .....4......20...... | **AT THE OXFORD UNION**.................................................. Decca LF 1330 |

**SUSANNA HOFFS** US singer (born 17/1/1957, Newport Beach, CA); she was lead singer with Bangles from 1981 until they disbanded in 1989. She appeared in the films *The Allnighter* and *Austin Powers: International Man Of Mystery* (her husband M Jay Roach was the film's director).

| 06/04/1991.....56......2...... | WHEN YOU'RE A BOY....................................................... Columbia 4672021 |

**CHRISTOPHER HOGWOOD** – see **ACADEMY OF ANCIENT MUSIC**

**HOLE** US rock group formed by Courtney Love (born Love Michelle Harrison, 9/7/1965, San Francisco, CA, guitar/vocals), Caroline Rue (drums), Jill Emery (bass) and Eric Erlandson (born 9/1/1963, Los Angeles, CA, guitar). Emery and Rue left in 1992 and were replaced by Kristen Pfaff (bass) and Patty Schemel (born 24/4/1967, Seattle, WA, drums); Pfaff died from a heroin overdose shortly after and was replaced by Melissa Auf Der Maur (born 17/3/1972, Montreal, Canada). Schemel left and was replaced by Samantha Maloney. Auf Der Maur left to join the Smashing Pumpkins. Courtney Love, widow of Nirvana's Kurt Cobain, became an actress, appearing in *Man On The Moon* and *The People Versus Larry Flint*. In September 2001 she sued Universal Music Group and the surviving members of Nirvana (Dave Grohl and Krist Novoselic) seeking to get all rights to their recordings. In June that year she had sued Grohl and Novoselic seeking the dissolution of Nirvana LLC, a company that had split the group's rights among the three parties. She had been successful in getting the release of *You Know You're Right* on a box set blocked, claiming the track was not crucial to the set's success. These suits were in conjunction with her own action against UMG in which she claimed her Geffen Records contract was terminated once the label was sold to UMG. She also claimed UMG had withheld $3.1 million in Nirvana royalties. Hole disbanded in May 2002.

| 12/10/1991.....59......1...... | PRETTY ON THE INSIDE.................................................... City Slang E 04071 |
| 23/04/1994.....13......5...... | LIVE THROUGH THIS..................................................... City Slang EFA 049352 |
| 19/09/1998.....11......4...... | CELEBRITY SKIN......................................................... Geffen GED 25164 |

**BILLIE HOLIDAY** US singer (born Eleanora Harris, 7/4/1915, Philadelphia, PA), she grew up in Baltimore, MD until moving with her mother to New York after her father had deserted them. After being raped at the age of eleven, Billie turned to prostitution, for which both she and her mother were arrested and charged, Billie being imprisoned on Ryker's Island. Upon release from prison she began to appear in various clubs in New York, where she quickly attained a veritable reputation. She was spotted by John Hammond in 1933, and recorded tracks with Benny Goodman, headlining at the Apollo Theater in Harlem in 1934. She sang with Count Basie's band between 1935 and 1937 and then joined Artie Shaw, although touring as a black female singer with a white band was not without its problems, not least whenever the band played in the South. By 1939, however, she had struck out on her own, helped by John Hammond and club owner Barney Josephson, proving a star attraction at the latter's Café Society and made a series of recordings for the Commodore label that ensured her reputation as perhaps the greatest jazz singer of all time. As her star rose, however, so did her dependency on drugs. By the 1940s she was hooked on opium and heroin, and it was claimed that out of weekly earnings of $1,000 (then a huge sum for a black female performer to be earning) half was being spent on her habit. In 1947 she was sent to the Federal Reformatory in West Virginia, her own manager having been responsible for her arraignment. Thereafter her life embraced trouble on a regular basis and her drug convictions made it impossible for her to work in any club where alcohol was on sale. She was arrested again in 1949 and 1956, although she was not charged with the latter offence. In May 1958 she was admitted to hospital suffering from heart and liver disease and since the police believed both to have been brought on by drug and alcohol abuse, they placed her under arrest. She died on 17/7/1959. She has a star on the Hollywood Walk of Fame. She was married twice during her lifetime, to Jimmy Monroe in 1941 (they divorced in 1957) and then to Louis McKay, as well as having numerous affairs throughout her career. She published her autobiography *Lady Sings The Blues* in 1956 that subsequently formed the basis of the film of the same name, with Diana Ross in the role of Billie Holiday, for which she earned an Oscar nomination.

| 16/11/1985.....60.....10......● | THE LEGEND OF BILLIE HOLIDAY............................................. MCA BHTV 1 |
| 06/09/1997.....63......1...... | LADY DAY – THE VERY BEST OF BILLIE HOLIDAY................................. Columbia MOODCD 52 |

O Silver disc ● Gold disc ✪ Platinum disc (additional platinum units are indicated by a figure following the symbol) ❶⁹ Number of weeks album topped the UK chart

## JOOLS HOLLAND

UK singer/pianist (born Julian Holland, 24/1/1958, London); he was a founder member of Squeeze in 1974 and left in 1980 to form the Millionaires with Mike Paice (saxophone), Pino Palladino (bass) and Martin Deegan (drums). He went solo in 1983 and combined this with TV work, becoming one of the presenters of *The Tube*. He rejoined Squeeze in 1985 and remained until 1990. He hosted his own TV series *Later* and formed the Rhythm & Blues Orchestra in 1994 as well as recording with Jamiroquai later. He was awarded an OBE in the Queen's 2003 Birthday Honours List.

| | | | | | |
|---|---|---|---|---|---|
| 05/05/1990 | 71 | 1 | | WORLD OF HIS OWN | I.R.S. EIRSA 1018 |
| 26/10/1996 | 38 | 2 | | SEX & JAZZ & ROCK & ROLL | Coliseum HF 51CD |
| 25/10/1997 | 50 | 1 | | LIFT THE LID | Coalition 3984205252 |
| 01/12/2001 | 8 | 37 | ◆² | **SMALL WORLD BIG BAND** This and the above two hits credited to **JOOLS HOLLAND AND HIS R&B ORCHESTRA** | WSM 0927426562 |
| 30/11/2002 | 17 | 14 | ◆ | MORE FRIENDS – SMALL WORLD BIG BAND 2 | WSM 0927494192 |
| 29/11/2003 | 39 | 9 | ● | JACK O THE GREEN – SMALL WORLD BIG BAND **JOOLS HOLLAND AND HIS R&B ORCHESTRA** | Radar RADAR001CD |

## HOLLIES

UK group formed in Manchester in 1961 by Allan Clarke (born Harold Allan Clarke, 5/4/1942, Salford, vocals), Graham Nash (born 2/2/1942, Blackpool, guitar), Eric Haydock (born 3/2/1943, Stockport, bass) and Don Rathbone (drums) as the Fourtones. They added another guitarist and changed their name to the Deltas, then settled on the Hollies in 1962. As the second guitarist did not want to turn professional he was replaced by Tony Hicks (born 16/12/1943, Nelson) in 1963; Rathbone moved to management and was replaced by Bobby Elliott (born 8/12/1942, Burnley). They made their first record in 1963 for Parlophone. Haydock left in 1966 and was replaced by Bernie Calvert (born 16/9/1942, Brierfield). Nash left in 1968 to link up with David Crosby and Stephen Stills, and Terry Sylvester (born 8/1/1945, Liverpool) replaced him. Nash, Hicks, Clarke, Elliott and Haydock reunited in 1982, with all but Haydock recording together in 1983.

| | | | | | |
|---|---|---|---|---|---|
| 15/02/1964 | 2 | 25 | | **STAY WITH THE HOLLIES** | Parlophone PMC 1220 |
| 02/10/1965 | 8 | 14 | | **HOLLIES** | Parlophone PMC 1261 |
| 16/07/1966 | 16 | 8 | | WOULD YOU BELIEVE | Parlophone PMC 7008 |
| 17/12/1966 | 23 | 7 | | FOR CERTAIN BECAUSE | Parlophone PCS 17011 |
| 17/06/1967 | 13 | 10 | | EVOLUTION | Parlophone PCS 7022 |
| 17/08/1968 | ❶⁷ | 27 | | **THE HOLLIES' GREATEST** | Parlophone PCS 7057 |
| 17/05/1969 | 3 | 7 | | **HOLLIES SING DYLAN** | Parlophone PCS 7078 |
| 28/11/1970 | 30 | 5 | | CONFESSIONS OF THE MIND | Parlophone PCS 7117 |
| 16/03/1974 | 38 | 3 | | HOLLIES | Polydor 2383 262 |
| 19/03/1977 | 4 | 12 | ● | **HOLLIES LIVE HITS** | Polydor 3283 428 |
| 22/07/1978 | 2 | 20 | ● | **20 GOLDEN GREATS** | EMI EMTV 11 |
| 01/10/1988 | 51 | 5 | | ALL THE HITS AND MORE | EMI EM 1301 |
| 03/04/1993 | 15 | 7 | ● | THE AIR THAT I BREATHE – THE BEST OF THE HOLLIES | EMI CDEMTV 74 |
| 05/04/2003 | 21 | 4 | ○ | GREATEST HITS | EMI 5820122 |

## MARK HOLLIS

UK singer/guitarist/keyboard player (born 1955, London), he was lead singer and front man with Talk Talk, a group he formed in 1981 with his elder brother Ed, Paul Webb, Lee Harris and Simon Bremner. The group effectively disbanded in 1991 but it was to be another seven years before Hollis released his first solo record.

| | | | | | |
|---|---|---|---|---|---|
| 14/02/1998 | 53 | 1 | | MARK HOLLIS | Polydor 5376882 |

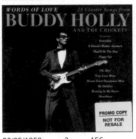

## BUDDY HOLLY

US singer (born Charles Hardin Holley, 7/9/1936, Lubbock, TX) who began his career recording country music until the success of Elvis Presley dictated a musical change. He formed a duo with Bob Montgomery and recorded a number of demos as Buddy and Bob (with Larry Welborn on bass), with Decca expressing interest in signing Holly as a solo artist. Holly formed a new band with Sonny Curtis and Don Guess, touring as Buddy Holly & The Two-Tunes (recordings of this time later appeared as Buddy Holly & The Three-Tunes: drummer Jerry Allison having joined the line-up). In February 1957 Buddy gathered The Crickets (Allison, Niki Sullivan and Joe B Mauldin) to re-record *That'll Be The Day*, the success of which landed Holly a solo deal with Coral, a subsidiary of the Brunswick label the Crickets recorded for. He split with the Crickets in 1958 and thereafter recorded solo. On 3/2/1959 he, Ritchie Valens and the Big Bopper were killed when their plane crashed near Mason City, IA. It was later reported that the crash was due to pilot error: after a successful take-off, pilot Roger Peterson experienced vertigo and flew straight into the ground. Buddy Holly was inducted into the Rock & Roll Hall of Fame in 1986.

| | | | | | |
|---|---|---|---|---|---|
| 02/05/1959 | 2 | 156 | | **THE BUDDY HOLLY STORY** | Coral LVA 9105 |
| 15/10/1960 | 7 | 14 | | **THE BUDDY HOLLY STORY VOLUME 2** | Coral LVA 9127 |
| 21/10/1961 | 5 | 14 | | **THAT'LL BE THE DAY** | Ace Of Hearts AH 3 |
| 06/04/1963 | 2 | 31 | | **REMINISCING** | Coral LVA 9212 |
| 13/06/1964 | 3 | 16 | | **BUDDY HOLLY SHOWCASE** | Coral LVA 9222 |
| 26/06/1965 | 13 | 6 | | HOLLY IN THE HILLS This and the above hit credited to **BUDDY HOLLY AND THE CRICKETS** | Coral LVA 9227 |
| 15/07/1967 | 9 | 40 | | **BUDDY HOLLY'S GREATEST HITS** | Ace Of Hearts AH 148 |
| 12/04/1969 | 13 | 1 | | GIANT **BUDDY HOLLY AND THE CRICKETS** | MCA MUPS 371 |
| 21/08/1971 | 32 | 6 | | BUDDY HOLLY'S GREATEST HITS | Coral CP 8 |
| 12/07/1975 | 42 | 3 | | BUDDY HOLLY'S GREATEST HITS | Coral CDLM 8007 |
| 11/03/1978 | ❶³ | 20 | ◆ | **20 GOLDEN GREATS BUDDY HOLLY AND THE CRICKETS** | EMI EMTV 8 |
| 08/09/1984 | 100 | 1 | | BUDDY HOLLY'S GREATEST HITS | MCA MCL 1618 |
| 18/02/1989 | 8 | 11 | ● | **TRUE LOVE WAYS** | Telstar STAR 2339 |
| 20/02/1993 | ❶¹ | 9 | ● | **WORDS OF LOVE BUDDY HOLLY AND THE CRICKETS** | Polygram TV 5144872 |
| 07/12/1996 | 24 | 8 | ● | THE VERY BEST OF BUDDY HOLLY | Dino DINCD 133 |

28/08/1999 . . . . . 25 . . . . . 3 . . . . . .     THE VERY BEST OF BUDDY HOLLY AND THE CRICKETS **BUDDY HOLLY AND THE CRICKETS** . . . . . . . . . . . Universal Music TV 1120462

**DAVID HOLMES** UK singer (born 14/2/1969, Belfast); he also recorded as The Disco Evangelists and Death Before Disco. He runs the clubs Sugar Sweet and Exploding Plastic Inevitable.

22/07/1995 . . . . . 51 . . . . . . 1 . . . . . .     THIS FILM'S CRAP, LET'S SLASH THE SEATS . . . . . . . . . . . . . . . . . . . . . . . . . . . . . . . . . . . . . . Go Discs 8286312
13/09/1997 . . . . . 34 . . . . . 2 . . . . . O     LET'S GET KILLED . . . . . . . . . . . . . . . . . . . . . . . . . . . . . . . . . . . . . . . . . . . . . . . . . . . . Go Discs 5391002
24/06/2000 . . . . . 22 . . . . . 2 . . . . . .     BOW DOWN TO THE EXIT SIGN . . . . . . . . . . . . . . . . . . . . . . . . . . . . . . . . . . . . . . . . . . . . Go Beat 5438662

**JOHN HOLT** Jamaican reggae singer (born 1947, Kingston); he originally recorded with the Paragons, leaving them in the late 1960s to go solo (although he had first recorded solo in 1963 with *I Cried A Tear* for the Beverley label).

01/02/1975 . . . . . 42 . . . . . 2 . . . . . .     A THOUSAND VOLTS OF HOLT . . . . . . . . . . . . . . . . . . . . . . . . . . . . . . . . . . . . . . . . . . . . Trojan TRLS 75

**HOME** UK vocal/instrumental group formed by Laurie Wisefield (guitar/vocals), Mick Stubbs (guitar, keyboards/vocals), Cliff Williams (bass/vocals), Clive John (keyboards), Johnny Weider (violin) and Mick Cook (drums/vocals). Wisefield was later in Wishbone Ash.

11/11/1972 . . . . . 41 . . . . . 1 . . . . . .     DREAMER . . . . . . . . . . . . . . . . . . . . . . . . . . . . . . . . . . . . . . . . . . . . . . . . . . . . . . . . . . CBS 67522

**HONEYCRACK** UK rock group formed in August 1994 by CJ (born Chris Jagdhar, guitar/vocals), Mark McRae (guitar), Pete Clark (bass), Willie Dowling (keyboards) and Hugh Degenhardt (drums). They disbanded in 1997.

01/06/1996 . . . . . 34 . . . . . 1 . . . . . .     PROZIAC . . . . . . . . . . . . . . . . . . . . . . . . . . . . . . . . . . . . . . . . . . . . . . . . . . . . . . . . . . Epic 4842302

**HONEYDRIPPERS** UK/US group formed in 1984 by Robert Plant (born 20/8/1948, West Bromwich, lead vocals), Jimmy Page (born 9/1/1944, Heston, guitar), Nile Rodgers (born 19/9/1952, New York, bass) and Jeff Beck (born 24/6/1944, Wallington, guitar), with Tony Thompson on drums. Page and Plant were ex-members of Led Zeppelin, Rodgers and Thompson were ex-Chic and Beck was with The Yardbirds, having also enjoyed a solo career. The project was abandoned after one album.

01/12/1984 . . . . . 56 . . . . . 10 . . . . . .     THE HONEYDRIPPERS VOLUME ONE . . . . . . . . . . . . . . . . . . . . . . . . . . . . . . . . . . . . . . . Es Paranza 790220

**HONEYZ** UK vocal group formed by Heavenli Abdi, Celena Cherry (born 26/4/1977, London) and Naima Belkhaiti (born 4/12/1973, Avignon, France). Heavenli left in early 1999 and was replaced by ex-Solid HarmoniE singer Mariama Goodman (born 25/12/1977, London). By August 2000 Heavenli returned. Celena later linked with ex-Kleshay member Alani Gibbon to form Anotherside.

05/12/1998 . . . . . 33 . . . . . 22 . . . . . ●     WONDER NO. 8 . . . . . . . . . . . . . . . . . . . . . . . . . . . . . . . . . . . . . . . . . . . . . . . . . . . . . Mercury 5588142

**HOOBASTANK** US rock group formed in Agoura Hills, CA in 1994 by Douglas Robb (vocals), Dan Estrin (guitar), Markku Lappalainen (bass) and Chris Hesse (drums).

05/06/2004 . . . . . 41 . . . . . 4+ . . . . . .     THE REASON . . . . . . . . . . . . . . . . . . . . . . . . . . . . . . . . . . . . . . . . . . . . . . . . . . . . . . . Mercury 9862261

**JOHN LEE HOOKER** US singer/guitarist (born 22/8/1917, Clarksdale, MS) who was taught to play the guitar by his grandfather. He made his debut recording in 1948 and was still recording in the 1990s with his *Mr Lucky* album making him the oldest artist to have reached the top three of the charts (he was 74 at the time). He was inducted into the Rock & Roll Hall of Fame in 1991. He has won four Grammys including Best Traditional Blues Recording in 1989 with Bonnie Raitt for *I'm In The Mood* and Best Pop Collaboration with Vocals in 1997 with Van Morrison for *Don't Look Back*. He died on 21/6/2001 and has a star on the Hollywood Walk of Fame.

04/02/1967 . . . . . 34 . . . . . 2 . . . . . .     HOUSE OF THE BLUES . . . . . . . . . . . . . . . . . . . . . . . . . . . . . . . . . . . . . . . . . . . . . . . . Marble Arch MAL 663
11/11/1989 . . . . . 63 . . . . . 8 . . . . . ●     THE HEALER . . . . . . . . . . . . . . . . . . . . . . . . . . . . . . . . . . . . . . . . . . . . . . . . . . . . . . Silvertone ORELP 508
21/09/1991 . . . . . 3 . . . . . 10 . . . . . ●     **MR. LUCKY** . . . . . . . . . . . . . . . . . . . . . . . . . . . . . . . . . . . . . . . . . . . . . . . . . . . . . . Silvertone ORELP 519
07/11/1992 . . . . . 15 . . . . . 4 . . . . . ●     BOOM BOOM . . . . . . . . . . . . . . . . . . . . . . . . . . . . . . . . . . . . . . . . . . . . . . . . . . . . . . Pointblank VPBCD 12
04/03/1995 . . . . . 23 . . . . . 5 . . . . . .     CHILL OUT 1995 Grammy Award for Best Traditional Blues Album . . . . . . . . . . . . . . . . . . . . Pointblank VPBCD 22
22/03/1997 . . . . . 63 . . . . . 2 . . . . . .     DON'T LOOK BACK 1997 Grammy Award for Best Traditional Blues Album . . . . . . . . . . . . . . . . Pointblank VPBCD 39

**HOOTIE AND THE BLOWFISH** US rock group formed at the University of South Carolina by Darius Rycker (vocals), Mark Bryan (guitar), Dean Felber (bass) and Jim 'Son' Sonefield (drums). The group was named Best New Artist at the 1995 Grammy Awards and also won Best Pop Performance by a Duo or Group with Vocal category for *Let Her Cry* the same year.

18/03/1995 . . . . . 12 . . . . . 11 . . . . . ●     CRACKED REAR VIEW ▲[8] ◆[16] . . . . . . . . . . . . . . . . . . . . . . . . . . . . . . . . . . . . . . . . . Atlantic 7826132
04/05/1996 . . . . . 9 . . . . . 16 . . . . . O     **FAIRWEATHER JOHNSON** ▲[2] . . . . . . . . . . . . . . . . . . . . . . . . . . . . . . . . . . . . . . . . . Atlantic 7567828852
26/09/1998 . . . . . 15 . . . . . 3 . . . .     MUSICAL CHAIRS . . . . . . . . . . . . . . . . . . . . . . . . . . . . . . . . . . . . . . . . . . . . . . . . . . . Atlantic 7567831362

**HOPE OF THE STATES** UK rock group formed in Chichester by Sam Herlihy (guitar/vocals), Jimi Lawrence (guitar), Ant Theaker (guitar/keyboards), Paul Wilson (bass), Mike Sidell (violin) and Simon Jones (drums). Lawrence was found hanging in a recording studio on 15/1/2004.

19/06/2004 . . . . . 21 . . . . . 2+ . . . . . .     THE LOST RIOTS . . . . . . . . . . . . . . . . . . . . . . . . . . . . . . . . . . . . . . . . . . . . . . . . . . . . Sony Music 5172649

**MARY HOPKIN** UK singer (born 3/5/1950, Pontardawe, Wales) who won *Opportunity Knocks* in 1968, an event spotted by model Twiggy who recommended her to Paul McCartney and the Apple label. Her debut single launched the label, along with The Beatles' own *Hey Jude* (her single replaced The Beatles at #1). She married producer Tony Visconti in 1971, but the relationship ended in 1981. In 1983 she joined with Julian Lloyd Webber, Bill Lovelady and Peter Skellern to form Oasis, a group that scored one hit album.

01/03/1969 . . . . . 3 . . . . . 9 . . . . . .     **POSTCARD** . . . . . . . . . . . . . . . . . . . . . . . . . . . . . . . . . . . . . . . . . . . . . . . . . . . . . . . Apple SAPCOR 5

### JAMES HORNER

**JAMES HORNER** US composer/arranger/conductor (born 14/8/1953, Los Angeles, CA), he studied at the Royal College of Music in London and later back in LA at both USC and UCLA. He has made his name as a composer of film music, with *Star Trek II, 48 Hours, Cocoon, Alien, Honey I Shrunk The Kids, An American Tail, Patriot Games* and *Titanic*. He has won four Grammy Awards: Song of the Year in 1987 with Barry Mann and Cynthia Weil for *Somewhere Out There*, which also won the award for Best Song Written Specifically for a Motion Picture or TV having been featured in *An American Tail,* Best Album of Original Instrumental Background Score written for a Motion Picture or TV in 1990 for *Glory* and Song of the Year in 1998 with Will Jennings for *My Heart Will Go On*. *My Heart Will Go On* also won the 1997 Oscar for Best Film Song.

| 23/09/1995 | 27 | 9 | | BRAVEHEART ◇ **LONDON SYMPHONY ORCHESTRA, CONDUCTOR JAMES HORNER** Original soundtrack to the film | Decca 4482952 |
| 31/01/1998 | ❶³ | 55 | ✪³ | **TITANIC** Original soundtrack to the film ◇⁵ ▲¹⁶ ◆¹¹ | Sony Classical SK 63213 |
| 12/09/1998 | 10 | 18 | | **BACK TO TITANIC** | Sony Classical SK 60691 |

### BRUCE HORNSBY AND THE RANGE

**BRUCE HORNSBY AND THE RANGE** US singer (born 23/11/1954, Williamsburg, VA); he moved to Los Angeles, CA in 1980 at the suggestion of Michael McDonald. He joined Sheena Easton's backing band in 1983 and formed the Range in 1984 with David Mansfield (guitar), Joe Puerta (bass), John Molo (drums) and George Marinelli (guitar). Mansfield was later replaced by Peter Harris who left in 1990. Hornsby filled in for Brent Mydland of the Grateful Dead when Mydland died. The group was named Best New Artist at the 1986 Grammy Awards. Bruce has since won two more Grammys: Best Bluegrass Recording in 1989 with the Nitty Gritty Dirt Band for *The Valley Road* and Best Pop Instrumental Performance in 1993 with Branford Marsalis for *Barcelona Mona*.

| 13/09/1986 | 16 | 26 | ○ | THE WAY IT IS | RCA PL 89901 |
| 14/05/1988 | 18 | 18 | ● | SCENES FROM THE SOUTHSIDE | RCA PL 86686 |
| 30/06/1990 | 23 | 7 | ○ | A NIGHT ON THE TOWN | RCA PL 82041 |
| 08/05/1993 | 32 | 3 | | HARBOR LIGHTS | RCA 07863661142 |

### JANE HORROCKS

**JANE HORROCKS** UK actress (born 18/1/1964, Rossendale Valley, Lancashire), she attended the Royal Academy of Dramatic Art before joining the Royal Shakespeare Company. She was first known for the TV show *Absolutely Fabulous* and Tesco commercials as a long-suffering daughter to Prunella Scales' mother. The play *The Rise And Fall Of Little Voice* was written especially for her.

| 21/10/2000 | 63 | 1 | | FURTHER ADVENTURES OF LITTLE VOICE | Liberty 5287542 |

### HORSE

**HORSE** UK group formed by Horse McDonald (vocals), George Hutchison (guitar), Angela McAlinden (guitar), Graham Brierton (bass), Steve Vantsis (bass), Steve Cooke (keyboards) and and Steve Cochrane (drums).

| 23/06/1990 | 44 | 2 | | THE SAME SKY | Echo Chamber EST 2123 |
| 13/11/1993 | 42 | 2 | | GOD'S HOME MOVIE | Oxygen MCD 10935 |

### HORSLIPS

**HORSLIPS** Irish group formed in Dublin in 1970 by Sean Fenn (guitar/vocals), Barry Devlin (bass/vocals), Charles O'Connor (violin, mandolin/vocals), Jim Lockhart (flute/tin whistle/keyboards/vocals) and Eamonn Carr (drums/vocals). They later added Gus Guest and Declan Sinnott (both on guitar), although the group effectively disbanded in 1980. Their hit album was inspired by the story of Tuatha De Danann's conquest of ancient pre-Christian Ireland.

| 30/04/1977 | 39 | 3 | | THE BOOK OF INVASIONS – A CELTIC SYMPHONY | DJM DJF 20498 |

### HOT CHOCOLATE

**HOT CHOCOLATE** UK group formed in London in 1969 by Patrick Olive (born 22/3/1947, Grenada, percussion), Ian King (drums) and Franklyn De Allie (guitar), subsequently adding Errol Brown (born 12/11/1948, Kingston, Jamaica, vocals), Tony Wilson (born 8/10/1947, Trinidad, bass) and Larry Ferguson (born 14/4/1948, Nassau, Bahamas, piano). They recorded their first single for Apple (a version of *Give Peace A Chance*) in 1969 before signing with RAK in 1970 and enjoying their first hit as songwriters, penning *Bet Yer Life I Do* for labelmates Herman's Hermits. De Allie was replaced by Harvey Hinsley (born 19/1/1948, Northampton) in 1970, Tony Connor (born 6/4/1947, Romford) replaced King on drums in 1973. Co-songwriter Wilson left in 1976, with Brown assuming full writing control. In 1987 the group announced they had split, and Brown went solo. Brown was awarded an MBE in the Queen's 2003 Birthday Honours List.

| 15/11/1975 | 34 | 7 | ○ | HOT CHOCOLATE | RAK SRAK 516 |
| 07/08/1976 | 32 | 7 | ○ | MAN TO MAN | RAK SRAK 522 |
| 20/11/1976 | 6 | 35 | ● | **GREATEST HITS** | RAK SRAK 524 |
| 08/04/1978 | 30 | 8 | ○ | EVERY 1'S A WINNER | RAK SRAK 531 |
| 15/12/1979 | 3 | 19 | ✪ | **20 HOTTEST HITS** | RAK EMTV 22 |
| 25/09/1982 | 24 | 7 | | MYSTERY | RAK SRAK 549 |
| 21/02/1987 | ❶¹ | 28 | ✪ | **THE VERY BEST OF HOT CHOCOLATE** | RAK EMTV 42 |
| 20/03/1993 | ❶¹ | 42 | ✪ | **THEIR GREATEST HITS** | EMI CDEMTV 73 |

### HOT HOT HEAT

**HOT HOT HEAT** Canadian rock group formed in Vancouver, British Columbia in 1999; they were re-formed in 2001 by Steve Bays (keyboards/vocals), Dante DeCaro (guitar), Dustin Hawthorne (bass) and Paul Hawley (drums).

| 12/04/2003 | 35 | 2 | | MAKE UP THE BREAKDOWN | B Unique 5046646202 |

### HOTHOUSE FLOWERS

**HOTHOUSE FLOWERS** Irish folk-rock group formed in Dublin in 1986 by Liam O'Maonlai (born 7/11/1964, Dublin, vocals/keyboards), Fiachna O'Braonain (born 27/11/1965, Dublin, guitar), Peter O'Toole (born 1/4/1965, Dublin, bass), Jerry Fehily (born 29/8/1963, Bishops Town, drums) and Leo Barnes (born 5/10/1965, Dublin, saxophone). Named after an album title by Wynton Marsalis.

| DATE | POS | WKS | BPI | ALBUM TITLE | LABEL & NUMBER |
|---|---|---|---|---|---|
| 18/06/1988 | 2 | 19 | ● | PEOPLE | London LONLP 58 |
| 16/06/1990 | 5 | 21 | ● | HOME | London 8281971 |
| 20/03/1993 | 7 | 11 | ○ | SONGS FROM THE RAIN | London 8283502 |

**HOTRODS** – see EDDIE AND THE HOTRODS

**STEVEN HOUGHTON** UK actor/singer (born 1972, Sheffield), best known as Gregg Blake in TV's *London's Burning*. He has also appeared in *Bugs* and *Indian Summer* and has used both spellings (Steven and Stephen) of his first name as an actor.

| 29/11/1997 | 21 | 7 | | STEVEN HOUGHTON | RCA 74321542592 |

**HOUND DOG AND THE MEGAMIXERS** UK production group.

| 01/12/1990 | 34 | 9 | | THE GREATEST EVER JUNIOR PARTY MEGAMIX | Pop & Arts PATLP 201 |

**HOUSE OF LOVE** UK rock group formed in London by Guy Chadwick (guitar/vocals), Terry Bickers (guitar), Chris Groothuizen (bass) and Pete Evans (drums). Bickers left in 1989 and was replaced by Simon Walker. Walker left in 1992.

| 10/03/1990 | 8 | 10 | | HOUSE OF LOVE | Fontana 8422931 |
| 10/11/1990 | 49 | 1 | | THE HOUSE OF LOVE | Fontana 8469781 |
| 18/07/1992 | 34 | 2 | | BABE RAINBOW | Fontana 5125492 |
| 03/07/1993 | 38 | 1 | | AUDIENCE WITH THE MIND | Fontana 5148802 |

**HOUSE OF PAIN** US rap group formed in Los Angeles, CA by Erik 'Everlast' Schrody, 'Danny Boy' O'Connor and Leor 'DJ Lethal' DiMant. Everlast subsequently recorded solo for Tommy Boy.

| 21/11/1992 | 73 | 1 | ● | HOUSE OF PAIN | XL Recordings XLCD 111 |
| 30/07/1994 | 8 | 6 | | SAME AS IT EVER WAS | XL Recordings XLCD 115 |

**HOUSEMARTINS** UK group formed in Hull, Humberside in 1984 by Paul Heaton (born 9/5/1962, Birkenhead, guitar/vocals), Stan Cullimore (born 6/4/1962, Hull, bass), Hugh Whitaker (drums) and Ted Key (vocals). Norman Cook (born Quentin Cook, 31/7/1963, Brighton) replaced Key in 1985. Whitaker left in 1987 and was replaced by Dave Hemingway (born 20/9/1960, Hull). The group was named Best British Newcomers at the 1987 BRIT Awards. They dissolved in 1989; Heaton formed the Beautiful South, and Cook recorded solo, subsequently forming Beats International and Freakpower and recording as Fatboy Slim. In 1993 Hugh Whitaker was sent to prison for six years for assaulting James Hewitt with an axe and setting fire to his house on three occasions.

*Now that's what I call quite good*

*The Housemartins*

| 05/07/1986 | 3 | 41 | ✪ | LONDON 0 HULL 4 | Go Discs AGOLP 7 |
| 27/12/1986 | 84 | 1 | | THE HOUSEMARTINS' CHRISTMAS SINGLES BOX | Go Discs GOD 816 |
| 03/10/1987 | 9 | 18 | ● | THE PEOPLE WHO GRINNED THEMSELVES TO DEATH | Go Discs AGOLP 9 |
| 21/05/1988 | 8 | 11 | ● | NOW THAT'S WHAT I CALL QUITE GOOD | Go Discs AGOLP 11 |
| 10/04/2004 | 29 | 3 | | THE BEST OF | Go Discs 9818214 |

**MARQUES HOUSTON** US singer (born 4/8/1981, Los Angeles, CA). Previously in Immature, he went solo in 2003.

| 14/02/2004 | 73 | 1 | | MH | Elektra 7559629352 |

**WHITNEY HOUSTON** US singer (born 9/8/1963, Newark, NJ) who is the daughter of soul singer Cissy Houston and a cousin of Dionne Warwick. She began her career singing gospel and modelling for the likes of *Vogue* before moving into session work for Chaka Khan and Lou Rawls, among others. Signed by Arista in 1983, she released her debut album in 1985 and continued her career as a model, having appeared on numerous front covers. She married singer Bobby Brown on 18/7/1992 and gave birth to their daughter Bobbi in March 1993. She has won six Grammy Awards: Best Pop Vocal Performance in 1985 for *Saving All My Love For You*, Best Pop Vocal Performance in 1987 for *I Wanna Dance With Somebody (Who Loves Me)*, Record of the Year and Best Pop Vocal Performance in 1993 for *I Will Always Love You*, Album of the Year in 1993 for *The Bodyguard* (which in the UK is listed as a various artists album) and Best Rhythm & Blues Vocal Performance in 1999 for *It's Not Right But It's Okay*. She was also named Best R&B Artist at the 1999 MTV Europe Music Awards.

| 14/12/1985 | 2 | 119 | ✪4 | WHITNEY HOUSTON ▲14 ◆13 | Arista 206978 |
| 13/06/1987 | ❶6 | 101 | ✪6 | WHITNEY ▲11 | Arista 208141 |
| 17/11/1990 | 4 | 29 | ✪ | I'M YOUR BABY TONIGHT | Arista 211039 |
| 04/01/1997 | 35 | 7 | | THE PREACHER'S WIFE ◇ Soundtrack from the 1996 film *The Preacher's Wife* | Arista 74321441252 |
| 28/11/1998 | 4 | 67 | ✪3 | MY LOVE IS YOUR LOVE ◇4 | Arista 07822190372 |
| 27/05/2000 | ❶2 | 50 | ✪4 | THE GREATEST HITS ◇3 | Arista 74321757392 |
| 16/02/2002 | 22 | 3 | | LOVE, WHITNEY | Arista 74321910272 |

**STEVE HOWE** UK guitarist/singer (born 8/4/1947, London), he began his career with The Syndicats in 1963 and later played with The Incrowd (that later changed its name to Tomorrow) and Bodast before working in PP Arnold's backing group. He replaced Pete Banks in Yes in 1970, also recording two solo albums during his time with the group. He later linked with Steve Hackett, Max Bacon, Phil Spalding and Jonathon Mover in GTR and then Jon Anderson, Bill Bruford and Rick Wakeman in Anderson Bruford Wakeman Howe. See also Anderson Bruford Wakeman Howe.

| DATE | POS | WKS | BPI | ALBUM TITLE | LABEL & NUMBER |
|------|-----|-----|-----|-------------|----------------|
| 15/11/1975 | 22 | 4 | ○ | BEGINNINGS | Atlantic K 50151 |
| 24/11/1979 | 68 | 2 | | THE STEVE HOWE ALBUM | Atlantic K 50621 |

**HUDDERSFIELD CHORAL SOCIETY** UK choir formed in Huddersfield, Yorkshire they were conducted by Owain Harwell Hughes and also featured organist David Bell.

| DATE | POS | WKS | BPI | ALBUM TITLE | LABEL & NUMBER |
|------|-----|-----|-----|-------------|----------------|
| 15/03/1986 | 8 | 10 | ● | THE HYMNS ALBUM | EMI EMTV 43 |
| 13/12/1986 | 29 | 4 | ● | THE CAROLS ALBUM | EMI EMTV 40 |

**HUE AND CRY** UK duo formed by Glasgow-born brothers Pat (born 10/3/1964) and Greg Kane (11/9/1966) who first recorded for Stampede in 1986.

| DATE | POS | WKS | BPI | ALBUM TITLE | LABEL & NUMBER |
|------|-----|-----|-----|-------------|----------------|
| 07/11/1987 | 22 | 11 | ○ | SEDUCED AND ABANDONED | Circa 2 |
| 10/12/1988 | 10 | 48 | ● | REMOTE/THE BITTER SUITE | Circa 6 |
| 29/06/1991 | 10 | 9 | | STARS CRASH DOWN | Circa 15 |
| 29/08/1992 | 33 | 2 | | TRUTH AND LOVE | Fidelity FIDELCD 1 |
| 10/04/1993 | 27 | 4 | | LABOURS ON LOVE – THE BEST OF HUE AND CRY | Circa HACCD 1 |

**ALAN HULL** UK singer/guitarist/pianist (born 20/2/1945, Newcastle-upon-Tyne), a founding member of Downtown Faction, later called Lindisfarne. They disbanded in 1973, Hull going solo, but re-formed in 1978. He died on 17/11/1995 from a heart attack.

| DATE | POS | WKS | BPI | ALBUM TITLE | LABEL & NUMBER |
|------|-----|-----|-----|-------------|----------------|
| 28/07/1973 | 29 | 3 | | PIPEDREAM | Charisma CAS 1069 |

**HUMAN LEAGUE** UK group formed in 1977 by Martyn Ware (born 19/5/1956, Sheffield, keyboards), Ian Craig Marsh (born 11/11/1956, Sheffield, keyboards), Addy Newton and Phil Oakey (born 2/10/1955, Leicester, vocals and synthesizer) as the Future, changing to Human League later the same year (the name was taken from a science-fiction computer game). Newton left soon after, with Adrian Wright (born 30/6/1956) his replacement, although his initial role within the group was to look after visuals. Signed to Fast Product Records in 1978, the group was switched to Virgin in 1979. Ware and Marsh left in 1980 to form Heaven 17. Oakley recruited Ian Burden (born 24/12/1957, bass), Joanne Catherall (born 18/9/1962, Sheffield, vocals) and Susanne Sulley (born 22/3/1963, Sheffield, vocals), later adding Jo Callis (born 2/5/1955) on synthesizer. Oakey also launched a solo career. The group was named Best British Newcomer at the inaugural BRIT Awards in 1982.

| DATE | POS | WKS | BPI | ALBUM TITLE | LABEL & NUMBER |
|------|-----|-----|-----|-------------|----------------|
| 31/05/1980 | 16 | 42 | ● | TRAVELOGUE | Virgin V 2160 |
| 22/08/1981 | 34 | 23 | ● | REPRODUCTION | Virgin V 2133 |
| 24/10/1981 | ❶⁴ | 72 | ✪³ | DARE | Virgin V 2192 |
| 17/07/1982 | 3 | 52 | ✪ | LOVE AND DANCING LEAGUE UNLIMITED ORCHESTRA | Virgin OVED 6 |
| 19/05/1984 | 3 | 18 | ● | HYSTERIA | Virgin V 2315 |
| 20/09/1986 | 7 | 6 | ● | CRASH | Virgin V 2391 |
| 12/11/1988 | 3 | 24 | ✪² | GREATEST HITS | Virgin HLTV 1 |
| 29/09/1990 | 24 | 2 | | ROMANTIC? | Virgin V 2624 |
| 04/02/1995 | 6 | 12 | ● | OCTOPUS | East West 4509987502 |
| 11/11/1995 | 28 | 8 | ● | GREATEST HITS | Virgin CDV 2792 |
| 18/08/2001 | 44 | 1 | | SECRETS | Papillon BTFLYCD 0019 |
| 27/09/2003 | 24 | 3 | ○ | THE VERY BEST OF | Virgin HLCDX2 |

**HUMBLE PIE** UK rock group formed in London in 1969 by Peter Frampton (born 22/4/1950, Beckenham, guitar/vocals), Steve Marriott (born 30/1/1947, London, guitar/vocals), Greg Ridley (born 23/10/1947, Carlisle, Cumbria, bass) and Jerry Shirley (born 4/2/1952, drums), all of whom had been with other groups – the three principal members having been with The Herd, Small Faces and Spooky Tooth respectively. Frampton left for a solo career in 1971 and was replaced by Dave 'Clem' Clempson (born 5/9/1949). The group split in 1975, briefly re-forming in 1980. Marriott was killed in a house fire on 20/4/1991.

| DATE | POS | WKS | BPI | ALBUM TITLE | LABEL & NUMBER |
|------|-----|-----|-----|-------------|----------------|
| 06/09/1969 | 32 | 1 | | AS SAFE AS YESTERDAY IS | Immediate IMSP 025 |
| 22/01/1972 | 32 | 2 | | ROCKING AT THE FILLMORE | A&M AMLH 63506 |
| 15/04/1972 | 28 | 5 | | SMOKIN' | A&M AMLS 64342 |
| 07/04/1973 | 34 | 2 | | EAT IT | A&M AMLS 6004 |

### ENGELBERT HUMPERDINCK
**ENGELBERT HUMPERDINCK** UK singer (born Arnold George Dorsey, 2/5/1936, Madras, India) who made his first recordings for Decca in 1958 as Gerry Dorsey. In 1965 he met Tom Jones' manager Gordon Mills, who suggested he change his name to Engelbert Humperdinck (a 19th-century German composer), which considerably improved his fortune. He also broke in the USA to where he relocated and went on the cabaret circuit and hosted his own TV variety show. He has a star on the Hollywood Walk of Fame.

| DATE | POS | WKS | BPI | ALBUM TITLE | LABEL & NUMBER |
|---|---|---|---|---|---|
| 20/05/1967 | 6 | 58 | | **RELEASE ME** | Decca SKL 4868 |
| 25/11/1967 | 3 | 33 | | **THE LAST WALTZ** | Decca SKL 4901 |
| 03/08/1968 | 3 | 45 | | **A MAN WITHOUT LOVE** | Decca SKL 4939 |
| 01/03/1969 | 3 | 8 | | **ENGELBERT** | Decca SKL 4985 |
| 06/12/1969 | 5 | 23 | | **ENGELBERT HUMPERDINCK** | Decca SKL 5030 |
| 11/07/1970 | 17 | 11 | | WE MADE IT HAPPEN | Decca SKL 5054 |
| 18/09/1971 | 48 | 1 | | ANOTHER TIME, ANOTHER PLACE | Decca SKL 5097 |
| 26/02/1972 | 45 | 1 | | LIVE AT THE RIVIERA LAS VEGAS | Decca TXS 105 |
| 21/12/1974 | ❶³ | 34 | ● | **ENGELBERT HUMPERDINCK – HIS GREATEST HITS** | Decca SKL 5198 |
| 04/05/1985 | 35 | 10 | | GETTING SENTIMENTAL | Telstar STAR 2254 |
| 04/04/1987 | 35 | 9 | | THE ENGELBERT HUMPERDINCK COLLECTION | Telstar STAR 2294 |
| 10/06/1995 | 16 | 6 | | LOVE UNCHAINED | EMI CDEMTV 94 |
| 08/04/2000 | 5 | 14 | ● | **AT HIS VERY BEST** | Universal TV 8449742 |
| 20/10/2001 | 42 | 2 | | I WANT TO WAKE UP WITH YOU | Universal TV 0149462 |
| 20/03/2004 | 4 | 12 | ● | **HIS GREATEST LOVE SONGS** | Universal TV 9817857 |

### HUNDRED REASONS
**HUNDRED REASONS** UK five-piece rock group formed in Surrey by Colin Doran (vocals), Larry Hibbitt (guitar), Paul Townsend (guitar), Andy Gilmour (bass) and Andy Bews (drums). They were named Best New British Band at the 2000 Kerrang! Awards.

| DATE | POS | WKS | ALBUM TITLE | LABEL & NUMBER |
|---|---|---|---|---|
| 01/06/2002 | 6 | 7 | **IDEAS ABOVE OUR STATION** | Columbia 5081482 |
| 13/03/2004 | 20 | 2 | SHATTERPROOF IS NOT A CHALLENGE | Columbia 5136932 |

### IAN HUNTER
**IAN HUNTER** UK singer (born 3/6/1946, Shrewsbury), he auditioned for Mott The Hoople in 1969 and was taken on as lead singer. He collapsed suffering from exhaustion in 1974, prompting the group to disband. He had recovered by 1975 and went solo.

| DATE | POS | WKS | ALBUM TITLE | LABEL & NUMBER |
|---|---|---|---|---|
| 12/04/1975 | 21 | 15 | IAN HUNTER | CBS 80710 |
| 29/05/1976 | 29 | 4 | ALL AMERICAN ALIEN BOY | CBS 81310 |
| 05/05/1979 | 49 | 3 | YOU'RE NEVER ALONE WITH A SCHIZOPHRENIC | Chrysalis CHR 1214 |
| 26/04/1980 | 61 | 2 | WELCOME TO THE CLUB | Chrysalis CJT 6 |
| 29/08/1981 | 79 | 2 | SHORT BACK 'N' SIDES | Chrysalis CHR 1326 |

### HURRAH!
**HURRAH!** UK group formed in Newcasatle-Upon-Tyne by Paul Handyside (guitar), Taffy Hughes (guitar) and Dave Porthouse (bass), later adding Steve Price (drums).

| DATE | POS | WKS | ALBUM TITLE | LABEL & NUMBER |
|---|---|---|---|---|
| 28/02/1987 | 71 | 1 | TELL GOD I'M HERE | Kitchenware 208201 |

### HURRICANE #1
**HURRICANE #1** UK group formed by Andy Bell (born 11/8/1970, Cardiff, guitar) following the demise of Ride and featuring Gaz Farmer (drums), Will Pepper (bass) and Alex Lowe (vocals). In November 1999 Bell joined Gay Dad, but a few days later joined Oasis.

| DATE | POS | WKS | ALBUM TITLE | LABEL & NUMBER |
|---|---|---|---|---|
| 27/09/1997 | 11 | 2 | HURRICANE #1 | Creation CRECD 206 |
| 01/05/1999 | 55 | 1 | ONLY THE STRONG SURVIVE | Creation CRECD 237 |

### HURRICANES
**HURRICANES** – see **JOHNNY AND THE HURRICANES**

### HUSKER DU
**HUSKER DU** US punk group formed in Minneapolis, MN in 1979 by Bob Mould (born 16/10/1960, Malone, NY, guitar/vocals), Greg Norton (bass) and Grant Hart (drums), named after a Norwegian board game *Do you remember?*, making their debut single in 1981. They disbanded in 1988 after Hart's dismissal, Mould and Norton then recording solo. Mould formed Sugar in 1991.

| DATE | POS | WKS | ALBUM TITLE | LABEL & NUMBER |
|---|---|---|---|---|
| 14/02/1987 | 72 | 1 | WAREHOUSE: SONGS AND STORIES | Warner Brothers 925 5441 |

### HYBRID
**HYBRID** UK trio of producers formed in Swansea by Mike Truman, Chris Healings and Lee Mullin. They have worked extensively with Julee Cruise and later toured with Moby as the opening act on his US tour.

| DATE | POS | WKS | ALBUM TITLE | LABEL & NUMBER |
|---|---|---|---|---|
| 25/09/1999 | 45 | 1 | WIDE ANGLE | Distinctive DISNCD 54 |

### PHYLLIS HYMAN
**PHYLLIS HYMAN** US singer (born 1949, Pittsburgh, PA) who began her career as a fashion model before being discovered singing by Norman Connors. After appearing as a guest singer on his album with Michael Henderson, she landed a solo contract with Buddah Records and was initially placed with veteran producer Thom Bell. She later recorded for Philadelphia International, Arista, EMI and Zoo and appeared on Broadway in a number of musicals. She committed suicide on 30/6/1995.

| DATE | POS | WKS | ALBUM TITLE | LABEL & NUMBER |
|---|---|---|---|---|
| 20/09/1986 | 97 | 1 | LIVING ALL ALONE | Philadelphia International PHIL 4001 |

### HYPNOSIS
**HYPNOSIS** UK studio group formed by Stewart and Bradley James.

| DATE | POS | WKS | BPI | ALBUM TITLE | LABEL & NUMBER |
|---|---|---|---|---|---|
| 17/08/1996 | 16 | 12 | ● | VOICES OF TRANQUILLITY | Dino DINCD 123 |
| 15/03/1997 | 32 | 4 | | VOICES OF TRANQUILLITY – VOLUME 2 | Dino DINCD 135 |

# I

**I AM KLOOT** UK group from Manchester: John Bramwell (guitar/vocals), Pete Jobson (guitar/bass) and Andy Hargreaves (drums).

27/09/2003 . . . . . 68 . . . . . . 1 . . . . . . I AM KLOOT . . . . . . . . . . . . . . . . . . . . . . . . . . . . . . . . . . . . . . . . . . . . . . . . . . . . . . . . . . . . . Echo ECHCD 46

**I-LEVEL** UK funk group formed by Sam Jones, Joe Dworniak and Duncan Bridgeman.

09/07/1983 . . . . . 50 . . . . . . 4 . . . . . . I-LEVEL . . . . . . . . . . . . . . . . . . . . . . . . . . . . . . . . . . . . . . . . . . . . . . . . . . . . . . . . . . . . . . . . . . . . . Virgin V 2270

**IAN VAN DAHL** Belgian producer/songwriter AnneMie Coene who was given the nickname 'Ian' when she was a child. The vocals on her debut hit were not by an 'Ian' but by a female singer, Marsha. By the second single it was revealed that the 'group' was the brainchild of producers Christophe Chantiz and Erik Vanspauwen.

08/06/2002 . . . . . 7 . . . . . . 7 . . . . . . **ACE** . . . . . . . . . . . . . . . . . . . . . . . . . . . . . . . . . . . . . . . . . . . . . . . . . . . . . . . . . . . . . . NuLife 74321934812

**ICE CUBE** US rapper (born O'Shea Jackson, 15/6/1969, Los Angeles) and founder member of NWA (Niggaz With Attitude), which he left in 1990 to form his own 'posse', Lench Mob. He also began acting, appearing in the 1991 film *Boyz N The Hood*.

28/07/1990 . . . . . 48 . . . . . . 5 . . . . . . AMERIKKA'S MOST WANTED . . . . . . . . . . . . . . . . . . . . . . . . . . . . . . . . . . . . . . . . . . . . Fourth & Broadway BRLP 551
09/03/1991 . . . . . 66 . . . . . . 3 . . . . . . KILL AT WILL . . . . . . . . . . . . . . . . . . . . . . . . . . . . . . . . . . . . . . . . . . . . . . . . . . . . . . . . . Fourth & Broadway BRLM 572
05/12/1992 . . . . . 73 . . . . . . 1 . . . . . . ○ THE PREDATOR ▲[1] . . . . . . . . . . . . . . . . . . . . . . . . . . . . . . . . . . . . . . . . . . . . . . . . . . . . Fourth & Broadway BRCD 592
18/12/1993 . . . . . 52 . . . . . . 1 . . . . . . LETHAL INJECTION . . . . . . . . . . . . . . . . . . . . . . . . . . . . . . . . . . . . . . . . . . . . . . . . . . Fourth & Broadway BRCD 609
01/04/2000 . . . . . 56 . . . . . . 1 . . . . . . WAR & PEACE – VOLUME II . . . . . . . . . . . . . . . . . . . . . . . . . . . . . . . . . . . . . . . . . . . . . . . . Priority CDPTY 183

**ICE-T** US rapper (born Tracy Morrow, 16/2/1958, Newark, NJ) who took his name from black exploitation writer Iceberg Slim. He also began a career as an actor, appearing in the films *New Jack City* (1991) and *Looters* (1992) with Ice Cube. He previously recorded for Sire Records but was thrown off the label following the outcry (led by shareholder Charlton Heston) over the single *Cop Killer* by Body Count, which Ice-T wrote and produced. He won the 1990 Grammy Award for Best Rap Performance by a Group with Melle Mel, Daddy Kane and Kool Moe Dee for *Back On The Block* by Quincy Jones.

21/10/1989 . . . . . 42 . . . . . . 2 . . . . . . THE ICEBERG/FREEDOM OF SPEECH . . . . . . . . . . . . . . . . . . . . . . . . . . . . . . . . . . . . . . . . . . . . . . Sire WX 316
25/05/1991 . . . . . 38 . . . . . . 4 . . . . . . ○ O.G. ORIGINAL GANGSTER . . . . . . . . . . . . . . . . . . . . . . . . . . . . . . . . . . . . . . . . . . . . . . . . . Sire WX 412
03/04/1993 . . . . . 15 . . . . . . 7 . . . . . . ● HOME INVASION . . . . . . . . . . . . . . . . . . . . . . . . . . . . . . . . . . . . . . . . . . . . . . . . . . Rhyme Syndicate RSYND 1
08/06/1996 . . . . . 26 . . . . . . 2 . . . . . . VI: RETURN OF THE REAL . . . . . . . . . . . . . . . . . . . . . . . . . . . . . . . . . . . . . . . . . . . . . . Rhyme Syndicate RSYND 3

**ICEHOUSE** Australian rock group formed in 1980 by Iva Davies (born 22/5/1955, multi-instrumentalist/vocals), Bob Kretshmer (guitar), Guy Pratt (guitar), Andy Qunta (keyboards), Michael Hoste (keyboards) and John Lloyd (drums) as Flowers. Icehouse was the Flowers' first album title, derived from Australian slang for a mental hospital.

05/03/1983 . . . . . 64 . . . . . . 6 . . . . . . LOVE IN MOTION . . . . . . . . . . . . . . . . . . . . . . . . . . . . . . . . . . . . . . . . . . . . . . . . . . . . . Chrysalis CHR 1390
02/04/1988 . . . . . 93 . . . . . . 1 . . . . . . MAN OF COLOURS . . . . . . . . . . . . . . . . . . . . . . . . . . . . . . . . . . . . . . . . . . . . . . . . . . . . Chrysalis CHR 1592

**ICICLE WORKS** UK rock group formed in Liverpool in 1980 by Ian McNabb (born 3/11/1960, Liverpool, guitar/vocals), Chris Layhe (bass) and Chris Sharrock (drums). The group took their name from a sci-fi book. McNabb later recorded solo.

31/03/1984 . . . . . 24 . . . . . . 6 . . . . . . THE ICICLE WORKS . . . . . . . . . . . . . . . . . . . . . . . . . . . . . . . . . . . . . . . . . . . . . . . . . Beggars Banquet BEGA 50
28/09/1985 . . . . . 55 . . . . . . 3 . . . . . . THE SMALL PRICE OF A BICYCLE . . . . . . . . . . . . . . . . . . . . . . . . . . . . . . . . . . . . . . . . . Beggars Banquet BEGA 61
01/03/1986 . . . . . 52 . . . . . . 2 . . . . . . SEVEN SINGLES DEEP . . . . . . . . . . . . . . . . . . . . . . . . . . . . . . . . . . . . . . . . . . . . . . . . Beggars Banquet BEGA 71
21/03/1987 . . . . . 28 . . . . . . 4 . . . . . . IF YOU WANT TO DEFEAT YOUR ENEMY SING HIS SONG . . . . . . . . . . . . . . . . . . . . . . . Beggars Banquet BEGA 78
14/05/1988 . . . . . 40 . . . . . . 3 . . . . . . BLIND . . . . . . . . . . . . . . . . . . . . . . . . . . . . . . . . . . . . . . . . . . . . . . . . . . . . . . . . . . . . Beggars Banquet IWA 2
05/09/1992 . . . . . 60 . . . . . . 1 . . . . . . THE BEST OF THE ICICLE WORKS . . . . . . . . . . . . . . . . . . . . . . . . . . . . . . . . . . . . . . . Beggars Banquet BEGA 124CD

**IDLEWILD** UK group formed in Edinburgh by Roddy Woomble (vocals), Rod Jones (guitar), Bob Fairfoull (bass) and Colin Newton (drums).

07/11/1998 . . . . . 53 . . . . . . 1 . . . . . . HOPE IS IMPORTANT . . . . . . . . . . . . . . . . . . . . . . . . . . . . . . . . . . . . . . . . . . . . . . . . . . . . Food 4971322
22/04/2000 . . . . . 15 . . . . . . 4 . . . . . . ○ 100 BROKEN WINDOWS . . . . . . . . . . . . . . . . . . . . . . . . . . . . . . . . . . . . . . . . . . . . . . . . . . Food FOODCD 32
27/07/2002 . . . . . 3 . . . . . . 8 . . . . . . ● **THE REMOTE PART** . . . . . . . . . . . . . . . . . . . . . . . . . . . . . . . . . . . . . . . . . . . . . . . . . Parlophone 5402432

### BILLY IDOL
UK singer (born William Broad, 30/11/1955, Stanmore, Middlesex) and an early follower of punk rock and in the TV audience when the Sex Pistols had their notorious interview with Bill Grundy. He formed Generation X with Tony James, John Towe and Bob Andrews in 1976, quitting in 1981 for a solo career masterminded by Kiss manager Bill Aucoin. A February 1990 motorcycle smash in LA broke his right leg and left wrist.

| | | | | | |
|---|---|---|---|---|---|
| 08/06/1985 | 7 | 34 | ✪ | VITAL IDOL | Chrysalis CUX 1502 |
| 28/09/1985 | 36 | 11 | ○ | REBEL YELL | Chrysalis CHR 1450 |
| 01/11/1986 | 8 | 20 | ● | WHIPLASH SMILE | Chrysalis CDL 1514 |
| 02/07/1988 | 2 | 25 | ✪ | IDOL SONGS: 11 OF THE BEST | Chrysalis BILTVD 1 |
| 12/05/1990 | 15 | 8 | ○ | CHARMED LIFE | Chrysalis CHR 1735 |
| 10/07/1993 | 20 | 2 | | CYBERPUNK | Chrysalis CDCHR 6000 |

### FRANK IFIELD
UK singer (born 30/11/1937, Coventry, raised in Australia) who began his career at the age of fifteen on Australian radio and TV where he had become a sizeable star before he came to the UK to try his luck. He signed to the UK Columbia label in 1959, working with producer Norrie Paramour.

| | | | | |
|---|---|---|---|---|
| 16/02/1963 | 3 | 36 | I'LL REMEMBER YOU | Columbia 33SX 1467 |
| 21/09/1963 | 3 | 32 | BORN FREE | Columbia 33SX 1462 |
| 28/03/1964 | 10 | 12 | BLUE SKIES | Columbia 33SX 1588 |
| 19/12/1964 | 9 | 3 | GREATEST HITS | Columbia 33SX 1633 |

### ENRIQUE IGLESIAS
Spanish singer (born 8/5/1975, Madrid), son of fellow singer Julio Iglesias. He began his professional career in 1995 and won the 1996 Grammy Award for Best Latin Pop Recording for *Enrique Iglesias*. When *Hero* hit #1, Julio and Enrique became the first father and son to top the UK singles chart.

| | | | | | |
|---|---|---|---|---|---|
| 26/01/2002 | ❶² | 71 | ✪⁴ | ESCAPE ◇² | Interscope 4931822 |
| 06/12/2003 | 13 | 12 | ● | SEVEN | Interscope 9861477 |

### JULIO IGLESIAS
Spanish singer (born 23/9/1943, Madrid) who planned a career as a goalkeeper with football team Real Madrid until a car accident left him temporarily paralysed. He learned to play the guitar in hospital. Initially popular within the Spanish-speaking world, he subsequently recorded in seven languages and became a worldwide star. He won the 1987 Grammy Award for Best Latin Pop Recording for *Un Hombre Solo,* and has a star on the Hollywood Walk of Fame. Both Julio's sons, Enrique (see above entry) and Julio Jr, have successful recording careers.

| | | | | | |
|---|---|---|---|---|---|
| 07/11/1981 | 43 | 5 | | DE NINA A MUJER | CBS 85063 |
| 28/11/1981 | 5 | 28 | ● | BEGIN THE BEGUINE | CBS 85462 |
| 16/10/1982 | 14 | 14 | ● | AMOR | CBS 25103 |
| 02/07/1983 | 5 | 17 | ● | JULIO | CBS 10038 |
| 01/09/1984 | 14 | 14 | ○ | 1100 BEL AIR PLACE | CBS 86308 |
| 19/10/1985 | 61 | 4 | | LIBRA | CBS 26623 |
| 03/09/1988 | 33 | 14 | ● | NON STOP | CBS 4609901 |
| 01/12/1990 | 27 | 20 | ● | STARRY NIGHT | CBS 4672841 |
| 28/05/1994 | 6 | 37 | ✪ | CRAZY ◇ | Columbia 4747382 |
| 12/08/1995 | 6 | 6 | | LA CARRETERA ◇ | Columbia 4807042 |

○ Silver disc  ● Gold disc  ✪ Platinum disc (additional platinum units are indicated by a figure following the symbol)  ❶⁹ Number of weeks album topped the UK chart

| 30/11/1996 | 56 | 3 | ○ | TANGO ◇ | Columbia 4866752 |
| 07/11/1998 | 18 | 9 | ● | MY LIFE: GREATEST HITS ◇ | Columbia 4910902 |
| 22/07/2000 | 32 | 3 | | NOCHE DE CUATRO LUNAS | Columbia 4974222 |
| 19/07/2003 | 64 | 1 | | LOVE SONGS | Columbia 5126042 |

**IMAGINATION** UK group formed in London in 1980 by Leee John (born John Lesley McGregor, 23/6/1957, London, vocals/keyboards), Ashley Ingram (born 27/11/1960, Northampton, bass/vocals) and Errol Kennedy (born in Montego Bay, Jamaica, drummer).

| 24/10/1981 | 20 | 53 | ● | BODY TALK | R&B RBLP 1001 |
| 11/09/1982 | 7 | 29 | ● | IN THE HEAT OF THE NIGHT | R&B RBLP 1002 |
| 14/05/1983 | 9 | 20 | ● | NIGHT DUBBING | R&B RBDUB 1 |
| 12/11/1983 | 25 | 8 | ● | SCANDALOUS | R&B RBLP 1004 |
| 12/08/1989 | 4 | 12 | ● | IMAGINATION – ALL THE HITS | Stylus SMR 985 |

**NATALIE IMBRUGLIA** Australian singer (born 4/2/1975, Sydney) who was initially famous for playing Beth in TV's *Neighbours,* before launching a singing career. It was originally claimed that her debut single *Torn* was written especially for her but it was later revealed to be a cover version of a Norwegian hit by Trine Rein of two years earlier, although this did not prevent the song from winning the 1998 MTV Europe Music Award for Best Song. She won Best International Female and Best International Newcomer at the 1999 BRIT Awards, took part in the *It's Only Rock 'N' Roll* project for the Children's Promise charity and starred in the 2003 film *Johnny English.*

| 06/12/1997 | 5 | 87 | ✪³ | LEFT OF THE MIDDLE ◇² | RCA 74321571382 |
| 17/11/2001 | 15 | 15 | ● | WHITE LILIES ISLAND | RCA 74321891212 |

**IMMACULATE FOOLS** UK pop group formed by Kevin Weatherall, his brother Paul, Andy Ross and his brother Peter, plus Barry Wickens.

| 11/05/1985 | 65 | 2 | | HEARTS OF FORTUNE | A&M AMA 5030 |

**IN TUNE** UK studio group formed by Stewart and Bradley James.

| 17/06/1995 | 21 | 3 | | ACOUSTIC MOODS | Global Television RADCD 13 |

**INCANTATION** UK group formed by Forbes Henderson (guitar), Tony Hinnigan (quenas/sikus/tarka/percussion/guitar/guitarron/pinkillo), Simon Rogers (charango/guitar/tiple/percussion), Chris Swithinbank (sikus/voice guitar/guitar/guitarron) and Mike Taylor (quenas/sikus/anata/bombo). They later contributed to the soundtracks to the films *The Mission* (1986) and *Patriot Games* (1992).

| 11/12/1982 | 9 | 26 | ● | CACHARPAYA (PANPIPES OF THE ANDES) | Beggars Banquet BEGA 39 |
| 17/12/1983 | 61 | 7 | | DANCE OF THE FLAMES | Beggars Banquet BEGA 49 |
| 28/12/1985 | 28 | 19 | ○ | THE BEST OF INCANTATION: MUSIC FROM THE ANDES | West Five CODA 19 |

**INCOGNITO** UK jazz-funk group formed in 1981 by ex-Light Of The World bass player Paul 'Tubbs' Williams with Peter Hinds (keyboards), Jean Paul Maunick (guitar) and Jeff Dunn (drums). Their later line-up featured Maunick, Hinds, Thomas Dyani-Akuru (percussion), Randy Hope-Taylor (bass), Graham Harvey (keyboards), Patrick Clahar (saxophone), Kevin Robinson (trumpet), Fayyaz Virgi (trombone), Andy Gangadeen (drums) and Maysa Leak (vocals). They won the 2001 MOBO Award for Best Jazz Act.

| 18/04/1981 | 28 | 8 | | JAZZ FUNK | Ensign ENVY 504 |
| 27/07/1991 | 44 | 2 | | INSIDE LIFE | Talkin Loud 8485461 |
| 04/07/1992 | 41 | 2 | | TRIBES, VIBES AND SCRIBES | Talkin Loud 5123632 |
| 06/11/1993 | 55 | 2 | | POSITIVITY | Talkin Loud 5182602 |
| 17/06/1995 | 11 | 4 | | 100 DEGREES AND RISING | Talkin Loud 5280002 |
| 01/06/1996 | 56 | 1 | | REMIXED | Talkin Loud 5323092 |

**INCREDIBLE STRING BAND** UK folk group formed in Glasgow in 1965 by Mike Heron (born 12/12/1942, Glasgow), Robin Williamson (born 24/11/1943, Edinburgh) and Clive Palmer, taking their name from the club where they met, 'Clive's Incredible Folk Club'. The original trio disbanded after the release of their debut album in 1966, but Heron and Williamson re-formed the following year as a duo and retained the name. By 1970 the line-up also featured Licorice McKechnie and Rose Simpson, although they departed the following year. They were replaced by Malcolm Le Maistre and Gerald Dott. The group disbanded in 1974.

| 21/10/1967 | 25 | 5 | | 5,000 SPIRITS OR THE LAYERS OF THE ONION | Elektra EUKS 257 |
| 06/04/1968 | 5 | 21 | | THE HANGMAN'S BEAUTIFUL DAUGHTER | Elektra EVKS7 258 |
| 20/07/1968 | 34 | 3 | | THE INCREDIBLE STRING BAND | Elektra EKL 254 |

| | | | | | |
|---|---|---|---|---|---|
| 24/01/1970 | 30 | 1 | | CHANGING HORSES | Elektra EKS 74057 |
| 09/05/1970 | 30 | 4 | | I LOOKED UP | Elektra 2469 002 |
| 31/10/1970 | 34 | 2 | | U | Elektra 2665 001 |
| 30/10/1971 | 46 | 1 | | LIQUID ACROBAT AS REGARDS THE AIR | Island ILPS 9172 |

**INCUBUS** US group formed in Calabasas, CA in 1991 by Brandon Boyd (vocals/percussion), Mike Einziger (guitar), Dirk Lance (bass), Jose Pasillas (drums) and DJ Chris Kilmore (turntables).

| | | | | | |
|---|---|---|---|---|---|
| 03/11/2001 | 15 | 4 | ● | MORNING VIEW | Epic 5040612 |
| 14/02/2004 | 6 | 4 | | **A CROW LEFT OF THE MURDER** | Epic 5150473 |

**INDIGO GIRLS** US duo formed by Amy Ray (born 12/4/1964, Decatur, GA, guitar/vocals) and Emily Saliers (born 22/7/1963, New Haven, CT, guitar/vocals). The pair met at school when they were aged ten and eleven respectively. Initially known as The B Band and then Saliers And Ray, they changed to The Indigo Girls whilst at university. Their first recordings were on their own J Ellis Records imprint (the name was in honour of an English teacher) and they signed with Epic in 1988. They won the 1989 Grammy Award for Best Contemporary Folk Recording for *Indigo Girls*.

| | | | | | |
|---|---|---|---|---|---|
| 11/06/1994 | 66 | 1 | | SWAMP OPHELIA | Epic 4759312 |
| 15/07/1995 | 43 | 2 | | 4.5 THE BEST OF THE INDIGO GIRLS | Epic 4804392 |

**INFA RIOT** UK vocal/instrumental group formed in 1979 by Lee Wilson (vocals), Barry Damery (guitar), Floyd Wilson (bass) and Mark Reynolds (drums). They made their first recordings in 1981 on the *Strength Through Oi* compilation and signed with Secret Records soon after. They shortened their name to The Infas in 1984 but disbanded in 1986.

| | | | | | |
|---|---|---|---|---|---|
| 07/08/1982 | 42 | 4 | | STILL OUT OF ORDER | Secret SEC 7 |

**JAMES INGRAM** US singer (born 1956, Akron, OH) who moved to Los Angeles in 1973, became the keyboard player for Leon Haywood and then formed Revelation Funk. He was signed by Quincy Jones after the latter heard a demo, and appeared on *The Dude* album. He has won two Grammy Awards: Best Rhythm & Blues Vocal Performance in 1981 for *One Hundred Ways* and Best Rhythm & Blues Vocal Performance in 1984 with Michael McDonald for *Yah Mo Be There*.

| | | | | | |
|---|---|---|---|---|---|
| 31/03/1984 | 25 | 17 | | IT'S YOUR NIGHT | Warner Brothers 9239701 |
| 30/08/1986 | 72 | 2 | | NEVER FELT SO GOOD | Qwest WX 44 |

**INME** UK rock group with Dave McPherson (guitar/vocals), Joe Morgan (bass/vocals) and Simon Taylor (drums).

| | | | | | |
|---|---|---|---|---|---|
| 08/02/2003 | 15 | 2 | | OVERGROWN EDEN | Music For Nations CDMFN275 |

**INNER CIRCLE** Jamaican group originally formed in 1968 by brothers Roger 'Fat Man' (lead guitar) and Ian 'Munty' Lewis (bass). They re-formed in 1972 with Calvin McKensie (drums), Bernard 'Touter' Harvey and Charles Farquharson (keyboards) being added to the line-up. Singer Jacob Miller joined in 1974 and they signed with Capitol in 1977, then Island in 1978. Miller was killed in a car crash on 21/2/1980. The group won the 1993 Grammy Award for Best Reggae Album for *Bad Boys*.

| | | | | | |
|---|---|---|---|---|---|
| 29/05/1993 | 44 | 2 | | BAD TO THE BONE | Magnet 9031776772 |

**INNER CITY** US dance duo Kevin Saunderson (born 9/5/1964, New York, keyboards) and Paris Grey (from Glencove, IL, vocals). Dennis White, who later enjoyed a chart career as Static Revenger, joined in 1989. Saunderson later recorded as Reese Project.

| | | | | | |
|---|---|---|---|---|---|
| 20/05/1989 | 3 | 30 | ✪ | **PARADISE** | 10 Records DIX 81 |
| 10/02/1990 | 17 | 6 | | PARADISE REMIXED | 10 Records XID 81 |
| 11/07/1992 | 52 | 1 | | PRAISE | 10 Records 4718862 |
| 15/05/1993 | 33 | 2 | | TESTAMENT '93 | 10 Records CDOVD 438 |

**INNOCENCE** UK group Mark Jolley (guitar), his sister Anna (vocals) and Brian Harris (percussion) who also recorded as Circuit, Gee Morris also being a member briefly.

| | | | | | |
|---|---|---|---|---|---|
| 10/11/1990 | 24 | 19 | ● | BELIEF | Cooltempo CTLP 20 |
| 31/10/1992 | 66 | 1 | | BUILD | Cooltempo CTCD 26 |

**INSPIRAL CARPETS** UK dance-rock group formed in Oldham, Manchester in 1987 by Clint Boon (born 28/6/1959, Oldham, organ), Stephen Holt (vocals), David Swift (bass), Graham Lambert (born 10/7/1964, Oldham, guitar) and Craig Gill (born 5/12/1971, Manchester, drums). Holt and Swift were replaced by Tom Hingley (born 9/7/1965, Oxford) and Martyn 'Bungle' Walsh (born 8/7/1968, Manchester) respectively.

| | | | | | |
|---|---|---|---|---|---|
| 05/05/1990 | 2 | 21 | | LIFE | Cow DUNG 8 |
| 04/05/1991 | 5 | 6 | ○ | **THE BEAST INSIDE** | Cow DUNG 14 |
| 17/10/1992 | 17 | 3 | | REVENGE OF THE GOLDFISH | Cow DUNG 19 |
| 19/03/1994 | 10 | 3 | | **DEVIL HOPPING** | Cow LDUNG 25CD |
| 30/09/1995 | 17 | 3 | | THE SINGLES | Cow CDMOOTEL 3 |
| 31/05/2003 | 65 | 1 | | COOL AS | Mute DUNG30CD |

**INSPIRATIONAL CHOIR** US gospel choir whose full name is The Inspirational Choir Of The Pentecostal First Born Church Of The Living God, with the label also crediting the Royal Choral Society. The choir, fronted by John Francis, also performed with Madness on their hit *Wings Of A Dove*.

| | | | | | |
|---|---|---|---|---|---|
| 18/01/1986 | 59 | 4 | | SWEET INSPIRATION | Portrait PRT 10048 |

**INSPIRATIONS** UK studio group fronted by keyboard player Neil Palmer.

| | | | | | |
|---|---|---|---|---|---|
| 29/04/1995 | 10 | 10 | | **PAN PIPE INSPIRATIONS** | Pure Music PMCD 7011 |

○ Silver disc ● Gold disc ✪ Platinum disc (additional platinum units are indicated by a figure following the symbol) ●⁹ Number of weeks album topped the UK chart

| | | | | | |
|---|---|---|---|---|---|
| 23/09/1995 | 10 | 8 | | PAN PIPE DREAMS | Pure Music PMCD 7016 |
| 11/11/1995 | 37 | 4 | | PURE EMOTIONS | Pure Music PMCD 7023 |
| 06/04/1996 | 23 | 6 | | PAN PIPE IMAGES | Telstar TCD 2819 |
| 12/10/1996 | 37 | 7 | | THE VERY BEST OF THE PAN PIPES | Telstar TCD 2845 |

### INTI ILLIMANI-GUAMARY
Chilean panpipe group formed in 1967 by Jorge Coulon, Horacio Duran, Renato Freyggang, Jose Seves, Marcelo Coulon, Max Berru, Horacio Salinas and Pedro Villagra. Their political views led to them being exiled from Chile in 1973 for fifteen years and they relocated to Rome. They came to worldwide prominence after appearing on the 1988 Amnesty International Tour with the likes of Sting, Peter Gabriel and Bruce Springsteen. Berru left the group in 1996.

| | | | | | |
|---|---|---|---|---|---|
| 17/12/1983 | 62 | 7 | | THE FLIGHT OF THE CONDOR Original soundtrack to the TV series | BBC REB 440 |

### INXS
Australian rock group formed in 1977 by Tim Farris (born 16/8/1957, Perth, guitar), Andrew Farris (born 27/3/1959, Perth, keyboards), Jon Farris (born 10/8/1961, Perth, drums/vocals), Michael Hutchence (born 22/1/1962, Sydney, vocals), Kirk Pengilly (born 4/7/1958, Sydney, guitar/saxophone/vocals) and Garry Beers (born 22/6/1957, Sydney, bass/vocals) as the Farris Brothers. The name INXS came at the suggestion of Midnight Oil manager Garry Morris in 1979. After their debut recording on Deluxe, from 1983 they concentrated on the international market, signing with Atlantic for the US with a top 30 hit in 1983, and making their UK breakthrough in 1985. Hutchence was named Best International Male at the 1991 BRIT Awards, when the band was also named Best International Group. Hutchence – who appeared in the 1987 film *Dogs In Space* – was found hanged in a Sydney hotel room on 22/11/1997. Despite a suicide verdict there is considerable speculation that he died after an autoerotic sex act went wrong. At the time he had been working on a solo album with producer Andy Gill. In June 2004 the group announced that they were to hold a worldwide reality TV competition to find a new lead singer.

| | | | | | |
|---|---|---|---|---|---|
| 08/02/1986 | 48 | 15 | | LISTEN LIKE THIEVES | Mercury MERH 82 |
| 28/11/1987 | 9 | 103 | ✪³ | KICK | Mercury MERH 114 |
| 06/10/1990 | 2 | 44 | ✪ | X | Mercury 8466681 |
| 16/11/1991 | 8 | 9 | | LIVE BABY LIVE | Mercury 5105801 |
| 15/08/1992 | ❶¹ | 33 | ● | WELCOME TO WHEREVER YOU ARE | Mercury 5125072 |
| 13/11/1993 | 3 | 8 | ● | FULL MOON, DIRTY HEARTS | Mercury 5186382 |
| 12/11/1994 | 3 | 22 | ✪ | INXS – THE GREATEST HITS ◇² | Mercury 5262302 |
| 19/04/1997 | 16 | 3 | | ELEGANTLY WASTED | Mercury 5346132 |
| 26/10/2002 | 15 | 3 | | DEFINITIVE | Mercury 0633562 |

### IQ
UK group formed in Southampton in 1981 by Peter Nicholls (vocals), Mike Holmes (guitar), Martin Orford (keyboards), Tim Esau (bass) and Mark Rideout (drums).

| | | | | | |
|---|---|---|---|---|---|
| 22/06/1985 | 72 | 1 | | THE WAKE | Sahara SAH 136 |

### IRON MAIDEN
UK heavy metal group (named after a medieval instrument of torture) formed in 1976 by Steve Harris (born 12/3/1957, Leytonstone, London, bass), Dave Murray (born 23/12/1958, London, guitar), Paul Di'anno (vocals) and Doug Sampson (drums). Tony Parsons joined in November 1979 but was replaced in January 1980 by Dennis Stratton (born 9/11/1954, London), at the same time as the drummer's stool was vacated by Sampson and taken by Clive Burr (born 8/3/1958). Before the year was out Stratton had left, being replaced by Adrian Smith (born 27/2/1957, London). Di'anno left in 1981 and was replaced by Bruce Dickinson (born 7/8/1958, Worksop, Nottinghamshire), after which they broke big on both sides of the Atlantic. Gurr left in 1983 and was replaced by Nicko McBrain (born 5/6/1954, London). Smith left in 1990 and was replaced by Janick Gers (born 27/1/1957, Hartlepool, Cleveland).

| | | | | | |
|---|---|---|---|---|---|
| 26/04/1980 | 4 | 15 | ✪ | IRON MAIDEN | EMI EMC 3330 |
| 28/02/1981 | 12 | 8 | ● | KILLERS | EMI EMC 3357 |
| 10/04/1982 | ❶² | 31 | ● | THE NUMBER OF THE BEAST | EMI EMC 3400 |
| 28/05/1983 | 3 | 18 | ✪ | PIECE OF MIND | EMI EMA 800 |
| 15/09/1984 | 2 | 13 | ● | POWERSLAVE | EMI POWER 1 |
| 15/06/1985 | 71 | 2 | | IRON MAIDEN | Fame FA 4131211 |
| 26/10/1985 | 2 | 14 | ● | LIVE AFTER DEATH | EMI RIP 1 |
| 11/10/1986 | 3 | 11 | ● | SOMEWHERE IN TIME | EMI EMC 3512 |
| 20/06/1987 | 98 | 1 | | THE NUMBER OF THE BEAST | Fame FA 3178 |
| 23/04/1988 | ❶¹ | 18 | ● | SEVENTH SON OF A SEVENTH SON | EMI EMD 1006 |
| 24/02/1990 | 10 | 4 | | RUNNING/SANCTUARY | EMI IRN 1 |
| 03/03/1990 | 10 | 3 | | WOMEN IN UNIFORM/TWILIGHT ZONE | EMI IRN 2 |
| 10/03/1990 | 5 | 3 | | PURGATORY/MAIDEN JAPAN | EMI IRN 3 |
| 17/03/1990 | 3 | 2 | | RUN TO THE HILLS/THE NUMBER OF THE BEAST | EMI IRN 4 |
| 24/03/1990 | 7 | 2 | | FLIGHT OF ICARUS/THE TROOPER | EMI IRN 5 |
| 31/03/1990 | 11 | 2 | | 2 MINUTES TO MIDNIGHT/ACES HIGH | EMI IRN 6 |
| 07/04/1990 | 9 | 2 | | RUNNING FREE (LIVE)/RUN TO THE HILLS (LIVE) | EMI IRN 7 |
| 14/04/1990 | 9 | 2 | | WASTED YEARS/STRANGER IN A STRANGE LAND | EMI IRN 8 |
| 21/04/1990 | 10 | 3 | | CAN I PLAY WITH MADNESS/THE EVIL THAT MEN DO | EMI IRN 9 |
| 28/04/1990 | 11 | 2 | | THE CLAIRVOYANT/INFINITE DREAMS (LIVE) This and the above nine entries are double 12-inch singles that were ineligible for the singles chart | EMI IRN 10 |
| 13/10/1990 | 2 | 14 | ● | NO PRAYER FOR THE DYING | EMI EMD 1017 |

| | | | | ALBUM TITLE | LABEL & NUMBER |
|---|---|---|---|---|---|
| 23/05/1992 | ❶¹ | 5 | ● | **FEAR OF THE DARK** | EMI CDEMD 1032 |
| 03/04/1993 | 3 | 4 | | **A REAL LIVE ONE** | EMI CDEMD 1042 |
| 30/10/1993 | 12 | 3 | | A REAL DEAD ONE | EMI CDEMD 1048 |
| 20/11/1993 | 23 | 1 | | LIVE AT DONNINGTON | EMI CDDON 1 |
| 14/10/1995 | 8 | 4 | | **THE X FACTOR** | EMI CDEMD 1087 |
| 05/10/1996 | 16 | 5 | ○ | THE BEST OF THE BEAST | EMI CDEMDX 1097 |
| 04/04/1998 | 16 | 2 | | VIRTUAL XI | EMI 4939152 |
| 10/06/2000 | 7 | 4 | ○ | **BRAVE NEW WORLD** | EMI 5266052 |
| 06/04/2002 | 15 | 3 | | ROCK IN RIO | EMI 5386430 |
| 16/11/2002 | 57 | 1 | ○ | EDWARD THE GREAT – THE GREATEST HITS | EMI 05431032 |
| 20/09/2003 | 2 | 5 | | **DANCE OF DEATH** | EMI 5923402 |

**GREGORY ISAACS** Jamaican reggae singer (born 1951, Kingston) who became known through his recordings for Success Records (owned by Rupie Edwards) in the early 1970s. He formed his own African Museum label with Errol Dunkley in 1973. A series of tours made him a star in both the UK and US and he signed with Virgin's Front Line label in 1980, switching to Pre the following year.

| | | | | | |
|---|---|---|---|---|---|
| 12/09/1981 | 93 | 1 | | MORE GREGORY | Pre PREX 9 |
| 04/09/1982 | 32 | 5 | | NIGHT NURSE | Island ILPS 9721 |

**CHRIS ISAAK** US singer (born 26/6/1956, Stockton, CA) who went to college in Japan and made cameo appearances in the films *Married To The Mob* (1988) and *Silence Of The Lambs* (1991).

| | | | | | |
|---|---|---|---|---|---|
| 26/01/1991 | 3 | 30 | ✪ | **WICKED GAME** | Reprise WX 406 |
| 24/04/1993 | 12 | 5 | | SAN FRANCISCO DAYS | Reprise 9362451162 |
| 03/06/1995 | 27 | 3 | | FOREVER BLUE | Reprise 9362458452 |

**ISLEY BROTHERS** US R&B vocal group formed as a quartet in Cincinnati, OH in 1955 by brothers Rudolph (born 1/4/1939, Cincinnati), Ronald (born 21/5/1941, Cincinnati), O'Kelly (born 25/12/1937, Cincinnati) and Vernon Isley. Vernon was killed in a bicycle accident but they re-formed as a trio. The group moved to New York and recorded for Teenage Records and other labels before signing to RCA in 1959 and working with Hugo & Luigi on *Shout*, which sold a million copies. After recording for Atlantic, Bang and United Artists they set up the T-Neck label (named after Teaneck, the area where they lived) and recorded *Testify* with Jimi Hendrix. They joined Motown in 1965, enjoying considerable success, especially in the UK, before leaving the label in 1969 and reviving T-Neck. The group was extended by younger brothers Marvin (born 18/8/1953, bass/percussion) and Ernie (born 7/3/1952, guitar/drums), and cousin Chris Jasper (keyboards). In 1984 the younger brothers and Jasper left to form Isley Jasper Isley (signed to Epic), the older brothers retaining the Isley Brothers moniker. Jasper recorded solo in 1988. O'Kelly died from a heart attack on 31/3/1986. Ernie, Marvin and Ronald recorded together again in 1992, the year the group were inducted into the Rock & Roll Hall of Fame. The group won the 1969 Grammy Award for Best Rhythm & Blues Vocal Performance by a Group for *It's Your Thing*.

| | | | | | |
|---|---|---|---|---|---|
| 14/12/1968 | 23 | 6 | | THIS OLD HEART OF MINE | Tamla Motown STML 11034 |
| 14/08/1976 | 50 | 5 | | HARVEST FOR THE WORLD | Epic EPC 81268 |
| 14/05/1977 | 46 | 2 | | GO FOR YOUR GUNS | Epic EPC 86027 |
| 24/06/1978 | 50 | 1 | | SHOWDOWN | Epic EPC 86039 |
| 05/03/1988 | 41 | 10 | | GREATEST HITS | Telstar STAR 2306 |

**IT BITES** UK rock group formed in Cumbria by Francis Dunnery (guitar/vocals), John Beck (keyboards), Dick Nolan (bass) and Bob Dalton (drums).

| | | | | | |
|---|---|---|---|---|---|
| 06/09/1986 | 35 | 5 | | THE BIG LAD IN THE WINDMILL | Virgin V 2378 |
| 02/04/1988 | 43 | 3 | | ONCE AROUND THE WORLD | Virgin V 2456 |
| 24/06/1989 | 40 | 3 | | EAT ME IN ST LOUIS | Virgin V 2591 |
| 31/08/1991 | 59 | 1 | | THANK YOU AND GOODNIGHT | Virgin VGD 24233 |

**IT'S A BEAUTIFUL DAY** US group formed in San Francisco, CA by David LaFlamme (violin), Patti Santos (vocals), Hal Wagenet (guitar), Linda LaFlamme (keyboards), Mitchell Holman (bass) and Val Fluentes (drums), who took their name to reflect the weather. Santos was killed in a car crash on 14/12/1989.

| | | | | | |
|---|---|---|---|---|---|
| 23/05/1970 | 58 | 1 | | IT'S A BEAUTIFUL DAY | CBS 63722 |
| 18/07/1970 | 45 | 2 | | MARRYING MAIDEN | CBS 66236 |

**IT'S IMMATERIAL** UK duo formed in Liverpool by John Campbell and Jarvis Whitehead.

| | | | | | |
|---|---|---|---|---|---|
| 27/09/1986 | 62 | 3 | | LIFE'S HARD AND THEN YOU DIE | Siren SIRENLP 4 |

# J

**JA RULE** US rapper Jeffrey Atkins (born 29/2/1977, New York City). Also in The Murderers with Black Child, Tah Murdah and Vita. He won the 2002 MOBO Award for Best Hip Hop Act.

| | | | | |
|---|---|---|---|---|
| 27/10/2001 | 3 | 50 | ✪ | PAIN IS LOVE ▲² .......................................Def Jam 5864372 |
| 30/11/2002 | 14 | 13 | ● | THE LAST TEMPTATION .................................Def Jam 0635432 |
| 15/11/2003 | 51 | 2 | | BLOOD IN MY EYE .....................................Def Jam 9861329 |

**FREDDIE JACKSON** US singer (born 2/10/1956, Harlem, NYC); he began as a backing singer for Melba Moore, Evelyn King and Angela Bofill before singing lead with Mystic Merlin. After one album he went solo, later appearing in the film *Def By Temptation*.

| | | | | |
|---|---|---|---|---|
| 18/05/1985 | 27 | 22 | ○ | ROCK ME TONIGHT ................................Capitol EJ 2403161 |
| 08/11/1986 | 30 | 15 | | JUST LIKE THE FIRST TIME ...........................Capitol EST 2023 |
| 30/07/1988 | 24 | 9 | | DON'T LET LOVE SLIP AWAY .........................Capitol EST 2067 |
| 17/11/1990 | 48 | 2 | | DO ME AGAIN ....................................Capitol EST 2134 |

**JANET JACKSON** US singer (born 16/5/1966, Gary, IN) who is the youngest of the nine Jackson children. She appeared with her brothers at seven, but started her TV career as an actress, appearing in *Good Times*, *Diff'rent Strokes* and *Fame*. She signed with A&M in 1982. She was briefly married to James DeBarge in 1984. With her *Rhythm Nation 1814* album in 1991, she was the first artist to have seven Top 5 singles from one album in the USA. She has won five Grammy Awards: Best Music Video Long Form in 1989 for *Rhythm Nation*, Best Rhythm & Blues Song in 1993 with James Harris III and Terry Lewis for *That's The Way Love Goes*, Best Music Video Short Form in 1995 with Michael Jackson for *Scream*, Best Music Video Short Form in 1997 for *Got 'Till It's Gone* and Best Dance Recording in 2001 for *All For You*. She was named Best Female at the 1997 MTV Europe Music Awards and appeared in the 2000 film *Nutty Professor II: The Klumps*. She has a star on the Hollywood Walk of Fame.

| | | | | |
|---|---|---|---|---|
| 05/04/1986 | 8 | 72 | ✪ | **CONTROL ▲²** .........................................A&M AMA 5106 |
| 14/11/1987 | 20 | 14 | ● | CONTROL – THE REMIXES ...........................Breakout MIXLP 1 |
| 30/09/1989 | 4 | 43 | ✪ | **RHYTHM NATION 1814 ▲⁴** ...........................A&M AMA 3920 |
| 29/05/1993 | ❶² | 57 | ✪² | **JANET ▲⁶** ..........................................Virgin CDV 2720 |
| 14/10/1995 | 2 | 21 | ✪² | **DESIGN OF A DECADE 1986–1996** ◇ ................A&M 5404222 |
| 18/10/1997 | 6 | 43 | ✪ | **THE VELVET ROPE** ◇ ▲¹ ...........................Virgin CDV 2860 |
| 05/05/2001 | 2 | 18 | ● | **ALL FOR YOU ▲¹** ...................................Virgin CDVX 2950 |
| 10/04/2004 | 32 | 2 | ○ | DAMITA JO .......................................Virgin CDVUS 251 |

**JERMAINE JACKSON** US singer (born 11/12/1954, Gary, IN); he is the fourth of nine children and was a member of the Jackson 5 from their formation in 1963 until they left Motown for Epic in 1975 (replaced by Randy). Married to Motown founder Berry Gordy's daughter Hazel in 1973 (divorced 1987), he stayed with the company, going solo. Moving to Arista in 1984, production credits included a track on Whitney Houston's debut album. Rejoining brothers in 1984 for *Victory*, he also made their biographical TV mini series.

| | | | |
|---|---|---|---|
| 31/05/1980 | 22 | 6 | LET'S GET SERIOUS ...............................Motown STML 12127 |
| 12/05/1984 | 57 | 6 | DYNAMITE .........................................Arista 206 317 |

**JOE JACKSON** UK singer (born 11/8/1954, Burton-on-Trent) who played with Johnny Dankworth and the National Youth Jazz Orchestra before joining Arms & Legs. He left in 1977 to become Musical Director to Coffee & Cream, recording his solo debut in 1978. He relocated to New York in 1982 and won the 2000 Grammy Award for Best Pop Instrumental Album for *Symphony No.1*.

| | | | | |
|---|---|---|---|---|
| 17/03/1979 | 40 | 11 | ○ | LOOK SHARP .....................................A&M AMLH 64743 |
| 13/10/1979 | 12 | 16 | ● | I'M THE MAN .....................................A&M AMLH 64794 |
| 18/10/1980 | 42 | 3 | | BEAT CRAZY ......................................A&M AMLH 64837 |
| 04/07/1981 | 14 | 14 | | JUMPIN' JIVE **JOE JACKSON'S JUMPIN' JIVE** ..........A&M AMLH 68530 |
| 03/07/1982 | 3 | 27 | ● | **NIGHT AND DAY** ................................A&M AMLH 64906 |
| 07/04/1984 | 14 | 14 | ○ | BODY AND SOUL ..................................A&M AMLX 65000 |

▲⁹ Number of weeks album topped the US chart  ◆¹² RIAA Diamond Awards  ◇³ IFPI Platinum Europe Awards

| 05/04/1986 | 41 | 5 | | BIG WORLD | A&M JWA 3 |
|---|---|---|---|---|---|
| 07/05/1988 | 66 | 2 | | LIVE 1980–1986 | A&M AMA 6706 |
| 29/04/1989 | 36 | 3 | | BLAZE OF GLORY | A&M AMA 5249 |
| 15/09/1990 | 7 | 9 | ● | **STEPPING OUT – THE VERY BEST OF JOE JACKSON** | A&M 3970521 |
| 11/05/1991 | 41 | 2 | | LAUGHTER AND LUST | Virgin America VUSLP 34 |

**MICHAEL JACKSON** US singer (born 29/8/1958, Gary, IN); he is the seventh of nine children and was lead singer with the Jackson 5 at the age of five. A parallel solo career began at Motown in 1971, and he later appeared as the Scarecrow in *The Wiz*. Relaunching himself in 1979, he became one of the biggest acts in the world – 1982's *Thriller* album sold over 50 million worldwide. Filming a Pepsi commercial in January 1984, his hair was set alight by a spark from a pyrotechnic leading to second degree burns of the skull; he donated the $1.5 million compensation to the Brotman Memorial Hospital where he had been treated. In 1985 he bought ATV publishing, controlling more than 250 Lennon and McCartney songs. He married Elvis Presley's daughter Lisa Marie in 1994, divorced in 1996, and married Debbie Rowe in November 1996, with whom he had two children (Prince Michael Jr and Paris Michael Katherine) – they filed for divorce in October 1999. He also had a second son by an un-named woman. Michael has won six BRIT Awards including Best International Male in 1984, 1988 and 1989, and an Artist of a Generation Award in 1996, the year he performed at the ceremony. He launched the MJJ record label with acts such as Brownstone and 3T. In 1984 he won eight Grammy Awards, the most by one artist in a single year until equalled by Carlos Santana in 2000. He signed the biggest ever recording deal, worth a reported $1 billion, with Sony in 1991. Accused of child molestation, he settled out of court in 1994. Thirteen Grammies include: Best Rhythm & Blues Vocal Performance in 1979 for *Don't Stop Till You Get Enough*; Best Rhythm & Blues Vocal Performance and Best Rhythm & Blues Song in 1983 for *Billie Jean*; Record of the Year and Best Rock Vocal Performance in 1983 for *Beat It*; Best Pop Vocal Performance in 1983 for *Thriller*; Best Recording for Children in 1983 for *E.T. The Extra-Terrestrial*; Producer of the Year in 1983; Best Video Album in 1984 for *Making Michael Jackson's 'Thriller'*; Song of the Year in 1985 with Lionel Richie for *We Are The World;* and Best Music Video Short Form in 1989 for *Leave Me Alone*. He was inducted into the Rock & Roll Hall of Fame in 2001. He has two stars on the Hollywood Walk of Fame for his contribution to recording and radio. In 2003 there were further child molestation charges and he was subsequently charged.

| 03/06/1972 | 37 | 5 | | GOT TO BE THERE | Tamla Motown STML 11205 |
|---|---|---|---|---|---|
| 13/01/1973 | 17 | 7 | ○ | BEN | Tamla Motown STML 11220 |
| 29/09/1979 | 5 | 187 | ✪6 | **OFF THE WALL** The album changed its catalogue number to 4500861 during its chart run | Epic EPC 84368 |
| 04/07/1981 | 11 | 18 | ○ | BEST OF MICHAEL JACKSON | Motown STMR 9009 |
| 18/07/1981 | 29 | 8 | | ONE DAY IN YOUR LIFE | Motown STML 12158 |
| 11/12/1982 | ❶8 | 196 | ✪11 | **THRILLER** ▲37 ◆26 1983 Grammy Award for Album of the Year and the 1984 BRIT Award for Best Album. The album is the best-selling album of all time, with worldwide sales in excess of 50 million copies | Epic EPC 85930 |
| 12/02/1983 | 82 | 2 | | E.T. THE EXTRA TERRESTRIAL | MCA 7000 |
| 09/07/1983 | ❶3 | 58 | ✪ | **18 GREATEST HITS** MICHAEL JACKSON PLUS THE JACKSON FIVE | Telstar STAR 2232 |
| 03/12/1983 | 66 | 3 | | MICHAEL JACKSON 9 SINGLE PACK | Epic MJ 1 |
| 09/06/1984 | 9 | 14 | ● | **FAREWELL MY SUMMER LOVE** | Motown ZL 72227 |
| 15/11/1986 | 21 | 10 | | DIANA ROSS. MICHAEL JACKSON. GLADYS KNIGHT. STEVIE WONDER. THEIR VERY BEST BACK TO BACK **DIANA ROSS/MICHAEL JACKSON/GLADYS KNIGHT/STEVIE WONDER** | PrioriTyV PTVR 2 |
| 12/09/1987 | ❶5 | 125 | ✪13 | **BAD** ▲6 | Epic EPC 4502901 |
| 31/10/1987 | 12 | 24 | ✪ | LOVE SONGS **DIANA ROSS AND MICHAEL JACKSON** When multi-artist packages were excluded from the main chart, this album featured on the compilation chart | Telstar STAR 2298 |
| 26/12/1987 | 27 | 25 | ✪ | THE MICHAEL JACKSON MIX | Stylus SMR 745 |
| 30/07/1988 | 91 | 1 | | SOUVENIR SINGLES PACK | Epic MJ 5 |
| 30/11/1991 | ❶1 | 96 | ✪6 | **DANGEROUS** ▲4 | Epic 4658021 |
| 29/02/1992 | 53 | 2 | | MOTOWN'S GREATEST HITS | Motown 5300142 |
| 15/08/1992 | 32 | 3 | | TOUR SOUVENIR PACK | Epic MJ 4 |
| 24/06/1995 | ❶1 | 78 | ✪4 | **HISTORY – PAST PRESENT AND FUTURE BOOK 1** ◇6 ▲2 | Epic 4747092 |
| 24/05/1997 | ❶2 | 16 | ● | **BLOOD ON THE FLOOR – HISTORY IN THE MIX** ◇2 | Epic 4875002 |
| 19/07/1997 | 5 | 12 | ● | **THE BEST OF MICHAEL JACKSON AND THE JACKSON FIVE** MICHAEL JACKSON AND THE JACKSON FIVE | Polygram TV 5308042 |
| 10/11/2001 | ❶1 | 12 | ✪ | **INVINCIBLE** ◇2 ▲1 | Epic 4951782 |
| 24/11/2001 | 15 | 16 | | GREATEST HITS – HISTORY VOLUME 1 Single CD version of Epic 4747092 | Epic 5018692 |
| 29/11/2003 | ❶1 | 29 | ✪4 | **NUMBER ONES** ◇ | Epic 5138002 |

**MILLIE JACKSON** US R&B singer (born 15/7/1944, Thompson, GA); she was a model in New Jersey before turning to singing in 1964. Her 1970 debut disc was for Spring, with whom she had over 30 R&B hits, eight also making the pop charts. Best known for her *Caught Up* and *Still Caught Up* albums that explored extra-marital affairs, she later recorded country songs, and with Isaac Hayes.

| 18/02/1984 | 59 | 5 | | E.S.P | Sire 250382 |
|---|---|---|---|---|---|
| 06/04/1985 | 81 | 2 | | LIVE AND UNCENSORED | Important TADLP 001 |

## JACKSON 5/JACKSONS
US group formed in Gary, IN as a trio in 1963 by Jackie (born Sigmund, 4/5/1951, Gary), Tito (born Toriano, 15/10/1953, Gary) and Jermaine Jackson (born 11/12/1954, Gary) as the Jackson Family. Younger brothers Marlon (born 12/3/1957, Gary) and Michael (born 29/8/1958, Gary) joined soon after and they began working as the Jackson 5. They supported Gladys Knight & The Pips in 1967, who recommended them to Motown's Berry Gordy, although their debut record was on Steeltown in 1968. They signed with Motown in 1968, initially a one-year deal. They left for Epic in 1975, Motown retaining both the name Jackson 5 and Jermaine (replaced by youngest brother Randy, born 29/10/1961, Gary). Three sisters (Janet, LaToya and Rebbie) also backed the group, and all recorded solo. Jermaine returned in 1984 for the *Victory* album and tour. Marlon left in 1987 to go solo, with Jackie, Tito, Jermaine and Randy in the line-up since 1989. They were inducted into the Rock & Roll Hall of Fame in 1997 and have a star on the Hollywood Walk of Fame.

| 21/03/1970 | 16 | 4 | | DIANA ROSS PRESENTS THE JACKSON FIVE | Tamla Motown STML 11142 |
|------------|----|----|----|------|------|
| 15/08/1970 | 22 | 6 | | ABC | Tamla Motown STML 11156 |
| 07/10/1972 | 26 | 14 | O | GREATEST HITS | Tamla Motown STML 11212 |
| 18/11/1972 | 16 | 8 | O | LOOKIN' THROUGH THE WINDOWS This and the above three hits credited to **JACKSON 5** | Tamla Motown STML 11214 |
| 16/07/1977 | 54 | 1 | | THE JACKSONS | Epic EPC 86009 |
| 03/12/1977 | 45 | 1 | | GOIN' PLACES | Epic EPC 86035 |
| 05/05/1979 | 33 | 7 | | DESTINY | Epic EPC 83200 |
| 11/10/1980 | 13 | 16 | ● | TRIUMPH | Epic EPC 86112 |
| 12/12/1981 | 53 | 9 | | THE JACKSONS LIVE | Epic EPC 88562 |
| 09/07/1983 | ❶³ | 58 | ✪ | **18 GREATEST HITS MICHAEL JACKSON PLUS THE JACKSON FIVE** | Telstar STAR 2232 |
| 21/07/1984 | 3 | 13 | | **VICTORY** | Epic EPC 86303 |
| 01/07/1989 | 39 | 3 | | 2300 JACKSON ST | Epic 4633521 |
| 19/07/1997 | 5 | 12 | ● | **THE BEST OF MICHAEL JACKSON AND THE JACKSON FIVE MICHAEL JACKSON AND THE JACKSON FIVE** | Polygram TV 5308042 |

## JADE
US female vocal trio formed in Los Angeles, CA by Joi Marshall, Tonya Kelly and Di Reed.

| 29/05/1993 | 43 | 3 | | JADE TO THE MAX | Giant 74321148002 |
|------------|----|----|----|------|------|

## MICK JAGGER
UK singer (born 26/7/1943, Dartford); he was lead singer with The Rolling Stones since they began in 1962. He appeared in the film *Ned Kelly* in 1970 (during which he was accidentally shot!) and married Bianca Rose Perez Moreno de Macias in 1971 and model Jerry Hall in 1990 (although in 1999 they were in divorce talks, Jagger claiming their Hindu ceremony was not a recognised marriage). Featured on the cover of *Rolling Stone* sixteen times, more than any other artist, he was knighted in the 2002 Queen's Birthday Honours List.

| 16/03/1985 | 6 | 11 | O | **SHE'S THE BOSS** | CBS 86310 |
|------------|----|----|----|------|------|
| 26/09/1987 | 26 | 5 | | PRIMITIVE COOL | CBS 4601231 |
| 20/02/1993 | 12 | 4 | | WANDERING SPIRIT | Atlantic 7567824362 |
| 01/12/2001 | 44 | 4 | O | GODDESS IN THE DOORWAY | Virgin CDVUS 214 |

## JAHEIM
US hip hop artist/rapper (born Jaheim Hoagland, 28/5/1978, New Brunswick, NJ). His grandfather Victor Hoagland was once in The Drifters. Jaheim won the Apollo Theater Talent Contest three times when he was just fifteen.

| 07/04/2001 | 50 | 1 | | GHETTO LOVE | WEA 9362474522 |
|------------|----|----|----|------|------|

## JAIMESON
UK keyboard player (born Jamie Williams, 1975, London) who also records as Jameson, Kinetic Rock Steady, DJ Infinity and 2 Deep.

| 21/02/2004 | 42 | 2 | | THINK ON YOUR FEET | V2/J-Did JAD1021722 |
|------------|----|----|----|------|------|

## JAKATTA
UK producer Dave Lee. He also records as Joey Negro, Li Kwan, Akubu, Hed Boys (with Andrew Livingstone), Z Factor and Raven Maize.

| 26/10/2002 | 12 | 4 | O | VISIONS | Rulin' RULINCD 01 |
|------------|----|----|----|------|------|

## JAM
UK group formed in Woking in 1976 by Paul Weller (born John Weller, 25/5/1958, Woking, guitar/vocals), Steve Brookes (guitar), Bruce Foxton (born 1/9/1955, Woking, bass) and Rick Buckler (born Paul Richard Buckler, 6/12/1955, Woking, drums). Brookes left before the year's end, the group signing with Polydor in 1977 for a £6,000 advance. At the forefront of the UK mod revival, they were unable to break in the USA. They disbanded in 1982, Weller launching Style Council and then going solo, Foxton recording solo and joining the re-formed Stiff Little Fingers, and Buckler joining Time UK.

| 28/05/1977 | 20 | 18 | | IN THE CITY | Polydor 2383 447 |
|------------|----|----|----|------|------|
| 26/11/1977 | 22 | 5 | O | THIS IS THE MODERN WORLD | Polydor 2383 475 |
| 11/11/1978 | 6 | 17 | ● | **ALL MOD CONS** | Polydor POLD 5008 |
| 24/11/1979 | 4 | 19 | ● | **SETTING SONS** | Polydor POLD 5028 |
| 06/12/1980 | 2 | 19 | ● | **SOUND EFFECTS** | Polydor POLD 5035 |
| 20/03/1982 | ❶¹ | 24 | ● | **THE GIFT** | Polydor POLD 5055 |
| 18/12/1982 | 2 | 15 | ● | **DIG THE NEW BREED** | Polydor POLD 5075 |
| 27/08/1983 | 100 | 1 | | IN THE CITY (Re-issue) | Polydor SPELP 27 |

▲⁹ Number of weeks album topped the US chart   ◆¹² RIAA Diamond Awards   ◇³ IFPI Platinum Europe Awards

| | DATE | POS | WKS | BPI | ALBUM TITLE | LABEL & NUMBER |
|---|---|---|---|---|---|---|
| | 22/10/1983 | 2 | 30 | ✪ | **SNAP** | Polydor SNAP 1 |
| | 13/07/1991 | 2 | 21 | ● | **GREATEST HITS** | Polydor 8495541 |
| | 18/04/1992 | 15 | 4 | | EXTRAS | Polydor 5131772 |
| | 06/11/1993 | 28 | 2 | | LIVE JAM | Polydor 5196672 |
| | 27/07/1996 | 58 | 1 | | THE JAM COLLECTION | Polydor 5314932 |
| | 07/06/1997 | 8 | 4 | | **DIRECTION REACTION CREATION** | Polydor 5371432 |
| | 25/10/1997 | 9 | 10 | | **THE VERY BEST OF THE JAM** | Polydor 5374232 |
| | 18/05/2002 | 3 | 7 | ● | **THE SOUND OF** | Polydor 5897812 |
| | 15/06/2002 | 33 | 2 | | AT THE BBC | Polydor 5896902 |

**JAM AND SPOON FEATURING PLAVKA** German instrumental/production duo Jam El Mar (Rolf Ellmer) and DJ Mark Spoon (Markus Loeffel) with Plavka singing lead. Jam and Spoon also recorded as Tokyo Ghetto Pussy and later as Storm.

| | DATE | POS | WKS | BPI | ALBUM TITLE | LABEL & NUMBER |
|---|---|---|---|---|---|---|
| | 19/02/1994 | 71 | 1 | | TRIPTOMATIC FAIRYTALES | Epic 4749282 |

**JAMELIA** UK singer (born Jamelia Davis, 1/10/1981, Birmimgham), she signed with Parlophone at the age of fifteen.

| | DATE | POS | WKS | BPI | ALBUM TITLE | LABEL & NUMBER |
|---|---|---|---|---|---|---|
| | 08/07/2000 | 39 | 2 | | DRAMA | Parlophone Rhythm Series 5272272 |
| | 11/10/2003 | 4 | 16 | ● | **THANK YOU** | Parlophone 5837772 |

**JAMES** UK group formed in Manchester in 1983 by Tim Booth (born 4/2/1960, lead vocals), Jim Glennie (born 10/10/1963, guitar), Danny Ryan (vocals), James Gott (guitar) and Gavin Whelan (drums). Initially signed with Factory, they joined Sire in 1986. Whelan left in 1990, replaced by Dave Boynton-Power (born 29/1/1961) and added Saul Davies (born 28/6/1965, guitar/violin), Andy Diagram (trumpet) and Mark Hunter (born 5/11/1968, keyboards) shortly before joining Fontana. Larry Gott (born 24/7/1957) joined in 1991.

| | DATE | POS | WKS | BPI | ALBUM TITLE | LABEL & NUMBER |
|---|---|---|---|---|---|---|
| | 02/08/1986 | 68 | 2 | | STUTTER | Blanco Y Negro JIMLP 1 |
| | 08/10/1988 | 90 | 1 | | STRIP MINE | Sire JIMLP 2 |
| | 16/06/1990 | 2 | 34 | ● | **GOLD MOTHER** | Fontana 8485951 |
| | 29/02/1992 | 2 | 14 | ● | **SEVEN** | Fontana 5109322 |
| | 09/10/1993 | 3 | 16 | ○ | **LAID** | Fontana 5149432 |
| | 24/09/1994 | 11 | 2 | | WAH WAH **JAMES AND BRIAN ENO** | Fontana 5228272 |
| | 08/03/1997 | 9 | 19 | ● | **WHIPLASH** | Fontana 5343542 |
| | 04/04/1998 | ❶¹ | 53 | ✪ | **THE BEST OF JAMES** | Fontana 5368982 |
| | 23/10/1999 | 2 | 11 | | **MILLIONAIRES** | Mercury 5467892 |
| | 14/07/2001 | 11 | 3 | ○ | PLEASED TO MEET YOU | Mercury 5861462 |

**RICK JAMES** US R&B singer (born James Ambrose Johnson, 1/2/1948, Buffalo, NY); he formed the Mynah Birds in 1965 with Neil Young, Bruce Palmer and Goldie McJohn and signed with Motown, although nothing was released, partly due to his arrest for draft evasion! Moving to London in 1970 he formed Main Line, before returning to the States and signing with Motown a second time, this time solo. He also formed The Stony City Band and the Mary Jane Girls, and produced such acts as Teena Marie and Eddie Murphy. Rick James died on 6/8/2004.

| | DATE | POS | WKS | BPI | ALBUM TITLE | LABEL & NUMBER |
|---|---|---|---|---|---|---|
| | 24/07/1982 | 93 | 2 | | THROWIN' DOWN | Motown STML 12167 |

**WENDY JAMES** UK singer (born 21/6/1966, London); she was formerly lead vocalist with Transvision Vamp.

| | DATE | POS | WKS | BPI | ALBUM TITLE | LABEL & NUMBER |
|---|---|---|---|---|---|---|
| | 20/03/1993 | 43 | 1 | | NOW AIN'T THE TIME FOR YOUR TEARS | MCA MCD 10800 |

**JAMIROQUAI** UK jazz-funk group formed in London in 1992 by Jason 'Jay' Kay (born 30/12/1969, Manchester, vocals), Simon Katz (born 16/5/1971, Nottingham, guitar), Toby Smith (born 29/10/1970, London, keyboards), Stuart Zender (born 18/3/1974, Philadelphia, PA, bass), Derrick McKenzie (born 27/3/1962, London, drums) and Wallace Buchanan (born 27/11/1965, London, didgeridoo). After one single for Acid Jazz they signed with Sony. Zender left in 1998. Kay was engaged for a time to TV presenter Denise Van Outen, and was in the *It's Only Rock 'N' Roll* project for the Children's Promise charity. The group won the 1997 Grammy Award for Best Pop Performance by a Group for *Virtual Insanity*.

| | DATE | POS | WKS | BPI | ALBUM TITLE | LABEL & NUMBER |
|---|---|---|---|---|---|---|
| | 26/06/1993 | ❶³ | 32 | ✪ | **EMERGENCY ON PLANET EARTH** | Sony S2 4740692 |
| | 29/10/1994 | 2 | 29 | ✪ | **THE RETURN OF THE SPACE COWBOY** | Sony S2 4778132 |
| | 21/09/1996 | 2 | 74 | ✪³ | **TRAVELLING WITHOUT MOVING** ◇ 1997 MOBO Award for Best Album | Sony S2 4839992 |
| | 26/06/1999 | ❶¹ | 29 | ✪ | **SYNKRONIZED** ◇ | Sony S2 4945172 |
| | 15/09/2001 | ❶² | 51 | ✪² | **A FUNK ODYSSEY** ◇ | Sony S2 5040692 |

**JAN AND DEAN** US duo Jan Berry (born 3/4/1941, Los Angeles, CA) and Dean Torrence (born 10/3/1940, Los Angeles) who formed the Barons in 1957 with four school friends. When they left school Berry, Torrence and Arnie Ginsburg continued, recording

*Jennie Lee* in Berry's garage, which was released by Arwin Records as Jan & Arnie (Torrence was away in the army reserve at the time) and hit #8 on the US charts. As Torrence returned, Ginsburg joined the navy, Torrence taking his role in the duo. Berry ended up in a coma after a car smash on 12/4/1966, ending the partnership, but they reunited in 1973, 1975 and 1978 Berry died on 27/3/2004.

| | | | | | |
|---|---|---|---|---|---|
| 12/07/1980 | 67 | 2 | | THE JAN AND DEAN STORY | K-Tel NE 1084 |

### JANE'S ADDICTION
US rock group formed in Los Angeles, CA in 1986 by Perry Farrell (born Perry Bernstein, 29/3/1959, New York, vocals), Dave Navarro (born 6/6/1967, Santa Monica, CA, guitar), Eric Avery (born 6/6/1967, Los Angeles, bass) and Stephen Perkins (born 13/9/1967, Los Angeles, drums). Their debut album was for Triple X in 1987, signing with Warner's in 1988. They split in 1992, Farrell and Perkins forming Porno For Pyros, but re-formed (minus Avery, replaced by Red Hot Chili Peppers' Michael 'Flea' Balzary) in 1997. Navarro joined Red Hot Chilli Peppers in 1993. They are named after a prostitute who introduced Farrell to Navarro and Avery.

| | | | | | |
|---|---|---|---|---|---|
| 08/09/1990 | 37 | 2 | ◇ | RITUAL DE LO HABITUAL | Warner Brothers WX 306 |
| 02/08/2003 | 14 | 3 | ◇ | STRAYS | Parlophone 5921980 |

### JAPAN
UK group formed in London in 1977 by David Sylvian (born David Batt, 23/2/1958, London, guitar/vocals), Steve Jansen (born Stephen Batt, 1/12/1959, London, drums), Richard Barbieri (born 30/11/1957, keyboards) and Mick Karn (born Anthony Michaelides, 24/7/1958, London, bass), later adding Rob Dean on guitar. Winning a talent contest, they signed with Ariola-Hansa, debuting in 1978. Switching to Virgin in 1980, Dean left the following year. They disbanded in 1982, Sylvian and Karn going solo. Karn also joined ex-Bauhaus Peter Murphy for one album as Dali's Car. Sylvian, Karn, Jansen and Barbieri reunited in 1991 as Rain Tree Crow.

| | | | | | |
|---|---|---|---|---|---|
| 09/02/1980 | 53 | 8 | ● | QUIET LIFE | Ariola Hansa AHAL 8011 |
| 15/11/1980 | 45 | 10 | ● | GENTLEMEN TAKE POLAROIDS | Virgin V 2180 |
| 26/09/1981 | 26 | 46 | ● | ASSEMBLAGE | Hansa HANLP 1 |
| 28/11/1981 | 12 | 50 | ● | TIN DRUM | Virgin V 2209 |
| 18/06/1983 | 5 | 14 | ● | **OIL ON CANVAS** | Virgin VD 2513 |
| 08/12/1984 | 45 | 7 | ● | EXORCISING GHOSTS | Virgin VGD 3510 |

### JEFF JARRATT AND DON REEDMAN
UK /Australian arrangers. Jarratt was previously an engineer and producer at Abbey Road Studios, Reedman working in the record industry, compiling albums for the likes of K-Tel and CBS before launching Focus Music International.

| | | | | | |
|---|---|---|---|---|---|
| 22/11/1980 | 39 | 8 | ◇ | MASTERWORKS | K-Tel ONE 1093 |

### JEAN-MICHEL JARRE
French synthesizer player (born 24/8/1948, Lyon); he abandoned musical studies in 1967 to experiment with synthesizers. He married actress Charlotte Rampling in 1976. In 1981 Jean-Michel was the first Western artist to perform in China.

| | | | | | |
|---|---|---|---|---|---|
| 20/08/1977 | 2 | 24 | ✪ | **OXYGENE** | Polydor 2310 555 |
| 16/12/1978 | 11 | 26 | ● | EQUINOXE | Polydor POLD 5007 |
| 06/06/1981 | 6 | 17 | ● | **MAGNETIC FIELDS** | Polydor POLS 1033 |
| 15/05/1982 | 6 | 17 | ● | **THE CONCERTS IN CHINA** | Polydor PODV 3 |
| 12/11/1983 | 14 | 29 | ● | THE ESSENTIAL JEAN-MICHEL JARRE | Polydor PROLP 3 |
| 24/11/1984 | 47 | 14 | ◇ | ZOOLOOK | Polydor POLH 15 |
| 12/04/1986 | 9 | 38 | | **RENDEZ-VOUS** | Polydor POLH 27 |
| 18/07/1987 | 18 | 15 | ◇ | IN CONCERT LYONS/HOUSTON | Polydor POLH 36 |
| 08/10/1988 | 2 | 13 | ● | **REVOLUTIONS** | Polydor POLH 45 |
| 14/10/1989 | 16 | 4 | ◇ | JARRE LIVE | Polydor 8412581 |
| 23/06/1990 | 14 | 10 | | WAITING FOR COUSTEAU | Dreyfus 8436141 |
| 26/10/1991 | 14 | 12 | ● | IMAGES – THE BEST OF JEAN-MICHEL JARRE | Dreyfus 5113061 |
| 05/06/1993 | 11 | 8 | | CHRONOLOGIE | Polydor 5193732 |
| 28/05/1994 | 60 | 1 | | CHRONOLOGIE PART 6 | Polydor 5195792 |
| 01/03/1997 | 11 | 5 | | OXYGENE 7–13 | Epic 4869842 |
| 23/05/1998 | 50 | 2 | | ODYSSEY THROUGH 02 | Epic 4897642 |
| 12/02/2000 | 37 | 1 | | METAMORPHOSES | Epic 4960222 |

**MAURICE JARRE** French composer (born 13/9/1924, Lyon); he studied at the Paris Conservatoire in 1944, later joining the house orchestra for the Jean Louis Barrault Theatre. He began composing for films in 1951, his famous scores incuding *The Longest Day, Lawrence Of Arabia* (for which he won an Academy Award), *Dr Zhivago* (another Oscar winner), *Ryan's Daughter, Fatal Attraction, A Passage To India* (his third Oscar winner) and *Witness*.

| | | | |
|---|---|---|---|
| 10/09/1966 .....3 .....106 ..... | **DOCTOR ZHIVAGO** Original soundtrack to the film. 1966 Grammy Award for Best Original Score Written for a Motion Picture or TV Show ...........................................................................MGM C 8007 |

**AL JARREAU** US singer (born 12/3/1940, Milwaukee, WI) who was a resident singer at San Francisco, CA nightclub in the 1960s with George Duke, his pianist. Signed to Reprise in 1975, he has won six Grammy Awards: Best Jazz Vocal Performance in 1977 for *Look To The Rainbow*, Best Jazz Vocal Performance in 1978 for *All Fly Home*, Best Recording for Children in 1980 with various others for *In Harmony*, Best Pop Vocal Performance in 1981 for *Breaking Away*, Best Jazz Vocal Performance in 1981 for *Blue Rondo A La Turk* and Best Rhythm & Blues Vocal Performance in 1992 for *Heaven And Earth*. He has a star on the Hollywood Walk of Fame.

| | |
|---|---|
| 05/09/1981 .....60 .....8 ...... | BREAKING AWAY ...............................................................Warner Brothers K 56917 |
| 30/04/1983 .....39 .....18 ...... | JARREAU .........................................................................Warner International U 0070 |
| 17/11/1984 .....81 .....1 ...... | HIGH CRIME ...............................................................................WEA 2508071 |
| 13/09/1986 .....45 .....10 ...... | L IS FOR LOVER ...............................................................WEA International 2530801 |

**JAY-Z** US rapper (born Jason Shawn Carter, Brooklyn, NYC); he later formed Payroll Records with Fanatic and Ski and appeared in the film *Streets Is Watching*. He won the 1998 Grammy Award for Best Rap Album for *Volume 2 – Hard Knock Life* and the 1999 MOBO Award for Best International Hip Hop Act.

| | |
|---|---|
| 29/09/2001 .....30 .....4 ......● | THE BLUEPRINT ▲³ ...............................................Roc-A-Fella/Def Jam 5863962 |
| 30/03/2002 .....37 .....2 ...... | THE BEST OF BOTH WORLDS **R KELLY & JAY-Z** ...........................................Jive 9223512 |
| 30/03/2002 .....65 .....1 ...... | CHAPTER ONE ...............................................................Roc-A-Fella 74321920462 |
| 30/11/2002 .....23 .....7 ......● | THE BLUEPRINT 2 THE GIFT & THE CURSE ▲¹ ...............................Def Jam 0633812 |
| 29/11/2003 .....34 .....7 ......● | THE BLACK ALBUM ▲² ...............................................Roc-A-Fella 9861121 |

**JAYHAWKS** US group formed in Minneapolis, MN by Marc Olson (guitar/vocals), Gary Louris (guitar/vocals), Marc Perlman (bass) and Ken Callaghan (drums), later adding Benmont Tench on keyboards.

| | |
|---|---|
| 25/02/1995 .....41 .....1 ...... | TOMORROW THE GREEN GRASS ...............................American Recordings 74321236802 |
| 03/05/1997 .....61 .....1 ...... | SOUND OF LIES ...............................................American Recordings 4917962 |
| 20/05/2000 .....60 .....1 ...... | SMILE ...............................................................................Columbia 4979712 |
| 19/04/2003 .....70 .....1 ...... | RAINY DAY MUSIC ...............................................American Recordings 0771362 |

**DJ JAZZY JEFF AND THE FRESH PRINCE** US rap duo formed in Philadelphia, PA by DJ Jeff Townes (born 22/1/1965) and Will Smith (born 25/9/1968, Philadelphia). Smith is also an actor, appearing in the comedy *Fresh Prince Of Bel Air* and films including *Independence Day* and *Men In Black*. Smith later recorded solo. The pair have won two Grammy Awards: Best Rap Performance in 1988 for *Parents Just Don't Understand* and Best Rap Performance by a Duo in 1991 for *Summertime*.

| | |
|---|---|
| 28/02/1987 .....97 .....1 ...... | ROCK THE HOUSE ...............................................................Champion CHAMP 1004 |
| 21/05/1988 .....68 .....2 ...... | HE'S THE DJ, I'M THE RAPPER ...............................................................Jive HIP 61 |
| 14/09/1991 .....69 .....1 ...... | HOMEBASE ...............................................................................Jive HIP 116 |
| 11/12/1993 .....50 .....6 ...... | CODE RED **JAZZY JEFF AND THE FRESH PRINCE** ...............................................Jive CHIP 140 |
| 16/05/1998 .....20 .....5 ...... | GREATEST HITS ...............................................................................Jive 0518482 |

**WYCLEF JEAN** US rapper (born17/10/1972, Haiti) who was also in The Fugees and Refugee Allstars. He launched Clef Records in 2000.

| | |
|---|---|
| 05/07/1997 .....40 .....6 ...... | THE CARNIVAL ...............................................................................Columbia 4874422 |
| 02/09/2000 .....5 .....15 ......● | **THE ECLEFTIC – TWO SIDES TO A BOOK** ...............................................Columbia 4979792 |
| 20/07/2002 .....30 .....2 ...... | MASQUERADE – MESSAGE TO THE STREET ...............................................Columbia 5078542 |

**JEFFERSON AIRPLANE** US rock group formed in San Francisco, CA in 1965 by Marty Balin (born Martyn Buchwald, 30/1/1942, Cincinnati, OH, vocals), Paul Kantner (born 12/3/1941, San Francisco , guitar), Jorma Kaukonen (born 23/12/1940, Washington DC, guitar), Bob Harvey (bass), Jerry Peloguin (drums) and Sigue Anderson (vocals) as Jefferson Airplane. They added singer Grace Slick (born Grace Wing, 30/10/1939, Chicago, IL) in 1965, and replaced Harvey with Jack Casady (born 13/4/1944, Washington DC) the same year. They first recorded for RCA in 1966. They changed their name to Jefferson Starship in 1974, shortened to Starship in 1985 after the departure of Kantner. Grace Slick left in 1978 owing to alcohol problems but returned in 1981, only to depart for good in 1988. Jefferson Airplane reunited in 1989 with the original 1966 line-up. The group (as Jefferson Airplane) was inducted into the Rock & Roll Hall of Fame in 1996.

| | |
|---|---|
| 28/06/1969 .....38 .....1 ...... | BLESS ITS POINTED LITTLE HEAD ...............................................RCA SF 8019 |
| 07/03/1970 .....34 .....7 ...... | VOLUNTEERS ...............................................................................RCA SF 8076 |
| 02/10/1971 .....42 .....1 ...... | BARK ...............................................................................Grunt FTR 1001 |
| 02/09/1972 .....30 .....1 ...... | LONG JOHN SILVER ...............................................................Grunt FTR 1007 |
| 31/07/1976 .....30 .....2 ...... | SPITFIRE ...............................................................................Grunt RFL 1557 |

| DATE | POS | WKS | BPI | ALBUM TITLE | LABEL & NUMBER |
|------|-----|-----|-----|-------------|----------------|
| 09/02/1980 | 22 | 11 | | FREEDOM AT POINT ZERO | Grunt FL 13452 |
| 18/07/1987 | 26 | 5 | | NO PROTECTION **STARSHIP** | Grunt 86413 |

**JELLYBEAN** US producer (born John Benitez, 7/11/1957, South Bronx, NYC) who began as a DJ, then remixing. In the early 1980s he began producing and recording under his own name, signing with Liberty in 1984. He appeared as a DJ in the film *Nighthawks*.

| DATE | POS | WKS | BPI | ALBUM TITLE | LABEL & NUMBER |
|------|-----|-----|-----|-------------|----------------|
| 31/10/1987 | 15 | 28 | ● | JUST VISITING THIS PLANET | Chrysalis CHR 1569 |
| 03/09/1988 | 16 | 7 | ○ | ROCKS THE HOUSE! | Chrysalis CJB 1 |

**JELLYFISH** US rock group formed in San Francisco, CA by Andy Sturmer (drums/vocals), Jason Faulkner (guitar), Chris Manning (bass) and Roger Manning (keyboards).

| DATE | POS | WKS | BPI | ALBUM TITLE | LABEL & NUMBER |
|------|-----|-----|-----|-------------|----------------|
| 22/05/1993 | 21 | 2 | | SPILT MILK | Charisma CDCUS 20 |

**KATHERINE JENKINS** UK mezzo soprano singer (born 29/6/1980, Neath, South Wales) who graduated from the Royal Academy of Music in 2002 and worked as a music teacher before going solo.

| DATE | POS | WKS | BPI | ALBUM TITLE | LABEL & NUMBER |
|------|-----|-----|-----|-------------|----------------|
| 17/04/2004 | 31 | 4 | | PREMIERE | UCJ 9866064 |

**JESUS AND MARY CHAIN** UK group formed in Scotland in 1983 by William Reid (born 28/10/1958, Glasgow, guitar/vocals), Jim Reid (born 29/12/1961, Glasgow, guitar/vocals), Douglas Hart (bass) and Murray Dalglish (drums) as the Poppy Seeds. Moving to London in 1984, Bobby Gillespie (ex-Primal Scream) replaced Dalglish. Debuted on Creation in 1984 signing with Blanco Y Negro in 1985. By 1992 the line-up was the Reid brothers, Ben Laurie (guitar), Mathew Parkin (bass) and Barry Blacker (drums).

| DATE | POS | WKS | BPI | ALBUM TITLE | LABEL & NUMBER |
|------|-----|-----|-----|-------------|----------------|
| 30/11/1985 | 31 | 10 | ● | PSYCHOCANDY | Blanco Y Negro BYN 7 |
| 12/09/1987 | 5 | 7 | ● | **DARKLANDS** | Blanco Y Negro BYN 11 |
| 30/04/1988 | 9 | 7 | ● | **BARBED WIRE KISSES** | Blanco Y Negro BYN 15 |
| 21/10/1989 | 11 | 4 | ○ | AUTOMATIC | Blanco Y Negro BYN 20 |
| 04/04/1992 | 14 | 5 | | HONEY'S DEAD | Blanco Y Negro 9031765542 |
| 24/07/1993 | 15 | 3 | | THE SOUND OF SPEED | Blanco Y Negro 4509931052 |
| 27/08/1994 | 13 | 3 | | STONED AND DETHRONED | Blanco Y Negro 4509967172 |
| 13/06/1998 | 47 | 1 | | MUNKI | Creation CRECD 232 |

**JESUS JONES** UK group formed in 1986 by Mike Edwards (born 22/6/1964, London, guitar/vocals), Gen (born Simon Matthews, 23/4/1964, Devizes, drums) and Al Jaworski (born 31/1/1966, Plymouth) as Big Colour, becoming Jesus Jones in 1988. Added Jerry De Borg (born 30/10/1963, London, guitar/vocals) and Iain 'Barry D' Baker (born 29/9/1965, Carshalton, keyboards/samples) in 1988, and signed with the Food label.

| DATE | POS | WKS | BPI | ALBUM TITLE | LABEL & NUMBER |
|------|-----|-----|-----|-------------|----------------|
| 14/10/1989 | 31 | 3 | ○ | LIQUIDIZER | Food FOODLP 3 |
| 09/02/1991 | ❶[1] | 24 | ● | **DOUBT** | Food FOODLP 5 |
| 06/02/1993 | 6 | 4 | | **PERVERSE** | Food FOODCD 8 |

**JESUS LIZARD** US rock group formed in 1989 by David Yow (vocals), David Sims (bass) and Duane Denison (guitar) with a drum machine, though later joined by Mac McNeilly (drums). Yow and Sims had previously been with Scratch Acid.

| DATE | POS | WKS | BPI | ALBUM TITLE | LABEL & NUMBER |
|------|-----|-----|-----|-------------|----------------|
| 10/09/1994 | 64 | 1 | | DOWN | Touch And Go TG 131CD |

**JET** Australian group from Melbourne with Nic Cester (guitar/vocals), Cameron Muncy (guitar/vocals), Mark Wilson (bass) and Chris Cester (drums/vocals).

| DATE | POS | WKS | BPI | ALBUM TITLE | LABEL & NUMBER |
|------|-----|-----|-----|-------------|----------------|
| 27/09/2003 | 14 | 19+ | ● | GET BORN | Elektra 7559628922 |

**JETHRO TULL** UK group formed in Luton in 1967 by Ian Anderson (born 10/8/1947, Edinburgh, vocals/flute), Glenn Cornick (born 24/4/1947, Barrow-in-Furness, bass), Mick Abrahams (born 7/4/1943, guitar) and Clive Bunker (born 12/12/1946, Blackpool, drums) and named after the 18th-century agriculturist. Their debut single was in 1968 on MGM; by the end of the year Abrahams left (to form Blodwyn Pig) and was replaced by Martin Barre (born 17/11/1946, Birmingham). John Evans (in Anderson's first band, the Blades, in 1963) joined on keyboards in 1970, with another ex-Blade, Jeffrey Hammond-Hammond, replacing Cornick later that year. Bunker left in 1971 and was replaced by Barriemore Barlow. Hammond-Hammond left in 1976 and was replaced by John Glascock, who died after open-heart surgery on 17/11/1979, his replacement being Dave Pegg (born 2/11/1947, Birmingham). The line-up on their 20th anniversary tour was Anderson, Barre, Pegg, Doane Perry and Martin Allcock.

| DATE | POS | WKS | BPI | ALBUM TITLE | LABEL & NUMBER |
|------|-----|-----|-----|-------------|----------------|
| 02/11/1968 | 10 | 22 | | **THIS WAS** | Island ILPS 9085 |
| 09/08/1969 | ❶[5] | 29 | | **STAND UP** | Island ILPS 9103 |
| 09/05/1970 | 3 | 13 | | **BENEFIT** | Island ILPS 9123 |
| 03/04/1971 | 4 | 21 | | **AQUALUNG** | Island ILPS 9145 |
| 18/03/1972 | 5 | 14 | | **THICK AS A BRICK** ▲[2] | Chrysalis CHR 1003 |
| 15/07/1972 | 8 | 11 | | **LIVING IN THE PAST** | Chrysalis CJT 1 |
| 28/07/1973 | 13 | 8 | ○ | A PASSION PLAY ▲[1] | Chrysalis CHR 1040 |
| 02/11/1974 | 14 | 4 | | WAR CHILD | Chrysalis CHR 1067 |
| 27/09/1975 | 20 | 6 | ○ | MINSTREL OF THE GALLERY | Chrysalis CHR 1082 |
| 31/01/1976 | 44 | 5 | ● | M.U. THE BEST OF JETHRO TULL | Chrysalis CHR 1078 |
| 15/05/1976 | 25 | 10 | | TOO OLD TO ROCK 'N' ROLL TOO YOUNG TO DIE | Chrysalis CHR 1111 |
| 19/02/1977 | 13 | 12 | | SONGS FROM THE WOOD | Chrysalis CHR 1132 |
| 29/04/1978 | 20 | 10 | ○ | HEAVY HORSES | Chrysalis CHR 1175 |

▲[9] Number of weeks album topped the US chart ◆[12] RIAA Diamond Awards ◇[3] IFPI Platinum Europe Awards

| DATE | POS | WKS | BPI | ALBUM TITLE | LABEL & NUMBER |
|------|-----|-----|-----|-------------|----------------|
| 14/10/1978 | 17 | 8 | O | LIVE BURSTING OUT | Chrysalis CJT 4 |
| 06/10/1979 | 27 | 4 | | STORM WATCH | Chrysalis CDL 1238 |
| 06/09/1980 | 25 | 5 | | A | Chrysalis CDL 1301 |
| 17/04/1982 | 27 | 19 | O | BROADSWORD AND THE BEAST | Chrysalis CDL 1380 |
| 15/09/1984 | 18 | 5 | | UNDER WRAPS | Chrysalis CDL 1461 |
| 02/11/1985 | 63 | 3 | O | ORIGINAL MASTERS | Chrysalis JTTV 1 |
| 19/09/1987 | 19 | 10 | ● | CREST OF A KNAVE 1988 Grammy Award for Best Hard Rock/Metal Performance | Chrysalis CDL 1590 |
| 09/07/1988 | 78 | 1 | | 20 YEARS OF JETHRO TULL | Chrysalis TBOX 1 |
| 02/09/1989 | 18 | 6 | O | ROCK ISLAND | Chrysalis CHR 1708 |
| 14/09/1991 | 27 | 3 | | CATFISH RISING | Chrysalis CHNR 1886 |
| 26/09/1992 | 34 | 2 | | A LITTLE LIGHT MUSIC | Chrysalis CCD 1954 |
| 16/09/1995 | 20 | 3 | | ROOTS TO BRANCHES | Chrysalis CDCHR 6109 |
| 29/06/1999 | 53 | 1 | | AQUALUNG | Chrysalis CD25 AQUA1 |
| 04/09/1999 | 44 | 1 | | J-TULL DOT COM | Papillion BTFLYCD 0001 |

**JETS** UK group formed by brothers Bobby, Ray and Tony Cotton.

| 10/04/1982 | 30 | 6 | | 100 PERCENT COTTON | EMI EMC 3399 |
|------|-----|-----|-----|-------------|----------------|

**JETS** US group formed in Minneapolis, MN by eight brothers and one sister – Leroy, Eddie, Eugene, Haini, Rudy, Kathi, Elizabeth and Moana Wolfgramm. Eugene left in 1988, forming Boys Club with Joe Pasquale, although he went under the name Gene Hunt in this venture. The Wolfgramms' parents are from Tonga.

| 11/04/1987 | 57 | 4 | | CRUSH ON YOU | MCA MCF 3312 |
|------|-----|-----|-----|-------------|----------------|

**JOAN JETT AND THE BLACKHEARTS** US singer (born Joan Larkin, 22/9/1960, Philadelphia, PA) who was guitarist with the all-girl Runaways from 1975 until 1978, forming the Blackhearts with Ricky Bird (guitar), Gary Ryan (bass) and Lee Crystal (drums) in 1980. She appeared in the 1987 film *Light Of Day* as leader of the band The Barbusters.

| 08/05/1982 | 25 | 7 | | I LOVE ROCK 'N' ROLL | Epic EPC 85686 |
|------|-----|-----|-----|-------------|----------------|

**JEWEL** US singer/guitarist (born Jewel Kilcher, 23/5/1974, Payson, UT, raised in Homer, Alaska); she studied opera in Illinois before moving to California and going solo. Her 1995 debut album sold over 8 million copies in the USA alone.

| 28/11/1998 | 54 | 1 | | SPIRIT | Atlantic 7567829502 |
|------|-----|-----|-----|-------------|----------------|
| 09/03/2002 | 34 | 3 | | THIS WAY | Atlantic 7567835192 |

**JICKS** – see STEPHEN MALKMUS

**JIMMY EAT WORLD** US group from Mesa, AZ with Jim Adkins (guitar/vocals), Tom Linton (guitar/vocals), Rick Burch (bass) and Zach Lind (drums). First recorded for Wooden Blue in 1994, then Christie Front Drive, Emery and Blueprint before Capitol in 1996.

| 09/02/2002 | 62 | 4 | | BLEED AMERICAN | DreamWorks 4503482 |
|------|-----|-----|-----|-------------|----------------|

**JIVE BUNNY AND THE MASTERMIXERS** UK production/mixing group with Andy Pickles, Les Hemstock, John Pickles and Ian Morgan.

| 09/12/1989 | 2 | 22 | ✪³ | JIVE BUNNY – THE ALBUM | Telstar STAR 2390 |
|------|-----|-----|-----|-------------|----------------|
| 08/12/1990 | 23 | 7 | ● | IT'S PARTY TIME | Telstar STAR 2449 |

**JJ72** Irish rock group formed by Mark Greaney (guitar/vocals), Hillary Woods (bass) and Fergal Matthews (drums). Despite much speculation, their name doesn't represent anything at all!

| 09/09/2000 | 16 | 20 | ● | JJ72 | Lakota LAK CD0017 |
|------|-----|-----|-----|-------------|----------------|
| 26/10/2002 | 20 | 2 | | I TO SKY | Lakota 5095292 |

**JOBOXERS** UK group formed by Dig Wayne (born 20/7/1958, vocals), Rob Marche (born 13/10/1962, Bristol, guitar), Dave Collard (born 17/1/1961, Bristol, keyboards), Chris Bostock (born 23/11/1962, Bristol, bass) and Sean McLusky (born 5/5/1961, Bristol, drums) evolving from Subway Sect. They disbanded in 1986.

| 24/09/1983 | 18 | 5 | | LIKE GANGBUSTERS | RCA BOXXLP 1 |
|------|-----|-----|-----|-------------|----------------|

**JODECI** US R&B vocal group formed by two sets of brothers: Joel 'JoJo' (born 10/6/1971, Charlotte, NC) and Cedric 'K-Ci' Hailey (born 2/9/1969, Charlotte) and Dalvin (born 23/7/1971, Newport News, VA) and Donald 'DeVante Swing' DeGrate. The Hailey brothers later recorded as K-Ci and Jojo whilst Dalvin DeGrate recorded solo.

| 29/07/1995 | 4 | 8 | | THE SHOW THE AFTER-PARTY THE HOTEL | Uptown MCD 11258 |
|------|-----|-----|-----|-------------|----------------|

**JOE** US singer (born Joseph Lewis Thomas, 1972, Cuthbert, GA) who was discovered singing in church by producer Vincent Henry.

| 12/02/1994 | 53 | 1 | | EVERYTHING | Mercury 5188072 |
|------|-----|-----|-----|-------------|----------------|
| 09/08/1997 | 26 | 4 | O | ALL THAT I AM | Jive CHIP 183 |
| 29/04/2000 | 46 | 4 | | MY NAME IS JOE | Jive 9220352 |
| 08/05/2004 | 73 | 3 | | AND THEN | Jive 82876586402 |

O Silver disc  ● Gold disc  ✪ Platinum disc (additional platinum units are indicated by a figure following the symbol)  ❶⁹ Number of weeks album topped the UK chart

**BILLY JOEL** US singer (born 9/5/1949, Hicksville, NY); he formed the Echoes in 1964, who became the Emeralds then the Lost Souls. He joined the Hassles in 1967 and when they split in 1969 he formed Attila with drummer Jon Small, making one album for Epic before going solo. His debut album was released on Family Productions in 1971. When the album failed (mainly through bad mastering and mixing) he played piano at a lounge club, was spotted by Columbia and signed with them in 1973. He married Elizabeth Weber (who became his manager) in 1973 and supermodel Christie Brinkley in 1985, both ending in divorce. He was inducted into the Rock & Roll Hall of Fame in 1999. He has won six Grammy Awards including: Record of the Year and Song of the Year in 1978 for *Just The Way You Are;* Best Rock Vocal Performance in 1980 for *Glass Houses;* and Best Recording for Children in 1982 with various others for *In Harmony 2.*

| DATE | POS | WKS | BPI | ALBUM TITLE | LABEL & NUMBER |
|------|-----|-----|-----|-----------|----------------|
| 25/03/1978 | 25 | 40 | ● | THE STRANGER ◆[10] | CBS 82311 |
| 25/11/1978 | 10 | 43 | ● | **52ND STREET** 1979 Grammy Awards for Album of the Year and Best Pop Vocal Performance | CBS 83181 |
| 22/03/1980 | 9 | 24 | ● | **GLASS HOUSES** | CBS 86108 |
| 10/10/1981 | 57 | 3 | | SONGS IN THE ATTIC | CBS 85273 |
| 02/10/1982 | 27 | 8 | | NYLON CURTAIN | CBS 85959 |
| 10/09/1983 | 2 | 95 | ☺[3] | **AN INNOCENT MAN** | CBS 25554 |
| 04/02/1984 | 95 | 1 | | COLD SPRING HARBOUR | CBS 32400 |
| 23/06/1984 | 98 | 1 | | PIANO MAN | CBS 32002 |
| 20/07/1985 | 7 | 39 | ☺ | **GREATEST HITS VOLUME 1 & VOLUME II** ◆[21] | CBS 88666 |
| 16/08/1986 | 38 | 10 | ○ | THE BRIDGE | CBS 86323 |
| 28/11/1987 | 92 | 1 | | KOHYEPT – LIVE IN LENINGRAD | CBS 4604071 |
| 04/11/1989 | 5 | 25 | ☺ | **STORM FRONT** | CBS 4656581 |
| 14/08/1993 | 3 | 26 | ☺ | **RIVER OF DREAMS** | Columbia 4738722 |
| 01/11/1997 | 23 | 4 | ○ | GREATEST HITS VOLUME III | Columbia 4882362 |
| 13/06/1998 | 33 | 4 | | GREATEST HITS – VOLUMES I, II & III | Columbia 4912742 |
| 27/05/2000 | 68 | 1 | | 2000 YEARS – THE MILLENNIUM CONCERT | Columbia 4979812 |
| 31/03/2001 | 4 | 24 | ☺ | **THE ULTIMATE COLLECTION** | Columbia SONYTV 98CD |

**ELTON JOHN** UK singer/pianist (born Reginald Kenneth Dwight, 25/3/1947, Pinner); he joined Bluesology in 1961. They turned professional in 1965, supporting visiting US R&B acts before becoming Long John Baldry's backing band. He left in 1967 (adopting his name from group members Elton Dean and John Baldry) to go solo and met up with lyricist Bernie Taupin. He recorded his first single (via Philips) in 1968 and signed with DJM in 1969. He launched the Rocket label in 1973 and publishing company Big Pig in 1974. Later he became Chairman of Watford FC. He married recording engineer Renate Blauer in 1984 (ended in divorce). He sang a re-written version of *Candle In The Wind* at the funeral of Diana, Princess of Wales, the only time he performed the song live. The single, with advance orders of 8.7 million, entered the US chart at #1 and sold over 11 million copies, only the seventh time a record had entered at pole position, Elton being the first artist to enter the US album charts at #1 (the single also topped the Canadian charts for 45 weeks, spent 18 months in the Top 3 and 30 months in the Top 10, earning 19 platinum awards). He won the Best Male Award at the 1991 BRIT Awards and Outstanding Contribution Award in 1986 (jointly with Wham!) and 1995, and The Freddie Mercury Award (in recognition of his charity work) at the 1998 BRIT Awards. He was awarded a CBE in 1996 and a knighthood in the 1998 New Year's Honours List. He was inducted into the Rock & Roll Hall of Fame in 1994. He took part in the Perfect Day project for the BBC's Children In Need charity. In 2000 the *Original Broadway Cast Album Of Aida*, written by Elton and Tim Rice, won the Grammy Award for Best Musical Show Album. His *Candle In The Wind 1997/Something About The Way You Look Tonight* is one of only five singles to have sold over two million copies in the UK. He has a star on the Hollywood Walk of Fame.

| DATE | POS | WKS | BPI | ALBUM TITLE | LABEL & NUMBER |
|------|-----|-----|-----|-----------|----------------|
| 23/05/1970 | 11 | 14 | | ELTON JOHN | DJM DJLPS 406 |
| 16/01/1971 | 6 | 20 | | **TUMBLEWEED CONNECTION** | DJM DJLPS 410 |
| 01/05/1971 | 20 | 2 | | THE ELTON JOHN LIVE ALBUM 17-11-70 | DJM DJLPS 414 |
| 20/05/1972 | 41 | 2 | | MADMAN ACROSS THE WATER | DJM DJLPH 420 |
| 03/06/1972 | 2 | 23 | | **HONKEY CHATEAU** ▲[5] | DJM DJLPH 423 |
| 10/02/1973 | ❶[6] | 42 | | **DON'T SHOOT ME I'M ONLY THE PIANO PLAYER** ▲[2] | DJM DJLPH 427 |
| 03/11/1973 | ❶[2] | 84 | ☺ | **GOODBYE YELLOW BRICK ROAD** ▲[8] | DJM DJLPO 1001 |
| 13/07/1974 | ❶[2] | 18 | ● | **CARIBOU** ▲[4] | DJM DJLPH 439 |
| 23/11/1974 | ❶[11] | 84 | ☺ | **ELTON JOHN'S GREATEST HITS** ▲[10] ◆[16] | DJM DJLPH 442 |
| 07/06/1975 | 2 | 24 | ● | **CAPTAIN FANTASTIC AND THE BROWN DIRT COWBOY** ▲[7] | DJM DJLPX 1 |
| 08/11/1975 | 5 | 12 | ● | **ROCK OF THE WESTIES** ▲[3] | DJM DJLPH 464 |
| 15/05/1976 | 6 | 9 | ○ | HERE AND THERE | DJM DJLPH 473 |
| 06/11/1976 | 3 | 15 | ● | **BLUE MOVES** | Rocket ROSP 1 |
| 15/10/1977 | 6 | 24 | ● | **GREATEST HITS VOLUME 2** | DJM DJH 20520 |
| 04/11/1978 | 8 | 26 | ● | **A SINGLE MAN** | Rocket TRAIN 1 |
| 20/10/1979 | 41 | 3 | | VICTIM OF LOVE | Rocket HISPD 125 |
| 08/03/1980 | 56 | 2 | | LADY SAMANTHA | DJM 22085 |
| 31/05/1980 | 12 | 13 | | 21 AT 33 | Rocket HISPD 126 |
| 25/10/1980 | 24 | 13 | ● | THE VERY BEST OF ELTON JOHN | K-Tel NE 1094 |
| 30/05/1981 | 12 | 12 | ○ | THE FOX | Rocket TRAIN 16 |
| 17/04/1982 | 13 | 12 | ○ | JUMP UP | Rocket HISPD 127 |
| 06/11/1982 | 39 | 13 | | LOVE SONGS | TV Records TVA 3 |
| 11/06/1983 | 7 | 73 | ☺ | **TOO LOW FOR ZERO** | Rocket HISPD 24 |
| 30/06/1984 | 2 | 23 | ☺ | **BREAKING HEARTS** | Rocket HISPD 25 |
| 16/11/1985 | 3 | 23 | ☺ | **ICE ON FIRE** | Rocket HISPD 26 |

▲[9] Number of weeks album topped the US chart ◆[12] RIAA Diamond Awards ◇[3] IFPI Platinum Europe Awards

| | DATE | POS | WKS | BPI | ALBUM TITLE | LABEL & NUMBER |
|---|---|---|---|---|---|---|
| | 15/11/1986 | 24 | 9 | ● | LEATHER JACKETS | Rocket EJLP 1 |
| | 12/09/1987 | 43 | 7 | | LIVE IN AUSTRALIA **ELTON JOHN AND THE MELBOURNE SYMPHONY ORCHESTRA** | Rocket EJBXL 1 |
| | 16/07/1988 | 18 | 6 | ○ | REG STRIKES BACK | Rocket EJLP 3 |
| | 23/09/1989 | ●5 | 42 | ✪3 | **SLEEPING WITH THE PAST** | Rocket 8388391 |
| | 10/11/1990 | ●2 | 96 | ✪9 | **THE VERY BEST OF ELTON JOHN** | Rocket 8469471 |
| | 27/06/1992 | 2 | 18 | ● | **THE ONE** | Rocket 5123602 |
| | 04/12/1993 | 5 | 18 | ✪ | **DUETS ELTON JOHN AND VARIOUS ARTISTS** | Rocket 5184782 |
| | 01/04/1995 | 3 | 14 | ● | **MADE IN ENGLAND** ◇ | Rocket 5261852 |
| | 18/11/1995 | 4 | 48 | ✪3 | **LOVE SONGS** ◇5 | Rocket 5287882 |
| | 11/10/1997 | 3 | 23 | ✪ | **THE BIG PICTURE** | Rocket 5362662 |
| | 03/04/1999 | 29 | 2 | | ELTON JOHN AND TIM RICE'S AIDA **ELTON JOHN AND FRIENDS** | Rocket 5246512 |
| | 25/11/2000 | 7 | 13 | ✪ | **ONE NIGHT ONLY – THE GREATEST HITS** | Mercury 5483342 |
| | 13/10/2001 | 2 | 34 | ✪2 | **SONGS FROM THE WEST COAST** ◇ | Rocket 5863302 |
| | 20/10/2001 | 41 | 4 | | GOODBYE YELLOW BRICK ROAD | Rocket 5281592 |
| | 23/11/2002 | 3 | 51 | ✪4 | **THE GREATEST HITS 1970–2002** ◇2 | Mercury 634992 |

**JOHNNY HATES JAZZ** UK group formed by Clark Datchler (keyboards/vocals), Calvin Hayes (keyboards/drums) and Mike Nocito (guitar/bass). Hayes, son of producer Mickie Most, was briefly engaged to Kim Wilde. Datchler left in 1988, replaced by Phil Thomalley (born 5/1/1964, Worlington, Suffolk).

| | DATE | POS | WKS | BPI | ALBUM TITLE | LABEL & NUMBER |
|---|---|---|---|---|---|---|
| | 23/01/1988 | ●1 | 39 | ✪2 | **TURN BACK THE CLOCK** | Virgin V 2475 |

**JOHNNY AND THE HURRICANES** US group formed in Toledo, OH in 1958 by John Pocisk 'Paris' (sax), Paul Tesluk (organ), Dave Yorko (guitar), Lionel 'Butch' Mattice (bass) and Tony Kaye (drums) as the Orbits. Kaye left in 1959, replaced by Bo Savich.

| | DATE | POS | WKS | BPI | ALBUM TITLE | LABEL & NUMBER |
|---|---|---|---|---|---|---|
| | 03/12/1960 | 18 | 1 | | STORMSVILLE | London HAI 2269 |
| | 01/04/1961 | 14 | 4 | | BIG SOUND OF JOHNNY AND THE HURRICANES | London HAK 2322 |

**ANDREAS JOHNSON** Swedish singer (born Lund) of jazz musician parents who was lead singer with Planet Waves, going solo when the group disbanded after one album.

| | DATE | POS | WKS | BPI | ALBUM TITLE | LABEL & NUMBER |
|---|---|---|---|---|---|---|
| | 19/02/2000 | 46 | 2 | | LIEBLING | WEA 3984269142 |

**HOLLY JOHNSON** UK singer (born William Johnson, 19/2/1960, Khartoum, Sudan); he was with Big In Japan before leaving for an unsuccessful solo career. He formed the Hollycaust, and then Frankie Goes To Hollywood in 1980 where he was lead singer. He left the group in 1987 to resume his solo career, this time with more success. In 1993 it was revealed he was HIV positive.

| | DATE | POS | WKS | BPI | ALBUM TITLE | LABEL & NUMBER |
|---|---|---|---|---|---|---|
| | 06/05/1989 | ●1 | 17 | ✪ | **BLAST** | MCA MCG 6042 |

**LINTON KWESI JOHNSON** Jamaican poet (born 24/8/1952, Chapeltown); he emigrated to London in 1963, where he got a degree in sociology at Goldsmith's College. After publishing the books *Voices Of The Living And The Dead* in 1974 and *Dread Beat And Blood* the following year, both of which were written in a patois style; he set about recording his poems to reggae music in 1977 and would later set up his own label, LKJ and publish a third book of poetry.

| | DATE | POS | WKS | BPI | ALBUM TITLE | LABEL & NUMBER |
|---|---|---|---|---|---|---|
| | 30/06/1979 | 66 | 1 | | FORCE OF VICTORY | Island ILPS 9566 |
| | 31/05/1980 | 46 | 5 | | BASS CULTURE | Island ILPS 9605 |
| | 10/03/1984 | 73 | 2 | | MAKING HISTORY | Island ILPS 9770 |

**PAUL JOHNSON** UK singer who was a member of Paradise before going solo. He later recorded with Mica Paris.

| | DATE | POS | WKS | BPI | ALBUM TITLE | LABEL & NUMBER |
|---|---|---|---|---|---|---|
| | 04/07/1987 | 63 | 2 | | PAUL JOHNSON | CBS 4506401 |
| | 16/09/1989 | 70 | 1 | | PERSONAL | CBS 4632841 |

**JAMES A JOHNSTON** US male musician (born James Alan Johnston, 1954, St Louis, MI); he was raised in Connecticut.

| | DATE | POS | WKS | BPI | ALBUM TITLE | LABEL & NUMBER |
|---|---|---|---|---|---|---|
| | 13/11/1999 | 44 | 9 | ● | WORLD WRESTLING FEDERATION – THE MUSIC – VOLUME 4 | Koch International 333612 |
| | 10/03/2001 | 11 | 8 | ● | WORLD WRESTLING FEDERATION – THE MUSIC – VOLUME 5 | Koch KOCCD8830 |

**BRIAN JOHNSTONE** UK radio and TV commentator (born 24/6/1912, Little Berkhamstead, Hertfordshire); he made his name as a cricket commentator with the BBC, joing them in 1946 and remaining for 48 years. He died on 5/1/1994.

| | DATE | POS | WKS | BPI | ALBUM TITLE | LABEL & NUMBER |
|---|---|---|---|---|---|---|
| | 05/03/1994 | 46 | 3 | | AN EVENING WITH JOHNNERS | Listen For Pleasure LFP 7742 |

**JOJO** – see K-CI AND JOJO

**AL JOLSON** US singer (born Asa Yoelson, 26/3/1886, Snrednicke, Lithuania, although some sources list his place of birth as St Petersburg in Russia); he emigrated to the USA shortly before the turn of the century and settled with his family in Washington DC. He began his career in 1906 and made his film debut in 1916, although it was his 1926 appearance in *April Showers*, for which he recorded three numbers, that led to a starring role in *The Jazz Singer* and lasting fame. As well as film and record success, Jolson was a major star of radio and made some of the earliest TV pilot shows. On 23/10/1950 he began complaining of chest pains (he had previously had one lung removed) and died soon after. On the night he died they turned off the lights on Broadway and stopped the traffic in Times Square in tribute. He was married four times during his life, including dancer Ruby Keeler, his third wife with whom he made a couple of films, and X-ray technician Erle Galbraith, who became his fourth wife. He has a star on the Hollywood Walk of Fame for his contribution to recording, a second for motion pictures and a third star for radio.

| | DATE | POS | WKS | BPI | ALBUM TITLE | LABEL & NUMBER |
|---|---|---|---|---|---|---|
| | 14/03/1981 | 18 | 7 | | 20 GOLDEN GREATS | MCA MCTV 4 |
| | 17/12/1983 | 67 | 4 | ○ | THE AL JOLSON COLLECTION | Ronco RON LP 5 |

○ Silver disc ● Gold disc ✪ Platinum disc (additional platinum units are indicated by a figure following the symbol) ●9 Number of weeks album topped the UK chart

## JON AND VANGELIS
UK/Greek duo of ex-Yes Jon Anderson (born 25/10/1944, Accrington) and Vangelis (born Evangelos Papathanassiou, 29/3/1943, Valos, Greece). Anderson had also recorded solo, Vangelis was a founder member of Aphrodite's Child.

| Date | Pos | Wks | BPI | Album Title | Label & Number |
|------|-----|-----|-----|-------------|----------------|
| 26/01/1980 | 4 | 11 | ● | **SHORT STORIES** | Polydor POLD 5030 |
| 11/07/1981 | 17 | 8 | | THE FRIENDS OF MR. CAIRO | Polydor POLD 5039 |
| 23/01/1982 | 6 | 15 | ● | **THE FRIENDS OF MR. CAIRO** Re-issue of Polydor POLD 5039 with an extra track | Polydor POLD 5053 |
| 02/07/1983 | 22 | 10 | | PRIVATE COLLECTION | Polydor POLH 4 |
| 11/08/1984 | 42 | 9 | | THE BEST OF JON AND VANGELIS | Polydor POLH 6 |

## ALED JONES
UK choirboy (born1971, Llandegfan, Wales); he made a duet with himself. The first half of the song, *What Can You Tell Me?*, was recorded while he was still a child star and shelved until his voice had broken, then he added his baritone half. He later became a regular on the Chris Moyles show on Radio 1.

| Date | Pos | Wks | BPI | Album Title | Label & Number |
|------|-----|-----|-----|-------------|----------------|
| 27/04/1985 | 6 | 43 | ✪ | **VOICES FROM THE HOLY LAND** | BBC REC 564 |
| 29/06/1985 | 2 | 44 | ✪ | **ALL THROUGH THE NIGHT** | BBC REH 569 |
| 23/11/1985 | 11 | 10 | ● | ALED JONES WITH THE BBC WELSH CHORUS This and the above two hits credited to **ALED JONES WITH THE BBC WELSH CHOIR** | 10 Records AJ 1 |
| 22/02/1986 | 36 | 6 | | WHERE E'ER YOU WALK | 10 Records DIX 21 |
| 12/07/1986 | 25 | 16 | ○ | PIE JESU | 10 Records AJ 2 |
| 29/11/1986 | 18 | 11 | ● | AN ALBUM OF HYMNS | Telstar STAR 2272 |
| 14/03/1987 | 52 | 6 | ○ | ALED (MUSIC FROM THE TV SERIES) | 10 Records AJ 3 |
| 05/12/1987 | 59 | 5 | | THE BEST OF ALED JONES | 10 Records AJ 5 |
| 26/10/2002 | 27 | 9 | ● | ALED | UCJ 0644792 |
| 11/10/2003 | 21 | 7 | ● | HIGHER | UCJ 9865579 |

## DONELL JONES
US singer (born Detroit, MI) who was first known as a songwriter with hits for Usher, Madonna, Brownstone and 702. He signed with LaFace in 1996.

| Date | Pos | Wks | BPI | Album Title | Label & Number |
|------|-----|-----|-----|-------------|----------------|
| 29/01/2000 | 47 | 3 | | WHERE I WANNA BE | LaFace 73008260602 |
| 22/06/2002 | 62 | 2 | | LIFE GOES ON | Arista ARI 147602 |

## GLENN JONES
US R&B singer (born1961, Jacksonville, FL); he sang gospel music as a child and joined The Bivens Specials whilst at school. He then formed The Modulations and was subsequently invited to California to record two albums with the Reverend James Cleveland. He moved into secular music in 1981 with Norman Connors and landed a solo deal with RCA in 1983. He switched to Jive in 1986 and later recorded for Atlantic and SAR.

| Date | Pos | Wks | BPI | Album Title | Label & Number |
|------|-----|-----|-----|-------------|----------------|
| 31/10/1987 | 62 | 1 | | GLENN JONES | Jive HIP 51 |

## GRACE JONES
US singer (born 15/5/1952, Spanishtown, Jamaica) who moved to Syracuse at the age of twelve. First a model and actress, she appeared in the film *Gordon's War*. She returned to acting in the 1990s; films include *McGinsey's Island* and *View To A Kill*.

| Date | Pos | Wks | BPI | Album Title | Label & Number |
|------|-----|-----|-----|-------------|----------------|
| 30/08/1980 | 45 | 2 | | WARM LEATHERETTE | Island ILPS 9592 |
| 23/05/1981 | 35 | 16 | | NIGHTCLUBBING | Island ILPS 9624 |
| 20/11/1982 | 15 | 22 | | LIVING MY LIFE | Island ILPS 9722 |
| 09/11/1985 | 12 | 8 | | SLAVE TO THE RHYTHM | ZTT GRACE 1 |
| 14/12/1985 | 4 | 30 | ● | **ISLAND LIFE** | Island GJ 1 |
| 29/11/1986 | 61 | 2 | ○ | INSIDE STORY | Manhattan MTL 1007 |

### HOWARD JONES
UK singer (born John Howard Jones, 23/2/1955, Southampton); he played with Warrior, the Bicycle Thieves and Skin Tight before signing to WEA in 1983 as a solo artist. He opened a vegetarian restaurant in New York in 1987.

| 17/03/1984 | ❶² | 57 | ✪ | HUMAN'S LIB | WEA WX 1 |
| 08/12/1984 | 15 | 33 | ● | THE 12" ALBUM | WEA WX 14 |
| 23/03/1985 | 2 | 25 | ● | DREAM INTO ACTION | WEA WX 15 |
| 25/10/1986 | 10 | 4 | ● | ONE TO ONE | WEA WX 68 |
| 01/04/1989 | 64 | 1 | | CROSS THAT LINE | WEA WX 225 |
| 05/06/1993 | 36 | 2 | | THE BEST OF HOWARD JONES | East West 4509927012 |

### JACK JONES
US singer (born 14/1/1938, Los Angeles); the son of actress Irene Hervey and actor/singer Allan Jones, he began singing whilst at school and upon graduating in 1957 joined his father's act. He was with the act for eight months before going solo, signing with Kapp Records in 1961, and also serving a six month spell in the Air Force. He remained with Kapp until 1967 when he switched to RCA (the label his father had been with when he scored his 1938 hit *The Donkey Serenade*) and continued to record a series of light pop songs. Numerous appearances on TV and live concerts have maintained his popularity across the decades. He has won two Grammy Awards: Best Solo Vocal Performance in 1961 for *Lollipops And Roses* and Best Solo Vocal Performance in 1963 for *Wives And Lovers*. He has a star on the Hollywood Walk of Fame.

| 29/04/1972 | 9 | 6 | | A SONG FOR YOU | RCA Victor SF 8228 |
| 03/06/1972 | 7 | 36 | ● | BREAD WINNERS | RCA Victor SF 8280 |
| 07/04/1973 | 8 | 10 | | TOGETHER | RCA Victor SF 8342 |
| 23/02/1974 | 10 | 5 | | HARBOUR | RCA Victor APLI 0408 |
| 19/02/1977 | 41 | 5 | | THE FULL LIFE | RCA Victor PL 12067 |
| 21/05/1977 | 10 | 8 | | ALL TO YOURSELF | RCA TVL 2 |

### NORAH JONES
US singer/pianist (born 30/3/1979, NYC) who is the daughter of Ravi Shankar. She worked with the Wax Poetic before forming her own band with Jesse Harris (guitar), Lee Alexander (bass) and Dan Rieser (drums). She was named International Breakthrough Artist at the 2003 BRIT Awards. Five days later she collected five Grammy Awards including Best New Artist, Record of the Year and Best Female Vocal Performance for *Don't Know Why*. *Don't Know Why* also won the Song of the Year award for writer Jesse Harris. *Come Away With Me* was named Best Engineered Album for S Husky Hoskulds and Jay Newland and Producer of the Year for Arif Mardin. She also won the 2002 MOBO Award for Best Jazz Act.

| 11/05/2002 | ❶⁴ | 112+ | ✪⁷ | COME AWAY WITH ME ◇⁵ ▲⁴ 2002 Grammy Awards for Album of the Year, Record of the Year and Best Pop Vocal Album . . . . . . . . . . |
| | | | | . . . . . . . . . . . . . . . . . . . . . . . . . . . . . . . . . . . . . . . . . . . . . . . . . . . . . . . . . . . . . . . . . . Parlophone 5386092 |
| 21/02/2004 | ❶² | 19+ | ✪² | FEELS LIKE HOME ◇² ▲⁶ . . . . . . . . . . . . . . . . . . . . . . . . . . . . . . . . . . . . . . . . . . . . . . . . . . . . . Blue Note 5983660 |

### QUINCY JONES
US producer/ keyboard player (born Quincy Delight Jones Jr, 14/3/1933, Chicago, IL) and raised in Seattle. A trumpeter with Lionel Hampton from 1950, in 1961 he became musical director of Mercury Records, later promoted to Vice President. He produced Lesley Gore's *It's My Party* (his first US #1) and later Michael Jackson's albums, including *Thriller*. He nearly died from a cerebral aneurysm in 1974 but recovered and set up the Qwest label in 1981. He composed the themes to films and TV series including *Ironside*. Previously married to Jeri Caldwell, Ulla Anderson and Peggy Lipton he had a child by Natassja Kinski. His nineteen Grammy Awards include: Best Instrumental Arrangement in 1963 for Count Basie's *I Can't Stop Lovin' You*; Best Instrumental Jazz Performance in 1969 for *Walking In Space*; Best Contemporary Instrumental Performance in 1971 for *Smackwater Jack*; Best Instrumental Arrangement in 1973 for *Summer In The City*; Best Instrumental Arrangement in 1976 with Robert Freedman for *The Wiz*; Best Instrumental Arrangement in 1980 with Jerry Hay for George Benson's *Dinorah, Dinorah*; Best Rhythm & Blues Vocal Performance by a Duo in 1981 for *The Dude*; Best Instrumental Arrangement in 1981 for *Velas*; Best Arrangement Accompanying Singers in 1981 with Jerry Hey for *Ai No Corrida*; Best Instrumental Arrangement in 1984 for *Grace (Gymnastics Theme)*; Best Jazz Fusion Performance in 1990 for *Birdland*; Best Arrangement on an Instrumental in 1990 with Ian Prince, Rod Temperton and Jerry Hey for *Birdland*; Best Instrumental Arrangement Accompanying Vocals in 1990 with Jerry Hey, Glen Ballard and Cliff Magness for *The Places You Find Love*; Best Large Jazz Ensemble Performance in 1993 with Miles Davis for *Miles And Quincy Live At Montreux*; Best Spoken Word Album in 2001 for *Q: The Autobiography of Quincy Jones*; and Producer of the Year in 1981, 1983 and 1990. He has a star on the Hollywood Walk of Fame.

| 18/04/1981 | 19 | 25 | ○ | THE DUDE | A&M AMLK 63721 |
| 20/03/1982 | 41 | 4 | | THE BEST | A&M AMLH 68542 |

| 18/08/1984 ..... 41 ...... 8 ...... | L.A. IS MY LADY **FRANK SINATRA WITH THE QUINCY JONES ORCHESTRA** ............................................. Qwest 925145 |
| 20/01/1990 ..... 26 ..... 12 ...... ● | BACK ON THE BLOCK 1990 Grammy Award for Album of the Year ....................................................... Qwest WX 313 |

## RICKIE LEE JONES
US singer (born 8/11/1954, Chicago, IL); she moved to Los Angeles, CA in 1977. She has won two Grammy Awards: Best New Artist in 1979 and Best Jazz Vocal Performance by a Duo in 1989 with Dr John for *Makin' Whoopee*.

| 16/06/1979 ..... 18 ..... 19 ...... ○ | RICKY LEE JONES ............................................................ Warner Brothers K 56628 |
| 08/08/1981 ..... 37 ..... 11 ...... ○ | PIRATES .................................................................. Warner Brothers K 56816 |
| 02/07/1983 ..... 51 ...... 3 ...... | GIRL AT HER VOLCANO ....................................................... Warner Brothers 9238051 |
| 13/08/1984 ..... 40 ...... 4 ...... | THE MAGAZINE .............................................................. Warner Brothers 9251171 |
| 07/10/1989 ..... 50 ...... 2 ...... | FLYING COWBOYS ............................................................ Geffen WX 309 |

## TAMMY JONES
UK country singer, born in Bangor, N.Wales, first seen widely on a TV talent show. She later recorded for Monarch and Blue Waters.

| 12/07/1975 ..... 38 ...... 5 ...... | LET ME TRY AGAIN .......................................................... Epic EPC 80853 |

## TOM JONES
UK singer (born Thomas Jones Woodward, 7/6/1940, Pontypridd, Wales); he formed his own group Tommy Scott & The Senators in 1963, recording tracks for EMI. Spotted supporting Mandy Rice-Davies by manager Gordon Mills in 1964, who suggested the name Tom Jones and secured a deal with Decca. With his own US TV series, he moved to California in 1969, performing regularly in Las Vegas. He was awarded the OBE in the 1999 New Year's Honours List. He was named Best New Artist at the 1965 Grammy Awards and Best British Male Solo Artist at the 2000 BRIT Awards. He was in the *Perfect Day* project for the BBC's Children In Need charity and has a star on the Hollywood Walk of Fame.

| 05/06/1965 ..... 11 ...... 5 ...... | ALONG CAME JONES ......................................................... Decca LK 6693 |
| 08/10/1966 ..... 23 ...... 8 ...... | FROM THE HEART ........................................................... Decca LK 4814 |
| 08/04/1967 .... 3 ..... 49 ...... | **GREEN GREEN GRASS OF HOME** ................................................ Decca SKL 4855 |
| 24/06/1967 .... 6 ..... 90 ...... | **LIVE AT THE TALK OF THE TOWN** ............................................. Decca SKL 4874 |
| 30/12/1967 .... 5 ..... 49 ...... | **13 SMASH HITS** ........................................................... Decca SKL 4909 |
| 27/07/1968 ..... ●² ..... 29 ...... | **DELILAH** ................................................................. Decca SKL 4946 |
| 21/12/1968 .... 4 ...... 9 ...... | **HELP YOURSELF** ........................................................... Decca SKL 4982 |
| 28/06/1969 ..... 2 ..... 20 ...... | **THIS IS TOM JONES** ....................................................... Decca SKL 5007 |
| 15/11/1969 ..... 2 ..... 45 ...... | **TOM JONES LIVE IN LAS VEGAS** .............................................. Decca SKL 5032 |
| 25/04/1970 .... 4 ..... 18 ...... | **TOM** .................................................................... Decca SKL 5045 |
| 14/11/1970 ..... 10 ..... 10 ...... | **I WHO HAVE NOTHING** ...................................................... Decca SKL 5072 |
| 29/05/1971 ..... 9 ...... 7 ...... | **SHE'S A LADY** ............................................................ Decca SKL 5089 |
| 27/11/1971 ..... 27 ...... 5 ...... | LIVE AT CAESAR'S PALACE .................................................... Decca D 1/11/2 |
| 24/06/1972 ..... 17 ...... 4 ...... | CLOSE UP .................................................................. Decca SKL 5132 |
| 23/06/1973 ..... 31 ...... 1 ...... | THE BODY AND SOUL OF TOM JONES ............................................. Decca SKL 5162 |
| 05/01/1974 ..... 15 ..... 13 ...... | GREATEST HITS ............................................................. Decca SKL 5176 |
| 22/03/1975 ..... ●⁴ ..... 21 ...... ● | **20 GREATEST HITS** ........................................................ Decca TJD 1/11/2 |
| 07/10/1978 ..... 12 ...... 9 ...... ● | I'M COMING HOME ........................................................... Lotus WH 5001 |
| 16/05/1987 ..... 16 ..... 12 ...... | THE GREATEST HITS ......................................................... Telstar STAR 2296 |
| 13/05/1989 ..... 34 ...... 3 ...... | AT THIS MOMENT ............................................................ Jive TOMTV 1 |
| 08/07/1989 ..... 46 ...... 4 ...... | AFTER DARK ................................................................ Stylus SMR 978 |
| 06/04/1991 ..... 44 ...... 4 ...... | CARRYING A TORCH .......................................................... Dover ADD 20 |
| 27/06/1992 ..... 8 ...... 6 ...... ● | **THE COMPLETE TOM JONES** .................................................. The Hit Label 8442862 |
| 26/11/1994 ..... 55 ...... 1 ...... | THE LEAD AND HOW TO SWING IT .............................................. ZTT 6544924982 |
| 14/11/1998 ..... 26 ...... 6 ...... | THE ULTIMATE HITS COLLECTION ............................................... Polygram TV 8449012 |
| 09/10/1999 ..... ●³ ..... 65 ...... ✪⁴ | **RELOAD** ◇ ................................................................ Gut GUTCD 009 |
| 16/11/2002 ..... 36 ...... 2 ...... | MR JONES ................................................................. V2 VVR 1021072 |
| 01/03/2003 ..... 2 ..... 14 ...... ✪ | **GREATEST HITS** ........................................................... Universal TV 8828632 |

## TREVOR JONES
UK composer/arranger (born 23/3/1949, Cape Town, South Africa).

| 05/07/1986 ..... 38 ...... 2 ...... | LABYRINTH Original soundtrack to the film. ................................. EMI America AML 3104 |

## JANIS JOPLIN
US singer (born 19/1/1943, Port Arthur, TX); she began her career in 1961 and would later join the Waller Creek Boys before moving to San Francisco. She moved back to Texas in 1965 in order to wean herself off her addiction to amphetamines and then returned to San Francisco to front Big Brother And The Holding Company, a role she was to hold for two years. She then assembled her own band, The Joplinaires, which subsequently changed name to the Kozmic Blues Band, with Sam Andrew (guitar/vocals), Bill King (keyboards), Brad Campbell (bass), Terry Clements (saxophone), Marcus Doubleday (trumpet) and Roy Markowitz (drums). Problems with drugs and alcohol returned, and the group (or rather Joplin herself) became known for erratic performances and disbanded in 1970. Joplin assembled another group, the Full Tilt Boogie Band; with Brad Campbell, John Till (guitar), Richard Bell (keyboards), Ken Pearson (keyboards) and Clark Pierson (drums), which toured with Grateful Dead and had begun work on a debut album when Joplin died from a heroin overdose on 4/10/1970. Released posthumously *Pearl* gave rise to the US #1 hit *Me And Bobby McGee*, a song written by Kris Kristofferson which has since become something of a standard. She was inducted into the Rock & Roll Hall of Fame in 1995.

| 17/04/1971 ..... 50 ...... 1 ...... | PEARL ▲⁹ .................................................................. CBS 64188 |

▲⁹ Number of weeks album topped the US chart  ◆¹² RIAA Diamond Awards  ◇³ IFPI Platinum Europe Awards

| DATE | POS | WKS | BPI | ALBUM TITLE | LABEL & NUMBER |
|---|---|---|---|---|---|
| 22/07/1972 | 30 | 6 | | JANIS JOPLIN IN CONCERT | CBS 67241 |
| 29/08/1998 | 26 | 4 | | THE ULTIMATE COLLECTION | Columbia SONYTV 52CD |

**MONTELL JORDAN** US R&B singer (born 3/12/1968, Los Angeles, CA). Graduating from Pepperdine University, he spent the next seven years trying to get a record deal. Six-foot-eight-inches tall, he appeared in the film *The Nutty Professor*.

| DATE | POS | WKS | BPI | ALBUM TITLE | LABEL & NUMBER |
|---|---|---|---|---|---|
| 24/06/1995 | 53 | 2 | | THIS IS HOW WE DO IT | RAL 5271792 |
| 14/09/1996 | 66 | 1 | | MORE TO TELL | Def Jam 5331912 |

**RONNY JORDAN** UK guitarist (born Ronnie Simpson, 29/11/1962, London); he made his first solo album in 1991 for Island Records. He won the 2000 MOBO Award with Mos Def for Best Jazz Act.

| DATE | POS | WKS | BPI | ALBUM TITLE | LABEL & NUMBER |
|---|---|---|---|---|---|
| 07/03/1992 | 52 | 4 | | THE ANTIDOTE | Island CID 9988 |
| 09/10/1993 | 49 | 2 | | THE QUIET REVOLUTION | Island CID 8009 |
| 03/09/1994 | 58 | 1 | | BAD BROTHERS **RONNY JORDAN MEETS DJ KRUSH** | Island IMCD 8024 |

**JOURNEY** US rock group formed in 1973 by Neal Schon (born 27/2/1954, guitar), George Tickner (guitar), Gregg Rolie (keyboards), Ross Valory (bass) and Aynsley Dunbar (drums). Tickner left in 1978, replaced by Steve Perry (born 22/1/1949, Hanford, CA, vocals). Rolie left in 1980, replaced by Jonathan Cain (born 26/2/1950). By 1986 the group was Schon, Cain and Perry, and after one more album they split with Schon and Cain, joining John Waite. Journey re-formed in 1996 with Perry, Schon, Cain, Valory and Steve Smith (drums).

| DATE | POS | WKS | BPI | ALBUM TITLE | LABEL & NUMBER |
|---|---|---|---|---|---|
| 20/03/1982 | 32 | 16 | | ESCAPE ▲¹ | CBS 85138 |
| 19/02/1983 | 6 | 8 | | **FRONTIERS** | CBS 25261 |
| 06/08/1983 | 100 | 1 | | EVOLUTION | CBS 32342 |
| 24/05/1986 | 22 | 5 | | RAISED ON RADIO | CBS 26902 |

**JOY DIVISION** UK group formed in Manchester in 1976 by Ian Curtis (born 15/7/1956, Macclesfield, vocals), Bernard Sumner (born Bernard Albrecht, 4/1/1956, Salford, guitar), Peter Hook (born 13/12/1956, Salford) and Steve Brotherdale (drums) as the Stiff Kittens, making their live debut as Warsaw. Brotherdale left in 1977, replaced by Stephen Morris (born 28/10/1957, Macclesfield) shortly before they changed name again to Joy Division (taken from the Nazi-concentration camp novel *House Of Dolls*). Curtis committed suicide on 18/5/1980 with the surviving members re-emerging as New Order.

| DATE | POS | WKS | BPI | ALBUM TITLE | LABEL & NUMBER |
|---|---|---|---|---|---|
| 26/07/1980 | 6 | 8 | | **CLOSER** | Factory FACT 25 |
| 30/08/1980 | 71 | 1 | | UNKNOWN PLEASURES | Factory FACT 10 |
| 17/10/1981 | 5 | 12 | | **STILL** | Factory DFACT 40 |
| 23/07/1988 | 7 | 8 | | **1977–1980 SUBSTANCE** | Factory FAC 250 |
| 01/07/1995 | 16 | 3 | | PERMANENT: JOY DIVISION 1995 | London 8286242 |
| 07/02/1998 | 70 | 1 | | HEART AND SOUL | London 3984290402 |

**JTQ** – see **JAMES TAYLOR QUARTET**

**JUDAS PRIEST** UK heavy rock group formed in 1969 by Ken 'KK' Downing (born 25/8/1951, Birmingham, guitar) and Ian Hill (born 20/1/1952, Birmingham, bass). By 1971 the line-up consisted of Downing, Hill, Rob Halford (born 25/8/1951, Birmingham, vocals), John Hinch (drums), adding second guitarist Glenn Tipton (born 25/10/1948, Birmingham) in 1974. They signed with Gull in 1974 and replaced Hinch with Alan Moore. They switched to CBS in 1977. They are named after a Bob Dylan album track, *The Ballad Of Frankie Lee And Judas Priest*. Rob Halford later launched a solo career, hitting the US album chart in 2001 with *Resurrection*.

| DATE | POS | WKS | BPI | ALBUM TITLE | LABEL & NUMBER |
|---|---|---|---|---|---|
| 14/05/1977 | 23 | 6 | | SIN AFTER SIN | CBS 82008 |
| 25/02/1978 | 27 | 5 | | STAINED CLASS | CBS 82430 |
| 11/11/1978 | 32 | 9 | | KILLING MACHINE | CBS 83135 |
| 06/10/1979 | 10 | 8 | | **UNLEASHED IN THE EAST** | CBS 83852 |
| 19/04/1980 | 4 | 17 | ○ | **BRITISH STEEL** | CBS 84160 |
| 07/03/1981 | 14 | 5 | ○ | POINT OF ENTRY | CBS 84834 |
| 17/07/1982 | 11 | 9 | | SCREAMING FOR VENGEANCE | CBS 85941 |
| 28/01/1984 | 19 | 5 | | DEFENDERS OF THE FAITH | CBS 25713 |
| 19/04/1986 | 33 | 4 | | TURBO | CBS 26641 |
| 13/06/1987 | 47 | 2 | | PRIEST… LIVE | CBS 4506391 |
| 28/05/1988 | 24 | 5 | | RAM IT DOWN | CBS 4611081 |
| 22/09/1990 | 26 | 2 | | PAINKILLER | CBS 4672901 |
| 08/05/1993 | 37 | 1 | | METAL WORKS 73–93 | Columbia 4730502 |

**JUDGE DREAD** UK singer (born Alex Hughes, 1945, Kent); he worked as a wrestler, bouncer and debt collector before fronting a mobile roadshow in the style of many Jamaican artists, singing over backing tapes. All his hits were banned by radio and TV because of the earthy lyrical content. He died from a heart attack whilst performing on stage on 13/3/1998.

| DATE | POS | WKS | BPI | ALBUM TITLE | LABEL & NUMBER |
|---|---|---|---|---|---|
| 06/12/1975 | 26 | 12 | | BEDTIME STORIES | Cactus CTLP 113 |
| 07/03/1981 | 51 | 2 | | 40 BIG ONES | Creole BIG 1 |

## JUICY LUCY
UK rock group formed in 1969 by Glenn Campbell (guitar/mandolin/percussion/vocals), Peter Dobson (drums), Keith Ellis (bass/vocals), Neil Hubbard (guitar), Chris Mercer (saxophone/keyboards) and Ray Owen (vocals). Later members included Mick Moody (guitar), Paul Williams (percussion/vocals), Rod Coombes (drums) and Jim Leverton (bass). They split in 1973.

| | | | | | |
|---|---|---|---|---|---|
| 18/04/1970 | 41 | 4 | | JUICY LUCY | Vertigo VO 2 |
| 21/11/1970 | 53 | 1 | | LIE BACK AND ENJOY IT | Vertigo 6360 014 |

## GARY JULES
US singer (born Gary Jules Aguirre, San Diego, CA); he was a member of Origin before going solo. He first came to prominence working with Michael Andrews.

| | | | | | |
|---|---|---|---|---|---|
| 31/01/2004 | 12 | 3 | | TRADING SNAKEOIL FOR WOLFTICKETS | Adventure/Sanctuary SANDP 252 |

## JULUKA
UK/South African group formed by Johnny Clegg (born 13/7/1953, Rochdale) who moved to South Africa in 1959 and formed Juluka (Zulu for 'sweat') with Sipho Mchunu in 1976. He formed Savuka in 1986.

| | | | | | |
|---|---|---|---|---|---|
| 23/07/1983 | 50 | 3 | | SCATTERLINGS | Safari SHAKA 1 |

## JUMPIN' JIVE – see JOE JACKSON

## JUNGLE BROTHERS
US rap group with Mike G (Michael Small), Afrika Baby Bam (Nathaniel Hall) and DJ Sammy B (Sammy Burwell) who have collaborated with De La Soul and A Tribe Called Quest.

| | | | | | |
|---|---|---|---|---|---|
| 03/02/1990 | 41 | 3 | | DONE BY THE FORCES OF NATURE | Eternal WX 332 |

## JUNIOR
UK singer (born Norman Giscombe, 10/11/1961, London); he made his record debut in 1982, later recording in the USA.

| | | | | | |
|---|---|---|---|---|---|
| 05/06/1982 | 28 | 14 | | JI | Mercury MERS 3 |

## JUNIOR SENIOR
Danish vocal duo Jeeper Mortensen and Jeppe Breum..

| | | | | | |
|---|---|---|---|---|---|
| 22/03/2003 | 29 | 3 | | D D DON'T DON'T STOP THE BEAT | Mercury FROG 0262CD |

## JURASSIC 5
US rap group formed in Los Angeles, CA by MC Mark 7even, MC Charli 2na, MC Zaakir, MC Akil, producer Cut Chemist and DJ Nu-Mark. The six had previously been in Unity Committee and Rebels of Rhythm before releasing *Unified Rebelution*.

| | | | | | |
|---|---|---|---|---|---|
| 13/06/1998 | 70 | 1 | ● | JURASSIC 5 | Pan PAN 015CD |
| 01/07/2000 | 23 | 3 | | QUALITY CONTROL | Interscope 4907102 |
| 19/10/2002 | 46 | 2 | | POWER IN NUMBERS | Interscope 4934372 |

# K

### K-CI AND JOJO
US duo of brothers Gedric 'K-Ci' (born 2/9/1969, Charlotte, NC) and Joel 'JoJo' Hailey (born 10/6/1971, Charlotte), both also in Jodeci, and are grandsons of Temptations' member Ron Tyson.

| | | | |
|---|---|---|---|
| 28/06/1997 | 51 | 2 | LOVE ALWAYS .................................................. MCA MCD 11613 |
| 03/07/1999 | 56 | 1 | IT'S REAL ...................................................... MCA MCD 11975 |

### K-KLASS
UK vocal/instrumental group formed by Andy Williams, Carl Thomas, Paul Roberts and Russ Morgan, with Bobbi Depasois providing vocals.

| | | | |
|---|---|---|---|
| 04/06/1994 | 73 | 1 | UNIVERSAL ........................................... Deconstruction CDPCSDX 149 |

### KACI
US singer (born Kaci Lynn Battaglia, 3/10/1987, Seminole, FL); she moved to Los Angeles at ten to pursue an acting career, subsequently presenting a Disney Christmas TV special. She made her first demo record at the age of eleven.

| | | | |
|---|---|---|---|
| 16/02/2002 | 47 | 2 | PARADISE ........................................................ Curb 0927402912 |

### JOSHUA KADISON
US singer (born 8/2/1965, Los Angeles, CA).

| | | | |
|---|---|---|---|
| 27/05/1995 | 45 | 4 | PAINTED DESERT SERENADE ..................................... SBK SBKCD 22 |

A SWINGIN' SAFARI
BERT KAEMPFERT AND HIS ORCHESTRA

### BERT KAEMPFERT
German orchestra leader/producer (born 16/10/1923, Hamburg); he was best known as the first to produce The Beatles, on the German sessions with Tony Sheridan that resulted in a belated UK hit after the group were superstars. He died in Spain whilst on holiday on 21/6/1980.

| | | | | |
|---|---|---|---|---|
| 05/03/1966 | 4 | 22 | | BYE BYE BLUES ....................................... Polydor LPHM 84086 |
| 16/04/1966 | 27 | 1 | | BEST OF BERT KAEMPFERT .............................. Polydor LPHM 84012 |
| 28/05/1966 | 20 | 15 | | SWINGING SAFARI ..................................... Polydor LPHM 46384 |
| 30/07/1966 | 13 | 26 | | STRANGERS IN THE NIGHT ............................... Polydor LPHM 84053 |
| 04/02/1967 | 33 | 3 | | RELAXING SOUND OF BERT KAEMPFERT .................... Polydor 583501 |
| 18/02/1967 | 25 | 18 | | BERT KAEMPFERT – BEST SELLER ......................... Polydor 583551 |
| 29/04/1967 | 36 | 5 | | HOLD ME ............................................ Polydor 184072 |
| 26/08/1967 | 24 | 5 | | KAEMPFERT SPECIAL ................................... Polydor 236207 |
| 19/06/1971 | 49 | 1 | | ORANGE COLOURED SKY ................................ Polydor 2310 091 |
| 05/07/1980 | 17 | 8 | O | SOUNDS SENSATIONAL ................................ Polydor POLTB 10 |

### KAJAGOOGOO
UK group from Leighton Buzzard with Steve Askew (guitar), Nick Beggs (born 15/12/1961, bass), Limahl (born Chris Hamill, 19/12/1958, his stage name an anagram of his real name, lead singer), Stuart Neale (keyboards) and Jez Strode (drums). Limahl went solo in 1983, Beggs taking over as lead singer. Later a trio, they shortened their name to Kaja. Beggs was later in Ellis, Beggs & Howard before becoming an A&R man in the record industry.

| | | | | |
|---|---|---|---|---|
| 30/04/1983 | 5 | 20 | O | WHITE FEATHERS ....................................... EMI EMC 3433 |
| 02/06/1984 | 35 | 3 | | ISLANDS ............................................... EMI KAJA 1 |

### NICK KAMEN
UK singer (born 15/4/1962, London); he was first noticed via a Levi Jeans ad, stripping off in a laundrette, backed by Marvin Gaye's *I Heard It Through The Grapevine*. Madonna helped him get a recording deal.

| | | | |
|---|---|---|---|
| 18/04/1987 | 34 | 7 | NICK KAMEN ...................................................... WEA WX 84 |

### KANE GANG
UK group formed in Newcastle-upon-Tyne by Martin Bramer (vocals), Paul Woods (vocals) and Dave Brewis (guitar) and named after the film *Citizen Kane*. Debuting in 1983, a year later they teamed with hit producer Pete Wingfield.

| | | | |
|---|---|---|---|
| 23/02/1985 | 21 | 8 | THE BAD AND LOWDOWN WORLD OF THE KANE GANG .......... Kitchenware KWLP 2 |
| 08/08/1987 | 41 | 4 | MIRACLE ...................................................... Kitchenware KWLP 7 |

### MICK KARN
UK singer/bass player (born Anthony Michaelide, 24/7/1958, London) who was a founder member of Japan in 1977. When they disbanded in 1982, he went solo, then formed short-lived Dali's Car with Peter Murphy before returning to a solo career.

| | | | |
|---|---|---|---|
| 20/11/1982 | 74 | 3 | TITLES ......................................................... Virgin V 2249 |

○ Silver disc ● Gold disc ✪ Platinum disc (additional platinum units are indicated by a figure following the symbol) ❶9 Number of weeks album topped the UK chart

| | | | | |
|---|---|---|---|---|
| 28/02/1987.....89......1...... | | | | DREAMS OF REASON PRODUCE MONSTERS. . . . . . . . . . . . . . . . . . . . . . . . . . . . . . . . . . . . . . . . . . . . Virgin V 2389 |

**KATRINA AND THE WAVES** UK-based US group with Katrina Leskanich (vocals), Vince de la Cruz (bass), Alex Cooper (drums) and Kimberley Rew (guitar). *Love Shine A Light* won the 1997 Eurovision Song Contest, the UK's first success since 1981.

| | |
|---|---|
| 08/06/1985.....28......6...... | KATRINA AND THE WAVES . . . . . . . . . . . . . . . . . . . . . . . . . . . . . . . . . . . . . . . . . . . . . . . . . . . . . . . . . . Capitol KTW 1 |
| 10/05/1986.....70......1...... | WAVES . . . . . . . . . . . . . . . . . . . . . . . . . . . . . . . . . . . . . . . . . . . . . . . . . . . . . . . . . . . . . . . . . . . . . Capitol EST 2010 |

**KAVANA** UK singer (born Anthony Kavanagh, 4/11/1977), he achieved his breakthrough after supporting Boyzone on tour.

| | |
|---|---|
| 10/05/1997.....29......2...... | KAVANA . . . . . . . . . . . . . . . . . . . . . . . . . . . . . . . . . . . . . . . . . . . . . . . . . . . . . . . . . . . . . . . . . Nemesis CDNMS 1 |

**KC AND THE SUNSHINE BAND** US disco group formed in Florida in 1973 by Harry Casey (born 31/1/1951, Hialeah, FL, keyboards/vocals) and Richard Finch (born 25/1/1954, Indianapolis, IN, bass) as KC & The Sunshine Junkanoo Band. With a flexible line-up between seven- and eleven-strong, Casey and Finch were the primary writers, also writing for others on the TK label, including George McCrae with *Rock Your Baby*. They won a 1975 Grammy for Best Rhythm & Blues Song with Willie Clarke and Betty Wright for *Where Is The Love*. Former guitarist Jerome Smith was crushed to death by a bulldozer on 28/7/2000. They have a star on the Hollywood Walk of Fame.

| | |
|---|---|
| 30/08/1975.....26......7...... | KC AND THE SUNSHINE BAND . . . . . . . . . . . . . . . . . . . . . . . . . . . . . . . . . . . . . . . . . . . . . . . . . Jay Boy JSL 9 |
| 01/03/1980.....10......6......O | **GREATEST HITS**. . . . . . . . . . . . . . . . . . . . . . . . . . . . . . . . . . . . . . . . . . . . . . . . . . . . . . . . . . . TK TKR 83385 |
| 27/08/1983.....46......4...... | ALL IN A NIGHT'S WORK . . . . . . . . . . . . . . . . . . . . . . . . . . . . . . . . . . . . . . . . . . . . . . . . . . . . . Epic EPC 85847 |

**KEANE** UK group formed in Sussex by Tom Chaplin (vocals), Tim Rice-Oxley (keyboards) and Richard Hughes (drums).

| | |
|---|---|
| 22/05/2004 ....❶⁴.....6+......✧² | **HOPES AND FEARS** . . . . . . . . . . . . . . . . . . . . . . . . . . . . . . . . . . . . . . . . . . . . . . . . . . . . . . . Island CID 8145 |

**RONAN KEATING** Irish singer (born 3/3/1977, Dublin); he was lead singer with Boyzone. He also went into management with Westlife and took part in the *It's Only Rock 'N' Roll* project for the Children's Promise charity.

| | |
|---|---|
| 12/08/2000 ....❶².....56......✧⁴ | **RONAN** ◇² . . . . . . . . . . . . . . . . . . . . . . . . . . . . . . . . . . . . . . . . . . . . . . . . . . . . . . . . . . . Polydor 5491032 |
| 01/06/2002 ....❶¹.....40......✧² | **DESTINATION** ◇ . . . . . . . . . . . . . . . . . . . . . . . . . . . . . . . . . . . . . . . . . . . . . . . . . . . . . . . Polydor 5897892 |
| 29/11/2003.....21.....17...... | TURN IT ON . . . . . . . . . . . . . . . . . . . . . . . . . . . . . . . . . . . . . . . . . . . . . . . . . . . . . . . . . . . Polydor 9865882 |

**KEEL** US rock group formed by Ron Keel (vocals), Marc Ferrari (guitar), Brian Jay (guitar), Kenny Chaisson (bass) and Dwain Miller (drums). Their hit album was produced by Kiss member Gene Simmons.

| | |
|---|---|
| 17/05/1986.....83......2...... | THE FINAL FRONTIER . . . . . . . . . . . . . . . . . . . . . . . . . . . . . . . . . . . . . . . . . . . . . . . . . . . . . Vertigo VERH 33 |

**HOWARD KEEL** US singer (born Harold Clifford Keel, 13/4/1919, Gillespie OH) who first came to prominence as an actor, appearing in such films as *Annie Get Your Gun* (1950), *Showboat* (1951), *Kiss Me Kate* and *Calamity Jane* (both 1953) and *Seven Brides For Seven Brothers* (1954). He was later a regular on TV, including the series *Dallas*. He has a star on the Hollywood Walk of Fame.

| | |
|---|---|
| 14/04/1984 .....6......19...... | **AND I LOVE YOU SO** . . . . . . . . . . . . . . . . . . . . . . . . . . . . . . . . . . . . . . . . . . . . . . . . . . Warwick WW 5137 |
| 09/11/1985.....20.....12......● | REMINISCING – THE HOWARD KEEL COLLECTION . . . . . . . . . . . . . . . . . . . . . . . . . . . . . . . Telstar STAR 2259 |
| 26/03/1988.....51......5...... | JUST FOR YOU. . . . . . . . . . . . . . . . . . . . . . . . . . . . . . . . . . . . . . . . . . . . . . . . . . . . . . . . . Telstar STAR 2318 |

**KELIS** US singer (born Kelis Rogers, 21/8/1980, Harlem, NYC). She won the 2001 BRIT Award for Best International Newcomer and has also recorded with Moby.

| | |
|---|---|
| 11/03/2000.....43.....13......● | KALEIDOSCOPE . . . . . . . . . . . . . . . . . . . . . . . . . . . . . . . . . . . . . . . . . . . . . . . . . . . . . . Virgin CDVUS 167 |
| 17/01/2004.....11....15+......● | TASTY. . . . . . . . . . . . . . . . . . . . . . . . . . . . . . . . . . . . . . . . . . . . . . . . . . . . . . . . . . . . . . Virgin CDV 2978 |

**R KELLY** US singer (born Robert Kelly, 8/1/1969, Chicago, IL). He formed Public Announcement, a group of backing singers and dancers, but scored as a solo. He signed with Jive in 1991; he also writes and produces. A rumoured marriage to singer Aaliyah in August 1994 was deemed a publicity hoax on her part. He received the Outstanding Achievement Award at the 2001 MOBOs and has won three Grammy Awards: Best Rhythm & Blues Song, Best Male Rhythm & Blues Vocal Performance and Best Song Written Specifically for a Motion Picture in 1997, all for *I Believe I Can Fly*.

| | |
|---|---|
| 29/02/1992.....67......1...... | BORN INTO THE 90'S **R KELLY AND PUBLIC ANNOUNCEMENT** . . . . . . . . . . . . . . . . . . . . . . . . . . . . . Jive CHIP 123 |
| 27/11/1993.....20.....44......● | 12 PLAY. . . . . . . . . . . . . . . . . . . . . . . . . . . . . . . . . . . . . . . . . . . . . . . . . . . . . . . . . . . . . . Jive CHIP 144 |
| 25/11/1995.....18.....10......● | R KELLY ▲¹ . . . . . . . . . . . . . . . . . . . . . . . . . . . . . . . . . . . . . . . . . . . . . . . . . . . . . . . . . . . Jive CHIP 166 |

| DATE | POS | WKS | BPI | ALBUM TITLE | LABEL & NUMBER |
|---|---|---|---|---|---|
| 21/11/1998 | 27 | 26 | ✪ | R ◇ | Jive 0517932 |
| 18/11/2000 | 21 | 3 | ● | TP-2.COM ▲[1] | Jive 9220262 |
| 30/03/2002 | 37 | 2 | | THE BEST OF BOTH WORLDS **R KELLY & JAY-Z** | Jive 9223512 |
| 01/03/2003 | 10 | 22 | ● | **CHOCOLATE FACTORY** ▲[1] The album was originally to be called *Loveland* but after bootleg copies began appearing, R Kelly recorded an entirely new album. Six tracks from the abandoned *Loveland* project are featured as a bonus CD on this release | Jive 9225082 |
| 04/10/2003 | 4 | 30 | ✪[2] | THE R IN R&B – GREATEST HITS VOLUME 1 | Jive 82876561792 |

### FELICITY KENDAL
UK fitness instructor (born 25/9/1946, Otton, Warwickshire); her main claim to fame is as an actress, notably in the TV series *The Good Life* as Barbara Good.

| DATE | POS | WKS | BPI | ALBUM TITLE | LABEL & NUMBER |
|---|---|---|---|---|---|
| 19/06/1982 | 29 | 47 | ● | SHAPE UP AND DANCE WITH FELICITY KENDAL (VOLUME ONE) | Lifestyle LEG 1 |

### KENICKIE
UK group formed in Sunderland in 1984 by Lauren Laverne (vocals), Marie Du Santiago (guitar), Emmy-Kate Montrose (bass) and Lauren's brother Johnny X (drums). The band is named after a character in *Grease*. Laverne later worked with Mint Royale and as a DJ for XFM.

| DATE | POS | WKS | BPI | ALBUM TITLE | LABEL & NUMBER |
|---|---|---|---|---|---|
| 24/05/1997 | 9 | 3 | | AT THE CLUB | Emidisc ADISCCD 002 |
| 12/09/1998 | 32 | 2 | | GET IN | EMI 4958512 |

### BRIAN KENNEDY
Irish singer/songwriter (born 12/10/1966, Belfast); ex-Van Morrison's Blues & Soul Revue, he co-writes with many other writers.

| DATE | POS | WKS | BPI | ALBUM TITLE | LABEL & NUMBER |
|---|---|---|---|---|---|
| 31/03/1990 | 64 | 1 | | THE GREAT WAR OF WORDS | RCA PL 74475 |
| 19/10/1996 | 19 | 3 | ○ | A BETTER MAN | RCA 74321409132 |

### NIGEL KENNEDY
UK violinist (born 28/12/1956, Brighton); he studied at the Yehudi Menuhin School and the Julliard School before making his Festival Hall debut in 1977. Within classical circles he is recognised for his playing and recording of the Elgar Concerto and Vivaldi's *Four Seasons*, but his ability to mix classical music with jazz and rock has widened his appeal.

| DATE | POS | WKS | BPI | ALBUM TITLE | LABEL & NUMBER |
|---|---|---|---|---|---|
| 01/03/1986 | 97 | 1 | | ELGAR: VIOLIN CONCERTO **NIGEL KENNEDY WITH THE LONDON PHILHARMONIC ORCHESTRA** | EMI EMX 4120581 |
| 07/10/1989 | 3 | 81 | ✪[2] | **VIVALDI: THE FOUR SEASONS NIGEL KENNEDY WITH THE ENGLISH CHAMBER ORCHESTRA** | EMI NIGE 2 |
| 05/05/1990 | 28 | 15 | ● | MENDELSSOHN/BRUCH/SCHUBERT **NIGEL KENNEDY WITH JEFFREY TATE CONDUCTING THE ENGLISH CHAMBER ORCHESTRA** | HMV 7496631 |
| 06/04/1991 | 16 | 12 | ● | BRAHMS: VIOLIN CONCERTO **NIGEL KENNEDY WITH THE LONDON PHILHARMONIC ORCHESTRA** | EMI NIGE 3 |
| 22/02/1992 | 56 | 1 | | JUST LISTEN **NIGEL KENNEDY WITH THE LONDON PHILHARMONIC ORCHESTRA CONDUCTED BY SIMON RATTLE** | EMI Classics CDNIGE 4 |
| 21/11/1992 | 40 | 6 | | BEETHOVEN VIOLIN CONCERTO, CORIOLAN OVERTURE **NIGEL KENNEDY WITH KLAUS TENNSTEDT CONDUCTING THE NORTH GERMAN RADIO SYMPHONY ORCHESTRA** | EMI Classics CDC 7545742 |
| 29/06/1996 | 67 | 1 | | KAFKA | EMI CDEMD 1095 |
| 06/11/1999 | 51 | 6 | | CLASSIC KENNEDY **NIGEL KENNEDY WITH THE ENGLISH CHAMBER ORCHESTRA** | EMI Classics CDC 5568902 |
| 02/11/2002 | 71 | 1 | | GREATEST HITS | EMI Classics 5574112 |

### KENNY
UK pop group formed by Richard Driscoll (vocals), Jan Style (guitar), Christopher Lacklison (keyboards), Chris Redburn (bass) and Andy Walton (drums); their hits also featuring session musicians including Chris Spedding.

| DATE | POS | WKS | BPI | ALBUM TITLE | LABEL & NUMBER |
|---|---|---|---|---|---|
| 17/01/1976 | 56 | 1 | | THE SOUND OF SUPER K | RAK SRAK 518 |

### GERARD KENNY
US singer/songwriter (born 8/7/1947, New York City).

| DATE | POS | WKS | BPI | ALBUM TITLE | LABEL & NUMBER |
|---|---|---|---|---|---|
| 21/07/1979 | 19 | 4 | | MADE IT THROUGH THE RAIN | RCA Victor PL 25218 |

### KERBDOG
Irish group originally formed in Kilkenny by Cormac Battle (guitar/vocals), Colin Fenelly (bass), Billy Dalton (guitar) and Darragh Butler (drums) as Rollercoaster. Dalton left in 1995 and the group continued as a trio.

| DATE | POS | WKS | BPI | ALBUM TITLE | LABEL & NUMBER |
|---|---|---|---|---|---|
| 12/04/1997 | 64 | 1 | | ON THE TURN | Fontana 5329992 |

### NIK KERSHAW
UK singer/writer/guitarist/keyboard player (born 1/3/1958, Bristol) who debuted in 1980 in Fusion. Later a songwriter, he wrote hits for Let Loose, The Hollies and Chesney Hawkes.

| DATE | POS | WKS | BPI | ALBUM TITLE | LABEL & NUMBER |
|---|---|---|---|---|---|
| 10/03/1984 | 5 | 61 | ✪ | HUMAN RACING | MCA MCF 3197 |

○ Silver disc   ● Gold disc   ✪ Platinum disc (additional platinum units are indicated by a figure following the symbol)   ❶[9] Number of weeks album topped the UK chart

| | | | | | |
|---|---|---|---|---|---|
| 01/12/1984 | 8 | 36 | ✪ | THE RIDDLE | MCA MCF 3245 |
| 08/11/1986 | 47 | 3 | ○ | RADIO MUSICOLA | MCA MCG 6016 |

**KEY SESSIONS QUARTET** UK studio group.

| | | | | | |
|---|---|---|---|---|---|
| 20/03/2004 | 54 | 2 | | THE PIANO SESSIONS | T2/Telstar TCD3387 |

**ALICIA KEYS** US singer (born 25/1/1981, Manhattan) who began songwriting aged fourteen, having played the piano since the age of seven. Signed by Arista Records in 1998, she followed label boss Clive Davies when he set up J Records, with a debut album in 2001 that sold 50,000 copies on its first day of release. Alicia had previously contributed to the soundtrack to *Shaft*. Five Grammy Awards in 2002 included Song of the Year, Best R&B Song and Best R&B Vocal Performance for *Fallin'*, and Best New Artist. She also won the 2002 MTV Europe Music Award for Best R&B Act.

| | | | | | |
|---|---|---|---|---|---|
| 22/09/2001 | 6 | 79 | ✪³ | SONGS IN A MINOR ◇ ▲³ 2001 Grammy Award for Best R&B Album and the 2002 MOBO Award for Best Album | J Records 80813200022 |
| 13/12/2003 | 13 | 29+ | ✪ | THE DIARY OF ALICIA KEYS ◇ ▲² | J Records 82876586202 |

**NUSRAT FATEH ALI KHAN/MICHAEL BROOK** Pakistani singer and Canadian producer/composer/multi-instrumentalist (though best known for his guitar playing). Khan (born 13/10/1948, Lyallpur, Pakistan); one of the most popular qawwali singers to have emerged from the Indian subcontinent, he was one of the first to incorporate Western rhythms into his music. Michael Brook studied at York University in Toronto and was first introduced to Indian music by trumpeter Jon Hassell. He has since worked with Youssou N'Dour, Bryan Ferry, Brian Eno and earned an Oscar nomination for his music to *Fires Of Kuwait*. Khan died on 16/8/1997.

| | | | | | |
|---|---|---|---|---|---|
| 06/04/1996 | 65 | 1 | | NIGHT SONG | Realworld CDRW 50 |

**CHAKA KHAN** US singer (born Yvette Marie Stevens, 23/3/1953, Great Lakes, IL); she replaced Paulette McWilliams as lead singer in Ask Rufus in 1972. She signed solo with Atlantic in 1978, leaving the group in 1980 after fulfiling her contractual obligations. Her sister Taka Boom fronted Undisputed Truth. She has won six Grammy Awards: Best Rhythm & Blues Vocal Performance in 1983 for *Chaka Khan,* Best Arrangement for Two or More Voices in 1983 with Arif Mardin for *Be Bop Medley,* Best Rhythm & Blues Vocal Performance in 1984 for *I Feel For You* (which also won the Best Rhythm & Blues Song category for writer Prince), Best Rhythm & Blues Vocal Performance by a Duo in 1990 with Ray Charles for *I'll Be Good To You,* Best Rhythm & Blues Vocal Performance in 1992 for *The Woman I Am* and Best Traditional R&B Vocal Performance in 2002 with The Funk Brothers for *What's Going On*. Chaka was given a Lifetime Achievement Award at the 2002 MOBO Awards.

| | | | | | |
|---|---|---|---|---|---|
| 21/04/1984 | 64 | 5 | | STOMPIN' AT THE SAVOY **RUFUS AND CHAKA KHAN** | Warner Brothers 9236791 |
| 20/10/1984 | 15 | 22 | ● | I FEEL FOR YOU | Warner Brothers 9251621 |
| 09/08/1986 | 77 | 2 | | DESTINY | Warner Brothers WX 45 |
| 03/06/1989 | 14 | 15 | ● | LIFE IS A DANCE – THE REMIX PROJECT | Warner Brothers WX 268 |
| 04/09/1999 | 62 | 1 | | BEST OF CHAKA KHAN – I'M EVERY WOMAN | warner.esp 9362475072 |

**KID ROCK** US rapper (born Robert Ritchie, 17/1/1971, Romeo, MI); he formed break dance crew the Furious Funkers, worked with Boogie Down Productions, producing his debut album in 1990. He took part in the *It's Only Rock 'N' Roll* project for the Children's Promise charity.

| | | | | | |
|---|---|---|---|---|---|
| 10/06/2000 | 73 | 1 | | THE HISTORY OF ROCK | East West 7567833142 |

**KIDS FROM 'FAME'** US group, a spin-off from the TV series that featured Debbie Allen (as Lydia), Carlo Imperato (Danny), Valerie Landsburg (Doris), Carol Mayo (Coco), Lori Singer (Julie) and Gene Anthony Ray (Leroy). The series itself was inspired by the film *Fame*, the title track of which was a UK #1 by Irene Cara (for the TV series the same number was sung by Erica Gimpel). Ray suffered a stroke in June 2003 and died on 14/11/2003.

| | | | | | |
|---|---|---|---|---|---|
| 24/07/1982 | ❶¹² | 45 | ✪ | THE KIDS FROM FAME | BBC REP 447 |
| 16/10/1982 | 2 | 21 | ✪ | THE KIDS FROM FAME AGAIN | RCA RCALP 6057 |
| 26/02/1983 | 8 | 28 | ○ | THE KIDS FROM FAME LIVE | RCA KIDLP 003 |
| 14/05/1983 | 14 | 16 | | THE KIDS FROM FAME SONGS | BBC KIDLP 004 |
| 20/08/1983 | 28 | 7 | | THE KIDS FROM FAME SING FOR YOU | BBC KIDLP 005 |

**KILLERS** US rock group formed in Las Vegas, NE by Brandon Flowers (vocals), David Keuning (guitar), Mark Stoermer (bass) and Ronnie Vannucci (drums).

| | | | | | |
|---|---|---|---|---|---|
| 19/06/2004 | 6 | 2+ | ○ | **HOT FUSS** | Lizard King LIZARD011 |

---

▲⁹ Number of weeks album topped the US chart   ◆¹² RIAA Diamond Awards   ◇³ IFPI Platinum Europe Awards

## KILLING JOKE
UK group formed in London in 1979 by Jeremy 'Jaz' Coleman (born 26/2/1960, Cheltenham, vocals), 'Big' Paul Ferguson (born 31/3/1958, High Wycombe, drums), Geordie (born K Walker 18/12/1958, Newcastle, guitar) and Martin 'Pig Youth' Glover (born 27/12/1960, Africa).

| | | | | |
|---|---|---|---|---|
| 25/10/1980 . . . . . 39 . . . . . 4 . . . . . . | KILLING JOKE . . . . . . . . . . . . . . . . . . . . . . . . . . . . . . . . . . . . . . . . . . . . . . . Polydor EGMD 545 |
| 20/06/1981 . . . . . 42 . . . . . 4 . . . . . . | WHAT'S THIS FOR . . . . . . . . . . . . . . . . . . . . . . . . . . . . . . . . . . . . . . . . . . . . . . E.G. EGMD 550 |
| 08/05/1982 . . . . . 12 . . . . . 6 . . . . . . | REVELATIONS . . . . . . . . . . . . . . . . . . . . . . . . . . . . . . . . . . . . . . . . . . . . . . . . . E.G. EGMD 3 |
| 27/11/1982 . . . . . 66 . . . . . 2 . . . . . . | HA' – KILLING JOKE LIVE . . . . . . . . . . . . . . . . . . . . . . . . . . . . . . . . . . . . . . . . E.G. EGMDT 4 |
| 23/07/1983 . . . . . 29 . . . . . 3 . . . . . . | FIRE DANCES . . . . . . . . . . . . . . . . . . . . . . . . . . . . . . . . . . . . . . . . . . . . . . . . . . E.G. EGMD 5 |
| 09/03/1985 . . . . . 11 . . . . . 9 . . . . . . ○ | NIGHT TIME . . . . . . . . . . . . . . . . . . . . . . . . . . . . . . . . . . . . . . . . . . . . . . . . . . E.G. EGLP 61 |
| 22/11/1986 . . . . . 54 . . . . . 1 . . . . . . | BRIGHTER THAN A THOUSAND SUNS . . . . . . . . . . . . . . . . . . . . . . . . . . . . . . E.G. EGLP 66 |
| 09/07/1988 . . . . . 92 . . . . . 1 . . . . . . | OUTSIDE THE GATE . . . . . . . . . . . . . . . . . . . . . . . . . . . . . . . . . . . . . . . . . . E.G. EGLP 73 |
| 06/08/1994 . . . . . 16 . . . . . 3 . . . . . . | PANDEMONIUM . . . . . . . . . . . . . . . . . . . . . . . . . . . . . . . . . . . . . . . . . . Butterfly BFLCD 9 |
| 13/04/1996 . . . . . 71 . . . . . 1 . . . . . . | DEMOCRACY . . . . . . . . . . . . . . . . . . . . . . . . . . . . . . . . . . . . . . . . . . . Butterfly BFLCD 17 |
| 09/08/2003 . . . . . 43 . . . . . 1 . . . . . . | KILLING JOKE . . . . . . . . . . . . . . . . . . . . . . . . . . . . . . . . . . . . . . . . . . . . Zuma ZUMACD002 |

## KILLS
UK duo formed in 2001 by VV (Alison Mosshart, vocals) and Hotel (Jamie Hince).

| | |
|---|---|
| 22/03/2003 . . . . . 47 . . . . . . 1 . . . . . . | KEEP ON YOUR MEAN SIDE . . . . . . . . . . . . . . . . . . . . . . . . . . . . . Domino Recordings WIGCD 124 |

## KILLSWITCH ENGAGE
US rock group formed in 1999 by Jesse Leach (vocals), Joel Stroetzel (guitar), Mike D'Antonio (bass) and Adam Dutkiewitz (drums). Leach was replaced in 2002 by Howard Jones.

| | |
|---|---|
| 22/05/2004 . . . . . 40 . . . . . . 1 . . . . . . | THE END OF HEARTACHE . . . . . . . . . . . . . . . . . . . . . . . . . . . . . . . . . . . . . . . . Roadrunner RR83732 |

## KIMERA WITH THE LONDON SYMPHONY ORCHESTRA
Korean female singer.

| | |
|---|---|
| 26/10/1985 . . . . . 38 . . . . . . 4 . . . . . . | HITS ON OPERA . . . . . . . . . . . . . . . . . . . . . . . . . . . . . . . . . . . . . . . . . . . . . . . Stylus SMR 8505 |

## KING
UK group formed in Coventry by ex-Reluctant Stereotypes Paul King (born 20/1/1960, Coventry, vocals), Mick Roberts (keyboards), Tony Wall (bass) and Jim Jackal (born Jim Lantsbery, guitar). King later went solo before becoming a presenter on VH-1.

| | |
|---|---|
| 09/02/1985 . . . . . 6 . . . . . . 21 . . . . . . ● | STEPS IN TIME . . . . . . . . . . . . . . . . . . . . . . . . . . . . . . . . . . . . . . . . . . . . . . . . . . . CBS 26095 |
| 23/11/1985 . . . . . 16 . . . . . 11 . . . . . . ● | BITTER SWEET . . . . . . . . . . . . . . . . . . . . . . . . . . . . . . . . . . . . . . . . . . . . . . . . . . . CBS 86320 |

## BB KING
US singer/guitarist (born Riley B King, 16/9/1925, Itta Bena, MS) who initially picked cotton alongside his parents and sang gospel in his spare time. In 1945 he moved to Memphis, sharing a room with a cousin, Bukka White (though he was unable to pay off his debts to the plantation owner until 1948) and busking on street corners. Appearing on radio stations KWEM and WDIA, the latter billed him as the 'Beale Street Blues Boy' (amended to Blues Boy King and then BB King); he debuted for Bullet Records in 1949. He was inducted into the Rock & Roll Hall of Fame in 1987 and twelve Grammy Awards include: Best Rhythm and Blues Solo Vocal Performance, Male in 1970 for *The Thrill Is Gone;* Best Traditional Blues Recording in 1983 for *Blues 'N' Jazz;* Best Traditional Blues Recording in 1985 for *My Guitar Sings The Blues;* Best Traditional Blues Recording in 1990 for *Live At San Quentin;* Best Traditional Blues Album in 1991 for *Live At The Apollo;* Best Traditional Blues Album in 1993 for *Blues Summit;* Best Rock Instrumental in 1996 with Jimmie Vaughan, Eric Clapton, Bonnie Raitt, Robert Cray, Buddy Guy, Dr John and Art Neville for *SRV Shuffle;* Best Traditional Blues in 1999 for *Blues On The Bayou;* Best Pop Collaboration With Vocals in 2000 with Dr John for *Is You Is, Or Is You Ain't (My Baby);* Best Pop Instrumental Performance in 2002 for *Auld Lang Syne* and Best Traditional Blues Album the same year for *A Christmas Celebration Of Hope.* He also won the 1998 MOBO Award for Lifetime Achievement. His guitar, usually a Gibson 335 or Gibson 355, was nicknamed 'Lucille' after a live date in Twist, AZ in the late 1940s. A fight broke out, a stove was knocked over and the building caught fire. BB rescued his guitar, later discovering the fight had been over a woman, Lucille. He has a star on the Hollywood Walk of Fame.

| | |
|---|---|
| 25/08/1979 . . . . . 60 . . . . . 5 . . . . . . | TAKE IT HOME . . . . . . . . . . . . . . . . . . . . . . . . . . . . . . . . . . . . . . . . . . . . . . . MCA MCF 3010 |
| 01/05/1999 . . . . . 24 . . . . . 4 . . . . . . | HIS DEFINITIVE GREATEST HITS . . . . . . . . . . . . . . . . . . . . . . . . . . . . . . . . . Universal TV 5473402 |
| 24/06/2000 . . . . . 15 . . . . . 15 . . . . . . ● | RIDING WITH THE KING ◇ **B.B. KING AND ERIC CLAPTON** 2000 Grammy for Best Traditional Blues Album . . . . Reprise 9362476122 |

## BEN E KING
US singer (born Benjamin Earl Nelson, 23/9/1938, Henderson, NC) who was with the Four B's and Moonglows before the Five Crowns in 1957. Drifters' manager George Treadwell hired the Crowns as the new Drifters in 1958, King singing lead on hits before being sacked for complaining about low wages. He went solo, signing with Atco five months later. He was later in The Soul Clan with Solomon Burke, Arthur Conley, Don Covay and Joe Tex.

| | |
|---|---|
| 01/07/1967 . . . . . 30 . . . . . 3 . . . . . . | SPANISH HARLEM . . . . . . . . . . . . . . . . . . . . . . . . . . . . . . . . . . . . . . . . . . . . . Atlantic 590001 |
| 14/03/1987 . . . . . 14 . . . . . 8 . . . . . . ● | STAND BY ME (THE ULTIMATE COLLECTION) . . . . . . . . . . . . . . . . . . . . . . . . . . . . Atlantic WX 90 |
| 20/10/1990 . . . . . 15 . . . . . 16 . . . . . . | THE VERY BEST OF BEN E KING AND THE DRIFTERS . . . . . . . . . . . . . . . . . . . . . Telstar STAR 2373 |
| 07/11/1998 . . . . . 41 . . . . . 3 . . . . . . . . . | THE VERY BEST OF BEN E KING AND THE DRIFTERS This and the above hit credited to **BEN E KING AND THE DRIFTERS** . . . . . . . . . . . . |
| | . . . . . . . . . . . . . . . . . . . . . . . . . . . . . . . . . . . . . . . . . . . . . . . . . . . Warner.esp/Global TV RADCD 108 |

## CAROLE KING
US singer (born Carole Klein, 9/2/1942, Brooklyn, NYC); she began songwriting in 1958, teaming with lyricist (and future husband) Gerry Goffin on four US #1s: *Will You Love Me Tomorrow, Go Away Little Girl, Take Good Care Of My Baby* and *The Loco-Motion.* Her debut solo record was in 1959; she resumed her career in 1967 following divorce from Goffin. She won four 1971 Grammy Awards including Record of the Year for *It's Too Late* and Song of the Year for *You've Got A Friend.*

| 24/07/1971 . . . . . 4 . . . . . 90 . . . . . | TAPESTRY ▲15 ◆10 1971 Grammy Awards for Album of the Year and Best Pop Vocal Performance . . . . . . . . . . . . . . A&M AMLS 2025 |
| 15/01/1972 . . . . . 18 . . . 10 . . . . . | MUSIC ▲3 . . . . . . . . . . . . . . . . . . . . . . . . . . . . . . . . . . . . . . . . . . . . . . . . . . . . . . . . . . . . . . . . A&M AMLH 67013 |
| 02/12/1972 . . . . . 40 . . . . . 2 . . . . . | RHYMES AND REASONS . . . . . . . . . . . . . . . . . . . . . . . . . . . . . . . . . . . . . . . . . . . . . . . . . . . . . . . . . Ode 77016 |
| 07/02/1998 . . . . . 24 . . . . . 3 . . . . . | TAPESTRY Re-issue of A&M AMLS 2025 . . . . . . . . . . . . . . . . . . . . . . . . . . . . . . . . . . . . . . . . . . Epic CD 82308 |
| 30/09/2000 . . . . . 31 . . . . . 3 . . . . . | NATURAL WOMAN – THE VERY BEST OF . . . . . . . . . . . . . . . . . . . . . . . . . . . . . . . . . . . . Columbia SONYTV 93CD |

**DIANA KING** Jamaican singer (born 8/11/1970, St Catherine's); played local clubs for eight years then toured as a backing singer with Shabba Ranks, relocating to New York in the process. She was signed as a solo artist by Sony in 1995.

| 12/08/1995 . . . . . 50 . . . . . . 2 . . . . . . | TOUGHER THAN LOVE . . . . . . . . . . . . . . . . . . . . . . . . . . . . . . . . . . . . . . . . . . . . . . . . . . . . Columbia 4777562 |

**EVELYN KING** US singer (born 29/6/1960, The Bronx, NYC); she moved to Philadelphia, PA in 1970. Discovered by producer T Life covering for her sister, who was a cleaner at Sigma Studios.

| 11/09/1982 . . . . . 35 . . . . . 9 . . . . . . | GET LOOSE . . . . . . . . . . . . . . . . . . . . . . . . . . . . . . . . . . . . . . . . . . . . . . . . . . . . . . . . . . . . . RCA RCALP 3093 |

**MARK KING** UK singer/bass player (born 20/10/1958, Cowes, Isle of Wight); he founded Level 42 in 1980 with Phil Gould, Boon Gould and Mike Lindup and launched a parallel solo career in 1984. Level 42 disbanded in 1995 and King concentrated on his solo career and session work thereafter.

| 21/07/1984 . . . . . 77 . . . . . . 2 . . . . . . | INFLUENCES . . . . . . . . . . . . . . . . . . . . . . . . . . . . . . . . . . . . . . . . . . . . . . . . . . . . . . . . . . . . . . Polydor MKLP 1 |

**SOLOMON KING** US singer (born Lexington, KY); he later based himself in the UK in Prestwick, Manchester

| 22/06/1968 . . . . . 40 . . . . 1 . . . . . . | SHE WEARS MY RING . . . . . . . . . . . . . . . . . . . . . . . . . . . . . . . . . . . . . . . . . . . . . . . . . . . . . Columbia SCX 6250 |

**KING ADORA** UK rock group formed in Birmingham, West Midlands by Matt Browne (guitar/vocals), Martyn Nelson (guitar/vocals), Robbie Grimmitt (bass) and Dan Dabrowski (drums).

| 02/06/2001 . . . . . 30 . . . . . . 1 . . . . . . | VIBRATE YOU . . . . . . . . . . . . . . . . . . . . . . . . . . . . . . . . . . . . . . . . . . . . . . . . . . . . Superior Quality RQS 13CD |

**KING CRIMSON** UK rock group formed in 1969 by Robert Fripp (born 11/4/1945, Wimbourne, Dorset, guitar), Ian McDonald (born 25/6/1946, London, keyboards), Greg Lake (born 10/11/1948, Bournemouth, bass) and Mike Giles (born 1/3/1942, Bournemouth, drums), with Pete Sinfield as lyricist. McDonald and Giles left after the second album (to form a duo), soon followed by Greg Lake (forming Emerson Lake and Palmer) and were replaced by Gordon Haskell (bass/vocals), Mel Collins (saxophone) and Andy McCullough (drums). Haskell quit two days after completing their third album, replaced by Ian Wallace, whilst Boz Burrell (born 1/8/1946, Lincoln) was recruited as lead singer (beating Bryan Ferry, among others, at the audition). Fripp assembled a new King Crimson in July 1972 with John Wetton (born 12/7/1949, Derby, bass/vocals), Bill Bruford (born 17/5/1948, London, drums), Jamie Muir (percussion) and David Cross (flute/violin). Muir left in February 1973 after injuring himself and reportedly entered a monastery. Fripp disbanded the group in September 1974 to go solo, although he used the name again in 1981 with Bruford, Adrian Belew (guitar) and Tony Levin (bass) for three albums over the next three years. He revived them again in 1993 with Levin, Belew, Jerry Marotta, Trey Gunn and Stick for a series of live dates, culminating in a new album in 1995. Fripp married fellow singer Toyah Wilcox in 1986. Wetton and Bruford were also members of U.K.

| 01/11/1969 . . . . . 5 . . . . . . 18 . . . . . . | **IN THE COURT OF THE CRIMSON KING** . . . . . . . . . . . . . . . . . . . . . . . . . . . . . . . . . . . . . . . . . . Island ILPS 9111 |
| 30/05/1970 . . . . . 4 . . . . . . 13 . . . . . . | **IN THE WAKE OF POSEIDON** . . . . . . . . . . . . . . . . . . . . . . . . . . . . . . . . . . . . . . . . . . . . . . . . Island ILPS 9127 |
| 16/01/1971 . . . . . 30 . . . . . 1 . . . . . | LIZARD . . . . . . . . . . . . . . . . . . . . . . . . . . . . . . . . . . . . . . . . . . . . . . . . . . . . . . . . . . . . . . . . Island ILPS 9141 |
| 08/01/1972 . . . . . 30 . . . . . 1 . . . . . | ISLANDS . . . . . . . . . . . . . . . . . . . . . . . . . . . . . . . . . . . . . . . . . . . . . . . . . . . . . . . . . . . . . . . Island ILPS 9175 |
| 07/04/1973 . . . . . 20 . . . . . 4 . . . . . | LARKS' TONGUES IN ASPIC . . . . . . . . . . . . . . . . . . . . . . . . . . . . . . . . . . . . . . . . . . . . . . . . . Island ILPS 9230 |
| 13/04/1974 . . . . . 28 . . . . . 2 . . . . . | STARLESS AND BIBLE BLACK . . . . . . . . . . . . . . . . . . . . . . . . . . . . . . . . . . . . . . . . . . . . . . . Island ILPS 9275 |
| 26/10/1974 . . . . . 45 . . . . . 1 . . . . . | RED . . . . . . . . . . . . . . . . . . . . . . . . . . . . . . . . . . . . . . . . . . . . . . . . . . . . . . . . . . . . . . . . . . . Island ILPS 9308 |
| 10/10/1981 . . . . . 41 . . . . . 4 . . . . . | DISCIPLINE . . . . . . . . . . . . . . . . . . . . . . . . . . . . . . . . . . . . . . . . . . . . . . . . . . . . . . . . . . . . E.G. EGLP 49 |
| 26/06/1982 . . . . . 39 . . . . . 5 . . . . . | BEAT . . . . . . . . . . . . . . . . . . . . . . . . . . . . . . . . . . . . . . . . . . . . . . . . . . . . . . . . . . . . . . . . . . . E.G. EGLP 51 |
| 31/03/1984 . . . . . 30 . . . . . 4 . . . . . | THREE OF A PERFECT PAIR . . . . . . . . . . . . . . . . . . . . . . . . . . . . . . . . . . . . . . . . . . . . . . . . . . E.G. EGLP 55 |
| 15/04/1995 . . . . . 58 . . . . . 1 . . . . . | THRAK . . . . . . . . . . . . . . . . . . . . . . . . . . . . . . . . . . . . . . . . . . . . . . . . . . . . . . . . . . . . . . . . Virgin KCCDY 1 |

**KING KURT** UK rock group formed in 1983 by Bert, Rory Lyons, Maggit, John Reddington, Smeg and Thwack, produced by Dave Edmunds. By 1985 Bert and Reddington had left, replaced by Dick Crippen and Jim Piper.

| 10/12/1983 . . . . . 99 . . . . . 1 . . . . . | OOH WALLAH WALLAH . . . . . . . . . . . . . . . . . . . . . . . . . . . . . . . . . . . . . . . . . . . . . . . . . . . . Stiff SEEZ 52 |
| 08/03/1986 . . . . . 50 . . . . . 4 . . . . . | BIG COCK . . . . . . . . . . . . . . . . . . . . . . . . . . . . . . . . . . . . . . . . . . . . . . . . . . . . . . . . . . . . . . . Stiff SEEZ 62 |

**KING'S X** US trio formed by Doug Pinnick (bass/vocals), Ty Taboo (guitar) and Jerry Gaskell (drums) as The Edge, changing their name when they relocated to Houston, TX. They signed with Megaforce in 1988.

| 01/07/1989 . . . . . 52 . . . . . 1 . . . . . | GRETCHEN GOES TO NEBRASKA . . . . . . . . . . . . . . . . . . . . . . . . . . . . . . . . . . . . . . . . . . Megaforce WX 279 |
| 10/11/1990 . . . . . 70 . . . . . 1 . . . . . | FAITH HOPE LOVE . . . . . . . . . . . . . . . . . . . . . . . . . . . . . . . . . . . . . . . . . . . . . . . . . . . Megaforce 7567821451 |
| 28/03/1992 . . . . . 46 . . . . . 1 . . . . . | KING'S X . . . . . . . . . . . . . . . . . . . . . . . . . . . . . . . . . . . . . . . . . . . . . . . . . . . . . . . . . . . . Atlantic 7567805062 |
| 12/02/1994 . . . . . 49 . . . . . 1 . . . . . | DOGMAN . . . . . . . . . . . . . . . . . . . . . . . . . . . . . . . . . . . . . . . . . . . . . . . . . . . . . . . . . . . Atlantic 7567825582 |

**KINGDOM COME** German/US rock group formed by Lenny Wolf (vocals), Danny Stag (guitar), Rick Steier (guitar), Johnny Frank (bass) and James Kottak (drums). By 1991 it was effectively Wolf recording solo with studio musicians.

| 26/03/1988 . . . . . 43 . . . . . 6 . . . . . | KINGDOM COME . . . . . . . . . . . . . . . . . . . . . . . . . . . . . . . . . . . . . . . . . . . . . . . . . . . . . . . Polydor KCLP 1 |
| 13/05/1989 . . . . . 25 . . . . . 4 . . . . . | IN YOUR FACE . . . . . . . . . . . . . . . . . . . . . . . . . . . . . . . . . . . . . . . . . . . . . . . . . . . . . . . . Polydor 8391921 |

**KINGMAKER** UK group formed in Hull in 1990 by Lawrence 'Loz' Hardy (born 14/9/1970, Manchester, guitar/vocals), Myles Howell (born 23/1/1971, Rugby, bass) and John Andrew (born 27/5/1963, Hull, drums). First on Sacred Heart, switching to Scorch in 1991.

| | | | | |
|---|---|---|---|---|
| 19/10/1991 . . . . . 29 . . . . . 3 . . . . . . | EAT YOURSELF WHOLE . . . . . . . . . . . . . . . . . . . . . . . . . . . . . . . . . . . . . . . . . . . . . . . . . . . . . . . . . . . . . . . . Scorch CHR 1878 |
| 29/05/1993 . . . . . 15 . . . . . . 7 . . . . . . | SLEEPWALKING . . . . . . . . . . . . . . . . . . . . . . . . . . . . . . . . . . . . . . . . . . . . . . . . . . . . . . . . . . . . . . . . . . Scorch CDCHR 6014 |

### CHOIR OF KING'S COLLEGE, CAMBRIDGE UK choir formed at King's College, Cambridge.

| | |
|---|---|
| 11/12/1971 . . . . . 38 . . . . . . 3 . . . . . . | THE WORLD OF CHRISTMAS . . . . . . . . . . . . . . . . . . . . . . . . . . . . . . . . . . . . . . . . . . . . . . . . . . . . . . . . . . . . . Argo SPAA 104 |

### KINGS OF CONVENIENCE Norwegian duo from Bergen, Erik Glambek Boe (guitar/vocals) and Erlend Oye (guitar).

| | |
|---|---|
| 10/02/2001 . . . . . 72 . . . . . . 1 . . . . . . | QUIET IS THE NEW LORD . . . . . . . . . . . . . . . . . . . . . . . . . . . . . . . . . . . . . . . . . . . . . . . . . . . . . . . . . . Source SOURCD 019 |

### KINGS OF LEON US rock group formed in Tennessee by Caleb Followhill (guitar/vocals), his brothers Jared (bass) and Nathan (drums) and cousin Matthew (guitar).

| | |
|---|---|
| 19/07/2003 . . . . . 3 . . . . . . 24 . . . . . ● | **YOUTH AND YOUNG MANHOOD** . . . . . . . . . . . . . . . . . . . . . . . . . . . . . . . . . . . . . . . . . . . . . . . . . . . Hand Me Down HMD27 |

### KINGS OF SWING ORCHESTRA Australian studio orchestra.

| | |
|---|---|
| 29/05/1982 . . . . . 28 . . . . . 11 . . . . . . | SWITCHED ON SWING . . . . . . . . . . . . . . . . . . . . . . . . . . . . . . . . . . . . . . . . . . . . . . . . . . . . . . . . . . . . . . K-Tel ONE 1166 |

### KINKS UK group formed in London in 1962 by Ray Davies (born 21/6/1944, Muswell Hill, London, guitar/vocals), his brother Dave (born 3/2/1947, Muswell Hill), Pete Quaife (born 31/12/1943, Tavistock, bass) and John Start (drums) as the Ray Davies Quartet. As the Ravens in 1963, Start was replaced with Mick Avory (born 15/2/1944, London) and on 31/12/1963 they appeared as The Kinks for the first time, signing with Pye in 1964. Numerous personnel changes came in the 1970s, Dave Davies recording solo. Ray Davies appeared in the film *Absolute Beginners*. They were inducted into the Rock & Roll Hall of Fame in 1990. In 2004, Ray Davies was shot by a mugger in New Orleans but survived, barely days after he was awarded the CBE.

| | |
|---|---|
| 17/10/1964 . . . . . 3 . . . . . . 25 . . . . . | **KINKS** . . . . . . . . . . . . . . . . . . . . . . . . . . . . . . . . . . . . . . . . . . . . . . . . . . . . . . . . . . . . . . . . . . . . . . . Pye NPL 18096 |
| 13/03/1965 . . . . . 3 . . . . . . 15 . . . . . | **KINDA KINKS** . . . . . . . . . . . . . . . . . . . . . . . . . . . . . . . . . . . . . . . . . . . . . . . . . . . . . . . . . . . . . . . . Pye NPL 18112 |
| 04/12/1965 . . . . . 9 . . . . . . 12 . . . . . | **KINDA KONTROVERSY** . . . . . . . . . . . . . . . . . . . . . . . . . . . . . . . . . . . . . . . . . . . . . . . . . . . . . . . Pye NPL 18131 |
| 10/09/1966 . . . . . 5 . . . . . . 31 . . . . . | **WELL RESPECTED KINKS** . . . . . . . . . . . . . . . . . . . . . . . . . . . . . . . . . . . . . . . . . . . . . . . . . . Marble Arch MAL 612 |
| 05/11/1966 . . . . . 12 . . . . . 11 . . . . . | FACE TO FACE . . . . . . . . . . . . . . . . . . . . . . . . . . . . . . . . . . . . . . . . . . . . . . . . . . . . . . . . . . . . . . . . . Pye NPL 18149 |
| 14/10/1967 . . . . . 35 . . . . . 2 . . . . . | SOMETHING ELSE BY THE KINKS . . . . . . . . . . . . . . . . . . . . . . . . . . . . . . . . . . . . . . . . . . . . . . Pye NSPL 18193 |
| 02/12/1967 . . . . . 9 . . . . . . 11 . . . . . | **SUNNY AFTERNOON** . . . . . . . . . . . . . . . . . . . . . . . . . . . . . . . . . . . . . . . . . . . . . . . . . . . . Marble Arch MAL 716 |
| 23/10/1971 . . . . . 21 . . . . . 4 . . . . . | GOLDEN HOUR OF THE KINKS . . . . . . . . . . . . . . . . . . . . . . . . . . . . . . . . . . . . . . . . . . Pye Golden Hour GH 501 |
| 14/10/1978 . . . . . 19 . . . . . 6 . . . . . | 20 GOLDEN GREATS . . . . . . . . . . . . . . . . . . . . . . . . . . . . . . . . . . . . . . . . . . . . . . . . . . . . . . . . . Ronco RPL 2031 |
| 05/11/1983 . . . . . 96 . . . . . 1 . . . . . | KINKS GREATEST HITS – DEAD END STREET . . . . . . . . . . . . . . . . . . . . . . . . . . . . . . . . . . . . . . PRT KINK 1 |
| 16/09/1989 . . . . . 35 . . . . . 7 . . . . . ● | THE ULTIMATE COLLECTION . . . . . . . . . . . . . . . . . . . . . . . . . . . . . . . . . . . . . . . . . Castle Communications CTVLP 001 |
| 18/09/1993 . . . . . 18 . . . . . 7 . . . . . ● | THE DEFINITIVE COLLECTION . . . . . . . . . . . . . . . . . . . . . . . . . . . . . . . . . . . . . . . . . . . . . . . Polygram TV 5164652 |
| 12/04/1997 . . . . . 42 . . . . . 3 . . . . . | THE VERY BEST OF THE KINKS . . . . . . . . . . . . . . . . . . . . . . . . . . . . . . . . . . . . . . . . . . . . . . . Polygram TV 5375542 |
| 08/06/2002 . . . . . 32 . . . . . 4 . . . . . ○ | THE ULTIMATE COLLECTION . . . . . . . . . . . . . . . . . . . . . . . . . . . . . . . . . . . . . . . . . . . . . . . . Sanctuary SANDD 109 |

### KATHY KIRBY UK singer (born 20/10/1940, Ilford). First noticed on tour with Cliff Richard and the Shadows in 1960, she became a regular on TV's *Stars And Garters*. She also had her own series on the BBC.

| | |
|---|---|
| 04/01/1964 . . . . . 11 . . . . . . 8 . . . . . . | 16 HITS FROM 'STARS AND GARTERS' . . . . . . . . . . . . . . . . . . . . . . . . . . . . . . . . . . . . . . . . . . . . . Decca LK 5475 |

### DOMINIC KIRWAN Irish singer (born 5/6/1960, Omagh, County Tyrone).

| | |
|---|---|
| 01/11/1997 . . . . . 54 . . . . . . 1 . . . . . . | THE MUSIC'S BACK . . . . . . . . . . . . . . . . . . . . . . . . . . . . . . . . . . . . . . . . . . . . . . . . . . . . . . . . . . . . Ritz RZCD 0084 |

### KISS US heavy rock group formed in New York in 1972 by Gene Simmons (born Chaim Witz, 25/8/1949, Haifa, Israel, bass/vocals), Paul Stanley (born Paul Elsen, 20/1/1950, New York, guitar/vocals), Peter Criss (born Peter Crisscoula, 27/12/1947, Brooklyn, NYC, drums/vocals) and Ace Frehley (born Paul Frehley, 22/4/1951, The Bronx, NYC, guitar/vocals) as Wicked Lester, becoming Kiss in 1973. They signed with Casablanca in 1974 and built a solid following with elaborate stage costumes and faces masked with make-up. All four released solo albums simultaneously in 1978. Criss left in 1980, replaced by Anton Fig and then Eric Carr (born 12/7/1950, Brooklyn, NYC). Frehley left in 1982 after a car accident (resurfacing with Frehley's Comet), replaced by Vinnie Vincent (born Vincent Cusano). They appeared without make-up for the first time in 1983. Vincent left in 1984, replaced by Mark St John (born Mark Norton), he in turn replaced by Bruce Kulick in 1985. Carr died from cancer on 24/11/1991, replaced by Eric Singer. In 1996 Frehley and Criss returned for an MTV *Unplugged* show, the original four members making the reunion permanent, appearing in the 1999 film *Detroit Rock City*. By 2003 they consisted of Simmons, Criss, Stanley and Tommy Thayer. They have a star on the Hollywood Walk of Fame.

| | |
|---|---|
| 29/05/1976 . . . . . 22 . . . . . . 5 . . . . . . | DESTROYER . . . . . . . . . . . . . . . . . . . . . . . . . . . . . . . . . . . . . . . . . . . . . . . . . . . . . . . . . . . . . . . . Casablanca CBSP 4008 |
| 26/06/1976 . . . . . 49 . . . . . . 2 . . . . . . | ALIVE! . . . . . . . . . . . . . . . . . . . . . . . . . . . . . . . . . . . . . . . . . . . . . . . . . . . . . . . . . . . . . . . . . . . . . . Casablanca CBSP 401 |
| 17/12/1977 . . . . . 60 . . . . . . 1 . . . . . . | ALIVE . . . . . . . . . . . . . . . . . . . . . . . . . . . . . . . . . . . . . . . . . . . . . . . . . . . . . . . . . . . . . . . . . . . . . Casablanca CALD 5004 |
| 07/07/1979 . . . . . 50 . . . . . . 6 . . . . . . | DYNASTY . . . . . . . . . . . . . . . . . . . . . . . . . . . . . . . . . . . . . . . . . . . . . . . . . . . . . . . . . . . . . . . . . Casablanca CALH 2051 |
| 28/06/1980 . . . . . 48 . . . . . . 3 . . . . . . | UNMASKED . . . . . . . . . . . . . . . . . . . . . . . . . . . . . . . . . . . . . . . . . . . . . . . . . . . . . . . . . . . . . . . . . . . Mercury 6302 032 |
| 05/12/1981 . . . . . 51 . . . . . . 3 . . . . . . | THE ELDER . . . . . . . . . . . . . . . . . . . . . . . . . . . . . . . . . . . . . . . . . . . . . . . . . . . . . . . . . . . . . . . . . Casablanca 6302 163 |
| 26/06/1982 . . . . . 42 . . . . . . 6 . . . . . . | KILLERS . . . . . . . . . . . . . . . . . . . . . . . . . . . . . . . . . . . . . . . . . . . . . . . . . . . . . . . . . . . . . . . . . . . . . Casablanca CANL 1 |
| 06/11/1982 . . . . . 22 . . . . . . 4 . . . . . . | CREATURES OF THE NIGHT . . . . . . . . . . . . . . . . . . . . . . . . . . . . . . . . . . . . . . . . . . . . . . . . . . Casablanca CANL 4 |
| 08/10/1983 . . . . . 7 . . . . . . 7 . . . . . . | **LICK IT UP** . . . . . . . . . . . . . . . . . . . . . . . . . . . . . . . . . . . . . . . . . . . . . . . . . . . . . . . . . . . . . Casablanca VERL 9 |
| 06/10/1984 . . . . . 11 . . . . . . 4 . . . . . . | ANIMALIZE . . . . . . . . . . . . . . . . . . . . . . . . . . . . . . . . . . . . . . . . . . . . . . . . . . . . . . . . . . . . . . . . . . . Vertigo VERL 18 |

05/10/1985 . . . . . 12 . . . . . 3 . . . . . ASYLUM . . . . . . . . . . . . . . . . . . . . . . . . . . . . . . . . . . . . . . . . . . . . . . . . . . . . . . . . . . . . . . . . . . . . Vertigo VERH 32
07/11/1987 . . . . . 4 . . . . . . 14 . . . . . **CRAZY NIGHTS** . . . . . . . . . . . . . . . . . . . . . . . . . . . . . . . . . . . . . . . . . . . . . . . . . . . . . . . . . . . . . . . Vertigo VERH 49
10/12/1988 . . . . . 62 . . . . . 2 . . . . . SMASHES, THRASHES AND HITS . . . . . . . . . . . . . . . . . . . . . . . . . . . . . . . . . . . . . . . . . . . . . . . . . Vertigo 8367591
04/11/1989 . . . . . 35 . . . . . 2 . . . . . HOT IN THE SHADE . . . . . . . . . . . . . . . . . . . . . . . . . . . . . . . . . . . . . . . . . . . . . . . . . . . . . . . . . . . Fontana 8389131
23/05/1992 . . . . . 10 . . . . . 3 . . . . . **REVENGE** . . . . . . . . . . . . . . . . . . . . . . . . . . . . . . . . . . . . . . . . . . . . . . . . . . . . . . . . . . . . . . . . . . Mercury 8480372
29/05/1993 . . . . . 24 . . . . . 2 . . . . . ALIVE III . . . . . . . . . . . . . . . . . . . . . . . . . . . . . . . . . . . . . . . . . . . . . . . . . . . . . . . . . . . . . . . . . . . Mercury 5148272
23/03/1996 . . . . . 74 . . . . . 1 . . . . . MTV UNPLUGGED . . . . . . . . . . . . . . . . . . . . . . . . . . . . . . . . . . . . . . . . . . . . . . . . . . . . . . . . . . . Mercury 5289502
12/07/1997 . . . . . 58 . . . . . 2 . . . . . GREATEST HITS . . . . . . . . . . . . . . . . . . . . . . . . . . . . . . . . . . . . . . . . . . . . . . . . . . . . . . . . . Polygram TV 5361592
03/10/1998 . . . . . 47 . . . . . 1 . . . . . PSYCHO-CIRCUS . . . . . . . . . . . . . . . . . . . . . . . . . . . . . . . . . . . . . . . . . . . . . . . . . . . . . . . . . . Mercury 5589922

**KISSING THE PINK** UK group formed in 1981 by Nick Whitecross (guitar/vocals), Simon Aldridge (guitar/vocals), Peter Barnett (bass/vocals), Jon Kingsley-Hall (keyboards/vocals), George Stewart (keyboards/vocals), Jo Wells (saxophone/vocals) and Steve Cusack (drums).

04/06/1983 . . . . . 54 . . . . . 5 . . . . . NAKED . . . . . . . . . . . . . . . . . . . . . . . . . . . . . . . . . . . . . . . . . . . . . . . . . . . . . . . . . . . . . . . . . . . . . Magnet KTPL 1001

**KITCHENS OF DISTINCTION** UK group formed in London in 1986 by Patrick Fitzgerald (born 7/4/1964, Basle, Switzerland, bass/vocals), Julian Swales (born 23/3/1964, Gwent, Wales, guitar) and Dan Goodwin (born 22/7/1964, Salamanca, Spain, drums). They have also worked under the name of Toilets of Destruction.

30/03/1991 . . . . . 45 . . . . . 1 . . . . . STRANGE FREE WORLD . . . . . . . . . . . . . . . . . . . . . . . . . . . . . . . . . . . . . . . . . . . . . . . One Little Indian TPLP 19
15/08/1992 . . . . . 72 . . . . . 1 . . . . . THE DEATH OF COOL . . . . . . . . . . . . . . . . . . . . . . . . . . . . . . . . . . . . . . . . . . . . . . One Little Indian TPLP 39CD

**EARTHA KITT** US singer (born 26/1/1928, Columbia, SC, raised in New York, later relocating to Paris). Break came on Broadway in *New Faces Of 1952*; subsequent films included *The Mark Of The Hawk* (1958), *Naughty Knights* (1971) and *Erik The Viking* (1989). She was also Catwoman in the TV series *Batman*. She has a star on the Hollywood Walk of Fame.

11/02/1961 . . . . . 17 . . . . . 1 . . . . . REVISITED . . . . . . . . . . . . . . . . . . . . . . . . . . . . . . . . . . . . . . . . . . . . . . . . . . . . . . . . . . . . . . . . . London HA 2296

**MYLEENE KLASS** UK singer (born 6/4/1978, Norfolk); she was a founding member of Hear'say who went solo when they disbanded in September 2002.

01/11/2003 . . . . . 32 . . . . . 3 . . . . . ○ MOVING ON . . . . . . . . . . . . . . . . . . . . . . . . . . . . . . . . . . . . . . . . . . . . . . . . . . . . . . . . . . . . . . . . UCJ 9865632

**KLEEER** US R&B group formed in New York City by Paul Crutchfield (vocals/percussion), Richard Lee (guitar/keyboards), Norman Durham (bass) and Woddy Cunningham (drums) as heavy metal band Pipeline. Toured as The Universal Robot Band, brainchild of producer Patrick Adams, after which they became Kleeer. They later added David Frank (keyboards) and singers Isabelle Coles, Melanie Moore and Yvette Flowers. Lee, Durham and Cunningham were previously the backing group for The Choice Four in Baltimore, MD.

06/07/1983 . . . . . 96 . . . . . 1 . . . . . SEEKRET . . . . . . . . . . . . . . . . . . . . . . . . . . . . . . . . . . . . . . . . . . . . . . . . . . . . . . . . . . . . . . . . . . . Atlantic 7812541
12/10/1985 . . . . . 87 . . . . . 2 . . . . . THE ARTISTS VOLUME III **WOMACK AND WOMACK/THE O'JAYS/KLEEER/THE S.O.S. BAND** . . . . . . . . . . . . . . . . Street Sounds ARTIS 3

**KLF** UK duo of Bill Drummond (born William Butterworth, 29/4/1953, South Africa) and Jimmy Cauty (born 1954, London) who teamed up in 1987 and released records as The JAMs, Disco 2000, The Justified Ancients of Mu Mu, The Timelords, 1300 Drums Featuring The Unjustified Ancients Of Mu and KLF. They established the KLF Communication record label; KLF stands for Kopyright Liberation Front. The group disbanded in 1992, returning in 1997 as 2K. They were named Best UK Group (jointly with Simply Red) at the 1992 BRIT Awards.

16/03/1991 . . . . . 3 . . . . . . 46 . . . . . . ✪ **THE WHITE ROOM** . . . . . . . . . . . . . . . . . . . . . . . . . . . . . . . . . . . . . . . . . . . . KLF Communications JAMSLP 6

**EARL KLUGH** – see **GEORGE BENSON**

**KNACK** US rock group formed in Los Angeles, CA in 1978 by Doug Fieger (guitar/vocals), Bruce Gary (drums), Prescott Niles (bass) and Berton Averre (guitar), all ex-session players. They disbanded in 1982, re-forming in 1986 with Billy Ward replacing Gary.

04/08/1979 . . . . . 65 . . . . . 2 . . . . . GET THE KNACK ▲5 . . . . . . . . . . . . . . . . . . . . . . . . . . . . . . . . . . . . . . . . . . . . . . . . . . . . . . . . . Capitol EST 11948

**BEVERLEY KNIGHT** UK singer (born Beverley Smith, 22/3/1973, Wolverhampton); she began singing in church, becoming known via local pirate radio. MOBO Awards include 1998 and 1999 for Best R&B Act.

05/09/1998 . . . . . 42 . . . . . 14 . . . . . ● PRODIGAL SISTA 1999 MOBO Award for Best Album . . . . . . . . . . . . . . . . . . . . . . . . Parlophone Rhythm Series 4962962
23/03/2002 . . . . . 7 . . . . . . 24 . . . . . ● **WHO I AM** . . . . . . . . . . . . . . . . . . . . . . . . . . . . . . . . . . . . . . . . . . . . . . . . . . . . . . . . Parlophone Rhythm Series 5360320

**GLADYS KNIGHT AND THE PIPS** US family group formed in 1952 by Gladys (born 28/5/1944, Atlanta, GA), brother Merald (born 4/9/1942, Atlanta), sister Brenda and cousins William (born 2/6/1941, Atlanta) and Elenor Guest (born 1940). Another cousin, James 'Pips' Woods, gave them their name. Initially singing in church, they turned professional in 1957, recording a debut single in 1959. Brenda and Elenor left in 1959, replaced by another cousin, Edward Patten (born 2/8/1939, Atlanta), and Langston George. George left in 1962. They were the first act to appear on the US TV show *Soul Train*, on 17/8/1972. Legal wrangles stopped them recording together from 1977 to 1980: the Pips recorded two LPs for Casablanca and Gladys one for Buddah. They disbanded in 1989. Gladys appeared in the film *Pipe Dreams* in 1976. Elenor Guest died from heart failure on 23/8/1997. They were inducted into the Rock & Roll Hall of Fame in 1996. The group won three Grammy Awards: Best Pop Vocal Performance by a Group in 1973 for *Neither One Of Us*, Best Rhythm & Blues Vocal Performance by a Group in 1973 for *Midnight Train To Georgia* and Best Rhythm & Blues Vocal Performance by a Group in 1988 for *Love Overboard*. Gladys also won a Grammy Award in 1986 for Best Pop Vocal Performance by a Group with Dionne Warwick, Elton John and Stevie Wonder for *That's What Friends Are For* and the 2001 Grammy Award for Best Traditional R&B Album for *At Last*. Gladys has a star on the Hollywood Walk of Fame.

31/05/1975 . . . . . 20 . . . . . 15 . . . . . ○ I FEEL A SONG . . . . . . . . . . . . . . . . . . . . . . . . . . . . . . . . . . . . . . . . . . . . . . . . . . . . . . . . . . . Buddah BDLP 4030
28/02/1976 . . . . . 6 . . . . . . 43 . . . . . ● **THE BEST OF GLADYS KNIGHT & THE PIPS** . . . . . . . . . . . . . . . . . . . . . . . . . . . . . . . . . . . . . . . Buddah BDLH 5013

▲9 Number of weeks album topped the US chart ◆12 RIAA Diamond Awards ◇3 IFPI Platinum Europe Awards

| DATE | POS | WKS | BPI | ALBUM TITLE | LABEL & NUMBER |
|------|-----|-----|-----|-------------|----------------|
| 16/07/1977 | 42 | 3 | | STILL TOGETHER | Buddah BDLH 5014 |
| 12/11/1977 | 3 | 22 | ✪ | **30 GREATEST** | K-Tel NE 1004 |
| 04/10/1980 | 16 | 6 | ○ | A TOUCH OF LOVE | K-Tel NE 1090 |
| 04/02/1984 | 43 | 5 | | THE COLLECTION – 20 GREATEST HITS | Starblend NITE 1 |
| 15/11/1986 | 21 | 10 | | DIANA ROSS. MICHAEL JACKSON. GLADYS KNIGHT. STEVIE WONDER. THEIR VERY BEST BACK TO BACK **DIANA ROSS/MICHAEL JACKSON/GLADYS KNIGHT/STEVIE WONDER** | PrioriTyV PTVR 2 |
| 27/02/1988 | 80 | 1 | | ALL OUR LOVE | MCA MCF 3409 |
| 28/10/1989 | 12 | 10 | ● | THE SINGLES ALBUM | Polygram TV GKTV 1 |
| 29/03/1997 | 69 | 2 | | THE SINGLES ALBUM | Polygram TV 8420032 |

**KNIGHTSBRIDGE STRINGS** UK studio orchestra assembled after the success of 101 Strings. The Knightsbridge Strings name was also used by the US label Monument.

| DATE | POS | WKS | BPI | ALBUM TITLE | LABEL & NUMBER |
|------|-----|-----|-----|-------------|----------------|
| 25/06/1960 | 20 | 1 | | STRING SWAY | Top Rank BUY 017 |

**DAVID KNOPFLER** UK singer/guitarist (born 27/12/1952, Glasgow) who is the younger brother of Mark Knopfler; both founder members of Dire Straits in 1977. He stayed with the group until July 1980 when he left to go solo.

| DATE | POS | WKS | BPI | ALBUM TITLE | LABEL & NUMBER |
|------|-----|-----|-----|-------------|----------------|
| 19/11/1983 | 82 | 1 | | RELEASE | Peach River DAVID 1 |

**MARK KNOPFLER** UK singer/guitarist (born 12/8/1949, Glasgow) who formed Dire Straits in 1977. He began solo projects in 1983 with the theme to the film *Local Hero,* also forming The Notting Hillbillies in 1986. He was awarded an OBE in the 2000 New Year's Honours List. Mark has collected five Grammy Awards: two as a member of Dire Straits and Best Country Instrumental Performance in 1985 with Chet Atkins for *Cosmic Square Dance,* Best Country Vocal Performance in 1990 with Chet Atkins for *Poor Boy Blues* and Best Country Instrumental Performance in 1990 with Chet Atkins for *So Soft Your Goodbye.*

| DATE | POS | WKS | BPI | ALBUM TITLE | LABEL & NUMBER |
|------|-----|-----|-----|-------------|----------------|
| 16/04/1983 | 14 | 11 | ○ | LOCAL HERO Original soundtrack to the film | Vertigo VERL 4 |
| 20/10/1984 | 65 | 3 | | CAL Original soundtrack to the film | Vertigo VERH 17 |
| 24/11/1990 | 41 | 11 | | NECK AND NECK ◇ | CBS 4674351 |
| 06/04/1996 | 9 | 17 | ● | **GOLDEN HEART** ◇ | Vertigo 5147322 |
| 07/10/2000 | 4 | 13 | ● | **SAILING TO PHILADELPHIA** ◇² | Mercury 5429812 |
| 12/10/2002 | 7 | 5 | ○ | **THE RAGPICKER'S DREAM** | Mercury 0632932 |

**BEYONCE KNOWLES** US singer (born 18/9/1981, Houston, TX) who was also lead singer with Destiny's Child. She also launched an acting career, appearing in the film *Austin Powers – Goldmember.* She won the 2003 MTV Europe Music Awards for Best R&B Female and Best Song with Jay-Z for *Crazy In Love.* Beyonce has also won five Grammy Awards, including: Best R&B Performance by a Duo or Group with Vocals with Luther Vandross for *The Closer I Get To You,* Best R&B Song (for writers Shawn Carter, Rich Harrison, Beyonce Knowles and Eugene Record) and Best Rap/Sung Collaboration with Jay-Z for *Crazy In Love* and Best Female R&B Vocal Performance for *Dangerously In Love* all in 2003. She was also named Best International Female at the 2004 BRIT Awards.

| DATE | POS | WKS | BPI | ALBUM TITLE | LABEL & NUMBER |
|------|-----|-----|-----|-------------|----------------|
| 05/07/2003 | ❶⁵ | 48 | ✪² | **BEYONCE** ◇ ▲¹ 2003 Grammy Award for Best Contemporary R&B Album | Columbia 5093952 |

**FRANKIE KNUCKLES** US singer (born 18/1/1955, the South Bronx, NYC) and a club DJ from 1971. He eventually owned his own club and became a noted remixer. He then launched his own recording career, and won the 1997 Grammy Award for Best Remixer.

| DATE | POS | WKS | BPI | ALBUM TITLE | LABEL & NUMBER |
|------|-----|-----|-----|-------------|----------------|
| 17/08/1991 | 59 | 2 | | BEYOND THE MIX | Virgin America VUSLP 6 |

**JOHN KONGOS** South African singer/multi-instrumentalist born in Johannesburg. He settled in the UK in 1966 and led a group called Scrub. He left in 1969 to go solo, with Dawn Records and then Fly, where he was produced by Gus Dudgeon. Kongos was later a top session musician and also scored the film *The Greek Tycoon.*

| DATE | POS | WKS | BPI | ALBUM TITLE | LABEL & NUMBER |
|------|-----|-----|-----|-------------|----------------|
| 15/01/1972 | 29 | 2 | | KONGOS | Fly HIFLY 7 |

**KOOL AND THE GANG** US group formed in New Jersey in 1964 by Robert 'Kool' Bell (born 8/10/1950, Youngstown, OH, bass), brother Ronald (born 1/11/1951, Youngstown, sax), Robert 'Spike' Mickens (trumpet), Dennis 'Dee Tee' Thomas (sax), Woody Sparrow (guitar) and Rick Westfield (keyboards) as the Jazziacs. Line-up and name-changes settled as Kool & The Gang in 1968, signing with De-Lite in 1969. They added singer James 'JT' Taylor (born 16/8/1953, South Carolina) and with producer Deodato moved from funk into mainstream. Taylor went solo in 1988, later returning. They won the 2003 MOBO Award for Outstanding Achievement.

| DATE | POS | WKS | BPI | ALBUM TITLE | LABEL & NUMBER |
|------|-----|-----|-----|-------------|----------------|
| 21/11/1981 | 10 | 20 | ● | SOMETHING SPECIAL | De-Lite DSR 001 |
| 02/10/1982 | 49 | 10 | | AS ONE | De-Lite DSR 3 |
| 07/05/1983 | 4 | 23 | ● | **TWICE AS KOOL** | Polystar PROLP 2 |
| 14/01/1984 | 18 | 23 | ○ | IN THE HEART | De-Lite DSR 4 |
| 15/12/1984 | 47 | 25 | ○ | EMERGENCY | De-Lite DSR 6 |
| 12/11/1988 | 28 | 13 | ● | THE SINGLES COLLECTION | De-Lite KGTV 1 |
| 27/10/1990 | 50 | 1 | | KOOL LOVE | Telstar STAR 2435 |
| 26/06/2004 | 56 | 1+ | | THE HITS – RELOADED | Unique Corp/Virgin/EMI VTDCD618 |

**KORGIS** UK duo Andy Davis (drums/guitar) and James Warren (bass/guitar/vocals), both ex-Stackridge, joined by Phil Harrison (keyboards/percussion) and Stuart Gordon (guitar/violin).

○ Silver disc ● Gold disc ✪ Platinum disc (additional platinum units are indicated by a figure following the symbol) ❶⁹ Number of weeks album topped the UK chart

26/07/1980 ..... 40 ...... 4 ...... DUMB WAITERS ....................................................................... Rialto TENOR 104

**KORN** US rock group formed in Bakersfield, CA in 1993 by Jonathan 'HIV' Davis (born 18/1/1971, Bakersfield, vocals), Brian 'Head' Welch (born 19/6/1970, Torrance, CA, guitar), James 'Munky' Shaffer (born 6/6/1970, Rosedale, CA, guitar), Reggie 'Fieldy Snuts' Arvizu (bass) and David Silveria (drums). They won the 1999 Grammy Award for Best Video Short Form for *Freak On A Leash* and the 2002 award for Best Metal Performance for *Here To Stay*.

26/10/1996 ..... 32 ...... 2 ...... LIFE IS PEACHY ..................................................................... Epic 4853696
29/08/1998 ..... 5 ...... 4 ...... **FOLLOW THE LEADER** ▲[1] ........................................................... Epic 4912212
27/11/1999 ..... 37 ...... 1 ...... ISSUES ▲[1] ......................................................................... Epic 4963592
22/06/2002 ..... 4 ...... 9 ...... ● **UNTOUCHABLES** .................................................................... Epic 5017702
06/12/2003 ..... 53 ...... 1 ...... TAKE A LOOK IN THE MIRROR ........................................................... Epic 05133253

**KOSHEEN** UK production duo from Bristol, with Markee 'Substance' Morrison and Darren 'Decoder' Beale plus singer Sian Evans.
29/09/2001 ..... 8 ...... 23 ...... ● **RESIST** ......................................................................... Moksha/Arista 74321880812
23/08/2003 ..... 7 ...... 6 ...... ● **KOKOPELLI** ...................................................................... Moksha/Arista 82876527232

**KRAFTWERK** German group formed in 1970 by Ralf Hutter (born 20/8/1946, Krefeld), Florian Schneider-Esleben (born 7/4/1947, Dusseldorf), Klaus Dinger and Thomas Homann, taking their name from the German for power plant. Dinger and Homann left in 1971, replaced two years later by Klaus Roeder-Bartos (born 31/5/1952, Berchtesgaden) and Wolfgang Flur (born 17/7/1947, Frankfurt).

17/05/1975 ..... 4 ...... 18 ...... ○ **AUTOBAHN** ....................................................................... Vertigo 6360 620
20/05/1978 ..... 9 ...... 13 ...... ● **THE MAN-MACHINE** ................................................................. Capitol EST 11728
23/05/1981 ..... 15 ...... 22 ...... ○ COMPUTER WORLD ..................................................................... EMI EMC 3370
06/02/1982 ..... 49 ...... 7 ...... TRANS-EUROPE EXPRESS ................................................................. Capitol EST 11603
22/06/1985 ..... 61 ...... 3 ...... AUTOBAHN Re-issue of Vertigo 6360 620 ................................................ Parlophone AUTO 1
15/11/1986 ..... 58 ...... 2 ...... ELECTRIC CAFÉ ........................................................................ EMI EMD 1001
22/06/1991 ..... 15 ...... 6 ...... ○ THE MIX ............................................................................ EMI EM 1408
16/08/2003 ..... 21 ...... 2 ...... TOUR DE FRANCE SOUNDTRACKS ........................................................... EMI 5917082

**DIANA KRALL** Canadian female pianist and singer (born 16/11/1964, Nanaimo, British Columbia); she studied the piano at the age of four and was performing regularly at fifteen. Her devotion to jazz music was inspired by her father's record collection and after studying at Berklee during the 1980s she relocated to New York. She first recorded for Justin Time.

12/06/1999 ..... 72 ...... 1 ...... WHEN I LOOK IN YOUR EYES 1999 Grammy Award for Best Jazz Vocal Album ................. Verve IMP 13042
29/09/2001 ..... 23 ...... 7 ...... THE LOOK OF LOVE ◇ ................................................................... Verve 5498462
23/11/2002 ..... 30 ...... 6 ...... A NIGHT IN PARIS 2002 Grammy Award for Best Jazz Vocal Album ......................... Verve 0653692
24/04/2004 ..... 4 ...... 8 ...... **THE GIRL IN THE OTHER ROOM** ....................................................... Verve 9862063

**BILLY J KRAMER AND THE DAKOTAS** UK singer (born William Ashton, 19/8/1943, Bootle) who was a British Rail apprentice fitter when signed by Brian Epstein in 1963. Epstein put Kramer with Manchester group the Dakotas — Mike Maxfield (born 23/2/1944, Manchester, guitar), Robin MacDonald (born 18/7/1943, Nairn, Scotland, rhythm guitar), Ray Jones (born 22/10/1939, Oldham, bass) and Tony Mansfield (born Anthony Bookbinder, 28/5/1943, Salford, drums) — recording various Lennon and McCartney compositions. Lennon suggested adding the 'J' to distinguish him from others with the same surname. The Dakotas split in 1968; by 1971 Kramer was recording under his real name.

16/11/1963 ..... 11 ...... 17 ...... LISTEN TO BILLY J KRAMER ............................................................. Parlophone PMC 1209

**ALISON KRAUSS AND UNION STATION** US singer/fiddle player (born 23/7/1971, Champaign, IL); she learned classical music from the age of five and by twelve was awarded the Most Promising Fiddle Player by the Society for the Preservation of Bluegrass Music. After a two year spell with Silver Rail she signed with Rounder Records, and Silver Rail changed name to Union Station. The group comprise Dan Tyminski (guitar), Ron Block (banjo), Adam Steffey (mandolin) and Barry Bales (bass). Fourteen Grammy Awards include: Best Bluegrass Recording (vocal or instrumental) in 1990 for *I've Got That Old Feeling*; Best Bluegrass Album in 1992 for *Every Time You Say Goodbye*; Best Southern Gospel, Country Gospel or Bluegrass Gospel Album in 1994 with The Cox Family for *I Know Who Holds Tomorrow*; Best Country Singer, Female in 1995 for *Baby, Now That I've Found You*; Best Country Collaboration with Vocals in 1995 with Shenandoah for *Somewhere In The Vicinity Of The Heart*; Best Country Collaboration in 1996 with Vince Gill and Union Station for *High Lonesome Sound*; Best Country Instrumental Performance with Union Station for *Little Liza Jane* from *So Long So Wrong*; Best Country Performance By A Duo Or Group With Vocal in 1997 with Union Station for *Looking In The Eyes Of Love* from *So Long So Wrong*; Best Bluegrass Album the same year for *So Long So Wrong*; Best Country Vocal Collaboration in 1998 with Clint Black, Joe Diffie, Merle Haggard, Emmylou Harris, Patty Loveless, Earl Scruggs, Ricky Skaggs, Marty Stuart, Pam Tillis, Randy Travis, Travis Tritt and Dwight Yoakam for *Same Old Train*; and Best Country Performance by a Duo or Group with Vocal in 2001 for *The Lucky One*. Alison and Union Station's recording of *The Lucky One* earned writer Robert Lee Castleman the 2001 Grammy Award for Best Country Song. She then won the 2003 Awards for Best Country Collaboration with Vocal with James Taylor for *How's The World Treating You* and Best Bluegrass Album for *Live*.

25/08/2001 ..... 72 ...... 1 ...... NEW FAVOURITE 2001 Grammy Award for Best Bluegrass Album .............................. Rounder ROUCD 0495

▲[9] Number of weeks album topped the US chart ◆[12] RIAA Diamond Awards ◇[3] IFPI Platinum Europe Awards

### LENNY KRAVITZ
US singer/multi-instrumentalist (born 26/5/1964, New York); he was self-taught on guitar, bass, piano and drums as a child. Family moved to Los Angeles, CA in 1977 when his mother, actress Roxie Kravitz, landed a TV role. He went into acting, appearing in a Bill Cosby special before leaving home at 16 to pursue a musical career, initially as Romeo Blue. Signed with Virgin in 1989. He was named Best International Male at the 1994 BRIT Awards. He has won four Grammy Awards: Best Male Rock Vocal Performance in 1998 for *Fly Away*, Best Male Rock Vocal Performance in 1999 for *American Woman*, Best Male Rock Vocal Performance in 2000 for *Again* and Best Male Rock Vocal Performance in 2001 for *Dig In*.

| DATE | POS | WKS | BPI | ALBUM TITLE | LABEL & NUMBER |
|---|---|---|---|---|---|
| 26/05/1990 | 56 | 4 | ● | LET LOVE RULE | Virgin America VUSLP 10 |
| 13/04/1991 | 8 | 27 | ✪ | **MAMA SAID** | Virgin America VUSLP 31 |
| 13/03/1993 | ❶² | 47 | ✪ | **ARE YOU GONNA GO MY WAY** | Virgin CDVUS 60 |
| 23/05/1995 | 5 | 4 | ● | **CIRCUS** | Virgin CDVUS 86 |
| 23/05/1998 | 18 | 13 | ● | 5 ◇ | Virgin CDVUS 140 |
| 04/11/2000 | 12 | 17 | ✪ | GREATEST HITS ◇ | Virgin CDVUSX 183 |
| 10/11/2001 | 55 | 1 | | LENNY ◇ | Virgin CDVUS 213 |
| 29/05/2004 | 74 | 1 | | BAPTISM | Virgin CDVUS 252 |

### KREUZ
UK vocal group with Sean Cummings, Wayne Lawes and Ricardo Reid.

| DATE | POS | WKS | BPI | ALBUM TITLE | LABEL & NUMBER |
|---|---|---|---|---|---|
| 18/03/1995 | 48 | 2 | | KREUZ KONTROL | Diesel DESCD 01 |

### KRIS KROSS
US teenage rap duo Mack Daddy (born Chris Kelly, 1/5/1978) and Daddy Mack (born Chris Smith, 10/1/1979).

| DATE | POS | WKS | BPI | ALBUM TITLE | LABEL & NUMBER |
|---|---|---|---|---|---|
| 27/06/1992 | 31 | 8 | | TOTALLY KROSSED OUT ▲² | Columbia 4714342 |

### KRIS KRISTOFFERSON
US singer/songwriter (born 22/6/1936, Brownsville, TX); he came to England to study at Oxford University during the 1950s and was initially signed by Larry Parnes. He then spent five years in the US Army before leaving in 1965 to pursue a career as a songwriter. While working as a cleaner at CBS studios in Nashville, he got the first of his songs recorded; Jerry Lee Lewis covering *Once More With Feeling*. His later compositions have included *Me And Bobby McGee* (a hit for Janis Joplin originally recorded by Roger Miller), *Help Me Make It Through The Night* (Gladys Knight), *One Day At A Time* (Lena Martell) and *For The Good Times* (Perry Como). He made his film debut in 1971 in *Cisco Pike* and has since appeared in *Pat Garrett And Billy The Kid* (with Bob Dylan), *A Star Is Born* (with Barbra Streisand), *Convoy* and *Millennium,* among others. He also worked as member of The Highwaymen (with Willie Nelson, Johnny Cash and Waylon Jennings) and was married to fellow singer Rita Coolidge between 1973 and 1980. He has won three Grammy Awards: Best Country Song in 1971 for *Help Me Make It Through The Night,* Best Country & Western Performance by Duo or Group with Rita Coolidge for *From The Bottle To The Bottom* in 1973 and for *Lover Please* in 1975.

| DATE | POS | WKS | BPI | ALBUM TITLE | LABEL & NUMBER |
|---|---|---|---|---|---|
| 06/05/1978 | 35 | 4 | | NATURAL ACT **KRIS KRISTOFFERSON AND RITA COOLIDGE** | A&M AMLH 64690 |

### KROKUS
Swiss rock group formed in Soluthurn in 1974 by Chris Von Rohr (vocals), Fernando Von Arb (guitar), Tommy Keifer (guitar), Jurg Naegeli (bass) and Freddie Steady (drums). Von Rohr switched to bass following the arrival of lead singer Marc Storace. By 1983 they consisted of Storace, Von Arb, Von Rohr, Mark Kohler (guitar) and Steve Pace (drums). Pace left in 1984 and was replaced by Jeff Klaven. Rohr also left the group in 1984.

| DATE | POS | WKS | BPI | ALBUM TITLE | LABEL & NUMBER |
|---|---|---|---|---|---|
| 21/02/1981 | 44 | 4 | | HARDWARE | Ariola ARL 5064 |
| 20/02/1982 | 28 | 5 | | ONE VICE AT A TIME | Ariola SPART 1189 |
| 16/04/1983 | 74 | 2 | | HEADHUNTER | Ariola 205 255 |

### KRS-ONE
US rapper (born Lawrence Kris Parker, 1966, The Bronx, NYC) who was with Boogie Down Productions with Scott LaRock before going solo when LaRock was shot to death. His name is an acronym for Knowledge Reigns Supreme Over Nearly Everyone; he later recorded with Goldie.

| DATE | POS | WKS | BPI | ALBUM TITLE | LABEL & NUMBER |
|---|---|---|---|---|---|
| 31/05/1997 | 58 | 1 | | I GOT NEXT | Jive CHIP 179 |

### K7
US rapper (born Louis Sharpe, New York City); he is also a member of TKA with Anthony Ortiz and Ralph Cruz. His backing group, The Swing Kids, feature Prophet, Los, Non-Stop and Tre Deuce.

| DATE | POS | WKS | BPI | ALBUM TITLE | LABEL & NUMBER |
|---|---|---|---|---|---|
| 05/02/1994 | 27 | 3 | | SWING BATTA SWING | Big Life BLRCD 27 |

### KULA SHAKER
UK rock group formed in 1994 by Crispian Mills (born 18/1/1973, London, guitar/vocals), Jay Darlington (born 3/5/1969, Sidcup, keyboards), Alonzo Bevin (born 24/10/1970, London, bass), Paul Winter-Hart (born 19/9/1971, London, drums) and Saul Dismont (vocals) as The Kays, name-changing to the Lovely Lads, and then Kula Shaker in 1995 (although minus Dismont). Won The City new band contest, signing with Columbia twelve days later. Named Best British Newcomer at the 1997 BRIT Awards. Mills is the son of actress Hayley Mills and grandson of actor Sir John Mills. They split in September 1999, Mills going solo.

| DATE | POS | WKS | BPI | ALBUM TITLE | LABEL & NUMBER |
|---|---|---|---|---|---|
| 28/09/1996 | ❶² | 44 | ✪² | **K** ◇ | Columbia SHAKER 1CD |
| 20/03/1999 | 9 | 10 | ● | **PEASANTS, PIGS & ASTRONAUTS** | Columbia SHAKER 2CD |

### CHARLIE KUNZ
US pianist (born 18/8/1896, Allentown, PA) who played piano from the age of six, forming his own semi-pro band at sixteen. He came to England in 1922 (having spent World War I making shells), forming his own band in the early 1930s. Such was his popularity during World War II that he was the subject of German propaganda attempts to discredit him, including Goebbels claiming he was really a German and had left the UK to fight with the German Army in Russia, and claims that his piano playing during radio broadcasts contained morse code messages for the Germans! He died from respiratory problems on 17/3/1958.

| DATE | POS | WKS | BPI | ALBUM TITLE | LABEL & NUMBER |
|---|---|---|---|---|---|
| 14/06/1969 | 9 | 11 | | **THE WORLD OF CHARLIE KUNZ** | Decca SPA 15 |

# L

**L.A. GUNS** US rock group formed in Los Angeles, CA in 1987 by Phil Lewis (vocals), Tracii Guns (guitar), Mick Cripps (guitar), Kelly Nickels (bass) and Steve Riley (drums). Guns had previously been a member of Guns N' Roses. The group disbanded in 1995 with Guns forming Killing Machine and Lewis forming Filthy Lucre.

| | | | |
|---|---|---|---|
| 05/03/1988.....73......1...... | L.A. GUNS. ...................................................................................... | Vertigo VERH 55 |
| 30/09/1989.....45......2...... | COCKED AND LOADED ............................................................................... | Vertigo 8385921 |
| 13/07/1991.....44......1...... | HOLLYWOOD VAMPIRES ............................................................................. | Mercury 8496041 |

**LA'S** UK rock group formed in Liverpool in 1986 by Lee Mavers (born 2/8/1962, Liverpool, guitar/vocals), John Power (born 14/9/1967, bass), Paul Hemmings (guitar) and John Timson (drums). They signed with Go Discs in 1987. By the time of their debut release in 1989 the line-up also included Neil Mavers on drums and Peter James 'Cammy' Cammel on guitar.

| | | | |
|---|---|---|---|
| 13/10/1990.....30.....20......○ | THE LA'S. ...................................................................................... | Go Discs 8282021 |

**PATTI LABELLE** US singer (born Patricia Holt, 24/5/1944, Philadelphia, PA); she was a member of LaBelle from 1962 to 1976 when the departure of Nona Hendryx brought the group to an end. Patti went solo, also appearing in films and musicals, including *A Soldier's Story*. She won the 1998 Grammy Award for Best Rhythm & Blues Traditional Vocal Performance for *Live! One Night Only* and has a star on the Hollywood Walk of Fame.

| | | | |
|---|---|---|---|
| 24/05/1986.....30.....17......○ | WINNER IN YOU ▲[1] ............................................................................ | MCA MCF 3319 |

**LADYSMITH BLACK MAMBAZO** South African group founded by lead vocalist Joseph Shabalala in 1960 (named after Shabalala's hometown and in honour of vocal group Black Mambazo, which means black axe). They turned professional in 1971, but they were relatively unknown outside their homeland until Paul Simon invited them to perform on his 1986 *Graceland* album. Shabalala was shot to death on 10/12/1991.

| | | | |
|---|---|---|---|
| 11/04/1987.....34......11......○ | SHAKA ZULU 1987 Grammy Award for Best Traditional Folk Recording ............................... | Warner Brothers WX 94 |
| 22/11/1997.....53......16......● | HEAVENLY ........................................................................................ | A&M 5407902 |
| 03/10/1998.....2.....34......○³ | **THE BEST OF LADYSMITH BLACK MAMBAZO – THE STAR AND WISEMAN** ............................... | Polygram TV 5652982 |
| 16/10/1999.....15......5...... | IN HARMONY ...................................................................................... | Universal Music TV 1537392 |
| 12/05/2001.....37......3...... | THE ULTIMATE COLLECTION .......................................................................... | Universal Music TV 5566822 |

**CLEO LAINE** UK singer (born Clementina Campbell, 28/10/1927, Southall, London) who began her career in 1952. Married to bandleader Johnny Dankworth, she was made a Dame in 1997. She won the 1985 Grammy Award for Best Jazz Vocal Performance for *Cleo At Carnegie – The 10th Anniversary Concert*.

| | | | |
|---|---|---|---|
| 07/01/1978.....18......22......○ | BEST OF FRIENDS **CLEO LAINE AND JOHN WILLIAMS** .............................................. | RCA Victor RS 1094 |
| 02/12/1978.....68......1...... | CLEO. ........................................................................................... | Arcade ADEP 37 |
| 31/05/1980.....15......14......● | SOMETIMES WHEN WE TOUCH **CLEO LAINE AND JAMES GALWAY** ..................................... | RCA PL 25296 |

**FRANKIE LAINE** US singer (born Frank Paul LoVecchio, 30/3/1913, Chicago, IL) who was in the choir at the Immaculate Conception Church in Chicago before leaving school for a career in show business. He was a dance instructor and singing waiter before he got his break replacing Perry Como as singer with the Freddie Carlone Band in 1937. He first recorded solo for Exclusive in 1945, and acted in films such as *When You're Smiling, Bring Your Smile Along* and *Rock 'Em Cowboy*. After his hits came to an end he toured in cabaret, and by the mid-1980s had retired to San Diego, California with his wife, former actress Nanette Gray. He has a star on the Hollywood Walk of Fame for his contribution to recording, and a second for TV.

| | | | |
|---|---|---|---|
| 24/06/1961 .....7.....23...... | **HELL BENT FOR LEATHER** ....................................................................... | Philips BBL 7468 |
| 24/09/1977 .....7......6......○ | **THE VERY BEST OF FRANKIE LAINE** ............................................................... | Warwick PR 5032 |

**GREG LAKE** UK singer (born 10/11/1948, Bournemouth, Dorset) who was in King Crimson before forming eponymous band with Keith Emerson and Carl Palmer. He began recording solo whilst still a member of Emerson, Lake & Palmer.

| | | | |
|---|---|---|---|
| 17/10/1981.....62......3...... | GREG LAKE. ...................................................................................... | Chrysalis CHR 1357 |

**LAMB** UK dance duo Louise Rhodes and Andrew Barlow who first linked in 1994. The pair are also in demand as remixers.

| | | | |
|---|---|---|---|
| 29/05/1999.....37......1...... | FEAR OF FOURS ................................................................................... | Fontana 5588212 |

| 20/10/2001 | 54 | 1 | | WHAT SOUND | Mercury 5865382 |

### ANNABEL LAMB UK singer (born 1961, Surrey); she was a nurse before becoming a singer.

| 28/04/1984 | 84 | 1 | | THE FLAME | A&M AMLX 68564 |

### LAMBCHOP US group formed by Kurt Wagner (vocals), Deanna Varagona (vocals), Paul Niehaus (vocals), Bill Killebrew (guitar), Jonathan Marx (saxophone), John Delworth (keyboards), Mike Doster (bass), Marc Trovillion (bass), Steve Goodhue (drums), Allen Lowrey (drums) and C Scott Chase (percussion).

| 19/02/2000 | 60 | 1 | | NIXON | City Slang 201522 |
| 02/03/2002 | 38 | 2 | | IS A WOMAN | City Slang 201902 |
| 21/02/2004 | 45 | 2 | | AW C'MON/NO YOU C'MON | City Slang 5958900 |

### LAMBRETTAS UK mod-revival group formed in Brighton by Jaz Bird (guitar/vocals), Mark Ellis (bass/vocals), Doug Sanders (guitar/vocals) and Paul Wincer (drums). They disbanded in 1981.

| 05/07/1980 | 28 | 8 | | BEAT BOYS IN THE JET AGE | Rocket TRAIN 10 |

### CHARLIE LANDSBOROUGH UK singer (born 21/10/1941, Wrexham, N.Wales).

| 12/10/1996 | 49 | 6 | | WITH YOU IN MIND | Ritz RITZBCD 0078 |
| 08/11/1997 | 42 | 3 | | FURTHER DOWN THE ROAD | Ritz RZCD 0085 |
| 10/10/1998 | 41 | 2 | | THE VERY BEST OF CHARLIE LANDSBOROUGH | Ritz RZCD 0087 |
| 02/10/1999 | 39 | 4 | | STILL CAN'T SAY GOODBYE | Ritz RZCD 0092 |
| 16/08/2003 | 37 | 6 | | SMILE | Telstar Premiere TPECD5516 |

### LANDSCAPE UK technopop group formed by Richard James Burgess (drums), Chris Heaton (keyboards), Andy 'Captain Whorlix' Pask (bass), Peter Thomas (trombone and percussion) and John Walters (saxophone/percussion). Burgess later became a top producer.

| 21/03/1981 | 16 | 13 | | FROM THE TEA ROOMS OF MARS … TO THE HELLHOLES OF URANUS | RCA RCALP 5003 |

### RONNIE LANE AND SLIM CHANCE UK group formed by Ronnie Lane (born 1/4/1946, Plaistow, London), formerly a member of The Faces, and featuring Steve Bingham (bass), Benny Gallagher (accordion/bass/guitar), Jimmy Jewell (saxophone), Billy Livsey (keyboards), Graham Lyle (banjo/guitar/mandolin/vocals), Ken Slaven (fiddle) and Kevin Westlake (guitar). Gallagher and Lyle had previously been members of McGuinness Flint and would go on to record as a duo. Lane died from multiple sclerosis on 4/6/1997.

| 17/08/1974 | 48 | 1 | | ANYMORE FOR ANYMORE | GM GML 1013 |
| 15/10/1977 | 44 | 3 | | ROUGH MIX **PETE TOWNSEND AND RONNIE LANE** | Polydor 2442 147 |

### k.d. lang Canadian singer (born Kathryn Dawn Lang, 2/11/1961, Consort, Alberta); as a country artist she released her first album in 1983 (in Canada only) and signed with Sire in 1987. She won the Best International Female award at the 1995 BRIT Awards, and has won four Grammy Awards including: Best Country Vocal Collaboration in 1988 with Roy Orbison for *Crying*; Best Country Vocal Performance in 1989 for *Absolute Torch And Twang;* and Best Female Pop Vocal Performance in 1992 for *Constant Craving.*

| 28/03/1992 | 3 | 52 | ✪ | **INGENUE** | Sire 7599268402 |
| 13/11/1993 | 36 | 2 | | EVEN COWGIRLS GET THE BLUES Original soundtrack to the film | Sire 9362454332 |
| 14/10/1995 | 7 | 5 | O | **ALL YOU CAN EAT** | Warner Brothers 9362460342 |
| 12/07/1997 | 19 | 3 | | DRAG | Warner Brothers 9362466232 |
| 15/07/2000 | 17 | 6 | | INVINCIBLE SUMMER | Warner Brothers 9362476052 |
| 05/07/2003 | 33 | 3 | | A WONDERFUL WORLD **TONY BENNETT AND K.D. LANG** 2003 Grammy Award for Best Traditional Pop Vocal Album | Columbia 5098702 |

### THOMAS LANG UK singer (born Tom Jones, Liverpool) who was a joiner for British Rail before recording. His backing band featured David Hughes, John Murphy, Andrew Redhead, Paul Thomas and Mark Vormawah.

| 20/02/1988 | 92 | 1 | | SCALLYWAG JAZ | Epic 4509961 |

### MARIO LANZA US singer (born Alfredo Arnold Cocozza, 31/1/1921, Philadelphia, PA) whose stage surname was his mother's maiden name. Debuting on screen in 1949 in *That Midnight Kiss,* he was considered one of the world's finest operatic tenors. He died in Rome on 7/10/1959. He has two stars on the Hollywood Walk of Fame, for his contribution to recording and motion pictures.

| 11/08/1956 | 5 | 1 | | **SONGS FROM THE STUDENT PRINCE AND OTHER FAMOUS MELODIES** | HMV ALP 1186 |
| 06/12/1958 | 4 | 21 | | **THE STUDENT PRINCE/THE GREAT CARUSO** Original soundtracks to the films | RCA RB 16113 |
| 23/07/1960 | 3 | 15 | | **THE GREAT CARUSO** | RCA RB 16112 |
| 09/01/1971 | 39 | 1 | | THE GREATEST HITS VOLUME 1 | RCA Victor LSB 4000 |
| 03/09/1981 | 29 | 11 | ● | THE LEGEND OF MARIO LANZA | K-Tel NE 1110 |
| 14/11/1987 | 49 | 8 | O | A PORTRAIT OF MARIO LANZA | Stylus SMR 741 |
| 12/03/1994 | 13 | 7 | | MARIO LANZA – THE ULTIMATE COLLECTION | RCA Victor 74321185742 |
| 12/06/2004 | 41 | 3+ | | THE DEFINITIVE COLLECTION | BMG 82876614032 |

### LARD US group formed by Jello Biafra (born Eric Boucher, 17/6/1958, Denver, CO), Al Jourgensen, Paul Barker and Jeff Ward. Biafra had previously been a member of The Dead Kennedys.

| 06/10/1990 | 69 | 1 | | THE LAST TEMPTATION OF REID | Alternative Tentacles VIRUS 84 |

### LASGO Belgian production group formed by Peter Luts and David Vervoort and fronted by singer Evi Goffin.

| 07/09/2002 | 30 | 3 | | SOME THINGS | Positiva 5419362 |

O Silver disc   ● Gold disc   ✪ Platinum disc (additional platinum units are indicated by a figure following the symbol)   ❶⁹ Number of weeks album topped the UK chart

**JAMES LAST** German orchestra leader (born Hans Last, 17/4/1929, Bremen) who joined the Hans-Gunther Osterreich Radio Bremen Dance Orchestra in 1946 as a bass player. After a spell fronting the Becker-Last Ensemble he was in-house arranger for Polydor Records, recording his first album, *Non-Stop Dancing* in 1965. His blend of well-known tunes over a dance beat proved immensely popular across Europe, and by 1990 he had released more than 50 albums of a similar style, selling more than 50 million copies. He later started working with a variety of guest musicians and singers, including Astrud Gilberto and Richard Clayderman.

| DATE | POS | WKS | BPI | ALBUM TITLE | LABEL & NUMBER |
|---|---|---|---|---|---|
| 15/04/1967 | 6 | 48 | | THIS IS JAMES LAST | Polydor 104678 |
| 22/07/1967 | 27 | 10 | | HAMMOND A-GO-GO | Polydor 249043 |
| 26/08/1967 | 32 | 2 | | LOVE THIS IS MY SONG | Polydor 583553 |
| 26/08/1967 | 35 | 1 | | NON-STOP DANCING | Polydor 236203 |
| 22/06/1968 | 32 | 3 | | JAMES LAST GOES POP | Polydor 249160 |
| 08/02/1969 | 40 | 1 | | DANCING '68 VOLUME 1 | Polydor 249216 |
| 31/05/1969 | 13 | 1 | | TRUMPET A-GO-GO | Polydor 249239 |
| 09/08/1969 | 26 | 1 | | NON-STOP DANCING '69 | Polydor 249294 |
| 24/01/1970 | 27 | 3 | | NON-STOP DANCING '69/2 | Polydor 249354 |
| 23/05/1970 | 26 | 1 | | NON-STOP EVERGREENS | Polydor 249370 |
| 11/07/1970 | 44 | 1 | | CLASSICS UP TO DATE | Polydor 249371 |
| 11/07/1970 | 67 | 1 | | NON-STOP DANCING '70 | Polydor 237104 |
| 24/10/1970 | 45 | 4 | | VERY BEST OF JAMES LAST | Polydor 2371 054 |
| 08/05/1971 | 21 | 4 | | NON-STOP DANCING '71 | Polydor 2371 111 |
| 26/06/1971 | 38 | 1 | | SUMMER HAPPENING | Polydor 2371 133 |
| 18/09/1971 | 47 | 1 | | BEACH PARTY 2 | Polydor 2371 211 |
| 02/10/1971 | 17 | 14 | | YESTERDAY'S MEMORIES | Contour 2870 117 |
| 16/10/1971 | 30 | 3 | | NON-STOP DANCING 12 | Polydor 2371 141 |
| 19/02/1972 | 32 | 2 | | NON-STOP DANCING 13 | Polydor 2371 189 |
| 04/03/1972 | 22 | 3 | | POLKA PARTY | Polydor 2371 190 |
| 29/04/1972 | 13 | 6 | | JAMES LAST IN CONCERT | Polydor 2371 191 |
| 24/06/1972 | 45 | 1 | | VOODOO PARTY | Polydor 2371 235 |
| 16/09/1972 | 49 | 1 | | CLASSICS UP TO DATE VOLUME 2 | Polydor 184061 |
| 30/09/1972 | 32 | 2 | | LOVE MUST BE THE REASON | Polydor 2371 281 |
| 27/01/1973 | 19 | 12 | | THE MUSIC OF JAMES LAST | Polydor 2683 010 |
| 24/02/1973 | 12 | 9 | | JAMES LAST IN RUSSIA | Polydor 2371 293 |
| 24/02/1973 | 27 | 3 | | NON-STOP DANCING VOLUME 14 | Polydor 2371 319 |
| 28/07/1973 | 24 | 5 | ○ | OLE | Polydor 2371 384 |
| 01/09/1973 | 34 | 2 | ○ | NON-STOP DANCING VOLUME 15 | Polydor 2371 376 |
| 20/04/1974 | 43 | 2 | ○ | NON-STOP DANCING VOLUME 16 | Polydor 2371 444 |
| 29/06/1974 | 49 | 1 | ○ | IN CONCERT VOLUME 2 | Polydor 2371 320 |
| 23/11/1974 | 39 | 2 | ○ | GOLDEN MEMORIES | Polydor 2371 472 |
| 26/07/1975 | 5 | 16 | ● | **TEN YEARS NON-STOP JUBILEE** | Polydor 2660 111 |
| 02/08/1975 | 60 | 1 | | VIOLINS IN LOVE | K-Tel 1 |
| 22/11/1975 | 3 | 19 | ● | **MAKE THE PARTY LAST** | Polydor 2371 612 |
| 08/05/1976 | 54 | 1 | | CLASSICS UP TO DATE VOLUME 3 | Polydor 2371 538 |
| 06/05/1978 | 49 | 4 | | EAST TO WEST | Polydor 2630 092 |
| 14/04/1979 | 2 | 45 | ○² | **LAST THE WHOLE NIGHT LONG** | Polydor PTD 001 |
| 23/08/1980 | 56 | 3 | ● | THE BEST FROM 150 GOLD RECORDS | Polydor 2681 211 |
| 01/11/1980 | 12 | 18 | ○ | CLASSICS FOR DREAMING | Polydor POLTV 11 |
| 14/02/1981 | 41 | 5 | | ROSES FROM THE SOUTH | Polydor 2372 051 |
| 21/11/1981 | 18 | 13 | ● | HANSIMANIA | Polydor POLTV 14 |
| 28/11/1981 | 88 | 2 | ● | LAST FOREVER | Polydor 2630 135 |
| 05/03/1983 | 57 | 3 | | BLUEBIRD | Polydor POLD 5072 |
| 30/04/1983 | 56 | 2 | | NON-STOP DANCING '83 – PARTY POWER | Polydor POLD 5094 |
| 30/04/1983 | 42 | 5 | | THE BEST OF MY GOLD RECORDS | Polydor PODV 7 |
| 03/12/1983 | 52 | 8 | ○ | THE GREATEST SONGS OF THE BEATLES | Polydor POLD 5119 |
| 24/03/1984 | 21 | 11 | | THE ROSE OF TRALEE AND OTHER IRISH FAVOURITES | Polydor POLD 5131 |
| 13/10/1984 | 74 | 2 | | PARADISE | Polydor POLD 5163 |
| 08/12/1984 | 68 | 9 | ● | JAMES LAST IN SCOTLAND | Polydor POLD 5166 |
| 14/09/1985 | 11 | 27 | ○ | LEAVE THE BEST TO LAST | Polydor PROLP 7 |
| 18/04/1987 | 22 | 11 | ● | BY REQUEST | Polydor POLH 34 |
| 26/11/1988 | 38 | 8 | ● | DANCE DANCE DANCE | Polydor JLTV 1 |
| 14/04/1990 | 12 | 12 | ● | CLASSICS BY MOONLIGHT | Polydor 8432181 |
| 15/06/1991 | 10 | 11 | ● | **POP SYMPHONIES** | Polydor 8494291 |
| 09/11/1991 | 14 | 15 | ○ | TOGETHER AT LAST RICHARD CLAYDERMAN AND JAMES LAST | Decca Delpine 5115251 |
| 12/09/1992 | 23 | 5 | ○ | VIVA ESPANA | Polygram TV 5172202 |
| 20/11/1993 | 12 | 10 | ● | JAMES LAST PLAYS ANDREW LLOYD WEBBER | Polydor 5199102 |

▲⁹ Number of weeks album topped the US chart   ◆¹² RIAA Diamond Awards   ◇³ IFPI Platinum Europe Awards

| 19/11/1994 | 28 | 7 | ● | IN HARMONY **RICHARD CLAYDERMAN AND JAMES LAST** | Polydor 5238242 |
| 18/11/1995 | 36 | 7 | | THE VERY BEST OF JAMES LAST AND HIS ORCHESTRA | Polydor 5295562 |
| 28/03/1998 | 32 | 3 | | POP SYMPHONIES 2 | Polydor 5396242 |
| 24/04/1999 | 18 | 5 | | COUNTRY ROADS | Polydor 5474022 |
| 03/11/2001 | 29 | 4 | | PLAYS ABBA | Polydor 5891982 |
| 06/09/2003 | 44 | 3 | | THE CLASSICAL COLLECTION | UCJ 9810457 |

**LATIN QUARTER** UK group formed in 1983 by Steve Skaith (guitar/vocals), Richard Wright (guitar) and Mike Jones (lyrics), adding Yona Dunsford (keyboards/vocals), Carol Douet (vocals), Greg Harewood (bass), Steve Jeffries (keyboards) and Richard Stevens (drums). Stevens and Jeffries left in 1987, replaced by Martin Lascalles (keyboards) and Darren Abraham (drums).

| 01/03/1986 | 91 | 2 | | MODERN TIMES | Rockin' Horse RHLP 1 |
| 06/06/1987 | 96 | 1 | | MICK AND CAROLINE | Rockin' Horse 208 142 |

**CYNDI LAUPER** US singer (born 20/6/1953, Queens, NYC) who joined local group Doc West as lead vocalist in 1974, then Flyer for three years. She formed Blue Angel with John Turi in 1978, releasing one album before disbanding and then signed as a solo artist with Portrait in 1983. She 'appeared' in an episode of *The Simpsons*, singing the US national anthem, and also appeared in the 1988 film *Vibes* and won the 1984 Grammy Award for Best New Artist.

| 18/02/1984 | 16 | 32 | ● | SHE'S SO UNUSUAL | Portrait PRT 25792 |
| 11/10/1986 | 25 | 12 | ○ | TRUE COLOURS | Portrait PRT 26948 |
| 01/07/1989 | 9 | 12 | | **A NIGHT TO REMEMBER** | Epic 4624991 |
| 27/11/1993 | 56 | 1 | | HAT FULL OF STARS | Epic 4730542 |
| 03/09/1994 | 2 | 34 | ✪² | **TWELVE DEADLY CYNS... AND THEN SOME** ◇ | Epic 4773632 |
| 22/02/1997 | 59 | 1 | | SISTERS OF AVALON | Epic 4853702 |

**LAUREL AND HARDY** UK/US comedy duo Stan Laurel (born Arthur Stanley Jefferson, 16/6/1890, Ulverston, Cumbria) and Oliver 'Babe' Hardy (born Oliver Norvell Hardy, 18/1/1892, Harlem, GA). Although they appeared in the same films from 1919 (*The Lucky Dog* being one of the first), they didn't team up until 1926, with *Putting Pants On Philip* (1927) regarded as their first official film (although *Duck Soup* was released first). Hardy died on 7/8/1957 after a stroke the previous September, Laurel from a heart attack on 23/2/1965. They have separate stars on the Hollywood Walk of Fame.

| 06/12/1975 | 55 | 4 | | THE GOLDEN AGE OF HOLLYWOOD COMEDY | United Artists UAG 29676 |

**AVRIL LAVIGNE** Canadian singer (born 27/9/1984, Napanee, Ontario) who was discovered by Antonio 'LA' Reid. At seventeen years and three months, she was the youngest female artist to have topped the UK album chart.

| 14/09/2002 | ●³ | 58 | ✪⁵ | **LET GO** ◇² | Arista 74321949312 |
| 05/06/2004 | ●¹ | 4+ | ✪⁵ | **UNDER MY SKIN** ▲¹ | Arista 82876617872 |

**LAW** UK duo formed by Paul Rodgers (born 12/12/1949, Middlesbrough, piano/vocals) and Kenny Jones (born 16/9/1948, London, drums), with their debut album also featuring Pino Palladino (bass) and Chris Rea (guitar). Rodgers had previously been in Free, Bad Company, The Firm and recorded solo. Jones had been in the Small Faces, and replaced Keith Moon in The Who. Rea enjoyed a successful solo career whilst Palladino was a member of Paul Young's backing group.

| 06/04/1991 | 61 | 1 | | THE LAW | Atlantic 7567821951 |

**JOEY LAWRENCE** US singer/actor (born 20/4/1976, Philadelphia, PA) who acted from the age of three. He appeared on *Gimme A Break* and *Blossom*.

| 31/07/1993 | 39 | 3 | | JOEY LAWRENCE | EMI CDEMC 3657 |

**SYD LAWRENCE** UK orchestra leader (born 1925); he formed his orchestra in 1966 having previously been a member of the BBC Northern Dance Orchestra. He led the group for 30 years before retiring in 1996, handing over leadership to lead trombonist Chris Dean. Syd Lawrence died on 5/5/1998.

| 08/08/1970 | 14 | 4 | | MORE MILLER AND OTHER BIG BAND MAGIC | Philips 6642 001 |
| 25/12/1971 | 43 | 2 | | MUSIC OF GLENN MILLER IN SUPER STEREO | Philips 6641 017 |
| 25/12/1971 | 31 | 2 | | SYD LAWRENCE WITH THE GLENN MILLER SOUND | Fontana SFL 13178 |
| 26/02/1972 | 34 | 1 | | SOMETHING OLD, SOMETHING NEW | Philips 6308 090 |

**RONNIE LAWS** US saxophonist/singer (born 3/10/1950, Houston, TX); he learned to play the saxophone at the age of twelve, encouraged by elder brother Hubert who was a member of The Crusaders. Ronnie later spent eighteen months in the horn section of Earth, Wind & Fire before going solo in 1975. Brother Hubert and sisters Debra and Eloise also enjoyed successful solo careers.

| 17/10/1981 | 100 | 1 | | SOLID GROUND | Liberty LBG 30336 |

**LAYO AND BUSHWACKA** UK dance group duo formed in London by Layo Paskin and Matthew 'Buskwacka' Benjamin. The pair are co-owner and resident DJ at The End respectively.

| 13/07/2002 | 61 | 1 | | NIGHT WORKS | XL Recordings XLCD 154 |

○ Silver disc  ● Gold disc  ✪ Platinum disc (additional platinum units are indicated by a figure following the symbol)  ●⁹ Number of weeks album topped the UK chart

### DOUG LAZY
US rapper/producer (born Gene Finlay) who made one album as radio DJ Mean Gene before becoming a producer.

| 10/03/1990 | 65 | 1 | | DOUG LAZY GETTIN' CRAZY | Atlantic 7567820661 |
|---|---|---|---|---|---|

### KELE LE ROC
UK singer (born Kelly Briggs, 5/10/1978, Jamaica) who later worked with Basement Jaxx, appearing on their hit *Romeo*. She won the 1999 MOBO Awards for Best Newcomer.

| 10/04/1999 | 44 | 2 | | EVERYBODY'S SOMEBODY | Wild Card 5596662 |
|---|---|---|---|---|---|

### LEAGUE UNLIMITED ORCHESTRA – see HUMAN LEAGUE

### LEAVES
Icelandic group formed in Reykjavik by Arna Gudjonsson (guitar/vocals), Arnar Olafsson (guitar/accordion), Hallur Hallson (bass) and Bjarni Grimsson (drums).

| 31/08/2002 | 71 | 1 | | BREATHE | B Unique 0927487392 |
|---|---|---|---|---|---|

### LED ZEPPELIN
UK rock group formed in 1968 by Robert Plant (born 20/8/1948, West Bromwich, lead vocals), Jimmy Page (born 9/1/1944, Heston, guitar), John Paul Jones (born John Baldwin, 3/6/1946, Sidcup, bass) and John Bonham (born 31/5/1948, Birmingham, drums) as the New Yardbirds. The name changed shortly after, suggested by The Who's Keith Moon (although it wasn't meant to be complimentary, he thought they would 'go down like a lead balloon', hence the subtle change). Bonham died, choking in his sleep, on 25/9/1980; the group disbanded two months later. They briefly re-formed for Live Aid in 1985, Phil Collins guesting on drums. In 1970, during a Danish tour, they were forbidden to use their name at a Copenhagen gig after Eva von Zeppelin (relative of airship designer Ferdinand von Zeppelin) threatened to sue! They were inducted into the Rock & Roll Hall of Fame in 1995.

| 12/04/1969 | 6 | 79 | | **LED ZEPPELIN** ◆10 | Atlantic 588171 |
|---|---|---|---|---|---|
| 08/11/1969 | ❶1 | 138 | | **LED ZEPPELIN 2** ▲7 ◆12 The album changed its catalogue number to Atlantic K 40037 during its chart run | Atlantic 588198 |
| 07/11/1970 | ❶4 | 40 | | **LED ZEPPELIN 3** ▲4 | Atlantic 2401 002 |
| 27/11/1971 | ❶2 | 69 | | **FOUR SYMBOLS (LED ZEPPELIN 4)** ◆22 The album changed its catalogue number to Atlantic K 50008 during its chart run. This album was variously known as *The Fourth Led Zeppelin Album, Runes, The New Led Zeppelin Album, Led Zeppelin Four* and *Symbols* during its chart run | Atlantic 2401 012 |
| 14/04/1973 | ❶2 | 13 | ✪ | **HOUSE OF THE HOLY** ▲2 ◆11 | Atlantic K 50014 |
| 15/03/1975 | ❶1 | 27 | ✪ | **PHYSICAL GRAFFITI** ▲6 ◆15 | Swan Song SSK 89400 |
| 24/04/1976 | ❶1 | 14 | ● | **PRESENCE** ▲2 | Swan Song SSK 59402 |
| 06/11/1976 | ❶1 | 15 | ✪ | **THE SONG REMAINS THE SAME** Original soundtrack to the film | Swan Song SSK 59402 |
| 08/09/1979 | ❶2 | 16 | ● | **IN THROUGH THE OUT DOOR** ▲7 | Swan Song SSK 59410 |
| 04/12/1982 | 4 | 7 | ○ | **CODA** | Swan Song A 0051 |
| 27/10/1990 | 10 | 45 | ✪2 | **REMASTERS** | Atlantic ZEP 1 |
| 10/11/1990 | 48 | 2 | | LED ZEPPELIN (BOX SET) | Atlantic 7567821441 |
| 09/10/1993 | 56 | 1 | | LED ZEPPELIN BOXED SET II | Atlantic 7567824772 |
| 29/11/1997 | 23 | 7 | ○ | BBC SESSIONS | Atlantic 7567830612 |
| 01/04/2000 | 40 | 1 | | LATTER DAYS – THE BEST OF – VOLUME 2 | Atlantic 7567832782 |
| 01/04/2000 | 55 | 1 | | EARLY DAYS – THE BEST OF – VOLUME ONE | Atlantic 7567832682 |
| 08/03/2003 | 11 | 23 | ● | VERY BEST OF – EARLY DAYS AND LATTER DAYS | Atlantic 7567836195 |
| 07/06/2003 | 5 | 7 | ● | **HOW THE WEST WAS WON** ▲1 Triple-disc live album that was originally recorded in Long Beach and Los Angeles in 1972 | Atlantic 7567835872 |

### BRENDA LEE
US singer (born Brenda Mae Tarplay, 11/12/1944, Lithonia, GA) who began singing when she was six and signed with Decca in 1956. In 1959 a Paris date was cancelled when the promoter discovered her age. Her manager put out a story that she was a 32-year-old midget and then received even more publicity denying it! Still touring in the 1990s, she was inducted in the Rock & Roll Hall of Fame in 2002.

| 24/11/1962 | 20 | 2 | | ALL THE WAY | Brunswick LAT 8383 |
|---|---|---|---|---|---|
| 16/02/1963 | 13 | 9 | | BRENDA – THAT'S ALL | Brunswick LAT 8516 |
| 13/04/1963 | 8 | 20 | | **ALL ALONE AM I** | Brunswick LAT 8530 |
| 16/07/1966 | 21 | 2 | | BYE BYE BLUES | Brunswick LAT 8649 |
| 01/11/1980 | 15 | 11 | ● | LITTLE MISS DYNAMITE – BRENDA LEE | Warwick WW 5083 |
| 07/01/1984 | 65 | 4 | | 25TH ANNIVERSARY | MCA MCLD 609 |
| 30/03/1985 | 16 | 9 | ● | THE VERY BEST OF BRENDA LEE | MCA LETV 1 |
| 15/10/1994 | 20 | 7 | | THE VERY BEST OF BRENDA LEE… WITH LOVE | Telstar TCD 2738 |

### PEGGY LEE
US singer (born Norma Jean Egstrom, 26/5/1920, Jamestown, ND); she began as a jazz singer with a number of bands before going solo in 1943, making her film debut in 1950 in *Mister Music*. She was married four times, to Jack Del Rio, Dewey Martin, Dave Barbour and Brad Dexter. Numerous films included *Johnny Guitar, The Jazz Singer* and *Pete Kelly's Blues* (for which she was nominated for an Oscar for Best Supporting Actress). She suffered a stroke in October 1988 but recovered to collect a Grammy's Lifetime Achievement Award in 1995. She provided the singing voice to the Walt Disney animated film *The Lady And The Tramp* and was later awarded $4 million in video sale royalties after taking the company to court. She won the 1969 Grammy Award for Best Female Solo Vocal Performance for *Is That All There Is?* Her hit *Fever,* which has been covered by artists ranging from Helen Shapiro, Madonna and Ronnie Laws, was co-written by Eddie Cooley and John Davenport. Davenport was in fact a *nom de plume* of Otis Blackwell, who was under contract to Jay-Dee at the time. Peggy later sued Universal Music for underpaid royalties on her

original Decca recordings. She won a settlement in January 2002, but died from cancer four days later on 22/1/2002. She has a star on the Hollywood Walk of Fame.

| 04/06/1960 . . . . . 8 . . . . 15 . . . . . | **LATIN A LA LEE** . . . . . . . . . . . . . . . . . . . . . . . . . . . . . . . . . . . . . . . . . . . . . . . . . . . . . . . . . . . . . . . . . . . . . . Capitol T 1290 |
| 11/06/1960 . . . . 16 . . . . . 6 . . . . . | BEAUTY AND THE BEAT **PEGGY LEE AND GEORGE SHEARING** . . . . . . . . . . . . . . . . . . . . . . . . . . . . . . . . . . . . . . . . . . . . Capitol T 1219 |
| 20/05/1961 . . . . 18 . . . . . 1 . . . . . | BEST OF PEGGY LEE VOLUME 2 . . . . . . . . . . . . . . . . . . . . . . . . . . . . . . . . . . . . . . . . . . . . . . . . . . . . . . . . Brunswick LAT 8355 |
| 21/10/1961 . . . . 20 . . . . . 1 . . . . . | BLACK COFFEE . . . . . . . . . . . . . . . . . . . . . . . . . . . . . . . . . . . . . . . . . . . . . . . . . . . . . . . . . . . . . . . . . . . Ace Of Hearts AH 5 |

## RAYMOND LEFEVRE French orchestra leader (born 1922, Paris) popular in Europe, who also had US hits during his career.

| 07/10/1967 . . . . 10 . . . . . 7 . . . . . | **RAYMOND LEFEVRE** . . . . . . . . . . . . . . . . . . . . . . . . . . . . . . . . . . . . . . . . . . . . . . . . . . . . . . . . . . . . . . . . . Major Minor MMLP 4 |
| 17/02/1968 . . . . 37 . . . . . 2 . . . . . | RAYMOND LEFEVRE VOLUME 2 . . . . . . . . . . . . . . . . . . . . . . . . . . . . . . . . . . . . . . . . . . . . . . . . . . . . . . . Major Minor SMLP 13 |

## LEFTFIELD UK instrumental/production duo formed by Neil Barnes and Paul Daley (previously with A Man Called Adam). The group was originally Barnes recording solo and issued one single for Outer Rhythm, *Not Forgotten*. Legal problems with Outer Rhythm prevented the pair from recording for a while and they made their names as remixers. They later set up the Hard Hands label and also recorded as Herbal Infusion. They split in February 2002.

| 11/02/1995 . . . . . 3 . . . . . 94 . . . . . . ✪ | **LEFTISM** . . . . . . . . . . . . . . . . . . . . . . . . . . . . . . . . . . . . . . . . . . . . . . . . . . . . . . . . . . . . . . . . . . . Hard Hands HANDCD 2 |
| 02/10/1999 . . . . ❶¹ . . . . 20 . . . . . . ✪ | **RHYTHM AND STEALTH** . . . . . . . . . . . . . . . . . . . . . . . . . . . . . . . . . . . . . . . . . . . . . . . . . . . . . . . . . . . Hard Hands HANDCD 4 |

## TOM LEHRER US comic singer (born 9/4/1928, New York City); he graduated from Harvard University and later returned there to teach mathematics. It was at Harvard that he first wrote satirical songs, performing them for colleagues. He recorded twelve songs and initially had 400 copies pressed on his own Lehrer label. The album's success led him to tour the country, and by the end of the 1950s he had recorded a further three albums. Although he stopped touring in 1960, his albums continued to sell and he switched to the nationally distributed Reprise in 1965. He returned to teaching in the late 1970s.

| 08/11/1958 . . . . . 7 . . . . . 19 . . . . . | **SONGS BY TOM LEHRER** . . . . . . . . . . . . . . . . . . . . . . . . . . . . . . . . . . . . . . . . . . . . . . . . . . . . . . . . . . . . . . Decca LF 1311 |
| 25/06/1960 . . . . . 7 . . . . . 7 . . . . . | **AN EVENING WASTED WITH TOM LEHRER** . . . . . . . . . . . . . . . . . . . . . . . . . . . . . . . . . . . . . . . . . . . . . . . . . Decca LK 4332 |

## DENISE LEIGH AND JANE GILCHRIST UK vocal duo formed by Denise Leigh (born 19/5/1971, Audley) and Jane Gilchrist (born 18/12/1965, Coventry). The pair first came to prominence on the Channel 4 programme *Opratunity*.

| 08/11/2003 . . . . 60 . . . . . 2 . . . . . . ○ | OPRATUNITY WINNERS . . . . . . . . . . . . . . . . . . . . . . . . . . . . . . . . . . . . . . . . . . . . . . . . . . . . . . . EMI Classics 05575942 |

## LEMAR UK male singer (born Lemar Obika, London) who was first known as a competitor on BBC TV's *Fame Academy*. He was named Best Urban Act at the 2004 BRIT Awards.

| 06/12/2003 . . . . 16 . . . . . 19 . . . . . . ✪ | DEDICATED . . . . . . . . . . . . . . . . . . . . . . . . . . . . . . . . . . . . . . . . . . . . . . . . . . . . . . . . . . . . . . . . . . . . Sony Music 5137912 |

## LEMON JELLY UK production/DJ duo Nick Franglen and Fred Deakin.

| 02/11/2002 . . . . 20 . . . . . 6 . . . . . . ● | LOST HORIZONS . . . . . . . . . . . . . . . . . . . . . . . . . . . . . . . . . . . . . . . . . . . . . . . . . . . . . . . . . . . . . . Impotent Fury IFXLCD 160 |

## LEMONHEADS US rock group formed in Boston, MA as the Whelps in 1985 by Evan Dando (born 4/3/1967, Boston, guitar/vocals), Ben Deily and Jesse Peretz. Dando adopted the name Lemonheads before settling on a line-up of himself, Nic Dalton (bass) and David Ryan (drums). The Lemonheads signed with Atlantic in 1990.

| 01/08/1992 . . . . 33 . . . . . 16 . . . . . . ● | IT'S A SHAME ABOUT RAY . . . . . . . . . . . . . . . . . . . . . . . . . . . . . . . . . . . . . . . . . . . . . . . . . . . . . . . . Atlantic 7567824602 |
| 23/10/1993 . . . . . 5 . . . . . 14 . . . . . . ● | **COME ON FEEL THE LEMONHEADS** . . . . . . . . . . . . . . . . . . . . . . . . . . . . . . . . . . . . . . . . . . . . . . . . . . Atlantic 7567825372 |
| 12/10/1996 . . . . 28 . . . . . 2 . . . . . | CAR BUTTON CLOTH . . . . . . . . . . . . . . . . . . . . . . . . . . . . . . . . . . . . . . . . . . . . . . . . . . . . . . . . . . . . . Atlantic 7567927262 |

## JOHN LENNON UK male singer (born John Winston Lennon, 9/10/1940, Woolton, Liverpool) and founding member of The Beatles. He began solo projects whilst still in the group, including an appearance in the film *How I Won The War* in 1967, writing a number of books and his debut solo album *Two Virgins* in 1968. He married Cynthia Powell in 1962 and met Yoko Ono in 1966, marrying her in Gibraltar in 1969. He formed the Plastic Ono Band in 1969 and moved to New York in 1971, although he was involved in a lengthy battle with US immigration until a resident visa was issued in 1976. He stopped recording in 1975 to become a 'house-husband' but returned to the studio in 1980. His return album *Double Fantasy* had just been released when he was shot dead outside his New York apartment by Mark David Chapman on 8/12/1980. In the immediate aftermath he scored three #1s in eight weeks, including *(Just Like) Starting Over*, which had already slipped down the charts to #21 at the time of his death. Awarded the MBE in 1964, he returned it in 1969 in protest at the UK's involvement in Nigeria-Biafra, their support for the USA in Vietnam and 'against *Cold Turkey* slipping down the charts'. His son Julian by Cynthia also recorded solo, whilst his son Sean by Yoko is a promising musician. Inducted into the Rock & Roll Hall of Fame in 1994 (as had The Beatles in 1988), he has a star on the Hollywood Walk of Fame.

| 16/01/1971 . . . . 11 . . . . . 11 . . . . . | JOHN LENNON AND THE PLASTIC ONO BAND **JOHN LENNON WITH THE PLASTIC ONO BAND** . . . . . . . . . . . . . . . . . Apple PCS 7124 |
| 30/10/1971 . . . . ❶² . . . . 101 . . . . . | **IMAGINE** ▲¹ **JOHN LENNON WITH THE PLASTIC ONO BAND (WITH THE FLUX FIDDLERS)** The album changed its catalogue number to Parlophone PAS 10004 during its chart run . . . . . . . . . . . . . . . . . . . . . . . . . . . . . . . . . . . . . . . . . . . . . . . . . . . . . Apple PAS 10004 |
| 14/10/1972 . . . . 11 . . . . . 6 . . . . . | SOMETIME IN NEW YORK CITY **JOHN AND YOKO LENNON WITH THE PLASTIC ONO BAND & ELEPHANT'S MEMORY** . Apple PCSP 716 |
| 08/12/1973 . . . . 13 . . . . . 12 . . . . . . ● | MIND GAMES . . . . . . . . . . . . . . . . . . . . . . . . . . . . . . . . . . . . . . . . . . . . . . . . . . . . . . . . . . . . . . . . . . . . . Apple PCS 7165 |
| 19/10/1974 . . . . . 6 . . . . . 10 . . . . . . ○ | **WALLS AND BRIDGES** ▲¹ . . . . . . . . . . . . . . . . . . . . . . . . . . . . . . . . . . . . . . . . . . . . . . . . . . . . . . . . . . . Apple PCTC 253 |
| 08/03/1975 . . . . . 6 . . . . . 28 . . . . . . ● | **ROCK 'N' ROLL** . . . . . . . . . . . . . . . . . . . . . . . . . . . . . . . . . . . . . . . . . . . . . . . . . . . . . . . . . . . . . . . . . . Apple PCS 7169 |

| DATE | POS | WKS | BPI | ALBUM TITLE | LABEL & NUMBER |
|---|---|---|---|---|---|
| 08/03/1975 | 8 | 29 | ● | **SHAVED FISH** | Apple PCS 7173 |
| 22/11/1980 | ❶² | 36 | ✪ | **DOUBLE FANTASY** ▲⁸ JOHN LENNON AND YOKO ONO 1981 Grammy Award for Album of the Year | Geffen K 99131 |
| 20/11/1982 | ❶⁶ | 43 | ✪³ | **THE JOHN LENNON COLLECTION** | Parlophone EMTV 37 |
| 04/02/1984 | 3 | 13 | ● | **MILK AND HONEY – A HEART PLAY** JOHN LENNON AND YOKO ONO | Polydor POLH 5 |
| 08/03/1986 | 55 | 3 | | JOHN LENNON LIVE IN NEW YORK CITY | Parlophone PCS 7031 |
| 22/10/1988 | 64 | 6 | ● | IMAGINE JOHN LENNON The album also includes tracks by The Beatles | Parlophone PCSP 722 |
| 08/11/1997 | 4 | 37 | ✪² | **LENNON LEGEND – THE VERY BEST OF JOHN LENNON** ◇² | Parlophone 8219542 |
| 14/11/1998 | 62 | 1 | | THE JOHN LENNON ANTHOLOGY | Capitol 8306142 |
| 26/02/2000 | 51 | 1 | | IMAGINE | Parlophone 5248582 |

**JULIAN LENNON** UK singer (born John Charles Julian Lennon, 8/4/1963, Liverpool); he is the son of John Lennon and the first child to be born to any of The Beatles. Paul McCartney penned *Hey Jude* in his honour.

| DATE | POS | WKS | BPI | ALBUM TITLE | LABEL & NUMBER |
|---|---|---|---|---|---|
| 03/11/1984 | 20 | 15 | ○ | VALOTTE | Charisma JLLP 1 |
| 05/04/1986 | 93 | 1 | | THE SECRET VALUE OF DAYDREAMING | Charisma CAS 1171 |
| 05/10/1991 | 42 | 4 | | HELP YOURSELF | Virgin V 2668 |

**ANNIE LENNOX** UK singer (born 25/12/1954, Aberdeen) who met Dave Stewart in 1971 and teamed up with him in Catch, the Tourists and then the Eurythmics. She took a two-year sabbatical from the group in 1979, enabling Stewart to undertake a number of solo projects, but they disbanded in 1991. She returned as a solo artist in 1992. One of the biggest winners at the BRIT Awards, including the Best British Female award in 1984, 1986, 1989, 1990 (all as lead singer with the Eurythmics), and 1993 and 1996. The Eurythmics received the Outstanding Contribution to British Music Award at the 1999 BRITs. She re-formed The Eurythmics with Stewart in 1999. She also took part in the *It's Only Rock 'N' Roll* project for the Children's Promise charity. Having won one Grammy Award whilst a member of The Eurythmics, she has gone on to collect a further two awards,: Best Music Video Long Form in 1992 for *Diva* and Best Female Pop Vocal Performance in 1995 for *No More 'I Love Yous'*. She won the Oscar in 2004 for Best Original Score for *Return Of The King* and Best Original Song with Fran Walsh and Howard Shore for *Into The West* from *Lord Of The Rings – Return Of The King*.

| DATE | POS | WKS | BPI | ALBUM TITLE | LABEL & NUMBER |
|---|---|---|---|---|---|
| 18/04/1992 | ❶² | 80 | ✪⁴ | **DIVA** 1993 BRIT Award for Best Album | RCA PD 75326 |
| 18/03/1995 | ❶¹ | 49 | ✪² | **MEDUSA** ◇² | RCA 74321257172 |
| 21/06/2003 | 3 | 14 | ● | **BARE** | RCA 82876524052 |

**DEKE LEONARD** UK singer/guitarist (born Roger Leonard) who was a member of Lucifer And The Corncrakers, The Jets, The Blackjacks, The Smokeless Zone and The Dream before joining The Bystanders in 1968, the group then changing their name to Man. He left in 1972 to go solo, rejoining them in 1974 where he remained until they disbanded in 1976. He has since recorded solo, joined Man at their various revivals and also had a spell as a journalist.

| DATE | POS | WKS | BPI | ALBUM TITLE | LABEL & NUMBER |
|---|---|---|---|---|---|
| 13/04/1974 | 50 | 1 | | KAMIKAZE | United Artists UAG 29544 |

**PAUL LEONI** UK pan flute player he also worked with Phil Coulter.

| DATE | POS | WKS | BPI | ALBUM TITLE | LABEL & NUMBER |
|---|---|---|---|---|---|
| 24/09/1983 | 17 | 19 | ○ | FLIGHTS OF FANCY | Nouveau Music NML 1002 |

**KRISTIAN LEONTIOU** UK male singer and songwriter (born in 1982, London).

| DATE | POS | WKS | BPI | ALBUM TITLE | LABEL & NUMBER |
|---|---|---|---|---|---|
| 12/06/2004 | 31 | 3+ | ○ | SOME DAY SOON | Polydor 9866206 |

**LES RHYTHMES DIGITALES** UK multi-instrumentalist Stuart Price who uses the French-sounding name Jacques Lu Cont for Les Rhythmes Digitales. He was born in Paris, but only because his parents were on holiday there from Reading!

| DATE | POS | WKS | BPI | ALBUM TITLE | LABEL & NUMBER |
|---|---|---|---|---|---|
| 05/06/1999 | 53 | 1 | | DARKDANCER | Wall Of Sound WALLCD 021 |

**LESS THAN JAKE** US rock group formed in Gainesville, FL by Chris DeMakes (guitar/vocals), Roger Manganelli (bass) and Vinnie Fiorello (drums).

| DATE | POS | WKS | BPI | ALBUM TITLE | LABEL & NUMBER |
|---|---|---|---|---|---|
| 31/05/2003 | 37 | 2 | | ANTHEM | Sire 9362484852 |

**LET LOOSE** UK vocal trio Richie Wermerling, Rob Jeffrey and Lee Murray.

| DATE | POS | WKS | BPI | ALBUM TITLE | LABEL & NUMBER |
|---|---|---|---|---|---|
| 19/11/1994 | 20 | 14 | ○ | LET LOOSE | Mercury 5260182 |
| 05/10/1996 | 42 | 1 | | ROLLERCOASTER | Mercury 5329552 |

**LEVEL 42** UK group formed in London in 1980 by Mark King (born 20/10/1958, Cowes, Isle of Wight, vocals/bass), Phil Gould (born 28/2/1957, Hong Kong, drums), Boon Gould (born 4/3/1955, Shanklin, Isle of Wight, guitar) and Mike Lindup (born 17/3/1959, London, keyboards/vocals). They debuted on the Elite label before signing to Polydor. The Gould brothers both left in 1987, replaced by Gary Husband (drums) and Alan Murphy (guitar). By 1991 they had a nucleus of King and Lindup with lead guitarist Jakko Jakszyk. They disbanded in 1995. Named from a Douglas Adams novel, *The Hitchhikers Guide To The Galaxy*, in which '42' was the answer to 'the meaning of life, the universe and everything'. Murphy died from AIDS-related pneumonia on 19/10/1989. Mark King has also recorded solo.

| DATE | POS | WKS | BPI | ALBUM TITLE | LABEL & NUMBER |
|---|---|---|---|---|---|
| 29/08/1981 | 20 | 18 | ○ | LEVEL 42 | Polydor POLS 1036 |
| 10/04/1982 | 46 | 6 | | THE EARLY TAPES JULY–AUGUST 1980 | Polydor POLS 1064 |
| 18/09/1982 | 17 | 16 | ○ | THE PURSUIT OF ACCIDENTS | Polydor POLD 5067 |

▲⁹ Number of weeks album topped the US chart   ◆¹² RIAA Diamond Awards   ◇³ IFPI Platinum Europe Awards

| DATE | POS | WKS | BPI | ALBUM TITLE | LABEL & NUMBER |
|------|-----|-----|-----|-------------|----------------|
| 03/09/1983 | 9 | 13 | ● | STANDING IN THE LIGHT | Polydor POLD 5110 |
| 13/10/1984 | 14 | 8 | ○ | TRUE COLOURS | Polydor POLH 10 |
| 06/07/1985 | 28 | 5 | | A PHYSICAL PRESENCE | Polydor POLH 23 |
| 26/10/1985 | 3 | 72 | ✪² | WORLD MACHINE | Polydor POLH 25 |
| 28/03/1987 | 2 | 54 | ✪² | RUNNING IN THE FAMILY | Polydor POLH 42 |
| 01/10/1988 | 2 | 11 | ● | STARING AT THE SUN | Polydor POLH 50 |
| 18/11/1989 | 5 | 15 | ✪ | LEVEL BEST | Polydor LEVTV 1 |
| 14/09/1991 | 3 | 5 | ○ | GUARANTEED | RCA PL 75005 |
| 26/03/1994 | 8 | 3 | | FOREVER NOW | RCA 74321189962 |
| 07/11/1998 | 41 | 2 | | THE VERY BEST OF LEVEL 42 | Polydor 5593732 |

**LEVELLERS** UK group formed in Brighton in 1988 by Mark Chadwick (born 23/6/1966, Munster, Germany, vocals/banjo/guitar), Alan Miles (vocals/guitar/mandolin/harmonica), Jeremy Cunningham (born 2/6/1965, Cuckfield, bass /bouzouki), Jon Sevink (born 15/5/1965, Harlow, violin) and Charlie Heather (born 2/2/1964, Beckenham, drums), and signed with HAG in 1989. Miles left in 1990, replaced by Simon Friend (born 17/5/1967, London).

| DATE | POS | WKS | BPI | ALBUM TITLE | LABEL & NUMBER |
|------|-----|-----|-----|-------------|----------------|
| 19/10/1991 | 14 | 30 | ● | LEVELLING THE LAND | China WOL 1022 |
| 04/09/1993 | 2 | 14 | ● | LEVELLERS | China WOLCD 1034 |
| 09/09/1995 | ❶¹ | 14 | ● | ZEITGEIST | China WOLCD 1064 |
| 31/08/1996 | 13 | 4 | | BEST LIVE – HEADLIGHTS WHITE LINES BLACK TAR RIVERS | China WOLCDX 1074 |
| 06/09/1997 | 5 | 6 | ● | MOUTH TO MOUTH | China 0630198562 |
| 07/11/1998 | 15 | 11 | ● | ONE WAY OF LIFE – THE BEST OF THE LEVELLERS | China 0521732 |
| 16/09/2000 | 28 | 2 | | HELLO PIG | China 8573843392 |

**LEVERT** US soul group from Ohio formed by Gerald (born 13/7/1966, Cleveland, OH) and Sean Levert (born 28/9/1969, Cleveland), and Marc Gordon. The Levert brothers are the sons of O'Jay vocalist Eddie Levert. They first recorded for Tempre in 1985 and have since become in demand as producers. Gerald Levert subsequently recorded solo. The group appeared in the 1991 Film *New Jack City*.

| DATE | POS | WKS | BPI | ALBUM TITLE | LABEL & NUMBER |
|------|-----|-----|-----|-------------|----------------|
| 29/08/1987 | 86 | 1 | | THE BIG THROWDOWN | Atlantic 7817731 |

**JAMES LEVINE** – see JOSE CARRERAS, PLACIDO DOMINGO, LUCIANO PAVAROTTI

**LEVITATION** UK group formed by Terry Bickers (vocals), Bic Hayes (guitar), Bob White (keyboards), Laurence O'Keefe (bass) and Dave Francollini (drums).

| DATE | POS | WKS | BPI | ALBUM TITLE | LABEL & NUMBER |
|------|-----|-----|-----|-------------|----------------|
| 16/05/1992 | 45 | 1 | | NEED FOR NOT | Rough Trade R 2862 |

**CJ LEWIS** UK reggae singer Steven James Lewis.

| DATE | POS | WKS | BPI | ALBUM TITLE | LABEL & NUMBER |
|------|-----|-----|-----|-------------|----------------|
| 03/09/1994 | 44 | 2 | ○ | DOLLARS | Black Market MCD 11131 |

**DONNA LEWIS** UK singer/guitarist (born in Cardiff, South Glamorgan), moved to New York where she began playing in piano bars.

| DATE | POS | WKS | BPI | ALBUM TITLE | LABEL & NUMBER |
|------|-----|-----|-----|-------------|----------------|
| 12/10/1996 | 52 | 1 | | NOW IN A MINUTE | Atlantic 7567827622 |

**HUEY LEWIS AND THE NEWS** US singer (born Hugh Creg III, 5/7/1950, New York); he joined Clover in 1976 and formed The News in 1980, with Chris Hayes (born 24/11/1957, California, guitar), Mario Cipollina (born 10/11/1954, California, bass), Bill Gibson (born 13/11/1951, California, drums), Sean Hopper (born 31/3/1953 California, keyboards) and Johnny Colla (born 2/7/1952, California, saxophone/guitar). They won the 1985 Grammy Award for Best Video Long Form for *The Heart Of Rock 'N' Roll*. They were also named Best International Group at the 1986 BRIT Awards.

| DATE | POS | WKS | BPI | ALBUM TITLE | LABEL & NUMBER |
|------|-----|-----|-----|-------------|----------------|
| 14/09/1985 | 23 | 24 | ● | SPORTS ▲¹ | Chrysalis CHR 1412 |
| 20/09/1986 | 8 | 52 | ✪² | FORE! ▲¹ | Chrysalis CDL 1534 |
| 06/08/1988 | 12 | 8 | ● | SMALL WORLD | Chrysalis CDL 1622 |
| 18/05/1991 | 39 | 2 | | HARD AT PLAY | Chrysalis CHR 1847 |
| 21/11/1992 | 23 | 8 | ○ | THE HEART OF ROCK AND ROLL – BEST OF HUEY LEWIS AND THE NEWS | Chrysalis CDCHR 1934 |

**JERRY LEE LEWIS** US singer (born 29/9/1935, Ferriday, LA) who taught himself piano, aged nine. He debuted for Sun in 1956 (his single was banned for being vulgar); his film debut was in *Disc Jockey Jamboree* (1957). He was known as 'The Killer' and well known for his marriages, one of which caused the cancellation of his UK tour in 1958 when it was revealed that his 'wife' Myra Gale was his thirteen-year-old cousin and he was not yet divorced from his second wife (also a bigamous marriage!). The 1989 film *Great Balls Of Fire* with Dennis Quaid is the story of his early career. He was inducted into the Rock & Roll Hall of Fame in 1986. He won the 1986

Grammy Award for Best Spoken Word Recording with others for *Interviews From The Class Of '55*. He has a star on the Hollywood Walk of Fame.

02/06/1962 . . . . . 14 . . . . . . 6 . . . . . . JERRY LEE LEWIS VOLUME 2 . . . . . . . . . . . . . . . . . . . . . . . . . . . . . . . . . . . . . . . . . . . . . . . . . . London HA 2440

## LINDA GAIL LEWIS – see VAN MORRISON

## LINDA LEWIS UK singer/songwriter born in London in 1950. In the early 1970s she was one of the top session singers working with artists such as David Bowie and Cat Stevens. She first recorded solo in 1971 for Bell.

09/08/1975 . . . . . 40 . . . . . . 4 . . . . . . NOT A LITTLE GIRL ANYMORE. . . . . . . . . . . . . . . . . . . . . . . . . . . . . . . . . . . . . . . . . . . . . . . . . . . . Arista ARTY 109

## RAMSEY LEWIS US pianist (born 27/5/1935, Chicago, IL); he formed the Gentlemen of Swing in 1956 with Eldes Young (bass) and Isaac 'Red' Holt (drums), changing their name to the Ramsey Lewis Trio upon signing with Chess. Young and Holt left in 1965 to form the Young-Holt Trio. Lewis re-formed his group the following year with Maurice White (drums) and Cleveland Eaton (bass). White left in 1970 to launch Earth, Wind & Fire; Eaton went solo. Lewis has won three Grammy Awards: Best Jazz Performance in 1965 for *The 'In' Crowd,* Best Rhythm & Blues Group Performance in 1965 for *Hold It Right There* and Best Rhythm & Blues Instrumental Performance in 1973 for *Hang On Sloopy*. His *Love Notes* album also won the 1977 Grammy Award for Best Album Package.

21/05/1966 . . . . . 20 . . . . . . 4 . . . . . . HANG ON RAMSEY . . . . . . . . . . . . . . . . . . . . . . . . . . . . . . . . . . . . . . . . . . . . . . . . . . . . . . . . . . Chess CRL 4520

## LFO UK instrumental group formed by Jez Varley (keyboards), Mark Bell (keyboards/programming), Simon Hartley (drums) and Richie Brook (keyboards). They later added singer Susie Thorpe. The initials stand for Low Frequency Oscillation.

03/08/1991 . . . . . 42 . . . . 2 . . . . . . FREQUENCIES . . . . . . . . . . . . . . . . . . . . . . . . . . . . . . . . . . . . . . . . . . . . . . . . . . . . . . . . . Warp WARPLP 3
10/02/1996 . . . . . 44 . . . . . . 1 . . . . . . ADVANCE . . . . . . . . . . . . . . . . . . . . . . . . . . . . . . . . . . . . . . . . . . . . . . . . . . . . . . . . . . Warp WARPCD 39

## LIBERTINES UK rock group formed in London by Carl Barat (guitar/vocals), Pete Doherty (guitar/vocals), John Hassall (bass) and Gary Powell (drums). Doherty was sacked in June 2003 because of a drug habit. He was later sentenced to six months in prison (reduced to two on appeal) for committing a burglary at Carl Barat's flat.

02/11/2002 . . . . . 35 . . . . . . 3 . . . . . ● UP THE BRACKET. . . . . . . . . . . . . . . . . . . . . . . . . . . . . . . . . . . . . . . . . . . . . . . . . . Rough Trade RTRADECD 065

## LIBERTY X UK vocal group formed by Kelli Young (born 7/4/1981, Derby), Tony Lundon (born 13/4/1979, Galway, Ireland), Jessica Taylor (born 23/6/1980), Michelle Heaton (born 19/7/1980) and Kevin Simm (born 5/9/1980). The five were the runners-up in the Popstars TV series that gave rise to Hear'Say. Although they became the first group called Liberty to register a hit single, the name had previously been claimed by another group and in March 2002 they were forced to amend their name to Liberty X.

08/06/2002 . . . . . 3 . . . . . . 58 . . . . . . ◎² **THINKING IT OVER** . . . . . . . . . . . . . . . . . . . . . . . . . . . . . . . . . . . . . . . . . . . . . . . . . . . . . V2 VVR 1017782
15/11/2003 . . . . . 12 . . . . . . 4 . . . . . . BEING SOMEBODY . . . . . . . . . . . . . . . . . . . . . . . . . . . . . . . . . . . . . . . . . . . . . . . . . . . . . . V2 VVR 1023562

## LIGHT OF THE WORLD UK funk group formed in 1978 by Canute 'Kenny' Wellington (trumpet), David 'Baps' Baptiste (trumpet), Jean Paul 'Bluey' Maunick (guitar), Everton McCalla (drums), Neville 'Breeze' McKreith (guitar), Chris Etienne (percussion), Paul 'Tubbs' Williams (bass) and Peter Hinds (keyboards). Splitting in 1981, Beggar & Co and Incognito were formed by ex-members.

24/01/1981 . . . . . 73 . . . . . . 1 . . . . . . ROUND TRIP . . . . . . . . . . . . . . . . . . . . . . . . . . . . . . . . . . . . . . . . . . . . . . . . . . . . . . . . Ensign ENVY 14

## GORDON LIGHTFOOT Canadian singer (born 17/11/1938, Orillia, Ontario) who became a member of the Swinging Singing Eight in 1958. He recorded his solo debut in 1961 and relaunched his solo career in 1965 after finding success as a songwriter.

20/05/1972 . . . . . 44 . . . . . . 1 . . . . . . DON QUIXOTE . . . . . . . . . . . . . . . . . . . . . . . . . . . . . . . . . . . . . . . . . . . . . . . . . . . . . . . Reprise K 44166
17/08/1974 . . . . . 45 . . . . . . 1 . . . . . . SUNDOWN ▲² . . . . . . . . . . . . . . . . . . . . . . . . . . . . . . . . . . . . . . . . . . . . . . . . . . . . . . . Reprise K 54020

## LIGHTHOUSE FAMILY UK group formed in Newcastle in 1993 by Tunde Baiyewu (born 25/11/1968, London, vocals) and Paul Tucker (born 12/8/1968, Crystal Palace, London, keyboards). The pair met whilst studying at college in Newcastle.

18/11/1995 . . . . . 3 . . . . . 154 . . . . . ◎⁶ **OCEAN DRIVE** ◇² . . . . . . . . . . . . . . . . . . . . . . . . . . . . . . . . . . . . . . . . . . . . . . . . . . . . Wild Card 5237872
01/11/1997 . . . . . 2 . . . . . . 73 . . . . . ◎⁴ **POSTCARDS FROM HEAVEN** ◇² . . . . . . . . . . . . . . . . . . . . . . . . . . . . . . . . . . . . . . . . . . Wild Card 5395162
01/12/2001 . . . . . 7 . . . . . . 18 . . . . . ◎ **WHATEVER GETS YOU THROUGH THE DAY** ◇ . . . . . . . . . . . . . . . . . . . . . . . . . . . . . . . Wild Card 5894122
30/11/2002 . . . . . 23 . . . . . . 6 . . . . . ● GREATEST HITS . . . . . . . . . . . . . . . . . . . . . . . . . . . . . . . . . . . . . . . . . . . . . . . . . . . . . Wild Card 0654482
19/04/2003 . . . . . 9 . . . . . . 12 . . . . . ◎ **THE VERY BEST OF**. . . . . . . . . . . . . . . . . . . . . . . . . . . . . . . . . . . . . . . . . . . . . . . . . . Wild Card 0761662

---

▲⁹ Number of weeks album topped the US chart   ◆¹² RIAA Diamond Awards   ◇³ IFPI Platinum Europe Awards

**LIGHTNING SEEDS** UK group formed by ex-Big In Japan member Ian Broudie (born 4/8/1958, Liverpool). Initially a one-man band, it now features four members: Broudie, Martin Campbell (ex-Rain, bass), Chris Sharrock (ex-Icicle Works, drums) and Paul Hemmings (ex-La's, guitar). Broudie also took part in the *Perfect Day* project for the BBC's Children In Need charity.

| 10/02/1990 | 50 | 2 | | CLOUDCUCKOOLAND | Ghetto GHETT 3 |
| 18/04/1992 | 53 | 1 | ○ | SENSE | Virgin CDV 2690 |
| 17/09/1994 | 12 | 58 | ✪ | JOLLIFICATION | Epic 4772379 |
| 18/05/1996 | 27 | 9 | ○ | PURE LIGHTNING SEEDS | Virgin CDV 2805 |
| 23/11/1996 | 11 | 26 | ● | DIZZY HEIGHTS | Epic 4866402 |
| 22/11/1997 | 5 | 41 | ✪² | **LIKE YOU DO... THE BEST OF LIGHTNING SEEDS** | Epic 4890342 |
| 04/12/1999 | 46 | 2 | | TILT | Epic 4962632 |

**LIL' KIM** US rapper (born Kimberly Jones, NYC) who is also a member of Junior M.A.F.I.A. She won the 2001 Grammy Award for Best Pop Collaboration with Vocals with Christina Aguilera, Mya and Pink for *Lady Marmalade*.

| 08/07/2000 | 67 | 1 | | THE NOTORIOUS KIM | Atlantic 7567928402 |

**LIL' LOUIS** US singer (born Louis Burns, Chicago, IL; he is the son of blues guitarist Bobby Sims (who played with BB King and Bobby Bland) and began his career as a DJ at the age of thirteen. He has also recorded as Black Magic and as part of Lil' Mo Yin Yang.

| 26/08/1989 | 35 | 5 | | FRENCH KISSES | ffrr 8281701 |

**LIMAHL** UK singer (born Christopher Hamill, 19/12/1958) whose stage name is an anagram of his surname. He first came to prominence as lead vocalist with Kajagoogoo and went solo six months after the group achieved their chart breakthrough.

| 01/12/1984 | 63 | 3 | | DON'T SUPPOSE | EMI PLML 1 |

**ALISON LIMERICK** UK singer born in London in 1959 who began her career in musicals and appeared in the show *Starlight Express* before launching a solo career.

| 04/04/1992 | 53 | 2 | | AND STILL I RISE | Arista 262365 |

**LIMP BIZKIT** US rock group formed in Florida in 1994 by Fred Durst (born 20/8/1971, Jacksonville, FL, vocals), Sam Rivers (bass), Wes Borland (guitar) and John Otto (drums), later adding DJ Lethal (Leor DiMant) to the line-up. Wes Borland left in October 2001 and was replaced by Mike Smith. Three awards at the 2001 MTV Europe Music Awards include: Best Group and Best Website.

| 03/07/1999 | 10 | 37 | ● | **SIGNIFICANT OTHER** ◇ ▲⁴ | Interscope IND 90335 |
| 09/09/2000 | 50 | 5 | | THREE DOLLAR BILL Y'ALL | Interscope IND 90124 |
| 28/10/2000 | ❶¹ | 48 | ✪² | **CHOCOLATE STARFISH AND THE HOT DOG FLAVOURED WATER** ◇² ▲² 2001 MTV Europe Music Award for Best Album ......... Interscope 4907932 |
| 04/10/2003 | 7 | 5 | ● | **RESULTS MAY VARY** | Interscope 9860976 |

**LINDISFARNE** UK group formed in Newcastle in 1967 by Alan Hull (born 20/2/1945, Newcastle-upon-Tyne, vocals/guitar/piano), Simon Cowe (born 1/4/1948, Jesmind Dene, guitar), Ray Jackson (born 12/12/1948, Wallsend, harmonica/mandolin), Rod Clements (born 17/11/1947, North Shields, bass/violin) and Ray Laidlaw (born 28/5/1948, North Shields, drums) as Downtown Faction. They changed their name the following year, Lindisfarne being an island off Northumberland. The group split in 1973 but reunited in 1978. Hull died on 17/11/1995 from a heart attack.

| 30/10/1971 | ❶⁴ | 56 | | **FOG ON THE TYNE** | Charisma CAS 1050 |
| 15/01/1972 | 8 | 30 | | **NICELY OUT OF TUNE** | Charisma CAS 1025 |
| 30/09/1972 | 5 | 10 | | **DINGLY DELL** | Charisma CAS 1057 |
| 11/08/1973 | 25 | 6 | | LINDISFARNE LIVE | Charisma CLASS 2 |
| 18/10/1975 | 55 | 1 | | FINEST HOUR | Charisma CAS 1108 |
| 24/06/1978 | 22 | 11 | ○ | BACK AND FOURTH | Mercury 9109 609 |

| 09/12/1978 | 71 | 1 | | MAGIC IN THE AIR | Mercury 6641 877 |
| 23/10/1982 | 59 | 3 | | SLEEPLESS NIGHTS | LMP GET 1 |

**LINKIN PARK** US rock group formed in Los Angeles by Chester Bennington (born 20/3/1976, vocals), Mike Shinoda (born 11/2/1977, raps/vocals), Joseph Hahn (born 15/3/1977, DJ), Brad Delson (born 1/12/1977, guitar), Dave 'Phoenix' Ferrel (born 8/2/1977, bass) and Rob Bourdon (born 20/1/1979, drums). They were awarded Best Group and Best Hard Rock Act at the 2002 MTV Europe Music Awards.

| 20/01/2001 | 4 | 77 | ✪³ | HYBRID THEORY ◇³ | Warner Brothers 9362477552 |
| 10/08/2002 | 3 | 8 | | REANIMATION | Warner Brothers 9362483542 |
| 05/04/2003 | ❶¹ | 33 | ✪ | METEORA ◇ ▲² | Warner Brothers 9362484612 |
| 06/12/2003 | 47 | 3 | ○ | LIVE IN TEXAS | Warner Brothers WB 485632 |

**LINX** UK funk duo formed by David Grant (born 8/8/1956, Hackney, London) and Sketch (born Peter Martin, 1954, Antigua). They signed a deal with Chrysalis on the strength of a self-financed debut disc. They disbanded in 1982 and Grant went solo.

| 28/03/1981 | 8 | 19 | ○ | INTUITION | Chrysalis CHR 1332 |
| 31/10/1981 | 35 | 4 | | GO AHEAD | Chrysalis CHR 1358 |

**LIONROCK** UK producer Justin Robertson. A group was later assembled, which included MC Buzz B.

| 20/04/1996 | 30 | 2 | | AN INSTINCT FOR DETECTION | Deconstruction 74321342812 |
| 28/03/1998 | 73 | 1 | | CITY DELIRIOUS | Concrete HARD 32CDX |

**LIQUID GOLD** UK disco group with Ellie Hope (vocals), Syd Twynham (guitar), Ray Knott (bass), Tom Marshall (keyboards) and Wally Rothe (drums). The group came second in the UK heat of the 1981 Eurovision Song Contest.

| 16/08/1980 | 34 | 3 | | LIQUID GOLD | Polo POLP 101 |

**LISA LISA AND CULT JAM WITH FULL FORCE** US group formed by Lisa Lisa (born Lisa Velez, 15/1/1967), Mark Hughes and Alex 'Spanador' Mosely, with all their hits written and produced by Full Force. Full Force are a US rap and hip hop group formed in New York by brothers Lucien 'Lou', Paul Anthony and Brian 'B-Fine' George and cousins Curtis Bedeau, Gerald Charles and Junior 'Shy-Shy' Clark. Originally formed as the Amplifiers, they were re-named in 1978. They were first known for producing Lisa Lisa & Cult Jam and later worked with artists as diverse as James Brown and Samantha Fox.

| 21/09/1985 | 96 | 1 | | LISA LISA AND CULT JAM WITH FULL FORCE | CBS 26593 |

**LIT** US group formed in California by A Jay Popoff (vocals), Jeremy Popoff (guitar), Kevin Blades (bass) and Allen Shellenberger (drums).

| 10/07/1999 | 55 | 1 | | A PLACE IN THE SUN | RCA 07863677752 |

**LITTLE ANGELS** UK heavy rock group formed by Toby Jepson (vocals), Bruce J Dickinson (guitar), Mark Plunkett (bass), Jim Dickinson (keyboards) and Michael Lee (drums). After a number of releases on Powerstation they signed with Polydor in 1988.

| 02/03/1991 | 17 | 6 | | YOUNG GODS | Polydor 8478461 |
| 06/02/1993 | ❶¹ | 5 | ○ | JAM | Polydor 5176422 |
| 23/04/1994 | 20 | 2 | | LITTLE OF THE PAST | Polydor 5219362 |
| 02/07/1994 | 18 | 2 | | TOO POSH TO MOSH, TOO GOOD TO LAST? | Essential ESSCD 213 |

**LITTLE FEAT** US group formed by Lowell George (born 13/4/1945, Los Angeles, CA), Bill Payne (born 12/3/1949, Waco, TX, keyboards), Roy Estrada (bass) and Richie Haywood (drums); they signed with Warner Brothers in 1970. Estrada left in 1972 and was replaced by Kenny Gradney, with Paul Barrere (born 3/7/1948, Burbank, CA, guitar) and Sam Clayton (percussion) joining at the same time. They disbanded in 1978, George going solo, but he died from a heart attack on 29/6/1979. The group re-formed in 1989 with Craig Fuller, ex-Pure Prairie League, taking George's place.

| 06/12/1975 | 36 | 3 | ○ | THE LAST RECORD ALBUM | Warner Brothers K 56156 |
| 21/05/1977 | 8 | 11 | ○ | TIME LOVES A HERO | Warner Brothers K 56349 |
| 11/03/1978 | 43 | 1 | | WAITING FOR COLUMBUS | Warner Brothers K 66075 |
| 01/12/1979 | 46 | 3 | | DOWN ON THE FARM | Warner Brothers K 56667 |
| 08/08/1981 | 76 | 1 | | HOY-HOY! | Warner Brothers K 66100 |

**LITTLE STEVEN** US singer/guitarist (born Steven Van Zandt, 22/11/1950, Boston, MA) who began with Steel Mill (featuring Bruce Springsteen) and then went on tour backing The Dovells. After a spell in Southside Johnny And The Asbury Jukes, he joined Bruce Springsteen's E Street Band in 1975 and stayed for six years. He left in 1981 to form Little Steven And The Disciples of Soul. He masterminded The Artists United Against Apartheid single *Sun City,* and worked with the likes of Gary US Bonds, Lone Justice and Ronnie Spector as producer.

| 06/11/1982 | 73 | 2 | | MEN WITHOUT WOMEN **LITTLE STEVEN AND THE DISCIPLES OF SOUL** | EMI America 3027 |
| 06/06/1987 | 52 | 2 | | FREEDOM NO COMPROMISE | Manhattan MTL 1010 |

---

**LITTLE VILLAGE** UK/US group formed by Nick Lowe (born 25/3/1949, Woodbridge, Suffolk, guitar/vocals), Ry Cooder (born 15/3/1947, Los Angeles, CA, guitar/vocals), John Hiatt (born 1952, Indianapolis, IN, guitar/vocals) and session drummer Jim Keltner.

| | | | | |
|---|---|---|---|---|
| 29/02/1992.....23......4...... | LITTLE VILLAGE ............................................................... Reprise 7599267132 |

**LIVE** US group formed in York, PA in 1991 by Ed Kowalcyzk (born 17/7/1971, Lancaster, PA, vocals), Patrick Dahlheimer (born 30/5/1971, York, bass), Chad Taylor (born 24/11/1970, York, guitar) and Chad Gracey (born 23/7/1971, York, drums). They signed with Radioactive in 1991.

| | |
|---|---|
| 15/07/1995.....37......6......O | THROWING COPPER ▲[1] ............................................... Radioactive RAD 10997 |
| 29/03/1997.....31......2...... | SECRET SAMADHI ▲[1] .................................................. Radioactive RAD 11590 |
| 16/10/1999.....56......1...... | THE DISTANCE TO HERE .................................................. Radioactive RAD 11966 |

**LIVIN' JOY** Italian dance group assembled by brothers Venturi and Giovanni Visnadi featuring the vocals of US singer Janice Robinson. The brothers are also responsible for Alex Party. Robinson left in 1996 and was replaced by fellow US singer Tameka Starr.

| | |
|---|---|
| 16/11/1996.....41......2...... | DON'T STOP MOVIN' ................................................... Undiscovered MCD 60023 |

**LIVING COLOUR** US rock group formed in New York in 1984 by Vernon Reid (born 22/8/1958, London, guitar), Corey Glover (born 6/11/1964, New York, vocals), Manuel 'Muzz' Skillings (born 6/1/1960, New York) and William Calhoun (born 22/7/1964, New York, drums). Glover appeared in the film *Platoon*. Skillings left in 1992, replaced by Doug Wimbush (born 22/9/1956, Hartford, CT). They won two Grammy Awards before they disbanded in 1995, Best Hard Rock Performance (Vocal or Instrumental) in 1989 for *Cult Of Personality* and in 1990 Best Hard Rock Performance (Vocal or Instrumental) for *Time's Up*. Vernon Reid later recorded solo.

| | |
|---|---|
| 15/09/1990.....20......19...... | TIME'S UP ............................................................... Epic 4669201 |
| 06/03/1993.....19......3...... | STAIN ................................................................... Epic 4728562 |

**LIVING IN A BOX** UK group formed by Richard Darbyshire (born 8/3/1960, Stockport, vocals), Marcus Vere (born 29/1/1962, keyboards) and Anthony 'Tich' Critchlow (drums). Darbyshire later recorded solo.

| | |
|---|---|
| 09/05/1987.....25......19......● | LIVING IN A BOX........................................................ Chrysalis CDL 1547 |
| 08/07/1989.....21......16......● | GATECRASHING ......................................................... Chrysalis CDL 1676 |

**LL COOL J** US rapper (born James Todd Smith, 14/1/1968, Queens, NY) who began rapping at the age of nine. His stage name is an abbreviation for Ladies Love Cool James. He appeared in the films *Krush Groove, Toys, Halloween H2O, B\*A\*P\*S, In Too Deep* and *Deep Blue Sea*. He has won two Grammy Awards: Best Rap Solo Performance in 1991 for *Mama Said Knock You Out* and Best Rap Solo Performance in 1996 for *Hey Lover*. He went into semi-retirement musically in 1997 to concentrate on his film career, appearing in *Kingdom Come* and *Any Given Sunday*. He returned to recording in 2000 with the album *The G.O.A.T.* (UK title *The Greatest Of All Time*).

| | |
|---|---|
| 15/02/1986.....71......1...... | RADIO ................................................................. Def Jam DEF 26745 |
| 13/06/1987.....54......19...... | BIGGER AND DEFFER .................................................... Def Jam 4505151 |
| 08/07/1989.....43......3...... | WALKING WITH A PANTHER................................................ Def Jam 4651121 |
| 13/10/1990.....49......2...... | MAMA SAID KNOCK YOU OUT ............................................ Def Jam 4673151 |
| 17/04/1993.....74......1...... | 14 SHOTS TO THE DOME ................................................. Def Jam 4736782 |
| 16/11/1996.....23......8...... | ALL WORLD ............................................................. Def Jam 5343032 |
| 25/10/1997.....37......4...... | PHENOMENON ......................................................... Def Jam 5391862 |
| 23/09/2000.....29......2...... | THE GREATEST OF ALL TIME ▲[1] ........................................ Def Jam 5429972 |
| 02/11/2002.....26......3...... | 10 .................................................................... Def Jam 0632192 |

**KELLY LLORENNA** UK singer, born in Manchester, who began her career (aged eighteen) with N-Trance before going solo.

| | |
|---|---|
| 07/12/2002.....62......2......O | ALL CLUBBED UP – THE BEST OF KELLY LLORENNA ............................... Universal TV 0666082 |

**ANDREW LLOYD WEBBER** UK composer/producer (born 22/3/1948, London); he first met lyricist and law student Tim Rice whilst both were studying at Magdalene College in Oxford; Lloyd Webber was studying music. Their first composition was *The Likes Of Us* and by 1967 they had completed their first musical, *Joseph And The Amazing Technicolor Dreamcoat*, which was first performed at a London school in 1968. Four years later, a West-End run and numerous provincial versions later, Lloyd Webber and Rice were regarded as the brightest musical talents of their era. Success continued with *Jesus Christ Superstar* (although religious groups expressed their outrage), which won a Grammy and seven Tony Awards during its US run. After a brief hiccup (*Jeeves*) it was back to the blockbuster for *Evita*, the story of Argentinean political leader Eva Peron, which gave rise to the international smash by Julia Covington, *Don't Cry For Me Argentina*. *Evita* had not yet finished its run when Lloyd Webber's next smash opened, with *Cats*, and in particular the song *Memory*, proving memorable. By now Lloyd Webber was working less and less with Rice and instead had utilised the lyrics of such writers as Don Black, Trevor Nunn and even TS Eliot (*Cats* was based on Eliot's book *Old Possum's Book of Practical Cats*). In 1982 Lloyd Webber made theatrical history when *Song And Dance* opened on Broadway and in the West End, for with *Evita* and *Cats* still performing in front of sell-out crowds, Lloyd Webber was the only composer to have three shows playing in the two major theatrical centres simultaneously. With Lloyd Webber having formed the Really Useful Company (where Prince Edward was at one time employed as tea boy!) and virtually underwriting his own shows, the success continued unabated: *Starlight Express, Phantom Of The Opera, Aspects Of Love* and *Sunset Boulevard* ensured Lloyd Webber's name was at the forefront of the genre. Virtually all of his shows have been revived over the years, further adding to his status as one of the most powerful men in the world of musical theatre. It was in this capacity that he was awarded a knighthood, although he has also written outside a theatrical environment, as the success of *Friends For Life*, the theme to the 1992 Barcelona Olympics would confirm. He has been married three times, including to singer Sarah Brightman, who performed the lead role in *Phantom Of The Opera*. He has won two Grammy Awards including Best Cast Show Album in 1980 with Tim Rice for *Evita*. The pair also won the 1996 Oscar for Best Film Song for *You Must Love Me* from *Evita*. He has a star on the Hollywood Walk of Fame.

| | |
|---|---|
| 11/02/1978 .....2......19......✪ | **VARIATIONS** ANDREW LLOYD WEBBER FEATURING CELLIST JULIAN LLOYD WEBBER ............................ MCA MCF 2824 |

O Silver disc  ● Gold disc  ✪ Platinum disc (additional platinum units are indicated by a figure following the symbol)  ❶[9] Number of weeks album topped the UK chart

23/03/1985 ..... 4 ..... 18 ..... ✪   **ANDREW LLOYD WEBBER: REQUIEM** PLACIDO DOMINGO, SARAH BRIGHTMAN, PAUL MILES-KINGSTON, WINCHESTER CATHEDRAL CHOIR AND THE ENGLISH CHAMBER ORCESTRA CONDUCTED BY LORIN MAAZEL 1975 Grammy Award for Best Contemporary Composition ............................................................................................................. HMV ALW 1

### JULIAN LLOYD WEBBER
UK cellist (born 1951), younger brother of Andrew Lloyd Webber. He was also a member of Oasis with Mary Hopkin, Bill Lovelady and Peter Skellern.

| 11/02/1978 ..... 2 ..... 19 ..... ✪ | **VARIATIONS** ............................................................................................ MCA MCF 2824 |
| 14/09/1985 ..... 59 ..... 5 ..... | PIECES .......................................................................................... Polydor PROLP 6 |
| 21/02/1987 ..... 94 ..... 1 ..... | ELGAR CELLO CONCERTO ........................................................................ Philips 4163541 |
| 27/10/1990 ..... 15 ..... 13 ..... ● | LLOYD WEBBER PLAYS LLOYD WEBBER ........................................................... Philips 4322911 |

### LO FIDELITY ALLSTARS
UK group formed by Wrekked Train (Dave Randall, vocals), Albino Priest (decks), A One Man Crowd Called Gentile (bass), the Slammer (drums), Sheriff John Stone (keyboards) and the Many Tentacles (engineering/keyboards). Randall left in December 1998. They later recorded with Pigeonhed, a rock group from Seattle formed by Shawn Smith and Steve Fisk.

06/06/1998 ..... 15 ..... 4 .....   HOW TO OPERATE WITH A BLOWN MIND ........................................................ Skint BRASSIC 8CD

### TONE LOC
US rapper (born Anthony Smith, 3/3/1966, Los Angeles, CA) who formed Triple A at school before going solo. *Loc'ed After Dark* was the first rap album to top US charts. His name originates from the Spanish nickname 'Antonio Loco'. He starred in the film *Ace Ventura: Pet Detective*.

25/03/1989 ..... 22 ..... 16 .....   LOC'ED AFTER DARK ▲¹ ....................................................................... Delicious BRLP 526

### JOSEF LOCKE
Irish singer (born Joseph McLaughlin, 23/3/1917, Londonderry); he served in the Irish Guards from the age of sixteen (he lied about his age in order to enlist, adding two years) and the Palestine Police before returning to Ireland in the 1930s and enlisting in the Royal Ulster Constabulary. It was here that his singing ambitions were rekindled and he took to touring as the 'Singing Bobby', becoming a celebrity on both sides of the Irish Sea. He appeared on radio in 1949 and was later a major TV celebrity. He also made five Royal Command Performances and was at the peak of his career in 1958 when he ran into trouble with the Inland Revenue, declining to meet their demands (he 'escaped' to Ireland). He disappeared from the public view for a considerable time, although his tax liabilities were eventually settled and he retired to County Kildare. He was the subject of the film *Hear My Song* and appeared in a number of films himself, including *Holidays With Pay*. He died on 15/10/1999.

| 28/06/1969 ..... 29 ..... 1 ..... | THE WORLD OF JOSEF LOCKE TODAY ............................................................. Decca SPA 21 |
| 21/03/1992 ..... 7 ..... 17 ..... ● | **HEAR MY SONG (THE BEST OF JOSEF LOCKE)** ................................................... EMI CDGO 2034 |
| 27/06/1992 ..... 41 ..... 2 ..... | TAKE A PAIR OF SPARKLING EYES ............................................................... EMI CDGO 2038 |

### JOHN LODGE
UK singer/guitarist (born 20/7/1945, Birmingham); he joined The Moody Blues in 1966 and then launched a parallel solo career as well as working with fellow Moody Blue member Justin Hayward.

| 29/03/1975 ..... 4 ..... 18 ..... | **BLUE JAYS** JUSTIN HAYWARD AND JOHN LODGE .............................................. Threshold THS 12 |
| 19/02/1977 ..... 38 ..... 2 ..... | NATURAL AVENUE .............................................................................. Decca TXS 120 |

### LISA LOEB AND NINE STORIES
US group based in New York and formed by Lisa Loeb (vocals), Tim Bright (guitar), Joe Quigley (bass) and Jonathan Feinberg (drums). Lisa won the Best International Newcomer award at the 1995 BRIT Awards.

07/10/1995 ..... 39 ..... 2 .....   TAILS ......................................................................................... Geffen GED 24734

### NILS LOFGREN
US singer/guitarist (born 21/6/1951, Chicago, IL); he first recorded as Paul Dowell And The Dolphin before forming Grin in the 1970s. After a spell with Neil Young's Crazy Horse, he was going to replace Mick Taylor in The Rolling Stones but signed solo with A&M instead. In 1984 he joined Bruce Springsteen's E Street Band, but still recorded solo for Towerbell and Essential.

| 17/04/1976 ..... 8 ..... 11 ..... ○ | **CRY TOUGH** ................................................................................ A&M AMLH 64573 |
| 26/03/1977 ..... 30 ..... 4 ..... | I CAME TO DANCE .............................................................................. A&M AMLH 64628 |
| 05/11/1977 ..... 38 ..... 2 ..... | NIGHT AFTER NIGHT ............................................................................ A&M AMLH 68439 |
| 26/09/1981 ..... 50 ..... 3 ..... | NIGHT FADES AWAY ....................................................................... Backstreet/A&M MCF 3121 |
| 01/05/1982 ..... 100 ..... 1 ..... | A RHYTHM ROMANCE ........................................................................... A&M AMLH 68543 |
| 06/07/1985 ..... 36 ..... 7 ..... | FLIP .......................................................................................... Towerbell TOWLP 11 |
| 05/04/1986 ..... 86 ..... 1 ..... | CODE OF THE ROAD ........................................................................... Towerbell TOWDLP 17 |
| 27/04/1991 ..... 61 ..... 1 ..... | SILVER LINING ................................................................................. Essential ESSLP 145 |

### JOHNNY LOGAN
Irish singer (born Sean Sherrard, Australia) who became a naturalised Irishman. He is the only artist to have won the Eurovision Song Contest on more than one occasion.

22/08/1987 ..... 83 ..... 1 .....   HOLD ME NOW ................................................................................. CBS 4510731

### LOLLY
UK teenage singer Anna Klumby (born 27/6/1978, Sutton Coldfield).

02/10/1999 ..... 21 ..... 12 ..... ●   MY FIRST ALBUM ............................................................................. Polydor 5479622

### LONDON BOYS
UK duo Dennis Fuller and Edem Ephraim who relocated to Germany before finding success in the hi-nrg market.

29/07/1989 ..... 2 ..... 29 ..... ✪   **THE TWELVE COMMANDMENTS OF DANCE** ...................................................... WEA WX 278

### LONDON PHILHARMONIC CHOIR
UK choir formed in 1947 as successor to the Philharmonic Choir (that had itself been formed in 1919).

| 03/12/1960 ..... 10 ..... 7 ..... | **THE MESSIAH** LONDON PHILHARMONIC CHOIR WITH THE LONDON ORCHESTRA CONDUCTED BY WALTER SUSSKIND ............ |
| | ................................................................................... Pye Golden Guinea GGL 0062 |
| 13/11/1976 ..... 10 ..... 10 ..... ○ | **SOUND OF GLORY** ............................................................................ Arcade ADEP 25 |

▲⁹ Number of weeks album topped the US chart   ◆¹² RIAA Diamond Awards   ◇³ IFPI Platinum Europe Awards

| | | | | | |
|---|---|---|---|---|---|
| 13/04/1991 | 54 | 3 | | PRAISE – 18 CHORAL MASTERPIECES This and the above hit credited to **LONDON PHILHARMONIC CHOIR WITH THE NATIONAL PHILHARMONIC ORCHESTRA CONDUCTED BY JOHN ALDISS** | Pop & Arts PATLP 301 |

## LONDON PHILHARMONIC ORCHESTRA
UK orchestra formed in 1932 by Thomas Beecham, who led the orchestra until 1939. Later conductors included Sir Adrian Boult, Sir John Pritchard, Bernard Haitink, Sir Georg Solti and Klaus Tennstedt and in 1964 it became resident orchestra for the Glyndebourne Festival Opera. Beecham later formed the Royal Philharmonic Orchestra.

| | | | | | |
|---|---|---|---|---|---|
| 23/04/1960 | 15 | 4 | | RAVEL'S BOLERO | London HAV 2189 |
| 08/04/1961 | 12 | 1 | | VICTORY AT SEA | Pye Golden Guinea GGL 0073 |
| 21/05/1983 | 7 | 17 | ○ | **DRESSED FOR THE OCCASION** CLIFF RICHARD & THE LONDON PHILHARMONIC ORCHESTRA | EMI EMC 3432 |
| 01/03/1986 | 97 | 1 | | ELGAR: VIOLIN CONCERTO **NIGEL KENNEDY WITH THE LONDON PHILHARMONIC ORCHESTRA** | EMI EMX 4120581 |
| 07/03/1987 | 73 | 4 | ● | THE MISSION Original soundtrack to the film **ENNIO MORRICONE WITH THE LONDON PHILHARMONIC ORCHESTRA** | Virgin V 2402 |
| 28/10/1989 | 47 | 7 | | CLASSIC BLUE **JUSTIN HAYWARD WITH MIKE BATT AND THE LONDON PHILHARMONIC ORCHESTRA** | Trax MODEM 1040 |
| 06/04/1991 | 16 | 12 | ● | BRAHMS: VIOLIN CONCERTO **NIGEL KENNEDY WITH THE LONDON PHILHARMONIC ORCHESTRA** | EMI NIGE 3 |
| 22/02/1992 | 56 | 1 | | JUST LISTEN **NIGEL KENNEDY WITH THE LONDON PHILHARMONIC ORCHESTRA CONDUCTED BY SIMON RATTLE** | EMI Classics CDNIGE 4 |

## LONDON SYMPHONY ORCHESTRA
UK orchestra formed in 1904 (the oldest surviving London orchestra) by members of the Queen's Hall Orchestra, with Hans Richter its first conductor. In 1912 it became the first UK orchestra to tour North America and made its first recordings in 1920. The LSO also scored a US top ten hit with their theme from *Star Wars*, written and conducted by John Williams, and also recorded as The Armada Orchestra, a disco group! The Royal Choral Society was formed in 1871 as the Royal Albert Hall Choral Society (and it is also the oldest surviving choral society in London) and was renamed in 1888.

| | | | | | |
|---|---|---|---|---|---|
| 18/03/1972 | 13 | 7 | | TOP TV THEMES | Studio Two STWO 372 |
| 16/12/1972 | 2 | 21 | | **THE STRAUSS FAMILY** LONDON SYMPHONY ORCHESTRA CONDUCTED BY CYRIL ORNADEL Original soundtrack to the film | Polydor 2659 014 |
| 05/07/1975 | 52 | 1 | | MUSIC FROM 'EDWARD VII' Original soundtrack to the TV series | Polydor 2659 041 |
| 18/12/1976 | 49 | 1 | | THE SNOW GOOSE **SPIKE MILLIGAN WITH THE LONDON SYMPHONY ORCHESTRA** | RCA Victor RS 1088 |
| 21/01/1978 | 21 | 12 | ● | STAR WARS **JOHN WILLIAMS AND THE LONDON SYMPHONY ORCHESTRA** Original soundtrack to the film | 20th Century BTD 541 |
| 08/07/1978 | 3 | 39 | ✪ | **CLASSIC ROCK** | K-Tel ONE 1009 |
| 10/02/1979 | 26 | 8 | | CLASSIC ROCK – THE SECOND MOVEMENT | K-Tel NE 1039 |
| 05/01/1980 | 34 | 5 | ● | RHAPSODY IN BLACK | K-Tel ONE 1063 |
| 01/08/1981 | 5 | 23 | ● | **CLASSIC ROCK – ROCK CLASSICS** LONDON SYMPHONY ORCHESTRA WITH THE ROYAL CHORAL SOCIETY | K-Tel ONE 1123 |
| 27/11/1982 | 35 | 11 | ● | THE BEST OF CLASSIC ROCK | K-Tel ONE 1080 |
| 27/08/1983 | 40 | 9 | ○ | CLASSIC ROCK – ROCK SYMPHONIES This and the above hit credited to **LONDON SYMPHONY ORCHESTRA WITH THE ROYAL CHORAL SOCIETY AND THE ROGER SMITH CHORALE** | K-Tel ONE 1243 |
| 26/10/1985 | 38 | 4 | | HITS ON OPERA **KIMERA WITH THE LONDON SYMPHONY ORCHESTRA** | Stylus SMR 8505 |
| 16/11/1985 | 13 | 15 | ● | THE POWER OF CLASSIC ROCK **LONDON SYMPHONY ORCHESTRA WITH THE ROYAL CHORAL SOCIETY AND THE ROGER SMITH CHORALE** | Portrait PRT 10049 |
| 14/11/1987 | 32 | 16 | | CLASSIC ROCK COUNTDOWN | CBS MOOD 3 |
| 18/11/1989 | 51 | 6 | ● | CLASSIC ROCK – THE LIVING YEARS | CBS MOOD 9 |
| 18/01/1992 | 24 | 8 | | WIND OF CHANGE – CLASSIC ROCK **LONDON SYMPHONY ORCHESTRA WITH THE ROYAL CHORAL SOCIETY** | Columbia MOODCD 19 |
| 19/11/1994 | 55 | 2 | | THE WORKS OF RICE AND LLOYD WEBBER | Vision VISCD 4 |
| 23/09/1995 | 27 | 9 | | BRAVEHEART ◇ **LONDON SYMPHONY ORCHESTRA, CONDUCTOR JAMES HORNER** Original soundtrack to the film | Decca 4482952 |
| 25/10/1997 | 34 | 2 | | PAUL McCARTNEY'S STANDING STONE **LONDON SYMPHONY ORCHESTRA CONDUCTED BY LAURENCE FOSTER** | EMI Classics CDC 5564842 |
| 27/03/1999 | 34 | 2 | | RETURN TO THE CENTRE OF THE EARTH **RICK WAKEMAN: LONDON SYMPHONY ORCHESTRA: ENGLISH CHAMBER CHOIR: NARRATED BY PATRICK STEWART** | EMI Classics CDC 5567632 |
| 15/05/1999 | 8 | 17 | ● | **STAR WARS – THE PHANTOM MENACE** JOHN WILLIAMS & THE LONDON SYMPHONY ORCHESTRA Original soundtrack to the film | Sony Classical SK 61816 |

## LONDON WELSH MALE VOICE CHOIR
UK choir based in London.

| | | | | | |
|---|---|---|---|---|---|
| 05/09/1981 | 61 | 10 | | SONGS OF THE VALLEYS | K-Tel NE 1117 |

## LONDONBEAT
US/Trinidadian R&B vocal trio with Jimmy Helms (born 1944, Florida), George Chandler (born in Atlanta, GA) and Jimmy Chambers (born 20/1/1946, Trinidad).

| | | | | | |
|---|---|---|---|---|---|
| 13/10/1990 | 34 | 6 | ○ | IN THE BLOOD | AnXious ZL 74810 |

## LONE JUSTICE
US group formed in Los Angeles, CA by Maria McKee (born 17/8/1964, Los Angeles, vocals), Ryan Hedgecock (guitar), Benmont Tench (keyboards), Marvin Etzioni (bass) and Don Effington (drums). By 1986 the line-up was McKee, Shayne Fontayne (guitar), Bruce Brody (keyboards), Greg Sutton (bass) and Rudy Richardson (drums). They disbanded in 1987 and McKee went solo.

| | | | | | |
|---|---|---|---|---|---|
| 06/07/1985 | 49 | 2 | | LONE JUSTICE | Geffen GEF 26288 |
| 08/11/1986 | 84 | 3 | | SHELTER | Geffen WX 73 |

○ Silver disc  ● Gold disc  ✪ Platinum disc (additional platinum units are indicated by a figure following the symbol)  ❶⁹ Number of weeks album topped the UK chart

### LONE STAR
UK group formed by Ken Driscoll (vocals), Tony Smith (guitar), Paul 'Tonka' Chapman (guitar), Rick Worsnop (keyboards), Peter Hurley (bass) and Dixie Lee (drums). By the time of their second album, Driscoll was replaced by John Sloman. They split in 1978 and Chapman joined UFO.

| 02/10/1976 | 47 | 1 | | LONE STAR | Epic EPC 81545 |
| 17/09/1977 | 36 | 6 | | FIRING ON ALL SIX | CBS 82213 |

### LONG RYDERS
US group formed in 1981 as The Long Riders by Sid Griffin (guitar/vocals), Barry Shank (bass/vocals) and Matt Roberts (drums), all previously in The Unclaimed. Steve Wynn (guitar) joined later but was replaced by Stephen McCarthy. By 1983 the line-up was Griffin, McCarthy, Des Brewer (bass) and Greg Sowders (drums), Brewer was replaced by Tom Stevens. They split in 1987.

| 16/11/1985 | 66 | 1 | | STATE OF OUR UNION | Island ILPS 9802 |

### LONGPIGS
UK group formed in Sheffield in 1993 by Crispin Hunt (vocals), Richard Hawley (guitar), Simon Stafford (bass) and Dee Boyle (drums). They were initially signed by Elektra but did not release any records, switching to Mother Records in 1994.

| 11/05/1996 | 26 | 9 | | THE SUN IS OFTEN OUT | Mother MUMCD 9602 |
| 23/10/1999 | 33 | 1 | | MOBILE HOME | Mother MUMCD 9902 |

### JOE LONGTHORNE
UK singer (born 31/5/1955, Hull); he made his TV debut on *Junior Showtime* in 1970.

| 03/12/1988 | 16 | 12 | ● | THE JOE LONGTHORNE SONGBOOK | Telstar STAR 2353 |
| 29/07/1989 | 22 | 10 | | ESPECIALLY FOR YOU | Telstar STAR 2365 |
| 09/12/1989 | 44 | 4 | ● | THE JOE LONGTHORNE CHRISTMAS ALBUM | Telstar STAR 2385 |
| 13/11/1993 | 47 | 4 | | I WISH YOU LOVE | EMI CDEMC 3662 |
| 08/10/1994 | 57 | 2 | | LIVE AT THE ROYAL ALBERT HALL | Premier CDDPR 126 |

### LONGVIEW
UK group formed in Manchester by Rob McVey (guitar/vocals), Doug Morch (guitar), Aidan Banks (bass) and Matt Dadds (drums).

| 02/08/2003 | 45 | 2 | | MERCURY | 14th Floor 5046668862 |

### LOOP
UK group formed in 1986 by Robert 'Josh' Hampton (vocals), Glen (bass) and Bex (drums). Bex left the following year and was replaced by John Wills, with the group adding bassist John McKay and second guitarist James Endicott.

| 04/02/1989 | 51 | 1 | | FADE OUT | Chapter 22 CHAPLP 34 |
| 03/02/1990 | 39 | 1 | | A GILDED ETERNITY | Situation Two SITU 27 |

### LOOSE ENDS
UK soul group formed by Carl McIntosh (guitar/bass), Jane Eugene (vocals) and Steve Nichol (keyboards/ trumpet). Eugene and Nichol left in 1990 and were replaced by Linda Carriere and Sunay Suleyman. Their debut hit *Tell Me What You Want* was the first record by a UK group to top the US R&B charts, a feat they repeated with *Slow Down*. Carl McIntosh won the 1998 MOBO Award for Contribution to Black Music.

| 21/04/1984 | 46 | 9 | | A LITTLE SPICE | Virgin V 2301 |
| 20/04/1985 | 13 | 13 | ○ | SO WHERE ARE YOU? | Virgin V 2340 |
| 18/10/1986 | 15 | 8 | ○ | ZAGORA | Virgin V 2384 |
| 02/07/1988 | 52 | 4 | | THE REAL CHUCKEEBOO | Virgin V 2528 |
| 29/09/1990 | 19 | 5 | ○ | LOOK HOW LONG | 10 Records DIX 94 |
| 19/09/1992 | 40 | 2 | | TIGHTEN UP VOLUME 1 | 10 Records DIXCD 112 |

### JENNIFER LOPEZ
US singer (born 24/7/1970, New York); first known as an actress, she appeared in the TV series *ER, In Living Color, Hotel Malibu* and was later one of the voices in the film *Antz*. Her first marriage to model Ojani Noa ended in divorce in 1998. Briefly engaged to producer Sean 'Puff Daddy' Combs, both were arrested in December 1999 after a nightclub shooting, charged with illegal possession of a firearm, although charges against Lopez were later dropped. The engagement ended soon after and Jennifer married dancer Cris Judd in September 2001 (this second marriage also ended in divorce). After a brief engagement to actor Ben Affleck, Jennifer married fellow singer Marc Anthony in June 2004. She appeared in the films *Out Of Sight* and *The Cell* and in the title role of the 1995 film *Selena,* the biopic of murdered Mexican singer Selena Quintanilla-Perez. She has won three MTV Europe Music Awards: Best R&B Act in 2000 and Best Female in 2001 and 2002.

| 17/07/1999 | 14 | 30 | ● | ON THE 6 ◇ | Columbia 4949302 |
| 03/02/2001 | 2 | 48 | ✪ | J.LO ◇² ▲¹ | Epic 5005502 |
| 30/03/2002 | 4 | 27 | ✪ | J TO THA L-O! – THE REMIXES ▲² | Epic 5060242 |
| 07/12/2002 | 13 | 34 | ✪ | THIS IS ME...THEN ◇ | Epic 5101282 |

### TRINI LOPEZ
US singer (born Trinidad Lopez, 15/5/1937, Dallas, TX) who was discovered by Don Costa when performing at a club in Los Angeles. He later appeared in a number of films, including *The Dirty Dozen* and *Marriage On The Rocks*.

| 26/10/1963 | 7 | 25 | | **TRINI LOPEZ AT P.J.'S** | Reprise R 6093 |
| 25/03/1967 | 6 | 17 | | **TRINI LOPEZ IN LONDON** | Reprise RSLP 6238 |

### JEFF LORBER
US keyboard player (born 4/11/1952, Philadelphia, PA); he began playing the piano at the age of four and later studied at the Berklee College of Music. He later formed Jeff Lorber Fusion and has worked extensively as both a pianist and producer.

| 18/05/1985 | 97 | 2 | | STEP BY STEP | Club JABH 9 |

### L'ORCHESTRE ELECTRONIQUE
UK synthesizer orchestra.

| 29/10/1983.....75......1......● | SOUND WAVES.....................................................Nouveau Music NML 1005 |

**SOPHIA LOREN** – see PETER SELLERS

**LORDS OF THE UNDERGROUND** US rap group formed in Newark, NJ by Dupre 'Do It All' Kelly, Al 'Mr Funky' Wardrick and Bruce 'DJ Lord Jazz' Colston. Do It All and Mr Funky had both been solo artists before linking in Lords Of The Underground.

| 12/11/1994.....68......1...... | KEEPERS OF THE FUNK.........................................Pendulum CDCHR 6088 |

**LOS BRAVOS** Spanish/German group with Spaniards Manolo 'Manuel' Fernandez (born 29/9/1943, Seville, keyboards), Pablo 'Gomez' Samllehi (born 5/11/1943, Barcelona, drums), Antonio Martinez (born 3/10/1945, Madrid, guitar) and Miguel Vicens-Danus (born 21/6/1944, Palma de Mallona, bass) and German lead vocalist Mike Kogel (born 25/4/1945, Beuliu), whose Spanish language records caught the ear of Decca executive Ivor Raymonds. They were invited to London to record the English song *Black Is Black*.

| 08/10/1966.....29......1...... | BLACK IS BLACK.................................................Decca LK 4822 |

**LOS LOBOS** US group formed in Los Angeles, CA in 1974 by Spanish Americans David Hidalgo (guitar/accordion/vocals), Cesar Rosas (guitar/vocals), Conrad Lozano (bass) and Luis Perez (drums). Steve Berlin (saxophone) was added to the line-up in 1983. They contributed eight tracks to the *La Bamba* soundtrack, the film of Ritchie Valens' life. Named after the Spanish word for 'wolves', they have three Grammy Awards: Best Mexican–American Performance in 1983 for *Anselma,* Best Mexican–American Performance in 1989 for *La Pistola Y El Corazon* and Best Pop Instrumental Performance in 1995 for *Mariachi Suite*.

| 06/04/1985.....77......6...... | HOW WILL THE WOLF SURVIVE?.................................Slash SLMP 3 |
| 07/02/1987.....77......3...... | BY THE LIGHT OF THE MOON...................................Slash SLAP 13 |
| 22/08/1987.....24......15......● | LA BAMBA ▲2 Original soundtrack to the film................London LONLP 36 |

**LOS NINOS** UK instrumental group.

| 22/07/1995.....74......1...... . | FRAGILE – MYSTICAL SOUNDS OF THE PANPIPES ...............Pearls DPWKF 4253 |

**JOE LOSS ORCHESTRA** UK bandleader (born 22/6/1909, Liverpool) who became a professional musician in 1926 and by the 1940s was acknowledged as the king of the ballroom. He was awarded the OBE in 1978. He died on 6/6/1990.

| 30/10/1971.....24......10...... | ALL-TIME PARTY HITS...........................................MFP 5227 |

**LOST BOYZ** US rap group formed by Freaky Tah, Mr Cheeks, Pretty Lou and Spigg Nice. They signed with Uptown Records in 1995. Freaky Tah was murdered on 28/3/1999.

| 06/07/1996.....64......1...... | LEGAL DRUG MONEY.............................................MCA UND 50310 |

**LOSTPROPHETS** UK nu-metal group formed in Pontypridd, Wales in 1997 by Ian Watkins (vocals), Mike Lewis (guitar), Lee Glaze (guitar) and Mike Chiplin (drums). Watkins and Lewis are both ex-Public Disturbance. After signing with Visible Noise in 1999 they added Stuart Richardson (bass) and Jamie Oliver (decks) to the line-up, releasing *The Fake Sound Of Progress* in 2000. The album was remixed in 2001 after the group had signed with Columbia for the US.

| 02/03/2002.....44......8......● | THE FAKE SOUND OF PROGRESS.................................Visible Noise TORMENT 005CD |
| 14/02/2004 .....4......19......● | **START SOMETHING**............................................Visible Noise TORMENT 32 |

**LOTUS EATERS** UK group formed in Liverpool by Peter Coyle (vocals), Gerard Quinn (keyboards), Alan Wills (drums) and Jeremy Kelly (guitar). Coyle and Kelly had previously been in the Wild Swans.

| 16/06/1984.....96......1...... | NO SENSE OF SIN................................................Sylvan 206 263 |

**JAMES LOUGHRAN** – see BBC CONCERT ORCHESTRA

**LOUISE** UK R&B singer (born Louise Elizabeth Nurding, 4/11/1974, Lewisham, London) who was a founder member of Eternal before going solo in 1995. She is married to Tottenham and England footballer Jamie Redknapp, son of former West Ham United manager Harry Redknapp.

| 06/07/1996 .....7......31......✪ | **NAKED**......................................................EMI CDEMC 3748 |
| 18/10/1997 .....5......19......✪ | **WOMAN IN ME**..............................................EMI 8219032 |
| 12/08/2000.....12......4......○ | ELBOW BEACH...................................................1st Avenue 5276142 |
| 22/09/2001 .....9......5......○ | **CHANGING FACES – THE BEST OF**.............................1st Avenue 5349672 |

**JACQUES LOUSSIER** French pianist (born26/10/1934, Angers), a classically trained musician who found fame taking the works of Johann Sebastian Bach and giving them a jazz interpretation. He later formed a trio with Pierre Michelot and Christian Garros.

| 30/03/1985.....58......3...... | JACQUES LOUSSIER – THE BEST OF PLAY BACH...................Start STL 1 |

**LOVE** US rock group formed in 1965 by Bryan Maclean (born1947, Los Angeles, CA, guitar/vocals), Arthur Lee (born 1945, Memphis, TN, guitar/vocals), John Echols (born 1945, Memphis, guitar), Johnny Fleckenstein (bass) and Don Conka (drums) as The Grass Roots. Fleckenstein and Conka left soon after their formation, replaced by Ken Forssi (born 1947, Cleveland, OH) and Alban 'Snoopy' Pfisterer (born1947, Switzerland) respectively, the group linking with Elektra Records soon after. Maclean left in 1967 and the group was re-assembled with Arthur Lee, Jay Donnellan (guitar), Frank Fayad (bass) and George Suranovitch (drums).

| 24/02/1968.....24......6...... | FOREVER CHANGES..............................................Elektra EKS7 4013 |
| 16/05/1970.....29......2...... | OUT HERE.......................................................Harvest SHOW 3/4 |
| 03/03/2001.....63......1......○ | FOREVER CHANGES Re-issue of Elektra EKS7 4013..............Elektra 8122735372 |

○ Silver disc  ● Gold disc  ✪ Platinum disc (additional platinum units are indicated by a figure following the symbol)  ❶⁹ Number of weeks album topped the UK chart

**COURTNEY LOVE** US guitarist/singer (born Love Michelle Harrison, 9/7/1965, San Francisco, CA) who was previously a member of Hole. She is Kurt Cobain of Nirvana's widow and subsequently became an actress, appearing in *Man On The Moon* and *The People Versus Larry Flint.*

21/02/2004......56......1......  AMERICA'S SWEETHEART .................................................................. Virgin CDVUS 249

**GEOFF LOVE AND HIS ORCHESTRA** UK orchestra leader (born 4/9/1917, Todmorden, Yorkshire); he made his radio debut in 1937 and formed his own band in 1955 for the TV show *On The Town*. He began recording as Manuel & His Music of the Mountains in 1959, later becoming much in demand as an orchestra leader and arranger for artists such as Russ Conway, Connie Francis, Judy Garland and Frankie Vaughan, both in live concerts and on record. He died on 8/7/1991.

07/08/1971......11......20......  BIG WAR MOVIE THEMES .................................................................. MFP 5171
21/08/1971......38......3......  BIG WESTERN MOVIE THEMES .............................................................. MFP 5204
30/10/1971......28......5......  BIG LOVE MOVIE THEMES ................................................................ MFP 5221

**MONIE LOVE** UK singer (born Simone Johnson, 2/7/1970, London) who signed to Cooltempo in 1988. She relocated to Brooklyn, NYC and worked with various US rappers.

20/10/1990......30......3......  DOWN TO EARTH ..................................................................... Cooltempo CTLP 14

**LOVE AND MONEY** UK group formed by James Grant (guitar/vocals), Bobby Paterson (bass), Paul McGeechan (keyboards) and Stuart Kerr (drums). Kerr later left to join Texas.

29/10/1988......71......1......  STRANGE KIND OF LOVE ................................................................. Fontana SFLP 7
03/08/1991......41......1......  DOGS IN THE TRAFFIC ................................................................. Fontana 8489931

**LOVE/HATE** US heavy rock group formed by Jizzy Pearl (vocals), Jon E Love (guitar), Skid Rose (bass) and Joey Gold (drums).

07/03/1992......20......4......  WASTED IN AMERICA .................................................................. Columbia 4694532
24/07/1993......24......1......  LET'S RUMBLE ...................................................................... RCA 74321153112

**LOVE UNLIMITED ORCHESTRA** US studio orchestra assembled by producer Barry White (born 12/9/1944, Galveston, TX) and arranger Gene Page (born 13/9/1938). Saxophonist Kenny Gorelick later recorded as Kenny G. Page died on 24/8/1998 and White on 4/7/2003.

06/04/1974......50......1......O  RHAPSODY IN WHITE .............................................................. Pye International NSPL 28191

**LYLE LOVETT** US singer/songwriter/guitarist(born 1/11/1957, Houston, TX); he studied journalism and later German at Texas University. Signed by MCA in 1986 having previously worked with Nanci Griffith, whilst early recordings were aimed at the country market he later moved into other musical areas. After opening for Dire Straits on their 1992 world tour, in 1993 he married actress Julia Roberts, although this later ended in divorce. He has won four Grammy Awards including Best Country Vocal Performance, Male in 1989 for *Lyle Lovett and His Large Band*, Best Pop Vocal Collaboration in 1994 with Al Green for *Funny How Time Slips Away,* and Best Country Performance By A Duo Or Group With Vocal in 1994 with Asleep At The Wheel for *Blues For Dixie*.

08/10/1994......54......1......  I LOVE EVERYBODY.................................................................. MCA MCD 10808
29/06/1996......62......1......  THE ROAD TO ENSENADA 1996 Grammy Award for Best Country Album ....................... MCA MCD 11409

**LENE LOVICH** US singer (born Lili Premilovich, Detroit, MI) with a Yugoslavian father and an English mother. She was briefly a member of the Diversions before going solo. She also appeared in the films *Dandy* and *Cha-Cha*.

17/03/1979......35......11......  STATELESS........................................................................ Stiff SEEZ 7
02/02/1980......19......6......  FLEX ............................................................................ Stiff SEEZ 19

**LOVIN' SPOONFUL** US group formed in New York in 1965 by John Sebastian (born 17/3/1944, New York, guitar/vocals), Zal Yanovsky (born 19/12/1944, Toronto, Canada, guitar), Steve Boone (born 23/9/1943, Camphejeune, NC, bass) and Joe Butler (born 19/1/1943, New York, drums). Yanovsky left in 1967 and was replaced by Jerry Yester (keyboards). They disbanded in 1968. Their name supposedly refers to the average male ejaculation, although some sources credit a phrase from *Coffee Blues* by Mississippi John Hurt. They were inducted into the Rock & Roll Hall of Fame in 2000.

07/05/1966......8......11......  **DAYDREAM**...................................................................... Pye International NPL 28078

**NICK LOWE** UK singer (born 25/3/1949, Woodbridge, Suffolk) who was in Brinsley Schwarz from 1970–75 and then in Rockpile. He was a founder member of Little Village with Ry Cooder, John Hiatt and Jim Keltner but later achieved greater success as a producer.

11/03/1978......22......9......  THE JESUS OF COOL .................................................................. Radar RAD 1
23/06/1979......43......6......  LABOUR OF LUST .................................................................... Radar RAD 21
20/02/1982......99......2......  NICK THE KNIFE..................................................................... F-Beat XXLP 14

**LOWGOLD** UK group formed by Darren Ford (guitar/vocals), Dan Symons (guitar), Miles Willey (bass) and Scott Simon (drums). They signed with Nude Records in 1998 and released their debut album two years later.

24/02/2001......33......2......  JUST BACKWARD OF SQUARE .......................................................... Nude 17CD

**L7** US rock group formed in 1985 in California by Donita Sparks (guitar/vocals), Suzi Gardner (guitar/vocals), Jennifer Finch (bass/vocals) and Dee Plakas (drums). They later added former Belly bassist, Gail Greenwood, to the line-up.

02/05/1992......24......6......  BRICKS ARE HEAVY ................................................................... Slash 8283072
23/07/1994......26......2......  HUNGRY FOR STINK .................................................................. Slash 8285312

**LUCK AND NEAT** UK garage duo DJ Luck (Joel Samuels) and MC Neat (Michael Rose). MC Neat also recorded with N+G and Kallaghan. The pair later dropped their respective 'DJ' and 'MC' titles.

| 08/06/2002 | 34 | 2 | | IT'S ALL GOOD | Island CID 8117 |

**LUDACRIS** US rapper (born Chris Bridges, 11/9/1977, Champayne, IL) who was in the Loudmouth Hooligans before going solo.

| 29/06/2002 | 57 | 2 | | WORD OF MOUF | Def Jam 5864462 |
| 18/10/2003 | 44 | 4 | | CHICKEN N BEER ▲¹ | Def Jam 9861137 |

**LULU** UK singer (born Marie McDonald McLaughlin Lawrie, 3/11/1948, Glasgow) who joined the Gleneagles in 1963. The manager Marion Massey changed their name to Lulu & The Luvvers the same year. She married Maurice Gibb (of the Bee Gees) in 1969, was later divorced and married John Frieda. She appeared in the films *To Sir With Love* and *Gonks Go Beat* and recorded the theme to the James Bond film *The Man With The Golden Gun*. She was awarded an OBE in the 2000 Queen's Birthday Honours List.

| 25/09/1971 | 15 | 6 | | THE MOST OF LULU | MFP 5215 |
| 06/03/1993 | 67 | 1 | | INDEPENDENCE | Dome DOMECD 1 |
| 01/06/2002 | 4 | 9 | ● | TOGETHER | Mercury 630212 |
| 22/11/2003 | 35 | 2 | ○ | THE GREATEST HITS | Universal TV 9865879 |
| 27/03/2004 | 68 | 1 | | BACK ON TRACK | Mercury 9866136 |

**BOB LUMAN** US country singer (born 15/4/1937, Nacogdoches, TX) who made his first records in 1957 and later appeared in films, including *Carnival Rock*. He died from pneumonia on 27/12/1978.

| 14/01/1961 | 18 | 1 | | LET'S THINK ABOUT LIVING | Warner Brothers WM 4025 |

**LUMIDEE** US female rapper (born Lumidee Cedeno, 1984, Spanish Harlem, NYC).

| 16/08/2003 | 70 | 3 | | ALMOST FAMOUS | Universal 9860622 |

**LUNIZ** US rap duo Yukmouth (Jerold Ellis) and Knumskull (Garrick Husband).

| 16/03/1996 | 41 | 3 | | OPERATION STACKOLA | Virgin CDVUS 94 |

**LURKERS** UK group formed by Howard Wall (vocals), Pete Stride (guitar), Arturo Bassick (born Arthur Billingsley, bass) and Manic Esso (born Pete Haynes, drums). Bassick left soon after their formation, replaced by Kim Bradshaw and then Nigel Moore. They split in 1980, re-forming two years later with Stride, Moore, Mark Fincham (vocals) and Dan Tozer (drums). Esso and Bassick returned in 1988.

| 01/07/1978 | 57 | 1 | | FULHAM FALLOUT | Beggars Banquet BEGA 2 |

**LUSCIOUS JACKSON** US rock group formed by Gabby Glaser (born 21/12/1965, bass/vocals), Vivian Trimble (keyboards), Jill Cunniff (born 17/8/1966, guitar/vocals) and Kate Scheffenbach (born 5/1/1966, drums). They were named after Philadelphia '76ers basketball player Lucius Jackson.

| 26/04/1997 | 55 | 1 | | FEVER IN FEVER OUT | Grand Royal GR 038 |

**LUSH** UK rock group formed in London in 1988 by Miki Berenyo (born 18/3/1967, London, guitar/vocals), Emma Anderson (born 10/6/1967, London, guitar), Steve Rippon (bass) and Christopher Acland (born 7/9/1966, Lancaster, drums). Rippon left in 1991 and was replaced by Philip King (born 29/4/1960, London). Acland committed suicide on 17/10/1996.

| 08/02/1992 | 7 | 3 | | SPOOKY | 4AD CAD 2002CD |
| 25/06/1994 | 19 | 2 | | SPLIT | 4AD CAD 4011CD |
| 30/03/1996 | 8 | 5 | | LOVELIFE | 4AD CAD 6004CD |

**VERA LYNN** UK singer (born Vera Margaret Welsh, 20/3/1919, London) who began her singing career in her mid-teens, working briefly with Joe Loss and then Charlie Kunz before going solo in 1941. Her radio show *Sincerely Yours* was popular with UK servicemen around the world and led to her being dubbed 'the forces-sweetheart'. She made three films during the war: *We'll Meet Again* (the title track became her signature tune and one of the most famous songs of the war), *Rhythm Serenade* and *One Exciting Night*. She retained her popularity after the war and was awarded the OBE in 1969, subsequently becoming Dame Vera Lynn in 1975.

| 21/11/1981 | 25 | 12 | ● | 20 FAMILY FAVOURITES | EMI EMTV 28 |
| 09/09/1989 | 44 | 3 | | WE'LL MEET AGAIN | Telstar STAR 2369 |

**JEFF LYNNE** UK singer/guitarist (born 20/12/1947, Birmingham) who was a member of Roy Wood's group The Move in 1970, which subsequently became The Electric Light Orchestra the following year. When Wood left to form Wizzard after one album Lynne took over as leader and was responsible for penning most of their hits. He later became a member of The Traveling Wilburys with Bob Dylan, George Harrison, Roy Orbison and Tom Petty and collected the 1989 Grammy Award for Best Rock Performance by a Group with Vocals as a member of the Traveling Wilburys for *Traveling Wilburys Volume One* (the album was known as *Handle With Care* in the UK). He later recorded solo and also worked extensively as a producer, for George Harrison, Roy Orbison, Randy Newman and The Beatles on their *Anthology* series, among others.

| 04/08/1990 | 24 | 4 | | ARMCHAIR THEATRE | Reprise WX 347 |

**PHILIP LYNOTT** Irish singer/guitarist (born 20/8/1951, Dublin) who formed Thin Lizzy in 1969. The group recorded their first album in 1971. He launched a parallel solo career in 1980 and later formed Grand Slam. He died from heart failure on 4/1/1986 although he had been in a coma for eight days following a drug overdose before his death.

| 26/04/1980 | 28 | 6 | | SOLO IN SOHO | Vertigo 9102 038 |
| 14/11/1987 | 55 | 10 | | SOLDIER OF FORTUNE – THE BEST OF PHIL LYNOTT AND THIN LIZZY **PHIL LYNOTT AND THIN LIZZY** | Telstar STAR 2300 |

**LYNYRD SKYNYRD** US rock group formed in Jacksonville, FL in 1964 by Gary Rossington (born 4/12/1951, Jacksonville, guitar), Larry Jungstrom (bass), Bob Burns (drums), Ronnie Van Zant (born 15/1/1948, Jacksonville, vocals) and Allen Collins (born 19/7/1952, Jacksonville, guitar). They went under numerous names until settling on Lynyrd Skynyrd (after their school gym teacher

Leonard Skinner) in 1970. They added Leon Wilkeson (born 2/4/1952, bass) in 1972 and Steve Gaines (born 14/9/1949, Seneca, MO, guitar) in 1976. Van Zant and Gaines were killed, along with four other passengers (including Gaines' sister Cassie, a member of the backing group) in a plane crash on 20/10/1977 when their plane ran out of fuel, although Rossington, Collins, Powell and Wilkeson all survived. Rossington and Collins left to form the Rossington Collins Band in 1980, which disbanded in 1982. Collins was paralysed in a car crash in 1986 that killed his girlfriend Debra Jean Watts (and was sent to prison after being held responsible for the crash). He died from pneumonia on 23/1/1990. Rossington and Johnny Van Zant (younger brother of Ronnie) assembled a version of Lynyrd Skynyrd in 1987 for a tribute tour. And in 1991 Rossington, Van Zant, Artimus Pyle (drums), Wilkeson, Billy Powell (keyboards), Randall Hall (guitar), Ed King (bass) and Custer (drums) regrouped. Pyle left the group for a second time in 1993 and was replaced by Mike Estes whilst Custer left the following year and was replaced by Owen Hale. Wilkeson died from chronic liver and lung disease on 27/7/2001.

| DATE | POS | WKS | BPI | ALBUM TITLE | LABEL & NUMBER |
|------|-----|-----|-----|-----------|----------------|
| 03/05/1975 | 43 | 1 | | NUTHIN' FANCY | MCA MCF 2700 |
| 28/02/1976 | 34 | 5 | | GIMME BACK MY BULLETS | MCA MCF 2744 |
| 06/11/1976 | 17 | 4 | ○ | ONE MORE FOR THE ROAD | MCA MCPS 279 |
| 12/11/1977 | 13 | 4 | | STREET SURVIVORS | MCA MCG 3525 |
| 04/11/1978 | 50 | 1 | | SKYNYRD'S FIRST AND LAST | MCA MCG 3529 |
| 09/02/1980 | 49 | 4 | | GOLD AND PLATINUM | MCA MCSP 308 |

**LYTE FUNKIE ONES** US group formed by Richard Cronin, Brian Gillis and Bradley Fischetti.

| DATE | POS | WKS | BPI | ALBUM TITLE | LABEL & NUMBER |
|------|-----|-----|-----|-----------|----------------|
| 26/02/2000 | 62 | 1 | | LYTE FUNKY ONES | Logic 74321706832 |

## M PEOPLE
UK dance group formed by Michael Pickering (born 21/2/1954, Manchester), Paul Heard (born 5/10/1960, London) and Heather Small (born 20/1/1965, London). They won awards for Best Dance Act at the 1994 and 1995 BRIT Awards. Small later launched a parallel solo career and also took part in the *Perfect Day* project for the BBC's Children In Need charity.

| | | | | |
|---|---|---|---|---|
| 06/03/1993 | 53 | 2 | | NORTHERN SOUL . . . . . . . . . . . . . . . . . . . . . . . . . . . . . . . . . . . . . . . . . . . . . . . . . Deconstruction 74321117772 |
| 16/10/1993 | 2 | 87 | ✪³ | **ELEGANT SLUMMING** 1994 Mercury Music Prize . . . . . . . . . . . . . . . . . . . . . . . . . . . . . . . . . Deconstruction 74321166782 |
| 26/11/1994 | 4 | 115 | ✪⁵ | **BIZARRE FRUIT/BIZARRE FRUIT II** ◇² *Bizarre Fruit II* is a remix album that was listed with *Bizarre Fruit* from 9/12/1995 . . . . . . . . . . |
| | | | | . . . . . . . . . . . . . . . . . . . . . . . . . . . . . . . . . . . . . . . . . . . . . . . . . . . . . . . . . Deconstruction 74321240812 |
| 16/09/1995 | 26 | 3 | | NORTHERN SOUL Re-issue of Deconstruction 74321117772 . . . . . . . . . . . . . . . . . . . . . . . . . . . . . . . . . RCA PD 75157 |
| 25/10/1997 | 2 | 40 | ✪² | **FRESCO** ◇ . . . . . . . . . . . . . . . . . . . . . . . . . . . . . . . . . . . . . . . . . . . . . . . . . . . . . . . M People 74321524902 |
| 14/11/1998 | 2 | 33 | ✪³ | **THE BEST OF M PEOPLE** ◇ . . . . . . . . . . . . . . . . . . . . . . . . . . . . . . . . . . . . . . . . . . . . . . M People 74321613872 |

## TIMO MAAS
German producer /DJ (born in Hanover) who was first known as a DJ at the Tunnel Club in Hamburg before recording solo.

| | | | |
|---|---|---|---|
| 16/03/2002 | 41 | 3 | LOUD . . . . . . . . . . . . . . . . . . . . . . . . . . . . . . . . . . . . . . . . . . . . . . . . . . . . . . . . . Perfecto PERFALB 08CD |

## MAC BAND FEATURING THE McCAMPBELL BROTHERS
US group formed in Flint, MI by brothers Charles, Kelvin, Ray and Derrick McCampbell (vocals), Mark Harper (guitar), Rodney Frazier (keyboards), Ray Flippin (bass) and Slye Fuller (drums). MAC stands for Men After Christ.

| | | | |
|---|---|---|---|
| 20/08/1988 | 61 | 3 | THE MAC BAND . . . . . . . . . . . . . . . . . . . . . . . . . . . . . . . . . . . . . . . . . . . . . . . . . . . . . . . MCA MCC 6032 |

## McALMONT AND BUTLER
UK duo of ex-Thieves David McAlmont and ex-Suede Bernard Butler (born 1/5/1970). David McAlmont later recorded solo.

| | | | |
|---|---|---|---|
| 09/12/1995 | 33 | 8 | THE SOUND OF McALMONT AND BUTLER . . . . . . . . . . . . . . . . . . . . . . . . . . . . . . . . . . . . . . . . Hut CDHUT 32 |
| 24/08/2002 | 18 | 2 | BRING IT BACK . . . . . . . . . . . . . . . . . . . . . . . . . . . . . . . . . . . . . . . . . . . . . . . . . . . . Chrysalis 5399772 |

## FRANKIE McBRIDE
Irish singer (born in Omagh, County Tyrone); formerly lead singer with the Polka Dots, he was the first Irish showband singer to make the UK singles Top Twenty.

| | | | |
|---|---|---|---|
| 17/02/1968 | 29 | 3 | FRANKIE McBRIDE . . . . . . . . . . . . . . . . . . . . . . . . . . . . . . . . . . . . . . . . . . . . . . . . . . . . Emerald SLD 28 |

## MACC LADS
UK vocal/instrumental group that has featured Muttley McLad (bass/vocals), The Beater (guitar/vocals), Philip 'Fast Fret' McCavity (guitar/vocals), Johnny Mard (guitar/vocals), Chorley the Hord (drums/vocals), Stez Styx (drums/vocals), Winston Dread (drums/vocals), Al O'Peesha (guitar/vocals), Cheeky Monkey (drums/vocals) and Uncle Nobby (guitar/vocals).

| | | | |
|---|---|---|---|
| 07/10/1989 | 72 | 1 | FROM BEER TO ETERNITY . . . . . . . . . . . . . . . . . . . . . . . . . . . . . . . . . . . . . . . . . . . . . . . . Hectic House HHLP 12 |

## PAUL McCARTNEY
UK singer (born James Paul McCartney, 18/6/1942, Liverpool) who was founding member of The Beatles with John Lennon and co-wrote most of their material. He released his first solo album in 1970, forming Wings the following year with wife Linda (keyboards/vocals), Denny Laine (guitar/vocals) and Denny Seiwell (drums). Henry McCullough (guitar) joined in 1972. Seiwell and McCullough left in 1973. The band became a five-piece again in 1974 with the addition of Jimmy McCullough and Geoff Britton (Britton left in 1975 and was replaced by Joe English). English and McCullough left in 1977, the group disbanding in 1981. Paul starred in the 1984 film *Give My Regards To Broad Street*. One of pop music's most honoured performers, he received the 1983 award for Best British Male at the BRIT Awards, the Sony Award for Technical Excellence at the 1983 BRIT Awards, countless Ivor Novello awards for his songwriting, the Outstanding Contribution Award at the 1983 BRIT Awards (as a Beatle), an MBE in 1964 (also as a Beatle) and was knighted in the 1996 New Year's Honours list. Linda died from breast cancer on 17/4/1998. He was inducted into the Rock & Roll Hall of Fame in 1999 (The Beatles were inducted in 1988). Having won ten Grammy Awards as a Beatle, three more included Best Arrangement Accompanying Singers in 1971 for *Uncle Albert/Admiral Halsey* and Best Rock Instrumental Performance in 1979 for *Rockestra Theme*. He has had more UK #1s than any other artist – seventeen were as a Beatle and four solo. *Mull Of Kintyre/Girls' School* is one of only five records to have sold more than 2 million copies in the UK. In July 2001 he was engaged to model Heather Mills (she had lost part of a leg after being hit by a police motorcycle), the pair marrying during 2002. In January 2002 he was named as pop

music's first billionaire, his assets estimated at £1.1 billion. In December 2002 an argument with John Lennon's widow Yoko Ono ensued over changing the credit to a number of songs from Lennon/McCartney to McCartney/Lennon.

| DATE | POS | WKS | BPI | ALBUM TITLE | LABEL & NUMBER |
|---|---|---|---|---|---|
| 02/05/1970 | 2 | 32 | | **McCARTNEY** ▲[3] | Apple PCS 7102 |
| 05/06/1971 | ❶[2] | 24 | | **RAM** PAUL AND LINDA McCARTNEY | Apple PAS 10003 |
| 18/12/1971 | 11 | 9 | | WINGS WILDLIFE **WINGS** | Apple PCS 7142 |
| 19/05/1973 | 5 | 16 | ● | **RED ROSE SPEEDWAY** ▲[3] | Apple PCTC 251 |
| 15/12/1973 | ❶[7] | 125 | ✪ | **BAND ON THE RUN** ▲[4] This and the above hit credited to **PAUL McCARTNEY AND WINGS** | Apple PAS 10007 |
| 21/06/1975 | ❶[2] | 29 | ✪ | **VENUS AND MARS** ▲[1] | Apple PCTC 254 |
| 17/04/1976 | 2 | 35 | ● | **WINGS AT THE SPEED OF SOUND** ▲[7] | Apple PAS 10010 |
| 15/01/1977 | 8 | 22 | ● | **WINGS OVER AMERICA** ▲[1] | Parlophone PAS 720 |
| 15/04/1978 | 4 | 23 | ● | **LONDON TOWN** | Parlophone PAS 10012 |
| 16/12/1978 | 5 | 32 | ✪ | **WINGS GREATEST HITS** | Parlophone PCTC 256 |
| 23/06/1979 | 6 | 15 | ● | **BACK TO THE EGG** This and the above five hits credited to **WINGS** | Parlophone PCTC 257 |
| 31/05/1980 | ❶[2] | 18 | ● | **McCARTNEY II** | Parlophone PCTC 258 |
| 07/03/1981 | 34 | 4 | | THE McCARTNEY INTERVIEW | EMI CHAT 1 |
| 08/05/1982 | ❶[2] | 27 | ● | **TUG OF WAR** ▲[3] | Parlophone PCTC 259 |
| 12/11/1983 | 4 | 23 | ✪ | **PIPES OF PEACE** | Parlophone PCTC 1652301 |
| 03/11/1984 | ❶[1] | 21 | ✪ | **GIVE MY REGARDS TO BROAD STREET** Original soundtrack to the film | Parlophone PCTC 2 |
| 13/09/1986 | 8 | 6 | ● | **PRESS TO PLAY** | Parlophone PCSD 103 |
| 14/11/1987 | 2 | 21 | ✪[3] | **ALL THE BEST!** | Parlophone PMTV 1 |
| 17/06/1989 | ❶[1] | 20 | ✪ | **FLOWERS IN THE DIRT** | Parlophone PCSD 106 |
| 17/11/1990 | 17 | 11 | ● | TRIPPING THE LIVE FANTASTIC | Parlophone PCST 7346 |
| 01/06/1991 | 7 | 3 | | **UNPLUGGED – THE OFFICIAL BOOTLEG** | Parlophone PCSD 116 |
| 12/10/1991 | 63 | 1 | | CHOBA B CCCP (THE RUSSIAN ALBUM) | Parlophone CDPCSD 117 |
| 13/02/1993 | 5 | 4 | ○ | **OFF THE GROUND** | Parlophone CDPCSD 125 |
| 20/11/1993 | 34 | 2 | | PAUL IS LIVE | Parlophone PDPCSD 147 |
| 17/05/1997 | 2 | 15 | ✪ | **FLAMING PIE** | Parlophone CDPCSD 171 |
| 27/03/1999 | 69 | 1 | | BAND ON THE RUN PAUL McCARTNEY AND WINGS | Parlophone 4991762 |
| 16/10/1999 | 12 | 11 | ● | RUN DEVIL RUN | Parlophone 5223512 |
| 19/05/2001 | 5 | 7 | ● | **WINGSPAN – HITS AND HISTORY** | Parlophone 5328762 |
| 24/11/2001 | 46 | 1 | ○ | DRIVING RAIN | Parlophone 5355102 |
| 29/03/2003 | 5 | 13 | ● | **BACK IN THE WORLD** | Parlophone 5830052 |

**KIRSTY MacCOLL** UK singer (born 10/10/1959) who was the daughter of folk singer/songwriter Ewan MacColl (he wrote 1972 Song of the Year Grammy Award winner *The First Time Ever I Saw Your Face*) and married to producer Steve Lillywhite. Signed to Stiff at sixteen, she was also a songwriter, penning *They Don't Know* for Tracy Ullman. She was hit by a speedboat in the Caribbean and died on 19/12/2000.

| DATE | POS | WKS | BPI | ALBUM TITLE | LABEL & NUMBER |
|---|---|---|---|---|---|
| 20/05/1989 | 34 | 12 | ○ | KITE | Virgin KMLP 1 |
| 06/07/1991 | 17 | 8 | | ELECTRIC LANDLADY | Virgin V 2663 |
| 12/03/1994 | 46 | 2 | | TITANIC DAYS | ZTT 4509947112 |
| 18/03/1995 | 6 | 27 | ● | **GALORE – THE BEST OF KIRSTY MacCOLL** | Virgin CDV 2763 |
| 01/04/2000 | 39 | 9 | ○ | TROPICAL BRAINSTORM | V2 VVR 1009872 |

**DEL McCOURY BAND** – see **STEVE EARLE**

**VAN McCOY** US producer/orchestra leader (born 6/1/1944, Washington DC) who was singer with numerous groups before going solo in 1959. He was more successful as a songwriter and producer, especially with Gladys Knight & The Pips, The Drifters, The Stylistics, Jackie Wilson, Peaches And Herb and Faith Hope & Charity. He won the 1975 Grammy Award for Best Pop Instrumental Performance for *The Hustle*. He died from a heart attack on 6/7/1979.

| DATE | POS | WKS | BPI | ALBUM TITLE | LABEL & NUMBER |
|---|---|---|---|---|---|
| 05/07/1975 | 32 | 11 | | DISCO BABY | Avco 9109 004 |

**GEORGE McCRAE** US singer (born 19/10/1944, West Palm Beach, FL) who was with the Jivin' Jets before marrying Gwen McCrae and working and recording as a duet. His #1 hit *Rock Your Baby* had been intended for Gwen but she failed to show for the recording session – it went on to sell more than eleven million copies worldwide.

| DATE | POS | WKS | BPI | ALBUM TITLE | LABEL & NUMBER |
|---|---|---|---|---|---|
| 03/08/1974 | 13 | 28 | ○ | ROCK YOUR BABY | Jay Boy JSL 3 |
| 13/09/1975 | 54 | 1 | | GEORGE McCRAE | Jay Boy JSL 10 |

**IAN McCULLOCH** UK singer (born 5/5/1959, Liverpool) in The Crucial Three with Pete Wylie and Julian Cope. He formed Echo And The Bunnymen in 1978. They disbanded in 1988, McCulloch going solo, before re-forming in 1996.

| DATE | POS | WKS | BPI | ALBUM TITLE | LABEL & NUMBER |
|---|---|---|---|---|---|
| 07/10/1989 | 18 | 3 | | CANDLELAND | WEA WX 303 |
| 21/03/1992 | 46 | 1 | | MYSTERIO | East West 9031762642 |

**MARTINE McCUTCHEON** UK singer (born 14/5/1976, London) who is best known as an actress playing Tiffany Raymond/Mitchell in *Eastenders*. Her character was killed in a road accident in 1999. By 2001 she was concentrating on acting again, appearing in the stage musical *My Fair Lady* in London.

| DATE | POS | WKS | BPI | ALBUM TITLE | LABEL & NUMBER |
|---|---|---|---|---|---|
| 18/09/1999 | 2 | 20 | ✪ | **YOU, ME & US** | Innocent CDSIN 4 |
| 25/11/2000 | 25 | 14 | ● | WISHING | Innocent CDSIN 7 |
| 14/12/2002 | 55 | 2 | ○ | MUSICALITY | Liberty 5805492 |

▲[9] Number of weeks album topped the US chart   ◆[12] RIAA Diamond Awards   ◇[3] IFPI Platinum Europe Awards

## JANE McDONALD

UK singer (born 4/4/1963, Wakefield); she is best known as the resident singer on board *The Galaxy* in the BBC TV documentary *The Cruise Ship*. She is the first artist to have an album debut at #1 on the charts without first having a hit single.

| DATE | POS | WKS | BPI | ALBUM TITLE | LABEL & NUMBER |
|---|---|---|---|---|---|
| 25/07/1998 | ❶³ | 27 | ✪ | JANE McDONALD | Focus Music International FMCD 001 |
| 17/06/2000 | 6 | 9 | ● | INSPIRATION | Universal TV 1578612 |
| 27/10/2001 | 24 | 3 | | LOVE AT THE MOVIES | Universal TV 0149472 |

## MICHAEL McDONALD

US singer (born 2/12/1952, St Louis, MO) who recorded solo in 1972 before joining Steely Dan in 1974 and the Doobie Brothers the following year. He went solo again when the group disbanded in 1982. Michael won three Grammy Awards with the Doobie Brothers and two during his time with the group: for Song of the Year in 1979 with Kenny Loggins for *What A Fool Believes* and Best Arrangement Accompanying Vocalist in 1979 for *What A Fool Believes*.

| DATE | POS | WKS | BPI | ALBUM TITLE | LABEL & NUMBER |
|---|---|---|---|---|---|
| 22/11/1986 | 6 | 35 | ✪ | SWEET FREEDOM: BEST OF MICHAEL McDONALD | Warner Brothers WX 67 |
| 26/05/1990 | 35 | 4 | | TAKE IT TO HEART | Reprise WX 285 |
| 17/03/2001 | 21 | 6 | | THE VERY BEST OF | Rhino 8122735302 |
| 17/05/2003 | 29 | 4 | | MOTOWN | Universal TV 9800233 |

## BOBBY McFERRIN

US singer (born 11/3/1950, New York) who began singing professionally in the mid-1970s and signed with Elektra Musician in 1980. His debut album was released in 1982. He has won ten Grammy Awards: Best Jazz Vocal Performance in 1985 with Jon Hendricks for *Another Night In Tunisia*; Best Arrangement for Two or More Voices in 1985 with Cheryl Bentyne for *Another Night In Tunisia*; Best Jazz Vocal Performance in 1986 for *'Round Midnight*; Best Jazz Vocal Performance in 1987 for *What Is This Thing Called Love*; Best Recording for Children in 1987 with Jack Nicholson for *The Elephant's Child*; Record of the Year, Song of the Year and Best Pop Vocal Performance in 1988 for *Don't Worry Be Happy*; Best Jazz Vocal Performance in 1988 for *Brothers*; and Best Jazz Vocal Performance in 1992 for *'Round Midnight*.

| DATE | POS | WKS | BPI | ALBUM TITLE | LABEL & NUMBER |
|---|---|---|---|---|---|
| 29/10/1988 | 92 | 1 | | SIMPLE PLEASURES | Manhattan MTL 1018 |

## KATE AND ANNA McGARRIGLE

Canadian vocal duo with sisters Kate (born 1944, St Sauveur, Monteal) and Anna McGarrigle (born 1946, St Sauveur); they were first known as songwriters, with Linda Ronstadt covering *Heart Like A Wheel* in 1974. They were signed by Warner Brothers soon after and later recorded for the Hannibal label. They effectively stopped recording in 1982 to raise their families, returning to the studio in 1990.

| DATE | POS | WKS | BPI | ALBUM TITLE | LABEL & NUMBER |
|---|---|---|---|---|---|
| 26/02/1977 | 35 | 4 | | DANCER WITH BRUISED KNEES | Warner Brothers K 56356 |

## SHANE MacGOWAN AND THE POPES

UK singer (born 25/12/1957, Tunbridge Wells, Kent, raised in Tipperary) who was with the Nipple Erectors before forming the Pogues. He went solo in 1993 and was in the *Perfect Day* project for BBC's Children In Need charity. The Popes was a studio group featuring contributions from Bernie 'The Undertaker' France (bass), Paul McGuiness (guitar), Johnny Depp (guitar), Kieran 'Mo' O'Hagan (guitar), Brian Robertson (guitar), Rick Trevan (horns), Sarah Jane Tuff (horns), Dick Cuthell (horns), Paul Taylor (horns), John Sheahan (fiddle/whistle), Colm O'Maonlai (whistle), Tom MacAnimal (banjo), Barney McKenna (banjo), Jem Finer (banjo), Siobhan Sheahan (harp), Tomas Lynch (Uillean pipe) and Danny Pope (drums), with a touring group later being assembled.

| DATE | POS | WKS | BPI | ALBUM TITLE | LABEL & NUMBER |
|---|---|---|---|---|---|
| 29/10/1994 | 37 | 2 | | THE SNAKE | ZTT 4509981042 |
| 08/11/1997 | 59 | 1 | | THE CROCK OF GOLD | ZTT MACG 002CD |

## MARY MacGREGOR

US singer (born 6/5/1948, St Paul, MN) who worked as a session singer before going solo.

| DATE | POS | WKS | BPI | ALBUM TITLE | LABEL & NUMBER |
|---|---|---|---|---|---|
| 23/04/1977 | 59 | 1 | | TORN BETWEEN TWO LOVERS | Ariola America AAS 1504 |

## McGUINNESS FLINT

UK group formed in 1969 by ex-Manfred Mann Tom McGuinness (born 2/12/1941, London, guitar/vocals), Hughie Flint (born 15/3/1942, drums), Benny Gallagher (born in Largs, guitar/vocals), Graham Lyle (born in Largs, guitar/vocals) and Dennis Coulson (keyboards). Gallagher and Lyle went on to record as a duo and with Ronnie Lane in Slim Chance.

| DATE | POS | WKS | BPI | ALBUM TITLE | LABEL & NUMBER |
|---|---|---|---|---|---|
| 23/01/1971 | 9 | 10 | | McGUINNESS FLINT | Capitol EAST 22625 |

## MACHINE HEAD

US rock group formed in Oakland, CA in 1992 by Robb Flynn (guitar/vocals), Logan Mader (guitar), Adam Duce (bass) and Chris Kontos (drums).

| DATE | POS | WKS | BPI | ALBUM TITLE | LABEL & NUMBER |
|---|---|---|---|---|---|
| 20/08/1994 | 25 | 3 | ○ | BURN MY EYES | Roadrunner RR 90169 |
| 05/04/1997 | 16 | 3 | | THE MORE THINGS CHANGE… | Roadrunner RR 88602 |
| 21/08/1999 | 13 | 2 | | THE BURNING RED | Roadrunner RR 86512 |
| 13/10/2001 | 34 | 1 | | SUPERCHARGER | Roadrunner 12085005 |

## DUFF McKAGAN

US singer/bass player (born Michael McKagan, 5/2/1964, Seattle, WA); a founder member of Guns N' Roses in 1985, he launched a parallel solo career in 1993. He was in more than 30 other bands beore Guns N' Roses, including The Fartz, Silly Killers and Thankless Dogs.

| DATE | POS | WKS | BPI | ALBUM TITLE | LABEL & NUMBER |
|---|---|---|---|---|---|
| 09/10/1993 | 27 | 2 | | BELIEVE IN ME | Geffen GED 24605 |

## MARIA McKEE

US singer (born 17/8/1964, Los Angeles, CA) who followed her half-brother, ex-Love Bryan MacLean, into the recording industry. By the early 1980s Maria and Bryan were working together in the Maria McKee Band, which later changed name to the Bryan MacLean Band and disbanded in 1985. Maria then formed Lone Justice before going solo in 1987.

| DATE | POS | WKS | BPI | ALBUM TITLE | LABEL & NUMBER |
|---|---|---|---|---|---|
| 24/06/1989 | 49 | 3 | | MARIA McKEE | Geffen WX 270 |
| 12/06/1993 | 26 | 3 | | YOU GOTTA SIN TO GET SAVED | Geffen GED 24508 |

## KENNETH McKELLAR

UK singer/arranger (born 1927, Paisley) who was popular in his homeland of Scotland from the 1950s and a regular on the EP charts when separate charts were compiled.

| DATE | POS | WKS | BPI | ALBUM TITLE | LABEL & NUMBER |
|---|---|---|---|---|---|
| 28/06/1969 | 27 | 7 | | THE WORLD OF KENNETH McKELLAR | Decca SPA 11 |

○ Silver disc ● Gold disc ✪ Platinum disc (additional platinum units are indicated by a figure following the symbol) ❶⁹ Number of weeks album topped the UK chart

| | | | |
|---|---|---|---|
| 31/01/1970.....45......3...... | ECO DI NAPOLI.................................................................................... Decca SKL 5018 |

**BILLY MacKENZIE** UK singer (born 27/3/1957, Dundee); a founder member of The Associates with Alan Rankin, he re-formed the group following Rankine's departure. MacKenzie subsequently signed solo with Nude but was found dead in a garden shed on 22/1/1997. Although his death was believed to be suicide following his mother's death, he had recently signed a six-album deal.

18/10/1997.....64......1...... BEYOND THE SUN ...................................................................................... Nude 8CD

**CRAIG McLACHLAN AND CHECK 1-2** Australian actor/singer (born 1/9/1965) who first came to prominence as Henry Ramsey in *Neighbours*. He later relocated to the UK and appeared in the musical *Grease*.

21/07/1990.....10.....11...... **CRAIG MCLACHLAN AND CHECK 1-2** ....................................................... Epic 4663471

**SARAH McLACHLAN** Canadian vocalist (born 28/1/1968, Halifax, Nova Scotia) who was adopted and brought up by Jack and Dorice McLachlan, although it is believed that Judy James, a Nova Scotian jewellery craftswoman, was her biological mother. She has three Grammy Awards: Best Pop Instrumental Performance in 1997 for *Last Dance*, Best Female Pop Vocal Performance in 1997 for *Building A Mystery* and Best Female Pop Vocal Performance in 1999 for *I Will Remember You*.

17/10/1998.....47......2...... SURFACING ......................................................................................... Arista 189702
14/02/2004.....33.....13......● AFTERGLOW ................................................................................... Arista 82876596712

**MALCOLM McLAREN** UK producer (born 22/1/1946, London) who is best known as manager of The Sex Pistols, Bow Wow Wow and Adam Ant among others. The World Famous Supreme Team are a US vocal/rapping group formed by Jade, Anjou, Tammy, Rockafella and Asia. The Bootzilla Orchestra was founded by ex-Parliament/Funkedlic William 'Bootsy' Collins.

04/06/1983.....18.....17......○ DUCK ROCK ........................................................................................ Charisma MMLP 1
26/05/1984.....44......4...... WOULD YA LIKE MORE SCRATCHIN' **MALCOLM MCLAREN AND THE WORLD FAMOUS SUPREME TEAM SHOW** .... Charisma CLAM1
29/12/1984.....47......8...... FANS ................................................................................................. Charisma MMDL 2
15/07/1989.....30.....11...... WALTZ DARLING **MALCOLM MCLAREN AND THE BOOTZILLA ORCHESTRA** ...................................... Epic 4607361
20/08/1994.....44......1...... PARIS ................................................................................................ No! NOCD 101

**BITTY McLEAN** UK singer (born 1972, Birmingham); he was a tape operator and later co-producer for UB40 before going solo.

19/02/1994.....19.....11......● JUST TO LET YOU KNOW .......................................................................... Brilliant BRILCD 1

**DON McLEAN** US singer (born 2/10/1945, New Rochelle, NY) who began performing in 1968 and made his debut album in 1970. The hit *Killing Me Softly With His Song* was written about him.

11/03/1972 .....3.....54......○ AMERICAN PIE ▲[7] ............................................................................ United Artists UAS 29285
17/06/1972.....16.....12...... TAPESTRY Originally released in 1970 without success .................................. United Artists UAS 29350
24/11/1973.....42......2...... PLAYIN' FAVOURITES.............................................................................. United Artists UAG 29528
14/06/1980.....19......9...... CHAIN LIGHTNING .............................................................................. EMI International INS 3025
27/09/1980 .....4.....12......● **THE VERY BEST OF DON MCLEAN**.......................................................... United Artists UAG 30314
15/04/2000.....30......3...... AMERICAN PIE – THE GREATEST HITS ......................................................... Capitol 5258472

**ANDY McNABB** UK soldier who was a member of the SAS (Special Air Services) regiment and fought in the Gulf War. His hit album is an audio adaptation of his autobiography of the same name.

21/05/1994.....45......2...... BRAVO TWO ZERO.............................................................................. Polygram TV 5222002

**IAN McNABB** UK singer/guitarist (born 3/11/1960, Liverpool) who formed Icicle Works in 1980 with Chris Layhe and Chris Sharrock and recorded five albums with the group before going solo.

30/01/1993.....51......1...... TRUTH AND BEAUTY ........................................................................... This Way Up 5143782
16/07/1994.....29......2...... HEAD LIKE A ROCK................................................................................ This Way Up 5222982
18/05/1996.....30......2...... MERSEYBEAST .................................................................................... This Way Up 5242152

**LUTRICIA McNEAL** US singer (born in Oklahoma City, KS) who moved to Sweden where she first had Top Ten hits.

25/07/1998.....16.....16...... LUTRICIA McNEAL ............................................................................. Wildstar CDWILD 5X

**RITA MacNEIL** Canadian folk singer (born 1944, Big Pond, Cape Breton) who first became known at the 1985 Tokyo Expo.

24/11/1990.....32......4......○ REASON TO BELIEVE ............................................................................ Polydor 8471061

**TOM McRAE** UK singer/songwriter (born in Chelmsford) whose parents were Church of England vicars. He studied music politics at London Guildhall University and recorded his debut album in 2001.

15/02/2003.....26......2...... JUST LIKE BLOOD ................................................................................ DB DB006CDLP

**IAN McSHANE** UK singer/actor (born1942); he is best known as an actor in such films as *The Wild And The Willing* (1962), *The Battle Of Britain* (1968) and *Ransom* (1974).He is also a familiar face on UK TV, most notably as *Lovejoy*, which he also produced.

| | | | | | |
|--|--|--|--|--|--|
| 21/11/1992.....40......7......O | | | | FROM BOTH SIDES NOW.................................................................. Polygram TV 5176192 |

**RALPH McTELL** UK singer/songwriter/guitarist (born Ralph May, 3/12/1944, Farnborough) who made his debut recording in 1968. He named himself after blues singer Blind Willie McTell.

18/11/1972.....36......1...... NOT TILL TOMORROW................................................................. Reprise K 44210
02/03/1974.....31......4......O EASY......................................................................... Reprise K 54013
15/02/1975.....13.....12......O STREETS..................................................................... Warner Brothers K 56105

**CHRISTINE McVIE** UK singer/keyboard player (born Christine Perfect, 12/7/1943, Birmingham); she was in Shades Of Blues before joining Chicken Shack in 1967. After marrying John McVie of Fleetwood Mac she left Chicken Shack and briefly formed the Christine Perfect Band (in response to *Melody Maker* poll that elected her Female Singer of the Year in 1969). In 1970 she joined the expanding Fleetwood Mac in place of Peter Green. She remained in the band although her marriage ended, going solo in 1984.

11/02/1984.....58......4...... CHRISTINE McVIE............................................................. Warner Brothers 9250591

**DAVID McWILLIAMS** UK singer/songwriter (born 4/7/1945, Belfast); he recorded his first single in 1966 and signed with manager Phil Solomon, who also looked after Them and The Bachelors. His three hit albums were produced by Mike Leander,who later produced Gary Glitter. He died on 8/1/2002 at the age of 56.

10/06/1967.....38......2...... DAVID McWILLIAMS SINGS....................................................... Major Minor MMLP 2
04/11/1967.....23......6...... DAVID McWILLIAMS VOLUME 2.................................................... Major Minor MMLP 10
09/03/1968.....39......1...... DAVID McWILLIAMS VOLUME 3.................................................... Major Minor MMLP 11

**MAD SEASON** UK group formed by Mark Lanegan (vocals), Layne Stanley (guitar/vocals), Mike McCready (guitar), Barrett Martin (acoustic bass/vibraphone/marimba/cello/drums/percussion) and John Baker Saunders (bass).

25/03/1995.....41......1...... ABOVE...................................................................... Columbia 4785072

**MADDER ROSE** US group formed in Manhattan, NYC by Billy Cote (vocals), Mary Lorson (guitar), Matt Verta-Ray (bass) and Johnny Kick (drums). Verta-Ray left the group in 1994 and was replaced by Chris Giammalvo.

09/04/1994.....52......2...... PANIC ON.................................................................... Atlantic 7567825812

**MADHOUSE** French production group formed by Bambi Mukendi and Stephane Durand and fronted by Turkish singer Buse Unlu who was 20 years of age at the time of their debut hit.

31/08/2002.....57......1...... ABSOLUTELY MAD............................................................... Serious SERRCD 001

**MADISON AVENUE** Australian dance duo formed by producer Andy Van Dorsselaar and singer Cheyne Coates.

04/11/2000.....74......1...... THE POLYESTER EMBASSY........................................................ VC Recordings CDVCR 7

**MADNESS** UK group formed in 1976 by Mike Barson (born 21/4/1958, London, keyboards), 'Chrissie Boy' Foreman (born 8/8/1958, London, guitar), Lee 'Kix' Thompson (born 5/10/1957, London, saxophone/vocals), John Hasler (drums), Chas Smash (born Cathal Smyth, 14/1/1959, London, horns), Suggs (born Graham McPherson, 13/1/1961, Hastings, vocals), Bedders (born Mark Bedford, 24/8/1961, London, bass) and Dan 'Woody' Woodgate (born 19/10/1960, London, drums) as The Invaders. They name-changed to Madness (after a Prince Buster song) in 1979 and signed a one-off deal with 2-Tone before linking with Stiff. They launched the Zarjazz label in 1984. Suggs later recorded solo and became a TV presenter. The group re-formed in 1999.

03/11/1979.....2.....78......✪ ONE STEP BEYOND......................................................... Stiff SEEZ 17
04/10/1980.....2.....46......✪ ABSOLUTELY............................................................... Stiff SEEZ 29
10/10/1981.....5.....29......● MADNESS 7................................................................ Stiff SEEZ 39
01/05/1982....❶³....88......✪ COMPLETE MADNESS......................................................... Stiff HIT-TV 1
13/11/1982.....10.....22......● THE RISE AND FALL........................................................ Stiff SEEZ 46
03/03/1984.....6.....19......O KEEP MOVING.............................................................. Stiff SEEZ 53
12/10/1985.....16......9......O MAD NOT MAD............................................................... Zarjazz JZLP 1
06/12/1986.....29......8......● UTTER MADNESS............................................................ Zarjazz JZLP 2
07/05/1988.....65......1...... THE MADNESS............................................................... Virgin V 2507
07/03/1992....❶³....96......✪³ DIVINE MADNESS........................................................... Virgin CDV 2692
14/11/1992.....22......9...... MADSTOCK!................................................................ Go Discs 8283672
13/06/1998.....19......5......● THE HEAVY HEAVY HITS..................................................... Virgin CDV 2862
13/11/1999.....17......2...... WONDERFUL................................................................ Virgin CDV 2889
02/11/2002.....45......2...... OUR HOUSE – THE ORIGINAL SONGS.......................................... Virgin CDV 2965

O Silver disc  ● Gold disc  ✪ Platinum disc (additional platinum units are indicated by a figure following the symbol)  ❶⁹ Number of weeks album topped the UK chart

## MADONNA

**MADONNA** US singer (born Madonna Louise Ciccone, 16/8/1958, Bay City, MI) who was with Patrick Hernandez's Revue before forming Breakfast Club in 1979. Her first records were backing Otto Van Wernherr in 1980, before signing solo with Sire in 1982. She made her lead film debut in *Desperately Seeking Susan* (1985), and later appeared in *Dick Tracy* (1990), *A League Of Their Own* (1992), *Body Of Evidence* (1993), *Evita* (1996) and *The Next Best Thing* (2000). As Eva Peron in *Evita*, she wore 85 costumes, 39 hats, 45 pairs of shoes and 56 pairs of earrings. She married actor Sean Penn in 1985; they divorced in 1989. She launched the Maverick label in 1992. Moving to London in 1999 with her daughter, Lourdes Maria Ciccone Leon, she married Guy Ritchie in January 2001, with whom she had a son, Rocco. While Sheena Easton was the first to record a James Bond theme and appear on screen, in 2002 Madonna was the first to perform the theme and appear in the film, in *Die Another Day*. She has won six Grammy Awards including: Best Music Video Long Form in 1991 for *Blond Ambition World Tour Live,* Best Pop Dance Performance, Best Recording Package and Best Music Video Short Form in 1998 for *Ray Of Light,* and Best Song for a Motion Picture in 1999 for *Beautiful Stranger*. She was named Best International Female artist at the 2001 BRIT Awards, her first such award. Four MTV Europe Music Awards include Best Female in 1998 and 2000 and Best Dance Act in 2000.

| DATE | POS | WKS | BPI | ALBUM TITLE | LABEL & NUMBER |
|------|-----|-----|-----|-----------|----------------|
| 11/02/1984 | 6 | 123 | ✪ | **MADONNA** The album changed its catalogue number to Sire WX 22 and its title to *The First Album* during its chart run . | Sire 923867 |
| 24/11/1984 | ❶² | 152 | ✪³ | **LIKE A VIRGIN** ▲³ ◆¹⁰ The album changed its catalogue number to Sire WX 20 during its chart run | Sire 925157 |
| 12/07/1986 | ❶⁶ | 85 | ✪⁷ | **TRUE BLUE** ▲⁵ | Sire WX 54 |
| 28/11/1987 | 5 | 16 | ✪ | **YOU CAN DANCE** | Sire WX 76 |
| 01/04/1989 | ❶² | 70 | ✪⁴ | **LIKE A PRAYER** ▲⁶ | Sire WX 239 |
| 02/06/1990 | 2 | 20 | ✪ | **I'M BREATHLESS** | Sire WX 351 |
| 24/11/1990 | ❶⁹ | 207 | ✪¹² | **THE IMMACULATE COLLECTION** ◆¹⁰ | Sire WX 370 |
| 24/10/1992 | 2 | 38 | ✪² | **EROTICA** | Maverick 9362450312 |
| 05/11/1994 | 2 | 27 | ✪ | **BEDTIME STORIES** ◇² | Maverick 9362457672 |
| 18/11/1995 | 3 | 29 | ✪³ | **SOMETHING TO REMEMBER** ◇³ | Maverick 9362461002 |
| 09/11/1996 | ❶¹ | 36 | ✪² | **EVITA** ◇² Original soundtrack to the film | Warner Brothers 9362464322 |
| 14/03/1998 | ❶² | 116 | ✪⁵ | **RAY OF LIGHT** ◇⁷ 1998 Grammy Award for Best Pop Album, 1998 MTV Europe Music Award for Best Album . | Maverick 9362468472 |
| 30/09/2000 | ❶² | 64 | ✪⁵ | **MUSIC** ◇⁵ ▲¹ | Maverick 9362479212 |
| 24/11/2001 | 2 | 24 | ✪² | **GHV2** ◇² | Maverick 9362480002 |
| 03/05/2003 | ❶¹ | 19 | ✪ | **AMERICAN LIFE** ◇ ▲¹ | Maverick 9362484542 |

## LISA MAFFIA

**LISA MAFFIA** UK rapper (born 1979) who is also a member of So Solid Crew. She won the 2003 MOBO Awards for Best UK Act (jointly with Big Brovaz) and Best Garage Act.

| DATE | POS | WKS | BPI | ALBUM TITLE | LABEL & NUMBER |
|------|-----|-----|-----|-----------|----------------|
| 23/08/2003 | 44 | 1 | | FIRST LADY | Independiente ISOM 39CD |

## MAGAZINE

**MAGAZINE** UK group formed in 1977 by ex-Buzzcocks Howard Devoto (born Howard Trafford, vocals), John McGeoch (guitar), Barry Adamson (bass), Bob Dickinson (keyboards) and Martin Jackson (drums). Dickinson left late 1977, Dave Formula his eventual replacement. Jackson left in 1978 and was replaced by John Doyle. McGeoch left in 1980 and was replaced by Robin Simon, who was replaced shorty after by Ben Mandelson. Devoto's departure in May 1981 brought the group to an end. McGeoch died on 4/3/2004.

| DATE | POS | WKS | BPI | ALBUM TITLE | LABEL & NUMBER |
|------|-----|-----|-----|-----------|----------------|
| 24/06/1978 | 29 | 8 | | REAL LIFE | Virgin V 2100 |
| 14/04/1979 | 38 | 8 | | SECONDHAND DAYLIGHT | Virgin V 2121 |
| 10/05/1980 | 28 | 4 | | CORRECT USE OF SOAP | Virgin V 2156 |
| 13/12/1980 | 69 | 1 | | PLAY | Virgin V 2184 |
| 27/06/1981 | 39 | 3 | | MAGIC, MURDER AND THE WEATHER | Virgin V 2200 |

## MAGNA CARTA

**MAGNA CARTA** UK vocal/instrumental rock group formed in 1969 by Chris Simpson, Lyell Tranter and Glen Stuart, although by 2001 the group was the duo of Chris and Linda Simpson. They also recorded for Philips, Fontana and Ariola during their career.

| DATE | POS | WKS | BPI | ALBUM TITLE | LABEL & NUMBER |
|------|-----|-----|-----|-----------|----------------|
| 08/08/1970 | 55 | 2 | | SEASONS | Vertigo 6360 003 |

## MAGNUM

**MAGNUM** UK heavy metal band formed in Birmingham, West Midlands in 1976 by Bob Catley (vocals), Tony Clarkin (guitar/vocals), Wally Lowe (bass), Mark Stanway (keyboards) and Mickey Barker (drums).

| DATE | POS | WKS | BPI | ALBUM TITLE | LABEL & NUMBER |
|------|-----|-----|-----|-----------|----------------|
| 16/09/1978 | 58 | 1 | | KINGDOM OF MADNESS | Jet JETLP 210 |
| 19/04/1980 | 34 | 5 | | MARAUDER | Jet JETLP 230 |
| 06/03/1982 | 17 | 7 | | CHASE THE DRAGON | Jet JETLP 235 |
| 21/05/1983 | 38 | 4 | | THE ELEVENTH HOUR | Jet JETLP 240 |
| 25/05/1985 | 24 | 7 | ● | ON A STORYTELLER'S NIGHT | FM WKFM LP 34 |
| 04/10/1986 | 24 | 5 | | VIGILANTE | Polydor POLD 5198 |
| 09/04/1988 | 5 | 9 | ○ | **WINGS OF HEAVEN** | Polydor POLD 5221 |
| 21/07/1990 | 9 | 5 | | **GOODNIGHT L.A.** | Polydor 8435681 |
| 14/09/1991 | 50 | 1 | | THE SPIRIT | Polydor 5111691 |
| 24/10/1992 | 27 | 2 | | SLEEPWALKING | Music For Nations CDMFN 143 |
| 18/06/1994 | 57 | 1 | | ROCK ART | EMI CDEMD 1066 |

## SEAN MAGUIRE

**SEAN MAGUIRE** UK actor/singer (born 18/4/1976) who appeared in children's TV programmes such as *Grange Hill* as Terence Ratcliffe, *Dangerfield* as Marty Dangerfield and *Eastenders* as Aidan Brosnan. After a brief record career, he returned to TV in *Sunburn* and the US TV series *Off Centre*.

| DATE | POS | WKS | BPI | ALBUM TITLE | LABEL & NUMBER |
|------|-----|-----|-----|-----------|----------------|
| 26/11/1994 | 75 | 1 | | SEAN MAGUIRE | Parlophone CDPCSDX 164 |
| 15/06/1996 | 43 | 2 | | SPIRIT | Parlophone CDPCSD 169 |

## MAHAVISHNU ORCHESTRA

**MAHAVISHNU ORCHESTRA** UK/US jazz-rock group formed in 1972 by John McLaughlin (born 4/1/1942, Yorkshire, guitar), Jan Hammer (born 17/4/1948, Prague, Czech Republic, keyboards), Jerry Goodman (violin), Rick Laird (born 5/2/1941, Dublin, bass) and Billy Cobham (born 16/5/1944, Panama, drums). McLaughlin disbanded the group in 1974 and re-formed it in 1975 with Jean-

▲⁹ Number of weeks album topped the US chart ◆¹² RIAA Diamond Awards ◇³ IFPI Platinum Europe Awards

Luc Ponty (born 29/9/1940, Avranches, France, violin), Gayle Moran (keyboards) and Narada Michael Walden (born 23/4/1952, Kalamazoo, MI, drums). Ponty left later the same year, replaced by Stu Goldberg (keyboards). They effectively disbanded a second time by the end of the decade, Walden enjoying success as a solo artist and producer – most notably for Whitney Houston among others.

| 31/03/1973 | 20 | 5 | | BIRDS OF FIRE | CBS 65321 |
| 28/07/1973 | 7 | 9 | | **LOVE, DEVOTION, SURRENDER CARLOS SANTANA AND THE MAHAVISHNU ORCHESTRA** | CBS 69037 |

### MAI TAI
Dutch group formed in Amsterdam in 1983 by Jettie Wells, Carolien De Windt and Mildred Douglas, all from Guyana.

| 06/07/1985 | 91 | 1 | | HISTORY | Holt Melt V 2359 |

### MAJESTICS
UK vocal group assembled for theTV series *Tutti Frutti*. The series featured Richard Wilson (as Eddie Clockerty), Maurice Roeves (Vincent Driver), Emma Thompson (Suzy Kettles), Stuart McGugan (Bomba MacAteer), Jake D'Arcy (Fud O'Donnell), Ron Donachie (Dennis Sproul), Robbie Coltrane (Danny Mglone), Katy Murphy (Janice Toner), Fiona Chalmers (Glenna McFadden) and Anne Kidd (Noreen Driver).

| 04/04/1987 | 64 | 4 | | TUTTI FRUTTI | BBC REN 629 |

### STEPHEN MALKMUS
US singer/guitarist (born 30/5/1963, Santa Monica, CA) who was in Pavement from 1989 to 2000 before going solo. He subsequently formed The Jicks as his backing group with John Moen and Joanna Bolme. Elastica's Justine Frischmann later joined on an ad hoc basis.

| 24/02/2001 | 49 | 1 | | STEPHEN MALKMUS | Domino WIGCD 90 |
| 29/03/2003 | 63 | 1 | | PIG LIB **STEPHEN MALMUS AND THE JICKS** | Domino WIGCD 122X |

### TIMMY MALLETT – see BOMBALURINA FEATURING TIMMY MALLETT

### YNGWIE J MALMSTEEN
Swedish guitarist (born 30/6/1963, Stockholm) who began playing the guitar at the age of eight and formed his first group, Powerhouse, at thirteen. The following year he formed Rising, taking the name in honour of the group Rainbow and put together a demo tape. It was heard by veteran producer Mike Varney who took Malmsteen to Los Angeles and got him into Ron Keel's group Steeler. He subsequently spent a short time with Alcatrazz before going solo with Polydor in 1984. Yngwie then launched his own group, Rising Force (named after his debut solo album) with Jeff Scott Soto (vocals), Jens Johansson (keyboards), Marcel Jacob (bass) and Anders Johansson (drums), Soto later being replaced by Mark Boals. A serious road accident put the group on hold for eighteen months before being reassembled in 1987 with Joe Lynn Turner on vocals. Turner was sacked in 1989 and was replaced by Goran Edman.

| 21/05/1988 | 27 | 7 | | ODYSSEY | Polydor POLD 5224 |
| 04/11/1989 | 65 | 1 | | TRIAL OF FIRE – LIVE IN LENINGRAD | Polydor 8397261 |
| 28/04/1990 | 43 | 2 | | ECLIPSE | Polydor 8434611 |
| 29/02/1992 | 57 | 1 | | FIRE AND ICE | Elektra 7559611372 |

### MAMA'S BOYS
Irish group formed in 1978 by brothers John (bass/vocals), Pat (guitar) and Tommy McManus (drums), adding singer Keith Murrell in 1987. By 1991 he had departed, replaced by Mike Wilson. Tommy died from a lung infection on 16/11/1994.

| 06/04/1985 | 55 | 4 | | POWER AND PASSION | Jive HIP 24 |

### MAMAS AND THE PAPAS
US group originally formed as the New Journeymen in St Thomas in the Virgin Islands in 1963 by John Phillips (born 30/8/1935, Parris Island, SC), Holly Michelle Gilliam Phillips (born 4/6/1945, Long Beach, CA) and Dennis 'Denny' Doherty (born 29/11/1941, Halifax, Novia Scotia), later adding Cass Elliot (born Ellen Naomi Cohen, 19/9/1941, Baltimore, MD) and becoming the Mamas & The Papas. They moved to Los Angeles, CA in 1964. They split in 1968, Mama Cass going solo. They reunited briefly in 1971 and then re-formed in 1982 with Phillips, Doherty, Phillips' daughter McKenzie and Spanky McFarlane. Michelle and John's daughter Chyna was later in Wilson Phillips. The group was inducted into the Rock & Roll Hall of Fame in 1998. Cass Elliot died from a heart attack on 29/7/1974. John Phillips died from heart failure on 18/3/2001.

| 25/06/1966 | 3 | 18 | | IF YOU CAN BELIEVE YOUR EYES AND EARS ▲[1] | RCA Victor RD 7803 |
| 28/01/1967 | 24 | 6 | | CASS, JOHN, MICHELLE, DENNY | RCA Victor SF 7639 |
| 24/06/1967 | 4 | 22 | | **MAMAS AND PAPAS DELIVER** | RCA Victor SF 7880 |
| 26/04/1969 | 7 | 2 | ○ | **HITS OF GOLD** | Stateside S 5007 |
| 18/06/1977 | 6 | 13 | | **THE BEST OF THE MAMAS AND PAPAS** | Arcade ADEP 30 |
| 28/01/1995 | 14 | 6 | | CALIFORNIA DREAMIN' – THE VERY BEST OF THE MAMAS AND THE PAPAS | Polygram TV 5239732 |
| 06/09/1997 | 30 | 4 | | CALIFORNIA DREAMIN' – GREATEST HITS OF THE MAMAS AND THE PAPAS | Telstar TV TTVCD 2931 |

### MAMBAS – see MARC ALMOND

### MAN
UK group formed in Wales by Micky Jones (born 7/6/1946, Merthyr Tydfil, guitar/vocals), Deke Leonard (guitar), Clive John (guitar /keyboards), Ray Williams (bass) and Jeff Jones, previously known as The Bystanders. By 1972 the line-up was Micky Jones, Clive John, Will Youatt (born Michael Youatt, 16/2/1950, Swansea, bass/vocals), Phil Ryan (born 21/10/1946, Port Talbot, keyboards) and Terry Williams (born 11/1/1948, Swansea, drums). Deke Leonard returned in 1974, but the group dissolved in 1976. The name was revived in the late 1980s by Jones, Leonard, Martin Ace (an ex-member of the group, bass) and John 'Pugwash' Weathers (drums). Deke Leonard also enjoyed solo success.

| 20/10/1973 | 23 | 3 | | BACK INTO THE FUTURE | United Artists UAD 60053/4 |
| 25/05/1974 | 24 | 4 | | RHINOS WINOS AND LUNATICS | United Artists UAG 29631 |

○ Silver disc ● Gold disc ✪ Platinum disc (additional platinum units are indicated by a figure following the symbol) ●[9] Number of weeks album topped the UK chart

| | | | | | |
|---|---|---|---|---|---|
| 11/10/1975 | 25 | 2 | | MAXIMUM DARKNESS | United Artists UAG 29872 |
| 17/04/1976 | 40 | 2 | | WELSH COLLECTION | MCA MCF 2753 |

## MANCHESTER BOYS CHOIR UK choir formed in Manchester.

| | | | | | |
|---|---|---|---|---|---|
| 21/12/1985 | 80 | 2 | ○ | THE NEW SOUND OF CHRISTMAS | K-Tel ONE 1314 |

## HENRY MANCINI
US orchestra leader (born 16/4/1924, Cleveland, OH, raised in Pennsylvania) who attended the Juillard School of Music in New York and became in-house composer for Universal Pictures in 1952. He has won twenty Grammy Awards, more than any other artist, for Album of the Year and Best Arrangement in 1958 for *The Music From Peter Gunn,* Best Performance by an Orchestra and Best Arrangement in 1960 for *Mr Lucky,* Best Jazz Performance by a Large Group in 1960 for *The Blues And The Beat,* Song of the Year (with Johnny Mercer), Record of the Year and Best Arrangement in 1961 for *Moon River,* Best Performance by an Orchestra and Best Soundtrack Album in 1961 for *Breakfast At Tiffany's,* Best Instrumental Arrangement in 1962 for *Baby Elephant Walk,* Record of the Year, Song of the Year (again with Johnny Mercer) and Best Background Arrangement in 1963 for *The Days Of Wine And Roses,* Best Instrumental Composition, Best Instrumental Performance and Best Instrumental Arrangement in 1964 for *The Pink Panther Theme,* Best Instrumental Arrangement in 1969 for *Romeo And Juliet* and Best Contemporary Instrumental Performance and Best Instrumental Arrangement in 1970 for *Theme From 'Z'.* He also won four Oscars. He died from cancer on 14/6/1994. He has a star on the Hollywood Walk of Fame.

| | | | | | |
|---|---|---|---|---|---|
| 16/10/1976 | 26 | 8 | ● | HENRY MANCINI | Arcade ADEP 24 |
| 30/06/1984 | 96 | 1 | | MAMMA **LUCIANO PAVAROTTI WITH THE HENRY MANCINI ORCHESTRA** | Decca 411959 |
| 08/12/1984 | 62 | 6 | | IN THE PINK **JAMES GALWAY AND HENRY MANCINI** | RCA Red Seal RL 85315 |
| 13/12/1986 | 46 | 8 | ○ | THE HOLLYWOOD MUSICALS **JOHNNY MATHIS AND HENRY MANCINI** | CBS 4502581 |

## MANFRED MANN
UK group formed in London in 1962 by Manfred Mann (born Michael Lubowitz, 21/10/1940, Johannesburg, South Africa, keyboards), Mike Hugg (born 11/8/1942, Andover, drums), Paul Jones (born Paul Pond, 24/2/1942, Portsmouth, vocals), Mike Vickers (born 18/4/1941, Southampton, guitar) and Dave Richmond (bass) as the Mann-Hugg Blues Brothers, also adding a horn section. They name-changed in 1963 and signed to HMV. Richmond left in 1964 and was replaced by Tom McGuinness (born 2/12/1941, London). Jones went solo in 1966 and was replaced by Mike D'Abo (born 1/3/1944, Letchworth), Rod Stewart unsuccessfully auditioning for the job. They disbanded in 1969, Mann forming Manfred Mann's Earth Band in 1971 with Mick Rogers (guitar/vocals), Colin Pattenden (bass) and Chris Slade (drums).

| | | | | | |
|---|---|---|---|---|---|
| 19/09/1964 | 3 | 24 | | **FIVE FACES OF MANFRED MANN** | HMV CLP 1731 |
| 23/10/1965 | 7 | 11 | | **MANN MADE** | HMV CLP 1911 |
| 17/09/1966 | 11 | 18 | | MANN MADE HITS | HMV CLP 3559 |
| 29/10/1966 | 22 | 4 | | AS IS | Fontana TL 5377 |
| 21/01/1967 | 40 | 1 | | SOUL OF MANN | HMV CSD 3594 |
| 18/09/1976 | 10 | 9 | ○ | **THE ROARING SILENCE** | Bronze ILPS 9357 |
| 17/06/1978 | 33 | 6 | | WATCH | Bronze BRON 507 |
| 24/03/1979 | 30 | 8 | | ANGEL STATION This and the above two hits credited to **MANFRED MANN'S EARTH BAND** | Bronze BRON 516 |
| 15/09/1979 | 9 | 14 | ● | **SEMI-DETACHED SUBURBAN** | EMI EMTV 19 |
| 26/02/1983 | 87 | 1 | | SOMEWHERE IN AFRIKA **MANFRED MANN'S EARTH BAND** | Bronze BRON 543 |
| 23/01/1993 | 23 | 4 | | AGES OF MANN – 22 CLASSIC HITS OF THE 60'S | Polygram TV 5143622 |
| 10/09/1994 | 69 | 1 | | THE VERY BEST OF MANFRED MANN'S EARTH BAND **MANFRED MANN'S EARTH BAND** | Arcade ARC 3100162 |

## MANHATTAN TRANSFER
US vocal group formed in New York in 1972 by Tim Hauser (born 1940, New York), Alan Paul (born 1949, New Jersey), Janis Siegel (born 1953, Brooklyn, NYC) and Cheryl Bentyne. Bentyne left in 1979 and was replaced by Laurel Masse (born 1954). They won eight Grammy Awards: Best Jazz Fusion Performance in 1980 for *Birdland,* Best Pop Vocal Performance by a Group in 1981 for *Boy From New York City,* Best Jazz Vocal Performance by a Group in 1981 for *Until I Met You (Corner Pocket),* Best Jazz Vocal Performance by a Group in 1982 for *Route 66,* Best Jazz Vocal Performance by a Group in 1983 for *Why Not!,* Best Jazz Vocal Performance by a Group in 1985 for *Vocalese,* Best Pop Vocal Performance by a Group in 1988 for *Brasil* and Best Contemporary Jazz Performance in 1991 for *Sassy.*

| | | | | | |
|---|---|---|---|---|---|
| 12/03/1977 | 12 | 20 | | COMING OUT | Atlantic K 50291 |
| 19/03/1977 | 49 | 7 | ● | MANHATTAN TRANSFER | Atlantic K 50138 |
| 25/02/1978 | 10 | 34 | ● | **PASTICHE** | Atlantic K 50444 |
| 11/11/1978 | 4 | 17 | ✪ | **LIVE** | Atlantic K 50540 |
| 17/11/1979 | 63 | 3 | | EXTENSIONS | Atlantic K 50674 |
| 18/02/1984 | 53 | 4 | | BODIES AND SOULS | Atlantic 7801041 |

## MANHATTANS
US R&B vocal group formed in Jersey City, NJ in 1962 by George 'Smitty' Smith (born 16/11/1943), Winfred 'Blue' Lovett (born 16/11/1943), Edward 'Sonny' Bivins (born 15/1/1942), Kenneth 'Wally' Kelly (born 9/1/1943) and Richard Taylor (born 1940). Smith died from meningitis on 16/12/1970, replaced by Gerald Alston (born 8/11/1942). Taylor became a Muslim (adopting the name Abdul Rashid Tallah), left the group in 1976 and died on 7/12/1987. Alston later recorded solo. They won the 1980 Grammy Award for Best Rhythm & Blues Vocal Performance by a Group for the single *Shining Star.*

| | | | | |
|---|---|---|---|---|
| 14/08/1976.....37......3...... | | | | MANHATTANS . . . . . . . . . . . . . . . . . . . . . . . . . . . . . . . . . . . . . . . . . . . . . . . . . . . . CBS 81513 |

**MANIC STREET PREACHERS** UK group formed in Blackwood, Gwent in 1988 by James Dean Bradfield (born 21/2/1969, Newport, Gwent, guitar/vocals), Nicky Wire (born Nick Jones, 20/1/1969, Tredegar, Gwent, bass), Sean Moore (born 30/7/1970, Pontypool, Gwent, drums) and Richey 'Manic' Edwards (born 22/12/1966, Blackwood, rhythm guitar); they all graduated from Swansea University. They funded their debut in 1989, signing with CBS/Columbia in 1990. Edwards disappeared in February 1995, with his passport, credit cards and car being found near a notorious suicide spot at the Severn Bridge. Despite sightings in Wales and India, he was officially declared dead in 2002. The group hass won four BRIT Awards including Best Group in 1997 and 1999.

| | |
|---|---|
| 22/02/1992.....13......17......● | GENERATION TERRORISTS. . . . . . . . . . . . . . . . . . . . . . . . . . . . . . . . . . . . . . . . . . . Columbia 4710602 |
| 03/07/1993 .....8......11......○ | **GOLD AGAINST THE SOUL** . . . . . . . . . . . . . . . . . . . . . . . . . . . . . . . . . . . . . . . . Columbia 4640642 |
| 10/09/1994 .....6......4 | **THE HOLY BIBLE** . . . . . . . . . . . . . . . . . . . . . . . . . . . . . . . . . . . . . . . . . . . . . . . Epic 4774219 |
| 01/06/1996 .....2......82......✪² | **EVERYTHING MUST GO** ◇ 1997 BRIT Award for Best Album . . . . . . . . . . . . . . . . . . . Epic 4839302 |
| 26/09/1998 ...●³.....60......✪³ | **THIS IS MY TRUTH TELL ME YOURS** ◇ 1999 BRIT Award for Best Album . . . . . . . . . . . Epic 4917039 |
| 31/03/2001 .....2......14 | **KNOW YOUR ENEMY** . . . . . . . . . . . . . . . . . . . . . . . . . . . . . . . . . . . . . . . . . . . . Epic 5018802 |
| 09/11/2002 .....4......12......✪ | **FOREVER DELAYED – THE GREATEST HITS** . . . . . . . . . . . . . . . . . . . . . . . . . . . . . . Epic 5095519 |
| 26/07/2003 .....11......3 | LIPSTICK TRACES – A SECRET HISTORY OF . . . . . . . . . . . . . . . . . . . . . . . . . . . . . . Epic 5123862 |

**BARRY MANILOW** US singer (born Barry Alan Pincus, 17/6/1946, Brooklyn, NYC) who was musical director for Bette Midler and a jingle writer before going solo, first recording as Featherbed. He won the 1978 Grammy Award for Best Pop Vocal Performance for the single *Copacabana (At The Copa)*. He has a star on the Hollywood Walk of Fame.

| | |
|---|---|
| 23/09/1978.....12......28......○ | EVEN NOW. . . . . . . . . . . . . . . . . . . . . . . . . . . . . . . . . . . . . . . . . . . . . . . . . . . . Arista SPART 1047 |
| 03/03/1979 .....3......151......✪ | **MANILOW MAGIC – THE BEST OF BARRY MANILOW** . . . . . . . . . . . . . . . . . . . . . . . . Arista ARTV 2 |
| 20/10/1979.....18......7......● | ONE VOICE . . . . . . . . . . . . . . . . . . . . . . . . . . . . . . . . . . . . . . . . . . . . . . . . . . Arista SPART 1106 |
| 29/11/1980 .....5......34......✪ | **BARRY** . . . . . . . . . . . . . . . . . . . . . . . . . . . . . . . . . . . . . . . . . . . . . . . . . . . . . Arista DLART 2 |
| 25/04/1981.....62......1 | GIFT SET . . . . . . . . . . . . . . . . . . . . . . . . . . . . . . . . . . . . . . . . . . . . . . . . . . . . . Arista BOX 1 |
| 03/10/1981.....5......26......✪ | **IF I SHOULD LOVE AGAIN** . . . . . . . . . . . . . . . . . . . . . . . . . . . . . . . . . . . . . . . . Arista BMAN 1 |
| 01/05/1982 ...●¹.....23......✪ | **BARRY LIVE IN BRITAIN** . . . . . . . . . . . . . . . . . . . . . . . . . . . . . . . . . . . . . . . . . Arista ARTV 4 |
| 27/11/1982.....7......9......● | **I WANNA DO IT WITH YOU** . . . . . . . . . . . . . . . . . . . . . . . . . . . . . . . . . . . . . . . . Arista BMAN 2 |
| 08/10/1983.....10......12......● | **A TOUCH MORE MAGIC** . . . . . . . . . . . . . . . . . . . . . . . . . . . . . . . . . . . . . . . . . Arista BMAN 3 |
| 01/12/1984.....28......6......○ | 2.00 A.M. PARADISE CAFE... . . . . . . . . . . . . . . . . . . . . . . . . . . . . . . . . . . . . . . . . Arista 206 496 |
| 16/11/1985.....40......6......○ | MANILOW . . . . . . . . . . . . . . . . . . . . . . . . . . . . . . . . . . . . . . . . . . . . . . . . . . . RCA PL 87044 |
| 20/02/1988.....81......1 | SWING STREET . . . . . . . . . . . . . . . . . . . . . . . . . . . . . . . . . . . . . . . . . . . . . . . . Arista 208860 |
| 20/05/1989.....20......4 | SONGS TO MAKE THE WHOLE WORLD SING. . . . . . . . . . . . . . . . . . . . . . . . . . . . Arista 209927 |
| 17/03/1990.....19......3 | LIVE ON BROADWAY . . . . . . . . . . . . . . . . . . . . . . . . . . . . . . . . . . . . . . . . . . . . Arista 303785 |
| 30/06/1990.....13......7 | THE SONGS 1975–1990. . . . . . . . . . . . . . . . . . . . . . . . . . . . . . . . . . . . . . . . . . . Arista 303868 |
| 02/11/1991.....53......3 | SHOWSTOPPERS . . . . . . . . . . . . . . . . . . . . . . . . . . . . . . . . . . . . . . . . . . . . . . Arista 212091 |
| 03/04/1993.....36......7 | HIDDEN TREASURES . . . . . . . . . . . . . . . . . . . . . . . . . . . . . . . . . . . . . . . Arista 74321135682 |
| 27/11/1993.....37......6......○ | THE PLATINUM COLLECTION – GREATEST HITS . . . . . . . . . . . . . . . . . . . . . Arista 74321175452 |
| 05/11/1994.....54......2 | SINGIN' WITH THE BIG BANDS . . . . . . . . . . . . . . . . . . . . . . . . . . . . . . . . Arista 07822187712 |
| 30/11/1996.....66......2 | SUMMER OF '78 . . . . . . . . . . . . . . . . . . . . . . . . . . . . . . . . . . . . . . . . . . Arista 07822188092 |
| 21/11/1998.....72......2 | BARRY SINGS SINATRA . . . . . . . . . . . . . . . . . . . . . . . . . . . . . . . . . . . . . Arista 07822190332 |
| 25/05/2002.....18......3 | HERE AT THE MAYFLOWER. . . . . . . . . . . . . . . . . . . . . . . . . . . . . . . . . . . Columbia COJ 21022 |
| 20/03/2004 .....8......7 | **ULTIMATE MANILOW** . . . . . . . . . . . . . . . . . . . . . . . . . . . . . . . . . . . . . . . Arista 82876604552 |

**AIMEE MANN** US singer/songwriter (born 9/8/1960, Richmond, VA) who was in punk group Young Snakes before leading 'Til Tuesday. She went solo in 1990 and married singer Michael Penn (brother of actors Sean, Christopher and Eileen) in December 1997.

| | |
|---|---|
| 18/09/1993.....39......1 | WHATEVER . . . . . . . . . . . . . . . . . . . . . . . . . . . . . . . . . . . . . . . . . . . . . . . Imago 72787210172 |
| 11/11/1995.....51......1 | I'M WITH STUPID. . . . . . . . . . . . . . . . . . . . . . . . . . . . . . . . . . . . . . . . . . . Geffen GED 24951 |
| 14/09/2002.....72......1 | LOST IN SPACE . . . . . . . . . . . . . . . . . . . . . . . . . . . . . . . . . . . . . . . . . . . . . V2 VVR 1020882 |

**ROBERTO MANN** UK orchestra leader who also recorded *Accordion Sounds*.

| | |
|---|---|
| 09/12/1967.....19......9 | GREAT WALTZES. . . . . . . . . . . . . . . . . . . . . . . . . . . . . . . . . . . . . . . . . . . . . Deram SML 1010 |

**SHELLY MANNE** US drummer (born 11/6/1920, New York City) who played the saxophone before switching to drums and working with various bands during the late 1930s and early 1940s. Was with Stan Kenton's band from 1946 to 1952, by when he was considered one of the best drummers of his generation. He appeared on countless recording sessions for other artists and assembled

the *My Fair Lady* project (jazz versions of tunes from the musical) with Leroy Vinnegar and Andre Previn. By the end of the 1950s his working band featured Joe Gordon (trumpet), Richie Kamuca (saxophone), Monty Budwig (bass) and Vic Feldman (piano/vibes). He opened his own club in Los Angeles, Shelly's Manne-Hole, in 1960, where he performed regularly. He died on 26/9/1984.

18/06/1960 . . . . . 20 . . . . . . 1 . . . . . . MY FAIR LADY . . . . . . . . . . . . . . . . . . . . . . . . . . . . . . . . . . . . . . . . . . . . . . . . . . . . . . . . . . . . Vogue LAC 12100

**MANOWAR** US heavy metal group formed in 1981 by Eric Adams (vocals), Ross 'The Boss' Funicello (guitar), Joey Demaio (bass) and Donnie Hamzik (drums). After one album for Liberty Records they signed with Music For Nations in 1982, with Scott Columbus replacing Hamzik on drums at the same time. Ross The Boss left the group in 1988 and Columbus left in 1990.

18/02/1984 . . . . . 83 . . . . . . 2 . . . . . . HAIL TO ENGLAND . . . . . . . . . . . . . . . . . . . . . . . . . . . . . . . . . . . . . . . . . . . . . . . . . . . . Music For Nations MFN 19
06/10/1984 . . . . . 73 . . . . . . 1 . . . . . . SIGN OF THE HAMMER . . . . . . . . . . . . . . . . . . . . . . . . . . . . . . . . . . . . . . . . . . . . . . . . . . . . 10 Records DIX 10

**MANSUN** UK group formed in Chester in 1995 by Paul Draper (born 26/9/1972, Liverpool, guitar/vocals), Stove King (born 8/1/1974, Ellesmere Port, bass) and Dominic Chad (born 5/6/1973, Cheltenham, guitar/vocals) as Grey Lantern, later changing their name to A Man Called Sun. Discovering a group named A Man Called Adam, the name was shortened to Mansun (their debut release listed their name as Manson, which had the estate of Charles Manson threatening legal action). Andie Rathbone (born 8/9/1971, drums) joined in 1996.

01/03/1997 . . . . ❶[1] . . . . 19 . . . . . . ● **ATTACK OF THE GREY LANTERN** . . . . . . . . . . . . . . . . . . . . . . . . . . . . . . . . . . . . . . . . . . . . Parlophone CDPCS 7387
19/09/1998 . . . . 6 . . . . . . 4 . . . . . . ● **SIX** . . . . . . . . . . . . . . . . . . . . . . . . . . . . . . . . . . . . . . . . . . . . . . . . . . . . . . . . . . . . Parlophone 4967232
26/08/2000 . . . . . 12 . . . . . . 4 . . . . . . ○ LITTLE KIX . . . . . . . . . . . . . . . . . . . . . . . . . . . . . . . . . . . . . . . . . . . . . . . . . . . . . . . . . . . . Parlophone 5277822

**MANTOVANI** UK orchestra leader (born Annunzio Paolo Mantovani, 15/11/1905, Venice, Italy) who moved to England with his parents in 1921. He formed his own orchestra in the early 1930s, had his first US hit in 1935 and was still in the album charts in the 1970s. He was given the Ivor Novello Oustanding Personal Services to Popular Music Award in 1956. He died in Kent on 29/3/1980. He has a star on the Hollywood Walk of Fame.

21/02/1959 . . . . . 4 . . . . . . 12 . . . . . . **CONTINENTAL ENCORES** . . . . . . . . . . . . . . . . . . . . . . . . . . . . . . . . . . . . . . . . . . . . . . . . Decca LK 4298
18/02/1961 . . . . . 16 . . . . . . 2 . . . . . . CONCERT SPECTACULAR . . . . . . . . . . . . . . . . . . . . . . . . . . . . . . . . . . . . . . . . . . . . . . . Decca LK 4377
16/04/1966 . . . . . 3 . . . . . . 15 . . . . . . **MANTOVANI MAGIC** . . . . . . . . . . . . . . . . . . . . . . . . . . . . . . . . . . . . . . . . . . . . . . . . . . . Decca LK 7949
15/10/1966 . . . . . 24 . . . . . . 3 . . . . . . MR MUSIC – MANTOVANI . . . . . . . . . . . . . . . . . . . . . . . . . . . . . . . . . . . . . . . . . . . . . . Decca LK 4809
14/01/1967 . . . . . 10 . . . . . . 43 . . . . . . **MANTOVANI'S GOLDEN HITS** . . . . . . . . . . . . . . . . . . . . . . . . . . . . . . . . . . . . . . . . . . Decca SKL 4818
30/09/1967 . . . . . 37 . . . . . . 1 . . . . . . HOLLYWOOD . . . . . . . . . . . . . . . . . . . . . . . . . . . . . . . . . . . . . . . . . . . . . . . . . . . . . . . . Decca SKL 4887
14/06/1969 . . . . . 6 . . . . . . 31 . . . . . . **THE WORLD OF MANTOVANI** . . . . . . . . . . . . . . . . . . . . . . . . . . . . . . . . . . . . . . . . . . . . Decca SPA 1
04/10/1969 . . . . . 4 . . . . . . 19 . . . . . . **THE WORLD OF MANTOVANI VOLUME 2** . . . . . . . . . . . . . . . . . . . . . . . . . . . . . . . . . . Decca SPA 36
16/05/1970 . . . . . 16 . . . . . . 8 . . . . . . MANTOVANI TODAY . . . . . . . . . . . . . . . . . . . . . . . . . . . . . . . . . . . . . . . . . . . . . . . . . Decca SKL 5003
26/02/1972 . . . . . 44 . . . . . . 1 . . . . . . TO LOVERS EVERYWHERE . . . . . . . . . . . . . . . . . . . . . . . . . . . . . . . . . . . . . . . . . . . . Decca SKL 5112
03/11/1979 . . . . . 9 . . . . . . 13 . . . . . . ✪ **20 GOLDEN GREATS** . . . . . . . . . . . . . . . . . . . . . . . . . . . . . . . . . . . . . . . . . . . . . . . Warwick WW 5067
16/03/1985 . . . . . 52 . . . . . . 3 . . . . . . MANTOVANI MAGIC . . . . . . . . . . . . . . . . . . . . . . . . . . . . . . . . . . . . . . . . . . . . . . . . . Telstar STAR 2237

**MANTRONIX** US rap duo formed in New York by songwriters/producers Curtis Mantronik (born Kurtis Kahleel, 4/9/1965, Jamaica) and MC Tee (born Tooure Embden). They signed with Sleeping Bag Records in 1985. Embden joined the US Air Force in 1989, replaced by Bryce Wilson and DJ Dee. Wilson later formed Groove Theory. They split in 1992, Kahleel returning as Kurtis Mantronik.

29/03/1986 . . . . . 45 . . . . . . 3 . . . . . . THE ALBUM . . . . . . . . . . . . . . . . . . . . . . . . . . . . . . . . . . . . . . . . . . . . . . . . . . . . . . . . 10 Records DIX 37
13/12/1986 . . . . . 66 . . . . . . 3 . . . . . . MUSICAL MADNESS . . . . . . . . . . . . . . . . . . . . . . . . . . . . . . . . . . . . . . . . . . . . . . . . . . 10 Records DIX 50
02/04/1988 . . . . . 39 . . . . . . 3 . . . . . . IN FULL EFFECT . . . . . . . . . . . . . . . . . . . . . . . . . . . . . . . . . . . . . . . . . . . . . . . . . . . . 10 Records DIX 74
17/02/1990 . . . . . 18 . . . . . . 6 . . . . . . ○ THIS SHOULD MOVE YA . . . . . . . . . . . . . . . . . . . . . . . . . . . . . . . . . . . . . . . . . . . . . . . Capitol EST 2117
30/03/1991 . . . . . 36 . . . . . . 2 . . . . . . THE INCREDIBLE SOUND MACHINE . . . . . . . . . . . . . . . . . . . . . . . . . . . . . . . . . . . . Capitol EST 2139

**MANUEL AND HIS MUSIC OF THE MOUNTAINS** UK orchestra leader (born Geoff Love, 4/9/1917, Todmorden, Yorkshire) who debuted on radio in 1937, forming his own band in 1955 for the TV show *On The Town*. He began recording as Manuel & His Music Of The Mountains in 1959, later becoming a much-in-demand orchestra leader/arranger for artists such as Russ Conway, Connie Francis, Judy Garland and Frankie Vaughan, both in live concerts and on record. He died on 8/7/1991.

10/09/1960 . . . . . 17 . . . . . . 1 . . . . . . MUSIC OF THE MOUNTAINS . . . . . . . . . . . . . . . . . . . . . . . . . . . . . . . . . . . . . . . . . . Columbia 33SX 1212
07/08/1971 . . . . . 18 . . . . . 19 . . . . . . THIS IS MANUEL . . . . . . . . . . . . . . . . . . . . . . . . . . . . . . . . . . . . . . . . . . . . . . . . . . . Studio Two STWO 5
31/01/1976 . . . . . 3 . . . . . . 18 . . . . . . ○ **CARNIVAL** . . . . . . . . . . . . . . . . . . . . . . . . . . . . . . . . . . . . . . . . . . . . . . . . . . . . . . . Studio Two 337

**ROOTS MANUVA** UK rapper Rodney Hylton Smith; he won the 1999 MOBO Award for Best Hip Hop Act.

25/08/2001 . . . . . 33 . . . . . . 3 . . . . . . ○ RUN COME SAVE ME . . . . . . . . . . . . . . . . . . . . . . . . . . . . . . . . . . . . . . . . . . . . . . . . . . . Big Dada BDCD 032
20/07/2002 . . . . . 75 . . . . . . 1 . . . . . . DUB COME SAVE ME . . . . . . . . . . . . . . . . . . . . . . . . . . . . . . . . . . . . . . . . . . . . . . . . . Big Dada BDCD 040

**PHIL MANZANERA** UK singer/guitarist (born Philip Targett Adams, 31/1/1951, London); he joined Roxy Music in 1972 as a replacement for Davy O'List and began a parallel solo career in 1975.

24/05/1975 . . . . . 40 . . . . . . 1 . . . . . . DIAMOND HEAD . . . . . . . . . . . . . . . . . . . . . . . . . . . . . . . . . . . . . . . . . . . . . . . . . . . . . . Island ILPS 9315

▲[9] Number of weeks album topped the US chart   ◆[12] RIAA Diamond Awards   ◇[3] IFPI Platinum Europe Awards

### MARC AND THE MAMBAS – see MARC ALMOND

### MARCY PLAYGROUND
US rock group formed by John Wozniak (born 19/1/1971, guitar/vocals), Dylan Keefe (born 11/4/1970, bass) and Dan Rieser (drums). The group was formed at the Marcy Open School in Minneapolis, MN, hence their name.

| DATE | POS | WKS | BPI | ALBUM TITLE | LABEL & NUMBER |
|---|---|---|---|---|---|
| 09/05/1998 | 61 | 1 | | MARCY PLAYGROUND | EMI 85335692 |

### ROSE MARIE
Irish singer (born 1962) who was a hairdresser when she got a break on TV talent shows *New Faces* and *Search For A Star*.

| DATE | POS | WKS | BPI | ALBUM TITLE | LABEL & NUMBER |
|---|---|---|---|---|---|
| 13/04/1985 | 30 | 13 | | ROSE MARIE SINGS JUST FOR YOU | A.1 RMTV 1 |
| 24/05/1986 | 62 | 3 | | SO LUCKY | A.1 RMLP 2 |
| 14/11/1987 | 22 | 11 | ● | SENTIMENTALLY YOURS | Telstar STAR 2302 |
| 19/11/1988 | 52 | 7 | ● | TOGETHER AGAIN | Telstar STAR 2333 |
| 23/03/1996 | 51 | 1 | | MEMORIES OF HOME | Telstar TCD 2788 |

### MARILLION
UK group formed in Aylesbury in 1978 by Doug Irvine (bass), Mick Pointer (born 22/7/1956, drums) and Steve Rothery (born 25/11/1959, Brampton, Yorkshire, guitar) as Silmarillion (title of a JRR Tolkien novel). They shortened their name in 1979, adding keyboard player Brian Jelliman. Irvine left in 1980, shortly before Fish (born Derek Dick, 25/4/1958, Dalkeith, Midlothian, vocals) and Diz Minnitt (bass) joined. Fish, later to record solo, was the focal point during more changes. They signed with EMI in 1982.

| DATE | POS | WKS | BPI | ALBUM TITLE | LABEL & NUMBER |
|---|---|---|---|---|---|
| 26/03/1983 | 7 | 31 | ✪ | SCRIPT FOR A JESTER'S TEAR | EMI EMC 3429 |
| 24/03/1984 | 5 | 20 | ● | FUGAZI | EMI EMC 2400851 |
| 17/11/1984 | 8 | 22 | ● | REAL TO REEL | EMI JEST 1 |
| 29/06/1985 | ❶¹ | 41 | ✪ | MISPLACED CHILDHOOD | EMI MRL 2 |
| 04/07/1987 | 2 | 15 | ● | CLUTCHING AT STRAWS | EMI EMD 1002 |
| 23/07/1988 | 64 | 6 | | B SIDES THEMSELVES | EMI EMS 1295 |
| 10/12/1988 | 25 | 6 | ● | THE THIEVING MAGPIE | EMI MARIL 1 |
| 07/10/1989 | 7 | 4 | ● | SEASON'S END | EMI EMD 1011 |
| 06/07/1991 | 7 | 7 | | HOLIDAYS IN EDEN | EMI EMD 1022 |
| 20/06/1992 | 27 | 2 | | A SINGLES COLLECTION 1982–1992 | EMI CDEMD 1033 |
| 19/02/1994 | 10 | 4 | | BRAVE | EMI CDEMC 1054 |
| 08/07/1995 | 16 | 2 | | AFRAID OF SUNLIGHT | EMI CDEMD 1079 |
| 06/04/1996 | 37 | 1 | | MADE AGAIN | EMI CDEMD 1094 |
| 03/05/1997 | 27 | 2 | | THIS STRANGE ENGINE | Raw Power RAWCD 121 |
| 03/10/1998 | 35 | 1 | | RADIATION | Raw Power RAWCD 126 |
| 30/10/1999 | 53 | 1 | | MARILLION.COM | Raw Power RAWCD 144 |

### MARILYN MANSON
US singer (born Brian Warner, 5/1/1969, Canton, OH) whose backing group comprises John 5 (born John Lowery, guitar), Twiggy Ramirez (born Jeordie White, 20/6/1972, bass), Madonna Wayne Gacy (born Stephen Bier, keyboards) and Ginger Fish (born Kenny Wilson, drums). Previous members included Olivia Newton-Bundy (born Brian Tutinuck, bass), Zsa Zsa Speck (born Perry Pandrea, keyboards), Zim Zum (born Michael Linton, guitar), Daisy Berkowitz (born Scott Mitchell, 28/4/1968, guitar) and Sara Lee Lucas (born Freddy Streithorst, drums).

| DATE | POS | WKS | BPI | ALBUM TITLE | LABEL & NUMBER |
|---|---|---|---|---|---|
| 26/10/1996 | 73 | 1 | | ANTICHRIST SUPERSTAR | Interscope IND 90086 |
| 26/09/1998 | 8 | 4 | | MECHANICAL ANIMAL ▲¹ | Interscope IND 90273 |
| 27/11/1999 | 61 | 1 | | THE LAST TOUR ON EARTH | Interscope 4905242 |
| 25/11/2000 | 23 | 2 | | HOLY WOOD | Nothing 4908592 |
| 24/05/2003 | 4 | 7 | ● | THE GOLDEN AGE OF GROTESQUE ▲¹ | Interscope 9800082 |

### MARION
UK rock group formed by Jamie Harding (vocals), Anthony Grantham (guitar), Phil Cunningham (guitar), Julian Phillips (bass) and Murad Mousa (drums).

| DATE | POS | WKS | BPI | ALBUM TITLE | LABEL & NUMBER |
|---|---|---|---|---|---|
| 17/02/1996 | 10 | 2 | | THIS WORLD AND BODY | London 8286952 |

### YANNIS MARKOPOULOS
Greek male orchestra leader and composer. His debut hit album featured the theme and incidental music from the TV series of the same name.

| DATE | POS | WKS | BPI | ALBUM TITLE | LABEL & NUMBER |
|---|---|---|---|---|---|
| 26/08/1978 | 22 | 8 | | WHO PAYS THE FERRYMAN | BBC REB 315 |

### MARKY MARK AND THE FUNKY BUNCH
US singer (born Mark Wahlberg, 5/6/1971, Boston, MA) and younger brother of New Kid On The Block Donnie Wahlberg. The Funky Bunch are led by DJ Terry Yancey. Mark Wahlberg later became an actor, appearing in *Boogie Nights* (1998) and the remake of *Planet Of The Apes* (2001).

| DATE | POS | WKS | BPI | ALBUM TITLE | LABEL & NUMBER |
|---|---|---|---|---|---|
| 05/10/1991 | 61 | 1 | | MUSIC FOR THE PEOPLE | Interscope 7567917371 |

○ Silver disc  ● Gold disc  ✪ Platinum disc (additional platinum units are indicated by a figure following the symbol)  ❶⁹ Number of weeks album topped the UK chart

### BOB MARLEY AND THE WAILERS
Jamaican singer (born 6/2/1945, St Ann's, although his passport had date of birth as 6/4/1945) who first recorded in 1961. He formed the Wailin' Wailers in 1964 with Peter Tosh (born Winston McIntosh, 19/10/1944, Westmoreland), Bunny Livingston (born Neville O'Riley, 10/4/1947, Kingston, who changed his name again to Bunny Wailer), Junior Braithwaite, Cherry Smith and Beverley Kelso. Marley left Jamaica in 1966, returning in 1967 to set up the Wailin' Soul label, reuniting with Tosh and Wailer. He signed with Island in 1972, adding Aston 'Family Man' Barrett and his brother Carlton to the rhythm section. Tosh and Wailer left in 1974. Eric Clapton's cover of *I Shot The Sheriff* attracted attention to Marley, who became reggae's biggest star. He survived an assassination attempt in December 1976 (although he, his wife Rita and manager Don Taylor all suffered gunshot wounds, prompting Marley to leave Jamaica for eighteen months) but died from cancer on 11/5/1981. Pete Tosh was shot to death during a robbery at his home on 11/9/1987. (Tosh laughed as three men broke into his house, for which he was viciously beaten. When the intruders found insufficient valuables in the house, they shot three people through the back of the head, including Tosh. It was later suggested that the robbery was carried out merely to cover up a feud.) Carlton Barrett was shot to death on 17/4/1987 by a gunman hired by his wife and her lover. Junior Braithwaite was shot and killed by intruders in his home in 1999. Bob Marley was inducted into the Rock & Roll Hall of Fame in 1994. Pete Tosh won the 1987 Grammy Award for Best Reggae Recording for *No Nuclear War*. Bunny Wailer won the 1990 award for *Time Will Tell – A Tribute To Bob Marley*, the 1994 award for *Crucial Roots Classics* and the 1996 award for *Hall Of Fame – A Tribute To Bob Marley's 50th Anniversary*, all in the same category. Bob Marley has a star on the Hollywood Walk of Fame.

| DATE | POS | WKS | BPI | ALBUM TITLE | LABEL & NUMBER |
|---|---|---|---|---|---|
| 04/10/1975 | 43 | 5 | ● | NATTY DREAD | Island ILPS 9281 |
| 20/12/1975 | 38 | 5 | ○ | LIVE | Island ILPS 9376 |
| 08/05/1976 | 15 | 13 | ● | RASTAMAN VIBRATION | Island ILPS 9383 |
| 11/06/1977 | 8 | 56 | ● | **EXODUS** | Island ILPS 9498 |
| 01/04/1978 | 4 | 24 | ● | **KAYA** | Island ILPS 9517 |
| 16/12/1978 | 40 | 11 | | BABYLON BY BUS | Island ISLD 11 |
| 13/10/1979 | 20 | 6 | | SURVIVAL | Island ILPS 9542 |
| 28/06/1980 | 6 | 17 | | UPRISING | Island ILPS 9596 |
| 25/07/1981 | 68 | 6 | | LIVE AT THE LYCEUM This is the same album as Island ILPS 9376 under a different title | Island ILPS 9376 |
| 28/05/1983 | 5 | 19 | | **CONFRONTATION** | Island ILPS 9760 |
| 19/05/1984 | ❶[12] | 330 | ✪[6] | **LEGEND – THE BEST OF BOB MARLEY AND THE WAILERS** ◆[10] | Island/Tuff Gong BMWX 1 |
| 28/06/1986 | 54 | 3 | | REBEL MUSIC | Island ILPS 9843 |
| 03/10/1992 | 10 | 5 | ○ | **SONGS OF FREEDOM** BOB MARLEY | Tuff Gong TGCBX 1 |
| 03/06/1995 | 5 | 8 | ● | **NATURAL MYSTIC** ◇ | Tuff Gong BMWCD 2 |
| 04/09/1999 | 40 | 3 | | THE SUN IS SHINING BOB MARLEY VS FUNKSTAR DELUXE This was an import single that was ineligible for the singles chart | Club Tools 0066735 CLU |
| 02/06/2001 | 5 | 15 | ● | **ONE LOVE – THE VERY BEST OF** ◇ | Tuff Gong BMWCD 3 |
| 07/07/2001 | 75 | 1 | | LIVELY UP YOURSELF BOB MARLEY | Music Collection 12691 |
| 10/11/2001 | 24 | 8 | | ONE LOVE | Tuff Gong 5865512 |
| 05/06/2004 | 51 | 2 | | ROOTS OF A LEGEND | Trojan TJODX 176 |

### LENE MARLIN
Norwegian singer/songwriter (born Lene Marlin Pederson, 17/8/1980, Tromso) who began playing guitar at the age of fifteen. She was named Best Nordic Act at the 1999 MTV Europe Music Awards.

| DATE | POS | WKS | BPI | ALBUM TITLE | LABEL & NUMBER |
|---|---|---|---|---|---|
| 25/03/2000 | 18 | 34 | ✪ | PLAYING MY GAME ◇ | Virgin CDVIR 83 |

### MAROON 5
US group formed in Los Angeles, CA in 1999 by Adam Levine (guitar/vocals), James Valentine (guitar), Jesse Carmichael (keyboards), Mickey Madden (bass) and Ryan Dusick (drums).

| DATE | POS | WKS | BPI | ALBUM TITLE | LABEL & NUMBER |
|---|---|---|---|---|---|
| 31/01/2004 | 2 | 19+ | ✪ | **SONGS ABOUT JANE** | J Records 82876584302 |

### NEVILLE MARRINER AND THE ACADEMY OF ST MARTIN IN THE FIELDS
UK conductor with the chamber orchestra of St Martin In The Fields. Marriner and the academy won two Grammy Awards including Best Classical Performance, Choral (other than opera) for *Haydn: The Creation* in 1981.

| DATE | POS | WKS | BPI | ALBUM TITLE | LABEL & NUMBER |
|---|---|---|---|---|---|
| 06/04/1985 | 64 | 6 | | AMADEUS Original soundtrack to the film. 1984 Grammy Award for Best Classical Album | London LONDP 6 |

### MARS VOLTA
US group formed in El Paso, TX in 2001 by Cedric 'Bixler' Zavala (vocals), Omar Rodriguez-Lopez (guitar), Juan Alderate (bass), Isaiah Owens (keyboards) and Jon Theodore (drums). Bixler and Rodriguez had previously been in At The Drive In.

| DATE | POS | WKS | BPI | ALBUM TITLE | LABEL & NUMBER |
|---|---|---|---|---|---|
| 05/07/2003 | 43 | 1 | | DE-LOUSED IN THE COMATORIUM | Universal 9860460 |

### BERNIE MARSDEN
UK singer/guitarist who was at various times a member of Babe Ruth, UFO and Whitesnake and launched a parallel solo career in the early 1980s. His album also featured contributions from Don Airey (keyboards), Neil Murray and Jack Bruce (bass) and Ian Paice, Cozy Powell and Simon Phillips (drums). He later formed SOS that evolved into Alaska.

| DATE | POS | WKS | BPI | ALBUM TITLE | LABEL & NUMBER |
|---|---|---|---|---|---|
| 05/09/1981 | 71 | 2 | | LOOK AT ME NOW | Parlophone PCF 7217 |

### KYM MARSH
UK singer (born 13/6/1976, Wiston) who is famous for winning a place in the group Hear'say on the TV show *Popstars*. She had previously sung with Solar Stone and left Hear'Say in January 2002 for a solo career.

| DATE | POS | WKS | BPI | ALBUM TITLE | LABEL & NUMBER |
|---|---|---|---|---|---|
| 02/08/2003 | 9 | 3 | | **STANDING TALL** | Universal 9800035 |

### AMANDA MARSHALL
Canadian singer/songwriter (born 1972, Toronto); she enrolled at the Toronto Royal Conservatory of Music to study classical music then developed an interest in jazz. She later had a spell opening for the Jeff Healey Band before releasing her debut album in 1996.

| DATE | POS | WKS | BPI | ALBUM TITLE | LABEL & NUMBER |
|---|---|---|---|---|---|
| 03/08/1996 | 47 | 2 | | AMANDA MARSHALL | Epic 4837912 |

▲[9] Number of weeks album topped the US chart　◆[12] RIAA Diamond Awards　◇[3] IFPI Platinum Europe Awards

### LENA MARTELL
UK singer (born Helen Thomson, Glasgow) who was in Billy McGregor's band before going solo. Her records were produced by manager George Elrick. Despite six hit albums, she registered only one hit single, the #1 *One Day At A Time*.

| | | | | |
|---|---|---|---|---|
| 25/05/1974 | 35 | 2 | | THAT WONDERFUL SOUND OF LENA MARTELL | Pye SPL 18427 |
| 08/01/1977 | 13 | 16 | ● | THE BEST OF LENA MARTELL | Pye NSPL 18506 |
| 27/05/1978 | 12 | 19 | ● | THE LENA MARTELL COLLECTION | Ronco RTL 2028 |
| 20/10/1979 | 5 | 18 | ✪ | **LENA'S MUSIC ALBUM** | Pye N 123 |
| 19/04/1980 | 9 | 9 | ● | **BY REQUEST** | Ronco RTL 2046 |
| 29/11/1980 | 23 | 7 | ● | BEAUTIFUL SUNDAY | Ronco RTL 2052 |

### MARTHA AND THE MUFFINS
Canadian group formed by Martha Johnson (keyboards), Carl Finkle (bass), Mark Gane (guitar), Tim Gane (drums), Andy Haas (saxophone) and Martha Ladly (guitar/keyboards/trombone). They disbanded in 1982, Johnson and Gane re-forming as M+M in 1984.

| | | | | |
|---|---|---|---|---|
| 15/03/1980 | 34 | 6 | | METRO MUSIC | Dindisc DID 1 |

### MARTIKA
US singer (born Marta Marrera, 18/5/1969, Whittier, CA) with Cuban parents; as a child she was in the musical *Annie* and vaious TV shows.

| | | | | |
|---|---|---|---|---|
| 16/09/1989 | 11 | 37 | ✪ | MARTIKA | CBS 4633551 |
| 07/09/1991 | 15 | 15 | ● | MARTIKA'S KITCHEN | Columbia 4671891 |

### BILLIE RAY MARTIN
German singer (born Birgit Dieckmann, Hamburg); she came to the UK in 1985 and was lead vocalist with Electribe 101 before going solo.

| | | | | |
|---|---|---|---|---|
| 03/02/1996 | 47 | 2 | | DEADLINE FOR MY MEMORIES | Magnet 0630121802 |

### DEAN MARTIN
US singer/actor (born Dino Paul Crocetti, 7/6/1917, Steubenville, OH) who moved to California in 1937, singing in local clubs. Teamed with comedian Jerry Lewis in 1946, they made sixteen films together, by which time Martin was established as a star in his own right. He was one of the first artists on Frank Sinatra's Reprise label (as befitted one of the infamous 'Ratpack', a hard-living and hard-drinking group comprising Sinatra, Martin, Sammy Davis Jr and Peter Crawford). He died from cancer on 25/12/1995. He has three stars on the Hollywood Walk of Fame, for his contribution to recording, motion pictures and TV.

| | | | | |
|---|---|---|---|---|
| 13/05/1961 | 18 | 1 | | THIS TIME I'M SWINGING | Capitol T 1442 |
| 25/02/1967 | 35 | 1 | | AT EASE WITH DEAN | Reprise RSLP 6322 |
| 04/11/1967 | 39 | 1 | | WELCOME TO MY WORLD | Philips DBL 001 |
| 12/10/1968 | 40 | 1 | | DEAN MARTIN'S GREATEST HITS VOLUME I | Reprise RSLP 6301 |
| 22/02/1969 | 9 | 8 | | **GENTLE ON MY MIND** | Reprise RSLP 6330 |
| 22/02/1969 | 9 | 1 | | **THE BEST OF DEAN MARTIN** | Capitol ST 21194 |
| 27/11/1971 | 45 | 1 | | WHITE CHRISTMAS **NAT 'KING' COLE AND DEAN MARTIN** | MFP 5224 |
| 13/11/1976 | 7 | 11 | ● | **20 ORIGINAL DEAN MARTIN HITS** | Reprise K 54066 |
| 05/06/1999 | 5 | 29 | ✪ | **THE VERY BEST OF DEAN MARTIN – THE CAPITOL & REPRISE YEARS** | EMI 4967212 |
| 26/08/2000 | 40 | 2 | | THE VERY BEST OF VOLUME 2 | Capitol 5277712 |
| 16/02/2002 | 24 | 3 | ○ | LOVE SONGS | Capitol 5377482 |
| 10/01/2004 | 59 | 2 | | VERY BEST OF | EMI 5920802 |

### GEORGE MARTIN
UK producer (born 3/1/1926, London) who trained at the Guildhall School of Music and joined EMI in 1950 as a junior A&R man. In 1955 he became head of Parlophone, a label that at the time had Shirley Bassey, Matt Monro, The Vipers, Temperance 7 and various comedy acts on their books. It was the latter category that was to provide him with his biggest hits in the late 1950s and early 1960s, with Peter Sellers registering three hits (the biggest of which was *Goodness Gracious Me* with Sophia Loren), Charlie Drake four (including *Splish Splash*) and Bernard Cribbins two (*Right Said Fred* and *Hole In The Ground*). In May 1962 he signed The Beatles to the label, although he had not been entirely impressed by their audition; and one of his first moves was to suggest the replacement of drummer Pete Best, who Martin felt was was little more than competent on his instrument. Over the next eight years Martin was to become almost a fifth Beatle, making sense of the group's grand recording plans and making them happen in the studio. Having been pivotal in the international success enjoyed by The Beatles (and other artists George signed to Parlophone in their wake, including Billy J Kramer, Cilla Black, Cliff Bennett & The Rebel Rousers, The Cougars, The Hollies, The Fourmost, The Paramounts and Simon Scott), he left EMI in 1965 to set up his own AIR London studio with Ron Richards and John Burgess, although he was still a regular visitor to Abbey Road Studios as The Beatles wouldn't record anywhere else. He also undertook projects for acts away from Parlophone, including America, Gerry & The Pacemakers, Jeff Beck and Stackridge. A second AIR studio was opened on the Caribbean island of Montserrat and soon became a preferred choice for many an act, including Paul McCartney, The Rolling Stones and Dire Straits, before the island was hit by a hurricane in 1989. He was knighted in 1996 and inducted into the Rock & Roll Hall of Fame in 1999. He won the 1973 Grammy Award for Best Arrangement Accompanying Singers for Paul McCartney's *Live And Let Die* and was given a NARAS Trustee Award in 1995. The Beatles' *Yellow Submarine* album was largely performed by The George Martin Orchestra.

| | | | | |
|---|---|---|---|---|
| 04/04/1998 | 5 | 13 | ● | **IN MY LIFE** Features contributions from Jim Carrey, Phil Collins, Celine Dion and Robbie Williams | Echo ECHCD 020 |

## JUAN MARTIN WITH THE ROYAL PHILHARMONIC ORCHESTRA
Spanish classical guitarist with the Royal Philharmonic Orchestra.

| 11/02/1984 | 21 | 9 | | SERENADE | K-Tel NE 1267 |

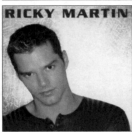

## RICKY MARTIN
Puerto Rican singer (born Enrique Martin Morales, 24/12/1971, Hato Rey) who was in the boy group Menudo before becoming an actor on Mexican TV and working on Broadway in *Les Miserables*. He was named Best Male at the 2000 MTV Europe Music Awards.

| 12/06/1999 | 2 | 48 | ✪ | RICKY MARTIN ◇² ▲¹ | Columbia 4944060 |
| 18/11/2000 | 14 | 21 | ✪ | SOUND LOADED ◇ | Columbia 4977692 |
| 01/12/2001 | 42 | 6 | ● | THE BEST OF | Columbia 5050192 |

## JOHN MARTYN
UK singer/guitarist (born Iain McGeachy, 11/9/1948, Glasgow) who was trained as a teenager by folk artist Hamish Imlach and was signed by Island Records in 1968, the first white solo artist on the label. His first two albums (released within ten months) were well-received, as were his next two, recorded with his new wife Beverly Kutner as John And Beverly Martyn. Despite critical acclaim commercial success eluded him and his *Live At Leeds* album released in 1975 was initially only available via mail order from Martyn at his Hastings home (he and his wife personally signed each copy ordered), although it was later issued by Island. He remained with Island until 1981 when he switched to WEA/Geffen for two albums and then released another DIY album, *Philentrophy* before returning to Island. He has since recorded for Permanent, Go Discs and Independiente.

| 04/02/1978 | 54 | 1 | | ONE WORLD | Island ILPS 9492 |
| 01/11/1980 | 54 | 2 | | GRACE AND DANGER | Island ILPS 9560 |
| 26/09/1981 | 25 | 7 | | GLORIOUS FOOL | Geffen K 99178 |
| 04/09/1982 | 20 | 7 | | WELL KEPT SECRET | WEA K 99255 |
| 17/11/1984 | 57 | 2 | | SAPPHIRE | Island ILPS 9779 |
| 08/03/1986 | 28 | 4 | | PIECE BY PIECE | Island ILPS 9807 |
| 10/10/1992 | 65 | 2 | | COULDN'T LOVE YOU MORE | Permanent PERMCD 9 |
| 10/08/1996 | 32 | 3 | | AND. | Go Discs 8287982 |
| 04/04/1998 | 51 | 1 | | THE CHURCH WITH ONE BELL | Independiente ISOM 3CD |
| 03/06/2000 | 66 | 1 | | GLASGOW WALKER | Independiente ISOM 15CD |

## HANK MARVIN
UK singer/guitarist (born Brian Rankin, 28/10/1941, Newcastle-upon-Tyne) who was co-founder of Cliff Richard 's backing group the Drifters, later renamed the Shadows. He went solo when they split in 1968.

| 22/11/1969 | 14 | 2 | | HANK MARVIN | Columbia SCX 6352 |
| 03/04/1971 | 30 | 4 | | MARVIN, WELCH AND FARRAR **HANK MARVIN, BRUCE WELCH AND JOHN FARRAR** | Regal Zonophone SRZA 8502 |
| 20/03/1982 | 66 | 3 | | WORDS AND MUSIC | Polydor POLD 5054 |
| 31/10/1992 | 18 | 10 | ● | INTO THE LIGHT | Polydor 5171482 |
| 20/11/1993 | 17 | 9 | ● | HEARTBEAT | Polygram TV 5213222 |
| 22/10/1994 | 19 | 11 | ● | THE BEST OF HANK MARVIN AND THE SHADOWS **HANK MARVIN AND THE SHADOWS** | Polygram TV 5238212 |
| 18/11/1995 | 33 | 7 | ● | HANK PLAYS CLIFF | Polygram TV 5294262 |
| 23/11/1996 | 34 | 7 | ● | HANK PLAYS HOLLY | Polygram TV 5337132 |
| 05/04/1997 | 71 | 1 | | HANKS PLAYS LIVE | Polygram TV 5374282 |
| 22/11/1997 | 41 | 6 | ○ | PLAY ANDREW LLOYD WEBBER AND TIM RICE | Polygram TV 5394792 |
| 14/11/1998 | 56 | 5 | ○ | VERY BEST OF HANK MARVIN AND THE SHADOWS – THE FIRST 40 YEARS This and the above hit credited to **HANK MARVIN AND THE SHADOWS** | Polygram TV 5592112 |
| 15/04/2000 | 17 | 5 | | MARVIN AT THE MOVIES | Universal TV 1570572 |
| 20/04/2002 | 10 | 6 | | **GUITAR PLAYER** | Universal TV 0171242 |

## RICHARD MARX
US singer/songwriter (born 16/9/1963, Chicago, IL) who was a jingle writer before joining Lionel Richie's group as a backing singer. He went solo in 1987 and married Cynthia Rhodes of Animotion in August 1989. He won the 2003 Grammy Award for Song of the Year for *Dance With My Father* with co-writer Luther Vandross.

| 09/04/1988 | 68 | 2 | | RICHARD MARX | Manhattan MTL 1017 |
| 20/05/1989 | 8 | 12 | ● | **REPEAT OFFENDER ▲¹** | EMI-USA MTL 1043 |
| 16/11/1991 | 7 | 20 | ● | **RUSH STREET** | Capitol ESTU 2158 |

▲⁹ Number of weeks album topped the US chart ◆¹² RIAA Diamond Awards ◇³ IFPI Platinum Europe Awards

| | | | |
|---|---|---|---|
| 19/02/1994.....11......5...... | PAID VACATION ................................................................ | Capitol CDESTU 2208 |
| 21/02/1998.....34......3...... | GREATEST HITS................................................................. | Capitol 8219142 |

**MARXMAN** UK left-wing political rap group formed by MC Hollis, Big Shouts and Phrase with musician Oisin 'Ollie' Lunny. Their debut single *Sad Affair* was banned by the BBC for being sympathetic to the IRA.

03/04/1993.....69......1......    33 REVOLUTIONS PER MINUTE ............................................... Talkin Loud 5145382

**MARY JANE GIRLS** US vocal group formed in 1983 by Joanne 'Jo-Jo' McDuffie, Candice 'Candi' Ghant, Kim 'Maxi' Wuletich and Cherri Wells. Wells was later replaced by Yvette 'Corvette' Marina.

28/05/1983.....51......9......    MARY JANES GIRLS ......................................................... Gordy STML 12189

**JOHN MASON** UK male fiddler and conductor (born in Troon, Ayrshire) who helped form the Scottish Fiddle Orchestra in 1980 and is currently its Director General. Also a qualified lawyer, he was awarded an MBE in 1987.

27/12/1975.....50......1......    STRINGS OF SCOTLAND ................................................... Philips 6382 108

**MASE** US rapper (born Mason Betha, 24/3/1970, Jacksonville, FL) who was discovered by Puff Daddy. He appeared on tracks by various other artists in the Puff Daddy stable before launching his own solo career in 1997. He later recorded with Puff Daddy, The Notorious B.I.G., Total, Brandy, BLACKstreet and Mya.

| | | |
|---|---|---|
| 24/01/1998.....53......7...... | HARLEM WORLD ▲² ....................................................... | Puff Daddy 8612730172 |
| 24/07/1999.....47......2...... | DOUBLE UP ............................................................... | Puff Daddy 74321674332 |

**MASSED WELSH CHOIRS** UK male-voice choir.

09/08/1969 .....5......7......    **CYMANSA GANN**........................................................ BBC REC 53M

**MASSIVE ATTACK** UK R&B group formed in Bristol in 1987 by 3-D (born Robert Del Naja, 21/1/1965, Brighton, vocals), Mushroom (born Andrew Vowles, 10/11/1967, Bristol, keyboards) and Daddy G (born Grant Marshall, 18/12/1959, Bristol, keyboards); they were all previously in the Wild Bunch. They were named Best Dance Act at the 1996 BRIT Awards. Mushroom left the group in September 1999.

| | | |
|---|---|---|
| 20/04/1991.....13......84......✪² | BLUE LINES ............................................................. | Wild Bunch WBRCD 1 |
| 08/10/1994 .....4......78......✪ | **PROTECTION/NO PROTECTION** *No Protection* is a remix album that was listed with *Protection* from 4/3/1995. | Wild Bunch WBRCD 2 |
| 02/05/1998.....●²......54......✪ | MEZZANINE ◇ .......................................................... | Circa WBRCDX 4 |
| 22/02/2003.....●¹......6......● | **100TH WINDOW** ....................................................... | Virgin CDV 2967 |

**MASTERMIXERS** — see JIVE BUNNY AND THE MASTERMIXERS

**MATCHBOX** UK rock 'n' roll revival group formed in 1971 by Fred Poke (bass), Jimmy Redhead, Steve Bloomfield (guitar), Wiffle Smith (vocals), Rusty Lipton (piano) and Bob Burgos (drums). Redhead left after their 1973 debut single, returning in 1979, when Graham Fenton (vocals) also joined. Dick Callan replaced Bloomfield for live appearances from 1980 onwards.

| | | |
|---|---|---|
| 02/02/1980.....44......5...... | MATCHBOX .............................................................. | Magnet MAG 5031 |
| 11/10/1980.....23......9......○ | MIDNITE DYNAMOS....................................................... | Magnet MAG 5036 |

**MATCHBOX 20** US group with Rob Thomas (born 14/2/1972, vocals), Kyle Cook (born 29/8/1975, guitar/vocals), Adam Gaynor (born 26/11/1963, guitar/vocals), Brian Yale (born 14/11/1968, bass) and Paul Doucette (born 22/8/1972, drums). Thomas was later in Santana and won three Grammy Awards in 1999 – Song Of The Year, Record Of The Year and Best Pop Collaboration with Vocals, all for *Smooth*.

| | | |
|---|---|---|
| 25/04/1998.....50......1......○ | YOURSELF OR SOMEONE LIKE YOU ◆¹² ...................................... | Atlantic 7567927212 |
| 03/06/2000.....31......2......○ | MAD SEASON BY MATCHBOX 20 ........................................... | Atlantic 7567833392 |
| 08/03/2003.....31......2...... | MORE THAN YOU THINK YOU ARE.......................................... | Atlantic ATL 836122 |

**MIREILLE MATHIEU** French singer (born 22/7/1946, Avignon) discovered by Johnny Stark who made her first recordings for Barclay in 1965. She has since proved to be one of France's biggest stars and appeared in the 1973 film *La Bonne Annee*.

02/03/1968.....39......1......    MIREILLE MATHIEU ...................................................... Columbia SCX 6210

## JOHNNY MATHIS

US singer (born John Royce Mathis, 30/9/1935, San Francisco, CA) who was a promising athlete at school, taking part in trials for the US Olympic team at the high jump. He was discovered by George Avakian and initially recorded jazz-style records in 1956, switching to pop ballads at the suggestion of Mitch Miller. In the early 1980s he worked with Chic's producers Nile Rodgers and Bernard Edwards, although nothing was ever released. He has a star on the Hollywood Walk of Fame.

| DATE | POS | WKS | BPI | ALBUM TITLE | LABEL & NUMBER |
|------|-----|-----|-----|-------------|----------------|
| 08/11/1958 | 6 | 2 | | WARM | Fontana TBA TFL 5015 |
| 24/01/1959 | 10 | 1 | | SWING SOFTLY | Fontana TBA TFL 5039 |
| 13/02/1960 | 10 | 2 | | RIDE ON A RAINBOW | Fontana TFL 5061 |
| 10/12/1960 | 6 | 10 | | RHYTHMS AND BALLADS OF BROADWAY | Fontana SET 101 |
| 17/06/1961 | 18 | 1 | | I'LL BUY YOU A STAR | Fontana TFL 5143 |
| 16/05/1970 | 23 | 10 | | RAINDROPS KEEP FALLING ON MY HEAD | CBS 63587 |
| 03/04/1971 | 27 | 5 | | LOVE STORY | CBS 64334 |
| 09/09/1972 | 40 | 3 | | FIRST TIME EVER I SAW YOUR FACE | CBS 64930 |
| 16/12/1972 | 49 | 1 | | MAKE IT EASY ON YOURSELF | CBS 65161 |
| 08/03/1975 | 18 | 11 | O | I'M COMING HOME | CBS 65690 |
| 05/04/1975 | 39 | 2 | | THE HEART OF A WOMAN | CBS 80533 |
| 26/07/1975 | 13 | 10 | O | WHEN WILL I SEE YOU AGAIN | CBS 80738 |
| 03/07/1976 | 14 | 12 | ● | I ONLY HAVE EYES FOR YOU | CBS 81329 |
| 19/02/1977 | 31 | 5 | | GREATEST HITS VOLUME IV | CBS 86022 |
| 18/06/1977 | ❶⁴ | 40 | ✪ | THE JOHNNY MATHIS COLLECTION | CBS 10003 |
| 17/12/1977 | 55 | 1 | O | SWEET SURRENDER | CBS 86036 |
| 29/04/1978 | 3 | 19 | ● | YOU LIGHT UP MY LIFE | CBS 86055 |
| 26/08/1978 | 16 | 11 | ● | THAT'S WHAT FRIENDS ARE FOR JOHNNY MATHIS AND DENIECE WILLIAMS | CBS 86068 |
| 07/04/1979 | 38 | 5 | | THE BEST DAYS OF MY LIFE | CBS 86080 |
| 03/11/1979 | 59 | 4 | O | MATHIS MAGIC | CBS 86103 |
| 08/03/1980 | ❶² | 15 | ● | TEARS AND LAUGHTER | CBS 10019 |
| 12/07/1980 | 20 | 8 | | ALL FOR YOU | CBS 86115 |
| 19/09/1981 | 9 | 16 | ● | CELEBRATION | CBS 10028 |
| 15/05/1982 | 34 | 7 | | FRIENDS IN LOVE | CBS 85652 |
| 17/09/1983 | 5 | 16 | ● | UNFORGETTABLE: A MUSICAL TRIBUTE TO NAT KING COLE JOHNNY MATHIS AND NATALIE COLE | CBS 10042 |
| 15/09/1984 | 45 | 3 | | A SPECIAL PART OF ME | CBS 25475 |
| 13/12/1986 | 46 | 8 | O | THE HOLLYWOOD MUSICALS JOHNNY MATHIS AND HENRY MANCINI | CBS 4502581 |

## MATT BIANCO

UK pop group formed by Mark Reilly (born 20/2/1960, High Wycombe, vocals), Basia (born Basha Trzetrzelewska, 30/9/1954, Jaworzno, Poland, vocals) and Danny White (born 26/8/1959, High Wycombe, keyboards). Reilly and White are both ex-Blue Rondo A La Turk. Basia later went solo.

| DATE | POS | WKS | BPI | ALBUM TITLE | LABEL & NUMBER |
|------|-----|-----|-----|-------------|----------------|
| 08/09/1984 | 35 | 39 | ● | WHOSE SIDE ARE YOU ON | WEA WX 7 |
| 22/03/1986 | 26 | 13 | O | MATT BIANCO | WEA WX 35 |
| 09/07/1988 | 23 | 13 | ● | INDIGO | WEA WX 181 |
| 03/11/1990 | 49 | 2 | | THE BEST OF MATT BIANCO | East West WX 376 |

## KATHY MATTEA

US singer (born 21/6/1959, Cross Lane, WV); she sang with a bluegrass group before moving to Nashville where she initially worked as a tour guide at the Country Music Hall of Fame. Working as a session singer on numerous jingles, she joined Bobby Goldsboro's touring group before signing with Mercury. She was named Female Singer of the Year in 1989 and 1990 by the Country Music Association.

| DATE | POS | WKS | BPI | ALBUM TITLE | LABEL & NUMBER |
|------|-----|-----|-----|-------------|----------------|
| 15/04/1995 | 61 | 1 | | READY FOR THE STORM (FAVOURITE CUTS) | Mercury 5280062 |
| 08/02/1997 | 65 | 1 | | LOVE TRAVELS | Mercury 5328992 |

## CERYS MATTHEWS

UK singer (born 11/4/1969, Cardiff) who was lead vocalist with Catatonia. In September 2001 she returned from a rehabilitation unit and announced she was leaving the group to go solo, subsequently moving to the US.

| DATE | POS | WKS | BPI | ALBUM TITLE | LABEL & NUMBER |
|------|-----|-----|-----|-------------|----------------|
| 31/05/2003 | 30 | 5 | | COCKAHOOP | Blanco Y Negro 2564603062 |

## MATTHEWS' SOUTHERN COMFORT

UK singer/guitarist (born Ian Matthew McDonald, 16/6/1946, Scunthorpe) who was an apprentice footballer with Bradford City. Turning to music, he co-founded Fairport Convention, then Matthews' Southern Comfort in 1969 with Mark Griffiths (guitar), Carl Barnwell (guitar), Gordon Huntley (steel guitar), Andy Leigh (bass) and Ramon Duffy (drums).

| DATE | POS | WKS | BPI | ALBUM TITLE | LABEL & NUMBER |
|------|-----|-----|-----|-------------|----------------|
| 25/07/1970 | 52 | 4 | | SECOND SPRING | Uni UNLS 112 |

## MAVERICKS

US country group from Florida formed by Raul Malo (guitar/vocals), Robert Reynolds (bass) and Paul Deakin (drums), adding Nick Kane (guitar) in 1994. After a self-financed 1990 debut album, they were signed by MCA before they finished their audition. They won the 1995 Grammy Award for Best Country Performance by a Group for *Here Comes The Rain*. Reynolds married country singer Trisha Yearwood in 1995.

| DATE | POS | WKS | BPI | ALBUM TITLE | LABEL & NUMBER |
|------|-----|-----|-----|-------------|----------------|
| 11/05/1996 | 56 | 1 | O | MUSIC FOR ALL OCCASIONS | MCA MCD 11344 |
| 14/03/1998 | 10 | 48 | ✪ | TRAMPOLINE | MCA Nashville UMD 80456 |

▲⁹ Number of weeks album topped the US chart  ◆¹² RIAA Diamond Awards  ◇³ IFPI Platinum Europe Awards

04/12/1999.....40......9......●    THE BEST OF THE MAVERICKS ............................................. Mercury 1701202
04/10/2003.....65......2......    MAVERICKS ............................................. Sanctuary SANCD 192

**MAX Q** Australian duo Michael Hutchence (born 22/1/1962, Sydney) and Ollie Olsen. Hutchence was in INXS and Olsen in No at the time of their hit. Hutchence was found hanged in a Sydney hotel room on 22/11/1997, a suicide verdict later being returned, although it was speculated that he died after an autoerotic sex act went wrong. He had been working on a solo album with producer Andy Gill at the time.
04/11/1989.....69......1......    MAX Q ............................................. Mercury 8389421

**MAXWELL** US R&B singer (born Maxwell Menard, 23/5/1974, Brooklyn, NYC) with West Indian and Puerto Rican parents.
13/04/1996.....39.....10......●    URBAN SUITE ............................................. Columbia 4836992
26/07/1997.....45......2......    MTV UNPLUGGED (EP) ............................................. Columbia 4882922
04/07/1998.....11......6......    EMBRYA ............................................. Columbia 4894202
22/09/2001.....46......2......    NOW ▲1 ............................................. Columbia 4974542

**MAXX** UK/Swedish/German vocal/instrumental group formed by Dakota O'Neill, Dawhite, George Torpey and Gary Bokoe.
23/07/1994.....66......1......    TO THE MAXXIMUM ............................................. Pulse 8 PULSE 15CD

**BRIAN MAY** UK singer/guitarist (born 19/7/1947, Twickenham) who made his first guitar in 1963. He recorded with The Others, turning down a career in astronomy for music, before joining Queen in 1970. As well as his solo work he also co-wrote and co-produced the 1991 Comic Relief three-track charity CD *The Stonk*.
12/11/1983.....35......4......    STAR FLEET PROJECT **BRIAN MAY AND FRIENDS** ............................................. EMI SFLT 1078061
10/10/1992 .....6.....14......●    **BACK TO THE LIGHT** ............................................. Parlophone CDPCSD 123
19/02/1994.....20......3......    LIVE AT BRIXTON ACADEMY **BRIAN MAY BAND** ............................................. Parlophone CDPCSD 150
13/06/1998.....23......2......    ANOTHER WORLD ............................................. Parlophone 4949732

**SIMON MAY** UK orchestra leader/songwriter especially known for his TV themes, most notably *Howard's Way* and hits for Anita Dobson (based on the theme to *Eastenders*) and *Benny's Theme* for Paul Henry of *Crossroads*.
27/09/1986.....59......7......    SIMON'S WAY ............................................. BBC REB 594

**JOHN MAYALL** UK singer/multi-instrumentalist (born 29/11/1933, Macclesfield, Cheshire); he formed his first group Powerhouse in 1955, which disbanded when Mayall had to undertake National Service. He eventually moved to London and formed the Blues Syndicate, a group that evolved into the Bluesbreakers. Among the many musicians who have passed through its ranks are Jack Bruce, Eric Clapton, Mick Fleetwood, Hughie Flint, Andy Fraser, Peter Green, Keef Hartley, Henry Lowther, John McVie and Mick Taylor. Mayall is rightly regarded as one of the pioneers of the UK blues boom of the 1960s and 1970s. He recorded his debut album in 1965 and was a regular on the album charts on both sides of the Atlantic for the next ten years or so. He continued to record and tour throughout the next two decades and returned to the charts in 1993, with his debut album for Silvertone.

30/07/1966 .....6.....17......    **BLUES BREAKERS** ............................................. Decca LK 4804
04/03/1967.....10.....19......    **A HARD ROAD** This and the above hit credited to **JOHN MAYALL AND THE BLUESBREAKERS**. ............................................. Decca SKL 4853
23/09/1967 .....8.....14......    **CRUSADE** ............................................. Decca SKL 4890
25/11/1967.....24......5......    THE BLUES ALONE ............................................. Ace Of Clubs SCL 1243
16/03/1968.....27......9......    THE DIARY OF A BAND VOLUME 1 ............................................. Decca SKL 4918
16/03/1968.....28......5......    THE DIARY OF A BAND VOLUME 2 This and the above hit credited to **JOHN MAYALL AND THE BLUESBREAKERS**. ..... Decca SKL 4919
20/07/1968 .....3.....17......    **BARE WIRES** ............................................. Decca SKL 4945
18/01/1969.....33......3......    BLUES FROM LAUREL CANYON ............................................. Decca SKL 4972
23/08/1969.....14......7......    LOOKING BACK ............................................. Decca SKL 5010
15/11/1969.....11......7......    THE TURNING POINT ............................................. Polydor 583571
11/04/1970 .....9......8......    **EMPTY ROOMS** ............................................. Polydor 583580
12/12/1970.....50......1......    U.S.A. UNION ............................................. Polydor 2425 020
26/06/1971.....31......2......    BACK TO THE ROOTS ............................................. Polydor 2657 005
17/04/1993.....61......1......    WAKE UP CALL ............................................. Silvertone ORECD 527

**JOHN MAYER** US singer (born16/10/1977, Atlanta, GA) who attended Berklee College of Music before releasing his debut album in 1999.
25/10/2003.....74......1......    HEAVIER THINGS ............................................. Columbia 5134722

**CURTIS MAYFIELD** US singer (born 3/6/1942, Chicago, IL) who joined the Impressions in 1957, writing many of their hits, as well as hits for Jerry Butler and others. He formed the Curtom label in 1968 with Emanuel Thomas (they adopted the slogan 'We're A Winner' from the last Impressions single on ABC) and went solo in 1970, being replaced in the Impressions by Leroy Hutson. He scored and appeared in the films *Superfly* (1972), its follow-up *Superfly TNT* (1973) and *Short Eyes* (1976). On 13/8/1990 he was performing outdoors in Brooklyn, NYC when the wind blew a lighting rig on top of him, leaving him paralysed from the neck down. The accident also led to diabetes, resulting in his right leg being amputated in 1998. He died on 26/12/1999 as a result of the injuries received in 1990 (although he had recorded one further album in 1996). He was awarded the Lifetime Achievement Award Grammy in 1995 and was inducted into the Rock & Roll Hall of Fame in 1999.
31/03/1973.....26......2......    SUPERFLY ▲4 Original soundtrack to the film ............................................. Buddah 2318 065

| | | | | | |
|---|---|---|---|---|---|
| 15/02/1997 | 44 | 2 | | NEW WORLD ORDER | Warner Brothers 9362463482 |

### MAZE FEATURING FRANKIE BEVERLY
US group formed in Philadelphia, PA in 1971 by Frankie Beverly (born 6/12/1946, Philadelphia) as Raw Soul, changing their name when they moved to San Francisco, CA. The line-up at the time of their debut album was Beverly (vocals), Wayne Thomas (guitar), Sam Porter (keyboards), Philip Woo (keyboards), Wayne 'Ziggy' Lindsay (keyboards), Robin Duke (bass), Roame Lowery (congas/vocals), McKinley 'Bug' Williams (percussion/vocals) and Aguna G Sun (drums).

| | | | | | |
|---|---|---|---|---|---|
| 07/05/1983 | 38 | 6 | | WE ARE ONE | Capitol EST 12262 |
| 09/03/1985 | 41 | 12 | | CAN'T STOP THE LOVE | Capitol MAZE 1 |
| 27/09/1986 | 70 | 2 | | LIVE IN LOS ANGELES | Capitol ESTSP 24 |
| 16/09/1989 | 43 | 5 | | SILKY SOUL | Warner Brothers WX 301 |

### MAZZY STAR
US duo Hope Sandoval (vocals) and David Roback (guitar). Roback had previously been with Rain Parade and Sandoval with Going Home.

| | | | | | |
|---|---|---|---|---|---|
| 09/10/1993 | 68 | 1 | | SO TONIGHT THAT I MIGHT SEE | Capitol CDEST 2206 |
| 16/11/1996 | 57 | 1 | | AMONG MY SWAN | Capitol CDEST 2288 |

### MC TUNES
UK rapper from Manchester (born Nicky Lockett) who later formed the Dust Junkys.

| | | | | | |
|---|---|---|---|---|---|
| 13/10/1990 | 26 | 3 | | THE NORTH AT ITS HEIGHTS | ZTT 3 |

### VAUGHAN MEADER
US comedian (born 20/3/1936, Boston, MA); his debut hit album also featured contributions from Earl Doud, Bob Booker, Norma MacMillan and Naomi Brossart in a parody of the then US President John F Kennedy and his family.

| | | | | | |
|---|---|---|---|---|---|
| 29/12/1962 | 12 | 8 | | THE FIRST FAMILY ▲[12] 1962 Grammy Awards for Album of the Year and Best Comedy Performance | London HAA 8048 |

### MEAT LOAF
US singer (born Marvin Lee Aday, 27/9/1951, Dallas, TX) who formed Meat Loaf Soul in 1966 before appearing in the stage musical *Hair*. He linked with Cheryl Murphy to form Stoney & Meat Loaf, with a debut US hit on the Motown label Rare Earth. He first met Jim Steinman in 1974, Steinman later penning the classic *Bat Out Of Hell* album. He appeared in a number of films, including *Roadie* (1979) and *Americathon* (1979). He won the 1993 Grammy Award for Best Rock Vocal Performance for *I'd Do Anything For Love (But I Won't Do That)*.

| | | | | | |
|---|---|---|---|---|---|
| 11/03/1978 | 9 | 474 | ✪[7] | **BAT OUT OF HELL** ◆[14] | Epic EPC 82419 |
| 12/09/1981 | ❶[2] | 46 | ✪ | **DEAD RINGER** | Epic EPC 83645 |
| 07/05/1983 | 7 | 23 | ● | **MIDNIGHT AT THE LOST AND FOUND** | Epic EPC 25243 |
| 10/11/1984 | 8 | 16 | ● | **BAD ATTITUDE** | Arista 206 619 |
| 26/01/1985 | 2 | 80 | ✪ | **HITS OUT OF HELL** The album changed its catalogue number to 4504471 during its chart run | Epic EPC 26156 |
| 11/10/1986 | 28 | 6 | ○ | **BLIND BEFORE I STOP** | Arista 207 741 |
| 07/11/1987 | 60 | 2 | | **LIVE' AT WEMBLEY** | RCA 208599 |
| 25/11/1989 | 9 | 12 | ● | **HEAVEN AND HELL** MEAT LOAF/BONNIE TYLER The album subsequently charted on the compilation chart | Telstar STAR 2361 |
| 18/09/1993 | ❶[11] | 59 | ✪[6] | **BAT OUT OF HELL II – BACK INTO HELL** ▲[1] | Virgin CDV 2710 |
| 22/10/1994 | 33 | 4 | | **ALIVE IN HELL** | Pure Music PMCD 7002 |
| 11/11/1995 | 3 | 27 | ✪ | **WELCOME TO THE NEIGHBOURHOOD** ◇ | Virgin CDV 2799 |
| 14/11/1998 | 14 | 34 | ✪ | **THE VERY BEST OF MEAT LOAF** | Virgin/Sony TV CDV 2868 |
| 03/05/2003 | 4 | 14 | ● | **COULDN'T HAVE SAID IT BETTER** | Mercury 0761192 |

### GLENN MEDEIROS
US singer (born 24/6/1970, Hawaii) who received his first break winning a local radio talent contest. He later recorded with Bobby Brown and Ray Parker Jr.

| | | | | | |
|---|---|---|---|---|---|
| 08/10/1988 | 63 | 2 | | NOT ME | London LONLP 68 |

### MEDIAEVAL BAEBES
Multi-national vocal group formed in 1996 by Katharine Blake, Teresa Casella, Audrey Evans, Marie Findlay, Nicole Frobusch, Ruth Galloway, Karen Lupton, Claire Ravel, Cylindra Sapphire, Carmen Schneider, Nichole Sleet and Rachel Van Asch.

| | | | | | |
|---|---|---|---|---|---|
| 29/11/1997 | 62 | 6 | ○ | SALVA NOS | Venture CDVE 935 |
| 31/10/1998 | 73 | 1 | | WORLDES BLYSSE | Venture CDVE 941 |

### MEDICS – see DOCTOR AND THE MEDICS

### MEGA CITY FOUR
UK thrash pop group formed in 1982 by Wiz (Darren Brown, guitar/vocals), Danny Brown (guitar), Gerry Bryant (bass) and Chris Jones (drums) as Capricorn, changing their name to Mega City Four in 1986.

| | | | | | |
|---|---|---|---|---|---|
| 17/06/1989 | 67 | 1 | | TRANZOPHOBIA | Decoy DYL 3 |
| 07/03/1992 | 41 | 1 | | SEBASTAPOL ROAD | Big Life MEGCD 1 |
| 22/05/1993 | 57 | 1 | | MAGIC BULLETS | Big Life MEGCD 3 |

### MEGADETH
US heavy rock group formed in Los Angeles, CA in 1983 by Dave Mustaine (born 13/9/1963, La Mesa, CA, lead guitar/vocals), Dave Ellefson (born 12/11/1964, Jackson, MN, bass), Gar Samuelson (drums) and Chris Poland (guitar). Samuelson and Poland left in 1987 and were replaced by Jeff Young and Chuck Behler. Young and Behler were replaced in 1990 by Marty Friedman (born

---

▲[9] Number of weeks album topped the US chart   ◆[12] RIAA Diamond Awards   ◇[3] IFPI Platinum Europe Awards

8/12/1962, Washington DC, guitar) and Nick Menza (born 23/7/1964, Munich, Germany, drums). Menza left in 1984 and was replaced by Jimmy DeGrasso. Mustaine had previously been with Metallica.

| | | | | | |
|---|---|---|---|---|---|
| 26/03/1988 | 18 | 5 | | SO FAR, SO GOOD… SO WHAT! | Capitol EST 2053 |
| 06/10/1990 | 8 | 4 | O | **RUST IN PEACE** | Capitol EST 2132 |
| 18/07/1992 | 5 | 8 | O | **COUNTDOWN TO EXTINCTION** | Capitol CDESTU 2175 |
| 25/03/1995 | 6 | 5 | | **YOUTHANASIA/HIDDEN TREASURE** *Hidden Treasure* is a bonus album that was listed with *Youthanasia* from 25/3/1995. ......... Capitol CDEST 2244 |
| 19/07/1997 | 38 | 1 | | CRYPTIC WRITINGS | Capitol CDEST 2297 |
| 18/09/1999 | 29 | 2 | | RISK | Capitol 4991340 |
| 26/05/2001 | 45 | 1 | | THE WORLD NEEDS A HERO | Metal Is MISCD 006 |

## ZUBIN MEHTA
Indian conductor (born 29/4/1936, Bombay); he studied in Vienna and then won the Liverpool International Conductors' Competition in 1958. He has served with the Montreal Symphony Orchestra, Los Angeles Philharmonic Orchestra, the Israel Philharmonic Orchestra and the New York Philharmonic Orchestra.

| | | | | |
|---|---|---|---|---|
| 10/09/1994 | ●[1] | 26 | ✪[2] | **THE THREE TENORS IN CONCERT 1994 JOSE CARRERAS, PLACIDO DOMINGO AND LUCIANO PAVAROTTI WITH MEHTA** ............ Teldec 4509962002 |
| 23/12/2000 | 57 | 2 | | THE THREE TENORS CHRISTMAS **CARRERAS/DOMINGO/PAVAROTTI FEATURING MEHTA** ............... Sony Classical SK 89131 |

## MEL AND KIM
UK duo of sisters Mel (born 11/7/1967) and Kim Appleby (born in 1962). Both previously models, Mel died from spinal cancer on 18/1/1990 and Kim began a solo career.

| | | | | | |
|---|---|---|---|---|---|
| 25/04/1987 | 3 | 25 | ✪ | **F.L.M.** | Supreme SU 2 |

## MELANIE
US singer (born Melanie Safka, 3/2/1947, Long Island, NY) who recorded her debut single in 1967 and later formed the record company Neighbourhood Records with her husband Peter Schekeryk. She also recorded with The Edwin Hawkins Singers.

| | | | | |
|---|---|---|---|
| 19/09/1970 | 5 | 27 | **CANDLES IN THE RAIN** | Buddah 2318 009 |
| 16/01/1971 | 22 | 11 | LEFTOVER WINE | Buddah 2318 011 |
| 29/05/1971 | 9 | 9 | **THE GOOD BOOK** | Buddah 2322 001 |
| 08/01/1972 | 14 | 14 | GATHER ME | Buddah 2322 002 |
| 01/04/1972 | 19 | 6 | GARDEN IN THE CITY | Buddah 2318 054 |
| 07/10/1972 | 23 | 2 | THE FOUR SIDES OF MELANIE | Buddah 2659 013 |

## MELBOURNE SYMPHONY ORCHESTRA – see ELTON JOHN

## JOHN MELLENCAMP
US singer (born 7/10/1951, Seymour, IN) who made his album debut in 1976. He was named Johnny Cougar by David Bowie's manager Tony De Fries. He won the 1982 Grammy Award for Best Rock Vocal Performance for *Hurts So Good*.

| | | | | |
|---|---|---|---|---|
| 06/11/1982 | 37 | 6 | AMERICAN FOOL ▲[9] **JOHN COUGAR** | Riva RVLP 16 |
| 03/03/1984 | 92 | 1 | UH-HUH | Riva RIVL 1 |
| 03/10/1987 | 31 | 12 | THE LONESOME JUBILEE | Mercury MERH 109 |
| 27/05/1989 | 25 | 4 | BIG DADDY This and above two hits credited to **JOHN COUGAR MELLENCAMP** | Mercury MERH 8382201 |
| 19/10/1991 | 39 | 2 | WHENEVER WE WANTED | Mercury 5101511 |
| 18/09/1993 | 37 | 2 | HUMAN WHEELS | Mercury 5180882 |
| 17/01/1998 | 25 | 4 | THE BEST THAT I COULD DO 1978–1988 | Mercury 5367382 |

## KATIE MELUA
Georgian singer (born in 1984); she was raised in Northern Ireland and subsequently discovered by Mike Batt.

| | | | | |
|---|---|---|---|---|
| 15/11/2003 | ●[6] | 33+ | ✪[3] | **CALL OFF THE SEARCH** | Dramatico DRAMCD 0002 |

## MEMBERS
UK rock group formed in Camberley in 1977 by Jean-Marie Carroll (guitar), Gary Baker (guitar), Adrian Lillywhite (drums), Chris Payne (bass) and Nicky Tesco (vocals). Baker left in 1978 and was replaced by Nigel Bennett.

| | | | | |
|---|---|---|---|---|
| 28/04/1979 | 45 | 5 | AT THE CHELSEA NIGHTCLUB | Virgin V 2120 |

## MEMPHIS HORNS – see ROBERT CRAY BAND

O Silver disc ● Gold disc ✪ Platinum disc (additional platinum units are indicated by a figure following the symbol) ●[9] Number of weeks album topped the UK chart

## MEN AT WORK

MEN AT WORK Australian rock group formed in Melbourne in 1979 by Colin Hay (born 29/6/1953, Scotland, guitar/vocals), Ron Strykert (born 18/8/1957, guitar), Greg Ham (born 27/9/1953, saxophone/keyboards/flute), John Rees (bass) and Jerry Speiser (drums). Hay recorded solo in 1987 as Colin James Hay. The group was named Best New Artist at the 1982 Grammy Awards.

| | | | | | |
|---|---|---|---|---|---|
| 15/01/1983 | ❶⁵ | 44 | ✪ | BUSINESS AS USUAL ▲¹⁵ | Epic EPC 85669 |
| 30/04/1983 | 8 | 27 | ● | CARGO | Epic EPC 25372 |

MEN THEY COULDN'T HANG UK group formed by Cush (vocals), Paul Simmonds (guitar), Shanne (bass), Phil (guitar/vocals) and his brother John (drums). They first signed with Imp in 1984. They added Nick Muir in 1990, disbanding soon after. They re-formed in 1996 with the addition of Kenny Harris (drums).

| | | | | | |
|---|---|---|---|---|---|
| 27/07/1985 | 91 | 2 | | NIGHT OF A THOUSAND CANDLES | Imp FIEND 50 |
| 08/11/1986 | 68 | 2 | | HOW GREEN IS THE VALLEY | MCA MCF 3337 |
| 23/04/1988 | 41 | 2 | | WAITING FOR BONAPARTE | Magnet MAGL 5075 |
| 06/05/1989 | 39 | 2 | | SILVER TOWN | Silvertone ORELP 503 |
| 01/09/1990 | 53 | 1 | | THE DOMINO CLUB | Silvertone ORELP 512 |

MEN WITHOUT HATS Canadian techno-rock group formed in Montreal, Quebec by brothers Ivan (vocals), Stefan (guitar) and Colin Doroschuk (keyboards) and Allan McCarthy (drums).

| | | | | | |
|---|---|---|---|---|---|
| 12/11/1983 | 96 | 1 | | RHYTHM OF YOUTH | Statik STATLP 10 |

MENSWEAR UK rock group formed in 1994 by Johnny Dean (born 12/12/1971, Salisbury, vocals), Chris Gentry (born 23/2/1977, Southend, guitar), Stuart Black (born 1/4/1974, London, bass), Matt Everett (born 13/8/1972, Birmingham, drums) and Simon White (born 1/7/1977, Birmingham, guitar). They performed on *Top Of The Pops* before even releasing a single. Everett left in 1997 and was briefly replaced by Tud Tudgate, the group disbanding soon after.

| | | | | | |
|---|---|---|---|---|---|
| 21/10/1995 | 11 | 6 | | NUISANCE | Laurel 8286792 |

NATALIE MERCHANT US singer (born 26/10/1963, Jamestown, NY); she was lead singer with 10,000 Maniacs from 1981–1990 when she went solo, signing with Elektra in 1992 (who promptly dropped 10,000 Maniacs from their roster). Natalie assembled her own backing group, comprising Jennifer Turner (guitar), Barry Maguire (guitar and bass) and Peter Yanowitz (drums).

| | | | | | |
|---|---|---|---|---|---|
| 01/07/1995 | 39 | 2 | | TIGERLILY | Elektra 7559617452 |
| 13/06/1998 | 52 | 1 | | OPHELIA | Elektra 7559621962 |

FREDDIE MERCURY UK singer (born Farookh Bulsara, 5/9/1946, Zanzibar, Tanzania) who moved to the UK in 1959, joining Queen as lead vocalist in 1970 and releasing his first single (as Larry Lurex) in 1973, shortly before Queen had their debut release. He launched a parallel solo career in 1984. With Queen he won the Outstanding Contribution Award at the 1990 BRIT Awards. Following his death Queen's *Bohemian Rhapsody* was named Best British Single and Mercury was posthumously awarded the Outstanding Contribution Award at the 1992 BRIT Awards. Only John Lennon (solo in 1982 and 1983 as a Beatle) had previously been awarded two Outstanding Contribution Awards. Mercury died from AIDS on 24/11/1991.

| | | | | | |
|---|---|---|---|---|---|
| 11/05/1985 | 6 | 23 | ● | MR BAD GUY | CBS 86312 |
| 22/10/1988 | 15 | 8 | ○ | BARCELONA FREDDIE MERCURY AND MONTSERRAT CABALLÉ | Polydor POLH 44 |
| 28/11/1992 | 4 | 25 | ✪² | THE FREDDIE MERCURY ALBUM | Parlophone CDPCSD 124 |
| 04/11/2000 | 13 | 9 | ● | SOLO | Parlophone 5280472 |

MERCURY REV US rock group originally formed by David Baker (guitar/vocals), Jonathan Donahue (guitar), Grasshopper (real name Sean Mackowiak, guitar/clarinet), Suzanne Thorpe (flute), Dave Fridmann (bass) and Jimmy Chambers (drums).

| | | | | | |
|---|---|---|---|---|---|
| 12/06/1993 | 43 | 1 | | BOCES | Beggars Banquet BBQCD 140 |
| 17/10/1998 | 27 | 12 | ● | DESERTER'S SONG | V2 VVR 1002772 |
| 08/09/2001 | 11 | 4 | | ALL IS DREAM | V2 VVR 1017528 |

MERLE AND ROY UK vocal/instrumental duo Merle and Roy Griffiths.

| | | | | | |
|---|---|---|---|---|---|
| 26/09/1987 | 74 | 5 | | REQUESTS | Myndd Mawr RMBR 8713 |

MERSEYBEATS UK group formed in Liverpool in 1960 as the Mavericks, changing their name to the Pacifics and finally the Merseybeats in 1962. The charting line-up was John Banks, Tony Crane, Johnny Gustafson and Aaron Williams. They disbanded in 1966, with Crane and another ex-Merseybeat, Billy Kinsley, forming The Merseys.

| | | | | | |
|---|---|---|---|---|---|
| 20/06/1964 | 12 | 9 | | THE MERSEYBEATS | Fontana TL 5210 |

**METALLICA** US heavy metal group formed in Los Angeles, CA in 1981 by Lars Ulrich (born 26/12/1963, Copenhagen, Denmark, drums), James Hetfield (born 3/8/1963, Los Angeles, vocals), Dave Mustaine (born 13/9/1963, La Mesa, CA, guitar) and Ron McGovney (bass). McGovney left in 1982 and was replaced by Cliff Burton (born 10/2/1962). Mustaine left in 1983 to form Megadeth and was replaced by Kirk Hammett (born 18/11/1962, San Francisco, CA). Burton was killed on 27/9/1986 when the tour bus crashed in Sweden; he was replaced by Jason Newsted (born 4/3/1963). They have won seven Grammy Awards including: Best Metal Performance (Vocal or Instrumental) in 1989 for *One*; Best Metal Performance (Vocal or Instrumental) in 1990 for *Stone Cold Crazy*; Best Metal Performance in 1998 for *Better Than You*; Best Hard Rock Performance in 1999 for *Whiskey In The Jar*; Best Rock Instrumental Performance with Michael Kamen and the San Francisco Symphony Orchestra for *The Call Of The Ktulu*; and Best Metal Performance for *St Anger*.

| | | | | |
|---|---|---|---|---|
| 11/08/1984 . . . . . 87 . . . . . . 2 . . . . . ● | RIDE THE LIGHTNING . . . . . . . . . . . . . . . . . . . . . . . . . . . . . . . . . . . . . . . . . . . . . . . . . . . . . . . . . . . . . . . . . . . Music For Nations MFN 27 |
| 15/03/1986 . . . . . 41 . . . . . . 4 . . . . . ● | MASTER OF PUPPETS . . . . . . . . . . . . . . . . . . . . . . . . . . . . . . . . . . . . . . . . . . . . . . . . . . . . . . . . . . . . . . . . . . . Music For Nations MFN 60 |
| 17/09/1988 . . . . . 4 . . . . . . 6 . . . . . ○ | ... AND JUSTICE FOR ALL . . . . . . . . . . . . . . . . . . . . . . . . . . . . . . . . . . . . . . . . . . . . . . . . . . . . . . . . . . . . . . . . Vertigo VERH 61 |
| 19/05/1990 . . . . . 56 . . . . . . 1 . . . . . | THE GOOD THE BAD AND THE LIVE: THE 6 ½ YEARS ANNIVERSARY COLLECTION . . . . . . . . . . . . . . . . . . . . . . . Vertigo 8754871 |
| 24/08/1991 . . . . . ❶¹ . . . . 72 . . . . . ✪ | METALLICA ▲⁴ ◆¹³ 1991 Grammy Award for Best Metal Performance with Vocal . . . . . . . . . . . . . . . . . . Vertigo 5100221 |
| 11/12/1993 . . . . . 54 . . . . . . 1 . . . . . | LIVE SHIT – BINGE AND PURGE This is a box set containing two CDs, three videos and a book . . . . . . . . . . . . . . . . . Vertigo 5187250 |
| 15/06/1996 . . . . . ❶¹ . . . . 18 . . . . . ● | LOAD ◇² ▲⁴ . . . . . . . . . . . . . . . . . . . . . . . . . . . . . . . . . . . . . . . . . . . . . . . . . . . . . . . . . . . . . . . . . . . . . . . . Vertigo 5326182 |
| 05/10/1996 . . . . . 47 . . . . . . 1 . . . . . | HERO OF THE DAY . . . . . . . . . . . . . . . . . . . . . . . . . . . . . . . . . . . . . . . . . . . . . . . . . . . . . . . . . . . . . . . . . . . Vertigo METCY 13 |
| 29/11/1997 . . . . . 4 . . . . . . 9 . . . . . ● | RELOAD ◇ ▲¹ . . . . . . . . . . . . . . . . . . . . . . . . . . . . . . . . . . . . . . . . . . . . . . . . . . . . . . . . . . . . . . . . . . . . . . Vertigo 5364092 |
| 05/12/1998 . . . . . 29 . . . . . . 2 . . . . . | GARAGE INC. ◇ . . . . . . . . . . . . . . . . . . . . . . . . . . . . . . . . . . . . . . . . . . . . . . . . . . . . . . . . . . . . . . . . . . . . . Vertigo 5383512 |
| 04/12/1999 . . . . . 33 . . . . . . 2 . . . . . | S&M ◇² . . . . . . . . . . . . . . . . . . . . . . . . . . . . . . . . . . . . . . . . . . . . . . . . . . . . . . . . . . . . . . . . . . . . . . . . . Vertigo 5487972 |
| 14/06/2003 . . . . . 3 . . . . . 11 . . . . . ● | ST ANGER ◇ ▲¹ . . . . . . . . . . . . . . . . . . . . . . . . . . . . . . . . . . . . . . . . . . . . . . . . . . . . . . . . . . . . . . . . . . . . . Vertigo 9865403 |

**METEORS** UK group formed by Paul Fenech (guitar/vocals) and Nigel Lewis (double bass/vocals) as Rock Therapy. They added Mark Robertson (drums) in 1980 and became Raw Deal at the time they signed with Alligator Records. They changed their name again to The Meteors. By 1982 only Fenech remained from the original line-up, adding Mick White (bass), Russell Jones (guitar) and later Steve Meadham (drums). White left in 1983, was briefly replaced by Rick Ross and then by Ian 'Spider' Cubitt. Neville Hunt (bass) joined in 1985, with Cubitt leaving soon after to be ultimately replaced by Lee Brown. Mark Howe later took over on drums.

| | |
|---|---|
| 26/02/1983 . . . . . 53 . . . . . . 3 . . . . . . | WRECKIN' CREW . . . . . . . . . . . . . . . . . . . . . . . . . . . . . . . . . . . . . . . . . . . . . . . . . . . . . . . . . . . . . . . . . . . . . . . . . I.D. NOSE 1 |

**METHOD MAN** US rapper (born Clifford Smith, 1971, Staten Island, NYC) who is a member of rap supergroup Wu-Tang Clan and is also known as Johnny Blaze, Meth Tical, Shakwon, The MZA and Ticallion Stallion.

| | |
|---|---|
| 28/11/1998 . . . . . 49 . . . . . . 1 . . . . . . | TICAL 2000: JUDGEMENT DAY . . . . . . . . . . . . . . . . . . . . . . . . . . . . . . . . . . . . . . . . . . . . . . . . . . . . . . . . . . . . . Def Jam 5589202 |
| 09/10/1999 . . . . . 45 . . . . . . 3 . . . . . . | BLACK OUT! **METHOD MAN AND REDMAN**. . . . . . . . . . . . . . . . . . . . . . . . . . . . . . . . . . . . . . . . . . . . . . . . . Def Jam 5466092 |
| 29/05/2004 . . . . . 29 . . . . . . 3 . . . . . . | TICAL 0 – THE PREQUEL . . . . . . . . . . . . . . . . . . . . . . . . . . . . . . . . . . . . . . . . . . . . . . . . . . . . . . . . . . . . . . . . . Def Jam 9862641 |

**MEZZOFORTE** Icelandic group formed in 1977 by Johann Asmundsson (bass), Gunnlauger Briem (drums), Eythor Gunnarsson (keyboards), Fridrik Karlsson (guitar) and Kristin Svavarsson (saxophone).

| | |
|---|---|
| 05/03/1983 . . . . . 23 . . . . . . 9 . . . . . . | SURPRISE SURPRISE . . . . . . . . . . . . . . . . . . . . . . . . . . . . . . . . . . . . . . . . . . . . . . . . . . . . . . . . . . . . . . . . . . . Steinar STELP 02 |
| 02/07/1983 . . . . . 95 . . . . . . 1 . . . . . . | CATCHING UP WITH MEZZOFORTE . . . . . . . . . . . . . . . . . . . . . . . . . . . . . . . . . . . . . . . . . . . . . . . . . . . . . . . . Steinar STELP 03 |

**M.G.'S** – see **BOOKER T AND THE M.G.'S**

**GEORGE MICHAEL** UK singer (born Georgios Panayiotou, 25/6/1963, London) who formed the Executive in 1979 with Andrew Ridgeley, the group later becoming Wham! He began recording solo while still in the group (*Careless Whisper* being released in the US as Wham! Featuring George Michael) before splitting the group in 1986. Legal wrangles with his record company stopped any new material from 1992 until 1996, when he switched to Virgin. He won the Best British Male Award at the 1988 and 1997 BRIT Awards and the 1996 MTV Europe Music Award for Best Male. Whilst with Wham! he had collected the Best British Group award in 1985 and an Outstanding Contribution award (jointly with Elton John) in 1986. Two Grammy Awards include Best Rhythm & Blues Vocal Performance by a Duo in 1987 with Aretha Franklin for *I Knew You Were Waiting (For Me)*.

| | |
|---|---|
| 14/11/1987 . . . . ❶¹ . . . . 77 . . . . . ✪⁴ | FAITH ▲¹² ◆¹⁰ 1988 Grammy Award for Album of the Year. . . . . . . . . . . . . . . . . . . . . . . . . . . . . . . . . . . . . Epic 4600001 |
| 15/09/1990 . . . . ❶¹ . . . . 57 . . . . . ✪⁴ | LISTEN WITHOUT PREJUDICE VOLUME 1 1991 BRIT Award for Best Album. . . . . . . . . . . . . . . . . . . . . . . . Epic 4672951 |
| 25/05/1996 . . . . ❶³ . . . . 99 . . . . . ✪⁶ | OLDER/OLDER & UPPER ◇⁴ *Older & Upper* is a remix album . . . . . . . . . . . . . . . . . . . . . . . . . . . . . . . Virgin CDVX 2802 |
| 21/11/1998 . . . . ❶⁸ . . . . 66 . . . . . ✪⁷ | LADIES & GENTLEMEN – THE BEST OF GEORGE MICHAEL ◇⁶ . . . . . . . . . . . . . . . . . . . . . . . . . . . . . . Epic 4927052 |
| 18/12/1999 . . . . . 2 . . . . . 17 . . . . . ✪² | SONGS FROM THE LAST CENTURY ◇² . . . . . . . . . . . . . . . . . . . . . . . . . . . . . . . . . . . . . . . . . . . . . . . . Virgin CDVX 2920 |
| 27/03/2004 . . . . ❶¹ . . . 14+ . . . . ✪² | PATIENCE ◇ . . . . . . . . . . . . . . . . . . . . . . . . . . . . . . . . . . . . . . . . . . . . . . . . . . . . . . . . . . . . . . . . . . . . . . . Aegean 5154022 |

**PRAS MICHEL** US rapper (born Prakazrel 'Pras' Micheal, 19/10/1972, NYC) who was also in The Fugees. He won the 1998 MOBO Award for Best International Single with Ol' Dirty Bastard and Mya for *Ghetto Superstar (That Is What You Are)*.

| | |
|---|---|
| 14/11/1998 . . . . . 44 . . . . . . 3 . . . . . . | GHETTO SUPERSTAR . . . . . . . . . . . . . . . . . . . . . . . . . . . . . . . . . . . . . . . . . . . . . . . . . . . . . . . . . . . . . . . . . . . Columbia 4914892 |

**KEITH MICHELL** Australian actor/singer (born 1/12/1926, Adelaide) who was famous for his portrayal of Henry VIII in the TV drama *The Merry Wives of Henry VIII*.

| | |
|---|---|
| 09/02/1980 . . . . . 28 . . . . . 12 . . . . . ○ | CAPTAIN BEAKY AND HIS BAND . . . . . . . . . . . . . . . . . . . . . . . . . . . . . . . . . . . . . . . . . . . . . . . . . . . . . . . . . . Polydor 2383 462 |

**MICHELLE** UK singer (born Michelle McManus, 1980, Bailleston, Lanarkshire); she won the 2003 *Pop Idols* TV competition.

| | | | | |
|---|---|---|---|---|
| 28/02/2004 ..... 3 ...... 7 ...... ● | | | | THE MEANING OF LOVE ............................................................... S 82876590662 |

**BETTE MIDLER** US singer (born 1/12/1944, Paterson, NJ, raised in Hawaii) who moved to New York in 1966, appearing on Broadway before starting a singing career in 1969. Barry Manilow was her pianist during her early career. She later appeared in numerous films, including 1979's *The Rose,* for which she was nominated for an Oscar. She has won four Grammy Awards including Best New Artist in 1973, Best Recording for Children in 1980 with various others for *In Harmony* and Record of the Year in 1989 for *Wind Beneath My Wings* (which also won Song of the Year for writers Larry Henley and Jeff Silbar). She has a star on the Hollywood Walk of Fame.

| | | | | |
|---|---|---|---|---|
| 08/03/1980 ..... 68 ...... 1 ...... | THE ROSE Original soundtrack to the film, 1980 Grammy Award for Best Pop Vocal Performance ............... Atlantic K 50681 |
| 15/07/1989 ..... 21 ...... 9 ...... ● | BEACHES Original soundtrack to the film ................................................. Atlantic 7819931 |
| 13/07/1991 ..... 5 ...... 11 ...... ● | SOME PEOPLE'S LIVES ................................................................ Atlantic 7567821291 |
| 15/02/1992 ..... 75 ...... 1 ...... | FOR THE BOYS Original soundtrack to the film ........................................... Atlantic 7567823292 |
| 30/10/1993 ..... 3 ...... 15 ...... ✪ | EXPERIENCE THE DIVINE – GREATEST HITS ............................................... Atlantic 7567824972 |
| 25/11/1995 ..... 55 ...... 4 ...... | BETTE OF ROSES ..................................................................... Atlantic 7567828232 |

**MIDNIGHT OIL** Australian rock group formed in 1976 by Jim Moginie (guitar), Rob Hirst (drums), Martin Rotsey (guitar), Andrew 'Bear' James (bass) and Peter Garrett (vocals). James left in 1980 and was replaced by Peter Gilford, who left in 1987 and was replaced by Dwayne 'Bones' Hillman. Garrett later ran for the Australian Senate for the Nuclear Disarmament Party (he polled over 200,000 votes and was only narrowly defeated).

| | | | | |
|---|---|---|---|---|
| 25/06/1988 ..... 19 ...... 16 ...... ● | DIESEL AND DUST ..................................................................... CBS 4600051 |
| 10/03/1990 ..... 28 ...... 3 ...... | BLUE SKY MINING ..................................................................... CBS 4656531 |
| 01/05/1993 ..... 27 ...... 2 ...... | EARTH AND SUN AND MOON ............................................................. Columbia 4736052 |

**MIDNIGHT STAR** US R&B group formed at Kentucky State University in 1976 by Reggie Calloway (trumpet), Vincent Calloway (trombone), Belinda Lipscomb (lead vocals), Melvin Watson, Boaz 'Bo' Watson, Jeffrey Cooper, Kenneth Gentry, Bobby Lovelace and William Simmons. The Calloway brothers left in 1987 to form Calloway.

| | | | | |
|---|---|---|---|---|
| 02/02/1985 ..... 85 ...... 2 ...... | PLANETARY INVASION ................................................................. Solar MCF 3251 |
| 05/07/1986 ..... 42 ...... 4 ...... | HEADLINES .......................................................................... Solar MCF 3322 |

**MIGHTY LEMON DROPS** UK group formed in Wolverhampton by Paul Marsh (guitar/vocals), David Newton (guitar), Tony Linehan (bass) and Keith Rowley (drums). They signed with Chrysalis' Blue Guitar imprint in 1985.

| | | | | |
|---|---|---|---|---|
| 04/10/1986 ..... 58 ...... 2 ...... | HAPPY HEAD ......................................................................... Blue Guitar AZLP 1 |
| 27/02/1988 ..... 34 ...... 3 ...... | THE WORLD WITHOUT END .............................................................. Blue Guitar AZLP 4 |

**MIGHTY MIGHTY BOSSTONES** US rock group formed in 1985 by Nate Albert (guitar), Dicky Barrett, Joe Gittleman (bass), Tim "Johnny Vegas" Burton (saxophone), Josh Dulcimer (drums) and "Bosstone" Ben Carr as The Bosstones. By 1990 the group had become the Mighty Mighty Bosstones and added drummer Joe Sirois and the beefed-up 'Hurtin' For Certain' horns, comprised of Vegas, trombonist and barrel-chested baritone Dennis Brockenborough and co-saxman Kevin Lenear.

| | | | | |
|---|---|---|---|---|
| 16/05/1998 ..... 40 ...... 2 ...... | LET'S FACE IT ........................................................................ Mercury 5344722 |

**MIGHTY MORPH'N POWER RANGERS** US vocal group assembled by Kussa Mahchi, Shuki Levy and Haim Saban to record an accompanying album to the third series of the TV series *Power Rangers*.

| | | | | |
|---|---|---|---|---|
| 24/12/1994 ..... 50 ...... 3 ...... O | POWER RANGERS – THE ALBUM – A ROCK ADVENTURE ....................................... RCA 74321252982 |

**MIKE AND THE MECHANICS** UK rock group formed by Genesis member Mike Rutherford (born 2/10/1950, Guildford, guitar) in 1986 with ex-Ace Paul Carrack (born 22/4/1951, Sheffield, keyboards/vocals), ex-Sad Café Paul Young (vocals), Peter Van Hooke (drums) and Adrian Lee (keyboards). Young died from a heart attack on 17/7/2000.

| | | | | |
|---|---|---|---|---|
| 15/03/1986 ..... 78 ...... 3 ...... | MIKE AND THE MECHANICS ............................................................. WEA WX 49 |
| 26/11/1988 ..... 2 ...... 19 ...... ● | THE LIVING YEARS ..................................................................... WEA WX 203 |
| 27/04/1991 ..... 11 ...... 7 ...... O | WORD OF MOUTH ...................................................................... Virgin V 2662 |
| 18/03/1995 ..... 9 ...... 33 ...... ● | BEGGAR ON A BEACH OF GOLD .......................................................... Virgin CDV 2772 |
| 02/03/1996 ..... 67 ...... 2 ...... | THE LIVING YEARS ..................................................................... Atlantic K 2560042 |
| 16/03/1996 ..... 3 ...... 31 ...... ✪² | HITS ................................................................................ Virgin CDV 2797 |
| 12/06/1999 ..... 14 ...... 4 ...... | MIKE AND THE MECHANICS ............................................................. Virgin CDV 2885 |
| 19/06/2004 ..... 61 ...... 1 ...... | REWIRED ............................................................................ Virgin CDVX 2984 |

**JOHN MILES** UK singer/multi-instrumentalist (born 23/4/1949, Jarrow) who was a guest singer with the Alan Parsons Project, Parsons having produced Miles' debut album in 1975. His first job after leaving school was making lavatory signs.

| | | | | |
|---|---|---|---|---|
| 27/03/1976 ..... 9 ...... 10 ...... O | REBEL .............................................................................. Decca SKL 5231 |
| 26/02/1977 ..... 37 ...... 3 ...... O | STRANGER IN THE CITY ................................................................ Decca TXS 118 |

▲⁹ Number of weeks album topped the US chart ◆¹² RIAA Diamond Awards ◇³ IFPI Platinum Europe Awards

| | | | | | |
|---|---|---|---|---|---|
| 01/04/1978 | 43 | 5 | | ZARAGON | Decca TXS 126 |
| 21/04/1979 | 46 | 5 | | MORE MILES PER HOUR | Decca TXS 135 |
| 29/08/1981 | 96 | 2 | | MILES HIGH | EMI EMC 3374 |

## ROBERT MILES
Italian DJ (born Roberto Concina, 3/11/1969, Fleurier, Switzerland) whose debut single, originally released in Italy in 1994, was recorded in a studio built by the artist in Venice. He was named Best International Newcomer at the 1997 BRIT Awards.

| | | | | | |
|---|---|---|---|---|---|
| 22/06/1996 | 7 | 48 | ✪ | DREAMLAND ◇ | Deconstruction 74321391262 |
| 06/12/1997 | 42 | 3 | | 23AM | Deconstruction 74321541132 |

## CHRISTINA MILIAN
US singer (born 26/9/1981, New Jersey, raised in Maryland);s she started as an actress in the TV shows *Sister Sister* and *Clueless* and worked for the Walt Disney Company. She wrote a number of hits, including Jennifer Lopez's *Play*, before going solo.

| | | | | | |
|---|---|---|---|---|---|
| 02/02/2002 | 23 | 11 | O | CHRISTINA MILIAN | Def Soul 5867392 |
| 12/06/2004 | 21 | 3+ | | IT'S ABOUT TIME | Def Jam UK 9862835 |

## MILK INCORPORATED
Belgian vocal/production group formed by Regi Penxten, Ivo Donkers and Filip Van Dueren with singer Nikki Van Lier. Van Lier was subsequently replaced by Sofie Winters, Ann Vervoort and then Linda Mertens.

| | | | | | |
|---|---|---|---|---|---|
| 05/10/2002 | 47 | 1 | | MILK INC. | Positiva 5419532 |

## DOMINIC MILLER
US guitarist (born 1960, Buenos Aires, Argentina); he moved to Racine, Wisconsin in 1970. After attending London's Guildhall School of Music he became a session guitarist, work for Phil Collins and Sting among others. He is a member of Sting's touring group.

| | | | | | |
|---|---|---|---|---|---|
| 14/06/2003 | 38 | 3 | | SHAPES | BBC Music WMSF60702 |

## FRANKIE MILLER
UK singer/songwriter/guitarist (born 1950, Glasgow) who moved to London in 1971 and was a member of the short-lived group Jude. He recorded his debut solo album in 1973 with backing provided by Brinsley Schwarz.

| | | | | | |
|---|---|---|---|---|---|
| 14/04/1979 | 54 | 1 | | FALLING IN LOVE | Chrysalis CHR 1220 |

## GLENN MILLER AND HIS ORCHESTRA
US orchestra leader/trombonist (born 1/3/1904, Clarinda, IA) who first learned to play the cornet and mandolin and then trombone, playing for the Grant City, MO town band. He formed his own orchestra in 1937 and four years later he was the top band leader in the world: when *Billboard* published the first ever sales chart in July 1940 he had three of the top ten places. He entered the US forces in 1942 as a captain and was later promoted to major, touring the UK during World War II. He worked on films including *Sun Valley Serenade* (1941) and *Orchestra Wives* (1942). On 15/12/1944 while en route to France his plane disappeared over the Channel. It was later believed that a bomber returning home had jettisoned its bombs, one striking Miller's plane (although one book claimed he died of a heart attack in a French brothel). *The Glenn Miller Story* starring James Stewart was made in 1953. His 1939 recording *In The Mood* won a special Grammy Hall of Fame award. He has a star on the Hollywood Walk of Fame.

| | | | | | |
|---|---|---|---|---|---|
| 28/01/1961 | 10 | 18 | | GLENN MILLER PLAYS SELECTIONS FROM 'THE GLENN MILLER STORY' AND OTHER HITS | RCA 27068 0023 |
| 05/07/1969 | 5 | 14 | | THE BEST OF GLENN MILLER | RCA International 1002 |
| 06/09/1969 | 30 | 2 | | NEARNESS OF YOU | RCA International INTS 1019 |
| 25/04/1970 | 18 | 17 | | A MEMORIAL 1944–1969 | RCA Victor GM 1 |
| 25/12/1971 | 28 | 2 | | THE REAL GLENN MILLER AND HIS ORCHESTRA PLAY THE ORIGINAL MUSIC OF THE FILM 'THE GLENN MILLER STORY' AND OTHER HITS This is a re-titled re-issue of RCA 27068 0023 | RCA International NTS 1157 |
| 14/02/1976 | 41 | 5 | | A LEGENDARY PERFORMER | RCA Victor DPM 2065 |
| 14/02/1976 | 53 | 2 | | A LEGENDARY PERFORMER VOLUME 2 | RCA Victor CPL 11349 |
| 09/04/1977 | 4 | 8 | | THE UNFORGETTABLE GLENN MILLER | RCA Victor TVL 1 |
| 20/03/1993 | 11 | 6 | | THE ULTIMATE GLENN MILLER | Bluebird 74321131372 |
| 25/02/1995 | 22 | 6 | O | THE LOST RECORDINGS | Happy Days CDHD 4012 |
| 18/10/2003 | 43 | 2 | | IN THE MOOD – THE DEFINITIVE GLENN MILLER | BMG 82876560302 |

## STEVE MILLER BAND
US rock group formed in San Francisco, CA in 1966 by Steve Miller (born 5/10/1943, Milwaukee, WI, guitar/vocals), James 'Curley' Cooke (guitar/vocals), Lonnie Turner (bass/vocals) and Tim Davis (drums/vocals). They signed to Capitol in 1967 and recorded their debut album in 1968. The group has a star on the Hollywood Walk of Fame.

| | | | | | |
|---|---|---|---|---|---|
| 12/06/1976 | 11 | 17 | ● | FLY LIKE AN EAGLE | Mercury 9286 177 |
| 04/06/1977 | 12 | 12 | O | BOOK OF DREAMS | Mercury 9286 456 |
| 19/06/1982 | 10 | 16 | O | ABRACADABRA | Mercury 6302 204 |
| 07/05/1983 | 79 | 2 | | STEVE MILLER BAND LIVE! | Mercury MERL 18 |
| 06/10/1990 | 34 | 3 | | THE BEST OF 1968–1973 | Capitol EST 2133 |
| 10/10/1998 | 58 | 1 | | GREATEST HITS | Polygram TV 5592402 |

## MILLI VANILLI
French/German vocal duo produced by Frank Farian (who previously produced Boney M) with Rob Pilatus (born 8/6/1965) and Fabrice Morvan. Rob and Fab (as they became known) were later involved in financial wrangles with Farian, revealing they had not sung on either of their first two hits, the actual vocalists being Charles Shaw, John Davis and Brad Howe. They were forced to give back their 1989 Best New Artist Grammy Award as a result. Pilatus was found dead from a drug overdose on 3/4/1998.

| | | | | | |
|---|---|---|---|---|---|
| 28/10/1989 | 6 | 25 | ✪ | ALL OR NOTHING/2 X 2 *2 X 2* is a remix album that was added to *All Or Nothing* from 25/11/1989 | Cooltempo CTLP 11 |

O Silver disc  ● Gold disc  ✪ Platinum disc (additional platinum units are indicated by a figure following the symbol)  ❶⁹ Number of weeks album topped the UK chart

### MILLICAN AND NESBITT
UK vocal duo Alan Millican and Tom Nesbitt; they were coalminers who won the TV talent show *Opportunity Knocks*.

| | | | | | |
|---|---|---|---|---|---|
| 23/03/1974 | 3 | 21 | ● | MILLICAN AND NESBITT | Pye NSPL 18428 |
| 04/01/1975 | 23 | 3 | ● | EVERYBODY KNOWS MILLICAN AND NESBITT | Pye NSPL 18446 |

### SPIKE MILLIGAN
UK comedian (born Terence Alan Milligan 16/4/1918, Ahmed Nagar, India) who was a writer and performer in *The Goons* radio series. Later as an actor, he appeared in (and often writing) such films as *Adolf Hitler My Part In His Downfall*, *The Last Remake Of Beau Geste*, *A Man About The House* and *The Life Of Brian*. He also starred in and wrote numerous TV series and was knighted in the 2001 New Year's Honours list. He died from liver failure on 27/2/2002.

| | | | | | |
|---|---|---|---|---|---|
| 25/11/1961 | 11 | 4 | | MILLIGAN PRESERVED | Parlophone PMC 1152 |
| 18/04/1964 | 20 | 1 | | HOW TO WIN AN ELECTION HARRY SECOMBE, PETER SELLERS AND SPIKE MILLIGAN | Philips AL 3464 |
| 18/12/1976 | 49 | 1 | | THE SNOW GOOSE SPIKE MILLIGAN WITH THE LONDON SYMPHONY ORCHESTRA | RCA Victor RS 1088 |

### MILLTOWN BROTHERS
UK rock group formed in Burnley, Lancashire by Matt Nelson (vocals), Simon Nelson (guitar), James Fraser (bass), Nian Brindle (drums) and Barney James (keyboards).

| | | | | |
|---|---|---|---|---|
| 23/03/1991 | 27 | 5 | SLINKY | A&M 3953461 |

### MINDBENDERS
UK group formed in Manchester in 1963 by Wayne Fontana as his backing group, comprising Eric Stewart (born 20/1/1945, Manchester, lead guitar/vocals), Bob Lang (born 10/1/1946, Manchester, bass) and Ric Rothwell (born Eric Rothwell, 11/3/1944, Stockport, drums). Fontana left acrimoniously to go solo in 1965, the group adding Graham Gouldman in 1968. Gouldman and Stewart were later members of 10 CC.

| | | | | |
|---|---|---|---|---|
| 20/02/1965 | 18 | 1 | WAYNE FONTANA AND THE MINDBENDERS WAYNE FONTANA & THE MINDBENDERS | Fontana TL 5230 |
| 25/06/1966 | 28 | 4 | THE MINDBENDERS | Fontana TL 5324 |

### MINDFUNK
US rock group formed in 1989 by Partick Dubar (vocals), Jason Coppola (guitar), Louis Svitek (guitar), John Monte (bass) and Reed St Mark (drums) and signed by Epic the same year. They were dropped in 1992 (hence the title of their debut hit album for Megaforce) at which point Coppola and St Mark left to be replaced by Jason Everman and Shawn Johnson respectively.

| | | | | |
|---|---|---|---|---|
| 15/05/1993 | 60 | 1 | DROPPED | Megaforce CDZAZ 3 |

### ZODIAC MINDWARP AND THE LOVE REACTION
UK heavy rock group formed in 1986 by Zodiac Mindwarp (born Mark Manning, vocals), Cobalt Stargazer (guitar), Kid Chaos (bass) and Slam Thunderhide (drums). They disbanded in 1989.

| | | | | |
|---|---|---|---|---|
| 05/03/1988 | 20 | 5 | TATTOOED BEAT MESSIAH | Mercury ZODLP 1 |

### MINI POPS
UK children's vocal group assembled by producer Martin Wyatt and TV programme-maker Mike Mansfield. The group featured Zoe Hart, Joanna Wyatt, Joanna Fisher, Abby Kimber and Paul Hardy.

| | | | | | |
|---|---|---|---|---|---|
| 26/12/1981 | 63 | 7 | ● | MINIPOPS | K-Tel NE 1102 |
| 19/02/1983 | 54 | 5 | | WE'RE THE MINIPOPS | K-Tel ONE 1187 |

### MINISTRY
US rock group formed by Alain Jourgensen (guitar/keyboards/vocals), Paul Barker (bass/keyboards) and Bill Reiflin (drums). Reiflin left the group in 1994 and was replaced by Ray Washam. Jourgensen is also a member of The Revolting Cocks.

| | | | | |
|---|---|---|---|---|
| 25/07/1992 | 33 | 5 | PSALM 69 | Sire 7599267272 |
| 10/02/1996 | 43 | 1 | FILTH PIG | Warner Brothers 9362458382 |

### LIZA MINNELLI
US actress/singer (born 12/3/1946, Los Angeles, CA) who is the daughter of singer Judy Garland and film director Vincente Minnelli. She hit the UK album charts for the first time in 1973, almost ten years after her US breakthrough. She debuted in public at the age of two-and-a-half in the 1949 film *The Good Old Summer Time* (which also starred her mother). Her debut hit single was written and produced by the Pet Shop Boys. In October 2000 she was discovered in a coma and rushed to hospital, recovering a few days later (she was reunited with her estranged step-sister Lorna Luft as a result). She has been married four times: to singer/songwriter Peter Allen (he won the 1982 Best Film Song Oscar with Burt Bacharach, Carole Bayer Sager and Christopher Cross for *Arthur's Theme* and died from an AIDS-related illness on 18/6/1992) in 1967, filmmaker Jack Haley in 1974, sculptor Mark Gero in 1979 and producer David Gest in November 2001. She has a star on the Hollywood Walk of Fame and won Best Actress Oscar in 1972 for *Cabaret*.

| | | | | | |
|---|---|---|---|---|---|
| 07/04/1973 | 9 | 15 | | LIZA WITH A 'Z' | CBS 65212 |
| 16/06/1973 | 45 | 1 | | THE SINGER | CBS 65555 |
| 21/10/1989 | 6 | 10 | ● | RESULTS | Epic 4655111 |
| 06/07/1996 | 58 | 1 | | GENTLY | Angel CDQ 8354702 |

### DANNII MINOGUE
Australian singer/actress (born 20/10/1970, Melbourne) who was first known via the TV series *Skyways* at the age of seven (a star in Australia before older sister Kylie) and later *Home And Away*. She was engaged to racing driver Jacques Villeneuve (her marriage to actor Julian McMahon lasted a year) although the pair had split up by January 2001.

| | | | | | |
|---|---|---|---|---|---|
| 15/06/1991 | 8 | 20 | ● | LOVE AND KISSES | MCA 10340 |
| 16/10/1993 | 52 | 1 | | GET INTO YOU | MCA MCD 10909 |
| 20/09/1997 | 57 | 1 | | GIRL | Eternal 3984205492 |
| 29/03/2003 | 8 | 7 | ● | NEON NIGHTS | London 2564600032 |

## KYLIE MINOGUE
Australian singer/actress (born 28/5/1968, Melbourne) whose first acting role was in *The Sullivans* in 1979, later appearing in the hit TV series *Neighbours* as Charlene. She hit #1 in Australia with *The Loco-Motion* in 1987, travelling to London to record with Stock Aitken Waterman. When *Kylie! – The Album* hit the #1 spot on 27/8/1988 she was the youngest woman to have topped the UK album charts. Kylie won two awards at the inaugural Top Of The Pops Awards in 2001: Best Tour and Best Single for *Can't Get You Out Of My Head*. Her two BRIT Awards in 2002 included Best International Female, the same year she won MTV Europe Music Awards for Best Dance and Best Pop Act. She won the 2003 Grammy Award for Best Dance Recording for *Come Into My World*. Kylie is Dannii Minogue's elder sister.

| | | | | |
|---|---|---|---|---|
| 16/07/1988 | ❶⁶ | 67 | ✪⁶ | **KYLIE! – THE ALBUM** . . . . . . PWL HF 3 |
| 21/10/1989 | ❶¹ | 33 | ✪⁴ | **ENJOY YOURSELF** . . . . . . PWL HF 9 |
| 24/11/1990 | 9 | 22 | ● | **RHYTHM OF LOVE** . . . . . . PWL HF 18 |
| 26/10/1991 | 15 | 12 | | LET'S GO TO IT . . . . . . PWL HF 21 |
| 05/09/1992 | ❶¹ | 10 | ○ | **KYLIE'S GREATEST HITS** . . . . . . PWL International HFCD 25 |
| 01/10/1994 | 4 | 15 | ● | **KYLIE MINOGUE** . . . . . . Deconstruction 74321227492 |
| 04/04/1998 | 10 | 4 | | **KYLIE MINOGUE** . . . . . . Deconstruction 74321517272 |
| 15/08/1998 | 63 | 1 | | MIXES . . . . . . Deconstruction 74321587152 |
| 28/10/2000 | 41 | 1 | | HITS PLUS . . . . . . Deconstruction 74321785342 |
| 07/10/2000 | 2 | 28 | ✪ | **LIGHT YEARS** . . . . . . Parlophone 5284002 |
| 13/10/2001 | ❶² | 70 | ✪⁵ | **FEVER** ◇³ 2002 BRIT Award for Best International Album . . . . . . Parlophone 5358042 |
| 30/11/2002 | 20 | 11 | ✪ | GREATEST HITS 87–92 . . . . . . PWL 9224682 |
| 29/11/2003 | 6 | 14 | ✪ | **BODY LANGUAGE** . . . . . . Parlophone 5957582 |

## MIRAGE
UK studio group created by producer Nigel Wright and featuring the vocals of Kiki Billy.

| | | | | |
|---|---|---|---|---|
| 26/12/1987 | 7 | 15 | ● | **THE BEST OF MIRAGE: JACK MIX '88** . . . . . . Stylus SMR 746 |
| 25/06/1988 | 7 | 12 | ● | **JACK MIX IN FULL EFFECT** . . . . . . Stylus SMR 856 |
| 07/01/1989 | 34 | 6 | | ROYAL MIX '89 . . . . . . Stylus SMR 871 |

## MIRAGE
UK studio group.

| | | | |
|---|---|---|---|
| 23/09/1995 | 25 | 3 | CLASSIC GUITAR MOODS . . . . . . Polygram TV 5290562 |

## MIS-TEEQ
UK R&B group formed by Alesha Dixon (born 7/10/1979, Welwyn Garden City), Su-Elise Nash (born 27/10/1978, Harlesden, London), Sabrina Washington (born 22/5/1981, West Dulwich, London) and Zena Playford. Co-lead singer Zena left the group after their first single due to illness but later went solo. They won the 2002 MOBO Award for Best British Garage Act.

| | | | | |
|---|---|---|---|---|
| 10/11/2001 | 3 | 31 | ✪ | **LICKIN' ON BOTH SIDES** . . . . . . Inferno/Telstar TCD 3212 |
| 12/04/2003 | 6 | 21 | ● | **EYE CANDY** . . . . . . Telstar TCD 3304 |

## MISSION
UK group formed in 1986 by Wayne Hussey (born Jerry Lovelock, 26/5/1959, Bristol, guitar/vocals) and Craig Adams (born 4/4/1962, Otley, bass) following the temporary demise of Sisters Of Mercy and also featuring Simon Hinkler (guitar) and Mick Brown (drums). Hinkler left in 1990 and was replaced by guitarist Paul Etchells in 1991.

| | | | | |
|---|---|---|---|---|
| 22/11/1986 | 14 | 20 | ○ | GOD'S OWN MEDICINE . . . . . . Mercury MERH 102 |
| 04/07/1987 | 35 | 4 | | THE FIRST CHAPTER . . . . . . Mercury MISH 1 |
| 12/03/1988 | 2 | 9 | ● | **CHILDREN** . . . . . . Mercury MISH 2 |
| 17/02/1990 | 7 | 8 | ● | **CARVED IN SAND** . . . . . . Mercury 8422511 |
| 03/11/1990 | 28 | 2 | | GRAINS OF SAND . . . . . . Mercury 8469371 |
| 04/07/1992 | 23 | 2 | | MASQUE . . . . . . Vertigo 5121212 |
| 19/02/1994 | 49 | 1 | | SUM AND SUBSTANCE . . . . . . Vertigo 5184472 |
| 25/02/1995 | 58 | 1 | | NEVERLAND . . . . . . Neverland SMEECD 001 |
| 15/06/1996 | 73 | 1 | | BLUE . . . . . . Equator SMEECD 002 |

## MRS MILLS
UK pianist Gladys Mills who worked extensively with Geoff Love. She died in February 1978.

| | | | |
|---|---|---|---|
| 10/12/1966 | 17 | 7 | COME TO MY PARTY . . . . . . Parlophone PMC 7010 |
| 28/12/1968 | 32 | 3 | MRS MILLS PARTY PIECES . . . . . . Parlophone PCS 7066 |
| 13/12/1969 | 23 | 2 | LET'S HAVE ANOTHER PARTY . . . . . . Parlophone PCS 7035 |
| 06/11/1971 | 49 | 1 | I'M MIGHTY GLAD . . . . . . MFP 5225 |

## MR BIG
US group from San Francisco, CA with Eric Martin (vocals), Paul Gilbert (guitar), Billy Sheehan (bass) and Pat Torpey (drums).

| | | | |
|---|---|---|---|
| 22/07/1989 | 60 | 1 | MR BIG . . . . . . Atlantic 7819901 |
| 13/04/1991 | 28 | 12 | LEAN INTO IT . . . . . . Atlantic 7567822091 |
| 02/10/1993 | 61 | 1 | BUMP AHEAD . . . . . . Atlantic 7567824952 |

## MR BUNGLE
US group with Mike Patton (born 27/1/1968, Eureka, CA, vocals), Trey Spruance (guitar), Trevor Dunn (bass) and Danny Heifetz (drums). Patton later joined Faith No More, ending Mr Bungle as a live act, later returning and reviving the group.

| | | | |
|---|---|---|---|
| 21/09/1991 | 57 | 1 | MR BUNGLE . . . . . . London 8282671 |

## MR MISTER
US rock group formed in Phoenix, AZ by Richard Page (bass/vocals), Steve George (keyboards), Pat Mastelotto (drums) and Steve Farris (guitar) and relocated to Los Angeles, CA. Farris left in 1989 and was replaced by Buzzy Feiten.

○ Silver disc ● Gold disc ✪ Platinum disc (additional platinum units are indicated by a figure following the symbol) ❶⁹ Number of weeks album topped the UK chart

| 15/02/1986 | 6 | 24 | ● | **WELCOME TO THE REAL WORLD** ▲[1] | RCA PL 89647 |

**MR SCRUFF** UK dance artist (born Andrew Carthy, 10/2/1972, Macclesfield).

| 21/09/2002 | 29 | 2 | ○ | TROUSER JAZZ | Ninja Tune ZENCD 65 |

**GEORGE MITCHELL MINSTRELS** UK choir leader (born 27/2/1917, Stirling, Scotland); he initially intended qualifying as an accountant, joining the Royal Army Pay Corps in World War II. Whilst there he organised a choir and following his demobilisation in 1947 assembled the George Mitchell Choir for the radio programme *Cabin In The Cotton*. He changed the name of the choir to the George Mitchell Glee Club in 1949, by which time it featured some 32 singers and was regularly on the radio and on tour. Having made their first Royal Variety Performance in 1950 they were one of the first groups to feature regularly on variety TV. It was in 1957 that they were first shown wearing their 'black-face' make-up (it was in fact red make-up, but the presence of green filters on the cameras made it appear black) and the following year Mitchell and producer George Innes came up with the concept of *Black and White Minstrel Show*. The show ran for almost 20 years on peak time TV before finally being axed by the BBC (they felt it might be racially offensive, although no known complaints were ever received). A version of the show toured on and off for the next fourteen years, although by 1992 complaints from the Commission for Racial Equality meant that none of the cast could appear black-faced.

| 26/11/1960 | ❶[6] | 142 | | **THE BLACK AND WHITE MINSTREL SHOW** | HMV CLP 1399 |
| 21/10/1961 | ❶[8] | 64 | | **ANOTHER BLACK AND WHITE MINSTREL SHOW** | HMV CLP 1460 |
| 20/10/1962 | ❶[2] | 26 | | **ON STAGE WITH THE GEORGE MITCHELL MINSTRELS** | HMV CLP 1599 |
| 02/11/1963 | 6 | 18 | | **ON TOUR WITH THE GEORGE MITCHELL MINSTRELS** | HMV CLP 1667 |
| 12/12/1964 | 6 | 7 | | **SPOTLIGHT ON THE GEORGE MITCHELL MINST6RELS** | HMV CLP 1803 |
| 04/12/1965 | 9 | 7 | | **MAGIC OF THE MINSTRELS** | HMV CLP 1917 |
| 26/11/1966 | 11 | 11 | | HERE COME THE MINSTRELS | HMV CLP 3579 |
| 16/12/1967 | 26 | 2 | | SHOWTIME | HMV CSD 3642 |
| 14/12/1968 | 33 | 1 | | SING THE IRVING BERLIN SONGBOOK | Columbia SCX 6267 |
| 19/12/1970 | 32 | 4 | | THE MAGIC OF CHRISTMAS | Columbia SCX 6431 |
| 19/11/1977 | 10 | 10 | | **30 GOLDEN GREATS** GEORGE MITCHELL MINSTRELS WITH THE JOE LOSS ORCHESTRA | EMI EMTV 7 |

**JONI MITCHELL** Canadian singer (born Roberta Joan Anderson, 7/11/1943, Fort McLeod, Alberta); she relocated to New York and adopted her married name (she married Chuck Mitchell in June 1965 although the marriage was later dissolved) for a stage name. She recorded her debut album in 1968 with David Crosby handling production and was inducted in to the Rock & Roll Hall of Fame in 1997. She has won five Grammy Awards including Best Folk Recording in 1969 for *Clouds* and Best Arrangement Accompanying Singers in 1974 with Tom Scott for *Down To You*.

| 06/06/1970 | 8 | 25 | | LADIES OF THE CANYON | Reprise RSLP 6376 |
| 24/07/1971 | 3 | 18 | | BLUE | Reprise K 44128 |
| 16/03/1974 | 14 | 11 | | COURT AND SPARK | Asylum SYLA 8756 |
| 01/02/1975 | 34 | 4 | | MILES OF AISLES | Asylum SYSP 902 |
| 27/12/1975 | 14 | 10 | | THE HISSING OF SUMMER LAWNS | Asylum SYLA 8763 |
| 11/12/1976 | 11 | 5 | ○ | HEJIRA | Asylum K 53053 |
| 21/01/1978 | 20 | 7 | ○ | DON JUAN'S RECKLESS DAUGHTER | Asylum K 63003 |
| 14/07/1979 | 24 | 7 | | MINGUS | Asylum K 53091 |
| 04/10/1980 | 63 | 3 | | SHADOWS AND LIGHT | Elektra K 62030 |
| 04/12/1982 | 32 | 8 | | WILD THINGS RUN FAST | Geffen GEF 25102 |
| 30/11/1985 | 57 | 3 | | DOG EAT DOG | Geffen GEF 26455 |
| 02/04/1988 | 26 | 7 | | CHALK FARM IN A RAIN STORM | Geffen WX 141 |
| 09/03/1991 | 25 | 5 | | NIGHT RIDE HOME | Geffen GEF 24302 |
| 05/11/1994 | 53 | 2 | | TURBULENT INDIGO 1995 Grammy Award for Best Pop Album and Best Album Package with Robbie Cavolina | Reprise 9362457862 |
| 10/10/1998 | 57 | 1 | | TAMING THE TIGER | Reprise 9362464512 |
| 11/03/2000 | 50 | 2 | | BOTH SIDES NOW 2000 Grammy Award for Best Traditional Pop Album | Reprise 9362476202 |

**MN8** UK vocal R&B group formed by KG, Kule-T, Dee-Tails and G-Man.

| 27/05/1995 | 13 | 4 | ○ | TO THE NEXT LEVEL | Columbia 4802802 |

**MOBB DEEP** US rap duo formed in Queens, NY by Havoc and The Prodigy. They have also worked with The Large Professor, Big Noyd, Das EFX, Bounty Killer, Ghostface Killer and various other rap acts.

| 23/11/1996 | 67 | 1 | | HELL ON EARTH | Loud 74321425582 |

▲[9] Number of weeks album topped the US chart ◆[12] RIAA Diamond Awards ◇[3] IFPI Platinum Europe Awards

**MOBY** US singer (born Richard Melville Hall, 11/9/1966, New York) nicknamed Moby because he is an ancestor of Herman Melville, the author of the Captain Ahab whaling story *Moby Dick*. His track *Thousand* (the B-side to *I Feel It*) earned him a place in the *Guinness Book Of Records*: at 1,015 beats per minute it is the fastest single ever. He won the 2000 MTV Europe Music Award for Best Video for *Natural Blues* and the 2002 award for Best Website.

| | | | | | | |
|---|---|---|---|---|---|---|
| 27/01/1996 | 21 | 7 | | EVERYTHING IS WRONG/MIXED & REMIXED | Mute LCDSTUMM 130 |
| 05/10/1996 | 38 | 1 | | ANIMAL RIGHTS | Mute CDSTUMM 150 |
| 29/05/1999 | ❶5 | 81 | ✪5 | PLAY ◇4 | Mute CDSTUMM 172 |
| 01/07/2000 | 54 | 2 | | I LIKE TO SCORE | Mute CDSTUMM 168 |
| 04/11/2000 | 24 | 3 | | PLAY/THE B SIDES | Mute LCDSTUMM 172 |
| 25/05/2002 | ❶1 | 34 | ✪ | **18** ◇ | Mute CDSTUMM 202 |

**MOCK TURTLES** UK rock group formed in Manchester in 1987 by former Judge Happiness member Martin Coogan (guitar/vocals) with Steve Green (bass), Krzysztof Korab (keyboards) and Steve Cowen (drums). Martin Glyn Murray (guitar) joined in 1989. When he left for an acting career the group disbanded.

| | | | | | |
|---|---|---|---|---|---|
| 25/05/1991 | 54 | 1 | | TURTLE SOUP | Imaginary ILLUSION 012 |
| 27/07/1991 | 33 | 3 | | TWO SIDES | Siren SRNLP31 |

**MODERN EON** UK vocal/instrumental group from Liverpool with Alex Johnson, Danny Hampson, Bob Wakelin, Tim Lever and Cliff Hewitt.

| | | | | | |
|---|---|---|---|---|---|
| 13/06/1981 | 65 | 1 | | FICTION TALES | Dindisc DID 11 |

**MODERN ROMANCE** UK pop group formed as the Leyton Buzzards, changing their name in 1980 to Modern Romance. The line-up at the time of their success was Geoff Deane (born 10/12/1954, vocals), Paul Gendler (born 11/8/1960, guitar), Robbie James (born 3/10/1962, keyboards), David Jaymes (born 28/11/1954, bass), Andy Kyriacou (born 19/4/1958, drums) and John du Prez (trumpet). Deane left at the end of 1982 and was replaced by Michael Mullins (born 9/11/1956). They disbanded in 1985.

| | | | | | |
|---|---|---|---|---|---|
| 16/04/1983 | 53 | 7 | | TRICK OF THE LIGHT | WEA X 0127 |
| 03/12/1983 | 45 | 6 | ● | PARTY TONIGHT | Ronco RONLP 3 |

**MODERN TALKING** German duo Thomas Anders and Dieter Bohlen.

| | | | | | |
|---|---|---|---|---|---|
| 11/10/1986 | 76 | 3 | | READY FOR ROMANCE | RCA PL 71133 |

**MOFFATTS** Canadian vocal group with Scott Moffatt (born 30/3/1984) and his triplet brothers Clint, Dave and Bob (born 8/3/1985).

| | | | | | |
|---|---|---|---|---|---|
| 06/03/1999 | 62 | 1 | | CHAPTER 1: A NEW BEGINNING | Chrysalis 4992072 |

**MOGWAI** UK group formed in Glasgow in 1996 by Stuart Braithwaite (guitar/vocals), Dominic Aitchison (guitar), John Cummings (guitar) and Martin Bulloch (drums). After releases on independent labels they added Brendan O'Hare in time for their debut album for Chemikal Underground, although he left after the recording sessions were complete.

| | | | | | |
|---|---|---|---|---|---|
| 08/11/1997 | 75 | 1 | | YOUNG TEAM | Chemikal Underground CHEM 018CD |
| 10/04/1999 | 29 | 2 | | COME ON, DIE YOUNG | Chemikal Underground CHEM 033CD |
| 12/05/2001 | 23 | 2 | | ROCK ACTION | Southpaw PAW CD1 |
| 21/06/2003 | 47 | 2 | | HAPPY SONGS FOR HAPPY PEOPLE | PIAS Recordings PIASX035CD |

**MOIST** Canadian group formed in Vancouver in 1992 by David Usher (guitar/vocals), Jeff Pearce (bass), Mark Makoway (guitar), Kevin Young (keyboards) and Paul Wilcox (drums). Their February 1994 own-label self-funded debut was picked up by EMI Canada a month later.

| | | | | | |
|---|---|---|---|---|---|
| 26/08/1995 | 49 | 3 | | SILVER TOWN | Chrysalis CDCHR 6080 |

**MOLLY HATCHET** US rock group formed in Jacksonville, FL in 1975 by Danny Joe Brown (vocals), Dave Hlubeck (guitar), Steve Holland (guitar), Duane Roland (guitar), Bonner Thomas (bass) and Bruce Crump (drums), named after a 17th-century lady who beheaded her lovers with an axe after sleeping with them. Brown left in 1980, replaced by Jimmy Farrar, Brown returning in 1982. Holland and Thomas left in 1983, replaced by John Galvin (keyboards) and Rick West (bass). Hlubeck left in 1989, replaced by Bobby Ingram.

| | | | | | |
|---|---|---|---|---|---|
| 25/01/1986 | 94 | 1 | | DOUBLE TROUBLE – LIVE | Epic EPC 88670 |

**MOLOKO** UK/Irish vocal/instrumental duo formed in Sheffield in 1993 by Mark Brydon and Roisin Murphy. They were named after a drug-laced milk drink in the Anthony Burgess novel and 1971 Stanley Kubrick film *A Clockwork Orange*. Murphy later recorded with Boris Dlugosch and The Psychedelic Waltons.

| | | | | | |
|---|---|---|---|---|---|
| 05/09/1998 | 64 | 1 | | I AM NOT A DOCTOR | Echo ECHCD 021 |
| 22/04/2000 | 3 | 26 | ✪ | **THINGS TO MAKE AND DO** | Echo ECHCD 31 |
| 15/03/2003 | 18 | 3 | ○ | STATUES | Echo ECHCD 44 |

**MONACO** UK duo Peter Hook (born 13/2/1956, Salford) and David Potts (born in Manchester). Hook was previously bass player with New Order, and first teamed up with Potts in Revenge in 1990.

○ Silver disc ● Gold disc ✪ Platinum disc (additional platinum units are indicated by a figure following the symbol) ❶9 Number of weeks album topped the UK chart

21/06/1997 . . . . . 11 . . . . . 3 . . . . . .      MUSIC FOR PLEASURE. . . . . . . . . . . . . . . . . . . . . . . . . . . . . . . . . . . . . . . . . . . . . . . . . . . . . Polydor 5372422

### MONEY MARK
US rapper (born Mark Ramos Nishita, Detroit, MI) who first became known with The Beastie Boys, effectively becoming the fourth, unofficial member after recording with them in 1988. His debut album, recorded at home, originally appeared as a set of three ten-inch singles released by Los Angeles label Love Kit before being re-issued on Mo Wax.

09/09/1995 . . . . . 35 . . . . . 2 . . . . . .      MARK'S KEYBOARD REPAIR . . . . . . . . . . . . . . . . . . . . . . . . . . . . . . . . . . . . . . . . . . . . . . . . Mo Wax MW 034CD
16/05/1998 . . . . . 17 . . . . . 4 . . . . . .      PUSH THE BUTTON . . . . . . . . . . . . . . . . . . . . . . . . . . . . . . . . . . . . . . . . . . . . . . . . . . . . Mo Wax MW 090CD

### ZOOT MONEY AND THE BIG ROLL BAND
UK R&B artist (born George Bruno, 17/7/1942, Bournemouth, piano/vocals) who formed the Big Roll Band in 1961 with Roger Collis (guitar), Kevin Drake (saxophone), Johnny King (bass) and Peter Brooks (drums). By 1963 they were Money, Andy Somers (later as Summers, a member of The Police, guitar), Nick Newall (saxophone) and Colin Allen (drums), later adding Paul Williams (bass) and Clive Burrows (saxophone). Burrows left in 1966 and was replaced by Johnny Almond. Money (and Andy Somers) joined Eric Burdon's New Animals in 1968. Money has also appeared in various TV dramas.

15/10/1966 . . . . . 23 . . . . . 3 . . . . . .      ZOOT . . . . . . . . . . . . . . . . . . . . . . . . . . . . . . . . . . . . . . . . . . . . . . . . . . . . . . . . . . . . . Columbia SCX 6075

### MONICA
US singer (born Monica Arnold, 24/10/1980, Atlanta, GA) who was discovered winning a talent contest. She recorded her debut album at fourteen. With Brandy she won the 1998 Grammy Award for Best Rhythm & Blues Performance by a Duo for the single *The Boy Is Mine*.

25/07/1998 . . . . . 52 . . . . . 10 . . . . . .      THE BOY IS MINE . . . . . . . . . . . . . . . . . . . . . . . . . . . . . . . . . . . . . . . . . . . . . . . . . . . . . Arista 07822190112

### MONKEES
UK/US group formed in Los Angeles, CA in 1965 by writer/director/producer Bob Rafelson and Bert Schneider for a TV series. From 437 applicants, the four chosen were Davy Jones (born 30/12/1945, Manchester) who had appeared on UK TV in *Coronation Street* and *Z Cars*, Michael Nesmith (born 30/12/1942, Houston, TX), Peter Tork (born Peter Thorkelson, 13/2/1944, Washington DC) and Mickey Dolenz (born 8/3/1945, Los Angeles). The TV series ran from 1966 to 1968, with a film, *Head*, in 1968. Tork left in 1968, the group continuing as a trio until 1969 when they disbanded. They re-formed in 1986 minus Nesmith and again in 1996 with all four original members. They took their name in honour of The Beatles. Tork served three months in prison for possession of hashish in the early 1970s. They have a star on the Hollywood Walk of Fame.

28/01/1967 . . . . ❶⁷ . . . . 36 . . . . . .      THE MONKEES ▲¹³ . . . . . . . . . . . . . . . . . . . . . . . . . . . . . . . . . . . . . . . . . . . . . . RCA Victor SF 7844
15/04/1967 . . . . ❶² . . . . 25 . . . . . .      MORE OF THE MONKEES ▲¹⁸ . . . . . . . . . . . . . . . . . . . . . . . . . . . . . . . . . . . . . . RCA Victor SF 7868
08/07/1967 . . . . . 2 . . . . . . 19 . . . . . .      HEADQUARTERS ▲¹ . . . . . . . . . . . . . . . . . . . . . . . . . . . . . . . . . . . . . . . . . . . . . . RCA Victor SF 7886
13/01/1968 . . . . . 5 . . . . . . 11 . . . . . .      PISCES, AQUARIUS, CAPRICORN & JONES LTD. ▲⁵ . . . . . . . . . . . . . . . . . . . . . RCA Victor SF 7912
28/11/1981 . . . . . 99 . . . . . 1 . . . . . .      THE MONKEES. . . . . . . . . . . . . . . . . . . . . . . . . . . . . . . . . . . . . . . . . . . . . . . . . . . . . Arista DARTY 12
15/04/1989 . . . . . 12 . . . . . 9 . . . . . .      HEY HEY IT'S THE MONKEES – GREATEST HITS . . . . . . . . . . . . . . . . . . . . . . . . . . . K-Tel NE 1432
22/03/1997 . . . . . 15 . . . . . 10 . . . . . .      HERE THEY COME: THE GREATEST HITS OF THE MONKEES . . . . . . . . . . . . . . . . . . . . . . . warner.esp/Telstar 9548352182
10/03/2001 . . . . . 15 . . . . . 7 . . . . . . ●      THE DEFINITIVE . . . . . . . . . . . . . . . . . . . . . . . . . . . . . . . . . . . . . . . . . . . . . . . . . . . warner.esp 8573866922

### MONKEY MAFIA
UK production duo Daniel Peppe and Jon Carter. Carter initially recorded as Artery and Junior Cartier and is married to Radio 1 DJ Sara Cox, while Peppe records as Agent Dan and Themroc.

16/05/1998 . . . . . 69 . . . . . 1 . . . . . .      SHOOT THE BOSS . . . . . . . . . . . . . . . . . . . . . . . . . . . . . . . . . . . . . . . . . . . . . . . . Heavenly HVNLP 21CD

### MONKS OF AMPLEFORTH ABBEY UK monastic choir.
17/06/1995 . . . . . 73 . . . . . 2 . . . . . .      VISION OF PEACE . . . . . . . . . . . . . . . . . . . . . . . . . . . . . . . . . . . . . . . . . . . . . . . . Classic FM CFMCD 1783

### MONO UK vocal/instrumental duo Siobahn De Mare (vocals) and Martin Virgo (all instruments).
08/08/1998 . . . . . 71 . . . . . 1 . . . . . .      FORMICA BLUES . . . . . . . . . . . . . . . . . . . . . . . . . . . . . . . . . . . . . . . . . . . . . . . . . . . Echo ECHDD 017

### MONOCHROME SET
UK group formed in 1978 by Bid (guitar/vocals) and Lester Square (guitar), adding Andy Warren (bass) in 1979. They later added Jeremy Harrington (bass) and J D Haney (drums). Numerous changes included Carrie Booth (keyboards), Nick Wesolowski (drums) and Foz (guitar) among the arrivals and Lex Crane and Morris Windsor among the departures. They disbanded in 1985, although Bid, Lester, Warren and Orson Presence (guitar/keyboards) re-formed in 1989.

03/05/1980 . . . . . 62 . . . . . 4 . . . . . .      STRANGE BOUTIQUE . . . . . . . . . . . . . . . . . . . . . . . . . . . . . . . . . . . . . . . . . . . . . . . . . Dindisc DID 4

### TONY MONOPOLY
Australian singer who first came to prominence winning the TV series *Opportunity Knocks and* later appeared in the West End show *Moby Dick*. A one-time competitor in the *Song For Europe* competition (he sang *Leave A Little Town* in 1977) he died in 1995 at the age of 50.

12/06/1976 . . . . . 25 . . . . . 4 . . . . . .      TONY MONOPOLY . . . . . . . . . . . . . . . . . . . . . . . . . . . . . . . . . . . . . . . . . . . . . . . . . . BUK BULP 2000

### MATT MONRO
UK singer (born Terence Parsons, 1/12/1932, London) who was a bus driver who sang in his spare time, usually under the name Al Jordan until adopting the name Monro, supposedly in honour of Winifred Atwell's father. After singing on a Camay commercial he was asked by George Martin to perform on a Peter Sellers album and was noticed for his Frank Sinatra impersonation. He represented the UK in the 1964 Eurovision Song Contest, coming second behind Italy with *I Love The Little Things,* which failed to chart in the UK. He moved to the US in 1965 and died from liver cancer on 7/2/1985.

07/08/1965 . . . . . 20 . . . . . 1 . . . . . .      I HAVE DREAMED . . . . . . . . . . . . . . . . . . . . . . . . . . . . . . . . . . . . . . . . . . . . . . . . . Parlophone PMC 1250
17/09/1966 . . . . . 25 . . . . . 2 . . . . . .      THIS IS THE LIFE . . . . . . . . . . . . . . . . . . . . . . . . . . . . . . . . . . . . . . . . . . . . . . . . . . . . Capitol T 2540
26/08/1967 . . . . . 30 . . . . . 1 . . . . . .      INVITATION TO THE MOVIES . . . . . . . . . . . . . . . . . . . . . . . . . . . . . . . . . . . . . . . . . . Capitol ST 2730

▲⁹ Number of weeks album topped the US chart  ◆¹² RIAA Diamond Awards  ◇³ IFPI Platinum Europe Awards

15/03/1980 ..... 5 ...... 11 ...... ●   **HEARTBREAKERS** .................................................................................. EMI EMTV 23

**MONSTER MAGNET** US rock group formed in New Jersey in 1989 by Dave Wyndorf (guitar/vocals), John McBain (guitar), Joe Calandra (bass), Jon Kleinman (drums) and Tim Cronin (visuals/propaganda). McBain left in 1993 and was replaced by Ed Mundell.

01/04/1995 ..... 51 ...... 1 ......   DOPES TO INFINITY ........................................................................... A&M 5403152
13/06/1998 ..... 65 ...... 1 ......   POWERTRIP .................................................................................. A&M 5409082

**MONTROSE** US rock group formed in 1973 by Ronnie Montrose (guitar), Sammy Hagar (born 13/10/1947, Monterey, CA, vocals), Bill Church (bass) and Denny Carmassi (drums). Church left in 1974, replaced by Alan Fitzgerald, while Hagar was sacked in 1975 (promptly going solo) and replaced by Bob James, with Jim Alcivar joining on keyboards at the same time. Ronnie Montrose dissolved the group in 1976 and initially went solo as a jazz-rock artist before forming Gamma. In 1983 he resumed a solo career.

15/06/1974 ..... 43 ...... 1 ......   MONTROSE .......................................................................... Warner Brothers K 46276

**MONTY PYTHON'S FLYING CIRCUS** UK film/TV comedy team formed by John Cleese (born 27/10/1939, Weston-super-Mare), Graham Chapman (born 8/1/1941, Leicester), Terry Jones (born 1/2/1942, Colwyn Bay), Terry Gilliam (born 22/11/1940, Minneapolis, MN), Eric Idle (born 29/3/1943, South Shields) and Michael Palin (born 5/5/1943, Sheffield). Most of the Python songs were written in conjunction with Neil Innes (born 9/12/1944, Danbury). Chapman died from throat cancer on 4/10/1989. Palin was awarded a CBE in the 2000 New Year's Honours List. The theme to the TV series was John Phillip Sousa's *Liberty Bell March*.

30/10/1971 ..... 26 ...... 3 ......   ANOTHER MONTY PYTHON RECORD ........................................................ Charisma CAS 1049
27/01/1973 ..... 39 ...... 3 ......   MONTY PYTHON'S PREVIOUS RECORD ...................................................... Charisma CAS 1063
23/02/1974 ..... 49 ...... 2 ......   THE MONTY PYTHON MATCHING TIE AND HANDKERCHIEF ..................................... Charisma CAS 1080
27/07/1974 ..... 19 ...... 8 ...... ○   MONTY PYTHON LIVE AT DRURY LANE ....................................................... Charisma CLASS 4
09/08/1975 ..... 45 ...... 4 ......   THE ALBUM OF THE SOUNDTRACK OF THE TRAILER OF THE FILM OF MONTY PYTHON AND THE HOLY GRAIL
  Original soundtrack to the film ............................................................... Charisma CAS 1003
24/11/1979 ..... 63 ...... 3 ......   MONTY PYTHON'S LIFE OF BRIAN Original soundtrack to the film ....................... Warner Brothers K 56751
18/10/1980 ..... 13 ...... 8 ......   MONTY PYTHON'S CONTRACTUAL OBLIGATION ALBUM ...................................... Charisma CAS 1152
16/11/1991 ..... 62 ...... 2 ......   MONTY PYTHON SINGS **MONTY PYTHON** .................................................... Virgin MONT 1

**MOODY BLUES** UK group formed in Birmingham in 1964 by Denny Laine (born Brian Hines, 29/10/1944, Tyseley, Birmingham), Ray Thomas (born 29/12/1942, Stourport-on-Severn), Mike Pinder (born 27/12/1941, Birmingham), Graeme Edge (born 30/3/1942, Roxeter) and Clint Warwick (born Clinton Eccles, 25/6/1940) as the Moody Blues Five. Laine and Warwick left in 1966 and the group disbanded, quickly re-forming with the three remaining members and Justin Hayward (born 14/10/1946, Swindon) and John Lodge (born 20/7/1945, Birmingham). Pinder left in 1978 and was replaced by Patrick Moraz (born 24/6/1948). Laine joined Wings in 1971 and Hayward, Lodge and Thomas recorded projects outside the group. They launched the Threshold label in 1970. Originally called M&B5, after the local Mitchell & Butler brewery sponsored them, later the M became Moody, the B Blues and the 5 was dropped. They appeared in *The Simpsons*, apprehending Homer Simpson and Ned Flanders trying to run out on their new wives in Las Vegas.

27/01/1968 ..... 27 ...... 16 ......   DAYS OF FUTURE PASSED ................................................................... Deram SML 707
03/08/1968 ..... 5 ...... 32 ......   **IN SEARCH OF THE LOST CHORD** ........................................................... Deram SML 711
03/05/1969 .... ❶² ..... 73 ......   **ON THE THRESHOLD OF A DREAM** .......................................................... Deram SML 1035
06/12/1969 ..... 2 ...... 44 ......   **TO OUR CHILDREN'S CHILDREN'S CHILDREN** .................................................. Threshold THS 1
15/08/1970 .... ❶⁷ ..... 19 ......   **A QUESTION OF BALANCE** .................................................................. Threshold THS 3
07/08/1971 .... ❶¹ ..... 21 ......   **EVERY GOOD BOY DESERVES FAVOUR** ....................................................... Threshold THS 5
02/12/1972 ..... 5 ...... 18 ......   **SEVENTH SOJOURN** ▲⁵ ..................................................................... Threshold THS 7
16/11/1974 ..... 14 ...... 18 ...... ●   THIS IS THE MOODY BLUES ................................................................. Threshold MB 1/2
24/06/1978 ..... 6 ...... 18 ...... ●   **OCTAVE** ................................................................................... Decca TXS 129
10/11/1979 ..... 15 ...... 10 ...... ●   OUT OF THIS WORLD ......................................................................... K-Tel NE 1051
23/05/1981 ..... 7 ...... 19 ...... ○   **LONG DISTANCE VOYAGER** ▲³ .............................................................. Threshold TXS 139
10/09/1983 ..... 15 ...... 8 ......   THE PRESENT ............................................................................... Threshold TXS 140
10/05/1986 ..... 24 ...... 6 ......   THE OTHER SIDE OF LIFE .................................................................. Threshold POLD 5190
25/06/1988 ..... 21 ...... 5 ......   SUR LA MER ................................................................................ Polydor POLH 43
20/01/1990 ..... 71 ...... 1 ......   GREATEST HITS ............................................................................. Threshold 8406591
13/07/1991 ..... 54 ...... 2 ......   KEYS OF THE KINGDOM ...................................................................... Threshold 8494331
05/10/1996 ..... 13 ...... 15 ...... ●   THE VERY BEST OF THE MOODY BLUES .................................................... Polygram TV 5358002
22/04/2000 ..... 19 ...... 6 ......   THE VERY BEST OF/STRANGE TIMES .......................................................... Universal TV 5414242
11/05/2002 ..... 27 ...... 4 ......   THE VERY BEST OF ........................................................................ Universal Music TV 5833442

**IAN MOOR** UK singer (born in Elloughton, Humberside) who started singing after signing up for a Government sponsored training scheme in cabaret entertainment, as well as working as a laboratory technician! Known via winning the TV talent contest *Stars In Their Eyes* performing *Lady In Red* as Chris De Burgh (after Moor won the Champion of Champions final, De Burgh joined him on stage to perform the song).

07/10/2000 ..... 38 ...... 2 ......   NATURALLY ............................................................................. BMG TV 74321783862

**CHRISTY MOORE** Irish singer (born 7/5/1945, Dublin); he began as a semi-professional, working on building sites during the day and performing in clubs at night. He made his debut album in 1969 and then formed Planxty, an Irish folk group, with Donal Lunny, Liam O'Flynn and Andy Irvine. He returned to a solo career in 1975, and rejoined the revived Planxty towards the end of the 1970s

before departing a second time in 1981, along with Lunny, to form Moving Hearts. This venture lasted a little over a year before Moore went solo once again.

| 04/05/1991 | 49 | 3 | | SMOKE AND STRONG WHISKEY | Newbury CM 21 |
| 21/09/1991 | 69 | 1 | | THE CHRISTY MOORE COLLECTION 81–91 | East West WX 434 |
| 06/11/1993 | 66 | 2 | | KING PUCK | Equator ATLASCD 003 |
| 14/09/1996 | 35 | 2 | | GRAFFITI TONGUE | Grapevine GRACD 215 |

**DUDLEY MOORE** UK comedian/actor/pianist/singer (born 19/4/1935, Dagenham, Essex); he was first known as a musician, playing semi-professionally in jazz clubs before linking with Vic Lewis. He formed his own Dudley Moore Trio in the early 1960s and combined his musical pursuits with comedy, appearing in the touring comedy show *Beyond The Fringe*. He achieved national prominence through his comedy series with Peter Cook, *Not Only... But Also* before acting took precedence and he moved to Hollywood, appearing in such films as *10* (alongside Bo Derek) and *Arthur* (Liza Minnelli). He linked up with Cook again in 1976 for the *Derek And Clive* albums that proved immensely successful despite no radio play. The pair won the 1974 Grammy Award for Best Spoken Word Recording for *Good Evening*. Dudley Moore was awarded a CBE in the 2001 Queen's Birthday Honours List. He was married four times to actresses Suzy Kendall, Tuesday Weld, Brogan Lane and heiress Nicole Rothschild and died from brain disease on 27/3/2002. He has a star on the Hollywood Walk of Fame.

| 04/12/1965 | 11 | 9 | | THE OTHER SIDE OF DUDLEY MOORE | Decca LK 4732 |
| 21/05/1966 | 25 | 1 | | ONCE MOORE WITH COOK **PETER COOK AND DUDLEY MOORE** | Decca LK 4785 |
| 11/06/1966 | 13 | 10 | | GENUINE DUD **DUDLEY MOORE TRIO** | Decca LK 4788 |
| 18/09/1976 | 12 | 25 | O | DEREK AND CLIVE LIVE | Island ILPS 9434 |
| 24/12/1977 | 18 | 8 | O | COME AGAIN This and the above hit credited to **PETER COOK AND DUDLEY MOORE** | Virgin V 2094 |
| 26/01/1991 | 38 | 5 | | ORCHESTRA! **SIR GEORG SOLTI AND DUDLEY MOORE** | Decca 4308361 |

**GARY MOORE** UK singer/guitarist (born 4/4/1952, Belfast) who formed his first band, Skid Row, in 1968 before joining Thin Lizzy in 1974. Later a member of Colosseum II, he rejoined Thin Lizzy, recording his debut solo album at the same time. Moore also joined Jack Bruce and Ginger Baker to form BBM.

| 03/02/1979 | 70 | 1 | | BACK ON THE STREETS | MCA MCF 2853 |
| 16/10/1982 | 30 | 6 | | CORRIDORS OF POWER | Virgin V 2245 |
| 18/02/1984 | 12 | 7 | | VICTIMS OF THE FUTURE | 10 Records DIX 2 |
| 13/10/1984 | 32 | 3 | | WE WANT MOORE? | 10 Records GMDL 1 |
| 14/09/1985 | 12 | 8 | O | RUN FOR COVER | 10 Records DIX 16 |
| 12/07/1986 | 99 | 1 | | ROCKIN' EVERY NIGHT | 10 Records XID 1 |
| 14/03/1987 | 8 | 14 | O | **WILD FRONTIER** | 10 Records DIX 56 |
| 11/02/1989 | 23 | 5 | O | AFTER THE WAR | Virgin V 2575 |
| 07/04/1990 | 13 | 26 | ✪ | STILL GOT THE BLUES | Virgin V 2612 |
| 21/03/1992 | 4 | 13 | ● | **AFTER HOURS** | Virgin CDV 2684 |
| 22/05/1993 | 8 | 5 | ● | **BLUES ALIVE** | Virgin CDVX 2716 |
| 26/11/1994 | 33 | 6 | ● | BALLADS AND BLUES 1982–1994 | Virgin CDV 2768 |
| 10/06/1995 | 14 | 5 | | BLUES FOR GREENEY | Virgin CDV 2784 |
| 07/06/1997 | 43 | 2 | | DARK DAYS IN PARADISE | Virgin CDV 2826 |
| 31/10/1998 | 54 | 1 | | OUT IN THE FIELDS – THE VERY BEST OF GARY MOORE | Virgin CDVX 2871 |
| 24/03/2001 | 53 | 1 | | BACK TO THE BLUES | Sanctuary SANCD 072 |

**MANDY MOORE** US singer (born 10/4/1984, Nashua, NH) whose family moved to Orlando, FL when she was two months old. She appeared in the 2002 film *A Walk To Remember*.

| 20/05/2000 | 52 | 1 | | I WANNA BE WITH YOU | Epic 4982769 |

**M.O.P.** US rap duo formed in Brownsville, Brooklyn in 1993 by Lil' Fame and Billy Danzenie. The name stands for Mashed Out Posse. They later recorded with Busta Rhymes.

| 25/08/2001 | 40 | 3 | | WARRIOZ | Epic 4982772 |

**PATRICK MORAZ** Swiss keyboard player (born 24/6/1948, Morges); he had been a member of Refugee before replacing Rick Wakeman in Yes. He later recorded with fellow Yes member Bill Bruford and also appeared on albums by Steve Howe and The Moody Blues.

| 10/04/1976 | 28 | 7 | | PATRICK MORAZ | Charisma CDS 4002 |
| 23/07/1977 | 44 | 1 | | OUT IN THE SUN | Charisma CDS 4007 |

## MORCHEEBA
UK psychedelic blues group formed by brothers Paul and Ross Godfrey and lead vocalist Skye Edwards. Edwards took part in the *Perfect Day* project for the BBC's Children In Need charity.

| | | | | | |
|---|---|---|---|---|---|
| 12/04/1997 | 57 | 3 | O | WHO CAN YOU TRUST? | Indochina ZEN 009CD |
| 28/03/1998 | 18 | 71 | ✪ | **BIG CALM** | Indochina ZEN 017CDX |
| 22/07/2000 | 6 | 14 | ● | **FRAGMENTS OF FREEDOM** | East West 8573840272 |
| 13/07/2002 | 7 | 8 | O | **CHARANGO** | East West 0927469632 |
| 12/07/2003 | 6 | 12 | ● | **PARTS OF THE PROCESS** | East West 5046658702 |

## MORDRED
US rock group formed in San Francisco, CA in 1985 by Scott Holderby (vocals), Danny White (guitar), James Sanguinetti (guitar), Art Liboon (bass) and Gannon Hall (drums). They added DJ Aaron 'Pause' Vaughn in 1990.

| | | | | |
|---|---|---|---|---|
| 16/02/1991 | 70 | 1 | | IN THIS LIFE | Noise International NO 1591 |

## ALANIS MORISSETTE
Canadian singer (born Nadine Morissette, 1/6/1974, Ottawa, Ontario) who began her career as an actress, appearing on Nickelodeon TV in 1984. She recorded her first single at eleven, and by 1992 was recording material similar to Paula Abdul. She switched styles in 1994 following a teaming with songwriter Glen Ballard and signed with Madonna's Maverick label. She won Best International Newcomer at the 1996 BRIT Awards and Best Female at the 1996 MTV Europe Music Awards. She has won seven Grammy Awards including Best Female Rock Singer and Best Rock Song (with Glen Ballard) in 1995 for *You Oughta Know*, Best Music Video Long Form in 1997 for *Jagged Little Pill Live* and Best Rock Song and Best Female Rock Vocal Performance in 1998 for *Uninvited*. *Jagged Little Pill* has sold in excess of 29 million copies worldwide, the most by any female performer.

| | | | | | |
|---|---|---|---|---|---|
| 26/08/1995 | ❶[11] | 172 | ✪[10] | **JAGGED LITTLE PILL** ◇[7] ▲[12] ◆[16] 1996 Grammy Awards for Album of the Year and Best Rock Album | Maverick 9362459012 |
| 14/11/1998 | 3 | 21 | ✪ | **SUPPOSED FORMER INFATUATION JUNKIE** ◇[2] ▲[2] | Maverick 9362470942 |
| 04/12/1999 | 56 | 5 | O | MTV UNPLUGGED ◇ | Maverick 9362475892 |
| 16/03/2002 | 2 | 10 | ● | **UNDER RUG SWEPT** ◇ ▲[1] | Maverick 9362482722 |
| 29/05/2004 | 8 | 4 | O | **SO CALLED CHAOS** | Maverick 9362487732 |

## ENNIO MORRICONE
Italian orchestra leader/conductor/composer (born 11/10/1928, Rome) who scored over 400 films and TV themes during his long and illustrious career, including the 1964 film *A Fistful Of Dollars,* for which he is best known. He won the 1987 Grammy Award for Best Album of Original Instrumental Background Score Written for a Motion Picture for *The Untouchables*. He has been nominated for five Oscars, although winning none.

| | | | | | |
|---|---|---|---|---|---|
| 12/10/1968 | 2 | 18 | | **THE GOOD, THE BAD AND THE UGLY** Original soundtrack to the film | United Artists SULP 1197 |
| 05/03/1977 | 43 | 2 | | MOSES Original soundtrack to the film | Pye 28503 |
| 02/05/1981 | 23 | 5 | | THIS IS ENNIO MORRICONE | EMI THIS 33 |
| 09/05/1981 | 29 | 6 | | CHI MAI | BBC REH 414 |
| 07/03/1987 | 73 | 4 | ● | THE MISSION **ENNIO MORRICONE WITH THE LONDON PHILHARMONIC ORCHESTRA** Original soundtrack to the film, which gained a 1986 Oscar nomination | Virgin V 2402 |
| 30/09/2000 | 48 | 1 | | THE VERY BEST OF | Virgin CDV 2929 |
| 10/04/2004 | 69 | 1 | | MOVIE MASTERPIECES | BMG 82876596932 |

## MARK MORRISON
UK R&B singer (born 3/5/1972, Hanover, Germany) who was raised in Leicester and also spent a number of years in Florida before returning to England in 1993. He was jailed for three months in 1997 for threatening an off-duty policeman with a stun gun and later arrested and held in custody for failing to turn up at court on three occasions: when the case came before court he was sentenced to a further year in prison. He won the 1996 MOBO Award for Best R&B Act.

| | | | | | |
|---|---|---|---|---|---|
| 04/05/1996 | 4 | 38 | ● | **RETURN OF THE MACK** | WEA 0630145862 |
| 27/09/1997 | 50 | 1 | | ONLY GOD CAN JUDGE ME | WEA 0630195392 |

## VAN MORRISON
UK singer (born George Ivan Morrison, 31/8/1945, Belfast) who joined his first band Deannie Sands And The Javelins at twelve and two years later joined The Monarchs. He formed Them in 1963, disbanding the group in 1966 following a traumatic US tour. He signed solo with Bert Bern's Bang label in 1967 and scored a US top ten hit with *Brown Eyed Girl*. He has achieved considerably more success as an album artist. He was presented with the Outstanding Contribution Award at the 1994 BRIT Awards and in 1996 was awarded an MBE. He was inducted into the Rock & Roll Hall of Fame in 1993 and won the 1997 Grammy Award for Best Pop Collaboration with Vocals with John Lee Hooker for *Don't Look Back*.

| DATE | POS | WKS | BPI | ALBUM TITLE | LABEL & NUMBER |
|------|-----|-----|-----|-------------|----------------|
| 18/04/1970 | 32 | 2 | | MOONDANCE | Warner Brothers WS 1835 |
| 11/08/1973 | 22 | 3 | | HARD NOSE THE HIGHWAY | Warner Brothers K 46242 |
| 16/11/1974 | 41 | 1 | O | VEEDON FLEECE | Warner Brothers K 56068 |
| 07/05/1977 | 23 | 5 | | A PERIOD OF TRANSITION | Warner Brothers K 56322 |
| 21/10/1978 | 27 | 6 | O | WAVELENGTH | Warner Brothers K 56526 |
| 08/09/1979 | 21 | 9 | O | INTO THE MUSIC | Vertigo 9120 852 |
| 20/09/1980 | 53 | 3 | | COMMON ONE | Mercury 6302 021 |
| 27/02/1982 | 31 | 14 | | BEAUTIFUL VISION | Mercury 6302 122 |
| 26/03/1983 | 14 | 8 | | INARTICULATE SPEECH OF THE HEART | Mercury MERL 16 |
| 03/03/1984 | 47 | 4 | | LIVE AT THE GRAND OPERA HOUSE BELFAST | Mercury MERL 36 |
| 09/02/1985 | 25 | 5 | | A SENSE OF WONDER | Mercury MERH 54 |
| 02/08/1986 | 27 | 5 | | NO GURU, NO METHOD, NO TEACHER | Mercury MERH 94 |
| 19/09/1987 | 26 | 6 | | POETIC CHAMPIONS COMPOSE | Mercury MERH 110 |
| 02/07/1988 | 18 | 7 | | IRISH HEARTBEAT **VAN MORRISON AND THE CHIEFTAINS** | Mercury MERH 124 |
| 10/06/1989 | 13 | 14 | ● | AVALON SUNSET | Polydor 8392621 |
| 07/04/1990 | 4 | 87 | ● | **THE BEST OF VAN MORRISON** | Polydor 8419701 |
| 20/10/1990 | 5 | 14 | ● | **ENLIGHTENMENT** | Polydor 8471001 |
| 21/09/1991 | 5 | 6 | O | **HYMNS TO THE SILENCE** | Polydor 8490261 |
| 27/02/1993 | 31 | 3 | | THE BEST OF VAN MORRISON VOLUME 2 | Polydor 5177602 |
| 12/06/1993 | 4 | 9 | O | **TOO LONG IN EXILE** | Exile 5192192 |
| 30/04/1994 | 8 | 5 | | **A NIGHT IN SAN FRANCISCO** | Polydor 5212902 |
| 24/06/1995 | 5 | 15 | ● | **DAYS LIKE THIS** | Exile 5273072 |
| 15/03/1997 | 10 | 7 | O | **THE HEALING GAME** | Exile 5371012 |
| 27/06/1998 | 20 | 3 | | THE PHILOSOPHER'S STONE | Exile 5317892 |
| 20/03/1999 | 11 | 16 | ● | BACK ON TOP | Pointblank VPBCD 50 |
| 29/01/2000 | 14 | 3 | | THE SKIFFLE SESSIONS – LIVE IN BELFAST **VAN MORRISON/LONNIE DONEGAN/CHRIS BARBER** | Venture CDVE 945 |
| 07/10/2000 | 34 | 2 | | YOU WIN AGAIN **VAN MORRISON/LINDA GAIL LEWIS** | Pointblank VPBCD 54 |
| 25/05/2002 | 6 | 6 | O | **DOWN THE ROAD** | Exile 5891772 |
| 01/11/2003 | 43 | 2 | | WHAT'S WRONG WITH THIS PICTURE | Blue Note 5901672 |

**MORRISSEY** UK singer (born Steven Morrissey, 22/5/1959, Davyhulme) who was a journalist for *Record Mirror* before forming The Smiths with Johnny Marr in 1982. He went solo in 1988. He has also recorded with Siouxsie of Siouxsie And The Banshees.

| DATE | POS | WKS | BPI | ALBUM TITLE | LABEL & NUMBER |
|------|-----|-----|-----|-------------|----------------|
| 26/03/1988 | ❶[1] | 20 | ● | **VIVA HATE** | HMV CSD 3787 |
| 27/10/1990 | 9 | 4 | O | **BONA DRAG** | HMV CLP 3788 |
| 16/03/1991 | 8 | 4 | O | **KILL UNCLE** | HMV CSD 3789 |
| 08/08/1992 | 4 | 5 | | **YOUR ARSENAL** | HMV CDCSD 3790 |
| 22/05/1993 | 13 | 2 | | BEETHOVEN WAS DEAF | HMV CDSCD 3791 |
| 26/03/1994 | ❶[1] | 5 | ● | **VAUXHALL AND I** | Parlophone CDPCSD 148 |
| 18/02/1995 | 15 | 2 | | WORLD OF MORRISSEY | Parlophone CDPCSD 163 |
| 09/09/1995 | 4 | 3 | O | **SOUTHPAW GRAMMAR** | RCA Victor 74321299532 |
| 23/08/1997 | 8 | 3 | | **MALADJUSTED** | Island CID 8059 |
| 20/09/1997 | 26 | 4 | | THE BEST OF SUEDEHEAD | EMI CDEMC 3771 |
| 29/05/2004 | 2 | 5+ | ● | **YOU ARE THE QUARRY** | Attack ATKDX001 |

**MORRISSEY MULLEN** UK instrumental duo of Dick Morrissey (born 9/5/1940, Horley, Surrey, saxophone) and Jim Mullen (born 26/11/1945, Glasgow, guitar). They first worked together in Herbie Mann's band and later backed the Average White Band before launching Morrissey Mullen in 1980. Morrissey died from cancer on 8/11/2000.

| DATE | POS | WKS | BPI | ALBUM TITLE | LABEL & NUMBER |
|------|-----|-----|-----|-------------|----------------|
| 18/07/1981 | 43 | 5 | | BADNESS | Beggars Banquet BEGA 27 |
| 03/04/1982 | 47 | 5 | | LIFE ON THE WIRE | Beggars Banquet BEGA 33 |
| 23/04/1983 | 95 | 1 | | IT'S ABOUT TIME | Beggars Banquet BEGA 44 |

**WENDY MOTEN** US singer (born in Memphis, TN) who is one of six children born to Elder James and Viola Moten. She began her singing career in the church, performing at the Grace Tabernacle Church and St Stephen's B Church.

| DATE | POS | WKS | BPI | ALBUM TITLE | LABEL & NUMBER |
|------|-----|-----|-----|-------------|----------------|
| 19/03/1994 | 42 | 2 | | WENDY MOTEN | EMI CDMTL 1073 |

**MOTHER EARTH** UK jazz funk group formed by Matt Deighton (guitar/vocals), Simon Bartholomew (guitar), Neil Corcoran (bass), Bryn Barklam (keyboards) and Chris White (drums).

| DATE | POS | WKS | BPI | ALBUM TITLE | LABEL & NUMBER |
|------|-----|-----|-----|-------------|----------------|
| 05/03/1994 | 45 | 2 | | THE PEOPLE TREE | Acid Jazz JAZIDCD 083 |

**MOTHERS OF INVENTION** US rock group formed by singer, songwriter, multi-instrumentalist, producer, author and journalist Frank Zappa (born 21/12/1940, Baltimore, MD) with Roy Collins (vocals), Roy Estrada (bass) and Jimmy Carl Black (drums) as The Soul Giants. They changed their name to Mothers (the 'Of Invention' being added at the insistence of the record company) in 1966. Zappa would also lead a solo career, but still remained at the helm of The Mothers' and released albums prolifically under both banners for the rest of his life. In November 1991 it was revealed he was suffering from prostrate cancer and he died on 4/12/1993.

| | | | | |
|---|---|---|---|---|
| 29/06/1968 . . . . . 32 . . . . . . 5 . . . . . . | WE'RE ONLY IN IT FOR THE MONEY The cover was done as a parody of The Beatles' *Sgt Pepper's Lonely Hearts Club Band* and depicts the following personalities: Tom Wilson, Don Preston (waxwork), Billy Mundi (waxwork), Jimmy Carl Black (waxwork), Ian Underwood (waxwork), Frank Zappa (waxwork), Roy Estrada, Billy Mundi, Bunk Gardner, Jimmy Carl Black, Don Preston, Ian Underwood, Frank Zappa, Gail Zappa, Moon Unit Zappa, Cal Schenkel, Lisa Cohen, Jimi Hendrix, Unknown, Gabriel (Portrait Of A Countess), Big Mama Thornton, Chester Field, Phantom Of The Opera, Frank Zappa Sr, Billy Porter, Joe Casey, Nancy Sinatra, Bob Norton, Dial Soapman, H. Bosch (Garden Of Earthly Delights), Coach Ware, David St John, Sandy Hurvitz, Lyndon B Johnson, Mary Martin, Sue Cole, Bunk Garnder (waxwork), Medalo Bops, The Statue Of Liberty, A Dallas policeman, Unknown, John Zacherle, Unknown, Pope Pius IV, Rodan, Elroy Pie, Herb Cohen, Itallo Paollozi, Unknown, Elvis Presley, Nosferatu, George Liberace, Eddie Haskel, Ed Wynn, Lloyd Price, Rod Serling, Rick Blaufeld, Eric Burdon, Pauline Butcher, Sunbeam Shaver, Captain Beefheart, Albert Einstein, Cindy, Sue Gross, Tommy Marlowe, Harry S Truman, Admiral Byrd, Lynn Lascaro, Sgt Fury, Cal Schenkel, Katherine C Thurston, David Crosby, Butterinman, Theda Bara, John Sloatman Jr, Jacqueline Beer, Jeff Sklarow, Lee Harvey Oswald, Gracie Allen, Dottie Dribble, Unknown, Metalman, Barbie And Ken and Ludwig Von Beethoven . . . . . . . . . . . . . . . . . . . . . . . . . . . . . . . . . . . . Verve SVLP 9199 |
| 28/03/1970 . . . . . 17 . . . . . . 3 . . . . . . | BURNT WEENY SANDWICH . . . . . . . . . . . . . . . . . . . . . . . . . . . . . . . . . . . . . . . . . . . . . . . . Reprise RSLP 6370 |
| 03/10/1970 . . . . . 28 . . . . . . 4 . . . . . . | WEASELS RIPPED MY FLESH . . . . . . . . . . . . . . . . . . . . . . . . . . . . . . . . . . . . . . . . . . . . . . Reprise RSLP 2028 |

**MOTLEY CRUE** US heavy rock group formed in Los Angeles, CA in 1981 by Nikki Sixx (born Frank Carlton Serafino Ferrano, 11/12/1958, San Jose, CA, bass), Tommy Lee (born Thomas Lee Bass, 3/10/1962, Athens, Greece, drums), Vince Neil (born Vincent Neil Wharton, 8/2/1961, Hollywood, CA, vocals) and Mick Mars (born Bob Deal, 3/4/1955, Terre Haute, guitar). On 8/12/1984 a car driven by Neil was involved in a crash, killing Hanoi Rocks drummer Nicholas 'Razzle' Dingley and injuring two others, for which Neil was jailed and fined. Neil was sacked from the group in 1992 (and issued a $5 million lawsuit for breach of contract) and replaced by John Corabi (born 26/4/1959, Philadelphia, PA), although Corabi later left (replaced by the returning Neil) and launched a $7 million lawsuit for breach of contract. Lee was married to actress Heather Locklear and then *Baywatch* actress Pamela Anderson (both marriages ended in divorce, although Lee and Anderson later remarried). Lee was sentenced to six months for assaulting Pamela Anderson during their first marriage and subsequently jailed a second time for breaching the terms of his parole after being caught drinking. Sixx was married to *Playboy* Playmate Brandi Brandt and then *Baywatch* actress Donna D'Errico. Neil married mud wrestler Sharisse Rudell.

| | | | | | |
|---|---|---|---|---|---|
| 13/07/1985 . . . . . 36 . . . . . . 3 . . . . . . | THEATRE OF PAIN . . . . . . . . . . . . . . . . . . . . . . . . . . . . . . . . . . . . . . . . . . . . . . . . . . . . . . . Elektra EKT 8 |
| 30/05/1987 . . . . . 14 . . . . . . 11 . . . . . . ○ | GIRLS, GIRLS, GIRLS . . . . . . . . . . . . . . . . . . . . . . . . . . . . . . . . . . . . . . . . . . . . . . . . . . . . . Elektra EKT 39 |
| 16/09/1989 . . . . . 4 . . . . . . 7 . . . . . . ● | **DR. FEELGOOD** ▲² . . . . . . . . . . . . . . . . . . . . . . . . . . . . . . . . . . . . . . . . . . . . . . . . . . . . . . Elektra EKT 59 |
| 19/10/1991 . . . . . 20 . . . . . . 3 . . . . . . | DECADE OF DECADENCE '81–'91 . . . . . . . . . . . . . . . . . . . . . . . . . . . . . . . . . . . . . . . . . . . Elektra EKT 95 |
| 26/03/1994 . . . . . 17 . . . . . . 2 . . . . . . | MOTLEY CRUE . . . . . . . . . . . . . . . . . . . . . . . . . . . . . . . . . . . . . . . . . . . . . . . . . . . Elektra 7559615342 |

**MOTORHEAD** UK heavy rock group formed in 1975 by Lemmy (born Ian Kilmister, 24/12/1945, Stoke-on-Trent) after he had been sacked from Hawkwind. The original line-up was Lemmy (bass/vocals), Larry Wallis (guitar) and Lucas Fox (drums). Fox was replaced by Philthy Animal (born Phil Taylor, 21/9/1954, Chesterfield) in 1975 and 'Fast' Eddie Clarke (born 5/10/1950, guitar) joined just before Wallis left in 1976. Clarke left in 1982 and was replaced by Brian Robertson (born 12/9/1956, Glasgow). Robertson and Taylor left in 1983 and were replaced by Phil Campbell (born 7/5/1961, Pontypridd) and Wurzel (born Michael Burston, 23/10/1949, Cheltenham). Taylor briefly returned but left again in 1992, this time being replaced by Mikkey Dee (born 31/10/1963, Olundby, Sweden). The group also recorded with Girlschool/Headgirl.

| | | | | | |
|---|---|---|---|---|---|
| 24/09/1977 . . . . . 43 . . . . . . 5 . . . . . . ○ | MOTORHEAD . . . . . . . . . . . . . . . . . . . . . . . . . . . . . . . . . . . . . . . . . . . . . . . . . . . . . . . Chiswick WIK 2 |
| 24/03/1979 . . . . . 24 . . . . . . 11 . . . . . . ○ | OVERKILL . . . . . . . . . . . . . . . . . . . . . . . . . . . . . . . . . . . . . . . . . . . . . . . . . . . . . . . . . Bronze BRON 515 |
| 27/10/1979 . . . . . 12 . . . . . . 13 . . . . . . ○ | BOMBER . . . . . . . . . . . . . . . . . . . . . . . . . . . . . . . . . . . . . . . . . . . . . . . . . . . . . . . . . . Bronze BRON 523 |
| 08/12/1979 . . . . . 65 . . . . . . 2 . . . . . . | ON PAROLE . . . . . . . . . . . . . . . . . . . . . . . . . . . . . . . . . . . . . . . . . . . . . . . . . . . . United Artists LBR 1004 |
| 08/11/1980 . . . . . 4 . . . . . . 16 . . . . . . ● | **ACE OF SPADES** . . . . . . . . . . . . . . . . . . . . . . . . . . . . . . . . . . . . . . . . . . . . . . . . . . . . Bronze BRON 531 |
| 27/06/1981 . . . . . ❶¹ . . . . . . 21 . . . . . . ● | **NO SLEEP 'TIL HAMMERSMITH** . . . . . . . . . . . . . . . . . . . . . . . . . . . . . . . . . . . . . . . . . Bronze BRON 535 |
| 17/04/1982 . . . . . 6 . . . . . . 9 . . . . . . ○ | **IRONFIST** . . . . . . . . . . . . . . . . . . . . . . . . . . . . . . . . . . . . . . . . . . . . . . . . . . . . . . . . Bronze BRNA 539 |
| 26/02/1983 . . . . . 71 . . . . . . 2 . . . . . . | WHAT'S WORDS WORTH . . . . . . . . . . . . . . . . . . . . . . . . . . . . . . . . . . . . . . . . . . . . . . . . Big Beat NED 2 |
| 04/06/1983 . . . . . 20 . . . . . . 4 . . . . . . | ANOTHER PERFECT DAY . . . . . . . . . . . . . . . . . . . . . . . . . . . . . . . . . . . . . . . . . . . . . . . Bronze BRON 546 |
| 15/09/1984 . . . . . 14 . . . . . . 6 . . . . . . ○ | NO REMORSE . . . . . . . . . . . . . . . . . . . . . . . . . . . . . . . . . . . . . . . . . . . . . . . . . . . Bronze PROTV MOTOR 1 |
| 09/08/1986 . . . . . 21 . . . . . . 4 . . . . . . | ORGASMATRON . . . . . . . . . . . . . . . . . . . . . . . . . . . . . . . . . . . . . . . . . . . . . . . . . . . . . . GWR GWLP 1 |
| 05/09/1987 . . . . . 34 . . . . . . 3 . . . . . . | ROCK 'N' ROLL . . . . . . . . . . . . . . . . . . . . . . . . . . . . . . . . . . . . . . . . . . . . . . . . . . . . . GWR GWLP 14 |
| 15/10/1988 . . . . . 79 . . . . . . 1 . . . . . . | NO SLEEP AT ALL . . . . . . . . . . . . . . . . . . . . . . . . . . . . . . . . . . . . . . . . . . . . . . . . . . . . . GWR GWR 31 |
| 02/02/1991 . . . . . 24 . . . . . . 4 . . . . . . | 1916 . . . . . . . . . . . . . . . . . . . . . . . . . . . . . . . . . . . . . . . . . . . . . . . . . . . . . . . . . . . . Epic 4674811 |
| 08/08/1992 . . . . . 60 . . . . . . 1 . . . . . . | MARCH OR DIE . . . . . . . . . . . . . . . . . . . . . . . . . . . . . . . . . . . . . . . . . . . . . . . . . . . . . . Epic 4717232 |
| 09/09/2000 . . . . . 52 . . . . . . 1 . . . . . . | THE BEST OF MOTORHEAD . . . . . . . . . . . . . . . . . . . . . . . . . . . . . . . . . . . . . . . . . . . . Metal Is MISDD 002 |

**MOTORS** UK rock group formed by Nick Garvey (born 26/4/1951, Stoke-on-Trent, guitar), Andy McMaster (born 27/7/1947, Glasgow, guitar), Rob Hendry (guitar) and Ricky Wernham (aka Ricky Slaughter, drums). Hendry left soon after their formation and was replaced by Bram Tchaikovsky (born Peter Bramall, 10/11/1950, Lincolnshire). The group dissolved by the end of the 1970s.

| | | | | |
|---|---|---|---|---|
| 15/10/1977 . . . . . 46 . . . . . . 5 . . . . . . | THE MOTORS . . . . . . . . . . . . . . . . . . . . . . . . . . . . . . . . . . . . . . . . . . . . . . . . . . . . . . Virgin V 2089 |
| 03/06/1978 . . . . . 60 . . . . . . 1 . . . . . . | APPROVED BY THE MOTORS . . . . . . . . . . . . . . . . . . . . . . . . . . . . . . . . . . . . . . . . . . . . Virgin V 2101 |

**MOTT THE HOOPLE** UK rock group formed in 1968 by Overend Watts (born Peter Watts, 13/5/1949, Birmingham, bass), Dale 'Buffin' Griffin (born 24/10/1948, Ross-on-Wye, drums), Verden Allen (born 26/5/1944, keyboards), Mick Ralphs (born 31/5/1944, Hereford, guitar) and Stan Tippins (vocals) as the Shakedown Sound. Tippins was replaced the following year by Ian Hunter (born 3/6/1946, Oswestry) shortly after the group signed with Island Records. They were on the verge of splitting in 1972 having had little

success, when David Bowie urged them to carry on and record a couple of tracks he had written. Allen left in 1972, Ralphs in 1973 (replaced by Luther Grosvenor, born 23/12/1949, Evesham). Grosvenor left in 1974 and was replaced by former David Bowie guitarist Mick Ronson (born 26/5/1949, Hull), although the group disbanded three months later. Hunter and Ronson formed the Hunter-Ronson Band, which lasted six months before splitting (they re-formed in 1990). Mott The Hoople were named after a 1967 novel by Willard Manus. Ronson died from cancer 29/4/1993.

| | | | | | |
|---|---|---|---|---|---|
| 02/05/1970 | 66 | 1 | | MOTT THE HOOPLE | Island ILPS 9108 |
| 17/10/1970 | 48 | 2 | | MAD SHADOWS | Island ILPS 9119 |
| 17/04/1971 | 44 | 2 | | WILD LIFE | Island ILPS 9144 |
| 23/09/1972 | 21 | 4 | | ALL THE YOUNG DUDES | CBS 65184 |
| 11/08/1973 | 7 | 15 | ○ | **MOTT THE HOOPLE** | CBS 65184 |
| 13/04/1974 | 11 | 5 | ● | THE HOOPLE | CBS 69062 |
| 23/11/1974 | 32 | 2 | | MOTT THE HOOPLE – LIVE | CBS 69093 |
| 04/10/1975 | 45 | 1 | | DRIVE ON | CBS 69154 |

**BOB MOULD** US singer/guitarist (born 16/10/1960, Malone, NY) who was a founding member and leader of Husker Du in 1979 with Greg Norton and Grant Hart. When the group dissolved in 1988, Mould went solo (as did Norton) and formed his own record company, SOL (Singles Only Label). In 1991 he formed Sugar with David Barbe and Malcolm Travi, then went solo again in 1995 when they split.

| | | | | | |
|---|---|---|---|---|---|
| 11/05/1996 | 52 | 1 | | BOB MOULD | Creation CRECD 188 |
| 05/09/1998 | 58 | 1 | | THE LAST DOG AND PONY SHOW | Creation CRECD 215 |

**MOUNTAIN** US rock group formed by Leslie West (born Leslie Weinstein, 22/10/1945, Queens, NYC, guitar), Felix Pappalardi (born 1939, The Bronx, NYC, bass), Steve Knight (keyboards) and Corky Laing (drums), after Pappalardi had produced West's solo album *Mountain*. After four albums the group temporarily disbanded, returning in 1974 with West, Pappalardi, Bob Mann (keyboards) and Alan Schwartzberg (drums). Laing returned the following year, although Mountain disbanded a second time soon after. In 1985 West, Laing and Mark Clarke (bass) revived the group a third time. Pappalardi was shot to death in the neck whilst in bed by his wife and songwriting partner Gail Collins on 17/4/1983. Although she claimed the gun had accidentally discharged and was acquitted of second degree murder, she was convicted of criminal negligent homicide and sentenced to serve between sixteen months and four years in prison. Pappalardi's father, Felix Pappalardi Sr, later launched a lawsuit against Collins for 'wilfully and maliciously' shooting his son.

| | | | | | |
|---|---|---|---|---|---|
| 05/06/1971 | 43 | 1 | | NANTUCKET SLEIGHRIDE | Island ILPS 9148 |
| 08/07/1972 | 21 | 3 | | THE ROAD GOES EVER ON | Island ILPS 9199 |

**NANA MOUSKOURI** Greek singer (born 10/10/1936, Athens) who began recording in 1959 and relocated to Germany in 1960 to break into the European market. After scoring several European hits, Nana undertook a US college tour in 1967 in an attempt to crossover into the US. Despite her nationality she represented Luxembourg in the 1963 Eurovision Song Contest.

| | | | | | |
|---|---|---|---|---|---|
| 07/06/1969 | 10 | 105 | | **OVER AND OVER** | Fontana S 5511 |
| 04/04/1970 | 10 | 25 | | **THE EXQUISITE NANA MOUSKOURI** | Fontana STL 5536 |
| 10/10/1970 | 68 | 1 | | RECITAL '70 | Fontana 6312 003 |
| 03/04/1971 | 16 | 15 | | TURN ON THE SUN | Fontana 6312 008 |
| 29/07/1972 | 29 | 11 | | BRITISH CONCERT | Fontana 6651 003 |
| 28/04/1973 | 29 | 11 | | SONGS FROM HER TV SERIES | Fontana 6312 036 |
| 28/09/1974 | 38 | 6 | | SPOTLIGHT ON NANA MOUSKOURI | Fontana 6641 197 |
| 10/07/1976 | 3 | 16 | ● | **PASSPORT** | Philips 9101 061 |
| 22/02/1986 | 19 | 10 | ○ | ALONE | Philips PHH 3 |
| 08/10/1988 | 44 | 8 | ● | THE MAGIC OF NANA MOUSKOURI | Philips NMTV 1 |
| 03/03/2001 | 39 | 5 | | AT HER VERY BEST | Philips 5485492 |

**MOVE** UK rock group formed in Birmingham in 1966 by Roy Wood (born Ulysses Wood, 8/11/1946, Birmingham, guitar/vocals), Carl Wayne (born 18/8/1944, Birmingham, vocals), Bev Bevan (born 24/11/1944, Birmingham, drums), Christopher 'Ace' Kefford (born 10/12/1946, Birmingham, bass) and Trevor Burton (born 9/3/1944, Birmingham, lead guitar). Kefford left in 1968, Burton in 1969 and Wayne in 1970. Their replacements were Rick Price and Jeff Lynne (born 20/12/1947, Birmingham, guitar/vocals). By 1971 the Move began evolving into the Electric Light Orchestra, a transformation completed in 1972.

| | | | | | |
|---|---|---|---|---|---|
| 13/04/1968 | 15 | 9 | | MOVE | Regal Zonophone SLPZ 1002 |

## ALISON MOYET
UK singer (born Genevieve Alison Moyet, 18/6/1961, Basildon) who had sung with a number of Southend groups before accepting an invitation from Vince Clarke (ex-Depeche Mode) to help form Yazoo in 1982. The group split after two albums, with Moyet going solo. After going into semi-retirement in 1995 she returned in 2001, appearing in the West End musical *Chicago*. She has twice been a winner at the BRIT Awards, having won the Best British Female Award in 1985 and 1988.

| | | | | |
|---|---|---|---|---|
| 17/11/1984 | ❶¹ | 84 | ✪⁴ | **ALF** ............................................................. CBS 26229 |
| 18/04/1987 | 2 | 52 | ✪² | **RAINDANCING** ................................................. CBS 4501521 |
| 04/05/1991 | 11 | 6 | ○ | HOODOO ........................................................ Columbia 4682721 |
| 02/04/1994 | 24 | 4 | | ESSEX ........................................................... Columbia 4759552 |
| 03/06/1995 | ❶¹ | 35 | ✪ | **SINGLES** ....................................................... Columbia 4806632 |
| 22/09/2001 | 16 | 4 | ○ | THE ESSENTIAL .................................................. Columbia STVCD 123 |
| 31/08/2002 | 18 | 9 | ○ | HOMETIME ..................................................... Sanctuary SANCD 128 |

## MS DYNAMITE
UK garage singer (born Niomi McLean-Daley, 1981), she won the 2002 MOBO Awards for Best British Act, Best Newcomer and Best Single for *It Takes More*. She also won the 2002 Mercury Music Prize, and two 2003 BRIT Awards: Best British Female Solo Artist and Best British Urban Act.

| | | | | |
|---|---|---|---|---|
| 22/06/2002 | 10 | 42 | ✪ | **A LITTLE DEEPER** 2002 Mercury Music Prize ............................ Polydor 5899552 |

## MTUME
US R&B group formed in 1980 by James Mtume (born in Philadelphia, PA, previously with Miles Davis' group) and featuring Tawatha Agee, Ed Moore and Roger Parker at the time of their hit. Mtume and Reggie Lucas won the 1980 Grammy Award for Best Rhythm & Blues Song for *Never Knew Love Like This Before*, a hit for Stephanie Mills.

| | | | | |
|---|---|---|---|---|
| 06/10/1984 | 85 | 1 | | YOU, ME AND HE .................................................. Epic EPC 26077 |

## MUD
UK pop group formed in 1966 by Les Gray (born 9/4/1946, Carshalton, vocals), Rob Davis (born 1/10/1947, Carshalton, guitar/vocals), Dave Mount (born 3/3/1947, Carshalton, drums/vocals) and Ray Stiles (born 20/11/1946, Carshalton, bass/vocals). They turned professional in 1968 and in 1972 were spotted by producer Mickie Most, who signed them to his label with songwriters Nicky Chinn and Mike Chapman. Gray later recorded solo and Stiles joined the Hollies. Davis later wrote dance hits including Coco's *I Need A Miracle* and Spiller's *Groovejet*. Gray died from cancer on 21/2/2004.

| | | | | |
|---|---|---|---|---|
| 28/09/1974 | 8 | 35 | ● | **MUD ROCK** ...................................................... RAK SRAK 508 |
| 26/07/1975 | 6 | 12 | ● | **MUD ROCK VOLUME 2** ............................................. RAK SRAK 513 |
| 01/11/1975 | 25 | 6 | ○ | MUD'S GREATEST HITS .............................................. RAK STRAK 6755 |
| 27/12/1975 | 33 | 5 | ○ | USE YOUR IMAGINATION ........................................ Private Stock PVLP 1003 |

## MUDHONEY
US group formed in Seattle, WA by Mark Arm (vocals), Steve Turner (guitar), Matt Lukin (bass) and Dan Peters (drums). Arm and Turner had previously been in Green River and Thrown Ups, Lukin in The Melvins and Peters in Bundles Of Hiss.

| | | | | |
|---|---|---|---|---|
| 31/08/1991 | 34 | 2 | | EVERY GOOD BOY DESERVES FUDGE ................................... Sub-Pop SP 18160 |
| 17/10/1992 | 39 | 2 | | PIECE OF CAKE ................................................... Reprise 9362450902 |
| 08/04/1995 | 70 | 1 | | MY BROTHER THE COW ............................................. Reprise 9362458402 |

## MULL HISTORICAL SOCIETY
UK group formed in Scotland in 2000 by Colin MacIntyre (guitar/vocals) and Alan Malloy (bass). They signed with independent label Tugboat the same year.

| | | | | |
|---|---|---|---|---|
| 27/10/2001 | 43 | 1 | | LOSS ......................................................... Blanco Y Negro 0927413072 |
| 15/03/2003 | 19 | 3 | | US ........................................................... Blanco Y Negro 0927499562 |

## GERRY MULLIGAN AND BEN WEBSTER
US instrumental duo Gerry Mulligan (born 6/4/1927, New York City, baritone saxophone) and Ben Webster (born 27/3/1909, Kansas City, MO, tenor saxophone). Mulligan had begun his career playing the piano before switching to sax, first making his name as an arranger, working with the likes of Gene Krupa and Claude Thornhill. He later played with Miles Davis, Stan Kenton, Chet Baker, Dave Brubeck, Stan Getz, Paul Desmond and others. He died from complications brought on by a knee infection on 20/1/1996. Webster also studied the piano before switching to the saxophone, a move that took place in 1930. After working with Bennie Moten, Fletcher Henderson and Andy Kirk he joined Duke Ellington's band in 1940, although three years later he formed his own outfit. He returned to Ellington towards the end of the decade, this stay being equally brief, and thereafter he toured almost exclusively as a solo artist. He died on 20/9/1973. Gerry Mulligan won the 1981 Grammy Award for Best Jazz Performance by a Big Band with his orchestra for *Walk On The Water*.

| | | | | |
|---|---|---|---|---|
| 24/09/1960 | 15 | 1 | | GERRY MULLIGAN MEETS BEN WEBSTER ................................... HMV CLP 1373 |

## SHAWN MULLINS
US singer/acoustic guitarist (born 8/3/1968, Atlanta, GA) who also runs the SMG independent record label. He later became a member of The Thorns with Matthew Sweet and Pete Droge.

| | | | | |
|---|---|---|---|---|
| 20/03/1999 | 60 | 1 | | SOUL'S CORE ..................................................... Columbia 4930372 |

## SAMANTHA MUMBA
Irish singer (born 18/1/1983, Dublin) with a Zambian aircraft engineer father and Irish office worker mother. She was just fifteen when she first signed with Wild Card. She later made her film debut in 2002 in *The Time Machine*.

| | | | | |
|---|---|---|---|---|
| 11/11/2000 | 9 | 16 | ● | **GOTTA TELL YOU** ................................................. Wild Card 5492262 |

## MUNGO JERRY
UK group formed in the late 1960s as a skiffle and pub-rock group by Ray Dorset (born 21/3/1946, Middlesex, guitar/vocals), Colin Earl (keyboards), Paul King (banjo/guitar) and Mike Cole (bass). Cole left in 1971 and was replaced by John Godfrey. King and Earl left in 1972 and were replaced by Jon Pope (keyboards) and Tim Reeves (drums). After their chart career ended Dorset recorded solo and also teamed up with Peter Green (ex-Fleetwood Mac) and Vincent Crane (ex-Atomic Rooster) as Katmandu. As a songwriter he penned Kelly Marie's chart topper *Feels Like I'm In Love*.

08/08/1970 . . . . . 13 . . . . . . 6 . . . . . . MUNGO JERRY . . . . . . . . . . . . . . . . . . . . . . . . . . . . . . . . . . . . . . . . . . . . . . . . . . . . . . . . . . . . Dawn DNLS 3008
04/11/1978 . . . . . 14 . . . . . . 8 . . . . . . ELECTRONICALLY TESTED. . . . . . . . . . . . . . . . . . . . . . . . . . . . . . . . . . . . . . . . . . . . . . . . . . . . . . . Dawn DNLS 3020

## MUNROS FEATURING DAVID METHREN
UK instrumental group with an album of traditional Scottish melodies.

27/06/1998 . . . . . 46 . . . . . . 3 . . . . . . THE LONE PIPER . . . . . . . . . . . . . . . . . . . . . . . . . . . . . . . . . . . . . . . . . . . . . . . . . . . . . . . . . . . . . . Virgin VTCD 185

## MUPPETS
US puppet group created for TV by Jim Henson (born 24/9/1936, Greenville, MS). Henson had already achieved considerable success with *Sesame Street* aimed at children. The Muppets were aimed at an older market and featured Kermit The Frog, Miss Piggy, Fozzie Bear, Animal (who enjoyed a solo hit), Gonzo and others. Henson died from pneumonia on 16/5/1990. The Muppets have won eight Grammy Awards, all in the Best Recording for Children category: in 1977, 1978, 1979, 1980, 1981, 1985, 1986 and 1998. Both Jim Henson and Kermit The Frog have a star on the Hollywood Walk of Fame.

11/06/1977 . . . . ❶[1] . . . 35 . . . . . ● **THE MUPPET SHOW** . . . . . . . . . . . . . . . . . . . . . . . . . . . . . . . . . . . . . . . . . . . . . . . . . . . . . . . . . . . . . Pye NSPH 19
25/02/1978 . . . . . 16 . . . . . 10 . . . . . . ○ THE MUPPET SHOW VOLUME 2 . . . . . . . . . . . . . . . . . . . . . . . . . . . . . . . . . . . . . . . . . . . . . . . . . . . . . . . Pye NSPH 21

## MURDERDOLLS
US rock group formed by Joey Jordison (guitar), Tripp Eisen (guitar), Wednesday 13 (vocals), Eric Griffin (bass) and Ben Graves (drums). Jordison is also a member of Slipknot while Eisen is a member of Static-X.

31/08/2002 . . . . . 40 . . . . . . 1 . . . . . . BEYOND THE VALLEY OF THE MURDERDOLLS. . . . . . . . . . . . . . . . . . . . . . . . . . . . . . . . . . . . Roadrunner RR 84262

## PETER MURPHY
UK singer (born 11/7/1957, Northampton) who was a founding member of Bauhaus in 1978 and remained with the group until they split in 1983. After a brief spell as one half of Dali's Car (with ex-Japan Mick Karn) he went solo, later forming The 100 Men as his backing group. This band featured Peter Bonas (guitar), Paul Statham (keyboards and guitar) and Eddie Branch (bass). He dissolved the band in 1992 and continued with his solo career.

26/07/1986 . . . . . 82 . . . . . . 1 . . . . . . SHOULD THE WORLD FAIL TO FALL APART . . . . . . . . . . . . . . . . . . . . . . . . . . . . . . . . . . . . . . Beggars Banquet BEGA 69

## ANNE MURRAY
Canadian singer (born Moma Anne Murray, 20/6/1945, Springhill, Nova Scotia); she was a physical education teacher before becoming a professional singer. She made her first record in 1969. She has won four Grammy Awards: Best Country & Western Vocal Performance in 1974 for *Love Song;* Best Pop Vocal Performance in 1978 for *You Needed Me;* Best Country Vocal Performance in 1980 for *Could I Have This Dance;* and Best Country Vocal Performance in 1983 for *A Little Good News.* She has a star on the Hollywood Walk of Fame.

03/10/1981 . . . . . 14 . . . . . 10 . . . . . . ○ THE VERY BEST OF ANNE MURRAY . . . . . . . . . . . . . . . . . . . . . . . . . . . . . . . . . . . . . . . . . . . . . . . . . Capitol EMTV 31

## PAULINE MURRAY AND THE INVISIBLE GIRLS
UK singer (ex-Penetration) with an all-male (despite their name) group that at times featured Robert Blamire (guitar), Vini Reilly, Bernard Sumner, John Maher, Wayne Hussey and Martin Hannett.

11/10/1980 . . . . . 25 . . . . . . 4 . . . . . . PAULINE MURRAY AND THE INVISIBLE GIRLS . . . . . . . . . . . . . . . . . . . . . . . . . . . . . . . . . . . . Elusive 2394 227

## MUSE
UK rock group formed in Teignmouth by Matt Bellamy (guitar/vocals), Chris Wolstenholme (bass) and Dominic Howard (drums). They were originally called Gothic Plague, Fixed Penalty and Rocket Baby Dolls. Named Best Newcomer in the 2000 NME Premier Awards, they were initially signed by Maverick Records in the US.

16/10/1999 . . . . . 29 . . . . . 16 . . . . . . ● SHOWBIZ. . . . . . . . . . . . . . . . . . . . . . . . . . . . . . . . . . . . . . . . . . . . . . . . . . . . . . . . . . . . . . . Mushroom MUSH 59CD
30/06/2001 . . . . . 3 . . . . . 24 . . . . . . ✪ **ORIGIN OF SYMMETRY** . . . . . . . . . . . . . . . . . . . . . . . . . . . . . . . . . . . . . . . . . . . . . . . . . . . . Mushroom MUSH 93CD
13/07/2002 . . . . . 10 . . . . . . 4 . . . . . . ○ **HULLABALOO** . . . . . . . . . . . . . . . . . . . . . . . . . . . . . . . . . . . . . . . . . . . . . . . . . . . . . . . . . . . Mushroom MUSH 105CDXX
04/10/2003 . . . . ❶[1] . . . 35 . . . . . . ✪ **ABSOLUTION** . . . . . . . . . . . . . . . . . . . . . . . . . . . . . . . . . . . . . . . . . . . . . . . . . . . . . . . . . Taste Media Ltd 5046685872

## MUSIC
UK rock group formed in Leeds by Robert Harvey (vocals), Adam Nutter (guitar), Stuart Coleman (bass) and Phil Jordan (drums).

14/09/2002 . . . . . 4 . . . . . 5 . . . . . . ● **THE MUSIC** . . . . . . . . . . . . . . . . . . . . . . . . . . . . . . . . . . . . . . . . . . . . . . . . . . . . . . . . . . . . . . Hut CDHUTX 76

## MUSIC STUDENTS – see IAN DURY AND THE BLOCKHEADS

## MUSICAL YOUTH
UK reggae group formed by Dennis Seaton (lead vocals), Kelvin (guitar) and his brother Michael Grant (keyboards) and Patrick (bass) and his brother Junior Waite (drums), all five of whom attended Duddeston Manor School in Birmingham. At the time of their debut hit their ages ranged from eleven to sixteen. Patrick Waite, who later served time in prison for drug offences, died after collapsing at a friend's house and hitting his head on 18/2/1993 at the age of 24 years.

04/12/1982 . . . . . 24 . . . . . 22 . . . . . . ● THE YOUTH OF TODAY . . . . . . . . . . . . . . . . . . . . . . . . . . . . . . . . . . . . . . . . . . . . . . . . . . . . . . MCA YOULP 1

▲[9] Number of weeks album topped the US chart ◆[12] RIAA Diamond Awards ◇[3] IFPI Platinum Europe Awards

**MUTTON BIRDS** New Zealand vocal/instrumental group formed in 1990 by Don McGlashan (guitar/vocals), David Long (guitar), Alan Gregg (bass) and Ross Burge (drums). After releasing their debut album on their own Bag Records imprint they signed with Virgin in 1993. Gregg left the group in 1999 and was replaced by Tony Fisher.

12/07/1997 . . . . . 64 . . . . . . 1 . . . . . . ENVY OF ANGELS . . . . . . . . . . . . . . . . . . . . . . . . . . . . . . . . . . . . . . . . . . . . . . . . . . . . . . . . . . . . . . . . . Virgin CDVIR 55

**MY BLOODY VALENTINE** UK rock group formed in Northern Ireland in 1984 by Kevin Shields (born 21/5/1963, New York, guitar/vocals), Colin O'Ciosoig (born 31/10/1964, Dublin, drums), Dave Conway (vocals) and Tina (keyboards). They later added Belinda Butcher (born 16/9/1961, London, vocals) and Debbie Googe (born 24/10/1962, Somerset, bass).

23/11/1991 . . . . . 24 . . . . . . 2 . . . . . . LOVELESS . . . . . . . . . . . . . . . . . . . . . . . . . . . . . . . . . . . . . . . . . . . . . . . . . . . . . . . . . . . . . . . . . . . . . Creation CRELP 060

**MY LIFE STORY** UK group formed by Jake Shillingford. For live dates the group is augmented by an eleven-piece orchestra.

22/03/1997 . . . . . 36 . . . . . . 1 . . . . . . THE GOLDEN MILE . . . . . . . . . . . . . . . . . . . . . . . . . . . . . . . . . . . . . . . . . . . . . . . . . . . . . . . . . Parlophone CDPCSY 7386

**MY MORNING JACKET** US rock group formed in Louisville, KY by Jim James (vocals), Johnny Quaid (guitar), Two-Tone Tommy (bass), Danny Cash (keyboards) and Patrick Hallahhhan (drums); they first recorded for Darla Records in 1999.

20/09/2003 . . . . . 62 . . . . . . 1 . . . . . . IT STILL MOVES . . . . . . . . . . . . . . . . . . . . . . . . . . . . . . . . . . . . . . . . . . . . . . . . . . . . . . . . . . . . . RCA 82876559252

**MY VITRIOL** UK rock group formed by Som Wijay-Wardner (born in Sri Lanka, guitar/vocals), Seth Taylor (guitar), Carolyn Bannister (bass) and Ravi Kesevaram (drums), taking the group's name from a passage in Graham Greene's book *Brighton Rock*. They first recorded for ORG Records before being snapped up by Infectious.

17/03/2001 . . . . . 24 . . . . . . 2 . . . . . . FINELINES . . . . . . . . . . . . . . . . . . . . . . . . . . . . . . . . . . . . . . . . . . . . . . . . . . . . . . . . . . . . Infectious INFECT 96CDX

**BILLIE MYERS** UK singer (born 14/6/1971, Coventry) of English and Jamaican parentage.

02/05/1998 . . . . . 19 . . . . . . 9 . . . . . . GROWING PAINS . . . . . . . . . . . . . . . . . . . . . . . . . . . . . . . . . . . . . . . . . . . . . . . . . . . . . . . . . . . . Universal UND 53100

**ALANNAH MYLES** Canadian singer (born 25/12/1955, Toronto, raised in Buckhorn, Canada); she won the 1990 Grammy Award for Best Female Rock Vocal Performance for *Black Velvet*.

28/04/1990 . . . . . 3 . . . . . . 21 . . . . . . ● **ALANNAH MYLES** . . . . . . . . . . . . . . . . . . . . . . . . . . . . . . . . . . . . . . . . . . . . . . . . . . . . . . . . . . . . Atlantic 7819561

# N

**'N SYNC** US vocal group formed in Orlando, FL by James Lance 'Lantsen' Bass (born 4/5/1979, Clinton, MS), Joshua Scott 'JC' Chasez (born 8/8/1976, Washington DC), Joseph 'Joey' Anthony Fatone (born 28/1/1977, Brooklyn, NY), Christopher Alan Kirkpatrick (born 17/10/1971, Clarion, PA) and Justin Randall Timberlake (born 31/1/1981, Memphis, TN). The name is derived from the last letters of the members' first names: JustiN, ChriS, JoeY, LantseN and JC. In 1999 ex-manager Louis J. Pearlman, his company Trans Continental Media, Trans Continental Records and BMG (which owns Trans Continental Records) launched a $150 million lawsuit claiming the group and Jive Records were using the name 'N Sync illegally. It was eventually settled out of court. Justin Timberlake allegedly got engaged to Britney Spears in June 2000; they actually got engaged a year later in July 2001 and split in March 2002. Bass briefly trained as an astronaut in 2002. Fatone appeared in the film *My Big Fat Greek Wedding*. Timberlake went solo in 2002 and Chasez in 2004.

| | | | | |
|---|---|---|---|---|
| 17/07/1999 | 30 | 2 | | N SYNC ◆10 ................................................................... Northwestside 74321681902 |
| 01/04/2000 | 14 | 22 | ● | NO STRINGS ATTACHED ▲8 ◆11 ......................................................... Jive 9220272 |
| 04/08/2001 | 12 | 8 | ● | CELEBRITY ▲1 ........................................................................ Jive 9222032 |

**N-TYCE** UK female R&B vocal group formed by Donna Stubbs, Chantal Kerzner, Ario Odubore and Michelle Robinson.

| | | | |
|---|---|---|---|
| 20/06/1998 | 44 | 1 | ALL DAY EVERY DAY ................................................................ Telstar TCD 2945 |

**JIMMY NAIL** UK singer (born James Michael Aloysius Bradford, 16/3/1954, Newcastle-upon-Tyne); he first came to prominence as an actor, appearing in the TV series *Auf Wiedersehen Pet* as Oz and later in *Spender* and *Crocodile Shoes*, both of which he also wrote. He also appeared in the films *Evita* and *Still Crazy*.

| | | | | |
|---|---|---|---|---|
| 08/08/1992 | 2 | 12 | ● | GROWING UP IN PUBLIC ............................................................ East West 4509901442 |
| 03/12/1994 | 2 | 31 | ✪3 | CROCODILE SHOES .................................................................. East West 4509985562 |
| 18/11/1995 | 8 | 15 | ✪ | BIG RIVER ......................................................................... East West 0630128232 |
| 30/11/1996 | 10 | 13 | ✪ | CROCODILE SHOES II ............................................................... East West 0630169352 |
| 18/10/1997 | 8 | 14 | ● | THE NAIL FILE – THE BEST OF JIMMY NAIL ............................................ East West 3984207392 |

**NAILBOMB** Brazilian/US duo formed by Max Cavalera (guitar/vocals) and Alex Newport (guitar/vocals). Cavalera was also a member of Sepultura whilst Newport was with Fudge Tunnel. They were originally called Hate, then Sickman and finally Nailbomb.

| | | | |
|---|---|---|---|
| 02/04/1994 | 62 | 1 | POINT BLANK ...................................................................... Roadrunner RR 90552 |

**NAPALM DEATH** UK rock group formed in Birmingham in 1981 by Lee Dorrian (vocals), Bill Steer (guitar), Shane Embury (bass) and Mick Harris (drums). Aside from being in Napalm Death the members have side projects: Steer is a also member of Carcass, Embury with Unseen Terror and Harris with Extreme Noise Terror.

| | | | |
|---|---|---|---|
| 15/09/1990 | 67 | 1 | HARMONY CORRUPTION ............................................................... Earache MOSH 19 |
| 30/05/1992 | 58 | 1 | UTOPIA BANISHED ................................................................... Earache MOSH 53CD |
| 03/02/1996 | 74 | 1 | DIATRIBES ......................................................................... Earache MOSH 141CDD |

**NAS** US singer (born Nasir Jones, 14/9/1974, Long Island, NY) who made his recording debut in 1989. He is also a member of The Firm with AZ, Foxy Brown and Dawn Robinson.

| | | | | |
|---|---|---|---|---|
| 13/07/1996 | 38 | 6 | | IT WAS WRITTEN ▲4 ................................................................ Columbia 4841962 |
| 17/04/1999 | 31 | 4 | | I AM... ▲2 ........................................................................ Columbia 4894192 |
| 25/01/2003 | 57 | 6 | ○ | GOD'S SON ........................................................................ Columbia 5098115 |

**GRAHAM NASH** UK singer/guitarist (born 2/2/1942, Blackpool) who formed the Two Teens with Allan Clarke in 1955; the pair later changed their name to Ricky And Dane and toured as part of the Kirk Stephens And The Deltas revue. They left in 1961 to form The Hollies with Tony Hicks, Eric Haydock and Don Rathbone. Nash left in 1968 to join David Crosby and Stephen Stills and remained with the group (expanded at times by the inclusion of Neil Young and reduced at others when Stills and Young left) until 1982 when he was tempted back into The Hollies. This was a brief reunion and Nash returned to working with Crosby and Stills, although his solo career has often dovetailed group commitments.

| | | | |
|---|---|---|---|
| 26/06/1971 | 13 | 8 | SONGS FOR BEGINNERS .............................................................. Atlantic 2401 011 |
| 13/05/1972 | 13 | 5 | GRAHAM NASH AND DAVID CROSBY **GRAHAM NASH AND DAVID CROSBY** ...................... Atlantic K 50011 |

▲9 Number of weeks album topped the US chart ◆12 RIAA Diamond Awards ◇3 IFPI Platinum Europe Awards

### JOHNNY NASH
US singer (born 19/8/1940, Houston, TX) who began his recording career in 1958, scoring a number of US hits with pop material. He set up the Jad and Joda labels in 1965 and in 1968 began recording regularly in Jamaica. He appeared in a number of films, including *Take A Giant Step*, *Key Witness* and the Swedish sex film *Love Is Not A Game!*

| | | | | | |
|---|---|---|---|---|---|
| 05/08/1972 | 39 | 6 | | I CAN SEE CLEARLY NOW | CBS 64860 |
| 10/12/1977 | 18 | 11 | ● | JOHNNY NASH COLLECTION | Epic EPC 10008 |

### NASH THE SLASH
Canadian singer/multi-instrumentalist who won't reveal his true name and appears on stage with his head swathed in bandages to disguise himself. He was a member of FM with Cameron Hawkins before going solo in 1978.

| | | | | |
|---|---|---|---|---|
| 21/02/1981 | 61 | 1 | CHILDREN OF THE NIGHT | Dindisc DID 9 |

### NATASHA
UK singer (full name Natasha England) who was previously a member of The Flirts before going solo in 1980.

| | | | | |
|---|---|---|---|---|
| 09/10/1982 | 53 | 3 | CAPTURED | Towerbell TOWLP 2 |

### ULTRA NATE
US singer (born Ultra Nate Wyche, 1968, Havre De Grace, MD) who was raised in Boston, MA and Baltimore, MD. She began her career with the Basement Boys and made her debut album in 1989. She is also a member of Stars On 54, a group assembled to record parts of the soundtrack to the film *54*.

| | | | | |
|---|---|---|---|---|
| 09/05/1998 | 17 | 4 | SITUATION: CRITICAL | AM:PM 5408242 |

### NATIONAL BRASS BAND
UK brass band.

| | | | | | |
|---|---|---|---|---|---|
| 10/05/1980 | 15 | 10 | ○ | GOLDEN MEMORIES | K-Tel ONE 1075 |

### NAUGHTY BY NATURE
US rap group from New Jersey comprising Anthony 'Treach' Criss, Vincent Brown and Kier 'DJ KG' Gist. Treach appeared in the film *Jason's Lyric* and married Sandra 'Pepa' Denton of Salt-N-Pepa in 1999. The group also appeared in the films *The Meteor Man* and *Who's The Man*.

| | | | | |
|---|---|---|---|---|
| 06/03/1993 | 40 | 2 | 19 NAUGHTY III | Big Life BLRCD 23 |
| 27/05/1995 | 20 | 3 | POVERTY'S PARADISE 1995 Grammy Award for Best Rap Album | Big Life BLRCD 28 |

### NAZARETH
UK rock group formed in Dunfermline in 1969 by Dan McCafferty (lead vocals), Manny Charlton (guitar), Pete Agnew (bass) and Darrell Sweet (born 16/5/1947, Bournemouth, drums). McCafferty released his debut solo album in 1975 and went solo when the group disbanded in the mid-1980s. They reunited in 1992. Sweet died from a heart attack on 30/4/1999.

| | | | | | |
|---|---|---|---|---|---|
| 26/05/1973 | 11 | 25 | | RAZAMANAZ | Mooncrest CREST 1 |
| 24/11/1973 | 10 | 7 | | **LOUD 'N' PROUD** | Mooncrest CREST 4 |
| 18/05/1974 | 13 | 3 | | RAMPANT | Mooncrest CREST 15 |
| 13/12/1975 | 54 | 1 | ○ | GREATEST HITS | Mooncrest TOPS 108 |
| 03/02/1979 | 34 | 9 | | NO MEAN CITY | Mooncrest TOPS 123 |
| 28/02/1981 | 60 | 3 | | THE FOOL CIRCLE | NEMS NEWL 6019 |
| 03/10/1981 | 78 | 3 | | NAZARETH LIVE | NEMS NELD 102 |

### NEARLY GOD
UK rapper Tricky (real name Adrian Thaws).

| | | | | |
|---|---|---|---|---|
| 04/05/1996 | 10 | 4 | **NEARLY GOD – POEMS** | Durban Poison DPCD 1001 |

### NED'S ATOMIC DUSTBIN
UK rock group formed in Stourbridge in 1988 by Jonn Penney (vocals), Rat (guitar), Matt Cheslin (bass), Alex Griffin (bass) and Dan Warton (drums).

| | | | | | |
|---|---|---|---|---|---|
| 09/02/1991 | 72 | 1 | | BITE | Rough Trade Germany RTD 14011831 |
| 13/04/1991 | 4 | 5 | ○ | **GOD FODDER** | Furtive 4681121 |
| 31/10/1992 | 13 | 2 | | ARE YOU NORMAL? | Furtive 4726332 |

### VINCE NEIL
US singer (born Vince Neil Wharton, 8/2/1961, Los Angeles, CA) and a founder member of Motley Crue in 1981. In 1992 he was sacked; the reason given was that motor racing had become his main priority. Neil rejected this and issued a $5 million lawsuit against the band for breach of contract, although he went solo during the litigation. By 1997 he had rejoined Motley Crue, replacing his replacement John Corabi (who issued a $7 million lawsuit against the band also for breach of contract but he did not name Neil as a defendant). On 8/12/1984 a car driven by Neil was involved in a crash, killing Hanoi Rocks drummer Nicholas 'Razzle' Dingley and injuring two others. Neil was jailed for twenty days, ordered to serve 200 hours community service and to pay $2.6 million in compensation. He appeared in the film *The Adventures Of Ford Fairlane* in 1990 and is married to mud wrestler Sharisse Rudell.

| | | | | |
|---|---|---|---|---|
| 08/05/1993 | 44 | 1 | EXPOSED | Warner Brothers 9362452602 |

### NELLY
US rapper (born Cornell Haynes, 2/11/1974, Travis, TX) who relocated to St Louis. He won two Grammy Awards in 2002; Best Male Rap Solo Performance for *Hot In Herre* and Best Rap/Sung Collaboration with Kelly Rowland for *Dilemma* and one the following year for Best Rap Performance by a Duo or Group with P Diddy and Murphy Lee for *Shake Ya Tailfeather*.

| | | | | | |
|---|---|---|---|---|---|
| 03/02/2001 | 14 | 31 | ● | COUNTRY GRAMMAR ▲5 | Universal 1578572 |
| 13/07/2002 | 2 | 38 | ✪2 | **NELLYVILLE** ◇ ▲4 | Universal 0186902 |

### BILL NELSON
UK singer/multi-instrumentalist (born 18/12/1948, Wakefield) who formed Be Bop Deluxe in 1971, which he fronted for most of the decade. When they disbanded in 1978, Nelson formed Red Noise for a brief time and then went solo. He proved in demand as a producer and session musician and appeared on recordings by the likes of The Skids, A Flock Of Seagulls and David Sylvian.

| 24/02/1979 | 33 | 5 | SOUND ON SOUND **BILL NELSON'S RED NOISE** | Harvest SHSP 4095 |
| 23/05/1981 | 7 | 6 | **QUIT DREAMING AND GET ON THE BEAM** | Mercury 6359 055 |
| 03/07/1982 | 28 | 4 | THE LOVE THAT WHIRLS (DIARY OF A THINKING HEART) | Mercury WHIRL 3 |
| 14/05/1983 | 30 | 5 | CHIMERA | Mercury MERB 19 |
| 03/05/1986 | 91 | 1 | GETTING THE HOLY GHOST ACROSS | Portrait PRT 26602 |

### PHYLLIS NELSON
US singer (born Jacksonville, FL) and a member of family group the Nelson Five. She was later a backing singer for Major Harris and Philly Cream. Her son Marc also enjoyed a recording career.

| 20/04/1985 | 29 | 10 | MOVE CLOSER | Carrere CAL 203 |

### SHARA NELSON
UK singer/songwriter (born London) who began her career with Massive Attack before going solo in 1993.

| 02/10/1993 | 22 | 9 | ● | WHAT SILENCE KNOWS | Cooltempo CTCD 35 |
| 07/10/1995 | 44 | 2 | | FRIENDLY FIRE | Cooltempo CTCD 48 |

### NENA
German rock group formed in Berlin by Gabriele 'Nena' Kerner (born 26/3/1960) and featuring Rolf Brendel (drums), Jurgen Dehmel (bass), Joern-Uwe Fahrenkrog-Peterson (keyboards) and Carlo Karges (guitar).

| 24/03/1984 | 31 | 5 | NENA | Epic EPC 25925 |

### N*E*R*D
US hip hop group The Neptunes, formed by Pharrell Williams and Chad Hugo. Based in Virginia, Williams and Hugo first came to prominence as songwriters, penning and producing hits for Kelis, Ol' Dirty Bastard and Jay-Z. The name stands for No-one Ever Really Dies. They won the 2002 and 2003 MOBO Awards for Best Producers and the 2003 Grammy Award in the same category.

| 17/08/2002 | 28 | 18 | ● | IN SEARCH OF | Virgin CDVUSX 216 |
| 03/04/2004 | 4 | 13+ | ● | **FLY OR DIE** | Virgin CDVUS 250 |

### ROBBIE NEVIL
US singer/songwriter/guitarist (born 10/1/1961, Los Angeles, CA); he appeared in TV series *Beverly Hills 90210*.

| 13/06/1987 | 93 | 1 | C'EST LA VIE | Manhattan MTL 1006 |

### NEVILLE BROTHERS
US group formed in New Orleans, LA in 1978 by Art (born 17/12/1937, New Orleans, keyboards/vocals), Charles (born 28/12/1938, New Orleans, saxophone/flute), Aaron (born 24/1/1941, New Orleans, keyboards/vocals) and Cyril Neville (born 10/1/1948, New Orleans, vocals). All had previously been heavily involved in the New Orleans music scene: Art had formed The Meters, Aaron had sung with The Avalons and Charles and Cyril had been members of various bands. They won the 1989 Grammy Award for Best Pop Instrumental Performance for *Healing Chant* from the album *Yellow Moon*. Additionally, Aaron Neville won the 1989 Grammy Award for Best Pop Vocal Performance by a Duo or Group with Linda Ronstadt for *Don't Know Much,* Best Pop Vocal Performance by a Duo or Group with Linda Ronstadt the following year for *All My Life* and Best Country Vocal Collaboration in 1994 with Trisha Yearwood for *I Fall To Pieces.* Art won the 1996 Grammy Award for Best Rock instrumental with Jimmie Vaughan, Eric Clapton, Bonnie Raitt, Robert Cray, B.B. King, Buddy Guy and Dr. John for *SRV Shuffle.*

| 18/08/1990 | 35 | 3 | BROTHER'S KEEPER | A&M 3953121 |

### NEW BOHEMIANS – see EDIE BRICKELL AND THE NEW BOHEMIANS

### NEW EDITION
US R&B vocal group formed in Boston, MA in 1982 by manager and producer Maurice Starr and comprising Ricky Bell (born 18/9/1967, Boston), Michael Bivins (born 10/8/1968, Boston), Bobby Brown (born 5/2/1969, Roxbury, MA), Ronald DeVoe (born 17/11/1967, Boston) and Ralph Tresvant (born 16/5/1968, Boston). They were all aged between thirteen and fifteen at the time of their formation and were moulded as an '80s version of the Jackson 5. The group split acrimoniously with Starr in 1984. Brown left in 1987 for a solo career, being replaced by Johnny Gill (born 22/5/1966, Washington DC). Bell, Bivins and DeVoe recorded as Bell Biv Devoe in 1990, whilst both Tresvant and Gill recorded solo. All six members reunited in 1996. Starr later created New Kids On The Block.

| 14/09/1996 | 22 | 3 | HOME AGAIN ▲¹ | MCA MCD 11480 |

### NEW FAST AUTOMATIC DAFFODILS
UK group formed in Manchester in 1988 by Andy Spearpoint (vocals), Dolan Hewison (guitar), Justin Crawford (bass), Perry Saunders (drums) and Icarus Wilson-Wright (percussion). They signed with Play It Again Sam in 1989.

| 17/11/1990 | 49 | 1 | PIGEON HOLE | Play It Again Sam BIAS 185 |
| 24/10/1992 | 57 | 1 | BODY EXIT MIND | Play It Again Sam BIAS 205CD |

### NEW FOUND GLORY
US rock group formed in Coral Springs, FL by Jordan Pundik (vocals), Chad Gilbert (guitar), Steve Klein (guitar), Ian Grushka (bass) and Cyrus Bolooki (drums).

| 29/06/2002 | 10 | 8 | **STICKS AND STONES** | MCA 1129722 |
| 29/05/2004 | 27 | 2 | CATALYST | Geffenr 9862440 |

### NEW KIDS ON THE BLOCK
US vocal group formed in 1984 by manager and producer Maurice Starr as a 'white New Edition' and comprising Donnie Wahlberg (born 17/8/1969, Dorchester, MA), Danny Wood (born 14/5/1969, Boston, MA), Jordan Knight (born 17/5/1970, Worcester, MA), his brother Jonathan (born 29/11/1968, Worcester) and Joey McIntyre (born 31/12/1972, Needham, MA). Originally called Nynuk, they changed to New Kids On The Block on signing with CBS Records' Black Division. They shortened their name to New Kids and then NKOTB in 1993. They disbanded in 1995 with McIntyre and Jordan Knight subsequently recording solo and Wahlberg and Wood becoming producers. McIntyre also became an actor, appearing in the film *The Fantasticks*.

| | | | | |
|---|---|---|---|---|
| 09/12/1989 | 2 | 41 | ✪² | HANGIN' TOUGH ▲² ............................................................................ CBS 4608741 |
| 30/06/1990 | ❶¹ | 31 | ✪ | STEP BY STEP ▲¹ .............................................................................. CBS 4666861 |
| 03/11/1990 | 6 | 13 | ● | NEW KIDS ON THE BLOCK ....................................................................... CBS 4675041 |
| 15/12/1990 | 13 | 5 | ● | MERRY, MERRY CHRISTMAS ...................................................................... CBS 4659071 |
| 02/03/1991 | 15 | 11 | | NO MORE GAMES/THE REMIX ALBUM ....................................................... Columbia 4674941 |
| 21/12/1991 | 50 | 4 | | H.I.T.S. ................................................................................. Columbia 4694381 |
| 12/03/1994 | 36 | 1 | | FACE THE MUSIC **NKOTB** ............................................................... Columbia 4743592 |

### NEW MODEL ARMY
UK rock group formed in Bradford in 1980 by Justin 'Slade The Leveller' Sullivan (born 8/4/1956, Jordans, guitar/vocals), Jason 'Moose' Harris (born 22/9/1958, Colchester, bass) and Robb Heaton (born 6/7/1961, Knutsford, drums). The group attracted considerable controversy from *Top Of The Pops* for wearing t-shirts with the slogan 'Only Stupid Bastards Use Heroin'. The group took their name from the army raised by Oliver Cromwell in the English Civil War.

| | | | |
|---|---|---|---|
| 12/05/1984 | 73 | 5 | VENGEANCE ..................................................................................... Abstract ABT 008 |
| 25/05/1985 | 22 | 3 | NO REST FOR THE WICKED ......................................................................... EMI NMAL 1 |
| 11/10/1986 | 45 | 3 | THE GHOST OF CAIN .............................................................................. EMI EMC 3516 |
| 18/02/1989 | 20 | 3 | THUNDER AND CONSOLATION ...................................................................... EMI EMC 3552 |
| 06/10/1990 | 23 | 2 | IMPURITY ........................................................................................ EMI EMC 3581 |
| 22/06/1991 | 43 | 2 | RAW MELODY MAN ................................................................................ EMI EMC 3595 |
| 10/04/1993 | 22 | 2 | THE LOVE OF HOPELESS CAUSES .................................................................... Epic 4735622 |
| 25/04/1998 | 72 | 1 | STRANGE BROTHERHOOD .......................................................................... Eagle EAGCD 021 |

### NEW MUSIK
UK technopop group formed by Clive Gates (keyboards), Tony Hibbert (bass), Tony Mansfield (guitar/keyboards/vocals) and Phil Towner (drums). Mansfield later became a successful producer (Captain Sensible and Naked Eyes).

| | | | |
|---|---|---|---|
| 17/05/1980 | 35 | 9 | FROM A TO B. ................................................................................... GTO GTLP 041 |
| 14/03/1981 | 68 | 2 | ANYWHERE. ..................................................................................... GTO GTLP 044 |

### NEW ORDER
UK group formed in 1980 following the sudden demise of Joy Division (brought about by Ian Curtis' suicide) and comprising Barney Sumner (born Bernard Dicken, 4/1/1956, Salford, guitar/vocals), Peter Hook (born 13/2/1956, Manchester, bass) and Stephen Morris (born 28/10/1957, Macclesfield, drums), adding Gillian Gilbert (born 27/1/1961, Macclesfield, keyboards) to the line-up five months later. Sumner later formed Electronic. The group won the 1998 BRIT Award for Best Video for *True Faith*.

| | | | | |
|---|---|---|---|---|
| 28/11/1981 | 30 | 10 | | MOVEMENT ................................................................................... Factory FACT 50 |
| 14/05/1983 | 4 | 29 | | **POWER, CORRUPTION AND LIES** ............................................................... Factory FACT 75 |
| 25/05/1985 | 7 | 10 | | **LOW-LIFE**. .................................................................................. Factory FACT 100 |
| 11/10/1986 | 9 | 5 | | **BROTHERHOOD** ............................................................................. Factory FACT 150 |
| 29/08/1987 | 3 | 37 | ✪ | **SUBSTANCE** ................................................................................ Factory FACT 200 |
| 11/02/1989 | ❶¹ | 14 | ● | **TECHNIQUE** ................................................................................ Factory FACT 275 |
| 22/02/1992 | 33 | 2 | ○ | BBC RADIO 1 LIVE IN CONCERT. ................................................. Windsong International WINCD 011 |
| 15/05/1993 | ❶¹ | 19 | ● | **REPUBLIC** ..................................................................................... London 8284132 |
| 17/07/1993 | 32 | 2 | | SUBSTANCE .................................................................................... London 5200082 |
| 03/12/1994 | 4 | 17 | ✪ | **(THE BEST OF) NEW ORDER/(THE REST OF) NEW ORDER** *(the rest of) New Order* is a remix album of *(the best of) New Order* that was listed from 2/9/1995. ................................. Centredate Co 8285802 |
| 08/09/2001 | 6 | 4 | ● | **GET READY** ............................................................................... London 8573896212 |

### NEW POWER GENERATION
US group formed by Prince as his backing group in 1991 and featuring Levi Seacer Jr (guitar), Tony M (raps), Tommy Barbarella (keyboards), Kirk Johnson (percussion/vocals), Damon Dickson (percussion/vocals), Sonny T (bass/vocals), Michael B (drums), Rosie Gaines (vocals) and Mayte Garcia (vocals and later Prince's wife), with Prince penning and producing their releases. By 1997 the group was fronted by Tora Tora (a pseudonym for Prince). Gaines later went solo.

| | | | |
|---|---|---|---|
| 08/04/1995 | 11 | 3 | EXODUS. ........................................................................................ NPG 0061032 |
| 11/07/1998 | 38 | 2 | NEWPOWER SOUL. ............................................................................ NPG 74321605982 |

## NEW RADICALS
US rock group fronted by singer/songwriter Gregg Alexander (born Grosse Pointe, MI). After brief success, Alexander announced he was leaving the group in order to concentrate on writing and producing on a freelance basis.

| | | | | | |
|---|---|---|---|---|---|
| 17/04/1999 | 10 | 14 | ● | **MAYBE YOU'VE BEEN BRAINWASHED TOO** ........................................ | MCA MCD 11858 |

## NEW SEEKERS
UK/Australian group formed by Keith Potger after the demise of The Seekers in 1969. The line-up for their hits consisted of Eve Graham (born 19/4/1943, Perth), Lyn Paul (born 16/2/1949, Manchester), Peter Doyle (born 28/7/1949, Melbourne), Marty Kristian (born 27/5/1947, Leipzig, Germany) and Paul Layton (born 4/8/1947, Beaconsfield). Doyle left in 1974 and was replaced by Peter Oliver (born 15/1/1952, Southampton). Disbanding in 1975, each member went solo (Kristian joined Prima Donna, UK's entrant in the 1980 Eurovision Song Contest). They re-formed in 1975 (minus Paul). Doyle died from cancer in Australia on 22/10/2001.

| | | | | | |
|---|---|---|---|---|---|
| 05/02/1972 | 40 | 4 | | NEW COLOURS .................................................. | Polydor 2383 066 |
| 01/04/1972 | 2 | 25 | | **WE'D LIKE TO TEACH THE WORLD TO SING** .......................... | Polydor 2883 103 |
| 12/08/1972 | 35 | 4 | | NEVER ENDING SONG OF LOVE ................................... | Polydor 2383 126 |
| 14/10/1972 | 23 | 5 | | CIRCLES ...................................................... | Polydor 2442 102 |
| 21/04/1973 | 47 | 2 | | NOW ......................................................... | Polydor 2383 195 |
| 30/03/1974 | 12 | 9 | ○ | TOGETHER .................................................... | Polydor 2383 264 |

## NEW WORLD THEATRE ORCHESTRA
UK orchestra assembled by Cyril Stapleton.

| | | | | | |
|---|---|---|---|---|---|
| 24/12/1960 | 20 | 1 | | LET'S DANCE TO THE HITS OF THE 30'S AND 40'S .................. | Pye Golden Guinea GGL 0026 |

## NEWCLEUS
US rap group formed in Brooklyn, NY by Ben 'Cozmo D' Cenad and his sister Yvette with Bob 'Chilly B' Crafton and his sister Monique.

| | | | | | |
|---|---|---|---|---|---|
| 25/08/1984 | 84 | 2 | | JAM ON REVENGE ............................................... | Sunnyview SVLP 6600 |

## BOB NEWHART
US comedian born in 1923 who proved equally popular on both TV and on record. He went on to appear in a number of films, including *Catch 22, Hell Is For Heroes, Hot Millions, On A Clear Day You Can See Forever* and *Cold Turkey*. He hosted his own TV series in the US from 1972–77. He has won three Grammy Awards including Best New Artist and Best Comedy Performance, Spoken Word for *Button Down Mind Strikes Back*, all in 1960. He has a star on the Hollywood Walk of Fame.

| | | | | | |
|---|---|---|---|---|---|
| 01/10/1960 | 2 | 37 | | **THE BUTTON-DOWN MIND OF BOB NEWHART** ▲[14] 1960 Grammy Award for Album of the Year ........ | Warner Brothers WM 4010 |

## ANTHONY NEWLEY
UK singer/actor (born 24/9/1931, Hackney, London) who was a successful child actor. He starred in *Vice Versa* with Petula Clark and began his singing career after appearing in the film *Idle On Parade,* the story of a singer conscripted into the army (topical because of Terry Dene and Elvis Presley). He and Leslie Bricusse were successful songwriters, penning the lyrics to *Goldfinger* for Shirley Bassey, the film *Willy Wonka And The Chocolate Factory* and the musicals *The Good Old Bad Old Days* and *Stop The World – I Want To Get Off* (featuring *What Kind Of Fool Am I?*) as well as appearing in films such as *Dr Doolittle*. He was married to actress Joan Collins (their daughter Tara Newley released her debut record in 1994), and died from cancer on 14/4/1999.

| | | | | | |
|---|---|---|---|---|---|
| 14/05/1960 | 19 | 2 | | LOVE IS A NOW AND THEN THING ................................ | Decca LK 4343 |
| 08/07/1961 | 5 | 12 | | **TONY** ....................................................... | Decca LK 4406 |
| 28/09/1963 | 10 | 10 | | **FOOL BRITANNIA** ANTHONY NEWLEY, PETER SELLERS, JOAN COLLINS ... | Ember CEL 902 |

## OLIVIA NEWTON-JOHN

UK singer (born 26/9/1948, Cambridge) who moved to Melbourne, Australia at the age of five. She won a talent contest in 1964; the prize was a trip to the UK but she postponed it for a year to finish school. She came over with Pat Carroll and performed as Pat & Olivia, remaining when Carroll's visa expired. She recorded her debut single in 1966 (for Decca), was a member of Toomorrow and in 1971 sang her first duet with Cliff Richard. She signed to Pye International (via Festival Records in Australia) in 1971 and appeared in the films *Grease* and *Xanadu*. It was revealed in 1992 that she had breast cancer. She has won four Grammy Awards: Best Country & Western Vocal Performance in 1973 for *Let Me Be There*; Record of the Year and Best Pop Vocal Performances in 1974 for *I Honestly Love You* and Video of the Year in 1982 for *Physical*. She was voted Female Vocalist of the Year in 1975 by the Country Music Association, the first UK artist to be afforded the honour. Not everyone in the CMA agreed and some members defected to form the Association of Country Entertainers. She has a star on the Hollywood Walk of Fame.

| | | | | | |
|---|---|---|---|---|---|
| 02/03/1974 | 37 | 3 | | MUSIC MAKES MY DAY ........................................... | Pye NSPL 28186 |
| 29/06/1974 | 40 | 2 | | LONG LIVE LOVE ............................................... | EMI EMC 3028 |
| 26/04/1975 | 37 | 2 | | HAVE YOU NEVER BEEN MELLOW ▲[1] .............................. | EMI EMC 3069 |
| 29/05/1976 | 49 | 4 | | COME ON OVER ................................................ | EMI EMC 3124 |
| 27/08/1977 | 60 | 1 | | MAKING A GOOD THING BETTER. .................................. | EMI EMC 3192 |
| 21/01/1978 | 19 | 9 | ● | GREATEST HITS ................................................ | EMI EMA 785 |
| 09/12/1978 | 30 | 9 | ● | TOTALLY HOT ................................................. | EMI EMA 789 |
| 19/07/1980 | 2 | 17 | ● | **XANADU** Original soundtrack to the film OLIVIA NEWTON-JOHN/ELECTRIC LIGHT ORCHESTRA ... | Jet LX 526 |
| 31/10/1981 | 11 | 22 | ● | PHYSICAL ..................................................... | EMI EMC 3386 |
| 23/10/1982 | 8 | 38 | ✪ | **GREATEST HITS** ............................................. | EMI EMTV 36 |
| 08/03/1986 | 66 | 3 | | SOUL KISS .................................................... | Mercury MERH 77 |
| 25/07/1992 | 12 | 6 | | BACK TO BASICS – THE ESSENTIAL COLLECTION 1971–1992 .......... | Mercury 5126412 |
| 04/02/1995 | 33 | 4 | | GAIA (ONE WOMAN'S JOURNEY) ................................... | D-Sharp DSHLCD 7017 |

## NICE
UK rock group formed in 1967 as PP Arnold's backing group before evolving into an autonomous band. They comprised Keith Emerson (born 2/11/1944, Todmorden, keyboards), Lee Jackson (born 8/1/1943, Newcastle-upon-Tyne, bass/vocals), Brian 'Blinky' Davison (born 25/5/1942, Leicester, guitar/vocals) and David O'List (born 13/12/1948, London, drums). O'List left in 1968; the remaining members continued as a trio until disbanding in 1970. Emerson then became a founding member of Emerson Lake & Palmer.

| | | | | | |
|---|---|---|---|---|---|
| 13/09/1969 | 3 | 6 | | **NICE** ....................................................... | Immediate IMSP 026 |

▲[9] Number of weeks album topped the US chart   ◆[12] RIAA Diamond Awards   ◇[3] IFPI Platinum Europe Awards

| 27/06/1970 . . . . . 2 . . . . . . 21 . . . . . . | FIVE BRIDGES . . . . . . . . . . . . . . . . . . . . . . . . . . . . . . . . . . . . . . . . . . . . . . . . . . . . . . . . . . . . . . . . . . . . . . . . . Charisma CAS 1014 |
| 17/04/1971 . . . . . 5 . . . . . . 11 . . . . . . | ELEGY . . . . . . . . . . . . . . . . . . . . . . . . . . . . . . . . . . . . . . . . . . . . . . . . . . . . . . . . . . . . . . . . . . . . . . . . . . . . . . . . Charisma CAS 1030 |

### PAUL NICHOLAS
UK singer/actor (born Oscar Beuselinck, 3/12/1945, Peterborough) who was a pianist with the Savages in 1964 and later joined the musical *Hair* before going solo as Paul Dean. He changed his name briefly back to Oscar before settling on Paul Nicholas. A successful actor, he appeared in the TV series *Just Good Friends*, the musical *Cats* and the film *Sgt Pepper's Lonely Hearts Club Band*.

| 29/11/1986 . . . . . 30 . . . . . . 8 . . . . . . ○ | JUST GOOD FRIENDS . . . . . . . . . . . . . . . . . . . . . . . . . . . . . . . . . . . . . . . . . . . . . . . . . . . . . . . . . . . . . . . . . . . . . . K-Tel ONE 1334 |

### NICKELBACK
Canadian rock group formed in Vancouver in 1996 by Chad Kroeger (guitar/vocals), his brother Mike (bass), Ryan Peake (guitar/vocals) and Ryan Vikedal (drums). Chad Kroeger later recorded solo on the soundtrack to *Spiderman*.

| 19/01/2002 . . . . ❶² . . . . . . 67 . . . . . . ✪³ | SILVER SIDE UP ◇² . . . . . . . . . . . . . . . . . . . . . . . . . . . . . . . . . . . . . . . . . . . . . . . . . . . . . . . . . . . . . . . . . . Roadrunner 12084852 |
| 04/10/2003 . . . . . 5 . . . . . . 12 . . . . . . ● | THE LONG ROAD . . . . . . . . . . . . . . . . . . . . . . . . . . . . . . . . . . . . . . . . . . . . . . . . . . . . . . . . . . . . . . . . . . . . . . . Roadrunner RR 84005 |

### STEVIE NICKS
US singer (born 26/5/1948, Phoenix, AZ) who was raised in California. After performing with San Francisco-based group Fritz she formed a duo with boyfriend Lindsey Buckingham and they both subsequently joined Fleetwood Mac in 1975. Nicks stopped touring with the group in 1990 and left in 1993, although she has made appearances with them since.

| 08/08/1981 . . . . . 11 . . . . . . 16 . . . . . . | BELLA DONNA ▲¹ . . . . . . . . . . . . . . . . . . . . . . . . . . . . . . . . . . . . . . . . . . . . . . . . . . . . . . . . . . . . . . . . . . . . . . . WEA K 99169 |
| 02/07/1983 . . . . . 28 . . . . . . 19 . . . . . . ○ | THE WILD HEART . . . . . . . . . . . . . . . . . . . . . . . . . . . . . . . . . . . . . . . . . . . . . . . . . . . . . . . . . . . . . WEA International 2500711 |
| 14/12/1985 . . . . . 30 . . . . . . 22 . . . . . . ● | ROCK A LITTLE . . . . . . . . . . . . . . . . . . . . . . . . . . . . . . . . . . . . . . . . . . . . . . . . . . . . . . . . . . . . . . . . . . . . . Modern PCS 7300 |
| 10/06/1989 . . . . . 3 . . . . . . 14 . . . . . . ● | THE OTHER SIDE OF THE MIRROR . . . . . . . . . . . . . . . . . . . . . . . . . . . . . . . . . . . . . . . . . . . . . . . . . . . . . EMI EMD 1008 |
| 14/09/1991 . . . . . 15 . . . . . . 6 . . . . . . ● | TIMESPACE – THE BEST OF STEVIE NICKS . . . . . . . . . . . . . . . . . . . . . . . . . . . . . . . . . . . . . . . . . . . . . . . . EMI EMD 3595 |
| 04/06/1994 . . . . . 16 . . . . . . 3 . . . . . . | STREET ANGEL . . . . . . . . . . . . . . . . . . . . . . . . . . . . . . . . . . . . . . . . . . . . . . . . . . . . . . . . . . . . . . . . . . . . . EMI CDEMC 3671 |
| 12/05/2001 . . . . . 43 . . . . . . 2 . . . . . . | TROUBLE IN SHANGRI-LA . . . . . . . . . . . . . . . . . . . . . . . . . . . . . . . . . . . . . . . . . . . . . . . . . . . . . . . . . . Reprise 9362473722 |

### HECTOR NICOL
UK comedian born in Edinburgh who also composed a number of football songs, usually as tributes to either Hearts or Hibernian.

| 28/04/1984 . . . . . 92 . . . . . . 1 . . . . . . | BRAVO JULIET . . . . . . . . . . . . . . . . . . . . . . . . . . . . . . . . . . . . . . . . . . . . . . . . . . . . . . . . . . . . . . . . . . . . . . . . . Klub KLP 42 |

### NICOLE
German singer (full name Nicole Hohloch) who came to prominence at the age of seventeen by winning the 1982 Eurovision Song Contest with *A Little Peace*, beating the UK entry by Bardo into seventh place.

| 02/10/1982 . . . . . 85 . . . . . . 2 . . . . . . | A LITTLE PEACE . . . . . . . . . . . . . . . . . . . . . . . . . . . . . . . . . . . . . . . . . . . . . . . . . . . . . . . . . . . . . . . . . . . . . . CBS 85011 |

### NICOLETTE
UK singer born in Scotland and raised in Nigeria; she made her debut record for Shut Up And Dance in 1992.

| 10/08/1996 . . . . . 36 . . . . . . 2 . . . . . . | LET NO ONE LIVE RENT FREE IN YOUR HEAD . . . . . . . . . . . . . . . . . . . . . . . . . . . . . . . . . . . . . . . . Talkin Loud 5326342 |

### NIGHTCRAWLERS
UK instrumental/production duo Alysha Warren and John Reid.

| 30/09/1995 . . . . . 14 . . . . . . 5 . . . . . . | LET'S PUSH IT . . . . . . . . . . . . . . . . . . . . . . . . . . . . . . . . . . . . . . . . . . . . . . . . . . . . . . . . . . . . . . . . . Final Vinyl 74321309702 |

### NIGHTMARES ON WAX
UK dance duo comprising George 'E.A.S.E.' Evelyn and Kevin 'Boy Wonder' Harper. Vocalist Desoto later joined the group.

| 24/04/1999 . . . . . 71 . . . . . . 2 . . . . . . ○ | CAR BOOT SOUL . . . . . . . . . . . . . . . . . . . . . . . . . . . . . . . . . . . . . . . . . . . . . . . . . . . . . . . . . . . . . . . . Warp WARPCD 061 |
| 14/09/2002 . . . . . 47 . . . . . . 2 . . . . . . | MIND ELEVATION . . . . . . . . . . . . . . . . . . . . . . . . . . . . . . . . . . . . . . . . . . . . . . . . . . . . . . . . . . . . . . . . Warp WARPCD 95 |

### NILSSON
US singer (born Harry Edward Nelson III, 15/6/1941, Brooklyn, NY) who moved to Los Angeles to work for the Security First National Bank as a supervisor, writing songs in his spare time. The Monkees recorded one of his songs in 1967 that prompted RCA to sign him the following year (although his biggest hits were scored with other writers' material). He effectively retired from the music industry in the 1980s to concentrate on other business interests, including a film distribution company, although he recorded sporadically throughout the decade. He suffered a heart attack in February 1993 and died on 15/1/1994 without having fully recovered. He won two Grammy Awards during his career: Best Solo Vocal Performance in 1969 for *Everybody's Talkin'* and Best Pop Vocal Performance in 1972 for *Without You*.

| 29/01/1972 . . . . . 46 . . . . . . 1 . . . . . . | THE POINT Original soundtrack to the TV series . . . . . . . . . . . . . . . . . . . . . . . . . . . . . . . . . . . . . . . . . . RCA Victor SF 8166 |
| 05/02/1972 . . . . . 4 . . . . . . 22 . . . . . . | NILSSON SCHMILSSON . . . . . . . . . . . . . . . . . . . . . . . . . . . . . . . . . . . . . . . . . . . . . . . . . . . . . . . . . . . RCA Victor SF 8242 |
| 19/08/1972 . . . . . 41 . . . . . . 1 . . . . . . | SON OF SCHMILSSON . . . . . . . . . . . . . . . . . . . . . . . . . . . . . . . . . . . . . . . . . . . . . . . . . . . . . . . . . . . . RCA Victor SF 8297 |
| 28/07/1973 . . . . . 20 . . . . . 19 . . . . . . | A LITTLE TOUCH OF SCHMILSSON IN THE NIGHT . . . . . . . . . . . . . . . . . . . . . . . . . . . . . . . . . . . . . RCA Victor SF 8371 |

### NINA AND FREDERICK
Danish vocal duo formed by Baron Frederick Jan Gustav Floris van Pallandt (born 14/5/1934, Copenhagen) and his wife Baroness Nina Moller. They hosted their own TV series in the UK in the 1960s. They divorced in 1976. Frederick was shot to death by a robber on 15/5/1994. Nina was of the opinion that he had been the victim of a professional killing.

| 13/02/1960 . . . . . 9 . . . . . . 2 . . . . . . | NINA AND FREDERICK . . . . . . . . . . . . . . . . . . . . . . . . . . . . . . . . . . . . . . . . . . . . . . . . . . . . . . . . . . . . . Pye NPT 19023 |
| 29/04/1961 . . . . . 11 . . . . . . 4 . . . . . . | NINA AND FREDERICK . . . . . . . . . . . . . . . . . . . . . . . . . . . . . . . . . . . . . . . . . . . . . . . . . . . . . . . . . . . . Columbia COL 1314 |

**9 BELOW ZERO** UK group formed by Dennis Greaves (guitar/vocals), Peter Clark (bass/vocals), Mark Feltham (harmonica) and Kenny Bradley (drums). Bradley left after their debut album and was replaced by Stix Burkey. The group disbanded in the mid-1980s with Greaves subsequently becoming a member of The Truth, although Feltham re-formed 9 Below Zero at the end of the decade.

| 14/03/1981 | 56 | 6 | | DON'T POINT YOUR FINGER | A&M AMLH 68521 |
| 20/03/1982 | 38 | 6 | | THIRD DEGREE | A&M AMLH 68537 |

**NINE INCH NAILS** US rock group formed in Cleveland, OH in 1988 and fronted by Michael Trent Reznor (born 17/5/1965, Mercer, PA). By the 1990s the group was effectively Reznor working as a solo artist in the studio and employing musicians for live dates. The group has won two Grammy Awards: Best Metal Performance with Vocal in 1992 for *Wish* and Best Metal Performance in 1995 for *Happiness In Slavery*.

| 12/10/1991 | 67 | 1 | O | PRETTY HATE MACHINE | TVT ILPS 9973 |
| 17/10/1992 | 18 | 3 | | BROKEN | Interscope IMCD 8004 |
| 19/03/1994 | 9 | 4 | O | **THE DOWNWARD SPIRAL** | Island CID 8012 |
| 09/10/1999 | 10 | 4 | | **THE FRAGILE** ▲[1] | Island CIDD 8091 |
| 16/03/2002 | 54 | 1 | | AND ALL THAT COULD HAVE BEEN – LIVE | Nothing CIDD 8113 |

**999** UK rock group formed in London in 1977 by Nick Cash (born Keith Lucas, 6/5/1950, Gosport, guitar/vocals), Guy Days (guitar), John Watson (bass) and Pablo LaBrittain (drums). After a self-funded single release they signed with United Artists in late 1977 and issued their debut album in 1978. They also recorded for Radarscope and Polydor. Watson left in 1985 and was replaced by Danny Palmer.

| 25/03/1978 | 53 | 1 | | 999 | United Artists UAG 30199 |

**911** UK vocal trio assembled in 1996 by Lee Brennan (born 27/9/1975, Carlisle), Simon 'Spike' Dawbarn (born 5/8/1974, Warrington) and Jimmy Constable (born 21/9/1973, Liverpool) after they won GMTV's 'Search for the next big thing' contest. Brennan later went solo.

| 08/03/1997 | 13 | 17 | ● | THE JOURNEY | Virgin CDV 2820 |
| 18/07/1998 | 10 | 4 | O | **MOVING ON** | Virgin CDV 2852 |
| 06/02/1999 | 8 | 4 | O | **THERE IT IS** | Virgin CDV 2873 |
| 06/11/1999 | 40 | 1 | | THE GREATEST HITS AND A LITTLE MORE… | Virgin CDV 2899 |

**NIRVANA** US rock group formed in Seattle, WA in 1987 by Kurt Cobain (born 20/2/1967, Hoquiam, WA, guitar/vocals), Kris Novoselic (born 16/5/1965, Seattle, bass) and Dale Crover (drums) as Skid Row. They changed their name the same year firstly to Ed Ted & Fred, then to Fecal Matter and finally to Nirvana as it means 'the extinction of individuality and absorption into supreme spirit as Buddhist highest good.' They released their debut album in 1989 for Sub Pop and brought in drummer Dave Grohl (born 14/1/1969, Warren, OH) in 1990. They were named Best International Newcomers at the 1993 BRIT Awards. Cobain, who was married to Hole member Courtney Love, committed suicide on 5/4/1994 although his body wasn't discovered for three days. Grohl later formed The Foo Fighters.

| 05/10/1991 | 7 | 187 | ✪[2] | **NEVERMIND** ▲[2] ◆[10] Baby on the cover is four-month-old Spencer Elden | DGC 24425 |
| 07/03/1992 | 33 | 7 | | BLEACH | Tupelo TUPCD 6 |
| 26/12/1992 | 14 | 11 | ● | INCESTICIDE | Geffen GED 24504 |
| 25/09/1993 | ❶[1] | 43 | ● | **IN UTERO** ▲[1] | Geffen GED 24536 |
| 12/11/1994 | ❶[1] | 40 | ✪ | **UNPLUGGED IN NEW YORK** ◇[2] ▲[1] 1995 Grammy Award for Best Alternative Music Performance | Geffen GED 24727 |
| 12/10/1996 | 4 | 6 | ✪ | **FROM THE MUDDY BANKS OF THE WISHKAH** ▲[1] | Geffen GED 25105 |
| 09/11/2002 | 3 | 23 | ✪ | **NIRVANA** ◇ | Geffen 4935232 |

**NO DOUBT** US rock group formed in Anaheim, CA in 1986 by John Spence (born 1969, Orange County, CA, vocals), Eric Stefani (keyboards), Tony Kanal (born 27/8/1970, bass), Adrian Young (born 26/8/1969, drums) and Tom Dumont (born 11/1/1968, guitar). Spence committed suicide on 21/12/1987 by shooting himself in the head and was initially replaced by Alan Meade and then Gwen Stefani (born 3/10/1969, Anaheim). Stefani later recorded with Eve and won the 2001 Grammy Award for Best Rap/Sung Performance for *Let Me Blow Ya Mind*. The group won the 2002 Grammy Award for Best Pop Performance By A Duo Or Group With Vocal for *Hey Baby* and the 2003 Award for Best Pop Performance by a Duo or Group with Vocal for *Underneath It All*.

| 18/01/1997 | 3 | 44 | ✪ | **TRAGIC KINGDOM** ◇[2] ▲[9] ◆[10] | Interscope IND 90003 |
| 22/04/2000 | 31 | 2 | | RETURN OF SATURN | Interscope 4906382 |
| 16/02/2002 | 43 | 6 | O | ROCK STEADY | Interscope 4931582 |
| 13/12/2003 | 5 | 28 | ✪ | **THE SINGLES 1992–2003** | Interscope 9861382 |

**NO MERCY** US group featuring Marty Cintron on lead vocals and twins Ariel and Gabriel Hernandez. The group originally worked as waiters in Gloria Estefan's restaurant.

| 07/06/1997 | 17 | 4 | | MY PROMISE ◇ | Arista 74321466902 |

**NOFX** US group formed by Fat Mike, El Hife, Erik Ghint and Herb Reath Stinks.

| 10/02/1996 | 60 | 1 | | HEAVY PETTING ZOO | Epitaph 864572 |

▲[9] Number of weeks album topped the US chart   ◆[12] RIAA Diamond Awards   ◇[3] IFPI Platinum Europe Awards

| | | | | |
|---|---|---|---|---|
| 10/06/2000 . . . . . 50 . . . . . . 1 . . . . . . | PUMP UP THE VALUUM . . . . . . . . . . . . . . . . . . . . . . . . . . . . . . . . . . . . . . . . . . . . . . . . . . . . . . . . . Epitaph 65842 |
| 23/03/2002 . . . . . 75 . . . . . . 1 . . . . . . | SPLIT SERIES – VOLUME 3 **RANCID/NOFX** . . . . . . . . . . . . . . . . . . . . . . . . . . . . . . . . . . . . . . . . . . . . . . BYO 079CD |
| 17/05/2003 . . . . . 48 . . . . . . 1 . . . . . . | WAR ON ERRORISM . . . . . . . . . . . . . . . . . . . . . . . . . . . . . . . . . . . . . . . . . . . . . . . . . . . Fat Wreck FAT657CD |

**NOLANS** Irish group formed by sisters Anne (born 12/11/1950), Denise (born 1952), Linda (born 23/2/1959), Bernadette (born 17/10/1961) and Maureen Nolan (born 14/6/1954). Denise left the group for a solo career in 1978. Anne left the group to get married and was replaced by Coleen (born 12/3/1965). Anne returned and the group became a quintet for a while until Linda left to get married.

| | |
|---|---|
| 29/07/1978 . . . . . 3 . . . . . . 12 . . . . . . ● | **20 GIANT HITS NOLAN SISTERS** . . . . . . . . . . . . . . . . . . . . . . . . . . . . . . . . . . . . . . . . . . . . . . . . . . . Target TGS 502 |
| 19/01/1980 . . . . . 15 . . . . . . 13 . . . . . . ● | NOLANS . . . . . . . . . . . . . . . . . . . . . . . . . . . . . . . . . . . . . . . . . . . . . . . . . . . . . . . . . . . . . . . . . Epic 83892 |
| 25/10/1980 . . . . . 11 . . . . . 33 . . . . . . ● | MAKING WAVES . . . . . . . . . . . . . . . . . . . . . . . . . . . . . . . . . . . . . . . . . . . . . . . . . . . . . . . . . . . Epic EPC 10023 |
| 27/03/1982 . . . . 7 . . . . . . 10 . . . . . . ● | **PORTRAIT** . . . . . . . . . . . . . . . . . . . . . . . . . . . . . . . . . . . . . . . . . . . . . . . . . . . . . . . . . . . . . Epic EPC 10033 |
| 20/11/1982 . . . . . 52 . . . . . . 8 . . . . . . ○ | ALTOGETHER . . . . . . . . . . . . . . . . . . . . . . . . . . . . . . . . . . . . . . . . . . . . . . . . . . . . . . . . . . . . . Epic EPC 10037 |
| 17/11/1984 . . . . . 39 . . . . . . 8 . . . . . . ○ | GIRLS JUST WANNA HAVE FUN . . . . . . . . . . . . . . . . . . . . . . . . . . . . . . . . . . . . . . . . . . . . . . . Towerbell TOWLP 10 |

**NOMAD** UK duo formed by songwriter/producer/keyboard player Damon Rochefort (from Cardiff, South Glamorgan) and vocalist Sharon Dee Clarke, who previously recorded as FPI Project. Nomad is Damon spelt backwards. Rochefort also recorded as Spirits.

| | |
|---|---|
| 22/06/1996 . . . . 48 . . . . . . 2 . . . . . . | CHANGING CABINS . . . . . . . . . . . . . . . . . . . . . . . . . . . . . . . . . . . . . . . . . . . . . . . . . . . . Rumour RULCD 100 |

**NOREAGA** US male rapper (born Victor Santiago, New York City) who is a member of Capone-N-Noreaga and also records as N.O.R.E. He won the 1998 MOBO Award for Best International Hip Hop Act.

| | |
|---|---|
| 25/07/1998 . . . . . 72 . . . . . . 1 . . . . . . | N.O.R.E . . . . . . . . . . . . . . . . . . . . . . . . . . . . . . . . . . . . . . . . . . . . . . . . . . . Penalty Recordings PENCD 3077 |

### NORTH GERMAN RADIO SYMPHONY ORCHESTRA – see NIGEL KENNEDY

**NORTHERN UPROAR** UK rock group formed in Manchester by Leon Meya (born 31/5/1978, bass/vocals), Paul Kelly (born 19/9/1977, guitar), Jeff Fletcher (born 14/12/1977, guitar) and Keith Chadwick (born 30/5/1977, drums).

| | |
|---|---|
| 11/05/1996 . . . . . 22 . . . . . . 2 . . . . . . | NORTHERN UPROAR . . . . . . . . . . . . . . . . . . . . . . . . . . . . . . . . . . . . . . . . . . . . . . . . . . Heavenly HVNLP 012CD |

**NORTHSIDE** UK group: Warren 'Dermo' Dermody (vocals), Cliff Ogier (bass), Timmy Walsh (guitar) and Paul Walsh (drums).

| | |
|---|---|
| 29/06/1991 . . . . . 19 . . . . . . 3 . . . . . . | CHICKEN RHYTHMS . . . . . . . . . . . . . . . . . . . . . . . . . . . . . . . . . . . . . . . . . . . . . . . . . . . . . . . Factory FACT 310 |

**NOT THE NINE O'CLOCK NEWS** UK TV comedy series featuring Rowan Atkinson (born 6/1/1955, Newcastle-Upon-Tyne), Mel Smith, Pamela Stephenson and Griff Rhys Jones. The original series also featured Colin Bostock-Smith. Atkinson went on to write and star in *Blackadder* and *Mr Bean* whilst Smith and Jones linked up to write and perform *Alas Smith And Jones*. Atkinson, Smith and Jones also formed Talkback Productions.

| | |
|---|---|
| 08/11/1980 . . . . . 5 . . . . . . 23 . . . . . . ✪ | **NOT THE NINE O'CLOCK NEWS** . . . . . . . . . . . . . . . . . . . . . . . . . . . . . . . . . . . . . . . . . . . . . . . . . . BBC REB 400 |
| 17/10/1981 . . . . . 5 . . . . . . 24 . . . . . . ● | **NOT THE NINE O'CLOCK NEWS – HEDGEHOG SANDWICH** . . . . . . . . . . . . . . . . . . . . . . . . . . . . . . . . . . . . BBC REB 421 |
| 23/10/1982 . . . . . 63 . . . . . . 4 . . . . . . | THE MEMORY KINDA LINGERS . . . . . . . . . . . . . . . . . . . . . . . . . . . . . . . . . . . . . . . . . . . . . . . . . . BBC REF 453 |

**NOTORIOUS B.I.G.** US rapper (born Christopher Wallace, 21/5/1972, Brooklyn, NY) also known as Biggy Smallz. He originally recorded with rap group OGB and was then discovered by Mister Cee and subsequently signed by Puff Daddy. He was shot dead on 9/3/1997 after attending the *Soul Train* awards in circumstances similar to those of 2Pac, prompting rumours of a feud between East and West Coast rapping crews (recent evidence suggests possible involvement of the Los Angeles Police Department in his death).

| | |
|---|---|
| 05/04/1997 . . . . . 23 . . . . . 16 . . . . . . | LIFE AFTER DEATH ▲[4] ◆[10] . . . . . . . . . . . . . . . . . . . . . . . . . . . . . . . . . . . . . . . . . . Puff Daddy 78612730112 |
| 18/12/1999 . . . . . 70 . . . . . . 1 . . . . . . | BORN AGAIN ▲[1] . . . . . . . . . . . . . . . . . . . . . . . . . . . . . . . . . . . . . . . . . . . . . . . . . . . Puff Daddy 74321717182 |

**NOTTING HILLBILLIES** UK group formed in 1986 by Mark Knopfler (born 12/8/1949, Glasgow, guitar/vocals), Steve Phillips (guitar/vocals) and Brendan Croker (guitar/vocals), all three were old friends. Knopfler was also the frontman for Dire Straits and recruited manager Ed Bicknell as drummer for the Notting Hillbillies. He also brought in Guy Fletcher (guitar), Paul Franklin (steel guitar) and Marcus Cliff (bass) for the touring line-up. However, after just one album the Hillbillies returned to their day jobs.

| | |
|---|---|
| 17/03/1990 . . . . . 2 . . . . . . 14 . . . . . . ● | **MISSING… PRESUMED HAVING A GOOD TIME** . . . . . . . . . . . . . . . . . . . . . . . . . . . . . . . . . . . . . . . . Vertigo 8426711 |

**HEATHER NOVA** US singer/guitarist born on an island in the Bermuda Sound and raised on a sailboat in the Caribbean. She later relocated to London.

| | |
|---|---|
| 08/04/1995 . . . . . 72 . . . . . . 1 . . . . . . | OYSTER . . . . . . . . . . . . . . . . . . . . . . . . . . . . . . . . . . . . . . . . . . . . . . . . . . . . . . . . . . . Butterfly BFLCD 12 |
| 20/06/1998 . . . . . 55 . . . . . . 1 . . . . . . | SIREN . . . . . . . . . . . . . . . . . . . . . . . . . . . . . . . . . . . . . . . . . . . . . . . . . . . . . . . . . . . . . V2 VVR 1001872 |

**NU SHOOZ** US duo formed in Portland, OR by husband and wife John Smith and Valerie Day.

| | |
|---|---|
| 14/06/1986 . . . . . 32 . . . . . . 8 . . . . . . | POOLSIDE . . . . . . . . . . . . . . . . . . . . . . . . . . . . . . . . . . . . . . . . . . . . . . . . . . . . . . . . . . . . Atlantic WX 60 |

○ Silver disc  ● Gold disc  ✪ Platinum disc (additional platinum units are indicated by a figure following the symbol)  ●[9] Number of weeks album topped the UK chart

### NUCLEAR ASSAULT
US rock group formed in 1985 by John Conelly (guitar/vocals), Anthony Bramante (guitar), Dan Lilker (born 18/10/1964, Queens, NY, bass) and Glenn Evans (drums). Lilker had previously been a member of Anthrax.

| 07/10/1989 | 60 | 1 | | HANDLE WITH CARE | Under One Flag FLAG 35 |
|---|---|---|---|---|---|

### NUCLEUS
UK instrumental group formed in 1969 by Ian Carr (born 21/4/1933, Dumfries, trumpet), Chris Spedding (born 17/6/1944, Sheffield, guitar), Karl Jenkins (keyboards) and John Marshall (drums). Jenkins and Marshall left in 1972 to join Soft Machine and although they were eventually replaced the group was effectively a vehicle for Ian Carr. Nucleus dissolved in the early 1970s with Spedding going on to launch a solo career.

| 11/07/1970 | 46 | 1 | | ELASTIC ROCK | Vertigo 6360 006 |
|---|---|---|---|---|---|

### TED NUGENT
US singer/guitarist (born 13/12/1948, Detroit, MI) who was a member of The Royal Highboys and Lourdes before moving to Chicago where he formed The Amboy Dukes in 1964. They made their recording debut for Mainstream in 1967 as Ted Nugent And The Amboy Dukes and then recorded two albums for Frank Zappa's DiscReet label before The Amboy Dukes moniker was dropped and Nugent went solo with Epic. His backing group consisted of Derek St Holmes (guitar), Rob Grange (bass) and Cliff Davies (drums) and Nugent proved to be  an extremely popular live draw as well as a steady album seller. By 1978 St Holmes and Grange had left and been replaced by Charlie Huhn (guitar) and John Sauter (bass). In 1982 Nugent switched to Atlantic Records and assembled a new group that included Carmine Appice (drums) and Derek St Holmes (vocals). He linked with Tommy Shaw (guitar/vocals and previously a member of Styx), Jack Blades (bass and formerly of Night Ranger) and Michael Cartellone (drums) to form Damn Yankees.

| 04/09/1976 | 56 | 1 | | TED NUGENT | Epic EPC 81268 |
|---|---|---|---|---|---|
| 30/10/1976 | 33 | 2 | | FREE FOR ALL | Epic EPC 81397 |
| 02/07/1977 | 28 | 5 | | CAT SCRATCH FEVER | Epic EPC 82010 |
| 11/03/1978 | 47 | 2 | | DOUBLE LIVE GONZO! | Epic EPC 88282 |
| 14/06/1980 | 37 | 3 | | SCREAM DREAM | Epic EPC 86111 |
| 25/04/1981 | 75 | 1 | | INTENSITIES (IN 10 CITIES) | Epic EPC 84917 |

### GARY NUMAN
UK singer (born Gary Anthony James Webb, 8/3/1958, London) who formed Tubeway Army in 1977, with Paul 'Scarlett' Gardiner (bass) and Gerald 'Rael' Lidyard (drums). Numan quit his job with WH Smith on the day his debut release was issued in 1978. He formed the Numa label in 1984. A keen aviator, he attempted to fly around the world in his light aircraft in 1982 but was arrested in India on suspicion of spying. The charge was later dropped. Gardiner died from a drug overdose on 4/2/1984.

| 09/06/1979 | ❶¹ | 31 | ● | REPLICAS | Beggars Banquet BEGA 7 |
|---|---|---|---|---|---|
| 25/08/1979 | 14 | 10 | | TUBEWAY ARMY This and the above hit credited to **TUBEWAY ARMY** | Beggars Banquet BEGA 5 |
| 22/09/1979 | ❶² | 21 | ● | **THE PLEASURE PRINCIPLE** | Beggars Banquet BEGA 10 |
| 13/09/1980 | ❶¹ | 11 | ● | **TELEKON** | Beggars Banquet BEGA 19 |
| 02/05/1981 | 2 | 4 | | **LIVING ORNAMENTS 1979–1980** This is a boxed set containing *Living Ornaments 1979* and *Living Ornaments 1980* | Beggars Banquet BOX 1 |
| 02/05/1981 | 39 | 3 | | LIVING ORNAMENTS 1980 | Beggars Banquet BEGA 25 |
| 02/05/1981 | 47 | 3 | | LIVING ORNAMENTS 1979 | Beggars Banquet BEGA 24 |
| 12/09/1981 | 3 | 8 | | **DANCE** | Beggars Banquet BEGA 28 |
| 18/09/1982 | 8 | 6 | | **I, ASSASSIN** | Beggars Banquet BEGA 40 |
| 27/11/1982 | 45 | 7 | | NEW MAN NUMAN – THE BEST OF GARY NUMAN | TV Records TVA 7 |
| 24/09/1983 | 12 | 6 | | WARRIORS | Beggars Banquet BEGA 47 |
| 06/10/1984 | 29 | 4 | | THE PLAN 1978 **TUBEWAY ARMY AND GARY NUMAN** | Beggars Banquet BEGA 55 |
| 24/11/1984 | 45 | 3 | | BERSERKER | Numa 1001 |
| 13/04/1985 | 29 | 5 | | WHITE NOISE – LIVE | Numa NUMAD 1002 |
| 28/09/1985 | 24 | 5 | | THE FURY | Numa 1003 |
| 08/11/1986 | 59 | 2 | | STRANGE CHARM | Numa 1005 |
| 03/10/1987 | 43 | 3 | | EXHIBITION | Beggars Banquet BEGA 88 |
| 08/10/1988 | 48 | 2 | | METAL RHYTHM | Illegal ILP 035 |
| 08/07/1989 | 59 | 1 | | AUTOMATIC **SHARPE AND NUMAN** | Polydor 8395201 |
| 28/10/1989 | 55 | 1 | | SKIN MECHANIC | I.R.S. EIRSA 1019 |
| 30/03/1991 | 39 | 1 | | OUTLAND | I.R.S. EIRSA 1039 |
| 22/08/1992 | 42 | 1 | | MACHINE + SOUL | Numa NUMACD 1009 |
| 02/10/1993 | 70 | 1 | | BEST OF GARY NUMAN 1978–83 | Beggars Banquet BEGA 150CD |
| 30/03/1996 | 21 | 3 | | THE PREMIER HITS **GARY NUMAN/TUBEWAY ARMY** | Polygram TV 5311492 |
| 01/11/1997 | 48 | 1 | | EXILE | Eagle EAGCD 008 |
| 21/10/2000 | 58 | 1 | | PURE | Eagle EAGCD 078 |
| 01/06/2002 | 44 | 1 | | EXPOSURE – THE BEST OF 1977–2002 | Jagged Halo |

### NUYORICAN SOUL
US R&B group formed by Masters At Work (Little Louie Vega and Kenny 'Dope' Gonzalez) and featuring Roy Ayers, George Benson, Jocelyn Brown, Jazzy Jeff, India, Vincent Montana Jr, Eddie Palmieri and Tito Puente.

| 01/03/1997 | 25 | 2 | | NUYORICAN SOUL | Talkin Loud 5344512 |
|---|---|---|---|---|---|

**NWA** US rap group formed in Compton, Los Angeles, CA in 1987 by Ice Cube (born O'Shea Jackson, 15/6/1969, Los Angeles), Eric 'Eazy-E' Wright (born 7/9/1964, Compton), MC Ren (born Lorenzo Patterson, 16/6/1966, Los Angeles), Dr Dre (born Andre Young, 18/2/1965, Los Angeles) and DJ Yella (born Antoine Carraby, 11/12/1967, Los Angeles). Ice Cube, Dr Dre and Eazy-E all released solo recordings. The group's name stands for Niggaz With Attitude (although according to some sources it stands for No Whiteboys Allowed). Eazy-E died from an AIDS-related illness on 26/3/1995. The group's 1991 album *EFIL4ZAGGIN* (Niggaz4Life spelt backwards) was seized by the UK government under the Obscene Publications Act. Distributors Island Records went to court in order to get the ban overturned and were represented by Geoffrey Robertson QC, who had previously represented the infamous magazine *Oz* in 1971.

| | | | | | |
|---|---|---|---|---|---|
| 30/09/1989 | 41 | 4 | ○ | STRAIGHT OUTTA COMPTON | Fourth & Broadway BRLP 534 |
| 15/06/1991 | 25 | 2 | | EFIL4ZAGGIN ▲[1] | Fourth & Broadway BRLP 562 |
| 31/08/1996 | 56 | 1 | | GREATEST HITS | Priority CDPTY 126 |
| 05/07/2003 | 35 | 4 | | STRAIGHT OUTTA COMPTON | Priority 5379362 |

**MICHAEL NYMAN** UK composer/pianist (born 23/3/1944, London) who studied at the Royal Academy of Music and later King's College in London. Although he has made his name as the composer of film themes and scores, including *The Draughtsman's Contract* (1982), *The Cook, The Thief, His Wife And Her Lover* (1989) and *Prospero's Books* (1991), he has also composed various operas, including *The Man Who Mistook His Wife For A Hat*.

| | | | | | |
|---|---|---|---|---|---|
| 12/02/1994 | 31 | 15 | ● | THE PIANO Original soundtrack to the film | Venture CDVE 919 |

○ Silver disc  ● Gold disc  ✪ Platinum disc (additional platinum units are indicated by a figure following the symbol)  ●⁹ Number of weeks album topped the UK chart

# O

**O-TOWN** US group formed by Ashley Angel (born 1/8/1981), Jacob Underwood (born 25/4/1980), Trevor Penick (born 16/11/1979), Erik-Michael Estrada (born 23/9/1979) and Dan Miller (born 4/9/1980). They were the US winners of *Making The Band*.

| | | | |
|---|---|---|---|
| 18/08/2001 | 7 | 5 | |

O-TOWN ................................................................................................. J Records 80813200002

**PAUL OAKENFOLD** UK producer (born 30/8/1963, London) who also records as Perfecto Allstars, Element Four, Planet Perfecto and Movement 98 and is a member of Rise.

| | | | |
|---|---|---|---|
| 06/07/2002 | 25 | 12 | O |

BUNKKA. ....................................................................................................... Perfecto PERFALB 09CD

**PHILIP OAKEY AND GIORGIO MORODER** UK/Italian duo formed by Philip Oakey (born 2/10/1955, Leicester, vocals/synthesiser) and Giorgio Moroder (born 26/4/1940, Ortisel, synthesiser). Oakey had previously been leader of Human League whilst Moroder had been producer and chief songwriter for hits by Chicory Tip, Donna Summer, Blondie, David Bowie, Irene Cara, The Three Degrees and others. The pair had previously worked together on the soundtrack to *Electric Dreams*.

| | | | |
|---|---|---|---|
| 10/08/1985 | 52 | 5 | |

PHILIP OAKEY AND GIORGIO MORODER ............................................................... Virgin V 2351

**OASIS** UK group formed in 1983 by Mary Hopkin (born 3/5/1950, Pontardawe, Wales), Julian Lloyd Webber (born 1951, the younger brother of Andrew Lloyd Webber), Bill Lovelady and Peter Skellern (born 1947, Bury).

| | | | |
|---|---|---|---|
| 28/04/1984 | 23 | 14 | |

OASIS .................................................................................................................. WEA WX 3

**OASIS** UK group formed in Manchester by Liam Gallagher (born 21/9/1972, Manchester, vocals), Paul 'Bonehead' Arthurs (born 23/6/1965, Manchester, guitar), Tony McCarroll (drums) and Paul 'Guigsy' McGuigan (born 9/5/1971, Manchester, bass). With Liam's brother, ex-Inspiral Carpets roadie Noel (born 29/5/1967, Manchester, guitar), they were catapulted into stardom. McCarroll was sacked in 1995 (getting a £500,000 settlement from the group) and replaced by Alan White (born 26/5/1972, London). They won the 1995 award for Best UK Newcomer at the BRIT Awards and were the major winners of 1996 – awards included Best UK Group and Best Video (for *Wonderwall*). Three MTV Europe Music Awards include Best Group in 1996 and Best Rock Act in 1997. Liam Gallagher married actress Patsy Kensit in April 1997; they divorced in September 2000. Bonehead left in August 1999 and two weeks later Guigsy also quit. They were replaced by Andy Bell (born 11/8/1970, Cardiff), formerly of Ride and Hurricane #1 on bass, and Gem Archer (guitar). They launched Big Brother label in 2000. Noel Gallagher quit in May 2000 during a world tour, temporarily replaced by Matt Deighton, later returning. Nicole Appleton (a member of All Saints, later Appleton) and Liam had a son, Gene, in July 2001.

| | | | | |
|---|---|---|---|---|
| 10/09/1994 | ●¹ | 177 | ✪⁶ | DEFINITELY MAYBE ◇² ...................................................... Creation CRECD 169 |
| 14/10/1995 | ●¹⁰ | 145 | ✪¹³ | (WHAT'S THE STORY) MORNING GLORY? ◇⁶ 1996 BRIT Award for Best Album ........... Creation CRECD 189 |
| 16/11/1996 | 23 | 3 | | DEFINITELY MAYBE SINGLES BOX – SILVER ................................... Creation CREDM 002 |
| 16/11/1996 | 24 | 3 | | (WHAT'S THE STORY) MORNING GLORY? SINGLES BOX – GOLD...................... Creation CREEMG 002 |
| 30/08/1997 | ●⁵ | 36 | ✪⁶ | BE HERE NOW ◇³ .......................................................... Creation CRECD 219 |
| 14/11/1998 | 2 | 28 | O | THE MASTERPLAN ......................................................... Creation CRECD 241 |
| 11/03/2000 | ●¹ | 29 | ✪² | STANDING ON THE SHOULDER OF GIANTS ◇ ............................ Big Brother RKID CD002 |
| 17/06/2000 | 63 | 8 | | (WHAT'S THE STORY) MORNING GLORY? Re-issue ......................... Big Brother RKIDCD 008 |
| 25/11/2000 | 5 | 10 | ● | FAMILIAR TO MILLIONS ...................................................... Big Brother RKIDCD 005 |
| 13/07/2002 | ●¹ | 43 | ✪³ | HEATHEN CHEMISTRY ◇ .................................................... Big Brother RKIDCD 25 |

**OBITUARY** US rock group formed in Brandon, FL by John Tardy (vocals), Allen West (guitar), Trevor Peres (guitar), David Tucker (bass) and Donald Tardy (drums) as Xecutioner, although after discovering another group with the same name they switched to Obituary. West and Tucker left in 1992 and were replaced by James Murphy and Frank Watkins.

| | | | |
|---|---|---|---|
| 18/04/1992 | 52 | 1 | |
| 17/09/1994 | 65 | 1 | |

THE END COMPLETE .......................................................................... Roadrunner RC 920121
WORLD DEMISE ................................................................................... Roadrunner RR 89955

**BILLY OCEAN** UK singer (born Leslie Sebastian Charles, 21/1/1950, Trinidad) who moved to London at the age of four and signed with GTO in 1975. He later relocated to the USA and won the 1984 Grammy Award for Best Rhythm & Blues Vocal Performance for *Caribbean Queen (No More Love On The Run)*.

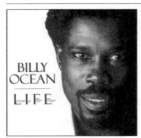

▲⁹ Number of weeks album topped the US chart ◆¹² RIAA Diamond Awards ◇³ IFPI Platinum Europe Awards

| DATE | POS | WKS | BPI | ALBUM TITLE | LABEL & NUMBER |
|---|---|---|---|---|---|
| 24/11/1984 | 9 | 59 | ● | SUDDENLY | Jive JIP 12 |
| 17/05/1986 | 2 | 32 | ● | LOVE ZONE | Jive HIP 35 |
| 19/03/1988 | 3 | 13 | ● | TEAR DOWN THESE WALLS | Jive HIP 57 |
| 28/10/1989 | 4 | 17 | ✪ | GREATEST HITS | Jive BOTV 1 |
| 16/08/1997 | 7 | 21 | ● | LOVE IS FOR EVER | Jive BOCD 2 |
| 15/02/2003 | 69 | 1 | | LET'S GET BACK TOGETHER – THE LOVE SONGS | Jive 9225232 |
| 19/06/2004 | 28 | 2+ | | ULTIMATE COLLECTION | Jive 82876614022 |

**OCEAN COLOUR SCENE** UK group formed by Simon Fowler (born 25/4/1965, Birmingham, guitar/vocals), Steve Craddock (born 22/8/1969, Birmingham, guitar/keyboards/vocals), Damon Minchella (born 1/6/1969, Liverpool, bass) and Oscar Harrison (born 15/4/1965, Birmingham, drums/keyboards). They took part in the *It's Only Rock 'N' Roll* project for the Children's Promise charity.

| DATE | POS | WKS | BPI | ALBUM TITLE | LABEL & NUMBER |
|---|---|---|---|---|---|
| 20/04/1996 | 2 | 73 | ✪3 | MOSELEY SHOALS ◇ | MCA MCD 60008 |
| 21/09/1996 | 54 | 2 | | OCEAN COLOUR SCENE | Fontana 5122692 |
| 15/03/1997 | 4 | 14 | ● | B-SIDES, SEASIDES & FREERIDES | MCA MCD 60034 |
| 27/09/1997 | ❶1 | 37 | ✪ | MARCHIN' ALREADY | MCA MCD 60053 |
| 25/09/1999 | 4 | 11 | ● | ONE FROM THE MODERN | Island CID 8090 |
| 21/04/2001 | 7 | 4 | ○ | MECHANICAL WONDER | Island CID 8104 |
| 17/11/2001 | 16 | 4 | ● | SONGS FROM THE FRONT ROW – THE BEST OF | Island CIDD 8111 |
| 19/07/2003 | 14 | 3 | ○ | NORTH ATLANTIC DRIFT | Sanctuary SANCD160 |
| 13/09/2003 | 75 | 1 | | ANTHOLOGY | Island 9807210 |

**OCEANIA** Australian group formed by Hinewehi Mohi (vocals) and former Killing Joke member Jaz Coleman (born Jeremy Coleman, Cheltenham, keyboard/vocals) and whose album was a collection of Aboriginal chants set to modern dance music!

| DATE | POS | WKS | BPI | ALBUM TITLE | LABEL & NUMBER |
|---|---|---|---|---|---|
| 23/10/1999 | 70 | 1 | | OCEANIA | Point Music 5367752 |

**OCEANIC** UK group formed by Siobhan Maher (vocals), Sarah Miller (vocals), Amanda Williams (vocals), Jorinda Williams (vocals), Jorinde Williams (vocals), Frank Crofts (keyboards) and David Harry (keyboards).

| DATE | POS | WKS | BPI | ALBUM TITLE | LABEL & NUMBER |
|---|---|---|---|---|---|
| 04/07/1992 | 49 | 2 | | THAT ALBUM BY OCEANIC | Dead Dead Good 4509900832 |

**DES O'CONNOR** UK singer (born 12/1/1932, London) who was a Butlin's Red Coat before making his stage debut in 1953. He compered *Sunday Night At The London Palladium* in the early 1960s, later hosting his own TV show and a revival of *Take Your Pick*.

| DATE | POS | WKS | BPI | ALBUM TITLE | LABEL & NUMBER |
|---|---|---|---|---|---|
| 07/12/1968 | 8 | 10 | | I PRETEND | Columbia SCX 6295 |
| 05/12/1970 | 40 | 4 | | WITH LOVE | Columbia SCX 6417 |
| 02/12/1972 | 25 | 6 | | SING A FAVOURITE SONG | Pye NSPL 18390 |
| 02/02/1980 | 17 | 7 | | JUST FOR YOU | Warwick WW 5071 |
| 13/10/1984 | 24 | 14 | ● | DES O'CONNOR NOW | Telstar STAR 2245 |
| 05/12/1992 | 63 | 4 | ○ | PORTRAIT | Columbia 4727302 |
| 17/11/2001 | 51 | 2 | | A TRIBUTE TO THE CROONERS | Decca 4704702 |

**HAZEL O'CONNOR** UK singer (born 16/5/1955, Coventry) who joined Albion Records in 1978, coming to prominence after appearing in the film *Breaking Glass* in 1980. She later appeared in *Car Trouble*.

| DATE | POS | WKS | BPI | ALBUM TITLE | LABEL & NUMBER |
|---|---|---|---|---|---|
| 09/08/1980 | 5 | 38 | ● | BREAKING GLASS Original soundtrack to the film | A&M AMLH 64820 |
| 12/09/1981 | 32 | 7 | | COVER PLUS | Albion ALB 108 |

**SINEAD O'CONNOR** Irish singer (born 12/12/1966, Glenageary) who started with local group Ton Ton Macoute. She first appeared on record on the soundtrack to *Captive,* releasing her debut in 1988. She was named Best International Newcomer at the 1991 BRIT Awards.

| DATE | POS | WKS | BPI | ALBUM TITLE | LABEL & NUMBER |
|---|---|---|---|---|---|
| 23/01/1988 | 27 | 20 | ● | THE LION AND THE COBRA | Ensign CHEN 7 |
| 24/03/1990 | ❶1 | 51 | ✪2 | I DO NOT WANT WHAT I HAVEN'T GOT ▲6 1990 Grammy Award for Best Alternative Music Performance | Ensign CHEN 14 |
| 26/09/1992 | 6 | 6 | | AM I NOT YOUR GIRL? | Ensign CCD 1952 |
| 24/09/1994 | 19 | 8 | ● | UNIVERSAL MOTHER | Ensign CDCHEN 34 |
| 22/11/1997 | 28 | 3 | ○ | SO FAR… THE BEST OF SINEAD O'CONNOR | Chrysalis 8215812 |

○ Silver disc ● Gold disc ✪ Platinum disc (additional platinum units are indicated by a figure following the symbol) ❶9 Number of weeks album topped the UK chart

| | | | | |
|---|---|---|---|---|
| 24/06/2000.....61......1...... | FAITH AND COURAGE .......................................................................... | Atlantic 7567833372 |
| 19/10/2002.....52......1...... | SEAN-NOS-NUA............................................................................. | R&M Entertainment RAMCD 001 |

**DANIEL O'DONNELL** Irish singer (born 12/12/1961, Kincasslagh, County Donegal) who is a hugely popular Irish country artist. He initially broke through in Scotland before becoming a major international concert attraction. He first recorded for Ritz in 1985. In 2002 he was awarded an MBE in the New Year's Honours List.

| | | | | |
|---|---|---|---|---|
| 15/10/1988.....56.....12......● | FROM THE HEART ........................................................................ | Telstar STAR 2327 |
| 28/10/1989.....43.....10...... | THOUGHTS OF HOME .................................................................... | Telstar STAR 2372 |
| 21/04/1990.....61......3...... | FAVOURITES .............................................................................. | Ritz RITZLP 052 |
| 17/11/1990.....46......7...... | THE LAST WALTZ......................................................................... | Ritz RITZALP 058 |
| 09/11/1991.....34.....14...... | THE VERY BEST OF DANIEL O'DONNELL.................................................... | Ritz RITZBLD 700 |
| 21/11/1992.....17......9...... | FOLLOW YOUR DREAM.................................................................... | Ritz RITZBCD 701 |
| 06/11/1993.....21.....10...... | A DATE WITH DANIEL – LIVE ............................................................. | Ritz RITZBCD 702 |
| 22/10/1994.....14.....11...... | ESPECIALLY FOR YOU ..................................................................... | Ritz RITZBCD 703 |
| 03/12/1994.....34......5...... | CHRISTMAS WITH DANIEL ............................................................... | Ritz RITZBCD 704 |
| 11/11/1995.....34......9...... | THE CLASSIC COLLECTION ............................................................... | Ritz RITZBCD 705 |
| 06/04/1996.....13......5...... | TIMELESS **DANIEL O'DONNELL AND MARY DUFF** ..................................... | Ritz RITZBCD 707 |
| 20/07/1996.....35......3...... | THE DANIEL O'DONNELL IRISH COLLECTION .............................................. | Ritz RITZCD 0080 |
| 26/10/1996.....11.....16...... | SONGS OF INSPIRATION .................................................................. | Ritz RITZBCD 709 |
| 08/11/1997.....11.....11...... | I BELIEVE ................................................................................. | Ritz RZBCD 710 |
| 31/10/1998......9.....10...... | **LOVE SONGS** .......................................................................... | Ritz RZBCD 715 |
| 02/10/1999.....10......8...... | **GREATEST HITS** ...................................................................... | Ritz RZBCD 716 |
| 28/10/2000......4.....10...... | **FAITH & INSPIRATION**................................................................ | Ritz RZBCD 717 |
| 01/12/2001.....27......5...... | LIVE LAUGH LOVE ....................................................................... | Rosette ROSCD 2002 |
| 02/11/2002.....19......3...... | YESTERDAY'S MEMORIES................................................................. | Rosette ROSCD 2020 |
| 22/03/2003......3.....10...... | **DANIEL IN BLUE JEANS** ............................................................... | DMG TV DMGTV001 |
| 25/10/2003.....11......6...... | AT THE END OF THE DAY................................................................. | Rosette ROSCD 2040 |
| 20/03/2004......3......8...... | **THE JUKEBOX YEARS** ................................................................. | DMG TV DMGTV005 |

**RYAN AND RACHEL O'DONNELL** Irish vocal and instrumental duo.

| | | | | |
|---|---|---|---|---|
| 16/03/2002.....17......4...... | THE CELTIC CHILLOUT ALBUM............................................................ | Decadance DECTV 001 |
| 30/11/2002.....37.....10...... | THE CELTIC CHILLOUT ALBUM This is a re-issue of Decadance DECTV 001 and was wrongly listed on the compilation albums chart for three weeks, peaking at #3 ............................................. | Decadance DECTV 007 |
| 22/03/2003.....37......3...... | THE CELTIC CHILLOUT ALBUM 2 ......................................................... | Decadance DECTV 009 |

**ODYSSEY** US R&B vocal group originally formed by sisters Lillian, Louise and Carmen Lopez as the Lopez Sisters. Carmen left in 1968, replaced by Tony Reynolds, who left in 1977, replaced by Bill McEarchern who in turn was replaced by Al Jackson.

| | | | | |
|---|---|---|---|---|
| 16/08/1980.....38......3...... | HANG TOGETHER ....................................................................... | RCA PL 13526 |
| 04/07/1981.....29......7...... | I'VE GOT THE MELODY .................................................................. | RCA RCALP 5028 |
| 03/07/1982.....21......9...... | HAPPY TOGETHER ...................................................................... | RCA RCALP 6036 |
| 20/11/1982.....69......5...... | THE MAGIC TOUCH OF ODYSSEY ........................................................ | Telstar STAR 2223 |
| 26/09/1987.....26......8......○ | THE GREATEST HITS .................................................................... | Stylus SMR 735 |

**ESTHER AND ABI OFARIM** Israeli husband and wife duo of Esther (born Esther Zaled, 13/6/1943, Safed) and Abi (born Abraham Reichstadt 5/10/1939, Tel Aviv) Ofarim. Esther represented Switzerland in the 1963 Eurovision Song Contest.

| | | | | |
|---|---|---|---|---|
| 24/02/1968......6.....20...... | **2 IN 3** ................................................................................ | Philips SBL 7825 |
| 12/07/1969.....29......4...... | OFARIM CONCERT – LIVE '69 ............................................................ | Philips XL 4 |

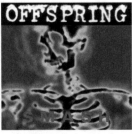

**OFFSPRING** US punk group formed in 1984 by songwriter Bryan Dexter Holland (born 29/12/1966, Orange County, CA, guitar/vocals), Greg Kriesel (born 20/1/1965, Glendale, CA, bass), Doug Thompson (vocals) and Jim Benton (drums) as Manic Subsidal. Thompson left, with Holland taking over as lead vocalist and Benton being replaced by James Lilja. Kevin 'Noodles' Wasserman (born 4/2/1963, Los Angeles, CA, guitar) joined shortly before they changed their name in 1985. Lilja left in 1987, replaced by Ron Welty (born 1/2/1971, Long Beach, CA). They were named Best Rock Act at the 1999 MTV Europe Music Awards.

| | | | | |
|---|---|---|---|---|
| 04/03/1995.....21.....34...... | SMASH ◇² ............................................................................... | Epitaph E 864322 |
| 15/02/1997.....17......3...... | IXNAY ON THE HOMBRE .................................................................. | Epitaph 64872 |

▲⁹ Number of weeks album topped the US chart    ◆¹² RIAA Diamond Awards    ◇³ IFPI Platinum Europe Awards

| | | | | | |
|---|---|---|---|---|---|
| 28/11/1998 | 10 | 44 | ✪ | AMERICANA ◇² | Columbia 4916562 |
| 25/11/2000 | 12 | 18 | ● | CONSPIRACY OF ONE ◇ | Columbia 4984819 |
| 13/12/2003 | 27 | 7 | | SPLINTER | Columbia 5122013 |

**MARY O'HARA** Irish harpist/singer (born 1935, Sligo) who spent twelve years in a Benedictine monastery before resuming a singing and playing career in 1974.

| | | | | | |
|---|---|---|---|---|---|
| 08/04/1978 | 37 | 3 | ○ | MARY O'HARA AT THE ROYAL FESTIVAL HALL | Chrysalis CHR 1159 |
| 01/12/1979 | 12 | 9 | ✪ | TRANQUILLITY | Warwick WW 5072 |

**O'JAYS** US R&B vocal group formed in 1958 by Eddie Levert (born 16/6/1942, Canton, OH), Walter Williams (born 25/8/1942, Canton), William Powell (born 20/1/1942, Canton), Bill Isles and Bobby Massey as the Triumphs. Later recording as the Mascots, they became the O'Jays (after Cleveland DJ Eddie O'Jay) in 1963. Isles left in 1965, Massey in 1972 and they continued as a trio. Powell gave up live work owing to ill health in 1975 (but continued to record with them), replaced by Sammy Strain (born 20/1/1942, Brooklyn, NYC). Powell died from cancer on 26/5/1977. Strain left in 1990, replaced by Nathaniel Best (born 13/12/1960, Miami, FL). Best left in 1996, replaced by Eric Grant. Levert's sons Gerald and Sean are members of Levert.

| | | | | | |
|---|---|---|---|---|---|
| 12/10/1985 | 87 | 2 | | THE ARTISTS VOLUME III WOMACK AND WOMACK/THE O'JAYS/KLEEER/THE S.O.S. BAND | Street Sounds ARTIS 3 |

**MIKE OLDFIELD** UK singer/multi-instrumentalist (born 15/5/1953, Reading) who released his first album in 1968 as Sallyangie with his sister Sally. He went solo in 1971 and his debut album came out in 1973, the first release on Virgin.

| | | | | | |
|---|---|---|---|---|---|
| 14/07/1973 | ●¹ | 278 | ✪⁷ | TUBULAR BELLS 1974 Grammy Award for Best Instrument Composition | Virgin V 2001 |
| 14/09/1974 | ●³ | 17 | ● | HERGEST RIDGE | Virgin V 2013 |
| 08/02/1975 | 17 | 7 | ○ | THE ORCHESTRAL TUBULAR BELLS MIKE OLDFIELD WITH THE ROYAL PHILHARMONIC ORCHESTRA | Virgin V 2026 |
| 15/11/1975 | 4 | 23 | ● | OMMADAWN | Virgin V 2043 |
| 20/11/1976 | 22 | 13 | ● | BOXED | Virgin V BOX 1 |
| 09/12/1978 | 14 | 17 | ✪ | INCANTATIONS | Virgin VDT 101 |
| 11/08/1979 | 16 | 9 | ○ | EXPOSED | Virgin VD 2511 |
| 08/12/1979 | 24 | 9 | ● | PLATINUM | Virgin V 2141 |
| 08/11/1980 | 27 | 12 | ● | QE 2 | Virgin V 2181 |
| 27/03/1982 | 7 | 27 | ● | FIVE MILES OUT | Virgin V 2222 |
| 04/06/1983 | 6 | 29 | ● | CRISES | Virgin V 2262 |
| 07/07/1984 | 15 | 16 | ● | DISCOVERY | Virgin V 2308 |
| 15/12/1984 | 97 | 1 | ○ | THE KILLING FIELDS Original soundtrack to the film | Virgin V 2328 |
| 02/11/1985 | 36 | 17 | ● | THE COMPLETE MIKE OLDFIELD | Virgin MOC 1 |
| 10/10/1987 | 29 | 5 | ● | ISLANDS | Virgin V 2466 |
| 22/07/1989 | 30 | 5 | | EARTH MOVING | Virgin V 2610 |
| 09/06/1990 | 49 | 2 | | AMAROK | Virgin V 2640 |
| 12/09/1992 | ●² | 30 | ✪² | TUBULAR BELLS II | WEA 4509906182 |
| 25/09/1993 | 5 | 10 | ● | ELEMENTS – THE BEST OF MIKE OLDFIELD | Virgin VTCD 18 |
| 03/12/1994 | 24 | 6 | ● | THE SONGS OF DISTANT EARTH | WEA 4509985812 |
| 07/09/1996 | 12 | 5 | ○ | VOYAGER | WEA 0630158962 |
| 12/09/1998 | 4 | 7 | ● | TUBULAR BELLS III | WEA 3984243492 |
| 05/06/1999 | 40 | 2 | | GUITARS | WEA 3984274012 |
| 16/06/2001 | 60 | 2 | | THE BEST OF TUBULAR BELLS | Virgin CDV 2936 |
| 07/06/2003 | 51 | 1 | | TUBULAR BELLS 2003 | WEA 2564602042 |

**OLIVE** UK group with ex-Simply Red Tim Kellett, Robin Taylor-Firth and vocalist Ruth-Ann Boyle.

| | | | | | |
|---|---|---|---|---|---|
| 31/05/1997 | 15 | 3 | | EXTRA VIRGIN | RCA 74321486872 |

**OMAR** UK singer (born Omar Lye Fook, 1969, Canterbury) who debuted with the Kongo label in 1990, then with Talkin' Loud in 1991.

| | | | | | |
|---|---|---|---|---|---|
| 14/07/1990 | 54 | 4 | | THERE'S NOTHING LIKE THIS | Kongo Dance KDLP 2 |
| 27/07/1991 | 19 | 6 | | THERE'S NOTHING LIKE THIS | Talkin Loud 5100211 |
| 24/10/1992 | 37 | 2 | | MUSIC MAKES MY DAY | Talkin Loud 5124012 |
| 02/07/1994 | 50 | 1 | | FOR PLEASURE | RCA 74321208532 |
| 16/08/1997 | 50 | 1 | | THIS IS NOT A LOVE SONG | RCA 74321496262 |

**OMNI TRIO** UK producer Rob Haigh.

| | | | | | |
|---|---|---|---|---|---|
| 11/02/1995 | 60 | 1 | | THE DEEPEST CUT – VOLUME 1 | Morning Shadow ASHADOW 1CD |
| 24/08/1996 | 43 | 1 | | THE HAUNTED SCIENCE | Morning Shadow ASHADOW 6CD |

○ Silver disc ● Gold disc ✪ Platinum disc (additional platinum units are indicated by a figure following the symbol) ●⁹ Number of weeks album topped the UK chart

**ONE DOVE** UK dance group with Ian Carmichael (born 1/6/1960, Glasgow), Jim McKinven (born 1959, Glasgow) and Dot Allison (born 17/8/1969, Edinburgh). McKinven had previously been in the Bluebells and Altered Images. Allison later went solo.

| | | | |
|---|---|---|---|
| 25/09/1993 | 30 | 2 | |

MORNING DOVE WHITE . . . . . . . . . . . . . . . . . . . . . . . . . . . . . . . . . . . . . . . . . . . . . . . . . . . . . . . . . . London 8283522

**1 GIANT LEAP** UK production group formed by Duncan Bridgeman and Jamie Catto. Catto is a member of Faithless, as is guest vocalist Maxi Jazz who appeared on their debut single with Robbie Williams.

27/04/2002 . . . . . 51 . . . . . . 3 . . . . . .
ONE GIANT LEAP. . . . . . . . . . . . . . . . . . . . . . . . . . . . . . . . . . . . . . . . . . . . . . . . . . . . . . . . Palm Pictures PALMCD 2077

**ONE HUNDRED & ONE STRINGS** German orchestra assembled by recording engineer Dick Miller in 1957, with Robert Lowden the first arranger. Their initial releases were on Miller's own Somerset label and they have since released more than 200 albums of their series of string-laden instrumentals.

26/09/1959 . . . . . 9 . . . . . . 7 . . . . . .
**GYPSY CAMPFIRES** . . . . . . . . . . . . . . . . . . . . . . . . . . . . . . . . . . . . . . . . . . . . . . . . Pye Golden Guinea GGL 0009
26/03/1960 . . . 17 . . . . . . 1 . . . . . .
THE SOUL OF SPAIN . . . . . . . . . . . . . . . . . . . . . . . . . . . . . . . . . . . . . . . . . . . . . . . . Pye Golden Guinea GGL 0017
16/04/1960 . . . . 10 . . . . . . 1 . . . . . .
**GRAND CANYON SUITE** . . . . . . . . . . . . . . . . . . . . . . . . . . . . . . . . . . . . . . . . . . . . . . . Pye Golden Guinea GGL 0048
27/08/1960 . . . . ❶⁵ . . . . 21 . . . . . .
**DOWN DRURY LANE TO MEMORY LANE** . . . . . . . . . . . . . . . . . . . . . . . . . . . . . . . . . . . . Pye Golden Guinea GGL 0061
15/10/1983 . . . . 32 . . . . . . 5 . . . . . .
MORNING NOON AND NIGHT . . . . . . . . . . . . . . . . . . . . . . . . . . . . . . . . . . . . . . . . . . . . . . . . Ronco RTL 2094

**ONE MINUTE SILENCE** UK group: Brian 'Yap' Barry (vocals), Chris Ignatiou (guitar), Glenn Diani (bass), Eddie Stratton (drums).

22/04/2000 . . . . . 61 . . . . . . 1 . . . . . .
BUY NOW … SAVED LATER . . . . . . . . . . . . . . . . . . . . . . . . . . . . . . . . . . . . . . . . . . . . . . . . . . V2 VVR 1012362

**ONE WORLD** UK group assembled by Kevin Godley (born 7/10/1945, Manchester), formerly of 10CC and Godley & Crème. The project featured contributions from Peter Gabriel, Robbie Robertson, Courtney Pine, Ryuichi Sakamoto, Sting, Clannad, Laurie Anderson, Bob Geldof, Terence Trent D'Arby, Howard Jones, Chrissie Hynde, Nusrat Fateh Ali Khan, Lou Reed, Dave Stewart, Joe Strummer, Suzanne Vega and many others.

09/06/1990 . . . . . 27 . . . . . . 3 . . . . . .
ONE WORLD ONE VOICE . . . . . . . . . . . . . . . . . . . . . . . . . . . . . . . . . . . . . . . . . . . . . . . . . . . . Virgin V 2632

**ALEXANDER O'NEAL** US singer (born 14/11/1954, Natchez, MS) who was the lead vocalist with Flyte Tyme that later became Time. He went solo in 1980 and later relocated to London.

The Greatest Hits Of Alexander O'Neal — This Thing Called Love

01/06/1985 . . . . . 19 . . . . . 18 . . . . . . ●
ALEXANDER O'NEAL. . . . . . . . . . . . . . . . . . . . . . . . . . . . . . . . . . . . . . . . . . . . . . . . . . . . . Tabu TBU 26485
08/08/1987 . . . . 4 . . . . 103 . . . . . ✪³
**HEARSAY/ALL MIXED UP** All Mixed Up is a remix album of Hearsay that was listed from 15/7/1989 . . . . . . . . . . . . . Tabu 4509361
17/12/1988 . . . . 53 . . . . . . 3 . . . . . .
MY GIFT TO YOU . . . . . . . . . . . . . . . . . . . . . . . . . . . . . . . . . . . . . . . . . . . . . . . . . . . . . . . Tabu 4631521
02/02/1991 . . . . . 2 . . . . 16 . . . . . . ●
**ALL TRUE MAN** . . . . . . . . . . . . . . . . . . . . . . . . . . . . . . . . . . . . . . . . . . . . . . . . . . . . . . . Tabu 4658821
30/05/1992 . . . . 4 . . . . 18 . . . . . . ●
**THIS THING CALLED LOVE – THE GREATEST HITS OF ALEXANDER O'NEAL** . . . . . . . . . . . . . . . . . . . . . . . Tabu 4717142
20/02/1993 . . . . . 14 . . . . . . 4 . . . . . .
LOVE MAKES NO SENSE . . . . . . . . . . . . . . . . . . . . . . . . . . . . . . . . . . . . . . . . . . . . . . . . . . . . Tabu 5495022

**ONLY ONES** UK group formed in 1976 by Peter Perrett (guitar/vocals), John Perry (guitar), Alan Mair (bass) and Mike Killie (drums) who signed with CBS in 1977. They disbanded in 1981 after being dropped by the label.

03/06/1978 . . . . . 56 . . . . . . 1 . . . . . .
THE ONLY ONES . . . . . . . . . . . . . . . . . . . . . . . . . . . . . . . . . . . . . . . . . . . . . . . . . . . . . . . . CBS 82830
31/03/1979 . . . . 42 . . . . . . 2 . . . . . .
EVEN SERPENTS SHINE . . . . . . . . . . . . . . . . . . . . . . . . . . . . . . . . . . . . . . . . . . . . . . . . . . . . . CBS 83451
03/05/1980 . . . . 37 . . . . . . 5 . . . . . .
BABY'S GOT A GUN . . . . . . . . . . . . . . . . . . . . . . . . . . . . . . . . . . . . . . . . . . . . . . . . . . . . . . . . CBS 84089

**YOKO ONO** Japanese singer (born 18/2/1933, Tokyo) who was married to John Lennon in 1969 and credited on most of his later songs, this delaying the release of some singles and albums. Her single was released in the aftermath of his murder in December 1980.

14/10/1972 . . . . . 11 . . . . . . 6 . . . . . .
SOMETIME IN NEW YORK CITY **JOHN AND YOKO LENNON WITH THE PLASTIC ONO BAND & ELEPHANT'S MEMORY** . . Apple PCSP 716
22/11/1980 . . . . ❶² . . . . 36 . . . . . . ✪
**DOUBLE FANTASY** JOHN LENNON AND YOKO ONO . . . . . . . . . . . . . . . . . . . . . . . . . . . . . . . . . Geffen K 99131
20/06/1981 . . . . 47 . . . . . . 2 . . . . . .
SEASON OF GLASS . . . . . . . . . . . . . . . . . . . . . . . . . . . . . . . . . . . . . . . . . . . . . . . . . . . . Geffen K 99164
04/02/1984 . . . . . 3 . . . . 13 . . . . . . ●
**MILK AND HONEY – A HEART PLAY** JOHN LENNON AND YOKO ONO. . . . . . . . . . . . . . . . . . . . . . . . Polydor POLH 5

**ONSLAUGHT** UK group formed in Bristol, Avon in 1983 by Paul Mahoney (vocals), Nigel Rocket (guitar), Jason Stallord (bass) and Steve Grice (drums). After a release on the indie label Cor, they were signed by Under One Flag, part of the Music For Nations group. Their debut for the label saw Sy Keeler join on vocals, Mahoney switching to bass and Stallord to rhythm guitar. Soon after the album release Mahoney left, replaced by James Hinder. Keeler and Stallord left before the recording of the next album, replaced by Rob Trottman and Steve Grimmett. Grimmett left in 1990, replaced by Tony O'Hara, and the group disbanded in 1991.

20/05/1989 . . . . . 46 . . . . . . 2 . . . . . .
IN SEARCH OF SANITY . . . . . . . . . . . . . . . . . . . . . . . . . . . . . . . . . . . . . . . . . . . . . . . . . . London 8281421

**ONYX** US rap group from New York, with Sticky Fingaz (born Kirk Jones), Big DS, Fredro Starr and Suave Sonny Caesar. After one single for Profile, switched to Columbia. Big DS left in 1995, Fredro Starr appeared in films, including Strapped, Dead Presidents and Clockers.

04/09/1993 . . . . . 59 . . . . . . 3 . . . . . .
BACDAFUCUP . . . . . . . . . . . . . . . . . . . . . . . . . . . . . . . . . . . . . . . . . . . . . . . . . . . . . . . Columbia 4729802

**OPERABABES** UK vocal duo Karen England and Rebecca Knight; they were first spotted busking in Covent Garden and invited to perform at the 2002 FA Cup Final.

| DATE | POS | WKS | BPI | ALBUM TITLE | LABEL & NUMBER |
|---|---|---|---|---|---|
| 08/06/2002 | 24 | 6 | | BEYOND IMAGINATION | Sony Classical SK89916 |

**OPM** US rock group formed by Matthew Lo (guitar/vocals), John Necro (bass) and Geoff Turney (drums).

| DATE | POS | WKS | BPI | ALBUM TITLE | LABEL & NUMBER |
|---|---|---|---|---|---|
| 21/07/2001 | 31 | 8 | O | MENACE TO SOBRIETY | Atlantic 7567929772 |

**ORANGE JUICE** UK group formed in Glasgow in 1977 by Edwyn Collins (born 23/8/1959, Edinburgh, guitar/vocals), David McClymont (bass), Steve Daly (drums) and James Kirk (guitar); they originally recorded for indie label Postcard. Kirk and Daly left in 1982 and were replaced by Malcolm Ross and Zeke Manyika. Collins later recorded solo.

| DATE | POS | WKS | BPI | ALBUM TITLE | LABEL & NUMBER |
|---|---|---|---|---|---|
| 06/03/1982 | 21 | 6 | | YOU CAN'T HIDE YOUR LOVE FOREVER | Polydor POLS 1057 |
| 20/11/1982 | 39 | 8 | | RIP IT UP | Polydor POLS 1076 |
| 10/03/1984 | 34 | 4 | | TEXAS FEVER | Polydor OJMLP 1 |

**ORB** UK house group formed in 1988 by Dr Alex Paterson (born Duncan Robert Alex Paterson, initials giving him his Dr title) and Jimmy Cauty. Cauty left in 1990 for KLF, Paterson assuming lead role. By 1996 they were Paterson, Andy Hughes and Thomas Fehlmann.

| DATE | POS | WKS | BPI | ALBUM TITLE | LABEL & NUMBER |
|---|---|---|---|---|---|
| 27/04/1991 | 29 | 5 | | THE ORB'S ADVENTURES BEYOND THE ULTRAWORLD | Big Life BLRDLP 5 |
| 18/07/1992 | ●[1] | 9 | | **U.F. ORB** | Big Life BLRCD 18 |
| 04/12/1993 | 23 | 2 | O | LIVE 93 | Island CIDD 8022 |
| 25/06/1994 | 6 | 4 | | **POMME FRITZ** | Inter-Modo ORBCD 1 |
| 01/04/1995 | 20 | 3 | | ORBVS TERRERVM | Island CIDX 8037 |
| 08/03/1997 | 19 | 3 | | ORBLIVION | Island CID 8055 |
| 17/10/1998 | 38 | 2 | | U.F. OFF – THE BEST OF ORB | Island CID 8078 |

**ROY ORBISON** US singer (born 23/4/1936, Vernon, TX) whose first group, the Wink Westerners, was formed in 1952. He released his debut record in 1955 with the Teen Kings for Je-Wel with his first solo recordings for Sun in 1956. He moved to Nashville to concentrate on songwriting in 1957, signing with RCA with little success before joining Monument. He later recorded as 'Lefty' in the Traveling Wilburys. His wife Claudette was killed in a motorcycle accident in 1966, whilst two of his three sons were killed in a fire in 1968. He died from a heart attack on 6/12/1988. He was inducted into the Rock & Roll Hall of Fame in 1987. He won four Grammy Awards: Best Country Performance by a Duo in 1980 with Emmylou Harris for *That Lovin' You Feelin' Again,* Best Spoken Word Documentary in 1986 with various others for *Interviews From The Class Of '55,* Best Country Vocal Collaboration in 1988 with k. d. lang for *Crying* and Best Pop Vocal Performance in 1990 for the single *Oh Pretty Woman.* He also collected the 1989 Grammy Award for Best Rock Performance by a Group with Vocals as a member of the Traveling Wilburys for *Traveling Wilburys Volume One* (the album was known as *Handle With Care* in the UK).

| DATE | POS | WKS | BPI | ALBUM TITLE | LABEL & NUMBER |
|---|---|---|---|---|---|
| 08/06/1963 | 15 | 8 | | LONELY AND BLUE | London HAU 2342 |
| 29/06/1963 | 17 | 3 | | CRYING | London HAU 2437 |
| 30/11/1963 | 6 | 58 | | IN DREAMS | London HAU 8108 |
| 25/07/1964 | 17 | 2 | | THE EXCITING SOUNDS OF ROY ORBISON | Ember NR 5013 |
| 05/12/1964 | 4 | 16 | | **OH PRETTY WOMAN** | London HAU 8207 |
| 25/09/1965 | 10 | 12 | | **THERE IS ONLY ONE ROY ORBISON** | London HAU 8252 |
| 26/02/1966 | 11 | 10 | | THE ORBISON WAY | London HAU 8279 |
| 24/09/1966 | 12 | 8 | | THE CLASSIC ROY ORBISON | London HAU 8297 |
| 22/07/1967 | 40 | 1 | | ORBISONGS | Monument SMO 5004 |
| 30/09/1967 | 40 | 1 | | ROY ORBISON'S GREATEST HITS | Monument SMO 5007 |
| 27/01/1973 | 39 | 3 | | ALL-TIME GREATEST HITS | Monument MNT 67290 |
| 29/11/1975 | ●[1] | 20 | ● | **THE BEST OF ROY ORBISON** | Arcade ADEP 19 |
| 18/07/1981 | 63 | 1 | | GOLDEN DAYS | Monument MNT 10026 |
| 04/07/1987 | 86 | 2 | O | IN DREAMS: THE GREATEST HITS | Virgin VGD 3514 |
| 29/10/1988 | ●[3] | 38 | ✪[2] | **THE LEGENDARY ROY ORBISON** | Telstar STAR 2330 |
| 11/02/1989 | 2 | 23 | ✪ | **MYSTERY GIRL** | Virgin V 2576 |
| 25/11/1989 | 51 | 3 | | A BLACK AND WHITE NIGHT | Virgin V 2601 |
| 03/11/1990 | 38 | 10 | | BALLADS – 22 CLASSIC LOVE SONGS | Telstar STAR 2441 |
| 28/11/1992 | 23 | 4 | | KING OF HEARTS | Virgin America CDVUS 58 |
| 16/11/1996 | 18 | 11 | ● | THE VERY BEST OF ROY ORBISON | Virgin CDV 2804 |
| 10/02/2001 | 4 | 10 | ● | **LOVE SONGS** | Virgin VTDCD 360 |

**WILLIAM ORBIT** UK producer (born William Wainwright) who also records as Bass-O-Matic and founded Guerilla and O Records. As a producer, he handled Madonna's *Ray Of Light* album. He was awarded Best Selling Classical Album for *Pieces In A Modern Style* at the inaugural Classical BRIT Awards in 2000. The eligibility of his album, from which the remixed *Barber's Adagio For Strings* was a big club and pop single, was the subject of considerable debate in the classical sector.

| DATE | POS | WKS | BPI | ALBUM TITLE | LABEL & NUMBER |
|---|---|---|---|---|---|
| 29/01/2000 | 2 | 14 | ● | **PIECES IN A MODERN STYLE** | WEA 3984289572 |

**ORBITAL** UK duo, brothers Paul (born 19/5/1968, Dartford) and Phil Hartnoll (born 9/1/1964, Dartford) who are named after the M25 – London's orbital motorway.

| DATE | POS | WKS | BPI | ALBUM TITLE | LABEL & NUMBER |
|---|---|---|---|---|---|
| 12/10/1991 | 71 | 1 | | ORBITAL | ffrr 8282481 |
| 05/06/1993 | 28 | 2 | | ORBITAL | Internal TRUCD 2 |
| 19/03/1994 | 32 | 2 | | PEEL SESSIONS | Internal LIECD 12 |
| 20/08/1994 | 4 | 4 | | **SNIVILISATION** | Internal Dance TRUCD 5 |

| | | | | | |
|------|-----|-----|-----|-------------|----------------|
| 11/05/1996 | 5 | 12 | ● | IN SIDES | Internal 8287632 |
| 25/01/1997 | 48 | 1 | | SATAN | Internal LIARX 37 |
| 17/04/1999 | 4 | 7 | O | **THE MIDDLE OF NOWHERE** | ffrr 5560762 |
| 12/05/2001 | 11 | 4 | O | THE ALTOGETHER | ffrr 8573877822 |
| 15/06/2002 | 36 | 3 | | WORK 1989–2002 | ffrr 0927461902 |

**ORCHESTRAL MANOEUVRES IN THE DARK** UK group formed in Liverpool in 1977 by Andy McCluskey (born 24/6/1959, Liverpool, vocals) and Paul Humphreys (born 27/2/1960, Liverpool, keyboards) as Id with Gary Hodgson (guitar), Steve Hollis (bass) and Malcolm Hughes (drums). They disbanded in 1978, re-forming the same year with the addition of Dave Hughes (keyboards) and Malcolm Homes (drums). They are also sometimes known as OMD.

| | | | | | |
|------|-----|-----|-----|-------------|----------------|
| 01/03/1980 | 27 | 29 | O | ORCHESTRAL MANOEUVRES IN THE DARK | Dindisc DID 2 |
| 01/11/1980 | 6 | 25 | ● | **ORGANISATION** | Dindisc DID 6 |
| 14/11/1981 | 3 | 39 | ✪ | **ARCHITECTURE AND MORALITY** | Dindisc DID 12 |
| 12/03/1983 | 5 | 13 | ● | **DAZZLE SHIPS** | Telegraph V 2261 |
| 12/05/1984 | 9 | 27 | ● | **JUNK CULTURE** | Virgin V 2310 |
| 29/06/1985 | 13 | 12 | O | CRUSH | Virgin V 2349 |
| 11/10/1986 | 15 | 7 | O | THE PACIFIC AGE | Virgin V 2398 |
| 12/03/1988 | 2 | 33 | ✪³ | **THE BEST OF O.M.D** | Virgin OMD 1 |
| 18/05/1991 | 3 | 29 | ✪ | **SUGAR TAX** | Virgin V 2648 |
| 26/06/1993 | 14 | 6 | | LIBERATOR | Virgin CDV 2715 |
| 14/09/1996 | 24 | 2 | | UNIVERSAL | Virgin CDV 2807 |
| 10/10/1998 | 16 | 4 | O | THE OMD SINGLES | Virgin CDV 2859 |

**ORCHESTRE NATIONALE DE LA RADIO DIFFUSION FRANCAISE** French orchestra conducted by Sir Thomas Beecham (born 29/4/1879, St Helens) who was largely a self-taught conductor. Inherited money enabled him to form the Beecham Symphony Orchestra in 1909 and with them he performed opera seasons at Covent Garden. In 1915 he formed the Beecham Opera Company that subsequently became the UK Opera Company. He was also responsible for founding the London Philharmonic Orchestra in 1932 and the Royal Philharmonic Orchestra in 1946. He died on 8/3/1961.

| | | | | | |
|------|-----|-----|-----|-------------|----------------|
| 26/03/1960 | 18 | 2 | | CARMEN | HMV ALP 1762/4 |

**ORIGINAL CAST RECORDING – MY FAIR LADY** UK cast recording of a stage show written by Allan Lerner and Frederick Loewe in 1956 as an adaptation of Bernard Shaw's play *Pygmalion*. This recording features Martine McCutcheon as Eliza, Jonathan Pryce as Higgins and Dennis Waterman as Doctor Dolittle.

| | | | | | |
|------|-----|-----|-----|-------------|----------------|
| 04/08/2001 | 73 | 1 | | MY FAIR LADY | First Night CASTCD 83 |

**STACIE ORRICO** US female singer born in Seattle, WA on 3/3/1986.

| | | | | | |
|------|-----|-----|-----|-------------|----------------|
| 04/10/2003 | 37 | 19 | ● | STACIE ORRICO | Virgin CDVUS 238 |

**BETH ORTON** UK singer/songwriter (born 1974, Norwich) who began her career guesting on albums by other artists, including The Chemical Brothers and William Orbit. She was named Best British Female Solo Artist at the 2000 BRIT Awards.

| | | | | | |
|------|-----|-----|-----|-------------|----------------|
| 26/10/1996 | 68 | 3 | | TRAILER PARK | Heavenly HVNLP 17CD |
| 27/03/1999 | 17 | 8 | | CENTRAL RESERVATION | Heavenly HVNLP 22CD |
| 10/08/2002 | 8 | 5 | O | **DAYBREAKER** | Heavenly HVNLP 37CD |
| 04/10/2003 | 45 | 2 | | PASS IN TIME – THE DEFINITIVE COLLECTION | Heavenly HVNLP 45CD |

**ORVILLE** – see **KEITH HARRIS**

**JEFFREY OSBORNE** US singer (born 9/3/1948, Providence, RI) who was the lead singer with LTD from 1970 to 1980 before going solo.

| | | | | | |
|------|-----|-----|-----|-------------|----------------|
| 05/05/1984 | 56 | 7 | | STAY WITH ME TONIGHT | A&M AMLX 64940 |
| 13/10/1984 | 59 | 3 | | DON'T STOP | A&M AMA 5017 |

**JOAN OSBORNE** US singer (born 8/7/1962, Anchorage, KY) who was a film student who took to singing as a dare at the Abilene Bar in New York in 1988. She formed the Womanly Hips label.

| | | | | | |
|------|-----|-----|-----|-------------|----------------|
| 09/03/1996 | 5 | 18 | ● | **RELISH** | Blues Gorilla 5266922 |

**KELLY OSBOURNE** UK singer (born 27/10/1984) who is the daughter of Ozzy and Sharon Osbourne.

| | | | | | |
|------|-----|-----|-----|-------------|----------------|
| 22/02/2003 | 31 | 2 | | SHUT UP | Epic 5094782 |

**OZZY OSBOURNE** UK singer (born John Osbourne, 3/12/1948, Birmingham) who was the lead singer with Black Sabbath from their formation in 1970 until leaving in 1980. He formed Blizzard of Oz with an ever-changing line-up. He appeared in the film *Trick Or Treat* in 1987. In 1982 he was banned from the city of San Antonio after being caught urinating on a wall of the monument to the

▲⁹ Number of weeks album topped the US chart   ◆¹² RIAA Diamond Awards   ◇³ IFPI Platinum Europe Awards

Alamo; the ban was finally lifted ten years later when he donated $20,000 towards its restoration. Osbourne also took part in the *It's Only Rock 'N' Roll* project for the Children's Promise charity. He won the 1993 Grammy Award for Best Metal Performance with vocal for *I Don't Want To Change The World*. He has a star on the Hollywood Walk of Fame.

| DATE | POS | WKS | BPI | ALBUM TITLE | LABEL & NUMBER |
|------|-----|-----|-----|-------------|----------------|
| 20/09/1980 | 7 | 8 | O | **OZZY OSBOURNE'S BLIZZARD OF OZ** | Jet JETLP 234 |
| 07/11/1981 | 14 | 12 | | DIARY OF A MADMAN | Jet JETLP 237 |
| 27/11/1982 | 21 | 6 | O | TALK OF THE DEVIL | Jet JETDP 401 |
| 10/12/1983 | 24 | 7 | O | BARK AT THE MOON | Epic EPC 25739 |
| 22/02/1986 | 8 | 10 | O | **THE ULTIMATE SIN** | Epic EPC 26404 |
| 23/05/1987 | 13 | 6 | | TRIBUTE | Epic 4504751 |
| 22/10/1988 | 23 | 4 | | NO REST FOR THE WICKED | Epic 4625811 |
| 17/03/1990 | 69 | 1 | | JUST SAY OZZY (LIVE) | Epic 4659401 |
| 19/10/1991 | 17 | 3 | | NO MORE TEARS | Epic 4678591 |
| 04/11/1995 | 22 | 3 | | OZZMOSIS | Epic 4810222 |
| 15/11/1997 | 68 | 1 | | THE OZZMAN COMETH – THE BEST OF OZZY OSBOURNE | Epic 4872602 |
| 27/10/2001 | 19 | 3 | | DOWN TO EARTH | Epic 4984742 |
| 15/03/2003 | 21 | 3 | | THE ESSENTIAL | Epic 5108402 |

### OSIBISA

**OSIBISA** Ghanaian/Nigerian group formed in the UK in the early 1970s by Teddy Osei, (flute/percussion), Kofi Ayivor (congas), Kiki Gyan (keyboards), Mike Odumosa (bass), Sol Amarifio (drums), Marc Tontoh (horns) and Wendell Richardson (guitar).

| DATE | POS | WKS | BPI | ALBUM TITLE | LABEL & NUMBER |
|------|-----|-----|-----|-------------|----------------|
| 22/05/1971 | 11 | 10 | | OSIBISA | MCA MDKS 8001 |
| 05/02/1972 | 11 | 7 | | WOYAYA | MCA MDKS 8005 |

### DONNY OSMOND

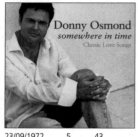

**DONNY OSMOND** US singer (born 9/12/1957, Ogden, UT) who joined the family vocal group in 1963, appearing on the *Andy Williams Show*. He first recorded solo in 1971 and later teamed with sister Marie. He returned with a new image and a US #2 in 1988.

| DATE | POS | WKS | BPI | ALBUM TITLE | LABEL & NUMBER |
|------|-----|-----|-----|-------------|----------------|
| 23/09/1972 | 5 | 43 | | **PORTRAIT OF DONNY** | MGM 2315 108 |
| 16/12/1972 | 7 | 24 | | **TOO YOUNG** | MGM 2315 113 |
| 26/05/1973 | 6 | 19 | ● | **ALONE TOGETHER** | MGM 2315 210 |
| 15/12/1973 | 4 | 13 | ● | **A TIME FOR US** | MGM 2315 273 |
| 08/02/1975 | 16 | 4 | O | DONNY | MGM 2315 314 |
| 02/10/1976 | 59 | 1 | | DISCOTRAIN | Polydor 2391 226 |
| 21/04/2001 | 10 | 3 | | **THIS IS THE MOMENT** | Decca Broadway 1587772 |
| 07/12/2002 | 12 | 10 | ✪ | SOMEWHERE IN TIME | Decca 0665302 |

### DONNY AND MARIE OSMOND

**DONNY AND MARIE OSMOND** US brother and sister duo Donny (born 9/12/1957, Ogden, UT) and Marie Osmond (born 13/10/1959, Ogden). They hosted their own TV show 1976–78, and appeared in the film *Goin' Coconuts* in 1978.

| DATE | POS | WKS | BPI | ALBUM TITLE | LABEL & NUMBER |
|------|-----|-----|-----|-------------|----------------|
| 02/11/1974 | 13 | 15 | O | I'M LEAVING IT ALL UP TO YOU | MGM 2315 307 |
| 26/07/1975 | 30 | 3 | | MAKE THE WORLD GO AWAY | MGM 2315 343 |
| 05/06/1976 | 48 | 1 | | DEEP PURPLE | Polydor 2391 220 |

### LITTLE JIMMY OSMOND

**LITTLE JIMMY OSMOND** US singer (born 16/4/1963, Canoga Park, CA) who is the youngest member of the Osmond family. After a brief singing career he turned his attentions to business, including tour promoting. He is also the youngest solo artist ever to top the UK single charts, a feat accomplished at the age of nine years eight months. His brother Donny holds second place, achieved when aged fourteen years and six months.

| DATE | POS | WKS | BPI | ALBUM TITLE | LABEL & NUMBER |
|------|-----|-----|-----|-------------|----------------|
| 17/02/1973 | 20 | 12 | | KILLER JOE | MGM 2315 157 |

### MARIE OSMOND

**MARIE OSMOND** US singer (born Olive Marie Osmond, 13/10/1959, Ogden, UT) who began performing with her brothers at fourteen. She teamed up with brother Donny for a number of hits and hosted their own TV show. She hosted her own show in 1980.

| DATE | POS | WKS | BPI | ALBUM TITLE | LABEL & NUMBER |
|------|-----|-----|-----|-------------|----------------|
| 09/02/1974 | 46 | 1 | | PAPER ROSES | MGM 2315 262 |

### OSMONDS

**OSMONDS** US family group formed in Ogden, UT in 1959 by Alan (born 22/6/1949, Ogden), Wayne (born 28/8/1951, Ogden), Merrill (born 30/4/1953, Ogden) and Jay Osmond (born 2/3/1955, Ogden) as the Osmond Brothers. In 1962 the group won a contract to appear on the weekly *Andy Williams Show* in 1962. They added brother Donny (born 9/10/1959, Ogden) to the line-up in 1963. The group later had their own UK TV series as well as a cartoon series. The original four brothers went on to record country music in the 1980s. The Osmonds have a star on the Hollywood Walk of Fame.

O Silver disc  ● Gold disc  ✪ Platinum disc (additional platinum units are indicated by a figure following the symbol)  ❶⁹ Number of weeks album topped the UK chart

| DATE | POS | WKS | BPI | ALBUM TITLE | LABEL & NUMBER |
|------|-----|-----|-----|-------------|----------------|
| 18/11/1972 | 13 | 22 | | OSMONDS LIVE | MGM 2315 117 |
| 16/12/1972 | 9 | 19 | | **CRAZY HORSES** | MGM 2315 123 |
| 25/08/1973 | 6 | 25 | ● | **THE PLAN** | MGM 2315 251 |
| 17/08/1974 | 5 | 20 | ● | **OUR BEST TO YOU** | MGM 2315 300 |
| 07/12/1974 | 13 | 9 | ○ | LOVE ME FOR A REASON | MGM 2315 312 |
| 14/06/1975 | 19 | 7 | ○ | I'M STILL GONNA NEED YOU | MGM 2315 342 |
| 10/01/1976 | 41 | 1 | ○ | AROUND THE WORLD – LIVE IN CONCERT | MGM 2659 044 |
| 20/04/1996 | 17 | 5 | | THE VERY BEST OF THE OSMONDS | Polydor 5270722 |
| 12/07/2003 | 4 | 11 | | **ULTIMATE COLLECTION** | Universal TV 9808355 |

**GILBERT O'SULLIVAN** Irish singer (born Raymond O'Sullivan, 1/12/1946, Waterford) who was in bands before having two songs recorded by the Tremeloes in 1967. He recorded as Gilbert for CBS in 1968, sending out demos. He was signed by Tom Jones/Engelbert Humperdinck manager Gordon Mills to MAM and renamed Gilbert O'Sullivan. Back with CBS in 1980, he later sued Mills over his original contract.

| DATE | POS | WKS | BPI | ALBUM TITLE | LABEL & NUMBER |
|------|-----|-----|-----|-------------|----------------|
| 25/09/1971 | 5 | 82 | | **GILBERT O'SULLIVAN HIMSELF** | MAM 501 |
| 18/11/1972 | ❶¹ | 64 | | **BACK TO FRONT** | MAM 502 |
| 06/10/1973 | 2 | 25 | ● | **I'M A WRITER NOT A FIGHTER** | MAM 505 |
| 26/10/1974 | 9 | 8 | ○ | **STRANGER IN MY OWN BACK YARD** | MAM MAMS 506 |
| 18/12/1976 | 13 | 11 | ○ | GREATEST HITS | MAM MAMA 2003 |
| 12/09/1981 | 98 | 1 | | 20 GOLDEN GREATS | K-Tel NE 1133 |
| 11/05/1991 | 50 | 4 | | NOTHING BUT THE BEST | Castle Communications CTVLP 107 |
| 27/03/2004 | 20 | 5 | ○ | THE BERRY VEST OF | EMI 5986722 |

**JOHN OTWAY AND WILD WILLY BARRETT** UK duo John Otway (born 2/10/1952, Aylesbury, vocals) and Wild Willy Barrett (guitar/fiddle).

| DATE | POS | WKS | BPI | ALBUM TITLE | LABEL & NUMBER |
|------|-----|-----|-----|-------------|----------------|
| 01/07/1978 | 44 | 1 | | DEEP AND MEANINGLESS | Polydor 2382 501 |

**OUI 3** US dance trio Blair Booth (vocals/programming), Philip Erb (keyboards) and Trevor Miles (rapping).

| DATE | POS | WKS | BPI | ALBUM TITLE | LABEL & NUMBER |
|------|-----|-----|-----|-------------|----------------|
| 07/08/1993 | 39 | 3 | | OUI LOVE YOU | MCA MCD 10833 |

**OUTHERE BROTHERS** US dance group formed by Malik E Martel, W Phillips, Hula Mahone and K Fingers. The CD that contained six mixes of their debut hit was reported to the Crown Prosecution Service for obscenity. The version in question, OHB Club Version, contained references to oral sex, although the CPS took no further action. Then the follow-up *Boom Boom Boom* also hit #1 and once again the club version on the CD attracted attention. The CPS also received a copy of the pair's album *1 Polish, 2 Biscuits And A Fish Sandwich* from Cleveland police, querying whether it contravened the Obscene Publications Act. Meanwhile the head of Wroughton Middle School in Gorleston, Norfolk, banned his pupils from bringing the record to the school! For publicity purposes, Hula and Malik assumed the roles of the brothers. They were later a production outfit, handling hits for Indo among others.

| DATE | POS | WKS | BPI | ALBUM TITLE | LABEL & NUMBER |
|------|-----|-----|-----|-------------|----------------|
| 27/05/1995 | 56 | 5 | | 1 POLISH 2 BISCUITS AND A FISH SANDWICH | Eternal 0630105852 |
| 30/12/1995 | 41 | 4 | | PARTY ALBUM This is a clean version of *1 Polish 2 Biscuits And A Fish Sandwich* | Eternal 0630127812 |

**OUTKAST** US rap duo formed in Atlanta, GA by Big Boi (born Antoine Patton) and Dre (born Andre Benjamin). Dre is the partner of fellow rapper Erykah Badu and the pair have a young son. The two also have outside interests: Big Boi runs Pitfall Kennels, which breeds and sells Pitbull Terriers, whilst Dre is a painter who runs Andre Classic Paintings! They first recorded for LaFace in 1994. The group has won six Grammy Awards including: Best Rap Performance by a Duo or Group in 2001 for *Ms Jackson,* Best Rap Performance by a Duo or Group in 2002 with Killer Mike for *The Whole World* and Best Urban/Alternative Performance in 2003 for *Hey Ya!*.

| DATE | POS | WKS | BPI | ALBUM TITLE | LABEL & NUMBER |
|------|-----|-----|-----|-------------|----------------|
| 20/01/2001 | 10 | 13 | | STANKONIA 2001 Grammy Award for Best Rap Album | Arista 73008260722 |
| 11/10/2003 | 8 | 38+ | ✪ | SPEAKERBOXXX/THE LOVE BELOW ◇ ▲⁷ 2003 Grammy Awards for Album of the Year and Best Rap Album | Arista 82876529052 |

**OVERLORD X** UK rapper who later teamed up with Cookie Crew, Demon Boyz, She Rockers and other leading UK rap acts to form Black Rhyme Organisation To Help Equal Rights (B.R.O.T.H.E.R.).

| DATE | POS | WKS | BPI | ALBUM TITLE | LABEL & NUMBER |
|------|-----|-----|-----|-------------|----------------|
| 04/02/1989 | 68 | 1 | | WEAPON IS MY LYRIC | Mango Street ILPS 9924 |

**MARK OWEN** UK singer (born 27/1/1974, Manchester) who was a founder member of Take That, staying with the group until they disbanded in 1996, then going solo. He also took part in the *It's Only Rock 'N' Roll* project for the Children's Promise charity.

| DATE | POS | WKS | BPI | ALBUM TITLE | LABEL & NUMBER |
|------|-----|-----|-----|-------------|----------------|
| 14/12/1996 | 33 | 11 | ● | GREEN MAN | RCA 74321435142 |
| 15/11/2003 | 59 | 1 | | IN YOUR OWN TIME | Universal MCD 60092 |

**OXIDE AND NEUTRINO** UK garage duo formed by Londoners Oxide (born Alex Rivers, seventeen at the time of their debut hit) and Neutrino (born Mark Oseitutu, eighteen at debut hit). Their first hit was an adaptation of the theme to the TV series *Casualty*, originally on a self-financed white label before being picked up by East West. They are also members of The So Solid Crew. They won the 2001 MOBO Award for Best Video for *Up Middle Finger*.

| DATE | POS | WKS | BPI | ALBUM TITLE | LABEL & NUMBER |
|------|-----|-----|-----|-------------|----------------|
| 06/05/2000 | 71 | 1 | | BOUND 4 DA RELOAD (CASUALTY) This was a 12-inch single deemed ineligible for the singles chart | East West OXIDE01T |

▲⁹ Number of weeks album topped the US chart ◆¹² RIAA Diamond Awards ◇³ IFPI Platinum Europe Awards

| 09/06/2001 | 11 | 19 | ● | EXECUTE | East West 8573885612 |
| 12/10/2002 | 28 | 2 | ○ | 2 STEPZ AHEAD | East West 5046607562 |

**OZRIC TENTACLES** UK group formed by Ed Wynne (guitar), his brother Roly (bass), Gavin Griffiths (bass), Joie Hinton (keyboards) and Nick Van Gelder (drums). They later added Tom Brookes (keyboards) and Paul Hankin (drums) to the line-up. Griffiths left in 1984, Brookes a year later. Van Gerlder left in 1987 and was replaced by Merv Peopler.

| 31/08/1991 | 70 | 1 | | STRANGEITUDE | Dovetail DOVELP 3 |
| 01/05/1993 | 11 | 4 | | JURASSIC SHIFT | Dovetail DOVELP 6 |
| 09/07/1994 | 18 | 2 | | ARBORESCENCE | Dovetail DOVELP 7 |

# P

**JIMMY PAGE** UK guitarist (born 9/1/1944, Heston) and founder member of Led Zeppelin in 1968, one of the most successful groups of all time. Page (ex-Yardbirds) and Robert Plant formed the Honeydrippers in 1984 and later undertook numerous solo projects. He won the 1998 Grammy Award for Best Hard Rock Song with Robert Plant for *Most High*.

| Date | Pos | Wks | |
|---|---|---|---|
| 27/02/1982 | 40 | 4 | DEATHWISH II Original soundtrack to the film . . . . . . . . . . . . . . . . . . . . . . . . . . . . . . . . . . . . . . . Swan Song SSK 59415 |
| 16/03/1985 | 44 | 4 | WHATEVER HAPPENED TO JUGULA? **ROY HARPER AND JIMMY PAGE** . . . . . . . . . . . . . . . . . . . . . . . . . Beggars Banquet BEGA 60 |
| 02/07/1988 | 27 | 6 | ● OUTRIDER . . . . . . . . . . . . . . . . . . . . . . . . . . . . . . . . . . . . . . . . . . . . . . . . . . . . . . . . . . . . . . Geffen WX 155 |
| 19/11/1994 | 7 | 13 | ● NO QUARTER – JIMMY PAGE AND ROBERT PLANT UNLEDDED . . . . . . . . . . . . . . . . . . . . . . . . . . . . . Fontana 5263622 |
| 02/05/1998 | 3 | 6 | **WALKING INTO CLARKSDALE** This and the above hit credited to **JIMMY PAGE AND ROBERT PLANT** . . . . . . . . . . . Mercury 5583242 |
| 22/07/2000 | 39 | 4 | LIVE AT THE GREEK **JIMMY PAGE AND THE BLACK CROWES** . . . . . . . . . . . . . . . . . . . . . . . . . . . . SPV Recordings SPV 09172022 |

**ELAINE PAIGE** UK singer (born Elaine Bickerstaff, 5/3/1948, Barnet) who was initially known for her lead role in *Evita,* although Julie Covington scored the hit single. She left the show after a few months in order to concentrate on a recording career.

| Date | Pos | Wks | |
|---|---|---|---|
| 01/05/1982 | 56 | 6 | ○ ELAINE PAIGE . . . . . . . . . . . . . . . . . . . . . . . . . . . . . . . . . . . . . . . . . . . . . . . . . . . . . . . . . . WEA K 58385 |
| 05/11/1983 | 2 | 48 | ✪² **STAGES** . . . . . . . . . . . . . . . . . . . . . . . . . . . . . . . . . . . . . . . . . . . . . . . . . . . . . . . . . . . . K-Tel NE 1262 |
| 20/10/1984 | 12 | 25 | ✪ CINEMA . . . . . . . . . . . . . . . . . . . . . . . . . . . . . . . . . . . . . . . . . . . . . . . . . . . . . . . . . . . . . K-Tel NE 1282 |
| 16/11/1985 | 8 | 20 | ✪ **LOVE HURTS** . . . . . . . . . . . . . . . . . . . . . . . . . . . . . . . . . . . . . . . . . . . . . . . . . . . . . . . . . WEA WX 28 |
| 29/11/1986 | 27 | 6 | ● CHRISTMAS . . . . . . . . . . . . . . . . . . . . . . . . . . . . . . . . . . . . . . . . . . . . . . . . . . . . . . . . . . . WEA WX 80 |
| 05/12/1987 | 14 | 15 | ✪ MEMORIES – THE BEST OF ELAINE PAIGE . . . . . . . . . . . . . . . . . . . . . . . . . . . . . . . . . . . . . . . Telstar STAR 2313 |
| 19/11/1988 | 51 | 8 | ● THE QUEEN ALBUM . . . . . . . . . . . . . . . . . . . . . . . . . . . . . . . . . . . . . . . . . . . . . . . . . . . . . Siren SRNLP 22 |
| 27/04/1991 | 36 | 4 | LOVE CAN DO THAT . . . . . . . . . . . . . . . . . . . . . . . . . . . . . . . . . . . . . . . . . . . . . . . . . . . . . RCA PL 74932 |
| 28/11/1992 | 22 | 9 | THE BEST OF ELAINE PAIGE AND BARBARA DICKSON **ELAINE PAIGE AND BARBARA DICKSON** . . . . . . . . . . . . . . Telstar TCD 2632 |
| 10/04/1993 | 71 | 1 | ROMANCE AND THE STAGE . . . . . . . . . . . . . . . . . . . . . . . . . . . . . . . . . . . . . . . . . . . . . . . RCA 74321136152 |
| 19/11/1994 | 46 | 3 | ○ PIAF . . . . . . . . . . . . . . . . . . . . . . . . . . . . . . . . . . . . . . . . . . . . . . . . . . . . . . . . . . . WEA 4509946412 |
| 01/07/1995 | 20 | 6 | ENCORE . . . . . . . . . . . . . . . . . . . . . . . . . . . . . . . . . . . . . . . . . . . . . . . . . . . . . . . . . WEA 0630104762 |
| 28/11/1998 | 60 | 4 | ON REFLECTION – THE VERY BEST OF ELAINE PAIGE . . . . . . . . . . . . . . . . . . . . . . . . . . . . . . Telstar TV/WEA TTVCD 2999 |
| 05/06/2004 | 35 | 4+ | CENTRE STAGE . . . . . . . . . . . . . . . . . . . . . . . . . . . . . . . . . . . . . . . . . . . . . . . . . . . . . WSM WSMCD171 |

**JENNIFER PAIGE** US singer/songwriter (born 3/9/1975, Atlanta, GA) who began performing duets with her brother at the age of eight and learned to play piano at ten. She moved to Los Angeles, CA in 1997.

| Date | Pos | Wks | |
|---|---|---|---|
| 31/10/1998 | 67 | 1 | JENNIFER PAIGE . . . . . . . . . . . . . . . . . . . . . . . . . . . . . . . . . . . . . . . . . . . . . . . . . . . . . E.A.R. 0039842ERE |

**PALE FOUNTAINS** UK group formed in Liverpool in 1981 by Michael Head (guitar/vocals), Chris McCaffrey (bass), Andy Diagram (trumpet) and Thomas Whelan (drums). They first recorded for the Operation Twilight label in 1982. The group disbanded in 1985; Head went on to form Shack with his brother John.

| Date | Pos | Wks | |
|---|---|---|---|
| 10/03/1984 | 85 | 2 | PACIFIC STREET . . . . . . . . . . . . . . . . . . . . . . . . . . . . . . . . . . . . . . . . . . . . . . . . . . . . . . Virgin V 2274 |
| 16/02/1985 | 94 | 1 | FROM ACROSS THE KITCHEN TABLE . . . . . . . . . . . . . . . . . . . . . . . . . . . . . . . . . . . . . . . . . . . . Virgin V 2333 |

**PALE SAINTS** UK group formed in Leeds in 1989 by Graeme Naysmith (born 9/2/1967, Edinburgh, guitar), Ian Masters (born 4/1/1964, Potters Bar, bass) and Chris Cooper (born 17/11/1966, Portsmouth, drums), with Ashley Horner (guitar) an occasional member. Horner was later replaced on a more permanent basis by Meriel Barham (born 15/10/1964).

| Date | Pos | Wks | |
|---|---|---|---|
| 24/02/1990 | 40 | 2 | THE COMFORTS OF MADNESS . . . . . . . . . . . . . . . . . . . . . . . . . . . . . . . . . . . . . . . . . . . . . . . 4AD CAD 0002 |
| 04/04/1992 | 61 | 1 | IN RIBBONS . . . . . . . . . . . . . . . . . . . . . . . . . . . . . . . . . . . . . . . . . . . . . . . . . . . . . . . . 4AD CAD 2004CD |

**PALLAS** UK rock group formed by Euan Lowson (vocals), Ronald Brown (keyboards/vocals), Neil Mathewson (guitar), Graeme Murray (bass) and Derek Forman (drums). Lowson was later replaced by Alan Reed.

| Date | Pos | Wks | |
|---|---|---|---|
| 25/02/1984 | 41 | 3 | SENTINEL . . . . . . . . . . . . . . . . . . . . . . . . . . . . . . . . . . . . . . . . . . . . . . . . . . . . . . . . Harvest SHSP 2400121 |
| 22/02/1986 | 70 | 1 | THE WEDGE . . . . . . . . . . . . . . . . . . . . . . . . . . . . . . . . . . . . . . . . . . . . . . . . . . . . . . . . Harvest SHVL 850 |

**PALMER** – see EMERSON, LAKE AND PALMER

**ROBERT PALMER** UK singer (born Alan Palmer, 19/1/1949, Scarborough) who joined the Alan Brown Set in 1969 before forming Vinegar Joe in 1971 and signing with Island. Palmer remained with Island as a solo artist when the group disbanded in 1974. He was lead singer for Power Station in 1985. He has won two Grammy Awards: Best Rock Vocal Performance in 1986 for *Addicted To Love* and Best Rock Vocal Performance in 1988 for *Simply Irresistible*. He died from a heart attack on 26/9/2003.

| DATE | POS | WKS | BPI | ALBUM TITLE | LABEL & NUMBER |
|---|---|---|---|---|---|
| 06/11/1976 | 46 | 1 | | SOME PEOPLE CAN DO WHAT THEY LIKE | Island ILPS 9420 |
| 14/07/1979 | 54 | 4 | | SECRETS | Island ILPS 9544 |
| 06/09/1980 | 31 | 8 | | CLUES | Island ILPS 9595 |
| 03/04/1982 | 32 | 6 | | MAYBE IT'S LIVE | Island ILPS 9665 |
| 23/04/1983 | 37 | 9 | | PRIDE | Island ILPS 9720 |
| 16/11/1985 | 5 | 37 | ● | **RIPTIDE** | Island ILPS 9801 |
| 09/07/1988 | 17 | 25 | ● | HEAVY NOVA | EMI EMD 1007 |
| 11/11/1989 | 7 | 17 | ✪ | **ADDICTIONS VOLUME 1** | Island ILPS 9944 |
| 17/11/1990 | 9 | 20 | ● | **DON'T EXPLAIN** | EMI EMDX 1018 |
| 04/04/1992 | 12 | 7 | ○ | ADDICTIONS VOLUME 2 | Island CIDTV 4 |
| 31/10/1992 | 32 | 3 | | RIDIN' HIGH | EMI CDEMD 1038 |
| 24/09/1994 | 25 | 4 | | HONEY | EMI CDEMD 1069 |
| 28/10/1995 | 4 | 21 | ✪ | **THE VERY BEST OF ROBERT PALMER** | EMI CDEMD 1088 |
| 16/11/2002 | 38 | 4 | | AT HIS VERY BEST | Universal TV 697812 |

**PANTERA** US heavy metal group formed in Arlington, TX in 1983 by Terry Glaze (guitar/vocals), 'Dimebag' Darrell Abbot (born 20/8/1966, Dallas, TX, guitar), Vince Abbott (born 11/3/1964, Dallas, drums) and Rex Rocker (born 27/7/1964, Graham, TX, bass). Glaze was replaced by Philip Anselmo (born 30/6/1968, New Orleans, LA) in 1988.

| DATE | POS | WKS | BPI | ALBUM TITLE | LABEL & NUMBER |
|---|---|---|---|---|---|
| 07/03/1992 | 64 | 1 | | VULGAR DISPLAYS OF POWER | Atco 7567917582 |
| 02/04/1994 | 3 | 4 | ○ | **FAR BEYOND DRIVEN ▲[1]** | Atco 7567923752 |
| 18/05/1996 | 17 | 3 | | THE GREAT SOUTHERN TRENDKILL | East West 7556199082 |
| 30/08/1997 | 54 | 1 | | OFFICIAL LIVE – 101 PROOF | East West 7559620682 |
| 08/04/2000 | 33 | 1 | | REINVENTING THE STEEL | Elektra 7559624512 |

**PAPA ROACH** US rock group formed in California in 1993 by Coby Dick (vocals), Jerry Horton (guitar), Will James (bass) and Dave Buckner (drums). James was replaced by Tobin Esperance in 1996.

| DATE | POS | WKS | BPI | ALBUM TITLE | LABEL & NUMBER |
|---|---|---|---|---|---|
| 13/01/2001 | 9 | 36 | ● | **INFEST** | DreamWorks 4502232 |
| 29/06/2002 | 4 | 7 | ● | **LOVE HATE TRAGEDY** | DreamWorks 4503672 |

**VANESSA PARADIS** French singer (born 22/12/1972, St Maur) who later became an actress. She made her screen debut in *Noce Blanche*.

| DATE | POS | WKS | BPI | ALBUM TITLE | LABEL & NUMBER |
|---|---|---|---|---|---|
| 07/11/1992 | 45 | 2 | | VANESSA PARADIS | Remark 5139542 |

**PARADISE LOST** UK death metal group formed in Yorkshire in 1989 by Nick Holmes (vocals), Gregor MacKintosh (guitar), Aaron Aedy (guitar), Stephen Edmonson (bass) and Mathew Archer (drums). They were originally signed by Peaceville. Archer left in 1994 and was replaced by Lee Morris.

| DATE | POS | WKS | BPI | ALBUM TITLE | LABEL & NUMBER |
|---|---|---|---|---|---|
| 24/06/1995 | 16 | 3 | | DRACONIAN TIMES | Music For Nations CDMFNX 184 |
| 26/07/1997 | 31 | 2 | | ONE SECOND | Music For Nations CDMFNX 222 |
| 19/06/1999 | 61 | 1 | | HOST | EMI 5205672 |

**MICA PARIS** UK singer (born Michelle Wallen, 27/4/1969, London) who was a member of the Spirit of Watts gospel choir and later toured and recorded with Hollywood Beyond. She went solo in 1988. In February 2001 her brother Jason Phillips was killed in a gangland-style shooting; three months later Mica was declared bankrupt.

| DATE | POS | WKS | BPI | ALBUM TITLE | LABEL & NUMBER |
|---|---|---|---|---|---|
| 03/09/1988 | 6 | 32 | ✪ | **SO GOOD** | Fourth & Broadway BRLP 525 |
| 27/10/1990 | 26 | 3 | ○ | CONTRIBUTION | Fourth & Broadway BRLP 558 |
| 26/06/1993 | 20 | 4 | | WHISPER A PRAYER | Fourth & Broadway BRCD 591 |
| 22/08/1998 | 59 | 1 | | BLACK ANGEL | Cooltempo 4958132 |

**PARIS ANGELS** Irish group formed by Rikki Turner, Jayne Gill, Paul 'Wags' Wagstaffe, Scott Carey and Mark Adge. Wags later became a member of Black Grape.

| DATE | POS | WKS | BPI | ALBUM TITLE | LABEL & NUMBER |
|---|---|---|---|---|---|
| 17/08/1991 | 37 | 2 | | SUNDEW | Virgin V 2667 |

**JOHN PARISH + POLLY JEAN HARVEY** UK guitarist Parish and singer Harvey (born 9/10/1969, Yeovil, Somerset) were members of PJ Harvey, the group launched by Polly in 1991. They met whilst members of Automatic Diamini in the late 1980s.

| DATE | POS | WKS | BPI | ALBUM TITLE | LABEL & NUMBER |
|---|---|---|---|---|---|
| 05/10/1996 | 46 | 1 | | DANCE HALL AT LOUSE POINT | Island CIDX 8051 |

○ Silver disc ● Gold disc ✪ Platinum disc (additional platinum units are indicated by a figure following the symbol) ●[9] Number of weeks album topped the UK chart

## GRAHAM PARKER AND THE RUMOUR
UK singer (born 18/11/1950, London) who was teamed up with the Rumour in 1975 and signed with Vertigo in 1976. The Rumour comprised Brinsley Schwarz (guitar), Bob Andrews (keyboards), Andrew Rodnar (bass) and Steve Goulding (drums).

| 27/11/1976 | 52 | 2 | | HEAT TREATMENT | Vertigo 6360 137 |
| 12/11/1977 | 19 | 4 | | STICK TO ME | Vertigo 9102 017 |
| 27/05/1978 | 14 | 5 | | PARKERILLA | Vertigo 6641 797 |
| 07/04/1979 | 18 | 8 | | SQUEEZING OUT SPARKS | Vertigo 9102 030 |
| 07/06/1980 | 11 | 10 | | THE UP ESCALATOR | Stiff SEEZ 23 |
| 27/03/1982 | 40 | 6 | | ANOTHER GREY AREA GRAHAM PARKER | RCA RCALP 6029 |

## RAY PARKER JR.
US singer/guitarist (born 1/5/1954, Detroit, MI) who learned to play the guitar whilst laid up with a broken leg and went on to become a prominent session guitarist in California, including spells working with Stevie Wonder, the Rolling Stones and Barry White. He formed Raydio in 1977 and began recording solo in 1982. He won the 1984 Grammy Award for Best Pop Instrumental Performance for *Ghostbusters*.

| 10/10/1987 | 40 | 7 | | AFTER DARK | Geffen WX 122 |

## ALEX PARKS
UK female singer (born 26/7/1984, Mount Hawke, Truro) who won the second series of *Fame Academy*.

| 06/12/2003 | 5 | 15 | ✪ | INTRODUCTION | Polydor 9866005 |

## JOHN PARR
UK singer/songwriter (born 18/11/1954, Nottingham) who appeared in the films *Bible!* and *Valet Girls* and wrote the themes to films such as *American Anthem* and *St Elmo's Fire*.

| 02/11/1985 | 60 | 2 | | JOHN PARR | London LONLP 12 |

## ALAN PARSONS PROJECT
UK producer/guitarist/keyboard player (born 1949) who worked as a staff engineer at Abbey Road Studios and made his reputation for engineering The Beatles' *Abbey Road* album, subsequently working on projects by artists such as Pink Floyd and Al Stewart. He then linked with songwriter Eric Woolfson in the Alan Parsons Project, adapting the works of Edgar Allan Poe and utilising a host of studio musicians.

| 28/08/1976 | 56 | 1 | O | TALES OF MYSTERY AND IMAGINATION | Charisma CDS 4003 |
| 13/08/1977 | 30 | 1 | O | I ROBOT | Arista SPARTY 1016 |
| 10/06/1978 | 49 | 4 | | PYRAMID | Arista SPART 1054 |
| 29/09/1979 | 74 | 1 | | EVE | Arista SPARTY 1100 |
| 15/11/1980 | 38 | 4 | | THE TURN OF A FRIENDLY CARD | Arista DLART 1 |
| 29/05/1982 | 27 | 11 | O | EYE IN THE SKY | Arista 204 666 |
| 26/11/1983 | 99 | 1 | | THE BEST OF THE ALAN PARSONS PROJECT | Arista APP 1 |
| 03/03/1984 | 24 | 8 | | AMMONIA AVENUE | Arista 206 100 |
| 23/02/1985 | 40 | 5 | | VULTURE CULTURE | Arista 206 577 |
| 14/02/1987 | 66 | 2 | | GAUDI | Arista 208 084 |

## PARTISANS
UK punk rock group formed in Bridgend by Robert 'Spike' Harrington (vocals), Andrew Lealand (guitar), Louise Wright (bass) and Mark 'Shark' Harris (drums).

| 19/02/1983 | 94 | 1 | | THE PARTISANS | No Future PUNK 4 |

## DOLLY PARTON
US singer (born 19/1/1946, Sevier County, TN); the fourth of twelve children, she made her own guitar at the age of five and sang on radio at eleven. She recorded her first single in 1955 for Gold Band and relocated to Nashville in 1964. She replaced Norma Jean on the Porter Wagoner TV show in 1967 and joined the Grand Ole Opry in 1968. She hosted her own TV variety show in 1976 and appeared in the films *9 To 5* and *Best Little Whorehouse In Texas* (her country #1 *I Will Always Love You* was featured in this film and later covered by Whitney Houston for *The Bodyguard*). She also appeared in an episode of *The Simpsons*, releasing all the male cast from a jail cell whilst on her way to sing at half time at the Super Bowl. She has won seven Grammy Awards including: Best Country Vocal Performance in 1978 for *Here You Come Again*; Best Country Song and Best Country Vocal Performance in 1981 for *9 To 5*; Best Country Vocal Collaboration in 1999 with Linda Ronstadt and Emmylou Harris for *After The Gold Rush*; Best Bluegrass Album in 2000 for *The Grass Is Blue*; and Best Female Country Vocal Performance in 2001 for *Shine*. She has a star on the Hollywood Walk of Fame.

| 25/11/1978 | 24 | 12 | ● | DOLLY PARTON/BOTH SIDES | Lotus WH 5006 |
| 07/09/1985 | 74 | 1 | | GREATEST HITS | RCA PL 84422 |
| 14/03/1987 | 60 | 4 | | TRIO DOLLY PARTON, LINDA RONSTADT AND EMMYLOU HARRIS 1987 Grammy Award for Best Country Performance by a Group | Warner Brothers 9254911 |
| 22/10/1994 | 65 | 2 | | THE GREATEST HITS | Telstar TCD 2739 |
| 08/11/1997 | 38 | 3 | | A LIFE IN MUSIC – ULTIMATE COLLECTION | RCA 74321443632 |
| 26/09/1998 | 41 | 3 | | HUNGRY AGAIN | MCA Nashville UMD 80522 |
| 24/02/2001 | 30 | 6 | O | LITTLE SPARROW | Sanctuary SANCD 074 |
| 03/03/2001 | 23 | 5 | | GOLD – THE HITS COLLECTION | RCA 74321840202 |
| 20/07/2002 | 37 | 5 | | HALOS AND HORNS | Sanctuary SANCD 126 |
| 02/08/2003 | 17 | 6 | | ULTIMATE | RCA 82876542012 |

## ALAN PARTRIDGE
UK comedian Steve Coogan (born 14/10/1965, Manchester) played Alan Partridge in the TV series. Partridge was the 'star' of a fictitious TV talk show that subsequently got relegated to local radio in Norfolk. Among Coogan's other comic creations are Tony Ferrino (who enjoyed a minor hit single with *Help Yourself/Bigamy At Christmas*) and Pauline Calf.

| 18/03/1995 | 41 | 3 | | KNOWING ME, KNOWING YOU 3 | BBC Canned Laughter ZBBC 1671CD |

**PARTRIDGE FAMILY** US group named after a TV series loosely based on the real life Cowsills. The Partridge Family members were Shirley (Shirley Jones, born 31/3/1934, Smithton, PA), Keith (David Cassidy, Jones' stepson, born 12/4/1950, New York), Laurie (Susan Dey), Danny (Danny Bomaduce), Christopher (Jeremy Gelbwaks) and Tracy (portrayed by Suzanne Crough), with only Jones and Cassidy appearing on the resultant records. The TV series began on ABC TV on 25/9/1970 and by the next month Bell Records had signed up the 'group', linking them with top songwriting teams. The series ended in 1974, by which time Cassidy was recording solo.

| | | | | |
|---|---|---|---|---|
| 08/01/1972.....46......2..... | UP TO DATE............................................................. Bell SBLL 143 |
| 22/04/1972.....14......7..... | THE PARTRIDGE FAMILY SOUND MAGAZINE............................... Bell BELLS 206 |
| 30/09/1972.....28......3..... | SHOPPING BAG.......................................................... Bell BELLS 212 |
| 09/12/1972.....45......1..... | CHRISTMAS CARD....................................................... Bell BELLS 214 |

**PASADENAS** UK soul group formed in 1987 by Jeff Aaron Brown (born 12/12/1964), Michael Milliner (born 16/2/1962), David Milliner (born 16/2/1962), John Andrew Banfield (born 4/12/1964) and Hammish Seelochan (born 11/8/1964), all of whom had previously been with dance outfit Finesse since 1982.

| | | | | |
|---|---|---|---|---|
| 22/10/1988 .....3......21......✪ | **TO WHOM IT MAY CONCERN**............................................ CBS 4628771 |
| 07/03/1992 .....6......11......○ | **YOURS SINCERELY**.................................................... Columbia 4712642 |

**PASSENGERS** Multinational album project that began as a combination between U2 and Brian Eno and which also featured guest appearances by Luciano Pavarotti, DJ Howie B and Japanese singer Holi.

| | |
|---|---|
| 18/11/1995.....12......5......● | ORIGINAL SOUNDTRACKS 1............................................... Island CID 8043 |

**PASSIONS** UK group formed in 1978 by Mitch Barker (vocals), Barbara Gogan (guitar/vocals), Clive Timperley (guitar/vocals), Claire Bidwell (bass) and Richard Williams (drums). Barker left in 1979 (owing to a broken leg), Bidwell left in 1980, replaced by David Agar. Timperley left in 1981, replaced by Kevin Armstrong, with Jeff Smith (keyboards) also joining. Armstrong left the following year and was replaced by Steve Wright.

| | |
|---|---|
| 03/10/1981.....92......1...... | THIRTY THOUSAND FEET OVER CHINA.................................... Polydor POLS 1041 |

**SEAN PAUL** Jamaican singer (born Sean Paul Henriques, 8/1/1975, Kingston). He won the 2002 MOBO Award for Best Reggae Act and the 2003 MTV Europe Music Award for Best New Act.

| | |
|---|---|
| 10/05/2003 .....2......45......✪2 | **DUTTY ROCK** ◇ 2003 Grammy Award for Best Reggae Album ......................... Atlantic 7567836202 |

**LUCIANO PAVAROTTI** Italian singer (born 12/10/1935, Modena) who made his professional debut as an operatic tenor in 1961 (in *Reggio Emilia*) and went on to become one of the leading operatic singers in the world. He has had two close brushes with death: in 1947 he suffered a blood infection and in 1975 survived an air crash in Milan. He has won five Grammy Awards including: Best Classical Performance Vocal Soloist in 1978 for *Hits From Lincoln Center*; Best Classical Performance Vocal Soloist in 1979 for *O Sole Mio*; Best Classical Performance Vocal Soloist in 1981 with Joan Sutherland and Marilyn Horne for *Live From Lincoln Center*; and Best Classical Performance Vocal Soloist in 1988 for *Luciano Pavarotti In Concert*. Mehta is the Indian conductor Zubin Mehta (born 29/4/1936, Bombay).

| | | | | |
|---|---|---|---|---|
| 15/05/1982.....95......1......● | PAVAROTTI'S GREATEST HITS............................................ Decca D 2362 |
| 30/06/1984.....96......1...... | MAMMA **LUCIANO PAVAROTTI WITH THE HENRY MANCINI ORCHESTRA**.............. Decca 411959 |
| 09/08/1986.....12......34......✪ | THE PAVAROTTI COLLECTION............................................ Stylus SMR 8617 |
| 16/07/1988.....63......8...... | THE NEW PAVAROTTI COLLECTION LIVE!................................... Stylus SMR 857 |
| 17/03/1990 ....●4.....72......✪3 | **THE ESSENTIAL PAVAROTTI**............................................. Decca 4302101 |
| 01/09/1990 ....●5.....78......✪5 | IN CONCERT **LUCIANO PAVAROTTI, PLACIDO DOMINGO AND JOSE CARRERAS** 1990 Grammy Award for Best Classical Performance Vocal Soloist ....................................... Decca 4304331 |
| 20/07/1991 ....●2.....28......✪ | **ESSENTIAL PAVAROTTI II**.............................................. Decca 4304701 |
| 15/02/1992.....19......7......○ | PAVAROTTI IN HYDE PARK............................................... Decca 4363202 |
| 04/09/1993.....23......4...... | TI AMO – PUCCINI'S GREATEST LOVE SONGS............................... Decca 4250992 |
| 12/02/1994.....44......4...... | MY HEART'S DELIGHT **LUCIANO PAVAROTTI WITH THE ROYAL PHILHARMONIC ORCHESTRA**....... Decca 4432602 |
| 10/09/1994 ....●1.....26......✪2 | **THE THREE TENORS IN CONCERT 1994** ◇3 **CARRERAS DOMINGO PAVAROTTI WITH ORCHESTRA CONDUCTED BY ZUBIN MEHTA**.......................................................... Teldec 4509962002 |
| 30/03/1996.....11......6...... | TOGETHER FOR THE CHILDREN OF BOSNIA.................................. Decca 4521002 |
| 14/12/1996.....45......4...... | PAVAROTTI AND FRIENDS FOR WAR CHILD **LUCIANO PAVAROTTI AND FRIENDS**......... Decca 4529002 |
| 25/10/1997.....39......5...... | THE ULTIMATE COLLECTION.............................................. Decca 4580002 |
| 29/08/1998.....14......6...... | THE THREE TENORS PARIS 1998 **CARRERAS DOMINGO PAVAROTTI WITH JAMES LEVINE**...... Decca 4605002 |
| 19/06/1999.....26......6...... | LOVE SONGS........................................................... Decca 4664002 |
| 23/12/2000.....57......2...... | THE THREE TENORS CHRISTMAS **CARRERAS/DOMINGO/PAVAROTTI FEATURING MEHTA**...... Sony Classical SK 89131 |
| 21/07/2001.....41......2...... | AMORE – THE LOVE ALBUM............................................... Decca 4701302 |
| 15/11/2003.....21......4...... | TI ADORO............................................................ Decca 4754602 |

**PAVEMENT** US rock group formed in California 1989 by Stephen Malkmus (born 1967, Santa Monica, CA, guitar/vocals) and Scott Kannberg (born 1967, Stockton, CA, guitar/vocals); Gary Young (drums) joined in 1990 and bass player Mark Ibold (born 1967, Cincinnati, OH) and second drummer Bob Nastanovich (born 1968, Rochester, NY) in 1991. Young left in 1993, replaced by Steve West (born 1967, Richmond, VA). They disbanded in 2000 and Malkmus and Kannberg both went solo.

| | |
|---|---|
| 25/04/1992.....72......1...... | SLANTED AND ENCHANTED................................................ Big Cat ABB 34CD |
| 03/04/1993.....30......2...... | WESTING (BY MUSKET AND SEXTANT)...................................... Big Cat ABBCD 40 |

| | | | | | |
|---|---|---|---|---|---|
| 26/02/1994 | 15 | 3 | | CROOKED RAIN CROOKED RAIN | Big Cat ABB 56CD |
| 22/04/1995 | 18 | 2 | | WOWEE ZOWEE | Big Cat ABB 84CD |
| 22/02/1997 | 27 | 2 | | BRIGHTEN THE CORNERS | Domino WIGCD 031 |
| 19/06/1999 | 19 | 3 | | TERROR TWILIGHT | Domino WIGCD 066 |

**TOM PAXTON** US folk singer/guitarist (born 31/10/1937, Chicago, IL) who attended the University of Oklahoma and moved to New York in 1960. He became a regular performer at the coffee houses of Greenwich Village before making his debut at the Gaslight. He failed an audition to join the Chad Mitchell Trio but they did record one of his compositions, *The Marvellous Toy* – their biggest hit in 1963. Tom was signed by Elektra in 1964 and remained with them for eight years before recording for Vanguard among others.

| | | | | | |
|---|---|---|---|---|---|
| 13/06/1970 | 23 | 5 | | NO. 6 | Elektra 2469 003 |
| 03/04/1971 | 18 | 4 | | THE COMPLEAT TOM PAXTON | Elektra EKD 2003 |
| 01/07/1972 | 47 | 1 | | PEACE WILL COME | Elektra K 44182 |

**PEARL JAM** US group formed in Seattle, WA in 1990 by Jeff Ament (born in Big Sandy, MT on 10/3/1963, bass), Stone Gossard (born in Seattle on 20/7/1966, guitar), Mike McCready (born in Seattle on 5/4/1965, guitar) and Eddie Vedder (born Edward Mueller in Evanston, IL on 23/12/1964, vocals), adding Dave Krusen (drums) the following year. Ament and Gossard had previously been members of Mother Love Bone, Green River and Temple Of The Dog, the latter group also including McCready and Vedder. Krusen left after the group's debut album had been completed and was replaced by Dave Abbruzzese (born on 17/5/1964). They signed with Epic in 1991. Abbruzzese left in 1994 and was replaced by Jack Irons (born in Los Angeles, CA on 18/7/1962). Pearl Jam portrayed the band Citizen Dick in the 1992 film *Singles*. The group won the 1995 Grammy Award for Best Hard Rock Performance for *Spin The Black Circle*. In 2000 the group released 25 albums in one week, one double album from each of 25 live dates recorded during their world tour of that year. Five of these charted in the USA in the same week at positions 103, 125, 134, 137 and 175 (and a further seven were only 2,000 sales short of also charting), including the album recorded at the Wembley Arena in London on 30/5/2000 at #137. According to statistics had the 25 albums been released as one album, then the sales would have been sufficient to chart at #13.

| | | | | | |
|---|---|---|---|---|---|
| 07/03/1992 | 18 | 65 | ● | TEN ◆12 | Epic 4688842 |
| 23/10/1993 | 2 | 24 | ● | VS ▲5 | Epic 4745492 |
| 03/12/1994 | 4 | 11 | ● | VITALOGY ▲1 | Epic 4778611 |
| 07/09/1996 | 3 | 5 | | NO CODE ▲2 | Epic 4844482 |
| 14/02/1998 | 7 | 7 | ○ | YIELD | Epic 4893652 |
| 05/12/1998 | 68 | 1 | | LIVE – ON TWO LEGS | Epic 4928592 |
| 27/05/2000 | 5 | 4 | | BINAURAL | Epic 4945902 |
| 23/11/2002 | 34 | 2 | | RIOT ACT | Epic 5100002 |

**DAVID PEASTON** US singer/songwriter born in St Louis, MO and brother of singer Fontella Bass, who was working as a schoolteacher in Brooklyn, NY when he entered the Apollo Theater amateur night. He won the talent contests for an entire year and repeated his winning streak on the TV series *Showtime At The Apollo* with a seven week run in 1987. He was snapped up by Geffen.

| | | | | | |
|---|---|---|---|---|---|
| 26/08/1989 | 66 | 1 | | INTRODUCING… DAVID PEASTON | Geffen 9242281 |

**PEBBLES** US singer (born Perri Alette McKissack, 29/8/1965, Oakland, CA) who was nicknamed 'Pebbles' because she resembled the cartoon character Pebbles Flintstone. She sang with Bill Summers before teaming up with Con Funk Shun and signed with MCA in 1987. She married producer and songwriter Antonio Reid in 1989; they later divorced. She later assembled and managed TLC.

| | | | | | |
|---|---|---|---|---|---|
| 14/05/1988 | 56 | 4 | | PEBBLES | MCA MCF 3418 |

**PEDDLERS** UK group formed in 1964 by Tab Martin (born 24/12/1944, Liverpool, bass), Trevor Morris (born 16/10/1943, Liverpool, drums) and Roy Phillips (born 5/5/1943, Poole, keyboards). The group disbanded in the mid-1970s with Martin becoming a session musician, Phillips emigrating to Australia and Morris joining Quantum Jump.

| | | | | | |
|---|---|---|---|---|---|
| 16/03/1968 | 27 | 13 | | FREE WHEELERS | CBS SBPG 63183 |
| 07/02/1970 | 16 | 3 | | BIRTHDAY | CBS 63682 |

**KEVIN PEEK** Australian guitarist who began as a percussionist at Adelaide Conservatorium of Music and later moved to London. He was a founding member of Sky in 1979 with John Williams, Tristram Fry, Herbie Flowers and Francis Monkman before launching a parallel solo career.

| | | | | | |
|---|---|---|---|---|---|
| 21/03/1981 | 52 | 2 | | AWAKENING | Ariola ARL 5065 |
| 13/10/1984 | 64 | 6 | | BEYOND THE PLANETS **KEVIN PEEK AND RICK WAKEMAN FEATURING JEFF WAYNE NARRATION PATRICK ALLEN** | Telstar STAR 2244 |

**MARTI PELLOW** UK singer (born Mark McLoughlin, 23/3/1966, Clydebank) who was lead singer with Vortex Motion, a group that subsequently became Wet Wet Wet. He left the group for a solo career in 1999.

| | | | | | |
|---|---|---|---|---|---|
| 07/07/2001 | 7 | 7 | ● | SMILE | Mercury 5860032 |
| 30/11/2002 | 34 | 8 | ● | SINGS THE HITS OF WET WET WET & SMILE | Universal TV 0632902 |
| 29/11/2003 | 66 | 1 | | BETWEEN THE COVERS | Universal TV 9812067 |

**TEDDY PENDERGRASS** US singer (born Theodore Pendergrass, 26/3/1950, Philadelphia, PA) who was a member of The Cadillacs before joining Harold Melvin & The Bluenotes (as did the rest of the group) in 1969. Initially the drummer, he became featured singer in 1970. Personality clashes with Melvin led him to go solo in 1976. A road accident on 18/3/1982 left him paralysed from the neck down, although he subsequently resumed his recording career. In 1982 he appeared in the film *Soup For One*. He won the 1982 Grammy Award for Best Recording for Children, along with Billy Joel, Bruce Springsteen, James Taylor, Kenny Loggins, Carly and Lucy Simon, Crystal Gayle, Lou Rawls, Deniece Williams, Janis Ian and Dr. John, for *In Harmony 2*.

| | | | | | |
|---|---|---|---|---|---|
| 13/07/1985 | 45 | 4 | | THE ARTISTS VOLUME 2 **LUTHER VANDROSS/TEDDY PENDERGRASS/CHANGE/ATLANTIC STARR** | Street Sounds ARTIS 2 |
| 21/05/1988 | 45 | 8 | | JOY | Elektra 9607751 |

20/03/2004 . . . . . 26 . . . . . . 3 . . . . . . 　SATISFACTION GUARANTEED: THE VERY BEST Also contains hits by Harold Melvin and the Bluenotes . . . . . . . . . . WSM WSMCD166

**PENETRATION** UK punk group formed in Durham, County Durham in 1977 by Pauline Murray (vocals), Gary Chaplin (guitar), Robert Blamire (bass) and Gary Smallman (drums). Chaplin left the following year and was replaced by Neale Floyd, but in October 1979 the group announced their decision to disband. Murray went on to form The Invisible Girls and later launched a solo career.

28/10/1978 . . . . . 22 . . . . . . 4 . . . . . . 　MOVING TARGETS . . . . . . . . . . . . . . . . . . . . . . . . . . . . . . . . . . . . . . . . . . . . . . . . . . . . . . . . . . . . . . . . . . . . . Virgin V 2109
06/10/1979 . . . . . 36 . . . . . . 4 . . . . . . 　COMING UP FOR AIR . . . . . . . . . . . . . . . . . . . . . . . . . . . . . . . . . . . . . . . . . . . . . . . . . . . . . . . . . . . . . . . . . . Virgin V 2131

**PENGUIN CAFÉ ORCHESTRA** UK instrumental group formed by Simon Jeffes (born on 19/2/1949, harmonium/ drums), Steve Nye (keyboards), Elizabeth Perry (violin), Gavyn Wright (violin), Bob Loveday (violin) Helen Liebmann (cello) and Neil Rennie (ukulele), although the group was effectively an outlet for leader Simon Jeffes. Jeffes died from a brain tumour on 10/12/1997.

04/04/1987 . . . . . 49 . . . . . . 5 . . . . . . 　SIGNS OF LIFE . . . . . . . . . . . . . . . . . . . . . . . . . . . . . . . . . . . . . . . . . . . . . . . . . . . . . . . . . . . . . . . Edition E.G. EGED 50

**CE CE PENISTON** US singer (born Cecelia Peniston, 6/9/1969, Dayton, OH) who moved to Phoenix in 1977, appeared in numerous talent and beauty contests, and was crowned Miss Black Arizona and Miss Galaxy in 1989. She then worked as a backing singer before launching a solo career and scoring a major debut hit with *Finally*, a song she had written whilst still at school.

08/02/1992 . . . . . 10 . . . . . 19 . . . . . O 　**FINALLY** . . . . . . . . . . . . . . . . . . . . . . . . . . . . . . . . . . . . . . . . . . . . . . . . . . . . . . . . . . . . . . . . . . . A&M 3971822
05/02/1994 . . . . . 31 . . . . . . 2 . . . . . . 　THOUGHT 'YA KNEW . . . . . . . . . . . . . . . . . . . . . . . . . . . . . . . . . . . . . . . . . . . . . . . . . . . . . . . . . . . . . A&M 5402012

**DAWN PENN** Jamaican singer (born Dawn Pickering, 1952, Kingston) discovered by Coxone Dodd and session singer for the likes of Johnny Nash before going solo. Her 1969 debut hit was written and recorded by Sonny and Cher. She has penned more than 400 songs.

09/07/1994 . . . . . 51 . . . . . . 2 . . . . . . 　NO, NO, NO . . . . . . . . . . . . . . . . . . . . . . . . . . . . . . . . . . . . . . . . . . . . . . . . . . . . . . . . . . . Big Beat 7567923652

**PENTANGLE** UK group formed in 1967 by Bert Jansch (born 3/11/1943, Glasgow, guitar), Jacqui McShee (vocals), John Renbourn (guitar/vocals), Danny Thompson (bass) and Terry Cox (drums). This version of Pentangle dissolved in 1972, but re-formed in 1984 with Mike Piggott replacing Renbourn. By 1991 Piggott had left and Nigel Portman-Smith (bass) and Gerry Conway (drums) had joined.

15/06/1968 . . . . . 21 . . . . . . 9 . . . . . . 　THE PENTANGLE . . . . . . . . . . . . . . . . . . . . . . . . . . . . . . . . . . . . . . . . . . . . . . . . . . . . . . Transatlantic TRA 162
01/11/1969 . . . . . 5 . . . . . 28 . . . . . . 　**BASKET OF LIGHT** . . . . . . . . . . . . . . . . . . . . . . . . . . . . . . . . . . . . . . . . . . . . . . . . . . . . . . Transatlantic TRA 205
12/12/1970 . . . . . 51 . . . . . . 2 . . . . . . 　CRUEL SISTER . . . . . . . . . . . . . . . . . . . . . . . . . . . . . . . . . . . . . . . . . . . . . . . . . . . . . . . Transatlantic TRA 228

**PEPSI AND SHIRLIE** UK duo formed by Lawrie 'Pepsi' DeMacque (born 10/12/1958, London) and Shirlie Holliman (born 18/4/1962, Watford). They first teamed up as backing singers and dancers for Wham!

07/11/1987 . . . . . 69 . . . . . . 2 . . . . . . 　ALL RIGHT NOW . . . . . . . . . . . . . . . . . . . . . . . . . . . . . . . . . . . . . . . . . . . . . . . . . . . . . . . . Polydor POLH 38

**A PERFECT CIRCLE** US rock group formed by Maynard James Keenan (vocals), Billy Howerdel (guitar), Troy Van Leeuwen (guitar), Paz Lenchantin (bass) and Josh Freese (drums). Keenan and Howerdel were ex-members of Tool and formed A Perfect Circle after Tool ran into legal difficulties with their record label.

03/06/2000 . . . . . 55 . . . . . . 1 . . . . . . 　MER DE NOMS . . . . . . . . . . . . . . . . . . . . . . . . . . . . . . . . . . . . . . . . . . . . . . . . . . . . . . . . . Virgin CDVUS 173
27/09/2003 . . . . . 37 . . . . . . 1 . . . . . . 　THIRTEENTH STEP . . . . . . . . . . . . . . . . . . . . . . . . . . . . . . . . . . . . . . . . . . . . . . . . . . . . . . . Virgin CDVUS 247

**CARL PERKINS** US singer (born Carl Lee Perkins, although his surname was misspelled on his birth certificate as Perkings, 9/4/1932, Tiptonville, TN) who was a member of the Perkins Brothers Band with brothers Jay (born 1930) and Clayton (born 1935) in 1950. He turned professional in 1954 and moved to Memphis to audition for Sun Records after hearing Elvis Presley. He joined Johnny Cash's touring band in 1967. The Beatles covered three of his songs in their early career (and earned Perkins more in royalties than he had earned from all his post-hit sales). Jay, a member of Carl's touring band, was badly injured in a car crash in 1956 (Carl was in the car at the time) and never fully recovered, dying on 21/10/1958. Clayton was also a member of the touring band, but was sacked in 1963 and shot himself on 25/12/1973. Carl Perkins was inducted into the Rock & Roll Hall of Fame in 1987. He won the 1986 Grammy Award for Best Spoken Word Recording with various others for *Interviews From The Class Of '55*. He died from a stroke on 19/1/1998.

15/04/1978 . . . . . 38 . . . . . . 3 . . . . . . 　OL' BLUE SUEDES IS BACK . . . . . . . . . . . . . . . . . . . . . . . . . . . . . . . . . . . . . . . . . . . . . . . . . . . . Jet UATV 30146

**LEE 'SCRATCH' PERRY** Jamaican singer (born Rainford Hugh Perry Hanover, 28/3/1936) who began as a talent scout and session organiser for Coxsone Dodd and first recorded solo in 1963. His early recording, *Chicken Scratch*, led to his nickname, although in 1968 he recorded *The Upsetter*, another of his nicknames. It was as The Upsetters that he organised the recording of *Return To Django* in 1969, a UK Top 40 hit. He set up the Upsetter label in Jamaica, with artists such as Dave Barker, The Stingers, The Bleechers and Junior Byles among the many that he brought to prominence. Perry also opened his own studio, Black Ark in 1974, where Bob Marley & The Wailers, Susan Cadogan and a host of seminal reggae giants recorded. The studio closed in 1980 when Perry set fire to it before coming to the UK. After a spell in The Netherlands, Switzerland and Britain he returned to Jamaica during the 1990s. He won the 2002 Grammy Award for Best Reggae Album for *Jamaican E.T.*

26/07/1997 . . . . . 49 . . . . . . 1 . . . . . . 　ARKOLOGY . . . . . . . . . . . . . . . . . . . . . . . . . . . . . . . . . . . . . . . . . . . . . . . . . . . . . Island Jamaica CRNCD 6

**STEVE PERRY** US singer (born 22/1/1949, Hanford, CA) who joined Journey as lead singer in 1978 as a replacement for George Tickner. Perry had already launched a solo career when Journey disbanded in 1986 , although he rejoined Journey in 1996 with Neal Schon, Jonathan Cain, Ross Valory and Steve Smith.

14/07/1984 . . . . . 59 . . . . . . 2 . . . . . . 　STREET TALK . . . . . . . . . . . . . . . . . . . . . . . . . . . . . . . . . . . . . . . . . . . . . . . . . . . . . . . . . . . . CBS 25967
27/08/1994 . . . . . 64 . . . . . . 1 . . . . . . 　FOR THE LOVE OF STRANGE MEDICINE . . . . . . . . . . . . . . . . . . . . . . . . . . . . . . . . . . . . . . . . . . Columbia 4771962

**PESHAY** UK producer Paul Pesce.

31/07/1999 . . . . . 63 . . . . . . 1 . . . . . . 　MILES FROM HOME . . . . . . . . . . . . . . . . . . . . . . . . . . . . . . . . . . . . . . . . . . . . . . . . . . . . . Island Blue PFA 1CD

○ Silver disc ● Gold disc ✪ Platinum disc (additional platinum units are indicated by a figure following the symbol) ●⁹ Number of weeks album topped the UK chart

### PESTALOZZI CHILDREN'S CHOIR
Multi-national children's choir; the group also worked with Paul McCartney on his *Pipes Of Peace* album.

| | | | | |
|---|---|---|---|---|
| 26/12/1981 | 65 | 2 | ● | SONGS OF JOY . . . . . . . . . . . . . . . . . . . . . . . . . . . . . . . . . . . . . . . . . . . . . . . . . . . . . . . . . . . . . . . . . . . . . K-Tel NE 1140 |

### PET SHOP BOYS
UK duo formed in 1981 by Neil Tennant (born 10/7/1954, Gosforth, Tyne and Wear, vocals) and Chris Lowe (born 4/10/1959, Blackpool, keyboards). Tennant was then assistant editor of *Smash Hits*, a position he held for a further two years whilst the pair wrote and made demos. They were signed by Epic for their debut release, *West End Girls*, which became a big European success but failed in the UK. They re-recorded the single for Parlophone and it took three months to make the top ten. In 1992 they launched the Spaghetti label. They won the 1987 BRIT Award for Best Single for *West End Girls* and were named Best British Group at the 1988 BRIT Awards.

| DATE | POS | WKS | BPI | ALBUM TITLE | LABEL & NUMBER |
|---|---|---|---|---|---|
| 05/04/1986 | 3 | 82 | ✪ | PLEASE | Parlophone PSB 1 |
| 29/11/1986 | 15 | 72 | ✪ | DISCO | EMI PRG 1001 |
| 19/09/1987 | 2 | 59 | ✪³ | PET SHOP BOYS, ACTUALLY | Parlophone PCSD 104 |
| 22/10/1988 | 2 | 39 | ✪² | INTROSPECTIVE | Parlophone PCS 7325 |
| 03/11/1990 | 2 | 14 | ✪ | BEHAVIOUR | Parlophone PCSD 113 |
| 16/11/1991 | 3 | 30 | ✪ | DISCOGRAPHY | Parlophone PMTV 3 |
| 09/10/1993 | ❶¹ | 22 | ✪ | VERY | Parlophone CDPCSD 143 |
| 24/09/1994 | 6 | 4 | | DISCO 2 | Parlophone CDPCSD 159 |
| 19/08/1995 | 2 | 5 | ○ | ALTERNATIVE | Parlophone CDPCSD 166 |
| 14/09/1996 | 4 | 8 | ● | BILINGUAL | Parlophone CDPCSD 170 |
| 23/10/1999 | 7 | 3 | ● | NIGHTLIFE | Parlophone 5218572 |
| 13/04/2002 | 7 | 4 | ○ | RELEASE | Parlophone 5385982 |
| 15/02/2003 | 36 | 1 | | DISCO 3 | Parlophone 5821402 |
| 06/12/2003 | 30 | 9 | ● | POPART – THE HITS | Parlophone 5950932 |

### PETER AND GORDON
UK duo formed in London in 1963 by Peter Asher (born 22/6/1944, London) and Gordon Waller (born 4/6/1945, Braemar, Scotland). Asher had been a child actor and is the brother of actress Jane Asher, Paul McCartney's one-time girlfriend. McCartney was invited to Peter & Gordon's first recording session in 1964 and wrote their two debut hits. The duo disbanded in 1967 with Asher moving into production.

| | | | | | |
|---|---|---|---|---|---|
| 20/06/1964 | 18 | 1 | | PETER AND GORDON | Columbia 33SX 1630 |

### PETER, PAUL AND MARY
US folk group formed in New York in 1961 by Peter Yarrow (born 31/5/1938, New York), Paul Stookey (born 30/11/1937, Baltimore, MD) and Mary Travers (born 7/11/1937, Louisville, KY), and assembled by future Bob Dylan manager Albert Grossman. They disbanded in the mid-1970s but re-formed in 1978. Yarrow later became a successful writer and producer. They won four Grammy Awards: Best Performance by a Vocal Group and Best Folk Recording in 1962 for *If I Had A Hammer* and Best Performance by a Vocal Group and Best Folk Recording in 1963 for *Blowin' In The Wind*.

| | | | | | |
|---|---|---|---|---|---|
| 04/01/1964 | 18 | 1 | | PETER PAUL AND MARY ▲⁷ | Warner Brothers WM 4064 |
| 21/03/1964 | 11 | 19 | | IN THE WIND ▲⁵ | Warner Brothers WM 8142 |
| 13/02/1965 | 20 | 2 | | IN CONCERT VOLUME 1 | Warner Brothers WM 8158 |
| 05/09/1970 | 60 | 4 | | TEN YEARS TOGETHER | Warner Brothers WS 2552 |

### PETERS AND LEE
UK duo of Lennie Peters (born 1939, London, piano/vocals) and Dianne Lee (born 1950, Sheffield, vocals) who first teamed up in 1970. Peters had been a pianist in a London pub; Lee half of a dance group called the Hailey Twins. They appeared on *Opportunity Knocks* in 1972, and proved a sensation, winning week after week and were then signed by Philips. Peters, uncle of Rolling Stone Charlie Watts and blind since he was sixteen, died of bone cancer on 10/10/1992.

| | | | | | |
|---|---|---|---|---|---|
| 30/06/1973 | ❶² | 55 | ● | WE CAN MAKE IT | Philips 6308 165 |
| 22/12/1973 | 9 | 48 | ● | BY YOUR SIDE | Philips 6308 192 |
| 21/09/1974 | 6 | 27 | ● | RAINBOW | Philips 6308 208 |
| 04/10/1975 | 2 | 32 | ● | FAVOURITES | Philips 9109 205 |
| 18/12/1976 | 44 | 4 | ○ | INVITATION | Philips 9101 027 |

## TOM PETTY AND THE HEARTBREAKERS
US singer (born 20/10/1953, Gainesville, FL) who formed his first group, the Sundowners, in 1968, later changing the name to the Epics and then Mudcrutch. The line-up comprised Petty (bass and guitar), Tommy Leadon (guitar), Mike Campbell (guitar) and Randall Marsh (drums). Signed by Shelter in 1973, they released only one single before the group split up in 1975, but Petty was retained and formed the Heartbreakers with Campbell, Benmont Tench (keyboards), Ron Blair (guitar), Jeff Jourard (guitar) and Stan Lynch (drums). Jourard left soon after. Petty subsequently became a member of The Traveling Wilburys. He collected the 1989 Grammy Award for Best Rock Performance by a Group with Vocals as a member of the Traveling Wilburys for *Traveling Wilburys Volume One* (the album was known as *Handle With Care* in the UK). Petty also won the 1995 Grammy Award for Best Male Rock Vocal Performance for *You Don't Know How It Feels*. He has a star on the Hollywood Walk of Fame.

| DATE | POS | WKS | BPI | ALBUM TITLE | LABEL & NUMBER |
|------|-----|-----|-----|-------------|----------------|
| 04/06/1977 | 24 | 12 | | TOM PETTY AND HEARTBREAKERS | Shelter ISA 5014 |
| 01/07/1978 | 34 | 5 | | YOU'RE GONNA GET IT | Island ISA 5017 |
| 17/11/1979 | 57 | 4 | | DAMN THE TORPEDOES | MCA MCF 3044 |
| 23/05/1981 | 32 | 5 | | HARD PROMISES | MCA MCF 3098 |
| 20/11/1982 | 45 | 4 | | LONG AFTER DARK | MCA MCF 3155 |
| 20/04/1985 | 23 | 6 | | SOUTHERN ACCENTS | MCA MCF 3260 |
| 02/05/1987 | 59 | 2 | | LET ME UP (I'VE HAD ENOUGH) | MCA MCG 6014 |
| 08/07/1989 | 8 | 16 | ● | **FULL MOON FEVER TOM PETTY** | MCA MCG 6034 |
| 20/07/1991 | 3 | 18 | ● | **INTO THE GREAT WIDE OPEN** | MCA 10317 |
| 13/11/1993 | 10 | 20 | ● | **GREATEST HITS ◆10** | MCA MCD 10964 |
| 12/11/1994 | 36 | 2 | | WILDFLOWERS | Warner Brothers 9362457592 |
| 24/08/1996 | 37 | 2 | | SHE'S THE ONE Original soundtrack to the film. | Warner Brothers 9362462852 |
| 01/05/1999 | 43 | 2 | | ECHO | Warner Brothers 9362472942 |
| 16/06/2001 | 14 | 6 | ○ | ANTHOLOGY – THROUGH THE YEARS | MCA 1701772 |

## PHARCYDE
US rap group formed in Los Angeles, CA by Romye 'Booty Brown' Robinson, Tre 'Slim Kid' Hardson, Imani 'Darky Boy' Wilcox, Derek 'Fat Lip' Stewart, DJ Mark Luv and J-Swift.

| DATE | POS | WKS | BPI | ALBUM TITLE | LABEL & NUMBER |
|------|-----|-----|-----|-------------|----------------|
| 21/08/1993 | 58 | 1 | | BIZARRE RIDE II THE PHARCYDE | Atlantic 7567922222 |
| 13/04/1996 | 46 | 1 | | LABCABINCALIFORNIA | Delicious Vinyl/Go Beat 8287332 |

## PHD
UK duo formed by classically trained pianist Tony Hymas and singer Jim Diamond (born 28/9/1953). Diamond later recorded solo.

| DATE | POS | WKS | BPI | ALBUM TITLE | LABEL & NUMBER |
|------|-----|-----|-----|-------------|----------------|
| 01/05/1982 | 33 | 8 | | P.H.D. | WEA K 99150 |

## BARRINGTON PHELOUNG
Australian conductor/arranger (born 1954, Sydney) who began his career playing in blues bands before moving to London, aged eighteen, to attend the Royal College of Music. He was appointed Musical Advisor to the London Contemporary Dance Theatre in 1979 before moving into film and TV work. His credits also include *Boon*, *The Politician's Wife*, *Truly Madly Deeply* and *Portrait Of A Marriage*.

| DATE | POS | WKS | BPI | ALBUM TITLE | LABEL & NUMBER |
|------|-----|-----|-----|-------------|----------------|
| 02/03/1991 | 4 | 30 | ✪ | **INSPECTOR MORSE – ORIGINAL MUSIC FROM THE TV SERIES** | Virgin VTLP 2 |
| 07/03/1992 | 18 | 12 | ○ | INSPECTOR MORSE VOLUME 2 – MUSIC FROM THE TV SERIES | Virgin Television VTCD 14 |
| 16/01/1993 | 20 | 11 | ○ | INSPECTOR MORSE VOLUME 3 | Virgin VTCD 16 |
| 25/11/2000 | 62 | 2 | | THE MAGIC OF INSPECTOR MORSE | Virgin VTDCD 353 |

## PHENOMENA
UK group formed by Tom Galley with his brother Neil (guitar), Glenn Hughes (vocals), Neil Murray (bass) and Cozy Powell (drums).

| DATE | POS | WKS | BPI | ALBUM TITLE | LABEL & NUMBER |
|------|-----|-----|-----|-------------|----------------|
| 06/07/1985 | 63 | 2 | | PHENOMENA | Bronze PM 1 |

## ARLENE PHILLIPS
UK fitness instructor and choreographer with musical accompaniment by the Funk Federation. She later choreographed films and musicals and was awarded the OBE in 2001.

| DATE | POS | WKS | BPI | ALBUM TITLE | LABEL & NUMBER |
|------|-----|-----|-----|-------------|----------------|
| 28/08/1982 | 41 | 24 | ● | KEEP IN SHAPE SYSTEM WITH ARLENE PHILLIPS | Supershape SUP 01 |
| 18/02/1984 | 100 | 1 | | KEEP IN SHAPE VOLUME 2. | Supershape SUP 2 |

## PHOTEK
UK jungle/drum and bass artist Rupert Parkes who began his career with a £2,000 loan from the Prince's Trust.

| DATE | POS | WKS | BPI | ALBUM TITLE | LABEL & NUMBER |
|------|-----|-----|-----|-------------|----------------|
| 15/06/1996 | 39 | 1 | | THE HIDDEN CAMERA | Science QEDCD 1 |
| 27/09/1997 | 30 | 2 | | MODUS OPERANDI | Science CDQED 1 |
| 26/09/1998 | 61 | 1 | | FORM & FUNCTION | Science CDQED 2 |

## PHOTOS
UK group from Worcestershire: Wendy Wu (vocals), Steve Eagles (guitar), Dave Sparrow (bass) and Oily Harrison (drums).

| DATE | POS | WKS | BPI | ALBUM TITLE | LABEL & NUMBER |
|------|-----|-----|-----|-------------|----------------|
| 21/06/1980 | 4 | 9 | | **THE PHOTOS** | CBS PHOTO 5 |

## EDITH PIAF
French singer (born Edith Giovanna Gassion, 19/12/1915, Paris) discovered singing on the streets by Louis Leplee, owner of a cabaret club. During the Second World War she was as important to French soldiers as Vera Lynn was to British, giving numerous concerts to French prisoners in Germany. After the war she had hits in both the US and UK charts. She died on 11/10/1963.

| DATE | POS | WKS | BPI | ALBUM TITLE | LABEL & NUMBER |
|------|-----|-----|-----|-------------|----------------|
| 26/09/1987 | 58 | 5 | | HEART AND SOUL | Stylus SMR 736 |

## PIGBAG
UK group formed in Cheltenham in 1980 by Chris Hamlyn (clarinet), Mark Smith (bass), Roger Freeman (trombone), James Johnstone (saxophone/guitar), Chris Lee (trumpet), Ollie Moore (saxophone), Simon Underwood (bass) and Andrew 'Chip' Carpenter (drums). Hamlyn left them in 1981, Freeman left in 1982, replaced by Oscar Verden, with Brian Nevill (drums) also joining. Singer Angela Jaeger joined in 1983 but the group disbanded soon after.

○ Silver disc ● Gold disc ✪ Platinum disc (additional platinum units are indicated by a figure following the symbol) ❶9 Number of weeks album topped the UK chart

| | | | | |
|---|---|---|---|---|
| 13/03/1982.....18.....14...... | | | | DR. HECKLE AND MR. JIVE. . . . . . . . . . . . . . . . . . . . . . . . . . . . . . . . . . . . . . . . . . . . . . . . . . . . . . . . . . . Y Records Y 17 |

**PILOT** UK group formed by David Paton (born 29/10/1951, Edinburgh, bass/guitar/vocals), Bill Lyall (born 26/3/1953, Edinburgh, keyboards/vocals), Stuart Tosh (born 26/9/1951, Aberdeen, drums/vocals) and Ian Bairnson (born 3/8/1953, Shetland Isles, guitar). When the group disbanded Bairnson, Paton and Tosh became part of the Alan Parsons Project (Parsons produced *January*) and Tosh later joined 10CC. Lyall died from an AIDS-related illness in December 1989.

| | |
|---|---|
| 31/05/1975.....48......1...... | SECOND FLIGHT . . . . . . . . . . . . . . . . . . . . . . . . . . . . . . . . . . . . . . . . . . . . . . . . . . . . . . . . . . . . . . . . EMI EMC 3075 |

**COURTNEY PINE** UK saxophonist (born 18/3/1964, London) who played with Dwarf Steps before providing musical backing for a number of reggae artists. He made his reputation in the jazz field, performing with the likes of Elvin Jones, Charlie Watts and Art Blakey. After turning down an opportunity to be in Art Blakey's Jazz Messengers he went solo in 1987. He later formed his own quartet with Kenny Kirkland (piano), Charnett Moffett (bass) and Marvin Smith (drums). He won the 1996 MOBO Award for Best Jazz Act.

| | |
|---|---|
| 25/10/1986.....39.....11......O | JOURNEY TO THE URGE WITHIN. . . . . . . . . . . . . . . . . . . . . . . . . . . . . . . . . . . . . . . . . . . . . . . . . . . . Island ILPS 9846 |
| 06/02/1988.....54......2...... | DESTINY'S SONGS AND THE IMAGE OF PURSUANCE . . . . . . . . . . . . . . . . . . . . . . . . . . . . . . . . . . . . . . . Anitlles AN 8275 |

**P!NK** US singer (born Alecia Moore, 8/9/1979, Philadelphia, PA) who was previously lead singer with Basic Instinct and then Choice before going solo. She attained her name because of her pink hair, although by the time of her fifth hit single had reverted to blonde. Pink won the 2001 Grammy Award for Best Pop Collaboration with Vocal with Christina Aguilera, Lil' Kim and Mya for *Lady Marmalade* and the 2003 Award for Best Female Rock Vocal Performance for *Trouble*. She also won the 2002 MTV Europe Music Award for Best Song for *Get The Party Started* and Best International Female Artist at the 2003 BRIT Awards.

| | |
|---|---|
| 27/05/2000.....13.....41......✪ | CAN'T TAKE ME HOME . . . . . . . . . . . . . . . . . . . . . . . . . . . . . . . . . . . . . . . . . . . . . . . . . . . . . . LaFace 73008260622 |
| 09/02/2002.....2.....73......✪⁵ | M!SSUNDAZTOOD ◇³ . . . . . . . . . . . . . . . . . . . . . . . . . . . . . . . . . . . . . . . . . . . . . . . . . . . . . . . Arista 07822147182 |
| 22/11/2003.....3.....22......✪ | TRY THIS ◇ . . . . . . . . . . . . . . . . . . . . . . . . . . . . . . . . . . . . . . . . . . . . . . . . . . . . . . . . . . . . . . Arista 82876571852 |

**PINK FAIRIES** UK group formed in 1970 by Twink (John Adler, drums), Paul Rudolph (guitar/vocals), Duncan Sanderson (bass/vocals) and Russell Hunter (drums). Twink left in 1971 and the group continued as a trio. Rudolph left in 1972 and was replaced by Larry Wallis. The group disbanded in 1974 but re-formed in 1975 with Sanderson, Hunter and Wallis being joined by Rudolph and Twink. Sanderson, Wallis and Hunter revived the name again in 1977 and added Martin Stone on vocals. A final incarnation of the group occurred in 1987 with Twink, Sanderson, Hunter and Wallis for one album.

| | |
|---|---|
| 29/07/1972.....48......1...... | WHAT A BUNCH OF SWEETIES. . . . . . . . . . . . . . . . . . . . . . . . . . . . . . . . . . . . . . . . . . . . . . . . . . . . Polydor 2383 132 |

**PINK FLOYD** UK rock group formed in London in 1965 by Roger Waters (born 6/9/1944, Great Bookham, vocals/bass), Rick Wright (born 28/7/1945, London, keyboards), Syd Barrett (born Roger Barrett, 6/1/1946, Cambridge, guitar/vocals) and Nick Mason (born 27/1/1945, Birmingham, drums) as Pink Floyd Sound (the name came from Georgia bluesmen Pink Anderson and Floyd Council). Barrett's erratic behaviour in 1968 led to Dave Gilmour (born 6/3/1947, Cambridge, guitar/vocals) replacing him. Their 1973 album *Dark Side Of The Moon* sold over 23 million copies worldwide, the most by a UK group, although this was matched by *The Wall*, which sold in excess of 23 million copies in the USA alone. Waters left in 1983 and made numerous attempts to prevent the remaining three from using the name Pink Floyd. They won the 1994 Grammy Award for Best Rock Instrumental Performance for *Marooned* and were inducted into the Rock & Roll Hall of Fame in 1996. Gilmour was awarded a CBE in the Queen's 2003 Honours List.

| | |
|---|---|
| 19/08/1967 .....6.....14...... | THE PIPER AT THE GATES OF DAWN . . . . . . . . . . . . . . . . . . . . . . . . . . . . . . . . . . . . . . . . . . . . . . . EMI SCX 6157 |
| 13/07/1968 .....9.....11...... | SAUCERFUL OF SECRETS . . . . . . . . . . . . . . . . . . . . . . . . . . . . . . . . . . . . . . . . . . . . . . . . . . . . . . Columbia SCX 6258 |
| 28/06/1969 .....9......5...... | MORE Original soundtrack to the film . . . . . . . . . . . . . . . . . . . . . . . . . . . . . . . . . . . . . . . . . . . . . . . Columbia SCX 6346 |
| 15/11/1969 .....5.....21...... | UMMAGUMMA. . . . . . . . . . . . . . . . . . . . . . . . . . . . . . . . . . . . . . . . . . . . . . . . . . . . . . . . . . . . . . Harvest SHDW 1/2 |
| 24/10/1970 .....❶¹.....23...... | ATOM HEART MOTHER. . . . . . . . . . . . . . . . . . . . . . . . . . . . . . . . . . . . . . . . . . . . . . . . . . . . . . . . . Harvest SHVL 781 |
| 07/08/1971.....32......6...... | RELICS . . . . . . . . . . . . . . . . . . . . . . . . . . . . . . . . . . . . . . . . . . . . . . . . . . . . . . . . . . . . . . . . . . Starline SRS 5071 |
| 20/11/1971.....3.....82...... | MEDDLE . . . . . . . . . . . . . . . . . . . . . . . . . . . . . . . . . . . . . . . . . . . . . . . . . . . . . . . . . . . . . . . . . Harvest SHVL 795 |
| 17/06/1972 .....6.....14......O | OBSCURED BY CLOUDS Original soundtrack to the film. . . . . . . . . . . . . . . . . . . . . . . . . . . . . . . . . . . Harvest SHSP 4020 |
| 31/03/1973 .....2.....351......✪⁷ | THE DARK SIDE OF THE MOON ▲¹ ◆¹⁵ . . . . . . . . . . . . . . . . . . . . . . . . . . . . . . . . . . . . . . . . . . Harvest SHVL 804 |
| 19/01/1974.....21.....20......● | A NICE PAIR This is a double album re-issue of *The Piper At The Gates Of Dawn* and *Saucerful Of Secrets* .... Harvest SHDW 403 |
| 27/09/1975 .....❶¹.....89......● | WISH YOU WERE HERE ▲² . . . . . . . . . . . . . . . . . . . . . . . . . . . . . . . . . . . . . . . . . . . . . . . . . . . . Harvest SHVL 814 |
| 19/02/1977 .....2.....33......● | ANIMALS . . . . . . . . . . . . . . . . . . . . . . . . . . . . . . . . . . . . . . . . . . . . . . . . . . . . . . . . . . . . . . . . Harvest SHVL 815 |
| 08/12/1979 .....3.....51......✪ | THE WALL ▲¹⁵ ◆²³ . . . . . . . . . . . . . . . . . . . . . . . . . . . . . . . . . . . . . . . . . . . . . . . . . . . . . . . . Harvest SHDW 411 |
| 05/12/1981.....37.....10...... | A COLLECTION OF GREAT DANCE SONGS . . . . . . . . . . . . . . . . . . . . . . . . . . . . . . . . . . . . . . . . . . . . Harvest SHVL 822 |
| 02/04/1983 .....❶².....25......● | THE FINAL CUT . . . . . . . . . . . . . . . . . . . . . . . . . . . . . . . . . . . . . . . . . . . . . . . . . . . . . . . . . . . . Harvest SHPF 1983 |
| 19/09/1987 .....3.....34......● | A MOMENTARY LAPSE OF REASON . . . . . . . . . . . . . . . . . . . . . . . . . . . . . . . . . . . . . . . . . . . . . . . . EMI EMD 1003 |
| 03/12/1988.....11.....12...... | DELICATE SOUND OF THUNDER . . . . . . . . . . . . . . . . . . . . . . . . . . . . . . . . . . . . . . . . . . . . . . . . . . EMI EQ 5009 |
| 09/04/1994 .....❶⁴.....51......✪² | THE DIVISION BELL ▲⁴ . . . . . . . . . . . . . . . . . . . . . . . . . . . . . . . . . . . . . . . . . . . . . . . . . . . . . . EMI CDEMD 1055 |
| 10/06/1995 .....❶².....21......● | PULSE ◇ ▲¹ . . . . . . . . . . . . . . . . . . . . . . . . . . . . . . . . . . . . . . . . . . . . . . . . . . . . . . . . . . . . . . EMI CDEMD 1078 |
| 09/03/1996.....48......2...... | RELICS . . . . . . . . . . . . . . . . . . . . . . . . . . . . . . . . . . . . . . . . . . . . . . . . . . . . . . . . . . . . . . . . . . EMI CDEMD 7082 |
| 16/08/1997.....44......2...... | THE PIPER AT THE GATES OF DAWN . . . . . . . . . . . . . . . . . . . . . . . . . . . . . . . . . . . . . . . . . . . . . . . EMI CDEMD 1073 |

▲⁹ Number of weeks album topped the US chart ◆¹² RIAA Diamond Awards ◇³ IFPI Platinum Europe Awards

| | | | | |
|---|---|---|---|---|
| 08/04/2000 | 15 | 5 | ○ | IS THERE ANYBODY OUT THERE? – LIVE ................................................................ EMI 5240752 |
| 17/11/2001 | 2 | 16 | ○² | **ECHOES – THE BEST OF PINK FLOYD** ◇² ........................................................... EMI 5361112 |
| 20/04/2002 | 64 | 5 | | THE WALL ...................................................................................................... EMI CDEMD 1071 |
| 12/04/2003 | 17 | 13 | | DARK SIDE OF THE MOON 30th anniversary re-issue of Harvest SHVL 804 ....................... EMI CDEMD 1064 |

### BILLIE PIPER
UK singer (born 9/9/1982, Swindon) who was fifteen years old at the time of her debut hit, having been singing since the age of four. She took part in the BRITS Trust *Thank Abba For The Music* project. In May 2001 she married former Virgin Radio DJ and entrepreneur Chris Evans and later became an actress.

| | | | | |
|---|---|---|---|---|
| 31/10/1998 | 14 | 23 | ✪ | HONEY TO THE B ............................................................................................. Innocent CDSIN 1 |
| 14/10/2000 | 14 | 4 | ○ | WALK OF LIFE .................................................................................................. Innocent CDSINX 3 |

### PIPS – see GLADYS KNIGHT AND THE PIPS

### PIRANHAS
UK group formed by 'Boring' Bob Grover (vocals), Johnny Helmer (guitar), Reginald Hornsbury (bass), Zoot Alors (saxophone) and Dick Slexia (drums).

| | | | | |
|---|---|---|---|---|
| 20/09/1980 | 69 | 3 | | PIRANHAS ....................................................................................................... Sire SRK 6098 |

### PIRATES
UK group formed in London in 1959 by Johnny Kidd (born Frederick Heath, 23/12/1939, London, vocals), Alan Caddy (guitar), Johnny Gordon (bass), Ken McKay (drums) and backing singers Mike West and Tom Brown. By 1962 the line-up comprised Mick Green (guitar), Johnny Spence (bass) and Frank Farley (drums). Although originally intended as a backing group for Johnny Kidd, The Pirates recorded without him from 1964. Green left in 1964 and was replaced by John Weider. The Pirates left Kidd in April 1966 with Kidd forming a new group, but when he was killed in a car crash on 7/10/1966 that group effectively ended. The original Pirates disbanded later in 1966 but re-formed in 1976 with Spence, Jon Morshead (guitar) and Farley. They disbanded again in 1982.

| | | | | |
|---|---|---|---|---|
| 19/11/1977 | 57 | 3 | | OUT OF THEIR SKULLS ....................................................................................... Warner Brothers K 56411 |

### PITCHSHIFTER
UK group formed in Nottingham by Jonathan Clayden (vocals), Jonathan Carter (guitar/programming), Mark Clayden (bass) and D (drums). They signed with Peaceville Records in 1991. By the time their debut album appeared D had departed and Stuart Toolin (guitar) joined. They subsequently added guitarist Jim Davies and also recorded for Earache and Geffen Records.

| | | | | |
|---|---|---|---|---|
| 03/06/2000 | 35 | 1 | | DEVIANT ........................................................................................................ MCA 1122542 |
| 11/05/2002 | 54 | 1 | | PSI ............................................................................................................... Mayan MYNCD 004 |

### GENE PITNEY
US singer (born 17/2/1941, Hartford, CT, raised in Rockville) who recorded his first single in 1959 and shortly after became a successful writer, penning *Rubber Ball* under the name Annie Orlowski (his wife's name) because of publishing difficulties. His other song writing credits include *He's A* Rebel (The Crystals), *Hello Mary Lou* (Ricky Nelson) and *Loneliness* (Des O'Connor). In 1961 he quit university to concentrate on music and signed with Musicor. He was inducted into the Rock & Roll Hall of Fame in 2002.

| | | | | |
|---|---|---|---|---|
| 11/04/1964 | 7 | 11 | | BLUE GENE ...................................................................................................... United Artists ULP 1061 |
| 06/02/1965 | 12 | 6 | | GENE PITNEY'S BIG SIXTEEN ............................................................................... Stateside SL 10118 |
| 20/03/1965 | 15 | 2 | | I'M GONNA BE STRONG ..................................................................................... Stateside SL 10120 |
| 20/11/1965 | 15 | 5 | | LOOKIN' THRU THE EYES OF LOVE ....................................................................... Stateside SL 10148 |
| 17/09/1966 | 13 | 17 | | NOBODY NEEDS YOUR LOVE ............................................................................... Stateside SL 10183 |
| 04/03/1967 | 39 | 1 | | YOUNG WARM AND WONDERFUL ....................................................................... Stateside SL 10194 |
| 22/04/1967 | 40 | 1 | | GENE PITNEY'S BIG SIXTEEN ............................................................................... Stateside SSL 10199 |
| 20/09/1969 | 8 | 9 | | **BEST OF GENE PITNEY** .................................................................................... Stateside SSL 10286 |
| 02/10/1976 | 6 | 14 | ● | **HIS 20 GREATEST HITS** ................................................................................... Arcade ADEP 22 |
| 20/10/1990 | 17 | 7 | ○ | BACKSTAGE – THE GREATEST HITS AND MORE ....................................................... Polydor 8471191 |
| 22/09/2001 | 40 | 2 | | THE ULTIMATE COLLECTION ............................................................................... Sequel NEECD 380 |

### PJ AND DUNCAN see ANT AND DEC

### PIXIES
US rock group formed in Boston, MA by Black Francis (born Charles Michael Kittridge Thompson IV, 1965, Long Beach, CA, guitar/vocals), Joey Santiago (born 10/6/1965, Manila, Philippines, guitar), Kim Deal (born 10/6/1961, Dayton, OH, bass) and David Lovering (born 6/12/1961, Boston, drums) as Pixies In Panoply. Francis subsequently changed his name to Frank Black and went solo in 1993. Deal was later a member of The Breeders.

| | | | | |
|---|---|---|---|---|
| 29/04/1989 | 8 | 9 | ● | **DOOLITTLE** .................................................................................................... 4AD CAD 905 |
| 25/08/1990 | 3 | 8 | ● | **BOSSANOVA** ................................................................................................. 4AD CAD 0010 |
| 05/10/1991 | 7 | 5 | ○ | **TROMPE LE MONDE** ....................................................................................... 4AD CAD 1014 |
| 18/10/1997 | 28 | 3 | | DEATH TO THE PIXIES ...................................................................................... 4AD DAD 7011CD |
| 18/10/1997 | 20 | 2 | | DEATH TO THE PIXIES – DELUXE EDITION ............................................................. 4AD DADD 7011CD |
| 18/07/1998 | 45 | 1 | | PIXIES AT THE BBC .......................................................................................... 4AD GAD 8013CD |
| 17/03/2001 | 53 | 1 | | THE COMPLETE B-SIDES ................................................................................... 4AD GAD 2103CD |
| 15/05/2004 | 16 | 5 | ○ | BEST OF – WAVE OF MUTILATION ....................................................................... 4AD CAD 2406CD |

**PLACEBO** UK rock group formed in London in 1994 by Brian Molko (guitar/vocals), Stefan Olsdal (bass) and Robert Schultzberg (drums). Schultzberg left in 1996 and was replaced by Steve Hewitt.

| | | | | | |
|---|---|---|---|---|---|
| 29/06/1996 | 5 | 13 | ● | **PLACEBO** | Elevator Music CDFLOORX 002 |
| 24/10/1998 | 7 | 17 | ✪ | **WITHOUT YOU I'M NOTHING** ◇ | Hut CDFLOOR 8 |
| 21/10/2000 | 6 | 5 | | **BLACK MARKET MUSIC** | Hut CDFLORXX 13 |
| 05/04/2003 | 11 | 10 | ● | SLEEPING WITH GHOSTS ◇ | Hut CDFLOOR 17 |
| 04/10/2003 | 50 | 1 | | SLEEPING WITH GHOSTS This is a 2CD Special Edition of Hut CDFLOOR 17 | Hut CDFLOORX 17 |

**PLANETS** UK classical fusion group formed by Ruth Miller (flute), Anne-Katherin Schirmer (classical and electric guitar), Beverley Jones (bass), Salima Williams (oboe/cor anglais), Jonathan Hill (violin), Lac-Hong Phi (cello), Ben Pugsley (classical, flamenco and electric guitar) and Michael Kruk (percussion).

| | | | | | |
|---|---|---|---|---|---|
| 02/03/2002 | 34 | 13 | ○ | CLASSICAL GRAFFITI | EMI/Dramatico CD5573162 |

**ROBERT PLANT** UK singer (born 20/8/1948, West Bromwich) who began his career with the New Memphis Bluesbreakers (a Birmingham-based group, despite their name), Crawling King Snakes and then Listen before going solo in 1967. He had spells with Band Of Joy and Hobstweedle before being invited to join Led Zeppelin in 1969 (he was not the original choice). In August 1975 he and his wife were in a serious car accident whilst on holiday in Rhodes, which forced Led Zeppelin to cancel plans for a world tour that year. The death of John Bonham in 1980 effectively brought Led Zeppelin to an end and Plant relaunched his solo career. In 1984 he and Jimmy Page formed The Honeydrippers with Jeff Beck and Nile Rodgers, and he has since recorded both solo and with Jimmy Page.

| | | | | | |
|---|---|---|---|---|---|
| 10/07/1982 | 2 | 15 | ○ | **PICTURES AT ELEVEN** | Swan Song SSK 59418 |
| 23/07/1983 | 7 | 14 | ● | **THE PRINCIPLE OF MOMENTS** | Atlantic 7901011 |
| 01/06/1985 | 19 | 4 | | SHAKEN 'N' STIRRED | Es Paranza 7902651 |
| 12/03/1988 | 10 | 7 | ● | **NOW AND ZEN** | Es Paranza WX 149 |
| 31/03/1990 | 15 | 9 | ○ | MANIC NIRVANA | Es Paranza WX 339 |
| 05/06/1993 | 6 | 8 | ○ | **FATE OF NATIONS** | Es Paranza 5148672 |
| 19/11/1994 | 7 | 13 | | **NO QUARTER – JIMMY PAGE AND ROBERT PLANT UNLEDDED** | Fontana 5263622 |
| 02/05/1998 | 3 | 6 | | **WALKING INTO CLARKSDALE** This and the above hit credited to **JIMMY PAGE AND ROBERT PLANT** | Mercury 5583242 |
| 06/07/2002 | 20 | 3 | | DREAMLAND | Mercury 5869632 |
| 15/11/2003 | 27 | 3 | | SIXTY SIX TO TIMBUKTU | Mercury 9813199 |

**PLASMATICS** US punk rock group formed in 1979 by former sex show star Wendy O. Williams (born 28/5/1949, Rochester, NY, vocals) with Richie Stotts (guitar), Wes Beech (guitar), Chosei Funahara (bass) and Stu Deutsch (drums). The group was the brainchild of pornographic mogul Rod Swenson – Wendy's stage 'outfit' was either see-through lingerie or topless with little more than strategically placed tape. After a number of recordings for Stiff and Capitol Records, the Plasmatics disbanded in 1982; Wendy subsequently went solo. She committed suicide on 6/4/1998.

| | | | | | |
|---|---|---|---|---|---|
| 11/10/1980 | 55 | 3 | | NEW HOPE FOR THE WRETCHED | Stiff SEEZ 24 |

**PLASTIK MAN** Canadian keyboard player Richie Hawtin. He also records as Fuse.

| | | | | | |
|---|---|---|---|---|---|
| 19/11/1994 | 58 | 1 | | MUSIK | Novamute NOMU 37CD |

**PLATTERS** US R&B vocal group formed in Los Angeles, CA in 1953 by Tony Williams (born 5/4/1928, Elizabeth, NJ, lead vocals), David Lynch (born 3/7/1929, St Louis, MO), Paul Robi (born 1931, New Orleans, LA), Herb Reed (born 1931, Kansas City, MO) and Zola Taylor (born 1934). The group was managed by Buck Ram (born Samuel Ram, 18/12/1908, Chicago, IL), who also penned *Only You*. Williams went solo in 1961, replaced by Sonny Turner. Williams' departure led to problems with Mercury, who initially refused to accept recordings without his lead vocal; Ram argued that their contract did not stipulate who should sing lead. Lynch died from cancer on 2/1/1981, Robi died from pancreatic cancer on 1/2/1989, Ram died on 1/1/1991 and Williams died from diabetes and emphysema on 14/8/1992. Due to the many personnel changes over the course of 25 years, numerous singers laid claim to the Platters name. The matter was settled in April 1999 when Herb Reed won ownership of the name. The group was inducted into the Rock & Roll Hall of Fame in 1990.

| | | | | | |
|---|---|---|---|---|---|
| 08/04/1978 | 8 | 13 | ○ | **20 CLASSIC HITS** | Mercury 9100 049 |

**PLAYERS ASSOCIATION** US dance group initially assembled as a studio aggregation by producer Danny Weiss and multi-instrumentalist Chris Hills. Performers on the hit included Chris Hills, Bob Berg (tenor saxophone), Bob Mover (alto saxophone), Karl Ratzer (guitar), Tom Harrell (trumpet), Pat Rebillot (keyboards), Mike Mandel (keyboards), Herb Bushler (bass), David Earle Johnson (percussion), Ray Mantilla (percussion), Gary Anderson (reeds), Marvin Stamm (trumpet), Victor Paz (trumpet) and Ed Byrne (trombone). A touring band was later formed. Weiss and Hills had previously recorded as Everything Is Everything and later recorded as Feel.

| | | | | | |
|---|---|---|---|---|---|
| 17/03/1979 | 54 | 4 | | TURN THE MUSIC UP | Vanguard VSD 79421 |

**PLAYN JAYN** UK vocal/instrumental group formed by Craig Lyndsey (vocals), Mike Jones (harmonica/vocals), Nick Jones (guitar), Erol Suleyman (bass) and Clive Francis (drums).

| | | | | | |
|---|---|---|---|---|---|
| 01/09/1984 | 93 | 1 | | FRIDAY THE 13TH (AT THE MARQUEE CLUB) | A&M JAYN 13 |

**PLIERS** – see **CHAKA DEMUS AND PLIERS**

**PM DAWN** US rap duo of brothers Atrell 'Prince B' Cordes (born 19/5/1970, Jersey City, NJ) and Jarrett 'DJ Minutemix' Cordes (born 17/7/1971, Jersey City). They began their recording career straight from leaving school. The group's name is defined as 'from the darkest hour comes the light'. They were named Best International Newcomers at the 1992 BRIT Awards.

14/09/1991 . . . . . 8 . . . . . . 12 . . . . . . ● **OF THE HEART, OF THE SOUL AND THE CROSS – THE UTOPIAN EXPERIENCE** . . . . . . . . . . . . . . . . . . . . . . . . . . . . . . . . . . Gee Street GEEA 7

03/04/1993 . . . . . 9 . . . . . . 5 . . . . . . ○ **THE BLISS ALBUM… ? (VIBRATIONS OF LOVE AND ANGER AND THE PONDERANCE OF LIFE AND EXISTENCE)** . . . . . Gee Street GEED 9

**P.O.D.** US Christian rock group formed in San Diego, CA in 1992 by Sonny Sandoval (vocals), Marcos Curiel (guitar), Traa Daniels (bass) and Noah 'Wuv' Bernado (drums). The group's name is short for Payable On Death.

19/01/2002 . . . . . 16 . . . . . . 6 . . . . . . SATELLITE . . . . . . . . . . . . . . . . . . . . . . . . . . . . . . . . . . . . . . . . . . . . . . . . . . . . . . . . . . . . . . . . . . . . . . . . . . . . . Atlantic 7567834752

**POGUES** UK group formed in London in 1983 by Shane MacGowan (born 25/12/1957, Tunbridge Wells, guitar/vocals), Jem Finer (born 20/7/1955, Stoke-on-Trent, banjo), James Fearnley (born 9/10/1954, Manchester, accordion), Andrew Ranken (born 13/11/1953, London, drums) and Caitlin O'Riordan (born 4/1/1965, Nigeria, bass) as Pogiue Mo Chone (Gaelic for 'kiss my arse'). They signed with Stiff in 1984, who shortened the name to make it less offensive. They later added Philip Chevron (born 17/6/1957, Dublin, guitar) and Peter 'Spider' Stacy (born 14/12/1958, Eastbourne, tin whistle), with ex-Clash member Joe Strummer (born John Mellors, 21/8/1952, Ankara, Turkey) becoming a member and taking over as lead singer when MacGowan was sacked. MacGowan later recorded solo.

03/11/1984 . . . . . 89 . . . . . 1 . . . . . . ○ RED ROSES FOR ME . . . . . . . . . . . . . . . . . . . . . . . . . . . . . . . . . . . . . . . . . . . . . . . . . . . . . . . . . . . . . . . . . . . . . Stiff SEEZ 55

17/08/1985 . . . . . 13 . . . . . 14 . . . . . . ● RUM, SODOMY AND THE LASH . . . . . . . . . . . . . . . . . . . . . . . . . . . . . . . . . . . . . . . . . . . . . . . . . . . . . . . . . . . . . . Stiff SEEZ 58

30/01/1988 . . . . . 3 . . . . . 16 . . . . . . ● **IF I SHOULD FALL FROM GRACE WITH GOD** . . . . . . . . . . . . . . . . . . . . . . . . . . . . . . . . . . . . . . . . . . . . . . . . . . . . . . Stiff NYR 1

29/07/1989 . . . . . 5 . . . . . 8 . . . . . . ● **PEACE AND LOVE** . . . . . . . . . . . . . . . . . . . . . . . . . . . . . . . . . . . . . . . . . . . . . . . . . . . . . . . . . . . . . . Pogue Mahone WX 247

13/10/1990 . . . . . 12 . . . . . 5 . . . . . . ○ HELL'S DITCH . . . . . . . . . . . . . . . . . . . . . . . . . . . . . . . . . . . . . . . . . . . . . . . . . . . . . . . . . . . . . . Pogue Mahone WX 366

12/10/1991 . . . . . 11 . . . . . 17 . . . . . . ○ THE BEST OF THE POGUES . . . . . . . . . . . . . . . . . . . . . . . . . . . . . . . . . . . . . . . . . . . . . . . . . . . . . . . . . . . . PM WX 430

11/09/1993 . . . . . 20 . . . . . 3 . . . . . . WAITING FOR HERB . . . . . . . . . . . . . . . . . . . . . . . . . . . . . . . . . . . . . . . . . . . . . . . . . . . . . . . . . . . . PM 4509934632

17/03/2001 . . . . . 18 . . . . . 19 . . . . . . ● THE VERY BEST OF . . . . . . . . . . . . . . . . . . . . . . . . . . . . . . . . . . . . . . . . . . . . . . . . . . . . . . . warner.esp 8573874592

**POINT BREAK** UK vocal group formed by Brett Adams (born 29/12/1976), David 'Ollie' Oliver (born 28/7/1976) and Declan Bennett (born 20/3/1981, Coventry). Brett and Ollie met working on the TV series *Byker Grove* (as Noddy and Marcus respectively).

19/08/2000 . . . . . 21 . . . . . 3 . . . . . . APOCADELIC . . . . . . . . . . . . . . . . . . . . . . . . . . . . . . . . . . . . . . . . . . . . . . . . . . . . . . . . . . . . . . . . . Eternal 8573828882

**POINTER SISTERS** US R&B vocal group formed in Oakland, CA in 1971 by sisters Anita (born 23/1/1948, Oakland), Bonnie (born 11/7/1950, Oakland), Ruth (born 19/3/1946, Oakland) and June (born 30/11/1954, Oakland) Pointer who first teamed up to sing at the church where their parents were ministers. They disbanded briefly in 1977; Bonnie signed solo with Motown and the remaining trio linked with Richard Perry's Planet label. The group appeared in the film *Car Wash*. They have won three Grammy Awards: Best Country & Western Performance by a Group in 1974 for *Fairy Tale,* Best Pop Vocal Performance by a Group in 1984 for *Jump (For My Love)* and Best Arrangement for Two or More Voices in 1984 for *Automatic*. The group has a star on the Hollywood Walk of Fame.

29/08/1981 . . . . . 21 . . . . . 13 . . . . . . BLACK AND WHITE . . . . . . . . . . . . . . . . . . . . . . . . . . . . . . . . . . . . . . . . . . . . . . . . . . . . . . . . . . . . . . Planet K 52300

05/05/1984 . . . . . 9 . . . . . 58 . . . . . . ● **BREAK OUT** . . . . . . . . . . . . . . . . . . . . . . . . . . . . . . . . . . . . . . . . . . . . . . . . . . . . . . . . . . . . . . . . Planet PL 84705

27/07/1985 . . . . . 34 . . . . . 7 . . . . . . CONTACT . . . . . . . . . . . . . . . . . . . . . . . . . . . . . . . . . . . . . . . . . . . . . . . . . . . . . . . . . . . . . . . . . . Planet PL 85457

29/07/1989 . . . . . 11 . . . . . 10 . . . . . . ● JUMP – THE BEST OF THE POINTER SISTERS . . . . . . . . . . . . . . . . . . . . . . . . . . . . . . . . . . . . . . . . . . . . RCA PL 90319

**POISON** US heavy rock group formed in Pittsburgh, PA in 1984 by Bret Michaels (born Bret Michael Sychak, 15/3/1963, Harrisburg, PA, vocals), Rikki Rockett (born Richard Ream, 9/8/1959, Mechanicsburg, PA, drums), Bobby Dall (born 2/11/1965, Miami, FL, bass) and Matt Smith (guitar) as Paris. They relocated to Los Angeles, CA (in an ambulance bought by Michaels for $700), replaced Smith with CC DeVille (born Bruce Anthony Johannesson, 14/5/1962, Brooklyn, NY) and name-changed to Poison. They signed with Enigma (through Capitol) in 1986. DeVille left in 1992, replaced by Richie Kotzen (born 3/2/1970, Birdsboro, PA), although he was fired after a year and replaced by Blues Saraceno (born 17/10/1971). They disbanded in 1994 and re-formed in 1999.

21/05/1988 . . . . . 18 . . . . . 21 . . . . . . ● OPEN UP AND SAY… AAH! . . . . . . . . . . . . . . . . . . . . . . . . . . . . . . . . . . . . . . . . . . . . . . . . . . . . . . Capitol EST 2059

21/07/1990 . . . . . 3 . . . . . 11 . . . . . . ● **FLESH AND BLOOD** . . . . . . . . . . . . . . . . . . . . . . . . . . . . . . . . . . . . . . . . . . . . . . . . . . . . . . . . Capitol EST 2126

14/12/1991 . . . . . 52 . . . . . 2 . . . . . . SWALLOW THIS LIVE . . . . . . . . . . . . . . . . . . . . . . . . . . . . . . . . . . . . . . . . . . . . . . . . . . . . . . . Capitol ESTU 2159

06/03/1993 . . . . . 20 . . . . . 3 . . . . . . NATIVE TONGUE . . . . . . . . . . . . . . . . . . . . . . . . . . . . . . . . . . . . . . . . . . . . . . . . . . . . . . . . Capitol CDESTU 2190

**POLECATS** UK group formed by Tim Worman (vocals), Martin Boorer (guitar), Philip Bloomberg (bass) and Neil Rooney (drums).

04/07/1981 . . . . . 28 . . . . . 2 . . . . . . POLECATS . . . . . . . . . . . . . . . . . . . . . . . . . . . . . . . . . . . . . . . . . . . . . . . . . . . . . . . . . . . . . . . . . . Vertigo 6359 057

## POLICE
UK/US rock group formed in London in 1977 by Stewart Copeland (born 16/7/1952, Alexandria, Egypt, drums), Sting (born Gordon Sumner, 2/10/1951, Wallsend, Tyne and Wear, vocals/bass) and Henry Padovani (guitar). The group funded the recording of their first single *Fall Out*. They added Andy Summers (born Andrew Somers, 31/12/1942, Poulton-le-Fylde, Lancashire) in June and Padovani left in August 1977. They signed with A&M in 1978. They were named Best British Group at the 1982 BRIT Awards and picked up an Outstanding Contribution Award in 1985. Police has won five Grammy Awards including: Best Rock Vocal Performance by a Group in 1981 for *Don't Stand So Close To Me*; Best Rock Instrumental Performance in 1982 for *Behind My Camel*; Best Pop Vocal Performance by a Group in 1983 for *Every Breath You Take* (for which Sting also won the Grammy for Best New Song of the Year). Sting began recording solo in 1985. Copeland recorded as Klark Kent and later formed Animal Logic. The group was inducted into the Rock & Roll Hall of Fame in 2003. Sting was awarded a CBE in the Queen's 2003 Birthday Honours List.

| | | | | | |
|---|---|---|---|---|---|
| 21/04/1979 | 6 | 96 | ✪ | OUTLANDOS D'AMOUR | A&M AMLH 68502 |
| 13/10/1979 | ❶⁴ | 74 | ✪ | REGGATTA DE BLANC 1980 Grammy Award for Best Rock Instrumental Performance | A&M AMLH 64792 |
| 11/10/1980 | ❶⁴ | 31 | ✪ | ZENYATTA MONDATTA | A&M AMLH 64831 |
| 10/10/1981 | ❶³ | 27 | ✪ | GHOST IN THE MACHINE | A&M AMLK 63730 |
| 25/06/1983 | ❶² | 48 | ✪ | SYNCHRONICITY ▲¹⁷ 1983 Grammy Award for Best Rock Vocal Performance by a Group | A&M AMLX 63735 |
| 08/11/1986 | ❶² | 55 | ✪⁴ | EVERY BREATH YOU TAKE – THE SINGLES | A&M EVERY 1 |
| 10/10/1992 | 10 | 21 | ● | GREATEST HITS | A&M 5400302 |
| 10/06/1995 | 25 | 3 | | LIVE! | A&M 5402222 |
| 22/11/1997 | ❶² | 50 | ✪ | THE VERY BEST OF STING AND THE POLICE ◇² STING AND THE POLICE | A&M 5404282 |

## SU POLLARD
UK actress (born 1949) best known for her role as Peggy Ollerenshaw in *Hi De Hi*.

| | | | | | |
|---|---|---|---|---|---|
| 22/11/1986 | 86 | 3 | ○ | SU | K-Tel NE 1327 |

## POLYPHONIC SPREE
US symphonic group formed in Dallas, TX by Tim DeLaughter with 24 other members. DeLaughter had previously been a member of Tripping Daisy and disbanded the group following the death of fellow member Wes Berggren.

| | | | | | |
|---|---|---|---|---|---|
| 12/07/2003 | 70 | 1 | | THE BEGINNING STAGES OF | 679 Recordings 2564603525 |

## IGGY POP
US singer (born James Jewel Osterberg, 21/4/1947, Muskegan, MI) who formed the Psychedelic Stooges in 1967 with his brother Scott and Ron Asheton. They disbanded in 1971, re-formed in 1972, disbanding for good in 1974. He later worked with Death In Vegas and also took part in the *It's Only Rock 'N' Roll* project for the Children's Promise charity.

| | | | | | |
|---|---|---|---|---|---|
| 09/04/1977 | 30 | 3 | | THE IDIOT | RCA Victor PL 12275 |
| 04/06/1977 | 44 | 2 | | RAW POWER IGGY POP AND THE STOOGES | Embassy 31464 |
| 01/10/1977 | 28 | 5 | | LUST FOR LIFE | RCA Victor PL 12488 |
| 19/05/1979 | 60 | 4 | | NEW VALUES | Arista SPART 1092 |
| 16/02/1980 | 62 | 2 | | SOLDIER | Arista SPART 1117 |
| 11/10/1986 | 43 | 7 | | BLAH BLAH BLAH | A&M AMA 5145 |
| 02/07/1988 | 61 | 1 | | INSTINCT | A&M AMA 5198 |
| 21/07/1990 | 50 | 2 | | BRICK BY BRICK | Virgin America VUSLP 19 |
| 25/09/1993 | 43 | 1 | | AMERICAN CAESAR | Virgin CDVUS 64 |
| 09/04/1977 | 30 | 3 | | THE IDIOT | RCA Victor PL 12275 |

## POP WILL EAT ITSELF
UK group formed in Wolverhampton in 1986 by Clint Mansell (born 7/11/1962, Coventry, guitar/vocals), Adam Mole (born 8/4/1962, Stourbridge, keyboards), Graham Crabbe (born 10/10/1964, Sutton Coldfield, drums) and Richard Marsh (born 4/3/1965, York, bass). They took their name from a headline in the *New Musical Express*. Robert 'Fuzz' Townshend (born 31/7/1964, Birmingham) joined on drums in 1992, with Crabbe moving to vocals.

| | | | | | |
|---|---|---|---|---|---|
| 13/05/1989 | 24 | 2 | | THIS IS THE DAY… THIS IS THE HOUR… THIS IS THIS? | RCA PL 74141 |
| 03/11/1990 | 33 | 3 | | CURE FOR SANITY | RCA PL 74828 |
| 19/09/1992 | 15 | 3 | | THE LOOKS OR THE LIFESTYLE | RCA 74321102650 |
| 06/03/1993 | 44 | 1 | | WEIRD'S BAR AND GRILLS | RCA 74321133432 |
| 06/11/1993 | 73 | 1 | | 16 DIFFERENT FLAVOURS OF HELL | RCA 74321153172 |
| 01/10/1994 | 11 | 2 | | DOS DEDOS MIS AMIGOS | Infectious INFECT 10CDX |
| 18/03/1995 | 25 | 2 | | TWO FINGERS MY FRIENDS? | Infectious INFECT 10CDRX |

## POPE JOHN PAUL II
Polish pontiff (born Karol Joseph Wojtyla, 18/5/1920, Katowice) who was an athletic young man with an ambition to be an actor. During the Second World War he helped Jews escape from Nazi hands in occupied Poland, entered the priesthood and was ordained on 1 November 1946. In 1958 he was named auxiliary bishop of Krakow and four years later made vicar capitular. Noted for his stand against communism, Pope Paul VI made him a cardinal in 1967. On 16 October 1978 he was named Pope John Paul II in succession to Pope John Paul I, the first Polish pope and the first non-Italian pope since Pope Adrian VI in 1522. In 1981 he was shot and injured as he entered St Peter's Square, but recovered after two months or so and even visited his would-be assassin in prison. He has visited most countries of the world whilst in office.

| | | | | | |
|---|---|---|---|---|---|
| 03/07/1982 | 71 | 4 | | JOHN PAUL II – THE PILGRIM POPE | BBC REB 445 |
| 10/12/1994 | 50 | 4 | | THE ROSARY POPE JOHN PAUL II/FATHER COLM KILCOYNE This is a double CD or cassette, one featuring the Rosary In Latin by Pope John Paul II, the other an English reading by Father Colm Kilcoyne | Pure Music PMCD 7009 |

## PORNO FOR PYROS
US rock group formed in 1992 by Perry Farrell (vocals), Peter DiStephano (guitar), Martyn Lenoble (bass) and Stephen Perkins (drums), following the demise of Farrell's previous group Jane's Addiction. The group were later joined by Matt Hyde (keyboards).

| | | | | | |
|---|---|---|---|---|---|
| 08/05/1993 | 13 | 3 | | PORNO FOR PYROS | Warner Brothers 9362452282 |

08/06/1996 . . . . . 40 . . . . . . 2 . . . . . . GOOD GOD'S URGE . . . . . . . . . . . . . . . . . . . . . . . . . . . . . . . . . . . . . . . . . . . . . . . . . . . . . . . . . . . . Warner Brothers 9362460522

**PORTISHEAD** UK group formed in Bristol in 1992 by Geoff Barrow (born 9/12/1971, Somerset, numerous instruments/producer), Beth Gibbons (born 4/1/1965, Devon, vocals), Adrian Utley (guitar) and Dave McDonald (sound engineer). Gibbons later recorded with Rustin Man.

03/09/1994 . . . . . 2 . . . . 71 . . . . . . ✪² **DUMMY** ◇ 1995 Mercury Music Prize. . . . . . . . . . . . . . . . . . . . . . . . . . . . . . . . . . . . . . . . . . . . . . . . . . . . . . . Go Beat 8285222
11/10/1997 . . . . . 2 . . . . 22 . . . . . . ● **PORTISHEAD** . . . . . . . . . . . . . . . . . . . . . . . . . . . . . . . . . . . . . . . . . . . . . . . . . . . . . . . . . . . . . . . . . . . . . . . . Go Beat 5391892
14/11/1998 . . . . . 40 . . . . . . 2 . . . . . . PNYC . . . . . . . . . . . . . . . . . . . . . . . . . . . . . . . . . . . . . . . . . . . . . . . . . . . . . . . . . . . . . . . . . . . . . . . . . . . . . . . . Go Beat 5594242

**SANDY POSEY** US singer (born Martha Sharp, 18/6/1947, Jasper, AL, raised in Arkansas) who worked as a session singer in Nashville and Memphis in the early 1960s.
11/03/1967 . . . . . 39 . . . . . . 1 . . . . . . BORN A WOMAN . . . . . . . . . . . . . . . . . . . . . . . . . . . . . . . . . . . . . . . . . . . . . . . . . . . . . . . . . . . . . . . . . . . . . MGM MGMCS 8035

**FRANK POURCEL** French orchestra leader/violinist (born 1/1/1915, Marseilles) who studied at the Paris Conservatoire before becoming leader of the French Fiddlers in the late 1940s. The group has also recorded as Franck Pourcel And His Rockin' Strings and by the early 1970s had sold over 15 million albums worldwide.
20/11/1971 . . . . . 8 . . . . . . 7 . . . . . . **THIS IS POURCEL**. . . . . . . . . . . . . . . . . . . . . . . . . . . . . . . . . . . . . . . . . . . . . . . . . . . . . . . . . . . . . . . . . . . Studio Two STWO 7

**COZY POWELL** UK drummer (born Colin Flooks, 29/12/1947, Cirencester) who was a member of Bedlam before recording solo. He retired from the music industry for a while, racing cars for Hitachi before joining Rainbow in 1975. He was killed in a road crash on 5/4/1998, with an autopsy revealing excess alcohol in his bloodstream.
26/01/1980 . . . . . 34 . . . . . 3 . . . . . OVER THE TOP . . . . . . . . . . . . . . . . . . . . . . . . . . . . . . . . . . . . . . . . . . . . . . . . . . . . . . . . . . . . . . . . . . Ariola ARL 5038
19/09/1981 . . . . 58 . . . . . . 4 . . . . . TILT . . . . . . . . . . . . . . . . . . . . . . . . . . . . . . . . . . . . . . . . . . . . . . . . . . . . . . . . . . . . . . . . . . . . . . . Polydor POLD 5047
28/05/1983 . . . . . 86 . . . . . . 1 . . . . . OCTOPUS . . . . . . . . . . . . . . . . . . . . . . . . . . . . . . . . . . . . . . . . . . . . . . . . . . . . . . . . . . . . . . . . . . . . . Polydor POLD 5093

**PETER POWELL** UK exercise instructor, born in 1951 in Worcestershire, who first came to prominence as a DJ on Radio 1 and later became an agent for a variety of celebrities, including his ex-wife Anthea Turner.
20/03/1982 . . . . . 9 . . . . . . 13 . . . . . ● **KEEP FIT AND DANCE**. . . . . . . . . . . . . . . . . . . . . . . . . . . . . . . . . . . . . . . . . . . . . . . . . . . . . . . . . . . . K-Tel NE 1167

**POWER STATION** UK/US rock group formed by Robert Palmer (born Alan Palmer, 19/1/1949, Scarborough, vocals), Tony Thompson (born 15/11/1954), drummer with Chic, John Taylor (born Nigel John Taylor, 20/6/1960, Birmingham), bass player with Duran Duran, and Andy Taylor (born16/2/1961, Wolverhampton), guitarist with Duran Duran, initially as a one-album outfit. Palmer left and was replaced by Michael Des Barres as the group wanted to work live. Palmer died from a heart attack on 26/9/2003. Thompson died from renal cell cancer on 12/11/2003.
06/04/1985 . . . . . 12 . . . . . 23 . . . . . ● THE POWER STATION . . . . . . . . . . . . . . . . . . . . . . . . . . . . . . . . . . . . . . . . . . . . . . . . . . . . . . . . . . . . Parlophone POST 1

**PRAYING MANTIS** UK group formed in London in 1977 by Tino Troy Neophytou (guitar/vocals), Robert Angelo (guitar), Chris Troy Neophytou (bass/vocals) and Mick Ransome (drums). By the time they signed with Arista in 1981 Angelo and Ransome had been replaced by Steve Carroll and Dave Potts respectively. Carroll left after their debut album for the label and was replaced by Bernie Shaw, with Jon Bavin (keyboards) joining at the same time. By the mid 1980s the band had become Stratus, although they re-formed as Praying Mantis in 1990 with both Troy Neophytou brothers, Paul Di'Anno (vocals), Dennis Stratton (guitar) and Bruce Bisland (drums).
11/04/1981 . . . . . 60 . . . . . . 2 . . . . . . TIME TELLS NO LIES . . . . . . . . . . . . . . . . . . . . . . . . . . . . . . . . . . . . . . . . . . . . . . . . . . . . . . . . . . . . Arista SPART 1153

**PREFAB SPROUT** UK rock group formed in Newcastle-upon-Tyne in 1982 by Paddy McAloon (born 7/6/1957, Consett, Co. Durham, guitar/vocals), his brother Martin (born 4/1/1962, Durham, bass), Wendy Smith (born 31/5/1963, Durham, guitar/vocals) and Mick Salmon (drums). They signed with Kitchenware in 1983. Salmon left in 1984, replaced by Graham Lant and then Neil Conti (born 12/2/1959, London).

17/03/1984 . . . . . 22 . . . . . . 7 . . . . . . SWOON. . . . . . . . . . . . . . . . . . . . . . . . . . . . . . . . . . . . . . . . . . . . . . . . . . . . . . . . . . . . . . . . . . . . . . . . . . Kitchenware KWLP 1
22/06/1985 . . . . . 21 . . . . 35 . . . . . ● STEVE McQUEEN . . . . . . . . . . . . . . . . . . . . . . . . . . . . . . . . . . . . . . . . . . . . . . . . . . . . . . . . . . . . . . . . Kitchenware KWLP 3
26/03/1988 . . . . . 5 . . . . . 24 . . . . . ● **FROM LANGLEY PARK TO MEMPHIS** . . . . . . . . . . . . . . . . . . . . . . . . . . . . . . . . . . . . . . . . . . . . . . . . . . . Kitchenware KWLP 9
01/07/1989 . . . . 18 . . . . . . 4 . . . . . ○ PROTEST SONGS. . . . . . . . . . . . . . . . . . . . . . . . . . . . . . . . . . . . . . . . . . . . . . . . . . . . . . . . . . . . . . . . Kitchenware KWLP 4
08/09/1990 . . . . . 7 . . . . . 17 . . . . . ● **JORDAN: THE COMEBACK** . . . . . . . . . . . . . . . . . . . . . . . . . . . . . . . . . . . . . . . . . . . . . . . . . . . . . . . . . Kitchenware KWLP 14
11/07/1992 . . . . . 3 . . . . . 13 . . . . . ● **A LIFE OF SURPRISES – THE BEST OF PREFAB SPROUT**. . . . . . . . . . . . . . . . . . . . . . . . . . . . . . . . . . . . Kitchenware 4718862
17/05/1997 . . . . 7 . . . . . 5 . . . . . . **ANDROMEDA HEIGHTS** . . . . . . . . . . . . . . . . . . . . . . . . . . . . . . . . . . . . . . . . . . . . . . . . . . . . . . . . . . . . Kitchenware KWCD 30

03/06/2001.....60......1...... THE GUNMAN AND OTHER STORIES .................................................................... Liberty 5326132

**PRESIDENTS OF THE UNITED STATES OF AMERICA** US trio formed in Seattle in 1994 by Chris Ballew (vocals/two-string guitar), Dave Dederer (vocals/three-string bass) and Dave Thiele (vocals/no-string drums). Thiele subsequently moved to Boston, MA and was replaced by Jason Finn. They disbanded in 1998.

13/01/1996.....14.....29......● THE PRESIDENTS OF THE UNITED STATES OF AMERICA ....................................................... Columbia 4810392
16/11/1996.....36......2...... II .......................................................................................................... Columbia 4850922

**ELVIS PRESLEY** US singer (born Elvis Aaron Presley, 8/1/1935, East Tupelo, MS, to Gladys and Vernon; his twin brother Jesse Garon was stillborn) who entered a singing contest in 1945 and came second behind Shirley Jones Gallentine. The family moved to Memphis in 1948 and upon graduation he worked as a truck driver at Crown Electric Co. He paid for his first recording (*My Happiness* and *That's When Your Heartaches Begin*) at Memphis Recording Service, a copy being later handed to Sam Phillips of Sun Records. He signed with Sun in 1954 and released his first single, *That's All Right* backed with *Blue Moon Of Kentucky* (catalogue number Sun 209), then signed with manager Colonel Tom Parker (born Andreas Cornelius Van Kuijk, 26/6/1909, Breda, Holland) in 1955 as bidding for his Sun contract got underway. He signed with RCA in November 1955, with Sun collecting $35,000 for Presley's contract and Presley himself $5,000 for future royalties on Sun material. His first single with RCA, *Heartbreak Hotel* backed with *I Was The One* (catalogue number RCA Victor 47-6420), topped the US charts for eight weeks. He was drafted into the US Army in 1958 (as US Private Presley 53310761) and subsequently stationed in Germany where he first met future wife Priscilla Beaulieu. He was demobbed in 1960. (The flight from Frankfurt made a refuelling stop at Prestwick Airport in Scotland, the only occasion Presley set foot in the UK. He did not tour outside the USA because Parker was an illegal immigrant and feared being refused re-entry; since this fact did not become public knowledge until after Presley's death, it has been suggested that Presley did not know of his manager's background.) He returned to the USA with his popularity having been maintained by a steady flow of releases. He married Priscilla in 1967 (their only child, Lisa Marie, was born in 1968). They divorced in 1973. He starred in 31 films (plus two others of live performances), beginning with *Love Me Tender* in 1956. His last recordings were made in April 1977 and his last live appearance was at the Market Square Arena, Indianapolis on 26/6/1977. He was found unconscious by girlfriend Ginger Alden on 16/8/1977 and pronounced dead on arrival at hospital. The cause of death was given as heart failure brought on by prescription drug abuse. Over 75,000 flocked to Graceland for his funeral; his body was laid next to his mother's at Forest Hills Cemetery in Memphis. After several break-ins, the body was moved to Graceland. He won three Grammy Awards including Best Inspirational Recording in 1972 for *He Touched Me*. He is the biggest selling solo artist in the world with sales of over 1 billion records. In 1993 the US postal service issued an Elvis Presley postage stamp; many were sent by fans to fictitious addresses so that they could be stamped 'Return To Sender'! Even 25 years after his death, there are more Elvis Presley fan clubs around the world (over 480) than for any other act. This is despite the fact that he recorded only in English and did only one concert outside the USA – in Canada in 1957. He was inducted into the Rock & Roll Hall of Fame in 1986 and has a star on the Hollywood Walk of Fame. Parker died from a stroke on 21/1/1997. In topping the charts (posthumously) with *A Little Less Conversation* Elvis became the first artist to top the UK singles chart eighteen times.

03/11/1956 .... ●[1].....16...... **ROCK 'N' ROLL** ...................................................................................................... HMV CLP 1093
04/05/1957 .... 3.....3...... **ROCK 'N' ROLL NO.2** ................................................................................................ HMV CLP 1105
31/08/1957 .... ●[3].....25...... **LOVING YOU** Original soundtrack to the film .................................................................. RCA RD 24001
26/10/1957 .... 3.....7...... **BEST OF ELVIS** .................................................................................................... HMV DLP 1159
30/11/1957 .... 2.....6...... **ELVIS'S CHRISTMAS ALBUM** ▲[4] ........................................................................ RCA RD 27052
13/09/1958 .... ●[7].....22...... **KING CREOLE** Original soundtrack to the film ................................................................ RCA RD 27086
11/10/1958 .... 2.....48...... **ELVIS' GOLDEN RECORDS** ....................................................................................... RCA RD 16069
08/11/1958 .... 4.....14...... **KING CREOLE** Original soundtrack to the film ................................................................ RCA RD 27086
04/04/1959 .... 4.....9...... **ELVIS (ROCK 'N' ROLL NO. 1)** .................................................................................. HMV CLP 1093
08/08/1959 .... 4.....15...... **A DATE WITH ELVIS** ............................................................................................. RCA RD 27128
18/06/1960 .... 4.....20...... **ELVIS' GOLDEN RECORDS VOLUME 2** ...................................................................... RCA RD 27159
23/07/1960 .... ●[1].....27...... **ELVIS IS BACK!** .................................................................................................. RCA RD 27171
10/12/1960 .... ●[22].....55...... **G.I. BLUES** Original soundtrack to the film ▲[10] .......................................................... RCA RD 27192
20/05/1961 .... 3.....25...... **HIS HAND IN MINE** ............................................................................................. RCA RD 27211
04/11/1961 .... 2.....18...... **SOMETHING FOR EVERYBODY** ▲[3] ....................................................................... RCA RD 27224
09/12/1961 .... ●[18].....65...... **BLUE HAWAII** Original soundtrack to the film ▲[20] ...................................................... RCA RD 27238
07/07/1962 .... ●[6].....25...... **POT LUCK** ........................................................................................................ RCA RD 27265
08/12/1962 .... 3.....17...... **ROCK 'N' ROLL NO. 2** .......................................................................................... RCA Victor RD 7528
26/01/1963 .... 2.....21...... **GIRLS! GIRLS! GIRLS!** Original soundtrack to the film ................................................... RCA Victor RD 7534
11/05/1963 .... 4.....21...... **IT HAPPENED AT THE WORLD'S FAIR** Original soundtrack to the film .............................. RCA Victor RD 7565
28/12/1963 .... 9.....14...... **FUN IN ACAPULCO** Original soundtrack to the film ....................................................... RCA Victor RD 7609
11/04/1964 .... 6.....13...... **ELVIS' GOLDEN RECORDS VOLUME 3** ...................................................................... RCA Victor RD 7630
04/07/1964 .... 5.....17...... KISSIN' COUSINS Original soundtrack to the film ............................................................ RCA Victor RD 7645
09/01/1965.....12......4...... ROUSTABOUT Original soundtrack to the film ▲[1] ........................................................ RCA Victor RD 7678
01/05/1965.....8......18...... GIRL HAPPY Original soundtrack to the film .................................................................. RCA Victor RD 7714
25/09/1965.....11......4...... FLAMING STAR AND SUMMER KISSES ...................................................................... RCA Victor RD 7723
04/12/1965.....8......8...... **ELVIS FOR EVERYONE** ........................................................................................... RCA Victor RD 7782
15/01/1966.....11......5...... HARLEM HOLIDAY Original soundtrack to the film .......................................................... RCA Victor RD 7767
30/04/1966.....11......5...... FRANKIE AND JOHNNY Original soundtrack to the film ..................................................... RCA Victor RD 7793
06/08/1966.....7......9...... **PARADISE HAWAIIAN STYLE** Original soundtrack to the film .......................................... RCA Victor RD 7810
26/11/1966.....17......6...... CALIFORNIA HOLIDAY Original soundtrack to the film ....................................................... RCA Victor RD 7820
08/04/1967.....11......14...... HOW GREAT THOU ART 1967 Grammy Award for Best Sacred Recording ............................ RCA Victor SF 7867
02/09/1967.....34......1...... DOUBLE TROUBLE Original soundtrack to the film ........................................................... RCA Victor SF 7892
20/04/1968.....39......1...... CLAMBAKE Original soundtrack to the film ................................................................... RCA Victor SD 7917

| DATE | POS | WKS | BPI | ALBUM TITLE | LABEL & NUMBER |
|------|-----|-----|-----|-------------|----------------|
| 03/05/1969 | 2 | 26 | | **ELVIS – NBC TV SPECIAL** Original TV soundtrack | RCA Victor RD 8011 |
| 05/07/1969 | 2 | 14 | | **ELVIS' SINGS FLAMING STAR** | RCA International INTS 1012 |
| 23/08/1969 | ❶¹ | 13 | | **FROM ELVIS IN MEMPHIS** | RCA Victor SF 8029 |
| 28/02/1970 | 36 | 1 | | PORTRAIT IN MUSIC | RCA Victor 558 |
| 14/03/1970 | 3 | 16 | | **FROM MEMPHIS TO VEGAS – FROM VEGAS TO MEMPHIS** | RCA Victor SF 8080/1 |
| 01/08/1970 | 2 | 18 | | **ON STAGE FEBRUARY 1970** | RCA Victor SF 8128 |
| 05/12/1970 | 21 | 11 | | ELVIS' GOLDEN RECORDS VOLUME 1 | RCA SF 8129 |
| 12/12/1970 | 49 | 2 | | WORLDWIDE 50 GOLD AWARD HITS VOLUME 1 – A TOUCH OF GOLD | RCA Victor LPM 6401 |
| 30/01/1971 | 12 | 41 | | THAT'S THE WAY IT IS Original soundtrack to the film | RCA Victor SF 8162 |
| 10/04/1971 | 6 | 9 | | **I'M 10,000 YEARS OLD – ELVIS COUNTRY** | RCA Victor SF 8172 |
| 24/07/1971 | 7 | 5 | | **LOVE LETTERS FROM ELVIS** | RCA Victor SF 8202 |
| 07/08/1971 | 5 | 21 | | **C'MON EVERYBODY** | RCA International INTS 1286 |
| 07/08/1971 | 20 | 4 | | YOU'LL NEVER WALK ALONE | RCA Camden CDM 1088 |
| 25/09/1971 | 38 | 2 | | ALMOST IN LOVE | RCA International INTS 1206 |
| 04/12/1971 | 7 | 5 | | **ELVIS CHRISTMAS ALBUM** | RCA International INTS 1126 |
| 18/12/1971 | 26 | 3 | | I GOT LUCKY | RCA International INTS 1322 |
| 27/05/1972 | 12 | 8 | | ELVIS NOW | RCA Victor SF 8266 |
| 03/06/1972 | 34 | 4 | | ROCK 'N' ROLL | RCA Victor SF 8233 |
| 03/06/1972 | 48 | 1 | | ELVIS FOR EVERYONE | RCA Victor SF 8232 |
| 15/07/1972 | 3 | 20 | | **ELVIS AS RECORDED AT MADISON SQUARE GARDEN** | RCA Victor SF 8296 |
| 12/08/1972 | 38 | 3 | | HE TOUCHED ME 1972 Grammy Award for Best Inspirational Recording | RCA Victor SF 8275 |
| 24/02/1973 | 11 | 10 | | ALOHA FROM HAWAII VIA SATELLITE Original TV soundtrack ▲¹ | RCA Victor DPS 2040 |
| 15/09/1973 | 16 | 4 | | ELVIS | RCA Victor SF 8378 |
| 02/03/1974 | 20 | 3 | | ELVIS – A LEGENDARY PERFORMER VOLUME 1 | RCA Victor CPLI 0341 |
| 25/05/1974 | 42 | 1 | | GOOD TIMES | RCA Victor APLI 0475 |
| 07/09/1974 | 44 | 1 | | ELVIS LIVE ON STAGE IN MEMPHIS | RCA Victor APLI 0606 |
| 22/02/1975 | 21 | 4 | | PROMISED LAND | RCA Victor APLI 0873 |
| 14/06/1975 | 48 | 3 | | TODAY | RCA Victor RS 1011 |
| 05/07/1975 | ❶¹ | 38 | ✪ | **ELVIS'S 40 GREATEST HITS** | Arcade ADEP 12 |
| 06/09/1975 | 16 | 13 | | THE ELVIS PRESLEY SUN COLLECTION | RCA Starcall HY 1001 |
| 19/06/1976 | 29 | 5 | | FROM ELVIS PRESLEY BOULEVARD, MEMPHIS, TENNESSEE | RCA Victor RS 1060 |
| 19/02/1977 | 12 | 11 | | ELVIS IN DEMAND | RCA Victor PL 42003 |
| 27/08/1977 | 3 | 15 | | **MOODY BLUE** | RCA Victor PL 12428 |
| 03/09/1977 | 7 | 9 | | **WELCOME TO MY WORLD** | RCA Victor PL 12274 |
| 03/09/1977 | 14 | 10 | | G.I. BLUES Original soundtrack to the film | RCA SF 5078 |
| 10/09/1977 | 49 | 2 | | BLUE HAWAII Original soundtrack to the film ▲²⁰ | RCA SF 8145 |
| 10/09/1977 | 27 | 4 | | ELVIS' GOLDEN RECORDS VOLUME 2 | RCA SF 8151 |
| 10/09/1977 | 30 | 4 | | HITS OF THE 70'S | RCA Victor LPLI 7527 |
| 10/09/1977 | 49 | 2 | | ELVIS' GOLDEN RECORDS VOLUME 3 | RCA SF 7630 |
| 10/09/1977 | 52 | 1 | | PICTURES OF ELVIS | RCA Starcall HY 1023 |
| 08/10/1977 | 31 | 2 | | THE SUN YEARS | Charly SUN 1001 |
| 15/10/1977 | 24 | 3 | | LOVING YOU | RCA Victor PL 42358 |
| 19/11/1977 | 13 | 11 | | ELVIS IN CONCERT Original TV soundtrack | RCA Victor PL 02578 |
| 22/04/1978 | 37 | 1 | | HE WALKS BESIDE ME | RCA Victor PL 12772 |
| 03/06/1978 | 47 | 4 | | THE '56 SESSIONS VOLUME 1 | RCA Victor PL 42101 |
| 02/09/1978 | 50 | 2 | | TV SPECIAL | RCA Victor PL 42370 |
| 11/11/1978 | 40 | 14 | | ELVIS'S 40 GREATEST HITS | RCA Victor PL 42691 |
| 03/02/1979 | 43 | 3 | | A LEGENDARY PERFORMER VOLUME 3 | RCA Victor PL 13082 |
| 05/05/1979 | 72 | 1 | | OUR MEMORIES OF ELVIS | RCA Victor PL 13279 |
| 24/11/1979 | 4 | 13 | ✪ | **LOVE SONGS** | K-Tel NE 1062 |
| 21/06/1980 | 32 | 5 | | ELVIS PRESLEY SINGS LEIBER AND STOLLER | RCA International INTS 5031 |
| 23/08/1980 | 21 | 4 | | ELVIS AARON PRESLEY | RCA ELVIS 25 |
| 23/08/1980 | 53 | 2 | | PARADISE HAWAIIAN STYLE Original soundtrack to the film | RCA International INTS 5037 |
| 29/11/1980 | 6 | 8 | ✪ | **INSPIRATION** | K-Tel NE 1101 |
| 14/03/1981 | 33 | 5 | | GUITAR MAN | RCA RCALP 5010 |
| 09/05/1981 | 47 | 4 | | THIS IS ELVIS PRESLEY Original soundtrack to the film | RCA RCALP 5029 |
| 28/11/1981 | 45 | 6 | ● | THE ULTIMATE PERFORMANCE | K-Tel NE 1141 |
| 13/02/1982 | 31 | 12 | | THE SOUND OF YOUR CRY | RCA RCALP 3060 |
| 06/03/1982 | 97 | 1 | | ELVIS PRESLEY EP PACK | RCA EP1 |
| 21/08/1982 | 62 | 5 | | ROMANTIC ELVIS – 20 LOVE SONGS/ROCKIN' ELVIS – THE SIXTIES 20 GREAT TRACKS | RCA RCALP 1000/1 |
| 18/12/1982 | 80 | 1 | | IT WON'T SEEM LIKE CHRISTMAS WITHOUT YOU | RCA International INTS 5235 |
| 30/04/1983 | 40 | 2 | | JAILHOUSE ROCK/LOVE IN LAS VEGAS | RCA RCALP 9020 |
| 20/08/1983 | 83 | 1 | | I WAS THE ONE | RCA RCALP 3105 |
| 03/12/1983 | 91 | 1 | | A LEGENDARY PERFORMER VOLUME 4 | RCA PL 84848 |
| 07/04/1984 | 71 | 3 | | I CAN HELP | RCA PL 89287 |
| 21/07/1984 | 69 | 2 | | THE FIRST LIVE RECORDINGS | RCA International PG 89387 |
| 26/01/1985 | 98 | 1 | | 20 GREATEST HITS VOLUME 2 | RCA International NL 89168 |
| 25/05/1985 | 92 | 1 | | RECONSIDER BABY | RCA PL 85418 |
| 12/10/1985 | 23 | 17 | ● | ELVIS PRESLEY – BALLADS: 18 CLASSIC LOVE SONGS | Telstar STAR 2264 |

◯ Silver disc  ● Gold disc  ✪ Platinum disc (additional platinum units are indicated by a figure following the symbol)  ❶⁹ Number of weeks album topped the UK chart

| DATE | POS | WKS | BPI | ALBUM TITLE | LABEL & NUMBER |
|------|-----|-----|-----|-------------|----------------|
| 29/08/1987 | 4 | 34 | ● | **PRESLEY – THE ALL TIME GREATEST HITS** | RCA PL 90100 |
| 28/01/1989 | 60 | 2 | | STEREO '57 (ESSENTIAL ELVIS VOLUME 2) | RCA PL 90250 |
| 21/07/1990 | 71 | 1 | | HITS LIKE NEVER BEFORE (ESSENTIAL ELVIS VOLUME 3) | RCA PL 90486 |
| 01/09/1990 | 62 | 1 | | THE GREAT PERFORMANCES | RCA PL 82227 |
| 24/08/1991 | 57 | 1 | | COLLECTORS GOLD | RCA PL 90574 |
| 22/02/1992 | 4 | 18 | ● | **FROM THE HEART – HIS GREATEST LOVE SONGS** | RCA PD 90642 |
| 10/09/1994 | 6 | 25 | ✪ | **THE ESSENTIAL COLLECTION** ◇ | RCA 74321228712 |
| 11/05/1996 | 42 | 3 | | ELVIS 56 | RCA 07863668562 |
| 07/06/1997 | 3 | 33 | ✪ | **ALWAYS ON MY MIND – ULTIMATE LOVE SONGS** | RCA 74321489842 |
| 28/02/1998 | 39 | 4 | | BLUE SUEDE SHOES | RCA 74321556282 |
| 02/12/2000 | 8 | 25 | ✪2 | **THE 50 GREATEST HITS** | RCA 74321811022 |
| 31/03/2001 | 50 | 3 | | THE LIVE GREATEST HITS | RCA 74321847082 |
| 24/11/2001 | 21 | 9 | | THE 50 GREATEST LOVE SONGS | RCA 74321900752 |
| 05/10/2002 | ❶2 | 32 | ✪2 | **ELV1S: 30 #1 HITS** ◇3 ▲3 | RCA 07863680792 |
| 18/10/2003 | 4 | 12 | | **2ND TO NONE** | RCA 82876570852 |
| 06/12/2003 | 41 | 5 | | CHRISTMAS PEACE | RCA 82876574892 |

**LISA MARIE PRESLEY** US singer (born 1/2/1968, Memphis, TN); she is the only child of legendary singer Elvis Presley and Priscilla Presley. Although she began writing songs at the age of eighteen, she did not pursue a musical career until into her 30s. She married Danny Keough in 1988 (by whom she had two children before they divorced), singer Michael Jackson in 1994 (they divorced in 1997) and actor Nicholas Cage in 2002 (they separated in 2003). Initially encouraged by producer Glen Ballard to return to music (he helped her get a contract with Capitol in 2000), she released her debut in 2003.

| | | | | | |
|------|-----|-----|-----|-------------|----------------|
| 26/07/2003 | 52 | 1 | | TO WHOM IT MAY CONCERN | Capitol 5905220 |

**PRETENDERS** UK/US rock group formed in 1978 by Chrissie Hynde (born 7/9/1951, Akron, OH, guitar/vocals), Pete Farndon (born 12/6/1952, Hereford, bass), Gerry Mackleduff (drums) and James Honeyman-Scott (born 4/11/1956, Hereford, guitar). After recording the first single Mackleduff was replaced by Martin Chambers (born 4/9/1951, Hereford). Farndon was fired in June 1982 and replaced by Billy Bremner (born 1947, Scotland, lead guitar) and Malcolm Foster (bass). Hynde had a daughter by Ray Davies (of the Kinks) and was due to marry him, but the vicar postponed the wedding after the pair argued just before the ceremony. Their relationship ended, and Hynde married Jim Kerr (Simple Minds) in 1984. By 1994 the group comprised Hynde, Chambers, Adam Seymour (guitar) and Andy Hobson (bass). Honeyman-Scott died from cocaine and heroin addiction on 16/6/1982. Farndon died from a drug overdose on 14/4/1983.

| DATE | POS | WKS | BPI | ALBUM TITLE | LABEL & NUMBER |
|------|-----|-----|-----|-------------|----------------|
| 19/01/1980 | ❶4 | 35 | ● | **PRETENDERS** | Real RAL 3 |
| 15/08/1981 | 7 | 27 | ○ | **PRETENDERS II** | Real SRK 3572 |
| 21/01/1984 | 11 | 16 | ● | LEARNING TO CRAWL | Real WX 2 |
| 01/11/1986 | 6 | 28 | ● | **GET CLOSE** | Real WX 64 |
| 07/11/1987 | 6 | 32 | ✪3 | **THE SINGLES** The album changed its label and catalogue number to WEA K 2422292 during its chart run | Real WX 135 |
| 26/05/1990 | 19 | 5 | ○ | PACKED! | WEA WX 346 |
| 21/05/1994 | 8 | 13 | ● | **LAST OF THE INDEPENDENTS** | WEA 4509958222 |
| 28/10/1995 | 23 | 4 | | THE ISLE OF VIEW | WEA 0630120592 |
| 29/05/1999 | 32 | 2 | | VIVA EL AMOR | WEA 3984271522 |
| 30/09/2000 | 21 | 8 | ● | GREATEST HITS | warner.esp 8573846072 |
| 31/05/2003 | 55 | 1 | | LOOSE SCREW | Eagle EAGCD256 |

**PRETTY THINGS** UK rock group formed in Sidcup in 1963 by Dick Taylor (born 28/1/1943, Dartford, lead guitar), Phil May (born 9/11/1944, Dartford, vocals), Viv Prince (born 9/8/1944, Loughborough, drums), Brian Pendleton (born 13/4/1944, Wolverhampton, rhythm guitar) and John Stax (born John Fullegar, 6/4/1944, Crayford, bass). They signed with Fontana the same year. Prince was replaced by Skip Alan (born Alan Skipper, 11/6/1948, London) in 1965. They then added Wally Allen (bass/vocals) and John Povey (born 20/8/1944, London, keyboards/vocals) to the line-up. The group disbanded in 1977 (following numerous personnel changes), but re-formed in 1980 with May, Taylor, Povey, Allen, Alan and Peter Tolson (born 10/9/1951, Bishops Stortford, guitar). Pendleton died from liver cancer on 16/5/2001.

| | | | | | |
|------|-----|-----|-----|-------------|----------------|
| 27/03/1965 | 6 | 10 | | **PRETTY THINGS** | Fontana TL 5239 |
| 27/06/1970 | 43 | 3 | | PARACHUTE | Harvest SHVL 774 |

**ALAN PRICE** UK singer/keyboard player (born 19/4/1941, Fairfield) who formed the Alan Price Trio in 1960 with Chas Chandler and John Steel. The group later evolved into the Alan Price Combo and then the Animals. He left them in 1965 to re-form the Combo with Boots Slade (bass), Roy Mills (drums), John Walters (trumpet), Terry Childs (saxophone), Steve Gregor (saxophone) and Pete Kirtley, changing the name to the Alan Price Set before the release of their first single.

| | | | | | |
|------|-----|-----|-----|-------------|----------------|
| 08/06/1974 | 9 | 10 | ○ | **BETWEEN TODAY AND YESTERDAY** | Warner Brothers K 56032 |

**CHARLEY PRIDE** US singer (born 18/3/1938 on a cotton farm, Sledge, MS – after his recording success he bought the farm) who began as a professional baseball player with Los Angeles Angels but switched to music when he was told he wasn't good enough. He signed with RCA in 1965 and has become the most successful black country music singer of all time, although it was initially planned to disguise his colour for fear of affecting sales. In 1967 he became the first black performer to appear at the Grand Ole Opry in 42 years, following DeFord Bailey in 1925 (the first black performer at the venue). He has won three Grammy Awards: Best Sacred Recording,

Musical in 1971 for *Did You Think To Pray,* Best Gospel Performance (Other Than Soul) also 1971 for *Let Me Live* and Best Country & Western Vocal Performance, Male in 1972 for *Charley Pride Sings Heart Songs.* He has a star on the Hollywood Walk of Fame.

| | | | | |
|---|---|---|---|---|
| 10/04/1971 | 29 | 1 | | CHARLEY PRIDE SPECIAL ....................................................................... RCA Victor SF 8171 |
| 28/05/1977 | 34 | 2 | | SHE'S JUST AN OLD LOVE TURNED MEMORY ........................................ RCA Victor PL 12261 |
| 03/06/1978 | 48 | 2 | ● | SOMEONE LOVES YOU HONEY ............................................................... RCA Victor PL 12478 |
| 26/01/1980 | 6 | 12 | ● | **GOLDEN COLLECTION** ................................................................................ K-Tel NE 1056 |

### MAXI PRIEST
UK singer (born Max Elliott, 10/6/1960, London) of Jamaican parentage. He was christened Max because his mother was a fan of Max Bygraves and took his professional name after his conversion to Rastafarianism. He began his career building sound systems and then he toured with the Saxon Assembly. His biggest solo hit was a record produced by Sly and Robbie in Jamaica. He later worked with Soul II Soul.

| | | | | |
|---|---|---|---|---|
| 06/12/1986 | 96 | 1 | | INTENTIONS ........................................................................................ 10 Records DIX 32 |
| 05/12/1987 | 25 | 15 | ● | MAXI .................................................................................................. 10 Records DIX 64 |
| 14/07/1990 | 11 | 13 | ● | BONAFIDE ........................................................................................... 10 Records DIX 92 |
| 09/11/1991 | 23 | 5 | ● | THE BEST OF ME ................................................................................ 10 Records DIX 111 |
| 14/11/1992 | 60 | 1 | | FE REAL ............................................................................................ 10 Records DIXCD 113 |

### PRIMAL SCREAM
UK rock group formed in Glasgow in 1984 by Bobby Gillespie (born 22/6/1964, Glasgow, vocals), the only constant member. The line-up has featured Robert Young, Andrew Innes, Henry Olsen, Tobay Toman, Jim Beattie, Hugo Nicolson, Martin Duffy, Denise Johnson and two DJs as it evolved from a metal band to a dance-fusion act. They signed with Creation in 1985, spent a brief spell at Warner's and then returned to Creation in 1989. They added ex-Stone Roses bass player Gary Mountfield in 1996. They took their name from Arthur Janov's book *Prisoner Of Pain* that referred to primal therapy.

| | | | | |
|---|---|---|---|---|
| 17/10/1987 | 62 | 1 | | SONIC FLOWER GROOVE ....................................................................... Elevation ELV 2 |
| 05/10/1991 | 8 | 30 | ● | **SCREAMADELICA** 1992 Mercury Music Prize ................................................ Creation CRELP 076 |
| 09/04/1994 | 2 | 18 | ● | **GIVE OUT, BUT DON'T GIVE UP** ................................................................. Creation CRECD 146 |
| 19/07/1997 | 2 | 10 | ● | **VANISHING POINT** ................................................................................ Creation CRECD 178 |
| 08/11/1997 | 43 | 1 | | ECHO DEK ........................................................................................... Creation CRECD 224 |
| 12/02/2000 | 3 | 10 | ● | **EXTERMINATOR** ................................................................................... Creation CRECD 239 |
| 17/08/2002 | 9 | 3 | | **EVIL HEAT** ......................................................................................... Columbia 5089232 |
| 15/11/2003 | 25 | 3 | | DIRTY HITS .......................................................................................... Columbia 5136039 |

### PRIMITIVES
UK group formed in 1985 by Keiron (vocals), Paul Court (guitar/vocals), Steve Dullaghan (bass) and Pete Tweedie (drums). Keiron was subsequently replaced by Australian singer Tracy Tracy and the group launched the Lazy label in 1988. Tweedie was subsequently replaced by Tig Williams and Dullaghan by Andy Hobson.

| | | | | |
|---|---|---|---|---|
| 09/04/1988 | 6 | 10 | ● | **LOVELY** ............................................................................................. Lazy PL 71688 |
| 02/09/1989 | 73 | 1 | | LAZY 86–88 ......................................................................................... Lazy 15 |
| 28/10/1989 | 33 | 2 | | PURE ................................................................................................. RCA PL 74252 |

### PRIMUS
US rock group formed in San Francisco, CA in 1984 by Les Claypool (bass/vocals), Todd Huth (guitar) and Tim 'Herb' Alexander (drums). Huth left the group before they recorded their debut and was replaced by Larry Lalonde. The group financed their debut recording and released it on their own Prawn Song label before signing with Interscope.

| | | | | |
|---|---|---|---|---|
| 08/05/1993 | 56 | 1 | | PORK SODA ......................................................................................... Interscope 7567922572 |

### PRINCE
US singer/guitarist/producer (born Prince Rogers Nelson, 7/6/1958, Minneapolis, MN) who began writing songs in 1970 and joined Grand Central in 1972 (with Prince's friend Andre Cymon). He formed Flyte Tyme in 1974 with Morris Day, Jellybean Johnson, Terry Lewis and Alexander O'Neal among the members. After a brief spell with 94 East (who also featured Colonel Abrams) he signed a solo deal with Warner's in 1977, with an agreement that he could produce himself, then almost unheard of in the industry, and his debut album appeared in 1988. One of the first black artists to receive extensive airplay on MTV, he later changed his name to a hieroglyphic (known as symbol) and then Artist Formerly Known As Prince (or AFKAP for short). Prince has won seven BRIT Awards including: Best International Male in 1985, 1992, 1993, 1995 and 1996. He also won an Oscar in 1984 for *Purple Rain* in the Best Original Song Score category. He married dancer Mayte Garcia on Valentine's Day in 1996, had the marriage annulled and then remarried her on Valentine's Day in 1999. He has won four Grammy Awards including: Best Rhythm & Blues Song in 1984 for *I Feel For You* and Best Rhythm & Blues Vocal Performance in 1986 for *Kiss.* He was inducted into the Rock & Roll Hall of Fame in 2004.

| | | | | |
|---|---|---|---|---|
| 21/07/1984 | 7 | 91 | ✪² | **PURPLE RAIN** Original soundtrack to the film ▲²⁴ ◆¹³ PRINCE AND THE REVOLUTION 1984 Grammy Awards for Best Rock Vocal Performance by a Group and Best Album of Original Score Written for a Motion Picture, and the 1985 BRIT Award for Best Soundtrack Album ............................................ Warner Brothers 9251101 |
| 08/09/1984 | 30 | 21 | ○ | 1999 ................................................................................................... Warner Brothers 9237201 |
| 04/05/1985 | 5 | 20 | ● | **AROUND THE WORLD IN A DAY** ▲³ .......................................................... Warner Brothers 9252861 |
| 12/04/1986 | 4 | 26 | ✪ | **PARADE – MUSIC FROM 'UNDER THE CHERRY MOON'** Original soundtrack to the film ............ Warner Brothers WX 39 |
| 11/04/1987 | 4 | 32 | ✪ | **SIGN 'O' THE TIMES** ............................................................................. Paisley Park WX 88 |
| 21/05/1988 | ❶¹ | 32 | ✪ | **LOVESEXY** ......................................................................................... Paisley Park WX 164 |
| 01/07/1989 | ❶¹ | 20 | ✪ | **BATMAN** Original soundtrack to the film ▲⁶ 1990 BRIT Award for Best Soundtrack Album .............. Warner Brothers WX 281 |

| DATE | POS | WKS | BPI | ALBUM TITLE | LABEL & NUMBER |
|---|---|---|---|---|---|
| 01/09/1990 | ❶¹ | 8 | ● | **GRAFFITI BRIDGE** | Paisley Park WX 361 |
| 24/08/1991 | 33 | 3 | | GETT OFF | Paisley Park 9401382 |
| 12/10/1991 | 2 | 57 | ◐ | **DIAMONDS AND PEARLS** | Paisley Park WX 432 |
| 17/10/1992 | ❶¹ | 21 | ◐ | **SYMBOLS** This and the above two hits credited to **PRINCE AND THE NEW POWER GENERATION** | Paisley Park 9362450372 |
| 25/09/1993 | 5 | 27 | ◐ | **THE HITS 1** | Paisley Park 9362454312 |
| 25/09/1993 | 5 | 28 | ◐ | **THE HITS 2** | Paisley Park 9362454352 |
| 25/09/1993 | 4 | 7 | ○ | **THE HITS/THE B-SIDES** | Paisley Park 9362454402 |
| 27/08/1994 | ❶¹ | 8 | ● | **COME** | Warner Brothers 9362457002 |
| 03/12/1994 | 36 | 3 | | THE BLACK ALBUM | Warner Brothers 9362457932 |
| 07/10/1995 | 4 | 5 | ● | **THE GOLD EXPERIENCE** | Warner Brothers 9362459992 |
| 20/07/1996 | 14 | 4 | | CHAOS AND DISORDER | Warner Brothers 9362463172 |
| 30/11/1996 | 18 | 6 | | EMANCIPATION | NPG CDEMD 1102 |
| 04/09/1999 | 47 | 1 | | THE VAULT… OLD FRIENDS 4 SALE | Warner Brothers 9362475222 |
| 11/08/2001 | 2 | 14 | ◐ | **THE VERY BEST OF PRINCE** | Warner Brothers 8122742722 |
| 01/05/2004 | 3 | 6 | ● | **MUSICOLOGY** | Columbia/NPG 5171659 |

### PRINCE CHARLES AND THE CITY BEAT BAND
US group formed in New York City; they also recorded for Greyhound and Solid Platinum Records.

| DATE | POS | WKS | BPI | ALBUM TITLE | LABEL & NUMBER |
|---|---|---|---|---|---|
| 30/04/1983 | 84 | 1 | | STONE KILLERS | Virgin V 2271 |

### PRINCESS
UK singer (real name Desiree Heslop) who was a backing singer for Osibisa, Evelyn Thomas and Precious Wilson before teaming up with Stock Aitken Waterman and the Supreme label. She later returned to being a backing singer, appearing on Vanilla Ice's *To The Extreme* album.

| DATE | POS | WKS | BPI | ALBUM TITLE | LABEL & NUMBER |
|---|---|---|---|---|---|
| 17/05/1986 | 15 | 14 | ○ | PRINCESS | Supreme SU1 |

### PRIORY OF THE RESURRECTION
UK group formed by a community of nuns from Chelmsford. Their album was inspired by the success of the earlier Gregorian Chants record.

| DATE | POS | WKS | BPI | ALBUM TITLE | LABEL & NUMBER |
|---|---|---|---|---|---|
| 31/03/2001 | 68 | 1 | | ETERNAL LIGHT – MUSIC OF INNER PEACE | Deutsche Grammophon 4710902 |

### PROBOT
US drummer (born Dave Grohl, 14/1/1969, Warren, OH) who was previously a member of Nirvana and leader of The Foo Fighters. The Probot project also features contributions from Cronos (of Venom), Max Cavalera, Lemmy (from Motorhead), Mike Dean, Kurt Brecht, Lee Dorrian, Wino (from Obsessed), Tom G Warrior (from Vovoid), Eric Wagner and King Diamond.

| DATE | POS | WKS | BPI | ALBUM TITLE | LABEL & NUMBER |
|---|---|---|---|---|---|
| 28/02/2004 | 34 | 2 | | PROBOT | Southern Lord STHL302 |

### P.J. PROBY
US singer (born James Marcus Smith, 6/11/1938, Houston, TX) who first recorded under the name Jeff Powers in 1958. Introduced by Jack Good to UK audiences in the TV special *Around The Beatles* in May 1964, he signed with Decca shortly after and was promoted in the USA as part of the UK invasion. He caused controversy when his trousers split during a live performance in Luton in 1965. In 1973 his fiancée Claudia Martin (daughter of Dean Martin) ran off with another man, prompting Proby to chase after the couple brandishing a gun. He fired off a couple of warning shots and was subsequently jailed for three months.

| DATE | POS | WKS | BPI | ALBUM TITLE | LABEL & NUMBER |
|---|---|---|---|---|---|
| 27/02/1965 | 16 | 3 | | I'M P.J. PROBY | Liberty LBY 1235 |

### PROCLAIMERS
UK duo formed by twin brothers Charlie and Craig Reid (born 5/3/1962, Edinburgh). They worked with Pete Wingfield on their second album, then took a break to help save Hibernian Football Club, becoming shareholders in the club.

| DATE | POS | WKS | BPI | ALBUM TITLE | LABEL & NUMBER |
|---|---|---|---|---|---|
| 09/05/1987 | 43 | 21 | ● | THIS IS THE STORY | Chrysalis CHR 1602 |
| 24/09/1988 | 6 | 27 | ◐ | **SUNSHINE ON LEITH** | Chrysalis CHR 1668 |
| 19/03/1994 | 8 | 6 | ○ | **HIT THE HIGHWAY** | Chrysalis CDCHR 6066 |
| 09/06/2001 | 61 | 1 | | PERSEVERE | Persevere PERSRECCD 04 |
| 25/05/2002 | 30 | 6 | ● | THE BEST OF | Chrysalis 5396822 |
| 27/09/2003 | 70 | 1 | | BORN INNOCENT | Persevere PERSRECCD 09 |

### PROCOL HARUM
UK rock group formed in 1959 by Gary Brooker (born 29/5/1945, Southend, vocals/piano), Robin Trower (born 9/3/1945, Southend, guitar), Chris Copping (born 29/8/1945, Southend, bass), Bob Scott (vocals) and Mick Brownlee (drums) as the Paramounts. Brownlee left when the group turned professional, replaced by Barry 'BJ' Wilson (born 18/3/1947, Southend). The Paramounts split in 1966 and re-formed as Procol Harum in 1967 with Brooker, Matthew Fisher (born 7/3/1946, Croydon, keyboards), Ray Royer (born 8/10/1945, guitar), Dave Knights (born 28/6/1945, London, bass) and Bobby Harrison (born 28/6/1943, drums). Following the success of their debut single Royer and Harrison were asked to leave and Trower and Wilson replaced them. There were numerous personnel changes up until 1977 when they disbanded. Wilson died from pneumonia in October 1990. The name is either derived from the Latin 'procul', meaning 'far from these things', or from the birth certificate of impresario Guy Steven's pedigree cat 'Procul Harun'. *A Whiter Shade Of Pale* was named Best Single (jointly with Queen's *Bohemian Rhapsody*) at the 1977 BRIT Awards.

| DATE | POS | WKS | BPI | ALBUM TITLE | LABEL & NUMBER |
|---|---|---|---|---|---|
| 19/07/1969 | 27 | 2 | | A SALTY DOG | Regal Zonophone SLRZ 1009 |
| 27/06/1970 | 49 | 1 | | HOME | Regal Zonophone SLRZ 1014 |
| 03/07/1971 | 42 | 1 | | BROKEN BARRICADES | Island ILPS 9158 |
| 06/05/1972 | 26 | 4 | | A WHITER SHADE OF PALE/A SALTY DOG This is a double re-issue of *A Whiter Shade Of Pale* and *A Salty Dog*, although the former was not previously a hit. | Fly Double Back TOOFA 7/8 |
| 06/05/1972 | 48 | 1 | | PROCOL HARUM LIVE IN CONCERT WITH THE EDMONTON SYMPHONY ORCHESTRA | Chrysalis CHR 1004 |
| 30/08/1975 | 41 | 2 | | PROCOL'S NINTH | Chrysalis CHR 1080 |

▲⁹ Number of weeks album topped the US chart   ◆¹² RIAA Diamond Awards   ◇³ IFPI Platinum Europe Awards

**PRODIGY** UK rave group formed in Essex in 1991 by Liam Howlett (born 21/8/1971, Braintree, musical instruments), Maxim Reality (born Keith Palmer, 21/3/1967, MC), Leeroy Thornhill (born 7/10/1969, Peterborough, dancer) and Keith Flint (born 17/9/1969, Braintree, vocals and dancer). The group was signed by Madonna's Maverick label for America. Prodigy was named Best Dance Act at the 1997 MOBO Awards and won the same category at the 1997 and 1998 BRIT Awards. The group has also won six MTV Europe Music Awards: Best Dance Act in 1994, 1996, 1997, 1998, Best Alternative Act in 1997 and Best Video for *Breathe* in 1997 (directed by Walter Stern). Howlett married ex-All Saints member Nicole Appleton in June 2002.

| | | | | |
|---|---|---|---|---|
| 10/10/1992 | 12 | 31 | ✪ | EXPERIENCE .................................................. XL Recordings XLCD 110 |
| 16/07/1994 | ❶¹ | 98 | ✪ | **MUSIC FOR THE JILTED GENERATION** ◇ ................... XL Recordings XLCD 114 |
| 12/07/1997 | ❶⁶ | 60 | ✪³ | **THE FAT OF THE LAND** ◇² ▲¹ .......................... XL Recordings XLCD 121 |

**PROJECT D** UK male synthesiser duo formed by Chris Cozens and Nick Magnus.

| | | | |
|---|---|---|---|
| 17/02/1990 | 13 | 11 | THE SYNTHESIZER ALBUM ............................... Telstar STAR 2371 |
| 29/09/1990 | 25 | 7 | SYNTHESIZER 2 ......................................... Telstar STAR 2428 |

**PRONG** US heavy metal group formed in New York by Tommy Victor (guitar/vocals), Mike Kirkland (bass) and Ted Parsons (drums). Kirkland left in 1991, replaced by Troy Gregory who soon left and was replaced by Paul Raven, with John Bechdel (keyboards) also joining. They disbanded in 1996.

| | | | |
|---|---|---|---|
| 12/02/1994 | 71 | 1 | CLEANSING ............................................ Epic 4747962 |

**PROPAGANDA** German synthesiser pop band formed in the UK by Claudia Brucken (vocals), Michael Mertens (percussion), Susanne Freytag (keyboards) and Ralf Dorper (keyboards). Brucken later married ZTT label boss Paul Morley and formed Act. The group left ZTT for Virgin in 1990, with Brucken remaining at ZTT for a solo career.

| | | | |
|---|---|---|---|
| 13/07/1985 | 16 | 12 | SECRET WISH ........................................... ZTT ZTTIQ 3 |
| 23/11/1985 | 82 | 2 | WISHFUL THINKING ..................................... ZTT ZTTIQ 20 |
| 09/06/1990 | 46 | 2 | 1234 .................................................. Virgin V 2625 |

**PROPELLERHEADS** UK dance duo formed by Alex Gifford (born 29/12/1963) and Will White (born 16/5/1973). Gifford had previously performed with The Grid.

| | | | | |
|---|---|---|---|---|
| 07/02/1998 | 6 | 13 | ● | **DECKSANDRUMSANDROCKANDROLL** ........................ Wall Of Sound WALLCD 015 |

**DOROTHY PROVINE** US singer (born 20/1/1937, Deadwood, SD) who was also an actress, appearing in the long-running TV series *77 Sunset Strip*.

| | | | |
|---|---|---|---|
| 02/12/1961 | 3 | 42 | **THE ROARING TWENTIES – SONGS FROM THE TV SERIES** ........... Warner Brothers WM 4035 |
| 10/02/1962 | 9 | 7 | **VAMP OF THE ROARING TWENTIES** .......................... Warner Brothers WM 4053 |

**PSYCHEDELIC FURS** UK rock group formed in 1979 by Richard Butler (born 5/6/1956, Kingston-upon-Thames, vocals), Vince Ely (drums), Roger Morris (guitar), Tim Butler (born 7/12/1958, Kingston-upon-Thames, bass) and Duncan Kilburn (woodwinds) and signed to CBS in 1980. They later added John Ashton (born 30/11/1957, guitar), although by the end of the 1980s the Furs were a trio of the Butler brothers and Ashton. They disbanded in 1993 with Richard Butler going on to form Love Spit Love.

| | | | | |
|---|---|---|---|---|
| 15/03/1980 | 18 | 6 | | PSYCHEDELIC FURS ...................................... CBS 84084 |
| 23/05/1981 | 30 | 9 | | TALK TALK TALK ........................................ CBS 84892 |
| 02/10/1982 | 20 | 6 | | FOREVER NOW .......................................... CBS 85909 |
| 19/05/1984 | 15 | 9 | | MIRROR MOVES ......................................... CBS 25950 |
| 14/02/1987 | 12 | 5 | ○ | MIDNIGHT TO MIDNIGHT ................................ CBS 4502561 |
| 13/08/1988 | 67 | 2 | | ALL OF THIS AND NOTHING .............................. CBS 4611101 |
| 18/11/1989 | 74 | 1 | | BOOK OF DAYS ......................................... CBS 4659821 |
| 13/07/1991 | 68 | 1 | | WORLD OUTSIDE ....................................... East West WX 422 |

**PUBLIC ENEMY** US rap group formed in 1984 by Chuck D (born Carlton Douglas Ridenhour, 1/8/1960, Long Island, NY), Hank Shocklee and Flavour Flav (born William Drayton, 16/3/1959 Long Island), later adding Professor Griff, Minister of Information (born Richard Griffin) and DJ Terminator X (born Norman Rogers, 25/8/1966, New York). They signed to Def Jam in 1986 and released their first album in 1987. Griff was sacked from the group in 1989 for allegedly making anti-Semitic remarks in a newspaper interview. The group took their name from the 1930s' FBI phrase 'Public Enemy Number One'.

| | | | | |
|---|---|---|---|---|
| 30/07/1988 | 8 | 9 | ○ | **IT TAKES A NATION OF MILLIONS TO HOLD US BACK** ................ Def Jam 4624151 |
| 28/04/1990 | 4 | 10 | ● | **FEAR OF A BLACK PLANET** ................................. Def Jam 4662811 |
| 19/10/1991 | 8 | 7 | ○ | **APOCALYPSE 91... THE ENEMY STRIKES BLACK** ................ Def Jam 4687511 |
| 03/10/1992 | 14 | 3 | | GREATEST MISSES ...................................... Def Jam 4720312 |
| 03/09/1994 | 12 | 3 | | MUSE SICK-N-HOUR MESS AGE ............................ Def Jam 5233622 |
| 16/05/1998 | 50 | 4 | | HE GOT GAME Original soundtrack to the film ................ Def Jam 5581302 |
| 31/07/1999 | 55 | 1 | | THERE'S A POISON GOIN' ON... .......................... PIAS Recordings PIASXCD 004 |

**PUBLIC IMAGE LTD.** UK rock group formed in 1978 by John Lydon (born 31/1/1956, London) who had just finished touring with Sex Pistols under the name Johnny Rotten, Keith Levene (ex-Clash), Jah Wobble (born John Wardle) and Jim Walker. They signed with the same label as the Sex Pistols and often released their records as P.I.L.

○ Silver disc ● Gold disc ✪ Platinum disc (additional platinum units are indicated by a figure following the symbol) ❶⁹ Number of weeks album topped the UK chart

| | | | | | |
|---|---|---|---|---|---|
| 23/12/1978 | 22 | 11 | ⭘ | PUBLIC IMAGE | Virgin V 2114 |
| 08/12/1979 | 18 | 8 | | METAL BOX | Virgin METAL 1 |
| 08/03/1980 | 46 | 2 | | SECOND EDITION OF PIL | Virgin VD 2512 |
| 22/11/1980 | 61 | 2 | | PARIS AU PRINTEMPS (PARIS IN THE SPRING) | Virgin V 2183 |
| 18/04/1981 | 11 | 5 | | FLOWERS OF ROMANCE | Virgin V 2189 |
| 08/10/1983 | 28 | 6 | | PIL LIVE IN TOKYO | Virgin VGD 3508 |
| 21/07/1984 | 56 | 2 | | THIS IS WHAT YOU WANT… THIS IS WHAT YOU GET | Virgin V 2309 |
| 15/02/1986 | 14 | 6 | | ALBUM/CASSETTE | Virgin V 2366 |
| 26/09/1987 | 40 | 2 | | HAPPY? | Virgin V 2455 |
| 10/06/1989 | 36 | 2 | | 9 | Virgin V 2588 |
| 10/11/1990 | 20 | 3 | | THE GREATEST HITS, SO FAR | Virgin V 2644 |
| 07/03/1992 | 46 | 2 | | THAT WHAT IS NOT | Virgin CDV 2681 |

**GARY PUCKETT AND THE UNION GAP** US singer/guitarist Gary Puckett (born 17/10/1942, Hibbing, MN) formed Union Gap in San Diego, CA in 1967, taking the name from the town of the same name in Washington. Other members included Kerry Chater (bass), Paul Whitebread (drums), Dwight Bement (saxophone) and Gary Withem (keyboards).

| | | | | | |
|---|---|---|---|---|---|
| 29/06/1968 | 24 | 4 | | UNION GAP | CBS 63342 |

**PUDDLE OF MUDD** US rock group formed by Wesley Scantlin (guitar/vocals), Paul Phillips (guitar/vocals), Douglas Ardito (bass/vocals) and Greg Upchurch (drums/vocals).

| | | | | | |
|---|---|---|---|---|---|
| 02/02/2002 | 12 | 36 | ✪ | COME CLEAN | Interscope 4930742 |

**PUFF DADDY** US rapper/record company boss/producer (born Sean Combs, 4/11/1970, New York) who launched the Bad Boy and Puff Daddy labels. He produced The Notorious B.I.G. and Mariah Carey. In September 1999 he was arrested after beating up a record company representative following an argument over a promotional video. In December 1999 he was arrested and charged with illegal possession of a firearm after a nightclub shooting left three people injured. He later amended his name to P Diddy. He has won three Grammy Awards including: Best Rap Performance by a Group in 1997 with Faith Evans and 112 for *I'll Be Missing You* and Best Rap Performance by a Duo or Group with P Diddy and Murphy Lee for *Shake Ya Tailfeather* in 2003. He has also won three MOBO Awards: Best Producer in 1997 and Best International Act and Outstanding Achievement in 1998.

| | | | | | |
|---|---|---|---|---|---|
| 02/08/1997 | 8 | 13 | ● | **NO WAY OUT** ◇ ▲⁴ 1997 Grammy Award for Best Rap Album | Puff Daddy 78612730122 |
| 04/09/1999 | 9 | 6 | ● | **FOREVER** | Puff Daddy 74321689052 |
| 08/06/2002 | 17 | 12 | ● | WE INVENTED THE REMIX **P DIDDY AND THE BAD BOY FAMILY** | Puff Daddy 74321945402 |

**PULP** UK rock group formed in 1981 by Jarvis Cocker (born 19/9/1963, Sheffield, guitar/vocals), Peter Dalton (keyboards), Jamie Pinchbeck (bass) and Wayne Furniss (drums). The line-up by 1992 consisted of Cocker, Russell Senior (born 18/5/1961, Sheffield, guitar), Candida Doyle (born 25/8/1963, Belfast, keyboards), Stephen Mackay (born 10/11/1966, Sheffield, bass) and Nicholas Banks (born 28/7/1965, Rotherham, drums). Senior left in 1995, replaced by Mark Webber (born 14/9/1970).

| | | | | | |
|---|---|---|---|---|---|
| 30/04/1994 | 9 | 43 | ● | **HIS 'N' HERS** | Island CID 8025 |
| 11/11/1995 | ❶¹ | 62 | ✪⁴ | **DIFFERENT CLASS** ◇ 1996 Mercury Music Prize | Island CID 8041 |
| 23/03/1996 | 10 | 6 | | **COUNTDOWN 1992–1983** | Nectar Masters NTMCDD 521 |
| 11/04/1998 | ❶¹ | 21 | ● | **THIS IS HARDCORE** | Island CID 8066 |
| 03/11/2001 | 6 | 3 | ⭘ | **WE LOVE LIFE** | Island CID 8110 |
| 30/11/2002 | 71 | 1 | | **HITS** | Island CID 8126 |

**PURESSENCE** UK group formed in Manchester by James Murdriezki (vocals), Tony Szuminski (drums), Neil McDonald (guitar) and Kevin Matthews (bass).

| | | | | | |
|---|---|---|---|---|---|
| 29/08/1998 | 36 | 2 | | ONLY FOREVER | Island CID 8064 |

**Q-TIPS** UK group formed by Paul Young (born 17/1/1956, Luton, vocals), Garth Watt-Roy (guitar), Ian Kewley (keyboards), Mick Pearl (bass), Steve Farr (saxophone), Stewart Blandamer (saxophone), Tony Hughes (trumpet) and Barry Watts (drums). Young and Pearl had previously been members of Streetband. The group disbanded in 1982 with Paul Young launching a solo career.

| 30/08/1980 | 50 | 1 | | Q-TIPS | Chrysalis CHR 1255 |

**QFX** UK producer Kirk Turnbull.

| 08/03/1997 | 62 | 1 | | ALIEN CHILD | Epidemic EPICD 9 |

**SUZI QUATRO** US singer and bass player (born Susan Kay Quatrocchio, 3/6/1950, Detroit, MI) who left school in 1964 and formed the Pleasure Seekers with her sisters, and later progressive rock act Cradle. In 1970 she relocated to London and signed with Mickie Most at RAK. She signed with Dreamland (the label set up by her hit writers Nicky Chinn and Mike Chapman) in 1980, but re-signed with RAK in 1983. Quatro also made her name as an actress, appearing as Leather Tuscadero in the TV series *Happy Days*.

| 13/10/1973 | 32 | 4 | O | SUZI QUATRO | RAK SRAK 505 |
| 26/04/1980 | 4 | 9 | ● | **SUZI QUATRO'S GREATEST HITS** | RAK EMTV 24 |

**FINLEY QUAYE** UK singer (born 25/3/1974, Edinburgh) of Ghanaian ancestry and from a musical background: he is Tricky's uncle, his father is a jazz composer and his brother, Caleb, is a top session guitarist. He was named Best Reggae Act at the 1997 MOBO Awards and Best British Male Artist at the 1998 BRIT Awards.

| 04/10/1997 | 3 | 56 | ✪ | **MAVERICK A STRIKE** | Epic 4887582 |
| 14/10/2000 | 35 | 2 | | VANGUARD | Epic 4997102 |
| 11/10/2003 | 56 | 1 | | MUCH MORE THAN LOVE | Sony Music 05125492 |

**QUEEN** UK group formed in London in 1970 by Brian May (born 19/7/1947, London, guitar), Roger Taylor (born Roger Meddows-Taylor, 26/1/1949, King's Lynn, Norfolk, drums), John Deacon (born 19/8/1951, Leicester, bass) and Freddie Mercury (born Farookh Bulsura, 5/9/1946, Zanzibar, Tanzania, vocals). They played their first date in 1971, signed with EMI in 1972 and were subsequently managed by Elton John's manager John Reid. All members undertook outside projects: Mercury recorded solo from 1985; Taylor produced actor Jimmy Nail; May formed the Immortals and he and Deacon worked with Elton John. Queen was the biggest hit at Live Aid in 1985. Mercury died from AIDS on 24/11/1991. The group was honoured with the Outstanding Contribution Award at the 1990 BRIT Awards, whilst *Bohemian Rhapsody* was named Best Single in 1992 (having won the same award in 1977 jointly with Procol Harum's *A Whiter Shade Of Pale*). Mercury was posthumously given a further Outstanding Contribution Award in 1992 (he and John Lennon being the only artists to have received it twice). *Bohemian Rhapsody* is one of only five singles to have sold more than 2 million copies in the UK. Inducted into the Rock & Roll Hall of Fame in 2001, Queen has a star on the Hollywood Walk of Fame.

| 23/03/1974 | 5 | 29 | ● | QUEEN 2 | EMI EMA 767 |
| 30/03/1974 | 24 | 18 | ● | QUEEN | EMI EMC 3006 |
| 23/11/1974 | 2 | 42 | ✪ | **SHEER HEART ATTACK** | EMI EMC 3061 |
| 13/12/1975 | ●4 | 50 | ✪ | **A NIGHT AT THE OPERA** | EMI EMTC 103 |
| 25/12/1976 | ●1 | 24 | ● | **A DAY AT THE RACES** | EMI EMTC 103 |
| 12/11/1977 | 4 | 20 | ● | **NEWS OF THE WORLD** | EMI EMA 784 |
| 25/11/1978 | 2 | 27 | ● | **JAZZ** | EMI EMA 788 |
| 07/07/1979 | 3 | 27 | ● | **LIVE KILLERS** | EMI EMSP 330 |
| 12/07/1980 | ●2 | 18 | ● | **THE GAME** ▲5 | EMI EMA 795 |
| 20/12/1980 | 10 | 15 | ● | **FLASH GORDON** Original soundtrack to the film | EMI EMC 3351 |
| 07/11/1981 | ●4 | 450 | ✪11 | **QUEEN'S GREATEST HITS** | Parlophone EMYV 30 |
| 15/05/1982 | 4 | 19 | ● | **HOT SPACE** | EMI EMA 797 |
| 10/03/1984 | 2 | 93 | ✪ | **THE WORKS** The album changed catalogue number to WORK1 during its chart run. | EMI EMC 240014 |
| 14/06/1986 | ●1 | 63 | ✪2 | **A KIND OF MAGIC** | EMI EU 3509 |
| 13/12/1986 | 3 | 43 | ✪ | **LIVE MAGIC** | EMI EMC 3519 |
| 03/06/1989 | ●1 | 32 | ✪ | **THE MIRACLE** | Parlophone PCSD 107 |
| 16/12/1989 | 67 | 1 | | QUEEN AT THE BEEB | Band Of Joy BOJLP 001 |
| 16/02/1991 | ●2 | 37 | ✪ | **INNUENDO** | Parlophone PCSD 115 |
| 09/11/1991 | ●5 | 106 | ✪8 | **GREATEST HITS II** | Parlophone PMTV 2 |
| 06/06/1992 | 2 | 15 | ● | **LIVE AT WEMBLEY** | Parlophone CDPCSP 725 |
| 19/11/1994 | 37 | 7 | | GREATEST HITS I & II | Parlophone CDPCSD 161 |
| 18/11/1995 | ●1 | 28 | ✪4 | **MADE IN HEAVEN** ◇5 | Parlophone CDPCSD 167 |
| 15/11/1997 | 7 | 12 | ✪ | **QUEEN ROCKS** | Parlophone 8230912 |
| 20/11/1999 | 5 | 19 | ✪ | **GREATEST HITS III** ◇ | Parlophone 5238942 |

○ Silver disc ● Gold disc ✪ Platinum disc (additional platinum units are indicated by a figure following the symbol) ●9 Number of weeks album topped the UK chart

| | | | | | |
|---|---|---|---|---|---|
| 25/11/2000 | 2 | 93 | ✪³ | GREATEST HITS I II & III ◇² | Parlophone 5298832 |
| 21/06/2003 | 38 | 2 | | LIVE AT WEMBLEY '86 | Parlophone 5904402 |

## QUEENS OF THE STONE AGE
US rock group formed by Josh Homme (guitar/vocals), Nick Oliveri, Dave Catching and Alfredo Hernandez (drums). By 2002 former Foo Fighters and Nirvana member Dave Grohl was drumming for the group.

| | | | | | |
|---|---|---|---|---|---|
| 02/09/2000 | 54 | 3 | O | RATED R | Interscope 4906832 |
| 07/09/2002 | 4 | 22 | O | SONGS FOR THE DEAF | Interscope 4934440 |

## QUEENSRYCHE
US heavy metal group formed in 1981 by Geoff Tate (born 14/1/1959, Stuttgart, vocals), Chris DeGarmo (born 14/6/1963, Wenatchee, WA, guitar), Michael Wilton (born 23/2/1962, San Francisco, CA, guitar), Eddie Jackson (born 29/1/1961, Robstown, TX, bass) Scott Rockenfield (born 15/6/1963, Seattle, WA, drums). All five had been classmates in Bellevue, WA.

| | | | | | |
|---|---|---|---|---|---|
| 29/09/1984 | 100 | 1 | | THE WARNING | EMI America EJ 2402201 |
| 26/07/1986 | 66 | 1 | | RAGE FOR ORDER | EMI America AML 3105 |
| 04/06/1988 | 58 | 3 | | OPERATION MINDCRIME | Manhattan MTL 1023 |
| 22/09/1990 | 13 | 3 | O | EMPIRE | EMI-USA MTL 1058 |
| 22/10/1994 | 13 | 3 | | PROMISED LAND | EMI CDMTL 1081 |
| 29/03/1997 | 46 | 1 | | HEAR IN THE NOW FRONTIER | EMI CDEMC 3764 |

## QUIET RIOT
US heavy metal group formed in 1975 by Kevin DuBrow (vocals), Randy Rhoads (guitar), Kelly Garni (bass) and Drew Forsyth (drums). Their first two albums were available only in Japan, after which Garni left and was replaced by Rudy Sarzo. Rhoads left in 1979 to join Ozzy Osbourne (and was later killed in a plane crash) and Quiet Riot disbanded. The group later re-formed with DuBrow, Sarxo, Carlos Cavazo (guitar) and Frankie Banali (drums). DuBrow left in 1988 and was replaced by Paul Shortino. After one more album the group disbanded a second time.

| | | | | | |
|---|---|---|---|---|---|
| 04/08/1984 | 71 | 1 | | CONDITION CRITICAL | Epic EPC 26075 |

## SINEAD QUINN
Irish singer (born 1980, Irvinestown) who studied musical technology at Hull University and appeared on TV's *Fame Academy*, finishing second behind David Sneddon.

| | | | | | |
|---|---|---|---|---|---|
| 26/07/2003 | 48 | 2 | | READY TO RUN | Fontana 9865367 |

## QUINTESSENCE
UK group formed by Raja Ram (born Ron Rothfield, flute/vocals), Shiva Shanker (also known as Shiva Jones, keyboards/vocals), Alan Mostert (guitar), Maha Dev (guitar), Sambhu Babaji (bass) and Jake Milton (drums).

| | | | | | |
|---|---|---|---|---|---|
| 27/06/1970 | 22 | 4 | | QUINTESSENCE | Island ILPS 9128 |
| 03/04/1971 | 43 | 1 | | DIVE DEEP | Island ILPS 9143 |
| 27/05/1972 | 50 | 1 | | SELF | RCA Victor SF 8273 |

## QUIREBOYS
UK heavy metal group formed in Newcastle-upon-Tyne in 1986 by Nigel Mogg (bass), Chris Johnstone (piano), Gus Bailey (guitar), Jonathon 'Spike' Grey (vocals) and Coze (drums). Originally known as the Queerboys, the name was quickly changed. They were joined by guitarist Ginger who left to form the Wildhearts and who was replaced by Guy 'Griff' Griffin. They released their first two singles on Survival, subsequently switching to Parlophone.

| | | | | | |
|---|---|---|---|---|---|
| 10/02/1990 | 2 | 15 | ● | A BIT OF WHAT YOU FANCY | Parlophone PCS 7335 |
| 27/03/1993 | 31 | 2 | | BITTER SWEET AND TWISTED | Parlophone CSPCSD 120 |

# R

## R & B ORCHESTRA – see JOOLS HOLLAND

**RACING CARS** UK group formed in Manchester in 1975 by ex-Mindbenders Bob Lang (born 10/1/1946, bass) and comprising Graham Headley Williams (guitar), Gareth 'Monty' Mortimer (vocals), Roy Edwards (bass) and Robert Wilding (drums), with Geraint Watkins (piano), Jerry Jumonville (saxophone) and Ray Ennis (guitar) also appearing on the sessions for their debut album.

| | | | |
|---|---|---|---|
| 19/02/1977.....39......6...... | DOWNTOWN MIDNIGHT................................................................Chrysalis CHR 1099 |

**RADIOHEAD** UK rock group formed in Oxford by Thom Yorke (born 7/10/1968, Wellingborough, guitar/vocals), Jonny Greenwood (born 5/11/1971, Oxford, guitar), his brother Colin (born 26/6/1969, Oxford, bass), Ed O'Brien (born 15/4/1968, Oxford, guitar) and Phil Selway (born 23/5/1967, Hemmingford Grey, drums) as On A Friday. The name changed in 1991 to Radiohead (the name came from a Talking Heads song).

| | | | | |
|---|---|---|---|---|
| 06/03/1993.....22.....82......✪ | PABLO HONEY.................................................................Parlophone CDPCS 7360 |
| 25/03/1995.....4.....160......✪³ | THE BENDS ◇.................................................................Parlophone CDPCS 7372 |
| 28/06/1997....❶²....75.....✪³ | OK COMPUTER ◇◇² 1997 Grammy Award for Best Alternative Music Performance...................Parlophone CDNODATA 02 |
| 14/10/2000....❶²....15......✪ | KID A ◇ ▲¹ 2000 Grammy Award for Best Alternative Music Album.................................Parlophone CDKIDA 1 |
| 16/06/2001....❶¹....12......● | AMNESIAC (Special Limited Edition) 2001 Grammy Award for Best Recording Package.............Parlophone CDSFHEIT 45101 |
| 24/11/2001.....23......2...... | I MIGHT BE WRONG Live mini album..............................................Parlophone CDFEIT 45104 |
| 21/06/2003....❶¹....14......✪ | HAIL TO THE THIEF.................................................................Parlophone 5848082 |
| 22/05/2004.....37......1...... | COM LAG 2+2=5.................................................................Parlophone TOCP 66280 |

**RAE AND CHRISTIAN** UK production duo formed in 1995 by Mark Rae and Steve Christian.

| | |
|---|---|
| 10/03/2001.....57......1...... | SLEEPWALKING.................................................................!K7 K7 096CD |

**GERRY RAFFERTY** UK singer/guitarist (born 16/4/1947, Paisley, Scotland) who joined the Humblebums in 1968 (a group that also included comic Billy Connolly), recording two albums for Transatlantic. The group disbanded in 1970 and Rafferty remained with Transatlantic for one solo album, released in 1971, before forming Stealers Wheel in 1972. He left them after recording their debut album, although he was persuaded back when *Stuck In The Middle With You* hit the top ten. He left again in 1975 and resurfaced as a solo artist in 1978. He later became a producer.

| | | | |
|---|---|---|---|
| 25/02/1978.....6.....37......● | CITY TO CITY ▲¹.................................................................United Artists UAS 30104 |
| 02/06/1979.....9.....24......● | NIGHT OWL.................................................................United Artists UAK 30238 |
| 26/04/1980.....15......9......○ | SNAKES AND LADDERS.................................................................United Artists UAK 30298 |
| 25/09/1982.....39......4...... | SLEEPWALKING.................................................................Liberty LBG 30352 |
| 21/05/1988.....43......4...... | NORTH AND SOUTH.................................................................London LONLP 55 |
| 13/02/1993.....73......1...... | A WING AND A PRAYER.................................................................A&M 5174952 |
| 28/10/1995.....17.....20......● | ONE MORE DREAM – THE VERY BEST OF GERRY RAFFERTY.....................................Polygram TV 5292792 |

**RAGE AGAINST THE MACHINE** US group formed in California in 1991 by Tom Morello (born 30/5//1964, New York, guitar), Brad Wilk (born 5/9/1968, Portland, OR, drums), Zack de la Rocha (born 13/1/1970, Long Beach, CA, vocals) and Timmy C (born Tim Commerford, bass). They signed with Epic in 1992 (having rejected advances from Madonna's Maverick label) and won the 1996 Grammy Award for Best Metal Performance for *Tire Me*. They disbanded in October 2000 but still won the 2000 Grammy Award for Best Hard Rock Performance for *Guerrilla Radio*, at the ceremony held in February 2001.

| | | | |
|---|---|---|---|
| 13/02/1993.....17.....43......● | RAGE AGAINST THE MACHINE.................................................................Epic 4722242 |
| 27/04/1996.....4......7......○ | EVIL EMPIRE ▲¹.................................................................Epic 4810262 |
| 13/11/1999.....23......2...... | THE BATTLE OF LOS ANGELES ▲¹.................................................................Epic 4919932 |

09/12/2000.....71......1...... RENEGADES.................................................................Epic 4999219

**RAGGA TWINS** UK vocal duo formed in 1990 by Flinty Badman and Deman Rocker.
01/06/1991.....26......5...... REGGAE OWES ME MONEY.....................................................Shut Up And Dance SUADLP 2

**RAGING SPEEDHORN** UK metal group formed in Corby, Northants in 1998 by Jon Loughlin (vocals), Frank Regan (vocals), Tony Loughlin (guitar), Gareth Smith (guitar), Darren Smith (bass/vocals) and Gordon Morrison (drums).
17/08/2002.....63......1...... WE WILL BE DEAD TOMORROW....................................................ZTT RSH 002CD

**RAH BAND** UK multi-instrumentalist Richard Anthony Hewson (born in Stockton-in-Tees) whose initials formed the name of the band. He was an arranger for Apple and was responsible for hits by Mary Hopkin, James Taylor and The Beatles.
06/04/1985.....60......6...... MYSTERY......................................................................RCA PL 70640

**RAHMAN** Indian composer (born AS Dileep Kumar, 6/1/1966, Madra) who followed his father into composing for films and adopted the name Allah Rakha Rahman after converting to Islam in 1988. He has won numerous Indian awards for his compositions, including the Padmashree from the Indian Government in 2000. He first came to the attention of western audiences after composing the music for the Andrew Lloyd Webber musical *Bombay Dreams*.
29/06/2002.....61......1...... RAHMAN/BOMBAY DREAMS......................................................Sony Classical 5084352

**RAILWAY CHILDREN** UK rock group formed in 1985 by Gary Newby (born 5/6/1966, Australia, guitar/vocals), Brian Bateman (born 3/8/1966, Wigan, guitar), Stephen Hull (born 7/7/1966, Wigan, bass) and Guy Keegan (born 16/6/1966, Wigan, drums). They added Tony Martin (keyboards) in 1987 and were initially linked with Factory Records, albeit without a contract. They signed with Virgin towards the end of the year, but had disbanded by 1995.
21/05/1988.....96......1...... RECURRENCE...................................................................Virgin V 2525
16/03/1991.....59......2...... NATIVE PLACE.................................................................Virgin V 2627

**RAIN PARADE** US rock group formed in Los Angeles, CA by David Roback (guitar/vocals), his brother Steve (bass/vocals), Matthew Puicci (guitar/vocals), Will Glenn (keyboards) and Eddie Kalwa (drums). David Roback and Kalwa left in 1984 and were replaced by John Thoman and Mark Marcum respectively.
29/06/1985.....78......1...... BEYOND THE SUNSET...........................................................Island IMA 17

**RAIN TREE CROW** UK group formed in 1991 by David Sylvian (born David Batt, 23/2/1958, London, guitar/vocals), Steve Jansen (born Stephen Batt, 1/12/1959, London, drums), Richard Barbieri (born 30/11/1957, keyboards) and Mick Karn (born Anthony Michaelides, 24/7/1958, London, bass). The four had previously been members of Japan from 1977–82, with Sylvian and Karn subsequently recording solo. Karn also linked with Peter Murphy (formerly of Bauhaus) to record one album as Dali's Car.
20/04/1991.....24......3...... RAIN TREE CROW..............................................................Virgin V 2659

**RAINBOW** UK heavy rock group formed in 1975 by ex-Deep Purple guitarist Ritchie Blackmore (born 14/4/1945, Weston-super-Mare), Ronnie James Dio (born 10/7/1949, Cortland, NY, vocals), Mickey Lee Soule (keyboards), Craig Gruber (bass) and Gary Driscoll (drums) as Ritchie Blackmore's Rainbow. Blackmore re-formed the group in 1976 with Dio, Tony Carey (born 16/10/1953, Fresno, CA, keyboards), Cozy Powell (born 29/12/1947, Cirencester, drums) and Jimmy Bain (bass). Bain was fired in 1977 and replaced by Mark Clarke. Carey and Clarke were fired in May 1977 and replaced by David Stone (keyboards) and Bob Daisley (bass). In 1978 Blackmore sacked all of the band except Powell and brought in Don Airey (keyboards), Graham Bonnet (born 12/12/1947, Skegness, vocals) and Roger Glover (born 30/11/1945, Brecon, Powys, bass). Powell resigned in 1980 (replaced by Bobby Rondinelli), Bonnet left a month later (replaced by Joe Lynn Turne), Airey left in 1981 (replaced by Dave Rosenthal) and Rondinelli left soon after (replaced by Chuck Burgi). Blackmore disbanded the group in 1984 and rejoined Deep Purple. Powell was killed in a car crash on 5/4/1998.

13/09/1975.....11......6......O RICHIE BLACKMORE'S RAINBOW...................................................Oyster OYA 2001
05/06/1976.....11......33......O RAINBOW RISING This and the above hit credited to **RICHIE BLACKMORE'S RAINBOW**.....................Polydor 2490 137
30/07/1977.....7......10......O **ON STAGE**..................................................................Polydor 2657 016
06/05/1978.....7......12......O **LONG LIVE ROCK 'N' ROLL**...................................................Polydor POLD 5002
18/08/1979.....6......37......● **DOWN TO EARTH**.............................................................Polydor POLD 5023
21/02/1981.....3......22......● **DIFFICULT TO CURE**.........................................................Polydor POLD 5036
08/08/1981.....91......2...... RICHIE BLACKMORE'S RAINBOW **RICHIE BLACKMORE'S RAINBOW**.......................Polydor 2940 141
21/11/1981.....14......17......● BEST OF RAINBOW..............................................................Polydor POLDV 2
24/04/1982.....5......14......O **STRAIGHT BETWEEN THE EYES**.................................................Polydor POLD 5056
17/09/1983.....11......6...... BENT OUT OF SHAPE.............................................................Polydor POLD 5116
08/03/1986.....31......4...... FINYL VINYL..................................................................Polydor PODV 8

**RAINDANCE** UK studio group formed by producers Bradley and Stewart James. They also recorded as School Of Excellence.
27/04/1996.....15......7......O RAINDANCE....................................................................Polygram TV 5298622

**BONNIE RAITT** US singer (born 8/11/1949, Burbank, CA) who signed with Warner Brothers in 1971, and whose debut album covered blues, R&B and country material. She went into semi-retirement in the mid-1980s (to battle alcoholism), but re-emerged at the end of the 1980s with a new record deal. She has won nine Grammy Awards including: Best Traditional Blues Recording in 1989 with John Lee Hooker for *I'm In The Mood,* Best Female Pop Vocal Performance in 1991 for *Something To Talk About,* Best Rock Performance by a Duo in 1991 with Delbert McClinton for *Good Man, Good Woman,* and Best Rock Instrumental in 1996 with

Jimmie Vaughan, Eric Clapton, Robert Cray, BB King, Buddy Guy, Dr John and Art Neville for *SRV Shuffle*. She was inducted into the Rock & Roll Hall of Fame in 2000 and has a star on the Hollywood Walk of Fame.

| | | | | |
|---|---|---|---|---|
| 28/04/1990 | 51 | 5 | NICK OF TIME ▲³ 1989 Grammy Awards for Album of the Year, Best Pop Vocal Performance and Best Rock Vocal Performance | Capitol EST 2095 |
| 06/07/1991 | 38 | 3 | LUCK OF THE DRAW 1991 Grammy Award for Best Rock Solo Vocal Performance | Capitol EST 2145 |
| 16/04/1994 | 26 | 5 | LONGING IN THEIR HEARTS ▲¹ 1994 Grammy Award for Best Pop Album | Capitol CDEST 2227 |
| 25/11/1995 | 69 | 1 | ROAD TESTED | Capitol CDEST 2274 |
| 18/04/1998 | 52 | 1 | FUNDAMENTAL | Capitol 8563972 |
| 24/05/2003 | 37 | 2 | THE BEST OF BONNIE RAITT 1989–2003 | Capitol 5821132 |

**RAKIM** US rapper (born William Griffin, 28/1/1968, Long Island, NY) originally with Erik B And Rakim with Eric Barrier. The pair later produced a number of acts for MCA including Jody Watley and appeared in the 1994 film *Gunmen*. Rakim later went solo.

| | | | | |
|---|---|---|---|---|
| 22/11/1997 | 72 | 1 | 18TH LETTER | Universal UD2 53111 |

**KAREN RAMIREZ** UK dance singer (born Karen Ramelize).

| | | | | |
|---|---|---|---|---|
| 01/08/1998 | 45 | 2 | DISTANT DREAMS | Manifesto 5369462 |

**RAMONES** US rock group formed in New York in 1974 by Johnny (born John Cummings, 8/10/1951, Long Island, NY, guitar), Joey (born Jeffrey Hyman, 19/5/1952, Forest Hills, NY, vocals) and Ritchie Ramone. Ritchie was soon replaced by Dee Dee (born Douglas Colvin, 18/9/1952, Fort Lee, VA, bass) and Tommy (born Thomas Erdelyi, 29/1/1952, Budapest, Hungary, drums) was added. They signed with Sire in 1975 and released their debut album in 1976. Tommy left the group in 1978 (but remained their producer) and was replaced by Marc Bell (born 15/7/1956, New York), who adopted the name Marky Ramone. Dee Dee left the group in 1989 and was replaced by CJ Ramone (born Christopher Joseph Ward, 8/10/1965, Long Island). The group disbanded in 1996. Joey Ramone died from cancer on 16/4/2001. Dee Dee Ramone was found dead from a drug overdose on 5/6/2002. The group was inducted into the Rock & Roll Hall of Fame in 2002.

| | | | | |
|---|---|---|---|---|
| 23/04/1977 | 45 | 1 | LEAVE HOME | Philips 9103 254 |
| 24/12/1977 | 60 | 2 | ROCKET TO RUSSIA | Sire 9103 255 |
| 07/10/1978 | 32 | 2 | ROAD TO RUIN | Sire SRK 6063 |
| 16/06/1979 | 27 | 8 | IT'S ALIVE | Sire SRK 26074 |
| 19/01/1980 | 14 | 8 | END OF THE CENTURY | Sire SRK 6077 |
| 26/01/1985 | 63 | 3 | TOO TOUGH TO DIE | Beggars Banquet BEGA 59 |
| 31/05/1986 | 38 | 2 | ANIMAL BOY | Beggars Banquet BEGA 70 |
| 10/10/1987 | 78 | 1 | HALFWAY TO SANITY | Beggars Banquet BEGA 89 |
| 19/08/1989 | 75 | 1 | BRAIN DRAIN | Chrysalis CHR 1725 |
| 08/07/1995 | 62 | 1 | ?ADIOS AMIGOS! | Chrysalis CDCHR 6104 |
| 09/06/2001 | 74 | 1 | HEY HO LET'S GO! – ANTHOLOGY | Rhino 8122758172 |

**RANCID** US rock group formed in 1989 by Tim 'Lint' Armstrong (guitar/vocals), Lars Frederiksen (guitar), Matt Freeman (bass) and Brett Reed (drums). Armstrong and Freeman were ex-Operation Ivy and formed Rancid when that band split up. Armstrong was later a member of The Transplants.

| | | | | |
|---|---|---|---|---|
| 02/09/1995 | 55 | 1 | … AND OUT COME THE WOLVES | Epitaph 864442 |
| 04/07/1998 | 32 | 2 | LIFE WON'T WAIT | Epitaph 64972 |
| 05/08/2000 | 68 | 1 | RANCID | Hellcat 04272 |
| 23/03/2002 | 75 | 1 | SPLIT SERIES – VOLUME 3 **RANCID/NOFX** | BYO 079CD |
| 06/09/2003 | 29 | 2 | INDESTRUCTIBLE | WEA 9362485392 |

**SHABBA RANKS** Jamaican singer (born Rexton Rawlson Fernando Gordon, 17/1/1966, Sturgetown) who began recording in 1980 as Jamaican DJ Don, building up a strong following on the island. He signed with Epic in 1990. While he was collecting his first Grammy Award thieves broke into his Jamaican home and virtually emptied it of all belongings.

| | | | | |
|---|---|---|---|---|
| 22/06/1991 | 51 | 2 | AS RAW AS EVER 1991 Grammy Award for Best Reggae Album | Epic 4681021 |
| 22/08/1992 | 71 | 2 | ROUGH AND READY VOL 1 | Epic 4714422 |
| 24/04/1993 | 38 | 6 | X-TRA NAKED 1992 Grammy Award for Best Reggae Album | Epic 4723332 |

**RAPTURE** US rock group formed in New York City in 1998 by Luke Jenner (guitar/vocals), Matt Safer (bass) and Vito Roccoforte (drums). They later added Gabriel Abdruzzi (multi-instruments).

| | | | | |
|---|---|---|---|---|
| 20/09/2003 | 32 | 2 | ECHOES | DFA/Output/Vertigo 9865447 |

**DIZZEE RASCAL** UK rapper (born Dylan Mills, London) who was eighteen at the time of his debut hit. He is also a member of The Roll Deep Crew.

| | | | | | |
|---|---|---|---|---|---|
| 02/08/2003 | 23 | 15 | ● | BOY IN DA CORNER 2003 Mercury Music Prize | XL Recordings XLCD170 |

**RASMUS** Finnish rock group formed in 1995 by schoolfriends Lauri Johannes Ylönen (born 23/4/1979, vocals), Eero Aleksi Heinonen (born 27/11/1979, guitar), Pauli Antero Rantasalmi (born 1/5/1979, guitar) and Aki Markus Hakala (born 28/10/1979, drums).

| | | | | | |
|---|---|---|---|---|---|
| 03/04/2004 | 10 | 13+ | ● | **DEAD LETTERS** | Motor 9806934 |

**ROLAND RAT SUPERSTAR** UK puppet first introduced on *TV AM*. Roland Rat's voice was supplied by David Claridge.

| | | | | |
|---|---|---|---|---|
| 15/12/1984 | 67 | 3 | THE CASSETTE OF THE ALBUM | Rodent RATL 1001 |

**RATT** US heavy metal group formed in Los Angeles in 1981 by Stephen Pearcy (vocals), Warren DiMartini (guitar), Robbin Crosby (guitar), Juan Croucier (bass) and Bobby Blotzer (drums). They signed with Atlantic in 1984; disbanded in 1993. Pearcy formed Arcade.

| DATE | POS | WKS | ALBUM TITLE | LABEL & NUMBER |
|------|-----|-----|-------------|----------------|
| 13/07/1985 | 50 | 2 | INVASION OF YOUR PRIVACY | Atlantic 7812571 |
| 25/10/1986 | 51 | 1 | DANCING UNDERCOVER | Atlantic 7816831 |
| 12/11/1988 | 82 | 1 | REACH FOR THE SKY | Atlantic 7819291 |
| 08/09/1990 | 55 | 1 | DETONATOR | Atlantic 7567821271 |

**SIMON RATTLE** – see NIGEL KENNEDY

**MARK RATTRAY** UK singer who first came to prominence by winning the TV talent contest *Opportunity Knocks* (he was the show's last ever winner).

| 08/12/1990 | 46 | 7 | MARK RATTRAY PERFORMS THE SONGS OF THE MUSICALS | Telstar STAR 2458 |
| 10/10/1992 | 55 | 1 | THE MAGIC OF THE MUSICALS **MARTI WEBB AND MARK RATTRAY** | Quality Television QTV 013 |

**RAVEN** UK rock group formed in Newcastle by John Gallagher (bass/vocals), his brother Mark (guitar) and Rob 'Wacko' Hunter (drums). The group relocated to the US where they signed with Atlantic. Hunter left in 1988 and was replaced by Joe Hasselvander.

| 17/10/1981 | 63 | 3 | ROCK UNTIL YOU DROP | Neat 001 |

**RAVEONETTES** Danish duo formed by Sune Rose Wagner (vocals) and Sharin Foo (bass/vocals), with Manoj Ramdas (guitar) and Jakob Hoyer (drums) appearing on live dates.

| 06/09/2003 | 43 | 1 | CHAIN GANG OF LOVE | Columbia 5123782 |

**SIMON RAYMONDE** – see HAROLD BUDD/ELIZABETH FRASER/ROBIN GUTHRIE/SIMON RAYMONDE

**CHRIS REA** UK singer (born 4/3/1951, Middlesbrough) who joined Magdelene as a replacement for David Coverdale in 1973 and recorded with them for Magnet. The group changed their name to the Beautiful Lovers but disbanded in 1977. Rea signed solo with Magnet and also appeared on Hank Marvin's solo project the same year. He later became an actor, starring in *Parting Shots* (1999).

| 28/04/1979 | 54 | 3 | DELTICS | Magnet MAG 5028 |
| 12/04/1980 | 60 | 1 | TENNIS | Magnet MAG 5032 |
| 03/04/1982 | 52 | 4 | CHRIS REA | Magnet MAGL 5040 |
| 18/06/1983 | 64 | 2 | WATER SIGN | Magnet MAGL 5048 |
| 21/04/1984 | 35 | 7 | WIRED TO THE MOON | Magnet MAGL 5057 |
| 25/05/1985 | 15 | 14 | ○ SHAMROCK DIARIES | Magnet MAGL 5062 |
| 26/04/1986 | 11 | 37 | ❂ ON THE BEACH | Magnet MAGL 5069 |
| 26/09/1987 | 2 | 46 | ❂ **DANCING WITH STRANGERS** | Magnet MAGL 5071 |
| 13/08/1988 | 37 | 10 | ON THE BEACH Re-issue of Magnet MAGL 5069 | Magnet WX 191 |
| 29/10/1988 | 5 | 51 | ❂3 **THE BEST OF CHRIS REA – NEW LIGHT THROUGH OLD WINDOWS** | WEA WX 200 |
| 11/11/1989 | ❶1 | 76 | ❂5 **THE ROAD TO HELL** | WEA WX 317 |
| 09/03/1991 | ❶3 | 37 | ❂2 **AUBERGE** | WEA 9031735801 |
| 14/11/1992 | 4 | 15 | ❂ **GOD'S GREAT BANANA SKIN** | East West 4509909952 |
| 13/11/1993 | 8 | 10 | ● **ESPRESSO LOGIC** | East West 4509943112 |
| 05/11/1994 | 3 | 18 | ❂ **THE BEST OF CHRIS REA** ◇ | East West 4509980402 |
| 23/11/1996 | 43 | 4 | ○ LA PASSION Original soundtrack to the film | East West 0630166952 |
| 31/01/1998 | 10 | 7 | ○ **THE BLUE CAFE** | East West 3984216882 |
| 20/11/1999 | 54 | 1 | THE ROAD TO HELL – PART 2 | East West 8573803992 |
| 14/10/2000 | 26 | 3 | KING OF THE BEACH | East West 8573850172 |
| 01/12/2001 | 69 | 1 | THE VERY BEST OF ◇ | East West 0927421282 |
| 28/09/2002 | 14 | 7 | ○ DANCING DOWN THE STONEY ROAD | Jazzee Blue JBLUECD 01X |
| 03/04/2004 | 27 | 3 | THE BLUE JUKEBOX | Jazzee Blue JBLUECD08X |

**EDDI READER** UK singer (born 28/8/1959, Glasgow) who was a street busker for eight years before fronting Fairground Attraction. She went solo in 1994 and won Best British Female at the 1995 BRIT Awards.

| 07/03/1992 | 34 | 2 | MIRMAMA | RCA PD 75156 |
| 02/07/1994 | 4 | 12 | ● **EDDI READER** | Blanco Y Negro 4509961772 |
| 20/07/1996 | 24 | 5 | CANDYFLOSS AND MEDICINE | Blanco Y Negro 0630151202 |
| 23/05/1998 | 49 | 2 | ANGELS & ELECTRICITY | Blanco Y Negro 3984228162 |

**REAL MCCOY** German/US trio: Olaf 'OJ' Jeglitza, Patricia 'Patsy' Petersen and Vanessa Mason. Petersen was later replaced by Lisa Cork.

| 20/05/1995 | 6 | 5 | **ANOTHER NIGHT – U.S. ALBUM** | Logic 74321280972 |

▲9 Number of weeks album topped the US chart  ◆12 RIAA Diamond Awards  ◇3 IFPI Platinum Europe Awards

## REAL PEOPLE
UK pop group formed in 1989 by Tony Griffiths (born 7/4/1966, Liverpool, bass/vocals), his brother Chris (born 30/3/1968, Liverpool, guitar/vocals), Sean Simpson (born 9/10/1969, Liverpool, guitar) and Tony Elson (born 2/1/1966, Liverpool, drums). A previous attempt known as Jo Jo And The Real People recorded with Stock Aitken Waterman without success.

| | | | | | |
|---|---|---|---|---|---|
| 18/05/1991 | 59 | 1 | | THE REAL PEOPLE | Columbia 4680841 |

## REAL THING
UK R&B group formed in Liverpool by Chris Amoo, Ray Lake, Dave Smith and Kenny Davis. They spent two years on the cabaret circuit and appeared on the TV talent show *Opportunity Knocks* before signing with Bell Records. Davis left and was replaced by Chris' brother Eddie, and the group switched to Pye after a brief spell with EMI. They appeared in the 1978 film *The Stud*. Remixed versions of their early hits revived interest in them and they recorded for Jive in 1986. Chris Amoo's Afghan hound Gable was Crufts Supreme Champion in 1987.

| | | | | | |
|---|---|---|---|---|---|
| 06/11/1976 | 34 | 3 | O | REAL THING | Pye NSPL 18507 |
| 07/04/1979 | 73 | 1 | | CAN YOU FEEL THE FORCE | Pye NSPH 18601 |
| 10/05/1980 | 56 | 2 | | 20 GREATEST HITS | K-Tel NE 1073 |
| 12/07/1986 | 24 | 11 | O | THE BEST OF THE REAL THING | West Five NRT 1 |

## REBEL MC
UK rapper/singer (born Mike West, 27/8/1965, Tottenham, London) who was an ex-member of Double Trouble And The Rebel MC. He later set up the Tribal Bass label and recorded as Conquering Lion.

| | | | | | |
|---|---|---|---|---|---|
| 28/04/1990 | 18 | 7 | | REBEL MUSIC | Desire LUVLP 5 |
| 13/07/1991 | 23 | 4 | | BLACK MEANING GOOD | Desire LUVLP 12 |

## REBEL ROUSERS – see CLIFF BENNETT AND THE REBEL ROUSERS

## REBELS – see DUANE EDDY AND THE REBELS

## IVAN REBROFF
Russian singer (born 31/7/1931).

| | | | | | |
|---|---|---|---|---|---|
| 16/06/1990 | 57 | 4 | | THE VERY BEST OF IVAN REBROFF | BBC REB 778 |

## RED BOX
UK group formed in 1982 by Simon Toulson-Clarke (guitar/vocals), Julian Close (saxophone), Martin Nickson (drums), Rob Legge (drums) and Paddy Talbot (keyboards). By the time of their hits the group were a duo of Toulson-Clarke and Close.

| | | | | | |
|---|---|---|---|---|---|
| 06/12/1986 | 73 | 4 | | THE CIRCLE AND THE SQUARE | Sire WX 79 |

## RED HOT CHILI PEPPERS
US rock group formed in Los Angeles, CA in 1978 by Anthony 'Antoine The Swann' Kiedis (born 1/11/1962, Grand Rapids, MI, vocals), Flea (born Michael Balzary, 16/10/1962, Melbourne, Australia, bass), Jack Irons (drums) and Hillel Slovak (guitar) as Los Faces and then Anthem. Slovak and Irons briefly left to join What Is This? and could not appear on the Peppers' first album for EMI America imprint Enigma in 1984. Slovak died of a drug overdose on 25/6/1988 and was replaced by John Frusciante (born 5/3/1970, New York). Irons left the same year and was replaced by Chad Smith (born 25/10/1962, St Paul, MN). Frusciante resigned in 1992 and was eventually replaced by Arik Marshall (born 13/2/1967, Los Angeles). Dave Navarro (born 7/6/1967, Santa Monica, CA) replaced Marshall in 1993. Navarro left the group in 1998 to go solo and was replaced by the returning Frusciante. The group appeared in an episode of the TV animation *The Simpsons,* performing *Give It Away* at both Moe's bar and at a Krusty The Klown special. The group has won two Grammy Awards: Best Hard Rock Performance with Vocal in 1992 for *Give It Away* and Best Rock Song in 1999 for *Scar Tissue*. They were also named Best Rock Act at the 2000 and 2002 MTV Europe Music Awards and collected the 2002 award for Best Live Act. They won their first BRIT Award in 2003 for Best International Group.

| | | | | | |
|---|---|---|---|---|---|
| 12/10/1991 | 25 | 84+ | ✪ | BLOOD SUGAR SEX MAGIK | Warner Brothers WX441 |
| 17/10/1992 | 23 | 4 | ● | WHAT HITS!? | EMI USA CDMTL 1071 |
| 19/11/1994 | 61 | 1 | | OUT IN LA | EMI CDMTL 1082 |
| 23/09/1995 | 2 | 11 | ● | ONE HOT MINUTE ◇ | Warner Brothers 9362457332 |
| 19/06/1999 | 5 | 123+ | ✪ | CALIFORNICATION ◇4 | Warner Brothers 9362473862 |
| 20/07/2002 | ❶5 | 69+ | ✪5 | BY THE WAY ◇3 | Warner Brothers 9362481402 |
| 29/11/2003 | 4 | 29+ | ✪2 | GREATEST HITS ◇ | Warner Brothers 9362485962 |

## RED HOUSE PAINTERS
US group formed by Mark Kozelek (guitar/vocals), Gordon Mack (guitar), Jerry Vessel (bass) and Anthony Koutsos (drums). They signed with 4AD in 1990. Despite the same titles their two hit albums are different.

| | | | | | |
|---|---|---|---|---|---|
| 05/06/1993 | 63 | 1 | | RED HOUSE PAINTERS | 4AD DAD 3008CD |
| 30/10/1993 | 68 | 1 | | RED HOUSE PAINTERS | 4AD CAD 3016CD |

## RED SNAPPER
UK group formed in 1993 by David Ayers (guitar), Ali Friend (double bass) and Richard Thair (drums). They funded their own debut EP.

| | | | | | |
|---|---|---|---|---|---|
| 21/09/1996 | 60 | 1 | | PRINCE BLIMEY | Warp WARPCD 45 |
| 10/10/1998 | 59 | 1 | | MAKING BONES | Warp WARPCD 056 |

## SHARON REDD
US singer (born 19/10/1945, Norfolk, VA) who began her career in musicals and landed the lead role in *Hair* in Australia. She signed as a solo artist with Prelude in 1980. She died from AIDS on 1/5/1992.

| | | | | | |
|---|---|---|---|---|---|
| 23/10/1982 | 59 | 5 | | REDD HOTT | Prelude PRL 25056 |

O Silver disc ● Gold disc ✪ Platinum disc (additional platinum units are indicated by a figure following the symbol) ❶9 Number of weeks album topped the UK chart

## OTIS REDDING

US singer (born 9/9/1941, Dawson, GA) who began his career backing Johnny Jenkins And The Pinetoppers and made his first recordings as Otis & The Shooters (The Shooters being The Pinetoppers) for Finer Arts. He went with Jenkins to Stax for a recording session and persuaded the label to let him use available studio time, subsequently releasing *These Arms Of Mine* on Volt (a Stax subsidiary). As Atlantic had paid for the Jenkins session they technically had Redding under contract (and signed him to their Atco label), but under a special arrangement all his early releases appeared on Volt. He was killed in a plane crash while en route to Madison, WI on 10/12/1967; the crash also killed most members of his backing group the Bar-Kays, the only survivor being Bar-Kay Ben Cauley. He won two Grammy Awards: Best Rhythm & Blues Song with Steve Cropper and Best Rhythm & Blues Performance in 1968, both for *Sittin' On The Dock Of The Bay* and was inducted into the Rock & Roll Hall of Fame in 1989.

| Date | Pos | Wks | BPI | Album | Label & Number |
|------|-----|-----|-----|-------|----------------|
| 19/02/1966 | 6 | 21 | | **OTIS BLUE: OTIS REDDING SINGS SOUL** | Atlantic ATL 5041 |
| 23/04/1966 | 30 | 1 | | THE GREAT OTIS REDDING SINGS SOUL BALLADS | Atlantic ATL 5029 |
| 23/07/1966 | 22 | 9 | | THE SOUL ALBUM | Atlantic 587011 |
| 21/01/1967 | 7 | 54 | | **OTIS BLUE: OTIS REDDING SINGS SOUL** | Atlantic ATL 5036 |
| 21/01/1967 | 23 | 16 | | COMPLETE AND UNBELIEVABLE… THE OTIS REDDING DICTIONARY OF SOUL | Atlantic 588050 |
| 29/04/1967 | 28 | 9 | | PAIN IN MY HEART | Atlantic 587042 |
| 01/07/1967 | 18 | 17 | | KING AND QUEEN **OTIS REDDING AND CARLA THOMAS** | Atlantic 589007 |
| 10/02/1968 | 2 | 43 | | **THE HISTORY OF OTIS REDDING** | Volt S 418 |
| 30/03/1968 | 14 | 16 | | OTIS REDDING IN EUROPE | Stax 589016 |
| 01/06/1968 | ❶¹ | 15 | | **DOCK OF THE BAY** | Stax 231001 |
| 12/10/1968 | 19 | 8 | | IMMORTAL OTIS REDDING | Atlantic 588113 |
| 11/09/1993 | 44 | 18 | | DOCK OF THE BAY – THE DEFINITIVE COLLECTION | Atlantic 9548317092 |
| 11/11/2000 | 26 | 8 | ● | THE VERY BEST OF | Atco 9548380872 |

## HELEN REDDY

Australian singer (born 25/10/1942, Melbourne) who made her stage debut at the age of four and later hosted her own TV series. She won a talent contest in 1966 that included a trip to New York and relocated to the city, later moving to Los Angeles, CA. Signed by Capitol in 1971, she won the 1972 Grammy Award for Best Pop Vocal Performance with *I Am Woman*. She has a star on the Hollywood Walk of Fame.

| Date | Pos | Wks | BPI | Album | Label & Number |
|------|-----|-----|-----|-------|----------------|
| 08/02/1975 | 17 | 9 | ○ | FREE AND EASY | Capitol EST 11348 |
| 14/02/1976 | 5 | 18 | ● | **THE BEST OF HELEN REDDY** | Capitol EST 11467 |

## REDHEAD KINGPIN AND THE FBI

US singer (born David Guppy, 1970, Englewood, NJ) who took his name from his red hair. Unlike most rappers, he does not swear on record as his mother is a serving police officer. FBI stands for For Black Intelligence and comprises DJ Wildstyle, Bo Roc, Lieutenant Squeak, Buzz and Poochie. They later changed their name to Private Investigations.

| Date | Pos | Wks | BPI | Album | Label & Number |
|------|-----|-----|-----|-------|----------------|
| 09/09/1989 | 35 | 3 | | A SHADE OF RED | 10 Records DIX 85 |

## REDMAN

US rapper (born Reggie Noble, Newark, NJ); he won the 2003 MOBO Award for Best Video with Christina Aguilera for *Dirrty*.

| Date | Pos | Wks | BPI | Album | Label & Number |
|------|-----|-----|-----|-------|----------------|
| 09/10/1999 | 45 | 3 | | BLACK OUT! **METHOD MAN AND REDMAN** | Def Jam 5466092 |
| 09/06/2001 | 57 | 4 | | MALPRACTICE | Def Jam 5483812 |

## REDSKINS

UK rock group formed in York by Chris Dean (who assumed the identity X Moore, guitar/vocals), Lloyd Dwyer (saxophone), Steve Nichol (trumpet), Martin Hewes (bass) and Nick King (drums) as No Swastikas. King was later replaced by Paul Hookham. They disbanded in 1986.

| Date | Pos | Wks | BPI | Album | Label & Number |
|------|-----|-----|-----|-------|----------------|
| 22/03/1986 | 31 | 4 | | NEITHER WASHINGTON NOR MOSCOW… | Decca FLP 1 |

## ALEX REECE

UK producer from London who is also a keyboard player, bass player, drummer and in demand as a remixer.

| Date | Pos | Wks | BPI | Album | Label & Number |
|------|-----|-----|-----|-------|----------------|
| 17/08/1996 | 19 | 5 | | SO FAR | Fourth & Broadway BRCD 621 |

## DAN REED NETWORK

US funk-rock group formed in Portland, OR by Dan Reed (vocals), Melvin Brannon II (bass), Brion James (guitar), Daniel Pred (drums) and Blake Sakamoto (keyboards).

| Date | Pos | Wks | BPI | Album | Label & Number |
|------|-----|-----|-----|-------|----------------|
| 04/11/1989 | 66 | 2 | | SLAM | Mercury 8388681 |
| 27/07/1991 | 15 | 4 | | THE HEAT | Mercury 8488551 |

## LOU REED

US singer (born Louis Firbank, 2/3/1943, Freeport, Long Island, NY) who was a founder member of Velvet Underground in 1965, leaving in 1970. He released his solo debut in 1972. He took part in the *Perfect Day* project for the BBC's Children In Need charity. He won the 1998 Grammy Award for Best Music Video Long Form for *Rock And Roll Heart*.

| Date | Pos | Wks | BPI | Album | Label & Number |
|------|-----|-----|-----|-------|----------------|
| 21/04/1973 | 13 | 25 | | TRANSFORMER | RCA Victor LSP 4807 |
| 20/10/1973 | 7 | 5 | ○ | **BERLIN** | RCA Victor RS 1002 |
| 16/03/1974 | 26 | 1 | | ROCK 'N' ROLL ANIMAL | RCA Victor APLI 0472 |

▲⁹ Number of weeks album topped the US chart   ◆¹² RIAA Diamond Awards   ◇³ IFPI Platinum Europe Awards

| DATE | POS | WKS | BPI | ALBUM TITLE | LABEL & NUMBER |
|---|---|---|---|---|---|
| 14/02/1976 | 52 | 1 | | CONEY ISLAND BABY | RCA Victor RS 1035 |
| 03/07/1982 | 91 | 2 | | TRANSFORMER | RCA International INTS 5061 |
| 09/06/1984 | 92 | 1 | | NEW SENSATIONS | RCA PL 84998 |
| 24/05/1986 | 69 | 1 | | MISTRIAL | RCA PL 87190 |
| 28/01/1989 | 14 | 22 | ● | NEW YORK | Sire WX 246 |
| 07/10/1989 | 29 | 5 | ○ | RETRO | RCA PL 90389 |
| 05/05/1990 | 22 | 5 | | SONGS FOR DRELLA **LOU REED AND JOHN CALE** | Sire WX 345 |
| 25/01/1992 | 6 | 6 | | **MAGIC AND LOSS** | Sire 7599266622 |
| 28/10/1995 | 56 | 4 | | THE BEST OF LOU REED AND THE VELVET UNDERGROUND **LOU REED AND THE VELVET UNDERGROUND** | Global Television RADCD 21 |
| 02/03/1996 | 26 | 2 | | SET THE TWILIGHT REELING | Warner Brothers 9362461592 |
| 07/02/1998 | 16 | 10 | | TRANSFORMER | RCA 74321601812 |
| 15/04/2000 | 54 | 1 | | ECSTASY | Reprise 9362474252 |
| 24/05/2003 | 31 | 3 | | NYC MAN | BMG 74321984012 |

### DON REEDMAN – see JEFF JARRATT AND DON REEDMAN

### REEF
UK rock group formed in Wolverhampton in 1993 by Gary Stringer (vocals), Kenwyn House (guitars), Jack Bessant (bass), Benmont Tench (keyboards) and Dominic Greensmith (drums) as Naked, name-changing upon signing with Sony.

| DATE | POS | WKS | BPI | ALBUM TITLE | LABEL & NUMBER |
|---|---|---|---|---|---|
| 01/07/1995 | 9 | 11 | ○ | **REPLENISH** | Sony S2 4806982 |
| 08/02/1997 | ❶¹ | 32 | ● | **GLOW** | Sony S2 4869402 |
| 01/05/1999 | 3 | 7 | | **RIDES** | Sony S2 4928822 |
| 02/09/2000 | 15 | 4 | | GETAWAY | Sony S2 4988912 |
| 08/02/2003 | 52 | 1 | | TOGETHER – THE BEST OF | Sony S2 5094352 |

### REEL 2 REAL FEATURING THE MAD STUNTMAN
US duo producer Erick 'More' Morillo and rapper Mark 'The Mad Stuntman' Quashie. Stuntman took his name from the Lee Majors character in *The Fall Guy* TV series. Morillo later launched the Subliminal label and was a member of Pianoheadz.

| DATE | POS | WKS | BPI | ALBUM TITLE | LABEL & NUMBER |
|---|---|---|---|---|---|
| 22/10/1994 | 8 | 8 | ● | **MOVE IT!** | Positiva CDTIVA 1003 |

### CONNOR REEVES
UK R&B singer (born 1971, London) who was initally known as a songwriter, penning tracks for Tina Turner, MN8, Brand New Heavies and Carleen Anderson. He later recorded with Mark Marrison.

| DATE | POS | WKS | BPI | ALBUM TITLE | LABEL & NUMBER |
|---|---|---|---|---|---|
| 06/12/1997 | 25 | 8 | ○ | EARTHBOUND | Wildstar CDWILD 3 |

### JIM REEVES

US country singer (born 20/8/1923, Panola County, TX) who hoped to become a professional baseball player with the St Louis Cardinals until an ankle injury ended his career. His year of birth is sometimes given as 1924 – the discrepancy occurred when Reeves lied about his age when trying out for the St Louis Cardinals. He became a DJ in Louisiana and made his first recordings for Macy's in 1950. He appeared in the 1963 film *Kimberley Jim*. He was killed in a plane crash in Nashville on 31/7/1964, although his body was not found for three days, despite over 500 people being involved in the search. He is buried in a specially landscaped area alongside Highway 79, along with his collie Cheyenne, who died in 1967.

| DATE | POS | WKS | BPI | ALBUM TITLE | LABEL & NUMBER |
|---|---|---|---|---|---|
| 28/03/1964 | 10 | 35 | | **GOOD 'N' COUNTRY** | RCA Camden CDN 5114 |
| 09/05/1964 | 3 | 23 | | **GENTLEMAN JIM** | RCA Victor RD 7541 |
| 15/08/1964 | 8 | 9 | | **A TOUCH OF VELVET** | RCA Victor RD 7521 |
| 15/08/1964 | 11 | 17 | | INTERNATIONAL JIM REEVES | RCA Victor RD 7577 |
| 22/08/1964 | 16 | 4 | | HE'LL HAVE TO GO | RCA Victor RD 27176 |
| 29/08/1964 | 10 | 10 | | **GOD BE WITH YOU** | RCA Victor RD 27193 |
| 29/08/1964 | 12 | 4 | | THE INTIMATE JIM REEVES | RCA Victor RD 7636 |
| 05/09/1964 | 2 | 52 | | **MOONLIGHT AND ROSES** | RCA Victor RD 7639 |
| 19/09/1964 | 12 | 5 | | COUNTRY SIDE OF JIM REEVES | RCA Camden CDN 5100 |
| 26/09/1964 | 17 | 3 | | WE THANK THEE | RCA Victor RD 7637 |
| 28/11/1964 | 4 | 17 | | **TWELVE SONGS OF CHRISTMAS** | RCA Victor RD 7663 |
| 30/01/1965 | 3 | 47 | | **THE BEST OF JIM REEVES** | RCA Victor RDC 7666 |
| 10/04/1965 | 12 | 5 | | HAVE I TOLD YOU LATELY THAT I LOVE YOU | RCA Camden CDN 5122 |
| 22/05/1965 | 16 | 4 | | THE JIM REEVES WAY | RCA Victor RD 7694 |
| 05/11/1966 | 2 | 34 | | **DISTANT DRUMS** | RCA Victor RD 7814 |
| 18/01/1969 | 15 | 5 | | A TOUCH OF SADNESS | RCA Victor RD 7978 |
| 05/07/1969 | ❶⁴ | 14 | | **ACCORDING TO MY HEART** | RCA International INTS 1013 |
| 23/08/1969 | 24 | 4 | | JIM REEVES AND SOME FRIENDS | RCA Victor SF 8022 |
| 29/11/1969 | 13 | 4 | | ON STAGE | RCA Victor SF 8047 |
| 26/12/1970 | 48 | 2 | | MY CATHEDRAL | RCA Victor SF 8146 |
| 03/07/1971 | 47 | 2 | | JIM REEVES WRITES YOU A RECORD | RCA Victor SF 8176 |
| 07/08/1971 | 9 | 21 | | **JIM REEVES' GOLDEN RECORDS** | RCA International INTS 1070 |
| 14/08/1971 | 8 | 15 | | **THE INTIMATE JIM REEVES** | RCA International INTS 1256 |
| 21/08/1971 | 35 | 5 | | GIRLS I HAVE KNOWN | RCA International INTS 1140 |
| 27/11/1971 | 3 | 6 | | **TWELVE SONGS OF CHRISTMAS** | RCA International INTS 1188 |

○ Silver disc ● Gold disc ✪ Platinum disc (additional platinum units are indicated by a figure following the symbol) ❶⁹ Number of weeks album topped the UK chart

| | | | | | |
|---|---|---|---|---|---|
| 27/11/1971 | 49 | 2 | | A TOUCH OF VELVET | RCA International INTS 1089 |
| 15/04/1972 | 32 | 5 | | MY FRIEND | RCA Victor SF 8258 |
| 20/09/1975 | ❶³ | 25 | ✪ | **40 GOLDEN GREATS** | Arcade ADEP 16 |
| 06/09/1980 | 53 | 4 | | COUNTRY GENTLEMAN | K-Tel NE 1088 |
| 08/08/1992 | 9 | 10 | | **THE DEFINITIVE JIM REEVES** | Arcade ARC 94982 |
| 28/09/1996 | 17 | 6 | ○ | THE ULTIMATE COLLECTION | RCA Victor 74321410872 |
| 05/07/2003 | 21 | 10 | | GENTLEMAN JIM – DEFINITIVE COLLECTION | RCA 82876530372 |

## VIC REEVES

UK singer/comedian (born Jim Moir, 24/1/1959, Darlington) who established himself as one of the top 'alternative' comedians in UK and has had his own series on national TV, with Bob Mortimer his usual sidekick.

| | | | | | |
|---|---|---|---|---|---|
| 16/11/1991 | 16 | 9 | ○ | I WILL CURE YOU | Sense SIGN 111 |

## NEIL REID

UK singer discovered singing at a Christmas party for old-age pensioners in 1968 who then worked various clubs, usually around school holidays. He won the TV talent show *Opportunity Knocks* three times at the age of eleven and later became the youngest artist to top the album charts with *Neil Reid*.

| | | | | | |
|---|---|---|---|---|---|
| 05/02/1972 | ❶³ | 16 | | **NEIL REID** | Decca SKL 5122 |
| 02/09/1972 | 47 | 2 | | SMILE | Decca SKL 5136 |

## R.E.M.

US rock group formed in Athens, GA in 1980 by Michael Stipe (born 4/1/1960, Decatur, GA, vocals), Peter Buck (born 6/12/1956, Berkeley, CA, guitar), Bill Berry (born 31/7/1958, Duluth, MN, drums) and Mike Mills (born 17/12/1956, Orange County, CA, bass), taking their name from the abbreviation for Rapid Eye Movement (a psychological term for the stage of sleep in which the most intense dreams occur). They made their first recording for Hib-Tone in 1981, signing with IRS in 1982 and linking with Warner's in 1988. The group has won the Best International Group at the BRIT Awards on three occasions: 1992, 1993 and 1995. They have also won three Grammy Awards including: Best Pop Performance by a Group with Vocal and Best Music Video Short Form in 1991, both for *Losing My Religion*.

| | | | | | |
|---|---|---|---|---|---|
| 28/04/1984 | 91 | 2 | | RECKONING | I.R.S. A 7045 |
| 29/06/1985 | 35 | 4 | | FABLES OF THE RECONSTRUCTION | I.R.S. MIRF 1003 |
| 06/09/1986 | 43 | 4 | | LIFE'S RICH PAGEANT | I.R.S. MIRG 1014 |
| 16/05/1987 | 60 | 2 | | DEAD LETTER OFFICE | I.R.S. SP 70054 |
| 26/09/1987 | 28 | 5 | | DOCUMENT | I.R.S. MIRG 1025 |
| 29/10/1988 | 69 | 3 | | EPONYMOUS | I.R.S. MIRG 1038 |
| 19/11/1988 | 27 | 22 | ✪ | GREEN | Warner Brothers WX 234 |
| 23/03/1991 | ❶¹ | 183 | ✪⁵ | **OUT OF TIME** ▲² 1991 Grammy Award for Best Alternative Music Album | Warner Brothers WX 404 |
| 10/10/1992 | 7 | 28 | ● | **THE BEST OF R.E.M** | I.R.S. MIRH 1 |
| 10/10/1992 | ❶⁴ | 179 | ✪⁶ | **AUTOMATIC FOR THE PEOPLE** | Warner Brothers 9362450552 |
| 08/10/1994 | ❶² | 56 | ✪³ | **MONSTER** ◇² ▲² | Warner Brothers 9362457632 |
| 21/09/1996 | ❶¹ | 20 | ✪ | **NEW ADVENTURES IN HI-FI** ◇ | Warner Brothers 9362463212 |
| 07/11/1998 | 2 | 29 | ✪ | UP ◇ | Warner Brothers 9362471122 |
| 26/05/2001 | ❶² | 15 | ✪ | REVEAL ◇ | Warner Brothers 9362479462 |
| 08/11/2003 | ❶¹ | 21 | ✪³ | **IN TIME – THE BEST OF – 1988–2003** ◇ | Warner Brothers 9362483812 |
| 08/11/2003 | 36 | 1 | | IN TIME – THE BEST OF – 1988–2003 LIMITED EDITION | Warner Brothers 9362486022 |

## REMBRANDTS

US vocal duo formed by Danny Wilde and Phil Solem who first linked in 1990. Solem left in 1996 and Wilde put together another band with Graham Edwards, Dorian Crozier and Mark Karan.

| | | | | | |
|---|---|---|---|---|---|
| 23/09/1995 | 14 | 5 | | LP | East West America 7559617522 |

## RENAISSANCE

UK rock group formed in 1969 by Keith Relf (born 22/3/1943, Richmond, harmonica/vocals), Jim McCarty (born 25/7/1943, Liverpool, drums), Louis Cennamo (bass), John Hawken (keyboards) and Jane Relf (vocals). Both Keith Relf and McCarty had been with the Yardbirds. By 1971 the group consisted of Jon Camp (bass), John Tout (keyboards), Terry Sullivan (drums) and Annie Haslam (vocals). Later members included Michael Dunford (guitar) and Andy Powell (guitar). The group disbanded in the early 1980s, although Haslam, Dunford and Jane Relf attempted to revive separate versions of the group bearing the name. Keith Relf died on 14/5/1976 after being electrocuted while playing his guitar at home.

| | | | | | |
|---|---|---|---|---|---|
| 21/02/1970 | 60 | 1 | | RENAISSANCE | Island ILPS 9114 |
| 19/08/1978 | 35 | 8 | ○ | A SONG FOR ALL SEASONS | Warner Brothers K 56460 |
| 02/06/1979 | 73 | 1 | | AZUR D'OR | Warner Brothers K 56633 |

## RENATO

UK duo formed by Renato Pagliari (born in Romania but based in Birmingham) and Renee (born Hilary Lester). Renato was working as a waiter at the time of his hit, whilst Renee left before the record became a hit, with the result that Val Penny had to mime for the accompanying video. Hilary returned for their second record, although Renato alone was credited with the hit album.

| | | | | | |
|---|---|---|---|---|---|
| 25/12/1982 | 26 | 14 | | SAVE YOUR LOVE | Lifestyle LEG 9 |

## RENEGADE SOUNDWAVE

UK dance group formed in London by Danny Briotett (bass), Carl Bonnie (guitar) and Gary Asquith (vocals) and initially signed with Rhythm King. Bonnie went solo in 1992.

| | | | | | |
|---|---|---|---|---|---|
| 24/03/1990 | 74 | 1 | | SOUNDCLASH | Mute STUMM 63 |

---

▲⁹ Number of weeks album topped the US chart   ◆¹² RIAA Diamond Awards   ◇³ IFPI Platinum Europe Awards

## REO SPEEDWAGON
US rock group formed in Champaign, IL in 1968 by Alan Gratzer (born 9/11/1948, Syracuse, NY, drums), Neal Doughty (born 29/7/1946, Evanston, IL, keyboards), Gary Richrath (born 18/10/1949, Peoria, IL, guitar), Terry Luttrell (vocals) and Craig Philbin (bass). They signed with Epic in 1970 and released their debut album in 1971. Kevin Cronin (born 6/10/1951, Evanston) replaced Luttrell as singer in 1972, briefly left the group at the end of the year but returned in 1976. Bruce Hall (born 3/5/1953, Champaign, IL) replaced Philbin in 1976. By 1990 the line-up consisted of Cronin, Doughty, Hall and new members Bryan Hitt, Dave Amato and Jesse Harms. They took their name from a 1911 fire engine.

25/04/1981 ..... 6 ..... 29 ...... O  **HI INFIDELITY ▲15** ................................................................ Epic EPC 84700
17/07/1982 ..... 29 ..... 7 ......  GOOD TROUBLE ................................................................ Epic EPC 85789

## REPUBLICA
UK rock group formed in London by Saffron (born Samantha Sprackling, 3/6/1968, Lagos, Nigeria, vocals), Tim Dorney (born 30/3/1965, Ascot, keyboards), Andy Todd (keyboards), Johnny Male (born 10/10/1963, Windsor, guitar) and ex-Bow Wow Wow Dave Barbarossa (drums). Barbarossa left Republica after their first album.

15/03/1997 ..... 4 ..... 36 ...... ●  **REPUBLICA** ................................................................ Deconstruction 74321410522
17/10/1998 ..... 37 ..... 2 ......  SPEED BALLADS ................................................................ Deconstruction 74321610462

## REVOLTING COCKS
US rock group formed by Alain Jourgenson, Richard 23 and Luc Van Acker, later adding William Rieflin. Richard 23 left in 1986 and was replaced by Chris Connelly. Later members of the group included Roland Barker, Mike Scaccia and Louie Svitek. Jourgenson is also a member of Ministry.

02/10/1993 ..... 39 ..... 1 ......  LINGER FICKEN' GOOD ................................................................ Devotion CDDVN 22

## REZILLOS
UK rock group formed in Edinburgh by Eugene Reynolds (born Alan Forbes, vocals), Fay Fife (born Sheila Hynde, vocals), Luke Warm (aka Jo Callis, guitar), Hi Fi Harris (born Mark Harris, guitar), Dr D.K. Smythe (bass), Angel Patterson (born Alan Patterson, drums) and Gale Warning (backing vocals). The group disbanded in 1978, with Fife and Reynolds forming the Revillos.

05/08/1978 ..... 16 ..... 10 ...... O  CAN'T STAND THE REZILLOS ................................................................ Sire K 56530
28/04/1979 ..... 30 ..... 5 ......  MISSION ACCOMPLISHED BUT THE BEAT GOES ON ................................................................ Sire SRK 6069

## BUSTA RHYMES
US rapper (born Trevor Smith, 20/5/1972, Brooklyn, NYC) who is also a member of rap group Leaders Of The New School And The Flipmode Squad.

30/03/1996 ..... 48 ..... 4 ......  THE COMING ................................................................ Elektra 7559617422
04/10/1997 ..... 34 ..... 5 ......  WHEN DISASTER STRIKES ................................................................ Elektra 7559622602
16/01/1999 ..... 54 ..... 7 ......  EXTINCTION LEVEL EVENT/FINAL WORLD FRONT ................................................................ Elektra 7559622112
01/07/2000 ..... 38 ..... 1 ......  ANARCHY ................................................................ Elektra 7559625172
29/09/2001 ..... 44 ..... 3 ......  TURN IT UP – THE VERY BEST OF ................................................................ Elektra 8122735802
23/03/2002 ..... 58 ..... 1 ......  GENESIS ................................................................ J Records 80813200092

## RIALTO
UK rock group formed in 1991 by Louis Eliot (vocals), Jonny Bull (guitar), Julian Taylor (bass), Pete Cuthbert (drums), Antony Christmas (drums) and Toby Hounsham (keyboards). They were originally formed in 1991 as Kinky Machine by Eliot and Bull.

25/07/1998 ..... 21 ..... 3 ......  RIALTO ................................................................ China 0630197452

## DAMIEN RICE
Irish singer/guitarist (born 1974, Celbridge, County Kildare) who was a member of Juniper before going solo.

02/08/2003 ..... 23 .... 34+ ..... ✪  O ................................................................ DRM/14th Floor DRM002CD

## CHARLIE RICH
US singer (born 14/12/1932, Colt, AR) who began his career performing jazz and blues, but made his breakthrough performing country music. He won the 1973 Grammy Award for Best Country & Western Vocal Performance for the single *Behind Closed Doors* (the song also won the Best Country Song award for writer Kenny O'Dell). He died from an acute blood clot on 25/7/1995.

23/03/1974 ..... 4 ..... 26 ...... ●  **BEHIND CLOSED DOORS** ................................................................ Epic 65716
13/07/1974 ..... 34 ..... 2 ......  VERY SPECIAL LOVE SONGS ................................................................ Epic 80031

## RICHIE RICH
UK singer who helped set up Gee Street Records with John Baker and the Stereo MC's. He later teamed up with the US rap and production group The Jungle Brothers.

22/07/1989 ..... 65 ..... 1 ......  I CAN MAKE YOU DANCE ................................................................ Gee Street GEEA 3

## TONY RICH PROJECT
US singer (born Anthony Jeffries, 19/11/1971, Detroit, MI) who began his career as a songwriter, penning four songs for Pebbles. Through her he was introduced to LA Reid (Pebbles' then husband) and signed with LaFace in 1994.

25/05/1996 ..... 27 ..... 10 ......  WORDS 1996 Grammy Award for Best Rhythm & Blues Album ................................................................ LaFace 73008260222

## RICH KIDS
UK rock group formed in London in 1977 by Glen Matlock (born 27/8/1956, London, bass/vocals), Steve New (guitar) and Rusty Egan (born 19/9/1957, drums), with Midge Ure (born 10/10/1953, Gambusland, Scotland, guitar/vocals) joining later. Matlock was ex-Sex Pistols, Ure ex-Slik. The group disbanded in 1978; Ure and Egan formed Visage, although Ure ultimately found greater success with Ultravox.

07/10/1978 ..... 51 ..... 1 ......  GHOST OF PRINCES IN TOWERS ................................................................ EMI EMC 3263

**CLIFF RICHARD** UK singer (born Harry Webb, 14/10/1940, Lucknow, India) who came to the UK in 1948. He joined the Dick Teague Skiffle Group in 1957, leaving in 1958 with drummer Terry Smart to form Harry Webb & The Drifters. He was renamed Cliff Richard prior to an engagement in Ripley that year. He auditioned for Norrie Paramour in August 1958 and signed with EMI, quitting his job with Atlas Lamps. He made his TV debut on Jack Good's *Oh Boy*, performing his debut release (originally released with *Schoolboy Crush* the A-side, *Move It* the B-side). His backing group in 1958 featured Hank Marvin, Bruce Welch, Ian Samwell and Terry Smart. He appeared in the 1959 film *Serious Charge*, then made numerous starring roles, and also appeared in the puppet film *Thunderbirds Are Go* (1966). The Drifters name-changed to The Shadows in 1959 to avoid confusion with the US R&B act of the same name. Richard later recorded inspirational material. He has received many awards and honours, including the Lifetime Achievement Award at the 35th Ivor Novello Awards (even though he isn't a songwriter), the Best British Male Award at the 1977 and 1982 BRIT Awards, the Outstanding Contribution Award at the 1989 BRIT Awards and, the crowning glory, a knighthood in 1995. In July 1996 he gave an impromptu 'concert' on Centre Court at the Wimbledon Tennis Championships when rain caused a delay. He performed four numbers with a 'backing group' that included tennis players Pam Shriver, Virginia Wade, Martina Navratilova, Hana Mandlikova, Conchita Martinez, Gigi Fernandez and Rosalyn Nideffer.

| DATE | POS | WKS | BPI | ALBUM TITLE | LABEL & NUMBER |
|---|---|---|---|---|---|
| 18/04/1959 | 4 | 31 | | **CLIFF** CLIFF RICHARD AND THE DRIFTERS | Columbia 33SX 1147 |
| 14/11/1959 | 2 | 36 | | **CLIFF SINGS** | Columbia 33SX 1192 |
| 15/10/1960 | 2 | 33 | | **ME AND MY SHADOWS** | Columbia 33SX 1261 |
| 22/04/1961 | 2 | 28 | | **LISTEN TO CLIFF** | Columbia 33SX 1320 |
| 21/10/1961 | ❶¹ | 16 | | **I'M 21 TODAY** | Columbia 33SX 1368 |
| 23/12/1961 | ❶⁶ | 42 | | **THE YOUNG ONES** Original soundtrack to the film | Columbia 33SX 1384 |
| 29/09/1962 | 3 | 21 | | **32 MINUTES AND 17 SECONDS** | Columbia 33SX 1431 |
| 26/01/1963 | ❶¹⁴ | 36 | | **SUMMER HOLIDAY** Original soundtrack to the film | Columbia 33SX 1472 |
| 13/07/1963 | 2 | 19 | | **CLIFF'S HIT ALBUM** | Columbia 33SX 1512 |
| 28/09/1963 | 8 | 10 | | **WHEN IN SPAIN** | Columbia 33SX 1541 |
| 11/07/1964 | 2 | 23 | | **WONDERFUL LIFE** Original soundtrack to the film | Columbia 33SX 1628 |
| 09/01/1965 | 13 | 5 | | ALADDIN AND HIS WONDERFUL LAMP This and the above ten hits credited to **CLIFF RICHARD AND THE SHADOWS** | Columbia 33SX 1676 |
| 17/04/1965 | 9 | 5 | | **CLIFF RICHARD** | Columbia 33SX 1709 |
| 14/08/1965 | 20 | 1 | | MORE HITS BY CLIFF | Columbia 33SX 1737 |
| 08/01/1966 | 19 | 1 | | LOVE IS FOREVER This and the above hit credited to **CLIFF RICHARD AND THE SHADOWS** | Columbia 33SX 1769 |
| 21/05/1966 | 9 | 12 | | **KINDA LATIN** | Columbia SX 6039 |
| 17/12/1966 | 6 | 18 | | **FINDERS KEEPERS** Original soundtrack to the film | Columbia SX 6079 |
| 07/01/1967 | 30 | 6 | | CINDERELLA | Columbia 33SX 6103 |
| 15/04/1967 | 23 | 9 | | DON'T STOP ME NOW | Columbia SCX 6133 |
| 11/11/1967 | 37 | 1 | | GOOD NEWS | Columbia SCX 6167 |
| 01/01/1968 | 29 | 2 | | CLIFF IN JAPAN | Columbia SCX 6244 |
| 16/11/1968 | 30 | 4 | | ESTABLISHED 1958 | Columbia SCX 6282 |
| 12/07/1969 | 5 | 17 | | **THE BEST OF CLIFF** This and the above hit credited to **CLIFF RICHARD AND THE SHADOWS** | Columbia SCX 6343 |
| 27/09/1969 | 24 | 3 | | SINCERELY | Columbia SCX 6357 |
| 12/12/1970 | 37 | 2 | | TRACKS 'N' GROOVES | Columbia SCX 6435 |
| 23/12/1972 | 49 | 2 | | THE BEST OF CLIFF VOLUME 2 **CLIFF RICHARD AND THE SHADOWS** | Columbia SCX 6519 |
| 19/01/1974 | 41 | 4 | | TAKE ME HIGH Original soundtrack to the film | EMI EMC 3016 |
| 29/05/1976 | 5 | 21 | ● | **I'M NEARLY FAMOUS** | EMI EMC 3122 |
| 26/03/1977 | 8 | 10 | | **EVERY FACE TELLS A STORY** | EMI EMC 3172 |
| 22/10/1977 | ❶¹ | 19 | ✪ | **40 GOLDEN GREATS** | EMI EMTV 6 |
| 04/03/1978 | 33 | 5 | | SMALL CORNERS | EMI EMC 3219 |
| 21/10/1978 | 25 | 3 | | GREEN LIGHT | EMI EMC 3231 |
| 17/02/1979 | 5 | 12 | ● | **THANK YOU VERY MUCH – REUNION CONCERT AT THE LONDON PALLADIUM** CLIFF RICHARD AND THE SHADOWS | EMI EMTV 15 |
| 15/09/1979 | 3 | 22 | ● | **ROCK 'N' ROLL JUVENILE** | EMI EMC 3307 |
| 13/09/1980 | 4 | 12 | ● | **I'M NO HERO** | EMI EMA 796 |
| 04/07/1981 | ❶⁵ | 43 | ✪ | **LOVE SONGS** | EMI EMTV 27 |
| 26/09/1981 | 4 | 25 | ✪ | **WIRED FOR SOUND** | EMI EMC 3377 |
| 04/09/1982 | 4 | 14 | ✪ | **NOW YOU SEE ME... NOW YOU DON'T** | EMI EMC 3415 |
| 21/05/1983 | 7 | 17 | ○ | **DRESSED FOR THE OCCASION** CLIFF RICHARD AND THE PHILHARMONIC ORCHESTRA | EMI EMC 3432 |
| 15/10/1983 | 7 | 24 | ● | **SILVER** | EMI EMC 1077871 |
| 14/07/1984 | 43 | 6 | | 20 ORIGINAL GREATS | EMI CRS 1 |
| 01/12/1984 | 43 | 5 | ○ | THE ROCK CONNECTION | EMI CLIF 2 |
| 26/09/1987 | 5 | 25 | ✪ | **ALWAYS GUARANTEED** | EMI EMD 1004 |
| 19/11/1988 | ❶² | 26 | ✪⁴ | **PRIVATE COLLECTION 1979–1988** | EMI CRTV 30 |
| 11/11/1989 | 7 | 21 | ✪ | **STRONGER** | EMI EMD 1012 |
| 17/11/1990 | 3 | 15 | ✪² | **FROM A DISTANCE... THE EVENT** | EMI CRTV 31 |
| 30/11/1991 | 10 | 7 | ✪ | **TOGETHER WITH CLIFF RICHARD** | EMI EMD 1028 |
| 01/05/1993 | ❶¹ | 15 | ● | **CLIFF RICHARD – THE ALBUM** | EMI CDEMD 1043 |
| 15/10/1994 | 3 | 21 | ✪ | **THE HIT LIST** | EMI CDEMTV 84 |
| 11/11/1995 | 15 | 9 | ● | SONGS FROM 'HEATHCLIFF' | EMI CDEMD 1091 |
| 24/08/1996 | 17 | 3 | | CLIFF AT THE MOVIES – 1959–1974 | EMI CDEMD 1096 |
| 02/08/1997 | 32 | 3 | | THE ROCK 'N' ROLL YEARS | EMI CDEMD 1109 |
| 31/10/1998 | 10 | 9 | | **REAL AS I WANNA BE** | EMI 4974062 |
| 21/10/2000 | 6 | 13 | ✪ | **THE WHOLE STORY – HIS GREATEST HITS** | EMI 5293222 |
| 17/11/2001 | 11 | 8 | ● | WANTED | Papillon WANTED 1 |
| 29/11/2003 | 9 | 6 | ✪ | **CLIFF AT CHRISTMAS** | EMI 5934982 |

**KEITH RICHARDS** UK male singer and guitarist (born 18/12/1943, Dartford, Kent) who was a founding member of The Rolling Stones in 1963 with Mick Jagger, Brian Jones, Bill Wyman, Ian Stewart and Charlie Watts. He and Jagger soon became the chief songwriters within the group.

| 15/10/1988 | 37 | 3 | | TALK IS CHEAP | Virgin V 2554 |
| 31/10/1992 | 45 | 1 | | MAIN OFFENDER | Virgin America CDVUS 59 |

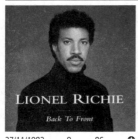

**LIONEL RICHIE** US singer (born 20/6/1949, Tuskegee, AL) who was a founding member of The Commodores in 1967 and quickly emerged as an accomplished songwriter, penning their biggest hits (usually ballads). He began writing for other artists in 1980, penning Kenny Rogers' hit *Lady* and left the group in 1982. He also co-wrote (with Michael Jackson) the USA For Africa single *We Are The World*. He has won four Grammy Awards including: Best Pop Vocal Performance in 1982 for *Truly,* Producer of the Year in 1984 with James Anthony Carmichael and Song of the Year in 1985 with Michael Jackson for *We Are The World*. He also won an Oscar for Best Original Song for *Say You Say Me* in 1985 and was given a Lifetime Achievement Award at the 1996 MOBO Awards. He has a star on the Hollywood Walk of Fame.

| 27/11/1982 | 9 | 86 | ✪ | LIONEL RICHIE | Motown STMA 8037 |
| 29/10/1983 | ❶³ | 154 | ✪³ | CAN'T SLOW DOWN ▲³ ◆¹⁰ 1984 Grammy Award for Album of the Year | Motown STMA 8041 |
| 23/08/1986 | 2 | 53 | ✪² | DANCING ON THE CEILING ▲² | Motown ZL 72412 |
| 06/06/1992 | ❶⁶ | 81 | ✪⁴ | BACK TO FRONT | Motown 5300182 |
| 20/04/1996 | 11 | 5 | ○ | LOUDER THAN WORDS | Mercury 5322412 |
| 31/01/1998 | 5 | 21 | ✪ | TRULY – THE LOVE SONGS ◇ | Motown 5308432 |
| 11/07/1998 | 31 | 3 | | TIME | Mercury 5585182 |
| 28/10/2000 | 6 | 24 | ✪ | RENAISSANCE ◇ | Mercury 5482222 |
| 07/12/2002 | 8 | 10 | ● | ENCORE | Mercury 0633482 |
| 22/11/2003 | 10 | 20 | ✪ | THE DEFINITIVE COLLECTION LIONEL RICHIE/THE COMMODORES | Universal TV 9861394 |
| 20/03/2004 | 5 | 7 | ● | JUST FOR YOU | Mercury 9861710 |

**JONATHAN RICHMAN AND THE MODERN LOVERS** US singer (born 16/5/1951, Boston, MA) who formed The Modern Lovers with Jerry Harrison (born 21/2/1949, Milwaukee, WI, guitar), Ernie Brooks (bass) and David Robinson (drums). By 1977 the Modern Lovers consisted of Leroy Radcliffe (guitar), Greg 'Curly' Kerenen (bass) and D Sharpe (drums).

| 27/08/1977 | 50 | 3 | | ROCK 'N' ROLL WITH THE MODERN LOVERS | Beserkeley BSERK 9 |

**RICHMOND STRINGS WITH THE MIKE SAMMES SINGERS** UK orchestra and vocal choir.

| 17/01/1976 | 18 | 7 | | MUSIC OF AMERICA | Ronco TRD 2016 |

**ADAM RICKITT** UK singer (born 29/5/1978, Crewe) who first came to prominence as an actor, playing the role of Nicky Tilsley in the TV soap *Coronation Street*.

| 30/10/1999 | 41 | 1 | | GOOD TIMES | Polydor 5431422 |

**FRANK RICOTTI ALL STARS** UK percussionist/vibe player (born 31/1/1949, London) who spent most of the 1970s as an accomplished session musician. The following decade he moved into film and TV soundtrack work as well as forming Paragonne.

| 24/12/1988 | 89 | 2 | | THE BEIDERBECKE COLLECTION | Dormouse DM 20CD |
| 14/01/1989 | 14 | 5 | ○ | THE BEIDERBECKE COLLECTION This was the album's placing in the compilation chart, where it was incorrectly listed | |
| | | | | | Dormouse DM 20CD |
| 26/06/1993 | 73 | 1 | | THE BEIDERBECKE COLLECTION | Dormouse DM 20CD |

**NELSON RIDDLE ORCHESTRA** US orchestra leader (born 1/6/1921, Oradell, NJ) who learned to play the trombone whilst a teenager and worked with many big bands during the late 1930s, including those of Charlie Spivak, Tommy Dorsey and Bob Crosby. He served in the army and then moved to California. By the end of the 1940s, after a spell at NBC, he joined Capitol Records as an in-house arranger. He worked on recordings by artists such as Nat King Cole and Frank Sinatra and then on various TV series and films. Later he worked with artists outside Capitol, including Ella Fitzgerald, Sammy Davis Jr, Peggy Lee, Jack Jones, Eddie Fisher, Shirley Bassey and Dinah Shore, among others. After a brief retirement spell in the 1970s he returned to work in the early 1980s, although he suffered ill health in his later years and died on 6/10/1985. He won three Grammy Awards: Best Composition in 1958 for *Cross Country Suite*, Best Instrumental Arrangement Accompanying Vocal in 1983 for Linda Ronstadt's *What's New* and Best Instrumental Arrangement Accompanying Vocal in 1985 for Linda Ronstadt's *Lush Life*. He also won an Academy Award (Oscar) in 1974 for his music to the film *The Great Gatsby*.

| 15/12/1962 | 12 | 7 | | LET'S FACE THE MUSIC SHIRLEY BASSEY WITH THE NELSON RIDDLE ORCHESTRA | Columbia 33SX 1454 |
| 26/10/1985 | 40 | 29 | ● | BLUE SKIES KIRI TE KAWANA WITH NELSON RIDDLE AND HIS ORCHESTRA | London KTKT 1 |
| 28/01/1984 | 31 | 5 | | WHAT'S NEW | Asylum 9602601 |
| 19/01/1985 | 100 | 1 | | LUSH LIFE This and the above hit credited to LINDA RONSTADT WITH THE NELSON RIDDLE ORCHESTRA | Asylum 9603871 |

**RIDE** UK rock group formed in Oxford by Mark Gardner (born 6/12/1969, Oxford, guitar/vocals), Andy Bell (born 11/8/1970, Cardiff, guitar/vocals), Stephan Queralt (born 4/2/1968, Oxford, bass) and Laurence Colbert (born 27/6/1970, Kingston, drums). All four had met whilst at art school. The group disbanded in 1996, with Bell forming Hurricane #1 and later joining Oasis, and Gardner and Colbert forming Animalhouse.

| 27/10/1990 | 11 | 5 | ○ | NOWHERE | Creation CRELP 074 |
| 21/03/1992 | 5 | 5 | ○ | GOING BLANK AGAIN | Creation CRECD 124 |

○ Silver disc  ● Gold disc  ✪ Platinum disc (additional platinum units are indicated by a figure following the symbol)  ❶⁹ Number of weeks album topped the UK chart

02/07/1994 . . . . . 5 . . . . . . 4 . . . . . . CARNIVAL OF LIGHT . . . . . . . . . . . . . . . . . . . . . . . . . . . . . . . . . . . . . . . . . . . . . . . . . . . . . . . . . . . . Creation CRECD 147
23/03/1996 . . . . . 21 . . . . . . 2 . . . . . TARANTULA . . . . . . . . . . . . . . . . . . . . . . . . . . . . . . . . . . . . . . . . . . . . . . . . . . . . . . . . . . . . . . . . . . . . Creation CRECD 180

### ANDRE RIEU
Dutch conductor and violinist (born 1949, Maastricht), who grew up listening to classical music and was taking fiddle lessons at the age of five. Known as 'the Waltz King of Europe' he is the conductor of the Strauss Opera.

22/04/2000 . . . . . 51 . . . . . . 2 . . . . CELEBRATION! . . . . . . . . . . . . . . . . . . . . . . . . . . . . . . . . . . . . . . . . . . . . . . . . . . . . . . . . . . . . . . . . . . Philips 5430692

### RIGHT SAID FRED
UK group formed in London in 1990 by Fred Fairbrass (born Christopher Abbott Bernard Fairbrass, 2/11/1956, East Grinstead, bass), his brother Richard (born 22/9/1953, East Grinstead, vocals) and Rob Manzoli (born 29/1/1954, London, guitar) following the failure of the brothers' previous group, the Actors. The group took their name from the Bernard Cribbins hit of the same name.

28/03/1992 . . . . ❶[1] . . . . 49 . . . . . . ✪[2] **UP** . . . . . . . . . . . . . . . . . . . . . . . . . . . . . . . . . . . . . . . . . . . . . . . . . . . . . . . . . . . . . . . . . . . . . . . . Tug SNOGCD 1
13/11/1993 . . . . . 35 . . . . . . 4 . . . . . . SEX AND TRAVEL . . . . . . . . . . . . . . . . . . . . . . . . . . . . . . . . . . . . . . . . . . . . . . . . . . . . . . . . . . . . . . . . . . Tug SNOGCD 2

### RIGHTEOUS BROTHERS
US vocal duo formed in 1962 by ex-Paramours Bill Medley (born 19/9/1940, Santa Ana, CA) and ex-Variations Bobby Hatfield (born 10/8/1940, Beaver Dam, WI). They were dubbed the Righteous Brothers by black marines. They first recorded for Moonglow in 1963 and were contracted to that label when Phil Spector expressed an interest in signing them (their US releases subsequently appeared on Philles, UK ones through London). Medley left in 1967 to go solo and Hatfield teamed up with Jimmy Walker but was not able to use the name Righteous Brothers for legal reasons. Hatfield and Medley re-formed in 1974. They were inducted into the Rock & Roll Hall of Fame in 2003. Hatfield was found dead in a hotel room on 5/11/2003 shortly before the pair were to perform on stage in Kalamazoo, MI.

01/12/1990 . . . . . 11 . . . . . 17 . . . . . . ✪ THE VERY BEST OF THE RIGHTEOUS BROTHERS: UNCHAINED MELODY . . . . . . . . . . . . . . . . . . . . . . . . . . . . . . . . . . Verve 8472481

### LeANN RIMES
US country singer (born 28/8/1982) who made her first album at the age of eleven for the independent Nor Va Jak label. She subsequently signed with Curb and her major label debut sold over 7 million copies in the US. She has also won two Grammy Awards including Best New Artist in 1996.

06/06/1998 . . . . . 11 . . . . . 22 . . . . . . ● SITTIN' ON TOP OF THE WORLD. . . . . . . . . . . . . . . . . . . . . . . . . . . . . . . . . . . . . . . . . . . . . . . . . . . . . Curb 5560682
14/04/2001 . . . . . 7 . . . . . 15 . . . . . . ● **I NEED YOU** . . . . . . . . . . . . . . . . . . . . . . . . . . . . . . . . . . . . . . . . . . . . . . . . . . . . . . . . . . . . . . . . . . Curb 8573876382
26/10/2002 . . . . . 14 . . . . . . 3 . . . . . . ○ TWISTED ANGEL . . . . . . . . . . . . . . . . . . . . . . . . . . . . . . . . . . . . . . . . . . . . . . . . . . . . . . . . . . . . . . . . . . Curb 5046611562
14/02/2004 . . . . . 2 . . . 20+ . . . . . ✪ **THE BEST OF** . . . . . . . . . . . . . . . . . . . . . . . . . . . . . . . . . . . . . . . . . . . . . . . . . . . . . . . . . . . . . . . . . . Curb 5046714812

### RIP RIG AND PANIC
UK/US group formed in 1980 by Gareth Sanger, Bruce Smith and Neneh Cherry (born 10/8/1964, Stockholm, Sweden). Smith later became a member of Public Image Ltd and Cherry launched a solo career.

26/06/1982 . . . . . 67 . . . . . . 3 . . . . . . I AM COLD . . . . . . . . . . . . . . . . . . . . . . . . . . . . . . . . . . . . . . . . . . . . . . . . . . . . . . . . . . . . . . . . . . . . . . . Virgin V 2228

### MINNIE RIPERTON
US singer (born 8/11/1947, Chicago, IL) who first recorded for Chess in 1966 under the name Andrea Davis and as a member of the Gems before joining Rotary Connection in 1967. She signed as a soloist with Janus in 1970 and switched to Epic in 1975. She died from cancer on 12/7/1979.

17/05/1975 . . . . . 33 . . . . . . 3 . . . . . . PERFECT ANGEL . . . . . . . . . . . . . . . . . . . . . . . . . . . . . . . . . . . . . . . . . . . . . . . . . . . . . . . . . . . . . . . . . . Epic EPC 80426

### ANGELA RIPPON
UK exercise instructor (born 12/10/1944, Redruth) who first came to prominence as a newsreader on BBC TV and then revealed another side to her talents with a dance routine conducted during the *Morecambe And Wise* TV series.

17/04/1982 . . . . . 8 . . . . . 26 . . . . . . ● **SHAPE UP AND DANCE FEATURING ANGELA RIPPON (VOLUME II)**. . . . . . . . . . . . . . . . . . . . . . . . . . . . . . . . . . . . . Lifestyle LEG 2

### RIVER CITY PEOPLE
UK group formed in Liverpool in 1986 by Siobhan Maher (born 11/1/1964, Liverpool, vocals), Tim Speed (born 17/11/1961, Chester, guitar), his brother Paul (born 27/10/1964, Chester, drums) and Dave Snell (bass). They were signed by EMI in 1988 but disbanded during the 1990s, with Paul and Tim going on to form Speed.

25/08/1990 . . . . . 23 . . . . . . 9 . . . . . SAY SOMETHING GOOD . . . . . . . . . . . . . . . . . . . . . . . . . . . . . . . . . . . . . . . . . . . . . . . . . . . . . . . . . EMI EMCX 3561
02/11/1991 . . . . . 56 . . . . . . 1 . . . . . THIS IS THE WORLD . . . . . . . . . . . . . . . . . . . . . . . . . . . . . . . . . . . . . . . . . . . . . . . . . . . . . . . . . . . . EMI EMC 3611

### RIVER DETECTIVES
UK male vocal and instrumental duo formed by Sam Corry and Dan O'Neill.

23/09/1989 . . . . . 51 . . . . . . 1 . . . . . SATURDAY NIGHT SUNDAY MORNING . . . . . . . . . . . . . . . . . . . . . . . . . . . . . . . . . . . . . . . . . . . . . . . . . WEA WX 2955

### DAVID ROACH
UK singer/saxophonist who later recorded with Michael Nyman and Philip Glass.

14/04/1984 . . . . . 73 . . . . . . 1 . . . . . . I LOVE SAX . . . . . . . . . . . . . . . . . . . . . . . . . . . . . . . . . . . . . . . . . . . . . . . . . . . . . . . . . . . . Nouveau Music NML 1006

### ROACHFORD
UK R&B group formed by Andrew Roachford (keyboards/vocals) and comprising Chris Taylor (drums), Hawi Gonwe (guitar) and Derrick Taylor (bass). They made their debut album for CBS in 1988.

23/07/1988 . . . . . 11 . . . . . 27 . . . . . . ○ ROACHFORD . . . . . . . . . . . . . . . . . . . . . . . . . . . . . . . . . . . . . . . . . . . . . . . . . . . . . . . . . . . . . . . . . . CBS 4606301
18/05/1991 . . . . . 20 . . . . . . 5 . . . . . GET READY! . . . . . . . . . . . . . . . . . . . . . . . . . . . . . . . . . . . . . . . . . . . . . . . . . . . . . . . . . . . . . . . Columbia 4681361
16/04/1994 . . . . . 25 . . . . . 21 . . . . . . ● PERMANENT SHADE OF BLUE. . . . . . . . . . . . . . . . . . . . . . . . . . . . . . . . . . . . . . . . . . . . . . . . . . . . . . Columbia 4758429
25/10/1997 . . . . . 19 . . . . . . 3 . . . . . FEEL . . . . . . . . . . . . . . . . . . . . . . . . . . . . . . . . . . . . . . . . . . . . . . . . . . . . . . . . . . . . . . . . . . . . Columbia 4885262

### MARTY ROBBINS
US singer (born Martin David Robinson, 26/9/1925, Glendale, AZ) who began his career in local clubs, usually under the name Jack Robinson as his mother disapproved of him performing at such venues. He first broke through on radio and then local TV, hosting his own *Western Caravan* on KPHO Phoenix. He made his first recordings for Columbia in 1952 and later appeared in eight films, including *Guns Of A Stranger* (1973). He also raced stock cars in Nashville. He won two Grammy Awards: Best Country & Western Performance in 1960 for *El Paso* and Best Country & Western Song in 1970 for *My Woman, My Woman, My Wife*. He suffered three heart attacks and died from cardiac arrest on 8/12/1982. He has a star on the Hollywood Walk of Fame.

▲[9] Number of weeks album topped the US chart   ◆[12] RIAA Diamond Awards   ◇[3] IFPI Platinum Europe Awards

| 13/08/1960.....20......1...... | | | | | GUNFIGHTER BALLADS AND TRAIL SONGS | Fontana TFL 5063 |
| 10/02/1979.....5......14......○ | | | | | **MARTY ROBBINS COLLECTION** | Lotus WH 5009 |

### JULIET ROBERTS
UK singer (born in London) who joined the reggae outfit Black Jade and then recorded solo for Bluebird. She was lead singer for Funk Masters on their top ten hit and later Working Week as well as maintaining a solo career.

| 02/04/1994.....65......1...... | NATURAL THING | Cooltempo CTCD 39 |

### PADDY ROBERTS
South African singer (born in1910) who trained as a lawyer in South Africa and served in the RAF during the Second World War. He was a pilot for BOAC after the war and later became a songwriter and singer. He died in London in September 1975.

| 26/09/1959.....8......5...... | **STRICTLY FOR GROWN UPS** | Decca LF 1322 |
| 17/09/1960.....16......1...... | PADDY ROBERTS TRIES AGAIN | Decca LK 4358 |

### B.A. ROBERTSON
UK singer/songwriter (born Brian Alexander Robertson, Glasgow) who was also responsible for penning hits by Brown Sauce and Mike + The Mechanics.

| 29/03/1980.....32......8...... | INITIAL SUCCESS | Asylum K 52216 |
| 04/04/1981.....61......2...... | BULLY FOR YOU | Asylum K 52275 |

### ROBBIE ROBERTSON
Canadian singer (born 5/7/1944, Toronto) who had previously been guitarist with Ronnie Hawkins' backing group and then guitarist and singer with The Band before launching a solo career.

| 14/11/1987.....23......14......● | ROBBIE ROBERTSON | Geffen WX 133 |
| 12/10/1991.....30......2...... | STORYVILLE | Geffen GEF 24303 |

### SMOKEY ROBINSON AND THE MIRACLES
US singer (born William Robinson, 19/2/1940, Detroit, MI) who formed the Matadors in 1954, changing the group's name to the Miracles at the suggestion of Berry Gordy. They made their first record for End in 1958, leased another product to Chess and became one of the first acts signed to Gordy's Motown company. Smokey wrote for many of the acts signed to the label, including the Temptations, Mary Wells and the Marvelettes. He was vice president of Motown from 1961–88 and wrote the company's theme song. He won the 1987 Grammy Award for Best Rhythm & Blues Vocal Performance for *Just To See Her*. He was inducted into the Rock & Roll Hall of Fame in 1987 and has a star on the Hollywood Walk of Fame.

| 20/06/1981.....17......10...... | BEING WITH YOU **SMOKEY ROBINSON** | Motown STML 12151 |
| 12/11/1988.....69......9...... | LOVE SONGS **MARVIN GAYE AND SMOKEY ROBINSON** | Telstar STAR 2331 |
| 14/11/1992.....65......2......○ | THE GREATEST HITS | Polygram TV 5301212 |

### TOM ROBINSON BAND
UK singer (born 1/7/1950, Cambridge) who formed his own band with Danny Kustow (guitar), 'Dolphon' Taylor (drums) and Mark Ambler (keyboards). He later moved to Germany.

| 03/06/1978.....4......12......● | **POWER IN THE DARKNESS** | EMI EMC 3226 |
| 24/03/1979.....18......6...... | TRB2 | EMI EMC 3296 |
| 29/09/1984.....21......5...... | HOPE AND GLORY **TOM ROBINSON** | Castaway ZL 70483 |

### PETE ROCK AND C.L. SMOOTH
US rap duo formed in Mount Vernon, NY by Peter 'Pete Rock' Phillips and Corey 'C.L. Smooth' Penn.

| 19/11/1994.....69......1...... | THE MAIN INGREDIENT | Elektra 7559616612 |

### ROCK GODDESS
UK rock group formed in London in 1977 by Jody Turner (guitar), her sister Julie (drums) and Tracey Lamb (bass), subsequently adding Kate Burbela (guitar). Lamb left in 1986 and was replaced by Dee O'Malley, who left the group in 1988 in order to start a family. Lamb later became a member of Girlschool.

| 12/03/1983.....65......2...... | ROCK GODDESS | A&M AMLH 68554 |
| 29/10/1983.....84......1...... | HELL HATH NO FURY | A&M AMLX 68560 |

### ROCKET FROM THE CRYPT
US group formed in San Diego, CA in 1990 by John 'Speedo' Reis (guitar/vocals), ND (guitar), Petey X (bass), Atom (drums), Apollo 9 (saxophone) and JC 2000 (trumpet).

| 03/02/1996.....41......3...... | SCREAM, DRACULA, SCREAM! | Elemental ELM 34CD |
| 18/07/1998.....63......1...... | RFTC | Elemental ELM 50CD |

### ROCKIN' BERRIES
UK group formed in Birmingham by Geoff Turton (born 11/3/1944, Birmingham, guitar), Clive Lea (born 16/2/1942, Birmingham, vocals), Bryan Charles 'Chuck' Botfield (born 14/11/1943, Birmingham, guitar), Roy Austin (born 27/12/1943, Birmingham, guitar) and Terry Bond (born 22/3/1943, Birmingham, drums). The group later recorded as The Berries while Turton recorded as Jefferson.

| 19/06/1965.....15......1...... | IN TOWN | Pye NPL 38013 |

### ROCKPILE
UK group formed by Dave Edmunds (born 15/4/1944, Cardiff, guitar/vocals), Nick Lowe (born 25/3/1949, Woodbridge, vocals), Billy Bremner (bass) and Terry Williams (drums). Edmunds and Williams are ex-Love Sculpture, Bremner is ex-Lulu And The Luvvers and Nick Lowe ex-Brinsley Schwarz. The name Rockpile was first used in 1972 as a solo album for Edmunds.

| 18/10/1980.....34......5...... | SECONDS OF PLEASURE | F-Beat XXLP 7 |

### ROCKSTEADY CREW
US singing/breakdancing group: Crazy Legs (born Richie Colon), Baby Love and Prince Ken Swift.

| 16/06/1984.....73......1...... | READY FOR BATTLE | Charisma RSC LP1 |

### ROCKWELL
US singer (born Kennedy Gordy, 15/3/1964, Detroit, MI) who is the son of Motown founder Berry Gordy.

○ Silver disc ● Gold disc ✪ Platinum disc (additional platinum units are indicated by a figure following the symbol) ●⁹ Number of weeks album topped the UK chart

25/02/1984.....52......5...... SOMEBODY'S WATCHING ME................................................................. Motown ZL 72147

## CLODAGH RODGERS
UK singer (born in Northern Ireland, later based in London) who made her debut in 1957 with Michael Holliday. She also recorded as Cloda Rodgers for Decca in 1962 and later recorded for Polydor and Precision.

13/09/1969.....27......1...... CLODAGH RODGERS................................................................. RCA Victor SF 8033

## PAUL RODGERS
UK singer (born 12/12/1949, Middlesbrough, Cleveland) who was a founding member of Free in 1968 with Andy Fraser, Paul Kossoff and Simon Kirke. He and Kirke then linked up in Bad Company in 1973; Rodgers was later a member of The Firm and The Law.

03/07/1993.....9......7...... **MUDDY WATER BLUES – A TRIBUTE TO MUDDY WATERS**................................ London 8284242
15/02/1997.....30......4...... NOW................................................................. SPV Recordings SPV 08544662

## RODS
US vocal/instrumental group formed by Garry Bordonaro, Carl Canedy, David Feinstein and Stephen Starmer.

24/07/1982.....75......4...... WILD DOGS................................................................. Arista SPART 1196

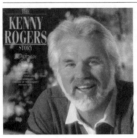

## KENNY ROGERS
US singer (born 21/8/1938, Houston, TX) who formed First Edition in 1967 with Mike Settle, Terry Williams and Thelma Camacho, all of whom had previously been members of the New Christy Minstrels. The group disbanded in 1974 with Rogers signing with Capitol as a solo artist in 1975. He has won three Grammy Awards: Best Country Vocal Performance in 1977 for *Lucille*, Best Country Vocal Performance in 1979 for *The Gambler* (which also won the Best Country Song category for writer Don Schlitz) and Best Country Vocal Performance by a Duo in 1987 with Ronnie Milsap for *Make No Mistake, She's Mine*. He has a star on the Hollywood Walk of Fame.

18/06/1977.....14......7...... KENNY ROGERS................................................................. United Artists UAS 30046
06/10/1979.....12......22......● THE KENNY ROGERS SINGLES ALBUM................................................. United Artists UAK 30263
09/02/1980.....7......10......● **KENNY**................................................................. United Artists UAG 30273
31/01/1981.....40......5...... LADY................................................................. Liberty LBG 30334
01/10/1983.....53......19...... EYES THAT SEE IN THE DARK................................................. RCA RCALP 6088
27/10/1984.....97......1...... WHAT ABOUT ME?................................................................. RCA PL 85043
27/07/1985.....4......29......✪ **THE KENNY ROGERS STORY**................................................. Liberty EMTV 39
25/09/1993.....16......5......○ DAYTIME FRIENDS – THE VERY BEST OF KENNY ROGERS.................... EMI CDEMTV 79
22/11/1997.....27......7......● LOVE SONGS................................................................. Virgin KENNYCD 1
29/05/1999.....14......6...... ALL THE HITS & ALL NEW LOVE SONGS................................. EMI 5207782

## ROLLING STONES
UK rock group formed in London in 1963 by Mick Jagger (born 26/7/1943, Dartford, vocals), Keith Richards (born 18/12/1943, Dartford, guitar), Brian Jones (born Lewis Brian Hopkin-Jones, 28/2/1942, Cheltenham, guitar), Bill Wyman (born William Perks, 24/10/1936, London, bass), Ian Stewart (born 1938, Pittenween, Scotland, keyboards) and Charlie Watts (born 2/6/1941, London), making their debut live appearance at the Flamingo Jazz Club on 14/1/1963. They signed with Decca in May 1963 and released their first single, a cover of Chuck Berry's *Come On,* in June (Decca rejected the first version of *Come On* as 'dreadful'). They made their first UK tour in 1963 supporting the Everly Brothers, Bo Diddley and Little Richard. Stewart appeared on many of their recordings but was not an official member of the group when they signed with Decca (he subsequently became road manager). Jones resigned from the group in June 1969 and drowned on 3/7/1969. He was replaced by Mick Taylor (born 17/1/1948, Welwyn Garden City). Taylor left in 1974 and was replaced by Ron Wood (born 1/6/1947, Hillingdon). The documentary film *Gimme Shelter* (1970) covers the events at the Altamont concert where fan Meredith Hunter was stabbed to death by Hell's Angels. Stewart died from a heart attack on 12/12/1985 in his doctor's waiting room. Wyman left in 1993. Jagger recorded solo and made appearances in a number of films, including *Ned Kelly* in 1970, and was knighted in the 2002 Queen's Birthday Honours List. The group was inducted into the Rock & Roll Hall of Fame in 1989. Jagger and Richards took part in the *It's Only Rock 'N' Roll* project for the Children's Promise charity. The group has won two Grammy Awards including the Best Music Video Short Form in 1994 for *Love Is Strong*.

25/04/1964....❶12....51...... **THE ROLLING STONES**................................................. Decca LK 4605
23/01/1965....❶10....37...... **ROLLING STONES NUMBER 2**......................................... Decca LK 4661
02/10/1965.....2......24...... **OUT OF OUR HEADS** ▲3................................................. Decca LK 4733
23/04/1966....❶8......28...... **AFTERMATH**................................................................. Decca LK 4786
12/11/1966.....4......43...... **BIG HITS (HIGH TIDE AND GREEN GRASS)**......................... Decca TXS 101
28/01/1967.....3......22...... **BETWEEN THE BUTTONS**................................................. Decca SKL 4852
23/12/1967.....3......13...... **THEIR SATANIC MAJESTIES REQUEST**......................... Decca TXS 103
21/12/1968.....3......12...... **BEGGARS BANQUET**................................................. Decca SKL 4955
27/09/1969.....2......37...... **THROUGH THE PAST DARKLY (BIG HITS VOLUME 2)**.......... Decca SKL 5019
20/12/1969....❶1......29......✪ **LET IT BLEED**................................................................. Decca SKL 5025
19/09/1970....❶2......15...... **GET YER YA-YA'S OUT!' – THE ROLLING STONES IN CONCERT**..... Decca SKL 5065
03/04/1971.....4......8...... **STONE AGE**................................................................. Decca SKL 5084
08/05/1971....❶5......25...... **STICKY FINGERS** ▲4................................................. Rolling Stones COC 59100
18/09/1971.....19......5...... GIMME SHELTER.................................................... Decca SKL 5101
11/03/1972.....14......8...... MILESTONES................................................................. Decca SKL 5098
10/06/1972....❶1......16...... **EXILE ON MAIN STREET** ▲4......................................... Rolling Stones COC 69100
11/11/1972.....41......1...... ROCK 'N' ROLLING STONES................................................. Decca SKL 5149
22/09/1973....❶2......14......● **GOAT'S HEAD SOUP** ▲4................................................. Rolling Stones COC 59101

▲9 Number of weeks album topped the US chart   ◆12 RIAA Diamond Awards   ◇3 IFPI Platinum Europe Awards

| DATE | POS | WKS | BPI | ALBUM TITLE | LABEL & NUMBER |
|---|---|---|---|---|---|
| 02/11/1974 | 2 | 9 | ● | IT'S ONLY ROCK 'N' ROLL ▲[1] | Rolling Stones COC 59103 |
| 28/06/1975 | 14 | 12 | | MADE IN THE SHADE | Rolling Stones COC 59104 |
| 28/06/1975 | 45 | 1 | | METAMORPHOSIS | Decca SKL 5212 |
| 29/11/1975 | 7 | 50 | ● | ROLLED GOLD – THE VERY BEST OF THE ROLLING STONES | Decca ROST 1/2 |
| 08/05/1976 | 2 | 14 | ● | BLACK AND BLUE ▲[4] | Rolling Stones COC 59106 |
| 08/10/1977 | 3 | 8 | ● | LOVE YOU LIVE | Rolling Stones COC 89101 |
| 05/11/1977 | 8 | 15 | | GET STONED | Arcade ADEP 32 |
| 24/06/1978 | 2 | 25 | ● | SOME GIRLS ▲[2] | Rolling Stones CUN 39108 |
| 05/07/1980 | ❶[2] | 18 | ● | EMOTIONAL RESCUE ▲[7] | Rolling Stones CUN 39111 |
| 12/09/1981 | 2 | 29 | ● | TATTOO YOU ▲[9] | Rolling Stones CUNS 39114 |
| 12/06/1982 | 4 | 18 | ● | STILL LIFE (AMERICAN CONCERTS 1981) | Rolling Stones CUN 39115 |
| 31/07/1982 | 94 | 3 | | IN CONCERT | Decca 6640 037 |
| 11/12/1982 | 24 | 12 | ● | STORY OF THE STONES | K-Tel NE 1201 |
| 19/11/1983 | 3 | 18 | ● | UNDERCOVER | Rolling Stones CUN 1654361 |
| 07/07/1984 | 23 | 18 | | REWIND 1971–1984 (THE BEST OF THE ROLLING STONES) | Rolling Stones 4501991 |
| 05/04/1986 | 4 | 10 | ● | DIRTY WORK | Rolling Stones CUN 86321 |
| 23/09/1989 | 2 | 18 | ● | STEEL WHEELS | Rolling Stones 4657521 |
| 07/07/1990 | 3 | 24 | ✪[2] | HOT ROCKS – THE GREATEST HITS 1964–1971 ◆[12] | London 8201401 |
| 20/04/1991 | 6 | 7 | ○ | FLASHPOINT | Rolling Stones 4681351 |
| 04/12/1993 | 16 | 28 | ✪[2] | JUMP BACK – THE BEST OF THE ROLLING STONES 1971–93 | Virgin CDV 2726 |
| 02/07/1994 | 74 | 1 | | STICKY FINGERS | Virgin CDVX 2730 |
| 23/07/1994 | ❶[1] | 24 | ◇ | VOODOO LOUNGE ◇ 1994 Grammy Award for Best Rock Album | Virgin CDV 2750 |
| 25/11/1995 | 9 | 11 | ● | STRIPPED ◇ | Virgin CDV 2801 |
| 11/10/1997 | 6 | 6 | ● | BRIDGES TO BABYLON ◇ | Virgin CDV 2840 |
| 14/11/1998 | 67 | 1 | | NO SECURITY | Virgin CDV 2880 |
| 12/10/2002 | 2 | 29 | ✪[2] | FORTY LICKS ◇ | Virgin Decca CDVDX 2964 |

**ROLLINS BAND** US group formed and fronted in 1987 by ex-Black Flag Henry Rollins (born Henry Garfield, 13/2/1961, Washington DC) with Chris Haskett, Andrew Weiss and Sim Cain. By 1999 the group consisted of Rollins, Jim Wilson (guitar), Marcus Blake (bass) and Jason Mackenroth (drums). Rollins won the 1994 Grammy Award for Best Spoken Word or Non-musical Album for *Get In The Van: On the Road with Black Flag*.

| DATE | POS | WKS | BPI | ALBUM TITLE | LABEL & NUMBER |
|---|---|---|---|---|---|
| 23/04/1994 | 22 | 2 | | WEIGHT | Imago 72787210342 |

**ROMAN HOLIDAY** UK group formed by Steve Lambert (vocals), his brother Rob (saxophone), Brian Bonhomme (guitar), Jon Durno (bass), Adrian York (keyboards), John Escott (trumpet) and Simon Cohen (drums).

| DATE | POS | WKS | BPI | ALBUM TITLE | LABEL & NUMBER |
|---|---|---|---|---|---|
| 22/10/1983 | 31 | 3 | | COOKIN' ON THE ROOF | Jive HIP 9 |

**ROMEO** UK rapper (born Marvin Dawkins) who is also a member of So Solid Crew.

| DATE | POS | WKS | BPI | ALBUM TITLE | LABEL & NUMBER |
|---|---|---|---|---|---|
| 23/11/2002 | 46 | 2 | ○ | SOLID LOVE | Relentless RELEN 006CD |

**RONDO VENEZIANO** Italian orchestra formed in 1980 by Gian Piero Reverberi (born29/7/1939, Genoa). The members all wear authentic 18th-century Italian costumes (complete with wigs) when performing.

| DATE | POS | WKS | BPI | ALBUM TITLE | LABEL & NUMBER |
|---|---|---|---|---|---|
| 05/11/1983 | 39 | 13 | ● | VENICE IN PERIL | Ferroway RON 1 |
| 10/11/1984 | 60 | 13 | | THE GENIUS OF VENICE | Ferroway RON 2 |
| 09/07/1988 | 34 | 7 | | VENICE IN PERIL Re-issue | Fanfare RON 1 |

**MICK RONSON** UK singer/guitarist (born 26/5/1949, Hull) who was in David Bowie's backing band before he became a member of Mott The Hoople in 1974, although the group disbanded three months later. He then teamed up with former Mott The Hoople singer Ian Hunter in the Hunter-Ronson Band. He was diagnosed as having cancer in 1991 and died on 29/4/1993.

| DATE | POS | WKS | BPI | ALBUM TITLE | LABEL & NUMBER |
|---|---|---|---|---|---|
| 16/03/1974 | 9 | 7 | | SLAUGHTER ON TENTH AVENUE | RCA Victor APL1 0353 |
| 08/03/1975 | 29 | 3 | | PLAY DON'T WORRY | RCA Victor APL1 0681 |

**LINDA RONSTADT** US singer (born 15/7/1946, Tucson, AZ) who formed the Three Ronstadts with her brother Mike and sister Suzi in 1960. They name-changed to the New Union Ramblers before Linda left to join the Kimmel Brothers. Bob Kimmel, Linda and Kenny Edwards then formed the Stone Poneys and recorded for Capitol. Ronstadt went solo in 1968 with her 1971 touring band, including future Eagles Glenn Frey, Bernie Leadon, Randy Meisner and Don Henley. She appeared in the 1983 film *The Pirates Of Penzance*, having also appeared in the Broadway production, and 'appeared' in an episode of the TV cartoon *The Simpsons*, singing the Plow King Theme jingle. She has won eleven Grammy Awards including: Best Country Vocal Performance in 1975 with *I Can't Help It (If I'm Still In Love With You)*; Best Recording for Children in 1980 with various others for *In Harmony*; Best Mexican-US Performance in 1988 for *Canciones De Mi Padre*; Best Pop Vocal Performance by a Duo in 1989 with Aaron Neville for *Don't Know Much*; Best Pop Vocal Performance by a Duo in 1990 with Aaron Neville for *All My Life*; Best Tropical Latin Album in 1992 for *Frenesi*; Best Mexican-American Album in 1992 for *Mas Canciones*; Best Children's Music in 1996 for *Dedicated To The One I Love*; and Best Country Vocal Collaboration in 1999 with Emmylou Harris and Dolly Parton for *After The Gold Rush*. Aaron Neville (born 21/1/1941, New Orleans, LA) was originally with the Hawketts before joining his brothers in the Neville Family Band; he then went solo.

| DATE | POS | WKS | BPI | ALBUM TITLE | LABEL & NUMBER |
|---|---|---|---|---|---|
| 04/09/1976 | 32 | 8 | ○ | HASTEN DOWN THE WIND 1976 Grammy Award for Best Pop Vocal Performance | Asylum K 53045 |
| 25/12/1976 | 37 | 9 | | GREATEST HITS | Asylum K 53055 |
| 01/10/1977 | 15 | 5 | | SIMPLE DREAMS ▲[5] | Asylum K 53065 |
| 14/10/1978 | 39 | 2 | ○ | LIVING IN THE USA ▲[1] | Asylum K 53085 |
| 08/03/1980 | 65 | 1 | | MAD LOVE | Asylum K 52210 |

| DATE | POS | WKS | BPI | ALBUM TITLE | LABEL & NUMBER |
|---|---|---|---|---|---|
| 28/01/1984 | 31 | 5 | | WHAT'S NEW | Asylum 9602601 |
| 19/01/1985 | 100 | 1 | | LUSH LIFE This and the above hit credited to **LINDA RONSTADT WITH THE NELSON RIDDLE ORCHESTRA** | Asylum 9603871 |
| 14/03/1987 | 60 | 4 | | TRIO **DOLLY PARTON, LINDA RONSTADT AND EMMYLOU HARRIS** 1987 Grammy Award for Best Country Performance by a Group | Warner Brothers 9254911 |
| 11/11/1989 | 43 | 8 | ● | CRY LIKE A RAINSTORM – HOWL LIKE THE WIND **LINDA RONSTADT FEATURING AARON NEVILLE** | Elektra EKT 76 |
| 11/10/2003 | 46 | 3 | | THE VERY BEST OF | Elektra 8122736052 |

### ROOTJOOSE

UK group formed in Cornwall by James Crowe (guitar/vocals), Rob Elton (guitar/vocals), Harry Collier (bass/vocals) and Fez (drums). They later changed their name to Rarebirds.

| DATE | POS | WKS | BPI | ALBUM TITLE | LABEL & NUMBER |
|---|---|---|---|---|---|
| 18/10/1997 | 58 | 1 | | RHUBARB | Rage RAGECD 6 |

### ROSE ROYCE

US soul group formed in Los Angeles, CA in 1972 by Kenji Chiba Brown (guitar), Lequient 'Duke' Jobe (bass), Victor Nix (keyboards), Kenny Copeland (trumpet), Freddie Dunn (trumpet), Michael Moore (saxophone) and Terral Santiel (congas). First known as Total Concept Unlimited, they were used by producer Norman Whitfield as Edwin Starr's backing band, later name-changing to Magic Wand and supporting Yvonne Fair, the Temptations and Undisputed Truth. They added lead singer Gwen Dickey and name-changed to Rose Royce in 1975. The first act to sign to Whitfield's eponymous label, their big break came with the recording of the soundtrack to the 1976 film *Car Wash*. Dickey left in 1977 and was replaced by Rose Norwalt. Dickey returned in 1978 for two years and was subsequently replaced by Ricci Benson. Nix left in 1977 (replaced by Michael Nash) and Brown left in 1980 (replaced by Walter McKinney). *Car Wash* won the 1976 Grammy Award for Best Album of Original Score Written for a Motion Picture. Jean Carn is a US singer born Sarah Jean Perkins in Columbus, GA.

| DATE | POS | WKS | BPI | ALBUM TITLE | LABEL & NUMBER |
|---|---|---|---|---|---|
| 22/10/1977 | 18 | 13 | ● | IN FULL BLOOM | Whitfield K 56394 |
| 30/09/1978 | 7 | 11 | ● | **STRIKES AGAIN** | Whitfield K 56257 |
| 22/09/1979 | 72 | 2 | | RAINBOW CONNECTION IV | Whitfield K 56714 |
| 01/03/1980 | ❶² | 34 | ✪ | **ROSE ROYCE GREATEST HITS** | Whitfield RRTV 1 |
| 13/10/1984 | 69 | 2 | | MUSIC MAGIC | Streetwave MKL 2 |
| 09/03/1985 | 65 | 4 | | THE ARTISTS VOLUME 1 **EARTH WIND & FIRE/JEAN CARN/ROSE ROYCE** | Street Sounds ARTIS 1 |

### ROSE TATTOO

Australian group formed in Sydney in 1977 by Angry Anderson (born Gary Stephen Anderson, 5/8/1948, vocals), Peter Wells (guitar/vocals), Michael Cocks (guitar), Mick 'Geordie' Leech (bass) and Dallas 'Digger' Royall (drums). They released their debut album in 1978. Cocks left in 1982 and was replaced by Robin Riley. Anderson and Leech then re-assembled the group with Greg Jordan (guitar), John Meyer (guitar) and Robert Bowron (drums) for one album before the group disbanded. Although another Rose Tattoo album appeared, this was a contractual obligation album that was effectively Anderson recording solo. The original line-up re-formed in 1993 (minus Royall who had died three years previously).

| DATE | POS | WKS | BPI | ALBUM TITLE | LABEL & NUMBER |
|---|---|---|---|---|---|
| 26/09/1981 | 40 | 4 | | ASSAULT AND BATTERY | Carrere CAL 127 |

### DIANA ROSS

US singer (born Diane Ernestine Ross, 26/3/1944, Detroit, MI) who joined the Primettes in 1959. The group subsequently became the Supremes when they were signed by Motown in 1960. She took over from Florence Ballard as lead singer and was given top billing in 1967. She left the group for a solo career in 1970 and was replaced by Jean Terrell. She appeared in films including the biopic of singer Billie Holiday *Lady Sings The Blues* (1972), for which she was nominated for an Oscar, *Mahogany* (1975), *The Wiz* (1978) and alongside Brandy in *Double Platinum* (1999). She left Motown in 1981, signing with RCA for the US and EMI/Capitol for the UK. She had a relationship with Motown founder Berry Gordy with whom she had a son. She has a star on the Hollywood Walk of Fame.

| DATE | POS | WKS | BPI | ALBUM TITLE | LABEL & NUMBER |
|---|---|---|---|---|---|
| 20/01/1968 | ❶³ | 60 | | **DIANA ROSS AND THE SUPREMES GREATEST HITS** ▲⁵ | Tamla Motown STML 11063 |
| 30/03/1968 | 6 | 18 | | **'LIVE' AT LONDON'S TALK OF THE TOWN** | Tamla Motown STML 11070 |
| 20/07/1968 | 30 | 2 | | REFLECTIONS This and the above two hits credited to **DIANA ROSS AND THE SUPREMES** | Tamla Motown STML 11073 |
| 25/01/1969 | ❶⁴ | 15 | | **DIANA ROSS AND THE SUPREMES JOIN THE TEMPTATIONS DIANA ROSS AND THE SUPREMES AND THE TEMPTATIONS** | Tamla Motown STML 11096 |
| 01/02/1969 | 8 | 6 | | **LOVE CHILD DIANA ROSS AND THE SUPREMES** | Tamla Motown STML 11095 |
| 28/06/1969 | 11 | 12 | | THE ORIGINAL SOUNDTRACK FROM TCB Original soundtrack to the TV series | Tamla Motown STML 11110 |
| 14/02/1970 | 28 | 4 | | TOGETHER This and the above hit credited to **DIANA ROSS AND THE SUPREMES AND THE TEMPTATIONS** | Tamla Motown STML 11122 |
| 24/10/1970 | 14 | 5 | | DIANA ROSS | Tamla Motown STML 11159 |
| 19/06/1971 | 31 | 3 | | EVERYTHING IS EVERYTHING | Tamla Motown STML 11178 |
| 09/10/1971 | 43 | 1 | | DIANA Original soundtrack to the TV series | Tamla Motown STMA 8001 |
| 09/10/1971 | 10 | 11 | ○ | **I'M STILL WAITING** | Tamla Motown STML 11193 |
| 11/11/1972 | 34 | 10 | ● | GREATEST HITS | Tamla Motown STMA 8006 |
| 01/09/1973 | 7 | 35 | ● | **TOUCH ME IN THE MORNING** | Tamla Motown STML 11239 |
| 27/10/1973 | 50 | 1 | | LADY SINGS THE BLUES ▲² Original soundtrack to the film | Tamla Motown TMSP 1131 |
| 19/01/1974 | 6 | 43 | ● | **DIANA AND MARVIN DIANA ROSS AND MARVIN GAYE** | Tamla Motown STMA 8015 |
| 02/03/1974 | 41 | 1 | | LAST TIME I SAW HIM | Tamla Motown STML 11255 |
| 08/06/1974 | 21 | 8 | | DIANA ROSS LIVE AT CAESAR'S PALACE | Tamla Motown STML 11248 |
| 27/03/1976 | 4 | 26 | ● | **DIANA ROSS** | Tamla Motown STML 12022 |
| 07/08/1976 | 2 | 29 | ● | **GREATEST HITS 2** | Tamla Motown STML 12036 |
| 19/03/1977 | 52 | 1 | ○ | AN EVENING WITH DIANA ROSS | Motown TMSP 6005 |
| 17/09/1977 | ❶⁷ | 34 | | **DIANA ROSS AND THE SUPREMES 20 GOLDEN GREATS DIANA ROSS AND THE SUPREMES** | Motown EMTV 5 |

▲⁹ Number of weeks album topped the US chart  ◆¹² RIAA Diamond Awards  ◇³ IFPI Platinum Europe Awards

| DATE | POS | WKS | BPI | ALBUM TITLE | LABEL & NUMBER |
|---|---|---|---|---|---|
| 04/08/1979 | 52 | 2 | | THE BOSS | Motown STML 12118 |
| 17/11/1979 | 2 | 29 | ✪ | **20 GOLDEN GREATS** | Motown EMTV 21 |
| 21/06/1980 | 12 | 32 | ● | DIANA | Motown STMA 8033 |
| 28/03/1981 | 26 | 10 | | TO LOVE AGAIN | Motown STML 12152 |
| 29/08/1981 | 78 | 2 | | DIANA AND MARVIN **DIANA ROSS AND MARVIN GAYE** Re-issue of Tamla Motown STML 8015 | Motown STMS 5001 |
| 07/11/1981 | 17 | 24 | ● | WHY DO FOOLS FALL IN LOVE | Capitol EST 26733 |
| 21/11/1981 | 21 | 31 | ✪ | ALL THE GREAT HITS | Motown STMA 8036 |
| 13/02/1982 | 43 | 6 | ○ | DIANA'S DUETS | Motown STML 12163 |
| 23/10/1982 | 33 | 12 | ○ | SILK ELECTRIC | Capitol EAST 27313 |
| 04/12/1982 | 5 | 17 | ✪ | **LOVE SONGS** | K-Tel NE 1200 |
| 16/07/1983 | 44 | 5 | | ROSS | Capitol EST 1867051 |
| 24/12/1983 | 8 | 31 | ● | **PORTRAIT** | Telstar STAR 2238 |
| 06/10/1984 | 40 | 5 | | SWEPT AWAY | Capitol ROSS 1 |
| 28/09/1985 | 11 | 19 | | EATEN ALIVE | Capitol ROSS 2 |
| 15/11/1986 | 21 | 10 | . | DIANA ROSS. MICHAEL JACKSON. GLADYS KNIGHT. STEVIE WONDER. THEIR VERY BEST BACK TO BACK **DIANA ROSS/ MICHAEL JACKSON/GLADYS KNIGHT/STEVIE WONDER** | PrioriTyV PTVR 2 |
| 30/05/1987 | 47 | 4 | | RED HOT RHYTHM 'N' BLUES | EMI EMC 3532 |
| 31/10/1987 | 12 | 24 | ✪ | LOVE SONGS **DIANA ROSS AND MICHAEL JACKSON** When multi-artist packages were excluded from the main chart, this album featured on the compilation chart | Telstar STAR 2298 |
| 21/01/1989 | 10 | 9 | ○ | **LOVE SUPREME DIANA ROSS AND THE SUPREMES** | Motown ZL 72701 |
| 27/05/1989 | 23 | 4 | ○ | WORKIN' OVERTIME | EMI EMD 1009 |
| 25/11/1989 | 34 | 6 | ● | GREATEST HITS LIVE | EMI EMDC 1001 |
| 14/12/1991 | 11 | 31 | ✪ | THE FORCE BEHIND THE POWER | EMI EMD 1023 |
| 29/02/1992 | 20 | 11 | | MOTOWN'S GREATEST HITS | Motown 5300132 |
| 24/04/1993 | 45 | 2 | | LIVE, STOLEN MOMENTS – THE LADY SINGS THE BLUES | EMI CDEMD 1044 |
| 30/10/1993 | ❶² | 67 | ✪⁴ | **ONE WOMAN – THE ULTIMATE COLLECTION** | EMI CDONE 1 |
| 25/12/1993 | 71 | 2 | | CHRISTMAS IN VIENNA **PLACIDO DOMINGO, DIANA ROSS & JOSE CARRERAS** | Sony Classical SK 53358 |
| 23/04/1994 | 58 | 1 | | DIANA EXTENDED – THE REMIXES | EMI CDDREX 1 |
| 26/11/1994 | 37 | 6 | ● | A VERY SPECIAL SEASON | EMI CDEMD 1075 |
| 16/09/1995 | 10 | 3 | | **TAKE ME HIGHER** | EMI CDEMD 1085 |
| 23/11/1996 | 42 | 7 | | VOICE OF LOVE | EMI CDEMD 1100 |
| 31/10/1998 | 35 | 4 | | 40 GOLDEN MOTOWN GREATS **DIANA ROSS AND THE SUPREMES** | Motown 5309612 |
| 20/11/1999 | 71 | 1 | | EVERY DAY IS A NEW DAY | EMI 5214762 |
| 17/11/2001 | 28 | 7 | ● | LOVE AND LIFE – THE VERY BEST OF | EMI/Universal TV 5358622 |
| 29/05/2004 | 26 | 3 | | THE NO 1'S **DIANA ROSS AND THE SUPREMES** | Motown 9818019 |

### RICKY ROSS
UK singer (born 22/12/1957, Dundee) who was a member of Deacon Blue before going solo.

| DATE | POS | WKS | BPI | ALBUM TITLE | LABEL & NUMBER |
|---|---|---|---|---|---|
| 15/06/1996 | 36 | 1 | | WHAT YOU ARE | Epic 4839982 |

### ROSTAL AND SCHAEFER
UK/French instrumental duo formed by Max Rostal (born 7/8/1905, Teschen, Austria) and Pierre Schaefer (born 14/8/1910, Nancy, France). Rostal was a UK violinist who began giving recitals from the age of six and was later a professor at the Berlin Hochschule and from 1958 at the Berne Conservatory. He died on 6/8/1991. Schaefer is a French composer and percussionist who worked for French radio from 1936–48 and later taught at the Paris Conservatoire.

| DATE | POS | WKS | BPI | ALBUM TITLE | LABEL & NUMBER |
|---|---|---|---|---|---|
| 14/07/1979 | 61 | 2 | | BEATLES CONCERTO | Parlophone PAS 10014 |

### DAVID LEE ROTH
US singer (born 10/10/1955, Bloomington, IN) who was lead singer with Van Halen from their formation in 1975 until 1985 when he left to go solo.

| DATE | POS | WKS | BPI | ALBUM TITLE | LABEL & NUMBER |
|---|---|---|---|---|---|
| 02/03/1985 | 91 | 2 | | CRAZY FROM THE HEAT | Warner Brothers 9252221 |
| 19/07/1986 | 28 | 9 | | EAT 'EM AND SMILE | Warner Brothers WX 56 |
| 06/02/1988 | 11 | 12 | ○ | SKYSCRAPER | Warner Brothers 9256711 |
| 26/01/1991 | 4 | 7 | ○ | **A LITTLE AIN'T ENOUGH** | Warner Brothers WX 403 |
| 19/03/1994 | 28 | 2 | | YOUR FILTHY LITTLE MOUTH | Reprise 9362453912 |

### ULI JON ROTH AND ELECTRIC SUN
German vocal/instrumental group formed in 1978 by Ulrich Roth, Clive Bunker, Ule Ritgen, Nicky Moore, Sidharta Gautama and Michael Flexig. Roth had previously been a member of The Scorpions.

| DATE | POS | WKS | BPI | ALBUM TITLE | LABEL & NUMBER |
|---|---|---|---|---|---|
| 23/02/1985 | 64 | 2 | | BEYOND THE ASTRAL SKIES | EMI ROTH 1 |

### THOMAS ROUND – see JUNE BRONHILL AND THOMAS ROUND

### DEMIS ROUSSOS
Greek singer (born 15/6/1947, Alexandria, Egypt) who was a member of Aphrodite's Child with Vangelis and Lucas Sideras from 1963 until they disbanded in the mid-1970s. He then went solo and became a big hit across Europe. He was one of the passengers hijacked and held hostage at Beirut Airport in 1985.

○ Silver disc  ● Gold disc  ✪ Platinum disc (additional platinum units are indicated by a figure following the symbol)  ❶⁹ Number of weeks album topped the UK chart

| | | | | | |
|---|---|---|---|---|---|
| 22/06/1974 | 2 | 68 | ✪ | FOREVER AND EVER | Philips 6325 021 |
| 19/04/1975 | 25 | 18 | ● | SOUVENIRS | Philips 6325 201 |
| 24/04/1976 | 4 | 34 | ● | HAPPY TO BE | Philips 9101 027 |
| 03/07/1976 | 39 | 6 | ● | MY ONLY FASCINATION | Philips 6325 094 |
| 16/04/1977 | 29 | 6 | ○ | THE MAGIC OF DEMIS ROUSSOS | Philips 9101 131 |
| 28/10/1978 | 36 | 11 | ○ | LIFE AND LOVE | Philips 9199 873 |
| 16/03/2002 | 17 | 4 | | FOREVER AND EVER – DEFINITIVE COLLECTION | Philips 5867702 |

### KELLY ROWLAND
US singer (born Kelendria Rowland, 11/2/1981, Houston, TX) and a member of Destiny's Child. She launched a parallel solo career in 2002. She won the 2002 Grammy Award for Best Rap/Song Collaboration with Nelly for *Dilemma* and got engaged to Dallas Cowboys football player Roy Williams in May 2003.

| | | | | | |
|---|---|---|---|---|---|
| 15/02/2003 | ❶[1] | 26 | ✪ | SIMPLY DEEP | Columbia 5096042 |

### ROXETTE
Swedish duo formed in 1986 by Per Gessle (born 12/2/1959, Halmstad, guitar/vocals) and Marie Fredriksson (born 29/5/1958, Ostra Ljungby, vocals). Gessle was ex-member of the group Gyllene Tyler while Fredriksson was a successful solo artist.

| | | | | | |
|---|---|---|---|---|---|
| 17/06/1989 | 4 | 53 | ✪ | LOOK SHARP! | EMI EMC 3557 |
| 13/04/1991 | 2 | 48 | ✪[2] | JOYRIDE | EMI EMD 1019 |
| 12/09/1992 | 2 | 17 | ● | TOURISM | EMI CDEMD 1036 |
| 23/04/1994 | 3 | 16 | ● | CRASH BOOM BANG ◇ | EMI CDEMD 1056 |
| 04/11/1995 | 5 | 20 | ✪ | DON'T BORE US, GET TO THE CHORUS! – GREATEST HITS ◇ | EMI CDXEMTV 98 |
| 10/04/1999 | 28 | 3 | | HAVE A NICE DAY | EMI 4994612 |
| 15/02/2003 | 11 | 4 | ○ | THE BALLAD HITS | Capitol 5427982 |

### ROXY MUSIC
UK group formed in 1971 by Bryan Ferry (born 26/9/1945, Washington, Tyne and Wear, vocals/keyboards), Andy Mackay (born 23/7/1946, London, saxophone), Brian Eno (born Brian Peter George St John le Baptiste de la Salle Eno, 15/5/1948, Woodbridge, synthesiser), Davy O'List (born 13/12/1950, London, guitar), Graham Simpson (bass) and Paul Thompson (born 13/5/1951, Jarrow, Northumberland). O'List left in 1972 and was replaced by Phil Manzanera (born Philip Targett Adams, 31/1/1951, London); Simpson was replaced by Rik Kenton the same year. Thereafter they went through a succession of bass guitarists, including John Porter, John Gustafson, John Wetton, Rik Kenton, Sal Maida, Rick Wills and Gary Tibbs (later a member of Adam And The Ants). They signed with management company EG in 1971, with their initial recordings licensed to Island. Ferry later recorded solo, while Eno moved into production. Eno was named Best Producer at the 1994 and 1996 BRIT Awards and also collected the 1992 Grammy Award with Daniel Lanois in the same category (jointly with Babyface).

| | | | | | |
|---|---|---|---|---|---|
| 29/07/1972 | 10 | 16 | ● | ROXY MUSIC | Island ILPS 9200 |
| 07/04/1973 | 4 | 27 | ● | FOR YOUR PLEASURE | Island ILPS 9232 |
| 01/12/1973 | ❶[1] | 17 | ● | STRANDED | Island ILPS 9252 |
| 30/11/1974 | 3 | 10 | ● | COUNTRY LIFE | Island ILPS 9303 |
| 08/11/1975 | 4 | 17 | ○ | SIREN | Island ILPS 9344 |
| 31/07/1976 | 6 | 12 | ○ | VIVA! ROXY MUSIC | Island ILPS 9400 |
| 19/11/1977 | 20 | 11 | ● | GREATEST HITS | Polydor 2302 073 |
| 24/03/1979 | 7 | 34 | ● | MANIFESTO | Polydor POLH 001 |
| 31/05/1980 | ❶[4] | 60 | ✪ | FLESH AND BLOOD | Polydor POLH 002 |
| 05/06/1982 | ❶[3] | 57 | ✪ | AVALON | Polydor EGLP 50 |
| 19/03/1983 | 26 | 7 | | MUSIQUE/THE HIGH ROAD | E.G. EGMLP 1 |
| 12/11/1983 | 23 | 25 | ● | ROXY MUSIC – THE ATLANTIC YEARS (1973–1980) | E.G. EGLP 54 |
| 26/04/1986 | ❶[5] | 77 | ✪ | STREET LIFE – 20 GREAT HITS | E.G. EGTV 1 |
| 19/11/1988 | 6 | 35 | ✪[3] | THE ULTIMATE COLLECTION | E.G. EGTV 2 |
| 04/11/1995 | 15 | 15 | ✪ | MORE THAN THIS – THE BEST OF BRYAN FERRY AND ROXY MUSIC This and the above two hits credited to **BRYAN FERRY AND ROXY MUSIC** | Virgin CDV 2791 |
| 23/06/2001 | 12 | 6 | ● | BEST OF | Virgin CDV 2939 |
| 19/06/2004 | 17 | 2+ | ○ | PLATINUM COLLECTION **BRYAN FERRY AND ROXY MUSIC** | Virgin BFRM1 |

### ROYAL PHILHARMONIC ORCHESTRA
UK orchestra formed in 1946 by Sir Thomas Beecham. Following his death in 1961 Rudolf Kempe became musical director. Sir Thomas Beecham and the Royal Philharmonic Orchestra won the 1960 Grammy Award for Best Classical Performance, Choral (including Oratorio) for *Handel's Messiah*. In 1966 Queen Elizabeth II conferred the Royal title on the orchestra. Among the musical directors since 1975 (when Kempe retired) are Andre Previn, Walter Weller and Vladimir Ashkenazy.

| DATE | POS | WKS | BPI | ALBUM TITLE | LABEL & NUMBER |
|---|---|---|---|---|---|
| 08/02/1975 | 17 | 7 | ○ | THE ORCHESTRAL TUBULAR BELLS **MIKE OLDFIELD WITH THE ROYAL PHILHARMONIC ORCHESTRA** | Virgin V 2026 |
| 08/01/1977 | 24 | 13 | ● | CLASSICAL GOLD | Ronco RTD 42020 |
| 23/12/1978 | 31 | 4 | | CLASSIC GOLD VOLUME 2 | Ronco RTD 42032 |
| 19/09/1981 | 4 | 43 | ✪ | **HOOKED ON CLASSICS** | K-Tel ONE 1146 |
| 31/07/1982 | 13 | 26 | ● | CAN'T STOP THE CLASSICS – HOOKED ON CLASSICS 2 | K-Tel ONE 1173 |
| 09/04/1983 | 19 | 15 | | JOURNEY THROUGH THE CLASSICS – HOOKED ON CLASSICS 3 This and the above two hits credited to **LOUIS CLARK CONDUCTING THE ROYAL PHILHARMONIC ORCHESTRA** | K-Tel ONE 1266 |
| 08/10/1983 | 30 | 9 | ○ | LOVE CLASSICS **ROYAL PHILHARMONIC ORCHESTRA CONDUCTED BY NICK PORTLOCK** | Nouveau Music NML 1003 |
| 10/12/1983 | 51 | 6 | ○ | THE BEST OF HOOKED ON CLASSICS **ROYAL PHILHARMONIC ORCHESTRA CONDUCTED BY LOUIS CLARK** | K-Tel ONE 1266 |
| 11/02/1984 | 21 | 9 | | SERENADE **JUAN MARTIN WITH THE ROYAL PHILHARMONIC ORCHESTRA** | K-Tel NE 1267 |
| 26/05/1984 | 95 | 2 | | AS TIME GOES BY **ROYAL PHILHARMONIC ORCHESTRA CONDUCTED BY HARRY RABINOVITZ** | Telstar STAR 2240 |
| 23/11/1985 | 17 | 18 | | THE CLASSIC TOUCH **RICHARD CLAYDERMAN WITH THE ROYAL PHILHARMONIC ORCHESTRA** | Decca SKL 5343 |
| 21/02/1987 | 94 | 1 | | ELGAR CELLO CONCERTO **JULIAN LLOYD WEBBER WITH THE ROYAL PHILHARMONIC ORCHESTRA CONDUCTED BY SIR YEHUDI MENUHIN** | Philips 4163541 |
| 26/11/1988 | 96 | 1 | | RHYTHM AND CLASSICS **LOUIS CLARK CONDUCTING THE ROYAL PHILHARMONIC ORCHESTRA** | Telstar STAR 2344 |
| 21/04/1990 | 72 | 1 | | OPERA EXTRAVAGANZA **ROYAL PHILHARMONIC ORCHESTRA, CHORUS ROYAL OPERA HOUSE, THE LONDON SYMPHONY ORCHESTRA, CONDUCTOR LUIS COBOS** | Epic MOOD 12 |
| 29/09/1990 | 39 | 4 | | MUSIC FOR THE LAST NIGHT OF THE PROMS **SIR CHARLES GROVES CONDUCTING THE ROYAL PHILHARMONIC ORCHESTRA AND CHORUS WITH SARAH WALKER (SOPRANO)** | Cirrus TVLP 501 |
| 27/10/1990 | 15 | 13 | ● | LLOYD WEBBER PLAYS LLOYD WEBBER **JULIAN LLOYD WEBBER WITH THE ROYAL PHILHARMONIC ORCHESTRA** | Philips 4322911 |
| 24/11/1990 | 29 | 7 | | MY CLASSIC COLLECTION **RICHARD CLAYDERMAN WITH THE ROYAL PHILHARMONIC ORCHESTRA** | Decca 8282281 |
| 05/10/1991 | 31 | 6 | ○ | SERIOUSLY CLASSIC **LOUIS CLARK CONDUCTING THE ROYAL PHILHARMONIC ORCHESTRA** | Virgin RPOLP 1 |
| 09/11/1991 | 3 | 36 | ✪² | **MICHAEL CRAWFORD PERFORMS ANDREW LLOYD WEBBER** MICHAEL CRAWFORD & THE ROYAL PHILHARMONIC ORCHESTRA | Telstar STAR 2544 |
| 14/11/1992 | 47 | 5 | ○ | THE VERY BEST OF RICHARD CLAYDERMAN **RICHARD CLAYDERMAN WITH THE ROYAL PHILHARMONIC ORCHESTRA** | Decca Delpine 8283362 |
| 12/02/1994 | 44 | 4 | | MY HEART'S DELIGHT **LUCIANO PAVAROTTI WITH THE ROYAL PHILHARMONIC ORCHESTRA** | Decca 4432602 |
| 30/07/1994 | 49 | 2 | | BIG SCREEN CLASSICS | Quality Television GIGSCD 1 |
| 13/04/1996 | 49 | 2 | | AMAZING **ELKIE BROOKS WITH THE ROYAL PHILHARMONIC ORCHESTRA** | Carlton Premiere 3036000282 |
| 26/06/2004 | 42 | 1+ | | SYMPHONIC ROCK | Virgin/EMI VTDCD620 |

### ROYKSOPP
Norwegian production duo formed in Tromso by Svein Berge and Torbjrn Brundtland. The group won the 2002 MTV Europe Music Award for Best Video for *Remind Me*.

| DATE | POS | WKS | BPI | ALBUM TITLE | LABEL & NUMBER |
|---|---|---|---|---|---|
| 24/08/2002 | 9 | 41 | ✪ | **MELODY AM** | Wall Of Sound WALLCD 027 |

### ROZALLA
Zambian singer (born Rozalla Miller, 18/3/1964, Ndola) who was lead singer with the Band Of Gypsies before going solo. She lives in Zimbabwe and London.

| DATE | POS | WKS | BPI | ALBUM TITLE | LABEL & NUMBER |
|---|---|---|---|---|---|
| 04/04/1992 | 20 | 4 | ○ | EVERYBODY'S FREE | Pulse 8 PULSECD 3 |

### RUBETTES
UK pop group formed in 1974 after the success of their debut single (sung by Paul Da Vinci). They comprised Alan Williams (born 22/12/1948, Welwyn Garden City, guitar/flute/piano), Tony Thorpe (born 20/7/1947, London, guitar/piano/drums), Mick Clarke (born 10/8/1946, Grimsby, Humberside, bass), Bill Hurd (born 11/8/1948, London, keyboards) and John Richardson (born 3/5/1948, Dagenham, drums), all of whom had been in Barry Blue's backing band. Williams was later a member of The Firm.

| DATE | POS | WKS | BPI | ALBUM TITLE | LABEL & NUMBER |
|---|---|---|---|---|---|
| 10/05/1975 | 41 | 1 | | WE CAN DO IT | Start ETAT 001 |

### JIMMY RUFFIN
US singer (born on 7/5/1939, Collinsville, MS) and older brother of David Ruffin who joined Motown in 1961, recording one single before he was drafted. He returned in 1963 and turned down the opportunity to join The Temptations, recommending his brother David instead. He later relocated to the UK and took part in the Paul Weller project Council Collective.

| DATE | POS | WKS | BPI | ALBUM TITLE | LABEL & NUMBER |
|---|---|---|---|---|---|
| 13/05/1967 | 32 | 6 | | THE JIMMY RUFFIN WAY | Tamla Motown STML 11048 |
| 01/06/1974 | 41 | 4 | | GREATEST HITS | Tamla Motown STML 11259 |

### RUFUS
US inter-racial R&B group formed in Chicago, IL in 1970 by Al Ciner (guitar), Charles Colbert (bass), Kevin Murphy (keyboards), Lee Graziano (drums), Paulette McWilliams (vocals), Ron Stockard and Dennis Belfield as Smoke, with Andre Fisher subsequently replacing Graziano. The group evolved from American Breed, and after further name (Ask Rufus and then Rufus) and personnel changes settled on a line-up of Chaka Khan (born Yvette Marie Stevens, 23/3/1953, Great Lakes, IL), Murphy, Tony Maiden (guitar), Dave Wolinski (keyboards), Bobby Watson (bass) and John Robinson (drums). Khan went solo in 1978. The group took their name from a help column in the US magazine *Mechanics Illustrated*, called 'Ask Rufus'. The group has won two Grammy Awards: Best Rhythm & Blues

Vocal Performance by a Group in 1974 for *Tell Me Something Good* and Best Rhythm & Blues Vocal Performance by a Group in 1983 for *Ain't Nobody*.

| | | | | | |
|---|---|---|---|---|---|
| 12/04/1975 | 48 | 2 | | RUFUSIZED | ABC ABCL 5063 |
| 21/04/1984 | 64 | 5 | | STOMPIN' AT THE SAVOY **RUFUS AND CHAKA KHAN** | Warner Brothers 9236791 |

### RUN D.M.C.
US rap group formed in New York in 1983 by Joseph 'Run' Simmons (born 24/11/1964, Queens, NYC), MC Darryl 'D' McDaniels (born 31/5/1964, Queens) and Jam Master Jay (born Jason Mizell, 21/1/1965, Queens). They signed with Profile the same year. Their eponymous debut album became the first rap album to achieve gold status in the US. Run's brother Russell Simmons co-founded Def Jam Records. Jason Mizell was shot to death on 31/10/2002.

| | | | | | |
|---|---|---|---|---|---|
| 26/07/1986 | 41 | 26 | ○ | RAISING HELL | Profile LONLP 21 |
| 04/06/1988 | 13 | 5 | | TOUGHER THAN LEATHER | Profile LONLP 38 |
| 15/05/1993 | 44 | 2 | | DOWN WITH THE KING | Profile FILECD 440 |
| 06/06/1998 | 31 | 3 | | TOGETHER FOREVER – GREATEST HITS 1983–1998 | Profile FILECD 474 |
| 26/04/2003 | 15 | 8 | | GREATEST HITS | Arista 74321980602 |

### TODD RUNDGREN
US singer (born 22/6/1948, Upper Darby, PA) who was in the groups Nazz and Utopia. He later became a successful producer, including Meat Loaf's *Bat Out Of Hell* album.

| | | | | | |
|---|---|---|---|---|---|
| 29/01/1977 | 27 | 6 | | RA | Bearsville K 55514 |
| 06/05/1978 | 42 | 3 | | HERMIT OF MINK HOLLOW | Bearsville K 55521 |

### BIC RUNGA
New Zealand singer (born 13/1/1976, Christchurch) of Chinese and Maori heritage. She made her first album in 1995.

| | | | | | |
|---|---|---|---|---|---|
| 03/04/2004 | 55 | 2 | | BEAUTIFUL COLLISION | Epic 5127279 |

### RUNRIG
UK group formed by Iain Bayne (born 22/1/1960, St Andrews), Bruce Guthro (born 31/8/1961, Canada), Rory MacDonald (born 27/7/1949, Dornoch, Scotland), Peter Wishart (born 3/3/1962, Dunfirmline), Malcolm Jones (born 12/7/1959, Inverness), Calum MacDonald (born 12/11/1953, Lochmaddy) and Donnie Munro (born 2/8/1953, Uig, Isle of Skye) who often record in Gaelic and who have established a big cult following in the US. Lead singer Donnie Munro stood for election in the 1997 General Election as a Labour candidate for Ross, Sky and Inverness West but lost to the Liberal Democrats. Wishart, however, was returned as the MP for North Tayside.

| | | | | | |
|---|---|---|---|---|---|
| 26/11/1988 | 61 | 2 | ● | ONCE IN A LIFETIME | Chrysalis CHR 1695 |
| 07/10/1989 | 11 | 4 | ● | SEARCHLIGHT | Chrysalis CHR 1713 |
| 22/06/1991 | 4 | 15 | ● | **THE BIG WHEEL** | Chrysalis CHR 1858 |
| 27/03/1993 | 2 | 6 | ○ | **AMAZING THINGS** | Chrysalis CDCHR 2000 |
| 26/11/1994 | 41 | 3 | | TRANSMITTING LIVE | Chrysalis CDCHR 6090 |
| 20/05/1995 | 45 | 2 | ○ | THE CUTTER AND THE CLAN | Chrysalis CCD 1669 |
| 18/11/1995 | 24 | 4 | | MARA | Chrysalis CDCHR 6111 |
| 19/10/1996 | 13 | 10 | ● | LONG DISTANCE – THE BEST OF RUNRIG | Chrysalis CDCHR 6116 |
| 23/05/1998 | 71 | 1 | | THE GAELIC COLLECTION 1973–1995 | Ridge RR 009 |
| 13/03/1999 | 29 | 2 | | IN SEARCH OF ANGELS | Ridge RR 010 |
| 26/05/2001 | 64 | 1 | | THE STAMPING GROUND | Ridge RR 16 |

### KATE RUSBY
UK singer/guitarist born in Barnsley; she grew up in a musical family and was introduced to folk music at an early age. At the age of fifteen she teamed up with fellow folk singer Kathryn Roberts and they recorded an album together. Kate launched a solo career in 1998 but also records with The Poozies.

| | | | | | |
|---|---|---|---|---|---|
| 09/06/2001 | 75 | 1 | | LITTLE LIGHTS | Pure PRCD 07 |

### RUSH
Canadian rock group formed in Toronto, Ontario in 1969 by Alex Lifeson (born Alex Zivojinovic, 27/8/1953, Fernie, British Columbia, guitar), Geddy Lee (born Gary Lee Weinrib, 29/7/1953, Toronto, vocals/bass) and John Rutsey (drums). They funded the release of their debut album on their own Moon label and were signed by Mercury as a result. Rutsey left in 1974 and was replaced by Neil Peart (born 12/9/1952, Hamilton, Ontario). They switched to Atlantic in 1989.

| | | | | | |
|---|---|---|---|---|---|
| 08/10/1977 | 22 | 4 | ● | FAREWELL TO KINGS | Mercury 9100 042 |
| 25/11/1978 | 14 | 6 | ○ | HEMISPHERES | Mercury 9100 059 |
| 26/01/1980 | 3 | 16 | ● | **PERMANENT WAVES** | Mercury 9100 071 |
| 21/02/1981 | 3 | 11 | ○ | **MOVING PICTURES** | Mercury 6337 160 |
| 07/11/1981 | 6 | 14 | ○ | **EXIT STAGE LEFT** | Mercury 6619 053 |
| 18/09/1982 | 3 | 9 | ○ | **SIGNALS** | Mercury 6337 243 |
| 28/04/1984 | 5 | 12 | ○ | **GRACE UNDER PRESSURE** | Vertigo VERH 12 |
| 09/11/1985 | 9 | 4 | ○ | **POWER WINDOWS** | Vertigo VERH 31 |
| 21/11/1987 | 10 | 4 | ○ | **HOLD YOUR FIRE** | Vertigo VERH 47 |
| 28/01/1989 | 12 | 4 | | A SHOW OF HANDS | Vertigo 8363461 |
| 09/12/1989 | 27 | 2 | ○ | PRESTO | Atlantic WX 327 |
| 13/10/1990 | 42 | 2 | | CHRONICLES | Vertigo CBTV 1 |

▲[9] Number of weeks album topped the US chart  ◆[12] RIAA Diamond Awards  ◇[3] IFPI Platinum Europe Awards

| | | | | |
|---|---|---|---|---|
| 14/09/1991.....10......4...... | ROLL THE BONES | Atlantic WX 436 |
| 30/10/1993.....14......3...... | COUNTERPARTS | Atlantic 7567825282 |
| 21/09/1996.....25......3...... | TEST FOR ECHO | Atlantic 7567829252 |
| 25/05/2002.....38......2...... | VAPOR TRAILS | Atlantic 7567835312 |

### JENNIFER RUSH
US singer (born Heidi Stern, 29/9/1960, Queens, NYC); she is the daughter of opera singer Maurice Stern. She had relocated to Germany by the time of her debut hit.

| | | | | |
|---|---|---|---|---|
| 16/11/1985.....7......35......✪ | JENNIFER RUSH | CBS 26488 |
| 03/05/1986.....32......5...... | MOVIN' | CBS 26710 |
| 18/04/1987.....48......3...... | HEART OVER MIND | CBS 4504701 |

### PATRICE RUSHEN
US singer/pianist (born 30/9/1954, Los Angeles, CA) who won the Monterey Jazz Festival in 1972 and was signed by Prestige as a result. She also played with Donald Byrd, Sonny Rollins and Abbey Lincoln before joining Lee Ritenour's group in 1977.

| | | | | |
|---|---|---|---|---|
| 01/05/1982.....24......14...... | STRAIGHT FROM THE HEART | Elektra K 52352 |
| 16/06/1984.....73......3...... | NOW | Elektra 960360 |

### BRENDA RUSSELL
US singer (born Brenda Gordon, Brooklyn, NYC) whose father was a member of the Ink Spots. She met her husband Brian Russell in Canada and as Brian & Brenda recorded two albums for Rocket Records, having been spotted by Elton John. Following her divorce in 1978 she recorded solo.

| | | | | |
|---|---|---|---|---|
| 23/04/1988.....77......4...... | GET HERE | A&M AMA 5178 |

### LEON RUSSELL
US singer/songwriter/producer/arranger/multi-instrumentalist (born 2/4/1941, Lawton, OK) who played with Jerry Lee Lewis and Ronnie Hawkins during the 1950s and became an in-demand session musician. Among his many credits are performances on hits by Frank Sinatra, Herb Alpert, Bobby Darin, The Byrds, Paul Revere and Delaney and Bonnie. He linked with Marc Benno to form Asylum Choir, launched Shelter Records and also maintained a solo career over the years. His song *This Masquerade*, covered by George Benson, won the 1976 Grammy Award for Record of the Year, the closest Russell had come to an award. He finally collected a Grammy Award in 2001 for Best Country Instrumental Performance for *Foggy Mountain Breakdown* with Earl Scruggs, Glen Duncan, Randy Scruggs, Steve Martin, Vince Gill, Marty Stuart, Gary Scruggs, Albert Lee, Paul Shaffer and Jerry Douglas.

| | | | | |
|---|---|---|---|---|
| 03/07/1971.....29......1...... | LEON RUSSELL AND THE SHELTER PEOPLE | A&M AMLS 65003 |

### MIKE RUTHERFORD
UK singer/guitarist (born i2/10/1950, Guildford) who was a founding member of Genesis in 1966 with Peter Gabriel, Tony Banks, Chas Stewart and Anthony Phillips and has remained a member ever since. In 1986 he formed Mike + The Mechanics with Paul Carrack, Paul Young, Peter Van Hooke and Adrian Lee, and he has also maintained a solo career.

| | | | | |
|---|---|---|---|---|
| 23/02/1980.....13......7...... | SMALLCREEP'S DAY | Charisma CAS 1149 |
| 18/09/1982.....23......4...... | ACTING VERY STRANGE | WEA K 99249 |

### RUTLES
UK group officially formed at 43 Egg Lane, Liverpool in 1959 by Ron Nasty (rhythm guitar/vocals), Dirk McQuickly (bass/vocals), Stig O'Hara (lead guitar/vocals) and Barry Wom (born Barrington Womble, drums/vocals), later acquiring a fifth member, Leppo (standing at the back of the stage). They were known as The Quarrelmen, name-changing to The Rutles in 1961. Unofficially, this was a parody of The Beatles assembled by ex-Bonzo Dog Neil Innes (born 9/12/1944, Danbury) and Monty Python member Eric Idle (born 29/3/1943, South Shields) for the TV documentary *All You Need Is Cash*.

| | | | | |
|---|---|---|---|---|
| 15/04/1978.....12......11......◯ | THE RUTLES | Warner Brothers K 56459 |

### RUTS
UK group formed by Malcolm Owen (vocals), Paul Fox (guitar/vocals), Dave Ruffy (drums) and John 'Segs' Jennings (bass). The group effectively came to an end after Owen's sudden death from a drug overdose on 14/7/1980.

| | | | | |
|---|---|---|---|---|
| 13/10/1979.....16......6...... | THE CRACK | Virgin V 2132 |
| 18/10/1980.....28......4...... | GRIN AND BEAR IT RUTS D.C | Virgin V 2188 |

### JOHN RUTTER
UK composer/conductor (born 1945, London) who was Director of Music at Clare College from 1975–79 and then formed the Cambridge Singers. He formed his own Collegium label in 1984 and was later awarded a Lambeth Doctorate of Music by the Archbishop of Canterbury in recognition of his contribution towards church music.

| | | | | |
|---|---|---|---|---|
| 02/11/2002.....75......1...... | THE COLLECTION | UCJ 4726222 |

### RZA
US rapper (born Robert Diggs, New York City) who is also a member of The Wu-Tang Clan and Gravediggaz rap groups.

| | | | | |
|---|---|---|---|---|
| 28/11/1998.....70......1...... | BOBBY DIGITAL IN STEREO | Gee Street GEE 1003802 |

◯ Silver disc ● Gold disc ✪ Platinum disc (additional platinum units are indicated by a figure following the symbol) ❶⁹ Number of weeks album topped the UK chart

**ROBIN S** US dance singer (born Robin Stone, Jamaica, NY).

04/09/1993 . . . . .34 . . . . . .3 . . . . . .  SHOW ME LOVE . . . . . . . . . . . . . . . . . . . . . . . . . . . . . . . . . . . . . . . . . . . . . . . . . . . . . . . . .Champion CHAMPCD 1028

**S CLUB JUNIORS** UK vocal group formed by Stacey McClean (born 17/2/1989, Blackpool), Calvin Goldspink (born 24/1/1989, Great Yarmouth), Rochelle Wiseman (born 21/3/1989, Barking), Aaron Renfree (born 19/12/1987, Truro), Jay Asforis (born 30/10/1989, Waltham Forest), Hannah Richings (born 30/11/1990, Birmingham), Daisy Evans (born 30/11/1989, Chadwell Heath) and Frankie Sandford (born 14/1/1989, Havering). They were assembled by Simon Fuller as a younger version of Fuller's other major act S Club 7 and were selected after over 10,000 children auditioned. When S Club 7/S Club disbanded in 2003, S Club Juniors became S Club 8.

02/11/2002 . . . . .5 . . . . . .13 . . . . . .✪  TOGETHER . . . . . . . . . . . . . . . . . . . . . . . . . . . . . . . . . . . . . . . . . . . . . . . . . . . . . . . . . . . . . . . .Polydor 0652502
25/10/2003 . . . . .13 . . . . . .4 . . . . . .  SUNDOWN **S CLUB 8** . . . . . . . . . . . . . . . . . . . . . . . . . . . . . . . . . . . . . . . . . . . . . . . . . . . . . . .Polydor 9865703

**S CLUB 7** UK vocal group formed by Paul Cattremole (born 7/3/1977), Jon Lee (born 26/4/1982), Rachel Stevens (born 9/4/1978), Joanne O'Meara (born 29/4/1979), Bradley McIntosh (born 8/8/1981), Hannah Spearitt (born 1/4/1981) and Tina Barrett (born 16/9/1976). The group was named Best British Newcomer at the 2000 BRIT Award and they took part in the *It's Only Rock 'N' Roll* project for the Children's Promise charity. Cattremole left in August 2002, and they shortened their name to S Club. They disbanded in May 2003, shortly after the release of their film *Seeing Double*.

16/10/1999 . . . . .2 . , . . .46 . . . . . .✪²  **S CLUB** ◇ . . . . . . . . . . . . . . . . . . . . . . . . . . . . . . . . . . . . . . . . . . . . . . . . . . . . . . . . . . . . . . .Polydor 5431032
24/06/2000 . . . ❶¹ . . . . .61 . . . . . .✪⁴  **7** ◇ . . . . . . . . . . . . . . . . . . . . . . . . . . . . . . . . . . . . . . . . . . . . . . . . . . . . . . . . . . . . . . . . . . . . . .Polydor 5438572
08/12/2001 . . . . .3 . . . . . .24 . . . . . .✪²  **SUNSHINE** ◇ . . . . . . . . . . . . . . . . . . . . . . . . . . . . . . . . . . . . . . . . . . . . . . . . . . . . . . . . . . . . . . .Polydor 5894092
07/12/2002 . . . . .17 . . . . .5 . . . . . .  **SEEING DOUBLE** . . . . . . . . . . . . . . . . . . . . . . . . . . . . . . . . . . . . . . . . . . . . . . . . . . . . . . . . . . . . . .Polydor 0654962
14/06/2003 . . . . .2 . . . . . .13 . . . . . .●  **BEST – THE GREATEST HITS OF** This and the above hit credited to **S CLUB** . . . . . . . . . . . . . . . . . . . . . .Polydor 9807374

**S-EXPRESS** UK dance group formed by producer/DJ Mark Moore, singer Michelle and vocalist/percussionis/dancer Chilo Harlo. The group later included female singer Sonique who subsequently enjoyed a successful solo career.

01/04/1989 . . . . .5 . . . . . .9 . . . . . .●  **ORIGINAL SOUNDTRACK** . . . . . . . . . . . . . . . . . . . . . . . . . . . . . . . . . . . . . . . . . . . . . . . . . . . . . .Rhythm King LEFTLP 8

**SABRES OF PARADISE** UK dance group formed by Andy Weatherall, Nina Walsh, Jagz Kooner and Gary Burns.

23/10/1993 . . . . .29 . . . . . .2 . . . . . .  SABRESONIC . . . . . . . . . . . . . . . . . . . . . . . . . . . . . . . . . . . . . . . . . . . . . . . . . . . . . . . . . . . . .Warp WARPCD 16
10/12/1994 . . . . .57 . . . . . .1 . . . . . .  HAUNTED DANCEHALL . . . . . . . . . . . . . . . . . . . . . . . . . . . . . . . . . . . . . . . . . . . . . . . . . . . . . .Warp WARPCD 26

**SACRED SPIRIT** German producer/composer The Fearsome Brave (real name Claus Zundel) who mixed the chants of North American Indians with contemporary beats. The album projects also featured the vocals of John Lee Hooker and Lightning Hopkins, among others. He also records as Divine Works.

01/04/1995 . . . . .9 . . . . . .27 . . . . . .✪  **CHANTS AND DANCES OF THE NATIVE AMERICAN INDIAN** ◇ . . . . . . . . . . . . . . . . . . . . . . . . . . . . . . . . . .Virgin CDV 2753
26/04/1997 . . . . .24 . . . . . .3 . . . . . .○  VOLUME 2 – CULTURE CLASH . . . . . . . . . . . . . . . . . . . . . . . . . . . . . . . . . . . . . . . . . . . . . . . .Virgin CDV 2827

**SAD CAFE** UK rock group formed in Manchester in 1976 by Paul Young (vocals), Ian Wilson (guitar), Mike Hehir (guitar), Lennie (saxophone), Vic Emerson (keyboards), John Stimpson (bass) and David Irving (drums). Stimpson was later their manager and was replaced by Des Tong. Young later joined Mike + The Mechanics and died from a heart attack on 17/7/2000.

01/10/1977 . . . . .56 . . . . . .1 . . . . . .  FANX TA RA . . . . . . . . . . . . . . . . . . . . . . . . . . . . . . . . . . . . . . . . . . . . . . . . . . . . . . . . .RCA Victor PL 25101
29/04/1978 . . . . .50 . . . . . .1 . . . . . .  MISPLACED IDEALS . . . . . . . . . . . . . . . . . . . . . . . . . . . . . . . . . . . . . . . . . . . . . . . . . . . .RCA Victor PL 25133
29/09/1979 . . . . .8 . . . . . .23 . . . . . .●  **FACADES** . . . . . . . . . . . . . . . . . . . . . . . . . . . . . . . . . . . . . . . . . . . . . . . . . . . . . . . . . . . . . .RCA PL 25249
25/10/1980 . . . . .46 . . . . . .5 . . . . . .○  SAD CAFE... . . . . . . . . . . . . . . . . . . . . . . . . . . . . . . . . . . . . . . . . . . . . . . . . . . . . . . . . . . .RCA SADLP 4
21/03/1981 . . . . .37 . . . . . .4 . . . . . .  LIVE . . . . . . . . . . . . . . . . . . . . . . . . . . . . . . . . . . . . . . . . . . . . . . . . . . . . . . . . . . . . . . . . . . .RCA SADLP 5
24/10/1981 . . . . .72 . . . . . .2 . . . . . .  OLE . . . . . . . . . . . . . . . . . . . . . . . . . . . . . . . . . . . . . . . . . . . . . . . . . . . . . . . . . . . . . . . . . .Polydor POLD 5045

▲⁹ Number of weeks album topped the US chart   ◆¹² RIAA Diamond Awards   ◇³ IFPI Platinum Europe Awards

**SADE** UK group formed in London in 1983 by Sade Adu (born Helen Folasade Adu, 16/1/1959, Ibadan, Nigeria), Stewart Matthewman (saxophone), Paul Denman (bass) and Andrew Hale (keyboards); they were all previously in Pride. Sade was signed solo to Epic in 1984, the band signing to her in turn. She appeared in the 1987 film *Absolute Beginners*. The backing group later recorded as Sweetback. Sade has won three Grammy Awards including Best New Artist in 1985 and Best Rhythm & Blues Performance by a Group in 1993 for *No Ordinary Love*. She was awarded an OBE in the 2002 New Year's Honours List.

| 28/07/1984 | .....2 | .....99 | .....✪⁴ | **DIAMOND LIFE** 1985 BRIT Award for Best Album ........................................... | .Epic EPC 26044 |
| 16/11/1985 | ....❶² | .....31 | .....✪² | **PROMISE** ▲² ....................................................................... | .Epic EPC 86318 |
| 14/05/1988 | .....3 | .....17 | .....✪ | **STRONGER THAN PRIDE** ............................................................. | .Epic 4604971 |
| 07/11/1992 | .....10 | .....27 | .....● | **LOVE DELUXE** ..................................................................... | .Epic 4726262 |
| 12/11/1994 | .....6 | .....16 | .....● | **THE BEST OF SADE** ◇² ............................................................. | .Epic 4777932 |
| 25/11/2000 | .....18 | .....21 | .....● | LOVERS ROCK ◇ 2001 Grammy Award for Best Pop Vocal Album ........................... | .Epic 5007662 |
| 02/03/2002 | .....51 | .....2 | | LOVERS LIVE ........................................................................ | .Epic 5061252 |

**ALESSANDRO SAFINA** Italian singer (born 1968, Sienna) who began his career as an opera singer and began incorporating rock music into his repertoire after being discovered by pianist and composer Romano Musumarra.

| 30/03/2002 | .....27 | .....2 | | SAFINA ............................................................................. | .Mercury 0167432 |

**BALLY SAGOO** Indian singer/record producer (born 1964); he produced his first single in 1990 and became house producer for the Oriental Star label.

| 09/11/1996 | .....63 | .....1 | | RISING FROM THE EAST ............................................................... | .Higher Ground 4850162 |

**SAILOR** UK group formed in 1974 by Georg Kajanus (guitar/vocals), Henry Marsh (keyboard/vocals), Grant Serpell (drums/vocals) and Phil Pickett (bass/vocals). Pickett later worked with Culture Club and wrote *Karma Chameleon*.

| 07/02/1976 | .....45 | .....8 | .....○ | TROUBLE ........................................................................... | .Epic EPC 69192 |

**GENERAL SAINT** – see **CLINT EASTWOOD AND GENERAL SAINT**

**SAINT ETIENNE** UK group formed in 1988 by Peter Wiggs (born 15/5/1966, Reigate) and Bob Stanley (born 25/12/1965, Horsham), with Moira Lambert of Faith Over Reason fronting their debut hit. Donna Savage of Dead Famous People sang the lead on their second hit before Sarah Cracknell (born12/4/1967, Chelmsford) became permanent vocalist in 1992; she later recorded solo.

| 26/10/1991 | .....34 | .....3 | | FOXBASE ALPHA ..................................................................... | .Heavenly HVNLP 1 |
| 06/03/1993 | .....7 | .....7 | | **SO TOUGH** ....................................................................... | .Heavenly HVNLP 6CD |
| 12/03/1994 | .....8 | .....4 | | **TIGER BAY** ...................................................................... | .Heavenly HVNLP 8CD |
| 25/11/1995 | .....17 | .....9 | .....○ | TOO YOUNG TO DIE – THE SINGLES ..................................................... | .Heavenly HVNLP 10CD |
| 27/01/1996 | .....50 | .....1 | | RESERECTION **SAINT ETIENNE DAHO** ................................................. | .Virgin DINSD 150 |
| 19/10/1996 | .....34 | .....2 | | CASINO CLASSICS ................................................................... | .Heavenly HVNLP 16CDL |
| 16/05/1998 | .....18 | .....3 | | GOOD HUMOUR ....................................................................... | .Creation CRECD 225 |
| 03/06/2000 | .....33 | .....1 | | SOUND OF WATER .................................................................... | .Mantra MNTCD 1018 |
| 19/10/2002 | .....55 | .....1 | | FINISTERRE ........................................................................ | .Mantra MNTCD 1033 |

**ST. GERMAIN** French group formed by Ludovic Navarre (conductor), Pascal Ohse (trumpet), Edouard Labor (saxophone/flute), Idrissa Diop (drums), Carneiro (percussion), Claudio De Qeiroz (baritone) and special guest Ernest Raglin.

| 20/05/2000 | .....73 | .....1 | .....● | TOURIST ◇ ......................................................................... | .Blue Note 5262012 |

**ST. PAUL'S BOYS CHOIR** UK boys choir.

| 29/11/1980 | .....36 | .....8 | | REJOICE ........................................................................... | .K-Tel NE 1064 |

**BUFFY SAINTE-MARIE** Canadian singer (born 20/2/1941, Piaport Indian Reserve, Saskatchewan) who is part North American Indian. She emerged during the late 1960s' folk boom. As a songwriter she penned *Until It's Time For You To Go*, a hit for both The Four Pennies and Elvis Presley. She was married at one time to record producer Jack Nitzsche who died in August 2000.

| 21/03/1992 | .....39 | .....2 | | COINCIDENCE (AND LIKELY STORIES) ................................................... | .Ensign CCD 1920 |

**RYUICHI SAKAMOTO** Japanese synthesizer player (born 17/1/1952, Tokyo); he was a member of The Yellow Magic Orchestra before going solo and later recording with ex-Japan David Sylvian. As an actor he appeared in *Merry Christmas Mr Lawrence* with David Bowie. He won an Oscar for his music to the (1987) film *The Last Emperor*. He also won the 1988 Grammy Award for Best Album of Original Instrumental Background Score written for a Motion Picture with David Byrne and Cong Su for *The Last Emperor*.

| 03/09/1983 | .....36 | .....9 | .....○ | MERRY CHRISTMAS MR LAWRENCE Original soundtrack to the film ......................... | .Virgin V 2276 |

**SALAD** UK/Dutch group with Marijne Van Der Vlugt (vocals), Paul Kennedy (guitar), Peter Brown (bass) and Rob Wakeman (drums).

| 27/05/1995 | .....16 | .....2 | | DRINK ME ........................................................................... | .Island Red CIRDX 1002 |

**SALT-N-PEPA** US rap duo formed in New York in 1985 by Salt (born Cheryl James, 28/3/1969, Brooklyn, NYC) and Pepa (born Sandra Denton, 9/11/1969, Kingston, Jamaica) as Super Nature, with a US R&B chart hit the same year, name-changing to Salt-N-Pepa

in 1986. They later launched Jireh Records. On stage they were usually augmented by DJ Spinderella, originally Latoya Hanson, then replaced by Deirdre Roper (born 3/8/1971, NYC) in 1988. Denton married Anthony 'Treach' Criss of Naughty By Nature in 1999. The group won the 1994 Grammy Award for Best Rap Performance by a Group for *None Of Your Business*.

| | | | | | |
|---|---|---|---|---|---|
| 06/08/1988 | 19 | 27 | ● | A SALT WITH A DEADLY PEPA | London FFRLP 3 |
| 12/05/1990 | 70 | 1 | | BLACKS' MAGIC | ffrr 8281641 |
| 06/07/1991 | 70 | 2 | | A BLITZ OF SALT-N-PEPA HITS (THE HITS REMIXED) | ffrr 8282491 |
| 19/10/1991 | 6 | 20 | ✪ | **THE GREATEST HITS** | ffrr 8282911 |
| 25/04/1992 | 37 | 2 | | RAPPED IN REMIXES | ffrr 8282972 |
| 23/04/1994 | 36 | 5 | | VERY NECESSARY | ffrr 8284542 |

### SALVATION ARMY UK instrumental/vocal group; the Salvation Army was originally formed by William Booth.

| | | | | | |
|---|---|---|---|---|---|
| 24/12/1977 | 16 | 5 | | BY REQUEST | Warwick WW 5038 |

### SAM AND DAVE US R&B vocal duo formed in 1961 by Sam Moore (born 12/10/1935, Miami, FL) and Dave Prater (born 9/5/1937, Ocilla, GA) and signed by Roulette in 1962. They switched to Atlantic in 1965, their material appearing on the Stax label. They won the 1967 Grammy Award for Best Rhythm & Blues Group Performance for *Soul Man*. They split in 1970, re-forming in 1972. Moore re-recorded *Soul Man* with Lou Reed as the theme to the film of the same name. Prater was killed in a car crash on 9/4/1988. They were inducted into the Rock & Roll Hall of Fame in 1992.

| | | | | | |
|---|---|---|---|---|---|
| 21/01/1967 | 35 | 7 | | HOLD ON I'M COMIN' | Atlantic 588045 |
| 22/04/1967 | 28 | 5 | | DOUBLE DYNAMITE | Stax 589003 |
| 23/03/1968 | 32 | 8 | | SOUL MAN | Stax 589015 |

### RICHIE SAMBORA US vocalist/guitarist (born 11/7/1959, New Jersey) who was a founder of Bon Jovi in 1983 and went solo from 1998.

| | | | | | |
|---|---|---|---|---|---|
| 14/09/1991 | 20 | 3 | | STRANGER IN THIS TOWN | Mercury 8488951 |
| 14/03/1998 | 24 | 2 | | UNDISCOVERED SOUL | Mercury 5369722 |

### SAMSON UK heavy metal group formed in 1978 by Paul Samson (guitar), Bruce Bruce (vocals), Chris Aylmer (bass) and Clive Burr (drums). Burr left soon after their formation to join Iron Maiden, replaced by Thundersticks. Bruce left in 1981 (assuming his real name of Bruce Dickinson, he resurfaced as lead singer with Iron Maiden), as did Thundersticks, with Nicky Moore (vocals) and Mel Gaynor (drums) replacements. Gaynor then left, with Pete Jupp his replacement. Aylmer left in 1984, replaced by Merv Goldsworthy. After Nicky Moore left in 1986 Samson disbanded the group and went solo, re-forming it in 1988. Samson died from cancer on 9/8/2002.

| | | | | | |
|---|---|---|---|---|---|
| 26/07/1980 | 34 | 6 | | HEAD ON | Gem GEMLP 108 |

### DAVID SANBORN US saxophonist (born 30/7/1945, Tampa, FL) who was raised in St Louis and played with Paul Butterfield's band before becoming an in-demand session musician. He provided the saxophone solo on David Bowie's *Young Americans,* among other tracks. In 1975 he recorded his debut album and has since combined his solo career with session work. He has won six Grammy Awards: Best Rhythm and Blues Instrumental Performance in 1981 for *All I Need Is You;* Best Jazz Fusion Performance (vocal or instrumental) in 1985 for *Straight To The Heart;* Best Jazz Fusion Performance (vocal or instrumental) in 1986 with for *Double Vision;* Best Rhythm and Blues Instrumental Performance in 1987 for *Chicago Song;* Best Pop Instrumental Performance in 1988 for *Close-Up;* and Best Contemporary Jazz Performance in 1999 for *Inside.*

| | | | | | |
|---|---|---|---|---|---|
| 14/03/1987 | 86 | 1 | | A CHANGE OF HEART | Warner Brothers 9254791 |

### ROGER SANCHEZ US producer/remixer (born 1/6/1967, NYC); he previously recorded as El Mariachi, Funk Junkeez and Transatlantic Soul and records as Roger S or the S Man in the USA and runs the R-Senal record label. He won the 2002 Grammy Award for Best Remixed Recording, Non-Classical for *Hella Good* by No Doubt.

| | | | | | |
|---|---|---|---|---|---|
| 11/08/2001 | 34 | 2 | | FIRST CONTACT | Defected SMAN 01CD |

### SANTANA US rock group formed in Los Angeles, CA in 1966 by a nucleus of Carlos Santana (born 20/7/1947, Autlan de Navarro, Mexico, guitar/vocals), Gregg Rolie (born 17/6/1947, Seattle, WA, keyboards) and David Brown (born 15/2/1947, New York, bass) as Santana Blues Band. They added percussionists Jose Chepitos Areas (born 17/6/1947, Leon, Nicaragua), Mike Carrabello and Mike Shrieve (born 6/7/1949, San Francisco, CA) in 1969 and shortened the name to Santana. They signed to CBS in 1969, and remained with the label until 1989 when Carlos launched the Guts & Grace label. There have been numerous personnel changes since, including most notably Neal Schon (born 27/2/1954, San Mateo, CA) on guitar who joined in 1971. Santana has won nine Grammy Awards including: Best Rock Instrumental Performance in 1988 for *Blues For Salvador;* Record of the Year and Best Pop Collaboration with Vocals in 1999 with Rob Thomas for *Smooth* (the song also won the Song of the Year award for writers Itaal Shur and Rob Thomas); Best Pop Group Performance in 1999 for *Maria Maria;* Best Pop Instrumental in 1999 for *El Farol;* Best Rock Group in 1999 with Everlast for *Put Your Lights On;* and Best Rock Instrumental in 1999 with Eric Clapton for *The Calling.* His eight awards in 1999 equalled Michael Jackson's tally of 1984. He also won the 2002 Grammy Award for Best Pop Collaboration With Vocals with Michelle Branch for *The Game Of Love* and the 2000 MOBO Award for Best World Music Act. He was inducted into the Rock & Roll Hall of Fame in 1998 and has a star on the Hollywood Walk of Fame.

| | | | | | |
|---|---|---|---|---|---|
| 02/05/1970 | 26 | 11 | | SANTANA | CBS 63815 |
| 28/11/1970 | 7 | 52 | ● | **ABRAXAS** ▲[6] | CBS 64807 |
| 13/11/1971 | 6 | 14 | | **SANTANA III** ▲[5] | CBS 69015 |
| 26/08/1972 | 29 | 4 | | CARLOS SANTANA AND BUDDY MILES LIVE **CARLOS SANTANA AND BUDDY MILES** | CBS 65142 |
| 25/11/1972 | 6 | 11 | | **CARAVANSERAI** | CBS 65299 |
| 28/07/1973 | 7 | 9 | | **LOVE, DEVOTION, SURRENDER CARLOS SANTANA AND MAHAVISHNU JOHN MCLAUGHLIN** | CBS 69037 |
| 08/12/1973 | 8 | 6 | ○ | **WELCOME** | CBS 69040 |
| 21/09/1974 | 14 | 15 | ● | GREATEST HITS | CBS 69081 |

▲[9] Number of weeks album topped the US chart  ◆[12] RIAA Diamond Awards  ◇[3] IFPI Platinum Europe Awards

| DATE | POS | WKS | BPI | ALBUM TITLE | LABEL & NUMBER |
|---|---|---|---|---|---|
| 02/11/1974 | 40 | 1 | | ILLUMINATIONS **CARLOS SANTANA AND ALICE COLTRANE** | CBS 69063 |
| 30/11/1974 | 18 | 5 | ○ | BORBOLETTA | CBS 69084 |
| 10/04/1976 | 21 | 9 | ○ | AMIGOS | CBS 86005 |
| 08/01/1977 | 27 | 3 | ○ | FESTIVAL | CBS 86020 |
| 05/11/1977 | 7 | 27 | ● | **MOONFLOWER** | CBS 88272 |
| 11/11/1978 | 17 | 16 | ● | INNER SECRETS | CBS 86075 |
| 24/03/1979 | 55 | 4 | | ONENESS – SILVER DREAMS GOLDEN REALITY **CARLOS SANTANA** | CBS 86037 |
| 27/10/1979 | 28 | 5 | ○ | MARATHON | CBS 86098 |
| 20/09/1980 | 65 | 2 | | THE SWING OF DELIGHT **CARLOS SANTANA** | CBS 22075 |
| 18/04/1981 | 33 | 4 | | ZEBOP! | CBS 84946 |
| 14/08/1982 | 35 | 7 | | SHANGO | CBS 85914 |
| 30/04/1983 | 84 | 3 | | HAVANA MOON **CARLOS SANTANA** | CBS 25350 |
| 23/03/1985 | 58 | 3 | | BEYOND APPEARANCES | CBS 86307 |
| 15/11/1986 | 50 | 8 | ● | VIVA! SANTANA – THE VERY BEST | K-Tel NE 1338 |
| 14/07/1990 | 68 | 1 | | SPIRITS DANCING IN THE FLESH | CBS 4669131 |
| 15/08/1998 | 12 | 26 | ● | THE ULTIMATE COLLECTION | Columbia SONYTV 47CD |
| 04/09/1999 | ❶² | 47 | ✪² | SUPERNATURAL ◇⁶ ▲¹² ◆¹⁴ 1999 Grammy Awards for Album of the Year and Best Rock Album | Arista 07822190802 |
| 02/11/2002 | 15 | 5 | | SHAMAN ◇ ▲¹ | Arista 74321959382 |

**PETER SARSTEDT** UK singer (born 10/12/1942); brother of Richard (who recorded as Eden Kane) and Clive (who recorded as Robin Sartsedt) Sarstedt. He still performs regularly in clubs around the country.

| | | | | | |
|---|---|---|---|---|---|
| 15/03/1969 | 8 | 4 | | **PETER SARSTEDT** | United Artists SULP 1219 |

**SASH!** German producer/DJ Sascha Lappessen and a dance group that features Thomas Ludke, Thomas Alisson and Ralf Kappmeier.

| | | | | | |
|---|---|---|---|---|---|
| 19/07/1997 | 6 | 38 | ✪ | **IT'S MY LIFE – THE ALBUM** | Multiply MULTYCD 1 |
| 05/09/1998 | 5 | 19 | ● | **LIFE GOES ON** | Multiply MULTYCD 2 |
| 29/04/2000 | 13 | 5 | | TRILENIUM | Multiply MULTY CD7 |
| 11/11/2000 | 33 | 3 | | ENCORE UNE FOIS – THE GREATEST HITS | Multiply MULTY CD10 |

**SASHA** UK producer (born Alexander Coe, 4/9/1969, Bangor, Wales, raised in Manchester); he was known as a remixer before signing a solo deal with DeConstruction.

| | | | | | |
|---|---|---|---|---|---|
| 12/03/1994 | 55 | 2 | | THE QAT COLLECTION | Deconstruction 74321191962 |
| 17/07/1999 | 18 | 3 | | XPANDER (EP) This was an EP that was too long to be eligible for the singles chart | Deconstruction 74321681992 |
| 17/08/2002 | 18 | 3 | | AIRDRAWN DAGGER | Arista 74321947862 |
| 26/06/2004 | 61 | 1+ | | INVOLVER | Global Underground GUSA001CDX |

**JOE SATRIANI** US guitarist (born 15/7/1957, Carle Place, NY); he began a solo career in 1984, although his work with other artists, including Greg Kihn, Mick Jagger and Deep Purple, made his reputation. He formed a touring band in 1988 with Stu Hamm (bass) and Jonathan Moyer (drums).

| | | | | | |
|---|---|---|---|---|---|
| 15/08/1992 | 13 | 6 | | THE EXTREMIST | Epic 4716722 |
| 06/11/1993 | 32 | 2 | | TIME MACHINE | Epic 4745152 |
| 14/10/1995 | 21 | 3 | | JOE SATRIANI | Epic 4811022 |
| 14/03/1998 | 32 | 2 | | CRYSTAL PLANET | Epic 4894732 |

**CHANTAY SAVAGE** US R&B singer/keyboard player (born Chicago, IL); she is the daughter of jazz musician parents. She had been a session backing singer for the likes of Kym Sims before going solo.

| | | | | | |
|---|---|---|---|---|---|
| 25/05/1996 | 66 | 1 | | I WILL SURVIVE (DOIN' IT MY WAY) | RCA 74321381622 |

**SAVAGE GARDEN** Australian duo Darren Hayes (vocals) and Daniel Jones (all instruments). Their debut album *Savage Garden* sold over 11 million copies worldwide. Jones later set up the Meridienmusik label and signed up Brisbane duo Aneiki – the label's first release. Hayes, meanwhile launched a solo career.

| | | | | | |
|---|---|---|---|---|---|
| 14/03/1998 | 2 | 68 | ✪² | **SAVAGE GARDEN** ◇² | Columbia 4871612 |
| 20/11/1999 | 7 | 64 | ✪³ | **AFFIRMATION** ◇ | Columbia 4949352 |

**TELLY SAVALAS** US singer/actor (born Aristotle Savalas, 21/1/1925, New York); he was in his late 30s when he became an actor, first on TV and then in films, before returning to TV where he created one of the best know detectives in *Kojak*. He died from cancer on 22/1/1994 and has a star on the Hollywood Walk of Fame.

| | | | | | |
|---|---|---|---|---|---|
| 22/03/1975 | 12 | 10 | ○ | TELLY | MCA MCF 2699 |

**SAVOY BROWN** UK group formed in 1966 by Kim Simmonds (born 6/12/1947, guitar), Brice Portius (vocals), Ray Chappell (bass), Bob Hall (piano), John O'Leary (harmonica) and Leo Manningham (drums) as The Savoy Brown Blues Band. O'Leary left after a

few months and was replaced by Martin Stone. After their debut album Simmonds re-formed the group with Hall, Chris Youlden (vocals), Dave Peverett (guitar/vocals), Rivers Jobe (bass) and Roger Earl (drums). This line up survived until 1970 when Simmonds put together a third version featuring Dave Walker (vocals), Paul Raymond (keyboards), Andy Pyle (bass) and Dave Bidwell (drums).

| 28/11/1970 | 50 | 1 | | LOOKIN' IN | Decca SKL 5066 |

### SAW DOCTORS
Irish rock group formed in Tuam, County Galway in 1987 by Leo Moran (vocals), Davy Corton (guitar/vocals), John 'Turps' Burke (mandolin/vocals), Pierce Doherty (bass) and John Donnelly (drums). Tony Lambert joined on keyboards in 1993 and later won £1 million on the Irish lottery.

| 08/06/1991 | 69 | 2 | | IF THIS IS ROCK AND ROLL, I WANT MY OLD JOB BACK | Solid ROCK 7 |
| 31/10/1992 | 33 | 2 | | ALL THE WAY FROM TUAM | Solid 4509911462 |
| 24/02/1996 | 6 | 5 | ● | **SAME OUL' TOWN** | Shamtown SAWDOC 004CD |
| 24/10/1998 | 24 | 2 | | SONGS FROM SUN STREET | Shamtown SAWDOC 006CD |
| 13/10/2001 | 58 | 1 | | VILLIANS | Shamtown SAWDOC 008CD |

### NITIN SAWHNEY
UK singer/producer who created *Secret Asians* with Sanjeev Bhaskar for BBC Radio and co-devised *Goodness Gracious Me*. He was named Best World Music Act at the 2001 MOBO Awards.

| 25/09/1999 | 44 | 2 | | BEYOND SKIN | Outcaste CASTE 9CD |
| 30/06/2001 | 40 | 1 | ◯ | PROPHESY | V2 VVR 1015912 |
| 26/07/2003 | 54 | 1 | | HUMAN | V2 VVR 1021852 |

### SAXON
UK heavy rock group formed in Yorkshire in 1977 by Peter 'Biff' Byford (born 5/1/1951, vocals), Paul Quinn (guitar), Graham Oliver (guitar), Steve Lawson (bass) and Pete Gill (drums). Gill left in 1980, replaced by Nigel Glockler.

| 12/04/1980 | 5 | 29 | ● | **WHEELS OF STEEL** | Carrere CAL 115 |
| 15/11/1980 | 11 | 13 | ● | STRONG ARM OF THE LAW | Carrere CAL 120 |
| 03/10/1981 | 9 | 11 | ◯ | **DENIM AND LEATHER** | Carrere CAL 128 |
| 22/05/1982 | 5 | 19 | ◯ | **THE EAGLE HAS LANDED** | Carrere CAL 157 |
| 26/03/1983 | 15 | 9 | | POWER AND THE GLORY | Carrere CAL 147 |
| 11/02/1984 | 18 | 7 | | CRUSADER | Carrere CAL 200 |
| 14/09/1985 | 36 | 4 | | INNOCENCE IS NO EXCUSE | Parlophone SAXON 2 |
| 27/09/1986 | 34 | 3 | | ROCK THE NATIONS | EMI EMC 3515 |
| 09/04/1988 | 49 | 2 | | DESTINY | EMI EMC 3543 |

### LEO SAYER
UK singer (born Gerard Hugh Sayer, 21/5/1948, Shoreham-by-Sea); he formed Jester in 1972, later changing the name to Patches. Songwriting with David Courtney the same year, they penned Roger Daltrey's solo debut before Sayer launched his own career under the guidance of Adam Faith. He later had his own BBC TV series. He won the 1977 Grammy Award for Best Rhythm & Blues Song with Vinnie Poncia for *You Make Me Feel Like Dancing*.

| 05/01/1974 | 2 | 22 | ◯ | **SILVER BIRD** | Chrysalis CHR 1050 |
| 26/10/1974 | 4 | 14 | ◯ | **JUST A BOY** | Chrysalis CHR 1068 |
| 20/09/1975 | 8 | 9 | ◯ | **ANOTHER YEAR** | Chrysalis CHR 1087 |
| 27/11/1976 | 4 | 66 | ✪ | **ENDLESS FLIGHT** | Chrysalis CHR 1125 |
| 22/10/1977 | 8 | 16 | ● | **THUNDER IN MY HEART** | Chrysalis CDL 1154 |
| 02/09/1978 | 15 | 25 | ● | LEO SAYER | Chrysalis CDL 1198 |
| 31/03/1979 | ❶³ | 37 | ✪ | **THE VERY BEST OF LEO SAYER** | Chrysalis CDL 1222 |
| 13/10/1979 | 44 | 4 | ● | HERE | Chrysalis CDL 1240 |
| 23/08/1980 | 15 | 9 | ◯ | LIVING IN A FANTASY | Chrysalis CDL 1297 |
| 08/05/1982 | 30 | 12 | | WORLD RADIO | Chrysalis CDL 1345 |
| 12/11/1983 | 15 | 18 | ● | HAVE YOU EVER BEEN IN LOVE | Chrysalis LEOTV 1 |
| 06/03/1993 | 26 | 4 | | ALL THE BEST | Chrysalis CDCHR 1980 |
| 20/02/1999 | 35 | 2 | | THE DEFINITIVE HITS COLLECTION | Polygram TV 5471152 |

### ALEXEI SAYLE
UK singer/comedian (born 7/8/1952, Liverpool); he has had his own TV series and appeared in a number of films, including *Gorky Park*, *Indiana Jones And The Last Crusade* and *Siesta*.

| 17/03/1984 | 62 | 5 | | THE FISH PEOPLE TAPES | Island IMA 9 |

▲⁹ Number of weeks album topped the US chart ◆¹² RIAA Diamond Awards ◇³ IFPI Platinum Europe Awards

**BOZ SCAGGS** US singer (born William Royce Scaggs, 8/6/1944, Ohio); he joined Steve Miller's band the Marksmen in 1959. He later formed Wigs which disbanded whilst on tour in Europe: Scaggs headed for Sweden and recorded his debut solo album, only available in Sweden. He returned to the USA in 1967, signing solo with Atlantic in 1969. After one album he switched to CBS. He won the 1976 Grammy Award for Best Rhythm & Blues Song with David Paich for *Lowdown*.

| | | | | | |
|---|---|---|---|---|---|
| 12/03/1977 | 37 | 24 | O | SILK DEGREES | CBS 81193 |
| 17/12/1977 | 55 | 1 | | DOWN TWO, THEN LEFT | CBS 86036 |
| 03/05/1980 | 52 | 4 | | MIDDLE MAN | CBS 86094 |

**SCARLET** UK female duo formed by Joe Youle (keyboards) and Cheryl Parker (vocals). They first met at school in Hull and began writing songs together at the age of sixteen.

| | | | | |
|---|---|---|---|---|
| 11/03/1995 | 59 | 2 | NAKED | WEA 4509976432 |

**SCARS** UK vocal/instrumental group formed in Scotland by Robert King, John Mackie, Paul Research and Steve McLaughlin.

| | | | | |
|---|---|---|---|---|
| 18/04/1981 | 67 | 3 | AUTHOR! AUTHOR! | Pre PREX 5 |

**MICHAEL SCHENKER GROUP** German/UK heavy metal group formed by Michael Schenker (born 10/1/1955, Savstedt, Germany), with a fluctuating line-up. Schenker had previously been the founder of The Scorpions and briefly a member of UFO before forming the Michael Schenker Group. He later shortened the group's name to MSG.

| | | | | | |
|---|---|---|---|---|---|
| 06/09/1980 | 8 | 8 | | MICHAEL SCHENKER GROUP | Chrysalis CHR 1302 |
| 19/09/1981 | 14 | 8 | O | MSG | Chrysalis CHR 1336 |
| 13/03/1982 | 5 | 11 | O | ONE NIGHT AT BUDOKAN | Chrysalis CTY 1375 |
| 23/10/1982 | 19 | 5 | | ASSAULT ATTACK | Chrysalis CHR 1393 |
| 10/09/1983 | 23 | 5 | | BUILT TO DESTROY | Chrysalis CHR 1441 |
| 23/06/1984 | 24 | 5 | | ROCK WILL NEVER DIE | Chrysalis CUX 1470 |
| 24/10/1987 | 65 | 2 | | PERFECT TIMING **MSG** | EMI EMC 3539 |

**SCHON** – see **SAMMY HAGARR**

**SCISSOR SISTERS** US rock group formed in New York City by Jake Shears (vocals), Babydaddy (keyboards/bass), Ana Matronic (vocals),Paddy Boom (drums), Derek G (guitar) and Del Marquis (guitar).

| | | | | | |
|---|---|---|---|---|---|
| 14/02/2004 | 5 | 20+ | ✪² | SCISSOR SISTERS | Polydor 9866058 |

**SCHOOL OF EXCELLENCE** UK instrumental duo formed by Stewart Bradley and James Bradley who also recorded as Raindance.

| | | | | |
|---|---|---|---|---|
| 28/10/1995 | 47 | 2 | PIANO MOODS | Dino DINCD 114 |

**SCOOCH** UK vocal group formed by Natalie Powers (born 26/7/1977, Birmingham), Caroline Barnes (born 15/4/1979, Leeds), Russ Spencer (born 1/3/1980, Bournemouth) and David Ducasse (born 3/11/1978, South Shields).

| | | | | |
|---|---|---|---|---|
| 19/08/2000 | 41 | 2 | FOUR SURE | Accolade 5278190 |

**SCOOTER** UK/German rock group formed in Hamburg by HP Baxter, Rick Jordan and Ferris Bueller as Celebrate The Nun before name-changing to Scooter. Bueller left in 1998, and was replaced by Axel Cohn.

| | | | | | |
|---|---|---|---|---|---|
| 13/04/1996 | 24 | 5 | | OUR HAPPY HARDCORE | Club Tools 0062282 CLU |
| 10/08/2002 | 6 | 14 | ● | PUSH THE BEAT FOR THIS JAM – THE SINGLES | Sheffield Tunes 0141172STU |
| 26/04/2003 | 20 | 4 | O | THE STADIUM TECHNO EXPERIENCE | Sheffield Tunes STU00147112CD |

**SCORPIONS** German heavy rock group formed in Hanover in 1971 by Klaus Meine (born 25/5/1948, Hanover, vocals), Rudolf Schenker (born 31/8/1948, Hildesheim, guitar), Michael Schenker (born 10/1/1955, Savstedt, guitar) and Rudy Lenners (drums). By 1980 the line-up was Meine, Rudolf Schenker, Mathias Jabs (born 25/10/1955, Hanover, guitar), Francis Bucholz (born 19/1/1950, bass) and Herman Rarebell (born 18/11/1949, Lubeck, drums). By 1999 James Kottak (born 26/12/1962, Louisville, KY) was drummer. One-time member Ulrich Roth later formed Electric Sun, whilst Michael Schenker formed the Michael Schenker Group.

| | | | | | |
|---|---|---|---|---|---|
| 21/04/1979 | 36 | 11 | | LOVE DRIVE | Harvest SHSP 4097 |
| 03/05/1980 | 23 | 6 | | ANIMAL MAGNETISM | Harvest SHSP 4113 |
| 10/04/1982 | 11 | 11 | | BLACKOUT | Harvest SHVL 823 |
| 24/03/1984 | 17 | 6 | | LOVE AT FIRST STING | Harvest ATAK 69 |
| 29/06/1985 | 18 | 8 | | WORLD WIDE LIVE | Harvest SCORP 1 |
| 14/05/1988 | 18 | 6 | | SAVAGE AMUSEMENT | Harvest SHSP 4125 |
| 17/11/1990 | 27 | 7 | O | CRAZY WORLD | Vertigo 8469081 |
| 25/09/1993 | 51 | 1 | | FACE THE HEAT | Mercury 5182802 |

**SCOTLAND WORLD CUP SQUAD** UK vocal group. Like their English counterparts, the Scottish football team has made records to capitalise on appearances in the World Cup. Also like England, they have had more success on the charts than on the field!

| | | | | |
|---|---|---|---|---|
| 25/05/1974 | 3 | 9 | EASY EASY | Polydor 2383 282 |

**BAND OF THE SCOTS GUARDS** UK military band; The Scots Guards were formed in 1642 by King Charles I with the formation of the band thought to have been in 1716.

| | | | | |
|---|---|---|---|---|
| 28/06/1969 | 25 | 2 | BAND OF THE SCOTS GUARDS | Fontana SFXL 54 |

### JACK SCOTT
Canadian singer (born Jack Scafone Jr, 28/1/1936, Windsor, Ontario); he moved to Michigan in 1946 and made his first recordings for ABC-Paramount in 1957. He later set up Ponie Records and recorded country material.

| 07/05/1960 | 7 | 11 | | I REMEMBER HANK WILLIAMS | Top Rank BUY 034 |
| 03/09/1960 | 11 | 1 | | WHAT IN THE WORLD'S COME OVER YOU | Top Rank BUY 024 |

### JILL SCOTT
US soul singer born in Philadelphia, PA in 1972.

| 29/07/2000 | 69 | 4 | ● | WHO IS JILL SCOTT – WORDS AND SOUNDS VOLUME 1 | Epic 4986252 |

### MIKE SCOTT
UK singer/multi-instrumentalist (born 14/12/1958, Edinburgh, Scotland); he was a founder member of The Waterboys in 1981 and launched a parallel solo career in 1995.

| 30/09/1995 | 23 | 2 | | BRING 'EM ALL IN | Chrysalis CDCHR 6108 |
| 11/10/1997 | 34 | 2 | | STILL BURNING | Chrysalis CDCHR 6122 |

### SCREAMING BLUE MESSIAHS
UK rock group formed by Bill Carter (guitar/vocals), Kenny Harris (drums) and Chris Thompson (bass). The group disbanded in 1989, Thompson and Harris going on to form Lerue.

| 17/05/1986 | 90 | 1 | | GUN-SHY | WEA WX 41 |

### SCREAMING TREES
US rock group formed in Ellensburg, WA by Gary Lee Connor (guitar), his brother Van Connor (bass), Mark Lanegan (vocals) and Mark Pickerell (drums). Pickerell was later replaced by Barrett Martin, whilst Lanegan later recorded solo.

| 20/07/1996 | 32 | 4 | | DUST | Epic 4839802 |

### SCREEN II
UK vocal/instrumental group formed by Richie Rufus and Vic Volocci whose hit album was a 12-inch doublepack single that was not eligible for the singles chart.

| 09/04/1994 | 36 | 1 | | LET THE RECORD SPIN | Cleveland City CLE 13015 |

### SCRITTI POLITTI
UK group formed in Leeds in 1977 by Green Gartside (born Green Strohmeyer-Gartside, 22/6/1956, Cardiff, vocals), Niall Jinks (bass) and Tom Morley (drums). Debuting in 1979 on their own St Pancras label, after a spell with Rough Trade they signed with Virgin in 1983 with the group now consisting of Green, David Gamson (keyboards) and Fred Maher (drums).

| 11/09/1982 | 12 | 7 | | SONGS TO REMEMBER | Rough Trade ROUGH 20 |
| 22/06/1985 | 5 | 19 | ● | CUPID AND PSYCHE 85 | Virgin V 2350 |
| 18/06/1988 | 8 | 11 | ● | PROVISION | Virgin V 2515 |
| 07/08/1999 | 33 | 2 | | ANOMIE & BONHOMIE | Virgin CDV 2884 |

### SEAHORSES
UK rock group formed by Chris Helme (born 22/7/1971, York, guitar), John Squire (born 24/11/1962, Manchester, guitar), Stuart Fletcher (born 16/1/1976, York, bass) and Andy Watts (drums). Ex-Stone Roses Squire denied any significance in the name being an anagram of 'he hates roses'!! He disbanded the group after their debut album and went solo.

| 07/06/1997 | 2 | 38 | ✪ | DO IT YOURSELF | Geffen GED 25134 |

### SEAL
UK singer (born Sealhenry Samuel, 19/2/1963, Paddington, London) who spent nearly ten years recording demos before meeting Adamski and co-writing *Killer*, a UK #1. On the strength of this he was signed by ZTT as a solo artist in 1990. He was the big winner at the 1992 BRIT Awards ceremony with three awards – Best Video (for *Crazy*), Best Album (*Seal*) and Best UK Male. He also won three Grammy Awards in 1996 for *Kiss From A Rose*: for Best Pop Vocal Performance, Record of the Year and Song of the Year. Seal also collected an International Achievement Award at the 1996 MOBO Awards.

| 01/06/1991 | ❶³ | 65 | ✪² | SEAL 1992 BRIT Award for Best Album | ZTT 9 |
| 04/06/1994 | ❶² | 64 | ✪² | SEAL II ◇ | ZTT 4509962562 |
| 28/11/1998 | 44 | 2 | ○ | HUMAN BEING | Warner Brothers 9362468282 |
| 27/09/2003 | 4 | 6 | | IV ◇ | Warner Brothers 9362485412 |

### SEARCHERS
UK group formed in Liverpool in 1961 by John McNally (born 30/8/1941, Liverpool, guitar/vocals), Mike Pender (born Michael Prendergast, 3/3/1942, Liverpool, guitar/vocals), Tony Jackson (born 16/7/1940, Liverpool, vocals/bass) and Norman McGarry (drums), with McGarry replaced by Chris Curtis (born Christopher Crummy, 26/8/1941, Oldham) in 1962. Jackson left in 1964, replaced by ex-Rebel Rousers Frank Allen (born Francis McNeice, 14/12/1943, Hayes), Curtis left in 1966, initially replaced by John Blunt (born 28/3/1947, Croydon), Blunt later replaced by Billy Adamson. Pender left in 1985 to form Mike Pender's Searchers (prompting a legal battle), replaced by Spencer James. Jackson died on 20/8/2003.

| 10/08/1963 | 2 | 44 | | MEET THE SEARCHERS | Pye NPL 18086 |
| 16/11/1963 | 5 | 21 | | SUGAR AND SPICE | Pye NPL 18089 |
| 30/05/1964 | 4 | 17 | | IT'S THE SEARCHERS | Pye NPL 18092 |
| 27/03/1965 | 8 | 5 | | SOUNDS LIKE THE SEARCHERS | Pye NPL 18111 |

▲⁹ Number of weeks album topped the US chart  ◆¹² RIAA Diamond Awards  ◇³ IFPI Platinum Europe Awards

### SEBADOH
US group formed in 1989 by Lou Barlow (guitar/bass/vocals), Jason Loewenstein (bass/guitar/vocals) and Bob Fay (drums). Fay left in 1998 and was replaced by Russ Pollard.

| DATE | POS | WKS | BPI | ALBUM TITLE | LABEL & NUMBER |
|---|---|---|---|---|---|
| 08/05/1993 | 63 | 1 | | BUBBLE AND SCRAPE | Domino WIGCD 4 |
| 03/09/1994 | 40 | 2 | | BAKESALE | Domino WIGCD 11 |
| 31/08/1996 | 38 | 1 | | HARMACY | Domino WIGCD 26 |
| 06/03/1999 | 45 | 1 | | THE SEBADOH | Domino WIGCD 057 |

### JON SECADA
US singer/songwriter (born Juan Secada, 4/10/1963, Havana, Cuba); he was raised in Miami, where he moved to in 1971 aged eight. First known as a songwriter, he penned six songs for Gloria Estefan, touring with her as a backing singer. He has a masters degree in jazz from Miami University. He has won two Grammy Awards: Best Latin Pop Album in 1992 for *Otro Dia Mas Sin Verte* and Best Latin Pop Performance in 1995 for *Amor*.

| DATE | POS | WKS | BPI | ALBUM TITLE | LABEL & NUMBER |
|---|---|---|---|---|---|
| 05/09/1992 | 20 | 11 | ● | JON SECADA | SBK SBKCD 19 |
| 04/06/1994 | 17 | 5 | | HEART, SOUL AND VOICE | SBK SBKCD 29 |

### HARRY SECOMBE
UK singer (born 8/9/1921, Swansea) who formed the Goons with Spike Milligan, Peter Sellers and Michael Bentine in 1949 and began his recording career in 1952. He later became presenter of the religious programme *Highway* on TV. He was appointed a CBE in 1963 and knighted in 1981. He died from cancer on 11/4/2001.

| DATE | POS | WKS | BPI | ALBUM TITLE | LABEL & NUMBER |
|---|---|---|---|---|---|
| 31/03/1962 | 16 | 1 | | SACRED SONGS | Philips RBL 7501 |
| 18/04/1964 | 20 | 1 | | HOW TO WIN AN ELECTION HARRY SECOMBE, PETER SELLERS AND SPIKE MILLIGAN | Philips AL 3464 |
| 22/04/1967 | 6 | 13 | | **SECOMBE'S PERSONAL CHOICE** | Philips BETS 707 |
| 07/08/1971 | 17 | 20 | | IF I RULED THE WORLD | Contour 6870 501 |
| 16/12/1978 | 8 | 12 | | **20 SONGS OF JOY** | Warwick WW 5052 |
| 05/12/1981 | 46 | 5 | | GOLDEN MEMORIES HARRY SECOMBE AND MOIRA ANDERSON | Warwick WW 5107 |
| 13/12/1986 | 45 | 5 | | HIGHWAY OF LIFE | Telstar STAR 2289 |
| 30/11/1991 | 46 | 5 | ○ | YOURS SINCERELY | Philips 5107321 |

### SECOND IMAGE
UK soul group formed in London by Simon Eyre (guitar), Weston Foster (guitar), Ozie Selcuck (guitar), Junior Bromfield (bass), Rem Fiori (keyboards), Frank Burke (trumpet) and Tom 'Zoot' Heritage (saxophone/flute). Bromfield and Burke designed their own skateboards and also represented the UK at the sport.

| DATE | POS | WKS | BPI | ALBUM TITLE | LABEL & NUMBER |
|---|---|---|---|---|---|
| 30/03/1985 | 100 | 1 | | STRANGE REFLECTIONS | MCA MCF 3255 |

### SECRET AFFAIR
UK mod revival group formed by Ian Page (vocals/trumpet/piano), David Cairns (guitar/vocals), Dennis Smith (bass/vocals) and Seb Shelton (drums). They also set up the I-Spy label. Shelton left in 1980, replaced by Paul Bultitude, although the group disbanded after a further two singles.

| DATE | POS | WKS | BPI | ALBUM TITLE | LABEL & NUMBER |
|---|---|---|---|---|---|
| 01/12/1979 | 41 | 8 | | GLORY BOYS | I-Spy 1 |
| 20/09/1980 | 48 | 4 | | BEHIND CLOSED DOORS | I-Spy 2 |
| 13/03/1982 | 84 | 3 | | BUSINESS AS USUAL | I-Spy 3 |

### NEIL SEDAKA
US singer (born 13/3/1939, Brooklyn, NYC); he began writing with Howard Greenfield in 1952 and was a member of the original Tokens in 1955. He began his own record career in 1957 with Legion, whilst still writing for other artists, and signed with RCA in 1958. His popularity in the US revived in the 1970s when he signed with Elton John's Rocket label. He has a star on the Hollywood Walk of Fame.

| DATE | POS | WKS | BPI | ALBUM TITLE | LABEL & NUMBER |
|---|---|---|---|---|---|
| 01/09/1973 | 13 | 10 | ○ | THE TRA-LA DAYS ARE OVER | MGM 2315 248 |
| 22/06/1974 | 17 | 10 | ○ | LAUGHTER IN THE RAIN | Polydor 2383 265 |
| 23/11/1974 | 48 | 1 | ○ | LIVE AT THE ROYAL FESTIVAL HALL | Polydor 2383 299 |
| 01/03/1975 | 31 | 6 | ○ | OVERNIGHT SUCCESS | Polydor 2442 131 |
| 10/07/1976 | 2 | 25 | ✪ | **LAUGHTER AND TEARS – THE BEST OF NEIL SEDAKA TODAY** | Polydor 2383 399 |
| 02/11/1991 | 10 | 16 | ✪ | **TIMELESS – THE VERY BEST OF NEIL SEDAKA** | Polydor 5114421 |
| 04/11/1995 | 23 | 9 | ● | CLASSICALLY SEDAKA | Vision VISCD 5 |
| 19/06/1999 | 33 | 3 | | THE VERY BEST OF NEIL SEDAKA | Universal Music TV 5646452 |

### SEEKERS
Australian group formed in Melbourne in the early 1960s by Judith Durham (born 3/7/1943, Melbourne, lead vocals), Keith Potger (born 2/3/1941, Columbo, Sri Lanka, guitar), Bruce Woodley (born 25/7/1942, Melbourne, Spanish guitar) and Athol Guy (born 5/1/1940, Victoria, bass). They disbanded in 1968 and Potger formed the New Seekers, although he wasn't in the group.

| | | | | | |
|---|---|---|---|---|---|
| 03/07/1965 | 5 | 36 | | **A WORLD OF OUR OWN** | Columbia 33SX 1722 |
| 03/07/1965 | 16 | 1 | | THE SEEKERS | Decca LK 4694 |
| 19/11/1966 | 3 | 67 | | **COME THE DAY** | Columbia SX 6093 |
| 25/11/1967 | 15 | 10 | | SEEKERS – SEEN IN GREEN | Columbia SCX 6193 |
| 14/09/1968 | 2 | 30 | | **LIVE AT THE TALK OF THE TOWN** | Columbia SCX 6278 |
| 16/11/1968 | ❶⁶ | 125 | | **THE BEST OF THE SEEKERS** | Columbia SCX 6268 |
| 23/04/1994 | 7 | 14 | | CARNIVAL OF HITS JUDITH DURHAM AND THE SEEKERS | EMI CDEMTV 83 |

## BOB SEGER AND THE SILVER BULLET BAND
US singer (born 6/5/1945, Dearborn, MI); he joined the Omens in 1964, first recording under his own name in 1966. He formed the Silver Bullet Band in 1975 with Drew Abbott (guitar), Robyn Robbins (keyboards), Alto Reed (saxophone), Chris Campbell (bass) and Charlie Allen Martin (drums). Campbell would be the only member to remain with the Silver Bullet Band for the next twenty years as they underwent personnel changes. The group won the 1980 Grammy Award for Best Rock Vocal Performance by a Group for *Against The Wind* and has a star on the Hollywood Walk of Fame. He was inducted into the Rock & Roll Hall of Fame in 2003.

| | | | | | |
|---|---|---|---|---|---|
| 03/06/1978 | 31 | 6 | ● | STRANGER IN TOWN | Capitol EAST 11698 |
| 15/03/1980 | 26 | 6 | | AGAINST THE WIND ▲⁶ | Capitol EAST 12041 |
| 26/09/1981 | 24 | 10 | | NINE TONIGHT | Capitol ESTSP 23 |
| 08/01/1983 | 45 | 10 | | THE DISTANCE | Capitol EST 12254 |
| 26/04/1986 | 35 | 6 | | LIKE A ROCK | Capitol EST 2011 |
| 21/09/1991 | 54 | 2 | | THE FIRE INSIDE | Capitol EST 2149 |
| 18/02/1995 | 6 | 12 | ● | **GREATEST HITS** | Capitol CDEST 2241 |

## SELECTER
UK ska group formed in Coventry in 1979 by Noel Davis (guitar), Prince Rimshot (born John Bradbury, drums) and Barry Jones (trombone). Following the success of their first record (B-side to The Specials debut), a touring group was assembled featuring Davis, Pauline Black (vocals), Crompton Amanor (drums), Charles Bainbridge (drums), Gappa Hendricks (keyboards), Desmond Brown (keyboards) and Charlie Anderson (bass), with Rico Rodriguez also appearing on their debut album. Black later recorded solo and hosted the children's TV show *Hold Tight*. The group re-formed in 1990.

| | | | | | |
|---|---|---|---|---|---|
| 23/02/1980 | 5 | 13 | ● | **TOO MUCH PRESSURE** | 2-Tone CDL TT 5002 |
| 07/03/1981 | 41 | 4 | | CELEBRATE THE BULLET | Chrysalis CHR 1306 |

## PETER SELLERS
UK comedian/actor (born Richard Henry Sellers, 8/9/1925, Southsea); he was a member of The Goons who later had international success as Inspector Clousseau in the *Pink Panther* series of films. He died from a heart attack on 24/7/1980.

| | | | | | |
|---|---|---|---|---|---|
| 14/02/1959 | 3 | 47 | | **THE BEST OF SELLERS** | Parlophone PMD 1069 |
| 12/12/1959 | 3 | 37 | | **SONGS FOR SWINGING SELLERS** | Parlophone PMC 1111 |
| 03/12/1960 | 5 | 18 | | **PETER AND SOPHIA** PETER SELLERS AND SOPHIA LOREN | Parlophone PMC 1131 |
| 28/09/1963 | 10 | 10 | | **FOOL BRITANNIA** ANTHONY NEWLEY, PETER SELLERS, JOAN COLLINS | Ember CEL 902 |
| 18/04/1964 | 20 | 1 | | HOW TO WIN AN ELECTION HARRY SECOMBE, PETER SELLERS AND SPIKE MILLIGAN | Philips AL 3464 |

## SEMISONIC
US group formed in Minnesota in 1993 by Dan Wilson (guitar/vocals), John Munson (bass) and Jake Slichter (drums).

| | | | | | |
|---|---|---|---|---|---|
| 24/07/1999 | 16 | 37 | ✪ | FEELING STRANGELY FINE | MCA MCD 11733 |
| 17/03/2001 | 13 | 4 | | ALL ABOUT CHEMISTRY | MCA 1125012 |

## SENSELESS THINGS
UK rock group formed by Mark Keds (guitar/vocals), Morgan Nicholls (bass) and Cass 'Cade' Browne (drums) as the Psychotics, changing their name in 1986. By 1987 Nicholls had switched to bass, Ben Harding taking over on guitar.

| | | | | | |
|---|---|---|---|---|---|
| 26/10/1991 | 66 | 1 | | THE FIRST OF TOO MANY | Epic 4691571 |
| 13/03/1993 | 37 | 1 | | EMPIRE OF THE SENSELESS | Epic 4735252 |

## SENSER
UK group formed in London in 1987 by Heitham Al-Sayed (raps/vocals/percussion), Nick Michaelson (guitar), Andy 'Awe' (DJ), Haggis (engineer), James Barrett (bass), John Morgan (drums) and Kersten Haigh (vocals/flute).

| | | | | | |
|---|---|---|---|---|---|
| 07/05/1994 | 4 | 5 | ○ | **STACKED UP** | Ultimate TOPPCD 008 |
| 02/05/1998 | 73 | 1 | | ASYLUM | Ultimate TOPPCD 064 |

## SEPULTURA
Brazilian heavy metal group formed in 1984 by Max Cavalera (born 4/8/1969, Belo Horizonte, guitar/vocals), Jairo T (guitar), Paolo Jr (born Paulo Xisto Pinto Jr, 30/4/1969, Belo Horizonte, bass) and Igor Cavalera (born 4/9/1970, Belo Horizonte, drums). The name is Portuguese for 'grave'. Jairo left in 1987, replaced by Andreas Kisser (born 24/8/1968, San Bernado Do Campo). Cavalera later formed Soulfly.

| | | | | | |
|---|---|---|---|---|---|
| 06/04/1991 | 40 | 2 | ○ | ARISE | Roadracer RO 93281 |
| 23/10/1993 | 11 | 4 | ● | CHAOS A.D. | Roadrunner RR 90002 |
| 09/03/1996 | 4 | 5 | ● | **ROOTS** | Roadrunner RR 89002 |
| 17/10/1998 | 40 | 1 | | AGAINST | Roadrunner RR 87002 |

▲⁹ Number of weeks album topped the US chart   ◆¹² RIAA Diamond Awards   ◇³ IFPI Platinum Europe Awards

### ERIC SERRA French conductor/composer born on 9/9/1959.

| | | | | | |
|---|---|---|---|---|---|
| 28/06/1997 | 58 | 2 | | THE FIFTH ELEMENT Original soundtrack to the film | Virgin CDVIR 63 |

### TAJA SEVELLE US singer/DJ (born Minneapolis, MN) discovered by Prince. After her debut album she moved to Los Angeles, CA and wrote with Burt Bacharach, Thom Bell and Nile Rodgers. By 1999 she was working with RJ Rice and was signed to 550 Music.

| | | | | | |
|---|---|---|---|---|---|
| 26/03/1988 | 48 | 4 | | TAJA SEVELLE | Paisley Park WX 165 |

### SEX PISTOLS UK punk rock group assembled in 1973 by manager Malcom McLaren with Paul Cook (born 20/7/1956, London, drums), Steve Jones (born 3/5/1955, London, guitar) and Glen Matlock (born 27/8/1956, London, bass) as the Swankers. After one gig they disbanded, but McLaren re-formed them, added Johnny Rotten (born John Lydon, 31/1/1956, London, vocals) and changed their name to the Sex Pistols in 1975. Signed by EMI in October 1976 for a £40,000 advance, they were dropped by the company in January 1977 after only one single as a result of their interview on the early evening TV show *Today* when, goaded by presenter Bill Grundy, they launched into an outburst of swearing. The following month Sid Vicious (born John Ritchie, 10/5/1957, London) replaced Matlock. They were signed by A&M on 10th March for a £75,000 advance. After protests by other acts on the label (most notably Rick Wakeman), they were dropped by A&M on 16th March without releasing a record, although copies of *God Save The Queen* were pressed. They were signed by Virgin in May 1977 for £15,000 advance. Their Virgin debut, *God Save The Queen*, was released on Jubilee Day. They disbanded in 1978 with Rotten forming Public Image Ltd. Vicious died from a drug overdose on 2/2/1979 whilst on bail for murdering his girlfriend Nancy Spungen (though recent evidence suggests that they may have been the victims of a robbery). The group re-formed in 1996 for a world tour.

| | | | | | |
|---|---|---|---|---|---|
| 12/11/1977 | ●² | 54 | ✪ | NEVER MIND THE BOLLOCKS, HERE'S THE SEX PISTOLS Later re-released with the catalogue number SPUNK 1 | Virgin V 2086 |
| 10/03/1979 | 7 | 33 | ● | THE GREAT ROCK 'N' ROLL SWINDLE Original soundtrack to the film | Virgin VD 2410 |
| 11/08/1979 | 6 | 10 | ○ | SOME PRODUCT – CARRI ON SEX PISTOLS | Virgin VR 2 |
| 16/02/1980 | 23 | 6 | ○ | FLOGGING A DEAD HORSE | Virgin V 2142 |
| 07/06/1980 | 16 | 11 | | THE GREAT ROCK 'N' ROLL SWINDLE Original soundtrack to the film | Virgin V 2168 |
| 17/10/1992 | 10 | 4 | ● | KISS THIS | Virgin CDV 2702 |
| 10/08/1996 | 26 | 2 | | FILTHY LUCRE LIVE | Virgin CDVUS 116 |
| 15/06/2002 | 29 | 3 | | JUBILEE | Virgin CDV 2961 |

### SHACK UK vocal/instrumental group formed in 1988 by Michael Head (vocals) with brother John (guitar). Shortly after finishing their second album, *Waterpistol*, the studio where it was recorded (Star Street in London) burned to the ground and the master tapes destroyed. A DAT copy was found, the album appearing four years later in 1995, by which time the group had disbanded and Michael Head had formed Strands. He revived Shack in 1999 with his brother John, Ren Perry (bass) and Iain Templeton (drums).

| | | | | | |
|---|---|---|---|---|---|
| 03/07/1999 | 25 | 2 | | H.M.S. FABLE | London 5561132 |
| 23/08/2003 | 55 | 1 | | HERE'S TOM WITH THE WEATHER | North Country NCCD 002 |

### SHADES OF RHYTHM UK production/instrumental group formed by Kevin Lancaster, Nick Slater and Rayan Hepburn.

| | | | | | |
|---|---|---|---|---|---|
| 17/08/1991 | 51 | 3 | | SHADES | ZTT 8 |

DANCE WITH THE SHADOWS / SOUND OF THE SHADOWS TWO ORIGINAL ALBUMS ON ONE C.D.

### SHADOWS UK group formed in 1960 by Hank Marvin (born Brian Rankin, 28/10/1941, Newcastle-upon-Tyne, lead guitar), Bruce Welch (born Bruce Cripps, 2/11/1941, Bognor Regis, rhythm guitar), Jet Harris (born Terence Harris, 6/7/1939, London, bass) and Tony Meehan (born Daniel Meehan, 2/3/1943, London) as The Drifters. The withdrawal of the record (*Feelin' Fine*) from the US market was forced by an injunction placed by the US R&B group The Drifters. The (UK) Drifters' second US release was credited the Four Jets but prompted a name-change to The Shadows. Meehan left in 1961, replaced by Brian Bennett (born 9/2/1940, London). Harris left in 1962, initially replaced by Brian 'Liquorice' Locking, who left in 1963 to become a Jehovah's Witness and was replaced by John Rostill (born 16/6/1942, Birmingham). They disbanded in 1968, re-forming on a number of occasions with Marvin, Welch, Bennett and John Farrar. Rostill died on 26/11/1973 after being accidentally electrocuted whilst playing guitar in his home studio. Welch discovered the body when he arrived to continue writing songs with Rostill.

| | | | | | |
|---|---|---|---|---|---|
| 18/04/1959 | 4 | 31 | | CLIFF CLIFF RICHARD & THE DRIFTERS | Columbia 33SX 1147 |
| 14/11/1959 | 2 | 36 | | CLIFF SINGS | Columbia 33SX 1192 |
| 15/10/1960 | 2 | 33 | | ME AND MY SHADOWS | Columbia 33SX 1261 |
| 22/04/1961 | 2 | 28 | | LISTEN TO CLIFF This and the above two hits credited to CLIFF RICHARD & THE SHADOWS | Columbia 33SX 1320 |
| 16/09/1961 | ●⁵ | 57 | | THE SHADOWS | Columbia 33SX 1374 |
| 21/10/1961 | ●¹ | 16 | | I'M 21 TODAY | Columbia 33SX 1368 |
| 23/12/1961 | ●⁶ | 42 | | THE YOUNG ONES Original soundtrack to the film | Columbia 33SX 1384 |
| 29/09/1962 | 3 | 21 | | 32 MINUTES AND 17 SECONDS This and the above two hits credited to CLIFF RICHARD & THE SHADOWS | Columbia 33SX 1431 |
| 13/10/1962 | ●⁷ | 38 | | OUT OF THE SHADOWS | Columbia 33SWX 1458 |
| 26/01/1963 | ●¹⁴ | 36 | | SUMMER HOLIDAY CLIFF RICHARD & THE SHADOWS Original soundtrack to the film | Columbia 33SX 1472 |
| 22/06/1963 | 2 | 49 | | THE SHADOWS' GREATEST HITS | Columbia 33SX 1522 |
| 13/07/1963 | 2 | 19 | | CLIFF'S HIT ALBUM | Columbia 33SX 1512 |
| 28/09/1963 | 8 | 10 | | WHEN IN SPAIN This and the above hit credited to CLIFF RICHARD & THE SHADOWS | Columbia 33SX 1541 |
| 09/05/1964 | 2 | 27 | | DANCE WITH THE SHADOWS | Columbia 33SX 1619 |
| 11/07/1964 | 2 | 23 | | WONDERFUL LIFE Original soundtrack to the film | Columbia 33SX 1628 |
| 09/01/1965 | 13 | 5 | | ALADDIN AND HIS WONDERFUL LAMP This and the above hit credited to CLIFF RICHARD & THE SHADOWS | Columbia 33SX 1676 |
| 17/07/1965 | 4 | 17 | | THE SOUND OF THE SHADOWS | Columbia 33SX 1736 |
| 14/08/1965 | 20 | 1 | | MORE HITS BY CLIFF | Columbia 33SX 1737 |
| 08/01/1966 | 19 | 1 | | LOVE IS FOREVER This and the above hit credited to CLIFF RICHARD & THE SHADOWS | Columbia 33SX 1769 |
| 21/05/1966 | 5 | 17 | | SHADOW MUSIC | Columbia SX 6041 |

| | | | | | |
|---|---|---|---|---|---|
| 15/07/1967 | 8 | 16 | | **JIGSAW** | Columbia SCX 6148 |
| 16/11/1968 | 30 | 4 | | ESTABLISHED 1958 | Columbia SCX 6282 |
| 12/07/1969 | 5 | 17 | | **THE BEST OF CLIFF** This and the above hit credited to **CLIFF RICHARD & THE SHADOWS** | Columbia SCX 6343 |
| 24/10/1970 | 30 | 4 | | SHADES OF ROCK | Columbia SCX 6420 |
| 23/12/1972 | 49 | 2 | | THE BEST OF CLIFF VOLUME II **CLIFF RICHARD & THE SHADOWS** | Columbia SCX 6519 |
| 13/04/1974 | 45 | 1 | | ROCKIN' WITH CURLY LEADS | EMI EMA 762 |
| 11/05/1974 | 48 | 6 | | THE SHADOWS' GREATEST HITS | Columbia SCX 1522 |
| 29/03/1975 | 30 | 5 | | SPECS APPEAL | EMI EMC 3066 |
| 12/02/1977 | ●6 | 43 | ✪ | **SHADOWS 20 GOLDEN GREATS** Holds the record for the biggest leap within the chart to the #1 spot, rising from #48 | EMI EMTV 3 |
| 15/09/1979 | ●3 | 43 | ✪ | **STRING OF HITS** | EMI EMC 3310 |
| 17/12/1979 | 5 | 12 | ● | **THANK YOU VERY MUCH – REUNION CONCERT AT THE LONDON PALLADIUM** **CLIFF RICHARD & THE SHADOWS** Columbia EMI EMTV 15 |
| 26/07/1980 | 16 | 8 | O | ANOTHER STRING OF HITS | EMI EMC 3339 |
| 13/09/1980 | 17 | 6 | O | CHANGE OF ADDRESS | Polydor 2442 179 |
| 19/09/1981 | 15 | 16 | O | HITS RIGHT UP YOUR STREET | Polydor POLD 5046 |
| 25/09/1982 | 24 | 6 | | LIFE IN THE JUNGLE/LIVE AT ABBEY ROAD | Polydor SHADS 1 |
| 22/10/1983 | 34 | 6 | | XXV | Polydor POLD 5120 |
| 17/11/1984 | 98 | 1 | | GUARDIAN ANGEL | Polydor POLD 5169 |
| 24/05/1986 | 6 | 19 | ● | **MOONLIGHT SHADOWS** | Polydor PROLP 8 |
| 24/10/1987 | 11 | 17 | ✪ | SIMPLY SHADOWS | Polydor SHAD 1 |
| 20/05/1989 | 11 | 9 | ● | STEPPIN' TO THE SHADOWS | Polydor SHAD 30 |
| 16/12/1989 | 12 | 9 | ● | AT THEIR VERY BEST | Polydor 8415201 |
| 13/10/1990 | 5 | 15 | ✪ | **REFLECTION** | Roll Over 8471201 |
| 16/11/1991 | 21 | 11 | ● | THEMES AND DREAMS | Polydor 5113741 |
| 15/05/1993 | 22 | 4 | | SHADOWS IN THE NIGHT – 16 CLASSIC TRACKS | Polygram TV 8437982 |
| 22/10/1994 | 19 | 11 | | THE BEST OF HANK MARVIN AND THE SHADOWS | Polygram TV 5238212 |
| 22/11/1997 | 41 | 6 | | PLAY ANDREW LLOYD WEBBER AND TIM RICE | Polygram TV 5394792 |
| 14/11/1998 | 56 | 5 | | VERY BEST OF HANK MARVIN AND THE SHADOWS – THE FIRST 40 YEARS This and the above two hits credited to **HANK MARVIN AND THE SHADOWS** | Polygram TV 5592112 |
| 12/08/2000 | 35 | 3 | | 50 GOLDEN GREATS | EMI 5275862 |
| 08/05/2004 | 7 | 8+ | ● | **LIFE STORY** | Universal TV 9817819 |

**SHAGGY** Jamaican singer (born Orville Richard Burrell, 22/10/1968, Kingston); he moved to New York at fifteen and formed the Sting International Posse. He later joined the US Marines, maintaining a parallel recording career. He won the 2001 MOBO Award for Best Reggae Act and the 2002 BRIT Award for Best International Male.

| | | | | | |
|---|---|---|---|---|---|
| 24/07/1993 | 67 | 1 | | PURE PLEASURE | Greensleeves GRELCD 184 |
| 14/10/1995 | 37 | 6 | O | BOOMBASTIC 1995 Grammy Award for Best Reggae Album | Virgin CDV 2782 |
| 17/02/2001 | ●1 | 47 | ✪3 | **HOT SHOT** ◇2 ▲6 | MCA 1122932 |
| 16/02/2002 | 20 | 5 | O | MR LOVER LOVER – THE BEST OF – PART 1 | Virgin VTCD 429 |
| 16/11/2002 | 54 | 2 | | LUCKY DAY | MCA 1131192 |

**SHAKATAK** UK group formed in London in 1980 by Bill Sharpe (keyboards), Jill Saward (vocals), Keith Winter (guitar), George Anderson (bass), Roger Odell (drums) and Nigel Wright (keyboards). Wright left the group but remained as producer. Sharpe later recorded with Gary Numan.

| | | | | | |
|---|---|---|---|---|---|
| 30/01/1982 | 35 | 17 | O | DRIVIN' HARD | Polydor POLS 1030 |
| 15/05/1982 | 4 | 28 | ● | **NIGHT BIRDS** | Polydor POLS 1059 |
| 27/11/1982 | 30 | 11 | ● | INVITATIONS | Polydor POLD 5068 |
| 22/10/1983 | 30 | 4 | | OUT OF THIS WORLD | Polydor POLD 5115 |
| 25/08/1984 | 17 | 9 | | DOWN ON THE STREET | Polydor POLD 5148 |
| 23/05/1985 | 82 | 3 | | LIVE! | Polydor POLH 21 |
| 22/10/1988 | 73 | 1 | | THE COOLEST CUTS | K-Tel NE 1422 |

**SHAKESPEARS SISTER** UK/US duo formed in 1989 by ex-Bananarama Siobhan Fahey (born 10/9/1958, London, vocals) and Marcella Detroit (born Marcella Levy, 21/6/1959, Detroit, MI, vocals/guitar/programming), who had toured and written with Eric Clapton. After a two year 'maternity' break following their debut hit, they disbanded in 1993, Detroit going solo. Fahey revived the name in 1996.

| | | | | | |
|---|---|---|---|---|---|
| 02/09/1989 | 9 | 8 | ● | **SACRED HEART** | London 8281311 |
| 29/02/1992 | 3 | 55 | ✪2 | **HORMONALLY YOURS** | London 8282262 |

**SHAKIN' PYRAMIDS** UK vocal/instrumental group formed in Glasgow by James G Creighton (guitar), Railroad Ken (guitar) and Dave Duncan (harmonica). The trio began their career busking before landing a contract with Virgin's Cuba Libra imprint. They later worked with Lonnie Donegan and disbanded after a second album, *Celts And Cobras*.

| 04/04/1981 .....48......4 ...... | | | | | SKIN 'EM UP ..................................................................Cuba Libra V 2199 |

**SHAKIRA** Colombian singer (born Shakira Isabel Mebarak Ripoll, 9/2/1977, Barranquilla); she was first known in the Spanish-speaking world before widening her appeal by recording in English. She won a Grammy Award in 2000 for Best Latin Pop Album for *Shakira – MTV Unplugged*.

| 23/03/2002 .....2......47......✪² | | | | | **LAUNDRY SERVICE** ◇⁴ ...................................................Epic SNY 639002 (import) |

**SHALAMAR** US group initially formed as a studio group in 1977. Following their debut success an actual group was assembled featuring Jody Watley (born 30/1/1959, Chicago, IL, god-daughter of Jackie Wilson), Jeffrey Daniels (born 24/8/1957, Los Angeles, CA) and Gerald Brown. Brown left in 1979, replaced by Howard Hewett (born 1/10/1955, Akron, OH). Both Watley and Daniel went solo in 1984, replaced by Delisa Davies and Micki Free. Hewitt left in 1985, replaced by Sydney Justin (previously a defensive back for US football side the Los Angeles Rams). Daniels was briefly married to singer Stephanie Mills. Hewett, Watley and Daniels reunited in 1996 to contribute to a Babyface single.

| 27/03/1982 .....6......72......✪ | | | | | **FRIENDS** ...............................................................Solar K 52345 |
| 11/09/1982 .....71......5 ...... | | | | | GREATEST HITS ..........................................................Solar SOLA 3001 |
| 30/07/1983 .....7......20......● | | | | | **THE LOOK** .............................................................Solar 960239 |
| 12/04/1986 .....5......24......● | | | | | **THE GREATEST HITS** ...................................................Stylus SMR 8615 |

**SHAM 69** UK rock group formed in 1977 by Jimmy Pursey (vocals), Dave Parsons (guitar), Albie Slider (bass) and Mark Cain (drums). Slider and Cain left in 1978, replaced by Dave Treganna and Rick Goldstein. They split in 1979, re-forming in 1980 for one album, then in 1987 attempted another comeback with a line-up of Pursey, Parsons, Andy Prince (bass), Ian Whitehead (drums), Tony Black (keyboards) and Linda Paganelli (saxophone). Pursey also recorded solo.

| 11/03/1978 .....25......8 ...... | | | | | TELL US THE TRUTH ......................................................Polydor 2383 491 |
| 02/12/1978 .....27......11......○ | | | | | THAT'S LIFE ............................................................Polydor POLD 5010 |
| 29/09/1979 .....8......8 ......○ | | | | | **THE ADVENTURES OF THE HERSHAM BOYS** ...................................Polydor POLD 5025 |

**SHAMEN** UK group formed in Scotland in 1985 by Colin Angus (born 24/8/1961, Aberdeen, vocals/bass), Derek MacKenzie (born 27/2/1964, Aberdeen), Keith MacKenzie (born 30/8/1961, Aberdeen) and Peter Stephenson (born 1/3/1962, Ayr). They signed with Moshka in 1987, adding sampling and keyboards player Will Sin (born William Sinnott, 23/12/1960, Glasgow) in 1987. The MacKenzie brothers left in 1988. Sin was drowned on 22/5/1991 whilst filming a video for *Pro-Gen*.

| 03/11/1990 .....31......10...... | | | | | EN-TACT ................................................................One Little Indian TPLP 22 |
| 28/09/1991 .....23......2 ...... | | | | | PROGENY ...............................................................One Little Indian TPLP 32 |
| 26/09/1992 .....3......35......✪ | | | | | **BOSS DRUM/DIFFERENT DRUM** *A Different Drum* is a remix album that was added to *Boss Drum* from 18/12/1993 ..............................................................One Little Indian TPLP 42CD |
| 20/11/1993 .....61......1 ...... | | | | | ON AIR – BBC SESSIONS ..................................................Band Of Joy BOJCD 006 |
| 04/11/1995 .....27......2 ...... | | | | | AXIS MUTATIS ..........................................................One Little Indian TPLP 52CDL |
| 02/05/1998 .....26......4 ...... | | | | | THE SHAMEN COLLECTION ................................................One Little Indian TPLP 72CDE |

**SHAMPOO** UK duo Jacqui Blake (born November 1974) and Carrie Askew (born May 1977) who first met at Plumstead Manor High School in London and first recorded for Icerink (Saint Etienne's label). Despite limited UK success, they were very popular in Japan.

| 05/11/1994 .....45......2 ...... | | | | | WE ARE SHAMPOO .......................................................Food FOODCD 12 |

**JIMMY SHAND AND HIS BAND** UK accordionist (born 29/1/1908, East Wenyss, Fife). A miner who was made redundant after the 1926 General Strike, he went to work in a music shop. He made his first recording in 1933. He was awarded the MBE in 1962 and was knighted in 1999. He died on 23/12/2000.

| 24/12/1983 .....97......2 ...... | | | | | FIFTY YEARS ON WITH JIMMY SHAND .....................................Ross WGR 062 |

**SHANICE** US R&B singer (born Shanice Wilson, 14/5/1973, Pittsburgh, PA) who debuted at the age of three and was singing with Ella Fitzgerald in a TV advertisement at eight. She signed with A&M in 1984 at the age of eleven, switching to Motown in 1989.

| 21/03/1992 .....21......4 ...... | | | | | INNER CHILD ...........................................................Motown 5300082 |

**SHANNON** US R&B singer (born Brenda Shannon Greene, 1958, Washington DC) who began in 1978 with the New York Jazz Ensemble. She sang with Brownstone in the early 1980s.

| 10/03/1984 .....52......12...... | | | | | LET THE MUSIC PLAY ....................................................Club JABL 1 |

**DEL SHANNON** US singer (born Charles Westover, 30/12/1934, Cooperville, MI). Shannon claimed his birthdate was in 1939 to improve his teen market appeal, an 'error' not revealed until years later. He signed with Big Top in 1960 and set up the Berlee label in 1963. His debut hit featured the 'musitron', a forerunner of the synthesizer developed by Max Crook. He died from a self-inflicted gunshot wound on 8/2/1990 having been prescribed the anti-depressant drug Prozac prior to his suicide. He was inducted into the Rock & Roll Hall of Fame in 1999.

| 11/05/1963 .....9......17...... | | | | | **HATS OFF TO LARRY** .....................................................London HAX 8071 |
| 02/11/1963 .....15......6 ...... | | | | | LITTLE TOWN FLIRT ......................................................London HAX 8091 |

○ Silver disc ● Gold disc ✪ Platinum disc (additional platinum units are indicated by a figure following the symbol) ●⁹ Number of weeks album topped the UK chart

**HELEN SHAPIRO** UK singer (born 28/9/1946, London); she signed with EMI whilst still at school and released her first single when aged fourteen. She appeared in the film *It's Trad Dad* and after her hits came to an end became an actress. She is the youngest female artist to have topped the UK single charts, a feat accomplished when she was fourteen years ten months.

| | | | | |
|---|---|---|---|---|
| 10/03/1962 | 2 | 25 | | TOPS WITH ME ................................................................................Columbia 33SX 1397 |

**FEARGAL SHARKEY** UK singer (born 13/8/1958, Londonderry, Northern Ireland); he was lead singer with the Undertones from their formation in 1975 until they split in 1983. He was the first artist to sign with Madness' Zarjazz label in 1984, switching to Virgin in 1985.

| | | | | |
|---|---|---|---|---|
| 23/11/1985 | 12 | 20 | ● | FEARGAL SHARKEY ................................................................................Virgin V 2360 |
| 20/04/1991 | 27 | 4 | | SONGS FROM THE MARDI GRAS ..........................................................Virgin V 2642 |

**SHARPE AND NUMAN** UK duo Bill Sharpe and Gary Numan (born Gary Anthony James Webb, 8/3/1958, London). Sharpe was keyboard player with Shakatak whilst Numan had formed Tubeway Army and enjoyed a successful solo career.

| | | | | |
|---|---|---|---|---|
| 08/07/1989 | 59 | 1 | | AUTOMATIC ................................................................................Polydor 8395201 |

**SANDIE SHAW** UK singer (born Sandra Goodrich, 26/2/1947, Dagenham). She was a machine operator when discovered by Adam Faith's manager Eve Taylor. Signed with Pye in 1964, her trademark of always singing barefoot was initially a publicity stunt devised by Taylor. She married fashion designer Jeff Banks in 1968 and later entertainment mogul Nik Powell.

| | | | | |
|---|---|---|---|---|
| 06/03/1965 | 3 | 13 | | SANDIE ................................................................................Pye NPL 18110 |
| 19/11/1994 | 64 | 1 | | NOTHING LESS THAN BRILLIANT ..........................................................Virgin VTCD 34 |

**GEORGE SHEARING** UK pianist (born 13/8/1919, London). Born blind, he learned piano from the age of three. After playing for names like Harry Parry and Stephane Grappelli, he moved to the USA in 1946 forming his own quartet, a group that would include Cal Tjader, Joe Pass, Gary Burton and Denzil Best among others. He also worked with numerous singers, including Peggy Lee, Nat 'King' Cole, Carmen McRae and Mel Torme, and also performed classical music. He has a star on the Hollywood Walk of Fame.

| | | | | |
|---|---|---|---|---|
| 11/06/1960 | 16 | 6 | | BEAUTY AND THE BEAT **PEGGY LEE AND GEORGE SHEARING** ........................Capitol T 1219 |
| 20/10/1962 | 8 | 7 | | **NAT 'KING' COLE SINGS AND THE GEORGE SHEARING QUARTET PLAYS NAT 'KING' COLE/GEORGE SHEARING QUARTET** Capitol W 1675 |

**SHED SEVEN** UK rock group formed in York in 1991 by Rick Witter (vocals), Tim Gladwin (bass), Paul Banks (guitar) and Alan Leach (drums). They fell out with their record label Polydor in 1999 and left in September of that year to sign with Artful.

| | | | | |
|---|---|---|---|---|
| 17/09/1994 | 16 | 2 | | CHANGE GIVER ................................................................................Polydor 5236152 |
| 13/04/1996 | 8 | 26 | ● | **A MAXIMUM HIGH** ................................................................................Polydor 5310392 |
| 13/06/1998 | 9 | 7 | | LET IT RIDE ................................................................................Polydor 5573592 |
| 12/06/1999 | 7 | 10 | ○ | **GOING FOR GOLD – THE GREATEST HITS** ................................................Polydor 5474422 |
| 19/05/2001 | 42 | 1 | | TRUTH BE TOLD ................................................................................Artful ARTFULCD 38 |

**SHEEP ON DRUGS** UK duo formed in London in 1991 by 'Dead' Lee Fraser (electronics/guitar) and 'King' Duncan Gil-Rodriguez (vocals). Lee later changed his name to Lee 303. They launched their own The Drug Squad label.

| | | | | |
|---|---|---|---|---|
| 10/04/1993 | 55 | 1 | | GREATEST HITS ................................................................................Transglobal CID 8006 |

**PETE SHELLEY** UK singer/guitarist (born Peter McNeish, 17/4/1955) who was a member of The Invisible Girle before going on to form The Buzzcocks. The group split in 1981 and he went solo. In 1986 he formed Zip and in 1990 re-formed The Buzzcocks.

| | | | | |
|---|---|---|---|---|
| 02/07/1983 | 42 | 4 | | XL – 1 ................................................................................Genetic XL 1 |

**VONDA SHEPARD** US singer (born 1963, NYC); her songs were first exposed via the TV show *Ally McBeal*. She was originally signed by Reprise but dropped after one release. She first hit the US charts in 1987 with a duet with Dan Hill (*Can't We Try*).

| | | | | |
|---|---|---|---|---|
| 17/10/1998 | 3 | 34 | ✪ | **SONGS FROM 'ALLY MCBEAL'** ◇² Original soundtrack to the TV programme ..................Epic 4911242 |
| 12/06/1999 | 39 | 2 | | BY 7.30 ................................................................................Epic 4945792 |
| 20/11/1999 | 9 | 13 | ● | **HEART & SOUL – NEW SONGS FROM ALLY MCBEAL** Original soundtrack to the TV programme ..................Epic 4950912 |

**SHERRICK** US singer (born 6/7/1957, Sacramento, CA) who backed Stevie Wonder, The Temptations and Rick James and such before going solo.

| | | | | |
|---|---|---|---|---|
| 29/08/1987 | 27 | 6 | | SHERRICK ................................................................................Warner Brothers WX 118 |

**BRENDAN SHINE** Irish male singer (born 2/6/1947, Ballinasloe, Dublin); he was a member of Kieran Kelly's Ceili Band before launching a solo career in 1971.

| | | | | |
|---|---|---|---|---|
| 12/11/1983 | 51 | 12 | ○ | THE BRENDAN SHINE COLLECTION ......................................................Play PLAYTV 1 |
| 03/11/1984 | 74 | 4 | | WITH LOVE ................................................................................Play PLAYTV 2 |
| 16/11/1985 | 81 | 7 | | MEMORIES ................................................................................Play PLAYTV 3 |
| 18/11/1989 | 62 | 6 | ○ | MAGIC MOMENTS ................................................................................Stylus SMR 991 |

**SHINING** UK group with Duncan Baxter (vocals), Simon Tong (guitar/keyboards), Dan MacBean (guitar), Simon Jones (born 29/7/1972, bass) and Mark Heaney (drums). Jones and Tong had previously been members of The Verve.

| | | | | |
|---|---|---|---|---|
| 28/09/2002 | 73 | 1 | | TRUE SKIES ................................................................................Zuma Recordings ZUMACD 001 |

**SHIREHORSES** UK vocal duo formed by Radio 1 DJs Mark Radcliffe (born 1958, Bolton) and Marc 'Lard' Riley (born Manchester). Their hit albums are basically satirical tributes to the leading bands of the day: thus their second album features contributions from Manic Street Sweepers, Radiohead, Robbie And William, and Dave Lee Travisty. The pair were named Radio DJs of the Year in 1998 by NME whilst their show won a Gold Sony Radio Award the same year.

| | | | | | |
|---|---|---|---|---|---|
| 15/11/1997 | 22 | 4 | | THE WORST ALBUM IN THE WORLD EVER... EVER! | East West 3984208512 |
| 26/05/2001 | 20 | 4 | | OUR KID EH | Columbia 5030492 |

**MICHELLE SHOCKED** US singer/guitarist (born Michelle Johnston, 24/2/1962, Dallas, TX). Her debut album *The Texas Campfire Tapes* was recorded on a Walkman at a campfire in Texas (crickets and passing lorries audible in the background). Later albums were recorded more conventionally. In 1995 she took legal action to be released from her contract with London after various disagreements.

| | | | | | |
|---|---|---|---|---|---|
| 10/09/1988 | 33 | 19 | ● | SHORT SHARP SHOCKED | Cooking Vinyl CVLP 1 |
| 18/11/1989 | 31 | 3 | | CAPTAIN SWING | Cooking Vinyl 8388781 |
| 11/04/1992 | 46 | 2 | | ARKANSAS TRAVELER | London 5121892 |

**SHOP ASSISTANTS** UK vocal/instrumental group formed in Edinburgh in 1983 by Alex Taylor (vocals), David Keegan (guitar), Sarah Kneale (bass), Ann Donald (drums) and Laura McBride (drums) as Buba And The Shop Assistants. After releases on Villa 21 and their own 53rd & 3rd label they signed with Chrysalis' Blue Guitar imprint. Donald was replaced by Joan Bride in 1986. The following year Taylor left to form Motorcycle Boy whilst Keegan became a skiing instructor. The band re-formed in 1989 with Keegan, Kneale, McPail (bass) and Margarita (drums). Keegan later joined The Pastels.

| | | | | | |
|---|---|---|---|---|---|
| 29/11/1986 | 100 | 1 | | SHOP ASSISTANTS | Blue Guitar AZLP 2 |

**HOWARD SHORE** Canadian conductor/composer who studied at the Berklee School of Music in Boston and recorded as a member of Lighthouse from 1969–72. He worked on the TV series *Saturday Night Live* as musical director from 1975–80 and began recording film scores in 1980. Since then he has composed the music to more than 50 films, including *Silence Of The Lambs*, *Philadelphia*, *Scanners*, *The Fly* and *After Hours*. He won an Oscar in 2004 for Best Original Song with Fran Walsh and Annie Lennox for *Into The West*.

| | | | | | |
|---|---|---|---|---|---|
| 05/01/2002 | 10 | 14 | O | THE LORD OF THE RINGS ◇ Original soundtrack to the film. 2002 Grammy Award for Best Score Soundtrack Album For A Motion Picture, Television Or Other Visual Media and 2002 Oscar for Best Original Score | Reprise 9362481102 |
| 11/01/2003 | 28 | 9 | ● | LORD OF THE RINGS – THE TWO TOWERS Original soundtrack to the film. 2003 Grammy Award for for Best Score Soundtrack Album For A Motion Picture, Television Or Other Visual Media | Reprise 9362484212 |
| 27/12/2003 | 34 | 11 | ● | LORD OF THE RINGS – RETURN OF THE KING Original soundtrack to the film. 2004 Oscar for Best Original Score | Reprise 9362486092 |

**SHOWADDYWADDY** UK rock 'n' roll revival group formed in Leicester in 1973 by Dave Bartram (vocals), Buddy Gask (vocals), Romeo Challenger (drums), Malcolm Allured (drums), Trevor Oakes (guitar), Russ Field (guitar), Rod Deas (bass) and Al James (bass). The group was formed by the amalgamation of two other groups, the Hammers and the Choice. They first came to prominence after winning *Opportunity Knocks* and were signed by Bell as a result.

| | | | | | |
|---|---|---|---|---|---|
| 07/12/1974 | 9 | 19 | | **SHOWADDYWADDY** | Bell BELLS 248 |
| 12/07/1975 | 7 | 17 | O | **STEP TWO** | Bell BELLS 256 |
| 29/05/1976 | 41 | 3 | O | TROCADERO | Bell SYBEL 8003 |
| 25/12/1976 | 4 | 26 | ✪ | **GREATEST HITS** | Arista ARTY 145 |
| 03/12/1977 | 20 | 10 | | RED STAR | Arista SPARTY 1023 |
| 09/12/1978 | ❶² | 17 | ✪ | **GREATEST HITS (1976–1978)** | Arista ARTV 1 |
| 10/11/1979 | 8 | 14 | ● | **CREPES AND DRAPES** | Arista ARTV 3 |
| 20/12/1980 | 33 | 8 | O | BRIGHT LIGHTS | Arista SPART 1142 |
| 07/11/1981 | 33 | 11 | ● | THE VERY BEST OF SHOWADDYWADDY | Arista SPART 1178 |
| 05/12/1987 | 90 | 1 | | THE BEST STEPS TO HEAVEN | Tiger SHTV 1 |

**SHRIEKBACK** UK group formed by Barry Andrews (vocals), Carl Marsh (guitar) and Dave Allen (bass). Marsh later left, the remaining pair recruiting Martyn Baker (drums) plus assorted session musicians and singers.

| | | | | | |
|---|---|---|---|---|---|
| 11/08/1984 | 85 | 1 | | JAM SCIENCE | Arista 206 416 |

**SHRIEVE** – see **SAMMY HAGAR**

**SHUT UP AND DANCE** UK hip hop/house duo formed in London in 1988 by Philip 'PJ' Johnson and Carl 'Smiley' Hyman. The duo also set up the Shut Up And Dance label.

| | | | | | |
|---|---|---|---|---|---|
| 27/06/1992 | 38 | 2 | | DEATH IS NOT THE END | Shut Up And Dance SUADCD 005 |

**SHY** UK vocal/instrumental group formed in Birmingham by Tony Mills (vocals), Steve Harris (guitar), Roy Davis (bass), Pat McKenna (keyboards) and Alan Kelly (drums). Mills later went on to join Siam.

| | | | | | |
|---|---|---|---|---|---|
| 11/04/1987 | 74 | 2 | | EXCESS ALL AREAS | RCA PL 71221 |

**LABI SIFFRE** UK singer (born 25/6/1945, London) with an English mother and Nigerian father. He spent some time working in Cannes, France before returning to the UK and going solo.

| | | | | | |
|---|---|---|---|---|---|
| 24/07/1971 | 47 | 1 | | SINGER AND THE SONG | Pye NSPL 28147 |
| 14/10/1972 | 46 | 1 | | CRYING, LAUGHING, LOVING, LYING | Pye NSPL 28163 |

### SIGUE SIGUE SPUTNIK
UK rock group formed in the mid-1980s by ex-Generation X Tony James (guitar), Martin Degville (vocals), Neal X (born Neil Whitmore, guitar), Chris Kavanagh (drums), Ray Mayhew (drums) and Miss Yana Ya Ya (keyboards). They disbanded in 1988, James joining Sisters Of Mercy.

| | | | |
|---|---|---|---|
| 09/08/1986 | 10 | 6 | FLAUNT IT ............................................................Parlophone PCS 7305 |
| 15/04/1989 | 53 | 1 | DRESS FOR EXCESS ...................................................Parlophone PCS 7328 |

### SIGUR ROS
Icelandic rock group formed in Reykjavic in 1994 by Jon Thor Birgisson (guitar/vocals), Georg Holm (bass) and August (drums). Kjartan Sveinsson (keyboards) joined in 1997 whilst August left in 1999, replaced by Orri Pall Dyrason. Their name means Victory Rose. An untitled track from their untitled album won the 2003 MTV Europe Music Award for Best Video.

| | | | |
|---|---|---|---|
| 26/08/2000 | 52 | 1 | AGAETIS BYRJUN ..........................................................Fat Cat FATCD 11 |
| 09/11/2002 | 49 | 1 | () Not only is this album unnamed, save for two symbols that look like brackets, the eight tracks on the album are all untitled ....... ............................................................................Fat Cat FATCD 22 |

### SILENCERS
UK group formed by Jimmie O'Neill (guitar/vocals), Cha Burns (guitar), Joe Donnelly (bass) and Martin Hanlin (drums).

| | | | |
|---|---|---|---|
| 23/03/1991 | 39 | 2 | DANCE TO THE HOLY MAN ..............................................RCA PL 74924 |
| 05/06/1993 | 52 | 1 | SECONDS OF PLEASURE .................................................RCA 74321141132 |

### SILVER BULLET
UK duo of Richard Brown and DJ Mo.

| | | | |
|---|---|---|---|
| 04/05/1991 | 38 | 2 | BRING DOWN THE WALLS NO LIMIT SQUAD RETURNS .....................Parlophone PCS 7350 |

### SILVER CONVENTION
German/US group initially formed as a studio project by producer Michael Kunze and writer/arranger Silvester Levay. Following the success of the single a group was assembled comprising singers Penny McLean, Ramona Wolf and Linda Thompson. Thompson left in 1976, replaced by Rhonda Heath, although the group had split by the end of the decade. The group won the 1975 Grammy Award for Best Rhythm & Blues Instrumental Performance for *Fly Robin Fly*.

| | | | |
|---|---|---|---|
| 25/06/1977 | 34 | 3 | SILVER CONVENTION: GREATEST HITS ...................................Magnet MAG 6001 |

### SILVER SUN
UK rock group formed in Darlington by James Broad (guitar/vocals), Paul Smith (guitar), Richard Kane (bass) and Richard Sayce (drums). Sayce left in 1999, replaced by Merlin Matthews. They later relocated to London.

| | | | |
|---|---|---|---|
| 24/05/1997 | 30 | 1 | SILVER SUN ............................................................Polydor 5372082 |
| 17/10/1998 | 74 | 1 | NEO WAVE .............................................................Polydor 5590852 |

### SILVERCHAIR
Australian rock group formed in Newcastle by Ben Gillies (born 24/11/1979, drums), Chris Joannou (born 10/11/1979, USA, bass) and Daniel Johns (born 22/4/1979, guitar/vocals) in 1992 as Innocent Criminals. After winning a national Talent Quest contest they recorded a single and video for Sony Australia (*Tomorrow* which reached #1 in their home country).

| | | | |
|---|---|---|---|
| 23/09/1995 | 49 | 1 | FROGSTOMP ...........................................................Murmur 4803402 |
| 15/02/1997 | 38 | 2 | FREAK SHOW ...........................................................Murmur 4871032 |
| 27/03/1999 | 29 | 2 | NEON BALLROOM .......................................................Murmur 4933092 |

### SILVERFISH
UK group formed in London by Lesley Rankine (vocals), Andrew 'The Fuzz' Duprey (guitar), Chris Powforth (bass) and Stuart Watson (drums). The group disbanded in 1993.

| | | | |
|---|---|---|---|
| 27/06/1992 | 65 | 1 | ORGAN FAN ...........................................................Creation CRECD 118 |

### CARLY SIMON
US singer (born 25/6/1945, New York) who began as one half of the Simon Sisters with sister Lucy. She made her first solo recordings in 1966, but had nothing released until 1971. She married James Taylor in 1972 and divorced in 1983. She won an Oscar in 1988 for *Let The River Run*, the theme to *Working Girl* in the Best Original Song category. She has also won four Grammy Awards: Best New Artist in 1971; Best Recording For Children in 1980 with various others for *In Harmony*; Best Recording for Children in 1982 with various others for *In Harmony 2;* and Best Song Written Specifically for a Motion Picture in 1989 for *Let The River Run*.

| | | | |
|---|---|---|---|
| 20/01/1973 | 3 | 26 | NO SECRETS ▲5 ........................................................Elektra K 42127 |
| 16/03/1974 | 19 | 9 | HOT CAKES ............................................................Elektra K 52005 |
| 09/05/1987 | 25 | 20 | ○   COMING AROUND AGAIN ...............................................Arista 208 140 |
| 03/09/1988 | 49 | 6 | GREATEST HITS LIVE ....................................................Arista 209 196 |
| 20/03/1999 | 22 | 6 | NOBODY DOES IT BETTER – THE VERY BEST OF CARLY SIMON ............warner.esp/Global TV RADCD 103 |
| 12/06/2004 | 25 | 3+ | REFLECTIONS – GREATEST HITS ..........................................Electro/Rhino 8122789702 |

### PAUL SIMON
US singer (born 13/10/1941, Newark, NJ). He met up with Art Garfunkel in 1955; they first recorded as Tom & Jerry for Big Records in 1957 (Garfunkel called himself Tom Graph, Simon was Jerry Landis). They first recorded as Simon & Garfunkel in 1964 and split in 1970. Simon had recorded as Jerry Landis, Tico and Tico & The Temples during his early career with Garfunkel and under his own name in 1970. Following the split with Garfunkel he remained with CBS, switching to Warner's in 1979. He married singer Edie Brickell in May 1992, having previously been married to actress Carrie Fisher (Princess Leia in *Star Wars*). He won five Grammy Awards with Garfunkel and three for his songwriting with the duo. Simon went on to win a further four in his own right (at the ceremony in 1975, he thanked Stevie Wonder, who had won the award two years previously, for not releasing an album that year!). Named Best International Male at the 1987 BRIT Awards, he was inducted into the Rock & Roll Hall of Fame in 2001 having previously been inducted in 1990 as a member of Simon & Garfunkel.

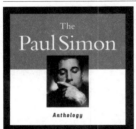

The Paul Simon

*Anthology*

| | | | |
|---|---|---|---|
| 26/02/1972 | ❶1 | 26 | PAUL SIMON ...........................................................CBS 69007 |
| 02/06/1973 | 4 | 22 | ●   THERE GOES RHYMIN' SIMON ............................................CBS 69035 |
| 01/11/1975 | 6 | 31 | ●   STILL CRAZY AFTER ALL THESE YEARS ▲1 1975 Grammy Awards for Album of the Year and Best Pop Vocal Performance ..CBS 86001 |
| 03/12/1977 | 6 | 15 | ●   GREATEST HITS, ETC .....................................................CBS 10007 |

▲9 Number of weeks album topped the US chart    ◆12 RIAA Diamond Awards    ◇3 IFPI Platinum Europe Awards

| DATE | POS | WKS | BPI | ALBUM TITLE | LABEL & NUMBER |
|------|-----|-----|-----|-------------|----------------|
| 30/08/1980 | 17 | 12 | ○ | ONE-TRICK PONY Original soundtrack to the film | Warner Brothers K 56846 |
| 12/11/1983 | 34 | 8 | | HEARTS AND BONES | Warner Brothers 9239421 |
| 13/09/1986 | ❶⁸ | 115 | ✪⁵ | GRACELAND 1986 Grammy Awards for Album of the Year and Record of the Year | Warner Brothers WX 52 |
| 24/01/1987 | 73 | 2 | | GREATEST HITS, ETC | CBS 4501661 |
| 05/11/1988 | 17 | 15 | ✪ | NEGOTIATIONS AND LOVE SONGS 1971–1986 | Warner Brothers WX 223 |
| 27/10/1990 | ❶² | 28 | ✪² | THE RHYTHM OF THE SAINTS | Warner Brothers WX 340 |
| 23/11/1991 | 60 | 1 | | PAUL SIMON'S CONCERT IN THE PARK – AUGUST 15TH 1991 | Warner Brothers WX 448 |
| 27/05/2000 | 6 | 12 | ● | GREATEST HITS/SHINING LIKE A NATIONAL GUITAR | Warner Brothers 9362477212 |
| 14/10/2000 | 20 | 4 | ○ | YOU'RE THE ONE | Warner Brothers 9362478442 |

## SIMON AND GARFUNKEL

US folk-rock duo formed by Paul Simon (born 13/10/1941, Newark, NJ) and Art Garfunkel (born 5/11/1941, Forest Hills, NY) who first teamed up at school in 1955. They recorded for Big Top in 1957 as Tom & Jerry (Garfunkel was Tom Graph, Simon was Jerry Landis) but split after leaving high school. Teaming again in 1960 as Simon & Garfunkel, their debut album was on CBS in 1964. They disbanded in 1970, Garfunkel concentrating on acting and Simon on a solo career. They have reunited for concerts and recorded their 1982 concert in Central Park. As a duo they won five Grammy Awards including Record of the Year and Best Contemporary Pop Vocal Performance by a Duo in 1968 for *Mrs Robinson,* and Record of the Year and Best Arrangement Accompanying Singers in 1970 for *Bridge Over Troubled Water.* Paul Simon was also awarded Grammy Awards for Best Original Score Written for a Motion Picture in 1968 for *The Graduate* and the Record of the Year and Best Contemporary Song in 1970 for *Bridge Over Troubled Water.* The pair also won two awards at the 1977 BRIT Awards: Best International Single and Album, both for *Bridge Over Troubled Water.* They were inducted into the Rock & Roll Hall of Fame in 1990.

| DATE | POS | WKS | BPI | ALBUM TITLE | LABEL & NUMBER |
|------|-----|-----|-----|-------------|----------------|
| 16/04/1966 | 13 | 104 | | SOUNDS OF SILENCE | CBS 62690 |
| 03/08/1968 | ❶⁷ | 77 | | BOOKENDS ▲⁷ | CBS 63101 |
| 31/08/1968 | 13 | 66 | | PARSLEY, SAGE, ROSEMARY AND THYME | CBS 62860 |
| 26/10/1968 | 3 | 71 | | THE GRADUATE ▲⁹ Original soundtrack to the film | CBS 70042 |
| 09/11/1968 | 24 | 6 | | WEDNESDAY MORNING 3 A.M. | CBS 63370 |
| 21/02/1970 | ❶⁴¹ | 307 | ✪ | BRIDGE OVER TROUBLED WATER ▲¹⁰ 1970 Grammy Award for Album of the Year | CBS 63699 |
| 22/07/1972 | 2 | 283 | ✪ | GREATEST HITS ◆¹³ | CBS 69003 |
| 04/04/1981 | 68 | 1 | ● | SOUNDS OF SILENCE Re-issue of CBS 62690 | CBS 32020 |
| 21/11/1981 | 4 | 80 | ✪³ | THE SIMON AND GARFUNKEL COLLECTION | CBS 10029 |
| 20/03/1982 | 6 | 43 | ● | THE CONCERT IN CENTRAL PARK | Geffen GEF 96008 |
| 30/11/1991 | 8 | 57 | ✪ | THE DEFINITIVE SIMON AND GARFUNKEL | Columbia MOODCD 21 |
| 05/02/2000 | 8 | 12 | | TALES FROM NEW YORK – THE VERY BEST OF SIMON & GARFUNKEL | Columbia SONYTV 81CD |
| 06/12/2003 | 25 | 11 | ● | THE ESSENTIAL | Columbia 5134702 |

## NINA SIMONE

US female singer (born Eunice Waymon, 21/2/1933, Tryon, SC); she scored her first US hit with *I Love You Porgy* in 1959. Towards the end of the 1960s she began devoting more time to political activities (including penning *To Be Young Gifted And Black,* which was a tribute to playwright Lorraine Hansberry) and subsequently relocated to France. She died on 21/4/2003.

| DATE | POS | WKS | BPI | ALBUM TITLE | LABEL & NUMBER |
|------|-----|-----|-----|-------------|----------------|
| 24/07/1965 | 18 | 3 | | I PUT A SPELL ON YOU | Philips BL 7671 |
| 15/02/1969 | 11 | 1 | | NUFF SAID | RCA Victor SF 7979 |
| 14/11/1987 | 56 | 8 | ● | MY BABY JUST CARES FOR ME | Charly CR 30217 |
| 16/07/1994 | 9 | 8 | ○ | FEELING GOOD – THE VERY BEST OF NINA SIMONE | Polygram TV 5226692 |
| 07/02/1998 | 12 | 10 | ● | BLUE FOR YOU – THE VERY BEST OF NINA SIMONE | Global Television RADCD 84 |
| 21/06/2003 | 27 | 3 | | GOLD | UCJ 9808087 |

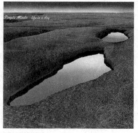

## SIMPLE MINDS

UK rock group formed in Glasgow in 1978 by Jim Kerr (born 9/7/1959, Glasgow, vocals), Charlie Burchill (born 27/11/1959, Glasgow, guitar), Mike McNeil (born 20/7/1958, Glasgow, keyboards), Derek Forbes (born 22/6/1956, Glasgow, bass), Brian McGhee (drums) and Duncan Barnwell (guitar), most of whom had been in Johnny and the Self Abusers. They first recorded for Zoom in 1978, their product licensed to Arista, switching to Virgin in 1981. Barnwell left in 1978, but was not replaced. McGhee left in 1981 and was replaced by Kenny Hyslop (born 14/2/1951, Helensburgh, Strathclyde), Mark Ogeltree and then Mel Gaynor (born 29/5/1959, Glasgow). Forbes left in 1984 and was replaced by John Giblin. Kerr married Chrissie Hynde in 1984 and, following their divorce, married Patsy Kensit (of Eighth Wonder) in 1992. This also ended in divorce. By 1995 the line-up was Kerr, Burchill, Foster, Mark Taylor (keyboards/acoustic guitar) and Mark Schulman (drums). In 1999 Kerr joined a consortium (along with Kenny Dalglish) taking over Glasgow Celtic Football Club.

| DATE | POS | WKS | BPI | ALBUM TITLE | LABEL & NUMBER |
|------|-----|-----|-----|-------------|----------------|
| 05/05/1979 | 30 | 6 | | LIFE IN A DAY | Zoom ZULP 1 |
| 27/09/1980 | 41 | 3 | | EMPIRES AND DANCE | Arista SPART 1140 |
| 12/09/1981 | 11 | 7 | ● | SONS AND FASCINATIONS/SISTERS FEELINGS CALL | Arista V 2207 |
| 27/02/1982 | 45 | 7 | | CELEBRATION | Virgin SPART 1183 |
| 25/09/1982 | 3 | 52 | ✪ | NEW GOLD DREAM (81,82,83,84) | Arista V 2230 |
| 18/02/1984 | ❶¹ | 57 | ✪ | SPARKLE IN THE RAIN | Virgin V 2300 |
| 02/11/1985 | ❶¹ | 83 | ✪³ | ONCE UPON A TIME | Virgin V 2364 |
| 06/06/1987 | ❶¹ | 26 | ✪² | LIVE IN THE CITY OF LIGHT | Virgin V SMDL 1 |
| 13/05/1989 | ❶¹ | 28 | ✪² | STREET FIGHTING YEARS | Virgin MINDS 1 |
| 20/04/1991 | 2 | 25 | ✪ | REAL LIFE | Virgin V 2660 |
| 24/10/1992 | ❶³ | 39 | ✪³ | GLITTERING PRIZE 81/92 | Virgin SMTVD 1 |
| 11/05/1995 | 2 | 14 | ● | GOOD NEWS FROM THE NEXT WORLD | Virgin CDV 2760 |
| 28/03/1998 | 19 | 3 | | NEAPOLIS | Chrysalis 4937122 |

○ Silver disc  ● Gold disc  ✪ Platinum disc (additional platinum units are indicated by a figure following the symbol)  ❶⁹ Number of weeks album topped the UK chart

| 17/11/2001 | 34 | 4 | ● | THE BEST OF SIMPLE MINDS | Virgin CDVD 2953 |

**SIMPLY RED** UK group fronted by singer/songwriter Mick Hucknall (born 8/6/1960, Manchester). He had formed new-wave band the Frantic Elevators in 1979, disbanding it in 1984 in favour of the soul-styled Simply Red. The initial line-up featured Hucknall, David Fryman, Eddie Sherwood, Ojo and Mog. The following year Hucknall re-formed the group with Fritz McIntyre (born 2/9/1958, Birmingham, keyboards), Tim Kellet (born 23/7/1964, Knaresborough, horns), Tony Bowers (born 31/10/1956, bass), Sylvan Richardson (guitar) and Chris Joyce (born 10/11/1957, Manchester, drums). Richardson left in 1987, replaced by Aziz Ibrahim, with Ian Kirkham (saxophone) and Janette Sewell (vocals) also joining. Sewell and Ibrahim left in 1988, Heitor TP joining on guitar. The line-up in 1996 was Hucknall, McIntyre, Heitor, Joyce and Ian Kirkham (keyboards). Hucknall was named Best British Male at the 1993 BRIT Awards whilst the group have won the Best British Group category in 1992 (jointly with KLF) and 1993. Hucknall also won the 1997 MOBO Award for Outstanding Achievement.

| 26/10/1985 | 2 | 130 | ✪³ | PICTURE BOOK | Elektra EKT 27 |
| 21/03/1987 | 2 | 60 | ✪³ | MEN AND WOMEN | WEA WX 85 |
| 25/02/1989 | ❶⁷ | 84 | ✪⁷ | A NEW FLAME | WEA WX 242 |
| 12/10/1991 | ❶¹² | 134 | ✪¹² | STARS | East West WX 427 |
| 21/10/1995 | ❶³ | 47 | ✪⁵ | LIFE ◇³ | East West 0630120692 |
| 24/02/1996 | 28 | 6 | | A NEW FLAME | East West 2446892 |
| 24/02/1996 | 33 | 5 | | PICTURE BOOK | East West 9031769932 |
| 02/03/1996 | 50 | 3 | | MEN AND WOMEN This and the above two albums are re-issues | East West 2420712 |
| 19/10/1996 | ❶² | 52 | ✪⁵ | GREATEST HITS ◇³ | East West 0630165522 |
| 30/05/1998 | ❶² | 26 | ✪² | BLUE ◇ | East West 3984230972 |
| 13/11/1999 | 6 | 17 | ✪ | LOVE AND THE RUSSIAN WINTER ◇ | East West 8573803592 |
| 25/11/2000 | 27 | 6 | ● | IT'S ONLY LOVE | East West 8573855372 |
| 05/04/2003 | 2 | 35 | ✪² | HOME ◇ | Simply Red.com SRA 001CD |

**JESSICA SIMPSON** US singer (born 10/7/1980, Dallas, TX); she moved to Los Angeles, making her debut album at seventeen. She married fellow singer Nick Lachey of 98 Degrees in 2002 (their marriage was the subject of the MTV documentary *The Newlyweds*).

| 06/05/2000 | 36 | 2 | | SWEET KISSES | Columbia 4949332 |
| 01/05/2004 | 36 | 5 | | IN THIS SKIN | Columbia SNY865602 |

**SIMPSONS** US cartoon TV series that first appeared in April 1987 as a short slot in Tracey Ullman's comedy show, leading to the Simpsons being given their own series. Created by Matt Groening, the family consists of Homer (the father, voice supplied by Dan Castellaneta), Marge (mother, Julie Kavner), Bart (son, Nancy Cartwright), Lisa (daughter, Yeardley Smith) and Maggie (youngest daughter, Liz Taylor). Aside from the success of the Simpsons themselves on the pop charts, a slew of acts have also 'appeared' in the programme, including Michael Jackson, Barry White, Tom Jones, Red Hot Chili Peppers, Sting, Ringo Starr, Spinal Tap, Aerosmith, Radiohead, Paul and Linda McCartney and Tony Bennett and more recently Britney Spears and 'N Sync. They have a star on the Hollywood Walk of Fame.

| 02/02/1991 | 6 | 30 | ● | THE SIMPSONS SING THE BLUES | Geffen 7599243081 |
| 12/09/1998 | 18 | 2 | ○ | THE SIMPSONS – SONGS IN THE KEY OF SPRINGFIELD | Rhino 8122759852 |

**JOYCE SIMS** US singer (born 1959, Rochester, NY) who worked in a hamburger bar, signing with Sleeping Bag Records in 1986.

| 09/01/1988 | 5 | 24 | ● | COME INTO MY LIFE | London LONLP 47 |
| 16/09/1989 | 64 | 1 | | ALL ABOUT LOVE | ffrr 8281291 |

**KYM SIMS** US singer (born 28/12/1966, Chicago, IL); she began as a jingle singer and also recorded with Ce Ce Peniston.

| 18/04/1992 | 39 | 2 | | TOO BLIND TO SEE IT | Atco 7567921042 |

**FRANK SINATRA** US singer (born 12/12/1915, Hoboken, NJ) who joined Harry James' band in 1939 and then Tommy Dorsey in 1940. He went solo in 1942 with Columbia, later switching to Capitol and forming the Reprise label in 1961. He began his film career in 1941 in *Las Vegas Nights* and landed his first starring role in *Higher And Higher* in 1943. He sold Reprise to Warner Brothers in 1963 and was made Vice President and Consultant of Warner Brothers Picture Corp. the same year. He won an Oscar for the film *From Here To Eternity* (for Best Supporting Actor) in 1953. He won eight Grammy Awards including Album of the Year in 1965 for *September Of My Years* and Record of the Year and Best Male Solo Vocal Performance in 1966 for *Strangers In The Night*. His daughter Nancy Sinatra is also an actress and singer. Frank died from a heart attack after a lengthy illness on 14/5/1998. He has star on the Hollywood Walk of Fame for his contribution to recording, a second star for motion pictures and a third star for TV.

| 28/07/1956 | ❶³ | 35 | | SONGS FOR SWINGING LOVERS | Capitol LCT 6106 |
| 16/02/1957 | ❶⁴ | 13 | | THIS IS SINATRA! | Capitol LCT 6123 |
| 25/05/1957 | 2 | 9 | | CLOSE TO YOU | Capitol LCT 6130 |
| 20/07/1957 | 3 | 7 | | FRANKIE | Philips BBL 7168 |
| 07/09/1957 | ❶⁷ | 18 | | A SWINGIN' AFFAIR! | Capitol LCT 6135 |
| 01/03/1958 | 3 | 5 | | WHERE ARE YOU? | Capitol LCT 6152 |
| 21/06/1958 | 3 | 12 | | THIS IS SINATRA (VOLUME 2) | Capitol LCT 6155 |
| 13/09/1958 | 2 | 26 | | COME FLY WITH ME ▲⁵ | Capitol LCT 6154 |
| 29/11/1958 | 8 | 1 | | FRANK SINATRA STORY | Fontana TFL 5030 |

▲⁹ Number of weeks album topped the US chart   ◆¹² RIAA Diamond Awards   ◇³ IFPI Platinum Europe Awards

| DATE | POS | WKS | BPI | ALBUM TITLE | LABEL & NUMBER |
|---|---|---|---|---|---|
| 13/12/1958 | 5 | 13 | | **FRANK SINATRA SINGS FOR ONLY THE LONELY** ▲⁵ 1958 Grammy Award for Best Album Cover | Capitol LCT 6168 |
| 16/05/1959 | 2 | 30 | | **COME DANCE WITH ME! FRANK SINATRA WITH BILLY MAY AND HIS ORCHESTRA** 1959 Grammy Awards for Album of the Year and Best Vocal Performance (it also won a Special Trustees Award for Artists & Repertoire Contribution) | Capitol LCT 6179 |
| 22/08/1959 | 5 | 8 | | **LOOK TO YOUR HEART** | Capitol LCT 6181 |
| 11/06/1960 | 6 | 9 | | **COME BACK TO SORRENTO** | Fontana TFL 5082 |
| 29/10/1960 | 5 | 17 | | **SWING EASY** | Capitol W 587 |
| 21/01/1961 | 4 | 28 | | **NICE 'N EASY** ▲⁹ | Capitol W 1417 |
| 15/07/1961 | 18 | 1 | | SINATRA SOUVENIR | Fontana TFL 5138 |
| 19/08/1961 | 6 | 10 | | **WHEN YOUR LOVER HAS GONE** | Encore ENC 101 |
| 23/09/1961 | 6 | 8 | | **SINATRA'S SWINGING SESSION!!! AND MORE** | Capitol W 1491 |
| 28/10/1961 | 8 | 8 | | **SINATRA SWINGS** | Reprise R 1002 |
| 25/11/1961 | 7 | 9 | | **SINATRA PLUS** | Fontana SET 303 |
| 16/12/1961 | 8 | 9 | | **RING-A-DING-DING** | Reprise R 1001 |
| 17/02/1962 | 13 | 4 | | COME SWING WITH ME | Capitol W 1594 |
| 07/04/1962 | 10 | 12 | | **I REMEMBER TOMMY…** | Reprise R 1003 |
| 09/06/1962 | 6 | 20 | | **SINATRA AND STRINGS** | Reprise R 1004 |
| 27/10/1962 | 12 | 9 | | GREAT SONGS FROM GREAT BRITAIN | Reprise R 1006 |
| 29/12/1962 | 14 | 11 | | SINATRA WITH SWINGING BRASS | Reprise R 1005 |
| 23/02/1963 | 2 | 23 | | **SINATRA-BASIE FRANK SINATRA AND COUNT BASIE** | Reprise R 1008 |
| 27/07/1963 | 8 | 18 | | **CONCERT SINATRA** | Reprise R 1009 |
| 05/10/1963 | 9 | 24 | | **SINATRA'S SINATRA** | Reprise R 1010 |
| 19/09/1964 | 17 | 4 | | IT MIGHT AS WELL BE SWING **FRANK SINATRA AND COUNT BASIE AND HIS ORCHESTRA** | Reprise R 1012 |
| 20/03/1965 | 20 | 1 | | SOFTLY AS I LEAVE YOU | Reprise R 1013 |
| 22/01/1966 | 9 | 19 | | **A MAN AND HIS MUSIC** 1966 Grammy Award for Album of the Year | Reprise R 1016 |
| 21/05/1966 | 18 | 8 | | MOONLIGHT SINATRA | Reprise R 1018 |
| 02/07/1966 | 4 | 18 | | **STRANGERS IN THE NIGHT** ▲¹ | Reprise R 1017 |
| 01/10/1966 | 7 | 18 | | **IN CONCERT: SINATRA AT 'THE SANDS'** | Reprise RLP 1019 |
| 03/12/1966 | 26 | 2 | | FRANK SINATRA SINGS SONGS FOR PLEASURE | MFP 1120 |
| 25/02/1967 | 22 | 12 | | THAT'S LIFE | Reprise RSLP 1020 |
| 07/10/1967 | 28 | 5 | | FRANK SINATRA | Reprise RSLP 1022 |
| 19/10/1968 | 8 | 38 | | **GREATEST HITS** | Reprise RSLP 1025 |
| 07/12/1968 | 17 | 10 | | BEST OF FRANK SINATRA | Capitol ST 21140 |
| 07/06/1969 | 2 | 59 | | **MY WAY** | Reprise RSLP 1029 |
| 04/10/1969 | 18 | 7 | | A MAN ALONE – THE WORDS AND MUSIC OF ROD McKUEN | Reprise RSLP 1030 |
| 09/05/1970 | 14 | 9 | | WATERTOWN | Reprise RSLP 1031 |
| 12/12/1970 | 6 | 40 | | **GREATEST HITS VOLUME 2** | Reprise RSLP 1032 |
| 05/06/1971 | 9 | 9 | | **SINATRA AND COMPANY** | Reprise RSLP 1033 |
| 27/11/1971 | 35 | 1 | | FRANK SINATRA SINGS RODGERS AND HART | Starline SRS 5083 |
| 08/01/1972 | 29 | 3 | | GREATEST HITS VOLUME 2 | Reprise K 44018 |
| 08/01/1972 | 35 | 1 | | MY WAY | Reprise K 44015 |
| 01/12/1973 | 12 | 13 | ● | OL' BLUE EYES IS BACK | Warner Brothers K 44249 |
| 17/08/1974 | 35 | 3 | ○ | SOME NICE THINGS I'VE MISSED | Reprise K 54020 |
| 15/02/1975 | 30 | 2 | ○ | SINATRA – THE MAIN EVENT LIVE Original TV soundtrack | Reprise K 54031 |
| 14/06/1975 | 30 | 3 | ○ | THE BEST OF OL' BLUE EYES | Reprise K 54042 |
| 19/03/1977 | ❶² | 18 | ✪ | **PORTRAIT OF SINATRA** | Reprise K 64039 |
| 13/05/1978 | 4 | 11 | ● | **20 GOLDEN GREATS** | Capitol EMTV 10 |
| 18/08/1984 | 41 | 8 | | L.A. IS MY LADY **FRANK SINATRA WITH THE QUINCY JONES ORCHESTRA** | Qwest 925145 |
| 22/03/1986 | 13 | 12 | ✪ | NEW YORK, NY (GREATEST HITS) | Warner Brothers WX 32 |
| 04/10/1986 | 40 | 5 | | THE FRANK SINATRA COLLECTION | Capitol EMTV 41 |
| 06/11/1993 | 5 | 14 | ✪ | **DUETS** | Capitol CDEST 2218 |
| 26/11/1994 | 29 | 6 | | DUETS II 1995 Grammy Award for Best Traditional Pop Album | Capitol CDEST 2245 |
| 11/03/1995 | 56 | 1 | | THIS IS FRANK SINATRA 1953–1957 | MFP CDDL 1275 |
| 02/12/1995 | 49 | 5 | | SINATRA 80TH – ALL THE BEST | Capitol CDESTD 2 |
| 16/08/1997 | 7 | 129 | ✪⁵ | **MY WAY – THE BEST OF FRANK SINATRA** ◇³ | Reprise 9362467122 |
| 30/05/1998 | 63 | 2 | | SONGS FOR SWINGING LOVERS | Capitol CDP 7465702 |
| 24/06/2000 | 10 | 7 | ● | **CLASSIC SINATRA** | Capitol 5235022 |
| 09/02/2002 | 6 | 9 | ● | **A FINE ROMANCE – THE LOVE SONGS OF FRANK SINATRA** | Reprise 8122735892 |

**NANCY SINATRA** US singer (born 8/6/1940, Jersey City, NY) who is the first child of Frank and Nancy Sinatra. She moved with her parents to Los Angeles, CA whilst still a child. She sang with her father and Elvis Presley on TV in 1959, signing with Reprise in 1961. Her various film appearances included *Marriage On The Rocks* with her father and Dean Martin. She married singer Tommy Sands in 1960, but they divorced in 1965.

| DATE | POS | WKS | BPI | ALBUM TITLE | LABEL & NUMBER |
|---|---|---|---|---|---|
| 16/04/1966 | 12 | 9 | | BOOTS | Reprise R 6202 |
| 18/06/1966 | 17 | 3 | | HOW DOES THAT GRAB YOU | Reprise R 6207 |
| 29/06/1968 | 17 | 12 | | NANCY AND LEE **NANCY SINATRA AND LEE HAZLEWOOD** | Reprise RSLP 6273 |
| 10/10/1970 | 39 | 3 | | NANCY'S GREATEST HITS | Reprise RSLP 6409 |
| 25/09/1971 | 42 | 1 | | NANCY AND LEE | Reprise K 44126 |
| 29/01/1972 | 31 | 4 | | DID YOU EVER This and the above hit credited to **NANCY SINATRA AND LEE HAZLEWOOD** | RCA Victor SF 8240 |

## SINFONIA OF LONDON – see HOWARD BLAKE CONDUCTING THE SINFONIA OF LONDON

### TALVIN SINGH
UK male DJ/producer who grew up in London but was sent to India at the age of sixteen to pursue a classical education. He returned to the UK in the late 1980s and worked as a session musician for the likes of Sun Ra, Bjork, Future Sound of London and The Indigo Girls. In 1995 he founded the Anokha club in London.

| DATE | POS | WKS | BPI | ALBUM TITLE | LABEL & NUMBER |
|---|---|---|---|---|---|
| 18/09/1999 | 41 | 4 | O | OK 1999 Mercury Music Prize | Island CID 8075 |
| 07/04/2001 | 57 | 1 | | HA | Island CID 8103 |

### SINITTA
US singer (born Sinitta Renay Malone, 19/10/1966, Seattle, WA) based in the UK. She is the daughter of Miquel Brown and began her career performing in musicals.

| | | | | | |
|---|---|---|---|---|---|
| 26/12/1987 | 34 | 19 | ● | SINITTA! | Fanfare BOYLP 1 |
| 09/12/1989 | 52 | 4 | ● | WICKED | Fanfare FARE 2 |

### SIOUXSIE AND THE BANSHEES
UK punk group formed in London in 1976 by Siouxsie Sioux (born Susan Dallion, 27/5/1957, Bromley, vocals), Steve 'Havoc' Severin (born Steven Bailey, 25/9/1955, London, bass), Sid Vicious (born John Ritchie, 10/5/1957, London, drums) and Marco Pirroni (born 27/4/1959, London, guitar). They disbanded after one gig, Vicious joining the Sex Pistols and Pirroni later joining Adam & The Ants. Sioux and Severin re-formed with Pete Fenton (guitar) and Kenny Morris (drums) in 1977. Fenton left after four months, replaced by John McKay. Morris and McKay left in 1979, replaced by Budgie (born Peter Clark, 21/8/1957, St Helens, drums) and an on-loan Robert Smith from The Cure. John McGeoch joined on guitar but left in 1982, Smith again filling in. He was eventually replaced by John Carruthers in 1984. Two years later Carruthers left, replaced by John Klein, with Martin McCarrick added on keyboards. They split in 1996. Sioux and Budgie, who later married, also recorded as the Creatures. Severin later linked with Robert Smith in a one-off project The Glove.

| | | | | | |
|---|---|---|---|---|---|
| 02/12/1978 | 12 | 11 | O | THE SCREAM | Polydor POLD 5009 |
| 22/09/1979 | 13 | 5 | O | JOIN HANDS | Polydor POLD 5024 |
| 16/08/1980 | 5 | 6 | O | KALEIDOSCOPE | Polydor 2442 177 |
| 27/06/1981 | 7 | 17 | O | JU JU | Polydor POLS 1034 |
| 12/12/1981 | 21 | 26 | ● | ONCE UPON A TIME – THE SINGLES | Polydor POLS 1056 |
| 13/11/1982 | 11 | 11 | O | A KISS IN THE DREAMHOUSE | Polydor POLD 5064 |
| 03/12/1983 | 29 | 10 | O | NOCTURNE | Wonderland SHAH 1 |
| 16/06/1984 | 15 | 6 | | HYENA | Wonderland SHELP 2 |
| 26/04/1986 | 13 | 6 | | TINDERBOX | Wonderland SHELP 3 |
| 14/03/1987 | 15 | 8 | O | THROUGH THE LOOKING GLASS | Wonderland SHELP 4 |
| 17/09/1988 | 20 | 5 | O | PEEPSHOW | Wonderland SHELP 5 |
| 22/06/1991 | 25 | 4 | | SUPERSTITION | Wonderland 8477311 |
| 17/10/1992 | 26 | 2 | | TWICE UPON A TIME – THE SINGLES | Wonderland 5171602 |
| 28/01/1995 | 33 | 2 | | THE RAPTURE | Wonderland 5237252 |

### SISQO
US singer (born Mark Andrews, 9/11/1977, Baltimore, MD); he is also a member of Dru Hill.

| | | | | | |
|---|---|---|---|---|---|
| 26/02/2000 | 15 | 36 | ● | UNLEASH THE DRAGON | Def Soul 5469392 |
| 04/08/2001 | 22 | 5 | O | RETURN OF DRAGON | Def Soul 5864182 |

### SISSEL
Norwegian singer/keyboard player (born Sissel Kyrkjebo, 1969, Bergen) who first came to prominence singing at the 1994 Winter Olympics in Lillehammer. She contributed to James Horner's soundtrack to Titanic and also recorded with Warren G.

| | | | | | |
|---|---|---|---|---|---|
| 20/05/1995 | 58 | 1 | | DEEP WITHIN MY SOUL | Mercury 5267752 |

### SISTER SLEDGE
US R&B vocal group formed in Philadelphia, PA by sisters Kathy (born 6/1/1959, Philadelphia), Joni (born 1957, Philadelphia), Kim (born 21/8/1958, Philadelphia) and Debbie Sledge (born 9/7/1955, Philadelphia). They began as The Sisters Sledge for the Money Back label in 1971, worked as backing singers and signed with Cotillion in 1974. Kathy Sledge later recorded solo.

| | | | | | |
|---|---|---|---|---|---|
| 12/05/1979 | 7 | 39 | ● | WE ARE FAMILY | Atlantic K 50587 |
| 22/06/1985 | 19 | 11 | O | WHEN THE BOYS MEET THE GIRLS | Atlantic 7812551 |
| 05/12/1987 | 72 | 3 | | FREAK OUT CHIC AND SISTER SLEDGE | Telstar STAR 2319 |
| 20/02/1993 | 19 | 5 | O | THE VERY BEST OF SISTER SLEDGE 1973–1993 | Atlantic 9548318132 |

### SISTERHOOD
UK group formed by Andrew Eldritch (born Andrew Taylor, 15/5/1959, Ely), ex-Sisters Of Mercy member, who released this album under the name Sisterhood to prevent his former group from utilising the name 'sister' – they became The Mission instead. Eldritch subsequently re-formed Sisters Of Mercy.

| | | | | | |
|---|---|---|---|---|---|
| 26/07/1986 | 90 | 1 | | GIFT | Merciful Release SIS 020 |

### SISTERS OF MERCY
UK rock group formed in Leeds in 1980 by Andrew Eldritch (born Andrew Taylor, 15/5/1959, Ely, vocals), Gary Marx (born Mark Pearman, guitar) and a drum machine called Doktor Avalanche. They set up the Merciful Release label the same year. They added Ben Gunn (guitar) and Craig Adams (born 4/4/1962, Otley, Yorkshire, bass) in 1980 in order to perform live. Gunn left in 1983, replaced by Wayne Hussey (born Jerry Lovelock, 26/5/1958, Bristol). They temporarily split in 1985, Hussey and Adams going on to form The Mission and Eldritch adopting the name Sisterhood for one album. Eldritch re-formed the group in 1987 with Patricia Morrison (born 14/1/1962), and by 1990 the line-up was Eldritch, Tony James (ex-Sigue Sigue Sputnik, guitar), Tim Bricheno (born 6/7/1963, Huddersfield, guitar) and Andreas Bruhn (born 5/11/1967, Hamburg, Germany, drums). James left in 1991.

| | | | | | |
|---|---|---|---|---|---|
| 23/03/1985 | 14 | 8 | ● | FIRST AND LAST AND ALWAYS | Merciful Release MR 337L |
| 28/11/1987 | 9 | 20 | ● | FLOODLAND | Merciful Release MR 441L |

| 03/11/1990 | 11 | 4 | O | VISION THING | Merciful Release MR 449L |
| 09/05/1992 | 5 | 5 | O | **SOME GIRLS WANDER BY MISTAKE** | Merciful Release 9031764762 |
| 04/09/1993 | 14 | 5 | | GREATEST HITS VOLUME 1 | Merciful Release 4509935792 |

**SIX BY SEVEN** UK rock group formed in Nottingham by Chris Olley (guitar/vocals), Sam Hempton (guitar), James Flower (keyboards/saxophone), Paul Douglas (bass) and Chris Davis (drums). Hempton left the group after the Glastonbury Festival in 2000.

| 23/03/2002 | 69 | 1 | | THE WAY I FEEL TODAY | Mantra MNTCD 1027 |

**SIXPENCE NONE THE RICHER** US group formed in Austin, TX by Leigh Nash (born Leigh Bingham, New Braunfels, TX, vocals), Matt Slocum (guitar), Sean Kelly (guitar), Justin Cary (bass) and Dale Baker (drums). Nash later recorded solo and contributed to the soundtrack for the film *Bounce*.

| 26/06/1999 | 27 | 3 | | SIXPENCE NONE THE RICHER | Elektra 7559624202 |

**60FT DOLLS** UK vocal/instrumental group from Newport, Wales with Richard Parfitt (guitar/vocals), Mike Cole (bass/vocals) and Carl Bevan (drums).

| 08/06/1996 | 36 | 2 | | THE BIG 3 | Indolent DOLLSCD 004 |

**RONI SIZE REPRAZENT** UK dance group from Bristol, formed by Roni Size (born Ryan Williams, 29/10/1969, Bristol) with Krust, DJ Die, Suv, MC Dynamite and singer Onallee. They won the 1997 MOBO Award for Best Jungle Act. Size and DJ Die are also in Breakbeat Era. Size later formed the Full Cycle label.

| 05/07/1997 | 8 | 34 | ● | **NEW FORMS** 1997 Mercury Music Prize | Talkin Loud 5349342 |
| 21/10/2000 | 15 | 4 | O | IN THE MODE | Talkin Loud 5480762 |
| 02/11/2002 | 72 | 1 | | TOUCHING DOWN **RONI SIZE** | Full Cycle FCYCDLP 010 |

**PETER SKELLERN** UK singer (born 1947, Bury); he sang with Harlan County before signing solo with Decca. He later linked with Julian Lloyd Webber, Mary Hopkin and Bill Lovelady in 1983 to form Oasis, a group who scored one hit album.

| 09/09/1978 | 48 | 3 | O | SKELLERN | Mercury 9109 701 |
| 08/12/1979 | 23 | 20 | ● | ASTAIRE | Mercury 9102 702 |
| 04/12/1982 | 67 | 5 | | A STRING OF PEARLS | Mercury MERL 10 |
| 01/04/1995 | 50 | 3 | | STARDUST MEMORIES | WEA 4509981322 |

**SKID ROW** UK rock group formed in Belfast in 1968 by Gary Moore (born 4/4/1952, Belfast, guitar), Phil Lynott (vocals), Brendan Shields (bass) and Noel Bridgemann (drums). Lynott left soon after to form Thin Lizzy with the remaining trio continuing and relocating to London after they signed with CBS. They disbanded after two albums with Moore going on to form an eponymous band.

| 10/10/1970 | 30 | 3 | | SKID | CBS 63965 |

**SKID ROW** US heavy rock group formed in New Jersey in 1986 by Rachel Bolan (born 9/2/1964, bass), Dave Sabo (born 16/9/1962, guitar), Rob Affuso (born 1/3/1963, drums), Scotti Hill (born 31/5/1964, guitar) and Sebastian Bach (born Sebastian Bierk, 3/4/1968, Bahamas, vocals). They signed with Atlantic Records in 1988.

| 02/09/1989 | 30 | 16 | ● | SKID ROW | Atlantic 7819361 |
| 22/06/1991 | 5 | 9 | O | **SLAVE TO THE GRIND** ▲[1] | Atlantic WX 423 |
| 08/04/1995 | 8 | 3 | | **SUBHUMAN RACE** | Atlantic 7567827302 |

**SKIDS** UK rock group formed in Scotland in 1977 by Stuart Adamson (born 11/4/1958, Manchester, guitar), Bill Simpson (bass), Tom Kellichan (drums) and Richard Jobson (vocals). Simpson and Webb left in 1980, replaced by Russell Webb and Mike Baillie. Adamson left in 1981 to form Big Country. After Big Country disbanded in 2000 Adamson became a country singer/songwriter but on 17/12/2001 his body was found hanged in a hotel room in Hawaii – he had been dead for two days. He had been depressed after his second marriage collapsed and had been declared missing from Nashville by his wife on 26/11/2001. Arranging to meet her, he changed his mind and flew to Honolulu and checked into a hotel on 4th December, rarely venturing out of his room thereafter.

| 17/03/1979 | 19 | 10 | | SCARED TO DANCE | Virgin V 2116 |
| 27/10/1979 | 32 | 5 | | DAYS IN EUROPA | Virgin V 2138 |
| 27/09/1980 | 9 | 5 | | **THE ABSOLUTE GAME** | Virgin V 2174 |
| 08/06/2002 | 71 | 1 | | GREATEST HITS **BIG COUNTRY AND THE SKIDS** | Universal TV 5869892 |

**SKIN** German/UK rock group formed in Hamburg by Neville MacDonald (vocals), Myke Gray (born 12/5/1968, London, guitar), Andy Robbins (bass) and Dicki Fliszar (drums) as Taste, name-changing as another group had the same name. Gray and Robbins had previously been in Jagged Edge.

| 14/05/1994 | 9 | 3 | | **SKIN** | Parlophone CDPCSD 151 |
| 06/04/1996 | 38 | 1 | | LUCKY | Parlophone CDPCSD 168 |
| 13/09/1997 | 72 | 1 | | EXPERIENCE ELECTRIC | Recall SRECD 705 |

**SKIN** UK singer (born Deborah Anne Dyer, 3/8/1967, London); she had previously been lead vocalist with Skunk Anansie. She took part in the *It's Only Rock 'N' Roll* project for the Children's Promise charity.

| 14/06/2003 | 43 | 2 | | FLESHWOUNDS | EMI 5841592 |

O Silver disc  ● Gold disc  ✪ Platinum disc (additional platinum units are indicated by a figure following the symbol)  ❶[9] Number of weeks album topped the UK chart

### SKUNK ANANSIE
UK rock group formed in London in 1994 by Skin (born Deborah Anne Dyer, 3/8/1967, London, vocals), Ace (born Martin Ivor Kent, 30/3/1967, Cheltenham, guitar), Cass Lewis (born Richard Keith Lewis, 1/9/1960, London, bass) and Mark Richardson (born 28/5/1970, Leeds, drums). Skin took part in the *It's Only Rock 'N' Roll* project for the Children's Promise charity.

| 30/09/1995 | 8 | 32 | ✪ | PARANOID & SUNBURNT | One Little Indian TPLP 55CD |
| 19/10/1996 | 9 | 55 | ✪ | STOOSH | One Little Indian TPLP 85CDL |
| 03/04/1999 | 16 | 14 | ● | POST ORGASMIC CHILL ◇ | Virgin CDV 2881 |

### SKY
UK rock group formed in 1978 by John Williams (born 24/4/1941, Melbourne, Australia, guitar), Herbie Flowers (bass), Francis Monkman (keyboards), Kevin Peek (guitar) and Tristan Fry (drums). Monkman left in 1980 and was replaced by Steve Gray; Williams left in 1983.

| 02/06/1979 | 9 | 56 | ✪ | SKY | Ariola ARLH 5022 |
| 26/04/1980 | ❶² | 53 | ✪ | SKY 2 | Ariola Hansa ADSKY 2 |
| 28/03/1981 | 3 | 23 | ● | SKY 3 | Ariola ASKY 3 |
| 03/04/1982 | 7 | 22 | ● | SKY 4 – FORTHCOMING | Ariola ASKY 4 |
| 22/01/1983 | 14 | 14 | ○ | SKY FIVE LIVE | Ariola 302 171 |
| 03/12/1983 | 44 | 10 | ○ | CADMIUM | Ariola 205 885 |
| 12/05/1984 | 15 | 18 | ● | MASTERPIECES – THE VERY BEST OF SKY | Telstar STAR 2241 |
| 13/04/1985 | 63 | 6 | | THE GREAT BALLOON RACE | Epic EPC 26419 |

### SKYY
US soul group formed in Brooklyn, NY by Solomon Roberts Jr (guitar/vocals), Denise Dunning-Crawford (vocals), Delores Dunning-Milligan (vocals), Bonnie Dunning (vocals), Anibal Anthony (guitar), Gerald La Bon (bass), Larry Greenberg (keyboards) and Tommy McConnel (drums). After providing the backing to Charles Earland on his *Let The Music Play* they signed with Salsoul and enjoyed a hit single (released in the UK under New York Skyy to avoid confusion with Sky) written and produced by Randy Muller. Denise, Delores and Bonnie are sisters.

| 21/06/1986 | 85 | 1 | | FROM THE LEFT SIDE | Capitol EST 2014 |

### SLADE
UK rock group formed in Wolverhampton in 1969 by Noddy Holder (born Neville Holder, 15/6/1950, Walsall, guitar/vocals), Dave Hill (born 4/4/1952, Fleet Castle, guitar), Don Powell (born 10/9/1950, Bilston, drums) and Jimmy Lea (born 14/6/1952, Wolverhampton, bass/piano), all four having originally teamed up in the 'N Betweens in 1966. They name-changed to Ambrose Slade in 1969, adopted a 'skinhead' look and released a debut album with Fontana. They shortened their name to Slade the same year and switched to Polydor in 1970. They split in 1988 but re-formed in 1991. Holder later became an actor, appearing in the TV series *The Grimleys*. He was awarded an MBE in the 2000 New Year's Honours List.

| 08/04/1972 | 2 | 58 | | SLADE ALIVE! | Polydor 2383 101 |
| 09/12/1972 | ❶³ | 34 | | SLAYED? | Polydor 2383 163 |
| 06/10/1973 | ❶⁴ | 24 | ● | SLADEST | Polydor 2442 119 |
| 23/02/1974 | ❶¹ | 16 | ● | OLD NEW BORROWED AND BLUE | Polydor 2383 261 |
| 14/12/1974 | 6 | 18 | ● | SLADE IN FLAME Original soundtrack to the film | Polydor 2442 126 |
| 27/03/1976 | 14 | 4 | | NOBODY'S FOOL | Polydor 2383 377 |
| 22/11/1980 | 21 | 15 | ● | SLADE SMASHES | Polydor POLTV 13 |
| 21/03/1981 | 25 | 4 | | WE'LL BRING THE HOUSE DOWN | Cheapskate SKATE 1 |
| 28/11/1981 | 68 | 2 | | TILL DEAF US DO PART | RCA RCALP 6021 |
| 18/12/1982 | 58 | 3 | | SLADE ON STAGE | RCA RCALP 3107 |
| 24/12/1983 | 49 | 13 | | THE AMAZING KAMIKAZE SYNDROME | RCA PL 70116 |
| 09/06/1984 | 89 | 1 | | SLADE'S GREATZ | Polydor SLAD 1 |
| 06/04/1985 | 60 | 2 | | ROGUES GALLERY | RCA PL 70604 |
| 30/11/1985 | 34 | 7 | ● | CRACKERS' – THE SLADE CHRISTMAS PARTY ALBUM | Telstar STAR 2271 |
| 09/05/1987 | 98 | 1 | | YOU BOYZ MAKE BIG NOIZE | RCA PL 71260 |
| 23/11/1991 | 34 | 5 | | WALL OF HITS | Polydor 5116121 |

▲⁹ Number of weeks album topped the US chart  ◆¹² RIAA Diamond Awards  ◇³ IFPI Platinum Europe Awards

25/01/1997 .....19......5 ......     GREATEST HITS – FEEL THE NOIZE ........................................................................Polydor 5371052

**SLASH'S SNAKEPIT** US group formed by Slash (born Saul Hudson 23/7/1965, Stoke-on-Trent, guitar) of Guns 'N' Roses, with contributions from Gilbey Clarke (guitar), Mike Inez (bass), Dizzy Reed (keyboards), Matt Sorum (drums), Paulinho Da Costa (percussion) and singers Eric Dover and The Party Girls.

25/02/1995 .....15......4 ......     IT'S FIVE O'CLOCK SOMEWHERE .................................................................Geffen GED 24730

**SLAUGHTER** US rock group formed in Las Vegas, NV in 1988 by Mark Slaughter (vocals), Tim Kelly (guitar), Dana Strum (bass) and Blas Elias (drums). Slaughter and Strum were previously in Vinnie Vincent's Invasion. Kelly was killed in a car crash on 5/2/1998.

23/05/1992 .....64......1 ......     THE WILD LIFE .....................................................................................Chrysalis CCD 1911

**SLAYER** US rock group formed in Huntington Beach, CA in 1982 by Tom Araya (bass/vocals), Kerry King (guitar), Jeff Hanneman (guitar) and Dave Lombardo (drums). Lombardo left in 1982, replaced by Paul Bostaph.

| | | | | | |
|---|---|---|---|---|---|
| 02/05/1987 | 47 | 3 | | REIGN IN BLOOD | London LONLP 34 |
| 23/07/1988 | 25 | 4 | O | SOUTH OF HEAVEN | London LONLP 63 |
| 06/10/1990 | 18 | 3 | | SEASONS IN THE ABYSS | Def US 8468711 |
| 02/11/1991 | 29 | 2 | | DECADE OF AGGRESSION – LIVE | Def US 5106051 |
| 15/10/1994 | 15 | 4 | | DIVINE INTERVENTION | American Recordings 74321236772 |
| 01/06/1996 | 31 | 2 | | UNDISPUTED ATTITUDE | American Recordings 74321357592 |
| 20/06/1998 | 27 | 2 | | DIABOLUS IN MUSICA | American Recordings 4913022 |
| 22/09/2001 | 31 | 1 | | GOD HATES US ALL | Mercury 5863312 |

**PERCY SLEDGE** US singer (born 25/11/1941, Leighton, AL); a member of the Esquires Combo before going solo in 1966. Recommended to Quin Ivy, owner of Norala Sound Studio, he wrote *When A Man Loves A Woman* around an Esquires song *Why Did You Leave Me Baby?*, with Cameron Lewis (bass) and Andrew Wright (organ), although session man Spooner Oldham has been credited for the organ sound. He later recorded for Capricorn (with a minor R&B hit *I'll Be Your Everything*), Monument and Pointblank.

14/03/1987 .....36......4 ......     WHEN A MAN LOVES A WOMAN (THE ULTIMATE COLLECTION) ...........................................Atlantic WX 89

**SLEEPER** UK group formed in London in 1992 by Louise Wener (born 30/7/1968, Ilford, guitar/vocals), Jon Stewart (born 12/9/1967, Sheffield, guitar), Kenediid 'Diid' Osman (born 10/4/1968, Mogadishu, Somalia, bass) and Andy Maclure (born 4/7/1970, Manchester, drums).

| | | | | | |
|---|---|---|---|---|---|
| 25/02/1995 | 5 | 11 | ● | **SMART** | Indolent SLEEPCD 007 |
| 18/05/1996 | 5 | 34 | ✪ | **THE IT GIRL** | Indolent SLEEPCD 012 |
| 25/10/1997 | 7 | 3 | O | **PLEASED TO MEET YOU** | Indolent SLEEPCD 016 |

**SLEEPY JACKSON** Australian group formed in Perth in 1997 by brothers Luke and Jesse Steele and Matt O'Connor.

26/07/2003 .....69......1 ......     LOVERS ...........................................................................................Virgin CDVIR 208

**SLEIGHRIDERS** UK studio group.

17/12/1983 ....100 .....1 ......     A VERY MERRY DISCO ................................................................................Warwick WW 5136

**GRACE SLICK** US singer (born Grace Wing, 30/10/1939, Chicago, IL); she was with Jefferson Airplane from 1965 until 1978 when alcohol problems saw her departure. She returned in 1981 and departed a second final time, in 1988.

31/05/1980 .....28......6 ......     DREAMS ..........................................................................................RCA PL 13544

**SLIK** UK pop group formed in Scotland by Midge Ure (born 10/10/1953, Cambuslang, guitar), Billy McIsaac (keyboards), Kenny Hyslop (drums) and Jim McGinlay (bass). Ure was later in the Rich Kids, Visage, Ultravox and recorded solo; Hyslop was later in Simple Minds.

12/06/1976 .....58......1 ......     SLIK ............................................................................................Bell SYBEL 8004

**SLIM CHANCE** – see **RONNIE LANE AND SLIM CHANCE**

**SLIPKNOT** US rock group formed in Des Moines, IA by DJ Sid Wilson, Joey Jordison (drums), Paul Gray (bass), Chris Fehn (percussion), James Root (guitar), Craig Jones (samples), Shawn Crahan (percussion), Mic Thompson (guitar) and Corey Taylor (vocals). Root and Taylor had previously been members of Stone Sour and revived the group in 2002 whilst Jordison formed Murderdolls.

| | | | | | |
|---|---|---|---|---|---|
| 10/07/1999 | 37 | 5 | ● | **SLIPKNOT** | Roadrunner RR 86555 |
| 08/09/2001 | ❶¹ | 7 | ● | **IOWA** | Roadrunner 12085642 |
| 05/06/2004 | 5 | 4+ | O | **VOLUME 3 (THE SUBLIMINAL VERSES)** | Roadrunner RR 83888 |

**SLITS** UK female punk group formed in 1976 by Ari-Up (vocals), Kate Korus (guitar), Suzi Gutsy (bass) and Palmolive (drums). Korus and Gutsy left soon after; they were replaced by Viv Albertine (guitar) and Tessa Pollitt (bass). Palmolive left in 1978 and was replaced by Budgie (born Peter Clark, 21/8/1957, St Helens). Budgie left to join Siouxsie & The Banshees in 1979 and was replaced by Bruce Smith. They split in 1981.

22/09/1979 .....30......5 ......     CUT ..............................................................................................Island ILPS 9573

**SLOWDIVE** UK group formed in 1989 by Rachel Goswell (born 16/5/1971, guitar/vocals), Neil Halstead (born 7/10/1970, Luton, guitar/vocals), Brook Christian Savill (born 6/12/1977, Bury, guitar), Nicholas Chaplin (born 23/12/1970, Slough, bass) and Adrian Sell (drums). Sell left soon after and was replaced by first Neil Carter and then Simon Scott (born 3/3/1971, Cambridge).

| | | | | | |
|---|---|---|---|---|---|
| 14/09/1991 | 32 | 2 | | JUST FOR A DAY | Creation CRELP 094 |
| 12/06/1993 | 51 | 1 | | SOUVLAKI | Creation CRECD 139 |

**SLY AND THE FAMILY STONE** US singer (born Sylvester Stewart, 15/3/1944, Dallas, TX); he formed Family Stone in 1966 with brother Freddie (born 5/6/1946, Dallas, guitar), sister Rosemary (born 21/3/1945, Vallejo, CA, vocals/piano), cousin Larry Graham (born 14/8/1946, Beaumont, TX, bass), Jerry Martini (born 1/10/1943, Colorado, saxophone), Cynthia Robinson (born 12/1/1946, Sacramento, CA, trumpet) and Greg Errico (born 1/9/1946, San Francisco, CA, drums). Graham left in 1972, forming Graham Central Station. Sly was jailed in 1989 for driving under the influence of cocaine. They were inducted into the Rock & Roll Hall of Fame in 1993.

05/02/1972 . . . . .31 . . . . . .2 . . . . . . THERE'S A RIOT GOIN' ON ▲² . . . . . . . . . . . . . . . . . . . . . . . . . . . . . . . . . . . . . . . . . . . . . . . . . . . . .Epic EPC 64613

**SLY AND ROBBIE** Jamaican duo Lowell 'Sly' Charles Dunbar (born 10/5/1952, Kingston, drums) and Robbie Shakespeare (born 27/9/1953, Kingston, bass) who first teamed up in the Aggravators. They received the 1998 Grammy Award for Best Reggae Performance for *Friends*.

09/05/1987 . . . . .35 . . . . . .5 . . . . . . RHYTHM KILLERS . . . . . . . . . . . . . . . . . . . . . . . . . . . . . . . . . . . . . . . . . . . . . . . . . . .Fourth & Broadway BRLP 512

**HEATHER SMALL** UK singer (born 20/1/1965, London); she was the lead singer with M People before going solo. She later recorded with Tom Jones.

10/06/2000 . . . . .12 . . . . . .4 . . . . . . PROUD . . . . . . . . . . . . . . . . . . . . . . . . . . . . . . . . . . . . . . . . . . . . . . . . . . . . . . . . . . . . .Arista 74321765482

**SMALL FACES** UK rock group formed in London in 1965 by Ronnie 'Plonk' Lane (born 1/4/1946, London, bass), Kenny Jones (born 16/9/1948, London, drums), Jimmy Winston (born James Langwith, 20/4/1945, London, organ) and Steve Marriott (born 30/1/1947, London, guitar/vocals). Winston left shortly after the group signed with Decca in 1965 and was replaced by Ian McLagan (born 12/5/1945, Middlesex). They disbanded in 1969 with Marriott subsequently forming Humble Pie and Lane, Jones and McLagan linking up with Ron Wood and Rod Stewart as the Faces. Marriott was killed in a house fire on 20/4/1991 whilst Lane died from multiple sclerosis on 4/6/1997.

| 14/05/1966 . . . . .3 . . . . . .25 . . . . . . | SMALL FACES . . . . . . . . . . . . . . . . . . . . . . . . . . . . . . . . . . . . . . . . . . . . . . . . . . . . . . . .Decca LK 4790 |
| 17/06/1967 . . . . .17 . . . . . .5 . . . . . . | FROM THE BEGINNING . . . . . . . . . . . . . . . . . . . . . . . . . . . . . . . . . . . . . . . . . . . . . . . . . . . .Decca LK 4879 |
| 01/07/1967 . . . . .21 . . . . . .17 . . . . . . | SMALL FACES . . . . . . . . . . . . . . . . . . . . . . . . . . . . . . . . . . . . . . . . . . . . . . . . . . .Immediate IMSP 008 |
| 15/06/1968 . . . ❶⁶ . . . . .19 . . . . . . | OGDEN'S NUT GONE FLAKE . . . . . . . . . . . . . . . . . . . . . . . . . . . . . . . . . . . . . . . . . . . .Immediate IMLP 012 |
| 11/05/1996 . . . . .66 . . . . . .1 . . . . . . | THE DECCA ANTHOLOGY 1965–1967 . . . . . . . . . . . . . . . . . . . . . . . . . . . . . . . . . . . . . . . .Decca 8445832 |
| 07/06/2003 . . . . .24 . . . . . .4 . . . . .○ | ULTIMATE COLLECTION . . . . . . . . . . . . . . . . . . . . . . . . . . . . . . . . . . . . . . . . . . .Sanctuary TDSAN004 |

**S\*M\*A\*S\*H** UK rock group formed in Welwyn Garden City by Ed Borrie (guitar/vocals), Rob Hague (drums) and Salvador Alessi (bass) as Smash At The Blues. They name-changed after spotting it misspelled on a hoarding.

02/04/1994 . . . . .28 . . . . . .3 . . . . . . S\*M\*A\*S\*H . . . . . . . . . . . . . . . . . . . . . . . . . . . . . . . . . . . . . . . . . . . . . . .Hi-Rise Recordings FLATMCD 2
17/09/1994 . . . . .59 . . . . . .1 . . . . . . SELF ABUSED . . . . . . . . . . . . . . . . . . . . . . . . . . . . . . . . . . . . . . . . . . . . . . .Hi-Rise Recordings FLATCD 6

**SMASHING PUMPKINS** US rock group formed in Chicago, IL in 1989 by Billy Corgan (born 17/3/1967, Chicago, guitar/vocals), James Iha (born 26/3/1968, Elk Grove, IL, guitar), D'Arcy Wretzky (born 1/5/1968, South Haven, MI, bass) and Jimmy Chamberlin (born 10/6/1964, Joliet, IL, drums). They signed with Caroline Records in the USA in 1991. On 12/7/1996 touring keyboard player Jonathan Melvoin died from a heroin overdose, Chamberlin just waking up in time from his own drug-induced sleep to alert paramedics; he was subsequently sacked for continued drug use. They added drummer Matt Walker and keyboard player Dennis Flemion the following month. The group won the 1996 MTV Europe Music Award for Best Rock Act and two Grammy Awards: Best Hard Rock Performance in 1996 for *Bullet With Butterfly Wings* and Best Hard Rock Performance in 1997 for *The End Is The Beginning Is The End*. In May 2000 the group announced they were to disband with Corgan forming a new group Zwan.

| 31/07/1993 . . . . .4 . . . . . .15 . . . . .● | SIAMESE DREAM . . . . . . . . . . . . . . . . . . . . . . . . . . . . . . . . . . . . . . . . . . . . . . . . . . . . . .Hut CDHUT 11 |
| 04/11/1995 . . . . .4 . . . . . .37 . . . . .✪ | MELLON COLLIE AND THE INFINITE SADNESS ▲¹ . . . . . . . . . . . . . . . . . . . . . . . . . . . . .Virgin CDHUTD 30 |
| 13/06/1998 . . . . .5 . . . . . .12 . . . . .● | ADORE . . . . . . . . . . . . . . . . . . . . . . . . . . . . . . . . . . . . . . . . . . . . . . . . . . . . . . . . . . . .Hut CDHUTX 51 |
| 11/03/2000 . . . . .7 . . . . . .4 . . . . .○ | MACHINA/THE MACHINES OF GOD . . . . . . . . . . . . . . . . . . . . . . . . . . . . . . . . . . . . . . .Hut CDHUT 59 |
| 01/12/2001 . . . . .28 . . . . . .3 . . . . .○ | ROTTEN APPLES – THE GREATEST HITS . . . . . . . . . . . . . . . . . . . . . . . . . . . . . . . . . . . . .Hut HUTD 70 |

**BRIAN SMITH AND HIS HAPPY PIANO** UK pianist.

19/09/1981 . . . . .97 . . . . . .1 . . . . . . PLAY IT AGAIN . . . . . . . . . . . . . . . . . . . . . . . . . . . . . . . . . . . . . . . . . . . . . . . . . . . . . . .Deram DS 047

**ELLIOTT SMITH** US singer/songwriter (born Portland, OR); he began writing songs at fourteen and later joined Heatmiser. He went solo in 1994 with the Cavity Search label, contributing music to the 1997 film *Good Will Hunting* (his track *Miss Misery* was nominated for an Oscar for Best Original Song). He signed with DreamWorks in 1998.

29/04/2000 . . . . .37 . . . . . .2 . . . . . . FIGURE 8 . . . . . . . . . . . . . . . . . . . . . . . . . . . . . . . . . . . . . . . . . . . . . . . . . . . . . .DreamWorks 4502252

**JIMMY SMITH** US organist (born 8/12/1925, Norristown, PA) who, after learning to play the piano and bass as a child, concentrated on Hammond organ, forming his own trio. He recorded for Blue Note in the 1950s, moving to Verve in 1962.

18/06/1966 . . . . .19 . . . . . .3 . . . . . . GOT MY MOJO WORKING . . . . . . . . . . . . . . . . . . . . . . . . . . . . . . . . . . . . . . . . . . . . . . . .Verve VLP 912

## KEELY SMITH

**KEELY SMITH** US singer (born Dorothy Keely Smith, 9/3/1932, Norfolk, VA); she married jazz trumpeter and singer Louis Prima in 1952 and recorded with both her husband and Frank Sinatra. Prima and Smith won the Best Performance by a Vocal Group Grammy Award in 1958 for *That Old Black Magic*. The couple divorced in 1961. She has a star on the Hollywood Walk of Fame.

16/01/1965 . . . . . 12 . . . . . . 9 . . . . . . LENNON-McCARTNEY SONGBOOK . . . . . . . . . . . . . . . . . . . . . . . . . . . . . . . . . . . . . . . . . . . . . . . . . . . . . . . . Reprise R 6142

## O.C. SMITH

**O.C. SMITH** US singer (born Ocie Lee Smith, 21/6/1936, Mansfield, LA) who replaced Joe Williams as singer in Count Basie's band in 1961. He began recording country music in 1965, switching to soul in 1973. He died from a heart attack on 23/11/2001.

17/08/1968 . . . . . 40 . . . . . . 1 . . . . . . HICKORY HOLLER REVISITED . . . . . . . . . . . . . . . . . . . . . . . . . . . . . . . . . . . . . . . . . . . . . . . . . . . . . . . . . . . . . . . . . . . . . . . . . . CBS 63362

## PATTI SMITH GROUP

**PATTI SMITH GROUP** US singer (born 31/12/1946, Chicago, IL); she debuted on record in 1974 for the Mer label. The group was Lenny Kaye (guitar), Richard Sohl (piano), Jay Dee Daughtery (drums) and Ivan Kral (guitar). Smith broke her neck when she fell off stage in Tampa, FL in 1977. They disbanded in 1980 after Patti had married Fred 'Sonic' Smith, formerly of the MC5, and retired to have a family. She resumed recording in 1988. Sohl died from a heart attack on 3/6/1990. Fred Smith died in 1995.

01/04/1978 . . . . . 16 . . . . . 14 . . . . . . O    EASTER . . . . . . . . . . . . . . . . . . . . . . . . . . . . . . . . . . . . . . . . . . . . . . . . . . . . . . . . . . . . . . . . . . . Arista SPART 1043
19/05/1979 . . . . . 41 . . . . . . 6 . . . . . . WAVE . . . . . . . . . . . . . . . . . . . . . . . . . . . . . . . . . . . . . . . . . . . . . . . . . . . . . . . . . . . . . . . . . . . . . . . . Arista SPART 1086
16/07/1988 . . . . . 70 . . . . . . 1 . . . . . . DREAM OF LIFE . . . . . . . . . . . . . . . . . . . . . . . . . . . . . . . . . . . . . . . . . . . . . . . . . . . . . . . . . . . . . . . . . . . Arista 209172
13/07/1996 . . . . . 44 . . . . . . 2 . . . . . . GONE AGAIN . . . . . . . . . . . . . . . . . . . . . . . . . . . . . . . . . . . . . . . . . . . . . . . . . . . . . . . . . . . . . . . . . Arista 07822187472
08/05/2004 . . . . . 70 . . . . . . 1 . . . . . . TRAMPIN' This and the above two hits credited to **PATTI SMITH** . . . . . . . . . . . . . . . . . . . . . . . . . . . . . . . . . . . . Columbia 5152159

## STEVEN SMITH AND FATHER

**STEVEN SMITH AND FATHER** UK instrumental duo (Steven played drums whilst his father played Hammond organ); they first came to prominence by winning the TV talent contest *Opportunity Knocks*.

13/05/1972 . . . . . 17 . . . . . 3 . . . . . . STEVEN SMITH AND FATHER AND 16 GREAT SONGS . . . . . . . . . . . . . . . . . . . . . . . . . . . . . . . . . . . . . . . Decca SKL 5128

## WILL SMITH

**WILL SMITH** US singer (born Willard Christopher Smith Jr, 25/9/1968, Philadelphia, PA); he first recorded as The Fresh Prince with DJ Jazzy Jeff, and as an actor appeared in the TV comedy *Fresh Prince Of Bel-Air* and the films *Independence Day*, *Men In Black* and *Wild Wild West*. He won two Grammy Awards whilst a member of DJ Jazzy Jeff and the Fresh Prince and went on to collect a further two awards: Best Rap Solo Performance in 1997 for *Men In Black* and Best Rap Solo Performance in 1998 for *Getting' Jiggy Wit It*. He has won two MTV Europe Music Awards: Best Rap Act in 1997 and Best Male in 1999. He also won the 1997 MOBO Award for Best Video for *Men In Black*.

06/12/1997 . . . . . 9 . . . . 70 . . . . . **☼**²    BIG WILLIE STYLE ◇² . . . . . . . . . . . . . . . . . . . . . . . . . . . . . . . . . . . . . . . . . . . . . . . . . . . . . . Columbia 4886622
27/11/1999 . . . . . 10 . . . . 15 . . . . . ☼    WILLENNIUM ◇ . . . . . . . . . . . . . . . . . . . . . . . . . . . . . . . . . . . . . . . . . . . . . . . . . . . . . . . . . . . Columbia 4949392
24/08/2002 . . . . . 24 . . . . . 2 . . . . . . BORN TO REIGN . . . . . . . . . . . . . . . . . . . . . . . . . . . . . . . . . . . . . . . . . . . . . . . . . . . . . . . . . . . . . . Columbia 5079552

## SMITH AND JONES

**SMITH AND JONES** UK comedy duo formed by Mel Smith (born 3/12/1952, London) and Griff Rhys Jones. The pair first came to prominence in the TV comedy series *Not The Nine O'Clock News,* with Pamela Stephenson and Rowan Atkinson, before linking up to write and perform their own series, *Alas Smith And Jones*. Smith later became a successful film director whilst he, Jones and Atkinson formed Talkback Productions, a TV production company.

15/11/1986 . . . . . 62 . . . . . . 8 . . . . . . SCRATCH AND SNIFF . . . . . . . . . . . . . . . . . . . . . . . . . . . . . . . . . . . . . . . . . . . . . . . . . . . . . . . . . 10 Records DIX 51

## SMITHS

**SMITHS** UK rock group formed in Manchester in 1982 by Johnny Marr (born John Maher, 31/10/1963, Manchester, guitar), Morrissey (born Stephen Morrissey, 22/5/1959, Manchester, vocals), Andy Rourke (born 1963, Manchester, bass) and Mike Joyce (born 1/6/1963, Manchester, drums). They signed with Rough Trade in 1983 and announced they were moving to EMI in 1987, although only Morrissey as a solo artist actually made the move. Marr subsequently formed Electronic.

03/03/1984 . . . . . 2 . . . . . . 33 . . . . . .   THE SMITHS . . . . . . . . . . . . . . . . . . . . . . . . . . . . . . . . . . . . . . . . . . . . . . . . . . . . . Rough Trade ROUGH 61
24/11/1984 . . . . . 7 . . . . . . 46 . . . . . ☼   HATFUL OF HOLLOW . . . . . . . . . . . . . . . . . . . . . . . . . . . . . . . . . . . . . . . . . . . . . . . . Rough Trade ROUGH 76
23/02/1985 . . . . ❶¹ . . . . 13 . . . . . . ●   MEAT IS MURDER . . . . . . . . . . . . . . . . . . . . . . . . . . . . . . . . . . . . . . . . . . . . . . . . . . Rough Trade ROUGH 81
28/06/1986 . . . . . 2 . . . . . . 22 . . . . . ●   THE QUEEN IS DEAD . . . . . . . . . . . . . . . . . . . . . . . . . . . . . . . . . . . . . . . . . . . . . . . Rough Trade ROUGH 96
07/03/1987 . . . . . 2 . . . . . . 15 . . . . . ●   THE WORLD WON'T LISTEN . . . . . . . . . . . . . . . . . . . . . . . . . . . . . . . . . . . . . . . . Rough Trade ROUGH 101
30/05/1987 . . . . 38 . . . . . . 5 . . . . . ●   LOUDER THAN BOMBS . . . . . . . . . . . . . . . . . . . . . . . . . . . . . . . . . . . . . . . . . . . Rough Trade ROUGH 255
10/10/1987 . . . . . 2 . . . . . . 17 . . . . . ●   STRANGEWAYS, HERE WE COME . . . . . . . . . . . . . . . . . . . . . . . . . . . . . . . . Rough Trade ROUGH 106
17/09/1988 . . . . . 2 . . . . . . 7 . . . . . ●   RANK . . . . . . . . . . . . . . . . . . . . . . . . . . . . . . . . . . . . . . . . . . . . . . . . . . . . . . . Rough Trade ROUGH 126
29/08/1992 . . . . ❶¹ . . . . . 9 . . . . . ●   BEST . . . 1 . . . . . . . . . . . . . . . . . . . . . . . . . . . . . . . . . . . . . . . . . . . . . . . . . . . . . WEA 4509903272
14/11/1992 . . . . 29 . . . . . . 5 . . . . . O   BEST . . . 2 . . . . . . . . . . . . . . . . . . . . . . . . . . . . . . . . . . . . . . . . . . . . . . . . . . . . . . . WEA 4509904062
04/03/1995 . . . . . 5 . . . . . . 9 . . . . . ☼   SINGLES . . . . . . . . . . . . . . . . . . . . . . . . . . . . . . . . . . . . . . . . . . . . . . . . . . . . . . . . . . WEA 4509990902
04/03/1995 . . . . 26 . . . . . . 3 . . . . . . HATFUL OF HOLLOW . . . . . . . . . . . . . . . . . . . . . . . . . . . . . . . . . . . . . . . . . . . . . . . . . WEA 4509918932
04/03/1995 . . . . 30 . . . . . . 4 . . . . . . THE QUEEN IS DEAD . . . . . . . . . . . . . . . . . . . . . . . . . . . . . . . . . . . . . . . . . . . . . . . . . WEA 4509918962
04/03/1995 . . . . 38 . . . . . . 4 . . . . . . STRANGEWAYS, HERE WE COME . . . . . . . . . . . . . . . . . . . . . . . . . . . . . . . . . . . . . . . WEA 4509918992

| | | | | | |
|---|---|---|---|---|---|
| 04/03/1995 | 39 | 2 | | MEAT IS MURDER | WEA 4509918952 |
| 04/03/1995 | 42 | 4 | | THE SMITHS | WEA 4509918922 |
| 04/03/1995 | 52 | 2 | | THE WORLD WON'T LISTEN | WEA 4509918982 |
| 14/10/2000 | 52 | 2 | | LOUDER THAN BOMBS This and the above six albums are all re-issues | WEA 4509938332 |
| 16/06/2001 | 30 | 4 | ● | THE VERY BEST OF | WEA 8573889482 |

**SMOKIE** UK pop group formed in 1968 by Chris Norman (vocals), Alan Silson (guitar), Terry Utley (bass) and Peter Spencer (drums) as Kindness. They name-changed to Smokey, amending the spelling to Smokie to avoid confusion with Smokey Robinson. Norman and Spencer were later successful as songwriters, penning hits for Kevin Keegan and the England World Cup Squad. Norman left, replaced by Alan Barton who was killed in a road crash in 1995.

| | | | | | |
|---|---|---|---|---|---|
| 01/11/1975 | 18 | 5 | O | SMOKIE/CHANGING ALL THE TIME | RAK SRAK 517 |
| 30/04/1977 | 6 | 22 | O | **GREATEST HITS** | RAK SRAK 526 |
| 04/11/1978 | 52 | 2 | O | THE MONTREUX ALBUM | RAK SRAK 6757 |
| 11/10/1980 | 23 | 13 | ● | SMOKIE'S HITS | RAK SRAK 540 |
| 17/03/2001 | 63 | 2 | | UNCOVERED – THE VERY BEST OF SMOKIE | Universal TV 0138172 |

**SNAP** US/German dance act assembled by producers Michael Muenzing and Luca Anzilotti, who appeared in the group as Benito Benitez and John 'Virgo' Garrett III, the other members being Turbo B (Durron Butler) and Penny Ford. Interviews for the group were handled by Jackie Harris owing to Ford's reluctance. Ford left in 1991 and was replaced by Thea Austin and then Niki Haris.

| | | | | | |
|---|---|---|---|---|---|
| 26/05/1990 | 10 | 39 | ● | **WORLD POWER** | Arista 210682 |
| 08/08/1992 | 8 | 15 | ● | **THE MADMAN'S RETURN** The album changed catalogue number to 74321128512 during its chart run | Logic 262552 |
| 15/10/1994 | 69 | 1 | | WELCOME TO TOMORROW | Arista 74321223842 |
| 07/09/1996 | 47 | 1 | | SNAP! ATTACK – THE BEST OF SNAP!/SNAP! ATTACK – THE REMIXES | Arista 74321384862 |

**SNEAKER PIMPS** UK rock group formed in 1992 by Liam Howe (keyboards) and Chris Corner (guitar) as F.R.I.S.K. They later added singer Keli Ali and name-changed to Sneaker Pimps. Ali left for a solo career in 1998.

| | | | | | |
|---|---|---|---|---|---|
| 31/08/1996 | 27 | 7 | ● | BECOMING X | Clean Up CUP 020CD |

**DAVID SNEDDON** UK singer (born 15/9/1978, Glasgow) who was winner of BBC TV's *Fame Academy;* he joined the show two weeks later than the other contestants as a replacement for Naomi Roper. In the final he received 3.5 million of the 6.9 million votes.

| | | | | | |
|---|---|---|---|---|---|
| 10/05/2003 | 5 | 5 | ● | **SEVEN YEARS – TEN WEEKS** | Fontana 9800063 |

**SNOOP DOGGY DOGG** US rapper (born Calvin Broadus, 20/10/1972, Long Beach, CA); he began rapping whilst serving a year in prison for selling cocaine, then was discovered by Dr Dre. He was arrested following a drive-by shooting and killing in 1993. He and his bodyguard were acquitted of murder in 1996, and as the jury could not agree on charges of manslaughter, the judge ordered a mistrial. As an actor he appeared in films including *Murder Was The Case, Half Baked* and *Hot Boyz.* He later formed rap supergroup 213 with Nate Dogg and Warren G.

| | | | | | |
|---|---|---|---|---|---|
| 11/12/1993 | 38 | 27 | ● | DOGGYSTYLE ▲3 | Death Row 6544922792 |
| 23/11/1996 | 15 | 11 | | THA DOGGFATHER ▲1 | Interscope INTD 90038 |
| 15/08/1998 | 28 | 3 | | DA GAMES IS TO BE SOLD, NOT TO BE TOLD ▲2 | Priority CDPTYX 153 |
| 05/06/1999 | 48 | 1 | | TOP DOGG | Priority CDPTY 171 |
| 05/05/2001 | 62 | 2 | ● | THA LAST MEAL | Priority CDPTY 199 |
| 10/05/2003 | 64 | 6 | ● | PAID THA COST TO BE THA BOSS This and the above two hits credited to **SNOOP DOGG** | Priority PRY391572 |

**SNOW** Canadian rapper/reggae singer (born Darren O'Brien, 30/10/1969, Toronto, Ontario). He was in prison awaiting trial for manslaughter (he was later acquitted) at the time of his debut hit.

| | | | | | |
|---|---|---|---|---|---|
| 17/04/1993 | 41 | 4 | | 12 INCHES OF SNOW | East West America 7567922072 |

**MARK SNOW** US composer/pianist (born 26/8/1946, Brooklyn, NYC). He relocated to Los Angeles, CA in 1974 and has written the scores to many TV series and films, including *The Day Lincoln Was Shot, Murder Between Friends* and *Hart To Hart.*

| | | | | | |
|---|---|---|---|---|---|
| 12/10/1996 | 42 | 2 | O | TRUTH AND THE LIGHT: MUSIC FROM THE X-FILES | Warner Brothers 9362462492 |

**SNOW PATROL** UK rock group formed in Dundee, Scotland by Gary Lightbody (guitar/vocals), Mark McClelland (bass/keyboards) and John Quinn (drums). They first recorded for Jeepster in 1998.

| | | | | | |
|---|---|---|---|---|---|
| 14/02/2004 | 3 | 20+ | ✪ | **FINAL STRAW** | Fiction 9865408 |

**SO SOLID CREW** UK rap/garage group that features 22 members, including MC Harvey, MC Romeo, Shane 'Kaish' Neil, Megaman, Jason 'G Man' Phillips, Ashley 'Asher D' Walters, Lisa Maffia and Dan Da Man. After live dates in November 2001 were marred by violence, including one at London's Astoria Theatre that resulted in a shooting, the rest of their UK tour was scrapped. They won the 2001 MOBO Awards for Best UK Garage Act and Best Newcomer, and the 2002 BRIT Award for Best Video for *21 Seconds.* In March 2002 Asher D was jailed for eighteen months for possessing a loaded revolver. In December 2002 Kaish and G Man were similarly questioned about gun and drug offences, with G Man being sentenced to four years for possessing a loaded firearm in June 2003.

| | | | | | |
|---|---|---|---|---|---|
| 01/12/2001 | 6 | 20 | ✪ | **THEY DON'T KNOW** | Independiente ISOM 27CD |
| 11/10/2003 | 70 | 1 | | 2ND VERSE | Independiente ISOM 35CD |

## SOFT CELL
UK techno-pop duo formed by Marc Almond (born Peter Marc Almond, 9/7/1957, Southport, vocals) and David Ball (born 3/5/1959, Blackpool, keyboards) who teamed up in 1979. They funded their debut release on their Big Frock label before signing with Some Bizzare in 1980. They split in 1984, Almond recording as Marc & The Mambas and solo, and Ball forming The Grid.

| 12/12/1981 | 5 | 46 | ✪ | NON-STOP EROTIC CABARET | Some Bizzare BZLP 2 |
| 26/06/1982 | 6 | 18 | ● | NON-STOP ECSTATIC DANCING | Some Bizzare BZX 1012 |
| 22/01/1983 | 5 | 10 | ● | THE ART OF FALLING APART | Some Bizzare BIZL 3 |
| 31/03/1984 | 12 | 5 | | THIS LAST NIGHT IN SODOM | Some Bizzare BIZL 6 |
| 20/12/1986 | 58 | 9 | | THE SINGLES ALBUM | Some Bizzare BZLP 3 |
| 01/06/1991 | 8 | 13 | | MEMORABILIA – THE SINGLES SOFT CELL AND MARC ALMOND | Mercury 8485121 |
| 13/04/2002 | 37 | 2 | | THE VERY BEST OF | Universal TV 5868342 |

## SOFT MACHINE
UK rock group formed in 1966 by Robert Wyatt (born 28/1/1945, Canterbury), Kevin Ayers (born 16/8/1945, Herne Bay), Daevid Allen, Mike Ratledge and Larry Nolan, although by 1967 the line-up was a trio of Wyatt, Ayers and Ratledge. By 1970 the line-up consisted of Wyatt, Ratledge, Hugh Hopper and Elton Dean. Wyatt left in 1971 to form Machine Mole and was first replaced by Phil Howard and then John Marshall. After numerous line-up changes, in 1984 the group comprised Karl Jenkins, John Marshall, Dave Macrae and Ray Warleigh.

| 04/04/1970 | 18 | 6 | | THIRD | CBS 66246 |
| 03/04/1971 | 32 | 2 | | FOURTH | CBS 64280 |

## SOLID SENDERS
UK vocal/instrumental group formed in 1977 by Wilko Johnson (guitar), John Potter (guitar), Steve Lewins (bass) and Alan Platt (drums). Johnson had previously been a member of Dr Feelgood and went on to join Ian Dury's backing band.

| 23/09/1978 | 42 | 3 | | SOLID SENDERS | Virgin V 2105 |

## DIANE SOLOMON
UK singer who later recorded for EMI.

| 09/08/1975 | 26 | 6 | | TAKE TWO | Philips 6308 236 |

## SIR GEORG SOLTI AND DUDLEY MOORE
UK duo formed by Sir Georg Solti and Dudley Moore. Solti was born in Budapest on 21/10/1912 and conducted the Budapest Opera in 1938 but was forced to leave the country in 1939. He later served as Musical Director at the Munich Opera (1946–52) and then Frankfurt (1952–61) before spending ten years at Covent Garden. In 1969 he was appointed Musical Director of the Chicago Symphony Orchestra. Moore (born 19/4/1935, Dagenham) first came to prominence as a musician, playing semi-professionally in jazz clubs before teaming up with Vic Lewis. He formed his own Dudley Moore Trio in the early 1960s and combined his musical pursuits with comedy, appearing in the touring comedy show *Beyond The Fringe*. He achieved national prominence through his comedy series with Peter Cook, *Not Only … But Also* before his acting career took precedence and he moved to Hollywood, appearing in such films as *10* (alongside Bo Derek) and *Arthur* (Liza Minnelli). He linked up with Peter Cook again in 1976 for the immensely successful *Derek And Clive* albums. Dudley Moore was awarded a CBE in the 2001 Queen's Birthday Honours List. Sir Georg Solti has won 29 Grammy Awards: Best Opera Recording in 1962 conducting the Rome Opera House Orchestra and Chorus for *Verdi: Aida*; Best Opera Recording in 1966 conducting the Vienna Philharmonic for *Wagner: Die Walkure*; Album of the Year, Classical in 1972 conducting the Chicago Symphony, Vienna Boys' Choir, Vienna State Opera Chorus, Vienna Singverein Chorus and soloists for *Mahler: Symphony No. 8 in E Flat Major*; Best Classical Performance, (conductor's award) in 1972 conducting the Chicago Symphony for *Mahler: Symphony No. 7 in E Minor*; Best Classical Performance, Choral (other than opera) in 1972 conducting the Chicago Symphony, Vienna Boys' Choir, Vienna State Opera Chorus, Vienna Singverein Chorus and soloists for *Mahler: Symphony No. 8 in E Flat Major*; Album of the Year, Classical and Best Classical Performance, (conductor's award) in 1974 conducting the Chicago Symphony for *Berlioz: Symphonie Fantastique*; Best Opera Recording in 1974 conducting the London Philharmonic for *Puccini: La Boheme*; Album of the Year, Classical in 1975 conducting the Chicago Symphony for *Beethoven: Symphonies*; Best Classical Performance, (conductor's award) in 1976 conducting the Chicago Symphony for *Strauss: Also Sprach Zarathustra*; Best Classical Performance, Choral (other than opera) in 1977 with Margaret Hillis, choral director, Chicago Symphony Chorus and Orchestra for *Verdi: Requiem*; Best Classical Performance, Choral (other than opera) in 1978 with Margaret Hillis, choral director, Chicago Symphony Chorus and Orchestra for *Beethoven: Missa Solemnis*; Album of the Year, Classical and Best Classical Orchestral Recording (conductor's award) in 1979 conducting the Chicago Symphony Orchestra for *Brahms: Symphonies*; Best Classical Performance, Choral (other than opera) in 1979 with Margaret Hillis, choral director, Chicago Symphony Chorus and Orchestra for *Brahms: A German Requiem*; Best Classical Orchestral Recording, (conductor's award) in 1980 conducting the Chicago Symphony for *Bruckner: Symphony No. 6 in A Major*; Best Classical Album and Best Classical Orchestral Recording (conductor's award) in 1981 conducting the Chicago Symphony Orchestra and Chorus for *Mahler: Symphony No. 2 in C Minor*; Best Classical Album and Best Classical Orchestral Recording, (conductor's award) in 1981 conducting the Chicago Symphony for *Mahler: Symphony No. 9 in D Major*; Best Classical Performance, Choral (other than opera) in 1982 with Margaret Hillis, chorus master and the Chicago Symphony Orchestra for *Berlioz: Damnation de Faust*; Best Classical Performance, Choral (other than opera) in 1983 with Margaret Hillis, chorus master and the Chicago Symphony Orchestrafor *Haydn: The Creation*; Best Opera Recording in 1985 conducting the Chicago Symphony Orchestra and Chorus for *Schoenberg: Moses und Aron*; Best Classical Orchestral Recording (conductor's award) in 1986 conducting the Chicago Symphony Orchestra for *Liszt: A Faust Symphony*; Best Classical Orchestral Recording, (conductor's award) in 1987 conducting the Chicago Symphony Orchestra for *Beethoven: Symphony No. 9 in D Minor*; Best Chamber Music Performance in 1988 with Murray Perahia, David Corkhill, and Evelyn Glennie for *Bartok: Sonata for 2 Pianos and Percussion, Brahms: Variation on a Theme by Joseph Haydn for 2 Pianos*; Best

○ Silver disc ● Gold disc ✪ Platinum disc (additional platinum units are indicated by a figure following the symbol) ●⁹ Number of weeks album topped the UK chart

Opera Recording in 1988 conducting the Vienna State Opera Choir and Vienna Philharmonic for *Wagner: Lohengrin*; Best Performance of a Choral Work in 1991 conducting the Chicago Symphony and Chorus for *Bach: Mass in B Minor*; Best Opera Recording in 1992 conducting the Vienna Philharmonic for *Richard Strauss: Die Frau Ohne Schatten*; and Best Opera Recording in 1997 with Ben Heppner: Herbert Lippert and Karita Mattila and the Chicago Symphony Chorus and Orchestra for *Wagner: Die Meistersinger Von Nurnberg*. Not surprisingly, this is the greatest tally of Grammy Awards won!

| 26/01/1991 | 38 | 5 | | ORCHESTRA! | Decca 4308361 |
|---|---|---|---|---|---|

### JIMMY SOMERVILLE
UK singer (born 22/6/1961, Glasgow) who was a founder member of Bronski Beat in 1984. He left the following year to form the Communards. They disbanded in 1988 and Somerville went solo in 1989.

| 09/12/1989 | 29 | 14 | ● | READ MY LIPS | London 8281661 |
|---|---|---|---|---|---|
| 24/11/1990 | 4 | 26 | | **THE SINGLES COLLECTION 1984/1990** | London 8282261 |
| 24/06/1995 | 38 | 2 | | DARE TO LOVE | London 8285402 |
| 22/09/2001 | 29 | 4 | | THE VERY BEST OF JIMMY SOMERVILLE BRONSKI BEAT AND THE COMMUNARDS **JIMMY SOMERVILLE BRONSKI BEAT & THE COMMUNARDS** | London 0927412582 |

### SONIA
UK singer (born Sonia Evans, 13/2/1971, Liverpool); after drama school she made a brief appearance in the TV comedy *Bread*. She introduced herself to producer Pete Waterman, securing a place on his TV show *Hitman And Her*, with Waterman writing and producing her early hits. She left PWL Management in 1991 and later represented the UK in the Eurovision Song Contest in 1993.

| 05/05/1990 | 7 | 10 | ● | **EVERYBODY KNOWS** | Chrysalis CHR 1734 |
|---|---|---|---|---|---|
| 19/10/1991 | 33 | 2 | | SONIA | IQ ZL 751675 |
| 29/05/1993 | 32 | 2 | | BETTER THE DEVIL YOU KNOW | Arista 74321149802 |

### SONIC BOOM
UK singer (born Pete Kember, 19/11/1965) who first adopted the name Sonic Boom whilst a member of Spacemen 3, which he had launched in 1982. He subsequently embarked on a solo career in 1990.

| 17/03/1990 | 65 | 1 | | SPECTRUM | Silvertone ORELP 56 |
|---|---|---|---|---|---|

### SONIC YOUTH
US rock group formed in the mid-1980s by Thurston Moore (born 25/7/1958, Coral Gables, FL, guitar), Kim Gordon (born 28/4/1953, New York, bass), Lee Renaldo (born 3/2/1956, New York, guitar) and Bob Bert (drums). Bert left in 1986, replaced by Steve Shelley (born 23/6/1962, Midland, MI). They switched to the Geffen label in 1990.

| 29/10/1988 | 99 | 1 | | DAYDREAM NATION | Blast First BFFP 34 |
|---|---|---|---|---|---|
| 04/02/1989 | 63 | 1 | | THE WHITEY ALBUM **CICCONE YOUTH** | Blast First BFFP 28 |
| 07/07/1990 | 32 | 2 | | GOO' | DGC 7599242971 |
| 04/05/1991 | 69 | 1 | | THE DIRTY BOOTS EP – PLUS 5 LIVE TRACKS | DGC 21634 |
| 01/08/1992 | 6 | 5 | | **DIRTY** | DGC DGCD 24485 |
| 21/05/1994 | 10 | 2 | | **EXPERIMENTAL JET SET, TRASH AND NO STAR** | Geffen GED 24632 |
| 14/10/1995 | 39 | 1 | | WASHING MACHINE | Geffen GED 24825 |
| 23/05/1998 | 38 | 1 | | A THOUSAND LEAVES | Geffen GED 25203 |

### SONIQUE
UK singer/DJ (born Sonia Clarke, London); she previously worked with Bass-O-Matic and S-Express before relaunching her solo career. She first recorded solo for Cooltempo Records whilst still a teenager and scored a big club hit with *Let Me Hold You*. Her UK #1 was re-released in the UK after it had hit the US Top Ten. She was named Best British Female Artist at the 2001 BRIT Awards.

| 24/06/2000 | 6 | 37 | ✪ | **HEAR MY CRY** ◇ | Universal 1592302 |
|---|---|---|---|---|---|

### SONNY AND CHER
US duo formed by Sonny Bono (born Salvatore Bono, 16/2/1935, Detroit, MI) and his wife Cher (born Cherilyn Sarkasian La Pierre, 20/5/1946, El Centro, CA). They first recorded together with Phil Spector as Caesar & Cleo in 1964, reverting to their real names in 1965. They were married in 1964, divorced 1965. Both recorded solo and appeared in films; Cher won an Oscar for her performance in *Moonstruck*. Sonny was killed in a skiing accident on 5/1/1998. They have a star on the Hollywood Walk of Fame.

| 16/10/1965 | 7 | 13 | | **LOOK AT US** | Atlantic ATL 5036 |
|---|---|---|---|---|---|
| 14/05/1966 | 15 | 7 | | THE WONDROUS WORLD OF SONNY AND CHER | Atlantic 587006 |

### S.O.S. BAND
US R&B group formed in Atlanta, GA by Mary Davis (vocals), Jason Bryant (keyboards), Abdul Raoof (trumpet), Billy Ellis (saxophone), John Simpson (bass), Bruno Speight (guitar), Jerome 'JT' Thomas (drums) and Willie 'Sonny' Killebrew (saxophone) as Santa Monica. They name-changed in 1980 (SOS stands for 'Sounds Of Success') upon signing with Tabu.

| 01/09/1984 | 29 | 10 | | JUST THE WAY YOU LIKE IT | Tabu TBU 26058 |
|---|---|---|---|---|---|
| 12/10/1985 | 87 | 2 | | THE ARTISTS VOLUME III **WOMACK AND WOMACK/THE O'JAYS/KLEEER/THE S.O.S. BAND** | Street Sounds ARTIS 3 |
| 17/05/1986 | 15 | 9 | | SANDS OF TIME | Tabu TBU 26863 |

### DAVID SOUL
US singer/actor (born David Solberg, 28/8/1943, Chicago, IL) who began his career as a folk singer, appearing on TV as 'The Covered Man' wearing a ski mask. As an actor he was best known as Ken Hutchinson in *Starsky & Hutch*. He also maintained a parallel career as a singer.

| 27/11/1976 | 2 | 28 | ● | **DAVID SOUL** | Private Stock PVLP 1012 |
|---|---|---|---|---|---|
| 17/09/1977 | 8 | 23 | ● | **PLAYING TO AN AUDIENCE OF ONE** | Private Stock PVLP 1026 |

### SOUL ASYLUM
US rock group formed in Minneapolis, MN in 1983 by Dave Pirner (born 16/4/1964, Green Bay, WI, guitar/vocals), Daniel Murphy (born 12/7/1962, Duluth, MN, guitar), Karl Mueller (born 27/7/1962, Minneapolis, bass) and Grant Young (born 5/1/1964, Iowa City, IA, drums). Young left in 1995 and was replaced by Sterling Campbell.

| 31/07/1993 | 27 | 25 | ● | GRAVE DANCERS UNION | Columbia 4722532 |
|---|---|---|---|---|---|
| 01/07/1995 | 22 | 4 | | LET YOUR DIM LIGHT SHINE | Columbia 4803202 |

### SOUL II SOUL
UK R&B group formed in London in 1982 as a sound system for dance clubs by Jazzie B (born Beresford Romeo, 26/1/1963, London) and Philip 'Daddae' Harvey (born 28/2/1964, London). Nellee Hooper (born Paul Andrew Hooper) joined in 1985, the group debuting on record in 1987. They achieved their chart breakthrough in 1989 with Caron Wheeler (born 19/1/1963, London) on lead vocals. Earlier lead singer Do'Reen (born Doreen Waddell, 1966, Southend) was killed on 1/3/2002 after being hit by a number of cars whilst trying to flee a shop after being caught shoplifting. The group has won two Grammy Awards: Best Rhythm & Blues Vocal Performance by a Group in 1989 for *Back To Life (However Do You Want Me),* and Best Rhythm & Blues Instrumental Performance in 1989 for *African Dance.* Jazzie B was given an Outstanding Contribution Award at the 1996 MOBO Awards.

| | | | | |
|---|---|---|---|---|
| 22/04/1989 | ●¹ | 60 | ✪ | **CLUB CLASSICS VOLUME ONE** ...................10 Records DIX 82 |
| 02/06/1990 | ●³ | 20 | ✪ | **VOLUME II (A NEW DECADE)** ...................10 Records DIX 90 |
| 25/04/1992 | 3 | 11 | ● | **VOLUME III JUST RIGHT** ...................10 Records DIXCD 100 |
| 27/11/1993 | 10 | 13 | ✪ | **VOLUME IV THE CLASSIC SINGLES 88–93** ...................Virgin CDV 2724 |
| 12/08/1995 | 13 | 4 | | VOLUME V – BELIEVE ...................Virgin CDV 2739 |

### SOULFLY
Brazilian/US rock group formed in 1996 by Max Cavalera (born 4/8/1969, Belo Horizonte, guitar/vocals), Jackson Bandeira (guitar), Marcello D Rapp (bass) and Roy 'Rata' Mayorga (drums). Cavalera had previously been a member of Sepultura and later worked with The Deftones.

| | | | |
|---|---|---|---|
| 02/05/1998 | 16 | 2 | SOULFLY ...................Roadrunner RR 87482 |
| 07/10/2000 | 45 | 1 | PRIMITIVE ...................Roadrunner RR 85655 |
| 06/07/2002 | 61 | 1 | 3 ...................Roadrunner RR 84555 |

### SOUNDGARDEN
US rock group formed in Seattle, WA in 1984 by Kim Thayil (born 4/9/1960, Seattle, guitar), Hiro Yamamoto (born 20/9/1968, Okinawa, Japan, bass), Chris Cornell (born 20/7/1964, Seattle, guitar/vocals) and Scott Sundquist (drums). Sundquist left soon after, replaced by Matt Cameron (born 28/11/1962, San Diego, CA). Yamamoto left in 1990 and was replaced by Ben 'Hunter' Shepherd (born 20/9/1968). They disbanded in 1997 with Chris Cornell going solo and later forming Audioslave. They won two Grammy Awards: Best Hard Rock Performance with Vocal in 1994 for *Black Hole Sun,* and Best Metal Performance with Vocal in 1994 for *Superunknown.*

| | | | | |
|---|---|---|---|---|
| 25/04/1992 | 39 | 2 | | BADMOTORFINGER ...................A&M 3953742 |
| 19/03/1994 | 4 | 24 | ● | **SUPERUNKNOWN ▲¹** ...................A&M 5402152 |
| 01/06/1996 | 7 | 6 | | **DOWN ON THE UPSIDE** ...................A&M 5405582 |

### SOUNDS OF BLACKNESS
US gospel choir formed in Minnesota in 1969 as the Macalester College Black Choir and which later came under the direction of former body builder Gary Hines (once crowned Mr Minnesota) in 1971. The 40-strong choir and 10-piece orchestra was eventually spotted by Jimmy Jam and Terry Lewis and provided backing vocals for Alexander O'Neill before recording their debut album. They won the 1991 Grammy Award for Best Gospel Album by a Choir for *The Evolution Of Gospel.*

| | | | |
|---|---|---|---|
| 30/04/1994 | 28 | 6 | AFRICA TO AMERICA: THE JOURNEY OF THE DRUM ...................A&M 5490092 |

### SOUNDS ORCHESTRAL
UK studio group assembled by producer John Schroeder and comprising John Pearson, Kenny Clare and Tony Reeves. Schroeder had previously been in-house producer for Oriole and later formed Alaska Records.

| | | | |
|---|---|---|---|
| 12/06/1965 | 17 | 1 | CAST YOUR FATE TO THE WIND ...................Piccadilly NPL 38041 |

### SOUP DRAGONS
UK rock group formed in Glasgow by Sean Dickinson (vocals), Jim McCulloch (guitar), Sushil Dade (bass) and Paul Quinn (drums).

| | | | | |
|---|---|---|---|---|
| 07/05/1988 | 60 | 1 | | THIS IS OUR ART ...................Siren WX 169 |
| 05/05/1990 | 7 | 15 | ○ | **LOVEGOD** ...................Raw TV Products SOUPLP 2 |
| 16/05/1992 | 74 | 1 | | HOTWIRED ...................Big Life BLRCD 15 |

### SOUTH BANK ORCHESTRA
UK orchestra conducted by Joseph Morovitz and Laurie Holloway on their hit album.

| | | | |
|---|---|---|---|
| 02/12/1978 | 47 | 6 | LILLIE Original TV soundtrack ...................Sounds MOR 516 |

### SPACE
French group originally put together as a studio group. The success of their single prompted the creation of a band, featuring Didier Marouani and Roland Romanelli (both on keyboards), Joe Hammer (drums) and singer Madeline Bell.

| | | | | |
|---|---|---|---|---|
| 17/09/1977 | 11 | 9 | ○ | MAGIC FLY ...................Pye International NSPL 28232 |

### SPACE
UK rock group formed in Liverpool by Tommy Scott (born 18/2/1967, Liverpool, bass/vocals), Andrew Parle (drums), James Murphy (guitar/vocals) and Francis Griffiths (keyboards). The group later recorded with Cerys Matthews of Catatonia.

| | | | | |
|---|---|---|---|---|
| 28/09/1996 | 5 | 42 | ✪ | **SPIDERS** ...................Gut GUTCD 1 |
| 21/03/1998 | 3 | 25 | ● | **TIN PLANET** ...................Gut GUTCD 005 |

### SPACEHOG
UK rock group formed in Leeds by brothers Ant (guitar/vocals) and Royston Langlands (vocals/bass), Richard Steel (guitar) and Jonny Cragg (drums).

| | | | |
|---|---|---|---|
| 15/02/1997 | 40 | 2 | RESIDENT ALIEN ...................Siren 7559618342 |

### SPACEMEN
UK group formed by Sonic Boom (born Peter Kember, 19/11/1965, Rugby, vocals), Jason Pierce (born 19/11/1965, Rugby, guitar/vocals), Pete Baines and Rosco as Spaceman 3. By the time of their hit album, Boom and Pierce were effectively working separately and split soon after. Boom launched a solo career and Pierce formed Spiritualized.

09/03/1991 . . . . .46 . . . . . .1 . . . . . . RECURRING . . . . . . . . . . . . . . . . . . . . . . . . . . . . . . . . . . . . . . . . . . . . . . . . . . . . . . .Fire FIRELP 23

**SPANDAU BALLET** UK pop group formed in London in 1976 by Tony Hadley (born 2/6/1960, London, vocals), Gary Kemp (born 16/10/1959, London, guitar), Steve Norman (born 25/3/1960, London, guitar), John Keeble (born 6/7/1959, London, drums) and Richard Miller as the Makers. They re-formed the following year as Spandau Ballet with Kemp, his brother Martin (born 10/10/1961, London, bass), Keeble, Hadley and Norman establishing their own 'New Romantic' image. They set up the Reformation label in 1980 with a licensing deal with Chrysalis. Both Kemp brothers appeared in the 1990 film *The Krays*. In 1998 Hadley, Norman and Keeble sued Gary Kemp, the chief songwriter, for a greater share of the royalties, but lost their case. They were awarded the Sony Technical Excellence Award at the 1984 BRIT Awards. Martin Kemp later concentrated on acting, appearing in the TV series *Eastenders* as Steve Owen. In 2003 Tony Hadley won ITV's *Reborn In The USA* competition.

| | | | | | |
|---|---|---|---|---|---|
| 14/03/1981 . . . . .5 . . . . .29 . . . . .● | **JOURNEY TO GLORY** . . . . . . . . . . . . . . . . . . . . . . . . . . . . . . . . . . . . . . . . . . . . . . . . .Reformation CHR 1331 |
| 20/03/1982 . . . . .15 . . . . .18 . . . . .● | DIAMOND . . . . . . . . . . . . . . . . . . . . . . . . . . . . . . . . . . . . . . . . . . . . . . . . . . . . . . . . .Reformation CDL 1353 |
| 12/03/1983 . . . .❶¹ . . . . .90 . . . . .✪ | **TRUE** . . . . . . . . . . . . . . . . . . . . . . . . . . . . . . . . . . . . . . . . . . . . . . . . . . . . . . . . . . . .Reformation CDL 1403 |
| 07/07/1984 . . . . .2 . . . . .39 . . . . .✪ | **PARADE** . . . . . . . . . . . . . . . . . . . . . . . . . . . . . . . . . . . . . . . . . . . . . . . . . . . . . . . . . .Reformation CDL 1473 |
| 16/11/1985 . . . . .3 . . . . .50 . . . . .✪² | **THE SINGLES COLLECTION** . . . . . . . . . . . . . . . . . . . . . . . . . . . . . . . . . . . . . . . . . . . . . . .Chrysalis SBTV 1 |
| 29/11/1986 . . . . .7 . . . . .19 . . . . .✪ | **THROUGH THE BARRICADES** . . . . . . . . . . . . . . . . . . . . . . . . . . . . . . . . . . . . . . . . . . .Reformation 4502591 |
| 30/09/1989 . . . . .31 . . . . .3 . . . . . . | HEART LIKE A SKY . . . . . . . . . . . . . . . . . . . . . . . . . . . . . . . . . . . . . . . . . . . . . . . . . . . . . . .CBS 4633181 |
| 28/09/1991 . . . . .44 . . . . .3 . . . . . . | THE BEST OF SPANDAU BALLET . . . . . . . . . . . . . . . . . . . . . . . . . . . . . . . . . . . . . . . . . . .Chrysalis CHR 1894 |
| 16/09/2000 . . . . .7 . . . . .20 . . . . .✪ | **GOLD – THE BEST OF** . . . . . . . . . . . . . . . . . . . . . . . . . . . . . . . . . . . . . . . . . . . . . . . . .Chrysalis 5267002 |
| 28/04/2001 . . . . .56 . . . . .3 . . . . . . | THE BEST OF . . . . . . . . . . . . . . . . . . . . . . . . . . . . . . . . . . . . . . . . . . . . . . . . . . . . . . .Chrysalis CCD 1894 |

**SPARKLE** US singer (born New York City) who was discovered by R Kelly. She won't reveal her full name although her first name is Stephanie. She was given the nickname 'Sparkle' by R Kelly after he spotted her wearing a distinctive sparkling jacket.

01/08/1998 . . . . .57 . . . . . .1 . . . . . . SPARKLE . . . . . . . . . . . . . . . . . . . . . . . . . . . . . . . . . . . . . . . . . . . . . . . . . . . . . . . . . . . . . .Jive 0521462

**SPARKLEHORSE** US group formed by Mark Linkous (vocals), David Charles (guitar/keyboards/drums), Bob Rupe (bass/vocals) and Johnny Hott (drums). In 1996 Linkous nearly died after mixing Valium with prescription anti-depressants and spent fourteen hours lying unconscious on the bathroom floor at his hotel.

| | |
|---|---|
| 18/05/1996 . . . . .58 . . . . . .1 . . . . . . | VIVADIXIESUBMARINETRANSMISSIONPLOT . . . . . . . . . . . . . . . . . . . . . . . . . . . . . . . . . . .Capitol CDEST 2280 |
| 01/08/1998 . . . . .30 . . . . . .2 . . . . . . | GOOD MORNING SPIDER . . . . . . . . . . . . . . . . . . . . . . . . . . . . . . . . . . . . . . . . . . . . . . . .Parlophone 4960142 |
| 23/06/2001 . . . . .49 . . . . . .1 . . . . . . | IT'S A WONDERFUL LIFE . . . . . . . . . . . . . . . . . . . . . . . . . . . . . . . . . . . . . . . . . . . . . . . . . .Capitol 5334272 |

**SPARKS** US rock group formed in Los Angeles, CA in 1968 by brothers Ron (born 12/8/1948, Culver City, CA, keyboards) and Russell Mael (born 5/10/1953, Santa Monica, CA, vocals) as Halfnelson. They evolved into Sparks by 1971 and featured both Mael brothers, Earle Mankay (guitar), Jim Mankay (bass) and Harley Fernstein (drums). The pair moved to the UK in 1973, enlisting Adrian Fisher (guitar), Martin Gordon (bass) and Dinky Diamond (drums) to re-form Sparks. They returned to the USA in 1976. Fisher died from a possible drugs overdose in May 2000.

| | |
|---|---|
| 01/06/1974 . . . . .4 . . . . .24 . . . . .● | **KIMONO MY HOUSE** . . . . . . . . . . . . . . . . . . . . . . . . . . . . . . . . . . . . . . . . . . . . . . . . . . .Island ILPS 9272 |
| 23/11/1974 . . . . .9 . . . . .13 . . . . .○ | **PROPAGANDA** . . . . . . . . . . . . . . . . . . . . . . . . . . . . . . . . . . . . . . . . . . . . . . . . . . . . . . .Island ILPS 9312 |
| 18/10/1975 . . . . .18 . . . . .4 . . . . . . | INDISCREET . . . . . . . . . . . . . . . . . . . . . . . . . . . . . . . . . . . . . . . . . . . . . . . . . . . . . . . .Island ILPS 9345 |
| 08/09/1979 . . . . .73 . . . . . .1 . . . . . . | NUMBER ONE IN HEAVEN . . . . . . . . . . . . . . . . . . . . . . . . . . . . . . . . . . . . . . . . . . . . . . . . . . .Virgin V 2115 |

**SPEAR OF DESTINY** UK rock group formed by Kirk Brandon (born 3/8/1956, London, guitar/vocals), Chris Bell (drums), Lasettes Ames (saxophone) and Stan Stammers (bass). Bell and Ames left in 1983, replaced by John Lennard and Nigel Preston. The group later added Alan St Clair (guitar) and Nicky Donnelly (saxophone).

| | |
|---|---|
| 23/04/1983 . . . . .62 . . . . . .2 . . . . . . | GRAPES OF WRATH . . . . . . . . . . . . . . . . . . . . . . . . . . . . . . . . . . . . . . . . . . . . . . . . . . . . . .Epic EPC 25318 |
| 28/04/1984 . . . . .22 . . . . . .7 . . . . . . | ONE EYED JACKS . . . . . . . . . . . . . . . . . . . . . . . . . . . . . . . . . . . . . . . . . . . . . . . .Burning Rome EPC 25836 |
| 07/09/1985 . . . . .11 . . . . . .7 . . . . . . | WORLD SERVICE . . . . . . . . . . . . . . . . . . . . . . . . . . . . . . . . . . . . . . . . . . . . . . . . .Burning Rome EPC 26514 |
| 02/05/1987 . . . . .16 . . . . .13 . . . . .○ | OUTLAND . . . . . . . . . . . . . . . . . . . . . . . . . . . . . . . . . . . . . . . . . . . . . . . . . . . . . . . . . . .Virgin DIX 59 |
| 16/05/1987 . . . . .53 . . . . . .3 . . . . . . | S.O.D. THE EPIC YEARS . . . . . . . . . . . . . . . . . . . . . . . . . . . . . . . . . . . . . . . . . . . . . . . . . . .Epic 4508721 |
| 22/10/1988 . . . . .37 . . . . . .3 . . . . . . | THE PRICE YOU PAY . . . . . . . . . . . . . . . . . . . . . . . . . . . . . . . . . . . . . . . . . . . . . . . . . . . . .Virgin V 2549 |

**SPEARHEAD** US hip hop group formed in San Francisco, CA by Michael Franti (vocals), Trinna Simmons (vocals), Sub Commander Ras Zulu (vocals), David James (guitar), Carl Young (keyboards), Oneida James (bass) and James Gray (drums). Franti had previously been a member of The Disposable Heroes Of Hiphoprisy.

29/03/1997 . . . . .68 . . . . . .1 . . . . . . CHOCOLATE SUPA HIGHWAY . . . . . . . . . . . . . . . . . . . . . . . . . . . . . . . . . . . . . . . . . . .Capitol CDEST 2293

**BILLIE JO SPEARS** US singer (born 14/1/1937, Beaumont, TX) who was discovered by Jack Rhodes, first recording for Abbot in 1953 as Billie Jo Moore. She began recording regularly for United Artists in 1964, and later occasionally with Brite Star and Cutlass.

| | |
|---|---|
| 11/09/1976 . . . . .47 . . . . . .2 . . . . . .○ | WHAT I'VE GOT IN MIND . . . . . . . . . . . . . . . . . . . . . . . . . . . . . . . . . . . . . . . . . . . . .United Artists UAS 29955 |
| 19/05/1979 . . . . .7 . . . . .17 . . . . . .○ | **THE BILLIE JO SPEARS SINGLES ALBUM** . . . . . . . . . . . . . . . . . . . . . . . . . . . . . . . . . .United Artists UAK 30231 |
| 21/11/1981 . . . . .17 . . . . . .9 . . . . . .● | COUNTRY GIRL . . . . . . . . . . . . . . . . . . . . . . . . . . . . . . . . . . . . . . . . . . . . . . . . . . . . . .Warwick WW 5109 |

**BRITNEY SPEARS** US singer (born 2/12/1981, Kentwood, LA); her first break was on the Disney Channel's *Mickey Mouse Club* at the age of eleven, having been turned down three years previously. She allegedly got engaged to Justin Timberlake of N' Sync in June 2000; it was later revealed that they got engaged in July 2001. At the same time she began filming her movie debut, *Cross Roads*. In September 2001 she fell foul of sponsors Pepsi Cola, with whom she had signed a £75 million deal, after she was photographed clutching a bottle of rival Coca Cola! She split with Timberlake in March 2002. She has won four MTV Europe Music Awards: Best Female; Best Breakthrough Artis; Best Song for *Baby One More Time;* and Best Pop Act, all in 1999. Britney is the youngest music icon to be given a star on the Hollywood Walk of Fame. In January 2004 she married former school friend Jason Alexander but a couple of days later revealed it was a drunken act and had the marriage annulled.

| | | | | | |
|---|---|---|---|---|---|
| 20/03/1999 | ....2 | .....85 | ....❂³ | ... BABY ONE MORE TIME ◇⁴ ▲⁶ ◆¹³ | Jive 0522172 |
| 27/05/2000 | ....2 | .....45 | ....❂³ | OOPS! I DID IT AGAIN ◇⁴ ▲¹ | Jive 9220392 |
| 17/11/2001 | ....4 | ....34 | ....❂ | BRITNEY ◇² ▲¹ | Jive 9222532 |
| 29/11/2003 | ....14 | ...31+ | ....❂ | IN THE ZONE ◇ ▲¹ | Jive 82876576442 |

**SPECIALS** UK ska group formed in Coventry in 1977 by Jerry Dammers (born Gerald Dankin, 22/5/1954, India, keyboards), Lynval Golding (born 7/7/1952, St Catherines, Jamaica, guitar), Terry Hall (born 19/3/1959, Coventry, vocals), Neville Staples (born 11/4/1956, Christiana, Jamaica, vocals), Roddy Radiation (born Rod Byers, guitar), Sir Horace Gentleman (born Horace Panter, bass) and a drummer named Silverton. Silverton left in 1978 and was replaced by John Bradbury. They funded the recording of their debut record and set up the 2 Tone label, distributed by Chrysalis. Staples, Hall and Golding left in 1981 to form the Fun Boy Three. In July 2001 the group's 1979 debut album, *The Specials*, re-charted on the album chart for the first time in more than twenty years after the RRP had been slashed to £2.99 and sold 11,000 copies in a single week (it re-charted at #22).

| | | | | | |
|---|---|---|---|---|---|
| 03/11/1979 | ....4 | ....45 | ....● | SPECIALS | 2-Tone CDL TT 5001 |
| 04/10/1980 | ....5 | ....19 | ....● | MORE SPECIALS SPECIALS AKA | 2-Tone CHR TT 5003 |
| 23/06/1984 | ....34 | ....6 | | IN THE STUDIO | 2-Tone CHR TT 5008 |
| 07/09/1991 | ....10 | ....9 | ....● | THE SPECIALS SINGLES | 2-Tone CHR TT 5010 |
| 07/07/2001 | ....22 | ....3 | | SPECIALS | Chrysalis CCD 5001 |

**PHIL SPECTOR** US producer (born Harvey Philip Spector, 26/12/1940, The Bronx, NY) who formed The Teddy Bears with Carol Connors and Marshall Leib and had an international hit with *To Know Him Is To Love Him* (Spector later put the words on his father's grave). After The Teddy Bears he teamed up with Lee Hazelwood and Lester Still as The Spectors Three, with little success. He then became a producer/ composer, working with the likes of Jerry Leiber and Mike Stoller, The Drifters, Ben E King, LaVern Baker and Ruth Brown before linking again with Lester Still to form Philles Records in 1961. He bought Still's share in the company and ran it single-handedly, overseeing hits for the likes of The Crystals and The Ronettes and creating the *A Christmas Gift For You* album (unfortunately, it came out at around the time of President John F Kennedy's assassination and got lost in the emotional aftermath). After the lack of domestic success for his masterpiece *River Deep Mountain High* by Ike and Tina Turner in 1966 (although it did reach the UK Top 5, prompting a vicious advertisement from Spector in the US trade press), Spector went into retirement, although he returned in 1969 to produce Sonny Charles & The Checkmates. He married Ronette member Ronnie Bennett in 1968 although this ended in divorce in 1974 (Spector made his first alimony payment of $1,300 to her in 26,000 nickels!). His involvement in The Beatles' *Abbey Road* album (he knocked incomplete tapes into shape, adding strings to *The Long And Winding Road*, much to the annoyance of Paul McCartney) caused controversy, but he continued to work with both John Lennon and George Harrison thereafter. He formed Warner-Spector with Warner Brothers that produced albums for Cher and Nilsson, but this was soon discarded, as was a link with Polydor, UK and the creation of Phil Spector International. By the mid-1980s he had become something of a recluse. He was inducted into the Rock & Roll Hall of Fame in 1989. He was charged with first degree murder on 3/2/2003 after a dead woman was found at his home in California.

| | | | | | |
|---|---|---|---|---|---|
| 23/12/1972 | ....21 | ....3 | | PHIL SPECTOR'S CHRISTMAS ALBUM | Apple SAPCOR 24 |
| 15/10/1977 | ....21 | ....10 | ....○ | PHIL SPECTOR'S ECHOES OF THE 60S | Phil Spector International 2307 013 |
| 25/12/1982 | ....96 | ....2 | | PHIL SPECTOR'S CHRISTMAS ALBUM | Phil Spector International 2307 005 |
| 10/12/1983 | ....19 | ....8 | ....● | PHIL SPECTOR'S GREATEST HITS/PHIL SPECTOR'S CHRISTMAS ALBUM | Impression PSLP 1/2 |
| 12/12/1987 | ....69 | ....6 | ....● | PHIL SPECTOR'S CHRISTMAS ALBUM | Chrysalis CDL 1625 |

**SPEEDWAY** UK rock group formed in Scotland by Jill Jackson (guitar/vocals), Dan Sells (guitar), Graeme Smillie (bass) and Jim Duguid (drums).

| | | | | | |
|---|---|---|---|---|---|
| 06/03/2004 | ....42 | ....1 | | SAVE YOURSELF | Innocent CDSIN12 |

**SPEEDY J** Dutch producer (born Jochem Paap, 1969, Rotterdam) who began his career as a DJ in the early 1980s and first recorded for the Plus 8 label. He has also recorded as Public Energy and Country And Western.

| | | | | | |
|---|---|---|---|---|---|
| 10/07/1993 | ....68 | ....1 | | GINGER | Warp WARPCD 14 |

**JON SPENCER BLUES EXPLOSION** US group assembled by producer Jon Spencer and featuring contributions from Rob K (vocals), Hollis Queens (vocals), Kurt Hoffman (saxophone) and Doug Easley (keyboards).

| | | | | | |
|---|---|---|---|---|---|
| 12/10/1996 | ....50 | ....1 | | NOW I GOT WORRY | Mute CDSTUMM 132 |
| 31/10/1998 | ....72 | ....1 | | ACME | Mute CDSTUMM 154 |

○ Silver disc ● Gold disc ❂ Platinum disc (additional platinum units are indicated by a figure following the symbol) ❶⁹ Number of weeks album topped the UK chart

**SPICE GIRLS** UK vocal group formed in June 1994 by Michelle Stephenson, Geraldine Halliwell (aka Geri/Ginger Spice, born 6/8/1972, Watford), Melanie Brown (aka Mel B/Scary Spice, born 29/5/1973, Leeds), Victoria Adams (aka Posh Spice, born 7/4/1974, Essex) and Melanie Chisholm (aka Mel C/Sporty Spice, born 12/1/1974, Liverpool) as Touch, later changing their name to The Spice Girls. Stephenson left after a month to return to university and was replaced by Emma Bunton (aka Baby Spice, born 21/1/1976, London). They were the first act to top the charts with their first six singles, repeating their success in the USA, topping the singles chart with *Wannabe* and then becoming the first female act in the UK to top the album charts. They appeared in the film *Spiceworld: The Movie* in 1997. They won four BRIT Awards: Best Single for *Wannabe* and Best Video for *Say You'll Be There*, both in 1997, a Special Achievement Award in 1998, and a Lifetime Achievement Award in 2000. They also won three MTV Europe Music Awards: Best Group in 1997 and 1998 and Best Pop Act in 1998. They took part in the England United recording for the 1998 World Cup Finals. Geri announced she was leaving the group for a solo career on 31/5/1998, although both Mel B (with Missy Misdemeanor Elliott) and Mel C (with Bryan Adams) preceded her into the charts. Victoria married Manchester United and England football star David Beckham in July 1999. Emma Bunton also recorded with Tin Tin Out whilst Victoria recorded with True Steppers and Dane Bowers. The group had a packet of crisps named after them by Walker's (the company sold over 16 million bags in its first year). The group also took part in the *It's Only Rock 'N' Roll* project for the Children's Promise charity. In June 2000 the girls were ordered to pay £45,000 to motor scooter company Aprilia. The order related to an earlier sponsorship deal the group signed in May 1998 where hundreds of 'Sonic Spice' scooters were produced featuring the likeness of all five girls. Three weeks after the deal was signed, Geri Halliwell left for a solo career. A subsequent appeal failed and the girls were left with a legal bill of nearly £1 million as a result.

| | | | | | |
|---|---|---|---|---|---|
| 16/11/1996 | ❶¹⁵ | 72 | ⊙¹⁰ | **SPICE** ▲⁵ ◇⁸ | Virgin CDV 2812 |
| 15/11/1997 | ❶³ | 55 | ⊙⁵ | **SPICEWORLD** ◇⁵ | Virgin CDV 2850 |
| 18/11/2000 | 2 | 8 | ⊙ | **FOREVER** | Virgin CDVX 2928 |

**SPIDER** US rock group formed in New York by Amanda Blue (vocals), Keith Lenthin (guitar), Holly Knight (keyboards), Jimmy Lowell (bass) and Anton Fig (drums). Knight later joined Device and subsequently went solo.

| | | | | | |
|---|---|---|---|---|---|
| 23/10/1982 | 75 | 1 | | ROCK 'N' ROLL GYPSIES | RCA RCALP 3101 |
| 07/04/1984 | 96 | 1 | | ROUGH JUSTICE | A&M AMLX 68563 |

**SPIN DOCTORS** US rock group formed in New York in 1987 by Chris Barron (born 5/2/1968, Hawaii, vocals), Eric Schenkman (born 12/12/1963, Massachusetts, guitar), Mark White (born 7/7/1962, New York, bass) and Aaron Comes (born 24/4/1968, Arizona, drums). They signed with Epic in 1990. Schenkman left in 1994, replaced by Anthony Krizan (born 25/8/1965, Plainfield, NJ). White left in 1998.

| | | | | | |
|---|---|---|---|---|---|
| 20/03/1993 | 2 | 48 | ⊙ | **POCKET FULL OF KRYPTONITE** | Epic 4682502 |
| 09/07/1994 | 3 | 9 | | **TURN IT UPSIDE DOWN** | Epic 4768862 |

**SPINAL TAP** UK/US rock group 'officially' formed in 1964 by Derek Smalls (played by Harry Shearer, born 23/12/1943, bass), David St Hubbins (played by Michael McKean, born 17/10/1947, vocals) and Nigel Tufnell (played by Christopher Guest, born 5/2/1948, guitar) as a beat combo, changing their name and musical style in 1967. During their career they had 22 names, never had a permanent drummer and charted only one album. In reality, the 'group' was a satire on heavy metal that was first aired on TV in the late 1970s and the subject of the 1984 film *This Is Spinal Tap*. They provided the voices of the Gorgons in the 1998 film *Small Soldiers*.

| | | | | | |
|---|---|---|---|---|---|
| 11/04/1992 | 51 | 2 | | BREAK LIKE THE WIND | MCA MCAD 10514 |

**SPINNERS** UK folk group formed in 1958 by Tony Davis (born 24/8/1930, Blackburn, banjo/guitar), Mick Groves (born 29/9/1936, Salford, guitar), Hughie Jones (born 21/7/1936, Liverpool, guitar/banjo) and Cliff Hall (born 11/9/1925, Cuba, guitar/harmonica), with 'Count' John McCormick (double bass) joining them in concert. The group disbanded in 1988.

| | | | | | |
|---|---|---|---|---|---|
| 05/09/1970 | 40 | 5 | | THE SPINNERS ARE IN TOWN | Fontana 6309 014 |
| 07/08/1971 | 14 | 12 | | SPINNERS LIVE PERFORMANCE | Contour 6870 502 |
| 13/11/1971 | 20 | 3 | | THE SWINGING CITY | Philips 6382 002 |
| 08/04/1972 | 33 | 4 | | LOVE IS TEASING | Columbia SCX 6493 |

**SPIRIT** US rock group formed in Los Angeles, CA by Jay Ferguson (born 10/5/1947, Burbank, CA, vocals), Randy California (born Randy Wolfe, 20/2/1951, Los Angeles, guitar), John Locke (born 25/9/1943, Los Angeles, keyboards), Mark Andes (born 19/2/1948, Philadelphia, PA, bass) and Ed 'Mr Skin' Cassidy (born 4/5/1931, Chicago, IL, drums) as Spirits Rebellious. Ferguson and Andes left in 1971 to form Jo Jo Gunne and were replaced by Al Staehely and Christian Staehely. California left at around the same time, but returned in 1976 (after a failed suicide attempt in which he jumped off a bridge into the River Thames) to team up with Cassidy and Larry Knight (bass) and in 1984 the original five members reunited. California was believed drowned after he disappeared whilst swimming near Hawaii with his son on 2/1/1997, with the authorities calling off the search owing to bad weather. His body has never been found.

| | | | | | |
|---|---|---|---|---|---|
| 18/04/1981 | 40 | 2 | | POTATO LAND | Beggars Banquet BEGA 23 |

**SPIRITUALIZED** UK group formed in 1990 by Jason Pierce (born 19/11/1965, Rugby, guitar/vocals), Mark Refoy (guitar), Willie Carruthers (bass) and John Mattock (drums), later adding Kate Radley (born 19/2/1965, piano/vocals). Pierce was previously in Spacemen 3, forming Spiritualized after falling out with the other spaceman, Sonic Boom. By 1995 their name had been extended to Spiritualized Electric Mainline and the group trimmed down to Jason Pierce, Kate Radley and Sean Cook (born 16/4/1969, bass/harmonica), although a year later the name shortened again to Spiritualized. They later launched their own Spaceman label.

| | | | | | |
|---|---|---|---|---|---|
| 11/04/1992 | 27 | 2 | | LAZER GUIDED MELODIES | Dedicated DEDCD 004 |
| 18/02/1995 | 20 | 2 | | PURE PHASE **SPIRITUALIZED ELECTRIC MAINLINE** | Dedicated DEDCD 017S |
| 28/06/1997 | 4 | 15 | ● | **LADIES & GENTLEMEN WE ARE FLOATING IN SPACE** | Dedicated DEDCD 034 |
| 07/11/1998 | 38 | 1 | | LIVE AT THE ROYAL ALBERT HALL | Deconstruction 74321622852 |
| 29/09/2001 | 3 | 4 | | **LET IT COME DOWN** | Spaceman OPM 001CD |
| 20/09/2003 | 25 | 2 | | AMAZING GRACE | Spaceman/Sanctuary SANCD 214X |

**SPITTING IMAGE** UK TV puppets created by Peter Fluck and Roger Law that lampooned political and public figures.

| | DATE | POS | WKS | BPI | ALBUM TITLE | LABEL & NUMBER |
|---|---|---|---|---|---|---|
| | 18/10/1986 | 55 | 3 | | SPIT IN YOUR EAR | Virgin V 2403 |

**SPLIT ENZ** New Zealand rock group formed in Auckland in 1972 by Tim Finn (born 25/6/1952, Te Awamuta, piano/vocals), Phil Judd (guitar/mandolin/vocals), Mike Chunn (born 8/6/1952, Auckland, bass/keyboards), Geoff Chunn (drums), Rob Gillies (saxophone), Miles Golding (violin) and Michael Howard (flute) as Split Ends. Moved to Australia in 1975 and name-changed to Split Enz, relocating to the UK in 1976. Later members included Tim's brother Neil (born 27/5/1958, Te Awamuta, guitar/vocals), Wally Wilkinson, Nigel Criggs (born 18/8/1949, bass), Malcolm Green (born 25/1/1953, drums), Paul Crowther (born 2/10/1949, Dunedin, drums) and Noel Crombie. Neil Finn later formed Crowded House, the brothers formed Finn and both subsequently recorded solo.

| 30/08/1980 | 42 | 8 | | TRUE COLOURS | A&M AMLH 64822 |
| 08/05/1982 | 71 | 1 | | TIME AND TIDE | A&M AMLH 64894 |

**SPOOKS** US hip hop group formed in 1995 by MCs Mr Booka-T aka Bookaso (born Booker T Tucker), Water Water aka Aqua Dinero, Hypno, JD aka Vengeance (born Joseph Davis) and singer Ming-Xia with the addition of a live band.

| 17/02/2001 | 25 | 12 | ◯ | S.I.O.S.O.S. VOLUME 1 | Epic 4982612 |

**SPOTNICKS** Swedish instrumental group formed in 1957 by Bo Winberg (born 27/3/1939, Gothenburg), Bob Lander (born 11/3/1942, Bo Starander), Bjorn Thelin (born 11/6/1942) and Ole Johannsson as The Frazers. They name-changed to The Spotnicks in 1961 and wore spacesuits on stage.

| 09/02/1963 | 20 | 1 | | OUT-A-SPACE | Oriole PS 40036 |

A Girl Called Dusty

**DUSTY SPRINGFIELD** UK singer (born Mary Isabel Catherine Bernadette O'Brien, 16/4/1939, Hampstead, London); she was a member of vocal trio the Lana Sisters before joining her brother Dion O'Brien and Tim Field in the Springfields in 1960. The group disbanded in 1963 and Dusty signed with Philips as a solo artist. She was the first act to appear on *Top of the Pops* on 1/1/1964, when she performed her debut hit *I Only Want To Be With You*. She relocated to the USA in 1972 and became an in-demand session singer. She was awarded the OBE in the 1999 New Year's Honours List; the presentation took place while Dusty was lying in hospital shortly before her death from breast cancer on 2/3/1999. She was inducted into the Rock & Roll Hall of Fame in 1999 (the ceremony was held eleven days after she died).

| 25/04/1964 | 6 | 23 | | A GIRL CALLED DUSTY | Philips BL 7594 |
| 23/10/1965 | 6 | 12 | | EVERYTHING'S COMING UP DUSTY | Philips RBL 1002 |
| 22/10/1966 | 2 | 36 | | GOLDEN HITS | Philips BL 7737 |
| 11/11/1967 | 40 | 1 | | WHERE AM I GOING? | Philips SBL 7820 |
| 21/12/1968 | 30 | 6 | | DUSTY… DEFINITELY | Philips SBL 7864 |
| 02/05/1970 | 35 | 2 | | FROM DUSTY… WITH LOVE | Philips SBL 7927 |
| 04/03/1978 | 41 | 2 | | IT BEGINS AGAIN | Mercury 9109 607 |
| 30/01/1988 | 14 | 10 | ● | DUSTY – THE SILVER COLLECTION | Phonogram DUSTV 1 |
| 07/07/1990 | 18 | 6 | ◯ | REPUTATION | Parlophone PCSD 111 |
| 14/05/1994 | 5 | 11 | ● | GOIN' BACK – THE VERY BEST OF DUSTY SPRINGFIELD 1962–1994 | Philips 8487892 |
| 08/07/1995 | 43 | 1 | | A VERY FINE LOVE | Columbia 4785082 |
| 07/11/1998 | 19 | 24 | ● | THE BEST OF DUSTY SPRINGFIELD | Mercury/Polygram TV 5383452 |
| 13/03/2004 | 25 | 4 | ◯ | THE LOOK OF LOVE | Universal TV 9816495 |

**RICK SPRINGFIELD** Australian singer (born 23/8/1949, Sydney) who was in Zoot before going solo in 1972. He later became a successful actor. He won the 1981 Grammy Award for Best Rock Vocal Performance for *Jessie's Girl*.

| 11/02/1984 | 41 | 4 | | LIVING IN OZ | RCA PL 84660 |
| 25/05/1985 | 68 | 3 | | TAO | RCA PL 85370 |
| 26/03/1988 | 80 | 1 | | ROCK OF LIFE | RCA PL 86620 |

BRUCE SPRINGSTEEN NEBRASKA

**BRUCE SPRINGSTEEN** US singer/guitarist (born Frederick Joseph Springsteen, 23/9/1949, Freehold, NJ); he joined the Castiles in 1965 and then Earth in 1967. He formed Child in 1969, who name-changed to Steel Mills shortly after, and assembled his first band in 1971. He signed with producers/managers Mike Appel and Jim Cretecos in 1972 shortly before linking with CBS and re-forming his band with David Sancious (keyboards), Garry Tallent (bass), Vini Lopez (drums), Clarence Clemons (saxophone) and Danny Federici (keyboards). They were renamed the E Street Band in 1973. Legal wrangles with Appel prevented the release of any new albums after *Born To Run* in 1975 to 1978, by which time Jon Landau had taken over as manager and co-producer. A motorcycle accident in April 1979 forced a three-month break and delayed his new album. He split with the E Street Band in 1989. He married actress Juliane Phillips in 1985, divorced in 1989 and then married former backing singer Patti Sciaffa in 1991. Bruce was named Best International Male at the 1986 BRIT Awards. He has won twelve Grammy Awards including: Best Recording for Children in 1982 with various others for *In Harmony 2*; Best; Rock Vocal Performance in 1984 for *Dancing In The Dark*; Best Rock Vocal Performance in 1997 for *Tunnel Of Love*; Song of the Year, Best Rock Song, Best Rock Vocal Performance and Best Song Written Specifically for a Motion Picture in 1994 for *Streets Of Philadelphia*; Best Contemporary Folk Performance in 1996 for *The Ghost Of Tom Joad*; Best Male Rock Vocal Performance and Best Rock Song for *The Rising* in 2002; and Best Rock Performance by a Duo or Group with Vocal with Warren Zevon for *Disorder In The House* in 2003. He was inducted into the Rock & Roll Hall of Fame in 1999. In 2000 he wrote and recorded *American Skin (41 Shots),* a song that criticised the New York police department over the shooting and killing of Amadiu Diallo. The African immigrant was hit by 19 of the 41 bullets fired at him by the police who mistook his wallet for a gun. Four policemen were later cleared of his murder. Following the song's release, the New York police department called for a boycott of Springsteen's concerts in the city.

◯ Silver disc  ● Gold disc  ✪ Platinum disc (additional platinum units are indicated by a figure following the symbol)  ❶⁹ Number of weeks album topped the UK chart

| 01/11/1975 | 17 | 50 | ✪ | BORN TO RUN | CBS 69170 |
| 17/06/1978 | 16 | 40 | ● | DARKNESS ON THE EDGE OF TOWN | CBS 86061 |
| 25/10/1980 | 2 | 88 | ● | THE RIVER ▲4 | CBS 88510 |
| 02/10/1982 | 3 | 19 | ○ | NEBRASKA | CBS 25100 |
| 16/06/1984 | ❶5 | 129 | ✪3 | BORN IN THE U.S.A. ▲7 ◆15 | CBS 86304 |
| 15/06/1985 | 41 | 10 | ○ | GREETINGS FROM ASBURY PARK | CBS 32210 |
| 15/06/1985 | 33 | 12 | ○ | THE WILD, THE INNOCENT AND THE E. STREET SHUFFLE | CBS 32363 |
| 22/11/1986 | 4 | 9 | ● | LIVE/1975–1985 ▲7 ◆13 BRUCE SPRINGSTEEN AND THE E. STREET BAND | CBS 4502271 |
| 17/10/1987 | ❶1 | 33 | ✪ | TUNNEL OF LOVE ▲1 | CBS 4602701 |
| 04/04/1992 | ❶1 | 17 | ● | HUMAN TOUCH | Columbia 4714232 |
| 04/04/1992 | 2 | 11 | ● | LUCKY TOWN | Columbia 4714242 |
| 24/04/1993 | 4 | 7 | ● | IN CONCERT – MTV UNPLUGGED | Columbia 4738602 |
| 11/03/1995 | ❶2 | 44 | ✪2 | GREATEST HITS ◇5 ▲2 | Columbia 4785552 |
| 25/11/1995 | 16 | 14 | ● | THE GHOST OF TOM JOAD ◇ | Columbia 4816502 |
| 21/11/1998 | 50 | 1 | | TRACKS | Columbia 4926052 |
| 24/04/1999 | 23 | 7 | | 18 TRACKS | Columbia 4942002 |
| 14/04/2001 | 12 | 6 | ○ | LIVE IN NEW YORK CITY BRUCE SPRINGSTEEN AND THE E. STREET BAND | Columbia 5000002 |
| 10/08/2002 | ❶1 | 16 | ● | THE RISING ◇ ▲2 2002 Grammy Award for Best Rock Album | Columbia 5080009 |
| 22/11/2003 | 28 | 2 | | THE ESSENTIAL Triple CD containing 42 songs. The album below is a double CD version containing 30 songs | Columbia 5137009 |
| 22/11/2003 | 32 | 7 | | THE ESSENTIAL | Columbia 5137002 |

**(SPUNGE)** UK group formed in 1994 by Alex Copeland (vocals), Damon Robins (guitar), Paul Gurney (guitar), Chris Murphy (bass) and Jeremy King (drums).

| 07/09/2002 | 48 | 1 | | THE STORY SO FAR | B Unique 0927487452 |

**SPYRO GYRA** US jazz-fusion group formed in Buffalo, NY in 1975 by Jay Beckenstein (born 14/5/1951, saxophone), Jeremy Wall (keyboards), Jim Kurzdorfer (bass), Tom Schuman (piano), Chet Catallo (guitar), Ed Konikoff (drums) and Richard Calandra (percussion). Catallo was later replaced by Jay Azzolina.

| 14/07/1979 | 11 | 16 | ○ | MORNING DANCE | Infinity INS 2003 |
| 23/02/1980 | 31 | 6 | | CATCHING THE SUN | MCA MCG 4009 |

**SQUEEZE** UK rock group formed in London in 1974 by Chris Difford (born 4/11/1954, London, guitar/vocals), Glenn Tilbrook (born 31/8/1957, London, guitar/vocals), Jools Holland (born Julian Holland, 24/1/1955, London, keyboards) and Paul Gunn (drums). Gunn left the same year and was replaced by Gilson Lavis (born 27/6/1951, Bedford), with bass player Harry Kakoulli joining at the same time. Kakoulli left in 1980 and was replaced by John Bentley (born 16/4/1951, London). Holland also left in 1980 and was replaced by Paul Carrack (born 22/4/1951, Sheffield). Carrack left in 1981 and was replaced by Don Snow (born 13/1/1957, Kenya). They split in 1982 and re-formed in 1985. Holland hosted the 1980s' TV series *The Tube* and subsequently *Later With Jools Holland*. He was awarded an OBE in the Queen's 2003 Birthday Honours List.

| 28/04/1979 | 45 | 11 | ○ | COOL FOR CATS | A&M AMLH 68503 |
| 16/02/1980 | 32 | 15 | | ARGY BARGY | A&M AMLH 64802 |
| 23/05/1981 | 19 | 26 | ○ | EAST SIDE STORY | A&M AMLH 64854 |
| 15/05/1982 | 20 | 7 | | SWEETS FROM A STRANGER | A&M AMLH 64899 |
| 06/11/1982 | 3 | 29 | ✪ | SINGLES – 45'S AND UNDER | A&M AMLH 68552 |
| 07/09/1985 | 31 | 7 | | COSI FAN TUTTI FRUTTI | A&M AMA 5085 |
| 19/09/1987 | 14 | 8 | ○ | BABYLON AND ON | A&M AMA 5161 |
| 23/09/1989 | 58 | 1 | | FRANK | A&M AMA 5278 |
| 07/04/1990 | 50 | 1 | | A ROUND AND A BOUT | I.R.S. DFCLP 1 |
| 07/09/1991 | 41 | 1 | | PLAY | Reprise WX 428 |
| 23/05/1992 | 6 | 13 | ● | GREATEST HITS | A&M 3971812 |
| 25/09/1993 | 26 | 4 | | SOME FANTASTIC PLACE | A&M 5401402 |
| 25/11/1995 | 50 | 1 | | RIDICULOUS | A&M 5404402 |
| 22/06/2002 | 8 | 6 | ● | THE BIG SQUEEZE – THE VERY BEST OF | Universal TV 4932532 |

**CHRIS SQUIRE** UK singer/bass guitarist (born 4/3/1948, London) who was a founder member of Yes in 1968 with Jon Anderson, Peter Banks, Bill Bruford and Tony Kaye. He worked outside the group with musicians such as Rick Wakeman, and launched a parallel solo career in 1975. Yes disbanded in 1981 with Squire joining Alan White, Trevor Rabin and Tony Kaye to form Cinema, although singer Rabin was replaced by Jon Anderson. As this was effectively a re-formed Yes, the curtain came down on Cinema and Yes was adopted as the group's name. By 1988 internal wrangles split the group apart. Squire lay claims to the name Yes – Anderson, Bruford, Wakeman and Howe resisted the temptation to call themselves No and instead recorded under their own names.

| 06/12/1975 | 25 | 7 | ○ | FISH OUT OF WATER | Atlantic K 50203 |

**JOHN SQUIRE** UK singer/guitarist (born 24/11/1962, Manchester); he was a member of Stone Roses before leaving to form The Seahorses. He disbanded the group after one album and went solo.

| 28/09/2002 | 17 | 2 | | TIME CHANGES EVERYTHING | North Country NCCDS 001 |

▲9 Number of weeks album topped the US chart   ◆12 RIAA Diamond Awards   ◇3 IFPI Platinum Europe Awards

**STAIND** US rock group formed in 1993 by Aaron Lewis (vocals), Mike Mushok (guitar) and Jon Wysocki (drums). They financed their own debut release, the cover of which nearly got them thrown off a Limp Bizkit tour because of the Satanic images. Limp Bizkit leader Fred Durst later relented and helped get them a deal with Flip Records.

| | | | | | |
|---|---|---|---|---|---|
| 01/09/2001 | ❶¹ | 26 | ✪ | **BREAK THE CYCLE** ▲³ | Elektra 7559626642 |
| 31/05/2003 | 16 | 3 | | **14 SHADES OF GREY** ▲¹ | Elektra 7559628822 |

**STANDS** UK group from Liverpool: Howie Payne (guitar/vocals), Luke Thomson (guitar), Dean Ravera (bass) and Steve Pilgrim (drums).

| | | | | |
|---|---|---|---|---|
| 06/03/2004 | 28 | 2 | ALL YEARS LEAVING | Echo ECHCD50 |

**LISA STANSFIELD** UK singer (born 11/4/1966, Rochdale); she formed Blue Zone in 1984 with Andy Morris (trumpet) and Ian Devaney (keyboards/trombone). They were signed by Rocking Horse in 1986 and released one album. Stansfield was invited to provide the lead vocals to Coldcut's third single in 1989 and its success gained her a solo deal with Arista via Big Life. She was named Best British Newcomer at the 1990 BRIT Awards and then Best British Female in 1991 and 1992.

| | | | | | |
|---|---|---|---|---|---|
| 02/12/1989 | 2 | 31 | ✪³ | **AFFECTION** | Arista 210379 |
| 23/11/1991 | 3 | 51 | ✪² | **REAL LOVE** | Arista 212300 |
| 20/11/1993 | 6 | 14 | ● | **SO NATURAL** | Arista 74321172312 |
| 05/04/1997 | 2 | 18 | | **LISA STANSFIELD** | Arista 74321458512 |
| 07/07/2001 | 38 | 2 | | **FACE UP** | Arista 74321863462 |
| 15/02/2003 | 3 | 9 | | **BIOGRAPHY – THE GREATEST HITS** | Arista 82876502222 |

**ALVIN STARDUST** UK singer (born Bernard William Jewry, 27/9/1942, London); he was road manager and occasional singer for Johnny Theakston & the Fentones when they made an audition tape as Shane Fenton & The Fentones. Theakston died soon after, Jewry assuming the Fenton name, signing with Parlophone in 1961. He quit recording in 1964, returning in 1973 as Alvin Stardust.

| | | | | | |
|---|---|---|---|---|---|
| 16/03/1974 | 4 | 12 | ● | **THE UNTOUCHABLE** | Magnet MAG 5001 |
| 21/12/1974 | 37 | 3 | ○ | ALVIN STARDUST | Magnet MAG 5004 |
| 04/10/1975 | 52 | 2 | | ROCK WITH ALVIN | Magnet MAG 5007 |

**ED STARINK** US synthesizer player who worked with The Chelsea Strings, London Starlight Orchestra and Jean Michel Jarre, and also produced albums for Demis Roussos.

| | | | | |
|---|---|---|---|---|
| 27/10/1990 | 22 | 5 | SYNTHESIZER GREATEST | Arcade ARC 938101 |
| 09/01/1993 | 29 | 6 | SYNTHESIZER GOLD | Arcade ARC 3100012 |

**FREDDIE STARR** UK comedian/singer (born Fred Smith, 9/1/1944, Liverpool); he began as a singer, making his first single for Decca in 1963. Nationally known via the TV series *Who Do You Do?* and then his own series, he later achieved notoriety for supposedly eating a fan's pet, prompting the classic *Sun* headline 'Freddie Starr Ate My Hamster'!

| | | | | | |
|---|---|---|---|---|---|
| 18/11/1989 | 10 | 9 | ● | **AFTER THE LAUGHTER** | Dover ADD 10 |
| 17/11/1990 | 33 | 7 | | THE WANDERER | Dover ADD 17 |

**KAY STARR** US singer (born Katherine LaVerne Starks, 21/7/1922, Dougherty, OK). She joined Joe Venuti's orchestra in 1937 and later Glenn Miller before going solo in 1945. Films included *Make Believe Ballroom* and *When You're Smiling*. She has a star on the Hollywood Walk of Fame.

| | | | | |
|---|---|---|---|---|
| 26/03/1960 | 16 | 1 | MOVIN' | Capitol 1254 |

**RINGO STARR** UK singer/drummer (born Richard Starkey, 7/7/1940, Liverpool); he was the drummer with Rory Storm & The Hurricanes until 1962 when he replaced Pete Best in The Beatles. He made his first solo album in 1970 and appeared in a number of films, including *Candy* (filmed in 1967, released in 1969), *Born To Boogie* and *That'll Be The Day*. He married Maureen Cox, and then actress Barbara Bach in 1981. He provided the voiceover to the children's TV series *Thomas The Tank Engine* and launched the Ring'O and Able record labels. He appeared in an episode of *The Simpsons,* replying to a fan letter from Marge twenty years after it was sent!

| | | | | | |
|---|---|---|---|---|---|
| 18/04/1970 | 7 | 6 | | **SENTIMENTAL JOURNEY** | Apple PCS 7101 |
| 08/12/1973 | 7 | 20 | ● | **RINGO** | Apple PCTC 252 |
| 07/12/1974 | 30 | 2 | ○ | GOODNIGHT VIENNA | Apple PMC 7168 |

**STARSAILOR** UK rock group formed in Chorley in 2000 by James Walsh (guitar/vocals), James Stelfox (bass), Barry Westhead (keyboards) and Ben Byrne (drums). The group took their name from a 1971 album by folk singer Tim Buckley.

| | | | | | |
|---|---|---|---|---|---|
| 20/10/2001 | 2 | 41 | ✪ | **LOVE IS HERE** | Chrysalis 5353502 |
| 27/09/2003 | 2 | 13 | ● | **SILENCE IS EASY** | EMI 5900072 |

**STARSHIP** – see JEFFERSON AIRPLANE

**STARSOUND** Dutch studio project assembled by ex-Golden Earring and producer Jaap Eggermont. The concept originally appeared on a US bootleg 12-inch called *Bits & Pieces* – sixteen minutes of segued hits from the 1960s, including some from The

Beatles. Since copyright matters ruled it out officially, Eggermont assembled studio musicians and singers to recreate the record (with Bas Muys, Okkie Huysdens and Hans Vermoulen singing the John Lennon, Paul McCartney and George Harrison vocals respectively).

| 16/05/1981 | ❶⁵ | 21 | ● | STARS ON 45 | CBS 86132 |
|---|---|---|---|---|---|
| 19/09/1981 | 18 | 6 | ● | STARS ON 45 VOLUME 2 | CBS 85181 |
| 03/04/1982 | 94 | 1 | | STARS MEDLEY | CBS 85651 |

## STARTRAX UK studio group assembled by Bruce Baxter.

| 01/08/1981 | 26 | 7 | | STARTRAX CLUB DISCO | Picksy KSYA 1001 |
|---|---|---|---|---|---|

## STATE OF THE HEART UK studio group.

| 16/03/1996 | 18 | 7 | ○ | PURE SAX | Virgin VTCD 78 |
|---|---|---|---|---|---|
| 12/10/1996 | 62 | 2 | | SAX AT THE MOVIES | Virgin VTCD 98 |

## STATIC-X US group formed by Wayne Static (guitar/vocals), Koicki Fukada (guitar), Tony Campos (bass) and Ken Jay (drums). They signed with Warner Brothers in 1998. Fukada left the group in 1999 and was replaced by Tripp Elsen.

| 23/06/2001 | 56 | 2 | | MACHINE | Warner Brothers 9362479482 |
|---|---|---|---|---|---|

## CANDI STATON US R&B singer (born Canzetta Maria Staton, 13/3/1943, Hanceville, AL); she was discovered by Bishop ML Jewell who formed the Jewell Gospel Trio with Candi, her sister Maggie and Naomi Harrison. Candi left at seventeen when she got married, but returned to music four children later, discovered a second time by Clarence Carter (who later became her second husband). She first recorded solo for Fame in 1969 and switched to Warner's in 1974. She later formed her own gospel label Beracah Records.

| 24/07/1976 | 34 | 3 | | YOUNG HEARTS RUN FREE | Warner Brothers K 56259 |
|---|---|---|---|---|---|

## STATUS QUO UK rock group formed in Beckenham in 1962 by Alan Lancaster (born 7/2/1949, Peckham, London, bass), Francis Rossi (born 29/4/1949, London, guitar/vocals), John Coghlan (born 19/9/1946, Dulwich, London, drums) and Jess Jaworski (organ) as the Spectres. Jaworski left in 1965 and was replaced by Roy Lynes (born 25/11/1943, Redhill). They signed to Pye via Piccadilly in 1966 (still as the Spectres), after three singles changing their name to Traffic Jam. After one single they changed to Status Quo, signing direct to Pye. Rick Parfitt (born Richard Harrison, 12/10/1948, Woking, guitar/vocals) joined at the same time. They switched to Vertigo in 1972. Lancaster left in 1984. They gained the Outstanding Contribution Award at the 1991 BRIT Awards, and also took part in the *It's Only Rock 'N' Roll* project for the Children's Promise charity. Rossi and Parfitt penned Manchester United's number one hit *Come On You Reds*. In 1991 the group entered the *Guinness Book Of Records* after playing four venues in one day (Sheffield International Centre, Glasgow Scottish Exhibition & Conference Centre, Birmingham National Exhibition Centre and Wembley Arena) as part of a 'Rock 'Til You Drop' tour to commemorate their 25th anniversary.

| 20/01/1973 | 5 | 37 | | PILEDRIVER | Vertigo 6360 082 |
|---|---|---|---|---|---|
| 09/06/1973 | 32 | 7 | ○ | THE BEST OF STATUS QUO | Pye NSPL 18402 |
| 06/10/1973 | ❶¹ | 28 | ● | HELLO | Vertigo 6360 098 |
| 18/05/1974 | 2 | 16 | ● | QUO | Vertigo 9102 001 |
| 01/03/1975 | ❶² | 27 | ● | ON THE LEVEL | Vertigo 9102 002 |
| 08/03/1975 | 20 | 6 | ○ | DOWN THE DUSTPIPE | Pye Golden Hour CH 604 |
| 20/03/1976 | ❶³ | 30 | ● | BLUE FOR YOU | Vertigo 9102 006 |
| 12/03/1977 | 3 | 14 | ● | STATUS QUO – LIVE | Vertigo 6641 580 |
| 26/11/1977 | 5 | 15 | ● | ROCKIN' ALL OVER THE WORLD | Vertigo 9102 014 |
| 11/11/1978 | 3 | 14 | ● | IF YOU CAN'T STAND THE HEAT | Vertigo 9102 027 |
| 20/10/1979 | 3 | 14 | ● | WHATEVER YOU WANT | Vertigo 9102 037 |
| 22/03/1980 | 3 | 48 | ✪ | 12 GOLD BARS | Vertigo QUO TV 1 |
| 25/10/1980 | 4 | 18 | ● | JUST SUPPOSIN' | Vertigo 6302 057 |
| 28/03/1981 | 2 | 13 | ● | NEVER TOO LATE | Vertigo 6302 104 |
| 10/10/1981 | 74 | 1 | | FRESH QUOTA | PRT DOW 2 |
| 24/04/1982 | ❶¹ | 20 | ● | 1982 | Vertigo 6302 169 |
| 13/11/1982 | 4 | 18 | ● | FROM THE MAKERS OF... | Vertigo PROLP 1 |
| 03/12/1983 | 9 | 22 | ● | BACK TO BACK | Vertigo VERH 10 |
| 04/08/1984 | 83 | 3 | | STATUS QUO LIVE AT THE N.E.C. | Vertigo 8189 471 |
| 01/12/1984 | 12 | 18 | ● | 12 GOLD BARS VOLUME TWO – (AND ONE) | Vertigo QUO TV 2 |
| 06/09/1986 | 7 | 23 | ● | IN THE ARMY NOW | Vertigo VERH 36 |
| 18/06/1988 | 12 | 5 | ● | AIN'T COMPLAINING | Vertigo VERH 58 |
| 02/12/1989 | 49 | 2 | ○ | PERFECT REMEDY | Vertigo 8420981 |
| 20/10/1990 | 2 | 25 | ✪² | ROCKING ALL OVER THE YEARS | Vertigo 8467971 |
| 05/10/1991 | 10 | 7 | | ROCK 'TIL YOU DROP | Vertigo 5103411 |
| 14/11/1992 | 37 | 1 | | LIVE ALIVE QUO | Polydor 5173672 |
| 03/09/1994 | 13 | 3 | | THIRSTY WORK | Polydor 5236072 |
| 17/02/1996 | 2 | 11 | ● | DON'T STOP – THE 30TH ANNIVERSARY ALBUM | Polygram TV 5310352 |
| 25/10/1997 | 13 | 6 | ○ | WHATEVER YOU WANT – THE VERY BEST OF STATUS QUO | Mercury TV 5535072 |
| 10/04/1999 | 26 | 2 | | UNDER THE INFLUENCE | Eagle EAGCD 076 |
| 29/04/2000 | 19 | 5 | | FAMOUS IN THE LAST CENTURY | Universal TV 1578142 |
| 05/10/2002 | 15 | 3 | ○ | HEAVY TRAFFIC | Universal TV 0187902 |
| 29/11/2003 | 44 | 2 | | RIFFS | Universal TV 9813909 |

### STEEL PULSE
UK reggae group formed in Birmingham in 1976 by David Hinds (born 15/6/1956, Birmingham, guitar/vocals), Basil Gabbidon (guitar/vocals) and Ronnie McQueen (bass), later adding Selwyn 'Bumbo' Brown (born 4/6/1958, London, keyboards), Steve 'Grizzly' Nesbitt (born 15/3/1948, Nevis, West Indies, drums), Fonso Martin (vocals) and Michael Riley (vocals). The group won the 1986 Grammy Award for Best Reggae Recording for *Babylon The Bandit*.

| | | | | |
|---|---|---|---|---|
| 05/08/1978 | 9 | 12 | | HANDSWORTH REVOLUTION | Island ILPS 9502 |
| 14/07/1979 | 42 | 6 | | TRIBUTE TO MARTYRS | Island ILPS 9568 |

### STEELEYE SPAN
UK folk-rock group formed in 1969 by ex-Fairport Convention Ashley Hutchings, Terry Woods, Gay Woods, Tim Hart and Maddy Prior. When they charted they were Tim Hart (born 9/1/1948, Lincoln, guitar/vocals), Maddy Prior (born 14/8/1947, Blackpool, vocals), Peter Knight (born 27/5/1947, London, vocals), Bob Johnson (born 17/3/1944, Enfield, London, guitar), Rick Kemp (born 15/11/1941, Little Hanford, Dorset, bass) and Nigel Pegrum (drums). Prior was made an MBE in the 2001 New Year's Honours list.

| | | | | |
|---|---|---|---|---|
| 10/04/1971 | 45 | 2 | | PLEASE TO SEE THE KING | B&C CAS 1029 |
| 14/10/1972 | 43 | 1 | | BELOW THE SALT | Chrysalis CHR 1008 |
| 28/04/1973 | 26 | 5 | ● | PARCEL OF ROGUES | Chrysalis CHR 1046 |
| 23/03/1974 | 13 | 13 | | NOW WE ARE SIX | Chrysalis CHR 1053 |
| 15/02/1975 | 21 | 4 | ○ | COMMONER'S CROWN | Chrysalis CHR 1071 |
| 25/10/1975 | 7 | 20 | ● | ALL AROUND MY HAT | Chrysalis CHR 1091 |
| 16/10/1976 | 41 | 3 | | ROCKET COTTAGE | Chrysalis CHR 1123 |

### TOMMY STEELE
UK singer (born Thomas Hicks, 17/12/1936, London); he was a member of skiffle group The Cavemen with Lionel Bart and Mike Pratt before being discovered singing in a coffee shop and signed by Decca. After appearing in the autobiographical *Tommy Steele Story* in 1957 he starred in a number of films and musicals, becoming an all-round entertainer. He was awarded an OBE in 1980. He has also published a novel (*The Final Run*), is a sculptor, and has had a painting exhibited at the Royal Academy.

| | | | | |
|---|---|---|---|---|
| 27/04/1957 | 5 | 1 | | TOMMY STEELE STAGE SHOW | Decca LF 1287 |
| 08/06/1957 | ❶⁴ | 21 | | THE TOMMY STEELE STORY | Decca LF 1288 |
| 12/04/1958 | ❶³ | 12 | | THE DUKE WORN JEANS Original soundtrack to the film | Decca LF 1308 |

### STEELY DAN
US pop group formed in Los Angeles, CA by Donald Fagen (born 10/1/1948, Passaic, NJ, vocals/keyboards), Walter Becker (born 20/2/1950, Queens, NYC, bass), Jeff 'Skunk' Baxter (born 13/12/1948, guitar), Jim Hodder (born 17/12/1947, Boston, MA, drums), David Palmer (vocals) and Denny Dias (guitar). Baxter later joined the Doobie Brothers, briefly replaced by Michael McDonald, who also went on to join the Doobie Brothers. Fagen and Becker, the nucleus of the group, parted company in 1981 but reunited in 1990. Hodder drowned on 5/6/1990. They took their name from the William Burroughs novel *The Naked Lunch*, Steely Dan being a steam-powered dildo. They have three Grammy Awards: Album of the Year and Best Pop Vocal Album for *Two Against Nature* and Best Pop Performance by a Duo or Group with Vocal for *Cousin Dupree* all in 2000. Additionally, their *Two Against Nature* album won the Best Engineered album award the same year. The group was inducted into the Rock & Roll Hall of Fame in 2001.

| | | | | |
|---|---|---|---|---|
| 30/03/1974 | 37 | 2 | ○ | PRETZEL LOGIC | Probe SPBA 6282 |
| 03/05/1975 | 13 | 6 | ○ | KATY LIED | ABC ABCL 5094 |
| 20/09/1975 | 38 | 1 | | CAN'T BUY A THRILL | ABC ABCL 5024 |
| 22/05/1976 | 11 | 13 | | ROYAL SCAM | ABC ABCL 5161 |
| 08/10/1977 | 5 | 10 | ○ | AJA | ABC ABCL 5225 |
| 02/12/1978 | 41 | 18 | | GREATEST HITS | ABC BLD 616 |
| 29/11/1980 | 27 | 12 | | GAUCHO | MCA MCF 3090 |
| 03/07/1982 | 44 | 6 | | GOLDEN HITS | MCA MCF 3145 |
| 26/10/1985 | 43 | 5 | ○ | REELIN' IN THE YEARS – THE VERY BEST OF STEELY DAN | MCA DANTV 1 |
| 10/10/1987 | 64 | 4 | | DO IT AGAIN – THE VERY BEST OF STEELY DAN | Telstar STAR 2297 |
| 20/11/1993 | 42 | 5 | | REMASTERED – THE BEST OF STEELY DAN | MCA MCD 10967 |
| 28/10/1995 | 62 | 1 | | ALIVE IN AMERICA | Giant 74321286912 |
| 11/03/2000 | 11 | 5 | | TWO AGAINST NATURE 2000 Grammy Awards for Album of the Year and Best Pop Vocal Album | Giant 74321621902 |
| 21/06/2003 | 21 | 3 | | EVERYTHING MUST GO | Reprise 9362484902 |

### WOUT STEENHUIS
Dutch guitarist; he later relocated to Broadstairs in Kent and died on 9/7/1985.

| | | | | |
|---|---|---|---|---|
| 21/11/1981 | 28 | 7 | | HAWAIIAN PARADISE/CHRISTMAS | Warwick WW 5106 |

### JIM STEINMAN
US singer/producer (born 1/11/1947, NYC); he was first known as the musical arranger for National Lampoon. He then wrote the *Bat Out Of Hell* album for Meat Loaf, produced by Todd Rundgren. Steinman intended producing the follow-up album, but with Meat Loaf unavailable at the time, ended up recording *Bad For Good*. He also produced hit albums for Bonnie Tyler and Barry Manilow and eventually resumed his relationship with Meat Loaf on *Dead Ringer* and *Bat Out Of Hell 2*.

| | | | | |
|---|---|---|---|---|
| 09/05/1981 | 7 | 25 | ○ | BAD FOR GOOD | Epic EPC 84361 |

### MARTIN STEPHENSON AND THE DAINTEES
UK singer/songwriter/guitarist (born 1965, Durham); he formed the Daintees in his teens, a line-up finally settling in 1985 with Anthony Dunn (bass/vocals), John Steel (keyboards) and Paul Smith (drums).

| | | | | |
|---|---|---|---|---|
| 17/05/1986 | 85 | 3 | | BOAT TO BOLIVIA | Kitchenware KWLP 5 |
| 16/04/1988 | 39 | 4 | | GLADSOME, HUMOUR AND BLUE | Kitchenware KWLP 8 |
| 19/05/1990 | 35 | 3 | | SALUTATION ROAD | Kitchenware 8281981 |
| 25/07/1992 | 68 | 1 | | THE BOY'S HEART | Kitchenware 8283242 |

## STEPPENWOLF

STEPPENWOLF Canadian rock group formed in 1967 by John Kay (born Joachim Krauledat, 12/4/1944, Tilsit, Germany, guitar/vocals), Michael Monarch (born 5/7/1950, Los Angeles, CA, guitar), Rushton Moreve (born 1948, Los Angeles, bass), Goldy McJohn (born John Goadsby, 2/5/1945, organ) and Jerry Edmonton (born Jerry McCrohan, 24/10/1946, drums) as Sparrow. They recorded one single for Columbia before relocating to Los Angeles, CA, name-changing to Steppenwolf and signing with Dunhill. Record producer Gabriel Mekler suggested the name, from a novel by Herman Hesse. Moreve left after their debut album, replaced by John Russell Morgan. Monarch and Morgan left in 1969, replaced by Larry Byrom (born 27/12/1948) and Nick St Nicholas (born Klaus Karl Kassbaum, 28/9/1943, Hamburg, Germany). They disbanded in 1972, re-forming two years later. Moreve was killed in a car crash on 1/7/1981. Edmonton was killed in a car crash on 28/11/1993.

| | | | | |
|---|---|---|---|---|
| 28/02/1970 | 43 | 4 | | MONSTER ................................................................Stateside SSL 5021 |
| 25/04/1970 | 59 | 2 | | STEPPENWOLF ..........................................................Stateside SSL 5020 |
| 04/07/1970 | 16 | 14 | | STEPPENWOLF LIVE ....................................................Stateside SSL 5029 |

## STEPS

STEPS UK vocal group formed by Faye Tozer (born 14/11/1975), Lee Latchford-Evans (born 28/1/1975), Claire Richards (born 17/8/1977), Ian Watkins (aka H, born 8/5/1976) and Lisa Scott-Lee (born 5/11/1975). They took part in the BRITS Trust *Thank Abba For The Music* project and the group received a Special Achievement Award for Best Selling Live Act at the 2000 BRIT Awards. They split in December 2001: Lisa Scott Lee announced plans to manage her three brothers' group 3SL, Faye Tozer recorded solo and Ian Watkins and Claire Richards forming H & Claire.

| | | | | |
|---|---|---|---|---|
| 26/09/1998 | 2 | 62 | ✪5 | STEP ONE ◇ ..........................................................Jive 0519112 |
| 06/11/1999 | ❶4 | 62 | ✪4 | STEPTACULAR ◇ ......................................................Ebul 0519442 |
| 11/11/2000 | 4 | 26 | ✪2 | BUZZ ..................................................................Ebul 9201172 |
| 27/10/2001 | ❶3 | 21 | ✪4 | GOLD – THE GREATEST HITS ............................................Ebul/Jive 9201412 |
| 07/12/2002 | 57 | 1 | | THE LAST DANCE ......................................................Jive 9201522 |

## STEREO MC'S

STEREO MC'S UK rap group formed in London by Rob Birch (born 11/6/1961, Nottingham), Nick 'The Head' Hallam (born 11/6/1960, Nottingham) and Owen 'If' Rossiter (born 20/3/1959, Newport), with singer Cath Coffey (born 1965, Kenya) joining them on tours. They were named Best British Group at the 1994 BRIT Awards.

| | | | | |
|---|---|---|---|---|
| 17/10/1992 | 2 | 52 | ✪ | CONNECTED 1994 BRIT Award for Best Album .....................Fourth & Broadway BRCD 589 |
| 09/06/2001 | 17 | 3 | ○ | DEEP DOWN AND DIRTY ................................................Island CID 8106 |

## STEREOLAB

STEREOLAB UK group formed in London in 1990 by Tim Gane (guitar), Letitia Sadier (vocals), Martin Kean (bass) and Joe Dilworth (drums), with Russell Yates (guitar) and Gina Morris (vocals) featuring in early live dates. The group formed their own Duophonic Ultra High Frequency label (the name Stereolab was taken from an imprint of the US hi-fi testing label – Vanguard). Mary Hansen (keyboards/vocals) joined the group in 1992 and Andy Ramsay replaced Dilworth. Duncan Brown (bass) and Sean O'Hagan (guitar) joined in 1993.

| | | | | |
|---|---|---|---|---|
| 18/09/1993 | 62 | 1 | | TRANSIENT RANDOM-NOISE BURSTS ......................................Duophonic UHF DUHFCD 02 |
| 20/08/1994 | 16 | 3 | | MARS AUDIAC QUINTET ................................................Duophonic UHF DUHFCD 05X |
| 29/04/1995 | 59 | 1 | | MUSIC FOR AMORPHOUS BODY STUDY CENTRE ..............................Duophonic UHF DUHFCD 08 |
| 16/09/1995 | 30 | 2 | | REFRIED ECTOPLASM (SWITCHED ON – VOLUME 2) ........................Duophonic UHF DUHFCD 09 |
| 30/03/1996 | 27 | 2 | | EMPEROR TOMATO KETCHUP ............................................Duophonic UHF DUHFCD 11 |
| 04/10/1997 | 19 | 2 | | DOTS AND LOOPS ....................................................Duophonic UHF DUHFCD 017 |

## STEREOPHONICS

STEREOPHONICS UK rock group formed in Aberdare in 1996 by Kelly Jones (born 3/6/1974, Aberdare, guitar/vocals), Richard Jones (born 23/5/1974, Aberdare, bass) and Stuart Cable (born 19/5/1970, Aberdare, drums) as Tragic Love Company, changing their name on signing with V2 in 1996. They were named Best British Newcomer at the 1998 BRIT Awards. Cable was sacked in September 2003 and temporarily replaced by Steve Gorman (formerly of Black Crowes).

| | | | | |
|---|---|---|---|---|
| 06/09/1997 | 6 | 117 | ✪2 | WORD GETS AROUND ..................................................V2 VVR 1000438 |
| 20/03/1999 | ❶1 | 101 | ✪5 | PERFORMANCE AND COCKTAILS ◇ ......................................V2 VVR 1004492 |
| 21/04/2001 | ❶5 | 87 | ✪5 | JUST ENOUGH EDUCATION TO PERFORM ◇2 ..............................V2 VVR 1015838 |
| 14/06/2003 | ❶1 | 36 | ✪2 | YOU GOTTA GO THERE TO COME BACK ..................................V2 VVR 1021902 |

**CAT STEVENS** UK singer (born Steven Georgiou, 21/7/1947, London) who was discovered by ex-Springfields turned producer Mike Hurst in 1966. He signed to Deram (an imprint of Decca designed as a showcase for UK talent) in July 1966 and switched to Island in 1970. He converted to the Islamic faith in 1977, taking the name Yusef Islam and retired from the music industry in 1979.

| DATE | POS | WKS | BPI | ALBUM TITLE | LABEL & NUMBER |
|------|-----|-----|-----|-------------|----------------|
| 25/03/1967 | 7 | 16 | | **MATTHEW AND SON** | Deram SML 1004 |
| 11/07/1970 | 63 | 4 | | MONA BONE JAKON | Island ILPS 9118 |
| 28/11/1970 | 20 | 39 | | TEA FOR THE TILLERMAN | Island ILPS 9135 |
| 02/10/1971 | 3 | 93 | | **TEASER AND THE FIRECAT** | Island ILPS 9154 |
| 07/10/1972 | 2 | 27 | ● | **CATCH BULL AT FOUR** ▲³ | Island ILPS 9206 |
| 21/07/1973 | 3 | 10 | ● | **FOREIGNER** | Island ILPS 9240 |
| 06/04/1974 | 3 | 15 | ● | **BUDDAH AND THE CHOCOLATE BOX** | Island ILPS 9274 |
| 19/07/1975 | 2 | 24 | ● | **GREATEST HITS** | Island ILPS 9310 |
| 14/05/1977 | 18 | 15 | ○ | IZITSO | Island ILPS 9451 |
| 03/02/1990 | 4 | 16 | ● | **THE VERY BEST OF CAT STEVENS** | Island CATV 1 |
| 27/11/1999 | 31 | 6 | ● | REMEMBER CAT STEVENS – THE ULTIMATE COLLECTION ◇ | Island CID 8079 |
| 25/10/2003 | 6 | 15 | ✪ | **THE VERY BEST OF CAT STEVENS** | Universal TV 9811208 |

**RACHEL STEVENS** UK singer (born 9/4/1978) and ex- S Club 7 member. She went solo when they disbanded in 2003.

| DATE | POS | WKS | BPI | ALBUM TITLE | LABEL & NUMBER |
|------|-----|-----|-----|-------------|----------------|
| 11/10/2003 | 9 | 6 | ● | **FUNKY DORY** | 19 9865702 |

**RAY STEVENS** US singer (born Ray Ragsdale, 24/1/1939, Clarksdale, GA) who started as a DJ at fifteen and began making novelty records in the early 1960s.

| DATE | POS | WKS | BPI | ALBUM TITLE | LABEL & NUMBER |
|------|-----|-----|-----|-------------|----------------|
| 26/09/1970 | 62 | 1 | | EVERYTHING IS BEAUTIFUL 1970 Grammy Award for Best Contemporary Vocal Performance | CBS 64074 |
| 13/09/1975 | 23 | 7 | | MISTY 1975 Grammy Award for Best Arrangement Accompanying Singer | Janus 9109 401 |

**SHAKIN' STEVENS** UK singer (born Michael Barratt, 4/3/1948, Ely, Wales) who began his career as lead singer with the Backbeats before changing the group's name (and his) to Shakin' Stevens and the Sunsets at the end of the 1960s. The group recorded unsuccessfully for a number of labels before disbanding in 1976. He then starred in the musical *Elvis* before launching a solo career recording similar-style music.

| DATE | POS | WKS | BPI | ALBUM TITLE | LABEL & NUMBER |
|------|-----|-----|-----|-------------|----------------|
| 15/03/1980 | 62 | 2 | | TAKE ONE! | Epic EPC 83978 |
| 04/04/1981 | 2 | 28 | ● | **THIS OLE HOUSE** | Epic EPC 84985 |
| 08/08/1981 | 34 | 5 | ● | SHAKIN' STEVENS | Hallmark SHM 3065 |
| 19/09/1981 | ❶¹ | 28 | ✪ | **SHAKY** | Epic EPC 10027 |
| 09/10/1982 | 3 | 18 | ✪ | **GIVE ME YOUR HEART TONIGHT** | Epic EPC 10035 |
| 26/11/1983 | 21 | 27 | ● | THE BOP WON'T STOP | Epic EPC 86301 |
| 17/11/1984 | 8 | 22 | ✪ | **SHAKIN' STEVENS GREATEST HITS** | Epic EPC 10047 |
| 16/11/1985 | 37 | 9 | ● | LIPSTICK POWDER AND PAINT | Epic EPC 26646 |
| 31/10/1987 | 59 | 7 | | LET'S BOOGIE | Epic 4601261 |
| 19/11/1988 | 42 | 8 | | A WHOLE LOTTA SHAKY | Epic MOOD 5 |
| 20/10/1990 | 65 | 2 | | THERE'S TWO KINDS OF MUSIC: ROCK 'N' ROLL! | Telstar STAR 2454 |
| 31/10/1992 | 57 | 2 | | THE EPIC YEARS **SHAKY** | Epic 4724222 |

**AL STEWART** UK singer (born 5/9/1945, Glasgow); he made his first recording in 1966 for Decca and his first album in 1967 for CBS, switching to RCA in 1977.

| DATE | POS | WKS | BPI | ALBUM TITLE | LABEL & NUMBER |
|------|-----|-----|-----|-------------|----------------|
| 11/04/1970 | 40 | 4 | | ZERO SHE FLIES | CBS 63848 |
| 05/02/1977 | 38 | 7 | ● | YEAR OF THE CAT | RCA Victor RS 1082 |
| 21/10/1978 | 39 | 1 | ○ | TIME PASSAGES | RCA Victor PL 25173 |
| 06/09/1980 | 55 | 6 | | 24 CARAT | RCA PL 25306 |
| 09/06/1984 | 83 | 2 | | RUSSIANS AND AMERICANS | RCA PL 70307 |

**ANDY STEWART** UK singer (born 20/12/1933, Scotland); he is best known as compere of TV's *White Heather Club*. Ill-health plagued his career and he later underwent a triple heart bypass. He was made an MBE in 1976; he died from a heart attack on 11/10/1993.

| DATE | POS | WKS | BPI | ALBUM TITLE | LABEL & NUMBER |
|------|-----|-----|-----|-------------|----------------|
| 03/02/1962 | 13 | 2 | | ANDY STEWART | Top Rank 35116 |

## DAVID A STEWART
UK singer/guitarist (born 9/9/1952, Sunderland); he was a founder member of Catch in 1977, the group later becoming the Tourists. When they split in 1980 he and Annie Lennox formed the Eurythmics, having a string of hits until Lennox took a sabbatical in 1990. Stewart was involved in various outside projects, including the Spiritual Cowboys in 1990. His marriage to former Bananarama's Siobhan Fahey in 1987 ended in divorce. He directed the 2000 film *Honest*, which starred All Saints' Natalie and Melanie Appleton and Melanie Blatt. He won the Best Producer category at the BRIT Awards on three occasions: 1986, 1987 and 1990. The Eurythmics received the Outstanding Contribution to British Music Award at the 1999 BRIT Awards and then re-formed.

| 07/04/1990 | 35 | 5 | | LILY WAS HERE Original soundtrack to the film | AnXious ZL 74233 |
| 15/09/1990 | 38 | 2 | | DAVE STEWART AND THE SPIRITUAL COWBOYS **DAVE STEWART AND THE SPIRITUAL COWBOYS** | RCA OB 74710 |

## JERMAINE STEWART
US R&B singer (born 7/9/1957, Columbus, OH, raised in Chicago, IL) who was a backing singer for Shalamar, the Temptations, Millie Jackson and Gladys Knight before signing solo with Arista. He died from liver cancer on 17/3/1996.

| 04/10/1986 | 49 | 4 | | FRANTIC ROMANTIC | 10 Records DIX 26 |
| 05/03/1988 | 32 | 8 | | SAY IT AGAIN | Sire SRNLP 14 |

## PATRICK STEWART – see ENGLISH CHAMBER ORCHESTRA

## ROD STEWART

UK singer (born 10/1/1945, Highgate, London) who was an apprentice footballer with Brentford FC. He quit after three weeks to travel around Europe busking, arriving back in the UK and joining the Five Dimensions in 1963. He was discovered by Long John Baldry and sang with his band before signing a solo deal with Decca in 1964 (he was dropped after one single). After spells with the Soul Agents and Steampacket, he spent two years with the Jeff Beck Group whilst still recording the odd solo single, although he also failed an audition to join Manfred Mann when Paul Jones left. He joined the Faces in 1969 and signed a solo deal with Phonogram, achieving his chart breakthrough two years later. He married actress Alana Hamilton in 1979 and divorced in 1984. He then married model Rachel Hunter in 1990 (which prompted the quote 'I found the girl I want, and it's all up to me now. I won't be putting my banana in anybody's fruit bowl from now on') although the pair subsequently separated. Rod was presented with the Outstanding Contribution Award at the 1993 BRIT Awards. He was inducted into the Rock & Roll Hall of Fame in 1994.

| 03/10/1970 | 62 | 1 | | GASOLINE ALLEY | Vertigo 6360 500 |
| 24/07/1971 | ❶⁶ | 81 | | EVERY PICTURE TELLS A STORY ▲⁴ | Mercury 6338 063 |
| 05/08/1972 | ❶² | 36 | | NEVER A DULL MOMENT | Philips 6499 153 |
| 25/08/1973 | ❶³ | 30 | ● | SING IT AGAIN ROD | Mercury 6499 484 |
| 26/01/1974 | 3 | 7 | | OVERTURE AND BEGINNERS **ROD STEWART & THE FACES** | Mercury 9100 001 |
| 19/10/1974 | ❶² | 20 | ● | SMILER | Mercury 9104 011 |
| 30/08/1975 | ❶⁷ | 88 | ✪ | ATLANTIC CROSSING | Warner Brothers K 56151 |
| 03/07/1976 | ❶² | 47 | ✪ | A NIGHT ON THE TOWN | Riva RVLP 1 |
| 16/07/1977 | 18 | 22 | ● | THE BEST OF ROD STEWART | Mercury 6643 030 |
| 19/11/1977 | 3 | 26 | ✪ | FOOT LOOSE AND FANCY FREE | Riva RVLP 5 |
| 21/01/1978 | 60 | 1 | ✪ | ATLANTIC CROSSING Re-issue | Riva RVLP 4 |
| 09/12/1978 | 3 | 31 | ● | BLONDES HAVE MORE FUN ▲³ | Riva RVLP 8 |
| 10/11/1979 | ❶⁵ | 74 | ✪ | ROD STEWART – GREATEST HITS VOL. 1 The album's label and catalogue number changed to Warner Brothers K 56744 during its chart run | Riva ROD TV 1 |
| 22/11/1980 | 4 | 13 | ✪ | FOOLISH BEHAVIOUR | Riva RVLP 11 |
| 14/11/1981 | 8 | 21 | ● | TONIGHT I'M YOURS | Riva RVLP 14 |
| 13/11/1982 | 35 | 5 | | ABSOLUTELY LIVE | Riva RVLP 17 |
| 18/06/1983 | 5 | 27 | ● | BODY WISHES | Warner Brothers 9238771 |
| 23/06/1984 | 8 | 17 | ○ | CAMOUFLAGE | Warner Brothers 9250951 |
| 05/07/1986 | 5 | 17 | ● | EVERY BEAT OF MY HEART | Warner Brothers WX 53 |
| 04/06/1988 | 11 | 8 | ● | OUT OF ORDER | Warner Brothers WX 152 |
| 25/11/1989 | 3 | 127 | ✪⁵ | THE BEST OF ROD STEWART | Warner Brothers WX 314 |
| 06/04/1991 | 2 | 27 | ✪ | VAGABOND HEART | Warner Brothers WX 408 |
| 07/11/1992 | 58 | 1 | | THE BEST OF ROD STEWART AND THE FACES 1971–1975 **ROD STEWART AND THE FACES** | Mercury 5141802 |
| 06/03/1993 | 3 | 9 | ● | ROD STEWART: LEAD VOCALIST | Warner Brothers 9362452582 |
| 05/06/1993 | 2 | 27 | ✪ | UNPLUGGED … AND SEATED | Warner Brothers 9362452892 |
| 10/06/1995 | 4 | 12 | ● | A SPANNER IN THE WORKS | Warner Brothers 9362458672 |
| 16/11/1996 | 8 | 19 | ● | IF WE FALL IN LOVE TONIGHT ◇ | Warner Brothers 9362464672 |
| 13/06/1998 | 2 | 11 | ● | WHEN WE WERE THE NEW BOYS | Atlantic 9362467922 |
| 07/04/2001 | 9 | 8 | ● | HUMAN | Atlantic ATL 83411 |
| 24/11/2001 | 7 | 30 | ✪ | THE STORY SO FAR – THE VERY BEST OF ◇ | Warner Brothers 8122735812 |
| 09/11/2002 | 8 | 18 | ✪ | IT HAD TO BE YOU – THE GREAT AMERICAN SONGBOOK | J Records 74321968672 |
| 01/11/2003 | 4 | 17 | ✪ | AS TIME GOES BY – THE GREAT AMERICAN SONGBOOK VOLUME 2 | J Records 82876574842 |
| 01/11/2003 | 13 | 5 | ● | CHANGING FACES – THE VERY BEST OF **ROD STEWART AND THE FACES** | Universal TV 9812604 |

## STIFF LITTLE FINGERS
Irish rock group formed by Jake Burns (guitar/vocals), Henry Cluney (guitar), Ali McMordie (bass) and Brian Falloon (drums). They formed the Rigid Digits label for their debut release.

| 03/03/1979 | 14 | 19 | ● | INFLAMMABLE MATERIAL | Rough Trade ROUGH 1 |
| 15/03/1980 | 8 | 10 | ○ | NOBODY'S HEROES | Chrysalis CHR 1270 |
| 20/09/1980 | 9 | 5 | ○ | HANX | Chrysalis CHR 1300 |
| 25/04/1981 | 14 | 8 | | GO FOR IT | Chrysalis CHX 1339 |
| 02/10/1982 | 24 | 6 | | NOW THEN… | Chrysalis CHR 1400 |

▲⁹ Number of weeks album topped the US chart ◆¹² RIAA Diamond Awards ◇³ IFPI Platinum Europe Awards

| | | | | | |
|---|---|---|---|---|---|
| 12/02/1983 | 19 | 9 | ○ | ALL THE BEST | Chrysalis CTY 1414 |

### CURTIS STIGERS
US singer (born 1968, Los Angeles, CA, raised in Boise ID); he formed the High Tops and moved to New York when they disbanded. He signed with Arista in 1991.

| | | | | | |
|---|---|---|---|---|---|
| 29/02/1992 | 7 | 50 | ✪² | CURTIS STIGERS | Arista 261953 |
| 01/07/1995 | 34 | 2 | | TIME WAS | Arista 74321282792 |

### STILLS
Canadian rock group formed in Montreal in 2000 with Tim Fletcher (vocals), Greg Paquet (guitar), Oliver Crow (bass) and Dave Hamelin (drums).

| | | | | | |
|---|---|---|---|---|---|
| 06/03/2004 | 66 | 1 | | LOGIC WILL BREAK YOUR HEART | 679 Recordings/Vice 7567836742 |

### STEPHEN STILLS
US singer (born 3/1/1945, Dallas, TX); he was a member of Buffalo Springfield and later formed Crosby Stills & Nash with David Crosby and Graham Nash. He also auditioned for the Monkees but was turned down because he had bad teeth. Manassas consisted of Stills, Chris Hillman (guitar/vocals), Al Perkins (guitar), Paul Harris (keyboards), Calvin Samuels (bass) and Dallas Taylor (drums), with Samuels being replaced by Kenny Pasarelli. (See also Crosby, Stills, Nash and Young.)

| | | | | | |
|---|---|---|---|---|---|
| 19/12/1970 | 30 | 1 | | STEPHEN STILLS | Atlantic 2401 004 |
| 14/08/1971 | 22 | 3 | | STEPHEN STILLS 2 | Atlantic 2401 013 |
| 20/05/1972 | 30 | 5 | | MANASSAS | Atlantic K 60021 |
| 19/05/1973 | 33 | 2 | | DOWN THE ROAD This and the above hit credited to **STEPHEN STILLS' MANASSAS** | Atlantic K 40440 |
| 26/07/1975 | 31 | 1 | | STILLS | CBS 69146 |
| 29/05/1976 | 54 | 2 | | ILLEGAL STILLS | CBS 81330 |
| 09/10/1976 | 12 | 5 | ○ | LONG MAY YOU RUN **STILLS-YOUNG BAND** | Reprise K 54081 |

### STILTSKIN
UK group formed in Glasgow by Ray Wilson (born 1969, Edinburgh, vocals), James Finnigan (bass), Peter Lawlor (guitar) and Ross McFarlane (drums). Their debut single was chosen for a Levi Jeans advertisement, the first time a classic had not been used. Wilson later became lead singer with Genesis.

| | | | | | |
|---|---|---|---|---|---|
| 29/10/1994 | 17 | 4 | | THE MIND'S EYE | White Water WWD 1 |

### STING
UK singer (born Gordon Sumner, 2/10/1951, Wallsend, Newcastle-upon-Tyne) who was in various local groups while teaching full time. He joined Police in 1977 as lead singer and bass player, emerging as chief songwriter. He began a parallel solo career in 1982 and after they disbanded in 1985 he formed a backing group, the Blue Turtles. He appeared in the films *Radio Man, Quadrophenia* and *Plenty*, among others. He was named Best British Male at the 1994 BRIT Awards, and received the Outstanding Contribution Award in 1985, as a member of Police. He then won a second Outstanding Contribution BRIT Award in 2002 as a solo artist. He appeared in an episode of *The Simpsons*, organising the charity record *We're Sending Our Love Down The Well*. Sting has won six Grammy Awards whilst with The Police (five with the group and one relating to his songwriting) and has gone on to win a further ten including: Best Rock Instrumental Performance in 1983 for *Brimstone And Treacle*; Best Video Long Form and Best Pop Vocal Performance in 1986 for *Bring On The Night*; Best Rock Song in 1991 for *Soul Cages*; Best Male Pop Vocal Performance in 1993 for *If I Ever Lose My Faith In You*; Best Music Video Long Form in 1993 for *Ten Summoner's Tales*; Best Pop Male Performance in 2000 for *She Walks This Earth (Soberana Rosa)*; and Best Pop Collaboration with Vocals with Mary J Blige in 2003 for *Whenever I Say Your Name*. He has a star on the Hollywood Walk of Fame and was awarded a CBE in Queen's 2003 Birthday Honours List.

| | | | | | |
|---|---|---|---|---|---|
| 29/06/1985 | 3 | 64 | ✪² | **THE DREAM OF BLUE TURTLES** | A&M DREAM 1 |
| 28/06/1986 | 16 | 12 | ○ | BRING ON THE NIGHT | A&M BRING 1 |
| 24/10/1987 | 1 | 47 | ✪ | **NOTHING LIKE THE SUN** 1988 BRIT Award for Best Album | A&M AMA 6402 |
| 02/02/1991 | ❶¹ | 16 | ● | **THE SOUL CAGES** | A&M 3964051 |
| 13/03/1993 | 2 | 60 | ✪² | **THE SUMMONER'S TALES** | A&M 5400752 |
| 19/11/1994 | 2 | 41 | ✪³ | **FIELDS OF GOLD – THE BEST OF STING 1984–1994** ◇⁴ | A&M 5403072 |
| 16/03/1996 | 4 | 27 | ✪ | **MERCURY FALLING** ◇ | A&M 5404862 |
| 22/11/1997 | ❶² | 50 | ✪ | **THE VERY BEST OF STING AND THE POLICE** ◇² **STING AND THE POLICE** | A&M 5404282 |
| 09/10/1999 | 5 | 44 | ✪ | **BRAND NEW DAY** ◇² 1999 Grammy Awards for Best Pop Album and Best Pop Male Performance | A&M 4904512 |
| 17/11/2001 | 3 | 15 | ● | **ALL THIS TIME** | A&M 4931802 |
| 04/10/2003 | 3 | 11 | ● | **SACRED LOVE** ◇ | A&M 9860619 |

### ANGIE STONE
US singer (born Angie Williams, Columbia, SC) who was previously a member of Vertical Hold and Sequence.

| | | | | | |
|---|---|---|---|---|---|
| 11/03/2000 | 62 | 3 | | BLACK DIAMOND | Arista 74321727752 |

### JOSS STONE
UK female soul singer (born Joscelyn Eve Stoker, 11/4/1987, Dover) who won the BBC talent show *Star For A Night* at the age of fourteen. Her debut album was produced by soul legend Betty Everett.

| | | | | | |
|---|---|---|---|---|---|
| 17/01/2003 | 4 | 24+ | ✪ | **THE SOUL SESSIONS** ◇ | Relentless CDREL2 |

## STONE ROSES

**STONE ROSES** UK rock group formed in Manchester in 1984 by Ian Brown (born 20/2/1963, Manchester, vocals), John Squire (born 24/11/1962, Manchester, guitar), Andy Couzens (guitar/vocals), Pete Garner (bass) and Alan 'Reni' Wren (born 10/4/1964, Manchester, drums). They signed with Thin Line in 1985, later recording for FM Revolver before Silvertone in 1988. Garner left in 1987, replaced by Gary 'Mani' Mountfield (born 16/11/1962, Manchester). A move to Geffen Records was delayed by an injunction taken out by Silvertone, although Stone Roses eventually signed a deal worth a reported $4 million in 1992. Wren left in 1995, replaced by Robbie Maddix. They disbanded in 1996. Brown later recorded solo, whilst Squire formed The Seahorses (denying there was any significance in the name being an anagram of 'he hates roses').

| DATE | POS | WKS | BPI | ALBUM TITLE | LABEL & NUMBER |
|------|-----|-----|-----|-------------|----------------|
| 13/05/1989 | 19 | 86 | ✪ | THE STONE ROSES | Silvertone ORELP 502 |
| 01/08/1992 | 32 | 3 | | TURNS INTO STONE | Silvertone ORECD 521 |
| 17/12/1994 | 4 | 28 | ✪ | **SECOND COMING** | Geffen GED 24503 |
| 27/05/1995 | 4 | 25 | ● | **THE COMPLETE STONE ROSES** | Silvertone ORECD 535 |
| 07/12/1996 | 58 | 1 | | GARAGE FLOWER | Silvertone GARAGECD 1 |
| 16/10/1999 | 26 | 3 | | STONE ROSES – 10TH ANNIVERSARY EDITION | Silvertone 0591242 |
| 11/11/2000 | 41 | 2 | ○ | THE REMIXES | Silvertone 9260152 |
| 16/11/2002 | 19 | 8 | ● | THE VERY BEST OF | Silvertone 9260382 |

**STONE SOUR** US group formed in Des Moines, IA in 1992 by Corey Taylor (vocals) and James Root (guitar). They disbanded when the pair joined Slipknot, revived in 2002 by Taylor, Root, Josh Rand (guitar), Sean Economaki (bass), Joel Ekman (drums) and DJ Sid Wilson.

| DATE | POS | WKS | BPI | ALBUM TITLE | LABEL & NUMBER |
|------|-----|-----|-----|-------------|----------------|
| 07/09/2002 | 41 | 1 | | STONE SOUR | Roadrunner RR 84252 |

**STONE TEMPLE PILOTS** US rock group formed in San Diego, CA in 1987 by Scott Weiland (born 27/10/1967, Santa Cruz, CA, vocals), Robert DeLeo (born 2/2/1966, New Jersey, bass), Dean DeLeo (born 23/8/1961, New Jersey, guitar) and Eric Krez (born 7/6/1966, Santa Cruz, drums) as Mighty Joe Young. They name-changed to Shirley Temple's Pussy before settling on Stone Temple Pilots in 1990, signing to Atlantic in 1992. They won the 1993 Grammy Award for Best Hard Rock Performance with Vocal for *Plush*.

| DATE | POS | WKS | BPI | ALBUM TITLE | LABEL & NUMBER |
|------|-----|-----|-----|-------------|----------------|
| 04/09/1993 | 27 | 8 | ○ | CORE | Atlantic 7567824182 |
| 18/06/1994 | 10 | 9 | ○ | **PURPLE** ▲[3] | Atlantic 7567826072 |
| 06/04/1996 | 31 | 2 | | TINY MUSIC… MUSIC FROM THE VATICAN GIFT SHOP | Atlantic 7567828712 |

**STONE THE CROWS** UK group formed by Maggie Bell (born 12/1/1945, Glasgow, vocals), Leslei Harvey (guitar), Jimmy Dewar (bass), John McGuinness (keyboards) and Colin Allen (drums). Dewar and McGuinness left and were replaced by Steve Thompson and Ronnie Leahy. On 3/5/1972 Harvey, younger brother of the Sensational Alex Harvey, was electrocuted whilst on stage at the Top Rank in Swansea. The group recorded one further album (with Jimmy McCulloch taking Harvey's place) but disbanded soon after.

| DATE | POS | WKS | BPI | ALBUM TITLE | LABEL & NUMBER |
|------|-----|-----|-----|-------------|----------------|
| 07/10/1972 | 33 | 3 | | CONTINUOUS PERFORMANCE | Polydor 2391 043 |

**IZZY STRADLIN' AND THE JU JU HOUNDS** US guitarist (born Jeffrey Isbell, 8/4/1962, Lafayette, IN) who was a founder member of Guns N' Roses in 1985 and remained with them until 1991. He then formed the Ju Ju Hounds with Rick Richards (guitar), Jimmy Ashhirst (bass) and Charlie Quintana (drums). After briefly standing in for Gilbey Clarke, his replacement in Guns N' Roses, when he broke his wrist in 1993, Stradlin' returned to the group on a more permanent basis in 1995.

| DATE | POS | WKS | BPI | ALBUM TITLE | LABEL & NUMBER |
|------|-----|-----|-----|-------------|----------------|
| 24/10/1992 | 52 | 1 | | IZZY STRADLIN' AND THE JU JU HOUNDS | Geffen GED 24490 |

**STRANGELOVE** UK group formed in 1991 by Patrick Duff (vocals), Alex Lee (guitar/keyboards), Julian Pransky-Poole (guitar), Joe Allen (bass) and John Langley (drums).

| DATE | POS | WKS | BPI | ALBUM TITLE | LABEL & NUMBER |
|------|-----|-----|-----|-------------|----------------|
| 13/08/1994 | 69 | 1 | | TIME FOR THE REST OF YOUR LIFE | Food FOODCD 11 |
| 29/06/1996 | 44 | 1 | | LOVE AND OTHER DEMONS | Food FOODCD 15 |
| 18/10/1997 | 67 | 1 | | STRANGELOVE | Food FOODCD 24 |

**STRANGLERS** UK punk-rock group formed in Surrey in 1974 by Hugh Cornwell (born 28/8/1949, London, guitar/vocals), Jet Black (born Brian Duffy, 26/8/1948, Ilford, drums) and Jean-Jacques Burnel (born 21/2/1952, London, vocals/bass), with Dave Greenfield (born 29/3/1949, Brighton, keyboards) joining the following year. Signed with United Artists in 1976, they were one of the first punk groups to link with a major company. They switched to Epic in 1982.

| DATE | POS | WKS | BPI | ALBUM TITLE | LABEL & NUMBER |
|------|-----|-----|-----|-------------|----------------|
| 30/04/1977 | 4 | 34 | ✪ | **STRANGLERS IV (RATTUS NORVEGICUS)** | United Artists UAG 30045 |
| 08/10/1977 | 2 | 19 | ● | **NO MORE HEROES** | United Artists UAG 30200 |
| 03/06/1978 | 2 | 18 | ● | **BLACK AND WHITE** | United Artists UAK 30222 |
| 10/03/1979 | 7 | 10 | ○ | **LIVE (X CERT)** | United Artists UAG 30224 |
| 06/10/1979 | 4 | 8 | ● | **THE RAVEN** | United Artists UAG 30262 |
| 21/02/1981 | 8 | 5 | | **THEMENINBLACK** | Liberty LBG 30313 |
| 21/11/1981 | 11 | 18 | ○ | **L.A. FOLIE** | Liberty LBG 30342 |
| 25/09/1982 | 12 | 16 | ○ | THE COLLECTION 1977–1982 | Liberty LBS 30353 |

▲[9] Number of weeks album topped the US chart  ◆[12] RIAA Diamond Awards  ◇[3] IFPI Platinum Europe Awards

| | | | | | | |
|---|------|-----|-----|-----|-------------|----------------|
| | 22/01/1983 | 4 | 11 | O | FELINE | Epic EPC 25237 |
| | 17/11/1984 | 14 | 10 | O | AURAL SCULPTURE | Epic EPC 26220 |
| | 20/09/1986 | 80 | 2 | | OFF THE BEATEN TRACK | Liberty LBG 5001 |
| | 08/11/1986 | 16 | 6 | | DREAMTIME | Epic EPC 26648 |
| | 20/02/1988 | 12 | 6 | ● | ALL LIVE AND ALL OF THE NIGHT | Epic 4652591 |
| | 18/02/1989 | 57 | 2 | | THE SINGLES – THE UA YEARS | EMI EM 1314 |
| | 17/03/1990 | 15 | 4 | O | 10 | Epic 4664831 |
| | 01/12/1990 | 4 | 47 | ✪ | **GREATEST HITS 1977–1990** | Epic 4675411 |
| | 19/09/1992 | 33 | 1 | | STRANGLERS IN THE NIGHT | Psycho WOLCD 1030 |
| | 27/05/1995 | 31 | 1 | | ABOUT TIME | When! WENCD 001 |
| | 08/02/1997 | 52 | 1 | | WRITTEN IN RED | When! WENCD 009 |
| | 22/06/2002 | 21 | 3 | O | PEACHES – THE VERY BEST OF | EMI 5402022 |
| | 28/02/2004 | 70 | 1 | | NORFOLK COAST | Liberty 5969512 |

### STRAWBERRY SWITCHBLADE

STRAWBERRY SWITCHBLADE UK punk duo by Rose McDowell (guitar/vocals) and Jill Bryson (guitar/vocals) who took their name from the title of an Orange Juice song. They disbanded in the late 1980s, Rose later recording as Candy Cane.

| | | | | | | |
|---|------|-----|-----|-----|-------------|----------------|
| | 13/04/1985 | 25 | 4 | | STRAWBERRY SWITCHBLADE | Korova KODE 11 |

### STRAWBS

STRAWBS UK folk-rock group formed in 1967 by Dave Cousins (born 7/1/1945, guitar/banjo/piano) and Tony Hooper as the Strawberry Hill Boys, shortening the name to Strawbs in 1970. The group at this time featured Cousins, Hooper, Richard Hudson (born 9/5/1948, London, drums/guitar/sitar), John Ford (born 1/7/1948, London, bass) and Rick Wakeman (born 18/5/1949, London, keyboards). Wakeman left in 1971 and was replaced by Blue Weaver (born 11/3/1947, Cardiff, guitar/autoharp/piano). Hooper left soon after, and was replaced by Dave Lambert (born 8/3/1949, Hounslow). Sandy Denny (born 6/1/1947, London) was also briefly a member. Hudson and Ford recorded as a duo, whilst Wakeman recorded solo and was a member of Yes.

| | | | | | | |
|---|------|-----|-----|-----|-------------|----------------|
| | 21/11/1970 | 27 | 2 | | JUST A COLLECTION OF ANTIQUES AND CURIOS | A&M AMLS 994 |
| | 17/07/1971 | 39 | 2 | | FROM THE WITCHWOOD | A&M AMLH 64304 |
| | 26/02/1972 | 11 | 12 | | GRAVE NEW WORLD | A&M AMLH 68078 |
| | 24/02/1973 | 2 | 12 | | **BUSTING AT THE SEAMS** | A&M AMLH 68144 |
| | 27/04/1974 | 35 | 3 | | HERO AND HEROINE | A&M AMLH 63607 |

### STRAY CATS

STRAY CATS US rockabilly group formed in New York by Brian Setzer (born 10/4/1959, Long Island, NYC, guitar/vocals), Lee Rocker (born Leon Drucher, 1961, bass) and Slim Jim Phantom (born Jim McDonnell, 20/3/1961, drums). They moved to the UK in 1979 and signed with Arista the same year. They disbanded in 1984 and reunited in 1986. Setzer and Phantom appeared in films: Setzer portrayed Eddie Cochran in La Bamba and Phantom appeared in Bird. Setzer later formed The Brian Setzer Orchestra. Slim Jim Phantom later joined Colonel Parker with Gilbey Clarke (ex-Guns N' Roses), Muddy Stardust (ex-L.A. Guns) and Teddy Andreadis (ex-Slash's Snakepit), the first contemporary act signed to actor Mel Gibson's Icon Records label.

| | | | | | | |
|---|------|-----|-----|-----|-------------|----------------|
| | 28/02/1981 | 6 | 22 | ● | **STRAY CATS** | Arista STRAY 1 |
| | 21/11/1981 | 48 | 4 | O | GONNA BALL | Arista STRAY 2 |
| | 03/09/1983 | 51 | 5 | | RANT 'N' RAVE WITH THE STRAY CATS | Arista STRAY 3 |
| | 08/04/1989 | 58 | 1 | | BLAST OFF | EMI MTL 1040 |

### STREETS

STREETS UK DJ Mike Skinner born in Birmingham but who later moved to London. He also records as Grafiti.

| | | | | | | |
|---|------|-----|-----|-----|-------------|----------------|
| | 06/04/2002 | 12 | 50 | ✪ | ORIGINAL PIRATE MATERIAL | Locked On/679 Recordings 0927435682 |
| | 22/05/2004 | 2 | 6+ | ✪ | **A GRAND DON'T COME FOR FREE** | Locked On/679 Recordings 2564615342 |

### STREETWALKERS

STREETWALKERS UK rock group formed by Roger Chapman (born 8/4/1942, Leicester, vocals) and Charlie Whitney (born 24/6/1944, Skipton, North Yorkshire, guitar), both of whom were in The Farinas in 1962 and then founder members of Family in 1967.

| | | | | | | |
|---|------|-----|-----|-----|-------------|----------------|
| | 12/06/1976 | 16 | 6 | | RED CARD | Vertigo 9102 010 |

### BARBRA STREISAND

BARBRA STREISAND US singer/actress (born Barbara Joan Streisand, 24/4/1942, Brooklyn, NYC); she began as an actress, appearing in the Broadway musical I Can Get It For You Wholesale in 1962. She made her film debut in Funny Girl in 1968 (for which she won the Oscar for Best Actress) and has since appeared in numerous films as well as undertaking production and directing. She has won eight Grammy Awards including: Album of the Year and Best Female Solo Vocal Performance in 1963 for The Barbra Streisand Album; Best Female Solo Vocal Performance in 1964 for People; Best Female Solo Vocal Performance in 1965 for My Name Is Barbra; Song of the Year with Paul Williams in 1977 Evergreen; Best Female Pop Vocal Performance in 1977 for Evergreen; and Best Pop Vocal Performance by a Duo in 1980 with Barry Gibb for Guilty. After winning an Oscar, an Emmy, several Grammies and a BRIT, she was awarded a special 'Star of the Decade' Tony award. She also has a star on the Hollywood Walk of Fame.

| | | | | | | |
|---|------|-----|-----|-----|-------------|----------------|
| | 22/01/1966 | 6 | 22 | | MY NAME IS BARBRA, TWO | CBS BPG 62603 |
| | 30/04/1966 | 19 | 3 | | FUNNY GIRL | Capitol W 2059 |
| | 10/05/1969 | 11 | 22 | | FUNNY GIRL Original soundtrack to the film | CBS 70044 |
| | 14/03/1970 | 45 | 2 | | HELLO DOLLY! Original soundtrack to the film | EMI Stateside SSL 10292 |
| | 04/04/1970 | 44 | 2 | | BARBRA STREISAND'S GREATEST HITS | CBS 63921 |
| | 17/04/1971 | 28 | 2 | | STONEY END | CBS 64269 |
| | 15/06/1974 | 49 | 1 | O | THE WAY WE WERE ▲2 | CBS 69057 |
| | 09/04/1977 | ❶2 | 54 | ✪ | **A STAR IS BORN** ▲6 Original soundtrack to the film | CBS 86021 |
| | 23/07/1977 | 32 | 9 | | STREISAND SUPERMAN | CBS 86030 |

O Silver disc  ● Gold disc  ✪ Platinum disc (additional platinum units are indicated by a figure following the symbol)  ❶9 Number of weeks album topped the UK chart

| 15/07/1978 | 50 | 1 | ○ | SONGBIRD | CBS 86060 |
| 17/03/1979 | ❶[4] | 30 | ✪ | **BARBRA STREISAND GREATEST HITS VOLUME 2** ▲[3] | CBS 10012 |
| 17/11/1979 | 25 | 13 | ● | WET | CBS 86104 |
| 11/10/1980 | ❶[2] | 82 | ✪ | **GUILTY** ▲[3] | CBS 86122 |
| 16/01/1982 | ❶[9] | 129 | ✪ | **LOVE SONGS** 1983 BRIT Award for Best Album | CBS 10031 |
| 19/11/1983 | 21 | 35 | ● | YENTL Original soundtrack to the film | CBS 86302 |
| 27/10/1984 | 15 | 12 | ● | EMOTION | CBS 86309 |
| 18/01/1986 | 3 | 16 | ● | **THE BROADWAY ALBUM** ▲[3] 1986 Grammy Award for Best Female Pop Vocal Performance | CBS 86322 |
| 30/05/1987 | 27 | 7 | ○ | ONE VOICE | CBS 4508901 |
| 03/12/1988 | 29 | 13 | ● | TILL I LOVED YOU | CBS 4629431 |
| 25/11/1989 | 22 | 23 | ● | A COLLECTION – GREATEST HITS… AND MORE | CBS 4658451 |
| 10/07/1993 | 4 | 17 | ● | **BACK TO BROADWAY** ▲[1] | Columbia 4738802 |
| 29/10/1994 | 63 | 1 | | BARBRA – THE CONCERT | Columbia 4775992 |
| 22/11/1997 | 12 | 12 | ● | HIGHER GROUND ▲[1] | Columbia 4885322 |
| 02/10/1999 | 12 | 9 | | A LOVE LIKE OURS | Columbia 4949342 |
| 30/09/2000 | 54 | 1 | | TIMELESS – LIVE IN CONCERT | Columbia 4974352 |
| 09/03/2002 | ❶[1] | 22 | ✪ | **THE ESSENTIAL** ◇ | Columbia 5062572 |
| 30/11/2002 | 30 | 6 | ● | DUETS | Columbia 5098129 |
| 08/11/2003 | 25 | 3 | | THE MOVIE ALBUM | Columbia 5134213 |

**STRINGS FOR PLEASURE** UK orchestra whose debut hit album featured a collection of songs written by Burt Bacharach.

| 04/12/1971 | 49 | 1 | | THE BEST OF BACHARACH | MFP 1334 |

**STROKES** US rock group formed in New York City in 1999 by Julian Casablancas (vocals), Nick Valensi (guitar), Albert Hammond (guitar), Nikolai Fraiture (bass) and Fabrizo Moretti (drums). They were named Best New International Act at the 2002 BRIT Awards.

| 08/09/2001 | 2 | 40 | ✪ | **IS THIS IT** | Rough Trade RTRADECD 030 |
| 01/11/2003 | 2 | 20 | ✪ | **ROOM ON FIRE** | Rough Trade RTRADECD 130 |

**JOE STRUMMER** UK singer/guitarist (born John Mellors, 21/8/1952, Ankara, Turkey); a founder of The Clash in 1976 after being lured from the R&B group The 101ers. He went solo in 1988 after the demise of The Clash and later fronted The Pogues and then formed The Mescaleros with Scott Shields, Martin Slattery, Pablo Cook and Tymonn Dogg, with Roger Daltrey also guesting on their album *Global A Go Go*. He also appeared in the films *Straight To Hell* and *Mystery Train*. He died from a heart attack on 22/12/2002.

| 14/10/1989 | 58 | 1 | | EARTHQUAKE WEATHER | Epic 4653471 |
| 30/10/1999 | 71 | 1 | | ROCK ART AND THE X-RAY STYLE | Mercury 5466542 |
| 28/07/2001 | 68 | 1 | | GLOBAL A GO GO | Hellcat 04402 |
| 01/11/2003 | 50 | 1 | | STREETCORE This and the above two hits credited to **JOE STRUMMER AND THE MESCALEROS** | Hellcat 04542 |

**AMY STUDT** UK singer/guitarist/pianist/songwriter (born 22/3/1986, London) who was discovered by Simon Fuller.

| 12/07/2003 | 18 | 11 | ● | FALSE SMILES | Polydor 9801074 |

**STYLE COUNCIL** UK group formed in 1983 by former Jam leader Paul Weller (born John Weller, 25/5/1958, Woking, guitar/vocals), ex-Merton Parkas keyboard player Mick Talbot (born 11/9/1958, London) and drummer Steve White (born 31/5/1965, London). The following year they added singer Dee C Lee (born Diane Sealey, 6/6/1961, London) as a full time member. Weller and Lee married in 1986. The Style Council disbanded in 1989. Weller went on to form the Paul Weller Movement and then to record solo.

| 24/03/1984 | 2 | 38 | ● | **CAFÉ BLEU** | Polydor TSCLP 1 |
| 08/06/1985 | ❶[1] | 22 | ● | **OUR FAVOURITE SHOP** | Polydor TSCLP 2 |
| 17/05/1986 | 8 | 8 | ○ | **HOME AND ABROAD** | Polydor TSCLP 3 |
| 14/02/1987 | 2 | 7 | ● | **THE COST OF LOVING** | Polydor TSCLP 4 |
| 02/07/1988 | 15 | 3 | ○ | CONFESSIONS OF A POP GROUP | Polydor TSCMC 5 |
| 18/03/1989 | 3 | 15 | ● | **THE SINGULAR ADVENTURES OF THE STYLE COUNCIL GREATEST HITS VOLUME 1** | Polydor TSCTV 1 |
| 10/07/1993 | 39 | 1 | | HERE'S SOME THAT GOT AWAY | Polydor 5193722 |
| 02/03/1996 | 60 | 1 | | THE STYLE COUNCIL COLLECTION | Polydor 5294832 |
| 02/09/2000 | 28 | 5 | | GREATEST HITS | Polydor 5579002 |

**STYLISTICS** US R&B vocal group formed in Philadelphia, PA in 1968 by the members of two groups, the Percussions and the Monarchs. They comprised Herb Murrell (born 27/4/1949, Lane, SC), James Dunn (born 4/2/1950, Philadelphia), Russell Thompkins Jr (born 21/3/1951, Philadelphia), Airrion Love (born 8/8/1949, Philadelphia) and James Smith (born 16/6/1950, New York). After local success with Sebring Records they were signed by Avco and teamed up initially with writer/producer Thom Bell and later with Van McCoy. Dunn left due to ill-health in 1978. They switched to Philadelphia International in 1980. When Smith later left they continued as a trio.

| | | | | | |
|---|---|---|---|---|---|
| 24/08/1974 | 42 | 3 | ○ | ROCKIN' ROLL BABY | Avco 6466 012 |
| 21/09/1974 | 26 | 14 | ○ | LET'S PUT IT ALL TOGETHER | Avco 6466 013 |
| 01/03/1975 | 36 | 1 | ○ | FROM THE MOUNTAIN | Avco 9109 002 |
| 05/04/1975 | ❶⁹ | 63 | ✪ | **THE BEST OF THE STYLISTICS** | Avco 9109 003 |
| 05/07/1975 | 5 | 23 | ● | **THANK YOU BABY** | Avco 9109 005 |
| 06/12/1975 | 26 | 9 | ○ | YOU ARE BEAUTIFUL | Avco 9109 006 |
| 12/06/1976 | 21 | 5 | ○ | FABULOUS | H&L 9109 008 |
| 18/09/1976 | ❶¹ | 21 | ● | **BEST OF THE STYLISTICS VOLUME 2** | H&L 9109 010 |
| 17/10/1992 | 34 | 3 | | THE GREATEST HITS OF THE STYLISTICS | Mercury 5129852 |

**STYX** US rock group formed in Chicago, IL in 1971 by Dennis De Young (born 18/2/1947, Chicago, keyboards/vocals), James Young (born 14/11/1948, Chicago, guitar/vocals), Chuck Panozzo (born 20/9/1947, Chicago, bass), his twin brother John (drums) and John Curulewski (guitar). Curulewski left in 1976, replaced by Tommy Shaw (born 11/9/1950, Montgomery, AL). They disbanded in 1984, and reunited in 1990. John Panozzo died from alcoholism on 16/7/1996.

| | | | | | |
|---|---|---|---|---|---|
| 03/11/1979 | 36 | 8 | | CORNERSTONE | A&M AMLK 63711 |
| 24/01/1981 | 8 | 8 | ○ | **PARADISE THEATER** ▲³ | A&M AMLH 63719 |
| 12/03/1983 | 67 | 6 | | KILROY WAS HERE | A&M AMLX 63734 |
| 05/05/1984 | 44 | 2 | | CAUGHT IN THE ACT | A&M AMLM 66704 |

**SUEDE** UK rock group formed in London in 1990 by Brett Anderson (born 27/9/1967, Haywards Heath, vocals), Mat Osman (born 9/10/1967, Haywards Heath) and Bernard Butler (born 1/5/1970, guitar). They signed with RMI the same year but left the label without any releases. They added drummer Simon Gilbert (born 23/5/1965, Stratford-on-Avon) to the line-up, signed with Nude Records in 1992 and later added Neil Codling on keyboards. Butler left in 1994 and was replaced by Richard Oakes (born 10/10/1976). In April 1992 they appeared on the cover of *Melody Maker*, even though they hadn't released any records.

| | | | | | |
|---|---|---|---|---|---|
| 10/04/1993 | ❶¹ | 22 | ● | **SUEDE** 1993 Mercury Music Prize | Nude 1CD |
| 22/10/1994 | 3 | 16 | ● | **DOG MAN STAR** | Nude 4778112 |
| 14/09/1996 | ❶¹ | 44 | ✪ | **COMING UP** | Nude 6CD |
| 18/10/1997 | 9 | 3 | | **SCI-FI LULLABIES** | Nude 9CD |
| 15/05/1999 | ❶¹ | 16 | ● | **HEAD MUSIC** | Nude 14CD |
| 12/10/2002 | 24 | 2 | | A NEW MORNING | Epic 5089569 |
| 01/11/2003 | 31 | 2 | | SINGLES | Sony Music 5136042 |

**SUGABABES** UK group formed by Keisha Buchanan (born 30/9/1985, London), Mutya Buena (born 21/5/1985, London) and Siobhan Donaghy (born 19/6/1984, London). Donaghy left the group for a solo career in August 2001 and was replaced by Heidi Range (born 23/5/1984), who had been a member of Atomic Kitten when they had first formed. Sugababes were named Best British Dance Act at the 2003 BRIT Awards.

| | | | | | |
|---|---|---|---|---|---|
| 23/12/2000 | 26 | 15 | ● | ONE TOUCH | London 8573861072 |
| 07/09/2002 | 2 | 40 | ✪² | **ANGELS WITH DIRTY FACES** ◇ | Island CID 8122 |
| 08/11/2003 | 3 | 29 | ✪² | **THREE** ◇ | Island CID 8137 |

**SUGAR** US rock group formed in 1991 by ex-Husker Du singer/writer Bob Mould (born 16/10/1960, Malone, NY, guitar/vocals), David Barbe (born 30/9/1963, Atlanta, GA, bass) and Malcolm Travis (born 15/2/1953, Niskayuna, NY, drums). They split in 1995.

| | | | | | |
|---|---|---|---|---|---|
| 19/09/1992 | 10 | 11 | ○ | **COPPER BLUE** | Creation CRECD 129 |
| 17/04/1993 | 3 | 5 | | **BEASTER** | Creation CRECD 153 |
| 17/09/1994 | 7 | 3 | | **FILE UNDER EASY LISTENING** | Creation CRECD 172 |

○ Silver disc ● Gold disc ✪ Platinum disc (additional platinum units are indicated by a figure following the symbol) ❶⁹ Number of weeks album topped the UK chart

## SUGAR RAY
US group formed in Orange County in 1995 by Mark Sayers McGrath (vocals), Rodney Sheppard (guitar), Murphy Karges (bass), Craig 'DJ Homocide' Bullock (born 17/12/1970, DJ) and Stan Frazier (born 23/4/1968, drums). They appeared in the 1997 film *Fathers' Day* with Billy Crystal and Robin Williams.

| | | | | |
|---|---|---|---|---|
| 19/06/1999 | 60 | 1 | | 14:59 .......................................................................................Atlantic 7567831512 |

## SUGARCUBES
Icelandic rock group formed in Reykjavik in 1986 by Bjork Gundmundsdottir (born 21/11/1965, Reykjavik, vocals/keyboards), Bragi Olaffson (born 11/8/1962, bass), Einar Orn Benediktsson (born 29/10/1962, Copenhagen, Denmark, vocals/trumpet), Margret Ornolfsdottir (born 21/11/1967, Reykjavik, keyboards), Sigtryggur Balduresson (born 2/10/1962, Stavanger, Norway, drums) and Thor Eldon (born 2/6/1962, Reykjavik, guitar). Bjork launched a solo career in 1992.

| | | | | |
|---|---|---|---|---|
| 07/05/1988 | 14 | 6 | | LIFE'S TOO GOOD .............................................................One Little Indian TPLP 5 |
| 14/10/1989 | 15 | 3 | | HERE TODAY, TOMORROW NEXT WEEK! ...................................One Little Indian TPLP 15 |
| 22/02/1992 | 16 | 4 | | STICK AROUND FOR JOY ...................................................One Little Indian TPLP 30CD |
| 17/10/1992 | 47 | 1 | | IT'S IT .......................................................................One Little Indian TPLP 40CD |

## SUGGS
UK singer (born Graham McPherson, 13/1/1961, Hastings) who was lead singer with Madness from 1978. He later managed the Farm and went solo in 1995. He also presents the TV pop quiz *Night Fever* on Channel 5.

| | | | | |
|---|---|---|---|---|
| 28/10/1995 | 14 | 5 | O | THE LONE RANGER ........................................................................WEA 0630124782 |

## SUICIDAL TENDENCIES
US vocal/instrumental group formed in Venice, CA in 1982 by Mike Muir (vocals). Members over the years have included Mark Dodson, Louiche Mayorga, Robert Trujillo, Brooks Wackerman, Mike Clark, Rocky George and Josh Paul.

| | | | | |
|---|---|---|---|---|
| 09/05/1987 | 81 | 1 | | JOIN THE ARMY ....................................................................................Virgin V 2424 |
| 21/07/1990 | 59 | 1 | | LIGHTS… CAMERA… REVOLUTION ..............................................................Epic 4665691 |

## SULTANS OF PING FC
Irish rock group formed in 1989 by Niall O'Flaherty (vocals), Paddy O'Connell (guitar), Morty McCarthy (drums) and Alan 'Dat' McFeely (bass).

| | | | | |
|---|---|---|---|---|
| 13/02/1993 | 26 | 2 | | CASUAL SEX IN THE CINEPLEX ..........................................................Rhythm King 4724952 |
| 05/03/1994 | 57 | 1 | | TEENAGE DRUG **SULTANS OF PING** ...........................................................Epic 4747162 |

## SUM 41
Canadian group formed in Ontario by Derick Whibley (guitar/vocals), Dave Baksh (guitar/vocals), Cone McCaslin (bass) and Steve Jocz (drums). They signed with Island Records in 1999.

| | | | | |
|---|---|---|---|---|
| 11/08/2001 | 7 | 43 | ✪ | **ALL KILLER NO FILLER** .....................................................................Island 5486622 |
| 07/12/2002 | 39 | 6 | O | DOES THIS LOOK INFECTED ...............................................................Mercury 0635590 |

## DONNA SUMMER
US singer (born Adrian Donna Gaines, 31/12/1948, Dorchester, MA); she began in the German production of *Hair*, relocating to Austria in 1971. She married actor Helmut Sommer, keeping an anglicised version of his name when they divorced. After meeting producer Giorgio Moroder she recorded solo for the Oasis label in 1973 and had numerous European hits, achieving a worldwide breakthrough in 1975. She appeared in the 1978 film *Thank God It's Friday* and married singer Bruce Sudano (of Brooklyn Dreams) in 1980. She has won five Grammy Awards: Best Rhythm & Blues Vocal Performance in 1978 for *Last Dance* (which also won the Best Rhythm & Blues Song category for writer Paul Jabara); Best Rock Vocal Performance in 1979 for *Hot Stuff*; Best Inspirational Performance in 1983 for *He's A Rebel*; Best Inspirational Performance in 1984 for *Forgive Me*; and Best Dance Recording in 1999 with Giorgio Moroder for *Carry On*. She has a star on the Hollywood Walk of Fame.

| | | | | |
|---|---|---|---|---|
| 31/01/1976 | 16 | 9 | ● | LOVE TO LOVE YOU BABY .................................................................GTO GTLP 008 |
| 22/05/1976 | 41 | 10 | ● | A LOVE TRILOGY ..........................................................................GTO GTLP 010 |
| 25/06/1977 | 3 | 23 | ● | **I REMEMBER YESTERDAY** ..............................................................GTO GTLP 025 |
| 26/11/1977 | 24 | 13 | ● | ONCE UPON A TIME .................................................................Casablanca CALD 5003 |
| 07/01/1978 | 4 | 18 | ● | **GREATEST HITS** ........................................................................GTO GTLP 028 |
| 21/10/1978 | 16 | 16 | ● | LIVE AND MORE ▲[1] .............................................................Casablanca CALD 5006 |
| 02/06/1979 | 23 | 23 | O | BAD GIRLS ▲[6] .....................................................................Casablanca CALD 5007 |
| 10/11/1979 | 24 | 22 | ● | ON THE RADIO – GREATEST HITS VOLUME 1 & 2 ▲[1] ....................Casablanca CALD 5008 |
| 01/11/1980 | 55 | 2 | | THE WANDERER ............................................................................Geffen K 99124 |
| 31/07/1982 | 13 | 16 | | DONNA SUMMER .................................................................Warner Brothers K 99163 |
| 16/07/1983 | 28 | 5 | | SHE WORKS HARD FOR THE MONEY ..........................................................Mercury MERL 21 |
| 15/09/1984 | 69 | 2 | | CATS WITHOUT CLAWS ...........................................................Warner Brothers 250806 |
| 25/03/1989 | 17 | 28 | ● | ANOTHER PLACE AND TIME .......................................................Warner Brothers WX 219 |
| 24/11/1990 | 24 | 9 | ● | THE BEST OF DONNA SUMMER .....................................................Warner Brothers WX 397 |
| 26/11/1994 | 37 | 2 | | ENDLESS SUMMER – GREATEST HITS ..........................................................Mercury 5262172 |
| 26/06/2004 | 16 | 1+ | | THE JOURNEY – THE VERY BEST OF DONNA SUMMER ..................................Mercury 9862858 |

## SUNDAYS
UK rock group formed in London in 1987 by David Gavurin (born 4/4/1963, guitar), Harriet Wheeler (born 26/6/1963, vocals), Paul Brindley (born 6/11/1963, bass) and Patrick Hannan (born 4/3/1966, drums).

| | | | | |
|---|---|---|---|---|
| 27/01/1990 | 4 | 8 | O | **READING WRITING AND ARITHMETIC** .......................................Rough Trade ROUGH 148 |
| 31/10/1992 | 15 | 3 | | BLIND .............................................................................Parlophone CDPCSD 121 |
| 04/10/1997 | 10 | 4 | O | **STATIC & SILENCE** ................................................................Parlophone CDEST 2300 |

## SUNSCREEM
UK group formed by Lucia Holm (vocals), Darren Woodford (guitar), Paul Carnell (keyboards), Rob Fricker (bass) and Sean Wright (drums).

---

▲[9] Number of weeks album topped the US chart   ◆[12] RIAA Diamond Awards   ◇[3] IFPI Platinum Europe Awards

| DATE | POS | WKS | BPI | ALBUM TITLE | LABEL & NUMBER |
|------|-----|-----|-----|-------------|----------------|
| 13/02/1993 | 33 | 5 | | 03 | Sony S2 4722182 |
| 30/03/1996 | 53 | 1 | | CHANGE OR DIE | Sony S2 4813132 |

**SUNSHINE BAND** – see KC AND THE SUNSHINE BAND

**SUPER FURRY ANIMALS** UK rock group formed in Cardiff in 1993 by Gruff Rhys (born 18/7/1970, Haverfordwest, guitar/vocals), Cian Claran (born 16/6/1976, Bangor, electronics/keyboards), Guto Pryce (born 4/9/1972, Cardiff, bass), Huw Bunford (born 15/9/1967, Cardiff, guitar/vocals) and Dafydd Ieuan (born 16/6/1976, Bangor, drums) who previously recorded for Ankst Records.

| DATE | POS | WKS | BPI | ALBUM TITLE | LABEL & NUMBER |
|------|-----|-----|-----|-------------|----------------|
| 01/06/1996 | 23 | 6 | | FUZZY LOGIC | Creation CRECD 190 |
| 06/09/1997 | 8 | 3 | | RADIATOR | Creation CRECD 214 |
| 05/12/1998 | 44 | 1 | | OUT SPACED | Creation CRECD 229 |
| 26/06/1999 | 10 | 9 | | GUERRILLA | Creation CRECD 242 |
| 27/05/2000 | 11 | 2 | | MWNG | Placid Casual PLC 03CD |
| 04/08/2001 | 3 | 7 | ● | RINGS AROUND THE WORLD | Epic 5024132 |
| 02/08/2003 | 4 | 4 | ○ | PHANTOM POWER | Epic 5123759 |

**SUPERGRASS** UK rock group: Danny Goffey (born 7/2/1974, Oxford, drums), Gareth 'Gaz' Coombes (born 8/3/1976, Oxford, guitar/vocals) and Mickey Quinn (born 17/12/1969, Oxford, bass). They made their first record for Nude Records in 1992 and signed with Parlophone in 1994. In 1995 they added Bob Coombes (born 27/4/1972, Oxford, keyboards) to the line-up. The group was named Best UK Newcomer at the 1996 BRIT Awards.

| DATE | POS | WKS | BPI | ALBUM TITLE | LABEL & NUMBER |
|------|-----|-----|-----|-------------|----------------|
| 27/05/1995 | ❶³ 36 | | ✪ | I SHOULD COCO | Parlophone CDPCS 7373 |
| 03/05/1997 | 2 | 25 | ✪ | IN IT FOR THE MONEY | Parlophone CDPCS 7388 |
| 02/10/1999 | 3 | 25 | ✪ | SUPERGRASS | Parlophone 5220562 |
| 12/10/2002 | 9 | 6 | ● | LIFE ON OTHER PLANETS | Parlophone 5418002 |
| 19/06/2004 | 4 | 2+ | ● | SUPERGRASS IS 10 – THE BEST OF 94–04 | Parlophone 5708602 |

**SUPERNATURALS** UK group formed by James McColl (guitar/lead vocals), Derek McManus (guitar), Mark Guthrie (bass), Ken McAlpine (keyboards) and Alan Tilston (drums). The group formed the OFL label before signing with Food.

| DATE | POS | WKS | BPI | ALBUM TITLE | LABEL & NUMBER |
|------|-----|-----|-----|-------------|----------------|
| 17/05/1997 | 9 | 4 | | IT DOESN'T MATTER ANYMORE | Food FOODCD 21 |
| 22/08/1998 | 21 | 3 | | A TUNE A DAY | Food 4995762 |

**SUPERTRAMP** UK rock group formed in 1969 by Richard Davies (born 22/7/1944, Swindon, vocals/keyboards), Roger Hodgson (born 21/3/1950, London, bass), Richard Palmer (born June 1947, Bournemouth, guitar) and Bob Miller (drums). They signed with A&M and added saxophonist Dave Winthrop (born 27/11/1948, New Jersey, USA) to the line-up in 1970. Palmer and Miller left in 1971 and were replaced by Kevin Currie (drums) and Frank Farrell (bass), with Hodgson switching to guitar. John Helliwell (born 15/2/1945, Todmorden, saxophone) and Bob C Benberg joined in 1973. Hodgson left for a solo career in 1982. They were named after a book by W H Davis, *Diary Of A Supertramp*.

| DATE | POS | WKS | BPI | ALBUM TITLE | LABEL & NUMBER |
|------|-----|-----|-----|-------------|----------------|
| 23/11/1974 | 4 | 22 | ● | CRIME OF THE CENTURY | A&M AMLS 68258 |
| 06/12/1975 | 20 | 15 | | CRISIS? WHAT CRISIS? | A&M AMLH 68347 |
| 23/04/1977 | 12 | 22 | ○ | EVEN IN THE QUIETEST MOMENTS… | A&M AMLK 64634 |
| 31/03/1979 | 3 | 53 | ✪ | BREAKFAST IN AMERICA ▲⁶ | A&M AMLK 63708 |
| 04/10/1980 | 7 | 17 | ● | PARIS | A&M AMLM 66702 |
| 06/11/1982 | 6 | 16 | ● | …FAMOUS LAST WORDS… ' | A&M AMLK 63732 |
| 25/05/1985 | 20 | 5 | | BROTHER WHERE YOU BOUND | A&M AMA 5014 |
| 18/10/1986 | 9 | 19 | ✪ | THE AUTOBIOGRAPHY OF SUPERTRAMP | A&M TRAMP 1 |
| 31/10/1987 | 93 | 1 | | FREE AS A BIRD | A&M AMA 5181 |
| 15/08/1992 | 24 | 4 | | THE VERY BEST OF SUPERTRAMP | A&M TRACD 1992 |
| 03/05/1997 | 74 | 1 | | SOME THINGS NEVER CHANGE | EMI CDCHR 6121 |
| 27/09/1997 | 8 | 6 | ● | THE VERY BEST OF SUPERTRAMP | Polygram TV 3970912 |

○ Silver disc  ● Gold disc  ✪ Platinum disc (additional platinum units are indicated by a figure following the symbol)  ❶⁹ Number of weeks album topped the UK chart

## SUPREMES

**SUPREMES** US R&B vocal group formed in 1959 by Mary Wilson (born 6/3/1944, Greenville, MS), Florence Ballard (born 30/6/1943, Detroit, MI) and Betty Travis as the Primettes, a sister group to manager Milton Jenkins' act the Primes (who became the Temptations). Diana Ross (born Diane Ross, 26/3/1944, Detroit) joined the same year, and Travis left to be replaced by Barbara Martin. They debuted on record for Lupine in 1960 shortly before signing with Motown, changing their name (at Berry Gordy's request) to Ballard's suggestion The Supremes. Martin left and the group remained a trio. Original lead Ballard was fired in 1967 and was replaced by Cindy Birdsong (born 15/12/1939, Camden, NJ). Ross went solo in 1970 and was replaced by Jean Terrell (born 26/11/1944, Texas, sister of boxer Ernie). Birdsong left in 1972 and was replaced by Lynda Laurence; Terrell left in 1973 to be replaced by Scherrie Payne (born 14/11/1944, Detroit, sister of Freda Payne). Laurence left in 1974 and was replaced by Susaye Greene. They disbanded in 1976, although Wilson formed a new Supremes with Karen Jackson and Karen Ragland. Ross and Wilson accepted an invitation to re-form the group for a series of live concerts in 2000. Ballard died on 21/2/1976 from a heart attack. They were inducted into the Rock & Roll Hall of Fame in 1988. Diana Ross was awarded a star on the Hollywood Walk of Fame in 1982, Mary Wilson in 1990.

| DATE | POS | WKS | BPI | ALBUM TITLE | LABEL & NUMBER |
|---|---|---|---|---|---|
| 05/12/1964 | 8 | 6 | | **MEET THE SUPREMES** | Stateside SL 10109 |
| 17/12/1966 | 15 | 21 | | **SUPREMES A GO-GO** ▲[2] | Tamla Motown STML 11039 |
| 13/05/1967 | 15 | 16 | | **THE SUPREMES SING MOTOWN** | Tamla Motown STML 11047 |
| 30/09/1967 | 25 | 7 | | **THE SUPREMES SING RODGERS AND HART** | Tamla Motown STML 11054 |
| 20/01/1968 | ❶[3] | 60 | | **DIANA ROSS AND THE SUPREMES GREATEST HITS** ▲[5] | Tamla Motown STML 11063 |
| 30/03/1968 | 6 | 18 | | **LIVE' AT LONDON'S TALK OF THE TOWN** | Tamla Motown STML 11070 |
| 20/07/1968 | 30 | 2 | | REFLECTIONS This and the above two hits credited to **DIANA ROSS AND THE SUPREMES** | Tamla Motown STML 11073 |
| 25/01/1969 | ❶[4] | 15 | | **DIANA ROSS AND THE SUPREMES JOIN THE TEMPTATIONS** DIANA ROSS AND THE SUPREMES AND THE TEMPTATIONS | |
| | | | | | TamlaMotown STML 11096 |
| 01/02/1969 | 8 | 6 | | **LOVE CHILD** DIANA ROSS AND THE SUPREMES | Tamla Motown STML 11095 |
| 28/06/1969 | 11 | 12 | | THE ORIGINAL SOUNDTRACK FROM TCB ▲[1] Original soundtrack to the TV series | Tamla Motown STML 11110 |
| 14/02/1970 | 28 | 4 | | TOGETHER This and the above hit credited to **DIANA ROSS AND THE SUPREMES AND THE TEMPTATIONS** | |
| | | | | | Tamla Motown STML 11122 |
| 29/05/1971 | 6 | 11 | | **THE MAGNIFICENT SEVEN** SUPREMES AND THE FOUR TOPS | Tamla Motown STML 11179 |
| 25/09/1971 | 40 | 1 | | TOUCH | Tamla Motown STML 11189 |
| 17/09/1977 | ❶[7] | 34 | | **DIANA ROSS AND THE SUPREMES 20 GOLDEN GREATS** | Motown EMTV 5 |
| 21/02/1989 | 10 | 9 | ◯ | **LOVE SUPREME** | Motown ZL 72701 |
| 31/10/1998 | 35 | 4 | | 40 GOLDEN MOTOWN GREATS | Motown 5309612 |
| 29/05/2004 | 26 | 3 | | THE NO 1'S This and the above three hits credited to **DIANA ROSS AND THE SUPREMES** | Motown 9818019 |

## SURVIVOR

**SURVIVOR** US rock group formed by Dave Bickler (keyboards/vocals), Jim Peterik (born 1/11/1950, keyboards/guitar/vocals), Frankie Sullivan (guitar/vocals), Gary Smith (drums) and Dennis Johnson (bass). Smith and Johnson left in 1981 and were replaced by Marc Droubay and Stephen Ellis. They won the 1982 Grammy Award for Best Rock Vocal Performance for *Eye Of The Tiger*. Bickler left in 1984 to be replaced by Jimi Jamison. Droubay and Ellis left in 1988. The group disbanded in 1989 and reunited in 1994.

| DATE | POS | WKS | BPI | ALBUM TITLE | LABEL & NUMBER |
|---|---|---|---|---|---|
| 21/08/1982 | 12 | 10 | | EYE OF THE TIGER | Scotti Brothers SCT 85845 |

## SUTHERLAND BROTHERS AND QUIVER

**SUTHERLAND BROTHERS AND QUIVER** UK folk-rock group formed in 1972 by Iain (guitar/vocals) and Gavin Sutherland (bass/vocals), Willie Wilson (drums/vocals), Bruce Thomas (bass), Pete Wood (keyboards) and Tim Renwick (guitar/vocals). The group disbanded in 1977.

| DATE | POS | WKS | BPI | ALBUM TITLE | LABEL & NUMBER |
|---|---|---|---|---|---|
| 15/05/1976 | 26 | 8 | ◯ | REACH FOR THE SKY | CBS 69191 |
| 09/10/1976 | 49 | 3 | ◯ | SLIPSTREAM | CBS 81593 |

## SWANS WAY

**SWANS WAY** UK group formed in Birmingham in 1982 by Rick Jones (double bass), Maggie De Monde (vocals) and Robert Shaw (guitar/vocals). De Monde and Shaw went on to form Scarlet Fantastic.

| DATE | POS | WKS | BPI | ALBUM TITLE | LABEL & NUMBER |
|---|---|---|---|---|---|
| 03/11/1984 | 88 | 1 | | THE FUGITIVE KIND | Balgier SWAN 1 |

## KEITH SWEAT

**KEITH SWEAT** US R&B singer/producer (born 22/7/1961, Harlem, NYC); he was a member of the Rhythm Makers and GQ before going solo. He appeared in the 1991 film *New Jack City* and later joined Gerald Levert and Johnny Gill to form Levert Sweat Gill.

| DATE | POS | WKS | BPI | ALBUM TITLE | LABEL & NUMBER |
|---|---|---|---|---|---|
| 29/10/1988 | 41 | 21 | ◯ | MAKE IT LAST FOREVER | Elektra 9607631 |
| 23/06/1990 | 47 | 4 | | I'LL GIVE ALL MY LOVE TO YOU | Vintertainment EKT 60 |
| 09/07/1994 | 20 | 4 | | GET UP ON IT | Elektra 7559615502 |
| 29/06/1996 | 36 | 2 | | KEITH SWEAT | Elektra 7559617072 |
| 03/10/1998 | 62 | 1 | | STILL IN THE GAME | Elektra 7559622622 |

## CLAIRE SWEENEY

**CLAIRE SWEENEY** UK singer (born 14/4/1972, Liverpool) who first came to prominence as an actress, appearing in the TV series *Brookside* as Lindsey Corkhill for two episodes in 1991 before leaving to sing on a cruise ship for four years. She returned to Brookside in 1995 and later appeared in the stage musical *Chicago* before launching a singing career.

| DATE | POS | WKS | BPI | ALBUM TITLE | LABEL & NUMBER |
|---|---|---|---|---|---|
| 27/07/2002 | 15 | 3 | | CLAIRE | T2 TCD 3254 |

## SWEET

**SWEET** UK pop group formed in London in 1968 by Brian Connolly (born Brian McManus, 5/10/1949, Hamilton, vocals), Mick Tucker (born 17/7/1949, London, drums), Steve Priest (born 23/2/1950, Hayes, bass) and Frank Torpey (guitar) as Sweetshop. After unsuccessful singles with Fontana and Parlophone, the group shortened their name and replaced Torpey with Andy Scott (born 30/6/1951, Wrexham). They signed with RCA in 1971. Connolly went solo in 1979 and the group dissolved in 1981. A series of heart attacks (including fourteen in one 24-hour spell) effectively brought Connolly's career to an end, and he died from kidney failure on 10/2/1997. After battling with leukaemia for five years, Mick Tucker died on 14/2/2002.

| DATE | POS | WKS | BPI | ALBUM TITLE | LABEL & NUMBER |
|---|---|---|---|---|---|
| 18/05/1974 | 27 | 2 | ● | SWEET FANNY ADAMS | RCA Victor LPI 5038 |
| 22/09/1984 | 49 | 6 | | SWEET SIXTEEN – IT'S IT'S… SWEET HITS | Anagram GRAM 16 |
| 20/01/1996 | 15 | 6 | | BALLROOM HITZ – THE VERY BEST OF SWEET | Polygram TV 5350012 |

▲[9] Number of weeks album topped the US chart ◆[12] RIAA Diamond Awards ◇[3] IFPI Platinum Europe Awards

### SWERVEDRIVER
UK group formed in 1990 by Adam Franklin (born 19/7/1968, guitar/vocals), Jimmy Hartridge (born 27/11/1967, guitar/vocals), Adi Vines (born 25/1/1968, bass) and Graham Bonner (born 28/4/1967, drums). By 1993 the group was a trio of Franklin, Hartridge and drummer Jez, Bonner and Vines going on to form Skyscraper.

| 12/10/1991 | 44 | 1 | | RAISE | Creation CRELP 093 |
| 09/10/1993 | 55 | 1 | | MEZCAL HEAD | Creation CCRE 143 |

### SWING OUT SISTER
UK jazz-pop group formed by Andy Connell (keyboards), Martin Jackson (percussion) and Corrine Drewery (vocals). Jackson left in 1989 and they continued as a duo. In 1994 they were joined by Derick Johnson (bass), Myke Wilson (drums), Tim Cansfield (guitar), John Thrikell (trumpet) and Gary Plumey (saxophone).

| 23/05/1987 | ❶² | 21 | ✪ | IT'S BETTER TO TRAVEL | Mercury OUTLP 1 |
| 20/05/1989 | 9 | 11 | ● | KALEIDOSCOPE WORLD | Fontana 8382931 |
| 16/05/1992 | 27 | 4 | | GET IN TOUCH WITH YOURSELF | Fontana 5122412 |

### SWINGLE SINGERS
US/French vocal group formed in 1963 by Ward Lamar Swingle (born 21/9/1927, Mobile, AL) who was a former conductor of Les Ballets De Paris. In 1973 he launched Swingle II. They won five Grammy Awards: Best New Artist and Best Performance by a Chorus for *Bach's Greatest Hits* in 1963; Best Performance by a Chorus in 1964 for *The Swingle Singers Going Baroque*; Best Performance by a Chorus in 1965 for *Anyone For Mozart?*; and Best Classical Performance, Choral (Other Than Opera) – Ward Swingle, choral master: Luciano Berio conducting the New York Philharmonic and Swingle Singers in 1969 for *Berio: Sinfonia*.

| 01/02/1964 | 13 | 18 | | JAZZ SEBASTIAN BACH | Philips BL 7572 |

### S.W.V.
US R&B vocal group formed by Cheryl 'Coko' Gamble (born 1974, lead vocals), Tamara 'Taj' Johnson (born 1974) and Leanne 'Lelee' Lyons (born 1976). The group's name is short for Sisters With Voices. Coko later recorded solo.

| 17/07/1993 | 17 | 17 | | IT'S ABOUT TIME | RCA 7863660742 |
| 04/05/1996 | 26 | 5 | | NEW BEGINNING | RCA 07863664872 |
| 16/08/1997 | 19 | 5 | | RELEASE SOME TENSION | RCA 74321496162 |

### SYBIL
US singer (born Sybil Lynch, 1963, Paterson, NJ); first known in Ce Ce & Company with Ce Ce Rogers before going solo in 1986.

| 05/09/1987 | 92 | 1 | | LET YOURSELF GO | Champion CHAMP 1009 |
| 24/02/1990 | 21 | 5 | | WALK ON BY | PWL HF 10 |
| 12/06/1993 | 13 | 6 | | GOOD 'N' READY | PWL International HFCD 28 |

### SYLVESTER
US singer (born Sylvester James, 6/9/1947, Los Angeles, CA). He joined the Cockettes in 1970 and signed solo with Blue Thumb in 1973. He formed the Two Tons of Fun (later known as the Weather Girls) and switched to Fantasy in 1977. He died from an AIDS-related illness on 16/12/1988.

| 23/06/1979 | 62 | 3 | | MIGHTY REAL | Fantasy FTA 3009 |

### DAVID SYLVIAN
UK singer (born David Batt, 23/2/1958, Lewisham) who was a founder member of Japan in 1977 until they disbanded in 1982 when he went solo.

| 07/07/1984 | 4 | 14 | ● | BRILLIANT TREES | Virgin V 2290 |
| 13/09/1986 | 24 | 5 | ○ | GONE TO EARTH | Virgin VDL 1 |
| 07/11/1987 | 37 | 2 | | SECRETS OF THE BEEHIVE | Virgin V 2471 |
| 02/04/1988 | 71 | 1 | | PLIGHT AND PREMONITION **DAVID SYLVAN AND HOLGAR CZUKAY** | Virgin VE 11 |
| 17/07/1993 | 21 | 2 | | THE FIRST DAY **DAVID SYLVAN AND ROBERT FRIPP** | Virgin CDVX 2712 |
| 10/04/1999 | 31 | 2 | | DEAD BEES ON A CAKE | Virgin CDV 2876 |
| 21/10/2000 | 57 | 1 | | EVERYTHING & NOTHING | Virgin CDVDX 2897 |

### SYMPHONIQUE
UK keyboard player Chris Cozens.

| 01/04/1995 | 21 | 4 | | MOODS SYMPHONIQUE 95 | Vision VISCD 10 |

### SYMPOSIUM
UK rock group formed in London in 1995 by Ross Cummins (vocals), William McGonagle (guitar), Hagop Tchaparian (guitar), Wojtek Godzisz (bass) and Joe Birch (drums).

| 08/11/1997 | 29 | 2 | | ONE DAY AT A TIME | Infectious INFECT 49CD |
| 30/05/1998 | 32 | 1 | | ON THE OUTSIDE | Infectious INFECT 056CD |

### SYNTHPHONIC VARIATIONS
UK studio group formed by Mitch Darton (guitar), Tristan Fry (percussion), Steve Gregory (saxophone), Bob Carter (keyboards), Nick Grennie-Smith (keyboards), Richard Williamson (keyboards), Ronnie Asprey (saxophone) and Steve Rance (programming).

| 01/11/1986 | 84 | 1 | | SEASONS | CBS 4501491 |

### SYSTEM OF A DOWN
US rock group formed in Los Angeles, CA by Serj Tankian (vocals), Daron Malakian (guitar), Shavo Odadjian (bass) and John Doolayan (drums). After a three-song demo attracted interest they signed with American (distributed by Columbia) in 1997 and released their eponymous debut album the following year.

| 08/09/2001 | 13 | 27 | ● | TOXICITY ▲¹ | Columbia 5015346 |
| 07/12/2002 | 56 | 1 | | STEAL THIS ALBUM | American Recordings 5102489 |

### SYSTEM 7
French/UK dance duo formed by Miquette Giraudy and Steve Hillage (born 2/8/1951, London). The group has also featured contributions from DJ Paul Oakenfold, Alex Paterson (of The Orb) and Simple Minds' Mike McNeil (born 20/7/1958, Glasgow).

| 20/06/1992 | 75 | 1 | | ALTITUDE | 10 Records TENG 403 |
| 20/03/1993 | 30 | 2 | | 777 | Wau BFLCD 1 |

○ Silver disc ● Gold disc ✪ Platinum disc (additional platinum units are indicated by a figure following the symbol) ❶⁹ Number of weeks album topped the UK chart

### T. REX

**T. REX** UK rock group formed in London in 1967 by Marc Bolan (born Mark Feld, 30/9/1947, Hackney, London, guitar/vocals), Steve Peregrine Took (born Stephen Porter, 28/7/1949, Eltham, percussion) and Ben Cartland. Took left in 1969 and was replaced by Mickey Finn (born 3/6/1947, Thornton Heath), with Steve Currie (bass) and Bill Legend (drums) also being recruited. *My People Were Fair And Had Sky In Their Hair* reached #1 in May 1972, almost four years after it was originally released – the longest time any album has ever taken to get to #1. Bolan appeared in the 1972 film *Born To Boogie*. He was killed when a car driven by his then-girlfriend Gloria Jones hit a tree on 16/9/1977. Took choked to death on a cherry on 27/10/1980 after eating 'magic mushrooms' that had numbed the senses in his throat. Currie was killed in a road crash on 28/4/1981. Finn died on 11/1/2003.

| Date | Peak | Weeks | | Title | Catalogue |
|---|---|---|---|---|---|
| 13/07/1968 | 15 | 9 | | MY PEOPLE WERE FAIR AND HAD SKY IN THEIR HAIR BUT NOW THEY'RE CONTENT TO WEAR STARS ON THEIR BROWS | Regal Zonophone SLRZ 1003 |
| 07/06/1969 | 12 | 3 | | UNICORN | Regal Zonophone S 1007 |
| 14/03/1970 | 21 | 6 | | A BEARD OF STARS This and the above two hits credited to **TYRANNOSAURUS REX** | Regal Zonophone SLRZ 1013 |
| 16/01/1971 | 13 | 24 | | T. REX | Fly HIFLY 2 |
| 07/08/1971 | 21 | 7 | | THE BEST OF T. REX | Flyback TON 2 |
| 09/10/1971 | **1**[8] | 44 | | **ELECTRIC WARRIOR** | Fly HIFLY 6 |
| 29/04/1972 | **1**[1] | 12 | | **PROPHETS, SEERS AND SAGES THE ANGELS OF THE AGES/MY PEOPLE WERE FAIR AND HAD SKY IN THEIR HAIR BUT NOW THEY'RE CONTENT TO WEAR STARS ON THEIR BROWS TYRANNOSAURUS REX** This is a double re-issue of *Prophets* and *My People*, although the former album was not previously a hit | Fly Double Back TOOFA 3/4 |
| 20/05/1972 | **1**[3] | 19 | | **BOLAN BOOGIE** | Fly HIFLY 8 |
| 05/08/1972 | 4 | 18 | | **THE SLIDER** | EMI BLN 5001 |
| 09/12/1972 | 44 | 2 | | A BEARD OF STARS/UNICORN | Cube TOOFA 9/10 |
| 31/03/1973 | 4 | 12 | | **TANX** | EMI BLN 5002 |
| 10/11/1973 | 32 | 3 | | GREAT HITS | EMI BLN 5003 |
| 16/03/1974 | 12 | 3 | | ZINC ALLOY AND THE HIDDEN RIDERS OF TOMORROW **MARC BOLAN AND T. REX** | EMI BLNA 7751 |
| 21/02/1976 | 50 | 1 | | FUTURISTIC DRAGON | EMI BLN 5004 |
| 09/04/1977 | 26 | 3 | | DANDY IN THE UNDERWORLD | EMI BLN 5005 |
| 30/06/1979 | 51 | 3 | | SOLID GOLD | EMI NUT 5 |
| 12/09/1981 | 35 | 6 | | T. REX IN CONCERT | Marc ABOLAN 1 |
| 07/11/1981 | 88 | 1 | | YOU SCARE ME TO DEATH | Cherry Red ERED 20 |
| 24/09/1983 | 83 | 3 | | DANCE IN THE MIDNIGHT This and the above hit credited to **MARC BOLAN** | Marc On Wax MARCL 501 |
| 04/05/1985 | 5 | 21 | ● | **BEST OF THE 20TH CENTURY BOY** | K-Tel NE 1297 |
| 28/09/1991 | 4 | 16 | ● | **THE ULTIMATE COLLECTION** | Telstar TCD 2539 |
| 07/10/1995 | 24 | 6 | | THE ESSENTIAL COLLECTION | Polygram TV 5259612 |
| 28/09/2002 | 18 | 8 | | THE ESSENTIAL COLLECTION This and the above three hits credited to **MARC BOLAN AND T. REX** | Universal TV 4934882 |

### TAKE THAT

**TAKE THAT** UK vocal group formed in Manchester in 1990 by Gary Barlow (born 20/1/1971, Frodsham), Howard Donald (born 27/4/1970, Manchester), Jason Orange (born 10/7/1974, Manchester), Mark Owen (born 27/1/1974, Oldham) and Robbie Williams (born 13/2/1974, Stoke-on-Trent) who took their name from a newspaper headline. Their initial single (*Do What U Like*) failed to chart but did secure them a major record deal with RCA. Williams had an acrimonious split with the group in 1995 and legal wrangles delayed his own solo career. The group announced they were to split in 1996 with their sign-off single *How Deep Is Your Love,* and with various solo projects awaiting the remaining members. The group won four BRIT Awards during their career: Best Single for *Could It Be Magic* in 1993, Best Single and Best Video for *Pray* in 1994 and Best Single for *Back For Good* in 1996, which was also their US chart debut. They also won two MTV Europe Music Awards: Best Group in 1994 and Best Live Act in 1995.

| Date | Peak | Weeks | Awards | Title | Catalogue |
|---|---|---|---|---|---|
| 05/09/1992 | 2 | 73 | ◇[2] | **TAKE THAT AND PARTY** | RCA 74321109 |
| 23/10/1993 | **1**[2] | 78 | ◇[4] | **EVERYTHING CHANGES** | RCA 74321169262 |
| 13/05/1995 | **1**[2] | 33 | ◇[2] | **NOBODY ELSE** ◇[2] | RCA 74321279092 |
| 26/08/1995 | 26 | 4 | | NOBODY ELSE (US VERSION) | Arista 07822188002 |
| 06/04/1996 | **1**[4] | 40 | ◇[3] | **GREATEST HITS** ◇[3] | RCA 74321355582 |

▲[9] Number of weeks album topped the US chart  ◆[12] RIAA Diamond Awards  ◇[3] IFPI Platinum Europe Awards

**TALK TALK** UK rock group formed in London in 1981 by Mark Hollis (born 1955, London, vocals/guitar/keyboards), Lee Harris (drums), Simon Bremner (keyboards) and Paul Webb (born 16/1/1962, bass). They signed with EMI the same year, with Bremner leaving in 1983. They switched to Polydor in 1990 but disbanded the following year.

| DATE | POS | WKS | BPI | ALBUM TITLE | LABEL & NUMBER |
|---|---|---|---|---|---|
| 24/07/1982 | 21 | 25 | ○ | THE PARTY'S OVER | EMI EMC 3413 |
| 25/02/1984 | 35 | 8 | | IT'S MY LIFE | EMI EMC 2400021 |
| 01/03/1986 | 8 | 21 | ● | **THE COLOUR OF SPRING** | EMI EMC 3506 |
| 24/09/1988 | 19 | 5 | ○ | SPIRIT OF EDEN | Parlophone PCSD 105 |
| 09/06/1990 | 3 | 21 | ● | **THE VERY BEST OF TALK TALK – NATURAL HISTORY** | Parlophone PCSD 109 |
| 06/04/1991 | 35 | 2 | | HISTORY REVISITED – THE REMIXES | Parlophone PCS 7349 |
| 28/09/1991 | 26 | 2 | | LAUGHING STOCK | Verve 8477171 |
| 08/02/1997 | 54 | 2 | | THE VERY BEST OF TALK TALK | EMI CDEMC 3763 |

**TALKING HEADS** US rock group formed in New York in 1974 by David Byrne (born 14/5/1952, Dumbarton, Scotland, guitar/vocals), Tina Weymouth (born 22/11/1950, Coronado, CA, bass) and Chris Frantz (born 8/5/1951, Fort Campbell, KY, drums). They signed with Sire in 1976 having added Jerry Harrison (born 21/2/1949, Milwaukee, WI, keyboards) to the line-up. Byrne won the 1988 Grammy Award for Best Album of Original Instrumental Background Score written for a Motion Picture with Ryuichi Sakamoto and Cong Su for *The Last Emperor*. The group was inducted into the Rock & Roll Hall of Fame in 2002.

| DATE | POS | WKS | BPI | ALBUM TITLE | LABEL & NUMBER |
|---|---|---|---|---|---|
| 25/02/1978 | 60 | 1 | | TALKING HEADS '77 | Sire 9103 328 |
| 29/07/1978 | 21 | 3 | | MORE SONGS ABOUT BUILDINGS AND FOOD | Sire K 56531 |
| 15/09/1979 | 33 | 5 | | FEAR OF MUSIC | Sire SRK 6076 |
| 01/11/1980 | 21 | 17 | ○ | REMAIN IN LIGHT | Sire SRK 6095 |
| 10/04/1982 | 22 | 5 | | THE NAME OF THIS BAND IS TALKING HEADS | Sire SRK 23590 |
| 18/06/1983 | 21 | 12 | | SPEAKING IN TONGUES | Sire K 9238831 |
| 27/10/1984 | 37 | 81 | ● | STOP MAKING SENSE | EMI TAH 1 |
| 29/06/1985 | 10 | 65 | ● | **LITTLE CREATURES** | EMI TAH 2 |
| 27/09/1986 | 7 | 9 | ● | **TRUE STORIES** | EMI EU 3511 |
| 26/03/1988 | 3 | 15 | ● | **NAKED** | EMI EMD 1005 |
| 24/10/1992 | 7 | 16 | ● | **ONCE IN A LIFETIME – THE BEST OF TALKING HEADS/SAND IN THE VASELINE** | EMI CDEQ 5010 |
| 18/09/1999 | 24 | 3 | | STOP MAKING SENSE | EMI 5224532 |

**TANGERINE DREAM** German group formed in 1968 by Edgar Froese (born 6/6/1944, Tilsit, guitar), Voker Hombach (flute/violin), Kirt Herkenber (bass) and Lanse Hapshash (drums). This line-up disbanded in 1969 and Froese recruited Konrad Schnitzler and Klaus Schulze, subsequently adding Christoph Franke and Steve Schroyder in 1971. Schroyder left in 1973 and was replaced by Peter Baumann. Baumann left in 1977 for a solo career and was replaced by Steve Jollife (who had briefly been a member in 1969) and added Klaus Kreiger at the same time. Franke left for a solo career in 1988 and was replaced by Ralf Wadephal.

| DATE | POS | WKS | BPI | ALBUM TITLE | LABEL & NUMBER |
|---|---|---|---|---|---|
| 20/04/1974 | 15 | 15 | ● | PHAEDRA | Virgin V 2010 |
| 05/04/1975 | 12 | 14 | ○ | RUBYCON | Virgin V 2025 |
| 20/12/1975 | 40 | 2 | ○ | RICOCHET | Virgin V 2044 |
| 13/11/1976 | 39 | 4 | ○ | STRATOSFEAR | Virgin V 2068 |
| 23/07/1977 | 25 | 7 | | SORCERER Original soundtrack to the film | MCA MCF 2806 |
| 19/11/1977 | 55 | 1 | | ENCORE | Virgin VD 2506 |
| 01/04/1978 | 37 | 4 | | CYCLONE | Virgin V 2097 |
| 17/02/1979 | 26 | 7 | | FORCE MAJEURE | Virgin V 2111 |
| 07/06/1980 | 36 | 5 | | TANGRAM | Virgin V 2147 |
| 18/04/1981 | 43 | 3 | | THIEF Original soundtrack to the film | Virgin V 2198 |
| 19/09/1981 | 43 | 5 | | EXIT | Virgin V 2212 |
| 10/04/1982 | 57 | 5 | | WHITE EAGLE | Virgin V 2226 |
| 05/11/1983 | 45 | 2 | | HYPERBOREA | Virgin V 2292 |
| 10/11/1984 | 90 | 1 | | POLAND | Jive Electro HIP 22 |

○ Silver disc  ● Gold disc  ✪ Platinum disc (additional platinum units are indicated by a figure following the symbol)  ❶⁹ Number of weeks album topped the UK chart

| | | | | | |
|---|---|---|---|---|---|
| 26/07/1986 | .97 | .1 | | UNDERWATER SUNLIGHT | Jive Electro HIP 40 |
| 27/06/1987 | .88 | .1 | | TYGER | Jive HIP 47 |

### TANK
UK group formed by Algy Ward (bass/vocals), Pete Brabbs (guitar) and Mark Brabbs (drums). The group disbanded in 1987 but re-formed in 1999 with Ward, Cliff Evans (guitar), Mick Tucker (guitar) and Bruce Bisland (drums).

| | | | | | |
|---|---|---|---|---|---|
| 13/03/1982 | .33 | .5 | | FILTH HOUNDS OF HADES | Kamaflage KAMLP 1 |

### BILL TARMEY
UK actor/singer (born William Cleworth Piddington, 4/4/1941, Manchester) whose most prominent role has been that of Jack Duckworth in the TV series *Coronation Street*.

| | | | | | |
|---|---|---|---|---|---|
| 27/11/1993 | .15 | .14 | ● | A GIFT OF LOVE | EMI CDEMC 3665 |
| 05/11/1994 | .28 | .9 | ○ | TIME FOR LOVE | EMI CDEMTV 85 |
| 18/05/1996 | .61 | .2 | | AFTER HOURS | EMI Premier PRMTVCD 2 |

### TASTE
Irish group formed in Cork in 1965 by Rory Gallagher (born 2/3/1949, Ballyshannon, County Donegal, guitar), Eric Kittringham (bass) and Norman Damery (drums). In 1968 Gallagher assembled a new line-up with Charlie McCracken (bass) and John Wilson (drums) but the group split in 1970. Gallagher then went solo. He died from complications brought on by a liver transplant on 14/6/1995.

| | | | | | |
|---|---|---|---|---|---|
| 07/02/1970 | .18 | .11 | | ON THE BOARDS | Polydor 583083 |
| 09/09/1972 | .41 | .1 | | TASTE – LIVE AT THE ISLE OF WIGHT | Polydor 2383 120 |

### JEFFREY TATE – see ENGLISH CHAMBER ORCHESTRA, NIGEL KENNEDY

### tATu
Russian vocal duo formed by Lena Katina (born Katina Elana Sergheeva, 4/10/1984, Moscow) and Julia Volkova Olegovna (born 20/2/1985, Moscow). Their name means This Girl Loves That Girl, reflecting their lesbian stance (later revealed as a marketing ploy instigated by their manager, especially when it was announced in May 2004 that Julia was pregnant by her long-term boyfriend).

| | | | | | |
|---|---|---|---|---|---|
| 25/01/2003 | .12 | .15 | ● | 200 KHM IN THE WRONG LANE ◇ | Interscope 0674562 |

### TAVARES
US R&B vocal group formed in New Bedford, MA in 1964 by brothers Ralph, Antone 'Chubby', Feliciano 'Butch', Arthur 'Pooch' and Perry Lee 'Tiny' Tavares as Chubby & The Turnpikes. They changed their name to Tavares in 1969.

| | | | | | |
|---|---|---|---|---|---|
| 21/08/1976 | .22 | .13 | | SKY HIGH | Capitol Soul EST 11533 |
| 01/04/1978 | .39 | .2 | ○ | THE BEST OF TAVARES | Capitol EST 11701 |

### ANDY TAYLOR
UK singer/guitarist (born 16/2/1961, Wolverhampton) who was a founder member of Duran Duran in 1978 and remained with the group until 1984. He then helped form Power Station with fellow Duran Duran member John Taylor, Robert Palmer and Tony Thompson. He launched a parallel solo career in 1987.

| | | | | | |
|---|---|---|---|---|---|
| 30/05/1987 | .61 | .1 | | THUNDER | MCA MCG 6018 |

### BECKY TAYLOR
UK singer (born 1988, London) who appeared in the West End musical *Les Miserables* at the age of seven, and won the British Arts Awards final for dancing at the age of nine. She was signed by EMI Classics a week after her father sent in a demo tape of her singing.

| | | | | | |
|---|---|---|---|---|---|
| 23/06/2001 | .67 | .1 | | A DREAM COME TRUE | EMI Classics CDC 5571422 |

### JAMES TAYLOR
US singer (born 12/3/1948, Boston, MA) who formed the Flying Machine in 1966. When they split in 1967 he moved to the UK and was signed as a solo artist to Apple Records, releasing one album before returning to the USA and signing with Warner's. He married Carly Simon in 1972 and was divorced in 1983. He appeared in an episode of *The Simpsons* offering advice when Homer became an astronaut. James has won seven Grammy Awards including: Best Pop Vocal Performance in 1971 for *You've Got A Friend*; Best Pop Vocal Performance in 1977 for *Handyman*; Best Recording For Children in 1980 with various others for *In Harmony*; Best Recording for Children in 1982 with various others for *In Harmony 2*; Best Male Pop Vocal Performance in 2001 for *Don't Let Me Be Lonely Tonight*; and Best Country Collaboration with Vocal in 2003 with Alison Krauss for *How's The World Treating You*. He was inducted into the Rock & Roll Hall of Fame in 2000.

| | | | | | |
|---|---|---|---|---|---|
| 21/11/1970 | .7 | .53 | | **SWEET BABY JAMES** | Warner Brothers ES 1843 |
| 29/05/1971 | .4 | .41 | | **MUD SLIDE SLIM AND THE BLUE HORIZON** | Warner Brothers WS 2561 |
| 08/01/1972 | .34 | .6 | | SWEET BABY JAMES | Warner Brothers K 46043 |
| 18/03/1972 | .49 | .1 | | MUD SLIDE SLIM AND THE BLUE HORIZON | Warner Brothers K 46085 |
| 09/12/1972 | .27 | .5 | | ONE MAN DOG | Warner Brothers K 46185 |
| 04/04/1987 | .53 | .5 | | CLASSIC SONGS | CBS/WEA JTV 1 |
| 21/06/1997 | .46 | .1 | | HOURGLASS 1997 Grammy Award for Best Pop Album | Columbia 4877482 |
| 24/08/2002 | .39 | .3 | | OCTOBER ROAD | Columbia 5032929 |
| 13/09/2003 | .4 | .7 | ● | **YOU'VE GOT A FRIEND – THE BEST OF** | Warner Brothers 8122738372 |

### JAMES TAYLOR QUARTET
UK jazz-funk trio of James Taylor, David Taylor and John Willmott formed in London in 1985 who have used various singers, although Noel McKoy became a permanent member in 1992. He was subsequently replaced by Yvonne Yaney. James Taylor had previously been a member of The Prisoners.

| | | | | | |
|---|---|---|---|---|---|
| 01/05/1993 | .36 | .3 | | SUPERNATURAL FEELING **JTQ WITH NOEL MCKOY** | Big Life BLRCD 21 |
| 29/10/1994 | .70 | .1 | | EXTENDED PLAY | Acid Jazz JAZID 110CD |
| 11/03/1995 | .63 | .1 | | IN THE HAND OF THE INEVITABLE | Acid Jazz JAZID CD115 |

### ROGER TAYLOR
UK singer/drummer (born Roger Meddows Taylor, 26/7/1949, King's Lynn, Norfolk) who was a founder member of Queen in 1970 and launched a parallel solo career in 1981.

| | | | | |
|---|---|---|---|---|
| 18/04/1981 | 18 | 5 | | FUN IN SPACE ....................................................................................... EMI EMC 3369 |
| 07/07/1984 | 30 | 4 | | STRANGE FRONTIER ..................................................................................... EMI RTA 1 |
| 17/09/1994 | 22 | 1 | | HAPPINESS? ................................................................. Parlophone CDPCSD 157 |
| 10/10/1998 | 53 | 1 | | ELECTRIC FIRE .................................................................... Parlophone 4967242 |

### KIRI TE KANAWA
New Zealand singer (born 6/3/1944, Gisborne) who sang at the 1981 wedding of HRH Prince Charles and Lady Diana Spencer. She was made a Dame of the British Empire in 1982.

| | | | | |
|---|---|---|---|---|
| 02/04/1983 | 57 | 1 | | CHANTS D'AUVERGNE VOLUME 1 **KIRI TE KANAWA WITH THE ENGLISH CHAMBER ORCHESTRA** ............... Decca SXDL 7604 |
| 26/10/1985 | 40 | 29 | ● | BLUE SKIES **KIRI TE KANAWA WITH NELSON RIDDLE AND HIS ORCHESTRA** ........................................ London KTKT 1 |
| 13/12/1986 | 47 | 4 | ● | CHRISTMAS WITH KIRI .............................................................. Decca PROLP 12 |
| 17/12/1988 | 70 | 3 | | KIRI ..................................................................................... K-Tel NE 1424 |
| 29/02/1992 | 23 | 10 | ○ | THE ESSENTIAL KIRI ............................................................... Decca 4362862 |
| 23/05/1992 | 73 | 1 | | KIRI SIDETRACKS – THE JAZZ ALBUM ................................................. Philips 4340922 |
| 09/04/1994 | 16 | 4 | ● | KIRI! .......................................................................... Polygram TV 4436002 |
| 10/11/2001 | 73 | 1 | | KIRI ......................................................................... EMI Classics CDC 5572312 |

### TEARDROP EXPLODES
UK rock group formed in Liverpool in 1978 by Julian Cope (born 21/10/1957, Deri, Mid-Glamorgan, vocals/bass), Paul Simpson (keyboards), Michael Simpson (guitar) and Gary Dwyer (drums) and signed with Zoo in 1979. Simpson left in 1979, replaced by Dave Balfe. They disbanded in 1982 with Cope recording solo. Balfe later formed Food records, discovering Blur and Shampoo before selling the label to EMI Records.

| | | | | |
|---|---|---|---|---|
| 18/10/1980 | 24 | 35 | ○ | KILIMANJARO ..................................................................... Mercury 6359 035 |
| 05/12/1981 | 29 | 6 | ○ | WILDER .......................................................................... Mercury 6359 056 |
| 14/04/1990 | 72 | 1 | | EVERYBODY WANTS TO SHAG… THE TEARDROP EXPLODES ....................... Fontana 8424391 |
| 15/08/1992 | 22 | 3 | | FLOORED GENIUS – THE BEST OF JULIAN COPE AND THE TEARDROP EXPLODES **JULIAN COPE AND THE TEARDROP EXPLODES** ................................................................. Island CID 8000 |

### TEARS FOR FEARS

UK group formed in 1981 by Roland Orzabal (born Roland Orzabal de la Quintana, 22/8/1961, Portsmouth, guitar/keyboards) and Curt Smith (born 24/6/1961, Bath, vocals/bass); they were both previously with Graduate, a five-piece ska band. Initially called History of Headaches, they took their name from Arthur Janov's book *Prisoners Of Pain* in which fears have to be confronted in order to be eliminated. They signed with Mercury in 1981 and worked with producer Chris Hughes (a former member of Adam and the Ants). The duo split in 1992 with Smith recording solo and Orzabal retaining the group name; by 2000 they had effectively re-formed. Smith later launched the Zerodisc label. The pair won the 1986 BRIT Award for Best Single for *Everybody Wants To Rule The World*.

| | | | | |
|---|---|---|---|---|
| 19/03/1983 | ❶[1] | 65 | ✪ | THE HURTING ...................................................................... Mercury MERS 17 |
| 09/03/1985 | 2 | 81 | ✪[3] | SONGS FROM THE BIG CHAIR ▲[5] ................................................. Mercury MERH 58 |
| 07/10/1989 | ❶[1] | 30 | ✪ | THE SEEDS OF LOVE ................................................................ Fontana 8387301 |
| 14/03/1992 | 2 | 37 | ✪[2] | TEARS ROLL DOWN (GREATEST HITS 1982–1992) ..................................... Fontana 5109392 |
| 19/06/1993 | 5 | 7 | ○ | ELEMENTAL ....................................................................... Mercury 5148752 |
| 28/10/1995 | 41 | 1 | | RAOUL AND THE KINGS OF SPAIN .................................................... Epic 4809822 |

### TECHNOTRONIC
Belgian dance group assembled by producer and DJ Jo 'Thomas DeQuincy' Bogaert and rapper Manuella 'Ya Kid K' Komosi with MC Eric. The group's videos also feature model Felly. They also recorded as Hi-Tek 3 Featuring Ya Kid K.

| | | | | |
|---|---|---|---|---|
| 06/01/1990 | 2 | 44 | ✪ | PUMP UP THE JAM .............................................................. Swanyard SYRLP 1 |
| 03/11/1990 | 7 | 14 | ● | TRIP ON THIS – REMIXES **TECHNOTRONIC AND HI TEK 3** ........................... Telstar STAR 2461 |
| 15/06/1991 | 27 | 4 | | BODY TO BODY .................................................................... ARS 4683421 |

### TEENAGE FANCLUB
UK rock group formed in Scotland in 1989 by Norman Blake (born 20/10/1965, Glasgow, guitar/vocals), Raymond McGinley (born 3/1/1964, Glasgow, guitar/vocals) and Francis MacDonald (born 21/11/1970, Bellshill, drums), later adding Gerard Love (born 31/8/1967, Motherwell, bass) to the line-up. Most of the band were ex-Boy Hairdressers. MacDonald left in 1989, replaced by Brendan O'Hare (born 16/1/1970, Motherwell). By 1995 Paul Quinn had taken over on drums.

| | | | | |
|---|---|---|---|---|
| 07/09/1991 | 53 | 2 | | THE KING .................................................................... Creation CRELP 096 |
| 16/11/1991 | 22 | 7 | | BANDWAGONESQUE ............................................................. Creation CRELP 106 |
| 16/10/1993 | 14 | 3 | | THIRTEEN ................................................................... Creation CRECD 144 |
| 10/06/1995 | 7 | 4 | | GRAND PRIX ................................................................. Creation CRECD 173 |
| 02/08/1997 | 3 | 5 | | SONGS FROM NORTHERN BRITAIN ............................................... Creation CRECD 196 |
| 04/11/2000 | 33 | 2 | | HOWDY ....................................................................... Columbia 5006222 |
| 08/02/2003 | 47 | 1 | | 4766 SECONDS: A SHORTCUT TO TEENAGE FANCLUB ........................... Poolside POOLS 3CD |

### TELETUBBIES
UK children's TV characters featuring Tinky Winky, Po, Dipsy and Laa-Laa. The characters are played by Dave Thompson, Pui Fan Lee, John Simmit and Nikky Sedley respectively. Simon Shelton replaced Thompson in 1998.

| | | | | |
|---|---|---|---|---|
| 04/04/1998 | 31 | 4 | | THE ALBUM ................................................... BBC Worldwide Music WMXU 00142 |

○ Silver disc ● Gold disc ✪ Platinum disc (additional platinum units are indicated by a figure following the symbol) ❶[9] Number of weeks album topped the UK chart

## TELEVISION
US rock group formed in New York in 1973 by Richard Hell (born Richard Myers, 2/10/1949, Lexington, KY, bass), Tom Verlaine (born Thomas Miller, 13/12/1949, New Jersey, guitar/vocals), Billy Ficca (drums) and Richard Lloyd (guitar). Hell left in 1975 and was replaced by Fred Smith (born 10/4/1948, New York). They disbanded in 1978, but re-formed in 1990.

| | | | | | |
|---|---|---|---|---|---|
| 26/03/1977 | 28 | 13 | | MARQUEE MOON | Elektra K 52046 |
| 29/04/1978 | 7 | 4 | | **ADVENTURE** | Elektra K 52072 |

## TEMPERANCE SEVEN
UK group formed in the 1950s by Captain Cephas Howard (trumpet/euphonium), Sheikh Haroun Wadi el John R T Davies (trombone/saxophone), Frank Paverty (sousaphone), Mr Philip 'Fingers' Harrison (saxophone), Alan Swainston-Cooper (clarinet), Canon Colin Bowles (piano), Brian Innes (drums), Dr John Grieves-Watson (banjo) and Whispering Paul McDowell (vocals).

| | | | | | |
|---|---|---|---|---|---|
| 13/05/1961 | 19 | 1 | | TEMPERANCE SEVEN PLUS ONE | Argo RG 11 |
| 25/11/1961 | 8 | 9 | | **TEMPERANCE SEVEN 1961** | Parlophone PMC 1152 |

## TEMPLE CHURCH CHOIR
UK male vocal group formed in London. The Temple Church is between Fleet Street and the River Thames and was established in the 12th century and consecrated in 1185. Although the church had a choir during the Middle Ages, the modern choir was not established until 1842 under the direction of John Calvert.

| | | | | | |
|---|---|---|---|---|---|
| 16/12/1961 | 8 | 3 | | **CHRISTMAS CAROLS** | HMV CLP 1309 |

## TEMPTATIONS
US R&B vocal group formed in 1960 by Eddie Kendricks (born 17/12/1939, Union Springs, AL), Paul Williams (born 2/7/1939, Birmingham, AL), Melvin Franklin (born David English, 12/10/1942, Montgomery, AL), Otis Williams (born Otis Miles, 30/10/1939, Texarkana, TX) and Eldridge Bryant from two other groups, The Primes and The Distants. They signed with Motown as The Elgins in 1961 and changed their name to The Temptations (suggested by Otis Williams). Bryant left in 1962 and was replaced by David Ruffin (born 18/1/1941, Meridian, MS). They scored their first hits with Smokey Robinson handling production and later switched to Norman Whitfield. Ruffin left in 1968 because the group would not give him individual credit as had happened with Diana Ross and the Supremes; he was replaced by Dennis Edwards (born 3/2/1943, Birmingham). Kendricks left in 1971, replaced by Richard Owens and then Damon Harris (born 3/7/1950, Baltimore, MD). Williams also left in 1971, replaced by Richard Street (born 5/10/1942, Detroit, MI). The group left Motown in 1976 for Atlantic but returned two albums later. By 1988 the line-up consisted of Otis Williams, Melvin Franklin, Richard Street, Dennis Edwards (who returned to the line-up in 1987) and Ron Tyson. Edwards subsequently left the group a second time and became embroiled in a legal dispute with them over the use of the name. Their line-up in 2001 was Otis Williams (last surviving original member), Ron Tyson, Barrington Henderson, Terry Weeks and Harry McGilberry. Paul Williams committed suicide on 17/8/1973, Ruffin died from a drugs overdose on 1/6/1991, Kendricks from cancer on 5/10/1992 and Franklin from emphysema on 23/2/1995. They won four Grammy Awards: Best Rhythm & Blues Group Performance in 1968 for *Cloud Nine*; Best Rhythm & Blues Group Performance, Best Rhythm & Blues Instrumental Performance and Best Rhythm & Blues Song in 1972, all for *Papa Was A Rolling Stone*; and Best Traditional Rhythm & Blues Vocal Album in 2000 for *Ear-Resistible*. The group was inducted into the Rock & Roll Hall of Fame in 1989 and has a star on the Hollywood Walk of Fame.

| | | | | |
|---|---|---|---|---|
| 24/12/1966 | 40 | 2 | GETTING READY | Tamla Motown STML 11035 |
| 11/02/1967 | 17 | 40 | TEMPTATIONS GREATEST HITS | Tamla Motown STML 11042 |
| 22/07/1967 | 20 | 4 | THE TEMPTATIONS LIVE! | Tamla Motown STML 11053 |
| 18/11/1967 | 19 | 18 | TEMPTATIONS WITH A LOT OF SOUL | Tamla Motown STML 11057 |
| 25/01/1969 | ❶⁴ | 15 | **DIANA ROSS AND THE SUPREMES JOIN THE TEMPTATIONS** | Tamla Motown STML 11096 |
| 28/06/1969 | 11 | 12 | THE ORIGINAL SOUNDTRACK FROM TCB ▲¹ This and the above hit credited to **DIANA ROSS AND THE SUPREMES AND THE TEMPTATIONS** | Tamla Motown STML 11110 |
| 20/09/1969 | 32 | 1 | CLOUD NINE | Tamla Motown STML 11109 |
| 14/02/1970 | 28 | 4 | TOGETHER **DIANA ROSS AND THE SUPREMES AND THE TEMPTATIONS** | Tamla Motown STML 11122 |
| 14/02/1970 | 20 | 4 | PUZZLE PEOPLE | Tamla Motown STML 11133 |
| 11/07/1970 | 56 | 1 | PSYCHEDELIC SHACK | Tamla Motown STML 11147 |
| 26/12/1970 | 35 | 12 | GREATEST HITS VOLUME 2 | Tamla Motown STML 11170 |
| 29/04/1972 | 34 | 2 | SOLID ROCK | Tamla Motown STML 11202 |
| 20/01/1973 | 19 | 7 | ALL DIRECTIONS | Tamla Motown STML 11218 |
| 07/07/1973 | 28 | 3 | MASTERPIECE | Tamla Motown STML 11229 |
| 08/12/1984 | 75 | 5 | TRULY FOR YOU | Motown ZL 72342 |
| 11/04/1992 | 8 | 9 | **MOTOWN'S GREATEST HITS** | Motown 5300152 |
| 27/01/2001 | 28 | 5 | AT THEIR VERY BEST This album was subsequently added to a similar compilation by The Four Tops and made the compilation chart, hitting #18 in March 2002 | Universal TV 135782 |

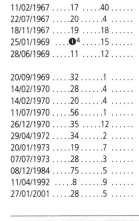

## 10 CC
UK rock group formed in 1972 by Eric Stewart (born 20/1/1945, Manchester, guitar/vocals), Graham Gouldman (born 10/5/1946, Manchester, guitar/vocals), Kevin Godley (born 7/10/1945, Manchester, vocals/drums) and Lol Creme (born 19/9/1947, Manchester, guitar/vocals). All four had previously been members of Hotlegs and had set up Strawberry Studios in Manchester. After working on two demos they were offered a deal with Jonathan King's UK label (he gave them their name – supposedly the amount of the average UK male ejaculation). Godley and Creme left in 1976 to form a new partnership; Gouldman and Stewart recruited Paul Burgess (drums), later adding Duncan Mackay (keyboards), Rick Fenn (guitar), Tony O'Malley (keyboards) and Stuart Tosh (drums) to the line-up. They disbanded in 1983.

| | | | | | |
|---|---|---|---|---|---|
| 01/09/1973 | 36 | 5 | ○ | 10 CC | UK UKAL 1005 |
| 15/06/1974 | 9 | 24 | ● | **SHEET MUSIC** | UK UKAL 1007 |
| 22/03/1975 | 4 | 40 | ● | **THE ORIGINAL SOUNDTRACK** | Mercury 9102 50Q |
| 07/06/1975 | 9 | 18 | ● | **GREATEST HITS OF 10 CC** | Decca UKAL 1012 |
| 31/01/1976 | 5 | 31 | ● | **HOW DARE YOU?** | Mercury 9102 501 |

| | | | | |
|---|---|---|---|---|
| 14/05/1977 | 3 | 21 | ● | **DECEPTIVE BENDS** .................................................. Mercury 9102 502 |
| 10/12/1977 | 14 | 15 | ● | LIVE AND LET LIVE ............................................... Mercury 6641 698 |
| 23/09/1978 | 3 | 15 | ● | **BLOODY TOURISTS** ................................................. Mercury 9102 503 |
| 06/10/1979 | 5 | 21 | ● | **GREATEST HITS 1972–1978** ........................................ Mercury 9102 504 |
| 05/04/1980 | 35 | 5 | | LOOK HEAR? ................................................... Mercury 9102 505 |
| 15/10/1983 | 70 | 2 | | WINDOW IN THE JUNGLE ........................................ Mercury MERL 28 |
| 29/08/1987 | 4 | 18 | ● | **CHANGING FACES – THE VERY BEST OF 10CC AND GODLEY AND CREME 10CC AND GODLEY AND CRÈME** ........... ProTV TGCLP 1 |
| 05/04/1997 | 37 | 4 | | THE VERY BEST OF 10CC ......................................... Mercury TV 5346122 |

**TEN CITY** US soul group formed in Chicago, IL by Byron Stingily (vocals), Herb Lawson (guitar) and Byron Burke (keyboards) as Ragtyme. They disbanded in 1994 and Stingily went solo.

| | | | | |
|---|---|---|---|---|
| 18/02/1989 | 22 | 12 | O | FOUNDATION ................................................... Atlantic WX 249 |

**TEN POLE TUDOR** UK punk rock group formed by Eddie Tenpole (born 6/12/1955, London, also known as Eddie Tudor-Pole), Garry Long (drums), Dick Crippen (bass) and Bob Kingston (guitar). Eddie later turned to acting and appeared in *Sid And Nancy* and *Absolute Beginners,* and recorded solo.

| | | | | |
|---|---|---|---|---|
| 09/05/1981 | 44 | 8 | | EDDIE, OLD BOB, DICK & GARRY ................................... Stiff SEEZ 31 |

**TEN SHARP** Dutch duo formed by Marcel Kapteijn (guitar/vocals) and Niels Hermes (keyboards), with Ton Groen (bass), Nick Bult (keyboards), Jelle Sieswerda (guitar), Bennie Top (drums) and Hubert Heeringa (saxophone) supplementing on live dates.

| | | | | |
|---|---|---|---|---|
| 09/05/1992 | 46 | 2 | | UNDER THE WATER-LINE .......................................... Columbia 4690702 |

**10,000 MANIACS** US group formed in Jamestown, NY in 1981 by Natalie Merchant (born 26/10/1963, Jamestown, vocals), Robert Buck (guitar), Steven Gustafson (bass), Dennis Drew (keyboards) and Jerome Augustyniak (drums) and signed by Elektra in 1985. In 1990 Merchant announced her intention to go solo, finally departing in 1992. Elektra promptly dropped the group from their roster! Buck died from liver failure on 19/12/2000 aged 42.

| | | | | |
|---|---|---|---|---|
| 27/05/1989 | 18 | 8 | O | BLIND MAN'S ZOO ............................................... Elektra EKT 57 |
| 10/10/1992 | 33 | 2 | | OUR TIME IN EDEN ............................................. Elektra 7559613852 |
| 06/11/1993 | 40 | 2 | | UNPLUGGED… AND SEATED ....................................... Elektra 7559615692 |

**TEN YEARS AFTER** UK rock group formed in Nottingham in 1965 by Alvin Lee (born 19/12/1944, Nottingham, guitar/vocals), Leo Lyons (born 30/11/1943, Standbridge, bass), Ric Lee (born 20/10/1945, Cannock, drums) and Chick Churchill (born 2/1/1949, Flint, Wales, keyboards) as The Jaybirds. They changed their name to Ten Years After in 1966 and signed with Decca in 1967. They stopped recording in 1975 and disbanded in 1980. In 2001 Ric Lee launched an investigation into the alleged missing royalty earnings from countless Woodstock compilations featuring the band's live or recorded versions of their perennial favourite *Goin' Home*.

| | | | | |
|---|---|---|---|---|
| 21/09/1968 | 26 | 7 | | UNDEAD ...................................................... Deram SML 1023 |
| 22/02/1969 | 6 | 5 | | **STONEDHENGE** ................................................. Deram SML 1029 |
| 04/10/1969 | 4 | 18 | | **SSSSH** ...................................................... Deram SML 1052 |
| 02/05/1970 | 4 | 27 | | **CRICKLEWOOD GREEN** ........................................... Deram SML 1065 |
| 09/01/1971 | 5 | 12 | | **WATT** ...................................................... Deram SML 1078 |
| 13/11/1971 | 36 | 1 | | A SPACE IN TIME ............................................... Chrysalis CHR 1001 |
| 07/10/1972 | 27 | 1 | | ROCK & ROLL MUSIC TO THE WORLD ............................... Chrysalis CHR 1009 |
| 28/07/1973 | 36 | 2 | | RECORDED LIVE ................................................. Chrysalis CHR 1049 |

**TENACIOUS D** US duo formed by comedians Kyle Glass (also known as KG or Kage) and Jack Black (also known as JB or Jables). Black had previously appeared in the film *Shallow Hal*.

| | | | | |
|---|---|---|---|---|
| 13/07/2002 | 38 | 31 | ● | TENACIOUS D .................................................. Epic 5077352 |

**KLAUS TENNSTEDT** – see NIGEL KENNEDY

**BRYN TERFEL** UK baritone singer (born Bryn Terfel Jones, 9/11/1965, Pantglas); he entered the London Guildhall School of Music in 1984 and graduated in 1989. He debuted at the Welsh National Opera in 1990 and two years later appeared at the Salzburg Festival. He won the Best Classical Vocal Grammy Award in 1996 for his album *Opera Arias*.

| | | | | |
|---|---|---|---|---|
| 16/11/1996 | 72 | 1 | | SOMETHING WONDERFUL ......................................... Deutsche Grammophon 4491632 |
| 28/10/2000 | 33 | 10 | O | WE'LL KEEP A WELCOME .......................................... Deutsche Grammophon 4635932 |
| 03/11/2001 | 49 | 2 | | SOME ENCHANTED EVENING ...................................... Deutsche Grammophon 4714252 |
| 08/11/2003 | 6 | 11 | ✪ | **BRYN** ...................................................... Deutsche Grammophon 4747032 |

**TERRAPLANE** UK vocal and instrumental group that featured Danny Bowes (vocals), Luke Morley (guitar) and Gary James (drums), all of whom went on to form Thunder in 1989.

| | | | | |
|---|---|---|---|---|
| 25/01/1986 | 74 | 1 | | BLACK AND WHITE .............................................. Epic EPC 26439 |

O Silver disc  ● Gold disc  ✪ Platinum disc (additional platinum units are indicated by a figure following the symbol)  ❶⁹ Number of weeks album topped the UK chart

## TAMMI TERRELL

**TAMMI TERRELL** US singer (born Tammy Montgomery, 21/1/1946, Philadelphia, PA) who made her first recordings for Wand in 1961 and toured with the James Brown Revue before signing as a solo artist with Motown. All her hits came whilst singing with Marvin Gaye: she would undoubtedly have gone on to enjoy solo success but for a brain tumour, first diagnosed after she collapsed on stage in 1967. Briefly married to boxer Ernie Terrell, she died on 16/3/1970. It has been widely claimed that her brain disorders were the result of regular beatings by someone within the Motown hierarchy. The accusations formed the basis of the novel *Number One With A Bullet* by former Marvin Gaye aide Elaine Jesmer. As Motown were unsuccessful in getting the book blocked, they bought the film rights and the project never saw light of day again.

22/08/1970 . . . . .60 . . . . . .4 . . . . . . GREATEST HITS **MARVIN GAYE AND TAMMI TERRELL** . . . . . . . . . . . . . . . . . . . . . . . . . . . . . . . . . . . . . . . . . . . Tamla Motown STML 11153

## TERRORVISION

**TERRORVISION** UK group formed in Bradford in 1986 by Tony Wright (born 6/5/1968, vocals), Mark Yates (born 4/4/1968, guitar), Leigh Marklew (born 10/8/1968, bass) and Shutty (born David Shuttleworth, 20/3/1967, drums) as Spoiled Bratz. They changed their name to Terrorvision in 1991 upon signing with EMI via their own Total Vegas label.

| | | | | |
|---|---|---|---|---|
15/05/1993 . . . . .75 . . . . . .1 . . . . . . FORMALDEHYDE . . . . . . . . . . . . . . . . . . . . . . . . . . . . . . . . . . . . . . . . . . . . . . . . . . . . . . . . . . . . . . . Total Vegas VEGASCD 1
30/04/1994 . . . . .18 . . . . .25 . . . . .● HOW TO MAKE FRIENDS AND INFLUENCE PEOPLE . . . . . . . . . . . . . . . . . . . . . . . . . . . . . . . . . . . . . . Total Vegas VEGASCD 2
23/03/1996 . . . . .8 . . . . . .12 . . . . .● **REGULAR URBAN SURVIVORS** . . . . . . . . . . . . . . . . . . . . . . . . . . . . . . . . . . . . . . . . . . . . . . . . . . . . Total Vegas VEGASCD 3
17/10/1998 . . . .34 . . . . . .2 . . . . . . SHAVING PEACHES . . . . . . . . . . . . . . . . . . . . . . . . . . . . . . . . . . . . . . . . . . . . . . . . . . . . . . . . . . . . Total Vegas 4996082
17/02/2001 . . . .48 . . . . . .1 . . . . . . GOOD TO GO . . . . . . . . . . . . . . . . . . . . . . . . . . . . . . . . . . . . . . . . . . . . . . . . . . . . . . . . . . . . . . . . . Papillion BTFLYCD 0011

## TODD TERRY

**TODD TERRY** US remixer/producer (born 18/4/1967, Brooklyn, NY) who was responsible for mixing hits by Everything But The Girl, Brownstone, 3T and Jimmy Somerville, among others, before going solo. He has also recorded as Swan Lake, Royal House, Gypsymen, T2 and Black Riot.

05/08/1995 . . . . .73 . . . . . .1 . . . . . . THE MINISTRY OF SOUND PRESENTS A DAY IN THE LIFE OF TODD TERRY . . . . . . . . . . . . . . . . . . . . . Sound Of Ministry SOMCD 2

## TESLA

**TESLA** US group formed in Sacramento, CA in 1985 by Jeff Keith (vocals), Tommy Skeoch (guitar/vocals), Frank Hannon (guitar/vocals), Brian Wheat (bass) and Troy Lucketta (drums) as City Kid. They name-changed in honour of the scientist Nikola Tesla.

11/02/1989 . . . . .34 . . . . . .2 . . . . . . THE GREAT RADIO CONTROVERSY . . . . . . . . . . . . . . . . . . . . . . . . . . . . . . . . . . . . . . . . . . . . . . . . .Geffen WX 244
02/03/1991 . . . . .59 . . . . . .1 . . . . . . FIVE MAN ACOUSTICAL JAM . . . . . . . . . . . . . . . . . . . . . . . . . . . . . . . . . . . . . . . . . . . . . . . . . . . . . .Geffen 9243111
21/09/1991 . . . .44 . . . . . .2 . . . . . . PSYCHOTIC SUPPER . . . . . . . . . . . . . . . . . . . . . . . . . . . . . . . . . . . . . . . . . . . . . . . . . . . . . . . . . .Geffen GEF 24424
03/09/1994 . . . .51 . . . . . .1 . . . . . . BUST A NUT . . . . . . . . . . . . . . . . . . . . . . . . . . . . . . . . . . . . . . . . . . . . . . . . . . . . . . . . . . . . . . . . .Geffen GED 24713

## TESTAMENT

**TESTAMENT** US rock group formed in San Francisco, CA as Legacy by Steve Souza (vocals), Derek Ramirez (guitar), Eric Peterson (guitar), Greg Christian (bass) and Louie Clemente (drums), with Alex Skolnick soon replacing Ramirez. Souza left a short while later and was replaced by Chuck Billy. Skolnick and Clemente left in 1992 and were replaced by Glen Alvelais and John Tempesta, although Alvelais left soon after and was replaced by James Murphy. Tempesta left in 1994 to join White Zombie and was replaced by John Dutte.

28/05/1988 . . . . .81 . . . . . .1 . . . . . . THE NEW ORDER . . . . . . . . . . . . . . . . . . . . . . . . . . . . . . . . . . . . . . . . . . . . . . . . . . . . . . . . . . . .Megaforce 7818491
19/08/1989 . . . .40 . . . . . .2 . . . . . . PRACTICE WHAT YOU PREACH . . . . . . . . . . . . . . . . . . . . . . . . . . . . . . . . . . . . . . . . . . . . . . . . . . . .Atlantic WX 297
06/10/1990 . . . .35 . . . . . .2 . . . . . . SOULS OF BLACK . . . . . . . . . . . . . . . . . . . . . . . . . . . . . . . . . . . . . . . . . . . . . . . . . . . . . . .Megaforce 7567821431
30/05/1992 . . . .48 . . . . . .1 . . . . . . THE RITUAL . . . . . . . . . . . . . . . . . . . . . . . . . . . . . . . . . . . . . . . . . . . . . . . . . . . . . . . . . . . . . . .Atlantic 7567823922

## TEXAS

**TEXAS** UK rock group formed in Glasgow in 1988 by Sharleen Spiteri (born 7/11/1967, Glasgow, vocals), Ally McErlaine (born 31/10/1968, Glasgow, guitar), Eddie Campbell (born 6/7/1965, keyboards), John McElhone (born 21/4/1963, Glasgow, bass) and Richard Hynd (born 17/6/1965, Aberdeen, drums). McElhone was previously a member of Altered Images and Hipsway.

25/03/1989 . . . . .3 . . . . . .30 . . . . .● SOUTHSIDE . . . . . . . . . . . . . . . . . . . . . . . . . . . . . . . . . . . . . . . . . . . . . . . . . . . . . . . . . . . . . . . . .Mercury 8381711
05/10/1991 . . . .32 . . . . . .4 . . . . . . MOTHERS HEAVEN . . . . . . . . . . . . . . . . . . . . . . . . . . . . . . . . . . . . . . . . . . . . . . . . . . . . . . . . . . . .Mercury 8485781
13/11/1993 . . . .18 . . . . . .2 . . . . .○ RICKS ROAD . . . . . . . . . . . . . . . . . . . . . . . . . . . . . . . . . . . . . . . . . . . . . . . . . . . . . . . . . . . . . . . . .Vertigo 5182522
15/02/1997 . . . ❶² . . . .102 . . . . ✪⁶ **WHITE ON BLONDE** ◇³ . . . . . . . . . . . . . . . . . . . . . . . . . . . . . . . . . . . . . . . . . . . . . . . . . . . . . . . . .Mercury 5343152
22/05/1999 . . . ❶¹ . . . . .47 . . . . ✪³ **THE HUSH** ◇² . . . . . . . . . . . . . . . . . . . . . . . . . . . . . . . . . . . . . . . . . . . . . . . . . . . . . . . . . . . . . . . .Mercury 5389722
04/11/2000 . . . ❶² . . . . .50 . . . . ✪⁶ **THE GREATEST HITS** ◇³ . . . . . . . . . . . . . . . . . . . . . . . . . . . . . . . . . . . . . . . . . . . . . . . . . . . . . . . .Mercury 5482622
01/11/2003 . . . . .5 . . . . .5 . . . . . . **CAREFUL WHAT YOU WISH FOR** . . . . . . . . . . . . . . . . . . . . . . . . . . . . . . . . . . . . . . . . . . . . . . . . . . . . . . .Mercury 9865712

## THA DOGG POUND

**THA DOGG POUND** US rap group formed by Snoop Doggy Dogg (born Calvin Broadus, 20/10/1972, Long Beach, CA), Delmar Arnaud (aka Dat Nigga Daz) and Ricardo Brown (aka Kurupt Tha Kingpin). Their debut album appeared at a time when Snoop Doggy Dogg was in prison awaiting trial for a drive-by shooting and killing in 1993. He and his bodyguard were subsequently acquitted of murder in 1996 and, as the jury could not agree on charges of manslaughter, the judge ordered a mistrial.

11/11/1995 . . . . .66 . . . . . .2 . . . . . . DOGG FOOD ▲¹ . . . . . . . . . . . . . . . . . . . . . . . . . . . . . . . . . . . . . . . . . . . . . . . . . . . . . . . . . . . . . . . .Death Row 5241772

## THAT PETROL EMOTION

**THAT PETROL EMOTION** UK group formed by Sean O'Neill (born 26/8/1957, Londonderry, guitar, previously known as John O'Neill), his brother Damian 'Dee' O'Neill (born 15/1/1961, Belfast, bass), Steve Mack (vocals), Reamman O'Gormain (guitar) and Ciaran McLaughlin (drums). The O'Neill brothers were previously members of The Undertones. Sean O'Neill left in 1989, Damian switched to guitar and John Marchini (bass) joined as his replacement. They were dropped by Virgin in 1992 and, after one release on their own Koogat label, disbanded in 1994.

| | | | | | |
|---|---|---|---|---|---|
| 10/05/1986 | 84 | 2 | | MANIC POP THRILL | Demon FIEND 70 |
| 23/05/1987 | 30 | 3 | | BABBLE | Polydor TPE LP 1 |
| 24/09/1988 | 53 | 2 | | END OF MILLENNIUM PSYCHOSIS BLUES | Virgin V 2550 |
| 21/04/1990 | 62 | 1 | | CHEMICRAZY | Virgin V 2618 |

**THE THE** UK rock group formed in 1980 by Matt Johnson (born 15/8/1961, London, guitar/vocals) with an ever-changing list of supporting musicians.

| | | | | | |
|---|---|---|---|---|---|
| 29/10/1983 | 27 | 5 | | SOUL MINING | Epic EPC 25525 |
| 29/11/1986 | 14 | 30 | ● | INFECTED | Some Bizzare EPC 26770 |
| 27/05/1989 | 4 | 9 | | **MIND BOMB** | Epic 4633191 |
| 06/02/1993 | 2 | 4 | | **DUSK** | Epic 4724682 |
| 19/06/1993 | 65 | 1 | | BURNING BLUE SOUL | 4AD HAD 113CD |
| 25/02/1995 | 28 | 2 | | HANKY PANKY | Epic 4781392 |
| 11/03/2000 | 45 | 1 | | NAKEDSELF | Nothing 4905102 |
| 01/06/2002 | 60 | 1 | | 45 RPM – THE SINGLES OF | Epic 5044699 |

**THEATRE OF HATE** UK rock group formed in 1981 by Kirk Brandon (born 3/8/1956, London, guitar/vocals), John Lennard (saxophone), Stan Stammers (bass), Bill Duffy (guitar) and Nigel Preston (drums). Duffy was later a member of The Cult whilst the bulk of the group later became Spear Of Destiny.

| | | | | | |
|---|---|---|---|---|---|
| 13/03/1982 | 17 | 6 | | WESTWORLD | Burning Rome TOH 1 |
| 18/08/1984 | 67 | 3 | | REVOLUTION | Burning Rome TOH 2 |

**THEAUDIENCE** UK rock group formed by Sophie Ellis Bextor (lead vocals), Kerin Smith (bass), Patrick Hannan (drums), Nyge Butler (keyboards) and Dean Molle (guitar). Billy Reeves had been a member of the group but left to concentrate on songwriting and later linked with Catherine Turner to form Yours. Sophie Ellis Bextor linked with Italian DJ Cristiano Spiller to form Spiller and then signed as a solo artist with Polydor in October 2000.

| | | | | | |
|---|---|---|---|---|---|
| 29/08/1998 | 22 | 2 | | THEAUDIENCE | Ellefre 5587712 |

**THEN JERICO** UK group formed by Mark Shaw (born 10/6/1961, Chesterfield, vocals), Scott Taylor (born 31/12/1961, Redhill, guitar), Rob Downes (born 7/12/1961, Cheadle Hulme, guitar), Jasper Stanthorpe (born 18/2/1958, Tonbridge, bass), Keith Airey (keyboards) and Steve Wren (born 26/10/1962, London, drums).

| | | | | | |
|---|---|---|---|---|---|
| 03/10/1987 | 35 | 7 | | FIRST (THE SOUND OF MUSIC) | London LONLP 26 |
| 04/03/1989 | 4 | 17 | | **THE BIG AREA** | London 8281221 |

**THERAPY?** UK rock band formed in Northern Ireland in 1989 by Andy Cairns (born 22/9/1965, Antrim, guitar/vocals), Michael McKeegan (born 25/3/1971, Antrim, bass) and Fyfe Ewing (drums). They launched the label Multifuckingnational when their original demos had been rejected by others, but signed with A&M in 1992. They later added Martin McCarrick (born 29/7/1962, Luton, guitar) and Graham Hopkins (born 20/12/1975, Dublin, drums).

| | | | | | |
|---|---|---|---|---|---|
| 08/02/1992 | 52 | 1 | | PLEASURE DEATH | Wiiija WIJ 11 |
| 14/11/1992 | 38 | 3 | | NURSE | A&M 5400442 |
| 19/02/1994 | 5 | 11 | ● | **TROUBLEGUM** | A&M 5401962 |
| 24/06/1995 | 9 | 7 | ○ | **INFERNAL LOVE** | A&M 5403792 |
| 11/04/1998 | 21 | 1 | | SEMI-DETACHED | A&M 5408912 |
| 30/10/1999 | 61 | 1 | | SUICIDE PACT – YOU FIRST | Ark 21 1539722 |

**THESE ANIMAL MEN** UK group formed in Brighton by Hooligan (born Julian Hewings, guitar/vocals), Patrick (bass), Boag (vocals) and Stevie (drums).

| | | | | | |
|---|---|---|---|---|---|
| 02/07/1994 | 39 | 2 | | TOO SUSSED? | Hi-Rise Recordings FLATMCD 4 |
| 08/10/1994 | 62 | 1 | | (COME ON, JOIN) THE HIGH SOCIETY | Hi-Rise Recordings FLATCD 8 |
| 25/03/1995 | 64 | 1 | | TAXI FOR THESE ANIMAL MEN | Hi-Rise Recordings FLATMCD 14 |

**THEY MIGHT BE GIANTS** US rock group formed in Boston, MA in 1983 by John Flansburgh (guitar/vocals) and John Linnell (accordion/keyboards/vocals), later adding Brian Doherty (drums), Tony Maimone (bass), Kurt Hoffman (saxophone) and Steven Bernstein (trumpet) to the line-up. Dan Hickey later replaced Doherty. The group won the 2001 Grammy Award for Best Song Written for a Motion Picture, Television or Other Visual Media for *Boss Of Me* from *Malcolm In The Middle*.

| | | | | | |
|---|---|---|---|---|---|
| 07/04/1990 | 14 | 12 | ○ | FLOOD | Elektra EKT 68 |

**THIN LIZZY** Irish rock group formed in Dublin in 1969 by Phil Lynott (born 20/8/1951, Dublin, vocals/bass), Brian Downey (born 27/1/1951, Dublin, drums) and Eric Bell (born 3/9/1947, Belfast, guitar). They signed with Decca in 1970. Bell left in 1972 and was briefly replaced by Gary Moore and then Scott Gorman (born 17/3/1951, Santa Monica, CA) and Brian Robertson (born 12/9/1956, Glasgow). Robertson left in 1980 and the group disbanded in 1983. Lynott recorded solo from 1980 and died from heart failure on 4/1/1986. According to legend, they took their name either from a kids' comic character or it was a reference to the Model-T Ford car.

| DATE | POS | WKS | BPI | ALBUM TITLE | LABEL & NUMBER |
|------|-----|-----|-----|-------------|----------------|
| 27/09/1975 | 60 | 1 | | FIGHTING | Vertigo 6360 121 |
| 10/04/1976 | 10 | 50 | ● | **JAILBREAK** | Vertigo 9102 008 |
| 06/11/1976 | 11 | 24 | ● | JOHNNY THE FOX | Vertigo 9102 012 |
| 01/10/1977 | 4 | 9 | ● | BAD REPUTATION | Vertigo 9102 016 |
| 17/06/1978 | 2 | 62 | ✪ | **LIVE AND DANGEROUS** | Vertigo 6641 807 |
| 05/05/1979 | 2 | 21 | ● | **BLACK ROSE (A ROCK LEGEND)** | Vertigo 9102 032 |
| 18/10/1980 | 7 | 7 | ◐ | **CHINATOWN** | Vertigo 6359 030 |
| 11/04/1981 | 6 | 13 | | **THE ADVENTURES OF THIN LIZZY** | Vertigo LIZTV 1 |
| 05/12/1981 | 38 | 8 | | RENEGADE | Vertigo 6359 083 |
| 12/03/1983 | 4 | 11 | ◐ | **THUNDER AND LIGHTNING** | Vertigo VERL 3 |
| 26/11/1983 | 29 | 6 | | LIFE – LIVE | Vertigo VERD 6 |
| 14/11/1987 | 55 | 10 | ● | SOLDIER OF FORTUNE – THE BEST OF PHIL LYNOTT AND THIN LIZZY **PHIL LYNOTT AND THIN LIZZY** | Telstar STAR 2300 |
| 16/02/1991 | 8 | 17 | | **DEDICATION – THE VERY BEST OF THIN LIZZY** | Vertigo 8481921 |
| 13/01/1996 | 18 | 11 | ◐ | WILD ONE – THE VERY BEST OF THIN LIZZY | Vertigo 5281132 |
| 19/06/2004 | 3 | 2+ | | **GREATEST HITS** | Universal TV 9821111 |

**3RD BASS** US rap group formed in Queens, NY by MC Serch (born Michael Berrin, 6/5/1967, Queens), Prime Minister Pete Nice (born Peter Nash, 5/2/1967, Brooklyn, NY) and DJ Richie Rich (real name Richard Lawson). They disbanded in 1992 with Nash and Lawson linking to form Prime Minister Pete Nice and DJ Daddy Rich, whilst Berrin became A&R Vice President for Wild Pitch Records.

| DATE | POS | WKS | BPI | ALBUM TITLE | LABEL & NUMBER |
|------|-----|-----|-----|-------------|----------------|
| 20/07/1991 | 46 | 1 | | DERELICTS OF DIALECT | Def Jam 4683171 |

**THIRD EAR BAND** UK vocal/instrumental group formed by Glenn Sweeny (drums), Paul Minns (oboe) and Richard Koss (violin), with Mel Davis (cello) also helping out on their debut album.

| DATE | POS | WKS | BPI | ALBUM TITLE | LABEL & NUMBER |
|------|-----|-----|-----|-------------|----------------|
| 27/06/1970 | 49 | 2 | | AIR, EARTH, FIRE, WATER | Harvest SHVL 773 |

**THIRD WORLD** Jamaican reggae group formed in Kingston in 1973 by Michael 'Ibo' Cooper (keyboards), Stephen 'Cat' Coore (guitar), Irving 'Carrot' Jarrett (percussion), Richie Daley (bass) and Carl Barovier (drums). By 1975 Willie 'Root' Stewart had taken over on drums and William 'Rugs' Clark joined as lead singer. By 1999 the group consisted of Richie Daley, William Clark, Stephen Coore, Leroy Romans, Lenworth Williams and Rupert Bent.

| DATE | POS | WKS | BPI | ALBUM TITLE | LABEL & NUMBER |
|------|-----|-----|-----|-------------|----------------|
| 21/10/1978 | 30 | 6 | | JOURNEY TO ADDIS | Island ILPS 9554 |
| 11/07/1981 | 37 | 9 | | ROCKS THE WORLD | CBS 85027 |
| 15/05/1982 | 87 | 3 | | YOU'VE GOT THE POWER | CBS 85563 |

**THIS MORTAL COIL** UK group formed by Ivo Watts-Russell, with contributions from Heidi Berry, Caroline Crawley, Kim Deal, Howard Devoto, Tanya Donelly and Gordon Sharp. Watts-Russell was the founder of 4AD Records and most of the contributors to This Mortal Coil were acts signed to the label.

| DATE | POS | WKS | BPI | ALBUM TITLE | LABEL & NUMBER |
|------|-----|-----|-----|-------------|----------------|
| 20/10/1984 | 38 | 4 | | IT'LL END IN TEARS | 4AD CAD 411 |
| 11/10/1986 | 53 | 3 | | FILIGREE AND SHADOW | 4AD DAD 609 |
| 04/05/1991 | 28 | 3 | | BLOOD | 4AD DAD 1005 |

**KENNY THOMAS** UK R&B singer/songwriter/keyboard player/producer from Essex who also played keyboards on an album by Sherman Hemsley and produced Laurie Roth.

| DATE | POS | WKS | BPI | ALBUM TITLE | LABEL & NUMBER |
|------|-----|-----|-----|-------------|----------------|
| 26/10/1991 | 3 | 23 | ✪ | **VOICES** | Cooltempo CTLP 24 |
| 25/09/1993 | 10 | 5 | ● | **WAIT FOR ME** | Cooltempo CTVD 36 |

**LILLO THOMAS** US singer (born Brooklyn, NY); he was an outstanding athlete as a child, later setting a world record for the 200 metres. He would have appeared at the 1984 Olympics but for a car crash in Brazil and pursued a musical career thereafter.

| DATE | POS | WKS | BPI | ALBUM TITLE | LABEL & NUMBER |
|------|-----|-----|-----|-------------|----------------|
| 02/05/1987 | 43 | 7 | | LILLO | Capitol EST 2031 |

**RAY THOMAS** UK guitarist (born 29/12/1942, Stourport-on-Severn) who was a founding member of The Moody Blues in 1964 with Denny Laine, Mike Pinder, Graeme Edge and Clint Warwick. He launched a parallel solo career in 1975.

| DATE | POS | WKS | BPI | ALBUM TITLE | LABEL & NUMBER |
|------|-----|-----|-----|-------------|----------------|
| 26/07/1975 | 23 | 3 | | FROM MIGHTY OAKS | Threshold THS 16 |

**RICHARD THOMPSON** UK singer/guitarist (born 3/4/1949, London) who was a founder member of Fairport Convention in 1966 with Ashley Hutchings, Simon Nicol, Judy Dyble, Ian Matthews and Shaun Frater. He remained with the group until 1971 and then formed a recording partnership with his wife Linda which ended when they separated in 1982. He then embarked on a solo career.

| DATE | POS | WKS | BPI | ALBUM TITLE | LABEL & NUMBER |
|------|-----|-----|-----|-------------|----------------|
| 27/04/1985 | 80 | 2 | | ACROSS A CROWDED ROOM | Polydor POLD 5175 |
| 18/10/1986 | 92 | 1 | | DARING ADVENTURES | Polydor POLD 5202 |
| 29/10/1988 | 89 | 1 | | AMNESIA | Capitol EST 2075 |
| 25/05/1991 | 32 | 3 | | RUMOUR AND SIGH | Capitol EST 2142 |
| 29/01/1994 | 23 | 3 | | MIRROR BLUE | Capitol CDEST 2207 |
| 20/04/1996 | 32 | 2 | | YOU? ME? US? | Capitol CDEST 2282 |
| 24/05/1997 | 69 | 1 | | INDUSTRY **RICHARD AND DANNY THOMPSON** | Parlophone CDPCS 7383 |
| 04/09/1999 | 28 | 2 | | MOCK TUDOR | Capitol 4988602 |
| 15/02/2003 | 52 | 1 | | THE OLD KIT BAG | Cooking Vinyl COOKCD251 |

▲⁹ Number of weeks album topped the US chart ◆¹² RIAA Diamond Awards ◇³ IFPI Platinum Europe Awards

### THOMPSON TWINS
UK/New Zealand group formed by Tom Bailey (born 18/6/1957, Halifax, vocals/keyboards), Joe Leeway (born 15/11/1957, London, percussion) and Alannah Currie (born 20/9/1959, Auckland, New Zealand, vocals/saxophone). They took their name from the detective twins in Herge's cartoon series *Tintin*. They first recorded for their own Dirty Discs label in 1980. Leeway left in 1986.

| | | | | |
| --- | --- | --- | --- | --- |
| 13/03/1982 | 48 | 3 | ✪ | SET ...................Tee TELP 2 |
| 26/02/1983 | 2 | 56 | ✪ | **QUICK STEP & SIDE KICK** ...................Arista 204 924 |
| 25/02/1984 | ●³ | 51 | ✪² | **INTO THE GAP** ...................Arista 205 971 |
| 28/09/1985 | 5 | 9 | ● | **HERE'S TO FUTURE DAYS** ...................Arista 207 164 |
| 02/05/1987 | 90 | 1 | | CLOSE TO THE BONE ...................Arista 208 143 |
| 10/03/1990 | 23 | 8 | ○ | THOMPSON TWINS – THE GREATEST HITS ...................Stylus SMR 92 |

### THORNS
US group formed by guitarists/vocalists Matthew Street (born 6/10/1964, Lincoln, NE), Shawn Mullins (born 8/3/1968, Atlanta, GA) and Peter Droge. All three had previously been solo artists before teaming up in The Thorns.

| | | | | |
| --- | --- | --- | --- | --- |
| 14/06/2003 | 68 | 1 | | THE THORNS ...................Columbia 5113732 |

### GEORGE THOROGOOD AND THE DESTROYERS
US guitarist (born 31/12/1952, Wilmington, DE) who formed The Destroyers in 1973, with Michael Lenn (bass), Jeff Simon (drums) and Ron Smith (guitar) who was an infrequent member. Their debut hit album was actually recorded in 1975, by which time Lenn had left and been replaced by Billy Blough. Smith left for good in 1980 and was replaced by Hank Carter (saxophone).

| | | | | |
| --- | --- | --- | --- | --- |
| 02/12/1978 | 67 | 1 | | GEORGE THOROGOOD AND THE DESTROYERS ...................Sonet SNTF 781 |

### THOUSAND YARD STARE
UK group formed in Windsor in 1988 by Stephen Barnes (vocals), Giles Duffy (guitar), Kevin Moxon (guitar), Sean McDonough (bass) and Dominic Bostock (drums).

| | | | | |
| --- | --- | --- | --- | --- |
| 07/03/1992 | 38 | 2 | | HANDS ON ...................Polydor 5130012 |

### 3 COLOURS RED
UK rock group featuring Pete Vuckovic (born 16/2/1971, Tiverton, vocals/bass), Chris McCormack (born 21/6/1973, South Shields, guitar), Ben Harding (born 31/1/1965, Stoke-on-Trent, guitar) and Keith Baxter (born 19/2/1971, Morecambe, drums). Chris McCormack is brother of The Wildhearts' Danny McCormack and launched the Limited record label in 1997.

| | | | | |
| --- | --- | --- | --- | --- |
| 24/05/1997 | 16 | 2 | | PURE ...................Creation CRECD 208 |
| 20/02/1999 | 17 | 2 | | REVOLT ...................Creation CRECD 227 |

### THREE DEGREES
US R&B vocal group, formed in Philadelphia, PA in 1963 by Fayette Pickney, Linda Turner and Shirley Porter. They scored their first hit for Swan in 1965. Turner and Porter left in 1966 and were replaced by Sheila Ferguson and Valerie Holiday. Ferguson left to become an actress in 1986 and was replaced by Victoria Wallace. The group appeared in the 1971 film *The French Connection*. It was claimed that they were Prince Charles' favourite group (they were tagged 'Charlie's Angels' at the time) and they performed at his 30th birthday celebration at Buckingham Palace.

| | | | | |
| --- | --- | --- | --- | --- |
| 10/08/1974 | 12 | 22 | ● | THREE DEGREES ...................Philadelphia International 65858 |
| 17/05/1975 | 6 | 16 | ● | **TAKE GOOD CARE OF YOURSELF** ...................Philadelphia International PIR 69137 |
| 24/02/1979 | 34 | 13 | ○ | NEW DIMENSIONS ...................Ariola ARLH 5012 |
| 03/03/1979 | 8 | 18 | ● | **A COLLECTION OF THEIR 20 GREATEST HITS** ...................Epic EPC 10013 |
| 15/12/1979 | 61 | 7 | | 3D ...................Ariola 3D 1 |
| 27/09/1980 | 9 | 15 | ● | **GOLD** ...................Ariola 3D 2 |

### 3LW
US vocal group formed in New Jersey by Kiely Alexis Williams (also known as Keylay Keylay, born 9/7/1986, Alexandria, VA), Naturi Cora Maria Naughton (born 20/5/1984, East Orange, NJ) and Adrienne Eliza Bailon (born 24/10/1983, of Puerto Rican and Ecuadorian descent). The group's name stands for Three Little Women. Naughton left in October 2002 and filed suit against her former bandmates and management company claiming she was forced out of the group.

| | | | | |
| --- | --- | --- | --- | --- |
| 16/06/2001 | 75 | 1 | | 3LW ...................Epic 4989142 |

### 3T
US R&B vocal trio formed in Los Angeles by Tariano 'Taj' Adaryll (born 4/8/1973, Hollywood, CA), Tarryll Adren (born 8/8/1975, Hollywood) and Tito Joe 'TJ' Jackson (born 16/7/1978, Hollywood). They are the sons of Tito Jackson and nephews of Michael Jackson.

| | | | | |
| --- | --- | --- | --- | --- |
| 24/02/1996 | 11 | 15 | ● | BROTHERHOOD ...................Epic 4816942 |

### THRILLS
Irish group formed in Dublin by Conor Deasey (vocals), Daniel Ryan (guitar), Padraic McMahon (bass), Kevin Horan (keyboards) and Ben Carrigan (drums).

| | | | | |
| --- | --- | --- | --- | --- |
| 12/07/2003 | 3 | 25 | ✪ | **SO MUCH FOR THE CITY** ...................Virgin CDV2974 |

### THROWING MUSES

US group formed in Newport, Long Island in 1986 by Kristin Hersh (born 1966, Atlanta, GA, guitar/vocals), her step sister Tanya Donelly (born 14/8/1966, Newport, guitar/vocals), Elaine Adamedes (bass) and David Narcizo (drums). Adamedes left and was replaced by Leslie Langston. The band then relocated to Boston, MA. Langston left in 1991 and was replaced by Fred Abong. Donelly, also a member of The Breeders, announced her departure in 1991 and by 1992 the group comprised Hersh, Narcizo and Bernard Georges (bass). They disbanded in 1993 but re-formed in 1994, although Hersh also undertook a solo career.

| DATE | POS | WKS | BPI | ALBUM TITLE | LABEL & NUMBER |
|------|-----|-----|-----|-------------|----------------|
| 04/02/1989 | 59 | 1 | | HUNKPAPA | 4AD CAD 901 |
| 02/03/1991 | 26 | 4 | | THE REAL RAMONA | 4AD CAD 1002 |
| 22/08/1992 | 13 | 3 | | RED HEAVEN | 4AD CAD 2013CD |
| 28/11/1992 | 74 | 1 | | THE CURSE | 4AD TAD 2019CD |
| 28/01/1995 | 10 | 3 | | **UNIVERSITY** | 4AD CADD 5002CD |
| 31/08/1996 | 36 | 1 | | LIMBO | 4AD CAD 6014CD |
| 29/03/2003 | 75 | 1 | | THROWING MUSES | 4AD CAD 2301CD |

### THUNDER

UK heavy rock group formed in 1989 by Danny Bowes (vocals), Luke Morley (guitar), Gary James (drums), Mark Lockhurst (bass) and Ben Matthews (guitar). Bowes, Morley and James were ex-members of Terraplane. Lockhurst left in 1993.

| DATE | POS | WKS | BPI | ALBUM TITLE | LABEL & NUMBER |
|------|-----|-----|-----|-------------|----------------|
| 17/03/1990 | 21 | 16 | ● | BACK STREET SYMPHONY | EMI EMC 3570 |
| 05/09/1992 | 2 | 10 | ● | **LAUGHING ON JUDGEMENT DAY** | EMI CDEMD 1035 |
| 04/02/1995 | 5 | 5 | | **BEHIND CLOSED DOORS** | EMI CDEMD 1076 |
| 07/10/1995 | 22 | 3 | | BEST OF THUNDER – THE FINEST HOUR (AND A BIT) | EMI CDEMD 1086 |
| 15/02/1997 | 14 | 3 | | THE THRILL OF IT ALL | Raw Power RAWCD 115 |
| 28/02/1998 | 35 | 1 | | LIVE | Eagle EDGCD 016 |
| 27/03/1999 | 49 | 1 | | GIVING THE GAME AWAY | Eagle EAGCD 046 |

### THURSDAY

US rock group formed in New Brunswick, NJ in 1998 by Geoff Rickly (vocals), Tom Keeley (guitar), Steve Pedulla (guitar), Tim Payne (bass) and Tucker Rule (drums). They first recorded for Eyeball Records.

| DATE | POS | WKS | BPI | ALBUM TITLE | LABEL & NUMBER |
|------|-----|-----|-----|-------------|----------------|
| 27/09/2003 | 62 | 1 | | WAR ALL THE TIME | Island 9860874 |

### TIESTO

Dutch male DJ Tijs Verwest (born 17/1/1969) who is also a member of Gouryella with Ferry Corsten.

| DATE | POS | WKS | BPI | ALBUM TITLE | LABEL & NUMBER |
|------|-----|-----|-----|-------------|----------------|
| 29/05/2004 | 54 | 2 | | JUST BE | Nebula NEBCD9010 |

### TIFFANY

US singer (born Tiffany Renee Darwish, 2/10/1971, Norwalk, CA) who started singing aged nine and was signed by her manager at the age of thirteen. She signed with MCA in 1986 and was sent out touring shopping malls to promote her debut album. She provided the voice of Judy Jetson in the film *Jetsons: The Movie* in 1990.

| DATE | POS | WKS | BPI | ALBUM TITLE | LABEL & NUMBER |
|------|-----|-----|-----|-------------|----------------|
| 27/02/1988 | 5 | 21 | ●² | **TIFFANY** ▲² | MCA MCF 3415 |
| 17/12/1988 | 56 | 6 | ○ | HOLD AN OLD FRIEND'S HAND | MCA MCF 3437 |

### TIGERTAILZ

US vocal/instrumental group formed in 1985 by Pepsi Tate, Jay Pepper, Steevie Jaimz and Ian Welsh. They subsequently added Ace Finchum and signed with Music For Nations in 1987. Jaimz left in 1987 and was replaced by Kim Hooker; Finchum left in 1991 and was replaced by Andy Skinner.

| DATE | POS | WKS | BPI | ALBUM TITLE | LABEL & NUMBER |
|------|-----|-----|-----|-------------|----------------|
| 07/04/1990 | 36 | 2 | | BEZERK | Music For Nations MFN 96 |

### TIGHT FIT

UK group originally assembled as session musicians to record their first two hits, inspired by the success of Starsound. A trio was put together in 1982 comprising Steve Grant, Julie Harris and Denise Gyngell, with Gyngell and Harris later replaced by Vicki Pemberton and Carol Stevens. Denise later married producer Pete Waterman.

| DATE | POS | WKS | BPI | ALBUM TITLE | LABEL & NUMBER |
|------|-----|-----|-----|-------------|----------------|
| 26/09/1981 | 38 | 4 | | BACK TO THE SIXTIES | Jive HIP 1 |
| 04/09/1982 | 87 | 2 | | TIGHT FIT | Jive HIP 2 |

### TIJUANA BRASS – see HERB ALPERT AND HIS TIJUANA BRASS

### TIK AND TOK

UK vocal/instrumental duo. They were ex-members of Shock, but also appeared as Ronnie and Reggie Dome and recorded with Gary Numan. Tik played guitars/keyboards/bass/vocals whilst Tok played keyboards/vocals.

| DATE | POS | WKS | BPI | ALBUM TITLE | LABEL & NUMBER |
|------|-----|-----|-----|-------------|----------------|
| 04/08/1984 | 89 | 2 | | INTOLERANCE | Survival SUR LP 008 |

### TANITA TIKARAM

UK singer (born 12/8/1969, Munster, Germany, of Malaysian and Fijian parentage) whose first album was produced by Rod Argent and Peter Van Hoote.

| DATE | POS | WKS | BPI | ALBUM TITLE | LABEL & NUMBER |
|------|-----|-----|-----|-------------|----------------|
| 24/09/1988 | 3 | 49 | ✪² | **ANCIENT HEART** | WEA WX 210 |
| 10/02/1990 | 3 | 7 | ● | **THE SWEET KEEPER** | East West WX 330 |
| 16/02/1991 | 19 | 4 | | EVERYBODY'S ANGEL | East West WX 401 |
| 25/02/1995 | 75 | 1 | | LOVERS IN THE CITY | East West 4509988042 |
| 19/09/1998 | 69 | 1 | | THE CAPPUCCINO SONGS | Mother MUMCD 9801 |

▲⁹ Number of weeks album topped the US chart  ◆¹² RIAA Diamond Awards  ◇³ IFPI Platinum Europe Awards

**JUSTIN TIMBERLAKE** US singer (born 31/1/1981, Memphis, TN) who was previously a member of N Sync before launching a solo career. He was briefly engaged to fellow singer Britney Spears and won the 2003 MOBO Award for Best R&B Act. He then won three 2003 MTV Europe Music Awards including Best Male and Best Pop. In the same year he won two Grammy Awards including Best Male Pop Vocal Performance for *Cry Me A River*. He has also won two BRIT Awards including Best International Male in 2004.

16/11/2002 ....❶7.....74......✪5    **JUSTIFIED** ◇ 2003 MTV Europe Music Award for Best Album. 2003 Grammy Award for Best Pop Vocal Album. 2004 BRIT Award for Best International Album .................................................................Jive 9224772

**TIMBUK 3** US duo formed by husband and wife Pat and Barbara Kooyman MacDonald and a tape machine. They first teamed up in Madison, WI in 1978 and are now based in Texas. They later added Wally Ingram on drums and Courtney Audain on bass.

14/02/1987 .....51......4 ......    GREETINGS FROM TIMBUK 3 ...............................................................I.R.S. MIRF 1015

**TIME** US soul group formed in 1981 by Prince and featuring Morris Day (vocals), Jesse Johnston (guitar), James 'Jimmy Jam' Harris (keyboards), Monte Moir (keyboards), Terry Lewis (bass) and Jellybean Johnson (drums). Harris, Moir and Lewis left in 1983 to form Flyte Time Productions (where they were responsible for albums by The SOS Band, Change, Alexander O'Neal and Janet Jackson). Time added Paul 'St Paul' Peterson and Jerome Benton in 1984 but the group disbanded later the same year. The original line-up plus Benton re-formed in 1990 whilst St Paul also enjoyed a solo career.

28/07/1990 .....66......1 ......    PANDEMONIUM ...........................................................Paisley Park WX 336

**TIME FREQUENCY** UK instrumental/production group formed by John Campbell and Debbie Muller.

18/06/1994 .....23......4 ......    DOMINATOR ...................................................Internal Affairs KGBD 500

**TIN MACHINE** UK/US rock group formed in 1989 by David Bowie (born David Robert Jones, 8/1/1947, Brixton, London) with Tony Sales (bass), Reeves Gabrels (born Boston, MA, guitar) and Hunt Sales (drums).

03/06/1989 .....3......9 ......●    **TIN MACHINE** ...................................................EMI USA MTLS 1044
14/09/1991 .....23......3 ......    TIN MACHINE II ................................................London 8282721

**TIN TIN OUT** UK instrumental/production duo formed by Darren Stokes and Lindsay Edwards.

05/10/1996 .....65......1 ......    ADVENTURES IN TIN TIN OUT LAND ................................VC Recordings VCRLPX 1

**TINDERSTICKS** UK rock group formed in Nottingham by Stuart Staples (born 14/11/1965, Nottingham, vocals), Dickon Hinchcliffe (born 9/7/1967, Nottingham, violin), Dave Boulter (born 27/2/1965, Nottingham, keyboards), Neil Fraser (born 22/11/1962, London, guitar), Mark Cornwill (born 15/5/1967, Nottingham, bass) and Al McCauley (born 2/8/1965, Nottingham, drums).

23/10/1993 .....56......1 ......    TINDERSTICKS ...............................................This Way Up 5183062
15/04/1995 .....13......3 ......    THE SECOND TINDERSTICKS ALBUM ...............................This Way Up 5263032
28/10/1995 .....32......1 ......    LIVE AT THE BLOOMSBURY THEATRE 12.3.95 .......................This Way Up 5285972
21/06/1997 .....37......2 ......    CURTAINS ...................................................This Way Up 5243442
18/09/1999 .....36......1 ......    SIMPLE PLEASURE .............................................Island CID 8085
02/06/2001 .....47......1 ......    CAN OUR LOVE .............................................RTM BBQCD 222X

**TLC** US female rap group formed by Tionne 'T-Boz' Watkins (born 26/4/1970, Des Moines, IA), Lisa 'Left Eye' Lopes (born 27/5/1971, Philadelphia, PA) and Rozonda 'Chilli' Thomas (born 27/2/1971, Atlanta, GA). They were founded and managed by Pebbles (then married to songwriter, producer and record label owner Antonio 'LA' Reid). Lopes was fined $10,000 and given five years probation in 1994 for setting fire to her boyfriend Andre Rison's home and vandalising his car, although the pair reconciled and he refused to press charges. In 1995 the group filed for Chapter 11 bankruptcy claiming liabilities of $3.5 million ($1.5 million of this related to an unpaid insurance claim by Lloyd's of London for Lopes' arson attack). Lisa Lopes later sang with a number of other acts, including Melanie C, and recorded solo, as did T-Boz. TLC won the 1999 MOBO Award for Best Video for *No Scrubs*. They also won five Grammy Awards including: Best Rhythm & Blues Group Performance in 1995 for *Creep*, Best Rhythm & Blues Song and Best Rhythm & Blues Group Performance in 1999 for *No Scrubs*, and Best Rhythm & Blues Album in 1999 for *Fanmail*. In 2000 the group was named Best International Group at the BRIT Awards. Lopes was killed in a car crash whilst on holiday in Honduras on 26/4/2002 and was awarded a posthumous Outstanding Achievement Award at the 2002 MOBO Awards.

20/05/1995 .....4......39......✪    **CRAZYSEXYCOOL** ◇ ◆11 1995 Grammy Award for Best Rhythm & Blues Album .........................LaFace 73008260092
06/03/1999 .....7......57......✪    **FANMAIL** ◇ ▲5 .............................................LaFace 73008260552
23/11/2002 .....45......1 ......    3D .............................................Arista 74321981502

**TOM TOM CLUB** US studio group assembled by Chris Frantz (born 8/5/1951, Fort Campbell, KY) and his wife Tina Weymouth (born 22/11/1950, Coronade, CA). The rest of the group comprised Stephen Stanley (keyboards) and Monty Brown (drums). Frantz and Weymouth were members of Talking Heads whilst Brown was with T-Connection.

24/10/1981 .....78......1 ......    TOM TOM CLUB ...............................................Island ILPS 9686

**TOMITA** Japanese synthesizer player (born Isao Tomita Tokyo, 1932) who grew up in both China and Japan. He graduated from Keio University in 1955 and began composing film and TV music. He formed Plasma Music in 1973 with Kinji Kitashoji and Mitsuo Miyamoto and recorded his debut solo album in 1974.

| 07/06/1975 | 17 | 20 | ● | SNOWFLAKES ARE DANCING | RCA Red Seal ARL 10488 |
| 16/08/1975 | 42 | 5 | | PICTURES AT AN EXHIBITION | RCA Red Seal ARL 10838 |
| 07/05/1977 | 41 | 6 | | HOLST: THE PLANETS | RCA Red Seal RL 11919 |
| 09/02/1980 | 66 | 2 | | TOMITA'S GREATEST HITS | RCA Red Seal RL 43076 |

**TONGUE 'N' CHEEK** UK R&B group, discovered by Total Contrast, who wrote and produced their debut album in 1990.

| 22/09/1990 | 45 | 3 | | THIS IS TONGUE 'N' CHEEK | Syncopate SYLP 6006 |

**TONY! TONI! TONE!** US R&B group from Oakland, CA formed by brothers Dwayne and Raphael Wiggins and cousin Timothy Christian. Wiggins also recorded as Raphael Saadiq and later joined Lucy Pearl with Dawn Robinson (of En Vogue) and Ali Shaheed Muhammad (of A Tribe Called Quest).

| 02/10/1993 | 66 | 1 | | SONS OF SOUL | Polydor 5149332 |

**TOOL** US rock group formed by Danny Carey, Justin Chancellor, Maynard James Keenan and Adam Jones. They won the 1997 Grammy Award for Best Metal Performance for *Aenema* and the 2001 Grammy Award for Best Metal Performance for *Schism*.

| 26/05/2001 | 16 | 3 | | LATERALUS ▲¹ | Tool Dissectional 9210132 |

**MARTINA TOPLEY BIRD** UK singer born in London in 1975; she was discovered by Tricky.

| 26/07/2003 | 70 | 1 | | QUIXOTIC | Independiente ISOM34CD |

**TOPLOADER** UK rock group formed in Eastbourne by Joseph Washbourn (born 24/12/1975, Sidcup, keyboards/vocals), Dan Hipgrave (born 5/8/1975, Brighton, guitar), Matt Knight (born 18/11/1972, Portsmouth, bass), Julian Deane (born 31/3/1971, Bristol, guitar) and Rob Green (born 24/10/1969, London, drums). Hipgrave is engaged to model and TV presenter Gail Porter.

| 03/06/2000 | 5 | 61 | ✪3 | ONKA'S BIG MOKA ◇ | Sony S2 4947802 |
| 31/08/2002 | 3 | 5 | | MAGIC HOTEL | Sony S2 5084712 |

**TOPOL** Israeli singer (born Chaim Topol, 9/9/1935, Tel Aviv) who came to prominence in the musical *Fiddler On The Roof*, later turned into a successful film. At the time of his birth Tel Aviv was part of Palestine.

| 11/05/1985 | 80 | 1 | | TOPOL'S ISRAEL | BBC REH 529 |

**BERNIE TORME** UK guitarist who played with Atomic Rooster, Ian Gillan and Mammoth. He also formed Desperado with former Twisted Sister singer Dee Snider, Clive Burr and Mark Russell.

| 03/07/1982 | 50 | 3 | | TURN OUT THE LIGHTS | Kamaflage KAMLP 2 |

**MEL TORME** US singer (born Melvin Howard, 13/9/1925, Chicago, IL) who made his name as a songwriter, singer and actor. Nicknamed The Velvet Fog (a moniker he was not happy with), The Kid With The Gauze In his Jaws and Mr Butterscotch, he made his film debut in 1944 in *Pardon My Rhythm* and hosted his own TV series in 1951. He won two Grammy Awards: Best Jazz Vocal Performance in 1982 with George Shearing for *An Evening With George Shearing And Mel Torme* and Best Jazz Vocal Performance in 1983 for *Top Drawer*. He died from a stroke on 15/6/1999. He has a star on the Hollywood Walk of Fame.

| 28/07/1956 | 3 | 4 | | MEL TORME AT 'THE CRESCENDO' | Vogue Coral LVA 9004 |
| 18/08/1956 | 3 | 4 | | MEL TORME WITH THE MARTY PAICH DEK-TETTE | London Jazz LTZ N 15009 |

**PETE TOSH** Jamaican singer (born Winston Hubert McIntosh, 19/10/1944, Westmoreland) who was a founder member of The Wailin' Wailers with Bob Marley, Bunny Livingston, Junior Braithwaite, Cherry Smith and Beverley Kelso in 1964; the group subsequently became The Wailers and backed Bob Marley on his hits. Tosh recorded solo throughout his time with Marley and later launched his own label, Intel Diplo HIM (short for Intelligent Diplomat for His Imperial Majesty). He won the 1987 Grammy Award for Best Reggae Recording for *No Nuclear War*, the first time reggae had been included as a separate category at the awards. On 11/9/1987 Tosh laughed as three men broke into his house, for which he was viciously beaten. When the intruders found insufficient valuables, they shot Tosh dead through the back of the head, and killed two others. It was later suggested the robbery was carried out to cover up a feud.

| 25/09/1976 | 54 | 1 | | LEGALIZE IT | Virgin V 2061 |

**TOTAL CONTRAST** UK R&B group formed in 1983 by Robin Achampong (bass/vocals) and Delroy Murray (keyboards/vocals). They later concentrated on production and songwriting.

| 08/03/1986 | 66 | 3 | | TOTAL CONTRAST | London LONLP 15 |

**TOTO** US rock group formed in Los Angeles, CA in 1978 by Bobby Kimball (born Robert Toteaux, 29/3/1947, Vinton, LA, vocals), Jeff Pocaro (born 1/4/1954, Hartford, CT, drums), his brother Steve (born 2/9/1957, Hartford, keyboards/vocals), David Hungate (bass), Steve Lukather (born 21/10/1957, Los Angeles, guitar) and David Paich (born 25/6/1954, Los Angeles, keyboards/vocals), all of whom were noted session musicians. They were named after Dorothy's dog in the film *The Wizard Of Oz*. Hungate left in 1983, replaced by Mike Pocaro (born 29/5/1955, Hartford). Kimball left in 1984, was initially replaced by Dennis 'Fergie' Frederiksen (born 15/5/1951) and then by Joseph Williams. Steve Pocaro left in 1988. Jeff Pocaro died on 5/8/1992 from heart failure brought about by drugs, although it was claimed he suffered an allergic reaction to garden pesticides (an autopsy found no traces of pesticide in his body). David Paich has won four Grammy Awards: Best Rhythm & Blues Song in 1976 with Boz Scaggs for *Lowdown,* Best Arrangement for Voices in 1982 for *Rosanna,* Best Instrumental Arrangement Accompanying Vocals in 1982 with Jerry Hey for *Rosanna,* and Best Engineered Recording in 1982 with Steve Pocaro and others for *Toto IV*. Steve Lukather won the 1982 Grammy Award for Best Rhythm & Blues Song with Jay Graydon and Bill Champlin for *Turn Your Love Around* and the 2001 Grammy Award for Best Pop Instrumental Album with Larry Carlton for *No Substitutions – Live In Osaka*. The group won three Grammy Awards including: Record of the Year in 1982 for *Rosanna* and Producer of the Year in 1982.

| 31/03/1979 | 37 | 5 | | TOTO | CBS 83148 |

▲⁹ Number of weeks album topped the US chart  ◆¹² RIAA Diamond Awards  ◇³ IFPI Platinum Europe Awards

| | | | | | | |
|---|---|---|---|---|---|---|
| | 26/02/1983 | 4 | 30 | ● | **TOTO IV** 1982 Grammy Award for Album of the Year | CBS 85529 |
| | 17/11/1984 | 67 | 2 | | ISOLATION | CBS 86305 |
| | 20/09/1986 | 99 | 1 | | FAHRENHEIT | CBS 57091 |
| | 09/04/1988 | 73 | 1 | | THE SEVENTH ONE | CBS 4604651 |

**ALI FARKA TOURE AND RY COODER** Malian/US duo formed in 1992 by Ali Farka Toure (guitar/vocals) and Ry Cooder (born 15/3/1947, Los Angeles, CA, guitar/vocals). They assembled a group featuring Clarence 'Gatemouth' Brown (viola), Hamma Sankare (calabash/vocals), Oumar Toure (conga/vocals), John Patitucci (bass) and Jim Keltner (drums).

| | | | | | | |
|---|---|---|---|---|---|---|
| | 09/04/1994 | 44 | 3 | | TALKING TIMBUKTU 1994 Grammy Award for Best World Music Album | World Circuit WCD 040 |

**TOURISTS** UK rock group formed in 1977 by Dave Stewart (born 9/9/1952, Sunderland), Annie Lennox (born 25/12/1954, Aberdeen) and Peet Coombes as Catch. They changed their name in 1979 to Tourists with the addition of Jim Toomey (drums) and Eddie Chin (bass) but disbanded in 1980 with Lennox and Stewart forming the Eurythmics.

| | | | | | | |
|---|---|---|---|---|---|---|
| | 14/07/1979 | 72 | 1 | | THE TOURISTS | Logo GO 1018 |
| | 03/11/1979 | 23 | 16 | O | REALITY EFFECT | Logo GO 1019 |
| | 22/11/1980 | 75 | 1 | | LUMINOUS BASEMENT | RCA Red Seal RCALP 5001 |

**PETE TOWNSHEND** UK singer (born 19/5/1945, London) and a founder member of The Who. He recorded his first solo album in 1972. Awarded a Lifetime Achievement Award at the 1983 BRIT Awards. He also won the 1993 Grammy Award for Best Music Show Album for *The Who's Tommy – Original Cast Recording*.

| | | | | | | |
|---|---|---|---|---|---|---|
| | 21/10/1972 | 30 | 2 | | WHO CAME FIRST | Track 2408 201 |
| | 15/10/1977 | 44 | 3 | | ROUGH MIX **PETE TOWNSHEND AND RONNIE LANE** | Polydor 2442 147 |
| | 03/05/1980 | 11 | 14 | O | EMPTY GLASS | Atco K 50699 |
| | 03/07/1982 | 32 | 8 | | ALL THE BEST COWBOYS HAVE CHINESE EYES | Atco K 50889 |
| | 30/11/1985 | 70 | 1 | | WHITE CITY A NOVEL | Atco 2523921 |

**TOY DOLLS** UK trio formed in Sunderland in 1980 by Olga, Flip and Happy Bob. They later composed the theme to *Razzmatazz*.

| | | | | | | |
|---|---|---|---|---|---|---|
| | 25/05/1985 | 71 | 1 | | A FAR OUT DISC | Volume VOLP 2 |

**TOYAH** UK singer (born Toyah Ann Wilcox, 18/5/1958, Birmingham) who was one of the most successful new-wave female singers and later appeared in the films *Jubilee* and *Quadrophenia*. Married to Robert Fripp, she later became a successful TV presenter.

| | | | | | | |
|---|---|---|---|---|---|---|
| | 14/06/1980 | 40 | 4 | | THE BLUE MEANING | Safari IEYA 666 |
| | 17/01/1981 | 22 | 14 | O | TOYAH! TOYAH! TOYAH! | Safari LIVE 2 |
| | 30/05/1981 | 2 | 46 | ● | **ANTHEM** | Safari VOOR 1 |
| | 19/06/1982 | 6 | 12 | O | **THE CHANGELING** | Safari VOOR 9 |
| | 13/11/1982 | 20 | 6 | | WARRIOR ROCK – TOYAH ON TOUR | Safari TNT 1 |
| | 05/11/1983 | 28 | 7 | | LOVE IS THE LAW | Safari VOOR 10 |
| | 25/02/1984 | 43 | 4 | | TOYAH! TOYAH! TOYAH! | K-Tel NE 1268 |
| | 03/08/1985 | 24 | 4 | | MINX | Portrait PRT 26415 |

**T'PAU** UK rock group formed in Shrewsbury in 1986 by Carol Decker (born 10/9/1957, London, vocals), Ronnie Rogers (born 13/3/1959, Shrewsbury, guitar), Paul Jackson (born 8/8/1961, Shrewsbury, bass), Tim Burgess (born 6/10/1961, Shrewsbury, drums), Michael Chetwood (born 26/8/1954, Shrewsbury, keyboards) and Taj Wyzgowski (guitar). The group was named after a *Star Trek* character. Wyzgowski left in 1988 and was replaced by Dean Howard. They disbanded in 1994 with Decker going solo.

| | | | | | | |
|---|---|---|---|---|---|---|
| | 26/09/1987 | ❶[1] | 59 | ✪4 | **BRIDGE OF SPIES** | Siren SIRENLP 8 |
| | 05/11/1988 | 4 | 17 | ✪ | **RAGE** | Siren SRNLP 20 |
| | 22/06/1991 | 10 | 7 | O | **THE PROMISE** | Siren SRNLP 32 |
| | 27/02/1993 | 35 | 2 | | HEART AND SOUL – THE VERY BEST OF T'PAU | Virgin TPAUD 1 |

**TQ** US rapper (born Terrance Quaites, Mobile, AL) who moved with his family to Compton in California and was subsequently influenced by NWA, among other rap acts. He was briefly lead singer with Coming Of Age before going solo.

| | | | | | | |
|---|---|---|---|---|---|---|
| | 08/05/1999 | 27 | 7 | | THEY NEVER SAW ME COMING | Epic 4914032 |
| | 20/05/2000 | 32 | 2 | | THE SECOND COMING | Epic 4977602 |

### IAN TRACEY WITH THE LIVERPOOL CATHEDRALS' CHOIRS
UK conductor with the male and female vocal choirs of Liverpool's cathedrals.

21/03/1992 . . . . . 62 . . . . . . 3 . . . . . .  YOUR FAVOURITE HYMNS . . . . . . . . . . . . . . . . . . . . . . . . . . . . . . . . . . . . . . . . . . . . . . . . . . . . . . . . . . . Virgin Classics 7912092

### TRACIE
UK singer (full name Tracie Young) discovered by Paul Weller and signed with his Respond label in 1983.

30/06/1984 . . . . . 64 . . . . . . 2 . . . . . .  FAR FROM THE HURTING KIND . . . . . . . . . . . . . . . . . . . . . . . . . . . . . . . . . . . . . . . . . . . . . . . . . . . . . . . . . Respond RRL 502

### TRAFFIC
UK rock group formed in 1967 by Steve Winwood (born 12/5/1948, Birmingham, vocals/keyboards/guitar), Dave Mason (born 10/5/1947, Worcester, guitar/vocals), Chris Wood (born 24/6/1944, Birmingham, flute/saxophone) and Jim Capaldi (born 24/8/1944, Evesham, drums/vocals) following Winwood's departure from the Spencer Davis Group. The group disbanded in 1974 with Winwood and Capaldi subsequently recording solo. Wood died from liver failure on 12/7/1983. They were inducted into the Rock & Roll Hall of Fame in 2004.

| | | | | | |
|---|---|---|---|---|---|
| 30/12/1967 | 8 | 16 | | **MR. FANTASY** . . . . . . . . . . . . . . . . . . . . . . . . . . . . . . . . . . . . . . . . . . . . . . . . . . . . . . . . . . . . . . . . . . . . . . . . . . . | Island ILP 9061 |
| 26/10/1968 | 9 | 8 | | TRAFFIC . . . . . . . . . . . . . . . . . . . . . . . . . . . . . . . . . . . . . . . . . . . . . . . . . . . . . . . . . . . . . . . . . . . . . . . . . . . . . . | Island ILPS 9081 |
| 08/08/1970 | 11 | 9 | | JOHN BARLEYCORN MUST DIE . . . . . . . . . . . . . . . . . . . . . . . . . . . . . . . . . . . . . . . . . . . . . . . . . . . . . . . . . . . . . | Island ILPS 9116 |
| 24/11/1973 | 40 | 3 | | TRAFFIC – ON THE ROAD . . . . . . . . . . . . . . . . . . . . . . . . . . . . . . . . . . . . . . . . . . . . . . . . . . . . . . . . . . . . . . . | Island ISLD 2 |
| 28/09/1974 | 31 | 1 | | WHEN THE EAGLE FLIES . . . . . . . . . . . . . . . . . . . . . . . . . . . . . . . . . . . . . . . . . . . . . . . . . . . . . . . . . . . . . . . . . | Island ILPS 9273 |
| 21/05/1994 | 29 | 4 | | FAR FROM HOME . . . . . . . . . . . . . . . . . . . . . . . . . . . . . . . . . . . . . . . . . . . . . . . . . . . . . . . . . . . . . . . . . . . . . . . | Virgin CDV 2727 |

### TRAIN
US rock group formed in San Francisco, CA in 1994 by Patrick Monahan (vocals), Ron Hotchkiss (guitar/vocals), Jim Stafford (guitar), Charlie Colin (bass) and Scott Underwood (drums). Although initially signed by Columbia Records, they were effectively farmed out to Aware Records before recording their debut album in 1998. They won two Grammy Awards in 2001 for *Drops Of Jupiter*: Best Rock Song for writers Charlie Colin, Rob Hotchkiss, Pat Monahan, Jimmy Stafford and Scott Underwood and Best Instrumental Arrangement Accompanying Singers for arranger Paul Buckmaster.

18/08/2001 . . . . . 8 . . . . . . 9 . . . . . . ●  **DROPS OF JUPITER** . . . . . . . . . . . . . . . . . . . . . . . . . . . . . . . . . . . . . . . . . . . . . . . . . . . . . . . . . . . . . . . . Columbia 5023069

### TRANSGLOBAL UNDERGROUND
UK group formed by Count Dubulah (bass/samples), Natacha Atlas (vocals), Alex Kasiek (keyboards) and Man Tu (drums).

| | | | | | |
|---|---|---|---|---|---|
| 30/10/1993 | 45 | 1 | | DREAM OF 100 NATIONS . . . . . . . . . . . . . . . . . . . . . . . . . . . . . . . . . . . . . . . . . . . . . . . . . . . . . . . . . . . . . . . | Nation NR 021CD |
| 29/10/1994 | 40 | 1 | | INTERNATIONAL TIMES . . . . . . . . . . . . . . . . . . . . . . . . . . . . . . . . . . . . . . . . . . . . . . . . . . . . . . . . . . . . . . . . | Nation NATCD 38 |
| 25/05/1996 | 62 | 1 | | PSYCHIC KARAOKE . . . . . . . . . . . . . . . . . . . . . . . . . . . . . . . . . . . . . . . . . . . . . . . . . . . . . . . . . . . . . . . . . . . | Nation NRCD 1067 |

### TRANSVISION VAMP
UK rock group formed by singer Wendy James (born 21/1/1966, London, vocals), Nick Christian Sayer (born 1/8/1964, guitar), Tex Axile (born 30/7/1963, keyboards), Dave Parsons (born 2/7/1962, bass) and Pol Burton (born 1/7/1964, drums). James later went solo whilst Parsons became a member of Bush.

| | | | | | |
|---|---|---|---|---|---|
| 15/10/1988 | 4 | 32 | ● | **POP ART** . . . . . . . . . . . . . . . . . . . . . . . . . . . . . . . . . . . . . . . . . . . . . . . . . . . . . . . . . . . . . . . . . . . . . . . . . . | MCA MCF 3421 |
| 08/07/1989 | ❶¹ | 26 | ✪ | **VELVETEEN** . . . . . . . . . . . . . . . . . . . . . . . . . . . . . . . . . . . . . . . . . . . . . . . . . . . . . . . . . . . . . . . . . . . . . . . | MCA MCG 6050 |

### TRASH CAN SINATRAS
UK group formed in Glasgow in 1987 by Frank Reader (guitar/vocals), John Douglas (guitar), Paul Livingston (guitar), George McDaid (bass) and Stephen Douglas (drums). McDaid left in 1992 and was replaced by David Hughes. Reader is the brother of Fairground Attraction's Eddi Reader.

| | | | | | |
|---|---|---|---|---|---|
| 07/07/1990 | 74 | 1 | | CAKE . . . . . . . . . . . . . . . . . . . . . . . . . . . . . . . . . . . . . . . . . . . . . . . . . . . . . . . . . . . . . . . . . . . . . . . . . . . . . | Go Discs 8282011 |
| 15/05/1993 | 50 | 1 | | I'VE SEEN EVERYTHING . . . . . . . . . . . . . . . . . . . . . . . . . . . . . . . . . . . . . . . . . . . . . . . . . . . . . . . . . . . . . . . | Go Discs 8284082 |

### TRAVELING WILBURYS
UK/US group formed in 1988 by George Harrison (born 24/2/1943, Liverpool, who assumed the names Nelson and Spike for the Wilburys), Roy Orbison (born 23/4/1936, Vernon, TX, Lefty), Tom Petty (born 20/10/1953, Gainesville, FL, Charlie T Junior or Muddy), Bob Dylan (born 24/5/1941, Duluth, MN, Lucky or Boo) and Jeff Lynne (born 30/12/1947, Birmingham, Otis or Clayton). Orbison died from a heart attack on 6/12/1988, Harrison from cancer on 29/11/2001.

| | | | | | |
|---|---|---|---|---|---|
| 05/11/1988 | 16 | 35 | ✪ | THE TRAVELING WILBURYS VOLUME 1 1989 Grammy Award for Best Rock Performance by a Group. Originally known as *Handle With Care* in the UK . . . . . . . . . . . . . . . . . . . . . . . . . . . . . . . . | Wilbury WX 224 |
| 10/11/1990 | 14 | 9 | ● | THE TRAVELING WILBURYS VOLUME 3 . . . . . . . . . . . . . . . . . . . . . . . . . . . . . . . . . . . . . . . . . . . . . . . . . . . . | Wilbury WX 384 |

### PAT TRAVERS
Canadian male singer/guitarist (born 1954, Toronto, Ontario ) who began his professional career in his brother's group before settling in London during the 1970s. He formed a group with Peter 'Mars' Cowling (bass) and Ron Dyke (drums), with Dyke being replaced first by Nicko McBrain and then by Clive Edwards. Travers went into retirement from 1984–90.

02/04/1977 . . . . . 40 . . . . . . 3 . . . . . .  MAKIN' MAGIC . . . . . . . . . . . . . . . . . . . . . . . . . . . . . . . . . . . . . . . . . . . . . . . . . . . . . . . . . . . . . . . . . . . . . . Polydor 2383 436

### TRAVIS
UK rock quartet formed in Glasgow in 1990 by Francis Healy (born 23/7/1973, Stafford, guitar/vocals), Douglas Payne (born 14/11/1972, Glasgow, guitar), Andrew Dunlop (born 1/3/1972, Glasgow, bass) and Neil Primrose (born 20/2/1972, Glasgow, drums). They were named Best British Group at the 2000 and 2002 BRIT Awards.

20/09/1997 . . . . . 9 . . . . . . 16 . . . . . . ●  **GOOD FEELING** . . . . . . . . . . . . . . . . . . . . . . . . . . . . . . . . . . . . . . . . . . . . . . . . . . . . . . . . . . . . . . . . . . . . Independiente ISOM 1CD

| | DATE | POS | WKS | BPI | ALBUM TITLE | LABEL & NUMBER |
|---|---|---|---|---|---|---|

05/06/1999 .....❶⁹ ....102 .....✪⁹ THE MAN WHO ◇³ 2000 BRIT Award for Best Album ........................................Independiente ISOM 9CDX
23/06/2001 .....❶³ ....54 .....✪⁴ THE INVISIBLE BAND ◇ ................................................................Independiente ISOM 25CD
25/10/2003 .....3 ....11 .....✪ 12 MEMORIES ........................................................................Independiente ISOM 40CD

**RANDY TRAVIS** US singer (born Randy Bruce Traywick, 4/5/1959, Marshville, NC) who was frequently in trouble with the law as a teenager for drunkenness, theft, drugs and motoring offences (one for speeding at 135 miles per hour). He was on probation in 1977 when he got a break at the Country City club in Charlotte and was subsequently signed by Warner Brothers in 1984. He has won four Grammy Awards including: Best Country Vocal Performance, Male in 1987 for *Always And Forever*, Best Country Vocal collaboration in 1998 with Clint Black, Joe Diffie, Merle Haggard, Emmylou Harris, Alison Krauss, Patty Loveless, Earl Scruggs, Ricky Skaggs, Marty Stuart, Pam Tillis, Travis Tritt and Dwight Yoakam for *Same Old Train*, and Best Southern, Country or Bluegrass Gospel Album in 2003 for *Rise And Shine*.
06/08/1988 .....64 ......2 ...... OLD 8 X 10 1988 Grammy Award for Best Country Vocal Performance, Male ..........................Warner Brothers WX 162

**JOHN TRAVOLTA** US singer/actor (born 18/2/1954, Englewood, NJ) who first became known in the film *Saturday Night Fever*. He then appeared in *Grease, Look Who's Talking, Face/Off* and many others. He has a star on the Hollywood Walk of Fame.
23/12/1978 .....40 ......6 ......● SANDY .................................................................................Midsong POLD 5014

**TREMELOES** UK group formed in 1959 by Brian Poole (born 2/11/1941, Barking, guitar/vocals), Alan Blakley (born 1/4/1942, Bromley, drums), Alan Howard (born 17/10/1941, Dagenham, saxophone) and Brian Scott (lead guitar), later adding Dave Munden (born 12/12/1943, Dagenham) on drums and switching Blakley to rhythm guitar, Howard to bass and allowing Poole to sing. They added Rick West (born Richard Westwood, 7/5/1943, Dagenham, lead guitar) in 1961 and signed with Decca in 1962. They split from Poole in 1966, by which time they comprised Blakely, Munden, West and Len 'Chips' Hawkes (born 11/11/1946, London). The group disbanded in 1974, by which time Blakley and Howard had established themselves as successful songwriters, but re-formed in the 1980s for numerous concerts. Blakley died from cancer on 10/6/1996.
03/06/1967 .....15 ......7 ...... HERE COMES THE TREMELOES ..............................................................CBS SBPG 63017

**RALPH TRESVANT** US singer (born 16/5/1968, Boston, MA) and a founder member of New Edition in 1981. He went solo when the group disbanded in 1989.
23/02/1991 .....37 ......3 ...... RALPH TRESVANT ........................................................................MCA MCG 6120

**A TRIBE CALLED QUEST** US rap group formed by rappers Q-Tip (born Jonathan Davis, 10/4/1970, Brooklyn, NY) and Phife Dog (born Malik Taylor, 20/11/1970, Brooklyn) and sound system controller Ali Shaheed Muhammad (born 11/8/1970, New York). Q-Tip has also recorded solo. Ali Shaheed Muhammad later became a member of Lucy Pearl with Dawn Robinson (of En Vogue) and Raphael Saadiq (of Tony! Toni! Tone!).
19/05/1990 .....54 ......2 ...... PEOPLE'S INSTINCTIVE TRAVELS… ..........................................................Jive HIP 96
12/10/1991 .....58 ......1 ...... THE LOW END THEORY ....................................................................Jive HIP 117
27/11/1993 .....70 ......1 ...... MIDNIGHT MARAUDERS .....................................................................Jive CHIP 143
10/08/1996 .....28 ......4 ...... BEATS, RHYMES AND LIFE ▲¹ ..............................................................Jive CHIP 170
10/10/1998 .....38 ......1 ...... THE LOVE MOVEMENT ......................................................................Jive 0521032

**OBIE TRICE** US male rapper (born 14/11/1978, Detroit, MI); he was discovered by Eminem.
11/10/2003 .....11 ......8 ...... CHEERS ...............................................................................Interscope 9860986

**TRICKY** UK rapper (born Adrian Thaws, 27/1/1968, Bristol, Avon) who began his career contributing tracks to Massive Attack and made his debut single in 1994. He also recorded under the names Nearly God and Starving Souls.
04/03/1995 .....3 ....35 ......● MAXINQUAYE ...........................................................................Fourth & Broadway BRCD 610
23/11/1996 .....30 ......2 ...... PRE-MILLENNIUM TENSION .................................................................Fourth & Broadway BRCDX 623
06/06/1998 .....23 ......2 ...... ANGELS WITH DIRTY FACES ................................................................Island CID 8071
28/08/1999 .....22 ......2 ...... JUXTAPOSE **TRICKY WITH DJ MUGGS AND GREASE** ..............................................Island CID 8087
14/07/2001 .....34 ......2 ...... BLOWBACK .............................................................................Anti/Epitaph 65962

**TRIFFIDS** Australian group formed in Perth by David McComb (guitar/keyboards/vocals), 'Evil' Graham Lee (guitar), Jill Burt (keyboards/vocals), Robert McComb (guitar/violin/vocals), Martyn Casey (bass) and Alsy MacDonald (drums).
22/04/1989 .....63 ......1 ...... THE BLACK SWAN ........................................................................Island ILPS 9928

**TRINITY** – see **JULIE DRISCOLL, BRIAN AUGER AND THE TRINITY**

**TRIUMPH** Canadian rock group formed in Toronto in 1975 by Rik Emmett (guitar/vocals), Mike Levine (bass/keyboards) and Gil Moore (drums). Emmett left the group in 1988, replaced by Phil Xenides, with Moore becoming lead singer.
10/05/1980 .....61 ......5 ...... PROGRESSIONS OF POWER ..................................................................RCA PL 13524
03/10/1981 .....64 ......3 ...... ALLIED FORCES .........................................................................RCA RCALP 6002

**TROGGS** UK rock group formed in Andover in 1964 by Howard Mansfield (guitar/vocals), Reg Presley (born Reginald Ball, 12/6/1943, Andover, bass), Dave Wright (guitar) and Ronnie Bond (born Ronald Bullis, 4/5/1943, Andover, drums) as the Troglodytes. Wright and Mansfield left soon after and was replaced by Pete Staples (born 3/5/1944, Andover) and Chris Britton (born 21/1/1945, Watford). As Staples played bass Presley switched to lead vocals. They signed with manager Larry Page in 1965 who leased their releases first to CBS then to Fontana. Ball adopted the name of Presley as a publicity stunt in 1966. Bond died on 13/11/1992.
30/07/1966 .....6 ......16 ...... **FROM NOWHERE… THE TROGGS** ............................................................Fontana TL 5355
25/02/1967 .....10 .....11 ...... **TROGGLODYNAMITE** .....................................................................Page One POL 001
05/08/1967 .....24 ......5 ...... THE BEST OF THE TROGGS .................................................................Page One FOR 001

○ Silver disc ● Gold disc ✪ Platinum disc (additional platinum units are indicated by a figure following the symbol) ❶⁹ Number of weeks album topped the UK chart

16/07/1994 .....27 ......3 ...... GREATEST HITS ...................................................................Polygram TV 5227392

### TROUBADOURS DU ROI BAUDOUIN
Zairian male and female vocal group formed by Father Uudo Haazen, a Belgian priest who went to the Congo in the 1950s.

22/05/1976 .....59 ......1 ...... MISSA LUBA ...................................................................Philips SBL 7592

### TROUBLE FUNK
US funk group formed in Washington DC by Mack Carey (percussion/vocals), with Robert Reed (keyboards), James Avery (keyboards), Chester Davis (guitar), Tony Fisher (bass), Taylor Reed (trumpet), David Rudd (saxophone), Gerald Reed (trombone), Robert Reed (trombone), Timothy David (percussion) and Emmett Nixon (drums).

08/11/1986 .....75 ......2 ...... SAY WHAT! ...................................................................Fourth & Broadway DCLP 101
05/09/1987 .....54 ......2 ...... TROUBLE OVER HERE, TROUBLE OVER THERE ...................................Fourth & Broadway BRLP 513

### ROBIN TROWER
UK singer/guitarist (born 9/3/1945, Southend) who was a member of The Paramounts from 1963–66 and then went on to form Procol Harum in 1967. He left the group in 1971 and formed Jude with Frankie Miller, Jim Dewar and Clive Bunker. He disbanded this group a short while later and formed The Robin Trower Band with Dewar and Reg Isidore (drums). Isidore left in 1974 and was replaced by Bill Lordan. Trower was a member of BLT in 1981 with Jack Bruce and Bill Lordan, although in 1983 he re-assembled his own group with Dewar, David Bronze (bass), Alan Clarke (drums) and Bobby Clouter (drums). The line-up by the time they switched to Atlantic Records comprised Trower, Bronze, Davey Pattison (vocals) and Pete Thompson (drums).

01/03/1975 .....26 ......4 ...... FOR EARTH BELOW ...................................................................Chrysalis CHR 1073
13/03/1976 .....15 ......6 ...... ROBIN TROWER LIVE ...................................................................Chrysalis CHR 1089
30/10/1976 .....31 ......1 ...... LONG MISTY DAYS ...................................................................Chrysalis CHR 1107
29/10/1977 .....58 ......1 ...... IN CITY DREAMS ...................................................................Chrysalis CHR 1148
16/02/1980 .....61 ......4 ...... VICTIMS OF THE FURY ...................................................................Chrysalis CHR 1215

### TRUTH HURTS
US R&B singer Shari Watson (from St Louis, MO).

24/08/2002 .....61 ......4 ...... TRUTHFULLY SPEAKING ...................................................................Interscope 4933312

### TUBES
US rock group formed in Phoenix, AZ in the late 1960s and relocated to San Francisco, CA in the early 1970s. They comprised Rick Anderson (born 1/8/1947, St Paul, MN, bass), Bill 'Sputnick' Spooner (born 16/4/1949, Phoenix, guitar), Vince Welnick (born 21/2/1951, Phoenix, keyboards), 'Fee' Waybill (born John Waldo, 17/9/1950, Omaha, NE, vocals), Michael Cotten (born 25/1/1950, Kansas City, MO, synthesizer), Prairie Prince (born 7/5/1950, Charlotte, NC, drums), Roger Steen (born 13/11/1949, Pipestone, MN, guitar) and Re Styles (born 3/3/1950, guitar/vocals). They signed with A&M in 1975. Welnick later joined the Grateful Dead.

04/03/1978 .....38 ......1 ...... WHAT DO YOU WANT FROM LIFE ...................................................................A&M AMS 68460
02/06/1979 .....40 ......5 ...... REMOTE CONTROL ...................................................................A&M AMLH 64751
04/06/1983 .....77 ......1 ...... OUTSIDE INSIDE ...................................................................Capitol EST 12260

### TURIN BRAKES
UK male duo formed in South London by Olly Knights and Gale Paridjanian.

17/03/2001 .....27 ......18 ......● THE OPTIMIST ...................................................................Source SOURCD 023
15/03/2003 .....4 ......11 ......● **ETHER SONG** ...................................................................Source CDSOUR 054

### IKE AND TINA TURNER
US husband and wife duo formed by Ike (born Izear Turner, 5/11/1931, Clarksdale, MS) and Tina Turner (born Annie Mae Bullock, 26/11/193, Brownsville, TN). They met in 1956 when Ike's band the Kings of Rhythm took a residency at a club in St Louis. They married in 1958 and at Ike's suggestion she took the stage name Tina. They first recorded as Ike & Tina Turner in 1960 for Sue Records. The backing band became the Ike & Tina Turner Revue and assembled three backing singers as the Ikettes. They linked with Phil Spector in 1966 (the lack of success in the US for *River Deep* prompted Spector to shut down his Philles label and go into semi-retirement) and later recorded for Blue Thumb. They separated in 1975, divorced in 1978 and officially ended their professional relationship in October 1976. Tina later went solo. Ike Turner served 18 months of a four-year prison sentence for driving under the influence of cocaine (in a later interview, he claimed to have spent $11 million on his habit). They were inducted into the Rock & Roll Hall of Fame in 1991. They won the 1971 Grammy Award for Best Rhythm & Blues Vocal Performance by a Duo for *Proud Mary*.

01/10/1966 .....27 ......1 ...... RIVER DEEP – MOUNTAIN HIGH ...................................................................London HAU 8298

### RUBY TURNER
UK singer (born 1958, Jamaica, raised in Birmingham) who formed her first band with Bob Lamb, Billy Paul and Geoff Pearse before signing with Jive in 1985. She later became a noted session singer, appearing on albums by UB40, Lulu and Joshua Kadison and sang with Full Flava. She also became an actress, appearing in *Eastenders*.

18/10/1986 .....47 ......11 ......○ WOMEN HOLD UP HALF THE SKY ...................................................................Jive HIP 36
08/10/1988 .....22 ......6 ......○ THE MOTOWN SONG BOOK ...................................................................Jive HIP 58
17/02/1990 .....74 ......2 ...... PARADISE ...................................................................Jive HIP 89

### TINA TURNER
US singer (born Annie Mae Bullock, 26/11/1939, Brownsville, TN) who teamed up with Ike Turner in 1956, becoming a singer with his Kings of Rhythm group. Following their marriage in 1958 she adopted the stage name Tina Turner and recorded as Ike & Tina Turner from 1960 until their professional relationship dissolved in 1976. She signed with Capitol in 1982 as a solo artist. She appeared in numerous films, including *Mad Max 3 – Beyond Thunderdome*. Her autobiography *I, Tina* was turned into the film *What's Love Got To Do With It* with Angela Bassett as Tina and Lawrence Fishburne as Ike. She was inducted into the Rock & Roll Hall of Fame in 1991 (as part of Ike & Tina Turner). She won one Grammy Award with Ike and six further awards including: Record of the Year and Best Pop Vocal Performance in 1984 for *What's Love Got To Do With It* (which also won the Song of the Year award for writers Graham Lyle and Terry Britten); Best Rock Vocal Performance in 1984 for *Better Be Good To Me*; Best Rock Vocal Performance in 1985 for *Out Of The Living*; and Best Rock Vocal Performance in 1986 for *Back Where You Started*. She also won the 1999 MOBO Award for Lifetime Achievement. She has a star on the Hollywood Walk of Fame.

▲⁹ Number of weeks album topped the US chart   ◆¹² RIAA Diamond Awards   ◇³ IFPI Platinum Europe Awards

| DATE | POS | WKS | BPI | ALBUM TITLE | LABEL & NUMBER |
|---|---|---|---|---|---|
| 30/06/1984 | 2 | 147 | ✪[3] | PRIVATE DANCER | Capitol TINA 1 |
| 20/09/1986 | 2 | 49 | ✪ | BREAK EVERY RULE | Capitol EST 2018 |
| 02/04/1988 | 8 | 13 | ● | LIVE IN EUROPE 1988 Grammy Award for Best Rock Vocal Performance | Capitol ESTD 1 |
| 30/09/1989 | ❶[1] | 78 | ✪[5] | FOREIGN AFFAIR | Capitol ESTU 2103 |
| 12/10/1991 | 2 | 141 | ✪[8] | SIMPLY THE BEST | Capitol ESTV 1 |
| 19/06/1993 | ❶[1] | 33 | ✪ | WHAT'S LOVE GOT TO DO WITH IT Original soundtrack to the film | Parlophone CDPCSD 128 |
| 13/04/1996 | 4 | 41 | ✪[2] | WILDEST DREAMS ◇[2] | Parlophone CDEST 2279 |
| 13/11/1999 | 9 | 19 | ✪ | TWENTY FOUR SEVEN◇ | Parlophone 5231802 |

**TURTLES** US group formed in Los Angeles, CA by Howard Kaylan (born 22/6/1947, New York, vocals), Al Nichol (born 31/3/1946, Winston Salem, NC, guitar), Jim Tucker (born 17/10/1946, Los Angeles, guitar), Chuck Portz (born 28/3/1945, Santa Monica, CA, bass), Mark Volman (born 19/4/1947, Los Angeles, vocals) and Don Murray (born 8/11/1945, Los Angeles, drums) as the Nightriders, later name-changing to the Crossfires. They became The Turtles upon signing with White Whale in 1965. Murray left in 1966, replaced by John Barbata (born 1/4/1946, New Jersey). Portz left soon after, replaced by Jim Pons (born 14/3/1943, Santa Monica). Barbata left in 1969, replaced by John Seiter (born 17/8/1944, St Louis, MO). The group disbanded in 1970. Murray set up a computer graphics company and died on 22/3/1996 from complications brought on by surgery.

| DATE | POS | WKS | BPI | ALBUM TITLE | LABEL & NUMBER |
|---|---|---|---|---|---|
| 22/07/1967 | 18 | 9 | | HAPPY TOGETHER | London HAU 8330 |

**SHANIA TWAIN** Canadian country singer (born Eilleen Regina Edwards, 28/8/1965, Windsor, Ontario) whose stage name means 'I'm on my way' in the Ojibwa Indian language. She signed with Mercury in 1992 and released her first single in 1993. She married record producer Robert John 'Mutt' Lange in 1993 and gave birth to their first son, Eja, in August 2001. Her *Come On Over* album is the biggest selling CD by a solo female artist, with sales of 26 million worldwide by March 2000. She has won five Grammy Awards including Best Country Song (written with her husband) and Best Female Country Vocal Performance in 1998 for *You're Still The One*, Best Country Song in 1999 for *Come On Over,* and Best Female Country Vocal Performance in 1999 for *Man! I Feel Like A Woman.*

| DATE | POS | WKS | BPI | ALBUM TITLE | LABEL & NUMBER |
|---|---|---|---|---|---|
| 21/03/1998 | ❶[11] | 138 | ✪[10] | COME ON OVER ◇[7] ◆[19] | Mercury 1700812 |
| 18/03/2000 | 7 | 25 | ✪ | THE WOMAN IN ME ◆[12] 1995 Grammy Award for Best Country Album | Mercury 5228862 |
| 15/07/2000 | 62 | 2 | | WILD & WICKED | RWP RWPCD1123 |
| 30/11/2002 | 4 | 45 | ✪[2] | UP! ◇[2] ▲[5] ◆[10] | Mercury 1703442 |

**TWEENIES** UK children's TV characters featuring Jake, Fizz, Milo, Bella and Doodles the dog.

| DATE | POS | WKS | BPI | ALBUM TITLE | LABEL & NUMBER |
|---|---|---|---|---|---|
| 25/11/2000 | 56 | 4 | ○ | FRIENDS FOREVER | BBC Music/Polydor WMSF 60362 |
| 01/12/2001 | 34 | 5 | | THE CHRISTMAS ALBUM | BBC Music WMSF 60482 |

**TWEET** US singer (real name Charlene Keys) who was discovered by and sang with Missy Elliott and Ja Rule before going solo.

| DATE | POS | WKS | BPI | ALBUM TITLE | LABEL & NUMBER |
|---|---|---|---|---|---|
| 25/05/2002 | 15 | 5 | | SOUTHERN HUMMINGBIRD | Elektra 7559627462 |

**TWELFTH NIGHT** UK group formed in Reading by Andy Sears (born 16/1/1960, vocals), Andy Revell (born 21/2/1958, guitar), Clive Mitten (born 24/2/1959, bass/keyboards), Rick Battersby (keyboards) and Brian Devoil (born 20/7/1954, drums).

| DATE | POS | WKS | BPI | ALBUM TITLE | LABEL & NUMBER |
|---|---|---|---|---|---|
| 27/10/1984 | 83 | 2 | | ART AND ILLUSION | Music For Nations MFN 36 |

**TWENTY 4 SEVEN FEATURING CAPTAIN HOLLYWOOD** German duo formed by Stay-C and Stella with Captain Hollywood (real name Tony Harrison).

| DATE | POS | WKS | BPI | ALBUM TITLE | LABEL & NUMBER |
|---|---|---|---|---|---|
| 19/01/1991 | 69 | 2 | | STREET MOVES | BCM 3124 |

**TWIGGY** UK singer (born Lesley Hornby, 1949, London); she first came to prominence as a model during the 1960s.

| DATE | POS | WKS | BPI | ALBUM TITLE | LABEL & NUMBER |
|---|---|---|---|---|---|
| 21/08/1976 | 33 | 8 | ○ | TWIGGY | Mercury 9102 600 |
| 30/04/1977 | 35 | 3 | | PLEASE GET MY NAME RIGHT | Mercury 9102 601 |

**TWISTA** US rapper (born Carl Mitchell, Chicago, IL) who also recorded with Speed Knot Mobstaz.

| DATE | POS | WKS | BPI | ALBUM TITLE | LABEL & NUMBER |
|---|---|---|---|---|---|
| 28/02/2004 | 47 | 11 | | KAMIKAZE ▲[1] | Atlantic 7567835982 |

**TWISTED SISTER** US heavy rock group formed in New York in 1982 by Dee Snider (vocals), Jay Jay French (guitar), Eddie Ojeda (guitar), Mark Mendoza (bass) and AJ Pero (drums). Pero left in 1987, replaced by Joey Franco, although the group disbanded later the same year. Snider later appeared in the film *Strangeland*.

| DATE | POS | WKS | BPI | ALBUM TITLE | LABEL & NUMBER |
|---|---|---|---|---|---|
| 25/09/1982 | 70 | 3 | | UNDER THE BLADE | Secret SECX 9 |
| 07/05/1983 | 14 | 9 | | YOU CAN'T STOP ROCK 'N' ROLL | Atlantic A 0074 |
| 16/06/1984 | 34 | 5 | | STAY HUNGRY | Atlantic 7801561 |
| 14/12/1985 | 95 | 1 | | COME OUT AND PLAY | Atlantic 7812751 |
| 25/07/1987 | 57 | 2 | | LOVE IS FOR SUCKERS | Atlantic WX 120 |

**2 IN A ROOM** US dance duo formed by rapper Rafael 'Dose' Vargas and remixer Roger 'Rog Nice' Pauletta who teamed up in Washington Heights in New York.

| DATE | POS | WKS | BPI | ALBUM TITLE | LABEL & NUMBER |
|---|---|---|---|---|---|
| 02/03/1991 | 73 | 1 | | WIGGLE IT | SBK SBKLP 11 |

○ Silver disc  ● Gold disc  ✪ Platinum disc (additional platinum units are indicated by a figure following the symbol)  ❶[9] Number of weeks album topped the UK chart

## 2 UNLIMITED
Dutch dance duo formed by Anita Dels (born 28/12/1971, Amsterdam) and Ray 'Kid Ray' Slijngaard (born 28/6/1971, Amsterdam) who teamed up in 1991 with Belgian production duo Phil Wilde and Jean-Paul De Coster. Wilde and De Coster had previously been responsible for Bizz Nizz.

| DATE | POS | WKS | BPI | ALBUM TITLE | LABEL & NUMBER |
|------|-----|-----|-----|-------------|----------------|
| 07/03/1992 | 37 | 3 | | GET READY | PWL Continental HFCD 23 |
| 22/05/1993 | ❶¹ | 21 | | **NO LIMITS** | PWL Continental HFCD 27 |
| 18/06/1994 | ❶¹ | 9 | ● | **REAL THINGS** ◇ | PWL Continental HFCD 38 |
| 11/11/1995 | 27 | 5 | | HITS UNLIMITED | PWL Continental HF 47CD |

## 2PAC
US rapper/actor Tupac Amara Shakur (born Lesane Crooks, 16/6/1971, Brooklyn, NY) who was a member of Digital Underground. He had numerous brushes with the law, including a gun battle with two off-duty policemen, an assault on Allen Hughes of Menace II Society, receiving a jail sentence for a sexual abuse conviction and causing the death of a six-year old child when his gun accidentally discharged. He was shot five times, had $40,000 stolen, and survived during a robbery in Manhattan in 1994. Two years later, on 7/9/1996 he was shot four times whilst travelling to the boxing match between Mike Tyson and Bruce Seldon in Las Vegas and died as a result of gunshot wounds on 13/9/1996. He also recorded as Makaveli and appeared in films such as *Nothing But Trouble*, *Poetic Justice* and *Above The Rim*. He won the 1996 MOBO Award for Best Video for *California Love*.

| DATE | POS | WKS | BPI | ALBUM TITLE | LABEL & NUMBER |
|------|-----|-----|-----|-------------|----------------|
| 09/03/1996 | 32 | 7 | ○ | ALL EYEZ ON ME ▲² | Death Row 5242492 |
| 16/11/1996 | 53 | 1 | | THE DOM KILLUMINATI – THE SEVEN DAY THEORY **MAKAVELI** | Death Row IND 90039 |
| 06/12/1997 | 44 | 1 | | R U STILL DOWN? (REMEMBER ME) | Jive CHIP 195 |
| 08/08/1998 | 65 | 1 | | IN HIS OWN WORDS | Eagle EAGCD 050 |
| 12/12/1998 | 17 | 35 | ✪ | GREATEST HITS | Jive 0522662 |
| 08/01/2000 | 75 | 1 | | STILL I RISE **2 PAC AND OUTLAWZ** | Interscope 4904132 |
| 21/04/2001 | 33 | 17 | ○ | UNTIL THE END OF TIME ▲¹ | Interscope 4908402 |
| 14/12/2002 | 68 | 1 | | BETTER DAYZ | Interscope 4970702 |
| 22/11/2003 | 62 | 1 | | RESURRECTION Original soundtrack to the film | Interscope 9861159 |

## TYGERS OF PAN TANG
UK rock group formed in Whitley Bay in 1979 by Jess Cox (vocals), Robb Weir (guitar), Rocky (bass) and Brian Dick (drums). They added John Sykes (guitar) in 1980, with Cox leaving the group at the end of the same year, replaced by Jon Deverill. Sykes left in 1981, replaced by Fred Purser, but the group disbanded in 1983. Deverill and Dick re-formed the group in 1985 with Steve Lamb (guitar), Neil Shepard (guitar) and Dave Donaldson (bass), although after two albums they disbanded again in 1987. They took their name from the Michael Moorcock novel *Stormbringer*.

| DATE | POS | WKS | BPI | ALBUM TITLE | LABEL & NUMBER |
|------|-----|-----|-----|-------------|----------------|
| 30/08/1980 | 18 | 5 | | WILD CAT | MCA MCF 3075 |
| 18/04/1981 | 33 | 4 | | SPELLBOUND | MCA MCF 3104 |
| 21/11/1981 | 51 | 3 | | CRAZY NIGHTS | MCA MCF 3123 |
| 28/08/1982 | 13 | 8 | | THE CAGE | MCA MCF 3150 |

## BONNIE TYLER
UK singer (born Gaynor Hopkins, 8/6/1951, Swansea) who was a club singer before being discovered by producers Steve Wolfe and Ronnie Scott.

| DATE | POS | WKS | BPI | ALBUM TITLE | LABEL & NUMBER |
|------|-----|-----|-----|-------------|----------------|
| 16/04/1983 | ❶¹ | 45 | ○ | **FASTER THAN THE SPEED OF NIGHT** | CBS 25304 |
| 17/05/1986 | 24 | 12 | | SECRET DREAMS AND FORBIDDEN FIRE | CBS 86319 |
| 29/11/1986 | 24 | 17 | | THE GREATEST HITS | Telstar STAR 2291 |
| 21/05/1988 | 78 | 1 | | HIDE YOUR HEART | CBS 4601251 |
| 25/11/1989 | 9 | 12 | | **HEAVEN AND HELL MEAT LOAF/BONNIE TYLER** | Telstar STAR 2361 |
| 14/07/2001 | 18 | 4 | ○ | THE GREATEST HITS | Sanctuary/Sony TV SANCD 082 |

## TYPE O NEGATIVE
US rock group formed in New York in 1988 by Peter Steele (bass/vocals), Kenny Hickey (guitar), Josh Silver (keyboards) and Johnny Kelly (drums). Steele had previously been a member of Carnivore.

| DATE | POS | WKS | BPI | ALBUM TITLE | LABEL & NUMBER |
|------|-----|-----|-----|-------------|----------------|
| 14/09/1996 | 26 | 1 | | OCTOBER RUST | Roadrunner RR 88742 |
| 02/10/1999 | 49 | 1 | | WORLD COMING DOWN | Roadrunner RR 86602 |

## JUDIE TZUKE
UK singer (born Judie Myers, 3/4/1955, London) who reverted to the former surname of her Polish father when she launched a singing career. She first recorded with Mike Paxman as Tzuke and Paxo in 1975 before joining Elton John's Rocket label. She formed Big Moon Records in 1996.

| DATE | POS | WKS | BPI | ALBUM TITLE | LABEL & NUMBER |
|------|-----|-----|-----|-------------|----------------|
| 04/08/1979 | 14 | 17 | ● | WELCOME TO THE CRUISE | Rocket TRAIN 7 |
| 10/05/1980 | 7 | 11 | ● | **SPORTS CAR** | Rocket TRAIN 9 |
| 16/05/1981 | 17 | 10 | | I AM PHOENIX | Rocket TRAIN 15 |
| 17/04/1982 | 19 | 10 | | SHOOT THE MOON | Chrysalis CDL 1382 |
| 30/10/1982 | 39 | 4 | | ROAD NOISE – THE OFFICIAL BOOTLEG | Chrysalis CTY 1405 |
| 01/10/1983 | 26 | 5 | | RITMO | Chrysalis CDL 1442 |
| 15/06/1985 | 35 | 3 | | THE CAT IS OUT | Legacy LLP 102 |
| 29/04/1989 | 57 | 1 | | TURNING STONES | Polydor 8390871 |

▲⁹ Number of weeks album topped the US chart ◆¹² RIAA Diamond Awards ◇³ IFPI Platinum Europe Awards

LABOUR of LOVE — UB40

## UB40

**UB40** UK reggae group formed in Birmingham in 1978 by Ali Campbell (born 15/2/1959, Birmingham, vocals/rhythm guitar), Earl Falconer (born 23/1/1959, Birmingham, bass), Robin Campbell (born 25/12/1954, Birmingham, guitar/vocals), Mickey Virtue (born 19/1/1957, Birmingham, keyboards), Brian Travers (born 7/2/1959, Birmingham, saxophone), Jim Brown (born 20/11/1957, Birmingham, drums), Norman Hassan (born 26/1/1957, Birmingham, percussion) and Yomi Babayemi (percussion), taking their name from the unemployment benefit form. Babayemi was deported to Nigeria after only two live dates and Astro (born Terence Wilson, 24/6/1957, Birmingham, reggae toaster/singer) joined them shortly before they began recording in 1979. They left indie label Graduate in 1980 (in protest against an anti-apartheid song, *Burden Of Shame*, being deleted from the South African release of their debut album *Signing Off*) and set up DEP International through Virgin. Falconer was jailed for six months in July 1988 for driving offences (he was driving with over twice the legal alcohol limit and his brother was killed) and the group were forced to use a replacement bass player for their world tour. Ali Campbell recorded solo in the 1990s. The group appeared in the 1997 film *Speed 2 – Cruise Control*.

| | | | | |
|---|---|---|---|---|
| 06/09/1980 | 2 | 71 | ✪ | SIGNING OFF ...................................................................................Graduate GRAD LP2 |
| 06/06/1981 | 2 | 38 | ✪ | **PRESENT ARMS** .............................................................................DEP International LPDEP 1 |
| 10/10/1981 | 38 | 7 | | PRESENT ARMS IN DUB .....................................................................DEP International LPDEP 2 |
| 28/08/1982 | 17 | 8 | | THE SINGLES ALBUM ..........................................................................Graduate GRADLSP 3 |
| 09/10/1982 | 4 | 8 | ● | UB 44 .........................................................................................DEP International LPDEP 3 |
| 26/02/1983 | 44 | 5 | | UB40 LIVE .....................................................................................DEP International LPDEP 4 |
| 24/09/1983 | ❶¹ | 76 | ✪² | **LABOUR OF LOVE** ...........................................................................DEP International LPDEP 5 |
| 20/10/1984 | 3 | 14 | ○ | **GEFFERY MORGAN...** .......................................................................DEP International DEP 6 |
| 14/09/1985 | 14 | 23 | | BAGGARIDDIM ..............................................................................DEP International LPDEP 10 |
| 09/08/1986 | 8 | 20 | ● | **RAT IN THE KITCHEN** .....................................................................DEP International LPDEP 11 |
| 07/11/1987 | 3 | 132 | ✪⁶ | **THE BEST OF UB40 – VOLUME ONE** .......................................................DEP International UBTV 1 |
| 23/07/1988 | 12 | 12 | ● | UB40 .........................................................................................DEP International LPDEP 13 |
| 09/12/1989 | 3 | 69 | ✪³ | **LABOUR OF LOVE II** .......................................................................DEP International LPDEP 14 |
| 24/07/1993 | ❶⁷ | 37 | ✪² | **PROMISES AND LIES** .......................................................................DEP International DEPCD 15 |
| 12/11/1994 | 5 | 15 | ● | **LABOUR OF LOVE – VOLUMES I AND II** ..................................................DEP International DEPDD 1 |
| 11/11/1995 | 12 | 11 | ✪ | THE BEST OF UB40 – VOLUME TWO .......................................................DEP International DUBTV 2 |
| 12/07/1997 | 7 | 9 | ○ | **GUNS IN THE GHETTO** .....................................................................DEP International CADEP 16 |
| 24/10/1998 | 8 | 12 | ● | **LABOUR OF LOVE III** .......................................................................DEP International DEPCD 18 |
| 04/11/2000 | 7 | 23 | ✪ | **THE VERY BEST OF – 1980–2000** ◇ ..............................................................Virgin DUBTVX 3 |
| 03/11/2001 | 29 | 2 | | COVER UP .................................................................................................Virgin DEPCD 19 |
| 14/06/2003 | 7 | 16 | ● | **LABOUR OF LOVE – VOLUMES I, II & III** ....................................................Virgin 5847242 |
| 15/11/2003 | 49 | 2 | | HOME GROWN ..............................................................................DEP International DEPCD 22 |

## UFO

**UFO** UK/German heavy metal group formed by Phil Mogg (born 1951, London, vocals), Mick Bolton (guitar), Pete Way (bass) and Andy Parker (drums) as Hocus Pocus, changing their name to UFO in 1969. Michael Schenker (born 10/1/1955, Savstedt, Germany) replaced Bolton in 1974, remaining with the group until 1979 when he rejoined the Scorpions, Paul Chapman being his replacement. They added Paul Raymond (keyboards) in 1977, and disbanded in 1983. Re-forming in 1985 without success, Way and Mogg attempted another revival in 1991.

| | | | | |
|---|---|---|---|---|
| 04/06/1977 | 54 | 2 | | LIGHTS OUT ...................................................................................Chrysalis CHR 1127 |
| 15/07/1978 | 26 | 7 | | OBSESSION ....................................................................................Chrysalis CHR 1182 |
| 10/02/1979 | 8 | 11 | ○ | **STRANGERS IN THE NIGHT** ...................................................................Chrysalis CJT 5 |
| 19/01/1980 | 11 | 7 | ○ | NO PLACE TO RUN .............................................................................Chrysalis CDL 1239 |
| 24/01/1981 | 19 | 5 | | THE WILD THE WILLING AND THE INNOCENT ...............................................Chrysalis CHR 1307 |
| 20/02/1982 | 8 | 6 | | **MECHANIX** .....................................................................................Chrysalis CHR 1360 |
| 12/02/1983 | 32 | 4 | | MAKING CONTACT .............................................................................Chrysalis CHR 1402 |
| 03/09/1983 | 39 | 4 | | HEADSTONE – THE BEST OF UFO .............................................................Chrysalis CTY 1437 |
| 16/11/1985 | 74 | 2 | | MISDEMEANOUR ...............................................................................Chrysalis CHR 1518 |

## UGLY KID JOE

**UGLY KID JOE** US rock group formed in California by Whitfield Crane (vocals), Klaus Eichstadt (guitar), Roger Lahr (guitar), Cordell Crockett (bass) and Mark Davis (drums). In 1992 Lahr was replaced by Dave Fortman. Davis left in 1994 and was replaced by Shannon Larkin.

| | | | |
|---|---|---|---|
| 13/06/1992 | 9 | 13 | **AS UGLY AS THEY WANNA BE** .................................................................Mercury 8688232 |
| 12/09/1992 | 11 | 24 | AMERICA'S LEAST WANTED ...................................................................Vertigo 5125712 |
| 17/06/1995 | 25 | 5 | MENACE TO SOBRIETY ........................................................................Mercury 5282622 |

○ Silver disc  ● Gold disc  ✪ Platinum disc (additional platinum units are indicated by a figure following the symbol)   ❶⁹ Number of weeks album topped the UK chart

## U.K.
UK group formed in 1977 by Allan Holdsworth (guitar), Eddie Jobson (keyboards/violin), John Wetton (born 12/7/19, Derby, bass/vocals) and Bill Bruford (born 17/5/1948, London, drums). Holsworth and Bruford left after one album, Bruford being replaced by Terry Bozzio. They disbanded in 1979.

| 27/05/1978 | 43 | 3 | | U.K | Polydor 2302 080 |
|------------|----|----|--|-----|------------------|

## U.K. SUBS
UK group formed in London in 1976 by Charlie Harper (born David Charles Perez, 25/4/1944, London, vocals), Nicky Garratt (guitar), Paul Slack (bass) and Pete Davies (drums). Harper also recorded solo.

| 13/10/1979 | 21 | 6 | | ANOTHER KIND OF BLUES | Gem GEMLP 100 |
|------------|----|----|--|----------------------|---------------|
| 19/04/1980 | 18 | 9 | | BRAND NEW AGE | Gem GEMLP 106 |
| 27/09/1980 | 8 | 6 | | **CRASH COURSE** | Gem GEMLP 111 |
| 21/02/1981 | 18 | 5 | | DIMINISHED RESPONSIBILITY | Gem GEMLP 112 |

## TRACEY ULLMAN
UK singer (born 30/12/1959, Burham, Buckinghamshire) who first came to prominence in the BBC TV show *Three Of A Kind* with David Copperfield and Lenny Henry. She launched a record career after meeting the wife of Stiff Records' boss. She appeared in a number of films and then relocated to the US where she starred in her own TV series.

| 03/12/1983 | 14 | 20 | O | YOU BREAK MY HEART IN 17 PLACES | Stiff SEEZ 51 |
|------------|----|----|---|--------------------------------|---------------|
| 08/12/1984 | 92 | 2 | | YOU CAUGHT ME OUT | Stiff SEEZ 56 |

## ULTIMATE KAOS
UK R&B vocal group formed in London by Haydon Eshun, Ryan Elliot, Jomo Baxter, Nicky Grant and Jayde Delpratt Spence.

| 29/04/1995 | 51 | 1 | | ULTIMATE KAOS | Wild Card 5274442 |
|------------|----|----|--|---------------|-------------------|

## ULTRA
UK group formed by James Hearn (born 19/6/1976, vocals), Michael Harwood (born 12/12/1975, guitar), Nick Keynes (born 3/5/1974, bass) and Jon O'Mahoney (born 10/8/1974, drums).

| 06/02/1999 | 37 | 2 | | ULTRA | East West 3984222452 |
|------------|----|----|--|-------|----------------------|

## ULTRA-SONIC
UK instrumental/production duo formed in 1990 by Rodger Hughes and Mallorca Lee. Lee was later a member of Public Domain.

| 11/11/1995 | 58 | 1 | | GLOBALTEKNO | Clubscene DCSR 007 |
|------------|----|----|--|-------------|--------------------|

## ULTRA VIVID SCENE
US singer Kurt Ralske who later assembled a working band, with Ralske on guitar/vocals, Jack Daley (bass) and Julian Klepacz (drums) as the nucleus.

| 19/05/1990 | 58 | 1 | | JOY 1967–1990 | 4AD CAD 005 |
|------------|----|----|--|---------------|-------------|

## ULTRAMARINE
UK dance duo formed in London by Paul Hammond (born 12/12/1965, Chelmsford, Essex, bass/keyboards) and Ian Cooper (born 15/8/1966, Derby, guitars/programming). They first recorded in 1989 for the Belgian label Les Disques Du Crepuscule, then Brainiak and Rough Trade, before switching to Blanco Y Negro.

| 04/09/1993 | 49 | 1 | | UNITED KINGDOMS | blanco y negro 4509934252 |
|------------|----|----|--|-----------------|----------------------------|

## ULTRASOUND
UK group formed by Andy 'Tiny' Wood (guitar/vocals), Richard Green (guitar), Vanessa West (bass), Matt Jones (keyboards and programmes) and Andy Pearce (drums).

| 01/05/1999 | 23 | 1 | | EVERYTHING PICTURE | Nude 12CD |
|------------|----|----|--|--------------------|-----------|

## ULTRAVOX
UK group formed in 1973 by John Foxx and Chris Cross (born Christopher St John, 14/7/1952, London, bass/synthesizer), who were joined by Warren Cann (born 20/5/1952, Victoria, Canada, drums) and Steve Shears (guitar), as Tiger Lily. Billy Currie (born 1/4/1952, Huddersfield, synthesizer/piano) joined prior to their debut recording, and the group's name changed to Ultravox in 1976. Foxx went solo in 1979 and ex-Slik and Visage member Midge Ure (born 10/10/1953, Cambuslang, Scotland, guitar/vocals) replaced him. They moved from Island to Chrysalis in 1980, where later Ure pursued a solo career. Ure was one of the prime movers behind Band Aid with Bob Geldof. Tony Fenneller was recruited as lead singer in 1993.

| 19/07/1980 | 3 | 72 | ✪ | VIENNA | Chrysalis CHR 1296 |
|------------|---|----|---|--------|--------------------|
| 19/09/1981 | 4 | 23 | ● | RAGE IN EDEN | Chrysalis CDL 1338 |
| 23/10/1982 | 6 | 30 | ● | QUARTET | Chrysalis CDL 1394 |
| 22/10/1983 | 9 | 15 | ● | MONUMENT – THE SOUNDTRACK | Chrysalis CUX 1452 |
| 14/04/1984 | 8 | 26 | ● | LAMENT | Chrysalis CDL 1459 |
| 10/11/1984 | 2 | 53 | ✪³ | THE COLLECTION | Chrysalis UTV 1 |
| 25/10/1986 | 9 | 6 | ● | U-VOX | Chrysalis CDL 1545 |
| 06/03/1993 | 10 | 6 | O | IF I WAS: THE VERY BEST OF MIDGE URE AND ULTRAVOX | Chrysalis CDCHR 1987 |
| 10/11/2001 | 45 | 2 | | THE VERY BEST OF This and the above hit credited to **MIDGE URE AND ULTRAVOX** | EMI 5358112 |

## UNBELIEVABLE TRUTH
UK group with Andy Yorke (guitar/vocals), Jason Moulster (bass) and Nigel Powell (drums). Yorke is the brother of Radiohead's Thom Yorke.

| 23/05/1998 | 21 | 2 | | ALMOST HERE | Virgin CDVX 2849 |
|------------|----|----|--|-------------|------------------|

▲⁹ Number of weeks album topped the US chart   ◆¹² RIAA Diamond Awards   ◇³ IFPI Platinum Europe Awards

**UNCLE KRACKER** US DJ/rapper (born Matthew Shafer, 6/6/1974, Mount Clemens, MI) who is also a member of Twisted Brown Trucker, Kid Rock's backing group.

22/09/2001 . . . . .40 . . . . . .3 . . . . . . DOUBLE WIDE . . . . . . . . . . . . . . . . . . . . . . . . . . . . . . . . . . . . . . . . . . . . . . . . . . . . . . . . . . . . . . . . . . . . . . . . . . . . . . . .Atlantic 7567832792

**UNDERCOVER** UK group formed by John Matthews (vocals), John Jules (bass) and Steve McCutcheon (keyboards). McCutcheon later linked with Wayne Hector to form a successful songwriting partnership.

05/12/1992 . . . . .26 . . . . . .9 . . . . . . CHECK OUT THE GROOVE . . . . . . . . . . . . . . . . . . . . . . . . . . . . . . . . . . . . . . . . . . . . . . . . . . . . . . . . . . . . . . . .PWL International HFCD 26

**UNDERTONES** UK group formed in Londonderry, Northern Ireland in 1975 by Feargal Sharkey (born 13/8/1958, Londonderry, vocals) and John O'Neill (born 26/8/1957, Londonderry, guitar) and including Damian 'Dee' O'Neill (born 15/1/1961, Belfast, guitar), Michael Bradley (born 13/8/1959, Londonderry, bass) and Billy Doherty (drums). They released their debut single on local independent label Good Vibrations. Radio exposure on John Peel's show attracted major record company interest, with the manager-less group negotiating a deal with Sire and re-issuing *Teenage Kicks*. They launched the Ardeck label in 1981 but disbanded in 1983, with Sharkey going solo (he was the first signing to Madness' Zarjazz label). The O'Neill brothers later formed That Petrol Emotion.

| | | | | | |
|---|---|---|---|---|---|
| 19/05/1979 | .13 | .21 | | THE UNDERTONES | Sire SRK 6071 |
| 26/04/1980 | .6 | .10 | | **HYPNOTISED** | Sire SRK 6088 |
| 16/05/1981 | .17 | .6 | | POSITIVE TOUCH | Ardeck ARD 103 |
| 19/03/1983 | .43 | .5 | | THE SIN OF PRIDE | Ardeck ARD 104 |
| 10/12/1983 | .67 | .4 | | ALL WRAPPED UP | Ardeck ARD 1654281/3 |
| 14/06/1986 | .96 | .1 | | CHER O'BOWLIES – PICK OF THE UNDERTONES **UNDERTONES FEATURING FEARGAL SHARKEY** | Ardeck EMS 1172 |
| 25/09/1993 | .45 | .3 | | THE BEST OF THE UNDERTONES – TEENAGE KICKS | Castle Communications CTVCD 121 |
| 13/09/2003 | .35 | .2 | | TEENAGE KICKS – THE BEST OF | Sanctuary TVSAN005 |

**UNDERWORLD** UK group formed in Romford, Essex in the late 1980s by Karl Hyde (born 10/5/1957, Worcester, guitar/vocals), Alfie Thomas, Rick Smith (born 25/5/1959, Ammanford, Wales, keyboards), Baz Allen and John Warwicker. By 1992 the band comprised Hyde, Smith and Darren Emerson (born 3/4/1971, Hornchurch, Essex, keyboards). Emerson left in April 2000 and recorded with Sasha.

| | | | | | |
|---|---|---|---|---|---|
| 05/02/1994 | .12 | .4 | ● | DUBNOBASSWITHMYHEADMAN | Junior Boy's Own JBOCD 1 |
| 23/03/1996 | .9 | .28 | ● | **SECOND TOUGHEST IN THE INFANTS** | Junior Boy's Own JBOCD 4 |
| 13/03/1999 | .3 | .12 | ● | **BEAUCOUP FISH** | JBO 1005438 |
| 16/09/2000 | .22 | .3 | | EVERYTHING EVERYTHING | JBO 1012548 |
| 28/09/2002 | .16 | .3 | | A HUNDRED DAYS OFF | JBO 1020102 |
| 05/10/2002 | .53 | .2 | | DUBNOBASSWITHMYHEADMAN | JBO 1001992 |
| 15/11/2003 | .43 | .2 | | 1992–2002 | JBO 1024698 |

**UNION** UK/Dutch group and the 1991 England rugby team. Following the successes of football teams with cup final records, Union and the England team recorded the traditional rugby song *Swing Low* as their anthem for the 1991 World Cup held in England.

26/10/1991 . . . . .17 . . . . . .6 . . . . . . WORLD IN UNION . . . . . . . . . . . . . . . . . . . . . . . . . . . . . . . . . . . . . . . . . . . . . . . . . . . . . . . . . . . . . . . . . . . . . . . . . .Columbia 4690471

**UNKLE** UK DJ/production duo formed by Josh Davis and James Lavelle.

| | | | | | |
|---|---|---|---|---|---|
| 21/01/1995 | .73 | .1 | | THE TIME HAS COME (EP) | Mo Wax MW 028P |
| 05/09/1998 | .4 | .9 | ● | **PSYENCE FICTION** | Mo Wax MW 085CD |
| 04/10/2003 | .24 | .2 | | NEVER, NEVER, LAND | Mo Wax MWU 001CDX |

**UNTOUCHABLES** US group formed by Chuck Askerneese (vocals), Clyde Grimes (guitar/vocals), Derek Breakfield (bass), Brewster (keyboards) and various drummers.

13/07/1985 . . . . .51 . . . . . .7 . . . . . . WILD CHILD . . . . . . . . . . . . . . . . . . . . . . . . . . . . . . . . . . . . . . . . . . . . . . . . . . . . . . . . . . . . . . . . . . . . . . . . . . . . . . . . . . . .Stiff SEEZ 57

**DAWN UPSHAW/THE LONDON SINFONIETTA/DAVID ZINMAN** US soprano singer (born 1960, Nashville, TN) with US conductor, David Zinman. Upshaw made her debut at the New York Metropolitan in 1985.

23/01/1993 . . . . .6 . . . . . .18 . . . . . .● **GORECKI: SYMPHONY NO. 3** . . . . . . . . . . . . . . . . . . . . . . . . . . . . . . . . . . . . . . . . . . . . . . . . . . . . . . . . . .Elektra Nonsuch 755979822

**URBAN COOKIE COLLECTIVE** UK vocal/instrumental group formed by Rohan Heath, Diane Charlemagne, Marty and DJ Pete Hayes.

26/03/1994 . . . . .28 . . . . . .2 . . . . . . HIGH ON A HAPPY VIBE . . . . . . . . . . . . . . . . . . . . . . . . . . . . . . . . . . . . . . . . . . . . . . . . . . . . . . . . . . . . . . . . . . . .Pulse 8 PULSE 13CD

**URBAN SPECIES** UK rap group formed in London in the 1980s by Mintos (real name Peter Akinrinola) and DJ Renegade (real name Winston Small), joined later by Dr Slim (real name Rodney Green).

07/05/1994 . . . . .43 . . . . . .2 . . . . . . LISTEN . . . . . . . . . . . . . . . . . . . . . . . . . . . . . . . . . . . . . . . . . . . . . . . . . . . . . . . . . . . . . . . . . . . . . . . . . . . . . . . . . . . . . .Talkin Loud 5186482

**MIDGE URE** UK singer (born 10/10/1953, Cambuslang, Scotland) who was a member of Slik and Visage and formed the Rich Kids with ex-Sex Pistol member Glen Matlock before joining Ultravox in 1979. He ran his own solo career in tandem from 1982 and co-wrote (with Bob Geldof) the Band Aid single *Do They Know It's Christmas?* He was subsequently active in staging Live Aid in 1985.

| | | | | | |
|---|---|---|---|---|---|
| 19/10/1985 | .2 | .15 | ● | **THE GIFT** | Chrysalis CHR 1508 |
| 10/09/1988 | .30 | .3 | | ANSWERS TO NOTHING | Chrysalis CHR 1649 |
| 28/09/1991 | .36 | .2 | | PURE | Arista 211922 |
| 06/03/1993 | .10 | .6 | ○ | **IF I WAS: THE VERY BEST OF MIDGE URE AND ULTRAVOX** | Chrysalis CDCHR 1987 |
| 10/11/2001 | .45 | .2 | | THE VERY BEST OF This and the above hit credited to **MIDGE URE AND ULTRAVOX** | EMI 5358112 |

○ Silver disc ● Gold disc ✪ Platinum disc (additional platinum units are indicated by a figure following the symbol) ❶⁹ Number of weeks album topped the UK chart

## URIAH HEAP

UK rock group formed by David Byron (born 29/1/1947, Epping, vocals), Mick Box (born 8/6/1947, London, guitar/vocals), Ken Hensley (born 24/8/1945, London, guitar/keyboards/vocals) and Paul Newton (born 1946, Andover, bass), with Alex Napier and then Nigel Olsson on drums. They took their name from a character in Charles Dickens' *David Copperfield*. Drummer Keith Baker recorded one album for the group before departing and being replaced by Lee Kerslake. Mark Clarke replaced Newton in 1971 but was himself replaced three months later by Gary Thain (born 15/5/1948, Wellington, New Zealand. Thain was sacked in 1975 and replaced by John Wetton. He left the following year, Hensley departed midway through a tour of the USA and Byron was forced out soon after, with the group drafting in John Lawton (vocals) and Trevor Bolder (bass). By the end of the 1970s the group comprised Box, Kerslake, Peter Goalby (vocals), John Sinclair (keyboards) and Bob Daisley (bass). Daisley left in 1983 and was replaced by the returning Trevor Bolder. Later members included Bernie Shaw (vocals) and Phil Lanzon (keyboards). Gary Thain died from a drug overdose on 19/3/1976 and David Byron, who recorded solo following his departure from the group, died on 28/2/1985.

| DATE | POS | WKS | BPI | ALBUM TITLE | LABEL & NUMBER |
|---|---|---|---|---|---|
| 13/11/1971 | 39 | 1 | | LOOK AT YOURSELF | Island ILPS 9169 |
| 10/06/1972 | 20 | 11 | | DEMONS AND WIZARDS | Bronze ILPS 9193 |
| 02/12/1972 | 28 | 3 | | THE MAGICIAN'S BIRTHDAY | Bronze ILPS 9213 |
| 19/05/1973 | 23 | 8 | O | URIAH HEEP LIVE | Island ISLD 1 |
| 29/09/1973 | 18 | 3 | O | SWEET FREEDOM | Island ILPS 9245 |
| 29/06/1974 | 23 | 3 | O | WONDERWORLD | Bronze ILPS 9280 |
| 05/07/1975 | 7 | 6 | O | **RETURN TO FANTASY** | Bronze ILPS 9335 |
| 12/06/1976 | 55 | 1 | | HIGH AND MIGHTY | Island ILPS 9384 |
| 22/03/1980 | 37 | 3 | | CONQUEST | Bronze BRON 524 |
| 17/04/1982 | 34 | 6 | | ABOMINOG | Bronze BRON 538 |
| 18/06/1983 | 46 | 4 | | HEAD FIRST | Bronze BRON 545 |
| 06/04/1985 | 79 | 2 | | EQUATOR | Portrait PRT 26414 |

## URUSEI YATSURA

UK group formed by Graham Kemp (born 3/12/1968, guitar/vocals), Fergus Lawrie (born 23/11/1968, guitar/vocals), Elaine Graham (born 1970, bass) and Ian Graham (born 19/10/1972, drums).

| DATE | POS | WKS | BPI | ALBUM TITLE | LABEL & NUMBER |
|---|---|---|---|---|---|
| 14/03/1998 | 64 | 1 | | SLAIN BY | CHE 3984222212 |

## USA FOR AFRICA

Multinational group inspired by the success of Band Aid. Veteran singer Harry Belafonte put together a US version with a song written by Lionel Richie and Michael Jackson, produced by Quincy Jones and released as USA For Africa (which stood for United Support of Artists), and featuring (in order) Lionel Richie, Stevie Wonder, Paul Simon, Kenny Rogers, James Ingram, Tina Turner, Billy Joel, Michael Jackson, Diana Ross, Dionne Warwick, Willie Nelson, Al Jarreau, Bruce Springsteen, Kenny Loggins, Steve Perry, Daryl Hall, Huey Lewis, Cyndi Lauper, Kim Carnes, Bob Dylan and Ray Charles. The record was named Record of the Year and Best Pop Vocal Performance by a Group at the 1985 Grammy Awards (and was also Song of the Year for writers Michael Jackson and Lionel Richie). It also won the Best Video Short Form with *We Are The World: The Video Event*. The resultant album featured previously unreleased tracks by Bruce Springsteen, Prince, Huey Lewis & The News, Chicago, Tina Turner, Pointer Sisters, Kenny Rogers and Steve Perry and the Canadian charity single by Northern Lights.

| DATE | POS | WKS | BPI | ALBUM TITLE | LABEL & NUMBER |
|---|---|---|---|---|---|
| 25/05/1985 | 31 | 5 | | WE ARE THE WORLD | CBS USAID F1 |

## USHER

US singer (born Usher Raymond, 14/10/1978, Chattanooga, TN) who began his recording career in 1994 aged fifteen. His *8701* album, released in July 2001, was to have been issued six months earlier as *All About U* but was withdrawn after pre-release copies became available on the internet. He won the 2001 Grammy Award for Best Male Rhythm & Blues Vocal Performance for *U Remind Me* and the 2002 award for Best Male Rhythm & Blues Vocal Performance for *U Don't Have To Call*.

| DATE | POS | WKS | BPI | ALBUM TITLE | LABEL & NUMBER |
|---|---|---|---|---|---|
| 17/01/1998 | 16 | 18 | ● | MY WAY | LaFace 73008260432 |
| 21/07/2001 | ❶[1] | 39 | ✪ | 8701 2001 MOBO Awards for Best Album and Best Rhythm & Blues Act | LaFace 74321874712 |
| 03/04/2004 | ❶[1] | 13+ | ✪ | **CONFESSIONS** ▲[9] ◇ | Arista 82876609902 |

## US3

UK duo of Mel Simpson (keyboards) and Geoff Wilkinson (samples). They first linked on another jazz sample experiment *And The Band Played Boogie* that was released on Coldcut's Ninja Tune label. It came to the attention of Blue Note Records since most of the samples came from their repertoire, and the pair were invited to produce a legitimate version with access to the entire catalogue. The resulting album featured rappers Tukka Yoot, Kobie Powell and Rahsaan and jazz musicians Gerald Presencer, Dennisa Rollins, Tony Remy and Steve Williamson.

| DATE | POS | WKS | BPI | ALBUM TITLE | LABEL & NUMBER |
|---|---|---|---|---|---|
| 31/07/1993 | 40 | 6 | | HAND ON THE TORCH/JAZZ MIXES | Blue Note CDEST 2195 |

## UTAH SAINTS

UK production/instrumental duo formed by Jez Willis (born 14/8/1963, Brampton, Cumbria) and Tim Garbutt (born 6/1/1969, London) who were both previously members of MDMA.

| DATE | POS | WKS | BPI | ALBUM TITLE | LABEL & NUMBER |
|---|---|---|---|---|---|
| 05/06/1993 | 10 | 15 | O | UTAH SAINTS | ffrr 8283792 |

## U.T.F.O.

US rap group formed in Brooklyn, NY by Shawn Fequiere, Fred Reeves, Jeffrey Campbell and Maurice Bailey, with their name standing for Untouchable Force Organization. Their debut hit was a 12-inch single deemed ineligible for the singles chart.

| DATE | POS | WKS | BPI | ALBUM TITLE | LABEL & NUMBER |
|---|---|---|---|---|---|
| 16/03/1985 | 72 | 1 | | ROXANNE ROXANNE (6 TRACK VERSION) | Streetwave XKHAN 506 |

---

▲[9] Number of weeks album topped the US chart   ◆[12] RIAA Diamond Awards   ◇[3] IFPI Platinum Europe Awards

**UTOPIA** US group formed in 1974 by Todd Rundgren (born 22/6/1948, Philadelphia, PA), with a line-up in 1977 comprising Kasim Sulton (bass), Roger Powell (keyboards) and John 'Willie' Wilcox (drums).

| | | | | |
|---|---|---|---|---|
| 01/10/1977 | 59 | 1 | | OOPS! SORRY WRONG PLANET ....................................................................Bearsville K 53517 |
| 16/02/1980 | 57 | 2 | | ADVENTURES IN UTOPIA ....................................................................Island ILPS 9602 |

**U2** Irish rock group initially formed in school in 1976 by Bono (born Paul Hewson, 10/5/1960, Dublin, vocals), The Edge (born David Evans, 8/8/1961, Wales, guitar), Adam Clayton (born 13/3/1960, Chinnor, Oxfordshire, bass), Larry Mullen Jr (born 31/10/1961, Dublin, drums) and Dick Evans (guitar) as Feedback. The name was changed to the Hype, Evans left to form the Virgin Prunes and there was a final name change to U2. After a talent contest win they signed to CBS Ireland in 1978 (CBS in the UK did not take up their option, with Island snapping them up in 1980 following live dates), and by 1987 they were world stars. Bono subsequently recorded with Clannad and Frank Sinatra, The Edge solo and Clayton and Mullen did film score work in the 1990s. They won the Best International Group Award at the 1988, 1989, 1990, 1998 and 2001 BRIT Awards, and a special award for Best Live Act in 1993, subsequently being awarded the Outstanding Contribution Award at the 2001 ceremony. They have also won fourteen Grammy Awards including: Best Rock Performance by a Group in 1988 for *Desire*; Best Performance Music Video in 1988 for *Where The Streets Have No Name*; Best Music Video Long Form in 1994 for *Zoo TV – Live From Sydney*; Record of the Year, Song of the Year and Best Rock Group Performance with Vocal in 2000, all for *Beautiful Day*; Record of the Year in 2001 for *Walk On*; Best Rock Performance by a Duo or Group with Vocal in 2001 for *Elevation*; and Best Pop Performance by a Duo or Group with Vocal in 2001 for *Stuck In A Moment You Can't Get Out Of*. The group has also won two MTV Europe Music Awards: Best Group in 1995 and Best Live Act in 1997. Additionally, Bono was awarded the Free Your Mind Award in 1999 in recognition of his charitable work.

| | | | | |
|---|---|---|---|---|
| 29/08/1981 | 52 | 31 | ● | BOY ....................................................................Island ILPS 9646 |
| 24/10/1981 | 11 | 42 | ✪ | OCTOBER ....................................................................Island ILPS 9680 |
| 12/03/1983 | ●¹ | 147 | ✪² | **WAR** ....................................................................Island ILPS 9733 |
| 03/12/1983 | 2 | 203 | ✪³ | **U2 LIVE 'UNDER A BLOOD RED SKY'** ....................................................................Island IMA 3 |
| 13/10/1984 | ●² | 130 | ✪² | **THE UNFORGETTABLE FIRE** ....................................................................Island U 25 |
| 27/07/1985 | 11 | 16 | ○ | WIDE AWAKE IN AMERICA ....................................................................Island 902791A |
| 21/03/1987 | ●² | 156 | ✪⁵ | **THE JOSHUA TREE** ▲⁹ ◆¹⁰ 1987 Grammy Awards for Album of the Year and Best Rock Performance by a Group ........Island U 26 |
| 20/02/1988 | 100 | 1 | | THE JOSHUA TREE SINGLES Contains four 7-inch singles: *With Or Without You, I Still Haven't Found What I'm Looking For, Where The Streets Have No Name* and *In God's Country* ....................................Island U2 PK 1 |
| 22/10/1988 | ●¹ | 61 | ✪⁴ | **RATTLE AND HUM** ▲⁶ ....................................................................Island U2 7 |
| 30/11/1991 | 2 | 87 | ✪⁴ | **ACHTUNG BABY** ▲¹ 1992 Grammy Award for Best Rock Performance ....................................Island U 28 |
| 17/07/1993 | ●¹ | 31 | ✪ | **ZOOROPA** ▲² 1993 Grammy Award for Best Alternative Music Album ....................................Island CIDU 29 |
| 15/03/1997 | ●¹ | 35 | ✪ | **POP** ◇² ▲¹ ....................................................................Island CIDU 210 |
| 14/11/1998 | ●¹ | 12 | ✪ | **THE BEST OF 1980–1990 & B SIDES** ....................................................................Island CIDDU 211 |
| 21/11/1998 | 4 | 65 | ✪⁵ | **THE BEST OF 1980–1990** ◇⁶ Owing to chart rules, this and the above compilation had separate chart entries ....Island CIDU 211 |
| 11/11/2000 | ●¹ | 62 | ✪³ | **ALL THAT YOU CAN'T LEAVE BEHIND** ◇⁴ 2001 Grammy Award for Best Rock Performance ....................Island CIDU 212 |
| 16/11/2002 | 2 | 12 | ✪² | **THE BEST OF 1990–2000 & B-SIDES** ◇² ....................................................................Island CIDTU 213 |
| 23/11/2002 | 37 | 11 | | THE BEST OF 1990–2000 ....................................................................Island CIDU 213 |

# V

**STEVE VAI** US singer/guitarist (born 6/6/1960, Long Island, NY) who formed his first group whilst still at school. He later studied at the Berklee College of Music in Boston, MA and then relocated to Los Angeles, CA. He joined Frank Zappa's backing band at the age of eighteen and later played with Alcatrazz, David Lee Roth and Whitesnake before going solo He won the 1993 Grammy Award for Best Rock Instrumental Performance with Zappa's Universe Rock Group Featuring Steve Vai, for *Sofa* from *Zappa's Universe*.

| | | | |
|---|---|---|---|
| 02/06/1990 | ....8 | .....10 | .....O |
| 07/08/1993 | ....17 | ......6 | |
| 15/04/1995 | ....39 | ......2 | |
| 28/09/1996 | ....41 | ......2 | |

PASSION AND WARFARE ................................................................Food For Thought GRUB 17
SEX AND RELIGION .........................................................................Relativity 4729472
ALIEN LOVE SECRETS .......................................................................Relativity 4785862
FIRE GARDEN ............................................................................Epic 4850622

**HOLLY VALANCE** Australian singer (born Holly Vukadinovic, 11/5/1983, Melbourne) who first came to prominence as an actress, starring in *Neighbours* as Felicity 'Flick' Scully.

| | | | |
|---|---|---|---|
| 26/10/2002 | ....9 | .....11 | .....● |
| 22/11/2003 | ....60 | ......1 | |

FOOTPRINTS .............................................................................London 0927493722
STATE OF MIND ...........................................................................London 5046701625

**FRANKIE VALLI** – see **FOUR SEASONS**

**VAN DER GRAAF GENERATOR** UK rock group formed in Manchester in 1967 by Peter Hammill (vocals), Nick Peame (keyboards), Keith Ellis (bass) and Chris Judge-Smith (drums). It was Judge-Smith who suggested the group's name, but he was soon replaced by Guy Evans, whilst Peame was replaced by Hugh Banton. Ellis left in 1969 to be replaced by Nic Potter, and David Jackson (woodwinds) was added to the line-up. Graham Smith joined in 1976 at the same time Banton and Jackson left. Hammill launched a parallel solo career in 1971 but Van Der Graaf Generator finally disbanded in 1978.

| | | | |
|---|---|---|---|
| 25/04/1970 | ....47 | ......2 | |

THE LEAST WE CAN DO IS WAVE TO EACH OTHER ...................................................Charisma CAS 1007

**PAUL VAN DYK** German DJ/remixer (born 16/12/1971, Eisenhüttenstadt) who also worked with Toni Halliday and Cosmic Baby, the latter in a group called Visions Of Shiva. He is also a member of Humate.

| | | | |
|---|---|---|---|
| 17/06/2000 | ....12 | ......3 | |

OUT THERE & BACK ........................................................................Deviant DVNT 37DCD

**VAN HALEN** US rock group formed in Pasadena, California in 1974 by David Lee Roth (born 10/10/1955, Bloomington, IN, lead vocals), Alex Van Halen (born 8/5/1955, Nijmegen, Holland, drums), Eddie Van Halen (born 26/1/1957, Nijmegen, guitar) and Michael Anthony (born Michael Sobolewski, 20/6/1955, Chicago, IL, bass). Roth quit in 1985 to go solo. Warner Brothers advised the Van Halen brothers not to retain the group name but they ignored the advice and recruited Sammy Hagar (born 13/10/1947, Monterey, CA) as lead singer. The cover to Van Halen's *For Unlawful Carnal Knowledge* album contained a telephone number that had previously belonged to a friend of Eddie Van Halen, one Steve Ripley. By the time the album was released, the number belonged to the McNutt family of Tulsa, Oklahoma, who launched a $2.068 million lawsuit for emotional distress against Warner Brothers and Van Halen.

| | | | |
|---|---|---|---|
| 27/05/1978 | ....34 | .....11 | .....● |
| 14/04/1979 | ....23 | ......7 | |
| 05/04/1980 | ....15 | ......7 | |
| 23/05/1981 | ....49 | ......4 | |
| 01/05/1982 | ....36 | ......5 | |
| 04/02/1984 | ....15 | .....24 | .....● |
| 05/04/1986 | ....16 | .....18 | .....O |
| 04/06/1988 | ....16 | .....12 | .....O |
| 29/06/1991 | ....12 | ......5 | |
| 06/03/1993 | ....24 | ......4 | |
| 04/02/1995 | ....8 | ......3 | |
| 09/11/1996 | ....45 | ......1 | |
| 28/03/1998 | ....43 | ......1 | |

VAN HALEN ◆[10] ..........................................................................Warner Brothers K 56470
VAN HALEN II .............................................................................Warner Brothers K 56616
WOMEN AND CHILDREN FIRST ................................................................Warner Brothers K 56793
FAIR WARNING ............................................................................Warner Brothers K 56899
DIVER DOWN .............................................................................Warner Brothers K 57003
1984 ◆[10] .................................................................................Warner Brothers 9239851
5150 ▲[3] .................................................................................Warner Brothers WS 5150
OU812 ▲[4] ...............................................................................Warner Brothers WX 177
FOR UNLAWFUL CARNAL KNOWLEDGE ▲[3] 1991 Grammy Award for Best Hard Rock Performance .......Warner Brothers WX 420
LIVE: RIGHT HERE, RIGHT NOW ...............................................................Warner Brothers 9362451982
BALANCE ▲[1] ..............................................................................Warner Brothers 9362457602
THE BEST OF VAN HALEN – VOLUME 1 ▲[1] .......................................................Warner Brothers 9362464742
VAN HALEN 3 .............................................................................Warner Brothers 9362466622

**ARMAND VAN HELDEN** US producer/remixer (born 1972, Boston, MA) who worked with Nuyorican Soul and CJ Bolland.

| | | | |
|---|---|---|---|
| 10/04/1999 | ....22 | ......6 | .....O |
| 10/06/2000 | ....38 | ......1 | |

2 FUTURE 4 U .............................................................................ffrr 5560902
KILLING PURITANS ........................................................................ffrr 8573833192

### DENISE VAN OUTEN
UK singer (born 27/5/1974, Basildon) who was a member of Those Two Girls before presenting TV's *The Big Breakfast*.

| | | | | | |
|---|---|---|---|---|---|
| 26/04/2003 | 34 | 2 | | TELL ME ON A SUNDAY Soundtrack to the London show starring Denise Van Outen | Really Useful 0761742 |

### LUTHER VANDROSS

US singer (born 20/4/1951, New York) who began his professional career as a commercial jingles singer, graduating to being one of New York's top session singers on records by David Bowie, Bette Midler, Barbra Streisand, Carly Simon, Change and many others. He formed his own group Luther who were signed to Cotillion (a division of Atlantic) but dropped after two albums. The success of the Change album enabled him to secure a new recording contract with Epic and retain production control, which led to him becoming one of the top R&B singers of the late-1980s and 1990s. He appeared in the 1993 film *The Meteor Man*. He has won eight Grammy Awards including: Best Rhythm & Blues Vocal Performance in 1990 for *Here And Now*; Best Rhythm & Blues Song (with Marcus Miller and Teddy Van), and Best Rhythm & Blues Vocal Performance in 1991 for *Power Of Love-Love Power*; Best Rhythm & Blues Vocal Performance in 1996 for *Your Secret Love*; Song of the Year (with co-writer Richard Marx) and Best Male Rhythm & Blues Vocal Performance in 2003 for *Dance With My Father*; and Best Rhythm & Blues Performance by a Duo or Group with Vocals with Beyoncé for *The Closer I Get To You* the same year. He was also given a Lifetime Achievement Award at the 2001 MOBO Awards. On 8/6/1987 his drummer Yogi Horton committed suicide by jumping out of a 17th-floor window in New York City after a performance at Madison Square Garden.

| DATE | POS | WKS | BPI | ALBUM TITLE | LABEL & NUMBER |
|---|---|---|---|---|---|
| 21/01/1984 | 42 | 8 | | BUSY BODY | Epic EPC 25608 |
| 06/04/1985 | 19 | 10 | | THE NIGHT I FELL IN LOVE | Epic EPC 26387 |
| 13/07/1985 | 45 | 4 | | THE ARTISTS VOLUME 2 **LUTHER VANDROSS/TEDDY PENDERGRASS/CHANGE/ATLANTIC STARR** | Street Sounds ARTIS 2 |
| 01/11/1986 | 3 | 99 | ✪² | **GIVE ME THE REASON** | Epic 4501341 |
| 21/02/1987 | 41 | 30 | | NEVER TOO MUCH | Epic EPC 32807 |
| 04/07/1987 | 23 | 16 | ✪ | FOREVER, FOR ALWAYS, FOR LOVE | Epic EPC 25013 |
| 16/04/1988 | 78 | 4 | | BUSY BODY | Epic 4601831 |
| 29/10/1988 | 3 | 22 | ● | **ANY LOVE** | Epic 4629081 |
| 11/11/1989 | 14 | 13 | | BEST OF LUTHER VANDROSS – BEST OF LOVE | Epic 4658011 |
| 25/05/1991 | 9 | 9 | ○ | **POWER OF LOVE** | Epic 4680121 |
| 12/06/1993 | 11 | 5 | | NEVER LET ME GO | Epic 4735982 |
| 01/10/1994 | ❶¹ | 28 | ✪ | **SONGS** | Epic 4766562 |
| 28/10/1995 | 12 | 14 | ● | GREATEST HITS 1981–1995 | Epic 4811002 |
| 19/10/1996 | 14 | 4 | ○ | YOUR SECRET LOVE | Epic 6638382 |
| 11/10/1997 | 56 | 2 | | ONE NIGHT WITH YOU – THE BEST OF LOVE | Epic 4888882 |
| 22/08/1998 | 42 | 1 | | I KNOW | EMI 8460892 |
| 16/02/2002 | 72 | 2 | | THE ESSENTIAL LUTHER VANDROSS | Epic 5050252 |
| 05/07/2003 | 41 | 15 | ○ | DANCE WITH MY FATHER ▲¹ 2003 Grammy Award for Best Rhythm & Blues Album | J Records 82876540732 |
| 23/08/2003 | 18 | 6 | | THE ESSENTIAL LUTHER VANDROSS | Epic 5133532 |

### VANESSA-MAE
UK classical violinist (born Vanessa-Mae Nicholson, 27/10/1968, Singapore) who is now resident in the UK.

| DATE | POS | WKS | BPI | ALBUM TITLE | LABEL & NUMBER |
|---|---|---|---|---|---|
| 25/02/1995 | 11 | 21 | ● | THE VIOLIN PLAYER ◇ | EMI CDC 5550892 |
| 02/11/1996 | 47 | 2 | | CLASSICAL ALBUM 1 | EMI Premier CDC 5553952 |
| 08/11/1997 | 27 | 5 | ○ | STORM | EMI 8218002 |
| 07/02/1998 | 56 | 3 | | CHINA GIRL – THE CLASSICAL ALBUM 2 | EMI Classics CDC 5564832 |
| 26/05/2001 | 58 | 2 | | SUBJECT TO CHANGE | EMI 5331002 |

### VANGELIS

Greek keyboard player (born Evangelos Papathanassiou, 29/3/1943, Valos) who moved to Paris in the early 1960s, forming Aphrodite's Child with Demis Roussos in 1968. Based in London from the mid-1970s, he worked with Jon Anderson as Jon And Vangelis. In 1981 he received an Oscar for *Chariots Of Fire*.

| DATE | POS | WKS | BPI | ALBUM TITLE | LABEL & NUMBER |
|---|---|---|---|---|---|
| 10/01/1976 | 31 | 7 | | HEAVEN AND HELL | RCA Victor RS 1025 |
| 09/10/1976 | 18 | 6 | | ALBEDO 0.39 | RCA Victor RS 1080 |
| 18/04/1981 | 5 | 97 | ✪ | **CHARIOTS OF FIRE** ▲⁴ Original soundtrack to the film | Polydor POLS 1026 |
| 05/05/1984 | 39 | 9 | | CHARIOTS OF FIRE Original soundtrack to the film. Re-issue of Polydor POLS 1026 | Polydor POLD 5160 |
| 13/10/1984 | 55 | 4 | | SOIL FESTIVITIES | Polydor POLH 11 |
| 30/03/1985 | 69 | 2 | | MASK | Polydor POLH 19 |
| 22/07/1989 | 11 | 13 | ● | THEMES | Polydor VGTV 1 |
| 24/10/1992 | 33 | 6 | ● | 1492 – THE CONQUEST OF PARADISE Original soundtrack to the film | East West 4509910142 |
| 18/06/1994 | 20 | 6 | ● | BLADERUNNER Original soundtrack to the film | East West 4509965742 |
| 02/03/1996 | 58 | 1 | | VOICES | East West 0630127862 |
| 20/04/1996 | 14 | 6 | | PORTRAIT (SO LONG AGO, SO CLEAR) ◇ | Polydor 5311542 |
| 08/11/2003 | 20 | 7 | ● | ODYSSEY – THE DEFINITIVE COLLECTION | Universal TV 9813149 |

## VANILLA FUDGE
US psychedelic rock group formed in New York in 1966 by Mark Stein (born 11/3/1947, New Jersey, keyboards/vocals), Vinnie Martell (born 11/11/1945, New York, guitar), Tim Bogart (born 27/8/1944, Richfield, NJ, bass) and Joey Brennan (drums). Brennan was soon replaced by Carmine Appice (born 15/12/1946, New York). They disbanded in 1970.

| | | | | | |
|---|---|---|---|---|---|
| 04/11/1967 | 31 | 3 | | VANILLA FUDGE | Atlantic 588086 |

## VANILLA ICE
US rapper (born Robert Van Winkle, 31/10/1968, Miami Lakes, FL) who appeared in the 1991 films *Cool As Ice* and *Teenage Mutant Ninja Turtles II*.

| | | | | | |
|---|---|---|---|---|---|
| 15/12/1990 | 4 | 20 | ✪ | TO THE EXTREME ▲16 | SBK SBKLP 9 |
| 06/07/1991 | 35 | 3 | | EXTREMELY LIVE | SBK SBKLP 12 |

## VAPORS
UK pub-rock group formed by David Fenton (vocals), Ed Bazalgette (guitar), Steve Smith (bass) and Howard Smith (drums). When the group disbanded, Fenton became a pub landlord in Woking.

| | | | | | |
|---|---|---|---|---|---|
| 07/06/1980 | 44 | 6 | | NEW CLEAR DAYS | United Artists UAG 30300 |

## VARDIS
UK group formed in Wakefield, Yorkshire by Steve Zodiac (guitar/vocals), Alan Selway (bass) and Gary Pearson (drums) as Quo Vardis, dropping the 'Quo' in 1979. Selway left in 1982 and was replaced by Terry Horbury.

| | | | | | |
|---|---|---|---|---|---|
| 01/11/1980 | 52 | 1 | | 100 MPH | Logo MOGO 4012 |

## FRANKIE VAUGHAN
UK singer (born Frank Abelson, 3/2/1928, Liverpool) whose chart success was equalled by that as a top cabaret act. He appeared in the film *Let's Make Love* with Marilyn Monroe in 1960 (and turned down the opportunity of a romantic liaison with her during filming!) and was awarded the OBE in 1965. He was also awarded a CBE in the 1996 New Year's Honours list. He died on 17/9/1999.

| | | | | | |
|---|---|---|---|---|---|
| 05/09/1959 | 6 | 2 | | FRANKIE VAUGHAN AT THE LONDON PALLADIUM | Philips BDL 7330 |
| 04/11/1967 | 40 | 1 | | FRANKIE VAUGHAN SONGBOOK | Philips DBL 001 |
| 25/11/1967 | 22 | 8 | | THERE MUST BE A WAY | Columbia SCX 6200 |
| 12/11/1977 | 24 | 9 | ● | 100 GOLDEN GREATS | Ronco RTDX 2021 |

## SARAH VAUGHAN
US singer (born 27/3/1924, Newark, NJ) who studied piano from 1931–39, won a talent contest at the Apollo Theater in 1942 and with it an engagement with the Earl Hines band as singer and second pianist. Her record debut was in 1944, the same year she joined Billy Eckstine's band. She married trumpeter George Treadwell in 1947 (subsequently her manager), and later married Clyde Atkins and Waymon Reed. She won the 1982 Grammy Award for Best Female Jazz Performance for *Gershwin Live* and died from cancer on 3/4/1990. She has two stars on the Hollywood Walk of Fame.

| | | | | | |
|---|---|---|---|---|---|
| 26/03/1960 | 19 | 1 | | NO COUNT – SARAH | Mercury MMC 14021 |

## STEVIE RAY VAUGHAN AND DOUBLE TROUBLE
US group formed by Stevie Ray Vaughan (born 3/10/1954, Dallas, TX, guitar/vocals), Lou Ann Barton (vocals), Reese Wynans (keyboards), Tommy Shannon (bass) and Chris Layton (drums). Vaughan was previously a member of The Nightcrawlers, Paul Ray And The Cobras, Triple Threat Revue and had also played with David Bowie, Eric Clapton, James Brown and Bob Dylan, among others. Shortly after performing in concert with Eric Clapton in Troy, Wisconsin on 27/8/1990 Stevie Ray was killed in a helicopter crash. He had convinced his brother to give up his seat so that he could make a quick return to Chicago. Flying in dense fog, the helicopter crashed into a man-made ski slope just a mile from the venue, killing all on board instantly. Stevie Ray won four Grammy Awards including: Best Traditional Blues Recording in 1984 with John Hammond, Sugar Blue, Koko Taylor & the Blues Machine, Luther "Guitar Junior" Johnson, J.B. Hutto & the New Hawks and his own band Double Trouble for *Blues Explosion*; Best Rock Instrumental Performance with Double Trouble for *Little Wing* from *The Sky Is Crying;* and Best Contemporary Blues Album in 1992, also for *The Sky Is Crying*.

| | | | | | |
|---|---|---|---|---|---|
| 15/07/1989 | 63 | 1 | | IN STEP 1989 Grammy Award for Best Contemporary Blues Recording | Epic 4633951 |

## VAUGHAN BROTHERS
US male duo formed by Stevie Ray Vaughan (see above) and his brother Jimmie (born 20/3/1951 Dallas, TX). Jimmie had been a member of The Fabulous Thunderbirds.

| | | | | | |
|---|---|---|---|---|---|
| 20/10/1990 | 63 | 1 | | FAMILY STYLE | Epic 4670141 |

## BOBBY VEE
US singer (born Robert Velline, 30/4/1943, Fargo, ND) inspired by Buddy Holly; he formed the Shadows in 1958, filling in for Holly, the Big Bopper and Ritchie Valens in Fargo the night after the fatal plane crash. The group recorded their first single in 1959, financing the session themselves, which led to a contract with Liberty Records (Vee signed a solo deal at the same time). He appeared in numerous films and was still appearing on the 'oldies' circuit into the 1990s.

The Very Best Of Bobby Vee

| | | | | | |
|---|---|---|---|---|---|
| 24/02/1962 | 7 | 8 | | TAKE GOOD CARE OF MY BABY | London HAG 2428 |
| 31/03/1962 | 20 | 1 | | HITS OF THE ROCKIN' 50'S | London HAG 2406 |
| 27/10/1962 | 2 | 27 | | BOBBY VEE MEETS THE CRICKETS BOBBY VEE AND THE CRICKETS | Liberty LBY 1086 |
| 12/01/1963 | 10 | 11 | | A BOBBY VEE RECORDING SESSION | Liberty LBY 1084 |
| 20/04/1963 | 10 | 14 | | BOBBY VEE'S GOLDEN GREATS | Liberty LBY 1112 |
| 05/10/1963 | 15 | 2 | | THE NIGHT HAS A THOUSAND EYES | Liberty LIB 1139 |
| 19/04/1980 | 5 | 10 | ● | THE BOBBY VEE SINGLES ALBUM | United Artists UAG 30253 |

**SUZANNE VEGA** US singer (born 12/8/1959, New York) who began her career on the New York folk circuit, signing with A&M in 1984. Her debut album the following year was greeted with critical acclaim. Her biggest hit (*Tom's Diner*) was remixed by UK remixers DNA who sampled Vega's original. Initially only on bootleg, it was then snapped up by Vega's own company A&M! Vega was apparently less than happy with the release. She took part in the *Perfect Day* project for the BBC's Children In Need charity.

| | | | | |
|---|---|---|---|---|
| 19/10/1985 .....11 .....71 ......✪ | SUZANNE VEGA ............................................................A&M AMA 5072 |
| 09/05/1987 .....2 .....39 ......✪ | **SOLITUDE STANDING** ..................................................A&M SUZLP 2 |
| 28/04/1990 .....7 ......7 ......● | **DAYS OF OPEN HAND** 1990 Grammy Award for Best Album Package (with Len Peltier and Jeffrey) ................A&M 3952931 |
| 19/09/1992 .....20 .....4 ......○ | 99.9 F ................................................................A&M 5400122 |
| 08/03/1997 .....43 .....3 ...... | NINE OBJECTS OF DESIRE .............................................A&M 5405832 |
| 31/10/1998 .....46 .....3 ...... | TRIED AND TRUE – THE BEST OF SUZANNE VEGA ...........................A&M 5409452 |
| 19/07/2003 .....27 .....5 ...... | RETROSPECTIVE – THE BEST OF .........................................UMTV 9808884 |

**ROSIE VELA** US singer (born 18/12/1952, Galveston, TX) who made her name as a model, later appearing in the films *Heaven's Gate* and *Inside Edge*.

| 31/01/1987 .....20 .....11 ......○ | ZAZU ................................................................A&M AMA 5016 |

**VELVET REVOLVER** US rock group formed in 2002 by former Guns N' Roses members Slash (born Saul Hudson, 23/7/1965, Stoke-on-Trent, guitar), Michael 'Duff' McKagan (born 5/2/1964, Seattle, bass) and Matt Sorum (born 19/11/1960, drums), later adding Dave Kushner (guitar) and Scott Weiland (born 27/10/1967, Santa Cruz, CA, vocals) who was formerly a member of Stone Temple Pilots.

| 19/06/2004 .....11 .....2+ ...... | CONTRABAND ▲¹ ...................................................RCA 82876628352 |

**VELVET UNDERGROUND** US rock group formed in New York in 1965 by Lou Reed (born 2/3/1942, Freeport, Long Island, NY, guitar/vocals), John Cale (born 9/3/1940, Cryant, various instruments), Sterling Morrison (born 29/8/1942, East Meadow, Long Island, guitar) and Angus MacLise (drums), who suggested the group's name which he had seen on a paperback book. However, MacLise left soon after and was replaced by Maureen Tucker. The group met Andy Warhol the same year, who played an integral part in their development, including introducing them to lead singer Nico (born Christa Paffgen, 16/10/1938, Cologne, Germany). Nico left after one album and then Warhol lost interest. Cale left in 1969 to be replaced by Billy Yule and Reed left in 1970 for a solo career, although the group carried on for a further two years before disbanding. There was a brief reunion in 1991 and a live album was made in 1993. Nico fell off her bicycle whilst on holiday in Ibiza and subsequently died of a brain haemorrhage on 18/7/1988. Morrison died from Non-Hodgkin's lymphoma on 30/8/1995. The group was inducted into the Rock & Roll Hall of Fame in 1996.

| 23/02/1985 .....47 ......4 ...... | V.U ................................................................Polydor POLD 5167 |
| 13/11/1993 .....70 ......1 ...... | LIVE MCMXCIII ........................................................Sire 9362454642 |
| 28/10/1995 .....56 ......4 ...... | THE BEST OF LOU REED AND THE VELVET UNDERGROUND **LOU REED AND THE VELVET UNDERGROUND** .Global Television RADCD 21 |
| 06/07/2002 .....59 ......1 ...... | VELVET UNDERGROUND AND NICO **VELVET UNDERGROUND AND NICO** ...................Polydor 823902 |

**VENGABOYS** Multinational group initially formed by DJs Danski (Dennis Van Den Driesschen) and DJ Delmundo (Wessel Van Diepen), later joined by singers and dancers Kim, Robin, Roy and Denice. Robin left in 1999 and was replaced by Yorick. Danski and Delmundo also recorded as Nakatomi.

| 03/04/1999 .....6 .....49 ......✪² | THE PARTY ALBUM! ..................................................Positiva 4993472 |
| 25/03/2000 .....9 .....28 ......● | THE PLATINUM ALBUM ...............................................Positiva 5259530 |

**VENOM** UK heavy metal group formed in Newcastle in the late-1970s by Conrad 'Cronos' Lant (bass/vocals), Jeff 'Mantas' Dunn (guitar) and Tony 'Abaddon' Bray (drums). Dunn left in 1985 and was replaced by Matt Hickey and Jimmy Clare. Lant left soon after for a solo career, taking Hickey and Clare with him, with Dunn returning and bringing in Tony 'The Demolition Risk' Dolan (bass/vocals) and Al Barnes (guitar). Barnes left in 1991 and was replaced by Steve 'War Maniac' White, although he left soon after. By 1996 Lant had returned to link up with Dunn, Bray and Dolan.

| 21/04/1984 .....64 ......1 ...... | AT WAR WITH SATAN ..................................................Neat 1015 |
| 13/04/1985 .....99 ......1 ...... | POSSESSED .........................................................Neat 1024 |

**ANTHONY VENTURA ORCHESTRA** Swiss orchestra leader who has worked with Carlos Franzetti, Alfred Gonzalez, Dan Kincaid, Eric Loffswold and Jim Snidero.

| 20/01/1979 .....44 ......4 ...... | DREAM LOVER .......................................................Lotus WH 5007 |

### TOM VERLAINE
US singer (born Thomas Miller, 13/12/1949, Mount Morris, NJ) who formed the Neon Boys in 1968 with Richard Hell and Billy Ficca, although the group eventually evolved into Television. In 1978 Television disbanded with Verlaine pursuing a solo career. However, Television was revived in 1991.

14/03/1987 .....99 ......1 ...... FLASH LIGHT ..................................................................................Fontana SFLP 1

### VERUCA SALT
US group formed in Chicago, IL in 1992 by Nina Gordon (guitar/vocals), Louise Post (guitar/vocals), Steve Lack (bass) and Jim Shapiro (drums). They made their first recordings for Minty Fresh in 1993 and subsequently linked with Geffen Records (who had already snapped up Jim Powers, the founder of Minty Fresh Records).

15/10/1994 .....47 ......2 ...... AMERICAN THIGHS ......................................................Hi-Rise Recordings FLATCD 9

### VERVE
UK group formed in 1989 by Richard Ashcroft (born 11/9/1971, Wigan, vocals), Peter Salisbury (born 24/9/1971, drums), Simon Jones (born 29/7/1972, bass) and Nick McCabe (born 14/7/1971, guitar). Their debut album was released in 1993. They were named Best British Group and Best Producer at the 1998 BRIT Awards. They disbanded in April 1999 with Ashcroft going solo and Jones joining The Shining.

03/07/1993 .....27 ......2 ..... A STORM IN HEAVEN ....................................................................Hut CDHUT 10
15/07/1995 .....13 .....11 ......● A NORTHERN SOUL ....................................................................Hut DGHUT 27
11/10/1997 ....❶¹² ....102 .....✿⁸ URBAN HYMNS ◇⁴ 1998 BRIT Award for Best Album ..................................Hut CDHUT 45

### VEX RED
UK rock group formed in Aldershot by Terry Abbott (guitar/vocals), Keith Lambert (bass/programming), Ant Forbes (guitar/keyboards), Nick Goulding (guitar/bass) and Ben Calvert (drums).

16/03/2002 .....48 ......1 ...... START WITH A STRONG AND PERSISTENT .....................................Virgin CDVUS 215

### VIBRATORS
UK punk rock group formed by Knox (born Ian Carnochan, 4/4/1945, guitar/vocals), John Ellis (born on 1/6/1952, guitar), Pat Collier (born October 1951, bass) and Eddie (born 1/4/1951, drums), later adding Chris Spedding (born 17/6/1944, Sheffield). Their main claim to fame was that they were to have supported the Sex Pistols on their Anarchy In The UK tour but pulled out following the furore over the Pistols' TV appearance with Bill Grundy!

25/06/1977 .....49 ......5 ...... PURE MANIA ......................................................................Epic EPC 82907
29/04/1978 .....33 ......2 ...... V2 ...............................................................................Epic EPC 82495

### VICE SQUAD
UK group formed in Bristol in 1978 by Beki Bondage (born Rebecca Bond, vocals), Dave Bateman (guitar), Mark Hambly (bass) and Shane Baldwin (drums). Bondage left in 1984 to form Ligotage and later Beki And The Bomshells whilst Vice Squad recruited Lia (vocals) and Sooty (guitar) for one album before disbanding in 1985.

24/10/1981 .....32 ......5 ...... NO CAUSE FOR CONCERN ...........................................Zonophone ZEM 103
22/05/1982 .....47 ......5 ...... STAND STRONG STAND PROUD ......................................Riot City ZEM 104

### SID VICIOUS
UK male singer (born John Ritchie, 10/5/1957, London) who replaced Glen Matlock in The Sex Pistols in February 1977. He was not part of the group that outraged the nation on the *Today* TV programme with Bill Grundy, but Vicious soon set about ensuring his own notoriety (a glass throwing incident at the 100 Club Punk Rock Festival left a female member of the audience blinded). Vicious took a second drugs overdose (he'd been hospitalised in January 1978) shortly after the Sex Pistols announced they were splitting up in 1978. For the rest of that year, Vicious, living with his girlfriend Nancy Spungen in New York, maintained a low profile, although he and Spungen were front-page news in October when she was found stabbed to death. Vicious had called the police but was then arrested and charged with her murder and placed in the detoxification unit of a New York prison (recent evidence suggests that they may have been the victims of a robbery). Malcolm McLaren got him out on bail but Vicious himself died at a New York party on 2/2/1979 from fluid on the lungs caused by a heroin overdose. It was later revealed that the drugs had been bought and supplied by Vicious' own mother. A film entitled *Sid And Nancy* with Gary Oldman and Chloe Webb in the lead roles was released in 1986.

15/12/1979 .....30 ......8 ......○ SID SINGS ..............................................................................Virgin V 2144

### VIENNA PHILHARMONIC ORCHESTRA CONDUCTED BY ARAM KHACHATURIAN
Austrian orchestra conducted by Aram Khachaturian. They also scored a hit single with the theme to the TV series *The Onedin Line*.

22/01/1972 .....16 .....15 ...... SPARTACUS Original soundtrack to the film ....................................Decca SXL 6000

### VIENNA SYMPHONY ORCHESTRA
Austrian orchestra formed in 1900 and consolidated in 1921; their first official conductor was Ferdinand Lowe, who held the position for 24 years. In 1938 the orchestra became the city's municipal orchestra, and after the Second World War Herbert Von Karajan assumed the role of musical director.

04/04/1987 .....43 ......4 ...... SYMPHONIC ROCK WITH THE VIENNA SYMPHONY ORCHESTRA ..............Stylus SMR 730

### VILLAGE PEOPLE
US group formed in New York by French producer Jacques Morali, each member representing gay stereotypes (although only one was actually gay): Randy Jones (cowboy), David 'Scar' Hodo (construction worker), Felipe Rose (Red Indian), Glenn Hughes (leather biker), Alexander Briley (soldier) and Victor Willis (policeman). Willis was later replaced by Ray Simpson (brother of Valerie Ashford). The group appeared in the film *Can't Stop The Music*. Morali died from AIDS on 15/11/1991 (his mother, who had dressed him as a girl whilst he was growing up, was barred from his funeral in Paris). Hughes died from lung cancer on 14/3/2001 at the age of 51. Although he had left the group in 1995, he asked to be buried wearing his biker outfit.

| DATE | POS | WKS | BPI | ALBUM TITLE | LABEL & NUMBER |
|------|-----|-----|-----|-------------|----------------|
| 27/01/1979 | 24 | 9 | | CRUISIN' | Mercury 9109 614 |
| 12/05/1979 | 14 | 19 | ● | GO WEST | Mercury 9109 621 |
| 16/08/1980 | 9 | 8 | ○ | **CAN'T STOP THE MUSIC** Original soundtrack to the film | Mercury 6399 051 |
| 18/12/1993 | 72 | 1 | | THE BEST OF THE VILLAGE PEOPLE | Bell 74321178312 |

**GENE VINCENT** US singer (born Vincent Eugene Craddock, 11/2/1935, Norfolk, VA) who was discharged from the US Navy in 1956 following a motorcycle accident and had to wear a steel brace thereafter. He made debut recordings in 1956 with his group the Blue Caps: Cliff Gallup (guitar), Willie Williams (guitar), Jack Neal (bass) and Dickie Harrell (drums). They scored a US top ten hit with the B-side *Be Bop A Lula*. They split in 1958 (Vincent had been unable to pay them their wages, which prompted the Musicians Union to withdraw his card). He was injured in the car crash that killed Eddie Cochran in 1960. Vincent died from a bleeding ulcer on 12/9/1970, Gallup died from a heart attack on 9/10/1988 aged 58 years. Gene Vincent was inducted into the Rock & Roll Hall of Fame in 1998.

| DATE | POS | WKS | BPI | ALBUM TITLE | LABEL & NUMBER |
|------|-----|-----|-----|-------------|----------------|
| 16/07/1960 | 12 | 2 | | CRAZY TIMES | Capitol T 1342 |

**VINNIE VINCENT** US guitarist/singer (real name Vincent Cusano) who joined Kiss in 1983 as a replacement for Ace Frehley. He left the following year and was replaced by Mark St John. He went solo and subsequently formed Vinnie Vincent's Invasion.

| DATE | POS | WKS | BPI | ALBUM TITLE | LABEL & NUMBER |
|------|-----|-----|-----|-------------|----------------|
| 28/05/1988 | 51 | 2 | | ALL SYSTEMS GO | Chrysalis CHR 1626 |

**VINES** Australian rock group formed by Craig Nicholls (guitar/vocals), Ryan Griffiths (guitar), Patrick Matthews (bass) and David Olliffe (drums). Olliffe appeared on their debut album but left the group as he disliked touring and was replaced by Hamish Rosser.

| DATE | POS | WKS | BPI | ALBUM TITLE | LABEL & NUMBER |
|------|-----|-----|-----|-------------|----------------|
| 20/07/2002 | 3 | 7 | ● | **HIGHLY EVOLVED** | Heavenly HVNLP 36CD |
| 03/04/2004 | 29 | 2 | | WINNING DAYS | Heavenly HVNLP 48CD |

**BOBBY VINTON** US singer (born Stanley Robert Vinton, 16/4/1935, Canonsburg, PA) who formed his own band, The Tempos, whilst still at high school. The band recorded two albums for Epic. Vinton went solo in 1962 and had his own TV series from 1975–78. He has a star on the Hollywood Walk of Fame.

| DATE | POS | WKS | BPI | ALBUM TITLE | LABEL & NUMBER |
|------|-----|-----|-----|-------------|----------------|
| 17/11/1990 | 67 | 2 | | BLUE VELVET | Epic 4675701 |

**VIOLENT FEMMES** US rock group formed in Milwaukee, WI by Gordon Gano (born 7/6/1963, New York, guitar/vocals), Brian Ritchie (born 21/11/1960, Milwaukee, bass) and Victor De Lorenzo (born 25/10/1954, Racine, WI, drums). Gano is also a member of Mercy Seat, whilst both Ritchie and De Lorenzo have recorded solo.

| DATE | POS | WKS | BPI | ALBUM TITLE | LABEL & NUMBER |
|------|-----|-----|-----|-------------|----------------|
| 01/03/1986 | 81 | 1 | | THE BLIND LEADING THE NAKED | Slash SLAP 10 |

**VIOLINSKI** UK instrumental group formed by Electric Light Orchestra member Mik Kaminski and also featuring Michael D'Albuquerque, Baz Dunnery, John Hodson, Paul Mann, John Marcangelo, Iain Whitmore and Andrew Brown.

| DATE | POS | WKS | BPI | ALBUM TITLE | LABEL & NUMBER |
|------|-----|-----|-----|-------------|----------------|
| 26/05/1979 | 49 | 1 | | NO CAUSE FOR ALARM | Jet JETLU 219 |

**VISAGE** UK electronic dance group formed by Steve Strange (born Steve Harrington, 28/5/1959), Rusty Egan (born 19/9/1957) and Midge Ure. Ure later left to join Ultravox, with Strange and Egan opening London's Camden Palace venue.

| DATE | POS | WKS | BPI | ALBUM TITLE | LABEL & NUMBER |
|------|-----|-----|-----|-------------|----------------|
| 24/01/1981 | 13 | 29 | ○ | VISAGE | Polydor 2490 157 |
| 03/04/1982 | 6 | 16 | ○ | **THE ANVIL** | Polydor POLD 5050 |
| 19/11/1983 | 38 | 11 | ● | FADE TO GREY – THE SINGLES COLLECTION | Polydor POLD 5117 |
| 03/11/1984 | 79 | 2 | | BEAT BOY | Polydor POLH 12 |

**VIXEN** US heavy rock group formed in Los Angeles, CA in 1986 by Janet Gardner (vocals), Janet Kushnemund (guitar), Pia Koko (bass) and Roxy Petrucci (drums). Koko left before their record debut and was replaced by Share Pedersen (bass). Pedersen later joined Contraband.

| DATE | POS | WKS | BPI | ALBUM TITLE | LABEL & NUMBER |
|------|-----|-----|-----|-------------|----------------|
| 08/10/1988 | 66 | 1 | | VIXEN | Manhattan MTL 1028 |
| 18/08/1990 | 20 | 4 | | REV IT UP | EMI USA MTL 1054 |

**VOICE OF THE BEEHIVE** UK/US group formed by Tracey Bryn (guitar/vocals), her sister Melissa Brooke Belland (guitar), Mick Jones (guitar), Dan Woodgate (drums) and Mark Bedford (bass). They first signed with the Food label.

| DATE | POS | WKS | BPI | ALBUM TITLE | LABEL & NUMBER |
|------|-----|-----|-----|-------------|----------------|
| 02/07/1988 | 13 | 13 | | LET IT BEE | London LONLP 57 |
| 24/08/1991 | 17 | 13 | ○ | HONEY LINGERS | London 8282591 |

**VON BONDIES** US rock group formed in Detroit, MI by Jason Stollsteimer (guitar/vocals), Marcie Bolen (guitar), Carrie Smith (bass) and Don Blum (drums).

| DATE | POS | WKS | BPI | ALBUM TITLE | LABEL & NUMBER |
|------|-----|-----|-----|-------------|----------------|
| 21/02/2004 | 36 | 2 | | PAWN SHOPPE HEART | Sire 9362485492 |

**HERBERT VON KARAJAN** Austrian conductor (born 5/4/1908, Salzburg) who made his debut conducting *Figaro* in Ulm in 1928 and went on to conduct at the Stadtisches Thearte in Ulm (1928–33), at Aachen (1934–38) and the Berlin Staatsoper (1938–42). His membership of the Nazi Party during the Second World War meant that he was not permitted to work until 1947, but in 1955 he was made principal conductor of the Berlin Philharmonic. He resigned in 1989 and died later the same year. He won three Grammy Awards: Best Opera Recording in 1964 conducting the Vienna Philharmonic Orchestra and Chorus on *Carmen*, Best Opera Recording in 1969 conducting the Berlin Philharmonic Orchestra on *Wagner: Siegfried* and Best Classical Performance, Conductors Award in 1978 conducting the Berlin Philharmonic on *Beethoven: Symphonies*.

| DATE | POS | WKS | BPI | ALBUM TITLE | LABEL & NUMBER |
|------|-----|-----|-----|-------------|----------------|
| 26/09/1970 | 51 | 2 | | BEETHOVEN TRIPLE CONCERTO **BERLIN PHILHARMONIC ORCHESTRA CONDUCTED BY HERBERT VON KARAJAN – SOLOIST DAVID OISTRAKH (VIOLIN), MSTISLAV ROSTROPOVICH (CELLO), SVIATOSLAU RICHTER (PIANO)** | HMV ASD 2582 |
| 16/04/1988 | 51 | 5 | | THE ESSENTIAL KARAJAN | Deutsche Grammophon HVKTV 1 |
| 03/08/1991 | 52 | 2 | | HOLST: THE PLANETS | Deutsche Grammophon 4352891 |

○ Silver disc ● Gold disc ✪ Platinum disc (additional platinum units are indicated by a figure following the symbol) ●⁹ Number of weeks album topped the UK chart

07/10/1995 .....30......8 ...... KARAJAN: ADAGIO .................................................................Deutsche Grammophon 4452822
13/04/1996 .....63.......1 ...... ADAGIO 2 This and the above two hits credited to **HERBERT VON KARAJAN CONDUCTING THE BERLIN PHILHARMONIC ORCHESTRA** .................................................Deutsche Grammophon 4495152

### ANNE SOFIE VON OTTER
Swedish female soprano (born 9/5/1955, Stockholm) who studied at the Guildhall School of Music and Drama and made her Covent Garden debut in 1985.

31/03/2001 .....67......1 ...... FOR THE STARS **ANNE SOFIE VON OTTER MEETS ELVIS COSTELLO** ...........................Deutsche Grammophon 4695302

### VOW WOW
Japanese/US group formed by Genki Hitomi (vocals), Kyoji Yamamoto (guitar), Rei Atsumi (keyboards), Neil Murray (bass) and Toshi Niimi (drums).

18/03/1989 .....75......1 ...... HELTER SKELTER ........................................................................................Arista 209691

### VOYAGE
French/UK group comprising Marc Chantereau (keyboards/vocals), Pierre-Alain Dahan (drums/vocals), Slim Pezin (guitar/vocals), Sylvia Mason (lead vocals) and Sauveur Mallia (bass).

09/09/1978 .....59......1 ...... VOYAGE .........................................................................................GTO GTLP 030

**WAH!** UK rock group formed in Liverpool in 1979 by Pete Wylie after being in the Crucial Three with Julian Cope and Ian McCulloch.

| | | | |
|---|---|---|---|
| 18/07/1981 | 33 | 5 | NAH=POO-THE ART OF BLUFF ....................................................Eternal CLASSIC 1 |
| 04/08/1984 | 28 | 6 | A WORD TO THE WISE GUY **MIGHTY WAH!** ....................................Beggars Banquet BEGA 54 |

**JOHN WAITE** UK singer (born 4/7/1955, London) who was lead singer with the Babys and Bad English before going solo in 1981.

| | | | |
|---|---|---|---|
| 10/11/1984 | 64 | 3 | NO BREAKS ....................................................EMI America WAIT 1 |

**TOM WAITS** US singer/pianist (born 7/12/1949, Pomona, CA); he played small clubs in Los Angeles before being signed by Frank Zappa's manager Herb Cohen. He signed with Asylum after a 1973 debut album and stayed with them for ten years, moving to Island Records in 1983. He has also appeared in a number of films, including *Rumble Fish, Down By Law, Candy Mountain* and *Cold Feet*.

| | | | |
|---|---|---|---|
| 08/10/1983 | 62 | 3 | SWORDFISHTROMBONE ....................................................Island ILPS 9762 |
| 19/10/1985 | 29 | 5 | RAIN DOGS ....................................................Island ILPS 9803 |
| 05/09/1987 | 20 | 5 | FRANK'S WILD YEARS ....................................................Island ITW 3 |
| 08/10/1988 | 84 | 1 | BIG TIME ....................................................Island ITW 4 |
| 19/09/1992 | 26 | 3 | BONE MACHINE 1992 Grammy Award for Best Alternative Music Album ....................Island CID 9993 |
| 20/11/1993 | 47 | 2 | THE BLACK RIDER ....................................................Island CID 8021 |
| 27/06/1998 | 63 | 1 | BEAUTIFUL MALADIES 1983–1993: THE ISLAND YEARS ....................Island 5245192 |
| 01/05/1999 | 9 | 5 | **MULE VARIATIONS** 1999 Grammy Award for Best Contemporary Folk Album ....................Epitaph 65472 |
| 18/05/2002 | 20 | 2 | ALICE ....................................................Anti 66322 |
| 18/05/2002 | 21 | 2 | BLOOD MONEY ....................................................Anti 66292 |

**RICK WAKEMAN** UK keyboard player (born 18/5/1949, London); he was in The Strawbs and Yes before going solo, making his name with a series of concept albums. *The Myths And Legends Of King Arthur And The Knights Of The Round Table* was subsequently staged with a full orchestra and choir on ice at Wembley's Empire Pool! After surviving a minor heart attack and combating alcoholism he formed his own label, Moon Records, later rejoining Yes. He launched another label, Ambient Records, and recorded a series of relaxation cassettes with fellow Isle of Man inhabitant Norman Wisdom. He is known for his collections of fountain pens, first issue Billy Bunter novels and other books, as featured in the TV series *Collectors Lot*. See also Anderson Bruford Wakeman Howe.

| | | | | |
|---|---|---|---|---|
| 24/02/1973 | 7 | 22 | | THE SIX WIVES OF HENRY VIII ....................................................A&M AMLH 64361 |
| 18/05/1974 | ❶¹ | 30 | ● | **JOURNEY TO THE CENTRE OF THE EARTH RICK WAKEMAN WITH THE LONDON SYMPHONY ORCHESTRA** ........A&M AMLH 63621 |
| 12/04/1975 | 2 | 28 | ● | **THE MYTHS AND LEGENDS OF KING ARTHUR AND THE KNIGHTS OF THE ROUND TABLE RICK WAKEMAN WITH THE** |
| | | | | **ENGLISH CHAMBER CHOIR AND CHOIR** ....................................................A&M AMLH 64515 |
| 24/04/1976 | 9 | 9 | | **NO EARTHLY CONNECTION** ....................................................A&M AMLH 64583 |
| 12/02/1977 | 14 | 9 | ○ | WHITE ROCK ....................................................A&M AMLH 64614 |
| 03/12/1977 | 25 | 5 | | CRIMINAL RECORD ....................................................A&M AMLK 64660 |
| 02/06/1979 | 25 | 10 | | RHAPSODIES ....................................................A&M AMLX 68508 |
| 27/06/1981 | 24 | 9 | | 1984 ....................................................Charisma CDS 4022 |
| 13/10/1984 | 64 | 6 | | BEYOND THE PLANETS **KEVIN PEEK & RICK WAKEMAN FEATURING JEFF WAYNE** NARRATION PATRICK ALLEN ....Telstar STAR 2244 |
| 16/05/1987 | 94 | 1 | | THE GOSPELS ....................................................Stylus SMR 729 |
| 27/03/1999 | 34 | 2 | | RETURN TO THE CENTRE OF THE EARTH **RICK WAKEMAN: LONDON SYMPHONY ORCHESTRA: ENGLISH** |
| | | | | **CHAMBER CHOIR: NARRATED BY PATRICK STEWART** ....................................................EMI Classics CDC 5567632 |

**NARADA MICHAEL WALDEN** US singer/producer (born Michael Anthony Walden, 23/4/1952, Kalamazoo, MI) who was a drummer with the Mahavishnu Orchestra 1973–1975 before going solo. Later a successful writer and producer, he was given the name Narada (which means 'supreme musician') by Sri Chinmoy. He has won two Grammy Awards: Best Rhythm & Blues Song in 1985 for *Freeway Of Love* and Producer of the Year in 1987.

| | | | |
|---|---|---|---|
| 14/05/1988 | 60 | 5 | DIVINE EMOTION **NARADA** ....................................................Atlantic WX 172 |

○ Silver disc  ● Gold disc  ✪ Platinum disc (additional platinum units are indicated by a figure following the symbol)  ❶⁹ Number of weeks album topped the UK chart

### WALKER BROTHERS
US vocal group formed in 1964 by Noel Scott Engel (born 9/1/1944, Hamilton, OH), John Maus (born 12/11/1943, NYC) and Gary Leeds (born 3/9/1944, Glendale, CA), all adopting Walker as a stage surname. Signed by Smash in the US, they disbanded in 1967, by which time both John and Gary had begun solo careers. They re-formed in 1976 for three albums.

| DATE | POS | WKS | BPI | ALBUM TITLE | LABEL & NUMBER |
|---|---|---|---|---|---|
| 18/12/1965 | 3 | 36 | | TAKE IT EASY | Philips BL 7691 |
| 03/09/1966 | 3 | 23 | | PORTRAIT | Philips SBL 7732 |
| 18/03/1967 | 6 | 15 | | IMAGES | Philips SBL 7770 |
| 16/09/1967 | 9 | 19 | | WALKER BROTHERS' STORY | Philips DBL 002 |
| 21/02/1976 | 49 | 3 | | NO REGRETS | GTO GTLP 007 |
| 25/01/1992 | 4 | 12 | ● | NO REGRETS – THE BEST OF SCOTT WALKER AND THE WALKER BROTHERS | Fontana 5108312 |
| 15/07/2000 | 55 | 1 | | NO REGRETS – THE BEST OF 1965–1976 This and the above hit credited to **SCOTT WALKER AND THE WALKER BROTHERS** | Universal TV 5108312 |

### SCOTT WALKER
US singer (born Noel Scott Engel, 9/1/1944, Hamilton, OH) who was a member of the Walker Brothers from 1964. The group disbanded in 1967, re-forming in 1976.

| DATE | POS | WKS | BPI | ALBUM TITLE | LABEL & NUMBER |
|---|---|---|---|---|---|
| 16/09/1967 | 3 | 17 | | SCOTT | Philips SBL 7816 |
| 20/04/1968 | ❶¹ | 18 | | SCOTT 2 | Philips SBL 7840 |
| 05/04/1969 | 3 | 4 | | SCOTT 3 | Philips S 7882 |
| 05/07/1969 | 7 | 3 | | SONGS FROM HIS TV SERIES | Philips SBL 7900 |
| 31/03/1984 | 60 | 2 | | CLIMATE HUNTER | Virgin V 2303 |
| 25/01/1992 | 4 | 12 | ● | NO REGRETS – THE BEST OF SCOTT WALKER AND THE WALKER BROTHERS Scott Walker and the Walker Brothers | Fontana 5108312 |
| 20/05/1995 | 27 | 1 | | TILT | Fontana 5268592 |
| 15/07/2000 | 55 | 1 | | NO REGRETS – THE BEST OF 1965–1976 **SCOTT WALKER AND THE WALKER BROTHERS** | Universal TV 5108312 |

### WALLFLOWERS
US rock group formed in Los Angeles, CA by Jakob Dylan (son of Bob Dylan, vocals), Michael Ward (guitar), Rami Jaffe (keyboards), Greg Richling (bass) and Mario Calire (drums). Their single *One Headlight* won the 1997 Grammy Award for Best Rock Performance By A Duo Or Group with Vocal, plus Best Rock Song for writer Jakob Dylan

| DATE | POS | WKS | BPI | ALBUM TITLE | LABEL & NUMBER |
|---|---|---|---|---|---|
| 21/06/1997 | 58 | 2 | | BRINGING DOWN THE HORSE | Interscope IND 90055 |

### BOB WALLIS AND HIS STORYVILLE JAZZ BAND
UK singer/trumpeter (born 3/6/1934, Bridlington) who formed The Storyville Jazz Band in 1950. He died on 10/1/1997.

| DATE | POS | WKS | BPI | ALBUM TITLE | LABEL & NUMBER |
|---|---|---|---|---|---|
| 11/06/1960 | 20 | 1 | | EVERYBODY LOVES SATURDAY NIGHT | Top Rank BUY 023 |

### JOE WALSH
US singer (born 20/11/1947, Wichita, KS) who was in The James Gang 1969–71 and The Eagles 1975–82, fronting his own band in between. He also tried twice for the nomination of Vice President in the US Presidential race.

| DATE | POS | WKS | BPI | ALBUM TITLE | LABEL & NUMBER |
|---|---|---|---|---|---|
| 17/04/1976 | 28 | 3 | | YOU CAN'T ARGUE WITH A SICK MIND | Anchor ABCL 5156 |
| 10/06/1978 | 16 | 17 | ○ | BUT SERIOUSLY FOLKS | Asylum K 53081 |

### WANG CHUNG
UK rock group formed in 1980 by Jack Hues (guitar/keyboards/vocals), Nick Feldman (bass) and Darren Costin (drums) as Huang Chung. They recorded for Arista, changing name and label in 1982. Costin left in 1985 and they continued as a duo.

| DATE | POS | WKS | BPI | ALBUM TITLE | LABEL & NUMBER |
|---|---|---|---|---|---|
| 21/04/1984 | 34 | 5 | | POINTS ON THE CURVE | Geffen GEF 25589 |

### WANNADIES
Swedish rock group formed in 1989 by Par Wiksten (guitar/vocals), Stefan Schonfeldt (guitar), Fredrik Schonfeldt (bass), Cristina Bergmark (percussion) and Gunnar Karlsson (drums).

| DATE | POS | WKS | BPI | ALBUM TITLE | LABEL & NUMBER |
|---|---|---|---|---|---|
| 17/05/1997 | 37 | 3 | | BAGSY ME | Indolent 74321429822 |
| 18/03/2000 | 73 | 1 | | YEAH | Indolent 74321687022 |

### WAR
– see ERIC BURDON AND WAR

### STEPHEN WARBECK
UK conductor/arranger/producer (born 21/10/1953), he has also worked with The Prague Philharmonic, Russell Watson and wrote scores to such films as *Shakespeare In Love, Quills* and *Christmas Carol*. He won an Oscar in 1998 for Best Original Score for *Shakespeare In Love*.

| DATE | POS | WKS | BPI | ALBUM TITLE | LABEL & NUMBER |
|---|---|---|---|---|---|
| 19/05/2001 | 30 | 5 | | CAPTAIN CORELLI'S MANDOLIN Original soundtrack to the film | Decca 4676782 |

### CLIFFORD T. WARD
UK singer (born 10/2/1946, Kidderminster) who was a schoolteacher before recording for John Peel's Dandelion label in the early 1970s. After over twenty years suffering from multiple sclerosis, he died from pneumonia on 18/12/2001.

| DATE | POS | WKS | BPI | ALBUM TITLE | LABEL & NUMBER |
|---|---|---|---|---|---|
| 21/07/1973 | 40 | 3 | | HOME THOUGHTS | Charisma CAS 1066 |
| 16/02/1974 | 42 | 2 | | MANTLE PIECES | Charisma CAS 1077 |

### MICHAEL WARD
UK singer, first known via *Opportunity Knocks*, the TV show's youngest ever winner.

| DATE | POS | WKS | BPI | ALBUM TITLE | LABEL & NUMBER |
|---|---|---|---|---|---|
| 05/01/1974 | 26 | 3 | | INTRODUCING MICHAEL WARD | Philips 6308 189 |

▲⁹ Number of weeks album topped the US chart   ◆¹² RIAA Diamond Awards   ◇³ IFPI Platinum Europe Awards

**WARLOCK** German rock group formed by Doro (born Dorothee Pesch in Dusseldorf, 3/6/1964, vocals), Rudy Graft (guitar), Peter Szigeti (guitar), Frank Rittel (bass) and Michael Eurich (drums). Graft left in 1986, replaced by Niko Arvantis. The original line-up dissolved when Pesch left to live in New York. A new line-up was assembled with Eurich, Tommy Bolan (guitar) and Tommy Henriksen (bass) and later Niko Arvantis. This line-up lasted for one album before disbanding. A 1989 album was credited to Doro and Warlock, although this was ostensibly a solo album, since when Doro has pursued a solo career.

14/11/1987 . . . . . 54 . . . . . . 2 . . . . . . TRIUMPH AND AGONY . . . . . . . . . . . . . . . . . . . . . . . . . . . . . . . . . . . . . . . . . . . . . . . . . . . . . Vertigo VERH 50

**WARM JETS** UK rock group formed by Louis Jones (guitar/vocals), Paul Noble (guitar/sound effects), Colleen Brown (bass) and Ed Grimshaw (drums). Brown was subsequently replaced by Aki Shibahara.

07/03/1998 . . . . . 40 . . . . . . 1 . . . . . . FUTURE SIGNS . . . . . . . . . . . . . . . . . . . . . . . . . . . . . . . . . . . . . . . . . . . . . . . . . . . . . . . . . Island 5243542

**JENNIFER WARNES** US singer (born 3/3/1947, Seattle, WA) who appeared in the Smothers Brothers TV show as Jennifer Warren before playing the lead role in the musical *Hair* in 1968. She signed with Decca in 1968 and later with Reprise and Arista. She has won two Grammy Awards: Best Vocal Performance by a Duo in 1982 with Joe Cocker for *Up Where We Belong* and Best Vocal Performance by a Duo in 1987 with Bill Medley for *(I've Had) The Time Of My Life*.

18/07/1987 . . . . . 33 . . . . . 12 . . . . . . ○ FAMOUS BLUE RAINCOAT – SONGS OF LEONARD COHEN . . . . . . . . . . . . . . . . . . . . . . . . . . . RCA PL 90048

**WARRANT** US heavy rock group formed in Los Angeles, CA by Jani Lane (born 1/2/1964, Akron, OH, vocals), Erik Turner (born 31/3/1964, Omaha, NE, guitar), Joey Allan (born 23/6/1964, Fort Wayne, IN, guitar), Jerry Dixon (born 15/9/1967, Pasadena, CA, bass) and Steven Sweet (born 29/10/1965, Weadsworth, OH, drums). They signed with Columbia in 1988. Lane went solo in 1992, later returning. Allen and Sweet also left and were replaced by Rick Steier and James Kottak.

19/09/1992 . . . . . 74 . . . . . . 1 . . . . . . DOG EAT DOG . . . . . . . . . . . . . . . . . . . . . . . . . . . . . . . . . . . . . . . . . . . . . . . . . . . . . Columbia 4720332

**DIONNE WARWICK** US singer (born Marie Dionne Warrick, 12/12/1940, East Orange, NJ) who formed the Gospelaires with sister Dee Dee, cousin Cissy Houston and Doris Troy, working as backing singers in New York. Heard by Burt Bacharach on a Drifters session in 1961, she was signed by Scepter in 1962. Her name was misspelled on the Scepter contract, hence her stage name (she was also briefly Dionne Warwicke, adding the 'e' after a visit to a psychic). She made her acting debut in the 1969 film *Slave* and also launched her own label, Sonday, distributed through Scepter. She has won five Grammy Awards: Best Female Solo Vocal Performance in 1968 for *Do You Know The Way To San Jose,* Best Contemporary Vocal Performance in 1970 for *I'll Never Fall In Love Again,* Best Pop Vocal Performance in 1979 for *I'll Never Love This Way Again,* Best Rhythm & Blues Vocal Performance in 1979 for *Déjà Vu* and Best Pop Vocal Performance by a Group in 1986 with Elton John, Gladys Knight and Stevie Wonder for *That's What Friends Are For*. She has a star on the Hollywood Walk of Fame.

23/05/1964 . . . . . 14 . . . . . 10 . . . . . . PRESENTING DIONNE WARWICK . . . . . . . . . . . . . . . . . . . . . . . . . . . . . . . . . . . . . . . . . . . . Pye NPL 28037
07/05/1966 . . . . . 8 . . . . . . 11 . . . . . . **BEST OF DIONNE WARWICK** . . . . . . . . . . . . . . . . . . . . . . . . . . . . . . . . . . . . . . . . . . . . . . Pye NPL 28078
04/02/1967 . . . . . 39 . . . . . . 2 . . . . . . HERE WHERE THERE IS LOVE . . . . . . . . . . . . . . . . . . . . . . . . . . . . . . . . . . . . . . . . . . . . Pye NPL 28096
18/05/1968 . . . . . 10 . . . . . 13 . . . . . . **VALLEY OF THE DOLLS** . . . . . . . . . . . . . . . . . . . . . . . . . . . . . . . . . . . . . . . . . . . . . . Pye NSPL 28114
23/05/1970 . . . . . 31 . . . . . 26 . . . . . . GREATEST HITS VOLUME 1 . . . . . . . . . . . . . . . . . . . . . . . . . . . . . . . . . . . . . . . . . . . . . Wand WNS 1
06/06/1970 . . . . . 28 . . . . . 14 . . . . . . GREATEST HITS VOLUME 2 . . . . . . . . . . . . . . . . . . . . . . . . . . . . . . . . . . . . . . . . . . . . . Wand WNS 2
30/10/1982 . . . . . 3 . . . . . . 33 . . . . . . ✪ **HEARTBREAKER** . . . . . . . . . . . . . . . . . . . . . . . . . . . . . . . . . . . . . . . . . . . . . . . . . . Arista 204 974
21/05/1983 . . . . . 11 . . . . . 17 . . . . . . ● THE DIONNE WARWICK COLLECTION . . . . . . . . . . . . . . . . . . . . . . . . . . . . . . . . . . . . Arista DIONE 1
29/10/1983 . . . . . 60 . . . . . . 3 . . . . . . SO AMAZING . . . . . . . . . . . . . . . . . . . . . . . . . . . . . . . . . . . . . . . . . . . . . . . . . . . . Arista 205 755
23/02/1985 . . . . . 86 . . . . . . 2 . . . . . . WITHOUT YOUR LOVE . . . . . . . . . . . . . . . . . . . . . . . . . . . . . . . . . . . . . . . . . . . . . . Arista 206 571
06/01/1990 . . . . . 6 . . . . . . 13 . . . . . . ● **LOVE SONGS** . . . . . . . . . . . . . . . . . . . . . . . . . . . . . . . . . . . . . . . . . . . . . . . . . . . Arista 410441
10/12/1994 . . . . . 60 . . . . . . 2 . . . . . . CHRISTMAS IN VIENNA II **DIONNE WARWICK PLACIDO DOMINGO** . . . . . . . . . . . . . . . . . . Sony Classical SK 64304
14/12/1996 . . . . . 58 . . . . . . 4 . . . . . . THE ESSENTIAL COLLECTION . . . . . . . . . . . . . . . . . . . . . . . . . . . . . . . . . . Global Television RADCD 48
03/08/2002 . . . . . 32 . . . . . . 4 . . . . . . ○ HEARTBREAKER – THE VERY BEST OF . . . . . . . . . . . . . . . . . . . . . . . . . . . . . WSM/BMG WSMCD 101

**WAS (NOT WAS)** US rock group formed in Detroit, MI in 1980 by Don Was (born Don Fagenson, 13/9/1952, Detroit, bass/synthesizer/vocals) and David Was (born David Weiss, 26/10/1952, Detroit, keyboards/vocals) with guest vocals from Sweet Pea Atkinson (born 20/9/1945, Oberlin, OH), Donald Ray Mitchell (born 12/4/1957, Detroit) and Sir Harry Bowens (born 8/10/1949, Detroit). They first recorded for Ze Records. Don Was was named Producer of the Year at the 1994 Grammy Awards.

09/04/1988 . . . . . 47 . . . . . . 6 . . . . . . WHAT UP DOG? . . . . . . . . . . . . . . . . . . . . . . . . . . . . . . . . . . . . . . . . . . . . . . . . . . . Fontana SFLP 4
21/07/1990 . . . . . 35 . . . . . . 6 . . . . . . ARE YOU OK? . . . . . . . . . . . . . . . . . . . . . . . . . . . . . . . . . . . . . . . . . . . . . . . . . . . Fontana 8463511
13/06/1992 . . . . . 61 . . . . . . 3 . . . . . . HELLO DAD I'M IN JAIL . . . . . . . . . . . . . . . . . . . . . . . . . . . . . . . . . . . . . . . . . . . . . Fontana 5124642

**GENO WASHINGTON AND THE RAM JAM BAND** US singer (born in Evansville, IN) who came to the UK while serving in the US Air Force and began singing while still in service. He remained in the UK and formed the Ram Jam Band with Pete Gage (guitar), Lionel Kingham (saxophone), Buddy Beadle (saxophone), Jeff Wright (organ), John Roberts (bass) and Herb Prestige (drums). He later returned to the US, forming a rock trio, while Gage joined Vinegar Joe.

10/12/1966 . . . . . 5 . . . . . . 38 . . . . . . **HAND CLAPPIN' – FOOT STOMPIN' – FUNKY BUTT – LIVE!** . . . . . . . . . . . . . . . . . . . . . . . Piccadilly NPL 38026
23/09/1967 . . . . . 8 . . . . . . 13 . . . . . . **HIPSTERS, FLIPSTERS, AND FINGER POPPIN' DADDIES** . . . . . . . . . . . . . . . . . . . . . . . . . Piccadilly NSPL 38032

**GROVER WASHINGTON JR** US saxophonist (born 12/12/1943, Buffalo, NY); he played sax from childhood. A prolific session musician, he debuted on album for Kudu in 1971. He died from a heart attack while recording a TV appearance on 17/12/1999.

09/05/1981 . . . . . 34 . . . . . . 9 . . . . . . ○ WINELIGHT 1981 Grammy Award for Best Jazz Fusion Performance . . . . . . . . . . . . . . . . . . . . Elektra K 52262
19/12/1981 . . . . . 98 . . . . . . 1 . . . . . . COME MORNING . . . . . . . . . . . . . . . . . . . . . . . . . . . . . . . . . . . . . . . . . . . . . . . . . . Elektra K 52337

## W.A.S.P.
US rock group formed in 1982 by Blackie Lawless (born Steve Duren, 4/9/1954, Florida, vocals/bass), Chris Holmes (born 23/6/1961, guitar), Randy Piper (guitar) and Tony Richards (drums). Piper and Richards left, replaced by Steve Riley and Johnny Rod (Lawless moving to guitar). Holmes left in 1990, and Lawless later recorded solo. Their name is an acronym for We Are Sexual Perverts.

| DATE | POS | WKS | BPI | ALBUM TITLE | LABEL & NUMBER |
|------|-----|-----|-----|-------------|----------------|
| 08/09/1984 | 51 | 2 | | W.A.S.P. | Capitol EJ 2401951 |
| 09/11/1985 | 48 | 1 | | THE LAST COMMAND | Capitol WASP 2 |
| 08/11/1986 | 53 | 3 | | INSIDE THE ELECTRIC CIRCUS | Capitol EST 2025 |
| 26/09/1987 | 23 | 4 | | LIVE IN THE RAW | Capitol EST 2040 |
| 15/04/1989 | 8 | 10 | O | **THE HEADLESS CHILDREN** | Capitol EST 2087 |
| 20/06/1992 | 21 | 2 | | THE CRIMSON IDOL | Parlophone CDPCSD 118 |
| 06/11/1993 | 69 | 1 | | FIRST BLOOD… LAST CUTS | Capitol CDESTFG 2217 |
| 01/07/1995 | 52 | 1 | | STILL NOT BLACK ENOUGH | Raw Power RAWCD 103 |

## WATERBOYS
UK rock group formed in London in 1981 by Mike Scott (born 14/12/1958, Edinburgh, guitar/vocals) and Anthony Thistlewaite (born 31/8/1955, Leicester, multi-instrumentalist), signing with Ensign. They later added guitarist Karl Wallinger (born 19/10/1957, Prestatyn, Wales), fiddler Steve Wickham and drummer Kevin Wilkinson. Wallinger left in 1986, forming World Party.

| DATE | POS | WKS | BPI | ALBUM TITLE | LABEL & NUMBER |
|------|-----|-----|-----|-------------|----------------|
| 16/06/1984 | 100 | 1 | | A PAGAN PLACE | Ensign ENCL 3 |
| 28/09/1985 | 37 | 17 | O | THIS IS THE SEA | Ensign ENCL 5 |
| 29/10/1988 | 13 | 19 | ● | FISHERMAN'S BLUES | Ensign CHEN 5 |
| 22/09/1990 | 5 | 6 | | **ROOM TO ROAM** | Ensign CHEN 16 |
| 11/05/1991 | 2 | 16 | ● | **BEST OF THE WATERBOYS '81–'91** | Ensign CHEN 19 |
| 05/06/1993 | 5 | 10 | O | **DREAM HARDER** | Geffen GED 24476 |
| 07/10/2000 | 47 | 1 | | A ROCK IN THE WEARY LAND | RCA 74321783052 |
| 21/07/2001 | 57 | 1 | | THIS IS THE SEA | Ensign CCD 1543 |
| 21/06/2003 | 74 | 1 | | UNIVERSAL HALL | Puck PUCK1 |

## WATERFRONT
UK duo formed in Cardiff, South Glamorgan with singer Chris Duffy and guitarist Phil Cilla

| DATE | POS | WKS | BPI | ALBUM TITLE | LABEL & NUMBER |
|------|-----|-----|-----|-------------|----------------|
| 12/08/1989 | 45 | 3 | | WATERFRONT | Polydor 8379701 |

## ROGER WATERS
UK singer (born 6/9/1944, Great Bookham) who was a founder member of Pink Floyd in 1965, leaving the group in 1983. He first recorded solo in 1970 with the soundtrack to *The Body*.

| DATE | POS | WKS | BPI | ALBUM TITLE | LABEL & NUMBER |
|------|-----|-----|-----|-------------|----------------|
| 12/05/1984 | 13 | 11 | | THE PROS AND CONS OF HITCH-HIKING | Harvest SHVL 240105 |
| 27/06/1987 | 25 | 7 | | RADIO K.A.O.S | EMI KAOS 1 |
| 22/09/1990 | 27 | 3 | | THE WALL – LIVE IN BERLIN **ROGER WATERS AND VARIOUS ARTISTS** | Mercury 8466111 |
| 19/09/1992 | 8 | 4 | O | **AMUSED TO DEATH** | Columbia 4687612 |

## ADAM WATKISS
UK singer who was a carpenter before winning TV talent contest *This Is The Moment*. He was previously in I.D.O.L.S. (The Infirmary Dramatic, Operatic and Literary Society) in Leicester with sisters Kate and Sarah. He performed at the 2001 Royal Variety Show.

| DATE | POS | WKS | BPI | ALBUM TITLE | LABEL & NUMBER |
|------|-----|-----|-----|-------------|----------------|
| 15/12/2001 | 65 | 3 | O | THIS IS THE MOMENT | UMTV/Decca 0166082 |

## JODY WATLEY
US singer (born 30/1/1959, Chicago, IL) who was a dancer on TV's *Soul Train* and then a singer with Shalamar from 1978 until 1983, when she went solo. She won the 1987 Grammy Award for Best New Artist.

| DATE | POS | WKS | BPI | ALBUM TITLE | LABEL & NUMBER |
|------|-----|-----|-----|-------------|----------------|
| 05/09/1987 | 62 | 2 | | JODY WATLEY | MCA MCG 6024 |
| 27/05/1989 | 39 | 2 | | LARGER THAN LIFE | MCA MCG 6044 |

## NIGEL WATSON AND THE SPLINTER GROUP – see PETER GREEN

## RUSSELL WATSON
UK operatic singer (born 20/11/1966, although he routinely knocks six years off his age); his debut album *The Voice* went double platinum in March 2001 (sales in excess of 600,000), the first classical album to do so since 1998.

| DATE | POS | WKS | BPI | ALBUM TITLE | LABEL & NUMBER |
|------|-----|-----|-----|-------------|----------------|
| 07/10/2000 | 5 | 36 | ✪² | **THE VOICE** 2001 Classical BRIT Awards for Best Selling Debut Album and Album of the Year | Decca 4672512 |
| 10/11/2001 | 6 | 21 | ✪² | **ENCORE** | Decca 4703002 |
| 30/11/2002 | 13 | 8 | ✪ | REPRISE | Decca 4731002 |

## WAX
US/UK duo formed by Andrew Gold (born 2/8/1951, Burbank, CA) and Graham Gouldman (born 10/5/1946, Manchester). Gold had previously enjoyed solo success while Gouldman had been in Hotlegs, a group that evolved into 10 CC.

| DATE | POS | WKS | BPI | ALBUM TITLE | LABEL & NUMBER |
|------|-----|-----|-----|-------------|----------------|
| 12/09/1987 | 59 | 3 | | AMERICAN ENGLISH | RCA PL 71430 |

## ANTHONY WAY
UK singer (born 1982, London) who was discovered as a soprano chorister at St Paul's Cathedral choir and appeared in the role of Henry Ashworth in the TV production *The Choir*. His debut hit album also featured the choir of Gloucester Cathedral whilst *Wings Of A Dove* was recorded with his friends and teachers in Uppingham.

| DATE | POS | WKS | BPI | ALBUM TITLE | LABEL & NUMBER |
|------|-----|-----|-----|-------------|----------------|
| 08/04/1995 | 3 | 12 | ● | **THE CHOIR – MUSIC FROM THE TV SERIES ANTHONY WAY AND STANISLAS SYREWICZ** | Decca 4481652 |

▲⁹ Number of weeks album topped the US chart  ◆¹² RIAA Diamond Awards  ◇³ IFPI Platinum Europe Awards

| | | | | | |
|---|---|---|---|---|---|
| 09/12/1995 | 61 | 3 | ○ | THE CHOIRBOY | Permanent PERMCD 41 |
| 14/12/1996 | 59 | 3 | | THE CHOIRBOY'S CHRISTMAS | Decca 4550502 |
| 15/03/1997 | 69 | 1 | | WINGS OF A DOVE | Decca 4556452 |

### WAY OUT WEST
UK dance duo formed by Nick Warren and Jody Wisternoff, both of whom began as DJs. The pair first got together in 1993 and signed with Deconstruction in 1994.

| | | | | | |
|---|---|---|---|---|---|
| 13/09/1997 | 42 | 1 | | WAY OUT WEST | Deconstruction 74321501952 |
| 01/09/2001 | 61 | 1 | | INTENSIFY | Distinctive Breaks DISNCD 76 |

### JEFF WAYNE
US producer/songwriter/keyboard player (born in NYC) who was David Essex's producer in the 1970s. His debut hit album was a musical adaptation of HG Wells' classic novel featuring narration by Richard Burton and contributions from David Essex, Justin Hayward, Julie Covington and Phil Lynott among others. *Spartacus* featured contributions from Jimmy Helms, Anthony Hopkins, Incantation, Catherine Zeta Jones, Alan King, Ladysmith Black Mambazo, Jo Partridge and Chris Thompson.

| | | | | | |
|---|---|---|---|---|---|
| 01/07/1978 | 5 | 235 | ✪4 | JEFF WAYNE'S MUSICAL VERSION OF THE WAR OF THE WORLDS | CBS 96000 |
| 13/10/1984 | 64 | 6 | | BEYOND THE PLANETS **KEVIN PEEK & RICK WAKEMAN FEATURING JEFF WAYNE NARRATION PATRICK ALLEN** | Telstar STAR 2244 |
| 03/10/1992 | 36 | 2 | | SPARTACUS | Columbia 4720302 |
| 06/07/1996 | 23 | 21 | | JEFF WAYNE'S MUSICAL VERSION OF THE WAR OF THE WORLDS | Columbia CDX 96000 |
| 19/10/1996 | 64 | 2 | | HIGHLIGHTS FROM JEFF WAYNE'S MUSICAL VERSION OF THE WAR OF THE WORLDS | Columbia 32356 |
| 22/04/2000 | 64 | 1 | | JEFF WAYNE'S MUSICAL VERSION OF THE WAR OF THE WORLDS – ULLADUBULLA – THE REMIX ALBUM | Columbia SONYTV 74CD |

### WAYSTED
UK rock group formed in 1982 by Pete Way (bass), Ian 'Fin' Muir (vocals), Ronnie Kayfield (guitar), Paul Raymond (guitar/keyboards) and Frank Noon (drums). Way had previously been in UFO and then Fastway before forming Waysted. Raymond was fired after their first album, replaced by Barry Benedetta, who lasted one tour before he too was fired, along with Kayfield and Noon. Neil Shepherd (guitar) lasted for one album before being replaced by Paul Chapman. Other members along the way have included Jimmy DiLella (guitar /keyboards), Jerry Shirley (drums), Johnny DiTeodora (drums), Danny Vaughan (vocals), Erik Gamans (guitar), Jon Deverill (vocals) before the band dissolved in 1987. Way then rejoined a revived UFO.

| | | | | | |
|---|---|---|---|---|---|
| 08/10/1983 | 78 | 3 | | VICES | Chrysalis CHR 1438 |
| 22/09/1984 | 73 | 2 | | WAYSTED | Music For Nations MFN 31 |

### WEATHER PROPHETS
UK group formed by Pete Astor (guitar/vocals), Greenwood Goulding (bass), Ooisin Little (bass) and Dave Morgan (drums).

| | | | | | |
|---|---|---|---|---|---|
| 09/05/1987 | 67 | 2 | | MAYFLOWER | Elevation ELV 1 |

### WEATHER REPORT
US jazz-rock group formed by Joe Zawinul (born 7/7/1932, Vienna, Austria, keyboards), Wayne Shorter (born 25/8/1933, Newark, NJ, reeds), Airto Moreira (born 5/8/1941, Itaipolis, Brazil, percussion) and Miroslav Vitous (born 6/12/1947, Prague, Czechoslovakia, bass). Zawinul and Shorter had previously been in Miles Davis' band, and later added Eric Gavatt (drums) and Um Romao (percussion) to the Weather Report line-up. Jaco Pastorius (born John Francis Pastorius, 1/12/1951, Norristown, PA, bass) joined in 1976 and left in 1982. They dissolved in 1986 with Zawinul forming Weather Update with Steve Khan (guitar) and Pete Erskine (drums). The group has won one Grammy Award: Best Jazz Fusion Performance Vocal or Instrumental in 1979 for *8.30*.

| | | | | | |
|---|---|---|---|---|---|
| 23/04/1977 | 43 | 6 | | HEAVY WEATHER | CBS 81775 |
| 11/11/1978 | 47 | 3 | | MR. GONE | CBS 82775 |
| 27/02/1982 | 88 | 2 | | WEATHER REPORT | CBS 85326 |
| 24/03/1984 | 54 | 1 | | DOMINO THEORY | CBS 25839 |

### MARTI WEBB
UK singer (born 1944, London) who was selected by composer Andrew Lloyd-Webber and lyricist Don Black to front the TV musical *Tell Me On A Sunday,* Webber's first project after his split with Tim Rice. She had previously replaced Elaine Paige in *Evita*.

| | | | | | |
|---|---|---|---|---|---|
| 16/02/1980 | 2 | 23 | ● | TELL ME ON A SUNDAY | Polydor POLD 5031 |
| 28/09/1985 | 55 | 4 | | ENCORE | Starblend BLEND 1 |
| 06/12/1986 | 65 | 5 | | ALWAYS THERE | BBC REB 619 |
| 10/10/1992 | 55 | 1 | | THE MAGIC OF THE MUSICALS **MARTI WEBB AND MARK RATTRAY** | Quality Television QTV 013 |

### WEDDING PRESENT
UK rock group formed in 1984 by David Gedge (born 23/4/1960, Leeds, guitar/vocals), Pete Solowka (born in Manchester, guitar), Keith Gregory (born 2/1/1963, Darlington, bass) and Paul Charman (born in Brighton, drums). Debuting on their own Reception label, they signed with RCA in 1989. Charman left soon after their debut and was replaced by Simon Smith (born 3/5/1965, Lincolnshire). Solowka left in 1991 and was replaced by Paul Dorrington. In 1992 they released a single a month, each making the top 40 for one week. Their album *Mini* was not listed in *Music Week* as it was originally considered a budget release. The chart was amended the following week to compensate.

| | | | | | |
|---|---|---|---|---|---|
| 24/10/1987 | 47 | 2 | | GEORGE BEST | Reception LEEDS 001 |
| 23/07/1988 | 42 | 3 | | TOMMY | Reception LEEDS 2 |
| 29/04/1989 | 22 | 3 | | UKRAINSKI VISTUIP V JOHNA PEELA | RCA PL 74104 |
| 04/11/1989 | 22 | 3 | | BIZZARO | RCA PL 74302 |

| DATE | POS | WKS | BPI | ALBUM TITLE | LABEL & NUMBER |
|------|-----|-----|-----|-------------|----------------|
| 08/06/1991 | 13 | 3 | | SEA MONSTERS | RCA PL 75012 |
| 20/06/1992 | 22 | 2 | | HIT PARADE 1 | RCA PD 75343 |
| 16/01/1993 | 19 | 2 | | HIT PARADE 2 | RCA 74321127752 |
| 24/09/1994 | 47 | 1 | | WATUSI | Island CID 8014 |
| 03/02/1996 | 40 | 1 | | MINI | Cooking Vinyl COOKCD 094 |
| 21/09/1996 | 36 | 1 | | SATURNALIA | Cooking Vinyl COOKCD 099 |

**WEE PAPA GIRL RAPPERS** UK rap duo Ty Tim and Total S (real names Samantha and Sandra Lawrence).

| DATE | POS | WKS | BPI | ALBUM TITLE | LABEL & NUMBER |
|------|-----|-----|-----|-------------|----------------|
| 05/11/1988 | 39 | 3 | | THE BEAT, THE RHYME AND THE NOISE | Jive HIP 67 |

**BERT WEEDON** UK guitarist (born 10/5/1921, London) who made his recording debut for Parlophone in 1956. He then became an in-demand session musician and signed with the Top Rank label in 1959.

| DATE | POS | WKS | BPI | ALBUM TITLE | LABEL & NUMBER |
|------|-----|-----|-----|-------------|----------------|
| 16/07/1960 | 18 | 1 | | KING SIZE GUITAR | Top Rank BUY 026 |
| 23/10/1976 | ❶[1] | 25 | ● | **22 GOLDEN GUITAR GREATS** | Warwick WW 5019 |

**WEEZER** US rock group formed in Los Angeles, CA in 1992 by Rivers Cuomo (born 1971, Connecticut, guitar/vocals), Brian Bell (born in Tennessee, guitar), Matt Sharp (bass) and Patrick Wilson (born in Buffalo, NY, drums). They signed with DGC Records in June 1993.

| DATE | POS | WKS | BPI | ALBUM TITLE | LABEL & NUMBER |
|------|-----|-----|-----|-------------|----------------|
| 04/03/1995 | 23 | 11 | | WEEZER | Geffen GED 24629 |
| 12/10/1996 | 43 | 1 | | PINKERTON | Geffen GED 25007 |
| 26/05/2001 | 31 | 4 | | THE GREEN ALBUM | Geffen 4930612 |
| 25/05/2002 | 16 | 3 | | MALADROIT | Geffen 4933252 |

**GILLIAN WELCH** US singer/guitarist (born 1968, Los Angeles, CA); she attended the Berklee School of Music in Boston, MA and made her debut album in 1996.

| DATE | POS | WKS | BPI | ALBUM TITLE | LABEL & NUMBER |
|------|-----|-----|-----|-------------|----------------|
| 14/06/2003 | 65 | 1 | | SOUL JOURNEY | WEA 5046668682 |

**PAUL WELLER** UK singer (born John Paul Weller, 25/5/1958, Woking) who was a founder member of the Jam in 1976 and also wrote most of their material. They split in 1982 and Weller formed the Style Council with Mick Talbot, later adding Weller's wife Dee C Lee (born Diane Sealey). He launched the Respond label with artists such as The Questions and Tracie Young. Weller disbanded the Style Council in 1989 and emerged in 1990 with the Paul Weller Movement. He was named Best British Male at the 1995 and 1996 BRIT Awards.

| DATE | POS | WKS | BPI | ALBUM TITLE | LABEL & NUMBER |
|------|-----|-----|-----|-------------|----------------|
| 12/09/1992 | 8 | 7 | | **PAUL WELLER** | Go Discs 8283432 |
| 18/09/1993 | 2 | 51 | ✪ | **WILD WOOD** | Go Discs 8284352 |
| 24/09/1994 | 13 | 5 | | LIVE WOOD | Go Discs 8285612 |
| 27/05/1995 | ❶[1] | 87 | ✪[4] | **STANLEY ROAD** ◇ | Go Discs 8286192 |
| 05/07/1997 | 2 | 13 | ● | **HEAVY SOUL** | Island CID 8058 |
| 21/11/1998 | 7 | 19 | ✪ | **MODERN CLASSICS – THE GREATEST HITS** | Island CID 8080 |
| 22/04/2000 | 2 | 8 | ● | **HELIOCENTRIC** | Island CID 8093 |
| 20/10/2001 | 3 | 16 | ✪ | **DAYS OF SPEED** | Independiente ISOM 26CD |
| 28/09/2002 | ❶[1] | 7 | ● | **ILLUMINATION** | Independiente ISOM 33CDL |
| 06/09/2003 | 22 | 3 | | FLY ON THE WALL – B SIDES & RARITIES | Island 0635272 |

**WENDY AND LISA** US soul duo Wendy Melvoin (born 1964, guitar) and Lisa Coleman (born 1960, keyboards), who teamed up in 1986 following the demise of Prince's backing group the Revolution. They had been childhood friends in Los Angeles, CA.

| DATE | POS | WKS | BPI | ALBUM TITLE | LABEL & NUMBER |
|------|-----|-----|-----|-------------|----------------|
| 10/10/1987 | 84 | 2 | | WENDY AND LISA | Virgin V 2444 |
| 18/03/1989 | 45 | 2 | | FRUIT AT THE BOTTOM | Virgin V 2580 |
| 04/08/1990 | 33 | 3 | | EROICA | Virgin V 2633 |

**KANYE WEST** US rapper born in Chicago, IL, he first worked with Roc-A-Fella as a producer before going solo.

| DATE | POS | WKS | BPI | ALBUM TITLE | LABEL & NUMBER |
|------|-----|-----|-----|-------------|----------------|
| 28/02/2004 | 13 | 18+ | ● | THE COLLEGE DROPOUT | Roc-A-Fella 9861739 |

**HAYLEY WESTENRA** New Zealand singer (born 1987, Christchurch); she was discovered at the age of eleven.

| DATE | POS | WKS | BPI | ALBUM TITLE | LABEL & NUMBER |
|------|-----|-----|-----|-------------|----------------|
| 27/09/2003 | 7 | 24 | ✪[2] | **PURE** | Decca 4753302 |

---

▲[9] Number of weeks album topped the US chart   ◆[12] RIAA Diamond Awards   ◇[3] IFPI Platinum Europe Awards

**WESTLIFE** Irish vocal group formed by Nicky Byrne (born 9/10/1978, Dublin), Shane Filan (born 5/7/1979, Sligo), Kian Egan (born 29/4/1980, Sligo), Bryan McFadden (born 12/4/1980, Dublin) and Mark Feehily (born 28/5/1980, Sligo). Called Westside, they had to change their name because of a US group of the same name. Co-managed by Boyzone's Ronan Keating, they were the first 'boy band' to have their first two hit singles enter the charts at #1. They were also the first group to have their first seven singles all hit #1 (and achieving seven #1s quicker than any other act ever, including Elvis Presley). They were named Best Pop Act at the 2001 and 2002 BRIT Awards, having previously won the Select UK & Ireland Award at the 2000 MTV Europe Music Awards. McFadden left in March 2004, with the group subsequently announcing a TV reality competition to find a replacement for the recording of their next album.

| | | | | |
|---|---|---|---|---|
| 13/11/1999 | .....2 | .....69 | .....✪⁴ | WESTLIFE ◇² ................................................................RCA 74321713212 |
| 18/11/2000 | ...❶¹ | .....28 | .....✪⁶ | COAST TO COAST ◇² .......................................................RCA 74321808312 |
| 24/11/2001 | ...❶¹ | .....35 | .....✪⁴ | WORLD OF OUR OWN ◇² ...................................................RCA 74321903082 |
| 23/11/2002 | ...❶¹ | .....34 | .....✪⁴ | UNBREAKABLE – THE GREATEST HITS VOLUME 1 ...............................S 74321975902 |
| 06/12/2003 | ...❶¹ | .....18 | .....✪² | TURNAROUND ◇ .............................................................S 82876557412 |

**WESTMINSTER ABBEY CHOIR/CONDUCTOR: MARTIN NEARY** UK choir.

| | | | |
|---|---|---|---|
| 20/09/1997 | .....34 | ......4 | JOHN TAVERNER: INNOCENCE ............................................Sony Classical SK 66613 |
| 12/09/1998 | .....58 | .....3 | PERFECT PEACE ....................................................Sony Classical SONYTV 49CDS |

**WESTWORLD** UK/US vocal/instrumental group formed by Derwood Andrews, Elizabeth Westwood and Ralph Jezzard.

| | | | |
|---|---|---|---|
| 05/09/1987 | .....49 | ......2 | WHERE THE ACTION IS .........................................................RCA PL 71429 |

**WET WET WET** UK group formed in Glasgow in 1982 by Graeme Clark (born 15/4/1966, Glasgow, bass), Tom Cunningham (born 22/6/1965, Glasgow, drums), Neil Mitchell (born 8/6/1967, Helensburgh, keyboards) and Marti Pellow (born Mark McLoughlin, 23/3/1966, Clydebank, vocals) as Vortex Motion. They launched the Precious Organisation label in 1984, signing with Phonogram in 1985. They were named Best British Newcomer at the 1988 BRIT Awards. Cunningham was sacked in 1997 and Pellow went solo in 1999. They took their name from a line in the Scritti Politti song *Getting Having And Holding*.

| | | | | |
|---|---|---|---|---|
| 03/10/1987 | ...❶¹ | .....72 | .....✪⁵ | POPPED IN SOULED OUT ........................................Precious Organisation JWWWL 1 |
| 19/11/1988 | .....3 | .....13 | .....✪ | THE MEMPHIS SESSIONS .......................................Precious Organisation JWWWL 2 |
| 11/11/1989 | .....2 | .....26 | .....✪² | HOLDING BACK THE RIVER .....................................Precious Organisation 8420111 |
| 08/02/1992 | ...❶² | .....25 | .....✪ | HIGH ON THE HAPPY SIDE ......................................Precious Organisation 5104272 |
| 29/05/1993 | ...10 | ......4 | | LIVE AT THE ROYAL ALBERT HALL ............................Precious Organisation 5147742 |
| 20/11/1993 | ...❶⁵ | .....67 | .....✪⁴ | END OF PART ONE (THEIR GREATEST HITS) ◇³ ................Precious Organisation 5184772 |
| 22/04/1995 | ...❶³ | .....45 | .....✪³ | PICTURE THIS ◇ ..............................................Precious Organisation 5268512 |
| 12/04/1997 | .....2 | .....26 | .....✪ | 10 .......................................................Precious Organisation 5363192 |

**WE'VE GOT A FUZZBOX AND WE'RE GONNA USE IT** UK rock group formed in Birmingham in 1985 by Maggie Dunne (vocals/keyboards/guitar), Jo Dunne (bass/piano), Vickie Perks (vocals) and Tina O'Neill (drums). Later called just Fuzzbox, they disbanded in 1990.

| | | | |
|---|---|---|---|
| 26/08/1989 | .....5 | ......6 | .......O | BIG BANG .......................................................................WEA WX 282 |

**WHALE** Swedish group formed by Cia Berg (vocals), her fiancé Henrik Schyffert (guitar) and Gordon Cyrus (bass). They said their debut hit *Hobo Humpin' Slobo Babe* was dedicated to 'affluent women who bring homeless men home to have their way with them'. The accompanying video won director Mark Pellington the 1994 MTV Europe Music Award for Best Director.

| | | | |
|---|---|---|---|
| 12/08/1995 | .....42 | ......2 | WE CARE ........................................................................Hut DGHUT 25 |

**WHAM!** UK pop group formed in 1981 by George Michael (born Georgios Panayiotou, 25/6/1963, Bushey) and Andrew Ridgeley (born 26/1/1963, Bushey). Signed by Innervision in 1982, they recruited backing singers Shirlie Holliman (born 18/4/1962, Watford) and Mandy Washburn (soon replaced by Dee C Lee, born Diane Sealey) in 1984. They switched to Epic in 1984 following a court case against Innervision, by which time Dee C Lee had gone solo and been replaced by Pepsi DeMacque (born 10/12/1958, London). They split in 1986 with a farewell concert at Wembley Stadium, Michael and Ridgeley later recording solo, while Pepsi and Shirlie also recorded as a duo. Michael and Ridgeley reunited for a concert in Rio in 1991. They were named Best British Group at the 1985 BRIT Awards and picked up an Outstanding Contribution Award at the 1986 ceremony, jointly with Elton John.

| | | | | |
|---|---|---|---|---|
| 09/07/1983 | ...❶² | .....116 | .....✪³ | FANTASTIC! .............................................................Inner Vision IVL 25328 |
| 18/11/1984 | ...❶² | .....72 | .....✪⁴ | MAKE IT BIG ▲³ ...............................................................Epic EPC 86311 |
| 19/07/1986 | .....2 | .....47 | .....✪ | THE FINAL ....................................................................Epic EPC 88681 |
| 06/12/1997 | .....4 | .....24 | .....✪² | THE BEST OF WHAM!... IF YOU WERE THERE ◇ ..................................Epic 4890202 |

**WHEATUS** US rock group formed in Long Island, NY by Brendan Brown (guitar/vocals), Rich Leigey (bass), Phil A Jimenez (guitar) and Peter Brown (Brendan's brother, drums). Leigey was replaced by Mike McCabe in July 2000.

| 03/03/2001 | 7 | 30 | ● | WHEATUS | Columbia 4996052 |
|---|---|---|---|---|---|

**CARON WHEELER** UK singer (born 19/1/1963, London), in Soul II Soul before going solo with RCA. She won a 1989 Grammy Award with Soul II Soul for Best Rhythm & Blues Vocal Performance by a Group for *Back To Life (However Do You Want Me)*.

| 13/10/1990 | 14 | 5 | O | UK BLAK | RCA PL 74751 |
|---|---|---|---|---|---|

**BILL WHELAN** Irish composer Bill Whelan fronting the RTE Orchestra. The riverdance first came to prominence during the 1994 Eurovision Song Contest when Ireland, represented by Paul Harrington and Charlie McGettigan, had triumphed with *Rock 'N' Roll Kids*, prompting a number of riverdance shows across the country.

| 25/03/1995 | 31 | 38 | ✪ | MUSIC FROM RIVERDANCE – THE SHOW | Celtic Heartbeat 75678061112 |
|---|---|---|---|---|---|

**WHIGFIELD** Danish model (born Sannie Charlotte Carlson, 11/4/1970, Skaelskor); she became the first artist to debut on the singles chart at number one with *Saturday Night*.

| 01/07/1995 | 13 | 7 | O | WHIGFIELD | Systematic 8286512 |
|---|---|---|---|---|---|

**WHISPERS** US R&B vocal group formed in Los Angeles, CA in 1964 by Wallace Scott (born 23/9/1943, Fort Worth, TX ), his twin brother Walter, Nicholas Caldwell (born 5/4/1944, Loma Linda, CA), Marcus Hutson (born 8/1/1943, Kansas City, MO) and Gordy Harmon. They first recorded for Dore in 1964, with their R&B chart breakthrough on Janus in 1970. They signed to Soul Train in 1975, by which time Harmon had left, replaced by Leavell Degree (born 31/7/1948, New Orleans, LA). Soul Train became Solar (Sound of Los Angeles Records) in 1977. The group later signed with Capitol Records.

| 14/03/1981 | 42 | 5 | | IMAGINATION | Solar SOLA 7 |
|---|---|---|---|---|---|
| 06/06/1987 | 63 | 4 | | JUST GETS BETTER WITH TIME | Solar MCF 3381 |

**ALAN WHITE** UK drummer (born 14/6/1949, Pelton, Durham), previously with saxophonist Johnny Almond, guitarist Steve Howe and Bell And Arc, and replaced Bill Bruford in Yes.

| 13/03/1976 | 41 | 4 | | RAMSHACKLED | Atlantic K 50217 |
|---|---|---|---|---|---|

**BARRY WHITE** US singer/producer (born 12/9/1944, Galveston, TX) who formed the Atlantics in 1963 and then (with Carl Carlton) the Majestics in 1964. His first solo singles were for Downey in 1965 and Jeep (as Barry Lee) before becoming A&R man for Mustang and Bronco in 1966. Discovering Love Unlimited in 1968, he formed a production company to handle them, linking with 20th Century Records in 1972. He first recorded as Barry White in 1973, forming the Love Unlimited Orchestra in 1974. As a youth he served three months in prison for stealing 300 tyres from a car dealer. Early in his career he wrote songs for *The Banana Splits* TV series. He published an autobiography *Insights On Life & Love* (1999). Grammy Awards were Best Male Rhythm & Blues Vocal Performance and Best Rhythm & Blues Traditional Vocal Performance in 1999, both for *Staying Power*. He died from kidney failure on 4/7/2003.

| 09/03/1974 | 18 | 17 | ● | STONE GON' | Pye NSPL 28186 |
|---|---|---|---|---|---|
| 02/11/1974 | 4 | 34 | ● | **CAN'T GET ENOUGH** ▲[1] | 20th Century BT 444 |
| 26/04/1975 | 12 | 15 | O | JUST ANOTHER WAY TO SAY I LOVE YOU | 20th Century BT 466 |
| 22/11/1975 | 18 | 12 | ● | GREATEST HITS | 20th Century BTH 8000 |
| 21/02/1976 | 22 | 14 | O | LET THE MUSIC PLAY | 20th Century BT 502 |
| 09/04/1977 | 17 | 7 | | BARRY WHITE'S GREATEST HITS VOLUME 2 | 20th Century BTH 8001 |
| 10/02/1979 | 46 | 4 | | THE MAN | 20th Century BT 571 |
| 21/12/1985 | 34 | 10 | O | HEART AND SOUL | K-Tel NE 1316 |
| 17/10/1987 | 74 | 6 | | THE RIGHT NIGHT AND BARRY WHITE | Breakout AMA 5154 |
| 02/07/1988 | 5 | 116 | ✪[5] | **THE COLLECTION** ◇[4] The album changed its label and catalogue number to 8347902 during its chart run. It was this version that qualified for an IFPI Platinum Europe Award | Mercury BWTV 1 |
| 11/02/1995 | 44 | 3 | | THE ICON IS LOVE | A&M 5402802 |
| 15/02/2003 | 21 | 3 | | LOVE SONGS | Universal TV 0686422 |

**KARYN WHITE** US singer (born 14/10/1965, Los Angeles, CA) who was a touring backing singer with O'Bryan and recorded with Jeff Lorber in 1986. She landed a solo deal with Warner's in 1988 and is married to producer Terry Lewis.

| 11/03/1989 | 20 | 27 | ● | KARYN WHITE | Warner Brothers WX 235 |
|---|---|---|---|---|---|
| 21/09/1991 | 31 | 3 | | RITUAL OF LOVE | Warner Brothers WX 411 |

**SNOWY WHITE** UK singer/guitarist (raised on the Isle of Wight) who played guitar with Pink Floyd's live band. He worked with Peter Green and joined Thin Lizzy in 1979. He left in 1982 to go solo.

| 11/02/1984 | 21 | 4 | | WHITE FLAMES | Towerbell TOWLP 3 |
|---|---|---|---|---|---|
| 09/02/1985 | 88 | 1 | | SNOWY WHITE | Towerbell TOWLP 8 |

**TONY JOE WHITE** US singer (born 23/7/1943, Oak Grove, LA) who, as a songwriter, penned Brook Benton's US hit *Rainy Night In Georgia* and *Polk Salad Annie*, later a hit for Elvis Presley.

| 26/09/1970 | 63 | 1 | | TONY JOE | CBS 63800 |
|---|---|---|---|---|---|

### WHITE LION
US rock group formed in New York City by Mike Tramp (vocals), Vito Bratta (guitar), James Lomenzo (bass) and Greg D'Angelo (drums). Lomenzo and D'Angelo left in 1991, replaced by Tommy Caradonna and Jimmy DeGrasso respectively.

| | POS | WKS | | ALBUM TITLE | LABEL & NUMBER |
|---|---|---|---|---|---|
| 01/07/1989 | 47 | 1 | | BIG GAME | Atlantic WX 277 |
| 20/04/1991 | 31 | 2 | | MANE ATTRACTION | Atlantic WX 415 |

### WHITE STRIPES
US rock duo formed in Detroit, MI in 1997 by (apparent) brother and sister Jack (born 9/7/1975, guitar/vocals) and Meg White (born 16/12/1974, drums). They later revealed they weren't brother and sister but husband and wife, their 1996 marriage certificate showing Jack's real name to be John Anthony Gillis. They divorced in March 2000. They were awarded the 2003 MTV Europe Music Award for Best Rock Act. They won two Grammy Awards in 2003 including Best Rock Song for *7 Nation Army*. They were named Best International Group at the 2004 BRIT Awards.

| | POS | WKS | | ALBUM TITLE | LABEL & NUMBER |
|---|---|---|---|---|---|
| 18/08/2001 | 55 | 17 | ● | WHITE BLOOD CELLS | Sympathy For The Record Industry SFTRI 660CD |
| 12/04/2003 | ❶² | 46 | ✪² | **ELEPHANT** 2003 Grammy Award for Best Alternative Music Album | XL Recordings XLCD 162 |

### WHITE ZOMBIE
US group formed by Rob Zombie (born Rob Straker, 12/1/1966, vocals), Tom Guay (guitar), Sean Yseult (bass) and Ivan DePlume (drums). Guay was later replaced by John Ricci.

| | POS | WKS | | ALBUM TITLE | LABEL & NUMBER |
|---|---|---|---|---|---|
| 27/05/1995 | 25 | 6 | | ASTRO CREEP 2000 – SONGS OF LOVE, DESTRUCTION AND OTHER SYNTHETIC DELUSIONS OF THE ELECTRIC HEAD | Geffen GED 24806 |

### WHITEOUT
UK vocal/instrumental group formed by Andrew Caldwell, Paul Carroll, Eric Lindsay and Stuart Smith.

| | POS | WKS | | ALBUM TITLE | LABEL & NUMBER |
|---|---|---|---|---|---|
| 01/07/1995 | 71 | 1 | | BITE IT | Silvertone ORECD 536 |

### WHITESNAKE
UK heavy rock group formed in 1978 by David Coverdale (born 22/9/1949, Saltburn-by-the-Sea, Cleveland, vocals), Mickey Moody (guitar), Bernie Marsden (guitar), Brian Johnston (keyboards), Neil Murray (bass) and John Dowie (drums). Coverdale had been in Deep Purple, leaving them in 1976 and making two solo albums as Whitesnake. Marsden later recorded solo.

| | POS | WKS | | ALBUM TITLE | LABEL & NUMBER |
|---|---|---|---|---|---|
| 18/11/1978 | 50 | 2 | | TROUBLE | EMI International INS 3022 |
| 13/10/1979 | 29 | 7 | | LOVE HUNTER | United Artists UAG 30264 |
| 07/06/1980 | 6 | 15 | ● | **READY AND WILLING** | United Artists UAG 30302 |
| 08/11/1980 | 5 | 15 | ✪ | **LIVE AT THE HEART OF THE CITY** | United Artists SNAKE 1 |
| 18/04/1981 | 2 | 23 | ● | **COME AN' GET IT** | Liberty LBG 30327 |
| 27/11/1982 | 9 | 9 | ○ | **SAINTS 'N' SINNERS** | Liberty LBG 30354 |
| 11/02/1984 | 9 | 7 | | **SLIDE IT IN** | Liberty LBG 2400001 |
| 11/04/1987 | 8 | 57 | ✪ | **WHITESNAKE 1987** | EMI EMC 3528 |
| 25/11/1989 | 10 | 10 | ● | **SLIP OF THE TONGUE** | EMI EMD 1013 |
| 16/07/1994 | 4 | 12 | ● | **GREATEST HITS** | EMI CDEMD 1065 |
| 21/06/1997 | 34 | 2 | | RESTLESS HEART **DAVID COVERDALE AND WHITESNAKE** | EMI CDEMD 1104 |
| 05/04/2003 | 44 | 3 | | THE BEST OF WHITESNAKE | EMI 5812452 |

### SLIM WHITMAN
US singer (born Otis Dewey Whitman Jr, 20/1/1924, Tampa, FL) who was a shipfitter when he turned professional in 1948. After his UK #1 *Rose Marie*, as one of the first country artists to tour the UK he was largely responsible for introducing country music to UK audiences. His concentration on the UK market marred his US chart career, but he was still having UK album hits into the 1970s. He appeared in the 1957 film *Jamboree* and has a star on the Hollywood Walk of Fame.

| | POS | WKS | | ALBUM TITLE | LABEL & NUMBER |
|---|---|---|---|---|---|
| 14/12/1974 | 44 | 2 | ○ | HAPPY ANNIVERSARY | United Artists UAS 29670 |
| 31/01/1976 | ❶⁶ | 17 | ● | **THE VERY BEST OF SLIM WHITMAN** | United Artists UAS 29898 |
| 15/01/1977 | ❶⁴ | 14 | ● | **RED RIVER VALLEY** | United Artists UAS 29993 |
| 15/10/1977 | 2 | 13 | ● | **HOME ON THE RANGE** | United Artists UATV 30102 |
| 13/01/1979 | 27 | 6 | ● | GHOST RIDERS IN THE SKY | United Artists UATV 30202 |
| 22/12/1979 | 18 | 7 | ● | SLIM WHITMAN'S 20 GREATEST LOVE SONGS | United Artists UAG 30270 |
| 27/09/1997 | 54 | 2 | | THE VERY BEST OF SLIM WHITMAN – 50ᵀᴴ ANNIVERSARY COLLECTION | United Artists CDEMC 3772 |

### ROGER WHITTAKER
Kenyan singer (born 22/3/1936, Nairobi) who came to the UK (his parents were of British origin) to attend university, turning to music after graduating in 1960. He hosted a radio series that led to his biggest hit *The Last Farewell*. He invited listeners to submit lyrics that he would put to music; Ron Webster, a Birmingham silversmith, penned *The Last Farewell*.

| | POS | WKS | | ALBUM TITLE | LABEL & NUMBER |
|---|---|---|---|---|---|
| 27/06/1970 | 23 | 1 | | I DON'T BELIEVE IN IF ANYMORE | Columbia SCX 6404 |

○ Silver disc  ● Gold disc  ✪ Platinum disc (additional platinum units are indicated by a figure following the symbol)  ❶⁹ Number of weeks album topped the UK chart

| | | | | | |
|---|---|---|---|---|---|
| 03/04/1971 | ....45 | ....2 | | NEW WORLD IN THE MORNING | Columbia SCX 6456 |
| 06/09/1975 | ....5 | ....42 | ● | **THE VERY BEST OF ROGER WHITTAKER** | Columbia SCX 6560 |
| 15/05/1976 | ....27 | ....7 | ○ | THE SECOND ALBUM OF THE VERY BEST OF ROGER WHITTAKER | EMI EMC 3117 |
| 09/12/1978 | ....52 | ....5 | | ROGER WHITTAKER SINGS THE HITS | Columbia SCX 6601 |
| 04/08/1979 | ....24 | ....9 | ● | 20 ALL TIME GREATS | Polydor POLTV 8 |
| 07/02/1981 | ....18 | ....14 | ○ | THE ROGER WHITTAKER ALBUM | K-Tel NE 1105 |
| 27/12/1986 | ....89 | ....1 | | SKYE BOAT SONG AND OTHER GREAT SONGS | Tembo TMB 113 |
| 23/05/1987 | ....15 | ....19 | ● | HIS FINEST COLLECTION | Tembo RWTV 1 |
| 23/09/1989 | ....20 | ....10 | ○ | HOME LOVIN' MAN | Tembo RWTV 2 |
| 11/05/1996 | ....74 | ....1 | | A PERFECT DAY – HIS GREATEST HITS AND MORE | RCA 74321371562 |
| 07/02/2004 | ....21 | ....5 | | NOW AND THEN – GREATEST HITS 1964 – 2004 | BMG 82876588332 |

**WHO** UK rock group formed in London in 1962 by Roger Daltrey (born 1/4/1944, London, vocals), Pete Townshend (born 19/5/1945, London, guitar), John Entwistle (born 9/10/1944, London, bass) and Doug Sandom (drums) as the Detours, name-changing to the High Numbers in 1964 and recruiting Keith Moon (born 23/8/1947, London) as drummer. They became The Who in 1964 because manager Kit Lambert thought that 'High Numbers' on a poster would suggest it was a bingo session. They signed with Brunswick in 1965. Moon died on 7/9/1978 from a drug overdose (at Flat 12, 9 Curzon Street, London, the apartment where Mama Cass had died four years previously). He was replaced by ex-Small Faces Kenny Jones (born 16/9/1948, London). In 1979 eleven fans were trampled to death in Cincinnati during a stampede for unreserved seats. Their 1969 album *Tommy* was made into a film in 1975, as was 1973's *Quadrophenia* in 1979. They split in 1983, re-forming for Live Aid in 1985. Entwistle, Daltrey and Townshend reunited in 1989 for a North American tour. They were presented with the Outstanding Contribution Award at the 1988 BRIT Awards, while Pete Townshend was given the Lifetime Achievement Award in 1983. They were inducted into the Rock & Roll Hall of Fame in 1990. The group appeared in an episode of *The Simpsons*, giving a concert on the wall that marked the boundary between Old Springfield and the breakaway city established by Homer Simpson. Entwistle died on 27/6/2002.

| | | | | | |
|---|---|---|---|---|---|
| 25/12/1965 | ....5 | ....11 | | **THE WHO SINGS MY GENERATION** | Brunswick LAT 8616 |
| 17/12/1966 | ....4 | ....17 | | **A QUICK ONE** | Reaction 593002 |
| 13/01/1968 | ....13 | ....11 | | THE WHO SELL-OUT | Track 613002 |
| 07/06/1969 | ....2 | ....9 | | **TOMMY** | Track 613013/4 |
| 06/06/1970 | ....3 | ....21 | | **LIVE AT LEEDS** | Track 2406 001 |
| 11/09/1971 | ❶¹ | ....13 | | **WHO'S NEXT** | Track 2408 102 |
| 18/12/1971 | ....9 | ....8 | | **MEATY, BEATY, BIG AND BOUNCY** | Track 2406 006 |
| 17/11/1973 | ....2 | ....13 | ● | **QUADROPHENIA** | Track 2647 013 |
| 26/10/1974 | ....10 | ....4 | ○ | **ODDS AND SODS** | Track 2406 116 |
| 23/08/1975 | ....30 | ....2 | | TOMMY Original soundtrack to the film | Track 2657 007 |
| 18/10/1975 | ....7 | ....6 | ● | **THE WHO BY NUMBERS** | Polydor 2490 129 |
| 09/10/1976 | ....2 | ....18 | ● | **THE STORY OF THE WHO** | Polydor 2683 069 |
| 09/12/1978 | ....6 | ....9 | ● | **WHO ARE YOU** | Polydor WHOD 5004 |
| 30/06/1979 | ....26 | ....13 | ○ | THE KIDS ARE ALRIGHT Original soundtrack to the film | Polydor 2675 174 |
| 06/10/1979 | ....23 | ....16 | ○ | QUADROPHENIA Original soundtrack to the film | Polydor 2625 037 |
| 25/10/1980 | ....20 | ....7 | | MY GENERATION | Virgin V 2179 |
| 28/03/1981 | ....2 | ....9 | ○ | **FACE DANCES** | Polydor WHOD 5037 |
| 11/09/1982 | ....11 | ....6 | | IT'S HARD | Polydor WHOD 5066 |
| 17/11/1984 | ....48 | ....4 | | WHO'S LAST | MCA WHO 1 |
| 12/10/1985 | ....44 | ....6 | | THE WHO COLLECTION | Impression IMDP 4 |
| 19/03/1988 | ....10 | ....11 | ● | **WHO'S BETTER, WHO'S BEST** | Polydor WTV 1 |
| 19/11/1988 | ....71 | ....4 | ● | THE WHO COLLECTION | Stylus SMR 570 |
| 24/03/1990 | ....59 | ....1 | | JOIN TOGETHER | Virgin VDT 102 |
| 16/07/1994 | ....48 | ....1 | | 30 YEARS OF MAXIMUM R&B | Polydor 5217512 |
| 04/03/1995 | ....59 | ....1 | | LIVE AT LEEDS | Polydor 5271692 |
| 06/07/1996 | ....47 | ....2 | | QUADROPHENIA This and the above hit are re-issues | Polydor 5319712 |
| 24/08/1996 | ....11 | ....6 | ● | MY GENERATION – THE VERY BEST OF THE WHO | Polydor 5331502 |
| 26/02/2000 | ....24 | ....2 | | BBC SESSIONS | BBC Music/Polydor 5477272 |
| 21/09/2002 | ....47 | ....1 | | MY GENERATION | MCA 1129262 |
| 02/11/2002 | ....17 | ....5 | ● | THE ULTIMATE COLLECTION | Polydor 0653002 |
| 12/07/2003 | ....72 | ....1 | | LIVE AT THE ROYAL ALBERT HALL | SPV Recordings SPV09374882 |
| 15/05/2004 | ....5 | ....7+ | | **THEN AND NOW** | Polydor 9866577 |

**JANE WIEDLIN** US singer/songwriter/guitarist (born 20/5/1958, Oconomowoc, WI); she was a guitarist with all-girl group The Go-Go's, who split in 1985.

| | | | | | |
|---|---|---|---|---|---|
| 24/09/1988 | ....48 | ....3 | | FUR | Manhattan MTL 1029 |

**WILCO** US group formed by Daniel Corrigan (vocals), Jeff Tweedy (bass/vocals), John Stirratt (keyboards/vocals), Max Johnston (banjo/fiddle), Lloyd Maines (guitar), Brian Henneman (guitar) and Ken Coomer (drums).

| | | | | | |
|---|---|---|---|---|---|
| 11/07/1998 | ....34 | ....2 | | MERMAID AVENUE **BILLY BRAGG AND WILCO** | Elektra 7559622042 |
| 20/03/1999 | ....38 | ....2 | | SUMMERTEETH | Reprise 9362472822 |
| 10/06/2000 | ....61 | ....1 | | MERMAID AVENUE – VOLUME 2 **BILLY BRAGG AND WILCO** | Elektra 7559625222 |
| 04/05/2002 | ....40 | ....1 | | YANKEE HOTEL FOXTROT | Nonesuch 7559796692 |
| 03/04/2004 | ....50 | ....1 | | A GHOST IS BORN | Nonesuch 7559798092 |

**WILD HORSES** UK group formed by Rick Steier (vocals), John Levesque (guitar/vocals), Chris Lester (bass/vocals), Jeff Pilson (bass), Darren Wharton (keyboards) and James Kottak (drums).

26/04/1980 . . . . .38 . . . . . .4 . . . . . . WILD HORSES . . . . . . . . . . . . . . . . . . . . . . . . . . . . . . . . . . . . . . . . . . . . . . . . . . . . . . . . . . .EMI EMC 3324

**EUGENE WILDE** US singer (born Ronald Bloomfield, Miami, FL) with the family group La Voyage, which became Tight Connection and recorded for TK in the 1970s. Wilde recorded solo in 1979, at the same time that the group changed their name to Simplicious. Both acts were signed to the same label. Wilde later recorded for MCA and as a songwriter penned tracks for the likes of Britney Spears.

08/12/1984 . . . . .67 . . . . . .4 . . . . . . EUGENE WILDE . . . . . . . . . . . . . . . . . . . . . . . . . . . . . . . . . . . . . . . . . . . . . . . . . . . . . . . . . .Fourth & Broadway BRLP 502

**KIM WILDE** UK singer (born Kim Smith, 18/11/1960, London) who began as backing vocalist for her father Marty on live dates. She signed with RAK in 1980, her early material written by brother Ricky and produced by him and Marty, and switched to MCA in 1984. Engaged to Mickie Most's son Calvin Hayes (of Johnny Hates Jazz) for a time, she was named Best British Female at the 1983 BRIT Awards

| | | | | |
|---|---|---|---|---|
| 11/07/1981 . . . . .3 . . . . . .14 . . . . . ● | KIM WILDE . . . . . . . . . . . . . . . . . . . . . . . . . . . . . . . . . . . . . . . . . . . . . . . . . . . . . . . . . . . . . . . .RAK SRAK 544 |
| 22/05/1982 . . .19 . . . . .11 . . . . .○ | SELECT . . . . . . . . . . . . . . . . . . . . . . . . . . . . . . . . . . . . . . . . . . . . . . . . . . . . . . . . . . . . . . . . . . . .RAK SRAK 548 |
| 26/11/1983 . . . . .90 . . . . . .1 . . . . . . | CATCH AS CATCH CAN . . . . . . . . . . . . . . . . . . . . . . . . . . . . . . . . . . . . . . . . . . . . . . . . . . . .RAK SRAK 165408 |
| 17/11/1984 . . . . .66 . . . . . .2 . . . . . . | TEASES AND DARES . . . . . . . . . . . . . . . . . . . . . . . . . . . . . . . . . . . . . . . . . . . . . . . . . . . . . . .MCA MCF 3250 |
| 18/05/1985 . . . . .78 . . . . . .4 . . . . . . | THE VERY BEST OF KIM WILDE . . . . . . . . . . . . . . . . . . . . . . . . . . . . . . . . . . . . . . . . . . . . . . . . .RAK WILDE 1 |
| 15/11/1986 . . . . .73 . . . . . .5 . . . . . . | ANOTHER STEP The album changed its catalogue number to KIML 1 during its chart run . . . . .MCA MCF 3339 |
| 25/06/1988 . . . . .8 . . . . . .38 . . . . .✪ | CLOSE . . . . . . . . . . . . . . . . . . . . . . . . . . . . . . . . . . . . . . . . . . . . . . . . . . . . . . . . . . . . . . . . . .MCA MCG 6030 |
| 26/05/1990 . . . . .37 . . . . . .3 . . . . . . | LOVE MOVES . . . . . . . . . . . . . . . . . . . . . . . . . . . . . . . . . . . . . . . . . . . . . . . . . . . . . . . . . . . . .MCA MCG 6088 |
| 30/05/1992 . . . . .21 . . . . . .3 . . . . . . | LOVE IS . . . . . . . . . . . . . . . . . . . . . . . . . . . . . . . . . . . . . . . . . . . . . . . . . . . . . . . . . . . . . . . .MCA MCAD 10625 |
| 25/09/1993 . . . . .11 . . . . . .7 . . . . . ● | THE SINGLES COLLECTION 1981–1993 . . . . . . . . . . . . . . . . . . . . . . . . . . . . . . . . . . . . . . . . . .MCA MCD 10921 |

**WILDHEARTS** UK group formed by Ginger (born David Walls, 17/12/1964, South Shields, guitar/vocals), Danny McCormack (born 28/2/1972, South Shields, bass/vocals), Jeff Streatham (born 8/6/1973, Southampton, guitar) and Richie Battersby (born 29/6/1968, Birmingham, drums). They originally signed with East West in 1992, consisting of Ginger, Mark Kedds, CJ and Willie Dowling, the latter two going on to form Honeycrack. Danny McCormack is the brother of 3 Colours Red's Chris McCormack.

| | | |
|---|---|---|
| 11/09/1993 . . . . .46 . . . . . .1 . . . . . . | EARTH VS THE WILDHEARTS . . . . . . . . . . . . . . . . . . . . . . . . . . . . . . . . . . . . . . . . . .East West 4509932012 |
| 03/06/1995 . . . . .6 . . .4 . . . . . . | P.H.U.Q . . . . . . . . . . . . . . . . . . . . . . . . . . . . . . . . . . . . . . . . . . . . . . . . . . . . . . . . . . . .East West 0630104372 |
| 01/06/1996 . . . . .16 . . . . . .2 . . . . . . | FISHING FOR LUCKIES . . . . . . . . . . . . . . . . . . . . . . . . . . . . . . . . . . . . . . . . . . . . . . . . .East West 0630148559 |
| 08/11/1997 . . . . .41 . . . . . .1 . . . . . . | ENDLESS, NAMELESS . . . . . . . . . . . . . . . . . . . . . . . . . . . . . . . . . . . . . . . . . . . . . . . . . .Mushroom MUSH 13CD |
| 06/09/2003 . . . . .54 . . . . . .1 . . . . . . | THE WILDHEARTS MUST BE DESTROYED . . . . . . . . . . . . . . . . . . . . . . . . . . . . . . . . . . . . . . . .Gut GUTCD25 |

**WILEY** UK male rapper (born in London) who was formerly a member of Pay As U Go and Roll Deep Crew.

08/05/2004 . . . . .45 . . . . . .1 . . . . . . TREDDIN' ON THIN ICE . . . . . . . . . . . . . . . . . . . . . . . . . . . . . . . . . . . . . . . . . . . . . . . . .XL Recordings XLCD 178

**COLM WILKINSON** Irish singer (born 5/6/1944, Dublin); he appeared in both the London and Broadway presentations of the stage show *Les Miserables* as well as other musicals such as *Evita* and *Jekyll and Hyde*.

10/06/1989 . . . . .27 . . . . . .6 . . . . . . STAGE HEROES . . . . . . . . . . . . . . . . . . . . . . . . . . . . . . . . . . . . . . . . . . . . . . . . . . . . . . . . . . . . .RCA BL 74105

**ALYSON WILLIAMS** US singer (born in Harlem, NYC); she is the daughter of trumpeter Bobby Booker. She was a backing singer before joining High Fashion in 1982. She debuted solo for Profile in 1986.

25/03/1989 . . . . .29 . . . . .21 . . . . . ● RAW . . . . . . . . . . . . . . . . . . . . . . . . . . . . . . . . . . . . . . . . . . . . . . . . . . . . . . . . . . . . . . . . . . . . .Def Jam 4632931

**ANDY WILLIAMS** US singer (born Howard Andrew Williams, 3/12/1928, Wall Lake, IA), who sang with his three brothers on radio before moving with the family to California. The group then teamed up with comedienne Kay Thompson for six years before Williams went solo in 1952. He appeared on Steve Allen's *Tonight* show for two and half years and hosted his own TV show from 1959, introducing the Osmonds to the record-buying public. He has a star on the Hollywood Walk of Fame.

| | | |
|---|---|---|
| 26/06/1965 . . . . .4 . . .46 . . . . . . | ALMOST THERE . . . . . . . . . . . . . . . . . . . . . . . . . . . . . . . . . . . . . . . . . . . . . . . . . . . . . . . . .CBS BPG 62533 |
| 07/08/1965 . . . . .16 . . . . . .1 . . . . . . | CAN'T GET USED TO LOSING YOU . . . . . . . . . . . . . . . . . . . . . . . . . . . . . . . . . . . . . . . . . .CBS BPG 62146 |
| 19/03/1966 . . . . .11 . . . . . .6 . . . . . . | MAY EACH DAY . . . . . . . . . . . . . . . . . . . . . . . . . . . . . . . . . . . . . . . . . . . . . . . . . . . . . . . . . .CBS BPG 62658 |
| 30/04/1966 . . . . .30 . . . . . .1 . . . . . . | GREAT SONGS FROM MY FAIR LADY . . . . . . . . . . . . . . . . . . . . . . . . . . . . . . . . . . . . . . . . . .CBS BPG 62430 |
| 23/07/1966 . . . . .24 . . . . . .4 . . . . . . | SHADOW OF YOUR SMILE . . . . . . . . . . . . . . . . . . . . . . . . . . . . . . . . . . . . . . . . . . . . . . . . . . . .CBS 62633 |
| 29/07/1967 . . . . .22 . . . . .11 . . . . . . | BORN FREE . . . . . . . . . . . . . . . . . . . . . . . . . . . . . . . . . . . . . . . . . . . . . . . . . . . . . . . . . . . . .CBS SBPG 63027 |

○ Silver disc ● Gold disc ✪ Platinum disc (additional platinum units are indicated by a figure following the symbol)  ❶⁹ Number of weeks album topped the UK chart

| DATE | POS | WKS | BPI | ALBUM TITLE | LABEL & NUMBER |
|------|-----|-----|-----|-------------|----------------|
| 11/05/1968 | ❶¹ | 22 | | **LOVE ANDY** | CBS 63167 |
| 06/07/1968 | 4 | 17 | | **HONEY** | CBS 63311 |
| 26/07/1969 | 22 | 9 | | HAPPY HEART | CBS 63614 |
| 27/12/1969 | 13 | 12 | | GET TOGETHER WITH ANDY WILLIAMS | CBS 63800 |
| 24/01/1970 | 22 | 10 | | ANDY WILLIAMS' SOUND OF MUSIC | CBS 66214 |
| 11/04/1970 | ❶⁵ | 116 | | **ANDY WILLIAMS GREATEST HITS** | CBS 63920 |
| 20/06/1970 | 7 | 48 | | **CAN'T HELP FALLING IN LOVE** | CBS 64067 |
| 05/12/1970 | 10 | 6 | | **ANDY WILLIAMS SHOW** | CBS 64127 |
| 03/04/1971 | ❶² | 25 | | **HOME LOVING MAN** | CBS 64286 |
| 31/07/1971 | 11 | 11 | | LOVE STORY | CBS 64467 |
| 29/04/1972 | 26 | 3 | | THE IMPOSSIBLE DREAM | CBS 67236 |
| 29/07/1972 | 11 | 16 | | LOVE THEME FROM 'THE GODFATHER' | CBS 64869 |
| 19/12/1972 | 23 | 10 | | GREATEST HITS VOLUME 2 | CBS 65151 |
| 22/12/1973 | 3 | 26 | ● | **SOLITAIRE** | CBS 65638 |
| 15/06/1974 | 7 | 11 | ○ | **THE WAY WE WERE** | CBS 80152 |
| 11/10/1975 | 60 | 1 | | THE OTHER SIDE OF ME | CBS 69152 |
| 28/01/1978 | 2 | 17 | ● | **REFLECTIONS** | CBS 10006 |
| 27/10/1984 | 22 | 10 | ● | GREATEST LOVE CLASSICS | EMI ANDY 1 |
| 07/11/1992 | 51 | 3 | | THE BEST OF ANDY WILLIAMS | Dino DINCD 50 |
| 10/04/1999 | 39 | 3 | | IN THE LOUNGE WITH… ANDY WILLIAMS | Columbia 4945082 |
| 19/02/2000 | 27 | 7 | | THE VERY BEST OF ANDY WILLIAMS | Columbia SONYTV 78CD |
| 06/07/2002 | 32 | 2 | | THE ESSENTIAL ANDY WILLIAMS | Columbia 5084142 |

**DENIECE WILLIAMS** US singer (born June Deniece Chandler, 3/6/1951, Gary, IN) who first recorded for Toddlin' Town in the late 1960s. She was backing singer in Stevie Wonder's group Wonderlove 1972–75. With songwriting ambitions, her first hit was intended for Earth Wind & Fire until persuaded by producer Maurice White to record it herself. She later recorded gospel material for Sparrow. She has won five Grammy Awards: Best Recording for Children in 1982 with various others for *In Harmony 2*, Best Gospel Performance by a Duo in 1986 with Sandi Patti for *They Say*, Best Soul Gospel Performance in 1986 for *I Surrender*, Best Gospel Performance in 1987 for *I Believe In You* and Best Pop/Contemporary Gospel Performance in 1998 for *This Is My Song*.

| DATE | POS | WKS | BPI | ALBUM TITLE | LABEL & NUMBER |
|------|-----|-----|-----|-------------|----------------|
| 21/05/1977 | 31 | 12 | ○ | THIS IS NIECEY | CBS 81869 |
| 26/08/1978 | 16 | 11 | ● | THAT'S WHAT FRIENDS ARE FOR **JOHNNY MATHIS AND DENIECE WILLIAMS** | CBS 86068 |

**DON WILLIAMS** US male singer (born 27/5/1939, Floydada, TX); he was originally in Strangers Two with Lofton Kline and then, with the addition of Susan Taylor, became The Poco-Seco Singers and were managed by Albert Grossman, Bob Dylan's manager. After a number of pop hits, Kline left the group and was replaced by a number of alternative singers, but further success eluded them. Taylor then left for a solo career and Don Williams went to work for a publishing company (he wrote a number of songs for her debut), before accepting an invitation to record solo by JMI. Success on the country charts prompted ABC/Dot to snap him up and he converted that success onto the pop charts. He later joined Capitol Records and appeared in a number of films, including *Smokey & The Bandit 2*.

| DATE | POS | WKS | BPI | ALBUM TITLE | LABEL & NUMBER |
|------|-----|-----|-----|-------------|----------------|
| 10/07/1976 | 29 | 15 | ○ | GREATEST HITS VOLUME 1 | ABC ABCL 5147 |
| 19/02/1977 | 13 | 20 | ● | VISIONS | ABC ABCL 5200 |
| 15/10/1977 | 27 | 5 | ○ | COUNTRY BOY | ABC ABCL 5233 |
| 05/08/1978 | 2 | 38 | ✪ | **IMAGES** | K-Tel NE 1033 |
| 05/08/1978 | 58 | 1 | ○ | YOU'RE MY BEST THING | ABC ABCD 5127 |
| 04/11/1978 | 28 | 8 | | EXPRESSIONS | ABC ABCL 5253 |
| 22/09/1979 | 29 | 12 | | NEW HORIZONS | K-Tel NE 1048 |
| 15/12/1979 | 58 | 4 | | PORTRAIT | MCA MCS 3045 |
| 06/09/1980 | 36 | 5 | | I BELIEVE IN YOU | MCA MCF 3077 |
| 18/07/1981 | 33 | 7 | | ESPECIALLY FOR YOU | MCA MCF 3114 |
| 17/04/1982 | 69 | 3 | | LISTEN TO THE RADIO | MCA MCF 3135 |
| 23/04/1983 | 52 | 1 | | YELLOW MOON | MCA MCF 3159 |
| 15/10/1983 | 22 | 13 | ○ | LOVE STORIES | K-Tel NE 1252 |
| 26/05/1984 | 65 | 4 | | CAFÉ CAROLINA | MCA MCF 3225 |

**IRIS WILLIAMS** UK singer (born 20/4/1944, Pontypridd, Wales).

| DATE | POS | WKS | BPI | ALBUM TITLE | LABEL & NUMBER |
|------|-----|-----|-----|-------------|----------------|
| 22/12/1979 | 69 | 4 | ● | HE WAS BEAUTIFUL | Columbia SCX 6627 |

**JOHN WILLIAMS** Australian guitarist (born 24/4/1941, Melbourne) who formed Sky with Steve Gray, Herbie Flowers, Kevin Peek and Tristan Fry in 1979 and left in 1984. He has recorded in a wide variety of musical styles.

| DATE | POS | WKS | BPI | ALBUM TITLE | LABEL & NUMBER |
|------|-----|-----|-----|-------------|----------------|
| 03/10/1970 | 46 | 1 | | PLAYS SPANISH MUSIC | CBS 72860 |
| 07/02/1976 | 20 | 9 | ● | RODRIGO: CONCERTO DE ARANJUEZ **JOHN WILLIAMS WITH THE ENGLISH CHAMBER ORCHESTRA CONDUCTED BY DANIEL BARENBOIM** | CBS 79369 |
| 07/01/1978 | 18 | 22 | ○ | BEST OF FRIENDS **CLEO LIANE AND JOHN WILLIAMS** | RCA Victor RS 1094 |
| 17/06/1978 | 23 | 5 | ○ | TRAVELLING | Cube HIFLY 27 |
| 30/06/1979 | 5 | 22 | | **BRIDGES** | Lotus WH 5015 |

▲⁹ Number of weeks album topped the US chart  ◆¹² RIAA Diamond Awards  ◇³ IFPI Platinum Europe Awards

04/08/1979 . . . . .64 . . . . . .3 . . . . . .     CAVATINA . . . . . . . . . . . . . . . . . . . . . . . . . . . . . . . . . . . . . . . . . . . . . . . . . . . . . . . . . . . . . . . . . . .Cube HIFLY 32

26/10/1996 . . . . .54 . . . . . .3 . . . . . .     JOHN WILLIAMS PLAYS THE MOVIES . . . . . . . . . . . . . . . . . . . . . . . . . . . . . . . . . . . . . . . . . . .Sony Classical S2K 62784

**JOHN WILLIAMS** US orchestra leader (born 8/2/1932, New York) who found fame as a composer of themes to films, including *Jaws* (1975), *Star Wars* (1977), *Close Encounters Of The Third Kind* (1977), *Raiders Of The Lost Ark* (1981) and *Jurassic Park* (1993), winning numerous Oscars. He has won eighteen Grammy Awards including: Best Chamber Music Performance in 1972 with Julian Bream for *Julian And John;* Best Pop Instrumental Performance in 1977 for *Star Wars;* Best Instrumental Composition in 1977 for *Main Theme From Star Wars;* Best Instrumental Composition in 1978 for *Theme From Close Encounters Of The Third Kind;* Best Instrumental Composition and Best Album of Original Score Written for a Motion Picture in 1979 for *Theme From Superman;* Best Instrumental Composition and Best Album of Original Score Written for a Motion Picture in 1980 for *The Empire Strikes Back;* Best Album of Original Score Written for a Motion Picture in 1981 for *Raiders Of The Lost Ark;* Best Instrumental Arrangement and Best Instrumental Composition in 1982 for *Flying (Theme From E.T. The Extra-Terrestrial);* Best Instrumental Composition for a Motion Picture in 1994 for *Schindler's List;* Best Instrumental Composition for a Motion Picture in 1998 for *Saving Private Ryan;* and Best Instrumental Composition for *Theme From Angela's Ashes.*

31/01/1976 . . . . .55 . . . . . .1 . . . . . .     JAWS Original soundtrack to the film. 1975 Grammy Award for Best Album of Original Score Written for a Motion Picture . . . . . . . . . . . . . . . . . . . . . . . . . . . . . . . . . . . . . . . . . . . . . . . . . . . . . . . . . . . . . . . . . . . . .MCA MCF 2716

21/01/1978 . . . . .21 . . . .12 . . . . . .     STAR WARS **JOHN WILLIAMS AND THE LONDON SYMPHONY ORCHESTRA** Original soundtrack to the film. 1977 Grammy Award for Best Album of Original Score Written for a Motion Picture . . . . . . . . . . . . . . . . . . . . . . .20th Century BTD 541

29/04/1978 . . . . .40 . . . . . .6 . . . . . .     CLOSE ENCOUNTERS OF THE THIRD KIND Original soundtrack to the film. 1978 Grammy Award for Best Album of Original Score Written for a Motion Picture . . . . . . . . . . . . . . . . . . . . . . . . . . . . . . . . . . . . . . . . . . . . . .Arista DLART 2001

25/12/1982 . . . . .47 . . . .10 . . . . . .O     E.T. THE EXTRA-TERRESTRIAL Original soundtrack to the film. 1982 Grammy Award for Best Album of Original Score Written for a Motion Picture . . . . . . . . . . . . . . . . . . . . . . . . . . . . . . . . . . . . . . . . . . . . . . . . . . . .MCA MCF 3160

25/06/1983 . . . . .85 . . . . . .5 . . . . . .     RETURN OF THE JEDI Original soundtrack to the film . . . . . . . . . . . . . . . . . . . . . . . . . . . . . . . . . . . .RSO RSD 5023

31/07/1993 . . . . .42 . . . . . .5 . . . . . .     JURASSIC PARK Original soundtrack to the film . . . . . . . . . . . . . . . . . . . . . . . . . . . . . . . . . . . . . . .MCA MCD 10859

02/04/1994 . . . . .59 . . . . . .2 . . . . . .     SCHINDLER'S LIST Original soundtrack to the film . . . . . . . . . . . . . . . . . . . . . . . . . . . . . . . . . . . . . . . .MCA MCD 10969

15/05/1999 . . . . .8 . . . .17 . . . . . .●     **STAR WARS EPISODE I: THE PHANTOM MENACE** Original soundtrack to the film . . . . . . . . . . . .Sony Classical SK 61816

10/11/2001 . . . . .19 . . . . . .7 . . . . . .●     HARRY POTTER Original soundtrack to the film . . . . . . . . . . . . . . . . . . . . . . . . . . . . . . . . . .Atlantic 7567930865

11/05/2002 . . . . .15 . . . . . .5 . . . . . .     STAR WARS EPISODE II: ATTACK OF THE CLONES **JOHN WILLIAMS & THE LONDON SYMPHONY ORCHESTRA** Original soundtrack to the film . . . . . . . . . . . . . . . . . . . . . . . . . . . . . . . . . . . . . . . . . . . . . . . . . . . . . . . . . . . . . . . . . . . . . . . . .Sony Classical SK89965

---

**KATHRYN WILLIAMS** UK singer/songwriter/guitarist (born 1974, Liverpool); her first album *Dog Leap Stairs* cost just £80 to record, released on her own Caw Records label (named after the sound a crow makes). Her second album *Little Black Numbers* cost £3,000 and was later licensed to EastWest. Her touring group features Alex Tustin (percussion), Laura Reid (cello), David Scott (Spanish guitar) and Jonny Bridgwood (double bass).

15/09/2001 . . . . .70 . . . . . .1 . . . . . .     LITTLE BLACK NUMBERS . . . . . . . . . . . . . . . . . . . . . . . . . . . . . . . . . . . . . . . . . . . . . . . . . .East West 8573899242

12/10/2002 . . . . .56 . . . . . .2 . . . . . .     OLD LOW LIGHT . . . . . . . . . . . . . . . . . . . . . . . . . . . . . . . . . . . . . . . . . . . . . . . . . . . . . . . . .East West 0927475522

---

**LUCINDA WILLIAMS** US singer/songwriter (born 26/1/1953, Lake Charles, LA); she made her debut album for Folkways in 1979 and later recorded for Rough Trade, RCA, American Recordings and Mercury. She has won three Grammy Awards: Best Country Song in 1993 for *Passionate Kisses*, Best Contemporary Folk Album in 1998 for *Car Wheels On A Gravel Road* and Best Female Rock Vocal Performance in 2001 for *Get Right With God*.

16/06/2001 . . . . .63 . . . . . .1 . . . . . .     ESSENCE . . . . . . . . . . . . . . . . . . . . . . . . . . . . . . . . . . . . . . . . . . . . . . . . . . . . . . . . . . . . .Lost Highway 1701972

19/04/2003 . . . . .48 . . . . . .1 . . . . . .     WORLD WITHOUT TEARS . . . . . . . . . . . . . . . . . . . . . . . . . . . . . . . . . . . . . . . . . . . . . . . . . .Lost Highway 1703552

---

**ROBBIE WILLIAMS** UK singer (born 13/2/1974, Stoke-on-Trent) who was a founding member of Take That in 1991 until an acrimonious split in 1995. His solo career was then delayed by legal wrangles. He was named Best British Male at the 1999 BRIT Awards as well as winning both the Best Single and Best Video awards for *Angels* and *Millennium* respectively. He repeated the Best Single and Best Video at the 2000 BRIT Awards for *She's The One*. The following year he won a further three awards, collecting Best British Male, Best British Single and Best Video, the last two for *Rock DJ*. He repeated his success as Best British Male in 2002 and 2003. In so doing he became the most successful artist of all time at the BRIT Awards having collected thirteen awards: four as a member of Take That and ten solo. He has also won three MTV Europe Music Awards: Best Male in 1998 and 2001 and Best Song in 2000 for *Rock DJ*. Robbie also took part in the *It's Only Rock 'N' Roll* project for the Children's Promise charity. On 22/2/2001 he was attacked during a show at Stuttgart by a 20 year old with a history of mental problems who punched him and pushed into the photographer's pit. After the assailant had been hustled away by security, Robbie resumed the show by telling the audience that he hadn't fancied his attacker! In February 2002 he was ordered to pay £200,000 for copyright infringement after portions of the song *Jesus In A Camper Van* on his *I've Been Expecting You* album were found to have been lifted from a 1973 song by Loudon Wainwright III. The song was ordered to be removed from all subsequent pressings of the album. In November 2002 he re-signed with EMI in a deal worth £80 million.

11/10/1997 . . . .●² . . . .123 . . . . .✪⁸     **LIFE THRU A LENS** ◇³ . . . . . . . . . . . . . . . . . . . . . . . . . . . . . . . . . . . . . . . . . . . . . . . . . . . .Chrysalis CDCHR 6127

07/11/1998 . . . .●³ . . . .98 . . . . .✪⁹     **I'VE BEEN EXPECTING YOU** ◇⁴ . . . . . . . . . . . . . . . . . . . . . . . . . . . . . . . . . . . . . . . . . . .Chrysalis 4978372

09/09/2000 . . . .●³ . . . .62 . . . . .✪⁸     **SING WHEN YOU'RE WINNING** ◇⁴ . . . . . . . . . . . . . . . . . . . . . . . . . . . . . . . . . . . . . . . . .Chrysalis 5293942

01/12/2001 . . . .●⁷ . . . .38 . . . . .✪⁷     **SWING WHEN YOU'RE WINNING** ◇⁴ . . . . . . . . . . . . . . . . . . . . . . . . . . . . . . . . . . . . . . . .Chrysalis 5368262

30/11/2002 . . . .●⁷ . . . .50 . . . . .✪⁶     **ESCAPOLOGY** ◇⁵ . . . . . . . . . . . . . . . . . . . . . . . . . . . . . . . . . . . . . . . . . . . . . . . . . . . . . . .EMI 5439942

11/10/2003 . . . . .2 . . . . . .17 . . . . . .✪     **LIVE AT KNEBWORTH** ◇² . . . . . . . . . . . . . . . . . . . . . . . . . . . . . . . . . . . . . . . . . . . . . . . . . .Chrysalis 5946372

---

**VANESSA WILLIAMS** US singer (born 18/3/1963, Tarrytown, NY) who was the first black woman to be crowned Miss America in 1984. She was stripped of the title when nude photographs of her appeared in *Penthouse* magazine. She later became an actress, appearing in the TV series *Melrose Place* and later films such as *New Jack City* (1991), *Soul Food* (1997), *Hoodlum* (1997) and *Dance With Me* (1998).

25/04/1992 . . . . .24 . . . . . .4 . . . . . .     THE COMFORT ZONE . . . . . . . . . . . . . . . . . . . . . . . . . . . . . . . . . . . . . . . . . . . . . . . . . . . . . .Polydor 5112672

## WENDY O WILLIAMS
US singer (born 28/5/1949, Rochester, NY); she began her career as a performer in sex shows and then formed The Plasmatics in 1979 with Richie Stotts (guitar), Wes Beech (guitar), Chosei Funahara (bass) and Stu Deutsch (drums). The 'group' was the brainchild of pornographic mogul Rod Swenson, with Wendy's stage 'outfit' being either see-through lingerie or topless with little more than strategically placed tape. After records for Stiff and Capitol the Plasmatics disbanded in 1982 with Wendy going solo. She committed suicide on 6/4/1998.

30/06/1984 ....100 .....1 ......   W.O.W ...................................................................Music For Nations MFN 24

## ANN WILLIAMSON
UK singer who also recorded religious material.

15/02/1986 .....16 .......9 ......   PRECIOUS MEMORIES .....................................................................Emerald ERTV 1
06/02/1988 .....58 ......4 ......   COUNT YOUR BLESSINGS ..............................................................Emerald Gem ERTV 2

## SONNY BOY WILLIAMSON
US guitarist/harmonica player/singer (born Alex Ford – his name sometimes given as Aleck Ford – 5/12/1899, Glendora, MS) who is also known as Rice Miller, the name being adopted from his childhood nickname and stepfather's surname. He toured the Deep South under the name Little Boy Blue and later worked with many leading blues artists of the era, including Elmore James, Big Boy Crudup, Robert Johnson and Howlin' Wolf. He first took to using the name Sonny Boy Williamson in 1941, despite the presence of another artist of the same name. When John Lee Williamson, the original Sonny Boy was murdered in 1948, Rice Miller/Little Boy Blue claimed the name for himself. After recording for a series of small labels in Arkansas and Mississippi, Sonny Boy linked with Chess/Checker in Chicago, IL, scoring three R&B hits whilst with the label. His reputation overseas was made with a series of live concerts in Europe during the early 1960s, including a number of dates with Chris Barber and he subsequently recorded with The Yardbirds, The Animals and Brian Auger. He died on 25/5/1965.

20/06/1964 .....20 ......1 ......   DOWN AND OUT BLUES .....................................................................Pye NPL 28036

## WILLING SINNERS – see MARC ALMOND

## BRUCE WILLIS
US singer/actor (born 19/3/1955, Penns Grove, NJ) who first became known via the role of David Addison in the TV series *Moonlighting*. He later appeared in the *Die Hard* films and many others, and married actress Demi Moore in 1987 although this later ended in divorce. He is one of the partners in the Planet Hollywood chain of restaurants.

18/04/1987 .....4 ......28 ......●   **THE RETURN OF BRUNO** ...............................................................Motown ZL 72571

## BRIAN WILSON
US keyboardist/bassist/singer (born 20/6/1942, Hawthorne, CA); a founding member of The Beach Boys, he stopped touring with the group in 1964 to concentrate on songwriting, with Glen Campbell being his replacement. He made his first solo recording in 1966 with the single *Caroline No*, finally issuing an album in 1988 with *Love And Mercy*. His second album *Sweet Insanity* was rejected by his record label Sire for being 'pathetic', whilst his debut hit album was inspired by a TV documentary of the same name. His daughters Carnie and Wendy Wilson are members of Wilson Phillips.

16/09/1995 .....59 ......1 ......   I JUST WASN'T MADE FOR THESE TIMES ......................................MCA MCD 11270
27/06/1998 .....30 ......2 ......   IMAGINATION ..................................................................Giant 74321573032

## MARI WILSON
UK singer (born 29/9/1957, London) whose original backing band were known as the Imaginations but were forced to change their name to the Wilsations and included Julia Fordham.

26/02/1983 .....24 ......9 ......   SHOW PEOPLE .......................................................Compact Organisation COMP 2

## WILSON PHILLIPS
US vocal trio formed in Los Angeles, CA by Chyna Phillips (born 12/2/1968, Los Angeles) and sisters Carnie (born 29/4/1968, Los Angeles) and Wendy Wilson (born 16/10/1969, Los Angeles). Phillips is the daughter of ex-Mamas & Papas John and Michelle Phillips, while the Wilson sisters are daughters of Beach Boy Brian Wilson. They disbanded in 1992 with the Wilson sisters recording as a duo and Phillips going solo. Carnie Wilson later hosted her own TV talk show.

30/06/1990 .....7 ......32 ......✪   **WILSON PHILLIPS** ........................................................................SBK SBKLP 5
13/06/1992 .....6 ......6 ......○   **SHADOWS AND LIGHT** ...............................................................SBK SBKCD 18

## WIN
UK group formed in Scotland by Davey Henderson (guitar/keyboards/vocals), Russell Burn (keyboards/vocals), Emmanuel Shoniwa (bass/guitar/keyboards/vocals), Simon Smeeton (guitar/bass/keyboards/vocals) and Ian Stoddart (drums/vocals). After 1987's debut album they added William Perry (keyboards/vocals), disbanding after a second album. Henderson later sang lead with Nectarine No 9.

04/04/1987 .....51 ......1 ......   UH! TEARS BABY .......................................................................Swampland LONLP 31

## MARIO WINANS
US singer (born 1981, Detroit, MI), brother of Carvin, Marvin, Ronald, BeBe and CeCe Winans, although he was not a member of the family group. Also known as Yellowman, he originally sang gospel music and also recorded for Motown.

01/05/2004 .....3 .....9+ ......✪   **HURT NO MORE** ..........................................................................Bad Boy 9862494

## WINDJAMMER
US R&B group formed in New Orleans by Kevin McLin (guitar), Roy Paul Joseph (guitar), Chris Severin (bass), Darrell Winchester (drums), Carl Dennis (vocals) and Fred McCray (keyboards). They originally recorded as Windstorm.

25/08/1984 .....82 ......1 ......   WINDJAMMER II ..............................................................................MCA MCF 3231

---

▲⁹ Number of weeks album topped the US chart    ◆¹² RIAA Diamond Awards    ◇³ IFPI Platinum Europe Awards

**BARBARA WINDSOR** UK singer (born Barbara Deeks, 1937, London) who is best known as an actress, appearing in many of the hugely successful *Carry On* films alongside the likes of Sid James and Kenneth Williams. She currently plays the role of Peggy Mitchell in the long-running TV series *Eastenders*.

03/04/1999 . . . . .45 . . . . . .2 . . . . . .　YOU'VE GOT A FRIEND . . . . . . . . . . . . . . . . . . . . . . . . . . . . . . . . . . . . . . . . . . . . . . . . . . . . . . . . . . . . . . . . . . .Telstar TV TTVCD 3034

**AMY WINEHOUSE** UK singer (born 1984, London).

01/11/2003 . . . . .13 . . . . .16 . . . . . .● FRANK . . . . . . . . . . . . . . . . . . . . . . . . . . . . . . . . . . . . . . . . . . . . . . . . . . . . . . . . . . . . . . . . . . . . . . . . . . . . . . . . . . . .Island 9812918

**JOSH WINK** US singer (born Joshua Winkleman, Philadelphia, PA) who has also recorded as Firefly, Just King & Wink, Winc, Size 9, E-Culture and Winx.

21/09/1996 . . . . .43 . . . . . .1 . . . . . .　LEFT ABOVE THE CLOUDS . . . . . . . . . . . . . . . . . . . . . . . . . . . . . . . . . . . . . . . . . . . . . . . . . . . . . . . . . . . . . . . . .XL Recordings XLCD 119

**JOHNNY WINTER** US singer/guitarist (born 23/2/1944, Leland, MS); the older brother of Edgar Winter, he made his recording debut in 1960 as Johnny And The Jammers. He then formed Winter, a group that also featured Tommy Shannon (bass) and John Turner (drums), before linking with The McCoys in 1970. He is also a sought-after producer, making albums with Muddy Waters among others.

16/05/1970 . . . . .59 . . . . . .2 . . . . . .　SECOND WINTER . . . . . . . . . . . . . . . . . . . . . . . . . . . . . . . . . . . . . . . . . . . . . . . . . . . . . . . . . . . . . . . . . . . . . . . . .CBS 66321
31/10/1970 . . . . .29 . . . . . .4 . . . . . .　JOHNNY WINTER AND... . . . . . . . . . . . . . . . . . . . . . . . . . . . . . . . . . . . . . . . . . . . . . . . . . . . . . . . . . . . . . . . . . . . .CBS 64117
15/05/1971 . . . . .20 . . . . . .6 . . . . . .　JOHNNY WINTER AND... LIVE . . . . . . . . . . . . . . . . . . . . . . . . . . . . . . . . . . . . . . . . . . . . . . . . . . . . . . . . . . . . . . . . .CBS 64289

**RUBY WINTERS** US R&B singer (born in Louisville, KY) who was more successful in the UK than in the US. She first recorded for the Diamond label in 1967.

10/06/1978 . . . . .27 . . . . . .7 . . . . . .　RUBY WINTERS . . . . . . . . . . . . . . . . . . . . . . . . . . . . . . . . . . . . . . . . . . . . . . . . . . . . . . . . . . . . . . . . . . . . . . .Creole CRLP 512
23/06/1979 . . . . .31 . . . . .10 . . . . . .○ SONGBIRD . . . . . . . . . . . . . . . . . . . . . . . . . . . . . . . . . . . . . . . . . . . . . . . . . . . . . . . . . . . . . . . . . . . . . . . . . . . . . .K-Tel NE 1045

**STEVE WINWOOD** UK singer (born 12/5/1948, Birmingham) who was lead singer with the Spencer Davis Group until 1967, when he left to form Traffic. His first release under his own name was in 1971. He won the 1986 Grammy Awards for Record of the Year and Best Pop Vocal Performance, both for *Higher Love*.

09/07/1977 . . . . .12 . . . . . .9 . . . . . .　STEVE WINWOOD . . . . . . . . . . . . . . . . . . . . . . . . . . . . . . . . . . . . . . . . . . . . . . . . . . . . . . . . . . . . . . . . . . . . . . .Island ILPS 9494
10/01/1981 . . . . .13 . . . . .20 . . . . . .○ ARC OF A DIVER . . . . . . . . . . . . . . . . . . . . . . . . . . . . . . . . . . . . . . . . . . . . . . . . . . . . . . . . . . . . . . . . . . . . . . .Island ILPS 9576
14/08/1982 . . . . . .6 . . . . .13 . . . . . .● **TALKING BACK TO THE NIGHT** . . . . . . . . . . . . . . . . . . . . . . . . . . . . . . . . . . . . . . . . . . . . . . . . . . . . . . . . . . . .Island ILPS 9777
12/07/1986 . . . . . .8 . . . . .42 . . . . . .● **BACK IN THE HIGH LIFE** . . . . . . . . . . . . . . . . . . . . . . . . . . . . . . . . . . . . . . . . . . . . . . . . . . . . . . . . . . . . . . . .Island ILPS 9844
07/11/1987 . . . . .12 . . . . .17 . . . . . .● CHRONICLES . . . . . . . . . . . . . . . . . . . . . . . . . . . . . . . . . . . . . . . . . . . . . . . . . . . . . . . . . . . . . . . . . . . . . . . . . .Island SSW 1
02/07/1988 . . . . . .4 . . . . .16 . . . . . .● **ROLL WITH IT ▲¹** . . . . . . . . . . . . . . . . . . . . . . . . . . . . . . . . . . . . . . . . . . . . . . . . . . . . . . . . . . . . . . . . . . . . . . . .Virgin V 2532
17/11/1990 . . . . .26 . . . . . .3 . . . . . .　REFUGEES OF THE HEART . . . . . . . . . . . . . . . . . . . . . . . . . . . . . . . . . . . . . . . . . . . . . . . . . . . . . . . . . . . . . . . . .Virgin V 2650
14/06/1997 . . . . .32 . . . . . .2 . . . . . .　JUNCTION SEVEN . . . . . . . . . . . . . . . . . . . . . . . . . . . . . . . . . . . . . . . . . . . . . . . . . . . . . . . . . . . . . . . . . . . . . .Virgin CDV 2832

**WIRE** UK group formed in 1976 by Colin Newman (born 16/9/1954, Salisbury, guitar/vocals), George Gill (guitar), Bruce Gilbert (born 18/5/1946, Watford, guitar), Graham Lewis (born 22/2/1953, Grantham, bass/vocals) and Robert Gotobed (born Mark Field, 1951, Leicester, drums). Gill was sacked soon after they started, the group continuing as a four-piece, although producer Mike Thorne often acted as the fifth member. They disbanded in 1980, with Newman going solo. Wire was revived in 1985 and recorded again in 1987. Gotobed left in 1990 and they continued as a trio, slightly amending their name to Wir.

07/10/1978 . . . . .48 . . . . . .1 . . . . . .　CHAIRS MISSING . . . . . . . . . . . . . . . . . . . . . . . . . . . . . . . . . . . . . . . . . . . . . . . . . . . . . . . . . . . . . . . . . . . . . . .Harvest SHSP 4093
13/10/1979 . . . . .39 . . . . . .1 . . . . . .　154 . . . . . . . . . . . . . . . . . . . . . . . . . . . . . . . . . . . . . . . . . . . . . . . . . . . . . . . . . . . . . . . . . . . . . . . . . . . . . . . . . .Harvest SHSP 4105
09/05/1987 . . . . .87 . . . . . .1 . . . . . .　THE IDEAL COPY . . . . . . . . . . . . . . . . . . . . . . . . . . . . . . . . . . . . . . . . . . . . . . . . . . . . . . . . . . . . . . . . . . . . . . . .Mute STUMM 42

**WISHBONE ASH** UK group formed in 1966 by Steve Upton (born 24/5/1946, Wrexham, drums), Martin Turner (born 1/10/1947, Torquay, Devon, bass/vocals) and Glen Turner (guitar) as Tanglewood. Glen Turner was replaced by Ted Turner (born David Turner, 2/8/1950) and with the addition of Andy Powell (born 8/2/1950, guitar) they became Wishbone Ash. Ted Turner left in 1974, replaced by Laurie Wisefield. Martin Turner left in 1980, replaced by John Wetton, with singers Claire Hamill and Trevor Bolder briefly joining at the same time. By 1987 the original quartet of Upton, Martin Turner, Ted Turner and Andy Powell had re-formed.

23/01/1971 . . . . .34 . . . . . .2 . . . . . .　WISHBONE ASH . . . . . . . . . . . . . . . . . . . . . . . . . . . . . . . . . . . . . . . . . . . . . . . . . . . . . . . . . . . . . . . . . . . . . . .MCA MKPS 2014
09/10/1971 . . . . .14 . . . . . .9 . . . . . .　PILGRIMAGE . . . . . . . . . . . . . . . . . . . . . . . . . . . . . . . . . . . . . . . . . . . . . . . . . . . . . . . . . . . . . . . . . . . . . . . . .MCA MDKS 8004
20/05/1972 . . . . . .3 . . . . .20 . . . . . .　**ARGUS** . . . . . . . . . . . . . . . . . . . . . . . . . . . . . . . . . . . . . . . . . . . . . . . . . . . . . . . . . . . . . . . . . . . . . . . . . . . . .MCA MDKS 8006
26/05/1973 . . . . .12 . . . . .10 . . . . . .　WISHBONE FOUR . . . . . . . . . . . . . . . . . . . . . . . . . . . . . . . . . . . . . . . . . . . . . . . . . . . . . . . . . . . . . . . . . . . . . . .MCA MDKS 8011
30/11/1974 . . . . .16 . . . . . .5 . . . . . .○ THERE'S THE RUB . . . . . . . . . . . . . . . . . . . . . . . . . . . . . . . . . . . . . . . . . . . . . . . . . . . . . . . . . . . . . . . . . . . . . . .MCA MCF 2585

| | | | | | |
|---|---|---|---|---|---|
| 03/04/1976 | 36 | 2 | | LOCKED IN | MCA MCF 2750 |
| 27/11/1976 | 22 | 3 | | NEW ENGLAND | MCA MCG 3523 |
| 29/10/1977 | 31 | 4 | | FRONT PAGE NEWS | MCA MCG 3524 |
| 28/10/1978 | 43 | 3 | | NO SMOKE WITHOUT FIRE | MCA MCG 3528 |
| 02/02/1980 | 41 | 4 | | JUST TESTING | MCA MCF 3052 |
| 01/11/1980 | 40 | 3 | | LIVE DATES II | MCA MCG 4012 |
| 25/04/1981 | 61 | 5 | | NUMBER THE BRAVE | MCA MCF 3103 |
| 16/10/1982 | 22 | 5 | | TWIN BARRELS BURNING | AVM ASH 1 |

**BILL WITHERS** US singer (born 4/7/1938, Slab Fork, WV); he worked for Lockhead Aircraft fitting toilets, writing songs in his spare time, when he met with Booker T Jones, who got him a contract with Sussex Records in 1970. He is married to actress Denise Nicholas. He has won three Grammy Awards: Best Rhythm & Blues Song in 1971 for *Ain't No Sunshine,* Best Rhythm & Blues Song in 1981 with William Salter and Ralph MacDonald for *Just The Two Of Us* and Best Rhythm & Blues Song in 1987 for *Lean On Me*.

| | | | | | |
|---|---|---|---|---|---|
| 11/02/1978 | 27 | 5 | | MENAGERIE | CBS 82265 |
| 15/06/1985 | 60 | 1 | | WATCHING YOU, WATCHING ME | CBS 26200 |
| 17/09/1988 | 90 | 4 | | GREATEST HITS | CBS 32343 |

**WITNESS** UK group formed in 1997 by Gerard Starkie (vocals), Ray Chan (guitar), Dylan Keeton (bass), Julian Pransky (guitar/keyboards) and John Langley (drums).

| | | | | | |
|---|---|---|---|---|---|
| 24/07/1999 | 59 | 1 | | BEFORE THE CALM | Island CID 8084 |
| 04/08/2001 | 62 | 1 | | UNDER A SUN | Island CID 8107 |

**WIZZARD** UK rock group formed in 1972 by Roy Wood (born Ulysses Adrian Wood, 8/11/1946, Birmingham) after chart success with the Move and Electric Light Orchestra. They comprised Wood (vocals/guitar), Rick Price (bass), Hugh McDowell (cello), Nick Pentelow (saxophone), Mike Burney (saxophone), Bill Hunt (keyboards), Keith Smart (drums) and Charlie Grima (drums). They split in 1975, by which time Wood had already begun recording solo.

| | | | | | |
|---|---|---|---|---|---|
| 19/05/1973 | 29 | 7 | | WIZZARD BREW | Harvest SHSP 4025 |
| 17/08/1974 | 19 | 4 | O | INTRODUCING EDDY AND THE FALCONS | Warner Brothers K 52029 |

**ANDREW WK** US singer (born Andrew Wilkes-Kryer, Los Angeles, CA) who moved to Michigan with his family at the age of five. Apparently the WK stood for 'White Killer' (a notorious US serial killer), 'Wild Kid' or 'Want Kicks', depending on his mood. First recording for Bulb Records in 2000, he was spotted by Foo Fighter Dave Grohl, who invited him to be opening act on their US tour.

| | | | | | |
|---|---|---|---|---|---|
| 24/11/2001 | 71 | 1 | | I GET WET | Mercury 5865882 |

**JAH WOBBLE'S INVADERS OF THE HEART** UK singer/multi-instrumentalist (born John Wardle, 1962, London) previously in Public Image Limited. He formed Invaders Of The Heart with Justin Adams (guitar) and Mark Ferda (keyboards) in 1987.

| | | | | | |
|---|---|---|---|---|---|
| 28/05/1994 | 13 | 5 | | TAKE ME TO GOD | Island CID 8017 |
| 14/10/1995 | 71 | 1 | | SPINNER **BRIAN ENO AND JAH WOBBLE** | All Saints ASCD 023 |

**WOLFGANG PRESS** UK group formed by Mick Allen (vocals), Andrew Gray (guitar) and Mark Cox (keyboards).

| | | | | | |
|---|---|---|---|---|---|
| 04/02/1995 | 75 | 1 | | FUNKY LITTLE DEMONS | 4AD CADD 4016CD |

**WOLFSBANE** UK group from Tamworth with Blaze Bayley (vocals), Jase Edwards (guitar), Jeff Hateley (bass) and Steve Ellet (drums).

| | | | | | |
|---|---|---|---|---|---|
| 05/08/1989 | 48 | 1 | | LIVE FAST, DIE FAST | Def US 8384861 |
| 20/10/1990 | 48 | 1 | | ALL'S BREAKING LOOSE… | Def US 8469671 |
| 19/10/1991 | 53 | 1 | | DOWN FALL THE GOOD GUYS | Def US 5104131 |

**BOBBY WOMACK** US singer (born 4/3/1944, Cleveland, OH) who joined the family gospel group the Womack Brothers (with Cecil, Curtis, Harris and Friendly Jr) in 1959. After playing guitar in Sam Cooke's backing group in 1960, he reunited with his brothers as the Valentinos and signed with Cooke's SAR label in 1961. He first recorded solo for the Him label in 1965. He married Cooke's widow Barbara in 1965 (just three months after Sam's funeral, at which he turned up wearing Sam's clothes) and divorced in 1970.

| | | | | | |
|---|---|---|---|---|---|
| 28/04/1984 | 31 | 8 | | THE POET II | Motown ZL 72205 |
| 28/09/1985 | 28 | 7 | | SO MANY RIVERS | MCA MCF 3282 |

**WOMACK AND WOMACK** US husband and wife duo Cecil Womack (born 1947, Cleveland, OH) and Linda Cooke Womack (born 1953). Cecil (Bobby's brother) was previously in the Valentinos with his brothers, while Linda is Sam Cooke's daughter.

| | | | | | |
|---|---|---|---|---|---|
| 21/04/1984 | 45 | 13 | | LOVE WARS | Elektra 960293 |
| 22/06/1985 | 56 | 2 | | RADIO M.U.S.C. MAN | Elektra EKT 6 |
| 12/10/1985 | 87 | 2 | | THE ARTISTS VOLUME III **WOMACK AND WOMACK/THE O'JAYS/KLEEER/THE S.O.S. BAND** | Street Sounds ARTIS 3 |
| 27/08/1988 | 4 | 37 | ✪ | **CONSCIENCE** | Fourth & Broadway BRLP 519 |

**WOMBLES** UK puppet characters created by Elizabeth Beresford and turned into a children's TV series with Bernard Cribbins narrating. The theme song had been written by Mike Batt (born 6/2/1950, Southampton) and, following the success of the series, Batt dressed up as Orinoco for TV appearances (as part of the agreement with the estate of Elizabeth Beresford, he was not allowed to be seen wearing the body without the head of the outfit at any time). The 'group' featured Orinoco (saxophone/vocals), Wellington (guitar), Madame Cholet (bass), Great Uncle Bulgaria (violin) and Bungo (drums).

| | | | | | |
|---|---|---|---|---|---|
| 02/03/1974 | 19 | 17 | ● | WOMBLING SONGS | CBS 65803 |
| 13/07/1974 | 18 | 31 | ● | REMEMBER YOU'RE A WOMBLE | CBS 80191 |
| 21/12/1974 | 17 | 6 | ● | KEEP ON WOMBLING | CBS 80526 |

| | | | | |
|---|---|---|---|---|
| 08/01/1977 | 29 | 1 | | 20 WOMBLING GREATS .................................................. Warwick PR 5022 |
| 18/04/1998 | 26 | 3 | | THE BEST WOMBLES ALBUM SO FAR – VOLUME 1 ............................ Columbia 4895622 |

**STEVIE WONDER** US singer (born Steveland Judkins, although his mother later remarried and he was given the surname Morris, 13/5/1950, Saginaw, MI) who was blinded soon after birth when too much oxygen was pumped into his incubator. He learned to play percussion, harmonica and piano as a child, and was introduced to Motown by Miracle Ronnie White. He signed with Motown in 1960, releasing his first singles as Little Stevie Wonder (named by Berry Gordy) in 1962. He made his film debut in 1964 in *Bikini Beach*. He married singer Syreeta Wright in 1970, the couple later divorcing. He assumed full artistic control from 1971 and formed his own backing group Wonderlove. A car crash in 1973 left him in a coma for four days. In February 1999 he became Dr Stevie Wonder after being awarded an honorary doctorate from the University of Alabama in Birmingham. He has won nineteen Grammy Awards including: Best Pop Vocal Performance in 1973 for *You Are The Sunshine Of My Life;* Best Rhythm & Blues Song and Best Rhythm & Blues Vocal Performance in 1973 for *Superstition;* Best Rhythm & Blues Song in 1974 for *Living For The City;* Best Rhythm & Blues Vocal Performance in 1974 for *Boogie On Reggae Woman;* Best Rhythm & Blues Vocal Performance in 1976 for *I Wish;* Producer of the Year in 1976; Best Pop Vocal Performance by a Group in 1986 with Dionne Warwick, Elton John and Gladys Knight for *That's What Friends Are For;* Best R&B Singer and Best R&B Song in 1995 for *For Your Love;* Best R&B Male Vocal Performance in 1998 for *St Louis Blues;* Best Instrumental Arrangement with Vocals in 1998 with Herbie Hancock and Robert Sadin for *St Louis Blues;* and Best R&B Performance By A Duo Or Group With Vocal in 2002 with Take 6 for *Love's In Need Of Love Today*. His three Album of the Year awards came with three consecutive releases: when Paul Simon won the award in 1975 he thanked Stevie Wonder for not releasing an album that year! Stevie was inducted into the Rock & Roll Hall of Fame in 1989, and has a star on the Hollywood Walk of Fame.

| | | | | |
|---|---|---|---|---|
| 07/09/1968 | 25 | 10 | | STEVIE WONDER'S GREATEST HITS ...................................... Tamla Motown STML 11075 |
| 13/12/1969 | 17 | 2 | | MY CHERIE AMOUR ................................................... Tamla Motown STML 11128 |
| 12/02/1972 | 30 | 4 | | GREATEST HITS VOLUME 2 ............................................. Tamla Motown STML 11196 |
| 03/02/1973 | 16 | 48 | ● | TALKING BOOK ...................................................... Tamla Motown STMA 8007 |
| 01/09/1973 | 8 | 55 | ● | **INNERVISIONS** 1973 Grammy Award for Album of the Year ............... Tamla Motown STMA 8011 |
| 17/08/1974 | 5 | 16 | ● | **FULFILLINGNESS' FIRST FINALE** ▲² 1974 Grammy Awards for Album of the Year and Best Pop Vocal Performance ....................................................... Tamla Motown STMA 8019 |
| 16/10/1976 | 2 | 54 | ✪ | **SONGS IN THE KEY OF LIFE** ▲¹⁴ 1976 Grammy Awards for Album of the Year and Best Pop Vocal Performance. He later gave the latter award to Otis Blackwell in recognition of Blackwell's songwriting skills ........ Tamla Motown TMSP 6002 |
| 10/11/1979 | 8 | 15 | ● | **JOURNEY THROUGH THE SECRET LIFE OF PLANTS** ......................... Motown TMSP 6009 |
| 08/11/1980 | 2 | 55 | ✪ | **HOTTER THAN JULY** ................................................ Motown STMA 8035 |
| 22/05/1982 | 8 | 17 | ● | **ORIGINAL MUSIQUARIUM 1** ........................................... Motown TMSP 6012 |
| 22/09/1984 | 2 | 19 | ✪ | **WOMAN IN RED STEVIE WONDER AND FEATURING DIONNE WARWICK** Original soundtrack to the film ........ Motown ZL 72285 |
| 24/11/1984 | 20 | 10 | ● | LOVE SONGS – 16 CLASSIC HITS ....................................... Telstar STAR 2251 |
| 28/09/1985 | 5 | 16 | ● | **IN SQUARE CIRCLE** 1985 Grammy Award for Best Rhythm & Blues Vocal Performance ...... Motown ZL 72005 |
| 15/11/1986 | 21 | 10 | | DIANA ROSS. MICHAEL JACKSON. GLADYS KNIGHT. STEVIE WONDER. THEIR VERY BEST BACK TO BACK |
| | | | | **DIANA ROSS/MICHAEL JACKSON/GLADYS KNIGHT/STEVIE WONDER** ............... PrioriTyV PTVR2 |
| 28/11/1987 | 33 | 4 | ● | CHARACTERS ........................................................ RCA ZL 72001 |
| 08/06/1991 | 56 | 1 | | JUNGLE FEVER Original soundtrack to the film .......................... Motown ZL 71750 |
| 25/03/1995 | 8 | 4 | | **CONVERSATION PEACE** .............................................. Motown 5302382 |
| 23/11/1996 | 19 | 12 | | SONG REVIEW – A GREATEST HITS COLLECTION ◇ .......................... Motown 5307572 |
| 09/11/2002 | 16 | 29 | ● | THE DEFINITIVE COLLECTION .......................................... Universal TV 0665022 |

**WAYNE WONDER** Jamaican singer (born VonWayne Charles, 26/7/1972, Franklin Town) who recorded his debut single in 1985. He won the 2003 MOBO Award for Best Reggae Act.

| | | | | |
|---|---|---|---|---|
| 28/06/2003 | 40 | 7 | | NO HOLDING BACK ................................................... Atlantic/VP 7567836282 |

**WONDER STUFF** UK rock group formed in Birmingham in 1985 by Miles Hunt (born 29/7/1966, Birmingham, guitar/vocals), Malcolm Treece (guitar/vocals), Martin Gilks (drums) and Rob Jones (born 1964, bass). Jones left in 1990 and the group added Martin Bell (fiddle) and Paul Clifford (bass). Jones died from a drug overdose on 30/7/1993. They disbanded in 1994.

| | | | | |
|---|---|---|---|---|
| 27/08/1988 | 18 | 7 | ○ | THE EIGHT LEGGED GROOVE MACHINE .................................... Polydor GONLP 1 |
| 14/10/1989 | 5 | 8 | ● | **HUP** ............................................................. Polydor 8411871 |
| 08/06/1991 | 3 | 23 | ● | **NEVER LOVED ELVIS** ............................................... Polydor 8472521 |
| 16/10/1993 | 4 | 5 | ○ | **CONSTRUCTION FOR THE MODERN IDIOT** ................................ Polydor 5198942 |
| 08/10/1994 | 8 | 4 | | **IF THE BEATLES HAD READ HUNTER… THE SINGLES** ...................... Polydor 5213972 |
| 29/07/1995 | 74 | 1 | | LIVE IN MANCHESTER ................................................. Windsong WINCD 074X |

**ROY WOOD** UK singer (born Ulysses Adrian Wood, 8/11/1946, Birmingham) who formed the Move in 1966 and then Electric Light Orchestra in 1971 with Jeff Lynne. Wood lost interest in this project and announced the formation of Wizzard the following year, disbanding that group in 1975. He had begun recording as a solo artist in 1972.

| | | | | |
|---|---|---|---|---|
| 18/08/1973 | 15 | 8 | | BOULDERS ........................................................... Harvest SHVL 803 |
| 24/07/1982 | 37 | 6 | | THE SINGLES ........................................................ Speed 1000 |

**WOODENTOPS** UK group formed in Northampton by Rolo McGinty (guitar/vocals), Simon Mawby (guitar), Alice Thompson (keyboards), Frank De Freitas (bass) and Benny Staples (drums). After one single with the Food label in 1984 they switched to Rough Trade in 1985.

| | | | | |
|---|---|---|---|---|
| 12/07/1986 | 35 | 4 | | GIANT .............................................................. Rough Trade ROUGH 87 |
| 05/03/1988 | 48 | 2 | | WOODEN FOOT COPS ON THE HIGHWAY .................................... Rough Trade ROUGH 127 |

## EDWARD WOODWARD

**EDWARD WOODWARD** UK singer (born 1/6/1930, Croydon) who was best known as a stage and TV actor, appearing in the long-running series *Callan* 1967–73, and later the US TV series *The Equalizer*. His film credits include *Where There's A Will* (1954), *Becket* (1964), *The File Of The Golden Goose* (1969), *Young Winston* (1973), *Stand Up Virgin Soldiers* (1977), *Hands Of A Murder* (1990) and *Mister Johnson* (1991).

| DATE | POS | WKS | BPI | ALBUM TITLE | LABEL & NUMBER |
|---|---|---|---|---|---|
| 06/06/1970 | 53 | 2 | | THIS MAN ALONE | DJM DJLPS 405 |
| 19/08/1972 | 20 | 10 | | THE EDWARD WOODWARD ALBUM | Jam JAL 103 |

**WOOLPACKERS** UK group featuring members of the cast and the props man from the TV series *Emmerdale* – Zak Dingle, his girlfriend Lisa, Vic Windsor and Terry. The Woolpack is the name of the public house in the series.

| 14/12/1996 | 26 | 10 | | EMMERDANCE | RCA 74321444052 |
| 29/11/1997 | 48 | 3 | | THE GREATEST LINE DANCING PARTY ALBUM | RCA 74321512272 |

**WORKING WEEK** UK group formed by Simon Booth (guitar), Larry Stabins (various reeds) and fronted by singer Juliet Roberts. Roberts later went solo.

| 06/04/1985 | 23 | 9 | | WORKING NIGHTS | Virgin V 2343 |
| 27/09/1986 | 72 | 1 | | COMPANEROS | Virgin V 2397 |

**WORLD OF TWIST** UK group formed in Sheffield in 1985 by James Fry (vocals), Gordon King (guitar), Andrew Hobson (bass), Tony Ogden (drums) and a horn section. The group was re-formed in 1989 by Ogden, King and Hobson with Alan Frost (keyboards), Julia 'MC Shells', Angela Reilly and Nick Sanderson (drums).

| 09/11/1991 | 50 | 1 | | QUALITY STREET | Circa 17 |

**WORLD PARTY** UK singer/guitarist/keyboard player Karl Wallinger (born 19/10/1957, Leicester) who had previously been a member of the Waterboys and left in 1986 in order to set up World Party.

| 21/03/1987 | 56 | 4 | | PRIVATE REVOLUTION | Chrysalis CHEN 4 |
| 19/05/1990 | 36 | 10 | O | GOODBYE JUMBO | Ensign CHEN 10 |
| 08/05/1993 | 2 | 8 | ● | **BANG!** | Ensign CDCHEN 33 |
| 28/06/1997 | 34 | 2 | | EGYPTOLOGY | Chrysalis CDCHR 6124 |
| 02/09/2000 | 64 | 1 | | DUMBING UP | Papillion BTFLYCD 0006 |

**WRECKLESS ERIC** UK singer (born Eric Goulden, Newhaven, Sussex); he began his career during the late 1970s and effectively retired in the early part of the 1980s before recording under his own name. He later formed The Len Bright Combo with Russ Wilkins and Bruce Band (drums) and then Le Beat Group Electrique with Andre Barreau (bass) and Catfish Truton (drums).

| 01/04/1978 | 46 | 1 | | WRECKLESS ERIC | Stiff SEEZ 6 |
| 08/03/1980 | 30 | 4 | | BIG SMASH | Stiff SEEZ 21 |

**RICK WRIGHT** UK keyboard player (born 28/7/1945, London); a founding member of Pink Floyd in 1965, he launched a parallel solo career in 1996.

| 19/10/1996 | 61 | 1 | | BROKEN CHINA | EMI CDEMD 1098 |

**WU-TANG CLAN** US rap group formed in Staten Island, NYC by Shallah Raekwon (born Corey Woods, 12/1/1968), Method Man (born Clifford Smith, 1/4/1971, Staten Island), Genius/GZA (born Gary Grice, 22/8/1966, Brooklyn, NYC), Ol' Dirty Bastard (born Russell Jones, 15/11/1968, Brooklyn), Inspectah Deck (born Jason Hunter), Ghostface Killah (born Dennis Coles, 9/5/1970, Staten Island, aka Tony Starks and Ironman), U-God (born Lamont Hawkins), RZA (born Robert Diggs) and Masta Killa (born Elgin Turner). In 1995 they added fellow rapper Cappadonna (born 1969, Brooklyn).

| 14/06/1997 | ●[1] | 10 | O | **WU-TANG FOREVER** ▲[1] | Loud 74321457682 |
| 02/12/2000 | 19 | 13 | ● | THE W | Epic 4995762 |

**KLAUS WUNDERLICH** German organist (born 1930, Chemnitz); he began working in the local opera but soon switched to popular music. His series of Hammond and Moog led albums have proved extremely popular the world over. He died on 28/10/1997.

| 30/08/1975 | 27 | 8 | | THE HIT WORLD OF KLAUS WUNDERLICH | Decca SPA 434 |
| 20/05/1978 | 28 | 4 | | THE UNIQUE KLAUS WUNDERLICH SOUND | Decca DBC 5/5 |
| 26/05/1979 | 43 | 5 | | THE FANTASTIC SOUND OF KLAUS WUNDERLICH | Lotus LH 5013 |
| 17/03/1984 | 81 | 2 | | ON THE SUNNY SIDE OF THE STREET | Polydor POLD 5133 |

**WURZELS** UK comedy/vocal trio first formed in 1966 by Tommy Banner, Tony Bayliss and Pete Budd as backing group for folk singer and comedian Adge Cutler. Cutler was killed in a car crash in 1974 but the group continued, with Banner and Budd later joined by Amos Morgan and Squire Wintour.

| 11/03/1967 | 38 | 4 | | ADGE CUTLER AND THE WURZELS | Columbia SX 6126 |
| 03/07/1976 | 15 | 20 | O | COMBINE HARVESTER | One Up OU 2138 |
| 02/04/1977 | 32 | 5 | O | GOLDEN DELICIOUS | EMI NTS 122 |

**WWF SUPERSTARS** US/UK wrestlers from the World Wrestling Federation featuring the likes of Hulk Hogan, Sid Justice, Sergeant Slaughter and The Undertaker.

| 17/04/1993 | 10 | 5 | | **WRESTLEMANIA – THE ALBUM** | Arista 74321138062 |

**BILL WYMAN** UK singer (born William Perks, 24/10/1936, London) who joined the Rolling Stones in 1962, quitting in 1993. He married model Mandy Smith in 1989, shortly after opening his own Sticky Fingers restaurant (the name was taken from a Stones album title). The couple were divorced in 1992. He later formed Bill Wyman's Rhythm Kings with Georgie Fame in the line-up.

▲[9] Number of weeks album topped the US chart ◆[12] RIAA Diamond Awards ◇[3] IFPI Platinum Europe Awards

| | | | | |
|---|---|---|---|---|

08/06/1974 . . . . .39 . . . . . .1 . . . . . . MONKEY GRIP . . . . . . . . . . . . . . . . . . . . . . . . . . . . . . . . . . . . . . . . . . . . . . . . . . . . . . . . . . . . . . . . . .Rolling Stones COC 59102
10/04/1982 . . . . .55 . . . . . .6 . . . . . . BILL WYMAN . . . . . . . . . . . . . . . . . . . . . . . . . . . . . . . . . . . . . . . . . . . . . . . . . . . . . . . . . . . . . . . . . . . . .A&M AMLH 68540
27/05/2000 . . . . .52 . . . . . .1 . . . . . . GROOVIN **BILL WYMAN'S RHYTHM KINGS** . . . . . . . . . . . . . . . . . . . . . . . . . . . . . . . . . . . . . . . . . . . . . . . . . . .Papillion BTFLYCD 003

**TAMMY WYNETTE** US singer (born Virginia Wynette Pugh, 5/5/1942, Itawamba County, MS) who was discovered by Billy Sherrill and signed to Epic in 1967. She established herself as country music's top female performer with over fifteen #1s on the country charts (although never making #1 in the pop charts, the #11 for *Justified And Ancient* and #19 for *Stand By Your Man* her best showing). She married construction worker Euple Byrd in 1959, guitarist Don Chapel (he sold nude photographs of her), singer George Jones from 1969 until 1975 and estate agent Michael Tomlin (for 44 days), all of these marriages ending in d.i.v.o.r.c.e. She also took part in the *Perfect Day* project for the BBC's Children In Need charity. She died after a lengthy illness on 6/4/1998 with her death diagnosed as having been caused by a blood clot in a lung. Her family was unconvinced and got the body exhumed for an autopsy prior to launching a $50 million lawsuit against her doctor and then manager/husband George Richey (he was later dropped from the lawsuit after giving his consent to the autopsy). The autopsy found the cause of death to have been a blood clot to a lung. She won two Grammy Awards: Best Country & Western Vocal Performance in 1967 for *I Don't Want To Play House* and Best Country & Western Vocal Performance in 1969 for *Stand By Your Man*.

17/05/1975 . . . . .4 . . . . . .23 . . . . . .O **THE BEST OF TAMMY WYNETTE** . . . . . . . . . . . . . . . . . . . . . . . . . . . . . . . . . . . . . . . . . . . . . . . . . . . . . .Epic EPC 63578
21/06/1975 . . . . .13 . . . . . .7 . . . . . .O STAND BY YOUR MAN . . . . . . . . . . . . . . . . . . . . . . . . . . . . . . . . . . . . . . . . . . . . . . . . . . . . . . . . . . . . .Epic EPC 69141
17/12/1977 . . . . .3 . . . . . .11 . . . . . .● **20 COUNTRY CLASSICS** . . . . . . . . . . . . . . . . . . . . . . . . . . . . . . . . . . . . . . . . . . . . . . . . . . . . . . . . . . . . .CBS PR 5040
04/02/1978 . . . . .43 . . . . . .3 . . . . . . COUNTRY GIRL MEETS COUNTRY BOY . . . . . . . . . . . . . . . . . . . . . . . . . . . . . . . . . . . . . . . . . . . . . . .Warwick PR 5039
06/06/1987 . . . . .45 . . . . . .5 . . . . . .O ANNIVERSARY – 20 YEARS OF HITS . . . . . . . . . . . . . . . . . . . . . . . . . . . . . . . . . . . . . . . . . . . . . . . . . .Epic 4503931

○ Silver disc  ● Gold disc  ✪ Platinum disc (additional platinum units are indicated by a figure following the symbol)  ❶⁹ Number of weeks album topped the UK chart

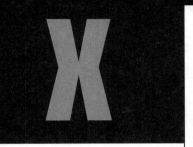

**X**

| | | |
|---|---|---|
| 06/09/2003 . . . . . 31 . . . . . 2 . . . . . | | |

**RICHARD X** UK producer/remixer (born in Whalley, Lancashire) who also records as Girls On Top.
RICHARD X PRESENTS HIS X-FACTOR VOLUME 1 . . . . . . . . . . . . . . . . . . . . . . . . . . . . . . . . . . . . . . . . . . . . . . Virgin CDRICH1

**X MAL DEUTSCHLAND** German rock group formed in Hamburg in 1980 by Anja Huwe (vocals), Manuela Rickers (guitar), Fiona Sangster (keyboards), Rita Simon (bass) and Caro May (drums), although Simon and May were later replaced by Wolfgang Ellerbrock and Manuela Zwingmann respectively. They first signed with 4AD in 1982. Zwingmann left after two singles and was replaced by Peter Bellendir.
07/07/1984 . . . . . 86 . . . . . . 1 . . . . . . TOCSIN . . . . . . . . . . . . . . . . . . . . . . . . . . . . . . . . . . . . . . . . . . . . . . . . . . . . . . . . . . . . . . . . . . . . . . . 4AD CAD 407

**X-PRESS 2** UK acid house group formed by Darren 'Rocky' Rock, Darren 'Diesel' House and Ashley 'Daddy Ash' Beedle. Beedle also records as the Black Science Orchestra, Rocky and Diesel as The Problem Kids.
04/05/2002 . . . . . 15 . . . . . . 3 . . . . . . MUZIKIZUM . . . . . . . . . . . . . . . . . . . . . . . . . . . . . . . . . . . . . . . . . . . . . . . . . . . . . . . . . . . . . . . Skint BRASSIC 23CD

**X-RAY SPEX** UK punk rock group formed in 1977 by Poly Styrene (born Marion Ellis, vocals), Paul Dean (bass), Paul 'BP' Harding (drums), Lora Logic (saxophone) and Jack 'Airport' Stafford (guitar). Styrene later went solo with limited success.
09/12/1978 . . . . . 30 . . . . . 14 . . . . . . GERM FREE ADOLESCENTS . . . . . . . . . . . . . . . . . . . . . . . . . . . . . . . . . . . . . . . . . . . . . . EMI International INS 3023

**XTC** UK group formed by Andy Partridge (born 1/11/1953, Valletta, Malta, guitar/vocals), Colin Moulding (born 17/8/1955, Swindon, bass/vocals), Dave Gregory (born 21/9/1952, Swindon, keyboards) and Terry Chambers (drums). They stopped touring in 1982 to concentrate on studio work. Partridge later released singles as Buster Gonad And The Jolly Testicles.

| | | | |
|---|---|---|---|
| 11/02/1978 . . . . . 38 . . . . . . 4 . . . . . | WHITE MUSIC . . . . . . . . . . . . . . . . . . . . . . . . . . . . . . . . . . . . . . . . . . . . . . . . . . . . . . . . . . . . Virgin V 2095 | | |
| 28/10/1978 . . . . . 21 . . . . . . 3 . . . . . | GO 2 . . . . . . . . . . . . . . . . . . . . . . . . . . . . . . . . . . . . . . . . . . . . . . . . . . . . . . . . . . . . . . . . . . . Virgin V 2108 | | |
| 01/09/1979 . . . . . 34 . . . . . . 7 . . . . . | DRUMS AND WIRES . . . . . . . . . . . . . . . . . . . . . . . . . . . . . . . . . . . . . . . . . . . . . . . . . . . . . . . Virgin V 2129 | | |
| 20/09/1980 . . . 16 . . . . . . 7 . . . . . . ○ | BLACK SEA . . . . . . . . . . . . . . . . . . . . . . . . . . . . . . . . . . . . . . . . . . . . . . . . . . . . . . . . . . . . . Virgin V 2173 | | |
| 20/02/1982 . . . . . 5 . . . . 11 . . . . . . ○ | **ENGLISH SETTLEMENT** . . . . . . . . . . . . . . . . . . . . . . . . . . . . . . . . . . . . . . . . . . . . . . . . . . . Virgin V 2223 | | |
| 13/11/1982 . . . . . 54 . . . . . . 3 . . . . . | WAXWORKS — SOME SINGLES (1977–1982) . . . . . . . . . . . . . . . . . . . . . . . . . . . . . . . . . . . Virgin V 2251 | | |
| 10/09/1983 . . . . . 51 . . . . . . 4 . . . . . | MUMMER . . . . . . . . . . . . . . . . . . . . . . . . . . . . . . . . . . . . . . . . . . . . . . . . . . . . . . . . . . . . . Virgin V 2264 | | |
| 27/10/1984 . . . . . 38 . . . . . . 2 . . . . . | THE BIG EXPRESS . . . . . . . . . . . . . . . . . . . . . . . . . . . . . . . . . . . . . . . . . . . . . . . . . . . . . . . Virgin V 2325 | | |
| 08/11/1986 . . . . . 90 . . . . . . 1 . . . . . | SKYLARKING . . . . . . . . . . . . . . . . . . . . . . . . . . . . . . . . . . . . . . . . . . . . . . . . . . . . . . . . . . . Virgin V 2399 | | |
| 11/03/1989 . . . . . 28 . . . . . . 3 . . . . . | ORANGES AND LEMONS . . . . . . . . . . . . . . . . . . . . . . . . . . . . . . . . . . . . . . . . . . . . . . . . . . Virgin V 2581 | | |
| 09/05/1992 . . . . . 28 . . . . . . 2 . . . . . | NONSUCH . . . . . . . . . . . . . . . . . . . . . . . . . . . . . . . . . . . . . . . . . . . . . . . . . . . . . . . . . . . Virgin CDV 2699 | | |
| 28/09/1996 . . . . . 33 . . . . . . 2 . . . . . | FOSSIL FUEL — THE XTC SINGLES COLLECTION 1977–1992 . . . . . . . . . . . . . . . . . . . . Virgin CDVDX 2811 | | |
| 06/03/1999 . . . . . 42 . . . . . . 1 . . . . . | APPLE VENUS — VOLUME 1 . . . . . . . . . . . . . . . . . . . . . . . . . . . . . . . . . . . . . . . . . . Cooking Vinyl COOKCD 172 | | |
| 03/06/2000 . . . . . 40 . . . . . . 1 . . . . . | APPLE VENUS — VOLUME 2 **XTC/WASP STAR** . . . . . . . . . . . . . . . . . . . . . . . . . Cooking Vinyl COOKCD 194 | | |

**XZIBIT** US rapper (born Alvin Nathaniel Joiner, Detroit, MI, raised in New Mexico) who was originally a member of The Likwit Crew with Tha Alkaholiks and King T. He made his album debut in 1996 for Loud Records, before linking with Dr. Dre.

| | | |
|---|---|---|
| 10/02/2001 . . . . . 27 . . . . 11 . . . . . . ○ | RESTLESS . . . . . . . . . . . . . . . . . . . . . . . . . . . . . . . . . . . . . . . . . . . . . . . . . . . . . . . . . . . . . . Epic 4989132 | |
| 12/10/2002 . . . . . 43 . . . . . . 2 . . . . . | MAN VS MACHINE . . . . . . . . . . . . . . . . . . . . . . . . . . . . . . . . . . . . . . . . . . . . . . . . . . . . . . . . Epic 5047539 | |

# Y

**Y&T** US rock group formed in San Francisco, CA during the 1970s by Dave Meniketti (guitar/vocals), Joey Alves (guitar), Philip Kennemore (bass) and Leonard Haze (drums) as Yesterday And Today, subsequently shortening their name to Y&T. Haze left in 1986 and was replaced by Jimmy DeGrasso; Alves left in 1989 and was replaced by Stef Burns. They disbanded in 1990.

| | | | |
|---|---|---|---|
| 11/09/1982 | 53 | 8 | BLACK TIGER .........................................................................A&M AMLH 64910 |
| 10/09/1983 | 35 | 4 | MEAN STREAK .........................................................................A&M AMLX 64960 |
| 18/08/1984 | 33 | 3 | IN ROCK WE TRUST ...................................................................A&M AMLX 65007 |

**YANNI** Greek composer/keyboard player (born 14/11/1954, Kalamata) who moved to the USA in 1972 to study psychology at the University of Minnesota and later moved to Los Angeles. His albums for the Private Music label made him a star in both the USA and in Greece. His album *Yanni Live At The Acropolis*, 1993 (the first time he performed live in Greece) is his best-selling album worldwide.

| | | | |
|---|---|---|---|
| 04/04/1998 | 40 | 2 | TRIBUTE ...............................................................................Virgin CDVUS 135 |

**YARDBIRDS** UK rock group formed in 1963 by Keith Relf (born 22/3/1943, Richmond, vocals), Anthony 'Top' Topham (guitar), Chris Dreja (born 11/11/1945, Surbiton, guitar), Paul 'Sam' Samwell-Smith (born 8/5/1943, Richmond, bass) and Jim McCarty (born 25/7/1943, Liverpool, drums), taking their name from a Jack Kerouac book. Topham left soon after and was replaced by Eric Clapton (born Eric Clapp, 30/3/1945, Ripley, Surrey), who in turn left in 1965 and was replaced by Jeff Beck (born 24/6/1944, Wallington, Surrey). Samwell-Smith left in 1966 and was replaced by Jimmy Page (born 9/1/1944, Heston, Middlesex). They disbanded in July 1968, Page forming The New Yardbirds in the October, which evolved into Led Zeppelin. Relf died on 14/5/1976, electrocuted while playing his guitar at home. The group was inducted into the Rock & Roll Hall of Fame in 1992.

| | | | |
|---|---|---|---|
| 23/07/1966 | 20 | 8 | YARDBIRDS ............................................................................Columbia SX 6063 |

**YAZOO** UK group formed by former Depeche Mode keyboard player Vince Clarke (born 3/7/1960, South Woodford) and singer Alison 'Alf' Moyet (born Genevieve Alison Moyet, 18/6/1961, Basildon, Essex). Clarke went on to front Assembly and then Erasure and Moyet pursued a successful solo career. The group won the 1983 BRIT Award for Best British Newcomer.

| | | | |
|---|---|---|---|
| 04/09/1982 | 2 | 63 | ✪ | UPSTAIRS AT ERIC'S .................................................................Mute STUMM 7 |
| 16/07/1983 | ❶² | 20 | ● | YOU AND ME BOTH ..................................................................Mute STUMM 12 |
| 18/09/1999 | 22 | 3 | ONLY YAZOO – THE BEST OF YAZOO ...................................................Mute CDMUTEL 6 |

**YAZZ** UK singer (born Yasmin Evans, 19/5/1963, London) who was formerly a model before recording with Suzette Smithson and Austin Howards as Biz in 1983, scoring a number of club hits. She later fronted *Doctorin' The House* with Coldcut's Matt Black and Jonathan Moore, before launching her own career with Big Life, the label set up by her future husband Jazz Summers.

| | | | |
|---|---|---|---|
| 26/11/1988 | 3 | 32 | ✪² | WANTED/WANTED – THE REMIXES .................................................Big Life YAZZLP 1 |

**YEAH YEAH YEAH** US rock group formed in New York City by Karen Orzolek (vocals), Nick Zinner (guitar) and Brian Chase (drums).

| | | | |
|---|---|---|---|
| 10/05/2003 | 13 | 6 | ○ | FEVER TO TELL ........................................................................Dress Up 0760612 |

**TRISHA YEARWOOD** US singer (born 19/9/1964, Monticello, GA ) who was a backing singer when she was discovered by Garth Brooks and invited to provide vocals on his *No Fences* album. Trisha subsequently opened for him on his 1991 US tour and the exposure led to her becoming the first female singer to top the country charts with her debut single, *She's In Love With The Boy*. By 1994 she had written her autobiography (although it was largely 'ghosted'), and the following year married Robert Reynolds from The Mavericks, although the marriage ended in 1999. She recorded the original version of *How Do I Live*, which was featured in the Nicolas Cage film *Con Air*; LeAnn Rimes scored the bigger hit with a cover version. Trisha has won three Grammy Awards: Best Country Vocal Collaboration in 1994 with Aaron Neville for *I Fall To Pieces*, Best Country Collaboration With Vocals in 1997 with Garth Brooks for *In Another's Eyes* and Best Female Country Vocal Performance the same year for *How Do I Live*.

| | | | |
|---|---|---|---|
| 25/07/1998 | 36 | 2 | WHERE YOUR ROAD LEADS .....................................................MCA Nashville UMD 80513 |

**YELLO** Swiss trio formed in Zurich in 1979 by Dieter Meiler (horns/vocals), Boris Blank (keyboards) and Carlos Peron (keyboards). Meiler had previously been in the Swiss national golf team.

| | | | |
|---|---|---|---|
| 21/05/1983 | 65 | 2 | YOU GOTTA SAY YES TO ANOTHER EXCESS ...............................................Stiff SEEZ 48 |

○ Silver disc  ● Gold disc  ✪ Platinum disc (additional platinum units are indicated by a figure following the symbol)  ◉ Albums released prior to 1973 that are known to have sold over 1 million copies in the UK

| 06/04/1985 | 92 | 1 | | STELLA | Elektra EKT 1 |
| 04/07/1987 | 48 | 3 | | ONE SECOND | Mercury MERH 100 |
| 10/12/1988 | 56 | 7 | ○ | FLAG | Mercury 8367781 |
| 29/06/1991 | 37 | 2 | | BABY | Mercury 8487911 |

**BRYN YEMM** UK gospel/inspirational singer born in Brynmawr, Wales to an Italian mother.

| 09/06/1984 | 57 | 2 | | HOW DO I LOVE THEE | Lifestyle LEG 17 |
| 07/07/1984 | 67 | 8 | | HOW GREAT THOU ART | Lifestyle LEG 15 |
| 22/12/1984 | 95 | 2 | | THE BRYN YEMM CHRISTMAS COLLECTION | Bay 104 |
| 26/10/1985 | 85 | 2 | | MY TRIBUTE – BRYN YEMM INSPIRATIONAL ALBUM | Word WSTR 9665 |

**YES** UK rock group formed in London in 1968 by Jon Anderson (born 25/10/1944, Accrington, vocals), Peter Banks, Tony Kaye, Chris Squire (born 4/3/1948, London, bass) and Bill Bruford (born 17/5/1948, London, drums). Banks and Kaye departed in 1971 and were replaced by Steve Howe (born 8/4/1947, London, guitar) and Rick Wakeman (born 18/5/1949, London, keyboards). Bruford joined King Crimson in 1972 and was replaced by Alan White (born 14/6/1949, Pelton, Durham). Wakeman left in 1974 but returned in 1976 when his replacement Patrick Moraz quit. Both Wakeman and Anderson left in 1980 with their replacements being ex-Buggles members Trevor Horn and Geoff Downes, although Yes disbanded soon after. They re-formed in 1983 with Anderson, Kaye, Squire, White and Trevor Rabin. The group won the 1984 Grammy Award for Best Rock Instrumental Performance for *Cinema*. Anderson, Bruford, Wakeman and Howe also combined to record as Anderson Bruford Wakeman Howe, and Bruford was also a member of U.K.

| 01/08/1970 | 45 | 3 | | TIME AND A WORD | Atlantic 2400 006 |
| 03/04/1971 | 7 | 29 | | **THE YES ALBUM** | Atlantic 2400 101 |
| 04/12/1971 | 7 | 17 | ◎ | **FRAGILE** | Atlantic 2409 019 |
| 23/09/1972 | 4 | 13 | ◎ | **CLOSE TO THE EDGE** | Atlantic K 50012 |
| 26/05/1973 | 7 | 13 | | YESSONGS | Atlantic K 60045 |
| 22/12/1973 | ❶² | 15 | ● | TALES FROM TOPOGRAPHIC OCEANS | Atlantic K 80001 |
| 21/12/1974 | 4 | 11 | | RELAYER | Atlantic K 50096 |
| 29/03/1975 | 27 | 7 | | YESTERDAYS | Atlantic K 50048 |
| 30/07/1977 | ❶² | 28 | ● | **GOING FOR THE ONE** | Atlantic K 50379 |
| 07/10/1978 | 8 | 11 | | TORMATO | Atlantic K 50518 |
| 30/08/1980 | 2 | 8 | ○ | DRAMA | Atlantic K 50736 |
| 10/01/1981 | 22 | 9 | ○ | YESSHOWS | Atlantic K 60142 |
| 26/11/1983 | 16 | 28 | ● | 90125 | Atco 790125 |
| 29/03/1986 | 44 | 3 | | 9012 LIVE: THE SOLOS | Atco 790 4741 |
| 10/10/1987 | 17 | 5 | | BIG GENERATOR | Atco WEX 70 |
| 11/05/1991 | 7 | 6 | | **UNION** | Arista 211558 |
| 02/04/1994 | 20 | 4 | | TALK | London 8284892 |
| 09/11/1996 | 48 | 1 | | KEYS TO ASCENSION | Essential EDFCD 417 |
| 15/11/1997 | 62 | 1 | | KEYS TO ASCENSION 2 | Essential EDFCD 457 |
| 02/10/1999 | 36 | 1 | | THE LADDER | Eagle EAGCD 088 |
| 22/09/2001 | 71 | 1 | | MAGNIFICATION | Eagle EAGCD 189 |
| 09/08/2003 | 10 | 7 | ○ | **THE ULTIMATE YES – 35TH ANNIVERSARY** | WSM 8122737022 |

**DWIGHT YOAKAM** US singer/guitarist (born 23/10/1956, Pikeville, KY) who played in various clubs in Los Angeles as well as working as a truck driver. He first recorded for Oak Records and then Enigma, before joining Warner Brothers' Reprise label in 1984. A regular on the US country charts since 1986, he finally made his national breakthrough in 1993. His film appearances include *Red Rock West* (1993) and *Sling Blade* (1996). He has won two Grammy Awards: Best Country Vocal Performance in 1993 for *Ain't That Lonely Yet* and Best Country Vocal Collaboration in 1998 with Clint Black, Joe Diffie, Merle Haggard, Emmylou Harris, Alison Krauss, Patty Loveless, Earl Scruggs, Ricky Skaggs, Marty Stuart, Pam Tillis, Randy Travis and Travis Tritt for *Same Old Train*.

| 09/05/1987 | 51 | 3 | | HILLBILLY DELUXE | Reprise WX 106 |
| 13/08/1988 | 87 | 1 | | BUENAS NOCHES FROM A LONELY ROOM | Reprise WX 193 |

**FARON YOUNG** US country singer/guitarist (born 25/2/1932, Shreveport, LA) who scored over 30 top ten hits on the US country charts and later appeared in numerous films. He committed suicide by shooting himself in the head on 10/12/1996.

| 28/10/1972 | 27 | 5 | | IT'S FOUR IN THE MORNING | Mercury 6338 095 |

**NEIL YOUNG** Canadian singer (born 12/11/1945, Toronto) who formed the Mynah Birds (featuring Rick James as lead singer) in the early 1960s. Moving to Los Angeles, CA in 1966 and joining Stephen Stills' band Buffalo Springfield, he signed a solo deal with Reprise in 1969. In 1970 he joined Crosby Stills And Nash, initially for live work only but has recorded with them periodically for twenty years. He was inducted into the Rock & Roll Hall of Fame in 1995.

| DATE | POS | WKS | BPI | ALBUM TITLE | LABEL & NUMBER |
|---|---|---|---|---|---|
| 31/10/1970 | 7 | 68 | | AFTER THE GOLDRUSH | Reprise RSLP 6383 |
| 04/03/1972 | ●¹ | 34 | | HARVEST ▲² | Reprise K 54005 |
| 27/10/1973 | 20 | 2 | | TIME FADES AWAY | Warner Brothers K 54010 |
| 10/08/1974 | 42 | 2 | O | ON THE BEACH | Reprise K 54014 |
| 05/07/1975 | 48 | 1 | | TONIGHT'S THE NIGHT | Reprise K 54040 |
| 27/12/1975 | 44 | 2 | O | ZUMA NEIL YOUNG AND CRAZY HORSE | Reprise K 54057 |
| 09/10/1976 | 12 | 5 | | LONG MAY YOU RUN STILLS-YOUNG BAND | Reprise K 54081 |
| 09/07/1977 | 17 | 8 | O | AMERICAN STARS 'N' BARS | Reprise K 54088 |
| 17/12/1977 | 46 | 5 | O | DECADE | Reprise K 64037 |
| 28/10/1978 | 42 | 3 | O | COMES A TIME | Reprise K 54099 |
| 14/07/1979 | 13 | 13 | | RUST NEVER SLEEPS | Reprise K 54105 |
| 01/12/1979 | 55 | 3 | ● | LIVE RUST This and the above hit credited to NEIL YOUNG AND CRAZY HORSE | Reprise K 64041 |
| 15/11/1980 | 34 | 3 | | HAWKS AND DOVES | Reprise K 54109 |
| 14/11/1981 | 69 | 3 | | RE-AC-TOR NEIL YOUNG AND CRAZY HORSE | Reprise K 54116 |
| 05/02/1983 | 29 | 5 | | TRANS | Geffen GEF 25019 |
| 03/09/1983 | 50 | 3 | | EVERYBODY'S ROCKIN' NEIL YOUNG AND THE SHOCKING PINKS | Geffen GEF 25590 |
| 14/09/1985 | 39 | 3 | | OLD WAYS | Geffen GEF 26377 |
| 02/08/1986 | 52 | 2 | | LANDING ON WATER | Geffen 9241091 |
| 04/07/1987 | 71 | 1 | | LIFE NEIL YOUNG AND CRAZY HORSE | Geffen WX 109 |
| 30/04/1988 | 56 | 3 | | THIS NOTE'S FOR YOU NEIL YOUNG AND THE BLUE NOTES | WEA WX 168 |
| 21/10/1989 | 17 | 5 | O | FREEDOM | Reprise WX 257 |
| 22/09/1990 | 15 | 5 | O | RAGGED GLORY | Reprise WX 374 |
| 02/11/1991 | 20 | 3 | O | WELD This and the above hit credited to NEIL YOUNG AND CRAZY HORSE | Reprise 7599266711 |
| 14/11/1992 | 9 | 18 | ● | HARVEST MOON | Reprise 9362450572 |
| 23/01/1993 | 69 | 1 | | LUCKY THIRTEEN | Geffen GED 24452 |
| 26/06/1993 | 4 | 13 | ● | UNPLUGGED | Reprise 9362453102 |
| 27/08/1994 | 2 | 7 | ● | SLEEPS WITH ANGELS NEIL YOUNG AND CRAZY HORSE | Reprise 9362457492 |
| 08/07/1995 | 4 | 9 | O | MIRROR BALL | Reprise 9362459342 |
| 06/07/1996 | 17 | 5 | | BROKEN ARROW | Reprise 9362462912 |
| 28/06/1997 | 36 | 2 | | YEAR OF THE HORSE | Reprise 9362466522 |
| 06/05/2000 | 10 | 4 | | SILVER AND GOLD This and the above hit credited to NEIL YOUNG AND CRAZY HORSE | Reprise 9362473052 |
| 20/04/2002 | 24 | 3 | | ARE YOU PASSIONATE | Reprise 9362481112 |
| 27/07/2002 | 15 | 13 | ● | DECADE Remastered version of Reprise K 64037 | Reprise 7599272332 |
| 26/07/2003 | 42 | 1 | | ON THE BEACH Remastered version of Reprise K 54014 | Reprise 9362484972 |
| 30/08/2003 | 24 | 3 | | GREENDALE NEIL YOUNG AND CRAZY HORSE | Reprise 9362485432 |

**PAUL YOUNG** UK singer (born 17/1/1956, Luton) who was an apprentice at Vauxhall Cars when he formed Streetband, who scored with the novelty *Toast*. After two albums the group disbanded, Young taking two members (John Gifford and Mick Pearl) and forming Q-Tips, a 1960s-influenced R&B outfit. After two years he went solo, releasing his debut (*Iron Out The Rough Spots*) in November 1982. He was named Best British Newcomer in 1984 and Best British Male at the 1985 BRIT Awards He also won the 1986 BRIT Award for Best Video for *Every Time You Go Away*.

| DATE | POS | WKS | BPI | ALBUM TITLE | LABEL & NUMBER |
|---|---|---|---|---|---|
| 30/07/1983 | ●⁵ | 119 | ✪³ | NO PARLEZ | CBS 25521 |
| 06/04/1985 | ●¹ | 49 | ✪² | THE SECRET OF ASSOCIATION | CBS 26234 |
| 01/11/1986 | 4 | 17 | ✪ | BETWEEN TWO FIRES | CBS 4501501 |
| 16/06/1990 | 4 | 11 | ● | OTHER VOICES | CBS 4669171 |
| 14/09/1991 | ●¹ | 27 | ✪³ | FROM TIME TO TIME – THE SINGLES COLLECTION | Columbia 4688251 |
| 23/10/1993 | 27 | 2 | | THE CROSSING | Columbia 4739282 |
| 26/11/1994 | 64 | 2 | | REFLECTIONS | Vision VISCD 1 |
| 31/05/1997 | 39 | 2 | | PAUL YOUNG | East West 0630186192 |
| 21/06/2003 | 27 | 3 | | THE ESSENTIAL | Sony Music 5122992 |

**WILL YOUNG** UK singer (born 20/1/1979) who studied politics at Exeter University and musical theatre at the Arts Educational School in London before beating 10,000 entrants to win the TV series *Pop Idol*, and the prize of a recording contract with BMG. He polled over 5 million votes in the final with Gareth Gates, and his debut single sold 385,483 copies on its first day of release and 1,108,269 copies in its first week. In so doing it became the biggest-selling first-week single by a debut artist and the second biggest-selling first-week single of all time (only Elton John's *Candle In The Wind* tribute to Princess Diana has sold more). Young was named British Breakthrough Artist at the 2003 BRIT Awards.

| DATE | POS | WKS | BPI | ALBUM TITLE | LABEL & NUMBER |
|---|---|---|---|---|---|
| 19/10/2002 | ●² | 19 | ✪² | FROM NOW ON | S 74321969592 |
| 13/12/2003 | ●² | 29+ | ✪⁴ | FRIDAY'S CHILD ◇ | S 82876557462 |

**YOUNG DISCIPLES** UK jazz-funk group formed by Mark 'O' and Femi, with Carleen Anderson and MC Mell 'O' providing the vocals. Anderson and Mark 'O' subsequently recorded solo. Later Anderson joined The Brand New Heavies and went on to re-record *Apparently Nothin'*.

31/08/1991 .....21......5 ......O      ROAD TO FREEDOM . . . . . . . . . . . . . . . . . . . . . . . . . . . . . . . . . . . . . . . . . . . . . . . . . . . . . . . . .Talkin Loud 5100971

**YOUNG GODS** Swiss rock group formed in 1985 by Franz Reise, Use Drums and Alain Mono.

15/02/1992 .....54 ......1 ......      T.V. SKY . . . . . . . . . . . . . . . . . . . . . . . . . . . . . . . . . . . . . . . . . . . . . . . . . . . . . . . . . . . .Play It Again Sam PIAS 201CD

**YOUNG HEART ATTACK** US rock group formed in Austin, TX in 2001 by Jennifer Stephens (vocals), Chris Hodge (guitar/vocals), Frenchie (guitar), Steven Hall (bass) and Joey Shuffield (drums).

24/04/2004 .....71 ......1 ......      MOUTHFUL OF LOVE . . . . . . . . . . . . . . . . . . . . . . . . . . . . . . . . . . . . . . . . . . . . . . . . . . . . . .XL Recordings XLCD173

**SYDNEY YOUNGBLOOD** US singer (born Sydney Ford, 1960, San Antonio, TX) who joined the US Army and was stationed in Germany before coming to the UK to launch his singing career.

28/10/1989 .....23 .....17 ......●      FEELING FREE . . . . . . . . . . . . . . . . . . . . . . . . . . . . . . . . . . . . . . . . . . . . . . . . . . . . . . . . . . . . . . . .Circa 9

**FRANK ZAPPA** US singer/songwriter/multi-instrumentalist/producer/author/journalist (born 21/12/1940, Baltimore, MD) who began his career as a drummer with R&B group The Ramblers and first began writing when he joined another R&B group, the Soul Giants. The group featured Zappa, Roy Collins (vocals), Roy Estrada (bass) and Jimmy Carl Black (drums). Eventually they changed their name to Mothers (the record company insisted that 'Of Invention' was added to the name) in 1966. In 1968 they recorded *We're Only In It For The Money*, complete with a parody of The Beatles' *Sgt Pepper* sleeve (the sleeve featured 86 'personalities', including Harry S. Truman, Ludwig Van Beethoven and a Dallas policeman), perhaps their best-known album. Always prolific, Zappa combined writing and recording with the Mothers Of Invention with a parallel solo career, hitting the UK charts in 1970 with *Hot Rats*. The following year a fire destroyed the group's equipment whilst they were performing in Montreux (the event was commemorated by Deep Purple in the song *Smoke On The Water*), whilst later the same year an incident at the Rainbow Theatre left Zappa in a wheelchair for almost a year (the jealous boyfriend of a fan, Trevor Howell, pushed Zappa off the stage, breaking his ankle in several places and fracturing his skull). Whilst some of Zappa's work was controversial (a Broadway musical called *Thing Fish* had AIDS, homophobia and racism as its theme), he was highly regarded throughout the musical world. He won three Grammy Awards: Best Rock Instrumental Performance in 1987 for *Jazz From Hell,* Best Rock Instrumental Performance in 1993 with Zappa's Universe Rock Group Featuring Steve Vai for *Sofa,* and Best Boxed Album Package with Gail Zappa in 1995 for *Civilization Phaze III*. He was also made Cultural Liaison Officer with the West by Czechoslovakia in 1990 and the following year announced plans to run for US President as an independent candidate in the 1992 elections, a move that prompted several death threats. In the event he never stood because in November 1991 it was revealed that he was suffering from prostate cancer and he died on 4/12/1993.

| | | | | |
|---|---|---|---|---|
| 28/02/1970 | 9 | 27 | | **HOT RATS** ..................................................................... Reprise RSLP 6356 |
| 19/12/1970 | 43 | 1 | | CHUNGA'S REVENGE ........................................................... Reprise RSLP 2030 |
| 06/05/1978 | 55 | 1 | | ZAPPA IN NEW YORK ........................................................... Discreet K 69204 |
| 10/03/1979 | 32 | 7 | | SHEIK YERBOUTI ................................................................. CBS 88339 |
| 13/10/1979 | 62 | 3 | | JOE'S GARAGE ACT I ............................................................ CBS 86101 |
| 19/01/1980 | 75 | 1 | | JOE'S GARAGE ACTS II & III ..................................................... CBS 88475 |
| 16/05/1981 | 55 | 4 | | TINSEL TOWN REBELLION ........................................................ CBS 88516 |
| 24/10/1981 | 51 | 2 | | YOU ARE WHAT YOU IS .......................................................... CBS 88560 |
| 19/06/1982 | 61 | 4 | | SHIP ARRIVING TOO LATE TO SAVE A DROWNING WITCH .......................... CBS 85804 |
| 18/06/1983 | 87 | 1 | | THE MAN FROM UTOPIA ......................................................... CBS 25251 |
| 27/10/1984 | 53 | 2 | | THEM OR US .................................................................... EMI FZD 1 |
| 30/04/1988 | 82 | 2 | | GUITAR ......................................................................... Zappa ZAPPA 6 |
| 02/09/1995 | 45 | 2 | | STRICTLY COMMERCIAL – THE BEST OF FRANK ZAPPA ............................ Rykodisc RCD 40600 |

**LENA ZAVARONI** UK singer (born 4/11/1963, Rothesay, Scotland) who first came to prominence aged ten when she won TV's *Opportunity Knocks*. She later became a successful TV presenter but died on 1/10/1999 after suffering from an eating disorder.

| | | | |
|---|---|---|---|
| 23/03/1974 | 8 | 5 | **MA** ............................................................................ Philips 6308 201 |

**ZERO 7** UK production duo formed by Henry Binns and Sam Hardaker. Both began their careers working in a London recording studio, then moved on to remixing (adopting their working name Zero 7 from a nightclub in Honduras) and recorded their debut in 1999. Their debut album also featured contributions from vocalists Sophie Barker, Sia Furler and Mozez.

| | | | | |
|---|---|---|---|---|
| 05/05/2001 | 28 | 43 | ● | SIMPLE THINGS ................................................................. Ultimate Dilemma UDRCD 016 |
| 13/03/2004 | 3 | 14 | ● | **WHEN IT FALLS** ................................................................ Ultimate Dilemma 5046709875 |

**WARREN ZEVON** US singer (born 24/1/1947, Chicago, IL) who made his debut album in 1969 and also wrote the score for a number of films. He died from cancer on 7/9/2003. He has won two Grammy Awards including Best Rock Performance by a Duo or Group with Vocal in 2003 with Bruce Springsteen for *Disorder In The House.*

| | | | |
|---|---|---|---|
| 27/09/2003 | 57 | 1 | THE WIND 2003 Grammy Award for Best Contemporary Folk Album ...................................... Rykodisc RCD 17001 |

**ZHANE** US duo of Renee Neufville and Jean Norris who formed whilst at Temple University in Philadelphia, PA.

| | | | |
|---|---|---|---|
| 10/05/1997 | 52 | 1 | SATURDAY NIGHT ............................................................... Motown 5307512 |

**HANS ZIMMER** German composer (born 1957, Frankfurt) who began his professional career writing jingles for TV commercials before writing the score for his first film, *Eureka* in 1981. He went onto become one of the most prolific film theme composers around. During 1988 he composed the score for no fewer than fourteen films. His credits include *Rain Man* (for which he was nominated for an Oscar; he believes he didn't win because he was only 30 years of age at the time!), *Bird On A Wire, Days Of Thunder, The Assassin, Thelma And Louise, Gladiators, Hannibal* and *Pearl Harbor*. He has won three Grammy Awards (where age obviously isn't a consideration): Best Instrumental Arrangement Accompanying Vocal with Andrae Crouch and Lebo Morake for *Circle of Life* from *The Lion King*, Best Musical Album For Children with Mark Mancina, Jay Rifkin and Chris Thomas in 1994 for *The Lion King* and Best Instrumental Composition for a Movie or TV in 1995 for *Crimson Tide*.

| | | | | | |
|---|---|---|---|---|---|
| 27/05/2000 | 17 | 16 | | GLADIATOR **HANS ZIMMER & LISA GERRARD** Original soundtrack to the film | Decca 4670942 |
| 03/03/2001 | 74 | 2 | | HANNIBAL Original soundtrack to the film | Decca 4676962 |
| 16/06/2001 | 50 | 2 | ○ | PEARL HARBOR **GREENAWAY/ZIMMER** Original soundtrack to the film | Hollywood 9362481132 |

**ZION TRAIN** UK group formed in London in 1990 by Molara (vocals), Neil Perch (DJ/bass), David Tench (trumpet), Colin Cod (keyboards) and Chris (trombone). Their debut release was issued on their own Zion Records; they signed with China Records in 1995.

| | | | | | |
|---|---|---|---|---|---|
| 13/07/1996 | 56 | 1 | | GROW TOGETHER | China WOLCD 1071 |

**ZOE** UK singer (born Zoe Jayne Pollack, 1970) who began her career as a backing vocalist for the likes of Bananarama before launching a solo career.

| | | | | | |
|---|---|---|---|---|---|
| 07/12/1991 | 67 | 1 | | SCARLET, RED AND BLUE | M&G 5114431 |

**ROB ZOMBIE** US singer (born Robert Cummings, 12/1/1966, Haverhill, MA) who formed White Zombie in 1985. He worked as a bike messenger, porn magazine art director and production assistant for a children's TV series before concentrating on music full time. He went solo in 1998 and the success of his debut album prompted the end of White Zombie.

| | | | | | |
|---|---|---|---|---|---|
| 05/09/1998 | 37 | 2 | | HELLBILLY DELUXE | Geffen GED 25212 |

**ZUCCHERO** Italian singer/guitarist (born Adelmo Fornaciari, 1956) who began his career training to become a veterinary surgeon. He was nicknamed 'Zucchero' (Italian for sugar) as a child.

| | | | | | |
|---|---|---|---|---|---|
| 18/05/1991 | 29 | 4 | | ZUCCHERO | London EVERY 1 |

**ZUTONS** UK group formed in Liverpool in 2002 by David McCabe (vocals), Boyan Chowdhury (guitar), Russell Pritchard (bass), Abi Harding (saxophone) and Sean Payne (drums).

| | | | | | |
|---|---|---|---|---|---|
| 01/05/2004 | 13 | 4 | ○ | WHO KILLED THE ZUTONS? | Deltasonic DLTCD019 |

**ZWAN** US rock group formed by Billy Corgan (born 17/3/1967, Chicago, IL, vocals), David Pajo (guitar), Matt Sweeney (guitar), Paz Lenchantin (bass) and Jimmy Chamberlin (drums). Corgan and Chamberlin were previously in Smashing Pumpkins. The group disbanded in September 2003.

| | | | | | |
|---|---|---|---|---|---|
| 22/02/2003 | 33 | 2 | | MARY STAR OF THE SEA | Reprise WB 484252 |

**ZZ TOP** US rock group formed in Houston, TX in 1969 by Billy Gibbons (born 16/12/1949, Houston, guitar/vocals), Dusty Hill (born 19/5/1949, Dallas, TX, bass/vocals) and Frank Beard (born 11/6/1949, Frankston, TX, drums), adopting their name from Texas bluesman ZZ Hill. Gibbons and Hill stopped shaving in 1979, giving the group their distinctive image (Beard, despite his name, is the clean-shaven member). The group appeared in the 1990 film *Back To The Future III*. They were inducted into the Rock & Roll Hall of Fame in 2004.

| | | | | | |
|---|---|---|---|---|---|
| 12/07/1975 | 60 | 1 | | FANDANGO! | London SHU 8482 |
| 08/08/1981 | 88 | 2 | | EL LOCO | Warner Brothers K 56929 |
| 30/04/1983 | 3 | 137 | ✪³ | **ELIMINATOR** ◆¹⁰ | Warner Brothers W 3774 |
| 09/11/1985 | 2 | 40 | ✪ | **AFTERBURNER** | Warner Brothers WX 27 |
| 27/10/1990 | 8 | 7 | ○ | **RECYCLER** | Warner Brothers WX 390 |
| 25/04/1992 | 5 | 17 | ● | **GREATEST HITS** | Warner Brothers 7599268462 |
| 05/02/1994 | 3 | 5 | | **ANTENNA** ◇ | RCA 74321152602 |
| 21/09/1996 | 32 | 2 | | RHYTHMEEN | RCA 74321394662 |

# COMPILATIONS, FILM SOUNDTRACKS, STAGE & STUDIO CAST RECORDINGS & OTHER ALBUMS

As mentioned earlier in this book, the British Album Chart was split into two in January 1989, with single-artist albums making up the Top 75 and compilation albums having their own twenty-place chart.

Up until then compilations, soundtracks, studio and stage recordings, and any other albums that were not accredited to a single artist found their way onto the main chart. Since then, most of these albums have featured on the compilation chart. Thus, where a compilation album has two entries in this listing, the first entry is the record's performance on the main chart (prior to 1989) and the second its performance on the compilation chart. A broken line divides the main and compilation chart entries.

There have been anomalies along the way. Albums that have combined the hits of Meat Loaf and Bonnie Tyler, for instance, appeared on the main chart prior to January 1989 and on the compilation chart thereafter, but Frank Sinatra and Tom Jones's respective duets albums have featured on the main chart only.

It had been my intention to list each compilation album under the label on which it appeared. The recent influx of co-operative albums, whereby the label credit that appears on the album and in *Music Week* might read Universal/EMI/Virgin, makes this a little more difficult. I then intended listing each of these albums under the label name that appears first on the credits, but when the catalogue number is an EMI or Virgin one rather than Universal, it made more sense to list the album under the EMI/Virgin entry. In case of difficulty, please refer to the index!

## A&M
US record label formed in 1962 by Herb Alpert and Jerry Moss as Carnival Records, operating out of Alpert's garage and as an outlet for Alpert's own recordings. Alpert began concentrating on other artists on the label in 1969, the same year they opened their own UK office (the A&M label first appeared in the UK in 1967), with international success coming from the likes of The Carpenters and Captain & Tennille, The Police and Bryan Adams. The label was sold to Polygram for $500 million in 1989.

| 02/05/1987 | 76 | 3 | | PRINCE'S TRUST TENTH ANNIVERSARY BIRTHDAY PARTY | A&M AMA 3906 |
| 22/08/1987 | 44 | 3 | | THE PRINCE'S TRUST CONCERT 1987 | A&M PTA 1987 |
| 05/12/1987 | 40 | 5 | ● | SPECIAL OLYMPICS – A VERY SPECIAL CHRISTMAS | A&M AMA 3911 |

| 23/12/1989 | 19 | 1 | | SPECIAL OLYMPICS – A VERY SPECIAL CHRISTMAS | A&M AMA 3911 |
| 29/09/1990 | ❶[1] | 6 | ● | **SLAMMIN'** | A&M SLAMM 1 |
| 20/04/1991 | 12 | 3 | | RAGE – MAKE SOME NOISE | A&M AMTV 1 |
| 29/06/1991 | ❶[5] | 21 | ● | **WINGS OF LOVE** | A&M 8455062 |
| 04/11/1995 | 18 | 1 | | THE HACIENDA – PLAY BY 01/96 | A&M 5404452 |

## ABKO
US label formed by former Sam Cooke, Donovan, Rolling Stones and (briefly) Beatles manager Allen Klein.

| 26/10/1996 | 12 | 1 | | THE ROLLING STONES ROCK AND ROLL CIRCUS | ABKCO 12682 |

## ABSTRACT UK punk label.

| 27/03/1982 | 48 | 8 | | PUNK AND DISORDERLY | Abstract AABT 100 |

## ACE OF HEARTS UK label.

| 16/05/1964 | 19 | 1 | | OUT CAME THE BLUES | Ace Of Hearts AH 72 |

## ACID JAZZ
UK jazz funk label formed in 1987 by Ed Piller and Radio London DJ Gilles Peterson. Peterson later went on to form Talkin' Loud.

| 29/05/1993 | 16 | 1 | | BEST OF ACID JAZZ VOLUME 2 | Acid Jazz JAZIDCD 66 |

## ALL AROUND THE WORLD UK label formed in Blackburn by Matt Cadman.

| 22/08/1998 | 9 | 2 | | **ROCK THE DANCEFLOOR** | All Around The World GLOBECD 9 |
| 03/04/1999 | 7 | 1 | | **ROCK THE DANCEFLOOR 2** | All Around The World GLOBECD 11 |
| 30/06/2001 | 19 | 1 | | ROCK THE DANCEFLOOR VOLUME 5 | All Around The World GLOBECD 21 |
| 21/06/2003 | 17 | 1 | | ROCK THE DANCEFLOOR 8 | All Around The World GLOBECD 43 |

## ALTERNATIVE TENTACLES US underground label formed in 1979 by Dead Kennedys founder Jello Biafra.

| 09/05/1992 | 15 | 1 | | VIRUS 100 – ALTERNATIVE TENTACLES | Alternative Tentacles 100CD |

## ANAGRAM UK punk label that later became part of Cherry Red Records.

| 04/09/1982 | 91 | 2 | | PUNK AND DISORDERLY (FURTHER CHARGES) | Anagram GRAM 001 |

## APPLE
UK label formed by The Beatles in 1968, initially as an outlet for their own recordings and subsequently signing such acts as Badfinger, Mary Hopkin and Billy Preston.

| 22/01/1972 | ❶[1] | 13 | | **CONCERT FOR BANGLADESH (RECORDED LIVE)** | Apple STCX 3385 |

## ARCADE
UK label formed in 1972, inspired by the success of K-Tel with TV-advertised albums of current and/or recent hits by original artists.

| 29/07/1972 | ❶[6] | 24 | | **20 FANTASTIC HITS** | Arcade 2891 001 |
| 29/11/1972 | 2 | 14 | | **20 FANTASTIC HITS VOLUME 2** | Arcade 2891 002 |
| 07/04/1973 | 2 | 15 | | **40 FANTASTIC HITS FROM THE 50'S AND 60'S** | Arcade ADEP 3/4 |
| 26/05/1973 | 3 | 8 | | **20 FANTASTIC HITS VOLUME 3** | Arcade ADEP 5 |
| 15/11/1975 | 5 | 11 | | **DISCO HITS '75** | Arcade ADEP 18 |
| 26/03/1977 | 16 | 10 | | ROCK ON | Arcade ADEP 27 |
| 04/06/1977 | 56 | 1 | | RULE BRITANNIA | Arcade ADEP 29 |
| 23/02/1980 | 58 | 2 | | FIRST LOVE | Arcade ADEP 41 |

| 12/01/1991 | 19 | 2 | | POP CLASSICS – 28 CLASSIC TRACKS | Arcade ARC 944421 |
| 30/03/1991 | 5 | 10 | | **SOFT METAL BALLADS** | Arcade ARC 933501 |
| 08/06/1991 | 9 | 8 | | **IT STARTED WITH A KISS** | Arcade ARC 910301 |
| 13/07/1991 | 4 | 9 | | **THE HEAT IS ON** | Arcade ARC 925401 |
| 31/08/1991 | 7 | 5 | | **DANCE CLASSICS VOLUME 2** | Arcade ARC 925511 |
| 31/08/1991 | 8 | 4 | | **DANCE CLASSICS VOLUME 1** | Arcade ARC 925501 |

| | | | | | | |
|---|---|---|---|---|---|---|
| 21/09/1991 | ❶² | | 6 | | GROOVY GHETTO | Arcade ARC 925601 |
| 02/11/1991 | 15 | | 2 | | GROOVY GHETTO – ALL THE RAGE | Arcade ARC 925701 |
| 14/12/1991 | 11 | | 6 | | CHRISTMAS LOVE SONGS | Arcade ARC 948201 |
| 29/02/1992 | 8 | | 4 | | GROOVY GHETTO 2 | Arcade ARC 948102 |
| 04/04/1992 | 16 | | 2 | | THE ESSENTIAL CHILL | Arcade 948902 |
| 18/07/1992 | 7 | | 6 | | ONE LOVE – THE VERY BEST OF REGGAE | Arcade ARC 94961 |
| 13/02/1993 | 9 | | 5 | | ROCK ROMANCE | Arcade 3011132 |
| 07/05/1994 | 13 | | 3 | | WOW! – LET THE MUSIC LIFT YOU UP | Arcade ARC 3100112 |
| 13/08/1994 | 11 | | 7 | | COMMITTED TO SOUL | Arcade ARC 3100142 |

### ARIOLA
German label formed in 1958 and subsequently sold to the media giant Bertelsmann. The company opened its own UK office in 1977 and was later integrated into the BMG company.

| | | | | | |
|---|---|---|---|---|---|
| 08/10/1988 | 35 | 5 | | BROTHERS IN RHYTHM | Ariola 303374 |
| 11/02/1989 | 15 | 2 | | RARE 3 | Ariola 209498 |

### ARISTA
US label that began life as Bell in the 1950s, the record division of the Columbia Pictures company. It enjoyed its first burst of success during the mid-1960s thanks to the stewardship of Larry Uttal in the US and went on to enjoy similar success in the first half of the 1970s thanks to Uttal and his UK counterpart Dick Leahy (the UK company had first surfaced independently in 1968). The arrival of Clive Davis (formerly of US giant CBS) in 1974 with his Arista imprint saw the Bell label being subsequently dropped (Uttal left to form Private Stock, whilst Leahy did similarly with GTO in the UK). Arista was bought by Bertelsmann in 1979, although Davis remained in almost complete control for a further two decades or so, masterminding such signings as Whitney Houston and Kenny G and overseeing the careers of Barry Manilow and Curtis Stigers, among others. Davis left the company as the new century began to launch J Records and was replaced by Antonio 'LA' Reid.

| | | | | | |
|---|---|---|---|---|---|
| 03/11/1979 | 75 | 1 | | MODS MAYDAY 79 | Arista FOUR 1 |
| 30/08/2003 | 2 | 8 | ● | THE NEPTUNES PRESENTS THE CLONES ▲¹ | Arista 82876533862 |

### ATLANTIC
US label formed in 1947 by Herb Abramson and Ahmet Ertegun, initially as an outlet for specialist jazz and R&B. The arrival of producer (and shareholder) Jerry Wexler and Ahmet's brother Nesuhi in the early 1950s (whilst Abramson was doing national service) saw the label expand its activities considerably over the next decade or so, subsequently signing distribution deals with the likes of Stax. Whilst its initial success came as a champion of black American music, it was also an important outlet for much rock music during the 1960s and 70s, including Led Zeppelin, Vanilla Fudge (on its Atco imprint), Cream, Iron Butterfly and Crosby Stills & Nash. Atlantic was sold to Warner Brothers to become part of the Warner-Elektra-Asylum conglomerate in 1968.

| | | | | | |
|---|---|---|---|---|---|
| 02/04/1966 | 12 | 27 | | SOLID GOLD SOUL | Atlantic ATL 5048 |
| 05/11/1966 | 22 | 19 | | MIDNIGHT SOUL | Atlantic 587 021 |
| 14/06/1969 | 16 | 15 | | THIS IS SOUL | Atlantic 643 301 |
| 25/03/1972 | 25 | 1 | | THE NEW AGE OF ATLANTIC | Atlantic K 20024 |
| 22/06/1974 | 23 | 7 | | ATLANTIC BLACK GOLD | Atlantic K 40550 |
| 03/04/1976 | 17 | 6 | ○ | BY INVITATION ONLY | Atlantic K 60112 |
| 11/04/1981 | 39 | 2 | | CONCERTS FOR THE PEOPLE OF KAMPUCHEA | Atlantic K 60153 |
| 02/02/1985 | 78 | 7 | | THIS IS SOUL | Atlantic SOUL 1 |
| 06/06/1987 | 9 | 23 | ✪ | ATLANTIC SOUL CLASSICS | Atlantic WX 105 |
| 18/06/1988 | 84 | 2 | | ATLANTIC SOUL BALLADS | Atlantic WX 98 |

### AZULI
UK house dance label formed in 1990 by Dave Piccioni.

| | | | | | |
|---|---|---|---|---|---|
| 19/02/2000 | 17 | 1 | | BLACKMARKET PRESENTS 2 STEP | Azuli A2CD 004 |
| 15/06/2002 | 20 | 1 | | ANOTHER LATE NIGHT – GROOVE ARMADA | Azuli ALNCD 05 |

### B UNIQUE
UK record label formed in London.

| | | | | | |
|---|---|---|---|---|---|
| 26/10/2002 | 2 | 3 | ○ | NME IN ASSOCIATION WITH WAR CHILD PRESENTS 1 LOVE | B Unique 0927493712 |

### BBC
UK label formed as the record division of the British Broadcasting Corporation.

| | | | | | |
|---|---|---|---|---|---|
| 04/01/1975 | 21 | 5 | | BBC TV'S BEST OF TOP OF THE POPS | Super Beeb BELP 001 |
| 22/10/1977 | 39 | 3 | ○ | 10 YEARS OF HITS – RADIO ONE | Super Beeb DBEDP 002 |
| 08/10/1988 | 10 | 7 | ● | ONES ON 1 | BBC REF 693 |
| 17/06/1989 | 7 | 4 | | RAY MOORE – A PERSONAL CHOICE | BBC STAR 2352 |
| 14/10/2000 | 20 | 1 | | BBC COUNTRY HITS | BBC 74321789652 |

### BEECHWOOD
UK label formed in Ashford, Kent.

| | | | | | |
|---|---|---|---|---|---|
| 11/05/1991 | 10 | 3 | | THE BEST OF INDIE TOP 20 | Beechwood Music BOTT 1 |
| 09/03/1996 | 20 | 1 | | THIS IS… SWING | Beechwood Music BEBOXCD 1 |
| 13/07/1996 | 18 | 1 | | THIS IS… HOUSE | Beechwood Music BEBOXCD 4 |

| DATE | POS | WKS | BPI | ALBUM TITLE | LABEL & NUMBER |
|------|-----|-----|-----|-------------|----------------|
| 12/07/1997 | 19 | 1 | | THIS IS… CLUB NATION | Beechwood Music BEBOXCD 13 |
| 11/10/1997 | 13 | 3 | | THIS IS… IBIZA | Beechwood Music BEBOXCD 14 |
| 31/01/1998 | 10 | 3 | | **THIS IS… SPEED GARAGE** | Beechwood Music BEBOXCD 17 |
| 21/03/1998 | 19 | 1 | | THIS IS… CLUB NATION 2 | Beechwood Music BEBOXCD 18 |
| 26/09/1998 | 16 | 2 | | THIS IS… IBIZA 98 | Beechwood Music BEBOXCD 22 |
| 30/01/1999 | 14 | 2 | | THIS IS… R&B | Beechwood Music BEBOXCD 25 |
| 05/06/1999 | 17 | 1 | | THIS IS… IBIZA 2000 | Beechwood Music BEBOXCD 28 |
| 17/07/1999 | 19 | 1 | | THIS IS… TRANCE | Beechwood Music BEBOXCD 30 |
| 05/02/2000 | 19 | 1 | | THIS IS… TRANCELIFE | Beechwood Music BEBOXCD 35 |
| 19/02/2000 | 10 | 2 | | **SLINKY – TECH-NIQUE** | Beechwood Music SLINKYYCD 002 |
| 01/07/2000 | 20 | 1 | | SLINKY FACTOR 3 | Beechwood Music SLINKYCD 03L |

**BEGGARS BANQUET** UK label formed in 1977 on the back of the punk explosion, with The Lurkers their first signing.

| DATE | POS | WKS | BPI | ALBUM TITLE | LABEL & NUMBER |
|------|-----|-----|-----|-------------|----------------|
| 21/11/1981 | 72 | 3 | | SLIP STREAM | Beggars Banquet BEGA 31 |
| 15/05/1982 | 88 | 1 | | SEX SWEAT AND BLOOD | Beggars Banquet BEGA 34 |
| 11/09/1982 | 44 | 4 | | THE BEST OF BRITISH JAZZ FUNK VOLUME 2 | Beggars Banquet BEGA 41 |

**BEYOND** UK dance label.

| DATE | POS | WKS | BPI | ALBUM TITLE | LABEL & NUMBER |
|------|-----|-----|-----|-------------|----------------|
| 06/03/1993 | 20 | 1 | | AMBIENT DUB VOLUME 2 – EARTH JUICE | Beyond RABDCD 3 |

**BIG BEAT**

| DATE | POS | WKS | BPI | ALBUM TITLE | LABEL & NUMBER |
|------|-----|-----|-----|-------------|----------------|
| 21/07/1984 | 88 | 3 | | ROCKABILLY PSYCHOS AND THE GARAGE DISEASE | Big Beat WIK 18 |

**BMG** German label (full name Bertelsmann Music Group) originally formed in 1835 as a publisher of hymn books and bibles and which grew to become one of the largest media companies in the world with interests in TV and radio, book publishing, newspapers and magazines and music. It owns labels such as RCA, Arista and Ariola.

| DATE | POS | WKS | BPI | ALBUM TITLE | LABEL & NUMBER |
|------|-----|-----|-----|-------------|----------------|
| 14/10/2000 | 7 | 4 | | **CD UK** | UMTV/Sony TV/Global 74321792852 |
| 28/10/2000 | 6 | 4 | | **STREET VIBES 6** | Sony TV/BMG TV 74321792512 |
| 25/11/2000 | 17 | 2 | | HEARTBEAT – 10TH ANNIVERSARY ALBUM | BMG TV Projects 74321789632 |
| 30/12/2000 | 9 | 2 | | **MOTOWN MANIA** | BMGTV/UMTV MCD 60075 |
| 03/02/2001 | 9 | 3 | | **CD:UK – MORE WICKED HITS** | UMTV/Sony TV/Global 74321826692 |
| 31/03/2001 | 4 | 5 | | **MUSIC – THE DEFINITIVE HITS COLLECTION** | BMG/Sony/Telstar/WSM MUSICCD 1 |
| 23/06/2001 | 7 | 3 | | **MUSIC – THE DEFINITIVE HITS COLLECTION 2** | BMG/Sony/Telstar/WSM MUSICCD 2 |
| 08/09/2001 | 4 | 6 | | **STREET VIBES 8** | BMG/Sony/Telstar 74321879472 |
| 29/09/2001 | ❶² | 6 | | **HITS 50** | BMG/Sony/Telstar/WSM HUTSCD 501 |
| 15/12/2001 | 4 | 11 | | **CHRISTMAS HITS** | BMG/Sony/Telstar/WSM HITSCDX 01 |
| 15/12/2001 | 10 | 6 | | **HITS 51** | BMG/Sony/Telstar/WSM HITSCD 511 |
| 19/01/2002 | 20 | 1 | | THE RHYTHMS OF A NATION | BMG TV Projects 74321910092 |
| 06/04/2002 | 2 | 9 | | **HITS 52** | BMG/Sony/Telstar/WSM HITSCD 521 |
| 25/05/2002 | 13 | 2 | | URBAN VIBES | BMG TV Projects 74321941932 |
| 10/08/2002 | 2 | 11 | | **HITS 53** | BMG/Sony/Telstar/WSM HITSCD 531 |
| 02/11/2002 | ❶² | 4 | ○ | **HITS 54** | BMG/Sony/Telstar/WSM HITSCD 541 |
| 30/11/2002 | 4 | 10 | ✪ | **HUGE HITS 2003** | BMG/Sony/Telstar/WSM HITSCD 2003 |
| 15/02/2003 | 8 | 2 | | **LATE NIGHT LOVE** | Sony TV/BMG TV 82876503442 |
| 01/03/2003 | 5 | 4 | | **BRIT AWARDS ALBUM** | BMG 82876504062 |
| 12/04/2003 | ❶² | 9 | | **HITS 55** | BMG/Sony/Telstar/WSM HITSCD 551 |
| 26/07/2003 | ❶¹ | 6 | ● | **HITS 56** | BMG/Sony/Telstar HITSCD 561 |
| 02/08/2003 | 6 | 4 | ○ | **DAVE PEARCE DANCE ANTHEMS – SUMMER 2003** | BMG/MOS/Telstar INSPCD31 |
| 06/09/2003 | 8 | 6 | | **SK8ER ROCK** | BMG/Telstar TV/UMTV 82876552512 |
| 01/11/2003 | 3 | 4 | | **HUGE HITS 2004 – THE VERY BEST OF HITS** | BMG/Sony/Telstar/WSM 82876573442 |
| 13/12/2003 | 5 | 6 | | **HITS 57** | BMG/Sony/Telstar/WSM 82876573832 |
| 14/02/2004 | ❶¹ | 4 | | **BEAUTIFUL** | BMG TV Projects 82876592692 |
| 28/02/2004 | ❶¹ | 3 | | **THE BRIT AWARDS ALBUM 2004** | BMG 82876590892 |
| 13/03/2004 | ❶¹ | 5 | ○ | **HIT 40 UK** | BMG/Sony/Telstar/WSM 5046720232 |
| 20/03/2004 | 5 | 4 | | **NATURAL WOMAN** | BMG TV/Sony TV 82876606672 |
| 17/04/2004 | 15 | 2 | | FOX KIDS PARTY HITS | BMG TV/Jive 82876608142 |
| 12/06/2004 | ❶¹ | 3+ | | **HITS 58** | BMG/Sony/Telstar/WSM 5046738352 |
| 19/06/2004 | 11 | 2+ | | WE LOVE MAMBO | BMG TV Projects 82876622552 |
| 26/06/2004 | 19 | 1+ | | CRUISE CONTROL | BMG TV/UMTV 82876624302 |

**BREAK DOWN** UK drum and bass label.

| DATE | POS | WKS | BPI | ALBUM TITLE | LABEL & NUMBER |
|------|-----|-----|-----|-------------|----------------|
| 17/09/1994 | 14 | 3 | | DRUM AND BASS SELECTION 2 | Break Down BDRCD 003 |
| 13/07/1996 | 13 | 3 | | MAX POWER – MAX BASS | Break Down BDRCD 15 |

**BREAKOUT** UK label formed as a dance imprint of A&M Records.

| DATE | POS | WKS | BPI | ALBUM TITLE | LABEL & NUMBER |
|------|-----|-----|-----|-------------|----------------|
| 03/09/1988 | 90 | 2 | | HOUSE HALLUCINATIONS (PUMP UP LONDON VOLUME 1) | Breakout HOSA 9002 |

**BRUNSWICK** US label formed in Chicago, IL in 1921 by a player-piano and billiard table manufacturer, the Brunswick-Balke-Collender Company. Brunswick enjoyed its initial success through its 'race' records imprint Vocalion, although by the end of the decade

▲⁹ Number of weeks album topped the US chart ◆¹² RIAA Diamond Awards ◇³ IFPI Platinum Europe Awards

artists such as Bing Crosby and the Mills Brothers had been brought in by A&R Director Jack Kapp. The Great Depression saw the company sold in 1931 to the American Record Corporation and Kapp left soon after to found Decca, with Brunswick continuing as a label for a further seven years until ARC was bought by CBS and discontinued. It was revived in 1957 by Bob Thiele of Decca and over the next three years became a renowned outlet for soul music, most notably with Jackie Wilson. It was bought by Wilson's manager Nat Tarnopol in 1960 and enjoyed considerable success for the next fifteen or so years, although Tarnopol's subsequent prosecution in the 1976 payola scandal (which also claimed Kenny Gamble) saw its importance diminished. Although it disappeared in the 1980s it was subsequently revived by Tarnopol's son during the 1990s as a re-issue company.

| 05/10/2002 | 15 | 1 | | ANGEL BEACH | Brunswick CDORB 1 |
| 26/07/2003 | 16 | 2 | | ANGEL BEACH – THE SECOND WAVE | Orb Recordings CDORB 4 |

## BUSINESS

| 16/06/1990 | 18 | 1 | | LOVERS FOR LOVERS VOLUME 3 | Business WBRLP 903 |

## CACTUS UK reggae label.

| 31/01/1976 | 53 | 1 | | REGGAE CHARTBUSTERS 75 | Cactus CTLP 114 |

## CAPITOL US label formed in California in 1942 by Johnny Mercer, Glenn Wallichs and Buddy De Sylva as Liberty Records, changing their name to Capitol when the directors held their first meeting. Initial success came from the likes of Nat King Cole and later signings Frank Sinatra and Dean Martin. In 1955 UK company EMI took a controlling interest in the company, although Capitol retained their autonomy (so much so that when The Beatles first exploded in the early 1960s, Capitol passed on them for being 'too British'). EMI bought the rest of the company in 1979.

| 18/02/1989 | 16 | 2 | | CAPITOL CLASSICS VOLUME 1 | Capitol EMS 1316 |
| 13/11/1999 | 6 | 10 | ● | **THE BEST OF BOND... JAMES BOND** | Capitol 5232942 |
| 08/12/2001 | 2 | 7 | ✪ | **THE BEST OF THE RAT PACK** | Capitol 5364522 |
| 30/11/2002 | 15 | 2 | ● | THE BEST OF BOND... JAMES BOND | Capitol 5405542 |
| 14/12/2002 | 15 | 3 | ● | CHRISTMAS WITH THE RAT PACK | Capitol 5422102 |

## CASTLE COMMUNICATIONS UK re-issue label that subsequently became part of the Sanctuary Group.

| 07/07/1990 | 4 | 11 | ● | **THE ULTIMATE 60S COLLECTION** | Castle Communications CTVLP 305 |
| 12/01/1991 | 14 | 6 | | THE ULTIMATE BLUES COLLECTION | Castle Communications CTVLP 206 |
| 08/08/1992 | 4 | 8 | | **JAZZ ON A SUMMER'S DAY** | Castle Communications CTVCD 108 |
| 10/10/1992 | 6 | 6 | | **BLOCKBUSTER – THE SENSATIONAL 70S** | Castle Communications CTVCD 209 |
| 05/06/1993 | 7 | 5 | | **ONE ORIGINAL STEP BEYOND** | Castle Communications CTVCD 115 |
| 03/07/1993 | 13 | 3 | | MONSTER HITS OF DANCE | Castle Communications CTVCD 220 |
| 30/10/1993 | 18 | 2 | | GOING UNDERGROUND | Castle Communications CTVCD 123 |

CIGARETTES AND ALCOHOL
40 MODERN ANTHEMS

FEATURING
MANIC STREET PREACHERS • TRAVIS • OASIS • THE CLASH • THE STONE ROSES
ROBBIE WILLIAMS • THE HAPPY MONDAYS • MADNESS • TOPLOADER

## CBS/COLUMBIA US label formed in Washington in 1877 as the Columbia Phonograph Company. After spells owned by Louis Sterling and the American Record Company ownership passed to the radio network Columbia Broadcasting Systems in 1938. The first company to manufacture 33rpm albums, it rose to become the largest record company in the world. It first established itself in the UK in 1963 following the acquisition of Oriole. Whilst US releases were invariably on the Columbia imprint, the fact that EMI owned the brand name meant UK releases were on CBS until the name was purchased from EMI towards the end of the 1980s. CBS/Columbia was sold to the Japanese electronic company Sony in 1989 for $2 billion.

| 20/05/1967 | 20 | 30 | | THRILL TO THE SENSATIONAL SOUND OF SUPER STEREO | CBS PR 5 |
| 28/06/1969 | 15 | 5 | | ROCK MACHINE I LOVE YOU | CBS SPR 26 |
| 28/06/1969 | 18 | 7 | | THE ROCK MACHINE TURNS YOU ON | CBS SPR 22 |
| 20/05/1972 | 10 | 9 | | **THE MUSIC PEOPLE** | CBS 66315 |
| 21/10/1978 | 10 | 11 | ● | **SATIN CITY** | CBS 10010 |
| 02/06/1979 | 6 | 12 | ○ | **THIS IS IT** | CBS 10014 |
| 19/04/1980 | 37 | 6 | ○ | FIRST LADIES OF COUNTRY | CBS 10018 |
| 21/06/1980 | 27 | 6 | | KILLER WATTS | CBS KW1 |
| 04/04/1981 | 55 | 3 | | BITTER SUITE | CBS 22082 |
| 16/10/1982 | 4 | 92 | ✪ | **REFLECTIONS** | CBS 10034 |
| 22/10/1983 | 15 | 21 | ● | IMAGINATIONS | CBS 10044 |
| 01/12/1984 | ❶[7] | 36 | ✪[3] | **THE HITS ALBUM** | CBS/WEA HITS 1 |
| 13/04/1985 | ❶[6] | 21 | ✪[2] | **THE HITS ALBUM 2** | CBS/WEA HITS 2 |
| 20/04/1985 | 90 | 2 | | CLUB CLASSICS VOLUME 2 | CBS VAULT 2 |
| 07/12/1985 | 2 | 21 | ✪[2] | **HITS 3** | CBS/WEA HITS 3 |
| 29/03/1986 | ❶[4] | 21 | ✪ | **HITS 4** | CBS/WEA/RCA/Ariola HITS 4 |
| 22/11/1986 | ❶[2] | 25 | ✪[3] | **HITS 5** | CBS/WEA/RCA/Ariola HITS 5 |
| 14/03/1987 | 4 | 19 | ✪ | **MOVE CLOSER** | CBS MOOD 1 |
| 27/06/1987 | 13 | 9 | ● | THE HOLIDAY ALBUM | CBS MOOD 2 |
| 25/07/1987 | ❶[1] | 19 | ✪[3] | **HITS 6** | CBS/WEA/BMG HITS 6 |
| 05/12/1987 | 2 | 17 | ✪[3] | **HITS 7** | CBS/WEA/RCA/Ariola HITS 7 |
| 30/04/1988 | ❶[4] | 26 | ✪ | **NITE FLITE** | CBS MOOD 4 |

○ Silver disc  ● Gold disc  ✪ Platinum disc (additional platinum units are indicated by a figure following the symbol)  ❶[9] Number of weeks album topped the UK chart

| DATE | POS | WKS | BPI | ALBUM TITLE | LABEL & NUMBER |
|---|---|---|---|---|---|
| 30/07/1988 | 2 | 13 | ✪ | HITS 8 | CBS/WEA/BMG HITS 8 |
| 17/12/1988 | 5 | 4 | | THE HITS ALBUM 9 | CBS/WEA/BMG HITS 9 |
| 14/01/1989 | 4 | 7 | | THE HITS ALBUM 9 | CBS/WEA/BMG HITS 9 |
| 04/03/1989 | 2 | 32 | ✪ | CHEEK TO CHEEK | CBS MOOD 6 |
| 13/05/1989 | ❶² | 26 | | NITE FLITE 2 | CBS MOOD 8 |
| 03/06/1989 | ❶⁶ | 13 | ✪ | THE HITS ALBUM 10 | CBS/WEA/BMG HITS 10 |
| 02/12/1989 | 2 | 14 | ✪² | MONSTER HITS | CBS/WEA/BMG HITS 11 |
| 30/12/1989 | 15 | 6 | | LAMBADA | CBS 4660551 |
| 24/03/1990 | ❶² | 37 | ✪² | JUST THE TWO OF US | CBS MOOD 11 |
| 09/06/1990 | 3 | 11 | ● | NITE FLITE 3 – BEING WITH YOU | CBS MOOD 14 |
| 11/08/1990 | 2 | 10 | | SNAP! IT UP – MONSTER HITS 2 | CBS/WEA/BMG HITS 12 |
| 29/12/1990 | 2 | 8 | | THE HIT PACK: THE BEST OF CHART MUSIC | CBS/WEA/BMG COMPC 1 |
| 10/08/1991 | ❶² | 9 | | THE HITS ALBUM 15 | CBS/WEA/BMG HITS 15 |
| 02/02/1991 | ❶² | 23 | ● | THINKING OF YOU… | Columbia MOOD 15 |
| 02/02/1991 | 9 | 3 | | THE FISH AND THE TREE AND THE BIRD AND THE BELL | Columbia 4678801 |
| 30/03/1991 | 12 | 3 | | EVERYBODY DANCE NOW | Columbia 4680501 |
| 20/04/1991 | 4 | 23 | ● | FREE SPIRIT – 17 CLASSIC ROCK BALLADS | Columbia MOODS 16 |
| 20/04/1991 | 10 | 5 | | YOU'RE THE INSPIRATION – 16 ROMANTIC LOVE SONGS | Columbia MOOD 17 |
| 10/08/1991 | 3 | 10 | ● | SIMPLY… LOVE | Columbia MOOD 17 |
| 17/08/1991 | ❶³ | 25 | ● | THE SOUND OF THE SUBURBS | Columbia MOOD 18 |
| 29/02/1992 | 11 | 5 | | THE SOUND OF THE CITY | Columbia MOODCD 22 |
| 27/06/1992 | ❶⁴ | 14 | ● | HEARTBEAT (MUSIC FROM THE TV SERIES) | Columbia 4719002 |
| 27/06/1992 | 3 | 6 | | HARD FAX | Columbia SETVCD 1 |
| 04/07/1992 | 11 | 6 | | THE BOYS ARE BACK IN TOWN | Columbia MOODCD 23 |
| 03/10/1992 | 10 | 5 | | SOMETHING IN THE AIR | Columbia SETVCD 2 |
| 31/10/1992 | ❶² | 23 | ✪ | THE ULTIMATE COUNTRY COLLECTION | Columbia MOODCD 26 |
| 21/11/1992 | 6 | 2 | | HARD FAX 2 – TWICE THE VICE! | Columbia SETVCD 3 |
| 29/05/1993 | ❶¹ | 23 | ✪ | ORIGINALS | Columbia MOODCD 29 |
| 21/08/1993 | 8 | 4 | | AFTER DARK | Columbia SETVCD 5 |
| 15/01/1994 | 14 | 2 | | TRUE LOVE WAYS | Columbia MOODCD 28 |
| 12/02/1994 | 8 | 4 | | SECRET LOVERS | Columbia SETVCD 4 |
| 19/03/1994 | 4 | 10 | ● | ORIGINALS 2 | Columbia MOODCD 31 |
| 23/07/1994 | 6 | 5 | ● | SOUL SEARCHING | Columbia MOODCD 34 |
| 28/01/1995 | ❶¹ | 16 | ● | THE BEST OF HEARTBEAT | Columbia MOODCD 37 |
| 04/03/1995 | 10 | 2 | | THE AWARDS 1995 | Columbia MOODCD 39 |
| 27/05/1995 | 4 | 6 | ● | TOP GEAR 2 | Columbia MOODCD 41 |
| 10/06/1995 | ❶² | 6 | ● | TOP OF THE POPS 1 | Columbia MOODCD 1 |
| 01/07/1995 | 3 | 5 | | MUNDO LATINO | Columbia SONYTV 2CD |
| 08/07/1995 | 5 | 3 | | PURE ATTRACTION | Columbia SONYTV 1CD |
| 16/09/1995 | 12 | 4 | | HEAVEN AND HELL | Columbia 4736662 |
| 30/09/1995 | ❶⁶ | 17 | ✪ | HEARTBEAT – FOREVER YOURS | Columbia SONYTV 8CD |
| 02/12/1995 | 14 | 7 | ● | TOP OF THE POPS 2 | Columbia SONYTV 9CD |
| 17/02/1996 | 6 | 4 | | BRIT AWARDS '96 | Columbia SONYTV 10CD |
| 15/06/1996 | 6 | 3 | | RAP FLAVAS | Columbia SONYTV 15CD |
| 28/09/1996 | 10 | 3 | | TOP OF THE POPS – THE CUTTING EDGE | Columbia SONYTV 19CD |
| 02/11/1996 | 4 | 17 | | THE ALL TIME GREATEST LOVE SONGS… | Columbia SONYTV 21CD |
| 02/11/1996 | 10 | 2 | | TAKE A BREAK | Columbia SONYTV 20CD |
| 22/02/1997 | 2 | 6 | | THE '97 BRIT AWARDS | Columbia SONYTV 23CD |
| 29/03/1997 | 5 | 6 | | THE ALL TIME GREATEST COUNTRY SONGS | Columbia SONYTV 24CD |
| 17/05/1997 | 4 | 12 | ● | WHAT A FEELING | Columbia SONYTV 26CD |
| 31/05/1997 | 15 | 2 | | BOYS | Columbia SONYTV 27CD |
| 18/10/1997 | 12 | 3 | | IT'S A SIXTIES NIGHT | Columbia SONYTV 32CD |
| 01/11/1997 | 4 | 14 | | THE ALL TIME GREATEST LOVE SONGS… VOLUME II | Columbia SONYTV 34CD |
| 07/02/1998 | 11 | 5 | | THE BRIT AWARDS 1998 | Columbia SONYTV 36CD |
| 07/03/1998 | ❶¹ | 13 | ● | FANTASTIC 80'S! | Columbia SONYTV 37CD |
| 21/03/1998 | 4 | 9 | ● | OH! WHAT A NIGHT | Columbia SONYTV 38CD |
| 28/03/1998 | 7 | 6 | | PERFECT DAY | Columbia SONYTV 42CD |
| 23/05/1998 | 4 | 7 | | FANTASTIC 80'S! 2 | Columbia SONYTV 45CD |
| 27/06/1998 | 8 | 3 | | ALLEZ! OLA! OLE! | Columbia SONYTV 46CD |
| 25/07/1998 | 12 | 3 | | SUMMER DANCE '98 | Columbia SONYTV 50CD |
| 08/08/1998 | 13 | 2 | | ANOTHER PERFECT DAY | Columbia SONYTV 51CD |
| 29/08/1998 | 14 | 2 | | FANTASTIC DANCE! | Columbia MOODCD 58 |
| 03/10/1998 | 8 | 4 | | FANTASTIC 70'S! | Columbia SONYTV 54CD |
| 14/11/1998 | 11 | 2 | | FANTASTIC 80'S! 3 | Columbia SONYTV 57CD |
| 28/11/1998 | 6 | 14 | ✪ | THE ALL TIME GREATEST LOVE SONGS OF THE 60'S, 70'S, 80'S & 90'S VOLUME III | Columbia SONYTV 56CD |
| 13/02/1999 | 3 | 7 | ● | THE 1999 BRIT AWARDS | Columbia SONYTV 61CD |
| 27/02/1999 | 17 | 1 | | THIS IS NOIZE | Columbia SONYTV 60CD |
| 20/03/1999 | ❶¹ | 2 | | ESPECIALLY FOR YOU | Columbia SONYTV 62CD |

▲⁹ Number of weeks album topped the US chart   ◆¹² RIAA Diamond Awards   ◇³ IFPI Platinum Europe Awards

| DATE | POS | WKS | BPI | ALBUM TITLE | LABEL & NUMBER |
|------|-----|-----|-----|-------------|----------------|
| 08/05/1999 | 9 | 4 | | THE NEW SOUL ALBUM | Columbia SONYTV 63CD |
| 05/06/1999 | 2 | 27 | ✪ | MUSIC TO WATCH GIRLS BY | Columbia SONYTV 67CD |
| 10/07/1999 | 12 | 3 | | THE ALL TIME GREATEST POP ALBUM | Columbia SONYTV 68CD |
| 04/09/1999 | 11 | 4 | | VIVA! LATINO | Columbia SONYTV 73CD |
| 20/11/1999 | 10 | 4 | | MORE MUSIC TO WATCH GIRLS BY | Columbia SONYTV 75CD |
| 04/03/2000 | 3 | 3 | | THE 2000 BRIT AWARDS | Columbia SONYTV 83CD |
| 08/04/2000 | 4 | 4 | | FOR YOU – 20 SONGS ESPECIALLY FOR YOU | Columbia SONYTV 84CD |
| 29/04/2000 | 16 | 2 | | TV 2000 | Columbia SONYTV 82CD |
| 24/06/2000 | 7 | 10 | ● | CIGARETTES AND ALCOHOL | Columbia SONYTV 87CD |
| 01/07/2000 | 17 | 1 | | IBIZA – THE STORY SO FAR | Columbia SONYTV 86CD |
| 29/07/2000 | 14 | 1 | | SUMMER BREEZE | Columbia SONYTV 89CD |
| 29/07/2000 | 19 | 1 | | CAFE MAMBO – THE REAL SOUND OF IBIZA | Columbia SONYTV 90CD |
| 02/09/2000 | 10 | 3 | ● | FANTASTIC 80'S – GO FOR IT | Columbia SONYTV 92CD |
| 18/11/2000 | 14 | 1 | ○ | JAMIE OLIVER'S COOKIN' – MUSIC TO COOK BY | Columbia SONYTV 95CD |
| 20/01/2001 | 4 | 5 | ○ | R&B MASTERS | Columbia STVCD 102 |
| 24/02/2001 | 15 | 7 | | BRIT AWARDS 2001 – ALBUM OF THE YEAR | Columbia STVCD 105 |
| 03/03/2001 | 17 | 1 | | CORROSION | Columbia STVCD 103 |
| 28/04/2001 | 18 | 1 | | ALL TIME GREATEST MOVIE SONGS 2001 | Columbia STVCD 113 |
| 05/05/2001 | 20 | 1 | ● | MUSIC TO WATCH GIRLS BY VOLUME 3 | Columbia SONYTV 96CD |
| 09/06/2001 | 18 | 1 | | LET THE MUSIC PLAY – 80'S GROOVE | Columbia STVCD 108 |
| 23/06/2001 | 18 | 1 | | MUSIC TO WATCH MOVIES BY | Columbia STVCD 114 |
| 07/07/2001 | 7 | 5 | ○ | INDEPENDENT WOMAN | Columbia STVCD 117 |
| 14/07/2001 | 12 | 2 | | R&B MASTERS 2 | Columbia STVCD 118 |
| 11/08/2001 | ❶[1] | 19 | ✪[2] | THE CLASSIC CHILLOUT ALBUM | Columbia STVCD 115 |
| 15/09/2001 | 10 | 4 | | CIGARETTES AND ALCOHOL VOLUME 2 | Columbia STVCD 122 |
| 03/11/2001 | 9 | 3 | ○ | SCHOOL DISCO.COM | Columbia 5048792 |
| 08/12/2001 | 13 | 6 | ● | THE CLASSIC CHILLOUT ALBUM 2 | Columbia STVCD 129 |
| 16/02/2002 | 9 | 3 | | R&B LOVESONGS | Columbia STVCD 135 |
| 23/02/2002 | ❶[2] | 8 | ● | SCHOOL DISCO.COM – SPRING TERM | Columbia 5062972 |
| 23/02/2002 | 7 | 3 | ○ | BRIT AWARDS 2002 – ALBUM OF THE YEAR | Columbia STVCD 134 |
| 20/04/2002 | 6 | 3 | | WWF – FORCEABLE ENTRY | Columbia 5079182 |
| 04/05/2002 | 5 | 5 | | ALTERNATIVE EIGHTIES | Columbia STVCD 141 |
| 08/06/2002 | 15 | 1 | | CIGARETTES AND ALCOHOL – SATURDAY NIGHT | Columbia STVCD 143 |
| 29/06/2002 | 11 | 4 | | CLUB TROPICANA | Columbia STVCD 145 |
| 13/07/2002 | 2 | 6 | | SCHOOL DISCO.COM – SUMMER HOLIDAY | Columbia 5084632 |
| 13/07/2002 | 18 | 1 | | ALTERNATIVE 60s | Columbia STVCD 144 |
| 03/08/2002 | 5 | 7 | ● | THE NEW CLASSIC CHILLOUT ALBUM | Columbia STVCD 148 |
| 21/09/2002 | 14 | 1 | | ALTERNATIVE 90s | Columbia STVCD 150 |
| 19/10/2002 | 15 | 1 | | BAD GIRLS | Columbia STVCD 152 |
| 26/10/2002 | 10 | 2 | | GET THE PARTY STARTED | Columbia STVCD 156 |
| 26/07/2003 | 7 | 5 | ● | THE VERY BEST OF THE FANTASTIC 80'S | Columbia STVCD 166 |
| 24/01/2004 | 11 | 1 | | WWE ORIGINALS | Columbia 5151163 |

**CHAMPAGNE** UK label formed by record company executive Dave McAleer as an imprint within DJM.

| DATE | POS | WKS | BPI | ALBUM TITLE | LABEL & NUMBER |
|------|-----|-----|-----|-------------|----------------|
| 04/04/1981 | 32 | 5 | | RE-MIXTURE | Champagne CHAMP 1 |

**CHAMPION** UK dance label.

| DATE | POS | WKS | BPI | ALBUM TITLE | LABEL & NUMBER |
|------|-----|-----|-----|-------------|----------------|
| 08/11/1986 | 66 | 2 | | ULTIMATE TRAX VOLUME 1 | Champion CHAMP 1003 |
| 07/03/1987 | 50 | 2 | | ULTIMATE TRAX VOLUME 2 | Champion CHAMP 1005 |
| 18/07/1987 | 69 | 2 | | ULTIMATE TRAX 3 – BATTLE OF THE DJS | Champion CHAMP 1008 |

**CHARM** UK reggae label.

| DATE | POS | WKS | BPI | ALBUM TITLE | LABEL & NUMBER |
|------|-----|-----|-----|-------------|----------------|
| 21/04/1990 | 14 | 4 | | PURE LOVERS VOLUME 1 | Charm CLP 101 |
| 22/09/1990 | 12 | 3 | | PURE LOVERS VOLUME 2 | Charm CLP 102 |
| 06/04/1991 | 16 | 2 | | PURE LOVERS VOLUME 3 | Charm CLP 103 |
| 02/11/1991 | 19 | 1 | | PURE LOVERS VOLUME 4 | Charm CLP 104 |
| 25/07/1992 | 17 | 1 | | JUST RAGGA | Charm CDCD 4 |
| 29/08/1992 | 13 | 3 | | PURE LOVERS VOLUME 5 | Charm CCDJS 105 |
| 27/02/1993 | 19 | 1 | | JUST RAGGA VOLUME III | Charm CRCD 16 |
| 01/05/1993 | 17 | 1 | | PURE LOVERS VOLUME 6 | Charm CCDJS 106 |

**CHRYSALIS** UK label formed in 1967 by Terry Ellis and Chris Wright as Chrysalis Artists (the name being an amalgamation of the two names), a management company. The record label was founded the following year and achieved success with Jethro Tull, Blodwyn Pig and Ten Years After. Ellis went to the USA to set up an operation there in 1975 and helped the label sign international acts such as Blondie and Pat Benatar, although Ellis and Wright had a number of disagreements and Ellis left the company in 1985, later forming Imago Records. Chrysalis later branched out to encompass TV and radio interests and Wright sold the record label to EMI. He later returned to music after forming Echo Music.

| DATE | POS | WKS | BPI | ALBUM TITLE | LABEL & NUMBER |
|------|-----|-----|-----|-------------|----------------|
| 25/05/1985 | 2 | 16 | ✪ | OUT NOW! 28 HOT HITS | Chrysalis/MCA OUTV 1 |
| 26/10/1985 | 3 | 12 | ✪ | OUT NOW!! 2 – 28 HOT HITS | Chrysalis/MCA OUTV 2 |

○ Silver disc ● Gold disc ✪ Platinum disc (additional platinum units are indicated by a figure following the symbol) ❶[9] Number of weeks album topped the UK chart

| 03/11/1990 | 6 | 3 | ○ | RED, HOT AND BLUE | Chrysalis CHR 1799 |
| 13/11/1993 | 4 | 10 | ● | SMASH HITS '93 – 40 TOP CHARTIN' GROOVES | Chrysalis CDCHR 6058 |

## CLASSIC FM UK label formed by radio station Classic FM.

| 20/04/1996 | 13 | 4 | | HALL OF FAME | Classic FM CFMCD 7 |
| 16/10/1999 | 11 | 7 | ● | RELAX… | Classic FM CFMCD 30 |
| 06/05/2000 | 10 | 8 | ● | HALL OF FAME 2000 | Classic FM CFMCD 31 |
| 04/11/2000 | 7 | 8 | ● | RELAX MORE | Classic FM CFMCD 32 |
| 14/04/2001 | 16 | 3 | ○ | THE SOUND OF CLASSIC FM | Classic FM CFMMC 33 |
| 27/10/2001 | 9 | 6 | ● | TIME TO RELAX | Classic FM CFMCD 34 |
| 06/04/2002 | 14 | 6 | | CLASSIC FM HALL OF FAME – GOLD | Classic FM CFMCD 36 |
| 02/11/2002 | 9 | 7 | ● | CLASSIC FM – SMOOTH CLASSICS | Classic FM CFMCD 37 |
| 01/11/2003 | 10 | 4 | | SMOOTH CLASSICS – DO NOT DISTURB | Classic FM CFMCD 38 |
| 24/04/2004 | 15 | 2 | | HALL OF FAME – THE GREAT COMPOSERS | Classic FM CFMCD 40 |

## CLUB UK label formed as an imprint of Phonogram.

| 03/09/1983 | 55 | 2 | | COME WITH CLUB (CLUB TRACKS VOLUME 2) | Club CLUBL 002 |

## CONCEPT UK rap label.

| 12/03/1994 | 9 | 7 | ○ | RAP ATTACK | Concept MOODCD 32 |

## CONCRETE UK dance label.

| 10/02/1996 | 16 | 1 | | BRIT HOP AND AMYL HOUSE | Concrete HARD 10LPCD |

## CONIFER UK classical label acquired by BMG in 1995.

| 21/11/1998 | 17 | 1 | ● | ONLY CLASSICAL ALBUM YOU'LL EVER NEED | Conifer 75605513322 |

## COOKIE JAR UK dance label formed as an imprint of Polygram Records.

| 14/12/1991 | 3 | 8 | ● | STEAMIN' – HARDCORE '92 | Cookie Jar JARTV 1 |
| 21/03/1992 | 2 | 9 | ○ | TECHNOSTATE | Cookie Jar JARCD 2 |
| 23/05/1992 | ❶² | 8 | ● | THE RAVE GENER8TOR | Cookie Jar JARCD 3 |
| 05/09/1992 | 2 | 7 | ○ | THE RAVE GENER8TOR 2 | Cookie Jar JARCD 4 |
| 28/11/1992 | 3 | 11 | ● | RAVE 92 | Cookie Jar JARCD 5 |
| 27/03/1993 | 6 | 5 | | UNDERGROUND VOLUME 1 | Cookie Jar JARCD 6 |
| 07/08/1993 | 7 | 5 | ○ | JAMMIN' | Cookie Jar JARCD 7 |
| 11/09/1993 | 12 | 2 | | FULL ON DANCE | Cookie Jar JARCD 8 |
| 06/11/1993 | 8 | 2 | | SOUL BEAT | Cookie Jar JARCD 9 |
| 27/11/1993 | 3 | 9 | ● | FULL ON DANCE '93 | Cookie Jar JARCD 10 |

## COOLTEMPO UK R&B label formed as an imprint of EMI.

| 01/08/1987 | 37 | 6 | | FIERCE | Cooltempo CTLP 4 |
| 01/07/1989 | 18 | 2 | | THIS IS GARAGE | Cooltempo CTLP 12 |

## COWBOY UK dance label formed in London.

| 08/05/1993 | 18 | 1 | | COWBOY COMPILATION – THE ALBUM VOLUME 1 | Cowboy RODEOCD 1 |

## CREOLE UK label formed in London by Larry Lawrence.

| 24/08/1985 | 48 | 6 | ● | 20 HOLIDAY HITS | Creole CTV 1 |

## DANCE POOL UK label formed in the early 1990s as an imprint of CBS/Sony.

| 25/09/1999 | 19 | 2 | | IBIZA – THE CLOSING PARTY | Dance Pool DP2 CD |

## DEBUT

| 27/06/1992 | 18 | 1 | | JUNGLE TEKNO VOLUME 1 | Debut CDTOT 5 |

## DECADANCE

| 20/04/2002 | 9 | 4 | | PURE CLASSICAL CHILLOUT | Decadance DECTV 002 |
| 20/07/2002 | 10 | 4 | | PURE GLOBAL CHILLOUT | Decadance DECTV 003 |

▲⁹ Number of weeks album topped the US chart  ◆¹² RIAA Diamond Awards  ◇³ IFPI Platinum Europe Awards

| | | | | |
|---|---|---|---|---|
| 09/11/2002 . . . . . 8 . . . . . . 3 . . . . . . | **THE CELTIC CHILLOUT ALBUM** This was wrongly listed on the compilation albums chart and was later switched to the main chart with the artist credit to Ryan & Rachel O'Donnell . . . . . . . . . . . . . . . . . . . . . . . . . Decadance DEDCTV 007 |
| 16/11/2002 . . . . . 9 . . . . . . 12 . . . . . | **CLASSICAL CHILLOUT GOLD** . . . . . . . . . . . . . . . . . . . . . . . . . . . . . . . . . . . . . . . . . . . Decadance DECTV 005 |
| 08/02/2003 . . . . . 10 . . . . . 4 . . . . . | **THE CLASSICAL LOVE ALBUM** . . . . . . . . . . . . . . . . . . . . . . . . . . . . . . . . . . . . . . . . . Decadance DECTV 008 |
| 31/05/2003 . . . . . 6 . . . . . . 4 . . . . . | **PIANO MOODS** . . . . . . . . . . . . . . . . . . . . . . . . . . . . . . . . . . . . . . . . . . . . . . . . . Decadance DECTV 010 |
| 12/07/2003 . . . . . 15 . . . . . 2 . . . . . | THE VERY BEST OF LATIN JAZZ . . . . . . . . . . . . . . . . . . . . . . . . . . . . . . . . . . . . . . . . Decadance DECTV 011 |
| 11/10/2003 . . . . . 16 . . . . . 1 . . . . . | THE ULTIMATE OLD SKOOL ALBUM . . . . . . . . . . . . . . . . . . . . . . . . . . . . . . . . . . . . Decadance DECSIX 011 |
| 18/10/2003 . . . . . 7 . . . . . . 3 . . . . . | **GUITAR MOODS** . . . . . . . . . . . . . . . . . . . . . . . . . . . . . . . . . . . . . . . . . . . . . . . . Decadance DECTV 017 |
| 25/10/2003 . . . . . 6 . . . . . . 4 . . . . . | **THE VERY BEST OF COUNTRY GOLD** . . . . . . . . . . . . . . . . . . . . . . . . . . . . . . . . . . . . . Decadance DECTV 012 |
| 15/11/2003 . . . . . 13 . . . . . 3 . . . . . | THE VERY BEST OF CLASSICAL CHILLOUT GOLD . . . . . . . . . . . . . . . . . . . . . . . . . . . . . . Decadance DECTV 013 |
| 07/02/2004 . . . . . 9 . . . . . . 3 . . . . . | **ROCK 'N' ROLL LOVE SONGS** . . . . . . . . . . . . . . . . . . . . . . . . . . . . . . . . . . . . . . . . Decadance DECTV 018 |
| 06/03/2004 . . . . . 9 . . . . . . 2 . . . . . | **ELECTRIC MOODS** . . . . . . . . . . . . . . . . . . . . . . . . . . . . . . . . . . . . . . . . . . . . . . Decadance DECTV020 |

**DECCA** UK label formed in 1929 by Edward Lewis as a natural progression from the company's interest as a gramophone manufacturer. It launched its own US operation in 1934 and also the London and later Deram imprints. The US operation was sold to MCA in 1961 whilst the UK operation was sold to Polygram following Lewis's death in 1979.

| | | | | |
|---|---|---|---|---|
| 08/02/1964 . . . . . 20 . . . . . 1 . . . . . | READY STEADY GO . . . . . . . . . . . . . . . . . . . . . . . . . . . . . . . . . . . . . . . . . . . . . . . . . Decca LK 4577 |
| 28/06/1969 . . . . . 24 . . . . . 6 . . . . . | THE WORLD OF BLUES POWER . . . . . . . . . . . . . . . . . . . . . . . . . . . . . . . . . . . . . . . . . Decca SPA 14 |
| 05/07/1969 . . . . . 13 . . . . . 11 . . . . . | THE WORLD OF BRASS BANDS . . . . . . . . . . . . . . . . . . . . . . . . . . . . . . . . . . . . . . . . . Decca SPA 20 |
| 06/09/1969 . . . . . 7 . . . . . . 5 . . . . . | **THE WORLD OF HITS VOLUME 2** . . . . . . . . . . . . . . . . . . . . . . . . . . . . . . . . . . . . . . . . Decca SPA 35 |
| 20/09/1969 . . . . . 17 . . . . . 2 . . . . . | THE WORLD OF PROGRESSIVE MUSIC (WOWIE ZOWIE) . . . . . . . . . . . . . . . . . . . . . . . . . . . . Decca SPA 34 |
| 20/09/1969 . . . . . 29 . . . . . 2 . . . . . | THE WORLD OF PHASE 4 STEREO . . . . . . . . . . . . . . . . . . . . . . . . . . . . . . . . . . . . . . . . Decca SPA 32 |
| 07/08/1971 . . . . . 10 . . . . . 22 . . . . . | **THE WORLD OF YOUR 100 BEST TUNES** . . . . . . . . . . . . . . . . . . . . . . . . . . . . . . . . . . . . Decca SPA 112 |
| 09/10/1971 . . . . . 9 . . . . . . 13 . . . . . | **THE WORLD OF YOUR 100 BEST TUNES VOLUME 2** . . . . . . . . . . . . . . . . . . . . . . . . . . . . . Decca SPA 155 |
| 27/09/1975 . . . . . 41 . . . . . 4 . . . . . | THE WORLD OF YOUR 100 BEST TUNES VOLUME 10 . . . . . . . . . . . . . . . . . . . . . . . . . . . . . Decca SPA 400 |
| 13/12/1975 . . . . . 21 . . . . . 5 . . . . . | THE TOP 25 FROM YOUR 100 BEST TUNES . . . . . . . . . . . . . . . . . . . . . . . . . . . . . . . . . . Decca HBT 1112 |

| | | | | |
|---|---|---|---|---|
| 01/06/1991 . . . . **❶**[2] . . . 23 . . . . . ● | **THE ESSENTIAL MOZART** . . . . . . . . . . . . . . . . . . . . . . . . . . . . . . . . . . . . . . . . . . . Decca 4333231 |
| 16/11/1991 . . . . . 2 . . . . . . 28 . . . . . ✪ | **ESSENTIAL OPERA** . . . . . . . . . . . . . . . . . . . . . . . . . . . . . . . . . . . . . . . . . . . . . . Decca 4338221 |
| 26/09/1992 . . . . . 9 . . . . . . 4 . . . . . | **ESSENTIAL BALLET** . . . . . . . . . . . . . . . . . . . . . . . . . . . . . . . . . . . . . . . . . . . . . . Decca 4366582 |
| 12/06/1993 . . . . . 8 . . . . . . 6 . . . . . ○ | **CLASSIC COMMERCIALS** . . . . . . . . . . . . . . . . . . . . . . . . . . . . . . . . . . . . . . . . . . . Decca 4406382 |
| 06/11/1993 . . . . . 17 . . . . . 2 . . . . . ○ | ESSENTIAL OPERA 2 . . . . . . . . . . . . . . . . . . . . . . . . . . . . . . . . . . . . . . . . . . . . . . Decca 4409472 |
| 06/06/1998 . . . . . 13 . . . . . 4 . . . . . | THE GREATEST CLASSICAL STARS ON EARTH . . . . . . . . . . . . . . . . . . . . . . . . . . . . . . . . Decca 4603902 |
| 02/09/2000 . . . . . 14 . . . . . 2 . . . . . | CALM . . . . . . . . . . . . . . . . . . . . . . . . . . . . . . . . . . . . . . . . . . . . . . . . . . . . . . . . Decca 4673512 |
| 10/11/2001 . . . . . 16 . . . . . 1 . . . . . | THE ULTIMATE MOVIE ALBUM . . . . . . . . . . . . . . . . . . . . . . . . . . . . . . . . . . . . . . . . . Decca 5857122 |
| 24/11/2001 . . . . . 2 . . . . . . 7 . . . . . ✪ | **CLASSICS 2002** . . . . . . . . . . . . . . . . . . . . . . . . . . . . . . . . . . . . . . . . . . . . . . . . Decca 4721092 |
| 30/03/2002 . . . . . 6 . . . . . . 3 . . . . . | **VOICES** . . . . . . . . . . . . . . . . . . . . . . . . . . . . . . . . . . . . . . . . . . . . . . . . . . . . . Decca 4722562 |
| 24/08/2002 . . . . . 12 . . . . . 4 . . . . . | CLASSIC ADS . . . . . . . . . . . . . . . . . . . . . . . . . . . . . . . . . . . . . . . . . . . . . . . . . . Decca 04724162 |
| 30/11/2002 . . . . . 17 . . . . . 3 . . . . . ● | CLASSICS 2003 . . . . . . . . . . . . . . . . . . . . . . . . . . . . . . . . . . . . . . . . . . . . . . . . . Decca 4726812 |
| 01/03/2003 . . . . . 4 . . . . . . 9 . . . . . ● | **THE VERY BEST OF RELAXING CLASSICS** . . . . . . . . . . . . . . . . . . . . . . . . . . . . . . . . . . Decca 4738672 |
| 29/03/2003 . . . . . 8 . . . . . . 3 . . . . . | **TIMELESS** . . . . . . . . . . . . . . . . . . . . . . . . . . . . . . . . . . . . . . . . . . . . . . . . . . . Decca 0391862 |
| 09/08/2003 . . . . . 19 . . . . . 1 . . . . . | GEORGE GERSHWIN – THE BEST OF . . . . . . . . . . . . . . . . . . . . . . . . . . . . . . . . . . . . . . Decca 9809662 |
| 18/10/2003 . . . . . 10 . . . . . 3 . . . . . | **WORLD IN UNION 2003** . . . . . . . . . . . . . . . . . . . . . . . . . . . . . . . . . . . . . . . . . . . Decca 4761240 |

**DECONSTRUCTION** UK label formed in 1988 by Keith Blackhurst, Mike Pickering (of M People) and Pete Hadfield. After a brief spell with EMI the label switched distribution to BMG.

| | | | | |
|---|---|---|---|---|
| 14/10/1989 . . . . . 4 . . . . . . 6 . . . . . | **ITALIA – DANCE MUSIC FROM ITALY** . . . . . . . . . . . . . . . . . . . . . . . . . . . . . . . . . . . . . Deconstruction 64289 |
| 27/02/1993 . . . . . 18 . . . . . 2 . . . . . | FULL ON – A YEAR IN THE LIFE OF HOUSE . . . . . . . . . . . . . . . . . . . . . . . . . . . . . . . . . . Deconstruction 74321128032 |
| 06/05/1995 . . . . . 3 . . . . . . 17 . . . . . ● | **CREAM LIVE** . . . . . . . . . . . . . . . . . . . . . . . . . . . . . . . . . . . . . . . . . . . . . . . . . . Deconstruction 74321272192 |
| 26/08/1995 . . . . . 17 . . . . . 1 . . . . . | DECONSTRUCTION CLASSICS – A HISTORY OF DANCE MUSIC . . . . . . . . . . . . . . . . . . . . . . . Deconstruction 74321299002 |
| 11/11/1995 . . . . . 2 . . . . . . 3 . . . . . ○ | **CREAM ANTHEMS** . . . . . . . . . . . . . . . . . . . . . . . . . . . . . . . . . . . . . . . . . . . . . . . Deconstruction 74321328162 |
| 06/07/1996 . . . . . 3 . . . . . . 5 . . . . . ○ | **CREAM LIVE – TWO** . . . . . . . . . . . . . . . . . . . . . . . . . . . . . . . . . . . . . . . . . . . . . . Deconstruction 74321391252 |
| 29/03/1997 . . . . . 16 . . . . . 1 . . . . . | CREAM SEPERATES – THE COLLECTION . . . . . . . . . . . . . . . . . . . . . . . . . . . . . . . . . . . . Deconstruction 74321463782 |
| 15/11/1997 . . . . . 11 . . . . . 2 . . . . . | CREAM ANTHEMS '97 . . . . . . . . . . . . . . . . . . . . . . . . . . . . . . . . . . . . . . . . . . . . . . Deconstruction 74321529622 |

**DEF JAM** US label formed in New York in 1984 by Rick Rubin and Russell Simmons, with LL Cool J and Beastie Boys among his initial signings. Rubin also became a successful producer for the likes of Red Hot Chili Peppers and Tom Petty & The Heartbreakers. Rubin and Simmons eventually split with Rubin relocating to Los Angeles and forming Def American (later American Recordings).

| | | | | |
|---|---|---|---|---|
| 08/08/1987 . . . . . 19 . . . . . 7 . . . . . | KICK IT – THE DEF JAM SAMPLER VOLUME 1 . . . . . . . . . . . . . . . . . . . . . . . . . . . . . . . . . Def Jam KICKIT 1 |
| 07/04/2001 . . . . . 7 . . . . . . 5 . . . . . ○ | **WESTWOOD** . . . . . . . . . . . . . . . . . . . . . . . . . . . . . . . . . . . . . . . . . . . . . . . . . . Def Jam UK 5643732 |
| 12/01/2002 . . . . . 19 . . . . . 1 . . . . . ● | WESTWOOD 2 . . . . . . . . . . . . . . . . . . . . . . . . . . . . . . . . . . . . . . . . . . . . . . . . . . Def Jam 5866192 |
| 28/09/2002 . . . . . 2 . . . . . . 7 . . . . . ● | **WESTWOOD 3** . . . . . . . . . . . . . . . . . . . . . . . . . . . . . . . . . . . . . . . . . . . . . . . . . Def Jam 0696762 |
| 10/04/2004 . . . . . 2 . . . . . . 8 . . . . . ● | **WESTWOOD – THE JUMP OFF** . . . . . . . . . . . . . . . . . . . . . . . . . . . . . . . . . . . . . . . . Def Jam 9817185 |

**DEF SOUL** UK label.

| | | | | |
|---|---|---|---|---|
| 03/02/2001 . . . . . 3 . . . . . . 3 . . . . . ○ | **THE LICK – PRESENTED BY TREVOR NELSON** . . . . . . . . . . . . . . . . . . . . . . . . . . . . . . . . Def Soul 5201682 |

**DEFECTED**

○ Silver disc  ● Gold disc  ✪ Platinum disc (additional platinum units are indicated by a figure following the symbol)  **❶**[9] Number of weeks album topped the UK chart

| | | | | | |
|---|---|---|---|---|---|
| 25/03/2000 | 18 | 1 | | SESSIONS TEN – SUBLIMINAL SESSIONS | Defected DEFSESS 1 |

**DERAM** UK label formed in 1966 as an imprint to Decca Records and intended for 'alternative' artists.

| | | | | | |
|---|---|---|---|---|---|
| 30/05/1981 | 51 | 5 | | STRENGTH THROUGH OI! | Deram SKIN 1 |

**DEUTSCHE GRAMMOPHON** German classical label formed in Hanover in 1898 by inventer Emile Berliner. The company was restructured following liquidation in 1937.

| | | | | | |
|---|---|---|---|---|---|
| 13/10/1990 | 6 | 9 | ● | **ESSENTIAL CLASSICS** | Deutsche Grammophon 4315411 |
| 28/03/1992 | 7 | 5 | | **LIVING CLASSICS** | Deutsche Grammophon 4356432 |
| 11/05/2002 | 17 | 2 | | MOZART GOLD – THE ESSENTIAL COLLECTION | Deutsche Grammophon 472342 |
| 10/05/2003 | 16 | 1 | | CLASSICAL GOLD | Deutsche Grammophon 4745412 |

**DINO** UK re-issue and TV marketing label formed in 1989; it closed in 1997.

| | | | | | |
|---|---|---|---|---|---|
| 02/12/1989 | 3 | 14 | | **THAT LOVING FEELING** | Dino DINTV 5 |
| 03/03/1990 | 5 | 26 | | **THAT LOVING FEELING VOLUME 2** | Dino DINTV 7 |
| 23/06/1990 | 3 | 8 | | **LEATHER AND LACE** | Dino DINTV 9 |
| 11/08/1990 | 9 | 9 | | **THE SUMMER OF LOVE** | Dino DINTV 10 |
| 06/10/1990 | ❶³ | 31 | | **THAT LOVING FEELING VOLUME 3** | Dino DINTV 11 |
| 10/11/1990 | 14 | 4 | | LEATHER AND LACE – THE SECOND CHAPTER | Dino DINTV 12 |
| 24/11/1990 | 4 | 29 | | **ROCK 'N' ROLL LOVE SONGS** | Dino DINTV 13 |
| 29/12/1990 | 16 | 3 | | BACHARACH AND DAVID – THEY WRITE THE SONGS | Dino DINTV 13 |
| 09/02/1991 | 6 | 8 | | **TRACKS OF MY TEARS (SMOKEY ROBINSON – WRITER AND PERFORMER)** | Dino DINTV 17 |
| 30/03/1991 | 2 | 9 | | **HARDCORE UPROAR** | Dino DINTV 20 |
| 06/04/1991 | 3 | 14 | | **THAT LOVING FEELING VOLUME 4** | Dino DINTV 19 |
| 01/06/1991 | 4 | 5 | | **LOVE SUPREME** | Dino DINTV 19 |
| 15/06/1991 | ❶¹ | 15 | | **THE RHYTHM DIVINE** | Dino DINTV 22 |
| 13/07/1991 | 2 | 10 | | **HARDCORE DANCEFLOOR** | Dino DINTV 24 |
| 27/07/1991 | 8 | 6 | | **CHIC AND ROSE ROYCE – THEIR GREATEST HITS SIDE BY SIDE** | Dino DINTV 23 |
| 03/08/1991 | 6 | 7 | | **LA FREEWAY** | Dino DINTV 25 |
| 12/10/1991 | 3 | 6 | | **WE WILL ROCK YOU** | Dino DINTV 26 |
| 19/10/1991 | 2 | 15 | | **THAT LOVING FEELING VOLUME 5** | Dino DINTV 28 |
| 02/11/1991 | ❶⁴ | 16 | | **HARDCORE ECSTASY** | Dino DINTV 29 |
| 02/11/1991 | 6 | 5 | | **THE RHYTHM DIVINE VOLUME 2** | Dino DINTV 27 |
| 23/11/1991 | 6 | 23 | | **MORE ROCK 'N' ROLL LOVE SONGS** | Dino DINTV 30 |
| 07/12/1991 | 8 | 9 | | **PARTY MIX** | Dino DINTV 32 |
| 28/12/1991 | ❶¹ | 10 | | **ESSENTIAL HARDCORE** | Dino DINTV 33 |
| 14/03/1992 | 2 | 9 | | **HEAVENLY HARDCORE** | Dino DINCD 35 |
| 28/03/1992 | 3 | 10 | | **BREAKING HEARTS** | Dino DINCD 34 |
| 18/04/1992 | 2 | 7 | | **COLD SWEAT** | Dino DINCD 36 |
| 02/05/1992 | 4 | 11 | | **HEARTLANDS** | Dino DINCD 37 |
| 20/06/1992 | 3 | 4 | | **LET'S TALK ABOUT LOVE** | Dino DINCD 39 |
| 11/07/1992 | 11 | 2 | | PRECIOUS | Dino DINCD 38 |
| 18/07/1992 | 10 | 6 | | **MIDNIGHT CRUISING** | Dino DINCD 37 |
| 01/08/1992 | 5 | 7 | | **UNDER SPANISH SKIES** | Dino DINCD 41 |
| 22/08/1992 | 8 | 6 | | **THE ORIGINALS!** | Dino DINCD 45 |
| 29/08/1992 | 7 | 5 | | **TRANCE DANCE** | Dino DINCD 43 |
| 19/09/1992 | ❶¹ | 13 | | **SIXTIES BEAT** | Dino DINCD 42 |
| 17/10/1992 | ❶² | 6 | | **ENERGY RUSH** | Dino DINCD 53 |
| 24/10/1992 | 5 | 6 | | **THE GREATEST VOICES** | Dino DINCD 44 |
| 14/11/1992 | 19 | 1 | | SWING HITS | Dino DINCD 46 |
| 28/11/1992 | 14 | 5 | | ROCK 'N' ROLL IS HERE TO STAY | Dino DINCD 48 |
| 05/12/1992 | 10 | 7 | | **STOMPIN' PARTY** | Dino DINCD 52 |
| 12/12/1992 | 7 | 7 | | **ENERGY RUSH II** | Dino DINCD 55 |
| 12/12/1992 | 8 | 12 | | **MEMORIES ARE MADE OF THIS** | Dino DINCD 47 |
| 30/01/1993 | 3 | 6 | | **ENERGY RUSH LEVEL 3** | Dino DINCD 57 |
| 13/02/1993 | ❶¹ | 38 | | **BLUES BROTHER SOUL SISTER** | Dino DINCD 56 |
| 10/04/1993 | ❶³ | 12 | | **ENERGY RUSH PRESENTS DANCE HITS 93** | Dino DINCD 59 |
| 05/06/1993 | 2 | 6 | | **ENERGY RUSH PHASE 4** | Dino DINCD 65 |
| 10/07/1993 | 9 | 8 | | **HEART FULL OF SOUL** | Dino DINCD 63 |

▲⁹ Number of weeks album topped the US chart   ◆¹² RIAA Diamond Awards   ◇³ IFPI Platinum Europe Awards

| DATE | POS | WKS | BPI | ALBUM TITLE | LABEL & NUMBER |
|---|---|---|---|---|---|
| 17/07/1993 | 8 | 8 | | BLUES BROTHER SOUL SISTER VOLUME 2 | Dino DINCD 61 |
| 24/07/1993 | 2 | 8 | | ENERGY RUSH DANCE HITS 93 (2ND DIMENSION) | Dino DINCD 62 |
| 04/09/1993 | 3 | 12 | | THAT LOVING FEELING VOLUME VI | Dino DINCD 64 |
| 11/09/1993 | 3 | 5 | | ENERGY RUSH FACTOR 5 | Dino DINCD 66 |
| 18/09/1993 | 2 | 7 | | RAVE GENERATION | Dino DINCD 68 |
| 25/09/1993 | 11 | 3 | | MORE THAN UNPLUGGED | Dino DINCD 69 |
| 16/10/1993 | 3 | 13 | | ENERGY RUSH PRESENTS DANCE HITS OF THE YEAR | Dino DINCD 70 |
| 16/10/1993 | 8 | 2 | | PLANET ROCK | Dino DINCD 67 |
| 23/10/1993 | 4 | 4 | | FUTURESHOCK – 20 FURIOUS DANCE TUNES | Dino DINCD 71 |
| 23/10/1993 | 11 | 3 | | COUNTRY WOMEN | Dino DINCD 72 |
| 27/11/1993 | 14 | 5 | | AS TIME GOES BY | Dino DINCD 77 |
| 04/12/1993 | 2 | 21 | | THE VERY BEST OF THAT LOVING FEELING | Dino DINCD 78 |
| 04/12/1993 | 5 | 7 | | ENERGY RUSH – SAFE SIX | Dino DINCD 74 |
| 04/12/1993 | 14 | 6 | | KEEP ON DANCING | Dino DINCD 80 |
| 25/12/1993 | 11 | 9 | | LOVE IN THE SIXTIES | Dino DINCD 81 |
| 29/01/1994 | 5 | 3 | | RAVE GENERATION 2 | Dino DINCD 75 |
| 19/02/1994 | 6 | 3 | | SOUL MATE | Dino DINCD 82 |
| 12/03/1994 | 5 | 4 | | ENERGY RUSH – EURO DANCE HITS 94 | Dino DINCD 76 |
| 02/04/1994 | 2 | 5 | | ENERGY RUSH 7 | Dino DINCD 79 |
| 09/04/1994 | 2 | 12 | | IT'S ELECTRIC | Dino DINCD 73 |
| 07/05/1994 | 2 | 12 | | BLUES BROTHER SOUL SISTER VOLUME 3 | Dino DINCD 85 |
| 28/05/1994 | ●[1] | 8 | | ENERGY RUSH – XTERMIN8 | Dino DINCD 84 |
| 04/06/1994 | 8 | 6 | | WONDERFUL WORLD | Dino DINCD 89 |
| 23/07/1994 | 9 | 5 | | THE BEST OF ROCK 'N' ROLL LOVE SONGS | Dino DINCD 91 |
| 30/07/1994 | 13 | 3 | | START – THE BEST OF BRITISH | Dino DINCD 92 |
| 06/08/1994 | 3 | 8 | | ENERGY RUSH DANCE HITS 94 | Dino DINCD 95 |
| 13/08/1994 | 4 | 10 | | THAT LOVING FEELING VOLUME VII | Dino DINCD 83 |
| 03/09/1994 | 3 | 8 | | DANCE MASSIVE | Dino DINCD 94 |
| 17/09/1994 | 7 | 6 | | WHEN A MAN LOVES A WOMAN | Dino DINCD 88 |
| 10/12/1994 | 3 | 17 | | ROCK ANTHEMS | Dino DINCD 101 |
| 17/12/1994 | 8 | 6 | | DANCE MASSIVE 2 | Dino DINCD 103 |
| 07/01/1995 | 17 | 2 | | THE ULTIMATE JUNGLE COLLECTION | Dino DINCD 105 |
| 11/02/1995 | 3 | 4 | | ENERGY RUSH K9 | Dino DINCD 102 |
| 11/03/1995 | 2 | 9 | | PURE SWING | Dino DINCD 97 |
| 08/04/1995 | 5 | 8 | | DRIVE TIME | Dino DINCD 96 |
| 27/05/1995 | 4 | 5 | | SKA MANIA | Dino DINCD 86 |
| 10/06/1995 | 2 | 5 | | DANCE MASSIVE 95 | Dino DINCD 87 |
| 10/06/1995 | 4 | 5 | | PURE SWING TWO | Dino DINCD 98 |
| 24/06/1995 | 19 | 1 | | REGGAE MASSIVE | Dino DINCD 93 |
| 15/07/1995 | 7 | 5 | | RAVE ANTHEMS | Dino DINCD 104 |
| 22/07/1995 | 4 | 7 | | DRIVE TIME 2 | Dino DINCD 99 |
| 19/08/1995 | 7 | 5 | | THE AMERICAN DINER | Dino DINCD 107 |
| 02/09/1995 | 3 | 8 | | PURE SWING III | Dino DINCD 109 |
| 21/10/1995 | 7 | 4 | | THE GREATEST DANCE ALBUM OF ALL TIME | Dino DINCD 108 |
| 28/10/1995 | 17 | 1 | | SPIRITUALLY IBIZA | Dino DINCD 111 |
| 18/11/1995 | ●[1] | 7 | | PURE SWING IV | Dino DINCD 116 |
| 25/11/1995 | 11 | 7 | | THE VERY BEST OF BLUES BROTHER SOUL SISTER | Dino DINCD 115 |
| 09/12/1995 | 16 | 4 | | THE GREATEST SOUL ALBUM OF ALL TIME | Dino DINCD 113 |
| 06/01/1996 | 4 | 6 | | DRIVETIME 3 | Dino DINCD 119 |
| 06/01/1996 | 6 | 5 | | PURE SWING 5 | Dino DINCD 117 |
| 30/03/1996 | 7 | 7 | | EIGHTIES SOUL WEEKENDER | Dino DINCD 122 |
| 13/04/1996 | 9 | 3 | | PURE SWING 96 | Dino DINCD 120 |
| 11/05/1996 | 10 | 4 | | ROCK ANTHEMS – VOLUME 2 | Dino DINCD 110 |
| 22/06/1996 | 9 | 3 | | PURE JAZZ MOODS – COOL JAZZ FOR A SUMMERS DAY | Dino DINCD 126 |
| 31/08/1996 | 8 | 3 | | DRIVE TIME 4 | Dino DINCD 128 |
| 07/09/1996 | 16 | 3 | | THE VERY BEST OF CAJUN – 40 HOT CAJUN CLASSICS | Dino DINCD 127 |
| 17/05/1997 | 18 | 1 | | THE VERY BEST OF BRASS | Dino DINCD 139 |

### DISCO DEMAND
UK label formed by Dave McAleer as an imprint of Pye Records.

| DATE | POS | WKS | BPI | ALBUM TITLE | LABEL & NUMBER |
|---|---|---|---|---|---|
| 15/03/1975 | 30 | 1 | | SOLID SOUL SENSATIONS | Disco Demand DDLP 5001 |

### DJ INTERNATIONAL

| DATE | POS | WKS | BPI | ALBUM TITLE | LABEL & NUMBER |
|---|---|---|---|---|---|
| 20/09/1986 | 52 | 12 | | THE HOUSE SOUND OF CHICAGO | DJ International LONLP 22 |
| 18/04/1987 | 38 | 7 | | THE HOUSE SOUND OF CHICAGO VOLUME 2 | DJ International LONLP 32 |
| 31/10/1987 | 36 | 4 | | JACKMASTER VOLUME 1 | DJ International JACKLP 501 |
| 13/02/1988 | 38 | 3 | | JACKMASTER VOLUME 2 | DJ International JACKLP 502 |

### DMC

| DATE | POS | WKS | BPI | ALBUM TITLE | LABEL & NUMBER |
|---|---|---|---|---|---|
| 18/03/2000 | 16 | 1 | | GROOVE ARMADA – BACK TO MINE | DMC BACKCD 4 |

○ Silver disc  ● Gold disc  ✪ Platinum disc (additional platinum units are indicated by a figure following the symbol)  ●[9] Number of weeks album topped the UK chart

| | | | | |
|---|---|---|---|---|
| 28/10/2000 . . . . . 19 . . . . . . 1 . . . . . . | | | | FAITHLESS – BACK TO MINE . . . . . . . . . . . . . . . . . . . . . . . . . . . . . . . . . . . . . . . . . . . . . . . . . . DMC BACKCD 5 |

## DMG TV

| | | | | |
|---|---|---|---|---|
| 26/04/2003 . . . . . 4 . . . . . . 6 . . . . . . | | | | LET'S GROOVE . . . . . . . . . . . . . . . . . . . . . . . . . . . . . . . . . . . . . . . . . . . . . . . . . . DMG TV/Sony TV DMGTV 002E |
| 17/04/2004 . . . . . 9 . . . . . . 3 . . . . . . | | | | FANTASTIC NO 1'S OF THE SEVENTIES . . . . . . . . . . . . . . . . . . . . . . . . . . . . . . . . . . . . . . . . . DMG TV DSTV002 |

## DOVER  UK re-issue and TV marketing label formed in 1988; it closed in 1992.

| | | | | |
|---|---|---|---|---|
| 29/10/1988 . . . . . 6 . . . . . . 11 . . . . . . ✪ | | | | SMASH HITS PARTY '88 . . . . . . . . . . . . . . . . . . . . . . . . . . . . . . . . . . . . . . . . . . . . . . . . . . . . . Dover ADD 5 |
| 14/01/1989 . . . . . 12 . . . . . 5 . . . . . . ✪ | | | | SMASH HITS PARTY '88 . . . . . . . . . . . . . . . . . . . . . . . . . . . . . . . . . . . . . . . . . . . . . . . . . . . . . Dover ADD 5 |
| 04/03/1989 . . . . . 2 . . . . . . 10 . . . . . ● | | | | AND ALL BECAUSE THE LADY LOVES… . . . . . . . . . . . . . . . . . . . . . . . . . . . . . . . . . . . . . . . . . . . . . Dover ADD 6 |
| 28/10/1989 . . . . . ❶³ . . . . 14 . . . . . ✪ | | | | SMASH HITS PARTY '89 – 30 SMASH HITS . . . . . . . . . . . . . . . . . . . . . . . . . . . . . . . . . . . . . . . . . . Dover ADD 8 |
| 10/02/1990 . . . . . 2 . . . . . . 15 . . . . . ● | | | | ALL BY MYSELF . . . . . . . . . . . . . . . . . . . . . . . . . . . . . . . . . . . . . . . . . . . . . . . . . . . . . . . Dover ADD 12 |
| 14/07/1990 . . . . . ❶² . . . . 10 . . . . . ● | | | | SMASH HITS – RAVE! . . . . . . . . . . . . . . . . . . . . . . . . . . . . . . . . . . . . . . . . . . . . . . . . . . . . Dover ADD 14 |
| 22/09/1990 . . . . . 2 . . . . . . 6 . . . . . . ● | | | | JUST SEVENTEEN – GET KICKIN' . . . . . . . . . . . . . . . . . . . . . . . . . . . . . . . . . . . . . . . . . . . . . Dover ADD 16 |
| 03/11/1990 . . . . . 2 . . . . . . 14 . . . . . ✪ | | | | SMASH HITS 1990 . . . . . . . . . . . . . . . . . . . . . . . . . . . . . . . . . . . . . . . . . . . . . . . . . . . . Dover ADD 18 |
| 24/11/1990 . . . . . 7 . . . . . . 8 . . . . . . | | | | A TON OF HITS – THE BEST OF STOCK AITKEN WATERMAN . . . . . . . . . . . . . . . . . . . . . . . . . . . . . Dover ADD 19 |
| 20/04/1991 . . . . . 4 . . . . . . 6 . . . . . . | | | | RED HOT METAL – 18 ROCK CLASSICS . . . . . . . . . . . . . . . . . . . . . . . . . . . . . . . . . . . . . . . . . Dover ADD 21 |
| 25/05/1991 . . . . . ❶² . . . . 9 . . . . . . | | | | SMASH HITS – MASSIVE! . . . . . . . . . . . . . . . . . . . . . . . . . . . . . . . . . . . . . . . . . . . . . . . . Dover ADD 24 |
| 08/06/1991 . . . . . 13 . . . . . 5 . . . . . . | | | | ALL BY MYSELF VOLUME 2 . . . . . . . . . . . . . . . . . . . . . . . . . . . . . . . . . . . . . . . . . . . . . . . Dover ADD 23 |
| 14/09/1991 . . . . . 2 . . . . . . 7 . . . . . . ○ | | | | MOMENTS IN SOUL . . . . . . . . . . . . . . . . . . . . . . . . . . . . . . . . . . . . . . . . . . . . . . . . . . . . Dover ADD 25 |
| 26/10/1991 . . . . . 3 . . . . . . 16 . . . . . ✪ | | | | SMASH HITS 1991 . . . . . . . . . . . . . . . . . . . . . . . . . . . . . . . . . . . . . . . . . . . . . . . . . . . . Dover ADD 28 |
| 16/05/1992 . . . . . 4 . . . . . . 7 . . . . . . | | | | THE GREATEST MOMENTS IN SOUL . . . . . . . . . . . . . . . . . . . . . . . . . . . . . . . . . . . . . . . . . . . Dover CCD 33 |
| 12/12/1992 . . . . . 5 . . . . . . 8 . . . . . . ● | | | | SMASH HITS '92 – 40 BIG HITS! SORTED! . . . . . . . . . . . . . . . . . . . . . . . . . . . . . . . . . . . . . Dover ADDCD 35 |

## DREAMSCAPE

| | | | | |
|---|---|---|---|---|
| 17/06/1995 . . . . . 20 . . . . . . 1 . . . . . . | | | | RADIO DREAMSCAPE – VOLUME 1 . . . . . . . . . . . . . . . . . . . . . . . . . . . . . . . . . . . . . . . Dreamscape DREAMCD 01 |

## EARTH

| | | | | |
|---|---|---|---|---|
| 16/11/1996 . . . . . 19 . . . . . . 1 . . . . . . | | | | LTJ BUKEM PRESENTS EARTH – VOLUME 1 . . . . . . . . . . . . . . . . . . . . . . . . . . . . . . . . . . . . Earth EARTHCD 001 |

## EAST WEST  US label formed in 1955 as a subsidiary of Atlantic; it was relaunched in 1989.

| | | | | |
|---|---|---|---|---|
| 12/10/1991 . . . . . 16 . . . . . . 2 . . . . . . | | | | I'M YOUR FAN – THE SONGS OF LEONARD COHEN . . . . . . . . . . . . . . . . . . . . . . . . . . . . . . . . . East West WX 444 |
| 26/06/1993 . . . . . 17 . . . . . . 1 . . . . . . ○ | | | | DISCO INFERNO . . . . . . . . . . . . . . . . . . . . . . . . . . . . . . . . . . . . . . . . . . . . . . . . . East West 9548319632 |
| 18/05/2002 . . . . . 10 . . . . . . 2 . . . . . . | | | | HEARTLESS CREW PRESENTS CRISP BISCUIT . . . . . . . . . . . . . . . . . . . . . . . . . . . . . . . . East West 0927460172 |
| 22/06/2002 . . . . . 10 . . . . . . 2 . . . . . . ○ | | | | DRIVIN' WITH JOHNNIE WALKER . . . . . . . . . . . . . . . . . . . . . . . . . . . . . . . . . . . . . . . . East West 0927473132 |

## ECHO/V2  UK labels formed by Chris Wright (Echo) and Richard Branson (V2). Wright had previously been a founder of Chrysalis whilst Branson had founded Virgin Records.

| | | | | |
|---|---|---|---|---|
| 02/03/2002 . . . . . 4 . . . . . . 4 . . . . . . | | | | ACOUSTIC . . . . . . . . . . . . . . . . . . . . . . . . . . . . . . . . . . . . . . . . . . . . . . . . . . . . Echo/V2 Music ECV21 |
| 22/06/2002 . . . . . 14 . . . . . . 2 . . . . . . | | | | ACOUSTIC 2 . . . . . . . . . . . . . . . . . . . . . . . . . . . . . . . . . . . . . . . . . . . . . . . . . . Echo/V2 Music ECV22 |
| 24/01/2004 . . . . . 2 . . . . . . 9 . . . . . . ● | | | | BEST OF ACOUSTIC . . . . . . . . . . . . . . . . . . . . . . . . . . . . . . . . . . . . . . . . . . . . . . Echo/V2 Music ECV24 |

## ELEVATE

| | | | | |
|---|---|---|---|---|
| 11/04/1992 . . . . . 11 . . . . . . 3 . . . . . . | | | | RAVE 2 – STRICTLY HARDCORE . . . . . . . . . . . . . . . . . . . . . . . . . . . . . . . . . . . . . . . . . . Elevate ELVCD 02 |
| 08/08/1992 . . . . . 17 . . . . . . 2 . . . . . . | | | | RAVING MAD . . . . . . . . . . . . . . . . . . . . . . . . . . . . . . . . . . . . . . . . . . . . . . . . . . . Elevate CDELV 01 |
| 27/02/1993 . . . . . 17 . . . . . . 3 . . . . . . | | | | THE WIND DOWN ZONE . . . . . . . . . . . . . . . . . . . . . . . . . . . . . . . . . . . . . . . . . . . . . . Elevate CDELV 04 |

## ELF

| | | | | |
|---|---|---|---|---|
| 13/06/1992 . . . . ❶¹ . . . . 6 . . . . . . ● | | | | EARTHRISE – THE RAINFOREST ALBUM . . . . . . . . . . . . . . . . . . . . . . . . . . . . . . . . . . . . . . . . . . Elf 5154192 |

## EMI  UK label formed in 1898 by William Barry Owen and Trevor Williams as the Gramophone Company to exploit and market Emile Berliner's gramophone. The company opened its own pressing plant at Hayes in 1908 and two years later adopted the distinctive 'His Master's Voice' name and logo with Francis Barraud's dog and gramophone painting. After acquiring various labels during the 1920s (including Parlophone and Pathe) the Depression of 1931 saw it merge with Columbia (a company with no connection to the US label of the same name) to form EMI (Electrical & Musical Industries). It bought a controlling interest in Capitol in 1955 to obtain an a US presence and bought the rest of the company outright in 1979 (the same year EMI was taken over by Thorn). Other labels purchased include Liberty/United Artists/Blue Note in 1980, Chrysalis, IRS, Food, Roulette and Virgin in 1992, the latter deal costing £510 million.

| | | | | |
|---|---|---|---|---|
| 21/06/1969 . . . . . 15 . . . . . 14 . . . . . . | | | | IMPACT . . . . . . . . . . . . . . . . . . . . . . . . . . . . . . . . . . . . . . . . . . . . . . . . . . . . . . . . . . EMI STWO 2 |
| 02/06/1973 . . . . . ❶³ . . . . 11 . . . . . . | | | | PURE GOLD . . . . . . . . . . . . . . . . . . . . . . . . . . . . . . . . . . . . . . . . . . . . . . . . . . . . . . . . EMI EMK 251 |
| 18/11/1978 . . . . . ❶³ . . . . 23 . . . . . . ✪ | | | | DON'T WALK – BOOGIE . . . . . . . . . . . . . . . . . . . . . . . . . . . . . . . . . . . . . . . . . . . . . . . . . . EMI EMTV 13 |
| 21/04/1979 . . . . . 2 . . . . . . 14 . . . . . ● | | | | COUNTRY LIFE . . . . . . . . . . . . . . . . . . . . . . . . . . . . . . . . . . . . . . . . . . . . . . . . . . . . . . EMI EMTV 16 |
| 02/06/1979 . . . . . 19 . . . . . . 6 . . . . . . | | | | KNUCKLE SANDWICH . . . . . . . . . . . . . . . . . . . . . . . . . . . . . . . . . . . . . . . . . . . . . . . . . . . EMI EMYV 18 |
| 15/12/1979 . . . . . 13 . . . . . . 8 . . . . . . ● | | | | ALL ABOARD . . . . . . . . . . . . . . . . . . . . . . . . . . . . . . . . . . . . . . . . . . . . . . . . . . . . . . . EMI EMTX 101 |
| 23/02/1980 . . . . . 16 . . . . . . 7 . . . . . . | | | | METAL FOR MUTHAS . . . . . . . . . . . . . . . . . . . . . . . . . . . . . . . . . . . . . . . . . . . . . . . . . . EMI EMC 3318 |

▲⁹ Number of weeks album topped the US chart  ◆¹² RIAA Diamond Awards  ◇³ IFPI Platinum Europe Awards

| VAR | DATE | POS | WKS | BPI | ALBUM TITLE | LABEL & NUMBER |
|---|---|---|---|---|---|---|
| | 14/06/1980 | 58 | 1 | | METAL FOR MUTHAS VOLUME 2 | EMI EMC 3337 |
| | 13/03/1982 | 11 | 8 | ● | 20 WITH A BULLET | EMI EMTV 32 |
| | 10/12/1983 | ●[5] | 50 | ✪[3] | NOW, THAT'S WHAT I CALL MUSIC | EMI/Virgin NOW 1 |
| | 07/04/1984 | ●[5] | 38 | ✪[2] | NOW, THAT'S WHAT I CALL MUSIC II | EMI/Virgin NOW 2 |
| | 26/05/1984 | 5 | 15 | ● | THEN CAME ROCK 'N' ROLL | EMI THEN 1 |
| | 11/08/1984 | ●[8] | 30 | ✪[2] | NOW, THAT'S WHAT I CALL MUSIC III | EMI/Virgin NOW 3 |
| | 08/12/1984 | 2 | 43 | ✪ | NOW, THAT'S WHAT I CALL MUSIC 4 | EMI/Virgin NOW 4 |
| | 01/06/1985 | 3 | 14 | ● | NOW DANCE – THE 12" MIXES | EMI/Virgin NOD 1 |
| | 13/07/1985 | 84 | 2 | | KERRANG! KOMPILATION – 24 ROCK MASTERS. | EMI/Virgin KER 1 |
| | 17/08/1985 | ●[5] | 21 | ✪[2] | NOW, THAT'S WHAT I CALL MUSIC 5 | EMI/Virgin NOW 5 |
| | 30/11/1985 | ●[2] | 22 | ✪[4] | NOW – THE CHRISTMAS ALBUM | EMI/Virgin NOX 1 |
| | 07/12/1985 | ●[4] | 40 | ✪[4] | NOW, THAT'S WHAT I CALL MUSIC 6 | EMI/Virgin NOW 6 |
| | 19/07/1986 | 7 | 9 | ✪ | NOW – THE SUMMER ALBUM – 30 SUMMER HITS | EMI/Virgin SUMMER 1 |
| | 23/08/1986 | ●[5] | 21 | ✪[2] | NOW, THAT'S WHAT I CALL MUSIC 7 | EMI/Virgin NOW 7 |
| | 08/11/1986 | 2 | 13 | ● | NOW DANCE '86 | EMI/Virgin NOD 2 |
| | 29/11/1986 | 65 | 4 | | NOW, THAT'S WHAT I CALL MUSIC '86 | EMI/Virgin/Polygram CDNOW 86 |
| | 06/12/1986 | ●[6] | 23 | ✪[4] | NOW, THAT'S WHAT I CALL MUSIC 8 | EMI/Virgin/Polygram NOW 8 |
| | 04/04/1987 | ●[5] | 26 | ✪[2] | NOW, THAT'S WHAT I CALL MUSIC 9 | EMI/Virgin/Polygram NOW 9 |
| | 03/10/1987 | 5 | 10 | | NOW! SMASH HITS | EMI/Virgin/Polygram NOSH 1 |
| | 05/12/1987 | ●[6] | 21 | ✪[4] | NOW THAT'S WHAT I CALL MUSIC 10 | EMI/Virgin/Polygram NOW 10 |
| | 05/03/1988 | 5 | 21 | ✪ | UNFORGETTABLE | EMI EMTV 44 |
| | 02/04/1988 | ●[3] | 17 | ✪[2] | NOW THAT'S WHAT I CALL MUSIC 11 | EMI/Virgin/Polygram NOW 11 |
| | 23/07/1988 | ●[5] | 17 | ✪[2] | NOW THAT'S WHAT I CALL MUSIC 12 | EMI/Virgin/Polygram NOW 12 |
| | 22/10/1988 | 27 | 12 | ✪ | THE CLASSIC EXPERIENCE | EMI EMTVD 45 |
| | 03/12/1988 | ●[4] | 6 | ✪[4] | NOW THAT'S WHAT I CALL MUSIC 13 | EMI/Virgin/Polygram NOW 13 |
| | 03/12/1988 | 59 | 5 | ● | HELLO CHILDREN… EVERYWHERE | EMI EM 1307 |
| | 14/01/1989 | ●[1] | 15 | ✪[4] | NOW THAT'S WHAT I CALL MUSIC 13 | EMI/Virgin/Polygram NOW 13 |
| | 14/01/1989 | 8 | 58 | ✪ | THE CLASSIC EXPERIENCE | EMI EMTVD 45 |
| | 28/01/1989 | 18 | 1 | | UNFORGETTABLE | EMI EMTV 44 |
| | 18/03/1989 | ●[1] | 15 | ● | UNFORGETTABLE 2 | EMI EMTV 46 |
| | 01/04/1989 | ●[7] | 18 | ✪[2] | NOW THAT'S WHAT I CALL MUSIC 14 | EMI/Virgin/Polygram NOW 14 |
| | 15/07/1989 | ●[6] | 14 | ✪ | NOW DANCE '89 – THE 12" MIXES | EMI/Virgin/Polygram NOD 3 |
| | 26/08/1989 | ●[5] | 13 | ✪ | NOW THAT'S WHAT I CALL MUSIC 15 | EMI/Virgin/Polygram NOW 15 |
| | 30/09/1989 | 2 | 10 | ● | IS THIS LOVE | EMI EMTV 47 |
| | 18/11/1989 | ●[1] | 12 | | THE 80'S ALBUM – THE ALBUM OF THE DECADE | EMI EMTVD 48 |
| | 02/12/1989 | ●[7] | 15 | ✪[3] | NOW THAT'S WHAT I CALL MUSIC 16 | EMI/Virgin/Polygram NOW 15 |
| | 09/12/1989 | 2 | 16 | ● | IT'S CHRISTMAS | EMI EMTV 49 |
| | 10/03/1990 | ●[4] | 14 | ✪ | NOW DANCE 901 – 20 SMASH DANCE HITS – THE 12" MIXES | EMI/Virgin/Polygram NOD 4 |
| | 05/05/1990 | ●[5] | 15 | ✪ | NOW THAT'S WHAT I CALL MUSIC 17 | EMI/Virgin/Polygram NOW 17 |
| | 26/05/1990 | ●[4] | 32 | ● | CLASSIC EXPERIENCE II | EMI EMTVD 50 |
| | 28/07/1990 | ●[3] | 13 | ✪ | NOW DANCE 902 | EMI/Virgin/Polygram NOD 5 |
| | 04/08/1990 | 8 | 7 | | THE WILD ONE | EMI EMTV 52 |
| | 20/10/1990 | ●[3] | 18 | ✪ | MISSING YOU – AN ALBUM OF LOVE | EMI EMTV 53 |
| | 10/11/1990 | ●[2] | 9 | ● | NOW DANCE 903 – THE 12" MIXES | EMI/Virgin/Polygram NOD 6 |
| | 17/11/1990 | 6 | 9 | ● | TRULY UNFORGETTABLE | EMI EMTVD 55 |
| | 01/12/1990 | ●[5] | 18 | ✪[3] | NOW! THAT'S WHAT I CALL MUSIC 18 | EMI/Virgin/Polygram NOW 18 |
| | 01/12/1990 | 12 | 4 | ● | THE BEST FROM THE MGM MUSICALS. | EMI EMTV 56 |
| | 16/02/1991 | 2 | 11 | ● | MISSING YOU 2 – AN ALBUM OF LOVE | EMI EMTV 57 |
| | 23/02/1991 | ●[3] | 12 | ✪ | AWESOME!! – 20 MASSIVE HITS | EMI/Virgin/Polygram EVP 58 |
| | 06/04/1991 | ●[5] | 16 | ✪ | NOW! THAT'S WHAT I CALL MUSIC 19 | EMI/Virgin/Polygram NOW 19 |
| | 11/05/1991 | 3 | 14 | ● | CLASSIC EXPERIENCE III | EMI EMTVD 59 |
| | 05/10/1991 | ●[3] | 9 | ● | NOW DANCE 91 | EMI/Virgin/Polygram NOD 7 |
| | 26/10/1991 | 7 | 6 | ● | SEXUAL HEALING | EMI EMTV 60 |
| | 02/11/1991 | 2 | 11 | ● | AWESOME! 2 | EMI/Virgin/Polygram EVP 1 |
| | 30/11/1991 | ●[7] | 18 | ✪[3] | NOW THAT'S WHAT I CALL MUSIC! 20 | EMI/Virgin/Polygram NOW 20 |
| | 30/11/1991 | 14 | 7 | ● | A CLASSICAL CHRISTMAS | EMI EMTV 62 |
| | 25/01/1992 | ●[4] | 15 | ● | THE ULTIMATE RAVE | EMI/Virgin/Polygram CDEVP 2 |
| | 22/02/1992 | 2 | 11 | | TENDER LOVE – 17 ROMANTIC LOVE SONGS | EMI CDEMTV 64 |
| | 22/02/1992 | 5 | 7 | ○ | THE CLASSIC ROMANCE | EMI CDEMTV 63 |
| | 25/04/1992 | ●[5] | 13 | ✪ | NOW THAT'S WHAT I CALL MUSIC! 21 | EMI/Virgin/Polygram CDNOW 21 |
| | 08/08/1992 | ●[8] | 14 | ✪ | NOW THAT'S WHAT I CALL MUSIC! 22 | EMI/Virgin/Polygram CDNOW 22 |
| | 22/08/1992 | 2 | 9 | ● | MAXIMUM RAVE | EMI CDEMTV 65 |
| | 12/09/1992 | 2 | 11 | ● | THE BEST OF JAMES BOND – 30TH ANNIVERSARY COLLECTION | EMI CDBOND 007 |
| | 17/10/1992 | 2 | 5 | | WICKED! | EMI CDEMTV 66 |
| | 31/10/1992 | 8 | 4 | | SMASHIE AND NICEY PRESENT LET'S ROCK! | EMI CDEMTV 67 |
| | 14/11/1992 | 3 | 11 | ● | NOW DANCE 92 | EMI/Virgin/Polygram CDNOD 8 |
| | 21/11/1992 | 2 | 15 | ✪ | IT'S CHRISTMAS TIME | EMI CDEMTV 69 |
| | 28/11/1992 | ●[5] | 18 | ✪[3] | NOW THAT'S WHAT I CALL MUSIC! 23 | EMI/Virgin/Polygram CDNOW 23 |

○ Silver disc  ● Gold disc  ✪ Platinum disc (additional platinum units are indicated by a figure following the symbol)  ●[9] Number of weeks album topped the UK chart

| DATE | POS | WKS | BPI | ALBUM TITLE | LABEL & NUMBER |
|---|---|---|---|---|---|
| 05/12/1992 | 17 | 2 | | FOREVER | EMI CDEMTV 70 |
| 30/01/1993 | 2 | 8 | | THE MEGA RAVE | EMI/Virgin/Polygram CDEVP 3 |
| 20/02/1993 | 4 | 8 | ● | SOUL MOODS | EMI CDEMTV 71 |
| 13/03/1993 | 2 | 8 | ● | MEGA DANCE – THE POWER ZONE | EMI/Virgin/Polygram CDEVP 4 |
| 27/03/1993 | 9 | 6 | | CLASSIC EXPERIENCE IV | EMI CDEMTVD 72 |
| 10/04/1993 | 6 | 6 | ○ | LOADED | EMI/Virgin/Polygram CDEVP 5 |
| 17/04/1993 | 3 | 6 | ○ | MEGA DANCE 2 – THE ENERGY ZONE | EMI/Virgin/Polygram CDEVP 6 |
| 08/05/1993 | ●[6] | 13 | ✪ | NOW THAT'S WHAT I CALL MUSIC! 24 | EMI/Virgin/Polygram CDNOW 24 |
| 26/06/1993 | ●[2] | 9 | | NOW DANCE 93 | EMI/Virgin/Polygram CDNOD 9 |
| 03/07/1993 | 11 | 4 | | INNA DANCEHALL STYLE | EMI CDEMTV 76 |
| 14/08/1993 | ●[5] | 10 | ✪ | NOW THAT'S WHAT I CALL MUSIC! 25 | EMI/Virgin/Polygram CDNOW 25 |
| 04/09/1993 | 10 | 5 | ○ | NOW THAT'S WHAT I CALL MUSIC! 1983 | EMI/Virgin/Polygram CDNOW 1983 |
| 04/09/1993 | 13 | 4 | ○ | NOW THAT'S WHAT I CALL MUSIC! 1984 | EMI/Virgin/Polygram CDNOW 1984 |
| 04/09/1993 | 15 | 4 | ○ | NOW THAT'S WHAT I CALL MUSIC! 1985 | EMI/Virgin/Polygram CDNOW 1985 |
| 04/09/1993 | 16 | 2 | | NOW THAT'S WHAT I CALL MUSIC! 1986 | EMI/Virgin/Polygram CDNOW 1986 |
| 04/09/1993 | 17 | 2 | | NOW THAT'S WHAT I CALL MUSIC! 1987 | EMI/Virgin/Polygram CDNOW 1987 |
| 18/09/1993 | 8 | 6 | | BACK TO THE 70'S | EMI CDEMTV 77 |
| 25/09/1993 | 14 | 2 | | NOW THAT'S WHAT I CALL MUSIC! 1992 | EMI/Virgin/Polygram CDNOW 1992 |
| 25/09/1993 | 20 | 1 | | NOW THAT'S WHAT I CALL MUSIC! 1988 | EMI/Virgin/Polygram CDNOW 1988 |
| 09/10/1993 | ●[1] | 8 | ● | NOW THAT'S WHAT I CALL MUSIC! 1993 | EMI/Virgin/Polygram CDNOW 1993 |
| 30/10/1993 | ●[1] | 6 | ● | NOW DANCE – THE BEST OF '93 | EMI/Virgin/Polygram CDNOD 10 |
| 06/11/1993 | 12 | 3 | | LET'S GO DISCO | EMI CDEMTV 78 |
| 27/11/1993 | ●[8] | 15 | ✪[3] | NOW THAT'S WHAT I CALL MUSIC! 26 | EMI/Virgin/Polygram CDNOW 26 |
| 27/11/1993 | 17 | 1 | ○ | IT TAKES TWO – LOVE'S GREATEST DUETS | EMI CDEMTV 80 |
| 29/01/1994 | ●[2] | 7 | ● | NOW DANCE 94 VOLUME 1 | EMI/Virgin/Polygram CDNOD 11 |
| 26/02/1994 | 6 | 3 | | THE BRIT AWARDS | EMI CDAWARD 1 |
| 19/03/1994 | 6 | 6 | | NOW! THAT'S WHAT I CALL LOVE | EMI/Virgin/Polygram CDEVP 7 |
| 19/03/1994 | 8 | 5 | | NOW DANCE 94 VOLUME 2 | EMI/Virgin/Polygram CDNOD 12 |
| 09/04/1994 | ●[4] | 15 | ✪ | NOW THAT'S WHAT I CALL MUSIC! 27 | EMI/Virgin/Polygram CDNOW 27 |
| 25/06/1994 | 14 | 5 | | TRANQUILLITY | EMI CDC 5552432 |
| 02/07/1994 | ●[2] | 8 | | NOW DANCE – SUMMER 94 | EMI/Virgin/Polygram CDNOD 13 |
| 13/08/1994 | ●[5] | 13 | ✪[2] | NOW THAT'S WHAT I CALL MUSIC! 28 | EMI/Virgin/Polygram CDNOW 28 |
| 08/10/1994 | 10 | 4 | | CLUB TOGETHER | EMI CDEMC 3692 |
| 15/10/1994 | ●[4] | 8 | ✪ | NOW THAT'S WHAT I CALL MUSIC! 1994 | EMI/Virgin/Polygram CDNOW 1994 |
| 29/10/1994 | 8 | 5 | | MISSING YOU | EMI CDEMTVD 86 |
| 26/11/1994 | ●[9] | 13 | ✪[5] | NOW THAT'S WHAT I CALL MUSIC! 29 | EMI/Virgin/Polygram CDNOW 29 |
| 26/11/1994 | 4 | 12 | ✪ | THE BEST COUNTRY ALBUM IN THE WORLD... EVER! | EMI CDEMTVD 93 |
| 10/12/1994 | 4 | 9 | ● | NOW DANCE – THE BEST OF 94 | EMI/Virgin/Polygram CDNOD 14 |
| 10/12/1994 | 10 | 4 | ● | THAT'S CHRISTMAS | EMI CDEMTV 88 |
| 11/03/1995 | 8 | 4 | ○ | UNLACED | EMI CDEMTV 90 |
| 01/04/1995 | 3 | 6 | ● | NOW DANCE 95 | EMI/Virgin/Polygram CDNOD 15 |
| 22/04/1995 | ●[4] | 12 | ✪[2] | NOW THAT'S WHAT I CALL MUSIC! 30 | EMI/Virgin/Polygram CDNOW 30 |
| 29/04/1995 | 9 | 4 | | CLUB TOGETHER 2 | EMI CDEMC 3704 |
| 15/07/1995 | 6 | 6 | ● | THE BEST CLASSICAL ALBUM IN THE WORLD... EVER! | EMI CDEMTVD 93 |
| 22/07/1995 | 8 | 4 | | MOST EXCELLENT DANCE | EMI CDMXD 1 |
| 29/07/1995 | 3 | 5 | | NOW DANCE SUMMER 95 | EMI/Virgin/Polygram CDNOD 16 |
| 29/07/1995 | 18 | 3 | | DEDICATED TO PLEASURE | EMI CDEMTV 91 |
| 12/08/1995 | ●[4] | 12 | ✪[2] | NOW THAT'S WHAT I CALL MUSIC! 31 | EMI/Virgin/Polygram CDNOW 31 |
| 23/09/1995 | 16 | 3 | | TECHNO NIGHTS AMBIENT DAWN | EMI CDEMTV 97 |
| 14/10/1995 | 2 | 6 | ✪ | NOW THAT'S WHAT I CALL MUSIC! 1995 | EMI/Virgin/Polygram CDNOW 1995 |
| 28/10/1995 | 12 | 2 | | THAT'S ROCK 'N' ROLL | EMI CDEMTVD 100 |
| 04/11/1995 | 11 | 6 | ● | THAT'S COUNTRY | EMI CDEMTV 103 |
| 11/11/1995 | ●[1] | 7 | | THE GREATEST PARTY ALBUM UNDER THE SUN! | EMI TV CDEMTVD 107 |
| 25/11/1995 | ●[6] | 15 | ✪[4] | NOW THAT'S WHAT I CALL MUSIC! 32 | EMI/Virgin/Polygram CDNOW 32 |
| 16/12/1995 | 15 | 2 | | THAT'S CHRISTMAS | EMI TV CDEMTVD 105 |
| 02/03/1996 | 8 | 4 | ○ | THE GREATEST DANCE ALBUM UNDER THE SUN! | EMI TV CDEMTVD 115 |
| 09/03/1996 | 9 | 5 | ○ | THE BEST OF THE NINETIES... SO FAR | EMI TV CDEMTVD 116 |
| 16/03/1996 | 11 | 2 | | BABY LOVE | EMI TV CDEMTV 117 |
| 30/03/1996 | ●[5] | 13 | ✪[2] | NOW THAT'S WHAT I CALL MUSIC! 33 | EMI/Virgin/Polygram CDNOW 33 |
| 11/05/1996 | 8 | 3 | ○ | MIX'O'MATIC | EMI TV CDEMTVD 123 |
| 18/05/1996 | 12 | 2 | | LOST PROPERTY | EMI TV CDEMTVD 122 |
| 01/06/1996 | 17 | 2 | | COMMON GROUND | EMI Premier PRMTVCD 1 |
| 08/06/1996 | 7 | 3 | | CLUB TOGETHER 3 | EMI TV CDEMTVD 124 |
| 15/06/1996 | 17 | 2 | | LOVERMAN | EMI TV CDEMTVD 125 |
| 20/07/1996 | ●[4] | 8 | ● | BIG MIX 96 | EMI TV/warner.esp CDEMTVD 129 |
| 24/08/1996 | ●[7] | 15 | ✪[3] | NOW THAT'S WHAT I CALL MUSIC! 34 | EMI/Virgin/Polygram CDNOW 34 |
| 28/09/1996 | 7 | 4 | | BIG MIX '96 – VOLUME 2 | EMI TV/warner.esp CDEMTVD 131 |
| 09/11/1996 | 15 | 1 | | EASY MOODS | EMI TV CDEMTVD 137 |
| 30/11/1996 | ●[7] | 18 | ✪[5] | NOW THAT'S WHAT I CALL MUSIC! 35 | EMI/Virgin/Polygram CDNOW 35 |

▲[9] Number of weeks album topped the US chart   ◆[12] RIAA Diamond Awards   ◇[3] IFPI Platinum Europe Awards

| DATE | POS | WKS | BPI | ALBUM TITLE | LABEL & NUMBER |
|---|---|---|---|---|---|
| 30/11/1996 | 13 | 4 | ● | GREATEST NON-STOP PARTY UNDER THE SUN | EMI TV CDEMTVD 149 |
| 07/12/1996 | 16 | 3 | ● | LOVE AT THE MOVIES… THE ALBUM | EMI TV/Sony TV CDEMTVD 144 |
| 28/12/1996 | 20 | 2 | ○ | THE DOG'S… ! | EMI TV CDEMTVD 143 |
| 05/04/1997 | ❶³ | 16 | ✪² | **NOW THAT'S WHAT I CALL MUSIC! 36** | EMI/Virgin/Polygram CDNOW 36 |
| 26/07/1997 | ❶⁴ | 16 | ✪² | **NOW THAT'S WHAT I CALL MUSIC! 37** | EMI/Virgin/Polygram CDNOW 37 |
| 01/11/1997 | ❶¹ | 6 | ✪ | **NOW DANCE 97** | EMI/Virgin CDNOD 17 |
| 29/11/1997 | ❶² | 17 | | **NOW THAT'S WHAT I CALL MUSIC! 38** | EMI/Virgin/Polygram CDNOW 38 |
| 18/04/1998 | ❶⁸ | 17 | | **NOW THAT'S WHAT I CALL MUSIC! 39** | EMI/Virgin/Polygram CDNOW 39 |
| 25/04/1998 | 14 | 1 | | TWENTIETH CENTURY BLUES | EMI 4946312 |
| 16/05/1998 | 19 | 1 | | A SONG FOR EUROTRASH | EMI 4950622 |
| 15/08/1998 | ❶⁴ | 14 | ✪³ | **NOW THAT'S WHAT I CALL MUSIC! 40** | EMI/Virgin/Polygram CDNOW 40 |
| 07/11/1998 | 3 | 5 | ● | **NOW DANCE 98** | EMI/Virgin CDNOD 18 |
| 05/12/1998 | ❶⁷ | 18 | ✪⁵ | **NOW THAT'S WHAT I CALL MUSIC! 41** | EMI/Virgin/Polygram CDNOW 41 |
| 10/04/1999 | ❶⁷ | 16 | ✪³ | **NOW THAT'S WHAT I CALL MUSIC! 42** | EMI/Virgin/Universal Music TV CDNOW 42 |
| 31/07/1999 | ❶⁴ | 15 | ✪³ | **NOW THAT'S WHAT I CALL MUSIC! 43** | EMI/Virgin/Universal Music TV CDNOW 43 |
| 30/10/1999 | ❶¹ | 8 | ✪ | **NOW DANCE 2000** | EMI/Virgin VTDCD 267 |
| 04/12/1999 | ❶⁸ | 18 | ✪⁷ | **NOW THAT'S WHAT I CALL MUSIC! 44** | EMI/Virgin/Universal Music TV CDNOW 44 |
| 29/04/2000 | ❶⁶ | 15 | ✪³ | **NOW THAT'S WHAT I CALL MUSIC! 45** | EMI/Virgin/Universal CDNOW 45 |
| 05/08/2000 | ❶⁴ | 16 | ✪³ | **NOW THAT'S WHAT I CALL MUSIC! 46** | EMI/Virgin/Universal CDNOW 46 |
| 18/11/2000 | 6 | 4 | ● | **Q AWARDS: THE ALBUM** | EMI/Virgin/Universal VTDCDX 330 |
| 02/12/2000 | ❶⁷ | 18 | ✪⁶ | **NOW THAT'S WHAT I CALL MUSIC! 47** | EMI/Virgin/Universal CDNOW 47 |
| 02/12/2000 | 4 | 10 | ✪ | **THE CLASSICAL ALBUM 2001** | EMI/Virgin/Universal CLCD 2 |
| 09/12/2000 | 2 | 8 | ✪ | **NOW THE CHRISTMAS ALBUM** | EMI/Virgin/Universal CDNOX 2 |
| 20/01/2001 | 2 | 6 | ● | **THE GREATEST NO 1 SINGLES** | EMI/Virgin/Universal VTDCD 357 |
| 21/04/2001 | ❶³ | 15 | ✪³ | **NOW THAT'S WHAT I CALL MUSIC! 48** | EMI/Virgin/Universal CDNOW 48 |
| 09/06/2001 | 2 | 7 | ● | **SMASH HITS SUMMER 2001** | EMI/Virgin/Universal VTDCD 373 |
| 11/08/2001 | ❶⁶ | 14 | ✪³ | **NOW THAT'S WHAT I CALL MUSIC! 49** | EMI/Virgin/Universal CDNOW 49 |
| 17/11/2001 | 2 | 14 | ✪ | **THE BEST AIR GUITAR ALBUM IN THE WORLD… EVER!** | EMI/Virgin/Universal VTDCD 416 |
| 01/12/2001 | ❶⁷ | 14 | ✪⁶ | **NOW THAT'S WHAT I CALL MUSIC! 50** | EMI/Virgin/Universal CDNOW 50 |
| 22/12/2001 | 5 | 8 | ● | **SMASH HITS 2002** | EMI/Virgin/Universal VTDCD 398 |
| 06/04/2002 | ❶³ | 17 | ✪³ | **NOW THAT'S WHAT I CALL MUSIC! 51** | EMI/Virgin/Universal CDNOW 51 |
| 03/08/2002 | ❶⁴ | 14 | ✪³ | **NOW THAT'S WHAT I CALL MUSIC! 52** | EMI/Virgin/Universal CDNOW 52 |
| 14/09/2002 | ❶⁵ | 10 | ✪ | **SMASH HITS – LET's PARTY** | EMI/Virgin/Universal VTDCD 503 |
| 23/11/2002 | 5 | 11 | ✪ | **50 YEARS OF THE GREATEST HIT SINGLES** | EMI/Virgin/Universal VTDCDX 491 |
| 30/11/2002 | ❶⁷ | 15 | ✪⁴ | **NOW THAT'S WHAT I CALL MUSIC! 53** | EMI/Virgin/Universal CDNOW 53 |
| 30/11/2002 | 2 | 11 | ✪² | **THE BEST AIR GUITAR ALBUM IN THE WORLD 2** | EMI/Virgin/Universal VTDCD 488 |
| 11/01/2003 | 20 | 1 | | SMASH HITS 2003 | EMI/Virgin/Universal VTDCD 492 |
| 22/02/2003 | 2 | 5 | ● | **I LUV SMASH HITS** | EMI/Virgin/Universal VTDCD 511 |
| 26/04/2003 | ❶⁷ | 14 | ✪² | **NOW THAT'S WHAT I CALL MUSIC! 54** | EMI/Virgin/Universal CDNOW 54 |
| 02/08/2003 | ❶⁵ | 15 | ✪² | **NOW THAT'S WHAT I CALL MUSIC! 55** | EMI/Virgin/Universal CDNOW 55 |
| 09/08/2003 | 9 | 3 | ○ | **ONE STEP BEYOND** | EMI Virgin/Sanctuary VTDCDX 546 |
| 30/08/2003 | 2 | 8 | ● | **NEW WOMAN – THE NEW COLLECTION 2003** | EMI/BMG/Telstar VTDCD576 |
| 11/10/2003 | ❶³ | 17 | ✪ | **NOW DECADES** | EMI/Virgin/Universal VTDCD 580 |
| 01/11/2003 | 8 | 2 | ○ | **SMASH HITS – LET'S PARTY ON** | EMI/Virgin/Universal VTDCD 581 |
| 29/11/2003 | ❶⁷ | 15 | ✪⁵ | **NOW THAT'S WHAT I CALL MUSIC! 56** | EMI/Virgin/Universal CDNOW 56 |
| 06/12/2003 | 14 | 9 | ● | **THE BEST AIR GUITAR ALBUM EVER III** | EMI/Virgin/Universal VTDCD 557 |
| 13/12/2003 | 15 | 3 | | I LOVE CHRISTMAS | EMI/Virgin/Universal VTDCDX 560 |
| 21/02/2004 | 7 | 3 | ○ | **I LUV SMASH HITS 2004** | EMI/Virgin/Universal VTDCD 563 |
| 27/03/2004 | 3 | 12 | ● | **BEST OF R&B** | EMI/Sony TV VTDCD 604 |
| 17/04/2004 | ❶⁸ | 11+ | ✪³ | **NOW THAT'S WHAT I CALL MUSIC! 57** | EMI/Virgin/Universal CDNOW 57 |
| 19/06/2004 | 2 | 2+ | ○ | **ENGLAND – THE ALBUM** | EMI TV/Sony TV VTCD 621 |

**EMPORIO** UK budget label formed as an imprint of Music Collection International.

| DATE | POS | WKS | BPI | ALBUM TITLE | LABEL & NUMBER |
|---|---|---|---|---|---|
| 16/06/2001 | 14 | 1 | | PAVAROTTI/DOMINGO/CARRERAS | Emporio EMTBX 320 |

**EPIC** US label formed in 1953 as an imprint of the Columbia label. It achieved its initial success with gospel and country recordings before beginning to encompass many different styles. In the UK it was initially dependent on its American material before launching its own artist & repertoire division, with success from artists as diverse as Wham! and Shakin' Stevens.

| DATE | POS | WKS | BPI | ALBUM TITLE | LABEL & NUMBER |
|---|---|---|---|---|---|
| 02/07/1983 | 85 | 2 | | DANCE MIX – DANCE HITS VOLUME 1 | Epic EPC 25564 |
| 24/09/1983 | 51 | 3 | | DANCE MIX – DANCE HITS VOLUME 2 | Epic DM 2 |
| 03/03/1984 | 70 | 1 | | DANCE MIX – DANCE HITS VOLUME 3 | Epic DM 3 |
| 03/03/1984 | 73 | 1 | | ELECTRO SHOCK VOLTAGE ONE | Epic VOLT 1 |
| 16/06/1984 | 4 | 22 | ● | **AMERICAN HEARTBEAT** | Epic EPC 10045 |
| 16/06/1984 | 99 | 1 | | DANCE MIX – DANCE HITS VOLUME 4 | Epic DM 4 |
| 08/03/1986 | 2 | 14 | ● | **HITS FOR LOVERS** | Epic EPC 10050 |
| 09/11/1991 | 14 | 2 | | MELLOW MADNESS | Epic MOOD 20 |
| 18/07/1992 | 6 | 5 | | **RED HOT + DANCE** | Epic 4718212 |
| 29/08/1992 | 5 | 11 | | **ROMANCING THE SCREEN** | Epic 4719012 |

○ Silver disc  ● Gold disc  ✪ Platinum disc (additional platinum units are indicated by a figure following the symbol)  ❶⁹ Number of weeks album topped the UK chart

| DATE | POS | WKS | BPI | ALBUM TITLE | LABEL & NUMBER |
|---|---|---|---|---|---|
| 06/09/1997 | 19 | 1 | | MIX HEAVEN '97 | Epic SONYTV 31CD |
| 17/10/1998 | 3 | 4 | | **VH1 DIVAS LIVE** | Epic SONYTV 55CD |
| 05/05/2001 | 10 | 2 | ○ | **ALLY MCBEAL – FOR ONCE IN MY LIFE** | Epic 5005772 |

### ERATO French classical label formed in 1881.

| DATE | POS | WKS | BPI | ALBUM TITLE | LABEL & NUMBER |
|---|---|---|---|---|---|
| 11/07/1992 | 14 | 5 | | THE ULTIMATE OPERA COLLECTION | Erato 2292457972 |

### ESSENTIAL RECORDINGS

| DATE | POS | WKS | BPI | ALBUM TITLE | LABEL & NUMBER |
|---|---|---|---|---|---|
| 06/05/2000 | 8 | 4 | | **ESSENTIAL SELECTION SPRING 2000** | Essential Recordings 8573828142 |
| 09/09/2000 | 11 | 3 | | ESSENTIAL SELECTION IBIZA 2000 | Essential Recordings 8573847842 |

### EXPANSION UK soul label formed in 1987 in King's Lynn by music journalist Ralph Tee and Les McCutcheon.

| DATE | POS | WKS | BPI | ALBUM TITLE | LABEL & NUMBER |
|---|---|---|---|---|---|
| 24/04/1993 | 20 | 1 | | WINNER'S CIRCLE | Expansion CDEXP 2 |

### FAME

| DATE | POS | WKS | BPI | ALBUM TITLE | LABEL & NUMBER |
|---|---|---|---|---|---|
| 08/12/1984 | 75 | 3 | | THE CHRISTMAS CAROL COLLECTION | Fame WHS 413000 |

### FANFARE

| DATE | POS | WKS | BPI | ALBUM TITLE | LABEL & NUMBER |
|---|---|---|---|---|---|
| 12/11/1988 | 16 | 9 | ✪ | THE HIT FACTORY VOLUME 2 | Fanfare/PWL HF 4 |
| 14/01/1989 | 13 | 3 | | THE HIT FACTORY VOLUME 2 | Fanfare/PWL HF 4 |
| 15/07/1989 | 3 | 10 | ● | **THE HIT FACTORY VOLUME 3** | Fanfare/PWL HF 8 |
| 23/09/1989 | 3 | 6 | ● | **JUST SEVENTEEN – HEARTBEATS** | Fanfare FARE 1 |

### FANTAZIA

| DATE | POS | WKS | BPI | ALBUM TITLE | LABEL & NUMBER |
|---|---|---|---|---|---|
| 05/12/1992 | 13 | 5 | | FANTAZIA – THE FIRST TASTE | Fantazia FANTA 001 |
| 24/07/1993 | 17 | 3 | | FANTAZIA – TWICE AS NICE | Fantazia FANTA 002CD |
| 25/06/1994 | 16 | 2 | | FANTAZIA III – MADE IN HEAVEN | Fantazia FANTA 005CD |
| 29/04/1995 | 6 | 6 | | **THE HOUSE COLLECTION – VOLUME 2** | Fantazia FHC 002CD |
| 30/09/1995 | 4 | 7 | ● | **THE HOUSE COLLECTION – VOLUME 3** | Fantazia FHC 3DL |
| 17/02/1996 | 3 | 10 | ● | **THE HOUSE COLLECTION – CLUB CLASSICS** | Fantazia FHCC 1CDL |
| 29/06/1996 | 2 | 9 | ○ | **FANTAZIA PRESENT THE HOUSE COLLECTION 4** | Fantazia FHC 4CDL |
| 14/09/1996 | 4 | 8 | | **THE HOUSE COLLECTION CLUB CLASSICS – 2** | Fantazia FHCCC 2CDL |
| 08/03/1997 | 3 | 7 | ○ | **THE HOUSE COLLECTION – VOLUME 5** | Fantazia FHC 5CD |
| 07/06/1997 | 4 | 6 | | **CLUB CLASSICS – VOLUME 3** | Fantazia FHCCC 3CD |
| 27/09/1997 | 10 | 3 | ○ | **THE HOUSE COLLECTION 6 – PAUL OAKENFOLD/PAUL COSFORD** | Fantazia FHC 6CD |
| 21/02/1998 | 2 | 5 | ○ | **FANTAZIA – BRITISH ANTHEMS** | Fantazia FBA 1CD |

### FEVERPITCH

| DATE | POS | WKS | BPI | ALBUM TITLE | LABEL & NUMBER |
|---|---|---|---|---|---|
| 16/09/1995 | 14 | 2 | | TRADE | Feverpitch FVRCD 1001 |
| 20/04/1996 | 11 | 3 | | TRADE – VOLUME TWO | Feverpitch FVRCD 2 |
| 09/11/1996 | 19 | 1 | | TRADE – VOLUME THREE | Feverpitch FVRCD 3 |
| 12/04/1997 | 15 | 2 | | TRADE – VOLUME FOUR | Feverpitch FVRCD 5 |

### FFRR UK label formed by journalist and DJ Pete Tong as an imprint within London Records. The label was closed in 2002.

| DATE | POS | WKS | BPI | ALBUM TITLE | LABEL & NUMBER |
|---|---|---|---|---|---|
| 30/01/1988 | 40 | 4 | | THE HOUSE SOUND OF CHICAGO VOLUME 3 | ffrr FFRLP 1 |
| 27/08/1988 | 70 | 7 | | THE HOUSE SOUND OF LONDON VOLUME 4 | ffrr FFRDP 4 |
| 01/10/1988 | 58 | 2 | | BALEARIC BEATS VOLUME 1 | ffrr FFRLP 5 |
| 20/01/1996 | 12 | 3 | ○ | ESSENTIAL MIX – TONG COX SASHA OAKENFOLD | ffrr 8287042 |
| 20/04/1996 | 14 | 1 | | LTJ BUKEM PRESENTS LOGICAL PROGRESSION | ffrr 8287472 |
| 11/05/1996 | 6 | 3 | | **ESSENTIAL MIX 2 – TONG, MACKINTOSH...** | ffrr 5354312 |
| 10/08/1996 | 12 | 2 | | METALHEADZ – PLATINUM BREAKZ | ffrr 8287832 |
| 07/09/1996 | 12 | 3 | | ESSENTIAL MIX 3 – TONG, SEAMAN, JULES ETC | ffrr 5358292 |
| 15/11/1997 | 10 | 2 | ● | **PETE TONG ESSENTIAL SELECTION – WINTER 97** | ffrr 5550932 |
| 18/04/1998 | 4 | 7 | ● | **PETE TONG ESSENTIAL SELECTION** | ffrr 5557862 |
| 08/08/1998 | 8 | 5 | ○ | **CARL COX – NON STOP 98/01** | ffrr 5560302 |
| 29/08/1998 | 2 | 7 | ● | **PETE TONG ESSENTIAL SELECTION – SUMMER 1998 (3 CD)** | ffrr 5560422 |
| 29/08/1998 | 4 | 9 | ● | **PETE TONG ESSENTIAL SELECTION – SUMMER 1998** | ffrr 5560422 |

▲[9] Number of weeks album topped the US chart  ◆[12] RIAA Diamond Awards  ◇[3] IFPI Platinum Europe Awards

| DATE | POS | WKS | BPI | ALBUM TITLE | LABEL & NUMBER |
|---|---|---|---|---|---|
| 05/12/1998 | 11 | 6 | ● | ESSENTIAL SELECTION '98 – PETE TONG/PAUL OAKENFOLD | ffrr 5659642 |
| 09/01/1999 | 13 | 5 | | ESSENTIAL SELECTION '98 – PETE TONG/PAUL OAKENFOLD | ffrr 5659642 |
| 20/03/1999 | 3 | 6 | | **PETE TONG – ESSENTIAL SELECTION – SPRING 1999** | ffrr 5560842 |
| 20/03/1999 | 13 | 3 | | PETE TONG – ESSENTIAL SELECTION – SPRING 1999 | ffrr 5560882 |
| 31/07/1999 | 7 | 3 | ● | **PETE TONG ESSENTIAL SELECTION – IBIZA 99** This is a three-CD version of the album listed below. The two albums were listed separately in the chart | ffrr 3984290822 |
| 31/07/1999 | 11 | 5 | ● | PETE TONG ESSENTIAL SELECTION – IBIZA 99 | ffrr 3984290832 |
| 30/10/1999 | 13 | 2 | | CARL COX – NON STOP 2000 | ffrr 8573804212 |
| 13/11/1999 | 10 | 3 | ● | **ESSENTIAL MILLENNIUM – PETE TONG FATBOY SLIM PAUL OAKENFOLD** | ffrr 8573806292 |

## FIRM

| DATE | POS | WKS | BPI | ALBUM TITLE | LABEL & NUMBER |
|---|---|---|---|---|---|
| 11/01/1997 | 10 | 4 | | **WORLD DANCE – THE DRUM + BASS EXPERIENCE** | Firm FIRMCD 10 |

## 4AD UK label formed in 1980 by Ivo Watts-Russell and Peter Kent, both of whom had previously worked at Beggars Banquet. Indeed, Beggars Banquet loaned the new label (initially called Axis) £2,000 to establish itself. Kent later left to set up another label, Situation 2.

| DATE | POS | WKS | BPI | ALBUM TITLE | LABEL & NUMBER |
|---|---|---|---|---|---|
| 11/07/1987 | 53 | 2 | | LONELY IS AN EYESORE | 4AD CAD 703 |

## 4 BEAT UK dance label.

| DATE | POS | WKS | BPI | ALBUM TITLE | LABEL & NUMBER |
|---|---|---|---|---|---|
| 20/01/1996 | 11 | 2 | | UNITED – VOLUME 3 | 4 Beat FBRCD 334 |
| 25/05/1996 | 17 | 1 | | UNITED DANCE – VOLUME FOUR | 4 Beat FBRCD 335 |
| 09/11/1996 | 20 | 1 | | UNITED – VOLUME 5 | 4 Beat FBRCD 336 |
| 26/04/1997 | 10 | 3 | | **UNITED – VOLUME 6** | 4 Beat FBRCD 337 |

## FOURTH & BROADWAY

| DATE | POS | WKS | BPI | ALBUM TITLE | LABEL & NUMBER |
|---|---|---|---|---|---|
| 07/03/1992 | 13 | 2 | | THE REBIRTH OF COOL, TOO | Fourth & Broadway BRCD 582 |
| 15/05/1993 | 9 | 4 | | **THE REBIRTH OF COOL III** | Fourth & Broadway BRCD 590 |

## FREESTYLE

| DATE | POS | WKS | BPI | ALBUM TITLE | LABEL & NUMBER |
|---|---|---|---|---|---|
| 03/10/1998 | 7 | 3 | | **BROTHER'S GONNA WORK IT OUT** | Freestyle XDUSTCDX 101 |

## FRESH

| DATE | POS | WKS | BPI | ALBUM TITLE | LABEL & NUMBER |
|---|---|---|---|---|---|
| 03/06/1995 | 20 | 1 | | FRESHEN UP VOLUME 1 | Fresh FRSHCD 1 |

## GATECRASHER

| DATE | POS | WKS | BPI | ALBUM TITLE | LABEL & NUMBER |
|---|---|---|---|---|---|
| 20/10/2001 | 6 | 4 | ○ | **GATECRASHER DIGITAL** | Gatecrasher Music GATECD 1 |
| 02/02/2002 | 2 | 3 | | **GATECRASHER EXPERIENCE** | Gatecrasher GATECD 2 |
| 04/05/2002 | 8 | 2 | | **GATECRASHER DIGITAL TRANCE** | Gatecrasher GATECD 3 |

## GLOBAL TELEVISION

| DATE | POS | WKS | BPI | ALBUM TITLE | LABEL & NUMBER |
|---|---|---|---|---|---|
| 17/12/1994 | 11 | 5 | ● | SOUNDS OF THE SEVENTIES | Global Television RADCD 01 |
| 17/12/1994 | 13 | 4 | | HITS, HITS AND MORE DANCE HITS | Global Television RADCD 02 |
| 21/01/1995 | 2 | 7 | ● | **SOFT REGGAE** | Global Television RADCD 04 |
| 18/02/1995 | 6 | 6 | | **NEW SOUL REBELS** | Global Television RADCD 05 |
| 25/02/1995 | ●[3] | 9 | | **ON A DANCE TIP** | Global Television RADCD 07 |
| 04/03/1995 | 8 | 4 | | **GIRLS AND GUITARS** | Global Television RADCD 06 |
| 15/04/1995 | 8 | 4 | ● | **FIFTY NUMBER ONES OF THE '60S** | Global Television RADCD 08 |
| 22/04/1995 | 4 | 5 | ○ | **CLUB CLASS** | Global Television RADCD 10 |
| 22/04/1995 | 5 | 5 | ○ | **INTO THE EIGHTIES** | Global Television RADCD 09 |
| 20/05/1995 | ●[3] | 7 | ● | **ON A DANCE TIP 2** | Global Television RADCD 12 |
| 17/06/1995 | 3 | 4 | ● | **DANCE BUZZ** | Global Television RADCD 17 |
| 01/07/1995 | 2 | 6 | | **CHARTBUSTERS** | Global Television RADCD 15 |
| 01/07/1995 | 13 | 2 | | GREAT SEX | Global Television RADCD 16 |
| 15/07/1995 | 11 | 2 | | THEMES AND DREAMS | Global Television RADCD 11 |
| 29/07/1995 | 7 | 8 | | **NATURAL WOMAN** | Global Television RADCD 14 |
| 12/08/1995 | 2 | 5 | | **SUMMER DANCE PARTY** | Global Television RADCD 18 |
| 26/08/1995 | 2 | 5 | | **HITZ BLITZ** | Global Television RADCD 20 |
| 23/09/1995 | 2 | 6 | | **DANCE TIP 3** | Global Television RADCD 20 |
| 30/09/1995 | 9 | 6 | | **DRIVING ROCK** | Global Television RADCD 03 |
| 28/10/1995 | 7 | 5 | | **NIGHTFEVER** | Global Television RADCD 24 |

○ Silver disc   ● Gold disc   ✪ Platinum disc (additional platinum units are indicated by a figure following the symbol)   ●[9] Number of weeks album topped the UK chart

| DATE | POS | WKS | BPI | ALBUM TITLE | LABEL & NUMBER |
|---|---|---|---|---|---|
| 18/11/1995 | 3 | 12 | ◐ | **DANCE TIP '95** | Global Television RADCD 27 |
| 23/12/1995 | ❶⁵ | 14 | ◐ | **HITS 96** | Global Television RADCD 30 |
| 17/02/1996 | 9 | 4 | ○ | **VYBIN' – YOUNG SOUL REBELS** | Global Television RADCD 19 |
| 02/03/1996 | 7 | 3 | | **DANCE TIP 4** | warner.esp TV/Global TV RADCD 26 |
| 06/04/1996 | 12 | 3 | | COUNTRY GOLD | Global Television RADCD 25 |
| 27/04/1996 | 6 | 4 | ○ | **UNTITLED** | Global Television RADCD 32 |
| 04/05/1996 | 2 | 5 | ● | **VYBIN' 3 – NEW SOUL REBELS** | Global Television RADCD 33 |
| 11/05/1996 | 6 | 4 | ○ | **DANCE MIX UK** | Global Television RADCD 37 |
| 18/05/1996 | ❶⁹ | 16 | ◐ | **NEW HITS 96** | Global TV/Warner TV RADCD 36 |
| 25/05/1996 | 10 | 3 | ○ | **NATURAL WOMAN – VOLUME 2** | Global Television RADCD 28 |
| 15/06/1996 | 5 | 5 | | **THE BEST OF ACID JAZZ** | Global Television RADCD 35 |
| 13/07/1996 | 4 | 6 | | **NO GREATER LOVE** | Global Television RADCD 34 |
| 20/07/1996 | 15 | 1 | | SHADES OF SOUL | Global Television RADCD 40 |
| 27/07/1996 | 7 | 5 | | **VYBIN' 4** | Global Television RADCD 38 |
| 03/08/1996 | 6 | 6 | | **UNTITLED 2** | Global Television RADCD 39 |
| 17/08/1996 | 9 | 6 | ○ | **THE ULTIMATE LINE DANCING ALBUM** | Global Television RADCD 41 |
| 14/09/1996 | 10 | 4 | | **DANCE MIX 2** | Global Television RADCD 42 |
| 19/10/1996 | 2 | 21 | ◐ | **HEARTBEAT – NUMBER 1 LOVE SONGS OF THE '60S** | Global Television RADCD 46 |
| 16/11/1996 | 12 | 2 | | THE BEST OF VYBIN' | Sony TV/Global TV RADCD 45 |
| 16/11/1996 | 20 | 1 | | UNTITLED 3 | Global Television RADCD 44 |
| 30/11/1996 | 4 | 10 | ● | **THE ULTIMATE PARTY ANIMAL** | Global Television RADCD 47 |
| 21/12/1996 | 7 | 7 | | **DANCE TIP 2000** | warner.esp/Global TV RADCD 50 |
| 08/02/1997 | 7 | 8 | | **THE ULTIMATE LINE DANCING ALBUM** | Global Television RADCD 41 |
| 15/02/1997 | 13 | 4 | | BEST OF ACID JAZZ VOLUME 2 | Global TV/Polygram TV RADCD 52 |
| 15/03/1997 | 9 | 5 | ● | **GIRL POWER** | Global Television RADCD 56 |
| 05/04/1997 | 6 | 7 | ○ | **THE OLD SKOOL** | Polygram TV/Global TV RADCD 59 |
| 19/04/1997 | 6 | 4 | ○ | **KLUBHOPPIN'** | Global Television RADCD 60 |
| 26/04/1997 | ❶⁴ | 11 | ● | **NEW HITS 1997** | Global Television RADCD 67 |
| 24/05/1997 | 4 | 6 | | **CHARTBUSTERS** | Global Television RADCD 65 |
| 31/05/1997 | 14 | 3 | | MODROPHENIA | Global Television RADCD 62 |
| 28/06/1997 | 2 | 8 | | **THE ULTIMATE SUMMER PARTY ANIMAL** | Global Television RADCD 63 |
| 26/07/1997 | 12 | 2 | | THE OLD SKOOL REUNION | Polygram TV/Global TV RADCD 69 |
| 16/08/1997 | ❶³ | 12 | | **FRESH HITS 1997** | warner.esp/Global TV/Sony TV RADCD 70 |
| 30/08/1997 | 10 | 3 | | **DRIVE ON** | Global Television RADCD 55 |
| 06/09/1997 | 6 | 5 | | **THE BEST DANCE ALBUM OF THE YEAR** | Global Television RADCD 61 |
| 20/09/1997 | 12 | 3 | | PURE REGGAE | Global Television RADCD 71 |
| 18/10/1997 | 5 | 4 | ○ | **SPEED GARAGE ANTHEMS** | Global Television RADCD 78 |
| 01/11/1997 | ❶¹ | 7 | ◐ | **HUGE HITS 1997** | warner.esp/Global TV/Sony TV RADCD 75 |
| 01/11/1997 | 6 | 5 | ○ | **HEARTBEAT – LOVE ME TENDER** | Global Television RADCD 72 |
| 22/11/1997 | 4 | 15 | ◐ | **A PERFECT LOVE** | warner.esp/Global TV RADCD 80 |
| 20/12/1997 | 4 | 7 | | **BIG HITS** | warner.esp/Global TV/Sony TV RADCD 88 |
| 27/12/1997 | 3 | 13 | ● | **FUNKY DIVAS** | Global Television RADCD 77 |
| 17/01/1998 | ❶² | 7 | ● | **THE EIGHTIES MIX** | Global Television RADCD 85 |
| 17/01/1998 | 9 | 3 | | **SHADES OF SOUL** | Global Television RADCD 66 |
| 31/01/1998 | 8 | 3 | ○ | **ONE WORLD** | Global Television RADCD 74 |
| 21/02/1998 | 4 | 7 | ● | **DROP DEAD GORGEOUS** | Global Television RADCD 73 |
| 21/02/1998 | 5 | 8 | ○ | **SPEED GARAGE ANTHEMS – VOLUME 2** | Global Television RADCD 83 |
| 04/04/1998 | 5 | 4 | ○ | **CLUB CULTURE EXPOSED!** | Global Television RADCD 93 |
| 18/04/1998 | 5 | 5 | ○ | **URBAN RHYMES** | Global TV/Polygram TV RADCD 89 |
| 23/05/1998 | 13 | 3 | | THE BEST DANCE ALBUM OF THE YEAR | Global Television RADCD 97 |
| 30/05/1998 | 10 | 3 | | **DROP DEAD GORGEOUS 2** | Global Television RADCD 94 |
| 01/08/1998 | 7 | 4 | ○ | **SPEED GARAGE ANTHEMS IN IBIZA** | Global Television RADCD 98X |
| 08/08/1998 | 8 | 3 | ● | **HEART FULL OF SOUL** | warner.esp/Global TV RADCD 99 |
| 22/08/1998 | 6 | 7 | | **STREET VIBES** | warner.esp/Global TV/Sony Music TV RADCD 95 |
| 24/10/1998 | 2 | 5 | ● | **THE FEMALE TOUCH** | warner.esp/Global TV RADCD 107 |
| 21/11/1998 | 9 | 3 | ● | **A PERFECT LOVE II** | warner.esp/Global TV RADCD 105 |
| 28/11/1998 | 7 | 12 | | **HEARTBEAT – THE 60'S GOLD COLLECTION** | Global Television RADCD 90 |
| 05/12/1998 | 16 | 8 | ● | FUNKY DIVAS 2 | Global Television RADCD 106 |
| 16/01/1999 | 5 | 4 | | **STREET VIBES 2** | warner.esp/Global TV/Sony Music TV RADCD 116 |
| 13/02/1999 | 6 | 4 | | **THE GREATEST ROCK 'N' ROLL LOVE SONGS** | Global Television RADCD 115 |
| 06/03/1999 | 7 | 2 | ○ | **DISCO HOUSE** | Global Television RADCD 120 |
| 03/04/1999 | ❶¹ | 12 | ◐ | **NEW HITS 99.** | warner.esp/Global TV/Sony TV RADCD 121 |
| 10/04/1999 | 9 | 7 | ○ | **THE FEMALE TOUCH 2** | warner.esp/Global TV RADCD 117 |
| 01/05/1999 | 12 | 4 | | HEART FULL OF SOUL – 2 | warner.esp/Global TV RADCD 122 |
| 15/05/1999 | 15 | 3 | | THE VERY BEST OF LATIN JAZZ – 2 | Global Television RADCD 118 |
| 12/06/1999 | 5 | 5 | ● | **FAT DANCE HITS** | Global Television RADCD 125 |
| 12/06/1999 | 6 | 5 | ○ | **STREET VIBES 3** | warner.esp/Global TV/Sony Music TV RADCD 124 |
| 26/06/1999 | 20 | 2 | | MIDSUMMER CLASSICS | Global Television RADCD 127 |
| 03/07/1999 | ❶³ | 9 | | **FRESH HITS 99.** | warner.esp/Global Music TV/Sony Music TV RADCD 126 |

▲⁹ Number of weeks album topped the US chart  ◆¹² RIAA Diamond Awards  ◇³ IFPI Platinum Europe Awards

| DATE | POS | WKS | BPI | ALBUM TITLE | LABEL & NUMBER |
|---|---|---|---|---|---|
| 17/07/1999 | 14 | 2 | | UNDER LATIN SKIES | Global Television RADCD 130 |
| 24/07/1999 | 2 | 5 | | **IBIZA 99 – THE YEAR OF TRANCE** | Global Television RADCD 128 |
| 31/07/1999 | 12 | 4 | | SALSA FEVER! | Global Television RADCD 133 |
| 28/08/1999 | 11 | 2 | | IBIZA DEL MAR | Global Television RADCD 137 |
| 04/09/1999 | ❶² | 11 | | **BIG HITS 99** | warner.esp/Global TV/Sony TV RADCD 134 |
| 11/09/1999 | 13 | 3 | | SPEED GARAGE ANTHEMS 99 | Global Television RADCD 142 |
| 02/10/1999 | 6 | 5 | | **FAT POP HITS** | Global Television RADCD 135 |
| 09/10/1999 | 9 | 4 | | **ROCK THE WORLD** | Global Television RADCD 138 |
| 09/10/1999 | 11 | 2 | | IBIZA 99 – THE YEAR OF TRANCE – VOLUME TWO | Global Television RADCD 150 |
| 23/10/1999 | 14 | 2 | | AYIA NAPA – CLUBBERS PARADISE | Global Television RADCD 151 |
| 06/11/1999 | ❶⁴ | 13 | | **HUGE HITS 99** | warner.esp/Global TV/Sony TV RADCD 147 |
| 20/11/1999 | 19 | 1 | | FUNK SOUL BROTHER – THE BEST OF DANCE SOUL & SWING | Global Television RADCD 136 |
| 20/11/1999 | 20 | 1 | | THE BIGGEST CLUB ALBUM OF THE YEAR | Global Television RADCD 148 |
| 18/12/1999 | 9 | 8 | | **RADIO 2 – SONGS OF THE CENTURY** | Global TV RADCD 119 |
| 18/12/1999 | 2 | 12 | | **HITS 2000** | warner.esp/Global TV/Sony TV RADCD 154 |
| 15/01/2000 | 18 | 3 | | FUNKY DIVAS 3 | Global Television RADCD 141 |
| 15/01/2000 | 19 | 1 | ○ | DISCO FEVER | Global Television RADCD 131 |
| 18/03/2000 | 4 | 6 | | **STREET VIBES 4** | warner.esp/Global TV/Sony TV RADCD 146 |
| 29/04/2000 | 5 | 6 | | **A PERFECT LOVE III** | warner.esp/Universal TV/Global TV RADCD 149X |
| 13/05/2000 | 8 | 4 | | **SOUNDTRACK TO THE WEEKEND** | Global TV RADCD 162 |
| 03/06/2000 | 5 | 3 | | **CRUISIN' – THE BEST OF DRIVETIME** | Global TV RADCD 160 |
| 17/06/2000 | 18 | 1 | | ALL YOU NEED IS LOVE | Global Television RADCD 163 |
| 24/06/2000 | 2 | 8 | | **STREET VIBES 5** | Sony TV/Global TV RADCD 161 |
| 08/07/2000 | 10 | 5 | | **HEADRUSH** | Global Television RADCD 166 |
| 29/07/2000 | 16 | 2 | | TRASHED IN IBIZA | Global TV RADCD 169 |

## GLOBAL UNDERGROUND

| DATE | POS | WKS | BPI | ALBUM TITLE | LABEL & NUMBER |
|---|---|---|---|---|---|
| 25/04/1998 | 16 | 1 | | JOHN DIGWEED – SYDNEY | Global Underground GU 006CD |
| 06/06/1998 | 12 | 3 | | PAUL OAKENFOLD – NEW YORK | Global Underground GU 007CDX |
| 21/11/1998 | 18 | 1 | | SASHA – SAN FRANCISCO | Global Underground GU 009CD |
| 27/02/1999 | 16 | 1 | | DANNY TENEAGLIA LIVE IN ATHENS | Global Underground GU 010CDX |
| 19/06/1999 | 20 | 1 | | NICK WARREN – BUDAPEST | Global Underground GU 011CD |
| 02/10/1999 | 12 | 2 | | SASHA – IBIZA | Global Underground GU 013CDX |
| 22/04/2000 | 19 | 1 | | PROTOTYPE3 – SEB FONTAINE | Global Underground PRO 003CD |
| 27/05/2000 | 20 | 1 | | URUGUAY – DARREN EMERSON | Global Underground GUO 015CDX |
| 10/03/2001 | 14 | 1 | | JOHN DIGWEED – LOS ANGELES | Global Underground GUO 19CDX |
| 12/10/2002 | 18 | 1 | | JAMES LAVELLE – BARCELONA 023 | Global Underground GU 023CDX |

## GO! DISCS
UK label formed in 1983 by Andy MacDonald and subsequently bought by Polygram. MacDonald later set up Independiente.

| DATE | POS | WKS | BPI | ALBUM TITLE | LABEL & NUMBER |
|---|---|---|---|---|---|
| 16/09/1995 | ❶² | 7 | | **HELP – WAR CHILD** | Go! Discs 8286822 |

## GODSKITCHEN

| DATE | POS | WKS | BPI | ALBUM TITLE | LABEL & NUMBER |
|---|---|---|---|---|---|
| 25/01/2003 | 9 | 2 | | **GODSKITCHEN DIRECT** | Godskitchen GKCD 001 |
| 09/08/2003 | 18 | 1 | | GODSKITCHEN – WORLDWIDE | Godskitchen GKCD 002 |

## GOOD LOOKING

| DATE | POS | WKS | BPI | ALBUM TITLE | LABEL & NUMBER |
|---|---|---|---|---|---|
| 10/05/1997 | 12 | 2 | | BLAME PRESENT LOGICAL PROGRESSION LEVEL 2 | Good Looking GLRCD 002X |
| 11/10/1997 | 18 | 1 | | LTJ BUKEM PRESENTS EARTH – VOLUME TWO | Good Looking EARTHCD 002 |
| 16/05/1998 | 18 | 1 | | INTENSE PRESENTS LOGICAL PROGRESSION LEVEL 3 | Good Looking GLRCD 003 |

## GTO
UK label formed by former Bell Records managing director Dick Leahy, scoring success with UK signings Heatwave and licensing in Donna Summer's early hits. The label was later sold to CBS.

| DATE | POS | WKS | BPI | ALBUM TITLE | LABEL & NUMBER |
|---|---|---|---|---|---|
| 16/08/1975 | 30 | 5 | | NEVER TOO YOUNG TO ROCK | GTO GTLP 004 |

## GUERILLA

| DATE | POS | WKS | BPI | ALBUM TITLE | LABEL & NUMBER |
|---|---|---|---|---|---|
| 17/04/1993 | 18 | 1 | | DUB HOUSE DISCO 2000 | Guerilla GRCD 7 |

## GUT

| DATE | POS | WKS | BPI | ALBUM TITLE | LABEL & NUMBER |
|---|---|---|---|---|---|
| 26/06/2004 | 17 | 1+ | | COME ON ENGLAND | Gut GUTCD30 |

## HAPPY DAYS

| DATE | POS | WKS | BPI | ALBUM TITLE | LABEL & NUMBER |
|---|---|---|---|---|---|
| 13/05/1995 | 16 | 1 | | YOU MUST REMEMBER THIS | Happy Days CDHD 2656 |

## HARVEST
UK rock label formed in 1969 as an imprint of EMI by Malcolm Jones, with initial releases covering progressive and underground rock. It achieved its greatest success with mainstream rock, however, including Pink Floyd's 25 million-selling album *Dark Side Of The Moon*.

| DATE | POS | WKS | BPI | ALBUM TITLE | LABEL & NUMBER |
|---|---|---|---|---|---|
| 16/07/1977 | 24 | 5 | | THE ROXY LONDON WC2 (JAN–APR 77) | Harvest SHSP 4069 |
| 26/05/1979 | 13 | 12 | ● | A MONUMENT TO BRITISH ROCK | Harvest EMTV 17 |

○ Silver disc   ● Gold disc   ✪ Platinum disc (additional platinum units are indicated by a figure following the symbol)   ❶⁹ Number of weeks album topped the UK chart

## HEART & SOUL

| | | | | |
|---|---|---|---|---|
| 19/08/1989 ..... 2 ..... 12 ..... ● | HEART AND SOUL | Heart & Soul HASTV 1 |
| 17/02/1990 ..... 2 ..... 14 ..... ● | BODY AND SOUL – HEART AND SOUL II | Heart & Soul 8407761 |
| 04/08/1990 ..... 4 ..... 9 ..... ● | HEART AND SOUL III – HEART FULL OF SOUL | Heart & Soul 8450091 |
| 16/02/1991 ..... 2 ..... 12 ..... ● | SOUL REFLECTION | Heart & Soul 8453341 |

## HEAVEN MUSIC

| | | |
|---|---|---|
| 05/04/1997 ..... 12 ..... 4 ..... | HARDCORE HEAVEN – VOLUME ONE | Heaven Music HMLCD 101 |
| 09/07/1997 ..... 13 ..... 2 ..... | HARDCORE HEAVEN – VOLUME 2 | Heaven Music HMLCD 102 |
| 14/02/1998 ..... 12 ..... 2 ..... | HARDCORE HEAVEN – VOLUME 3 | Heaven Music HMLCD 103 |
| 08/08/1998 ..... 17 ..... 1 ..... | HARDCORE HEAVEN – VOLUME 4 | Heaven Music HMLCD 104 |
| 13/02/1999 ..... 17 ..... 4 ..... | HARDCORE HEAVEN – VOLUME 5 | Heaven Music HMLCD 105 |

## HEAVENLY UK label formed in 1990 by Jeff Barrett.

| | | |
|---|---|---|
| 25/05/1996 ..... 19 ..... 1 ..... | LIVE AT THE SOCIAL – VOLUME 1 | Heavenly HVNLP 13CD |

## HED KANDI

| | | |
|---|---|---|
| 27/09/2003 ..... 17 ..... 1 ..... | DISCO KANDI 05.03 | Hed KandFi HEDK 034 |
| 13/03/2004 ..... 18 ..... 1 ..... | DISCO HEAVEN 01.04 | Hed Kandi HEDK 037 |
| 01/05/2004 ..... 16 ..... 3 ..... | TWISTED DISCO 02.04 | Hed Kandi HEDK 038 |

## HI-LIFE/POLYDOR

| | | |
|---|---|---|
| 02/11/1996 ..... 17 ..... 1 ..... | THE SUMMER OF NINETY SIX – UP YER RONSON | Hi-Life/Polydor 5332422 |

## HIGHER GROUND

| | | |
|---|---|---|
| 12/04/1997 ..... 19 ..... 1 ..... | GROOVERIDER PRESENTS THE PROTOTYPE YEARS | Higher Ground 4872192 |

## THE HIT LABEL UK label formed by Chris Wright after he sold the Chrysalis label to EMI.

| | | |
|---|---|---|
| 27/06/1992 ..... 6 ..... 5 ..... ○ | Q THE BLUES | The Hit Label AHLCD 1 |
| 22/08/1992 ..... 9 ..... 5 ..... | SMASH HITS – PARTY ON! | The Hit Label CCD 34 |
| 17/10/1992 ..... 20 ..... 1 ..... | BEST OF CAPITAL GOLD – 24 CARAT CLASSIC HITS | The Hit Label AHLCD 2 |
| 28/11/1992 ..... 11 ..... 7 ..... ● | BIG! DANCE HITS OF 92 | The Hit Label AHLCD 4 |
| 05/12/1992 ..... 16 ..... 2 ..... ○ | REMEMBER WHEN SINGERS COULD SING | The Hit Label AHLCD 3 |
| 10/04/1993 ..... 14 ..... 4 ..... | Q RHYTHM AND BLUES | The Hit Label AHLCD 7 |
| 08/05/1993 ..... 3 ..... 8 ..... ● | THE LEGENDARY JOE BLOGGS ALBUM | The Hit Label AHLCD 10 |
| 31/07/1993 ..... 12 ..... 5 ..... | GET IT ON – GREATEST HITS OF THE 70'S | The Hit Label AHLCD 12 |
| 30/10/1993 ..... 15 ..... 2 ..... ○ | THE LEGENDARY JOE BLOGGS ALBUM 2 | The Hit Label AHLCD 13 |
| 13/11/1993 ..... 11 ..... 4 ..... ● | IT MUST BE LOVE | The Hit Label AHLCD 17 |
| 05/03/1994 ..... 9 ..... 4 ..... | THE BOYZ WHO SOULED THE WORLD | The Hit Label AHLCD 18 |
| 21/05/1994 ..... 20 ..... 1 ..... | Q COUNTRY | The Hit Label AHLCD 16 |
| 18/06/1994 ..... 12 ..... 5 ..... | KERRANG! THE ALBUM | The Hit Label AHLCD 21 |
| 27/08/1994 ..... 12 ..... 4 ..... | THE ULTIMATE GOLD COLLECTION | The Hit Label AHLCD 22 |
| 04/02/1995 ..... 13 ..... 4 ..... ● | ULTIMATE LOVE | The Hit Label AHLCD 24 |
| 18/02/1995 ..... 17 ..... 2 ..... ● | FEEL LIKE MAKING LOVE | The Hit Label AHLCD 25 |
| 08/07/1995 ..... 12 ..... 1 ..... | REGGAE GROOVE | The Hit Label ULTCD 020 |

## HMV UK label formed in 1899 by William Barry Owen, taking its name 'His Master's Voice' from the famous painting by Francis Barraud of a dog looking into a gramophone. In 1931 the company merged with Columbia to form EMI and later became the first UK label to issue 45rpm 7-inch discs, although after 1968 the label effectively disappeared apart from classical recordings. The label was revived for singer Morrissey's post-Smiths solo career.

| | | |
|---|---|---|
| 10/03/1962 ..... 19 ..... 1 ..... | GREAT MOTION PICTURE THEMES | HMV CLP 1508 |

## IGNITION

| | | |
|---|---|---|
| 13/11/1999 ..... 12 ..... 1 ..... | FIRE & SKILL – THE SONGS OF THE JAM | Ignition IGNCD 3 |

## IMMEDIATE UK label formed in 1965 by Rolling Stones' manager Andrew Loog Oldham and Tony Calder with a roster that included The Small Faces, The Nice and Chris Farlowe. The label filed for bankruptcy by the end of the decade.

| | | |
|---|---|---|
| 11/05/1968 ..... 40 ..... 1 ..... | BLUES ANYTIME | Immediate IMLP 014 |

---

**IMP CLASSICS** UK classical label formed by Pickwick Records, the name standing for Innovative Music Productions. The label was relaunched in 2004.

| | | | | | | |
|---|---|---|---|---|---|---|
| 11/04/1992 | 12 | 3 | | | DISCOVER THE CLASSICS VOLUME 2 | IMP Classics/Pickwick CDBOXD 22 |
| 11/04/1992 | 15 | 3 | | | DISCOVER THE CLASSICS VOLUME 1 | IMP Classics/Pickwick CDBOXD 21 |

## IMPRESSION

| | | | | | | |
|---|---|---|---|---|---|---|
| 16/10/1982 | 28 | 21 | ● | | BEST FRIENDS | Impression LP IMP 1 |
| 03/09/1983 | 13 | 8 | ○ | | SUNNY AFTERNOON | Impression LP IMP 2 |
| 26/11/1983 | 77 | 5 | | | PRECIOUS MOMENTS | Impression LP IMP 3 |
| 07/04/1984 | 24 | 12 | ○ | | ALWAYS AND FOREVER – THE COLLECTION | Impression LP IMP 4 |
| 21/07/1984 | 37 | 3 | | | WIPEOUT – 20 INSTRUMENTAL GREATS | Impression LP IMP 5 |
| 28/07/1984 | 90 | 1 | | | SUNNY AFTERNOON VOLUME TWO | Impression LP IMP 7 |
| 22/12/1984 | 91 | 1 | | | FRIENDS AGAIN | Impression LP IMP 8 |

## INCREDIBLE

| | | | | | |
|---|---|---|---|---|---|
| 31/10/1998 | 7 | 2 | | **GATECRASHER** | INCredible INC 2CDX |
| 06/03/1999 | 6 | 2 | | **NORTHERN EXPOSURE – SASHA + JOHN DIGWEED** | INCredible INC 4CD |
| 20/03/1999 | 14 | 3 | | INCREDIBLE SOUND OF TREVOR NELSON | INCredible INC 3CD |
| 10/04/1999 | 4 | 8 | | **GATECRASHER RED** | INCredible INC 5CD |
| 08/05/1999 | 16 | 2 | | GOLDIE – INCREDIBLE SOUND OF DRUM 'N' BASS | INCredible INC 6CD |
| 07/08/1999 | 3 | 6 | | **GATECRASHER WET** | INCredible INC 8CD |
| 20/11/1999 | 6 | 3 | | **GATECRASHER DISCO-TECH** | INCredible INC 11CD |
| 29/04/2000 | 9 | 4 | | **TREVOR NELSON'S RHYTHM NATION** | INCredible INC 15CD |
| 08/07/2000 | 13 | 2 | | COMMUNICATE – SASHA & DIGWEED | INCredible INC 14CDX |
| 12/08/2000 | 3 | 4 | | **GATECRASHER – GLOBAL SOUND SYSTEM** | INCredible INC 12CD |
| 19/08/2000 | 14 | 2 | | INCREDIBLE SOUND OF THE DREEM TEEM | INCredible INC 18CD |
| 09/12/2000 | 13 | 2 | | GATECRASHER – NATIONAL ANTHEMS | INCredible INC 22CDX |
| 07/04/2001 | 10 | 2 | ○ | **GATECRASHER DISCOTECH GENERATION** | INCredible 5020749 |
| 15/09/2001 | 11 | 4 | | GARAGE NATION | INCredible 5040712 |
| 29/09/2001 | 17 | 1 | | GODS KITCHEN – THE TRUE SOUND OF A CLUBBING SUMMER | INCredible 5044892 |
| 26/01/2002 | 5 | 3 | | **GODSKITCHEN JOURNEYS** | INCredible 5053252 |
| 30/03/2002 | 13 | 2 | | GODSKITCHEN – LIFE | INCredible 5076212 |
| 11/05/2002 | 9 | 2 | | **GARAGE NATION 02** | INCredible 5053242 |
| 24/08/2002 | 15 | 1 | | GODSKITCHEN – SUMMER TRANCE | INCredible 5089442 |

## INSPIRED

| | | | | | |
|---|---|---|---|---|---|
| 12/02/2000 | 8 | 4 | | **LOVED UP** | Inspired INSPCD 1 |
| 27/05/2000 | 7 | 3 | | **ULTIMATE AYIA NAPA** | Inspired INSPCD 2 |
| 07/10/2000 | 14 | 3 | | ULTIMATE IBIZA | Inspired INSPCD 3 |
| 03/02/2001 | 13 | 2 | | FEELS SO GOOD | Inspired INSPCD 5 |
| 09/06/2001 | 12 | 3 | | DANCESTAR 2001 | Inspired INSPCD 9 |
| 21/07/2001 | 18 | 1 | | DREAMSTATES | Inspired INSPCD 8 |
| 25/08/2001 | 3 | 9 | | **LOVIN' IT** | INCredible/Inspired INSPCD 12 |
| 22/09/2001 | 5 | 3 | | **BIG CLUB HITS** | Inspired INSPCD 13 |
| 03/11/2001 | 16 | 2 | | RAVE NATION | Inspired INSPCD 16 |
| 22/12/2001 | 11 | 7 | | LOVIN' IT 2 | INCredible/Inspired INSPCD 15 |
| 02/03/2002 | 5 | 3 | | **CLUB HITS 2002** | INCredible/Inspired INSPCD 17 |
| 05/10/2002 | 17 | 3 | | TUNE IN–CHILL OUT | Inspired INSPCD 23 |
| 26/10/2002 | 7 | 3 | | **ORIGINAL HARDCORE** | Inspired INSPCD 24 |
| 08/02/2003 | 12 | 2 | | CLUB HITS 2003 | Inspired/Sony TV INSPCD 25 |
| 08/03/2003 | 19 | 1 | | ORIGINAL HARDCORE – THE BATTLE | Inspired INSPCD 26 |
| 07/02/2004 | 19 | 1 | | ORIGINAL HARDCORE – THE NU BREED | Inspired INSPCD 34 |
| 28/02/2004 | 3 | 3 | | **ANTHEMS OF TRANCE** | Inspired/UMTV INSPCD35 |
| 06/03/2004 | 3 | 3 | | **DAVE PEARCE DANCE ANTHEMS SPRING 2004** | Inspired/BMG TV INSPCD033 |
| 13/03/2004 | 9 | 1 | | **JAZZ CAFE – THE SOUL MIX** | Inspired/UCJ INSPCD37 |
| 10/04/2004 | 8 | 3 | | **ANTHEMS OF HOUSE** | Inspired/UMTV INSPCD 36 |
| 08/05/2004 | 7 | 5 | | **ANTHEMS OF OLD SKOOL** | Inspired INSPCD 38 |

## ISLAND UK label formed by Chris Blackwell in 1961, although initial UK releases were issued on a variety of labels before Blackwell formed his own label imprint. The label was sold to A&M in 1989 and later absorbed into the Universal group.

| DATE | POS | WKS | BPI | ALBUM TITLE | LABEL & NUMBER |
|------|-----|-----|-----|-------------|----------------|
| 26/08/1967 | 37 | 19 | | CLUB SKA '67 | Island ILP 956 |
| 14/06/1969 | 18 | 10 | | YOU CAN ALL JOIN IN | Island IWPS 2 |
| 05/01/1980 | 33 | 6 | | THE SECRET POLICEMAN'S BALL | Island ILPS 9601 |
| 29/03/1980 | 53 | 6 | | CLUB SKA '67 | Island IRSP 4 |
| 16/06/1984 | 71 | 4 | | CREW CUTS | Island IMA 11 |
| 27/10/1984 | 95 | 2 | | CREW CUTS – LESSON 2 | Island IMA 14 |
| 18/07/1987 | 9 | 10 | ● | **THE ISLAND STORY** | Island ISL 25 |
| 03/11/1990 | 7 | 4 | ○ | **HAPPY DAZE... VOLUME 1** | Island ILPTV 1 |
| 06/04/1991 | 17 | 2 | | HAPPY DAZE VOLUME 2 | Island ILPTV 3 |
| 30/10/1993 | 5 | 6 | ● | **REGGAE 93** | Island CIDTV 7 |
| 27/08/1994 | 10 | 5 | ○ | **PURE REGGAE – VOLUME 1** | Island CIDTV 8 |

## JACK TRAX UK house dance label formed in 1987 by Damon D'Cruz. The label closed in 1992.

| DATE | POS | WKS | ALBUM TITLE | LABEL & NUMBER |
|------|-----|-----|-------------|----------------|
| 18/07/1987 | 83 | 2 | JACK TRAX – THE FIRST ALBUM | Jack Trax JTRAX 1 |
| 03/10/1987 | 61 | 2 | JACK TRAX – THE SECOND ALBUM | Jack Trax JTRAX 2 |
| 05/03/1988 | 49 | 4 | JACK TRAX – THE THIRD ALBUM | Jack Trax JTRAX 4 |

## JDJ

| DATE | POS | WKS | ALBUM TITLE | LABEL & NUMBER |
|------|-----|-----|-------------|----------------|
| 30/03/1996 | 11 | 2 | DANCE WARS – JUDGE JULES VS. JOHN KELLY | JDJ JDJCD 10 |

## JETSTAR UK reggae label originally formed in London in 1967 as Pama Records. It became Jet Star Phonographics in 1978.

| DATE | POS | WKS | ALBUM TITLE | LABEL & NUMBER |
|------|-----|-----|-------------|----------------|
| 30/03/1985 | 32 | 11 | REGGAE HITS VOLUME 1 | Jetstar JETLP 1001 |
| 26/10/1985 | 86 | 2 | REGGAE HITS VOLUME 2 | Jetstar JETLP 1002 |
| 04/06/1988 | 56 | 7 | REGGAE HITS VOLUME 4 | Jetstar JETLP 1004 |
| 17/12/1988 | 96 | 1 | REGGAE HITS VOLUME 5 | Jetstar JETLP 1005 |
| 05/08/1989 | 13 | 6 | REGGAE HITS VOLUME 6 | Jetstar JETLP 1006 |
| 23/12/1989 | 13 | 6 | REGGAE HITS VOLUME 7 | Jetstar JETLP 1007 |
| 30/06/1990 | 7 | 5 | **REGGAE HITS VOLUME 8** | Jetstar JETLP 1008 |
| 20/07/1991 | 6 | 7 | **REGGAE HITS VOLUME 10** | Jetstar JETLP 1010 |
| 18/04/1992 | 5 | 6 | **REGGAE HITS VOLUME 12** | Jetstar JECD 1012 |
| 28/08/1993 | 13 | 1 | REGGAE HITS VOLUME 14 | Jetstar JECD 1014 |
| 03/09/1994 | 9 | 8 | **JUNGLE HITS VOLUME 1** | Jetstar STRCD 1 |

## JIVE UK label formed in 1981 by South African Clive Calder as part of the Zomba Group. Jive opened a US office three years later and over the next decade or so enjoyed considerable success with US rap and gospel material. In the 1990s it became a force in pop circles thanks to artists such as Britney Spears and the Backstreet Boys. Zomba was sold to BMG in 2002 for $2.7 billion.

| DATE | POS | WKS | ALBUM TITLE | LABEL & NUMBER |
|------|-----|-----|-------------|----------------|
| 26/03/1988 | 70 | 2 | THE WORD VOLUME 2 | Jive HOP 220 |

## JUMPIN' & PUMPIN' UK dance label formed in 1989 as an imprint of Passion Music.

| DATE | POS | WKS | ALBUM TITLE | LABEL & NUMBER |
|------|-----|-----|-------------|----------------|
| 18/01/1992 | 20 | 1 | NOISE | Jumpin' & Pumpin' CDTOT 3 |
| 16/05/1992 | 11 | 3 | NOISE 2 | Jumpin' & Pumpin' CDTOT 4 |

## JUNIOR BOY'S OWN

| DATE | POS | WKS | ALBUM TITLE | LABEL & NUMBER |
|------|-----|-----|-------------|----------------|
| 13/08/1994 | 20 | 1 | JUNIOR BOY'S OWN COLLECTION | Junior Boy's Own JBOCD 2 |

## KASINO

| DATE | POS | WKS | ALBUM TITLE | LABEL & NUMBER |
|------|-----|-----|-------------|----------------|
| 16/02/1985 | 69 | 3 | STARGAZERS | Kasino KTV 1 |

## KNIGHT UK label formed as an imprint of Castle Communications.

| DATE | POS | WKS | ALBUM TITLE | LABEL & NUMBER |
|------|-----|-----|-------------|----------------|
| 18/05/1991 | 13 | 2 | SOUTHERN KNIGHTS | Knight KTVLP 1 |

## KOCH Austrian label formed in 1975 by Franz Koch, his son Michael launching the label in the USA in 1987 as Koch Entertainment.

| DATE | POS | WKS | BPI | ALBUM TITLE | LABEL & NUMBER |
|------|-----|-----|-----|-------------|----------------|
| 22/04/2000 | 20 | 1 | ○ | POKEMON – 2 B A MASTER | Koch 333622 |

▲⁹ Number of weeks album topped the US chart   ◆¹² RIAA Diamond Awards   ◇³ IFPI Platinum Europe Awards

**K-TEL** US label formed in Minneapolis as a pioneer of TV-advertised compilations, opening a UK company in 1972. The label effectively closed in the UK in 1990 although the company remains exploiting its back catalogue and licensing catalogue.

| DATE | POS | WKS | BPI | ALBUM TITLE | LABEL & NUMBER |
|------|-----|-----|-----|-------------|----------------|
| 10/06/1972 | ❶[8] | 28 | | **20 DYNAMIC HITS** | K-Tel TE 292 |
| 07/10/1972 | ❶[11] | 22 | | **20 ALL TIME GREATS OF THE 50'S** | K-Tel NE 490 |
| 25/11/1972 | 2 | 12 | | **25 DYNAMIC HITS VOLUME 2** | K-Tel TE 291 |
| 02/12/1972 | ❶[3] | 18 | | **25 ROCKIN' AND ROLLIN' GREATS** | K-Tel NE 493 |
| 31/03/1973 | ❶[2] | 11 | | **20 FLASHBACK GREATS OF THE SIXTIES** | K-Tel NE 494 |
| 21/04/1973 | 2 | 8 | | **BELIEVE IN MUSIC** | K-Tel TE 294 |
| 08/11/1975 | 19 | 7 | | GOOFY GREATS | K-Tel NE 707 |
| 13/12/1975 | 9 | 8 | ● | **40 SUPER GREATS** | K-Tel NE 708 |
| 31/01/1976 | 3 | 10 | | **MUSIC EXPRESS** | K-Tel TE 702 |
| 10/04/1976 | 3 | 13 | | **JUKE BOX JIVE** | K-Tel NE 709 |
| 17/04/1976 | 17 | 14 | | GREAT ITALIAN LOVE SONGS | K-Tel NE 303 |
| 15/05/1976 | 4 | 10 | | **HIT MACHINE** | K-Tel TE 713 |
| 05/06/1976 | 44 | 1 | | EUROVISION FAVOURITES | K-Tel NE 712 |
| 02/10/1976 | 30 | 1 | | SUMMER CRUISING | K-Tel NE 918 |
| 16/10/1976 | ❶[2] | 14 | | **SOUL MOTION** | K-Tel NE 930 |
| 16/10/1976 | 8 | 12 | | **COUNTRY COMFORT** | K-Tel NE 294 |
| 04/12/1976 | 3 | 14 | | **DISCO ROCKET** | K-Tel NE 948 |
| 11/12/1976 | 14 | 10 | | 44 SUPERSTARS | K-Tel NE 939 |
| 12/02/1977 | 2 | 18 | | **HEARTBREAKERS** | K-Tel NE 954 |
| 19/02/1977 | 5 | 9 | | **DANCE TO THE MUSIC** | K-Tel NE 957 |
| 07/05/1977 | 15 | 9 | | HIT ACTION | K-Tel NE 993 |
| 29/10/1977 | 12 | 7 | | SOUL CITY | K-Tel NE 1003 |
| 12/11/1977 | 3 | 24 | ✪ | **FEELINGS** | K-Tel NE 1006 |
| 26/11/1977 | ❶[6] | 20 | ✪ | **DISCO FEVER** | K-Tel NE 1014 |
| 21/01/1978 | 15 | 7 | | 40 NUMBER ONE HITS | K-Tel NE 1008 |
| 04/03/1978 | 6 | 8 | | **DISCO STARS** | K-Tel NE 1022 |
| 10/06/1978 | 10 | 6 | | **DISCO DOUBLE** | K-Tel NE 1024 |
| 08/07/1978 | 12 | 11 | | ROCK RULES | K-Tel RL 001 |
| 08/07/1978 | 47 | 2 | | THE WORLD'S WORST RECORD SHOW | Yuk/K-Tel NE 1023 |
| 19/08/1978 | 4 | 9 | ● | **STAR PARTY** | K-Tel NE 1034 |
| 04/11/1978 | 2 | 17 | ● | **EMOTIONS** | K-Tel NE 1035 |
| 25/11/1978 | 2 | 13 | ● | **MIDNIGHT HUSTLE** | K-Tel NE 1037 |
| 20/01/1979 | ❶[1] | 14 | | **ACTION REPLAY** | K-Tel NE 1040 |
| 07/04/1979 | 11 | 9 | | DISCO INFERNO | K-Tel NE 1043 |
| 05/05/1979 | 17 | 7 | | HI ENERGY | K-Tel NE 1044 |
| 22/09/1979 | 31 | 8 | | HOT TRACKS | K-Tel NE 1049 |
| 24/11/1979 | 10 | 10 | ● | **NIGHT MOVES** | K-Tel NE 1065 |
| 24/11/1979 | 35 | 8 | ● | TOGETHER | K-Tel NE 1053 |
| 12/01/1980 | 5 | 10 | ● | **VIDEO STARS** | K-Tel NE 1066 |
| 26/01/1980 | 17 | 5 | ○ | THE SUMMIT | K-Tel NE 1067 |
| 29/03/1980 | 6 | 8 | ● | **STAR TRACKS** | K-Tel NE 1070 |
| 26/04/1980 | 15 | 12 | ○ | GOOD MORNING AMERICA | K-Tel NE 1072 |
| 17/05/1980 | 9 | 17 | ● | **MAGIC REGGAE** | K-Tel NE 1074 |
| 17/05/1980 | 32 | 6 | ○ | HAPPY DAYS | K-Tel NE 1076 |
| 14/06/1980 | 3 | 10 | ● | **HOT WAX** | K-Tel NE 1082 |
| 27/09/1980 | 2 | 8 | ● | **MOUNTING EXCITEMENT** | K-Tel NE 1091 |
| 11/10/1980 | 6 | 16 | ✪ | **THE LOVE ALBUM** | K-Tel NE 1062 |
| 25/10/1980 | 15 | 14 | ● | AXE ATTACK | K-Tel NE 1100 |
| 15/11/1980 | 6 | 17 | ✪ | **CHART EXPLOSION** | K-Tel NE 1103 |
| 27/12/1980 | 25 | 10 | ● | NIGHTLIFE | K-Tel NE 1107 |
| 14/02/1981 | 17 | 6 | | HIT MACHINE | K-Tel NE 1113 |
| 21/03/1981 | 42 | 4 | | RHYTHM 'N' REGGAE | K-Tel NE 1115 |
| 25/04/1981 | 3 | 9 | ● | **CHARTBUSTERS 81** | K-Tel NE 1118 |
| 02/05/1981 | 31 | 6 | | AXE ATTACK 2 | K-Tel NE 1120 |
| 23/05/1981 | 6 | 15 | ● | **THEMES** | K-Tel NE 1122 |
| 29/08/1981 | 27 | 11 | ○ | CALIFORNIA DREAMING | K-Tel NE 1126 |
| 19/09/1981 | 29 | 5 | ○ | DANCE DANCE DANCE | K-Tel NE 1143 |
| 03/10/1981 | 32 | 11 | ● | THE PLATINUM ALBUM | K-Tel NE 1134 |

| DATE | POS | WKS | BPI | ALBUM TITLE | LABEL & NUMBER |
|---|---|---|---|---|---|
| 10/10/1981 | 10 | 15 | ● | LOVE IS... | K-Tel NE 1129 |
| 21/11/1981 | ❶¹ | 17 | ✪ | CHART HITS '81 | K-Tel NE 1142 |
| 09/01/1982 | 6 | 10 | | MODERN DANCE | K-Tel NE 1156 |
| 06/02/1982 | 2 | 12 | ● | DREAMING | K-Tel NE 1159 |
| 06/03/1982 | 2 | 12 | ✪ | ACTION TRAX | K-Tel NE 1162 |
| 01/05/1982 | 98 | 1 | | MIDNIGHT HOUR | K-Tel NE 1157 |
| 03/07/1982 | 17 | 7 | ○ | TURBO TRAX | K-Tel NE 1176 |
| 04/09/1982 | 83 | 1 | | THE NO. 1 SOUNDS OF THE SEVENTIES | K-Tel NE 1172 |
| 11/09/1982 | 2 | 14 | ● | CHARTBEAT/CHARTHEAT | K-Tel NE 1180 |
| 30/10/1982 | 28 | 8 | | THE LOVE SONGS ALBUM | K-Tel NE 1179 |
| 06/11/1982 | 11 | 17 | ✪ | CHART HITS '82 | K-Tel NE 1195 |
| 06/11/1982 | 26 | 8 | | DISCO DANCER | K-Tel NE 1190 |
| 18/12/1982 | 42 | 6 | ● | STREETSCENE | K-Tel NE 1183 |
| 15/01/1983 | 5 | 21 | ● | VISIONS | K-Tel ONE 1199 |
| 12/02/1983 | 46 | 12 | | HEAVY | K-Tel NE 1023 |
| 05/03/1983 | 3 | 9 | ○ | HOTLINE | K-Tel NE 1027 |
| 11/06/1983 | 7 | 9 | ○ | CHART STARS | K-Tel NE 1225 |
| 20/08/1983 | 79 | 3 | | COOL HEAT | K-Tel NE 1231 |
| 10/09/1983 | 5 | 6 | | HEADLINE HITS | K-Tel NE 1253 |
| 08/10/1983 | 3 | 16 | ● | THE TWO OF US | K-Tel NE 1222 |
| 08/10/1983 | 33 | 6 | | IMAGES | K-Tel NE 1254 |
| 12/11/1983 | 6 | 11 | ● | CHART HITS '83 VOLUME 1 AND 2 | K-Tel NE 1256 |
| 24/03/1984 | 15 | 11 | ● | NIGHT MOVES | K-Tel NE 1255 |
| 26/05/1984 | 4 | 11 | ● | HUNGRY FOR HITS | K-Tel NE 1272 |
| 23/06/1984 | 43 | 3 | | THE THEMES ALBUM | K-Tel NE 1257 |
| 28/07/1984 | 18 | 12 | ○ | BREAKDANCE, YOU CAN DO IT! | K-Tel ONE 1276 |
| 22/09/1984 | 7 | 16 | ● | ALL BY MYSELF | K-Tel NE 1273 |
| 01/12/1984 | 25 | 15 | ● | HOOKED ON NUMBER ONES – 100 NON-STOP HITS | K-Tel ONE 1285 |
| 02/02/1985 | 52 | 6 | | FOUR STAR COUNTRY | K-Tel NE 1278 |
| 02/03/1985 | 13 | 7 | ● | MODERN LOVE – 24 LOVE SONGS FOR TODAY | K-Tel NE 1286 |
| 05/10/1985 | 11 | 8 | ● | EXPRESSIONS – 24 BEAUTIFUL BALLADS | K-Tel NE 1307 |
| 09/11/1985 | 10 | 11 | ● | ROCK ANTHEMS | K-Tel NE 1309 |
| 09/11/1985 | 34 | 12 | | OVATION – THE BEST OF ANDREW LLOYD WEBBER | K-Tel ONE 1311 |
| 22/03/1986 | 38 | 4 | | MASTERS OF METAL | K-Tel NE 1295 |
| 12/04/1986 | 8 | 15 | ● | HEART TO HEART – 24 LOVE SONG DUETS | K-Tel NE 1318 |
| 19/04/1986 | 43 | 9 | ○ | ROCK ANTHEMS – VOLUME 2 | K-Tel NE 1319 |
| 05/07/1986 | 50 | 4 | | RAP IT UP – RAP'S GREATEST HITS | K-Tel NE 1324 |
| 19/07/1986 | 20 | 8 | ○ | DRIVE TIME USA – 22 SUMMER CRUISING GREATS | K-Tel NE 1321 |
| 18/10/1986 | 35 | 7 | ○ | DANCE HITS '86 | K-Tel NE 1344 |
| 01/11/1986 | 20 | 10 | | TOGETHER | K-Tel NE 1345 |
| 07/02/1987 | 15 | 14 | ○ | IMPRESSIONS – 15 INSTRUMENTAL IMAGES | K-Tel NE 1346 |
| 21/03/1987 | 36 | 7 | ○ | RHYTHM OF THE NIGHT | K-Tel NE 1348 |
| 21/03/1987 | 63 | 1 | | HITS REVIVAL | K-Tel Holland KTLP 2351 |
| 13/06/1987 | 10 | 10 | ● | FRIENDS AND LOVERS | K-Tel NE 1352 |
| 27/06/1987 | 10 | 9 | ● | HITS REVIVAL | K-Tel NE 1363 |
| 17/10/1987 | 38 | 5 | ○ | TRUE LOVE | K-Tel NE 1359 |
| 31/10/1987 | 9 | 21 | ✪ | FROM MOTOWN WITH LOVE | K-Tel NE 1381 |
| 14/11/1987 | 65 | 4 | ○ | ALWAYS | K-Tel NE 1377 |
| 19/12/1987 | 97 | 2 | | WOW WHAT A PARTY | K-Tel NE 1388 |
| 05/03/1988 | 13 | 10 | ● | HORIZONS | K-Tel NE 1360 |
| 30/04/1988 | 45 | 3 | | HITS REVIVAL 2: REPLAY | K-Tel NE 1405 |
| 14/05/1988 | 26 | 9 | | TSOP – THE SOUND OF PHILADELPHIA | K-Tel NE 1406 |
| 11/06/1988 | 12 | 12 | ● | THE HITS OF HOUSE ARE HERE | K-Tel NE 1419 |
| 15/10/1988 | 28 | 13 | ● | MOTOWN IN MOTION | K-Tel NE 1410 |
| 15/10/1988 | 83 | 4 | ○ | THE RETURN OF SUPERBAD | K-Tel NE 1421 |
| 05/11/1988 | 50 | 5 | | THE LOVERS | K-Tel NE 1426 |
| 26/11/1988 | 43 | 7 | ● | RAPPIN' UP THE HOUSE | K-Tel NE 1428 |
| 14/01/1989 | 19 | 1 | | RAPPIN' UP THE HOUSE | K-Tel NE 1428 |
| 04/02/1989 | 6 | 7 | | FROM MOTOWN WITH LOVE | K-Tel NE 1381 |
| 25/03/1989 | 10 | 5 | | HIP HOUSE – THE DEEPEST BEATS IN TOWN | K-Tel NE 1430 |
| 29/07/1989 | 5 | 8 | | GLAM SLAM | K-Tel NE 1434 |
| 23/09/1989 | 5 | 7 | | LOVE HOUSE | K-Tel NE 1446 |
| 30/09/1989 | 5 | 7 | | ETERNAL LOVE | K-Tel NE 1447 |
| 21/10/1989 | 6 | 7 | | RAP ATTACK | K-Tel NE 1450 |
| 25/11/1989 | 15 | 4 | | SEDUCTION | K-Tel NE 1451 |
| 10/03/1990 | 12 | 3 | | CAN U FEEL IT? – THE CHAMPION LEGEND | K-Tel ONE 1452 |
| 21/04/1990 | 6 | 12 | | HOOKED ON COUNTRY | K-Tel NE 1459 |

## LEGENDS IN
22/12/1990 . . . . . 16 . . . . . . 1 . . . . . .  CHRISTMAS GREATEST HITS . . . . . . . . . . . . . . . . . . . . . . . . . . . . . . . . . . . . . . . . . . . . . . . . . . . . Legends In LELP 501

## LIBERTY US label formed in 1955 by Al Bennett, Sy Waronker and Ted Keep with success coming from the likes of Bobby Vee, Eddie Cochran and Johnny Burnette. It bought the Imperial label in 1962 but was itself bought by United Artists in 1969.
27/03/1982 . . . . . 4 . . . . . . 13 . . . . . ●  **JAMES BOND'S GREATEST HITS** . . . . . . . . . . . . . . . . . . . . . . . . . . . . . . . . . . . . . . . . . . . . . . . . . Liberty EMTV 007

## LIFE AID ARMENIA UK charity label formed by John Dee to raise funds for Armenia after an earthquake in December 1988 left more than 50,000 dead.
21/04/1990 . . . . . 3 . . . . . . 10 . . . . . ●  **THE EARTHQUAKE ALBUM... ROCK AID ARMENIA** . . . . . . . . . . . . . . . . . . . . . . . . . . . . . . . . . . . . Life Aid Armenia AIDLP 001

## LIMBO UK trance music label formed in Glasgow in 1992.
18/05/1996 . . . . . 17 . . . . . . 1 . . . . . .  THE TUNNEL MIXES . . . . . . . . . . . . . . . . . . . . . . . . . . . . . . . . . . . . . . . . . . . . . . . . . . . . . . . . . Limbo LIMB 56CD

## LONDON UK label formed in 1947 in the USA by Decca Records as an outlet for its domestic releases. The label was introduced into the UK in 1949 and the company enjoyed almost two decades of success before beginning to fade. Sold, along with Decca, to Polygram in 1980 following the death of Decca founder Sir Edward Lewis the previous year, the London label was effectively revived in 1982. The name was sold to Warner Brothers in 2000.
10/06/1989 . . . . . 8 . . . . . . 5 . . . . . .  **FFRR – SILVER ON BLACK** . . . . . . . . . . . . . . . . . . . . . . . . . . . . . . . . . . . . . . . . . . . . . . . . . London 8281551
11/11/1989 . . . . . 8 . . . . . . 7 . . . . . ●  **DANCE DECADE – DANCE HITS OF THE 80'S** . . . . . . . . . . . . . . . . . . . . . . . . . . . . . . . . . . . . . . . . London DDTV 1
16/06/1990 . . . . . 4 . . . . . . 8 . . . . . ○  **THE NORTHERN BEAT** . . . . . . . . . . . . . . . . . . . . . . . . . . . . . . . . . . . . . . . . . . . . . . . . London 8409681
07/07/1990 . . . . . 20 . . . . . . 2 . . . . . .  MASSIVE 4 . . . . . . . . . . . . . . . . . . . . . . . . . . . . . . . . . . . . . . . . . . . . . . . . . . . . . . . . . London 8282101
08/02/1992 . . . . . 10 . . . . . . 1 . . . . . .  **ONLY FOR THE HEADSTRONG** . . . . . . . . . . . . . . . . . . . . . . . . . . . . . . . . . . . . . . . . . . . . London 8283032
20/06/1992 . . . . . 18 . . . . . . 1 . . . . . .  ONLY FOR THE HEADSTRONG II . . . . . . . . . . . . . . . . . . . . . . . . . . . . . . . . . . . . . . . . . . London 8283162
15/07/2000 . . . . . 18 . . . . . . 1 . . . . . .  G-A-Y . . . . . . . . . . . . . . . . . . . . . . . . . . . . . . . . . . . . . . . . . . . . . . . . . . . . . . . London 9548387682
26/08/2000 . . . . . 6 . . . . . . 4 . . . . . ○  **ARTFUL DODGER PRESENTS REWIND** . . . . . . . . . . . . . . . . . . . . . . . . . . . . . . . . . . . . . . London 8573844602
03/05/2003 . . . . . 6 . . . . . . 2 . . . . . ○  HOPE . . . . . . . . . . . . . . . . . . . . . . . . . . . . . . . . . . . . . . . . . . . . . . . . . . . . . . London 5046658462

## LOOSE END UK label established as an imprint of Arista Records.
11/08/1984 . . . . . 46 . . . . . . 5 . . . . . .  CHUNKS OF FUNK. . . . . . . . . . . . . . . . . . . . . . . . . . . . . . . . . . . . . . . . . . . . . . . . . . . Loose End CHUNK 1

## LOTUS
28/10/1978 . . . . . 24 . . . . . . 6 . . . . . .  ECSTASY. . . . . . . . . . . . . . . . . . . . . . . . . . . . . . . . . . . . . . . . . . . . . . . . . . . . . . . . . . . Lotus WH 5003

## MANGO UK label formed as an imprint of Island Records.
03/07/1993 . . . . . 3 . . . . . . 9 . . . . . ●  **ON A REGGAE TIP** . . . . . . . . . . . . . . . . . . . . . . . . . . . . . . . . . . . . . . . . . . . . . . . . . . . . Mango CIDTV 5

## MANIFESTO UK dance label formed as an imprint of Universal Records; it was closed down in 2002.

Café Del Mar Volumen Seis
Compiled by José Padilla

23/08/1997 . . . . . 18 . . . . . . 1 . . . . . .  CAFE DEL MAR IBIZA – VOLUMEN CUATRO . . . . . . . . . . . . . . . . . . . . . . . . . . . . . . . . . . . Manifesto 5539072
25/07/1998 . . . . . 16 . . . . . . 2 . . . . . .  CAFE DEL MAR IBIZA – VOLUMEN CINCO . . . . . . . . . . . . . . . . . . . . . . . . . . . . . . . . . . . Manifesto 5652282
21/08/1999 . . . . . 15 . . . . . . 2 . . . . . .  CAFE DEL MAR IBIZA – VOLUMEN SEIS. . . . . . . . . . . . . . . . . . . . . . . . . . . . . . . . . . . . . Manifesto 5648612
08/07/2000 . . . . . 14 . . . . . . 3 . . . . . .  CAFE DEL MAR – VOLUMEN SIETE. . . . . . . . . . . . . . . . . . . . . . . . . . . . . . . . . . . . . . . . Manifesto 5249122
30/06/2001 . . . . . 12 . . . . . . 3 . . . . . ○  I DEL MAR VOLUMEN OCHO . . . . . . . . . . . . . . . . . . . . . . . . . . . . . . . . . . . . . . . . . . . . Manifesto 5860592

## MARBLE ARCH UK label formed as a budget imprint of Pye Records.
10/02/1968 . . . . . 23 . . . . . . 3 . . . . . .  STARS OF '68 . . . . . . . . . . . . . . . . . . . . . . . . . . . . . . . . . . . . . . . . . . . . . . . . . . . . . Marble Arch MAL 762

## MARQUEE
04/05/1991 . . . . . 5 . . . . . . 6 . . . . . ○  **MARQUEE METAL** . . . . . . . . . . . . . . . . . . . . . . . . . . . . . . . . . . . . . . . . . . . . . . . . . . Marquee 8454171

## MASSIVE MUSIC
25/04/1998 . . . . . 16 . . . . . . 2 . . . . . .  101% SPEED GARAGE VOLUME 2 . . . . . . . . . . . . . . . . . . . . . . . . . . . . . . . . Massive Music MMCCD 011
17/04/1999 . . . . . 14 . . . . . . 5 . . . . . .  101% SPEED GARAGE ANTHEMS . . . . . . . . . . . . . . . . . . . . . . . . . . . . . . . . . Massive Music MMCCD 012

## MASTERCUTS UK label formed by Ian Dewhirst as an imprint within Beechwood Music.
28/09/1991 . . . . . 18 . . . . . . 2 . . . . . .  CLASSIC MELLOW MASTERCUTS VOLUME 1 . . . . . . . . . . . . . . . . . . . . . . . . . . . . . . . Mastercuts CUTSLP 3
21/03/1992 . . . . . 8 . . . . . . 5 . . . . . .  **NEW JACK SWING MASTERCUTS VOLUME 1** . . . . . . . . . . . . . . . . . . . . . . . . . . . . . . Mastercuts CUTSCD 5
16/05/1992 . . . . . 14 . . . . . . 3 . . . . . .  CLASSIC FUNK MASTERCUTS VOLUME 1 . . . . . . . . . . . . . . . . . . . . . . . . . . . . . . . . . Mastercuts CUTSCD 6
04/07/1992 . . . . . 18 . . . . . . 1 . . . . . .  CLASSIC JAZZ-FUNK MASTERCUTS VOLUME 3 . . . . . . . . . . . . . . . . . . . . . . . . . . . . . Mastercuts CUTSCD 7

○ Silver disc  ● Gold disc  ✪ Platinum disc (additional platinum units are indicated by a figure following the symbol)  ❶⁹ Number of weeks album topped the UK chart

| | | | |
|---|---|---|---|
| 15/08/1992 | 12 | 3 | CLASSIC MELLOW MASTERCUTS VOLUME 2 ............................................ Mastercuts CUTSCD 8 |
| 06/03/1993 | 16 | 3 | CLASSIC SALSOUL MASTERCUTS VOLUME 1 ........................................... Mastercuts CUTSCD 10 |
| 24/04/1993 | 14 | 3 | CLASSIC RARE GROOVE MASTERCUTS VOLUME 1 ...................................... Mastercuts CUTSCD 11 |
| 22/05/1993 | 16 | 1 | CLASSIC P-FUNK MASTERCUTS VOLUME 1 ............................................ Mastercuts CUTSCD 12 |
| 22/01/1994 | 19 | 2 | CLASSIC JAZZ-FUNK MASTERCUTS VOLUME 4 ......................................... Mastercuts CUTSCD 16 |
| 26/03/1994 | 18 | 1 | NEW JACK SWING VOLUME 3 ....................................................... Mastercuts CUTSCD 18 |
| 14/05/1994 | 18 | 1 | CLASSIC ELECTRO MASTERCUTS VOLUME 1 ........................................... Mastercuts CUTSCD 19 |
| 18/06/1994 | 11 | 2 | CLASSIC HOUSE MASTERCUTS VOLUME 1 ............................................. Mastercuts CUTSCD 20 |

## MASTERSOUND

28/03/1987 ..... 96 ...... 1
HEART OF SOUL VOLUME 1 ........................................................ Mastersound MASL 001

## MASTERWORKS

05/12/1992 ..... 18 ...... 3
TAKE 2: OPERA FAVOURITES/ORCHESTRAL CLASSICS .................................... Masterworks S2K 48226

## MAWSON AND WARSHAM

16/03/1991 ..... 10 ...... 3
**PETER HETHERINGTON: SONGS FROM THE HEART** ................................... Mawson And Warsham PHMC 2

## MCA
US label originally formed by Jules Stern in 1924 as a booking agency, the name standing for the Music Corporation of America. The MCA label first surfaced in 1962 following its acquisition of Decca USA, Brunswick and Vocalion, and later acquisitions included Geffen Records and Motown. MCA was sold to the Japanese company Matsushita in 1990 and again to Seagrams in 1996 for $5.7 billion and became part of the newly created Universal Music Group.

24/05/1980 ..... 60 ...... 2
PRECIOUS METAL ................................................................ MCA MCF 3069

23/04/1994 ..... 19 ...... 2
RHYTHM COUNTRY AND BLUES ...................................................... MCA MCD 10965
27/05/1995 ..... 9 ...... 3
**MORE BUMP 'N' GRIND** ....................................................... MCA MCD 11286
02/11/1996 ..... 18 ...... 1
THE TARANTINO COLLECTION ...................................................... MCA MCD 80325

## MCI
UK label formed as the music division of video distrubtors VCI, the name standing for Music Collection International.

04/03/1995 ..... 20 ...... 1
BORN TO BE WILD ............................................................... MCI Music MUSCD 001

## MERCURY
US label formed in Chicago in 1947 by Berl Adams, Irving Green and Art Talmadge. After acquiring the Majestic and Smash labels Mercury was sold to Philips in 1963 and later became part of the Universal Music Group.

02/07/1983 ..... 58 ...... 4
WIRED FOR CLUBS (CLUB TRACKS VOLUME 1) ......................................... Mercury CLUBL 1001
26/11/1983 ..... 6 ...... 17 ...... ●
**FORMULA 30** ................................................................ Mercury PROLP 4
14/06/1986 ..... 70 ...... 2
BEAT RUNS WILD ................................................................ Mercury WILD 1
01/11/1986 ..... 80 ...... 3 ...... ●
FORMULA THIRTY – 2 ............................................................ Mercury PROLP 9

26/10/1991 .... ❶[1] ..... 21 ...... ✪
**TWO ROOMS – CELEBRATING THE SONGS OF ELTON JOHN AND BERNIE TAUPIN** ........... Mercury 8457491
21/12/2002 ..... 2 ...... 7 ...... ✪
**FAME ACADEMY** .............................................................. Mercury 0636132
27/09/2003 ..... 9 ...... 4
**BEST OF CAFE DEL MAR** ...................................................... Mercury 9811381

## METROPOLE MUSIC

25/05/1996 ..... 10 ...... 3
**DANNY RAMPLING – LOVE GROOVE DANCE PARTY** .................................. Metropole Music LGCD 1
08/02/1997 ..... 17 ...... 2
DANNY RAMPLING – LOVE GROOVE DANCE PARTY ...................................... Metropole Music LGCD 2
07/06/1997 ..... 12 ...... 2
DANNY RAMPLING/LOVE GROOVE PARTY 5 & 6 ......................................... Metropole Music LGCD 3

## MFP
UK label formed as a budget imprint of EMI, the name standing for Music For Pleasure.

04/12/1971 ..... 49 ...... 1
BREAKTHROUGH .................................................................. MFP 1334

## MINISTRY OF SOUND
UK dance label formed in 1993 by James Palumbo which subsequently added the imprints Sound of Ministry, FSUK, Ride and Data and a joint venture label in Relentless as well as a successful London nightclub.

THE ANNUAL
MILLENNIUM EDITION
Mixed by Judge Jules & Tall Paul

11/09/1993 ..... 16 ...... 2
MINISTRY OF SOUND: THE SESSIONS VOLUME 1 ....................................... Ministry Of Sound MINSTCD 1
30/04/1994 ..... 6 ...... 5
**MINISTRY OF SOUND – THE SESSIONS VOLUME 2** ................................. Ministry Of Sound MINSTCD 002
22/10/1994 ..... 8 ...... 3
**MINISTRY OF SOUND – THE SESSIONS VOLUME 3** ................................. Ministry Of Sound MINSTCD 003
01/04/1995 ..... 19 ...... 1
THE FUTURE SOUND OF NEW YORK .................................................. Ministry Of Sound SOMCD 1
06/05/1995 ..... 9 ...... 5
**MINISTRY OF SOUND – THE SESSIONS 4** ....................................... Ministry Of Sound MINCDB 4
30/09/1995 ..... 15 ...... 5
MINISTRY OF SOUND SESSIONS – VOLUME 5 ......................................... Ministry Of Sound MINCD 5
25/11/1995 ..... 13 ...... 6
THE ANNUAL ................................................................... Ministry Of Sound ANNCD 95
16/03/1996 ..... 8 ...... 4
**MINISTRY OF SOUND SESSION SIX – FRANKIE KNUCKLES** .......................... Ministry Of Sound MINCD 6

---

▲[9] Number of weeks album topped the US chart    ◆[12] RIAA Diamond Awards    ◇[3] IFPI Platinum Europe Awards

| DATE | POS | WKS | BPI | ALBUM TITLE | LABEL & NUMBER |
|------|-----|-----|-----|-------------|----------------|
| 13/04/1996 | 5 | 6 | ○ | **DANCE NATION** | Ministry Of Sound DNCD 96 |
| 20/07/1996 | 4 | 8 | | **MINISTRY OF SOUND – DANCE NATION 2** | Ministry Of Sound DNCD 962 |
| 21/09/1996 | 9 | 6 | | **ONE HALF OF A WHOLE DECADE – 5 YEARS** | Ministry Of Sound MOS 5CD |
| 12/10/1996 | 7 | 4 | | **NORTHERN EXPOSURE – SASHA & JOHN DIGWEED** | Ministry Of Sound NECD 1 |
| 23/11/1996 | ❶⁵ | 24 | ✪² | **THE ANNUAL II – PETE TONG & BOY GEORGE** | Ministry Of Sound ANNCD 96 |
| 01/03/1997 | 4 | 4 | | **SESSIONS SEVEN** | Ministry Of Sound MINCD 7 |
| 29/03/1997 | ❶¹ | 10 | ● | **DANCE NATION 3 – PETE TONG & JUDGE JULES** | Ministry Of Sound DNCD 3 |
| 21/06/1997 | 12 | 3 | | MINISTRY OF SOUND CLASSICS MIXED BY JUDGE JULES | Ministry Of Sound CLACD 1 |
| 26/07/1997 | 11 | 3 | | SESSION EIGHT – TODD TERRY | Ministry Of Sound MINCD 8 |
| 13/09/1997 | 2 | 8 | ● | **DANCE NATION 4 – PETE TONG/BOY GEORGE** | Ministry Of Sound DNCD 4 |
| 27/09/1997 | 15 | 2 | | NORTHERN EXPOSURE 2 – SASHA & DIGWEED | Ministry Of Sound NECD 2 |
| 15/11/1997 | ❶² | 15 | ✪ | **THE ANNUAL III – PETE TONG & BOY GEORGE** | Ministry Of Sound ANNCD 97 |
| 14/03/1998 | 17 | 1 | | SESSIONS NINE – ERICK MORILLO | Ministry Of Sound MINCD 9 |
| 28/03/1998 | 2 | 9 | | **PETE TONG/BOY GEORGE – DANCE NATION 5** | Ministry Of Sound DNCD 5 |
| 04/07/1998 | 2 | 9 | | **CLUBBER'S GUIDE TO… IBIZA – JULES/TONG** | Ministry Of Sound MOSCD 1 |
| 05/09/1998 | ❶¹ | 9 | ● | **THE IBIZA ANNUAL** | Ministry Of Sound MOSCD 2 |
| 14/11/1998 | ❶² | 15 | ✪ | **THE ANNUAL IV – JUDGE JULES & BOY GEORGE** | Ministry Of Sound ANNCD 98 |
| 30/01/1999 | ❶² | 7 | | **CLUBBER'S GUIDE TO… NINETY NINE** | Ministry Of Sound MOSCD 3 |
| 27/03/1999 | ❶¹ | 11 | | **DANCE NATION 6 – TALL PAUL & BRANDON BLOCK** | Ministry Of Sound DNCD 6 |
| 15/05/1999 | 6 | 4 | | **GALAXY WEEKEND: MIXED BY BOY GEORGE & ALLISTER WHITEHEAD** | Ministry Of Sound GALCD 1 |
| 29/05/1999 | ❶³ | 9 | | **TRANCE NATION: MIXED BY SYSTEM F** | Ministry Of Sound TNCD 1 |
| 19/06/1999 | ❶² | 10 | ○ | **CLUBBER'S GUIDE TO IBIZA – SUMMER '99** | Ministry Of Sound MOSCD 4 |
| 07/08/1999 | 4 | 5 | ● | **CLUBBER'S GUIDE TO… TRANCE: MIXED BY ATB** | Ministry Of Sound MOSCD 5 |
| 28/08/1999 | ❶¹ | 8 | ● | **THE IBIZA ANNUAL: MIXED BY JUDGE JULES + TALL PAUL** | Ministry Of Sound MOSCD 6 |
| 09/10/1999 | ❶¹ | 6 | ● | **TRANCE NATION 2: MIXED BY FERRY CORSTEN** | Ministry Of Sound TNCD 2 |
| 30/10/1999 | 8 | 3 | | **GALAXY MIX – BOY GEORGE** | Ministry Of Sound GAL CD2 |
| 13/11/1999 | 2 | 15 | ✪ | **THE ANNUAL – MILLENNIUM EDITION** | Ministry Of Sound ANNCD 99 |
| 29/01/2000 | ❶² | 8 | | **CLUBBER'S GUIDE TO… 2000** | Ministry Of Sound MOSCD 7 |
| 26/02/2000 | ❶¹ | 7 | | **REWIND – THE SOUND OF UK GARAGE** | Ministry Of Sound MOSCD 8 |
| 08/04/2000 | ❶¹ | 5 | ● | **DANCE NATION – TALL PAUL/BRANDON BLOCK** | Ministry Of Sound DNCD 7 |
| 13/05/2000 | 2 | 6 | | **TRANCE NATION 3** | Ministry Of Sound TNCD 3 |
| 27/05/2000 | 14 | 2 | | GALAXY HIT MIX | Ministry Of Sound GALCD 3 |
| 10/06/2000 | ❶¹ | 7 | | **CLUBBER'S GUIDE TO IBIZA – SUMMER 2000** | Ministry Of Sound MOSCD 9 |
| 15/07/2000 | 20 | 1 | | HEADLINERS – TALL PAUL | Ministry Of Sound MINCD 11 |
| 22/07/2000 | 5 | 7 | | **AYIA NAPA THE ALBUM – SHANKS & BIGFOOT** | Ministry Of Sound MOSCD 10 |
| 02/09/2000 | ❶³ | 10 | ✪ | **THE IBIZA ANNUAL – SUMMER 2000** | Ministry Of Sound MOSCD 11L |
| 07/10/2000 | ❶⁴ | 7 | | **TRANCE NATION 4** | Ministry Of Sound TNCD 4 |
| 11/11/2000 | ❶² | 12 | ✪ | **THE ANNUAL 2000 – JUDGE JULES/TALL PAUL** | Ministry Of Sound ANNCD 2KL |
| 02/12/2000 | 9 | 7 | ● | **UK GARAGE – THE ALBUM** | Ministry Of Sound MOSCD 12 |
| 20/01/2001 | ❶² | 5 | | **CLUBBERS GUIDE TO 2001** | Ministry Of Sound MOSCD 13 |
| 17/02/2001 | ❶⁶ | 18 | ✪ | **THE CHILLOUT SESSION** | Ministry Of Sound MOSCD 15 |
| 24/02/2001 | 6 | 5 | | **REAL GARAGE – MIXED LIVE BY MASTERSTEPZ** | Ministry Of Sound MOSCD 16 |
| 03/03/2001 | 10 | 3 | | **HARD ENERGY** | Ministry Of Sound MOSCD 17 |
| 07/04/2001 | ❶² | 9 | | **THE ANNUAL – SPRING 2001** | Ministry Of Sound MOSCD 17 |
| 12/05/2001 | 4 | 5 | | **TRANCE NATION 5** | Ministry Of Sound TNCD 5 |
| 09/06/2001 | 4 | 5 | | **CLUBBERS GUIDE TO IBIZA – SUMMER 2001** | Ministry Of Sound MOSCD 18 |
| 16/06/2001 | 9 | 3 | | **AYIA NAPA – THE ALBUM 2001** | Ministry Of Sound MOSCD 19 |
| 23/06/2001 | 2 | 11 | ✪ | **THE CHILLOUT SESSION 2** | Ministry Of Sound MOSCD 20 |
| 01/09/2001 | 3 | 5 | | **IBIZA ANNUAL** | Ministry Of Sound MOSCD 21 |
| 08/09/2001 | 12 | 3 | | IBIZA CHILLOUT SESSION | Ministry Of Sound MOSCD 22 |
| 06/10/2001 | 4 | 4 | | **CLUB NATION** | Ministry Of Sound MOSCD 28 |
| 13/10/2001 | 2 | 7 | ● | **BACK TO THE OLD SKOOL** | Ministry Of Sound MOSCD 23 |
| 17/11/2001 | ❶¹ | 12 | ● | **THE ANNUAL 2002** | Ministry Of Sound ANCD 2K1 |
| 01/12/2001 | 11 | 2 | | BACK TO THE OLD SKOOL 2 | Ministry Of Sound MOSCD 29 |
| 19/01/2002 | ❶³ | 6 | ● | **CLUBBERS GUIDE TO 2002** | Ministry Of Sound MOSCD 27 |
| 16/02/2002 | 5 | 4 | | **ADDICTED TO BASS** | Ministry Of Sound MOSCD 36 |
| 16/02/2002 | 7 | 6 | | **THE KARMA COLLECTION** | Ministry Of Sound MOSCD 30 |
| 09/03/2002 | 7 | 3 | | **BACK TO THE OLD SKOOL – HIP HOP** | Ministry Of Sound MOSCD 32 |
| 23/03/2002 | 2 | 5 | | **TRANCE NATION** | Ministry Of Sound MOSCD 34 |
| 30/03/2002 | 20 | 1 | | BACK TO THE OLD SKOOL – DRUM & BASS | Ministry Of Sound MOSCD 38 |
| 06/04/2002 | 3 | 6 | | **SPRING ANNUAL 2002** | Ministry Of Sound MOSCD 35 |
| 27/04/2002 | 7 | 2 | | **CLUB NATION – MIAMI 2002** | Ministry Of Sound MOSCD 44 |
| 04/05/2002 | 4 | 5 | | **THE CHILLOUT SESSION – IBIZA 2002** | Ministry Of Sound MOSCD 40 |
| 18/05/2002 | 6 | 4 | | **BACK TO THE OLD SKOOL – IBIZA** | Ministry Of Sound MOSCD 40 |
| 25/05/2002 | 3 | 4 | | **21ST CENTURY DISCO** | Ministry Of Sound MOSCD 31 |
| 08/06/2002 | ❶¹ | 6 | | **CLUBBERS GUIDE TO IBIZA 2002** | Ministry Of Sound MOSCD 42 |
| 29/06/2002 | 3 | 4 | | **ADDICTED TO TRANCE** | Ministry Of Sound MOSCD 49 |
| 27/07/2002 | 9 | 3 | | **CLUB NATION IBIZA** | Ministry Of Sound MOSCD 47 |
| 24/08/2002 | 19 | 1 | | SORTED | Ministry Of Sound MOSCD 46 |

○ Silver disc   ● Gold disc   ✪ Platinum disc (additional platinum units are indicated by a figure following the symbol)   ❶⁹ Number of weeks album topped the UK chart

| DATE | POS | WKS | BPI | ALBUM TITLE | LABEL & NUMBER |
|------|-----|-----|-----|-------------|----------------|
| 31/08/2002 | 4 | 6 | | THE ANNUAL IBIZA 2002 | Ministry Of Sound MOSCD 50 |
| 28/09/2002 | 3 | 7 | | DANCE NATION ANTHEMS | Ministry Of Sound MOSCD 52 |
| 19/10/2002 | 9 | 2 | | TRANCE CLASSICS | Ministry Of Sound MOSCD 54 |
| 16/11/2002 | ❶1 | 11 | | THE ANNUAL 2003 | Ministry Of Sound ANCD 2K2 |
| 30/11/2002 | 20 | 1 | | THE CHILLOUT SESSION 2003 | Ministry Of Sound MOSCD 56 |
| 07/12/2002 | 18 | 1 | | TRANCE NATION 2003 | Ministry Of Sound MOSCD 55 |
| 18/01/2003 | ❶1 | 8 | | CLUBBERS GUIDE 2003 | Ministry Of Sound MOSCD 58 |
| 08/02/2003 | 17 | 2 | | THE KARMA COLLECTION 2003 | Ministry Of Sound MOSCD 59 |
| 15/03/2003 | 3 | 4 | | TRANCE NATION – FUTURE | Ministry Of Sound MOSCD 61 |
| 05/04/2003 | 9 | 3 | | LATE NIGHT SESSIONS | Ministry Of Sound MOSCD 64 |
| 12/04/2003 | 3 | 6 | | THE ANNUAL SPRING 2003 | Ministry Of Sound MOSCD 63 |
| 26/04/2003 | 2 | 10 | | BACK TO THE OLD SKOOL CLUB CLASSICS | Ministry Of Sound MOSCD 62 |
| 17/05/2003 | 8 | 4 | | TRANCE NATION DEEPER | Ministry Of Sound MOSCD 66 |
| 31/05/2003 | 10 | 3 | | CHILLOUT SESSION – SUMMER COLLECTION 2003 | Ministry Of Sound MOSCD 65 |
| 28/06/2003 | 2 | 7 | | CLUBBERS GUIDE TO SUMMER 2003 | Ministry Of Sound MOSCD 67 |
| 12/07/2003 | 4 | 3 | | BACK TO THE OLD SKOOL – IBIZA ANTHEMS | Ministry Of Sound MOSCD 70 |
| 02/08/2003 | 17 | 1 | | ELECTROTECH | Ministry Of Sound MIRCD 69 |
| 16/08/2003 | 16 | 2 | | ON THE BEACH | Ministry Of Sound MOSCD 71 |
| 06/09/2003 | 5 | 5 | | THE ANNUAL SUMMER 2003 | Ministry Of Sound MOSCD 73 |
| 20/09/2003 | 16 | 1 | | SMOOVE PRESENTS STREET BEATS | Ministry Of Sound MOSCD 72 |
| 27/09/2003 | 11 | 3 | | THE CHILLOUT SESSION – IBIZA SUNSETS | Ministry Of Sound MOSCD 68 |
| 11/10/2003 | 4 | 4 | | TRANCE NATION HARDER | Ministry Of Sound MOSCD 75 |
| 25/10/2003 | 10 | 2 | | HOUSE CLASSICS | Ministry Of Sound MOSCD 76 |
| 15/11/2003 | 2 | 13 | | THE ANNUAL 2004 | Ministry Of Sound ANCD2K3 |
| 29/11/2003 | 16 | 1 | | TRANCE NATION ANTHEMS – JUDGE JULES | Ministry Of Sound MOSCD 78 |
| 17/01/2004 | ❶3 | 5 | | CLUBBERS GUIDE – 2004 | Ministry Of Sound MOSCD 80 |
| 28/02/2004 | 2 | 7 | | FUNK SOUL CLASSICS | Ministry Of Sound MOSCD 84 |
| 20/03/2004 | 13 | 2 | | TRANCE NATION ELECTRIC – JUDGE JULES | Ministry Of Sound MOSCD 81 |
| 17/04/2004 | 19 | 1 | | THE SOUND OF SMOOVE | Ministry Of Sound/UMTV MOSCD 86 |
| 08/05/2004 | 6 | 5 | | ANNUAL SPRING 2004 | Ministry Of Sound MOSCD 87 |
| 05/06/2004 | 12 | 1 | | ACID JAZZ CLASSICS | Ministry Of Sound MOSCD 91 |
| 12/06/2004 | 8 | 2 | | REWIND GARAGE CLASSICS | Ministry Of Sound MOSCD 93 |
| 26/06/2004 | 9 | 1+ | | DISCO CLASSICS | Ministry Of Sound/UMTV MOSCD 81 |

## MIRACLE

| DATE | POS | WKS | BPI | ALBUM TITLE | LABEL & NUMBER |
|------|-----|-----|-----|-------------|----------------|
| 04/02/1995 | 5 | 4 | ○ | LOVE ETERNAL | Miracle MIRCD 0001 |

## MISS MONEYPENNY'S

| DATE | POS | WKS | BPI | ALBUM TITLE | LABEL & NUMBER |
|------|-----|-----|-----|-------------|----------------|
| 22/03/1997 | 12 | 1 | | GLAMOROUS ONE | Miss Moneypenny's MPENNYCD 1 |

## MORE PROTEIN
UK label formed by George O'Dowd (better known as Boy George, former lead singer with Culture Club).

| DATE | POS | WKS | BPI | ALBUM TITLE | LABEL & NUMBER |
|------|-----|-----|-----|-------------|----------------|
| 01/02/1992 | 20 | 1 | | CLOSET CLASSICS VOLUME 1 – MORE PROTEIN SAMPLER | More Protein CMMD 1 |

## TAMLA MOTOWN/MOTOWN
US R&B label formed in Detroit, MI in 1959 by Berry Gordy with an $800 loan from his family. The name was derived from Motortown, the nickname for Detroit since Henry Ford set up his production plant there at the end of the 19th century. The Motown company later formed a number of label imprints, including Rare Earth (a rock label), MoWest (following the company's relocation to California), Gordy and Workshop (a jazz label), but became primarily known for its stomping dance hits of the 1960s. It was sold to MCA in 1989 for $61 million and subsequently became part of the Universal Music Group.

| DATE | POS | WKS | BPI | ALBUM TITLE | LABEL & NUMBER |
|------|-----|-----|-----|-------------|----------------|
| 03/04/1965 | 16 | 4 | | A COLLECTION OF TAMLA MOTOWN HITS | Tamla Motown TML 11001 |
| 04/03/1967 | 33 | 3 | | 16 ORIGINAL BIG HITS – VOLUME 4 | Tamla Motown TML 11043 |
| 17/06/1967 | 11 | 40 | | TAMLA MOTOWN HITS VOLUME 5 | Tamla Motown TML 11050 |
| 21/10/1967 | 2 | 54 | | BRITISH MOTOWN CHARTBUSTERS | Tamla Motown TML 11055 |
| 10/02/1968 | 21 | 13 | | MOTOWN MEMORIES | Tamla Motown TML 11064 |
| 24/08/1968 | 32 | 2 | | TAMLA MOTOWN HITS VOLUME 6 | Tamla Motown STML 11074 |
| 30/11/1968 | 8 | 11 | | BRITISH MOTOWN CHARTBUSTERS VOLUME 2 | Tamla Motown STML 11082 |
| 25/10/1969 | ❶1 | 93 | ● | MOTOWN CHARTBUSTERS VOLUME 3 | Tamla Motown STML 11121 |
| 21/02/1970 | 56 | 1 | | COLLECTION OF BIG HITS VOLUME 8 | Tamla Motown STML 11130 |
| 24/10/1970 | ❶1 | 40 | | MOTOWN CHARTBUSTERS VOLUME 4 | Tamla Motown STML 11162 |
| 17/04/1971 | ❶3 | 36 | | MOTOWN CHARTBUSTERS VOLUME 5 | Tamla Motown STML 11181 |
| 23/10/1971 | 2 | 36 | | MOTOWN CHARTBUSTERS VOLUME 6 | Tamla Motown STML 11191 |
| 26/02/1972 | 22 | 4 | | MOTOWN MEMORIES | Tamla Motown STML 11200 |
| 18/03/1972 | 21 | 8 | ● | MOTOWN STORY | Tamla Motown TMSP 1130 |
| 25/11/1972 | 9 | 16 | | MOTOWN CHARTBUSTERS VOLUME 7 | Tamla Motown STML 11215 |

▲9 Number of weeks album topped the US chart ◆12 RIAA Diamond Awards ◇3 IFPI Platinum Europe Awards

| | | | | | |
|---|---|---|---|---|---|
| 03/11/1973 | 9 | 15 | ● | **MOTOWN CHARTBUSTERS VOLUME 8** | Tamla Motown STML 11246 |
| 26/10/1974 | 14 | 15 | | MOTOWN CHARTBUSTERS VOLUME 9 | Tamla Motown STML 11270 |
| 01/11/1975 | 8 | 35 | ● | **MOTOWN GOLD** | Tamla Motown STML 12003 |
| 05/11/1977 | 28 | 4 | ○ | MOTOWN GOLD VOLUME 2 | Motown STML 12070 |
| 07/10/1978 | 2 | 18 | ● | **BIG WHEELS OF MOTOWN** | Motown EMTV 12 |
| 02/02/1980 | ❶² | 23 | ● | **THE LAST DANCE** | Motown EMTV 20 |
| 02/08/1980 | 53 | 2 | | THE 20TH ANNIVERSARY ALBUM | Motown TMSP 6010 |
| 21/05/1988 | 3 | 18 | ● | **MOTOWN DANCE PARTY** | Motown ZC 72700 |
| 19/05/1990 | 10 | 7 | | **MOTOWN DANCE PARTY 2** | Motown ZL 72703 |
| 06/10/1990 | 3 | 10 | | **SOUL DECADE: THE SIXTIES** | Motown ZL 74816 |
| 24/10/1992 | 5 | 5 | ○ | **MOTOWN'S GREATEST LOVE SONGS** | Motown 5300062 |
| 12/11/1994 | 6 | 13 | ● | **MOTOWN – THE ULTIMATE HITS COLLECTION** | Motown 5304652 |
| 04/11/1995 | 19 | 1 | | MOTOWN – THE HITS COLLECTION – VOLUME 2 | Motown 5306042 |
| 12/09/1998 | 15 | 2 | | MOTOWN 40 FOREVER | Motown 5308492 |

## MOUNTAIN

| | | | | | |
|---|---|---|---|---|---|
| 03/07/1976 | 45 | 2 | | GOLDEN FIDDLE AWARDS 1976 | Mountain TOPC 5002 |

## MUSIC UNITES

| | | | | | |
|---|---|---|---|---|---|
| 12/03/1994 | 19 | 1 | | JOURNEYS BY DJ VOLUME 4 | Music Unites JDJCD 4 |

## NEEDLE

| | | | | | |
|---|---|---|---|---|---|
| 04/07/1987 | 46 | 4 | | DANCE MANIA VOLUME 1 | Needle DAMA 1 |
| 20/02/1988 | 81 | 2 | | MAD ON HOUSE VOLUME 1 | Needle MADD 1 |
| 14/05/1988 | 25 | 8 | | HOUSE HITS | Needle HOHI 88 |

**NEMS** UK label that was formed as a division of the NEMS company. NEMS (North End Music Stores) was the company owned by Brian Epstein that found lasting fame for discovering The Beatles, Cilla Black, Billy J Kramer and Gerry & The Pacemakers, among others, although all of these artists were signed to other labels and managed by NEMS. NEMS launched its own label in 1968 (after Epstein had died) with artists such as Cupid's Inspiration and later enjoyed success with rock act Black Sabbath.

| | | | | | |
|---|---|---|---|---|---|
| 12/12/1981 | 100 | 2 | | LIVE AND HEAVY | NEMS NEL 6020 |

## NETWORK

| | | | | | |
|---|---|---|---|---|---|
| 20/01/1996 | 16 | 2 | | RENAISSANCE – MIX COLLECTION – PART 2 | Network RENMIX 2CD |
| 13/04/1996 | 20 | 1 | | BACK TO BASICS – CUT THE CRAP | Network B2BCD 1 |

## NICE

| | | | | | |
|---|---|---|---|---|---|
| 14/09/1996 | 20 | 1 | | TRIBUTE TO THE SMALL FACES – LONG AGOS/WORLDS APART | Nice NYCE 1CD |

## NME/ISLAND

| | | | | | |
|---|---|---|---|---|---|
| 09/04/1988 | 37 | 8 | | SERGEANT PEPPER KNEW MY FATHER | NME/Island PELP 100 |

## NOUVEAU MUSIC

| | | | | | |
|---|---|---|---|---|---|
| 24/09/1983 | 61 | 2 | | CLASSIC THEMES | Nouveau Music NML 1001 |
| 02/06/1984 | 96 | 1 | | ESSENTIAL DISCO AND DANCE | Nouveau Music NML 1010 |
| 30/03/1985 | 91 | 1 | | DREAM MELODIES | Nouveau Music NML 1013 |

**NPG** US label formed by Prince; the name stands for New Power Generation.

| | | | | | |
|---|---|---|---|---|---|
| 20/08/1994 | 15 | 1 | | 1-800 NEW FUNK | NPG BR 7110062 |

**NUMA** UK label formed by Gary Numan.

| | | | | | |
|---|---|---|---|---|---|
| 22/03/1986 | 94 | 1 | | NUMA RECORDS YEAR 1 | Numa NUMA1004 |

**OLD GOLD** UK label formed as a re-issue label by Pickwick.

| | | | | | |
|---|---|---|---|---|---|
| 07/04/1990 | 18 | 1 | | LET'S DANCE – SOUND OF THE SIXTIES PART 1 | Old Gold OG 1702 |

**ORIOLE** UK label formed in the 1950s. An early outlet for Tamla Motown releases in the UK, it was subsequently bought by CBS.

| | | | | | |
|---|---|---|---|---|---|
| 24/08/1963 | 17 | 5 | | THE MERSEY BEAT VOLUME 1 | Oriole PS 40047 |

## PARKFIELD

| | | | | | |
|---|---|---|---|---|---|
| 28/07/1990 | 13 | 2 | | NOTHING COMPARES TO THIS | Parkfield PMLP 5020 |

**PARLOPHONE** UK label originally formed in Europe in 1911 as Parlophon by Carl Gesellschaaft Lindstrom. The company was taken over by the Dutch Transoceanic Trading Company in 1920, which in turn formed Parlophone Company Ltd in London in 1923. Two years later it linked with the Columbia label and subsequently became part of EMI in 1931. During the 1950s under the direction of George Martin it established a reputation for comedy recordings, subsequently ensuring its lasting place in music folklore with the signing of The Beatles in 1962.

| | | | | | |
|---|---|---|---|---|---|
| 22/06/1991 | 3 | 7 | ● | **IT'S COOL** | Parlophone PCSTV 1 |

| DATE | POS | WKS | BPI | ALBUM TITLE | LABEL & NUMBER |
|---|---|---|---|---|---|
| 04/07/1992 | 6 | 4 | ○ | DANCE ENERGY 4 – FEEL THE RHYTHM | Parlophone CDPMTV 4 |
| 03/09/1994 | 6 | 5 | | 60'S SOUL 90'S SOUL | Parlophone CDPCSTV 4 |

### PERFECTO
UK dance label formed by DJ and producer Paul Oakenfold.

| DATE | POS | WKS | BPI | ALBUM TITLE | LABEL & NUMBER |
|---|---|---|---|---|---|
| 01/08/1992 | 15 | 4 | | HARDCORE DJS… TAKE CONTROL | Perfecto 74321101812 |
| 09/11/1996 | 18 | 1 | | PERFECTO FLUORO: OAKENFOLD | Perfecto 0630166942 |
| 04/11/2000 | 12 | 2 | | PERFECTO PRESENTS PAUL OAKENFOLD – TRAVELLING | Perfecto PERFALB 02CD |
| 19/05/2001 | 20 | 1 | | TIMO MAAS – CONNECTED | Perfecto PERFALB 04CD |
| 25/08/2001 | 13 | 1 | | IBIZA – PAUL OAKENFOLD | Perfecto PERFALB 05CD |

### PHILIPS
Dutch label formed in Eindhoven in 1950 as Philips Phonographische Industries. The company bought US company Mercury Records in 1960 but linked with German company Siemens and their Deutsche Grammophon label in 1962 to form Phonogram. Later part of the Universal Music Group the label was revived as a classical label in the 1980s.

| DATE | POS | WKS | BPI | ALBUM TITLE | LABEL & NUMBER |
|---|---|---|---|---|---|
| 09/03/1963 | 4 | 19 | | ALL STAR FESTIVAL | Philips DL 99500 |
| 02/06/1973 | 9 | 11 | | 20 ORIGINAL CHART HITS | Philips TV 1 |
| 02/06/1973 | 36 | 1 | ○ | NICE 'N' EASY | Philips 6441 076 |
| 06/08/1977 | 11 | 12 | | NEW WAVE | Philips 5300 902 |
| 03/11/2001 | 10 | 3 | | UTOPIA – CHILLED CLASSICS | Philips 4720642 |

### PICKWICK
UK label formed in 1962; it was initially acting as a budget re-issue company for major labels such as CBS, RCA and EMI. It also launched the Hallmark label and scored with its *Top of the Pops* range and also instigated its own recordings. Sold to Carlton in 1992 and to Point in 1999, it virtually disappeared as a label during the 1990s, but was revived in 2002 following a period in receivership.

| DATE | POS | WKS | BPI | ALBUM TITLE | LABEL & NUMBER |
|---|---|---|---|---|---|
| 20/11/1993 | 4 | 12 | | THE VERY BEST OF DISNEY | Pickwick DISCD 471 |
| 05/11/1994 | 16 | 3 | ○ | THE LION KING SING-ALONG | Pickwick/Disney DSMCD 477 |
| 19/11/1994 | 9 | 4 | | THE VERY BEST OF DISNEY 2 | Pickwick/Disney DISCD 480 |

### POLYDOR
German label formed in 1924 as the pop music division of the classical company Deutsche Grammophon, which opened a UK office in 1956 and was initially used as an outlet for the company's European recordings. It began signing more of its own UK-based artists during the 1960s and also signed successful distribution deals with the likes of RSO and subsequently became part of the Universal Music Group.

| DATE | POS | WKS | BPI | ALBUM TITLE | LABEL & NUMBER |
|---|---|---|---|---|---|
| 10/12/1966 | 26 | 2 | | STEREO MUSICALE SHOWCASE | Polydor 104450 |
| 09/10/1971 | 24 | 4 | | THE A–Z OF EASY LISTENING | Polydor 2661 005 |
| 24/02/1979 | 45 | 3 | | 20 OF ANOTHER KIND | Polydor POLS 1006 |
| 19/05/1979 | 23 | 11 | | BOOGIE BUS | Polydor 9198 174 |
| 03/05/1980 | 7 | 14 | | CHAMPAGNE AND ROSES | Polydor ROSTV 1 |
| 30/08/1980 | 11 | 13 | ● | I AM WOMAN | Polydor WOMTV 1 |
| 11/10/1980 | 64 | 3 | | COUNTRY ROUND UP | Polydor KOWTV 1 |
| 18/10/1980 | 16 | 5 | | MONSTERS OF ROCK | Polydor 2488 810 |
| 06/12/1980 | 45 | 10 | ● | THE HITMAKERS | Polydor HOPTV 1 |
| 04/04/1981 | 3 | 13 | ● | ROLL ON | Polydor REDTV 1 |
| 17/10/1981 | 20 | 8 | ○ | MONSTER TRACKS | Polydor HOTTV 2 |
| 01/11/1986 | 58 | 5 | ● | SIMON BATES – OUR TUNE | Polydor PROLP 10 |
| 12/11/1988 | 3 | 9 | ○3 | ANDREW LLOYD WEBBER – THE PREMIER COLLECTION | Polydor ALWTV 1 |
| 14/01/1989 | ●1 | 55 | ○3 | ANDREW LLOYD WEBBER – THE PREMIER COLLECTION | Polydor ALWTV 1 |
| 04/02/1989 | ●4 | 21 | ○ | THE MARQUEE – 30 LEGENDARY YEARS | Polydor MOTV 1 |
| 31/03/1990 | 6 | 8 | | SKINBEAT – THE FIRST TOUCH | Polydor SKINL 101 |
| 18/08/1990 | ●2 | 10 | ● | KNEBWORTH – THE ALBUM | Polydor 843912 |
| 13/07/1991 | ●1 | 13 | ● | PURPLE RAINBOWS | Polydor/EMI 8455341 |
| 05/10/1991 | 6 | 5 | ○ | ABSOLUTION – ROCK THE ALTERNATIVE WAY | Polydor 8457471 |
| 20/11/1999 | 2 | 14 | ○2 | ABBAMANIA | Polydor/Universal Music TV 5433592 |
| 08/12/2001 | 5 | 5 | ● | ANDREW LLOYD WEBBER – GOLD | Polydor 5894922 |
| 06/09/2003 | 17 | 1 | | FAME ACADEMY – BEE GEES SPECIAL | Polydor 9865586 |
| 18/10/2003 | 2 | 4 | | FAME ACADEMY – THE FINALISTS | Polydor 9865835 |
| 01/11/2003 | ●1 | 3 | | GREASEMANIA | Polydor/S 9865823 |

**POLYGRAM** Dutch label formed in 1972 following the merger of Polydor and Phonogram. The label subsequently became part of the Universal Music Group.

| DATE | POS | WKS | BPI | ALBUM TITLE | LABEL & NUMBER |
|------|-----|-----|-----|-------------|----------------|
| 22/02/1992 | ❶² | 9 | ● | THE AWARDS 1992 | Polygram TV 5152072 |
| 21/03/1992 | ❶³ | 10 | | SOUL EMOTION | Polygram TV 5151882 |
| 02/05/1992 | 2 | 10 | ● | COUNTRY MOODS | Polygram TV 5152992 |
| 30/05/1992 | 7 | 3 | | BEATS RHYMES AND BASSLINES – THE BEST OF RAP | Polygram TV 5153842 |
| 06/06/1992 | 5 | 9 | ○ | POWER CUTS – ROCK'S GREATEST HITS | Polygram TV 5154152 |
| 20/06/1992 | ❶¹ | 20 | ● | MODERN LOVE | Polygram TV 5155182 |
| 18/07/1992 | 4 | 11 | ○ | DANCING ON SUNSHINE | Polygram TV/Virgin 5155192 |
| 01/08/1992 | 5 | 8 | | BLAME IT ON THE BOOGIE | Polygram TV 5155172 |
| 05/09/1992 | 5 | 5 | | READING – THE INDIE ALBUM | Polygram TV 5156482 |
| 20/02/1993 | 3 | 7 | ● | THE AWARDS 1993 | Polygram TV 5160752 |
| 27/03/1993 | 3 | 10 | ● | COUNTRY ROADS | Polygram TV 5161002 |
| 17/04/1993 | 8 | 6 | | MEGA-LO-MANIA | Polygram TV 5158132 |
| 24/04/1993 | 11 | 5 | | UNDER THE COVERS | Polygram TV 5160742 |
| 08/05/1993 | 3 | 8 | ● | MIDNIGHT MOODS – THE LIGHTER SIDE OF JAZZ | Polygram TV 5158162 |
| 05/06/1993 | 5 | 10 | ● | WOMAN TO WOMAN | Polygram TV 5161632 |
| 19/06/1993 | 7 | 4 | | THE GIFT OF SONG | Polygram TV 5160582 |
| 26/06/1993 | 4 | 7 | ● | SOUL INSPIRATION | Polygram TV 5162262 |
| 03/07/1993 | 7 | 6 | ○ | THE BLUES EXPERIENCE | Polygram TV 5162282 |
| 24/07/1993 | 10 | 4 | ○ | TEMPTED | Polygram TV 5163052 |
| 14/08/1993 | 9 | 9 | ○ | LEADERS OF THE PACK | Polygram TV 5163762 |
| 14/08/1993 | 15 | 3 | | ALL NIGHT LONG | Polygram TV 5163752 |
| 04/09/1993 | 9 | 3 | | PROGRESSION | Polygram TV 5163982 |
| 02/10/1993 | 16 | 2 | | ROUND MIDNIGHT | Polygram TV 5164712 |
| 09/10/1993 | 4 | 5 | ○ | DISCO DIVAS | Polygram TV 5164802 |
| 22/01/1994 | ❶¹ | 4 | ○ | THE SOUND OF KISS 100FM | Polygram TV 5164862 |
| 19/02/1994 | 4 | 6 | ● | THE MOVIES' GREATEST LOVE SONGS | Polygram TV 5166512 |
| 19/02/1994 | 11 | 3 | | DANCE DIVAS | Polygram TV 5166522 |
| 05/03/1994 | 8 | 3 | | FACE THE MUSIC – TORVILL AND DEAN | Polygram TV 8450652 |
| 12/03/1994 | ❶⁴ | 14 | ✪ | SOUL DEVOTION | Polygram TV 5166242 |
| 19/03/1994 | 2 | 7 | ● | I KNOW THEM SO WELL – TIM RICE | Polygram TV 5166502 |
| 09/04/1994 | 9 | 4 | ○ | WOMAN 2 WOMAN TWO | Polygram TV 5163302 |
| 23/04/1994 | 4 | 8 | ○ | ACOUSTIC MOODS | Polygram TV 5166592 |
| 07/05/1994 | ❶⁴ | 8 | ● | DANCE ZONE – LEVEL ONE | Polygram TV 5167142 |
| 21/05/1994 | 10 | 3 | | REMEMBER THEN – 30 DOO-WOP GREATS | Polygram TV 5167922 |
| 25/06/1994 | 2 | 9 | ● | THE ULTIMATE EIGHTIES | Polygram TV 5168312 |
| 02/07/1994 | 9 | 6 | ○ | ROCK THERAPY | Polygram TV 5168612 |
| 16/07/1994 | ❶² | 6 | ● | DANCE ZONE – LEVEL TWO | Polygram TV 5169122 |
| 23/07/1994 | 5 | 10 | ● | POWER AND SOUL | Polygram TV 5168962 |
| 27/08/1994 | 2 | 7 | ● | GROOVIN' | Polygram TV 5169682 |
| 10/09/1994 | 3 | 7 | ● | SATIN AND STEEL – WOMEN IN ROCK | Polygram TV 5169712 |
| 17/09/1994 | 3 | 6 | ● | SOUL NIGHTS | Polygram TV 5250052 |
| 01/10/1994 | 5 | 5 | ○ | SENSES | Polygram TV 5166272 |
| 08/10/1994 | ❶¹ | 6 | ● | DANCE ZONE – LEVEL THREE | Polygram TV 5250732 |
| 15/10/1994 | 17 | 1 | | AFTER MIDNIGHT | Polygram TV 5168712 |
| 29/10/1994 | 5 | 3 | ● | THE ULTIMATE 80'S BALLADS | Polygram TV 5251132 |
| 12/11/1994 | 2 | 12 | | DANCE ZONE '94 | Polygram TV 5251302 |
| 11/02/1995 | 3 | 6 | ● | ENDLESS LOVE | Polygram TV 5253412 |
| 25/02/1995 | 3 | 8 | | ELECTRIC DREAMS | Polygram TV 5254352 |
| 11/03/1995 | 11 | 3 | ○ | THE ESSENTIAL GROOVE | Polygram TV 5254382 |
| 25/03/1995 | ❶² | 8 | ✪ | DANCE ZONE LEVEL FOUR | Polygram TV 5169442 |
| 25/03/1995 | 14 | 3 | | EMERALD ROCK | Polygram TV 5169612 |
| 01/04/1995 | 2 | 5 | ● | TOGETHER | Polygram TV 5254612 |
| 08/04/1995 | 17 | 1 | | EVERY SONG TELLS A STORY | Polygram TV 5251702 |
| 15/04/1995 | 4 | 5 | ● | ROCKS OFF | Polygram TV 5254872 |
| 06/05/1995 | 8 | 5 | ○ | LET'S HEAR IT FOR THE GIRLS | Polygram TV 5165522 |
| 13/05/1995 | 4 | 5 | ○ | SHINE: 20 BRILLIANT INDIE HITS | Polygram TV 5255672 |
| 20/05/1995 | 3 | 6 | ● | SILK AND STEEL | Polygram TV 5255692 |
| 03/06/1995 | 8 | 3 | ○ | TEENAGE KICKS | Polygram TV 5253382 |

○ Silver disc  ● Gold disc  ✪ Platinum disc (additional platinum units are indicated by a figure following the symbol)  ❶⁹ Number of weeks album topped the UK chart

| DATE | POS | WKS | BPI | ALBUM TITLE | LABEL & NUMBER |
|---|---|---|---|---|---|
| 10/06/1995 | 8 | 4 | | WORLD IN UNION – ANTHEMS | Polygram TV 5278072 |
| 24/06/1995 | ●³ | 10 | ● | DANCE ZONE LEVEL FIVE | Polygram TV 5256332 |
| 01/07/1995 | 6 | 3 | O | SUNNY AFTERNOONS | Polygram TV 5256002 |
| 15/07/1995 | 5 | 7 | ● | THE NUMBER ONE CLASSIC SOUL ALBUM | Polygram TV 5256562 |
| 22/07/1995 | 14 | 2 | O | THE NUMBER ONE REGGAE ALBUM | Polygram TV 5256392 |
| 19/08/1995 | 7 | 4 | | ACOUSTIC FREEWAY | Polygram TV 5257352 |
| 26/08/1995 | 3 | 5 | O | THE NUMBER ONE 70'S ROCK ALBUM | Polygram TV 5257172 |
| 26/08/1995 | 5 | 4 | O | SUMMERTIME SOUL | Polygram TV 5258002 |
| 02/09/1995 | ●¹ | 7 | ● | DANCE ZONE LEVEL SIX | Polygram TV 5258602 |
| 02/09/1995 | 4 | 5 | ● | SHINE TOO | Polygram TV 5258582 |
| 23/09/1995 | 7 | 5 | O | ACOUSTIC ROCK | Polygram TV 5258962 |
| 14/10/1995 | 3 | 5 | ● | KISS IN IBIZA '95 | Polygram TV 5259112 |
| 04/11/1995 | 2 | 12 | ◉ | THE NUMBER ONE MOVIES ALBUM | Polygram TV 5259622 |
| 11/11/1995 | 8 | 4 | ● | DANCE ZONE '95 | Polygram TV 5350452 |
| 11/11/1995 | 16 | 2 | ● | THE NUMBER ONE ALL TIME ROCK ALBUM | Polygram TV 5350542 |
| 18/11/1995 | 13 | 6 | ● | SHINE 3 | Polygram TV 5259652 |
| 09/12/1995 | 4 | 13 | ◉² | THE NUMBER ONE CHRISTMAS ALBUM | Polygram TV 5259782 |
| 03/02/1996 | ●¹ | 10 | ● | SISTERS OF SWING | Polygram TV 5352252 |
| 10/02/1996 | 3 | 6 | O | SOFT ROCK | Polygram TV 5352482 |
| 10/02/1996 | 4 | 3 | ● | PASS THE VIBES | Polygram TV 5352212 |
| 10/02/1996 | 6 | 7 | ● | THE LOOK OF LOVE | Polygram TV 5351902 |
| 10/02/1996 | 7 | 8 | | CLASSIC MOODS | Polygram TV 4522492 |
| 17/02/1996 | ●¹ | 6 | ● | THE NUMBER ONE LOVE ALBUM | Polygram TV 5352622 |
| 02/03/1996 | 17 | 1 | | FREEWAY | Polygram TV 5259192 |
| 09/03/1996 | 3 | 6 | ● | SHINE 2 | Polygram TV 5353212 |
| 09/03/1996 | 7 | 5 | O | AMBIENT MOODS | Polygram TV 5259522 |
| 23/03/1996 | 3 | 5 | ● | THE BEST OF WOMAN TO WOMAN | Polygram TV 5353572 |
| 06/04/1996 | 2 | 7 | ● | CLUB MIX 96 | Polygram TV 5354122 |
| 27/04/1996 | 9 | 2 | | GO WITH THE FLOW – ESSENTIAL ACID JAZZ | Polygram TV 5352412 |
| 04/05/1996 | ●¹ | 5 | ● | DANCE ZONE LEVEL SEVEN | Polygram TV 5354272 |
| 11/05/1996 | ●¹ | 5 | ● | BOYZ OF SWING | Polygram TV 5354232 |
| 01/06/1996 | 3 | 4 | O | LADYKILLERS | Polygram TV 5355362 |
| 01/06/1996 | 4 | 3 | O | SISTERS OF SWING 2 | Polygram TV 5354752 |
| 08/06/1996 | 16 | 2 | | FUNKMASTER MIX | Polygram TV 5355762 |
| 15/06/1996 | 7 | 4 | ● | TRUEBRIT | Polygram TV 5354792 |
| 22/06/1996 | 2 | 5 | ● | MIX ZONE | Polygram TV 5355822 |
| 29/06/1996 | 8 | 3 | O | SUMMER VYBES | Polygram TV 5356442 |
| 06/07/1996 | 17 | 1 | | HORIZONS – 12 DREAMHOUSE ANTHEMS | Polygram TV 8287932 |
| 13/07/1996 | 5 | 3 | | KISS MIX '96 | Polygram TV 5357012 |
| 20/07/1996 | 2 | 9 | ● | SHINE 5 | Polygram TV 5356892 |
| 27/07/1996 | 10 | 4 | O | THE NUMBER ONE EIGHTIES ALBUM | Polygram TV 5356832 |
| 27/07/1996 | 12 | 3 | O | THE NUMBER ONE SUMMER ALBUM | Polygram TV 5356312 |
| 03/08/1996 | 2 | 8 | ● | CLUB MIX 96 – VOLUME 2 | Polygram TV 5357652 |
| 17/08/1996 | 16 | 2 | | THE NUMBER ONE COUNTRY ALBUM | Polygram TV 5357222 |
| 07/09/1996 | 5 | 4 | O | PURE DANCE '96 | Polygram TV 5357892 |
| 07/09/1996 | 6 | 4 | | THE SAX ALBUM | Polygram TV 5358052 |
| 14/09/1996 | 6 | 5 | O | BOYZ OF SWING II | Polygram TV 5357552 |
| 21/09/1996 | 4 | 6 | ● | DANCE ZONE LEVEL EIGHT | Polygram TV 5359032 |
| 05/10/1996 | 2 | 5 | ● | SHINE 6 | Polygram TV 5359202 |
| 12/10/1996 | 6 | 4 | | THE NUMBER ONE ACOUSTIC ROCK ALBUM | Polygram TV 5358142 |
| 19/10/1996 | ●⁴ | 8 | ● | KISS IN IBIZA '96 | Polygram TV 5359672 |
| 02/11/1996 | 12 | 1 | | THE NUMBER ONE RAP ALBUM | Polygram TV 5358112 |
| 16/11/1996 | 18 | 2 | | THE NUMBER ONE ROCK BALLADS ALBUM | Polygram TV 5359412 |
| 07/12/1996 | 13 | 7 | ● | SHINE 7 | Polygram TV 5530512 |
| 14/12/1996 | 11 | 5 | ● | HITS ZONE '97 | Polygram TV 5531872 |
| 21/12/1996 | 7 | 8 | ● | CLUB MIX 97 | Polygram TV 5532012 |
| 18/01/1997 | 2 | 16 | ● | THE NUMBER ONE MOTOWN ALBUM | Polygram TV 5307642 |
| 01/02/1997 | 2 | 6 | ● | WIRED | Polygram TV 5532572 |
| 08/02/1997 | 5 | 5 | O | CRUSH | Polygram TV 5532952 |
| 15/02/1997 | 3 | 5 | ● | AMOUR – THE ULTIMATE LOVE COLLECTION | Polygram TV 5533322 |
| 01/03/1997 | ●² | 6 | ● | CLUB MIX 97 – VOLUME 2 | Polygram TV 5533642 |
| 22/03/1997 | 11 | 2 | | DRUM & BASS MIX 97 | Polygram TV 5533952 |
| 29/03/1997 | 13 | 4 | | THE NUMBER ONE SCI-FI ALBUM | Polygram TV 5533602 |
| 05/04/1997 | 9 | 5 | | THE NUMBER ONE SKA ALBUM | Polygram TV 5534192 |
| 19/04/1997 | 2 | 7 | ● | KISS ANTHEMS | Polygram TV 5534792 |
| 03/05/1997 | 6 | 5 | ● | SHINE 8 | Polygram TV 5534252 |
| 10/05/1997 | 7 | 4 | O | SISTERS OF SWING III | Polygram TV/Global TV 5534652 |
| 17/05/1997 | 14 | 2 | | FUSED | Polygram TV 5534822 |
| 24/05/1997 | 12 | 4 | O | TRACKSPOTTING | Polygram TV 5534302 |

▲⁹ Number of weeks album topped the US chart ◆¹² RIAA Diamond Awards ◇³ IFPI Platinum Europe Awards

| | DATE | POS | WKS | BPI | ALBUM TITLE | LABEL & NUMBER |
|---|---|---|---|---|---|---|
| | 31/05/1997 | 7 | 3 | ○ | DANCE ZONE LEVEL NINE | Polygram TV 5377162 |
| | 07/06/1997 | 15 | 2 | | LADYKILLERS 2 | Polygram TV 5533812 |
| | 21/06/1997 | 6 | 5 | | MIXED EMOTIONS | Polygram TV 5536842 |
| | 28/06/1997 | 4 | 5 | ● | CLUB MIX 97 – VOLUME 3 | Polygram TV 5536912 |
| | 05/07/1997 | 3 | 8 | | KISS 100FM – SMOOTH GROOVES | Polygram TV 5333412 |
| | 12/07/1997 | 9 | 3 | ○ | SUGAR HITS! | Polygram TV 5536982 |
| | 02/08/1997 | 6 | 7 | ● | THE FIRST SUMMER OF LOVE | Polygram TV/Sony 5538622 |
| | 09/08/1997 | 3 | 6 | ● | KISS MIX '97 | Polygram TV 5538402 |
| | 23/08/1997 | 4 | 5 | | PETE TONG ESSENTIAL SELECTION – SUMMER 97 | Polygram TV 5538862 |
| | 30/08/1997 | 8 | 4 | | HITS ZONE SUMMER '97 | Polygram TV 5538262 |
| | 30/08/1997 | 15 | 2 | | DANGER ZONE | Polygram TV 5538702 |
| | 06/09/1997 | 14 | 2 | | THE NUMBER ONE DRIVE ALBUM | Polygram TV 5539402 |
| | 13/09/1997 | 7 | 4 | ○ | SHINE 9 | Polygram TV 5539752 |
| | 20/09/1997 | 13 | 3 | | THE NUMBER ONE JAZZ ALBUM | Polygram TV 5539372 |
| | 27/09/1997 | ❶[1] | 7 | ● | KISS IN IBIZA '97 | Polygram TV 5550352 |
| | 04/10/1997 | 10 | 4 | ○ | THE NUMBER ONE LINE DANCING ALBUM | Polygram TV 5538582 |
| | 11/10/1997 | 20 | 1 | | THE NUMBER ONE ROCK 'N' ROLL ALBUM | Polygram TV 5550172 |
| | 18/10/1997 | 9 | 3 | ○ | PURE DANCE '97 | Polygram TV 5550842 |
| | 01/11/1997 | 13 | 2 | ○ | THE NUMBER ONE SEVENTIES ALBUM | Polygram TV 5550542 |
| | 08/11/1997 | 17 | 1 | | HEART & SOUL | Polygram TV 5550632 |
| | 15/11/1997 | 18 | 1 | | HITS ZONE – THE BEST OF '97 | Polygram TV 5550702 |
| | 29/11/1997 | 6 | 7 | ● | KISS ANTHEMS '97 – 2 | Polygram TV 5550902 |
| | 13/12/1997 | 8 | 9 | ● | MASSIVE DANCE: 98 | warner.esp/Polygram TV/Global TV 5553432 |
| | 17/01/1998 | 20 | 1 | ● | SHINE – BEST OF 97 | Polygram TV 5550732 |
| | 07/02/1998 | ❶[1] | 7 | ● | ULTIMATE CLUB MIX | Polygram TV 5550962 |
| | 14/02/1998 | ❶[1] | 4 | ○ | LOVE – 39 ALL TIME LOVE CLASSICS | Polygram TV 5550602 |
| | 21/02/1998 | 10 | 4 | ○ | PURE ROCK BALLADS | Polygram TV 5555892 |
| | 28/02/1998 | 2 | 7 | ● | KISS SMOOTH GROOVES '98 | Polygram TV 5555742 |
| | 28/03/1998 | 10 | 3 | ○ | INTO THE BLUE | Polygram TV 5556652 |
| | 04/04/1998 | 15 | 2 | ○ | ULTIMATE DISCO MIX | Polygram TV 5556622 |
| | 11/04/1998 | 6 | 3 | ○ | UNDISPUTED | Polygram TV 5556952 |
| | 25/04/1998 | 6 | 4 | ○ | FRIDAY NIGHT FEVER | Polygram TV 5557332 |
| | 02/05/1998 | 18 | 1 | | CONNECTED | Polygram TV T21CD 1000 |
| | 09/05/1998 | 3 | 7 | ● | KISS GARAGE | Polygram TV 5558872 |
| | 16/05/1998 | 2 | 7 | ● | TOP OF THE POPS 1998 – VOLUME 1 | Polygram TV 5557132 |
| | 30/05/1998 | 4 | 7 | ○ | DAVE PEARCE PRESENTS DANCE ANTHEMS | Polygram TV 5559602 |
| | 27/06/1998 | 7 | 3 | ● | THE ULTIMATE SUMMER PARTY ALBUM | Polygram TV 5650502 |
| | 04/07/1998 | 3 | 8 | ● | MIXED EMOTIONS II | Polygram TV 5650342 |
| | 11/07/1998 | 5 | 5 | ○ | SISTERS OF SWING 98 | Polygram TV 5650762 |
| | 25/07/1998 | 4 | 4 | ● | KISS MIX '98 | Polygram TV 5652312 |
| | 01/08/1998 | 16 | 1 | | THE SUMMER OF LOVE GOES ON – SIXTIES | Polygram TV/Sony TV 5651312 |
| | 08/08/1998 | 4 | 11 | ● | RELAX! THE ULTIMATE 80'S MIX | Polygram TV 5652852 |
| | 15/08/1998 | 5 | 5 | ○ | ULTIMATE CLUB MIX 2 | Polygram TV 5652922 |
| | 29/08/1998 | 10 | 3 | ○ | SHINE 10 | Polygram TV 5650472 |
| | 05/09/1998 | 12 | 3 | | COOL GROOVES | Polygram TV 5651622 |
| | 12/09/1998 | 5 | 5 | ○ | POWER & SOUL | Polygram TV 5654422 |
| | 19/09/1998 | 2 | 7 | ● | KISS IN IBIZA '98 | Polygram TV 5654102 |
| | 26/09/1998 | 3 | 6 | ● | TOP OF THE POPS 1998 – VOLUME 2 | Polygram TV/BBC Music 5654362 |
| | 17/10/1998 | 5 | 3 | | DAVE PEARCE PRESENTS DANCE ANTHEMS VOLUME 2 | Polygram TV 5592622 |
| | 24/10/1998 | 13 | 2 | | MOBO 1998 – MUSIC OF BLACK ORIGIN | Polygram TV 5656592 |
| | 31/10/1998 | 12 | 1 | | THE BEST OF DRIVE TIME | Polygram TV 5654672 |
| | 07/11/1998 | 10 | 3 | ○ | SOUL | Polygram TV 5654332 |
| | 07/11/1998 | 13 | 1 | | ULTIMATE CLUB MIX – 98 | Polygram TV 5592782 |
| | 21/11/1998 | 5 | 17 | ✪ | WOMAN | Polygram TV/Sony TV 5654392 |
| | 28/11/1998 | 8 | 9 | ● | KISS ANTHEMS '98 | Polygram TV 5592652 |
| | 28/11/1998 | 11 | 2 | | TOP OF THE POPS – BEST OF 1998 | Polygram TV 5592752 |
| | 12/12/1998 | 5 | 20 | ✪ | MUSIC OF THE NIGHT | Polygram TV 5654962 |
| | 12/12/1998 | 11 | 7 | ✪ | THE ULTIMATE CHRISTMAS COLLECTION | Polygram TV 5654582 |
| | 09/01/1999 | 19 | 1 | ● | PARTY | Polygram TV 5654492 |
| | 06/02/1999 | 3 | 6 | ● | KISS SMOOTH GROOVES '99 | Polygram TV 5654452 |
| | 06/02/1999 | 8 | 3 | ○ | RELAX! THE ULTIMATE 80'S MIX – VOLUME 2 | Polygram TV 5640882 |
| | 13/02/1999 | ❶[1] | 12 | ✪ | LOVE SONGS | Polygram TV/warner.esp 5641122 |
| | 27/02/1999 | ❶[2] | 9 | ● | KISS HOUSE NATION | Polygram TV 5471862 |

## PORTRAIT UK label formed as an imprint of CBS.

| | DATE | POS | WKS | BPI | ALBUM TITLE | LABEL & NUMBER |
|---|---|---|---|---|---|---|
| | 16/08/1986 | 9 | 12 | ○ | THE HEAT IS ON – 16 TRACKS | Portrait PRT 10051 |
| | 16/08/1986 | 40 | 6 | | SUMMER DAYS, BOOGIE NIGHTS – 16 TRACKS | Portrait PRT 10052 |

## POSITIVA UK dance label formed in 1993 by Nick Halkes as an imprint of EMI. Halkes later went on to form Incentive Records.

| DATE | POS | WKS | BPI | ALBUM TITLE | LABEL & NUMBER |
|------|-----|-----|-----|-------------|----------------|
| 02/04/1994 | 15 | 1 | | PHASE ONE | Positiva CDTIVA 1002 |
| 26/04/1997 | 11 | 3 | | ACCESS ALL AREAS | Positiva CDTIVA 1015 |
| 24/05/2003 | 11 | 2 | | A DECADE OF DANCE | Positiva 5834792 |

### PRIORITY
US label formed in 1985 by Bryan Turner. The company was sold to EMI in 1997 for a total of $118 million.

| DATE | POS | WKS | BPI | ALBUM TITLE | LABEL & NUMBER |
|------|-----|-----|-----|-------------|----------------|
| 15/04/2000 | 13 | 8 | O | WWF AGGRESSION | Priority CDPTY 194 |

### PROTO

| DATE | POS | WKS | BPI | ALBUM TITLE | LABEL & NUMBER |
|------|-----|-----|-----|-------------|----------------|
| 26/11/1983 | 100 | 1 | | TWELVE INCHES OF PLEASURE | Proto 1 |

### PUMP

| DATE | POS | WKS | BPI | ALBUM TITLE | LABEL & NUMBER |
|------|-----|-----|-----|-------------|----------------|
| 20/07/1996 | 11 | 4 | | EIGHTIES SOUL WEEKENDER 2 | Pump DINCD 124 |
| 07/12/1996 | 17 | 3 | ● | THE VERY BEST OF PURE SWING | Pump DINCD 100 |
| 08/02/1997 | 10 | 3 | | SLOW JAMS | Pump DINCD 129 |
| 10/05/1997 | 15 | 2 | | EIGHTIES SOUL WEEKENDER 3 | Pump DINCD 138 |

### PURE MUSIC

| DATE | POS | WKS | BPI | ALBUM TITLE | LABEL & NUMBER |
|------|-----|-----|-----|-------------|----------------|
| 22/10/1994 | 9 | 4 | | THE LADY SINGS THE BLUES | Pure Music PMCD 7001 |
| 05/11/1994 | 11 | 4 | | THE GREATEST NUMBER ONES OF THE EIGHTIES | Pure Music PMCD 7003 |
| 11/02/1995 | ❶[2] | 11 | ● | DANCE MANIA 95 – VOLUME 1 | Pure Music PMCD 7008 |
| 08/04/1995 | ❶[2] | 9 | | DANCE MANIA 95 – VOLUME 2 | Pure Music PMCD 7010 |
| 15/07/1995 | ❶[3] | 7 | ● | DANCE MANIA 95 – VOLUME 3 | Pure Music PMCD 7013 |
| 30/09/1995 | 7 | 4 | | DANCE MANIA 95 – VOLUME 4 | Pure Music PMCD 7015 |
| 11/11/1995 | 5 | 11 | ● | THE BEST OF DANCE MANIA 95 | Pure Music PMCD 7025 |

### PURE SILK

| DATE | POS | WKS | BPI | ALBUM TITLE | LABEL & NUMBER |
|------|-----|-----|-----|-------------|----------------|
| 06/11/1999 | 15 | 2 | O | PURE SILK – A NEW DIMENSION | Pure Silk PURESCD 2 |
| 26/02/2000 | 12 | 3 | | PURE SILK – THE THIRD DIMENSION | Pure Silk PURESCD 3 |
| 01/07/2000 | 8 | 6 | | PURE SILK IN AYIA NAPA | Pure Silk PSRANCD 1 |
| 11/11/2000 | 20 | 1 | | GARAGE VIBES | Pure Silk VIBECD 1 |
| 09/06/2001 | 20 | 1 | | PURE SILK IN AYIA NAPA 2 | Pure Silk PSRANCD 2 |

### PYE
UK label formed in 1953 following the purchase of the Nixa label by the radio and TV manufacturer Pye. Following the further acquisition of Polygon Records (itself formed in 1949), Pye Records officially came into being in 1955. It launched the Pye International label in 1958 and Golden Guinea in the early 1960s, by which time the company was jointly owned by ATV (Associated Television). ATV acquired the rest of the company in 1966, but would lose the rights to the name Pye in 1980. Renamed PRT (Precision Records & Tapes) in 1980, the company was purchased by the Bell Group following its acquisition of ATV but in 1987 was subsequently sold to Roy Richards who reintroduced the Nixa label. It was subsequently sold again to Castle Communications in 1989 and later became part of the Sanctuary Group.

| DATE | POS | WKS | BPI | ALBUM TITLE | LABEL & NUMBER |
|------|-----|-----|-----|-------------|----------------|
| 09/05/1959 | 4 | 13 | | CURTAIN UP | Pye Nixa BRTH 0059 |
| 23/06/1962 | 13 | 7 | | HONEY HIT PARADE | Pye Golden Guinea GGL 0129 |
| 01/12/1962 | 19 | 2 | | ALL THE HITS BY ALL THE STARS | Pye Golden Guinea GGL 0162 |
| 07/09/1963 | 11 | 6 | | HITSVILLE | Pye Golden Guinea GGL 0202 |
| 14/09/1963 | 14 | 2 | | THE BEST OF RADIO LUXEMBOURG | Pye Golden Guinea GGL 0208 |
| 23/11/1963 | 20 | 1 | | HITSVILLE VOLUME 2 | Pye Golden Guinea GGL 0233 |
| 04/01/1964 | 15 | 3 | | THE BLUES VOLUME 1 | Pye NPL 28030 |
| 22/02/1964 | 16 | 4 | | FOLK FESTIVAL OF THE BLUES (LIVE RECORDING) | Pye NPL 28033 |
| 30/05/1964 | 16 | 3 | | THE BLUES VOLUME 2 | Pye NPL 28035 |
| 16/10/1971 | 36 | 1 | | PYE CHARTBUSTERS | Pye PCB 15000 |
| 18/12/1971 | 29 | 3 | | PYE CHARTBUSTERS VOLUME 2 | Pye PCB 15001 |

### QUALITY PRICE MUSIC

| DATE | POS | WKS | BPI | ALBUM TITLE | LABEL & NUMBER |
|------|-----|-----|-----|-------------|----------------|
| 04/11/1995 | 15 | 1 | ● | CLUB IBIZA | Quality Price Music QPMCD 1 |
| 30/03/1996 | 19 | 1 | | CLUB IBIZA SILVER EDITION | Quality Price Music QPMXCD 1 |
| 19/10/1996 | 19 | 1 | | CLUB IBIZA – VOLUME 2 | Quality Price Music QPMCD 6 |

### QUALITY TELEVISION

| DATE | POS | WKS | BPI | ALBUM TITLE | LABEL & NUMBER |
|------|-----|-----|-----|-------------|----------------|
| 15/02/1992 | 3 | 7 | | HIT THE DECKS VOLUME 1 – BATTLE OF THE DJS | Quality Price Music QTVCD 003 |
| 04/04/1992 | ❶[2] | 15 | | ALL WOMAN | Quality Price Music QTVCD 004 |
| 02/05/1992 | 3 | 8 | | TEMPTATION | Quality Price Music QTVCD 005 |
| 06/06/1992 | 4 | 6 | | THE SOUND OF SKA | Quality Price Music QTVCD 007 |
| 20/06/1992 | 7 | 4 | | TO HAVE AND TO HOLD – THE WEDDING ALBUM | Quality Price Music QTVCD 006 |
| 04/07/1992 | 3 | 6 | | HIT THE DECKS VOLUME 2 – BATTLE OF THE DJS | Quality Price Music QTVCD 008 |
| 11/07/1992 | 5 | 8 | | CELEBRATION – THE BEST OF REGGAE – 25 YEARS OF TROJAN | Quality Price Music QTVCD 0101 |
| 18/07/1992 | 16 | 3 | | DANGER ZONE VOLUME 1 | Quality Price Music QTVCD 009 |

▲[9] Number of weeks album topped the US chart ◆[12] RIAA Diamond Awards ◇[3] IFPI Platinum Europe Awards

| DATE | POS | WKS | BPI | ALBUM TITLE | LABEL & NUMBER |
|---|---|---|---|---|---|
| 12/09/1992 | 6 | 5 | | **THREE STEPS TO HEAVEN – ROCK 'N' ROLL LEGENDS** | Quality Price Music QTVCD 011 |
| 10/10/1992 | ❶[1] | 7 | | **ALL WOMAN 2** | Quality Price Music QTVCD 012 |
| 07/11/1992 | 3 | 4 | | **HIT THE DECKS VOLUME III** | Quality Price Music QTVCD 017 |
| 07/11/1992 | 4 | 7 | | **THE POWER OF LOVE** | Quality Price Music QTVCD 015 |
| 21/11/1992 | 7 | 14 | | **RARE GROOVE – DYNAMIC DISCO HITS** | Quality Price Music QTVCD 016 |
| 16/01/1993 | 19 | 1 | | ALL WOMAN – THE COMPLETE WOMAN | Quality Price Music QTVCD 019 |
| 30/01/1993 | 10 | 3 | | **THE NASHVILLE DREAM** | Quality Price Music QTVCD 014 |
| 08/05/1993 | 10 | 4 | | **GLAM MANIA** | Quality Price Music MANIACD 1 |
| 19/03/1994 | 2 | 11 | | **ALL WOMAN 3** | Quality Price Music ALLWOCD 3 |
| 03/12/1994 | 18 | 4 | | ALL WOMAN 4 | Quality Price Music ALLWOCD 4 |
| 07/10/1995 | 6 | 13 | | **THE BEST OF ALL WOMAN** | Quality Price Music BOWOCD 001 |

## R&S

| DATE | POS | WKS | BPI | ALBUM TITLE | LABEL & NUMBER |
|---|---|---|---|---|---|
| 16/11/1991 | 18 | 1 | | R&S RECORDS – ORDER TO DANCE | R&S RSLP 1 |
| 24/09/1994 | 16 | 1 | | IN ORDER TO DANCE 5 | R&S RS 94003CDXX |

## RCA

**RCA** US label formed in 1929. The Radio Corporation of America had, through its Victor label, the rights to the use of the famous dog and trumpet logo (the HMV logo for the UK). It launched the 45rpm single in 1949, later to become a worldwide standard for singles, but it was the signing of Elvis Presley in 1955 that enabled the company to become one of the most successful labels in the world. Sold to General Electric in 1985, the company was later purchased by the Bertelsmann company and became part of BMG.

| DATE | POS | WKS | BPI | ALBUM TITLE | LABEL & NUMBER |
|---|---|---|---|---|---|
| 28/05/1983 | 35 | 5 | | GET ON UP | RCA BSLP 5001 |
| 05/09/1987 | 80 | 1 | | RARE | RCA NL 90010 |
| 23/04/1988 | 88 | 1 | | RARE 2 | RCA PL 71681 |
| 13/05/1989 | 19 | 2 | | DIRTY DANCING – LIVE IN CONCERT | RCA BL 90336 |
| 24/06/1989 | 2 | 10 | | **RAINBOW WARRIORS** | RCA PL 74065 |
| 13/02/1993 | 6 | 10 | ○ | **CELTIC HEART** | RCA 74321131662 |
| 01/07/1995 | 13 | 4 | | PRIDE – THE VERY BEST OF SCOTLAND | RCA 74321284372 |
| 01/06/1996 | 10 | 6 | ○ | **THE BEAUTIFUL GAME – UEFA EURO '96** | RCA 74321382082 |
| 11/04/1998 | 19 | 1 | | EVERY WOMAN | RCA 74321573352 |

## REACHIN'

| DATE | POS | WKS | BPI | ALBUM TITLE | LABEL & NUMBER |
|---|---|---|---|---|---|
| 09/11/1991 | 18 | 2 | | RAVE | Reachin' REMULP 01 |

## REACT

| DATE | POS | WKS | BPI | ALBUM TITLE | LABEL & NUMBER |
|---|---|---|---|---|---|
| 22/06/1991 | 13 | 4 | | REACTIVATE VOLUME 1 – THE BELGIAN TECHNO ANTHEMS | React REACTLP 1 |
| 05/10/1991 | 9 | 4 | | **REACTIVATE VOLUME 2 – PHASERS ON FULL** | React REACTLP 2 |
| 16/05/1992 | 16 | 2 | | REACTIVATE VOLUME 4 – TECHNOVATION | React REACTCD 6 |
| 05/09/1992 | 18 | 2 | | REACTIVATE VOLUME 5 – PURE TRANCE AND TECHNO | React REACTCD 10 |
| 04/06/1994 | 20 | 1 | | FRESKA! | React REACTCD 39 |
| 24/09/1994 | 20 | 1 | | HOUSE NATION 1 | React REACTCD 48 |
| 03/06/1995 | 14 | 1 | | REACTIVATE 10 | React REACTCDX 060 |
| 12/08/1995 | 17 | 1 | | CAFE DEL MAR IBIZA – VOLUMEN DOS | React REACTCDL 062 |
| 10/08/1996 | 16 | 1 | | CAFE DEL MAR IBIZA – VOLUMEN TRES | React REACTCD 084 |
| 26/10/1996 | 14 | 1 | | REACTIVATE 11 – STINGER BEAT AND TECHNO RAYS | React REACTCDX 088 |
| 02/11/1996 | 16 | 1 | | LAURENT GARNIER – LABORATOIRE MIX | React REACTCD 87 |
| 10/05/1997 | 10 | 3 | | **BONKERS 2** | React REACTCD 101 |
| 21/06/1997 | 17 | 2 | | REACTIVATE 12 | React REACTCDX 102 |
| 01/11/1997 | 9 | 3 | ○ | **BONKERS 3 – JOURNEY INTO MADNESS** | React REACTCD 115 |
| 30/05/1998 | 8 | 4 | | **BONKERS 4 – WORLD FRENZY** | React REACTCD 122 |
| 07/11/1998 | 12 | 2 | | BONKERS 5 – ANARCHY IN THE UNIVERSE | React REACTCD 141 |
| 01/05/1999 | 10 | 4 | | **BONKERS 6 (WHEEL CRAZY)** | React REACTCD 150 |
| 16/10/1999 | 18 | 1 | | BONKERS 7 – MILLENNIUM MADNESS | React REACTCD 167 |
| 16/10/1999 | 18 | 3 | | TWICE AS NICE IN AYIA NAPA – DJ SPOONY | React REACTCD 164 |
| 17/05/2003 | 18 | 1 | | BONKERS X | React REACTCD 231 |
| 24/04/2004 | 7 | 4 | | **BONKERS 12** | React REACTCD 246 |

## REALLY USEFUL UK label formed by Andrew Lloyd Webber.

| DATE | POS | WKS | BPI | ALBUM TITLE | LABEL & NUMBER |
|---|---|---|---|---|---|
| 28/11/1992 | 2 | 11 | ✪ | **THE PREMIERE COLLECTION – ENCORE (ANDREW LLOYD WEBBER)** | Really Useful/Polydor 5173362 |

○ Silver disc ● Gold disc ✪ Platinum disc (additional platinum units are indicated by a figure following the symbol) ❶[9] Number of weeks album topped the UK chart

| DATE | POS | WKS | BPI | ALBUM TITLE | LABEL & NUMBER |
|---|---|---|---|---|---|
| 05/11/1994 | 3 | 18 | ✪² | THE VERY BEST OF ANDREW LLOYD WEBBER ◇ | Really Useful/Polydor 5238602 |
| 31/10/1998 | 3 | 4 | ● | SONGS FROM WHISTLE DOWN THE WIND | Really Useful/Polydor 5594412 |

**RECORD SHACK** UK record label formed by Jeff Weston. Record Shack began life as a record shop in Borehamwood before moving to London. Its first record was by Shakatak (who took their name from the shop), which was duly leased to Polydor.

| DATE | POS | WKS | BPI | ALBUM TITLE | LABEL & NUMBER |
|---|---|---|---|---|---|
| 08/09/1984 | 41 | 4 | | RECORD SHACK PRESENTS – VOLUME ONE | Record Shack RSTV 1 |

**REINFORCED**

| DATE | POS | WKS | BPI | ALBUM TITLE | LABEL & NUMBER |
|---|---|---|---|---|---|
| 29/05/1993 | 18 | 1 | | INFORCERS 3 | Reinforced RIVET 1242CD |

**RELENTLESS** UK urban label formed in 1999 as a joint venture between Shabs Jonaputra and Paul Franklyn with the Ministry of Sound label. The label went into liquidation in 2003.

| DATE | POS | WKS | BPI | ALBUM TITLE | LABEL & NUMBER |
|---|---|---|---|---|---|
| 26/01/2002 | 3 | 4 | | SO SOLID CREW – FUCK IT | Relentless REL 004CD |
| 09/03/2002 | 11 | 3 | | OLD SKOOL JUNGLE | Relentless RELEN 005CD |
| 27/07/2002 | 16 | 2 | | OLD SKOOL REGGAE | Relentless RELEN 008CD |

**RENNAISSANCE MUSIC**

| DATE | POS | WKS | BPI | ALBUM TITLE | LABEL & NUMBER |
|---|---|---|---|---|---|
| 18/10/1997 | 16 | 2 | | RENAISSANCE WORLDWIDE LONDON | Renaissance Music RENWW 1CD |
| 01/04/2000 | 18 | 1 | | RENAISSANCE – AWAKENING – DAVE SEAMAN | Renaissance Music RENCD 1 |
| 19/08/2000 | 20 | 1 | | RENAISSANCE IBIZA – MIXED BY DEEP DISH | Renaissance Records REN 2CD |
| 17/03/2001 | 17 | 1 | | PROGRESSION VOLUME 1 | Renaissance Music REN 3CD |
| 28/07/2001 | 2 | 5 | | RENAISSANCE IBIZA 2001 | Renaissance REN 5CD |

**REPRISE** US label formed by Frank Sinatra in 1960 after his contract with Capitol Records had expired. Aside from Sinatra, other artists linked to the label included Sammy Davis Jr and Dean Martin and the company was sold to Warner Brothers in 1963 as part of a deal that tied Frank Sinatra to the Warner Brothers film studio. It subsequently became part of the Warner Music Group.

| DATE | POS | WKS | BPI | ALBUM TITLE | LABEL & NUMBER |
|---|---|---|---|---|---|
| 22/11/2003 | 14 | 3 | | LIVE & SWINGING – THE ULTIMATE RAT PACK | Reprise 8122737362 |

**RESPOND** UK label formed by former Jam founder Paul Weller.

| DATE | POS | WKS | BPI | ALBUM TITLE | LABEL & NUMBER |
|---|---|---|---|---|---|
| 15/10/1983 | 50 | 3 | | RESPOND PACKAGE – LOVE THE REASON | Respond RRL 501 |

**RHYTHM KING**

| DATE | POS | WKS | BPI | ALBUM TITLE | LABEL & NUMBER |
|---|---|---|---|---|---|
| 06/06/1987 | 67 | 2 | | CHICAGO JACKBEAT VOLUME 2 | Rhythm King LEFTLP 2 |

**RITZ**

| DATE | POS | WKS | BPI | ALBUM TITLE | LABEL & NUMBER |
|---|---|---|---|---|---|
| 18/06/1983 | 37 | 6 | | TEARDROPS | Ritz RITZSP 399 |

**RONCO** Canadian label formed in the UK in 1972, having made its reputation in its home country for selling carpet cleaners and other household goods. Along with K-Tel it helped establish the concept of TV-marketed compilation albums, although it also branched out to releasing film soundtracks. It went into bankruptcy in 1984.

| DATE | POS | WKS | BPI | ALBUM TITLE | LABEL & NUMBER |
|---|---|---|---|---|---|
| 21/10/1972 | 2 | 13 | | 20 STAR TRACKS | Ronco PP 2001 |
| 23/06/1973 | ❶⁷ | 8 | | THAT'LL BE THE DAY | Ronco MR 2002/3 |
| 08/11/1975 | 17 | 8 | | BLAZING BULLETS | Ronco RTI 2012 |
| 06/12/1975 | 11 | 12 | ● | GREATEST HITS OF WALT DISNEY | Ronco RTD 2013 |
| 06/12/1975 | 39 | 5 | | A CHRISTMAS GIFT | Ronco P 12430 |
| 24/01/1976 | 9 | 5 | | STAR TRACKIN' 76 | Ronco RTL 2014 |
| 08/01/1977 | 24 | 12 | ✪ | CLASSICAL GOLD | Ronco RTD 42020 |
| 16/07/1977 | 57 | 1 | | SUPERGROUPS | Ronco RTL 2023 |
| 26/11/1977 | 26 | 13 | ● | BLACK JOY | Ronco RTL 2025 |
| 18/03/1978 | 5 | 7 | ✪² | BOOGIE NIGHTS | Ronco RTL 2027 |
| 18/11/1978 | 15 | 11 | ● | BOOGIE FEVER | Ronco RTL 2034 |
| 09/06/1979 | 54 | 3 | | ROCK LEGENDS | Ronco RTL 2037 |
| 03/11/1979 | 3 | 11 | ✪ | ROCK 'N' ROLLER DISCO | Ronco RTL 2040 |
| 08/12/1979 | 6 | 18 | ✪ | PEACE IN THE VALLEY | Ronco RTL 2043 |
| 22/12/1979 | 62 | 3 | | MILITARY GOLD | Ronco RTD 42042 |
| 25/10/1980 | 29 | 5 | | STREET LEVEL | Ronco RTL 2048 |
| 08/11/1980 | 9 | 12 | ● | COUNTRY LEGENDS | Ronco RTL 2050 |
| 15/11/1980 | 13 | 9 | ● | RADIOACTIVE | Ronco RTL 2049 |
| 29/11/1980 | 47 | 3 | ● | SPACE INVADERS | Ronco RTL 2051 |
| 06/12/1980 | 24 | 6 | ● | THE LEGENDARY BIG BANDS | Ronco RTL 2047 |
| 09/05/1981 | ❶¹ | 23 | ● | DISCO DAZE AND DISCO NITES | Ronco RTL 2057 A/B |
| 19/09/1981 | 2 | 17 | ✪ | SUPER HITS 1 & 2 | Ronco RTL 2058 A/B |
| 24/10/1981 | 27 | 11 | ● | COUNTRY SUNRISE/COUNTRY SUNSET | Ronco RTL 2057 A/B |
| 14/11/1981 | 44 | 9 | ● | ROCK HOUSE | Ronco RTL 2061 |
| 12/12/1981 | 44 | 5 | | MISTY MORNINGS | Ronco RTL 2066 |
| 12/12/1981 | 84 | 4 | | MEMORIES ARE MADE OF THIS | Ronco RTL 2062 |
| 19/12/1981 | 30 | 9 | ● | WE ARE MOST AMUSED (THE BEST OF BRITISH COMEDY) | Ronco/Charisma RTD 2067 |
| 26/12/1981 | 2 | 10 | ✪ | HITS, HITS, HITS | Ronco RTL 2063 |
| 24/04/1982 | 7 | 10 | ● | DISCO UK AND DISCO USA | Ronco RTL 2073 |

▲⁹ Number of weeks album topped the US chart ◆¹² RIAA Diamond Awards ◇³ IFPI Platinum Europe Awards

| | | | | |
|---|---|---|---|---|
| 15/05/1982 . . . . . 3 . . . . . . 10 . . . . . . ● | **CHARTBUSTERS 82** . . . . . . . . . . . . . . . . . . . . . . . . . . . . . . . . . . . . . . . . . . . . . . . . . . . . Ronco RTL 2074 |
| 03/07/1982 . . . . . 10 . . . . . . 8 . . . . . . ○ | **OVERLOAD** . . . . . . . . . . . . . . . . . . . . . . . . . . . . . . . . . . . . . . . . . . . . . . . . . . . . . . . . . Ronco RTL 2079 |
| 28/08/1982 . . . . . 25 . . . . . 10 . . . . . ○ | SOUL DAZE/SOUL NITES . . . . . . . . . . . . . . . . . . . . . . . . . . . . . . . . . . . . . . . . . . . . . . . Ronco RTL 2080 |
| 11/09/1982 . . . . . 4 . . . . . . 8 . . . . . . ● | BREAKOUT . . . . . . . . . . . . . . . . . . . . . . . . . . . . . . . . . . . . . . . . . . . . . . . . . . . . . . . . . . Ronco RTL 2081 |
| 30/10/1982 . . . . . 41 . . . . . 10 . . . . . ● | MUSIC FOR THE SEASONS . . . . . . . . . . . . . . . . . . . . . . . . . . . . . . . . . . . . . . . . . . . . . . Ronco RTL 2075 |
| 27/11/1982 . . . . . 30 . . . . . 7 . . . . . . ● | CHART WARS . . . . . . . . . . . . . . . . . . . . . . . . . . . . . . . . . . . . . . . . . . . . . . . . . . . . . . . . . Ronco RTL 2086 |
| 27/11/1982 . . . . . 38 . . . . . 7 . . . . . . ○ | THE GREAT COUNTRY MUSIC SHOW . . . . . . . . . . . . . . . . . . . . . . . . . . . . . . . . . . . . . . . Ronco RTD 2083 |
| 18/12/1982 . . . . . 49 . . . . . 10 . . . . . ● | THE BEST OF THE COMPOSERS: BEETHOVEN/STRAUSS/TCHAIKOVSKY/MOZART . . . . . . . . . . . . . Ronco RTL 2084 |
| 25/12/1982 . . . . . ❶² . . . . 17 . . . . . ✪ | **RAIDERS OF THE POP CHARTS** . . . . . . . . . . . . . . . . . . . . . . . . . . . . . . . . . . . . . . . . . . Ronco RTL 2088 |
| 19/03/1983 . . . . . 4 . . . . . . 13 . . . . . ● | **CHART RUNNERS** . . . . . . . . . . . . . . . . . . . . . . . . . . . . . . . . . . . . . . . . . . . . . . . . . . . Ronco RTL 2090 |
| 21/05/1983 . . . . . 5 . . . . . . 10 . . . . . ● | **CHART ENCOUNTERS OF THE HIT KIND** . . . . . . . . . . . . . . . . . . . . . . . . . . . . . . . . . . . Ronco RTL 2091 |
| 18/06/1983 . . . . . 12 . . . . . 13 . . . . . ● | LOVERS ONLY . . . . . . . . . . . . . . . . . . . . . . . . . . . . . . . . . . . . . . . . . . . . . . . . . . . . . . . Ronco RTL 2093 |
| 16/07/1983 . . . . . 11 . . . . . 10 . . . . . ● | HITS ON FIRE . . . . . . . . . . . . . . . . . . . . . . . . . . . . . . . . . . . . . . . . . . . . . . . . . . . . . . . Ronco RTL 2095 |
| 17/09/1983 . . . . . 4 . . . . . . 9 . . . . . . | **THE HIT SQUAD – CHART TRACKING** . . . . . . . . . . . . . . . . . . . . . . . . . . . . . . . . . . . . . Ronco RON LP 1 |
| 17/09/1983 . . . . . 28 . . . . . 7 . . . . . . | THE HIT SQUAD – NIGHT CLUBBING . . . . . . . . . . . . . . . . . . . . . . . . . . . . . . . . . . . . . . . Ronco RON LP 2 |
| 12/11/1983 . . . . . 12 . . . . . 11 . . . . . ● | THE HIT SQUAD – HITS OF '83 . . . . . . . . . . . . . . . . . . . . . . . . . . . . . . . . . . . . . . . . . . . Ronco RON LP 4 |
| 17/12/1983 . . . . . 6 . . . . . . 17 . . . . . ● | **GREEN VELVET** . . . . . . . . . . . . . . . . . . . . . . . . . . . . . . . . . . . . . . . . . . . . . . . . . . . . Ronco RON LP 6 |
| 07/01/1984 . . . . . 20 . . . . . 9 . . . . . . | CHART TREK VOLUMES 1 AND 2 . . . . . . . . . . . . . . . . . . . . . . . . . . . . . . . . . . . . . . . . . . Ronco RON LP 8 |
| 21/01/1984 . . . . . 8 . . . . . . 14 . . . . . | **SOMETIMES WHEN WE TOUCH** . . . . . . . . . . . . . . . . . . . . . . . . . . . . . . . . . . . . . . . . Ronco RON LP 9 |
| 24/03/1984 . . . . . 47 . . . . . . 6 . . . . . | BABY LOVE . . . . . . . . . . . . . . . . . . . . . . . . . . . . . . . . . . . . . . . . . . . . . . . . . . . . . . . . Ronco RON LP 11 |
| 07/04/1984 . . . . . 75 . . . . . . 2 . . . . . | DREAMS AND THEMES . . . . . . . . . . . . . . . . . . . . . . . . . . . . . . . . . . . . . . . . . . . . . . . Ronco RON LP 10 |

## ROUGH TRADE

UK label formed in London in 1978 by Geoff Travis which evolved from the Rough Trade retail outlet that had opened in 1976. Having established a reputation for being able to supply the leading punk imports, its first release in 1978 heralded the arrival of industrial rock. Travis later launched the Blanco Y Negro label.

| | | | | |
|---|---|---|---|---|
| 14/08/1982 . . . . . 66 . . . . . . 3 . . . . . | SOWETO . . . . . . . . . . . . . . . . . . . . . . . . . . . . . . . . . . . . . . . . . . . . . . . . . . . . . . . Rough Trade ROUGH 37 |

## RUMOUR

| | | | | |
|---|---|---|---|---|
| 16/09/1989 . . . . . 15 . . . . . . 4 . . . . . | WAREHOUSE RAVES . . . . . . . . . . . . . . . . . . . . . . . . . . . . . . . . . . . . . . . . . . . . . . Rumour RUMLD 101 |
| 31/03/1990 . . . . . 12 . . . . . . 5 . . . . . | WAREHOUSE RAVES 3 . . . . . . . . . . . . . . . . . . . . . . . . . . . . . . . . . . . . . . . . . . . . . . Rumour RUMLD 103 |
| 29/09/1990 . . . . . 13 . . . . . . 3 . . . . . | WAREHOUSE RAVES 4 . . . . . . . . . . . . . . . . . . . . . . . . . . . . . . . . . . . . . . . . . . . . . . Rumour RUMLD 104 |
| 11/05/1991 . . . . . 18 . . . . . . 1 . . . . . | WAREHOUSE RAVES 5 . . . . . . . . . . . . . . . . . . . . . . . . . . . . . . . . . . . . . . . . . . . . . . Rumour RUMLD 105 |
| 20/07/1991 . . . . . 20 . . . . . . 1 . . . . . | BREAKS, BASS AND BLEEPS 2 . . . . . . . . . . . . . . . . . . . . . . . . . . . . . . . . . . . . . . . . . . Rumour RAID 504 |
| 21/03/1992 . . . . . 16 . . . . . . 2 . . . . . | WAREHOUSE RAVES 6 . . . . . . . . . . . . . . . . . . . . . . . . . . . . . . . . . . . . . . . . . . . . . Rumour CDRUMD 106 |
| 18/04/1992 . . . . . 20 . . . . . . 1 . . . . . | BREAKS, BASS AND BLEEPS 4 . . . . . . . . . . . . . . . . . . . . . . . . . . . . . . . . . . . . . . . . . Rumour CDRAID 507 |
| 27/06/1992 . . . . . 20 . . . . . . 1 . . . . . | MOVIN' ON . . . . . . . . . . . . . . . . . . . . . . . . . . . . . . . . . . . . . . . . . . . . . . . . . . . . . Rumour RULCD 300 |
| 29/08/1992 . . . . . 20 . . . . . . 1 . . . . . | WAREHOUSE RAVES 7 . . . . . . . . . . . . . . . . . . . . . . . . . . . . . . . . . . . . . . . . . . . . . Rumour CDRUMD 107 |
| 26/09/1992 . . . . . 18 . . . . . . 1 . . . . . | TRANCE . . . . . . . . . . . . . . . . . . . . . . . . . . . . . . . . . . . . . . . . . . . . . . . . . . . . . . . Rumour CDRAID 508 |
| 24/10/1992 . . . . . 15 . . . . . . 2 . . . . . | MOVIN' ON 2 . . . . . . . . . . . . . . . . . . . . . . . . . . . . . . . . . . . . . . . . . . . . . . . . . . . . Rumour RULCD 301 |

## S RECORDS
UK label formed by record company executive Simon Cowell as an imprint within BMG.

| | | | | |
|---|---|---|---|---|
| 20/04/2002 . . . . ❶⁴ . . . . 10 . . . . . . ✪² | **POP IDOL – THE BIG BAND ALBUM** . . . . . . . . . . . . . . . . . . . . . . . . . . . . . . . . . . . . . . . . S 74321932412 |
| 20/12/2003 . . . . . 2 . . . . . . 3 . . . . . | THE IDOLS – THE XMAS FACTOR . . . . . . . . . . . . . . . . . . . . . . . . . . . . . . . . . . . . . . . . . S 82876581592 |

## SANCTUARY
UK label formed in 1977 by Andy Taylor and Rod Smallwood. The pair had first met in 1969 at college and formed Smallwood Taylor Enterprises in 1976, the company subsequently becoming Sanctuary a year later as an artist management company. It launched the label in the early 1990s and later acquired Castle Communications and its catalogue, including Pye and Immediate, later adding Trojan and CMC to form the Sanctuary Group.

| | | | | |
|---|---|---|---|---|
| 08/02/2003 . . . . . 2 . . . . . . 6 . . . . . . ● | **REGGAE LOVE SONGS: 50 JAMAICAN LOVERS CLASSICS** . . . . . . . . . . . . . . . . . . . . . . . . . . . Sanctuary TDSAN 001 |
| 17/04/2004 . . . . . 12 . . . . . . 3 . . . . . | THE ESSENTIAL ACOUSTIC ALBUM . . . . . . . . . . . . . . . . . . . . . . . . . . . . Sanctuary/BMG TV TDSAN010 |

## SATELLITE

| | | | | |
|---|---|---|---|---|
| 19/07/1997 . . . . . 20 . . . . . . 1 . . . . . | TUFF JAM PRESENTS UNDERGROUND FREQUENCIES – 1 . . . . . . . . . . . . . . . . . . . . . Satellite 74321494672 |
| 23/05/1998 . . . . . 14 . . . . . . 2 . . . . . | TUFF JAM PRESENTS UNDERGROUND FREQUENCIES – 2 . . . . . . . . . . . . . . . . . . . . . Satellite 74321564462 |

## SAVE THE CHILDREN FUND

| | | | | |
|---|---|---|---|---|
| 10/09/1966 . . . . . 6 . . . . . . 16 . . . . . | **STARS CHARITY FANTASIA SAVE THE CHILDREN FUND** . . . . . . . . . . . . . . . . . . . . . . . . . . . . . SCF PL 145 |

## SECRET

| | | | | |
|---|---|---|---|---|
| 31/10/1981 . . . . . 60 . . . . . . 4 . . . . . | CARRY ON OI! . . . . . . . . . . . . . . . . . . . . . . . . . . . . . . . . . . . . . . . . . . . . . . . . . . . . . . . . . Secret SEC 2 |
| 25/09/1982 . . . . . 54 . . . . . . 4 . . . . . | OI! OI! THAT'S YER LOT . . . . . . . . . . . . . . . . . . . . . . . . . . . . . . . . . . . . . . . . . . . . . . . . Secret SEC 5 |

## SERIOUS

| | | | | |
|---|---|---|---|---|
| 07/06/1986 . . . . . 17 . . . . . 10 . . . . . | UPFRONT 1 – 14 DANCE TRACKS . . . . . . . . . . . . . . . . . . . . . . . . . . . . . . . . . . . . . . . . . . . . Serious UPFT 1 |
| 23/08/1986 . . . . . 27 . . . . . . 6 . . . . . | UPFRONT 2 – 14 DANCE TRACKS . . . . . . . . . . . . . . . . . . . . . . . . . . . . . . . . . . . . . . . . . . . . Serious UPFT 2 |
| 01/11/1986 . . . . . 37 . . . . . . 5 . . . . . | UPFRONT 3 . . . . . . . . . . . . . . . . . . . . . . . . . . . . . . . . . . . . . . . . . . . . . . . . . . . . . . . . . . Serious UPFT 3 |
| 31/01/1987 . . . . . 21 . . . . . . 5 . . . . . | UPFRONT 4 . . . . . . . . . . . . . . . . . . . . . . . . . . . . . . . . . . . . . . . . . . . . . . . . . . . . . . . . . . Serious UPFT 4 |
| 28/03/1987 . . . . . 21 . . . . . . 6 . . . . . | UPFRONT 5 . . . . . . . . . . . . . . . . . . . . . . . . . . . . . . . . . . . . . . . . . . . . . . . . . . . . . . . . . . Serious UPFT 5 |
| 28/03/1987 . . . . . 95 . . . . . . 1 . . . . . | SERIOUS HIP-HOP 2 . . . . . . . . . . . . . . . . . . . . . . . . . . . . . . . . . . . . . . . . . . . . . . . . . . Serious SHOP 2 |

○ Silver disc　● Gold disc　✪ Platinum disc (additional platinum units are indicated by a figure following the symbol)　❶⁹ Number of weeks album topped the UK chart

| DATE | POS | WKS | BPI | ALBUM TITLE | LABEL & NUMBER |
|---|---|---|---|---|---|
| 23/05/1987 | 22 | 6 | | UPFRONT 6 | Serious UPFT 6 |
| 04/07/1987 | 55 | 12 | | THE BEST OF HOUSE VOLUME 1 | Serious BEHO 1 |
| 15/08/1987 | 31 | 4 | | UPFRONT 7 | Serious UPFT 7 |
| 12/09/1987 | 30 | 7 | | BEST OF HOUSE VOLUME 2 | Serious BEHO 2 |
| 17/10/1987 | 22 | 6 | | UPFRONT 8 | Serious UPFT 8 |
| 17/10/1987 | 81 | 1 | | HIP-HOP '87 | Serious HHOP 87 |
| 14/11/1987 | 61 | 3 | | BEST OF HOUSE VOLUME 3 | Serious BEHO 3 |
| 12/12/1987 | 77 | 4 | | BEST OF HOUSE MEGAMIX | Serious BOIT 1 |
| 19/12/1987 | 92 | 1 | | UPFRONT 9 | Serious UPFT 9 |
| 20/02/1988 | 59 | 2 | | DANCE MANIA VOLUME 2 | Serious DAMA 2 |
| 12/03/1988 | 27 | 8 | | BEST OF HOUSE VOLUME 4 | Serious BEHO 4 |
| 09/04/1988 | 45 | 5 | | UPFRONT 10 | Serious UPFT 10 |
| 14/05/1988 | 73 | 2 | | BEST OF HOUSE MEGAMIX VOLUME 2 | Serious BOIT 2 |
| 29/10/1988 | 93 | 1 | | ACID TRAX MAGAMIX VOLUME 1 | Serious DUIX 1 |
| 18/02/1989 | 15 | 1 | | UPFRONT 89 | Serious UPFT 89 |
| 21/09/2002 | 18 | 2 | | JUDGE JULES PRESENTS TRIED AND TESTED | Serious 0690572 |

### SHUT UP AND DANCE
UK hip hop and dance label formed by PJ and Smiley. They also record as Shut Up And Dance.

| DATE | POS | WKS | BPI | ALBUM TITLE | LABEL & NUMBER |
|---|---|---|---|---|---|
| 22/02/1992 | 20 | 1 | | SHUT UP AND DANCE | Shut Up And Dance SUADCOMPCD 001 |

### SIX6

| DATE | POS | WKS | BPI | ALBUM TITLE | LABEL & NUMBER |
|---|---|---|---|---|---|
| 01/10/1994 | 9 | 5 | ◯ | RENAISSANCE | SIX6 REMNIX 1CD |
| 06/07/1996 | 12 | 3 | | RENAISSANCE THE MIX COLLECTION – PART 3 | SIX6 RENMIXCD 3 |

### SLINKY MUSIC

| DATE | POS | WKS | BPI | ALBUM TITLE | LABEL & NUMBER |
|---|---|---|---|---|---|
| 17/02/2001 | 17 | 1 | | SLINKY PRESENTS SUPERCLUB DJ'S – GUY ORNADEL | Slinky Music SLINKYCD 005 |

### SOLAR SYSTEM

| DATE | POS | WKS | BPI | ALBUM TITLE | LABEL & NUMBER |
|---|---|---|---|---|---|
| 30/05/1987 | 70 | 1 | | THE SOLAR SYSTEM | Solar MCG 3338 |

### SOLID STATE

| DATE | POS | WKS | BPI | ALBUM TITLE | LABEL & NUMBER |
|---|---|---|---|---|---|
| 08/02/1997 | 16 | 1 | | HIP HOP DON'T STOP – 20 CLASSIC HIP HOP SUPERJAMS | Solid State SOLIDSCD 6 |
| 29/03/1997 | 17 | 2 | | HOUSE OF HANDBAG – NUOVO DISCO COLLECTION | Solid State SOLIDSCD 7 |

### SOME BIZARRE
UK label formed by Stevo (real name Steven Pearse), the manager of acts such as Soft Cell and The The.

| DATE | POS | WKS | BPI | ALBUM TITLE | LABEL & NUMBER |
|---|---|---|---|---|---|
| 14/03/1981 | 58 | 1 | | THE SOME BIZZARE ALBUM | Some Bizarre BZLP 1 |

### SONY
Japanese label formed in 1988 following the acquisition of CBS/Columbia for $2 billion by the electronic giant Sony.

| DATE | POS | WKS | BPI | ALBUM TITLE | LABEL & NUMBER |
|---|---|---|---|---|---|
| 25/11/1995 | 4 | 11 | ✪ | THIS YEAR'S LOVE IS FOREVER | Sony TV/Global TV MOODCD 42 |
| 13/04/1996 | 6 | 6 | | IT TAKES TWO | Sony TV/Global TV MOODCD 43 |
| 13/07/1996 | 17 | 1 | | MUNDO AFRIKA | Polygram TV/Sony TV MOODCD 44 |
| 31/08/1996 | 2 | 10 | ✪ | FRESH HITS 96 | warner.esp/Global TV/Sony TV MOODCD 46 |
| 09/11/1996 | ❶² | 12 | ✪ | HUGE HITS 1996 | warner.esp/Global TV/Sony TV MOODCD 50 |
| 30/11/1996 | 12 | 7 | ● | THIS YEAR'S LOVE (WILL LAST FOREVER) XXX | Sony TV/Global TV MOODCD 49 |
| 21/12/1996 | 2 | 13 | ✪ | HITS 97 | warner.esp/Global TV/Sony TV MOODCD 48 |
| 01/02/1997 | 3 | 5 | | ABSOLUTE GOLD | Sony TV SONYTV 22CD |
| 08/11/1997 | 7 | 4 | ● | THE ALL TIME GREATEST ROCK SONGS | Sony TV/warner.esp MOODCD 53 |
| 04/04/1998 | ❶² | 12 | ✪ | NEW HITS 98 | warner.esp/Global TV/Sony TV MOODCD 57 |
| 18/04/1998 | 18 | 1 | | LOVE TRAIN – THE SOUND OF PHILADELPHIA | Sony TV/MCI MOODCD 56 |
| 04/07/1998 | ❶⁶ | 17 | ✪ | FRESH HITS 98 | warner.esp/Global TV/Sony TV MOODCD 59 |
| 19/09/1998 | ❶⁵ | 9 | | BIG HITS 98 | warner.esp/Global TV/Sony TV MOODCD 60 |
| 07/11/1998 | ❶² | 11 | ✪ | HUGE HITS 1998 | warner.esp/Global TV/Sony TV MOODCD 62 |
| 07/11/1998 | 3 | 8 | ● | THE ALL TIME GREATEST MOVIE SONGS | Sony TV/Polygram TV MOODCD 61 |
| 19/12/1998 | 2 | 14 | ✪² | HITS 99 | warner.esp/Global TV/Sony TV MOODCD 64 |
| 26/06/1999 | 14 | 3 | | THE CELTIC COLLECTION | warner.esp/Columbia MOODCD 65 |
| 13/11/1999 | 7 | 4 | | THE ALL TIME GREATEST MOVIE SONGS – VOLUME TWO | Sony TV/Universal Music TV MOODCD 67 |
| 27/11/1999 | 9 | 8 | ✪ | THE ALL TIME GREATEST LOVE SONGS – VOLUME 4 | Sony TV/Universal Music TV MOODCD 68 |
| 20/05/2000 | 20 | 1 | | ALAN TITCHMARSH – IN A COUNTRY GARDEN | Sony Classical SONYTV 85CD |

▲⁹ Number of weeks album topped the US chart  ◆¹² RIAA Diamond Awards  ◇³ IFPI Platinum Europe Awards

| | 24/06/2000 | 17 | 1 | | AMERICAN DREAM | Sony TV/warner.esp MOODCD 69 |
| | 02/12/2000 | 20 | 1 | ✪ | THE ALL TIME GREATEST LOVE SONGS | Sony TV/Universal TV MOODCD 71 |
| | 13/10/2001 | 13 | 3 | | MOBO 2001 – THE ALBUM | BMG/Sony/Telstar MOODCD 72 |
| | 06/04/2002 | 11 | 2 | | THE CLASSIC SCORE | Sony TV/Decca MOODCD 73 |
| | 21/09/2002 | 4 | 6 | ○ | **KERRANG! 4 – THE ALBUM** | Sony TV/Universal TV 691442 |
| | 10/05/2003 | 8 | 4 | | **NU SOUL** | Sony Music STVCD 161 |
| | 14/06/2003 | 4 | 8 | ● | **ALWAYS & FOREVER** | Sony Music STVCD 163 |
| | 20/09/2003 | 8 | 3 | | **LET'S GROOVE AGAIN** | Sony Music STVCD 168 |
| | 27/09/2003 | 2 | 5 | | **HOT CITY NIGHTS** | Sony Music STVCD 167 |
| | 18/10/2003 | 4 | 4 | | **THE VERY BEST OF ALL WOMAN** | Sony/BMG/Telstar MOODCD 77 |
| | 25/10/2003 | 8 | 2 | | **ALWAYS & FOREVER II** | Sony Music TV STVCD 170 |
| | 14/02/2004 | 4 | 4 | | **MY HEART WILL GO ON** | Sony Music TV STVCD 173 |
| | 20/03/2004 | 14 | 3 | | FIRST LADIES OF COUNTRY | Sony TV/Universal TV MOODCD 81 |
| | 03/04/2004 | 10 | 2 | | **SOUL MAN** | Sony Music TV STVCD 177 |
| | 05/06/2004 | 2 | 4+ | | **MORE THAN A FEELING** | Sony Music TV STVCD 183 |
| | 12/06/2004 | 7 | 3+ | | **BACK TO THE 80S** | Sony Music TV STVCD 184 |
| | 19/06/2004 | 11 | 2+ | | HEROES | Sony Music TV STVCD 182 |

## SOUND DIMENSION

| | 05/08/1995 | 10 | 10 | ○ | **A RETROSPECTIVE OF HOUSE '91–'95 – VOLUME 1** | Sound Dimension SDIMCD 3 |
| | 13/01/1996 | 15 | 3 | ○ | A RETROSPECTIVE OF HOUSE '91–'95 – VOLUME 2 | Sound Dimension SDIMCD 4 |
| | 01/06/1996 | 9 | 2 | | **A RETROSPECTIVE OF HOUSE '91–'96 – VOLUME 3: JAY/KELLY/ANDERSON** | Sound Dimension SDIMCD 5 |
| | 07/09/1996 | 7 | 5 | | **A RETROSPECTIVE OF HOUSE '91–'96 – VOLUME 4** | Sound Dimension SDIMCD 6 |
| | 01/02/1997 | 18 | 2 | ○ | AN INTROSPECTIVE OF HOUSE: 1ST DIMENSION | Sound Dimension SDIMCD 7 |
| | 14/06/1997 | 9 | 4 | | **AN INTROSPECTIVE OF HOUSE: 2ND DIMENSION** | Sound Dimension SDIMCD 8 |
| | 13/09/1997 | 14 | 2 | | AN INTROSPECTIVE OF HOUSE: 3RD DIMENSION | Sound Dimension SDIMCD 9 |

## SOUTHERN FRIED
UK dance label formed by DJ and musician Fatboy Slim (born Quentin Cook, 31/7/1963, Brighton, also known as Norman Cook).

| | 09/03/2002 | 19 | 1 | | FATBOY SLIM – LIVE ON BRIGHTON BEACH | Southern Fried ECB 26CD |
| | 19/10/2002 | 11 | 2 | | BIG BEACH BOUTIQUE II | Southern Fried ECB 34CDX |

## SPRINGTIME

| | 12/12/1981 | 69 | 4 | | THE SECRET POLICEMAN'S OTHER BALL | Springtime HAHA 6003 |
| | 20/03/1982 | 29 | 5 | | THE SECRET POLICEMAN'S OTHER BALL (THE MUSIC) | Springtime HAHA 6004 |

## STARBLEND

| | 12/11/1983 | 89 | 2 | | IN TOUCH | Starblend STD 9 |
| | 23/06/1984 | 48 | 7 | | BROKEN DREAMS | Starblend SLTD 1 |
| | 27/04/1985 | 77 | 2 | | 12 X 12 MEGA MIXES | Starblend INCH 1 |
| | 03/08/1985 | 43 | 8 | | AMERICAN DREAMS | Starblend SLTD 12 |
| | 21/12/1985 | 94 | 1 | | CHRISTMAS AT THE COUNTRY STORE | Starblend NOEL 1 |
| | 12/07/1986 | 60 | 3 | | DISCOVER COUNTRY/DISCOVER NEW COUNTRY | Starblend DNC 1 |
| | 16/08/1986 | 38 | 8 | | HEARTBREAKERS – 18 CLASSICAL LOVE HITS | Starblend BLEND 3 |
| | 20/09/1986 | 88 | 1 | | ABSOLUTE ROCK 'N' ROLL | Starblend SLTD 15 |

## START

| | 15/04/1989 | 13 | 5 | | THE SONGS OF BOB DYLAN | START STDL 20 |

## STAX
US label formed in Memphis, TN in 1961 by Jim Stewart and his sister Estelle Axton, after an earlier label Satellite Records was forced to close after objections from another company with the same name. With subsidiary labels Enterprise and Volt, Stax became one of the leading R&B labels in the US thanks to artists such as Isaac Hayes and Booker T & The MGs. Initially linking with Atlantic, Stax was responsible for breaking Otis Redding but ended its association with Atlantic in 1968 and became part of the Gulf & Western group. Jim Stewart bought back the label in 1970 thanks to a loan from Polydor Records, but by 1976 the label was declared bankrupt and its back catalogue was bought by Fantasy Records.

| | 08/04/1967 | 10 | 16 | | **HIT THE ROAD STAX** | Stax 589005 |

## STIFF
UK new wave label formed in 1975 by Dave Robinson (a producer and promoter) and Andrew Jakeman (tour manager for Dr Feelgood) with a loan of £400 from Dr Feelgood singer Lee Brilleaux. After success with artists such as Madness, Elvis Costello and The

○ Silver disc  ● Gold disc  ✪ Platinum disc (additional platinum units are indicated by a figure following the symbol)  ●9 Number of weeks album topped the UK chart

Damned the company merged with Island Records in 1984 with Robinson appointed Managing Director of both labels, but the move was not a success and Stiff returned to being an independent in 1986 before being sold to ZTT for £300,000.

| DATE | POS | WKS | | ALBUM TITLE | LABEL & NUMBER |
|---|---|---|---|---|---|
| 11/03/1978 | 28 | 7 | | STIFF'S LIVE STIFFS | Stiff GET 1 |

## STOIC

| 16/06/1984 | 35 | 14 | | EMERALD CLASSICS | Stoic SRTV 1 |

## STREETWAVE/STREET SOUNDS
UK dance label formed by record company executive Morgan Khan. The company closed in 1988.

| DATE | POS | WKS | | ALBUM TITLE | LABEL & NUMBER |
|---|---|---|---|---|---|
| 23/10/1982 | 51 | 4 | | STREETNOISE VOLUME 1 | Streetwave STR 32234 |
| 19/02/1983 | 35 | 6 | | STREET SOUNDS EDITION 2 | Street Sounds STSND 002 |
| 23/04/1983 | 21 | 5 | | STREET SOUNDS EDITION 3 | Street Sounds STSND 003 |
| 25/06/1983 | 14 | 8 | | STREET SOUNDS EDITION 4 | Street Sounds STSND 004 |
| 13/08/1983 | 16 | 8 | | STREET SOUNDS EDITION 5 | Street Sounds STSND 005 |
| 08/10/1983 | 23 | 5 | | STREET SOUNDS EDITION 6 | Street Sounds STSND 006 |
| 22/10/1983 | 18 | 8 | | STREET SOUNDS ELECTRO 1 | Street Sounds ELCST 1 |
| 17/12/1983 | 48 | 4 | | STREET SOUNDS EDITION 7 | Street Sounds STSND 007 |
| 07/01/1984 | 49 | 7 | | STREET SOUNDS ELECTRO 2 | Street Sounds ELCST 2 |
| 03/03/1984 | 71 | 1 | | STREET SOUNDS HI-ENERGY NO 1 | Street Sounds HINRG 16 |
| 10/03/1984 | 22 | 7 | | STREET SOUNDS EDITION 8 | Street Sounds STSND 008 |
| 10/03/1984 | 24 | 10 | | STREET SOUNDS CRUCIAL ELECTRO | Street Sounds ELCST 999 |
| 07/04/1984 | 25 | 9 | | STREET SOUNDS ELECTRO 3 | Street Sounds ELCST 3 |
| 12/05/1984 | 22 | 5 | | STREET SOUNDS EDITION 9 | Street Sounds STSND 009 |
| 09/06/1984 | 25 | 9 | | STREET SOUNDS ELECTRO 4 | Street Sounds ELCST 4 |
| 30/06/1984 | 60 | 4 | | STREET SOUNDS UK ELECTRO | Street Sounds ELCST 1984 |
| 21/07/1984 | 91 | 3 | | LET THE MUSIC SCRATCH | Street Sounds MKL 1 |
| 11/08/1984 | 35 | 6 | | STREET SOUNDS CRUCIAL ELECTRO 2 | Street Sounds ELCST 100 |
| 18/08/1984 | 24 | 6 | | STREET SOUNDS EDITION 10 | Street Sounds STSND 010 |
| 06/10/1984 | 17 | 6 | | STREET SOUNDS ELECTRO 5 | Street Sounds ELCST 5 |
| 10/11/1984 | 48 | 4 | | STREET SOUNDS EDITION 11 | Street Sounds STSND 011 |
| 09/03/1985 | 24 | 10 | | STREET SOUNDS ELECTRO 6 | Street Sounds ELCST 6 |
| 18/05/1985 | 12 | 7 | | STREET SOUNDS ELECTRO 7 | Street Sounds ELCST 7 |
| 18/05/1985 | 23 | 4 | | STREET SOUNDS EDITION 12 | Street Sounds STSND 012 |
| 13/07/1985 | 23 | 5 | | STREET SOUNDS ELECTRO 8 | Street Sounds ELCST 8 |
| 17/08/1985 | 19 | 9 | | STREET SOUNDS EDITION 13 | Street Sounds STSND 013 |
| 17/08/1985 | 65 | 4 | | STREET SOUNDS N.Y. VS L.A. BEATS | Street Sounds ELCST 1001 |
| 05/10/1985 | 18 | 6 | | STREET SOUNDS ELECTRO 9 | Street Sounds ELCST 9 |
| 16/11/1985 | 43 | 3 | | STREET SOUNDS EDITION 14 | Street Sounds STSND 014 |
| 21/12/1985 | 58 | 8 | | STREET SOUNDS EDITION 15 | Street Sounds STSND 015 |
| 21/12/1985 | 72 | 6 | | STREET SOUNDS ELECTRO 10 | Street Sounds ELCST 10 |
| 29/03/1986 | 19 | 5 | | STREET SOUNDS HIP-HOP ELECTRO 11 | Street Sounds ELCST 11 |
| 05/04/1986 | 17 | 7 | | STREET SOUNDS EDITION 16 | Street Sounds STSND 016 |
| 21/06/1986 | 96 | 1 | | JAZZ JUICE 2 | Street Sounds SOUND 4 |
| 28/06/1986 | 28 | 4 | | STREET SOUNDS HIP-HOP ELECTRO 12 | Street Sounds ELCST 12 |
| 19/07/1986 | 35 | 5 | | STREET SOUNDS EDITION 17 | Street Sounds STSND 017 |
| 06/09/1986 | 23 | 5 | | STREET SOUNDS HIP-HOP ELECTRO 13 | Street Sounds ELCST 13 |
| 11/10/1986 | 20 | 5 | | STREET SOUNDS EDITION 18 | Street Sounds STSND 018 |
| 11/10/1986 | 40 | 3 | | STREET SOUNDS HIP-HOP ELECTRO 14 | Street Sounds ELCST 14 |
| 11/10/1986 | 88 | 1 | | JAZZ JUICE 3 | Street Sounds SOUND 5 |
| 15/11/1986 | 46 | 2 | | STREET SOUNDS HIP-HOP ELECTRO 15 | Street Sounds ELCST 15 |
| 06/12/1986 | 61 | 3 | | STREET SOUNDS EDITION 19 | Street Sounds STSND 019 |
| 24/01/1987 | 41 | 3 | | STREET SOUNDS CRUCIAL ELECTRO 3 | Street Sounds ELCST 1002 |
| 07/02/1987 | 61 | 3 | | STREET SOUNDS ANTHEMS – VOLUME 1 | Street Sounds MUSIC 5 |
| 14/02/1987 | 25 | 4 | | STREET SOUNDS EDITION 20 | Street Sounds STSND 020 |
| 13/06/1987 | 40 | 3 | | STREET SOUNDS HIP-HOP ELECTRO 16 | Street Sounds ELCST 16 |
| 04/07/1987 | 40 | 5 | | STREET SOUNDS DANCE MUSIC '87 | Street Sounds STSND 871 |
| 15/08/1987 | 38 | 3 | | STREET SOUNDS HIP-HOP 17 | Street Sounds ELCST 17 |
| 15/08/1987 | 97 | 1 | | JAZZ JUICE 5 | Street Sounds SOUND 8 |
| 12/09/1987 | 47 | 3 | | STREET SOUNDS 87 VOLUME 2 | Street Sounds STSND 872 |
| 12/09/1987 | 80 | 2 | | BEST OF WEST COAST HIP HOP | Street Sounds MACA 1 |
| 24/10/1987 | 67 | 1 | | STREET SOUNDS HIP-HOP 18 | Street Sounds ELCST 18 |
| 19/03/1988 | 39 | 4 | | STREET SOUNDS HIP-HOP 20 | Street Sounds ELCST 20 |
| 19/03/1988 | 73 | 2 | | STREET SOUNDS 88–1 | Street Sounds STSND 881 |
| 04/06/1988 | 87 | 1 | | STREET SOUNDS HIP-HOP 21 | Street Sounds ELCST 21 |

## STRICTLY UNDERGROUND

| 19/09/1992 | 20 | 1 | | ILLEGAL RAVE | Strictly Underground STHCCD 1 |

▲[9] Number of weeks album topped the US chart   ◆[12] RIAA Diamond Awards   ◇[3] IFPI Platinum Europe Awards

## STUDIO TWO

| | | | | | |
|---|---|---|---|---|---|
| 21/10/1967 ..... 2 ...... 19 ..... | | | | BREAKTHROUGH | Studio Two STWO 1 |
| 04/09/1971 ..... 39 ...... 4 ..... | | | | TOTAL SOUND | Studio Two STWO 4 |
| 30/10/1971 ..... 16 ...... 4 ..... | | | | STUDIO TWO CLASSICS | Studio Two STWO 6 |

## STYLUS UK label formed in 1985 by Tony Naughton following the collapse of Ronco Records where Naughton had been general manager. Another TV merchandising company, Stylus crashed in 1990.

| | | | | | |
|---|---|---|---|---|---|
| 03/08/1985 ..... 35 ...... 9 ..... ● | THE MAGIC OF TORVILL AND DEAN | Stylus SMR 8502 |
| 17/08/1985 ..... 15 ...... 8 ..... ○ | NIGHT BEAT | Stylus SMR 8501 |
| 24/08/1985 ..... 29 ...... 10 ..... ○ | DISCO BEACH PARTY | Stylus SMR 8503 |
| 14/12/1985 ..... 54 ...... 4 ..... ○ | VELVET WATERS | Stylus SMR 8507 |
| 28/12/1985 ..... 87 ...... 2 ..... | CHOICES OF THE HEART | Stylus SMR 8511 |
| 08/03/1986 ..... 7 ...... 9 ..... ○ | NIGHT BEAT II | Stylus SMR 8613 |
| 17/05/1986 ..... 17 ...... 10 ..... ○ | LET'S HEAR IT FOR THE GIRLS | Stylus SMR 8614 |
| 01/11/1986 ..... 26 ...... 9 ..... | BLACK MAGIC | Stylus SMR 619 |
| 08/11/1986 ..... 10 ...... 14 ..... ● | HIT MIX '86 | Stylus SMR 624 |
| 22/11/1986 ..... 74 ...... 4 ..... | CLASSICS BY CANDLELIGHT | Stylus SMR 620 |
| 14/03/1987 ..... 48 ...... 6 ..... | BANDS OF GOLD – THE SWINGING SIXTIES | Stylus SMR 726 |
| 21/03/1987 ..... 75 ...... 4 ..... | BANDS OF GOLD – THE SENSATIONAL SEVENTIES | Stylus SMR 727 |
| 28/03/1987 ..... 82 ...... 1 ..... | BANDS OF GOLD – THE ELECTRIC EIGHTIES | Stylus SMR 728 |
| 11/07/1987 ..... 3 ...... 44 ..... ✪ | SIXTIES MIX – 60 SEQUENCED HITS FROM THE SIXTIES | Stylus SMR 733 |
| 24/10/1987 ..... 18 ...... 17 ..... ● | THE HIT FACTORY: THE BEST OF STOCK AITKEN WATERMAN | Stylus SMR 740 |
| 21/11/1987 ..... 29 ...... 11 ..... ○ | HIT MIX – HITS OF THE YEAR | Stylus SMR 744 |
| 02/04/1988 ..... 5 ...... 13 ..... ● | HIP HOP AND RAPPING IN THE HOUSE | Stylus SMR 852 |
| 07/05/1988 ..... 14 ...... 20 ..... ● | SIXTIES MIX 2 | Stylus SMR 855 |
| 04/06/1988 ..... 29 ...... 11 ..... | BACK ON THE ROAD | Stylus SMR 854 |
| 30/07/1988 ..... 8 ...... 15 ..... ✪ | THE GREATEST EVER ROCK 'N' ROLL MIX | Stylus SMR 858 |
| 03/09/1988 ..... 3 ...... 13 ..... ● | RAP TRAX | Stylus SMR 859 |
| 01/10/1988 ..... 20 ...... 10 ..... ● | RARE GROOVE MIX – 70 SMASH HITS OF THE 70'S | Stylus SMR 863 |
| 22/10/1988 ..... 7 ...... 12 ..... ✪ | SOFT METAL | Stylus SMR 862 |
| 26/11/1988 ..... 48 ...... 7 ..... | HIT MIX '88 | Stylus SMR 865 |
| 17/12/1988 ..... 26 ...... 4 ..... | THE GREATEST HITS OF HOUSE | Stylus SMR 867 |
| 14/01/1989 ..... 5 ...... 9 ..... ● | THE GREATEST HITS OF HOUSE | Stylus SMR 867 |
| 14/01/1989 ..... 7 ...... 27 ..... ✪ | SOFT METAL | Stylus SMR 862 |
| 14/01/1989 ..... 15 ...... 2 ..... ● | HIT MIX '88 | Stylus SMR 865 |
| 18/02/1989 ..... 9 ...... 8 ..... | BEAT THIS – 20 HITS OF RHYTHM KING | Stylus SMR 973 |
| 11/03/1989 ..... 18 ...... 1 ..... | NEW ROOTS | Stylus SMR 972 |
| 25/03/1989 ..... 3 ...... 8 ..... ● | HIP HOUSE | Stylus SMR 974 |
| 22/04/1989 ..... 5 ...... 11 ..... ○ | THE SINGER AND THE SONG | Stylus SMR 975 |
| 27/05/1989 ..... 2 ...... 29 ..... ✪ | PRECIOUS METAL | Stylus SMR 976 |
| 24/06/1989 ..... 7 ...... 6 ..... ○ | DON'T STOP THE MUSIC | Stylus SMR 977 |
| 15/07/1989 ..... 4 ...... 11 ..... ● | HOT SUMMER NIGHTS | Stylus SMR 980 |
| 19/08/1989 ..... 9 ...... 7 ..... ○ | SUNSHINE MIX | Stylus SMR 986 |
| 26/08/1989 ..... 5 ...... 9 ..... | THE GREATEST EVER ROCK 'N' ROLL MIX | Stylus SMR 858 |
| 02/09/1989 ..... 7 ...... 6 ..... | MIDNIGHT LOVE | Stylus SMR 981 |
| 16/09/1989 ..... 6 ...... 10 ..... ○ | LEGENDS AND HEROES | Stylus SMR 987 |
| 21/10/1989 ..... 2 ...... 11 ..... ● | THE RIGHT STUFF – REMIX '89 | Stylus SMR 990 |
| 25/11/1989 ..... 13 ...... 8 ..... ● | JUKE BOX JIVE – ROCK 'N' ROLL GREATS | Stylus SMR 993 |
| 30/12/1989 ..... 2 ...... 10 ..... ● | WARE'S THE HOUSE? | Stylus SMR 997 |
| 13/01/1990 ..... ●⁵ ...... 23 ..... ✪ | PURE SOFT METAL | Stylus SMR 996 |
| 10/03/1990 ..... 2 ...... 15 ..... ● | THE RIGHT STUFF 2 – NOTHING BUT A HOUSE PARTY | Stylus SMR 998 |
| 26/05/1990 ..... 4 ...... 9 ..... | SIXTIES MIX 3 | Stylus SMR 021 |
| 20/10/1990 ..... 9 ...... 2 ..... | MOMENTS IN SOUL | Stylus SMR 023 |

## SUNDISSENTIAL

| | | | | | |
|---|---|---|---|---|---|
| 27/04/2002 ..... 16 ...... 1 ..... | SUNDISSENTIAL – HARDER FASTER | Sundissential SUNDICD 302 |

## SUPREME UNDERGROUND

| | | | | | |
|---|---|---|---|---|---|
| 08/03/1997 ..... 20 ...... 1 ..... | HARDCORE EXPLOSION '97 | Supreme Underground SUMCD 116 |

## TALKIN' LOUD UK acid jazz label formed by former Radio London DJ Gilles Peterson, who earlier helped form Acid Jazz Records.

| | | | | | |
|---|---|---|---|---|---|
| 30/01/1993 ..... 6 ...... 3 ..... | TALKIN LOUD TWO | Talkin Loud 5159362 |

## TELDEC German label formed in 1932 by the electrical company Telefunken following its acquisition of the assets of the bankrupt label Ultraphon. Initially called Telefunkenplatte, Teldec was created in 1948 following its merger with Decca and was subsequently bought by Warner Music Group in 1988.

| | | | | | |
|---|---|---|---|---|---|
| 21/11/1992 ..... 19 ...... 2 ..... ○ | SENSUAL CLASSICS | Teldec 4509900552 |

○ Silver disc  ● Gold disc  ✪ Platinum disc (additional platinum units are indicated by a figure following the symbol)  ●⁹ Number of weeks album topped the UK chart

**TELSTAR** UK label formed in 1982 by Neil Palmer and Sean O'Brien. Although it began as a compilation and TV merchandising company, it subsequently branched out to do its own recordings and launched the Multiply and Wildstar labels. The company went into liquidation in 2004.

| DATE | POS | WKS | BPI | ALBUM TITLE | LABEL & NUMBER |
|------|-----|-----|-----|-------------|----------------|
| 16/10/1982 | 7 | 6 | ● | CHART ATTACK | Telstar STAR 2221 |
| 06/11/1982 | 34 | 16 | ● | MIDNIGHT IN MOTOWN | Telstar STAR 2222 |
| 18/12/1982 | 89 | 1 | | DIRECT HITS | Telstar STAR 2226 |
| 08/01/1983 | 97 | 1 | | DANCIN' – 20 ORIGINAL MOTOWN MOVERS | Telstar STAR 2225 |
| 05/02/1983 | 68 | 5 | | INSTRUMENTAL MAGIC | Telstar STAR 2227 |
| 30/04/1983 | 28 | 6 | | 20 GREAT ITALIAN LOVE SONGS | Telstar STAR 2230 |
| 04/06/1983 | 20 | 12 | | IN THE GROOVE – THE 12 INCH DISCO PARTY | Telstar STAR 2228 |
| 12/11/1983 | 34 | 6 | | ROOTS REGGAE 'N' REGGAE ROCK | Telstar STAR 2233 |
| 19/11/1983 | 22 | 9 | | SUPERCHART '83 | Telstar STAR 2236 |
| 04/02/1984 | 10 | 22 | ● | **THE VERY BEST OF MOTOWN LOVE SONGS** | Telstar STAR 2239 |
| 26/05/1984 | 11 | 12 | | DON'T STOP DANCING | Telstar STAR 2242 |
| 13/10/1984 | 6 | 9 | ● | **HITS, HITS, HITS – 18 SMASH ORIGINALS** | Telstar STAR 2243 |
| 08/12/1984 | 20 | 12 | ● | LOVE SONGS – 16 CLASSIC LOVE SONGS | Telstar STAR 2246 |
| 15/12/1984 | 10 | 10 | | **GREEN VELVET** This is a re-issue of an album that originally appeared on Ronco | Telstar STAR 2252 |
| 07/09/1985 | 13 | 9 | | OPEN TOP CARS AND GIRLS IN T'SHIRTS | Telstar STAR 2257 |
| 16/11/1985 | ❶¹ | 17 | ✪ | **THE GREATEST HITS OF 1985** | Telstar STAR 2269 |
| 16/11/1985 | 7 | 18 | ✪ | **THE LOVE ALBUM – 16 CLASSIC LOVE SONGS** | Telstar STAR 2268 |
| 30/11/1985 | 64 | 5 | ● | THE PRINCE'S TRUST COLLECTION | Telstar STAR 2275 |
| 07/12/1985 | 33 | 7 | ● | PERFORMANCE – THE VERY BEST OF TIM RICE AND ANDREW LLOYD WEBBER | Telstar STAR 2262 |
| 07/12/1985 | 42 | 5 | | MORE GREEN VELVET | Telstar STAR 2267 |
| 18/10/1986 | 6 | 12 | ● | **THE CHART** | Telstar STAR 2278 |
| 01/11/1986 | 54 | 7 | | ROCK LEGENDS | Telstar STAR 2290 |
| 08/11/1986 | 8 | 13 | ● | **THE GREATEST HITS OF 1986** | Telstar STAR 2286 |
| 08/11/1986 | 14 | 16 | ● | LOVERS | Telstar STAR 2279 |
| 22/11/1986 | 19 | 22 | ● | SIXTIES MANIA | Telstar STAR 2287 |
| 06/12/1986 | 25 | 12 | ● | MOTOWN CHARTBUSTERS | Telstar STAR 2283 |
| 28/03/1987 | 23 | 8 | | THE DANCE CHART | Telstar STAR 2285 |
| 03/10/1987 | 27 | 7 | ● | TRACKS OF MY TEARS | Telstar STAR 2295 |
| 21/11/1987 | 12 | 11 | ● | THE GREATEST HITS OF 1987 | Telstar STAR 2309 |
| 28/11/1987 | 39 | 10 | ● | DANCE MIX '87 | Telstar STAR 2314 |
| 28/11/1987 | 41 | 10 | ● | ALWAYS AND FOREVER THE LOVE ALBUM | Telstar STAR 2301 |
| 28/11/1987 | 46 | 7 | ● | SIXTIES PARTY MEGAMIX ALBUM | Telstar STAR 2307 |
| 26/12/1987 | 10 | 12 | ● | **LIFE IN THE FAST LANE** | Telstar STAR 2315 |
| 26/12/1987 | 11 | 40 | ✪² | THE GREATEST LOVE | Telstar STAR 2316 |
| 01/10/1988 | 12 | 8 | ● | …AND THE BEST GOES ON | Telstar STAR 2338 |
| 05/11/1988 | 60 | 6 | | THE HEART AND SOUL OF ROCK AND ROLL | Telstar STAR 2351 |
| 12/11/1988 | 51 | 9 | ○ | THE LOVE ALBUM '88 | Telstar STAR 2332 |
| 19/11/1988 | 11 | 8 | ● | THE GREATEST HITS OF 1988 | Telstar STAR 2334 |
| 19/11/1988 | 33 | 8 | | BEST OF HOUSE '88 | Telstar STAR 2347 |
| 19/11/1988 | 79 | 5 | | INSTRUMENTAL GREATS | Telstar STAR 2341 |
| 03/12/1988 | 47 | 6 | ● | BACK TO THE SIXTIES | Telstar STAR 2348 |
| 03/12/1988 | 78 | 4 | ● | HYPERACTIVE | Telstar STAR 2328 |
| 17/12/1988 | 88 | 2 | | MORNING HAS BROKEN | Telstar STAR 2337 |
| 31/12/1988 | 37 | 2 | ● | THE GREATEST LOVE 2 | Telstar STAR 2352 |
| 14/01/1989 | 3 | 23 | ● | **THE GREATEST LOVE 2** | Telstar STAR 2352 |
| 14/01/1989 | 7 | 31 | ✪² | **THE GREATEST LOVE** | Telstar STAR 2316 |
| 14/01/1989 | 8 | 8 | | **THE GREATEST HITS OF 1988** | Telstar STAR 2334 |
| 14/01/1989 | 11 | 5 | | BEST OF HOUSE '88 | Telstar STAR 2347 |
| 14/01/1989 | 14 | 4 | | BACK TO THE SIXTIES | Telstar STAR 2348 |
| 14/01/1989 | 18 | 2 | ✪ | LOVE SONGS | Telstar STAR 2298 |
| 25/02/1989 | ❶¹ | 8 | ◉ | **THE BRITS – THE AWARDS 1989** | Telstar STAR 2346 |
| 04/03/1989 | ❶¹ | 15 | ● | **DEEP HEAT – 26 HOTTEST HOUSE HITS** | Telstar STAR 2345 |
| 22/04/1989 | 2 | 13 | ● | **DEEP HEAT – THE SECOND BURN** | Telstar STAR 2356 |
| 15/07/1989 | 9 | 9 | | **PROTECT THE INNOCENT** | Telstar STAR 2363 |
| 15/07/1989 | 12 | 4 | | RHYTHM OF THE SUN | Telstar STAR 2362 |
| 22/07/1989 | 2 | 13 | ● | **DEEP HEAT 3 – THE THIRD DEGREE** | Telstar STAR 2364 |
| 22/07/1989 | 6 | 10 | | **THIS IS SKA** | Telstar STAR 2366 |

▲⁹ Number of weeks album topped the US chart    ◆¹² RIAA Diamond Awards    ◇³ IFPI Platinum Europe Awards

| | DATE | POS | WKS | BPI | ALBUM TITLE | LABEL & NUMBER |
|---|---|---|---|---|---|---|
| | 23/09/1989 | ●[5] | 11 | ● | DEEP HEAT 4 – PLAY WITH FIRE | Telstar STAR 2388 |
| | 14/10/1989 | 4 | 10 | ● | MOTOWN HEARTBREAKERS | Telstar STAR 2343 |
| | 11/11/1989 | 4 | 18 | ● | THE GREATEST LOVE 3 | Telstar STAR 2384 |
| | 18/11/1989 | 2 | 19 | ✪ | NUMBER ONES OF THE EIGHTIES | Telstar STAR 2382 |
| | 18/11/1989 | 4 | 11 | ● | THE GREATEST HITS OF 1989 | Telstar STAR 2389 |
| | 25/11/1989 | 4 | 17 | ✪ | DEEP HEAT 1989 – FIGHT THE FLAME | Telstar STAR 2380 |
| | 25/11/1989 | 9 | 12 | ● | HEAVEN AND HELL | Telstar STAR 2361 |
| | 09/12/1989 | 15 | 5 | ● | SOFT ROCK | Telstar STAR 2397 |
| | 03/02/1990 | ●[2] | 11 | ● | DEEP HEAT 5 – FEED THE FEVER – 32 HOTTEST CLUB HITS | Telstar STAR 2411 |
| | 03/02/1990 | 13 | 4 | | NEW TRADITIONS | Telstar STAR 2399 |
| | 10/02/1990 | 6 | 11 | | MILESTONES – 20 ROCK OPERAS | Telstar STAR 2379 |
| | 24/02/1990 | 3 | 10 | ● | THE AWARDS 1990 | Telstar STAR 2368 |
| | 17/03/1990 | 16 | 3 | | PRODUCT 2378 | Telstar STAR 2378 |
| | 31/03/1990 | ●[2] | 14 | ● | DEEP HEAT 6 – THE SIXTH SENSE | Telstar STAR 2412 |
| | 12/05/1990 | 2 | 12 | ● | GET ON THIS! – 30 DANCE HITS VOLUME 1 | Telstar STAR 2420 |
| | 19/05/1990 | 2 | 12 | ● | A NIGHT AT THE OPERA | Telstar STAR 2414 |
| | 07/07/1990 | ●[1] | 9 | ● | DEEP HEAT 7 – SEVENTH HEAVEN | Telstar STAR 2422 |
| | 18/08/1990 | ●[4] | 12 | ● | MEGABASS | Telstar STAR 2425 |
| | 25/08/1990 | 3 | 9 | | GET ON THIS!!! 2 | Telstar STAR 2424 |
| | 25/08/1990 | 13 | 5 | | MOLTEN METAL | Telstar STAR 2429 |
| | 15/09/1990 | 9 | 7 | | COUNTRY'S GREATEST HITS | Telstar STAR 2433 |
| | 27/10/1990 | 3 | 5 | ● | DEEP HEAT 8 – THE HAND OF FATE | Telstar STAR 2447 |
| | 27/10/1990 | 4 | 19 | ● | THE GREATEST LOVE 4 | Telstar STAR 2400 |
| | 27/10/1990 | 9 | 6 | ● | THE FINAL COUNTDOWN – THE VERY BEST OF SOFT METAL | Telstar STAR 2431 |
| | 03/11/1990 | 10 | 4 | | RAVE | Telstar STAR 2453 |
| | 17/11/1990 | 4 | 14 | ● | THE GREATEST HITS OF 1990 | Telstar STAR 2439 |
| | 24/11/1990 | 3 | 12 | ✪ | DEEP HEAT 90 | Telstar STAR 2438 |
| | 24/11/1990 | 8 | 12 | ● | THE MOTOWN COLLECTION | Telstar STAR 2375 |
| | 01/12/1990 | 7 | 11 | ● | 60 NUMBER ONES OF THE SIXTIES | Telstar STAR 2432 |
| | 08/12/1990 | 5 | 17 | ● | THE VERY BEST OF GREATEST LOVE | Telstar STAR 2443 |
| | 08/12/1990 | 6 | 8 | ● | MEGABASS 2 | Telstar STAR 2448 |
| | 26/01/1991 | ●[2] | 7 | ● | DEEP HEAT 9 – NINTH LIFE – KISS THE BLISS | Telstar STAR 2470 |
| | 16/02/1991 | 7 | 6 | ● | THE BRITS 1991 – THE MAGIC OF BRITISH MUSIC | Telstar STAR 2481 |
| | 23/02/1991 | ●[3] | 20 | ● | UNCHAINED MELODIES | Telstar STAR 2480 |
| | 23/03/1991 | 15 | 4 | | DON'T STOP… DOOWOP! | Telstar STAR 2485 |
| | 30/03/1991 | 2 | 9 | ● | THIN ICE – THE FIRST STEP | Telstar STAR 2500 |
| | 13/04/1991 | 16 | 3 | | AFTER THE DANCE | Telstar STAR 2501 |
| | 11/05/1991 | 2 | 6 | | MASSIVE HITS | Telstar STAR 2505 |
| | 18/05/1991 | 3 | 8 | | UNCHAINED MELODIES – II | Telstar STAR 2515 |
| | 01/06/1991 | 2 | 7 | | DEEP HEAT 10 – THE AWAKENING | Telstar STAR 2490 |
| | 08/06/1991 | 3 | 8 | | MEGABASS 3 | Telstar STAR 2483 |
| | 22/06/1991 | 4 | 8 | | FAST FORWARD | Telstar STAR 2502 |
| | 03/08/1991 | ●[1] | 9 | | THIN ICE 2 – THE SECOND SHIVER | Telstar STAR 2535 |
| | 14/09/1991 | 10 | 4 | | Q – THE ALBUM VOLUME 1 | Telstar STAR 2522 |
| | 28/09/1991 | 4 | 6 | | MAKE YOU SWEAT | Telstar STAR 2542 |
| | 12/10/1991 | 8 | 5 | | BORN TO BE WILD | Telstar STAR 2524 |
| | 19/10/1991 | 5 | 11 | ● | IN LOVE – GREATEST LOVE 5 | Telstar STAR 2510 |
| | 02/11/1991 | 7 | 10 | | BURNING HEARTS | Telstar STAR 2492 |
| | 09/11/1991 | 2 | 15 | ✪ | THE BEST OF DANCE '91 | Telstar STAR 2537 |
| | 16/11/1991 | 4 | 13 | ● | THE GREATEST HITS OF 1991 | Telstar STAR 2536 |
| | 23/11/1991 | 6 | 14 | ● | LOVE AT THE MOVIES | Telstar STAR 2545 |
| | 23/11/1991 | 18 | 2 | | PUNK AND DISORDERLY – NEW WAVE 1976–1981 | Telstar STAR 2520 |
| | 30/11/1991 | 13 | 15 | ● | CLASSICAL MASTERS | Telstar STAR 2549 |
| | 07/12/1991 | 15 | 10 | | LEGENDS OF SOUL – A WHOLE STACK OF SOUL | Telstar STAR 2489 |
| | 21/12/1991 | 3 | 8 | ● | DEEP HEAT 11 – SPIRIT OF ECSTASY | Telstar STAR 2555 |
| | 15/02/1992 | 2 | 7 | | KAOS THEORY | Telstar STAR 2562 |
| | 15/02/1992 | 5 | 6 | | ALL THE BEST – LOVE DUETS VOLUME 1 | Telstar STAR 2557 |
| | 29/02/1992 | 15 | 3 | | GOLD – 18 EPIC SPORTING ANTHEMS | Telstar TCD 2563 |
| | 07/03/1992 | ●[2] | 10 | | THE ULTIMATE HARDCORE | Telstar TCD 2561 |
| | 11/04/1992 | 3 | 10 | | CLUB FOR HEROES | Telstar TCD 2566 |
| | 02/05/1992 | 2 | 8 | | KAOS THEORY 2 | Telstar TCD 2583 |
| | 02/05/1992 | 13 | 3 | | INDIE HITS | Telstar TCD 2578 |
| | 09/05/1992 | 11 | 6 | | FLIGHT OF THE CONDOR | Telstar TCD 2576 |
| | 23/05/1992 | 8 | 5 | | GARAGE CITY | Telstar TCD 2584 |
| | 06/06/1992 | 2 | 6 | | RAVING WE'RE RAVING | Telstar TCD 2567 |
| | 18/07/1992 | ●[2] | 8 | | KT3 – KAOS THEORY 3 | Telstar TCD 2593 |
| | 01/08/1992 | 9 | 4 | | THE DIVAS OF DANCE | Telstar TCD 2592 |
| | 08/08/1992 | 2 | 10 | | RAVE ALERT | Telstar TCD 2594 |
| | 19/09/1992 | 4 | 6 | | BLUE EYED SOUL | Telstar TCD 2591 |

○ Silver disc  ● Gold disc  ✪ Platinum disc (additional platinum units are indicated by a figure following the symbol)  ●[9] Number of weeks album topped the UK chart

| DATE | POS | WKS | BPI | ALBUM TITLE | LABEL & NUMBER |
|---|---|---|---|---|---|
| 10/10/1992 | 2 | 5 | | KAOS THEORY 4 | Telstar TCD 2605 |
| 17/10/1992 | 2 | 6 | | RAVE NATION | Telstar TCD 2607 |
| 17/10/1992 | 4 | 9 | | MORE THAN LOVE | Telstar TCD 2606 |
| 07/11/1992 | ❶² | 17 | | THE BEST OF DANCE '92 | Telstar TCD 2610 |
| 14/11/1992 | 4 | 15 | | CLASSIC LOVE | Telstar TCD 2620 |
| 14/11/1992 | 4 | 16 | | THE GREATEST HITS OF 1992 | Telstar TCD 2611 |
| 21/11/1992 | 13 | 1 | | ROCK N ROLL HEARTBEATS | Telstar TCD 2628 |
| 21/11/1992 | 16 | 1 | | MY GENERATION | Telstar TCD 2609 |
| 28/11/1992 | 5 | 11 | | THE GREATEST HITS OF DANCE | Telstar TCD 2616 |
| 19/12/1992 | 17 | 3 | | SONIC SYSTEM | Telstar TCD 2624 |
| 23/01/1993 | 19 | 2 | | MOVIE HITS | Telstar TCD 2615 |
| 20/02/1993 | ❶³ | 15 | ✪ | HITS 93 VOLUME 1 | Telstar TCD 2641 |
| 27/02/1993 | 5 | 15 | ● | COUNTRY LOVE | Telstar TCD 2645 |
| 10/04/1993 | 2 | 7 | ● | DEEP HEAT 93 VOLUME 1 | Telstar TCD 2651 |
| 29/05/1993 | 2 | 8 | ● | HITS 93 VOLUME 2 | Telstar TCD 2661 |
| 12/06/1993 | 19 | 2 | | THE PIG ATTRACTION FEATURING PINKY AND PERKY | Telstar TCD 2668 |
| 26/06/1993 | ❶¹ | 15 | ✪ | 100% DANCE | Telstar TCD 2667 |
| 03/07/1993 | 4 | 14 | ● | RAGGA HEAT REGGAE BEAT | Telstar TCD 2666 |
| 17/07/1993 | 4 | 7 | | FRESH DANCE 93 | Telstar TCD 2665 |
| 14/08/1993 | 2 | 9 | | HITS 93 VOLUME 3 | Telstar TCD 2681 |
| 18/09/1993 | ❶² | 7 | ● | DANCE ADRENALIN | Telstar TCD 2688 |
| 02/10/1993 | ❶⁴ | 9 | ✪ | 100% DANCE VOLUME 2 | Telstar TCD 2681 |
| 09/10/1993 | 5 | 5 | | LOVE IS RHYTHM | Telstar TCD 2683 |
| 09/10/1993 | 11 | 4 | | COUNTRY LOVE 2 | Telstar TCD 2682 |
| 06/11/1993 | ❶³ | 14 | ● | THE BEST OF DANCE '93 | Telstar TCD 2662 |
| 13/11/1993 | 4 | 13 | | THE GREATEST HITS OF 1993 | Telstar TCD 2663 |
| 20/11/1993 | 2 | 9 | ● | HITS 93 VOLUME 4 | Telstar CDHITS 934 |
| 20/11/1993 | 11 | 7 | ● | THE ALL TIME GREATEST HITS OF DANCE | Telstar TCD 2679 |
| 20/11/1993 | 16 | 8 | ● | THE GREATEST LOVE 6 – WITH LOVE FROM THE STARS | Telstar TCD 2686 |
| 11/12/1993 | 2 | 17 | ✪ | 100% REGGAE | Telstar TCD 2659 |
| 11/12/1993 | 7 | 9 | ● | 100% DANCE VOLUME 3 | Telstar TCD 2705 |
| 18/12/1993 | 9 | 4 | | A HEART OF GOLD | Telstar TCD 2692 |
| 08/01/1994 | 16 | 3 | | NO 1'S OF DANCE | Telstar TCD 2701 |
| 19/02/1994 | ❶³ | 10 | ● | DANCE HITS '94 – VOLUME 1 | Telstar TCD 2693 |
| 19/02/1994 | 2 | 6 | ● | LOVE OVER GOLD | Telstar TCD 2684 |
| 12/03/1994 | 3 | 10 | ● | 100% RAP | Telstar TCD 2694 |
| 19/03/1994 | 3 | 7 | ● | HITS 94 VOLUME 1 | Telstar/BMG CDHITS 941 |
| 09/04/1994 | 17 | 2 | | LOVE ON FILM | Telstar TCD 2545 |
| 16/04/1994 | 20 | 1 | | MOVIE HITS | Telstar TCD 2615 |
| 23/04/1994 | 2 | 7 | ● | 100% DANCE VOLUME 4 | Telstar TCD 2714 |
| 30/04/1994 | 4 | 14 | ✪ | 100% REGGAE VOLUME 2 | Telstar TCD 2716 |
| 07/05/1994 | 2 | 7 | | AWESOME DANCE | Telstar TCD 2721 |
| 11/06/1994 | ❶¹ | 8 | ● | DANCE HITS '94 VOLUME 2 | Telstar TCD 2720 |
| 02/07/1994 | 3 | 8 | ● | JAZZ MOODS | Telstar TCD 2722 |
| 23/07/1994 | ❶² | 11 | ● | IT'S THE ULTIMATE DANCE ALBUM | Telstar TCD 2725 |
| 23/07/1994 | 4 | 7 | ● | 100% SUMMER | Telstar TCD 2730 |
| 06/08/1994 | 6 | 7 | ● | 100% REGGAE VOLUME 3 | Telstar TCD 2724 |
| 24/09/1994 | 2 | 8 | ● | 100% HITS | Telstar TCD 2726 |
| 08/10/1994 | 5 | 14 | | 100% ACID JAZZ | Telstar TCD 2733 |
| 15/10/1994 | 11 | 2 | | THE ULTIMATE HITS ALBUM | Telstar/BMG CDHITS 942 |
| 29/10/1994 | 7 | 6 | ● | JUNGLE MANIA 94 | Telstar TCD 2735 |
| 29/10/1994 | 14 | 2 | | ULTIMATE REGGAE PARTY ALBUM! | Telstar TCD 2731 |
| 29/10/1994 | 18 | 1 | | JAZZ MOODS 2 | Telstar TCD 2740 |
| 05/11/1994 | 7 | 7 | | 100% PURE LOVE | Telstar TCD 2737 |
| 05/11/1994 | 10 | 5 | ● | THE BEST OF DANCE '94 | Telstar TCD 2743 |
| 12/11/1994 | 9 | 5 | ● | THE GREATEST HITS OF 1994 | Telstar TCD 2744 |
| 03/12/1994 | 9 | 7 | ● | SMASH HITS '94 | Telstar TCD 2750 |
| 10/12/1994 | 9 | 6 | ● | 100% CHRISTMAS | Telstar TCD 2754 |
| 24/12/1994 | 5 | 8 | ● | JUNGLE MANIA 2 | Telstar TCD 2756 |
| 07/01/1995 | 6 | 5 | | THE GREATEST LOVE EVER | Telstar TCD 2747 |
| 07/01/1995 | 11 | 3 | ● | THE BEST OF 100% DANCE | Telstar TCD 2752 |
| 14/01/1995 | 8 | 6 | | 100% CLASSICS | Telstar TCD 2757 |
| 28/01/1995 | 19 | 2 | | THE GREATEST HITS OF THE 90'S – PART 1 | Telstar TCD 2749 |
| 18/02/1995 | 16 | 4 | | 100% HOUSE CLASSICS – VOLUME 1 | Telstar TCD 2759 |
| 18/03/1995 | ❶¹ | 7 | ● | SMASH HITS '95 – VOLUME 1 | Telstar TCD 2764 |
| 25/03/1995 | 5 | 6 | | JUNGLE MANIA 3 | Telstar TCD 2762 |
| 06/05/1995 | 2 | 6 | | WARNING! DANCE BOOM | Telstar TCD 2763 |
| 17/06/1995 | 14 | 4 | | 100% ACID JAZZ – VOLUME 2 | Telstar TCD 2767 |
| 24/06/1995 | 4 | 5 | ● | SMASH HITS '95 – VOLUME 2 | Telstar TCD 2768 |

▲⁹ Number of weeks album topped the US chart ◆¹² RIAA Diamond Awards ◇³ IFPI Platinum Europe Awards

| DATE | POS | WKS | BPI | ALBUM TITLE | LABEL & NUMBER |
|---|---|---|---|---|---|
| 08/07/1995 | 7 | 2 | | **100% SUMMER '95** | Telstar TCD 2777 |
| 05/08/1995 | 4 | 5 | | **CLUB ZONE** | Telstar TCD 2779 |
| 05/08/1995 | 11 | 4 | | 100% SUMMER JAZZ | Telstar TCD 2781 |
| 02/09/1995 | 7 | 4 | ● | **WARNING! DANCE BOOM 2** | Telstar TCD 2783 |
| 02/09/1995 | 16 | 2 | | 100% CARNIVAL! | Telstar TCD 2782 |
| 07/10/1995 | 10 | 3 | | **CLUB ZONE 2** | Telstar TCD 2787 |
| 04/11/1995 | 10 | 3 | | **BEST SWING '95** | Telstar TCD 2789 |
| 18/11/1995 | 8 | 9 | | **THE GREATEST HITS OF 1995** | Telstar TCD 2792 |
| 06/01/1996 | 2 | 7 | ● | **BEST SWING 96** | Telstar TCD 2805 |
| 20/01/1996 | 20 | 1 | | 100% CLASSICS – VOLUME 2 | Telstar TCD 2800 |
| 17/02/1996 | 8 | 5 | | **OUR FRIENDS ELECTRIC** | Telstar TCD 2814 |
| 24/02/1996 | 16 | 2 | | THE GREATEST 90S DANCE HITS | Telstar TCD 2807 |
| 09/03/1996 | 6 | 5 | | **BEST SWING 96 – VOLUME 2** | Telstar TCD 2820 |
| 23/03/1996 | 4 | 8 | | **100% PURE GROOVE** | Telstar TCD 2818 |
| 13/04/1996 | 19 | 1 | | LOVE OVER GOLD 2 | Telstar TCD 2803 |
| 20/04/1996 | 12 | 3 | | TECHNOHEDZ – 20 FIRESTARTIN' TECHNO ANTHEMS | Telstar TCD 2823 |
| 27/04/1996 | 10 | 3 | | **LOVE II SWING** | Telstar TCD 2817 |
| 25/05/1996 | 3 | 6 | | **SWING MIX 96** | Telstar TCD 2831 |
| 08/06/1996 | 9 | 4 | | **MASSIVE DANCE MIX 96** | Telstar TCD 2830 |
| 08/06/1996 | 12 | 3 | | 100% PURE GROOVE 2 | Telstar TCD 2840 |
| 29/06/1996 | 4 | 16 | ● | **MOVIE KILLERS** | Telstar TCD 2836 |
| 29/06/1996 | 18 | 1 | | CAFE LATINO | Telstar TCD 2841 |
| 06/07/1996 | 7 | 9 | ● | **100% SUMMER MIX 96** | Telstar TCD 2843 |
| 13/07/1996 | 20 | 1 | | BEST SWING '96 – VOLUME 3 | Telstar TCD 2837 |
| 20/07/1996 | 20 | 1 | | FI ROCK | Telstar TCD 2835 |
| 21/09/1996 | 11 | 3 | | 100% DANCE HITS 96 | Telstar TCD 2826 |
| 28/09/1996 | 12 | 3 | | MAD FOR IT | Telstar TCD 2868 |
| 05/10/1996 | 11 | 4 | | 100% DRUM & BASS | Telstar TCD 2847 |
| 09/11/1996 | 9 | 4 | ○ | **THE MOTHER OF ALL SWING ALBUMS** | Telstar TCD 2877 |
| 09/11/1996 | 13 | 3 | ● | THE BEST OF DANCE '96 | Telstar TCD 2871 |
| 16/11/1996 | 4 | 9 | ● | **THE GREATEST HITS OF 1996 – THE STORY OF THE YEAR** | Telstar TCD 2873 |
| 18/01/1997 | 15 | 3 | | THE GREATEST CLASSICAL MOVIE ALBUM | Telstar TCD 2880 |
| 22/02/1997 | 7 | 5 | | **THE MOTHER OF ALL SWING MIX ALBUMS** | Telstar TCD 2890 |
| 08/03/1997 | 13 | 3 | | ONCE IN A LIFETIME | Telstar TCD 2889 |
| 10/05/1997 | 10 | 7 | | **SOUL SURVIVORS – 40 NORTHERN SOUL ANTHEMS** | Telstar TCD 2869 |
| 17/05/1997 | 5 | 7 | | **CLUB CUTS 97** | Telstar TCD 2898 |
| 14/06/1997 | 3 | 7 | | **CLUBLAND** | Telstar TV TCD 2912 |
| 21/06/1997 | 5 | 10 | ● | **SIXTIES SUMMER MIX** | Telstar TV TCD 2908 |
| 05/07/1997 | 5 | 10 | ● | **A DECADE OF IBIZA – 1987–1997** | Telstar TV TCD 2902 |
| 19/07/1997 | 2 | 7 | ● | **CLUB CUTS 97 – VOLUME 2** | Telstar TV TTVCD 2916 |
| 26/07/1997 | 8 | 6 | ○ | **100% SUMMER MIX 97** | Telstar TV TTVCD 2906 |
| 02/08/1997 | 11 | 5 | | THE MOTHER OF ALL SWING II | Telstar TV TTVCD 2896 |
| 16/08/1997 | 13 | 2 | ○ | PURE HITS '97 | Telstar TV TTVCD 2914 |
| 30/08/1997 | 5 | 5 | ○ | **THE GREATEST DANCE ALBUM EVER MADE** | Telstar TV TTVCD 2918 |
| 20/09/1997 | 16 | 4 | | MOONDANCE – THE ALBUM | Telstar TV TTVCD 2919 |
| 27/09/1997 | 6 | 4 | ○ | **CLUBLAND – VOLUME 2** | Telstar TV TTVCD 2928 |
| 11/10/1997 | 5 | 4 | ○ | **CLUB CUTS 97 – VOLUME 3** | Telstar TV TTVCD 2933 |
| 08/11/1997 | 6 | 4 | ● | **THE BEST OF DANCE '97** | Telstar TV TTVCD 2929 |
| 15/11/1997 | 2 | 12 | ✪ | **THE GREATEST HITS OF 1997** | Telstar TV TTVCD 2938 |
| 21/02/1998 | 17 | 1 | | MOVIE LOVERS | Telstar TCD 2876 |
| 07/03/1998 | 3 | 5 | ○ | **CLUBLIFE** | Telstar TV TTVCD 2946 |
| 07/03/1998 | 13 | 4 | | POWER OF A WOMAN | Telstar/warner.esp TTVCD 2950 |
| 21/03/1998 | 2 | 5 | ● | **THE BOX HITS 98** | Telstar TV TTVCD 2951 |
| 04/04/1998 | 5 | 6 | | **NON-STOP DANCE ANTHEMS** | Telstar TV TTVCD 2958 |
| 02/05/1998 | 2 | 7 | ● | **CLUB HITS 98** | Telstar TV TTVCD 2953 |
| 23/05/1998 | 3 | 6 | | **FANTAZIA – BRITISH ANTHEMS – SUMMERTIME** | Telstar TV FBA 2CD |
| 23/05/1998 | 14 | 3 | | STREET JAMS | Telstar TV/Polygram TV TTVCD 2963 |
| 13/06/1998 | ❶³ | 6 | ● | **THE BOX HITS 98 – VOLUME 2** | Telstar TV TTVCD 2974 |
| 20/06/1998 | 20 | 2 | | SMILE JAMAICA | Telstar TV TTVCD 2976 |
| 27/06/1998 | 13 | 2 | | BEST OF 100% PURE GROOVES | Telstar TV TTVCD 2957 |
| 04/07/1998 | 4 | 5 | | **NON STOP HITS** | Telstar TV TTVCD 2962 |
| 11/07/1998 | 5 | 7 | | **IBIZA ANTHEMS** | Telstar TV TTVCD 2965 |
| 18/07/1998 | 13 | 4 | | 100% SUMMER MIX 98 | Telstar TV TTVCD 2968 |
| 15/08/1998 | 19 | 1 | | SIXTIES SUMMER MIX 2 | Telstar TV TTVCD 2972 |
| 22/08/1998 | 13 | 2 | | CLUBLIFE 2 | Telstar TV TTVCD 2960 |
| 29/08/1998 | 8 | 9 | | **ULTIMATE COUNTRY: 40 COUNTRY GREATS** | Telstar TV TTVCD 2986 |
| 05/09/1998 | 19 | 1 | | NON STOP HITS – VOLUME 2 | Telstar TV TTVCD 2993 |
| 19/09/1998 | 17 | 2 | | SOUL SURVIVORS 2 | Telstar TV TTVCD 2992 |
| 10/10/1998 | 9 | 3 | | **SUNDANCE – CHAPTER ONE** | Telstar TV TTVCD 2989 |

○ Silver disc  ● Gold disc  ✪ Platinum disc (additional platinum units are indicated by a figure following the symbol)  ❶⁹ Number of weeks album topped the UK chart

| DATE | POS | WKS | BPI | ALBUM TITLE | LABEL & NUMBER |
|------|-----|-----|-----|-------------|----------------|
| 17/10/1998 | 2 | 4 | | BOX HITS 98 – VOLUME 3 | Telstar TV TTVCD 2988 |
| 31/10/1998 | 15 | 1 | | CARWASH | Telstar TV TTVCD 2998 |
| 07/11/1998 | 9 | 2 | | THE BEST OF DANCE '98 | Telstar TV TTVCD 3001 |
| 14/11/1998 | 3 | 12 | | THE GREATEST HITS OF 1998 | Telstar TV TTVCD 3002 |
| 05/12/1998 | 17 | 1 | ● | CHRIS TARRANT PRESENTS ULTIMATE PARTY MEGAMIX | Telstar TV TTVCD 3009 |
| 09/01/1999 | 6 | 6 | | THE BOX R&B HITS ALBUM | Telstar TV TTVCD 3008 |
| 30/01/1999 | 14 | 2 | | THE GREATEST LOVE | Telstar TV TTVCD 3006 |
| 06/02/1999 | ●² | 17 | ● | EUPHORIA | Telstar TV TTVCD 3007 |
| 13/03/1999 | 15 | 1 | | BORN TO BE WILD | Telstar TV TTVCD 3012 |
| 03/04/1999 | 4 | 10 | ● | THE CHILLOUT ALBUM | Telstar TV TTVCD 3037 |
| 10/04/1999 | 4 | 10 | ● | ESSENTIAL SOUNDTRACKS | Telstar TV TTVCD 3038 |
| 10/04/1999 | 10 | 5 | | BEST DANCE 99 | Telstar TV TTVCD 3036 |
| 24/04/1999 | 9 | 3 | | FUNKY HOUSE | Telstar TV TTVCD 3050 |
| 29/05/1999 | 2 | 6 | ● | DEEPER – EUPHORIA II: MIXED BY RED JERRY | Telstar TV TTVCD 3064 |
| 05/06/1999 | 3 | 5 | ● | NATIONAL ANTHEMS 99 | Telstar TV TTVCD 3051 |
| 03/07/1999 | 7 | 4 | | IBIZA ANTHEMS 2 | Telstar TV TTVCD 3054 |
| 10/07/1999 | 15 | 2 | | CHRIS TARRANT'S ULTIMATE SUMMER PARTY | Telstar TV TTVCD 3067 |
| 24/07/1999 | 10 | 3 | | ADRENALIN | Telstar TV TTVCD 3075 |
| 31/07/1999 | 14 | 4 | | THE CHILL OUT ALBUM – 2 | Telstar TV TTVCD 3076 |
| 14/08/1999 | 10 | 3 | | SUMMER DANCE ANTHEMS 99 | Telstar TV TTVCD 3077 |
| 04/09/1999 | 11 | 2 | | NATIONAL ANTHEMS 99 – VOLUME 2 | Telstar TV TTVCD 3081 |
| 11/09/1999 | 5 | 5 | ● | IBIZA EUPHORIA | Telstar TV TTVCD 3078 |
| 09/10/1999 | 16 | 1 | | CLUB HITS 99 | Telstar TV TTVCD 3079 |
| 06/11/1999 | 19 | 1 | | THE GREATEST HITS OF THE NINETIES | Telstar TV TTVCD 3084 |
| 13/11/1999 | 8 | 3 | | THE GREATEST HITS OF 1999 – THE STORY SO FAR | Telstar TV TTVCD 3087 |
| 25/12/1999 | 5 | 12 | ● | EUPHORIA – LEVEL 3 | Telstar TV TTVCD 3095 |
| 15/01/2000 | 4 | 11 | ● | BREAKDOWN | Telstar TV TTVCD 3098 |
| 12/02/2000 | ●¹ | 6 | | AYIA NAPA – FANTASY ISLAND | Telstar TV TTVCD 3115 |
| 18/03/2000 | 8 | 6 | | GARAGE ANTHEMS | Telstar TV TTVCD 3120 |
| 08/04/2000 | 13 | 4 | | SWITCHED ON | Telstar TV TTVCD 3086 |
| 15/04/2000 | 8 | 3 | | ESSENTIAL SOUNDTRACKS | Telstar TV TTVCD 3121 |
| 29/04/2000 | 3 | 6 | ● | PURE EUPHORIA – LEVEL 4 | Telstar TV TTVCD 3118 |
| 27/05/2000 | 9 | 3 | | BIG TUNES 2000 | Telstar TV TTVCD 3110 |
| 10/06/2000 | 4 | 7 | | CHILLED EUPHORIA | Telstar TV TTVCD 3127 |
| 10/06/2000 | 10 | 3 | | GARAGE NATION | Telstar TV TTVCD 3125 |
| 24/06/2000 | 14 | 2 | | LOVE ON A SUMMER'S DAY | Telstar TV TTVCD 3126 |
| 19/08/2000 | 4 | 5 | | IBIZA EUPHORIA – ALEX GOLD/AGNELLI & NELSON | Telstar TV TTVCD 3134 |
| 02/09/2000 | 4 | 7 | ● | BREAKDOWN – VERY BEST OF EUPHORIC DANCE | Telstar TV TTVCD 3133 |
| 02/09/2000 | 6 | 8 | | PURE R&B | Telstar TV TTVCD 3138 |
| 30/09/2000 | 9 | 4 | | THE COOL SOUND OF THE 70S | Telstar TV TTVCD 3148 |
| 07/10/2000 | 18 | 1 | | LOVE 2 DANCE | Telstar TV TTVCD 3140 |
| 25/11/2000 | 11 | 3 | ● | PURE R&B 2 | Telstar TV/BMG TV TTVCD 3153 |
| 02/12/2000 | 6 | 8 | ● | TRANCENDENTAL EUPHORIA | Telstar TV/BMG TV TTVCD 3155 |
| 02/12/2000 | 19 | 1 | | DISNEY'S GREATEST HITS | Telstar TV/BMG TV TTVCD 3151 |
| 16/12/2000 | 10 | 7 | ● | HARD HOUSE EUPHORIA | Telstar TV/BMG TV TTVCD 3152 |
| 23/12/2000 | 16 | 3 | | THE RECORD OF THE YEAR 2000 | Telstar TV TTVCD 3154 |
| 23/12/2000 | 19 | 1 | | ULTIMATE SIXTIES COLLECTION | Telstar TV TTVCD 3156 |
| 27/01/2001 | 5 | 6 | | DEEP & CHILLED EUPHORIA | Telstar TV/BMG TV TTVCD 3164 |
| 03/02/2001 | ●² | 8 | ● | BREAKDOWN – VERY BEST OF EUPHORIC DANCE | Telstar/BMG TTVCD 3158 |
| 17/02/2001 | 12 | 1 | | THE DREEM TEEM IN SESSION | Telstar/4 Liberty LIBTCD 008 |
| 17/02/2001 | 9 | 2 | | LOVE UNLIMITED – THE SOULFUL SOUND OF LOVE | Telstar TV/BMG TV TTVCD 3167 |
| 24/03/2001 | 10 | 3 | | THE ULTIMATE SOUL COLLECTION | Telstar TV/BMG TV TTVCD 3168 |
| 31/03/2001 | 8 | 5 | | THE VERY BEST EUPHORIC CHILLOUT MIXES | Telstar TV/BMG TV TTVCD 3175 |
| 31/03/2001 | 18 | 2 | | AYIA NAPA – RETURN TO FANTASY ISLAND | Telstar TV/BMG TV TTVCD 3157 |
| 14/04/2001 | 3 | 6 | ● | TRUE EUPHORIA | Telstar TV/BMG TV TTVCD 3176 |
| 28/04/2001 | 7 | 6 | | STREET VIBES 7 | Telstar TV/BMG TV 74321854882 |
| 09/06/2001 | 8 | 4 | | PURE R&B 3 | Telstar TV/BMG TV TTVCD 3188 |
| 09/06/2001 | 15 | 2 | | ESSENTIAL TRACKS | Telstar TV/BMG TV TTVCD 3182 |
| 30/06/2001 | 5 | 8 | | FUNKY DIVAS – THE VERY BEST IN SOUL DANCE AND R&B | Telstar TV/BMG TV TTVCD 3193 |
| 07/07/2001 | 9 | 3 | ○ | PURE HIP HOP | Telstar/ BMG/Sony TTVCD 3191 |
| 04/08/2001 | 2 | 4 | | BEST OF EUPHORIC DANCE – BREAKDOWN IBIZA | Telstar TV/BMG TV TTVCD 3195 |
| 25/08/2001 | 8 | 2 | | CHILLED OUT EUPHORIA | Telstar TV/BMG TV TTVCD 3189 |
| 15/09/2001 | 3 | 6 | | IBIZA EUPHORIA – DAVE PEARCE | Telstar/BMG TTVCD 3199 |
| 03/11/2001 | 12 | 2 | | HARD HOUSE EUPHORIA – TIDY BOYS VS LISA | Telstar TV/BMG TTVCD 3177 |
| 09/02/2002 | 20 | 1 | | SONGS FROM THE CHILLOUT LOUNGE | Telstar TV/BMG TTVCD 3230 |
| 16/02/2002 | 4 | 4 | | ELECTRO BREAKDANCE – THE REAL OLD SCHOOL REVIVAL | Telstar TV/BMG TTVCD 3240 |
| 02/03/2002 | 3 | 6 | | PURE GROOVE – THE VERY BEST 80'S SOUL FUNK GROOVES | Telstar TV/BMG TTVCD 3238 |
| 02/03/2002 | 6 | 4 | | WHITE LABEL EUPHORIA – JOHN OO FLEMING | Telstar TV/BMG TTVCD 3241 |
| 09/03/2002 | 2 | 5 | | THE VERY BEST OF ALL WOMAN | Telstar TV/BMG TTVCD 3242 |

▲[9] Number of weeks album topped the US chart   ◆[12] RIAA Diamond Awards   ◇[3] IFPI Platinum Europe Awards

| DATE | POS | WKS | BPI | ALBUM TITLE | LABEL & NUMBER |
|---|---|---|---|---|---|
| 30/03/2002 | 4 | 6 | ○ | **RUDE BOY REVIVAL** | Telstar TV/BMG TTVCD 3247 |
| 13/04/2002 | 5 | 6 | | **ELECTRIC – THE VERY BEST OF ELECTRONIC, NEW WAVE & SYNTH** | Telstar TV/BMG TTVCD 3246 |
| 04/05/2002 | 3 | 5 | | **ABSOLUTE EUPHORIA – DAVE PEARCE** | Telstar TV/BMG TTVCD 3251 |
| 25/05/2002 | 18 | 1 | | THE VERY BEST POP ALBUM | Telstar TV/BMG TTVCD 3260 |
| 22/06/2002 | 4 | 5 | | **VERY BEST OF EUPHORIC DANCE BREAKDOWN** | Telstar TV/BMG TTVCD 3262 |
| 06/07/2002 | 5 | 3 | | **EXTREME EUPHORIA – LISA LASHES** | Telstar TV/BMG TTVCD 3265 |
| 03/08/2002 | 16 | 3 | | SUMMER COUNTRY – 41 CLASSIC COUNTRY HITS FOR A MODERN WORLD | Telstar/BMG TTVCD 3273 |
| 17/08/2002 | ❶[1] | 12 | ● | **THE VERY BEST OF PURE R&B – THE SUMMER** | Telstar TV/BMG TTVCD 3244 |
| 24/08/2002 | 5 | 9 | ● | **SONGS TO MAKE YOU FEEL GOOD – 41 UPLIFTING CLASSICS** | Telstar TV/BMG TTVCD 3270 |
| 31/08/2002 | 10 | 3 | | **IBIZA EUPHORIA – MIXED BY DAVE PEARCE** | Telstar TV/BMG TTVCD 3274 |
| 28/09/2002 | 4 | 6 | ● | **FUNKY DIVAS – THE AUTUMN COLLECTION** | Telstar TV/BMG TTVCD 3290 |
| 05/10/2002 | 7 | 4 | | **PURE GROOVE – THE CLASSICS** | Telstar TV/BMG TTVCD 3256 |
| 02/11/2002 | 4 | 4 | | **VERY BEST EUPHORIC OLD SKOOL BREAKDOWN** | Telstar TV/BMG TTVCD 3282 |
| 09/11/2002 | 12 | 2 | | CHOOSE 80'S DANCE | Telstar TV/BMG TTVCD 3272 |
| 23/11/2002 | 3 | 5 | | **THE VERY BEST OF EUPHORIA – MATT DAREY** | Telstar TV/BMG TTVCD 3297 |
| 07/12/2002 | 11 | 10 | ● | THE VERY BEST OF PURE R&B – THE WINTER | Telstar TV/BMG TTVCD 3303 |
| 01/02/2003 | 6 | 3 | | **DEEPER SHADES OF EUPHORIA** | Telstar TV/BMG TTVCD 3285 |
| 08/02/2003 | 4 | 7 | | **VERY BEST OF DAVE PEARCE DANCE ANTHEMS** | Telstar TV/BMG TTVCD 3318 |
| 08/02/2003 | 11 | 3 | | THE FUNKIN' 80S | Telstar TV/BMG TTVCD 3301 |
| 08/03/2003 | 2 | 6 | | **THE VERY BEST EUPHORIC HOUSE BREAKDOWN** | Telstar TV/BMG TTVCD 3307 |
| 29/03/2003 | 3 | 6 | | **THE VERY BEST OF ALL WOMAN 2003** | Telstar TV/BMG TTVCD 3299 |
| 12/04/2003 | 2 | 10 | | **THE VERY BEST OF PURE R&B – SUMMER 2003** | Telstar TV/BMG TTVCD 3325 |
| 19/04/2003 | 12 | 3 | | WHITE LABEL EUPHORIA – LEVEL 2 | Telstar TV/BMG TTVCD 3327 |
| 17/05/2003 | 5 | 6 | | **ELECTRIC – LEVEL 2** | Telstar TV/BMG TTVCD 3329 |
| 17/05/2003 | 14 | 4 | | THE VERY BEST OF PURE HIP HOP | Telstar TV/BMG TTVCD 3328 |
| 14/06/2003 | 3 | 8 | | **THE VERY BEST OF DRIVE TIME** | Telstar TV/BMG TTVCD 3336 |
| 14/06/2003 | 4 | 5 | | **DARK SIDE OF THE 80'S** | Telstar TV/BMG TTVCD 3322 |
| 21/06/2003 | 10 | 2 | | **ROCKABILLY REVIVAL** | Telstar TV/BMG TTVCD 3341 |
| 28/06/2003 | 12 | 2 | | LATIN LEGENDS | Telstar TV/BMG TTVCD 3271 |
| 05/07/2003 | 8 | 3 | | **THE VERY BEST OF EUPHORIC DANCE BREAKDOWN** | Telstar TV/BMG TTVCD 3344 |
| 19/07/2003 | 6 | 3 | | **EXTREME EUPHORIA – LISA LASHES** | Telstar TV/BMG TTVCD 3346 |
| 02/08/2003 | 4 | 5 | | **THE VERY BEST OF STREET VIBES** | Telstar TV/BMG TTVCD 3330 |
| 30/08/2003 | 10 | 3 | | **ALL TIME CLASSICS SOUL HEARTBREAKERS** | Telstar TV/BMG TTVCD 3352 |
| 13/09/2003 | 12 | 4 | | BOMBAY MIX | Telstar TV/BMG TTVCD 3354 |
| 27/09/2003 | 8 | 4 | | **THE VERY BEST OF PURE DANCEHALL** | Telstar TV/BMG TTVCD 3353 |
| 08/11/2003 | 3 | 9 | | **THE VERY BEST OF PURE R&B – WINTER 2003** | Telstar TV/BMG TTVCD 3362 |
| 08/11/2003 | 9 | 3 | | **100% PURE OLD SKOOL CLUB CLASSICS** | Telstar TV/BMG TTVCD 3361 |
| 22/11/2003 | 14 | 1 | | EUPHORIA | Telstar TV/BMG TTVCD 3365 |
| 07/02/2004 | 2 | 7 | | **BLING** | Telstar TV/BMG TTVCD 3381 |
| 21/02/2004 | 10 | 1 | | **LOVE SONGS TO MAKE YOU FEEL GOOD** | Telstar TV/BMG TTVCD 3382 |
| 21/02/2004 | 17 | 1 | | VERY BEST OF EUPHORIC DISCO BREAKDOWN | Telstar TV/BMG TTVCD 3379 |
| 27/03/2004 | 16 | 1 | | LOVELY DAY | Telstar TV/EMI TV TTVCD 3384 |
| 10/04/2004 | 9 | 2 | | **LOVE BITES & SCHOOL NITES** | Telstar TV/BMG TTVCD 3385 |
| 12/06/2004 | 19 | 1 | | CRASH INDIE ANTHEMS 1982–2004 | Telstar TV/BMG TTVCD 3389 |

### TOMMY BOY
US label formed in New York in 1981 by Tom Silverman with a $5,000 loan from his parents.

| DATE | POS | WKS | | ALBUM TITLE | LABEL & NUMBER |
|---|---|---|---|---|---|
| 06/04/1985 | 44 | 6 | | TOMMY BOY GREATEST BEATS | Tommy Boy ILPS 9825 |

### TOPAZ

| DATE | POS | WKS | | ALBUM TITLE | LABEL & NUMBER |
|---|---|---|---|---|---|
| 22/05/1976 | 7 | 7 | | **A TOUCH OF COUNTRY** | Topaz TOC\R 1976 |
| 03/07/1976 | 57 | 1 | | A TOUCH OF CLASS | Topaz TOC 1976 |

### TOUCHDOWN

| DATE | POS | WKS | | ALBUM TITLE | LABEL & NUMBER |
|---|---|---|---|---|---|
| 13/03/1993 | 8 | 4 | | **D-FROST – 20 GLOBAL DANCE WARNINGS** | Touchdown CTVCD 114 |

### TOWERBELL
UK label formed by record company executive Bob England.

| DATE | POS | WKS | BPI | ALBUM TITLE | LABEL & NUMBER |
|---|---|---|---|---|---|
| 08/02/1986 | 10 | 11 | ● | **THE DANCE HITS ALBUM** | Towerbell TVLP 8 |
| 15/03/1986 | 44 | 9 | ● | THE CINEMA HITS ALBUM | Towerbell TVLP 9 |
| 17/05/1986 | 27 | 9 | ○ | SISTERS ARE DOIN' IT | Towerbell TVLP 11 |
| 07/06/1986 | 51 | 5 | ○ | TWO'S COMPANY | Towerbell TVLP 12 |
| 28/06/1986 | 25 | 8 | | DANCE HITS II | Towerbell TVLP 13 |
| 02/08/1986 | 15 | 9 | | THE ORIGINALS: 32 ALL-TIME CLASSIC GREATS | Towerbell TBDLP 14 |
| 09/08/1986 | 51 | 3 | | YOU'VE GOT TO LAUGH | Towerbell TVLP 15 |

### TRAX

| DATE | POS | WKS | BPI | ALBUM TITLE | LABEL & NUMBER |
|---|---|---|---|---|---|
| 17/12/1988 | 89 | 2 | | NOEL – CHRISTMAS SONGS AND CAROLS | Trax TRXLP 701 |
| 22/07/1989 | 19 | 1 | | DREAMS OF IRELAND | Trax MODEM 1035 |
| 17/02/1990 | 7 | 6 | ● | **ROCK OF AMERICA** | Trax MODEM 1036 |

| | | | | | |
|---|---|---|---|---|---|
| 19/05/1990 | 4 | 10 | ● | FREEDOM TO PARTY – FIRST LEGAL RAVE | Trax MODEM 1048 |
| 28/07/1990 | 9 | 6 | | SUMMER CHART PARTY | Trax BWTX 1 |
| 03/11/1990 | 16 | 2 | | FREEDOM 2 – THE ULTIMATE RAVE | Trax BWTX 4 |
| 17/11/1990 | 20 | 1 | | KARAOKE PARTY | Trax BETX 5 |
| 16/03/1991 | 7 | 9 | | KARAOKE PARTY II | Trax TXTV 1 |

## TROJAN
UK reggae label formed in 1969, taking its name from the nickname of Jamaican producer Duke Reid and established as a UK outlet for his Treasure Isle recordings. Its original founders were Chris Blackwell and Lee Gopthal, although Blackwell later left to form Island Records. Trojan went into receivership in 1975 and was later bought by the Sanctuary Group.

| | | | | | |
|---|---|---|---|---|---|
| 07/08/1971 | 20 | 7 | | TIGHTEN UP VOLUME 4 | Trojan TBL 163 |
| 21/08/1971 | 25 | 4 | | CLUB REGGAE | Trojan TBL 159 |
| 16/06/1984 | 89 | 1 | | 20 REGGAE CLASSICS | Trojan TRLS 222 |
| 03/08/2002 | 6 | 6 | ● | YOUNG GIFTED & BLACK | Trojan TJDDD 006 |

## TV RECORDS

| | | | | | |
|---|---|---|---|---|---|
| 02/10/1982 | 24 | 7 | | MODERN HEROES | TV Records TVA 1 |
| 09/10/1982 | 26 | 8 | | ENDLESS LOVE | TV Records TV 2 |
| 06/11/1982 | 19 | 7 | | FLASH TRACKS | TV Records PTVL 1 |
| 25/12/1982 | 71 | 3 | | PARTY FEVER/DISCO MANIA | TV Records TVA 5 |

## TVD ENTERTAINMENT

| | | | | | |
|---|---|---|---|---|---|
| 09/05/1998 | 12 | 3 | | OFF YER NUT!! | TVD Entertainment/Life On Mars TVDCD 1 |

## 2-TONE
UK label formed in 1979 by Jerry Dammers of The Specials as a label imprint within Chrysalis. Initially home to Dammers' own group, later acts included Selecter, Madness (for one single), The Beat and The Bodysnatchers, among others.

| | | | | | |
|---|---|---|---|---|---|
| 26/11/1983 | 51 | 9 | | THIS ARE TWO TONE | 2-Tone CHRTT 5007 |
| 05/08/1989 | 16 | 5 | | THE 2 TONE STORY | 2-Tone CHRTT 5009 |
| 23/10/1993 | 10 | 4 | | THE BEST OF 2 TONE | 2-Tone CDCHRTT 5012 |

## ULTRASOUND

| | | | | | |
|---|---|---|---|---|---|
| 15/07/1995 | 13 | 3 | | THE HOUSE OF HANDBAG | Ultrasound USCD 3 |
| 04/11/1995 | 16 | 2 | | THE HOUSE OF HANDBAG – AUTUMN/WINTER COLLECTION | Ultrasound USCD 4 |

## UNITED DANCE

| | | | | | |
|---|---|---|---|---|---|
| 18/01/1997 | 8 | 3 | | THE ANTHEMS '92–'97 | United Dance UNCD 003 |
| 12/07/1997 | 17 | 2 | | UNITED DANCE PRESENTS ANTHEMS 2 – '88–'92 | United Dance UMCD 004 |

## UNIVERSAL
Canadian label formed in 1995 following the acquisition of the MCA company by Seagrams and the subsequent creation of the Universal Music Group. In 2000 a $20 billion merger between Seagrams and French media company Vivendi created Vivendi Universal, the world's largest record company.

Latin Fever

38 Of The Hottest Sexy Summer Tunes
Including: Ricky Martin, Jennifer Lopez, Enrique Iglesias, Santana, Marc Anthony, Lou Bega, Stardust, Gloria Estefan, Gypsy Kings & Sergio Mendes

| | | | | | |
|---|---|---|---|---|---|
| 13/06/1998 | 2 | 6 | ● | MASSIVE DANCE: 98 – VOLUME 2 | warner.esp/Polygram TV/Global TV 5650632 |
| 17/10/1998 | 9 | 3 | | THE HEART OF THE 80S AND 90S | Universal MCD 60061 |
| 12/12/1998 | 5 | 9 | ● | MASSIVE DANCE: 99 | warner.esp/Polygram TV/Global TV 5655352 |
| 20/03/1999 | 5 | 3 | | THE LOVE SONGS OF BURT BACHARACH | Universal Music TV 5642652 |
| 27/03/1999 | 8 | 3 | | BLUES BROTHER SOUL SISTER CLASSICS | Universal Music TV 5641832 |
| 03/04/1999 | 3 | 5 | | MASSIVE DANCE: 99 – VOLUME TWO | warner.esp/Universal Music TV/Global TV 5643102 |
| 08/05/1999 | 2 | 7 | ● | KISS CLUBLIFE | Universal Music TV 5474662 |
| 22/05/1999 | 2 | 6 | ● | TOP OF THE POPS '99 – VOLUME ONE | BBC/Universal Music TV 5644592 |
| 29/05/1999 | 13 | 2 | | DANCING IN THE STREET | Universal Music TV 5495092 |
| 12/06/1999 | 10 | 5 | ○ | THE SOUND OF MAGIC | Universal Music TV 5644792 |
| 19/06/1999 | 16 | 2 | | SIXTIES SUMMER LOVE | Universal Music TV 5642712 |
| 26/06/1999 | 7 | 4 | ● | KISS SMOOTH GROOVES – SUMMER '99 | Universal Music TV 5645422 |
| 10/07/1999 | 2 | 4 | ● | THE BOX – DANCE HITS | Universal Music TV 5645482 |
| 17/07/1999 | 8 | 8 | ● | COUNTRY | Sony TV/Universal Music TV 5644822 |
| 24/07/1999 | 5 | 6 | ○ | DAVE PEARCE PRESENTS 40 CLASSIC DANCE ANTHEMS | Universal Music TV 5471962 |
| 31/07/1999 | 14 | 3 | | AFRODISIAC | Universal Music TV 5648502 |
| 21/08/1999 | 3 | 7 | ● | CLUB MIX 99 | Universal Music TV 5648922 |
| 04/09/1999 | 9 | 3 | | SISTERS OF SWING 99 | Universal Music TV 5649302 |
| 18/09/1999 | ❶[3] | 8 | ● | KISS IBIZA '99 | Universal Music TV 1537512 |

▲[9] Number of weeks album topped the US chart   ◆[12] RIAA Diamond Awards   ◇[3] IFPI Platinum Europe Awards

| DATE | POS | WKS | BPI | ALBUM TITLE | LABEL & NUMBER |
|------|-----|-----|-----|-------------|----------------|
| 25/09/1999 | ❶¹ | 8 | ✪ | **TOP OF THE POPS '99 – VOLUME TWO** | Universal Music TV 5450692 |
| 02/10/1999 | 5 | 5 | | **THE SOUND OF MAGIC LOVE** | Universal Music TV 5648842 |
| 16/10/1999 | ❶¹ | 6 | ○ | **LAND OF MY FATHERS** Official album of the Rugby World Cup | Universal Music TV 4665674 |
| 16/10/1999 | 10 | 2 | | **MOBO 1999** | Universal Music TV 5451432 |
| 23/10/1999 | 7 | 3 | | **DAVE PEARCE PRESENTS 40 CLASSIC DANCE ANTHEMS 2** | Universal Music TV 1539732 |
| 06/11/1999 | 20 | 1 | | THE 90'S | Universal Music TV 5453532 |
| 13/11/1999 | 4 | 19 | ✪ | **WOMAN 2** | Universal Music/Sony TV/Global TV 5451402 |
| 13/11/1999 | 5 | 3 | | **THE BOX DANCE HITS – VOLUME 2** | Universal Music TV 1537792 |
| 20/11/1999 | 17 | 2 | ✪ | THE NUMBER ONE DANCE PARTY ALBUM | Universal Music TV 5550572 |
| 27/11/1999 | 6 | 11 | ● | **KISS CLUBLIFE 2000** | Universal Music TV 5649422 |
| 11/12/1999 | 9 | 10 | ● | **MASSIVE DANCE HITS 2000** | warner.esp/Global TV/Universal Music TV 1570942 |
| 15/01/2000 | 14 | 1 | | CELEBRATION 2000 | Universal TV 5450662 |
| 05/02/2000 | 2 | 6 | ● | **CLUBMIX 2000** | Universal TV 5411542 |
| 12/02/2000 | ❶¹ | 7 | ✪ | **THE LOVE SONGS ALBUM** | warner.esp/Universal TV/Global TV 5412002 |
| 04/03/2000 | 3 | 6 | ● | **TOP OF THE POPS 2000 VOLUME 1** | Universal TV 5411972 |
| 11/03/2000 | 2 | 6 | ● | **CLUB 2K** | Universal TV 5413302 |
| 01/04/2000 | 3 | 4 | ○ | **KISS UK GARAGE – MIXED BY KARL BROWN** | Universal TV 5414782 |
| 01/04/2000 | 5 | 4 | | **THAT OLE DEVIL CALLED LOVE** | Universal TV 5456062 |
| 15/04/2000 | 3 | 7 | ● | **RELOADED** | Universal TV 5415512 |
| 15/04/2000 | 5 | 2 | ○ | **BOX DANCE HITS 2000** | Universal TV 5414592 |
| 29/04/2000 | 6 | 7 | | **THE CLASSICAL ALBUM** | Universal/Virgin/EMI 4671402 |
| 29/04/2000 | 15 | 2 | | TOP OF THE POPS 2 | Universal TV 5412742 |
| 06/05/2000 | 2 | 7 | ● | **KISS HOUSE NATION 2000** | Universal TV 1576052 |
| 20/05/2000 | 7 | 4 | ○ | **DAVE PEARCE PRESENTS 40 CLASSIC ANTHEMS – 3** | Universal Music TV 5418122 |
| 03/06/2000 | 3 | 5 | | **KISS SMOOTH GROOVES 2000** | Universal TV 5246682 |
| 10/06/2000 | 6 | 3 | | **DJ LUCK & MC NEAT PRESENTS** | Universal TV 5246852 |
| 10/06/2000 | 9 | 2 | ○ | **THE SOUND OF MAGIC VOLUME 2** | Universal TV 5414092 |
| 17/06/2000 | ❶¹ | 11 | ● | **TOP OF THE POPS 2000 VOLUME 2** | Universal TV 5246972 |
| 24/06/2000 | ❶³ | 11 | ✪ | **CLUB MIX IBIZA 2000** | Universal TV 5246822 |
| 24/06/2000 | 15 | 1 | | EURO 2000 – THE OFFICIAL ALBUM | Universal TV 1590902 |
| 22/07/2000 | ❶¹ | 7 | ● | **KISS CLUBLIFE SUMMER 2000** | Universal TV 5601122 |
| 29/07/2000 | 15 | 3 | | RESPECT – THE SOUNDTRACK TO THE SOUL GENERATION | warner.esp/Universal TV 5248624 |
| 05/08/2000 | 3 | 9 | ● | **LATIN FEVER** | Sony TV/Universal TV 5601282 |
| 12/08/2000 | 7 | 3 | ● | **CLUB 2K VOL. 2** | Universal TV/Ministry Of Sound 5601982 |
| 12/08/2000 | 11 | 3 | | THE REAL SOUND OF AYIA NAPA | Universal TV 5601092 |
| 19/08/2000 | 15 | 2 | | SUMMERTIME | Universal TV 5601932 |
| 09/09/2000 | 12 | 2 | | THE BOX | Universal TV 5602472 |
| 23/09/2000 | ❶² | 7 | ● | **KISS IBIZA 2000** | Universal TV 5603662 |
| 23/09/2000 | 11 | 2 | | HOT POP | Universal TV 5601322 |
| 30/09/2000 | 15 | 2 | | THE LATE NIGHT MIX | Universal TV 5606232 |
| 14/10/2000 | 3 | 5 | ○ | **MOBO 2000** | Universal TV 5606662 |
| 21/10/2000 | ❶¹ | 5 | ● | **CLUBMIX 2000 VOLUME 2** | Universal TV 5605872 |
| 28/10/2000 | 3 | 5 | ● | **THE HIT FACTORY** | Universal TV 5606692 |
| 04/11/2000 | 3 | 4 | ● | **KISS GARAGE PRESENT DJ LUCK & MC NEAT** | Universal TV 5605992 |
| 11/11/2000 | 4 | 4 | ● | **TOP OF THE POPS 2000 – VOL 3** | Universal TV 5605652 |
| 11/11/2000 | 6 | 13 | ✪ | **STEVE WRIGHT'S SUNDAY LOVE SONGS** | Universal TV 5602902 |
| 18/11/2000 | 10 | 2 | | **WOMAN 3** | Sony TV/Universal TV 5603632 |
| 18/11/2000 | 8 | 2 | | **KISS HOUSE NATION 2001** | Universal TV 5605932 |
| 02/12/2000 | 8 | 9 | ○ | **MUSIC OF THE MILLENNIUM VOL. 2** | EMI/Virgin/Universal 5602302 |
| 09/12/2000 | 18 | 3 | | MASSIVE DANCE 2001 | BMG/M.O.S/UMTV/Warners 5201102 |
| 03/02/2001 | 2 | 7 | ● | **RELOADED 2** | Universal TV 5602332 |
| 03/02/2001 | 10 | 2 | | **TOP OF THE POPS 2 – 70'S ROCK** | Universal TV 5606262 |
| 10/02/2001 | 2 | 7 | ● | **PASSION – SONGS FOR LOVERS** | warner.esp/Universal TV/Global TV 5207042 |
| 24/02/2001 | 3 | 8 | ● | **CLUB MIX 2001** | Universal TV 5209312 |
| 03/03/2001 | 4 | 4 | ○ | **TOP OF THE POPS 2001 – VOL 1** | Universal TV 5209862 |
| 10/03/2001 | 11 | 3 | | THE NATURAL BLUES ALBUM | Universal TV 5209392 |
| 17/03/2001 | 2 | 6 | ● | **KISS SMOOTH GROOVES 2001** | Universal TV 5208542 |
| 24/03/2001 | 7 | 3 | | **MAGIC** | Universal TV 5608982 |
| 31/03/2001 | 6 | 4 | | **CLUBBED** | Universal TV 5561892 |
| 07/04/2001 | 6 | 3 | | **MTV SELECT** | Universal TV 5563142 |
| 14/04/2001 | 4 | 8 | ● | **DJ LUCK & MC NEAT PRESENTS – II** | Universal TV 5563182 |
| 21/04/2001 | 12 | 2 | | KISS CLUBLIFE 2001 | Universal TV 5561922 |
| 05/05/2001 | 4 | 7 | ● | **DISCO FEVER** | Universal TV 5564082 |
| 26/05/2001 | 7 | 4 | ○ | **SUNSET IBIZA** | Universal TV 5566692 |
| 02/06/2001 | 7 | 3 | ○ | **PURE & SIMPLE** | Universal TV 5561222 |
| 23/06/2001 | 9 | 4 | ○ | **RELOADED 3** | Universal TV 5567342 |
| 23/06/2001 | 11 | 3 | ○ | **R&B SELECTOR** | Universal TV 5565202 |
| 23/06/2001 | 15 | 2 | | DANNY RAMPLING – LOVE GROOVE DANCE PARTY | Universal TV 5605902 |
| 07/07/2001 | 2 | 5 | ● | **PARTY IN THE PARK** | Universal TV 5850002 |

○ Silver disc   ● Gold disc   ✪ Platinum disc (additional platinum units are indicated by a figure following the symbol)   ❶⁹ Number of weeks album topped the UK chart

| DATE | POS | WKS | BPI | ALBUM TITLE | LABEL & NUMBER |
|---|---|---|---|---|---|
| 07/07/2001 | 18 | 1 | | MTV DANCE | Universal TV 5567252 |
| 14/07/2001 | 9 | 5 | ○ | KERRANG – THE ALBUM | WSM/Universal TV 564882 |
| 14/07/2001 | 4 | 4 | ● | TOP OF THE POPS – SUMMER 2001 | Universal TV 5566662 |
| 04/08/2001 | 8 | 3 | | CLUBBED – VOLUME 2 – MIXED BY JUDGE JULES | Universal TV 5568732 |
| 11/08/2001 | 2 | 8 | ● | CLUBMIX IBIZA | UMTV/Ministry Of Sound 5853332 |
| 11/08/2001 | 7 | 4 | ● | KISS SMOOTH GROOVES SUMMER 2001 | Universal TV 5851162 |
| 11/08/2001 | 11 | 4 | | ATOMIC 80'S | Universal TV 5851622 |
| 01/09/2001 | 9 | 2 | | DISCO FEVER – VOLUME 2 | Universal TV 5855102 |
| 08/09/2001 | 5 | 7 | ● | CLOSE TO YOU | Universal TV 5853742 |
| 08/09/2001 | 15 | 2 | | MTV HITS | Universal TV 5853922 |
| 29/09/2001 | 6 | 4 | ○ | KISS IN IBIZA 2001 | Universal TV 5855182 |
| 29/09/2001 | 17 | 1 | | GOD'S KITCHEN | Universal TV 5044892 |
| 06/10/2001 | 7 | 4 | ○ | DJ LUCK & MC NEAT PRESENT VOLUME 3 | Universal TV 5854302 |
| 13/10/2001 | 15 | 2 | | URBAN CHILL | Universal TV 5855872 |
| 27/10/2001 | 5 | 3 | ● | URBAN KISS | Universal TV 5854722 |
| 03/11/2001 | 8 | 3 | ● | TOP OF THE POPS – AUTUMN 2001 | Universal TV 5858752 |
| 17/11/2001 | 14 | 1 | | FEMALE | Sony TV/Universal TV 5857662 |
| 17/11/2001 | 11 | 2 | | PUMP UP THE VOLUME | Universal TV 5841642 |
| 17/11/2001 | 11 | 5 | ● | ALL TOGETHER NOW | Universal TV 5855712 |
| 24/11/2001 | 8 | 9 | ● | KERRANG! 2 – THE ALBUM | WSM/Universal TV 5857632 |
| 24/11/2001 | 12 | 3 | | STEVE WRIGHT'S SUNDAY LOVE SONGS VOLUME 2 | Universal TV 5856482 |
| 01/12/2001 | 7 | 10 | ✪ | MOTOWN GOLD | Universal TV 0163012 |
| 01/12/2001 | 16 | 1 | | R&B HITS | Universal TV 5855902 |
| 29/12/2001 | 4 | 7 | ● | KISS HITLIST 2002 | EMI/Virgin/Universal 5841812 |
| 12/01/2002 | 4 | 5 | ○ | THE LICK – TREVOR NELSON | Universal TV 5855042 |
| 02/02/2002 | 4 | 4 | ○ | RELOADED 4 | Universal TV 5840892 |
| 02/02/2002 | 7 | 2 | | CLUBBED 2002 – MIXED BY JUDGE JULES | Universal TV 5843552 |
| 09/02/2002 | ❶[1] | 5 | ● | CLUB MIX 2002 | Universal TV 5859562 |
| 09/02/2002 | 3 | 4 | ● | LOVE | Universal TV 5845252 |
| 23/02/2002 | 10 | 3 | | KISS SMOOTH GROOVES 2002 | Universal TV 5844942 |
| 09/03/2002 | 18 | 1 | | RAPPERS DELIGHT | Universal TV 5847272 |
| 16/03/2002 | ❶[2] | 9 | ● | SUPERCHARGED | UMTV/WSM 5848582 |
| 16/03/2002 | 20 | 1 | | TOGETHER | Universal TV 5858922 |
| 23/03/2002 | 7 | 4 | ○ | GIRLS SAY | Universal TV 5849012 |
| 30/03/2002 | 7 | 3 | ○ | MURDER ON THE DANCEFLOOR | Universal TV 5849672 |
| 30/03/2002 | 18 | 1 | | TEMPTATIONS/FOUR TOPS: AT THEIR BEST | Universal 5830142 |
| 13/04/2002 | 10 | 2 | | NEW JACK SWING | Universal TV 5749912 |
| 27/04/2002 | 6 | 4 | | SUPA FUNKY | Universal TV 5832352 |
| 11/05/2002 | 5 | 6 | ○ | SIMPLY ACOUSTIC | Sony TV/Universal TV 5848622 |
| 18/05/2002 | 4 | 5 | ○ | KERRANG! 3 – THE ALBUM | Universal TV 5845062 |
| 25/05/2002 | ❶[1] | 5 | ● | KISSTORY | Universal TV 5831082 |
| 25/05/2002 | 4 | 4 | ○ | TOP OF THE POPS SPRING 2002 | Universal TV 5832322 |
| 08/06/2002 | 16 | 1 | | BEAUTIFUL GAME | Universal TV 5848192 |
| 08/06/2002 | 20 | 1 | | TEENAGE KICKS | Universal TV 5832642 |
| 22/06/2002 | ❶[1] | 12 | ● | THE VERY BEST OF MTV UNPLUGGED | WSM/Universal TV 5835452 |
| 22/06/2002 | 3 | 6 | ● | URBAN KISS 2002 | Universal TV 5830412 |
| 22/06/2002 | 13 | 2 | | EMOTIONS | Universal TV 5832812 |
| 06/07/2002 | 7 | 20 | | THE VERY BEST OF SMOOTH JAZZ | Universal Classics & Jazz 5834902 |
| 06/07/2002 | ❶[3] | 12 | ✪ | CLUBLAND | Universal TV/Serious 5836012 |
| 13/07/2002 | 4 | 3 | ○ | PARTY IN THE PARK 2002 | Universal TV/Serious 5837632 |
| 27/07/2002 | 2 | 5 | | CLUBMIX IBIZA 2002 | Universal TV/Serious 5834602 |
| 27/07/2002 | 5 | 4 | | SEXY CRAZY COOL | Universal TV 5847282 |
| 17/08/2002 | 9 | 4 | | ROCK MONSTERS | Universal TV 5834142 |
| 31/08/2002 | 2 | 5 | | KISS HITLIST SUMMER 2002 | UMTV/Serious 690162 |
| 14/09/2002 | 13 | 2 | | KISSTORY IBIZA CLASSIC | Universal TV 0694552 |
| 21/09/2002 | 3 | 20 | ✪ | WHILE MY GUITAR GENTLY WEEPS | Universal TV 583442 |
| 28/09/2002 | 18 | 1 | | LOUNGIN' – MUSIC TO WATCH THE WORLD GO BY | UMTV/Serious 5832732 |
| 12/10/2002 | 17 | 1 | | SERIOUS CLUB HITS | UMTV/Serious 5834802 |
| 09/11/2002 | 10 | 2 | | A WOMAN'S TOUCH | Universal TV 0693582 |
| 16/11/2002 | 14 | 2 | | TOP OF THE POPS 2003 | Universal TV 695822 |
| 23/11/2002 | ❶[1] | 12 | ✪ | CLUBLAND II – THE RIDE OF YOUR LIFE | UMTV/AATW 0680632 |
| 23/11/2002 | 13 | 6 | ● | STEVE WRIGHT'S SUNDAY LOVE SONGS | Universal TV 699232 |
| 08/02/2003 | 8 | 8 | ● | FRIENDS REUNITED | Universal TV 0696342 |
| 15/02/2003 | ❶[2] | 6 | ● | LOVE – ETERNAL LOVESONGS | Universal TV 0686682 |
| 22/02/2003 | 12 | 4 | | THE LICK – BEST OF | Universal TV 0685402 |
| 01/03/2003 | ❶[1] | 6 | ● | CLUB MIX 2003 | Universal TV 0687152 |
| 15/03/2003 | 8 | 3 | | Q THE ALBUM | EMI/Virgin/Universal 0685042 |
| 22/03/2003 | 8 | 3 | | SMOOTH JAZZ 2 | UCJ 0694612 |
| 29/03/2003 | 6 | 3 | | TOP OF THE POPS SPRING 2003 | EMI/Virgin/Universal 0689752 |

▲[9] Number of weeks album topped the US chart   ◆[12] RIAA Diamond Awards   ◇[3] IFPI Platinum Europe Awards

| DATE | POS | WKS | BPI | ALBUM TITLE | LABEL & NUMBER |
|---|---|---|---|---|---|
| 05/04/2003 | 10 | 2 | | HEARTBEAT LOVE SONGS | Universal TV 0685512 |
| 12/04/2003 | 16 | 2 | | PURE DRUM & BASS | Universal TV 0689202 |
| 26/04/2003 | 2 | 10 | ● | CLUBLAND X-TREME | UMTV/AATW 0392142 |
| 10/05/2003 | 6 | 3 | | URBAN KISS 2003 | Universal TV 0391452 |
| 24/05/2003 | 2 | 9 | ● | KISS PRESENTS HIP HOP CLASSICS | Universal TV 9800273 |
| 07/06/2003 | 18 | 1 | | THE VERY BEST OF CHILLED CLASSICS | UCJ 0690452 |
| 14/06/2003 | 2 | 7 | ○ | THE QUIET STORM | Universal TV 9800257 |
| 28/06/2003 | 3 | 6 | | 60'S SOUL MIX | Universal TV 9808144 |
| 28/06/2003 | 10 | 4 | | MAGIC – SUMMER FEELING 2003 | Universal TV 9807671 |
| 05/07/2003 | ●³ | 15 | | CLUBLAND III | UMTV/AATW 9800267 |
| 05/07/2003 | 17 | 1 | | KERRANG! – HIGH VOLTAGE | UMTV/WSMS 0396382 |
| 12/07/2003 | 7 | 3 | | KISS HITLIST SUMMER 2003 | Universal TV 0396432 |
| 02/08/2003 | 10 | 5 | | THE PIANO AND THE SONG | Universal TV 9800254 |
| 09/08/2003 | 4 | 7 | | COUNTRY LOVE | Universal TV 9806791 |
| 09/08/2003 | 17 | 2 | | FEELIN' GOOD | UCJ 9809935 |
| 16/08/2003 | 3 | 8 | | RIDE DA RIDDIMS | Universal TV 9809706 |
| 16/08/2003 | 18 | 1 | | FRIENDS REUNITED – THE 90'S | Universal TV 9808782 |
| 23/08/2003 | 5 | 4 | | CAPITAL GOLD REGGAE CLASSICS | Universal TV 9808537 |
| 23/08/2003 | 15 | 1 | | WHAT A FEELING | Universal TV 9809318 |
| 30/08/2003 | ●³ | 9 | | KISS PRESENTS R&B COLLABORATIONS | Universal TV/Sony TV 0391412 |
| 06/09/2003 | 7 | 3 | | ANTHEM CLASSICS FROM CLUBLAND | UMTV/AATW 9811029 |
| 06/09/2003 | 11 | 3 | | TOP OF THE POPS SUMMER 2003 | Universal/EMI/Virgin 9810528 |
| 06/09/2003 | 12 | 3 | | KISS XXX HIP HOP | Universal TV 9865595 |
| 13/09/2003 | 7 | 4 | | KISSTORY URBAN CLASSICS | Universal TV 9811370 |
| 27/09/2003 | ●² | 7 | | CLUBMIX SUMMER 2003 | UMTV/AATW 9811192 |
| 04/10/2003 | 5 | 4 | | MOBO PRESENTS URBAN BEATS 2003 | Universal TV 9811773 |
| 11/10/2003 | 9 | 3 | | THE MICHAEL PARKINSON COLLECTION | UCJ 9811787 |
| 18/10/2003 | 15 | 1 | | URBAN FUSION | Universal TV 9811174 |
| 25/10/2003 | 13 | 1 | | 70'S SOUL MIX | Universal TV 9811527 |
| 08/11/2003 | 10 | 3 | | WHILE MY GUITAR GENTLY WEEPS II | Universal TV 9807760 |
| 15/11/2003 | ●¹ | 7 | ● | WESTWOOD – PLATINUM EDITION | Def Jam/Universal Music TV 9813338 |
| 15/11/2003 | 2 | 22 | ✪ | POP PARTY | EMI/Virgin/Universal 9812645 |
| 22/11/2003 | ●¹ | 18 | ✪ | CLUBLAND 4 | UMTV/AATW 9813598 |
| 29/11/2003 | 4 | 10 | ✪ | THE NUMBER ONE CLASSICAL ALBUM 2004 | UCJ 4761390 |
| 29/11/2003 | 7 | 11 | | KISS PRESENTS HOT JOINTS | Universal TV 9813698 |
| 29/11/2003 | 17 | 6 | | CAPITAL GOLD MOTOWN CLASSICS | Universal TV 9810954 |
| 07/02/2004 | ●¹ | 7 | ● | KISS SMOOTH R&B | Sony TV/Universal TV 9815795 |
| 14/02/2004 | ●² | 8 | ● | CLUBMIX 2004 | UMTV/AATW 9816475 |
| 14/02/2004 | 2 | 6 | ● | STEVE WRIGHT'S CHOCOLATES AND CHAMPAGNE | Universal TV 9826480 |
| 13/03/2004 | 5 | 6 | ○ | LEADERS OF THE PACK – 60'S GIRLS | Universal TV 9811326 |
| 20/03/2004 | ●¹ | 12 | ● | FLOORFILLERS | UMTV/AATW 9817728 |
| 20/03/2004 | 7 | 4 | | RIDE DA RIDDIMS 2 | Universal TV 9815623 |
| 03/04/2004 | 13 | 2 | | KISS PRESENTS LAYDEEZ WITH ATTITUDE | Universal TV 9818595 |
| 17/04/2004 | 3 | 10 | ● | POP PRINCESSES | Universal TV 9817531 |
| 17/04/2004 | 14 | 2 | | 60'S SOUL MIX 2 | Universal TV 9818833 |
| 01/05/2004 | 2 | 7 | ● | CLUBLAND X-TREME 2 | UMTV/AATW 9819336 |
| 22/05/2004 | 2 | 6+ | | KISS PRESENTS THE HIP HOP COLLECTION | Universal TV 9819774 |
| 22/05/2004 | 4 | 4 | | CAPITAL GOLD – JUST GREAT SONGS | Universal TV 9819149 |
| 05/06/2004 | 15 | 1 | | IN THE MOOD FOR LOVE | Universal TV 9820180 |
| 12/06/2004 | 9 | 3+ | | THIS IS THE MODERN WORLD | Universal TV 9819443 |
| 12/06/2004 | 11 | 1 | | THE NO. 1 OPERA ALBUM | UCJ 4762004 |
| 19/06/2004 | 4 | 2+ | | PURPLE RAINBOWS | EMI/Universal TV 9821194 |
| 19/06/2004 | 18 | 1 | | NEW BREED | Universal TV 9820091 |
| 26/06/2004 | 20 | 1+ | | JUST FOR YOU | Universal TV 9820026 |

## UNIVERSE

| DATE | POS | WKS | BPI | ALBUM TITLE | LABEL & NUMBER |
|---|---|---|---|---|---|
| 15/05/1993 | 13 | 2 | | UNIVERSE – WORLD TECHNO TRIBE | Universe VERSECD 1 |
| 10/06/1995 | 19 | 1 | | UNIVERSE PRESENTS THE TRIBAL GATHERING | Universe 8284522 |
| 19/10/1996 | 15 | 2 | | TRIBAL GATHERING '96 | Universe UNV 001CD |

## URBAN

| DATE | POS | WKS | BPI | ALBUM TITLE | LABEL & NUMBER |
|---|---|---|---|---|---|
| 14/11/1987 | 96 | 1 | | URBAN CLASSICS | Urban URBLP 4 |
| 24/09/1988 | 51 | 8 | | URBAN ACID | Urban URBLP 15 |
| 08/10/1988 | 86 | 3 | | ACID JAZZ AND OTHER ILLICIT GROOVES | Urban URBLP 16 |

**V2** UK label formed by Richard Branson, the former founder and owner of Virgin, after he sold Virgin to EMI Records.

| DATE | POS | WKS | BPI | ALBUM TITLE | LABEL & NUMBER |
|---|---|---|---|---|---|
| 24/05/1997 | 20 | 1 | | LOADED LOCK IN | V2 WR 1000222 |
| 14/06/1997 | 18 | 1 | | YOU'LL NEVER WALK ALONE | V2 WR 1000342 |

○ Silver disc ● Gold disc ✪ Platinum disc (additional platinum units are indicated by a figure following the symbol) ●⁹ Number of weeks album topped the UK chart

## VERTIGO
UK label formed in the late 1960s as a rock label by Philips; it later became part of the Universal Music Group.

| DATE | POS | WKS | BPI | ALBUM TITLE | LABEL & NUMBER |
|---|---|---|---|---|---|
| 21/06/1986 | 50 | 2 | | HEAR 'N' AID | Vertigo VERH 35 |
| 27/08/1988 | ❶¹ | 14 | ✪ | **HOT CITY NIGHTS** | Vertigo PROVTV 15 |
| 04/11/1989 | 3 | 14 | ● | **ROCK CITY NIGHT** | Vertigo RCNTV 1 |
| 28/09/1991 | 2 | 9 | ● | **THE POWER AND THE GLORY** | Vertigo 5103601 |

## VERVE
US jazz label formed in 1957 by producer Norman Granz, with artists of the calibre of Ella Fitzgerald (who was managed by Granz), Dizzy Gillespie and Oscar Peterson on its roster. The company was sold to MGM Records in 1961 for $3 million and under the direction of Creed Taylor (later to form his own CTI and Kudu labels) enjoyed considerable commercial success. In 1969 MGM and Verve were sold to Transcontinental Music and subsequently to Polygram, with Verve mainly being used as a re-issue label.

| DATE | POS | WKS | BPI | ALBUM TITLE | LABEL & NUMBER |
|---|---|---|---|---|---|
| 07/09/2002 | 14 | 1 | | CHILLED JAZZ | Verve 0692092 |
| 21/12/2002 | 13 | 2 | | THE JAZZ ALBUM 2003 | Verve 0680672 |
| 26/04/2003 | 12 | 3 | | DIVAS OF JAZZ | Verve 0394222 |

## VIRGIN
UK record company formed in 1973 by Richard Branson and Nik Powell. Branson had already run a mail order and retail operation and launched the record division in order to release Mike Oldfield's *Tubular Bells* album, which had been turned down by just about everyone else. The success of the album (it sold more than 5 million copies worldwide) saw the company gain a reputation for taking on left-field rock artists, until the 1980s when it achieved success with pop acts such as Culture Club and Human League. It would later acquire Charisma Records, form its own US outlet in Virgin America and launch other UK labels such as Ten, but in 1992 Branson sold Virgin Records to Thorn EMI for £510 million. Less than five years later Branson started again with V2.

| DATE | POS | WKS | BPI | ALBUM TITLE | LABEL & NUMBER |
|---|---|---|---|---|---|
| 22/11/1980 | 49 | 1 | | CASH COWS | Virgin MILK 1 |
| 17/04/1982 | 25 | 6 | | MUSIC OF QUALITY AND DISTINCTION (VOLUME 1) | Virgin V 2219 |
| 01/06/1985 | 61 | 3 | | MASSIVE – AN ALBUM OF REGGAE HITS | Virgin V 2346 |
| 19/01/1991 | 20 | 2 | | DANCE ENERGY | Virgin Television VTDLP 3 |
| 01/06/1991 | 6 | 5 | | **DANCE ENERGY 2** | Virgin Television VTLP 4 |
| 19/10/1991 | 2 | 22 | ✪² | **MOODS** | Virgin Television VTLP 5 |
| 30/11/1991 | 10 | 6 | ○ | **DANCE ENERGY 3** | Virgin Television VTLP 6 |
| 29/02/1992 | 4 | 10 | | **THREE MINUTE HEROES** | Virgin Television VTCD 9 |
| 16/05/1992 | 3 | 8 | ● | **MOODS 2** | Virgin Television VTCD 12 |
| 25/07/1992 | 2 | 12 | ● | **THE GREATEST DANCE ALBUM IN THE WORLD!** | Virgin Television VTCD 13 |
| 31/10/1992 | 7 | 5 | ○ | **NEW ROMANTIC CLASSICS** | Virgin Television VTCD 15 |
| 17/07/1993 | ❶⁴ | 19 | ✪² | **THE BEST DANCE ALBUM IN THE WORLD... EVER!** | Virgin Television VTDCD 17 |
| 23/10/1993 | 5 | 6 | | **THE SINGER AND THE SONG** | Virgin Television VTDCD 21 |
| 20/11/1993 | 3 | 12 | ✪ | **THE BEST DANCE ALBUM IN THE WORLD... EVER! 2** | Virgin Television VTDCD 22 |
| 04/12/1993 | 2 | 9 | ✪³ | **THE BEST CHRISTMAS ALBUM IN THE WORLD... EVER!** | Virgin Television VTDCD 23 |
| 29/01/1994 | ❶¹ | 9 | ● | **SWEET SOUL HARMONIES** | Virgin Television VTCD 20 |
| 26/02/1994 | 2 | 10 | ● | **DANCE TO THE MAX** | Virgin Television VTCD 24 |
| 12/03/1994 | 10 | 4 | ○ | **RAP TO THE MAX** | Virgin Television VTCD 25 |
| 30/04/1994 | 8 | 10 | ○ | **IN THE AIR TONIGHT** | Virgin Television VTDCD 26 |
| 07/05/1994 | ❶² | 31 | ✪² | **PURE MOODS** | Virgin Television VTCD 28 |
| 28/05/1994 | 4 | 8 | ● | **DANCE TO THE MAX 2** | Virgin Television VTCD 29 |
| 04/06/1994 | 4 | 10 | ✪ | **THE BEST REGGAE ALBUM IN THE WORLD... EVER!** | Virgin Television VTDCD 27 |
| 09/07/1994 | 8 | 5 | ○ | **SUPERFUNK** | Virgin Television VTDCD 30 |
| 30/07/1994 | 2 | 11 | ● | **THE BEST DANCE ALBUM IN THE WORLD... EVER! 3** | Virgin Television VTDCD 32 |
| 20/08/1994 | 10 | 2 | ○ | **SWEET SOUL HARMONIES 2** | Virgin Television VTCD 31 |
| 03/09/1994 | ❶³ | 24 | ✪³ | **THE BEST ROCK ALBUM IN THE WORLD... EVER!** | Virgin Television VTDCD 35 |
| 03/09/1994 | 12 | 3 | | DANCE TO THE MAX 3 | Virgin Television VTCD 33 |
| 29/10/1994 | 2 | 10 | ✪ | **THE BEST ROCK 'N' ROLL ALBUM IN THE WORLD... EVER!** | Virgin Television VTDCD 37 |
| 19/11/1994 | ❶¹ | 23 | ✪³ | **THE LOVE ALBUM** | Virgin Television VTDCD 38 |
| 19/11/1994 | 5 | 4 | ● | **THE BEST DANCE ALBUM IN THE WORLD... EVER! 4** | Virgin Television VTDCD 40 |
| 04/02/1995 | ❶¹ | 13 | ● | **THE BEST PUNK ALBUM IN THE WORLD... EVER!** | Virgin Television VTDCD 42 |
| 18/02/1995 | 8 | 5 | ○ | **DANCE '95** | Virgin Television VTCD 43 |
| 04/03/1995 | 11 | 3 | ○ | THE BEST FUNK ALBUM IN THE WORLD... EVER! | Virgin Television VTDCD 44 |
| 25/03/1995 | 8 | 2 | ○ | **CELTIC MOODS** | Virgin Television VTDCD 45 |
| 15/04/1995 | 3 | 8 | ● | **THE BEST ROCK ALBUM IN THE WORLD... EVER! II** | Virgin Television VTDCD 47 |
| 06/05/1995 | 2 | 9 | ● | **STREET SOUL** | Virgin Television VTDCD 41 |
| 10/06/1995 | 8 | 3 | ○ | **DANCE HEAT '95** | Virgin Television VTCD 50 |
| 17/06/1995 | 6 | 5 | | **CELTIC MOODS 2** | Virgin Television VTCD 52 |
| 15/07/1995 | 4 | 7 | ● | **THE BEST DANCE ALBUM IN THE WORLD... EVER! 5** | Virgin Television VTCD 55 |
| 15/07/1995 | 8 | 3 | ○ | **THE BLUES ALBUM** | Virgin Television VTDCD 54 |
| 22/07/1995 | ❶¹ | 11 | | **THE BEST SUMMER ALBUM IN THE WORLD... EVER!** | Virgin Television VTCD 57 |
| 29/07/1995 | 18 | 1 | | SUMMER SWING | Virgin Television VTDCD 53 |

| DATE | POS | WKS | BPI | ALBUM TITLE | LABEL & NUMBER |
|---|---|---|---|---|---|
| 19/08/1995 | 16 | 1 | | SERVE CHILLED | Virgin Television VTCD 56 |
| 02/09/1995 | 2 | 23 | ✪² | THE BEST ROCK BALLADS ALBUM IN THE WORLD... EVER! | Virgin Television VTDCD 60 |
| 02/09/1995 | 9 | 4 | ● | THIS IS CULT FICTION | Virgin Television VTCD 59 |
| 16/09/1995 | 2 | 8 | ✪ | THE BEST... ALBUM IN THE WORLD... EVER! | Virgin Television VTCD 58 |
| 21/10/1995 | 3 | 4 | ● | THE BEST DANCE ALBUM IN THE WORLD... 95! | Virgin Television VTCD 67 |
| 11/11/1995 | 7 | 4 | ● | THE BEST 80'S ALBUM IN THE WORLD... EVER! | Virgin Television VTCD 68 |
| 18/11/1995 | 2 | 16 | ✪² | THE LOVE ALBUM II | Virgin Television VTCD 69 |
| 18/11/1995 | 14 | 5 | ● | INSTRUMENTAL MOODS | Virgin Television VTCD 65 |
| 25/11/1995 | 5 | 8 | ● | THE BEST PARTY... EVER! | Virgin Television VTCD 71 |
| 02/12/1995 | 2 | 17 | ✪² | THE BEST SIXTIES ALBUM IN THE WORLD... EVER! | Virgin Television VTCD 66 |
| 10/02/1996 | ❶² | 12 | ✪² | THE BEST... ALBUM IN THE WORLD... EVER! 2 | Virgin VTDCD 76 |
| 24/02/1996 | ❶⁴ | 12 | ● | IN THE MIX 96 | Virgin VTDCD 77 |
| 23/03/1996 | 2 | 10 | ● | THE BEST RAP ALBUM IN THE WORLD... EVER! | Virgin VTDCD 75 |
| 13/04/1996 | 16 | 2 | ○ | THE BEST PUNK ALBUM IN THE WORLD... EVER! 2 | Virgin VTDCD 79 |
| 27/04/1996 | 2 | 7 | ● | THE BEST... ALBUM IN THE WORLD... EVER! 3 | Virgin VTDCD 84 |
| 18/05/1996 | 14 | 3 | | SHARPE – OVER THE HILLS & FAR AWAY | Virgin VTCD 81 |
| 25/05/1996 | 2 | 14 | ● | IN THE MIX 96 – 2 | Virgin VTDCD 85 |
| 01/06/1996 | 8 | 4 | ● | THE BEST ROCK ANTHEMS ALBUM IN THE WORLD... EVER! | Virgin VTDCD 83 |
| 15/06/1996 | 3 | 10 | ● | THE BEST SWING ALBUM IN THE WORLD... EVER! | Virgin VTDCD 86 |
| 15/06/1996 | 5 | 5 | ○ | SPIRITS OF NATURE | Virgin VTCD 87 |
| 29/06/1996 | 5 | 5 | ● | THE BEST FOOTIE ANTHEMS IN THE WORLD... EVER! | Virgin VTCD 94 |
| 29/06/1996 | 16 | 2 | | THE BIG HIT MIX | Virgin VTCD 96 |
| 27/07/1996 | 3 | 6 | ● | IN THE MIX – 90'S HITS | Virgin VTDCD 89 |
| 17/08/1996 | ❶¹ | 13 | ✪ | THE BEST DANCE ALBUM IN THE WORLD... EVER! 6 | Virgin VTDCD 91 |
| 17/08/1996 | 8 | 5 | ● | THE BEST JAZZ ALBUM IN THE WORLD... EVER! | Virgin VTDCD 93 |
| 17/08/1996 | 11 | 4 | | EVENING SESSION – PRIORITY TUNES | Virgin VTDCD 93 |
| 21/09/1996 | 15 | 3 | | THIS IS THE RETURN OF CULT FICTION | Virgin VTCD 112 |
| 28/09/1996 | 11 | 3 | | THE BEST OF MASTERCUTS | Virgin VTCD 101 |
| 12/10/1996 | ❶¹ | 6 | ● | IN THE MIX 96 – 3 | Virgin VTDCD 97 |
| 12/10/1996 | 16 | 1 | | WIPEOUT 2097: THE SOUNDTRACK | Virgin CDV 2815 |
| 26/10/1996 | 2 | 6 | | THE BEST... ALBUM IN THE WORLD... EVER! 4 | Virgin VTDCD 96 |
| 09/11/1996 | 10 | 10 | ● | THE BEST OPERA ALBUM IN THE WORLD... EVER! | Virgin VTDCD 100 |
| 09/11/1996 | 11 | 9 | ● | THE BEST IRISH ALBUM IN THE WORLD... EVER! | Virgin VTDCD 102 |
| 16/11/1996 | 2 | 13 | ✪ | THE LOVE ALBUM III | Virgin VTDCD 104 |
| 23/11/1996 | 2 | 15 | ✪² | THE BEST SIXTIES ALBUM IN THE WORLD... EVER! II | Virgin VTDCD 106 |
| 23/11/1996 | 9 | 3 | | THE BEST MIX ALBUM IN THE WORLD... EVER! | Virgin VTDCD 108 |
| 30/11/1996 | 2 | 19 | ✪³ | THE BEST CHRISTMAS ALBUM IN THE WORLD... EVER! | Virgin VTDCD 103 |
| 14/12/1996 | 8 | 7 | ● | SMASH HITS MIX '97 | Virgin VTDCD 110 |
| 08/02/1997 | ❶¹ | 11 | ● | IN THE MIX 97 | Virgin VTDCD 116 |
| 15/02/1997 | ❶¹ | 11 | ● | THE SOUL ALBUM | Virgin VTDCD 115 |
| 22/03/1997 | ❶¹ | 7 | ● | THE BEST... ALBUM IN THE WORLD... EVER! 5 | Virgin/EMI VTDCD 120 |
| 29/03/1997 | 2 | 7 | ● | GORGEOUS | Virgin VTDCD 121 |
| 26/04/1997 | 2 | 7 | ● | IN THE MIX 97 – 2 | Virgin/EMI VTDCD 132 |
| 17/05/1997 | 2 | 9 | ● | SPICE GIRLS PRESENT THE BEST GIRL POWER ALBUM IN THE WORLD... EVER! | Virgin/EMI VTDCD 123 |
| 24/05/1997 | 11 | 3 | ● | ELECTRONICA (FULL-ON BIG BEATS) | Virgin VTDCD 131 |
| 24/05/1997 | ❶² | 7 | ● | BIG MIX '97 | Warner/Virgin/EMI VTDCD 130 |
| 07/06/1997 | ❶¹ | 8 | ● | SMASH HITS – SUMMER '97 | Virgin/EMI VTDCD 144 |
| 14/06/1997 | ❶⁴ | 9 | ● | THE BEST CLUB ANTHEMS IN THE WORLD... EVER! | Virgin/EMI VTDCD 124 |
| 21/06/1997 | 9 | 6 | ● | THE BEST SCOTTISH ALBUM IN THE WORLD... EVER! | Virgin/EMI VTDCD 137 |
| 05/07/1997 | 3 | 9 | ● | THE BEST SUMMER ALBUM IN THE WORLD... EVER! | Virgin/EMI VTDCD 140 |
| 12/07/1997 | ❶² | 15 | ● | THE BEST DISCO ALBUM IN THE WORLD | Virgin/EMI VTDCD 143 |
| 19/07/1997 | 8 | 4 | ● | THE BEST... ALBUM IN THE WORLD... EVER! 6 | Virgin/EMI VTDCD 136 |
| 02/08/1997 | 2 | 6 | ● | IN THE MIX 97 – 3 | Virgin/EMI VTDCD 135 |
| 16/08/1997 | 2 | 11 | ● | THE BEST DANCE ALBUM IN THE WORLD... EVER! 7 | Virgin/EMI VTDCD 138 |
| 16/08/1997 | 5 | 6 | ● | THE BEST LATINO CARNIVAL IN THE WORLD... EVER! | Virgin/EMI VTDCD 152 |
| 30/08/1997 | 17 | 2 | | CAFE MAMBO | Virgin/EMI VTDCD 150 |
| 06/09/1997 | 10 | 3 | ○ | MORE! GIRLS' NIGHT OUT | Virgin/EMI VTDCD 149 |
| 20/09/1997 | 5 | 7 | ○ | CLUB HITS 97/98: SOUNDTRACK TO A SEASON | Virgin/EMI VTDCD 167 |
| 11/10/1997 | ❶¹ | 5 | ● | BIG MIX '97 – VOLUME 2 | Virgin/EMI/warner.esp VTDCD 172 |
| 25/10/1997 | ❶¹ | 10 | | THE BEST... ANTHEMS...EVER! | Virgin/EMI VTDCD 154 |
| 08/11/1997 | 10 | 16 | ✪ | THE MOST RELAXING CLASSICAL ALBUM IN THE WORLD... EVER! | Virgin/EMI VTDCD 155 |
| 15/11/1997 | 11 | 9 | ✪ | THE LOVE ALBUM IV | Virgin/EMI VTDCD 156 |
| 22/11/1997 | 3 | 12 | ✪ | THE BEST SIXTIES ALBUM IN THE WORLD... EVER! III | Virgin/EMI VTDCD 160 |
| 22/11/1997 | 13 | 9 | ● | THE BEST SEVENTIES ALBUM IN THE WORLD... EVER! | Virgin/EMI VTDCD 157 |
| 22/11/1997 | 16 | 3 | ● | NEW PURE MOODS | Virgin/EMI VTDCD 158 |
| 29/11/1997 | 7 | 11 | ● | THE BEST ROCK BALLADS ALBUM IN THE WORLD... EVER! II | Virgin/EMI VTDCD 159 |
| 06/12/1997 | 6 | 11 | ● | THE BEST CLUB ANTHEMS IN THE WORLD... EVER! 2 | Virgin/EMI VTDCD 169 |
| 06/12/1997 | 7 | 6 | ● | THE BEST PARTY IN THE WORLD... EVER! | Virgin/EMI VTDCD 161 |
| 13/12/1997 | 9 | 7 | ● | SMASH HITS '98 | Virgin/EMI VTDCD 164 |

○ Silver disc   ● Gold disc   ✪ Platinum disc (additional platinum units are indicated by a figure following the symbol)   ❶⁹ Number of weeks album topped the UK chart

| DATE | POS | WKS | BPI | ALBUM TITLE | LABEL & NUMBER |
|------|-----|-----|-----|-------------|----------------|
| 10/01/1998 | 3 | 6 | ○ | **MAXIMUM SPEED** | Virgin/EMI VTDCD 173 |
| 07/02/1998 | 3 | 8 | ● | **THE SOUL ALBUM II** | Virgin/EMI VTDCD 165 |
| 14/02/1998 | ❶² | 7 | ● | **IN THE MIX 98** | Virgin/EMI VTDCD 174 |
| 07/03/1998 | 10 | 5 | ○ | **CARIBBEAN UNCOVERED** | Virgin/EMI VTDCD 175 |
| 21/03/1998 | 2 | 7 | ● | **SUPERWOMAN** | Virgin/EMI VTDCD 179 |
| 04/04/1998 | 3 | 6 | ● | **CLUB NATION** | Virgin/EMI VTDCD 180 |
| 18/04/1998 | 3 | 10 | ● | **THE BEST... ANTHEMS... EVER! 2** | Virgin/EMI VTDCD 183 |
| 25/04/1998 | 6 | 5 | ○ | **THE BEST HIP HOP ANTHEMZ IN THE WORLD... EVER!** | Virgin/EMI VTDCD 184 |
| 02/05/1998 | 18 | 2 | | R.I.P. PRESENTS THE REAL SOUND OF UNDERGROUND | Virgin/EMI VTDCDX 178 |
| 16/05/1998 | 3 | 6 | ● | **THE BEST CLUB ANTHEMS IN THE WORLD... EVER! III** | Virgin/EMI VTDCD 187 |
| 30/05/1998 | 2 | 6 | ● | **SMASH HITS – SUMMER '98** | Virgin/EMI VTDCD 186 |
| 30/05/1998 | 7 | 5 | ● | **THE BEST DISCO ALBUM IN THE WORLD... EVER! 2** | Virgin/EMI VTDCD 191 |
| 27/06/1998 | 2 | 11 | ● | **THE BEST SIXTIES SUMMER ALBUM IN THE WORLD... EVER!** | Virgin/EMI VTDCD 200 |
| 27/06/1998 | 6 | 3 | ✪ | **ALL NEW – THE BEST FOOTIE ANTHEMS IN THE WORLD... EVER!** | Virgin/EMI VTCD 193 |
| 04/07/1998 | 6 | 4 | ● | **IN THE MIX 98 – 2** | Virgin/EMI VTDCD 195 |
| 11/07/1998 | 6 | 6 | ● | **THE BEST SUMMER PARTY ALBUM IN THE WORLD... EVER!** | Virgin/EMI VTDCD 194 |
| 18/07/1998 | 11 | 3 | | THE BEST ALBUM... IN THE WORLD... EVER! 7. | Virgin/EMI VTDCD 204 |
| 25/07/1998 | 2 | 9 | ● | **THE BEST DANCE ALBUM IN THE WORLD... EVER! 8** | Virgin/EMI VSCDT 196 |
| 15/08/1998 | 11 | 3 | | THE BEST RAVE ANTHEMS IN THE WORLD... EVER! | Virgin/EMI VTDCD 203 |
| 05/09/1998 | 17 | 2 | | WORLD MOODS | Virgin/EMI VTDCD 201 |
| 24/10/1998 | ❶¹ | 4 | ● | **IN THE MIX IBIZA** | Virgin/EMI VTDCD 228 |
| 31/10/1998 | ❶¹ | 5 | ● | **THE BEST CHART HITS ALBUM IN THE WORLD... EVER!** | Virgin/EMI VTDCD 225 |
| 07/11/1998 | 8 | 2 | | **CLUB NATION 2** | Virgin/EMI VTCDC 227 |
| 07/11/1998 | 12 | 9 | ● | THE MOST RELAXING CLASSICAL ALBUM IN THE WORLD... EVER! II | Virgin/EMI VTDCD 207 |
| 14/11/1998 | 3 | 18 | ✪ | **THE VERY BEST OF THE LOVE ALBUM** | Virgin/EMI VTDCD 213 |
| 14/11/1998 | 14 | 3 | ● | THE BEST COUNTRY BALLADS IN THE WORLD... EVER! | Virgin/EMI VTDCD 211 |
| 14/11/1998 | 19 | 1 | ○ | THE BEST... ANTHEMS... EVER! 3 | Virgin/EMI VTDCD 210 |
| 21/11/1998 | 10 | 2 | ● | **THE BEST ROCK ANTHEMS... EVER!** | Virgin/EMI VTDCD 215 |
| 21/11/1998 | 11 | 7 | ● | THE BEST SIXTIES ALBUM IN THE WORLD... EVER! IV. | Virgin/EMI VTDCD 216 |
| 28/11/1998 | 15 | 1 | ○ | CREAM ANTHEMS MIXED BY TALL PAUL AND SEB FONTAINE | Virgin/EMI VTDCDX 229 |
| 28/11/1998 | 16 | 2 | ● | BIGGEST 80'S HITS IN THE WORLD... EVER! | Virgin/EMI VTDCD 218 |
| 26/12/1998 | 10 | 4 | ● | **SMASH HITS '99!** | Virgin/EMI VTDCD 223 |
| 23/01/1999 | ❶¹ | 11 | ● | **THE BEST CLUB ANTHEMS 99 IN THE WORLD... EVER!** | Virgin/EMI VTDCD 221 |
| 13/02/1999 | 2 | 6 | ● | **THE BEST SIXTIES LOVE ALBUM... EVER!** | Virgin/EMI VTDCD 235 |
| 27/02/1999 | 5 | 4 | | **THE BEST CHART HITS IN THE WORLD... EVER! 99** | Virgin/EMI VTDCD 238 |
| 06/03/1999 | 13 | 2 | | DISCO: 1999 | Virgin/EMI VTDCD 239 |
| 13/03/1999 | 3 | 4 | ○ | **IN THE MIX 2000** | Virgin/EMI VTDCD 240 |
| 13/03/1999 | 6 | 4 | ○ | **THE '80S LOVE ALBUM** | Virgin/EMI VTDCD 241 |
| 27/03/1999 | 2 | 6 | ○ | **RESIDENT – 2 YEARS OF OAKENFOLD AT CREAM** | Virgin/EMI VTDCD 237 |
| 10/04/1999 | 13 | 4 | | MAXIMUM SPEED 99 | Virgin/EMI VTDCD 242 |
| 08/05/1999 | 5 | 4 | ○ | **THE BEST HOUSE ANTHEMS... EVER!** | Virgin/EMI VTDCD 245 |
| 15/05/1999 | 3 | 5 | ○ | **TRANCEFORMER** | Virgin/EMI VTDCDX 256 |
| 29/05/1999 | 9 | 3 | | **21ST CENTURY ROCK** | Virgin/EMI VTDCD 247 |
| 05/06/1999 | 3 | 5 | ○ | **SMASH HITS – SUMMER '99** | Virgin/EMI VTDCD 246 |
| 12/06/1999 | 2 | 7 | ● | **CREAM IBIZA – ARRIVALS** | Virgin/EMI VTDCD 249 |
| 10/07/1999 | 7 | 4 | ○ | **THE BEST TRANCE ANTHEMS... EVER!** | Virgin/EMI VTDCD 261 |
| 24/07/1999 | ❶¹ | 9 | ● | **THE BEST DANCE ALBUM IN THE WORLD... EVER! 9** | Virgin/EMI VTDCD 251 |
| 07/08/1999 | 2 | 11 | ✪ | **THE BEST IBIZA ANTHEMS... EVER!** | Virgin/EMI VTDCDX 254 |
| 28/08/1999 | 14 | 4 | ● | NEW WOMAN | Virgin/EMI VTDCD 248 |
| 04/09/1999 | 4 | 4 | ○ | **CLUB ANTHEMS 99** | Virgin/EMI VTDCD 281 |
| 18/09/1999 | 13 | 2 | | CREAM IBIZA – DEPARTURES | Virgin/EMI VTDCDX 266 |
| 18/09/1999 | 18 | 1 | | THE VERY BEST OF CLASSICAL EXPERIENCE. | Virgin/EMI VTDCD 252 |
| 25/09/1999 | 8 | 3 | | **TRANCEMIX 99 – A SPRITUAL JOURNEY THROUGH TIME AND SPACE** | Virgin/EMI VTDCDX 282 |
| 16/10/1999 | 7 | 4 | | **THE CHILLOUT MIX** | Virgin/EMI VTDCDX 283 |
| 23/10/1999 | 2 | 4 | ○ | **THE BEST PEPSI CHART ALBUM IN THE WORLD... EVER!** | Virgin/EMI VTDCD 268 |
| 06/11/1999 | 10 | 3 | ● | **THE BEST CLASSICAL ALBUM OF THE MILLENNIUM... EVER!** | Virgin/EMI VTDCDX 269 |
| 20/11/1999 | 8 | 15 | ● | **THE BEST LOVESONGS... EVER!** | Virgin/EMI VTDCDX 274 |
| 27/11/1999 | 2 | 14 | ✪ | **CREAM ANTHEMS 2000** | Virgin/EMI VTDCD 272 |
| 27/11/1999 | 16 | 2 | | THE SIXTIES | Virgin/EMI VTDCDX 270 |
| 04/12/1999 | 8 | 12 | ● | **THE BEST... AND FRIENDS ALBUM IN THE WORLD... EVER!** | Virgin/EMI VTDCD 286 |
| 04/12/1999 | 5 | 6 | ● | **THE BEST MILLENNIUM PARTY... EVER!** | Virgin/EMI VTDCD 278 |
| 11/12/1999 | 8 | 10 | ● | **THE BEST CLUB ANTHEMS 2000... EVER!** | Virgin/EMI VTDCD 271 |
| 11/12/1999 | 12 | 7 | ● | THE BEST MUSICALS ALBUM IN THE WORLD... EVER! | Virgin/EMI VTDCD 277 |
| 25/12/1999 | 7 | 7 | ● | **SMASH HITS 2000** | Virgin/EMI VTDCD 279 |
| 26/02/2000 | 4 | 5 | ● | **BEST DANCE ALBUM IN THE WORLD EVER! 2000** | Virgin/EMI VTDCD 291 |
| 18/03/2000 | 7 | 4 | ● | **BEST PEPSI CHART ALBUM... EVER! 2000** | Virgin/EMI VTDCD 300 |
| 18/03/2000 | 11 | 3 | ○ | IN THE MIX 2000 | Virgin/EMI VTDCD 290 |
| 18/03/2000 | 14 | 3 | | NUKLEUZ PRESENTS HARDHOUSE ANTHEMS | Virgin/EMI VTDCDX 293 |
| 25/03/2000 | 10 | 4 | | **UNDERGROUND EXPLOSION – THE REAL GARAGE MIX** | Virgin/EMI VTDCDX 299 |

▲⁹ Number of weeks album topped the US chart     ◆¹² RIAA Diamond Awards     ◇³ IFPI Platinum Europe Awards

| DATE | POS | WKS | BPI | ALBUM TITLE | LABEL & NUMBER |
|------|-----|-----|-----|-------------|----------------|
| 01/04/2000 | ❶[1] | 7 | ● | NEW WOMAN 2000 | Virgin/EMI VTDCD 289 |
| 01/04/2000 | 6 | 4 | ○ | MELTDOWN 2000 – BEST NEW TRANCE | Virgin VTDCDX 301 |
| 15/04/2000 | 11 | 3 | ○ | BEST JAZZ ALBUM IN THE WORLD… EVER! VOLUME 2 | Virgin VTDCD 294 |
| 22/04/2000 | ❶[1] | 5 | ○ | GIRLS 2K | Virgin/EMI VTDCD 303 |
| 29/04/2000 | 2 | 8 | ○ | CREAM LIVE | Virgin VTDCDX 304 |
| 13/05/2000 | 10 | 4 | ○ | THE BEST TV ADS… EVER! | Virgin/EMI VTCDX 306 |
| 03/06/2000 | 2 | 7 | ● | THE BEST CLUB ANTHEMS… EVER! 2K | Virgin/EMI VTDCD 297 |
| 17/06/2000 | 6 | 9 | | THE BEST SUMMER HOLIDAY EVER | Virgin/EMI VTDCD 307 |
| 17/06/2000 | 4 | 3 | | BEST FOOTIE ANTHEMS EVER | Virgin/EMI VTDCD 310 |
| 17/06/2000 | 10 | 4 | ○ | THE BEST EASY ALBUM EVER | Virgin/EMI VTDCD 296 |
| 24/06/2000 | 9 | 8 | ● | THE BEST PUB JUKEBOX IN THE WORLD EVER | Virgin/EMI VTDCD 308 |
| 01/07/2000 | 4 | 5 | ○ | CREAM IBIZA ARRIVALS | Virgin/EMI VTDCDX 311 |
| 01/07/2000 | 16 | 2 | | NUKLEUZ PRESENTS HARDHOUSE ANTHEMS VOL.2 | Virgin/EMI VTDCD 314 |
| 22/07/2000 | 3 | 7 | | SMASH HITS SUMMER 2000 | Virgin/EMI VTDCD 315 |
| 29/07/2000 | 18 | 2 | | CREAM RESIDENT – SEB FONTAINE | Virgin/EMI VTDCD 318 |
| 12/08/2000 | 2 | 8 | ● | BEST IBIZA ANTHEMS EVER 2K | Virgin/EMI VTDCDX 321 |
| 19/08/2000 | 5 | 6 | ● | NEW WOMAN SUMMER 2000 | Virgin/EMI VTDCD 322 |
| 02/09/2000 | 3 | 6 | ● | BEST DANCE ALBUM IN THE WORLD EVER – 10 | Virgin/EMI VTDCD 317 |
| 09/09/2000 | 5 | 4 | ○ | CREAMFIELDS | Virgin/EMI VTDCDX 351 |
| 09/09/2000 | 16 | 3 | | THE BEST PROMS ALBUM IN THE WORLD EVER! | Virgin/EMI VTDCD 232 |
| 23/09/2000 | 5 | 6 | ○ | IBIZA UNCOVERED II | Virgin/EMI VTDCD 324 |
| 30/09/2000 | 8 | 5 | ○ | THE BEST GARAGE ANTHEMS EVER | Virgin/EMI VTDCD 325 |
| 30/09/2000 | 10 | 4 | ○ | YOUNG GUNS GO FOR IT | Virgin/EMI VTDCD 346 |
| 07/10/2000 | 2 | 8 | ● | PEPSI CHART 2001 | Virgin/EMI VTDCD 331 |
| 07/10/2000 | 13 | 4 | | NUKLEUZ PTS – HARDHOUSE ANTHEMS 3 | Virgin/EMI VTCDX 354 |
| 04/11/2000 | ❶[1] | 13 | ✪ | NOW DANCE 2001 | Virgin/EMI VTDCD 349 |
| 18/11/2000 | 13 | 2 | | DECADES – STORY OF THE 60'S/70'S/80'S | Virgin/EMI VTDCD 337 |
| 25/11/2000 | ❶[1] | 12 | ✪ | CREAM ANTHEMS 2001 | Virgin/EMI VTDCDX 338 |
| 25/11/2000 | 4 | 14 | ✪ | THE NEW LOVE ALBUM | Virgin/EMI VTDCDX 339 |
| 25/11/2000 | 20 | 1 | ○ | THE BEST AND FRIENDS ALBUM IN THE WORLD | Virgin/EMI VTDCDX 333 |
| 09/12/2000 | 4 | 17 | ✪ | THE BEST CHRISTMAS ALBUM IN THE WORLD EVER | Virgin/EMI VTDCD 347 |
| 09/12/2000 | 12 | 6 | ● | THE BEST CLUB ANTHEMS 2001 EVER | Virgin/EMI VTDCD 342 |
| 16/12/2000 | 5 | 7 | ● | SMASH HITS 2001 | Virgin/EMI VTDCD 345 |
| 06/01/2001 | 19 | 1 | ● | THE BEST PARTY IN TOWN EVER | Virgin/EMI VTDCD 341 |
| 27/01/2001 | 6 | 3 | | NUKLEUZ PRESENTS BIG ROOM DJS | Virgin/EMI VTDCDX 358 |
| 17/02/2001 | 4 | 6 | | DANCE MASTERS | Virgin/EMI VTDCD 359 |
| 17/02/2001 | 3 | 10 | | I LOVE 80'S | Virgin/EMI VTDCD 361 |
| 24/02/2001 | 19 | 1 | | A FRENCH AFFAIR | Virgin/EMI VTDCD 356 |
| 03/03/2001 | 2 | 7 | ● | THE NEW PEPSI CHART ALBUM | Virgin/EMI VTDCD 362 |
| 03/03/2001 | 13 | 2 | | NUKLEUZ PRESENTS HARDHOUSE ANTHEMS 2001 | Virgin/EMI VTDCDX 364 |
| 24/03/2001 | ❶[1] | 8 | ● | NEW WOMAN 2001 | Virgin/EMI VTDCD 365 |
| 31/03/2001 | 2 | 6 | | NOW DANCE 2001 PART 2 | Virgin/EMI VTDCD 368 |
| 14/04/2001 | 5 | 8 | | CREAM LIVE | Virgin/EMI VTDCDX 369 |
| 28/04/2001 | 3 | 11 | ✪ | THE ALBUM | Virgin/EMI VTDCD 380 |
| 12/05/2001 | 10 | 3 | | THE BEST HARD HOUSE EVER | Virgin/EMI VTDCD 370 |
| 19/05/2001 | 17 | 2 | | THE BEST NORTHERN SOUL ALL-NIGHTER EVER | Virgin/EMI VTDCD 377 |
| 26/05/2001 | 5 | 4 | | CLUBBED OUT | Virgin/EMI VTDCDX 381 |
| 02/06/2001 | 9 | 3 | | I LOVE 70'S | Virgin/EMI VTDCD 372 |
| 09/06/2001 | 10 | 3 | ○ | I LOVE IBIZA | Virgin/EMI VTDCD 374 |
| 23/06/2001 | ❶[7] | 20 | ✪ | CAPITAL GOLD LEGENDS | Virgin/EMI VTDCD 382 |
| 07/07/2001 | 2 | 8 | ● | THE BEST SUMMER HOLIDAY 2001 EVER | Virgin/EMI VTDCDX 390 |
| 14/07/2001 | 19 | 1 | | THE CHILLOUT | Virgin/EMI VTDCD 388 |
| 21/07/2001 | 4 | 4 | ○ | BEST DANCE ALBUM IN THE WORLD EVER 11 | Virgin/EMI VTDCD 386 |
| 28/07/2001 | 3 | 6 | ● | UNBELIEVABLE | Virgin/EMI VTDCD 389 |
| 28/07/2001 | 10 | 2 | | UNCOVERED | Virgin/EMI VTDCD 384 |
| 18/08/2001 | 5 | 4 | ○ | THE BEST IBIZA ANTHEMS EVER 2001 | Virgin/EMI VTDCD 391 |
| 01/09/2001 | 7 | 3 | | CREAM IBIZA | Virgin/EMI VTDCX 376 |
| 01/09/2001 | 11 | 2 | | THE BEST CARNIVAL ALBUM EVER | Virgin/EMI VTDCD 411 |
| 22/09/2001 | 4 | 20 | ✪ | CLASSICAL CHILLOUT | Virgin/EMI VTDCD 408 |
| 06/10/2001 | 11 | 3 | | I LOVE 90S | Virgin/EMI VTDCD 410 |
| 13/10/2001 | 4 | 5 | ● | IT'S A GIRL THING | Virgin/EMI VTDCD 385 |
| 20/10/2001 | 10 | 2 | | Q ANTHEMS | Universal/Virgin/EMI VTDCD 409 |
| 20/10/2001 | ❶[2] | 7 | ✪ | PEPSI CHART 2002 | Virgin/EMI VTDCD 414 |
| 27/10/2001 | 12 | 1 | | MIXMAG PRESENTS BIG TUNES | Virgin/EMI VTDCD 412 |
| 03/11/2001 | ❶[3] | 5 | ● | NOW DANCE 2002 | Virgin/EMI VTDCD 393 |
| 17/11/2001 | 2 | 13 | ✪ | CAPITAL GOLD LEGENDS II | Virgin/EMI VTDCD 418 |
| 17/11/2001 | 7 | 6 | ● | THE OPERA ALBUM 2002 | Virgin/EMI VTDCD 417 |
| 24/11/2001 | 14 | 2 | ● | NEW WOMAN – LOVE SONGS | Virgin/EMI VTDCD 419 |
| 24/11/2001 | 18 | 1 | | CREAM ANTHEMS 2002 | Virgin/EMI VTDCDX 400 |

○ Silver disc  ● Gold disc  ✪ Platinum disc (additional platinum units are indicated by a figure following the symbol)  ❶[9] Number of weeks album topped the UK chart

| DATE | POS | WKS | BPI | ALBUM TITLE | LABEL & NUMBER |
|---|---|---|---|---|---|
| 08/12/2001 | 10 | 11 | ● | **PURE CHILLOUT** | Virgin/EMI VTDCD 420 |
| 15/12/2001 | 2 | 6 | ● | **I LOVE 2 PARTY** | Virgin/EMI VTDCD 421 |
| 12/01/2002 | 20 | 1 | ● | THE ALBUM 2 | Virgin/EMI VTDCD 394 |
| 09/02/2002 | ❶[1] | 5 | ○ | **BEST CLUB ANTHEMS 2002** | Virgin/EMI VTDCD 401 |
| 16/02/2002 | 2 | 3 | ● | **THE LOVE ALBUM CLASSICS** | Virgin/EMI VTDCDX 435 |
| 16/02/2002 | 10 | 3 | ○ | **CLASSICAL CHILLOUT 2** | Virgin/EMI VTDCD 437 |
| 23/02/2002 | 2 | 5 | ○ | **NEW PEPSI CHART 2002** | Virgin/EMI VTDCD 348 |
| 09/03/2002 | 20 | 1 | | UNBELIEVABLE TOO | Virgin/EMI VTDCD 436 |
| 16/03/2002 | ❶[1] | 3 | ● | **NEW WOMAN 2002** | Virgin/EMI VTDCD 438 |
| 16/03/2002 | 3 | 6 | ● | **NOW DANCE 2002 PART 2** | Virgin/EMI VTDCD 439 |
| 23/03/2002 | 11 | 1 | | PURE CELTIC CHILLOUT | Virgin/EMI VTDCD 443 |
| 30/03/2002 | 2 | 6 | ● | **CAPITAL GOLD LEGENDS III** | Virgin/EMI VTDCD 440 |
| 13/04/2002 | 8 | 6 | | **LADY SINGS THE BLUES** | Virgin/EMI VTDCD 426 |
| 20/04/2002 | 3 | 6 | | **CREAM ANTHEMS SPRING 2002** | Virgin/EMI VTDCDX 442 |
| 04/05/2002 | 7 | 4 | | **ELECTRIC DREAMS** | Virgin/EMI VTDCD 447 |
| 11/05/2002 | 3 | 4 | ○ | THE ALBUM 3 | Virgin/EMI VTDCD 441 |
| 18/05/2002 | 3 | 5 | | **FUTURE TRANCE** | Virgin/EMI VTDCDX 453 |
| 01/06/2002 | 3 | 5 | | **BEST UNOFFICIAL FOOTIE ANTHEMS EVER!** | Virgin/EMI VTDCDX 310 |
| 08/06/2002 | 12 | 3 | | PUNK – THE JUBILEE | Virgin/EMI VTDCD 452 |
| 15/06/2002 | ❶[1] | 7 | | **SMASH HITS SUMMER 2002** | Virgin/EMI VTDCD 456 |
| 15/06/2002 | 2 | 6 | | **BEST OF BRITISH** | Virgin/EMI VTDCD 302 |
| 22/06/2002 | ❶[1] | 6 | | **CAPITAL GOLD ROCK LEGENDS** | Virgin/EMI VTDCD 458 |
| 29/06/2002 | 8 | 2 | | CREAM BEACH 2002 | Virgin/EMI VTDCDX 464 |
| 06/07/2002 | 6 | 3 | | **PARTY AT THE PALACE** | Universal TV/Virgin/EMI VTDCD 463 |
| 13/07/2002 | 3 | 6 | | **THE BEST DANCE ALBUM EVER 2002** | Universal TV/Virgin/EMI VTDCD 476 |
| 20/07/2002 | 6 | 5 | | **THE BEST SIXTIES SUMMER PARTY EVER** | Universal TV/Virgin/EMI VTDCD 471 |
| 27/07/2002 | 7 | 2 | | I LOVE SUMMER | Universal TV/Virgin/EMI VTDCD 469 |
| 03/08/2002 | 3 | 6 | ● | **THE BEST CLUB ANTHEMS SUMMER 2002** | Universal TV/Virgin/EMI VTDCD 467 |
| 24/08/2002 | 4 | 5 | ● | **TRANCE MASTERS** | Virgin/EMI VTDCD 495 |
| 24/08/2002 | 18 | 1 | | FUTURE CHILL | Virgin/EMI VTDCDX 472 |
| 31/08/2002 | 8 | 3 | ○ | **HOLIDAY HITS – NON STOP EURO POP** | Virgin/EMI VTDCD 494 |
| 14/09/2002 | 2 | 6 | ● | **THE ALBUM 4** | Virgin/EMI VTDCD 481 |
| 21/09/2002 | 17 | 1 | | FUTURE TRANCE IBIZA | Virgin/EMI VTDCDX 507 |
| 05/10/2002 | 10 | 2 | | **RETRO DANCE MASTERS** | Virgin/EMI VTDCD 506 |
| 12/10/2002 | ❶[1] | 6 | ● | **NEW WOMAN – THE AUTUMN COLLECTION** | Virgin/EMI VTDCD 475 |
| 26/10/2002 | ❶[1] | 5 | ● | **NOW DANCE 2003** | Virgin/EMI VTDCD 479 |
| 26/10/2002 | 11 | 2 | | LADY SINGS THE BLUES – NIGHT & DAY | Virgin/EMI VTDCD 499 |
| 09/11/2002 | 2 | 13 | ✪ | **CAPITAL GOLD COUNTRY LEGENDS** | Virgin/EMI VTDCD 480 |
| 09/11/2002 | 5 | 3 | ● | **PEPSI CHART 2003** | Virgin/EMI VTDCD 478 |
| 16/11/2002 | 8 | 9 | ● | **CAPITAL GOLD SIXTIES LEGENDS** | Virgin/EMI VTDCD 485 |
| 16/11/2002 | 9 | 3 | ● | **THE BEST BANDS EVER** | Virgin/EMI VTDCD 508 |
| 16/11/2002 | 18 | 1 | ○ | CLASSICAL LEGENDS | Virgin/EMI VTDCD 489 |
| 07/12/2002 | 11 | 7 | ● | CAPITAL GOLD EIGHTIES LEGENDS | Virgin/EMI VTDCD 496 |
| 28/12/2002 | 11 | 3 | ● | I LOVE 2 PARTY 2003 | Virgin/EMI VTDCD 483 |
| 04/01/2003 | 17 | 1 | ● | BEST CLUB ANTHEMS 2003 | Virgin/EMI VTDCD 498 |
| 08/02/2003 | 2 | 4 | ● | **I LOVE U** | Virgin/EMI VTDCDX 493 |
| 15/02/2003 | 11 | 5 | ○ | THE BEST ONE HIT WONDERS IN THE WORLD | Virgin/EMI VTDCD 497 |
| 08/03/2003 | 20 | 1 | | SCOTLAND ROCKS | Virgin/EMI VTDCD 516 |
| 15/03/2003 | 7 | 3 | ○ | LIVE FOREVER – THE BEST OF BRITPOP | Virgin/EMI VTDCD 512 |
| 22/03/2003 | 11 | 2 | | FUTURE TRANCE 2003 | Virgin VTDCD 518 |
| 29/03/2003 | 6 | 4 | | **CAPITAL GOLD SOUL LEGENDS** | Virgin/EMI VTDCD 517 |
| 29/03/2003 | 5 | 9 | ● | **SUPER 70'S** | Virgin/EMI VTDCD 513 |
| 05/04/2003 | 2 | 5 | ● | **NEW WOMAN 2003** | Virgin/EMI VTDCD 514 |
| 12/04/2003 | 5 | 5 | ● | **NOW DANCE 2003 PART 2** | Virgin/EMI VTDCD 515 |
| 19/04/2003 | 9 | 2 | | **THE X LIST** | Virgin/EMI VTDCD 520 |
| 19/04/2003 | 15 | 1 | | THE VERY BEST OF CLASSICAL CHILLOUT | Virgin/EMI VTDCD 524 |
| 26/04/2003 | 7 | 5 | ● | **CAPITAL GOLD BRITISH LEGENDS** | Virgin/EMI VTDCD 519 |
| 10/05/2003 | 4 | 5 | ○ | **SMASH HITS – THE REUNION** | Virgin/EMI VTDCD 523 |
| 24/05/2003 | 19 | 2 | | CLASSICAL HEARTBREAKERS | Virgin/EMI VTDCD 522 |
| 31/05/2003 | 5 | 3 | ○ | **UP ALL NIGHT** | Virgin/EMI/Universal VTDCD 529 |
| 14/06/2003 | ❶³ | 37 | ✪³ | **POWER BALLADS** | Virgin/EMI VTDCD 413 |
| 14/06/2003 | 5 | 5 | | **SMASH HITS CHART SUMMER 2003** | Virgin/EMI/Universal VTDCD 530 |
| 14/06/2003 | 15 | 2 | | COOL SUMMER JAZZ | Virgin/EMI VTDCD 531 |
| 21/06/2003 | 9 | 2 | | **THE BEST PROG ROCK ALBUM IN THE WORLD** | Virgin/EMI VTDCD 533 |
| 05/07/2003 | 5 | 5 | ○ | **THE BEST SUMMER HOLIDAY EVER** | Virgin/EMI VTDCD 534 |
| 26/07/2003 | 5 | 6 | ● | **THE RETURN OF THE SUPER 70'S** | Virgin/EMI VTDCD 567 |
| 02/08/2003 | 13 | 2 | | BEST PANPIPES ALBUM IN THE WORLD... EVER! | Virgin/EMI VTDCD 545 |
| 09/08/2003 | 14 | 3 | ○ | GOOD VIBES | Virgin/EMI VTDCD 565 |
| 16/08/2003 | 3 | 4 | ○ | **THE BEST DANCE ALBUM IN THE WORLD EVER** | Virgin/EMI VTDCD 536 |

▲[9] Number of weeks album topped the US chart ◆[12] RIAA Diamond Awards ◇[3] IFPI Platinum Europe Awards

| DATE | POS | WKS | BPI | ALBUM TITLE | LABEL & NUMBER |
|---|---|---|---|---|---|
| 30/08/2003 | 20 | 1 | | THE BEST SMOOTH JAZZ EVER | Virgin/EMI VTDCDX 570 |
| 06/09/2003 | 16 | 3 | | THE ULTIMATE RELAXATION ALBUM | Virgin/EMI VTDCDX 577 |
| 20/09/2003 | 6 | 4 | ○ | **BITTERSWEET LOVESONGS** | Virgin/EMI VTDCD 574 |
| 11/10/2003 | 7 | 4 | ○ | **CAPITAL GOLD LAS VEGAS LEGENDS** | Virgin/EMI VTDCD 582 |
| 08/11/2003 | ❶¹ | 3 | ○ | **NOW DANCE 2004** | Virgin/EMI VTDCD 539 |
| 08/11/2003 | 13 | 1 | | BEST BANDS EVER 2004 | Virgin/EMI VTDCD 538 |
| 15/11/2003 | 5 | 7 | ● | **CAPITAL GOLD – LOVE LEGENDS** | Virgin/EMI VTDCD 553 |
| 15/11/2003 | 16 | 1 | | SUPER 60'S | Virgin/EMI VTDCD 547 |
| 22/11/2003 | 4 | 12 | ✪ | **SCHOOL REUNION – THE 80'S** | Virgin/EMI VTDCD 544 |
| 22/11/2003 | 15 | 3 | | CAPITAL GOLD – ROCK 'N' ROLL LEGENDS | Virgin/EMI VTDCD 554 |
| 22/11/2003 | 17 | 2 | ○ | COUNTRY BALLADS | Virgin/EMI VTDCD 556 |
| 10/01/2004 | 17 | 3 | ● | THE VERY BEST CLUB ANTHEMS EVER | Virgin/EMI VTDCDX 569 |
| 14/02/2004 | 2 | 3 | | **LOVE IS – THE ALBUM** | Virgin/EMI VTDCDX 596 |
| 06/03/2004 | 4 | 5 | ○ | **BEST HEAVY METAL ALBUM IN THE WORLD EVER** | Virgin/EMI VTDCD 598 |
| 20/03/2004 | 2 | 6 | ○ | **MEMORIES ARE MADE OF THIS** | Virgin/EMI VTDCD 602 |
| 20/03/2004 | ❶¹ | 7 | ● | **THE VERY BEST OF NEW WOMAN** | Virgin/EMI VTDCD 599 |
| 27/03/2004 | 20 | 1 | | PEACE – PURE CLASSICAL CALM | Virgin/EMI VTDCD 600 |
| 03/04/2004 | 4 | 4 | | **NOW DANCE** | Virgin/EMI VTDCD 607 |
| 10/04/2004 | 8 | 7 | ○ | **BEST WORSHIP SONGS EVER** | Virgin/EMI VTDCD 593 |
| 01/05/2004 | 5 | 8 | ● | **BACK TO THE MOVIES – HITS FROM THE FLIX** | Virgin/EMI VTDCD 611 |
| 08/05/2004 | 8 | 3 | | LATE NIGHT MOODS | Virgin/EMI VTDCD 609 |
| 22/05/2004 | 9 | 3 | | **TRANCE MASTERS** | Virgin/EMI VTDCDX 612 |
| 29/05/2004 | 9 | 2 | | **SUMMER IN THE SIXTIES** | Virgin/EMI VTDCD 613 |
| 05/06/2004 | 10 | 2 | | **SUPER 70'S ROCK** | Virgin/EMI VTDCD 614 |
| 19/06/2004 | ❶² | 2+ | ● | **BIGGER, BETTER POWER BALLADS** | Virgin/EMI VTDCD 619 |
| 26/06/2004 | 10 | 1+ | | **CAPITAL GOLD JAZZ LEGENDS** | Virgin/EMI/UCJ VTDCD 615 |

## VISION

| DATE | POS | WKS | BPI | ALBUM TITLE | LABEL & NUMBER |
|---|---|---|---|---|---|
| 04/03/1995 | 13 | 5 | | FLARED HITS AND PLATFORM SOUL | Vision VISCD 7 |
| 13/05/1995 | 6 | 5 | ○ | **DANCE NATION '95** | Vision VISCD 11 |
| 10/06/1995 | 18 | 2 | | LOVE WITH A REGGAE RHYTHM | Vision VISCD 13 |
| 09/09/1995 | 5 | 6 | ● | **THE BEST DANCE ALBUM OF THE YEAR!** | Vision VISCD 15 |

## VITAL SOUNDS

| DATE | POS | WKS | BPI | ALBUM TITLE | LABEL & NUMBER |
|---|---|---|---|---|---|
| 04/07/1992 | 17 | 2 | | RED HOT AND WHITE LABELS | Vital Sounds CDVIT 1 |
| 26/09/1992 | 13 | 2 | | RED HOT AND WHITE 2 | Vital Sounds CDVIT 2 |
| 29/05/1993 | 12 | 2 | | STRICTLY RAGGA | Vital Sounds CDVIT 3 |

## VOLUME

| DATE | POS | WKS | BPI | ALBUM TITLE | LABEL & NUMBER |
|---|---|---|---|---|---|
| 01/05/1993 | 19 | 1 | | VOLUME SIX | Volume 6VCD 6 |
| 02/10/1993 | 14 | 3 | | TRANCE EUROPE EXPRESS | Volume TEEXCD 1 |
| 11/06/1994 | 17 | 2 | | TRANCE EUROPE EXPRESS 2 | Volume TEEXCD 2 |

## WALT DISNEY US label formed by the Walt Disney film company, which had been formed in 1928.

| DATE | POS | WKS | BPI | ALBUM TITLE | LABEL & NUMBER |
|---|---|---|---|---|---|
| 22/11/1997 | 9 | 4 | | **DISNEY'S HIT SINGLES & MORE!** | Walt Disney WD 115632 |
| 28/11/1998 | 12 | 4 | | THE DISNEY EXPERIENCE | Walt Disney WD 608202 |
| 06/04/2002 | 15 | 2 | | THE MAGIC OF DISNEY – 20 SUPERSTAR HITS | Walt Disney 0927452545 |

## WARNER BROTHERS US label first formed in 1930 by the film company of the same name following its acquisition of Brunswick Records and two leading music publishers. This venture failed and was not revived until 1958 when the company launched a series of film- and TV-related releases. Warner Brothers bought Frank Sinatra's Reprise Records in 1963 as it expanded its roster and activities, although in 1967 it was sold to Seven Arts. Soon after Seven Arts had added the Atlantic label to its roster the parent company was sold to the Kinney Corporation (which had begun as a car park and funeral home operator), and with the acquisition of Elektra Records, WEA (Warner-Elektra-Atlantic) Records came into being. The corporate name later changed to Warner Communications.

| DATE | POS | WKS | BPI | ALBUM TITLE | LABEL & NUMBER |
|---|---|---|---|---|---|
| 25/03/1978 | 28 | 3 | | HOPE AND ANCHOR FRONT ROW FESTIVAL | Warner Brothers K 66077 |
| 21/07/1979 | ❶⁶ | 17 | ✪ | **THE BEST DISCO ALBUM IN THE WORLD** | Warner Brothers K 58062 |
| 14/05/1983 | 19 | 16 | | THE LAUGHTER AND TEARS COLLECTION | WEA LTC 1 |
| 04/08/1990 | 18 | 3 | | NOBODY'S CHILD – ROMANIAN ANGEL APPEAL | Warner Brothers WX 353 |
| 15/08/1992 | 15 | 2 | | BARCELONA GOLD | Warner Brothers 9362450462 |
| 18/02/1995 | 4 | 9 | | **THE ULTIMATE SOUL COLLECTION – 45 SOUL CLASSICS** | Warner Music 9548333402 |
| 05/05/1995 | 16 | 1 | | DISCO INFERNO | Warner Music UK 9548319632 |
| 28/10/1995 | 11 | 2 | ○ | THE ULTIMATE SOUL COLLECTION – VOLUME 2 | Warner Music 9548338402 |
| 06/04/1996 | 8 | 4 | | **SONGS IN THE KEY OF X** | Warner Brothers 9362460792 |

○ Silver disc  ● Gold disc  ✪ Platinum disc (additional platinum units are indicated by a figure following the symbol)  ❶⁹ Number of weeks album topped the UK chart

| DATE | POS | WKS | BPI | ALBUM TITLE | LABEL & NUMBER | VAR |
|---|---|---|---|---|---|---|
| 06/04/1996 | 10 | 5 | | TWELVE | warner.esp TV/Global TV 0630146802 | |
| 08/06/1996 | 4 | 5 | ○ | VIVA! EUROPOP | warner.esp TV/Global TV 0630152072 | |
| 02/11/1996 | 7 | 4 | ● | DISCO MIX 96 | warner.esp 9548348072 | |
| 15/02/1997 | 2 | 6 | ● | SIMPLY THE BEST LOVE SONGS | warner.esp 9548351122 | |
| 05/04/1997 | 7 | 6 | ○ | SIMPLY THE BEST CLASSIC SOUL | warner.esp 9548352042 | |
| 07/06/1997 | 14 | 2 | | SUMMER GROOVE | warner.esp 9548353822 | |
| 01/11/1997 | 7 | 4 | ● | ALL MY LOVE | Polygram TV/warner.esp 9548359482 | |
| 14/02/1998 | 2 | 6 | ● | SIMPLY THE BEST LOVE SONGS 2 | warner.esp 9548362252 | |
| 07/03/1998 | 5 | 4 | ○ | A LITTLE BLUES IN YOUR SOUL | warner.esp/Global TV 9548362232 | |
| 28/03/1998 | 9 | 3 | ○ | SIMPLY THE BEST DISCO | warner.esp 9548354282 | |
| 16/05/1998 | 6 | 5 | ○ | CLUBBIN' | warner.esp 9548364262 | |
| 11/07/1998 | 11 | 3 | | LIVE 4 EVER | Sony TV/warner.esp 9548364372 | |
| 15/08/1998 | 9 | 2 | | CLUB CLASS | warner.esp 3984245692 | |
| 22/08/1998 | 4 | 6 | ● | TOTALLY WICKED | warner.esp/Global TV/Sony Music TV 3984246352 | |
| 31/10/1998 | 14 | 2 | ○ | SIMPLY THE BEST CLASSICAL ANTHEMS | warner.esp 3984255442 | |
| 14/11/1998 | 17 | 2 | ○ | SIMPLY THE BEST RADIO HITS | warner.esp 9548369352 | |
| 06/02/1999 | 7 | 2 | ○ | TOTALLY WICKED TOO! | warner.esp/Global TV/Sony Music TV 9548372542 | |
| 10/04/1999 | 20 | 1 | | CLUBZONE – DANCING IN THE CITY | warner.esp/Radio City/3 Beat 3984270952 | |
| 19/06/1999 | 17 | 1 | | MUSIC FOR LIFE | warner.esp 9548376472 | |
| 10/07/1999 | 4 | 5 | ● | CLUB IBIZA | warner.esp 3984288992 | |
| 04/09/1999 | 13 | 3 | | DANCEMIX.UK.V1 | warner.esp 3984294752 | |
| 25/09/1999 | 5 | 5 | | THIS YEAR IN IBIZA | warner.esp 8573800372 | |
| 25/09/1999 | 17 | 1 | | CRAZY LITTLE THING CALLED LOVE | warner.esp/Global TV 9548379382 | |
| 02/10/1999 | 18 | 1 | | THE DEFINITIVE SOUND OF ATLANTIC SOUL | warner.esp 7567805959 | |
| 12/02/2000 | 2 | 15 | ● | PURE GARAGE | warner.esp WMMCD 001 | |
| 04/03/2000 | 4 | 5 | ● | DANCE HITS 2000 | warner.esp/Global TV/Sony TV WMMCD 003 | |
| 25/03/2000 | ❶² | 8 | ☆ | NEW HITS 2000 | warner.esp/Global TV/Sony TV WMMCD 004 | |
| 13/05/2000 | 5 | 7 | ● | TWICE AS NICE – SEXY & STYLISH | warner.esp WMMCD 005 | |
| 15/07/2000 | ❶² | 7 | ● | FRESH HITS – VOLUME 1 | warner.esp/Global TV/Sony TV WMMCD 008 | |
| 15/07/2000 | 2 | 11 | ○ | PURE GARAGE II | warner.esp WMMCD 007 | |
| 02/09/2000 | 8 | 3 | ○ | SPACE | warner.esp WMMCD 010 | |
| 09/09/2000 | 3 | 26 | ● | CHILLED IBIZA | warner.esp WMMCD 011 | |
| 16/09/2000 | 2 | 7 | ○ | FRESH HITS – VOL 2 | warner.esp WMMCD 012 | |
| 23/09/2000 | 6 | 7 | ○ | TWICE AS NICE – SUMMER OF LOVE | warner.esp WMMCD 013 | |
| 30/09/2000 | 4 | 8 | ● | HARD HOUSE NATION | warner.esp WMMCD 014 | |
| 04/11/2000 | 2 | 5 | | HUGE HITS 2000 | Warner/BMG TV/Sony TV WSMCD 015 | |
| 25/11/2000 | 2 | 11 | ● | PURE GARAGE III | warner.esp WSMCD 016 | |
| 25/11/2000 | 13 | 2 | ● | 60 NUMBER ONES OF THE 60'S | warner.esp WSMCD 017 | |
| 09/12/2000 | 11 | 6 | ● | THE CLUBBER'S BIBLE | warner.esp WSMCD 022 | |
| 16/12/2000 | 5 | 6 | ● | HARD HOUSE NATION – 2 | warner.esp WSMCD 023 | |
| 16/12/2000 | 3 | 9 | ☆ | HITS 2001 | BMG/Sony/Telstar/WSM WSMCD 019 | |
| 17/03/2001 | 3 | 6 | ● | PURE GARAGE IV | warner.esp WSMCD 030 | |
| 17/03/2001 | 7 | 3 | ○ | HARD HOUSE VOL.3 | warner.esp WSMCD 031 | |
| 28/04/2001 | 11 | 4 | | TWICE AS NICE – SEXY AND STYLISH | warner.esp WSMCD 034 | |
| 05/05/2001 | 6 | 5 | ○ | THE CLUBBER'S BIBLE II | warner.esp WSMCD 035 | |
| 12/05/2001 | 14 | 4 | | FUNKOLOGY – ONE NATION UNDER A GROOVE | warner.esp WSMCD 033 | |
| 19/05/2001 | 4 | 17 | ☆ | THE LOOK OF LOVE – THE BEST OF BURT BACHARACH | WSM/Universal TV 9547396245 | |
| 16/06/2001 | 17 | 3 | | FRANTIC | warner.esp WSMCD 039 | |
| 30/06/2001 | 16 | 1 | | URBAN RENEWAL – SONGS OF PHIL COLLINS | WEA 8573876372 | |
| 07/07/2001 | 12 | 4 | ○ | THE ARTFUL DODGER PRESENTS REWIND 2001 | WSM WSMCD 038 | |
| 14/07/2001 | 10 | 3 | | PURE HIP HOP – EXPLICIT BEATS | WSM/Universal TV WSMCD 041 | |
| 28/07/2001 | 14 | 2 | | DANCE PARADE IBIZA | WSM/Universal WSMCD 042 | |
| 04/08/2001 | 9 | 8 | ● | THE GREATEST 80'S SOUL WEEKENDER | WSM WSMCD 043 | |
| 04/08/2001 | 12 | 3 | ○ | SIMPLY THE BEST REGGAE ALBUM | WSM WSMCD 044 | |
| 18/08/2001 | 18 | 2 | | MTV IBIZA 2001 | WSM WSMCD 049 | |
| 01/09/2001 | 10 | 4 | | PURE FLAVA | WSM/Universal TV WSMCD 047 | |
| 08/09/2001 | 5 | 6 | ● | CHILLED IBIZA II | WSM WSMCD 045 | |
| 27/10/2001 | 19 | 1 | | TEENDREEM | WSM WSMCD 053 | |
| 10/11/2001 | 7 | 2 | ○ | PURE GARAGE V | WSM WSMCD 046 | |
| 24/11/2001 | 19 | 2 | ○ | HARD DANCE ANTHEMS | WSM WSMCD 055 | |
| 08/12/2001 | 17 | 1 | | ESSENTIAL SELECTION – CLUBBERS BIBLE | WSM WSMCD 052 | |
| 12/01/2002 | 3 | 7 | | JUNGLE MASSIVE | WSM WSMCD 060 | |
| 19/01/2002 | 9 | 4 | | TWICE AS NICE – ESSENTIAL GROOVES | WSM WSMCD 059 | |
| 09/02/2002 | ❶¹ | 6 | ● | LOVE SO STRONG | WSM WSMCD 051 | |
| 16/02/2002 | 12 | 3 | ○ | CLUBBED UP | WSM WSMCD 069 | |
| 02/03/2002 | 15 | 1 | ● | OCEAN'S ELEVEN | Warner Brothers 9362481122 | |
| 16/03/2002 | 7 | 3 | ○ | PURE GENIUS | WSM 0927450012 | |
| 16/03/2002 | 9 | 3 | ○ | SOUL BROTHERS | WSM WSMCD 065 | |
| 23/03/2002 | 15 | 2 | | FRANTIC 2002 | WSM WSMCD 066 | |

▲[9] Number of weeks album topped the US chart  ◆[12] RIAA Diamond Awards  ◇[3] IFPI Platinum Europe Awards

| DATE | POS | WKS | BPI | ALBUM TITLE | LABEL & NUMBER |
|---|---|---|---|---|---|
| 23/03/2002 | 17 | 1 | | JUNGLE MASSIVE – 21st CENTURY BREAKBEAT | warner.esp WSMCD 070 |
| 20/04/2002 | 14 | 2 | | INSTANT KARMA | WSM WSMCD 064 |
| 18/05/2002 | 14 | 3 | | BLUES AND SOUL MASTERS | WSM WSMCD 074 |
| 01/06/2002 | 12 | 3 | ○ | CHILLED IBIZA III | Warner Dance WSMCD 078 |
| 01/06/2002 | ❶¹ | 7 | ● | **THE BEST SUMMER ALBUM 2002** | Sony TV/WSM WSMCD 084 |
| 08/06/2002 | 4 | 7+ | ● | **JUMPERS 4 GOALPOSTS** | WSM WSMCD 081 |
| 08/06/2002 | 5 | 5 | ○ | **TWICE AS NICE PRESENTS URBAN FLAVAS** | Warner Dance WSMCD 079 |
| 15/06/2002 | 4 | 21 | ● | **THE ULTIMATE CHICK FLICK SOUNDTRACK** | WSM/Universal TV WSMCD 071 |
| 06/07/2002 | 17 | 1 | | CREWS CONTROL | Warner Dance WSMCD 077 |
| 13/07/2002 | 15 | 2 | | BACK IN THE DAY | Warner Dance WSMCD 090 |
| 27/07/2002 | 3 | 6 | ● | **BOOM SELECTION** | Sony TV/Warner Dance WSMCD 089 |
| 03/08/2002 | 9 | 3 | | **HANDS TO HEAVEN** | Warner Dance WSMCD 082 |
| 24/08/2002 | 8 | 4 | ○ | **THE ULTIMATE HEN NIGHT PARTY ALBUM** | WSM WSMCD 103 |
| 14/09/2002 | 8 | 4 | ○ | **GET UR FREAK ON** | Warner Dance WSMCD 062 |
| 14/09/2002 | 16 | 3 | | THE PAN PIPE CHILLOUT ALBUM | warner.esp WSMCD 106 |
| 28/09/2002 | 12 | 2 | | IBIZA HITMIX 2002 | Warner Dance WSMCD 073 |
| 12/10/2002 | 3 | 5 | ● | **TWICE AS NICE PRESENTS MOBO 2002** | Warner Dance WSMCD 110 |
| 02/11/2002 | 12 | 1 | | PURE GENIUS VOLUME 2 | WSM WSMCD 115 |
| 09/11/2002 | 11 | 1 | | PURE TRANCE | Warner Dance WSMCD 087 |
| 23/11/2002 | 2 | 19 | ✪ | **ALL TIME CLASSIC TEARJERKERS** | WSM WSMCD 116 |
| 23/11/2002 | 14 | 5 | | PLATINUM SOUL LEGENDS – 1960–1975 | WSM WSMCD 100 |
| 21/12/2002 | 4 | 9 | ● | **PURE GARAGE PLATINUM – THE VERY BEST OF** | Warner Dance WSMCD 120 |
| 11/01/2003 | 5 | 5 | ○ | **BASS BREAKS & BEATS 2003** | Warner Dance WSMCD 121 |
| 11/01/2003 | 13 | 1 | ○ | PARTY ANIMAL | WSM WSMCD 114 |
| 01/02/2003 | 5 | 6 | | **URBAN EXPLOSION** | INCredible/Warner Dance WSMCD 123 |
| 08/02/2003 | 4 | 4 | ● | **THE POWER OF LOVE** | Sony TV/WSM WSMCD 127 |
| 08/03/2003 | ❶² | 11 | ● | **THE VERY BEST OF MTV UNPLUGGED 2** | UMTV/WSM 5046623832 |
| 15/03/2003 | 11 | 2 | | STRANGE AND BEAUTIFUL | WSM WSMCD 122 |
| 22/03/2003 | 4 | 4 | ● | **CHICK FLICKS – THE SEQUEL** | UMTV/WSM WSMCD 126 |
| 22/03/2003 | 10 | 2 | | **SHAMROCKS AND SHENANIGANS** | WSM WSMCD 129 |
| 05/04/2003 | 4 | 3 | ○ | **SONGBIRDS** | WSM WSMCD 119 |
| 12/04/2003 | 8 | 5 | | TWICE AS NICE PRESENTS URBAN FLAVAS 2003 | Urban Explosion/WSM WSMCD 124 |
| 19/04/2003 | 7 | 2 | | **THE ULTIMATE SMOOCHY ALBUM** | WSM WSMCD 130 |
| 17/05/2003 | 10 | 3 | | **REPRESS – 80'S CLUB CLASSICS** | Warner Dance WSMCD 136 |
| 24/05/2003 | 3 | 5 | ● | **IBIZA – THE HISTORY OF HOUSE** | Warner Dance WSMCD 075 |
| 31/05/2003 | 11 | 2 | ○ | THE BEST SUMMER ALBUM 2003 | WSM/Sony WSMCD 133 |
| 07/06/2003 | 5 | 7 | ● | **ALL TIME CLASSIC ROCK 'N' ROLL TEARJERKERS** | WSM WSMCD 128 |
| 14/06/2003 | 3 | 13 | ● | **PURE URBAN ESSENTIALS** | Warner Dance/Sony TV WSMCD 132 |
| 26/07/2003 | 3 | 6 | ○ | **IBIZA – THE HISTORY OF CHILLOUT** | Warner Dance WSMCD 143 |
| 26/07/2003 | 20 | 1 | | SKATE TO HELL | WSM WSMCD 139 |
| 09/08/2003 | 6 | 4 | ○ | **IBIZA – THE HISTORY OF HARD DANCE** | Warner Dance WSMCD 144 |
| 30/08/2003 | 12 | 3 | | RE-PRESS – THE 70'S SOUL REVIVAL | Warner Dance WSMCD 146 |
| 13/09/2003 | 9 | 5 | ○ | **SWING CLASSICS** | Warner Dance WSMCD 149 |
| 25/10/2003 | 3 | 6 | ● | **HAIRBRUSH DIVAS** | WSM WSMCD 152 |
| 08/11/2003 | 2 | 19 | ✪ | **R&B LOVE** | Warner Dance/Sony TV WSMCD 148 |
| 15/11/2003 | 18 | 1 | | ALL TIME CLASSIC COUNTRY TEARJERKERS | WSM WSMCD 145 |
| 06/12/2003 | 5 | 1 | ✪ | **THE ULTIMATE CHICK FLICK LOVE SONGS** | UMTV/WSM WSMCD 154 |
| 06/12/2003 | 12 | 3 | ● | THE ULTIMATE CHEESE PARTY | WSM WSMCD 153 |
| 13/12/2003 | 4 | 10 | ● | **PURE URBAN ESSENTIALS 2** | Sony TV/Warner Dance WSMCD 150 |
| 10/01/2004 | 12 | 3 | | PURE GARAGE PRESENTS FOUR TO THE FLOOR | Warner Dance WSMCD 159 |
| 31/01/2004 | 3 | 6 | ○ | **DRUM & BASS ARENA** | Warner Dance WSMCD 160 |
| 20/03/2004 | 8 | 4 | ○ | **HAIRBRUSH DIVAS 2** | WSM WSMCD 164 |
| 24/04/2004 | 10 | 3 | | **SUPERBAD** | Warner Dance WSMCD 165 |
| 01/05/2004 | 8 | 3 | | **THE ULTIMATE FUNK PARTY** | WSM WSMCD 175 |
| 15/05/2004 | 8 | 4 | | **URBAN MUSIC FESTIVAL** | Warner Dance WSMCD 1667 |
| 29/05/2004 | 4 | 4 | | **LOVE HURTS** | warner.esp WSMCD172 |
| 12/06/2004 | 13 | 3+ | | CHILLED IBIZA GOLD | Warner Dance WSMCD 178 |
| 19/06/2004 | 7 | 2+ | | **IBIZA – THE HISTORY OF TRANCE** | Warner Dance WSMCD 169 |

## WARP

| DATE | POS | WKS | BPI | ALBUM TITLE | LABEL & NUMBER |
|---|---|---|---|---|---|
| 11/06/1994 | 16 | 2 | | ARTIFICIAL INTELLIGENCE | Warp WARPLTDCD 23 |

## WARWICK

| DATE | POS | WKS | BPI | ALBUM TITLE | LABEL & NUMBER |
|---|---|---|---|---|---|
| 29/11/1975 | 21 | 8 | | ALL-TIME PARTY HITS | Warwick WW 5001 |
| 17/04/1976 | 3 | 24 | | **INSTRUMENTAL GOLD** | Warwick WW 5012 |
| 29/05/1976 | 15 | 5 | | HAMILTON'S HOT SHOTS | Warwick WW 5014 |
| 08/01/1977 | 31 | 2 | | SONGS OF PRAISE | Warwick WW 5020 |
| 29/01/1977 | 19 | 5 | | HIT SCENE | Warwick PR 5023 |
| 25/11/1978 | 47 | 7 | | LOVE SONGS – 16 CLASSIC LOVE SONGS | Warwick WW 5046 |

○ Silver disc  ● Gold disc  ✪ Platinum disc (additional platinum units are indicated by a figure following the symbol)  ❶⁹ Number of weeks album topped the UK chart

| DATE | POS | WKS | BPI | ALBUM TITLE | LABEL & NUMBER |
|---|---|---|---|---|---|
| 02/12/1978 | 72 | 3 | | BLACK VELVET | Warwick WW 5047 |
| 07/04/1979 | 14 | 10 | | COUNTRY PORTRAITS | Warwick WW 5057 |
| 10/11/1979 | 42 | 5 | ● | 20 SMASH DISCO HITS (THE BITCH) | Warwick WW 5061 |
| 16/02/1980 | 46 | 3 | | COUNTRY GUITAR | Warwick WW 5070 |
| 14/11/1981 | 35 | 8 | | DISCO EROTICA | Warwick WW 5108 |
| 10/04/1982 | 68 | 3 | | PS I LOVE YOU | Warwick WW 5121 |
| 06/11/1982 | 24 | 10 | | HITS OF THE SCREAMING 60'S | Warwick WW 5124 |
| 22/12/1984 | 64 | 2 | | MERRY CHRISTMAS TO YOU | Warwick WW 5141 |

## WEST FIVE

| DATE | POS | WKS | BPI | ALBUM TITLE | LABEL & NUMBER |
|---|---|---|---|---|---|
| 18/10/1986 | 33 | 7 | ○ | THE POWER OF LOVE | West Five WEF 4 |

## WESTMOOR

| DATE | POS | WKS | BPI | ALBUM TITLE | LABEL & NUMBER |
|---|---|---|---|---|---|
| 24/03/1990 | 14 | 2 | | EMERALD CLASSICS VOLUMES I AND II | Westmoor WMTV 1 |

## WESTWAY DANCE

| DATE | POS | WKS | BPI | ALBUM TITLE | LABEL & NUMBER |
|---|---|---|---|---|---|
| 18/07/1998 | 15 | 3 | | ELEMENTS – SEB FONTAINE/TONY DE VIT | Westway Dance 3984238682 |

## WHITE ISLAND

| DATE | POS | WKS | BPI | ALBUM TITLE | LABEL & NUMBER |
|---|---|---|---|---|---|
| 14/10/2000 | 13 | 3 | | MTV IBIZA 2000 – THE PARTY | White Island MTVRCD 001 |

## WORLDS END

| DATE | POS | WKS | BPI | ALBUM TITLE | LABEL & NUMBER |
|---|---|---|---|---|---|
| 26/09/1992 | 17 | 1 | | VOLUME FOUR | Worlds End V 4CD |

## WORLDWIDE ULTIMATUM

| DATE | POS | WKS | BPI | ALBUM TITLE | LABEL & NUMBER |
|---|---|---|---|---|---|
| 15/03/1997 | 13 | 2 | | CARL COX – FACT 2 | Worldwide Ultimatum 0091022 |

## XL RECORDINGS UK dance label formed in 1991 by Richard Russell and Martin Mills.

| DATE | POS | WKS | BPI | ALBUM TITLE | LABEL & NUMBER |
|---|---|---|---|---|---|
| 14/09/1991 | 5 | 9 | | XL RECORDINGS – THE SECOND CHAPTER | XL Recordings XLLP 108 |
| 25/04/1992 | 6 | 8 | | THE THIRD CHAPTER | XL Recordings XLCD 109 |
| 06/03/1999 | 3 | 3 | | PRODIGY PRESENTS THE DIRTCHAMBER SESSIONS 1 | XL Recordings XLCD 128 |

## ZOMBA UK label initially formed in 1977 as a book publishing company by South African Clive Calder. It branched out into music in 1981 with the launch of Jive Records and was sold to BMG in 2002 for $2.7 billion.

| DATE | POS | WKS | BPI | ALBUM TITLE | LABEL & NUMBER |
|---|---|---|---|---|---|
| 24/10/1987 | 86 | 1 | | THE WORD | Zomba HOP 217 |

## ZTT UK label formed in 1983 by ex-Buggles member/producer Trevor Horn and his wife Jill Sinclair with music journalist Paul Morley.

| DATE | POS | WKS | BPI | ALBUM TITLE | LABEL & NUMBER |
|---|---|---|---|---|---|
| 19/10/1985 | 40 | 3 | | IQ 6: ZANG TUMB TUM SAMPLED | ZTT IQ 6 |

## FILM SOUNDTRACKS

| DATE | POS | WKS | BPI | ALBUM TITLE | LABEL & NUMBER |
|---|---|---|---|---|---|
| 28/07/1956 | ❶[3] | 162 | | OKLAHOMA! ▲[4] | Capitol LCT 6100 |
| 28/07/1956 | ❶[6] | 40 | | CAROUSEL | Capitol LCT 6105 |
| 25/08/1956 | 3 | 4 | | THE EDDY DUCHIN STORY ▲[1] | Brunswick LAT 8119 |
| 22/09/1956 | ❶[48] | 200 | | THE KING AND I ▲[1] | Capitol LCT 6108 |
| 22/12/1956 | 2 | 26 | | HIGH SOCIETY | Capitol LCT 6116 |
| 18/01/1958 | ❶[11] | 23 | | PAL JOEY | Capitol LCT 6148 |
| 08/02/1958 | 3 | 10 | | PYJAMA GAME | Philips BBL 7197 |
| 08/11/1958 | ❶[115] | 313 | | SOUTH PACIFIC ▲[31] | RCA RB 16065 |
| 31/01/1959 | 2 | 88 | | GIGI ▲[10] 1958 Grammy Award for Best Soundtrack Album | MGM C 770 |
| 10/10/1959 | 7 | 5 | | PORGY AND BESS 1959 Grammy Award for Best Soundtrack Album | Philips ABL 3282 |
| 23/01/1960 | 2 | 15 | | THE FIVE PENNIES | London HAU 2189 |
| 07/05/1960 | 2 | 31 | | CAN CAN | Capitol W 1301 |
| 05/11/1960 | 15 | 3 | | BEN HUR | MGM C 802 |
| 21/01/1961 | 17 | 1 | | NEVER ON SUNDAY | London HAT 2309 |
| 18/02/1961 | 9 | 10 | | SONG WITHOUT END | Pye Golden Guinea GGL 30169 |
| 29/04/1961 | 6 | 22 | | SEVEN BRIDES FOR SEVEN BROTHERS | MGM C 853 |
| 03/06/1961 | 17 | 1 | | EXODUS ▲[14] 1960 Grammy Award for Best Soundtrack Album | RCA RD 27210 |
| 11/11/1961 | 12 | 7 | | GLENN MILLER STORY | Ace Of Hearts AH 12 |
| 24/03/1962 | ❶[13] | 175 | | WEST SIDE STORY 1961 Grammy Award for Best Soundtrack Album | Philips BBL 7530 |

▲[9] Number of weeks album topped the US chart ◆[12] RIAA Diamond Awards ◇[3] IFPI Platinum Europe Awards

| DATE | POS | WKS | BPI | ALBUM TITLE | LABEL & NUMBER |
|------|-----|-----|-----|-------------|----------------|
| 28/04/1962 | 3 | 21 | | IT'S TRAD DAD | Columbia 33SX 1412 |
| 22/09/1962 | 14 | 9 | | THE MUSIC MAN ▲12 | Warner Brothers WB 4066 |
| 03/11/1962 | 14 | 7 | | PORGY AND BESS Re-issue of Philips ABL 3282 | CBS APG 60002 |
| 15/06/1963 | 20 | 2 | | JUST FOR FUN | Decca LK 4525 |
| 31/10/1964 | 9 | 51 | | MY FAIR LADY | CBS BPG 72237 |
| 16/01/1965 | 2 | 82 | | MARY POPPINS ▲14 1964 Grammy Award for Best Original Score Written for a Motion Picture or TV Show | HMV CLP 1794 |
| 10/04/1965 | ❶70 | 381 | ✪ | THE SOUND OF MUSIC ▲18 | RCA Victor RB 6616 |
| 29/07/1967 | 31 | 11 | | A MAN AND A WOMAN | United Artists SULP 1155 |
| 28/10/1967 | 9 | 19 | | THOROUGHLY MODERN MILLIE | Brunswick STA 8685 |
| 09/03/1968 | 5 | 51 | ● | THE JUNGLE BOOK | Disney ST 3948 |
| 21/09/1968 | 36 | 1 | | STAR! | Stateside SSL 10233 |
| 23/11/1968 | 4 | 107 | | OLIVER! | RCA Victor SB 6777 |
| 23/11/1968 | 37 | 1 | | CAMELOT | Warner Brothers WS 1712 |
| 08/02/1969 | 10 | 4 | | CHITTY CHITTY BANG BANG | United Artists SULP 1200 |
| 14/06/1969 | 3 | 67 | | 2001 – A SPACE ODYSSEY | MGM CS 8078 |
| 20/12/1969 | 2 | 67 | | EASY RIDER | Stateside SSL 5018 |
| 24/01/1970 | 25 | 26 | | THE JUNGLE BOOK Re-issue of Disney ST 3948 | Disney BVS 4041 |
| 07/02/1970 | 2 | 102 | | PAINT YOUR WAGON | Paramount SPFL 257 |
| 18/07/1970 | 35 | 19 | | WOODSTOCK ▲4 | Atlantic 2662 001 |
| 24/04/1971 | 10 | 33 | | LOVE STORY | Paramount SPFL 267 |
| 12/02/1972 | 4 | 46 | | CLOCKWORK ORANGE | Warner Brothers K 46127 |
| 08/04/1972 | 26 | 2 | | FIDDLER ON THE ROOF | United Artists UAD 60011/2 |
| 13/05/1972 | 20 | 2 | | 2001 – A SPACE ODYSSEY Re-issue of MGM CS 8078 | MGM 2315 034 |
| 25/11/1972 | 25 | 2 | | SOUTH PACIFIC Re-issue of RCA RB 16065 | RCA Victor SB 2011 |
| 31/03/1973 | 13 | 22 | | CABARET | Probe SPB 1052 |
| 14/04/1973 | 36 | 3 | | LOST HORIZON | Bell SYBEL 8000 |
| 22/09/1973 | 23 | 18 | | JESUS CHRIST SUPERSTAR ▲3 | MCA MDKS 8012/3 |
| 27/04/1974 | 37 | 1 | ○ | AMERICAN GRAFFITI | MCA MCSP 253 |
| 08/06/1974 | 32 | 1 | ○ | A TOUCH OF CLASS | Philips 6612 040 |
| 05/10/1974 | 47 | 3 | | SUNSHINE | MCA MCF 2566 |
| 05/04/1975 | 21 | 9 | ● | TOMMY | Polydor 2657 014 |
| 27/11/1976 | 23 | 7 | ● | ALL THIS AND WORLD WAR II | Riva RVLP 2 |
| 02/07/1977 | 59 | 1 | | THE BEST OF CAR WASH | MCA MCF 2799 |
| 11/03/1978 | ❶18 | 65 | ✪ | SATURDAY NIGHT FEVER ◆15 ▲24 1978 Grammy Award for Album of the Year | RSO 2658 123 |
| 22/04/1978 | 2 | 19 | ● | THE STUD | Ronco RTD 2029 |
| 06/05/1978 | 39 | 4 | | THE LAST WALTZ | Warner Brothers K 66076 |
| 20/05/1978 | 40 | 5 | ○ | THANK GOD IT'S FRIDAY | Casablanca TGIF 100 |
| 27/05/1978 | 37 | 7 | ○ | FM | MCA MCSP 284 |
| 08/07/1978 | ❶13 | 47 | ✪ | GREASE ▲12 | RSO RSD 2001 |
| 12/08/1978 | 38 | 2 | ○ | SGT. PEPPER'S LONELY HEARTS CLUB BAND | A&M AMLZ 66600 |
| 07/10/1978 | 52 | 1 | | CONVOY | Capitol EST 24590 |
| 31/03/1979 | 42 | 6 | | LEMON POPSICLE | Warwick WW 5050 |
| 09/06/1979 | 36 | 8 | | THAT SUMMER | Arista SPART 1088 |
| 30/06/1979 | 25 | 9 | | THE WORLD IS FULL OF MARRIED MEN | Ronco RTD 2038 |
| 14/07/1979 | 53 | 7 | | THE WARRIORS | A&M AMLH 64761 |
| 09/02/1980 | 45 | 7 | | SUNBURN | Warwick RTL 2044 |
| 16/02/1980 | 25 | 10 | | GOING STEADY | Warwick WW 5078 |
| 08/03/1980 | 48 | 7 | | THE WANDERERS | Gem GEMLP 103 |
| 06/09/1980 | ❶2 | 25 | ● | FAME | RSO 2479 253 |
| 14/02/1981 | 5 | 15 | ● | DANCE CRAZE | 2-Tone CHRTT 5004 |
| 17/07/1982 | 98 | 1 | | THE SOUND OF MUSIC Re-issue of RCA Victor RB 6616 | RCA International 5134 |
| 04/09/1982 | 42 | 7 | | ROCKY III | Liberty LBG 30351 |
| 04/09/1982 | 83 | 2 | | ANNIE | CBS 70219 |
| 11/09/1982 | 67 | 3 | | BRIMSTONE AND TREACLE | A&M AMLH 64915 |
| 12/02/1983 | 40 | 14 | | AN OFFICER AND A GENTLEMAN | Island ISTA 3 |
| 02/07/1983 | 9 | 30 | | FLASHDANCE ▲2 1983 Grammy Award, Best Album of Original Score Written for a Motion Picture or TV Show | Casablanca CANH 5 |
| 01/10/1983 | 14 | 8 | ○ | STAYING ALIVE | RSO RSBG 3 |
| 21/04/1984 | 7 | 25 | ● | FOOTLOOSE ▲10 | CBS 70246 |
| 21/04/1984 | 29 | 10 | | AGAINST ALL ODDS | Virgin V 2313 |
| 16/06/1984 | 6 | 29 | ● | BREAKDANCE | Polydor POLD 5147 |
| 07/07/1984 | 30 | 13 | | BEAT STREET | Atlantic 7801541 |
| 18/08/1984 | 46 | 7 | ○ | ELECTRIC DREAMS | Virgin V 2318 |
| 29/09/1984 | 24 | 25 | ● | GHOSTBUSTERS | Arista 206 559 |
| 12/01/1985 | 34 | 20 | | BREAKDANCE 2 – ELECTRIC BOOGALOO | Polydor POLD 5168 |
| 16/02/1985 | 24 | 32 | ● | BEVERLY HILLS COP ▲2 1985 Grammy Award for Best Album of Original Score Written for a Motion Picture or TV Show ................................ MCA MCF 3253 | |
| 11/01/1986 | 66 | 8 | | BACK TO THE FUTURE | MCA MCF 3285 |
| 01/02/1986 | 3 | 22 | ● | ROCKY IV | Scotti Brothers SCT 70272 |
| 05/04/1986 | 19 | 9 | ● | ABSOLUTE BEGINNERS | Virgin V 2386 |

| DATE | POS | WKS | BPI | ALBUM TITLE | LABEL & NUMBER |
|---|---|---|---|---|---|
| 11/10/1986 | 4 | 46 | ✪² | TOP GUN ▲⁵ 1987 BRIT Award for Best Soundtrack | CBS 70296 |
| 11/04/1987 | 59 | 26 | ✪² | THE BLUES BROTHERS | Atlantic K 50715 |
| 02/05/1987 | 90 | 2 | ○ | PLATOON | WEA WX 95 |
| 18/07/1987 | 71 | 5 | | BEVERLY HILLS COP II | MCA MCF 3383 |
| 01/08/1987 | 4 | 25 | ✪ | WHO'S THAT GIRL | Sire WX 102 |
| 03/10/1987 | 60 | 4 | | FULL METAL JACKET | Warner Brothers 9256131 |
| 31/10/1987 | 4 | 63 | ✪⁵ | DIRTY DANCING ◆¹¹ ▲¹⁸ | RCA BL 86408 |
| 16/01/1988 | 93 | 2 | ● | FLASHDANCE Re-issue of Casablanca CANH 5 | Mercury PRICE 111 |
| 20/02/1988 | 73 | 2 | | CRY FREEDOM | MCA MCG 6029 |
| 14/05/1988 | 3 | 27 | | MORE DIRTY DANCING | RCA BL 86965 |
| 24/09/1988 | 6 | 16 | | BUSTER 1989 BRIT Award for Best Soundtrack | Virgin V 2544 |
| 22/10/1988 | 50 | 9 | ● | GOOD MORNING VIETNAM | A&M AMA 3913 |
| 14/01/1989 | ❶² | 158 | ✪⁵ | DIRTY DANCING ◆¹¹ ▲¹⁸ | RCA BL 86408 |
| 14/01/1989 | 2 | 36 | ✪³ | BUSTER | Virgin V 2544 |
| 21/01/1989 | 7 | 29 | ● | GOOD MORNING VIETNAM | A&M AMA 3913 |
| 21/01/1989 | 4 | 80 | ✪² | THE BLUES BROTHERS | Atlantic K 50715 |
| 28/01/1989 | ❶¹ | 61 | ✪ | THE LOST BOYS | Atlantic 7817671 |
| 04/02/1989 | 2 | 15 | ● | COCKTAIL | Elektra EKT 54 |
| 04/02/1989 | 14 | 17 | ✪ | MORE DIRTY DANCING | RCA BL 86965 |
| 18/03/1989 | 13 | 3 | | SCANDAL | Parlophone PCS 7331 |
| 22/04/1989 | 4 | 34 | ✪² | TOP GUN | CBS 70296 |
| 15/07/1989 | 17 | 2 | | LICENCE TO KILL | MCA MCG 6051 |
| 22/07/1989 | 15 | 4 | | GHOSTBUSTERS II | MCA MCG 6051 |
| 10/03/1990 | 16 | 1 | | THE DELINQUENTS | PWL HF 11 |
| 26/05/1990 | 2 | 72 | ✪² | PRETTY WOMAN | EMI USA MTL 1052 |
| 23/06/1990 | 6 | 18 | ● | TEENAGE MUTANT NINJA TURTLES | SBK SBKLP 6 |
| 11/08/1990 | 4 | 15 | ● | DAYS OF THUNDER | Epic 4671591 |
| 27/10/1990 | 15 | 4 | | GHOST | MILAN A 620 |
| 02/02/1991 | 9 | 9 | | ROCKY V | Capitol EST 2137 |
| 02/03/1991 | 8 | 11 | | GREASE Re-issue of RSO RSD 2001 | Polydor 8179981 |
| 23/03/1991 | 19 | 1 | | THE GODFATHER PART III | Columbia 4678131 |
| 27/04/1991 | 16 | 5 | | NEW JACK CITY | Giant 7559244091 |
| 01/06/1991 | 6 | 15 | ○ | MERMAIDS | Epic 4678741 |
| 27/07/1991 | 3 | 14 | ○ | ROBIN HOOD: PRINCE OF THIEVES | Polydor 5110502 |
| 18/01/1992 | 3 | 8 | | BILL AND TED'S BOGUS JOURNEY | Interscope 7567917252 |
| 29/02/1992 | 13 | 7 | | MY GIRL | Epic 4692134 |
| 30/05/1992 | 5 | 11 | | WAYNE'S WORLD ▲² 1993 BRIT Award for Best Soundtrack | Reprise 7599258052 |
| 19/09/1992 | 16 | 1 | | MO' MONEY | Perspective 3610042 |
| 14/11/1992 | 17 | 2 | | BOOMERANG | LaFace 73008260062 |
| 28/11/1992 | ❶¹¹ | 80 | ✪⁷ | THE BODYGUARD ◆¹⁷ ▲²⁰ 1994 BRIT Award for Best Soundtrack | Arista 07822186992 |
| 30/01/1993 | 14 | 4 | | SISTER ACT | Hollywood HWDCD 9 |
| 13/02/1993 | 10 | 6 | | BRAM STOKER'S DRACULA | Columbia 4727462 |
| 20/03/1993 | 16 | 3 | | RESERVOIR DOGS | MCA MCD 10793 |
| 05/06/1993 | 13 | 3 | | INDECENT PROPOSAL | MCA MCD 10863 |
| 24/07/1993 | 16 | 6 | | THE LAST ACTION HERO | Columbia 4739902 |
| 18/09/1993 | 20 | 1 | | SLIVER | Virgin CDVMMX 11 |
| 16/10/1993 | 10 | 6 | ○ | SLEEPLESS IN SEATTLE ▲¹ | Epic 4735942 |
| 16/10/1993 | 16 | 3 | | JUDGEMENT NIGHT | Epic 4741832 |
| 08/01/1994 | 11 | 5 | | ALADDIN | Pickwick DSTCD 470 |
| 05/03/1994 | 17 | 1 | | WAYNE'S WORLD 2 | Warner Brothers WB 45485 |
| 12/03/1994 | 5 | 14 | ● | PHILADELPHIA ◇ | Epic 4749982 |
| 07/05/1994 | 18 | 1 | | ABOVE THE RIM | Interscope 6544923592 |
| 28/05/1994 | 5 | 21 | ✪ | FOUR WEDDINGS AND A FUNERAL | Vertigo 5167512 |
| 25/06/1994 | 13 | 5 | ● | THE CROW ▲¹ | Atlantic 7567825192 |
| 06/08/1994 | 18 | 1 | ○ | THE FLINTSTONES | MCA MCD 11045 |
| 22/10/1994 | 4 | 20 | | THE LION KING ◇³ ◆¹⁰ ▲¹⁰ | Mercury 5226902 |
| 22/10/1994 | 5 | 13 | ● | FORREST GUMP ◆¹² | Epic 4769412 |
| 05/11/1994 | 5 | 56 | ● | PULP FICTION ◇³ 1995 BRIT Award for Best Soundtrack | MCA MCD 11103 |
| 11/03/1995 | 10 | 6 | ○ | NATURAL BORN KILLERS | Interscope 6544924602 |
| 08/07/1995 | 19 | 1 | | BAD BOYS | Work 4804532 |
| 29/07/1995 | 11 | 4 | | BATMAN FOREVER 1996 BRIT Award for Best Soundtrack | Atlantic 7567827592 |
| 03/02/1996 | 8 | 5 | | WAITING TO EXHALE ◇ ▲⁵ | Arista 07822187962 |
| 03/02/1996 | 13 | 2 | | DANGEROUS MINDS ▲⁴ | MCA MCD 11228 |
| 02/03/1996 | 2 | 66 | ✪³ | TRAINSPOTTING ◇ 1997 BRIT Award for Best Soundtrack | EMI Premier CDEMC 3739 |
| 20/07/1996 | 18 | 1 | | MISSION: IMPOSSIBLE | Mother MUMCD 9603 |
| 19/10/1996 | 20 | 1 | | THE NUTTY PROFESSOR | Def Jam 5319112 |
| 29/03/1997 | 5 | 10 | ● | SPACE JAM | Atlantic 7567829792 |
| 05/04/1997 | 3 | 24 | ✪ | ROMEO + JULIET ◇ | Premier Soundtracks PRMDCD 28 |

▲⁹ Number of weeks album topped the US chart  ◆¹² RIAA Diamond Awards  ◇³ IFPI Platinum Europe Awards

| DATE | POS | WKS | BPI | ALBUM TITLE | LABEL & NUMBER |
|---|---|---|---|---|---|
| 03/05/1997 | 15 | 1 | | THE SAINT | Virgin CDVUD 126 |
| 02/08/1997 | 5 | 13 | ● | **MEN IN BLACK – THE ALBUM** ▲2 | Columbia 4881222 |
| 09/08/1997 | 18 | 1 | | SPAWN – THE ALBUM | Epic 4881182 |
| 13/09/1997 | ❶3 | 43 | ✪3 | **THE FULL MONTY** 1998 BRIT Award for Best Soundtrack | RCA Victor 09026689042 |
| 27/09/1997 | 11 | 5 | ○ | TRAINSPOTTING #2 | Premier Soundtracks PRMDCD 36 |
| 31/01/1998 | 19 | 1 | | BOOGIE NIGHTS | Premier Soundtracks 8556312 |
| 18/04/1998 | 11 | 7 | ○ | JACKIE BROWN | Maverick 9362468412 |
| 27/06/1998 | 15 | 4 | ○ | THE WEDDING SINGER | Maverick 9362468402 |
| 04/07/1998 | 18 | 3 | ● | CITY OF ANGELS ▲3 | Reprise 9362468672 |
| 18/07/1998 | 2 | 15 | | **GREASE** Second re-issue of RSO RSD 2001 | Polydor 0440412 |
| 25/07/1998 | 13 | 4 | | GODZILLA – THE ALBUM | Epic 4896102 |
| 12/09/1998 | 7 | 23 | ● | **LOCK, STOCK & TWO SMOKING BARRELS** | Island CID 8077 |
| 26/09/1998 | 19 | 2 | ○ | ARMAGEDDON ▲2 | Columbia 4913842 |
| 05/06/1999 | 4 | 19 | ✪ | **NOTTING HILL** ◇ 2000 BRIT Award for Best Soundtrack | Island 5462072 |
| 19/06/1999 | 14 | 3 | ○ | HUMAN TRAFFIC | London 5561092 |
| 26/06/1999 | 16 | 5 | ● | THE MATRIX ◇ | Maverick 9362474192 |
| 17/07/1999 | 6 | 11 | ● | **AUSTIN POWERS – THE SPY WHO SHAGGED ME** | Maverick 9362473842 |
| 11/09/1999 | 9 | 5 | ○ | **SOUTH PARK: BIGGER, LONGER & UNCUT** | Atlantic 7567831992 |
| 02/10/1999 | 17 | 1 | | MANUMISSION – THE MOVIE | Telstar TV TTVCD 3066 |
| 04/03/2000 | ❶3 | 8 | ● | **THE BEACH** | London 4344310792 |
| 25/03/2000 | 13 | 1 | | THE MILLION DOLLAR HOTEL | Island CID 8094 |
| 08/04/2000 | 8 | 5 | ● | **POKEMON – THE FIRST MOVIE** | Atlantic 7567832612 |
| 29/04/2000 | 4 | 7 | ● | **KEVIN AND PERRY – GO LARGE** | Virgin/EMI VTDCDX 298 |
| 01/07/2000 | 12 | 8 | ○ | MISSION IMPOSSIBLE 2 | Hollywood 0110302 HWR |
| 16/09/2000 | 11 | 3 | | SNATCH | Universal 5249992 |
| 21/10/2000 | 10 | 4 | | **BILLY ELLIOT** | Polydor 5493602 |
| 04/11/2000 | 16 | 3 | ○ | COYOTE UGLY ◇ | Curb/London 8573852542 |
| 14/04/2001 | 5 | 8 | ● | **SAVE THE LAST DANCE** | Hollywood 025422 HWR |
| 28/04/2001 | ❶7 | 30 | ✪3 | **BRIDGET JONES'S DIARY** | Mercury 5487962 |
| 21/07/2001 | 13 | 2 | | TOMB RAIDER | Elektra 7559626652 |
| 15/09/2001 | 2 | 12 | | **MOULIN ROUGE** ◇4 | Interscope 4905072 |
| 29/09/2001 | 20 | 2 | | THE FAST AND THE FURIOUS | Def Jam 5865062 |
| 27/10/2001 | 17 | 2 | ○ | AMERICAN PIE 2 | Universal 0163482 |
| 10/11/2001 | 8 | 2 | ● | **BRIDGET JONES'S DIARY 2** ◇2 | Mercury 5865982 |
| 26/01/2002 | 20 | 1 | ○ | O BROTHER WHERE ART THOU ▲2 2001 Grammy Award for Album of the Year | Mercury 1700692 |
| 02/03/2002 | 15 | 1 | ● | OCEAN'S ELEVEN | Warner Brothers 9362481122 |
| 16/03/2002 | 9 | 7 | | **MOULIN ROUGE – COLLECTORS EDITION** | Interscope 4932592 |
| 30/03/2002 | 5 | 7 | ● | **ALI G INDAHOUSE – DA SOUNDTRACK** | Island CID 8115 |
| 20/04/2002 | 15 | 2 | | 24 HOUR PARTY PEOPLE | London 0927449302 |
| 01/06/2002 | 14 | 6 | | SPIDER-MAN | Columbia 5075476 |
| 10/08/2002 | 14 | 2 | | AUSTIN POWERS IN GOLDMEMBER | Maverick 9362483492 |
| 09/11/2002 | ❶2 | 26 | ● | **8 MILE** ◇ ▲4 | Interscope 4935322 |
| 25/01/2003 | 4 | 12 | ● | **CHICAGO** 2003 Grammy Award for Best Compilation Soundtrack Album for a Motion Picture | Epic 5105322 |
| 17/05/2003 | 2 | 8 | ○ | **THE MATRIX RELOADED** | Maverick 9362484112 |
| 19/07/2003 | 12 | 2 | | CHARLIE'S ANGELS: FULL THROTTLE | Columbia 5123062 |
| 18/10/2003 | 17 | 1 | | BAD BOYS II ▲4 | Bad Boy 750327 |
| 25/10/2003 | 6 | 11 | ● | **KILL BILL VOLUME 1** | Maverick 9362485882 |
| 29/11/2003 | 2 | 23 | ● | **LOVE ACTUALLY** ◇ | Island 9814032 |
| 27/03/2004 | ❶2 | 14+ | | **ULTIMATE DIRTY DANCING** | RCA 82876555252 |
| 01/05/2004 | 13 | 4 | | KILL BILL VOLUME 2 | Maverick 9362486762 |

## STAGE AND STUDIO CAST RECORDINGS

| DATE | POS | WKS | BPI | ALBUM TITLE | LABEL & NUMBER |
|---|---|---|---|---|---|
| 04/08/1956 | 5 | 2 | | **SALAD DAYS (ORIGINAL LONDON STAGE CAST RECORDING)** | Oriole MG 20004 |
| 10/05/1958 | ❶19 | 155 | | **MY FAIR LADY (ORIGINAL BROADWAY STAGE CAST)** ▲15 | Philips RBL 1000 |
| 24/01/1959 | 3 | 27 | | **WEST SIDE STORY (ORIGINAL BROADWAY STAGE CAST)** ▲54 | Philips BBL 7277 |
| 26/03/1960 | 5 | 11 | | **FINGS AIN'T WOT THEY USED TO BE (ORIGINAL LONDON STAGE CAST)** | Decca LK 4346 |
| 26/03/1960 | 9 | 1 | | **AT THE DROP OF A HAT (ORIGINAL LONDON STAGE CAST)** | Parlophone PMC 1033 |
| 02/04/1960 | 2 | 27 | | **FLOWER DRUM SONG (ORIGINAL BROADWAY STAGE CAST)** ▲3 | Philips ABL 3302 |
| 07/05/1960 | 5 | 9 | | **FOLLOW THAT GIRL (ORIGINAL LONDON STAGE CAST)** | HMV CLP 1366 |

○ Silver disc  ● Gold disc  ✪ Platinum disc (additional platinum units are indicated by a figure following the symbol)  ❶9 Number of weeks album topped the UK chart

| DATE | POS | WKS | BPI | ALBUM TITLE | LABEL & NUMBER |
|---|---|---|---|---|---|
| 21/05/1960 | 6 | 13 | | **MOST HAPPY FELLA (ORIGINAL BROADWAY STAGE CAST)** | Philips BBL 7374 |
| 21/05/1960 | 18 | 1 | | MAKE ME AN OFFER (ORIGINAL LONDON STAGE CAST) | HMV CLP 1333 |
| 28/05/1960 | 10 | 3 | | **FLOWER DRUM SONG (ORIGINAL LONDON STAGE CAST)** | HMV CLP 1359 |
| 25/06/1960 | 12 | 1 | | SHOWBOAT (ORIGINAL STUDIO CAST RECORDING) | HMV CLP 1310 |
| 09/07/1960 | 19 | 1 | | MOST HAPPY FELLA (ORIGINAL LONDON STAGE CAST) | HMV CLP 1365 |
| 30/07/1960 | 14 | 1 | | WEST SIDE STORY (ORIGINAL BROADWAY STAGE CAST) | Philips SBBL 504 |
| 10/09/1960 | 4 | 91 | | **OLIVER! (ORIGINAL LONDON STAGE CAST)** | Decca LK 4359 |
| 11/03/1961 | 12 | 8 | | KING KONG (ORIGINAL SOUTH AFRICAN STAGE CAST) | Decca LK 4392 |
| 06/05/1961 | 8 | 13 | | **MUSIC MAN (ORIGINAL LONDON STAGE CAST)** | HMV CLP 1444 |
| 24/06/1961 | 4 | 19 | | **THE SOUND OF MUSIC (ORIGINAL BROADWAY STAGE CAST)** | Philips ABL 3370 |
| 22/07/1961 | 13 | 17 | | BEYOND THE FRINGE (ORIGINAL LONDON STAGE CAST) | Parlophone PMC 1145 |
| 22/07/1961 | 17 | 3 | | BYE BYE BIRDIE (ORIGINAL LONDON STAGE CAST) | Philips ABL 3385 |
| 29/07/1961 | 4 | 68 | | **THE SOUND OF MUSIC (ORIGINAL LONDON STAGE CAST)** | HMV CLP 1453 |
| 09/09/1961 | 8 | 14 | | **STOP THE WORLD – I WANT TO GET OFF (ORIGINAL LONDON STAGE CAST)** | Decca LK 4408 |
| 14/07/1962 | 7 | 21 | | **BLITZ (ORIGINAL LONDON STAGE CAST)** | HMV CLP 1569 |
| 18/05/1963 | 20 | 2 | | HALF A SIXPENCE (ORIGINAL LONDON STAGE CAST) | Decca LK 4521 |
| 03/08/1963 | 12 | 10 | | PICKWICK (ORIGINAL LONDON STAGE CAST) | Philips AL 3431 |
| 04/01/1964 | 19 | 1 | | MY FAIR LADY (ORIGINAL BROADWAY STAGE CAST) | CBS BPG 68001 |
| 22/02/1964 | 12 | 11 | | AT THE DROP OF ANOTHER HAT (ORIGINAL LONDON STAGE CAST) | Parlophone PMC 1216 |
| 03/10/1964 | 10 | 12 | | **CAMELOT (ORIGINAL BROADWAY STAGE CAST)** ▲6 | CBS APG 60001 |
| 16/01/1965 | 19 | 1 | | CAMELOT (ORIGINAL LONDON STAGE CAST ) | HMV CLP 1756 |
| 11/03/1967 | 4 | 50 | | **FIDDLER ON THE ROOF (ORIGINAL LONDON STAGE CAST)** | CBS SBPG 70030 |
| 28/12/1968 | 3 | 94 | | **HAIR (ORIGINAL LONDON STAGE CAST)** | Polydor 583043 |
| 30/08/1969 | 23 | 4 | | THE WORLD OF OLIVER (ORIGINAL LONDON STAGE CAST) Re-issue of Decca LK 4359 | Decca SPA 30 |
| 06/09/1969 | 29 | 3 | | HAIR (ORIGINAL BROADWAY STAGE CAST) ▲13 1968 Grammy Award for Best Original Cast Show Album. | RCA SF 7959 |
| 08/01/1972 | 6 | 20 | ● | **JESUS CHRIST SUPERSTAR (ORIGINAL STUDIO CAST RECORDING)** | MCA MKPS 2011/2 |
| 19/02/1972 | 25 | 17 | | GODSPELL (ORIGINAL LONDON STAGE CAST). | Arista BELLS 203 |
| 22/01/1977 | 4 | 35 | ✪ | **EVITA (ORIGINAL STUDIO CAST RECORDING)** | MCA MCX 503 |
| 17/06/1978 | 51 | 3 | | WHITE MANSIONS (ORIGINAL STUDIO CAST RECORDING) | A&M AMLX 64691 |
| 18/11/1978 | 24 | 18 | ✪ | EVITA (ORIGINAL LONDON STAGE CAST) | MCA MCF 3257 |
| 01/08/1981 | 6 | 26 | ○ | **CATS (ORIGINAL LONDON STAGE CAST)** | Polydor CATX 001 |
| 06/11/1982 | 38 | 7 | ○ | MACK AND MABEL (ORIGINAL BROADWAY STAGE CAST) | MCA MCL 1728 |
| 04/08/1984 | 21 | 9 | ○ | STARLIGHT EXPRESS (ORIGINAL LONDON STAGE CAST) | Starlight LNER 1 |
| 10/11/1984 | 10 | 16 | ● | **CHESS (ORIGINAL STUDIO CAST RECORDING)** | RCA PL 70500 |
| 18/05/1985 | 11 | 32 | ✪2 | WEST SIDE STORY (ORIGINAL STUDIO CAST RECORDING) | Deutsche Grammophon 41525 |
| 02/11/1985 | 87 | 3 | | CHESS PIECES (ORIGINAL STUDIO CAST RECORDING) | Telstar STAR 2274 |
| 15/02/1986 | 72 | 4 | | LES MISERABLES (ORIGINAL LONDON STAGE CAST) | First Night ENCORE 1 |
| 10/05/1986 | 72 | 6 | | HIGHLIGHTS FROM WEST SIDE STORY (ORIGINAL STUDIO CAST RECORDING) | Deutsche Grammophon 45963 |
| 17/05/1986 | 21 | 6 | | DAVE CLARK'S TIME: THE ALBUM (ORIGINAL STUDIO CAST RECORDING) | EMI AMPH 1 |
| 11/10/1986 | 5 | 24 | ✪ | **SOUTH PACIFIC (ORIGINAL STUDIO CAST RECORDING)** ▲31 | CBS SM 42205 |
| 21/02/1987 | ❶3 | 141 | ✪3 | **THE PHANTOM OF THE OPERA (ORIGINAL LONDON STAGE CAST)** | Really Useful PODV 3 |
| 13/06/1987 | 26 | 5 | | MATADOR (ORIGINAL STUDIO CAST RECORDING) | Epic VIVA 1 |
| 21/11/1987 | 41 | 12 | ● | MY FAIR LADY (ORIGINAL STUDIO CAST RECORDING) | Decca MFL 1 |
| 16/09/1989 | ❶1 | 29 | ✪ | **ASPECTS OF LOVE (ORIGINAL LONDON STAGE CAST)** | Really Useful/Polydor 8411261 |
| 24/02/1990 | 4 | 11 | ● | **MISS SAIGON (ORIGINAL LONDON STAGE CAST)** | Geffen WX 329 |
| 29/06/1991 | 59 | 1 | | FIVE GUYS NAMED MOE (ORIGINAL LONDON STAGE CAST) | First Night CAST 23 |
| 10/10/1992 | 57 | 2 | | THE KING AND I (ORIGINAL STUDIO CAST RECORDING) | Philips 4380072 |
| 10/04/1993 | 33 | 3 | | LEONARD BERNSTEIN'S WEST SIDE STORY (ORIGINAL STUDIO CAST RECORDING) | IMG IMGCD 1801 |
| 10/04/1993 | 42 | 2 | | THE NEW STARLIGHT EXPRESS (ORIGINAL LONDON STAGE CAST) | Really Useful/Polydor 5190412 |
| 11/09/1993 | 11 | 4 | | SUNSET BOULEVARD (ORIGINAL LONDON STAGE CAST) | Really Useful/Polydor 5197672 |
| 02/10/1993 | 20 | 3 | | GREASE (ORIGINAL LONDON STAGE CAST) | Epic 4746322 |
| 01/04/1995 | 36 | 3 | | OLIVER! (1994 LONDON CAST) (ORIGINAL LONDON STAGE CAST) | First Night CASTCD 47 |
| 11/05/1996 | 32 | 7 | | LES MISERABLES – 10TH ANNIVERSARY CONCERT (ORIGINAL LONDON STAGE CAST) | First Night ENCORECD 8 |
| 16/11/1996 | 58 | 1 | | MARTIN GUERRE (ORIGINAL LONDON STAGE CAST) | First Night CASTCD 70 |
| 14/12/1996 | 41 | 4 | | HEATHCLIFF LIVE (THE SHOW) (ORIGINAL LONDON STAGE CAST). | EMI CDEMDEUK 1099 |
| 27/06/1998 | 61 | 1 | | CHICAGO – THE MUSICAL (ORIGINAL LONDON STAGE CAST) | RCA Victor 09026631552 |
| 22/08/1998 | 17 | 6 | | SATURDAY NIGHT FEVER (ORIGINAL LONDON STAGE CAST) | Polydor 5579322 |
| 13/11/1999 | 56 | 2 | | MAMMA MIA! (ORIGINAL LONDON STAGE CAST). | Polydor 5431152 |
| 08/04/2000 | 60 | 1 | | THE ARISTOCATS – READ ALONG (ORIGINAL CAST RECORDING) | Walt Disney WD 713914 |

▲9 Number of weeks album topped the US chart  ◆12 RIAA Diamond Awards  ◇3 IFPI Platinum Europe Awards

## TV AND RADIO COMPILATIONS, SOUNDTRACKS AND SPIN-OFFS

| DATE | POS | WKS | BPI | ALBUM TITLE | LABEL & NUMBER |
|------|-----|-----|-----|-------------|----------------|
| 13/12/1958 | 9 | 14 | | **JACK GOOD'S 'OH BOY'** | Parlophone PMC 1072 |
| 04/03/1961 | 10 | 12 | | **HUCKLEBERRY HOUND** | Pye Golden Guinea GGL 004 |
| 02/03/1963 | 11 | 9 | | THAT WAS THE WEEK THAT WAS | Parlophone PMC 1197 |
| 28/03/1964 | 17 | 2 | | STARS FROM STARS AND GARTERS | Pye Golden Guinea GGL 0252 |
| 04/11/1972 | 16 | 7 | | THE BBC 1922–1972 | BBC 50 |
| 06/12/1975 | 21 | 6 | | SUPERSONIC | Stallion SSM 001 |
| 10/04/1976 | ●³ | 15 | ● | **ROCK FOLLIES** | Island ILPS 9362 |
| 11/03/1978 | 8 | 16 | | **FONZIE'S FAVOURITES** | Warwick WW 5037 |
| 08/04/1978 | 10 | 17 | ● | **PENNIES FROM HEAVEN** | World Records SH 266 |
| 01/07/1978 | 31 | 4 | | MORE PENNIES FROM HEAVEN | World Records SH 267 |
| 09/12/1978 | 65 | 3 | | STARS ON SUNDAY BY REQUEST | Corzon Sounds CSL 0081 |
| 14/02/1981 | 47 | 4 | ○ | THE HITCHHIKERS GUIDE TO THE GALAXY VOLUME 2 | Original ORA 54 |
| 01/08/1981 | 43 | 10 | | THE MUSIC OF THE COSMOS | RCA RCALP 5032 |
| 21/11/1981 | 50 | 12 | ○ | BRIDESHEAD REVISITED (CONDUCTED BY GEOFFREY BURGON) | Chrysalis CDL 1367 |
| 23/10/1982 | 85 | 3 | | ON THE AIR – 60 YEARS OF BBC THEME MUSIC | BBC REF 454 |
| 26/11/1983 | 54 | 6 | | REILLY ACE OF THEMES | Red Bus BUSLP 1004 |
| 04/02/1984 | 21 | 6 | | ORIGINAL MUSIC FROM AUF WIEDERSEHEN PET | Towerbell AUF 1 |
| 18/02/1984 | 30 | 6 | | THE TUBE | K-Tel NE 1261 |
| 08/09/1984 | 46 | 4 | | SONG AND DANCE | RCA BL 70480 |
| 18/05/1985 | 61 | 1 | | VICTORY IN EUROPE – BROADCASTS AND REPORTS FROM BBC CORRESPONDENTS | BBC REC 562 |
| 28/09/1985 | 26 | 13 | ○ | THE TV HITS ALBUM | Towerbell TVLP 3 |
| 26/10/1985 | 11 | 9 | ● | MUSIC FROM THE TELEVISION SERIES 'MIAMI VICE' | BBC REMV 584 |
| 16/11/1985 | 33 | 10 | ● | THE EASTENDERS SING-ALONG ALBUM | BBC REB 586 |
| 23/11/1985 | 34 | 6 | ● | TELLYHITS – 16 TOP TV THEMES | Stylus/BBC BBSR 508 |
| 01/02/1986 | 53 | 3 | | MISTRAL'S DAUGHTER | Carrere CAL 221 |
| 15/02/1986 | 6 | 11 | ● | **JONATHAN KING'S ENTERTAINMENT FROM THE U.S.A.** | Stylus SMR 6812 |
| 12/04/1986 | 19 | 7 | ○ | THE TV HITS ALBUM TWO – 16 ORIGINAL HIT-TV THEMES | Towerbell TVLP 10 |
| 05/07/1986 | 68 | 2 | | TELLYHITS 2 – 16 TOP TV THEMES | Stylus/BBC BBSR 616 |
| 18/10/1986 | 44 | 4 | | THE VERY BEST OF ENTERTAINMENT FROM THE U.S.A. VOLUME 2 | PrioriTyV UPTVR 1 |
| 06/12/1986 | 10 | 24 | ● | **MUSIC FROM THE BBC-TV SERIES 'THE SINGING DETECTIVE'** | BBC REN 608 |
| 27/06/1987 | 71 | 2 | | THE ROCK 'N' ROLL YEARS 1964–1967 | BBC REN 633 |
| 27/06/1987 | 77 | 1 | | THE ROCK 'N' ROLL YEARS 1968–1971 | BBC REN 634 |
| 27/06/1987 | 80 | 2 | | THE ROCK 'N' ROLL YEARS 1956–1959 | BBC REN 631 |
| 27/06/1987 | 84 | 1 | | THE ROCK 'N' ROLL YEARS 1960–1963 | BBC REN 632 |
| 03/10/1987 | 50 | 6 | | MOONLIGHTING 'THE TV SOUNDTRACK ALBUM' | MCA MCF 3386 |
| 17/10/1987 | 71 | 4 | | MIAMI VICE 2 | MCA MCG 6019 |
| 28/11/1987 | 39 | 6 | ○ | THE CHART SHOW – DANCE HITS 1987 | Chrysalis ADD 1 |
| 26/03/1988 | 16 | 8 | ○ | THE CHART SHOW – ROCK THE NATION | Dover ADD 2 |
| 01/10/1988 | 5 | 9 | ● | **MOONLIGHTING 2** | WEA WX 202 |
| 01/10/1988 | 95 | 1 | | MIAMI VICE III | MCA MCG 6033 |
| 20/05/1989 | 8 | 4 | ○ | **THE CHART SHOW – ROCK THE NATION 2** | Dover ADD 4 |
| 03/06/1989 | 4 | 7 | ○ | **THE CHART SHOW – DANCE MASTERS** | Dover ADD 7 |
| 23/09/1989 | 17 | 3 | | TV TUNES | K-Tel NE 1446 |
| 17/02/1990 | 8 | 13 | | **PENNIES FROM HEAVEN** | BBC REF 768 |
| 21/09/1991 | 13 | 3 | | THE OLD GREY WHISTLE TEST – THE BEST OF THE TEST | Windsong International OGWTLP 1 |
| 25/07/1992 | 8 | 10 | | **32 ONES ON ONE – RADIO 1'S 25TH ANNIVERSARY** | Connoisseur Collection ONECD 32 |
| 28/11/1992 | 11 | 10 | ● | GLADIATORS | Polygram TV 5158772 |
| 30/01/1993 | 7 | 10 | | **THE BEST OF THE CLASSICAL BITS** | Philips 4381662 |
| 13/02/1993 | 3 | 9 | | **HEAD OVER HEELS** | Telstar TCD 2510 |
| 13/03/1993 | 2 | 13 | ● | **LIPSTICK ON YOUR COLLAR – 28 ORIGINAL HITS OF THE 50S** | Polygram TV 5160862 |
| 17/04/1993 | 4 | 11 | ● | **THE CHART SHOW – THE ULTIMATE ROCK ALBUM** | The Hit Label AHLCD 9 |
| 03/07/1993 | 18 | 2 | | ROAD SHOW HITS (21 YEARS OF RADIO 1 FM ROAD SHOW) | Connoisseur Collection RSHCD 20 |
| 07/08/1993 | 8 | 5 | | **THE BIG BREAKFAST ALBUM** | Arcade ARC 3100082 |
| 02/10/1993 | 10 | 3 | ○ | **THE CHART SHOW – ULTIMATE ROCK 2** | The Hit Label AHLCD 13 |
| 23/10/1993 | 17 | 2 | | TALES FROM THE CITY | Polygram TV 5165152 |
| 20/11/1993 | 20 | 1 | | RETURN OF THE GLADIATORS | Polygram TV 5165172 |
| 04/06/1994 | 3 | 13 | ● | **TOP GEAR** | Epic MOODCD 33 |

○ Silver disc  ● Gold disc  ✪ Platinum disc (additional platinum units are indicated by a figure following the symbol)  ●⁹ Number of weeks album topped the UK chart

| DATE | POS | WKS | BPI | ALBUM TITLE | LABEL & NUMBER |
|------|-----|-----|-----|-------------|----------------|
| 16/07/1994 | 13 | 3 | | CHART SHOW – ULTIMATE BLUES ALBUM | The Hit Label AHLCD 19 |
| 22/10/1994 | 13 | 2 | | DR. HILARY JONES CLASSIC RELAXATION | Polygram TV 4458112 |
| 20/05/1995 | 18 | 2 | | THE CHART SHOW PRESENTS THE CHART MACHINE | Polygram TV 5250392 |
| 24/06/1995 | 17 | 1 | | TOP GEAR CLASSICS – TURBO CLASSICS | Deutsche Grammophon 4479412 |
| 05/08/1995 | 6 | 3 | ○ | **THE CHART SHOW DANCE ALBUM** | Polygram TV 5257682 |
| 18/11/1995 | 20 | 1 | | THE CORONATION STREET ALBUM | EMI Premier CDCOROTV 1 |
| 09/03/1996 | 11 | 4 | | TOP GEAR 3 | Columbia SONYTV 12CD |
| 17/08/1996 | 66 | 2 | | INDEPENDENCE DAY UK (RADIO SOUNDTRACK) | Speaking Volumes 5329634 |
| 09/11/1996 | 12 | 3 | ○ | TOP GEAR – ON THE ROAD AGAIN | EMI TV CDEMTVD 132 |
| 02/08/1997 | 12 | 1 | | AFTER THE BREAK | Columbia SONYTV 30CD |
| 13/09/1997 | ❶[4] | 10 | ✪ | **IBIZA UNCOVERED** | Virgin/EMI VTDCD 168 |
| 08/11/1997 | 10 | 2 | ● | **READY STEADY GO! – NUMBER ONE SIXTIES ALBUM** | Polygram TV 5539342 |
| 21/03/1998 | 5 | 5 | ● | **READY STEADY GO! – SIXTIES MOTOWN SOUND** | Polygram TV 5308652 |
| 22/08/1998 | 2 | 9 | | **IBIZA UNCOVERED 2** | Virgin/EMI VTDCD 202 |
| 26/09/1998 | 6 | 6 | ○ | **TOP GEAR ANTHEMS** | Virgin/EMI VTDCD 192 |
| 03/10/1998 | 13 | 2 | | STARSKY AND HUTCH PRESENTS | Virgin/EMI VTDCDX 205 |
| 05/12/1998 | 2 | 14 | ✪ | **CHEF AID – THE SOUTH PARK ALBUM** | Columbia 4917002 |
| 03/04/1999 | 12 | 3 | | LIVE & KICKING – VIEWERS CHOICE PART 1 | Virgin/EMI VTCD 244 |
| 17/04/1999 | 2 | 9 | | **QUEER AS FOLK – THE WHOLE THING SORTED** | Almighty ALMYCD 28 |
| 12/06/1999 | 3 | 11 | ● | **SONGS FROM DAWSON'S CREEK** | Columbia 4943692 |
| 28/08/1999 | 10 | 3 | | MTV IBIZA 99 | Columbia SONYTV 72CD |
| 02/10/1999 | 2 | 7 | ● | **IBIZA UNCOVERED – THE RETURN** | Virgin/EMI VTDCD 255 |
| 23/10/1999 | 12 | 1 | | SEX, CHIPS & ROCK 'N' ROLL | Virgin/EMI VTDCD 264 |
| 20/11/1999 | 7 | 2 | ● | **BUFFY THE VAMPIRE SLAYER – THE ALBUM** | Columbia 4966332 |
| 27/11/1999 | 2 | 16 | ✪[2] | **MUSIC OF THE MILLENNIUM** | Universal/Virgin/EMI 5453002 |
| 26/02/2000 | 5 | 5 | | **QUEER AS FOLK 2** | Channel 4 Music C4M 00012 |
| 11/03/2000 | 17 | 1 | | THE GRIMLEYS Original TV soundtrack | Global TV RADCD 157 |
| 26/08/2000 | 17 | 3 | | BIG BROTHER Original TV soundtrack | Channel 4 Music C4M 00062 |
| 28/10/2000 | 5 | 3 | | **SONGS FROM DAWSON'S CREEK – VOL 2** | Columbia 5009242 |
| 30/12/2000 | 18 | 1 | | MORE COLD FEET Original TV soundtrack | BMG TV Projects 74321789612 |
| 26/05/2001 | 15 | 2 | | TRIGGER HAPPY TV – SERIES 2 | Channel 4 Music C4M 00122 |
| 08/12/2001 | 13 | 8 | ● | COLD FEET Original TV soundtrack | Universal TV 5859132 |
| 15/03/2003 | ❶[3] | 10 | ✪ | **THE VERY BEST OF COLD FEET** | Universal TV 0688202 |
| 01/11/2003 | 12 | 2 | | BUFFY THE VAMPIRE SLAYER | Virgin/EMI VTCD 587 |
| 13/03/2004 | 6 | 6 | ● | **SEX AND THE CITY** | Sony Music TV STVCD 172 |
| 22/05/2004 | 14 | 2 | | THE OC | Warner Brothers 9362487672 |

## ANONYMOUS COVER VERSIONS

| DATE | POS | WKS | BPI | ALBUM TITLE | LABEL & NUMBER |
|------|-----|-----|-----|-------------|----------------|
| 29/02/1964 | 19 | 2 | | BEATLEMANIA | Top Six TSL 1 |
| 07/08/1971 | ❶[1] | 7 | | **HOT HITS 6** | MFP 5214 |
| 07/08/1971 | ❶[3] | 12 | | **TOP OF THE POPS VOLUME 18** | Hallmark SHM 745 |
| 07/08/1971 | 16 | 3 | | TOP OF THE POPS VOLUME 17 | Hallmark SHM 740 |
| 07/08/1971 | 46 | 2 | | MILLION SELLER HITS | MFP 5203 |
| 07/08/1971 | 48 | 1 | | HOT HITS 5 | MFP 5208 |
| 21/08/1971 | 36 | 3 | | SMASH HITS SUPREMES STYLE | MFP 5184 |
| 02/10/1971 | 3 | 9 | | **TOP OF THE POPS VOLUME 19** | Hallmark SHM 750 |
| 23/10/1971 | 3 | 9 | | **HOT HITS 7** | MFP 5236 |
| 06/11/1971 | 38 | 1 | | SMASH HITS COUNTRY STYLE | MFP 5228 |
| 13/11/1971 | ❶[1] | 8 | | **TOP OF THE POPS VOLUME 20** | Hallmark SHM 755 |
| 27/11/1971 | 35 | 2 | | NON STOP 20 VOLUME 4 | Plexium PXMS 1006 |
| 04/12/1971 | 21 | 3 | | SMASH HITS '71 | MFP 5229 |
| 11/12/1971 | 2 | 4 | | **HOT HITS 8** | MFP 5243 |
| 27/09/1975 | 21 | 7 | | 40 SINGALONG PUB SONGS | K-Tel NE 509 |
| 06/11/1976 | 21 | 6 | | FORTY MANIA | Ronco RDT 2018 |

## MISCELLANEOUS

| DATE | POS | WKS | BPI | ALBUM TITLE | LABEL & NUMBER |
|------|-----|-----|-----|-------------|----------------|
| 12/09/1970 | 34 | 4 | | EDINBURGH MILITARY TATTOO 1970 | Waverley SZLP 2121 |
| 18/09/1971 | 44 | 1 | | EDINBURGH MILITARY TATTOO 1971 | Waverley SZLP 2128 |
| 11/12/1971 | 48 | 1 | | ELECTRONIC ORGANS TODAY | Ad-Rhythm ADBS 1 |
| 08/12/1973 | 7 | 6 | | **MUSIC FOR A ROYAL WEDDING** Music from the wedding of HRH Princess Anne and Captain Mark Phillips | BBC REW 163 |
| 01/08/1981 | 84 | 1 | | ROYAL ROMANCE | Windsor WIN001 |
| 08/08/1981 | ❶[2] | 11 | ● | **THE OFFICIAL BBC ALBUM OF THE ROYAL WEDDING** Music from the wedding of HRH Prince Charles and Lady Diana Spencer | BBC REP 413 |
| 09/08/1986 | 55 | 1 | | ROYAL WEDDING Music from the wedding of HRH Prince Andrew and Sarah Ferguson | BBC REP 596 |
| 28/12/1991 | 20 | 1 | | TRIVIAL PURSUIT – THE MUSIC MASTER GAME | Telstar STAC 2550 |
| 27/09/1997 | 3 | 5 | | **DIANA PRINCESS OF WALES 1961–1997 – FUNERAL SERVICE** ◇ | BBC Worldwide Classics 4498002 |
| 13/12/1997 | ❶[4] | 10 | | **DIANA PRINCESS OF WALES – TRIBUTE** | Diana Memorial Fund WR 1001052 |
| 22/07/2000 | 20 | 1 | | HAPPY AND GLORIOUS Tribute album for HRH The Queen Mother's 100th birthday celebrations | Decca 4671002 |

▲[9] Number of weeks album topped the US chart  ◆[12] RIAA Diamond Awards  ◇[3] IFPI Platinum Europe Awards

# THE NUMBER ONE RECORDS LISTED CHRONOLOGICALLY 1956–2004

As can be seen from the listing, soundtracks in general and *South Pacific* in particular dominated the first few years of the chart, hitting the top of the charts on nine occasions and spending a total of 115 weeks at the summit. Its closest rival is *The Sound Of Music* which hit the top on no fewer than twelve occasions but 'only' managed to register 70 weeks at the summit.

With the advent of the rock 'n' roll age, no act has dominated the charts quite like The Beatles. Fifteen of their albums have topped the charts, with four of them spending twenty or more weeks at the top. With increased competition these days, it is unlikely any album (or act) will come this close again.

Here, however, are the albums that have achieved the honour of topping the British album charts, together with the week in which they moved to the top and how long they spent there.

## 1956

| 28 July | 2 | SONGS FOR SWINGING LOVERS | Frank Sinatra |
|---|---|---|---|
| 11 August | 2 | CAROUSEL | Original Soundtrack |
| 25 August | 1 | SONGS FOR SWINGING LOVERS | Frank Sinatra |
| 1 September | 4 | CAROUSEL | Original Soundtrack |
| 29 September | 2 | OKLAHOMA! | Original Soundtrack |
| 13 October | 2 | THE KING AND I | Original Soundtrack |
| 27 October | 1 | ROCK 'N' ROLL STAGE SHOWS | Bill Haley |
| 3 November | 1 | THE KING AND I | Original Soundtrack |
| 10 November | 1 | ELVIS PRESLEY ROCK 'N' ROLL | Elvis Presley |
| 17 November | 15 | THE KING AND I | Original Soundtrack |

## 1957

| 1 March | 1 | THIS IS FRANK SINATRA | Frank Sinatra |
|---|---|---|---|
| 8 March | 1 | THE KING AND I | Original Soundtrack |
| 15 March | 1 | THIS IS FRANK SINATRA | Frank Sinatra |
| 22 March | 1 | THE KING AND I | Original Soundtrack |
| 29 March | 1 | THIS IS FRANK SINATRA | Frank Sinatra |
| 5 April | 3 | THE KING AND I | Original Soundtrack |
| 26 April | 1 | THIS IS FRANK SINATRA | Frank Sinatra |
| 3 May | 5 | THE KING AND I | Original Soundtrack |
| 7 June | 1 | THE KING AND I/LOVE IS THE THING | Original Soundtrack/ Nat King Cole |
| 14 June | 1 | OKLAHOMA! | Original Soundtrack |
| 21 June | 4 | THE KING AND I | Original Soundtrack |
| 19 July | 3 | THE TOMMY STEELE STORY (OST) | Tommy Steele |
| 10 August | 3 | THE KING AND I | Original Soundtrack |
| 6 September | 2 | LOVING YOU (OST) | Original Soundtrack |
| 20 September | 7 | A SWINGIN' AFFAIR | Frank Sinatra |
| 8 November | 1 | LOVING YOU | Elvis Presley |
| 15 November | 11 | THE KING AND I | Original Soundtrack |

## 1958

| 1 February | 7 | PAL JOEY | Original Soundtrack |
|---|---|---|---|
| 21 March | 1 | THE KING AND I | Original Soundtrack |
| 28 March | 3 | PAL JOEY | Original Soundtrack |
| 18 April | 1 | PAL JOEY/THE DUKE WORE JEANS (OST) | Original Soundtrack/ Tommy Steele |
| 25 April | 2 | THE DUKE WORE JEANS (OST) | Tommy Steele |
| 9 May | 19 | MY FAIR LADY | Stage Cast Recording |
| 19 September | 7 | KING CREOLE (OST) | Elvis Presley |
| 8 November | 70 | SOUTH PACIFIC | Original Soundtrack |

## 1960

| 12 March | 1 | THE EXPLOSIVE FREDDY CANNON | Freddy Cannon |
|---|---|---|---|
| 19 March | 19 | SOUTH PACIFIC | Original Soundtrack |
| 30 July | 1 | ELVIS IS BACK! | Elvis Presley |
| 6 August | 5 | SOUTH PACIFIC | Original Soundtrack |
| 10 September | 5 | DOWN DURY LANE TO MEMORY LANE | 101 Strings |
| 15 October | 13 | SOUTH PACIFIC | Original Soundtrack |

## 1961

| 14 January | 7 | G.I. BLUES (OST) | Elvis Presley |
|---|---|---|---|
| 4 March | 1 | SOUTH PACIFIC | Original Soundtrack |
| 11 March | 3 | G.I. BLUES (OST) | Elvis Presley |
| 1 April | 1 | SOUTH PACIFIC | Original Soundtrack |
| 8 April | 12 | G.I. BLUES (OST) | Elvis Presley |
| 1 July | 4 | SOUTH PACIFIC | Original Soundtrack |
| 29 July | 1 | THE BLACK AND WHITE MINSTREL SHOW | George Mitchell Minstrels |
| 26 August | 1 | SOUTH PACIFIC | Original Soundtrack |
| 2 September | 1 | THE BLACK AND WHITE MINSTREL SHOW | George Mitchell Minstrels |
| 9 September | 1 | SOUTH PACIFIC | Original Soundtrack |
| 16 September | 1 | THE BLACK AND WHITE MINSTREL SHOW | George Mitchell Minstrels |
| 23 September | 4 | THE SHADOWS | Shadows |

| 21 October | 1 | THE BLACK AND WHITE MINSTREL SHOW | George Mitchell Minstrels |
|---|---|---|---|
| 28 October | 1 | THE SHADOWS | Shadows |
| 4 November | 1 | I'M 21 TODAY | Cliff Richard and The Shadows |
| 11 November | 8 | ANOTHER BLACK AND WHITE MINSTREL SHOW | George Mitchell Minstrels |

## 1962

| 6 January | 1 | BLUE HAWAII (OST) | Elvis Presley |
|---|---|---|---|
| 13 January | 6 | THE YOUNG ONES (OST) | Cliff Richard and The Shadows |
| 24 February | 17 | BLUE HAWAII (OST) | Elvis Presley |
| 23 June | 5 | WEST SIDE STORY | Original Soundtrack |
| 28 July | 5 | POT LUCK | Elvis Presley |
| 1 September | 1 | WEST SIDE STORY | Original Soundtrack |
| 8 September | 1 | POT LUCK | Elvis Presley |
| 15 September | 1 | WEST SIDE STORY | Original Soundtrack |
| 22 September | 1 | BEST OF BALL, BARBER AND BILK | Kenny Ball, Chris Barber & Acker Bilk |
| 29 September | 3 | WEST SIDE STORY | Original Soundtrack |
| 20 October | 1 | BEST OF BALL, BARBER AND BILK | Kenny Ball, Chris Barber & Acker Bilk |
| 27 October | 3 | OUT OF THE SHADOWS | Shadows |
| 17 November | 1 | WEST SIDE STORY | Original Soundtrack |
| 24 November | 1 | OUT OF THE SHADOWS | Shadows |
| 1 December | 2 | ON STAGE WITH THE GEORGE MITCHELL MINSTRELS | George Mitchell Minstrels |
| 15 December | 1 | WEST SIDE STORY | Original Soundtrack |
| 22 December | 1 | OUT OF THE SHADOWS | Shadows |
| 29 December | 2 | THE BLACK AND WHITE MINSTREL SHOW | George Mitchell Minstrels |

## 1963

| 12 January | 1 | WEST SIDE STORY | Original Soundtrack |
|---|---|---|---|
| 19 January | 2 | OUT OF THE SHADOWS | Shadows |
| 2 February | 14 | SUMMER HOLIDAY (OST) | Cliff Richard and The Shadows |
| 11 May | 30 | PLEASE PLEASE ME | Beatles |
| 7 December | 21 | WITH THE BEATLES | Beatles |

## 1964

| 2 May | 12 | THE ROLLING STONES | Rolling Stones |
|---|---|---|---|
| 25 July | 21 | A HARD DAY'S NIGHT | Beatles |
| 19 December | 7 | BEATLES FOR SALE | Beatles |

## 1965

| 6 February | 3 | ROLLING STONES NUMBER 2 | Rolling Stones |
|---|---|---|---|
| 27 February | 1 | BEATLES FOR SALE | Beatles |
| 6 March | 6 | ROLLING STONES NUMBER 2 | Rolling Stones |
| 17 April | 1 | THE FREEWHEELIN' BOB DYLAN | Bob Dylan |
| 24 April | 1 | ROLLING STONES NUMBER 2 | Rolling Stones |
| 1 May | 3 | BEATLES FOR SALE | Beatles |
| 22 May | 1 | THE FREEWHEELIN' BOB DYLAN | Bob Dylan |
| 29 May | 1 | BRINGING IT ALL BACK HOME | Bob Dylan |
| 5 June | 10 | THE SOUND OF MUSIC | Original Soundtrack |
| 14 August | 9 | HELP! | Beatles |
| 16 October | 10 | THE SOUND OF MUSIC | Original Soundtrack |
| 25 December | 9 | RUBBER SOUL | Beatles |

## 1966

| 19 February | 10 | THE SOUND OF MUSIC | Original Soundtrack |
|---|---|---|---|
| 30 April | 8 | AFTERMATH | Rolling Stones |
| 25 June | 7 | THE SOUND OF MUSIC | Original Soundtrack |
| 13 August | 7 | REVOLVER | Beatles |
| 1 October | 18 | THE SOUND OF MUSIC | Original Soundtrack |

## 1967

| 4 February | 7 | THE MONKEES | Monkees |
|---|---|---|---|

| DATE | WKS | TITLE | ARTIST |
|------|-----|-------|--------|
| 25 March | 7 | THE SOUND OF MUSIC | Original Soundtrack |
| 13 May | 1 | MORE OF THE MONKEES | Monkees |
| 20 May | 1 | THE SOUND OF MUSIC | Original Soundtrack |
| 27 May | 1 | MORE OF THE MONKEES | Monkees |
| 3 June | 1 | THE SOUND OF MUSIC | Original Soundtrack |
| 10 June | 23 | SGT PEPPER'S LONELY HEARTS CLUB BAND | Beatles |
| 18 November | 1 | THE SOUND OF MUSIC | Original Soundtrack |
| 25 November | 1 | SGT PEPPER'S LONELY HEARTS CLUB BAND | Beatles |
| 2 December | 3 | THE SOUND OF MUSIC | Original Soundtrack |
| 23 December | 2 | SGT PEPPER'S LONELY HEARTS CLUB BAND | Beatles |

## 1968

| DATE | WKS | TITLE | ARTIST |
|------|-----|-------|--------|
| 6 January | 3 | VAL DOONICAN ROCKS BUT GENTLY | Val Doonican |
| 27 January | 1 | THE SOUND OF MUSIC | Original Soundtrack |
| 3 February | 1 | SGT PEPPER'S LONELY HEARTS CLUB BAND | Beatles |
| 10 February | 1 | FOUR TOPS GREATEST HITS | Four Tops |
| 17 February | 3 | DIANA ROSS AND THE SUPREMES GREATEST HITS | Diana Ross and The Supremes |
| 9 March | 10 | JOHN WESLEY HARDING | Bob Dylan |
| 18 May | 1 | SCOTT 2 | Scott Walker |
| 25 May | 3 | JOHN WESLEY HARDING | Bob Dylan |
| 15 June | 1 | LOVE ANDY | Andy Williams |
| 22 June | 1 | DOCK OF THE BAY | Otis Redding |
| 29 June | 6 | OGDEN'S NUT GONE FLAKE | Small Faces |
| 10 August | 1 | DELILAH | Tom Jones |
| 17 August | 5 | BOOKENDS | Simon and Garfunkel |
| 21 September | 1 | DELILAH | Tom Jones |
| 28 September | 2 | BOOKENDS | Simon and Garfunkel |
| 12 October | 6 | THE HOLLIES' GREATEST | Hollies |
| 23 November | 1 | THE SOUND OF MUSIC | Original Soundtrack |
| 30 November | 1 | THE HOLLIES' GREATEST | Hollies |
| 7 December | 7 | THE BEATLES (WHITE ALBUM) | Beatles |

## 1969

| DATE | WKS | TITLE | ARTIST |
|------|-----|-------|--------|
| 25 January | 1 | THE BEST OF THE SEEKERS | Seekers |
| 1 February | 1 | THE BEATLES (WHITE ALBUM) | Beatles |
| 8 February | 1 | THE BEST OF THE SEEKERS | Seekers |
| 15 February | 4 | DIANA ROSS AND THE SUPREMES JOIN THE TEMPTATIONS | Diana Ross and The Supremes and The Temptations |
| 15 March | 2 | GOODBYE | Cream |
| 29 March | 2 | THE BEST OF THE SEEKERS | Seekers |
| 12 April | 1 | GOODBYE | Cream |
| 19 April | 1 | THE BEST OF THE SEEKERS | Seekers |
| 26 April | 1 | GOODBYE | Cream |
| 3 May | 1 | THE BEST OF THE SEEKERS | Seekers |
| 10 May | 2 | ON THE THRESHOLD OF A DREAM | Moody Blues |
| 24 May | 4 | NASHVILLE SKYLINE | Bob Dylan |
| 21 June | 3 | HIS ORCHESTRA, HIS CHORUS, HIS SINGERS, HIS SOUND | Ray Conniff |
| 12 July | 4 | ACCORDING TO MY HEART | Jim Reeves |
| 9 August | 3 | STAND UP | Jethro Tull |
| 30 August | 1 | FROM ELVIS IN MEMPHIS | Elvis Presley |
| 6 September | 2 | STAND UP | Jethro Tull |
| 20 September | 2 | BLIND FAITH | Blind Faith |
| 4 October | 11 | ABBEY ROAD | Beatles |
| 20 December | 1 | LET IT BLEED | Rolling Stones |
| 27 December | 6 | ABBEY ROAD | Beatles |

## 1970

| DATE | WKS | TITLE | ARTIST |
|------|-----|-------|--------|
| 7 February | 1 | LED ZEPPELIN 2 | Led Zeppelin |
| 14 February | 1 | MOTOWN CHARTBUSTERS VOLUME 3 | Various Artists |
| 21 February | 13 | BRIDGE OVER TROUBLED WATER | Simon and Garfunkel |

| DATE | WKS | TITLE | ARTIST |
|------|-----|-------|--------|
| 23 May | 3 | LET IT BE | Beatles |
| 13 June | 4 | BRIDGE OVER TROUBLED WATER | Simon and Garfunkel |
| 11 July | 1 | SELF PORTRAIT | Bob Dylan |
| 18 July | 5 | BRIDGE OVER TROUBLED WATER | Simon and Garfunkel |
| 22 August | 3 | A QUESTION OF BALANCE | Moody Blues |
| 12 September | 1 | COSMO'S FACTORY | Creedence Clearwater Revival |
| 19 September | 2 | GET YER YA-YA'S OUT!' – THE ROLLING STONES IN CONCERT | Rolling Stones |
| 3 October | 1 | BRIDGE OVER TROUBLED WATER | Simon and Garfunkel |
| 10 October | 1 | PARANOID | Black Sabbath |
| 17 October | 1 | BRIDGE OVER TROUBLED WATER | Simon and Garfunkel |
| 24 October | 1 | ATOM HEART MOTHER | Pink Floyd |
| 31 October | 1 | MOTOWN CHARTBUSTERS VOLUME 4 | Various Artists |
| 7 November | 3 | LED ZEPPELIN 3 | Led Zeppelin |
| 28 November | 1 | NEW MORNING | Bob Dylan |
| 5 December | 1 | GREATEST HITS | Andy Williams |
| 12 December | 1 | LED ZEPPELIN 3 | Led Zeppelin |
| 19 December | 4 | GREATEST HITS | Andy Williams |

## 1971

| DATE | WKS | TITLE | ARTIST |
|------|-----|-------|--------|
| 16 January | 11 | BRIDGE OVER TROUBLED WATER | Simon and Garfunkel |
| 3 April | 2 | HOME LOVING MAN | Andy Williams |
| 17 April | 3 | MOTOWN CHARTBUSTERS VOLUME 5 | Various Artists |
| 8 May | 4 | STICKY FINGERS | Rolling Stones |
| 5 June | 2 | RAM | Paul and Linda McCartney |
| 19 June | 1 | STICKY FINGERS | Rolling Stones |
| 26 June | 1 | TARKUS | Emerson, Lake & Palmer |
| 3 July | 5 | BRIDGE OVER TROUBLED WATER | Simon and Garfunkel |
| 7 August | 1 | HOT HITS 6 | Anonymous Cover Versions |
| 14 August | 1 | EVERY GOOD BOY DESERVES FAVOUR | Moody Blues |
| 21 August | 3 | TOP OF THE POPS VOLUME 18 | Anonymous Cover Versions |
| 11 September | 1 | BRIDGE OVER TROUBLED WATER | Simon and Garfunkel |
| 18 September | 1 | WHO'S NEXT | Who |
| 25 September | 1 | FIREBALL | Deep Purple |
| 2 October | 4 | EVERY PICTURE TELLS A STORY | Rod Stewart |
| 30 October | 2 | IMAGINE | John Lennon with the Plastic Ono Band (with the Flux Fiddlers) |
| 13 November | 2 | EVERY PICTURE TELLS A STORY | Rod Stewart |
| 27 November | 1 | TOP OF THE POPS VOLUME 20 | Anonymous Cover Versions |
| 4 December | 2 | FOUR SYMBOLS (LED ZEPPELIN 4) | Led Zeppelin |
| 18 December | 6 | ELECTRIC WARRIOR | T. Rex |

## 1972

| DATE | WKS | TITLE | ARTIST |
|------|-----|-------|--------|
| 29 January | 1 | CONCERT FOR BANGLADESH | Various Artists |
| 5 February | 2 | ELECTRIC WARRIOR | T. Rex |
| 19 February | 3 | NEIL REID | Neil Reid |
| 11 March | 1 | HARVEST | Neil Young |
| 18 March | 1 | PAUL SIMON | Paul Simon |
| 25 March | 4 | FOG ON THE TYNE | Lindisfarne |
| 22 April | 2 | MACHINE HEAD | Deep Purple |
| 6 May | 1 | PHROPHETS, SEERS AND SAGES THE ANGELS OF THE AGES/MY PEOPLE WERE FAIR AND HAD SKY IN THEIR HAIR BUT NOW THEY'RE CONTENT TO WEAR STARS ON THEIR BROWS | Tyrannosaurus Rex |
| 13 May | 1 | MACHINE HEAD | Deep Purple |
| 20 May | 3 | BOLAN BOOGIE | T. Rex |
| 10 June | 1 | EXILE ON MAIN STREET | Rolling Stones |
| 17 June | 8 | 20 DYNAMIC HITS | Various Artists |
| 12 August | 5 | 20 FANTASTIC HITS | Various Artists |
| 16 September | 2 | NEVER A DULL MOMENT | Rod Stewart |
| 30 September | 1 | 20 FANTASTIC HITS | Various Artists |
| 7 October | 8 | 20 ALL TIME HITS OF THE FIFTIES | Various Artists |
| 2 December | 3 | 25 ROCKIN' AND ROLLIN' GREATS | Various Artists |
| 23 December | 3 | 20 ALL TIME HITS OF THE FIFTIES | Various Artists |

## 1973

| DATE | WKS | TITLE | ARTIST |
|------|-----|-------|--------|
| 13 January | 1 | SLAYED? | Slade |

| DATE | WKS | TITLE | ARTIST |
|---|---|---|---|
| 20 January | 1 | **BACK TO FRONT** | Gilbert O'sullivan |
| 27 January | 2 | **SLAYED?** | Slade |
| 10 February | 6 | **DON'T SHOOT ME I'M ONLY THE PIANO PLAYER** | Elton John |
| 24 March | 1 | **MILLION DOLLAR BABIES** | Alice Cooper |
| 31 March | 2 | **20 FLASHBACK GREAT HITS OF THE SIXTIES** | Various Artists |
| 14 April | 2 | **HOUSE OF THE HOLY** | Led Zeppelin |
| 28 April | 1 | **OOH-LA-LA** | Faces |
| 5 May | 5 | **ALADDIN SANE** | David Bowie |
| 9 June | 3 | **PURE GOLD** | Various Artists |
| 30 June | 7 | **THAT'LL BE THE DAY** | Various Artists |
| 18 August | 2 | **WE CAN MAKE IT** | Peters and Lee |
| 1 September | 3 | **SING IT AGAIN ROD** | Rod Stewart |
| 22 September | 2 | **GOAT'S HEAD SOUP** | Rolling Stones |
| 6 October | 3 | **SLADEST** | Slade |
| 27 October | 1 | **HELLO** | Status Quo |
| 3 November | 5 | **PIN-UPS** | David Bowie |
| 8 December | 1 | **STRANDED** | Roxy Music |
| 15 December | 1 | **DREAMS ARE NUTHIN' MORE THAN WISHES** | David Cassidy |
| 22 December | 2 | **GOODBYE YELLOW BRICK ROAD** | Elton John |

## 1974

| DATE | WKS | TITLE | ARTIST |
|---|---|---|---|
| 5 January | 2 | **TALES FROM TOPOGRAPHIC OCEANS** | Yes |
| 19 January | 1 | **SLADEST** | Slade |
| 26 January | 1 | **AND I LOVE YOU SO** | Perry Como |
| 2 February | 4 | **THE SINGLES 1969–1973** | Carpenters |
| 2 March | 1 | **OLD NEW BORROWED AND BLUE** | Slade |
| 9 March | 11 | **THE SINGLES 1969–1973** | Carpenters |
| 25 May | 1 | **JOURNEY TO THE CENTRE OF THE EARTH** | Rick Wakeman |
| 1 June | 1 | **THE SINGLES 1969–1973** | Carpenters |
| 8 June | 4 | **DIAMOND DOGS** | David Bowie |
| 6 July | 1 | **THE SINGLES 1969–1973** | Carpenters |
| 13 July | 2 | **CARIBOU** | Elton John |
| 27 July | 7 | **BAND ON THE RUN** | Paul McCartney and Wings |
| 14 September | 3 | **HERGEST RIDGE** | Mike Oldfield |
| 5 October | 1 | **TUBULAR BELLS** | Mike Oldfield |
| 12 October | 1 | **ROLLIN'** | Bay City Rollers |
| 19 October | 1 | **SMILER** | Rod Stewart |
| 26 October | 1 | **ROLLIN'** | Bay City Rollers |
| 2 November | 1 | **SMILER** | Rod Stewart |
| 9 November | 2 | **ROLLIN'** | Bay City Rollers |
| 23 November | 11 | **ELTON JOHN'S GREATEST HITS** | Elton John |

## 1975

| DATE | WKS | TITLE | ARTIST |
|---|---|---|---|
| 8 February | 3 | **ENGELBERT HUMPERDINCK – HIS GREATEST HITS** | Engelbert Humperdinck |
| 1 March | 2 | **ON THE LEVEL** | Status Quo |
| 15 March | 1 | **PHYSICAL GRAFFITI** | Led Zeppelin |
| 22 March | 4 | **20 GREATEST HITS** | Tom Jones |
| 19 April | 2 | **THE BEST OF THE STYLISTICS** | Stylistics |
| 3 May | 3 | **ONCE UPON A STAR** | Bay City Rollers |
| 24 May | 5 | **THE BEST OF THE STYLISTICS** | Stylistics |
| 28 June | 1 | **VENUS AND MARS** | Wings |
| 5 July | 2 | **HORIZON** | Carpenters |
| 19 July | 1 | **VENUS AND MARS** | Wings |
| 26 July | 3 | **HORIZON** | Carpenters |
| 16 August | 2 | **THE BEST OF THE STYLISTICS** | Stylistics |
| 30 August | 5 | **ATLANTIC CROSSING** | Rod Stewart |
| 4 October | 1 | **WISH YOU WERE HERE** | Pink Floyd |
| 11 October | 2 | **ATLANTIC CROSSING** | Rod Stewart |
| 25 October | 3 | **40 GOLDEN GREATS** | Jim Reeves |
| 15 November | 1 | **WE ALL HAD DOCTOR'S PAPERS** | Max Boyce |
| 22 November | 5 | **40 GREATEST HITS** | Perry Como |
| 27 December | 2 | **A NIGHT AT THE OPERA** | Queen |

## 1976

| DATE | WKS | TITLE | ARTIST |
|---|---|---|---|
| 10 January | 1 | **40 GREATEST HITS** | Perry Como |
| 17 January | 2 | **A NIGHT AT THE OPERA** | Queen |
| 31 January | 1 | **THE BEST OF ROY ORBISON** | Roy Orbison |
| 7 February | 6 | **THE VERY BEST OF SLIM WHITMAN** | Slim Whitman |
| 20 March | 3 | **BLUE FOR YOU** | Status Quo |
| 10 April | 2 | **ROCK FOLLIES** | TV Soundtrack |
| 24 April | 1 | **PRESENCE** | Led Zeppelin |
| 1 May | 1 | **ROCK FOLLIES** | TV Soundtrack |
| 8 May | 9 | **GREATEST HITS** | Abba |
| 10 July | 2 | **A NIGHT ON THE TOWN** | Rod Stewart |
| 24 July | 10 | **20 GOLDEN GREATS** | Beach Boys |
| 2 October | 1 | **BEST OF THE STYLISTICS VOLUME 2** | Stylistics |
| 9 October | 1 | **STUPIDITY** | Dr. Feelgood |
| 16 October | 2 | **GREATEST HITS** | Abba |
| 30 October | 2 | **SOUL MOTION** | Various Artists |
| 13 November | 1 | **THE SONG REMAINS THE SAME (OST)** | Led Zeppelin |
| 20 November | 1 | **22 GOLDEN GUITAR GREATS** | Bert Weedon |
| 27 November | 6 | **20 GOLDEN GREATS** | Glen Campbell |

## 1977

| DATE | WKS | TITLE | ARTIST |
|---|---|---|---|
| 8 January | 1 | **A DAY AT THE RACES** | Queen |
| 15 January | 1 | **ARRIVAL** | Abba |
| 22 January | 4 | **RED RIVER VALLEY** | Slim Whitman |
| 19 February | 6 | **SHADOWS 20 GOLDEN GREATS** | Shadows |
| 2 April | 2 | **PORTRAIT OF SINATRA** | Frank Sinatra |
| 16 April | 9 | **ARRIVAL** | Abba |
| 18 June | 1 | **THE BEATLES AT THE HOLLYWOOD BOWL** | Beatles |
| 25 June | 1 | **THE MUPPET SHOW** | Muppets |
| 2 July | 2 | **A STAR IS BORN (OST)** | Barbra Streisand |
| 16 July | 4 | **THE JOHNNY MATHIS COLLECTION** | Johnny Mathis |
| 13 August | 2 | **GOING FOR THE ONE** | Yes |
| 27 August | 2 | **20 ALL TIME GREATS** | Connie Francis |
| 10 September | 1 | **ELVIS'S 40 GREATEST HITS** | Elvis Presley |
| 17 September | 7 | **DIANA ROSS AND THE SUPREMES 20 GOLDEN GREATS** | Diana Ross and The Supremes |
| 5 November | 1 | **40 GOLDEN GREATS** | Cliff Richard |
| 12 November | 2 | **NEVER MIND THE BOLLOCKS, HERE'S THE SEX PISTOLS** | Sex Pistols |
| 26 November | 2 | **THE SOUND OF BREAD** | Bread |
| 10 December | 6 | **DISCO FEVER** | Various Artists |

## 1978

| DATE | WKS | TITLE | ARTIST |
|---|---|---|---|
| 21 January | 1 | **THE SOUND OF BREAD** | Bread |
| 28 January | 1 | **RUMOURS** | Fleetwood Mac |
| 4 February | 7 | **THE ALBUM** | Abba |
| 25 March | 3 | **20 GOLDEN GREATS** | Buddy Holly and The Crickets |
| 15 April | 3 | **20 GOLDEN GREATS** | Nat 'King' Cole |
| 6 May | 18 | **SATURDAY NIGHT FEVER** | Various Artists |
| 9 September | 4 | **NIGHT FLIGHT TO VENUS** | Boney M |
| 7 October | 13 | **GREASE** | Original Soundtrack |

## 1979

| DATE | WKS | TITLE | ARTIST |
|---|---|---|---|
| 6 January | 2 | **GREATEST HITS (1976–1978)** | Showaddywaddy |
| 27 January | 3 | **DON'T WALK – BOOGIE** | Various Artists |
| 10 February | 1 | **ACTION REPLAY** | Various Artists |
| 17 February | 4 | **PARALLEL LINES** | Blondie |
| 17 March | 2 | **SPIRITS HAVING FLOWN** | Bee Gees |
| 31 March | 4 | **BARBRA STREISAND GREATEST HITS VOLUME 2** | Barbra Streisand |
| 28 April | 3 | **THE VERY BEST OF LEO SAYER** | Leo Sayer |
| 19 May | 4 | **VOULEZ-VOUS** | Abba |
| 16 June | 5 | **DISCOVERY** | Electric Light Orchestra |
| 21 July | 1 | **REPLICAS** | Tubeway Army |
| 28 July | 6 | **THE BEST DISCO ALBUM IN THE WORLD** | Various Artists |
| 8 September | 2 | **IN THROUGH THE OUT DOOR** | Led Zeppelin |

| DATE | WKS | TITLE | ARTIST |
|---|---|---|---|
| 22 September | 1 | THE PLEASURE PRINCIPLE | Gary Numan |
| 29 September | 1 | OCEANS OF FANTASY | Boney M |
| 6 October | 1 | THE PLEASURE PRINCIPLE | Gary Numan |
| 13 October | 1 | EAT TO THE BEAT | Blondie |
| 13 October | 4 | REGGATTA DE BLANC | Police |
| 10 November | 1 | TUSK | Fleetwood Mac |
| 17 November | 3 | GREATEST HITS VOLUME 2 | Abba |
| 8 December | 5 | ROD STEWART – GREATEST HITS VOL. 1 | |
| | | | Rod Stewart |

## 1980

| DATE | WKS | TITLE | ARTIST |
|---|---|---|---|
| 12 January | 1 | GREATEST HITS VOLUME 2 | Abba |
| 19 January | 4 | PRETENDERS | Pretenders |
| 16 February | 2 | THE LAST DANCE | Various Artists |
| 1 March | 3 | STRING OF HITS | Shadows |
| 22 March | 2 | TEARS AND LAUGHTER | Johnny Mathis |
| 5 April | 2 | DUKE | Genesis |
| 19 April | 2 | ROSE ROYCE GREATEST HITS | Rose Royce |
| 3 May | 2 | SKY 2 | Sky |
| 17 May | 2 | THE MAGIC OF BONEY M | Boney M |
| 31 May | 2 | McCARTNEY II | Paul McCartney |
| 14 June | 2 | PETER GABRIEL | Peter Gabriel |
| 28 June | 1 | FLESH AND BLOOD | Roxy Music |
| 5 July | 2 | EMOTIONAL RESCUE | Rolling Stones |
| 19 July | 2 | THE GAME | Queen |
| 2 August | 1 | DEEPEST PURPLE | Deep Purple |
| 9 August | 2 | BACK IN BLACK | AC/DC |
| 23 August | 3 | FLESH AND BLOOD | Roxy Music |
| 13 September | 1 | TELEKON | Gary Numan |
| 20 September | 1 | NEVER FOR EVER | Kate Bush |
| 27 September | 2 | SCARY MONSTERS AND SUPER CREEPS | |
| | | | David Bowie |
| 11 October | 4 | ZENYATTA MONDATTA | Police |
| 8 November | 2 | GUILTY | Barbra Streisand |
| 22 November | 9 | SUPER TROUPER | Abba |

## 1981

| DATE | WKS | TITLE | ARTIST |
|---|---|---|---|
| 24 January | 2 | KINGS OF THE WILD FRONTIER | Adam & The Ants |
| 7 February | 2 | DOUBLE FANTASY | John Lennon and Yoko Ono |
| 21 February | 3 | FACE VALUE | Phil Collins |
| 14 March | 10 | KINGS OF THE WILD FRONTIER | Adam & The Ants |
| 23 May | 5 | STARS ON 45 | Star Sound |
| 27 June | 1 | NO SLEEP 'TIL HAMMERSMITH | Motorhead |
| 4 July | 1 | DISCO DAZE & DISCO NITES | Various Artists |
| 11 July | 5 | LOVE SONGS | Cliff Richard |
| 15 August | 2 | THE OFFICIAL BBC ALBUM OF THE ROYAL WEDDING | |
| | | | TV Soundtrack |
| 29 August | 2 | TIME | Electric Light Orchestra |
| 12 September | 2 | DEAD RINGER | Meat Loaf |
| 26 September | 2 | ABACAB | Genesis |
| 10 October | 3 | GHOST IN THE MACHINE | Police |
| 31 October | 1 | DARE | Human League |
| 7 November | 1 | SHAKY | Shakin' Stevens |
| 14 November | 4 | QUEEN'S GREATEST HITS | Queen |
| 12 December | 1 | CHART HITS '81 | Various Artists |
| 19 December | 3 | THE VISITORS | Abba |

## 1982

| DATE | WKS | TITLE | ARTIST |
|---|---|---|---|
| 9 January | 3 | DARE | Human League |
| 30 January | 7 | LOVE SONGS | Barbra Streisand |
| 20 March | 1 | THE GIFT | Jam |
| 27 March | 2 | LOVE SONGS | Barbra Streisand |
| 10 April | 2 | THE NUMBER OF THE BEAST | Iron Maiden |
| 24 April | 1 | 1982 | Status Quo |
| 1 May | 1 | BARRY LIVE IN BRITAIN | Barry Manilow |
| 8 May | 2 | TUG OF WAR | Paul McCartney |
| 22 May | 2 | COMPLETE MADNESS | Madness |
| 5 June | 1 | AVALON | Roxy Music |
| 12 June | 1 | COMPLETE MADNESS | Madness |

| DATE | WKS | TITLE | ARTIST |
|---|---|---|---|
| 19 June | 2 | AVALON | Roxy Music |
| 3 July | 3 | THE LEXICON OF LOVE | ABC |
| 24 July | 1 | THE LEXICON OF LOVE = FAME | ABC=Original Soundtrack |
| 31 July | 1 | FAME | Original Soundtrack |
| 7 August | 8 | THE KIDS FROM FAME | Kids From Fame |
| 2 October | 4 | LOVE OVER GOLD | Dire Straits |
| 30 October | 4 | THE KIDS FROM FAME | Kids From Fame |
| 27 November | 1 | THE SINGLES – THE FIRST TEN YEARS | Abba |
| 4 December | 6 | THE JOHN LENNON COLLECTION | John Lennon |

## 1983

| DATE | WKS | TITLE | ARTIST |
|---|---|---|---|
| 15 January | 2 | RAIDERS OF THE POP CHARTS | Various Artists |
| 29 January | 5 | BUSINESS AS USUAL | Men At Work |
| 5 March | 1 | THRILLER | Michael Jackson |
| 12 March | 1 | WAR | U2 |
| 19 March | 1 | THRILLER | Michael Jackson |
| 26 March | 1 | THE HURTING | Tears For Fears |
| 2 April | 2 | THE FINAL CUT | Pink Floyd |
| 16 April | 1 | FASTER THAN THE SPEED OF NIGHT | Bonnie Tyler |
| 23 April | 3 | LET'S DANCE | David Bowie |
| 14 May | 1 | TRUE | Spandau Ballet |
| 21 May | 1 | THRILLER | Michael Jackson |
| 25 June | 2 | SYNCHRONICITY | Police |
| 9 July | 2 | FANTASTIC! | Wham! |
| 23 July | 2 | YOU AND ME BOTH | Yazoo |
| 6 August | 2 | THE VERY BEST OF THE BEACH BOYS | Beach Boys |
| 20 August | 3 | 18 GREATEST HITS | Michael Jackson Plus the Jackson Five |
| 10 September | 1 | THE VERY BEST OF THE BEACH BOYS | Beach Boys |
| 17 September | 1 | NO PARLEZ | Paul Young |
| 24 September | 1 | LABOUR OF LOVE | UB40 |
| 1 October | 2 | NO PARLEZ | Paul Young |
| 15 October | 1 | GENESIS | Genesis |
| 22 October | 3 | COLOUR BY NUMBERS | Culture Club |
| 12 November | 1 | CAN'T SLOW DOWN | Lionel Richie |
| 19 November | 2 | COLOUR BY NUMBERS | Culture Club |
| 3 December | 1 | SEVEN AND THE RAGGED TIGER | Duran Duran |
| 10 December | 1 | NO PARLEZ | Paul Young |
| 17 December | 4 | NOW! THAT'S WHAT I CALL MUSIC | Various Artists |

## 1984

| DATE | WKS | TITLE | ARTIST |
|---|---|---|---|
| 14 January | 1 | NO PARLEZ | Paul Young |
| 21 January | 1 | NOW! THAT'S WHAT I CALL MUSIC | Various Artists |
| 28 January | 1 | THRILLER | Michael Jackson |
| 4 February | 2 | TOUCH | Eurythmics |
| 18 February | 1 | SPARKLE IN THE RAIN | Simple Minds |
| 25 February | 3 | INTO THE GAP | Thompson Twins |
| 17 March | 2 | HUMAN'S LIB | Howard Jones |
| 31 March | 2 | CAN'T SLOW DOWN | Lionel Richie |
| 14 April | 5 | NOW! THAT'S WHAT I CALL MUSIC 2 | Various Artists |
| 19 May | 12 | LEGEND – THE BEST OF BOB MARLEY AND THE WAILERS | |
| | | | Bob Marley and The Wailers |
| 11 August | 8 | NOW! THAT'S WHAT I CALL MUSIC 3 | Various Artists |
| 6 October | 1 | TONIGHT | David Bowie |
| 13 October | 2 | THE UNFORGETTABLE FIRE | U2 |
| 27 October | 1 | STEELTOWN | Big Country |
| 3 November | 1 | GIVE MY REGARDS TO BROAD STREET (OST) | |
| | | | Paul McCartney |
| 10 November | 1 | WELCOME TO THE PLEASUREDOME | Frankie Goes To Hollywood |
| 17 November | 2 | MAKE IT BIG | Wham! |
| 1 December | 7 | THE HITS ALBUM/THE HITS TAPE | Various Artists |

## 1985

| DATE | WKS | TITLE | ARTIST |
|---|---|---|---|
| 19 January | 1 | ALF | Alison Moyet |
| 26 January | 3 | AGENT PROVOCATEUR | Foreigner |
| 16 February | 1 | BORN IN THE U.S.A. | Bruce Springsteen |
| 23 February | 1 | MEAT IS MURDER | Smiths |
| 2 March | 5 | NO JACKET REQUIRED | Phil Collins |
| 6 April | 1 | THE SECRET OF ASSOCIATION | Paul Young |

| DATE | WKS | TITLE | ARTIST |
|---|---|---|---|
| 13 April | 6 | **THE HITS ALBUM 2/THE HITS TAPE 2** | Various Artists |
| 25 May | 2 | **BROTHERS IN ARMS** | Dire Straits |
| 8 June | 1 | **OUR FAVOURITE SHOP** | Style Council |
| 15 June | 2 | **BOYS AND GIRLS** | Bryan Ferry |
| 29 June | 1 | **MISPLACED CHILDHOOD** | Marillion |
| 6 July | 4 | **BORN IN THE U.S.A.** | Bruce Springsteen |
| 3 August | 2 | **BROTHERS IN ARMS** | Dire Straits |
| 17 August | 5 | **NOW! THAT'S WHAT I CALL MUSIC 5** | Various Artists |
| 21 September | 1 | **LIKE A VIRGIN** | Madonna |
| 28 September | 2 | **HOUNDS OF LOVE** | Kate Bush |
| 12 October | 1 | **LIKE A VIRGIN** | Madonna |
| 19 October | 1 | **HOUNDS OF LOVE** | Kate Bush |
| 26 October | 1 | **THE LOVE SONGS** | George Benson |
| 2 November | 1 | **ONCE UPON A TIME** | Simple Minds |
| 9 November | 1 | **THE LOVE SONGS** | George Benson |
| 16 November | 2 | **PROMISE** | Sade |
| 30 November | 1 | **THE GREATEST HITS OF 1985** | Various Artists |
| 7 December | 2 | **NOW! THAT'S WHAT I CALL MUSIC 6** | Various Artists |
| 21 December | 2 | **NOW! – THE CHRISTMAS ALBUM** | Various Artists |

## 1986

| DATE | WKS | TITLE | ARTIST |
|---|---|---|---|
| 4 January | 2 | **NOW! THAT'S WHAT I CALL MUSIC 6** | Various Artists |
| 18 January | 10 | **BROTHERS IN ARMS** | Dire Straits |
| 29 March | 4 | **HITS 4** | Various Artists |
| 26 April | 5 | **STREET LIFE – 20 GREAT HITS** | Bryan Ferry and Roxy Music |
| 31 May | 2 | **SO** | Peter Gabriel |
| 14 June | 1 | **A KIND OF MAGIC** | Queen |
| 21 June | 3 | **INVISIBLE TOUCH** | Genesis |
| 12 July | 6 | **TRUE BLUE** | Madonna |
| 23 August | 5 | **NOW! THAT'S WHAT I CALL MUSIC 7** | Various Artists |
| 27 September | 1 | **SILK AND STEEL** | Five Star |
| 4 October | 5 | **GRACELAND** | Paul Simon |
| 8 November | 2 | **EVERY BREATH YOU TAKE – THE SINGLES** | Police |
| 22 November | 2 | **HITS 5** | Various Artists |
| 6 December | 6 | **NOW! THAT'S WHAT I CALL MUSIC 8** | Various Artists |

## 1987

| DATE | WKS | TITLE | ARTIST |
|---|---|---|---|
| 17 January | 2 | **THE WHOLE STORY** | Kate Bush |
| 31 January | 3 | **GRACELAND** | Paul Simon |
| 21 February | 3 | **PHANTOM OF THE OPERA** | Original London Cast |
| 14 March | 1 | **THE VERY BEST OF HOT CHOCOLATE** | Hot Chocolate |
| 21 March | 2 | **THE JOSHUA TREE** | U2 |
| 4 April | 5 | **NOW! THAT'S WHAT I CALL MUSIC 9** | Various Artists |
| 9 May | 2 | **KEEP YOUR DISTANCE** | Curiosity Killed the Cat |
| 23 May | 2 | **IT'S BETTER TO TRAVEL** | Swing Out Sister |
| 6 June | 1 | **LIVE IN THE CITY OF LIGHT** | Simple Minds |
| 13 June | 6 | **WHITNEY** | Whitney Houston |
| 25 July | 1 | **INTRODUCING THE HARDLINE ACCORDING TO TERENCE TRENT D'ARBY** | Terence Trent D'Arby |
| 1 August | 4 | **HITS 6** | Various Artists |
| 29 August | 1 | **HYSTERIA** | Def Leppard |
| 5 September | 1 | **HITS 6** | Various Artists |
| 12 September | 5 | **BAD** | Michael Jackson |
| 17 October | 1 | **TUNNEL OF LOVE** | Bruce Springsteen |
| 24 October | 1 | **NOTHING LIKE THE SUN** | Sting |
| 31 October | 2 | **TANGO IN THE NIGHT** | Fleetwood Mac |
| 14 November | 1 | **FAITH** | George Michael |
| 21 November | 1 | **BRIDGE OF SPIES** | T'pau |
| 28 November | 1 | **WHENEVER YOU NEED SOMEBODY** | Rick Astley |
| 5 December | 6 | **NOW! THAT'S WHAT I CALL MUSIC 10** | Various Artists |

## 1988

| DATE | WKS | TITLE | ARTIST |
|---|---|---|---|
| 16 January | 1 | **POPPED IN SOULED OUT** | Wet Wet Wet |
| 23 January | 1 | **TURN BACK THE CLOCK** | Johnny Hates Jazz |
| 30 January | 8 | **INTRODUCING THE HARDLINE ACCORDING TO TERENCE TRENT D'ARBY** | Terence Trent D'Arby |
| 26 March | 1 | **VIVA HATE** | Morrissey |
| 2 April | 3 | **NOW! THAT'S WHAT I CALL MUSIC 11** | Various Artists |
| 23 April | 1 | **SEVENTH SON OF A SEVENTH SON** | Iron Maiden |
| 30 April | 1 | **THE INNOCENTS** | Erasure |
| 7 May | 2 | **TANGO IN THE NIGHT** | Fleetwood Mac |
| 21 May | 1 | **LOVESEXY** | Prince |
| 28 May | 1 | **TANGO IN THE NIGHT** | Fleetwood Mac |
| 4 June | 4 | **NITE FLITE** | Various Artists |
| 2 July | 3 | **TRACY CHAPMAN** | Tracy Chapman |
| 23 July | 5 | **NOW! THAT'S WHAT I CALL MUSIC 12** | Various Artists |
| 27 August | 4 | **KYLIE! – THE ALBUM** | Kylie Minogue |
| 24 September | 1 | **HOT CITY NIGHTS** | Various Artists |
| 1 October | 2 | **NEW JERSEY** | Bon Jovi |
| 15 October | 1 | **FLYING COLOURS** | Chris De Burgh |
| 22 October | 1 | **RATTLE AND HUM** | U2 |
| 29 October | 3 | **MONEY FOR NOTHING** | Dire Straits |
| 19 November | 2 | **KYLIE! – THE ALBUM** | Kylie Minogue |
| 3 December | 3 | **NOW! THAT'S WHAT I CALL MUSIC 13** | Various Artists |
| 24 December | 2 | **PRIVATE COLLECTION – 1988** | Cliff Richard |

## 1989

| DATE | WKS | TITLE | ARTIST |
|---|---|---|---|
| 7 January | 1 | **NOW! THAT'S WHAT I CALL MUSIC 13** | Various Artists |
| 14 January | 1 | **THE INNOCENTS** | Erasure |
| 21 January | 3 | **THE LEGENDARY ROY ORBISON** | Roy Orbison |
| 11 February | 1 | **TECHNIQUE** | New Order |
| 18 February | 1 | **THE RAW AND THE COOKED** | Fine Young Cannibals |
| 25 February | 4 | **A NEW FLAME** | Simply Red |
| 25 March | 1 | **ANYTHING FOR YOU** | Gloria Estefan & Miami Music Machine |
| 1 April | 2 | **LIKE A PRAYER** | Madonna |
| 15 April | 2 | **WHEN THE WORLD KNOWS YOUR NAME** | Deacon Blue |
| 29 April | 1 | **A NEW FLAME** | Simply Red |
| 6 May | 1 | **BLAST** | Holly Johnson |
| 13 May | 1 | **STREET FIGHTING YEARS** | Simple Minds |
| 20 May | 2 | **TEN GOOD REASONS** | Jason Donovan |
| 3 June | 1 | **THE MIRACLE** | Queen |
| 10 June | 2 | **TEN GOOD REASONS** | Jason Donovan |
| 24 June | 1 | **FLOWERS IN THE DIRT** | Paul McCartney |
| 1 July | 1 | **BATMAN (OST)** | Prince |
| 8 July | 1 | **VELVETEEN** | Transvision Vamp |
| 15 July | 1 | **CLUB CLASSICS VOLUME ONE** | Soul II Soul |
| 22 July | 2 | **A NEW FLAME** | Simply Red |
| 5 August | 6 | **CUTS BOTH WAYS** | Gloria Estefan |
| 16 September | 1 | **ASPECTS OF LOVE** | Original London Cast |
| 23 September | 1 | **WE TOO ARE ONE** | Eurythmics |
| 30 September | 1 | **FOREIGN AFFAIR** | Tina Turner |
| 7 October | 1 | **THE SEEDS OF LOVE** | Tears For Fears |
| 14 October | 1 | **CROSSROADS** | Tracy Chapman |
| 21 October | 1 | **ENJOY YOURSELF** | Kylie Minogue |
| 28 October | 2 | **WILD!** | Erasure |
| 11 November | 3 | **THE ROAD TO HELL** | Chris Rea |
| 2 December | 8 | **... BUT SERIOUSLY** | Phil Collins |

## 1990

| DATE | WKS | TITLE | ARTIST |
|---|---|---|---|
| 27 January | 1 | **COLOUR** | Christians |
| 3 February | 7 | **... BUT SERIOUSLY** | Phil Collins |
| 24 March | 1 | **I DO NOT WANT WHAT I HAVEN'T GOT** | Sinead O'Connor |
| 31 March | 1 | **CHANGESTWOBOWIE** | David Bowie |
| 7 April | 2 | **ONLY YESTERDAY – RICHARD & KAREN CARPENTER'S GREATEST HITS** | Carpenters |
| 21 April | 1 | **BEHIND THE MASK** | Fleetwood Mac |
| 28 April | 5 | **ONLY YESTERDAY – RICHARD & KAREN CARPENTER'S GREATEST HITS** | Carpenters |
| 2 June | 3 | **VOLUME II (A NEW DECADE)** | Soul II Soul |
| 23 June | 1 | **THE ESSENTIAL PAVAROTTI** | Luciano Pavarotti |
| 30 June | 1 | **STEP BY STEP** | New Kids on the Block |
| 7 July | 3 | **THE ESSENTIAL PAVAROTTI** | Luciano Pavarotti |
| 28 July | 5 | **SLEEPING WITH THE PAST** | Elton John |
| 1 September | 1 | **GRAFFITI BRIDGE** | Prince |

| DATE | WKS | TITLE | ARTIST |
|------|-----|-------|--------|
| 8 September | 1 | IN CONCERT | Carreras Domingo Pavarotti Orchestra Del Maggio Musicale Fiorentino Orchestra Del Teatro Dell'opera Di Roma Zubin Mehta |
| 15 September | 1 | LISTEN WITHOUT PREJUDICE VOLUME 1 | George Michael |
| 22 September | 4 | IN CONCERT | Carreras Domingo Pavarotti Orchestra Del Maggio Musicale Fiorentino Orchestra Del Teatro Dell'opera Di Roma Zubin Mehta |
| 20 October | 1 | SOME FRIENDLY | Charlatans |
| 27 October | 2 | THE RHYTHM OF THE SAINTS | Paul Simon |
| 10 November | 2 | THE VERY BEST OF ELTON JOHN | Elton John |
| 24 November | 9 | THE IMMACULATE COLLECTION | Madonna |

## 1991

| DATE | WKS | TITLE | ARTIST |
|------|-----|-------|--------|
| 26 January | 1 | MCMXC A.D | Enigma |
| 2 February | 1 | THE SOUL CAGES | Sting |
| 9 February | 1 | DOUBT | Jesus Jones |
| 16 February | 2 | INNUENDO | Queen |
| 2 March | 1 | CIRCLE OF ONE | Oltea Adams |
| 9 March | 1 | AUBERGE | Chris Rea |
| 16 March | 1 | SPARTACUS | Farm |
| 23 March | 1 | OUT OF TIME | R.E.M. |
| 30 March | 9 | GREATEST HITS | Eurythmics |
| 1 June | 3 | SEAL | Seal |
| 22 June | 1 | GREATEST HITS | Eurythmics |
| 29 June | 6 | LOVE HURTS | Cher |
| 10 August | 2 | ESSENTIAL PAVAROTTI II | Luciano Pavarotti |
| 24 August | 1 | METALLICA | Metallica |
| 31 August | 2 | JOSEPH AND THE AMAZING TECHNICOLOUR DREAMCOAT | Jason Donovan/Original London Cast |
| 14 September | 1 | FROM TIME TO TIME – THE SINGLES COLLECTION | Paul Young |
| 21 September | 1 | ON EVERY STREET | Dire Straits |
| 28 September | 1 | USE YOUR ILLUSION II | Guns N' Roses |
| 5 October | 1 | WAKING UP THE NEIGHBOURS | Bryan Adams |
| 12 October | 2 | STARS | Simply Red |
| 26 October | 1 | CHORUS | Erasure |
| 2 November | 1 | STARS | Simply Red |
| 9 November | 1 | GREATEST HITS II | Queen |
| 16 November | 1 | SHEPHERD MOONS | Enya |
| 23 November | 1 | WE CAN'T DANCE | Genesis |
| 30 November | 1 | DANGEROUS | Michael Jackson |
| 7 December | 4 | GREATEST HITS II | Queen |

## 1992

| DATE | WKS | TITLE | ARTIST |
|------|-----|-------|--------|
| 4 January | 5 | STARS | Simply Red |
| 8 February | 2 | HIGH ON THE HAPPY SIDE | Wet Wet Wet |
| 22 February | 3 | STARS | Simply Red |
| 14 March | 3 | DIVINE MADNESS | Madness |
| 4 April | 1 | HUMAN TOUCH | Bruce Springsteen |
| 11 April | 1 | ADRENALIZE | Def Leppard |
| 18 April | 1 | DIVA | Annie Lennox |
| 25 April | 1 | UP | Right Said Fred |
| 2 May | 1 | WISH | Cure |
| 9 May | 1 | STARS | Simply Red |
| 16 May | 1 | 1992 – THE LOVE ALBUM | Carter – The Unstoppable Sex Machine |
| 23 May | 1 | FEAR OF THE DARK | Iron Maiden |
| 30 May | 1 | MICHAEL BALL | Michael Ball |
| 6 June | 6 | BACK TO FRONT | Lionel Richie |
| 18 July | 1 | U.F. ORB | Orb |
| 25 July | 3 | THE GREATEST HITS 1966–1992 | Neil Diamond |

| DATE | WKS | TITLE | ARTIST |
|------|-----|-------|--------|
| 15 August | 1 | WELCOME TO WHEREVER YOU ARE | Inxs |
| 22 August | 1 | WE CAN'T DANCE | Genesis |
| 29 August | 1 | BEST... 1 | Smiths |
| 5 September | 1 | KYLIE'S GREATEST HITS | Kylie Minogue |
| 12 September | 2 | TUBULAR BELLS II | Mike Oldfield |
| 26 September | 1 | THE BEST OF BELINDA VOLUME 1 | Belinda Carlisle |
| 3 October | 1 | GOLD – GREATEST HITS | Abba |
| 10 October | 1 | AUTOMATIC FOR THE PEOPLE | R.E.M. |
| 17 October | 1 | SYMBOLS | Prince and The New Power Generation |
| 24 October | 3 | GLITTERING PRIZE 81/92 | Simple Minds |
| 14 November | 1 | KEEP THE FAITH | Bon Jovi |
| 21 November | 1 | CHER'S GREATEST HITS: 1965–1992 | Cher |
| 28 November | 2 | POP! – THE FIRST 20 HITS | Erasure |
| 12 December | 6 | CHER'S GREATEST HITS: 1965–1992 | Cher |

## 1993

| DATE | WKS | TITLE | ARTIST |
|------|-----|-------|--------|
| 23 January | 2 | LIVE – THE WAY WE WALK VOLUME 2: THE LONGS | Genesis |
| 6 February | 1 | JAM | Little Angels |
| 13 February | 1 | PURE CULT | Cult |
| 20 February | 1 | WORDS OF LOVE | Buddy Holly and The Crickets |
| 27 February | 1 | WALTHAMSTOW | East 17 |
| 6 March | 1 | DIVA | Annie Lennox |
| 13 March | 2 | ARE YOU GONNA GO MY WAY | Lenny Kravitz |
| 27 March | 1 | THEIR GREATEST HITS | Hot Chocolate |
| 3 April | 1 | SONGS OF FAITH AND DEVOTION | Depeche Mode |
| 10 April | 1 | SUEDE | Suede |
| 17 April | 1 | BLACK TIE WHITE NOISE | David Bowie |
| 24 April | 1 | AUTOMATIC FOR THE PEOPLE | R.E.M. |
| 1 May | 1 | CLIFF RICHARD – THE ALBUM | Cliff Richard |
| 8 May | 1 | AUTOMATIC FOR THE PEOPLE | R.E.M. |
| 15 May | 1 | REPUBLIC | New Order |
| 22 May | 1 | AUTOMATIC FOR THE PEOPLE | R.E.M. |
| 29 May | 2 | JANET | Janet Jackson |
| 12 June | 1 | NO LIMITS | 2 Unlimited |
| 19 June | 1 | WHAT'S LOVE GOT TO DO WITH IT (OST) | Tina Turner |
| 26 June | 3 | EMERGENCY ON PLANET EARTH | Jamiroquai |
| 17 July | 1 | ZOOROPA | U2 |
| 24 July | 7 | PROMISES AND LIES | UB40 |
| 11 September | 1 | MUSIC BOX | Mariah Carey |
| 18 September | 1 | BAT OUT OF HELL II – BACK INTO HELL | Meat Loaf |
| 25 September | 1 | IN UTERO | Nirvana |
| 2 October | 1 | BAT OUT OF HELL II – BACK INTO HELL | Meat Loaf |
| 9 October | 1 | VERY | Pet Shop Boys |
| 16 October | 1 | BAT OUT OF HELL II – BACK INTO HELL | Meat Loaf |
| 23 October | 1 | EVERYTHING CHANGES | Take That |
| 30 October | 3 | BAT OUT OF HELL II – BACK INTO HELL | Meat Loaf |
| 20 November | 1 | BOTH SIDES OF THE STORY | Phil Collins |
| 27 November | 5 | BAT OUT OF HELL II – BACK INTO HELL | Meat Loaf |

## 1994

| DATE | WKS | TITLE | ARTIST |
|------|-----|-------|--------|
| 1 January | 1 | ONE WOMAN – THE ULTIMATE COLLECTION | Diana Ross |
| 8 January | 1 | EVERYTHING CHANGES | Take That |
| 15 January | 1 | SO FAR SO GOOD | Bryan Adams |
| 22 January | 1 | ONE WOMAN – THE ULTIMATE COLLECTION | Diana Ross |
| 29 January | 2 | TEASE ME | Chaka Demus & Pliers |
| 12 February | 1 | UNDER THE PINK | Tori Amos |
| 19 February | 1 | THE CROSS OF CHANGES | Enigma |
| 26 February | 4 | MUSIC BOX | Mariah Carey |
| 26 March | 1 | VAUXHALL AND I | Morrissey |
| 2 April | 1 | MUSIC BOX | Mariah Carey |
| 9 April | 4 | THE DIVISION BELL | Pink Floyd |
| 7 May | 1 | PARKLIFE | Blur |
| 14 May | 2 | OUR TOWN – THE GREATEST HITS OF DEACON BLUE | Deacon Blue |

| DATE | WKS | TITLE | ARTIST |
|---|---|---|---|
| 28 May | 1 | **I SAY I SAY I SAY** | Erasure |
| 4 June | 2 | **SEAL** | Seal |
| 18 June | 1 | **REAL THINGS** | 2 Unlimited |
| 25 June | 1 | **EVERYBODY ELSE IS DOING IT, SO WHY CAN'T WE?** | |
| | | | Cranberries |
| 2 July | 2 | **HAPPY NATION** | Ace Of Base |
| 16 July | 1 | **MUSIC FOR THE JILTED GENERATION** | Prodigy |
| 23 July | 1 | **VOODOO LOUNGE** | Rolling Stones |
| 30 July | 4 | **END OF PART ONE (THEIR GREATEST HITS)** | |
| | | | Wet Wet Wet |
| 27 August | 1 | **COME** | Prince |
| 3 September | 1 | **END OF PART ONE (THEIR GREATEST HITS)** | |
| | | | Wet Wet Wet |
| 10 September | 1 | **DEFINITELY MAYBE** | Oasis |
| 17 September | 1 | **THE THREE TENORS IN CONCERT** | Carreras Domingo Pavarotti |
| | | | With Orchestra Conducted B |
| | | | Y Zubin Mehta |
| 24 September | 1 | **FROM THE CRADLE** | Eric Clapton |
| 1 October | 1 | **SONGS** | Luther Vandross |
| 8 October | 2 | **MONSTER** | R.E.M. |
| 22 October | 3 | **CROSS THE ROAD – THE BEST OF BON JOVI** | |
| | | | Bon Jovi |
| 12 November | 1 | **UNPLUGGED IN NEW YORK** | Nirvana |
| 19 November | 2 | **CROSS THE ROAD – THE BEST OF BON JOVI** | |
| | | | Bon Jovi |
| 3 December | 1 | **CARRY ON UP THE CHARTS – THE BEST OF THE BEAUTIFUL SOUTH** | |
| | | | Beautiful South |
| 10 December | 1 | **LIVE AT THE BBC** | Beatles |
| 17 December | 6 | **CARRY ON UP THE CHARTS – THE BEST OF THE BEAUTIFUL SOUTH** | |
| | | | Beautiful South |

## 1995

| DATE | WKS | TITLE | ARTIST |
|---|---|---|---|
| 28 January | 6 | **THE COLOUR OF MY LOVE** | Celine Dion |
| 11 March | 1 | **GREATEST HITS** | Bruce Springsteen |
| 18 March | 1 | **MEDUSA** | Annie Lennox |
| 25 March | 1 | **ELASTICA** | Elastica |
| 1 April | 1 | **THE COLOUR OF MY LOVE** | Celine Dion |
| 8 April | 1 | **WAKE UP!** | Boo Radleys |
| 15 April | 1 | **GREATEST HITS** | Bruce Springsteen |
| 22 April | 3 | **PICTURE THIS** | Wet Wet Wet |
| 13 May | 2 | **NOBODY ELSE** | Take That |
| 27 May | 1 | **STANLEY ROAD** | Paul Weller |
| 3 June | 1 | **SINGLES** | Alison Moyet |
| 10 June | 2 | **PULSE** | Pink Floyd |
| 24 June | 1 | **HISTORY – PAST PRESENT AND FUTURE BOOK 1** | |
| | | | Michael Jackson |
| 1 July | 4 | **THESE DAYS** | Bon Jovi |
| 29 July | 3 | **I SHOULD COCO** | Supergrass |
| 19 August | 2 | **IT'S GREAT WHEN YOU'RE STRAIGHT… YEAH** | |
| | | | Black Grape |
| 2 September | 1 | **SAID AND DONE** | Boyzone |
| 9 September | 1 | **THE CHARLATANS** | Charlatans |
| 16 September | 1 | **ZEITGEIST** | Levellers |
| 23 September | 2 | **THE GREAT ESCAPE** | Blur |
| 7 October | 1 | **DAYDREAM** | Mariah Carey |
| 14 October | 1 | **(WHAT'S THE STORY) MORNING GLORY?** | |
| | | | Oasis |
| 21 October | 3 | **LIFE** | Simply Red |
| 11 November | 1 | **DIFFERENT CLASS** | Pulp |
| 18 November | 1 | **MADE IN HEAVEN** | Queen |
| 25 November | 7 | **ROBSON & JEROME** | Robson and Jerome |

## 1996

| DATE | WKS | TITLE | ARTIST |
|---|---|---|---|
| 13 January | 6 | **(WHAT'S THE STORY) MORNING GLORY?** | |
| | | | Oasis |
| 24 February | 1 | **EXPECTING TO FLY** | Bluetones |
| 2 March | 3 | **(WHAT'S THE STORY) MORNING GLORY?** | |
| | | | Oasis |
| 23 March | 1 | **FALLING INTO YOU** | Celine Dion |

| DATE | WKS | TITLE | ARTIST |
|---|---|---|---|
| 30 March | 1 | **ANTHOLOGY 2** | Beatles |
| 6 April | 4 | **GREATEST HITS** | Take That |
| 4 May | 2 | **JAGGED LITTLE PILL** | Alanis Morissette |
| 18 May | 1 | **1977** | Ash |
| 25 May | 3 | **OLDER/OLDER & UPPER** | George Michael |
| 15 June | 1 | **LOAD** | Metallica |
| 22 June | 1 | **18 TIL I DIE** | Bryan Adams |
| 29 June | 1 | **JAGGED LITTLE PILL** | Alanis Morissette |
| 6 July | 2 | **RECURRING DREAM – THE VERY BEST OF CROWDED HOUSE** | |
| | | | Crowded House |
| 20 July | 8 | **JAGGED LITTLE PILL** | Alanis Morissette |
| 14 September | 1 | **COMING UP** | Suede |
| 21 September | 1 | **NEW ADVENTURES IN HI-FI** | R.E.M. |
| 28 September | 2 | **K** | Kula Shaker |
| 12 October | 1 | **NATURAL** | Peter Andre |
| 19 October | 2 | **GREATEST HITS** | Simply Red |
| 2 November | 1 | **BLUE IS THE COLOUR** | Beautiful South |
| 9 November | 1 | **A DIFFERENT BEAT** | Boyzone |
| 16 November | 1 | **SPICE** | Spice Girls |
| 23 November | 2 | **TAKE TWO** | Robson and Jerome |
| 7 December | 8 | **SPICE** | Spice Girls |

## 1997

| DATE | WKS | TITLE | ARTIST |
|---|---|---|---|
| 1 February | 1 | **EVITA (OST)** | Madonna |
| 8 February | 1 | **GLOW** | Reef |
| 15 February | 1 | **WHITE ON BLONDE** | Texas |
| 22 February | 1 | **BLUR** | Blur |
| 1 March | 1 | **ATTACK OF THE GREY LANTERN** | Mansun |
| 8 March | 1 | **SPICE** | Spice Girls |
| 15 March | 1 | **POP** | U2 |
| 22 March | 4 | **SPICE** | Spice Girls |
| 19 April | 1 | **DIG YOUR OWN HOLE** | Chemical Brothers |
| 26 April | 1 | **ULTRA** | Depeche Mode |
| 3 May | 2 | **TELLIN' STORIES** | Charlatans |
| 17 May | 1 | **SPICE** | Spice Girls |
| 24 May | 2 | **BLOOD ON THE FLOOR – HISTORY IN THE MIX** | |
| | | | Michael Jackson |
| 7 June | 1 | **OPEN ROAD** | Gary Barlow |
| 14 June | 1 | **WU-TANG FOREVER** | Wu-Tang Clan |
| 21 June | 1 | **MIDDLE OF NOWHERE** | Hanson |
| 28 June | 2 | **OK COMPUTER** | Radiohead |
| 12 July | 6 | **THE FAT OF THE LAND** | Prodigy |
| 23 August | 1 | **WHITE ON BLONDE** | Texas |
| 30 August | 4 | **BE HERE NOW** | Oasis |
| 27 September | 1 | **MARCHIN' ALREADY** | Ocean Colour Scene |
| 4 October | 1 | **BE HERE NOW** | Oasis |
| 11 October | 5 | **URBAN HYMNS** | Verve |
| 15 November | 2 | **SPICEWORLD** | Spice Girls |
| 29 November | 1 | **LET'S TALK ABOUT LOVE** | Celine Dion |
| 13 December | 1 | **SPICEWORLD** | Spice Girls |
| 20 December | 2 | **LET'S TALK ABOUT LOVE** | Celine Dion |

## 1998

| DATE | WKS | TITLE | ARTIST |
|---|---|---|---|
| 3 January | 6 | **URBAN HYMNS** | Verve |
| 14 February | 1 | **TITANIC (OST)** | James Horner |
| 21 February | 1 | **URBAN HYMNS** | Verve |
| 28 February | 2 | **TITANIC (OST)** | James Horner |
| 14 March | 2 | **RAY OF LIGHT** | Madonna |
| 28 March | 1 | **LET'S TALK ABOUT LOVE** | Celine Dion |
| 4 April | 1 | **THE BEST OF JAMES** | James |
| 11 April | 1 | **THIS IS HARDCORE** | Pulp |
| 18 April | 2 | **LIFE THRU A LENS** | Robbie Williams |
| 2 May | 2 | **MEZZANINE** | Massive Attack |
| 16 May | 1 | **INTERNATIONAL VELVET** | Catatonia |
| 23 May | 1 | **VERSION 2.0** | Garbage |
| 30 May | 1 | **BLUE** | Simply Red |
| 6 June | 1 | **WHERE WE BELONG** | Boyzone |
| 13 June | 1 | **BLUE** | Simply Red |
| 20 June | 1 | **THE GOOD WILL OUT** | Embrace |

| DATE | WKS | TITLE | ARTIST |
|---|---|---|---|
| 27 June | 1 | **TALK ON CORNERS** | Corrs |
| 4 July | 1 | **FIVE** | Five |
| 11 July | 1 | **TALK ON CORNERS** | Corrs |
| 18 July | 1 | **HELLO NASTY** | Beastie Boys |
| 25 July | 3 | **JANE MCDONALD** | Jane Mcdonald |
| 15 August | 3 | **TALK ON CORNERS** | Corrs |
| 5 September | 2 | **WHERE WE BELONG** | Boyzone |
| 19 September | 1 | **TALK ON CORNERS** | Corrs |
| 26 September | 3 | **THIS IS MY TRUTH TELL ME YOURS** | Manic Street Preachers |
| 17 October | 1 | **HITS** | Phil Collins |
| 24 October | 2 | **QUENCH** | Beautiful South |
| 7 November | 1 | **I'VE BEEN EXPECTING YOU** | Robbie Williams |
| 14 November | 1 | **THE BEST OF – 1990 & B SIDES** | U2 |
| 21 November | 8 | **LADIES & GENTLEMEN – THE BEST OF GEORGE MICHAEL** George Michael | |

## 1999

| DATE | WKS | TITLE | ARTIST |
|---|---|---|---|
| 16 January | 1 | **I'VE BEEN EXPECTING YOU** | Robbie Williams |
| 23 January | 4 | **YOU'VE COME A LONG WAY, BABY** | Fatboy Slim |
| 20 February | 1 | **I'VE BEEN EXPECTING YOU** | Robbie Williams |
| 27 February | 3 | **TALK ON CORNERS** | Corrs |
| 20 March | 1 | **PERFORMANCE AND COCKTAILS** | Stereophonics |
| 27 March | 2 | **13** | Blur |
| 10 April | 1 | **TALK ON CORNERS** | Corrs |
| 17 April | 1 | **GOLD – GREATEST HITS** | Abba |
| 24 April | 1 | **EQUALLY CURSED AND BLESSED** | Catatonia |
| 1 May | 2 | **GOLD – GREATEST HITS** | Abba |
| 15 May | 1 | **HEAD MUSIC** | Suede |
| 22 May | 1 | **THE HUSH** | Texas |
| 29 May | 2 | **GOLD – GREATEST HITS** | Abba |
| 12 June | 2 | **BY REQUEST** | Boyzone |
| 26 June | 1 | **SYNKRONIZED** | Jamiroquai |
| 3 July | 1 | **SURRENDER** | Chemical Brothers |
| 10 July | 7 | **BY REQUEST** | Boyzone |
| 28 August | 2 | **THE MAN WHO** | Travis |
| 11 September | 3 | **COME ON OVER** | Shania Twain |
| 2 October | 1 | **RHYTHM AND STEALTH** | Leftfield |
| 9 October | 1 | **RELOAD** | Tom Jones |
| 16 October | 3 | **COME ON OVER** | Shania Twain |
| 6 November | 3 | **STEPTACULAR** | Steps |
| 27 November | 1 | **ALL THE WAY – A DECADE OF LOVE SONGS** Celine Dion | |
| 4 December | 1 | **STEPTACULAR** | Steps |
| 11 December | 5 | **COME ON OVER** | Shania Twain |

## 2000

| DATE | WKS | TITLE | ARTIST |
|---|---|---|---|
| 15 January | 5 | **THE MAN WHO** | Travis |
| 19 February | 3 | **RISE** | Gabrielle |
| 11 March | 1 | **STANDING ON THE SHOULDERS OF GIANTS** Oasis | |
| 18 March | 2 | **THE MAN WHO** | Travis |
| 1 April | 2 | **SUPERNATURAL** | Santana |
| 15 April | 5 | **PLAY** | Moby |
| 20 May | 1 | **RELOAD** | Tom Jones |
| 27 May | 2 | **THE GREATEST HITS** | Whitney Houston |
| 10 June | 1 | **CRUSH** | Bon Jovi |
| 17 June | 1 | **RELOAD** | Tom Jones |
| 24 June | 1 | **7** | S Club 7 |
| 1 July | 1 | **THE MARSHALL MATHERS LP** | Eminem |
| 8 July | 1 | **ALONE WITH EVERYBODY** | Richard Ashcroft |
| 15 July | 1 | **THE MARSHALL MATHERS LP** | Eminem |
| 22 July | 1 | **PARACHUTES** | Coldplay |
| 29 July | 2 | **IN BLUE** | Corrs |
| 12 August | 2 | **RONAN** | Ronan Keating |
| 26 August | 2 | **BORN TO DO IT** | Craig David |
| 9 September | 3 | **SING WHEN YOU'RE WINNING** | Robbie Williams |
| 30 September | 2 | **MUSIC** | Madonna |
| 14 October | 2 | **KID A** | Radiohead |
| 28 October | 1 | **SAINTS AND SINNERS** | All Saints |

| DATE | WKS | TITLE | ARTIST |
|---|---|---|---|
| 4 November | 1 | **THE GREATEST HITS** | Texas |
| 11 November | 1 | **ALL THAT YOU CAN'T LEAVE BEHIND** | U2 |
| 18 November | 1 | **COAST TO COAST** | Westlife |
| 25 November | 9 | **1** | Beatles |

## 2001

| DATE | WKS | TITLE | ARTIST |
|---|---|---|---|
| 27 January | 1 | **THE GREATEST HITS** | Texas |
| 3 February | 1 | **CHOCOLATE STARFISH AND THE HOT DOG** Limp Bizkit | |
| 10 February | 6 | **NO ANGEL** | Dido |
| 24 March | 2 | **SONGBIRD** | Eva Cassidy |
| 7 April | 2 | **POPSTARS** | Hear'say |
| 21 April | 2 | **JUST ENOUGH EDUCATION TO PERFORM** Stereophonics | |
| 5 May | 1 | **FREE ALL ANGELS** | Ash |
| 12 May | 2 | **SURVIVOR** | Destiny's Child |
| 26 May | 2 | **REVEAL** | R.E.M. |
| 9 June | 1 | **HOT SHOT** | Shaggy |
| 16 June | 1 | **AMNESIAC** | Radiohead |
| 23 June | 3 | **THE INVISIBLE BAND** | Travis |
| 21 July | 1 | **8701** | Usher |
| 28 July | 2 | **SURVIVOR** | Destiny's Child |
| 11 August | 1 | **WHITE LADDER** | David Gray |
| 18 August | 1 | **RIGHT NOW** | Atomic Kitten |
| 25 August | 1 | **WHITE LADDER** | David Gray |
| 1 September | 1 | **BREAK THE CYCLE** | Staind |
| 8 September | 1 | **IOWA** | Slipknot |
| 15 September | 2 | **A FUNK ODYSSEY** | Jamiroquai |
| 29 September | 1 | **THE ID** | Macy Gray |
| 6 October | 1 | **NO ANGEL** | Dido |
| 13 October | 2 | **FEVER** | Kylie Minogue |
| 27 October | 2 | **GOLD – THE GREATEST HITS** | Steps |
| 10 November | 1 | **INVINCIBLE** | Michael Jackson |
| 17 November | 1 | **GOLD – THE GREATEST HITS** | Steps |
| 24 November | 1 | **WORLD OF OUR OWN** | Westlife |
| 1 December | 7 | **SWING WHEN YOU'RE WINNING** | Robbie Williams |

## 2002

| DATE | WKS | TITLE | ARTIST |
|---|---|---|---|
| 19 January | 3 | **JUST ENOUGH EDUCATION TO PERFORM** Stereophonics | |
| 9 February | 1 | **COME WITH US** | Chemical Brothers |
| 16 February | 2 | **ESCAPE** | Enrique Iglesias |
| 2 March | 2 | **THE VERY BEST OF** | Sting & The Police |
| 16 March | 2 | **THE ESSENTIAL COLLECTION** | Barbra Streisand |
| 23 March | 2 | **SILVER SIDE UP** | Nickelback |
| 6 April | 4 | **A NEW DAY HAS COME** | Celine Dion |
| 4 May | 1 | **ALL RISE** | Blue |
| 11 May | 2 | **THE LAST BROADCAST** | Doves |
| 25 May | 1 | **18** | Moby |
| 1 June | 1 | **DESTINATION** | Ronan Keating |
| 8 June | 5 | **THE EMINEM SHOW** | Eminem |
| 13 July | 1 | **HEATHEN CHEMISTRY** | Oasis |
| 20 July | 3 | **BY THE WAY** | Red Hot Chili Peppers |
| 10 August | 1 | **THE RISING** | Bruce Springsteen |
| 17 August | 1 | **BY THE WAY** | Red Hot Chili Peppers |
| 31 August | 1 | **IMAGINE** | Eva Cassidy |
| 7 September | 2 | **A RUSH OF BLOOD TO THE HEAD** | Coldplay |
| 21 September | 1 | **FEELS SO GOOD** | Atomic Kitten |
| 28 September | 1 | **ILLUMINATION** | Paul Weller |
| 5 October | 2 | **ELV1S: 30 NUMBER 1 HITS** | Elvis Presley |
| 19 October | 2 | **FROM NOW ON** | Will Young |
| 2 November | 1 | **ONE BY ONE** | Foo Fighters |
| 9 November | 1 | **A NEW DAY AT MIDNIGHT** | David Gray |
| 16 November | 1 | **ONE LOVE** | Blue |
| 23 November | 1 | **UNBREAKABLE – THE GREATEST HITS VOLUME 1** Westlife | |
| 30 November | 6 | **ESCAPOLOGY** | Robbie Williams |

## 2003

| DATE | WKS | TITLE | ARTIST |
|------|-----|-------|--------|
| 11 January | 3 | LET GO | Avril Lavigne |
| 1 February | 2 | JUSTIFIED | Justin Timberlake |
| 15 February | 1 | SIMPLY DEEP | Kelly Rowland |
| 22 February | 1 | 100TH WINDOW | Massive Attack |
| 1 March | 2 | JUSTIFIED | Justin Timberlake |
| 8 March | 4 | COME AWAY WITH ME | Norah Jones |
| 5 April | 1 | METEORA | Linkin Park |
| 12 April | 2 | ELEPHANT | White Stripes |
| 26 April | 1 | A RUSH OF BLOOD TO THE HEAD | Coldplay |
| 3 May | 1 | AMERICAN LIFE | Madonna |
| 10 May | 1 | JUSTIFIED | Justin Timberlake |
| 17 May | 1 | THINK TANK | Blur |
| 24 May | 3 | JUSTIFIED | Justin Timberlake |
| 14 June | 1 | YOU GOTTA GO THERE TO COME BACK | Stereophonics |
| 21 June | 1 | HAIL TO THE THIEF | Radiohead |
| 28 June | 1 | FALLEN | Evanescence |
| 5 July | 5 | BEYONCE | Beyonce Knowles |
| 9 August | 1 | MAGIC AND MEDICINE | Coral |
| 16 August | 1 | ESCAPOLOGY | Robbie Williams |
| 23 August | 2 | AMERICAN TUNE | Eva Cassidy |
| 6 September | 4 | PERMISSION TO LAND | Darkness |
| 4 October | 1 | ABSOLUTION | Muse |
| 11 October | 4 | LIFE FOR RENT | Dido |
| 8 November | 1 | IN TIME – THE BEST OF – 1988–2003 | R.E.M. |
| 15 November | 1 | GUILTY | Blue |
| 22 November | 1 | LIFE FOR RENT | Dido |
| 29 November | 1 | NUMBER ONES | Michael Jackson |
| 6 December | 1 | TURNAROUND | Westlife |
| 13 December | 1 | FRIDAY'S CHILD | Will Young |
| 20 December | 3 | LIFE FOR RENT | Dido |

## 2004

| DATE | WKS | TITLE | ARTIST |
|------|-----|-------|--------|
| 10 January | 1 | FRIDAY'S CHILD | Will Young |
| 17 January | 2 | LIFE FOR RENT | Dido |
| 31 January | 3 | CALL OFF THE SEARCH | Katie Melua |
| 21 February | 2 | FEELS LIKE HOME | Norah Jones |
| 6 March | 3 | CALL OFF THE SEARCH | Katie Melua |
| 27 March | 1 | PATIENCE | George Michael |
| 3 April | 1 | CONFESSIONS | Usher |
| 10 April | 2 | ANASTACIA | Anastacia |
| 24 April | 2 | GREATEST HITS | Guns N' Roses |
| 8 May | 1 | D12 WORLD | D12 |
| 15 May | 1 | GREATEST HITS | Guns N' Roses |
| 22 May | 2 | HOPES AND FEARS | Keane |
| 5 June | 1 | UNDER MY SKIN | Avril Lavigne |
| 12 June | 1 | HOPES AND FEARS | Keane |
| 19 June | 1 | NO ROOTS | Faithless |
| 26 June | 1 | HOPES AND FEARS | Keane |

# THE NUMBER ONE COMPILATION RECORDS LISTED CHRONOLOGICALLY 1989–2004

This listing details compilation, soundtrack and stage recordings that have topped the charts since the creation of a separate compilation chart in 1989.

## 1989

| DATE | WKS | TITLE | ARTIST |
|---|---|---|---|
| 14 January | 1 | NOW! THAT'S WHAT I CALL MUSIC 13 | EMI/Virgin/Polygram |
| 21 January | 2 | ANDREW LLOYD WEBBER – THE PREMIERE COLLECTION | Polydor |
| 4 February | 4 | THE MARQUEE – THIRTY LEGENDARY YEARS | Polydor |
| 4 March | 1 | THE BRITS – THE AWARDS 1989 | Telstar |
| 11 March | 1 | THE PREMIERE COLLECTION | Really Useful |
| 18 March | 1 | DEEP HEAT | Telstar |
| 25 March | 1 | UNFORGETTABLE 2 | EMI |
| 1 April | 7 | NOW! THAT'S WHAT I CALL MUSIC 14 | EMI/Virgin/Polygram |
| 20 May | 2 | NITE FLITE 2 | CBS |
| 3 June | 6 | THE HITS ALBUM 10 | CBS/WEA/BMG |
| 15 July | 6 | NOW! DANCE '89 | EMI/Virgin |
| 26 August | 5 | NOW! THAT'S WHAT I CALL MUSIC 15 | EMI/Virgin/Polygram |
| 30 September | 5 | DEEP HEAT 4 – PLAY WITH FIRE | Telstar |
| 4 November | 3 | SMASH HITS PARTY '89 | Dover |
| 25 November | 1 | THE 80S – THE ALBUM OF THE DECADE | EMI |
| 2 December | 7 | NOW! THAT'S WHAT I CALL MUSIC 16 | EMI/Virgin/Polygram |

## 1990

| DATE | WKS | TITLE | ARTIST |
|---|---|---|---|
| 20 January | 2 | PURE SOFT METAL | Stylus |
| 3 February | 2 | DEEP HEAT 5 – FEED THE FEVER | Telstar |
| 17 February | 3 | PURE SOFT METAL | Stylus |
| 10 March | 4 | NOW DANCE 901 | EMI/Virgin/Polygram |
| 7 April | 2 | DEEP HEAT 6 – THE SIXTH SENSE | Telstar |
| 21 April | 2 | JUST THE TWO OF US | CBS |
| 5 May | 5 | NOW! THAT'S WHAT I CALL MUSIC 17 | EMI/Virgin/Polygram |
| 9 June | 4 | THE CLASSIC EXPERIENCE II | EMI |
| 7 July | 1 | DEEP HEAT 7 – SEVENTH HEAVEN | Telstar |
| 14 July | 2 | SMASH HITS – RAVE! | Dover |
| 28 July | 3 | NOW DANCE 902 | EMI/Virgin/Polygram |
| 18 August | 2 | KNEBWORTH – THE ALBUM | Polydor |
| 1 September | 4 | MEGABASS | Telstar |
| 29 September | 1 | SLAMMIN' | A&M |
| 6 October | 3 | THAT LOVING FEELING VOLUME 3 | Dino |
| 27 October | 3 | MISSING YOU – AN ALBUM OF LOVE | EMI |
| 17 November | 2 | NOW DANCE 903 | EMI/Virgin/Polygram |
| 1 December | 7 | NOW! THAT'S WHAT I CALL MUSIC 18 | EMI/Virgin/Polygram |

## 1991

| DATE | WKS | TITLE | ARTIST |
|---|---|---|---|
| 19 January | 2 | DIRTY DANCING (ORIGINAL SOUNDTRACK) | RCA |
| 2 February | 2 | DEEP HEAT 9 – THE NINTH LIFE | Telstar |
| 16 February | 1 | THE LOST BOYS (ORIGINAL SOUNDTRACK) | Atlantic |
| 23 February | 3 | AWESOME! | EMI |
| 16 March | 3 | UNCHAINED MELODIES | Telstar |
| 6 April | 5 | NOW! THAT'S WHAT I CALL MUSIC 19 | EMI/Virgin/Polygram |
| 11 May | 2 | THINKING OF YOU | Columbia |
| 25 May | 2 | SMASH HITS – MASSIVE | Dover |
| 8 June | 1 | THE ESSENTIAL MOZART | Decca |
| 15 June | 1 | THE RHYTHM DIVINE | Dino |
| 22 June | 1 | THE ESSENTIAL MOZART | Decca |
| 29 June | 5 | WINGS OF LOVE | A&M |
| 3 August | 1 | THIN ICE 2 – THE SECOND SHIVER | Telstar |
| 10 August | 1 | PURPLE RAINBOWS | Polydor |
| 17 August | 2 | THE HITS ALBUM 15 | Sony/BMG |
| 31 August | 3 | THE SOUND OF THE SUBURBS | Columbia |
| 21 September | 2 | GROOVY GHETTO | Arcade |
| 5 October | 3 | NOW! DANCE 91 | EMI/Virgin/Polygram |
| 26 October | 1 | TWO ROOMS – ELTON JOHN & BERNIE TAUPIN | Mercury |
| 2 November | 4 | HARDCORE ECSTASY | Dino |
| 30 November | 7 | NOW! THAT'S WHAT I CALL MUSIC 20 | EMI/Virgin/Polygram |

## 1992

| DATE | WKS | TITLE | ARTIST |
|---|---|---|---|
| 18 January | 1 | ESSENTIAL HARDCORE | Dino |
| 25 January | 4 | THE ULTIMATE RAVE | EMI/Virgin/Polygram |
| 22 February | 2 | THE AWARDS 1992 | Polygram TV |
| 7 March | 2 | THE ULTIMATE HARDCORE | Telstar |
| 21 March | 3 | SOUL EMOTION | Polygram |
| 11 April | 1 | ALL WOMAN | Quality Television |
| 25 April | 5 | NOW! THAT'S WHAT I CALL MUSIC 21 | EMI/Virgin/Polygram |
| 30 May | 2 | THE RAVE GENERATOR | Cookie Jar |
| 13 June | 1 | EARTHRISE – THE RAINFOREST ALBUM | Elf |
| 20 June | 1 | MODERN LOVE | Polygram |
| 27 June | 4 | HEARTBEAT | Columbia |
| 25 July | 2 | KT3 – THE KAOS THEORY | Telstar |
| 8 August | 8 | NOW! THAT'S WHAT I CALL MUSIC 22 | EMI/Virgin/Polygram |
| 3 October | 1 | SIXTIES BEAT | Dino |
| 10 October | 1 | ALL WOMAN 2 | Quality Television |
| 17 October | 2 | ENERGY RUSH | Dino |
| 31 October | 1 | THE ULTIMATE COUNTRY COLLECTION | Columbia |
| 7 November | 1 | THE BEST OF DANCE '92 | Telstar |
| 14 November | 1 | THE ULTIMATE COUNTRY COLLECTION | Columbia |
| 21 November | 1 | THE BEST OF DANCE '92 | Telstar |
| 28 November | 5 | NOW! THAT'S WHAT I CALL MUSIC 23 | EMI/Virgin/Polygram |

## 1993

| DATE | WKS | TITLE | ARTIST |
|---|---|---|---|
| 2 January | 8 | THE BODYGUARD (OST) | Arista |
| 27 February | 3 | HITS '93 VOLUME 1 | Telstar/BMG |
| 20 March | 2 | THE BODYGUARD (OST) | Arista |
| 3 April | 1 | BLUES BROTHER SOUL SISTER | Dino |
| 10 April | 3 | ENERGY RUSH PRESENTS DANCE HITS '93 | Dino |
| 1 May | 1 | THE BODYGUARD (OST) | Arista |
| 8 May | 6 | NOW! THAT'S WHAT I CALL MUSIC 24 | EMI/Virgin/Polygram |
| 19 June | 1 | ORIGINALS | Columbia |
| 26 June | 2 | NOW! DANCE '93 | EMI/Virgin/Polygram |
| 10 July | 1 | 100% DANCE | Telstar |
| 17 July | 4 | THE BEST DANCE ALBUM IN THE WORLD... EVER! | Virgin |
| 14 August | 5 | NOW! THAT'S WHAT I CALL MUSIC 25 | EMI/Virgin/Polygram |
| 18 September | 2 | DANCE ADRENALIN | Telstar |
| 2 October | 2 | 100% DANCE VOLUME 2 | Telstar |
| 16 October | 1 | NOW THAT'S WHAT I CALL MUSIC! 1993 | EMI/Virgin/Polygram |
| 23 October | 2 | 100% DANCE VOLUME 2 | Telstar |
| 6 November | 1 | NOW! DANCE – THE BEST OF '93 | EMI/Virgin/Polygram |
| 13 November | 2 | THE BEST OF DANCE '93 | Telstar |
| 27 November | 8 | NOW! THAT'S WHAT I CALL MUSIC 26 | EMI/Virgin/Polygram |

## 1994

| DATE | WKS | TITLE | ARTIST |
|---|---|---|---|
| 22 January | 1 | SOUND OF KISS FM | Polygram |
| 29 January | 2 | NOW! DANCE 94 VOLUME 1 | EMI/Virgin/Polygram |
| 12 February | 1 | SWEET SOUL HARMONIES | Virgin |
| 19 February | 3 | DANCE HITS 94 – VOLUME 1 | Telstar |
| 12 March | 4 | SOUL DEVOTION | Polygram |
| 9 April | 4 | NOW! THAT'S WHAT I CALL MUSIC 27 | EMI/Virgin/Polygram |
| 7 May | 4 | DANCE ZONE LEVEL ONE | Polygram |
| 4 June | 1 | ENERGY RUSH – XTERMIN8 | Dino |
| 11 June | 2 | DANCE HITS 94 – VOLUME 2 | Telstar |
| 18 June | 2 | PURE MOODS | Virgin |
| 2 July | 2 | NOW! DANCE – SUMMER 94 | EMI/Virgin |
| 16 July | 2 | DANCE ZONE LEVEL TWO | Polygram |
| 30 July | 2 | IT'S THE ULTIMATE DANCE ALBUM | Telstar |
| 13 August | 5 | NOW! THAT'S WHAT I CALL MUSIC 28 | EMI/Virgin/Polygram |
| 17 September | 3 | BEST ROCK ALBUM IN THE WORLD EVER | Virgin |
| 8 October | 1 | DANCE ZONE LEVEL THREE | Polygram |
| 15 October | 4 | NOW! THAT'S WHAT I CALL MUSIC 1994 | EMI/Virgin/Polygram |
| 12 November | 1 | BEST ROCK ALBUM IN THE WORLD EVER | Virgin |
| 19 November | 1 | THE LOVE ALBUM | Virgin |
| 26 November | 9 | NOW! THAT'S WHAT I CALL MUSIC 29 | EMI/Virgin/Polygram |

## 1995

| DATE | WKS | TITLE | ARTIST |
|------|-----|-------|--------|
| 28 January | 1 | BEST OF HEARTBEAT | Columbia |
| 4 February | 1 | BEST PUNK ALBUM IN THE WORLD... EVER! | Virgin |
| 11 February | 2 | DANCE MANIA 95 – VOLUME ONE | Pure Music |
| 25 February | 3 | ON A DANCE TIP | Global Television |
| 18 March | 1 | SMASH HITS 95 – VOLUME 1 | Telstar |
| 25 March | 2 | DANCE ZONE LEVEL FOUR | Polygram |
| 8 April | 2 | DANCE MANIA 95 – VOLUME TWO | Pure Music |
| 22 April | 4 | NOW! THAT'S WHAT I CALL MUSIC 30 | EMI/Virgin/Polygram |
| 20 May | 3 | ON A DANCE TIP 2 | Global Television |
| 10 June | 2 | TOP OF THE POPS 1 | Columbia |
| 24 June | 3 | DANCE ZONE LEVEL FIVE | Polygram |
| 15 July | 3 | DANCE MANIA 95 – VOLUME THREE | Pure Music |
| 5 August | 1 | THE BEST SUMMER ALBUM IN THE WORLD... EVER! | Virgin |
| 12 August | 4 | NOW! THAT'S WHAT I CALL MUSIC 31 | EMI/Virgin/Polygram |
| 9 September | 1 | DANCE ZONE LEVEL SIX | Polygram |
| 16 September | 2 | HELP – WAR CHILD | Go! Discs |
| 30 September | 6 | HEARTBEAT – FOREVER YOURS | Columbia |
| 11 November | 1 | THE GREATEST PARTY ALBUM UNDER THE SUN | EMI |
| 18 November | 1 | PURE SWING IV | Dino |
| 25 November | 6 | NOW! THAT'S WHAT I CALL MUSIC 32 | EMI/Virgin/Polygram |
| 23 December | 5 | HITS 96 | Global Television |

## 1996

| DATE | WKS | TITLE | ARTIST |
|------|-----|-------|--------|
| 3 February | 1 | SISTERS OF SWING | Polygram TV |
| 10 February | 2 | THE BEST... ALBUM IN THE WORLD... EVER! 2 | Virgin |
| 24 February | 1 | THE NUMBER ONE LOVE ALBUM | Polygram TV |
| 2 March | 4 | IN THE MIX 96 | Polygram TV |
| 30 March | 5 | NOW THAT'S WHAT I CALL MUSIC! 33 | EMI/Virgin/Polygram |
| 4 May | 1 | DANCE ZONE LEVEL SEVEN | Polygram TV |
| 11 May | 1 | BOYZ OF SWING | Polygram TV |
| 18 May | 9 | NEW HITS 96 | Global TV/ |
| 20 July | 4 | BIG MIX 96 | EMI TV/Warner |
| 17 August | 1 | THE BEST DANCE ALBUM IN THE WORLD... EVER! 6 | Virgin |
| 24 August | 7 | NOW THAT'S WHAT I CALL MUSIC! 34 | EMI/Virgin/Polygram |
| 12 October | 1 | IN THE MIX 96 – 3 | Virgin |
| 19 October | 4 | KISS IN IBIZA '96 | Polygram TV |
| 16 November | 2 | HUGE HITS 1996 | Warner.Esp/GLOBAL MUSIC TV/SONY MUSIC TV |
| 30 November | 7 | NOW THAT'S WHAT I CALL MUSIC! 35 | EMI/Virgin/Polygram |

## 1997

| DATE | WKS | TITLE | ARTIST |
|------|-----|-------|--------|
| 18 January | 4 | THE ANNUAL II – PETE TONG & BOY GEORGE | Ministry Of Sound |
| 15 February | 1 | IN THE MIX 97 | Virgin |
| 22 February | 1 | THE ANNUAL II – PETE TONG & BOY GEORGE | Warner.Esp/GLOBAL MUSIC TV/SONY MUSIC TV |
| 1 March | 2 | CLUB MIX 97 – VOLUME 2 | Polygram TV |
| 15 March | 1 | THE SOUL ALBUM | Virgin |
| 22 March | 1 | THE BEST... ALBUM IN THE WORLD... EVER! 5 | Virgin/EMI |
| 29 March | 1 | DANCE NATION 3 – PETE TONG & JUDGE JULES | Ministry Of Sound |
| 5 April | 3 | NOW THAT'S WHAT I CALL MUSIC! 36 | EMI/Virgin/Polygram |
| 26 April | 4 | NEW HITS 1997 | Telstar |
| 24 May | 2 | BIG MIX '97 | Warner/Virgin/EMI |
| 7 June | 1 | SMASH HITS – SUMMER '97 | Virgin/EMI |
| 14 June | 4 | THE BEST CLUB ANTHEMS IN THE WORLD... EVER! | Virgin/EMI |
| 12 July | 2 | THE BEST DISCO ALBUM IN THE WORLD | Virgin/EMI |
| 26 July | 4 | NOW THAT'S WHAT I CALL MUSIC! 37 | EMI/Virgin/Polygram |
| 23 August | 3 | FRESH HITS 1997 | Warner.Esp/GLOBAL MUSIC TV/SONY MUSIC TV |
| 13 September | 3 | IBIZA UNCOVERED (TELEVISION COMPILATION) | Virgin/EMI |
| 4 October | 1 | KISS IN IBIZA '97 | Polygram TV |
| 11 October | 1 | IBIZA UNCOVERED (TELEVISION COMPILATION) | Virgin/EMI |
| 18 October | 1 | BIG MIX '97 – VOLUME 2 | VIRGIN/EMI/Warner.Esp |
| 25 October | 1 | THE BEST... ANTHEMS... EVER! | Virgin/EMI |
| 1 November | 1 | NOW DANCE 97 | EMI/Virgin |
| 8 November | 1 | HUGE HITS 1997 | Warner.Esp/GLOBAL MUSIC TV/SONY MUSIC TV |
| 15 November | 2 | THE ANNUAL III – PETE TONG & BOY GEORGE | Ministry Of Sound |
| 29 November | 2 | NOW THAT'S WHAT I CALL MUSIC! 38 | EMI/Virgin/Polygram |
| 13 December | 4 | DIANA PRINCESS OF WALES – TRIBUTE (ROYAL COMPILATION ALBUM) | Diana Memorial Fund |

## 1998

| DATE | WKS | TITLE | ARTIST |
|------|-----|-------|--------|
| 10 January | 2 | NOW THAT'S WHAT I CALL MUSIC! 38 | EMI/Virgin/Polygram |
| 24 January | 2 | THE EIGHTIES MIX | Global Television |
| 7 February | 1 | ULTIMATE CLUB MIX | Polygram TV |
| 14 February | 1 | IN THE MIX 98 | Virgin/EMI |
| 21 February | 1 | LOVE | Polygram TV |
| 28 February | 1 | IN THE MIX 98 | Virgin/EMI |
| 7 March | 1 | FANTASTIC 80'S! | Columbia |
| 14 March | 3 | THE FULL MONTY (OST) | RCA Victor |
| 4 April | 2 | NEW HITS 98 | Warner.Esp/GLOBAL MUSIC TV/SONY MUSIC TV |
| 18 April | 8 | NOW THAT'S WHAT I CALL MUSIC! 39 | EMI/Virgin/Polygram |
| 13 June | 3 | THE BOX HITS 98 – VOLUME 2 | Telstar |
| 4 July | 6 | FRESH HITS 98 | Warner.Esp/GLOBAL MUSIC TV/SONY MUSIC TV |
| 15 August | 4 | NOW THAT'S WHAT I CALL MUSIC! 40 | EMI/Virgin/Polygram |
| 12 September | 1 | THE IBIZA ANNUAL | Ministry Of Sound |
| 19 September | 5 | BIG HITS 98 | Warner.Esp/GLOBAL MUSIC TV/SONY MUSIC TV |
| 24 October | 1 | IN THE MIX IBIZA | Virgin/EMI |
| 31 October | 1 | THE BEST CHART HITS ALBUM IN THE WORLD... EVER! | Virgin/EMI |
| 7 November | 1 | HUGE HITS 1998 | Warner.Esp/GLOBAL MUSIC TV/SONY MUSIC TV |
| 14 November | 2 | THE ANNUAL IV – JUDGE JULES & BOY GEORGE | Ministry Of Sound |
| 28 November | 1 | HUGE HITS 1998 | Warner.Esp/GLOBAL MUSIC TV/SONY MUSIC TV |
| 5 December | 7 | NOW THAT'S WHAT I CALL MUSIC! 41 | EMI/Virgin/Polygram |

## 1999

| DATE | WKS | TITLE | ARTIST |
|------|-----|-------|--------|
| 23 January | 1 | THE BEST CLUB ANTHEMS 99 IN THE WORLD... EVER! | Virgin/EMI |
| 30 January | 2 | CLUBBER'S GUIDE TO... NINETY NINE | Ministry Of Sound |
| 13 February | 1 | EUPHORIA | Telstar |
| 20 February | 1 | LOVE SONGS | Polygram TV/Warner Esp |
| 27 February | 1 | EUPHORIA | Telstar |
| 6 March | 2 | KISS HOUSE NATION | Polygram TV |
| 20 March | 1 | ESPECIALLY FOR YOU | Columbia |
| 27 March | 1 | DANCE NATION 6 – TALL PAUL & BRANDON BLOCK | Ministry Of Sound |
| 3 April | 1 | NEW HITS 99 | Warner.Esp/GLOBAL MUSIC TV/SONY MUSIC TV |
| 10 April | 7 | NOW THAT'S WHAT I CALL MUSIC! 42 | EMI/Virgin/Universal TV |
| 29 May | 3 | TRANCE NATION: MIXED BY SYSTEM F | Ministry Of Sound |
| 19 June | 2 | CLUBBER'S GUIDE TO IBIZA – SUMMER '99 | Ministry Of Sound |
| 3 July | 3 | FRESH HITS 99 | Warner.Esp/GLOBAL MUSIC TV/SONY MUSIC TV |
| 24 July | 1 | THE BEST DANCE ALBUM IN THE WORLD... EVER! 9 | Virgin/EMI |

| DATE | WKS | TITLE | ARTIST |
|---|---|---|---|
| 31 July | 4 | NOW THAT'S WHAT I CALL MUSIC! 43 | EMI/Virgin/Universal TV |
| 28 August | 1 | THE IBIZA ANNUAL: MIXED BY JUDGE JULES + TALL PAUL | |
| | | | Ministry Of Sound |
| 4 September | 2 | BIG HITS 99 | Warner.Esp/GLOBAL MUSIC TV/SONY MUSIC TV |
| 18 September | 3 | KISS IBIZA '99 | Universal Music TV |
| 9 October | 1 | TOP OF THE POPS '99 – VOLUME TWO | Universal Music TV |
| 16 October | 1 | TRANCE NATION 2: MIXED BY FERRY CORSTEN | |
| | | | Ministry Of Sound |
| 23 October | 1 | LAND OF MY FATHERS | Universal Music TV |
| 30 October | 1 | NOW DANCE 2000 | EMI/Virgin |
| 6 November | 4 | HUGE HITS 99 | Warner.Esp/GLOBAL MUSIC TV/SONY MUSIC TV |
| 4 December | 8 | NOW THAT'S WHAT I CALL MUSIC! 44 | EMI/Virgin/Universal TV |

## 2000

| DATE | WKS | TITLE | ARTIST |
|---|---|---|---|
| 29 January | 2 | CLUBBER'S GUIDE TO... 2000 | Ministry Of Sound |
| 12 February | 1 | AYIA NAPA – FANTASY ISLAND | Telstar TV |
| 19 February | 1 | THE LOVE SONGS ALBUM | Warner.Esp/UNIVERSAL TV/GLOBAL TV |
| 26 February | 1 | REWIND – THE SOUND OF UK GARAGE | Ministry Of Sound |
| 4 March | 3 | THE BEACH (ORIGINAL SOUNDTRACK) | London |
| 25 March | 2 | NEW HITS 2000 | Warner.Esp/GLOBAL TV/SONY TV |
| 8 April | 1 | NEW WOMAN 2000 | Virgin/EMI |
| 15 April | 1 | DANCE NATION – TALL PAUL/BRANDON BLOCK | |
| | | | Ministry Of Sound |
| 22 April | 1 | GIRLS 2K | Virgin/EMI |
| 29 April | 6 | NOW THAT'S WHAT I CALL MUSIC! 45 | EMI/Virgin/Universal |
| 10 June | 1 | CLUBBER'S GUIDE TO IBIZA – SUMMER 2000 | |
| | | | Ministry Of Sound |
| 17 June | 1 | TOP OF THE POPS 2000 – VOLUME 2 | Universal TV |
| 24 June | 3 | CLUB MIX IBIZA 2000 | Universal TV |
| 15 July | 2 | FRESH HITS – VOLUME 1 | Warner.Esp/GLOBAL TV/SONY TV |
| 29 July | 1 | KISS CLUBLIFE SUMMER 2000 | Universal TV |
| 5 August | 4 | NOW THAT'S WHAT I CALL MUSIC! 46 | EMI/Virgin/Universal |
| 2 September | 3 | THE IBIZA ANNUAL – SUMMER 2000 | Ministry Of Sound |
| 23 September | 2 | KISS IBIZA 2000 | Universal TV |
| 7 October | 3 | TRANCE NATION 4 | Ministry Of Sound |
| 28 October | 1 | CLUBMIX 2000 VOLUME 2 | Universal TV |
| 4 November | 1 | NOW DANCE 2001 | Virgin/EMI |
| 11 November | 2 | THE ANNUAL 2000 – JUDGE JULES/TALL PAUL | |
| | | | Ministry Of Sound |
| 25 November | 1 | CREAM ANTHEMS 2001 | Virgin/EMI |
| 2 December | 7 | NOW THAT'S WHAT I CALL MUSIC! 47 | EMI/Virgin/Universal |

## 2001

| DATE | WKS | TITLE | ARTIST |
|---|---|---|---|
| 20 January | 2 | CLUBBERS GUIDE TO 2001 | Ministry Of Sound |
| 3 February | 2 | BREAKDOWN – VERY BEST OF EUPHORIC DANCE | |
| | | | Telstar TV |
| 17 February | 6 | THE CHILL OUT SESSION | Ministry Of Sound |
| 31 March | 1 | NEW WOMAN 2001 | Virgin/EMI |
| 7 April | 2 | THE ANNUAL – SPRING 2001 | Ministry Of Sound |
| 21 April | 3 | NOW THAT'S WHAT I CALL MUSIC! 48 | EMI/Virgin/Universal |
| 12 May | 7 | BRIDGET JONES' DIARY (ORIGINAL SOUNDTRACK) | |
| | | | Mercury |
| 23 June | 7 | CAPITAL GOLD LEGENDS | Virgin/EMI |
| 11 August | 6 | NOW THAT'S WHAT I CALL MUSIC! 49 | EMI/Virgin/Universal |
| 29 September | 2 | HITS 50 | BMG/Sony/Telstar/WSM |
| 13 October | 1 | THE CLASSIC CHILLOUT ALBUM | Columbia |
| 20 October | 2 | PEPSI CHART 2002 | Virgin/EMI |
| 3 November | 3 | NOW DANCE 2002 | Virgin/EMI |
| 24 November | 1 | THE ANNUAL 2002 | Ministry Of Sound |
| 1 December | 7 | NOW THAT'S WHAT I CALL MUSIC! 50 | Virgin/EMI/Universal |

## 2002

| DATE | WKS | TITLE | ARTIST |
|---|---|---|---|
| 19 January | 3 | CLUBBERS GUIDE TO 2002 | Ministry Of Sound |
| 9 February | 1 | BEST CLUB ANTHEMS 2002 | Virgin/EMI |
| 16 February | 1 | CLUB MIX 2002 | Universal TV |
| 23 February | 1 | LOVE SO STRONG | WSM |
| 2 March | 2 | SCHOOL DISCO.COM – SPRING TERM | Columbia |
| 16 March | 1 | NEW WOMAN 2002 | Virgin/EMI |
| 23 March | 2 | SUPERCHARGED | UMTV/WSM |
| 6 April | 2 | NOW THAT'S WHAT I CALL MUSIC! 51 | Virgin/EMI/Universal |
| 20 April | 4 | POP IDOL – THE BIG BAND ALBUM | S |
| 18 May | 1 | NOW THAT'S WHAT I CALL MUSIC! 51 | Virgin/EMI/Universal |
| 25 May | 1 | KISSTORY | Universal TV |
| 1 June | 1 | THE BEST SUMMER ALBUM 2002 | Sony TV |
| 8 June | 1 | CLUBBERS GUIDE TO IBIZA 2002 | Ministry Of Sound |
| 22 June | 1 | CAPITAL GOLD ROCK LEGENDS | Virgin/EMI |
| 29 June | 1 | THE VERY BEST OF MTV UNPLUGGED | WSM/Universal |
| 6 July | 3 | CLUBLAND | Universal TV |
| 3 August | 4 | NOW THAT'S WHAT I CALL MUSIC! 52 | Virgin/EMI/Universal |
| 15 August | 1 | SMASH HITS SUMMER 2002 | Virgin/EMI |
| 7 September | 1 | THE VERY BEST OF PURE R&B – THE SUMMER | |
| | | | Telstar |
| 14 September | 5 | SMASH HITS – LET'S PARTY | EMI/Virgin/Universal |
| 19 October | 1 | NEW WOMAN – THE AUTUMN COLLECTION | |
| | | | Virgin/EMI |
| 26 October | 1 | NOW DANCE 2003 | Virgin |
| 2 November | 2 | HITS 54 | BMG TV |
| 16 November | 1 | THE ANNUAL 2003 | Ministry Of Sound |
| 23 November | 1 | CLUBLAND II – THE RIDE OF YOUR LIFE | Universal |
| 30 November | 7 | NOW THAT'S WHAT I CALL MUSIC! 53 | EMI |

## 2003

| DATE | WKS | TITLE | ARTIST |
|---|---|---|---|
| 18 January | 1 | CLUBBERS GUIDE 2003 | Ministry Of Sound |
| 25 January | 2 | 8 MILE (ORIGINAL SOUNDTRACK) | Interscope |
| 15 February | 1 | LOVE – ETERNAL LOVESONGS | Universal TV |
| 1 March | 1 | CLUB MIX 2003 | Universal TV |
| 8 March | 2 | THE VERY BEST OF MTV UNPLUGGED 2 | WSM/Universal |
| 22 March | 2 | THE VERY BEST OF COLD FEET (TELEVISION COMPILATION) | |
| | | | Universal TV |
| 12 April | 2 | HITS 55 | BMG TV |
| 26 April | 7 | NOW THAT'S WHAT I CALL MUSIC! 54 | EMI |
| 14 June | 3 | POWER BALLADS | Virgin/EMI |
| 5 July | 3 | CLUBLAND III | UMTV/AATW |
| 26 July | 1 | HITS 56 | BMG TV |
| 2 August | 5 | NOW THAT'S WHAT I CALL MUSIC! 55 | EMI |
| 6 September | 3 | KISS PRESENTS R&B COLLABORATIONS | |
| | | | Universal |
| 27 September | 2 | CLUBMIX SUMMER 2003 | UMTV/AATW |
| 11 October | 3 | NOW DECADES | EMI/Virgin/Universal |
| 1 November | 1 | GREASEMANIA | Polydor |
| 8 November | 1 | NOW DANCE 2004 | Virgin/EMI |
| 15 November | 1 | WESTWOOD – PLATINUM EDITION | Def Jam/Universal |
| 22 November | 1 | CLUBLAND 4 | UMTV/AATW |
| 29 November | 7 | NOW THAT'S WHAT I CALL MUSIC! 56 | EMI/Virgin/Universal |

## 2004

| DATE | WKS | TITLE | ARTIST |
|---|---|---|---|
| 18 January | 3 | CLUBBERS GUIDE – 2004 | Ministry Of Sound |
| 7 February | 1 | KISS SMOOTH R&B | Universal |
| 14 February | 1 | CLUBMIX 2004 | UMTV/AATW |
| 21 February | 1 | BEAUTIFUL | BMG TV |
| 28 February | 1 | THE BRIT AWARDS ALBUM 2003 | BMG |
| 6 March | 1 | CLUBMIX 2004 | UMTV/AATW |
| 13 March | 1 | HITS 40 UK | BMG |
| 20 March | 1 | FLOORFILLERS | UMTV/AATW |
| 27 March | 1 | THE VERY BEST OF NEW WOMAN | Virgin/EMI |
| 3 April | 2 | ULTIMATE DIRTY DANCING | RCA |
| 17 April | 7 | NOW THAT'S WHAT I CALL MUSIC! 57 | EMI/Virgin/Universal |
| 12 June | 1 | HITS 58 | BMG/Sony/Telstar/WSM |
| 19 June | 2 | POWER BALLADS II | BMG/Sony/Telstar/WSM |

# ALPHABETICAL LISTING OF THE ALBUMS

This section lists, in alphabetical order of album title, every chart hit since the first chart was compiled in 1958 through to today. Each album title is then followed by the full artist credit and the year in which the record first made its appearance on the charts.

Various artists albums are listed in alphabetical order and then show the label credit under which the album is listed in the main section. Of course, an authentic alphabetical listing would have *Now That's What I Call Music! 53* ahead of *Now That's What I Call Music! 2*, but it has been decided to list these chronologically rather than alphabetically.

Similarly, countless artists have released albums called *Greatest Hits*, *Best Of* or *Live*; these are also listed chronologically.

() SIGUR ROS 2002
A JETHRO TULL 1980
THE A LIST A1 2000
AALIYAH AALIYAH 2001
AARON CARTER AARON CARTER 1998
ABACAB GENESIS 1981
ABANDONED SHOPPING TROLLEY HOTLINE GOMEZ 2000
ABBA ABBA 1976
ABBAMANIA VARIOUS ARTISTS (POLYDOR) 1999
THE ABBEY DOWNSIDE ABBEY MONKS & CHOIRBOYS 1996
ABBEY ROAD BEATLES 1969
ABC JACKSON FIVE 1970
ABDUCTION EAT STATIC 1993
ABOMINOG URIAH HEEP 1982
ABOUT A BOY – OST BADLY DRAWN BOY 2002
ABOUT FACE DAVID GILMOUR 1984
ABOUT TIME STRANGLERS 1995
ABOUT TIME 2 CLOCK 1997
ABOVE MAD SEASON 1995
ABOVE THE RIM (OST) FILM SOUNDTRACK 1994
ABRACADABRA STEVE MILLER BAND 1982
ABRACADABRA ABC 1991
ABRAXAS SANTANA 1970
ABRIENDO PUERTAS GLORIA ESTEFAN 1995
ABSENT FRIENDS DIVINE COMEDY 2004
ABSOLUTE ABBA ABBA 1988
ABSOLUTE BEGINNERS (OST) FILM SOUNDTRACK 1986
ABSOLUTE EUPHORIA – DAVE PEARCE VARIOUS ARTISTS (TELSTAR) 2002
THE ABSOLUTE GAME SKIDS 1980
ABSOLUTE GOLD VARIOUS ARTISTS (SONY) 1997
ABSOLUTE ROCK 'N' ROLL VARIOUS ARTISTS (STARBLEND) 1986
ABSOLUTELY MADNESS 1980
ABSOLUTELY ABC 1990
ABSOLUTELY LIVE DOORS 1970
ABSOLUTELY LIVE ROD STEWART 1982
ABSOLUTELY MAD MADHOUSE 2002
ABSOLUTION MUSE 2003
ABSOLUTION – ROCK THE ALTERNATIVE WAY VARIOUS ARTISTS (POLYDOR) 1991
ABSTRACT EMOTIONS RANDY CRAWFORD 1986
ABSTRACT THEORY ABS 2003
AC/DC LIVE AC/DC 1992
ACCELERATOR FUTURE SOUND OF LONDON 1992
ACCESS ALL AREAS VARIOUS ARTISTS (POSITIVA) 1997
ACCIDENT OF BIRTH BRUCE DICKINSON 1997
ACCORDING TO MY HEART JIM REEVES 1969
ACE IAN VAN DAHL 2002
ACE A'S + KILLER B'S DODGY 1998
ACE OF SPADES MOTORHEAD 1980
ACES AND KINGS – THE BEST OF GO WEST GO WEST 1993
ACHTUNG BABY U2 1991
ACID JAZZ AND OTHER ILLICIT GROOVES VARIOUS ARTISTS (URBAN) 1988
ACID TRAX MAGAMIX VOLUME 1 VARIOUS ARTISTS (SERIOUS) 1988
ACKER MR ACKER BILK 1961
ACKER BILK'S OMNIBUS MR ACKER BILK 1960
ACME JON SPENCER BLUES EXPLOSION 1998
ACOUSTIC VARIOUS ARTISTS (ECHO) 2002
ACOUSTIC FREEWAY VARIOUS ARTISTS (POLYGRAM) 1995
ACOUSTIC MOODS VARIOUS ARTISTS (POLYGRAM) 1994
ACOUSTIC MOODS IN TUNE 1995
ACOUSTIC ROCK VARIOUS ARTISTS (POLYGRAM) 1995
ACOUSTIC SOUL INDIA ARIE 2001
ACOUSTIC 2 VARIOUS ARTISTS (ECHO/V2) 2002
ACROSS A CROWDED ROOM RICHARD THOMPSON 1985
ACROSS THE WIRE – LIVE IN NEW YORK COUNTING CROWS 1998
ACTING VERY STRANGE MIKE RUTHERFORD 1982
ACTION REPLAY VARIOUS ARTISTS (K-TEL) 1979
ACTION TRAX VARIOUS ARTISTS (K-TEL) 1982
ADAGIO 2 HERBERT VON KARAJAN CONDUCTING THE BERLIN PHILHARMONIC ORCHESTRA 1996
ADAM ADAM FAITH 1960

ADAM AND EVE CATHERINE WHEEL 1998
ADAM FAITH ADAM FAITH 1962
ADDICTED TO BASS VARIOUS ARTISTS (MINISTRY OF SOUND) 2002
ADDICTED TO TRANCE VARIOUS ARTISTS (MINISTRY OF SOUND) 2002
ADDICTIONS VOLUME 1 ROBERT PALMER 1989
ADDICTIONS VOLUME 2 ROBERT PALMER 1992
ADEVA ADEVA 1989
ADGE CUTLER AND THE WURZELS WURZELS 1967
ADIEMUS II – CANTATA MUNDI ADIEMUS 1997
ADIEMUS III – DANCES OF TIME ADIEMUS 1998
ADORE SMASHING PUMPKINS 1998
ADRENALIN VARIOUS ARTISTS (TELSTAR) 1999
ADRENALIZE DEF LEPPARD 1992
ADVANCE LFO 1996
ADVENTURE TELEVISION 1978
ADVENTURES IN TIN TIN OUT LAND TIN TIN OUT 1996
ADVENTURES IN UTOPIA UTOPIA 1980
THE ADVENTURES OF THE HERSHAM BOYS SHAM 69 1979
THE ADVENTURES OF THIN LIZZY THIN LIZZY 1981
AFFECTION LISA STANSFIELD 1989
AFFIRMATION SAVAGE GARDEN 1999
AFRAID OF SUNLIGHT MARILLION 1995
AFRICA TO AMERICA: THE JOURNEY OF THE DRUM SOUNDS OF BLACKNESS 1994
AFRODISIAC VARIOUS ARTISTS (UNIVERSAL) 1999
AFTER ALL THESE YEARS FOSTER & ALLEN 1986
AFTER DARK RAY PARKER JR 1987
AFTER DARK TOM JONES 1989
AFTER DARK VARIOUS ARTISTS (COLUMBIA) 1993
AFTER HOURS GARY MOORE 1992
AFTER HOURS BILL TARMEY 1996
AFTER MIDNIGHT VARIOUS ARTISTS (POLYGRAM) 1994
AFTER MURDER PARK AUTEURS 1996
AFTER THE BREAK TELEVISION COMPILATION 1997
AFTER THE DANCE VARIOUS ARTISTS (TELSTAR) 1991
AFTER THE GOLDRUSH NEIL YOUNG 1970
AFTER THE LAUGHTER FREDDIE STARR 1989
AFTER THE WAR GARY MOORE 1989
AFTERBURNER ZZ TOP 1985
AFTERGLOW CROWDED HOUSE 2000
AFTERGLOW SARAH McLACHLAN 2004
AFTERMATH ROLLING STONES 1966
AGAETIS BYRJUN SIGUR ROS 2000
AGAINST SEPULTURA 1998
AGAINST ALL ODDS (OST) FILM SOUNDTRACK 1984
AGAINST PERFECTION ADORABLE 1993
AGAINST THE WIND BOB SEGER & THE SILVER BULLET BAND 1980
AGE AIN'T NOTHING BUT A NUMBER AALIYAH 1994
THE AGE OF CONSENT BRONSKI BEAT 1984
THE AGE OF PLASTIC BUGGLES 1980
AGENT PROVOCATEUR FOREIGNER 1984
AGENTS OF FORTUNE BLUE OYSTER CULT 1976
AGES OF MANN – 22 CLASSIC HITS OF THE 60'S MANFRED MANN 1993
AGNUS DEI CHOIR OF NEW COLLEGE OXFORD/EDWARD HIGGINBOTTOM 1996
AGNUS DEI II CHOIR OF NEW COLLEGE OXFORD/EDWARD HIGGINBOTTOM 1998
AHEAD RINGS OUT BLODWYN PIG 1969
AIN'T COMPLAINING STATUS QUO 1988
AIN'T NO STOPPIN' – ENIGMA 1981
AIR CONDITIONING CURVED AIR 1970
THE AIR THAT I BREATHE – THE BEST OF THE HOLLIES HOLLIES 1993
AIR, EARTH, FIRE, WATER THIRD EAR BAND 1970
AIRDRAWN DAGGER SASHA 2002
AJA STEELY DAN 1977
AL AL GREEN 1992
AL GREEN'S GREATEST HITS AL GREEN 1975
THE AL JOLSON COLLECTION AL JOLSON 1983
ALADDIN (OST) FILM SOUNDTRACK 1994
ALADDIN AND HIS WONDERFUL LAMP CLIFF RICHARD & THE SHADOWS 1965

ALADDIN SANE DAVID BOWIE 1973
ALAN TITCHMARSH – IN A COUNTRY GARDEN VARIOUS ARTISTS (SONY) 2000
ALANNAH MYLES ALANNAH MYLES 1990
ALBEDO 0.39 VANGELIS 1976
THE ALBUM ABBA 1978
THE ALBUM MANTRONIX 1986
THE ALBUM TELETUBBIES 1998
THE ALBUM VARIOUS ARTISTS (VIRGIN) 2001
THE ALBUM BOB THE BUILDER 2001
THE ALBUM 2 VARIOUS ARTISTS (VIRGIN) 2002
THE ALBUM 3 VARIOUS ARTISTS (VIRGIN) 2002
THE ALBUM 4 VARIOUS ARTISTS (VIRGIN) 2002
THE ALBUM OF THE SOUNDTRACK OF THE TRAILER OF THE FILM OF MONTY PYTHON AND THE HOLY GRAIL (OST) MONTY PYTHON'S FLYING CIRCUS 1975
ALBUM OF THE YEAR FAITH NO MORE 1997
ALBUM/CASSETTE PUBLIC IMAGE LTD 1986
ALCHEMY – DIRE STRAITS LIVE DIRE STRAITS 1984
ALED ALED JONES 2002
ALED (MUSIC FROM THE TV SERIES) ALED JONES 1987
ALED JONES WITH THE BBC WELSH CHORUS ALED JONES WITH THE BBC WELSH CHORUS 1985
ALEXANDER O'NEAL ALEXANDER O'NEAL 1985
ALF ALISON MOYET 1984
ALI G INDAHOUSE – DA SOUNDTRACK FILM SOUNDTRACK 2002
ALICE TOM WAITS 2002
ALICE COOPER GOES TO HELL ALICE COOPER 1976
ALICE IN CHAINS ALICE IN CHAINS 1995
ALICE'S RESTAURANT ARLO GUTHRIE 1970
ALIEN CHILD QFX 1997
ALIEN LOVE SECRETS STEVE VAI 1995
ALIENS ATE MY BUICK THOMAS DOLBY 1988
ALISHA RULES THE WORLD ALISHA'S ATTIC 1996
ALIVE KISS 1977
ALIVE III KISS 1993
ALIVE IN AMERICA STEELY DAN 1995
ALIVE IN HELL MEAT LOAF 1994
ALIVE ON ARRIVAL STEVE FORBERT 1979
ALIVE! KISS 1976
ALIVE, SHE CRIED DOORS 1983
ALL ABOARD VARIOUS ARTISTS (EMI) 1979
ALL ABOUT CHEMISTRY SEMISONIC 2001
ALL ABOUT EVE ALL ABOUT EVE 1988
ALL ABOUT LOVE JOYCE SIMS 1989
ALL ALONE AM I BRENDA LEE 1963
ALL AMERICAN ALIEN BOY IAN HUNTER 1976
THE ALL AMERICAN REJECTS ALL-AMERICAN REJECTS 2003
ALL AROUND MY HAT STEELEYE SPAN 1975
ALL AROUND THE WORLD JASON DONOVAN 1993
ALL BY MYSELF VARIOUS ARTISTS (K-TEL) 1984
ALL BY MYSELF REGINA BELLE 1987
ALL BY MYSELF VARIOUS ARTISTS (DOVER) 1990
ALL BY MYSELF VOLUME 2 VARIOUS ARTISTS (DOVER) 1991
ALL CHANGE CAST 1995
ALL CLUBBED UP – THE BEST OF KELLY LLORENNA KELLY LLORENNA 2002
ALL DAY EVERY DAY N-TYCE 1998
ALL DIRECTIONS TEMPTATIONS 1973
ALL EYEZ ON ME 2PAC 1996
ALL FOR A SONG BARBARA DICKSON 1982
ALL FOR YOU JOHNNY MATHIS 1980
ALL FOR YOU JANET JACKSON 2001
ALL HITS ALL SAINTS 2001
ALL I REALLY WANT TO DO CHER 1965
ALL IN A NIGHT'S WORK KC & THE SUNSHINE BAND 1983
ALL IN THE MIND KENNY 'DOPE' PRESENTS THE BUCKETHEADS 1996
ALL IN THE NAME OF LOVE ATLANTIC STARR 1987
ALL IS DREAM MERCURY REV 2001
ALL KILLER NO FILLER SUM 41 2001
ALL LIVE AND ALL OF THE NIGHT STRANGLERS 1988
ALL MOD CONS JAM 1978

ALL MY LOVE VARIOUS ARTISTS (WARNER BROTHERS) 1997

ALL 'N' ALL EARTH WIND & FIRE 1978

ALL NEW – THE BEST FOOTIE ANTHEMS IN THE WORLD... EVER! – VARIOUS ARTISTS (VIRGIN) 1998

ALL NIGHT LONG VARIOUS ARTISTS (POLYGRAM) 1993

ALL OF THIS AND NOTHING PSYCHEDELIC FURS 1988

ALL OR NOTHING/2 X 2 MILLI VANILLI 1989

ALL OUR LOVE GLADYS KNIGHT & THE PIPS 1988

ALL OVER THE PLACE BANGLES 1985

ALL RIGHT NOW PEPSI & SHIRLIE 1987

ALL RISE BLUE 2001

ALL SAINTS ALL SAINTS 1997

ALL STAR FESTIVAL VARIOUS ARTISTS (PHILIPS) 1963

ALL SYSTEMS GO VINNIE VINCENT 1988

ALL THAT I AM JOE 1997

ALL THAT JAZZ BREATHE 1988

ALL THAT MATTERS MICHAEL BOLTON 1997

ALL THAT YOU CAN'T LEAVE BEHIND U2 2000

ALL THE BEST STIFF LITTLE FINGERS 1983

ALL THE BEST LEO SAYER 1993

ALL THE BEST – LOVE DUETS VOLUME 1 VARIOUS ARTISTS (TELSTAR) 1992

ALL THE BEST COWBOYS HAVE CHINESE EYES PETE TOWNSHEND 1982

ALL THE BEST! – PAUL McCARTNEY 1987

ALL THE FUN OF THE FAIR DAVID ESSEX 1975

ALL THE GREAT HITS DIANA ROSS 1981

ALL THE HITS EDDY GRANT 1984

ALL THE HITS & ALL NEW LOVE SONGS KENNY ROGERS 1999

ALL THE HITS AND MORE HOLLIES 1988

ALL THE HITS BY ALL THE STARS VARIOUS ARTISTS (PYE) 1962

ALL THE WAY BRENDA LEE 1962

ALL THE WAY... A DECADE OF SONGS CELINE DION 1999

ALL THE WAY FROM TUAM SAW DOCTORS 1992

ALL THE YOUNG DUDES MOTT THE HOOPLE 1972

ALL THINGS MUST PASS GEORGE HARRISON 1970

ALL THIS AND HEAVEN TOO ANDREW GOLD 1978

ALL THIS AND WORLD WAR II (OST) FILM SOUNDTRACK 1976

ALL THIS TIME STING 2001

ALL THIS USELESS BEAUTY ELVIS COSTELLO & THE ATTRACTIONS 1996

ALL THROUGH THE NIGHT ALED JONES WITH THE BBC WELSH CHORUS 1985

ALL TIME CLASSIC COUNTRY TEARJERKERS VARIOUS ARTISTS (WARNER BROTHERS) 2003

ALL TIME CLASSIC ROCK N ROLL TEARJERKERS VARIOUS ARTISTS (WARNER BROTHERS) 2003

ALL TIME CLASSIC SOUL HEARTBREAKERS VARIOUS ARTISTS (TELSTAR) 2003

ALL TIME CLASSIC TEARJERKERS VARIOUS ARTISTS (WARNER BROTHERS) 2002

THE ALL TIME GREATEST COUNTRY SONGS VARIOUS ARTISTS (COLUMBIA) 1997

THE ALL TIME GREATEST HITS OF DANCE VARIOUS ARTISTS (TELSTAR) 1993

THE ALL TIME GREATEST LOVE SONGS VARIOUS ARTISTS (SONY) 2000

THE ALL TIME GREATEST LOVE SONGS – VOLUME 4 VARIOUS ARTISTS (SONY) 1999

THE ALL TIME GREATEST LOVE SONGS OF THE 60'S, 70'S, 80'S & 90'S VOLUME III VARIOUS ARTISTS (COLUMBIA) 1998

THE ALL TIME GREATEST LOVE SONGS... – VARIOUS ARTISTS (COLUMBIA) 1996

THE ALL TIME GREATEST LOVE SONGS... VOLUME II VARIOUS ARTISTS (COLUMBIA) 1997

THE ALL TIME GREATEST MOVIE SONGS VARIOUS ARTISTS (SONY) 1998

THE ALL TIME GREATEST MOVIE SONGS – VOLUME TWO VARIOUS ARTISTS (SONY) 1999

ALL TIME GREATEST MOVIE SONGS 2001 VARIOUS ARTISTS (COLUMBIA) 2001

THE ALL TIME GREATEST POP ALBUM VARIOUS ARTISTS (COLUMBIA) 1999

THE ALL TIME GREATEST ROCK SONGS VARIOUS ARTISTS (SONY) 1997

ALL TO YOURSELF JACK JONES 1977

ALL TOGETHER NOW ARGENT 1972

ALL TOGETHER NOW VARIOUS ARTISTS (UNIVERSAL) 2001

ALL TRUE MAN ALEXANDER O'NEAL 1991

ALL WOMAN VARIOUS ARTISTS (QUALITY PRICE MUSIC) 1992

ALL WOMAN – THE COMPLETE WOMAN VARIOUS ARTISTS (QUALITY PRICE MUSIC) 1993

ALL WOMAN 2 VARIOUS ARTISTS (QUALITY PRICE MUSIC) 1992

ALL WOMAN 3 VARIOUS ARTISTS (QUALITY PRICE MUSIC) 1994

ALL WOMAN 4 VARIOUS ARTISTS (QUALITY PRICE MUSIC) 1994

ALL WORLD LL COOL J 1996

ALL WRAPPED UP UNDERTONES 1983

ALL YEARS LEAVING STANDS 2004

ALL YOU CAN EAT K.D. LANG 1995

ALL YOU NEED IS LOVE VARIOUS ARTISTS (GLOBAL) 2000

ALL 4 ONE ALL-4-ONE 1994

ALLEZ! OLA! OLE! – VARIOUS ARTISTS (COLUMBIA) 1998

ALLIED FORCES TRIUMPH 1981

THE ALLNIGHTER GLENN FREY 1985

ALL'S BREAKING LOOSE... – WOLFSBANE 1990

ALL TIME GREATEST HITS ROY ORBISON 1973

ALL TIME PARTY HITS JOE LOSS & HIS ORCHESTRA 1971

ALL TIME PARTY HITS VARIOUS ARTISTS (WARWICK) 1975

ALLY MCBEAL – FOR ONCE IN MY LIFE VARIOUS ARTISTS (EPIC) 2001

ALMA CARIBENA – CARIBBEAN SOUL GLORIA ESTEFAN 2000

ALMOST BLUE ELVIS COSTELLO & THE ATTRACTIONS 1981

ALMOST FAMOUS LUMIDEE 2003

ALMOST HERE UNBELIEVABLE TRUTH 1998

ALMOST IN LOVE ELVIS PRESLEY 1971

ALMOST THERE ANDY WILLIAMS 1965

ALOHA FROM HAWAII VIA SATELLITE (OST TV) ELVIS PRESLEY 1973

ALONE NANA MOUSKOURI 1986

ALONE TOGETHER DONNY OSMOND 1973

ALONE WITH EVERYBODY RICHARD ASHCROFT 2000

ALONG CAME JONES TOM JONES 1965

ALPHA ASIA 1983

ALPHABET CITY ABC 1987

ALTERNATIVE PET SHOP BOYS 1995

ALTERNATIVE EIGHTIES VARIOUS ARTISTS (COLUMBIA) 2002

ALTERNATIVE 90S VARIOUS ARTISTS (COLUMBIA) 2002

ALTERNATIVE 60'S VARIOUS ARTISTS (COLUMBIA) 2002

ALTITUDE SYSTEM 7 1992

ALTITUDE ALT 1995

ALTOGETHER NOLANS 1982

THE ALTOGETHER ORBITAL 2001

ALVIN STARDUST ALVIN STARDUST 1974

ALWAYS VARIOUS ARTISTS (K-TEL) 1987

ALWAYS HAZELL DEAN 1988

ALWAYS MICHAEL BALL 1993

ALWAYS & FOREVER ETERNAL 1993

ALWAYS & FOREVER VARIOUS ARTISTS (SONY) 2003

ALWAYS & FOREVER II VARIOUS ARTISTS (SONY) 2003

ALWAYS AND FOREVER – THE COLLECTION VARIOUS ARTISTS (IMPRESSION) 1984

ALWAYS AND FOREVER THE LOVE ALBUM VARIOUS ARTISTS (TELSTAR) 1987

ALWAYS GUARANTEED CLIFF RICHARD 1987

ALWAYS ON MY MIND – ULTIMATE LOVE SONGS ELVIS PRESLEY 1997

ALWAYS THERE MARTI WEBB 1986

AM I NOT YOUR GIRL? – SINEAD O'CONNOR 1992

AMADEUS (OST) NEVILLE MARRINER & THE ACADEMY OF ST. MARTIN IN THE FIELDS 1985

THE AMALGAMUT FILTER 2002

AMANDA MARSHALL AMANDA MARSHALL 1996

AMANDLA MILES DAVIS 1989

AMAROK MIKE OLDFIELD 1990

AMAZING ELKIE BROOKS WITH THE ROYAL PHILHARMONIC ORCHESTRA 1996

AMAZING DARTS DARTS 1978

AMAZING GRACE JUDY COLLINS 1985

AMAZING GRACE SPIRITUALIZED 2003

THE AMAZING KAMIKAZE SYNDROME SLADE 1983

AMAZING THINGS RUNRIG 1993

AMAZULU AMAZULU 1986

AMBIENT 4 ON LAND BRIAN ENO 1982

AMBIENT DUB VOLUME 2 – EARTH JUICE VARIOUS ARTISTS (BEYOND) 1993

AMBIENT MOODS VARIOUS ARTISTS (POLYGRAM) 1996

AMERICA HERB ALPERT & THE TIJUANA BRASS 1971

AMERICA AMERICA 1972

AMERICA'S SWEETHEART COURTNEY LOVE 2004

THE AMERICAN ADVENTURE ELECTRIC SOFT PARADE 2003

AMERICAN CAESAR IGGY POP 1993

THE AMERICAN DINER VARIOUS ARTISTS (DINO) 1995

AMERICAN DREAM VARIOUS ARTISTS (SONY) 2000

AMERICAN DREAMS VARIOUS ARTISTS (STARBLEND) 1985

AMERICAN ENGLISH WAX 1987

AMERICAN FOOL JOHN COUGAR 1982

AMERICAN GRAFFITI (OST) FILM SOUNDTRACK 1974

AMERICAN HEARTBEAT VARIOUS ARTISTS (EPIC) 1984

AMERICAN LIFE MADONNA 2003

AMERICAN PIE DON MCLEAN 1972

AMERICAN PIE – THE GREATEST HITS DON MCLEAN 2000

AMERICAN PIE 2 (OST) FILM SOUNDTRACK 2001

AMERICAN RECORDINGS TV – THE MAN COMES AROUND JOHNNY CASH 2004

AMERICAN STARS 'N' BARS NEIL YOUNG 1977

AMERICAN THIGHS VERUCA SALT 1994

AMERICAN TUNE EVA CASSIDY 2003

AMERICANA OFFSPRING 1998

AMERICA'S LEAST WANTED UGLY KID JOE 1992

AMERIKKA'S MOST WANTED ICE CUBE 1990

AMIGOS SANTANA 1976

AMIGOS PARA SIEMPRE (FRIENDS FOR LIFE) JOSE CARRERAS & SARAH BRIGHTMAN 1992

AMMONIA AVENUE ALAN PARSONS PROJECT 1984

AMNESIA RICHARD THOMPSON 1988

AMNESIAC RADIOHEAD 2001

AMONG MY SWAN MAZZY STAR 1996

AMONG THE LIVING ANTHRAX 1987

AMOR JULIO IGLESIAS 1982

AMORE – THE LOVE ALBUM LUCIANO PAVAROTTI 2001

AMORICA BLACK CROWES 1994

AMOUR – THE ULTIMATE LOVE COLLECTION VARIOUS ARTISTS (POLYGRAM) 1997

AMPLIFIED HEART EVERYTHING BUT THE GIRL 1994

AMUSED TO DEATH ROGER WATERS 1992

AN ALBUM OF HYMNS ALED JONES 1986

AN EMOTIONAL FISH AN EMOTIONAL FISH 1990

AN EVENING WASTED WITH TOM LEHRER TOM LEHRER 1960

AN EVENING WITH DIANA ROSS DIANA ROSS 1977

AN EVENING WITH JOHN DENVER JOHN DENVER 1975

AN EVENING WITH JOHNNERS BRIAN JOHNSTONE 1994

AN INNOCENT MAN BILLY JOEL 1983

AN INSTINCT FOR DETECTION LIONROCK 1996

AN INTROSPECTIVE OF HOUSE: 1ST DIMENSION VARIOUS ARTISTS (SOUND DIMENSION) 1997

AN INTROSPECTIVE OF HOUSE: 2ND DIMENSION VARIOUS ARTISTS (SOUND DIMENSION) 1997

AN INTROSPECTIVE OF HOUSE: 3RD DIMENSION VARIOUS ARTISTS (SOUND DIMENSION) 1997

AN OFFICER AND A GENTLEMAN (OST) FILM SOUNDTRACK 1983

THE ANALOGUE THEATRE C.J. BOLLAND 1996

ANAM CLANNAD 1990

ANARCHY CHUMBAWAMBA 1994

ANARCHY BUSTA RHYMES 2000

ANASTACIA ANASTACIA 2004

ANCIENT HEART TANITA TIKARAM 1988
AND JOHN MARTYN 1996
AND ALL BECAUSE THE LADY LOVES... – VARIOUS ARTISTS (DOVER) 1989
AND ALL THAT COULD HAVE BEEN – LIVE NINE INCH NAILS 2002
AND I LOVE YOU SO SHIRLEY BASSEY 1972
AND I LOVE YOU SO PERRY COMO 1973
AND I LOVE YOU SO HOWARD KEEL 1984
... AND JUSTICE FOR ALL METALLICA 1988
AND LOVE SAID NO – 1997–2004 H.I.M. 2004
AND NOW THE LEGACY BEGINS DREAM WARRIORS 1991
... AND OUT COME THE WOLVES RANCID 1995
AND STILL I RISE ALISON LIMERICK 1992
... AND THE BEST GOES ON VARIOUS ARTISTS (TELSTAR) 1988
AND THEN JOE 2004
... AND THEN THERE WERE THREE... – GENESIS 1978
ANDERSON BRUFORD WAKEMAN HOWE ANDERSON BRUFORD WAKEMAN HOWE 1989
ANDREW LLOYD WEBBER – GOLD VARIOUS ARTISTS (POLYDOR) 2001
ANDREW LLOYD WEBBER – THE PREMIER COLLECTION VARIOUS ARTISTS (POLYDOR) 1988
ANDREW LLOYD WEBBER: REQUIEM PLACIDO DOMINGO, SARAH BRIGHTMAN, PAUL MILES-KINGSTON, WINCHESTER CATHEDRAL CHOIR & THE ENGLISH CHAMBER 1985
ANDROMEDA HEIGHTS PREFAB SPROUT 1997
ANDY STEWART ANDY STEWART 1962
ANDY WILLIAMS GREATEST HITS ANDY WILLIAMS 1970
ANDY WILLIAMS SHOW ANDY WILLIAMS 1970
ANDY WILLIAMS' SOUND OF MUSIC ANDY WILLIAMS 1970
ANGEL BEACH VARIOUS ARTISTS (BRUNSWICK) 2002
ANGEL BEACH – THE SECOND WAVE VARIOUS ARTISTS (ORB RECORDINGS) 2003
ANGEL CLARE ART GARFUNKEL 1973
ANGEL DELIGHT FAIRPORT CONVENTION 1971
ANGEL DUST FAITH NO MORE 1992
ANGEL STATION MANFRED MANN'S EARTH BAND 1979
ANGELIC UPSTARTS ANGELIC UPSTARTS 1981
ANGELS & ELECTRICITY EDDI READER 1998
ANGELS WITH DIRTY FACES TRICKY 1998
ANGELS WITH DIRTY FACES SUGABABES 2002
ANIMAL BOY RAMONES 1986
ANIMAL MAGIC BLOW MONKEYS 1986
ANIMAL MAGNETISM SCORPIONS 1980
ANIMAL RIGHTS MOBY 1996
ANIMAL TRACKS ANIMALS 1965
ANIMALISMS ANIMALS 1966
ANIMALIZE KISS 1984
THE ANIMALS ANIMALS 1964
ANIMALS PINK FLOYD 1977
ANIMATION JON ANDERSON 1982
ANNIE (OST) FILM SOUNDTRACK 1982
ANNIVERSARY – 20 YEARS OF HITS TAMMY WYNETTE 1987
THE ANNUAL VARIOUS ARTISTS (MINISTRY OF SOUND) 1995
THE ANNUAL – MILLENNIUM EDITION VARIOUS ARTISTS (MINISTRY OF SOUND) 1999
THE ANNUAL – SPRING 2001 VARIOUS ARTISTS (MINISTRY OF SOUND) 2001
THE ANNUAL SPRING 2003 VARIOUS ARTISTS (MINISTRY OF SOUND) 2003
THE ANNUAL SUMMER 2003 VARIOUS ARTISTS (MINISTRY OF SOUND) 2003
THE ANNUAL 2003 VARIOUS ARTISTS (MINISTRY OF SOUND) 2002
THE ANNUAL 2004 VARIOUS ARTISTS (MINISTRY OF SOUND) 2003
THE ANNUAL 2002 VARIOUS ARTISTS (MINISTRY OF SOUND) 2001
THE ANNUAL IBIZA 2002 VARIOUS ARTISTS (MINISTRY OF SOUND) 2002

THE ANNUAL 2000 – JUDGE JULES/TALL PAUL VARIOUS ARTISTS (MINISTRY OF SOUND) 2000
THE ANNUAL II – PETE TONG & BOY GEORGE VARIOUS ARTISTS (MINISTRY OF SOUND) 1996
THE ANNUAL III – PETE TONG & BOY GEORGE VARIOUS ARTISTS (MINISTRY OF SOUND) 1997
THE ANNUAL IV – JUDGE JULES & BOY GEORGE VARIOUS ARTISTS (MINISTRY OF SOUND) 1998
ANOMIE & BONHOMIE SCRITTI POLITTI 1999
ANOTHER BLACK AND WHITE MINSTREL SHOW GEORGE MITCHELL MINSTRELS 1961
ANOTHER GREY AREA GRAHAM PARKER 1982
ANOTHER KIND OF BLUES U.K. SUBS 1979
ANOTHER LATE NIGHT – GROOVE ARMADA VARIOUS ARTISTS (AZULI) 2001
ANOTHER LEVEL BLACKSTREET 1996
ANOTHER LEVEL ANOTHER LEVEL 1998
ANOTHER MONTY PYTHON RECORD MONTY PYTHON'S FLYING CIRCUS 1971
ANOTHER MUSIC IN A DIFFERENT KITCHEN BUZZCOCKS 1978
ANOTHER NIGHT – U.S. ALBUM REAL MCCOY 1995
ANOTHER PAGE CHRISTOPHER CROSS 1983
ANOTHER PERFECT DAY MOTORHEAD 1983
ANOTHER PERFECT DAY VARIOUS ARTISTS (COLUMBIA) 1998
ANOTHER PLACE AND TIME DONNA SUMMER 1989
ANOTHER SIDE OF BOB DYLAN BOB DYLAN 1964
ANOTHER STEP KIM WILDE 1986
ANOTHER STRING OF HITS SHADOWS 1980
ANOTHER TICKET ERIC CLAPTON 1981
ANOTHER TIME, ANOTHER PLACE ENGELBERT HUMPERDINCK 1971
ANOTHER TIME, ANOTHER PLACE BRYAN FERRY 1974
ANOTHER WORLD BRIAN MAY 1998
ANOTHER YEAR LEO SAYER 1975
ANSWERS TO NOTHING MIDGE URE 1988
ANTENNA ZZ TOP 1994
ANTENNA CAVE IN 2003
ANTHEM TOYAH 1981
ANTHEM BLACK UHURU 1984
ANTHEM LESS THAN JAKE 2003
ANTHEM CLASSICS FROM CLUBLAND VARIOUS ARTISTS (UNIVERSAL) 2003
THE ANTHEMS '92 '97 VARIOUS ARTISTS (UNITED DANCE) 1997
ANTHEMS OF HOUSE VARIOUS ARTISTS (INSPIRED) 2004
ANTHEMS OF TRANCE VARIOUS ARTISTS (INSPIRED) 2004
THE ANTHOLOGY DEEP PURPLE 1985
ANTHOLOGY ALIEN ANT FARM 2001
ANTHOLOGY OCEAN COLOUR SCENE 2003
ANTHOLOGY – THE SOUNDS OF SCIENCE BEASTIE BOYS 1999
ANTHOLOGY – THROUGH THE YEARS TOM PETTY & HEARTBREAKERS 2001
ANTHOLOGY 1 BEATLES 1995
ANTHOLOGY 2 BEATLES 1996
ANTHOLOGY 3 BEATLES 1996
ANTICHRIST SUPERSTAR MARILYN MANSON 1996
THE ANTIDOTE RONNY JORDAN 1992
ANTMUSIC – THE VERY BEST OF ADAM ANT ADAM ANT 1993
ANUTHA ZONE DR. JOHN 1998
THE ANVIL VISAGE 1982
ANY LOVE LUTHER VANDROSS 1988
ANYMORE FOR ANYMORE RONNIE LANE & SLIM CHANCE 1974
ANYTHING DAMNED 1986
ANYTHING FOR YOU GLORIA ESTEFAN & MIAMI MUSIC MACHINE 1988
ANYTHING IS POSSIBLE DEBBIE GIBSON 1991
ANYTIME ANYWHERE RITA COOLIDGE 1977
ANYWAY FAMILY 1970
ANYWAYYAWANNA BEATMASTERS 1989
ANYWHERE NEW MUSIK 1981

APOCADELIC POINT BREAK 2000
APOCALYPSE 91... THE ENEMY STRIKES BLACK PUBLIC ENEMY 1991
APPETITE FOR DESTRUCTION GUNS N' ROSES 1987
APPLE VENUS – VOLUME 1 XTC 1999
APPLE VENUS – VOLUME 2 XTC/WASP STAR 2000
APPROVED BY THE MOTORS MOTORS 1978
APRIL MOON SAM BROWN 1990
AQUALUNG JETHRO TULL 1971
AQUALUNG JETHRO TULL 1999
AQUALUNG AQUALUNG 2002
AQUARIUM AQUA 1997
AQUARIUS AQUA 2000
ARBORESCENCE OZRIC TENTACLES 1994
ARC OF A DIVER STEVE WINWOOD 1981
ARCHETYPE FEAR FACTORY 2004
ARCHITECTURE AND MORALITY ORCHESTRAL MANOEUVRES IN THE DARK 1981
ARCHIVE 1967–1975 GENESIS 1998
ARCHIVE ONE DAVE CLARKE 1996
ARE YOU EXPERIENCED JIMI HENDRIX EXPERIENCE 1967
ARE YOU GONNA GO MY WAY LENNY KRAVITZ 1993
ARE YOU NORMAL? – NED'S ATOMIC DUSTBIN 1992
ARE YOU OK? – WAS (NOT WAS) 1990
ARE YOU PASSIONATE NEIL YOUNG 2002
ARE YOU READY? – BUCKS FIZZ 1982
ARENA DURAN DURAN 1984
ARETHA ARETHA FRANKLIN 1986
ARETHA NOW ARETHA FRANKLIN 1968
THE ARGUMENT FUGAZI 2001
ARGUS WISHBONE ASH 1972
ARGY BARGY SQUEEZE 1980
ARIA – THE OPERA ALBUM ANDREA BOCELLI 1998
ARISE SEPULTURA 1991
THE ARISTOCATS – READ ALONG ORIGINAL CAST RECORDING 2000
ARKANSAS TRAVELER MICHELLE SHOCKED 1992
ARKOLOGY LEE 'SCRATCH' PERRY 1997
ARMAGEDDON (OST) FILM SOUNDTRACK 1998
ARMCHAIR MELODIES DAVID GRAY & TOMMY TYCHO 1976
ARMCHAIR THEATRE JEFF LYNNE 1990
ARMED FORCES ELVIS COSTELLO & THE ATTRACTIONS 1979
AROUND THE FUR DEFTONES 1997
AROUND THE NEXT DREAM BBM 1994
AROUND THE WORLD – LIVE IN CONCERT OSMONDS 1976
AROUND THE WORLD – THE JOURNEY SO FAR EAST 17 1996
AROUND THE WORLD IN A DAY PRINCE 1985
ARRIVAL ABBA 1976
ART AND ILLUSION TWELFTH NIGHT 1984
THE ART GARFUNKEL ALBUM ART GARFUNKEL 1984
THE ART OF CHRIS FARLOWE CHRIS FARLOWE 1966
THE ART OF FALLING APART SOFT CELL 1983
THE ART OF WAR BONE THUGS-N-HARMONY 1997
ART OFFICIAL INTELLIGENCE: MOSIAC THUMP DE LA SOUL 2000
ARTFUL DODGER PRESENTS REWIND VARIOUS ARTISTS (LONDON) 2000
THE ARTFUL DODGER PRESENTS REWIND 2001 VARIOUS ARTISTS (WARNER BROTHERS) 2001
ARTIFICIAL INTELLIGENCE VARIOUS ARTISTS (WARP) 1994
THE ARTISTS VOLUME 1 EARTH WIND & FIRE/JEAN CARN/ROSE ROYCE 1985
THE ARTISTS VOLUME 2 LUTHER VANDROSS/TEDDY PENDERGRASS/CHANGE/ATLANTIC STARR 1985
THE ARTISTS VOLUME III WOMACK & WOMACK/THE O'JAYS/KLEEER/THE S.O.S. BAND 1985
AS IF TO NOTHING CRAIG ARMSTRONG 2002
AS IS MANFRED MANN 1966
AS IT HAPPENS DR. FEELGOOD 1979
AS ONE KOOL & THE GANG 1982
AS ONE DOUBLE TROUBLE 1990
AS RAW AS EVER SHABBA RANKS 1991
AS SAFE AS YESTERDAY IS HUMBLE PIE 1969

AS THE BAND TURNS ATLANTIC STARR 1985

AS TIME GOES BY ROYAL PHILHARMONIC ORCHESTRA CONDUCTED BY HARRY RABINOVITZ 1984

AS TIME GOES BY VARIOUS ARTISTS (DINO) 1993

AS TIME GOES BY BRYAN FERRY 1999

AS TIME GOES BY: THE GREAT AMERICAN SONGBOOK VOLUME 2 ROD STEWART 2003

AS UGLY AS THEY WANNA BE UGLY KID JOE 1992

ASHANTI ASHANTI 2002

ASIA ASIA 1982

ASK A WOMAN WHO KNOWS NATALIE COLE 2002

ASLEEP IN THE BACK ELBOW 2001

ASPECTS OF LOVE ORIGINAL LONDON STAGE CAST SOUNDTRACK 1989

ASQUARIUS CUD 1992

ASSAULT AND BATTERY ROSE TATTOO 1981

ASSAULT ATTACK MICHAEL SCHENKER GROUP 1982

ASSEMBLAGE JAPAN 1981

ASTAIRE PETER SKELLERN 1979

ASTONISHING SOUNDS, AMAZING MUSIC HAWKWIND 1976

ASTRO ASIA 1985

ASTRO CREEP 2000 – SONGS OF LOVE, DESTRUCTION AND OTHER SYNTHETIC DELUSIONS OF THE ELECTRIC HEAD WHITE ZOMBIE 1995

ASTRONAUTS AND HERETICS THOMAS DOLBY 1992

ASYLUM KISS 1985

ASYLUM SENSER 1998

AT EASE WITH DEAN DEAN MARTIN 1967

AT HER VERY BEST NANA MOUSKOURI 2001

AT HIS VERY BEST ENGELBERT HUMPERDINCK 2000

AT HIS VERY BEST ROBERT PALMER 2002

AT HIS VERY BEST LOUIS ARMSTRONG 2003

AT THE BBC JAM 2002

AT THE CHELSEA NIGHTCLUB MEMBERS 1979

AT THE CLUB KENICKIE 1997

AT THE CRESCENDO LOUIS ARMSTRONG 1956

AT THE DROP OF A HAT ORIGINAL LONDON STAGE CAST SOUNDTRACK 1960

AT THE DROP OF ANOTHER HAT ORIGINAL LONDON STAGE CAST SOUNDTRACK 1964

AT THE END OF THE CLICHE – CARL COX 1996

AT THE END OF THE DAY FUREYS & DAVEY ARTHUR 1985

AT THE END OF THE DAY DANIEL O'DONNELL 2003

AT THE END OF THE RAINBOW KEITH HARRIS, ORVILLE & CUDDLES 1983

AT THE OXFORD UNION GERARD HOFFNUNG 1960

AT THEIR VERY BEST SHADOWS 1989

AT THEIR VERY BEST TEMPTATIONS 2001

AT THIS MOMENT TOM JONES 1989

AT WAR WITH SATAN VENOM 1984

AT WORST... THE BEST OF BOY GEORGE & CULTURE CLUB BOY GEORGE/CULTURE CLUB 1993

ATLANTIC BLACK GOLD VARIOUS ARTISTS (ATLANTIC) 1974

ATLANTIC BRIDGE BILLY CONNOLLY 1976

ATLANTIC CROSSING ROD STEWART 1975

ATLANTIC REALM (OST TV) CLANNAD 1989

ATLANTIC SOUL BALLADS VARIOUS ARTISTS (ATLANTIC) 1988

ATLANTIC SOUL CLASSICS VARIOUS ARTISTS (ATLANTIC) 1987

ATOM HEART MOTHER PINK FLOYD 1970

ATOMIC 80'S VARIOUS ARTISTS (UNIVERSAL) 2001

ATOMIC ROOSTER ATOMIC ROOSTER 1970

ATOMIC/ATOMIX – THE VERY BEST OF BLONDIE BLONDIE 1998

ATTACK OF THE GREY LANTERN MANSUN 1997

ATTACK OF THE KILLER B'S ANTHRAX 1991

AUBERGE CHRIS REA 1991

AUDIENCE WITH THE MIND HOUSE OF LOVE 1993

AUDIO LESSNOVER DELIRIOUS? 2001

AUDIOSLAVE AUDIOSLAVE 2002

AUDIOWEB AUDIOWEB 1996

AUF DER MAUR AUF DER MAUR 2004

AUGUST ERIC CLAPTON 1986

AUGUST AND EVERYTHING AFTER COUNTING CROWS 1994

AURAL SCULPTURE STRANGLERS 1984

AUSTIN POWERS IN GOLDMEMBER (OST) FILM SOUNDTRACK 2002

AUSTIN POWERS – THE SPY WHO SHAGGED ME (OST) FILM SOUNDTRACK 1999

AUTHOR! AUTHOR! – SCARS 1981

AUTOAMERICAN BLONDIE 1980

AUTOBAHN KRAFTWERK 1975

THE AUTOBIOGRAPHY OF SUPERTRAMP SUPERTRAMP 1986

AUTOGEDDON JULIAN COPE 1994

AUTOMANIKK A GUY CALLED GERALD 1990

AUTOMATIC SHARPE & NUMAN 1989

AUTOMATIC JESUS & MARY CHAIN 1989

AUTOMATIC FOR THE PEOPLE R.E.M. 1992

AUTUMN '66 SPENCER DAVIS GROUP 1966

AVE MARIA – THE ALBUM LESLEY GARRET 1994

AVALANCHE THEA GILMORE 2003

AVALON ROXY MUSIC 1982

AVALON SUNSET VAN MORRISON 1989

AVERAGE WHITE BAND AVERAGE WHITE BAND 1975

AW C'MON/NO YOU C'MON LAMBCHOP 2004

AWAKE DREAM THEATER 1994

AWAKE AND BREATHE B*WITCHED 1999

AWAKENING KEVIN PEEK 1981

THE AWARDS 1990 VARIOUS ARTISTS (TELSTAR) 1990

THE AWARDS 1992 VARIOUS ARTISTS (POLYGRAM) 1992

THE AWARDS 1993 VARIOUS ARTISTS (POLYGRAM) 1993

THE AWARDS 1995 VARIOUS ARTISTS (COLUMBIA) 1995

AWESOME DANCE VARIOUS ARTISTS (TELSTAR) 1994

AWESOME! 2 VARIOUS ARTISTS (EMI) 1991

AWESOME!! – 20 MASSIVE HITS VARIOUS ARTISTS (EMI) 1991

AXE ATTACK VARIOUS ARTISTS (K-TEL) 1980

AXE ATTACK 2 VARIOUS ARTISTS (K-TEL) 1981

AXIS MUTATIS SHAMEN 1995

AXIS: BOLD AS LOVE JIMI HENDRIX EXPERIENCE 1967

AY FOND KISS FAIRGROUND ATTRACTION 1990

AYIA NAPA – CLUBBERS PARADISE VARIOUS ARTISTS (GLOBAL) 1999

AYIA NAPA – FANTASY ISLAND VARIOUS ARTISTS (TELSTAR) 2000

AYIA NAPA – RETURN TO FANTASY ISLAND VARIOUS ARTISTS (TELSTAR) 2001

AYIA NAPA – THE ALBUM 2001 VARIOUS ARTISTS (MINISTRY OF SOUND) 2001

AYIA NAPA THE ALBUM – SHANKS & BIGFOOT VARIOUS ARTISTS (MINISTRY OF SOUND) 2000

THE A-Z OF EASY LISTENING VARIOUS ARTISTS (POLYDOR) 1971

AZNAVOUR SINGS AZNAVOUR VOLUME 3 CHARLES AZNAVOUR 1974

AZUR D'OR RENAISSANCE 1979

B FOR BROTHERHOOD BROTHERHOOD OF MAN 1978

B SIDES THEMSELVES MARILLION 1988

B*WITCHED B*WITCHED 1998

THE B-52'S B-52'S 1979

BABBLE THAT PETROL EMOTION 1987

BABE RAINBOW HOUSE OF LOVE 1992

BABY YELLO 1991

BABY ANIMALS BABY ANIMALS 1992

BABY I'M A WANT YOU BREAD 1972

BABY I'M BORED EVAN DANDO 2003

BABY LOVE VARIOUS ARTISTS (RONCO) 1984

BABY LOVE VARIOUS ARTISTS (EMI) 1996

... BABY ONE MORE TIME BRITNEY SPEARS 1999

BABY THE STARS SHINE BRIGHT EVERYTHING BUT THE GIRL 1986

BABYLON AND ON SQUEEZE 1987

BABYLON BY BUS BOB MARLEY & THE WAILERS 1978

BABY'S GOT A GUN ONLY ONES 1980

BACCARA BACCARA 1978

BACDAFUCUP ONYX 1993

BACHARACH AND DAVID – THEY WRITE THE SONGS VARIOUS ARTISTS (DINO) 1990

THE BACHELORS AND 16 GREAT SONGS BACHELORS 1964

BACHELORS' GIRLS BACHELORS 1966

BACK AGAIN IN THE D.H.S.S. HALF MAN HALF BISCUIT 1987

BACK AND FOURTH LINDISFARNE 1978

BACK FOR THE ATTACK DOKKEN 1987

BACK HOME AGAIN JOHN DENVER 1974

BACK IN BLACK AC/DC 1980

BACK IN THE DAY VARIOUS ARTISTS (WARNER BROTHERS) 2002

BACK IN THE D.H.S.S. HALF MAN HALF BISCUIT 1986

BACK IN THE HIGH LIFE STEVE WINWOOD 1986

BACK IN THE WORLD PAUL McCARTNEY 2003

BACK INTO THE FUTURE MAN 1973

BACK ON THE BLOCK QUINCY JONES 1990

BACK ON THE ROAD VARIOUS ARTISTS (STYLUS) 1988

BACK ON THE STREETS GARY MOORE 1979

BACK ON TOP VAN MORRISON 1999

BACK ON TRACK LULU 2004

BACK STREET SYMPHONY THUNDER 1990

BACK TO BACK STATUS QUO 1983

BACK TO BACK DAVID ESSEX 1994

BACK TO BASICS BILLY BRAGG 1987

BACK TO BASICS – CUT THE CRAP VARIOUS ARTISTS (NETWORK) 1996

BACK TO BASICS – THE ESSENTIAL COLLECTION 1971–1992 OLIVIA NEWTON-JOHN 1992

BACK TO BROADWAY BARBRA STREISAND 1993

BACK TO FRONT GILBERT O'SULLIVAN 1972

BACK TO FRONT LIONEL RICHIE 1992

BACK TO SCHOOL (MINI MAGGIT) DEFTONES 2001

BACK TO THE BLUES GARY MOORE 2001

BACK TO THE EGG WINGS 1979

BACK TO THE FUTURE (OST) FILM SOUNDTRACK 1986

BACK TO THE LIGHT BRIAN MAY 1992

BACK TO THE MOVIES – HITS FROM THE FLIX VARIOUS ARTISTS (VIRGIN) 2001

BACK TO THE MYSTERY CITY HANOI ROCKS 1983

BACK TO THE OLD SKOOL VARIOUS ARTISTS (MINISTRY OF SOUND) 2001

BACK TO THE OLD SKOOL CLUB CLASSICS VARIOUS ARTISTS (MINISTRY OF SOUND) 2003

BACK TO THE OLD SKOOL – IBIZA VARIOUS ARTISTS (MINISTRY OF SOUND) 2003

BACK TO THE OLD SKOOL – IBIZA ANTHEMS VARIOUS ARTISTS (MINISTRY OF SOUND) 2003

BACK TO THE OLD SKOOL 2 VARIOUS ARTISTS (MINISTRY OF SOUND) 2001

BACK TO THE OLD SKOOL – DRUM & BASS VARIOUS ARTISTS (MINISTRY OF SOUND) 2002

BACK TO THE OLD SKOOL – HIP HOP VARIOUS ARTISTS (MINISTRY OF SOUND) 2002

BACK TO THE ROOTS JOHN MAYALL 1971

BACK TO THE 70'S VARIOUS ARTISTS (EMI) 1993

BACK TO THE SIXTIES TIGHT FIT 1981

BACK TO THE SIXTIES VARIOUS ARTISTS (TELSTAR) 1989

BACK TO TITANIC JAMES HORNER 1998

BACKBEAT BAND BACKBEAT 1994

BACKLASH BAD ENGLISH 1991

BACKLESS ERIC CLAPTON 1978

BACKSTAGE – THE GREATEST HITS AND MORE GENE PITNEY 1990

BACKSTREET BOYS BACKSTREET BOYS 1996

BACKSTREET'S BACK BACKSTREET BOYS 1997

BACKTRACKIN' – ERIC CLAPTON 1984

BAD MICHAEL JACKSON 1987

THE BAD AND LOWDOWN WORLD OF THE KANE GANG KANE GANG 1985

BAD ANIMALS HEART 1987

BAD ATTITUDE MEAT LOAF 1984

BAD BOYS (OST) FILM SOUNDTRACK 1995

BAD BOYS INC. BAD BOYS INC. 1994

BAD BOYS II (OST) FILM SOUNDTRACK 2003

BAD BROTHERS RONNY JORDAN MEETS DJ KRUSH 1994

BAD COMPANY BAD COMPANY 1974

BAD ENGLISH BAD ENGLISH 1989

BAD FOR GOOD JIM STEINMAN 1981

BAD GIRLS DONNA SUMMER 1979
BAD GIRLS VARIOUS ARTISTS (COLUMBIA) 2002
BAD NEWS BAD NEWS 1987
BAD REPUTATION THIN LIZZY 1977
BAD TO THE BONE INNER CIRCLE 1993
BAD VIBES LLOYD COLE 1993
BADLANDS BADLANDS 1989
BADMOTORFINGER SOUNDGARDEN 1992
BADNESS MORRISSEY MULLEN 1981
BADUIZM ERYKAH BADU 1997
BAG OF HITS FUN LOVIN' CRIMINALS 2002
BAGGARIDDIM UB40 1985
BAGSY ME WANNADIES 1997
BAKER GURVITZ ARMY BAKER-GURVITZ ARMY 1975
BAKESALE SEBADOH 1994
BALANCE VAN HALEN 1995
BALANCE OF POWER ELECTRIC LIGHT ORCHESTRA 1986
BALEARIC BEATS VOLUME 1 VARIOUS ARTISTS (FFRR) 1988
THE BALLAD HITS ROXETTE 2003
BALLAD OF EASY RIDER BYRDS 1970
BALLADS – 22 CLASSIC LOVE SONGS ROY ORBISON 1990
BALLADS AND BLUES 1982–1994 GARY MOORE 1994
BALLADS – THE LOVE SONG COLLECTION BOYZONE 2003
BALLBREAKER AC/DC 1995
BALLROOM HITZ – THE VERY BEST OF SWEET SWEET 1996
BALLS TO PICASSO BRUCE DICKINSON 1994
BALLYHOO – THE BEST OF ECHO AND THE BUNNYMEN
    ECHO & THE BUNNYMEN 1997
BANANARAMA BANANARAMA 1984
BANBA CLANNAD 1993
THE BAND BAND 1970
BAND OF GYPSIES JIMI HENDRIX 1970
BAND OF THE SCOTS GUARDS BAND OF THE SCOTS
    GUARDS 1969
BAND ON THE RUN PAUL McCARTNEY & WINGS 1973
BAND ON THE RUN PAUL McCARTNEY & WINGS 1999
BANDOLIER BUDGIE 1975
BANDS OF GOLD – THE ELECTRIC EIGHTIES VARIOUS
    ARTISTS (STYLUS) 1987
BANDS OF GOLD – THE SENSATIONAL SEVENTIES VARIOUS
    ARTISTS (STYLUS) 1987
BANDS OF GOLD – THE SWINGING SIXTIES VARIOUS
    ARTISTS (STYLUS) 1987
BANDSTAND FAMILY 1972
BANDWAGONESQUE TEENAGE FANCLUB 1991
BANG! – WORLD PARTY 1993
BANG! – GREATEST HITS OF FRANKIE GOES TO HOLLYWOOD
    FRANKIE GOES TO HOLLYWOOD 1993
BAPTISM LENNY KRAVITZ 2004
BARAFUNDLE GORKY'S ZYGOTIC MYNCI 1997
THE BARBARA DICKSON ALBUM BARBARA DICKSON 1980
THE BARBARA DICKSON SONGBOOK BARBARA DICKSON
    1985
BARBED WIRE KISSES JESUS & MARY CHAIN 1988
BARBRA – THE CONCERT BARBRA STREISAND 1994
BARBRA STREISAND GREATEST HITS VOLUME 2 BARBRA
    STREISAND 1979
BARBRA STREISAND'S GREATEST HITS BARBRA
    STREISAND 1970
BARCELONA FREDDIE MERCURY & MONTSERRAT
    CABALLE 1988
BARCELONA GOLD VARIOUS ARTISTS (WARNER BROTHERS)
    1992
BARCLAY JAMES HARVEST LIVE BARCLAY JAMES HARVEST
    1974
BARCLAY JAMES HARVEST XII BARCLAY JAMES HARVEST
    1978
BARE ANNIE LENNOX 2003
BARE WIRES JOHN MAYALL & THE BLUESBREAKERS 1968
BARK JEFFERSON AIRPLANE 1971
BARK AT THE MOON OZZY OSBOURNE 1983
BARRY BARRY MANILOW 1980
BARRY LIVE IN BRITAIN BARRY MANILOW 1982
BARRY SINGS SINATRA BARRY MANILOW 1998
BARRY WHITE'S GREATEST HITS VOLUME 2 BARRY
    WHITE 1977

THE BASEMENT TAPES BOB DYLAN 1975
BASKET OF LIGHT PENTANGLE 1969
BASS CULTURE LINTON KWESI JOHNSON 1980
BAT OUT OF HELL MEAT LOAF 1978
BAT OUT OF HELL II – BACK INTO HELL MEAT LOAF 1993
BATMAN (OST) DANNY ELFMAN 1989
BATMAN (OST) PRINCE 1989
BATMAN FOREVER (OST) FILM SOUNDTRACK 1995
BATTERIES NOT INCLUDED AFTER THE FIRE 1982
BATTLE HYMNS FOR CHILDREN SINGING HAYSI FANTAYZEE
    1983
THE BATTLE OF LOS ANGELES RAGE AGAINST THE
    MACHINE 1999
THE BATTLE RAGES ON... – DEEP PURPLE 1993
BAY OF KINGS STEVE HACKETT 1983
BAYOU COUNTRY CREEDENCE CLEARWATER REVIVAL
    1970
THE BBC 1922–1972 (TV AND RADIO EXTRACTS)
    TELEVISION AND RADIO COMPILATION 1972
BBC COUNTRY HITS VARIOUS ARTISTS (BBC) 2000
BBC RADIO 1 LIVE IN CONCERT NEW ORDER 1992
BBC SESSIONS LED ZEPPELIN 1997
BBC SESSIONS JIMI HENDRIX EXPERIENCE 1998
BBC SESSIONS WHO 2000
BBC TV'S BEST OF TOP OF THE POPS VARIOUS ARTISTS
    (SUPER BEEB) 1975
BE HERE NOW OASIS 1997
BE MY LOVE... AN ALBUM OF LOVE PLACIDO DOMINGO
    1990
BE NOT NOBODY VANESSA CARLTON 2002
BE SEEING YOU DR. FEELGOOD 1977
BE YOURSELF TONIGHT EURYTHMICS 1985
THE BEACH (OST) FILM SOUNDTRACK 2000
THE BEACH BOYS BEACH BOYS 1985
THE BEACH BOYS LOVE YOU BEACH BOYS 1977
BEACH BOYS PARTY BEACH BOYS 1966
BEACH BOYS TODAY BEACH BOYS 1966
BEACH PARTY 2 JAMES LAST 1971
BEACHES (OST) BETTE MIDLER 1989
A BEARD OF STARS TYRANNOSAURUS REX 1970
A BEARD OF STARS/UNICORN T. REX 1972
THE BEAST INSIDE INSPIRAL CARPETS 1991
BEASTER SUGAR 1993
BEAT KING CRIMSON 1982
BEAT BOY VISAGE 1984
BEAT BOYS IN THE JET AGE LAMBRETTAS 1980
BEAT CRAZY JOE JACKSON 1980
BEAT GIRL (OST) ADAM FAITH 1961
BEAT OF THE BRASS HERB ALPERT & THE TIJUANA BRASS
    1968
BEAT RUNS WILD VARIOUS ARTISTS (MERCURY) 1986
BEAT STREET (OST) FILM SOUNDTRACK 1984
BEAT THE CARROTT JASPER CARROTT 1981
BEAT THIS – 20 HITS OF RHYTHM KING VARIOUS ARTISTS
    (STYLUS) 1989
THE BEAT, THE RHYME AND THE NOISE WEE PAPA GIRL
    RAPPERS 1988
BEATLEMANIA ANONYMOUS COVER VERSIONS 1964
THE BEATLES (WHITE ALBUM) BEATLES 1968
THE BEATLES 1962–1966 BEATLES 1973
THE BEATLES 1967–1970 BEATLES 1973
THE BEATLES AT THE HOLLYWOOD BOWL BEATLES 1977
BEATLES BALLADS BEATLES 1980
BEATLES CONCERTO ROSTAL & SCHAEFER 1979
BEATLES FOR SALE BEATLES 1964
THE BEATLES TAPES BEATLES 1976
BEATS RHYMES AND BASSLINES – THE BEST OF RAP
    VARIOUS ARTISTS (POLYGRAM) 1992
BEATS, RHYMES AND LIFE A TRIBE CALLED QUEST 1996
BEATSONGS BLUE AEROPLANES 1991
BEAUCOUP FISH UNDERWORLD 1999
BEAUTIFUL VARIOUS ARTISTS (BMG) 2004
BEAUTIFUL COLLISION BIC RUNGA 2004
BEAUTIFUL DREAMS CHRIS DE BURGH 1995
BEAUTIFUL FREAK EELS 1997
BEAUTIFUL GAME VARIOUS ARTISTS (UNIVERSAL) 2002

THE BEAUTIFUL GAME – EUFA EURO '96 VARIOUS ARTISTS
    (RCA) 1996
BEAUTIFUL GARBAGE GARBAGE 2001
BEAUTIFUL INSANE ELECTRASY 1998
BEAUTIFUL MALADIES 1983–1993: THE ISLAND YEARS
    TOM WAITS 1998
BEAUTIFUL NOISE NEIL DIAMOND 1976
BEAUTIFUL SUNDAY LENA MARTELL 1980
BEAUTIFUL – THE REMIX ALBUM BLONDIE 1995
BEAUTIFUL VISION VAN MORRISON 1982
BEAUTIFUL WASTELAND CAPERCAILLIE 1997
BEAUTY AND THE BEAT PEGGY LEE & GEORGE SHEARING
    1960
BEAUTY ON A BACK STREET DARYL HALL & JOHN OATES
    1977
BEAUTY STAB ABC 1983
BEBEL GILBERTO BEBEL GILBERTO 2004
BECOME WHAT YOU ARE JULIANA HATFIELD THREE 1993
BECOMING X SNEAKER PIMPS 1996
BED FIVE THIRTY 1991
BEDTIME STORIES JUDGE DREAD 1975
BEDTIME STORIES MADONNA 1994
BEE GEE FIRST BEE GEES 1967
BEE GEES GREATEST BEE GEES 1979
BEEBOP MOPTOP DANNY WILSON 1989
BEETHOVEN TRIPLE CONCERTO BERLIN PHILHARMONIC
    ORCHESTRA CONDUCTED BY HERBERT VON
    KARAJAN – SOLOIST DAVID OISTRAKH (VIOLIN),
    MSTISLAV ROSTROPOVICH (CELLO), SVIATOSLAU
    RICHTER (PIANO) 1970
BEETHOVEN VIOLIN CONCERTO, CORIOLAN OVERTURE
    NIGEL KENNEDY WITH KLAUS TENNSTEDT
    CONDUCTING THE NORTH GERMAN RADIO
    SYMPHONY ORCHESTRA 1992
BEETHOVEN WAS DEAF MORRISSEY 1993
BEFORE AND AFTER TIM FINN 1993
BEFORE THE CALM WITNESS 1999
BEFORE THE FLOOD BOB DYLAN 1974
BEFORE THE RAIN ETERNAL 1997
BEG FOR MERCY G-UNIT 2003
BEGGAR ON A BEACH OF GOLD MIKE & THE MECHANICS
    1995
BEGGARS BANQUET ROLLING STONES 1968
BEGIN THE BEGUINE JULIO IGLESIAS 1981
THE BEGINNING STAGES OF POLYPHONIC SPREE 2003
BEGINNINGS STEVE HOWE 1975
BEGINNINGS – GREATEST HITS AND NEW SONGS CILLA
    BLACK 2003
BEHAVIOUR PET SHOP BOYS 1990
BEHIND CLOSED DOORS CHARLIE RICH 1974
BEHIND CLOSED DOORS SECRET AFFAIR 1980
BEHIND CLOSED DOORS THUNDER 1995
BEHIND THE MASK FLEETWOOD MAC 1990
BEHIND THE SUN ERIC CLAPTON 1985
BEHIND THE SUN CHICANE 2000
THE BEIDERBECKE COLLECTION FRANK RICOTTI ALL STARS
    1988
BEING SOMEBODY LIBERTY X 2003
BEING WITH YOU SMOKEY ROBINSON 1981
BELIEF INNOCENCE 1990
BELIEVE CHER 1998
BELIEVE DISTURBED 2002
BELIEVE IN ME DUFF McKAGAN 1993
BELIEVE IN MUSIC VARIOUS ARTISTS (K-TEL) 1973
BELIEVE YOU ME BLANCMANGE 1985
BELLA DONNA STEVIE NICKS 1981
BELLAMY BROTHERS BELLAMY BROTHERS 1976
THE BELLE STARS BELLE STARS 1983
BELOW THE SALT STEELEYE SPAN 1972
BEN MICHAEL JACKSON 1973
BEN HUR (OST) FILM SOUNDTRACK 1960
BEND SINISTER FALL 1986
THE BENDS RADIOHEAD 1995
BENEATH THE SURFACE GENIUS/GZA 1999
BENEFIT JETHRO TULL 1970
BENNY GOODMAN TODAY BENNY GOODMAN 1971

BENT OUT OF SHAPE RAINBOW 1983

BENTLEY RHYTHM ACE BENTLEY RHYTHM ACE 1997

BERLIN LOU REED 1973

BERNSTEIN IN BERLIN – BEETHOVEN SYMPHONY NO. 9 LEONARD BERNSTEIN 1990

THE BERRY VEST OF GILBERT O'SULLIVAN 2004

BERSERKER GARY NUMAN 1984

BERT KAEMPFERT – BEST SELLER BERT KAEMPFERT & HIS ORCHESTRA 1967

THE BEST QUINCY JONES 1982

THE BEST... ALBUM IN THE WORLD... EVER! 4 VARIOUS ARTISTS (VIRGIN) 1996

THE BEST 80'S ALBUM IN THE WORLD... EVER! – VARIOUS ARTISTS (VIRGIN) 1995

THE BEST AIR GUITAR ALBUM EVER III VARIOUS ARTISTS (EMI) 2003

THE BEST AIR GUITAR ALBUM IN THE WORLD... EVER! – VARIOUS ARTISTS (EMI) 2001

THE BEST AIR GUITAR ALBUM IN THE WORLD 2 VARIOUS ARTISTS (EMI) 2002

THE BEST ALBUM... IN THE WORLD... EVER! 7 VARIOUS ARTISTS (VIRGIN) 1998

THE BEST AND FRIENDS ALBUM IN THE WORLD VARIOUS ARTISTS (VIRGIN) 2000

THE BEST BANDS EVER VARIOUS ARTISTS (VIRGIN) 2002

BEST BANDS EVER 2004 VARIOUS ARTISTS (VIRGIN) 2003

THE BEST CARNIVAL ALBUM EVER VARIOUS ARTISTS (VIRGIN) 2001

THE BEST CHART HITS ALBUM IN THE WORLD... EVER! – VARIOUS ARTISTS (VIRGIN) 1998

THE BEST CHART HITS IN THE WORLD... EVER! 99 VARIOUS ARTISTS (VIRGIN) 1999

THE BEST CHRISTMAS ALBUM IN THE WORLD EVER VARIOUS ARTISTS (VIRGIN) 2000

THE BEST CHRISTMAS ALBUM IN THE WORLD... EVER! – VARIOUS ARTISTS (VIRGIN) 1993

THE BEST CHRISTMAS ALBUM IN THE WORLD... EVER! – VARIOUS ARTISTS (VIRGIN) 1996

THE BEST CLASSICAL ALBUM IN THE WORLD... EVER! – VARIOUS ARTISTS (EMI) 1995

THE BEST CLASSICAL ALBUM OF THE MILLENNIUM... EVER! – VARIOUS ARTISTS (VIRGIN) 1999

THE BEST CLUB ANTHEMS SUMMER 2002 VARIOUS ARTISTS (VIRGIN) 2002

THE BEST CLUB ANTHEMS 2000... EVER! – VARIOUS ARTISTS (VIRGIN) 1999

THE BEST CLUB ANTHEMS 2001 EVER VARIOUS ARTISTS (VIRGIN) 2000

BEST CLUB ANTHEMS 2002 VARIOUS ARTISTS (VIRGIN) 2002

THE BEST CLUB ANTHEMS 99 IN THE WORLD... EVER! – VARIOUS ARTISTS (VIRGIN) 1999

THE BEST CLUB ANTHEMS IN THE WORLD... EVER! – VARIOUS ARTISTS (VIRGIN) 1997

THE BEST CLUB ANTHEMS IN THE WORLD... EVER! 2 VARIOUS ARTISTS (VIRGIN) 1997

THE BEST CLUB ANTHEMS IN THE WORLD... EVER! III VARIOUS ARTISTS (VIRGIN) 1998

THE BEST CLUB ANTHEMS... EVER! 2K VARIOUS ARTISTS (VIRGIN) 2000

THE BEST COUNTRY ALBUM IN THE WORLD... EVER! – VARIOUS ARTISTS (EMI) 1994

THE BEST COUNTRY BALLADS IN THE WORLD... EVER! – VARIOUS ARTISTS (VIRGIN) 1998

THE BEST DANCE ALBUM EVER 2002 VARIOUS ARTISTS (VIRGIN) 2002

BEST DANCE ALBUM IN THE WORLD EVER – 10 VARIOUS ARTISTS (VIRGIN) 2000

BEST DANCE ALBUM IN THE WORLD EVER 11 VARIOUS ARTISTS (VIRGIN) 2001

BEST DANCE ALBUM IN THE WORLD EVER! 2000 VARIOUS ARTISTS (VIRGIN) 2000

THE BEST DANCE ALBUM IN THE WORLD... 95! – VARIOUS ARTISTS (VIRGIN) 1995

THE BEST DANCE ALBUM IN THE WORLD... EVER! – VARIOUS ARTISTS (VIRGIN) 1993

THE BEST DANCE ALBUM IN THE WORLD... EVER! 2 VARIOUS ARTISTS (VIRGIN) 1993

THE BEST DANCE ALBUM IN THE WORLD... EVER! 3 VARIOUS ARTISTS (VIRGIN) 1994

THE BEST DANCE ALBUM IN THE WORLD... EVER! 4 VARIOUS ARTISTS (VIRGIN) 1994

THE BEST DANCE ALBUM IN THE WORLD... EVER! 5 VARIOUS ARTISTS (VIRGIN) 1995

THE BEST DANCE ALBUM IN THE WORLD... EVER! 6 VARIOUS ARTISTS (VIRGIN) 1996

THE BEST DANCE ALBUM IN THE WORLD... EVER! 7 VARIOUS ARTISTS (VIRGIN) 1997

THE BEST DANCE ALBUM IN THE WORLD... EVER! 8 VARIOUS ARTISTS (VIRGIN) 1998

THE BEST DANCE ALBUM IN THE WORLD... EVER! 9 VARIOUS ARTISTS (VIRGIN) 1999

THE BEST DANCE ALBUM IN THE WORLD EVER VARIOUS ARTISTS (VIRGIN) 2003

THE BEST DANCE ALBUM OF THE YEAR VARIOUS ARTISTS (GLOBAL) 1997

THE BEST DANCE ALBUM OF THE YEAR VARIOUS ARTISTS (GLOBAL) 1998

THE BEST DANCE ALBUM OF THE YEAR! – VARIOUS ARTISTS (VISION) 1995

BEST DANCE 99 VARIOUS ARTISTS (TELSTAR) 1999

THE BEST DAYS OF MY LIFE JOHNNY MATHIS 1979

THE BEST DISCO ALBUM IN THE WORLD VARIOUS ARTISTS (WARNER BROTHERS) 1979

THE BEST DISCO ALBUM IN THE WORLD VARIOUS ARTISTS (VIRGIN) 1997

THE BEST DISCO ALBUM IN THE WORLD... EVER! 2 VARIOUS ARTISTS (VIRGIN) 1998

THE BEST EASY ALBUM EVER VARIOUS ARTISTS (VIRGIN) 2000

BEST FOOTIE ANTHEMS EVER VARIOUS ARTISTS (VIRGIN) 2000

THE BEST FOOTIE ANTHEMS IN THE WORLD... EVER! – VARIOUS ARTISTS (VIRGIN) 1996

BEST FRIENDS VARIOUS ARTISTS (IMPRESSION) 1982

BEST FRIENDS FOSTER & ALLEN 1997

THE BEST FROM 150 GOLD RECORDS JAMES LAST 1980

THE BEST FROM THE MGM MUSICALS VARIOUS ARTISTS (EMI) 1990

THE BEST FUNK ALBUM IN THE WORLD... EVER! – VARIOUS ARTISTS (VIRGIN) 1995

THE BEST GARAGE ANTHEMS EVER VARIOUS ARTISTS (VIRGIN) 2000

BEST – THE GREATEST HITS OF S CLUB 2003

THE BEST HARD HOUSE EVER VARIOUS ARTISTS (VIRGIN) 2001

BEST HEAVY METAL ALBUM IN THE WORLD EVER VARIOUS ARTISTS (VIRGIN) 2004

THE BEST HIP HOP ANTHEMZ IN THE WORLD... EVER! – VARIOUS ARTISTS (VIRGIN) 1998

THE BEST HOUSE ANTHEMS... EVER! – VARIOUS ARTISTS (VIRGIN) 1999

THE BEST IBIZA ANTHEMS EVER 2001 VARIOUS ARTISTS (VIRGIN) 2001

BEST IBIZA ANTHEMS EVER 2K VARIOUS ARTISTS (VIRGIN) 2000

THE BEST IBIZA ANTHEMS... EVER! – VARIOUS ARTISTS (VIRGIN) 1999

THE BEST IRISH ALBUM IN THE WORLD... EVER! – VARIOUS ARTISTS (VIRGIN) 1996

THE BEST JAZZ ALBUM IN THE WORLD... EVER! – VARIOUS ARTISTS (VIRGIN) 1996

BEST JAZZ ALBUM IN THE WORLD... EVER! – VARIOUS ARTISTS (VIRGIN) 2000

BEST KEPT SECRET SHEENA EASTON 1983

THE BEST LATINO CARNIVAL IN THE WORLD... EVER! – VARIOUS ARTISTS (VIRGIN) 1997

BEST LIVE – HEADLIGHTS WHITE LINES BLACK TAR RIVERS LEVELLERS 1996

THE BEST LOVESONGS... EVER! – VARIOUS ARTISTS (VIRGIN) 1999

THE BEST MILLENNIUM PARTY... EVER! – VARIOUS ARTISTS (VIRGIN) 1999

THE BEST MIX ALBUM IN THE WORLD... EVER! – VARIOUS ARTISTS (VIRGIN) 1996

BEST MOVES CHRIS DE BURGH 1981

THE BEST MUSICALS ALBUM IN THE WORLD... EVER! – VARIOUS ARTISTS (VIRGIN) 1999

THE BEST NORTHERN SOUL ALL NIGHTER EVER VARIOUS ARTISTS (VIRGIN) 2001

BEST OF ROXY MUSIC 2001

THE BEST OF RICKY MARTIN 2001

THE BEST OF SPANDAU BALLET 2001

THE BEST OF CORRS 2001

THE BEST OF PROCLAIMERS 2002

BEST OF BONNIE RAITT 2003

THE BEST OF DE LA SOUL 2003

THE BEST OF LEANN RIMES 2004

THE BEST OF FATS DOMINO 2004

THE BEST OF HOUSEMARTINS 2004

BEST OF R&B VARIOUS ARTISTS (EMI) 2004

BEST OF – VOLUME 2 BOB DYLAN 2000

THE BEST OF 10 YEARS – 32 SUPERHITS BONEY M 1986

THE BEST OF 100% DANCE VARIOUS ARTISTS (TELSTAR) 1995

BEST OF 100% PURE GROOVES VARIOUS ARTISTS (TELSTAR) 1998

THE BEST OF 1968–1973 STEVE MILLER BAND 1990

THE BEST OF 1969/1974 DAVID BOWIE 1998

THE BEST OF 1974/1979 DAVID BOWIE 1998

THE BEST OF 1980–1990 & B SIDES U2 1998

THE BEST OF 1990–2000 & B SIDES U2 2002

THE BEST OF 2 TONE VARIOUS ARTISTS (2 TONE) 1993

THE BEST OF ACID JAZZ VARIOUS ARTISTS (GLOBAL) 1996

BEST OF ACID JAZZ VOLUME 2 VARIOUS ARTISTS (ACID JAZZ) 1993

BEST OF ACID JAZZ VOLUME 2 VARIOUS ARTISTS (GLOBAL) 1997

BEST OF ACOUSTIC VARIOUS ARTISTS (ECHO/V2) 2004

THE BEST OF ALED JONES ALED JONES 1987

THE BEST OF ALL WOMAN VARIOUS ARTISTS (QUALITY PRICE MUSIC) 1995

THE BEST OF ANDY WILLIAMS ANDY WILLIAMS 1992

THE BEST OF ART OF NOISE ART OF NOISE 1988

THE BEST OF AZTEC CAMERA AZTEC CAMERA 1999

THE BEST OF BACHARACH STRINGS FOR PLEASURE 1971

BEST OF BALL, BARBER AND BILK KENNY BALL, CHRIS BARBER & ACKER BILK 1962

BEST OF BARBER AND BILK VOLUME 1 CHRIS BARBER & ACKER BILK 1961

BEST OF BARBER AND BILK VOLUME 2 CHRIS BARBER & ACKER BILK 1961

THE BEST OF BELINDA VOLUME 1 BELINDA CARLISLE 1992

BEST OF BERT KAEMPFERT BERT KAEMPFERT & HIS ORCHESTRA 1966

THE BEST OF BING BING CROSBY 1977

THE BEST OF BING CROSBY BING CROSBY 1996

THE BEST OF BLACK SABBATH BLACK SABBATH 2000

THE BEST OF BLONDIE BLONDIE 1981

THE BEST OF BOB DYLAN BOB DYLAN 1997

THE BEST OF BOND... JAMES BOND VARIOUS ARTISTS (CAPITOL) 1999

THE BEST OF BOND JAMES BOND VARIOUS ARTISTS (CAPITOL) 2002

THE BEST OF BONNIE RAITT 1989–2003 BONNIE RAITT 2003

THE BEST OF BOTH WORLDS R KELLY & JAY-Z 2002

BEST OF BOWIE DAVID BOWIE 2002

THE BEST OF BREAD BREAD 1972

THE BEST OF BREAD VOLUME 2 BREAD 1974

BEST OF BRITISH VARIOUS ARTISTS (VIRGIN/EMI) 2002

THE BEST OF BRITISH JAZZ FUNK VOLUME 2 VARIOUS ARTISTS (BEGGARS BANQUET) 1982

BEST OF CAFE DEL MAR VARIOUS ARTISTS (MERCURY) 2003

BEST OFCAPITAL GOLD – 24 CARAT CLASSIC HITS VARIOUS ARTISTS (THE HIT LABEL) 1992

THE BEST OF CAR WASH VARIOUS ARTISTS (MCA) 1977

BEST OF CHAKA KHAN – I'M EVERY WOMAN CHAKA KHAN 1999

BEST OF CHIC CHIC 1979

BEST OF CHRIS BARBER CHRIS BARBER 1960

THE BEST OF CHRIS REA CHRIS REA 1994

THE BEST OF CHRIS REA – NEW LIGHT THROUGH OLD WINDOWS CHRIS REA 1988

THE BEST OF CILLA BLACK CILLA BLACK 1968

THE BEST OF CLASSIC ROCK LONDON SYMPHONY ORCHESTRA WITH THE ROYAL CHORAL SOCIETY & THE ROGER SMITH CHORALE 1982

THE BEST OF CLIFF CLIFF RICHARD & THE SHADOWS 1969

THE BEST OF CLIFF VOLUME 2 CLIFF RICHARD & THE SHADOWS 1972

THE BEST OF CREAM CREAM 1969

THE BEST OF DANCE '91 VARIOUS ARTISTS (TELSTAR) 1991

THE BEST OF DANCE '92 VARIOUS ARTISTS (TELSTAR) 1992

THE BEST OF DANCE '93 VARIOUS ARTISTS (TELSTAR) 1993

THE BEST OF DANCE '94 VARIOUS ARTISTS (TELSTAR) 1994

THE BEST OF DANCE '96 VARIOUS ARTISTS (TELSTAR) 1996

THE BEST OF DANCE '97 VARIOUS ARTISTS (TELSTAR) 1997

THE BEST OF DANCE '98 VARIOUS ARTISTS (TELSTAR) 1998

THE BEST OF DANCE MANIA 95 VARIOUS ARTISTS (PURE MUSIC) 1995

THE BEST OF DARYL HALL AND JOHN OATES – LOOKING BACK DARYL HALL & JOHN OATES 1991

THE BEST OF DEAN MARTIN DEAN MARTIN 1969

THE BEST OF DEANNA DURBIN DEANNA DURBIN 1982

THE BEST OF DEL AMITRI – HATFUL OF RAIN DEL AMITRI 1998

BEST OF DIONNE WARWICK DIONNE WARWICK 1966

THE BEST OF DONNA SUMMER DONNA SUMMER 1990

THE BEST OF DRIVE TIME VARIOUS ARTISTS (POLYGRAM) 1998

THE BEST OF DUSTY SPRINGFIELD DUSTY SPRINGFIELD 1998

THE BEST OF EARTH WIND & FIRE VOLUME 1 EARTH WIND & FIRE 1978

THE BEST OF ELAINE PAIGE AND BARBARA DICKSON ELAINE PAIGE & BARBARA DICKSON 1992

BEST OF ELVIS ELVIS PRESLEY 1957

THE BEST OF ELVIS COSTELLO – THE MAN ELVIS COSTELLO & THE ATTRACTIONS 1985

BEST OF EN VOGUE EN VOGUE 1998

BEST OF EUPHORIC DANCE – BREAKDOWN IBIZA VARIOUS ARTISTS (TELSTAR) 2001

THE BEST OF EVERYTHING BUT THE GIRL EVERYTHING BUT THE GIRL 1996

BEST OF FRANK SINATRA FRANK SINATRA 1968

THE BEST OF FREE – ALL RIGHT NOW FREE 1991

BEST OF FRIENDS CLEO LAINE & JOHN WILLIAMS 1978

BEST OF GARY NUMAN 1978–83 GARY NUMAN 1993

BEST OF GENE PITNEY GENE PITNEY 1969

THE BEST OF GLADYS KNIGHT & THE PIPS GLADYS KNIGHT & THE PIPS 1976

THE BEST OF GLENN MILLER GLENN MILLER & HIS ORCHESTRA 1969

THE BEST OF HANK MARVIN AND THE SHADOWS HANK MARVIN & THE SHADOWS 1994

THE BEST OF HEARTBEAT VARIOUS ARTISTS (COLUMBIA) 1995

THE BEST OF HELEN REDDY HELEN REDDY 1976

THE BEST OF HOOKED ON CLASSICS ROYAL PHILHARMONIC ORCHESTRA CONDUCTED BY LOUIS CLARK 1983

BEST OF HOUSE '88 VARIOUS ARTISTS (TELSTAR) 1988

BEST OF HOUSE MEGAMIX VARIOUS ARTISTS (SERIOUS) 1987

BEST OF HOUSE MEGAMIX VOLUME 2 VARIOUS ARTISTS (SERIOUS) 1988

THE BEST OF HOUSE VOLUME 1 VARIOUS ARTISTS (SERIOUS) 1987

BEST OF HOUSE VOLUME 2 VARIOUS ARTISTS (SERIOUS) 1987

BEST OF HOUSE VOLUME 3 VARIOUS ARTISTS (SERIOUS) 1987

BEST OF HOUSE VOLUME 4 VARIOUS ARTISTS (SERIOUS) 1988

THE BEST OF HOWARD JONES HOWARD JONES 1993

THE BEST OF – IN A LIFETIME CLANNAD 2003

THE BEST OF INCANTATION: MUSIC FROM THE ANDES INCANTATION 1985

THE BEST OF INDIE TOP 20 VARIOUS ARTISTS (BEECHWOOD MUSIC) 1991

THE BEST OF JAMES JAMES 1998

THE BEST OF JAMES BOND – 30TH ANNIVERSARY COLLECTION VARIOUS ARTISTS (EMI) 1992

THE BEST OF JAMES BROWN – THE GODFATHER OF SOUL JAMES BROWN 1987

THE BEST OF JASPER CARROTT JASPER CARROTT 1978

THE BEST OF JIM REEVES JIM REEVES 1965

THE BEST OF JOHN DENVER JOHN DENVER 1974

BEST OF JOHN DENVER VOLUME 2 JOHN DENVER 1977

THE BEST OF JOHNNY CASH JOHNNY CASH 1976

THE BEST OF JON AND VANGELIS JON & VANGELIS 1984

THE BEST OF LADYSMITH BLACK MAMBAZO – THE STAR AND WISEMAN LADYSMITH BLACK MAMBAZO 1998

THE BEST OF LENA MARTELL LENA MARTELL 1977

THE BEST OF LOU REED AND THE VELVET UNDERGROUND LOU REED & THE VELVET UNDERGROUND 1995

BEST OF LUTHER VANDROSS – BEST OF LOVE LUTHER VANDROSS 1989

THE BEST OF M PEOPLE M PEOPLE 1998

THE BEST OF MARVIN GAYE MARVIN GAYE 1976

THE BEST OF MASTERCUTS VARIOUS ARTISTS (VIRGIN) 1996

THE BEST OF MATT BIANCO MATT BIANCO 1990

THE BEST OF ME MAXI PRIEST 1991

THE BEST OF ME BRYAN ADAMS 1999

THE BEST OF MICHAEL BALL MICHAEL BALL 1994

BEST OF MICHAEL JACKSON MICHAEL JACKSON 1981

THE BEST OF MICHAEL JACKSON AND THE JACKSON FIVE MICHAEL JACKSON & THE JACKSON FIVE 1997

THE BEST OF MIRAGE: JACK MIX '88 MIRAGE 1987

THE BEST OF MOTORHEAD MOTORHEAD 2000

THE BEST OF MY GOLD RECORDS JAMES LAST 1983

THE BEST OF NANCI GRIFFITH NANCI GRIFFITH 1993

THE BEST OF NAT 'KING' COLE NAT 'KING' COLE 1968

THE BEST OF NAT 'KING' COLE VOLUME 2 NAT 'KING' COLE 1970

THE BEST OF NEIL DIAMOND NEIL DIAMOND 1996

THE BEST OF NICK CAVE & THE BAD SEEDS NICK CAVE & THE BAD SEEDS 1998

THE BEST OF O.M.D. ORCHESTRAL MANOEUVRES IN THE DARK 1988

THE BEST OF OL' BLUE EYES FRANK SINATRA 1975

BEST OF PEGGY LEE VOLUME 2 PEGGY LEE 1961

THE BEST OF R.E.M. R.E.M. 1992

THE BEST OF RADIO LUXEMBOURG VARIOUS ARTISTS (PYE) 1963

BEST OF RAINBOW RAINBOW 1981

THE BEST OF RICHARD CLAYDERMAN RICHARD CLAYDERMAN 1997

THE BEST OF ROCK 'N' ROLL LOVE SONGS VARIOUS ARTISTS (DINO) 1994

THE BEST OF ROD STEWART ROD STEWART 1977

THE BEST OF ROD STEWART ROD STEWART 1989

THE BEST OF ROD STEWART AND THE FACES 1971–1975 ROD STEWART & THE FACES 1992

THE BEST OF ROY ORBISON ROY ORBISON 1975

THE BEST OF SADE SADE 1994

THE BEST OF SELLERS PETER SELLERS 1959

THE BEST OF SHIRLEY BASSEY SHIRLEY BASSEY 1992

THE BEST OF SIMPLE MINDS SIMPLE MINDS 2001

THE BEST OF SPANDAU BALLET SPANDAU BALLET 1991

THE BEST OF STATUS QUO STATUS QUO 1973

THE BEST OF SUEDEHEAD MORRISSEY 1997

THE BEST OF T. REX T. REX 1971

THE BEST OF TAMMY WYNETTE TAMMY WYNETTE 1975

THE BEST OF TAVARES TAVARES 1978

THE BEST OF THE ALAN PARSONS PROJECT ALAN PARSONS PROJECT 1983

THE BEST OF THE B-52'S – DANCE THIS MESS AROUND B-52'S 1990

BEST OF THE BEACH BOYS BEACH BOYS 1966

THE BEST OF THE BEACH BOYS BEACH BOYS 1995

BEST OF THE BEACH BOYS VOLUME 2 BEACH BOYS 1967

BEST OF THE BEACH BOYS VOLUME 3 BEACH BOYS 1968

THE BEST OF THE BEAST IRON MAIDEN 1996

BEST OF THE BEE GEES BEE GEES 1969

BEST OF THE BOOMTOWN RATS BOOMTOWN RATS 2004

THE BEST OF THE CHRISTIANS CHRISTIANS 1993

THE BEST OF THE CLASSICAL BITS TELEVISION COMPILATION 1993

THE BEST OF THE COMPOSERS: BEETHOVEN/STRAUSS/TCHAIKOVSKY/MOZART VARIOUS ARTISTS (RONCO) 1982

THE BEST OF THE DAMNED DAMNED 1981

BEST OF THE DOOLEYS DOOLEYS 1979

THE BEST OF THE DOORS DOORS 1998

BEST OF THE DUBLINERS DUBLINERS 1967

THE BEST OF THE EAGLES EAGLES 1985

THE BEST OF THE FACES FACES 1977

THE BEST OF THE FOUR TOPS FOUR TOPS 1982

BEST OF THE GOONS SHOWS GOONS 1959

BEST OF THE GOONS SHOWS VOLUME 2 GOONS 1960

THE BEST OF THE ICICLE WORKS ICICLE WORKS 1992

THE BEST OF THE MAMAS AND PAPAS MAMAS & THE PAPAS 1977

THE BEST OF THE MAVERICKS MAVERICKS 1999

THE BEST OF THE NINETIES... SO FAR VARIOUS ARTISTS (EMI) 1996

THE BEST OF THE POGUES POGUES 1991

THE BEST OF THE RAT PACK VARIOUS ARTISTS (CAPITOL) 2001

THE BEST OF THE REAL THING REAL THING 1986

THE BEST OF THE SEEKERS SEEKERS 1968

THE BEST OF THE STYLISTICS STYLISTICS 1975

BEST OF THE STYLISTICS VOLUME 2 STYLISTICS 1976

THE BEST OF THE TROGGS TROGGS 1967

THE BEST OF THE UNDERTONES – TEENAGE KICKS UNDERTONES 1993

THE BEST OF THE VILLAGE PEOPLE VILLAGE PEOPLE 1993

BEST OF THE WATERBOYS '81 '91 WATERBOYS 1991

BEST OF THE 20TH CENTURY BOY MARC BOLAN & T. REX 1985

BEST OF THUNDER – THE FINEST HOUR (AND A BIT) THUNDER 1995

BEST OF TONY CHRISTIE TONY CHRISTIE 1976

THE BEST OF TUBULAR BELLS MIKE OLDFIELD 2001

THE BEST OF UB40 – VOLUME ONE UB40 1987

THE BEST OF UB40 – VOLUME TWO UB40 1995

THE BEST OF VAN HALEN – VOLUME 1 VAN HALEN 1996

THE BEST OF VAN MORRISON VAN MORRISON 1990

THE BEST OF VAN MORRISON VOLUME 2 VAN MORRISON 1993

THE BEST OF VYBIN' – VARIOUS ARTISTS (GLOBAL) 1996

BEST OF – WAVE OF MUTILATION PIXIES 2004

BEST OF WEST COAST HIP HOP VARIOUS ARTISTS (STREET SOUNDS) 1987

THE BEST OF WHAM!... IF YOU WERE THERE WHAM! 1997

THE BEST OF WHITESNAKE WHITESNAKE 2003

THE BEST OF WOMAN TO WOMAN VARIOUS ARTISTS (POLYGRAM) 1996

THE BEST ONE HIT WONDERS IN THE WORLD VARIOUS ARTISTS (VIRGIN) 2003

THE BEST OPERA ALBUM IN THE WORLD... EVER! – VARIOUS ARTISTS (VIRGIN) 1996

BEST PANPIPES ALBUM IN THE WORLD... EVER! – VARIOUS ARTISTS (VIRGIN) 2003

THE BEST PARTY IN THE WORLD... EVER! – VARIOUS ARTISTS (VIRGIN) 1997

THE BEST PARTY IN TOWN EVER VARIOUS ARTISTS (VIRGIN) 2001

THE BEST PARTY... EVER! – VARIOUS ARTISTS (VIRGIN) 1995

THE BEST PEPSI CHART ALBUM IN THE WORLD... EVER! – VARIOUS ARTISTS (VIRGIN) 1999

BEST PEPSI CHART ALBUM... EVER! 2000 VARIOUS ARTISTS (VIRGIN) 2000

THE BEST PROG ROCK ALBUM IN THE WORLD VARIOUS ARTISTS (VIRGIN) 2003

THE BEST PROMS ALBUM IN THE WORLD EVER! – VARIOUS ARTISTS (VIRGIN) 2000

THE BEST PUB JUKEBOX IN THE WORLD EVER VARIOUS ARTISTS (VIRGIN) 2000

THE BEST PUNK ALBUM IN THE WORLD... EVER! – VARIOUS ARTISTS (VIRGIN) 1995

THE BEST PUNK ALBUM IN THE WORLD... EVER! 2 VARIOUS ARTISTS (VIRGIN) 1996

THE BEST RAP ALBUM IN THE WORLD... EVER! – VARIOUS ARTISTS (VIRGIN) 1996

THE BEST RAVE ANTHEMS IN THE WORLD... EVER! – VARIOUS ARTISTS (VIRGIN) 1998

THE BEST REGGAE ALBUM IN THE WORLD... EVER! – VARIOUS ARTISTS (VIRGIN) 1994

THE BEST ROCK ALBUM IN THE WORLD... EVER! – VARIOUS ARTISTS (VIRGIN) 1994

THE BEST ROCK ALBUM IN THE WORLD... EVER! II VARIOUS ARTISTS (VIRGIN) 1995

THE BEST ROCK ANTHEMS ALBUM IN THE WORLD... EVER! – VARIOUS ARTISTS (VIRGIN) 1996

THE BEST ROCK ANTHEMS... EVER! – VARIOUS ARTISTS (VIRGIN) 1998

THE BEST ROCK BALLADS ALBUM IN THE WORLD... EVER! – VARIOUS ARTISTS (VIRGIN) 1995

THE BEST ROCK BALLADS ALBUM IN THE WORLD... EVER! II VARIOUS ARTISTS (VIRGIN) 1997

THE BEST ROCK 'N' ROLL ALBUM IN THE WORLD... EVER! – VARIOUS ARTISTS (VIRGIN) 1994

THE BEST SCOTTISH ALBUM IN THE WORLD... EVER! – VARIOUS ARTISTS (VIRGIN) 1997

THE BEST SEVENTIES ALBUM IN THE WORLD... EVER! – VARIOUS ARTISTS (VIRGIN) 1997

BEST SHOTS PAT BENATAR 1987

THE BEST SIXTIES ALBUM IN THE WORLD... EVER! – VARIOUS ARTISTS (VIRGIN) 1995

THE BEST SIXTIES ALBUM IN THE WORLD... EVER! II VARIOUS ARTISTS (VIRGIN) 1996

THE BEST SIXTIES ALBUM IN THE WORLD... EVER! III VARIOUS ARTISTS (VIRGIN) 1997

THE BEST SIXTIES ALBUM IN THE WORLD... EVER! IV VARIOUS ARTISTS (VIRGIN) 1998

THE BEST SIXTIES LOVE ALBUM... EVER! – VARIOUS ARTISTS (VIRGIN) 1999

THE BEST SIXTIES SUMMER ALBUM IN THE WORLD... EVER! – VARIOUS ARTISTS (VIRGIN) 1998

THE BEST SIXTIES SUMMER PARTY EVER VARIOUS ARTISTS (VIRGIN) 2002

THE BEST SMOOTH JAZZ EVER VARIOUS ARTISTS (VIRGIN) 2003

THE BEST STEPS TO HEAVEN SHOWADDYWADDY 1987

THE BEST SUMMER ALBUM IN THE WORLD... EVER! – VARIOUS ARTISTS (VIRGIN) 1995

THE BEST SUMMER ALBUM IN THE WORLD... EVER! – VARIOUS ARTISTS (VIRGIN) 1997

THE BEST SUMMER ALBUM 2002 VARIOUS ARTISTS (WARNER BROTHERS) 2002

THE BEST SUMMER ALBUM 2003 VARIOUS ARTISTS (WARNER BROTHERS) 2003

THE BEST SUMMER HOLIDAY 2001 EVER VARIOUS ARTISTS (VIRGIN) 2001

THE BEST SUMMER HOLIDAY EVER VARIOUS ARTISTS (VIRGIN) 2000

THE BEST SUMMER HOLIDAY EVER VARIOUS ARTISTS (VIRGIN) 2003

THE BEST SUMMER PARTY ALBUM IN THE WORLD... EVER! – VARIOUS ARTISTS (VIRGIN) 1998

BEST SWING '95 VARIOUS ARTISTS (TELSTAR) 1995

BEST SWING 96 VARIOUS ARTISTS (TELSTAR) 1996

BEST SWING 96 – VOLUME 2 VARIOUS ARTISTS (TELSTAR) 1996

BEST SWING '96 – VOLUME 3 VARIOUS ARTISTS (TELSTAR) 1996

THE BEST SWING ALBUM IN THE WORLD... EVER! – VARIOUS ARTISTS (VIRGIN) 1996

THE BEST THAT I COULD DO 1978–1988 JOHN MELLENCAMP 1998

THE BEST TRANCE ANTHEMS... EVER! – VARIOUS ARTISTS (VIRGIN) 1999

THE BEST TV ADS... EVER! – VARIOUS ARTISTS (VIRGIN) 2000

BEST UNOFFICIAL FOOTIE ANTHEMS EVER! – VARIOUS ARTISTS (VIRGIN) 2002

THE BEST WOMBLES ALBUM SO FAR – VOLUME 1 WOMBLES 1998

BEST WORSHIP SONGS EVER VARIOUS ARTISTS (VIRGIN) 2004

THE BEST YEARS OF OUR LIVES STEVE HARLEY & COCKNEY REBEL 1975

THE BEST YEARS OF OUR LIVES NEIL DIAMOND 1989

THE BEST... ALBUM IN THE WORLD... EVER! – VARIOUS ARTISTS (VIRGIN) 1995

THE BEST... ALBUM IN THE WORLD... EVER! 2 VARIOUS ARTISTS (VIRGIN) 1996

THE BEST... ALBUM IN THE WORLD... EVER! 3 VARIOUS ARTISTS (VIRGIN) 1996

THE BEST... ALBUM IN THE WORLD... EVER! 5 VARIOUS ARTISTS (VIRGIN) 1997

THE BEST... ALBUM IN THE WORLD... EVER! 6 VARIOUS ARTISTS (VIRGIN) 1997

THE BEST... AND FRIENDS ALBUM IN THE WORLD... EVER! – VARIOUS ARTISTS (VIRGIN) 1999

BEST... 1 SMITHS 1992

BEST... 2 SMITHS 1992

THE BEST... ANTHEMS... EVER! – VARIOUS ARTISTS (VIRGIN) 1997

THE BEST... ANTHEMS... EVER! 2 VARIOUS ARTISTS (VIRGIN) 1998

THE BEST... ANTHEMS... EVER! 3 VARIOUS ARTISTS (VIRGIN) 1998

THE BETA BAND BETA BAND 1999

BETE NOIRE BRYAN FERRY 1987

BETTE OF ROSES BETTE MIDLER 1995

BETTER DAYZ 2PAC 2002

BETTER LIVING THROUGH CHEMISTRY FATBOY SLIM 1996

A BETTER MAN BRIAN KENNEDY 1996

BETTER THE DEVIL YOU KNOW SONIA 1993

BETTY HELMET 1994

BETWEEN 10TH AND 11TH CHARLATANS 1992

BETWEEN THE BUTTONS ROLLING STONES 1967

BETWEEN THE COVERS MARTI PELLOW 2003

BETWEEN THE LINES FIVE STAR 1987

BETWEEN THE LINES JASON DONOVAN 1990

BETWEEN THE SENSES HAVEN 2002

BETWEEN TODAY AND YESTERDAY ALAN PRICE 1974

BETWEEN TWO FIRES PAUL YOUNG 1986

BEVERLEY CRAVEN BEVERLEY CRAVEN 1991

BEVERLY HILLS COP (OST) FILM SOUNDTRACK 1985

BEVERLY HILLS COP II (OST) FILM SOUNDTRACK 1987

BEYONCE BEYONCE KNOWLES 2003

BEYOND APPEARANCES SANTANA 1985

BEYOND GOOD AND EVIL CULT 2001

BEYOND IMAGINATION OPERABABES 2002

BEYOND SKIN NITIN SAWHNEY 1999

BEYOND THE ASTRAL SKIES ULI JON ROTH & ELECTRIC SUN 1985

BEYOND THE FRINGE ORIGINAL LONDON STAGE CAST SOUNDTRACK 1961

BEYOND THE MIX FRANKIE KNUCKLES 1991

BEYOND THE PLANETS KEVIN PEEK & RICK WAKEMAN FEATURING JEFF WAYNE NARRATION PATRICK ALLEN 1984

BEYOND THE SUN BILLY MACKENZIE 1997

BEYOND THE SUNSET RAIN PARADE 1985

BEYOND THE VALLEY OF THE MURDERDOLLS MURDERDOLLS 2002

THE BEYONDNESS OF THINGS ENGLISH CHAMBER ORCHESTRA CONDUCTED BY JOHN BARRY 1999

BEZERK TIGERTAILZ 1990

THE BIBLE BIBLE 1989

THE BIG 3 60FT DOLLS 1996

THE BIG AREA THEN JERICO 1989

BIG BAM BOOM DARYL HALL & JOHN OATES 1984

BIG BAND PERCUSSION TED HEATH & HIS MUSIC 1962

BIG BANG WE'VE GOT A FUZZBOX & WE'RE GONNA USE IT 1989

BIG BEACH BOUTIQUE II VARIOUS ARTISTS (SOUTHERN FRIED) 2002

THE BIG BREAKFAST ALBUM TELEVISION COMPILATION 1993

BIG BROTHER OST TELEVISION SOUNDTRACK 2000

BIG CALM MORCHEEBA 1998

BIG CLUB HITS VARIOUS ARTISTS (INSPIRED) 2001

BIG COCK KING KURT 1986

BIG DADDY JOHN COUGAR MELLENCAMP 1989

THE BIG EXPRESS XTC 1984

BIG GAME WHITE LION 1989

BIG GENERATOR YES 1987

THE BIG HIT MIX VARIOUS ARTISTS (VIRGIN) 1996

BIG HITS VARIOUS ARTISTS (GLOBAL) 1997

BIG HITS (HIGH TIDE AND GREEN GRASS) ROLLING STONES 1966

BIG HITS 98 VARIOUS ARTISTS (SONY) 1998

BIG HITS 99 VARIOUS ARTISTS (GLOBAL) 1999

THE BIG LAD IN THE WINDMILL IT BITES 1986

BIG LOVE ALI CAMPBELL 1995

BIG LOVE MOVIE THEMES GEOFF LOVE & HIS ORCHESTRA 1971

BIG MIX 96 VARIOUS ARTISTS (EMI) 1996

BIG MIX '96 – VOLUME 2 VARIOUS ARTISTS (EMI) 1996

BIG MIX '97 VARIOUS ARTISTS (VIRGIN) 1997

BIG MIX '97 – VOLUME 2 VARIOUS ARTISTS (VIRGIN) 1997

THE BIG ONES FOUR SEASONS 1971

BIG ONES AEROSMITH 1994

THE BIG PICTURE ELTON JOHN 1997

(BIG RED LETTER DAY) BUFFALO TOM 1993

BIG RIVER JIMMY NAIL 1995

BIG SCIENCE LAURIE ANDERSON 1982

BIG SCREEN CLASSICS ROYAL PHILHARMONIC ORCHESTRA 1994

BIG SMASH WRECKLESS ERIC 1980

BIG SOUND OF JOHNNY AND THE HURRICANES JOHNNY & THE HURRICANES 1961

BIG SPENDER SHIRLEY BASSEY 1971

THE BIG SQUEEZE – THE VERY BEST OF SQUEEZE 2002

BIG THING DURANDURAN 1988

THE BIG THROWDOWN LEVERT 1987

BIG TIME TOM WAITS 1988

BIG TUNES 2000 VARIOUS ARTISTS (TELSTAR) 2000

BIG WAR MOVIE THEMES GEOFF LOVE & HIS ORCHESTRA 1971

BIG WESTERN MOVIE THEMES GEOFF LOVE & HIS ORCHESTRA 1971

THE BIG WHEEL RUNRIG 1991

BIG WHEELS OF MOTOWN VARIOUS ARTISTS (MOTOWN) 1978

BIG WILLIE STYLE WILL SMITH 1997

BIG WORLD JOE JACKSON 1986

BIG! DANCE HITS OF 92 VARIOUS ARTISTS (THE HIT LABEL) 1992

BIGGER AND DEFFER LL COOL J 1987

BIGGER THAN BOTH OF US DARYL HALL & JOHN OATES 1976

BIGGER, BETTER, FASTER, MORE! – 4 NON BLONDES 1993

BIGGEST 80'S HITS IN THE WORLD... EVER! – VARIOUS ARTISTS (VIRGIN) 1998

THE BIGGEST CLUB ALBUM OF THE YEAR VARIOUS ARTISTS (GLOBAL) 1999

BILINGUAL PET SHOP BOYS 1996

BILL AND TED'S BOGUS JOURNEY (OST) FILM SOUNDTRACK 1992

BILL WYMAN BILL WYMAN 1982

THE BILLIE JO SPEARS SINGLES ALBUM BILLIE JO SPEARS 1979

BILLY BILLY FURY 1963

BILLY AND ALBERT BILLY CONNOLLY 1987

BILLY ELLIOT (OST) FILM SOUNDTRACK 2000

THE BILLY FURY HIT PARADE BILLY FURY 1983

BINAURAL PEARL JAM 2000

BIOGRAPHY – THE GREATEST HITS LISA STANSFIELD 2003

BIOLOGICAL RADIO DREADZONE 1997

BIRDLAND BIRDLAND 1991

BIRDS OF FIRE MAHAVISHNU ORCHESTRA 1973

BIRDY (OST) PETER GABRIEL 1985

BIRTH, SCHOOL, WORK, DEATH GODFATHERS 1988

BIRTHDAY PEDDLERS 1970

A BIT OF WHAT YOU FANCY QUIREBOYS 1990

BITCHES BREW MILES DAVIS 1970

BITE ALTERED IMAGES 1983

BITE NED'S ATOMIC DUSTBIN 1991

BITE IT WHITEOUT 1995

BITTER SUITE VARIOUS ARTISTS (CBS) 1981

BITTER SUITES TO SUCCUBI CRADLE OF FILTH 2001

BITTER SWEET KING 1985

BITTER SWEET AND TWISTED QUIREBOYS 1993

BITTERSWEET BLU CANTRELL 2003

BITTERSWEET LOVESONGS VARIOUS ARTISTS (VIRGIN) 2003

BIZARRE FRUIT/BIZARRE FRUIT II M PEOPLE 1994

BIZARRE RIDE II THE PHARCYDE PHARCYDE 1993

BIZZARO WEDDING PRESENT 1989

BLACK BLACK 1991

THE BLACK ALBUM DAMNED 1980

THE BLACK ALBUM PRINCE 1994

THE BLACK ALBUM JAY-Z 2003

BLACK AND BLUE ROLLING STONES 1976

BLACK AND BLUE BACKSTREET BOYS 2000

BLACK AND WHITE STRANGLERS 1978

BLACK AND WHITE POINTER SISTERS 1981

BLACK AND WHITE TERRAPLANE 1986

THE BLACK AND WHITE MINSTREL SHOW GEORGE MITCHELL MINSTRELS 1960

A BLACK AND WHITE NIGHT ROY ORBISON 1989

BLACK ANGEL MICA PARIS 1998

BLACK CELEBRATION DEPECHE MODE 1986

BLACK CHERRY GOLDFRAPP 2003

BLACK COFFEE PEGGY LEE 1961

BLACK DIAMOND ANGIE STONE 2000

BLACK EYED MAN COWBOY JUNKIES 1992

BLACK IS BLACK LOS BRAVOS 1966

BLACK JOY VARIOUS ARTISTS (RONCO) 1977

BLACK LOVE AFGHAN WHIGS 1996

BLACK MAGIC VARIOUS ARTISTS (STYLUS) 1986

BLACK MARKET MUSIC PLACEBO 2000

BLACK MEANING GOOD REBEL MC 1991

BLACK MOSES ISAAC HAYES 1972

BLACK OUT! – METHOD MAN & REDMAN 1999

BLACK REBEL MOTORCYCLE CLUB BLACK REBEL MOTORCYCLE CLUB 2002

THE BLACK RIDER TOM WAITS 1993

BLACK ROSE (A ROCK LEGEND) THIN LIZZY 1979

BLACK SABBATH BLACK SABBATH 1970

BLACK SABBATH LIVE AT LAST BLACK SABBATH 1980

BLACK SABBATH VOLUME 4 BLACK SABBATH 1972

BLACK SEA XTC 1980

BLACK SECRET TECHNOLOGY A GUY CALLED GERALD 1995

BLACK SUNDAY CYPRESS HILL 1993

THE BLACK SWAN TRIFFIDS 1989

BLACK TIE WHITE NOISE DAVID BOWIE 1993

BLACK TIGER Y & T 1982

BLACK UHURU BLACK UHURU 1981

BLACK VELVET VARIOUS ARTISTS (WARWICK) 1978

BLACKMARKET PRESENTS 2 STEP VARIOUS ARTISTS (AZULI) 2000

BLACKOUT SCORPIONS 1982

BLACKS' MAGIC SALT-N-PEPA 1990

BLACKSTREET BLACKSTREET 1994

BLADERUNNER (OST) VANGELIS 1994

BLAH BLAH BLAH IGGY POP 1986

BLAM! – BROTHERS JOHNSON 1978

BLAME IT ON THE BOOGIE VARIOUS ARTISTS (POLYGRAM) 1992

BLAME PRESENT LOGICAL PROGRESSION LEVEL 2 VARIOUS ARTISTS (GOOD LOOKING) 1997

BLAST HOLLY JOHNSON 1989

BLAST OFF STRAY CATS 1989

BLAZE OF GLORY JOE JACKSON 1989

BLAZE OF GLORY/YOUNG GUNS II (OST) JON BON JOVI 1990

BLAZING BULLETS VARIOUS ARTISTS (RONCO) 1975

BLEACH NIRVANA 1992

BLEED AMERICAN JIMMY EAT WORLD 2002

BLESS ITS POINTED LITTLE HEAD JEFFERSON AIRPLANE 1969

BLESSED BURDEN CARLEEN ANDERSON 1998

BLIND ICICLE WORKS 1988

BLIND SUNDAYS 1992

BLIND BEFORE I STOP MEAT LOAF 1986

BLIND DOG AT ST. DUNSTAN'S CARAVAN 1976

BLIND FAITH BLIND FAITH 1969

THE BLIND LEADING THE NAKED VIOLENT FEMMES 1986

BLIND MAN'S ZOO 10,000 MANIACS 1989

BLIND MELON BLIND MELON 1994

BLING VARIOUS ARTISTS (TELSTAR) 2004

BLINK 182 BLINK 182 2003

THE BLISS ALBUM… ? (VIBRATIONS OF LOVE AND ANGER AND THE PONDERANCE OF LIFE AND EXISTENCE) PM DAWN 1993

BLISSED OUT BELOVED 1990

BLITZ ORIGINAL LONDON STAGE CAST SOUNDTRACK 1962

A BLITZ OF SALT N PEPA HITS (THE HITS REMIXED) SALT-N-PEPA 1991

BLOCKBUSTER – THE SENSATIONAL 70S VARIOUS ARTISTS (CASTLE COMMUNICATIONS) 1992

BLOKE ON BLOKE BILLY BRAGG 1997

BLONDE ON BLONDE BOB DYLAN 1966

BLONDES HAVE MORE FUN ROD STEWART 1978

BLONDIE BLONDIE 1979

BLOOD THIS MORTAL COIL 1991

BLOOD AND CHOCOLATE ELVIS COSTELLO & THE ATTRACTIONS 1986

BLOOD FROM STONE DARE 1991

BLOOD IN MY EYE JA RULE 2003

BLOOD MONEY TOM WAITS 2002

BLOOD ON THE FLOOR – HISTORY IN THE MIX MICHAEL JACKSON 1997

BLOOD ON THE TRACKS BOB DYLAN 1975

BLOOD SUGAR SEX MAGIK RED HOT CHILI PEPPERS 1991

BLOOD SWEAT AND TEARS BLOOD, SWEAT & TEARS 1969

BLOOD SWEAT AND TEARS 3 BLOOD, SWEAT & TEARS 1970

BLOOD, FIRE AND LIVE ALMIGHTY 1990

BLOODFLOWERS CURE 2000

BLOODY TOURISTS 10 CC 1978

BLOW UP YOUR VIDEO AC/DC 1988

BLOWBACK TRICKY 2001

BLUE JONI MITCHELL 1971

BLUE DOUBLE 1986

BLUE MISSION 1996

BLUE SIMPLY RED 1998

BLUE BELL KNOLL COCTEAU TWINS 1988

THE BLUE CAFE – CHRIS REA 1998

BLUE EYED SOUL VARIOUS ARTISTS (TELSTAR) 1992

BLUE FOR YOU STATUS QUO 1976

BLUE FOR YOU – THE VERY BEST OF NINA SIMONE NINA SIMONE 1998

BLUE GENE GENE PITNEY 1964

BLUE HAWAII (OST) ELVIS PRESLEY 1961

BLUE HAWAII (OST) ELVIS PRESLEY 1977

BLUE IS THE COLOUR BEAUTIFUL SOUTH 1996

BLUE JAYS JUSTIN HAYWARD & JOHN LODGE 1975

THE BLUE JUKEBOX CHRIS REA 2004

BLUE LIGHT, RED LIGHT HARRY CONNICK JR. 1991

BLUE LINES MASSIVE ATTACK 1991

THE BLUE MEANING TOYAH 1980

BLUE MOVES ELTON JOHN 1976

BLUE MURDER BLUE MURDER 1989

BLUE PRINT RORY GALLAGHER 1973

BLUE ROSES FROM THE MOONS NANCI GRIFFITH 1997

BLUE SKIES FRANK IFIELD 1964

BLUE SKIES KIRI TE KANAWA WITH NELSON RIDDLE & HIS ORCHESTRA 1985

BLUE SKY MINING MIDNIGHT OIL 1990

BLUE SUEDE SHOES ELVIS PRESLEY 1998

BLUE SUNSHINE GLOVE 1983

BLUE VELVET BOBBY VINTON 1990

BLUE VIEWS PAUL CARRACK 1996

THE BLUEBELLS – THE SINGLES COLLECTION BLUEBELLS 1993

BLUEBIRD JAMES LAST 1983

THE BLUEPRINT JAY-Z 2001

THE BLUEPRINT 2 THE GIFT & THE CURSE JAY-Z 2002

BLUES JIMI HENDRIX 1994

BLUES ERIC CLAPTON 1999

THE BLUES ALBUM VARIOUS ARTISTS (VIRGIN) 1995

BLUES ALIVE GARY MOORE 1993

THE BLUES ALONE JOHN MAYALL 1967

BLUES AND SOUL MASTERS VARIOUS ARTISTS (WSM) 2002

BLUES ANYTIME VARIOUS ARTISTS (IMMEDIATE) 1968

BLUES BREAKERS JOHN MAYALL WITH ERIC CLAPTON 1966

BLUES BROTHER SOUL SISTER VARIOUS ARTISTS (DINO) 1993

BLUES BROTHER SOUL SISTER CLASSICS VARIOUS ARTISTS (UNIVERSAL) 1999

BLUES BROTHER SOUL SISTER VOLUME 2 VARIOUS ARTISTS (DINO) 1993

BLUES BROTHER SOUL SISTER VOLUME 3 VARIOUS ARTISTS (DINO) 1994

THE BLUES BROTHERS (OST) FILM SOUNDTRACK 1987

THE BLUES EXPERIENCE VARIOUS ARTISTS (POLYGRAM) 1993

BLUES FOR ALLAH GRATEFUL DEAD 1975

BLUES FOR GREENEY GARY MOORE 1995

BLUES FROM LAUREL CANYON JOHN MAYALL 1969

THE BLUES VOLUME 1 VARIOUS ARTISTS (PYE) 1964

THE BLUES VOLUME 2 VARIOUS ARTISTS (PYE) 1964

BLUR BLUR 1997

BLUR: BEST OF BLUR 2000

BLURRING THE EDGES MEREDITH BROOKS 1997

BO DIDDLEY'S BEACH PARTY BO DIDDLEY 1964

BO DIDDLEY BO DIDDLEY 1963

BO DIDDLEY IS A GUNSLINGER BO DIDDLEY 1963

BO DIDDLEY RIDES AGAINS BO DIDDLEY 1963

BOAT TO BOLIVIA MARTIN STEPHENSON & THE DAINTEES 1986

THE BOATMAN'S CALL NICK CAVE & THE BAD SEEDS 1997

BOB DYLAN BOB DYLAN 1965

BOB DYLAN AT BUDOKAN BOB DYLAN 1979

BOB MOULD BOB MOULD 1996

BOBBIE GENTRY AND GLEN CAMPBELL BOBBIE GENTRY & GLEN CAMPBELL 1970

BOBBY BOBBY BROWN 1992

BOBBY CRUSH BOBBY CRUSH 1972

THE BOBBY CRUSH INCREDIBLE DOUBLE DECKER PARTY 101 GREAT SONGS BOBBY CRUSH 1982

BOBBY DIGITAL IN STEREO RZA 1998

BOBBY VEE MEETS THE CRICKETS BOBBY VEE & THE CRICKETS 1962

A BOBBY VEE RECORDING SESSION BOBBY VEE 1963

THE BOBBY VEE SINGLES ALBUM BOBBY VEE 1980

BOBBY VEE'S GOLDEN GREATS BOBBY VEE 1963

BOCES MERCURY REV 1993

BODIES AND SOULS MANHATTAN TRANSFER 1984

BODY AND SOUL JOE JACKSON 1984

BODY AND SOUL – HEART AND SOUL II VARIOUS ARTISTS (HEART & SOUL) 1990

THE BODY AND SOUL OF TOM JONES TOM JONES 1973

BODY EXIT MIND NEW FAST AUTOMATIC DAFFODILS 1992
BODY LANGUAGE KYLIE MINOGUE 2003
BODY TALK IMAGINATION 1981
BODY TO BODY TECHNOTRONIC 1991
BODY WISHES ROD STEWART 1983
THE BODYGUARD (OST) FILM SOUNDTRACK 1992
BOHEME DEEP FOREST 1995
BOING! – AIRHEAD 1992
BOLAN BOOGIE T. REX 1972
BOMBAY MIX VARIOUS ARTISTS (TELSTAR) 2003
BOMBER MOTORHEAD 1979
BON JOVI BON JOVI 1984
BONA DRAG MORRISSEY 1990
BONAFIDE MAXI PRIEST 1990
BONE MACHINE TOM WAITS 1992
BONKERS 2 VARIOUS ARTISTS (REACT) 1997
BONKERS X VARIOUS ARTISTS (REACT) 2003
BONKERS 3 – JOURNEY INTO MADNESS VARIOUS ARTISTS
(REACT) 1997
BONKERS 12 VARIOUS ARTISTS (REACT) 2004
BONKERS 4 – WORLD FRENZY VARIOUS ARTISTS (REACT)
1998
BONKERS 5 – ANARCHY IN THE UNIVERSE VARIOUS
ARTISTS (REACT) 1998
BONKERS 6 (WHEEL CRAZY) VARIOUS ARTISTS (REACT)
1999
BONKERS 7 – MILLENNIUM MADNESS VARIOUS ARTISTS
(REACT) 1999
BOOGIE BUS VARIOUS ARTISTS (POLYDOR) 1979
BOOGIE FEVER VARIOUS ARTISTS (RONCO) 1978
BOOGIE NIGHTS VARIOUS ARTISTS (RONCO) 1978
BOOGIE NIGHTS (OST) FILM SOUNDTRACK 1998
BOOGIE WITH CANNED HEAT CANNED HEAT 1968
BOOGIE WONDERLAND – THE VERY BEST OF EARTH WIND &
FIRE EARTH WIND & FIRE 1996
BOOK OF DAYS PSYCHEDELIC FURS 1989
BOOK OF DREAMS STEVE MILLER BAND 1977
THE BOOK OF INVASIONS – A CELTIC SYMPHONY HORSLIPS
1977
BOOKBINDER'S KID ELKIE BROOKS 1988
BOOKENDS SIMON & GARFUNKEL 1968
BOOM BOOM JOHN LEE HOOKER 1992
BOOM SELECTION VARIOUS ARTISTS (WARNER BROTHERS)
2002
BOOMANIA BETTY BOO 1990
BOOMBASTIC SHAGGY 1995
BOOMERANG (OST) FILM SOUNDTRACK 1992
BOOMTOWN RATS BOOMTOWN RATS 1977
BOOTH AND THE BAD ANGEL BOOTH & THE BAD ANGEL
1996
THE BOOTLEG SERIES VOLUMES 1 3 BOB DYLAN 1991
BOOTLEG SERIES VOLUME 6 BOB DYLAN 2004
THE BOOTLEG VERSIONS FUGEES 1996
BOOTS NANCY SINATRA 1966
BOP TILL YOU DROP RY COODER 1979
THE BOP WON'T STOP SHAKIN' STEVENS 1983
BORBOLETTA SANTANA 1974
BORDER LINE RY COODER 1980
BORN CHINA BLACK 1995
BORN BOND 2000
BORN A WOMAN SANDY POSEY 1967
BORN AGAIN BLACK SABBATH 1983
BORN AGAIN NOTORIOUS B.I.G. 1999
BORN DEAD BODY COUNT 1994
BORN FREE FRANK IFIELD 1963
BORN FREE ANDY WILLIAMS 1967
BORN IN THE U.S.A. BRUCE SPRINGSTEEN 1984
BORN INNOCENT PROCLAIMERS 2003
BORN INTO THE 90'S R KELLY & PUBLIC ANNOUNCEMENT
1992
BORN THIS WAY! – COOKIE CREW 1989
BORN TO BE WILD VARIOUS ARTISTS (TELSTAR) 1991
BORN TO BE WILD VARIOUS ARTISTS (MCI) 1995
BORN TO BE WILD VARIOUS ARTISTS (TELSTAR) 1999
BORN TO DO IT CRAIG DAVID 2000
BORN TO LOVE PEABO BRYSON & ROBERTA FLACK 1983

BORN TO REIGN WILL SMITH 2002
BORN TO RUN BRUCE SPRINGSTEEN 1975
BORN TO SING EN VOGUE 1990
BORROWED HEAVEN CORRS 2004
BORROWED TIME DIAMOND HEAD 1982
THE BOSS DIANA ROSS 1979
BOSS DRUM/DIFFERENT DRUM SHAMEN 1992
BOSSANOVA PIXIES 1990
BOSTON BOSTON 1977
BOSTON BOSTON 1981
BOTH SIDES NOW JONI MITCHELL 2000
BOTH SIDES OF THE STORY PHIL COLLINS 1993
BOULDERS ROY WOOD 1973
BOUNCE BON JOVI 2002
BOUNCING OFF THE SATELLITES B-52'S 1987
BOUND 4 DA RELOAD (CASUALTY) OXIDE & NEUTRINO
2000
BOW DOWN TO THE EXIT SIGN DAVID HOLMES 2000
BOWIE AT THE BEEB DAVID BOWIE 2000
BOWS AND ARROWS WALKMEN 2004
THE BOX VARIOUS ARTISTS (UNIVERSAL) 2000
BOX CAR RACER BOX CAR RACER 2002
THE BOX – DANCE HITS VARIOUS ARTISTS (UNIVERSAL)
1999
THE BOX DANCE HITS – VOLUME 2 VARIOUS ARTISTS
(UNIVERSAL) 1999
BOX DANCE HITS 2000 VARIOUS ARTISTS (UNIVERSAL)
2000
THE BOX HITS 98 VARIOUS ARTISTS (TELSTAR) 1998
THE BOX HITS 98 – VOLUME 2 VARIOUS ARTISTS (TELSTAR)
1998
BOX HITS 98 – VOLUME 3 VARIOUS ARTISTS (TELSTAR)
1998
THE BOX R&B HITS ALBUM VARIOUS ARTISTS (TELSTAR)
1999
BOXED MIKE OLDFIELD 1976
BOY U2 1981
BOY IN DA CORNER DIZZEE RASCAL 2003
THE BOY IS MINE MONICA 1998
THE BOY WITH THE ARAB STRAP BELLE & SEBASTIAN 1998
THE BOY WITH THE X-RAY EYES BABYLON ZOO 1996
THE BOYS BOYS 1977
BOYS VARIOUS ARTISTS (COLUMBIA) 1997
BOYS AND GIRLS BRYAN FERRY 1985
THE BOYS ARE BACK IN TOWN VARIOUS ARTISTS
(COLUMBIA) 1992
BOYS DON'T CRY CURE 1983
BOYS FOR PELE TORI AMOS 1996
THE BOY'S HEART MARTIN STEPHENSON & THE DAINTEES
1992
BOY'S NIGHT OUT FIRST CIRCLE 1987
BOYZ OF SWING VARIOUS ARTISTS (POLYGRAM) 1996
BOYZ OF SWING II VARIOUS ARTISTS (POLYGRAM) 1996
THE BOYZ WHO SOULED THE WORLD VARIOUS ARTISTS
(THE HIT LABEL) 1994
BPM... THE VERY BEST OF THE BEAT BEAT 1996
BRAHMS: VIOLIN CONCERTO NIGEL KENNEDY WITH THE
LONDON PHILHARMONIC ORCHESTRA 1991
BRAIN DRAIN RAMONES 1989
BRAIN SALAD SURGERY EMERSON, LAKE & PALMER 1973
BRAINWASHED GEORGE HARRISON 2002
BRAM STOKER'S DRACULA (OST) FILM SOUNDTRACK 1993
BRAND NEW AGE U.K. SUBS 1980
BRAND NEW BOOTS AND PANTIES BLOCKHEADS 2001
BRAND NEW DAY STING 1999
BRAND NEW HEAVIES BRAND NEW HEAVIES 1992
THE BRASS ARE COMIN' – HERB ALPERT & THE TIJUANA
BRASS 1970
BRASS CONSTRUCTION BRASS CONSTRUCTION 1976
BRASSED OFF (OST) GRIMETHORPE COLLIERY BAND 1998
BRAVE MARILLION 1994
BRAVE AND CRAZY MELISSA ETHERIDGE 1989
BRAVE NEW WORLD IRON MAIDEN 2000
BRAVEHEART (OST) LONDON SYMPHONY ORCHESTRA,
CONDUCTOR JAMES HORNER 1995
BRAVO JULIET HECTOR NICOL 1984

BRAVO TWO ZERO ANDY MCNABB 1994
BRAZILIAN LOVE AFFAIR GEORGE DUKE 1980
BREAD WINNERS JACK JONES 1972
BREAK EVERY RULE TINA TURNER 1986
BREAK LIKE THE WIND SPINAL TAP 1992
BREAK MACHINE BREAK MACHINE 1984
BREAK OUT POINTER SISTERS 1984
BREAK THE CYCLE STAIND 2001
BREAKAWAY ART GARFUNKEL 1975
BREAKAWAY GALLAGHER & LYLE 1976
BREAKDANCE (OST) FILM SOUNDTRACK 1984
BREAKDANCE 2 – ELECTRIC BOOGALOO (OST) FILM
SOUNDTRACK 1985
BREAKDANCE, YOU CAN DO IT! – VARIOUS ARTISTS (K-TEL)
1984
BREAKDOWN VARIOUS ARTISTS (TELSTAR) 2000
BREAKDOWN – VERY BEST OF EUPHORIC DANCE VARIOUS
ARTISTS (TELSTAR) 2000
BREAKFAST IN AMERICA SUPERTRAMP 1979
BREAKIN' OUT FAT LARRY'S BAND 1982
BREAKING AWAY AL JARREAU 1981
BREAKING AWAY JAKI GRAHAM 1986
BREAKING GLASS (OST) HAZEL O'CONNOR 1980
BREAKING HEARTS ELTON JOHN 1984
BREAKING HEARTS VARIOUS ARTISTS (DINO) 1992
BREAKING POINT CENTRAL LINE 1982
BREAKOUT VARIOUS ARTISTS (RONCO) 1982
BREAKS, BASS AND BLEEPS 2 VARIOUS ARTISTS
(RUMOUR) 1991
BREAKS, BASS AND BLEEPS 4 VARIOUS ARTISTS
(RUMOUR) 1992
BREAKTHROUGH VARIOUS ARTISTS (STUDIO TWO) 1967
BREAKTHROUGH VARIOUS ARTISTS (MFP) 1971
BREATHE FAITH HILL 2000
BREATHE LEAVES 2002
BREATHLESS CAMEL 1978
BREATHLESS KENNY G 1993
BRENDA – THAT'S ALL BRENDA LEE 1963
THE BRENDAN SHINE COLLECTION BRENDAN SHINE 1983
BREWING UP WITH BILLY BRAGG BILLY BRAGG 1984
BRICK BY BRICK IGGY POP 1990
BRICKS ARE HEAVY L7 1992
THE BRIDE STRIPPED BARE BRYAN FERRY 1978
BRIDESHEAD REVISITED (OST – TV – CONDUCTED BY
GEOFFREY BURGON) TELEVISION SOUNDTRACK 1981
THE BRIDGE BILLY JOEL 1986
THE BRIDGE ACE OF BASE 1995
BRIDGE OF SPIES T'PAU 1987
BRIDGE OVER TROUBLED WATER RAY CONNIFF 1970
BRIDGE OVER TROUBLED WATER SIMON & GARFUNKEL
1970
BRIDGES JOHN WILLIAMS 1979
BRIDGES TO BABYLON ROLLING STONES 1997
BRIDGET JONES'S DIARY (OST) FILM SOUNDTRACK 2001
BRIDGET JONES'S DIARY 2 (OST) FILM SOUNDTRACK
2001
BRIGADE HEART 1990
BRIGHT LIGHTS SHOWADDYWADDY 1980
BRIGHTEN THE CORNERS PAVEMENT 1997
BRIGHTER THAN A THOUSAND SUNS KILLING JOKE 1986
BRILLIANT TREES DAVID SYLVAN 1984
BRIMSTONE AND TREACLE (OST) FILM SOUNDTRACK 1982
BRING DOWN THE WALLS NO LIMIT SQUAD RETURNS
SILVER BULLET 1991
BRING 'EM ALL IN MIKE SCOTT 1995
BRING IT BACK MCALMONT & BUTLER 2002
BRING IT ON GOMEZ 1998
BRING IT ON ALISTAIR GRIFFIN 2004
BRING ON THE NIGHT STING 1986
BRINGING DOWN THE HORSE WALLFLOWERS 1997
BRINGING IT ALL BACK HOME BOB DYLAN 1965
THE BRIT AWARDS VARIOUS ARTISTS (EMI) 1994
BRIT AWARDS '96 VARIOUS ARTISTS (COLUMBIA) 1996
THE BRIT AWARDS 1998 VARIOUS ARTISTS (COLUMBIA)
1998
BRIT AWARDS ALBUM VARIOUS ARTISTS (BMG) 2003

THE BRIT AWARDS ALBUM 2004 VARIOUS ARTISTS (BMG) 2004
BRIT AWARDS 2001 – ALBUM OF THE YEAR VARIOUS ARTISTS (COLUMBIA) 2001
BRIT AWARDS '96 VARIOUS ARTISTS (COLUMBIA) 1996
BRIT HOP AND AMYL HOUSE VARIOUS ARTISTS (CONCRETE) 1996
BRITISH CONCERT NANA MOUSKOURI 1972
BRITISH MOTOWN CHARTBUSTERS VARIOUS ARTISTS (MOTOWN) 1967
BRITISH MOTOWN CHARTBUSTERS VOLUME 2 VARIOUS ARTISTS (MOTOWN) 1968
BRITISH STEEL JUDAS PRIEST 1980
BRITNEY BRITNEY SPEARS 2001
THE BRITS – THE AWARDS 1989 VARIOUS ARTISTS (TELSTAR) 1989
THE BRITS 1991 – THE MAGIC OF BRITISH MUSIC VARIOUS ARTISTS (TELSTAR) 1991
BROADCAST CUTTING CREW 1986
BROADSWORD AND THE BEAST JETHRO TULL 1982
THE BROADWAY ALBUM BARBRA STREISAND 1986
THE BROADWAY I LOVE PLACIDO DOMINGO WITH THE LONDON SYMPHONY ORCHESTRA CONDUCTED BY EUGENE KOHN 1991
BROKE HED P E 2000
BROKEN NINE INCH NAILS 1992
BROKEN ARROW NEIL YOUNG & CRAZY HORSE 1996
BROKEN BARRICADES PROCOL HARUM 1971
BROKEN CHINA RICK WRIGHT 1996
BROKEN DREAMS VARIOUS ARTISTS (STARBLEND) 1984
BROKEN ENGLISH MARIANNE FAITHFULL 1979
A BROKEN FRAME DEPECHE MODE 1982
BROTHAS DOOBIE FUNKDOOBIEST 1995
BROTHER SISTER BRAND NEW HEAVIES 1994
BROTHER WHERE YOU BOUND SUPERTRAMP 1985
BROTHERHOOD NEW ORDER 1986
BROTHERHOOD 3T 1996
BROTHERHOOD OF MAN BROTHERHOOD OF MAN 1978
BROTHERHOOD OF MAN SING 20 NUMBER ONE HITS BROTHERHOOD OF MAN 1980
BROTHERS AND SISTERS ALLMAN BROTHERS BAND 1973
BROTHER'S GONNA WORK IT OUT VARIOUS ARTISTS (FREESTYLE) 1998
BROTHERS IN ARMS DIRE STRAITS 1985
BROTHERS IN RHYTHM VARIOUS ARTISTS (ARIOLA) 1988
BROTHER'S KEEPER NEVILLE BROTHERS 1990
BROWN SUGAR D'ANGELO 1995
BRUTAL PLANET ALICE COOPER 2000
BRUTAL YOUTH ELVIS COSTELLO & THE ATTRACTIONS 1994
BRYN BRYN TERFEL 2003
THE BRYN YEMM CHRISTMAS COLLECTION BRYN YEMM 1984
B SIDES, SEASIDES & FREERIDES OCEAN COLOUR SCENE 1997
BUBBLE AND SCRAPE SEBADOH 1993
BUCKS FIZZ BUCKS FIZZ 1981
BUDDAH AND THE CHOCOLATE BOX CAT STEVENS 1974
BUDDY HOLLY SHOWCASE BUDDY HOLLY & THE CRICKETS 1964
THE BUDDY HOLLY STORY BUDDY HOLLY & THE CRICKETS 1959
THE BUDDY HOLLY STORY VOLUME 2 BUDDY HOLLY & THE CRICKETS 1960
BUDDY HOLLY'S GREATEST HITS BUDDY HOLLY 1967
BUDDY'S SONG (OST) CHESNEY HAWKES 1991
BUENA VISTA SOCIAL CLUB RY COODER 1997
BUENA VISTA SOCIAL CLUB PRESENTS IBRAHIM FERRER IBRAHIM FERRER 1999
BUENAS NOCHES FROM A LONELY ROOM DWIGHT YOAKAM 1988
THE BUFFALO SKINNERS BIG COUNTRY 1993
BUFFY THE VAMPIRE SLAYER TELEVISION SOUNDTRACK 2003
BUFFY THE VAMPIRE SLAYER – THE ALBUM TELEVISION SOUNDTRACK 1999
BUHLOONE MINDSTATE DE LA SOUL 1993

BUILD INNOCENCE 1992
BUILDING THE PERFECT BEAST DON HENLEY 1985
BUILT TO DESTROY MICHAEL SCHENKER GROUP 1983
BULLET FROM A GUN DEREK B 1988
BULLINAMINGVASE ROY HARPER 1977
BULLY FOR YOU B.A. ROBERTSON 1981
BUMMED HAPPY MONDAYS 1990
BUMP AHEAD MR. BIG 1993
BUNKKA PAUL OAKENFOLD 2002
BURN DEEP PURPLE 1974
BURN MY EYES MACHINE HEAD 1994
BURNED ELECTRAFIXION 1995
BURNIN' SKY BAD COMPANY 1977
BURNING BLUE SOUL THE THE 1981
BURNING FROM THE INSIDE BAUHAUS 1983
BURNING HEARTS VARIOUS ARTISTS (TELSTAR) 1991
THE BURNING RED MACHINE HEAD 1999
BURNT WEENY SANDWICH MOTHERS OF INVENTION 1970
BURY THE HATCHET CRANBERRIES 1999
BUSINESS AS USUAL SECRET AFFAIR 1982
BUSINESS AS USUAL MEN AT WORK 1983
BUSINESS AS USUAL E.P.M.D. 1991
BUSINESS OF PUNISHMENT CONSOLIDATED 1994
BUST A NUT TESLA 1994
BUSTED BUSTED 2002
BUSTER (OST) FILM SOUNDTRACK 1988
BUSTING AT THE SEAMS STRAWBS 1973
BUSY BODY LUTHER VANDROSS 1984
... BUT SERIOUSLY PHIL COLLINS 1989
BUT SERIOUSLY FOLKS... – JOE WALSH 1978
BUTTERFLY MARIAH CAREY 1997
THE BUTTON DOWN MIND OF BOB NEWHART BOB NEWHART 1960
BUY NOW... SAVED LATER ONE MINUTE SILENCE 2000
BUZZ STEPS 2000
BY 7.30 VONDA SHEPARD 1999
BY ALL MEANS BY ALL MEANS 1988
BY ALL MEANS NECESSARY BOOGIE DOWN PRODUCTIONS 1988
BY INVITATION ONLY VARIOUS ARTISTS (ATLANTIC) 1976
BY REQUEST SALVATION ARMY 1977
BY REQUEST LENA MARTELL 1980
BY REQUEST JAMES LAST 1987
BY REQUEST FOSTER & ALLEN 1993
BY REQUEST BOYZONE 1999
BY SPECIAL REQUEST – THE VERY BEST OF FOSTER & ALLEN 2003
BY THE LIGHT OF THE MOON LOS LOBOS 1987
BY THE WAY RED HOT CHILI PEPPERS 2002
BY YOUR SIDE PETERS & LEE 1973
BY YOUR SIDE BLACK CROWES 1999
BYE BYE BIRDIE ORIGINAL LONDON STAGE CAST SOUNDTRACK 1961
BYE BYE BLUES BERT KAEMPFERT & HIS ORCHESTRA 1966
BYE BYE BLUES BRENDA LEE 1966
BYRDS BYRDS 1973
C.C.S. C.C.S. 1972
C.M.B. COLOR ME BADD 1991
CA$HFLOW CA$HFLOW 1986
CABARET (OST) FILM SOUNDTRACK 1973
CACHARPAYA (PANPIPES OF THE ANDES) INCANTATION 1982
CADMIUM SKY 1983
CAFE BLEU STYLE COUNCIL 1984
CAFE CAROLINA DON WILLIAMS 1984
CAFE DEL MAR – VOLUMEN SIETE VARIOUS ARTISTS (MANIFESTO) 2000
CAFE DEL MAR IBIZA – VOLUMEN CINCO VARIOUS ARTISTS (MANIFESTO) 1998
CAFE DEL MAR IBIZA – VOLUMEN CUATRO VARIOUS ARTISTS (MANIFESTO) 1997
CAFE DEL MAR IBIZA – VOLUMEN DOS VARIOUS ARTISTS (REACT) 1995
CAFE DEL MAR IBIZA – VOLUMEN SEIS VARIOUS ARTISTS (MANIFESTO) 1999

CAFE DEL MAR IBIZA – VOLUMEN TRES VARIOUS ARTISTS (REACT) 1996
CAFE DEL MAR VOLUMEN OCHO VARIOUS ARTISTS (MANIFESTO) 2001
CAFE LATINO VARIOUS ARTISTS (TELSTAR) 1996
CAFE MAMBO VARIOUS ARTISTS (VIRGIN) 1997
CAFE MAMBO – THE REAL SOUND OF IBIZA VARIOUS ARTISTS (COLUMBIA) 2000
THE CAGE TYGERS OF PAN TANG 1982
CAHOOTS BAND 1971
CAKE TRASH CAN SINATRAS 1990
CAL (OST) MARK KNOPFLER 1984
CALIFORNIA DREAMIN' – GREATEST HITS OF THE MAMAS AND THE PAPAS MAMAS & THE PAPAS 1997
CALIFORNIA DREAMIN' – THE VERY BEST OF THE MAMAS AND THE PAPAS MAMAS & THE PAPAS 1995
CALIFORNIA DREAMING VARIOUS ARTISTS (K-TEL) 1981
CALIFORNIA HOLIDAY (OST) ELVIS PRESLEY 1966
CALIFORNICATION RED HOT CHILI PEPPERS 1999
CALL OFF THE SEARCH KATIE MELUA 2003
CALLING ALL STATIONS GENESIS 1997
CALLING CARD RORY GALLAGHER 1976
CALM VARIOUS ARTISTS (DECCA) 2000
CAMELOT ORIGINAL BROADWAY STAGE CAST SOUNDTRACK 1964
CAMELOT ORIGINAL LONDON STAGE CAST SOUNDTRACK 1965
CAMELOT (OST) FILM SOUNDTRACK 1968
CAMINO PALMERO CALLING 2002
CAMOUFLAGE ROD STEWART 1984
CAN CAN (OST) FILM SOUNDTRACK 1960
CAN I PLAY WITH MADNESS/THE EVIL THAT MEN DO IRON MAIDEN 1990
CAN OUR LOVE TINDERSTICKS 2001
CAN U FEEL IT? – THE CHAMPION LEGEND VARIOUS ARTISTS (K-TEL) 1990
CAN YOU DO ME GOOD DEL AMITRI 2002
CAN YOU FEEL THE FORCE REAL THING 1979
CAN YOU TELL WHAT IT IS YET? ROLF HARRIS 1997
CANADIAN PACIFIC GEORGE HAMILTON IV 1971
CANDLELAND IAN MCCULLOCH 1989
CANDLES HEATWAVE 1981
CANDLES IN THE RAIN MELANIE 1970
CANDYFLOSS AND MEDICINE EDDI READER 1996
CANDY O CARS 1979
CAN I BUS CANIBUS 1998
CANNED HEAT '70 CONCERT CANNED HEAT 1970
CANNED HEAT COOKBOOK CANNED HEAT 1970
CAN'T BE WITH YOU TONIGHT JUDY BOUCHER 1987
CAN'T BUY A THRILL STEELY DAN 1975
CAN'T GET ENOUGH BARRY WHITE 1974
CAN'T GET ENOUGH EDDY GRANT 1981
CAN'T GET USED TO LOSING YOU ANDY WILLIAMS 1965
CAN'T HELP FALLING IN LOVE ANDY WILLIAMS 1970
CAN'T SLOW DOWN LIONEL RICHIE 1983
CAN'T STAND THE REZILLOS REZILLOS 1978
CAN'T STOP THE CLASSICS – HOOKED ON CLASSICS 2 LOUIS CLARK CONDUCTING THE ROYAL PHILHARMONIC ORCHESTRA 1982
CAN'T STOP THE LOVE MAZE FEATURING FRANKIE BEVERLY 1985
CAN'T STOP THE MUSIC (OST) VILLAGE PEOPLE 1980
CAN'T TAKE ME HOME PINK 2000
CANTERBURY DIAMOND HEAD 1983
CANTO GREGORIANO CORO DE MUNJES DEL MONASTERIO BENEDICTINO DE SANTO DOMINGO DE SILOS 1994
CANTO NOEL CORO DE MUNJES DEL MONASTERIO BENEDICTINO DE SANTO DOMINGO DE SILOS 1994
CAPERCAILLIE CAPERCAILLIE 1994
CAPITAL GOLD BRITISH LEGENDS VARIOUS ARTISTS (VIRGIN) 2003
CAPITAL GOLD EIGHTIES LEGENDS VARIOUS ARTISTS (VIRGIN) 2002
CAPITAL GOLD LEGENDS VARIOUS ARTISTS (VIRGIN) 2001
CAPITAL GOLD LEGENDS II VARIOUS ARTISTS (VIRGIN) 2001

CAPITAL GOLD LEGENDS III VARIOUS ARTISTS (VIRGIN/EMI) 2002

CAPITAL GOLD – LOVE LEGENDS VARIOUS ARTISTS (VIRGIN) 2003

CAPITAL GOLD MOTOWN CLASSICS VARIOUS ARTISTS (UNIVERSAL) 2003

CAPITAL GOLD REGGAE CLASSICS VARIOUS ARTISTS (UNIVERSAL) 2003

CAPITAL GOLD ROCK LEGENDS VARIOUS ARTISTS (VIRGIN/EMI) 2002

CAPITAL GOLD – ROCK 'N' ROLL LEGENDS VARIOUS ARTISTS (VIRGIN) 2003

CAPITAL GOLD SIXTIES LEGENDS VARIOUS ARTISTS (VIRGIN) 2002

CAPITOL CLASSICS VOLUME 1 VARIOUS ARTISTS (CAPITOL) 1989

THE CAPPUCCINO SONGS TANITA TIKARAM 1998

CAPTAIN BEAKY AND HIS BAND KEITH MICHELL 1980

CAPTAIN CORELLI'S MANDOLIN (OST) STEPHEN WARBECK 2001

CAPTAIN FANTASTIC AND THE BROWN DIRT COWBOY ELTON JOHN 1975

CAPTAIN PARALYTIC AND THE BROWN ALE COWBOY MIKE HARDING 1978

CAPTAIN SWING MICHELLE SHOCKED 1989

CAPTURED NATASHA 1982

CAR BOOT SOUL NIGHTMARES ON WAX 1999

CAR BUTTON CLOTH LEMONHEADS 1996

CARAVANSERAI SANTANA 1972

CAREFUL WHAT YOU WISH FOR TEXAS 2003

CARGO MEN AT WORK 1983

CARIBBEAN GUITAR CHET ATKINS 1963

CARIBBEAN UNCOVERED VARIOUS ARTISTS (VIRGIN) 1998

CARIBOU ELTON JOHN 1974

CARL AND THE PASSIONS/SO TOUGH BEACH BOYS 1972

CARL COX – FACT 2 VARIOUS ARTISTS (WORLDWIDE ULTIMATUM) 1997

CARL COX – NON STOP 2000 VARIOUS ARTISTS (FFRR) 1999

CARL COX – NON STOP 98/01 VARIOUS ARTISTS (FFRR) 1998

CARLOS SANTANA AND BUDDY MILES LIVE CARLOS SANTANA & BUDDY MILES 1972

CARMEL 6 TRACK (EP) CARMEL 1983

CARMEN ORCHESTRE NATIONAL DE LA RADIO DIFFUSION FRANCAISE, CONDUCTED BY SIR THOMAS BEECHAM 1960

CARNIVAL MANUEL & THE MUSIC OF THE MOUNTAINS 1976

THE CARNIVAL WYCLEF JEAN 1997

CARNIVAL OF HITS JUDITH DURHAM & THE SEEKERS 1994

CARNIVAL OF LIGHT RIDE 1994

THE CAROLS ALBUM HUDDERSFIELD CHORAL SOCIETY 1986

CAROUSEL (OST) FILM SOUNDTRACK 1958

THE CARPENTERS CARPENTERS 1971

THE CARPENTERS COLLECTION RICHARD CLAYDERMAN 1995

CARROTT IN NOTTS JASPER CARROTT 1976

CARROTT'S LIB JASPER CARROTT 1982

CARRY ON OI! – VARIOUS ARTISTS (SECRET) 1981

CARRY ON UP THE CHARTS – THE BEST OF THE BEAUTIFUL SOUTH BEAUTIFUL SOUTH 1994

CARRYING A TORCH TOM JONES 1991

CARS CARS 1978

THE CARS GREATEST HITS CARS 1985

CARVED IN SAND MISSION 1990

CARWASH VARIOUS ARTISTS (TELSTAR) 1998

CASANOVA DIVINE COMEDY 1996

CASH COWS VARIOUS ARTISTS (VIRGIN) 1980

CASHMERE CASHMERE 1985

CASINO CLASSICS SAINT ETIENNE 1996

CASINO ROYALE (OST) BURT BACHARACH 1967

CASS, JOHN, MICHELLE, DENNY MAMAS & THE PAPAS 1967

THE CASSETTE OF THE ALBUM ROLAND RAT SUPERSTAR 1984

CASSIDY LIVE DAVID CASSIDY 1974

CAST OF THOUSANDS ELBOW 2003

CAST YOUR FATE TO THE WIND SOUNDS ORCHESTRAL 1965

CASUAL SEX IN THE CINEPLEX SULTANS OF PING F.C. 1993

CASUALLY DRESSED AND DEEP IN CONVERSATION FUNERAL FOR A FRIEND 2003

THE CAT IS OUT JUDIE TZUKE 1985

CAT SCRATCH FEVER TED NUGENT 1977

CATALYST NEW FOUND GLORY 2004

CATCH AS CATCH CAN KIM WILDE 1983

CATCH BULL AT FOUR CAT STEVENS 1972

CATCH US IF YOU CAN DAVE CLARK FIVE 1965

CATCHING THE SUN SPYRO GYRA 1980

CATCHING UP WITH MEZZOFORTE MEZZOFORTE 1983

CATFISH RISING JETHRO TULL 1991

CATS ORIGINAL LONDON STAGE CAST SOUNDTRACK 1981

CATS WITHOUT CLAWS DONNA SUMMER 1984

CAUGHT IN THE ACT STEVE GIBBONS BAND 1977

CAUGHT IN THE ACT STYX 1984

THE CAUTION HORSES COWBOY JUNKIES 1990

CAVATINA JOHN WILLIAMS 1979

CD UK VARIOUS ARTISTS (BMG) 2000

CD:UK – MORE WICKED HITS VARIOUS ARTISTS (BMG) 2001

CELEBRATE THE BULLET SELECTER 1981

CELEBRATION JOHNNY MATHIS 1981

CELEBRATION SIMPLE MINDS 1982

CELEBRATION – THE BEST OF REGGAE – 25 YEARS OF TROJAN VARIOUS ARTISTS (QUALITY PRICE MUSIC) 1992

CELEBRATION 2000 VARIOUS ARTISTS (UNIVERSAL) 2000

CELEBRATION! – ANDRE RIEU 2000

CELEBRITY N SYNC 2001

CELEBRITY SKIN HOLE 1998

CELINE DION CELINE DION 1998

THE CELTIC CHILLOUT ALBUM VARIOUS ARTISTS COMPILATION (DECADANCE) 2002

THE CELTIC CHILLOUT ALBUM RYAN & RACHEL O'DONNELL 2002

THE CELTIC CHILLOUT ALBUM 2 RYAN & RACHEL O'DONNELL 2003

THE CELTIC COLLECTION VARIOUS ARTISTS (SONY) 1999

CELTIC DREAMS CELTIC SPIRIT 1998

CELTIC HEART VARIOUS ARTISTS (RCA) 1993

CELTIC MOODS VARIOUS ARTISTS (VIRGIN) 1995

CELTIC MOODS 2 VARIOUS ARTISTS (VIRGIN) 1995

THE CELTS ENYA 1992

CENTERFIELD JOHN FOGERTY 1985

CENTRAL HEATING HEATWAVE 1978

CENTRAL RESERVATION BETH ORTON 1999

CENTRE STAGE DAVID ESSEX 1986

CENTRE STAGE MICHAEL BALL 2001

CENTRE STAGE ELAINE PAIGE 2004

CEREAL KILLER SOUNDTRACK GREEN JELLY 1993

CEREBRAL CAUSTIC FALL 1995

CEREMONY CULT 1991

C'EST CHIC CHIC 1979

C'EST LA VIE ROBBIE NEVIL 1987

C'EST POUR VIVRE CELINE DION 1997

CHA CHA CHA EMF 1995

CHAIN FAMILY STAND 1990

CHAIN GANG OF LOVE RAVEONETTES 2003

CHAIN LIGHTNING DON MCLEAN 1980

CHAIRMAN OF THE BOARD COUNT BASIE 1960

CHAIRS MISSING WIRE 1978

CHALK FARM IN A RAIN STORM JONI MITCHELL 1988

CHAMBER MUSIC COAL CHAMBER 1999

CHAMPAGNE AND ROSES VARIOUS ARTISTS (POLYDOR) 1980

CHANGE ALARM 1989

CHANGE EVERYTHING DEL AMITRI 1992

CHANGE GIVER SHED SEVEN 1994

CHANGE OF ADDRESS SHADOWS 1980

CHANGE OF HEART CHANGE 1984

A CHANGE OF HEART DAVID SANBORN 1987

CHANGE OF SEASON DARYL HALL & JOHN OATES 1990

CHANGE OR DIE SUNSCREEM 1996

THE CHANGELING TOYAH 1982

CHANGES JULIE FELIX 1966

CHANGESBOWIE DAVID BOWIE 1990

CHANGESONEBOWIE DAVID BOWIE 1976

CHANGESTWOBOWIE DAVID BOWIE 1981

CHANGING CABINS NOMAD 1996

CHANGING FACES BROS 1991

CHANGING FACES – THE BEST OF LOUISE 2001

CHANGING FACES – THE VERY BEST OF ROD STEWART & THE FACES 2003

CHANGING FACES – THE VERY BEST OF 10CC AND GODLEY AND CRÈME 10CC & GODLEY & CREME 1987

CHANGING HORSES INCREDIBLE STRING BAND 1970

CHANTS AND DANCES OF THE NATIVE AMERICAN INDIAN SACRED SPIRIT 1995

CHANTS D'AUVERGNE VOLUME 1 KIRI TE KANAWA WITH THE ENGLISH CHAMBER ORCHESTRA 1983

CHAOS A.D. SEPULTURA 1993

CHAOS AND DISORDER PRINCE 1996

CHAPTER ONE JAY-Z 2002

CHAPTER 1: A NEW BEGINNING MOFFATS 1999

CHAPTER TWO ASHANTI 2003

CHARACTERS STEVIE WONDER 1987

CHARANGO MORCHEEBA 2002

CHARIOTS OF FIRE (OST) VANGELIS 1981

THE CHARLATANS CHARLATANS 1995

CHARLEY PRIDE SPECIAL CHARLEY PRIDE 1971

CHARLOTTE CHURCH CHARLOTTE CHURCH 1999

CHARMED LIFE BILLY IDOL 1990

THE CHART VARIOUS ARTISTS (TELSTAR) 1986

CHART ATTACK VARIOUS ARTISTS (TELSTAR) 1982

CHART ENCOUNTERS OF THE HIT KIND VARIOUS ARTISTS (RONCO) 1983

CHART EXPLOSION VARIOUS ARTISTS (K-TEL) 1980

CHART HITS '81 VARIOUS ARTISTS (K-TEL) 1981

CHART HITS '82 VARIOUS ARTISTS (K-TEL) 1982

CHART HITS '83 VOLUME 1 AND 2 VARIOUS ARTISTS (K-TEL) 1983

CHART RUNNERS VARIOUS ARTISTS (RONCO) 1983

THE CHART SHOW – DANCE HITS 1987 TELEVISION COMPILATION 1987

THE CHART SHOW – DANCE MASTERS TELEVISION COMPILATION 1989

THE CHART SHOW – ROCK THE NATION TELEVISION COMPILATION 1988

THE CHART SHOW – ROCK THE NATION 2 TELEVISION COMPILATION 1989

THE CHART SHOW – THE ULTIMATE ROCK ALBUM TELEVISION COMPILATION 1993

CHART SHOW – ULTIMATE BLUES ALBUM TELEVISION COMPILATION 1993

THE CHART SHOW – ULTIMATE ROCK 2 TELEVISION COMPILATION 1993

THE CHART SHOW DANCE ALBUM TELEVISION COMPILATION 1995

THE CHART SHOW PRESENTS THE CHART MACHINE TELEVISION COMPILATION 1995

CHART STARS VARIOUS ARTISTS (K-TEL) 1983

CHART TREK VOLUMES 1 AND 2 VARIOUS ARTISTS (RONCO) 1984

CHART WARS VARIOUS ARTISTS (RONCO) 1982

CHARTBEAT/CHARTHEAT VARIOUS ARTISTS (K-TEL) 1982

CHARTBUSTERS VARIOUS ARTISTS (GLOBAL) 1995

CHARTBUSTERS VARIOUS ARTISTS (GLOBAL) 1997

CHARTBUSTERS 81 VARIOUS ARTISTS (K-TEL) 1981

CHARTBUSTERS 82 VARIOUS ARTISTS (RONCO) 1982

CHAS AND DAVE'S CHRISTMAS CAROL ALBUM CHAS & DAVE 1986

CHAS AND DAVE'S CHRISTMAS JAMBOREE BAG CHAS & DAVE 1981

CHAS AND DAVE'S GREATEST HITS CHAS & DAVE 1984

CHAS AND DAVE'S KNEES UP – JAMBOREE BAG NUMBER 2 CHAS & DAVE 1983

CHASE THE DRAGON MAGNUM 1982

CHEAP TRICK AT BUDOKAN CHEAP TRICK 1979

CHEAPNESS AND BEAUTY BOY GEORGE 1995

CHECK OUT THE GROOVE UNDERCOVER 1992

CHEEK TO CHEEK VARIOUS ARTISTS (CBS) 1989

CHEERS OBIE TRICE 2003

CHEF AID – THE SOUTH PARK ALBUM TELEVISION SOUNDTRACK 1998

THE CHEMICAL WEDDING BRUCE DICKINSON 1998

CHEMICRAZY THAT PETROL EMOTION 1990

CHER CHER 1988

CHER O'BOWLIES – PICK OF THE UNDERTONES UNDERTONES FEATURING FEARGAL SHARKEY 1986

CHERISH DAVID CASSIDY 1972

CHERISHED MEMORIES EDDIE COCHRAN 1963

CHER'S GREATEST HITS: 1965–1992 CHER 1992

CHESS ORIGINAL STUDIO CAST RECORDING 1984

CHESS PIECES ORIGINAL STUDIO CAST RECORDING 1985

CHET ATKINS WORKSHOP CHET ATKINS 1961

CHEWING THE FAT BLUE RONDO A LA TURK 1982

CHI MAI ENNIO MORRICONE 1981

CHIC AND ROSE ROYCE – THEIR GREATEST HITS SIDE BY SIDE VARIOUS ARTISTS (DINO) 1991

CHICAGO CHICAGO 1970

CHICAGO FILM SOUNDTRACK 2003

CHICAGO – THE MUSICAL ORIGINAL LONDON STAGE CAST SOUNDTRACK 1998

CHICAGO 16 CHICAGO 1982

CHICAGO 17 CHICAGO 1984

CHICAGO 3 CHICAGO 1971

CHICAGO 5 CHICAGO 1972

CHICAGO JACKBEAT VOLUME 2 VARIOUS ARTISTS (RHYTHM KING) 1987

THE CHICAGO STORY – COMPLETE GREATEST CHICAGO 2002

CHICAGO TRANSIT AUTHORITY CHICAGO TRANSIT AUTHORITY 1969

CHICAGO X CHICAGO 1976

CHICK FLICKS – THE SEQUEL VARIOUS ARTISTS (WARNER BROTHERS) 2003

CHICKEN N BEER LUDACRIS 2003

CHICKEN RHYTHMS NORTHSIDE 1991

CHICKENEYE DEEJAY PUNK-ROC 1998

CHILD IN TIME IAN GILLAN BAND 1976

CHILD IS THE FATHER TO THE MAN BLOOD, SWEAT & TEARS 1968

CHILDREN MISSION 1988

CHILDREN OF THE NIGHT NASH THE SLASH 1981

CHILDREN OF THE NIGHT 52ND STREET 1986

A CHILD'S ADVENTURE MARIANNE FAITHFULL 1983

CHILL OUT BLACK UHURU 1982

CHILL OUT JOHN LEE HOOKER 1995

THE CHILL OUT ALBUM – 2 VARIOUS ARTISTS (TELSTAR) 1999

THE CHILL OUT SESSION VARIOUS ARTISTS (MINISTRY OF SOUND) 2001

CHILLED EUPHORIA VARIOUS ARTISTS (TELSTAR) 2000

CHILLED IBIZA VARIOUS ARTISTS (WARNER BROTHERS) 2000

CHILLED IBIZA II VARIOUS ARTISTS (WARNER BROTHERS) 2001

CHILLED IBIZA III VARIOUS ARTISTS (WARNER BROTHERS) 2002

CHILLED JAZZ VARIOUS ARTISTS (VERVE) 2002

CHILLED OUT EUPHORIA VARIOUS ARTISTS (TELSTAR) 2001

THE CHILLOUT VARIOUS ARTISTS (VIRGIN) 2001

THE CHILLOUT ALBUM VARIOUS ARTISTS (TELSTAR) 1999

THE CHILLOUT MIX VARIOUS ARTISTS (VIRGIN) 1999

THE CHILLOUT SESSION – IBIZA SUNSETS VARIOUS ARTISTS (MINISTRY OF SOUND) 2003

THE CHILLOUT SESSION – IBIZA 2002 VARIOUS ARTISTS (MINISTRY OF SOUND) 2002

THE CHILLOUT SESSION 2 VARIOUS ARTISTS (MINISTRY OF SOUND) 2001

THE CHILLOUT SESSION 2003 VARIOUS ARTISTS (MINISTRY OF SOUND) 2002

CHILLOUT SESSION – SUMMER COLLECTION 2003 VARIOUS ARTISTS (MINISTRY OF SOUND) 2003

CHIMERA BILL NELSON 1983

THE CHIMES CHIMES 1990

CHINA CRISIS COLLECTION – THE VERY BEST OF CHINA CRISIS CHINA CRISIS 1990

CHINA DOLL FOXY BROWN 1999

CHINA GIRL – THE CLASSICAL ALBUM 2 VANESSA-MAE 1998

CHINATOWN THIN LIZZY 1980

CHINESE WALL PHILIP BAILEY 1985

CHIRPING CRICKETS CRICKETS 1958

CHITTY CHITTY BANG BANG (OST) FILM SOUNDTRACK 1969

CHOBA B CCCP (THE RUSSIAN ALBUM) PAUL McCARTNEY 1991

CHOCOLATE FACTORY R KELLY 2003

CHOCOLATE STARFISH AND THE HOT DOG FLAVOURED WATER LIMP BIZKIT 2000

CHOCOLATE SUPA HIGHWAY SPEARHEAD 1997

CHOICES – THE SINGLES COLLECTION BLOW MONKEYS 1989

CHOICES OF THE HEART VARIOUS ARTISTS (STYLUS) 1985

THE CHOIR – MUSIC FROM THE TV SERIES ANTHONY WAY & STANISLAS SYREWICZ 1995

THE CHOIRBOY ANTHONY WAY 1995

THE CHOIRBOY'S CHRISTMAS ANTHONY WAY 1996

CHOKE BEAUTIFUL SOUTH 1990

CHOOSE 80'S DANCE VARIOUS ARTISTS (TELSTAR) 2002

CHOOSE YOUR MASQUES HAWKWIND 1982

CHORUS ERASURE 1991

THE CHOSEN FEW DOOLEYS 1979

CHRIS BARBER BAND BOX NO. 2 CHRIS BARBER 1960

CHRIS REA CHRIS REA 1982

CHRIS TARRANT PRESENTS ULTIMATE PARTY MEGAMIX VARIOUS ARTISTS (TELSTAR) 1998

CHRIS TARRANT'S ULTIMATE SUMMER PARTY VARIOUS ARTISTS (TELSTAR) 1999

CHRIST THE ALBUM CRASS 1982

THE CHRISTIANS CHRISTIANS 1987

CHRISTINA AGUILERA CHRISTINA AGUILERA 1999

CHRISTINE MCVIE CHRISTINE MCVIE 1984

CHRISTINA MILIAN CHRISTINA MILIAN 2002

CHRISTMAS ELAINE PAIGE 1986

THE CHRISTMAS ALBUM NEIL DIAMOND 1992

THE CHRISTMAS ALBUM TWEENIES 2001

CHRISTMAS AT THE COUNTRY STORE VARIOUS ARTISTS (STARBLEND) 1985

CHRISTMAS CARD PARTRIDGE FAMILY 1972

CHRISTMAS CAROLS TEMPLE CHURCH CHOIR 1961

CHRISTMAS CAROLS FROM GUILDFORD CATHEDRAL GUILDFORD CATHEDRAL CHOIR CONDUCTOR: BARRY ROSE 1966

THE CHRISTMAS COLLECTION FOSTER & ALLEN 1990

A CHRISTMAS GIFT VARIOUS ARTISTS (RONCO) 1975

CHRISTMAS GREATEST HITS VARIOUS ARTISTS (LEGENDS IN) 1990

CHRISTMAS HITS VARIOUS ARTISTS (BMG) 2001

CHRISTMAS IN VIENNA PLACIDO DOMINGO, DIANA ROSS & JOSE CARRERAS 1993

CHRISTMAS IN VIENNA II DIONNE WARWICK PLACIDO DOMINGO 1994

CHRISTMAS LOVE SONGS VARIOUS ARTISTS (ARCADE) 1991

CHRISTMAS PEACE ELVIS PRESLEY 2003

CHRISTMAS WITH BING CROSBY BING CROSBY 1991

CHRISTMAS WITH DANIEL DANIEL O'DONNELL 1994

CHRISTMAS WITH KIRI KIRI TE KANAWA 1986

CHRISTMAS WITH NAT 'KING' COLE NAT 'KING' COLE 1988

CHRISTMAS WITH THE RAT PACK VARIOUS ARTISTS (CAPITOL) 2002

CHRISTOPHER CROSS CHRISTOPHER CROSS 1981

THE CHRISTY MOORE COLLECTION 81–91 CHRISTY MOORE 1991

CHROME CATHERINE WHEEL 1993

THE CHRONIC DR. DRE 2000

CHRONIC GENERATION CHRON GEN 1982

CHRONICLE OF THE BLACK SWORD HAWKWIND 1985

CHRONICLES STEVE WINWOOD 1987

CHRONICLES RUSH 1990

CHRONOLOGIE JEAN-MICHEL JARRE 1993

CHRONOLOGIE PART 6 JEAN-MICHEL JARRE 1994

CHUCK BERRY CHUCK BERRY 1963

CHUCK BERRY ON STAGE CHUCK BERRY 1963

CHUNGA'S REVENGE FRANK ZAPPA 1970

CHUNKS OF FUNK VARIOUS ARTISTS (LOOSE END) 1984

THE CHURCH OF HAWKWIND HAWKWIND 1982

THE CHURCH WITH ONE BELL JOHN MARTYN 1998

CIELI DE TOSCANA ANDREA BOCELLI 2001

CIGARETTES AND ALCOHOL VARIOUS ARTISTS (COLUMBIA) 2000

CIGARETTES AND ALCOHOL – SATURDAY NIGHT VARIOUS ARTISTS (COLUMBIA) 2002

CIGARETTES AND ALCOHOL VOLUME 2 VARIOUS ARTISTS (COLUMBIA) 2001

CILLA CILLA BLACK 1965

CILLA SINGS A RAINBOW CILLA BLACK 1966

CINDERELLA CLIFF RICHARD 1967

CINEMA ELAINE PAIGE 1984

THE CINEMA HITS ALBUM VARIOUS ARTISTS (TOWERBELL) 1986

THE CIRCLE AND THE SQUARE RED BOX 1986

CIRCLE OF ONE OLETA ADAMS 1990

CIRCLES NEW SEEKERS 1972

THE CIRCUS ERASURE 1987

CIRCUS LENNY KRAVITZ 1995

CIRCUS MARY BLACK 1995

CITY BABY ATTACKED BY RATS CHARGED GBH 1982

CITY DELIRIOUS LIONROCK 1998

CITY OF ANGELS (OST) FILM SOUNDTRACK 1998

CITY TO CITY GERRY RAFFERTY 1978

A CIVILISED MAN JOE COCKER 1984

THE CLAIRVOYANT/INFINITE DREAMS (LIVE) IRON MAIDEN 1990

CLAMBAKE (OST) ELVIS PRESLEY 1968

CLAPTON CHRONICLES – THE BEST OF ERIC CLAPTON ERIC CLAPTON 1999

THE CLASH CLASH 1977

CLASSIC ADS VARIOUS ARTISTS (DECCA) 2002

CLASSIC BLUE JUSTIN HAYWARD WITH MIKE BATT & THE LONDON PHILHARMONIC ORCHESTRA 1989

THE CLASSIC CHILLOUT ALBUM VARIOUS ARTISTS (COLUMBIA) 2001

THE CLASSIC CHILLOUT ALBUM 2 VARIOUS ARTISTS (COLUMBIA) 2001

THE CLASSIC COLLECTION DANIEL O'DONNELL 1995

CLASSIC COMMERCIALS VARIOUS ARTISTS (DECCA) 1993

CLASSIC ELECTRO MASTERCUTS VOLUME 1 VARIOUS ARTISTS (MASTERCUTS) 1994

THE CLASSIC EXPERIENCE VARIOUS ARTISTS (EMI) 1988

CLASSIC EXPERIENCE II VARIOUS ARTISTS (EMI) 1990

CLASSIC EXPERIENCE III VARIOUS ARTISTS (EMI) 1991

CLASSIC EXPERIENCE IV VARIOUS ARTISTS (EMI) 1993

CLASSIC FM HALL OF FAME – GOLD VARIOUS ARTISTS (CLASSIC FM) 2001

CLASSIC FM – SMOOTH CLASSICS VARIOUS ARTISTS (CLASSIC FM) 2002

CLASSIC FUNK MASTERCUTS VOLUME 1 VARIOUS ARTISTS (MASTERCUTS) 1992

CLASSIC GOLD VOLUME 2 ROYAL PHILHARMONIC ORCHESTRA 1978

CLASSIC GUITAR MOODS MIRAGE 1995

CLASSIC HOUSE MASTERCUTS VOLUME 1 VARIOUS ARTISTS (MASTERCUTS) 1994

CLASSIC JAZZ-FUNK MASTERCUTS VOLUME 3 VARIOUS ARTISTS (MASTERCUTS) 1992

CLASSIC JAZZ-FUNK MASTERCUTS VOLUME 4 VARIOUS ARTISTS (MASTERCUTS) 1994

CLASSIC KENNEDY NIGEL KENNEDY WITH THE ENGLISH CHAMBER ORCHESTRA 1999

CLASSIC LOVE VARIOUS ARTISTS (TELSTAR) 1992

CLASSIC MELLOW MASTERCUTS VOLUME 1 VARIOUS ARTISTS (MASTERCUTS) 1991

CLASSIC MELLOW MASTERCUTS VOLUME 2 VARIOUS ARTISTS (MASTERCUTS) 1992

CLASSIC MOODS VARIOUS ARTISTS (POLYGRAM) 1996

CLASSIC P FUNK MASTERCUTS VOLUME 1 VARIOUS ARTISTS (MASTERCUTS) 1993

CLASSIC RARE GROOVE MASTERCUTS VOLUME 1 VARIOUS ARTISTS (MASTERCUTS) 1993

CLASSIC ROCK LONDON SYMPHONY ORCHESTRA 1978

CLASSIC ROCK – ROCK CLASSICS LONDON SYMPHONY ORCHESTRA WITH THE ROYAL CHORAL SOCIETY 1981

CLASSIC ROCK – ROCK SYMPHONIES LONDON SYMPHONY ORCHESTRA WITH THE ROYAL CHORAL SOCIETY & THE ROGER SMITH CHORALE 1983

CLASSIC ROCK – THE LIVING YEARS LONDON SYMPHONY ORCHESTRA 1989

CLASSIC ROCK – THE SECOND MOVEMENT LONDON SYMPHONY ORCHESTRA 1979

CLASSIC ROCK COUNTDOWN LONDON SYMPHONY ORCHESTRA 1987

THE CLASSIC ROMANCE VARIOUS ARTISTS (EMI) 1992

THE CLASSIC ROY ORBISON ROY ORBISON 1966

CLASSIC SALSOUL MASTERCUTS VOLUME 1 VARIOUS ARTISTS (MASTERCUTS) 1993

THE CLASSIC SCORE VARIOUS ARTISTS (SONY) 2002

CLASSIC SINATRA FRANK SINATRA 2000

CLASSIC SONGS JAMES TAYLOR 1987

CLASSIC THEMES VARIOUS ARTISTS (NOUVEAU MUSIC) 1983

THE CLASSIC TOUCH RICHARD CLAYDERMAN WITH THE ROYAL PHILHARMONIC ORCHESTRA 1985

THE CLASSICAL ALBUM VARIOUS ARTISTS (UNIVERSAL) 2000

CLASSICAL ALBUM 1 VANESSA-MAE 1996

THE CLASSICAL ALBUM 2001 VARIOUS ARTISTS (EMI) 2000

CLASSICAL CHILLOUT VARIOUS ARTISTS (VIRGIN) 2001

CLASSICAL CHILLOUT GOLD VARIOUS ARTISTS COMPILATION (DECADANCE) 2002

CLASSICAL CHILLOUT 2 VARIOUS ARTISTS (VIRGIN) 2002

A CLASSICAL CHRISTMAS VARIOUS ARTISTS (EMI) 1991

THE CLASSICAL COLLECTION JAMES LAST 2003

CLASSICAL GOLD ROYAL PHILHARMONIC ORCHESTRA 1977

CLASSICAL GOLD VARIOUS ARTISTS (RONCO) 1977

CLASSICAL GOLD VARIOUS ARTISTS (DEUTSCHE GRAMMOPHON) 2003

CLASSICAL GRAFFITI PLANETS 2002

CLASSICAL HEARTBREAKERS VARIOUS ARTISTS (VIRGIN) 2003

CLASSICAL LEGENDS VARIOUS ARTISTS (VIRGIN) 2002

THE CLASSICAL LOVE ALBUM VARIOUS ARTISTS (DECADANCE) 2003

CLASSICAL MASTERS VARIOUS ARTISTS (TELSTAR) 1991

CLASSICAL MEDITATIONS JAMES GALWAY 1996

CLASSICALLY SEDAKA NEIL SEDAKA 1995

CLASSICS APHEX TWIN 1995

CLASSICS 2002 VARIOUS ARTISTS (DECCA) 2001

CLASSICS 2003 VARIOUS ARTISTS (DECCA) 2002

CLASSICS BY CANDLELIGHT VARIOUS ARTISTS (STYLUS) 1986

CLASSICS BY MOONLIGHT JAMES LAST 1990

CLASSICS FOR DREAMING JAMES LAST 1980

CLASSICS UP TO DATE JAMES LAST 1970

CLASSICS UP TO DATE VOLUME 2 JAMES LAST 1972

CLASSICS UP TO DATE VOLUME 3 JAMES LAST 1976

CLEANSING PRONG 1994

CLEAR BOMB THE BASS 1995

CLEO CLEO LAINE 1978

CLIFF CLIFF RICHARD & THE DRIFTERS 1959

CLIFF AT CHRISTMAS CLIFF RICHARD 2003

CLIFF AT THE MOVIES – 1959–1974 CLIFF RICHARD 1996

CLIFF IN JAPAN CLIFF RICHARD 1968

CLIFF RICHARD CLIFF RICHARD 1965

CLIFF RICHARD – THE ALBUM CLIFF RICHARD 1993

CLIFF SINGS CLIFF RICHARD & THE SHADOWS 1959

CLIFF'S HIT ALBUM CLIFF RICHARD & THE SHADOWS 1963

CLIMATE HUNTER SCOTT WALKER 1984

CLINTON FORD CLINTON FORD 1962

CLOCK WITHOUT HANDS NANCI GRIFFITH 2001

CLOCKWORK ORANGE (OST) FILM SOUNDTRACK 1972

CLODAGH RODGERS CLODAGH RODGERS 1969

CLOSE KIM WILDE 1988

CLOSE ENCOUNTERS OF THE THIRD KIND (OST) JOHN WILLIAMS 1978

CLOSE TO THE BONE THOMPSON TWINS 1987

CLOSE TO THE EDGE YES 1972

CLOSE TO YOU CARPENTERS 1971

CLOSE TO YOU FRANK SINATRA 1957

CLOSE TO YOU VARIOUS ARTISTS (UNIVERSAL) 2001

CLOSE UP TOM JONES 1972

CLOSE UP IN SWING ERROL GARNER 1962

CLOSER JOY DIVISION 1980

CLOSET CLASSICS VOLUME 1 – MORE PROTEIN SAMPLER VARIOUS ARTISTS (MORE PROTEIN) 1992

CLOUD NINE TEMPTATIONS 1969

CLOUD NINE GEORGE HARRISON 1987

CLOUDCUCKOOLAND LIGHTNING SEEDS 1990

CLUB 2K VARIOUS ARTISTS (UNIVERSAL) 2000

CLUB 2K VOL. 2 VARIOUS ARTISTS (UNIVERSAL) 2000

CLUB ANTHEMS 99 VARIOUS ARTISTS (VIRGIN) 1999

CLUB CLASS VARIOUS ARTISTS (GLOBAL) 1995

CLUB CLASS VARIOUS ARTISTS (WARNER BROTHERS) 1998

CLUB CLASSICS – VOLUME 3 VARIOUS ARTISTS (FANTAZIA) 1997

CLUB CLASSICS VOLUME 2 VARIOUS ARTISTS (CBS) 1985

CLUB CLASSICS VOLUME ONE SOUL II SOUL 1989

CLUB CULTURE EXPOSED! – VARIOUS ARTISTS (GLOBAL) 1998

CLUB CUTS 97 VARIOUS ARTISTS (TELSTAR) 1997

CLUB CUTS 97 – VOLUME 2 VARIOUS ARTISTS (TELSTAR) 1997

CLUB CUTS 97 – VOLUME 3 VARIOUS ARTISTS (TELSTAR) 1997

CLUB FOR HEROES VARIOUS ARTISTS (TELSTAR) 1992

CLUB HITS 97/98: SOUNDTRACK TO A SEASON VARIOUS ARTISTS (VIRGIN) 1997

CLUB HITS 98 VARIOUS ARTISTS (TELSTAR) 1998

CLUB HITS 99 VARIOUS ARTISTS (TELSTAR) 1999

CLUB HITS 2002 VARIOUS ARTISTS (INCREDIBLE) 2002

CLUB HITS 2003 VARIOUS ARTISTS (INSPIRED) 2003

CLUB IBIZA VARIOUS ARTISTS (QUALITY PRICE MUSIC) 1995

CLUB IBIZA VARIOUS ARTISTS (WARNER BROTHERS) 1999

CLUB IBIZA – VOLUME 2 VARIOUS ARTISTS (QUALITY PRICE MUSIC) 1996

CLUB IBIZA SILVER EDITION VARIOUS ARTISTS (QUALITY PRICE MUSIC) 1996

CLUB MIX 2001 VARIOUS ARTISTS (UNIVERSAL) 2001

CLUB MIX 2002 VARIOUS ARTISTS (UNIVERSAL) 2002

CLUB MIX 2003 VARIOUS ARTISTS (UNIVERSAL) 2003

CLUB MIX 96 VARIOUS ARTISTS (POLYGRAM) 1996

CLUB MIX 96 – VOLUME 2 VARIOUS ARTISTS (POLYGRAM) 1996

CLUB MIX 97 VARIOUS ARTISTS (POLYGRAM) 1996

CLUB MIX 97 – VOLUME 2 VARIOUS ARTISTS (POLYGRAM) 1997

CLUB MIX 97 – VOLUME 3 VARIOUS ARTISTS (POLYGRAM) 1997

CLUB MIX 99 VARIOUS ARTISTS (UNIVERSAL) 1999

CLUB MIX IBIZA 2000 VARIOUS ARTISTS (UNIVERSAL) 2000

CLUB NATION VARIOUS ARTISTS (VIRGIN) 1998

CLUB NATION VARIOUS ARTISTS (MINISTRY OF SOUND) 2001

CLUB NATION IBIZA VARIOUS ARTISTS (MINISTRY OF SOUND) 2002

CLUB NATION 2 VARIOUS ARTISTS (VIRGIN) 1998

CLUB NATION – MIAMI 2002 VARIOUS ARTISTS (MINISTRY OF SOUND) 2002

CLUB REGGAE VARIOUS ARTISTS (TROJAN) 1971

CLUB SKA '67 VARIOUS ARTISTS (ISLAND) 1967

CLUB SKA '67 VARIOUS ARTISTS (ISLAND) 1980

CLUB TOGETHER VARIOUS ARTISTS (EMI) 1994

CLUB TOGETHER 2 VARIOUS ARTISTS (EMI) 1995

CLUB TOGETHER 3 VARIOUS ARTISTS (EMI) 1996

CLUB TROPICANA VARIOUS ARTISTS (COLUMBIA) 2002

CLUB ZONE VARIOUS ARTISTS (TELSTAR) 1995

CLUB ZONE 2 VARIOUS ARTISTS (TELSTAR) 1995

CLUBBED VARIOUS ARTISTS (UNIVERSAL) 2001

CLUBBED – VOLUME 2 – MIXED BY JUDGE JULES VARIOUS ARTISTS (UNIVERSAL) 2001

CLUBBED OUT VARIOUS ARTISTS (VIRGIN) 2001

CLUBBED 2002 – MIXED BY JUDGE JULES VARIOUS ARTISTS (UNIVERSAL) 2002

CLUBBED UP VARIOUS ARTISTS (WARNER BROTHERS) 2002

THE CLUBBER'S BIBLE VARIOUS ARTISTS (WARNER BROTHERS) 2000

THE CLUBBER'S BIBLE II VARIOUS ARTISTS (WARNER BROTHERS) 2001

CLUBBER'S GUIDE TO… IBIZA – JULES/TONG VARIOUS ARTISTS (MINISTRY OF SOUND) 1998

CLUBBER'S GUIDE TO IBIZA – SUMMER '99 VARIOUS ARTISTS (MINISTRY OF SOUND) 1999

CLUBBER'S GUIDE TO IBIZA – SUMMER 2000 VARIOUS ARTISTS (MINISTRY OF SOUND) 2000

CLUBBERS GUIDE TO IBIZA – SUMMER 2001 VARIOUS ARTISTS (MINISTRY OF SOUND) 2001

CLUBBERS GUIDE TO IBIZA 2002 VARIOUS ARTISTS (MINISTRY OF SOUND) 2002

CLUBBER'S GUIDE TO… NINETY NINE VARIOUS ARTISTS (MINISTRY OF SOUND) 1999

CLUBBERS GUIDE TO SUMMER 2003 VARIOUS ARTISTS (MINISTRY OF SOUND) 2003

CLUBBER'S GUIDE TO… TRANCE: MIXED BY ATB VARIOUS ARTISTS (MINISTRY OF SOUND) 1999

CLUBBER'S GUIDE TO… 2000 VARIOUS ARTISTS (MINISTRY OF SOUND) 2000

CLUBBERS GUIDE TO 2001 VARIOUS ARTISTS (MINISTRY OF SOUND) 2001

CLUBBERS GUIDE TO 2002 VARIOUS ARTISTS (MINISTRY OF SOUND) 2002

CLUBBERS GUIDE 2003 VARIOUS ARTISTS (MINISTRY OF SOUND) 2002

CLUBBERS GUIDE – 2004 VARIOUS ARTISTS (MINISTRY OF SOUND) 2004

CLUBBIN' – VARIOUS ARTISTS (WARNER BROTHERS) 1998

CLUBLAND VARIOUS ARTISTS (TELSTAR) 1997

CLUBLAND VARIOUS ARTISTS (UNIVERSAL TV/SERIOUS) 2002

CLUBLAND II VARIOUS ARTISTS (UNIVERSAL) 2002

CLUBLAND III VARIOUS ARTISTS (UNIVERSAL) 2003

CLUBLAND 4 VARIOUS ARTISTS (UNIVERSAL) 2003

CLUBLAND – VOLUME 2 VARIOUS ARTISTS (TELSTAR) 1997

CLUBLAND X-TREME VARIOUS ARTISTS (UNIVERSAL) 2003

CLUBLAND X-TREME 2 VARIOUS ARTISTS (UNIVERSAL) 2004

CLUBLIFE VARIOUS ARTISTS (TELSTAR) 1998

CLUBLIFE 2 VARIOUS ARTISTS (TELSTAR) 1998

CLUBMIX 2000 VARIOUS ARTISTS (UNIVERSAL) 2000

CLUBMIX 2000 VOL.2 VARIOUS ARTISTS (UNIVERSAL) 2000

CLUBMIX 2004 VARIOUS ARTISTS (UNIVERSAL) 2004

CLUBMIX IBIZA VARIOUS ARTISTS (UNIVERSAL) 2001

CLUBMIX IBIZA 2002 VARIOUS ARTISTS (UNIVERSAL) 2002

CLUBMIX SUMMER 2003 VARIOUS ARTISTS (UNIVERSAL) 2003

CLUBZONE – DANCING IN THE CITY VARIOUS ARTISTS (WARNER BROTHERS) 1999

CLUES ROBERT PALMER 1980

CLUTCHING AT STRAWS MARILLION 1987

C'MON C'MON SHERYL CROW 2002
C'MON EVERYBODY ELVIS PRESLEY 1971
C'MON EVERYBODY EDDIE COCHRAN 1988
C'MON KIDS BOO RADLEYS 1996
COAST TO COAST WESTLIFE 2000
COCKAHOOP CERYS MATTHEWS 2003
COCKED AND LOADED L.A. GUNS 1989
COCKTAIL (OST) FILM SOUNDTRACK 1989
CODA LED ZEPPELIN 1982
CODE OF THE ROAD NILS LOFGREN 1986
CODE RED JAZZY JEFF & THE FRESH PRINCE 1993
CODE SELFISH FALL 1992
COHEN LIVE LEONARD COHEN 1994
COINCIDENCE (AND LIKELY STORIES) BUFFY SAINTE-
    MARIE 1992
COLD FEET (OST) TELEVISION SOUNDTRACK 2001
COLD SPRING HARBOUR BILLY JOEL 1984
COLD SWEAT VARIOUS ARTISTS (DINO) 1992
COLLABORATION GEORGE BENSON & EARL KLUGH 1987
THE COLLECTION ULTRAVOX 1984
THE COLLECTION BARRY WHITE 1988
COLLECTION RAY CHARLES 1990
THE COLLECTION LLOYD COLE 1999
COLLECTION TRACY CHAPMAN 2001
THE COLLECTION JOHN RUTTER 2002
THE COLLECTION – 20 GREATEST HITS GLADYS KNIGHT &
    THE PIPS 1984
THE COLLECTION – 24 ESSENTIAL HITS EARTH WIND &
    FIRE 1986
A COLLECTION – GREATEST HITS... AND MORE BARBRA
    STREISAND 1989
THE COLLECTION – THE 20 GREATEST HITS FOUR SEASONS
    1988
THE COLLECTION – THE VERY BEST OF BREAD AND DAVID
    GATES BREAD & DAVID GATES 1987
THE COLLECTION 1977–1982 STRANGLERS 1982
A COLLECTION OF BEATLES OLDIES BEATLES 1966
COLLECTION OF BIG HITS VOLUME 8 VARIOUS ARTISTS
    (MOTOWN) 1970
A COLLECTION OF GREAT DANCE SONGS PINK FLOYD 1981
A COLLECTION OF TAMLA MOTOWN HITS VARIOUS ARTISTS
    (MOTOWN) 1965
A COLLECTION OF THEIR 20 GREATEST HITS THREE
    DEGREES 1979
COLLECTORS GOLD ELVIS PRESLEY 1991
THE COLLECTOR'S SERIES VOLUME 1 CELINE DION 2000
THE COLLEGE DROPOUT KANYE WEST 2004
COLOSSEUM COLOSSEUM 1969
COLOSSEUM LIVE COLOSSEUM 1971
COLOUR CHRISTIANS 1990
THE COLOUR AND THE SHAPE FOO FIGHTERS 1997
COLOUR BY NUMBERS CULTURE CLUB 1983
COLOUR MY WORLD PETULA CLARK 1967
THE COLOUR OF MY LOVE CELINE DION 1994
THE COLOUR OF SPRING TALK TALK 1986
COLOURBOX COLOURBOX 1985
COLOURS ADAM F 1997
COM LAG 2+2=5 RADIOHEAD 2004
COMBAT ROCK CLASH 1982
COMBINE HARVESTER WURZELS 1976
COME PRINCE 1994
COME AGAIN PETER COOK & DUDLEY MOORE 1977
COME AN' GET IT WHITESNAKE 1981
COME AWAY WITH ME NORAH JONES 2002
COME BACK TO SORRENTO FRANK SINATRA 1960
COME CLEAN PUDDLE OF MUDD 2002
COME DANCE WITH ME! – FRANK SINATRA WITH BILLY
    MAY & HIS ORCHESTRA 1959
COME DOWN DANDY WARHOLS 1998
COME FIND YOURSELF FUN LOVIN' CRIMINALS 1996
COME FLY WITH ME MICHAEL BUBLE 2004
COME FLY WITH ME FRANK SINATRA 1958
COME INTO MY LIFE JOYCE SIMS 1988
COME MORNING GROVER WASHINGTON JR. 1981
COME MY WAY MARIANNE FAITHFULL 1965
COME ON FEEL THE LEMONHEADS LEMONHEADS 1993

COME ON OVER OLIVIA NEWTON-JOHN 1976
COME ON OVER SHANIA TWAIN 1998
COME ON, DIE YOUNG MOGWAI 1999
(COME ON, JOIN) THE HIGH SOCIETY THESE ANIMAL MEN
    1994
COME OUT AND PLAY TWISTED SISTER 1985
COME SWING WITH ME FRANK SINATRA 1962
COME TASTE THE BAND DEEP PURPLE 1975
COME THE DAY SEEKERS 1966
COME TO MY PARTY MRS. MILLS 1966
COME TOGETHER AS ONE WILL DOWNING 1989
COME WITH CLUB (CLUB TRACKS VOLUME 2) VARIOUS
    ARTISTS (CLUB) 1983
COME WITH US CHEMICAL BROTHERS 2002
COMEDY BLACK 1988
COMES A TIME NEIL YOUNG 1978
COMFORT IN SOUND FEEDER 2002
THE COMFORT ZONE VANESSA WILLIAMS 1992
COMFORTER COMPULSION 1994
THE COMFORTS OF MADNESS PALE SAINTS 1990
COMIC RELIEF PRESENTS UTTERLY UTTERLY LIVE! – COMIC
    RELIEF 1986
COMIN' ATCHA! – CLEOPATRA 1998
THE COMING BUSTA RHYMES 1996
COMING ALIVE AGAIN BARBARA DICKSON 1989
COMING AROUND AGAIN CARLY SIMON 1987
COMING BACK HARD AGAIN FAT BOYS 1988
COMING IN FOR THE KILL CLIMIE FISHER 1989
COMING OUT MANHATTAN TRANSFER 1977
COMING UP SUEDE 1996
COMING UP FOR AIR PENETRATION 1979
THE COMMITMENTS (OST) COMMITMENTS 1991
THE COMMITMENTS VOLUME 2 COMMITMENTS 1992
COMMITTED TO SOUL VARIOUS ARTISTS (ARCADE) 1994
COMMODORES LIVE! – COMMODORES 1978
COMMON GROUND VARIOUS ARTISTS (EMI) 1996
COMMON ONE VAN MORRISON 1980
COMMONER'S CROWN STEELEYE SPAN 1975
COMMUNARDS COMMUNARDS 1986
COMMUNICATE – SASHA & DIGWEED VARIOUS ARTISTS
    (INCREDIBLE) 2000
COMMUNIQUE DIRE STRAITS 1979
COMMUNITY MUSIC ASIAN DUB FOUNDATION 2000
COMO'S GOLDEN RECORDS PERRY COMO 1959
COMPANEROS WORKING WEEK 1986
COMPARSA DEEP FOREST 1998
COMPASS KUMPAS DALEK I 1980
THE COMPLEAT TOM PAXTON TOM PAXTON 1971
COMPLETE AND UNBELIEVABLE... THE OTIS REDDING
    DICTIONARY OF SOUL OTIS REDDING 1967
THE COMPLETE B SIDES PIXIES 2001
THE COMPLETE GLEN CAMPBELL GLEN CAMPBELL 1989
THE COMPLETE GREATEST HITS EAGLES 2003
COMPLETE MADNESS MADNESS 1982
THE COMPLETE MIKE OLDFIELD MIKE OLDFIELD 1985
THE COMPLETE PICTURE – THE VERY BEST OF DEBORAH
    HARRY AND BLONDIE DEBORAH HARRY & BLONDIE
    1991
THE COMPLETE STONE ROSES STONE ROSES 1995
THE COMPLETE TOM JONES TOM JONES 1992
COMPLETELY HOOKED – THE BEST OF DR. HOOK DR. HOOK
    1992
COMPOSITIONS ANITA BAKER 1990
COMPUTER WORLD KRAFTWERK 1981
CONCERT – THE CURE LIVE CURE 1984
CONCERT FOR BANGLADESH (RECORDED LIVE) VARIOUS
    ARTISTS (APPLE) 1972
A CONCERT FOR THE PEOPLE (BERLIN) BARCLAY JAMES
    HARVEST 1982
THE CONCERT IN CENTRAL PARK SIMON & GARFUNKEL
    1982
CONCERT SINATRA FRANK SINATRA 1963
CONCERT SPECTACULAR MANTOVANI & HIS ORCHESTRA
    1961
CONCERTO FOR GROUP AND ORCHESTRA DEEP PURPLE
    1970

CONCERTS FOR THE PEOPLE OF KAMPUCHEA VARIOUS
    ARTISTS (ATLANTIC) 1981
THE CONCERTS IN CHINA JEAN-MICHEL JARRE 1982
CONDITION CRITICAL QUIET RIOT 1984
CONEY ISLAND BABY LOU REED 1976
CONFESSIONS USHER 2004
CONFESSIONS OF A POP GROUP STYLE COUNCIL 1988
CONFESSIONS OF THE MIND HOLLIES 1970
CONFRONTATION BOB MARLEY & THE WAILERS 1983
CONGRATULATIONS, I'M SORRY GIN BLOSSOMS 1996
CONNECTED STEREO MC'S 1992
CONNECTED VARIOUS ARTISTS (POLYGRAM) 1998
CONNIE'S GREATEST HITS CONNIE FRANCIS 1961
CONQUEST URIAH HEEP 1980
CONSCIENCE WOMACK & WOMACK 1988
CONSCIENCE BELOVED 1993
CONSEQUENCES KEVIN GODLEY & LOL CRÈME 1977
CONSPIRACY DRIZABONE 1994
CONSPIRACY OF ONE OFFSPRING 2000
CONSTRICTOR ALICE COOPER 1986
CONSTRUCTION FOR THE MODERN IDIOT WONDERSTUFF
    1993
CONSTRUCTION TIME AGAIN DEPECHE MODE 1983
CONTACT POINTER SISTERS 1985
CONTENDERS EASTERHOUSE 1986
CONTINENTAL ENCORES MANTOVANI & HIS ORCHESTRA
    1959
THE CONTINO SESSIONS DEATH IN VEGAS 1999
CONTINUOUS PERFORMANCE STONE THE CROWS 1972
CONTRABAND VELVET REVOLVER 2004
CONTRIBUTION MICA PARIS 1990
CONTROL JANET JACKSON 1986
CONTROL – THE REMIXES JANET JACKSON 1987
CONVERSATION PEACE STEVIE WONDER 1995
CONVOY (OST) FILM SOUNDTRACK 1978
COOKIN' ON THE ROOF ROMAN HOLLIDAY 1983
COOL AS INSPIRAL CARPETS 2003
COOL FOR CATS SQUEEZE 1979
COOL GROOVES VARIOUS ARTISTS (POLYGRAM) 1998
COOL HEAT VARIOUS ARTISTS (K-TEL) 1983
THE COOL SOUND OF THE 70S VARIOUS ARTISTS (TELSTAR)
    2000
COOL SUMMER JAZZ VARIOUS ARTISTS (VIRGIN) 2003
COOL SUMMER REGGAE ASWAD 2002
THE COOLEST CUTS SHAKATAK 1988
COOLEYHIGHHARMONY BOYZ II MEN 1992
COP YER WHACK OF THIS BILLY CONNOLLY 1975
COPPER BLUE SUGAR 1992
COPPERHEAD ROAD STEVE EARLE 1988
COPPEROPOLIS GRANT LEE BUFFALO 1996
THE CORAL CORAL 2002
CORAL FANG DISTILLERS 2003
CORE STONE TEMPLE PILOTS 1993
CORNERSTONE STYX 1979
CORNERSTONES – JIMI HENDRIX 1967–1970 JIMI
    HENDRIX 1990
THE CORONATION STREET ALBUM TELEVISION
    COMPILATION 1995
CORRECT USE OF SOAP MAGAZINE 1980
CORRIDORS OF POWER GARY MOORE 1982
CORROSION VARIOUS ARTISTS (COLUMBIA) 2001
COSA NOSTRA BECK – OLA JEFF BECK 1969
COSI FAN TUTTI FRUTTI SQUEEZE 1985
COSMIC CARROTT JASPER CARROTT 1987
COSMIC THING B-52'S 1989
COSMIC WHEELS DONOVAN 1973
COSMO'S FACTORY CREEDENCE CLEARWATER REVIVAL
    1970
THE COST OF LOVING STYLE COUNCIL 1987
COULDN'T HAVE SAID IT BETTER MEAT LOAF 2003
COULDN'T LOVE YOU MORE JOHN MARTYN 1992
COUNT THREE AND PRAY BERLIN 1987
COUNT YOUR BLESSINGS ANN WILLIAMSON 1988
COUNTDOWN 1992-1983 PULP 1996
COUNTDOWN TO EXTINCTION MEGADETH 1992
COUNTERFEIT (EP) MARTIN L. GORE 1989

COUNTERPARTS RUSH 1993
COUNTRY VARIOUS ARTISTS (UNIVERSAL) 1999
COUNTRY BALLADS VARIOUS ARTISTS (VIRGIN) 2003
COUNTRY BOY DON WILLIAMS 1977
COUNTRY COMFORT VARIOUS ARTISTS (K-TEL) 1976
COUNTRY GENTLEMAN JIM REEVES 1980
COUNTRY GIRL BILLIE JO SPEARS 1981
COUNTRY GIRL MEETS COUNTRY BOY TAMMY WYNETTE 1978
COUNTRY GOLD VARIOUS ARTISTS (GLOBAL) 1996
COUNTRY GRAMMAR NELLY 2001
COUNTRY GUITAR VARIOUS ARTISTS (WARWICK) 1980
COUNTRY LEGENDS VARIOUS ARTISTS (RONCO) 1980
COUNTRY LEGENDS VARIOUS ARTISTS (VIRGIN) 2002
COUNTRY LIFE ROXY MUSIC 1974
COUNTRY LIFE VARIOUS ARTISTS (EMI) 1979
COUNTRY LOVE VARIOUS ARTISTS (TELSTAR) 1993
COUNTRY LOVE VARIOUS ARTISTS (UNIVERSAL) 2003
COUNTRY LOVE 2 VARIOUS ARTISTS (TELSTAR) 1993
COUNTRY MOODS VARIOUS ARTISTS (POLYGRAM) 1992
COUNTRY NUMBER ONE DON GIBSON 1980
COUNTRY PORTRAITS VARIOUS ARTISTS (WARWICK) 1979
COUNTRY ROADS VARIOUS ARTISTS (POLYGRAM) 1993
COUNTRY ROADS JAMES LAST 1999
COUNTRY ROUND UP VARIOUS ARTISTS (POLYDOR) 1980
COUNTRY SIDE OF JIM REEVES JIM REEVES 1964
COUNTRY SUNRISE/COUNTRY SUNSET VARIOUS ARTISTS (RONCO) 1981
COUNTRY WOMEN VARIOUS ARTISTS (DINO) 1993
COUNTRY'S GREATEST HITS VARIOUS ARTISTS (TELSTAR) 1990
COURT AND SPARK JONI MITCHELL 1974
THE COVENANT, THE SWORD AND THE ARM OF THE LAW CABARET VOLTAIRE 1985
COVER GIRL SHAWN COLVIN 1994
COVER PLUS HAZEL O'CONNOR 1981
COVER SHOT DAVID ESSEX 1993
COVER TO COVER JEFF HEALEY BAND 1995
COVER UP UB40 2001
COVERDALE PAGE COVERDALE PAGE 1993
COWBOY ERASURE 1997
COWBOY COMPILATION – THE ALBUM VOLUME 1 VARIOUS ARTISTS (COWBOY) 1993
COYOTE UGLY (OST) FILM SOUNDTRACK 2000
THE CRACK RUTS 1979
THE CRACKDOWN CABARET VOLTAIRE 1983
CRACKED REAR VIEW HOOTIE & THE BLOWFISH 1995
CRACKERS' – THE SLADE CHRISTMAS PARTY ALBUM SLADE 1985
CRAIG DOUGLAS CRAIG DOUGLAS 1960
CRAIG MCLACHLAN AND CHECK 1-2 CRAIG MCLACHLAN & CHECK 1 2 1990
CRANK ALMIGHTY 1994
CRASH HUMAN LEAGUE 1986
CRASH BOOM BANG ROXETTE 1994
CRASH COURSE U.K. SUBS 1980
CRASH LANDING JIMI HENDRIX 1975
CRAZY JULIO IGLESIAS 1994
CRAZY FROM THE HEAT DAVID LEE ROTH 1985
CRAZY HORSES OSMONDS 1972
CRAZY LITTLE THING CALLED LOVE VARIOUS ARTISTS (WARNER BROTHERS) 1999
CRAZY NIGHTS TYGERS OF PAN TANG 1981
CRAZY NIGHTS KISS 1987
CRAZY TIMES GENE VINCENT 1960
CRAZY WORLD SCORPIONS 1990
THE CRAZY WORLD OF ARTHUR BROWN CRAZY WORLD OF ARTHUR BROWN 1968
CRAZYSEXYCOOL TLC 1995
CREAM ANTHEMS VARIOUS ARTISTS (DECONSTRUCTION) 1995
CREAM ANTHEMS SPRING 2002 VARIOUS ARTISTS (VIRGIN) 2002
CREAM ANTHEMS 2000 VARIOUS ARTISTS (VIRGIN) 1999
CREAM ANTHEMS 2001 VARIOUS ARTISTS (VIRGIN) 2000
CREAM ANTHEMS 2002 VARIOUS ARTISTS (VIRGIN) 2001

CREAM ANTHEMS '97 VARIOUS ARTISTS (DECONSTRUCTION) 1997
CREAM ANTHEMS MIXED BY TALL PAUL AND SEB FONTAINE VARIOUS ARTISTS (VIRGIN) 1998
CREAM BEACH 2002 VARIOUS ARTISTS (VIRGIN/EMI) 2002
CREAM IBIZA VARIOUS ARTISTS (VIRGIN) 2001
CREAM IBIZA – ARRIVALS VARIOUS ARTISTS (VIRGIN) 1999
CREAM IBIZA – DEPARTURES VARIOUS ARTISTS (VIRGIN) 1999
CREAM IBIZA ARRIVALS VARIOUS ARTISTS (VIRGIN) 2000
CREAM LIVE VARIOUS ARTISTS (DECONSTRUCTION) 1995
CREAM LIVE VARIOUS ARTISTS (VIRGIN) 2000
CREAM LIVE VARIOUS ARTISTS (VIRGIN) 2001
CREAM LIVE – TWO VARIOUS ARTISTS (DECONSTRUCTION) 1996
THE CREAM OF ERIC CLAPTON ERIC CLAPTON & CREAM 1987
CREAM RESIDENT – SEB FONTAINE VARIOUS ARTISTS (VIRGIN) 2000
CREAM SEPERATES – THE COLLECTION VARIOUS ARTISTS (DECONSTRUCTION) 1997
CREAMFIELDS VARIOUS ARTISTS (VIRGIN) 2000
CREATING PATTERNS 4 HERO 2001
CREATURES OF THE NIGHT KISS 1982
THE CREEDENCE COLLECTION CREEDENCE CLEARWATER REVIVAL 1985
CRE OLE (BEST OF KID CREOLE AND COCONUTS) KID CREOLE & THE COCONUTS 1984
CREPES AND DRAPES SHOWADDYWADDY 1979
CREST OF A KNAVE JETHRO TULL 1987
CREW CUTS VARIOUS ARTISTS (ISLAND) 1984
CREW CUTS – LESSON 2 VARIOUS ARTISTS (ISLAND) 1984
CREWS CONTROL VARIOUS ARTISTS (WARNER DANCE) 2002
CRICKLEWOOD GREEN TEN YEARS AFTER 1970
CRIME OF THE CENTURY SUPERTRAMP 1974
CRIMINAL RECORD RICK WAKEMAN 1977
THE CRIMSON IDOL W.A.S.P. 1992
CRISES MIKE OLDFIELD 1983
CRISIS? WHAT CRISIS? – SUPERTRAMP 1975
THE CROCK OF GOLD SHANE MACGOWAN & THE POPES 1997
CROCODILE SHOES JIMMY NAIL 1994
CROCODILE SHOES II JIMMY NAIL 1996
CROCODILES ECHO & THE BUNNYMEN 1980
CROOKED RAIN CROOKED RAIN PAVEMENT 1994
CROSBY, STILLS AND NASH CROSBY, STILLS & NASH 1969
THE CROSS OF CHANGES ENIGMA 1994
CROSS PURPOSES BLACK SABBATH 1994
CROSS ROAD – THE BEST OF BON JOVI BON JOVI 1994
CROSS THAT LINE HOWARD JONES 1989
THE CROSSING BIG COUNTRY 1983
THE CROSSING PAUL YOUNG 1993
CROSSING THE RED SEA WITH THE ADVERTS ADVERTS 1978
CROSSROADS TRACY CHAPMAN 1989
THE CROW (OST) FILM SOUNDTRACK 1994
A CROW LEFT OF THE MURDER INCUBUS 2004
CRUEL SISTER PENTANGLE 1970
CRUELTY AND THE BEAST CRADLE OF FILTH 1998
CRUISIN' – VILLAGE PEOPLE 1979
CRUISIN' – THE BEST OF DRIVETIME VARIOUS ARTISTS (GLOBAL) 2000
CRUSADE JOHN MAYALL & THE BLUESBREAKERS 1967
CRUSADER SAXON 1984
CRUSADER CHRIS DE BURGH 1986
CRUSH ORCHESTRAL MANOEUVRES IN THE DARK 1985
CRUSH VARIOUS ARTISTS (POLYGRAM) 1997
CRUSH BON JOVI 2000
CRUSH ON YOU JETS 1987
CRUSHIN' – FAT BOYS 1987
CRY FAITH HILL 2002
CRY FREEDOM (OST) FILM SOUNDTRACK 1988
CRY LIKE A RAINSTORM – HOWL LIKE THE WIND LINDA RONSTADT FEATURING AARON NEVILLE 1989
CRY OF LOVE JIMI HENDRIX 1971

CRY TOUGH NILS LOFGREN 1976
CRYING ROY ORBISON 1963
CRYING, LAUGHING, LOVING, LYING LABI SIFFRE 1972
CRYPTIC WRITINGS MEGADETH 1997
THE CRYSTAL GAYLE SINGLES ALBUM CRYSTAL GAYLE 1980
CRYSTAL PLANET JOE SATRIANI 1998
CSN CROSBY, STILLS & NASH 1977
CUCKOO CURVE 1993
CUCUMBER CASTLE BEE GEES 1970
THE CULT CULT 1994
THE CULT OF ANT & DEC ANT & DEC 1997
THE CULT OF RAY FRANK BLACK 1996
CULTOSAURUS ERECTUS BLUE OYSTER CULT 1980
CULTURA BREED 77 2004
CUNNING STUNTS CARAVAN 1975
CUPID AND PSYCHE 85 SCRITTI POLITTI 1985
CURE FOR SANITY POP WILL EAT ITSELF 1990
CURED STEVE HACKETT 1981
A CURIOUS FEELING TONY BANKS 1979
THE CURSE THROWING MUSES 1992
THE CURSE OF BLONDIE BLONDIE 2003
CURTAIN UP VARIOUS ARTISTS (PYE) 1959
CURTAINS TINDERSTICKS 1997
CURTIS STIGERS CURTIS STIGERS 1992
CURVED AIR CURVED AIR 1971
CUT SLITS 1979
CUT THE CAKE AVERAGE WHITE BAND 1975
CUT THE CRAP CLASH 1985
CUTS BOTH WAYS GLORIA ESTEFAN 1989
CUTS LIKE A KNIFE BRYAN ADAMS 1986
THE CUTTER AND THE CLAN RUNRIG 1995
CUTTIN' HERBIE B BOYS 1984
CYBERPUNK BILLY IDOL 1993
CYCLONE TANGERINE DREAM 1978
CYMANSA GANN MASSED WELSH CHOIRS 1969
CYPRESS HILL III (TEMPLES OF BOOM) CYPRESS HILL 1995
D12 WORLD D12 2004
D D DON'T DON'T STOP THE BEAT JUNIOR SENIOR 2003
DA GAMES IS TO BE SOLD, NOT TO BE TOLD SNOOP DOGGY DOGG 1998
DA REAL WORLD MISSY 'MISDEMEANOR' ELLIOTT 1999
DADA ALICE COOPER 1983
DAISIES OF THE GALAXY EELS 2000
DAMITA JO JANET JACKSON 2004
DAMN RIGHT, I'VE GOT THE BLUES BUDDY GUY 1991
DAMN THE TORPEDOES TOM PETTY & HEARTBREAKERS 1979
DAMNATION AND A DAY CRADLE OF FILTH 2003
DAMNED DAMNED DAMNED DAMNED 1977
DANCE GARY NUMAN 1981
THE DANCE FLEETWOOD MAC 1997
DANCE '95 VARIOUS ARTISTS (VIRGIN) 1995
DANCE ADRENALIN VARIOUS ARTISTS (TELSTAR) 1993
DANCE BUZZ VARIOUS ARTISTS (GLOBAL) 1995
THE DANCE CHART VARIOUS ARTISTS (TELSTAR) 1987
DANCE CLASSICS VOLUME 1 VARIOUS ARTISTS (ARCADE) 1991
DANCE CLASSICS VOLUME 2 VARIOUS ARTISTS (ARCADE) 1991
DANCE CRAZE (OST) FILM SOUNDTRACK 1981
DANCE DANCE DANCE VARIOUS ARTISTS (K-TEL) 1981
DANCE DANCE DANCE JAMES LAST 1988
DANCE DECADE – DANCE HITS OF THE 80'S VARIOUS ARTISTS (LONDON) 1989
DANCE DIVAS VARIOUS ARTISTS (POLYGRAM) 1994
DANCE ENERGY VARIOUS ARTISTS (VIRGIN) 1991
DANCE ENERGY 2 VARIOUS ARTISTS (VIRGIN) 1991
DANCE ENERGY 3 VARIOUS ARTISTS (VIRGIN) 1991
DANCE ENERGY 4 – FEEL THE RHYTHM VARIOUS ARTISTS (PARLOPHONE) 1992
DANCE HALL AT LOUSE POINT JOHN PARISH & POLLY JEAN HARVEY 1996
DANCE HEAT '95 VARIOUS ARTISTS (VIRGIN) 1995
DANCE HITS 2000 VARIOUS ARTISTS (WARNER BROTHERS) 2000

DANCE HITS '86 VARIOUS ARTISTS (K-TEL) 1986
DANCE HITS '94 – VOLUME 1 VARIOUS ARTISTS (TELSTAR) 1994
DANCE HITS '94 VOLUME 2 VARIOUS ARTISTS (TELSTAR) 1994
THE DANCE HITS ALBUM VARIOUS ARTISTS (TOWERBELL) 1986
DANCE HITS II VARIOUS ARTISTS (TOWERBELL) 1986
DANCE IN THE MIDNIGHT MARC BOLAN 1983
DANCE INTO THE LIGHT PHIL COLLINS 1996
DANCE MANIA 95 – VOLUME 1 VARIOUS ARTISTS (PURE MUSIC) 1995
DANCE MANIA 95 – VOLUME 2 VARIOUS ARTISTS (PURE MUSIC) 1995
DANCE MANIA 95 – VOLUME 3 VARIOUS ARTISTS (PURE MUSIC) 1995
DANCE MANIA 95 – VOLUME 4 VARIOUS ARTISTS (PURE MUSIC) 1995
DANCE MANIA VOLUME 1 VARIOUS ARTISTS (NEEDLE) 1987
DANCE MANIA VOLUME 2 VARIOUS ARTISTS (SERIOUS) 1988
DANCE MASSIVE VARIOUS ARTISTS (DINO) 1994
DANCE MASSIVE 2 VARIOUS ARTISTS (DINO) 1994
DANCE MASSIVE 95 VARIOUS ARTISTS (DINO) 1995
DANCE MASTERS VARIOUS ARTISTS (VIRGIN) 2001
DANCE MIX – DANCE HITS VOLUME 1 VARIOUS ARTISTS (EPIC) 1983
DANCE MIX – DANCE HITS VOLUME 2 VARIOUS ARTISTS (EPIC) 1983
DANCE MIX – DANCE HITS VOLUME 3 VARIOUS ARTISTS (EPIC) 1984
DANCE MIX – DANCE HITS VOLUME 4 VARIOUS ARTISTS (EPIC) 1984
DANCE MIX 2 VARIOUS ARTISTS (GLOBAL) 1996
DANCE MIX '87 VARIOUS ARTISTS (TELSTAR) 1987
DANCE MIX UK VARIOUS ARTISTS (GLOBAL) 1996
DANCE NATION VARIOUS ARTISTS (MINISTRY OF SOUND) 1996
DANCE NATION ANTHEMS VARIOUS ARTISTS (MINISTRY OF SOUND) 2002
DANCE NATION – TALL PAUL/BRANDON BLOCK VARIOUS ARTISTS (MINISTRY OF SOUND) 2000
DANCE NATION 3 – PETE TONG & JUDGE JULES VARIOUS ARTISTS (MINISTRY OF SOUND) 1997
DANCE NATION 4 – PETE TONG/BOY GEORGE VARIOUS ARTISTS (MINISTRY OF SOUND) 1997
DANCE NATION 6 – TALL PAUL & BRANDON BLOCK VARIOUS ARTISTS (MINISTRY OF SOUND) 1999
DANCE NATION '95 VARIOUS ARTISTS (VISION) 1995
DANCE OF DEATH IRON MAIDEN 2003
DANCE OF THE FLAMES INCANTATION 1983
DANCE PARADE IBIZA VARIOUS ARTISTS (WARNER BROTHERS) 2001
DANCE TIP '95 VARIOUS ARTISTS (GLOBAL) 1995
DANCE TIP 2000 VARIOUS ARTISTS (GLOBAL) 1996
DANCE TIP 3 VARIOUS ARTISTS (GLOBAL) 1995
DANCE TIP 4 VARIOUS ARTISTS (GLOBAL) 1996
DANCE TO THE HOLY MAN SILENCERS 1991
DANCE TO THE MAX VARIOUS ARTISTS (VIRGIN) 1994
DANCE TO THE MAX 2 VARIOUS ARTISTS (VIRGIN) 1994
DANCE TO THE MAX 3 VARIOUS ARTISTS (VIRGIN) 1994
DANCE TO THE MUSIC VARIOUS ARTISTS (K-TEL) 1977
DANCE WARS – JUDGE JULES VS. JOHN KELLY VARIOUS ARTISTS (JDJ) 1996
DANCE WITH MY FATHER LUTHER VANDROSS 2003
DANCE WITH THE GUITAR MAN DUANNE EDDY 1963
DANCE WITH THE SHADOWS SHADOWS 1964
DANCE ZONE – LEVEL ONE VARIOUS ARTISTS (POLYGRAM) 1994
DANCE ZONE – LEVEL THREE VARIOUS ARTISTS (POLYGRAM) 1994
DANCE ZONE – LEVEL TWO VARIOUS ARTISTS (POLYGRAM) 1994
DANCE ZONE '94 VARIOUS ARTISTS (POLYGRAM) 1994
DANCE ZONE '95 VARIOUS ARTISTS (POLYGRAM) 1995

DANCE ZONE LEVEL EIGHT VARIOUS ARTISTS (POLYGRAM) 1996
DANCE ZONE LEVEL FIVE VARIOUS ARTISTS (POLYGRAM) 1995
DANCE ZONE LEVEL FOUR VARIOUS ARTISTS (POLYGRAM) 1995
DANCE ZONE LEVEL NINE VARIOUS ARTISTS (POLYGRAM) 1997
DANCE ZONE LEVEL SEVEN VARIOUS ARTISTS (POLYGRAM) 1996
DANCE ZONE LEVEL SIX VARIOUS ARTISTS (POLYGRAM) 1995
DANCE... YA KNOW IT! – BOBBY BROWN 1989
DANCEMIX.UK.V1 VARIOUS ARTISTS (WARNER BROTHERS) 1999
DANCER WITH BRUISED KNEES KATE & ANNA MCGARRIGLE 1977
DANCES WITH WOLVES (FILM SOUNDTRACK) JOHN BARRY 1991
DANCESTAR 2001 VARIOUS ARTISTS (INSPIRED) 2001
DANCIN' – 20 ORIGINAL MOTOWN MOVERS VARIOUS ARTISTS (TELSTAR) 1983
DANCIN' IN THE KEY OF LIFE STEVE ARRINGTON 1985
DANCIN' ON THE EDGE LITA FORD 1984
DANCING DOWN THE STONEY ROAD CHRIS REA 2002
DANCING IN THE STREET VARIOUS ARTISTS (UNIVERSAL) 1999
DANCING ON SUNSHINE VARIOUS ARTISTS (POLYGRAM) 1992
DANCING ON THE CEILING LIONEL RICHIE 1986
DANCING ON THE COUCH GO WEST 1987
DANCING '68 VOLUME 1 JAMES LAST 1969
DANCING UNDERCOVER RATT 1986
DANCING WITH STRANGERS CHRIS REA 1987
DANDY IN THE UNDERWORLD T. REX 1977
DANGER ZONE SAMMY HAGAR 1980
DANGER ZONE VARIOUS ARTISTS (POLYGRAM) 1997
DANGER ZONE VOLUME 1 VARIOUS ARTISTS (QUALITY PRICE MUSIC) 1992
DANGEROUS MICHAEL JACKSON 1991
DANGEROUS ACQUAINTANCES MARIANNE FAITHFULL 1981
DANGEROUS CURVES LITA FORD 1992
DANGEROUS MINDS (OST) FILM SOUNDTRACK 1996
DANGEROUS MUSIC ROBIN GEORGE 1985
DANIEL IN BLUE JEANS DANIEL O'DONNELL 2003
THE DANIEL O'DONNELL IRISH COLLECTION DANIEL O'DONNELL 1996
DANNY RAMPLING – LOVE GROOVE DANCE PARTY VARIOUS ARTISTS (METROPOLE) 1996
DANNY RAMPLING – LOVE GROOVE DANCE PARTY VARIOUS ARTISTS (METROPOLE) 1997
DANNY RAMPLING – LOVE GROOVE DANCE PARTY VARIOUS ARTISTS (UNIVERSAL) 2001
DANNY RAMPLING/LOVE GROOVE PARTY 5 & 6 VARIOUS ARTISTS (METROPOLE) 1997
DANNY TENEAGLIA LIVE IN ATHENS VARIOUS ARTISTS (GLOBAL UNDERGROUND) 1999
DARE HUMAN LEAGUE 1981
DARE TO LOVE JIMMY SOMERVILLE 1995
DARING ADVENTURES RICHARD THOMPSON 1986
DARK DAYS COAL CHAMBER 2002
DARK DAYS IN PARADISE GARY MOORE 1997
DARK SIDE OF THE 80'S VARIOUS ARTISTS (TELSTAR) 2003
THE DARK SIDE OF THE MOON PINK FLOYD 1973
DARKDANCER LES RHYTHMES DIGITALES 1999
DARKLANDS JESUS & MARY CHAIN 1987
DARKNESS ON THE EDGE OF TOWN BRUCE SPRINGSTEEN 1978
DARREN DAY DARREN DAY 1998
DART ATTACK DARTS 1979
DARTS DARTS 1977
A DATE WITH DANIEL – LIVE DANIEL O'DONNELL 1993
A DATE WITH ELVIS ELVIS PRESLEY 1959
A DATE WITH ELVIS CRAMPS 1986

A DATE WITH THE EVERLY BROTHERS EVERLY BROTHERS 1961
THE DATSUNS DATSUNS 2002
DAUGHTER OF TIME COLOSSEUM 1970
DAVE CLARK'S TIME THE ALBUM ORIGINAL STUDIO CAST RECORDING 1986
DAVE DEE, DOZY, BEAKY, MICK AND TICH DAVE DEE, DOZY, BEAKY, MICK & TICH 1966
DAVE PEARCE DANCE ANTHEMS SPRING 2004 VARIOUS ARTISTS (INSPIRED) 2004
DAVE PEARCE DANCE ANTHEMS – SUMMER 2003 VARIOUS ARTISTS (BMG) 2003
DAVE PEARCE PRESENTS 40 CLASSIC ANTHEMS – 3 VARIOUS ARTISTS (UNIVERSAL) 2000
DAVE PEARCE PRESENTS 40 CLASSIC DANCE ANTHEMS VARIOUS ARTISTS (UNIVERSAL) 1999
DAVE PEARCE PRESENTS 40 CLASSIC DANCE ANTHEMS 2 VARIOUS ARTISTS (UNIVERSAL) 1999
DAVE PEARCE PRESENTS DANCE ANTHEMS VARIOUS ARTISTS (POLYGRAM) 1998
DAVE PEARCE PRESENTS DANCE ANTHEMS VOLUME 2 VARIOUS ARTISTS (POLYGRAM) 1998
DAVE STEWART AND THE SPIRITUAL COWBOYS DAVE STEWART & THE SPIRITUAL COWBOYS 1990
DAVID BYRNE DAVID BYRNE 1994
DAVID ESSEX DAVID ESSEX 1974
THE DAVID ESSEX ALBUM DAVID ESSEX 1979
DAVID GATES AND BREAD: ESSENTIALS DAVID GATES & BREAD 1997
DAVID GILMOUR DAVID GILMOUR 1978
DAVID GRANT DAVID GRANT 1983
DAVID LIVE DAVID BOWIE 1974
DAVID MCWILLIAMS SINGS DAVID MCWILLIAMS 1967
DAVID MCWILLIAMS VOLUME 2 DAVID MCWILLIAMS 1967
DAVID MCWILLIAMS VOLUME 3 DAVID MCWILLIAMS 1968
DAVID SOUL DAVID SOUL 1976
DAWN OF THE DICKIES DICKIES 1979
DAWNRAZOR FIELDS OF THE NEPHILIM 1987
THE DAY BABYFACE 1996
A DAY AT THE RACES QUEEN 1976
A DAY IN THE LIFE ERIC BENET 1999
A DAY WITHOUT RAIN ENYA 2000
DAYBREAKER BETH ORTON 2002
DAYDREAM LOVIN' SPOONFUL 1966
DAYDREAM MARIAH CAREY 1995
DAYDREAM NATION SONIC YOUTH 1988
DAYS IN EUROPA SKIDS 1979
DAYS LIKE THIS VAN MORRISON 1995
DAYS OF FUTURE PASSED MOODY BLUES 1968
DAYS OF OPEN HAND SUZANNE VEGA 1990
DAYS OF SPEED PAUL WELLER 2001
DAYS OF THUNDER (OST) FILM SOUNDTRACK 1990
DAYTIME FRIENDS – THE VERY BEST OF KENNY ROGERS KENNY ROGERS 1993
DAZZLE SHIPS ORCHESTRAL MANOEUVRES IN THE DARK 1983
DE 7 DAVE EDMUNDS 1982
DE LA SOUL IS DEAD DE LA SOUL 1991
DE NINA A MUJER JULIO IGLESIAS 1981
DEAD BEES ON A CAKE DAVID SYLVIAN 1999
DEAD CITIES FUTURE SOUND OF LONDON 1996
DEAD ELVIS DEATH IN VEGAS 1997
DEAD LETTER OFFICE R.E.M. 1987
DEAD LETTERS RASMUS 2004
DEAD RINGER MEAT LOAF 1981
DEADLINE FOR MY MEMORIES BILLIE RAY MARTIN 1996
DEAN MARTIN'S GREATEST HITS VOLUME I DEAN MARTIN 1968
DEAR CATASTROPHE WAITRESS BELLE & SEBASTIAN 2003
DEAR PERRY PERRY COMO 1958
DEATH IS NOT THE END SHUT UP & DANCE 1992
DEATH OF A LADIES MAN LEONARD COHEN 1977
THE DEATH OF COOL KITCHENS OF DISTINCTION 1992
DEATH TO THE PIXIES PIXIES 1997
DEATH TO THE PIXIES – DELUXE EDITION PIXIES 1997
DEATH WALKS BEHIND YOU ATOMIC ROOSTER 1971

DEATHWISH II (OST) JIMMY PAGE 1982
DE LOUSED IN THE COMATORIUM MARS VOLTA 2003
DEBRAVATION DEBORAH HARRY 1993
DEBUT BJORK 1993
DECADE NEIL YOUNG 1977
DECADE DURAN DURAN 1989
DECADE OF AGGRESSION – LIVE SLAYER 1991
A DECADE OF DANCE VARIOUS ARTISTS (POSITIVA) 2003
DECADE OF DECADENCE '81 '91 MOTLEY CRUE 1991
A DECADE OF IBIZA – 1987–1997 VARIOUS ARTISTS (TELSTAR) 1997
DECADES – STORY OF THE 60'S/70'S/80'S VARIOUS ARTISTS (VIRGIN) 2000
THE DECCA ANTHOLOGY 1965–1967 SMALL FACES 1996
DECENCY DIESEL PARK WEST 1992
DECEPTION COLOUR FIELD 1987
DECEPTIVE BENDS 10 CC 1977
DECKSANDRUMSANDROCKANDROLL PROPELLERHEADS 1998
DECLAN DECLAN 2002
DECLARATION ALARM 1984
THE DECLINE OF BRITISH SEA POWER BRITISH SEA POWER 2003
DECONSTRUCTION CLASSICS – A HISTORY OF DANCE MUSIC VARIOUS ARTISTS (DECONSTRUCTION) 1995
DEDICATED LEMAR 2003
DEDICATED TO PLEASURE VARIOUS ARTISTS (EMI) 1995
DEDICATION BAY CITY ROLLERS 1976
DEDICATION GARY U.S. BONDS 1981
DEDICATION – THE VERY BEST OF THIN LIZZY THIN LIZZY 1991
DEEP & CHILLED EUPHORIA VARIOUS ARTISTS (TELSTAR) 2001
DEEP AND MEANINGLESS JOHN OTWAY & WILD WILLY BARRETT 1978
DEEP DOWN AND DIRTY STEREO MC'S 2001
DEEP FOREST DEEP FOREST 1994
DEEP HEAT – 26 HOTTEST HOUSE HITS VARIOUS ARTISTS (TELSTAR) 1989
DEEP HEAT – THE SECOND BURN VARIOUS ARTISTS (TELSTAR) 1989
DEEP HEAT 10 – THE AWAKENING VARIOUS ARTISTS (TELSTAR) 1991
DEEP HEAT 11 – SPIRIT OF ECSTASY VARIOUS ARTISTS (TELSTAR) 1991
DEEP HEAT 1989 – FIGHT THE FLAME VARIOUS ARTISTS (TELSTAR) 1989
DEEP HEAT 3 – THE THIRD DEGREE VARIOUS ARTISTS (TELSTAR) 1989
DEEP HEAT 4 – PLAY WITH FIRE VARIOUS ARTISTS (TELSTAR) 1989
DEEP HEAT 5 – FEED THE FEVER – 32 HOTTEST CLUB HITS VARIOUS ARTISTS (TELSTAR) 1990
DEEP HEAT 6 – THE SIXTH SENSE VARIOUS ARTISTS (TELSTAR) 1990
DEEP HEAT 7 – SEVENTH HEAVEN VARIOUS ARTISTS (TELSTAR) 1990
DEEP HEAT 8 – THE HAND OF FATE VARIOUS ARTISTS (TELSTAR) 1990
DEEP HEAT 9 – NINTH LIFE – KISS THE BLISS VARIOUS ARTISTS (TELSTAR) 1991
DEEP HEAT 90 VARIOUS ARTISTS (TELSTAR) 1990
DEEP HEAT 93 VOLUME 1 VARIOUS ARTISTS (TELSTAR) 1993
DEEP IN THE HEART OF NOWHERE BOB GELDOF 1986
DEEP PURPLE DONNY & MARIE OSMOND 1976
DEEP PURPLE IN ROCK DEEP PURPLE 1970
DEEP PURPLE LIVE DEEP PURPLE 1976
DEEP PURPLE LIVE IN LONDON DEEP PURPLE 1982
DEEP SEA SKIVING BANANARAMA 1983
DEEP WITHIN MY SOUL SISSEL 1995
DEEPER – EUPHORIA II: MIXED BY RED JERRY VARIOUS ARTISTS (TELSTAR) 1999
DEEPER SHADES OF EUPHORIA VARIOUS ARTISTS (TELSTAR) 2003
THE DEEPEST CUT – VOLUME 1 OMNI TRIO 1995

DEEPEST PURPLE DEEP PURPLE 1980
DEF DUMB AND BLONDE DEBORAH HARRY 1989
DEFECTOR STEVE HACKETT 1980
DEFENDERS OF THE FAITH JUDAS PRIEST 1984
DEFINITELY MAYBE OASIS 1994
DEFINITELY MAYBE SINGLES BOX – SILVER OASIS 1996
DEFINITIVE INXS 2002
THE DEFINITIVE MONKEES 2001
THE DEFINITIVE RAY CHARLES 2001
THE DEFINITIVE EVERLY BROTHERS 2002
THE DEFINITIVE DRIFTERS 2003
THE DEFINITIVE ALICE COOPER ALICE COOPER 2001
THE DEFINITIVE COLLECTION KINKS 1993
THE DEFINITIVE HITS COLLECTION LEO SAYER 1999
THE DEFINITIVE COLLECTION ABBA 2001
THE DEFINITIVE COLLECTION STEVIE WONDER 2002
THE DEFINITIVE COLLECTION LIONEL RICHIE/COMMODORES 2003
THE DEFINITIVE COLLECTION MARIO LANZA 2004
THE DEFINITIVE FRANKIE VALLI & THE FOUR SEASONS FRANKIE VALLI & THE FOUR SEASONS 2001
THE DEFINITIVE JIM REEVES JIM REEVES 1992
THE DEFINITIVE PATSY CLINE 1932–1963 PATSY CLINE 1992
THE DEFINITIVE SIMON AND GARFUNKEL SIMON & GARFUNKEL 1991
THE DEFINITIVE SOUND OF ATLANTIC SOUL VARIOUS ARTISTS (WARNER BROTHERS) 1999
DEFTONES DEFTONES 2003
DEHUMANIZER BLACK SABBATH 1992
DEJA VU CROSBY, STILL, NASH & YOUNG 1970
DEJA VU A.B.'S 1984
DELICATE SOUND OF THUNDER PINK FLOYD 1988
DELILAH TOM JONES 1968
THE DELINQUENTS (OST) FILM SOUNDTRACK 1990
DELIVER US FROM EVIL BUDGIE 1982
DELIVERANCE BABY D 1996
DELTICS CHRIS REA 1979
DEMANUFACTURE FEAR FACTORY 1995
DEMOCRACY KILLING JOKE 1996
DEMOLITION GIRLSCHOOL 1980
DEMOLITION RYAN ADAMS 2002
DEMONS AND WIZARDS URIAH HEEP 1972
DENIM AND LEATHER SAXON 1981
DEREK AND CLIVE LIVE PETER COOK & DUDLEY MOORE 1976
DEREK AND THE DOMINOS IN CONCERT DEREK & THE DOMINOS 1973
DERELICTS OF DIALECT 3RD BASS 1991
DES O'CONNOR NOW DES O'CONNOR 1984
DESENSITIZED DROWNING POOL 2004
DESERTER'S SONG MERCURY REV 1998
DESIGN OF A DECADE 1986–1996 JANET JACKSON 1995
DESIRE BOB DYLAN 1976
DESIRE WALKS ON HEART 1993
DESIRELESS EAGLE-EYE CHERRY 1998
DESOLATION ANGELS BAD COMPANY 1979
DESPERADO EAGLES 1975
DESPITE YOURSELF HEADSWIM 1998
DESTINATION RONAN KEATING 2002
DESTINATION ANYWHERE JON BON JOVI 1997
DESTINY JACKSONS 1979
DESTINY CHAKA KHAN 1986
DESTINY SAXON 1988
DESTINY GLORIA ESTEFAN 1996
DESTINY'S CHILD DESTINY'S CHILD 1998
DESTINY'S SONGS AND THE IMAGE OF PURSUANCE COURTNEY PINE 1988
DESTROYER KISS 1976
DETONATOR RATT 1990
DETROIT SPINNERS' SMASH HITS DETROIT SPINNERS 1977
DEUCE RORY GALLAGHER 1971
D'EUX – THE FRENCH ALBUM CELINE DION 1995
DEVIANT PITCH SHIFTER 2000
DEVIL HOPPING INSPIRAL CARPETS 1994

THE DEVIL IN SISTER GEORGE BOY GEORGE/JESUS LOVES YOU/CULTURE CLUB 1994
DEVILS NIGHT D12 2001
DEVINE TIME SIDNEY DEVINE 1976
D FROST – 20 GLOBAL DANCE WARNINGS VARIOUS ARTISTS (TOUCHDOWN) 1993
DIABOLUS IN MUSICA SLAYER 1998
DIAMOND SPANDAU BALLET 1982
DIAMOND DOGS DAVID BOWIE 1974
DIAMOND HEAD PHIL MANZANERA 1975
DIAMOND LIFE SADE 1984
DIAMONDS AND PEARLS PRINCE & THE NEW POWER GENERATION 1991
DIANA DIANA ROSS 1980
DIANA (OST TV) DIANA ROSS 1971
DIANA AND MARVIN DIANA ROSS & MARVIN GAYE 1974
DIANA EXTENDED – THE REMIXES DIANA ROSS 1994
DIANA PRINCESS OF WALES – TRIBUTE (ROYAL COMPILATION ALBUM) ROYAL COMPILATION ALBUM 1997
DIANA PRINCESS OF WALES 1961–1997 – FUNERAL SERVICE (ROYAL COMPILATION ALBUM) ROYAL COMPILATION ALBUM 1997
DIANA ROSS DIANA ROSS 1970
DIANA ROSS DIANA ROSS 1976
DIANA ROSS AND THE SUPREMES 20 GOLDEN GREATS DIANA ROSS & THE SUPREMES 1977
DIANA ROSS AND THE SUPREMES GREATEST HITS DIANA ROSS & THE SUPREMES 1968
DIANA ROSS AND THE SUPREMES JOIN THE TEMPTATIONS DIANA ROSS & THE SUPREMES & THE TEMPTATIONS 1969
DIANA ROSS LIVE AT CAESAR'S PALACE DIANA ROSS 1974
DIANA ROSS PRESENTS THE JACKSON FIVE JACKSON FIVE 1970
DIANA ROSS. MICHAEL JACKSON. GLADYS KNIGHT. STEVIE WONDER. THEIR VERY BEST BACK TO BACK DIANA ROSS/MICHAEL JACKSON/GLADYS KNIGHT/STEVIE WONDER 1986
DIANA'S DUETS DIANA ROSS 1982
THE DIARY OF A BAND VOLUME 1 JOHN MAYALL & THE BLUESBREAKERS 1968
THE DIARY OF A BAND VOLUME 2 JOHN MAYALL & THE BLUESBREAKERS 1968
DIARY OF A HOLLOW HORSE CHINA CRISIS 1989
DIARY OF A MADMAN OZZY OSBOURNE 1981
THE DIARY OF ALICIA KEYS ALICIA KEYS 2003
DIATRIBES NAPALM DEATH 1996
DID YOU EVER NANCY SINATRA & LEE HAZLEWOOD 1972
DIESEL AND DUST MIDNIGHT OIL 1988
A DIFFERENT BEAT BOYZONE 1996
DIFFERENT CLASS PULP 1995
A DIFFERENT KIND OF TENSION BUZZCOCKS 1979
DIFFERENT LIGHT BANGLES 1986
DIFFICULT SHAPES AND PASSIVE RHYTHMS SOME PEOPLE THINK IT'S FUN TO ENTERTAIN CHINA CRISIS 1982
DIFFICULT TO CURE RAINBOW 1981
DIFFORD AND TILBROOK DIFFORD & TILBROOK 1984
DIG THE NEW BREED JAM 1982
DIG YOUR OWN HOLE CHEMICAL BROTHERS 1997
DIGIMORTAL FEAR FACTORY 2001
DIMENSION INTRUSION FUSE 1993
DIMINISHED RESPONSIBILITY U.K. SUBS 1981
DINGLY DELL LINDISFARNE 1972
THE DIONNE WARWICK COLLECTION DIONNE WARWICK 1983
DIRE STRAITS DIRE STRAITS 1978
DIRECT HITS VARIOUS ARTISTS (TELSTAR) 1982
DIRECTION REACTION CREATION JAM 1997
DIRK WEARS WHITE SOX ADAM & THE ANTS 1981
DIRT ALICE IN CHAINS 1992
DIRTY SONIC YOUTH 1992
THE DIRTY BOOTS EP – PLUS 5 LIVE TRACKS SONIC YOUTH 1991
DIRTY DANCING – LIVE IN CONCERT VARIOUS ARTISTS (RCA) 1989

DIRTY DANCING (OST) FILM SOUNDTRACK 1987
DIRTY HITS PRIMAL SCREAM 2003
DIRTY VEGAS DIRTY VEGAS 2002
DIRTY WORK ROLLING STONES 1986
DISCIPLINE KING CRIMSON 1981
DISCO PET SHOP BOYS 1986
DISCO 3 PET SHOP BOYS 2003
DISCO 2 PET SHOP BOYS 1994
DISCO BABY VAN MCCOY & THE SOUL CITY SYMPHONY 1975
DISCO BEACH PARTY VARIOUS ARTISTS (STYLUS) 1985
DISCO DANCER VARIOUS ARTISTS (K-TEL) 1982
DISCO DAZE AND DISCO NITES VARIOUS ARTISTS (RONCO) 1981
DISCO DIVAS VARIOUS ARTISTS (POLYGRAM) 1993
DISCO DOUBLE VARIOUS ARTISTS (K-TEL) 1978
DISCO EROTICA VARIOUS ARTISTS (WARWICK) 1981
DISCO FEVER VARIOUS ARTISTS (K-TEL) 1977
DISCO FEVER VARIOUS ARTISTS (GLOBAL) 2000
DISCO FEVER VARIOUS ARTISTS (UNIVERSAL) 2001
DISCO FEVER – VOLUME 2 VARIOUS ARTISTS (UNIVERSAL) 2001
DISCO HEAVEN 01.04 VARIOUS ARTISTS (HED KANDI) 2004
DISCO HITS '75 VARIOUS ARTISTS (ARCADE) 1975
DISCO HOUSE VARIOUS ARTISTS (GLOBAL) 1999
DISCO INFERNO VARIOUS ARTISTS (K-TEL) 1978
DISCO INFERNO VARIOUS ARTISTS (EAST WEST) 1993
DISCO INFERNO VARIOUS ARTISTS (WARNER BROTHERS) 1995
DISCO KANDI 05.03 VARIOUS ARTISTS (HED KANDI) 2003
DISCO MIX 96 VARIOUS ARTISTS (WARNER BROTHERS) 1996
DISCO ROCKET VARIOUS ARTISTS (K-TEL) 1976
DISCO STARS VARIOUS ARTISTS (K-TEL) 1978
DISCO UK AND DISCO USA VARIOUS ARTISTS (RONCO) 1982
DISCO: 1999 VARIOUS ARTISTS (VIRGIN) 1999
DISCOGRAPHY PET SHOP BOYS 1991
DISCOTRAIN DONNY OSMOND 1976
DISCOVER GENE LOVES JEZEBEL 1986
DISCOVER COUNTRY/DISCOVER NEW COUNTRY VARIOUS ARTISTS (STARBLEND) 1986
DISCOVER THE CLASSICS VOLUME 1 VARIOUS ARTISTS (IMP) 1992
DISCOVER THE CLASSICS VOLUME 2 VARIOUS ARTISTS (IMP) 1992
DISCOVERY ELECTRIC LIGHT ORCHESTRA 1979
DISCOVERY MIKE OLDFIELD 1984
DISCOVERY DAFT PUNK 2001
DISGRACEFUL DUBSTAR 1995
DISINTEGRATION CURE 1989
THE DISNEY EXPERIENCE VARIOUS ARTISTS (WALT DISNEY) 1998
DISNEY'S GREATEST HITS VARIOUS ARTISTS (TELSTAR) 2000
DISNEY'S HIT SINGLES & MORE! – VARIOUS ARTISTS (WALT DISNEY) 1997
DISRAELI GEARS CREAM 1967
THE DISTANCE BOB SEGER & THE SILVER BULLET BAND 1983
THE DISTANCE TO HERE LIVE 1999
DISTANT DREAMS KAREN RAMIREZ 1998
DISTANT DRUMS JIM REEVES 1966
DISTANT THUNDER ASWAD 1988
DIVA ANNIE LENNOX 1992
DIVA – THE ULTIMATE COLLECTION MARIA CALLAS 1996
DIVAS LIVE VARIOUS ARTISTS (EPIC) 1998
THE DIVAS OF DANCE VARIOUS ARTISTS (TELSTAR) 1992
DIVAS OF JAZZ VARIOUS ARTISTS (VERVE) 2003
DIVE DEEP QUINTESSENCE 1971
DIVE IN DARIUS 2002
DIVER DOWN VAN HALEN 1982
DIVINE EMOTION NARADA 1988
DIVINE INTERVENTION SLAYER 1994
DIVINE MADNESS MADNESS 1992

DIVINE WORKS DIVINE WORKS 1997
DIVINYLS DIVINYLS 1991
THE DIVISION BELL PINK FLOYD 1994
DIZZY HEIGHTS LIGHTNING SEEDS 1996
DIZZY UP THE GIRL GOO GOO DOLLS 1999
DJ LUCK & MC NEAT PRESENT VOLUME 3 VARIOUS ARTISTS (UNIVERSAL) 2001
DJ LUCK & MC NEAT PRESENTS VARIOUS ARTISTS (UNIVERSAL) 2000
DJ LUCK & MC NEAT PRESENTS – II VARIOUS ARTISTS (UNIVERSAL) 2001
DO A RUNNER ATHLETICO SPIZZ 80 1980
DO IT AGAIN – THE VERY BEST OF STEELY DAN STEELY DAN 1987
DO IT FOR LOVE DARYL HALL & JOHN OATES 2003
DO IT YOURSELF IAN DURY & THE BLOCKHEADS 1979
DO IT YOURSELF SEAHORSES 1997
DO ME AGAIN FREDDIE JACKSON 1990
DOCK OF THE BAY OTIS REDDING 1968
DOCK OF THE BAY – THE DEFINITIVE COLLECTION OTIS REDDING 1993
DOCTOR ADAMSKI'S MUSICAL PHARMACY ADAMSKI 1990
DR. BYRD AND MR HYDE BYRDS 1969
DR. FEELGOOD MOTLEY CRUE 1989
DR. HECKLE AND MR. JIVE PIGBAG 1982
DR. HILARY JONES CLASSIC RELAXATION TELEVISION COMPILATION 1994
DR. HOOK LIVE IN THE UK DR. HOOK 1981
DR. HOOK'S GREATEST HITS DR. HOOK 1980
DOCTOR WHO – THE EVIL OF THE DALEKS RADIO SOUNDTRACK 1992
DOCTOR WHO – THE PARADISE OF DEATH RADIO SOUNDTRACK 1993
DOCTOR WHO – THE POWER OF THE DALEKS TELEVISION SOUNDTRACK 1993
DOCTOR ZHIVAGO (OST) MAURICE JARRE 1966
DOCUMENT R.E.M. 1987
THE DODGY ALBUM DODGY 1993
DOES THIS LOOK INFECTED SUM 41 2002
DOG EAT DOG JONI MITCHELL 1985
DOG EAT DOG WARRANT 1992
DOG MAN STAR SUEDE 1994
DOGG FOOD THA DOGG POUND 1995
DOGGYSTYLE SNOOP DOGGY DOGG 1993
DOGMAN KING'S X 1994
DOG'S HITS AND THE BOOTLEG ALBUM DOGS D'AMOUR 1991
DOGS IN THE TRAFFIC LOVE & MONEY 1991
THE DOG'S… ! – VARIOUS ARTISTS (EMI) 1996
DOLL REVOLUTION BANGLES 2003
THE DOLLAR ALBUM DOLLAR 1982
DOLLARS C.J. LEWIS 1994
DOLLY PARTON/BOTH SIDES DOLLY PARTON 1978
THE DOM KILLUMINATI – THE SEVEN DAY THEORY MAKAVELI 1996
DOMINATOR TIME FREQUENCY 1994
DOMINGO: ARIAS AND SPANISH SONGS PLACIDO DOMINGO 1992
THE DOMINO CLUB MEN THEY COULDN'T HANG 1990
DOMINO THEORY WEATHER REPORT 1984
DON JUAN'S RECKLESS DAUGHTER JONI MITCHELL 1978
DON QUIXOTE GORDON LIGHTFOOT 1972
DONE AND DUSTED DUST JUNKYS 1998
DONE BY THE FORCES OF NATURE JUNGLE BROTHERS 1990
DONNA SUMMER DONNA SUMMER 1982
DONNY DONNY OSMOND 1975
DON'T ASK TINA ARENA 1995
DON'T BE AFRAID OF THE DARK ROBERT CRAY BAND 1988
DON'T BE CRUEL BOBBY BROWN 1989
DON'T BORE US, GET TO THE CHORUS! – GREATEST HITS ROXETTE 1995
DON'T EXPLAIN ROBERT PALMER 1990
DON'T GET WEIRD ON ME BABE LLOYD COLE 1991
DON'T LET LOVE SLIP AWAY FREDDIE JACKSON 1988
DON'T LOOK ANY FURTHER DENNIS EDWARDS 1984
DON'T LOOK BACK BOSTON 1978

DON'T LOOK BACK JOHN LEE HOOKER 1997
DON'T MIND IF I DO CULTURE CLUB 1999
DON'T POINT YOUR FINGER 9 BELOW ZERO 1981
DON'T SHOOT ME I'M ONLY THE PIANO PLAYER ELTON JOHN 1973
DON'T STAND ME DOWN DEXYS MIDNIGHT RUNNERS 1985
DON'T STOP JEFFREY OSBORNE 1984
DON'T STOP – THE 30TH ANNIVERSARY ALBUM STATUS QUO 1996
DON'T STOP DANCING VARIOUS ARTISTS (TELSTAR) 1984
DON'T STOP ME NOW... – CLIFF RICHARD 1967
DON'T STOP MOVIN' – LIVIN' JOY 1996
DON'T STOP THE MUSIC VARIOUS ARTISTS (STYLUS) 1989
DON'T STOP... DOOWOP! – VARIOUS ARTISTS (TELSTAR) 1991
DON'T SUPPOSE LIMAHL 1984
DON'T SWEAT THE TECHNIQUE ERIC B & RAKIM 1992
DON'T THINK TWICE IT'S ALL RIGHT BARBARA DICKSON 1992
DON'T TRY THIS AT HOME BILLY BRAGG 1991
DON'T WALK – BOOGIE VARIOUS ARTISTS (EMI) 1978
DOOKIE GREEN DAY 1994
DOOLITTLE PIXIES 1989
DOOR TO DOOR CARS 1987
THE DOORS DOORS 1991
THE DOORS (OST) DOORS 1991
DOOWUTCHYALIKE/PACKET MAN DIGITAL UNDERGROUND 1990
DOPES TO INFINITY MONSTER MAGNET 1995
DOPPELGANGER KID CREOLE & THE COCONUTS 1983
DOPPELGANGER CURVE 1992
DOREMI FASOL LATIDO HAWKWIND 1972
DOS DEDOS MIS AMIGOS POP WILL EAT ITSELF 1994
DOTS AND LOOPS STEREOLAB 1997
DOUBLE BARREL DAVE & ANSIL COLLINS 1971
DOUBLE DEVINE SIDNEY DEVINE 1976
DOUBLE DYNAMITE SAM & DAVE 1967
DOUBLE FANTASY JOHN LENNON & YOKO ONO 1980
DOUBLE LIVE GARTH BROOKS 1998
DOUBLE LIVE GONZO! – TED NUGENT 1978
DOUBLE TROUBLE GILLAN 1981
DOUBLE TROUBLE – LIVE MOLLY HATCHETT 1986
DOUBLE TROUBLE (OST) ELVIS PRESLEY 1967
DOUBLE UP MASE 1999
DOUBLE VISION FOREIGNER 1978
DOUBLE WIDE UNCLE KRACKER 2001
DOUBT JESUS JONES 1991
DOUG LAZY GETTING' CRAZY DOUG LAZY 1990
DOUGHNUT IN GRANNY'S GREENHOUSE BONZO DOG DOO-DAH BAND 1969
DOWN JESUS LIZARD 1994
DOWN AND OUT BLUES SONNY BOY WILLIAMSON 1964
DOWN DRURY LANE TO MEMORY LANE 101 STRINGS 1960
DOWN FALL THE GOOD GUYS WOLFSBANE 1991
DOWN IN THE GROOVE BOB DYLAN 1988
DOWN MEXICO WAY HERB ALPERT & THE TIJUANA BRASS 1970
DOWN ON THE FARM LITTLE FEAT 1979
DOWN ON THE STREET SHAKATAK 1984
DOWN ON THE UPSIDE SOUNDGARDEN 1996
DOWN THE DUSTPIPE STATUS QUO 1975
DOWN THE ROAD STEPHEN STILLS' MANASSAS 1973
DOWN THE ROAD VAN MORRISON 2002
DOWN TO EARTH RAINBOW 1979
DOWN TO EARTH MONIE LOVE 1990
DOWN TO EARTH OZZY OSBOURNE 2001
DOWN TWO, THEN LEFT BOZ SCAGGS 1977
DOWN WITH THE KING RUN D.M.C. 1993
DOWNTOWN MIDNIGHT RACING CARS 1977
THE DOWNWARD SPIRAL NINE INCH NAILS 1994
DRACONIAN TIMES PARADISE LOST 1995
DRAG K.D. LANG 1997
DRAMA YES 1980
DRAMA JAMELIA 2000
DRASTIC PLASTIC BE-BOP DELUXE 1978

DRAWN FROM MEMORY EMBRACE 2000
DRAWN TO THE DEEP END GENE 1997
DREAM A DREAM CHARLOTTE CHURCH 2000
THE DREAM ACADEMY DREAM ACADEMY 1985
A DREAM COME TRUE BECKY TAYLOR 2001
DREAM EVIL DIO 1987
A DREAM FULFILLED WILL DOWNING 1991
DREAM HARDER WATERBOYS 1993
DREAM INTO ACTION HOWARD JONES 1985
DREAM LOVER ANTHONY VENTURA ORCHESTRA 1979
DREAM MELODIES VARIOUS ARTISTS (NOUVEAU MUSIC) 1985
DREAM OF 100 NATIONS TRANSGLOBAL UNDERGROUND 1993
DREAM OF A LIFETIME MARVIN GAYE 1985
THE DREAM OF BLUE TURTLES STING 1985
DREAM OF LIFE PATTI SMITH 1988
DREAM ON VOLUME 1 D:REAM 1993
DREAM POLICE CHEAP TRICK 1979
DREAM WORLD CROWN HEIGHTS AFFAIR 1978
DREAMBOAT ANNIE HEART 1977
DREAMER HOME 1972
DREAMING VARIOUS ARTISTS (K-TEL) 1982
THE DREAMING KATE BUSH 1982
DREAMING... – PATSY CLINE 1991
DREAMLAND BLACK BOX 1990
DREAMLAND AZTEC CAMERA 1993
DREAMLAND ROBERT MILES 1996
DREAMLAND ROBERT PLANT 2002
DREAMS GRACE SLICK 1980
DREAMS AND THEMES VARIOUS ARTISTS (RONCO) 1984
DREAMS ARE NUTHIN' MORE THAN WISHES DAVID CASSIDY 1973
DREAMS CAN COME TRUE – GREATEST HITS VOLUME 1 GABRIELLE 2001
DREAMS OF IRELAND VARIOUS ARTISTS (TRAX) 1989
DREAMS OF REASON PRODUCE MONSTERS MICK KARN 1987
DREAMSTATES VARIOUS ARTISTS (INSPIRED) 2001
DREAMTIME CULT 1984
DREAMTIME STRANGLERS 1986
THE DREEM TEEM IN SESSION VARIOUS ARTISTS (TELSTAR) 2001
DRESS FOR EXCESS SIGUE SIGUE SPUTNIK 1989
DRESSED FOR THE OCCASION CLIFF RICHARD & THE LONDON PHILHARMONIC ORCHESTRA 1983
DRILL YOUR OWN HOLE GAYE BYKERS ON ACID 1987
DRINK ME SALAD 1995
DRINKIN' AND COURTIN' – DUBLINERS 1968
DRINKING GASOLINE CABARET VOLTAIRE 1985
DRIVE ON MOTT THE HOOPLE 1975
DRIVE ON VARIOUS ARTISTS (GLOBAL) 1997
DRIVE TIME VARIOUS ARTISTS (DINO) 1995
DRIVE TIME 2 VARIOUS ARTISTS (DINO) 1995
DRIVE TIME 4 VARIOUS ARTISTS (DINO) 1996
DRIVE TIME USA – 22 SUMMER CRUISING GREATS VARIOUS ARTISTS (K-TEL) 1986
DRIVE THRU BOOTY FREAK POWER 1995
DRIVETIME 3 VARIOUS ARTISTS (DINO) 1996
DRIVIN' HARD SHAKATAK 1982
DRIVIN' ME WILD CLIFF BENNETT & THE REBEL ROUSERS 1966
DRIVIN' WITH JOHNNIE WALKER VARIOUS ARTISTS (EAST WEST) 2002
DRIVING RAIN PAUL McCARTNEY 2001
DRIVING ROCK VARIOUS ARTISTS (GLOBAL) 1995
DROP DEAD GORGEOUS VARIOUS ARTISTS (GLOBAL) 1998
DROP DEAD GORGEOUS 2 VARIOUS ARTISTS (GLOBAL) 1998
A DROP OF THE HARD STUFF DUBLINERS 1967
DROPPED MINDFUNK 1993
DROPS OF JUPITER TRAIN 2001
DRUGSTORE DRUGSTORE 1995
DRUKQS APHEX TWIN 2001
DRUM & BASS ARENA VARIOUS ARTISTS (WARNER BROTHERS) 2004

DRUM & BASS MIX 97 VARIOUS ARTISTS (POLYGRAM) 1997
DRUM AND BASS SELECTION 2 VARIOUS ARTISTS (BREAK DOWN) 1994
THE DRUM IS EVERYTHING CARMEL 1984
DRUMS AND WIRES XTC 1979
DRUMS ARE DANGEROUS DRUM CLUB 1994
DRUNK ENOUGH TO DANCE BOWLING FOR SOUP 2002
DRY PJ HARVEY 1992
D TRAIN D-TRAIN 1982
DUB COME SAVE ME ROOTS MANUVA 2002
DUB HOUSE DISCO 2000 VARIOUS ARTISTS (GUERILLA) 1993
DUB NO BASS WITH MY HEAD MAN UNDERWORLD 1994
THE DUBLINERS 25 YEARS CELEBRATION DUBLINERS 1987
DUCK ROCK MALCOLM MCLAREN 1983
THE DUDE QUINCY JONES 1981
DUETS ELTON JOHN & VARIOUS ARTISTS 1993
DUETS FRANK SINATRA 1993
DUETS BARBRA STREISAND 2002
DUETS & ARIAS ROBERTO ALAGNA/ANGELA GHEORGIU 1996
DUETS II FRANK SINATRA 1994
DUKE GENESIS 1980
THE DUKE WORE JEANS TOMMY STEELE 1958
DUMB WAITERS KORGIS 1980
DUMBING UP WORLD PARTY 2000
DUMMY PORTISHEAD 1994
DUOPHONIC CHARLES & EDDIE 1992
DUOTONES KENNY G 1987
DURAN DURAN DURAN DURAN 1981
DURAN DURAN (THE WEDDING ALBUM) DURAN DURAN 1993
DUSK THE THE 1993
DUSKY SAPPHO EP CARLEEN ANDERSON 1993
DUST SCREAMING TREES 1996
DUSTY – THE SILVER COLLECTION DUSTY SPRINGFIELD 1988
DUSTY... DEFINITELY DUSTY SPRINGFIELD 1968
DUTTY ROCK SEAN PAUL 2003
DUTY NOW FOR THE FUTURE DEVO 1979
DYLAN AND THE DEAD BOB DYLAN & THE GRATEFUL DEAD 1989
DYNAMITE JERMAINE JACKSON 1984
DYNASTY KISS 1979
E.1999 ETERNAL BONE THUGS-N-HARMONY 1996
E.C. WAS HERE ERIC CLAPTON 1975
E.S.P. MILLIE JACKSON 1984
E.S.P. BEE GEES 1987
E.T. – THE EXTRATERRESTRIAL (OST) JOHN WILLIAMS 1982
E.T. THE EXTRA TERRESTRIAL MICHAEL JACKSON 1983
THE EAGLE HAS LANDED SAXON 1982
EARLY DAYS – THE BEST OF – VOLUME ONE LED ZEPPELIN 2000
THE EARLY TAPES JULY AUGUST 1980 LEVEL 42 1982
EARTH AND SUN AND MOON MIDNIGHT OIL 1993
EARTH INFERNO FIELDS OF THE NEPHILIM 1991
EARTH MOVING MIKE OLDFIELD 1989
EARTH VS THE WILDHEARTS WILDHEARTS 1993
EARTHBOUND CONNOR REEVES 1997
EARTHLING DAVID BOWIE 1997
THE EARTHQUAKE ALBUM... ROCK AID ARMENIA VARIOUS ARTISTS (LIFE AID ARMENIA) 1990
EARTHQUAKE WEATHER JOE STRUMMER 1989
EARTHRISE – THE RAINFOREST ALBUM VARIOUS ARTISTS (ELF) 1992
EAST OF THE SUN, WEST OF THE MOON A-HA 1990
EAST SIDE STORY SQUEEZE 1981
EAST TO WEST JAMES LAST 1978
THE EASTENDERS SING ALONG ALBUM TELEVISION COMPILATION 1985
EASTER PATTI SMITH GROUP 1978
EASY RALPH MCTELL 1974
EASY EASY SCOTLAND FOOTBALL WORLD CUP SQUAD 1974 1974
EASY MOODS VARIOUS ARTISTS (EMI) 1996

EASY PIECES LLOYD COLE & THE COMMOTIONS 1985
EASY RIDER (OST) FILM SOUNDTRACK 1969
EAT 'EM AND SMILE DAVID LEE ROTH 1986
EAT IT HUMBLE PIE 1973
EAT ME IN ST LOUIS IT BITES 1989
EAT TO THE BEAT BLONDIE 1979
EAT YOURSELF WHOLE KINGMAKER 1991
EATEN ALIVE DIANA ROSS 1985
ECHO TOM PETTY & HEARTBREAKERS 1999
ECHO AND THE BUNNYMEN ECHO & THE BUNNYMEN 1987
ECHO DEK PRIMAL SCREAM 1997
ECHO PARK FEEDER 2001
ECHOES RAPTURE 2003
ECHOES – THE BEST OF PINK FLOYD PINK FLOYD 2001
ECHOES – THE COLLECTION LUDOVICO EINAUDI 2003
ECHOES OF GOLD ADRIAN BRETT 1979
ECLECTIC BIG COUNTRY 1996
THE ECLEFTIC – TWO SIDES TO A BOOK WYCLEF JEAN 2000
ECLIPSE YNGWIE J MAMLSTEEN 1990
ECO DI NAPOLI KENNETH MCKELLAR 1970
ECSTASY VARIOUS ARTISTS (LOTUS) 1978
ECSTASY LOU REED 2000
EDDI READER EDDI READER 1994
THE EDDIE COCHRAN MEMORIAL ALBUM EDDIE COCHRAN 1960
THE EDDIE COCHRAN SINGLES ALBUM EDDIE COCHRAN 1979
EDDIE, OLD BOB, DICK & GARRY TEN POLE TUDOR 1981
EDELWEISS VINCE HILL 1967
EDEN EVERYTHING BUT THE GIRL 1984
THE EDGAR BROUGHTON BAND EDGAR BROUGHTON BAND 1971
EDINBURGH MILITARY TATTOO 1970 MISCELLANEOUS 1970
EDINBURGH MILITARY TATTOO 1971 MISCELLANEOUS 1971
EDIZIOBE D'ORO FOUR SEASONS 1971
THE EDUCATION HOUR FALL 1982
EDUTAINMENT BOOGIE DOWN PRODUCTIONS 1990
EDWARD THE GREAT – THE GREATEST HITS IRON MAIDEN 2002
THE EDWARD WOODWARD ALBUM EDWARD WOODWARD 1972
EFIL4ZAGGIN N.W.A. 1991
EGO WAR AUDIOBULLYS 2003
EGYPTOLOGY WORLD PARTY 1997
THE EIGHT LEGGED GROOVE MACHINE WONDERSTUFF 1988
8 MILE FILM SOUNDTRACK 2002
808:88:98 808 STATE 1998
801 LIVE 801 1976
8701 USHER 2001
18 MOBY 2002
18 GREATEST HITS MICHAEL JACKSON PLUS THE JACKSON FIVE 1983
18 TIL I DIE BRYAN ADAMS 1996
18 TRACKS BRUCE SPRINGSTEEN 1999
18TH LETTER RAKIM 1997
THE 80'S ALBUM – THE ALBUM OF THE DECADE VARIOUS ARTISTS (EMI) 1989
THE '80S LOVE ALBUM VARIOUS ARTISTS (VIRGIN) 1999
THE EIGHTIES MIX VARIOUS ARTISTS (GLOBAL) 1998
EIGHTIES SOUL WEEKENDER VARIOUS ARTISTS (DINO) 1996
EIGHTIES SOUL WEEKENDER 2 VARIOUS ARTISTS (PUMP) 1996
EIGHTIES SOUL WEEKENDER 3 VARIOUS ARTISTS (PUMP) 1997
80 F AFTER THE FIRE 1980
EL CORAZON STEVE EARLE 1997
EL LOCO ZZ TOP 1981
ELAINE PAIGE ELAINE PAIGE 1982
ELASTIC ROCK NUCLEUS 1970
ELASTICA ELASTICA 1995
ELBOW BEACH LOUISE 2000

THE ELDER KISS 1981
ELECTRIBAL MEMORIES ELECTRIBE 101 1990
ELECTRIC CULT 1987
ELECTRIC VARIOUS ARTISTS (TELSTAR) 2002
ELECTRIC CAFE – KRAFTWERK 1986
ELECTRIC DREAMS VARIOUS ARTISTS (POLYGRAM) 1995
ELECTRIC DREAMS VARIOUS ARTISTS (VIRGIN) 2002
ELECTRIC DREAMS (OST) FILM SOUNDTRACK 1984
ELECTRIC FIRE ROGER TAYLOR 1998
ELECTRIC FOLKLORE LIVE ALARM 1988
ELECTRIC LADYLAND JIMI HENDRIX EXPERIENCE 1968
ELECTRIC LADYLAND JIMI HENDRIX 1997
ELECTRIC LANDLADY KIRSTY MACCOLL 1991
ELECTRIC – LEVEL 2 VARIOUS ARTISTS (TELSTAR) 2003
ELECTRIC LIGHT ORCHESTRA ELECTRIC LIGHT ORCHESTRA 1972
ELECTRIC LIGHT ORCHESTRA II ELECTRIC LIGHT ORCHESTRA 1973
ELECTRIC LIGHT ORCHESTRA PART TWO ELECTRIC LIGHT ORCHESTRA PART TWO 1991
ELECTRIC MOODS VARIOUS ARTISTS (DECADANCE) 2004
ELECTRIC ORGANS TODAY MISCELLANEOUS 1971
ELECTRIC TEPEE HAWKWIND 1992
ELECTRIC WARRIOR T. REX 1971
ELECTRIC YOUTH DEBBIE GIBSON 1989
ELECTRO BREAKDANCE VARIOUS ARTISTS (TELSTAR) 2002
ELECTRO GLIDE IN BLUE APOLLO FOUR FORTY 1997
ELECTRO SHOCK VOLTAGE ONE VARIOUS ARTISTS (EPIC) 1984
ELECTRONIC ELECTRONIC 1991
ELECTRONICA (FULL ON BIG BEATS) VARIOUS ARTISTS (VIRGIN) 1997
ELECTRONICALLY TESTED MUNGO JERRY 1978
ELECTRO SHOCK BLUES EELS 1998
ELECTROTECH VARIOUS ARTISTS (MINISTRY OF SOUND) 2003
ELEGANT SLUMMING M PEOPLE 1993
ELEGANTLY WASTED INXS 1997
ELEGY NICE 1971
ELEMENTAL TEARS FOR FEARS 1993
ELEMENTALZ BROTHERHOOD 1996
ELEMENTS – SEB FONTAINE/TONY DE VIT VARIOUS ARTISTS (WESTWAY) 1998
ELEMENTS – THE BEST OF MIKE OLDFIELD MIKE OLDFIELD 1993
ELEPHANT WHITE STRIPES 2003
ELEPHUNK BLACK EYED PEAS 2003
1100 BEL AIR PLACE JULIO IGLESIAS 1984
ELEVENTEEN DAISY CHAINSAW 1992
THE ELEVENTH HOUR MAGNUM 1983
ELGAR CELLO CONCERTO JULIAN LLOYD WEBBER WITH THE ROYAL PHILHARMONIC ORCHESTRA CONDUCTED BY SIR YEHUDI MENUHIN 1987
ELGAR/PAYNE SYMPHONY NO. 3 BBC SYMPHONY ORCHESTRA CONDUCTED BY ANDREW DAVIS 1998
ELGAR: VIOLIN CONCERTO NIGEL KENNEDY WITH THE LONDON PHILHARMONIC ORCHESTRA 1986
ELIMINATOR ZZ TOP 1983
ELITE HOTEL EMMYLOU HARRIS 1976
ELITE SYNCOPATIONS CHRIS BARBER 1960
ELIZIUM FIELDS OF THE NEPHILIM 1990
ELLA AT THE OPERA HOUSE ELLA FITZGERALD 1960
ELLA FITZGERALD SINGS THE IRVING BERLIN SONG BOOK ELLA FITZGERALD 1958
ELLA SINGS GERSHWIN ELLA FITZGERALD 1960
ELLA SINGS GERSHWIN VOLUME 5 ELLA FITZGERALD 1960
ELO'S GREATEST HITS ELECTRIC LIGHT ORCHESTRA 1979
ELTON JOHN ELTON JOHN 1970
ELTON JOHN AND TIM RICE'S AIDA ELTON JOHN & FRIENDS 1999
THE ELTON JOHN LIVE ALBUM 17-11-70 ELTON JOHN 1971
ELTON JOHN'S GREATEST HITS ELTON JOHN 1974
ELVIS ELVIS PRESLEY 1973
ELVIS – A LEGENDARY PERFORMER VOLUME 1 ELVIS PRESLEY 1974
ELVIS – NBC TV SPECIAL (OST TV) ELVIS PRESLEY 1969

ELVIS (ROCK 'N' ROLL NO. 1) ELVIS PRESLEY 1959
ELVIS 56 ELVIS PRESLEY 1996
ELVIS AARON PRESLEY ELVIS PRESLEY 1980
ELVIS AS RECORDED AT MADISON SQUARE GARDEN ELVIS PRESLEY 1972
ELVIS CHRISTMAS ALBUM ELVIS PRESLEY 1957
ELVIS CHRISTMAS ALBUM ELVIS PRESLEY 1971
ELVIS FOR EVERYONE ELVIS PRESLEY 1965
ELVIS' GOLDEN RECORDS ELVIS PRESLEY 1958
ELVIS' GOLDEN RECORDS VOLUME 1 ELVIS PRESLEY 1970
ELVIS' GOLDEN RECORDS VOLUME 2 ELVIS PRESLEY 1960
ELVIS' GOLDEN RECORDS VOLUME 3 ELVIS PRESLEY 1964
ELVIS IN CONCERT (OST TV) ELVIS PRESLEY 1977
ELVIS IN DEMAND ELVIS PRESLEY 1977
ELVIS IS BACK! – ELVIS PRESLEY 1960
ELVIS LIVE ON STAGE IN MEMPHIS ELVIS PRESLEY 1974
ELVIS NOW ELVIS PRESLEY 1972
ELVIS PRESLEY – BALLADS: 18 CLASSIC LOVE SONGS ELVIS PRESLEY 1985
ELVIS PRESLEY EP PACK ELVIS PRESLEY 1982
ELVIS PRESLEY SINGS LEIBER AND STOLLER ELVIS PRESLEY 1980
THE ELVIS PRESLEY SUN COLLECTION ELVIS PRESLEY 1975
ELVIS' SINGS FLAMING STAR ELVIS PRESLEY 1969
ELVIS'S 40 GREATEST HITS ELVIS PRESLEY 1975
ELV1S: 30 #1 HITS ELVIS PRESLEY 2002
EMANCIPATION PRINCE 1996
EMBRYA MAXWELL 1998
EMERALD CLASSICS VARIOUS ARTISTS (STOIC) 1984
EMERALD CLASSICS VOLUMES I AND II VARIOUS ARTISTS (WESTMOOR) 1990
EMERALD ROCK VARIOUS ARTISTS (POLYGRAM) 1995
EMERGENCY KOOL & THE GANG 1984
EMERGENCY ON PLANET EARTH JAMIROQUAI 1993
EMERSON, LAKE AND PALMER EMERSON, LAKE & PALMER 1970
EMERSON, LAKE AND POWELL EMERSON, LAKE & POWELL 1986
THE EMINEM SHOW EMINEM 2002
EMMERDANCE WOOLPACKERS 1996
EMOTION BARBRA STREISAND 1984
THE EMOTIONAL HOOLIGAN GARY CLAIL ON-U SOUND SYSTEM 1991
EMOTIONAL RESCUE ROLLING STONES 1980
EMOTIONS VARIOUS ARTISTS (K-TEL) 1978
EMOTIONS MARIAH CAREY 1991
EMOTIONS VARIOUS ARTISTS (UNIVERSAL) 2002
EMPEROR TOMATO KETCHUP STEREOLAB 1996
EMPIRE QUEENSRYCHE 1990
EMPIRE BURLESQUE BOB DYLAN 1985
EMPIRE OF THE SENSELESS SENSELESS THINGS 1993
EMPIRES AND DANCE SIMPLE MINDS 1980
EMPTY GLASS PETE TOWNSHEND 1980
EMPTY ROOMS JOHN MAYALL 1970
ENCHANTED MARC ALMOND 1990
ENCHANTMENT CHARLOTTE CHURCH 2001
ENCORE TANGERINE DREAM 1977
ENCORE MARTI WEBB 1985
ENCORE ELAINE PAIGE 1995
ENCORE RUSSELL WATSON 2001
ENCORE LIONEL RICHIE 2002
ENCORE UNE FOIS – THE GREATEST HITS SASH! 2000
THE END COMPLETE OBITUARY 1992
END HITS FUGAZI 1998
THE END OF HEARTACHE KILLSWITCH ENGAGE 2004
THE END OF INNOCENCE DON HENLEY 1989
END OF MILLENNIUM PSYCHOSIS BLUES THAT PETROL EMOTION 1988
END OF PART ONE (THEIR GREATEST HITS) WET WET WET 1993
END OF THE CENTURY RAMONES 1980
ENDLESS HEAVEN 17 1986
ENDLESS FLIGHT LEO SAYER 1976
ENDLESS HARMONY SOUNDTRACK BEACH BOYS 1998
ENDLESS LOVE VARIOUS ARTISTS (TV RECORDS) 1982
ENDLESS LOVE VARIOUS ARTISTS (POLYGRAM) 1995

ENDLESS SUMMER – GREATEST HITS DONNA SUMMER 1994
ENDLESS, NAMELESS WILDHEARTS 1997
ENEMA OF THE STATE BLINK 182 2000
ENERGIQUE BIZARRE INC 1992
ENERGY ORCHARD ENERGY ORCHARD 1990
ENERGY RUSH VARIOUS ARTISTS (DINO) 1992
ENERGY RUSH – EURO DANCE HITS 94 VARIOUS ARTISTS (DINO) 1994
ENERGY RUSH – SAFE SIX VARIOUS ARTISTS (DINO) 1993
ENERGY RUSH – XTERMIN8 VARIOUS ARTISTS (DINO) 1994
ENERGY RUSH 7 VARIOUS ARTISTS (DINO) 1994
ENERGY RUSH DANCE HITS 93 (2ND DIMENSION) VARIOUS ARTISTS (DINO) 1993
ENERGY RUSH DANCE HITS 94 VARIOUS ARTISTS (DINO) 1994
ENERGY RUSH FACTOR 5 VARIOUS ARTISTS (DINO) 1993
ENERGY RUSH II VARIOUS ARTISTS (DINO) 1992
ENERGY RUSH K9 VARIOUS ARTISTS (DINO) 1995
ENERGY RUSH LEVEL 3 VARIOUS ARTISTS (DINO) 1993
ENERGY RUSH PHASE 4 VARIOUS ARTISTS (DINO) 1993
ENERGY RUSH PRESENTS DANCE HITS 93 VARIOUS ARTISTS (DINO) 1993
ENERGY RUSH PRESENTS DANCE HITS OF THE YEAR VARIOUS ARTISTS (DINO) 1993
ENGELBERT ENGELBERT HUMPERDINCK 1969
ENGELBERT HUMPERDINCK ENGELBERT HUMPERDINCK 1969
ENGELBERT HUMPERDINCK – HIS GREATEST HITS ENGELBERT HUMPERDINCK 1974
THE ENGELBERT HUMPERDINCK COLLECTION ENGELBERT HUMPERDINCK 1987
ENGLAND HALF ENGLISH BILLY BRAGG & THE BLOKES 2002
ENGLISH SETTLEMENT XTC 1982
ENJOY YOURSELF KYLIE MINOGUE 1989
ENLIGHTENMENT VAN MORRISON 1990
EN TACT SHAMEN 1990
ENTER THE DRU DRU HILL 1998
ENTERTAINMENT GANG OF FOUR 1979
ENTREAT CURE 1991
ENTRODUCING... – DJ SHADOW 1996
ENVY OF ANGELS MUTTON BIRDS 1997
ENYA (OST TV) ENYA 1987
THE EPIC YEARS SHAKY 1992
EPONYMOUS R.E.M. 1988
THE EP'S 1992–1994 DAVID GRAY 2001
EQUALLY CURSED AND BLESSED CATATONIA 1999
EQUALS EXPLOSION EQUALS 1968
EQUATOR URIAH HEEP 1985
EQUINOXE JEAN-MICHEL JARRE 1978
ERASURE ERASURE 1995
ERIC BURDEN DECLARES WAR ERIC BURDON & WAR 1970
ERIC CARMEN ERIC CARMEN 1976
ERIC CLAPTON ERIC CLAPTON 1970
EROICA WENDY & LISA 1990
EROTICA MADONNA 1992
ERROL FLYNN DOGS D'AMOUR 1989
ESCAPE JOURNEY 1982
ESCAPE ENRIQUE IGLESIAS 2002
ESCAPE FROM TV JAN HAMMER 1987
ESCAPOLOGY ROBBIE WILLIAMS 2002
ESCM BT 1997
ESPECIALLY FOR YOU DON WILLIAMS 1981
ESPECIALLY FOR YOU JOE LONGTHORNE 1989
ESPECIALLY FOR YOU DANIEL O'DONNELL 1994
ESPECIALLY FOR YOU VARIOUS ARTISTS (COLUMBIA) 1999
ESPRESSO LOGIC CHRIS REA 1993
ESSENCE LUCINDA WILLIAMS 2001
THE ESSENTIAL ALISON MOYET 2001
THE ESSENTIAL BOB DYLAN 2001
THE ESSENTIAL BARBRA STREISAND 2002
THE ESSENTIAL LEONARD COHEN 2003
THE ESSENTIAL OZZY OSBOURNE 2003
THE ESSENTIAL PAUL YOUNG 2003

THE ESSENTIAL PERRY COMO 2003
THE ESSENTIAL BRUCE SPRINGSTEEN 2003
THE ESSENTIAL SIMON & GARFUNKEL 2003
THE ESSENTIAL ACOUSTIC ALBUM VARIOUS ARTISTS (SANCTUARY) 2004
THE ESSENTIAL ANDY WILLIAMS ANDY WILLIAMS 2002
ESSENTIAL BALLET VARIOUS ARTISTS (DECCA) 1992
THE ESSENTIAL CHILL VARIOUS ARTISTS (ARCADE) 1992
THE ESSENTIAL CLASH CLASH 2003
ESSENTIAL CLASSICS VARIOUS ARTISTS (DEUTSCHE GRAMMOPHON) 1990
THE ESSENTIAL COLLECTION ELVIS PRESLEY 1994
THE ESSENTIAL COLLECTION MARC BOLAN & T. REX 1995
THE ESSENTIAL COLLECTION DIONNE WARWICK 1996
THE ESSENTIAL COLLECTION DARYL HALL & JOHN OATES 2001
THE ESSENTIAL COLLECTION NEIL DIAMOND 2002
THE ESSENTIAL COLLECTION MARC BOLAN & T. REX 2002
ESSENTIAL DISCO AND DANCE VARIOUS ARTISTS (NOUVEAU MUSIC) 1984
THE ESSENTIAL DOMINGO PLACIDO DOMINGO 1989
ESSENTIAL ELLA ELLA FITZGERALD 1994
THE ESSENTIAL GROOVE VARIOUS ARTISTS (POLYGRAM) 1995
ESSENTIAL HARDCORE VARIOUS ARTISTS (DINO) 1991
THE ESSENTIAL JEAN MICHEL JARRE JEAN-MICHEL JARRE 1983
THE ESSENTIAL JOSE CARRERAS JOSE CARRERAS 1991
THE ESSENTIAL KARAJAN HERBERT VON KARAJAN 1988
THE ESSENTIAL KIRI KIRI TE KANAWA 1992
THE ESSENTIAL LUTHER VANDROSS LUTHER VANDROSS 2002
THE ESSENTIAL LUTHER VANDROSS LUTHER VANDROSS 2003
ESSENTIAL MILLENNIUM – PETE TONG FATBOY SLIM PAUL OAKENFOLD VARIOUS ARTISTS (FFRR) 1999
ESSENTIAL MIX – TONG COX SASHA OAKENFOLD VARIOUS ARTISTS (FFRR) 1996
ESSENTIAL MIX 2 – TONG, MACKINTOSH... – VARIOUS ARTISTS (FFRR) 1996
ESSENTIAL MIX 3 – TONG, SEAMAN, JULES ETC VARIOUS ARTISTS (FFRR) 1996
THE ESSENTIAL MOZART VARIOUS ARTISTS (DECCA) 1991
ESSENTIAL OPERA VARIOUS ARTISTS (DECCA) 1991
ESSENTIAL OPERA 2 VARIOUS ARTISTS (DECCA) 1993
THE ESSENTIAL PAVAROTTI LUCIANO PAVAROTTI 1990
ESSENTIAL PAVAROTTI II LUCIANO PAVAROTTI 1991
ESSENTIAL SELECTION – CLUBBERS BIBLE VARIOUS ARTISTS (WARNER BROTHERS) 2001
ESSENTIAL SELECTION '98 – PETE TONG/PAUL OAKENFOLD VARIOUS ARTISTS (FFRR) 1998
ESSENTIAL SELECTION IBIZA 2000 VARIOUS ARTISTS (ESSENTIAL RECORDINGS) 2000
ESSENTIAL SELECTION PRESENTS THE CLUBBER'S BIBLE THE SECOND COMING VARIOUS ARTISTS (INCREDIBLE) 2001
ESSENTIAL SELECTION SPRING 2000 VARIOUS ARTISTS (ESSENTIAL RECORDINGS) 2000
ESSENTIAL SOUNDTRACKS VARIOUS ARTISTS (TELSTAR) 1999
ESSENTIAL SOUNDTRACKS VARIOUS ARTISTS (TELSTAR) 2000
THE ESSENTIAL TONY BENNETT TONY BENNETT 1998
ESSENTIAL TRACKS VARIOUS ARTISTS (TELSTAR) 2001
ESSENTIALS – THE VERY BEST OF GEORGE BENSON GEORGE BENSON 1998
ESSEX ALISON MOYET 1994
ESTABLISHED 1958 CLIFF RICHARD & THE SHADOWS 1968
ESTE MUNDO GIPSY KINGS 1991
ETERNAL FLAME – THE BEST OF THE BANGLES BANGLES 2001
THE ETERNAL IDOL BLACK SABBATH 1987
ETERNAL LIGHT – MUSIC OF INNER PEACE PRIORY OF THE RESURRECTION 2001
ETERNAL LOVE VARIOUS ARTISTS (K-TEL) 1989
ETHER SONG TURIN BRAKES 2003

EUGENE WILDE EUGENE WILDE 1984
EUPHORIA DEF LEPPARD 1999
EUPHORIA VARIOUS ARTISTS (TELSTAR) 1999
EUPHORIA VARIOUS ARTISTS (TELSTAR) 2003
EUPHORIA – LEVEL 3 VARIOUS ARTISTS (TELSTAR) 1999
EUPHORIA MORNING CHRIS CORNELL 1999
EUREKA BIBLE 1988
EURO 2000 – THE OFFICIAL ALBUM VARIOUS ARTISTS (UNIVERSAL) 2000
EUROMAN COMETH JEAN-JACQUES BURNEL 1979
EUROPOP EIFFEL 65 2000
EUROVISION FAVOURITES VARIOUS ARTISTS (K-TEL) 1976
EURYTHMICS LIVE 1983–1989 EURYTHMICS 1993
EV3 EN VOGUE 1997
EVANGELINE EMMYLOU HARRIS 1981
EVE ALAN PARSONS PROJECT 1979
EVEN COW GIRLS GET THE BLUES (OST) K.D. LANG 1993
EVEN IN THE QUIETEST MOMENTS... – SUPERTRAMP 1977
EVEN NOW BARRY MANILOW 1978
EVEN SERPENT'S SHINE ONLY ONES 1979
EVENING FALLS RICHARD HARVEY & FRIENDS 1989
EVENING SESSION – PRIORITY TUNES VARIOUS ARTISTS (VIRGIN) 1996
EVENTIDE FAITH BROTHERS 1985
EVE OLUTION EVE 2002
EVERGREEN MR ACKER BILK 1978
EVERGREEN ECHO & THE BUNNYMEN 1997
EVERLASTING NATALIE COLE 1988
THE EVERLY BROTHERS EVERLY BROTHERS 1984
EVERLY BROTHERS REUNION CONCERT – LIVE AT THE ROYAL ALBERT HALL EVERLY BROTHERS 1984
EVERY BEAT OF MY HEART ROD STEWART 1986
EVERY BREATH YOU TAKE – THE SINGLES POLICE 1986
EVERY DAY IS A NEW DAY DIANA ROSS 1999
EVERY FACE TELLS A STORY CLIFF RICHARD 1977
EVERY GOOD BOY DESERVES FAVOUR MOODY BLUES 1971
EVERY GOOD BOY DESERVES FUDGE MUDHONEY 1991
EVERY HOME SHOULD HAVE ONE PATTI AUSTIN 1981
EVERY 1'S A WINNER HOT CHOCOLATE 1978
EVERY PICTURE TELLS A STORY ROD STEWART 1971
EVERY SONG TELLS A STORY VARIOUS ARTISTS (POLYGRAM) 1995
EVERY WOMAN VARIOUS ARTISTS (RCA) 1998
EVERYBODY HEAR'SAY 2001
EVERYBODY DANCE NOW VARIOUS ARTISTS (COLUMBIA) 1991
EVERYBODY ELSE IS DOING IT, SO WHY CAN'T WE? – CRANBERRIES 1993
EVERYBODY HERTZ AIR 2002
EVERYBODY KNOWS SONIA 1990
EVERYBODY KNOWS MILLICAN AND NESBITT MILLICAN & NESBITT 1975
EVERYBODY LOVES A NUT JOHNNY CASH 1966
EVERYBODY LOVES SATURDAY NIGHT BOB WALLIS & HIS STORYVILLE JAZZMEN 1960
EVERYBODY WANTS TO SHAG... THE TEARDROP EXPLODES TEARDROP EXPLODES 1990
EVERYBODY'S ANGEL TANITA TIKARAM 1991
EVERYBODY'S FREE ROZALLA 1992
EVERYBODY'S ROCKIN' – NEIL YOUNG & THE SHOCKING PINKS 1983
EVERYBODY'S SOMEBODY KELE LE ROC 1999
EVERYONE PLAY DARTS DARTS 1978
EVERYONE'S GOT ONE ECHOBELLY 1994
EVERYTHING CLIMIE FISHER 1988
EVERYTHING BANGLES 1988
EVERYTHING JOE 1994
EVERYTHING & NOTHING DAVID SYLVIAN 2000
EVERYTHING CHANGES TAKE THAT 1993
EVERYTHING EVERYTHING UNDERWORLD 2000
EVERYTHING IS BEAUTIFUL RAY STEVENS 1970
EVERYTHING IS BEAUTIFUL DANA 1980
EVERYTHING IS EVERYTHING DIANA ROSS 1971
EVERYTHING IS WRONG/MIXED & REMIXED MOBY 1996
EVERYTHING MUST GO MANIC STREET PREACHERS 1996
EVERYTHING MUST GO STEELY DAN 2003

EVERYTHING PICTURE ULTRASOUND 1999
EVERYTHING'S ALRIGHT FOREVER BOO RADLEYS 1992
EVERYTHING'S COMING UP DUSTY DUSTY SPRINGFIELD 1965
EVERYTHING'S EVENTUAL APPLETON 2003
EVIL EMPIRE RAGE AGAINST THE MACHINE 1996
EVIL HEAT PRIMAL SCREAM 2002
EVITA ORIGINAL LONDON STAGE CAST SOUNDTRACK 1978
EVITA ORIGINAL STUDIO CAST RECORDING 1977
EVITA (OST) MADONNA 1996
EVOLUTION HOLLIES 1967
EVOLUTION JOURNEY 1983
EVOLUTION OLETA ADAMS 1993
EVOLUTION BOYZ II MEN 1997
EVOLVER GRID 1994
EXCESS ALL AREAS SHY 1987
EXCITER DEPECHE MODE 2001
THE EXCITING SOUNDS OF ROY ORBISON ROY ORBISON 1964
EXECUTE OXIDE & NEUTRINO 2001
EX-EL 808 STATE 1991
EXHIBITION GARY NUMAN 1987
EXILE GARY NUMAN 1997
EXILE ON MAIN STREET ROLLING STONES 1972
EXIT TANGERINE DREAM 1981
EXIT O STEVE EARLE 1987
EXIT PLANET DUST CHEMICAL BROTHERS 1995
EXIT STAGE LEFT RUSH 1981
EXODUS BOB MARLEY & THE WAILERS 1977
EXODUS NEW POWER GENERATION 1995
EXODUS (OST) FILM SOUNDTRACK 1961
EXORCISING GHOSTS JAPAN 1984
EXPANSION TEAM DILATED PEOPLES 2002
EXPECTING TO FLY BLUETONES 1996
EXPERIENCE JIMI HENDRIX 1971
EXPERIENCE PRODIGY 1992
EXPERIENCE ELECTRIC SKIN 1997
EXPERIENCE HENDRIX – THE BEST JIMI HENDRIX 2000
EXPERIENCE HENDRIX – THE BEST OF JIMI HENDRIX JIMI HENDRIX 1997
EXPERIENCE THE DIVINE – GREATEST HITS BETTE MIDLER 1993
EXPERIMENTAL JET SET, TRASH AND NO STAR SONIC YOUTH 1994
EXPLOITED LIVE EXPLOITED 1981
EXPLOSIVE COMPANY AMEN CORNER 1969
THE EXPLOSIVE FREDDY CANNON FREDDY CANNON 1960
EXPOSED MIKE OLDFIELD 1979
EXPOSED VINCE NEIL 1993
EXPOSURE ROBERT FRIPP 1979
EXPOSURE – THE BEST OF 1977–2002 GARY NUMAN 2002
EXPRESS YOURSELF CLEARLY E.Y.C. 1994
EXPRESSIONS DON WILLIAMS 1978
EXPRESSIONS – 24 BEAUTIFUL BALLADS VARIOUS ARTISTS (K-TEL) 1985
THE EXQUISITE NANA MOUSKOURI NANA MOUSKOURI 1970
EXTENDED PLAY JAMES TAYLOR QUARTET 1994
EXTENSIONS MANHATTAN TRANSFER 1979
EXTERMINATOR PRIMAL SCREAM 2000
EXTINCTION LEVEL EVENT/FINAL WORLD FRONT BUSTA RHYMES 1999
EXTRA TEXTURE (READ ALL ABOUT IT) GEORGE HARRISON 1975
EXTRA VIRGIN OLIVE 1997
EXTRAS JAM 1992
EXTRATERRESTRIAL LIVE BLUE OYSTER CULT 1982
EXTREME EUPHORIA – LISA LASHES VARIOUS ARTISTS (TELSTAR TV/BMG) 2002
EXTREME II PORNAGRAFFITTI EXTREME 1991
EXTREMELY LIVE VANILLA ICE 1991
THE EXTREMIST JOE SATRIANI 1992
EXTRICATE FALL 1990
EYE CANDY MIS-TEEQ 2003
EYE IN THE SKY ALAN PARSONS PROJECT 1982

EYE OF THE HURRICANE ALARM 1987
EYE OF THE TIGER SURVIVOR 1982
EYES OF A WOMAN AGNETHA FALTSKOG 1985
EYES THAT SEE IN THE DARK KENNY ROGERS 1983
F.L.M. MEL & KIM 1987
FABLES OF THE RECONSTRUCTION R.E.M. 1985
FABRIQUE FASHION 1982
FABULOUS STYLISTICS 1976
FABULOUS DISASTER EXODUS 1989
FABULOUS SHIRLEY BASSEY SHIRLEY BASSEY 1961
THE FABULOUS SHIRLEY BASSEY SHIRLEY BASSEY 1971
FABULOUS STYLE OF THE EVERLY BROTHERS EVERLY
    BROTHERS 1960
FACADES SAD CAFE 1979
FACE DANCES WHO 1981
FACE THE HEAT SCORPIONS 1993
FACE THE MUSIC NKOTB 1994
FACE THE MUSIC – TORVILL AND DEAN VARIOUS ARTISTS
    (POLYGRAM) 1994
FACE TO FACE KINKS 1966
FACE TO FACE BARCLAY JAMES HARVEST 1987
FACE TO FACE – A LIVE RECORDING STEVE HARLEY &
    COCKNEY REBEL 1977
FACE UP LISA STANSFIELD 2001
FACE VALUE PHIL COLLINS 1981
FACES EARTH WIND & FIRE 1980
THE FACTS OF LIFE BLACK BOX RECORDER 2000
FADE OUT LOOP 1989
FADE TO GREY – THE SINGLES COLLECTION VISAGE 1983
FADED SEASIDE GLAMOUR DELAYS 2004
FAHRENHEIT TOTO 1986
FAIR WARNING VAN HALEN 1981
FAIRWEATHER JOHNSON HOOTIE & THE BLOWFISH 1996
FAIRY TALE DONOVAN 1965
FAITH CURE 1981
FAITH GEORGE MICHAEL 1987
FAITH & INSPIRATION DANIEL O'DONNELL 2000
FAITH ALIVE ADAM FAITH 1965
FAITH AND COURAGE SINEAD O'CONNOR 2000
FAITH HOPE LOVE KING'S X 1990
FAITHLESS – BACK TO MINE VARIOUS ARTISTS (DMC)
    2000
THE FAKE SOUND OF PROGRESS LOSTPROPHETS 2002
FALCO 3 FALCO 1986
FALLEN EVANESCENCE 2003
THE FALLING CARMEL 1986
FALLING FORWARD JULIA FORDHAM 1994
FALLING IN LOVE FRANKIE MILLER 1979
FALLING INTO YOU CELINE DION 1996
FALSE ACCUSATIONS ROBERT CRAY BAND 1985
FALSE SMILES AMY STUDT 2003
FAME (OST) FILM SOUNDTRACK 1980
FAME ACADEMY VARIOUS ARTISTS (MERCURY) 2002
FAME ACADEMY – BEE GEES SPECIAL VARIOUS ARTISTS
    (POLYDOR) 2003
FAME ACADEMY – THE FINALISTS VARIOUS ARTISTS
    (POLYDOR) 2003
FAME AND FASHION (BOWIE'S ALL TIME GREATEST HITS)
    DAVID BOWIE 1984
FAME AT LAST GEORGIE FAME 1964
FAMILIAR TO MILLIONS OASIS 2000
FAMILY ENTERTAINMENT FAMILY 1969
FAMILY FAVOURITES RUSS CONWAY 1959
FAMILY STYLE VAUGHAN BROTHERS 1990
FAMOUS BLUE RAINCOAT – SONGS OF LEONARD COHEN
    JENNIFER WARNES 1987
FAMOUS IN THE LAST CENTURY STATUS QUO 2000
... FAMOUS LAST WORDS... ' – SUPERTRAMP 1982
FANDANGO! ZZ TOP 1975
FANMAIL TLC 1999
FANS MALCOLM MCLAREN 1984
FANTASTIC 70'S! – VARIOUS ARTISTS (COLUMBIA) 1998
FANTASTIC 80'S – GO FOR IT VARIOUS ARTISTS
    (COLUMBIA) 2000
FANTASTIC 80'S! – VARIOUS ARTISTS (COLUMBIA) 1998
FANTASTIC 80'S! 2 VARIOUS ARTISTS (COLUMBIA) 1998

FANTASTIC 80'S! 3 VARIOUS ARTISTS (COLUMBIA) 1998
FANTASTIC DANCE! – VARIOUS ARTISTS (COLUMBIA) 1998
FANTASTIC NO 1'S OF THE SEVENTIES VARIOUS ARTISTS
    (DMG TV) 2004
THE FANTASTIC SOUND OF KLAUS WUNDERLICH KLAUS
    WUNDERLICH 1979
FANTASTIC STAR MARC ALMOND 1996
FANTASTIC! WHAM! 1983
FANTAZIA – BRITISH ANTHEMS VARIOUS ARTISTS
    (FANTAZIA) 1998
FANTAZIA – BRITISH ANTHEMS – SUMMERTIME VARIOUS
    ARTISTS (TELSTAR) 1998
FANTAZIA – THE FIRST TASTE VARIOUS ARTISTS
    (FANTAZIA) 1992
FANTAZIA – TWICE AS NICE VARIOUS ARTISTS (FANTAZIA)
    1993
FANTAZIA III – MADE IN HEAVEN VARIOUS ARTISTS
    (FANTAZIA) 1994
FANTAZIA PRESENT THE HOUSE COLLECTION 4 VARIOUS
    ARTISTS (FANTAZIA) 1996
FANX TA RA SAD CAFE 1977
FAR BEYOND DRIVEN PANTERA 1994
FAR FROM HOME TRAFFIC 1994
FAR FROM THE HURTING KIND TRACIE 1984
FAR FROM THE MADDENING CROWDS CHICANE 1997
A FAR OUT DISC TOY DOLLS 1985
FAREWELL ANGELINA JOAN BAEZ 1965
FAREWELL MY SUMMER LOVE MICHAEL JACKSON 1984
FAREWELL TO KINGS RUSH 1977
FASHION NUGGET CAKE 1997
THE FAST AND THE FURIOUS VARIOUS ARTISTS (DEF JAM)
    2002
FAST FORWARD VARIOUS ARTISTS (TELSTAR) 1991
FASTER THAN THE SPEED OF NIGHT BONNIE TYLER 1983
FASTWAY FASTWAY 1983
FAT DANCE HITS VARIOUS ARTISTS (GLOBAL) 1999
THE FAT OF THE LAND PRODIGY 1997
FAT OUT OF HELL ROY 'CHUBBY' BROWN 1996
FAT POP HITS VARIOUS ARTISTS (GLOBAL) 1999
FATBACK LIVE FATBACK BAND 1987
FATBOY SLIM – LIVE ON BRIGHTON BEACH VARIOUS
    ARTISTS (SOUTHERN FRIED) 2002
FATE FOR BREAKFAST ART GARFUNKEL 1979
FATE OF NATIONS ROBERT PLANT 1993
FATHER ABRAHAM IN SMURFLAND FATHER ABRAHAM &
    THE SMURFS 1978
FAVOURITES PETERS & LEE 1975
FAVOURITES DANIEL O'DONNELL 1990
FAWLTY TOWERS TELEVISION SOUNDTRACK 1979
FAWLTY TOWERS VOLUME 2 (TV ORIGINAL CAST)
    TELEVISION SOUNDTRACK 1981
FE REAL MAXI PRIEST 1992
FEAR OF A BLACK PLANET PUBLIC ENEMY 1990
FEAR OF FOURS LAMB 1999
FEAR OF MUSIC TALKING HEADS 1979
FEAR OF THE DARK IRON MAIDEN 1992
FEARGAL SHARKEY FEARGAL SHARKEY 1985
FEARLESS FAMILY 1971
FEARLESS EIGHTH WONDER 1988
FEAST CREATURES 1983
FEAST OF WIRE CALEXICO 2003
FEEL ROACHFORD 1997
FEEL LIKE MAKING LOVE VARIOUS ARTISTS (THE HIT
    LABEL) 1995
FEEL THIS JEFF HEALEY BAND 1992
FEELIN' GOOD VARIOUS ARTISTS (UNIVERSAL) 2003
FEELING FREE SYDNEY YOUNGBLOOD 1989
FEELING GOOD – THE VERY BEST OF NINA SIMONE NINA
    SIMONE 1994
FEELING STRANGELY FINE SEMISONIC 1999
FEELINGS VARIOUS ARTISTS (K-TEL) 1977
FEELS LIKE HOME NORAH JONES 2004
FEELS LIKE RAIN BUDDY GUY 1993
FEELS SO GOOD VARIOUS ARTISTS (INSPIRED) 2001
FEELS SO GOOD ATOMIC KITTEN 2002
FEETS DON'T FAIL ME NOW HERBIE HANCOCK 1979

FELICIANO JOSE FELICIANO 1968
FELINE STRANGLERS 1983
FELIX #1 FELIX 1993
FELLOW HOODLUMS DEACON BLUE 1991
FELT MOUNTAIN GOLDFRAPP 2001
FEMALE VARIOUS ARTISTS (UNIVERSAL) 2001
THE FEMALE TOUCH VARIOUS ARTISTS (GLOBAL) 1998
THE FEMALE TOUCH 2 VARIOUS ARTISTS (GLOBAL) 1999
FERMENT CATHERINE WHEEL 1992
FERRY ACROSS THE MERSEY GERRY & THE PACEMAKERS
    1965
FESTIVAL SANTANA 1977
FEVER KYLIE MINOGUE 2001
FEVER IN FEVER OUT LUSCIOUS JACKSON 1997
FEVER TO TELL YEAH YEAH YEAH 2003
FFRR – SILVER ON BLACK VARIOUS ARTISTS (LONDON)
    1989
FFWD FFWD 1994
FI ROCK VARIOUS ARTISTS (TELSTAR) 1996
FICTION COMSAT ANGELS 1982
FICTION TALES MODERN EON 1981
FIDDLER ON THE ROOF ORIGINAL LONDON STAGE CAST
    SOUNDTRACK
FIDDLER ON THE ROOF (OST) FILM SOUNDTRACK 1972
FIELDS OF GOLD – THE BEST OF STING 1984–1994 STING
    1994
FIERCE VARIOUS ARTISTS (COOLTEMPO) 1987
15 BIG ONES BEACH BOYS 1976
5TH DIMENSION BYRDS 1966
THE FIFTH ELEMENT (OST) ERIC SERRA 1997
50 GOLDEN GREATS SHADOWS 1980
THE 50 GREATEST HITS ELVIS PRESLEY 2000
THE 50 GREATEST LOVE SONGS ELVIS PRESLEY 2001
FIFTY NUMBER ONES OF THE '60S VARIOUS ARTISTS
    (GLOBAL) 1995
50 YEARS OF THE GREATEST HIT SINGLES VARIOUS
    ARTISTS (EMI) 2002
52ND STREET BILLY JOEL 1978
FIFTY YEARS ON WITH JIMMY SHAND JIMMY SHAND &
    HIS BAND 1983
THE '56 SESSIONS VOLUME 1 ELVIS PRESLEY 1978
FIGHTING THIN LIZZY 1975
FIGURE 8 ELLIOTT SMITH 2000
FILE UNDER EASY LISTENING SUGAR 1994
FILIGREE AND SHADOW THIS MORTAL COIL 1986
FILMS ABOUT GHOSTS – THE BEST OF COUNTING CROWS
    2004
FILTH HOUNDS OF HADES TANK 1982
FILTH PIG MINISTRY 1996
FILTHY LUCRE LIVE SEX PISTOLS 1996
FIN DE SIECLE DIVINE COMEDY 1998
THE FINAL WHAM! 1986
THE FINAL COUNTDOWN EUROPE 1986
THE FINAL COUNTDOWN – THE VERY BEST OF SOFT METAL
    VARIOUS ARTISTS (TELSTAR) 1990
THE FINAL CUT PINK FLOYD 1983
THE FINAL FRONTIER KEEL 1986
FINAL STRAW SNOW PATROL 2004
FINALLY CE CE PENISTON 1992
FINALLY BLACKSTREET 1999
FIND OUT STEVEN DANTE 1988
FIND YOUR WAY GABRIELLE 1993
FINDERS KEEPERS (OST) CLIFF RICHARD 1966
THE FINE ART OF SURFACING BOOMTOWN RATS 1979
A FINE ROMANCE – THE LOVE SONGS OF FRANK SINATRA
    2002
FINE YOUNG CANNIBALS FINE YOUNG CANNIBALS 1985
FINELINES MY VITRIOL 2001
THE FINEST FINE YOUNG CANNIBALS 1996
FINEST HOUR LINDISFARNE 1975
FINGS AIN'T WOT THEY USED TO BE ORIGINAL LONDON
    STAGE CAST SOUNDTRACK 1960
FINISTERRE SAINT ETIENNE 2002
FINN FINN 1995
FINYL VINYL RAINBOW 1986
FIRE ELECTRIC SIX 2003

FIRE & SKILL – THE SONGS OF THE JAM VARIOUS ARTISTS (IGNITION) 1999
FIRE AND ICE YNGWIE J MAMLSTEEN 1992
FIRE AND WATER FREE 1970
FIRE AND WATER DAVE GREENFIELD & JEAN-JACQUES BURNEL 1983
FIRE DANCES KILLING JOKE 1983
FIRE GARDEN STEVE VAI 1996
THE FIRE INSIDE BOB SEGER & THE SILVER BULLET BAND 1991
FIRE OF UNKNOWN ORIGIN BLUE OYSTER CULT 1981
FIREBALL DEEP PURPLE 1971
FIREWORKS JOSE FELICIANO 1970
FIREWORKS (SINGLES 1997–2002) EMBRACE 2002
FIRING ON ALL SIX LONE STAR 1977
THE FIRM FIRM 1985
FIRST (THE SOUND OF MUSIC) THEN JERICO 1987
FIRST AND LAST AND ALWAYS SISTERS OF MERCY 1985
FIRST BAND ON THE MOON CARDIGANS 1996
FIRST BLOOD... LAST CUTS W.A.S.P. 1993
THE FIRST BORN IS DEAD NICK CAVE & THE BAD SEEDS 1985
THE FIRST CHAPTER MISSION 1987
FIRST CONTACT ROGER SANCHEZ 2001
THE FIRST DAY DAVID SYLVAN & ROBERT FRIPP 1993
THE FIRST FAMILY VAUGHN MEADER 1962
FIRST LADIES OF COUNTRY VARIOUS ARTISTS (CBS) 1980
FIRST LADIES OF COUNTRY VARIOUS ARTISTS (SONY) 2004
FIRST LADY LISA MAFFIA 2003
THE FIRST LADY OF SOUL ARETHA FRANKLIN 1986
THE FIRST LIVE RECORDINGS ELVIS PRESLEY 1984
FIRST LOVE VARIOUS ARTISTS (ARCADE) 1980
FIRST LOVE MICHAEL BALL 1996
THE FIRST OF A MILLION KISSES FAIRGROUND ATTRACTION 1988
THE FIRST OF TOO MANY SENSELESS THINGS 1991
FIRST RAYS OF THE NEW RISING SUN JIMI HENDRIX 1997
FIRST STEP FACES 1970
THE FIRST SUMMER OF LOVE VARIOUS ARTISTS (POLYGRAM) 1997
FIRST TAKE ROBERTA FLACK 1972
FIRST TEN YEARS JOAN BAEZ 1971
FIRST TIME EVER I SAW YOUR FACE JOHNNY MATHIS 1972
THE FISH AND THE TREE AND THE BIRD AND THE BELL VARIOUS ARTISTS (COLUMBIA) 1991
FISH OUT OF WATER CHRIS SQUIRE 1975
THE FISH PEOPLE TAPES ALEXEI SAYLE 1984
FISH RISING STEVE HILLAGE 1975
FISHERMAN'S BLUES WATERBOYS 1988
FISHING FOR LUCKIES WILDHEARTS 1996
5 J.J. CALE 1979
5 LENNY KRAVITZ 1998
FIVE FIVE 1998
FIVE BRIDGES NICE 1970
FIVE FACES OF MANFRED MANN MANFRED MANN 1964
FIVE GUYS NAMED MOE ORIGINAL LONDON STAGE CAST SOUNDTRACK 1991
FIVE MAN ACOUSTICAL JAM TESLA 1991
FIVE MILES OUT MIKE OLDFIELD 1982
5150 VAN HALEN 1986
THE FIVE PENNIES (OST) FILM SOUNDTRACK 1960
5,000 SPIRITS OR THE LAYERS OF THE ONION INCREDIBLE STRING BAND 1967
FLAG YELLO 1988
THE FLAME ANNABEL LAMB 1984
FLAMENCO GUITAR MANITAS DE PLATA 1967
FLAMING PIE PAUL McCARTNEY 1997
FLAMING STAR AND SUMMER KISSES ELVIS PRESLEY 1965
FLARED HITS AND PLATFORM SOUL VARIOUS ARTISTS (VISION) 1995
FLASH JEFF BECK 1985
FLASH GORDON (FILM SOUNDTRACK) QUEEN 1980
FLASH LIGHT TOM VERLAINE 1987
FLASH TRACKS VARIOUS ARTISTS (TV RECORDS) 1982
FLASHDANCE (OST) FILM SOUNDTRACK 1983

FLASHPOINT ROLLING STONES 1991
THE FLAT EARTH THOMAS DOLBY 1984
FLAUNT IT SIGUE SIGUE SPUTNIK 1986
FLAUNT THE IMPERFECTION CHINA CRISIS 1985
FLEETWOOD MAC FLEETWOOD MAC 1968
FLEETWOOD MAC FLEETWOOD MAC 1976
FLEETWOOD MAC LIVE FLEETWOOD MAC 1980
FLESH AND BLOOD ROXY MUSIC 1980
FLESH AND BLOOD POISON 1990
FLESHWOUNDS SKIN 2003
FLEX LENE LOVICH 1980
FLICK OF THE SWITCH AC/DC 1983
FLIGHT OF ICARUS/THE TROOPER IRON MAIDEN 1990
FLIGHT OF THE CONDOR VARIOUS ARTISTS (TELSTAR) 1992
THE FLIGHT OF THE CONDOR (OST TV) INTI ILLIMANI-GUAMARY 1983
FLIGHTS OF FANCY PAUL LEONI 1983
THE FLINTSTONES (OST) FILM SOUNDTRACK 1994
FLIP NILS LOFGREN 1985
FLOATERS FLOATERS 1977
FLOCK FLOCK 1970
A FLOCK OF SEAGULLS A FLOCK OF SEAGULLS 1982
FLOGGING A DEAD HORSE SEX PISTOLS 1980
FLOOD THEY MIGHT BE GIANTS 1990
FLOODLAND SISTERS OF MERCY 1987
FLOOR FILLAS FLIP & FILL 2003
FLOORED GENIUS – THE BEST OF JULIAN COPE AND THE TEARDROP EXPLODES JULIAN COPE & THE TEARDROP EXPLODES 1992
FLOORFILLERS VARIOUS ARTISTS (UNIVERSAL) 2004
FLORAL DANCE BRIGHOUSE & RASTRICK BRASS BAND 1978
FLOWER DRUM SONG ORIGINAL BROADWAY STAGE CAST SOUNDTRACK 1960
FLOWER DRUM SONG ORIGINAL LONDON STAGE CAST SOUNDTRACK 1960
FLOWERS ACE OF BASE 1998
FLOWERS ECHO & THE BUNNYMEN 2001
FLOWERS IN THE DIRT PAUL McCARTNEY 1989
FLOWERS OF ROMANCE PUBLIC IMAGE LTD 1981
FLUSH THE FASHION ALICE COOPER 1980
FLY DIXIE CHICKS 1999
FLY LIKE AN EAGLE STEVE MILLER BAND 1976
FLY ON THE WALL AC/DC 1985
FLY ON THE WALL – B SIDES & RARITIES PAUL WELLER 2003
FLY OR DIE N*E*R*D 2004
FLYER NANCI GRIFFITH 1994
FLYING COLOURS CHRIS DE BURGH 1988
FLYING COWBOYS RICKIE LEE JONES 1989
FLYING LIZARDS FLYING LIZARDS 1980
FM (OST) FILM SOUNDTRACK 1978
FOCUS FOCUS 1975
FOCUS 3 FOCUS 1972
FOCUS AT THE RAINBOW FOCUS 1973
FOG ON THE TYNE LINDISFARNE 1971
FOLD YOUR HANDS CHILD YOU WALK LIKE A PEASANT BELLE & SEBASTIAN 2000
FOLK FESTIVAL OF THE BLUES (LIVE RECORDING) VARIOUS ARTISTS (PYE) 1964
FOLKLORE NELLY FURTADO 2003
FOLLOW THAT GIRL ORIGINAL LONDON STAGE CAST SOUNDTRACK 1960
FOLLOW THE LEADER ERIC B & RAKIM 1988
FOLLOW THE LEADER KORN 1998
FOLLOW YOUR DREAM DANIEL O'DONNELL 1992
FONTANELLE BABES IN TOYLAND 1992
FONZIE'S FAVOURITES TELEVISION COMPILATION 1978
FOO FIGHTERS FOO FIGHTERS 1995
FOOL BRITANNIA ANTHONY NEWLEY, PETER SELLERS, JOAN COLLINS 1963
THE FOOL CIRCLE NAZARETH 1981
FOOLISH BEHAVIOUR ROD STEWART 1980
FOOT LOOSE AND FANCY FREE ROD STEWART 1977
FOOTLOOSE (OST) FILM SOUNDTRACK 1984
FOOTPRINTS HOLLY VALANCE 2002

FOR CERTAIN BECAUSE HOLLIES 1966
FOR EARTH BELOW ROBIN TROWER 1975
FOR ONCE IN MY LIFE TONY BENNETT 1968
FOR PLEASURE OMAR 1994
FOR SOMEONE SPECIAL KEN DODD 1967
FOR THE BOYS (OST) BETTE MIDLER 1992
FOR THE GOOD TIMES PERRY COMO 1983
FOR THE LOVE OF STRANGE MEDICINE STEVE PERRY 1994
FOR THE STARS VON OTTER MEETS COSTELLO 2001
FOR THOSE ABOUT TO ROCK WE SALUTE YOU AC/DC 1981
FOR TO NEXT STEVE HILLAGE 1983
FOR TWISTERS ONLY CHUBBY CHECKER 1962
FOR UNLAWFUL CARNAL KNOWLEDGE VAN HALEN 1991
FOR YOU VARIOUS ARTISTS (COLUMBIA) 2000
FOR YOUR EARS ONLY BENTLEY RHYTHM ACE 2000
FOR YOUR PLEASURE ROXY MUSIC 1973
FORBIDDEN BLACK SABBATH 1995
THE FORCE BEHIND THE POWER DIANA ROSS 1991
FORCE MAJEURE TANGERINE DREAM 1979
FORCE OF VICTORY LINTON KWESI JOHNSON 1979
FORE! – HUEY LEWIS & THE NEWS 1986
FOREIGN AFFAIR TINA TURNER 1989
FOREIGNER CAT STEVENS 1973
FOREVER VARIOUS ARTISTS (EMI) 1992
FOREVER CRANES 1993
FOREVER DAMAGE 1997
FOREVER PUFF DADDY 1999
FOREVER SPICE GIRLS 2000
FOREVER AND EVER DEMIS ROUSSOS 1974
FOREVER AND EVER – DEFINITIVE COLLECTION DEMIS ROUSSOS 2002
FOREVER BLUE CHRIS ISAAK 1995
FOREVER CHANGES LOVE 1968
FOREVER CHANGES LOVE 2001
FOREVER DELAYED – THE GREATEST HITS MANIC STREET PREACHERS 2002
FOREVER ELLA ELLA FITZGERALD 1996
FOREVER FOR NOW HARRY CONNICK JR. 1993
FOREVER NOW PSYCHEDELIC FURS 1982
FOREVER NOW LEVEL 42 1994
FOREVER YOUR GIRL PAULA ABDUL 1989
FOREVER, FOR ALWAYS, FOR LOVE LUTHER VANDROSS 1987
FORGING AHEAD BAD MANNERS 1982
FORGIVEN, NOT FORGOTTEN CORRS 1996
FORM & FUNCTION PHOTEK 1998
FORMALDEHYDE TERRORVISION 1993
FORMICA BLUES MONO 1998
FORMULA 30 VARIOUS ARTISTS (MERCURY) 1983
FORMULA THIRTY – 2 VARIOUS ARTISTS (MERCURY) 1986
FORREST GUMP (OST) FILM SOUNDTRACK 1994
40 BIG ONES JUDGE DREAD 1981
40 FANTASTIC HITS FROM THE 50'S AND 60'S VARIOUS ARTISTS (ARCADE) 1973
FORTY FINGERS FRESHLY PACKED CHICKEN SHACK 1968
44 SUPERSTARS VARIOUS ARTISTS (K-TEL) 1976
40 GOLDEN GREATS JIM REEVES 1975
40 GOLDEN GREATS CLIFF RICHARD 1977
40 GOLDEN MOTOWN GREATS DIANA ROSS & THE SUPREMES 1998
40 GREATEST HERB ALPERT & THE TIJUANA BRASS 1977
40 GREATEST HITS PERRY COMO 1975
FORTY LICKS ROLLING STONES 2002
FORTY MANIA ANONYMOUS COVER VERSIONS 1976
40 NUMBER ONE HITS VARIOUS ARTISTS (K-TEL) 1978
41 HOLLYWOOD GREATS – THE BEST OF DORIS DAY 2002
40 SINGALONG PUB SONGS ANONYMOUS COVER VERSIONS 1975
40 SUPER GREATS VARIOUS ARTISTS (K-TEL) 1975
THE 49ERS 49ERS 1990
FOSSIL FUEL – THE XTC SINGLES COLLECTION 1977–1992 XTC 1996
FOSTERS AND ALLEN'S CHRISTMAS COLLECTION FOSTER & ALLEN 1989
FOTHERINGAY FOTHERINGAY 1970
FOUNDATION TEN CITY 1989

FOUNTAINS OF WAYNE FOUNTAINS OF WAYNE 1997
4 FOREIGNER 1981
IV CYPRESS HILL 1998
IV SEAL 2003
45 RPM – THE SINGLES OF THE THE 2002
458489 A SIDES FALL 1990
4.5 THE BEST OF THE INDIGO GIRLS INDIGO GIRLS 1995
THE FOUR SEASONS STORY FOUR SEASONS 1976
4766 SECONDS: A SHORTCUT TO TEENAGE FANCLUB
    TEENAGE FANCLUB 2003
THE FOUR SIDES OF MELANIE MELANIE 1972
461 OCEAN BOULEVARD ERIC CLAPTON 1974
FOUR STAR COUNTRY VARIOUS ARTISTS (K-TEL) 1985
FOUR SURE SCOOCH 2000
FOUR SYMBOLS (LED ZEPPELIN 4) LED ZEPPELIN 1971
4,000 WEEKS HOLIDAY IAN DURY & THE MUSIC STUDENTS
    1984
FOUR TOPS GREATEST HITS FOUR TOPS 1968
FOUR TOPS GREATEST HITS VOLUME 2 FOUR TOPS 1971
FOUR TOPS LIVE! – FOUR TOPS 1967
FOUR TOPS ON TOP FOUR TOPS 1966
THE FOUR TOPS STORY 1964–1972 FOUR TOPS 1973
FOUR WEDDINGS AND A FUNERAL (OST) FILM
    SOUNDTRACK 1994
FOUR CALENDAR CAFE – COCTEAU TWINS 1993
1492 – THE CONQUEST OF PARADISE (OST) VANGELIS
    1992
14 SHOTS TO THE DOME LL COOL J 1993
14 THINGS TO THINK ABOUT CHRIS FARLOWE 1966
14:59 SUGAR RAY 1999
FOURTH SOFT MACHINE 1971
4 TRACK DEMOS PJ HARVEY 1993
FOUR WAY STREET CROSBY, STILL, NASH & YOUNG 1971
14 SHADES OF GREY STAIND 2003
FOX FOX 1975
THE FOX ELTON JOHN 1981
FOX KIDS PARTY HITS VARIOUS ARTISTS (BMG) 2004
FOXBASE ALPHA SAINT ETIENNE 1991
FOXTROT GENESIS 1972
FRAGGLE ROCK FRAGGLES 1984
FRAGILE YES 1971
THE FRAGILE NINE INCH NAILS 1999
FRAGILE – MYSTICAL SOUNDS OF THE PANPIPES LOS
    NINOS 1995
FRAGMENTS OF FREEDOM MORCHEEBA 2000
FRAMPTON COMES ALIVE PETER FRAMPTON 1976
FRANK SQUEEZE 1989
FRANK AMY WINEHOUSE 2003
FRANK BLACK FRANK BLACK 1993
FRANK BLACK AND THE CATHOLICS FRANK BLACK 1998
FRANK SINATRA FRANK SINATRA 1967
THE FRANK SINATRA COLLECTION FRANK SINATRA 1986
FRANK SINATRA SINGS FOR ONLY THE LONELYCLOSE TO
    YOU CARPENTERS 19711958
FRANK SINATRA SINGS RODGERS AND HART FRANK
    SINATRA 1971
FRANK SINATRA SINGS SONGS FOR PLEASURE FRANK
    SINATRA 1966
FRANK SINATRA STORY FRANK SINATRA 1958
FRANKIE FRANK SINATRA 1957
FRANKIE AND JOHNNY (OST) ELVIS PRESLEY 1966
FRANKIE MCBRIDE FRANKIE MCBRIDE 1968
FRANKIE VAUGHAN AT THE LONDON PALLADIUM FRANKIE
    VAUGHAN 1959
FRANKIE VAUGHAN SONGBOOK FRANKIE VAUGHAN 1967
FRANK'S WILD YEARS TOM WAITS 1987
FRANTIC VARIOUS ARTISTS (WARNER BROTHERS) 2001
FRANTIC BRYAN FERRY 2002
FRANTIC ROMANTIC JERMAINE STEWART 1986
FRANTIC 2002 VARIOUS ARTISTS (WSM) 2002
FRANZ FERDINAND FRANZ FERDINAND 2004
FREAK OF NATURE ANASTACIA 2001
FREAK OUT CHIC & SISTER SLEDGE 1987
FREAK SHOW SILVERCHAIR 1997
FREDDIE AND THE DREAMERS FREDDIE & THE DREAMERS
    1963

THE FREDDIE MERCURY ALBUM FREDDIE MERCURY 1992
FREE RICK ASTLEY 1991
FREE ALL ANGELS ASH 2001
FREE AND EASY HELEN REDDY 1975
FREE AS A BIRD SUPERTRAMP 1987
FREE AT LAST FREE 1972
FREE FOR ALL TED NUGENT 1976
FREE LIVE! – FREE 1971
FREE ME EMMA BUNTON 2004
FREE PEACE SWEET DODGY 1996
FREE SPIRIT – 17 CLASSIC ROCK BALLADS VARIOUS
    ARTISTS (COLUMBIA) 1991
THE FREE STORY FREE 1974
FREE WHEELERS PEDDLERS 1968
FREEDOM NEIL YOUNG 1989
FREEDOM 2 – THE ULTIMATE RAVE VARIOUS ARTISTS
    (TRAX) 1990
FREEDOM AT POINT ZERO JEFFERSON STARSHIP 1980
FREEDOM NO COMPROMISE LITTLE STEVEN 1987
FREEDOM OF CHOICE DEVO 1980
FREEDOM TO PARTY – FIRST LEGAL RAVE VARIOUS ARTISTS
    (TRAX) 1990
FREEWAY VARIOUS ARTISTS (POLYGRAM) 1996
THE FREEWHEELIN' BOB DYLAN BOB DYLAN 1964
FREEZE FRAME J. GEILS BAND 1982
A FRENCH AFFAIR VARIOUS ARTISTS (VIRGIN) 2001
FRENCH KISSES LIL' LOUIS 1989
THE FRENZ EXPERIMENT FALL 1988
FREQUENCIES LFO 1991
FRESCO M PEOPLE 1997
FRESH CREAM CREAM 1966
FRESH DANCE 93 VARIOUS ARTISTS (TELSTAR) 1993
FRESH FRUIT FOR ROTTING VEGETABLES DEAD KENNEDYS
    1980
FRESH FRUIT IN FOREIGN PLACES KID CREOLE & THE
    COCONUTS 1982
FRESH HITS – VOL 1 VARIOUS ARTISTS (WARNER
    BROTHERS) 2000
FRESH HITS – VOL 2 VARIOUS ARTISTS (WARNER
    BROTHERS) 2000
FRESH HITS 1997 VARIOUS ARTISTS (GLOBAL) 1997
FRESH HITS 96 VARIOUS ARTISTS (SONY) 1996
FRESH HITS 98 VARIOUS ARTISTS (SONY) 1998
FRESH HITS 99 VARIOUS ARTISTS (WARNER BROTHERS)
    1999
FRESH HORSES GARTH BROOKS 1995
FRESH QUOTA STATUS QUO 1981
FRESH! – GINA G 1997
FRESHEN UP VOLUME 1 VARIOUS ARTISTS (FRESH) 1995
FRESKA! – VARIOUS ARTISTS (REACT) 1994
FRIDAY NIGHT FEVER VARIOUS ARTISTS (POLYGRAM) 1998
FRIDAY THE 13TH (AT THE MARQUEE CLUB) PLAYN JAYN
    1984
FRIDAY'S CHILD WILL YOUNG 2003
FRIED' – JULIAN COPE 1984
FRIEND OR FOE ADAM ANT 1982
FRIENDLY FIRE SHARA NELSON 1995
FRIENDS BEACH BOYS 1968
FRIENDS SHALAMAR 1982
FRIENDS AGAIN VARIOUS ARTISTS (IMPRESSION) 1984
FRIENDS AND LOVERS VARIOUS ARTISTS (K-TEL) 1987
FRIENDS AND LOVERS BERNARD BUTLER 1999
FRIENDS FOREVER TWEENIES 2000
FRIENDS IN LOVE JOHNNY MATHIS 1982
THE FRIENDS OF MR. CAIRO JON & VANGELIS 1981
FRIENDS REUNITED VARIOUS ARTISTS (UNIVERSAL) 2003
FRIENDS REUNITED – THE 90'S VARIOUS ARTISTS
    (UNIVERSAL) 2003
FROGSTOMP SILVERCHAIR 1995
FROM A DISTANCE... THE EVENT CLIFF RICHARD 1990
FROM A SPARK TO A FLAME – THE VERY BEST OF CHRIS DE
    BURGH CHRIS DE BURGH 1989
FROM A TO B NEW MUSIK 1980
FROM ACROSS THE KITCHEN TABLE PALE FOUNTAINS 1985
FROM BEER TO ETERNITY MACC LADS 1989
FROM BOTH SIDES NOW IAN MCSHANE 1992

FROM DUSTY... WITH LOVE DUSTY SPRINGFIELD 1970
FROM ELVIS IN MEMPHIS ELVIS PRESLEY 1969
FROM ELVIS PRESLEY BOULEVARD, MEMPHIS, TENNESSEE
    ELVIS PRESLEY 1976
FROM EVERY SPHERE ED HARCOURT 2003
FROM HER TO ETERNITY NICK CAVE FEATURING THE BAD
    SEEDS 1984
FROM HERE TO ETERNITY CLASH 1999
FROM LANGLEY PARK TO MEMPHIS PREFAB SPROUT 1988
FROM LUXURY TO HEARTACHE CULTURE CLUB 1986
FROM MEMPHIS TO VEGAS – FROM VEGAS TO MEMPHIS
    ELVIS PRESLEY 1970
FROM MIGHTY OAKS RAY THOMAS 1975
FROM MOTOWN WITH LOVE VARIOUS ARTISTS (K-TEL)
    1987
FROM NOW ON WILL YOUNG 2002
FROM NOWHERE... THE TROGGS TROGGS 1966
FROM SEA TO SHINING SEA JOHNNY CASH 1968
FROM THE BEGINNING SMALL FACES 1967
FROM THE BOTTOM UP BROWNSTONE 1995
FROM THE CHOIRGIRL HOTEL TORI AMOS 1998
FROM THE CRADLE ERIC CLAPTON 1994
FROM THE HEART TOM JONES 1966
FROM THE HEART DANIEL O'DONNELL 1988
FROM THE HEART – HIS GREATEST LOVE SONGS ELVIS
    PRESLEY 1992
FROM THE HEART OF TOWN GALLON DRUNK 1993
FROM THE INSIDE ALICE COOPER 1978
FROM THE LEFT SIDE SKYY 1986
FROM THE MAKERS OF... – STATUS QUO 1982
FROM THE MOUNTAIN STYLISTICS 1975
FROM THE MUDDY BANKS OF THE WISHKAH NIRVANA
    1996
FROM THE OFFICIAL BARCELONA GAMES CEREMONY
    PLACIDO DOMINGO, JOSE CARRERAS &
    MONTSERRAT CABALLE 1992
FROM THE TEA ROOMS OF MARS... TO THE HELLHOLES OF
    URANUS LANDSCAPE 1981
FROM THE WITCHWOOD STRAWBS 1971
FROM TIME TO TIME – THE SINGLES COLLECTION PAUL
    YOUNG 1991
FRONT PAGE NEWS WISHBONE ASH 1977
FRONTIERS JOURNEY 1983
FRUIT AT THE BOTTOM WENDY & LISA 1989
FUGAZI MARILLION 1984
THE FUGITIVE TONY BANKS 1983
THE FUGITIVE KIND SWANS WAY 1984
FULFILLINGNESS' FIRST FINALE STEVIE WONDER 1974
FULHAM FALLOUT LURKERS 1978
FULL CIRCLE BOYZ II MEN 2002
FULL CLIP: A DECADE OF GANG STARR GANG STARR 1999
FULL HOUSE FAIRPORT CONVENTION 1970
FULL HOUSE DOOLEYS 1980
THE FULL LIFE JACK JONES 1977
FULL METAL JACKET (OST) FILM SOUNDTRACK 1987
THE FULL MONTY (OST) FILM SOUNDTRACK 1997
FULL MOON BRANDY 2002
FULL MOON FEVER TOM PETTY 1989
FULL MOON, DIRTY HEARTS INXS 1993
FULL ON – A YEAR IN THE LIFE OF HOUSE VARIOUS ARTISTS
    (DECONSTRUCTION) 1993
FULL ON DANCE VARIOUS ARTISTS (COOKIE JAR) 1993
FULL ON DANCE '93 VARIOUS ARTISTS (COOKIE JAR) 1993
FULL ON... MASK HYSTERIA ALTERN 8 1992
FULLY QUALIFIED SURVIVOR MICHAEL CHAPMAN 1970
THE FUN BOY THREE FUN BOY THREE 1982
FUN IN ACAPULCO (OST) ELVIS PRESLEY 1963
FUN IN SPACE ROGER TAYLOR 1981
FUNDAMENTAL BONNIE RAIT 1998
A FUNK ODYSSEY JAMIROQUAI 2001
FUNK SOUL BROTHER – THE BEST OF DANCE SOUL & SWING
    VARIOUS ARTISTS (GLOBAL) 1999
FUNK SOUL CLASSICS VARIOUS ARTISTS (MINISTRY OF
    SOUND) 2004
THE FUNKIN' 80S VARIOUS ARTISTS (TELSTAR) 2003
FUNKMASTER MIX VARIOUS ARTISTS (POLYGRAM) 1996

FUNKOLOGY – ONE NATION UNDER A GROOVE VARIOUS ARTISTS (WARNER BROTHERS) 2001
FUNKY DIVAS EN VOGUE 1992
FUNKY DIVAS VARIOUS ARTISTS (GLOBAL) 1997
FUNKY DIVAS VARIOUS ARTISTS (TELSTAR) 2001
FUNKY DIVAS – THE AUTUMN COLLECTION VARIOUS ARTISTS (TELSTAR) 2002
FUNKY DIVAS 2 VARIOUS ARTISTS (GLOBAL) 1998
FUNKY DIVAS 3 VARIOUS ARTISTS (GLOBAL) 2000
FUNKY DORY RACHEL STEVENS 2003
FUNKY HOUSE VARIOUS ARTISTS (TELSTAR) 1999
FUNKY LITTLE DEMONS WOLFGANG PRESS 1995
FUNNY GIRL BARBRA STREISAND 1966
FUNNY GIRL (OST) BARBRA STREISAND 1969
FUR JANE WIEDLIN 1988
FUREYS FINEST FUREYS & DAVEY ARTHUR 1987
FURTHER GENEVA 1997
FURTHER ADVENTURES OF LITTLE VOICE JANE HORROCKS 2000
FURTHER DOWN THE ROAD CHARLIE LANDSBOROUGH 1997
FURTHEST FROM THE SUN FAMILY CAT 1992
THE FURY GARY NUMAN 1985
FUSED VARIOUS ARTISTS (POLYGRAM) 1997
THE FUTURE LEONARD COHEN 1992
FUTURE BLUES CANNED HEAT 1970
FUTURE CHILL VARIOUS ARTISTS (VIRGIN) 2002
FUTURE SHOCK GILLAN 1981
FUTURE SHOCK HERBIE HANCOCK 1983
FUTURE SIGNS WARM JETS 1998
THE FUTURE SOUND OF NEW YORK VARIOUS ARTISTS (MINISTRY OF SOUND) 1995
FUTURE TRANCE VARIOUS ARTISTS (VIRGIN) 2002
FUTURE TRANCE IBIZA VARIOUS ARTISTS (VIRGIN) 2002
FUTURE TRANCE 2003 VARIOUS ARTISTS (VIRGIN) 2003
FUTURESHOCK – 20 FURIOUS DANCE TUNES VARIOUS ARTISTS (DINO) 1993
FUTURISTIC DRAGON T. REX 1976
FUZZY GRANT LEE BUFFALO 1993
FUZZY LOGIC SUPER FURRY ANIMALS 1996
FYC FINE YOUNG CANNIBALS 1990
G FORCE KENNY G 1984
G N' R THE LIES, THE SEX, THE DRUGS, THE VIOLENCE, THE SHOCKING TRUTH GUNS N' ROSES 1988
G SIDES GORILLAZ 2002
G.I. BLUES (OST) ELVIS PRESLEY 1960
GABRIELLE GABRIELLE 1996
THE GAELIC COLLECTION 1973–1995 RUNRIG 1998
GAIA (ONE WOMAN'S JOURNEY) OLIVIA NEWTON-JOHN 1995
GALAXY HIT MIX VARIOUS ARTISTS (MINISTRY OF SOUND) 2000
GALAXY MIX – BOY GEORGE VARIOUS ARTISTS (MINISTRY OF SOUND) 1999
GALAXY WEEKEND: MIXED BY BOY GEORGE & ALLISTER WHITEHEAD VARIOUS ARTISTS (MINISTRY OF SOUND) 1999
GALLUS GUN 1992
GALORE – THE BEST OF KIRSTY MACCOLL KIRSTY MACCOLL 1995
GALORE – THE SINGLES 1987–1997 CURE 1997
THE GAME QUEEN 1980
GAMES B.B.E. 1998
GANGSTA'S PARADISE COOLIO 1995
GANGSTERS OF THE GROOVE – THE 90'S MIX HEATWAVE 1991
GAP BAND 8 GAP BAND 1987
GARAGE ANTHEMS VARIOUS ARTISTS (TELSTAR) 2000
GARAGE CITY VARIOUS ARTISTS (TELSTAR) 1992
GARAGE FLOWER STONE ROSES 1996
GARAGE INC. METALLICA 1998
GARAGE NATION VARIOUS ARTISTS (TELSTAR) 2000
GARAGE NATION VARIOUS ARTISTS (INCREDIBLE) 2001
GARAGE NATION 02 VARIOUS ARTISTS (INCREDIBLE) 2002
GARAGE VIBES VARIOUS ARTISTS (PURE SILK) 2000
GARBAGE GARBAGE 1995

THE GARDEN JOHN FOXX 1981
GARDEN IN THE CITY MELANIE 1972
GARY GLITTER'S GREATEST HITS GARY GLITTER 1976
GASOLINE ALLEY ROD STEWART 1970
GATECRASHER VARIOUS ARTISTS (INCREDIBLE) 1998
GATECRASHER DIGITAL TRANCE VARIOUS ARTISTS (GATECRASHER) 2000
GATECRASHER – GLOBAL SOUND SYSTEM VARIOUS ARTISTS (INCREDIBLE) 2000
GATECRASHER – NATIONAL ANTHEMS VARIOUS ARTISTS (INCREDIBLE) 2000
GATECRASHER DIGITAL VARIOUS ARTISTS (GATECRASHER) 2001
GATECRASHER DISCO TECH VARIOUS ARTISTS (INCREDIBLE) 1999
GATECRASHER EXPERIENCE VARIOUS ARTISTS (GATECRASHER) 2002
GATECRASHER RED VARIOUS ARTISTS (INCREDIBLE) 1999
GATECRASHER WET VARIOUS ARTISTS (INCREDIBLE) 1999
GATECRASHING LIVING IN A BOX 1989
GATHER ME MELANIE 1972
GATHERING OF FREAKS FREAK OF NATURE 1994
GAUCHO STEELY DAN 1980
GAUDI ALAN PARSONS PROJECT 1987
G A Y VARIOUS ARTISTS (LONDON) 2000
GAZE BEAUTIFUL SOUTH 2003
GEFFERY MORGAN... – UB40 1984
GENE PITNEY'S BIG SIXTEEN GENE PITNEY 1967
GENERATION TERRORISTS MANIC STREET PREACHERS 1992
GENERATION X GENERATION X 1978
GENESIS GENESIS 1983
GENESIS BUSTA RHYMES 2002
GENESIS LIVE GENESIS 1973
THE GENIUS OF VENICE RONDO VENEZIANO 1984
GENO DEXYS MIDNIGHT RUNNERS 1983
GENTLE ON MY MIND DEAN MARTIN 1969
GENTLE SHADES OF VAL DOONICAN VAL DOONICAN 1966
GENTLEMAN JIM JIM REEVES 1964
GENTLEMAN JIM – DEFINITIVE COLLECTION JIM REEVES 2003
GENTLEMEN AFGHAN WHIGS 1993
GENTLEMEN TAKE POLAROIDS JAPAN 1980
GENTLY LIZA MINNELLI 1996
GENUINE DUD DUDLEY MOORE TRIO 1966
GEOGADDI BOARDS OF CANADA 2002
THE GEORGE BENSON COLLECTION GEORGE BENSON 1981
GEORGE BEST WEDDING PRESENT 1987
GEORGE GERSHWIN – THE BEST OF VARIOUS ARTISTS (DECCA) 2003
GEORGE HARRISON GEORGE HARRISON 1979
GEORGE MCCRAE GEORGE MCCRAE 1975
GEORGE THOROGOOD AND THE DESTROYERS GEORGE THOROGOOD & THE DESTROYERS 1978
GEORGIA SATELLITES GEORGIA SATELLITES 1987
GERM FREE ADOLESCENTS X-RAY SPEX 1978
GERRY MULLIGAN MEETS BEN WEBSTER GERRY MULLIGAN & BEN WEBSTER 1960
GET A GRIP AEROSMITH 1993
GET BORN JET 2003
GET CARTER (OST) ROY BUDD 1998
GET CLOSE PRETENDERS 1986
GET EVEN BROTHER BEYOND 1988
GET HAPPY! – ELVIS COSTELLO & THE ATTRACTIONS 1980
GET HERE BRENDA RUSSELL 1988
GET IN KENICKIE 1998
GET IN TOUCH WITH YOURSELF SWING OUT SISTER 1992
GET INTO YOU DANNII MINOGUE 1993
GET IT ON – GREATEST HITS OF THE 70'S VARIOUS ARTISTS (THE HIT LABEL) 1993
GET LOOSE EVELYN KING 1982
GET NERVOUS PAT BENATAR 1982
GET ON THIS! – 30 DANCE HITS VOLUME 1 VARIOUS ARTISTS (TELSTAR) 1990
GET ON THIS!!! 2 VARIOUS ARTISTS (TELSTAR) 1990
GET ON UP VARIOUS ARTISTS (RCA) 1983

GET OUT AND WALK FARMER'S BOYS 1983
GET READY 2 UNLIMITED 1992
GET READY NEW ORDER 2001
GET READY! – ROACHFORD 1991
GET RHYTHM RY COODER 1987
GET RICH OR DIE TRYIN' – 50 CENT 2003
GET RIGHT INTAE HIM BILLY CONNOLLY 1975
GET STONED ROLLING STONES 1977
GET THAT FEELING JIMI HENDRIX & CURTIS KNIGHT 1968
GET THE KNACK KNACK 1979
GET THE PARTY STARTED VARIOUS ARTISTS (COLUMBIA) 2002
GET TOGETHER WITH ANDY WILLIAMS ANDY WILLIAMS 1969
GET UP ON IT KEITH SWEAT 1994
GET UR FREAK ON VARIOUS ARTISTS (WARNER BROTHERS) 2002
GET YER YA-YA'S OUT!' – THE ROLLING STONES IN CONCERT ROLLING STONES 1970
GETAHEAD CURIOSITY KILLED THE CAT 1989
THE GETAWAY CHRIS DE BURGH 1982
GETAWAY REEF 2000
GETT OFF PRINCE & THE NEW POWER GENERATION 1991
GETTIN' HIGH ON YOUR OWN SUPPLY APOLLO FOUR FORTY 1999
GETTING READY TEMPTATIONS 1966
GETTING SENTIMENTAL ENGELBERT HUMPERDINCK 1985
GETTING THE HOLY GHOST ACROSS BILL NELSON 1986
GETTING TO THIS BLODWYN PIG 1970
GHETTO BLASTER CRUSADERS 1984
GHETTO LOVE JAHEIM 2001
GHETTO MUSIC: THE BLUEPRINT OF HIP HOP BOOGIE DOWN PRODUCTIONS 1989
GHETTO SUPERSTAR PRAS MICHEL 1998
GHOST (OST) FILM SOUNDTRACK 1990
GHOST IN THE MACHINE POLICE 1981
GHOST OF A DOG EDIE BRICKELL & THE NEW BOHEMIANS 1990
THE GHOST OF CAIN NEW MODEL ARMY 1986
GHOST OF PRINCES IN TOWERS RICH KIDS 1978
THE GHOST OF TOM JOAD BRUCE SPRINGSTEEN 1995
GHOST RIDERS IN THE SKY SLIM WHITMAN 1979
GHOSTBUSTERS (OST) FILM SOUNDTRACK 1984
GHOSTBUSTERS II (OST) FILM SOUNDTRACK 1989
GIANT BUDDY HOLLY & THE CRICKETS 1969
GIANT WOODENTOPS 1986
GIANT STEPS BOO RADLEYS 1993
THE GIFT JAM 1982
THE GIFT MIDGE URE 1985
GIFT SISTERHOOD 1986
A GIFT FROM A FLOWER TO A GARDEN DONOVAN 1968
THE GIFT OF GAME CRAZY TOWN 2001
A GIFT OF LOVE BILL TARMEY 1993
THE GIFT OF SONG VARIOUS ARTISTS (POLYGRAM) 1993
GIFT SET BARRY MANILOW 1981
GIGI (OST) FILM SOUNDTRACK 1959
GILBERT O'SULLIVAN HIMSELF GILBERT O'SULLIVAN 1971
A GILDED ETERNITY LOOP 1990
GIMME BACK MY BULLETS LYNYRD SKYNYRD 1976
GIMME SHELTER ROLLING STONES 1971
GINGER SPEEDY J 1993
GINGER BAKER'S AIR FORCE GINGER BAKER'S AIR FORCE 1970
GINUWINE... THE BACHELOR GINUWINE 1998
GIPSY KINGS GIPSY KINGS 1989
GIRL DANNII MINOGUE 1997
GIRL AT HER VOLCANO RICKIE LEE JONES 1983
A GIRL CALLED DUSTY DUSTY SPRINGFIELD 1964
GIRL HAPPY (OST) ELVIS PRESLEY 1965
THE GIRL IN THE OTHER ROOM DIANA KRALL 2004
A GIRL LIKE ME EMMA BUNTON 2001
GIRL POWER VARIOUS ARTISTS (GLOBAL) 1997
GIRLS 2K VARIOUS ARTISTS (VIRGIN) 2000
GIRLS AND GUITARS VARIOUS ARTISTS (GLOBAL) 1995
GIRLS GIRLS GIRLS ELVIS COSTELLO 1989
GIRLS I HAVE KNOWN JIM REEVES 1971

GIRLS JUST WANNA HAVE FUN NOLANS 1984
GIRLS! GIRLS! GIRLS! (OST) ELVIS PRESLEY 1963
GIRLS, GIRLS, GIRLS MOTLEY CRUE 1987
GIRLS SAY VARIOUS ARTISTS (UNIVERSAL) 2002
GIVE 'EM ENOUGH ROPE CLASH 1978
GIVE ME CONVENIENCE DEAD KENNEDYS 1987
GIVE ME THE NIGHT GEORGE BENSON 1980
GIVE ME THE REASON LUTHER VANDROSS 1986
GIVE ME YOUR HEART TONIGHT SHAKIN' STEVENS 1982
GIVE MY REGARDS TO BROAD STREET (OST) PAUL
     McCARTNEY 1984
GIVE OUT, BUT DON'T GIVE UP PRIMAL SCREAM 1994
GIVING THE GAME AWAY THUNDER 1999
GIVING YOU THE BEST THAT I GOT ANITA BAKER 1988
GLAD ALL OVER AGAIN DAVE CLARK FIVE 1993
GLADIATOR HANS ZIMMER & LISA GERRARD 2000
GLADIATORS TELEVISION SOUNDTRACK 1992
GLADSOME, HUMOUR AND BLUE MARTIN STEPHENSON &
     THE DAINTEES 1988
GLAM MANIA VARIOUS ARTISTS (QUALITY PRICE MUSIC)
     1993
GLAM SLAM VARIOUS ARTISTS (K-TEL) 1989
GLAMOROUS ONE VARIOUS ARTISTS (MISS
     MONEYPENNY'S) 1997
GLASGOW NIGHT OUT GLEN DALY 1971
GLASGOW WALKER JOHN MARTYN 2000
GLASS HOUSES BILLY JOEL 1980
THE GLEN CAMPBELL ALBUM GLEN CAMPBELL 1970
GLEN CAMPBELL LIVE GLEN CAMPBELL 1970
GLEN CAMPBELL'S GREATEST HITS GLEN CAMPBELL 1971
GLENN JONES GLENN JONES 1987
GLENN MILLER PLAYS SELECTIONS FROM 'THE GLENN
     MILLER STORY' AND OTHER HITS (OST) GLENN
     MILLER & HIS ORCHESTRA 1961
GLENN MILLER STORY (OST) FILM SOUNDTRACK 1961
GLITTER GARY GLITTER 1972
GLITTER MARIAH CAREY 2001
GLITTERING PRIZE 81/92 SIMPLE MINDS 1992
GLOBAL A GO GO JOE STRUMMER & THE MESCALEROS
     2001
GLOBALTEKNO ULTRA-SONIC 1995
THE GLOBE BIG AUDIO DYNAMITE II 1991
THE GLOBE SESSIONS SHERYL CROW 1998
GLORIA! – GLORIA ESTEFAN 1998
GLORIOUS FOOL JOHN MARTYN 1981
GLORY BOYS SECRET AFFAIR 1979
THE GLORY OF GERSHWIN LARRY ADLER 1994
GLORY ROAD GILLAN 1980
GLOW REEF 1997
GO 2 XTC 1978
GO AHEAD LINX 1981
GO FOR IT STIFF LITTLE FINGERS 1981
GO FOR YOUR GUNS ISLEY BROTHERS 1977
GO POP! AGAIN SMURFS 1997
GO WEST VILLAGE PEOPLE 1979
GO WEST/BANGS AND CRASHES GO WEST 1985
GO WITH THE FLOW – ESSENTIAL ACID JAZZ VARIOUS
     ARTISTS (POLYGRAM) 1996
GO YOUR OWN WAY GARETH GATES 2003
GOAT'S HEAD SOUP ROLLING STONES 1973
GOD BE WITH YOU JIM REEVES 1964
GOD FODDER NED'S ATOMIC DUSTBIN 1991
GOD HATES US ALL SLAYER 2001
GOD SHUFFLED HIS FEET CRASH TEST DUMMIES 1994
GODDESS IN THE DOORWAY MICK JAGGER 2001
THE GODFATHER – THE VERY BEST OF JAMES BROWN 2002
THE GODFATHER PART III (OST) FILM SOUNDTRACK 1991
GOD'S GREAT BANANA SKIN CHRIS REA 1992
GOD'S HOME MOVIE HORSE 1993
GOD'S KITCHEN VARIOUS ARTISTS (UNIVERSAL) 2002
GOD'S OWN MEDICINE MISSION 1986
GOD'S SON NAS 2003
GODSKITCHEN DIRECT VARIOUS ARTISTS (GODSKITCHEN)
     2003
GODSKITCHEN JOURNEYS VARIOUS ARTISTS (INCREDIBLE)
     2002

GODSKITCHEN – LIFE VARIOUS ARTISTS (INCREDIBLE)
     2002
GODSKITCHEN – SUMMER TRANCE VARIOUS ARTISTS
     (INCREDIBLE) 2002
GODSKITCHEN – WORLDWIDE VARIOUS ARTISTS
     (GODSKITCHEN) 2003
GODSPELL ORIGINAL LONDON STAGE CAST SOUNDTRACK
     1972
GODZILLA – THE ALBUM (OST) FILM SOUNDTRACK 1998
GOIN' BACK – THE VERY BEST OF DUSTY SPRINGFIELD
     1962–1994 DUSTY SPRINGFIELD 1994
GOIN' PLACES JACKSONS 1977
GOING BLANK AGAIN RIDE 1992
GOING FOR GOLD – THE GREATEST HITS SHED SEVEN 1999
GOING FOR THE ONE YES 1977
GOING PLACES HERB ALPERT & THE TIJUANA BRASS 1966
GOING STEADY (OST) FILM SOUNDTRACK 1980
GOING UNDERGROUND VARIOUS ARTISTS (CASTLE
     COMMUNICATIONS) 1993
GOLD NEIL DIAMOND 1971
GOLD THREE DEGREES 1980
GOLD BARBARA DICKSON 1985
GOLD RYAN ADAMS 2001
GOLD ELLA FITZGERALD 2003
GOLD NINA SIMONE 2003
GOLD – 18 EPIC SPORTING ANTHEMS VARIOUS ARTISTS
     (TELSTAR) 1992
GOLD – THE BEST OF SPANDAU BALLET 2000
GOLD – GREATEST HITS ABBA 1992
GOLD – GREATEST HITS CARPENTERS 2000
GOLD – GREATEST HITS PERRY COMO 2001
GOLD – THE GREATEST HITS STEPS 2001
GOLD – THE HITS COLLECTION DOLLY PARTON 2001
GOLD AGAINST THE SOUL MANIC STREET PREACHERS 1993
GOLD AND IVORY DAVID ESSEX 1977
GOLD AND PLATINUM LYNYRD SKYNYRD 1980
THE GOLD EXPERIENCE PRINCE 1995
GOLD MOTHER JAMES 1990
GOLD ON SILVER BEVERLEY-PHILLIPS ORCHESTRA 1976
GOLD PLATED CLIMAX BLUES BAND 1976
GOLDEN AGE OF DONEGAN LONNIE DONEGAN 1962
GOLDEN AGE OF DONEGAN VOLUME 2 LONNIE DONEGAN
     1963
THE GOLDEN AGE OF GROTESQUE MARILYN MANSON 2003
THE GOLDEN AGE OF HOLLYWOOD COMEDY LAUREL &
     HARDY 1975
THE GOLDEN AGE OF WIRELESS THOMAS DOLBY 1982
GOLDEN ALL TIME HITS BACHELORS 1967
GOLDEN COLLECTION CHARLEY PRIDE 1980
GOLDEN DAYS ROY ORBISON 1981
GOLDEN DAYS FUREYS & DAVEY ARTHUR 1984
GOLDEN DELICIOUS WURZELS 1977
GOLDEN FIDDLE AWARDS 1976 VARIOUS ARTISTS
     (MOUNTAIN) 1976
GOLDEN GREATS IAN BROWN 1999
GOLDEN HEART MARK KNOPFLER 1996
GOLDEN HITS DUSTY SPRINGFIELD 1966
GOLDEN HITS DRIFTERS 1968
GOLDEN HITS STEELY DAN 1982
GOLDEN HITS OF SHIRLEY BASSEY SHIRLEY BASSEY 1968
GOLDEN HOUR OF THE KINKS KINKS 1971
GOLDEN MEMORIES JAMES LAST 1974
GOLDEN MEMORIES NATIONAL BRASS BAND 1980
GOLDEN MEMORIES HARRY SECOMBE & MOIRA
     ANDERSON 1981
THE GOLDEN MILE MY LIFE STORY 1997
GOLDEN RIBBONS DAWN 1974
THE GOLDEN SECTION JOHN FOXX 1983
GOLDEN STATE BUSH 2001
GOLDEN TREASURY OF BILK MR ACKER BILK 1961
THE GOLDEN YEARS GRACIE FIELDS 1975
GOLDEN YEARS DAVID BOWIE 1983
THE GOLDEN YEARS OF THE EVERLY BROTHERS – THEIR 24
     GREATEST HITS EVERLY BROTHERS 1993
GOLDIE – INCREDIBLE SOUND OF DRUM 'N' BASS VARIOUS
     ARTISTS (INCREDIBLE) 1999

GONE AGAIN PATTI SMITH 1996
GONE TO EARTH BARCLAY JAMES HARVEST 1977
GONE TO EARTH DAVID SYLVAN 1986
GONNA BALL STRAY CATS 1981
GONNA GET YOU FREEEZ 1983
GONNA MAKE YOU SWEAT C&C MUSIC FACTORY 1991
GOO' – SONIC YOUTH 1990
GOOD AS I BEEN TO YOU BOB DYLAN 1992
THE GOOD THE BAD THE UGLY FRANKEE 2004
THE GOOD BOOK MELANIE 1971
GOOD DEEDS AND DIRTY RAGS GOODBYE MR. MACKENZIE
     1989
GOOD FEELING TRAVIS 1997
GOOD GOD'S URGE PORNO FOR PYROS 1996
GOOD HUMOUR SAINT ETIENNE 1998
GOOD MORNING AMERICA VARIOUS ARTISTS (K-TEL) 1980
GOOD MORNING SPIDER SPARKLEHORSE 1998
GOOD MORNING VIETNAM (OST) FILM SOUNDTRACK
     1988
GOOD MOURNING ALKALINE TRIO 2003
GOOD 'N' COUNTRY JIM REEVES 1964
GOOD 'N' READY SYBIL 1993
GOOD NEWS CLIFF RICHARD 1967
GOOD NEWS FROM THE NEXT WORLD SIMPLE MINDS 1995
THE GOOD SON NICK CAVE & THE BAD SEEDS 1990
GOOD STUFF B-52'S 1992
THE GOOD THE BAD AND THE LIVE: THE 6 1/2 YEARS
     ANNIVERSARY COLLECTION METALLICA 1990
GOOD TIMES ELVIS PRESLEY 1974
GOOD TIMES ADAM RICKITT 1999
GOOD TO BE BACK NATALIE COLE 1989
GOOD TO GO TERRORVISION 2001
GOOD TO GO LOVER GWEN GUTHRIE 1986
GOOD TROUBLE REO SPEEDWAGON 1982
THE GOOD WILL OUT EMBRACE 1998
GOOD, BAD BUT BEAUTIFUL SHIRLEY BASSEY 1975
THE GOOD, THE BAD AND THE 4 SKINS 4-SKINS 1982
THE GOOD, THE BAD AND THE UGLY (OST) ENNIO
     MORRICONE 1968
GOOD VIBES VARIOUS ARTISTS (VIRGIN) 2003
GOODBYE CREAM 1969
GOODBYE DUBSTAR 1997
GOODBYE COUNTRY (HELLO NIGHTCLUB) GROOVE
     ARMADA 2001
GOODBYE CRUEL WORLD ELVIS COSTELLO & THE
     ATTRACTIONS 1984
GOODBYE GIRL DAVID GATES 1978
GOODBYE JUMBO WORLD PARTY 1990
GOODBYE YELLOW BRICK ROAD ELTON JOHN 1973
GOODBYE YELLOW BRICK ROAD ELTON JOHN 2001
GOODNIGHT L.A. MAGNUM 1990
GOODNIGHT VIENNA RINGO STARR 1974
GOOFY GREATS VARIOUS ARTISTS (K-TEL) 1975
GOOSEFAIR CHINA DRUM 1996
GORECKI: SYMPHONY NO. 3 DAWN UPSHAW
     (SOPRANO)/THE LONDON SINFONIETTA/DAVID
     ZINMAN (CONDUCTOR) 1993
GORGEOUS 808 STATE 1993
GORGEOUS VARIOUS ARTISTS (VIRGIN) 1997
GORGEOUS GEORGE EDWYN COLLINS 1995
GORILLAZ GORILLAZ 2001
GORKY 5 GORKY'S ZYGOTIC MYNCI 1998
GOSH IT'S BAD MANNERS BAD MANNERS 1981
THE GOSPELS RICK WAKEMAN 1987
GOT MY MOJO WORKING JIMMY SMITH 1966
GOT TO BE THERE MICHAEL JACKSON 1972
GOTTA GET THRU THIS DANIEL BEDINGFIELD 2002
GOTTA TELL YOU SAMANTHA MUMBA 2000
GOYA... A LIFE IN A SONG PLACIDO DOMINGO 1989
GRACE JEFF BUCKLEY 1994
GRACE AND DANGER JOHN MARTYN 1980
GRACE UNDER PRESSURE RUSH 1984
GRACELAND PAUL SIMON 1986
THE GRADUATE (OST) SIMON & GARFUNKEL 1968
GRAFFITI BRIDGE PRINCE 1990
GRAFFITI TONGUE CHRISTY MOORE 1996

**GRAHAM NASH AND DAVID CROSBY** GRAHAM NASH & DAVID CROSBY 1972
**GRAINS OF SAND** MISSION 1990
**GRAN TURISMO** CARDIGANS 1998
**GRAND CANYON SUITE** 101 STRINGS 1960
**GRAND CHAMP** DMX 2003
**A GRAND DON'T COME FOR FREE** STREETS 2004
**GRAND PRIX** TEENAGE FANCLUB 1995
**GRAPES OF WRATH** SPEAR OF DESTINY 1983
**GRASSHOPPER** J.J. CALE 1982
**GRATEFUL DEAD FROM THE MARS HOTEL** GRATEFUL DEAD 1974
**GRAVE DANCERS UNION** SOUL ASYLUM 1993
**GRAVE NEW WORLD** STRAWBS 1972
**A GRAVEYARD OF EMPTY BOTTLES** DOGS D'AMOUR 1989
**GRAVITY** JAMES BROWN 1986
**GREASE** ORIGINAL LONDON STAGE CAST SOUNDTRACK 1993
**GREASE (OST)** FILM SOUNDTRACK 1978
**GREASEMANIA** VARIOUS ARTISTS (S) 2003
**THE GREAT BALLOON RACE** SKY 1985
**THE GREAT CARUSO** MARIO LANZA 1960
**THE GREAT COUNTRY MUSIC SHOW** VARIOUS ARTISTS (RONCO) 1982
**THE GREAT DEPRESSION** DMX 2001
**THE GREAT EASTERN** DELGADOS 2000
**THE GREAT ESCAPE** BLUR 1995
**GREAT EXPECTATIONS** TASMIN ARCHER 1992
**GREAT HITS** T. REX 1973
**GREAT ITALIAN LOVE SONGS** VARIOUS ARTISTS (K-TEL) 1976
**GREAT MOTION PICTURE THEMES** VARIOUS ARTISTS (HMV) 1962
**THE GREAT OTIS REDDING SINGS SOUL BALLADS** OTIS REDDING 1966
**THE GREAT PERFORMANCES** ELVIS PRESLEY 1990
**THE GREAT RADIO CONTROVERSY** TESLA 1989
**THE GREAT ROCK 'N' ROLL SWINDLE (OST)** SEX PISTOLS 1979
**GREAT SEX** VARIOUS ARTISTS (GLOBAL) 1995
**GREAT SONGS FROM GREAT BRITAIN** FRANK SINATRA 1962
**GREAT SONGS FROM MY FAIR LADY** ANDY WILLIAMS 1966
**THE GREAT SOUTHERN TRENDKILL** PANTERA 1996
**GREAT WALTZES** ROBERTO MANN 1967
**THE GREAT WAR OF WORDS** BRIAN KENNEDY 1990
**GREATEST** DURAN DURAN 1998
**THE GREATEST 80'S SOUL WEEKENDER** VARIOUS ARTISTS (WARNER BROTHERS) 2001
**THE GREATEST 90S DANCE HITS** VARIOUS ARTISTS (TELSTAR) 1996
**THE GREATEST CLASSICAL MOVIE ALBUM** VARIOUS ARTISTS (TELSTAR) 1997
**THE GREATEST CLASSICAL STARS ON EARTH** VARIOUS ARTISTS (DECCA) 1998
**THE GREATEST DANCE ALBUM EVER MADE** VARIOUS ARTISTS (TELSTAR) 1997
**THE GREATEST DANCE ALBUM IN THE WORLD!** – VARIOUS ARTISTS (VIRGIN) 1992
**THE GREATEST DANCE ALBUM OF ALL TIME** VARIOUS ARTISTS (DINO) 1995
**THE GREATEST DANCE ALBUM UNDER THE SUN!** – VARIOUS ARTISTS (EMI) 1996
**THE GREATEST EVER JUNIOR PARTY MEGAMIX** HOUND DOG & THE MEGAMIXERS 1990
**THE GREATEST EVER ROCK 'N' ROLL MIX** VARIOUS ARTISTS (STYLUS) 1988
**GREATEST HITS** RAY CHARLES 1963
**GREATEST HITS** FRANK IFIELD 1964
**GREATEST HITS** BOB DYLAN 1967
**GREATEST HITS** MARVIN GAYE 1968
**GREATEST HITS** FRANK SINATRA 1968
**GREATEST HITS** MARVIN GAYE & TAMMI TERRELL 1970
**GREATEST HITS** BEACH BOYS 1970
**GREATEST HITS** HERB ALPERT & THE TIJUANA BRASS 1970
**GREATEST HITS** JACKSON FIVE 1972

**GREATEST HITS** DIANA ROSS 1972
**GREATEST HITS** FLEETWOOD MAC 1972
**GREATEST HITS** SIMON & GARFUNKEL 1972
**GREATEST HITS** JIMMY RUFFIN 1974
**GREATEST HITS** TOM JONES 1974
**GREATEST HITS** SANTANA 1974
**GREATEST HITS** NAZARETH 1975
**GREATEST HITS** CAT STEVENS 1975
**GREATEST HITS** BARRY WHITE 1975
**GREATEST HITS** HOT CHOCOLATE 1976
**GREATEST HITS** GILBERT O'SULLIVAN 1976
**GREATEST HITS** FOUR SEASONS 1976
**GREATEST HITS** ABBA 1976
**GREATEST HITS** GLITTER BAND 1976
**GREATEST HITS** LINDA RONSTADT 1976
**GREATEST HITS** SHOWADDYWADDY 1976
**GREATEST HITS** SMOKIE 1977
**GREATEST HITS** ROXY MUSIC 1977
**GREATEST HITS** HERMAN'S HERMITS 1977
**GREATEST HITS** COMMODORES 1978
**GREATEST HITS** DONNA SUMMER 1978
**GREATEST HITS** OLIVIA NEWTON-JOHN 1978
**GREATEST HITS** STEELY DAN 1978
**GREATEST HITS** CREEDENCE CLEARWATER REVIVAL 1979
**GREATEST HITS** KC & THE SUNSHINE BAND 1980
**GREATEST HITS** SHALAMAR 1982
**GREATEST HITS** OLIVIA NEWTON-JOHN 1982
**GREATEST HITS** MARVIN GAYE 1983
**GREATEST HITS** BUCKS FIZZ 1983
**GREATEST HITS** DOLLY PARTON 1985
**THE GREATEST HITS** BONNIE TYLER 1986
**THE GREATEST HITS** SHALAMAR 1986
**THE GREATEST HITS** TOM JONES 1987
**THE GREATEST HITS** ODYSSEY 1987
**GREATEST HITS** FLEETWOOD MAC 1988
**GREATEST HITS** HUMAN LEAGUE 1988
**GREATEST HITS** ISLEY BROTHERS 1988
**GREATEST HITS** LEONARD COHEN 1988
**GREATEST HITS** BILL WITHERS 1988
**GREATEST HITS** FIVE STAR 1989
**THE GREATEST HITS** ELECTRIC LIGHT ORCHESTRA 1989
**GREATEST HITS** BILLY OCEAN 1989
**GREATEST HITS** MOODY BLUES 1990
**GREATEST HITS** BANGLES 1990
**GREATEST HITS** EURYTHMICS 1991
**GREATEST HITS** JASON DONOVAN 1991
**GREATEST HITS** JAM 1991
**THE GREATEST HITS** SALT-N-PEPA 1991
**GREATEST HITS** ZZ TOP 1992
**THE GREATEST HITS** SMOKEY ROBINSON & THE MIRACLES 1992
**GREATEST HITS** GLORIA ESTEFAN 1992
**GREATEST HITS** POLICE 1992
**GREATEST HITS** SQUEEZE 1992
**GREATEST HITS** SHEEP ON DRUGS 1993
**GREATEST HITS** DORIS DAY 1993
**THE GREATEST HITS** BONEY M 1993
**GREATEST HITS** TOM PETTY & HEARTBREAKERS 1993
**THE GREATEST HITS** DOLLY PARTON 1994
**GREATEST HITS** TROGGS 1994
**GREATEST HITS** WHITESNAKE 1994
**GREATEST HITS** GIPSY KINGS 1994
**GREATEST HITS** BRUCE SPRINGSTEEN 1995
**GREATEST HITS** BOB SEGER & THE SILVER BULLET BAND 1995
**GREATEST HITS** ASWAD 1995
**GREATEST HITS** HUMAN LEAGUE 1995
**GREATEST HITS** TAKE THAT 1996
**GREATEST HITS** N.W.A. 1996
**GREATEST HITS** SIMPLY RED 1996
**GREATEST HITS** KISS 1997
**GREATEST HITS** ETERNAL 1997
**GREATEST HITS** KENNY G 1997
**GREATEST HITS** FOSTER & ALLEN 1998
**GREATEST HITS** STEVE MILLER BAND 1998
**GREATEST HITS** DAVID ESSEX 1998

**GREATEST HITS** 2PAC 1998
**GREATEST HITS** DJ JAZZY JEFF & THE FRESH PRINCE 1998
**GREATEST HITS** ARETHA FRANKLIN 1998
**GREATEST HITS** BEACH BOYS 1998
**GREATEST HITS** SMURFS 1998
**GREATEST HITS** RICHARD MARX 1998
**THE GREATEST HITS** CHER 1999
**GREATEST HITS** DANIEL O'DONNELL 1999
**GREATEST HITS** HAPPY MONDAYS 1999
**GREATEST HITS** JOE COCKER 1999
**GREATEST HITS** PRETENDERS 2000
**GREATEST HITS** LENNY KRAVITZ 2000
**GREATEST HITS** STYLE COUNCIL 2000
**THE GREATEST HITS** TEXAS 2000
**THE GREATEST HITS** WHITNEY HOUSTON 2000
**THE GREATEST HITS** BONNIE TYLER 2001
**GREATEST HITS** FIVE 2001
**GREATEST HITS** CURE 2001
**THE GREATEST HITS** EDDY GRANT 2001
**GREATEST HITS** MARIAH CAREY 2001
**THE GREATEST HITS** BONEY M 2001
**GREATEST HITS** BIG COUNTRY & THE SKIDS 2002
**GREATEST HITS** RICK ASTLEY 2002
**GREATEST HITS** CATATONIA 2002
**GREATEST HITS** BLONDIE 2002
**GREATEST HITS** NIGEL KENNEDY 2002
**GREATEST HITS** BJORK 2002
**GREATEST HITS** LIGHTHOUSE FAMILY 2002
**GREATEST HITS** TOM JONES 2003
**GREATEST HITS** HOLLIES 2003
**GREATEST HITS** RUN D.M.C. 2003
**THE GREATEST HITS** LULU 2003
**GREATEST HITS** GUNS N' ROSES 2004
**GREATEST HITS** RED HOT CHILI PEPPERS 2003
**GREATEST HITS** THIN LIZZY 2004
**THE GREATEST HITS** ATOMIC KITTEN 2004
**GREATEST HITS – CHAPTER ONE** BACKSTREET BOYS 2001
**GREATEST HITS – FEEL THE NOIZE** SLADE 1997
**GREATEST HITS I, II & III** QUEEN 2000
**GREATEST HITS – VOLUMES I, II & III** BILLY JOEL 1998
**GREATEST HITS (1976–1978)** SHOWADDYWADDY 1978
**THE GREATEST HITS 1966–1992** NEIL DIAMOND 1992
**THE GREATEST HITS 1970–2002** ELTON JOHN 2002
**GREATEST HITS 1972–1978** 10 CC 1979
**GREATEST HITS 1977–1990** STRANGLERS 1990
**GREATEST HITS 1980–1994** ARETHA FRANKLIN 1994
**GREATEST HITS 1981–1995** LUTHER VANDROSS 1995
**GREATEST HITS 1985–1995** MICHAEL BOLTON 1995
**GREATEST HITS 87–92** KYLIE MINOGUE 2002
**GREATEST HITS 2** DIANA ROSS 1976
**THE GREATEST HITS AND A LITTLE MORE...** – 911 1999
**THE GREATEST HITS COLLECTION** BANANARAMA 1988
**GREATEST HITS I & II** QUEEN 1994
**GREATEST HITS I II & III** QUEEN 2000
**GREATEST HITS II** QUEEN 1991
**GREATEST HITS III** QUEEN 1999
**GREATEST HITS LIVE** CARLY SIMON 1988
**GREATEST HITS LIVE** DIANA ROSS 1989
**GREATEST HITS OF ALL** GEORGE BENSON 2003
**GREATEST HITS OF 10 CC** 10 CC 1975
**THE GREATEST HITS OF 1985** VARIOUS ARTISTS (TELSTAR) 1985
**THE GREATEST HITS OF 1986** VARIOUS ARTISTS (TELSTAR) 1986
**THE GREATEST HITS OF 1987** VARIOUS ARTISTS (TELSTAR) 1987
**THE GREATEST HITS OF 1988** VARIOUS ARTISTS (TELSTAR) 1988
**THE GREATEST HITS OF 1989** VARIOUS ARTISTS (TELSTAR) 1989
**THE GREATEST HITS OF 1990** VARIOUS ARTISTS (TELSTAR) 1990
**THE GREATEST HITS OF 1991** VARIOUS ARTISTS (TELSTAR) 1991
**THE GREATEST HITS OF 1992** VARIOUS ARTISTS (TELSTAR) 1992

THE GREATEST HITS OF 1993 VARIOUS ARTISTS (TELSTAR) 1993

THE GREATEST HITS OF 1994 VARIOUS ARTISTS (TELSTAR) 1994

THE GREATEST HITS OF 1995 VARIOUS ARTISTS (TELSTAR) 1995

THE GREATEST HITS OF 1996 – THE STORY OF THE YEAR VARIOUS ARTISTS (TELSTAR) 1996

THE GREATEST HITS OF 1997 VARIOUS ARTISTS (TELSTAR) 1997

THE GREATEST HITS OF 1998 VARIOUS ARTISTS (TELSTAR) 1998

THE GREATEST HITS OF 1999 – THE STORY SO FAR VARIOUS ARTISTS (TELSTAR) 1999

THE GREATEST HITS OF DANCE VARIOUS ARTISTS (TELSTAR) 1992

THE GREATEST HITS OF HOUSE VARIOUS ARTISTS (STYLUS) 1988

THE GREATEST HITS OF THE 90'S – PART 1 VARIOUS ARTISTS (TELSTAR) 1995

THE GREATEST HITS OF THE NINETIES VARIOUS ARTISTS (TELSTAR) 1999

THE GREATEST HITS OF THE STYLISTICS STYLISTICS 1992

GREATEST HITS OF WALT DISNEY VARIOUS ARTISTS (RONCO) 1975

GREATEST HITS VOLUME 1 JOHNNY CASH 1969

THE GREATEST HITS VOLUME 1 MARIO LANZA 1971

GREATEST HITS VOLUME 1 DON WILLIAMS 1976

GREATEST HITS VOLUME 1 COCKNEY REJECTS 1980

GREATEST HITS VOLUME 1 SISTERS OF MERCY 1993

GREATEST HITS VOLUME 1 – DIONNE WARWICK 1970

GREATEST HITS VOLUME 1 & VOLUME II BILLY JOEL 1985

GREATEST HITS VOLUME 2 RAY CHARLES 1968

GREATEST HITS VOLUME 2 DIONNE WARWICK 1970

GREATEST HITS VOLUME 2 TEMPTATIONS 1970

GREATEST HITS VOLUME 2 FRANK SINATRA 1970

GREATEST HITS VOLUME 2 STEVIE WONDER 1972

GREATEST HITS VOLUME 2 ANDY WILLIAMS 1972

GREATEST HITS VOLUME 2 ELTON JOHN 1977

GREATEST HITS VOLUME 2 ABBA 1979

GREATEST HITS VOLUME 2 COCKNEY REJECTS 1980

GREATEST HITS VOLUME 2 MADONNA 2001

GREATEST HITS VOLUME 2 GLORIA ESTEFAN 2001

GREATEST HITS VOLUME 3 BOB DYLAN 1988

GREATEST HITS VOLUME 3 (LIVE AND LOUD) COCKNEY REJECTS 1981

GREATEST HITS VOLUME III BILLY JOEL 1997

GREATEST HITS VOLUME IV JOHNNY MATHIS 1977

GREATEST HITS, ETC. PAUL SIMON 1977

THE GREATEST HITS, SO FAR PUBLIC IMAGE LTD 1990

GREATEST HITS/SHINING LIKE A NATIONAL GUITAR PAUL SIMON 2000

THE GREATEST LINE DANCING PARTY ALBUM WOOLPACKERS 1997

THE GREATEST LOVE VARIOUS ARTISTS (TELSTAR) 1987

THE GREATEST LOVE VARIOUS ARTISTS (TELSTAR) 1999

THE GREATEST LOVE 2 VARIOUS ARTISTS (TELSTAR) 1988

THE GREATEST LOVE 3 VARIOUS ARTISTS (TELSTAR) 1989

THE GREATEST LOVE 4 VARIOUS ARTISTS (TELSTAR) 1990

THE GREATEST LOVE 6 – WITH LOVE FROM THE STARS VARIOUS ARTISTS (TELSTAR) 1993

GREATEST LOVE CLASSICS ANDY WILLIAMS 1984

THE GREATEST LOVE EVER VARIOUS ARTISTS (TELSTAR) 1995

GREATEST LOVE SONGS PLACIDO DOMINGO 1988

GREATEST MESSAGES GRANDMASTER FLASH & THE FURIOUS FIVE 1984

GREATEST MISSES PUBLIC ENEMY 1992

GREATEST MOMENTS CULTURE CLUB 1998

THE GREATEST MOMENTS IN SOUL VARIOUS ARTISTS (DOVER) 1992

THE GREATEST NO 1 SINGLES VARIOUS ARTISTS (EMI) 2001

GREATEST NON STOP PARTY UNDER THE SUN VARIOUS ARTISTS (EMI) 1996

THE GREATEST NUMBER ONES OF THE EIGHTIES VARIOUS ARTISTS (PURE MUSIC) 1994

THE GREATEST OF ALL TIME LL COOL J 2000

THE GREATEST PARTY ALBUM UNDER THE SUN! – VARIOUS ARTISTS (EMI) 1995

GREATEST REMIXES VOLUME I C&C MUSIC FACTORY 1992

THE GREATEST ROCK 'N' ROLL LOVE SONGS VARIOUS ARTISTS (GLOBAL) 1999

THE GREATEST SONGS OF THE BEATLES JAMES LAST 1983

THE GREATEST SOUL ALBUM OF ALL TIME VARIOUS ARTISTS (DINO) 1995

THE GREATEST STORY EVER TOLD BALAAM & THE ANGEL 1986

THE GREATEST VOICES VARIOUS ARTISTS (DINO) 1992

GREEN R.E.M. 1988

THE GREEN ALBUM WEEZER 2001

GREEN GREEN GRASS OF HOME TOM JONES 1967

GREEN LIGHT CLIFF RICHARD 1978

GREEN MAN MARK OWEN 1996

GREEN MIND DINOSAUR JR 1991

GREEN ONIONS BOOKER T & THE M.G.S 1964

GREEN RIVER CREEDENCE CLEARWATER REVIVAL 1970

GREEN VELVET VARIOUS ARTISTS (RONCO) 1983

GREEN VELVET VARIOUS ARTISTS (TELSTAR) 1984

GREEN VIRGIN STEVE HILLAGE 1978

GREENDALE NEIL YOUNG & CRAZY HORSE 2003

GREETINGS FROM ASBURY PARK BRUCE SPRINGSTEEN 1985

GREETINGS FROM TIMBUK 3 TIMBUK 3 1987

GREG LAKE GREG LAKE 1981

GREGORIAN MOODS DOWNSIDE ABBEY MONKS & CHOIRBOYS 1998

GREIG AND SCHUMANN PIANO CONCERTOS STEPHEN BISHOP 1972

GRETCHEN GOES TO NEBRASKA KING'S X 1989

THE GRIMLEYS – ORIGINAL TV SOUNDTRACK TELEVISION SOUNDTRACK 2000

GRIN AND BEAR IT RUTS D.C. 1980

GROOVE ARMADA – BACK TO MINE VARIOUS ARTISTS (DMC) 2000

GROOVERIDER PRESENTS THE PROTOTYPE YEARS VARIOUS ARTISTS (HIGHER GROUND) 1997

GROOVIN BILL WYMAN'S RHYTHM KINGS 2000

GROOVIN' – VARIOUS ARTISTS (POLYGRAM) 1994

GROOVUS MAXIMUS ELECTRIC BOYS 1992

GROOVY GHETTO VARIOUS ARTISTS (ARCADE) 1991

GROOVY GHETTO – ALL THE RAGE VARIOUS ARTISTS (ARCADE) 1991

GROOVY GHETTO 2 VARIOUS ARTISTS (ARCADE) 1992

GROW TOGETHER ZION TRAIN 1996

GROWING PAINS BILLIE MYERS 1998

GROWING UP IN PUBLIC JIMMY NAIL 1992

GRRR! IT'S BETTY BOO BETTY BOO 1992

GTR G.T.R. 1986

GUARANTEED LEVEL 42 1991

GUARDIAN ANGEL SHADOWS 1984

GUERRILLA SUPER FURRY ANIMALS 1999

GUILTY BARBRA STREISAND 1980

GUILTY BLUE 2003

GUITAR FRANK ZAPPA 1988

GUITAR MAN ELVIS PRESLEY 1981

GUITAR MOODS VARIOUS ARTISTS (DECADANCE) 2003

GUITAR PLAYER HANK MARVIN 2002

GUITARS MIKE OLDFIELD 1999

GUNFIGHTER BALLADS AND TRAIL SONGS MARTY ROBBINS 1960

THE GUNMAN AND OTHER STORIES PREFAB SPROUT 2001

GUNS IN THE GHETTO UB40 1997

GUN SHY SCREAMING BLUE MESSIAHS 1986

GUTTERFLOWER GOO GOO DOLLS 2002

GUYS 'N' DOLLS GUYS 'N' DOLLS 1975

GYPSY CAMPFIRES 101 STRINGS 1959

H.I.T.S. NEW KIDS ON THE BLOCK 1991

H.M.S. FABLE SHACK 1999

H.Q. ROY HARPER 1975

H2O DARYL HALL & JOHN OATES 1982

HA TALVIN SINGH 2001

HA' – KILLING JOKE LIVE KILLING JOKE 1982

THE HACIENDA – PLAY BY 01/96 VARIOUS ARTISTS (A&M) 1995

HADDAWAY – THE ALBUM HADDAWAY 1993

HAIL TO ENGLAND MANOWAR 1984

HAIL TO THE THIEF RADIOHEAD 2003

HAIR ORIGINAL BROADWAY STAGE CAST SOUNDTRACK 1969

HAIR ORIGINAL LONDON STAGE CAST SOUNDTRACK 1968

HAIRBRUSH DIVAS VARIOUS ARTISTS (WARNER BROTHERS) 2003

HAIRBRUSH DIVAS 2 VARIOUS ARTISTS (WARNER BROTHERS) 2004

HALF A SIXPENCE ORIGINAL LONDON STAGE CAST SOUNDTRACK 1963

HALFWAY BETWEEN THE GUTTER AND THE STARS FATBOY SLIM 2000

HALFWAY TO PARADISE BILLY FURY 1961

HALFWAY TO SANITY RAMONES 1987

HALL AND OATES DARYL HALL & JOHN OATES 1976

HALL AND OATES LIVE AT THE APOLLO WITH DAVID RUFFIN AND EDDIE KENDRICK DARYL HALL & JOHN OATES 1985

HALL OF FAME GEORGIE FAME 1967

HALL OF FAME VARIOUS ARTISTS (CLASSIC FM) 1996

HALL OF FAME – THE GREAT COMPOSERS VARIOUS ARTISTS (CLASSIC FM) 2004

HALL OF FAME 2000 VARIOUS ARTISTS (CLASSIC FM) 2000

HALL OF THE MOUNTAIN GRILL HAWKWIND 1974

HALOS AND HORNS DOLLY PARTON 2002

HAMBURGER CONCERTO FOCUS 1974

HAMILTON'S HOT SHOTS VARIOUS ARTISTS (WARWICK) 1976

HAMMER AND TONGS GOODBYE MR. MACKENZIE 1991

HAMMOND A GO GO JAMES LAST 1967

HANCOCK TONY HANCOCK 1962

HAND CLAPPIN' – FOOT STOMPIN' – FUNKY BUTT – LIVE! – GENO WASHINGTON 1966

HANDCREAM FOR A GENERATION CORNERSHOP 2002

HAND CUT BUCKS FIZZ 1983

HAND ON THE TORCH/JAZZ MIXES US3 1993

HANDCREAM FOR A GENERATION CORNERSHOP 2002

HANDLE WITH CARE NUCLEAR ASSAULT 1989

HANDS ON THOUSAND YARD STARE 1992

HANDS TO HEAVEN VARIOUS ARTISTS (WARNER BROTHERS) 2002

HANDSWORTH REVOLUTION STEEL PULSE 1978

HANG ON IN THERE BABY JOHNNY BRISTOL 1974

HANG ON RAMSEY RAMSEY LEWIS TRIO 1966

HANG TOGETHER ODYSSEY 1980

HANGIN' TOUGH NEW KIDS ON THE BLOCK 1989

THE HANGMAN'S BEAUTIFUL DAUGHTER INCREDIBLE STRING BAND 1968

HANK MARVIN HANK MARVIN 1969

HANK PLAYS CLIFF HANK MARVIN 1995

HANK PLAYS HOLLY HANK MARVIN 1996

HANKS PLAYS LIVE HANK MARVIN 1997

HANKY PANKY THE THE 1995

HANNIBAL (OST) HANS ZIMMER 2001

HANSIMANIA JAMES LAST 1981

HANX STIFF LITTLE FINGERS 1980

HAPPINESS BELOVED 1990

HAPPINESS? – ROGER TAYLOR 1994

HAPPINESS IN MAGAZINES GRAHAM COXON 2004

HAPPY AND GLORIOUS VARIOUS ARTISTS (DECCA) 2000

HAPPY ANNIVERSARY SLIM WHITMAN 1974

HAPPY BIRTHDAY ALTERED IMAGES 1981

HAPPY DAYS VARIOUS ARTISTS (K-TEL) 1980

HAPPY DAYS – THE BEST OF ROBSON AND JEROME ROBSON & JEROME 1997

HAPPY DAZE VOLUME 2 VARIOUS ARTISTS (ISLAND) 1991

HAPPY DAZE... VOLUME 1 VARIOUS ARTISTS (ISLAND) 1990

HAPPY FAMILIES BLANCMANGE 1982

HAPPY HEAD MIGHTY LEMON DROPS 1986

HAPPY HEART ANDY WILLIAMS 1969

HAPPY HOUR TED HAWKINS 1987
HAPPY IN HELL CHRISTIANS 1992
HAPPY MONDAYS – LIVE HAPPY MONDAYS 1991
HAPPY NATION ACE OF BASE 1993
HAPPY SONGS FOR HAPPY PEOPLE MOGWAI 2003
HAPPY TO BE DEMIS ROUSSOS 1976
HAPPY TOGETHER TURTLES 1967
HAPPY TOGETHER ODYSSEY 1982
HAPPY? – PUBLIC IMAGE LTD 1987
HARBOR LIGHTS BRUCE HORNBY & THE RANGE 1993
HARBOUR JACK JONES 1974
HARD AT PLAY HUEY LEWIS & THE NEWS 1991
HARD CANDY COUNTING CROWS 2002
HARD DANCE ANTHEMS VARIOUS ARTISTS (WARNER
    BROTHERS) 2001
A HARD DAY'S NIGHT BEATLES 1964
HARD ENERGY VARIOUS ARTISTS (MINISTRY OF SOUND)
    2001
HARD FAX VARIOUS ARTISTS (COLUMBIA) 1992
HARD FAX 2 – TWICE THE VICE! – VARIOUS ARTISTS
    (COLUMBIA) 1992
HARD HOUSE EUPHORIA VARIOUS ARTISTS (TELSTAR) 2000
HARD HOUSE EUPHORIA – TIDY BOYS VS LISA VARIOUS
    ARTISTS (TELSTAR) 2001
HARD HOUSE NATION VARIOUS ARTISTS (WARNER
    BROTHERS) 2000
HARD HOUSE NATION – 2 VARIOUS ARTISTS (WARNER
    BROTHERS) 2000
HARD HOUSE VOL.3 VARIOUS ARTISTS (WARNER
    BROTHERS) 2001
HARD NOSE ON THE HIGHWAY VAN MORRISON 1973
HARD PROMISES TOM PETTY & HEARTBREAKERS 1981
HARD RAIN BOB DYLAN 1976
A HARD ROAD JOHN MAYALL & THE BLUESBREAKERS 1967
HARD TO EARN GANG STARR 1994
THE HARD WAY STEVE EARLE & THE DUKES 1990
HARDCORE DANCEFLOOR VARIOUS ARTISTS (DINO) 1991
HARDCORE DJS... TAKE CONTROL VARIOUS ARTISTS
    (PERFECTO) 1992
HARDCORE ECSTASY VARIOUS ARTISTS (DINO) 1991
HARDCORE EXPLOSION '97 VARIOUS ARTISTS (SUPREME
    UNDERGROUND) 1997
HARDCORE HEAVEN – VOLUME 2 VARIOUS ARTISTS
    (HEAVEN MUSIC) 1997
HARDCORE HEAVEN – VOLUME 3 VARIOUS ARTISTS
    (HEAVEN MUSIC) 1998
HARDCORE HEAVEN – VOLUME 4 VARIOUS ARTISTS
    (HEAVEN MUSIC) 1998
HARDCORE HEAVEN – VOLUME 5 VARIOUS ARTISTS
    (HEAVEN MUSIC) 1999
HARDCORE HEAVEN – VOLUME ONE VARIOUS ARTISTS
    (HEAVEN MUSIC) 1997
HARDCORE UPROAR VARIOUS ARTISTS (DINO) 1991
HARDER... FASTER APRIL WINE 1980
HARDWARE KROKUS 1981
HARK THE HERALD ANGELS SING HAMBURG STUDENTS
    CHOIR 1960
HARLEM HOLIDAY (OST) ELVIS PRESLEY 1966
HARLEM WORLD MASE 1998
HARMACY SEBADOH 1996
HARMONY CORRUPTION NAPALM DEATH 1990
HARRY POTTER (OST) JOHN WILLIAMS 2001
HARRY'S BAR GORDON HASKELL 2002
HARVEST NEIL YOUNG 1972
HARVEST FOR THE WORLD ISLEY BROTHERS 1976
HARVEST MOON NEIL YOUNG 1992
HASTEN DOWN THE WIND LINDA RONSTADT 1976
HAT FULL OF STARS CYNDI LAUPER 1993
HAT TRICK AMERICA 1973
HATE DELGADOS 2002
HATFUL OF HOLLOW SMITHS 1984
HATS BLUE NILE 1989
HATS OFF TO LARRY DEL SHANNON 1963
HAUNTED DANCEHALL SABRES OF PARADISE 1994
THE HAUNTED SCIENCE OMNI TRIO 1996
HAUNTING MELODIES ELECTRIC WINDENSEMBLE 1984

HAVANA MOON CARLOS SANTANA 1983
HAVE A GOOD FOREVER... – COOL NOTES 1985
HAVE A LITTLE FAITH JOE COCKER 1994
HAVE A NICE DAY ROXETTE 1999
HAVE I TOLD YOU LATELY THAT I LOVE YOU JIM REEVES 1965
HAVE TWANGY GUITAR WILL TRAVEL DUANNE EDDY 1959
HAVE YOU EVER BEEN IN LOVE LEO SAYER 1983
HAVE YOU FED THE FISH BADLY DRAWN BOY 2002
HAVE YOU NEVER BEEN MELLOW OLIVIA NEWTON-JOHN
    1975
HAWAII HIGH LLAMAS 1996
HAWAIIAN PARADISE/CHRISTMAS WOUT STEENHUIS 1981
HAWKS AND DOVES NEIL YOUNG 1980
HAWKWIND HAWKWIND 1984
HE GOT GAME (OST) PUBLIC ENEMY 1998
HE TOUCHED ME ELVIS PRESLEY 1972
HE WALKS BESIDE ME ELVIS PRESLEY 1978
HE WAS BEAUTIFUL IRIS WILLIAMS 1979
HEAD FIRST URIAH HEEP 1983
HEAD LIKE A ROCK IAN MCNABB 1994
HEAD MUSIC SUEDE 1999
HEAD ON SAMSON 1980
THE HEAD ON THE DOOR CURE 1985
HEAD OVER HEELS COCTEAU TWINS 1983
HEAD OVER HEELS PAULA ABDUL 1995
HEAD OVER HEELS TELEVISION SOUNDTRACK 1993
HEADED FOR THE FUTURE NEIL DIAMOND 1986
HEADHUNTER KROKUS 1983
THE HEADLESS CHILDREN W.A.S.P. 1989
HEADLESS CROSS BLACK SABBATH 1989
HEADLINE HITS VARIOUS ARTISTS (K-TEL) 1983
HEADLINERS – TALL PAUL VARIOUS ARTISTS (MINISTRY OF
    SOUND) 2000
HEADLINES MIDNIGHT STAR 1986
HEADLINES AND DEADLINES – THE HITS OF A HA A-HA
    1991
HEADQUARTERS MONKEES 1967
HEADRUSH VARIOUS ARTISTS (GLOBAL) 2000
HEADSTONE – THE BEST OF UFO UFO 1983
THE HEALER JOHN LEE HOOKER 1989
THE HEALING GAME VAN MORRISON 1997
HEAR IN THE NOW FRONTIER QUEENSRYCHE 1997
HEAR MY CRY SONIQUE 2000
HEAR MY SONG (THE BEST OF JOSEF LOCKE) JOSEF LOCKE
    1992
HEAR 'N' AID VARIOUS ARTISTS (VERTIGO) 1986
HEAR NOTHING, SEE NOTHING, SAY NOTHING DISCHARGE
    1982
HEARSAY/ALL MIXED UP ALEXANDER O'NEAL 1987
HEART HEART 1985
HEART & SOUL VARIOUS ARTISTS (POLYGRAM) 1997
HEART & SOUL – NEW SONGS FROM ALLY MCBEAL (OST
    TV) VONDA SHEPARD 1999
HEART AND SOUL BARRY WHITE 1985
HEART AND SOUL EDITH PIAF 1987
HEART AND SOUL VARIOUS ARTISTS (HEART & SOUL) 1989
HEART AND SOUL JOY DIVISION 1998
HEART AND SOUL – THE VERY BEST OF T'PAU T'PAU 1993
HEART AND SOUL III – HEART FULL OF SOUL VARIOUS
    ARTISTS (HEART & SOUL) 1990
THE HEART AND SOUL OF ROCK AND ROLL VARIOUS
    ARTISTS (TELSTAR) 1988
HEART FULL OF SOUL VARIOUS ARTISTS (DINO) 1993
HEART FULL OF SOUL VARIOUS ARTISTS (GLOBAL) 1998
HEART FULL OF SOUL – 2 VARIOUS ARTISTS (GLOBAL) 1999
HEART IN MOTION AMY GRANT 1991
HEART LIKE A SKY SPANDAU BALLET 1989
HEART 'N' SOUL TINA CHARLES 1977
THE HEART OF A WOMAN JOHNNY MATHIS 1975
THE HEART OF CHICAGO CHICAGO 1989
THE HEART OF CHICAGO – 1967–1997 CHICAGO 1999
A HEART OF GOLD VARIOUS ARTISTS (TELSTAR) 1993
THE HEART OF ROCK AND ROLL – BEST OF HUEY LEWIS AND
    THE NEWS HUEY LEWIS & THE NEWS 1992
HEART OF SOUL VOLUME 1 VARIOUS ARTISTS
    (MASTERCUTS) 1987

HEART OF STONE CHER 1989
THE HEART OF THE 80S AND 90S VARIOUS ARTISTS
    (UNIVERSAL) 1998
HEART OVER MIND JENNIFER RUSH 1987
HEART STRINGS FOSTER & ALLEN 1992
HEART TO HEART – 20 HOT HITS RAY CHARLES 1980
HEART TO HEART – 24 LOVE SONG DUETS VARIOUS
    ARTISTS (K-TEL) 1986
HEART, SOUL AND VOICE JON SECADA 1994
HEARTBEAT HANK MARVIN 1993
HEARTBEAT – 10TH ANNIVERSARY ALBUM VARIOUS
    ARTISTS (BMG) 2000
HEARTBEAT – FOREVER YOURS VARIOUS ARTISTS
    (COLUMBIA) 1995
HEARTBEAT – LOVE ME TENDER VARIOUS ARTISTS
    (GLOBAL) 1997
HEARTBEAT LOVE SONGS VARIOUS ARTISTS (UNIVERSAL)
    2003
HEARTBEAT – NUMBER 1 LOVE SONGS OF THE '60S
    VARIOUS ARTISTS (GLOBAL) 1996
HEARTBEAT – THE 60'S GOLD COLLECTION VARIOUS
    ARTISTS (GLOBAL) 1998
HEARTBEAT (MUSIC FROM THE TV SERIES) VARIOUS
    ARTISTS (COLUMBIA) 1992
HEARTBEAT CITY CARS 1984
HEARTBEATS BARBARA DICKSON 1984
HEARTBREAK STATION CINDERELLA 1990
HEARTBREAKER FREE 1973
HEARTBREAKER DIONNE WARWICK 1982
HEARTBREAKER – THE VERY BEST OF DIONNE WARWICK
    2002
HEARTBREAKERS VARIOUS ARTISTS (K-TEL) 1977
HEARTBREAKERS MATT MONRO 1980
HEARTBREAKERS – 18 CLASSICAL LOVE HITS VARIOUS
    ARTISTS (STARBLEND) 1986
HEARTLANDS VARIOUS ARTISTS (DINO) 1992
HEARTLESS CREW PRESENTS CRISP BISCUIT VARIOUS
    ARTISTS (EAST WEST) 2002
HEARTLIGHT NEIL DIAMOND 1982
HEARTS AND BONES PAUL SIMON 1983
HEARTS AND FLOWERS JOAN ARMATRADING 1990
HEARTS OF FORTUNE IMMACULATE FOOLS 1985
HEARTWORK CARCASS 1993
THE HEAT DAN REED NETWORK 1991
THE HEAT TONI BRAXTON 2000
THE HEAT IS ON VARIOUS ARTISTS (ARCADE) 1991
THE HEAT IS ON – 16 TRACKS VARIOUS ARTISTS
    (PORTRAIT) 1986
HEAT TREATMENT GRAHAM PARKER & THE RUMOUR
    1976
HEATHCLIFF LIVE (THE SHOW) – ORIGINAL LONDON STAGE
    CAST SOUNDTRACK 1996
HEATHEN DAVID BOWIE 2002
HEATHEN CHEMISTRY OASIS 2002
HEAVEN DJ SAMMY 2003
HEAVEN AND HELL VANGELIS 1976
HEAVEN AND HELL BLACK SABBATH 1980
HEAVEN AND HELL MEAT LOAF/BONNIE TYLER 1989
HEAVEN AND HELL VARIOUS ARTISTS (TELSTAR) 1989
HEAVEN AND HELL VARIOUS ARTISTS (CLUMBIA) 1995
HEAVEN IS WAITING DANSE SOCIETY 1984
HEAVEN KNOWS JAKI GRAHAM 1985
HEAVEN ON EARTH BELINDA CARLISLE 1988
HEAVEN OR LAS VEGAS COCTEAU TWINS 1990
HEAVEN UP HERE ECHO & THE BUNNYMEN 1981
HEAVENLY LADYSMITH BLACK MAMBAZO 1997
HEAVENLY HARDCORE VARIOUS ARTISTS (DINO) 1992
HEAVIER THINGS JOHN MAYER 2003
HEAVY VARIOUS ARTISTS (K-TEL) 1983
THE HEAVY HEAVY HITS MADNESS 1998
HEAVY HORSES JETHRO TULL 1978
HEAVY NOVA ROBERT PALMER 1988
HEAVY PETTING ZOO NOFX 1996
HEAVY RHYME EXPERIENCE VOLUME 1 BRAND NEW
    HEAVIES 1992
HEAVY SOUL PAUL WELLER 1997

HEAVY TRAFFIC STATUS QUO 2002
HEAVY WEATHER WEATHER REPORT 1977
THE HEIGHT OF BAD MANNERS BAD MANNERS 1983
HEJIRA JONI MITCHELL 1976
HELIOCENTRIC PAUL WELLER 2000
HELL BENT FOR LEATHER FRANKIE LAINE 1961
HELL FREEZES OVER EAGLES 1994
HELL HATH NO FURY ROCK GODDESS 1983
HE'LL HAVE TO GO JIM REEVES 1964
HELL ON EARTH MOBB DEEP 1996
HELL TO PAY JEFF HEALEY BAND 1990
HELLBILLY DELUXE ROB ZOMBIE 1998
HELLO STATUS QUO 1973
HELLO CHILDREN... EVERYWHERE VARIOUS ARTISTS (EMI) 1988
HELLO DAD I'M IN JAIL WAS (NOT WAS) 1992
HELLO DOLLY LOUIS ARMSTRONG 1964
HELLO DOLLY! (OST) BARBRA STREISAND 1970
HELLO I'M JOHNNY CASH JOHNNY CASH 1970
HELLO NASTY BEASTIE BOYS 1998
HELLO PIG LEVELLERS 2000
HELLO, I MUST BE GOING PHIL COLLINS 1982
HELL'S DITCH POGUES 1990
HELP WAR CHILD VARIOUS ARTISTS (GO! DISCS) 1995
HELP YOURSELF TOM JONES 1968
HELP YOURSELF JULIAN LENNON 1991
HELP! – BEATLES 1965
HELTER SKELTER VOW WOW 1989
HEMISPHERES RUSH 1978
HENDRIX IN THE WEST JIMI HENDRIX 1972
HENRY MANCINI HENRY MANCINI 1976
HENRY'S DREAM NICK CAVE & THE BAD SEEDS 1992
HEPBURN HEPBURN 1999
HER BEST SONGS EMMYLOU HARRIS 1980
HERE LEO SAYER 1979
HERE AND THERE ELTON JOHN 1976
HERE COME THE MINSTRELS GEORGE MITCHELL MINSTRELS 1966
HERE COME THE WARM JETS BRIAN ENO 1974
HERE COMES THE TREMELOES TREMELOES 1967
HERE THEY COME: THE GREATEST HITS OF THE MONKEES MONKEES 1997
HERE TODAY, TOMORROW NEXT WEEK! – SUGARCUBES 1989
HERE WE COME A1 1999
HERE WHERE THERE IS LOVE DIONNE WARWICK 1967
HERE'S SOME THAT GOT AWAY STYLE COUNCIL 1993
HERE'S TO FUTURE DAYS THOMPSON TWINS 1985
HERE'S TOM WITH THE WEATHER SHACK 2003
HERGEST RIDGE MIKE OLDFIELD 1974
HERMAN'S HERMITS HERMAN'S HERMITS 1965
HERMIT OF MINK HOLLOW TODD RUNDGREN 1978
HERO AND HEROINE STRAWBS 1974
HERO OF THE DAY METALLICA 1996
HEROES DAVID BOWIE 1977
HEROES COMMODORES 1980
HEROES TO ZEROES BETA BAND 2004
HE'S THE DJ, I'M THE RAPPER DJ JAZZY JEFF & THE FRESH PRINCE 1988
HEY GLITTER BAND 1974
HEY HEY IT'S THE MONKEES – GREATEST HITS MONKEES 1989
HEY HO LET'S GO! – ANTHOLOGY RAMONES 2001
HEY STOOPID ALICE COOPER 1991
HI ENERGY VARIOUS ARTISTS (K-TEL) 1979
HI FI SERIOUS A 2002
HI INFIDELITY REO SPEEDWAGON 1981
HI LIFE – THE BEST OF AL GREEN AL GREEN 1988
HI TENSION HI TENSION 1979
HICKORY HOLLER REVISITED O.C. SMITH 1968
THE HIDDEN CAMERA PHOTEK 1996
HIDDEN TREASURES BARRY MANILOW 1993
HIDE YOUR HEART BONNIE TYLER 1988
HIDEAWAY DE'LACY 1995
HI FI COMPANION ALBUM RAY CONNIFF 1960
HIGH AND MIGHTY URIAH HEEP 1976

HIGH CIVILIZATION BEE GEES 1991
HIGH CRIME AL JARREAU 1984
HIGH LAND HARD RAIN AZTEC CAMERA 1983
HIGH 'N' DRY DEF LEPPARD 1981
HIGH ON A HAPPY VIBE URBAN COOKIE COLLECTIVE 1994
HIGH ON EMOTION – LIVE FROM DUBLIN CHRIS DE BURGH 1990
HIGH ON THE HAPPY SIDE WET WET WET 1992
HIGH PRIORITY CHERRELLE 1986
HIGH SOCIETY (OST) FILM SOUNDTRACK 1960
HIGHER ALED JONES 2003
HIGHER AND HIGHER – THE BEST OF HEAVEN 17 HEAVEN 17 1993
HIGHER GROUND BARBRA STREISAND 1997
THE HIGHER THEY CLIMB DAVID CASSIDY 1975
HIGHLIGHTS FROM JEFF WAYNE'S MUSICAL VERSION OF THE WAR OF THE WORLDS JEFF WAYNE 1996
HIGHLIGHTS FROM LAST NIGHT AT THE PROMS '82 BBC SYMPHONY ORCHESTRA, SINGS & SYMPHONY CHORUS CONDUCTED BY JAMES LOUGHRAN 1982
HIGHLIGHTS FROM WEST SIDE STORY ORIGINAL STUDIO CAST RECORDING 1986
HIGHLY EVOLVED VINES 2002
HIGHLY STRUNG STEVE HACKETT 1983
HIGHWAY FREE 1971
HIGHWAY 61 REVISITED BOB DYLAN 1965
HIGHWAY OF LIFE HARRY SECOMBE 1986
HIGHWAY SONG – BLACKFOOT LIVE BLACKFOOT 1982
HIGHWAY TO HELL AC/DC 1979
HILLBILLY DELUXE DWIGHT YOAKAM 1987
HINDA HINDA HICKS 1998
HINTERLAND AIM 2002
HIP HOP AND RAPPING IN THE HOUSE VARIOUS ARTISTS (STYLUS) 1988
HIP HOP DON'T STOP – 20 CLASSIC HIP HOP SUPERJAMS VARIOUS ARTISTS (SOLID STATE) 1997
HIP HOUSE VARIOUS ARTISTS (STYLUS) 1989
HIP HOP – THE DEEPEST BEATS IN TOWN VARIOUS ARTISTS (K-TEL) 1989
HIP HOP '87 VARIOUS ARTISTS (SERIOUS) 1987
HIPS AND MAKERS KRISTIN HERSH 1994
HIPSTERS, FLIPSTERS, AND FINGER POPPIN' DADDIES GENO WASHINGTON 1967
HIPSWAY HIPSWAY 1986
HIS 12 GREATEST HITS NEIL DIAMOND 1974
HIS 20 GREATEST HITS GENE PITNEY 1976
HIS DEFINITIVE GREATEST HITS B.B. KING 1999
HIS FINEST COLLECTION ROGER WHITTAKER 1987
HIS GREATEST HITS DAVID ESSEX 1991
HIS GREATEST LOVE SONGS CHARLES AZNAVOUR 1980
HIS GREATEST LOVE SONGS ENGELBERT HUMPERDINCK 2004
HIS HAND IN MINE ELVIS PRESLEY 1961
HIS LATEST AND GREATEST CHUCK BERRY 1964
HIS 'N' HERS PULP 1994
HIS ORCHESTRA, HIS CHORUS, HIS SINGERS, HIS SOUND RAY CONNIFF 1969
THE HISSING OF SUMMER LAWNS JONI MITCHELL 1975
HISTORY MAI TAI 1985
HISTORY – AMERICA'S GREATEST HITS AMERICA 1976
HISTORY – PAST PRESENT AND FUTURE BOOK 1 MICHAEL JACKSON 1995
HISTORY OF ERIC CLAPTON ERIC CLAPTON 1972
THE HISTORY OF OTIS REDDING OTIS REDDING 1968
THE HISTORY OF ROCK KID ROCK 2000
THE HISTORY OF THE BONZOS BONZO DOG DOO-DAH BAND 1974
HISTORY OF THE BYRDS BYRDS 1973
HISTORY REVISITED – THE REMIXES TALK TALK 1991
HIT PETER GABRIEL 2003
HIT ACTION VARIOUS ARTISTS (K-TEL) 1977
THE HIT FACTORY VARIOUS ARTISTS (UNIVERSAL) 2000
THE HIT FACTORY VOLUME 2 VARIOUS ARTISTS (FANFARE) 1988
THE HIT FACTORY VOLUME 3 VARIOUS ARTISTS (FANFARE) 1989

THE HIT FACTORY: THE BEST OF STOCK AITKEN WATERMAN VARIOUS ARTISTS (STYLUS) 1987
THE HIT LIST CLIFF RICHARD 1994
HIT MACHINE VARIOUS ARTISTS (K-TEL) 1976
HIT MACHINE VARIOUS ARTISTS (K-TEL) 1981
HIT MAKER – BURT BACHARACH BURT BACHARACH 1965
HIT MIX – HITS OF THE YEAR VARIOUS ARTISTS (STYLUS) 1987
HIT MIX '86 VARIOUS ARTISTS (STYLUS) 1986
HIT MIX '88 VARIOUS ARTISTS (STYLUS) 1988
HIT MIX '88 VARIOUS ARTISTS (STYLUS) 1989
HIT 'N' RUN GIRLSCHOOL 1981
THE HIT PACK: THE BEST OF CHART MUSIC VARIOUS ARTISTS (CBS) 1990
HIT PARADE PETULA CLARK 1967
HIT PARADE 1 WEDDING PRESENT 1992
HIT PARADE 2 WEDDING PRESENT 1993
HIT SCENE VARIOUS ARTISTS (WARWICK) 1977
THE HIT SQUAD – CHART TRACKING VARIOUS ARTISTS (RONCO) 1983
THE HIT SQUAD – HITS OF '83 VARIOUS ARTISTS (RONCO) 1983
THE HIT SQUAD – NIGHT CLUBBING VARIOUS ARTISTS (RONCO) 1983
HIT THE DECKS VOLUME 1 – BATTLE OF THE DJS VARIOUS ARTISTS (QUALITY PRICE MUSIC) 1992
HIT THE DECKS VOLUME 2 – BATTLE OF THE DJS VARIOUS ARTISTS (QUALITY PRICE MUSIC) 1992
HIT THE DECKS VOLUME III VARIOUS ARTISTS (QUALITY PRICE MUSIC) 1992
HIT THE HIGHWAY PROCLAIMERS 1994
HIT THE ROAD STAX VARIOUS ARTISTS (STAX) 1967
THE HIT WORLD OF KLAUS WUNDERLICH KLAUS WUNDERLICH 1975
THE HITCHHIKERS GUIDE TO THE GALAXY VOLUME 2 TELEVISION SOUNDTRACK 1981
THE HITMAKERS VARIOUS ARTISTS (POLYDOR) 1980
THE HITS GARTH BROOKS 1994
HITS MIKE AND THE MECHANICS 1996
HITS PHIL COLLINS 1998
HITS PULP 2002
THE HITS 1 PRINCE 1993
THE HITS 2 PRINCE 1993
HITS! THE VERY BEST OF ERASURE 2003
HITS 2000 VARIOUS ARTISTS (GLOBAL) 1999
HITS 2001 VARIOUS ARTISTS (WARNER BROTHERS) 2000
HITS 3 VARIOUS ARTISTS (CBS) 1985
HITS 4 VARIOUS ARTISTS (CBS) 1986
HITS 5 VARIOUS ARTISTS (CBS) 1986
HITS 6 VARIOUS ARTISTS (CBS) 1987
HITS 7 VARIOUS ARTISTS (CBS) 1987
HITS 8 VARIOUS ARTISTS (CBS) 1988
HITS 40 UK VARIOUS ARTISTS (BMG) 2004
HITS 50 VARIOUS ARTISTS (BMG) 2001
HITS 51 VARIOUS ARTISTS (BMG) 2001
HITS 52 VARIOUS ARTISTS (BMG) 2002
HITS 53 VARIOUS ARTISTS (BMG) 2002
HITS 54 VARIOUS ARTISTS (BMG) 2002
HITS 55 VARIOUS ARTISTS (BMG) 2003
HITS 56 VARIOUS ARTISTS (BMG) 2003
HITS 57 VARIOUS ARTISTS (BMG) 2003
HITS 93 VOLUME 1 VARIOUS ARTISTS (TELSTAR) 1993
HITS 93 VOLUME 2 VARIOUS ARTISTS (TELSTAR) 1993
HITS 93 VOLUME 3 VARIOUS ARTISTS (TELSTAR) 1993
HITS 93 VOLUME 4 VARIOUS ARTISTS (TELSTAR) 1993
HITS 94 VOLUME 1 VARIOUS ARTISTS (TELSTAR) 1994
HITS 96 VARIOUS ARTISTS (GLOBAL) 1995
HITS 97 VARIOUS ARTISTS (SONY) 1996
HITS 99 VARIOUS ARTISTS (SONY) 1998
THE HITS ALBUM VARIOUS ARTISTS (CBS) 1984
THE HITS ALBUM 10 VARIOUS ARTISTS (CBS) 1989
THE HITS ALBUM 15 VARIOUS ARTISTS (CBS) 1991
THE HITS ALBUM 1997 VARIOUS ARTISTS (WARNER BROTHERS) 1997
THE HITS ALBUM 2 VARIOUS ARTISTS (CBS) 1985
THE HITS ALBUM 9 VARIOUS ARTISTS (CBS) 1988

HITS FOR LOVERS VARIOUS ARTISTS (EPIC) 1986
HITS FOR NOW AND ALWAYS KEN DODD 1966
HITS LIKE NEVER BEFORE (ESSENTIAL ELVIS VOLUME 3) ELVIS PRESLEY 1990
HITS OF GOLD MAMAS & THE PAPAS 1969
THE HITS OF HOUSE ARE HERE VARIOUS ARTISTS (K-TEL) 1988
HITS OF THE 70'S ELVIS PRESLEY 1977
HITS OF THE ROCKIN' 50'S BOBBY VEE 1962
HITS OF THE SCREAMING 60'S VARIOUS ARTISTS (WARWICK) 1982
HITS OF THE SIXTIES BACHELORS 1966
HITS ON FIRE VARIOUS ARTISTS (RONCO) 1983
HITS ON OPERA KIMERA WITH THE LONDON SYMPHONY ORCHESTRA 1985
HITS OUT OF HELL MEAT LOAF 1985
HITS PLUS KYLIE MINOGUE 2000
THE HITS – RELOADED KOOL AND THE GANG 2004
HITS REVIVAL VARIOUS ARTISTS (K-TEL) 1987
HITS REVIVAL VARIOUS ARTISTS (K-TEL) 1987
HITS REVIVAL 2: REPLAY VARIOUS ARTISTS (K-TEL) 1988
HITS RIGHT UP YOUR STREET SHADOWS 1981
HITS UNLIMITED 2 UNLIMITED 1995
HITS ZONE – THE BEST OF '97 VARIOUS ARTISTS (POLYGRAM) 1997
HITS ZONE '97 VARIOUS ARTISTS (POLYGRAM) 1996
HITS ZONE SUMMER '97 VARIOUS ARTISTS (POLYGRAM) 1997
HITS, HITS AND MORE DANCE HITS VARIOUS ARTISTS (GLOBAL) 1994
HITS, HITS, HITS VARIOUS ARTISTS (RONCO) 1981
HITS, HITS, HITS – 18 SMASH ORIGINALS VARIOUS ARTISTS (TELSTAR) 1984
THE HITS/THE B SIDES PRINCE 1993
HITSVILLE VARIOUS ARTISTS (PYE) 1963
HITSVILLE VOLUME 2 VARIOUS ARTISTS (PYE) 1963
HITZ BLITZ VARIOUS ARTISTS (GLOBAL) 1995
HOLD AN OLD FRIEND'S HAND TIFFANY 1988
HOLD ME BERT KAEMPFERT & HIS ORCHESTRA 1967
HOLD ME LAURA BRANIGAN 1985
HOLD ME IN YOUR ARMS RICK ASTLEY 1988
HOLD ME NOW JOHNNY LOGAN 1987
HOLD ME, THRILL ME, KISS ME GLORIA ESTEFAN 1994
HOLD ON I'M COMIN' – SAM & DAVE 1967
HOLD OUT JACKSON BROWNE 1980
HOLD YOUR FIRE RUSH 1987
HOLDING BACK THE RIVER WET WET WET 1989
HOLES IN THE WALL ELECTRIC SOFT PARADE 2002
THE HOLIDAY ALBUM VARIOUS ARTISTS (CBS) 1987
HOLIDAY HITS – NON STOP EURO POP VARIOUS ARTISTS (VIRGIN) 2002
HOLIDAYS IN EDEN MARILLION 1991
HOLLAND BEACH BOYS 1973
HOLLIES HOLLIES 1965
HOLLIES HOLLIES 1974
THE HOLLIES' GREATEST HOLLIES 1968
HOLLIES LIVE HITS HOLLIES 1977
HOLLIES SING DYLAN HOLLIES 1969
HOLLY IN THE HILLS BUDDY HOLLY & THE CRICKETS 1965
HOLLYWOOD MANTOVANI & HIS ORCHESTRA 1967
HOLLYWOOD AND BROADWAY RICHARD CLAYDERMAN 1986
HOLLYWOOD GOLDEN CLASSICS JOSE CARRERAS 1991
THE HOLLYWOOD MUSICALS JOHNNY MATHIS & HENRY MANCINI 1986
HOLLYWOOD VAMPIRES L.A. GUNS 1991
HOLST: THE PLANETS TOMITA 1977
HOLST: THE PLANETS HERBERT VON KARAJAN CONDUCTING THE BERLIN PHILHARMONIC ORCHESTRA 1981
THE HOLY BIBLE MANIC STREET PREACHERS 1994
HOLY DIVER DIO 1983
THE HOLY GROUND MARY BLACK 1993
HOLY WOOD MARILYN MANSON 2000
HOME PROCOL HARUM 1970
HOME HOTHOUSE FLOWERS 1990

HOME DIXIE CHICKS 2003
HOME SIMPLY RED 2003
HOME AGAIN NEW EDITION 1996
HOME AND ABROAD STYLE COUNCIL 1986
HOME GROWN UB40 2003
HOME INVASION ICE-T 1993
HOME LOVIN' MAN ROGER WHITTAKER 1989
HOME LOVING MAN ANDY WILLIAMS 1971
HOME MOVIES – THE BEST OF EVERYTHING BUT THE GIRL EVERYTHING BUT THE GIRL 1993
HOME ON THE RANGE SLIM WHITMAN 1977
HOME RUN HARDFLOOR 1996
HOME THOUGHTS CLIFFORD T. WARD 1973
HOMEBASE DJ JAZZY JEFF & THE FRESH PRINCE 1991
HOMEBREW NENEH CHERRY 1992
HOMECOMING AMERICA 1972
HOMEGROWN DODGY 1994
HOMESICK DEACON BLUE 2001
HOMETIME ALISON MOYET 2002
HOMEWORK DEEP BLUE SOMETHING 1996
HOMEWORK DAFT PUNK 1997
HOMOGENIC BJORK 1997
HONEY ANDY WILLIAMS 1968
HONEY ROBERT PALMER 1994
HONEY HIT PARADE VARIOUS ARTISTS (PYE) 1962
HONEY LINGERS VOICE OF THE BEEHIVE 1991
HONEY TO THE B BILLIE PIPER 1998
THE HONEYDRIPPERS VOLUME ONE HONEYDRIPPERS 1984
HONEY'S DEAD JESUS & MARY CHAIN 1992
HONKEY CHATEAU ELTON JOHN 1972
HONKIN' ON BOBO AEROSMITH 2004
HOODOO ALISON MOYET 1991
HOOKED GREAT WHITE 1991
HOOKED ON CLASSICS LOUIS CLARK CONDUCTING THE ROYAL PHILHARMONIC ORCHESTRA 1981
HOOKED ON COUNTRY VARIOUS ARTISTS (K-TEL) 1990
HOOKED ON NUMBER ONES – 100 NON STOP HITS VARIOUS ARTISTS (K-TEL) 1988
THE HOOPLE MOTT THE HOOPLE 1974
HOORAY FOR BOOBIES BLOODHOUND GANG 2000
HOPE VARIOUS ARTISTS (LONDON) 2003
HOPE AND ANCHOR FRONT ROW FESTIVAL VARIOUS ARTISTS (WARNER BROTHERS) 1978
HOPE AND GLORY TOM ROBINSON 1984
HOPE IS IMPORTANT IDLEWILD 1998
HOPES AND DREAMS DAVID GRANT 1985
HOPES AND FEARS KEANE 2004
HORACE BROWN HORACE BROWN 1996
HORIZON CARPENTERS 1975
HORIZONS VARIOUS ARTISTS (K-TEL) 1988
HORIZONS – 12 DREAMHOUSE ANTHEMS VARIOUS ARTISTS (POLYGRAM) 1996
HORIZONTAL BEE GEES 1968
HORMONALLY YOURS SHAKESPEAR'S SISTER 1992
THE HORNS OF JERICO HI-JACK 1991
HOST PARADISE LOST 1999
HOT MELANIE B 2000
HOT AUGUST NIGHT NEIL DIAMOND 1977
HOT AUGUST NIGHT II NEIL DIAMOND 1987
HOT CAKES CARLY SIMON 1974
HOT CHOCOLATE HOT CHOCOLATE 1975
HOT CITY NIGHTS VARIOUS ARTISTS (VERTIGO) 1988
HOT CITY NIGHTS VARIOUS ARTISTS (SONY) 2003
HOT FUSS KILLERS 2004
HOT HITS 5 ANONYMOUS COVER VERSIONS 1971
HOT HITS 6 ANONYMOUS COVER VERSIONS 1971
HOT HITS 7 ANONYMOUS COVER VERSIONS 1971
HOT HITS 8 ANONYMOUS COVER VERSIONS 1971
HOT IN THE SHADE KISS 1989
HOT LOVE DAVID ESSEX 1980
HOT POP VARIOUS ARTISTS (UNIVERSAL) 2000
HOT RAIL CALEXICO 2000
HOT RATS FRANK ZAPPA 1970
HOT ROCKS – THE GREATEST HITS 1964–1971 ROLLING STONES 1990
HOT SHOT SHAGGY 2001

HOT SHOTS II BETA BAND 2001
HOT SPACE QUEEN 1982
HOT SUMMER NIGHTS VARIOUS ARTISTS (STYLUS) 1989
HOT TRACKS VARIOUS ARTISTS (K-TEL) 1979
HOT WAX VARIOUS ARTISTS (K-TEL) 1980
HOTEL CALIFORNIA EAGLES 1976
HOTLINE VARIOUS ARTISTS (K-TEL) 1983
HOTTER THAN JULY STEVIE WONDER 1980
HOTWIRED SOUP DRAGONS 1992
HOUNDS OF LOVE KATE BUSH 1985
THE HOUR OF BEWILDERBEAST BADLY DRAWN BOY 2000
HOURGLASS JAMES TAYLOR 1997
HOURS... – DAVID BOWIE 1999
HOUSE CLASSICS VARIOUS ARTISTS (MINISTRY OF SOUND) 2003
THE HOUSE COLLECTION – CLUB CLASSICS VARIOUS ARTISTS (FANTAZIA) 1996
THE HOUSE COLLECTION – VOLUME 2 VARIOUS ARTISTS (FANTAZIA) 1995
THE HOUSE COLLECTION – VOLUME 3 VARIOUS ARTISTS (FANTAZIA) 1995
THE HOUSE COLLECTION – VOLUME 5 VARIOUS ARTISTS (FANTAZIA) 1997
THE HOUSE COLLECTION 6 – PAUL OAKENFOLD/PAUL COSFORD VARIOUS ARTISTS (FANTAZIA) 1997
THE HOUSE COLLECTION CLUB CLASSICS – 2 VARIOUS ARTISTS (FANTAZIA) 1996
HOUSE HALLUCINATIONS (PUMP UP LONDON VOLUME 1) VARIOUS ARTISTS (BREAKOUT) 1988
HOUSE HITS VARIOUS ARTISTS (NEEDLE) 1988
HOUSE NATION 1 VARIOUS ARTISTS (REACT) 1994
THE HOUSE OF BLUE LIGHT DEEP PURPLE 1987
HOUSE OF DOLLS GENE LOVES JEZEBEL 1987
THE HOUSE OF HANDBAG VARIOUS ARTISTS (ULTRASOUND) 1995
THE HOUSE OF HANDBAG – AUTUMN/WINTER COLLECTION VARIOUS ARTISTS (ULTRASOUND) 1995
HOUSE OF HANDBAG – NUOVO DISCO COLLECTION VARIOUS ARTISTS (SOLID STATE) 1997
THE HOUSE OF LOVE HOUSE OF LOVE 1990
HOUSE OF LOVE HOUSE OF LOVE 1990
HOUSE OF PAIN HOUSE OF PAIN 1992
HOUSE OF THE BLUES JOHN LEE HOOKER 1967
HOUSE OF THE HOLY LED ZEPPELIN 1973
THE HOUSE SOUND OF CHICAGO VARIOUS ARTISTS (DJ INTERNATIONAL) 1986
THE HOUSE SOUND OF CHICAGO VOLUME 2 VARIOUS ARTISTS (DJ INTERNATIONAL) 1987
THE HOUSE SOUND OF CHICAGO VOLUME 3 VARIOUS ARTISTS (FFRR) 1988
THE HOUSE SOUND OF LONDON VOLUME 4 VARIOUS ARTISTS (FFRR) 1988
THE HOUSE WE BUILT ALISHA'S ATTIC 2001
THE HOUSEMARTINS' CHRISTMAS SINGLES BOX HOUSEMARTINS 1986
HOW 'BOUT US CHAMPAIGN 1981
HOW DARE YOU? – 10 CC 1976
HOW DO I LOVE THEE BRYN YEMM 1984
HOW DO YOU LIKE IT? – GERRY & THE PACEMAKERS 1963
HOW DOES THAT GRAB YOU NANCY SINATRA 1966
HOW GREAT THOU ART ELVIS PRESLEY 1967
HOW GREAT THOU ART BRYN YEMM 1984
HOW GREEN IS THE VALLEY MEN THEY COULDN'T HANG 1986
HOW MEN ARE HEAVEN 17 1984
HOW THE WEST WAS WON LED ZEPPELIN 2003
HOW TO BE A ZILLIONAIRE ABC 1985
HOW TO MAKE FRIENDS AND INFLUENCE PEOPLE TERRORVISION 1994
HOW TO OPERATE WITH A BLOWN MIND LO FIDELITY ALLSTARS 1998
HOW TO WIN AN ELECTION HARRY SECOMBE, PETER SELLERS & SPIKE MILLIGAN 1964
HOW WILL THE WOLF SURVIVE? – LOS LOBOS 1985
HOWDY TEENAGE FANCLUB 2000
HOY HOY! – LITTLE FEAT 1981

**HUCKLEBERRY HOUND** TELEVISION SOUNDTRACK 1961
**HUGE HITS 1996** VARIOUS ARTISTS (SONY) 1996
**HUGE HITS 1997** VARIOUS ARTISTS (GLOBAL) 1997
**HUGE HITS 1998** VARIOUS ARTISTS (SONY) 1998
**HUGE HITS 99** VARIOUS ARTISTS (GLOBAL) 1999
**HUGE HITS 2000** VARIOUS ARTISTS (WARNER BROTHERS) 2000
**HUGE HITS 2003** VARIOUS ARTISTS (BMG) 2002
**HUGE HITS 2004 – THE VERY BEST OF HITS** VARIOUS ARTISTS (BMG) 2003
**HUGGIN' AN' A KISSIN'** – BOMBALURINA FEATURING TIMMY MALLETT 1990
**HULLABALOO** MUSE 2002
**HUMAN** ROD STEWART 2001
**HUMAN** NITIN SAWHNEY 2003
**HUMAN BEING** SEAL 1998
**HUMAN CLAY** CREED 2001
**HUMAN CONDITIONS** RICHARD ASHCROFT 2002
**HUMAN RACING** NIK KERSHAW 1984
**HUMAN TOUCH** BRUCE SPRINGSTEEN 1992
**HUMAN TRAFFIC (OST)** FILM SOUNDTRACK 1999
**HUMAN WHEELS** JOHN MELLENCAMP 1993
**HUMAN'S LIB** HOWARD JONES 1984
**A HUNDRED DAYS OFF** UNDERWORLD 2002
**HUNDREDS AND THOUSANDS** BRONSKI BEAT 1985
**THE HUNGER** MICHAEL BOLTON 1990
**HUNGRY AGAIN** DOLLY PARTON 1998
**HUNGRY FOR HITS** VARIOUS ARTISTS (K-TEL) 1984
**HUNGRY FOR STINK** L7 1994
**HUNKPAPA** THROWING MUSES 1989
**HUNKY DORY** DAVID BOWIE 1972
**THE HUNTER** BLONDIE 1982
**HUNTING HIGH AND LOW** A-HA 1985
**HUP** WONDERSTUFF 1989
**HURRICANE #1** HURRICANE #1 1997
**HURT NO MORE (IMPORT)** MARIO WINANS 2004
**THE HURTING** TEARS FOR FEARS 1983
**THE HUSH** TEXAS 1999
**HYBRID THEORY** LINKIN PARK 2001
**HYENA** SIOUXSIE & THE BANSHEES 1984
**THE HYMNS ALBUM** HUDDERSFIELD CHORAL SOCIETY 1986
**HYMNS TO THE SILENCE** VAN MORRISON 1991
**HYMNS WE HAVE LOVED** PAT BOONE 1960
**HYMNS WE LOVE** PAT BOONE 1960
**HYPERACTIVE** VARIOUS ARTISTS (TELSTAR) 1988
**HYPERBOREA** TANGERINE DREAM 1983
**HYPNOTISED** UNDERTONES 1980
**HYPOCRISY IS THE GREATEST LUXURY** DISPOSABLE HEROES OF HIPHOPRISY 1992
**HYSTERIA** HUMAN LEAGUE 1984
**HYSTERIA** DEF LEPPARD 1987
**I AIN'T MOVIN'** – DES'REE 1994
**I AM** EARTH WIND & FIRE 1979
**I AM COLD** RIP RIG & PANIC 1982
**I AM KLOOT** I AM KLOOT 2003
**I AM KURIOUS, ORANJ** FALL 1988
**I AM NOT A DOCTOR** MOLOKO 1998
**I AM PHOENIX** JUDIE TZUKE 1981
**I AM WHAT I AM** SHIRLEY BASSEY 1984
**I AM WOMAN** VARIOUS ARTISTS (POLYDOR) 1980
**I AM...** – NAS 1999
**I BELIEVE** DANIEL O'DONNELL 1997
**I BELIEVE** TIM BURGESS 2003
**I BELIEVE IN YOU** DON WILLIAMS 1980
**I CAME TO DANCE** NILS LOFGREN 1977
**I CAN HELP** ELVIS PRESLEY 1984
**I CAN MAKE YOU DANCE** RICHIE RICH 1989
**I CAN SEE CLEARLY NOW** JOHNNY NASH 1972
**I CAN SEE YOUR HOUSE FROM HERE** CAMEL 1979
**I CAPRICORN** SHIRLEY BASSEY 1972
**... I CARE BECAUSE YOU DO** APHEX TWIN 1995
**I CARE 4 U** AALIYAH 2003
**I COULDN'T LIVE WITHOUT YOUR LOVE** PETULA CLARK 1966
**I DID WHAT I DID FOR MARIA** TONY CHRISTIE 1971

**I DO NOT WANT WHAT I HAVEN'T GOT** SINEAD O'CONNOR 1990
**I DON'T BELIEVE IN IF ANYMORE** ROGER WHITTAKER 1970
**I DON'T WANT TO PUT A HOLD ON YOU** BERNIE FLINT 1977
**I DON'T WANT YOU BACK** EAMON 2004
**I FEEL A SONG** GLADYS KNIGHT & THE PIPS 1975
**I FEEL ALRIGHT** STEVE EARLE 1996
**I FEEL FOR YOU** CHAKA KHAN 1984
**I FEEL NO FRET** AVERAGE WHITE BAND 1979
**I GET WET** ANDREW WK 2001
**I GOT LUCKY** ELVIS PRESLEY 1971
**I GOT NEXT** KRS ONE 1997
**I HAVE DREAMED** MATT MONRO 1965
**I HEAR TALK** BUCKS FIZZ 1984
**I JUST WASN'T MADE FOR THESE TIMES** BRIAN WILSON 1995
**I KNOW** LUTHER VANDROSS 1998
**I KNOW COS I WAS THERE** MAX BOYCE 1978
**I KNOW THEM SO WELL – TIM RICE** VARIOUS ARTISTS (POLYGRAM) 1994
**I LEFT MY HEART IN SAN FRANCISCO** TONY BENNETT 1965
**I LIKE TO SCORE** MOBY 2000
**I LOOKED UP** INCREDIBLE STRING BAND 1970
**I LOVE A PARTY** RUSS ABBOT 1985
**I LOVE CHRISTMAS** VARIOUS ARTISTS (EMI) 2003
**I LOVE COUNTRY MUSIC** VAL DOONICAN 1975
**I LOVE 80'S** VARIOUS ARTISTS (VIRGIN) 2001
**I LOVE EVERYBODY** LYLE LOVETT 1994
**I LOVE IBIZA** VARIOUS ARTISTS (VIRGIN) 2001
**I LOVE 90S** VARIOUS ARTISTS (VIRGIN) 2001
**I LOVE ROCK 'N' ROLL** JOAN JETT & THE BLACKHEARTS 1982
**I LOVE SAX** DAVID ROACH 1984
**I LOVE 70'S** VARIOUS ARTISTS (VIRGIN) 2001
**I LOVE SUMMER** VARIOUS ARTISTS (VIRGIN) 2002
**I LOVE 2 PARTY** VARIOUS ARTISTS (VIRGIN) 2001
**I LOVE 2 PARTY 2003** VARIOUS ARTISTS (VIRGIN) 2002
**I LOVE U** VARIOUS ARTISTS (VIRGIN) 2003
**I LUV SMASH HITS** VARIOUS ARTISTS (EMI) 2003
**I LUV SMASH HITS 2004** VARIOUS ARTISTS (EMI) 2004
**I MIGHT BE WRONG** RADIOHEAD 2001
**I NEED YOU** LEANN RIMES 2001
**I NEVER LOVED A MAN** ARETHA FRANKLIN 1967
**I ONLY HAVE EYES FOR YOU** JOHNNY MATHIS 1976
**I PRETEND** DES O'CONNOR 1968
**I PUT A SPELL ON YOU** NINA SIMONE 1965
**I REMEMBER HANK WILLIAMS** JACK SCOTT 1960
**I REMEMBER TOMMY... – FRANK SINATRA** 1962
**I REMEMBER YESTERDAY** DONNA SUMMER 1977
**I ROBOT** ALAN PARSONS PROJECT 1977
**I SAY I SAY I SAY** ERASURE 1994
**I SHOULD COCO** SUPERGRASS 1995
**I STAND ALONE** AGNETHA FALTSKOG 1988
**I TO SKY** JJ72 2002
**I WANNA BE WITH YOU** MANDY MOORE 2000
**I WANNA DO IT WITH YOU** BARRY MANILOW 1982
**I WANNA HAVE SOME FUN** SAMANTHA FOX 1989
**I WANT CANDY** BOW WOW WOW 1982
**I WANT TO LIVE** JOHN DENVER 1978
**I WANT TO WAKE UP WITH YOU** ENGELBERT HUMPERDINCK 2001
**I WANT YOU** MARVIN GAYE 1976
**I WAS THE ONE** ELVIS PRESLEY 1983
**I WAS WARNED** ROBERT CRAY 1992
**I WHO HAVE NOTHING** TOM JONES 1970
**I WILL ALWAYS LOVE YOU** JAMES GALWAY 1995
**I WILL CURE YOU** VIC REEVES 1991
**I WILL LOVE YOU ALL OF MY LIFE** FOSTER & ALLEN 1983
**I WILL SURVIVE (DOIN' IT MY WAY)** CHANTAY SAVAGE 1996
**I WILL WAIT FOR YOU** LESLEY GARRETT 2000
**I WISH YOU LOVE** JOE LONGTHORNE 1993
**I, ASSASSIN** GARY NUMAN 1982
**_ADIOS AMIGOS!** – RAMONES 1995
**IAN HUNTER** IAN HUNTER 1975

**IBIZA EUPHORIA – MIXED BY DAVE PEARCE** VARIOUS ARTISTS (TELSTAR) 2002
**IBIZA HITMIX 2002** VARIOUS ARTISTS (WARNER BROTHERS) 2002
**IBIZA – PAUL OAKENFOLD** VARIOUS ARTISTS (PERFECTO) 2001
**IBIZA – THE CLOSING PARTY** VARIOUS ARTISTS (DANCE POOL) 1999
**IBIZA – THE HISTORY OF CHILLOUT** VARIOUS ARTISTS (WARNER BROTHERS) 2003
**IBIZA – THE HISTORY OF HARD DANCE** VARIOUS ARTISTS (WARNER BROTHERS) 2003
**IBIZA – THE HISTORY OF HOUSE** VARIOUS ARTISTS (WARNER BROTHERS) 2003
**IBIZA – THE STORY SO FAR** VARIOUS ARTISTS (COLUMBIA) 2000
**IBIZA 99 – THE YEAR OF TRANCE** VARIOUS ARTISTS (GLOBAL) 1999
**IBIZA 99 – THE YEAR OF TRANCE – VOLUME TWO** VARIOUS ARTISTS (GLOBAL) 1999
**THE IBIZA ANNUAL** VARIOUS ARTISTS (MINISTRY OF SOUND) 1998
**IBIZA ANNUAL** VARIOUS ARTISTS (MINISTRY OF SOUND) 2001
**THE IBIZA ANNUAL – SUMMER 2000** VARIOUS ARTISTS (MINISTRY OF SOUND) 2000
**THE IBIZA ANNUAL: MIXED BY JUDGE JULES + TALL PAUL** VARIOUS ARTISTS (MINISTRY OF SOUND) 1999
**IBIZA ANTHEMS** VARIOUS ARTISTS (TELSTAR) 1998
**IBIZA ANTHEMS 2** VARIOUS ARTISTS (TELSTAR) 1999
**IBIZA CHILLOUT SESSION** VARIOUS ARTISTS (MINISTRY OF SOUND) 2001
**IBIZA DEL MAR** VARIOUS ARTISTS (GLOBAL) 1999
**IBIZA EUPHORIA** VARIOUS ARTISTS (TELSTAR) 1999
**IBIZA EUPHORIA – ALEX GOLD/AGNELLI & NELSON** VARIOUS ARTISTS (TELSTAR) 2000
**IBIZA EUPHORIA – DAVE PEARCE** VARIOUS ARTISTS (TELSTAR) 2001
**IBIZA UNCOVERED – THE RETURN** TELEVISION COMPILATION 1999
**IBIZA UNCOVERED** TELEVISION COMPILATION 1997
**IBIZA UNCOVERED 2** TELEVISION COMPILATION 1998
**IBIZA UNCOVERED II** VARIOUS ARTISTS (VIRGIN) 2000
**ICE CREAM FOR CROW** CAPTAIN BEEFHEART & HIS MAGIC BAND 1982
**ICE ON FIRE** ELTON JOHN 1985
**THE ICEBERG/FREEDOM OF SPEECH** ICE-T 1989
**THE ICICLE WORKS** ICICLE WORKS 1984
**THE ICON IS LOVE** BARRY WHITE 1995
**THE ID** MACY GRAY 2001
**I'D LIKE TO TEACH THE WORLD TO SING** RAY CONNIFF 1972
**IDEA** BEE GEES 1968
**THE IDEAL COPY** WIRE 1987
**THE IDEAL CRASH** DEUS 1999
**IDEAS ABOVE OUR STATION** HUNDRED REASONS 2002
**THE IDIOT** IGGY POP 1977
**IDLEWILD** EVERYTHING BUT THE GIRL 1988
**IDOL SONGS: 11 OF THE BEST** BILLY IDOL 1988
**THE IDOLS – THE XMAS FACTOR** VARIOUS ARTISTS (S) 2003
**IF I RULED THE WORLD** HARRY SECOMBE 1971
**IF I SHOULD FALL FROM GRACE WITH GOD** POGUES 1988
**IF I SHOULD LOVE AGAIN** BARRY MANILOW 1981
**IF I WAS: THE VERY BEST OF MIDGE URE AND ULTRAVOX** MIDGE URE/ULTRAVOX 1993
**IF MUSIC BE THE FOOD OF LOVE... PREPARE FOR INDIGESTION** DAVE DEE, DOZY, BEAKY, MICK & TICH 1967
**IF ONLY I COULD REMEMBER MY NAME** DAVID CROSBY 1971
**IF THE BEATLES HAD READ HUNTER... THE SINGLES** WONDERSTUFF 1994
**IF THIS IS ROCK AND ROLL, I WANT MY OLD JOB BACK** SAW DOCTORS 1991
**IF WE FALL IN LOVE TONIGHT** ROD STEWART 1996
**IF YOU CAN BELIEVE YOUR EYES AND EARS** MAMAS & THE PAPAS 1966

IF YOU CAN'T STAND THE HEAT STATUS QUO 1978
IF YOU HAPPY WITH YOU NEED DO NOTHING ALFIE 2001
IF YOU WANT BLOOD YOU'VE GOT IT AC/DC 1978
IF YOU WANT TO DEFEAT YOUR ENEMY SING HIS SONG ICICLE WORKS 1987
IF YOU'VE NEVER BEEN EMBRACE 2001
II BOYZ II MEN 1994
II PRESIDENTS OF THE UNITED STATES OF AMERICA 1996
III GUY 2000
III SIDES TO EVERY STORY EXTREME 1992
I LEVEL I-LEVEL 1983
I'LL BUY YOU A STAR JOHNNY MATHIS 1961
ILL COMMUNICATION BEASTIE BOYS 1994
I'LL GIVE ALL MY LOVE TO YOU KEITH SWEAT 1990
I'LL REMEMBER YOU FRANK IFIELD 1963
ILLEGAL RAVE VARIOUS ARTISTS (STRICTLY UNDERGROUND) 1992
ILLEGAL STILLS STEPHEN STILLS 1976
ILLUMINA ALISHA'S ATTIC 1998
ILLUMINATION PAUL WELLER 2002
ILLUMINATIONS CARLOS SANTANA & ALICE COLTRANE 1974
I'M 10,000 YEARS OLD – ELVIS COUNTRY ELVIS PRESLEY 1971
I'M 21 TODAY CLIFF RICHARD & THE SHADOWS 1961
I'M A WRITER NOT A FIGHTER GILBERT O'SULLIVAN 1973
I'M ALIVE JACKSON BROWNE 1993
I'M BREATHLESS MADONNA 1990
I'M COMING HOME JOHNNY MATHIS 1975
I'M COMING HOME TOM JONES 1978
I'M GLAD YOU'RE HERE WITH ME TONIGHT NEIL DIAMOND 1977
I'M GONNA BE STRONG GENE PITNEY 1965
I'M IN YOU PETER FRAMPTON 1977
I'M LEAVING IT ALL UP TO YOU DONNY & MARIE OSMOND 1974
I'M MIGHTY GLAD MRS. MILLS 1971
I'M NEARLY FAMOUS CLIFF RICHARD 1976
I'M NO HERO CLIFF RICHARD 1980
I'M NOT FOLLOWING YOU EDWYN COLLINS 1997
I'M P.J. PROBY P.J. PROBY 1965
I'M REAL JAMES BROWN 1988
I'M STILL GONNA NEED YOU OSMONDS 1975
I'M STILL WAITING DIANA ROSS 1971
I'M THE MAN JOE JACKSON 1979
I'M WITH STUPID AIMEE MANN 1995
I'M YOUR BABY TONIGHT WHITNEY HOUSTON 1990
I'M YOUR FAN – THE SONGS OF LEONARD COHEN VARIOUS ARTISTS (EAST WEST) 1991
I'M YOUR MAN LEONARD COHEN 1988
IMA BT 1995
IMAGES WALKER BROTHERS 1967
IMAGES DON WILLIAMS 1978
IMAGES VARIOUS ARTISTS (K-TEL) 1983
IMAGES GUITAR CORPORATION 1992
IMAGES – THE BEST OF JEAN MICHEL JARRE JEAN-MICHEL JARRE 1991
IMAGINATION WHISPERS 1981
IMAGINATION BRIAN WILSON 1998
IMAGINATION – ALL THE HITS IMAGINATION 1989
IMAGINATIONS VARIOUS ARTISTS (CBS) 1983
IMAGINE JOHN LENNON WITH THE PLASTIC ONO BAND (WITH THE FLUX FIDDLERS) 1971
IMAGINE JOHN LENNON 2000
IMAGINE EVA CASSIDY 2002
IMAGINE JOHN LENNON (OST) JOHN LENNON 1988
THE IMMACULATE COLLECTION MADONNA 1990
IMMORTAL OTIS REDDING OTIS REDDING 1968
IMPACT VARIOUS ARTISTS (EMI) 1969
IMPERIAL BEDROOM ELVIS COSTELLO & THE ATTRACTIONS 1982
IMPERIAL WIZARD DAVID ESSEX 1979
IMPLANT EAT STATIC 1994
THE IMPOSSIBLE DREAM ANDY WILLIAMS 1972
THE IMPOSSIBLE DREAM SENSATIONAL ALEX HARVEY BAND 1974

IMPRESSIONS – 15 INSTRUMENTAL IMAGES VARIOUS ARTISTS (K-TEL) 1987
IMPURITY NEW MODEL ARMY 1990
IN BLUE CORRS 2000
IN CITY DREAMS ROBIN TROWER 1977
IN CONCERT DEEP PURPLE 1980
IN CONCERT ROLLING STONES 1982
IN CONCERT LUCIANO PAVAROTTI, PLACIDO DOMINGO & JOSE CARRERAS 1990
IN CONCERT DOORS 1991
IN CONCERT – MTV UNPLUGGED BRUCE SPRINGSTEEN 1993
IN CONCERT LYONS/HOUSTON JEAN-MICHEL JARRE 1987
IN CONCERT VOLUME 1 PETER, PAUL & MARY 1965
IN CONCERT VOLUME 2 JAMES LAST 1974
IN CONCERT: SINATRA AT 'THE SANDS' – FRANK SINATRA 1966
IN DEEP ARGENT 1973
IN DREAMS ROY ORBISON 1963
IN DREAMS BRENDA COCHRANE 1991
IN DREAMS: THE GREATEST HITS ROY ORBISON 1987
IN FLIGHT GEORGE BENSON 1977
IN FOR THE KILL BUDGIE 1974
IN FULL BLOOM ROSE ROYCE 1977
IN FULL EFFECT MANTRONIX 1988
IN HARMONY RICHARD CLAYDERMAN & JAMES LAST 1994
IN HARMONY RICHARD CLAYDERMAN & JAMES LAST 1994
IN HARMONY LADYSMITH BLACK MAMBAZO 1999
IN HEARING OF ATOMIC ROOSTER ATOMIC ROOSTER 1971
IN HIS OWN WORDS 2PAC 1998
IN IT FOR THE MONEY SUPERGRASS 1997
IN LOVE – GREATEST LOVE 5 VARIOUS ARTISTS (TELSTAR) 1991
IN MY LIFE GEORGE MARTIN 1998
IN MYSTERIOUS WAYS JOHN FOXX 1985
IN NO SENSE/NONSENSE ART OF NOISE 1987
IN ON THE KILLTAKER FUGAZI 1993
IN ORDER TO DANCE 5 VARIOUS ARTISTS (R&S) 1994
IN OUR GUN GOMEZ 2002
IN OUR LIFETIME MARVIN GAYE 1981
IN PIECES GARTH BROOKS 1994
IN RIBBONS PALE SAINTS 1992
IN ROCK WE TRUST Y & T 1984
IN SEARCH OF N*E*R*D 2002
IN SEARCH OF ANGELS RUNRIG 1999
IN SEARCH OF SANITY ONSLAUGHT 1989
IN SEARCH OF SPACE HAWKWIND 1971
IN SEARCH OF THE LOST CHORD MOODY BLUES 1968
IN SIDES ORBITAL 1996
THE IN SOUND FROM WAY OUT! – BEASTIE BOYS 1996
IN SQUARE CIRCLE STEVIE WONDER 1985
IN STEP STEVIE RAY VAUGHAN & DOUBLE TROUBLE 1989
IN STEREO BOMFUNK MCS 2000
IN STYLE WITH THE CRICKETS CRICKETS 1961
IN THE AIR TONIGHT VARIOUS ARTISTS (VIRGIN) 1994
IN THE ARMY NOW STATUS QUO 1986
IN THE BEGINNING BLAZIN' SQUAD 2002
IN THE BLOOD LONDONBEAT 1990
IN THE CITY JAM 1977
IN THE COURT OF THE CRIMSON KING KING CRIMSON 1969
IN THE DARK GRATEFUL DEAD 1987
IN THE DYNAMITE JET SALOON DOGS D'AMOUR 1988
IN THE EYE OF THE STORM ROGER HODGSON 1984
IN THE FLAT FIELD BAUHAUS 1980
IN THE GROOVE – THE 12 INCH DISCO PARTY VARIOUS ARTISTS (TELSTAR) 1983
IN THE HAND OF THE INEVITABLE JAMES TAYLOR QUARTET 1995
IN THE HEART KOOL & THE GANG 1984
IN THE HEAT OF THE NIGHT IMAGINATION 1982
IN THE HEAT OF THE NIGHT PAT BENATAR 1985
IN THE LOUNGE WITH... ANDY WILLIAMS ANDY WILLIAMS 1999

IN THE MIX – 90'S HITS VARIOUS ARTISTS (VIRGIN) 1996
IN THE MIX 2000 VARIOUS ARTISTS (VIRGIN) 1999
IN THE MIX 2000 VARIOUS ARTISTS (VIRGIN) 2000
IN THE MIX 96 VARIOUS ARTISTS (VIRGIN) 1996
IN THE MIX 96 – 2 VARIOUS ARTISTS (VIRGIN) 1996
IN THE MIX 96 – 3 VARIOUS ARTISTS (VIRGIN) 1996
IN THE MIX 97 VARIOUS ARTISTS (VIRGIN) 1997
IN THE MIX 97 – 2 VARIOUS ARTISTS (VIRGIN) 1997
IN THE MIX 97 – 3 VARIOUS ARTISTS (VIRGIN) 1997
IN THE MIX 98 VARIOUS ARTISTS (VIRGIN) 1998
IN THE MIX 98 – 2 VARIOUS ARTISTS (VIRGIN) 1998
IN THE MIX IBIZA VARIOUS ARTISTS (VIRGIN) 1998
IN THE MODE RONI SIZE REPRAZENT 2000
IN THE MOOD – THE DEFINITIVE GLENN MILLER 2003
IN THE PINK JAMES GALWAY & HENRY MANCINI 1984
IN THE POCKET COMMODORES 1981
IN THE SKIES PETER GREEN 1979
IN THE STUDIO SPECIAL AKA 1984
IN THE WAKE OF POSEIDON KING CRIMSON 1970
IN THE WIND PETER, PAUL & MARY 1964
IN THE ZONE BRITNEY SPEARS 2003
IN THIS LIFE MORDRED 1991
IN THIS SKIN JESSICA SIMPSON 2004
IN THROUGH THE OUT DOOR LED ZEPPELIN 1979
IN TIME – THE BEST OF – 1988–2003 R.E.M. 2003
IN TOUCH VARIOUS ARTISTS (STARBLEND) 1983
IN TOWN ROCKIN' BERRIES 1965
IN UTERO NIRVANA 1993
IN VISIBLE SILENCE ART OF NOISE 1986
IN YOUR EYES GEORGE BENSON 1983
IN YOUR FACE KINGDOM COME 1989
IN YOUR MIND BRYAN FERRY 1977
IN YOUR OWN TIME MARK OWEN 2003
INARTICULATE SPEECH OF THE HEART VAN MORRISON 1983
INCANTATIONS MIKE OLDFIELD 1978
INCESTICIDE NIRVANA 1992
THE INCOMPARABLE ELLA ELLA FITZGERALD 1980
THE INCREDIBLE PLAN MAX BOYCE 1976
THE INCREDIBLE SHRINKING DICKIES DICKIES 1979
THE INCREDIBLE SOUND MACHINE MANTRONIX 1991
INCREDIBLE SOUND OF THE DREEM TEEM VARIOUS ARTISTS (INCREDIBLE) 2000
INCREDIBLE SOUND OF TREVOR NELSON VARIOUS ARTISTS (INCREDIBLE) 1999
THE INCREDIBLE STRING BAND INCREDIBLE STRING BAND 1968
INDECENT PROPOSAL (OST) FILM SOUNDTRACK 1993
INDEPENDENCE LULU 1993
INDEPENDENCE DAY (OST) DAVID ARNOLD 1996
INDEPENDENCE DAY UK RADIO SOUNDTRACK 1996
INDEPENDENT WOMAN VARIOUS ARTISTS (COLUMBIA) 2001
INDEPENDENT WORM SALOON BUTTHOLE SURFERS 1993
INDESTRUCTIBLE RANCID 2003
INDIAN SUMMER GO WEST 1992
INDIE HITS VARIOUS ARTISTS (TELSTAR) 1992
INDIGO MATT BIANCO 1988
INDISCREET SPARKS 1975
INDISCREET FM 1986
INDUSTRY RICHARD & DANNY THOMPSON 1997
INFECTED THE THE 1986
INFERNAL LOVE THERAPY? 1995
INFEST PAPA ROACH 2001
INFIDELS BOB DYLAN 1983
INFINITY GURU JOSH 1990
INFINITY WITHIN DEEE'LITE 1992
INFLAMMABLE MATERIAL STIFF LITTLE FINGERS 1979
INFLUENCES MARK KING 1984
INFORCERS 3 VARIOUS ARTISTS (REINFORCED) 1993
INFORMATION DAVE EDMUNDS 1983
INFOTAINMENT SCAN FALL 1993
INGENUE K.D. LANG 1992
INITIAL SUCCESS B.A. ROBERTSON 1980
INNA DANCEHALL STYLE VARIOUS ARTISTS (EMI) 1993
INNER CHILD SHANICE 1992

INNER SECRETS SANTANA 1978
INNERVISIONS STEVIE WONDER 1973
INNOCENCE IS NO EXCUSE SAXON 1985
INNOCENT EYES DELTA GOODREM 2003
THE INNOCENTS ERASURE 1988
INNUENDO QUEEN 1991
INSIDE INFORMATION FOREIGNER 1987
INSIDE JOB DON HENLEY 2000
INSIDE LIFE INCOGNITO 1991
INSIDE SHELLEY BERMAN SHELLEY BERMAN 1960
INSIDE STORY GRACE JONES 1986
INSIDE THE ELECTRIC CIRCUS W.A.S.P. 1986
INSOMNIAC GREEN DAY 1995
INSPECTOR MORSE – ORIGINAL MUSIC FROM THE TV
    SERIES BARRINGTON PHELOUNG 1991
INSPECTOR MORSE VOLUME 2 – MUSIC FROM THE TV
    SERIES BARRINGTON PHELOUNG 1992
INSPECTOR MORSE VOLUME 3 BARRINGTON PHELOUNG
    1993
INSPIRATION ELVIS PRESLEY 1980
INSPIRATION JANE MCDONALD 2000
INSPIRATIONS ELKIE BROOKS 1989
INSTANT KARMA VARIOUS ARTISTS (WSM) 2002
INSTANT PARTY EVERLY BROTHERS 1962
INSTINCT IGGY POP 1988
INSTRUMENTAL GOLD VARIOUS ARTISTS (WARWICK) 1976
INSTRUMENTAL GREATS VARIOUS ARTISTS (TELSTAR)
    1988
INSTRUMENTAL MAGIC VARIOUS ARTISTS (TELSTAR) 1983
INSTRUMENTAL MOODS VARIOUS ARTISTS (VIRGIN) 1995
INTELLIGENCE AND SACRIFICE ALEC EMPIRE 2002
INTENSE PRESENTS LOGICAL PROGRESSION LEVEL 3
    VARIOUS ARTISTS (GOOD LOOKING) 1998
INTENSIFY WAY OUT WEST 2001
INTENSITIES (IN 10 CITIES) TED NUGENT 1981
INTENTIONS MAXI PRIEST 1986
INTERGALACTIC SONIC 7'S ASH 2002
INTERMISSION DIO 1986
INTERNAL EXILE FISH 1991
INTERNATIONAL JIM REEVES JIM REEVES 1964
INTERNATIONAL SUPERHITS GREEN DAY 2001
INTERNATIONAL TIMES TRANSGLOBAL UNDERGROUND
    1994
INTERNATIONAL VELVET CATATONIA 1998
THE INTERNATIONALE BILLY BRAGG 1990
INTERPRETATIONS CARPENTERS 1994
INTERPRETER JULIAN COPE 1996
THE INTIMATE JIM REEVES JIM REEVES 1964
INTO THE BLUE VARIOUS ARTISTS (POLYGRAM) 1998
INTO THE DRAGON BOMB THE BASS 1988
INTO THE EIGHTIES VARIOUS ARTISTS (GLOBAL) 1995
INTO THE FIRE BRYAN ADAMS 1987
INTO THE GAP THOMPSON TWINS 1984
INTO THE GREAT WIDE OPEN TOM PETTY &
    HEARTBREAKERS 1991
INTO THE LABYRINTH DEAD CAN DANCE 1993
INTO THE LIGHT CHRIS DE BURGH 1986
INTO THE LIGHT GLORIA ESTEFAN 1991
INTO THE LIGHT HANK MARVIN 1992
INTO THE LIGHT DAVID COVERDALE 2000
INTO THE MUSIC VAN MORRISON 1979
INTO THE SKYLINE CATHY DENNIS 1993
INTOLERANCE TIK & TOK 1984
INTRODUCING EDDY AND THE FALCONS WIZZARD 1974
INTRODUCING MICHAEL WARD MICHAEL WARD 1974
INTRODUCING RICHARD CLAYDERMAN RICHARD
    CLAYDERMAN 1982
INTRODUCING THE HARDLINE ACCORDING TO TERENCE
    TRENT D'ARBY TERENCE TRENT D'ARBY 1987
INTRODUCING... DAVID PEASTON DAVID PEASTON 1989
INTRODUCTION ALEX PARKS 2003
INTROSPECTIVE PET SHOP BOYS 1988
INTUITION LINX 1981
INVASION OF YOUR PRIVACY RATT 1985
INVINCIBLE FIVE 1999
INVINCIBLE MICHAEL JACKSON 2001

INVINCIBLE SUMMER K.D. LANG 2000
THE INVISIBLE BAND TRAVIS 2001
INVISIBLE TOUCH GENESIS 1986
INVITATION PETERS & LEE 1976
INVITATION TO THE MOVIES MATT MONRO 1967
INVITATIONS SHAKATAK 1982
INVOLVER SASHA 2004
INXS – THE GREATEST HITS INXS 1994
IOWA SLIPKNOT 2001
IQ 6: ZANG TUMB TUM SAMPLED VARIOUS ARTISTS (ZTT)
    1985
IRISH HEARTBEAT VAN MORRISON & THE CHIEFTAINS
    1988
IRISH TOUR '74 RORY GALLAGHER 1974
IRON MAIDEN IRON MAIDEN 1980
IRONFIST MOTORHEAD 1982
IRONMAN GHOSTFACE KILLAH 1996
IRREPLACEABLE GEORGE BENSON 2004
IRV GOTTI PRESENTS THE INC IRV GOTTI PRESENTS THE
    INC 2002
IS A WOMAN LAMBCHOP 2002
IS THERE ANYBODY OUT THERE? – LIVE PINK FLOYD 2000
IS THERE ANYTHING ABOUT BRAND X 1982
IS THIS DESIRE? PJ HARVEY 1998
IS THIS IT STROKES 2001
IS THIS LOVE VARIOUS ARTISTS (EMI) 1989
ISDN FUTURE SOUND OF LONDON 1994
ISDN (REMIX) FUTURE SOUND OF LONDON 1995
ISLAND LIFE GRACE JONES 1985
THE ISLAND STORY VARIOUS ARTISTS (ISLAND) 1987
ISLANDS KING CRIMSON 1972
ISLANDS KAJAGOOGOO 1984
ISLANDS MIKE OLDFIELD 1987
THE ISLE OF VIEW PRETENDERS 1995
ISMISM KEVIN GODLEY & LOL CRÈME 1981
ISN'T IT GRAND BOYS CLANCY BROTHERS & TOMMY
    MAKEM 1966
THE ISNESS AMORPHOUS ANDROGYNOUS 2002
ISOLATION TOTO 1984
ISSUES KORN 1999
IT BEGINS AGAIN DUSTY SPRINGFIELD 1978
IT DOESN'T MATTER ANYMORE SUPERNATURALS 1997
THE IT GIRL SLEEPER 1996
IT GOES WITHOUT SAYING DUM DUMS 2000
IT HAD TO BE YOU – THE GREAT AMERICAN SONGBOOK
    ROD STEWART 2002
IT HAPPENED AT THE WORLD'S FAIR (OST) ELVIS PRESLEY
    1963
IT IS THE BUSINESS OF THE FUTURE TO BE DANGEROUS
    HAWKWIND 1993
IT MIGHT AS WELL BE SWING FRANK SINATRA & COUNT
    BASIE & HIS ORCHESTRA 1964
IT MUST BE HIM VIKKI CARR 1967
IT MUST BE LOVE VARIOUS ARTISTS (THE HIT LABEL) 1993
IT STARTED WITH A KISS VARIOUS ARTISTS (ARCADE)
    1991
IT STILL MOVES MY MORNING JACKET 2003
IT TAKES A NATION OF MILLIONS TO HOLD US BACK
    PUBLIC ENEMY 1988
IT TAKES A THIEF COOLIO 1994
IT TAKES TWO VARIOUS ARTISTS (SONY) 1996
IT TAKES TWO – LOVE'S GREATEST DUETS VARIOUS ARTISTS
    (EMI) 1993
IT WAS WRITTEN NAS 1996
IT WON'T SEEM LIKE CHRISTMAS WITHOUT YOU ELVIS
    PRESLEY 1982
ITALIA – DANCE MUSIC FROM ITALY VARIOUS ARTISTS
    (DECONSTRUCTION) 1989
ITCHY FEET JOHNNY CASH 1978
ITCHY FEET BLUES BAND 1981
IT'LL END IN TEARS THIS MORTAL COIL 1984
IT'S A BEAUTIFUL DAY IT'S A BEAUTIFUL DAY 1970
IT'S A BIG DADDY THING BIG DADDY 1989
IT'S A GAME BAY CITY ROLLERS 1977
IT'S A GIRL THING VARIOUS ARTISTS (VIRGIN) 2001
IT'S A MAN'S WORLD CHER 1995

IT'S A SHAME ABOUT RAY LEMONHEADS 1992
IT'S A SIXTIES NIGHT VARIOUS ARTISTS (COLUMBIA) 1997
IT'S A WONDERFUL LIFE SPARKLEHORSE 2001
IT'S ABOUT TIME JOHN DENVER 1983
IT'S ABOUT TIME MORRISSEY MULLEN 1983
IT'S ABOUT TIME SWV 1993
IT'S ABOUT TIME CHRISTINA MILIAN 2004
IT'S ALIVE RAMONES 1979
IT'S ALL ABOUT THE STRAGGLERS ARTFUL DODGER 2000
IT'S ALL GOOD LUCK & NEAT 2002
IT'S BETTER TO TRAVEL SWING OUT SISTER 1987
IT'S CHRISTMAS VARIOUS ARTISTS (EMI) 1989
IT'S CHRISTMAS TIME VARIOUS ARTISTS (EMI) 1992
IT'S COOL VARIOUS ARTISTS (PARLOPHONE) 1991
IT'S ELECTRIC VARIOUS ARTISTS (DINO) 1994
IT'S EVERLY TIME EVERLY BROTHERS 1960
IT'S FIVE O'CLOCK SOMEWHERE SLASH'S SNAKEPIT 1995
IT'S FOUR IN THE MORNING FARON YOUNG 1972
IT'S GREAT WHEN YOU'RE STRAIGHT... YEAH BLACK
    GRAPE 1995
IT'S HARD WHO 1982
IT'S IMPOSSIBLE PERRY COMO 1971
IT'S IT SUGARCUBES 1992
IT'S MAGIC SHIRLEY BASSEY 1971
IT'S MY LIFE TALK TALK 1984
IT'S MY LIFE – THE ALBUM SASH! 1997
IT'S ONLY A MOVIE FAMILY 1973
IT'S ONLY LOVE SIMPLY RED 2000
IT'S ONLY ROCK 'N' ROLL ROLLING STONES 1974
IT'S PARTY TIME JIVE BUNNY & THE MIXMASTERS 1990
IT'S REAL K-CI & JOJO 1999
IT'S THE SEARCHERS SEARCHERS 1964
IT'S THE TALK OF THE TOWN RAY CONNIFF 1960
IT'S THE ULTIMATE DANCE ALBUM VARIOUS ARTISTS
    (TELSTAR) 1994
IT'S TIME... – CLOCK 1995
IT'S TRAD MAN (OST) FILM SOUNDTRACK 1962
IT'S YOUR NIGHT JAMES INGRAM 1984
I'VE BEEN EXPECTING YOU ROBBIE WILLIAMS 1998
I'VE GOT A SONG FOR YOU SHIRLEY BASSEY 1966
I'VE GOT THE MELODY ODYSSEY 1981
I'VE NEVER BEEN TO ME CHARLENE 1982
I'VE SEEN EVERYTHING TRASH CAN SINATRAS 1993
IXNAY ON THE HOMBRE OFFSPRING 1997
IZITSO CAT STEVENS 1977
IZZY STRADLIN' AND THE JU JU HOUNDS IZZY STRADLIN' &
    THE JU JU HOUNDS 1992
J TO THA L O! – THE REMIXES JENNIFER LOPEZ 2002
J.LO JENNIFER LOPEZ 2001
JACK GOOD'S 'OH BOY' – TELEVISION COMPILATION 1958
JACK MIX IN FULL EFFECT MIRAGE 1988
JACK O THE GREEN – SMALL WORLD BIG BAND JOOLS
    HOLLAND & HIS R&B ORCHESTRA 2003
JACKPOT CHINGY 2004
JACK RABBIT SLIM STEVE FORBERT 1979
JACK TRAX – THE FIRST ALBUM VARIOUS ARTISTS (JACK
    TRAX) 1987
JACK TRAX – THE SECOND ALBUM VARIOUS ARTISTS (JACK
    TRAX) 1987
JACK TRAX – THE THIRD ALBUM VARIOUS ARTISTS (JACK
    TRAX) 1988
JACKIE BROWN (OST) FILM SOUNDTRACK 1998
JACKMASTER VOLUME 1 VARIOUS ARTISTS (DJ
    INTERNATIONAL) 1987
JACKMASTER VOLUME 2 VARIOUS ARTISTS (DJ
    INTERNATIONAL) 1988
THE JACKSONS JACKSONS 1977
THE JACKSONS LIVE JACKSONS 1982
JACQUES LOUSSIER – THE BEST OF PLAY BACH JACQUES
    LOUSSIER 1985
JADE TO THE MAX JADE 1993
JAGGED LITTLE PILL ALANIS MORISSETTE 1995
JAILBREAK THIN LIZZY 1976
JAILHOUSE ROCK/LOVE IN LAS VEGAS ELVIS PRESLEY 1983
JAM LITTLE ANGELS 1993
THE JAM COLLECTION JAM 1996

JAM ON REVENGE NEWCLEUS 1984

JAM SCIENCE SHRIEKBACK 1984

JAMBOREE BAG NUMBER 3 CHAS & DAVE 1985

JAMES BOND 007 – A VIEW TO A KILL (OST) JOHN BARRY 1985

JAMES BOND 007 – GOLDFINGER (OST) JOHN BARRY 1964

JAMES BOND 007 – THE LIVING DAYLIGHTS (OST) JOHN BARRY 1987

JAMES BOND'S GREATEST HITS VARIOUS ARTISTS (LIBERTY) 1982

JAMES GALWAY AND THE CHIEFTAINS IN IRELAND JAMES GALWAY & THE CHIEFTAINS 1987

THE JAMES GALWAY COLLECTION JAMES GALWAY 1982

JAMES GALWAY PLAYS SONGS FOR ANNIE JAMES GALWAY 1978

JAMES LAST GOES POP JAMES LAST 1968

JAMES LAST IN CONCERT JAMES LAST 1972

JAMES LAST IN RUSSIA JAMES LAST 1973

JAMES LAST IN SCOTLAND JAMES LAST 1984

JAMES LAST PLAYS ANDREW LLOYD WEBBER JAMES LAST 1993

JAMES LAVELLE – BARCELONA 023 VARIOUS ARTISTS COMPILATION (GLOBAL UNDERGROUND) 2002

JAMIE OLIVER'S COOKIN' – MUSIC TO COOK BY VARIOUS ARTISTS (COLUMBIA) 2000

JAMMIN' – VARIOUS ARTISTS (COOKIE JAR) 1993

THE JAN AND DEAN STORY JAN & DEAN 1980

JANE FONDA'S WORKOUT RECORD JANE FONDA 1983

JANE FONDA'S WORKOUT RECORD: NEW AND IMPROVED JANE FONDA 1984

JANE MCDONALD JANE MCDONALD 1998

JANET JANET JACKSON 1993

JANIS JOPLIN IN CONCERT JANIS JOPLIN 1972

JAPANESE WHISPERS: SINGLES NOV 82–NOV 83 CURE 1983

JAR OF FLIES/SAP ALICE IN CHAINS 1994

JARRE LIVE JEAN-MICHEL JARRE 1989

JARREAU AL JARREAU 1983

JAWS (OST) JOHN WILLIAMS 1976

JAZZ QUEEN 1978

THE JAZZ ALBUM 2003 VARIOUS ARTISTS (VERVE) 2002

JAZZ CAFE – THE SOUL MIX VARIOUS ARTISTS (INSPIRED) 2004

JAZZ CLASSICS LOUIS ARMSTRONG 1961

JAZZ FUNK INCOGNITO 1981

JAZZ JUICE 2 VARIOUS ARTISTS (STREET SOUNDS) 1986

JAZZ JUICE 3 VARIOUS ARTISTS (STREET SOUNDS) 1986

JAZZ JUICE 5 VARIOUS ARTISTS (STREET SOUNDS) 1987

JAZZ MOODS VARIOUS ARTISTS (TELSTAR) 1994

JAZZ MOODS 2 VARIOUS ARTISTS (TELSTAR) 1994

JAZZ ON A SUMMER'S DAY VARIOUS ARTISTS (CASTLE COMMUNICATIONS) 1992

JAZZ SAMBA STAN GETZ & CHARLIE BYRD 1963

JAZZ SEBASTIAN BACH SWINGLE SINGERS 1964

THE JAZZ SINGER (OST) NEIL DIAMOND 1980

JAZZMATAZZ GURU 1993

JAZZMATAZZ VOLUME II – THE NEW REALITY GURU 1995

JEALOUS ONES STILL ENVY (J.O.S.E.) FAT JOE 2002

JEFF BECK, TIM BOGERT & CARMINE APPICE JEFF BECK, TIM BOGERT & CARMINE APPICE 1973

JEFF WAYNE'S MUSICAL VERSION OF THE WAR OF THE WORLDS JEFF WAYNE 1978

JEFF WAYNE'S MUSICAL VERSION OF THE WAR OF THE WORLDS JEFF WAYNE 1996

JEFF WAYNE'S MUSICAL VERSION OF THE WAR OF THE WORLDS – ULLADUBULLA – THE REMIX ALBUM JEFF WAYNE 2000

JEHOVAHKILL JULIAN COPE 1992

JENNIFER PAIGE JENNIFER PAIGE 1998

JENNIFER RUSH JENNIFER RUSH 1985

JERKY VERSIONS OF THE DREAM HOWARD DEVOTO 1983

JERRY LEE LEWIS VOLUME 2 JERRY LEE LEWIS 1962

JESUS CHRIST SUPERSTAR ORIGINAL STUDIO CAST RECORDING 1972

JESUS CHRIST SUPERSTAR (OST) FILM SOUNDTRACK 1973

THE JESUS OF COOL NICK LOWE 1978

JEWEL MARCELLA DETROIT 1994

JI JUNIOR 1982

JIGSAW SHADOWS 1967

JIM DIAMOND JIM DIAMOND 1993

JIM REEVES AND SOME FRIENDS JIM REEVES 1969

JIM REEVES' GOLDEN RECORDS JIM REEVES 1971

THE JIM REEVES WAY JIM REEVES 1965

JIM REEVES WRITES YOU A RECORD JIM REEVES 1971

JIMI HENDRIX JIMI HENDRIX 1975

JIMI HENDRIX – THE ULTIMATE EXPERIENCE JIMI HENDRIX 1992

JIMI HENDRIX AT THE ISLE OF WIGHT JIMI HENDRIX 1971

THE JIMI HENDRIX CONCERTS JIMI HENDRIX 1982

THE JIMMY RUFFIN WAY JIMMY RUFFIN 1967

JINX RORY GALLAGHER 1982

JIVE BUNNY – THE ALBUM JIVE BUNNY & THE MIXMASTERS 1989

JJ72 JJ72 2000

JOAN ARMATRADING JOAN ARMATRADING 1976

JOAN BAEZ JOAN BAEZ 1965

JOAN BAEZ IN CONCERT VOLUME 2 JOAN BAEZ 1964

JOAN BAEZ NO. 5 JOAN BAEZ 1965

JOAN BAEZ ON VANGUARD JOAN BAEZ 1969

JOB LOT CHAS & DAVE 1983

JODY WATLEY JODY WATLEY 1987

JOE BROWN – LIVE JOE BROWN 1963

JOE BUDDEN JOE BUDDEN 2003

JOE COCKER/WITH A LITTLE HELP FROM MY FRIENDS JOE COCKER 1972

THE JOE LONGTHORNE CHRISTMAS ALBUM JOE LONGTHORNE 1989

THE JOE LONGTHORNE SONGBOOK JOE LONGTHORNE 1988

JOE SATRIANI JOE SATRIANI 1995

JOE'S GARAGE ACT I FRANK ZAPPA 1979

JOE'S GARAGE ACTS II & III FRANK ZAPPA 1980

JOEY LAWRENCE JOEY LAWRENCE 1993

JOHN BARLEYCORN MUST DIE TRAFFIC 1970

JOHN DENVER JOHN DENVER 1979

JOHN DENVER – COLLECTION JOHN DENVER 1984

JOHN DIGWEED – LOS ANGELES VARIOUS ARTISTS (GLOBAL UNDERGROUND) 2001

JOHN DIGWEED SYDNEY VARIOUS ARTISTS (GLOBAL UNDERGROUND) 1998

JOHN HANSON SINGS 20 SHOWTIME GREATS JOHN HANSON 1977

JOHN LENNON AND THE PLASTIC ONO BAND JOHN LENNON WITH THE PLASTIC ONO BAND 1971

THE JOHN LENNON ANTHOLOGY JOHN LENNON 1998

THE JOHN LENNON COLLECTION JOHN LENNON 1982

JOHN LENNON LIVE IN NEW YORK CITY JOHN LENNON 1986

JOHN PARR JOHN PARR 1985

JOHN PAUL II – THE PILGRIM POPE POPE JOHN PAUL II 1982

JOHN TAVERNER: INNOCENCE WESTMINSTER ABBEY CHOIR/CONDUCTOR: MARTIN NEARY 1997

JOHN WESLEY HARDING BOB DYLAN 1968

JOHN WILLIAMS PLAYS THE MOVIES JOHN WILLIAMS 1996

JOHNNY CASH JOHNNY CASH 1971

JOHNNY CASH AT FOLSOM PRISON JOHNNY CASH 1968

JOHNNY CASH AT SAN QUENTIN JOHNNY CASH 1969

THE JOHNNY CASH SHOW JOHNNY CASH 1970

THE JOHNNY MATHIS COLLECTION JOHNNY MATHIS 1977

JOHNNY NASH COLLECTION JOHNNY NASH 1977

JOHNNY THE FOX THIN LIZZY 1976

JOHNNY WINTER AND… – JOHNNY WINTER 1970

JOHNNY WINTER AND… LIVE JOHNNY WINTER 1971

JOIN BING AND SING ALONG BING CROSBY 1960

JOIN HANDS SIOUXSIE & THE BANSHEES 1979

JOIN THE ARMY SUICIDAL TENDENCIES 1987

JOIN TOGETHER WHO 1990

JOLLIFICATION LIGHTNING SEEDS 1994

JON SECADA JON SECADA 1992

JONATHAN BUTLER JONATHAN BUTLER 1987

JONATHAN KING'S ENTERTAINMENT FROM THE U.S.A. – TELEVISION COMPILATION 1986

JONATHAN LIVINGSTONE SEAGULL (OST) NEIL DIAMOND 1974

JORDAN: THE COMEBACK PREFAB SPROUT 1990

JOSE CARRERAS COLLECTION JOSE CARRERAS 1988

JOSE CARRERAS SINGS ANDREW LLOYD WEBBER JOSE CARRERAS 1989

JOSE FELICIANO JOSE FELICIANO 1969

JOSEPH AND THE AMAZING TECHNICOLOUR DREAMCOAT ORIGINAL LONDON STAGE CAST SOUNDTRACK 1991

JOSH GROBAN JOSH GROBAN 2003

THE JOSHUA TREE U2 1987

THE JOSHUA TREE SINGLES U2 1988

THE JOURNEY 911 1997

THE JOURNEY – THE VERY BEST OF DONNA SUMMER 2004

JOURNEY INWARDS LTJ BUKEM 2000

JOURNEY THROUGH THE CLASSICS – HOOKED ON CLASSICS 3 LOUIS CLARK CONDUCTING THE ROYAL PHILHARMONIC ORCHESTRA 1983

JOURNEY THROUGH THE SECRET LIFE OF PLANTS STEVIE WONDER 1979

JOURNEY TO ADDIS THIRD WORLD 1978

JOURNEY TO GLORY SPANDAU BALLET 1981

JOURNEY TO THE CENTRE OF THE EARTH RICK WAKEMAN WITH THE LONDON SYMPHONY ORCHESTRA 1974

JOURNEY TO THE URGE WITHIN COURTNEY PINE 1986

JOURNEYMAN ERIC CLAPTON 1989

JOURNEYS BY DJ VOLUME 4 VARIOUS ARTISTS (MUSIC UNITES) 1994

JOY TEDDY PENDERGRASS 1988

JOY 1967–1990 ULTRA VIVID SCENE 1990

A JOYFUL NOISE UNTO THE CREATOR GALLIANO 1992

JOYRIDE ROXETTE 1991

J-TULL DOT COM JETHRO TULL 1999

JU JU SIOUXSIE & THE BANSHEES 1981

JUBILEE SEX PISTOLS 2002

JUDGE JULES PRESENTS TRIED AND TESTED VARIOUS ARTISTS (SERIOUS) 2002

JUDGEMENT NIGHT (OST) FILM SOUNDTRACK 1993

JUDITH JUDY COLLINS 1975

JUDY AT CARNEGIE HALL JUDY GARLAND 1962

JUICY LUCY JUICY LUCY 1970

JUKE BOX JIVE VARIOUS ARTISTS (K-TEL) 1976

JUKE BOX JIVE – ROCK 'N' ROLL GREATS VARIOUS ARTISTS (STYLUS) 1989

THE JUKEBOX YEARS DANIEL O'DONNELL 2004

JULIA FORDHAM JULIA FORDHAM 1988

JULIAN COPE PRESENTS 20 MOTHERS JULIAN COPE 1995

THE JULIET LETTERS ELVIS COSTELLO & THE BRODSKY QUARTET 1993

JULIO JULIO IGLESIAS 1983

JUMP – THE BEST OF THE POINTER SISTERS POINTER SISTERS 1989

JUMP BACK – THE BEST OF THE ROLLING STONES 1971–93 ROLLING STONES 1993

JUMP UP ELTON JOHN 1982

JUMPERS 4 GOALPOSTS VARIOUS ARTISTS (WARNER BROTHERS) 2002

JUMPIN' JIVE JOE JACKSON'S JUMPIN' JIVE 1981

JUNCTION SEVEN STEVE WINWOOD 1997

THE JUNGLE BOOK (OST) FILM SOUNDTRACK 1968

THE JUNGLE BOOK (OST) FILM SOUNDTRACK 1970

JUNGLE FEVER (OST) STEVIE WONDER 1991

JUNGLE HITS VOLUME 1 VARIOUS ARTISTS (JETSTAR) 1994

JUNGLE MANIA 2 VARIOUS ARTISTS (TELSTAR) 1994

JUNGLE MANIA 3 VARIOUS ARTISTS (TELSTAR) 1995

JUNGLE MANIA 94 VARIOUS ARTISTS (TELSTAR) 1994

JUNGLE MASSIVE VARIOUS ARTISTS (WARNER BROTHERS) 2002

JUNGLE MASSIVE – 21ST CENTURY BREAKBEAT VARIOUS ARTISTS (WSM) 2002

JUNGLE TEKNO VOLUME 1 VARIOUS ARTISTS (DEBUT) 1992

JUNIOR BOY'S OWN COLLECTION VARIOUS ARTISTS (JUNIOR BOY'S OWN) 1994

**JUNK CULTURE** ORCHESTRAL MANOEUVRES IN THE DARK 1984

**JUNK SCIENCE** DEEP DISH 1998

**JUNKYARD** BIRTHDAY PARTY 1982

**JURASSIC 5** JURASSIC 5 1998

**JURASSIC PARK (OST)** JOHN WILLIAMS 1993

**JURASSIC SHIFT** OZRIC TENTACLES 1993

**JUST A BOY** LEO SAYER 1974

**JUST A COLLECTION OF ANTIQUES AND CURIOS** STRAWBS 1970

**JUST A GIGGLE** BARRON KNIGHTS 1980

**JUST ADD LIFE** ALMIGHTY 1996

**JUST ANOTHER WAY TO SAY I LOVE YOU** BARRY WHITE 1975

**JUST BACKWARD OF SQUARE** LOWGOLD 2001

**JUST BE** TIESTO 2004

**JUST CAN'T STOP IT** BEAT 1980

**JUST ENOUGH EDUCATION TO PERFORM** STEREOPHONICS 2001

**JUST FOR A DAY** SLOWDIVE 1991

**JUST FOR FUN (OST)** FILM SOUNDTRACK 1963

**JUST FOR YOU** DES O'CONNOR 1980

**JUST FOR YOU** HOWARD KEEL 1988

**JUST FOR YOU** LIONEL RICHIE 2004

**JUST GETS BETTER WITH TIME** WHISPERS 1987

**JUST GOOD FRIENDS** PAUL NICHOLAS 1986

**JUST LIKE BLOOD** TOM MCRAE 2003

**JUST LIKE THE FIRST TIME** FREDDIE JACKSON 1986

**JUST LISTEN** NIGEL KENNEDY WITH THE LONDON PHILHARMONIC ORCHESTRA CONDUCTED BY SIMON RATTLE 1992

**JUST LOVING YOU** ANITA HARRIS 1968

**JUST ONE NIGHT** ERIC CLAPTON 1980

**JUST PUSH PLAY** AEROSMITH 2001

**JUST RAGGA** VARIOUS ARTISTS (CHARM) 1992

**JUST RAGGA VOLUME III** VARIOUS ARTISTS (CHARM) 1993

**JUST SAY OZZY (LIVE)** OZZY OSBOURNE 1990

**JUST SEVENTEEN – GET KICKIN'** – VARIOUS ARTISTS (DOVER) 1990

**JUST SEVENTEEN – HEARTBEATS** VARIOUS ARTISTS (FANFARE) 1989

**JUST SUPPOSIN'** – STATUS QUO 1980

**JUST TESTING** WISHBONE ASH 1980

**JUST THE TWO OF US** VARIOUS ARTISTS (CBS) 1990

**JUST THE WAY YOU LIKE IT** S.O.S. BAND 1984

**JUST TO LET YOU KNOW** BITTY MCLEAN 1994

**JUST VISITING THIS PLANET** JELLYBEAN 1987

**JUSTIFIED** JUSTIN TIMBERLAKE 2002

**JUXTAPOSE** TRICKY WITH DJ MUGGS & GREASE 1999

**K** KULA SHAKER 1996

**KAEMPFERT SPECIAL** BERT KAEMPFERT & HIS ORCHESTRA 1967

**KAFKA** NIGEL KENNEDY 1996

**KAIZOKO BAN** ACCEPT 1986

**KALEIDOSCOPE** SIOUXSIE & THE BANSHEES 1980

**KALEIDOSCOPE** KELIS 2000

**KALEIDOSCOPE WORLD** SWING OUT SISTER 1989

**KAMAKIRIAD** DONALD FAGEN 1993

**KAMIKAZE** DEKE LEONARD 1974

**KAMIKAZE** TWISTA 2004

**KAOS – THE ANTI ACOUSTIC WARFARE** ADAM F 2001

**KAOS THEORY** VARIOUS ARTISTS (TELSTAR) 1992

**KAOS THEORY 2** VARIOUS ARTISTS (TELSTAR) 1992

**KAOS THEORY 4** VARIOUS ARTISTS (TELSTAR) 1992

**KARAJAN: ADAGIO** HERBERT VON KARAJAN CONDUCTING THE BERLIN PHILHARMONIC ORCHESTRA 1995

**KARAOKE PARTY** VARIOUS ARTISTS (TRAX) 1990

**KARAOKE PARTY II** VARIOUS ARTISTS (TRAX) 1991

**THE KARMA COLLECTION** VARIOUS ARTISTS (MINISTRY OF SOUND) 2002

**THE KARMA COLLECTION 2003** VARIOUS ARTISTS (MINISTRY OF SOUND) 2003

**KARYN WHITE** KARYN WHITE 1989

**KATRINA AND THE WAVES** KATRINA & THE WAVES 1985

**KATY LIED** STEELY DAN 1975

**KAVANA** KAVANA 1997

**KAYA** BOB MARLEY & THE WAILERS 1978

**KC AND THE SUNSHINE BAND** KC & THE SUNSHINE BAND 1975

**KEEP FIT AND DANCE** PETER POWELL 1982

**KEEP IN SHAPE SYSTEM WITH ARLENE PHILLIPS** ARLENE PHILLIPS 1982

**KEEP IN SHAPE VOLUME 2** ARLENE PHILLIPS 1984

**KEEP MOVING** MADNESS 1984

**KEEP ON DANCING** VARIOUS ARTISTS (DINO) 1993

**KEEP ON WOMBLING** WOMBLES 1974

**KEEP ON YOUR MEAN SIDE** KILLS 2003

**KEEP THE FAITH** BON JOVI 1992

**KEEP THE FAITH** FAITH EVANS 1998

**KEEP THE MUSIC PLAYING** SHIRLEY BASSEY 1991

**KEEP YOUR DISTANCE** CURIOSITY KILLED THE CAT 1987

**KEEP YOUR EYE ON ME** HERB ALPERT 1987

**KEEPER OF THE SEVEN KEYS PART 2** HELLOWEEN 1988

**KEEPERS OF THE FUNK** LORDS OF THE UNDERGROUND 1994

**KEEPING THE SUMMER ALIVE** BEACH BOYS 1980

**KEITH SWEAT** KEITH SWEAT 1996

**KENNY** KENNY ROGERS 1980

**KENNY BALL'S GOLDEN HITS** KENNY BALL 1963

**KENNY ROGERS** KENNY ROGERS 1977

**THE KENNY ROGERS SINGLES ALBUM** KENNY ROGERS 1979

**THE KENNY ROGERS STORY** KENNY ROGERS 1985

**KEROSENE HAT** CRACKER 1994

**KERRANG – THE ALBUM** VARIOUS ARTISTS (UNIVERSAL) 2001

**KERRANG! 2 – THE ALBUM** VARIOUS ARTISTS (UNIVERSAL) 2001

**KERRANG! 3 – THE ALBUM** VARIOUS ARTISTS (UNIVERSAL) 2002

**KERRANG! 4 – THE ALBUM** VARIOUS ARTISTS (UNIVERSAL) 2002

**KERRANG! – HIGH VOLTAGE** VARIOUS ARTISTS (UNIVERSAL) 2003

**KERRANG! KOMPILATION – 24 ROCK MASTERS** VARIOUS ARTISTS (EMI) 1985

**KERRANG! THE ALBUM** VARIOUS ARTISTS (THE HIT LABEL) 1994

**KEVIN AND PERRY – GO LARGE (OST)** FILM SOUNDTRACK 2000

**THE KEY** JOAN ARMATRADING 1983

**KEYS OF THE KINGDOM** MOODY BLUES 1991

**KEYS TO ASCENSION** YES 1996

**KEYS TO ASCENSION 2** YES 1997

**KICK** INXS 1987

**THE KICK INSIDE** KATE BUSH 1978

**KICK IT – THE DEF JAM SAMPLER VOLUME 1** VARIOUS ARTISTS (DEF JAM) 1987

**KICK UP THE FIRE AND LET THE FLAMES BREAK LOOSE** COOPER TEMPLE CLAUSE 2003

**KICKING AGAINST THE PRICKS** NICK CAVE & THE BAD SEEDS 1986

**KID A** RADIOHEAD 2000

**KIDOLOGY** GLAMMA KID 2000

**THE KIDS ARE ALRIGHT (OST)** WHO 1979

**THE KIDS FROM FAME** KIDS FROM FAME 1982

**THE KIDS FROM FAME AGAIN** KIDS FROM FAME 1982

**THE KIDS FROM FAME LIVE** KIDS FROM FAME 1983

**THE KIDS FROM FAME SING FOR YOU** KIDS FROM FAME 1983

**THE KIDS FROM FAME SONGS** KIDS FROM FAME 1983

**KIKI DEE** KIKI DEE 1977

**KILIMANJARO** TEARDROP EXPLODES 1980

**KILL AT WILL** ICE CUBE 1991

**KILL BILL VOLUME 1** FILM SOUNDTRACK 2003

**KILL BILL VOLUME 2** FILM SOUNDTRACK 2004

**KILL UNCLE** MORRISSEY 1991

**KILLER** ALICE COOPER 1972

**KILLER JOE** LITTLE JIMMY OSMOND 1973

**KILLER ON THE RAMPAGE** EDDY GRANT 1982

**KILLER WATTS** VARIOUS ARTISTS (CBS) 1980

**KILLERS** IRON MAIDEN 1981

**KILLERS** KISS 1982

**THE KILLING FIELDS (OST)** MIKE OLDFIELD 1984

**KILLING JOKE** KILLING JOKE 1980

**KILLING JOKE** KILLING JOKE 2003

**KILLING MACHINE** JUDAS PRIEST 1978

**KILLING ME SOFTLY** ROBERTA FLACK 1973

**KILLING PURITANS** ARMAND VAN HELDEN 2000

**KILLING TIME** TINA COUSINS 1999

**KILN HOUSE** FLEETWOOD MAC 1970

**KILROY WAS HERE** STYX 1983

**KIM APPLEBY** KIM APPLEBY 1990

**KIM WILDE** KIM WILDE 1981

**KIMONO MY HOUSE** SPARKS 1974

**KIND OF BLUE** MILES DAVIS 2001

**A KIND OF HUSH** CARPENTERS 1976

**A KIND OF MAGIC** QUEEN 1986

**KINDA KINKS** KINKS 1965

**KINDA KONTROVERSY** KINKS 1965

**KINDA LATIN** CLIFF RICHARD 1966

**THE KING** TEENAGE FANCLUB 1991

**KING** BELLY 1995

**THE KING AND I** ORIGINAL STUDIO CAST RECORDING 1992

**THE KING AND I (OST)** FILM SOUNDTRACK 1958

**KING AND QUEEN** OTIS REDDING & CARLA THOMAS 1967

**KING COTTON** FIVEPENNY PIECE 1976

**KING CREOLE (OST)** ELVIS PRESLEY 1958

**KING FOR A DAY, FOOL FOR A LIFETIME** FAITH NO MORE 1995

**KING KONG** ORIGINAL SOUTH AFRICAN STAGE CAST SOUNDTRACK 1961

**KING OF AMERICA** COSTELLO SHOW 1986

**KING OF FOOLS** DELIRIOUS? 1997

**KING OF HEARTS** ROY ORBISON 1992

**KING OF STAGE** BOBBY BROWN 1989

**KING OF THE BEACH** CHRIS REA 2000

**KING OF THE ROAD** BOXCAR WILLIE 1980

**KING PUCK** CHRISTY MOORE 1993

**KING SIZE GUITAR** BURT WEEDON 1960

**KINGDOM COME** KINGDOM COME 1988

**KINGDOM OF MADNESS** MAGNUM 1978

**KINGS OF THE WILD FRONTIER** ADAM & THE ANTS 1980

**KING'S X** KING'S X 1992

**KINGSIZE** BOO RADLEYS 1998

**KINGSIZE** FIVE 2001

**KINKS** KINKS 1964

**KINKS GREATEST HITS – DEAD END STREET** KINKS 1983

**KIRI** KIRI TE KANAWA 1988

**KIRI** KIRI TE KANAWA 2001

**KIRI SIDETRACKS – THE JAZZ ALBUM** KIRI TE KANAWA 1992

**KIRI! – KIRI TE KANAWA** 1994

**KISH KASH** BASEMENT JAXX 2003

**KISS 100FM – SMOOTH GROOVES** VARIOUS ARTISTS (POLYGRAM) 1997

**KISS ANTHEMS** VARIOUS ARTISTS (POLYGRAM) 1997

**KISS ANTHEMS '97 – 2** VARIOUS ARTISTS (POLYGRAM) 1997

**KISS ANTHEMS '98** VARIOUS ARTISTS (POLYGRAM) 1998

**KISS CLUBLIFE** VARIOUS ARTISTS (UNIVERSAL) 1999

**KISS CLUBLIFE 2000** VARIOUS ARTISTS (UNIVERSAL) 1999

**KISS CLUBLIFE 2001** VARIOUS ARTISTS (UNIVERSAL) 2001

**KISS CLUBLIFE SUMMER 2000** VARIOUS ARTISTS (UNIVERSAL) 2000

**KISS GARAGE** VARIOUS ARTISTS (POLYGRAM) 1998

**KISS GARAGE PRESENT DJ LUCK & MC NEAT** VARIOUS ARTISTS (UNIVERSAL) 2000

**KISS HITLIST SUMMER 2002** VARIOUS ARTISTS (UNIVERSAL) 2002

**KISS HITLIST SUMMER 2003** VARIOUS ARTISTS (UNIVERSAL) 2003

**KISS HITLIST 2002** VARIOUS ARTISTS (UNIVERSAL) 2002

**KISS HOUSE NATION** VARIOUS ARTISTS (POLYGRAM) 1999

**KISS HOUSE NATION 2000** VARIOUS ARTISTS (UNIVERSAL) 2000

**KISS HOUSE NATION 2001** VARIOUS ARTISTS (UNIVERSAL) 2000

KISS IBIZA 2000 VARIOUS ARTISTS (UNIVERSAL) 2000
KISS IBIZA '99 VARIOUS ARTISTS (UNIVERSAL) 1999
KISS IN IBIZA 2001 VARIOUS ARTISTS (UNIVERSAL) 2001
KISS IN IBIZA '95 VARIOUS ARTISTS (POLYGRAM) 1995
KISS IN IBIZA '96 VARIOUS ARTISTS (POLYGRAM) 1996
KISS IN IBIZA '97 VARIOUS ARTISTS (POLYGRAM) 1997
KISS IN IBIZA '98 VARIOUS ARTISTS (POLYGRAM) 1998
A KISS IN THE DREAMHOUSE SIOUXSIE & THE BANSHEES
    1982
KISS ME KISS ME KISS ME CURE 1987
KISS MIX '96 VARIOUS ARTISTS (POLYGRAM) 1996
KISS MIX '97 VARIOUS ARTISTS (POLYGRAM) 1997
KISS MIX '98 VARIOUS ARTISTS (POLYGRAM) 1998
KISS PRESENTS HIP HOP CLASSICS VARIOUS ARTISTS
    (UNIVERSAL) 2003
KISS PRESENTS HOT JOINTS VARIOUS ARTISTS
    (UNIVERSAL) 2003
KISS PRESENTS LAYDEEZ WITH ATTITUDE VARIOUS ARTISTS
    (UNIVERSAL) 2004
KISS PRESENTS R&B COLLABROATIONS VARIOUS ARTISTS
    (UNIVERSAL) 2003
KISS SMOOTH GROOVES – SUMMER '99 VARIOUS ARTISTS
    (UNIVERSAL) 1999
KISS SMOOTH GROOVES 2000 VARIOUS ARTISTS
    (UNIVERSAL) 2000
KISS SMOOTH GROOVES 2001 VARIOUS ARTISTS
    (UNIVERSAL) 2001
KISS SMOOTH GROOVES '98 VARIOUS ARTISTS
    (POLYGRAM) 1998
KISS SMOOTH GROOVES '99 VARIOUS ARTISTS
    (POLYGRAM) 1999
KISS SMOOTH GROOVES SUMMER 2001 VARIOUS ARTISTS
    (UNIVERSAL) 2001
KISS SMOOTH R&B VARIOUS ARTISTS (UNIVERSAL) 2004
KISS THE LIPS OF LIFE BRILLIANT 1986
KISS THE SKY TATYANA ALI 1999
KISS THIS SEX PISTOLS 1992
KISS UK GARAGE – MIXED BY KARL BROWN VARIOUS
    ARTISTS (UNIVERSAL) 2000
KISSIN' COUSINS (OST) ELVIS PRESLEY 1964
KISSING TO BE CLEVER CULTURE CLUB 1982
KISSTORY VARIOUS ARTISTS (UNIVERSAL) 2002
KISSTORY IBIZA CLASSIC VARIOUS ARTISTS (UNIVERSAL)
    2002
KISSTORY URBAN CLASSICS VARIOUS ARTISTS
    (UNIVERSAL) 2003
KITE KIRSTY MACCOLL 1989
KLUBHOPPIN' – VARIOUS ARTISTS (GLOBAL) 1997
KNEBWORTH – THE ALBUM VARIOUS ARTISTS (POLYDOR)
    1990
KNIFE AZTEC CAMERA 1984
KNOCK ON WOOD EDDIE FLOYD 1967
KNOCKED OUT LOADED BOB DYLAN 1986
KNOW YOUR ENEMY MANIC STREET PREACHERS 2001
KNOWING ME, KNOWING YOU 3 ALAN PARTRIDGE 1995
KNUCKLE SANDWICH VARIOUS ARTISTS (EMI) 1979
KOHYEPT – LIVE IN LENINGRAD BILLY JOEL 1987
KOJAK VARIETY ELVIS COSTELLO 1995
KOKOPELLI KOSHEEN 2003
KONGOS JOHN KONGOS 1972
KOO KOO DEBBIE HARRY 1981
KOOL LOVE KOOL & THE GANG 1990
KOOL AID BIG AUDIO DYNAMITE II 1990
KREUZ KONTROL KREUZ 1995
KT3 – KAOS THEORY 3 VARIOUS ARTISTS (TELSTAR) 1992
KYLIE MINOGUE KYLIE MINOGUE 1994
KYLIE MINOGUE KYLIE MINOGUE 1998
KYLIE! – THE ALBUM KYLIE MINOGUE 1988
KYLIE'S GREATEST HITS KYLIE MINOGUE 1992
L STEVE HILLAGE 1976
L KEVIN GODLEY & LOL CRÈME 1978
L IS FOR LOVER AL JARREAU 1986
L.A. FOLIE STRANGLERS 1981
L.A. GUNS L.A. GUNS 1988
L.A. IS MY LADY FRANK SINATRA WITH THE QUINCY
    JONES ORCHESTRA 1984

L.A. WOMAN DOORS 1971
L.A.M.F. HEARTBREAKERS 1977
LA (LIGHT ALBUM) BEACH BOYS 1979
LA BAMBA (OST) LOS LOBOS 1987
LA CARRETERA JULIO IGLESIAS 1995
LA FREEWAY VARIOUS ARTISTS (DINO) 1991
LA LUNA SARAH BRIGHTMAN 2001
LA PASSION (OST) CHRIS REA 1996
LA VERITE CLASSIX NOUVEAUX 1982
LABCABINCALIFORNIA PHARCYDE 1996
LABOUR OF LOVE UB40 1983
LABOUR OF LOVE – VOLUMES I AND II UB40 1994
LABOUR OF LOVE – VOLUMES I, II & III UB40 2003
LABOUR OF LOVE II UB40 1989
LABOUR OF LOVE III UB40 1998
LABOUR OF LUST NICK LOWE 1979
LABOURS ON LOVE – THE BEST OF HUE AND CRY HUE &
    CRY 1993
LABYRINTH (OST) TREVOR JONES 1986
LACE AND WHISKY ALICE COOPER 1977
THE LADDER YES 1999
LADIES & GENTLEMEN – THE BEST OF GEORGE MICHAEL
    GEORGE MICHAEL 1998
LADIES & GENTLEMEN WE ARE FLOATING IN SPACE
    SPIRITUALIZED 1997
LADIES NIGHT ATOMIC KITTEN 2003
LADIES OF THE CANYON JONI MITCHELL 1970
LADY KENNY ROGERS 1981
LADY DAY – THE VERY BEST OF BILLIE HOLIDAY BILLIE
    HOLIDAY 1997
LADY SAMANTHA ELTON JOHN 1980
THE LADY SINGS THE BLUES VARIOUS ARTISTS (PURE
    MUSIC) 1994
LADY SINGS THE BLUES VARIOUS ARTISTS (VIRGIN) 2002
LADY SINGS THE BLUES (OST) DIANA ROSS 1973
LADY SINGS THE BLUES – NIGHT & DAY VARIOUS ARTISTS
    (VIRGIN) 2002
LADY SOUL ARETHA FRANKLIN 1968
LADYKILLERS VARIOUS ARTISTS (POLYGRAM) 1996
LADYKILLERS 2 VARIOUS ARTISTS (POLYGRAM) 1997
LAID JAMES 1993
THE LAMB LIES DOWN ON BROADWAY GENESIS 1974
LAMBADA VARIOUS ARTISTS (CBS) 1989
LAMENT ULTRAVOX 1984
LAND COMSAT ANGELS 1983
LAND OF HOPE AND GLORY G.U.S. (FOOTWEAR) BAND &
    THE MORRISTON ORPHEUS CHOIR 1970
LAND OF MY FATHERS VARIOUS ARTISTS (UNIVERSAL)
    1999
LANDING ON WATER NEIL YOUNG 1986
LANDMARKS CLANNAD 1998
THE LANGUAGE OF LOVE EVERYTHING BUT THE GIRL 1990
LARGER THAN LIFE JODY WATLEY 1989
LARKS' TONGUES IN ASPIC KING CRIMSON 1973
THE LA'S LA'S 1990
LAS VEGAS LEGENDS VARIOUS ARTISTS (VIRGIN) 2003
LASER LOVE AFTER THE FIRE 1979
THE LAST ACTION HERO (OST) FILM SOUNDTRACK 1993
THE LAST BROADCAST DOVES 2002
THE LAST CALL ANTI-PASTI 1981
THE LAST COMMAND W.A.S.P. 1985
THE LAST DANCE VARIOUS ARTISTS (MOTOWN) 1980
THE LAST DANCE STEPS 2002
THE LAST DOG AND PONY SHOW BOB MOULD 1998
LAST FOREVER JAMES LAST 1981
LAST GOON SHOW OF ALL GOONS 1972
THE LAST IN LINE DIO 1984
LAST NIGHT AT THE PROMS COLIN DAVIS CONDUCTING
    THE BBC SYMPHONY ORCHESTRA, SINGERS &
    CHORUS 1969
LAST OF THE INDEPENDENTS PRETENDERS 1994
THE LAST RECORD ALBUM LITTLE FEAT 1975
LAST SPLASH BREEDERS 1993
THE LAST TEMPTATION ALICE COOPER 1994
THE LAST TEMPTATION JA RULE 2002
THE LAST TEMPTATION OF REID LARD 1990

LAST THE WHOLE NIGHT LONG JAMES LAST 1979
LAST TIME I SAW HIM DIANA ROSS 1974
THE LAST TOUR ON EARTH MARILYN MANSON 1999
LAST TRAIN TO LHASA BANCO DE GAIA 1995
THE LAST WALTZ ENGELBERT HUMPERDINCK 1967
THE LAST WALTZ DANIEL O'DONNELL 1990
LATE NIGHT GRANDE HOTEL NANCI GRIFFITH 1991
LATE NIGHT LOVE VARIOUS ARTISTS (BMG) 2003
THE LATE NIGHT MIX VARIOUS ARTISTS (UNIVERSAL) 2000
LATE NIGHT SAX AFTER DARK 1996
LATE NIGHT SESSIONS VARIOUS ARTISTS (MINISTRY OF
    SOUND) 2003
LATERALUS TOOL 2001
LATE SEPTEMBER DEEPEST BLUE 2004
LATIN A LA LEE PEGGY LEE 1960
LATIN FEVER VARIOUS ARTISTS (UNIVERSAL) 2000
LATIN LEGENDS VARIOUS ARTISTS (TELSTAR) 2003
LATTER DAYS – THE BEST OF – VOLUME 2 LED ZEPPELIN
    2000
LAUGH TERRY HALL 1997
LAUGHING AT THE PIECES DOCTOR & THE MEDICS 1986
LAUGHING ON JUDGEMENT DAY THUNDER 1992
LAUGHING STOCK TALK TALK 1991
LAUGHTER IAN DURY & THE BLOCKHEADS 1980
LAUGHTER AND LUST JOE JACKSON 1991
LAUGHTER AND TEARS – THE BEST OF NEIL SEDAKA TODAY
    NEIL SEDAKA 1976
THE LAUGHTER AND TEARS COLLECTION VARIOUS ARTISTS
    (WARNER BROTHERS) 1983
LAUGHTER IN THE RAIN NEIL SEDAKA 1974
LAUNDRY SERVICE SHAKIRA 2002
LAURENT GARNIER – LABORATOIRE MIX VARIOUS ARTISTS
    (REACT) 1996
THE LAW LAW 1991
LAWYERS IN LOVE JACKSON BROWNE 1983
LAZER GUIDED MELODIES SPIRITUALIZED 1992
LAZY 86–88 PRIMITIVES 1989
LE ROI EST MORT, VIVE LE ROI! – ENIGMA 1996
THE LEAD AND HOW TO SWING IT TOM JONES 1994
LEADERS OF THE PACK VARIOUS ARTISTS (POLYGRAM)
    1993
LEADERS OF THE PACK – 60'S GIRLS VARIOUS ARTISTS
    (UNIVERSAL) 2004
LEAN INTO IT MR. BIG 1991
LEARNING TO CRAWL PRETENDERS 1984
THE LEAST WE CAN DO IS WAVE TO EACH OTHER VAN DE
    GRAAF GENERATOR 1970
LEATHER AND LACE VARIOUS ARTISTS (DINO) 1990
LEATHER AND LACE – THE SECOND CHAPTER VARIOUS
    ARTISTS (DINO) 1990
LEATHER JACKETS ELTON JOHN 1986
LEAVE HOME RAMONES 1977
LEAVE THE BEST TO LAST JAMES LAST 1985
LED ZEPPELIN LED ZEPPELIN 1969
LED ZEPPELIN (BOX SET) LED ZEPPELIN 1990
LED ZEPPELIN 2 LED ZEPPELIN 1969
LED ZEPPELIN 3 LED ZEPPELIN 1970
LED ZEPPELIN BOXED SET II LED ZEPPELIN 1993
LEFT ABOVE THE CLOUDS JOSH WINK 1996
LEFT OF THE MIDDLE NATALIE IMBRUGLIA 1997
LEFTISM LEFTFIELD 1995
LEFTOVER WINE MELANIE 1971
LEGACY – THE GREATEST HITS COLLECTION BOYZ II MEN
    2002
LEGAL DRUG MONEY LOST BOYZ 1996
LEGALIZE IT PETER TOSH 1976
LEGEND – THE BEST OF BOB MARLEY AND THE WAILERS
    BOB MARLEY & THE WAILERS 1984
THE LEGEND – THE ESSENTIAL COLLECTION JOE COCKER
    1992
LEGEND (MUSIC FROM ROBIN OF SHERWOOD) CLANNAD
    1984
THE LEGEND OF BILLIE HOLIDAY BILLIE HOLIDAY 1985
THE LEGEND OF BOBBY DARIN – HIS GREATEST HITS
    BOBBY DARIN 1985
THE LEGEND OF MARIO LANZA MARIO LANZA 1981

LEGEND OF THE GLASS MOUNTAIN RON GOODWIN & HIS ORCHESTRA 1970
THE LEGENDARY BIG BANDS VARIOUS ARTISTS (RONCO) 1980
THE LEGENDARY JOE BLOGGS ALBUM VARIOUS ARTISTS (THE HIT LABEL) 1993
THE LEGENDARY JOE BLOGGS ALBUM 2 VARIOUS ARTISTS (THE HIT LABEL) 1993
A LEGENDARY PERFORMER GLENN MILLER & HIS ORCHESTRA 1976
A LEGENDARY PERFORMER VOLUME 2 GLENN MILLER & HIS ORCHESTRA 1976
A LEGENDARY PERFORMER VOLUME 3 ELVIS PRESLEY 1979
A LEGENDARY PERFORMER VOLUME 4 ELVIS PRESLEY 1983
THE LEGENDARY ROY ORBISON ROY ORBISON 1988
LEGENDS AND HEROES VARIOUS ARTISTS (STYLUS) 1989
LEGENDS OF SOUL – A WHOLE STACK OF SOUL VARIOUS ARTISTS (TELSTAR) 1991
LEISURE BLUR 1991
LEISURE NOISE GAY DAD 1999
LEMON POPSICLE (OST) FILM SOUNDTRACK 1979
THE LENA MARTELL COLLECTION LENA MARTELL 1978
LENA'S MUSIC ALBUM LENA MARTELL 1979
LENNON LEGEND – THE VERY BEST OF JOHN LENNON JOHN LENNON 1997
LENNON McCARTNEY SONGBOOK KEELY SMITH 1965
LENNY LENNY KRAVITZ 2001
LEO SAYER LEO SAYER 1978
LEON RUSSELL AND THE SHELTER PEOPLE LEON RUSSELL 1971
LEONARD BERNSTEIN'S WEST SIDE STORY ORIGINAL STUDIO CAST RECORDING 1993
LES MISERABLES – 10TH ANNIVERSARY CONCERT – ORIGINAL LONDON STAGE CAST SOUNDTRACK 1996
LES MISERABLES ORIGINAL LONDON STAGE CAST SOUNDTRACK 1986
LESLEY GARRETT LESLEY GARRET 1998
LET GO AVRIL LAVIGNE 2002
LET IT BE BEATLES 1970
LET IT BE – NAKED BEATLES 2003
LET IT BEE VOICE OF THE BEEHIVE 1988
LET IT BLEED ROLLING STONES 1969
LET IT COME DOWN SPIRITUALIZED 2001
LET IT RAIN TRACY CHAPMAN 2002
LET IT RIDE SHED SEVEN 1998
LET LOOSE LET LOOSE 1994
LET LOVE IN NICK CAVE & THE BAD SEEDS 1994
LET LOVE RULE LENNY KRAVITZ 1990
LET ME COME OVER BUFFALO TOM 1992
LET ME TRY AGAIN TAMMY JONES 1975
LET ME UP (I'VE HAD ENOUGH) TOM PETTY & HEARTBREAKERS 1987
LET NO ONE LIVE RENT FREE IN YOUR HEAD NICOLETTE 1996
LET THE MUSIC PLAY BARRY WHITE 1976
LET THE MUSIC PLAY SHANNON 1984
LET THE MUSIC PLAY – 80'S GROOVE VARIOUS ARTISTS (COLUMBIA) 2001
LET THE MUSIC SCRATCH VARIOUS ARTISTS (STREET SOUNDS) 1984
LET THE RECORD SPIN SCREEN II 1994
LET THE RHYTHM HIT 'EM ERIC B & RAKIM 1990
LET THEM EAT BINGO BEATS INTERNATIONAL 1990
LET THERE BE ROCK AC/DC 1977
LET US PLAY! – COLDCUT 1997
LET YOUR DIM LIGHT SHINE SOUL ASYLUM 1995
LET YOURSELF GO SYBIL 1987
LETHAL INJECTION ICE CUBE 1993
LET'S BOOGIE SHAKIN' STEVENS 1987
LET'S DANCE DAVID BOWIE 1983
LET'S DANCE – SOUND OF THE SIXTIES PART 1 VARIOUS ARTISTS (OLD GOLD) 1990
LET'S DANCE TO THE HITS OF THE 30'S AND 40'S NEW WORLD THEATRE ORCHESTRA 1960
LET'S FACE IT MIGHTY MIGHTY BOSSTONES 1998

LET'S FACE THE MUSIC SHIRLEY BASSEY WITH THE NELSON RIDDLE ORCHESTRA 1962
LET'S GET BACK TOGETHER – THE LOVE SONGS BILLY OCEAN 2003
LET'S GET IT ON MARVIN GAYE 1973
LET'S GET IT STARTED MC HAMMER 1991
LET'S GET KILLED DAVID HOLMES 1997
LET'S GET SERIOUS JERMAINE JACKSON 1980
LET'S GO DISCO VARIOUS ARTISTS (EMI) 1993
LET'S GO ROUND AGAIN – THE BEST OF AWB AVERAGE WHITE BAND 1994
LET'S GO TO IT KYLIE MINOGUE 1991
LET'S GROOVE VARIOUS ARTISTS (DMG TV) 2003
LET'S GROOVE AGAIN VARIOUS ARTISTS (SONY) 2003
LET'S HAVE ANOTHER PARTY MRS. MILLS 1969
LET'S HEAR IT FOR THE GIRLS VARIOUS ARTISTS (STYLUS) 1986
LET'S HEAR IT FOR THE GIRLS VARIOUS ARTISTS (POLYGRAM) 1995
LET'S MAKE THIS PRECIOUS – THE BEST OF DEXYS MIDNIGHT RUNNERS 2003
LET'S PUSH IT NIGHTCRAWLERS 1995
LET'S PUT IT ALL TOGETHER STYLISTICS 1974
LET'S RUMBLE LOVE/HATE 1993
LET'S STICK TOGETHER BRYAN FERRY 1976
LET'S TALK ABOUT LOVE VARIOUS ARTISTS (DINO) 1992
LET'S TALK ABOUT LOVE CELINE DION 1997
LET'S THINK ABOUT LIVING BOB LUMAN 1961
LETTIN' LOOSE HEAVY PETTIN' 1983
LEVEL 42 LEVEL 42 1981
LEVEL BEST LEVEL 42 1989
LEVELLERS LEVELLERS 1993
LEVELLING THE LAND LEVELLERS 1991
LEVITATION HAWKWIND 1980
THE LEXICON OF LOVE ABC 1982
LIBERATOR ORCHESTRAL MANOEUVRES IN THE DARK 1993
LIBERTY DURAN DURAN 1990
LIBRA JULIO IGLESIAS 1985
LICENCE TO KILL (OST) FILM SOUNDTRACK 1989
LICENSE TO ILL BEASTIE BOYS 1987
LICK – PRESENTED BY TREVOR NELSON VARIOUS ARTISTS (DEF JAM) 2001
THE LICK – BEST OF VARIOUS ARTISTS (UNIVERSAL) 2003
THE LICK – TREVOR NELSON VARIOUS ARTISTS (UNIVERSAL) 2002
LICK IT UP KISS 1983
LICK MY DECALS OFF BABY CAPTAIN BEEFHEART & HIS MAGIC BAND 1971
LICKIN' ON BOTH SIDES MIS-TEEQ 2001
LIE BACK AND ENJOY IT JUICY LUCY 1970
LIEBLING ANDREAS JOHNSON 2000
LIEGE AND LIEF FAIRPORT CONVENTION 1970
LIFE NEIL YOUNG & CRAZY HORSE 1987
LIFE INSPIRAL CARPETS 1990
LIFE CARDIGANS 1995
LIFE SIMPLY RED 1995
LIFE – LIVE THIN LIZZY 1983
LIFE AFTER DEATH NOTORIOUS B.I.G. 1997
LIFE AND LOVE DEMIS ROUSSOS 1978
LIFE FOR RENT DIDO 2003
LIFE GOES ON SASH! 1998
LIFE GOES ON DONELL JONES 2002
LIFE IN A DAY SIMPLE MINDS 1979
A LIFE IN MUSIC – ULTIMATE COLLECTION DOLLY PARTON 1997
LIFE IN THE FAST LANE VARIOUS ARTISTS (TELSTAR) 1987
LIFE IN THE JUNGLE/LIVE AT ABBEY ROAD SHADOWS 1982
LIFE IS A DANCE – THE REMIX PROJECT CHAKA KHAN 1989
LIFE IS PEACHY KORN 1996
LIFE MODEL BLUE AEROPLANES 1994
A LIFE OF SURPRISES – THE BEST OF PREFAB SPROUT PREFAB SPROUT 1992
LIFE ON OTHER PLANETS SUPERGRASS 2002
LIFE ON THE LINE EDDIE & THE HOT RODS 1977

LIFE ON THE WIRE MORRISSEY MULLEN 1982
LIFE THRU A LENS ROBBIE WILLIAMS 1997
A LIFE WITH BRIAN FLOWERED UP 1991
LIFE WON'T WAIT RANCID 1998
LIFEFORMS FUTURE SOUND OF LONDON 1994
LIFELINES A-HA 2002
LIFE'S A RIOT WITH SPY VS SPY BILLY BRAGG 1984
LIFE'S HARD AND THEN YOU DIE IT'S IMMATERIAL 1986
LIFE'S RICH PAGEANT R.E.M. 1986
LIFE'S TOO GOOD SUGARCUBES 1988
LIFE STORY SHADOWS 2004
LIFT THE LID JOOLS HOLLAND & HIS R&B ORCHESTRA 1997
LIFT YOUR SKINNY FISTS LIKE ANTENNAS TO GODSPEED YOU BLACK EMPEROR! 2000
LIGHT AT THE END OF THE TUNNEL DAMNED 1987
LIGHT UP THE NIGHT BROTHERS JOHNSON 1980
THE LIGHT USER SYNDROME FALL 1996
LIGHT YEARS KYLIE MINOGUE 2000
LIGHT YEARS – THE VERY BEST OF ELECTRIC LIGHT ORCHESTRA ELECTRIC LIGHT ORCHESTRA 1997
LIGHTS OUT UFO 1977
LIGHTS... CAMERA... REVOLUTION SUICIDAL TENDENCIES 1990
LIKE A PRAYER MADONNA 1989
LIKE A ROCK BOB SEGER & THE SILVER BULLET BAND 1986
LIKE A VIRGIN MADONNA 1984
LIKE GANGBUSTERS JOBOXERS 1983
LIKE THE DESERTS MISS THE RAIN EVERYTHING BUT THE GIRL 2002
LIKE YOU DO... THE BEST OF LIGHTNING SEEDS LIGHTNING SEEDS 1997
LILAC TIME JUNE BRONHILL & THOMAS ROUND 1960
LILLIE (OST TV) SOUTH BANK ORCHESTRA CONDUCTED BY JOSEPH MOROVITZ & LAURIE HOLLOWAY 1978
LILLO LILLO THOMAS 1987
LILY WAS HERE (OST) DAVID A STEWART 1990
LIMBO THROWING MUSES 1996
LINDISFARNE LIVE LINDISFARNE 1973
LINDY'S PARTY BOLSHOI 1987
LINE UP GRAHAM BONNET 1981
LINGALONGAMAX MAX BYGRAVES 1978
LINGER FICKEN' GOOD REVOLTING COCKS 1993
THE LION AND THE COBRA SINEAD O'CONNOR 1988
THE LION KING (OST) FILM SOUNDTRACK 1994
THE LION KING SING ALONG VARIOUS ARTISTS (PICKWICK) 1994
LIONEL RICHIE LIONEL RICHIE 1982
LIONHEART KATE BUSH 1978
LIONS BLACK CROWES 2001
LIPSTICK ON YOUR COLLAR – 28 ORIGINAL HITS OF THE 50S TELEVISION SOUNDTRACK 1993
LIPSTICK POWDER AND PAINT SHAKIN' STEVENS 1985
LIPSTICK TRACES – A SECRET HISTORY OF MANIC STREET PREACHERS 2003
LIQUID ACROBAT AS REGARDS THE AIR INCREDIBLE STRING BAND 1971
LIQUID GOLD LIQUID GOLD 1980
LIQUID SKIN GOMEZ 1999
LIQUID SWORDS GENIUS/GZA 1995
LIQUIDIZER JESUS JONES 1989
LISA LISA AND CULT JAM WITH FULL FORCE LISA LISA & CULT JAM WITH FULL FORCE 1985
LISA STANSFIELD LISA STANSFIELD 1997
LISTEN A FLOCK OF SEAGULLS 1983
LISTEN URBAN SPECIES 1994
LISTEN LIKE THIEVES INXS 1986
LISTEN TO BILLY J. KRAMER BILLY J. KRAMER WITH THE DAKOTAS 1963
LISTEN TO CLIFF CLIFF RICHARD & THE SHADOWS 1961
LISTEN TO THE RADIO DON WILLIAMS 1982
LISTEN WITHOUT PREJUDICE VOLUME 1 GEORGE MICHAEL 1990
A LITTLE AIN'T ENOUGH DAVID LEE ROTH 1991
A LITTLE BIT MORE DR. HOOK 1976

A LITTLE BIT OF MAMBO LOU BEGA 1999
A LITTLE BIT OF THIS, A LITTLE BIT OF THAT D-MOB 1989
LITTLE BLACK NUMBERS KATHRYN WILLIAMS 2001
A LITTLE BLUES IN YOUR SOUL VARIOUS ARTISTS (WARNER BROTHERS) 1998
LITTLE CREATURES TALKING HEADS 1985
A LITTLE DEEPER MS DYNAMITE 2002
LITTLE DREAMER PETER GREEN 1980
LITTLE EARTHQUAKES TORI AMOS 1992
LITTLE KIX MANSUN 2000
A LITTLE LIGHT MUSIC JETHRO TULL 1992
LITTLE LIGHTS KATE RUSBY 2001
LITTLE LOVE AFFAIRS NANCI GRIFFITH 1988
LITTLE MISS DYNAMITE – BRENDA LEE BRENDA LEE 1980
A LITTLE NIGHT MUSIC RICHARD CLAYDERMAN 1988
LITTLE OF THE PAST LITTLE ANGELS 1994
A LITTLE PEACE NICOLE 1982
LITTLE QUEEN HEART 1977
A LITTLE SOUTH OF SANITY AEROSMITH 1998
LITTLE SPARROW DOLLY PARTON 2001
A LITTLE SPICE LOOSE ENDS 1984
A LITTLE TOUCH OF SCHMILSSON IN THE NIGHT NILSSON 1973
LITTLE TOWN FLIRT DEL SHANNON 1963
LITTLE VILLAGE LITTLE VILLAGE 1992
LIVE BOB MARLEY & THE WAILERS 1975
LIVE MANHATTAN TRANSFER 1978
LIVE EAGLES 1980
LIVE SAD CAFE 1981
LIVE EUROPEANS 1984
LIVE THUNDER 1998
LIVE – ERA '87 '93 GUNS N' ROSES 1999
LIVE – ON TWO LEGS PEARL JAM 1998
LIVE – THE WAY WE WALK VOLUME 1: THE SHORTS GENESIS 1992
LIVE – THE WAY WE WALK VOLUME 2: THE LONGS GENESIS 1993
LIVE & KICKING – VIEWERS CHOICE PART 1 TELEVISION COMPILATION 1999
LIVE (X CERT) STRANGLERS 1979
LIVE 1975 – THE ROLLING THUNDER REVUE BOB DYLAN 2002
LIVE 1979 HAWKWIND 1980
LIVE 1980–1986 JOE JACKSON 1988
LIVE 4 EVER VARIOUS ARTISTS (WARNER BROTHERS) 1998
LIVE 93 ORB 1993
LIVE A PARIS CELINE DION 1996
LIVE AFTER DEATH IRON MAIDEN 1985
LIVE ALIVE QUO STATUS QUO 1992
LIVE AND DANGEROUS THIN LIZZY 1978
LIVE AND DIRECT ASWAD 1983
LIVE AND HEAVY VARIOUS ARTISTS (NEMS) 1981
LIVE AND LEARN ELKIE BROOKS 1979
LIVE AND LET LIVE 10 CC 1977
LIVE AND MORE DONNA SUMMER 1978
LIVE & SWINGING – THE ULTIMATE RAT PACK VARIOUS ARTISTS (REPRISE) 2003
LIVE AND UNCENSORED MILLIE JACKSON 1985
LIVE AT BRIXTON ACADEMY BRIAN MAY BAND 1994
LIVE AT CAESAR'S PALACE TOM JONES 1971
LIVE AT DONNINGTON IRON MAIDEN 1993
LIVE AT KNEBWORTH ROBBIE WILLIAMS 2003
LIVE AT LEEDS WHO 1970
LIVE' AT LONDON'S TALK OF THE TOWN DIANA ROSS & THE SUPREMES 1968
LIVE AT THE ALBANY EMPIRE FLYING PICKETS 1983
LIVE AT THE BBC BEATLES 1994
LIVE AT THE BBC DIRE STRAITS 1995
LIVE AT THE BBC FLEETWOOD MAC 1995
LIVE AT THE BLOOMSBURY THEATRE 12.3.95 TINDERSTICKS 1995
LIVE AT THE BRIXTON ACADEMY FAITH NO MORE 1991
LIVE AT THE GRAND OPERA HOUSE BELFAST VAN MORRISON 1984
LIVE AT THE GREEK JIMMY PAGE & THE BLACK CROWES 2000

LIVE AT THE HEART OF THE CITY WHITESNAKE 1980
LIVE AT THE HOLLYWOOD BOWL DOORS 1987
LIVE AT THE LONDON PALLADIUM BING CROSBY 1977
LIVE AT THE LYCEUM BOB MARLEY & THE WAILERS 1981
LIVE AT THE PALLADIUM CARPENTERS 1977
LIVE AT THE RIVIERA LAS VEGAS ENGELBERT HUMPERDINCK 1972
LIVE AT THE ROYAL ALBERT HALL WET WET WET WITH THE WREN ORCHESTRA 1993
LIVE AT THE ROYAL ALBERT HALL JOE LONGTHORNE 1994
LIVE AT THE ROYAL ALBERT HALL BOB DYLAN 1998
LIVE AT THE ROYAL ALBERT HALL SPIRITUALIZED 1998
LIVE AT THE ROYAL ALBERT HALL WHO 2003
LIVE AT THE ROYAL FESTIVAL HALL NEIL SEDAKA 1974
LIVE AT THE SOCIAL – VOLUME 1 VARIOUS ARTISTS (HEAVENLY) 1996
LIVE AT THE TALK OF THE TOWN TOM JONES 1967
LIVE AT THE TALK OF THE TOWN SEEKERS 1968
LIVE AT THE TALK OF THE TOWN SHIRLEY BASSEY 1970
LIVE AT TREORCHY MAX BOYCE 1975
LIVE AT TREORCHY MAX BOYCE 1978
LIVE AT WEMBLEY QUEEN 1992
'LIVE' AT WEMBLEY MEAT LOAF 1987
LIVE AT WEMBLEY '86 QUEEN 2003
LIVE BABY LIVE INXS 1991
LIVE BURSTING OUT JETHRO TULL 1978
LIVE CREAM CREAM 1970
LIVE CREAM VOLUME 2 CREAM 1972
LIVE DATES II WISHBONE ASH 1980
LIVE EVIL BLACK SABBATH 1983
LIVE FAST, DIE FAST WOLFSBANE 1989
LIVE FOREVER – THE BEST OF BRITPOP VARIOUS ARTISTS (VIRGIN) 2003
LIVE FROM EARTH PAT BENATAR 1983
THE LIVE GREATEST HITS ELVIS PRESLEY 2001
LIVE HERALD STEVE HILLAGE 1979
LIVE IN AUSTRALIA ELTON JOHN & THE MELBOURNE SYMPHONY ORCHESTRA 1987
LIVE IN BELFAST ROWAN ATKINSON 1981
LIVE IN EUROPE TINA TURNER 1988
LIVE IN LONDON JOHN DENVER 1976
LIVE IN LOS ANGELES MAZE FEATURING FRANKIE BEVERLY 1986
LIVE IN MANCHESTER WONDERSTUFF 1995
LIVE IN NEW YORK CITY BRUCE SPRINGSTEEN & THE E. STREET BAND 2001
LIVE IN TEXAS LINKIN PARK 2003
LIVE IN THE CITY OF LIGHT SIMPLE MINDS 1987
LIVE IN THE RAW W.A.S.P. 1987
LIVE IN THE UK HELLOWEEN 1989
LIVE IN YUGOSLAVIA ANTI-NOWHERE LEAGUE 1983
LIVE IT LIKE YOU LOVE IT CHARLATANS 2002
LIVE JAM JAM 1993
LIVE KILLERS QUEEN 1979
LIVE LAUGH LOVE DANIEL O'DONNELL 2001
LIVE MAGIC QUEEN 1986
LIVE MCMXCIII VELVET UNDERGROUND 1993
LIVE ON BROADWAY BARRY MANILOW 1990
LIVE ONE NIGHT ONLY BEE GEES 1998
LIVE RUST NEIL YOUNG & CRAZY HORSE 1979
LIVE SEEDS NICK CAVE & THE BAD SEEDS 1993
LIVE SHIT – BINGE AND PURGE METALLICA 1993
LIVE THROUGH THIS HOLE 1994
LIVE WOOD PAUL WELLER 1994
LIVE YOUR LIFE BE FREE BELINDA CARLISLE 1991
LIVE! – SHAKATAK 1985
LIVE! – POLICE 1995
LIVE! IN EUROPE RORY GALLAGHER 1972
LIVE! IN THE AIR AGE BE-BOP DELUXE 1977
LIVE! LIVE! LIVE! – BRYAN ADAMS 1994
LIVE, STOLEN MOMENTS – THE LADY SINGS THE BLUES DIANA ROSS 1993
LIVE/1975–1985 BRUCE SPRINGSTEEN & THE E. STREET BAND 1986
LIVE: RIGHT HERE, RIGHT NOW VAN HALEN 1993
LIVEANDIRECT ADAMSKI 1989

LIVELY UP YOURSELF BOB MARLEY 2001
LIVERPOOL FRANKIE GOES TO HOLLYWOOD 1986
LIVES IN THE BALANCE JACKSON BROWNE 1986
LIVING ALL ALONE PHYLLIS HYMAN 1986
LIVING CLASSICS VARIOUS ARTISTS (DEUTSCHE GRAMMOPHON) 1992
LIVING EYES BEE GEES 1981
LIVING IN A BOX LIVING IN A BOX 1987
LIVING IN A FANTASY LEO SAYER 1980
LIVING IN OZ RICK SPRINGFIELD 1984
LIVING IN THE MATERIAL WORLD GEORGE HARRISON 1973
LIVING IN THE PAST JETHRO TULL 1972
LIVING IN THE PRESENT FUTURE EAGLE-EYE CHERRY 2000
LIVING IN THE USA LINDA RONSTADT 1978
LIVING INSIDE YOUR LOVE GEORGE BENSON 1979
LIVING LEGENDS EVERLY BROTHERS 1977
LIVING MY LIFE GRACE JONES 1982
LIVING ON THE FAULT LINE DOOBIE BROTHERS 1977
LIVING ORNAMENTS 1979 GARY NUMAN 1981
LIVING ORNAMENTS 1979–1980 GARY NUMAN 1981
LIVING ORNAMENTS 1980 GARY NUMAN 1981
LIVING PROOF CHER 2001
THE LIVING YEARS MIKE & THE MECHANICS 1988
THE LIVING YEARS MIKE & THE MECHANICS 1996
LIZA WITH A 'Z' – LIZA MINNELLI 1973
LIZARD KING CRIMSON 1971
LLOYD COLE LLOYD COLE 1990
LLOYD WEBBER PLAYS LLOYD WEBBER JULIAN LLOYD WEBBER WITH THE ROYAL PHILHARMONIC ORCHESTRA 1990
LOAD METALLICA 1996
LOADED VARIOUS ARTISTS (EMI) 1993
LOADED LOCK IN VARIOUS ARTISTS (V2) 1997
LOADS – THE BEST OF THE HAPPY MONDAYS HAPPY MONDAYS 1995
LOCAL HERO (OST) MARK KNOPFLER 1983
LOC'ED AFTER DARK TONE LOC 1989
LOCK UP THE WOLVES DIO 1990
LOCK, STOCK & TWO SMOKING BARRELS (OST) FILM SOUNDTRACK 1998
LOCKED IN WISHBONE ASH 1976
LOCO FUN LOVIN' CRIMINALS 2001
LODGER DAVID BOWIE 1979
LOGIC WILL BREAK YOUR HEART STILLS 2004
LONDON D-INFLUENCE 1997
LONDON 0 HULL 4 HOUSEMARTINS 1986
LONDON CALLING CLASH 1979
LONDON TOWN WINGS 1978
LONDON WARSAW NEW YORK BASIA 1990
LONE JUSTICE LONE JUSTICE 1985
THE LONE PIPER MUNROS FEATURING DAVID METHREN 1998
THE LONE RANGER SUGGS 1995
LONE STAR LONE STAR 1976
LONELY AND BLUE ROY ORBISON 1963
LONELY IS AN EYESORE VARIOUS ARTISTS (4AD) 1987
THE LONESOME JUBILEE JOHN COUGAR MELLENCAMP 1987
LONG AFTER DARK TOM PETTY & HEARTBREAKERS 1982
LONG GONE BEFORE DAYLIGHT CARDIGANS 2003
THE LONG BLACK VEIL CHIEFTAINS 1995
LONG COLD WINTER CINDERELLA 1988
LONG DISTANCE – THE BEST OF RUNRIG RUNRIG 1996
LONG DISTANCE VOYAGER MOODY BLUES 1981
LONG JOHN SILVER JEFFERSON AIRPLANE 1972
LONG LIVE LOVE OLIVIA NEWTON-JOHN 1974
LONG LIVE ROCK 'N' ROLL RAINBOW 1978
LONG MAY YOU RUN STILLS-YOUNG BAND 1976
LONG MISTY DAYS ROBIN TROWER 1976
LONG PLAYER FACES 1971
THE LONG ROAD NICKELBACK 2003
THE LONG ROAD BACK PETER ANDRE 2004
THE LONG RUN EAGLES 1979
LONGING IN THEIR HEARTS BONNIE RAIT 1994
LONNIE LONNIE DONEGAN 1958

LONNIE DONEGAN SHOWCASE LONNIE DONEGAN 1956
THE LOOK SHALAMAR 1983
LOOK AT ME NOW BERNIE MARSDEN 1981
LOOK BETH NIELSEN CHAPMAN 2004
LOOK AT US SONNY & CHER 1965
LOOK AT YOURSELF URIAH HEEP 1971
LOOK HEAR? – 10 CC 1980
LOOK HOW LONG LOOSE ENDS 1990
LOOK INTO THE EYEBALL DAVID BYRNE 2001
THE LOOK OF LOVE VARIOUS ARTISTS (POLYGRAM) 1996
THE LOOK OF LOVE DIANA KRALL 2001
THE LOOK OF LOVE DUSTY SPRINGFIELD 2004
THE LOOK OF LOVE – THE BEST OF BURT BACHARACH
    VARIOUS ARTISTS (WARNER BROTHERS) 2001
LOOK OF LOVE – THE VERY BEST OF ABC ABC 2001
LOOK SHARP JOE JACKSON 1979
LOOK SHARP! – ROXETTE 1989
LOOK TO YOUR HEART FRANK SINATRA 1959
LOOKIN' IN SAVOY BROWN 1970
LOOKIN' THROUGH THE WINDOWS JACKSON FIVE 1972
LOOKIN' THRU THE EYES OF LOVE GENE PITNEY 1965
LOOKING BACK JOHN MAYALL 1969
LOOKING EAST JACKSON BROWNE 1996
LOOKING FORWARD CROSBY, STILL, NASH & YOUNG 1999
THE LOOKS OR THE LIFESTYLE POP WILL EAT ITSELF 1992
LOONEE TUNES BAD MANNERS 1980
LOOSE SCREW PRETENDERS 2003
LORD OF THE RINGS BO HANNSON 1972
THE LORD OF THE RINGS – OST HOWARD SHORE 2002
THE LORD OF THE RINGS – RETURN OF THE KING (OST)
    HOWARD SHORE 2003
THE LORD OF THE RINGS – THE TWO TOWERS – OST
    HOWARD SHORE 2003
LORD UPMINSTER IAN DURY & THE BLOCKHEADS 1981
LORE CLANNAD 1996
LOSS MULL HISTORICAL SOCIETY 2001
LOST BOYS FLYING PICKETS 1984
THE LOST BOYS (OST) FILM SOUNDTRACK 1989
LOST HORIZON (OST) FILM SOUNDTRACK 1973
LOST HORIZONS LEMON JELLY 2002
LOST IN SPACE AIMEE MANN 2002
LOST PROPERTY VARIOUS ARTISTS (EMI) 1996
THE LOST RECORDINGS GLENN MILLER & HIS ORCHESTRA
    1995
THE LOST RIOTS HOPE OF THE STATES 2004
LOST SIDES DOVES 2003
LOST SONGS 95–98 DAVID GRAY 2000
LOST SOULS DOVES 2000
LOST WITHOUT YOUR LOVE BREAD 1977
LOUD TIMO MAAS 2002
LOUD AND CLEAR SAMMY HAGAR 1980
LOUD 'N' PROUD NAZARETH 1973
LOUDER THAN BOMBS SMITHS 1987
LOUDER THAN WORDS LIONEL RICHIE 1996
LOUDMOUTH – THE BEST OF THE BOOMTOWN RATS AND
    BOB GELDOF BOOMTOWN RATS & BOB GELDOF 1994
LOUNGIN' – VARIOUS ARTISTS (UNIVERSAL) 2002
LOVE AZTEC CAMERA 1987
LOVE VARIOUS ARTISTS (POLYGRAM) 1998
LOVE VARIOUS ARTISTS (UNIVERSAL) 2002
LOVE ACTUALLY (OST) FILM SOUNDTRACK 2003
THE LOVE ALBUM VARIOUS ARTISTS (K-TEL) 1980
THE LOVE ALBUM DORIS DAY 1994
THE LOVE ALBUM VARIOUS ARTISTS (VIRGIN) 1994
THE LOVE ALBUM CLASSICS VARIOUS ARTISTS (VIRGIN)
    2002
THE LOVE ALBUM – 16 CLASSIC LOVE SONGS VARIOUS
    ARTISTS (TELSTAR) 1985
THE LOVE ALBUM '88 VARIOUS ARTISTS (TELSTAR) 1988
THE LOVE ALBUM II VARIOUS ARTISTS (VIRGIN) 1995
THE LOVE ALBUM III VARIOUS ARTISTS (VIRGIN) 1996
THE LOVE ALBUM IV VARIOUS ARTISTS (VIRGIN) 1997
LOVE ALWAYS K-CI & JOJO 1997
LOVE AND DANCING LEAGUE UNLIMITED ORCHESTRA
    1982
LOVE AND KISSES DANNII MINOGUE 1991

LOVE AND KISSES FROM BROTHERHOOD OF MAN 1976
LOVE AND LIFE DEFINITION OF SOUND 1991
LOVE & LIFE MARY J. BLIGE 2003
LOVE AND LIFE – THE VERY BEST OF DIANA ROSS 2001
LOVE AND OTHER DEMONS STRANGELOVE 1996
LOVE AND THE RUSSIAN WINTER SIMPLY RED 1999
LOVE AND THEFT BOB DYLAN 2001
LOVE ANDY ANDY WILLIAMS 1968
LOVE AT FIRST STING SCORPIONS 1984
LOVE AT THE GREEK NEIL DIAMOND 1977
LOVE AT THE MOVIES VARIOUS ARTISTS (TELSTAR) 1991
LOVE AT THE MOVIES JANE MCDONALD 2001
LOVE AT THE MOVIES... THE ALBUM VARIOUS ARTISTS
    (EMI) 1996
LOVE BEACH EMERSON, LAKE & PALMER 1978
LOVE BITES BUZZCOCKS 1978
LOVE BITES & SCHOOL NITES VARIOUS ARTISTS (TELSTAR)
    2004
LOVE BYRD DONALD BYRD 1981
LOVE CAN DO THAT ELAINE PAIGE 1991
LOVE CHILD DIANA ROSS & THE SUPREMES 1969
LOVE CLASSICS ROYAL PHILHARMONIC ORCHESTRA
    CONDUCTED BY NICK PORTLOCK 1983
LOVE DELUXE SADE 1992
LOVE DRIVE SCORPIONS 1979
LOVE ETERNAL VARIOUS ARTISTS (MIRACLE) 1995
LOVE – ETERNAL LOVESONGS VARIOUS ARTISTS
    (UNIVERSAL) 2003
LOVE FOR SALE BONEY M 1977
LOVE GAMES DRIFTERS 1975
LOVE HAS FOUND ITS WAY DENNIS BROWN 1982
LOVE HATE TRAGEDY PAPA ROACH 2002
LOVE HOUSE VARIOUS ARTISTS (K-TEL) 1989
LOVE HUNTER WHITESNAKE 1979
LOVE HURTS EVERLY BROTHERS 1982
LOVE HURTS ELAINE PAIGE 1985
LOVE HURTS CHER 1991
LOVE II SWING VARIOUS ARTISTS (TELSTAR) 1996
LOVE IN MOTION ICEHOUSE 1983
LOVE IN THE SIXTIES VARIOUS ARTISTS (DINO) 1993
LOVE IS... – VARIOUS ARTISTS (K-TEL) 1981
LOVE IS KIM WILDE 1992
LOVE IS A NOW AND THEN THING ANTHONY NEWLEY
    1960
LOVE IS FOR EVER BILLY OCEAN 1997
LOVE IS FOR SUCKERS TWISTED SISTER 1987
LOVE IS FOREVER CLIFF RICHARD & THE SHADOWS 1966
LOVE IS HELL PART 1 RYAN ADAMS 2003
LOVE IS HERE STARSAILOR 2001
LOVE IS RHYTHM VARIOUS ARTISTS (TELSTAR) 1993
LOVE IS TEASING SPINNERS 1972
LOVE IS – THE ALBUM VARIOUS ARTISTS (VIRGIN) 2004
LOVE IS THE LAW TOYAH 1983
LOVE IS THE THING NAT 'KING' COLE 1957
LOVE IT TO DEATH ALICE COOPER 1972
LOVE LETTERS FROM ELVIS ELVIS PRESLEY 1971
A LOVE LIKE OURS BARBRA STREISAND 1999
LOVE MAKES NO SENSE ALEXANDER O'NEAL 1993
LOVE ME AGAIN RITA COOLIDGE 1978
LOVE ME FOR A REASON OSMONDS 1974
LOVE ME TENDER JULIE ANDREWS 1983
LOVE METAL H.I.M. 2003
THE LOVE MOVEMENT A TRIBE CALLED QUEST 1998
LOVE MOVES KIM WILDE 1990
LOVE MUST BE THE REASON JAMES LAST 1972
LOVE NOT MONEY EVERYTHING BUT THE GIRL 1985
THE LOVE OF HOPELESS CAUSES NEW MODEL ARMY 1993
LOVE ON A SUMMER'S DAY VARIOUS ARTISTS (TELSTAR)
    2000
LOVE ON FILM VARIOUS ARTISTS (TELSTAR) 1994
LOVE ON THE AIRWAYS GALLAGHER & LYLE 1977
LOVE OVER GOLD DIRE STRAITS 1982
LOVE OVER GOLD VARIOUS ARTISTS (TELSTAR) 1994
LOVE OVER GOLD 2 VARIOUS ARTISTS (TELSTAR) 1996
LOVE SCENES CULT 1985
LOVE SCENES BEVERLEY CRAVEN 1993

LOVE SENSUALITY DEVOTION – GREATEST HITS ENIGMA
    2001
LOVE SO STRONG VARIOUS ARTISTS (WARNER BROTHERS)
    2002
LOVE SONGS BEATLES 1977
LOVE SONGS ELVIS PRESLEY 1979
LOVE SONGS NEIL DIAMOND 1981
LOVE SONGS CLIFF RICHARD 1981
LOVE SONGS CHICAGO 1982
LOVE SONGS ELTON JOHN 1982
LOVE SONGS DIANA ROSS 1982
LOVE SONGS COMMODORES 1982
LOVE SONGS BARBRA STREISAND 1982
LOVE SONGS SHIRLEY BASSEY 1982
THE LOVE SONGS GEORGE BENSON 1985
THE LOVE SONGS RANDY CRAWFORD 1987
LOVE SONGS DIANA ROSS & MICHAEL JACKSON 1987
LOVE SONGS MARVIN GAYE & SMOKEY ROBINSON 1988
LOVE SONGS VARIOUS ARTISTS (TELSTAR) 1989
LOVE SONGS MARVIN GAYE 1990
LOVE SONGS DIONNE WARWICK 1990
LOVE SONGS KENNY ROGERS 1997
LOVE SONGS CARPENTERS 1997
THE LOVE SONGS CHRIS DE BURGH 1997
LOVE SONGS DANIEL O'DONNELL 1998
LOVE SONGS ABBA 1998
LOVE SONGS VARIOUS ARTISTS (POLYGRAM) 1999
LOVE SONGS DR. HOOK 1999
LOVE SONGS LUCIANO PAVAROTTI 1999
THE LOVE SONGS MARVIN GAYE 2000
LOVE SONGS ROY ORBISON 2001
LOVE SONGS DEAN MARTIN 2002
LOVE SONGS NAT 'KING' COLE 2003
LOVE SONGS BARRY WHITE 2003
LOVE SONGS JULIO IGLESIAS 2003
LOVE SONGS – 16 CLASSIC HITS STEVIE WONDER 1984
LOVE SONGS – 16 CLASSIC LOVE SONGS VARIOUS ARTISTS
    (WARWICK) 1978
LOVE SONGS – 16 CLASSIC LOVE SONGS VARIOUS ARTISTS
    (TELSTAR) 1984
LOVE SONGS – THE VERY BEST OF FOSTER AND ALLEN
    VOLUME 2 FOSTER & ALLEN 1987
THE LOVE SONGS ALBUM VARIOUS ARTISTS (K-TEL) 1982
THE LOVE SONGS ALBUM MICHAEL CRAWFORD 1994
THE LOVE SONGS ALBUM VARIOUS ARTISTS (UNIVERSAL)
    2000
THE LOVE SONGS OF ANDREW LLOYD WEBBER RICHARD
    CLAYDERMAN 1989
THE LOVE SONGS OF BURT BACHARACH VARIOUS ARTISTS
    (UNIVERSAL) 1996
LOVE SONGS TO MAKE YOU FEEL GOOD VARIOUS ARTISTS
    (TELSTAR) 2004
LOVE STORIES DON WILLIAMS 1983
LOVE STORY ANDY WILLIAMS 1971
LOVE STORY JOHNNY MATHIS 1971
LOVE STORY RAY CONNIFF 1971
LOVE STORY LLOYD COLE 1995
LOVE STORY (OST) FILM SOUNDTRACK 1971
A LOVE STORY MICHAEL BALL 2003
LOVE SUPREME DIANA ROSS & THE SUPREMES 1989
LOVE SUPREME VARIOUS ARTISTS (DINO) 1991
THE LOVE THAT WHIRLS (DIARY OF A THINKING HEART)
    BILL NELSON 1982
LOVE – THE ESSENTIAL AL GREEN 2002
LOVE THEME FROM 'THE GODFATHER' – ANDY WILLIAMS
    1972
LOVE THIS IS MY SONG JAMES LAST 1967
LOVE TO LOVE YOU BABY DONNA SUMMER 1976
LOVE TRACKS GLORIA GAYNOR 1979
LOVE TRAIN – THE SOUND OF PHILADELPHIA VARIOUS
    ARTISTS (SONY) 1998
LOVE TRAVELS KATHY MATTEA 1997
A LOVE TRILOGY DONNA SUMMER 1976
LOVE 2 DANCE VARIOUS ARTISTS (TELSTAR) 2000
LOVE UNCHAINED ENGELBERT HUMPERDINCK 1995
LOVE UNLIMITED VARIOUS ARTISTS (TELSTAR) 2001

LOVE WARS WOMACK & WOMACK 1984
LOVE, WHITNEY WHITNEY HOUSTON 2002
LOVE WITH A REGGAE RHYTHM VARIOUS ARTISTS (VISION) 1995
LOVE YOU LIVE ROLLING STONES 1977
LOVE YOU TILL TUESDAY DAVID BOWIE 1984
LOVE ZONE BILLY OCEAN 1986
LOVE, DEVOTION, SURRENDER CARLOS SANTANA & MAHAVISHNU JOHN MCLAUGHLIN 1973
LOVE, LIFE AND FEELINGS SHIRLEY BASSEY 1976
LOVEBOAT ERASURE 2000
LOVEBOX GROOVE ARMADA 2002
LOVED UP VARIOUS ARTISTS (INSPIRED) 2000
LOVEGOD SOUP DRAGONS 1990
LOVELESS MY BLOODY VALENTINE 1991
LOVELIFE LUSH 1996
LOVELINES CARPENTERS 1990
LOVELY PRIMITIVES 1988
LOVELY DAY VARIOUS ARTISTS (TELSTAR) 2004
THE LOVER IN ME SHEENA EASTON 1989
LOVERMAN VARIOUS ARTISTS (EMI) 1996
LOVERS VARIOUS ARTISTS (TELSTAR) 1986
THE LOVERS VARIOUS ARTISTS (K-TEL) 1988
LOVERS SLEEPY JACKSON 2003
LOVERS FOR LOVERS VOLUME 3 VARIOUS ARTISTS (BUSINESS) 1990
LOVERS IN THE CITY TANITA TIKARAM 1995
LOVERS LIVE SADE 2002
LOVERS ONLY VARIOUS ARTISTS (RONCO) 1983
LOVERS ROCK SADE 2000
LOVE'S A PRIMA DONNA STEVE HARLEY & COCKNEY REBEL 1976
LOVES SONGS – THE VERY BEST OF RANDY CRAWFORD RANDY CRAWFORD 2000
LOVESCAPE NEIL DIAMOND 1991
LOVESEXY PRINCE 1988
LOVESONGS FOR UNDERDOGS TANYA DONELLY 1997
LOVIN' IT VARIOUS ARTISTS (INCREDIBLE) 2001
LOVIN' IT 2 VARIOUS ARTISTS (INCREDIBLE) 2001
LOVING YOU ELVIS PRESLEY 1957
LOVING YOU ELVIS PRESLEY 1977
LOW DAVID BOWIE 1977
THE LOW END THEORY A TRIBE CALLED QUEST 1991
LOW-LIFE NEW ORDER 1985
LP REMBRANDTS 1995
LTJ BUKEM PRESENTS EARTH – VOLUME 1 VARIOUS ARTISTS (EARTH) 1996
LTJ BUKEM PRESENTS EARTH – VOLUME TWO VARIOUS ARTISTS (GOOD LOOKING) 1997
LTJ BUKEM PRESENTS LOGICAL PROGRESSION VARIOUS ARTISTS (FFRR) 1996
LUCK OF THE DRAW BONNIE RAIT 1991
LUCKY SKIN 1996
LUCKY DAY SHAGGY 2002
LUCKY 13 SHADES OF VAL DOONICAN VAL DOONICAN 1964
LUCKY THIRTEEN NEIL YOUNG 1993
LUCKY TOWN BRUCE SPRINGSTEEN 1992
LUMINOUS BASEMENT TOURISTS 1980
LUSH LIFE LINDA RONSTADT WITH THE NELSON RIDDLE ORCHESTRA 1985
LUST FOR LIFE IGGY POP 1977
LUSTRA ECHOBELLY 1997
LUTRICIA MCNEAL LUTRICIA MCNEAL 1998
LUXEMBOURG BLUETONES 2003
THE LUXURY GAP HEAVEN 17 1983
LUXURY LINER EMMYLOU HARRIS 1977
LUXURY OF LIFE FIVE STAR 1985
LYTE FUNKIE ONES LYTE FUNKIE ONES 2000
M.U. THE BEST OF JETHRO TULL JETHRO TULL 1976
MA LENA ZAVARONI 1974
THE MAC BAND MAC BAND FEATURING THE MCCAMPBELL BROTHERS 1988
MACALLA CLANNAD 1985
MACHINA/THE MACHINES OF GOD SMASHING PUMPKINS 2000

MACHINE STATIC-X 2001
MACHINE + SOUL GARY NUMAN 1992
MACHINE GUN ETIQUETTE DAMNED 1979
MACHINE HEAD DEEP PURPLE 1972
MACHISMO CAMEO 1988
MACK AND MABEL ORIGINAL BROADWAY STAGE CAST SOUNDTRACK 1982
MAD DOGS AND ENGLISHMEN JOE COCKER 1970
MAD FOR IT VARIOUS ARTISTS (TELSTAR) 1996
MAD LOVE LINDA RONSTADT 1980
MAD NOT MAD MADNESS 1985
MAD ON HOUSE VOLUME 1 VARIOUS ARTISTS (NEEDLE) 1988
MAD SEASON BY MATCHBOX 20 MATCHBOX 20 2000
MAD SHADOWS MOTT THE HOOPLE 1970
MAD, BAD AND DANGEROUS TO KNOW DEAD OR ALIVE 1987
MADCAP LAUGHS SYD BARRETT 1970
MADE AGAIN MARILLION 1996
MADE IN AMERICA CARPENTERS 1981
MADE IN ENGLAND ELTON JOHN 1995
MADE IN HEAVEN QUEEN 1995
MADE IN JAPAN DEEP PURPLE 1973
MADE IN THE SHADE ROLLING STONES 1975
MADE IT THROUGH THE RAIN GERARD KENNY 1979
MADE TO LOVE MAGIC NICK DRAKE 2004
MADMAN ACROSS THE WATER ELTON JOHN 1972
THE MADMAN'S RETURN SNAP! 1992
THE MADNESS MADNESS 1988
MADNESS 7 MADNESS 1981
MADNESS, MONEY AND MUSIC SHEENA EASTON 1982
MADONNA MADONNA 1983
MADSTOCK! – MADNESS 1992
THE MAGAZINE RICKIE LEE JONES 1984
MAGGIE FOSTER & ALLEN 1983
MAGIC GILLAN 1982
MAGIC VARIOUS ARTISTS (UNIVERSAL) 2001
MAGIC AND LOSS LOU REED 1992
MAGIC AND MEDICINE CORAL 2003
MAGIC BULLETS MEGA CITY FOUR 1993
THE MAGIC FLUTE OF JAMES GALWAY JAMES GALWAY 1978
MAGIC FLY SPACE 1977
MAGIC HOTEL TOPLOADER 2002
MAGIC HOUR CAST 1999
MAGIC IN THE AIR LINDISFARNE 1978
THE MAGIC IS YOU SHIRLEY BASSEY 1979
MAGIC MOMENTS BRENDAN SHINE 1989
THE MAGIC OF BONEY M BONEY M 1980
THE MAGIC OF CHRISTMAS GEORGE MITCHELL MINSTRELS 1970
THE MAGIC OF DEMIS ROUSSOS DEMIS ROUSSOS 1977
THE MAGIC OF DISNEY – 20 SUPERSTAR HITS VARIOUS ARTISTS (WALT DISNEY) 2002
THE MAGIC OF FOSTER AND ALLEN (THEIR GREATEST HITS) FOSTER & ALLEN 1989
THE MAGIC OF INSPECTOR MORE BARRINGTON PHELOUNG 2000
THE MAGIC OF NANA MOUSKOURI NANA MOUSKOURI 1988
MAGIC OF THE MINSTRELS GEORGE MITCHELL MINSTRELS 1965
THE MAGIC OF THE MOVIES DORIS DAY 1999
THE MAGIC OF THE MUSICALS MARTI WEBB & MARK RATTRAY 1992
THE MAGIC OF TORVILL AND DEAN VARIOUS ARTISTS (STYLUS) 1985
THE MAGIC OF VAL DOONICAN VAL DOONICAN 1970
MAGIC REGGAE VARIOUS ARTISTS (K-TEL) 1980
MAGIC – SUMMER FEELING 2003 VARIOUS ARTISTS (UNIVERSAL) 2003
THE MAGIC TOUCH OF ODYSSEY ODYSSEY 1982
MAGIC, MURDER AND THE WEATHER MAGAZINE 1981
MAGICAL MYSTERY TOUR BEATLES 1968
MAGICAL RING CLANNAD 1983
THE MAGICIAN'S BIRTHDAY URIAH HEEP 1972

MAGNET ROBIN GIBB 2003
MAGNETIC FIELDS JEAN-MICHEL JARRE 1981
MAGNIFICATION YES 2001
THE MAGNIFICENT SEVEN SUPREMES & THE FOUR TOPS 1971
THE MAIN INGREDIENT PETE ROCK & C.L. SMOOTH 1994
MAIN OFFENDER KEITH RICHARDS 1992
MAINSTREAM LLOYD COLE & THE COMMOTIONS 1987
MAIRE MAIRE BRENNAN 1992
MAKE IT BIG WHAM! 1984
MAKE IT EASY ON YOURSELF JOHNNY MATHIS 1972
MAKE IT GOOD A1 2002
MAKE IT LAST FOREVER KEITH SWEAT 1988
MAKE ME AN OFFER ORIGINAL LONDON STAGE CAST SOUNDTRACK 1960
MAKE THE PARTY LAST JAMES LAST 1975
MAKE THE WORLD GO AWAY DONNY & MARIE OSMOND 1975
MAKE UP THE BREAKDOWN HOT HOT HEAT 2003
MAKE YOU SWEAT VARIOUS ARTISTS (TELSTAR) 1991
MAKE YOUR MOVE CAPTAIN & TENNILLE 1980
MAKIN' MAGIC PAT TRAVERS 1977
MAKING A GOOD THING BETTER OLIVIA NEWTON-JOHN 1977
MAKING BONES RED SNAPPER 1998
MAKING CONTACT UFO 1983
MAKING HISTORY LINTON KWESI JOHNSON 1984
MAKING LOVE AND MUSIC DR. HOOK 1977
MAKING MOVIES DIRE STRAITS 1980
MAKING TRACKS FIVEPENNY PIECE 1973
MAKING WAVES NOLANS 1980
MALACHI MALACHI CUSH 2003
MALADJUSTED MORRISSEY 1997
MALADROIT WEEZER 2002
MALPRACTICE DR. FEELGOOD 1975
MALPRACTICE REDMAN 2001
MAMA SAID LENNY KRAVITZ 1991
MAMA SAID KNOCK YOU OUT LL COOL J 1990
MAMAS AND PAPAS DELIVER MAMAS & THE PAPAS 1967
MAMBO SINUENDO RY COODER & MANUEL GALBAM 2003
MAMMA LUCIANO PAVAROTTI WITH THE HENRY MANCINI ORCHESTRA 1984
MAMMA MIA! – ORIGINAL LONDON STAGE CAST SOUNDTRACK 1999
MAMOUNA BRYAN FERRY 1994
THE MAN BARRY WHITE 1979
MAN NENEH CHERRY 1996
MAN ALIVE 4 OF US 1993
A MAN ALONE – THE WORDS AND MUSIC OF ROD MCKUEN FRANK SINATRA 1969
A MAN AND HIS MUSIC FRANK SINATRA 1966
THE MAN AND HIS MUSIC SAM COOKE 1986
A MAN AND A WOMAN (OST) FILM SOUNDTRACK 1967
THE MAN FROM UTOPIA FRANK ZAPPA 1983
MAN IN BLACK JOHNNY CASH 1971
THE MAN IN BLACK – DEFINITIVE COLLECTION JOHNNY CASH 1994
MAN IN BLACK – THE VERY BEST OF JOHNNY CASH 2002
MAN OF COLOURS ICEHOUSE 1988
MAN ON THE LINE CHRIS DE BURGH 1984
MAN TO MAN HOT CHOCOLATE 1976
MAN VS MACHINE XZIBIT 2002
THE MAN WHO TRAVIS 1999
THE MAN WHO SOLD THE WORLD DAVID BOWIE 1972
THE MAN WITH THE GOLDEN FLUTE JAMES GALWAY 1978
A MAN WITHOUT LOVE ENGELBERT HUMPERDINCK 1968
MANASSAS STEPHEN STILLS' MANASSAS 1972
MANE ATTRACTION WHITE LION 1991
MANGE TOUT BLANCMANGE 1984
MANHATTAN TRANSFER MANHATTAN TRANSFER 1977
MANHATTANS MANHATTANS 1976
MANIC NIRVANA ROBERT PLANT 1990
MANIC POP THRILL THAT PETROL EMOTION 1986
MANIFESTO ROXY MUSIC 1979
MANILOW BARRY MANILOW 1985

MANILOW MAGIC – THE BEST OF BARRY MANILOW BARRY MANILOW 1979
THE MAN MACHINE KRAFTWERK 1978
MANN MADE MANFRED MANN 1965
MANN MADE HITS MANFRED MANN 1966
MANNERS AND PHYSIQUE ADAM ANT 1990
MANTLE PIECES CLIFFORD T. WARD 1974
MANTOVANI MAGIC MANTOVANI & HIS ORCHESTRA 1966
MANTOVANI MAGIC MANTOVANI & HIS ORCHESTRA 1985
MANTOVANI TODAY MANTOVANI & HIS ORCHESTRA 1970
MANTOVANI'S GOLDEN HITS MANTOVANI & HIS ORCHESTRA 1967
MANUMISSION – THE MOVIE FILM SOUNDTRACK 1999
MANY HAPPY RETURNS – THE HITS GARY GLITTER 1992
MARA RUNRIG 1995
MARATHON SANTANA 1979
MARAUDER MAGNUM 1980
MARAUDER BLACKFOOT 1981
MARC COHN MARC COHN 1991
MARCH OR DIE MOTORHEAD 1992
MARCHIN' ALREADY OCEAN COLOUR SCENE 1997
MARCY PLAYGROUND MARCY PLAYGROUND 1998
THE MARIA CALLAS COLLECTION MARIA CALLAS 1987
MARIA MCKEE MARIA MCKEE 1989
MARIAH CAREY MARIAH CAREY 1990
MARIANNE FAITHFULL MARIANNE FAITHFULL 1965
MARILLION.COM MARILLION 1999
MARIO LANZA – THE ULTIMATE COLLECTION MARIO LANZA 1994
MARK HOLLIS MARK HOLLIS 1998
THE MARK II PURPLE SINGLES DEEP PURPLE 1979
MARK RATTRAY PERFORMS THE SONGS OF THE MUSICALS MARK RATTRAY 1990
THE MARK TOM & TRAVIS SHOW BLINK 182 2000
MARK'S KEYBOARD REPAIR MONEY MARK 1995
MAROON BARENAKED LADIES 2000
THE MARQUEE – 30 LEGENDARY YEARS VARIOUS ARTISTS (POLYDOR) 1989
MARQUEE METAL VARIOUS ARTISTS (MARQUE) 1991
MARQUEE MOON TELEVISION 1977
MARRYING MAIDEN IT'S A BEAUTIFUL DAY 1970
MARS AUDIAC QUINTET STEREOLAB 1994
THE MARSHALL MATHERS LP EMINEM 2000
MARTIKA MARTIKA 1989
MARTIKA'S KITCHEN MARTIKA 1991
MARTIN GUERRE ORIGINAL LONDON STAGE CAST SOUNDTRACK 1996
THE MARTYR MANTRAS JESUS LOVES YOU 1991
MARVIN AT THE MOVIES HANK MARVIN 2000
MARVIN, WELCH AND FARRAR HANK MARVIN, BRUCE WELCH & JOHN FARRAR 1971
MARY MARY J. BLIGE 1999
MARY JANES GIRLS MARY JANE GIRLS 1983
MARY O'HARA AT THE ROYAL FESTIVAL HALL MARY O'HARA 1978
MARY POPPINS (OST) FILM SOUNDTRACK 1965
MARY STAR OF THE SEA ZWAN 2003
MASK BAUHAUS 1981
MASK VANGELIS 1985
MASQUE MISSION 1992
MASQUERADE – MESSAGE TO THE STREET WYCLEF JEAN 2002
MASSIVE – AN ALBUM OF REGGAE HITS VARIOUS ARTISTS (VIRGIN) 1985
MASSIVE 4 VARIOUS ARTISTS (LONDON) 1990
MASSIVE DANCE 2001 VARIOUS ARTISTS (UNIVERSAL) 2000
MASSIVE DANCE HITS 2000 VARIOUS ARTISTS (UNIVERSAL) 1999
MASSIVE DANCE MIX 96 VARIOUS ARTISTS (TELSTAR) 1996
MASSIVE DANCE: 98 VARIOUS ARTISTS (WARNER BROTHERS) 1997
MASSIVE DANCE: 98 – VOLUME 2 VARIOUS ARTISTS (POLYGRAM) 1998

MASSIVE DANCE: 99 VARIOUS ARTISTS (POLYGRAM) 1998
MASSIVE DANCE: 99 – VOLUME TWO VARIOUS ARTISTS (POLYGRAM) 1999
MASSIVE HITS VARIOUS ARTISTS (TELSTAR) 1991
MASTER AND EVERYONE BONNIE PRINCE BILLY 2003
MASTER OF PUPPETS METALLICA 1986
MASTER OF REALITY BLACK SABBATH 1971
MASTERPIECE TEMPTATIONS 1973
MASTERPIECES – THE ESSENTIAL FLUTE OF JAMES GALWAY JAMES GALWAY 1993
MASTERPIECES – THE VERY BEST OF SKY SKY 1984
THE MASTERPLAN OASIS 1998
MASTERS OF METAL VARIOUS ARTISTS (K-TEL) 1986
MASTERWORKS JEFF JARRATT & DON REEDMAN 1980
MATA LEAO BIOHAZARD 1996
MATADOR ORIGINAL STUDIO CAST RECORDING 1987
MATCHBOX MATCHBOX 1980
MATHIS MAGIC JOHNNY MATHIS 1979
THE MATRIX (OST) FILM SOUNDTRACK 1999
THE MATRIX RELOADED FILM SOUNDTRACK 2003
MATT BIANCO MATT BIANCO 1986
MATTERS OF THE HEART TRACY CHAPMAN 1992
MATTHEW AND SON CAT STEVENS 1967
MAVERICK A STRIKE FINLEY QUAYE 1997
MAVERICKS MAVERICKS 2003
MAX POWER – MAX BASS VARIOUS ARTISTS (BREAK DOWN) 1996
MAX Q MAX Q 1989
MAXI MAXI PRIEST 1987
MAXIMUM DARKNESS MAN 1975
A MAXIMUM HIGH SHED SEVEN 1996
MAXIMUM JOY FRANKIE GOES TO HOLLYWOOD 2000
MAXIMUM RAVE VARIOUS ARTISTS (EMI) 1992
MAXIMUM SECURITY ALIEN SEX FIEND 1985
MAXIMUM SPEED VARIOUS ARTISTS (VIRGIN) 1998
MAXIMUM SPEED 99 VARIOUS ARTISTS (VIRGIN) 1999
MAXINQUAYE TRICKY 1995
MAY EACH DAY ANDY WILLIAMS 1966
MAYA BANCO DE GAIA 1994
MAYBE IT'S LIVE ROBERT PALMER 1982
MAYBE YOU SHOULD DRIVE BARENAKED LADIES 1994
MAYBE YOU'VE BEEN BRAINWASHED TOO NEW RADICALS 1999
MAYFLOWER WEATHER PROPHETS 1987
McCARTNEY PAUL McCARTNEY 1970
McCARTNEY II PAUL McCARTNEY 1980
THE McCARTNEY INTERVIEW PAUL McCARTNEY 1981
MCGUINNESS FLINT MCGUINNESS FLINT 1971
MCLEMORE AVENUE BOOKER T & THE M.G.S 1970
MCMXC A.D ENIGMA 1990
MCVICAR (OST) ROGER DALTREY 1980
ME AND BILLY WILLIAMS MAX BOYCE 1980
ME AND MR JOHNSON ERIC CLAPTON 2004
ME AND MY SHADOWS CLIFF RICHARD & THE SHADOWS 1960
ME MYSELF I JOAN ARMATRADING 1980
MEAN BUSINESS FIRM 1986
MEAN STREAK Y & T 1983
THE MEANING OF LOVE MICHELLE 2004
MEAT IS MURDER SMITHS 1985
MEATY, BEATY, BIG AND BOUNCY WHO 1971
MECHANICAL ANIMAL MARILYN MANSON 1998
MECHANICAL WONDER OCEAN COLOUR SCENE 2001
MECHANIX UFO 1982
MEDDLE PINK FLOYD 1971
MEDICINE 4 MY PAIN LYNDEN DAVID HALL 1998
MEDUSA ANNIE LENNOX 1995
MEET DANNY WILSON DANNY WILSON 1988
MEET THE BELLRAYS BELLRAYS 2002
MEET THE SEARCHERS SEARCHERS 1963
MEET THE SUPREMES SUPREMES 1964
MEGA DANCE – THE POWER ZONE VARIOUS ARTISTS (EMI) 1993
MEGA DANCE 2 – THE ENERGY ZONE VARIOUS ARTISTS (EMI) 1993
THE MEGA RAVE VARIOUS ARTISTS (EMI) 1993

MEGABASS VARIOUS ARTISTS (TELSTAR) 1990
MEGABASS 2 VARIOUS ARTISTS (TELSTAR) 1990
MEGABASS 3 VARIOUS ARTISTS (TELSTAR) 1991
MEGA LO MANIA VARIOUS ARTISTS (POLYGRAM) 1993
MEGATOP PHOENIX BIG AUDIO DYNAMITE 1989
MEISO DJ KRUSH 1995
MELLON COLLIE AND THE INFINITE SADNESS SMASHING PUMPKINS 1995
MELLOW GOLD BECK 1994
MELLOW MADNESS VARIOUS ARTISTS (EPIC) 1991
MELODY AM ROYKSOPP 2002
MELTDOWN ASH 2004
MELTDOWN 2000 – BEST NEW TRANCE VARIOUS ARTISTS (VIRGIN) 2000
MELTING POT CHARLATANS 1998
MEL TORME AT 'THE CRESCENDO' MEL TORME 1956
MEL TORME WITH TH MARTY PAICH DEK-TETTE MEL TORME 1956
MEMORABILIA – THE SINGLES SOFT CELL & MARC ALMOND 1991
A MEMORIAL 1944–1969 GLENN MILLER & HIS ORCHESTRA 1970
MEMORIAL BEACH A-HA 1993
MEMORIES BRENDAN SHINE 1985
MEMORIES FOSTER & ALLEN 1991
MEMORIES – THE BEST OF ELAINE PAIGE ELAINE PAIGE 1987
MEMORIES ARE MADE OF HITS PERRY COMO 1975
MEMORIES ARE MADE OF THIS RAY CONNIFF 1961
MEMORIES ARE MADE OF THIS VARIOUS ARTISTS (RONCO) 1981
MEMORIES ARE MADE OF THIS VARIOUS ARTISTS (DINO) 1992
MEMORIES ARE MADE OF THIS VARIOUS ARTISTS (DINO) 1994
MEMORIES ARE MADE OF THIS VARIOUS ARTISTS (VIRGIN) 2004
MEMORIES OF HOME ROSE MARIE 1996
THE MEMORY KINDA LINGERS NOT THE NINE O'CLOCK NEWS CAST 1982
THE MEMORY OF TREES ENYA 1995
THE MEMPHIS SESSIONS WET WET WET 1988
MEN AND WOMEN SIMPLY RED 1987
MEN AND WOMEN SIMPLY RED 1996
MEN IN BLACK – THE ALBUM FILM SOUNDTRACK 1997
MEN WITHOUT WOMEN LITTLE STEVEN & THE DISCIPLES OF SOUL 1982
THE MENACE ELASTICA 2000
MENACE TO SOBRIETY UGLY KID JOE 1995
MENACE TO SOBRIETY OPM 2001
MENAGERIE BILL WITHERS 1978
MENDELSSOHN/BRUCH/SCHUBERT NIGEL KENNEDY WITH JEFFREY TATE CONDUCTING THE ENGLISH CHAMBER ORCHESTRA 1990
MER DE NOMS A PERFECT CIRCLE 2000
MERCURY AMERICAN MUSIC CLUB 1993
MERCURY LONGVIEW 2003
MERCURY FALLING STING 1996
MERMAID AVENUE BILLY BRAGG & WILCO 1998
MERMAID AVENUE – VOLUME 2 BILLY BRAGG & WILCO 2000
MERMAIDS (OST) FILM SOUNDTRACK 1991
MERRY CHRISTMAS MARIAH CAREY 1994
MERRY CHRISTMAS MR LAWRENCE (OST) RYUICHI SAKAMOTO 1983
MERRY CHRISTMAS TO YOU VARIOUS ARTISTS (WARWICK) 1984
MERRY, MERRY CHRISTMAS NEW KIDS ON THE BLOCK 1990
THE MERSEY BEAT VOLUME 1 VARIOUS ARTISTS (ORIOLE) 1963
MERSEYBEAST IAN MCNABB 1996
THE MERSEYBEATS MERSEYBEATS 1964
MESOPOTAMIA B-52'S 1982
THE MESSAGE GRANDMASTER FLASH & THE FURIOUS FIVE 1982

**THE MESSIAH** LONDON PHILHARMONIC CHOIR WITH THE LONDON ORCHESTRA CONDUCTED BY WALTER SUSSKIND 1960

**METAL BOX** PUBLIC IMAGE LTD 1979

**METAL FOR MUTHAS** VARIOUS ARTISTS (EMI) 1980

**METAL FOR MUTHAS VOLUME 2** VARIOUS ARTISTS (EMI) 1980

**METAL HEART** ACCEPT 1985

**METAL RHYTHM** GARY NUMAN 1988

**METAL WORKS 73–93** JUDAS PRIEST 1993

**METALHEADZ – PLATINUM BREAKZ** VARIOUS ARTISTS (FFRR) 1996

**METALLICA** METALLICA 1991

**METAMATIC** JOHN FOXX 1980

**METAMORPHOSES** JEAN-MICHEL JARRE 2000

**METAMORPHOSIS** ROLLING STONES 1975

**METAMORPHOSIS** HILARY DUFF 2003

**METEORA** LINKIN PARK 2003

**METRO MUSIC** MARTHA & THE MUFFINS 1980

**MEZCAL HEAD** SWERVEDRIVER 1993

**MEZZAMORPHIS** DELIRIOUS? 1999

**MEZZANINE** MASSIVE ATTACK 1998

**MH** MARQUES HOUSTON 2004

**MI TIERRA** GLORIA ESTEFAN 1993

**MIAMI VICE 2** TELEVISION SOUNDTRACK 1987

**MIAMI VICE III** TELEVISION SOUNDTRACK 1988

**MIAOW** BEAUTIFUL SOUTH 1994

**MICHAEL BALL** MICHAEL BALL 1992

**MICHAEL BUBLÉ – MICHAEL BUBLÉ** 2003

**MICHAEL CRAWFORD PERFORMS ANDREW LLOYD WEBBER** MICHAEL CRAWFORD & THE ROYAL PHILHARMONIC ORCHESTRA 1991

**MICHAEL FLATLEY'S LORD OF THE DANCE** RONAN HARDIMAN 1996

**MICHAEL JACKSON 9 SINGLE PACK** MICHAEL JACKSON 1983

**THE MICHAEL JACKSON MIX** MICHAEL JACKSON 1987

**THE MICHEAL PARKINSON COLLECTION** VARIOUS ARTISTS (UNIVERSAL) 2003

**MICHAEL SCHENKER GROUP** MICHAEL SCHENKER GROUP 1980

**MICHELLE GAYLE** MICHELLE GAYLE 1994

**MICK AND CAROLINE** LATIN QUARTER 1987

**MICRO PHONIES** CABARET VOLTAIRE 1984

**MIDDLE CLASS REVOLT** FALL 1994

**MIDDLE MAN** BOZ SCAGGS 1980

**MIDDLE OF NOWHERE** HANSON 1997

**THE MIDDLE OF NOWHERE** ORBITAL 1999

**MIDIAN** CRADLE OF FILTH 2000

**MIDNIGHT AT THE LOST AND FOUND** MEAT LOAF 1983

**MIDNIGHT CRUISING** VARIOUS ARTISTS (DINO) 1992

**MIDNIGHT HOUR** VARIOUS ARTISTS (K-TEL) 1982

**MIDNIGHT HUSTLE** VARIOUS ARTISTS (K-TEL) 1978

**MIDNIGHT IN MOTOWN** VARIOUS ARTISTS (TELSTAR) 1982

**MIDNIGHT LIGHTNING** JIMI HENDRIX 1975

**MIDNIGHT LOVE** MARVIN GAYE 1982

**MIDNIGHT LOVE** VARIOUS ARTISTS (STYLUS) 1989

**MIDNIGHT MAGIC** COMMODORES 1979

**MIDNIGHT MARAUDERS** A TRIBE CALLED QUEST 1993

**MIDNIGHT MOODS – THE LIGHTER SIDE OF JAZZ** VARIOUS ARTISTS (POLYGRAM) 1993

**MIDNIGHT MOODS – THE LOVE COLLECTION** GEORGE BENSON 1991

**MIDNIGHT POSTCARDS** ADAM FAITH 1993

**MIDNIGHT SOUL** VARIOUS ARTISTS (ATLANTIC) 1966

**MIDNIGHT STROLL** ROBERT CRAY BAND WITH THE MEMPHIS HORNS 1990

**MIDNIGHT TO MIDNIGHT** PSYCHEDELIC FURS 1987

**MIDNITE DYNAMOS** MATCHBOX 1980

**MIDNITE VULTURES** BECK 1999

**MIDSUMMER CLASSICS** VARIOUS ARTISTS (GLOBAL) 1999

**MIGHTY JOE MOON** GRANT LEE BUFFALO 1994

**MIGHTY LIKE A ROSE** ELVIS COSTELLO 1991

**MIGHTY REAL** SYLVESTER 1979

**MIKE AND THE MECHANICS** MIKE & THE MECHANICS 1986

**MIKE AND THE MECHANICS** MIKE & THE MECHANICS 1996

**MIKE AND THE MECHANICS** MIKE & THE MECHANICS 1999

**MILES FROM HOME** PESHAY 1999

**MILES HIGH** JOHN MILES 1981

**MILES OF AISLES** JONI MITCHELL 1975

**MILESTONES** ROLLING STONES 1972

**MILESTONES – 20 ROCK OPERAS** VARIOUS ARTISTS (TELSTAR) 1990

**MILITARY GOLD** VARIOUS ARTISTS (RONCO) 1979

**MILK AND HONEY – A HEART PLAY** JOHN LENNON & YOKO ONO 1984

**MILK & KISSES** COCTEAU TWINS 1996

**MILK INC.** MILK INC. 2002

**MILLENNIUM** BACKSTREET BOYS 1999

**MILLICAN AND NESBITT** MILLICAN & NESBITT 1974

**MILLIGAN PRESERVED** SPIKE MILLIGAN 1961

**MILLION DOLLAR BABIES** ALICE COOPER 1973

**THE MILLION DOLLAR HOTEL (OST)** FILM SOUNDTRACK 2000

**A MILLION DOLLARS' WORTH OF TWANG** DUANNE EDDY 1961

**A MILLION DOLLARS' WORTH OF TWANG VOLUME 2** DUANNE EDDY 1962

**MILLION MILE REFLECTIONS** CHARLIE DANIELS BAND 1979

**MILLION SELLER HITS** ANONYMOUS COVER VERSIONS 1971

**MILLIONAIRES** JAMES 1999

**MIMOSA** FUN LOVIN' CRIMINALS 1999

**MIND ADVENTURES** DES'REE 1992

**MIND AND SOUL COLLABORATORS** BACK TO THE PLANET 1993

**MIND BOMB** THE THE 1989

**MIND ELEVATION** NIGHTMARES ON WAX 2002

**MIND GAMES** JOHN LENNON 1973

**THE MINDBENDERS** MINDBENDERS 1966

**THE MIND'S EYE** STILTSKIN 1994

**MINGUS** JONI MITCHELL 1979

**MINI** WEDDING PRESENT 1996

**MINIPOPS** MINIPOPS 1981

**MINISTRY OF SOUND – DANCE NATION 2** VARIOUS ARTISTS (MINISTRY OF SOUND) 1996

**MINISTRY OF SOUND – THE SESSIONS 4** VARIOUS ARTISTS (MINISTRY OF SOUND) 1995

**MINISTRY OF SOUND – THE SESSIONS VOLUME 2** VARIOUS ARTISTS (MINISTRY OF SOUND) 1994

**MINISTRY OF SOUND – THE SESSIONS VOLUME 3** VARIOUS ARTISTS (MINISTRY OF SOUND) 1994

**MINISTRY OF SOUND CLASSICS MIXED BY JUDGE JULES** VARIOUS ARTISTS (MINISTRY OF SOUND) 1997

**MINISTRY OF SOUND SESSION SIX – FRANKIE KNUCKLES** VARIOUS ARTISTS (MINISTRY OF SOUND) 1996

**MINISTRY OF SOUND SESSIONS – VOLUME 5** VARIOUS ARTISTS (MINISTRY OF SOUND) 1995

**MINISTRY OF SOUND: THE SESSIONS VOLUME 1** VARIOUS ARTISTS (MINISTRY OF SOUND) 1993

**THE MINISTRY OF SOUND PRESENTS A DAY IN THE LIFE OF TODD TERRY** TODD TERRY 1995

**MINOR EARTH MAJOR SKY** A-HA 2000

**MINSTREL OF THE GALLERY** JETHRO TULL 1975

**MINUTES** ELKIE BROOKS 1984

**MINX** TOYAH 1985

**MIRACLE** KANE GANG 1987

**THE MIRACLE** QUEEN 1989

**MIRAGE** FLEETWOOD MAC 1982

**MIRIELLE MATHIEU** MIRIELLE MATHIEU 1968

**MIRMAMA** EDDI READER 1992

**MIRROR BALL** NEIL YOUNG 1995

**MIRROR BLUE** RICHARD THOMPSON 1994

**MIRROR MAN** CAPTAIN BEEFHEART & HIS MAGIC BAND 1971

**MIRROR MOVES** PSYCHEDELIC FURS 1984

**MIRRORS** BLUE OYSTER CULT 1979

**MISDEMEANOUR** UFO 1985

**THE MISEDUCATION OF LAURYN HILL** LAURYN HILL 1998

**MISPLACED CHILDHOOD** MARILLION 1985

**MISPLACED IDEALS** SAD CAFÉ 1978

**MISS E. . . SO ADDICTIVE** MISSY 'MISDEMEANOR' ELLIOTT 2001

**MISS RANDY CRAWFORD – THE GREATEST HITS** RANDY CRAWFORD 1984

**MISS SAIGON** ORIGINAL LONDON STAGE CAST SOUNDTRACK 1990

**MISSA LUBA** TROUBADOURS DU ROI BAUDOUIN 1976

**MISSING YOU** VARIOUS ARTISTS (EMI) 1994

**MISSING YOU** DAVID ESSEX 1995

**MISSING YOU – AN ALBUM OF LOVE** VARIOUS ARTISTS (EMI) 1990

**MISSING YOU 2 – AN ALBUM OF LOVE** VARIOUS ARTISTS (EMI) 1991

**MISSING... PRESUMED HAVING A GOOD TIME** NOTTING HILLBILLIES 1990

**THE MISSION (OST)** ENNIO MORRICONE WITH THE LONDON PHILHARMONIC ORCHESTRA 1987

**MISSION ACCOMPLISHED BUT THE BEAT GOES ON** REZILLOS 1979

**MISSION IMPOSSIBLE 2 (OST)** FILM SOUNDTRACK 2000

**MISSION: IMPOSSIBLE (OST)** FILM SOUNDTRACK 1996

**M!SSUNDAZTOOD** PINK 2002

**MRS 'ARDIN'S KID** MIKE HARDING 1975

**MRS. MILLS PARTY PIECES** MRS. MILLS 1968

**MISTAKEN IDENTITY** KIM CARNES 1981

**MR BAD GUY** FREDDIE MERCURY 1985

**MR. BUNGLE** MR. BUNGLE 1991

**MR. FANTASY** TRAFFIC 1967

**MR. GONE** WEATHER REPORT 1978

**MISTER HEARTBREAK** LAURIE ANDERSON 1984

**MR JONES** TOM JONES 2002

**MR. LOVE PANTS** IAN DURY & THE BLOCKHEADS 1998

**MR LOVER LOVER – THE BEST OF – PART 1 –** SHAGGY 2002

**MR. LUCKY** JOHN LEE HOOKER 1991

**MR. MOONLIGHT** FOREIGNER 1994

**MR. MUSIC – MANTOVANI** MANTOVANI & HIS ORCHESTRA 1966

**MR. TAMBOURINE MAN** BYRDS 1965

**MR. UNIVERSE** GILLAN 1979

**MR. WONDERFUL** FLEETWOOD MAC 1968

**MR. BIG** MR. BIG 1989

**MISTRAL'S DAUGHTER (OST TV)** FILM SOUNDTRACK 1986

**MISTRIAL** LOU REED 1986

**MISTY** RAY STEVENS 1975

**MISTY MORNINGS** VARIOUS ARTISTS (RONCO) 1981

**THE MIX** KRAFTWERK 1991

**MIX HEAVEN '97** VARIOUS ARTISTS (EPIC) 1997

**MIX ZONE** VARIOUS ARTISTS (POLYGRAM) 1996

**MIXED EMOTIONS** VARIOUS ARTISTS (POLYGRAM) 1997

**MIXED EMOTIONS** BEVERLEY CRAVEN 1999

**MIXED EMOTIONS II** VARIOUS ARTISTS (POLYGRAM) 1998

**MIXED UP** CURE 1990

**MIXES** KYLIE MINOGUE 1998

**MIXMAG PRESENTS BIG TUNES** VARIOUS ARTISTS (VIRGIN) 2001

**MIX'O'MATIC** VARIOUS ARTISTS (EMI) 1996

**MO' MONEY (OST)** FILM SOUNDTRACK 1992

**MOB RULES** BLACK SABBATH 1981

**MOBILE HOME** LONGPIGS 1999

**MOBO 1998 – MUSIC OF BLACK ORIGIN** VARIOUS ARTISTS (POLYGRAM) 1998

**MOBO 1999** VARIOUS ARTISTS (UNIVERSAL) 1999

**MOBO 2000** VARIOUS ARTISTS (UNIVERSAL) 2000

**MOBO 2001 – THE ALBUM** VARIOUS ARTISTS (SONY) 2001

**MOBO PRESENTS URBAN BEATS 2003** VARIOUS ARTISTS (UNIVERSAL) 2003

**MOCK TUDOR** RICHARD THOMPSON 1999

**MODERN CLASSICS – THE GREATEST HITS** PAUL WELLER 1998

**MODERN DANCE** VARIOUS ARTISTS (K-TEL) 1982

**MODERN HEROES** VARIOUS ARTISTS (TV RECORDS) 1982

**MODERN LIFE IS RUBBISH** BLUR 1993

MODERN LOVE VARIOUS ARTISTS (POLYGRAM) 1992
MODERN LOVE – 24 LOVE SONGS FOR TODAY VARIOUS ARTISTS (K-TEL) 1985
MODERN MUSIC BE-BOP DELUXE 1976
MODERN SOUNDS IN COUNTRY AND WESTERN MUSIC RAY CHARLES 1962
MODERN TIMES LATIN QUARTER 1986
MODROPHENIA VARIOUS ARTISTS (GLOBAL) 1997
MODS MAYDAY 79 VARIOUS ARTISTS (ARISTA) 1979
MODUS OPERANDI PHOTEK 1997
MOLTEN METAL VARIOUS ARTISTS (TELSTAR) 1990
THE MOMENT KENNY G 1996
MOMENT IN TIME ROBSON GREEN 2002
MOMENT OF TRUTH GANG STARR 1998
A MOMENTARY LAPSE OF REASON PINK FLOYD 1987
MOMENTS IN SOUL VARIOUS ARTISTS (STYLUS) 1990
MOMENTS IN SOUL VARIOUS ARTISTS (DOVER) 1991
MONA BONE JAKON CAT STEVENS 1970
MONA LISA JUDITH DURHAM 1996
MONDO BONGO BOOMTOWN RATS 1981
MONEY & CIGARETTES ERIC CLAPTON 1983
MONEY FOR NOTHING DIRE STRAITS 1988
THE MONKEES MONKEES 1967
THE MONKEES MONKEES 1981
MONKEY GRIP BILL WYMAN 1974
MONKEY KONG A 1999
MONSTER STEPPENWOLF 1970
MONSTER R.E.M. 1994
MONSTER HITS VARIOUS ARTISTS (CBS) 1989
MONSTER HITS OF DANCE VARIOUS ARTISTS (CASTLE COMMUNICATIONS) 1993
MONSTER TRACKS VARIOUS ARTISTS (POLYDOR) 1981
MONSTERS OF ROCK VARIOUS ARTISTS (POLYDOR) 1980
MONTAGE KENNY G 1990
THE MONTREAUX ALBUM SMOKIE 1978
MONTROSE MONTROSE 1974
MONTY PYTHON LIVE AT DRURY LANE MONTY PYTHON'S FLYING CIRCUS 1974
THE MONTY PYTHON MATCHING TIE AND HANDKERCHIEF MONTY PYTHON'S FLYING CIRCUS 1974
MONTY PYTHON SINGS MONTY PYTHON 1991
MONTY PYTHON'S CONTRACTUAL OBLIGATION ALBUM MONTY PYTHON'S FLYING CIRCUS 1980
MONTY PYTHON'S LIFE OF BRIAN (OST) MONTY PYTHON'S FLYING CIRCUS 1979
MONTY PYTHON'S PREVIOUS RECORD MONTY PYTHON'S FLYING CIRCUS 1973
MONUMENT – THE SOUNDTRACK ULTRAVOX 1983
A MONUMENT TO BRITISH ROCK VARIOUS ARTISTS (HARVEST) 1979
MOODS NEIL DIAMOND 1972
MOODS VARIOUS ARTISTS (VIRGIN) 1991
MOODS 2 VARIOUS ARTISTS (VIRGIN) 1992
MOODS SYMPHONIQUE 95 SYMPHONIQUE 1995
MOODY BLUE ELVIS PRESLEY 1977
THE MOON AND THE MELODIES HAROLD BUDD, ELIZABETH FRASER, ROBIN GUTHRIE & SIMON RAYMONDE 1986
MOON MADNESS CAMEL 1976
MOON SAFARI AIR 1998
MOONDANCE VAN MORRISON 1970
MOONDANCE – THE ALBUM VARIOUS ARTISTS (TELSTAR) 1997
MOONFLOWER SANTANA 1977
MOONLIGHT AND ROSES JIM REEVES 1964
MOONLIGHT SHADOWS SHADOWS 1986
MOONLIGHT SINATRA FRANK SINATRA 1966
MOONLIGHTING "THE TV SOUNDTRACK ALBUM" – TELEVISION SOUNDTRACK 1987
MOONLIGHTING 2 TELEVISION SOUNDTRACK 1988
MOONTAN GOLDEN EARRING 1974
MORE (OST) PINK FLOYD 1969
MORE ABBA GOLD – MORE ABBA HITS ABBA 1993
MORE BOB DYLAN GREATEST HITS BOB DYLAN 1971
MORE BUMP 'N' GRIND VARIOUS ARTISTS (MCA) 1995
MORE CHUCK BERRY CHUCK BERRY 1963
MORE COLD FEET – OST TELEVISION SOUNDTRACK 2000

MORE DIRTY DANCING (OST) FILM SOUNDTRACK 1988
MORE FRIENDS – SMALL WORLD BIG BAND 2 JOOLS HOLLAND 2002
MORE GREAT SONG HITS FROM THE BACHELORS BACHELORS 1965
MORE GREEN VELVET VARIOUS ARTISTS (TELSTAR) 1985
MORE GREGORY GREGORY ISAACS 1981
MORE HITS BY CLIFF CLIFF RICHARD & THE SHADOWS 1965
MORE JUNK WILFRED BRAMBELL & HARRY H. CORBETT 1964
MORE MILES PER HOUR JOHN MILES 1979
MORE MILLER AND OTHER BIG BAND MAGIC SYD LAWRENCE 1970
MORE MINSTREL MELODIES BIG BEN BANJO BAND 1960
MORE MUSIC TO WATCH GIRLS BY VARIOUS ARTISTS (COLUMBIA) 1999
MORE OF THE HARD STUFF DUBLINERS 1967
MORE OF THE MONKEES MONKEES 1967
MORE PENNIES FROM HEAVEN TELEVISION SOUNDTRACK 1978
MORE ROCK 'N' ROLL LOVE SONGS VARIOUS ARTISTS (DINO) 1991
MORE SONGS ABOUT BUILDINGS AND FOOD TALKING HEADS 1978
MORE SONGS ABOUT LOVE AND HATE GODFATHERS 1989
MORE SPECIALS SPECIALS 1980
MORE THAN FRIENDS JONATHAN BUTLER 1989
MORE THAN LOVE VARIOUS ARTISTS (TELSTAR) 1992
MORE THAN THIS – THE BEST OF BRYAN FERRY AND ROXY MUSIC BRYAN FERRY & ROXY MUSIC 1995
MORE THAN UNPLUGGED VARIOUS ARTISTS (DINO) 1993
MORE THAN YOU THINK YOU ARE MATCHBOX 20 2003
THE MORE THINGS CHANGE... – MACHINE HEAD 1997
MORE TO TELL MONTELL JORDAN 1996
... MORE UNCHARTED HEIGHTS OF DISGRACE DOGS D'AMOUR 1993
MORE! GIRLS' NIGHT OUT VARIOUS ARTISTS (VIRGIN) 1997
MORNING COMES QUICKLY BARBARA DICKSON 1977
MORNING DANCE SPYRO GYRA 1979
MORNING DOVE WHITE ONE DOVE 1993
MORNING HAS BROKEN VARIOUS ARTISTS (TELSTAR) 1988
MORNING NOON AND NIGHT 101 STRINGS 1983
MORNING VIEW INCUBUS 2001
MOROCCAN ROLL BRAND X 1977
MORRISON HOTEL DOORS 1970
MOSAIQUE GIPSY KINGS 1989
MOSE ALIVE MOSE ALLISON 1966
MOSELEY SHOALS OCEAN COLOUR SCENE 1996
MOSES (OST) ENNIO MORRICONE 1977
MOST EXCELLENT DANCE VARIOUS ARTISTS (EMI) 1995
MOST HAPPY FELLA ORIGINAL BROADWAY STAGE CAST SOUNDTRACK 1960
MOST HAPPY FELLA ORIGINAL LONDON STAGE CAST SOUNDTRACK 1960
THE MOST OF HERMAN'S HERMITS HERMAN'S HERMITS 1971
THE MOST OF LULU LULU 1971
MOST OF THE ANIMALS ANIMALS 1966
THE MOST RELAXING CLASSICAL ALBUM IN THE WORLD... EVER! – VARIOUS ARTISTS (VIRGIN) 1997
THE MOST RELAXING CLASSICAL ALBUM IN THE WORLD... EVER! II VARIOUS ARTISTS (VIRGIN) 1998
THE MOST WONDERFUL TIME OF THE YEAR MICHAEL CRAWFORD 1999
MOTHER FIST AND HER FIVE DAUGHTERS MARC ALMOND & THE WILLING SINNERS 1987
MOTHER NATURE CALLS CAST 1997
THE MOTHER OF ALL SWING ALBUMS VARIOUS ARTISTS (TELSTAR) 1996
THE MOTHER OF ALL SWING II VARIOUS ARTISTS (TELSTAR) 1997
THE MOTHER OF ALL SWING MIX ALBUMS VARIOUS ARTISTS (TELSTAR) 1997
MOTHERS HEAVEN TEXAS 1991

MOTIVATION RADIO STEVE HILLAGE 1977
MOTLEY CRUE MOTLEY CRUE 1994
MOTORHEAD MOTORHEAD 1977
MOTORMOUTH BEN ELTON 1987
THE MOTORS MOTORS 1977
MOTORVATIN' – CHUCK BERRY 1977
MOTOWN MICHAEL MCDONALD 2003
MOTOWN – THE HITS COLLECTION – VOLUME 2 VARIOUS ARTISTS (MOTOWN) 1995
MOTOWN – THE ULTIMATE HITS COLLECTION VARIOUS ARTISTS (MOTOWN) 1994
MOTOWN 40 FOREVER VARIOUS ARTISTS (MOTOWN) 1998
MOTOWN CHARTBUSTERS VARIOUS ARTISTS (TELSTAR) 1986
MOTOWN CHARTBUSTERS VOLUME 3 VARIOUS ARTISTS (MOTOWN) 1969
MOTOWN CHARTBUSTERS VOLUME 4 VARIOUS ARTISTS (MOTOWN) 1970
MOTOWN CHARTBUSTERS VOLUME 5 VARIOUS ARTISTS (MOTOWN) 1971
MOTOWN CHARTBUSTERS VOLUME 6 VARIOUS ARTISTS (MOTOWN) 1971
MOTOWN CHARTBUSTERS VOLUME 7 VARIOUS ARTISTS (MOTOWN) 1972
MOTOWN CHARTBUSTERS VOLUME 8 VARIOUS ARTISTS (MOTOWN) 1973
MOTOWN CHARTBUSTERS VOLUME 9 VARIOUS ARTISTS (MOTOWN) 1974
THE MOTOWN COLLECTION VARIOUS ARTISTS (TELSTAR) 1990
MOTOWN DANCE PARTY VARIOUS ARTISTS (MOTOWN) 1988
MOTOWN DANCE PARTY 2 VARIOUS ARTISTS (MOTOWN) 1990
MOTOWN GOLD VARIOUS ARTISTS (MOTOWN) 1975
MOTOWN GOLD VARIOUS ARTISTS (UNIVERSAL) 2001
MOTOWN GOLD VOLUME 2 VARIOUS ARTISTS (MOTOWN) 1977
MOTOWN HEARTBREAKERS VARIOUS ARTISTS (TELSTAR) 1989
MOTOWN IN MOTION VARIOUS ARTISTS (K-TEL) 1988
MOTOWN MANIA VARIOUS ARTISTS (BMG) 2000
MOTOWN MEMORIES VARIOUS ARTISTS (MOTOWN) 1968
MOTOWN MEMORIES VARIOUS ARTISTS (MOTOWN) 1972
THE MOTOWN SONG BOOK RUBY TURNER 1988
MOTOWN STORY VARIOUS ARTISTS (MOTOWN) 1972
MOTOWN'S GREATEST HITS TEMPTATIONS 1992
MOTOWN'S GREATEST HITS MICHAEL JACKSON 1992
MOTOWN'S GREATEST HITS DIANA ROSS 1992
MOTOWN'S GREATEST LOVE SONGS VARIOUS ARTISTS (MOTOWN) 1992
MOTT THE HOOPLE MOTT THE HOOPLE 1970
MOTT THE HOOPLE MOTT THE HOOPLE 1973
MOTT THE HOOPLE – LIVE MOTT THE HOOPLE 1974
MOULIN ROUGE (OST) FILM SOUNDTRACK 2001
MOULIN ROUGE – COLLECTORS EDITION FILM SOUNDTRACK 2002
THE MOUNTAIN STEVE EARLE & THE DEL MCCOURY BAND 1999
MOUNTING EXCITEMENT VARIOUS ARTISTS (K-TEL) 1980
MOUTH TO MOUTH LEVELLERS 1997
MOUTHFUL OF LOVE YOUNG HEART ATTACK 2004
MOVE MOVE 1968
MOVE CLOSER PHYLLIS NELSON 1985
MOVE CLOSER VARIOUS ARTISTS (CBS) 1987
MOVE IT! – REEL 2 REAL FEATURING THE MAD STUNTMAN 1994
MOVE TO THIS CATHY DENNIS 1991
MOVE YOUR SKIN AND WHY NOT 1990
MOVEMENT NEW ORDER 1981
THE MOVIE ALBUM BARBRA STREISAND 2003
THE MOVIE ALBUM – AS TIME GOES BY NEIL DIAMOND 1998
MOVIE HITS VARIOUS ARTISTS (TELSTAR) 1993
MOVIE HITS VARIOUS ARTISTS (TELSTAR) 1994
MOVIE KILLERS VARIOUS ARTISTS (TELSTAR) 1996

MOVIE LOVERS VARIOUS ARTISTS (TELSTAR) 1998
MOVIE MASTERPIECES ENNIO MORRICONE 2004
THE MOVIES MICHAEL BALL 1998
THE MOVIES' GREATEST LOVE SONGS VARIOUS ARTISTS (POLYGRAM) 1994
MOVIN' – KAY STARR 1960
MOVIN' – JENNIFER RUSH 1986
MOVIN MELODIES ATB 2000
MOVIN' ON VARIOUS ARTISTS (RUMOUR) 1992
MOVIN' ON 2 VARIOUS ARTISTS (RUMOUR) 1992
MOVING MOUNTAINS JUSTIN HAYWARD 1985
MOVING ON OLETA ADAMS 1995
MOVING ON 911 1998
MOVING ON MYLEENE KLASS 2003
MOVING PICTURES RUSH 1981
MOVING TARGETS PENETRATION 1978
MOVING WAVES FOCUS 1972
MOZART GOLD – THE ESSENTIAL COLLECTION VARIOUS ARTISTS (DEUTSCHE GRAMMOPHON) 2002
MSG MICHAEL SCHENKER GROUP 1981
MTV DANCE VARIOUS ARTISTS (UNIVERSAL) 2001
MTV HITS VARIOUS ARTISTS (UNIVERSAL) 2001
MTV IBIZA 2000 – THE PARTY VARIOUS ARTISTS (WHITE ISLAND) 2000
MTV IBIZA 2001 VARIOUS ARTISTS (WARNER BROTHERS) 2001
MTV IBIZA 99 TELEVISION COMPILATION 1999
MTV SELECT VARIOUS ARTISTS (UNIVERSAL) 2001
MTV UNPLUGGED KISS 1996
MTV UNPLUGGED ALICE IN CHAINS 1996
MTV UNPLUGGED ALANIS MORISSETTE 1999
MTV UNPLUGGED (EP) MARIAH CAREY 1992
MTV UNPLUGGED (EP) MAXWELL 1997
MTV UNPLUGGED 2.0 LAURYN HILL 2002
MUCH LOVE SHOLA AMA 1997
MUCH MORE THAN LOVE FINLEY QUAYE 2003
MUD ROCK MUD 1974
MUD ROCK VOLUME 2 MUD 1975
MUD SLIDE SLIM AND THE BLUE HORIZON JAMES TAYLOR 1971
MUDDY WATER BLUES – A TRIBUTE TO MUDDY WATERS PAUL RODGERS 1993
MUD'S GREATEST HITS MUD 1975
MULE VARIATIONS TOM WAITS 1999
MUMMER XTC 1983
MUNDO AFRIKA VARIOUS ARTISTS (SONY) 1996
MUNDO LATINO VARIOUS ARTISTS (COLUMBIA) 1995
MUNGO JERRY MUNGO JERRY 1970
MUNKI JESUS & MARY CHAIN 1998
THE MUPPET SHOW MUPPETS 1977
THE MUPPET SHOW VOLUME 2 MUPPETS 1978
MURDER BALLADS NICK CAVE & THE BAD SEEDS 1996
MURDER ON THE DANCEFLOOR VARIOUS ARTISTS (UNIVERSAL) 2002
MUSCLE OF LOVE ALICE COOPER 1974
MUSE SICK N HOUR MESS AGE PUBLIC ENEMY 1994
MUSIC CAROLE KING 1972
MUSIC MADONNA 2000
THE MUSIC MUSIC 2002
MUSIC – THE DEFINITIVE HITS COLLECTION VARIOUS ARTISTS (BMG) 2001
MUSIC – THE DEFINITIVE HITS COLLECTION 2 VARIOUS ARTISTS (BMG) 2001
MUSIC BOX MARIAH CAREY 1993
MUSIC EXPRESS VARIOUS ARTISTS (K-TEL) 1976
MUSIC FOR A ROYAL WEDDING (ROYAL COMPILATION ALBUM) ROYAL COMPILATION ALBUM 1973
MUSIC FOR ALL OCCASIONS MAVERICKS 1996
MUSIC FOR AMORPHOUS BODY STUDY CENTRE STEREOLAB 1995
MUSIC FOR DANCING GRID 1995
MUSIC FOR FILMS BRIAN ENO 1978
MUSIC FOR LIFE VARIOUS ARTISTS (WARNER BROTHERS) 1999
MUSIC FOR PLEASURE MONACO 1997
MUSIC FOR THE JILTED GENERATION PRODIGY 1994

MUSIC FOR THE LAST NIGHT OF THE PROMS SIR CHARLES GROVES CONDUCTING THE ROYAL PHILHARMONIC ORCHESTRA & CHORUS WITH SARAH WALKER (SOPRANO) 1990
MUSIC FOR THE MASSES DEPECHE MODE 1987
MUSIC FOR THE PEOPLE MARKY MARK & THE FUNKY BUNCH 1991
MUSIC FOR THE SEASONS VARIOUS ARTISTS (RONCO) 1982
MUSIC FROM 'EDWARD VII' (OST TV) LONDON SYMPHONY ORCHESTRA 1975
MUSIC FROM RIVERDANCE – THE SHOW BILL WHEELAN 1995
MUSIC FROM THE BBC TV SERIES 'THE SINGING DETECTIVE' – TELEVISION SOUNDTRACK 1986
MUSIC FROM THE TELEVISION SERIES 'MIAMI VICE' – TELEVISION SOUNDTRACK 1985
MUSIC FROM 'TWIN PEAKS' – ANGELO BADALAMENTI 1990
MUSIC IN THE DOLLS HOUSE FAMILY 1968
MUSIC MAGIC ROSE ROYCE 1984
MUSIC MAKES MY DAY OLIVIA NEWTON-JOHN 1974
MUSIC MAKES MY DAY OMAR 1992
MUSIC MAN ORIGINAL LONDON STAGE CAST SOUNDTRACK 1961
THE MUSIC MAN (OST) FILM SOUNDTRACK 1962
MUSIC 'N' MOTION CHRISTINA GREGG 1978
MUSIC OF AMERICA RICHMOND STRINGS WITH THE MIKE SAMMES SINGERS 1976
MUSIC OF GLENN MILLER IN SUPER STEREO SYD LAWRENCE 1971
THE MUSIC OF JAMES LAST JAMES LAST 1973
THE MUSIC OF LOVE RICHARD CLAYDERMAN 1984
MUSIC OF QUALITY AND DISTINCTION (VOLUME 1) VARIOUS ARTISTS (VIRGIN) 1982
THE MUSIC OF RICHARD CLAYDERMAN RICHARD CLAYDERMAN 1983
THE MUSIC OF THE COSMOS TELEVISION SOUNDTRACK 1981
MUSIC OF THE MILLENNIUM TELEVISION COMPILATION 1999
MUSIC OF THE MILLENNIUM VOL. 2 VARIOUS ARTISTS (UNIVERSAL) 2000
MUSIC OF THE MOUNTAINS MANUEL & THE MUSIC OF THE MOUNTAINS 1960
MUSIC OF THE NIGHT VARIOUS ARTISTS (POLYGRAM) 1998
MUSIC OF THE SPHERES IAN BROWN 2001
THE MUSIC PEOPLE VARIOUS ARTISTS (CBS) 1972
MUSIC TO WATCH GIRLS BY VARIOUS ARTISTS (COLUMBIA) 1999
MUSIC TO WATCH GIRLS BY VOLUME 3 VARIOUS ARTISTS (COLUMBIA) 2001
MUSIC TO WATCH MOVIES BY VARIOUS ARTISTS (COLUMBIA) 2001
MUSICAL CHAIRS HOOTIE & THE BLOWFISH 1998
MUSICAL MADNESS MANTRONIX 1986
MUSICALITY MARTINE MCCUTCHEON 2002
THE MUSICALS MICHAEL BALL 1996
THE MUSIC'S BACK DOMINIC KIRWAN 1997
MUSICOLOGY PRINCE 2004
MUSIK PLASTIK MAN 1994
MUSIQUE/THE HIGH ROAD ROXY MUSIC 1983
MUST I PAINT YOU A PICTURE BILLY BRAGG 2003
MUSTN'T GRUMBLE CHAS & DAVE 1982
MUTATIONS BECK 1998
MUTINY (STUDIO CAST RECORDING) DAVID ESSEX, FRANK FINLAY & VARIOUS ARTISTS 1983
MUZIKIZUM X-PRESS 2 2002
MWNG SUPER FURRY ANIMALS 2000
MY AIM IS TRUE ELVIS COSTELLO 1977
MY BABY JUST CARES FOR ME NINA SIMONE 1987
MY BROTHER THE COW MUDHONEY 1995
MY CATHEDRAL JIM REEVES 1970
MY CHERIE AMOUR STEVIE WONDER 1969
MY CLASSIC COLLECTION RICHARD CLAYDERMAN WITH THE ROYAL PHILHARMONIC ORCHESTRA 1990

MY COLOURING BOOK AGNETHA FALTSKOG 2004
MY CONCERTO FOR YOU RUSS CONWAY 1960
MY FAIR LADY SHELLY MANNE 1960
MY FAIR LADY ORIGINAL CAST RECORDING 2001
MY FAIR LADY ORIGINAL BROADWAY STAGE CAST SOUNDTRACK 1958
MY FAIR LADY ORIGINAL STUDIO CAST RECORDING 1987
MY FAIR LADY (OST) FILM SOUNDTRACK 1964
MY FIRST ALBUM LOLLY 1999
MY FRIEND JIM REEVES 1972
MY GENERATION VARIOUS ARTISTS (TELSTAR) 1992
MY GENERATION – THE VERY BEST OF THE WHO WHO 1996
MY GIFT TO YOU ALEXANDER O'NEAL 1988
MY GIRL (OST) FILM SOUNDTRACK 1992
MY HEART WILL GO ON VARIOUS ARTISTS (SONY) 2004
MY HEART'S DELIGHT LUCIANO PAVAROTTI WITH THE ROYAL PHILHARMONIC ORCHESTRA 1994
MY HITS AND LOVE SONGS GLEN CAMPBELL 1999
MY LIFE MARY J. BLIGE 1994
MY LIFE FOR A SONG PLACIDO DOMINGO 1983
MY LIFE IN THE BUSH OF GHOSTS BRIAN ENO & DAVID BYRNE 1981
MY LIFE: GREATEST HITS JULIO IGLESIAS 1998
MY LOVE IS YOUR LOVE WHITNEY HOUSTON 1998
MY NAME IS BARBRA, TWO BARBRA STREISAND 1966
MY NAME IS JOE JOE 2000
MY NATION UNDERGROUND JULIAN COPE 1988
MY ONLY FASCINATION DEMIS ROUSSOS 1976
MY PEOPLE WERE FAIR AND HAD SKY IN THEIR HAIR BUT NOW THEY'RE CONTENT TO WEAR STARS ON THEIR BROWS TYRANNOSAURUS REX 1968
MY PROMISE NO MERCY 1997
MY SECRET PASSION – THE ARIAS MICHAEL BOLTON 1998
MY SOUL COOLIO 1997
MY TRIBUTE – BRYN YEMM INSPIRATIONAL ALBUM BRYN YEMM & THE GWENT CHORALE 1985
MY WAY FRANK SINATRA 1969
MY WAY USHER 1998
MY WAY – THE BEST OF FRANK SINATRA FRANK SINATRA 1997
MYSTERIES OF FUNK GROOVERIDER 1998
MYSTERIO IAN MCCULLOCH 1992
MYSTERY HOT CHOCOLATE 1982
MYSTERY RAH BAND 1985
MYSTERY GIRL ROY ORBISON 1989
MYSTERY WHITE BOY – LIVE 95–96 JEFF BUCKLEY 2000
THE MYTHS AND LEGENDS OF KING ARTHUR AND THE KNIGHTS OF THE ROUND TABLE RICK WAKEMAN 1975
N SYNC N SYNC 1999
N.O.R.E. NOREAGA 1998
NAH=POO THE ART OF BLUFF WAH! 1981
THE NAIL FILE – THE BEST OF JIMMY NAIL JIMMY NAIL 1997
NAKED KISSING THE PINK 1983
NAKED TALKING HEADS 1988
NAKED BLUE PEARL 1990
NAKED SCARLET 1995
NAKED LOUISE 1996
NAKED BABY PHOTOS BEN FOLDS FIVE 1998
THE NAKED RIDE HOME JACKSON BROWNE 2002
NAKED THUNDER IAN GILLAN 1990
NAKEDSELF THE THE 2000
THE NAME OF THIS BAND IS TALKING HEADS TALKING HEADS 1982
NANCY AND LEE NANCY SINATRA & LEE HAZLEWOOD 1968
NANCY AND LEE NANCY SINATRA & LEE HAZLEWOOD 1971
NANCY'S GREATEST HITS NANCY SINATRA 1970
NANTUCKET SLEIGHRIDE MOUNTAIN 1971
THE NASHVILLE DREAM VARIOUS ARTISTS (QUALITY PRICE MUSIC) 1993
NASHVILLE SKYLINE BOB DYLAN 1969
NAT 'KING' COLE SINGS AND THE GEORGE SHEARING QUARTET PLAYS NAT 'KING' COLE/GEORGE SHEARING QUARTET 1962

NATHAN MICHAEL SHAWN WANYA BOYZ II MEN 2000
NATIONAL ANTHEMS 99 VARIOUS ARTISTS (TELSTAR) 1999
NATIONAL ANTHEMS 99 – VOLUME 2 VARIOUS ARTISTS (TELSTAR) 1999
NATIVE PLACE RAILWAY CHILDREN 1991
NATIVE TONGUE POISON 1993
NATTY DREAD BOB MARLEY & THE WAILERS 1975
NATURAL PETER ANDRE 1996
NATURAL ACT KRIS KRISTOFFERSON & RITA COOLIDGE 1978
NATURAL AVENUE JOHN LODGE 1977
THE NATURAL BLUES ALBUM VARIOUS ARTISTS (UNIVERSAL) 2001
NATURAL BORN KILLERS (OST) FILM SOUNDTRACK 1995
NATURAL HIGH COMMODORES 1978
NATURAL MYSTIC BOB MARLEY & THE WAILERS 1995
NATURAL THING JULIET ROBERTS 1994
NATURAL WOMAN VARIOUS ARTISTS (GLOBAL) 1995
NATURAL WOMAN VARIOUS ARTISTS (BMG) 2004
NATURAL WOMAN – THE VERY BEST OF CAROLE KING 2000
NATURAL WOMAN – VOLUME 2 VARIOUS ARTISTS (GLOBAL) 1996
NATURALLY IAN MOOR 2000
THE NATURE OF THE BEAST APRIL WINE 1981
NAZARETH LIVE NAZARETH 1981
NEAPOLIS SIMPLE MINDS 1998
NEARLY GOD – POEMS NEARLY GOD 1996
NEARNESS OF YOU GLENN MILLER & HIS ORCHESTRA 1969
NEBRASKA BRUCE SPRINGSTEEN 1982
NECK AND NECK CHET ATKINS & MARK KNOPFLER 1990
NEED FOR NOT LEVITATION 1992
NEGOTIATIONS AND LOVE SONGS 1971–1986 PAUL SIMON 1988
NEIL REID NEIL REID 1972
NEITHER FISH NOR FLESH TERENCE TRENT D'ARBY 1989
NEITHER WASHINGTON NOR MOSCOW… – REDSKINS 1986
NELLYVILLE NELLY 2002
NENA NENA 1984
NEO WAVE SILVER SUN 1998
NEON BALLROOM SILVERCHAIR 1999
THE NEON HANDSHAKE HELL IS FOR HEROES 2003
NEON NIGHTS DANNII MINOGUE 2003
THE NEPHILIM FIELDS OF THE NEPHILIM 1988
THE NEPTUNES PRESENTS CLONES VARIOUS ARTISTS (ARISTA) 2003
NERVE NET BRIAN ENO 1992
NEVER A DULL MOMENT ROD STEWART 1972
NEVER CAN SAY GOODBYE GLORIA GAYNOR 1975
NEVER ENDING SONG OF LOVE NEW SEEKERS 1972
NEVER ENOUGH MELISSA ETHERIDGE 1992
NEVER FELT SO GOOD JAMES INGRAM 1986
NEVER FOR EVER KATE BUSH 1980
NEVER LET HER GO DAVID GATES 1975
NEVER LET ME DOWN DAVID BOWIE 1987
NEVER LET ME GO LUTHER VANDROSS 1993
NEVER LOVED ELVIS WONDERSTUFF 1991
NEVER MIND THE BOLLOCKS, HERE'S THE SEX PISTOLS SEX PISTOLS 1977
NEVER, NEVER, LAND UNKLE 2003
NEVER NEVER NEVER SHIRLEY BASSEY 1973
NEVER NEVERLAND ANNIHILATOR 1990
NEVER ON SUNDAY (OST) FILM SOUNDTRACK 1961
NEVER SAY DIE BLACK SABBATH 1978
NEVER S A Y NEVER BRANDY 1998
NEVER TOO LATE STATUS QUO 1981
NEVER TOO MUCH LUTHER VANDROSS 1987
NEVER TOO YOUNG TO ROCK VARIOUS ARTISTS (GTO) 1975
NEVERLAND MISSION 1995
NEVERMIND NIRVANA 1991
NEW ADVENTURES IN HI FI R.E.M. 1996
THE NEW AGE OF ATLANTIC VARIOUS ARTISTS (ATLANTIC) 1972

NEW BEGINNING SWV 1996
NEW BEGINNING STEPHEN GATELY 2000
NEW BOOTS AND PANTIES IAN DURY & THE BLOCKHEADS 1977
THE NEW CLASSIC CHILLOUT ALBUM VARIOUS ARTISTS (COLUMBIA) 2002
NEW CLEAR DAYS VAPORS 1980
NEW COLOURS NEW SEEKERS 1972
NEW DAY JANE HARRISON 1989
A NEW DAY AT MIDNIGHT DAVID GRAY 2002
A NEW DAY HAS COME CELINE DION 2002
A NEW DAY – LIVE IN LAS VEGAS CELINE DION 2004
NEW DIMENSIONS THREE DEGREES 1979
NEW ENGLAND WISHBONE ASH 1976
NEW FAVOURITE ALISON KRAUSS & UNION STATION 2001
A NEW FLAME SIMPLY RED 1989
A NEW FLAME SIMPLY RED 1996
NEW FORMS RONI SIZE REPRAZENT 1997
NEW FRONTIERS (EP) DJ HYPE PRESENTS GANJA KRU 1997
NEW FUNKY NATION BOO-YAA T.R.I.B.E. 1990
NEW GOLD DREAM (81,82,83,84) SIMPLE MINDS 1982
THE NEW GOODIES LP GOODIES 1975
NEW HITS 1997 VARIOUS ARTISTS (GLOBAL) 1997
NEW HITS 2000 VARIOUS ARTISTS (WARNER BROTHERS) 2000
NEW HITS 96 VARIOUS ARTISTS (GLOBAL) 1996
NEW HITS 98 VARIOUS ARTISTS (SONY) 1998
NEW HITS 99 VARIOUS ARTISTS (GLOBAL) 1999
NEW HOPE FOR THE WRETCHED PLASMATICS 1980
NEW HORIZONS DON WILLIAMS 1979
NEW JACK CITY (OST) FILM SOUNDTRACK 1991
NEW JACK SWING VARIOUS ARTISTS (UNIVERSAL) 2002
NEW JACK SWING MASTERCUTS VOLUME 1 VARIOUS ARTISTS (MASTERCUTS) 1992
NEW JACK SWING VOLUME 3 VARIOUS ARTISTS (MASTERCUTS) 1994
NEW JERSEY BON JOVI 1988
NEW KIDS ON THE BLOCK NEW KIDS ON THE BLOCK 1990
NEW LEE DORSEY LEE DORSEY 1966
THE NEW LOVE ALBUM VARIOUS ARTISTS (VIRGIN) 2000
NEW MAN NUMAN – THE BEST OF GARY NUMAN GARY NUMAN 1982
NEW MISERABLE EXPERIENCE GIN BLOSSOMS 1994
NEW MORNING BOB DYLAN 1970
A NEW MORNING SUEDE 2002
THE NEW ORDER TESTAMENT 1988
THE NEW PAVAROTTI COLLECTION LIVE! – LUCIANO PAVAROTTI 1988
THE NEW PEPSI CHART ALBUM VARIOUS ARTISTS (VIRGIN) 2001
NEW PURE MOODS VARIOUS ARTISTS (VIRGIN) 1997
NEW ROMANTIC CLASSICS VARIOUS ARTISTS (VIRGIN) 1992
NEW ROOTS VARIOUS ARTISTS (STYLUS) 1989
NEW SENSATIONS LOU REED 1984
NEW SKIN FOR THE OLD CEREMONY LEONARD COHEN 1974
THE NEW SOUL ALBUM VARIOUS ARTISTS (COLUMBIA) 1999
NEW SOUL REBELS VARIOUS ARTISTS (GLOBAL) 1995
THE NEW SOUND OF CHRISTMAS MANCHESTER BOYS CHOIR 1985
THE NEW STARLIGHT EXPRESS ORIGINAL LONDON STAGE CAST SOUNDTRACK 1993
NEW TRADITIONALISTS DEVO 1981
NEW TRADITIONS VARIOUS ARTISTS (TELSTAR) 1990
THE NEW TRANSISTOR HEROES BIS 1997
NEW VALUES IGGY POP 1979
NEW WAVE VARIOUS ARTISTS (PHILIPS) 1977
NEW WAVE AUTEURS 1993
NEW WOMAN VARIOUS ARTISTS (VIRGIN) 1999
NEW WOMAN – THE AUTUMN COLLECTION VARIOUS ARTISTS (VIRGIN) 2002
NEW WOMAN – LOVE SONGS VARIOUS ARTISTS (VIRGIN) 2001

NEW WOMAN – THE NEW COLLECTION 2003 VARIOUS ARTISTS (EMI) 2003
NEW WOMAN 2000 VARIOUS ARTISTS (VIRGIN) 2000
NEW WOMAN 2001 VARIOUS ARTISTS (VIRGIN) 2001
NEW WOMAN 2002 VARIOUS ARTISTS (VIRGIN) 2002
NEW WOMAN 2003 VARIOUS ARTISTS (VIRGIN) 2003
NEW WOMAN SUMMER 2000 VARIOUS ARTISTS (VIRGIN) 2000
NEW WORLD IN THE MORNING ROGER WHITTAKER 1971
NEW WORLD ORDER CURTIS MAYFIELD 1997
A NEW WORLD RECORD ELECTRIC LIGHT ORCHESTRA 1976
NEW YORK LOU REED 1989
NEW YORK, NEW YORK (GREATEST HITS) FRANK SINATRA 1986
NEWPOWER SOUL NEW POWER GENERATION 1998
NEWS OF THE WORLD QUEEN 1977
NEXT SENSATIONAL ALEX HARVEY BAND 1975
NEXUS ANOTHER LEVEL 1999
NICE NICE 1969
NICE 'N EASY FRANK SINATRA 1961
NICE 'N' EASY VARIOUS ARTISTS (PHILIPS) 1973
A NICE PAIR PINK FLOYD 1974
NICELY OUT OF TUNE LINDISFARNE 1972
NICK BERRY NICK BERRY 1986
NICK BERRY NICK BERRY 1992
NICK KAMEN NICK KAMEN 1987
NICK OF TIME BONNIE RAIT 1990
NICK THE KNIFE NICK LOWE 1982
NICK WARREN – BUDAPEST VARIOUS ARTISTS (GLOBAL UNDERGROUND) 1999
NIGHT AFTER NIGHT NILS LOFGREN 1977
NIGHT AND DAY JOE JACKSON 1982
A NIGHT AT THE MOVIES DAVID ESSEX 1997
A NIGHT AT THE OPERA QUEEN 1975
A NIGHT AT THE OPERA VARIOUS ARTISTS (TELSTAR) 1990
NIGHT BEAT VARIOUS ARTISTS (STYLUS) 1985
NIGHT BEAT II VARIOUS ARTISTS (STYLUS) 1986
NIGHT BIRDS SHAKATAK 1982
NIGHT CALLS JOE COCKER 1992
NIGHT DUBBING IMAGINATION 1983
NIGHT FADES AWAY NILS LOFGREN 1981
NIGHT FLIGHT JUSTIN HAYWARD 1980
NIGHT FLIGHT BUDGIE 1981
NIGHT FLIGHT TO VENUS BONEY M 1978
NIGHT GALLERY BARRON KNIGHTS 1978
THE NIGHT HAS A THOUSAND EYES BOBBY VEE 1963
THE NIGHT I FELL IN LOVE LUTHER VANDROSS 1985
A NIGHT IN PARIS DIANA KRALL 2002
A NIGHT IN SAN FRANCISCO VAN MORRISON 1994
NIGHT MOVES VARIOUS ARTISTS (K-TEL) 1979
NIGHT MOVES VARIOUS ARTISTS (K-TEL) 1984
NIGHT NURSE GREGORY ISAACS 1982
NIGHT OF A THOUSAND CANDLES MEN THEY COULDN'T HANG 1985
NIGHT ON MY SIDE GEMMA HAYES 2002
A NIGHT ON THE TOWN ROD STEWART 1976
A NIGHT ON THE TOWN BRUCE HORNBY & THE RANGE 1990
NIGHT OUT ELLEN FOLEY 1979
NIGHT OWL GERRY RAFFERTY 1979
NIGHT PEOPLE CLASSIX NOUVEAUX 1981
NIGHT RIDE HOME JONI MITCHELL 1991
NIGHT SONG NUSRAT FATEH ALI KHAN/MICHAEL BROOK 1996
NIGHT TIME KILLING JOKE 1985
A NIGHT TO REMEMBER CYNDI LAUPER 1989
NIGHT WORKS LAYO & BUSHWACKA 2002
NIGHTCLUBBING GRACE JONES 1981
NIGHTFEVER VARIOUS ARTISTS (GLOBAL) 1995
THE NIGHTFLY DONALD FAGEN 1982
NIGHTFREAK AND THE SONS OF BECKER CORAL 2004
NIGHTLIFE VARIOUS ARTISTS (K-TEL) 1980
NIGHTLIFE PET SHOP BOYS 1999
NIGHTLINE RANDY CRAWFORD 1983
NIGHTSHIFT COMMODORES 1985

NILSSON SCHMILSSON NILSSON 1972
NIMROD GREEN DAY 1997
NINA AND FREDERICK NINA & FREDERICK 1960
NINA AND FREDERICK NINA & FREDERICK 1961
9 PUBLIC IMAGE LTD 1989
NINE LIVES AEROSMITH 1997
999 999 1978
90125 YES 1983
9012 LIVE: THE SOLOS YES 1986
NINE OBJECTS OF DESIRE SUZANNE VEGA 1997
NINE TONIGHT BOB SEGER & THE SILVER BULLET BAND 1981
1984 RICK WAKEMAN 1981
1984 VAN HALEN 1984
1984 (FOR THE LOVE OF BIG BROTHER) (OST) EURYTHMICS 1984
1984–1989 LLOYD COLE & THE COMMOTIONS 1989
1982 STATUS QUO 1982
19 NAUGHTY III NAUGHTY BY NATURE 1993
THE 1999 BRIT AWARDS VARIOUS ARTISTS (COLUMBIA) 1999
1999 PRINCE 1984
1999 CASSIUS 1999
1992 – THE LOVE ALBUM CARTER – THE UNSTOPPABLE SEX MACHINE 1992
1992–2002 UNDERWORLD 2003
1979–1983 BAUHAUS 1985
1977 ASH 1996
1977–1980 SUBSTANCE JOY DIVISION 1988
1916 MOTORHEAD 1991
THE 90'S VARIOUS ARTISTS (UNIVERSAL) 1999
NINETY 808 STATE 1989
99.9 F SUZANNE VEGA 1992
THE '97 BRIT AWARDS VARIOUS ARTISTS (COLUMBIA) 1997
NINTH HERB ALPERT & THE TIJUANA BRASS 1968
NIRVANA NIRVANA 2002
NITE FLITE VARIOUS ARTISTS (CBS) 1988
NITE FLITE 2 VARIOUS ARTISTS (CBS) 1989
NITE FLITE 3 – BEING WITH YOU VARIOUS ARTISTS (CBS) 1990
NIXON LAMBCHOP 2000
THE NO 1 DANCE PARTY ALBUM VARIOUS ARTISTS (UNIVERSAL) 1999
NO 1'S OF DANCE VARIOUS ARTISTS (TELSTAR) 1994
NO ANGEL DIDO 2000
NO BREAKS JOHN WAITE 1984
NO CAUSE FOR ALARM VIOLINSKI 1979
NO CAUSE FOR CONCERN VICE SQUAD 1981
NO CODE PEARL JAM 1996
NO COUNT – SARAH SARAH VAUGHAN 1960
NO EARTHLY CONNECTION RICK WAKEMAN 1976
NO EXIT BLONDIE 1999
NO FREE LUNCH GREEN ON RED 1985
NO GOATS, NO GLORY GOATS 1994
NO GREATER LOVE VARIOUS ARTISTS (GLOBAL) 1996
NO GURU, NO METHOD, NO TEACHER VAN MORRISON 1986
NO HOLDING BACK WAYNE WONDER 2003
NO JACKET REQUIRED PHIL COLLINS 1985
NO LIMITS 2 UNLIMITED 1993
NO MEAN CITY NAZARETH 1979
NO MORE DRAMA MARY J. BLIGE 2001
NO MORE GAMES/THE REMIX ALBUM NEW KIDS ON THE BLOCK 1991
NO MORE HEROES STRANGLERS 1977
NO MORE SHALL WE PART NICK CAVE & THE BAD SEEDS 2001
NO MORE TEARS OZZY OSBOURNE 1991
NO MORE THE FOOL ELKIE BROOKS 1986
NO NEED TO ARGUE CRANBERRIES 1994
NO ORDINARY WORLD JOE COCKER 1999
NO PARLEZ PAUL YOUNG 1983
NO PLACE LIKE HOME BIG COUNTRY 1991
NO PLACE TO RUN UFO 1980
NO PRAYER FOR THE DYING IRON MAIDEN 1990

NO PROTECTION STARSHIP 1987
NO QUARTER – JIMMY PAGE AND ROBERT PLANT UNLEDDED JIMMY PAGE & ROBERT PLANT 1994
NO REASON TO CRY ERIC CLAPTON 1976
NO REGRETS WALKER BROTHERS 1976
NO REGRETS – THE BEST OF 1965–1976 SCOTT WALKER & THE WALKER BROTHERS 2000
NO REGRETS – THE BEST OF SCOTT WALKER AND THE WALKER BROTHERS SCOTT WALKER & THE WALKER BROTHERS 1992
NO REMORSE MOTORHEAD 1984
NO RESERVATIONS APACHE INDIAN 1993
NO REST FOR THE WICKED NEW MODEL ARMY 1985
NO REST FOR THE WICKED OZZY OSBOURNE 1988
NO ROOTS FAITHLESS 2004
NO SECRETS CARLY SIMON 1973
NO SECURITY ROLLING STONES 1998
NO SENSE OF SIN LOTUS EATERS 1984
NO SLEEP AT ALL MOTORHEAD 1988
NO SLEEP 'TIL HAMMERSMITH MOTORHEAD 1981
NO SMOKE WITHOUT FIRE WISHBONE ASH 1978
NO STRINGS ATTACHED N SYNC 2000
NO WAY OUT PUFF DADDY 1997
NO, NO, NO DAWN PENN 1994
THE NO. 1 SOUNDS OF THE SEVENTIES VARIOUS ARTISTS (K-TEL) 1982
THE NO.1'S DIANA ROSS AND THE SUPREMES 2004
NO. 10 UPPING STREET BIG AUDIO DYNAMITE 1986
NO. 6 TOM PAXTON 1970
NOBODY DOES IT BETTER – THE VERY BEST OF CARLY SIMON CARLY SIMON 1999
NOBODY ELSE TAKE THAT 1995
NOBODY ELSE (US VERSION) TAKE THAT 1995
NOBODY NEEDS YOUR LOVE GENE PITNEY 1966
NOBODY'S CHILD – ROMANIAN ANGEL APPEAL VARIOUS ARTISTS (WARNER BROTHERS) 1990
NOBODY'S FOOL SLADE 1976
NOBODY'S HEROES STIFF LITTLE FINGERS 1980
NOBODY'S PERFECT DEEP PURPLE 1988
NOCHE DE CUATRO LUNAS JULIO IGLESIAS 2000
NOCTURAMA NICK CAVE & THE BAD SEEDS 2003
NOCTURNE SIOUXSIE & THE BANSHEES 1983
A NOD'S AS GOOD AS A WINK... TO A BLIND HORSE FACES 1971
NOEL – CHRISTMAS SONGS AND CAROLS VARIOUS ARTISTS (TRAX) 1988
NOISE VARIOUS ARTISTS (JUMPIN' & PUMPIN') 1992
NOISE 2 VARIOUS ARTISTS (JUMPIN' & PUMPIN') 1992
NOLA DOWN 1995
NOLANS NOLANS 1980
NON STOP JULIO IGLESIAS 1988
NON STOP 20 VOLUME 4 ANONYMOUS COVER VERSIONS 1971
NON STOP HITS VARIOUS ARTISTS (TELSTAR) 1998
NON STOP HITS – VOLUME 2 VARIOUS ARTISTS (TELSTAR) 1998
NON STOP DANCE ANTHEMS VARIOUS ARTISTS (TELSTAR) 1998
NON STOP DANCING JAMES LAST 1967
NON STOP DANCING 12 JAMES LAST 1971
NON STOP DANCING 13 JAMES LAST 1972
NON STOP DANCING '69 JAMES LAST 1969
NON STOP DANCING '69/2 JAMES LAST 1970
NON STOP DANCING '70 JAMES LAST 1970
NON STOP DANCING '71 JAMES LAST 1971
NON STOP DANCING '83 – PARTY POWER JAMES LAST 1983
NON STOP DANCING VOLUME 14 JAMES LAST 1973
NON STOP DANCING VOLUME 15 JAMES LAST 1973
NON STOP DANCING VOLUME 16 JAMES LAST 1974
NON STOP ECSTATIC DANCING SOFT CELL 1982
NON STOP EROTIC CABARET SOFT CELL 1981
NON STOP EVERGREENS JAMES LAST 1970
NONSUCH XTC 1992
NORFOLK COAST STRANGLERS 2004
NORTH ELVIS COSTELLO 2003

NORTH AND SOUTH GERRY RAFFERTY 1988
THE NORTH AT ITS HEIGHTS MC TUNES 1990
NORTH ATLANTIC DRIFT OCEAN COLOUR SCENE 2003
NORTH OF A MIRACLE NICK HEYWARD 1983
THE NORTH STAR RODDY FRAME 1998
THE NORTH STAR GRASSMAN AND THE RAVENS SANDY DENNY 1971
THE NORTHERN BEAT VARIOUS ARTISTS (LONDON) 1990
NORTHERN EXPOSURE – SASHA & JOHN DIGWEED VARIOUS ARTISTS (MINISTRY OF SOUND) 1996
NORTHERN EXPOSURE – SASHA + JOHN DIGWEED VARIOUS ARTISTS (INCREDIBLE) 1999
NORTHERN EXPOSURE 2 – SASHA & DIGWEED VARIOUS ARTISTS (MINISTRY OF SOUND) 1997
NORTHERN SOUL M PEOPLE 1993
A NORTHERN SOUL VERVE 1995
NORTHERN STAR MELANIE C 1999
NORTHERN UPROAR NORTHERN UPROAR 1996
NORTHWINDS DAVID COVERDALE 1982
NOT A LITTLE GIRL ANYMORE LINDA LEWIS 1975
NOT FRAGILE BACHMAN-TURNER OVERDRIVE 1974
NOT ME GLENN MEDEIROS 1988
NOT SATISFIED ASWAD 1982
NOT THAT I'M BIASED MAX BOYCE 1979
NOT THAT KIND ANASTACIA 2000
NOT THE NINE O'CLOCK NEWS NOT THE NINE O'CLOCK NEWS CAST 1980
NOT THE NINE O'CLOCK NEWS – HEDGEHOG SANDWICH NOT THE NINE O'CLOCK NEWS CAST 1981
NOT TILL TOMORROW RALPH MCTELL 1972
NOTHIN' BUT THE BLUE ELKIE BROOKS 1994
NOTHING BUT THE BEST GILBERT O'SULLIVAN 1991
NOTHING COMPARES TO THIS VARIOUS ARTISTS (PARKFIELD) 1990
NOTHING LESS THAN BRILLIANT SANDIE SHAW 1994
NOTHING LIKE THE SUN STING 1987
NOTORIOUS DURAN DURAN 1986
THE NOTORIOUS BYRD BROTHERS BYRDS 1968
THE NOTORIOUS KIM LIL' KIM 2000
NOTTING HILL (OST) FILM SOUNDTRACK 1999
NOW NEW SEEKERS 1973
NOW PATRICE RUSHEN 1984
NOW PAUL RODGERS 1997
NOW MAXWELL 2001
NOW – THE CHRISTMAS ALBUM VARIOUS ARTISTS (EMI) 1985
NOW – THE SUMMER ALBUM – 30 SUMMER HITS VARIOUS ARTISTS (EMI) 1986
NOW AIN'T THE TIME FOR YOUR TEARS WENDY JAMES 1993
NOW AND THEN CARPENTERS 1973
NOW AND THEN – GREATEST HITS 1964–2004 ROGER WHITTAKER 2004
NOW AND ZEN ROBERT PLANT 1988
NOW DANCE VARIOUS ARTISTS (VIRGIN) 2004
NOW DANCE – SUMMER 94 VARIOUS ARTISTS (EMI) 1994
NOW DANCE – THE 12" MIXES VARIOUS ARTISTS (EMI) 1985
NOW DANCE – THE BEST OF '93 VARIOUS ARTISTS (EMI) 1993
NOW DANCE – THE BEST OF 94 VARIOUS ARTISTS (EMI) 1994
NOW DANCE 2000 VARIOUS ARTISTS (EMI) 1999
NOW DANCE 2001 VARIOUS ARTISTS (VIRGIN) 2000
NOW DANCE 2001 PART 2 VARIOUS ARTISTS (VIRGIN) 2001
NOW DANCE 2002 VARIOUS ARTISTS (VIRGIN) 2001
NOW DANCE 2002 PART 2 VARIOUS ARTISTS (VIRGIN) 2002
NOW DANCE 2003 VARIOUS ARTISTS (VIRGIN) 2002
NOW DANCE 2003 PART 2 VARIOUS ARTISTS (VIRGIN) 2003
NOW DANCE 2004 VARIOUS ARTISTS (VIRGIN) 2003
NOW DANCE '86 VARIOUS ARTISTS (EMI) 1986
NOW DANCE '89 – THE 12" MIXES VARIOUS ARTISTS (EMI) 1989

NOW DANCE 901 – 20 SMASH DANCE HITS – THE 12"
MIXES VARIOUS ARTISTS (EMI) 1990
NOW DANCE 902 VARIOUS ARTISTS (EMI) 1990
NOW DANCE 903 – THE 12" MIXES VARIOUS ARTISTS
(EMI) 1990
NOW DANCE 91 VARIOUS ARTISTS (EMI) 1991
NOW DANCE 92 VARIOUS ARTISTS (EMI) 1992
NOW DANCE 93 VARIOUS ARTISTS (EMI) 1993
NOW DANCE 94 VOLUME 1 VARIOUS ARTISTS (EMI) 1994
NOW DANCE 94 VOLUME 2 VARIOUS ARTISTS (EMI) 1994
NOW DANCE 95 VARIOUS ARTISTS (EMI) 1995
NOW DANCE 97 VARIOUS ARTISTS (EMI) 1997
NOW DANCE 98 VARIOUS ARTISTS (EMI) 1998
NOW DANCE SUMMER 95 VARIOUS ARTISTS (EMI) 1995
NOW DECADES VARIOUS ARTISTS (EMI) 2003
NOW I GOT WORRY JON SPENCER BLUES EXPLOSION 1996
NOW I'M A COWBOY AUTEURS 1994
NOW IN A MINUTE DONNA LEWIS 1996
NOW OR NEVER BLAZIN' SQUAD 2003
NOW SMASH HITS VARIOUS ARTISTS (EMI) 1987
NOW THAT'S WHAT I CALL LOVE VARIOUS ARTISTS (EMI)
1994
NOW THAT'S WHAT I CALL MUSIC 10 VARIOUS ARTISTS
(EMI) 1987
NOW THAT'S WHAT I CALL MUSIC 11 VARIOUS ARTISTS
(EMI) 1988
NOW THAT'S WHAT I CALL MUSIC 12 VARIOUS ARTISTS
(EMI) 1988
NOW THAT'S WHAT I CALL MUSIC 13 VARIOUS ARTISTS
(EMI) 1988
NOW THAT'S WHAT I CALL MUSIC 13 VARIOUS ARTISTS
(EMI) 1989
NOW THAT'S WHAT I CALL MUSIC 14 VARIOUS ARTISTS
(EMI) 1989
NOW THAT'S WHAT I CALL MUSIC 15 VARIOUS ARTISTS
(EMI) 1989
NOW THAT'S WHAT I CALL MUSIC 16 VARIOUS ARTISTS
(EMI) 1989
NOW THAT'S WHAT I CALL MUSIC 17 VARIOUS ARTISTS
(EMI) 1990
NOW THAT'S WHAT I CALL MUSIC 18 VARIOUS ARTISTS
(EMI) 1990
NOW THAT'S WHAT I CALL MUSIC 19 VARIOUS ARTISTS
(EMI) 1991
NOW THAT'S WHAT I CALL MUSIC 1983 VARIOUS ARTISTS
(EMI) 1993
NOW THAT'S WHAT I CALL MUSIC 1984 VARIOUS ARTISTS
(EMI) 1993
NOW THAT'S WHAT I CALL MUSIC 1985 VARIOUS ARTISTS
(EMI) 1993
NOW THAT'S WHAT I CALL MUSIC 1986 VARIOUS ARTISTS
(EMI) 1993
NOW THAT'S WHAT I CALL MUSIC 1987 VARIOUS ARTISTS
(EMI) 1993
NOW THAT'S WHAT I CALL MUSIC 1988 VARIOUS ARTISTS
(EMI) 1993
NOW THAT'S WHAT I CALL MUSIC 1992 VARIOUS ARTISTS
(EMI) 1993
NOW THAT'S WHAT I CALL MUSIC 1993 VARIOUS ARTISTS
(EMI) 1993
NOW THAT'S WHAT I CALL MUSIC 1994 VARIOUS ARTISTS
(EMI) 1994
NOW THAT'S WHAT I CALL MUSIC 1995 VARIOUS ARTISTS
(EMI) 1995
NOW THAT'S WHAT I CALL MUSIC 20 VARIOUS ARTISTS
(EMI) 1991
NOW THAT'S WHAT I CALL MUSIC 21 VARIOUS ARTISTS
(EMI) 1992
NOW THAT'S WHAT I CALL MUSIC 22 VARIOUS ARTISTS
(EMI) 1992
NOW THAT'S WHAT I CALL MUSIC 23 VARIOUS ARTISTS
(EMI) 1992
NOW THAT'S WHAT I CALL MUSIC 24 VARIOUS ARTISTS
(EMI) 1993
NOW THAT'S WHAT I CALL MUSIC 25 VARIOUS ARTISTS
(EMI) 1993

NOW THAT'S WHAT I CALL MUSIC 26 VARIOUS ARTISTS
(EMI) 1993
NOW THAT'S WHAT I CALL MUSIC 27 VARIOUS ARTISTS
(EMI) 1994
NOW THAT'S WHAT I CALL MUSIC 28 VARIOUS ARTISTS
(EMI) 1994
NOW THAT'S WHAT I CALL MUSIC 29 VARIOUS ARTISTS
(EMI) 1994
NOW THAT'S WHAT I CALL MUSIC 30 VARIOUS ARTISTS
(EMI) 1995
NOW THAT'S WHAT I CALL MUSIC 31 VARIOUS ARTISTS
(EMI) 1995
NOW THAT'S WHAT I CALL MUSIC 32 VARIOUS ARTISTS
(EMI) 1995
NOW THAT'S WHAT I CALL MUSIC 33 VARIOUS ARTISTS
(EMI) 1996
NOW THAT'S WHAT I CALL MUSIC 34 VARIOUS ARTISTS
(EMI) 1996
NOW THAT'S WHAT I CALL MUSIC 35 VARIOUS ARTISTS
(EMI) 1996
NOW THAT'S WHAT I CALL MUSIC 36 VARIOUS ARTISTS
(EMI) 1997
NOW THAT'S WHAT I CALL MUSIC 37 VARIOUS ARTISTS
(EMI) 1997
NOW THAT'S WHAT I CALL MUSIC 38 VARIOUS ARTISTS
(EMI) 1997
NOW THAT'S WHAT I CALL MUSIC 39 VARIOUS ARTISTS
(EMI) 1998
NOW THAT'S WHAT I CALL MUSIC 40 VARIOUS ARTISTS
(EMI) 1998
NOW THAT'S WHAT I CALL MUSIC 41 VARIOUS ARTISTS
(EMI) 1998
NOW THAT'S WHAT I CALL MUSIC 42 VARIOUS ARTISTS
(EMI) 1999
NOW THAT'S WHAT I CALL MUSIC 43 VARIOUS ARTISTS
(EMI) 1999
NOW THAT'S WHAT I CALL MUSIC 44 VARIOUS ARTISTS
(EMI) 1999
NOW THAT'S WHAT I CALL MUSIC 45 VARIOUS ARTISTS
(EMI) 2000
NOW THAT'S WHAT I CALL MUSIC 46 VARIOUS ARTISTS
(EMI) 2000
NOW THAT'S WHAT I CALL MUSIC 47 VARIOUS ARTISTS
(EMI) 2000
NOW THAT'S WHAT I CALL MUSIC 48 VARIOUS ARTISTS
(EMI) 2001
NOW THAT'S WHAT I CALL MUSIC 49 VARIOUS ARTISTS
(EMI) 2001
NOW THAT'S WHAT I CALL MUSIC 50 VARIOUS ARTISTS
(EMI) 2001
NOW THAT'S WHAT I CALL MUSIC! 51 VARIOUS ARTISTS
(EMI) 2002
NOW THAT'S WHAT I CALL MUSIC! 52 VARIOUS ARTISTS
(EMI) 2002
NOW THAT'S WHAT I CALL MUSIC! 53 VARIOUS ARTISTS
(EMI) 2002
NOW THAT'S WHAT I CALL MUSIC! 54 VARIOUS ARTISTS
(EMI) 2003
NOW THAT'S WHAT I CALL MUSIC! 55 VARIOUS ARTISTS
(EMI) 2003
NOW THAT'S WHAT I CALL MUSIC! 56 VARIOUS ARTISTS
(EMI) 2003
NOW THAT'S WHAT I CALL MUSIC! 57 VARIOUS ARTISTS
(EMI) 2004
NOW THAT'S WHAT I CALL QUITE GOOD HOUSEMARTINS
1988
NOW THE CHRISTMAS ALBUM VARIOUS ARTISTS (EMI)
2000
NOW THEN... – STIFF LITTLE FINGERS 1982
NOW VOYAGER BARRY GIBB 1984
NOW WE ARE SIX STEELEYE SPAN 1974
NOW WE MAY BEGIN RANDY CRAWFORD 1980
NOW YOU SEE ME... NOW YOU DON'T CLIFF RICHARD
1982
NOW, THAT'S WHAT I CALL MUSIC VARIOUS ARTISTS (EMI)
1983

NOW, THAT'S WHAT I CALL MUSIC 2 VARIOUS ARTISTS
(EMI) 1984
NOW, THAT'S WHAT I CALL MUSIC 3 VARIOUS ARTISTS
(EMI) 1984
NOW, THAT'S WHAT I CALL MUSIC 4 VARIOUS ARTISTS
(EMI) 1984
NOW, THAT'S WHAT I CALL MUSIC 5 VARIOUS ARTISTS
(EMI) 1985
NOW, THAT'S WHAT I CALL MUSIC 6 VARIOUS ARTISTS
(EMI) 1985
NOW, THAT'S WHAT I CALL MUSIC 7 VARIOUS ARTISTS
(EMI) 1986
NOW, THAT'S WHAT I CALL MUSIC 8 VARIOUS ARTISTS
(EMI) 1986
NOW, THAT'S WHAT I CALL MUSIC '86 VARIOUS ARTISTS
(EMI) 1986
NOW, THAT'S WHAT I CALL MUSIC 9 VARIOUS ARTISTS
(EMI) 1987
NOW? – VIC DAMONE 1981
NOWHERE RIDE 1990
NU-CLEAR SOUNDS ASH 1998
NU FLOW BIG BROVAZ 2002
NU SOUL VARIOUS ARTISTS (SONY) 2003
NUDE CAMEL 1981
NUFF SAID NINA SIMONE 1969
NUISANCE MENSWEAR 1995
NUKLEUZ PTS – HARDHOUSE ANTHEMS 3 VARIOUS
ARTISTS (VIRGIN) 2000
NUKLEUZ PRESENTS BIG ROOM DJS VARIOUS ARTISTS
(VIRGIN) 2001
NUKLEUZ PRESENTS HARDHOUSE ANTHEMS VARIOUS
ARTISTS (VIRGIN) 2000
NUKLEUZ PRESENTS HARDHOUSE ANTHEMS 2001
VARIOUS ARTISTS (VIRGIN) 2001
NUKLEUZ PRESENTS HARDHOUSE ANTHEMS VOL.2
VARIOUS ARTISTS (VIRGIN) 2000
NUMA RECORDS YEAR 1 VARIOUS ARTISTS (NUMA) 1986
NUMBER 8 J.J. CALE 1983
THE NUMBER OF THE BEAST IRON MAIDEN 1987
THE NUMBER ONE ACOUSTIC ROCK ALBUM VARIOUS
ARTISTS (POLYGRAM) 1996
THE NUMBER ONE ALL TIME ROCK ALBUM VARIOUS
ARTISTS (POLYGRAM) 1995
THE NUMBER ONE CHRISTMAS ALBUM VARIOUS ARTISTS
(POLYGRAM) 1995
THE NUMBER ONE CLASSICAL ALBUM 2004 VARIOUS
ARTISTS (UNIVERSAL) 2003
THE NUMBER ONE CLASSIC SOUL ALBUM VARIOUS
ARTISTS (POLYGRAM) 1995
THE NUMBER ONE COUNTRY ALBUM VARIOUS ARTISTS
(POLYGRAM) 1996
THE NUMBER ONE DRIVE ALBUM VARIOUS ARTISTS
(POLYGRAM) 1997
THE NUMBER ONE EIGHTIES ALBUM VARIOUS ARTISTS
(POLYGRAM) 1996
NUMBER ONE IN HEAVEN SPARKS 1979
THE NUMBER ONE JAZZ ALBUM VARIOUS ARTISTS
(POLYGRAM) 1997
THE NUMBER ONE LINE DANCING ALBUM VARIOUS
ARTISTS (POLYGRAM) 1997
THE NUMBER ONE LOVE ALBUM VARIOUS ARTISTS
(POLYGRAM) 1996
THE NUMBER ONE MOTOWN ALBUM VARIOUS ARTISTS
(POLYGRAM) 1997
THE NUMBER ONE MOVIES ALBUM VARIOUS ARTISTS
(POLYGRAM) 1995
THE NUMBER ONE RAP ALBUM VARIOUS ARTISTS
(POLYGRAM) 1996
THE NUMBER ONE REGGAE ALBUM VARIOUS ARTISTS
(POLYGRAM) 1995
THE NUMBER ONE ROCK BALLADS ALBUM VARIOUS
ARTISTS (POLYGRAM) 1996
THE NUMBER ONE ROCK 'N' ROLL ALBUM VARIOUS
ARTISTS (POLYGRAM) 1997
THE NUMBER ONE SCI FI ALBUM VARIOUS ARTISTS
(POLYGRAM) 1997

THE NUMBER ONE SEVENTIES ALBUM VARIOUS ARTISTS (POLYGRAM) 1997
THE NUMBER ONE 70'S ROCK ALBUM VARIOUS ARTISTS (POLYGRAM) 1995
THE NUMBER ONE SKA ALBUM VARIOUS ARTISTS (POLYGRAM) 1997
THE NUMBER ONE SUMMER ALBUM VARIOUS ARTISTS (POLYGRAM) 1996
#1S MARIAH CAREY 1998
NUMBER ONES MICHAEL JACKSON 2003
NUMBER ONES OF THE EIGHTIES VARIOUS ARTISTS (TELSTAR) 1989
NUMBER 10 J.J. CALE 1992
NUMBER THE BRAVE WISHBONE ASH 1981
NURSE THERAPY? 1992
NURSERY CRYME GENESIS 1974
NUT CRACKER SUITE DUKE ELLINGTON 1961
NUTHIN' FANCY LYNYRD SKYNYRD 1975
NUT CRACKER SUITE DUKE ELLINGTON 1961
NUTHIN' FANCY LYNYRD SKYNYRD 1975
THE NUTTY PROFESSOR (OST) FILM SOUNDTRACK 1996
NUYORICAN SOUL NUYORICAN SOUL 1997
NYC MAN LOU REED 2003
NYLON CURTAIN BILLY JOEL 1982
O DAMIEN RICE 2003
O BROTHER WHERE ART THOU (OST) FILM SOUNDTRACK 2002
O YEAH – ULTIMATE HITS AEROSMITH 2002
0898: BEAUTIFUL SOUTH BEAUTIFUL SOUTH 1992
05:22:09:12 OFF FRONT 242 1993
0141 632 6326 GUN 1997
06:21:03:11 UP EVIL FRONT 242 1993
O.G. ORIGINAL GANGSTER ICE-T 1991
O3 SUNSCREEM 1993
OASIS OASIS 1984
OBSCURED BY CLOUDS (OST) PINK FLOYD 1972
OBSESSION UFO 1978
OBSOLETE FEAR FACTORY 1998
OCEAN COLOUR SCENE OCEAN COLOUR SCENE 1996
OCEAN DRIVE LIGHTHOUSE FAMILY 1995
OCEAN RAIN ECHO & THE BUNNYMEN 1984
OCEAN'S ELEVEN FILM SOUNDTRACK 2002
OCEANIA OCEANIA 1999
OCEANS OF FANTASY BONEY M 1979
OCTAVE MOODY BLUES 1978
OCTOBER U2 1981
OCTOBER LOAD JAMES TAYLOR 2002
OCTOBER RUST TYPE O NEGATIVE 1996
OCTOBERON BARCLAY JAMES HARVEST 1976
OCTOPUS COZY POWELL 1983
OCTOPUS HUMAN LEAGUE 1995
ODDS AND SODS WHO 1974
O DE LAY BECK 1996
ODESSA BEE GEES 1969
ODYSSEY YNGWIE J MAMLSTEEN 1988
ODYSSEY – THE DEFINITIVE COLLECTION VANGELIS 2003
ODYSSEY THROUGH O2 JEAN-MICHEL JARRE 1998
OEDIPUS SCHMOEDIPUS BARRY ADAMSON 1996
OF THE HEART, OF THE SOUL AND THE CROSS – THE UTOPIAN EXPERIENCE PM DAWN 1991
OFARIM CONCERT – LIVE '69 ESTHER & ABI OFARIM 1969
OFF THE BEATEN TRACK STRANGLERS 1986
OFF THE BONE CRAMPS 1983
OFF THE GROUND PAUL McCARTNEY 1993
OFF THE WALL MICHAEL JACKSON 1979
OFF YER NUT!! – VARIOUS ARTISTS (TVD) 1998
THE OFFICIAL BBC ALBUM OF THE ROYAL WEDDING (ROYAL COMPILATION ALBUM) ROYAL COMPILATION ALBUM 1981
OFFICIAL BOOTLEG ALBUM BLUES BAND 1980
OFFICIAL LIVE – 101 PROOF PANTERA 1997
OGDEN'S NUT GONE FLAKE SMALL FACES 1968
OH MERCY BOB DYLAN 1989
OH PRETTY WOMAN ROY ORBISON 1964
OH! WHAT A NIGHT VARIOUS ARTISTS (COLUMBIA) 1998
OI! OI! THAT'S YER LOT VARIOUS ARTISTS (SECRET) 1982
OIL ON CANVAS JAPAN 1983
OK TALVIN SINGH 1999

OK COMPUTER RADIOHEAD 1997
OK KEN? – CHICKEN SHACK 1969
OKLAHOMA! (OST) FILM SOUNDTRACK 1958
OL' BLUE EYES IS BACK FRANK SINATRA 1973
OL' BLUE SUEDES IS BACK CARL PERKINS 1978
OLD 8 X 10 RANDY TRAVIS 1988
OLD FOUR EYES IS BACK MIKE HARDING 1977
OLD GOLDEN THROAT JOHNNY CASH 1968
THE OLD GREY WHISTLE TEST – THE BEST OF THE TEST TELEVISION COMPILATION 1991
THE OLD KIT BAG RICHARD THOMPSON 2003
OLD LOW LIGHT KATHRYN WILLIAMS 2002
OLD NEW BORROWED AND BLUE SLADE 1974
THE OLD SKOOL VARIOUS ARTISTS (GLOBAL) 1997
OLD SKOOL JUNGLE VARIOUS ARTISTS (RELENTLESS) 2002
OLD SKOOL REGGAE VARIOUS ARTISTS (RELENTLESS) 2002
THE OLD SKOOL REUNION VARIOUS ARTISTS (GLOBAL) 1997
OLD WAYS NEIL YOUNG 1985
OLDER/OLDER & UPPER GEORGE MICHAEL 1996
OLE JAMES LAST 1973
OLE SAD CAFÉ 1981
OLIAS OF SUNHILLOW JON ANDERSON 1976
OLIVER! (1994 LONDON CAST) – ORIGINAL LONDON STAGE CAST SOUNDTRACK 1995
OLIVER! – ORIGINAL LONDON STAGE CAST SOUNDTRACK 1960
OLIVER! (OST) FILM SOUNDTRACK 1968
OLYMPIAN GENE 1995
THE OMD SINGLES ORCHESTRAL MANOEUVRES IN THE DARK 1998
OMMADAWN MIKE OLDFIELD 1975
ON ECHOBELLY 1995
ON A DANCE TIP VARIOUS ARTISTS (GLOBAL) 1995
ON A DANCE TIP 2 VARIOUS ARTISTS (GLOBAL) 1995
ON A DAY LIKE TODAY BRYAN ADAMS 1998
ON A REGGAE TIP VARIOUS ARTISTS (MANGO) 1993
ON A STORYTELLER'S NIGHT MAGNUM 1985
ON AIR – BBC SESSIONS SHAMEN 1993
ON EAGLE'S WINGS MICHAEL CRAWFORD 1998
ON EVERY STREET DIRE STRAITS 1991
ON HOW LIFE IS MACY GRAY 1999
ON PAROLE MOTORHEAD 1979
ON REFLECTION – THE VERY BEST OF ELAINE PAIGE ELAINE PAIGE 1998
ON STAGE JIM REEVES 1969
ON STAGE RAINBOW 1977
ON STAGE FEBRUARY 1970 ELVIS PRESLEY 1970
ON STAGE WITH THE GEORGE MITCHELL MINSTRELS GEORGE MITCHELL MINSTRELS 1962
ON THE 6 JENNIFER LOPEZ 1999
ON THE AIR – 60 YEARS OF BBC THEME MUSIC (TV & RADIO COMPILATION) TELEVISION AND RADIO COMPILATION 1982
ON THE BEACH NEIL YOUNG 1974
ON THE BEACH CHRIS REA 1986
ON THE BEACH VARIOUS ARTISTS (MINISTRY OF SOUND) 2003
ON THE BOARDS TASTE 1970
ON THE BORDER EAGLES 1974
ON THE LEVEL STATUS QUO 1975
ON THE LINE GARY U.S. BONDS 1982
ON THE LOOSE DEUCE 1995
ON THE NIGHT DIRE STRAITS 1993
ON THE OUTSIDE SYMPOSIUM 1998
ON THE RADIO – GREATEST HITS VOLUME 1 & 2 DONNA SUMMER 1979
ON THE RIVIERA GIBSON BROTHERS 1980
ON THE SUNNY SIDE OF THE STREET KLAUS WUNDERLICH 1984
ON THE THRESHOLD OF A DREAM MOODY BLUES 1969
ON THE TURN KERBDOG 1997
ON THE WATERS BREAD 1970
ON THROUGH THE NIGHT DEF LEPPARD 1980
ON TOUR DELANEY & BONNIE & FRIENDS 1970
ON TOUR DAVID ESSEX 1976

ON TOUR WITH THE GEORGE MITCHELL MINSTRELS GEORGE MITCHELL MINSTRELS 1963
ONCE AROUND THE WORLD IT BITES 1988
ONCE IN A LIFETIME RUNRIG 1988
ONCE IN A LIFETIME VARIOUS ARTISTS (TELSTAR) 1997
ONCE IN A LIFETIME – THE BEST OF TALKING HEADS/SAND IN THE VASELINE TALKING HEADS 1992
ONCE MOORE WITH COOK PETER COOK & DUDLEY MOORE 1966
ONCE MORE INTO THE BLEACH DEBBIE HARRY & BLONDIE 1988
ONCE UPON A STAR BAY CITY ROLLERS 1975
ONCE UPON A TIME DONNA SUMMER 1977
ONCE UPON A TIME SIMPLE MINDS 1985
ONCE UPON A TIME – THE SINGLES SIOUXSIE & THE BANSHEES 1981
ONCE UPON THE CROSS DEICIDE 1995
ONE BEE GEES 1989
THE ONE ELTON JOHN 1992
1 BEATLES 2000
THE ONE AND ONLY BILLY FURY BILLY FURY 1983
ONE BY ONE FOO FIGHTERS 2002
ONE CAREFUL OWNER MICHAEL BALL 1994
ONE DAY AT A TIME SYMPOSIUM 1997
ONE DAY AT A TIME FOSTER & ALLEN 1999
ONE DAY IN YOUR LIFE MICHAEL JACKSON 1981
ONE EYED JACKS SPEAR OF DESTINY 1984
THE ONE FOR ME MR ACKER BILK 1976
ONE FROM THE MODERN OCEAN COLOUR SCENE 1999
ONE GIANT LEAP ONE GIANT LEAP 2002
ONE HALF OF A WHOLE DECADE – 5 YEARS VARIOUS ARTISTS (MINISTRY OF SOUND) 1996
ONE HEAD, TWO ARMS, TWO LEGS DAWN OF THE REPLICANTS 1998
ONE HEART CELINE DION 2003
ONE HOT MINUTE RED HOT CHILI PEPPERS 1995
154 WIRE 1979
101 DEPECHE MODE 1989
101 DAMNATIONS CARTER – THE UNSTOPPABLE SEX MACHINE 1991
101% SPEED GARAGE ANTHEMS VARIOUS ARTISTS (MASSIVE MUSIC) 1999
101% SPEED GARAGE VOLUME 2 VARIOUS ARTISTS (MASSIVE MUSIC) 1998
100 BROKEN WINDOWS IDLEWILD 2000
100 DEGREES AND RISING INCOGNITO 1995
100 GOLDEN GREATS MAX BYGRAVES 1976
100 GOLDEN GREATS FRANKIE VAUGHAN 1977
100 GOLDEN GREATS FOSTER & ALLEN 1995
100 MPH VARDIS 1980
100% ACID JAZZ VARIOUS ARTISTS (TELSTAR) 1994
100% ACID JAZZ – VOLUME 2 VARIOUS ARTISTS (TELSTAR) 1995
100% CARNIVAL! – VARIOUS ARTISTS (TELSTAR) 1995
100% CHRISTMAS VARIOUS ARTISTS (TELSTAR) 1994
100% CLASSICS VARIOUS ARTISTS (TELSTAR) 1995
100% CLASSICS – VOLUME 2 VARIOUS ARTISTS (TELSTAR) 1996
100% COLOMBIAN FUN LOVIN' CRIMINALS 1998
100 PERCENT COTTON JETS 1982
100% DANCE VARIOUS ARTISTS (TELSTAR) 1993
100% DANCE HITS 96 VARIOUS ARTISTS (TELSTAR) 1996
100% DANCE VOLUME 2 VARIOUS ARTISTS (TELSTAR) 1993
100% DANCE VOLUME 3 VARIOUS ARTISTS (TELSTAR) 1993
100% DANCE VOLUME 4 VARIOUS ARTISTS (TELSTAR) 1994
100% DRUM & BASS VARIOUS ARTISTS (TELSTAR) 1996
100% GINUWINE GINUWINE 1999
100% HITS VARIOUS ARTISTS (TELSTAR) 1994
100% HOUSE CLASSICS – VOLUME 1 VARIOUS ARTISTS (TELSTAR) 1995
100% PURE GROOVE VARIOUS ARTISTS (TELSTAR) 1996
100% PURE GROOVE 2 VARIOUS ARTISTS (TELSTAR) 1996
100% PURE LOVE VARIOUS ARTISTS (TELSTAR) 1994

**100% PURE OLD SKOOL CLUB CLASSICS** VARIOUS ARTISTS (TELSTAR) 2003

**100% RAP** VARIOUS ARTISTS (TELSTAR) 1994

**100% REGGAE** VARIOUS ARTISTS (TELSTAR) 1993

**100% REGGAE VOLUME 2** VARIOUS ARTISTS (TELSTAR) 1994

**100% REGGAE VOLUME 3** VARIOUS ARTISTS (TELSTAR) 1994

**100% SUMMER** VARIOUS ARTISTS (TELSTAR) 1994

**100% SUMMER '95** VARIOUS ARTISTS (TELSTAR) 1995

**100% SUMMER JAZZ** VARIOUS ARTISTS (TELSTAR) 1995

**100% SUMMER MIX 96** VARIOUS ARTISTS (TELSTAR) 1996

**100% SUMMER MIX 97** VARIOUS ARTISTS (TELSTAR) 1997

**100% SUMMER MIX 98** VARIOUS ARTISTS (TELSTAR) 1998

**100TH WINDOW** MASSIVE ATTACK 2003

**ONE IN A MILLION** AALIYAH 1996

**ONE LOVE** DELAKOTA 1998

**ONE LOVE** BOB MARLEY & THE WAILERS 2001

**1 LOVE** VARIOUS ARTISTS (B UNIQUE) 2002

**ONE LOVE** BLUE 2002

**ONE LOVE – THE VERY BEST OF** BOB MARLEY & THE WAILERS 2001

**ONE LOVE – THE VERY BEST OF REGGAE** VARIOUS ARTISTS (ARCADE) 1992

**ONE MAN DOG** JAMES TAYLOR 1972

**ONE MAN SHOW** MIKE HARDING 1976

**ONE MORE CAR ONE MORE RIDER** ERIC CLAPTON 2002

**ONE MORE DREAM – THE VERY BEST OF GERRY RAFFERTY** GERRY RAFFERTY 1995

**ONE MORE FOR THE ROAD** LYNYRD SKYNYRD 1976

**ONE NATION UNDER A GROOVE** FUNKADELIC 1978

**ONE NIGHT AT BUDOKAN** MICHAEL SCHENKER GROUP 1982

**ONE NIGHT ONLY – THE GREATEST HITS** ELTON JOHN 2000

**ONE NIGHT WITH YOU – THE BEST OF LOVE** LUTHER VANDROSS 1997

**ONE NIL** NEIL FINN 2001

**ONE OF THE BOYS** ROGER DALTREY 1977

**ONE OF THESE NIGHTS** EAGLES 1975

**ONE ON ONE** CHEAP TRICK 1982

**ONE ORIGINAL STEP BEYOND** VARIOUS ARTISTS (CASTLE COMMUNICATIONS) 1993

**ONE PIECE AT A TIME** JOHNNY CASH 1976

**1 POLISH 2 BISCUITS AND A FISH SANDWICH** OUTHERE BROTHERS 1995

**ONE SECOND** YELLO 1987

**ONE SECOND** PARADISE LOST 1997

**ONE STEP BEYOND** MADNESS 1979

**ONE STEP BEYOND** VARIOUS ARTISTS (EMI) 2003

**ONE STEP CLOSER** DOOBIE BROTHERS 1980

**THE ONE THING** MICHAEL BOLTON 1993

**ONE TO ONE** HOWARD JONES 1986

**ONE TOUCH** SUGABABES 2000

**1234** PROPAGANDA 1990

**ONE VICE AT A TIME** KROKUS 1982

**ONE VOICE** BARRY MANILOW 1979

**ONE VOICE** BARBRA STREISAND 1987

**ONE WAY OF LIFE – THE BEST OF THE LEVELLERS** LEVELLERS 1998

**ONE WILD NIGHT – LIVE 1985–2001** BON JOVI 2001

**ONE WOMAN – THE ULTIMATE COLLECTION** DIANA ROSS 1993

**ONE WORLD** JOHN MARTYN 1978

**ONE WORLD** JOHN DENVER 1986

**ONE WORLD** VARIOUS ARTISTS (GLOBAL) 1998

**ONE WORLD ONE VOICE** ONE WORLD 1990

**1–800 NEW FUNK** VARIOUS ARTISTS (NPG) 1994

**ONENESS – SILVER DREAMS GOLDEN REALITY** CARLOS SANTANA 1979

**ONES ON 1** VARIOUS ARTISTS (BBC) 1988

**ONE TRICK PONY (OST)** PAUL SIMON 1980

**ONKA'S BIG MOKA** TOPLOADER 2000

**ONLY A WOMAN LIKE YOU** MICHAEL BOLTON 2002

**ONLY CLASSICAL ALBUM YOU'LL EVER NEED** VARIOUS ARTISTS (CONIFER) 1998

**ONLY EVERYTHING** JULIANA HATFIELD 1995

**ONLY FOR THE HEADSTRONG** VARIOUS ARTISTS (LONDON) 1992

**ONLY FOR THE HEADSTRONG II** VARIOUS ARTISTS (LONDON) 1992

**ONLY FOREVER** PURESSENCE 1998

**ONLY GOD CAN JUDGE ME** MARK MORRISON 1997

**ONLY HUMAN** DINA CARROLL 1996

**THE ONLY ONES** ONLY ONES 1978

**ONLY THE STRONG SURVIVE** HURRICANE #1 1999

**ONLY YAZOO – THE BEST OF YAZOO** YAZOO 1999

**ONLY YESTERDAY – RICHARD & KAREN CARPENTER'S GREATEST HITS** CARPENTERS 1990

**ONLY YOU** HARRY CONNICK JR. 2004

**OOH LAS VEGAS** DEACON BLUE 1990

**OOH WALLAH WALLAH** KING KURT 1983

**OOH YEAH! –** DARYL HALL & JOHN OATES 1988

**OOH LA LA** FACES 1973

**OOPS! I DID IT AGAIN** BRITNEY SPEARS 2000

**OOPS! SORRY WRONG PLANET** UTOPIA 1977

**OPEN** STEVE HILLAGE 1979

**OPEN ALL NIGHT** GEORGIA SATELLITES 1988

**OPEN HEART ZOO** MARTIN GRECH 2002

**OPEN ROAD** JULIE DRISCOLL, BRIAN AUGER & THE TRINITY 1968

**OPEN ROAD** DONOVAN 1970

**OPEN ROAD** GARY BARLOW 1997

**OPEN TOP CARS AND GIRLS IN T'SHIRTS** VARIOUS ARTISTS (TELSTAR) 1985

**OPEN UP AND SAY... AAH! –** POISON 1988

**THE OPERA ALBUM 2002** VARIOUS ARTISTS (VIRGIN) 2001

**THE OPERA BAND** AMICI FOREVER 2003

**OPERA EXTRAVAGANZA** THE ROYAL PHILHARMONIC ORCHESTRA, CHORUS ROYAL OPERA HOUSE, THE LONDON SYMPHONY ORCHESTRA, CONDUCTOR LUIS COBOS 1990

**OPERATION MINDCRIME** QUEENSRYCHE 1988

**OPERATION STACKOLA** LUNIZ 1996

**OPHELIA** NATALIE MERCHANT 1998

**OPERATUNITY WINNERS** DENISE LEIGH & JANE GILCHRIST 2003

**THE OPTIMIST** TURIN BRAKES 2001

**ORANGE COLOURED SKY** BERT KAEMPFERT & HIS ORCHESTRA 1971

**ORANGES AND LEMONS** XTC 1989

**THE ORBISON WAY** ROY ORBISON 1966

**ORBISONGS** ROY ORBISON 1967

**ORBITAL** ORBITAL 1991

**ORBITAL** ORBITAL 1993

**ORBLIVION** ORB 1997

**THE ORB'S ADVENTURES BEYOND THE ULTRAWORLD** ORB 1991

**ORBVS TERRERVM** ORB 1995

**ORCHESTRA! –** SIR GEORG SOLTI & DUDLEY MOORE 1991

**ORCHESTRAL MANOEUVRES IN THE DARK** ORCHESTRAL MANOEUVRES IN THE DARK 1980

**THE ORCHESTRAL TUBULAR BELLS** MIKE OLDFIELD WITH THE ROYAL PHILHARMONIC ORCHESTRA 1975

**ORDINARY MAN** DAY ONE 2000

**ORGAN FAN** SILVERFISH 1992

**ORGANIC** JOE COCKER 1996

**ORGANISATION** ORCHESTRAL MANOEUVRES IN THE DARK 1980

**ORGASMATRON** MOTORHEAD 1986

**ORIGIN OF SYMMETRY** MUSE 2001

**ORIGINAL FLAVA** BRAND NEW HEAVIES 1994

**ORIGINAL GREATEST HITS** EVERLY BROTHERS 1970

**ORIGINAL HARDCORE** VARIOUS ARTISTS (INSPIRED) 2002

**ORIGINAL HARDCORE – THE BATTLE** VARIOUS ARTISTS (INSPIRED) 2003

**ORIGINAL HARDCORE – THE NU BREED** VARIOUS ARTISTS (INSPIRED) 2004

**ORIGINAL MASTERS** JETHRO TULL 1985

**ORIGINAL MUSIC FROM AUF WIEDERSEHEN PET** TELEVISION SOUNDTRACK 1984

**ORIGINAL MUSIQUARIUM 1** STEVIE WONDER 1982

**ORIGINAL PIRATE MATERIAL** STREETS 2002

**THE ORIGINAL SOUNDTRACK** 10 CC 1975

**ORIGINAL SOUNDTRACK** S-EXPRESS 1989

**THE ORIGINAL SOUNDTRACK FROM TCB (OST TV)** DIANA ROSS & THE SUPREMES & THE TEMPTATIONS 1969

**ORIGINAL SOUNDTRACKS 1** PASSENGERS 1995

**ORIGINALS** VARIOUS ARTISTS (COLUMBIA) 1993

**ORIGINALS 2** VARIOUS ARTISTS (COLUMBIA) 1994

**THE ORIGINALS! –** VARIOUS ARTISTS (DINO) 1992

**THE ORIGINALS: 32 ALL TIME CLASSIC GREATS** VARIOUS ARTISTS (TOWERBELL) 1986

**OSIBISA** OSIBISA 1971

**OSMONDS LIVE** OSMONDS 1972

**THE OTHER CHET ATKINS** CHET ATKINS 1961

**THE OTHER MAN'S GRASS IS ALWAYS GREENER** PETULA CLARK 1968

**OTHER PEOPLE'S SONGS** ERASURE 2003

**THE OTHER SIDE** LYNDEN DAVID HALL 2000

**THE OTHER SIDE OF DUDLEY MOORE** DUDLEY MOORE 1965

**THE OTHER SIDE OF LIFE** MOODY BLUES 1986

**THE OTHER SIDE OF ME** ANDY WILLIAMS 1975

**THE OTHER SIDE OF THE MIRROR** STEVIE NICKS 1989

**OTHER VOICES** PAUL YOUNG 1990

**OTHER VOICES/OTHER ROOMS** NANCI GRIFFITH 1993

**OTIS BLUE: OTIS REDDING SINGS SOUL** OTIS REDDING 1966

**OTIS REDDING IN EUROPE** OTIS REDDING 1968

**OTO** FLUKE 1995

**O TOWN** O-TOWN 2001

**OU812** VAN HALEN 1988

**OUI LOVE YOU** OUI 3 1993

**OUR BEST TO YOU** OSMONDS 1974

**OUR FAVOURITE SHOP** STYLE COUNCIL 1985

**OUR FRIENDS ELECTRIC** VARIOUS ARTISTS (TELSTAR) 1996

**OUR HAPPY HARDCORE** SCOOTER 1996

**OUR HOUSE – THE ORIGINAL SONGS** MADNESS 2002

**OUR KID EH** SHIREHORSES 2001

**OUR MEMORIES OF ELVIS** ELVIS PRESLEY 1979

**OUR TIME IN EDEN** 10,000 MANIACS 1992

**OUR TOWN – THE GREATEST HITS OF DEACON BLUE** DEACON BLUE 1994

**OUT CAME THE BLUES** VARIOUS ARTISTS (ACE OF HEARTS) 1964

**OUT HERE** LOVE 1970

**OUT IN LA** RED HOT CHILI PEPPERS 1994

**OUT IN THE FIELDS – THE VERY BEST OF GARY MOORE** GARY MOORE 1998

**OUT IN THE SUN** PATRICK MORAZ 1977

**OUT NOW! 28 HOT HITS** VARIOUS ARTISTS (CHRYSALIS) 1985

**OUT NOW!! 2 – 28 HOT HITS** VARIOUS ARTISTS (CHRYSALIS) 1985

**OUT OF AFRICA (OST)** JOHN BARRY 1986

**OUT OF HERE** CORDUROY 1994

**OUT OF ORDER** ROD STEWART 1988

**OUT OF OUR HEADS** ROLLING STONES 1965

**OUT OF SEASON** BETH GIBBONS & RUSTIN MAN 2002

**OUT OF THE BLUE** ELECTRIC LIGHT ORCHESTRA 1977

**OUT OF THE BLUE** DEBBIE GIBSON 1988

**OUT OF THE CRADLE** LINDSEY BUCKINGHAM 1992

**OUT OF THE SHADOWS** SHADOWS 1962

**OUT OF THEIR SKULLS** PIRATES 1977

**OUT OF THIS WORLD** MOODY BLUES 1979

**OUT OF THIS WORLD** SHAKATAK 1983

**OUT OF THIS WORLD** EUROPE 1988

**OUT OF TIME** R.E.M. 1991

**OUT ON THE STREET** DAVID ESSEX 1976

**OUT SPACED** SUPER FURRY ANIMALS 1998

**OUT THERE & BACK** PAUL VAN DYK 2000

**OUT A SPACE** SPOTNICKS 1963

**OUTLAND** SPEAR OF DESTINY 1987

**OUTLAND** GARY NUMAN 1991

**OUTLANDOS D'AMOUR** POLICE 1979

OUTRIDER JIMMY PAGE 1988
OUTROSPECTIVE FAITHLESS 2001
OUTSIDE DAVID BOWIE 1995
OUTSIDE INSIDE TUBES 1983
OUTSIDE THE GATE KILLING JOKE 1988
OUTTA SIGHT OUTTA MIND DATSUNS 2004
OVATION – THE BEST OF ANDREW LLOYD WEBBER VARIOUS
    ARTISTS (K-TEL) 1985
OVER AND OVER NANA MOUSKOURI 1969
OVER THE TOP COZY POWELL 1980
OVERGROWN EDEN INME 2003
OVERKILL MOTORHEAD 1979
OVERLOAD VARIOUS ARTISTS (RONCO) 1982
OVERNIGHT SUCCESS NEIL SEDAKA 1975
OVERTURE AND BEGINNERS ROD STEWART & THE FACES
    1974
OVO PETER GABRIEL 2000
THE OWNERZ GANG STARR 2003
OXYGENE JEAN-MICHEL JARRE 1977
OXYGENE 7 13 JEAN-MICHEL JARRE 1997
OYSTER HEATHER NOVA 1995
THE OZZMAN COMETH – THE BEST OF OZZY OSBOURNE
    OZZY OSBOURNE 1997
OZZMOSIS OZZY OSBOURNE 1995
OZZY OSBOURNE'S BLIZZARD OF OZ OZZY OSBOURNE'S
    BLIZZARD OF OZ 1980
P.H.D. P.H.D. 1982
P.H.U.Q. WILDHEARTS 1995
PABLO HONEY RADIOHEAD 1993
PACER AMPS 1995
THE PACIFIC AGE ORCHESTRAL MANOEUVRES IN THE
    DARK 1986
PACIFIC STREET PALE FOUNTAINS 1984
PACK UP YOUR TROUBLES RUSS CONWAY 1958
PACKED! – PRETENDERS 1990
PADDY ROBERTS TRIES AGAIN PADDY ROBERTS 1960
A PAGAN PLACE WATERBOYS 1984
PAID IN FULL ERIC B & RAKIM 1987
PAID THA COST TO BE THA BOSS SNOOP DOGG 2003
PAID VACATION RICHARD MARX 1994
PAIN IN MY HEART OTIS REDDING 1967
PAIN IS LOVE JA RULE 2001
PAINKILLER JUDAS PRIEST 1990
PAINKILLER BABES IN TOYLAND 1993
PAINT THE SKY WITH STARS – THE BEST OF ENYA ENYA
    1997
PAINT YOUR WAGON (OST) FILM SOUNDTRACK 1970
PAINTED DESERT SERENADE JOSHUA KADISON 1995
PAINTED FROM MEMORY ELVIS COSTELLO WITH BURT
    BACHARACH 1998
PAINTING IT RED BEAUTIFUL SOUTH 2000
PAL JOEY (OST) FILM SOUNDTRACK 1960
THE PAN PIPE CHILLOUT ALBUM VARIOUS ARTISTS
    (WARNER BROTHERS) 2002
PAN PIPE DREAMS INSPIRATIONS 1995
PAN PIPE IMAGES INSPIRATIONS 1996
PAN PIPE INSPIRATIONS INSPIRATIONS 1995
PAN PIPE MOODS FREE THE SPIRIT 1995
PAN PIPE MOODS IN PARADISE FREE THE SPIRIT
    1996
PAN PIPE MOODS TWO FREE THE SPIRIT 1995
PAN PIPES – ROMANCE OF IRELAND JOHN ANDERSON
    ORCHESTRA 1995
PANDEMONIUM TIME 1990
PANDEMONIUM KILLING JOKE 1994
PANDEMONIUM B2K 2003
PANIC ON MADDER ROSE 1994
PAN ORAMA FLASH & THE PAN 1983
PAPA LOVES MAMBO – THE VERY BEST OF PERRY COMO
    2004
PAPER MONSTERS DAVE GAHAN 2003
PAPER ROSES MARIE OSMOND 1974
PAPER SCISSORS STONE CATATONIA 2001
PARACHUTE PRETTY THINGS 1970
PARACHUTES COLDPLAY 2000
PARADE SPANDAU BALLET 1984

PARADE – MUSIC FROM 'UNDER THE CHERRY MOON' (OST)
    PRINCE 1986
PARADISE JAMES LAST 1984
PARADISE INNER CITY 1989
PARADISE RUBY TURNER 1990
PARADISE KACI 2002
PARADISE HAWAIIAN STYLE (OST) ELVIS PRESLEY 1966
PARADISE LOST HERD 1968
PARADISE REMIXED INNER CITY 1990
PARADISE THEATER STYX 1981
PARALLEL LINES BLONDIE 1978
PARANOID BLACK SABBATH 1970
PARANOID BLACK SABBATH 2002
PARANOID & SUNBURNT SKUNK ANANSIE 1995
PARCEL OF ROGUES STEELEYE SPAN 1973
PARCEL OF ROGUES BARBARA DICKSON 1994
PARIS SUPERTRAMP 1980
PARIS CURE 1993
PARIS MALCOLM MCLAREN 1994
PARIS AU PRINTEMPS (PARIS IN THE SPRING) PUBLIC
    IMAGE LTD 1980
PARKERILLA GRAHAM PARKER & THE RUMOUR 1978
PARKLIFE BLUR 1994
PARSLEY, SAGE, ROSEMARY AND THYME SIMON &
    GARFUNKEL 1968
THE PARTISANS PARTISANS 1983
THE PARTRIDGE FAMILY SOUND MAGAZINE PARTRIDGE
    FAMILY 1972
PARTS OF THE PROCESS MORCHEEBA 2003
PARTY VARIOUS ARTISTS (POLYGRAM) 1999
PARTY ALBUM OUTHERE BROTHERS 1995
THE PARTY ALBUM! – VENGABOYS 1999
PARTY AT THE PALACE VARIOUS ARTISTS (VIRGIN) 2002
PARTY CRAZY BLACK LACE 1986
PARTY DOLL AND OTHER FAVOURITES MARY CHAPIN
    CARPENTER 1999
PARTY FEVER/DISCO MANIA VARIOUS ARTISTS (TV
    RECORDS) 1982
PARTY IN THE PARK VARIOUS ARTISTS (UNIVERSAL) 2001
PARTY IN THE PARK 2002 VARIOUS ARTISTS (UNIVERSAL)
    2002
PARTY MIX VARIOUS ARTISTS (DINO) 1991
THE PARTY MIX ALBUM B-52'S 1981
PARTY PARTY – 16 GREAT PARTY ICEBREAKERS BLACK
    LACE 1984
PARTY PARTY 2 BLACK LACE 1985
PARTY TIME RUSS CONWAY 1960
PARTY TIME CHEEKY GIRLS 2003
PARTY TONIGHT MODERN ROMANCE 1983
THE PARTY'S OVER TALK TALK 1982
PASS IN TIME – THE DEFINITIVE COLLECTION BETH ORTON
    2003
PASS THE VIBES VARIOUS ARTISTS (POLYGRAM) 1996
PASSAGE CARPENTERS 1977
PASSION PETER GABRIEL 1989
PASSION JOSE CARRERAS 1996
PASSION VARIOUS ARTISTS (UNIVERSAL) 2001
PASSION AND WARFARE STEVE VAI 1990
A PASSION PLAY JETHRO TULL 1973
PASSPORT NANA MOUSKOURI 1976
PAST MASTERS VOLUME 1 BEATLES 1988
PAST MASTERS VOLUME 2 BEATLES 1988
PASTICHE MANHATTAN TRANSFER 1978
PASTPRESENT CLANNAD 1989
PAT BOONE ORIGINALS PAT BOONE 1976
PAT GARRETT & BILLY THE KID (OST) BOB DYLAN 1973
PATASHNIK BIOSPHERE 1994
PATIENCE GEORGE MICHAEL 2004
PATRICK MORAZ PATRICK MORAZ 1976
PATRIOT GAMES GUNSHOT 1993
PAUL HARDCASTLE PAUL HARDCASTLE 1985
PAUL IS LIVE PAUL McCARTNEY 1993
PAUL JOHNSON PAUL JOHNSON 1987
PAUL McCARTNEY'S LIVERPOOL ORATORIO CARL DAVIS &
    THE ROYAL LIVERPOOL PHILHARMONIC ORCHESTRA
    & CHOIR 1991

PAUL McCARTNEY'S STANDING STONE LONDON
    SYMPHONY ORCHESTRA CONDUCTED BY LAURENCE
    FOSTER 1997
PAUL OAKENFOLD – NEW YORK VARIOUS ARTISTS (GLOBAL
    UNDERGROUND) 1998
PAUL SIMON PAUL SIMON 1972
PAUL SIMON'S CONCERT IN THE PARK – AUGUST 15TH
    1991 PAUL SIMON 1991
PAUL WELLER PAUL WELLER 1992
PAUL YOUNG PAUL YOUNG 1997
PAULINE PAULINE HENRY 1994
PAULINE MURRAY AND THE INVISIBLE GIRLS PAULINE
    MURRAY & THE INVISIBLE GIRLS 1980
PAUL'S BOUTIQUE BEASTIE BOYS 1989
PAVAROTTI AND FRIENDS FOR WAR CHILD LUCIANO
    PAVAROTTI & FRIENDS 1996
THE PAVAROTTI COLLECTION LUCIANO PAVAROTTI 1986
PAVAROTTI IN HYDE PARK LUCIANO PAVAROTTI 1992
PAVAROTTI/DOMINGO/CARRERAS VARIOUS ARTISTS
    (EMPORIO) 2001
PAVAROTTI'S GREATEST HITS LUCIANO PAVAROTTI 1982
PAWN SHOPPE HEART VON BONDIES 2004
PAWNSHOP GUITARS GILBY CLARKE 1994
PEACE EURYTHMICS 1999
PEACE AND LOVE POGUES 1989
PEACE AT LAST BLUE NILE 1996
PEACE IN OUR TIME BIG COUNTRY 1988
PEACE IN THE VALLEY VARIOUS ARTISTS (RONCO)
    1979
PEACE – PURE CLASSICAL CALM VARIOUS ARTISTS
    (VIRGIN) 2004
PEACE WILL COME TOM PAXTON 1972
PEACEFUL JOURNEY HEAVY D & THE BOYZ 1991
PEACHES – THE VERY BEST OF STRANGLERS 2002
PEARL JANIS JOPLIN 1971
PEARL HARBOR (OST) GREENAWAY/ZIMMER 2001
PEARLS ELKIE BROOKS 1981
PEARLS II ELKIE BROOKS 1982
PEASANTS, PIGS & ASTRONAUTS KULA SHAKER 1999
PEBBLES PEBBLES 1988
PEEL SESSIONS ORBITAL 1994
PEEPSHOW SIOUXSIE & THE BANSHEES 1988
PEGGY SUICIDE JULIAN COPE 1991
PELICAN WEST HAIRCUT 100 1982
PELOTON DELGADOS 1998
PENDULUM CREEDENCE CLEARWATER REVIVAL 1971
PENNIES FROM HEAVEN TELEVISION SOUNDTRACK 1978
PENNIES FROM HEAVEN TELEVISION SOUNDTRACK 1990
THE PENTANGLE PENTANGLE 1968
PENTHOUSE AND PAVEMENT HEAVEN 17 1981
PENTHOUSE TAPES SENSATIONAL ALEX HARVEY BAND
    1976
PEOPLE HOTHOUSE FLOWERS 1988
PEOPLE MOVE ON BERNARD BUTLER 1998
THE PEOPLE TREE MOTHER EARTH 1994
THE PEOPLE WHO GRINNED THEMSELVES TO DEATH
    HOUSEMARTINS 1987
PEOPLE'S INSTINCTIVE TRAVELS... – A TRIBE CALLED
    QUEST 1990
PEPSI CHART 2001 VARIOUS ARTISTS (VIRGIN) 2000
PEPSI CHART 2002 VARIOUS ARTISTS (VIRGIN) 2001
PEPSI CHART 2003 VARIOUS ARTISTS (VIRGIN) 2002
PERFECT ANGEL MINNIE RIPERTON 1975
PERFECT DAY VARIOUS ARTISTS (COLUMBIA) 1998
A PERFECT DAY – HIS GREATEST HITS AND MORE ROGER
    WHITTAKER 1996
A PERFECT LOVE VARIOUS ARTISTS (GLOBAL) 1997
A PERFECT LOVE II VARIOUS ARTISTS (GLOBAL) 1998
A PERFECT LOVE III VARIOUS ARTISTS (GLOBAL) 2000
PERFECT PEACE WESTMINSTER ABBEY
    CHOIR/CONDUCTOR: MARTIN NEARY 1998
PERFECT REMEDY STATUS QUO 1989
PERFECT STRANGERS DEEP PURPLE 1984
PERFECT TIMING KIKI DEE 1981
PERFECT TIMING MSG 1987
PERFECTLY GOOD GUITAR JOHN HIATT 1993

PERFECTO FLUORO:OAKENFOLD VARIOUS ARTISTS (PERFECTO) 1996
PERFECTO PRESENTS PAUL OAKENFOLD – TRAVELLING VARIOUS ARTISTS (PERFECTO) 2000
PERFORMANCE – THE VERY BEST OF TIM RICE AND ANDREW LLOYD WEBBER VARIOUS ARTISTS (TELSTAR) 1985
PERFORMANCE AND COCKTAILS STEREOPHONICS 1999
PERHAPS ASSOCIATES 1985
PERHAPS LOVE PLACIDO DOMINGO & JOHN DENVER 1981
PERILOUS JOURNEY GORDON GILTRAP 1978
A PERIOD OF TRANSITION VAN MORRISON 1977
PERMANENT SHADE OF BLUE ROACHFORD 1994
PERMANENT VACATION AEROSMITH 1987
PERMANENT WAVES RUSH 1980
PERMANENT: JOY DIVISION 1995 JOY DIVISION 1995
PERMISSION TO LAND DARKNESS 2003
PERRY PERRY COMO 1974
PERSEVERE PROCLAIMERS 2001
PERSISTENCE OF TIME ANTHRAX 1990
PERSONAL PAUL JOHNSON 1989
THE PERSUADERS JOHN BARRY 1972
PERVERSE JESUS JONES 1993
PET SHOP BOYS, ACTUALLY PET SHOP BOYS 1987
PET SOUNDS BEACH BOYS 1966
PETE TONG – ESSENTIAL SELECTION – SPRING 1999 VARIOUS ARTISTS (FFRR) 1999
PETE TONG ESSENTIAL SELECTION VARIOUS ARTISTS (FFRR) 1998
PETE TONG ESSENTIAL SELECTION – IBIZA 99 VARIOUS ARTISTS (FFRR) 1999
PETE TONG ESSENTIAL SELECTION – SUMMER 1998 VARIOUS ARTISTS (FFRR) 1998
PETE TONG ESSENTIAL SELECTION – SUMMER 97 VARIOUS ARTISTS (POLYGRAM) 1997
PETE TONG ESSENTIAL SELECTION – WINTER 97 VARIOUS ARTISTS (FFRR) 1997
PETE TONG/BOY GEORGE – DANCE NATION 5 VARIOUS ARTISTS (MINISTRY OF SOUND) 1998
PETER AND GORDON PETER & GORDON 1964
PETER AND SOPHIA PETER SELLERS & SOPHIA LOREN 1960
PETER COX PETER COX 1997
PETER GABRIEL PETER GABRIEL 1977
PETER GABRIEL PETER GABRIEL 1978
PETER GABRIEL PETER GABRIEL 1980
PETER GABRIEL PETER GABRIEL 1982
PETER GABRIEL PLAYS LIVE PETER GABRIEL 1983
PETER HETHERINGTON: SONGS FROM THE HEART VARIOUS ARTISTS (MAWSON & WARSHAM) 1991
PETER PAUL AND MARY PETER, PAUL & MARY 1964
PETER SARSTEDT PETER SARSTEDT 1969
PHAEDRA TANGERINE DREAM 1974
THE PHANTOM OF THE OPERA ORIGINAL LONDON STAGE CAST SOUNDTRACK 1987
PHANTOM POWER SUPER FURRY ANIMALS 2003
PHANTASMAGORIA CURVED AIR 1972
PHANTASMAGORIA DAMNED 1985
PHASE ONE VARIOUS ARTISTS (POSITIVA) 1994
PHENOMENA PHENOMENA 1985
PHENOMENON LL COOL J 1997
PHIL COULTER'S IRELAND PHIL COULTER 1985
PHIL EVERLY PHIL EVERLY 1983
PHIL FEARON AND GALAXY PHIL FEARON & GALAXY 1984
PHIL SPECTOR'S CHRISTMAS ALBUM PHIL SPECTOR 1972
PHIL SPECTOR'S ECHOES OF THE 60'S PHIL SPECTOR 1977
PHIL SPECTOR'S GREATEST HITS/PHIL SPECTOR'S CHRISTMAS ALBUM PHIL SPECTOR 1983
PHILADELPHIA (OST) FILM SOUNDTRACK 1994
PHILIP OAKEY AND GIORGIO MORODER PHILIP OAKEY & GIORGIO MORODER 1985
PHILOPHOBIA ARAB STRAP 1998
THE PHILOSOPHER'S STONE VAN MORRISON 1998
PHOENIX DAN FOGELBERG 1980
THE PHOTOS PHOTOS 1980

PHYSICAL OLIVIA NEWTON-JOHN 1981
PHYSICAL GRAFFITI LED ZEPPELIN 1975
A PHYSICAL PRESENCE LEVEL 42 1985
PIAF ELAINE PAIGE 1994
THE PIANO (OST) MICHAEL NYMAN 1994
THE PIANO AND THE SONG VARIOUS ARTISTS (UNIVERSAL) 2003
PIANO MAN BILLY JOEL 1984
PIANO MOODS SCHOOL OF EXCELLENCE 1995
PIANO MOODS VARIOUS ARTISTS (DECADANCE) 2003
THE PIANO SESSIONS KEY SESSIONS QUARTET 2004
THE PICK OF BILLY CONNOLLY BILLY CONNOLLY 1981
THE PICK, THE SICKLE AND THE SHOVEL GRAVEDIGGAZ 1997
PICKLED EGGS & SHERBET ALL SEEING I 1999
PICKWICK ORIGINAL LONDON STAGE CAST SOUNDTRACK 1963
PICTURE BOOK SIMPLY RED 1985
PICTURE BOOK SIMPLY RED 1996
A PICTURE OF YOU JOE BROWN & THE BRUVVERS 1962
PICTURE PERFECT MORNING EDIE BRICKELL 1994
PICTURE THIS WET WET WET 1995
PICTURES AT AN EXHIBITION EMERSON, LAKE & PALMER 1971
PICTURES AT AN EXHIBITION TOMITA 1975
PICTURES AT ELEVEN ROBERT PLANT 1982
PICTURES OF ELVIS ELVIS PRESLEY 1977
PIE JESU ALED JONES 1986
PIECE BY PIECE JOHN MARTYN 1986
PIECE OF CAKE MUDHONEY 1992
PIECE OF MIND IRON MAIDEN 1983
PIECES JULIAN LLOYD WEBBER & THE LONDON SYMPHONY ORCHESTRA 1985
PIECES IN A MODERN STYLE WILLIAM ORBIT 2000
PIECES OF HANCOCK TONY HANCOCK 1960
THE PIG ATTRACTION FEATURING PINKY AND PERKY PINKY & PERKY 1993
PIG LIB STEPHEN MALMUS & THE JICKS 2003
PIGEON HOLE NEW FAST AUTOMATIC DAFFODILS 1990
PIL LIVE IN TOKYO PUBLIC IMAGE LTD 1983
PILEDRIVER STATUS QUO 1973
PILGRIM ERIC CLAPTON 1998
PILGRIMAGE WISHBONE ASH 1971
THE PILLAGE CAPPADONNA 1998
PILLS 'N' THRILLS AND BELLYACHES HAPPY MONDAYS 1990
PILLS 'N' THRILLS AND BELLYACHES HAPPY MONDAYS 2002
PINK BUBBLES GO APE HELLOWEEN 1991
PINKERTON WEEZER 1996
PINKY BLUE ALTERED IMAGES 1982
PIN UPS DAVID BOWIE 1973
PIOUHGD BUTTHOLE SURFERS 1991
THE PIOUS BIRD OF GOOD OMEN FLEETWOOD MAC 1969
PIPEDREAM ALAN HULL 1973
THE PIPER AT THE GATES OF DAWN PINK FLOYD 1967
PIPES OF PEACE PAUL McCARTNEY 1983
PIRANHAS PIRANHAS 1980
PIRATES RICKIE LEE JONES 1981
PISCES, AQUARIUS, CAPRICORN & JONES LTD. MONKEES 1968
PIXIES AT THE BBC PIXIES 1998
A PLACE IN THE SUN LIT 1999
A PLACE IN THE WORLD MARY CHAPIN CARPENTER 1996
A PLACE ON EARTH – THE GREATEST HITS BELINDA CARLISLE 1999
PLACEBO PLACEBO 1996
PLACIDO DOMINGO COLLECTION PLACIDO DOMINGO 1986
THE PLAGUE DEMON 1983
THE PLAN OSMONDS 1973
THE PLAN 1978 TUBEWAY ARMY & GARY NUMAN 1984
PLANET ROCK VARIOUS ARTISTS (DINO) 1993
PLANET WAVES BOB DYLAN 1974
PLANETARY INVASION MIDNIGHT STAR 1985
PLASTIC LETTERS BLONDIE 1978
PLATINUM MIKE OLDFIELD 1979

THE PLATINUM ALBUM VARIOUS ARTISTS (K-TEL) 1981
THE PLATINUM ALBUM VENGABOYS 2000
THE PLATINUM COLLECTION BARBARA DICKSON 2004
THE PLATINUM COLLECTION BRYAN FERRY 2004
THE PLATINUM COLLECTION PHIL COLLINS 2004
THE PLATINUM COLLECTION – GREATEST HITS BARRY MANILOW 1993
PLATINUM SOUL LEGENDS – 1960–1975 VARIOUS ARTISTS (WARNER BROTHERS) 2002
PLATOON (OST) FILM SOUNDTRACK 1987
PLAY MAGAZINE 1980
PLAY SQUEEZE 1991
PLAY MOBY 1999
PLAY ANDREW LLOYD WEBBER AND TIM RICE HANK MARVIN & THE SHADOWS 1997
PLAY DIRTY GIRLSCHOOL 1983
PLAY DON'T WORRY MICK RONSON 1975
PLAY GAMES DOG EAT DOG 1996
PLAY IT AGAIN BRIAN SMITH & HIS HAPPY PIANO 1981
PLAY/THE B SIDES MOBY 2000
PLAY TO WIN GABRIELLE 2004
PLAYED BODINES 1987
PLAYIN' FAVOURITES DON MCLEAN 1973
PLAYING MY GAME LENE MARLIN 2000
PLAYING TO AN AUDIENCE OF ONE DAVID SOUL 1977
PLAYING WITH A DIFFERENT SEX AU PAIRS 1981
PLAYS ABBA JAMES LAST 2001
PLAYS SPANISH MUSIC JOHN WILLIAMS 1970
PLEASE PET SHOP BOYS 1986
PLEASE DON'T TOUCH STEVE HACKETT 1978
PLEASE GET MY NAME RIGHT TWIGGY 1977
PLEASE HAMMER DON'T HURT 'EM MC HAMMER 1990
PLEASE PLEASE ME BEATLES 1963
PLEASE TO SEE THE KING STEELEYE SPAN 1971
PLEASE YOURSELF BANANARAMA 1993
PLEASED TO MEET YOU SLEEPER 1997
PLEASED TO MEET YOU JAMES 2001
PLEASURE GIRLS AT OUR BEST 1981
PLEASURE AND PAIN DR. HOOK 1979
PLEASURE DEATH THERAPY? 1992
PLEASURE ONE HEAVEN 17 1986
THE PLEASURE PRINCIPLE GARY NUMAN 1979
PLIGHT AND PREMONITION DAVID SYLVAN & HOLGAR CZUKAY 1988
THE PLOT THICKENS GALLIANO 1994
PNYC PORTISHEAD 1998
POCKET FULL OF KRYPTONITE SPIN DOCTORS 1993
A POCKETFUL OF DREAMS BIG FUN 1990
POD BREEDERS 1990
POEMS, PRAYERS AND PROMISES JOHN DENVER 1973
THE POET II BOBBY WOMACK 1984
POETIC CHAMPIONS COMPOSE VAN MORRISON 1987
THE POINT (OST TV) NILSSON 1972
POINT BLANK BONFIRE 1989
POINT BLANK NAILBOMB 1994
POINT OF ENTRY JUDAS PRIEST 1981
POINTLESS NOSTALGIC JAMIE CULLUM 2004
POINTS ON THE CURVE WANG CHUNG 1984
POISON BELL BIV DEVOE 1990
POKEMON – 2 B A MASTER VARIOUS ARTISTS (KOCH) 2000
POKEMON – THE FIRST MOVIE (OST) FILM SOUNDTRACK 2000
POLAND TANGERINE DREAM 1984
POLECATS POLECATS 1981
POLKA PARTY JAMES LAST 1972
THE POLYESTER EMBASSY MADISON AVENUE 2000
POLYTHENE FEEDER 1997
POMME FRITZ ORB 1994
POOLSIDE NU SHOOZ 1986
POP U2 1997
POP ART TRANSVISION VAMP 1988
POP CLASSICS – 28 CLASSIC TRACKS VARIOUS ARTISTS (ARCADE) 1991
POP IDOL – THE BIG BAND ALBUM VARIOUS ARTISTS (S) 2002

POP LIFE BANANARAMA 1991
POP PARTY VARIOUS ARTISTS (UNIVERSAL) 2003
POP PRINCESSES VARIOUS ARTISTS (UNIVERSAL) 2004
POP SAID DARLING BUDS 1989
POP SYMPHONIES JAMES LAST 1991
POP SYMPHONIES 2 JAMES LAST 1998
POP TRASH DURAN DURAN 2000
POP! – THE FIRST 20 HITS ERASURE 1992
POPART – THE HITS PET SHOP BOYS 2003
POPPED IN SOULED OUT WET WET WET 1987
POPSTARS HEAR'SAY 2001
POPULAR MUSIC FROM TV FILM & OPERA MARIA CALLAS 2000
PORCELAIN JULIA FORDHAM 1989
PORCUPINE ECHO & THE BUNNYMEN 1983
PORGY AND BESS (OST) FILM SOUNDTRACK 1959
PORK SODA PRIMUS 1993
PORNO FOR PYROS PORNO FOR PYROS 1993
PORNOGRAPHY CURE 1982
PORTISHEAD PORTISHEAD 1997
PORTRAIT WALKER BROTHERS 1966
PORTRAIT DON WILLIAMS 1979
PORTRAIT NOLANS 1982
PORTRAIT DIANA ROSS 1983
PORTRAIT DES O'CONNOR 1992
PORTRAIT (SO LONG AGO, SO CLEAR) VANGELIS 1996
PORTRAIT IN MUSIC ELVIS PRESLEY 1970
PORTRAIT IN MUSIC BURT BACHARACH 1971
PORTRAIT OF A LEGEND SAM COOKE 2003
PORTRAIT OF DONNY DONNY OSMOND 1972
A PORTRAIT OF DORIS DAY DORIS DAY 1989
A PORTRAIT OF ELLA FITZGERALD ELLA FITZGERALD 1988
A PORTRAIT OF MARIO LANZA MARIO LANZA 1987
PORTRAIT OF SINATRA FRANK SINATRA 1977
POSITIVE REACTION CAVEMAN 1991
POSITIVE TOUCH UNDERTONES 1981
POSITIVITY INCOGNITO 1993
POSSESSED VENOM 1985
POST BJORK 1995
POST HISTORIC MONSTERS CARTER – THE UNSTOPPABLE SEX MACHINE 1993
POST ORGASMIC CHILL SKUNK ANANSIE 1999
POST/TELEGRAM BJORK 1996
POSTCARD MARY HOPKIN 1969
POSTCARDS FROM HEAVEN LIGHTHOUSE FAMILY 1997
POT LUCK ELVIS PRESLEY 1962
POTATO LAND SPIRIT 1981
POVERTY'S PARADISE NAUGHTY BY NATURE 1995
POWER & SOUL VARIOUS ARTISTS (POLYGRAM) 1998
POWER AND PASSION MAMA'S BOYS 1985
POWER AND SOUL VARIOUS ARTISTS (POLYGRAM) 1994
POWER AND THE GLORY SAXON 1983
THE POWER AND THE GLORY VARIOUS ARTISTS (VERTIGO) 1991
POWER BALLADS VARIOUS ARTISTS (VIRGIN) 2003
POWER CUTS – ROCK'S GREATEST HITS VARIOUS ARTISTS (POLYGRAM) 1992
POWER IN NUMBERS JURASSIC 5 2002
POWER IN THE DARKNESS TOM ROBINSON BAND 1978
POWER OF A WOMAN ETERNAL 1995
POWER OF A WOMAN VARIOUS ARTISTS (TELSTAR) 1998
THE POWER OF CLASSIC ROCK LONDON SYMPHONY ORCHESTRA WITH THE ROYAL CHORAL SOCIETY & THE ROGER SMITH CHORALE 1985
THE POWER OF GLORIA GAYNOR GLORIA GAYNOR 1986
THE POWER OF LOVE VARIOUS ARTISTS (WEST FIVE) 1986
POWER OF LOVE LUTHER VANDROSS 1991
THE POWER OF LOVE VARIOUS ARTISTS (QUALITY PRICE MUSIC) 1992
THE POWER OF LOVE VARIOUS ARTISTS (WARNER BROTHERS) 2003
POWER OF TEN CHRIS DE BURGH 1992
POWER RANGERS – THE ALBUM – A ROCK ADVENTURE MIGHTY MORPH'N POWER RANGERS 1994
THE POWER STATION POWER STATION 1985
POWER THEMES 90 F.A.B. 1990

POWER WINDOWS RUSH 1985
POWER, CORRUPTION AND LIES NEW ORDER 1983
POWERAGE AC/DC 1978
POWERLIGHT EARTH WIND & FIRE 1983
POWERSLAVE IRON MAIDEN 1984
POWERTRIP MONSTER MAGNET 1998
POWERTRIPPIN' – ALMIGHTY 1993
PRACTICE WHAT YOU PREACH TESTAMENT 1989
PRAISE INNER CITY 1992
PRAISE – 18 CHORAL MASTERPIECES LONDON PHILHARMONIC CHOIR WITH THE NATIONAL PHILHARMONIC ORCHESTRA CONDUCTED BY JOHN ALDISS 1991
THE PREACHERS WIFE (OST) WHITNEY HOUSTON 1997
PRECIOUS VARIOUS ARTISTS (DINO) 1992
PRECIOUS MEMORIES ANN WILLIAMSON 1986
PRECIOUS METAL VARIOUS ARTISTS (MCA) 1980
PRECIOUS METAL VARIOUS ARTISTS (STYLUS) 1989
PRECIOUS MOMENTS VARIOUS ARTISTS (IMPRESSION) 1983
PRECIOUS TIME PAT BENATAR 1981
THE PREDATOR ICE CUBE 1992
THE PREMIER HITS GARY NUMAN/TUBEWAY ARMY 1996
PREMIERE KATHERINE JENKINS 2004
THE PREMIERE COLLECTION – ENCORE (ANDREW LLOYD WEBBER) VARIOUS ARTISTS (REALLY USEFUL) 1992
PREMIERS SYMPTOMES AIR 1999
PRE MILLENNIUM TENSION TRICKY 1996
PRESENCE LED ZEPPELIN 1976
THE PRESENT MOODY BLUES 1983
PRESENT ARMS UB40 1981
PRESENT ARMS IN DUB UB40 1981
A PRESENT FOR EVERYONE BUSTED 2003
PRESENTING DIONNE WARWICK DIONNE WARWICK 1964
THE PRESIDENTS OF THE UNITED STATES OF AMERICA PRESIDENTS OF THE UNITED STATES OF AMERICA 1996
PRESLEY – THE ALL TIME GREATEST HITS ELVIS PRESLEY 1987
PRESS TO PLAY PAUL McCARTNEY 1986
PRESTO RUSH 1989
THE PRETENDER JACKSON BROWNE 1976
PRETENDERS PRETENDERS 1980
PRETENDERS II PRETENDERS 1981
PRETTY HATE MACHINE NINE INCH NAILS 1991
PRETTY ON THE INSIDE HOLE 1991
PRETTY THINGS PRETTY THINGS 1965
PRETTY WOMAN (OST) FILM SOUNDTRACK 1990
PRETZEL LOGIC STEELY DAN 1974
THE PRICE YOU PAY SPEAR OF DESTINY 1988
PRIDE ROBERT PALMER 1983
PRIDE – THE VERY BEST OF SCOTLAND VARIOUS ARTISTS (RCA) 1995
PRIEST... LIVE JUDAS PRIEST 1987
PRIMITIVE NEIL DIAMOND 1984
PRIMITIVE SOULFLY 2000
PRIMITIVE COOL MICK JAGGER 1987
PRINCE BLIMEY RED SNAPPER 1996
PRINCE CHARMING ADAM & THE ANTS 1981
THE PRINCE'S TRUST COLLECTION VARIOUS ARTISTS (TELSTAR) 1985
THE PRINCE'S TRUST CONCERT 1987 VARIOUS ARTISTS (A&M) 1987
PRINCE'S TRUST TENTH ANNIVERSARY BIRTHDAY PARTY VARIOUS ARTISTS (A&M) 1987
PRINCESS PRINCESS 1986
THE PRINCIPLE OF MOMENTS ROBERT PLANT 1983
PRISONERS IN PARADISE EUROPE 1991
PRIVATE AUDITION HEART 1982
PRIVATE COLLECTION JON & VANGELIS 1983
PRIVATE COLLECTION 1979–1988 CLIFF RICHARD 1988
PRIVATE DANCER TINA TURNER 1984
PRIVATE EYES DARYL HALL & JOHN OATES 1982
PRIVATE PRACTICE DR. FEELGOOD 1978
PRIVATE REVOLUTION WORLD PARTY 1987
PROBOT PROBOT 2004

PROCOL HARUM LIVE IN CONCERT WITH THE EDMONTON SYMPHONY ORCHESTRA PROCOL HARUM 1972
PROCOL'S NINTH PROCOL HARUM 1975
PRODIGAL SISTA BEVERLEY KNIGHT 1998
PRODIGY PRESENTS THE DIRTCHAMBER SESSIONS 1 VARIOUS ARTISTS (XL RECORDINGS) 1999
PRODUCT 2378 VARIOUS ARTISTS (TELSTAR) 1990
PROGENY SHAMEN 1991
PROGRESSION VARIOUS ARTISTS (POLYGRAM) 1993
PROGRESSION VOL.1 VARIOUS ARTISTS (RENAISSANCE) 2001
PROGRESSIONS OF POWER TRIUMPH 1980
PROMISE SADE 1985
THE PROMISE T'PAU 1991
PROMISED LAND ELVIS PRESLEY 1975
PROMISED LAND QUEENSRYCHE 1994
PROMISES AND LIES UB40 1993
PROPAGANDA SPARKS 1974
PROPHESY NITIN SAWHNEY 2001
PROPHETS, SEERS AND SAGES THE ANGELS OF THE AGES/MY PEOPLE WERE FAIR AND HAD SKY IN THEIR HAIR BUT NOW THEY'RE CONTENT TO WEAR STARS ON THEIR BROWS TYRANNOSAURUS REX 1972
THE PROS AND CONS OF HITCH HIKING ROGER WATERS 1984
PROTECT THE INNOCENT VARIOUS ARTISTS (TELSTAR) 1989
PROTECTION MASSIVE ATTACK 1994
PROTECTION/NO PROTECTION MASSIVE ATTACK 1995
PROTEST SONGS PREFAB SPROUT 1989
PROTOTYPE3 – SEB FONTAINE VARIOUS ARTISTS (GLOBAL UNDERGROUND) 2000
PROUD HEATHER SMALL 2000
PROVISION SCRITTI POLITTI 1988
PROVOCATIVE JOHNNY GILL 1993
PROZIAC HONEYCRACK 1996
PS I LOVE YOU VARIOUS ARTISTS (WARWICK) 1982
PSALM 69 MINISTRY 1992
PSYCHE – THE ALBUM PJ & DUNCAN 1994
PSYCHEDELIC FURS PSYCHEDELIC FURS 1980
PSYCHEDELIC SHACK TEMPTATIONS 1970
PSYCHIC KARAOKE TRANSGLOBAL UNDERGROUND 1996
PSYCHOCANDY JESUS & MARY CHAIN 1985
PSYCHO CIRCUS KISS 1998
THE PSYCHOMODO COCKNEY REBEL 1974
PSYCHOTIC SUPPER TESLA 1991
PSYENCE FICTION UNKLE 1998
PSI PITCHSHIFTER 2002
PUBLIC IMAGE PUBLIC IMAGE LTD 1978
PULP FICTION (OST) FILM SOUNDTRACK 1994
PULSE PINK FLOYD 1995
PUMP AEROSMITH 1989
PUMP AEROSMITH 1995
PUMP UP THE JAM TECHNOTRONIC 1990
PUMP UP THE VALUUM NOFX 2000
PUMP UP THE VOLUME VARIOUS ARTISTS (UNIVERSAL) 2001
PUNCH THE CLOCK ELVIS COSTELLO & THE ATTRACTIONS 1983
PUNK AND DISORDERLY VARIOUS ARTISTS (ABSTRACT) 1982
PUNK AND DISORDERLY – NEW WAVE 1976–1981 VARIOUS ARTISTS (TELSTAR) 1991
PUNK AND DISORDERLY (FURTHER CHARGES) VARIOUS ARTISTS (ANAGRAM) 1982
PUNK – THE JUBILEE VARIOUS ARTISTS (VIRGIN) 2002
PUNK'S NOT DEAD EXPLOITED 1981
PURE PRIMITIVES 1989
PURE MIDGE URE 1991
PURE 3 COLOURS RED 1997
PURE GARY NUMAN 2000
PURE HAYLEY WESTENRA 2003
PURE & SIMPLE VARIOUS ARTISTS (UNIVERSAL) 2001
PURE ATTRACTION VARIOUS ARTISTS (COLUMBIA) 1995
PURE CELTIC CHILLOUT VARIOUS ARTISTS (VIRGIN/EMI) 2002

PURE CHILLOUT VARIOUS ARTISTS (VIRGIN) 2001
PURE CLASSICAL CHILLOUT VARIOUS ARTISTS (DECADANCE) 2002
PURE CULT CULT 1993
PURE DANCE '96 VARIOUS ARTISTS (POLYGRAM) 1996
PURE DANCE '97 VARIOUS ARTISTS (POLYGRAM) 1997
PURE DRUM & BASS VARIOUS ARTISTS (UNIVERSAL) 2003
PURE EMOTIONS INSPIRATIONS 1995
PURE EUPHORIA – LEVEL 4 VARIOUS ARTISTS (TELSTAR) 2000
PURE FLAVA VARIOUS ARTISTS (WARNER BROTHERS) 2001
PURE GARAGE VARIOUS ARTISTS (WARNER BROTHERS) 2000
PURE GARAGE II VARIOUS ARTISTS (WARNER BROTHERS) 2000
PURE GARAGE III VARIOUS ARTISTS (WARNER BROTHERS) 2000
PURE GARAGE IV VARIOUS ARTISTS (WARNER BROTHERS) 2001
PURE GARAGE V VARIOUS ARTISTS (WARNER BROTHERS) 2001
PURE GARAGE PLATINUM – THE VERY BEST OF VARIOUS ARTISTS (WARNER BROTHERS) 2002
PURE GARAGE PRESENTS FOUR ON THE FLOOR VARIOUS ARTISTS (WARNER BROTHERS) 2004
PURE GENIUS VARIOUS ARTISTS (WARNER BROTHERS) 2002
PURE GENIUS VOLUME 2 VARIOUS ARTISTS (WARNER BROTHERS) 2002
PURE GLOBAL CHILLOUT VARIOUS ARTISTS (DECADANCE) 2002
PURE GOLD VARIOUS ARTISTS (EMI) 1973
PURE GROOVE VARIOUS ARTISTS (TELSTAR) 2002
PURE GROOVE – THE CLASSICS VARIOUS ARTISTS (TELSTAR) 2002
PURE HIP HOP VARIOUS ARTISTS (TELSTAR) 2001
PURE HIP HOP – EXPLICIT BEATS VARIOUS ARTISTS (WARNER BROTHERS) 2001
PURE HITS '97 VARIOUS ARTISTS (TELSTAR) 1997
PURE JAZZ MOODS – COOL JAZZ FOR A SUMMERS DAY VARIOUS ARTISTS (DINO) 1996
PURE LIGHTNING SEEDS LIGHTNING SEEDS 1996
PURE LOVERS VOLUME 1 VARIOUS ARTISTS (CHARM) 1990
PURE LOVERS VOLUME 2 VARIOUS ARTISTS (CHARM) 1990
PURE LOVERS VOLUME 3 VARIOUS ARTISTS (CHARM) 1991
PURE LOVERS VOLUME 4 VARIOUS ARTISTS (CHARM) 1991
PURE LOVERS VOLUME 5 VARIOUS ARTISTS (CHARM) 1992
PURE LOVERS VOLUME 6 VARIOUS ARTISTS (CHARM) 1993
PURE MANIA VIBRATORS 1977
PURE MOODS VARIOUS ARTISTS (VIRGIN) 1994
PURE PHASE SPIRITUALIZED ELECTRIC MAINLINE 1995
PURE PLEASURE SHAGGY 1993
PURE R&B VARIOUS ARTISTS (TELSTAR) 2000
PURE R&B 2 VARIOUS ARTISTS (TELSTAR) 2000
PURE R&B 3 VARIOUS ARTISTS (TELSTAR) 2001
PURE REGGAE VARIOUS ARTISTS (GLOBAL) 1997
PURE REGGAE VOLUME 1 VARIOUS ARTISTS (ISLAND) 1994
PURE ROCK BALLADS VARIOUS ARTISTS (POLYGRAM) 1998
PURE SAX STATE OF THE HEART 1996
PURE SILK – A NEW DIMENSION VARIOUS ARTISTS (PURE SILK) 1999
PURE SILK – THE THIRD DIMENSION VARIOUS ARTISTS (PURE SILK) 2000
PURE SILK IN AYIA NAPA VARIOUS ARTISTS (PURE SILK) 2000
PURE SILK IN AYIA NAPA 2 VARIOUS ARTISTS (PURE SILK) 2001
PURE SOFT METAL VARIOUS ARTISTS (STYLUS) 1990
PURE SWING VARIOUS ARTISTS (DINO) 1995
PURE SWING 5 VARIOUS ARTISTS (DINO) 1996
PURE SWING 96 VARIOUS ARTISTS (DINO) 1996
PURE SWING III VARIOUS ARTISTS (DINO) 1995
PURE SWING IV VARIOUS ARTISTS (DINO) 1995
PURE SWING TWO VARIOUS ARTISTS (DINO) 1995
PURE TRANCE VARIOUS ARTISTS (WARNER BROTHERS) 2002

PURE URBAN ESSENTIALS VARIOUS ARTISTS (WARNER BROTHERS) 2003
PURE URBAN ESSENTIALS 2 VARIOUS ARTISTS (WARNER BROTHERS) 2003
PURGATORY/MAIDEN JAPAN IRON MAIDEN 1990
PURPENDICULAR DEEP PURPLE 1996
PURPLE STONE TEMPLE PILOTS 1994
PURPLE RAIN (OST) PRINCE & THE REVOLUTION 1984
PURPLE RAINBOWS VARIOUS ARTISTS (POLYDOR) 1991
THE PURSUIT OF ACCIDENTS LEVEL 42 1982
PUSH BROS 1988
PUSH THE BEAT FOR THIS JAM – THE SINGLES SCOOTER 2002
PUSH THE BUTTON MONEY MARK 1998
PUTTIN' ON THE STYLE – THE GREATEST HITS LONNIE DONEGAN 2003
PUTTING ON THE STYLE LONNIE DONEGAN 1978
PUZZLE PEOPLE TEMPTATIONS 1970
PXR 5 HAWKWIND 1979
PYE CHARTBUSTERS VARIOUS ARTISTS (PYE) 1971
PYE CHARTBUSTERS VOLUME 2 VARIOUS ARTISTS (PYE) 1971
PYRAMID ALAN PARSONS PROJECT 1978
PYROMANIA DEF LEPPARD 1983
Q THE ALBUM VARIOUS ARTISTS (EMI) 2003
Q – THE ALBUM VOLUME 1 VARIOUS ARTISTS (TELSTAR) 1991
Q ANTHEMS VARIOUS ARTISTS (VIRGIN) 2001
Q AWARDS: THE ALBUM VARIOUS ARTISTS (EMI) 2000
Q COUNTRY VARIOUS ARTISTS (THE HIT LABEL) 1994
Q RHYTHM AND BLUES VARIOUS ARTISTS (THE HIT LABEL) 1993
Q THE BLUES VARIOUS ARTISTS (THE HIT LABEL) 1992
Q: ARE WE NOT MEN? A: NO WE ARE DEVO DEVO 1978
THE QAT COLLECTION SASHA 1994
QE 2 MIKE OLDFIELD 1980
QUADROPHENIA WHO 1973
QUADROPHENIA (OST) WHO 1979
QUADROPHENIA WHO 1996
QUALITY CONTROL JURASSIC 5 2000
QUALITY STREET WORLD OF TWIST 1991
QUARK STRANGENESS AND CHARM HAWKWIND 1977
QUARTER MOONS IN A TEN CENT TOWN EMMYLOU HARRIS 1978
QUARTET ULTRAVOX 1982
QUEEN – QUEEN 1974
QUEEN 2 QUEEN 1974
THE QUEEN ALBUM ELAINE PAIGE 1988
QUEEN AT THE BEEB QUEEN 1989
THE QUEEN IS DEAD SMITHS 1986
QUEEN OF SOUL – THE VERY BEST OF ARETHA FRANKLIN ARETHA FRANKLIN 1994
QUEEN ROCKS QUEEN 1997
QUEEN'S GREATEST HITS QUEEN 1981
QUEER AS FOLK – THE WHOLE THING SORTED TELEVISION SOUNDTRACK 1999
QUEER AS FOLK 2 TELEVISION SOUNDTRACK 2000
QUENCH BEAUTIFUL SOUTH 1998
? (THE BEST OF NEW ORDER)/? (THE REST OF NEW ORDER) NEW ORDER 1994
A QUESTION OF BALANCE MOODY BLUES 1970
A QUICK ONE WHO 1966
QUICK STEP & SIDE KICK THOMPSON TWINS 1983
QUICKSILVER DJ QUICKSILVER 1998
QUIET IS THE NEW LORD KINGS OF CONVENIENCE 2001
QUIET LIFE JAPAN 1980
THE QUIET REVOLUTION RONNY JORDAN 1993
QUIET REVOLUTION CHRIS DE BURGH 1999
THE QUIET STORM VARIOUS ARTISTS (UNIVERSAL) 2003
QUINTESSENCE QUINTESSENCE 1970
QUIT DREAMING AND GET ON THE BEAM BILL NELSON 1981
QUIXOTIC MARTINA TOPLEY BIRD 2003
QUO STATUS QUO 1974
R R KELLY 1998

THE R IN R&B – GREATEST HITS VOLUME 1 R KELLY 2003
R KELLY R KELLY 1995
R U STILL DOWN? (REMEMBER ME) 2PAC 1997
R&B HITS VARIOUS ARTISTS (UNIVERSAL) 2001
R&B LOVE VARIOUS ARTISTS (WARNER BROTHERS) 2003
R&B LOVESONGS VARIOUS ARTISTS (COLUMBIA) 2002
R&B MASTERS VARIOUS ARTISTS (COLUMBIA) 2001
R&B MASTERS 2 VARIOUS ARTISTS (COLUMBIA) 2001
R&B SELECTOR VARIOUS ARTISTS (UNIVERSAL) 2001
R&S RECORDS – ORDER TO DANCE VARIOUS ARTISTS (R&S) 1991
R.I.P. PRESENTS THE REAL SOUND OF UNDERGROUND VARIOUS ARTISTS (VIRGIN) 1998
RA TODD RUNDGREN 1977
RABBITS ON AND ON JASPER CARROTT 1975
RADAR EARTHLING 1995
RADIATION MARILLION 1998
RADIATOR SUPER FURRY ANIMALS 1997
RADIO LL COOL J 1986
RADIO 2 – SONGS OF THE CENTURY VARIOUS ARTISTS (GLOBAL) 1999
RADIO DREAMSCAPE – VOLUME 1 VARIOUS ARTISTS (DREAMSCAPE) 1995
RADIO K.A.O.S. ROGER WATERS 1987
RADIO M.U.S.C. MAN WOMACK & WOMACK 1985
RADIO MUSICOLA NIK KERSHAW 1986
RADIO ONE JIMI HENDRIX 1989
RADIO SESSIONS CURVE 1993
RADIOACTIVE VARIOUS ARTISTS (RONCO) 1980
RAFI'S REVENGE ASIAN DUB FOUNDATION 1998
RAGE T'PAU 1988
RAGE – MAKE SOME NOISE VARIOUS ARTISTS (A&M) 1991
RAGE AGAINST THE MACHINE RAGE AGAINST THE MACHINE 1993
RAGE FOR ORDER QUEENSRYCHE 1986
RAGE IN EDEN ULTRAVOX 1981
RAGGA HEAT REGGAE BEAT VARIOUS ARTISTS (TELSTAR) 1993
RAGGED GLORY NEIL YOUNG & CRAZY HORSE 1990
THE RAGPICKER'S DREAM MARK KNOPFLER 2002
RAHMAN: BOMBAY DREAMS RAHMAN/ORIGINAL SOUND RECORDING 2002
RAIDERS OF THE POP CHARTS VARIOUS ARTISTS (RONCO) 1982
RAIN DANCES CAMEL 1977
RAIN DOGS TOM WAITS 1985
RAIN TREE CROW RAIN TREE CROW 1991
RAINBOW PETERS & LEE 1974
RAINBOW NEIL DIAMOND 1974
RAINBOW MARIAH CAREY 1999
RAINBOW CONNECTION IV ROSE ROYCE 1979
RAINBOW DOME MUSIC STEVE HILLAGE 1979
RAINBOW FRIDGE (OST) JIMI HENDRIX 1971
RAINBOW RISING RICHIE BLACKMORE'S RAINBOW 1976
RAINBOW WARRIORS VARIOUS ARTISTS (RCA) 1989
RAINDANCE RAINDANCE 1996
RAINDANCING ALISON MOYET 1987
RAINDROPS KEEP FALLING ON MY HEAD JOHNNY MATHIS 1970
RAINGODS WITH ZIPPOS FISH 1999
RAINTOWN DEACON BLUE 1987
RAINY DAY MUSIC JAYHAWKS 2003
THE RAINY SEASON MARC COHN 1993
RAISE EARTH WIND & FIRE 1981
RAISE SWERVEDRIVER 1991
RAISE YOUR FIST AND YELL ALICE COOPER 1987
RAISED ON RADIO JOURNEY 1986
RAISED THE PRESSURE ELECTRONIC 1996
RAISING HELL FATBACK BAND 1976
RAISING HELL RUN D.M.C. 1986
RALPH TRESVANT RALPH TRESVANT 1991
RAM PAUL & LINDA McCARTNEY 1971
RAM IT DOWN JUDAS PRIEST 1988
RAMPANT NAZARETH 1974
RAMSHACKLED ALAN WHITE 1976
RANCID RANCID 2000

RANK SMITHS 1988
RANT 'N' RAVE WITH THE STRAY CATS STRAY CATS 1983
RAOUL AND THE KINGS OF SPAIN TEARS FOR FEARS 1995
RAP ATTACK VARIOUS ARTISTS (K-TEL) 1989
RAP ATTACK VARIOUS ARTISTS (CONCEPT) 1994
RAP FLAVAS VARIOUS ARTISTS (COLUMBIA) 1996
RAP IT UP – RAP'S GREATEST HITS VARIOUS ARTISTS (K-TEL) 1986
RAP TO THE MAX VARIOUS ARTISTS (VIRGIN) 1994
RAP TRAX VARIOUS ARTISTS (STYLUS) 1988
RAPPED IN REMIXES SALT-N-PEPA 1992
RAPPERS DELIGHT VARIOUS ARTISTS (UNIVERSAL) 2002
RAPPIN' UP THE HOUSE VARIOUS ARTISTS (K-TEL) 1988
RAPTURE ANITA BAKER 1986
THE RAPTURE SIOUXSIE & THE BANSHEES 1995
RARE DAVID BOWIE 1983
RARE VARIOUS ARTISTS (RCA) 1987
RARE 2 VARIOUS ARTISTS (RCA) 1988
RARE 3 VARIOUS ARTISTS (ARIOLA) 1989
RARE GROOVE – DYNAMIC DISCO HITS VARIOUS ARTISTS (QUALITY PRICE MUSIC) 1992
RARE GROOVE MIX – 70 SMASH HITS OF THE 70'S VARIOUS ARTISTS (STYLUS) 1988
RARITIES BEATLES 1979
RASTAMAN VIBRATION BOB MARLEY & THE WAILERS 1976
RAT IN THE KITCHEN UB40 1986
RATED R QUEENS OF THE STONE AGE 2000
RATTLE AND HUM U2 1988
RATTLESNAKES LLOYD COLE & THE COMMOTIONS 1984
RAVE VARIOUS ARTISTS (TELSTAR) 1990
RAVE VARIOUS ARTISTS (REACHIN') 1991
RAVE 2 – STRICTLY HARDCORE VARIOUS ARTISTS (ELEVATE) 1992
RAVE 92 VARIOUS ARTISTS (COOKIE JAR) 1992
RAVE ALERT VARIOUS ARTISTS (TELSTAR) 1992
RAVE ANTHEMS VARIOUS ARTISTS (DINO) 1995
THE RAVE GENER8TOR VARIOUS ARTISTS (COOKIE JAR) 1992
THE RAVE GENER8TOR 2 VARIOUS ARTISTS (COOKIE JAR) 1992
RAVE GENERATION VARIOUS ARTISTS (DINO) 1993
RAVE GENERATION 2 VARIOUS ARTISTS (DINO) 1994
RAVE NATION VARIOUS ARTISTS (TELSTAR) 1992
RAVE NATION VARIOUS ARTISTS (INSPIRED) 2001
RAVEL'S BOLERO LONDON PHILHARMONIC ORCHESTRA 1960
THE RAVEN STRANGLERS 1979
RAVING MAD VARIOUS ARTISTS (ELEVATE) 1992
RAVING WE'RE RAVING VARIOUS ARTISTS (TELSTAR) 1992
RAW ALYSON WILLIAMS 1989
RAW ALARM 1991
THE RAW AND THE COOKED FINE YOUNG CANNIBALS 1989
RAW LIKE SUSHI NENEH CHERRY 1989
RAW MEAT FOR THE BALCONY BILLY CONNOLLY 1978
RAW MELODY MAN NEW MODEL ARMY 1991
RAW POWER IGGY POP & THE STOOGES 1977
RAY FRAZIER CHORUS 1991
RAY CHARLES – LIVING LEGEND RAY CHARLES 1993
RAY MOORE – A PERSONAL CHOICE RAY MOORE & VARIOUS ARTISTS 1989
RAY OF LIGHT MADONNA 1998
RAYMOND LEFEVRE RAYMOND LEFEVRE 1967
RAYMOND LEFEVRE VOLUME 2 RAYMOND LEFEVRE 1968
RAZAMANAZ NAZARETH 1973
RAZORBLADE SUITCASE BUSH 1997
THE RAZOR'S EDGE AC/DC 1990
RE PRESS – THE 70'S SOUL REVIVAL VARIOUS ARTISTS (WARNER BROTHERS) 2003
REACH FOR THE SKY SUTHERLAND BROTHERS & QUIVER 1976
REACH FOR THE SKY RATT 1988
REACH OUT FOUR TOPS 1967
REACH OUT BURT BACHARACH 1970
REACH THE BEACH FIXX 1983
REACHING TO THE CONVERTED BILLY BRAGG 1999

REACTIVATE 10 VARIOUS ARTISTS (REACT) 1995
REACTIVATE 11 – STINGER BEAT AND TECHNO RAYS VARIOUS ARTISTS (REACT) 1996
REACTIVATE 12 VARIOUS ARTISTS (REACT) 1997
REACTIVATE VOLUME 1 – THE BELGIAN TECHNO ANTHEMS VARIOUS ARTISTS (REACT) 1991
REACTIVATE VOLUME 2 – PHASERS ON FULL VARIOUS ARTISTS (REACT) 1991
REACTIVATE VOLUME 4 – TECHNOVATION VARIOUS ARTISTS (REACT) 1992
REACTIVATE VOLUME 5 – PURE TRANCE AND TECHNO VARIOUS ARTISTS (REACT) 1992
RE AC TOR NEIL YOUNG & CRAZY HORSE 1981
READ MY LIPS JIMMY SOMERVILLE 1989
READ MY LIPS SOPHIE ELLIS BEXTOR 2001
READING – THE INDIE ALBUM VARIOUS ARTISTS (POLYGRAM) 1992
READING WRITING AND ARITHMETIC SUNDAYS 1990
READY BLUES BAND 1980
READY AND WILLING WHITESNAKE 1980
READY FOR BATTLE ROCKSTEADY CREW 1984
READY FOR ROMANCE MODERN TALKING 1986
READY FOR THE STORM (FAVOURITE CUTS) KATHY MATTEA 1995
READY STEADY GO VARIOUS ARTISTS (DECCA) 1964
READY STEADY GO! – NUMBER ONE SIXTIES ALBUM TELEVISION COMPILATION 1997
READY STEADY GO! – SIXTIES MOTOWN SOUND TELEVISION COMPILATION 1998
READY TO RUN SINEAD QUINN 2003
REAL BELINDA CARLISLE 1993
REAL AS I WANNA BE CLIFF RICHARD 1998
THE REAL CHUCKEEBOO LOOSE ENDS 1988
A REAL DEAD ONE IRON MAIDEN 1993
REAL GARAGE – MIXED LIVE BY MASTERSTEPZ VARIOUS ARTISTS (MINISTRY OF SOUND) 2001
THE REAL GLENN MILLER AND HIS ORCHESTRA PLAY THE ORIGINAL MUSIC OF THE FILM 'THE GLENN MILLER STORY' AND OTHER HITS (OST) GLENN MILLER & HIS ORCHESTRA 1971
REAL LIFE MAGAZINE 1978
REAL LIFE SIMPLE MINDS 1991
REAL LIVE BOB DYLAN 1984
A REAL LIVE ONE IRON MAIDEN 1993
REAL LOVE LISA STANSFIELD 1991
THE REAL PEOPLE REAL PEOPLE 1991
THE REAL RAMONA THROWING MUSES 1991
THE REAL SOUND OF AYIA NAPA VARIOUS ARTISTS (UNIVERSAL) 2000
REAL THING REAL THING 1976
THE REAL THING FAITH NO MORE 1990
REAL THINGS 2 UNLIMITED 1994
REAL TO REEL MARILLION 1984
REALITY DAVID BOWIE 2003
REALITY EFFECT TOURISTS 1979
THE REALITY OF MY SURROUNDINGS FISHBONE 1991
REANIMATION LINKIN PARK 2002
REASON MELANIE C 2003
THE REASON HOOBASTANK 2004
REASON TO BELIEVE RITA MCNEIL 1990
REASONS TO BE CHEERFUL – THE VERY BEST OF IAN DURY AND THE BLOCKHEADS IAN DURY & THE BLOCKHEADS 1999
REBEL JOHN MILES 1976
REBEL MUSIC BOB MARLEY & THE WAILERS 1986
REBEL MUSIC REBEL MC 1990
REBEL SOULS ASWAD 1984
REBEL YELL BILLY IDOL 1985
THE REBIRTH OF COOL III VARIOUS ARTISTS (FOURTH & BROADWAY) 1993
THE REBIRTH OF COOL, TOO VARIOUS ARTISTS (FOURTH & BROADWAY) 1992
RECITAL '70 NANA MOUSKOURI 1970
RECKLESS BRYAN ADAMS 1985
RECKONING R.E.M. 1984
RECONSIDER BABY ELVIS PRESLEY 1985

THE RECORD OF THE YEAR 2000 VARIOUS ARTISTS (TELSTAR) 2000
RECORD SHACK PRESENTS – VOLUME ONE VARIOUS ARTISTS (RECORD SHACK) 1984
RECORDED LIVE TEN YEARS AFTER 1973
RECORDS: THE BEST OF FOREIGNER FOREIGNER 1982
RECOVERING THE SATELLITES COUNTING CROWS 1996
RECURRENCE RAILWAY CHILDREN 1988
RECURRING SPACEMEN 3 1991
RECURRING DREAM – THE VERY BEST OF CROWDED HOUSE CROWDED HOUSE 1996
RECYCLER ZZ TOP 1990
RED KING CRIMSON 1974
RED BLACK UHURU 1981
RED COMMUNARDS 1987
RED AND GOLD FAIRPORT CONVENTION 1989
RED CARD STREETWALKERS 1976
RED DIRT GIRL EMMYLOU HARRIS 2000
RED HEAVEN THROWING MUSES 1992
RED HOT + DANCE VARIOUS ARTISTS (EPIC) 1992
RED HOT AND WHITE 2 VARIOUS ARTISTS (VITAL SOUNDS) 1992
RED HOT AND WHITE LABELS VARIOUS ARTISTS (VITAL SOUNDS) 1992
RED HOT METAL – 18 ROCK CLASSICS VARIOUS ARTISTS (DOVER) 1991
RED HOT RHYTHM 'N' BLUES DIANA ROSS 1987
RED HOUSE PAINTERS RED HOUSE PAINTERS 1993
RED HOUSE PAINTERS RED HOUSE PAINTERS 1993
RED MEDICINE FUGAZI 1995
RED RIVER VALLEY SLIM WHITMAN 1977
RED ROSE SPEEDWAY PAUL McCARTNEY & WINGS 1973
RED ROSES FOR ME POGUES 1984
THE RED SHOES KATE BUSH 1993
RED STAR SHOWADDYWADDY 1977
RED, HOT AND BLUE VARIOUS ARTISTS (CHRYSALIS) 1990
REDD HOTT SHARON REDD 1982
REEL LIFE BOY MEETS GIRL 1989
REELIN' IN THE YEARS – THE VERY BEST OF STEELY DAN STEELY DAN 1985
REFLECTION SHADOWS 1990
REFLECTIONS DIANA ROSS & THE SUPREMES 1968
REFLECTIONS ANDY WILLIAMS 1978
REFLECTIONS GEORGE HAMILTON IV 1979
REFLECTIONS VARIOUS ARTISTS (CBS) 1982
REFLECTIONS FOSTER & ALLEN 1987
REFLECTIONS PAUL YOUNG 1994
REFELCTIONS – GREATEST HITS CARLY SIMON 2004
REFRIED ECTOPLASM (SWITCHED ON – VOLUME 2) STEREOLAB 1995
REFUGEES OF THE HEART STEVE WINWOOD 1990
REG STRIKES BACK ELTON JOHN 1988
REGENERATION DIVINE COMEDY 2001
REGGAE 93 VARIOUS ARTISTS (ISLAND) 1993
REGGAE CHARTBUSTERS 75 VARIOUS ARTISTS (CACTUS) 1976
REGGAE GROOVE VARIOUS ARTISTS (THE HIT LABEL) 1995
REGGAE HITS VOLUME 1 VARIOUS ARTISTS (JETSTAR) 1985
REGGAE HITS VOLUME 10 VARIOUS ARTISTS (JETSTAR) 1991
REGGAE HITS VOLUME 12 VARIOUS ARTISTS (JETSTAR) 1992
REGGAE HITS VOLUME 14 VARIOUS ARTISTS (JETSTAR) 1993
REGGAE HITS VOLUME 2 VARIOUS ARTISTS (JETSTAR) 1985
REGGAE HITS VOLUME 4 VARIOUS ARTISTS (JETSTAR) 1988
REGGAE HITS VOLUME 5 VARIOUS ARTISTS (JETSTAR) 1988
REGGAE HITS VOLUME 6 VARIOUS ARTISTS (JETSTAR) 1989
REGGAE HITS VOLUME 7 VARIOUS ARTISTS (JETSTAR) 1989
REGGAE HITS VOLUME 8 VARIOUS ARTISTS (JETSTAR) 1990
REGGAE LOVE SONGS: 50 JAMAICAN LOVERS CLASSICS VARIOUS ARTISTS (SANCTUARY) 2003
REGGAE MASSIVE VARIOUS ARTISTS (DINO) 1995
REGGAE OWES ME MONEY RAGGA TWINS 1991
REGGATTA DE BLANC POLICE 1979
REGULAR URBAN SURVIVORS TERRORVISION 1996

REGULATE... G FUNK ERA WARREN G 1994
REI MOMO DAVID BYRNE 1989
REIGN IN BLOOD SLAYER 1987
REILLY ACE OF THEMES TELEVISION SOUNDTRACK 1983
REINVENTING THE STEEL PANTERA 2000
REJOICE ST. PAUL'S BOYS' CHOIR 1980
RELATIONSHIP OF COMMAND AT THE DRIVE IN 2000
RELAX MORE VARIOUS ARTISTS (CLASSIC FM) 2000
RELAX! THE ULTIMATE 80'S MIX VARIOUS ARTISTS (POLYGRAM) 1998
RELAX! THE ULTIMATE 80'S MIX – VOLUME 2 VARIOUS ARTISTS (POLYGRAM) 1999
RELAX... – VARIOUS ARTISTS (CLASSIC FM) 1999
RELAXING SOUND OF BERT KAEMPFERT BERT KAEMPFERT & HIS ORCHESTRA 1967
RELAYER YES 1974
RELEASE DAVID KNOPFLER 1983
RELEASE PET SHOP BOYS 2002
RELEASE ME ENGELBERT HUMPERDINCK 1967
RELEASE SOME TENSION SWV 1997
RELICS PINK FLOYD 1971
RELICS PINK FLOYD 1996
RELISH JOAN OSBORNE 1996
RELOAD METALLICA 1997
RELOAD TOM JONES 1999
RELOADED VARIOUS ARTISTS (UNIVERSAL) 2000
RELOADED 2 VARIOUS ARTISTS (UNIVERSAL) 2001
RELOADED 3 VARIOUS ARTISTS (UNIVERSAL) 2001
RELOADED 4 VARIOUS ARTISTS (UNIVERSAL) 2002
REMAIN IN LIGHT TALKING HEADS 1980
REMANUFACTURE – CLONING TECHNOLOGY FEAR FACTORY 1997
REMASTERED – THE BEST OF STEELY DAN STEELY DAN 1993
REMASTERS LED ZEPPELIN 1990
REMEDY BASEMENT JAXX 1999
REMEMBER CAT STEVENS – THE ULTIMATE COLLECTION CAT STEVENS 1999
REMEMBER ME THIS WAY GARY GLITTER 1974
REMEMBER THEN – 30 DOO WOP GREATS VARIOUS ARTISTS (POLYGRAM) 1994
REMEMBER WHEN SINGERS COULD SING VARIOUS ARTISTS (THE HIT LABEL) 1996
REMEMBER YOU'RE A WOMBLE WOMBLES 1974
REMEMBER YOU'RE MINE FOSTER & ALLEN 1988
REMINISCING BUDDY HOLLY & THE CRICKETS 1963
REMINISCING FOSTER & ALLEN 1986
REMINISCING – THE HOWARD KEEL COLLECTION HOWARD KEEL 1985
THE REMIX ALBUM – DIAMONDS ARE FOREVER SHIRLEY BASSEY 2000
REMIXED INCOGNITO 1996
THE REMIXES STONE ROSES 2000
THE REMIXES GROOVE ARMADA 2000
THE REMIXES MARIAH CAREY 2003
RE MIXTURE VARIOUS ARTISTS (CHAMPAGNE) 1981
REMOTE CONTROL TUBES 1979
THE REMOTE PART IDLEWILD 2002
REMOTE/THE BITTER SUITE HUE & CRY 1988
RENAISSANCE RENAISSANCE 1970
RENAISSANCE ASWAD 1988
RENAISSANCE VARIOUS ARTISTS (SIX6) 1994
RENAISSANCE LIONEL RICHIE 2000
RENAISSANCE – AWAKENING – DAVE SEAMAN VARIOUS ARTISTS (RENAISSANCE) 2000
RENAISSANCE – MIX COLLECTION – PART 2 VARIOUS ARTISTS (NETWORK) 1996
RENAISSANCE IBIZA – MIXED BY DEEP DISH VARIOUS ARTISTS (RENAISSANCE) 2000
RENAISSANCE IBIZA 2001 VARIOUS ARTISTS (RENAISSANCE) 2001
RENAISSANCE THE MIX COLLECTION – PART 3 VARIOUS ARTISTS (SIX6) 1996
RENAISSANCE WORLDWIDE LONDON VARIOUS ARTISTS (RENAISSANCE) 1997
RENDEZ-VOUS JEAN-MICHEL JARRE 1986

RENEGADE THIN LIZZY 1981
RENEGADES BRASS CONSTRUCTION 1984
RENEGADES RAGE AGAINST THE MACHINE 2000
REPEAT OFFENDER RICHARD MARX 1989
REPEAT WHEN NECESSARY DAVE EDMUNDS 1979
REPLENISH REEF 1995
REPLICAS TUBEWAY ARMY 1979
REPRESS – 80'S CLUB CLASSICS VARIOUS ARTISTS (WARNER BROTHERS) 2003
REPRISE RUSSELL WATSON 2002
REPRODUCTION HUMAN LEAGUE 1981
REPTILE ERIC CLAPTON 2001
REPUBLIC NEW ORDER 1993
REPUBLICA REPUBLICA 1997
REPUTATION DUSTY SPRINGFIELD 1990
REQUESTS MERLE & ROY 1987
RESERECTION SAINT ETIENNE DAHO 1996
RESERVOIR DOGS (OST) FILM SOUNDTRACK 1993
RESIDENT – 2 YEARS OF OAKENFOLD AT CREAM VARIOUS ARTISTS (VIRGIN) 1999
RESIDENT ALIEN SPACEHOG 1997
RESIST KOSHEEN 2001
RESPECT VARIOUS ARTISTS (UNIVERSAL) 2000
RESPECT – THE VERY BEST OF ARETHA FRANKLIN 2002
RESPECT YOURSELF JOE COCKER 2002
RESPOND PACKAGE – LOVE THE REASON VARIOUS ARTISTS (RESPOND) 1983
RESTLESS XZIBIT 2001
RESTLESS AND WILD ACCEPT 1983
RESTLESS HEART DAVID COVERDALE & WHITESNAKE 1997
RESULTS LIZA MINNELLI 1989
RESULTS MAY VARY LIMP BIZKIT 2003
RESURRECTION E 17 1998
RESURRECTION (OST) 2PAC 2003
RETRO LOU REED 1989
RETRO ACTIVE DEF LEPPARD 1993
RETRO DANCE MASTERS VARIOUS ARTISTS (VIRGIN) 2002
RETROSPECTIVE – THE BEST OF SUZANNE VEGA 2003
A RETROSPECTIVE OF HOUSE '91 '95 – VOLUME 1 VARIOUS ARTISTS (SOUND DIMENSION) 1995
A RETROSPECTIVE OF HOUSE '91 '95 – VOLUME 2 VARIOUS ARTISTS (SOUND DIMENSION) 1996
A RETROSPECTIVE OF HOUSE '91 '96 – VOLUME 3: JAY/KELLY/ANDERSON VARIOUS ARTISTS (SOUND DIMENSION) 1996
A RETROSPECTIVE OF HOUSE '91 '96 – VOLUME 4 VARIOUS ARTISTS (SOUND DIMENSION) 1996
THE RETURN OF BRUNO BRUCE WILLIS 1987
RETURN OF DRAGON SISQO 2001
RETURN OF SATURN NO DOUBT 2000
THE RETURN OF SUPERBAD VARIOUS ARTISTS (K-TEL) 1988
RETURN OF THE GLADIATORS TELEVISION COMPILATION 1993
RETURN OF THE JEDI (OST) JOHN WILLIAMS 1983
RETURN OF THE MACK MARK MORRISON 1996
THE RETURN OF THE SPACE COWBOY JAMIROQUAI 1994
THE RETURN OF THE SUPER 70'S VARIOUS ARTISTS (VIRGIN) 2003
RETURN TO FANTASY URIAH HEEP 1975
RETURN TO THE CENTRE OF THE EARTH RICK WAKEMAN; LONDON SYMPHONY ORCHESTRA; ENGLISH CHAMBER CHOIR; NARRATED BY PATRICK STEWART 1999
RETURN TO THE LAST CHANCE SALOON BLUETONES 1998
RETURN TO THE VALLEY OF THE GO GO'S GO-GO'S 1995
REUNION BLACK SABBATH 1998
REV IT UP VIXEN 1990
REVEAL R.E.M. 2001
REVELATIONS KILLING JOKE 1982
REVELATIONS GENE 1999
REVENGE EURYTHMICS 1986
REVENGE KISS 1992
REVENGE OF THE GOLDFISH INSPIRAL CARPETS 1992
REVERENCE FAITHLESS 1996
REVISITED EARTHA KITT 1961

REVOLT 3 COLOURS RED 1999
REVOLUTION THEATRE OF HATE 1984
THE REVOLUTION TONIGHT BLUE OYSTER CULT 1983
REVOLUTIONS JEAN-MICHEL JARRE 1988
REVOLVER BEATLES 1966
REWIND – THE SOUND OF UK GARAGE VARIOUS ARTISTS (MINISTRY OF SOUND) 2000
REWIND 1971–1984 (THE BEST OF THE ROLLING STONES) ROLLING STONES 1984
REWIRED MIKE AND THE MECHANICS 2004
RFTC ROCKET FROM THE CRYPT 1998
RHAPSODIES RICK WAKEMAN 1979
RHAPSODY AND BLUE CRUSADERS 1980
RHAPSODY IN BLACK LONDON SYMPHONY ORCHESTRA 1980
RHAPSODY IN WHITE LOVE UNLIMITED ORCHESTRA 1974
RHINESTONE COWBOY GLEN CAMPBELL 1975
RHINOS WINOS AND LUNATICS MAN 1974
RHUBARB ROOTJOOSE 1999
RHYMES AND REASONS CAROLE KING 1972
RHYMES AND REASONS JOHN DENVER 1973
RHYTHM AND CLASSICS LOUIS CLARK CONDUCTING THE ROYAL PHILHARMONIC ORCHESTRA 1988
RHYTHM AND STEALTH LEFTFIELD 1999
RHYTHM COUNTRY AND BLUES VARIOUS ARTISTS (MCA) 1994
THE RHYTHM DIVINE VARIOUS ARTISTS (DINO) 1991
THE RHYTHM DIVINE VOLUME 2 VARIOUS ARTISTS (DINO) 1991
RHYTHM KILLERS SLY & ROBBIE 1987
RHYTHM 'N' REGGAE VARIOUS ARTISTS (K-TEL) 1981
RHYTHM NATION 1814 JANET JACKSON 1989
RHYTHM OF LIFE PAUL HAIG 1983
RHYTHM OF LOVE KYLIE MINOGUE 1990
RHYTHM OF LOVE ANITA BAKER 1994
RHYTHM OF THE NIGHT DEBARGE 1985
RHYTHM OF THE NIGHT VARIOUS ARTISTS (K-TEL) 1987
THE RHYTHM OF THE NIGHT CORONA 1995
THE RHYTHM OF THE SAINTS PAUL SIMON 1990
RHYTHM OF THE SUN VARIOUS ARTISTS (TELSTAR) 1989
RHYTHM OF YOUTH MEN WITHOUT HATS 1983
A RHYTHM ROMANCE NILS LOFGREN 1982
RHYTHMEEN ZZ TOP 1996
RHYTHMS AND BALLADS OF BROADWAY JOHNNY MATHIS 1960
THE RHYTHMS OF A NATION VARIOUS ARTISTS (BMG) 2002
RIALTO RIALTO 1998
RICH AND POOR RANDY CRAWFORD 1989
RICHARD CHAMBERLAIN SINGS RICHARD CHAMBERLAIN 1963
RICHARD CLAYDERMAN – CHRISTMAS RICHARD CLAYDERMAN 1984
RICHARD D JAMES ALBUM APHEX TWIN 1996
RICHARD MARX RICHARD MARX 1988
RICHARD X PRESENTS HIS X FACTOR VOLUME 1 RICHARD X 2003
RICHIE BLACKMORE'S RAINBOW RICHIE BLACKMORE'S RAINBOW 1975
RICKS ROAD TEXAS 1993
RICKIE LEE JONES RICKIE LEE JONES 1979
RICKY MARTIN RICKY MARTIN 1999
RICOCHET TANGERINE DREAM 1975
RID OF ME PJ HARVEY 1993
THE RIDDLE NIK KERSHAW 1984
RIDE A ROCK HORSE ROGER DALTREY 1975
RIDE DA RIDDIMS VARIOUS ARTISTS (UNIVERSAL) 2003
RIDE DA RIDDIMS 2 VARIOUS ARTISTS (UNIVERSAL) 2004
RIDE ON A RAINBOW JOHNNY MATHIS 1960
RIDE THE LIGHTNING METALLICA 1984
RIDES REEF 1999
RIDICULOUS SQUEEZE 1995
RIDIN' HIGH ROBERT PALMER 1992
RIDING WITH THE KING B.B. KING & ERIC CLAPTON 2000
RIFFS STATUS QUO 2003
RIGHT HERE RIGHT NOW FIERCE 1999
THE RIGHT MOMENT BARBARA DICKSON 1986

THE RIGHT NIGHT AND BARRY WHITE BARRY WHITE 1987
RIGHT NOW ATOMIC KITTEN 2000
THE RIGHT STUFF – REMIX '89 VARIOUS ARTISTS (STYLUS) 1989
THE RIGHT STUFF 2 – NOTHING BUT A HOUSE PARTY VARIOUS ARTISTS (STYLUS) 1990
RING CONNELLS 1995
RING OF CHANGES BARCLAY JAMES HARVEST 1983
RING A DING DING FRANK SINATRA 1961
RINGO RINGO STARR 1973
RINGS AROUND THE WORLD SUPER FURRY ANIMALS 2001
RIO DURAN DURAN 1982
RIOT ACT PEARL JAM 2002
RIP IT UP ORANGE JUICE 1982
RIPE BANDERAS 1991
RIPTIDE ROBERT PALMER 1985
RISE HERB ALPERT 1979
RISE GABRIELLE 1999
THE RISE AND FALL MADNESS 1982
THE RISE AND FALL OF ZIGGY STARDUST AND THE SPIDERS FROM MARS DAVID BOWIE 1972
RISE AND SHINE ASWAD 1994
RISING DR. HOOK 1980
THE RISING BRUCE SPRINGSTEEN 2002
RISING FOR THE MOON FAIRPORT CONVENTION 1975
RISING FROM THE EAST BALLY SAGOO 1996
RISK MEGADETH 1999
RISOTTO FLUKE 1997
RISQUE CHIC 1979
RITMO JUDIE TZUKE 1983
THE RITUAL TESTAMENT 1992
RITUAL DE LO HABITUAL JANE'S ADDICTION 1990
RITUAL OF LOVE KARYN WHITE 1991
THE RIVER BRUCE SPRINGSTEEN 1980
RIVER DEEP – MOUNTAIN HIGH IKE & TINA TURNER 1966
RIVER OF DREAMS BILLY JOEL 1993
ROACHFORD ROACHFORD 1988
THE ROAD AND THE MILES MAX BOYCE 1978
THE ROAD GOES EVER ON MOUNTAIN 1972
THE ROAD GOES ON FOREVER ALLMAN BROTHERS BAND 1976
ROAD HAWKS HAWKWIND 1976
ROAD NOISE – THE OFFICIAL BOOTLEG JUDIE TZUKE 1982
ROAD SHOW HITS (21 YEARS OF RADIO 1 FM ROAD SHOW) VARIOUS ARTISTS (CONNOISSEUR COLLECTION) 1993
ROAD TESTED BONNIE RAIT 1995
THE ROAD TO ENSENADA LYLE LOVETT 1996
ROAD TO FREEDOM YOUNG DISCIPLES 1991
THE ROAD TO FREEDOM CHRIS DE BURGH 2004
THE ROAD TO HELL CHRIS REA 1989
THE ROAD TO HELL – PART 2 CHRIS REA 1999
ROAD TO RUIN RAMONES 1978
THE ROARING SILENCE MANFRED MANN'S EARTH BAND 1976
THE ROARING TWENTIES – SONGS FROM THE TV SERIES DOROTHY PROVINE 1961
ROBBIE ROBERTSON ROBBIE ROBERTSON 1987
THE ROBERT JOHNSON SONGBOOK PETER GREEN WITH NIGEL WATSON & THE SPLINTER GROUP 1998
ROBERTA FLACK AND DONNY HATHAWAY ROBERTA FLACK & DONNY HATHAWAY 1980
ROBERTA FLACK'S GREATEST HITS ROBERTA FLACK 1984
ROBIN HOOD: PRINCE OF THIEVES (OST) FILM SOUNDTRACK 1991
ROBIN TROWER LIVE ROBIN TROWER 1976
ROBSON & JEROME ROBSON & JEROME 1995
ROCK & ROLL MUSIC TO THE WORLD TEN YEARS AFTER 1972
ROCK A LITTLE STEVIE NICKS 1985
ROCK ACTION MOGWAI 2001
ROCK AIN'T DEAD HEAVY PETTIN' 1985
ROCK ANTHEMS VARIOUS ARTISTS (K-TEL) 1985
ROCK ANTHEMS VARIOUS ARTISTS (DINO) 1994
ROCK ANTHEMS – VOLUME 2 VARIOUS ARTISTS (K-TEL) 1986

ROCK ANTHEMS – VOLUME 2 VARIOUS ARTISTS (DINO) 1996
ROCK AROUND THE CLOCK BILL HALEY 1956
ROCK AROUND THE CLOCK BILL HALEY & HIS COMETS 1968
ROCK ART MAGNUM 1994
ROCK ART AND THE X-RAY STYLE JOE STRUMMER & THE MESCALEROS 1999
ROCK CITY NIGHT VARIOUS ARTISTS (VERTIGO) 1989
THE ROCK CONNECTION CLIFF RICHARD 1984
ROCK FOLLIES TELEVISION SOUNDTRACK 1976
ROCK GODDESS ROCK GODDESS 1983
ROCK HOUSE VARIOUS ARTISTS (RONCO) 1981
ROCK IN RIO IRON MAIDEN 2002
A ROCK IN THE WEARY LAND WATERBOYS 2000
ROCK ISLAND JETHRO TULL 1989
ROCK LEGENDS VARIOUS ARTISTS (RONCO) 1979
ROCK LEGENDS VARIOUS ARTISTS (TELSTAR) 1986
ROCK MACHINE I LOVE YOU VARIOUS ARTISTS (CBS) 1969
THE ROCK MACHINE TURNS YOU ON VARIOUS ARTISTS (CBS) 1969
ROCK ME BABY DAVID CASSIDY 1973
ROCK ME TONIGHT FREDDIE JACKSON 1985
ROCK MONSTERS VARIOUS ARTISTS (UNIVERSAL) 2002
ROCK 'N' ROLL ELVIS PRESLEY 1956
ROCK 'N' ROLL ELVIS PRESLEY 1972
ROCK 'N' ROLL JOHN LENNON 1975
ROCK 'N' ROLL MOTORHEAD 1987
ROCK N ROLL RYAN ADAMS 2003
ROCK 'N' ROLL ANIMAL LOU REED 1974
ROCK 'N' ROLL DUDES GLITTER BAND 1975
ROCK 'N' ROLL GYPSIES SPIDER 1982
ROCK N ROLL HEARTBEATS VARIOUS ARTISTS (TELSTAR) 1992
ROCK 'N' ROLL IS HERE TO STAY VARIOUS ARTISTS (DINO) 1992
ROCK 'N' ROLL JUVENILE CLIFF RICHARD 1979
ROCK 'N' ROLL LOVE SONGS VARIOUS ARTISTS (DINO) 1990
ROCK 'N' ROLL LOVE SONGS VARIOUS ARTISTS (DECADANCE) 2004
ROCK 'N' ROLL MILLION SELLERS CONNIE FRANCIS 1960
ROCK 'N' ROLL MUSIC BEATLES 1976
ROCK 'N' ROLL NO. 2 ELVIS PRESLEY 1957
ROCK 'N' ROLL NO. 2 ELVIS PRESLEY 1962
ROCK 'N' ROLL WITH THE MODERN LOVERS JONATHAN RICHMAN & THE MODERN LOVERS 1977
THE ROCK 'N' ROLL YEARS CLIFF RICHARD 1997
THE ROCK 'N' ROLL YEARS 1956–1959 TELEVISION COMPILATION 1987
THE ROCK 'N' ROLL YEARS 1960–1963 TELEVISION COMPILATION 1987
THE ROCK 'N' ROLL YEARS 1964–1967 TELEVISION COMPILATION 1987
THE ROCK 'N' ROLL YEARS 1968–1971 TELEVISION COMPILATION 1987
ROCK 'N' ROLLER DISCO VARIOUS ARTISTS (RONCO) 1979
ROCK 'N' ROLL STAGE SHOWS BILL HALEY 1956
ROCK 'N' ROLLING STONES ROLLING STONES 1972
ROCK 'N' SOUL (PART ONE) DARYL HALL & JOHN OATES 1983
ROCK OF AMERICA VARIOUS ARTISTS (TRAX) 1990
ROCK OF LIFE RICK SPRINGFIELD 1988
ROCK OF THE WESTIES ELTON JOHN 1975
ROCK ON DAVID ESSEX 1973
ROCK ON VARIOUS ARTISTS (ARCADE) 1977
ROCK PEBBLES AND SAND STANLEY CLARKE 1980
ROCK ROMANCE VARIOUS ARTISTS (ARCADE) 1993
ROCK RULES VARIOUS ARTISTS (K-TEL) 1979
ROCK STEADY NO DOUBT 2002
ROCK THE DANCEFLOOR VARIOUS ARTISTS (ALL AROUND THE WORLD) 1998
ROCK THE DANCEFLOOR VOLUME 5 VARIOUS ARTISTS (ALL AROUND THE WORLD) 2001
ROCK THE DANCEFLOOR 2 VARIOUS ARTISTS (ALL AROUND THE WORLD) 1999

ROCK THE DANCEFLOOR 8 VARIOUS ARTISTS (ALL AROUND THE WORLD) 2003
ROCK THE HOUSE DJ JAZZY JEFF & THE FRESH PRINCE 1987
ROCK THE HOUSE 'LIVE' – HEART 1991
ROCK THE JOINT BILL HALEY 1957
ROCK THE NATIONS SAXON 1986
ROCK THE WORLD FIVE STAR 1988
ROCK THE WORLD VARIOUS ARTISTS (GLOBAL) 1999
ROCK THERAPY VARIOUS ARTISTS (POLYGRAM) 1994
ROCK 'TIL YOU DROP STATUS QUO 1991
ROCK UNTIL YOU DROP RAVEN 1981
ROCK WILL NEVER DIE MICHAEL SCHENKER GROUP 1984
ROCK WITH ALVIN ALVIN STARDUST 1975
ROCK YOUR BABY GEORGE MCCRAE 1974
ROCKABILLY PSYCHOS AND THE GARAGE DISEASE VARIOUS ARTISTS (BIG BEAT) 1984
ROCKABILLY REVIVAL VARIOUS ARTISTS (TELSTAR) 2003
ROCKBIRD DEBBIE HARRY 1986
ROCKET COTTAGE STEELEYE SPAN 1976
ROCKET TO RUSSIA RAMONES 1977
ROCKIN' ALL OVER THE WORLD STATUS QUO 1977
ROCKIN' EVERY NIGHT GARY MOORE 1986
ROCKIN' ROLL BABY STYLISTICS 1974
ROCKIN' THE SUBURBS BEN FOLDS 2001
ROCKIN' WITH CURLY LEADS SHADOWS 1974
ROCKING ALL OVER THE YEARS STATUS QUO 1990
ROCKING AT THE FILLMORE HUMBLE PIE 1972
ROCKS OFF VARIOUS ARTISTS (POLYGRAM) 1995
ROCKS THE HOUSE! – JELLYBEAN 1988
ROCKS THE WORLD THIRD WORLD 1981
ROCKY III (OST) FILM SOUNDTRACK 1982
ROCKY IV (OST) FILM SOUNDTRACK 1986
THE ROCKY MOUNTAIN COLLECTION JOHN DENVER 1997
ROCKY MOUNTAIN HIGH JOHN DENVER 1973
ROCKY V (OST) FILM SOUNDTRACK 1991
ROD STEWART – GREATEST HITS VOL. 1 ROD STEWART 1979
ROD STEWART: LEAD VOCALIST ROD STEWART 1993
RODRIGO: CONCERTO DE ARANJUEZ JOHN WILLIAMS WITH THE ENGLISH CHAMBER ORCHESTRA CONDUCTED BY DANIEL BARENBOIM 1976
THE ROGER WHITTAKER ALBUM ROGER WHITTAKER 1981
ROGER WHITTAKER SINGS THE HITS ROGER WHITTAKER 1978
ROGUES GALLERY SLADE 1985
ROLL ON VARIOUS ARTISTS (POLYDOR) 1981
ROLL THE BONES RUSH 1991
ROLL WITH IT STEVE WINWOOD 1988
ROLLED GOLD – THE VERY BEST OF THE ROLLING STONES ROLLING STONES 1975
ROLLERCOASTER LET LOOSE 1996
ROLLIN' – BAY CITY ROLLERS 1974
THE ROLLING STONES ROLLING STONES 1964
ROLLING STONES NUMBER 2 ROLLING STONES 1965
THE ROLLING STONES ROCK AND ROLL CIRCUS ROLLING STONES AND VARIOUS ARTISTS 1996
ROMANCE DAVID CASSIDY 1985
ROMANCE AND THE STAGE ELAINE PAIGE 1993
ROMANCING THE SCREEN VARIOUS ARTISTS (EPIC) 1992
ROMANTIC CALLAS – THE BEST OF MARIA CALLAS 2001
ROMANTIC ELVIS – 20 LOVE SONGS/ROCKIN' ELVIS – THE SIXTIES 20 GREAT TRACKS ELVIS PRESLEY 1982
ROMANTIC GUITAR PAUL BRETT 1980
ROMANTIC? – HUMAN LEAGUE 1990
ROMANZA ANDREA BOCELLI 1997
ROMEO + JULIET (OST) FILM SOUNDTRACK 1997
RONAN RONAN KEATING 2000
ROOM ON FIRE STROKES 2003
ROOM TO ROAM WATERBOYS 1990
ROOT DOWN (EP) BEASTIE BOYS 1995
ROOTS SEPULTURA 1996
ROOTS OF A LEGEND BOB MARLEY AND THE WAILERS 2004
ROOTS REGGAE 'N' REGGAE ROCK VARIOUS ARTISTS (TELSTAR) 1983

ROOTS TO BRANCHES JETHRO TULL 1995
ROOTY BASEMENT JAXX 2001
ROPIN' THE WIND GARTH BROOKS 1992
RORY GALLAGHER RORY GALLAGHER 1971
THE ROSARY POPE JOHN PAUL II/FATHER COLM KILCOYNE 1994
THE ROSE (OST) BETTE MIDLER 1980
ROSE GARDEN LYNN ANDERSON 1971
ROSE MARIE SINGS JUST FOR YOU ROSE MARIE 1985
THE ROSE OF TRALEE AND OTHER IRISH FAVOURITES JAMES LAST 1984
ROSE ROYCE GREATEST HITS ROSE ROYCE 1980
ROSES FROM THE SOUTH JAMES LAST 1981
ROSS DIANA ROSS 1983
ROTTEN APPLES – THE GREATEST HITS SMASHING PUMPKINS 2001
ROTTERS CLUB HATFIELD & THE NORTH 1975
ROUGH AND READY VOL 1 SHABBA RANKS 1992
ROUGH DIAMONDS BAD COMPANY 1982
ROUGH JUSTICE SPIDER 1984
ROUGH MIX PETE TOWNSHEND & RONNIE LANE 1977
ROUND AMEN CORNER AMEN CORNER 1968
A ROUND AND A BOUT SQUEEZE 1990
ROUND MIDNIGHT VARIOUS ARTISTS (POLYGRAM) 1993
ROUND MIDNIGHT ELKIE BROOKS 1993
ROUND TRIP LIGHT OF THE WORLD 1981
ROUNDS FOUR TET 2003
ROUSTABOUT (OST) ELVIS PRESLEY 1965
ROXANNE ROXANNE (6 TRACK VERSION) U.T.F.O. 1985
THE ROXY LONDON WC2 (JAN APR 77) VARIOUS ARTISTS (HARVEST) 1977
ROXY MUSIC ROXY MUSIC 1972
ROXY MUSIC – THE ATLANTIC YEARS (1973–1980) ROXY MUSIC 1983
ROY ORBISON'S GREATEST HITS ROY ORBISON 1967
ROYAL MIX '89 MIRAGE 1989
ROYAL ROMANCE (ROYAL COMPILATION ALBUM) ROYAL COMPILATION ALBUM 1981
ROYAL SCAM STEELY DAN 1976
ROYAL WEDDING (ROYAL COMPILATION ALBUM) ROYAL COMPILATION ALBUM 1986
RUBBER SOUL BEATLES 1965
RUBY WINTERS RUBY WINTERS 1978
RUBYCON TANGERINE DREAM 1975
RUDE BOY REVIVAL VARIOUS ARTISTS (TELSTAR) 2002
RUFUSIZED RUFUS 1975
RULE BRITANNIA VARIOUS ARTISTS (ARCADE) 1977
RUM, SODOMY AND THE LASH POGUES 1985
RUMOUR AND SIGH RICHARD THOMPSON 1991
RUMOURS FLEETWOOD MAC 1977
RUN COME SAVE ME ROOTS MANUVA 2001
RUN DEVIL RUN PAUL McCARTNEY 1999
RUN FOR COVER GARY MOORE 1985
RUN TO THE HILLS/THE NUMBER OF THE BEAST IRON MAIDEN 1990
RUN WITH THE PACK BAD COMPANY 1976
RUNAWAY HORSES BELINDA CARLISLE 1989
RUNNING FREE (LIVE)/RUN TO THE HILLS (LIVE) IRON MAIDEN 1990
RUNNING IN THE FAMILY LEVEL 42 1987
RUNNING ON EMPTY JACKSON BROWNE 1978
RUNNING/SANCTUARY IRON MAIDEN 1990
A RUSH OF BLOOD TO THE HEAD COLDPLAY 2002
RUSH STREET RICHARD MARX 1991
RUSS ABBOT'S MADHOUSE RUSS ABBOT 1983
RUSS CONWAY PRESENTS 24 PIANO GREATS RUSS CONWAY 1977
RUSSIAN ROULETTE ACCEPT 1986
RUSSIANS AND AMERICANS AL STEWART 1984
RUST IN PEACE MEGADETH 1990
RUST NEVER SLEEPS NEIL YOUNG & CRAZY HORSE 1979
THE RUTLES RUTLES 1978
S AWFUL NICE RAY CONNIFF 1960
S CLUB S CLUB 7 1999
S WONDERFUL 'S MARVELLOUS RAY CONNIFF 1962
S&M METALLICA 1999

S*M*A*S*H S*M*A*S*H 1994
S.I.O.S.O.S. VOLUME 1 SPOOKS 2001
S.O.D. THE EPIC YEARS SPEAR OF DESTINY 1987
S.R.O. HERB ALPERT & THE TIJUANA BRASS 1967
SABBATH BLOODY SABBATH BLACK SABBATH 1973
SABOTAGE BLACK SABBATH 1975
SABRESONIC SABRES OF PARADISE 1993
SACHA DISTEL SACHA DISTEL 1970
SACRED ARIAS ANDREA BOCELLI 1999
SACRED HEART DIO 1985
SACRED HEART SHAKESPEARS SISTER 1989
SACRED LOVE STING 2003
SACRED SONGS HARRY SECOMBE 1962
SACRIFICE BLACK WIDOW 1970
SAD CAFÉ – SAD CAFÉ 1980
SAFINA ALESSANDRO SAFINA 2002
SAHB STORIES SENSATIONAL ALEX HARVEY BAND 1976
SAID AND DONE BOYZONE 1995
SAILING TO PHILADELPHIA MARK KNOPFLER 2000
THE SAINT (OST) FILM SOUNDTRACK 1997
ST ANGER METALLICA 2003
SAINT JULIAN JULIAN COPE 1987
SAINTS & SINNERS ALL SAINTS 2000
SAINTS 'N' SINNERS WHITESNAKE 1982
SALSA FEVER! – VARIOUS ARTISTS (GLOBAL) 1999
A SALT WITH A DEADLY PEPA SALT-N-PEPA 1988
A SALTY DOG PROCOL HARUM 1969
SALUTATION ROAD MARTIN STEPHENSON & THE DAINTEES 1990
SALVA NOS MEDIAEVAL BAEBES 1997
SAMANTHA FOX SAMANTHA FOX 1987
SAME AS IT EVER WAS HOUSE OF PAIN 1994
SAME OUL' TOWN SAW DOCTORS 1996
THE SAME SKY HORSE 1990
SAMMY DAVIS JR AT THE COCONUT GROVE SAMMY DAVIS 1963
SAMMY HAGAR SAMMY HAGAR 1987
SAMURAI GRAND PRIX 1983
SAN FRANCISCO AMERICAN MUSIC CLUB 1994
SAN FRANCISCO DAYS CHRIS ISAAK 1993
SANDIE SANDIE SHAW 1965
SANDINISTA CLASH 1980
SANDS OF TIME S.O.S. BAND 1986
SANDY JOHN TRAVOLTA 1978
SANTA MONICA '72 DAVID BOWIE 1994
SANTANA SANTANA 1970
SANTANA III SANTANA 1971
SAPPHIRE JOHN MARTYN 1984
SASHA – IBIZA VARIOUS ARTISTS (GLOBAL UNDERGROUND) 1999
SASHA – SAN FRANCISCO VARIOUS ARTISTS (GLOBAL UNDERGROUND) 1998
SATAN ORBITAL 1997
SATCHMO PLAYS KING OLIVER LOUIS ARMSTRONG 1960
SATELLITE P.O.D. 2002
SATELLITES BIG DISH 1991
SATIN CITY VARIOUS ARTISTS (CBS) 1978
SATIN THE STEEL – WOMEN IN ROCK VARIOUS ARTISTS (POLYGRAM) 1994
SATISFACTION GUARANTEED: THE VERY BEST TEDDY PENDERGRASS 2004
SATISFY MY SOUL PAUL CARRACK 2000
SATURDAY NIGHT ZHANE 1997
SATURDAY NIGHT FEVER ORIGINAL LONDON STAGE CAST SOUNDTRACK 1998
SATURDAY NIGHT FEVER (OST) FILM SOUNDTRACK 1978
SATURDAY NIGHT SUNDAY MORNING RIVER DETECTIVES 1989
SATURNALIA WEDDING PRESENT 1996
SATURNZ RETURN GOLDIE 1998
SAUCERFUL OF SECRETS PINK FLOYD 1968
SAVAGE EURYTHMICS 1987
SAVAGE AMUSEMENT SCORPIONS 1988
SAVAGE GARDEN SAVAGE GARDEN 1998
SAVE THE LAST DANCE (OST) FILM SOUNDTRACK 2001
SAVE YOUR LOVE RENATO 1982

SAVE YOURSELF SPEEDWAY 2004
SAVED BOB DYLAN 1980
SAVED MY LIFE TODD EDWARDS 1996
THE SAX ALBUM VARIOUS ARTISTS (POLYGRAM) 1996
SAX AT THE MOVIES STATE OF THE HEART 1996
SAX MOODS BLOWING FREE 1995
SAX MOODS – VOLUME 2 BLOWING FREE 1996
SAX-A GO GO CANDY DULFER 1993
SAXUALITY CANDY DULFER 1990
SAY IT AGAIN JERMAINE STEWART 1988
SAY SOMETHING GOOD RIVER CITY PEOPLE 1990
SAY WHAT! – TROUBLE FUNK 1986
SAY YOU WILL FLEETWOOD MAC 2003
SCALLYWAG JAZ THOMAS LANG 1988
SCANDAL (OST) FILM SOUNDTRACK 1989
SCANDALOUS IMAGINATION 1983
SCARED TO DANCE SKIDS 1979
SCARLET AND OTHER STORIES ALL ABOUT EVE 1989
SCARLET, RED AND BLUE ZOE 1991
SCARLET'S WALK TORI AMOS 2002
SCARY MONSTERS AND SUPER CREEPS DAVID BOWIE 1980
SCATTERLINGS JULUKA 1983
SCENES FROM THE SECOND STORY GOD MACHINE 1993
SCENES FROM THE SOUTHSIDE BRUCE HORNBY & THE RANGE 1988
SCHINDLER'S LIST (OST) JOHN WILLIAMS 1994
SCHIZOPHONIC GERI HALLIWELL 1999
SCHIZOPHRENIC JC CHASEZ 2004
SCHOOL DISCO.COM VARIOUS ARTISTS (COLUMBIA) 2001
SCHOOL DISCO.COM – SUMMER HOLIDAY VARIOUS ARTISTS (COLUMBIA) 2002
SCHOOL REUNION – THE 80'S VARIOUS ARTISTS (VIRGIN) 2003
SCHOOL'S OUT ALICE COOPER 1972
SCHUBERT DIP EMF 1991
SCIENCE & NATURE BLUETONES 2000
SCIENCE OF THE GODS EAT STATIC 1997
THE SCIENCE OF THINGS BUSH 1999
SCI FI LULLABIES SUEDE 1997
SCISSOR SISTERS SCISSOR SISTERS 2004
SCISSORS CUT ART GARFUNKEL 1981
THE SCORE FUGEES 1996
SCORPIO RISING DEATH IN VEGAS 2002
SCORPION EVE 2001
SCOTCH ON THE ROCKS BAND OF THE BLACK WATCH 1976
SCOTLAND ROCKS VARIOUS ARTISTS (VIRGIN) 2003
SCOTT SCOTT WALKER 1967
SCOTT 2 SCOTT WALKER 1968
SCOTT 3 SCOTT WALKER 1969
SCOTTISH LOVE SONGS CORRIES 1970
SCOUNDREL DAYS A-HA 1986
SCRATCH AND SNIFF SMITH & JONES 1986
THE SCREAM SIOUXSIE & THE BANSHEES 1978
SCREAM DREAM TED NUGENT 1980
SCREAM IF YOU WANT TO GO FASTER GERI HALLIWELL 2001
SCREAM, DRACULA, SCREAM! – ROCKET FROM THE CRYPT 1996
SCREAMADELICA PRIMAL SCREAM 1991
SCREAMING BLUE MURDER GIRLSCHOOL 1982
SCREAMING FOR VENGEANCE JUDAS PRIEST 1982
THE SCREEN BEHIND THE MIRROR ENIGMA 2000
SCREEN GEMS ELKIE BROOKS 1984
SCRIPT FOR A JESTER'S TEAR MARILLION 1983
SEA CHANGE BECK 2002
SEA MONSTERS WEDDING PRESENT 1991
THE SEA OF LOVE ADVENTURES 1988
SEA OF TRANQUILLITY PHIL COULTER 1984
SEAL SEAL 1991
SEAL II SEAL 1994
SEAN MAGUIRE SEAN MAGUIRE 1994
SEAN NOS NUA SINEAD O'CONNOR 2002
SEARCHING FOR THE YOUNG SOUL REBELS DEXYS MIDNIGHT RUNNERS 1980
SEARCHLIGHT RUNRIG 1989

SEASON OF GLASS YOKO ONO 1981
SEASONS MAGNA CARTA 1970
SEASONS BING CROSBY 1977
SEASONS SYNTHPHONIC VARIATIONS 1986
SEASON'S END MARILLION 1989
SEASONS IN THE ABYSS SLAYER 1990
THE SEBADOH SEBADOH 1999
SEBASTAPOL ROAD MEGA CITY FOUR 1992
SECOMBE'S PERSONAL CHOICE HARRY SECOMBE 1967
THE SECOND ALBUM SPENCER DAVIS GROUP 1966
THE SECOND ALBUM OF THE VERY BEST OF ROGER
    WHITTAKER ROGER WHITTAKER 1976
SECOND COMING STONE ROSES 1994
THE SECOND COMING TQ 2000
SECOND EDITION OF PIL PUBLIC IMAGE LTD 1980
SECOND FLIGHT PILOT 1975
SECOND LIGHT DREADZONE 1995
SECOND SIGHTING FREHLEY'S COMET 1988
SECOND SPRING MATTHEWS' SOUTHERN COMFORT 1970
THE SECOND TINDERSTICKS ALBUM TINDERSTICKS 1995
2ND TO NONE ELVIS PRESLEY 2003
SECOND TOUGHEST IN THE INFANTS UNDERWORLD 1996
2ND VERSE SO SOLID CREW 2003
SECOND WINTER JOHNNY WINTER 1970
SECONDHAND DAYLIGHT MAGAZINE 1979
SECONDS OF PLEASURE ROCKPILE 1980
SECONDS OF PLEASURE SILENCERS 1993
SECONDS OUT GENESIS 1977
SECRET COMBINATION RANDY CRAWFORD 1981
SECRET DREAMS AND FORBIDDEN FIRE BONNIE TYLER
    1986
A SECRET HISTORY – THE BEST OF DIVINE COMEDY DIVINE
    COMEDY 1999
SECRET LOVERS VARIOUS ARTISTS (COLUMBIA) 1994
SECRET MESSAGES ELECTRIC LIGHT ORCHESTRA 1983
THE SECRET OF ASSOCIATION PAUL YOUNG 1985
SECRET PEOPLE CAPERCAILLIE 1993
THE SECRET POLICEMAN'S BALL VARIOUS ARTISTS
    (ISLAND) 1980
THE SECRET POLICEMAN'S OTHER BALL VARIOUS ARTISTS
    (SPRINGTIME) 1981
THE SECRET POLICEMAN'S OTHER BALL (THE MUSIC)
    VARIOUS ARTISTS (SPRINGTIME) 1982
SECRET SAMADHI LIVE 1997
SECRET SECRETS JOAN ARMATRADING 1985
THE SECRET VALUE OF DAYDREAMING JULIAN LENNON
    1986
SECRET WISH PROPAGANDA 1985
SECRET WORLD LIVE PETER GABRIEL 1994
SECRETS ROBERT PALMER 1979
SECRETS WILTON FELDER FEATURING BOBBY WOMACK &
    INTRODUCING ALLTRINA GRAYSON 1985
SECRETS TONI BRAXTON 1996
SECRETS HUMAN LEAGUE 2001
SECRETS OF THE BEEHIVE DAVID SYLVAN 1987
SEDUCED AND ABANDONED HUE & CRY 1987
SEDUCTION VARIOUS ARTISTS (K-TEL) 1989
SEE JUNGLE! SEE JUNGLE! GO JOIN YOUR GANG YEAH CITY
    ALL OVER! GO APE CRAZY BOW WOW WOW 1981
SEE THE LIGHT JEFF HEALEY BAND 1989
SEE THIS THROUGH AND LEAVE COOPER TEMPLE CLAUSE
    2002
THE SEEDS OF LOVE TEARS FOR FEARS 1989
SEEING DOUBLE S CLUB 2002
THE SEEKERS SEEKERS 1965
SEEKERS – SEEN IN GREEN SEEKERS 1967
SEEKRET KLEEER 1985
THE SEER BIG COUNTRY 1986
SEIZE THE TIME FUN DA MENTAL 1994
SELECT KIM WILDE 1982
SELECTED AMBIENT WORKS VOLUME II APHEX TWIN 1994
SELF QUINTESSENCE 1972
SELF ABUSED S*M*A*S*H 1994
SELF CONTROL LAURA BRANIGAN 1984
SELF PORTRAIT BOB DYLAN 1970
SELLING ENGLAND BY THE POUND GENESIS 1973

SELMA SONGS BJORK 2000
SEMI DETACHED THERAPY? 1998
SEMI DETACHED SUBURBAN MANFRED MANN 1979
SEMINAL LIVE FALL 1989
SENSATIONAL MICHELLE GAYLE 1997
SENSATIONAL ALEX HARVEY BAND LIVE SENSATIONAL
    ALEX HARVEY BAND 1975
SENSE LIGHTNING SEEDS 1992
SENSE AND SENSUALITY AU PAIRS 1982
A SENSE OF WONDER VAN MORRISON 1985
SENSES VARIOUS ARTISTS (POLYGRAM) 1994
SENSUAL CLASSICS VARIOUS ARTISTS (TELDEC) 1992
THE SENSUAL WORLD KATE BUSH 1989
SENTIMENTAL JOURNEY RINGO STARR 1970
SENTIMENTALLY YOURS ROSE MARIE 1987
SENTIMENTO ANDREA BOCELLI 2002
SENTINEL PALLAS 1984
SEPTEMBER MORN NEIL DIAMOND 1980
SERENADE NEIL DIAMOND 1974
SERENADE JUAN MARTIN WITH THE ROYAL
    PHILHARMONIC ORCHESTRA 1984
SERENITY CULTURE BEAT 1993
SERGEANT PEPPER KNEW MY FATHER VARIOUS ARTISTS
    (NME) 1988
SERIOUS CLUB HITS VARIOUS ARTISTS (UNIVERSAL)
    2002
SERIOUS HIP HOP 2 VARIOUS ARTISTS (SERIOUS) 1987
SERIOUS HITS... LIVE! – PHIL COLLINS 1990
SERIOUSLY ORCHESTRA LOUIS CLARK CONDUCTING THE
    ROYAL PHILHARMONIC ORCHESTRA 1991
SERVE CHILLED VARIOUS ARTISTS (VIRGIN) 1995
SESSION EIGHT – TODD TERRY VARIOUS ARTISTS
    (MINISTRY OF SOUND) 1997
A SESSION WITH THE DAVE CLARK FIVE DAVE CLARK FIVE
    1964
SESSIONS NINE – ERICK MORILLO VARIOUS ARTISTS
    (MINISTRY OF SOUND) 1998
SESSIONS SEVEN VARIOUS ARTISTS (MINISTRY OF
    SOUND) 1997
SESSIONS TEN – SUBLIMINAL SESSIONS VARIOUS
    ARTISTS (DEFECTED) 2000
SET THOMPSON TWINS 1982
SET THE CONTROLS FOR THE HEART OF THE BASS BASS-O-
    MATIC 1990
SET THE TWILIGHT REELING LOU REED 1996
SETTING SONS JAM 1979
SEVEN JAMES 1992
7 S CLUB 7 2000
SEVEN ENRIQUE IGLESIAS 2003
SEVEN AGES OF ACKER MR ACKER BILK 1960
SEVEN AND THE RAGGED TIGER DURAN DURAN 1983
SEVEN BRIDES FOR SEVEN BROTHERS (OST) FILM
    SOUNDTRACK 1961
777 SYSTEM 7 1993
SEVEN SINGLES DEEP ICICLE WORKS 1986
SEVEN TEARS GOOMBAY DANCE BAND 1982
SEVEN THE HARD WAY PAT BENATAR 1985
78000 FAHRENHEIT BON JOVI 1985
SEVEN YEARS – TEN WEEKS DAVID SNEDDON 2003
SEVENS GARTH BROOKS 1997
17 SECONDS CURE 1980
THE SEVENTH ONE TOTO 1988
SEVENTH SOJOURN MOODY BLUES 1972
SEVENTH SON OF A SEVENTH SON IRON MAIDEN 1988
SEVENTH STAR BLACK SABBATH FEATURING TONY IOMMI
    1986
70'S SOUL MIX VARIOUS ARTISTS (UNIVERSAL) 2003
SEX & JAZZ & ROCK & ROLL JOOLS HOLLAND & HIS R&B
    ORCHESTRA 1996
SEX AND RELIGION STEVE VAI 1993
SEX AND THE CITY TELEVISION AND RADIO COMPILATION
    2004
SEX AND TRAVEL RIGHT SAID FRED 1993
SEX MACHINE – THE VERY BEST OF JAMES BROWN JAMES
    BROWN 1991
SEX PACKETS DIGITAL UNDERGROUND 1990

SEX SWEAT AND BLOOD VARIOUS ARTISTS (BEGGARS
    BANQUET) 1982
SEX, CHIPS & ROCK 'N' ROLL TELEVISION SOUNDTRACK
    1999
SEXTET A CERTAIN RATIO 1982
SEXUAL HEALING VARIOUS ARTISTS (EMI) 1991
SEXY CRAZY COOL VARIOUS ARTISTS (UNIVERSAL) 2002
SGT PEPPER'S LONELY HEARTS CLUB BAND BEATLES 1967
SGT. PEPPER'S LONELY HEARTS CLUB BAND (OST) FILM
    SOUNDTRACK 1978
A SHADE OF RED REDHEAD KINGPIN & THE F.B.I. 1989
SHADES J.J. CALE 1981
SHADES SHADES OF RHYTHM 1991
SHADES OF GREEN FOSTER & ALLEN 1997
SHADES OF ROCK SHADOWS 1970
SHADES OF SOUL VARIOUS ARTISTS (GLOBAL) 1996
SHADES OF SOUL VARIOUS ARTISTS (GLOBAL) 1998
SHADOW DANCING ANDY GIBB 1978
SHADOW MUSIC SHADOWS 1966
SHADOW OF YOUR SMILE ANDY WILLIAMS 1966
THE SHADOWS SHADOWS 1961
SHADOWS 20 GOLDEN GREATS SHADOWS 1977
SHADOWS AND LIGHT JONI MITCHELL 1980
SHADOWS AND LIGHT WILSON PHILLIPS 1992
SHADOWS COLLIDE WITH PEOPLE JOHN FRUSCIANTE 2004
SHADOWS ON THE WALL GORDON HASKELL 2002
THE SHADOWS' GREATEST HITS SHADOWS 1963
SHADOWS IN THE NIGHT – 16 CLASSIC TRACKS SHADOWS
    1993
SHAFT ISAAC HAYES 1971
SHAKA ZULU LADYSMITH BLACK MAMBAZO 1987
SHAKE YOU DOWN GREGORY ABBOTT 1987
SHAKE YOUR MONEY MAKER BLACK CROWES 1991
SHAKEN AND STIRRED DAVID ARNOLD 1997
SHAKEN 'N' STIRRED ROBERT PLANT 1985
SHAKESPEARE ALABAMA DIESEL PARK WEST 1989
SHAKIN' STEVENS SHAKIN' STEVENS 1981
SHAKIN' STEVENS GREATEST HITS SHAKIN' STEVENS 1984
SHAKING THE TREE – GOLDEN GREATS PETER GABRIEL
    1990
SHAKY SHAKIN' STEVENS 1981
SHAMAN SANTANA 2002
SHAME BRAD 1993
SHAME AND SIN ROBERT CRAY BAND 1993
THE SHAMEN COLLECTION SHAMEN 1998
SHAMROCK DIARIES CHRIS REA 1985
SHAMROCKS AND SHENANIGANS VARIOUS ARTISTS
    (WARNER BROTHERS) 2003
SHANGO SANTANA 1982
SHANGRI LA ANIMAL NIGHTLIFE 1985
SHAPE UP AND DANCE FEATURING ANGELA RIPPON
    (VOLUME II) ANGELA RIPPON 1982
SHAPE UP AND DANCE WITH FELICITY KENDAL (VOLUME
    ONE) FELICITY KENDAL 1982
SHAPE UP AND DANCE WITH SUZANNE DANDO SUZANNE
    DANDO 1984
SHAPES DOMINIC MILLER 2003
SHARE MY WORLD MARY J. BLIGE 1997
SHARPE – OVER THE HILLS & FAR AWAY VARIOUS ARTISTS
    (VIRGIN) 1996
SHATTERPROOF IS NOT A CHALLENGE HUNDRED REASONS
    2004
SHAVED FISH JOHN LENNON 1975
SHAVING PEACHES TERRORVISION 1998
SHE HARRY CONNICK JR. 1994
SHE WAS ONLY A GROCER'S DAUGHTER BLOW MONKEYS
    1987
SHE WEARS MY RING SOLOMON KING 1968
SHE WORKS HARD FOR THE MONEY DONNA SUMMER
    1983
SHEER GREED GIRL 1980
SHEER HEART ATTACK QUEEN 1974
SHEER MAGIC MR ACKER BILK 1977
SHEET MUSIC 10 CC 1974
SHEIK YERBOUTI FRANK ZAPPA 1979
SHELTER LONE JUSTICE 1986

SHELTER BRAND NEW HEAVIES 1997
SHENANIGANS GREEN DAY 2002
SHEPHERD MOONS ENYA 1991
SHER OO CILLA BLACK 1968
SHERRICK SHERRICK 1987
SHERRY FOUR SEASONS 1963
SHERYL CROW SHERYL CROW 1996
SHE'S A LADY TOM JONES 1971
SHE'S JUST AN OLD LOVE TURNED MEMORY CHARLEY PRIDE 1977
SHE'S SO UNUSUAL CYNDI LAUPER 1984
SHE'S THE BOSS MICK JAGGER 1985
SHE'S THE ONE (OST) TOM PETTY & HEARTBREAKERS 1996
SHIFT WORK FALL 1991
SHINE AVERAGE WHITE BAND 1980
SHINE FRIDA 1984
SHINE MARY BLACK 1997
SHINE BOND 2002
SHINE – BEST OF 97 VARIOUS ARTISTS (POLYGRAM) 1998
SHINE (OST) DAVID HIRSCHFELDER 1997
SHINE 10 VARIOUS ARTISTS (POLYGRAM) 1998
SHINE 2 VARIOUS ARTISTS (POLYGRAM) 1996
SHINE 3 VARIOUS ARTISTS (POLYGRAM) 1995
SHINE 5 VARIOUS ARTISTS (POLYGRAM) 1996
SHINE 6 VARIOUS ARTISTS (POLYGRAM) 1996
SHINE 7 VARIOUS ARTISTS (POLYGRAM) 1996
SHINE 8 VARIOUS ARTISTS (POLYGRAM) 1997
SHINE 9 VARIOUS ARTISTS (POLYGRAM) 1997
SHINE TOO VARIOUS ARTISTS (POLYGRAM) 1995
SHINE: 20 BRILLIANT INDIE HITS VARIOUS ARTISTS (POLYGRAM) 1995
SHIP ARRIVING TOO LATE TO SAVE A DROWNING WITCH FRANK ZAPPA 1982
SHIRLEY SHIRLEY BASSEY 1961
SHIRLEY BASSEY SHIRLEY BASSEY 1962
SHIRLEY BASSEY AT THE PIGALLE SHIRLEY BASSEY 1965
THE SHIRLEY BASSEY COLLECTION SHIRLEY BASSEY 1972
THE SHIRLEY BASSEY SINGLES ALBUM SHIRLEY BASSEY 1975
SHIRLEY BASSEY SINGS ANDREW LLOYD WEBBER SHIRLEY BASSEY 1993
SHIRLEY BASSEY SINGS THE MOVIES SHIRLEY BASSEY 1995
SHOOT FROM THE HIP SOPHIE ELLIS BEXTOR 2003
SHOOT THE BOSS MONKEY MAFIA 1998
SHOOT THE MOON JUDIE TZUKE 1982
SHOOTENANNY EELS 2003
SHOOTING RUBBERBANDS AT THE STARS EDIE BRICKELL & THE NEW BOHEMIANS 1989
SHOOTING STAR ELKIE BROOKS 1978
SHOOTING STARS DOLLAR 1979
SHOP ASSISTANTS SHOP ASSISTANTS 1986
SHOPPING BAG PARTRIDGE FAMILY 1972
A SHORT ALBUM ABOUT LOVE DIVINE COMEDY 1997
SHORT BACK 'N' SIDES IAN HUNTER 1981
SHORT SHARP SHOCKED MICHELLE SHOCKED 1988
SHORT STORIES JON & VANGELIS 1980
SHOT OF LOVE BOB DYLAN 1981
SHOULD THE WORLD FAIL TO FALL APART PETER MURPHY 1986
THE SHOUTING STAGE JOAN ARMATRADING 1988
SHOVE IT CROSS 1988
SHOW ME LOVE ROBIN S 1993
THE SHOW MUST GO ON SHIRLEY BASSEY 1996
A SHOW OF HANDS RUSH 1989
SHOW PEOPLE MARI WILSON 1983
SHOW SOME EMOTION JOAN ARMATRADING 1977
THE SHOW THE AFTER PARTY THE HOTEL JODECI 1995
SHOWADDYWADDY SHOWADDYWADDY 1974
SHOWBIZ CURE 1993
SHOWBIZ CUD 1994
SHOWBIZ MUSE 1999
SHOWBOAT ORIGINAL STUDIO CAST RECORDING 1960
SHOWDOWN ISLEY BROTHERS 1978
SHOWSTOPPERS BARRY MANILOW 1991
SHOWTIME GEORGE MITCHELL MINSTRELS 1967

SHUT UP KELLY OSBOURNE 2003
SHUT UP AND DANCE PAULA ABDUL 1990
SHUT UP AND DANCE VARIOUS ARTISTS (SHUT UP & DANCE) 1992
SHUT UP AND DIE LIKE AN AVIATOR STEVE EARLE & THE DUKES 1991
SHUTTERED ROOM FIXX 1982
SIAMESE DREAM SMASHING PUMPKINS 1993
SID SINGS SID VICIOUS 1979
SIGN 'O' THE TIMES PRINCE 1987
SIGN OF THE HAMMER MANOWAR 1984
SIGNALS RUSH 1982
SIGNIFICANT OTHER LIMP BIZKIT 1999
SIGNING OFF UB40 1980
SIGNS OF LIFE PENGUIN CAFÉ ORCHESTRA 1987
S'IL SUFFISAIT D'AIMER CELINE DION 1998
SILENCE IS EASY STARSAILOR 2003
SILK AND STEEL FIVE STAR 1986
SILK AND STEEL VARIOUS ARTISTS (POLYGRAM) 1995
SILK DEGREES BOZ SCAGGS 1977
SILK ELECTRIC DIANA ROSS 1982
SILKY SOUL MAZE FEATURING FRANKIE BEVERLY 1989
SILVER CLIFF RICHARD 1983
SILVER AND GOLD A.S.A.P 1989
SILVER AND GOLD NEIL YOUNG 2000
SILVER BIRD LEO SAYER 1974
SILVER CONVENTION: GREATEST HITS SILVER CONVENTION 1977
SILVER LINING NILS LOFGREN 1991
SILVER SIDE UP NICKELBACK 2002
SILVER SUN SILVER SUN 1997
SILVER TOWN MEN THEY COULDN'T HANG 1989
SILVER TOWN MOIST 1995
THE SIMON AND GARFUNKEL COLLECTION SIMON & GARFUNKEL 1981
SIMON BATES – OUR TUNE VARIOUS ARTISTS (POLYDOR) 1986
SIMON'S WAY SIMON MAY ORCHESTRA 1986
SIMPLE DREAMS LINDA RONSTADT 1977
SIMPLE PLEASURE TINDERSTICKS 1999
SIMPLE PLEASURES BOBBY MCFERRIN 1988
SIMPLE THINGS ZERO 7 2001
SIMPLY ACOUSTIC VARIOUS ARTISTS (UNIVERSAL) 2002
SIMPLY DEEP KELLY ROWLAND 2003
SIMPLY SHADOWS SHADOWS 1987
SIMPLY THE BEST TINA TURNER 1991
SIMPLY THE BEST CLASSIC SOUL VARIOUS ARTISTS (WARNER BROTHERS) 1997
SIMPLY THE BEST CLASSICAL ANTHEMS VARIOUS ARTISTS (WARNER BROTHERS) 1998
SIMPLY THE BEST DISCO VARIOUS ARTISTS (WARNER BROTHERS) 1998
SIMPLY THE BEST LOVE SONGS VARIOUS ARTISTS (WARNER BROTHERS) 1997
SIMPLY THE BEST LOVE SONGS 2 VARIOUS ARTISTS (WARNER BROTHERS) 1998
SIMPLY THE BEST RADIO HITS VARIOUS ARTISTS (WARNER BROTHERS) 1998
SIMPLY THE BEST REGGAE ALBUM VARIOUS ARTISTS (WARNER BROTHERS) 2001
SIMPLY… LOVE VARIOUS ARTISTS (COLUMBIA) 1991
THE SIMPSONS – SONGS IN THE KEY OF SPRINGFIELD SIMPSONS 1997
THE SIMPSONS SING THE BLUES SIMPSONS 1991
SIN AFTER SIN JUDAS PRIEST 1977
THE SIN OF PRIDE UNDERTONES 1983
SINATRA – THE MAIN EVENT LIVE (OST TV) FRANK SINATRA 1975
SINATRA 80TH – ALL THE BEST FRANK SINATRA 1995
SINATRA AND COMPANY FRANK SINATRA 1971
SINATRA AND STRINGS FRANK SINATRA 1962
SINATRA PLUS FRANK SINATRA 1961
SINATRA SOUVENIR FRANK SINATRA 1961
SINATRA SWINGS FRANK SINATRA 1961
SINATRA WITH SWINGING BRASS FRANK SINATRA 1962
SINATRA BASIE FRANK SINATRA & COUNT BASIE 1963

SINATRA'S SINATRA FRANK SINATRA 1963
SINATRA'S SWINGING SESSION!!! AND MORE FRANK SINATRA 1961
SINCE I LEFT YOU AVALANCHES 2001
SINCE YOU'VE BEEN GONE DAMAGE 2001
SINCERE MJ COLE 2000
SINCERELY CLIFF RICHARD 1969
SING A FAVOURITE SONG DES O'CONNOR 1972
SING ALONG WITH MAX MAX BYGRAVES 1972
SING ALONG WITH MAX VOLUME 2 MAX BYGRAVES 1972
SING BROTHER SING EDGAR BROUGHTON BAND 1970
SING IT AGAIN ROD ROD STEWART 1973
SING LOFTY DON ESTELLE & WINDSOR DAVIES 1976
SING SOMETHING SIMPLE CLIFF ADAMS SINGERS 1960
SING SOMETHING SIMPLE CLIFF ADAMS SINGERS 1962
SING SOMETHING SIMPLE CLIFF ADAMS SINGERS 1982
SING SOMETHING SIMPLE '76 CLIFF ADAMS SINGERS 1976
SING THE IRVING BERLIN SONGBOOK GEORGE MITCHELL MINSTRELS 1968
SING THE SPARROW AFI 2003
SING WHEN YOU'RE WINNING ROBBIE WILLIAMS 2000
SINGALONGAMAX VOLUME 3 MAX BYGRAVES 1973
SINGALONGAMAX VOLUME 4 MAX BYGRAVES 1973
SINGALONGAWARYEARS MAX BYGRAVES 1989
SINGALONGAWARYEARS VOLUME 2 MAX BYGRAVES 1989
SINGALONGPARTY SONG MAX BYGRAVES 1973
SINGALONGXMAS MAX BYGRAVES 1974
THE SINGER LIZA MINNELLI 1973
SINGER AND THE SONG LABI SIFFRE 1971
THE SINGER AND THE SONG VARIOUS ARTISTS (STYLUS) 1989
THE SINGER AND THE SONG VARIOUS ARTISTS (VIRGIN) 1993
SINGIN' WITH THE BIG BANDS BARRY MANILOW 1994
SINGING TO MY BABY EDDIE COCHRAN 1960
SINGING TO MY BABY EDDIE COCHRAN 1963
THE SINGLE FACTOR CAMEL 1982
SINGLE LIFE CAMEO 1985
A SINGLE MAN ELTON JOHN 1978
THE SINGLES ROY WOOD 1982
THE SINGLES PRETENDERS 1987
SINGLES SMITHS 1995
THE SINGLES INSPIRAL CARPETS 1995
SINGLES ALISON MOYET 1995
THE SINGLES BLUETONES 2002
SINGLES SUEDE 2003
THE SINGLES 1992–2003 NO DOUBT 2003
SINGLES 93 03 CHEMICAL BROTHERS 2003
SINGLES – 45'S AND UNDER SQUEEZE 1982
THE SINGLES – THE FIRST TEN YEARS ABBA 1982
THE SINGLES – THE UA YEARS STRANGLERS 1989
THE SINGLES 1969–1973 CARPENTERS 1974
THE SINGLES 1974–1978 CARPENTERS 1978
THE SINGLES 81–85 DEPECHE MODE 1985
THE SINGLES 86–98 DEPECHE MODE 1998
THE SINGLES ALBUM UB40 1982
THE SINGLES ALBUM JIMI HENDRIX 1983
THE SINGLES ALBUM SOFT CELL 1986
THE SINGLES ALBUM GLADYS KNIGHT & THE PIPS 1989
THE SINGLES ALBUM GLADYS KNIGHT & THE PIPS 1997
THE SINGLES COLLECTION SPANDAU BALLET 1985
THE SINGLES COLLECTION KOOL & THE GANG 1988
THE SINGLES COLLECTION CLASH 1991
THE SINGLES COLLECTION FOUR TOPS 1992
THE SINGLES COLLECTION CONNIE FRANCIS 1993
THE SINGLES COLLECTION DAVID BOWIE 1993
THE SINGLES COLLECTION 1981–1993 KIM WILDE 1993
A SINGLES COLLECTION 1982–1992 MARILLION 1992
THE SINGLES COLLECTION 1984/1990 JIMMY SOMERVILLE 1990
SINGLES OF THE 90S ACE OF BASE 1999
SINGS GREATEST PALACE MUSIC BONNIE PRINCE BILLY 2004
SINGS THE HITS OF WET WET WET & SMILE MARTI PELLOW 2002

THE SINGULAR ADVENTURES OF THE STYLE COUNCIL GREATEST HITS VOLUME 1 STYLE COUNCIL 1989
SINITTA! – SINITTA 1987
SINNER DROWNING POOL 2002
SIOGO BLACKFOOT 1983
SIREN ROXY MUSIC 1975
SIREN HEATHER NOVA 1998
SIRIUS CLANNAD 1987
SISTER ACT (OST) FILM SOUNDTRACK 1993
SISTERS BLUEBELLS 1984
SISTERS ARE DOIN' IT VARIOUS ARTISTS (TOWERBELL) 1986
SISTERS OF AVALON CYNDI LAUPER 1997
SISTERS OF SWING VARIOUS ARTISTS (POLYGRAM) 1996
SISTERS OF SWING 2 VARIOUS ARTISTS (POLYGRAM) 1996
SISTERS OF SWING 98 VARIOUS ARTISTS (POLYGRAM) 1998
SISTERS OF SWING 99 VARIOUS ARTISTS (UNIVERSAL) 1999
SISTERS OF SWING III VARIOUS ARTISTS (POLYGRAM) 1997
SITTIN' ON TOP OF THE WORLD LEANN RIMES 1998
SITUATION: CRITICAL ULTRA NATE 1998
SIX MANSUN 1998
SIX WHEELS ON MY WAGON FLUKE 1993
THE SIX WIVES OF HENRY VIII RICK WAKEMAN 1973
SIXPENCE NONE THE RICHER SIXPENCE NONE THE RICHER 1999
16 DIFFERENT FLAVOURS OF HELL POP WILL EAT ITSELF 1993
16 HITS FROM 'STARS AND GARTERS' – KATHY KIRBY 1964
16 LOVER'S LANE GO-BETWEENS 1988
16 ORIGINAL BIG HITS – VOLUME 4 VARIOUS ARTISTS (MOTOWN) 1967
SIXTEEN STONE BUSH 1996
THE SIXTIES VARIOUS ARTISTS (VIRGIN) 1999
SIXTIES BEAT VARIOUS ARTISTS (DINO) 1992
SIXTIES MANIA VARIOUS ARTISTS (TELSTAR) 1986
SIXTIES MIX – 60 SEQUENCED HITS FROM THE SIXTIES VARIOUS ARTISTS (STYLUS) 1987
SIXTIES MIX 2 VARIOUS ARTISTS (STYLUS) 1988
SIXTIES MIX 3 VARIOUS ARTISTS (STYLUS) 1990
SIXTIES PARTY MEGAMIX ALBUM VARIOUS ARTISTS (TELSTAR) 1987
60'S SOUL MIX VARIOUS ARTISTS (UNIVERSAL) 2003
60'S SOUL MIX 2 VARIOUS ARTISTS (UNIVERSAL) 2004
60'S SOUL 90'S SOUL VARIOUS ARTISTS (PARLOPHONE) 1994
SIXTIES SUMMER LOVE VARIOUS ARTISTS (UNIVERSAL) 1999
SIXTIES SUMMER MIX VARIOUS ARTISTS (TELSTAR) 1997
SIXTIES SUMMER MIX 2 VARIOUS ARTISTS (TELSTAR) 1998
60 NUMBER ONES OF THE SIXTIES VARIOUS ARTISTS (TELSTAR) 1990
60 NUMBER ONE'S OF THE 60'S VARIOUS ARTISTS (WARNER BROTHERS) 2000
SIXTY SIX TO TIMBUKTU ROBERT PLANT 2003
SIZE ISN'T EVERYTHING BEE GEES 1993
SKA MANIA VARIOUS ARTISTS (DINO) 1995
SKA 'N' B BAD MANNERS 1980
SKATE TO HELL VARIOUS ARTISTS (WARNER BROTHERS) 2003
SK8ER ROCK VARIOUS ARTISTS (BMG) 2003
SKELLERN PETER SKELLERN 1978
SKETCHES FOR MY SWEETHEART THE DRUNK JEFF BUCKLEY 1998
SKID SKID ROW 1970
SKID ROW SKID ROW 1989
SKIDIP EEK-A-MOUSE 1982
THE SKIFFLE SESSIONS – LIVE IN BELFAST VAN MORRISON/LONNIE DONEGAN/CHRIS BARBER 2000
SKIN SKIN 1994
SKIN 'EM UP SHAKIN' PYRAMIDS 1981

SKIN MECHANIC GARY NUMAN 1989
SKINBEAT – THE FIRST TOUCH VARIOUS ARTISTS (POLYDOR) 1984
SKULL & BONES CYPRESS HILL 2000
SKUNKWORTHS BRUCE DICKINSON 1996
SKY SKY 1979
SKY 2 SKY 1980
SKY 3 SKY 1981
SKY 4 – FORTHCOMING SKY 1982
SKY FIVE LIVE SKY 1983
SKY HIGH TAVARES 1976
THE SKY IS TOO HIGH GRAHAM COXON 1998
SKYE BOAT SONG AND OTHER GREAT SONGS ROGER WHITTAKER 1986
SKYLARKING XTC 1986
SKYNYRD'S FIRST AND LAST LYNYRD SKYNYRD 1978
THE SKY'S GONE OUT BAUHAUS 1982
SKYSCRAPER DAVID LEE ROTH 1988
SLADE ALIVE! – SLADE 1972
SLADE IN FLAME (OST) SLADE 1974
SLADE ON STAGE SLADE 1982
SLADE SMASHES SLADE 1980
SLADE'S GREATZ SLADE 1984
SLADEST SLADE 1973
SLAIN BY URUSEI YATSURA 1998
SLAM DAN REED NETWORK 1989
SLAMMIN' – VARIOUS ARTISTS (A&M) 1990
SLANG DEF LEPPARD 1996
SLANTED AND ENCHANTED PAVEMENT 1992
SLAUGHTER ON TENTH AVENUE MICK RONSON 1974
SLAVE TO LOVE BRYAN FERRY 2000
SLAVE TO THE GRIND SKID ROW 1991
SLAVE TO THE RHYTHM GRACE JONES 1985
SLAVES AND MASTERS DEEP PURPLE 1990
SLAYED? – SLADE 1972
SLEEP NO MORE COMSAT ANGELS 1981
SLEEPING WITH GHOSTS PLACEBO 2003
SLEEPING WITH THE PAST ELTON JOHN 1989
SLEEPLESS IN SEATTLE (OST) FILM SOUNDTRACK 1993
SLEEPLESS NIGHTS LINDISFARNE 1982
SLEEPS WITH ANGELS NEIL YOUNG & CRAZY HORSE 1994
SLEEPWALKING GERRY RAFFERTY 1982
SLEEPWALKING MAGNUM 1992
SLEEPWALKING KINGMAKER 1993
SLEEPWALKING RAE & CHRISTIAN 2001
SLEEPY EYED BUFFALO TOM 1995
SLEIGHT OF HAND JOAN ARMATRADING 1986
SLICKER THAN YOUR AVERAGE CRAIG DAVID 2002
THE SLIDE AREA RY COODER 1982
SLIDE IT IN WHITESNAKE 1984
THE SLIDER T. REX 1972
SLIK SLIK 1976
SLIM SHADY EMINEM 1999
SLIM WHITMAN'S 20 GREATEST LOVE SONGS SLIM WHITMAN 1979
SLINKY MILLTOWN BROTHERS 1991
SLINKY – TECH NIQUE VARIOUS ARTISTS (BEECHWOOD MUSIC) 2000
SLINKY FACTOR 3 VARIOUS ARTISTS (BEECHWOOD MUSIC) 2000
SLINKY PRESENTS SUPERCLUB DJ'S – GUY ORNADEL VARIOUS ARTISTS (SLINKY MUSIC) 2001
SLIP OF THE TONGUE WHITESNAKE 1989
SLIP STREAM VARIOUS ARTISTS (BEGGARS BANQUET) 1981
SLIPKNOT SLIPKNOT 1999
SLIPPERY WHEN WET BON JOVI 1986
SLIPSTREAM SUTHERLAND BROTHERS & QUIVER 1976
SLIVER – FILM SOUNDTRACK 1993
SLOW JAMS VARIOUS ARTISTS (PUMP) 1997
SLOW TRAIN COMING BOB DYLAN 1979
SLOWHAND ERIC CLAPTON 1977
SMALL CORNERS CLIFF RICHARD 1978
SMALL FACES SMALL FACES 1966
SMALL FACES SMALL FACES 1967
THE SMALL PRICE OF A BICYCLE ICICLE WORKS 1985

SMALL WORLD HUEY LEWIS & THE NEWS 1988
SMALL WORLD BIG BAND JOOLS HOLLAND 2001
SMALLCREEP'S DAY MIKE RUTHERFORD 1980
SMART SLEEPER 1995
SMASH OFFSPRING 1995
SMASH HITS CHART SUMMER 2003 VARIOUS ARTISTS (VIRGIN) 2003
SMASH HITS PARTY '88 VARIOUS ARTISTS (DOVER) 1988
SMASH HITS PARTY '89 – 30 SMASH HITS VARIOUS ARTISTS (DOVER) 1989
SMASH HITS JIMI HENDRIX EXPERIENCE 1968
SMASH HITS – MASSIVE! – VARIOUS ARTISTS (DOVER) 1991
SMASH HITS – PARTY ON! – VARIOUS ARTISTS (THE HIT LABEL) 1992
SMASH HITS – RAVE! – VARIOUS ARTISTS (DOVER) 1990
SMASH HITS – SUMMER '97 VARIOUS ARTISTS (VIRGIN) 1997
SMASH HITS – SUMMER '98 VARIOUS ARTISTS (VIRGIN) 1998
SMASH HITS – SUMMER '99 VARIOUS ARTISTS (VIRGIN) 1999
SMASH HITS 1990 VARIOUS ARTISTS (DOVER) 1990
SMASH HITS 1991 VARIOUS ARTISTS (DOVER) 1991
SMASH HITS 2000 VARIOUS ARTISTS (VIRGIN) 1999
SMASH HITS 2001 VARIOUS ARTISTS (VIRGIN) 2000
SMASH HITS 2002 VARIOUS ARTISTS (EMI) 2001
SMASH HITS '71 ANONYMOUS COVER VERSIONS 1971
SMASH HITS '92 – 40 BIG HITS! SORTED! – VARIOUS ARTISTS (DOVER) 1992
SMASH HITS '93 – 40 TOP CHARTIN' GROOVES VARIOUS ARTISTS (CHRYSALIS) 1993
SMASH HITS '94 VARIOUS ARTISTS (TELSTAR) 1994
SMASH HITS '95 – VOLUME 1 VARIOUS ARTISTS (TELSTAR) 1995
SMASH HITS '95 – VOLUME 2 VARIOUS ARTISTS (TELSTAR) 1995
SMASH HITS '98 VARIOUS ARTISTS (VIRGIN) 1997
SMASH HITS '99! – VARIOUS ARTISTS (VIRGIN) 1998
SMASH HITS COUNTRY STYLE ANONYMOUS COVER VERSIONS 1971
SMASH HITS – LET'S PARTY VARIOUS ARTISTS (EMI) 2002
SMASH HITS – LET'S PARTY ON VARIOUS ARTISTS (EMI) 2003
SMASH HITS MIX '97 VARIOUS ARTISTS (VIRGIN) 1996
SMASH HITS SUMMER 2000 VARIOUS ARTISTS (VIRGIN) 2000
SMASH HITS SUMMER 2001 VARIOUS ARTISTS (EMI) 2001
SMASH HITS SUMMER 2002 VARIOUS ARTISTS (VIRGIN/EMI) 2002
SMASH HITS SUPREMES STYLE ANONYMOUS COVER VERSIONS 1971
SMASH HITS – THE REUNION VARIOUS ARTISTS (VIRGIN) 2003
SMASHES, THRASHES AND HITS KISS 1988
SMASHIE AND NICEY PRESENT LET'S ROCK! – VARIOUS ARTISTS (EMI) 1992
SMELL OF FEMALE CRAMPS 1983
SMILE NEIL REID 1972
SMILE JAYHAWKS 2000
SMILE MARTI PELLOW 2001
SMILE CHARLIE LANDSBOROUGH 2003
SMILE JAMAICA VARIOUS ARTISTS (TELSTAR) 1998
SMILER ROD STEWART 1974
SMILEY SMILE BEACH BOYS 1967
THE SMITHS SMITHS 1984
SMOKE AND STRONG WHISKEY CHRISTY MOORE 1991
SMOKIE/CHANGING ALL THE TIME SMOKIE 1975
SMOKIE'S HITS SMOKIE 1980
SMOKIN' – HUMBLE PIE 1972
SMOOTH CLASSICS – DO NOT DISTURB VARIOUS ARTISTS (CLASSIC FM) 2003
SMOOTH JAZZ 2 VARIOUS ARTISTS (UNIVERSAL) 2003
SMOOVE PRESENTS STREET BEATS VARIOUS ARTISTS (MINISTRY OF SOUND) 2003
SMURF'S CHRISTMAS PARTY SMURFS 1996

THE SMURFS GO POP! – SMURFS 1996
THE SMURFS HITS '97 – VOLUME 1 SMURFS 1997
SNAFU EAST OF EDEN 1970
THE SNAKE SHANE MACGOWAN & THE POPES 1994
SNAKES AND LADDERS GERRY RAFFERTY 1980
SNAP JAM 1983
SNAP CRACKLE AND BOP JOHN COOPER CLARKE 1980
SNAP! ATTACK – THE BEST OF SNAP!/SNAP! ATTACK – THE
    REMIXES SNAP! 1996
SNAP! IT UP – MONSTER HITS 2 VARIOUS ARTISTS (CBS)
    1990
SNATCH (OST) FILM SOUNDTRACK 2000
SNEAKIN' SUSPICION DR. FEELGOOD 1977
SNIVILISATION ORBITAL 1994
THE SNOW GOOSE CAMEL 1975
THE SNOW GOOSE SPIKE MILLIGAN WITH THE LONDON
    SYMPHONY ORCHESTRA 1976
SNOWFLAKES ARE DANCING TOMITA 1975
THE SNOWMAN HOWARD BLAKE CONDUCTING THE
    SINFONIA OF LONDON 1984
SNOWY WHITE SNOWY WHITE 1985
SO PETER GABRIEL 1986
SO AMAZING DIONNE WARWICK 1983
SO-CALLED CHAOS ALANIS MORISSETTE 2004
SO CLOSE DINA CARROLL 1993
SO FAR CROSBY, STILL, NASH & YOUNG 1974
SO FAR ALEX REECE 1996
SO FAR AWAY CHORDS 1980
SO FAR SO GOOD BRYAN ADAMS 1993
SO FAR, SO GOOD... SO WHAT! – MEGADETH 1988
SO FAR... THE BEST OF SINEAD O'CONNOR SINEAD
    O'CONNOR 1997
SO GOOD MICA PARIS 1988
SO LUCKY ROSE MARIE 1986
SO MANY RIVERS BOBBY WOMACK 1985
SO MUCH FOR THE AFTERGLOW EVERCLEAR 1998
SO MUCH FOR THE CITY THRILLS 2003
SO NATURAL LISA STANSFIELD 1993
SO RED THE ROSE ARCADIA 1985
SO SOLID CREW – F**K IT VARIOUS ARTISTS (RELENTLESS)
    2002
SO TONIGHT THAT I MIGHT SEE MAZZY STAR 1993
SO TOUGH SAINT ETIENNE 1993
SO WHERE ARE YOU? – LOOSE ENDS 1985
THE SOFT BULLETIN FLAMING LIPS 1999
SOFT METAL VARIOUS ARTISTS (STYLUS) 1988
SOFT METAL BALLADS VARIOUS ARTISTS (ARCADE) 1991
SOFT REGGAE VARIOUS ARTISTS (GLOBAL) 1995
SOFT ROCK VARIOUS ARTISTS (TELSTAR) 1989
SOFT ROCK VARIOUS ARTISTS (POLYGRAM) 1996
SOFTLY AS I LEAVE YOU FRANK SINATRA 1965
SOFTLY WITH THESE SONGS – THE BEST OF ROBERTA FLACK
    ROBERTA FLACK 1994
SOGNO ANDREA BOCELLI 1999
SOIL FESTIVITIES VANGELIS 1984
THE SOLAR SYSTEM VARIOUS ARTISTS (SOLAR) 1987
SOLD BOY GEORGE 1987
SOLDIER IGGY POP 1980
SOLDIER OF FORTUNE – THE BEST OF PHIL LYNOTT AND
    THIN LIZZY PHIL LYNOTT & THIN LIZZY 1987
SOLID GROUNDHOGS 1974
SOLID ASHFORD & SIMPSON 1985
SOLID BOND GRAHAM BOND 1970
SOLID BRONZE – GREAT HITS BEAUTIFUL SOUTH 2001
SOLID GOLD T. REX 1979
SOLID GOLD GANG OF FOUR 1981
SOLID GOLD SOUL VARIOUS ARTISTS (ATLANTIC) 1966
SOLID GROUND RONNIE LAWS 1981
SOLID LOVE ROMEO 2002
SOLID ROCK TEMPTATIONS 1972
SOLID SENDERS SOLID SENDERS 1978
SOLID SOUL SENSATIONS VARIOUS ARTISTS (DISCO
    DEMAND) 1975
SOLITAIRE ANDY WILLIAMS 1973
SOLITUDE STANDING SUZANNE VEGA 1987
SOLITUDE/SOLITAIRE PETER CETERA 1986

SOLO FREDDIE MERCURY 2000
SOLO CONCERT BILLY CONNOLLY 1974
SOLO IN SOHO PHIL LYNOTT 1980
THE SOME BIZARRE ALBUM VARIOUS ARTISTS (SOME
    BIZARRE) 1981
SOME DAY SOON KRISTIAN LEONTIOU 2004
SOME ENCHANTED EVENING BLUE OYSTER CULT 1978
SOME ENCHANTED EVENING BRYN TERFEL 2001
SOME FANTASTIC PLACE SQUEEZE 1993
SOME FRIENDLY CHARLATANS 1990
SOME GAVE ALL BILLY RAY CYRUS 1992
SOME GIRLS ROLLING STONES 1978
SOME GIRLS WANDER BY MISTAKE SISTERS OF MERCY
    1992
SOME GREAT REWARD DEPECHE MODE 1984
SOME MORE OF ME POEMS AND SONGS PAM AYRES 1976
SOME NICE THINGS I'VE MISSED FRANK SINATRA 1974
SOME OF ME POEMS AND SONGS PAM AYRES 1976
SOME OF MY BEST FRIENDS ARE SONGS VAL DOONICAN
    1977
SOME OTHER SUCKER'S PARADE DEL AMITRI 1997
SOME PEOPLE CAN DO WHAT THEY LIKE ROBERT PALMER
    1976
SOME PEOPLE'S LIVES BETTE MIDLER 1991
SOME PRODUCT – CARRI ON SEX PISTOLS SEX PISTOLS
    1979
SOME RAINY MORNING ROBERT CRAY 1995
SOME THINGS LASGO 2002
SOME THINGS NEVER CHANGE SUPERTRAMP 1997
SOMEBODY'S WATCHING ME ROCKWELL 1984
SOMEONE LOVES YOU HONEY CHARLEY PRIDE 1978
SOMETHING SHIRLEY BASSEY 1970
SOMETHING ELSE SHIRLEY BASSEY 1971
SOMETHING ELSE BY THE KINKS KINKS 1967
SOMETHING FOR EVERYBODY ELVIS PRESLEY 1961
SOMETHING IN THE AIR VARIOUS ARTISTS (COLUMBIA)
    1992
SOMETHING OLD, SOMETHING NEW SYD LAWRENCE 1972
SOMETHING SPECIAL KOOL & THE GANG 1981
SOMETHING SPECIAL – 100 GOLDEN LOVE SONGS FOSTER
    & ALLEN 1996
SOMETHING TO REMEMBER MADONNA 1995
SOMETHING UP MY SLEEVE SUZY BOGGUSS 1993
SOMETHING WICKED THIS WAY COMES HERBALISER 2002
SOMETHING WONDERFUL BRYN TERFEL 1996
SOMETHING'S GOING ON FRIDA 1982
SOMETIME IN NEW YORK CITY JOHN LENNON WITH THE
    PLASTIC ONO BAND & ELEPHANT'S MEMORY 1972
SOMETIMES WHEN WE TOUCH CLEO LAINE & JAMES
    GALWAY 1980
SOMETIMES WHEN WE TOUCH VARIOUS ARTISTS (RONCO)
    1984
SOMETIMES YOU WIN DR. HOOK 1979
SOMEWHERE IN AFRIKA MANFRED MANN'S EARTH BAND
    1983
SOMEWHERE IN ENGLAND GEORGE HARRISON 1981
SOMEWHERE IN TIME IRON MAIDEN 1986
SOMEWHERE IN TIME DONNY OSMOND 2002
SOMEWHERE MY LOVE RAY CONNIFF 1967
SOMEWHERE SOON HIGH 1990
SON OF SCHMILSSON NILSSON 1972
SONG AND DANCE TELEVISION SOUNDTRACK 1984
THE SONG AND DANCE MEN MAX BYGRAVES 1978
A SONG FOR ALL SEASONS RENAISSANCE 1978
A SONG FOR EUROTRASH VARIOUS ARTISTS (EMI) 1998
A SONG FOR ME FAMILY 1970
A SONG FOR YOU JACK JONES 1972
A SONG FOR YOU CARPENTERS 1972
SONG OF SEVEN JON ANDERSON 1980
THE SONG REMAINS THE SAME (OST) LED ZEPPELIN 1976
SONG REVIEW – A GREATEST HITS COLLECTION STEVIE
    WONDER 1996
SONG WITHOUT END (OST) FILM SOUNDTRACK 1961
SONGBIRD BARBRA STREISAND 1978
SONGBIRD RUBY WINTERS 1979
SONGBIRD EVA CASSIDY 2001

SONGBIRDS VARIOUS ARTISTS (WARNER BROTHERS) 2003
SONGBOOK – A LIFETIME OF MUSIC DAVID GATES 2002
SONGS LUTHER VANDROSS 1994
SONGS ABOUT JANE MAROON 5 2004
SONGS BY TOM LEHRER TOM LEHRER 1958
SONGS FOR A TAILOR JACK BRUCE 1969
SONGS FOR A WINTER'S NIGHT GEORGE HAMILTON IV
    1982
SONGS FOR BEGINNERS GRAHAM NASH 1971
SONGS FOR DRELLA LOU REED & JOHN CALE 1990
SONGS FOR SWINGING LOVERS FRANK SINATRA 1958
SONGS FOR SWINGING SELLERS PETER SELLERS 1959
SONGS FOR THE DEAF QUEENS OF THE STONE AGE 2002
SONGS FROM A ROOM LEONARD COHEN 1969
SONGS FROM 'ALLY MCBEAL' (OST TV) VONDA SHEPARD
    1998
SONGS FROM AN AMERICAN MOVIE VOLUME 1
    EVERCLEAR 2000
SONGS FROM AN AMERICAN MOVIE VOLUME 2
    EVERCLEAR 2001
SONGS FROM DAWSON'S CREEK – VOL 2 TELEVISION
    SOUNDTRACK 2000
SONGS FROM DAWSON'S CREEK TELEVISION
    SOUNDTRACK 1999
SONGS FROM 'HEATHCLIFF' – CLIFF RICHARD 1995
SONGS FROM HER TV SERIES NANA MOUSKOURI 1973
SONGS FROM HIS TV SERIES SCOTT WALKER 1969
SONGS FROM MY SKETCHBOOK VAL DOONICAN 1990
SONGS FROM NORTHERN BRITAIN TEENAGE FANCLUB
    1997
SONGS FROM STAGE AND SCREEN MICHAEL CRAWFORD &
    THE LONDON SYMPHONY ORCHESTRA 1987
SONGS FROM SUN STREET SAW DOCTORS 1998
SONGS FROM THE BIG CHAIR TEARS FOR FEARS 1985
SONGS FROM THE CHILLOUT LOUNGE VARIOUS ARTISTS
    (TELSTAR) 2002
SONGS FROM THE FRONT ROW – THE BEST OF OCEAN
    COLOUR SCENE 2001
SONGS FROM THE LAST CENTURY GEORGE MICHAEL 1999
SONGS FROM THE MARDI GRAS FEARGAL SHARKEY 1991
SONGS FROM THE MIRROR FISH 1991
SONGS FROM THE OTHER SIDE CHARLATANS 2002
SONGS FROM THE RAIN HOTHOUSE FLOWERS 1993
SONGS FROM THE STUDENT PRINCE AND OTHER FAMOUS
    MELODIES MARIO LANZA 1956
SONGS FROM THE WEST COAST ELTON JOHN 2001
SONGS FROM THE WOOD JETHRO TULL 1977
SONGS FROM WHISTLE DOWN THE WIND VARIOUS
    ARTISTS (REALLY USEFUL) 1998
SONGS IN A MINOR ALICIA KEYS 2001
SONGS IN THE ATTIC BILLY JOEL 1981
SONGS IN THE KEY OF LIFE STEVIE WONDER 1976
SONGS IN THE KEY OF X VARIOUS ARTISTS (WARNER
    BROTHERS) 1996
THE SONGS 1975–1990 BARRY MANILOW 1990
SONGS OF A LIFETIME BING CROSBY 1979
THE SONGS OF BOB DYLAN VARIOUS ARTISTS (START)
    1989
THE SONGS OF DISTANT EARTH MIKE OLDFIELD 1994
SONGS OF FAITH AND DEVOTION DEPECHE MODE 1993
SONGS OF FREEDOM BOB MARLEY 1992
SONGS OF INSPIRATION DANIEL O'DONNELL 1996
SONGS OF JOY NIGEL BROOKS SINGERS 1975
SONGS OF JOY PESTALOZZI CHILDREN'S CHOIR 1981
SONGS OF LEONARD COHEN LEONARD COHEN 1968
SONGS OF LOVE RICHARD CLAYDERMAN 1987
SONGS OF LOVE PLACIDO DOMINGO 2000
SONGS OF LOVE AND HATE LEONARD COHEN 1971
SONGS OF OUR HERITAGE DUANNE EDDY 1960
SONGS OF PRAISE VARIOUS ARTISTS (WARWICK) 1977
SONGS OF SANCTUARY ADIEMUS 1995
SONGS OF THE FREE GANG OF FOUR 1982
SONGS OF THE SEASHORE JAMES GALWAY 1979
SONGS OF THE VALLEYS LONDON WELSH MALE VOICE
    CHOIR 1981
THE SONGS THAT GOT AWAY SARAH BRIGHTMAN 1989

SONGS TO LEARN AND SING ECHO & THE BUNNYMEN 1985

SONGS TO MAKE THE WHOLE WORLD SING BARRY MANILOW 1989

SONGS TO MAKE YOU FEEL GOOD VARIOUS ARTISTS (TELSTAR) 2002

SONGS TO REMEMBER SCRITTI POLITTI 1982

SONGS TO SING IN YOUR BATH RUSS CONWAY 1959

SONGS WE LOVE TO SING FOSTER & ALLEN 1994

SONGWRITER JUSTIN HAYWARD 1977

SONIA SONIA 1991

SONIC ATTACK HAWKWIND 1981

SONIC FLOWER GROOVE PRIMAL SCREAM 1987

SONIC SYSTEM VARIOUS ARTISTS (TELSTAR) 1992

SONIC TEMPLE CULT 1989

SONNY SIDE OF CHER CHER 1966

SONS AND FASCINATIONS/SISTERS FEELINGS CALL SIMPLE MINDS 1981

SONS OF SOUL TONY! TONI! TONE! 1993

SOONER OR LATER BBMAK 2001

SOPHISTICATED BOOM BOOM DEAD OR ALIVE 1984

SOPHTWARE SLUMP GRANDADDY 2000

SOPRANO IN HOLLYWOOD LESLEY GARRET 1996

SOPRANO IN RED LESLEY GARRET 1995

A SOPRANO INSPIRED LESLEY GARRET 1997

THE SOPRANO'S GREATEST HITS LESLEY GARRET 1997

SORCERER (OST) TANGERINE DREAM 1977

SORTED VARIOUS ARTISTS (MINISTRY OF SOUND) 2002

SOUL VARIOUS ARTISTS (POLYGRAM) 1998

THE SOUL ALBUM OTIS REDDING 1966

THE SOUL ALBUM VARIOUS ARTISTS (VIRGIN) 1997

THE SOUL ALBUM II VARIOUS ARTISTS (VIRGIN) 1998

SOUL ALONE DARYL HALL 1993

SOUL BEAT VARIOUS ARTISTS (COOKIE JAR) 1993

SOUL BROTHERS VARIOUS ARTISTS (WARNER BROTHERS) 2002

THE SOUL CAGES STING 1991

SOUL CITY VARIOUS ARTISTS (K-TEL) 1977

SOUL DAZE/SOUL NITES VARIOUS ARTISTS (RONCO) 1982

SOUL DECADE: THE SIXTIES VARIOUS ARTISTS (MOTOWN) 1990

SOUL DESTRUCTION ALMIGHTY 1991

SOUL DEVOTION VARIOUS ARTISTS (POLYGRAM) 1994

SOUL EMOTION VARIOUS ARTISTS (POLYGRAM) 1992

SOUL INSPIRATION VARIOUS ARTISTS (POLYGRAM) 1993

SOUL JOURNEY GILLIAN WELCH 2003

SOUL KISS OLIVIA NEWTON-JOHN 1986

SOUL MAN VARIOUS ARTISTS (SONY) 2004

SOUL MATE VARIOUS ARTISTS (DINO) 1994

SOUL MEN SAM & DAVE 1968

SOUL MINING THE THE 1983

SOUL MOODS VARIOUS ARTISTS (EMI) 1993

SOUL MOTION VARIOUS ARTISTS (K-TEL) 1976

SOUL NIGHTS VARIOUS ARTISTS (POLYGRAM) 1994

SOUL OF MANN MANFRED MANN 1967

THE SOUL OF SPAIN 101 STRINGS 1960

SOUL PROVIDER MICHAEL BOLTON 1990

SOUL REFLECTION VARIOUS ARTISTS (HEART & SOUL) 1991

SOUL SEARCHING VARIOUS ARTISTS (COLUMBIA) 1994

SOUL SEARCHING TIME AVERAGE WHITE BAND 1976

THE SOUL SESSIONS JOSS STONE 2004

SOUL SURVIVORS – 40 NORTHERN SOUL ANTHEMS VARIOUS ARTISTS (TELSTAR) 1997

SOUL SURVIVORS 2 VARIOUS ARTISTS (TELSTAR) 1998

SOULFLY SOULFLY 1998

SOULJACKER EELS 2001

SOUL'S CORE SHAWN MULLINS 1999

SOULS OF BLACK TESTAMENT 1990

SOUND EFFECTS JAM 1980

SOUND LOADED RICKY MARTIN 2000

THE SOUND OF JAM 2002

THE SOUND OF BREAD BREAD 1977

THE SOUND OF CLASSIC FM VARIOUS ARTISTS (CLASSIC FM) 2001

THE SOUND OF FURY BILLY FURY 1960

SOUND OF GLORY LONDON PHILHARMONIC CHOIR WITH THE NATIONAL PHILHARMONIC ORCHESTRA CONDUCTED BY JOHN ALDISS 1976

THE SOUND OF KISS 100FM VARIOUS ARTISTS (POLYGRAM) 1994

SOUND OF LIES JAYHAWKS 1997

THE SOUND OF MAGIC VARIOUS ARTISTS (UNIVERSAL) 1999

THE SOUND OF MAGIC LOVE VARIOUS ARTISTS (UNIVERSAL) 2000

THE SOUND OF MAGIC VOLUME 2 VARIOUS ARTISTS (UNIVERSAL) 2000

THE SOUND OF MCALMONT AND BUTLER MCALMONT & BUTLER 1995

SOUND OF MUSIC ADICTS 1982

THE SOUND OF MUSIC ORIGINAL BROADWAY STAGE CAST SOUNDTRACK 1961

THE SOUND OF MUSIC ORIGINAL LONDON STAGE CAST SOUNDTRACK 1961

THE SOUND OF MUSIC (OST) FILM SOUNDTRACK 1965

SOUND OF PIBROCH CORRIES 1972

THE SOUND OF SKA VARIOUS ARTISTS (QUALITY PRICE MUSIC) 1992

THE SOUND OF SMOOVE VARIOUS ARTISTS (MINISTRY OF SOUND) 2004

THE SOUND OF SPEED JESUS & MARY CHAIN 1993

THE SOUND OF SUPER K KENNY 1976

THE SOUND OF THE CITY VARIOUS ARTISTS (COLUMBIA) 1992

THE SOUND OF THE SHADOWS SHADOWS 1965

THE SOUND OF THE SUBURBS VARIOUS ARTISTS (COLUMBIA) 1991

SOUND OF THE UNDERGROUND GIRLS ALOUD 2003

SOUND OF THE WHITE NOISE ANTHRAX 1993

SOUND OF WATER SAINT ETIENNE 2000

THE SOUND OF YOUR CRY ELVIS PRESLEY 1982

SOUND ON SOUND BILL NELSON'S RED NOISE 1979

SOUND VENTURE GEORGIE FAME 1966

SOUND WAVES L'ORCHESTRE ELECTRONIQUE 1983

SOUNDCLASH RENEGADE SOUNDWAVE 1990

SOUNDS GENTLE VAL DOONICAN 1969

SOUNDS LIKE HERB ALPERT & THE TIJUANA BRASS 1967

SOUNDS LIKE THE SEARCHERS SEARCHERS 1965

SOUNDS OF SILENCE SIMON & GARFUNKEL 1966

SOUNDS OF THE SEVENTIES VARIOUS ARTISTS (GLOBAL) 1994

SOUNDS SENSATIONAL BERT KAEMPFERT & HIS ORCHESTRA 1980

SOUNDTRACK RECORDINGS FROM THE FILM 'JIMI HENDRIX' (OST) JIMI HENDRIX 1973

SOUNDTRACK TO THE WEEKEND VARIOUS ARTISTS (GLOBAL) 2000

SOUP BLIND MELON 1995

SOURCE TAGS AND CODES AND YOU WILL KNOW US BY THE TRAIL OF DEAD 2002

SOUTH OF HEAVEN SLAYER 1988

SOUTH PACIFIC ORIGINAL STUDIO CAST RECORDING 1986

SOUTH PACIFIC (OST) FILM SOUNDTRACK 1958

SOUTH PARK: BIGGER, LONGER & UNCUT (OST) FILM SOUNDTRACK 1999

SOUTHERN ACCENTS TOM PETTY & HEARTBREAKERS 1985

THE SOUTHERN DEATH CULT SOUTHERN DEATH CULT 1983

SOUTHERN FREEZ FREEEZ 1981

THE SOUTHERN HARMONY AND MUSICAL COMPANION BLACK CROWES 1992

SOUTHERN HUMMINGBIRD TWEET 2002

SOUTHERN KNIGHTS VARIOUS ARTISTS (KNIGHT) 1991

SOUTHERN NIGHTS GLEN CAMPBELL 1977

SOUTHPAW GRAMMAR MORRISSEY 1995

SOUTHSIDE TEXAS 1989

SOUVENIR SINGLES PACK MICHAEL JACKSON 1988

SOUVENIRS DEMIS ROUSSOS 1975

SOUVENIRS FOSTER & ALLEN 1990

SOUVLAKI SLOWDIVE 1993

SOWETO VARIOUS ARTISTS (ROUGH TRADE) 1982

SPACE VARIOUS ARTISTS (WARNER BROTHERS) 2000

SPACE BANDITS HAWKWIND 1990

A SPACE IN TIME TEN YEARS AFTER 1971

SPACE INVADERS VARIOUS ARTISTS (RONCO) 1980

SPACE JAM (OST) FILM SOUNDTRACK 1997

SPACE ODDITY DAVID BOWIE 1972

SPACE RITUAL ALIVE HAWKWIND 1973

THE SPAGHETTI INCIDENT? – GUNS N' ROSES 1993

SPANISH HARLEM BEN E. KING 1967

SPANISH TRAIN AND OTHER STORIES CHRIS DE BURGH 1985

A SPANNER IN THE WORKS ROD STEWART 1995

SPANNERS BLACK DOG 1995

SPARKLE SPARKLE 1998

SPARKLE IN THE RAIN SIMPLE MINDS 1984

SPARTACUS VIENNA PHILHARMONIC ORCHESTRA CONDUCTED BY ARAM KHACHATURIAN 1972

SPARTACUS FARM 1991

SPARTACUS JEFF WAYNE 1992

SPAWN – THE ALBUM (OST) FILM SOUNDTRACK 1997

SPEAK AND SPELL DEPECHE MODE 1981

SPEAKERBOXXX/THE LOVE BELOW OUTKAST 2003

SPEAKING IN TONGUES TALKING HEADS 1983

SPEAKING WITH THE ANGEL MARY BLACK 1999

SPECIAL BEAT SERVICE BEAT 1982

SPECIAL FORCES ALICE COOPER 1981

SPECIAL OLYMPICS – A VERY SPECIAL CHRISTMAS VARIOUS ARTISTS (A&M) 1987

A SPECIAL PART OF ME JOHNNY MATHIS 1984

SPECIALLY FOR YOU DUANE EDDY 1959

SPECIALS SPECIALS 1979

SPECIALS SPECIALS 2001

THE SPECIALS SINGLES SPECIALS 1991

SPECS APPEAL SHADOWS 1975

SPECTRAL MORNINGS STEVE HACKETT 1979

SPECTRES BLUE OYSTER CULT 1978

SPECTRUM SONIC BOOM 1990

SPEED BALLADS REPUBLICA 1998

SPEED GARAGE ANTHEMS VARIOUS ARTISTS (GLOBAL) 1997

SPEED GARAGE ANTHEMS – VOLUME 2 VARIOUS ARTISTS (GLOBAL) 1998

SPEED GARAGE ANTHEMS 99 VARIOUS ARTISTS (GLOBAL) 1999

SPEED GARAGE ANTHEMS IN IBIZA VARIOUS ARTISTS (GLOBAL) 1998

SPELLBOUND TYGERS OF PAN TANG 1981

SPELLBOUND PAULA ABDUL 1991

SPICE SPICE GIRLS 1996

SPICE GIRLS PRESENT THE BEST GIRL POWER ALBUM IN THE WORLD... EVER! – VARIOUS ARTISTS (VIRGIN) 1997

SPICEWORLD SPICE GIRLS 1997

SPIDER MAN (OST) FILM SOUNDTRACK 2002

SPIDERS SPACE 1996

SPIKE ELVIS COSTELLO 1989

SPILT MILK JELLYFISH 1993

SPIN DARREN HAYES 2002

SPINNER BRIAN ENO & JAH WOBBLE 1995

THE SPINNERS ARE IN TOWN SPINNERS 1970

SPINNERS LIVE PERFORMANCE SPINNERS 1971

SPIRIT JOHN DENVER 1976

THE SPIRIT MAGNUM 1991

SPIRIT SEAN MAGUIRE 1996

SPIRIT JEWEL 1998

SPIRIT OF EDEN TALK TALK 1988

SPIRIT OF RELAXATION DREAMKEEPER 1997

SPIRIT OF ST LOUIS ELLEN FOLEY 1981

SPIRIT OF THE IRISH DUBLINERS 2003

SPIRIT OF TRANQUILLITY HARMONIUM 1998

SPIRIT – STALLION OF THE CIMARRON – OST BRYAN ADAMS 2002

THE SPIRIT ROOM MICHELLE BRANCH 2002

SPIRITCHASER DEAD CAN DANCE 1996

SPIRITS DANCING IN THE FLESH SANTANA 1990

SPIRITS HAVING FLOWN BEE GEES 1979

SPIRITS OF NATURE VARIOUS ARTISTS (VIRGIN) 1996

**SPIRITUALLY IBIZA** VARIOUS ARTISTS (DINO) 1995
**SPIT IN YOUR EAR** SPITTING IMAGE 1986
**SPITFIRE** JEFFERSON STARSHIP 1976
**SPLINTER** OFFSPRING 2003
**SPLINTER GROUP** PETER GREEN 1997
**SPLIT** GROUNDHOGS 1971
**SPLIT** LUSH 1994
**SPLIT SERIES – VOLUME 3** RANCID/NOFX 2002
**SPLIT THE DIFFERENCE** GOMEZ 2004
**SPOOKY** LUSH 1992
**SPORTS** HUEY LEWIS & THE NEWS 1985
**SPORTS CAR** JUDIE TZUKE 1980
**THE SPOTLIGHT KID** CAPTAIN BEEFHEART & HIS MAGIC BAND 1972
**SPOTLIGHT ON NANA MOUSKOURI** NANA MOUSKOURI 1974
**SPOTLIGHT ON THE GEORGE MITCHELL MINST6RELS** GEORGE MITCHELL MINSTRELS 1964
**SPRING ANNUAL 2002** VARIOUS ARTISTS (MINISTRY OF SOUND) 2002
**SPYBOY** EMMYLOU HARRIS 1998
**SPYGLASS GUEST** GREENSLADE 1974
**SQUARE THE CIRCLE** JOAN ARMATRADING 1992
**SQUEEZING OUT SPARKS** GRAHAM PARKER & THE RUMOUR 1979
**SSSSH** TEN YEARS AFTER 1969
**STACIE ORRICO** STACIE ORRICO 2003
**STACKED UP** SENSER 1994
**THE STADIUM TECHNO EXPERIENCE** SCOOTER 2003
**STAGE** DAVID BOWIE 1978
**STAGE FRIGHT** BAND 1970
**STAGE HEROES** COLM WILKINSON 1989
**STAGE STRUCK** RORY GALLAGHER 1980
**STAGES** ELAINE PAIGE 1983
**STAGE STRUCK** DAVID ESSEX 1982
**STAIN** LIVING COLOUR 1993
**STAINED CLASS** JUDAS PRIEST 1978
**STAKES IS HIGH** DE LA SOUL 1996
**STAMPEDE** DOOBIE BROTHERS 1975
**THE STAMPING GROUND** RUNRIG 2001
**STAND BY ME (THE ULTIMATE COLLECTION)** BEN E. KING & THE DRIFTERS 1987
**STAND BY YOUR MAN** TAMMY WYNETTE 1975
**STAND STRONG STAND PROUD** VICE SQUAD 1982
**STAND UP** JETHRO TULL 1969
**STANDARDS** ALARM 1990
**STANDING HAMPTON** SAMMY HAGAR 1982
**STANDING IN THE LIGHT** LEVEL 42 1983
**STANDING ON A BEACH – THE SINGLES** CURE 1986
**STANDING ON THE SHOULDER OF GIANTS** OASIS 2000
**STANDING TALL** CRUSADERS 1981
**STANDING TALL** KYM MARSH 2003
**STANKONIA** OUTKAST 2001
**STANLEY ROAD** PAUL WELLER 1995
**STAR** BELLY 1993
**STAR FLEET PROJECT** BRIAN MAY & FRIENDS 1983
**A STAR IS BORN (OST)** BARBRA STREISAND 1977
**STAR PARTY** VARIOUS ARTISTS (K-TEL) 1978
**STAR PORTRAIT** JOHNNY CASH 1972
**STAR TRACKIN' 76** VARIOUS ARTISTS (RONCO) 1976
**STAR TRACKS** VARIOUS ARTISTS (K-TEL) 1980
**STAR WARS EPISODE II – OST** LONDON SYMPHONY ORCHESTRA/JOHN WILLIAMS 2002
**STAR WARS – THE PHANTOM MENACE (OST)** JOHN WILLIAMS 1999
**STAR WARS (OST)** JOHN WILLIAMS 1978
**STAR! (OST)** FILM SOUNDTRACK 1968
**STARDUST** PAT BOONE 1958
**STARDUST MEMORIES** PETER SKELLERN 1995
**STARGAZERS** VARIOUS ARTISTS (KASINO) 1985
**STARING AT THE SUN** LEVEL 42 1988
**STARLESS AND BIBLE BLACK** KING CRIMSON 1974
**STARLIGHT EXPRESS** ORIGINAL LONDON STAGE CAST SOUNDTRACK 1984
**STARRY EYED AND BOLLOCK NAKED** CARTER – THE UNSTOPPABLE SEX MACHINE 1994

**STARRY NIGHT** JULIO IGLESIAS 1990
**STARS** SIMPLY RED 1991
**STARS AND TOPSOIL – A COLLECTION 1982–1990** COCTEAU TWINS 2000
**STARS CHARITY FANTASIA SAVE THE CHILDREN FUND** VARIOUS ARTISTS (SCF) 1966
**STARS CRASH DOWN** HUE & CRY 1991
**STARS FROM STARS AND GARTERS** TELEVISION COMPILATION 1964
**STARS MEDLEY** STARSOUND 1982
**STARS OF '68** VARIOUS ARTISTS (MARBLE ARCH) 1968
**STARS ON 45** STARSOUND 1981
**STARS ON 45 VOLUME 2** STARSOUND 1981
**STARS ON SUNDAY BY REQUEST** TELEVISION COMPILATION 1978
**STARS – THE BEST OF 1992–2002** CRANBERRIES 2002
**THE STARS WE ARE** MARC ALMOND 1988
**STARSKY AND HUTCH PRESENTS** TELEVISION COMPILATION 1998
**START SOMETHING** LOSTPROPHETS 2004
**START – THE BEST OF BRITISH** VARIOUS ARTISTS (DINO) 1994
**START WITH A STRONG AND PERSISTENT** VEX RED 2002
**STARTRAX CLUB DISCO** STARTRAX 1981
**STATE OF EUPHORIA** ANTHRAX 1988
**STATE OF MIND** HOLLY VALANCE 2003
**STATE OF OUR UNION** LONG RYDERS 1985
**STATE OF THE WORLD ADDRESS** BIOHAZARD 1994
**STATELESS** LENE LOVICH 1979
**STATIC & SILENCE** SUNDAYS 1997
**STATION TO STATION** DAVID BOWIE 1976
**STATIONARY TRAVELLER** CAMEL 1984
**STATUES** MOLOKO 2003
**STATUS QUO – LIVE** STATUS QUO 1977
**STATUS QUO LIVE AT THE N.E.C.** STATUS QUO 1984
**STAY HUNGRY** TWISTED SISTER 1984
**STAY ON THESE ROADS** A-HA 1988
**STAY STICK!** CRAMPS 1990
**STAY WITH ME** REGINA BELLE 1989
**STAY WITH ME TONIGHT** JEFFREY OSBORNE 1984
**STAY WITH THE HOLLIES** HOLLIES 1964
**STAYING ALIVE (OST)** FILM SOUNDTRACK 1983
**STEADY DIET OF NOTHIMG** FUGAZI 1991
**STEAL THIS ALBUM** SYSTEM OF A DOWN 2002
**STEAL YOUR FACE** GRATEFUL DEAD 1976
**STEAM** EAST 17 1994
**STEAMIN' – HARDCORE '92** VARIOUS ARTISTS (COOKIE JAR) 1991
**STEEL WHEELS** ROLLING STONES 1989
**STEELTOWN** BIG COUNTRY 1984
**STELLA** YELLO 1985
**STEP BY STEP** JEFF LORBER 1985
**STEP BY STEP** NEW KIDS ON THE BLOCK 1990
**STEP IN THE ARENA** GANG STARR 1991
**STEP ONE** STEPS 1998
**STEP TWO** SHOWADDYWADDY 1975
**STEPHEN MALKMUS** STEPHEN MALKMUS 2001
**STEPHEN STILLS** STEPHEN STILLS 1970
**STEPHEN STILLS 2** STEPHEN STILLS 1971
**STEPPENWOLF** STEPPENWOLF 1970
**STEPPENWOLF LIVE** STEPPENWOLF 1970
**STEPPIN' TO THE SHADOWS** SHADOWS 1989
**STEPPING OUT – THE VERY BEST OF JOE JACKSON** JOE JACKSON 1990
**STEPS IN TIME** KING 1985
**STEPTACULAR** STEPS 1999
**STEPTOE AND SON** WILFRED BRAMBELL & HARRY H. CORBETT 1963
**STEPTOE AND SON** WILFRED BRAMBELL & HARRY H. CORBETT 1964
**STEREO '57 (ESSENTIAL ELVIS VOLUME 2)** ELVIS PRESLEY 1989
**STEREO MUSICALE SHOWCASE** VARIOUS ARTISTS (POLYDOR) 1966
**THE STEVE HOWE ALBUM** STEVE HOWE 1979
**STEVE MCQUEEN** PREFAB SPROUT 1985

**STEVE MILLER BAND LIVE!** – STEVE MILLER BAND 1983
**STEVE WINWOOD** STEVE WINWOOD 1977
**STEVE WRIGHT'S CHOCOLATES AND CHAMPAGNE** VARIOUS ARTISTS (UNIVERSAL) 2004
**STEVE WRIGHT'S SUNDAY** VARIOUS ARTISTS (UNIVERSAL) 2002
**STEVE WRIGHT'S SUNDAY LOVE SONGS** VARIOUS ARTISTS (UNIVERSAL) 2000
**STEVE WRIGHT'S SUNDAY LOVE SONGS VOLUME 2** VARIOUS ARTISTS (UNIVERSAL) 2001
**STEVEN HOUGHTON** STEVEN HOUGHTON 1997
**STEVIE WONDER'S GREATEST HITS** STEVIE WONDER 1968
**STICK AROUND FOR JOY** SUGARCUBES 1992
**STICK TO ME** GRAHAM PARKER & THE RUMOUR 1977
**STICKS AND STONES** NEW FOUND GLORY 2002
**STICKY FINGERS** ROLLING STONES 1971
**STIFF UPPER LIP** AC/DC 2000
**STIFF'S LIVE STIFFS** VARIOUS ARTISTS (STIFF) 1978
**STIGMA** EMF 1992
**STILETTO** LITA FORD 1990
**STILL** JOY DIVISION 1981
**STILL BURNING** MIKE SCOTT 1997
**STILL CAN'T SAY GOODBYE** CHARLIE LANDSBOROUGH 1999
**STILL CLIMBING** BROWNSTONE 1997
**STILL CRAZY AFTER ALL THESE YEARS** PAUL SIMON 1975
**STILL GOT THE BLUES** GARY MOORE 1990
**STILL I RISE** 2PAC & OUTLAWZ 2000
**STILL IN THE GAME** KEITH SWEAT 1998
**STILL LIFE (AMERICAN CONCERTS 1981)** ROLLING STONES 1982
**STILL NOT BLACK ENOUGH** W.A.S.P. 1995
**STILL OUT OF ORDER** INFA RIOT 1982
**STILL SEXY – THE ALBUM** ERROL BROWN 2001
**STILL TOGETHER** GLADYS KNIGHT & THE PIPS 1977
**STILL WATERS** BEE GEES 1997
**STILL WATERS RUN DEEP** FOUR TOPS 1970
**STILLS** STEPHEN STILLS 1975
**THE STING (OST)** MARVIN HAMLISCH 1974
**STOLEN MOMENTS** JOHN HIATT 1990
**STOMPIN' AT THE SAVOY** RUFUS & CHAKA KHAN 1984
**STOMPIN' PARTY** VARIOUS ARTISTS (DINO) 1992
**STONE AGE** ROLLING STONES 1971
**STONE GON'** – BARRY WHITE 1974
**STONE KILLERS** PRINCE CHARLES & THE CITY BEAT BAND 1983
**THE STONE ROSES** STONE ROSES 1989
**STONE ROSES – 10TH ANNIVERSARY EDITION** STONE ROSES 1999
**STONE SOUR** STONE SOUR 2002
**STONED AND DETHRONED** JESUS & MARY CHAIN 1994
**STONED RAIDERS** CYPRESS HILL 2001
**STONEDHENGE** TEN YEARS AFTER 1969
**STONES** NEIL DIAMOND 1971
**STONES IN THE ROAD** MARY CHAPIN CARPENTER 1994
**STONEY END** BARBRA STREISAND 1971
**STOOSH** SKUNK ANANSIE 1996
**STOP MAKING SENSE** TALKING HEADS 1984
**STOP THAT TRAIN** CLINT EASTWOOD & GENERAL SAINT 1983
**STOP THE WORLD** BLACK, ROCK & RON 1989
**STOP THE WORLD – I WANT TO GET OFF** ORIGINAL LONDON STAGE CAST SOUNDTRACK 1961
**STOP!** – SAM BROWN 1989
**STORIES FROM THE CITY STORIES FROM THE SEA** PJ HARVEY 2000
**STORIES OF JOHNNY** MARC ALMOND 1985
**STORM** VANESSA-MAE 1997
**STORM BRINGER** DEEP PURPLE 1974
**STORM FRONT** BILLY JOEL 1989
**A STORM IN HEAVEN** VERVE 1993
**STORM WATCH** JETHRO TULL 1979
**STORMS** NANCI GRIFFITH 1989
**STORMSVILLE** JOHNNY & THE HURRICANES 1960
**THE STORY OF A YOUNG HEART** A FLOCK OF SEAGULLS 1984

THE STORY OF THE CLASH – VOLUME 1 CLASH 1988
STORY OF THE STONES ROLLING STONES 1982
THE STORY OF THE WHO WHO 1976
THE STORY SO FAR (SPUNGE) 2002
THE STORY SO FAR – THE VERY BEST OF ROD STEWART 2001
STORYTELLING BELLE & SEBASTIAN 2002
STORYVILLE ROBBIE ROBERTSON 1991
STR8 OFF THA STREETZ OF MUTHAPHUKKIN COMPTON EAZY-E 1996
STRAIGHT DOGS D'AMOUR 1990
STRAIGHT BETWEEN THE EYES RAINBOW 1982
STRAIGHT FROM THE HEART PATRICE RUSHEN 1982
STRAIGHT OUTTA COMPTON N.W.A. 1989
STRAIGHT OUTTA COMPTON N.W.A. 2003
STRAIGHT SHOOTER BAD COMPANY 1975
STRANDED ROXY MUSIC 1973
STRANGE AND BEAUTIFUL VARIOUS ARTISTS (WARNER BROTHERS) 2003
STRANGE ANGELS KRISTIN HERSH 1998
STRANGE BEHAVIOUR DURAN DURAN 1999
STRANGE BOUTIQUE MONOCHROME SET 1980
STRANGE BROTHERHOOD NEW MODEL ARMY 1998
STRANGE CHARM GARY NUMAN 1986
STRANGE FREE WORLD KITCHENS OF DISTINCTION 1991
STRANGE FRONTIER ROGER TAYLOR 1984
STRANGE KIND OF LOVE LOVE & MONEY 1988
STRANGE LITTLE GIRLS TORI AMOS 2001
STRANGE REFLECTIONS SECOND IMAGE 1985
STRANGE TIMES CHAMELEON 1986
STRANGE WEATHER MARIANNE FAITHFULL 1987
STRANGEITUDE OZRIC TENTACLES 1991
STRANGELOVE STRANGELOVE 1997
THE STRANGER BILLY JOEL 1978
STRANGER IN MY OWN BACK YARD GILBERT O'SULLIVAN 1974
STRANGER IN THE CITY JOHN MILES 1977
STRANGER IN THIS TOWN RICHIE SAMBORA 1991
STRANGER IN TOWN BOB SEGER & THE SILVER BULLET BAND 1978
STRANGER ON THE SHORE MR ACKER BILK 1962
STRANGERS IN THE NIGHT FRANK SINATRA 1966
STRANGERS IN THE NIGHT BERT KAEMPFERT & HIS ORCHESTRA 1966
STRANGERS IN THE NIGHT UFO 1979
STRANGEWAYS, HERE WE COME SMITHS 1987
STRANGLERS IN THE NIGHT STRANGLERS 1992
STRANGLERS IV (RATTUS NORVEGICUS) STRANGLERS 1977
STRATOSFEAR TANGERINE DREAM 1976
THE STRAUSS FAMILY (OST) LONDON SYMPHONY ORCHESTRA CONDUCTED BY CYRIL ORNADEL 1972
STRAW DONKEY... THE SINGLES CARTER – THE UNSTOPPABLE SEX MACHINE 1995
STRAWBERRIES DAMNED 1982
STRAWBERRY SWITCHBLADE STRAWBERRY SWITCHBLADE 1985
STRAY AZTEC CAMERA 1990
STRAY CATS STRAY CATS 1981
STRAYS JANE'S ADDICTION 2003
STREET ANGEL STEVIE NICKS 1994
STREET DREAMS FABOLOUS 2003
STREET FIGHTING YEARS SIMPLE MINDS 1989
STREET JAMS VARIOUS ARTISTS (TELSTAR) 1998
STREET LEGAL BOB DYLAN 1978
STREET LEVEL VARIOUS ARTISTS (RONCO) 1980
STREET LIFE CRUSADERS 1979
STREET LIFE – 20 GREAT HITS BRYAN FERRY & ROXY MUSIC 1986
STREET MACHINE SAMMY HAGAR 1979
STREET MOVES TWENTY 4 SEVEN FEATURING CAPTAIN HOLLYWOOD 1991
STREET PARTY CHAS 'N' DAVE 1995
STREET SOUL VARIOUS ARTISTS (VIRGIN) 1995
STREET SOUNDS 87 VOLUME 2 VARIOUS ARTISTS (STREET SOUNDS) 1987

STREET SOUNDS 88 1 VARIOUS ARTISTS (STREET SOUNDS) 1988
STREET SOUNDS ANTHEMS – VOLUME 1 VARIOUS ARTISTS (STREET SOUNDS) 1987
STREET SOUNDS CRUCIAL ELECTRO VARIOUS ARTISTS (STREET SOUNDS) 1984
STREET SOUNDS CRUCIAL ELECTRO 2 VARIOUS ARTISTS (STREET SOUNDS) 1984
STREET SOUNDS CRUCIAL ELECTRO 3 VARIOUS ARTISTS (STREET SOUNDS) 1987
STREET SOUNDS DANCE MUSIC '87 VARIOUS ARTISTS (STREET SOUNDS) 1987
STREET SOUNDS EDITION 10 VARIOUS ARTISTS (STREET SOUNDS) 1984
STREET SOUNDS EDITION 11 VARIOUS ARTISTS (STREET SOUNDS) 1984
STREET SOUNDS EDITION 12 VARIOUS ARTISTS (STREET SOUNDS) 1985
STREET SOUNDS EDITION 13 VARIOUS ARTISTS (STREET SOUNDS) 1985
STREET SOUNDS EDITION 14 VARIOUS ARTISTS (STREET SOUNDS) 1985
STREET SOUNDS EDITION 15 VARIOUS ARTISTS (STREET SOUNDS) 1985
STREET SOUNDS EDITION 16 VARIOUS ARTISTS (STREET SOUNDS) 1986
STREET SOUNDS EDITION 17 VARIOUS ARTISTS (STREET SOUNDS) 1986
STREET SOUNDS EDITION 18 VARIOUS ARTISTS (STREET SOUNDS) 1986
STREET SOUNDS EDITION 19 VARIOUS ARTISTS (STREET SOUNDS) 1986
STREET SOUNDS EDITION 2 VARIOUS ARTISTS (STREET SOUNDS) 1983
STREET SOUNDS EDITION 20 VARIOUS ARTISTS (STREET SOUNDS) 1987
STREET SOUNDS EDITION 3 VARIOUS ARTISTS (STREET SOUNDS) 1983
STREET SOUNDS EDITION 4 VARIOUS ARTISTS (STREET SOUNDS) 1983
STREET SOUNDS EDITION 5 VARIOUS ARTISTS (STREET SOUNDS) 1983
STREET SOUNDS EDITION 6 VARIOUS ARTISTS (STREET SOUNDS) 1983
STREET SOUNDS EDITION 7 VARIOUS ARTISTS (STREET SOUNDS) 1983
STREET SOUNDS EDITION 8 VARIOUS ARTISTS (STREET SOUNDS) 1984
STREET SOUNDS EDITION 9 VARIOUS ARTISTS (STREET SOUNDS) 1984
STREET SOUNDS ELECTRO 1 VARIOUS ARTISTS (STREET SOUNDS) 1983
STREET SOUNDS ELECTRO 10 VARIOUS ARTISTS (STREET SOUNDS) 1985
STREET SOUNDS ELECTRO 2 VARIOUS ARTISTS (STREET SOUNDS) 1984
STREET SOUNDS ELECTRO 3 VARIOUS ARTISTS (STREET SOUNDS) 1984
STREET SOUNDS ELECTRO 4 VARIOUS ARTISTS (STREET SOUNDS) 1984
STREET SOUNDS ELECTRO 5 VARIOUS ARTISTS (STREET SOUNDS) 1984
STREET SOUNDS ELECTRO 6 VARIOUS ARTISTS (STREET SOUNDS) 1985
STREET SOUNDS ELECTRO 7 VARIOUS ARTISTS (STREET SOUNDS) 1985
STREET SOUNDS ELECTRO 8 VARIOUS ARTISTS (STREET SOUNDS) 1985
STREET SOUNDS ELECTRO 9 VARIOUS ARTISTS (STREET SOUNDS) 1985
STREET SOUNDS HI ENERGY NO 1 VARIOUS ARTISTS (STREET SOUNDS) 1984
STREET SOUNDS HIP HOP 17 VARIOUS ARTISTS (STREET SOUNDS) 1987
STREET SOUNDS HIP HOP 18 VARIOUS ARTISTS (STREET SOUNDS) 1987

STREET SOUNDS HIP HOP 20 VARIOUS ARTISTS (STREET SOUNDS) 1988
STREET SOUNDS HIP HOP 21 VARIOUS ARTISTS (STREET SOUNDS) 1988
STREET SOUNDS HIP HOP ELECTRO 11 VARIOUS ARTISTS (STREET SOUNDS) 1986
STREET SOUNDS HIP HOP ELECTRO 12 VARIOUS ARTISTS (STREET SOUNDS) 1986
STREET SOUNDS HIP HOP ELECTRO 13 VARIOUS ARTISTS (STREET SOUNDS) 1986
STREET SOUNDS HIP HOP ELECTRO 14 VARIOUS ARTISTS (STREET SOUNDS) 1986
STREET SOUNDS HIP HOP ELECTRO 15 VARIOUS ARTISTS (STREET SOUNDS) 1986
STREET SOUNDS HIP HOP ELECTRO 16 VARIOUS ARTISTS (STREET SOUNDS) 1987
STREET SOUNDS N.Y. VS L.A. BEATS VARIOUS ARTISTS (STREET SOUNDS) 1985
STREET SOUNDS UK ELECTRO VARIOUS ARTISTS (STREET SOUNDS) 1984
STREET SURVIVORS LYNYRD SKYNYRD 1977
STREET TALK STEVE PERRY 1984
STREET VIBES VARIOUS ARTISTS (GLOBAL) 1998
STREET VIBES 2 VARIOUS ARTISTS (GLOBAL) 1999
STREET VIBES 3 VARIOUS ARTISTS (GLOBAL) 1999
STREET VIBES 4 VARIOUS ARTISTS (GLOBAL) 2000
STREET VIBES 5 VARIOUS ARTISTS (GLOBAL) 2000
STREET VIBES 6 VARIOUS ARTISTS (BMG) 2000
STREET VIBES 7 VARIOUS ARTISTS (TELSTAR) 2001
STREET VIBES 8 VARIOUS ARTISTS (BMG) 2001
STREETCORE JOE STRUMMER & THE MESCALEROS 2003
STREETNOISE VOLUME 1 VARIOUS ARTISTS (STREET SOUNDS) 1982
STREETS RALPH MCTELL 1975
STREETSCENE VARIOUS ARTISTS (K-TEL) 1982
STREETSOUL GURU'S JAZZMATAZZ 2000
STREISAND SUPERMAN BARBRA STREISAND 1977
STRENGTH ALARM 1985
STRENGTH ENUFF Z'NUFF 1991
STRENGTH THROUGH OI! – VARIOUS ARTISTS (DERAM) 1981
STRICTLY COMMERCIAL – THE BEST OF FRANK ZAPPA FRANK ZAPPA 1995
STRICTLY FOR GROWN UPS PADDY ROBERTS 1959
STRICTLY RAGGA VARIOUS ARTISTS (VITAL SOUNDS) 1993
STRIKES AGAIN ROSE ROYCE 1978
STRING ALONG WITH NAT 'KING' COLE NAT 'KING' COLE 1961
STRING OF HITS SHADOWS 1979
A STRING OF PEARLS PETER SKELLERN 1982
A STRING OF TONY'S HITS TONY BENNETT 1966
STRING SWAY KNIGHTSBRIDGE STRINGS 1960
STRINGS OF SCOTLAND JOHN MASON 1975
STRINGS OF SCOTLAND MISCELLANEOUS 1975
STRIP ADAM ANT 1983
STRIP MINE JAMES 1988
STRIPPED CHRISTINA AGUILERA 2002
STRIPPED ROLLING STONES 1995
STRIVE TO SURVIVE CAUSING LEAST SUFFERING POSSIBLE A FLUX OF PINK INDIANS 1983
STRONG ARM OF THE LAW SAXON 1980
STRONG PERSUADER ROBERT CRAY BAND 1986
STRONGER CLIFF RICHARD 1989
STRONGER THAN PRIDE SADE 1988
STRONGER TOGETHER D-SIDE 2004
THE STUD (OST) FILM SOUNDTRACK 1978
THE STUDENT PRINCE JOHN HANSON 1960
THE STUDENT PRINCE/THE GREAT CARUSO (OST) MARIO LANZA 1958
THE STUDENT PRINCE/THE VAGABOND KING JOHN HANSON 1961
STUDIO TWO CLASSICS VARIOUS ARTISTS (STUDIO TWO) 1971
STUMBLE INTO GRACE EMMYLOU HARRIS 2003
THE STUN (CARROTT TELLS ALL) JASPER CARROTT 1983
STUNT BARENAKED LADIES 1999

STUPID STUPID STUPID BLACK GRAPE 1997
STUPIDITY DR. FEELGOOD 1976
STUTTER JAMES 1986
THE STYLE COUNCIL COLLECTION STYLE COUNCIL 1996
SU SU POLLARD 1986
SUBHUMAN RACE SKID ROW 1995
SUBJECT TO CHANGE VANESSA-MAE 2001
SUBSTANCE NEW ORDER 1987
SUBSTANCE NEW ORDER 1993
SUDDENLY BILLY OCEAN 1984
SUE FRAZIER CHORUS 1989
SUEDE SUEDE 1993
SUGAR AND SPICE SEARCHERS 1963
SUGAR HITS! – VARIOUS ARTISTS (POLYGRAM) 1997
SUGAR TAX ORCHESTRAL MANOEUVRES IN THE DARK
    1991
SUICIDE PACT – YOU FIRST THERAPY? 1999
SUITS FISH 1994
SULK ASSOCIATES 1982
SULTANS OF SWING – THE VERY BEST OF DIRE STRAITS
    DIRE STRAITS 1998
SUM AND SUBSTANCE MISSION 1994
SUMDAY GRANDADDY 2003
SUMMER BREEZE VARIOUS ARTISTS (COLUMBIA) 2000
SUMMER CHART PARTY VARIOUS ARTISTS (TRAX) 1990
SUMMER COUNTRY VARIOUS ARTISTS (TELSTAR) 2002
SUMMER CRUISING VARIOUS ARTISTS (K-TEL) 1976
SUMMER DANCE '98 VARIOUS ARTISTS (COLUMBIA) 1998
SUMMER DANCE ANTHEMS 99 VARIOUS ARTISTS
    (TELSTAR) 1999
SUMMER DANCE PARTY VARIOUS ARTISTS (GLOBAL) 1995
SUMMER DAYS (AND SUMMER NIGHTS) BEACH BOYS
    1966
SUMMER DAYS, BOOGIE NIGHTS – 16 TRACKS VARIOUS
    ARTISTS (PORTRAIT) 1986
SUMMER DREAMS – 28 CLASSIC TRACKS BEACH BOYS
    1990
SUMMER GROOVE VARIOUS ARTISTS (WARNER
    BROTHERS) 1997
SUMMER HAPPENING JAMES LAST 1971
SUMMER HOLIDAY (OST) CLIFF RICHARD & THE SHADOWS
    1963
SUMMER OF '78 BARRY MANILOW 1996
THE SUMMER OF LOVE VARIOUS ARTISTS (DINO) 1990
THE SUMMER OF LOVE GOES ON – SIXTIES VARIOUS
    ARTISTS (POLYGRAM) 1998
THE SUMMER OF NINETY SIX – UP YER RONSON VARIOUS
    ARTISTS (HI-LIFE) 1996
SUMMER SWING VARIOUS ARTISTS (VIRGIN) 1995
SUMMER VYBES VARIOUS ARTISTS (POLYGRAM) 1996
SUMMERTEETH WILCO 1999
SUMMERTIME VARIOUS ARTISTS (UNIVERSAL) 2000
SUMMERTIME SOUL VARIOUS ARTISTS (POLYGRAM) 1995
THE SUMMIT VARIOUS ARTISTS (K-TEL) 1980
THE SUN IS OFTEN OUT LONGPIGS 1996
THE SUN IS SHINING BOB MARLEY VS FUNKSTAR DELUXE
    1999
THE SUN YEARS ELVIS PRESLEY 1977
SUNBURN (OST) FILM SOUNDTRACK 1980
SUNBURST FINISH BE-BOP DELUXE 1976
SUNDANCE – CHAPTER ONE VARIOUS ARTISTS (TELSTAR)
    1998
SUNDAY 8PM FAITHLESS 1998
SUNDEW PARIS ANGELS 1991
SUNDISSENTIAL – HARDER FASTER VARIOUS ARTISTS
    (SUNDISSENTIAL) 2002
SUNDOWN GORDON LIGHTFOOT 1974
SUNDOWN S CLUB 8 2003
SUNFLOWER BEACH BOYS 1970
SUNLIGHT HERBIE HANCOCK 1978
SUNMACHINE DARIO G 1998
SUNNY AFTERNOON KINKS 1967
SUNNY AFTERNOON VARIOUS ARTISTS (IMPRESSION)
    1983
SUNNY AFTERNOON VOLUME TWO VARIOUS ARTISTS
    (IMPRESSION) 1984

SUNNY AFTERNOONS VARIOUS ARTISTS (POLYGRAM)
    1995
SUNSET BOULEVARD ORIGINAL LONDON STAGE CAST
    SOUNDTRACK 1993
SUNSET IBIZA VARIOUS ARTISTS (UNIVERSAL) 2001
SUNSETS ON EMPIRE FISH 1997
SUNSHINE S CLUB 7 2001
SUNSHINE (OST) FILM SOUNDTRACK 1974
SUNSHINE MIX VARIOUS ARTISTS (STYLUS) 1989
THE SUNSHINE OF YOUR SMILE MIKE BERRY 1981
SUNSHINE ON LEITH PROCLAIMERS 1988
SUNSHINE SUPERMAN DONOVAN 1967
SUPA FUNKY VARIOUS ARTISTS (UNIVERSAL) 2002
SUPER HITS 1 & 2 VARIOUS ARTISTS (RONCO) 1981
SUPER 60'S VARIOUS ARTISTS (VIRGIN) 2003
SUPER TROUPER ABBA 1980
SUPERBAD VARIOUS ARTISTS (WARNER BROTHERS) 2004
SUPERCHARGED VARIOUS ARTISTS (UNIVERSAL) 2002
SUPERCHARGER MACHINE HEAD 2001
SUPERCHART '83 VARIOUS ARTISTS (TELSTAR) 1983
SUPERFLY (OST) CURTIS MAYFIELD 1973
SUPERFUNK VARIOUS ARTISTS (VIRGIN) 1994
SUPERGRASS SUPERGRASS 1999
SUPERGRASS IS 10 – THE BEST OF 94–04 SUPERGRASS
    2004
SUPERGROUPS VARIOUS ARTISTS (RONCO) 1977
SUPERNATURAL DES'REE 1998
SUPERNATURAL SANTANA 1999
SUPERNATURAL FEELING JAMES TAYLOR QUARTET 1993
SUPERNATURE CERRONE 1978
SUPERSONIC TELEVISION COMPILATION 1975
SUPERSTITION SIOUXSIE & THE BANSHEES 1991
SUPERUNKNOWN SOUNDGARDEN 1994
SUPERWOMAN VARIOUS ARTISTS (VIRGIN) 1998
SUPPOSED FORMER INFATUATION JUNKIE ALANIS
    MORISSETTE 1998
SUPREMES A GO GO SUPREMES 1966
THE SUPREMES SING MOTOWN SUPREMES 1967
THE SUPREMES SING RODGERS AND HART SUPREMES
    1967
SUR LA MER MOODY BLUES 1988
SURFACING SARAH MCLACHLAN 1998
SURFER GIRL BEACH BOYS 1967
SURFIN' USA BEACH BOYS 1965
SURF'S UP BEACH BOYS 1971
SURPRISE SURPRISE MEZZOFORTE 1983
SURRENDER CHEMICAL BROTHERS 1999
SURVIVAL BOB MARLEY & THE WAILERS 1979
SURVIVOR DESTINY'S CHILD 2001
SUZANNE VEGA SUZANNE VEGA 1985
SUZI QUATRO SUZI QUATRO 1973
SUZI QUATRO'S GREATEST HITS SUZI QUATRO 1980
SWAGGER BLUE AEROPLANES 1990
SWAGGER GUN 1994
SWALLOW THIS LIVE POISON 1991
SWAMP OPHELIA INDIGO GIRLS 1994
SWANSONG CARCASS 1996
SWEET BABY JAMES JAMES TAYLOR 1970
SWEET DANNY WILSON DANNY WILSON 1991
SWEET DREAMS PATSY CLINE 1991
SWEET DREAMS (ARE MADE OF THIS) EURYTHMICS 1983
SWEET FANNY ADAMS SWEET 1974
SWEET FREEDOM URIAH HEEP 1973
SWEET FREEDOM: BEST OF MICHAEL MCDONALD MICHAEL
    MCDONALD 1986
SWEET INSPIRATION CILLA BLACK 1970
SWEET INSPIRATION INSPIRATIONAL CHOIR 1986
THE SWEET KEEPER TANITA TIKARAM 1990
SWEET KISSES JESSICA SIMPSON 2000
SWEET LOVE – THE VERY BEST OF ANITA BAKER 2002
SWEET SIXTEEN – IT'S IT'S... SWEET HITS SWEET 1984
SWEET SOUL HARMONIES VARIOUS ARTISTS (VIRGIN)
    1994
SWEET SOUL HARMONIES 2 VARIOUS ARTISTS (VIRGIN)
    1994
SWEET SURRENDER JOHNNY MATHIS 1977

SWEET THINGS GEORGIE FAME 1966
SWEETS FROM A STRANGER SQUEEZE 1982
SWEPT JULIA FORDHAM 1991
SWEPT AWAY DIANA ROSS 1984
SWIMMER BIG DISH 1986
SWING BATTA SWING K7 1994
SWING CLASSICS VARIOUS ARTISTS (WARNER BROTHERS)
    2003
SWING EASY FRANK SINATRA 1960
SWING HITS VARIOUS ARTISTS (DINO) 1992
SWING MIX 96 VARIOUS ARTISTS (TELSTAR) 1996
THE SWING OF DELIGHT CARLOS SANTANA 1980
SWING SOFTLY JOHNNY MATHIS 1959
SWING STREET BARRY MANILOW 1988
SWING WHEN YOU'RE WINNING ROBBIE WILLIAMS 2001
A SWINGIN' AFFAIR! FRANK SINATRA 1957
SWINGIN' WITH RAYMOND CHUMBAWAMBA 1995
SWINGIN' WITH THE BIG BAND BIG BAND 2002
THE SWINGING CITY SPINNERS 1971
SWINGING SAFARI BERT KAEMPFERT & HIS ORCHESTRA
    1966
SWITCHED ON VARIOUS ARTISTS (TELSTAR) 2000
SWITCHED ON SWING KINGS OF SWING ORCHESTRA
    1982
SWOON PREFAB SPROUT 1984
SWORDFISHTROMBONE TOM WAITS 1983
SYD LAWRENCE WITH THE GLENN MILLER SOUND SYD
    LAWRENCE 1971
SYMBOLS PRINCE & THE NEW POWER GENERATION 1992
SYMPHONIC ROCK ROYAL PHILHARMONIC ORCHESTRA
    2004
SYMPHONIC ROCK WITH THE VIENNA SYMPHONY
    ORCHESTRA VIENNA SYMPHONY ORCHESTRA 1987
SYMPHONIES FOR THE SEVENTIES WALDO DE LOS RIOS
    1971
SYMPHONY OR DAMN TERENCE TRENT D'ARBY 1993
SYNCHRO SYSTEM KING SUNNY ADE & HIS AFRICAN
    BEATS 1983
SYNCHRONICITY POLICE 1983
SYNKRONIZED JAMIROQUAI 1999
SYNTHESIZER 2 PROJECT D 1990
THE SYNTHESIZER ALBUM PROJECT D 1990
SYNTHESIZER GOLD ED STARINK 1993
SYNTHESIZER GREATEST ED STARINK 1990
T. REX T. REX 1971
T. REX IN CONCERT T. REX 1981
T.V. SKY YOUNG GODS 1992
TADPOLES BONZO DOG DOO-DAH BAND 1969
TAILS LISA LOEB & NINE STORIES 1995
TAJA SEVELLE TAJA SEVELLE 1988
TAKE A BREAK VARIOUS ARTISTS (COLUMBIA) 1996
TAKE A LOOK NATALIE COLE 1993
TAKE A LOOK IN THE MIRROR KORN 2003
TAKE A LOOK OVER YOUR SHOULDER (REALITY) WARREN G
    1997
TAKE A PAIR OF SPARKLING EYES JOSEF LOCKE 1992
TAKE DIS CREDIT TO THE NATION 1994
TAKE FAT AND PARTY ROY 'CHUBBY' BROWN 1995
TAKE GOOD CARE OF MY BABY BOBBY VEE 1962
TAKE GOOD CARE OF YOURSELF THREE DEGREES 1975
TAKE IT EASY WALKER BROTHERS 1965
TAKE IT HOME B.B. KING 1979
TAKE IT TO HEART MICHAEL MCDONALD 1990
TAKE ME HIGH (OST) CLIFF RICHARD 1974
TAKE ME HIGHER DIANA ROSS 1995
TAKE ME TO GOD JAH WOBBLE'S INVADERS OF THE HEART
    1994
TAKE MY TIME SHEENA EASTON 1981
TAKE OFF YOUR PANTS AND JACKET BLINK 182 2001
TAKE ONE! – SHAKIN' STEVENS 1980
TAKE THAT AND PARTY TAKE THAT 1992
TAKE THE HEAT OFF ME BONEY M 1977
TAKE THEM ON ON YOUR OWN BLACK REBEL
    MOTORCYCLE CLUB 2003
TAKE TWO DIANE SOLOMON 1975
TAKE TWO ROBSON & JEROME 1996

TAKIN' IT TO THE STREETS DOOBIE BROTHERS 1976
TAKING ON THE WORLD GUN 1989
TALES FROM NEW YORK – THE VERY BEST OF SIMON & GARFUNKEL SIMON & GARFUNKEL 2000
TALES FROM THE CITY TELEVISION COMPILATION 1993
TALES FROM TOPOGRAPHIC OCEANS YES 1973
TALES OF A LIBRARIAN TORI AMOS 2003
TALES OF MYSTERY AND IMAGINATION ALAN PARSONS PROJECT 1976
TALK YES 1994
TALK IS CHEAP KEITH RICHARDS 1988
TALK OF THE DEVIL OZZY OSBOURNE 1982
TALK ON CORNERS CORRS 1997
TALK TALK TALK PSYCHEDELIC FURS 1981
TALKIE WALKIE AIR 2004
TALKIN LOUD TWO VARIOUS ARTISTS (TALKIN LOUD) 1993
TALKING BACK TO THE NIGHT STEVE WINWOOD 1982
TALKING BOOK STEVIE WONDER 1973
TALKING HEADS '77 TALKING HEADS 1978
TALKING TIMBUKTU ALI FARKA TOURE & RY COODER 1994
TALKING WITH THE TAXMAN ABOUT POETRY BILLY BRAGG 1986
TALLULAH GO-BETWEENS 1987
TAMING THE TIGER JONI MITCHELL 1998
TAMLA MOTOWN HITS VOLUME 5 VARIOUS ARTISTS (MOTOWN) 1967
TAMLA MOTOWN HITS VOLUME 6 VARIOUS ARTISTS (MOTOWN) 1968
TANGO JULIO IGLESIAS 1996
TANGO IN THE NIGHT FLEETWOOD MAC 1987
TANGRAM TANGERINE DREAM 1980
TANTO TEMPO BEBEL GILBERTO 2002
TANX T. REX 1973
TAO RICK SPRINGFIELD 1985
TAP ROOT MANUSCRIPT NEIL DIAMOND 1971
TAPESTRY CAROLE KING 1971
TAPESTRY DON MCLEAN 1972
A TAPESTRY OF DREAMS CHARLES AZNAVOUR 1974
THE TARANTINO COLLECTION VARIOUS ARTISTS (MCA) 1996
TARANTULA RIDE 1996
TARKUS EMERSON, LAKE & PALMER 1971
TASTE – LIVE AT THE ISLE OF WIGHT TASTE 1972
A TASTE OF HONEY MR ACKER BILK 1963
TASTY KELIS 2004
TATTOO RORY GALLAGHER 1973
TATTOO YOU ROLLING STONES 1981
TATTOOED BEAT MESSIAH ZODIAC MINDWARP & THE LOVE REACTION 1988
TATTOOED MILLIONAIRE BRUCE DICKINSON 1990
TAXI BRYAN FERRY 1993
TAXI FOR THESE ANIMAL MEN THESE ANIMAL MEN 1995
TEA FOR THE TILLERMAN CAT STEVENS 1970
TEACH THE WORLD TO LAUGH BARRON KNIGHTS 1979
TEAR DOWN THESE WALLS BILLY OCEAN 1988
TEARDROPS VARIOUS ARTISTS (RITZ) 1983
TEARS AND LAUGHTER JOHNNY MATHIS 1980
TEARS OF HAPPINESS KEN DODD 1965
TEARS OF STONE CHIEFTAINS 1999
TEARS ROLL DOWN (GREATEST HITS 1982–1992) TEARS FOR FEARS 1992
TEASE ME CHAKA DEMUS & PLIERS 1993
TEASER AND THE FIRECAT CAT STEVENS 1971
TEASES AND DARES KIM WILDE 1984
TECHNICAL ECSTASY BLACK SABBATH 1976
TECHNIQUE NEW ORDER 1989
TECHNO NIGHTS AMBIENT DAWN VARIOUS ARTISTS (EMI) 1995
TECHNOHEDZ – 20 FIRESTARTIN' TECHNO ANTHEMS VARIOUS ARTISTS (TELSTAR) 1996
TECHNOSTATE VARIOUS ARTISTS (COOKIE JAR) 1992
TED NUGENT TED NUGENT 1976
TEENAGE DEPRESSION EDDIE & THE HOT RODS 1976
TEENAGE DRUG SULTANS OF PING 1994
TEENAGE KICKS VARIOUS ARTISTS (POLYGRAM) 1995

TEENAGE KICKS VARIOUS ARTISTS (UNIVERSAL) 2002
TEENAGE KICKS – THE BEST OF UNDERTONES 2003
TEENAGE MUTANT NINJA TURTLES (OST) FILM SOUNDTRACK 1990
TEENAGE WARNING ANGELIC UPSTARTS 1979
TEENAGER OF THE YEAR FRANK BLACK 1994
TEENDREEM VARIOUS ARTISTS (WARNER BROTHERS) 2001
TELEKON GARY NUMAN 1980
TELL GOD I'M HERE HURRAH! 1987
TELL IT TO MY HEART TAYLOR DAYNE 1988
TELL ME IT'S NOT TRUE 'FROM THE MUSICAL BLOOD BROTHERS' – BARBARA DICKSON 1983
TELL ME ON A SUNDAY MARTI WEBB 1980
TELL ME ON A SUNDAY DENISE VAN OUTEN 2003
TELL US THE TRUTH SHAM 69 1978
TELLIN' STORIES CHARLATANS 1997
TELLY TELLY SAVALAS 1975
TELLYHITS – 16 TOP TV THEMES TELEVISION COMPILATION 1985
TELLYHITS 2 – 16 TOP TV THEMES TELEVISION COMPILATION 1986
TEMPERAMENTAL EVERYTHING BUT THE GIRL 1999
TEMPERANCE SEVEN 1961 TEMPERANCE SEVEN 1961
TEMPERANCE SEVEN PLUS ONE TEMPERANCE SEVEN 1961
TEMPTATION VARIOUS ARTISTS (QUALITY PRICE MUSIC) 1992
TEMPTATIONS/FOUR TOPS: AT THEIR BEST VARIOUS ARTISTS (UNIVERSAL) 2002
TEMPTATIONS GREATEST HITS TEMPTATIONS 1967
THE TEMPTATIONS LIVE! – TEMPTATIONS 1967
TEMPTATIONS WITH A LOT OF SOUL TEMPTATIONS 1967
TEMPTED VARIOUS ARTISTS (POLYGRAM) 1993
10 STRANGLERS 1990
TEN PEARL JAM 1992
10 WET WET WET 1997
10 LL COOL J 2002
10 CC 10 CC 1973
TEN GOOD REASONS JASON DONOVAN 1989
TEN MORE TURNIPS FROM THE TIP IAN DURY & THE BLOCKHEADS 2002
TEN NEW SONGS LEONARD COHEN 2001
TEN SHORT SONGS ABOUT LOVE GARY CLARK 1993
TEN SUMMONER'S TALES STING 1993
10,000 HZ LEGEND AIR 2001
10 TO 23 JOSE FELICIANO 1970
TEN YEARS NON STOP JUBILEE JAMES LAST 1975
10 YEARS OF HITS – RADIO ONE VARIOUS ARTISTS (SUPER BEEB) 1977
TEN YEARS TOGETHER PETER, PAUL & MARY 1970
TENACIOUS D TENACIOUS D 2002
TENDER LOVE – 17 ROMANTIC LOVE SONGS VARIOUS ARTISTS (EMI) 1992
TENDER PREY NICK CAVE & THE BAD SEEDS 1988
TENDERLY GEORGE BENSON 1989
TENEMENT SYMPHONY MARC ALMOND 1991
TENNESSEE MOON (THE NASHVILLE COLLECTION) NEIL DIAMOND 1996
TENNIS CHRIS REA 1980
TERENCE TRENT D'ARBY'S VIBRATOR TERENCE TRENT D'ARBY 1995
TERMINATOR 2 (OST) BRAD FIEDEL 1991
TERRAPIN STATION GRATEFUL DEAD 1977
TERROR TWILIGHT PAVEMENT 1999
TEST FOR ECHO RUSH 1996
TESTAMENT '93 INNER CITY 1993
TESTIFY PHIL COLLINS 2002
TESTIMONY DANA GLOVER 2003
TEXAS FEVER ORANGE JUICE 1984
THA DOGGFATHER SNOOP DOGGY DOGG 1996
THA LAST MEAL SNOOP DOGG 2001
THANK CHRIST FOR THE BOMB GROUNDHOGS 1970
THANK GOD IT'S FRIDAY (OST) FILM SOUNDTRACK 1978
THANK YOU DURAN DURAN 1995
THANK YOU JAMELIA 2003

THANK YOU AND GOODNIGHT IT BITES 1991
THANK YOU BABY STYLISTICS 1975
THANK YOU FOR THE MUSIC ABBA 1983
THANK YOU FOR THE YEARS SHIRLEY BASSEY 2003
THANK YOU VERY MUCH – REUNION CONCERT AT THE LONDON PALLADIUM CLIFF RICHARD & THE SHADOWS 1979
THANKFUL KELLY CLARKSON 2003
THANKS BUT I'LL EAT IT HERE LOWELL GEORGE 1979
THAT ALBUM BY OCEANIC OCEANIC 1992
THAT LOVING FEELING VINCE HILL 1978
THAT LOVING FEELING VARIOUS ARTISTS (DINO) 1989
THAT LOVING FEELING VOLUME 2 VARIOUS ARTISTS (DINO) 1990
THAT LOVING FEELING VOLUME 3 VARIOUS ARTISTS (DINO) 1990
THAT LOVING FEELING VOLUME 4 VARIOUS ARTISTS (DINO) 1991
THAT LOVING FEELING VOLUME 5 VARIOUS ARTISTS (DINO) 1991
THAT LOVING FEELING VOLUME VI VARIOUS ARTISTS (DINO) 1993
THAT LOVING FEELING VOLUME VII VARIOUS ARTISTS (DINO) 1994
THAT OLE DEVIL CALLED LOVE VARIOUS ARTISTS (UNIVERSAL) 2000
THAT SUMMER (OST) FILM SOUNDTRACK 1979
THAT WAS THE WEEK THAT WAS TELEVISION SOUNDTRACK 1963
THAT WHAT IS NOT PUBLIC IMAGE LTD 1992
THAT WONDERFUL SOUND OF LENA MARTELL LENA MARTELL 1974
THAT'LL BE THE DAY BUDDY HOLLY & THE CRICKETS 1961
THAT'LL BE THE DAY (OST) FILM SOUNDTRACK 1973
THAT'S ALL BOBBY DARIN 1960
THAT'S CHRISTMAS VARIOUS ARTISTS (EMI) 1994
THAT'S CHRISTMAS VARIOUS ARTISTS (EMI) 1995
THAT'S COUNTRY VARIOUS ARTISTS (EMI) 1995
THAT'S LIFE FRANK SINATRA 1967
THAT'S LIFE SHAM 69 1978
THAT'S RIGHT GEORGE BENSON 1996
THAT'S ROCK 'N' ROLL VARIOUS ARTISTS (EMI) 1995
THAT'S THE WAY IT IS (OST) ELVIS PRESLEY 1971
THAT'S WHAT FRIENDS ARE FOR JOHNNY MATHIS & DENIECE WILLIAMS 1978
THAT'S WHAT LIFE IS ALL ABOUT BING CROSBY 1975
THEATRE OF PAIN MOTLEY CRUE 1985
THEAUDIENCE THEAUDIENCE 1998
THEIR FIRST LP SPENCER DAVIS GROUP 1966
THEIR GREATEST HITS FOUR TOPS 1990
THEIR GREATEST HITS HOT CHOCOLATE 1993
THEIR GREATEST HITS – THE RECORD BEE GEES 2001
THEIR GREATEST HITS 1971–1975 EAGLES 1976
THEIR SATANIC MAJESTIES REQUEST ROLLING STONES 1967
THEM OR US FRANK ZAPPA 1984
THEMENINBLACK STRANGLERS 1981
THEMES VARIOUS ARTISTS (K-TEL) 1981
THEMES VANGELIS 1989
THE THEMES ALBUM VARIOUS ARTISTS (K-TEL) 1984
THEMES AND DREAMS SHADOWS 1991
THEMES AND DREAMS VARIOUS ARTISTS (GLOBAL) 1995
THEN AND NOW DAVID CASSIDY 2001
THEN AND NOW WHO 2004
THEN CAME ROCK 'N' ROLL VARIOUS ARTISTS (EMI) 1984
THEN PLAY ON FLEETWOOD MAC 1969
THERE AND BACK JEFF BECK 1980
THERE GOES RHYMIN' SIMON PAUL SIMON 1973
THERE IS NOTHING LEFT TO LOSE FOO FIGHTERS 1999
THERE IS ONLY ONE ROY ORBISON ROY ORBISON 1965
THERE IT IS 911 1999
THERE MUST BE A WAY FRANKIE VAUGHAN 1967
THERE YOU'LL BE FAITH HILL 2001
THERE'S A POISON GOIN' ON... – PUBLIC ENEMY 1999
THERE'S A RIOT GOIN' ON SLY & THE FAMILY STONE 1972
THERE'S NOTHING LIKE THIS OMAR 1990

THERE'S ONE IN EVERY CROWD ERIC CLAPTON 1975
THERE'S SOMETHING GOING ON BABYBIRD 1998
THERE'S THE RUB WISHBONE ASH 1974
THERE'S TWO KINDS OF MUSIC: ROCK 'N' ROLL! – SHAKIN' STEVENS 1990
THESE ARE MY MOUNTAINS ALEXANDER BROTHERS 1966
THESE ARE MY SONGS PETULA CLARK 1967
THESE ARE MY SONGS MOIRA ANDERSON 1970
THESE ARE SPECIAL TIMES CELINE DION 1998
THESE DAYS BON JOVI 1995
THESE DREAMS – GREATEST HITS HEART 1997
THESE FOOLISH THINGS BRYAN FERRY 1973
THEY DON'T KNOW SO SOLID CREW 2001
THEY NEVER SAW ME COMING TQ 1999
THEY SAID IT COULDN'T BE DONE GRANDMASTER FLASH 1985
THICK AS A BRICK JETHRO TULL 1972
THIEF (OST) TANGERINE DREAM 1981
THE THIEVING MAGPIE MARILLION 1988
THIN ICE – THE FIRST STEP VARIOUS ARTISTS (TELSTAR) 1991
THIN ICE 2 – THE SECOND SHIVER VARIOUS ARTISTS (TELSTAR) 1991
A THING CALLED LOVE JOHNNY CASH 1972
THINGS TO MAKE AND DO MOLOKO 2000
THINK ON YOUR FEET JAIMESON 2004
THINK TANK BLUR 2003
THINKING ABOUT MYSELF COSMIC BABY 1994
THINKING IT OVER LIBERTY X 2002
THINKING OF YOU… – VARIOUS ARTISTS (COLUMBIA) 1991
THIRD SOFT MACHINE 1970
THE THIRD CHAPTER VARIOUS ARTISTS (XL RECORDINGS) 1992
THIRD DEGREE 9 BELOW ZERO 1982
THIRD STAGE BOSTON 1986
THIRSTY WORK STATUS QUO 1994
THIRTEEN TEENAGE FANCLUB 1993
13 BLUR 1999
13 SMASH HITS TOM JONES 1967
THIRTEEN TALES FROM URBAN BOHEMIA DANDY WARHOLS 2000
THIRTEENTH STEP A PERFECT CIRCLE 2003
30 GOLDEN GREATS GEORGE MITCHELL MINSTRELS WITH THE JOE LOSS ORCHESTRA 1977
30 GREATEST GLADYS KNIGHT & THE PIPS 1977
30 SMASH HITS OF THE WAR YEARS BAND & CHORUS OF HER MAJESTY'S GUARDS DIVISION 1975
30 SOMETHING CARTER – THE UNSTOPPABLE SEX MACHINE 1991
THIRTY THOUSAND FEET OVER CHINA PASSIONS 1981
THIRTY THREE AND A THIRD GEORGE HARRISON 1976
33 REVOLUTIONS PER MINUTE MARXMAN 1993
32 MINUTES AND 17 SECONDS CLIFF RICHARD & THE SHADOWS 1962
32 ONES ON ONE – RADIO 1'S 25TH ANNIVERSARY VARIOUS ARTISTS (CONNOISSEUR COLLECTION) 1992
30 YEARS OF MAXIMUM R&B WHO 1994
THIS ARE TWO TONE VARIOUS ARTISTS (2 TONE) 1983
THIS DESERT LIFE COUNTING CROWS 1999
THIS FILM'S CRAP, LET'S SLASH THE SEATS DAVID HOLMES 1995
THIS FIRE PAULA COLE 1997
THIS IS … CLUB NATION VARIOUS ARTISTS (BEECHWOOD MUSIC) 1997
THIS IS … CLUB NATION 2 VARIOUS ARTISTS (BEECHWOOD MUSIC) 1998
THIS IS … HOUSE VARIOUS ARTISTS (BEECHWOOD MUSIC) 1996
THIS IS … IBIZA VARIOUS ARTISTS (BEECHWOOD MUSIC) 1997
THIS IS … IBIZA 2000 VARIOUS ARTISTS (BEECHWOOD MUSIC) 1999
THIS IS … IBIZA 98 VARIOUS ARTISTS (BEECHWOOD MUSIC) 1998

THIS IS … R&B VARIOUS ARTISTS (BEECHWOOD MUSIC) 1999
THIS IS … SPEED GARAGE VARIOUS ARTISTS (BEECHWOOD MUSIC) 1998
THIS IS … SWING VARIOUS ARTISTS (BEECHWOOD MUSIC) 1996
THIS IS … TRANCE VARIOUS ARTISTS (BEECHWOOD MUSIC) 1999
THIS IS BIG AUDIO DYNAMITE BIG AUDIO DYNAMITE 1985
THIS IS CHAQUITO CHAQUITO & QUEDO BRASS 1968
THIS IS CULT FICTION VARIOUS ARTISTS (VIRGIN) 1995
THIS IS DARIN BOBBY DARIN 1960
THIS IS DESMOND DEKKER DESMOND DEKKER 1969
THIS IS ELVIS PRESLEY (OST) ELVIS PRESLEY 1981
THIS IS ENNIO MORRICONE ENNIO MORRICONE 1981
THIS IS FRANK SINATRA 1953–1957 FRANK SINATRA 1995
THIS IS GARAGE VARIOUS ARTISTS (COOLTEMPO) 1989
THIS IS HANCOCK TONY HANCOCK 1960
THIS IS HANCOCK TONY HANCOCK 1963
THIS IS HARDCORE PULP 1998
THIS IS HOW WE DO IT MONTELL JORDAN 1995
THIS IS IT VARIOUS ARTISTS (CBS) 1979
THIS IS JAMES LAST JAMES LAST 1967
THIS IS MANUEL MANUEL & THE MUSIC OF THE MOUNTAINS 1971
THIS IS ME… THEN JENNIFER LOPEZ 2002
THIS IS MY LIFE – THE GREATEST HITS SHIRLEY BASSEY 2000
THIS IS MY TRUTH TELL ME YOURS MANIC STREET PREACHERS 1998
THIS IS NIECEY DENIECE WILLIAMS 1977
THIS IS NOIZE VARIOUS ARTISTS (COLUMBIA) 1999
THIS IS NOT A LOVE SONG OMAR 1997
THIS IS NOT A TEST MISSY ELLIOTT 2003
THIS IS OUR ART SOUP DRAGONS 1988
THIS IS POURCEL FRANK POURCEL 1971
THIS IS SKA VARIOUS ARTISTS (TELSTAR) 1989
THIS IS SINATRA! FRANK SINATRA 1957
THIS IS SINATRA (VOLUME 2) FRANK SINATRA 1958
THIS IS SOUL VARIOUS ARTISTS (ATLANTIC) 1969
THIS IS SOUL VARIOUS ARTISTS (ATLANTIC) 1985
THIS IS THE DAY… THIS IS THE HOUR… THIS IS THIS? – POP WILL EAT ITSELF 1989
THIS IS THE LIFE MATT MONRO 1966
THIS IS THE MODERN WORLD JAM 1977
THIS IS THE MOMENT ADAM WATKISS 2001
THIS IS THE MOMENT DONNY OSMOND 2001
THIS IS THE MOODY BLUES MOODY BLUES 1974
THIS IS THE REMIX DESTINY'S CHILD 2002
THIS IS THE RETURN OF CULT FICTION VARIOUS ARTISTS (VIRGIN) 1996
THIS IS THE SEA WATERBOYS 1985
THIS IS THE SEA WATERBOYS 2001
THIS IS THE STORY PROCLAIMERS 1987
THIS IS THE WORLD RIVER CITY PEOPLE 1991
THIS IS TOM JONES TOM JONES 1969
THIS IS TONGUE 'N' CHEEK TONGUE 'N' CHEEK 1990
THIS IS VAL DOONICAN VAL DOONICAN 1971
THIS IS WHAT YOU WANT… THIS IS WHAT YOU GET PUBLIC IMAGE LTD 1984
THIS IS WHERE I CAME IN BEE GEES 2001
THIS IS… TRANCELIFE VARIOUS ARTISTS (BEECHWOOD MUSIC) 2000
THIS KIND OF LOVE PHIL FEARON & GALAXY 1985
THIS LAST NIGHT IN SODOM SOFT CELL 1984
THIS LEFT FEELS RIGHT BON JOVI 2003
THIS MAN ALONE EDWARD WOODWARD 1970
THIS NATION'S SAVING GRACE FALL 1985
THIS NOTE'S FOR YOU NEIL YOUNG & THE BLUE NOTES 1988
THIS OLD HEART OF MINE ISLEY BROTHERS 1968
THIS OLE HOUSE SHAKIN' STEVENS 1981
THIS SHOULD MOVE YA MANTRONIX 1990
THIS STRANGE ENGINE MARILLION 1997

THIS THING CALLED LOVE – THE GREATEST HITS OF ALEXANDER O'NEAL ALEXANDER O'NEAL 1992
THIS TIME ENGLAND WORLD CUP SQUAD 1982
THIS TIME AROUND HANSON 2000
THIS TIME I'M SWINGING DEAN MARTIN 1961
THIS TIME IT'S PERSONAL MICHAEL BALL 2000
THIS TIME THE FIRST FOUR YEARS CULTURE CLUB 1987
THIS WAS JETHRO TULL 1968
THIS WAY JEWEL 2002
THIS WAY UP CHRIS DE BURGH 1994
THIS WORLD AND BODY MARION 1996
THIS YEAR IN IBIZA VARIOUS ARTISTS (WARNER BROTHERS) 1999
THIS YEAR'S LOVE (WILL LAST FOREVER) XXX VARIOUS ARTISTS (SONY) 1996
THIS YEAR'S LOVE IS FOREVER VARIOUS ARTISTS (SONY) 1995
THIS YEAR'S MODEL ELVIS COSTELLO 1978
THOMPSON TWINS – THE GREATEST HITS THOMPSON TWINS 1990
THE THORNS THORNS 2003
THOROUGHLY MODERN MILLIE (OST) FILM SOUNDTRACK 1967
THOUGHT 'YA KNEW CE CE PENISTON 1994
THOUGHTS OF HOME DANIEL O'DONNELL 1989
THOUGHTS OF LOVE SHIRLEY BASSEY 1976
A THOUSAND LEAVES SONIC YOUTH 1998
A THOUSAND VOLTS OF HOLT JOHN HOLT 1975
THRAK KING CRIMSON 1995
3 SOULFLY 2002
3 CAR GARAGE – INDIE RECORDINGS 95–96 HANSON 1998
THREE SUGABABES 2003
THREE CHORD OPERA NEIL DIAMOND 2001
3D THREE DEGREES 1979
3D TLC 2002
THREE DEGREES THREE DEGREES 1974
THREE DOLLAR BILL Y'ALL LIMP BIZKIT 2000
THE THREE E.P.'S BETA BAND 1998
3 FEET HIGH AND RISING DE LA SOUL 1989
THREE HEARTS IN THE HAPPY ENDING MACHINE DARYL HALL 1986
THREE IMAGINARY BOYS CURE 1979
THREE LIGHT YEARS ELECTRIC LIGHT ORCHESTRA 1979
3LW 3LW 2001
THREE MINUTE HEROES VARIOUS ARTISTS (VIRGIN) 1992
THREE OF A PERFECT PAIR KING CRIMSON 1984
THREE SIDES LIVE GENESIS 1982
THREE SNAKES AND ONE CHARM BLACK CROWES 1996
THREE STEPS TO HEAVEN – ROCK 'N' ROLL LEGENDS VARIOUS ARTISTS (QUALITY PRICE MUSIC) 1992
THE THREE TENORS CHRISTMAS CARRERAS/DOMINGO/PAVAROTTI FEATURING MEHTA 2000
THE THREE TENORS IN CONCERT 1994 CARRERAS DOMINGO PAVAROTTI WITH ORCHESTRA CONDUCTED BY ZUBIN MEHTA 1994
THE THREE TENORS IN CONCERT 1994 JOSE CARRERAS, PLACIDO DOMINGO & LUCIANO PAVROTTI WITH MEHTA 1994
THE THREE TENORS PARIS 1998 CARRERAS DOMINGO PAVAROTTI WITH JAMES LEVINE 1998
3 YEARS, 5 MONTHS AND 2 DAYS IN THE LIFE OF… – ARRESTED DEVELOPMENT 1992
THE THRILL OF IT ALL THUNDER 1997
THRILL TO THE SENSATIONAL SOUND OF SUPER STEREO VARIOUS ARTISTS (CBS) 1967
THRILLER EDDIE & THE HOT RODS 1979
THRILLER MICHAEL JACKSON 1982
THRILLER THEMES CHAQUITO ORCHESTRA 1972
THROUGH A BIG COUNTRY – GREATEST HITS BIG COUNTRY 1990
THROUGH THE BARRICADES SPANDAU BALLET 1986
THROUGH THE EVIL CLAYTOWN TROUPE 1989
THROUGH THE FIRE HAGAR, SCHON, AARONSON, SHRIEVE 1984

THROUGH THE LOOKING GLASS SIOUXSIE & THE BANSHEES 1987
THROUGH THE PAST DARKLY (BIG HITS VOLUME 2) ROLLING STONES 1969
THROUGH THE STORM ARETHA FRANKLIN 1989
THROUGH THE YEARS CILLA BLACK 1993
THROWIN' DOWN RICK JAMES 1982
THROWING COPPER LIVE 1995
THROWING MUSES THROWING MUSES 2003
THUNDER ANDY TAYLOR 1987
THUNDER AND CONSOLATION NEW MODEL ARMY 1989
THUNDER AND LIGHTNING THIN LIZZY 1983
THUNDER IN MY HEART LEO SAYER 1977
TI ADORO LUCIANO PAVAROTTI 2003
TI AMO – PUCCINI'S GREATEST LOVE SONGS LUCIANO PAVAROTTI 1993
TICAL 0 – THE PREQUEL METHOD MAN 2004
TICAL 2000: JUDGEMENT DAY METHOD MAN 1998
TICKET TO RIDE CARPENTERS 1972
TIFFANY TIFFANY 1988
TIGER BAY SAINT ETIENNE 1994
TIGERLILY NATALIE MERCHANT 1995
TIGERMILK BELLE & SEBASTIAN 1999
TIGHT FIT TIGHT FIT 1982
TIGHTEN UP VOLUME 1 LOOSE ENDS 1992
TIGHTEN UP VOLUME 4 VARIOUS ARTISTS (TROJAN) 1971
TIGHTEN UP 88 BIG AUDIO DYNAMITE 1988
TILL DEAF US DO PART SLADE 1981
TILL DEATH DO US PART CYPRESS HILL 2004
TILL I LOVED YOU BARBRA STREISAND 1988
TILL WE HAVE FACES STEVE HACKETT 1984
TILT COZY POWELL 1981
TILT SCOTT WALKER 1995
TILT LIGHTNING SEEDS 1999
TIME ELECTRIC LIGHT ORCHESTRA 1981
THE TIME BROS 1989
TIME FLEETWOOD MAC 1995
TIME PETER ANDRE 1997
TIME LIONEL RICHIE 1998
TIME AFTER TIME EVA CASSIDY 2001
TIME AND A WORD YES 1970
TIME AND TIDE SPLIT ENZ 1982
TIME AND TIDE BASIA 1988
TIME CHANGES EVERYTHING JOHN SQUIRE 2002
TIME FADES AWAY NEIL YOUNG 1973
TIME FOR LOVE BILL TARMEY 1994
TIME FOR THE REST OF YOUR LIFE STRANGELOVE 1994
A TIME FOR US DONNY OSMOND 1973
TIME FURTHER OUT DAVE BRUBECK 1962
THE TIME HAS COME (EP) UNKLE 1995
TIME HONOURED GHOST BARCLAY JAMES HARVEST 1975
THE TIME IS NEAR KEEF HARTLEY BAND 1970
TIME LOVES A HERO LITTLE FEAT 1977
TIME MACHINE JOE SATRIANI 1993
TIME OUT DAVE BRUBECK QUARTET 1960
TIME OUT OF MIND BOB DYLAN 1997
TIME PASSAGES AL STEWART 1978
TIME PIECES – THE BEST OF ERIC CLAPTON ERIC CLAPTON 1982
TIME SEX LOVE MARY CHAPIN CARPENTER 2001
TIME TELLS NO LIES PRAYING MANTIS 1981
TIME TO CELEBRATE RUSS CONWAY 1959
TIME TO RELAX VARIOUS ARTISTS (CLASSIC FM) 2001
TIME WAS CURTIS STIGERS 1995
TIME, LOVE AND TENDERNESS MICHAEL BOLTON 1991
TIMELESS GOLDIE 1995
TIMELESS DANIEL O'DONNELL & MARY DUFF 1996
TIMELESS SARAH BRIGHTMAN 1997
TIMELESS – LIVE IN CONCERT BARBRA STREISAND 2000
TIMELESS – THE CLASSICS VOLUME 2 MICHAEL BOLTON 1999
TIMELESS – THE VERY BEST OF NEIL SEDAKA NEIL SEDAKA 1991
TIMELESS (THE CLASSICS) MICHAEL BOLTON 1992
TIMELESS FLIGHT STEVE HARLEY & COCKNEY REBEL 1976

TIMEPIECES – THE BEST OF ERIC CLAPTON ERIC CLAPTON 2000
THE TIMES THEY ARE A CHANGIN' – BOB DYLAN 1964
TIME'S UP LIVING COLOUR 1990
TIMESPACE – THE BEST OF STEVIE NICKS STEVIE NICKS 1991
TIMING IS EVERYTHING CHRIS DE BURGH 2002
TIMO MAAS – CONNECTED VARIOUS ARTISTS (PERFECTO) 2001
TIN DRUM JAPAN 1981
TIN MACHINE TIN MACHINE 1989
TIN MACHINE II TIN MACHINE 1991
TIN PLANET SPACE 1998
TINDERBOX SIOUXSIE & THE BANSHEES 1986
TINDERSTICKS TINDERSTICKS 1993
TINSEL TOWN REBELLION FRANK ZAPPA 1981
TINY MUSIC… MUSIC FROM THE VATICAN GIFT SHOP STONE TEMPLE PILOTS 1996
TITANIC (OST) JAMES HORNER 1998
TITANIC DAYS KIRSTY MACCOLL 1994
TITLE OF RECORD FILTER 1999
TITLE TK BREEDERS 2002
TITLES MICK KARN 1982
TO BRING YOU MY LOVE PJ HARVEY 1995
TO HAVE AND TO HOLD – THE WEDDING ALBUM VARIOUS ARTISTS (QUALITY PRICE MUSIC) 1992
TO LOVE AGAIN DIANA ROSS 1981
TO LOVERS EVERYWHERE MANTOVANI & HIS ORCHESTRA 1972
TO OUR CHILDREN'S CHILDREN'S CHILDREN MOODY BLUES 1969
TO RIDE, SHOOT STRAIGHT AND SPEAK THE TRUTH ENTOMBED 1997
TO SEE THE LIGHTS GENE 1996
TO THE 5 BOROUGHS BEASTIE BOYS 2004
TO THE EXTREME VANILLA ICE 1990
TO THE FAITHFUL DEPARTED CRANBERRIES 1996
TO THE LIMIT JOAN ARMATRADING 1978
TO THE MAXXIMUM MAXX 1994
TO THE MOON CAPERCAILLIE 1995
TO THE NEXT LEVEL MN8 1995
TO THE TOP ASWAD 1986
TO VENUS AND BACK TORI AMOS 1999
TO WHOM IT MAY CONCERN PASADENAS 1988
TO WHOM IT MAY CONCERN LISA MARIE PRESLEY 2003
TOCA FRAGMA 2001
TOCSIN X MAL DEUTSCHLAND 1984
TODAY ELVIS PRESLEY 1975
TOGETHER DIANA ROSS & THE SUPREMES & THE TEMPTATIONS 1970
TOGETHER JACK JONES 1973
TOGETHER NEW SEEKERS 1974
TOGETHER VARIOUS ARTISTS (K-TEL) 1979
TOGETHER VARIOUS ARTISTS (K-TEL) 1986
TOGETHER VARIOUS ARTISTS (POLYGRAM) 1995
TOGETHER VARIOUS ARTISTS (UNIVERSAL) 2002
TOGETHER LULU 2002
TOGETHER S CLUB JUNIORS 2002
TOGETHER AGAIN ROSE MARIE 1988
TOGETHER ALONE CROWDED HOUSE 1993
TOGETHER AT LAST RICHARD CLAYDERMAN & JAMES LAST 1991
TOGETHER FOR THE CHILDREN OF BOSNIA LUCIANO PAVAROTTI 1996
TOGETHER FOREVER – GREATEST HITS 1983–1998 RUN D.M.C. 1998
TOGETHER – THE BEST OF REEF 2003
TOGETHER WITH CLIFF RICHARD CLIFF RICHARD 1991
TOM TOM JONES 1970
TOM JONES LIVE IN LAS VEGAS TOM JONES 1969
TOM PETTY AND HEARTBREAKERS TOM PETTY & HEARTBREAKERS 1977
TOM TOM CLUB TOM TOM CLUB 1981
TOMB RAIDER (OST) FILM SOUNDTRACK 2001
TOMITA'S GREATEST HITS TOMITA 1980
TOMMY WHO 1969

TOMMY WEDDING PRESENT 1988
TOMMY (OST) WHO 1975
TOMMY (OST) FILM SOUNDTRACK 1975
TOMMY BOY GREATEST BEATS VARIOUS ARTISTS (TOMMY BOY) 1985
TOMMY STEELE STAGE SHOW TOMMY STEELE 1957
THE TOMMY STEELE STORY TOMMY STEELE 1957
TOMORROW BELONGS TO ME SENSATIONAL ALEX HARVEY BAND 1975
TOMORROW THE GREEN GRASS JAYHAWKS 1995
A TON OF HITS – THE BEST OF STOCK AITKEN WATERMAN VARIOUS ARTISTS (DOVER) 1990
TONGUES AND TAILS SOPHIE B HAWKINS 1992
TONI BRAXTON TONI BRAXTON 1994
TONIC FOR THE TROOPS BOOMTOWN RATS 1978
TONIGHT DAVID BOWIE 1984
TONIGHT I'M YOURS ROD STEWART 1981
TONIGHT'S THE NIGHT NEIL YOUNG 1975
TONY ANTHONY NEWLEY 1961
TONY CHRISTIE – LIVE TONY CHRISTIE 1975
TONY HADLEY TONY HADLEY 1997
TONY JOE TONY JOE WHITE 1970
TONY MAKES IT HAPPEN TONY BENNETT 1967
TONY MONOPOLY TONY MONOPOLY 1976
TONY'S GREATEST HITS TONY BENNETT 1967
TOO BLIND TO SEE IT KYM SIMS 1992
TOO HOT TO HANDLE HEATWAVE 1977
TOO LEGIT TO QUIT HAMMER 1991
TOO LONG IN EXILE VAN MORRISON 1993
TOO LOW FOR ZERO ELTON JOHN 1983
TOO MUCH PRESSURE SELECTER 1980
TOO OLD TO ROCK 'N' ROLL TOO YOUNG TO DIE JETHRO TULL 1976
TOO POSH TO MOSH, TOO GOOD TO LAST? – LITTLE ANGELS 1994
TOO SUSSED? – THESE ANIMAL MEN 1994
TOO TOUGH TO DIE RAMONES 1985
TOO WICKED ASWAD 1990
TOO YOUNG DONNY OSMOND 1972
TOO YOUNG TO DIE – THE SINGLES SAINT ETIENNE 1995
TOONAGE CARTOONS 1999
TOO RYE AY KEVIN ROWLAND & DEXY'S MIDNIGHT RUNNERS 1982
THE TOP CURE 1984
THE TOP 25 FROM YOUR 100 BEST TUNES VARIOUS ARTISTS (DECCA) 1975
TOP DOGG SNOOP DOGG 1999
TOP GEAR – ON THE ROAD AGAIN TELEVISION COMPILATION 1996
TOP GEAR TELEVISION COMPILATION 1994
TOP GEAR 2 VARIOUS ARTISTS (COLUMBIA) 1995
TOP GEAR 3 TELEVISION COMPILATION 1996
TOP GEAR ANTHEMS TELEVISION COMPILATION 1998
TOP GEAR CLASSICS – TURBO CLASSICS TELEVISION COMPILATION 1995
TOP GUN (OST) FILM SOUNDTRACK 1986
TOP KATZ – THE ALBUM PJ & DUNCAN 1995
TOP OF THE POPS – AUTUMN 2001 VARIOUS ARTISTS (UNIVERSAL) 2001
TOP OF THE POPS – BEST OF 1998 VARIOUS ARTISTS (POLYGRAM) 1998
TOP OF THE POPS 2003 VARIOUS ARTISTS (UNIVERSAL) 2002
TOP OF THE POPS SPRING 2002 VARIOUS ARTISTS (UNIVERSAL) 2002
TOP OF THE POPS – SUMMER 2001 VARIOUS ARTISTS (UNIVERSAL) 2001
TOP OF THE POPS SUMMER 2003 VARIOUS ARTISTS (UNIVERSAL) 2003
TOP OF THE POPS – THE CUTTING EDGE VARIOUS ARTISTS (COLUMBIA) 1996
TOP OF THE POPS 1 VARIOUS ARTISTS (COLUMBIA) 1995
TOP OF THE POPS 1998 – VOLUME 1 VARIOUS ARTISTS (POLYGRAM) 1998
TOP OF THE POPS 1998 – VOLUME 2 VARIOUS ARTISTS (POLYGRAM) 1998

TOP OF THE POPS 2 VARIOUS ARTISTS (COLUMBIA) 1995

TOP OF THE POPS 2 VARIOUS ARTISTS (UNIVERSAL) 2000

TOP OF THE POPS 2 – 70'S ROCK VARIOUS ARTISTS (UNIVERSAL) 2001

TOP OF THE POPS 2000 – VOL 3 VARIOUS ARTISTS (UNIVERSAL) 2000

TOP OF THE POPS 2000 VOLUME 1 VARIOUS ARTISTS (UNIVERSAL) 2000

TOP OF THE POPS 2000 VOLUME 2 VARIOUS ARTISTS (UNIVERSAL) 2000

TOP OF THE POPS 2001 – VOL 1 VARIOUS ARTISTS (UNIVERSAL) 2001

TOP OF THE POPS '99 – VOLUME ONE VARIOUS ARTISTS (UNIVERSAL) 1999

TOP OF THE POPS '99 – VOLUME TWO VARIOUS ARTISTS (UNIVERSAL) 1999

TOP OF THE POPS VOLUME 17 ANONYMOUS COVER VERSIONS 1971

TOP OF THE POPS VOLUME 18 ANONYMOUS COVER VERSIONS 1971

TOP OF THE POPS VOLUME 19 ANONYMOUS COVER VERSIONS 1971

TOP OF THE POPS VOLUME 20 ANONYMOUS COVER VERSIONS 1971

TOP PRIORITY RORY GALLAGHER 1979

TOP TV THEMES LONDON SYMPHONY ORCHESTRA 1972

TOPOL'S ISRAEL TOPOL 1985

TOPS WITH ME HELEN SHAPIRO 1962

TORMATO YES 1978

TORMENT AND TOREROS MARC & THE MAMBAS 1983

TORN BETWEEN TWO LOVERS MARY MACGREGOR 1977

TOTAL CONTRAST TOTAL CONTRAST 1986

TOTAL SOUND VARIOUS ARTISTS (STUDIO TWO) 1971

TOTALLY HOT OLIVIA NEWTON-JOHN 1978

TOTALLY KROSSED OUT KRIS KROSS 1992

TOTALLY WICKED VARIOUS ARTISTS (WARNER BROTHERS) 1998

TOTALLY WICKED TOO! – VARIOUS ARTISTS (WARNER BROTHERS) 1999

TOTO TOTO 1979

TOTO IV TOTO 1983

TOUCH SUPREMES 1971

TOUCH EURYTHMICS 1983

TOUCH DANCE EURYTHMICS 1984

TOUCH 'EM WITH LOVE BOBBIE GENTRY 1969

TOUCH ME GARY GLITTER 1973

TOUCH ME SAMANTHA FOX 1986

TOUCH ME IN THE MORNING DIANA ROSS 1973

A TOUCH MORE MAGIC BARRY MANILOW 1983

A TOUCH OF BLUE DAVID CASSIDY 2003

A TOUCH OF CLASS VARIOUS ARTISTS (TOPAZ) 1976

A TOUCH OF CLASS (OST) FILM SOUNDTRACK 1974

A TOUCH OF COUNTRY VARIOUS ARTISTS (TOPAZ) 1976

A TOUCH OF LOVE GLADYS KNIGHT & THE PIPS 1980

A TOUCH OF MUSIC IN THE NIGHT MICHAEL CRAWFORD 1993

A TOUCH OF SADNESS JIM REEVES 1969

A TOUCH OF VELVET JIM REEVES 1964

TOUCH SENSITIVE BRUCE FOXTON 1984

TOUCHED BY JESUS ALL ABOUT EVE 1991

TOUCHING DOWN RONI SIZE 2002

TOUGH IT OUT FM 1989

TOUGHER THAN LEATHER RUN D.M.C. 1988

TOUGHER THAN LOVE DIANA KING 1995

TOUR DE FRANCE SOUNDTRACKS KRAFTWERK 2003

TOUR SOUVENIR PACK MICHAEL JACKSON 1992

TOURISM ROXETTE 1992

TOURIST ST. GERMAIN 2000

THE TOURISTS TOURISTS 1979

TOXICITY SYSTEM OF A DOWN 2001

TOYAH! TOYAH! TOYAH! – TOYAH 1981

TOYAH! TOYAH! TOYAH! – TOYAH 1984

TP 2.COM R KELLY 2000

TRACK RECORD JOAN ARMATRADING 1983

TRACKS BRUCE SPRINGSTEEN 1998

TRACKS 'N' GROOVES CLIFF RICHARD 1970

TRACKS OF MY TEARS VARIOUS ARTISTS (TELSTAR) 1987

TRACKS OF MY TEARS (SMOKEY ROBINSON – WRITER AND PERFORMER) VARIOUS ARTISTS (DINO) 1991

TRACKSPOTTING VARIOUS ARTISTS (POLYGRAM) 1997

TRACY CHAPMAN TRACY CHAPMAN 1988

TRADE VARIOUS ARTISTS (FEVERPITCH) 1995

TRADE – VOLUME FOUR VARIOUS ARTISTS (FEVERPITCH) 1997

TRADE – VOLUME THREE VARIOUS ARTISTS (FEVERPITCH) 1996

TRADE – VOLUME TWO VARIOUS ARTISTS (FEVERPITCH) 1996

TRADING SECRETS WITH THE MOON ADVENTURES 1990

TRADING SNAKEOIL FOR WOLFTICKETS GARY JULES 2004

TRAFFIC TRAFFIC 1968

TRAFFIC – ON THE ROAD TRAFFIC 1973

TRAGIC KINGDOM NO DOUBT 1997

TRAILER PARK BETH ORTON 1996

TRAINS, BOATS AND PLANES FRANK & WALTERS 1992

TRAINSPOTTING #2 (OST) FILM SOUNDTRACK 1997

TRAINSPOTTING (OST) FILM SOUNDTRACK 1996

THE TRA LA DAYS ARE OVER NEIL SEDAKA 1973

TRAMPIN' PATTI SMITH 2004

TRAMPOLINE MAVERICKS 1998

TRANCE VARIOUS ARTISTS (RUMOUR) 1992

TRANCE CLASSICS VARIOUS ARTISTS (MINISTRY OF SOUND) 2002

TRANCE DANCE VARIOUS ARTISTS (DINO) 1992

TRANCE EUROPE EXPRESS VARIOUS ARTISTS (VOLUME) 1993

TRANCE EUROPE EXPRESS 2 VARIOUS ARTISTS (VOLUME) 1994

TRANCE MASTERS VARIOUS ARTISTS (VIRGIN) 2002

TRANCE NATION VARIOUS ARTISTS (MINISTRY OF SOUND) 2002

TRANCE NATION ANTHEMS – JUDGE JULES VARIOUS ARTISTS (MINISTRY OF SOUND) 2003

TRANCE NATION DEEPER VARIOUS ARTISTS (MINISTRY OF SOUND) 2003

TRANCE NATION ELECTRIC – JUDGE JULE VARIOUS ARTISTS (MINISTRY OF SOUND) 2004

TRANCE NATION – FUTURE VARIOUS ARTISTS (MINISTRY OF SOUND) 2003

TRANCE NATION HARDER VARIOUS ARTISTS (MINISTRY OF SOUND) 2003

TRANCE NATION 2: MIXED BY FERRY CORSTEN VARIOUS ARTISTS (MINISTRY OF SOUND) 1999

TRANCE NATION 3 VARIOUS ARTISTS (MINISTRY OF SOUND) 2000

TRANCE NATION 4 VARIOUS ARTISTS (MINISTRY OF SOUND) 2000

TRANCE NATION 5 VARIOUS ARTISTS (MINISTRY OF SOUND) 2001

TRANCE NATION: MIXED BY SYSTEM F VARIOUS ARTISTS (MINISTRY OF SOUND) 1999

TRANCE NATION 2003 VARIOUS ARTISTS (MINISTRY OF SOUND) 2002

TRANCEFORMER VARIOUS ARTISTS (VIRGIN) 1999

TRANCEMIX 99 – A SPRITUA; JOURNEY THROUGH TIME AND SPACE VARIOUS ARTISTS (VIRGIN) 1999

TRANCENDENTAL EUPHORIA VARIOUS ARTISTS (TELSTAR) 2000

TRANQUILLITY MARY O'HARA 1979

TRANQUILLITY VARIOUS ARTISTS (EMI) 1994

TRANS NEIL YOUNG 1982

TRANSCENDENTAL BLUES STEVE EARLE 2000

TRANS EUROPE EXPRESS KRAFTWERK 1982

TRANSFORMER LOU REED 1973

TRANSIENT RANDOM NOISE BURSTS STEREOLAB 1993

TRANSMITTING LIVE RUNRIG 1994

TRANZOPHOBIA MEGA CITY FOUR 1989

TRASH ALICE COOPER 1989

TRASHED IN IBIZA VARIOUS ARTISTS (GLOBAL) 2000

THE TRAVELING WILBURYS VOLUME 1 TRAVELING WILBURYS 1988

THE TRAVELING WILBURYS VOLUME 3 TRAVELING WILBURYS 1990

TRAVELLING JOHN WILLIAMS 1978

TRAVELLING LIGHT LESLEY GARRETT 2001

TRAVELLING WITHOUT MOVING JAMIROQUAI 1996

TRAVELOGUE HUMAN LEAGUE 1980

TRB2 TOM ROBINSON BAND 1979

TREASURE COCTEAU TWINS 1984

TREDDIN' ON THIN ICE WILEY 2004

TRESPASS GENESIS 1984

TREVOR NELSON'S RHYTHM NATION VARIOUS ARTISTS (INCREDIBLE) 2000

TRIAL OF FIRE – LIVE IN LENINGRAD YNGWIE J MAMLSTEEN 1989

TRIBAL GATHERING '96 VARIOUS ARTISTS (UNIVERSE) 1996

TRIBES, VIBES AND SCRIBES INCOGNITO 1992

TRIBUTE OZZY OSBOURNE 1987

TRIBUTE YANNI 1998

TRIBUTE TO MARTYRS STEEL PULSE 1979

A TRIBUTE TO THE CROONERS DES O'CONNOR 2001

TRIBUTE TO THE SMALL FACES – LONG AGOS/WORLDS APART VARIOUS ARTISTS (NICE) 1996

TRICK OF THE LIGHT MODERN ROMANCE 1983

A TRICK OF THE TRAIL GENESIS 1976

TRICK OR TREAT PAUL BRADY 1991

TRIED AND TRUE – THE BEST OF SUZANNE VEGA SUZANNE VEGA 1998

TRIGGER HAPPY TV – SERIES 2 VARIOUS ARTISTS (CHANNEL 4 MUSIC) 2001

TRILENIUM SASH! 2000

TRILOGY EMERSON, LAKE & PALMER 1972

TRINI LOPEZ AT P.J.'S TRINI LOPEZ 1963

TRINI LOPEZ IN LONDON TRINI LOPEZ 1967

TRIO DOLLY PARTON, LINDA RONSTADT & EMMYLOU HARRIS 1987

TRIP ON THIS – REMIXES TECHNOTRONIC & HI TEK 3 1990

TRIPPING THE LIVE FANTASTIC PAUL McCARTNEY 1990

TRIPTOMATIC FAIRYTALES JAM & SPOON 1994

TRIUMPH JACKSONS 1980

TRIUMPH AND AGONY WARLOCK 1987

TRIVIAL PURSUIT – THE MUSIC MASTER GAME MISCELLANEOUS 1991

TROCADERO SHOWADDYWADDY 1976

TROGGLODYNAMITE TROGGS 1967

TROMPE LE MONDE PIXIES 1991

TROOPS OF TOMORROW EXPLOITED 1982

TROPICAL BRAINSTORM KIRSTY MACCOLL 2000

TROPICAL GANGSTERS KID CREOLE & THE COCONUTS 1982

TROPICO PAT BENATAR 1984

TROUBADOUR J.J. CALE 1976

TROUBLE SAILOR 1976

TROUBLE WHITESNAKE 1978

TROUBLE IN SHANGRI LA STEVIE NICKS 2001

TROUBLE OVER HERE, TROUBLE OVER THERE TROUBLE FUNK 1987

THE TROUBLE WITH BEING MYSELF MACY GRAY 2003

TROUBLEGUM THERAPY? 1994

TROUSER JAZZ MR. SCRUFF 2002

TROUT MASK REPLICA CAPTAIN BEEFHEART & HIS MAGIC BAND 1969

TRUANT ALIEN ANT FARM 2003

TRUE – SPANDAU BALLET 1983

TRUE BALLADS TONY HADLEY 2003

TRUE BLUE MADONNA 1986

TRUE COLOURS SPLIT ENZ 1980

TRUE COLOURS LEVEL 42 1984

TRUE COLOURS CYNDI LAUPER 1986

TRUE CONFESSIONS BANANARAMA 1986

TRUE EUPHORIA VARIOUS ARTISTS (TELSTAR) 2001

TRUE LOVE VARIOUS ARTISTS (K-TEL) 1987

TRUE LOVE PAT BENATAR 1991

TRUE LOVE WAYS BUDDY HOLLY 1989

TRUE LOVE WAYS VARIOUS ARTISTS (COLUMBIA) 1994

**TRUE SKIES** SHINING 2002
**TRUE SPIRIT** CARLEEN ANDERSON 1994
**TRUE STORIES** TALKING HEADS 1986
**TRUEBRIT** VARIOUS ARTISTS (POLYGRAM) 1996
**TRULY – THE LOVE SONGS** LIONEL RICHIE 1998
**TRULY FOR YOU** TEMPTATIONS 1984
**TRULY UNFORGETTABLE** VARIOUS ARTISTS (EMI) 1990
**TRUMPET A GO GO** JAMES LAST 1969
**TRUNK FUNK – THE BEST OF THE BRAND NEW HEAVIES** BRAND NEW HEAVIES 1999
**TRUST** ELVIS COSTELLO & THE ATTRACTIONS 1981
**TRUST** BROTHER BEYOND 1989
**TRUTH AND BEAUTY** IAN MCNABB 1993
**TRUTH AND LOVE** HUE & CRY 1992
**TRUTH AND THE LIGHT: MUSIC FROM THE X FILES** MARK SNOW 1996
**TRUTH BE TOLD** SHED SEVEN 2001
**TRUTHDARE DOUBLEDARE** BRONSKI BEAT 1986
**TRUTHFULLY SPEAKING** TRUTH HURTS 2002
**TRY A LITTLE KINDNESS** GLEN CAMPBELL 1970
**TRY THIS** PINK 2003
**TRY WHISTLING THIS** NEIL FINN 1998
**TSOP – THE SOUND OF PHILADELPHIA** VARIOUS ARTISTS (K-TEL) 1988
**THE TUBE** TELEVISION COMPILATION 1984
**TUBEWAY ARMY** TUBEWAY ARMY 1979
**TUBTHUMPER** CHUMBAWAMBA 1997
**TUBULAR BELLS** MIKE OLDFIELD 1973
**TUBULAR BELLS II** MIKE OLDFIELD 1992
**TUBULAR BELLS III** MIKE OLDFIELD 1998
**TUESDAY NIGHT MUSIC CLUB** SHERYL CROW 1994
**TUFF JAM PRESENTS UNDERGROUND FREQUENCIES – 1** VARIOUS ARTISTS (SATELLITE) 1997
**TUFF JAM PRESENTS UNDERGROUND FREQUENCIES – 2** VARIOUS ARTISTS (SATELLITE) 1998
**TUG OF WAR** PAUL A-Z 1982
**TUMBLEWEED CONNECTION** ELTON JOHN 1971
**A TUNE A DAY** SUPERNATURALS 1998
**TUNE IN CHILL OUT** VARIOUS ARTISTS (INSPIRED) 2002
**THE TUNNEL MIXES** VARIOUS ARTISTS (LIMBO) 1996
**TUNNEL OF LOVE** BRUCE SPRINGSTEEN 1987
**TURBO** JUDAS PRIEST 1986
**TURBO TRAX** VARIOUS ARTISTS (K-TEL) 1982
**TURBULENT INDIGO** JONI MITCHELL 1994
**TURN BACK THE CLOCK** JOHNNY HATES JAZZ 1988
**TURN IT ON** RONAN KEATING 2003
**TURN IT ON AGAIN – THE HITS** GENESIS 1999
**TURN IT UP – THE VERY BEST OF** BUSTA RHYMES 2001
**TURN IT UPSIDE DOWN** SPIN DOCTORS 1994
**THE TURN OF A FRIENDLY CARD** ALAN PARSONS PROJECT 1980
**TURN OF THE TIDE** BARCLAY JAMES HARVEST 1981
**TURN ON THE RADIO** CHANGE 1985
**TURN ON THE SUN** NANA MOUSKOURI 1971
**TURN OUT THE LIGHTS** BERNIE TORME 1982
**TURN THE DARK OFF** HOWIE B 1997
**TURN THE MUSIC UP** PLAYERS ASSOCIATION 1979
**TURN, TURN, TURN** BYRDS 1966
**TURNAROUND** WESTLIFE 2003
**THE TURNING POINT** JOHN MAYALL 1969
**TURNING STONES** JUDIE TZUKE 1989
**TURNS INTO STONE** STONE ROSES 1992
**TURTLE SOUP** MOCK TURTLES 1991
**TUSK** FLEETWOOD MAC 1979
**TUTTI FRUTTI** MAJESTICS 1987
**TUTU** MILES DAVIS 1986
**TV 2000** VARIOUS ARTISTS (COLUMBIA) 2000
**THE TV HITS ALBUM** TELEVISION COMPILATION 1985
**THE TV HITS ALBUM TWO – 16 ORIGINAL HIT TV THEMES** TELEVISION COMPILATION 1986
**TV SPECIAL** ELVIS PRESLEY 1978
**TV TUNES** TELEVISION COMPILATION 1989
**TWANGIN' –** DAVE EDMUNDS 1981
**THE TWANG'S THE THANG** DUANNE EDDY 1960
**TWANGY GUITAR – SILKY STRINGS** DUANNE EDDY 1962
**TWELVE** VARIOUS ARTISTS (WARNER BROTHERS) 1996

**THE TWELVE COMMANDMENTS OF DANCE** LONDON BOYS 1989
**TWELVE DEADLY CYNS... AND THEN SOME** CYNDI LAUPER 1994
**12 GOLD BARS** STATUS QUO 1980
**12 GOLD BARS VOLUME TWO – (AND ONE)** STATUS QUO 1984
**12 GREATEST HITS VOLUME 2** NEIL DIAMOND 1982
**TWELVE INCHES OF PLEASURE** VARIOUS ARTISTS (PROTO) 1983
**12 INCHES OF SNOW** SNOW 1993
**12 MEMORIES** TRAVIS 2003
**TWELVE MONTHS, ELEVEN DAYS** GARY BARLOW 1999
**TWELVE OF THOSE SONGS** SHIRLEY BASSEY 1968
**12 PLAY** R KELLY 1993
**TWELVE SONGS OF CHRISTMAS** JIM REEVES 1964
**12 X 12 MEGA MIXES** VARIOUS ARTISTS (STARBLEND) 1985
**THE 12" ALBUM** HOWARD JONES 1984
**THE 20TH ANNIVERSARY ALBUM** VARIOUS ARTISTS (MOTOWN) 1980
**TWENTIETH CENTURY BLUES** VARIOUS ARTISTS (EMI) 1998
**20 ALL TIME EUROVISION FAVOURITES** NIGEL BROOKS SINGERS 1976
**20 ALL TIME GREATEST** PETULA CLARK 1977
**20 ALL TIME GREATS** CONNIE FRANCIS 1977
**20 ALL TIME GREATS** ROGER WHITTAKER 1979
**20 ALL TIME GREATS OF THE 50'S** VARIOUS ARTISTS (K-TEL) 1972
**20 CLASSIC HITS** PLATTERS 1978
**20 COUNTRY CLASSICS** TAMMY WYNETTE 1977
**20 DYNAMIC HITS** VARIOUS ARTISTS (K-TEL) 1972
**20 FAMILY FAVOURITES** VERA LYNN 1981
**20 FANTASTIC HITS** VARIOUS ARTISTS (ARCADE) 1972
**20 FANTASTIC HITS VOLUME 2** VARIOUS ARTISTS (ARCADE) 1972
**20 FANTASTIC HITS VOLUME 3** VARIOUS ARTISTS (ARCADE) 1973
**25TH ANNIVERSARY** BRENDA LEE 1984
**25TH ANNIVERSARY ALBUM** SHIRLEY BASSEY 1978
**21ST CENTURY DISCO** VARIOUS ARTISTS (MINISTRY OF SOUND) 2002
**21ST CENTURY ROCK** VARIOUS ARTISTS (VIRGIN) 1999
**25 DYNAMIC HITS VOLUME 2** VARIOUS ARTISTS (K-TEL) 1972
**25 GOLDEN GREATS** BACHELORS 1979
**25 ROCKIN' AND ROLLIN' GREATS** VARIOUS ARTISTS (K-TEL) 1972
**25 THUMPING GREAT HITS** DAVE CLARK FIVE 1978
**25 YEARS** HAWKLORDS 1978
**20 FLASHBACK GREATS OF THE SIXTIES** VARIOUS ARTISTS (K-TEL) 1973
**24 CARAT** AL STEWART 1980
**24 CARAT PURPLE** DEEP PURPLE 1975
**24 HOUR PARTY PEOPLE (OST)** VARIOUS ARTISTS (LONDON) 2002
**24 NIGHTS** ERIC CLAPTON 1991
**24 ORIGINAL HITS** DRIFTERS 1975
**TWENTY FOUR SEVEN** TINA TURNER 1999
**20 GIANT HITS** NOLAN SISTERS 1978
**20 GOLDEN GREATS** GLEN CAMPBELL 1976
**20 GOLDEN GREATS** BEACH BOYS 1976
**20 GOLDEN GREATS** BUDDY HOLLY & THE CRICKETS 1978
**20 GOLDEN GREATS** KINKS 1978
**20 GOLDEN GREATS** NEIL DIAMOND 1978
**20 GOLDEN GREATS** HOLLIES 1978
**20 GOLDEN GREATS** NAT 'KING' COLE 1978
**20 GOLDEN GREATS** FRANK SINATRA 1978
**20 GOLDEN GREATS** MANTOVANI & HIS ORCHESTRA 1979
**20 GOLDEN GREATS** DORIS DAY 1979
**20 GOLDEN GREATS** DIANA ROSS 1979
**20 GOLDEN GREATS** DION & THE BELMONTS 1980
**20 GOLDEN GREATS** ADAM FAITH 1981
**20 GOLDEN GREATS** AL JOLSON 1981
**20 GOLDEN GREATS** GILBERT O'SULLIVAN 1981
**20 GOLDEN GREATS OF KEN DODD** KEN DODD 1980

**20 GREAT ITALIAN LOVE SONGS** VARIOUS ARTISTS (TELSTAR) 1983
**20 GREATEST HITS** TOM JONES 1975
**20 GREATEST HITS** REAL THING 1980
**20 GREATEST HITS** BEATLES 1982
**20 GREATEST HITS VOLUME 2** ELVIS PRESLEY 1985
**20 GREATEST LOVE SONGS** NAT 'KING' COLE 1982
**20 HOLIDAY HITS** VARIOUS ARTISTS (CREOLE) 1985
**20 HOTTEST HITS** HOT CHOCOLATE 1979
**20 OF ANOTHER KIND** VARIOUS ARTISTS (POLYDOR) 1979
**21 AT 33** ELTON JOHN 1980
**20 ORIGINAL CHART HITS** VARIOUS ARTISTS (PHILIPS) 1973
**20 ORIGINAL DEAN MARTIN HITS** DEAN MARTIN 1976
**20 ORIGINAL GREATS** CLIFF RICHARD 1984
**20 REGGAE CLASSICS** VARIOUS ARTISTS (TROJAN) 1984
**20 SMASH DISCO HITS (THE BITCH)** VARIOUS ARTISTS (WARWICK) 1979
**20 SONGS OF JOY** HARRY SECOMBE 1978
**20 STAR TRACKS** VARIOUS ARTISTS (RONCO) 1972
**26 MIXES FOR CASH** APHEX TWIN 2003
**23AM** ROBERT MILES 1997
**2300 JACKSON ST** JACKSONS 1989
**22 GOLDEN GUITAR GREATS** BURT WEEDON 1976
**20 WITH A BULLET** VARIOUS ARTISTS (EMI) 1982
**20 WOMBLING GREATS** WOMBLES 1977
**20 YEARS OF JETHRO TULL** JETHRO TULL 1988
**20/20** BEACH BOYS 1969
**20/20** GEORGE BENSON 1985
**25** HARRY CONNICK JR. 1993
**TWENTYSOMETHING** JAMIE CULLUM 2003
**TWICE AS KOOL** KOOL & THE GANG 1983
**TWICE AS NICE – ESSENTIAL GROOVES** VARIOUS ARTISTS (WARNER BROTHERS) 2002
**TWICE AS NICE PRESENTS URBAN FLAVAS** VARIOUS ARTISTS (WARNER BROTHERS) 2002
**TWICE AS NICE PRESENTS URBAN FLAVAS 2003** VARIOUS ARTISTS (WARNER BROTHERS) 2003
**TWICE AS NICE – SEXY & STYLISH** VARIOUS ARTISTS (WARNER BROTHERS) 2000
**TWICE AS NICE – SEXY AND STYLISH** VARIOUS ARTISTS (WARNER BROTHERS) 2001
**TWICE AS NICE – SUMMER OF LOVE** VARIOUS ARTISTS (WARNER BROTHERS) 2000
**TWICE AS NICE IN AYIA NAPA – DJ SPOONY** VARIOUS ARTISTS (REACT) 1999
**TWICE AS NICE PRESENTS MOBO 2002** VARIOUS ARTISTS (WARNER BROTHERS) 2002
**TWICE THE LOVE** GEORGE BENSON 1988
**TWICE UPON A TIME – THE SINGLES** SIOUXSIE & THE BANSHEES 1992
**TWIGGY** TWIGGY 1976
**TWILIGHT OF IDOLS** FASHION 1984
**TWIN BARRELS BURNING** WISHBONE ASH 1982
**TWIST** FAT LADY SINGS 1991
**TWIST WITH CHUBBY CHECKER** CHUBBY CHECKER 1962
**TWISTED** DEL AMITRI 1995
**TWISTED ANGEL** LEANN RIMES 2002
**TWISTED DISCO 02.04** VARIOUS ARTISTS (HED KANDI) 2004
**TWISTED TENDERNESS** ELECTRONIC 1999
**TWISTIN' AND TWANGIN' –** DUANNE EDDY 1962
**TWO** CALLING 2004
**2.00 A.M. PARADISE CAFÉ –** BARRY MANILOW 1984
**TWO AGAINST NATURE** STEELY DAN 2000
**TWO BAD DJ** CLINT EASTWOOD & GENERAL SAINT 1982
**TWO CAN PLAY THAT GAME** BOBBY BROWN 1995
**TWO DAYS AWAY** ELKIE BROOKS 1977
**TWO FACES OF FAME** GEORGIE FAME 1967
**TWO FINGERS MY FRIENDS?** – POP WILL EAT ITSELF 1995
**2 FUTURE 4 U** ARMAND VAN HELDEN 1999
**200 KHM IN THE WRONG LANE** TATU 2003
**2 IN 3** ESTHER & ABI OFARIM 1968
**2,000,000 VOICES** ANGELIC UPSTARTS 1981
**2 MINUTES TO MIDNIGHT/ACES HIGH** IRON MAIDEN 1990
**THE TWO OF US** VARIOUS ARTISTS (K-TEL) 1983

TWO PAGES 4 HERO 1998
TWO ROOMS – CELEBRATING THE SONGS OF ELTON JOHN AND BERNIE TAUPIN VARIOUS ARTISTS (MERCURY) 1991
TWO SEVENS CLASH CULTURE 1978
TWO SIDES MOCK TURTLES 1991
TWO SIDES OF THE FOUR PENNIES FOUR PENNIES 1964
2 STEPZ AHEAD OXIDE & NEUTRINO 2002
TWO STEPS FROM THE MOVE HANOI ROCKS 1984
2001 DR. DRE 1999
2001 – A SPACE ODYSSEY (OST) FILM SOUNDTRACK 1969
THE 2000 BRIT AWARDS VARIOUS ARTISTS (COLUMBIA) 2000
2000 YEARS – THE MILLENNIUM CONCERT BILLY JOEL 2000
THE 2 TONE STORY VARIOUS ARTISTS (2 TONE) 1989
2 X 45 CABARET VOLTAIRE 1982
TWO'S COMPANY VARIOUS ARTISTS (TOWERBELL) 1986
TYGER TANGERINE DREAM 1987
TYR BLACK SABBATH 1990
TYRANNY FOR YOU FRONT 242 1991
U INCREDIBLE STRING BAND 1970
U GOT 2 KNOW CAPPELLA 1994
U.F. OFF – THE BEST OF ORB ORB 1998
U.F. ORB ORB 1992
U.K. U.K. 1978
U.S.A. UNION JOHN MAYALL 1970
U2 LIVE 'UNDER A BLOOD RED SKY' – U2 1983
UB 44 UB40 1982
UB40 UB40 1988
UB40 LIVE UB40 1983
UGLY BEAUTIFUL BABYBIRD 1996
UH! TEARS BABY WIN 1987
UH HUH JOHN COUGAR MELLENCAMP 1984
UH HUH HER PJ HARVEY 2004
UH OH DAVID BYRNE 1992
UK BLAK CARON WHEELER 1990
UK GARAGE – THE ALBUM VARIOUS ARTISTS (MINISTRY OF SOUND) 2000
UKRAINSKI VISTUIP V JOHNA PEELA WEDDING PRESENT 1989
ULTIMATE DOLLY PARTON 2003
ULTIMATE TONI BRAXTON 2003
ULTIMATE AYIA NAPA VARIOUS ARTISTS (INSPIRED) 2000
THE ULTIMATE BLUES COLLECTION VARIOUS ARTISTS (CASTLE COMMUNICATIONS) 1991
THE ULTIMATE CHEESE PARTY VARIOUS ARTISTS (WARNER BROTHERS) 2003
THE ULTIMATE CHICK FLICK LOVE SONGS VARIOUS ARTISTS (WARNER BROTHERS) 2003
THE ULTIMATE CHICK FLICK SOUNDTRACK VARIOUS ARTISTS (WSM/UNIVERSAL) 2002
THE ULTIMATE CHRISTMAS COLLECTION VARIOUS ARTISTS (POLYGRAM) 1998
ULTIMATE CLUB MIX VARIOUS ARTISTS (POLYGRAM) 1998
ULTIMATE CLUB MIX – 98 VARIOUS ARTISTS (POLYGRAM) 1998
ULTIMATE CLUB MIX 2 VARIOUS ARTISTS (POLYGRAM) 1998
THE ULTIMATE COLLECTION BRYAN FERRY & ROXY MUSIC 1988
THE ULTIMATE COLLECTION ROXY MUSIC 1988
THE ULTIMATE COLLECTION KINKS 1989
THE ULTIMATE COLLECTION MARC BOLAN & T. REX 1991
THE ULTIMATE COLLECTION LOUIS ARMSTRONG 1994
THE ULTIMATE COLLECTION NEIL DIAMOND 1996
THE ULTIMATE COLLECTION JIM REEVES 1996
THE ULTIMATE COLLECTION CLANNAD 1997
THE ULTIMATE COLLECTION LUCIANO PAVAROTTI 1997
THE ULTIMATE COLLECTION JANIS JOPLIN 1998
THE ULTIMATE COLLECTION SANTANA 1998
THE ULTIMATE COLLECTION NAT 'KING' COLE 1999
THE ULTIMATE COLLECTION EARTH WIND & FIRE 1999
THE ULTIMATE COLLECTION LADYSMITH BLACK MAMBAZO 2001

THE ULTIMATE COLLECTION GENE PITNEY 2001
THE ULTIMATE COLLECTION CHRIS DE BURGH 2001
THE ULTIMATE COLLECTION ELECTRIC LIGHT ORCHESTRA 2001
THE ULTIMATE COLLECTION BILLY JOEL 2001
THE ULTIMATE COLLECTION BILLY JOEL 2002
THE ULTIMATE COLLECTION PETULA CLARK 2002
THE ULTIMATE COLLECTION KINKS 2002
THE ULTIMATE COLLECTION WHO 2002
ULTIMATE COLLECTION SMALL FACES 2003
ULTIMATE COLLECTION OSMONDS 2003
THE ULTIMATE COLLECTION EMERSON, LAKE & PALMER 2004
ULTIMATE COLLECTION BILLY OCEAN 2004
THE ULTIMATE COUNTRY COLLECTION VARIOUS ARTISTS (COLUMBIA) 1992
ULTIMATE COUNTRY: 40 COUNTRY GREATS VARIOUS ARTISTS (TELSTAR) 1998
ULTIMATE DIRTY DANCING FILM SOUNDTRACK 2004
ULTIMATE DISCO MIX VARIOUS ARTISTS (POLYGRAM) 1998
THE ULTIMATE EIGHTIES VARIOUS ARTISTS (POLYGRAM) 1994
THE ULTIMATE 80'S BALLADS VARIOUS ARTISTS (POLYGRAM) 1994
THE ULTIMATE FUNK PARTY VARIOUS ARTISTS (WARNER BROTHERS) 2004
THE ULTIMATE GLENN MILLER GLENN MILLER & HIS ORCHESTRA 1993
THE ULTIMATE GOLD COLLECTION VARIOUS ARTISTS (THE HIT LABEL) 1994
THE ULTIMATE GUITAR COLLECTION JULIAN BREAM 1996
THE ULTIMATE HARDCORE VARIOUS ARTISTS (TELSTAR) 1992
THE ULTIMATE HEN NIGHT PARTY ALBUM VARIOUS ARTISTS (WARNER BROTHERS) 2002
THE ULTIMATE HITS ALBUM VARIOUS ARTISTS (TELSTAR) 1994
THE ULTIMATE HITS COLLECTION TOM JONES 1998
ULTIMATE IBIZA VARIOUS ARTISTS (INSPIRED) 2000
THE ULTIMATE JUNGLE COLLECTION VARIOUS ARTISTS (DINO) 1995
ULTIMATE KAOS ULTIMATE KAOS 1995
THE ULTIMATE LINE DANCING ALBUM VARIOUS ARTISTS (GLOBAL) 1996
ULTIMATE LOVE VARIOUS ARTISTS (THE HIT LABEL) 1995
ULTIMATE MANILOW BARRY MANILOW 2004
THE ULTIMATE MOVIE ALBUM VARIOUS ARTISTS (DECCA) 2001
THE ULTIMATE OLD SKOOL ALBUM VARIOUS ARTISTS (DECADANCE) 2003
THE ULTIMATE OPERA COLLECTION VARIOUS ARTISTS (ERATO) 1992
THE ULTIMATE PARTY ANIMAL VARIOUS ARTISTS (GLOBAL) 1996
THE ULTIMATE PERFORMANCE ELVIS PRESLEY 1981
THE ULTIMATE RAVE VARIOUS ARTISTS (EMI) 1992
ULTIMATE REGGAE PARTY ALBUM! – VARIOUS ARTISTS (TELSTAR) 1994
THE ULTIMATE RELAXATION ALBUM VARIOUS ARTISTS (VIRGIN) 2003
THE ULTIMATE SIN OZZY OSBOURNE 1986
THE ULTIMATE 60S COLLECTION VARIOUS ARTISTS (CASTLE COMMUNICATIONS) 1990
ULTIMATE SIXTIES COLLECTION VARIOUS ARTISTS (TELSTAR) 2000
THE ULTIMATE SMOOCHY ALBUM VARIOUS ARTISTS (WARNER BROTHERS) 2003
THE ULTIMATE SOUL COLLECTION VARIOUS ARTISTS (TELSTAR) 2001
THE ULTIMATE SOUL COLLECTION – 45 SOUL CLASSICS VARIOUS ARTISTS (WARNER BROTHERS) 1995
THE ULTIMATE SOUL COLLECTION – VOLUME 2 VARIOUS ARTISTS (WARNER BROTHERS) 1995
THE ULTIMATE SUMMER PARTY ALBUM VARIOUS ARTISTS (POLYGRAM) 1998

THE ULTIMATE SUMMER PARTY ANIMAL VARIOUS ARTISTS (GLOBAL) 1997
ULTIMATE TRAX 3 – BATTLE OF THE DJS VARIOUS ARTISTS (CHAMPION) 1987
ULTIMATE TRAX VOLUME 1 VARIOUS ARTISTS (CHAMPION) 1986
ULTIMATE TRAX VOLUME 2 VARIOUS ARTISTS (CHAMPION) 1987
THE ULTIMATE YES – 35TH ANNIVERSARY YES 2003
ULTRA DEPECHE MODE 1997
ULTRA ULTRA 1999
ULTRA OBSCENE BREAKBEAT ERA 1999
ULTRAVIOLET ALL ABOUT EVE 1992
ULTRAVIOLET ED ALLEYNE-JOHNSON 1994
UMMAGUMMA PINK FLOYD 1969
THE UNAUTHORIZED BIOGRAPHY OF REINHOLD MESSNER BEN FOLDS FIVE 1999
UNBELIEVABLE VARIOUS ARTISTS (VIRGIN) 2001
UNCHAINED MELODIES VARIOUS ARTISTS (TELSTAR) 1991
UNCHAINED MELODIES – II VARIOUS ARTISTS (TELSTAR) 1991
UNBELIEVABLE TOO VARIOUS ARTISTS (VIRGIN) 2002
UNBREAKABLE – THE GREATEST HITS VOLUME 1 WESTLIFE 2002
UNCOVERED VARIOUS ARTISTS (VIRGIN) 2001
UNCOVERED – THE VERY BEST OF SMOKIE SMOKIE 2001
UNDEAD TEN YEARS AFTER 1968
UNDER A RAGING MOON ROGER DALTREY 1985
UNDER A SUN WITNESS 2001
UNDER CONSTRUCTION MISSY ELLIOTT 2002
UNDER LATIN SKIES VARIOUS ARTISTS (GLOBAL) 1999
UNDER MY SKIN AVRIL LAVIGNE 2004
UNDER RUG SWEPT ALANIS MORISSETTE 2002
UNDER SPANISH SKIES VARIOUS ARTISTS (DINO) 1992
UNDER THE BLADE TWISTED SISTER 1982
UNDER THE COVERS VARIOUS ARTISTS (POLYGRAM) 1993
UNDER THE INFLUENCE STATUS QUO 1999
UNDER THE PINK TORI AMOS 1994
UNDER THE RED SKY BOB DYLAN 1990
UNDER THE WATER LINE TEN SHARP 1992
UNDER WRAPS JETHRO TULL 1984
UNDERCOVER ROLLING STONES 1983
UNDERGROUND EXPLOSION – THE REAL GARAGE MIX VARIOUS ARTISTS (VIRGIN) 2000
UNDERGROUND VOLUME 1 VARIOUS ARTISTS (COOKIE JAR) 1993
THE UNDERTONES UNDERTONES 1979
UNDERWATER SUNLIGHT TANGERINE DREAM 1986
UNDISCOVERED SOUL RICHIE SAMBORA 1998
UNDISPUTED VARIOUS ARTISTS (POLYGRAM) 1998
UNDISPUTED ATTITUDE SLAYER 1996
UNEQUALLED EQUALS EQUALS 1967
THE UNEXPECTED GUEST DEMON 1982
THE UNEXPECTED SONGS – SURRENDER SARAH BRIGHTMAN 1995
UNFINISHED MONKEY BUSINESS IAN BROWN 1998
UNFORGETTABLE VARIOUS ARTISTS (EMI) 1988
UNFORGETTABLE – WITH LOVE NATALIE COLE 1991
UNFORGETTABLE 2 VARIOUS ARTISTS (EMI) 1989
THE UNFORGETTABLE FIRE U2 1984
THE UNFORGETTABLE GLENN MILLER GLENN MILLER & HIS ORCHESTRA 1977
UNFORGETTABLE NAT 'KING' COLE NAT 'KING' COLE 1965
THE UNFORGETTABLE NAT 'KING' COLE NAT 'KING' COLE 1991
UNFORGETTABLE: A MUSICAL TRIBUTE TO NAT KING COLE JOHNNY MATHIS & NATALIE COLE 1983
UNHALFBRICKING FAIRPORT CONVENTION 1969
UNICORN TYRANNOSAURUS REX 1969
UNION TONI CHILDS 1989
UNION YES 1991
UNION GAP GARY PUCKETT & THE UNION GAP 1968
THE UNIQUE KLAUS WUNDERLICH SOUND KLAUS WUNDERLICH 1978
UNISON CELINE DION 1995
UNITED – VOLUME 3 VARIOUS ARTISTS (FOURBEAT) 1996

UNITED – VOLUME 5 VARIOUS ARTISTS (4 BEAT) 1996
UNITED – VOLUME 6 VARIOUS ARTISTS (4 BEAT) 1997
UNITED DANCE – VOLUME FOUR VARIOUS ARTISTS (4 BEAT) 1996
UNITED DANCE PRESENTS ANTHEMS 2 – '88 '92 VARIOUS ARTISTS (UNITED DANCE) 1997
UNITED KINGDOMS ULTRAMARINE 1993
UNIVERSAL K-KLASS 1994
UNIVERSAL ORCHESTRAL MANOEUVRES IN THE DARK 1996
UNIVERSAL HALL WATERBOYS 2003
UNIVERSAL MOTHER SINEAD O'CONNOR 1994
UNIVERSAL SOLDIER DONOVAN 1967
UNIVERSE – WORLD TECHNO TRIBE VARIOUS ARTISTS (UNIVERSE) 1993
UNIVERSE PRESENTS THE TRIBAL GATHERING VARIOUS ARTISTS (UNIVERSE) 1995
UNIVERSITY THROWING MUSES 1995
UNKNOWN PLEASURES JOY DIVISION 1980
UNKNOWN TERRITORY BOMB THE BASS 1991
UNLACED VARIOUS ARTISTS (EMI) 1995
UNLEASH THE DRAGON SISQO 2000
UNLEASHED IN THE EAST JUDAS PRIEST 1979
UN LED ED DREAD ZEPPELIN 1990
UNMASKED KISS 1980
UNPLUGGED ERIC CLAPTON 1992
UNPLUGGED NEIL YOUNG 1993
UNPLUGGED ARRESTED DEVELOPMENT 1993
UNPLUGGED BOB DYLAN 1995
UNPLUGGED BRYAN ADAMS 1997
UNPLUGGED CORRS 1999
UNPLUGGED – THE OFFICIAL BOOTLEG PAUL McCARTNEY 1991
UNPLUGGED IN NEW YORK NIRVANA 1994
UNPLUGGED... AND SEATED ROD STEWART 1993
UNPLUGGED... AND SEATED 10,000 MANIACS 1993
THE UNRECORDED JASPER CARROTT JASPER CARROTT 1979
UNRELEASED AND REVAMPED CYPRESS HILL 1996
UNTIL THE END OF TIME 2PAC 2001
UNTITLED BYRDS 1970
UNTITLED MARC & THE MAMBAS 1982
UNTITLED VARIOUS ARTISTS (GLOBAL) 1996
UNTITLED 2 VARIOUS ARTISTS (GLOBAL) 1996
UNTITLED 3 VARIOUS ARTISTS (GLOBAL) 1996
THE UNTOUCHABLE ALVIN STARDUST 1974
UNTOUCHABLES KORN 2002
UNUSUAL HEAT FOREIGNER 1991
UP ABC 1989
UP RIGHT SAID FRED 1992
UP R.E.M. 1998
UP PETER GABRIEL 2002
UP SHANIA TWAIN 2002
UP ALL NIGHT EAST 17 1995
UP ALL NIGHT VARIOUS ARTISTS (VIRGIN) 2003
UP AT THE LAKE CHARLATANS 2004
THE UP ESCALATOR GRAHAM PARKER & THE RUMOUR 1980
UP ON THE ROOF – SONGS FROM THE BRILL BUILDING NEIL DIAMOND 1993
UP THE BRACKET LIBERTINES 2002
UP TO DATE PARTRIDGE FAMILY 1972
UP TO OUR HIPS CHARLATANS 1994
UPFRONT 1 – 14 DANCE TRACKS VARIOUS ARTISTS (SERIOUS) 1986
UPFRONT 10 VARIOUS ARTISTS (SERIOUS) 1988
UPFRONT 2 – 14 DANCE TRACKS VARIOUS ARTISTS (SERIOUS) 1986
UPFRONT 3 VARIOUS ARTISTS (SERIOUS) 1986
UPFRONT 4 VARIOUS ARTISTS (SERIOUS) 1987
UPFRONT 5 VARIOUS ARTISTS (SERIOUS) 1987
UPFRONT 6 VARIOUS ARTISTS (SERIOUS) 1987
UPFRONT 7 VARIOUS ARTISTS (SERIOUS) 1987
UPFRONT 8 VARIOUS ARTISTS (SERIOUS) 1987
UPFRONT 89 VARIOUS ARTISTS (SERIOUS) 1989
UPFRONT 9 VARIOUS ARTISTS (SERIOUS) 1987

UPRISING BOB MARLEY & THE WAILERS 1980
THE UPS AND DOWNS STEPHEN 'TIN TIN' DUFFY 1985
UPSTAIRS AT ERIC'S YAZOO 1982
URBAN ACID VARIOUS ARTISTS (URBAN) 1988
URBAN BEACHES CACTUS WORLD NEWS 1986
URBAN CHILL VARIOUS ARTISTS (UNIVERSAL) 2001
URBAN CLASSICS VARIOUS ARTISTS (URBAN) 1987
URBAN EXPLOSION VARIOUS ARTISTS (WARNER BROTHERS) 2003
URBAN FUSION VARIOUS ARTISTS (UNIVERSAL) 2003
URBAN HYMNS VERVE 1997
URBAN KISS VARIOUS ARTISTS (UNIVERSAL) 2001
URBAN KISS 2002 VARIOUS ARTISTS (UNIVERSAL) 2002
URBAN KISS 2003 VARIOUS ARTISTS (UNIVERSAL) 2003
URBAN RENEWAL – SONGS OF PHIL COLLINS VARIOUS ARTISTS (WARNER BROTHERS) 2001
URBAN RHYMES VARIOUS ARTISTS (GLOBAL) 1998
URBAN SUITE MAXWELL 1996
URBAN VIBES VARIOUS ARTISTS (BMG) 2002
URIAH HEEP LIVE URIAH HEEP 1973
URUGUAY – DARREN EMERSON VARIOUS ARTISTS (GLOBAL UNDERGROUND) 2000
US PETER GABRIEL 1992
US MULL HISTORICAL SOCIETY 2003
US AND US ONLY CHARLATANS 1999
USE YOUR ILLUSION I GUNS N' ROSES 1991
USE YOUR ILLUSION II GUNS N' ROSES 1991
USE YOUR IMAGINATION MUD 1975
UTAH SAINTS UTAH SAINTS 1993
UTOPIA – CHILLED CLASSICS VARIOUS ARTISTS (PHILIPS) 2001
UTOPIA BANISHED NAPALM DEATH 1992
UTTER MADNESS MADNESS 1986
U-VOX ULTRAVOX 1986
V DEEP BOOMTOWN RATS 1982
V.U. VELVET UNDERGROUND 1985
V2 VIBRATORS 1978
VACATION GO-GO'S 1982
VAGABOND HEART ROD STEWART 1991
VAL VAL DOONICAN 1968
VAL DOONICAN ROCKS BUT GENTLY VAL DOONICAN 1967
VALENTINE ROY HARPER 1974
VALENTYNE SUITE COLOSSEUM 1969
VALHALLA AVENUE FATIMA MANSIONS 1992
VALLEY OF THE DOLLS DIONNE WARWICK 1968
VALLEY OF THE DOLLS GENERATION X 1979
VALOTTE JULIAN LENNON 1984
VAMP OF THE ROARING TWENTIES DOROTHY PROVINE 1962
VAN HALEN VAN HALEN 1978
VAN HALEN 3 VAN HALEN 1998
VAN HALEN II VAN HALEN 1979
VANESSA PARADIS VANESSA PARADIS 1992
VANGUARD FINLEY QUAYE 2000
VANILLA FUDGE VANILLA FUDGE 1967
VANISHING POINT PRIMAL SCREAM 1997
VAPOR TRAILS RUSH 2002
VARIATIONS ANDREW LLOYD WEBBER FEATURING CELLIST JULIAN LLOYD WEBBER 1978
VARIOUS POSITIONS LEONARD COHEN 1985
VAULT – THE GREATEST HITS 1980–1995 DEF LEPPARD 1995
THE VAULT... OLD FRIENDS 4 SALE PRINCE 1999
VAUXHALL AND I MORRISSEY 1994
VEEDON FLEECE VAN MORRISON 1974
THE VEGETARIANS OF LOVE BOB GELDOF 1990
VEHICLES & ANIMALS ATHLETE 2003
THE VELVET ROPE JANET JACKSON 1997
VELVET UNDERGROUND AND NICO VELVET UNDERGROUND AND NICO 2002
VELVET WATERS VARIOUS ARTISTS (STYLUS) 1985
VELVETEEN TRANSVISION VAMP 1989
VENGEANCE NEW MODEL ARMY 1984
VENICE IN PERIL RONDO VENEZIANO 1983
VENICE IN PERIL RONDO VENEZIANO 1988
VENUS AND MARS WINGS 1975

VERDI ANDREA BOCELLI 2000
VERMIN IN ERMINE MARC ALMOND & THE WILLING SINNERS 1984
VERSION 2.0 GARBAGE 1998
VERTICAL SMILES BLACKFOOT 1984
VERTIGO GROOVE ARMADA 1999
THE VERTIGO OF BLISS BIFFY CLYRO 2003
VERY PET SHOP BOYS 1993
THE VERY BEST CLUB ANTHEMS EVER VARIOUS ARTISTS (VIRGIN) 2004
THE VERY BEST EUPHORIC CHILLOUT MIXES VARIOUS ARTISTS (TELSTAR) 2001
THE VERY BEST EUPHORIC HOUSE BREAKDOWN VARIOUS ARTISTS (TELSTAR) 2003
VERY BEST EUPHORIC OLD SKOOL BREAKDOWN VARIOUS ARTISTS (TELSTAR) 2002
THE VERY BEST OF ENNIO MORRICONE 2000
THE VERY BEST OF OTIS REDDING 2000
THE VERY BEST OF SMITHS 2001
THE VERY BEST OF POGUES 2001
THE VERY BEST OF MICHAEL MCDONALD 2001
THE VERY BEST OF DINA CARROLL 2001
THE VERY BEST OF BANANARAMA 2001
THE VERY BEST OF BRONSKI BEAT 2001
THE VERY BEST OF MIDGE URE & ULTRAVOX 2001
THE VERY BEST OF EAGLES 2001
THE VERY BEST OF CHRIS REA 2001
THE VERY BEST OF SOFT CELL 2002
THE VERY BEST OF MOODY BLUES 2002
THE VERY BEST OF FLEETWOOD MAC 2002
THE VERY BEST OF STONE ROSES 2002
THE VERY BEST OF LIGHTHOUSE FAMILY 2003
THE VERY BEST OF HUMAN LEAGUE 2003
THE VERY BEST OF LINDA RONSTADT 2003
THE VERY BEST OF SHERYL CROW 2003
THE VERY BEST OF CAT STEVENS 2003
THE VERY BEST OF CHER 2003
THE VERY BEST OF DEAN MARTIN 2004
THE VERY BEST OF BAY CITY ROLLERS 2004
THE VERY BEST OF – 1980–2000 UB40 2000
THE VERY BEST OF 10CC 10 CC 1997
THE VERY BEST OF ADAM AND THE ANTS ADAM & THE ANTS 1999
THE VERY BEST OF ALL WOMAN VARIOUS ARTISTS (TELSTAR) 2002
THE VERY BEST OF ALL WOMAN VARIOUS ARTISTS (SONY) 2003
THE VERY BEST OF ANDREW LLOYD WEBBER VARIOUS ARTISTS (REALLY USEFUL) 1994
THE VERY BEST OF ANDY WILLIAMS ANDY WILLIAMS 2000
THE VERY BEST OF ANNE MURRAY ANNE MURRAY 1981
THE VERY BEST OF ART GARFUNKEL – ACROSS AMERICA ART GARFUNKEL 1996
THE VERY BEST OF BARBARA DICKSON BARBARA DICKSON 1986
THE VERY BEST OF BEN E. KING & THE DRIFTERS BEN E. KING & THE DRIFTERS 1998
THE VERY BEST OF BEN E. KING AND THE DRIFTERS BEN E. KING & THE DRIFTERS 1998
THE VERY BEST OF BLUES BROTHER SOUL SISTER VARIOUS ARTISTS (DINO) 1995
THE VERY BEST OF BRASS VARIOUS ARTISTS (DINO) 1997
THE VERY BEST OF BRENDA LEE BRENDA LEE 1985
THE VERY BEST OF BRENDA LEE... WITH LOVE BRENDA LEE 1994
THE VERY BEST OF BUDDY HOLLY BUDDY HOLLY 1996
THE VERY BEST OF BUDDY HOLLY AND THE CRICKETS BUDDY HOLLY & THE CRICKETS 1999
THE VERY BEST OF CAJUN – 40 HOT CAJUN CLASSICS VARIOUS ARTISTS (DINO) 1996
THE VERY BEST OF CAT STEVENS CAT STEVENS 1990
THE VERY BEST OF CAT STEVENS CAT STEVENS 2003
THE VERY BEST OF CHARLIE LANDSBOROUGH CHARLIE LANDSBOROUGH 1998
THE VERY BEST OF CHER 2003

THE VERY BEST OF CHILLED CLASSICS VARIOUS ARTISTS (UNIVERSAL) 2003
THE VERY BEST OF CHRIS DE BURGH CHRIS DE BURGH 1984
THE VERY BEST OF CILLA BLACK CILLA BLACK 1983
THE VERY BEST OF CLASSICAL CHILLOUT VARIOUS ARTISTS (VIRGIN) 2003
THE VERY BEST OF CLASSICAL CHILLOUT GOLD VARIOUS ARTISTS (DECADANCE) 2003
THE VERY BEST OF CLASSICAL EXPERIENCE VARIOUS ARTISTS (VIRGIN) 1999
THE VERY BEST OF COLD FEET TELEVISION AND RADIO COMPILATION 2003
THE VERY BEST OF COUNTRY GOLD VARIOUS ARTISTS (DECADANCE) 2003
THE VERY BEST OF DANIEL O'DONNELL DANIEL O'DONNELL 1991
VERY BEST OF DAVE PEARCE DANCE ANTHEMS VARIOUS ARTISTS (TELSTAR) 2003
THE VERY BEST OF DAVID BOWIE DAVID BOWIE 1981
THE VERY BEST OF DAVID ESSEX DAVID ESSEX 1982
THE VERY BEST OF DEAN MARTIN – THE CAPITOL & REPRISE YEARS DEAN MARTIN 1999
VERY BEST OF DEEP PURPLE DEEP PURPLE 1998
THE VERY BEST OF DEXY'S MIDNIGHT RUNNERS DEXYS MIDNIGHT RUNNERS 1991
THE VERY BEST OF DISNEY VARIOUS ARTISTS (PICKWICK) 1993
THE VERY BEST OF DISNEY 2 VARIOUS ARTISTS (PICKWICK) 1994
THE VERY BEST OF DOLLAR DOLLAR 1982
THE VERY BEST OF DON MCLEAN DON MCLEAN 1980
THE VERY BEST OF DRIVE TIME VARIOUS ARTISTS (TELSTAR) 2003
VERY BEST OF – EARLY DAYS AND LATTER DAYS LED ZEPPELIN 2003
THE VERY BEST OF EARTH WIND & FIRE EARTH WIND & FIRE 1992
VERY BEST OF EDDIE COCHRAN EDDIE COCHRAN 1970
THE VERY BEST OF ELKIE BROOKS ELKIE BROOKS 1986
THE VERY BEST OF ELTON JOHN ELTON JOHN 1980
THE VERY BEST OF ELTON JOHN ELTON JOHN 1990
THE VERY BEST OF ELVIS COSTELLO ELVIS COSTELLO 1999
THE VERY BEST OF ELVIS COSTELLO AND THE ATTRACTIONS ELVIS COSTELLO & THE ATTRACTIONS 1994
THE VERY BEST OF ENTERTAINMENT FROM THE U.S.A. VOLUME 2 TELEVISION COMPILATION 1986
THE VERY BEST OF EUPHORIA – MATT DAREY VARIOUS ARTISTS (TELSTAR) 2002
VERY BEST OF EUPHORIC DANCE BREAKDOWN VARIOUS ARTISTS (TELSTAR) 2002
VERY BEST OF EUPHORIC DANCE BREAKDOWN VARIOUS ARTISTS (TELSTAR) 2003
VERY BEST OF EUPHORIC DISCO BREAKDOWN VARIOUS ARTISTS (TELSTAR) 2004
VERY BEST OF FATS DOMINO FATS DOMINO 1970
THE VERY BEST OF FOREIGNER FOREIGNER 1992
THE VERY BEST OF FOSTER AND ALLEN FOSTER & ALLEN 1984
THE VERY BEST OF FRANKIE LAINE FRANKIE LAINE 1977
THE VERY BEST OF FRANKIE VALLI AND THE FOUR SEASONS FRANKIE VALLI & THE FOUR SEASONS 1992
THE VERY BEST OF GREATEST LOVE VARIOUS ARTISTS (TELSTAR) 1990
VERY BEST OF HANK MARVIN AND THE SHADOWS – THE FIRST 40 YEARS HANK MARVIN & THE SHADOWS 1998
THE VERY BEST OF HERB ALPERT HERB ALPERT 1991
THE VERY BEST OF HOT CHOCOLATE HOT CHOCOLATE 1987
THE VERY BEST OF IVAN REBROFF IVAN REBROFF 1990
VERY BEST OF JAMES LAST JAMES LAST 1970
THE VERY BEST OF JAMES LAST AND HIS ORCHESTRA JAMES LAST 1995
THE VERY BEST OF JIMMY SOMERVIILE BRONSKI BEAT AND THE COMMUNARDS JIMMY SOMERVILLE BRONSKI BEAT & THE COMMUNARDS 2001

THE VERY BEST OF JOAN ARMATRADING JOAN ARMATRADING 1991
THE VERY BEST OF KIKI DEE KIKI DEE 1994
THE VERY BEST OF KIM WILDE KIM WILDE 1985
THE VERY BEST OF LATIN JAZZ VARIOUS ARTISTS (DECADANCE) 2003
THE VERY BEST OF LATIN JAZZ – 2 VARIOUS ARTISTS (GLOBAL) 1999
THE VERY BEST OF LEO SAYER LEO SAYER 1979
THE VERY BEST OF LEVEL 42 LEVEL 42 1998
THE VERY BEST OF LOUIS ARMSTRONG LOUIS ARMSTRONG 1982
THE VERY BEST OF MANFRED MANN'S EARTH BAND MANFRED MANN'S EARTH BAND 1994
THE VERY BEST OF MARVIN GAYE MARVIN GAYE 1994
THE VERY BEST OF MARVIN GAYE MARVIN GAYE 2001
THE VERY BEST OF MEAT LOAF MEAT LOAF 1998
THE VERY BEST OF MICHAEL BALL IN CONCERT AT THE ROYAL ALBERT HALL MICHAEL BALL 1999
THE VERY BEST OF MILES DAVIS MILES DAVIS 1996
THE VERY BEST OF MOTOWN LOVE SONGS VARIOUS ARTISTS (TELSTAR) 1984
THE VERY BEST OF MTV UNPLUGGED VARIOUS ARTISTS (UNIVERSAL) 2002
THE VERY BEST OF MTV UNPLUGGED 2 VARIOUS ARTISTS (WARNER BROTHERS) 2003
THE VERY BEST OF NEIL DIAMOND NEIL DIAMOND 1983
THE VERY BEST OF NEIL SEDAKA NEIL SEDAKA 1999
THE VERY BEST OF NEW WOMAN VARIOUS ARTISTS (VIRGIN) 2004
THE VERY BEST OF PATSY CLINE PATSY CLINE 1996
THE VERY BEST OF PRINCE PRINCE 2001
THE VERY BEST OF PURE DANCEHALL VARIOUS ARTISTS (TELSTAR) 2003
THE VERY BEST OF PURE HIP HOP VARIOUS ARTISTS (TELSTAR) 2003
THE VERY BEST OF PURE R&B – THE SUMMER VARIOUS ARTISTS (TELSTAR) 2002
THE VERY BEST OF PURE R&B – THE WINTER VARIOUS ARTISTS (TELSTAR) 2002
THE VERY BEST OF PURE R&B – SUMMER 2003 VARIOUS ARTISTS (TELSTAR) 2003
THE VERY BEST OF PURE R&B – WINTER 2003 VARIOUS ARTISTS (TELSTAR) 2003
THE VERY BEST OF PURE SWING VARIOUS ARTISTS (PUMP) 1996
THE VERY BEST OF RANDY CRAWFORD RANDY CRAWFORD 1993
THE VERY BEST OF RICHARD CLAYDERMAN RICHARD CLAYDERMAN WITH THE ROYAL PHILHARMONIC ORCHESTRA 1992
THE VERY BEST OF RELAXING CLASSICS VARIOUS ARTISTS (DECCA) 2003
THE VERY BEST OF RITA COOLIDGE RITA COOLIDGE 1981
THE VERY BEST OF ROBERT PALMER ROBERT PALMER 1995
THE VERY BEST OF ROGER WHITTAKER ROGER WHITTAKER 1975
THE VERY BEST OF ROY ORBISON ROY ORBISON 1996
THE VERY BEST OF SHOWADDYWADDY SHOWADDYWADDY 1981
THE VERY BEST OF SISTER SLEDGE 1973–1993 SISTER SLEDGE 1993
THE VERY BEST OF SLIM WHITMAN SLIM WHITMAN 1976
THE VERY BEST OF SLIM WHITMAN – 50TH ANNIVERSARY COLLECTION SLIM WHITMAN 1997
THE VERY BEST OF SMOOTH JAZZ VARIOUS ARTISTS (UNIVERSAL) 2002
THE VERY BEST OF STING AND THE POLICE STING & THE POLICE 1997
THE VERY BEST OF STREET VIBES VARIOUS ARTISTS (TELSTAR) 2003
THE VERY BEST OF SUPERTRAMP SUPERTRAMP 1992
THE VERY BEST OF SUPERTRAMP SUPERTRAMP 1997
THE VERY BEST OF TALK TALK TALK TALK 1997
THE VERY BEST OF TALK TALK – NATURAL HISTORY TALK TALK 1990

THE VERY BEST OF THAT LOVING FEELING VARIOUS ARTISTS (DINO) 1993
THE VERY BEST OF THE BEACH BOYS BEACH BOYS 1983
THE VERY BEST OF THE BEACH BOYS BEACH BOYS 2001
THE VERY BEST OF THE BEE GEES BEE GEES 1990
THE VERY BEST OF THE COMMODORES COMMODORES 1995
THE VERY BEST OF THE COMMODORES – 16 CLASSIC TRACKS COMMODORES 1985
THE VERY BEST OF THE DRIFTERS DRIFTERS 1986
THE VERY BEST OF THE EAGLES EAGLES 1994
THE VERY BEST OF THE ELECTRIC LIGHT ORCHESTRA ELECTRIC LIGHT ORCHESTRA 1994
THE VERY BEST OF THE EVERLY BROTHERS EVERLY BROTHERS 1974
THE VERY BEST OF THE FANTASTIC 80'S VARIOUS ARTISTS (COLUMBIA) 2003
THE VERY BEST OF THE JAM JAM 1997
THE VERY BEST OF THE KINKS KINKS 1997
THE VERY BEST OF THE LOVE ALBUM VARIOUS ARTISTS (VIRGIN) 1998
THE VERY BEST OF THE MOODY BLUES MOODY BLUES 1996
THE VERY BEST OF THE OSMONDS OSMONDS 1996
THE VERY BEST OF THE PAN PIPES INSPIRATIONS 1996
THE VERY BEST OF THE RIGHTEOUS BROTHERS: UNCHAINED MELODY RIGHTEOUS BROTHERS 1990
THE VERY BEST OF TONY BENNETT – 20 GREATEST HITS TONY BENNETT 1977
THE VERY BEST OF VOLUME 2 DEAN MARTIN 2000
THE VERY BEST OF/STRANGE TIMES MOODY BLUES 2000
THE VERY BEST POP ALBUM VARIOUS ARTISTS (TELSTAR) 2002
A VERY FINE LOVE DUSTY SPRINGFIELD 1995
A VERY MERRY DISCO SLEIGHRIDERS 1983
VERY NECESSARY SALT-N-PEPA 1994
VERY SPECIAL LOVE SONGS CHARLIE RICH 1974
A VERY SPECIAL SEASON DIANA ROSS 1994
VESPERTINE BJORK 2001
VI: RETURN OF THE REAL ICE-T 1996
VIAGGIO ITALIANO ANDREA BOCELLI 1999
VIBRATE YOU KING ADORA 2001
VIC DAMONE SINGS THE GREAT SONGS VIC DAMONE 1983
VICES WAYSTED 1983
VICTIM OF LOVE ELTON JOHN 1979
VICTIMS OF CIRCUMSTANCES BARCLAY JAMES HARVEST 1984
VICTIMS OF THE FURY ROBIN TROWER 1980
VICTIMS OF THE FUTURE GARY MOORE 1984
VICTORIA BECKHAM VICTORIA BECKHAM 2001
VICTORIALAND COCTEAU TWINS 1986
VICTORY JACKSONS 1984
VICTORY AT SEA LONDON PHILHARMONIC ORCHESTRA 1961
VICTORY IN EUROPE – BROADCASTS AND REPORTS FROM BBC CORRESPONDENTS RADIO SOUNDTRACK 1985
VIDEO STARS VARIOUS ARTISTS (K-TEL) 1980
VIENNA ULTRAVOX 1980
VIGIL IN A WILDERNESS OF MIRRORS FISH 1990
VIGILANTE MAGNUM 1986
VILLIANS SAW DOCTORS 2001
VINTAGE MICHAEL BOLTON 2004
VIOLATOR DEPECHE MODE 1990
THE VIOLIN PLAYER VANESSA-MAE 1995
VIOLINS IN LOVE JAMES LAST 1975
THE VIRGIN SUICIDES – OST AIR 2000
VIRGINS AND PHILISTINES COLOUR FIELD 1985
VIRTUAL XI IRON MAIDEN 1998
VIRUS 100 – ALTERNATIVE TENTACLES VARIOUS ARTISTS (ALTERNATIVE TENTACLES) 1992
VISAGE VISAGE 1981
VISION OF PEACE MONKS OF AMPLEFORTH ABBEY 1995
VISION THING SISTERS OF MERCY 1990
VISIONS DON WILLIAMS 1977
VISIONS VARIOUS ARTISTS (K-TEL) 1983
VISIONS JAKATTA 2002
THE VISITORS ABBA 1981

VITAL IDOL BILLY IDOL 1985
VITALOGY PEARL JAM 1994
VIVA EL AMOR PRETENDERS 1999
VIVA ESPANA JAMES LAST 1992
VIVA HATE MORRISSEY 1988
VIVA! EUROPOP VARIOUS ARTISTS (WARNER BROTHERS) 1996
VIVA! LATINO VARIOUS ARTISTS (COLUMBIA) 1999
VIVA! ROXY MUSIC ROXY MUSIC 1976
VIVA! SANTANA – THE VERY BEST SANTANA 1986
VIVADIXIESUBMARINETRANSMISSIONPLOT SPARKLEHORSE 1996
VIVALDI: THE FOUR SEASONS NIGEL KENNEDY WITH THE ENGLISH CHAMBER ORCHESTRA 1989
VIVALDI'S THE FOUR SEASONS ACADEMY OF ANCIENT MUSIC (CONDUCTED BY CHRISTOPHER HOGWOOD) 1985
VIVE LE ROCK ADAM ANT 1985
VIXEN VIXEN 1988
THE VOICE BRENDA COCHRANE 1990
THE VOICE RUSSELL WATSON 2000
VOICE OF A GENERATION BLITZ 1982
VOICE OF AN ANGEL CHARLOTTE CHURCH 1998
THE VOICE OF CHURCHILL SIR WINSTON CHURCHILL 1965
VOICE OF LOVE DIANA ROSS 1996
THE VOICE OF RICHARD DIMBLEBY RICHARD DIMBLEBY 1966
VOICE OF THE HEART CARPENTERS 1983
VOICES KENNY THOMAS 1991
VOICES VANGELIS 1996
VOICES VARIOUS ARTISTS (DECCA) 2002
VOICES FROM THE HOLY LAND ALED JONES WITH THE BBC WELSH CHORUS 1985
VOICES OF TRANQUILLITY HYPNOSIS 1996
VOICES OF TRANQUILLITY – VOLUME 2 HYPNOSIS 1997
VOLARE – THE VERY BEST OF THE GIPSY KINGS GIPSY KINGS 1999
VOLUME 1 – SOUND MAGIC AFRO CELT SOUND SYSTEM 1996
VOLUME 2 – CULTURE CLASH SACRED SPIRIT 1997
VOLUME 2: RELEASE AFRO CELT SOUND SYSTEM 1999
VOLUME 8 – THE THREAT IS REAL! – ANTHRAX 1998
VOLUME FOUR VARIOUS ARTISTS (WORLDS END) 1992
VOLUME II (A NEW DECADE) SOUL II SOUL 1990
VOLUME III JUST RIGHT SOUL II SOUL 1992
VOLUME IV THE CLASSIC SINGLES 88–93 SOUL II SOUL 1993
VOLUME SIX VARIOUS ARTISTS (VOLUME) 1993
VOLUME 3 (THE SUBLIMINAL VERSES) SLIPKNOT 2004
VOLUME V – BELIEVE SOUL II SOUL 1995
VOLUNTEERS JEFFERSON AIRPLANE 1970
VOODOO D'ANGELO 2000
VOODOO CHILD – THE COLLECTION JIMI HENDRIX 2002
VOODOO HIGHWAY BADLANDS 1991
VOODOO LOUNGE ROLLING STONES 1994
VOODOO PARTY JAMES LAST 1972
VOULEZ-VOUS ABBA 1979
VOYAGE VOYAGE 1998
VOYAGE OF THE ACOLYTE STEVE HACKETT 1975
VOYAGER MIKE OLDFIELD 1996
VOYAGEUR ENIGMA 2003
VS PEARL JAM 1993
VULGAR DISPLAYS OF POWER PANTERA 1992
VULTURE CULTURE ALAN PARSONS PROJECT 1985
VYBIN' – YOUNG SOUL REBELS VARIOUS ARTISTS (GLOBAL) 1996
VYBIN' 3 – NEW SOUL REBELS VARIOUS ARTISTS (GLOBAL) 1996
VYBIN' 4 VARIOUS ARTISTS (GLOBAL) 1996
THE W WU-TANG CLAN 2000
W.A.S.P. W.A.S.P. 1984
W.O.W. WENDY O. WILLIAMS 1984
WAH WAH BRIAN ENO 1994
WAH WAH JAMES & BRIAN ENO 1994
WAIT FOR ME KENNY THOMAS 1993
WAITING FUN BOY THREE 1983

WAITING FOR BONAPARTE MEN THEY COULDN'T HANG 1988
WAITING FOR COLUMBUS LITTLE FEAT 1978
WAITING FOR COUSTEAU JEAN-MICHEL JARRE 1990
WAITING FOR HERB POGUES 1993
WAITING FOR THE FLOODS ARMOURY SHOW 1985
WAITING FOR THE PUNCHLINE EXTREME 1995
WAITING FOR THE SUN DOORS 1968
WAITING TO EXHALE (OST) FILM SOUNDTRACK 1996
THE WAKE IQ 1985
WAKE ME WHEN IT'S OVER FASTER PUSSYCAT 1989
WAKE UP AND SMELL THE COFFEE CRANBERRIES 2001
WAKE UP CALL JOHN MAYALL 1993
WAKE UP! – BOO RADLEYS 1995
THE WAKING HOUR DALI'S CAR 1984
WAKING HOURS DEL AMITRI 1990
WAKING UP THE NEIGHBOURS BRYAN ADAMS 1991
WAKING UP WITH THE HOUSE ON FIRE CULTURE CLUB 1984
A WALK ACROSS THE ROOFTOPS BLUE NILE 1984
WALK INTO LIGHT IAN ANDERSON 1983
WALK OF LIFE BILLIE PIPER 2000
WALK ON BOSTON 1994
WALK ON JOHN HIATT 1995
WALK ON BY SYBIL 1990
WALK RIGHT BACK WITH THE EVERLYS EVERLY BROTHERS 1975
WALK UNDER LADDERS JOAN ARMATRADING 1981
WALKER BROTHERS' STORY WALKER BROTHERS 1967
WALKING BACK HOME DEACON BLUE 1999
WALKING INTO CLARKSDALE JIMMY PAGE & ROBERT PLANT 1998
WALKING ON SUNSHINE (THE VERY BEST OF EDDY GRANT) EDDY GRANT 1989
WALKING WITH A PANTHER LL COOL J 1989
WALKING WOUNDED EVERYTHING BUT THE GIRL 1996
THE WALL PINK FLOYD 1979
THE WALL PINK FLOYD 2002
THE WALL – LIVE IN BERLIN ROGER WATERS & VARIOUS ARTISTS 1990
WALL OF HITS SLADE 1991
WALLS AND BRIDGES JOHN LENNON 1974
WALTERS ROOM BLACK SCIENCE ORCHESTRA 1996
WALTHAMSTOW EAST 17 1993
WALTZ DARLING MALCOLM MCLAREN & THE BOOTZILLA ORCHESTRA 1989
THE WANDERER DONNA SUMMER 1980
THE WANDERER FREDDIE STARR 1990
THE WANDERERS (OST) FILM SOUNDTRACK 1980
WANDERING SPIRIT MICK JAGGER 1993
WANTED CLIFF RICHARD 2001
WANTED/WANTED – THE REMIXES YAZZ 1988
WAR U2 1983
WAR ALL THE TIME THURSDAY 2003
WAR & PEACE – VOLUME II ICE CUBE 2000
WAR CHILD JETHRO TULL 1974
WAR HEROES JIMI HENDRIX 1972
WAR OF THE WORLDS JEFF WAYNE 1978
WAR ON ERRORISM NOFX 2003
WAREHOUSE RAVES VARIOUS ARTISTS (RUMOUR) 1989
WAREHOUSE RAVES 3 VARIOUS ARTISTS (RUMOUR) 1990
WAREHOUSE RAVES 4 VARIOUS ARTISTS (RUMOUR) 1990
WAREHOUSE RAVES 5 VARIOUS ARTISTS (RUMOUR) 1991
WAREHOUSE RAVES 6 VARIOUS ARTISTS (RUMOUR) 1992
WAREHOUSE RAVES 7 VARIOUS ARTISTS (RUMOUR) 1992
WAREHOUSE: SONGS AND STORIES HUSKER DU 1987
WARE'S THE HOUSE? – VARIOUS ARTISTS (STYLUS) 1989
WARM JOHNNY MATHIS 1958
WARM HERB ALPERT & THE TIJUANA BRASS 1969
WARM LEATHERETTE GRACE JONES 1980
THE WARNING QUEENSRYCHE 1984
WARNING GREEN DAY 2000
WARNING! DANCE BOOM VARIOUS ARTISTS (TELSTAR) 1995
WARNING! DANCE BOOM 2 VARIOUS ARTISTS (TELSTAR) 1995

WARRIOR ON THE EDGE OF TIME HAWKWIND 1975
WARRIOR ROCK – TOYAH ON TOUR TOYAH 1982
WARRIORS GARY NUMAN 1983
THE WARRIORS (OST) FILM SOUNDTRACK 1979
WARRIOZ M.O.P. 2001
WASHING MACHINE SONIC YOUTH 1995
WASTED IN AMERICA LOVE/HATE 1992
WASTED YEARS/STRANGER IN A STRANGE LAND IRON MAIDEN 1990
WASTED YOUTH GIRL 1982
WATCH MANFRED MANN'S EARTH BAND 1978
WATCHING YOU, WATCHING ME BILL WITHERS 1985
WATER MARK ART GARFUNKEL 1978
WATER SIGN CHRIS REA 1983
WATERFRONT WATERFRONT 1989
WATERLOO ABBA 1974
WATERMARK ENYA 1988
WATERTOWN FRANK SINATRA 1970
WATT TEN YEARS AFTER 1971
WATUSI WEDDING PRESENT 1994
WAVE PATTI SMITH GROUP 1979
WAVELENGTH VAN MORRISON 1978
WAVES KATRINA & THE WAVES 1986
WAXWORKS – SOME SINGLES (1977–1982) XTC 1982
WAY BEYOND BLUE CATATONIA 1996
THE WAY I FEEL TODAY SIX BY SEVEN 2002
THE WAY IT IS BRUCE HORNBY & THE RANGE 1986
WAY OF TODAY VIKKI CARR 1967
WAY OUT WEST WAY OUT WEST 1997
THE WAY TO THE SKY NEIL DIAMOND 1981
THE WAY WE WERE ANDY WILLIAMS 1974
THE WAY WE WERE BARBRA STREISAND 1974
WAYNE FONTANA AND THE MINDBENDERS WAYNE FONTANA & THE MINDBENDERS 1965
WAYNE'S WORLD (OST) FILM SOUNDTRACK 1992
WAYNE'S WORLD 2 (OST) FILM SOUNDTRACK 1994
WAYSTED WAYSTED 1984
WE ALL HAD DOCTOR'S PAPERS MAX BOYCE 1975
WE ARE FAMILY SISTER SLEDGE 1979
WE ARE IN LOVE HARRY CONNICK JR. 1990
WE ARE MOST AMUSED (THE BEST OF BRITISH COMEDY) VARIOUS ARTISTS (RONCO) 1981
WE ARE ONE MAZE FEATURING FRANKIE BEVERLY 1983
WE ARE SHAMPOO SHAMPOO 1994
WE ARE THE WORLD USA FOR AFRICA 1985
WE ARE... THE LEAGUE ANTI-NOWHERE LEAGUE 1982
WE CAN DO IT RUBETTES 1975
WE CAN MAKE IT PETERS & LEE 1973
WE CAN'T DANCE GENESIS 1991
WE CARE WHALE 1995
WE GET LETTERS (VOL.2) PERRY COMO 1958
WE HAVE ALL THE TIME IN THE WORLD – THE VERY BEST OF LOUIS ARMSTRONG LOUIS ARMSTRONG 1994
WE INVENTED THE REMIX P DIDDY & THE BAD BOY FAMILY 2002
WE LOVE LIFE PULP 2001
WE MADE IT HAPPEN ENGELBERT HUMPERDINCK 1970
WE MUST BELIEVE IN MAGIC CRYSTAL GAYLE 1978
WE ROCK HARD FREESTYLERS 1998
WE SOLD OUR SOUL FOR ROCK 'N' ROLL BLACK SABBATH 1976
WE THANK THEE JIM REEVES 1964
WE TOO ARE ONE EURYTHMICS 1989
WE WANT BILLY BILLY FURY 1963
WE WANT MOORE? – GARY MOORE 1984
WE WILL BE DEAD TOMORROW RAGING SPEEDHORN 2002
WE WILL ROCK YOU VARIOUS ARTISTS (DINO) 1991
WE WISH YOU A MERRY CHRISTMAS RAY CONNIFF 1962
WEAPON IS MY LYRIC OVERLORD X 1989
WEASELS RIPPED MY FLESH MOTHERS OF INVENTION 1970
WEATHER REPORT WEATHER REPORT 1982
WEATHERED CREED 2001
WE'D LIKE TO TEACH THE WORLD TO SING NEW SEEKERS 1972
THE WEDDING SINGER (OST) FILM SOUNDTRACK 1998

THE WEDGE PALLAS 1986
WEDNESDAY MORNING 3 A.M. SIMON & GARFUNKEL 1968
WEEKEND IN L.A. GEORGE BENSON 1978
WEEZER WEEZER 1995
WEIGHT ROLLINS BAND 1994
WEIRD SCENES INSIDE THE GOLD MINE DOORS 1972
WEIRD'S BAR AND GRILLS POP WILL EAT ITSELF 1993
WELCOME SANTANA 1973
WELCOME BACK MY FRIENDS TO THE SHOW THAT NEVER ENDS – LADIES AND GENTLEMEN: EMERSON, LAKE AND PALMER EMERSON, LAKE & PALMER 1974
WELCOME TO MY NIGHTMARE ALICE COOPER 1975
WELCOME TO MY WORLD DEAN MARTIN 1967
WELCOME TO MY WORLD ELVIS PRESLEY 1977
WELCOME TO POPPY'S FUN LOVIN' CRIMINALS 2003
WELCOME TO THE BEAUTIFUL SOUTH BEAUTIFUL SOUTH 1989
WELCOME TO THE CLUB IAN HUNTER 1980
WELCOME TO THE CRUISE JUDIE TZUKE 1979
WELCOME TO THE MONKEYHOUSE DANDY WARHOLS 2003
WELCOME TO THE NEIGHBOURHOOD MEAT LOAF 1995
WELCOME TO THE PLEASUREDOME FRANKIE GOES TO HOLLYWOOD 1984
WELCOME TO THE REAL WORLD MR. MISTER 1986
WELCOME TO TOMORROW SNAP! 1994
WELCOME TO WHEREVER YOU ARE INXS 1992
WELD NEIL YOUNG & CRAZY HORSE 1991
WE'LL BRING THE HOUSE DOWN SLADE 1981
WE'LL KEEP A WELCOME BRYN TERFEL 2000
WELL KEPT SECRET JOHN MARTYN 1982
WE'LL MEET AGAIN VERA LYNN 1989
WELL PLEASED CHAS & DAVE 1984
WELL RESPECTED KINKS KINKS 1966
WELL, WELL SAID THE ROCKING CHAIR DEAN FRIEDMAN 1978
WELSH COLLECTION MAN 1976
WENDY AND LISA WENDY & LISA 1987
WENDY MOTEN WENDY MOTEN 1994
WE'RE ONLY IN IT FOR THE MONEY MOTHERS OF INVENTION 1968
WE'RE THE MINIPOPS MINIPOPS 1983
WEST SIDE STORY ORIGINAL BROADWAY STAGE CAST SOUNDTRACK 1959
WEST SIDE STORY ORIGINAL STUDIO CAST RECORDING 1985
WEST SIDE STORY (OST) FILM SOUNDTRACK 1962
WESTING (BY MUSKET AND SEXTANT) PAVEMENT 1993
WESTLIFE WESTLIFE 1999
WESTWOOD VARIOUS ARTISTS (DEF JAM) 2001
WESTWOOD 2 VARIOUS ARTISTS (DEF JAM) 2002
WESTWOOD 3 VARIOUS ARTISTS (DEF JAM) 2002
WESTWOOD – THE JUMP OFF VARIOUS ARTISTS (DEF JAM) 2004
WESTWOOD – PLATINUM EDITION VARIOUS ARTISTS (UNIVERSAL) 2003
WESTWORLD THEATRE OF HATE 1982
WET BARBRA STREISAND 1979
WE'VE GOTTA GET OUT OF THIS PLACE ANGELIC UPSTARTS 1980
WHALER SOPHIE B HAWKINS 1994
WHALES AND NIGHTINGALES JUDY COLLINS 1971
WHAMMY! – B-52'S 1983
WHA'PPEN BEAT 1981
WHAT A BUNCH OF SWEETIES PINK FAIRIES 1972
WHAT A FEELING VARIOUS ARTISTS (COLUMBIA) 1997
WHAT A FEELING VARIOUS ARTISTS (UNIVERSAL) 2003
WHAT A WONDERFUL WORLD LOUIS ARMSTRONG 1968
WHAT ABOUT ME? – KENNY ROGERS 1984
WHAT ARE YOU GOING TO DO WITH YOUR LIFE? – ECHO & THE BUNNYMEN 1999
WHAT DO YOU WANT FROM LIFE TUBES 1978
WHAT DOES ANYTHING MEAN? BASICALLY CHAMELEON 1985
WHAT GOES UP MIGHT COME DOWN DAVID GUNSON 1982
WHAT HITS!? – RED HOT CHILI PEPPERS 1992

WHAT IN THE WORLD'S COME OVER YOU JACK SCOTT 1960
WHAT IS BEAT? (THE BEST OF THE BEAT) BEAT 1983
WHAT I'VE GOT IN MIND BILLIE JO SPEARS 1976
WHAT MY HEART WANTS TO SAY GARETH GATES 2002
WHAT NOW MY LOVE HERB ALPERT & THE TIJUANA BRASS 1966
WHAT NOW MY LOVE SHIRLEY BASSEY 1971
WHAT PRICE PARADISE? – CHINA CRISIS 1986
WHAT SILENCE KNOWS SHARA NELSON 1993
WHAT SOUND LAMB 2001
WHAT UP DOG? – WAS (NOT WAS) 1988
WHAT WERE ONCE VICES ARE NOW HABITS DOOBIE BROTHERS 1974
WHAT YOU ARE RICKY ROSS 1996
WHAT YOU SEE IS WHAT YOU GET GLEN GOLDSMITH 1988
WHATEVER AIMEE MANN 1993
WHATEVER AND EVER AMEN BEN FOLDS FIVE 1997
WHATEVER GETS YOU THROUGH THE DAY LIGHTHOUSE FAMILY 2001
WHATEVER HAPPENED TO JUGULA? – ROY HARPER & JIMMY PAGE 1985
WHATEVER YOU SAY, SAY NOTHING DEACON BLUE 1993
WHATEVER YOU WANT STATUS QUO 1979
WHATEVER YOU WANT – THE VERY BEST OF STATUS QUO STATUS QUO 1997
WHAT'S BIN DID AND WHAT'D BIN HID DONOVAN 1965
WHAT'S GOING ON? – MARVIN GAYE 1999
WHAT'S INSIDE JOAN ARMATRADING 1995
WHAT'S LOVE GOT TO DO WITH IT (OST) TINA TURNER 1993
WHAT'S NEW LINDA RONSTADT WITH THE NELSON RIDDLE ORCHESTRA 1984
WHAT'S THAT NOISE COLDCUT 1989
WHAT'S THE 411? – MARY J. BLIGE 1993
(WHAT'S THE STORY) MORNING GLORY? OASIS 1995
(WHAT'S THE STORY) MORNING GLORY? OASIS 2000
(WHAT'S THE STORY) MORNING GLORY? SINGLES BOX – GOLD OASIS 1996
WHAT'S THIS FOR KILLING JOKE 1981
WHAT'S WORDS WORTH MOTORHEAD 1983
WHAT'S WRONG WITH THIS PICTURE VAN MORRISON 2003
WHEATUS WHEATUS 2001
WHEELS OF FIRE (DOUBLE: LIVE AND STUDIO) CREAM 1968
WHEELS OF FIRE (SINGLE: IN THE STUDIO) CREAM 1968
WHEELS OF STEEL SAXON 1980
WHEN A MAN LOVES A WOMAN VARIOUS ARTISTS (DINO) 1994
WHEN A MAN LOVES A WOMAN (THE ULTIMATE COLLECTION) PERCY SLEDGE 1987
WHEN DISASTER STRIKES BUSTA RHYMES 1997
WHEN I DREAM CRYSTAL GAYLE 1978
WHEN I LOOK IN YOUR EYES DIANA KRALL 1999
WHEN I WAS BORN FOR THE 7TH TIME CORNERSHOP 1997
WHEN I WAS CRUEL ELVIS COSTELLO 2002
WHEN IN SPAIN CLIFF RICHARD & THE SHADOWS 1963
WHEN IT FALLS ZERO 7 2004
WHEN THE BOYS MEET THE GIRLS SISTER SLEDGE 1985
WHEN THE EAGLE FLIES TRAFFIC 1974
WHEN THE PAWN. . . FIONA APPLE 2000
WHEN THE WORLD KNOWS YOUR NAME DEACON BLUE 1989
WHEN WE WERE THE NEW BOYS ROD STEWART 1998
WHEN WILL I SEE YOU AGAIN JOHNNY MATHIS 1975
WHEN YOU WERE SWEET SIXTEEN FUREYS & DAVEY ARTHUR 1982
WHEN YOUR LOVER HAS GONE FRANK SINATRA 1961
WHEN YOU'RE A BOY SUSANNA HOFFS 1991
WHENEVER WE WANTED JOHN MELLENCAMP 1991
WHENEVER YOU NEED SOMEBODY RICK ASTLEY 1987
WHERE AM I GOING? – DUSTY SPRINGFIELD 1967
WHERE ARE YOU? FRANK SINATRA 1958
WHERE ARE YOU GONNA BE TONIGHT? – WILLIE COLLINS 1986
WHERE E'ER YOU WALK ALED JONES 1986

WHERE I WANNA BE DONELL JONES 2000
WHERE THE ACTION IS WESTWORLD 1987
WHERE WE BELONG BOYZONE 1998
WHERE YOU BEEN DINOSAUR JR 1993
WHERE YOUR ROAD LEADS TRISHA YEARWOOD 1998
WHIGFIELD WHIGFIELD 1995
WHILE MY GUITAR GENTLY WEEPS VARIOUS ARTISTS (UNIVERSAL) 2002
WHILE MY GUITAR GENTLY WEEPS II VARIOUS ARTISTS (UNIVERSAL) 2003
WHILE THE CITY SLEEPS GEORGE BENSON 1986
WHIPLASH JAMES 1997
WHIPLASH SMILE BILLY IDOL 1986
WHIPPED CREAM AND OTHER DELIGHTS HERB ALPERT & THE TIJUANA BRASS 1966
WHIPPED! – FASTER PUSSYCAT 1992
WHIRLPOOL CHAPTERHOUSE 1991
THE WHISPER DAVID ESSEX 1983
WHISPER A PRAYER MICA PARIS 1993
WHISPERING JACK JOHN FARNHAM 1987
WHITE BLOOD CELLS WHITE STRIPES 2001
WHITE BOY WITH A FEATHER JASON DOWNS 2001
WHITE CHRISTMAS NAT 'KING' COLE & DEAN MARTIN 1971
WHITE CHRISTMAS BING CROSBY 1974
WHITE CITY A NOVEL PETE TOWNSHEND 1985
WHITE EAGLE TANGERINE DREAM 1982
WHITE FEATHERS KAJAGOOGOO 1983
WHITE FLAMES SNOWY WHITE 1984
WHITE LABEL EUPHORIA – JOHN 00 FLEMING VARIOUS ARTISTS (TELSTAR) 2002
WHITE LABEL EUPHORIA – LEVEL 2 VARIOUS ARTISTS (TELSTAR) 2003
WHITE LADDER DAVID GRAY 2000
WHITE LILIES ISLAND NATALIE IMBRUGLIA 2001
WHITE MAGIC FOR LOVERS DRUGSTORE 1998
WHITE MANSIONS ORIGINAL STUDIO CAST RECORDING 1978
WHITE MUSIC XTC 1978
WHITE NOISE – LIVE GARY NUMAN 1985
WHITE ON BLONDE TEXAS 1997
WHITE PONY DEFTONES 2000
WHITE ROCK RICK WAKEMAN 1977
THE WHITE ROOM KLF 1991
A WHITER SHADE OF PALE/A SALTY DOG PROCOL HARUM 1972
WHITESNAKE 1987 WHITESNAKE 1987
THE WHITEY ALBUM CICCONE YOUTH 1989
WHITEY FORD SINGS THE BLUES EVERLAST 1999
WHITNEY WHITNEY HOUSTON 1987
WHITNEY HOUSTON WHITNEY HOUSTON 1985
WHO ARE YOU WHO 1978
THE WHO BY NUMBERS WHO 1975
WHO CAME FIRST PETE TOWNSHEND 1972
WHO CAN YOU TRUST? – MORCHEEBA 1997
WHO CARES A LOT? – THE GREATEST HITS FAITH NO MORE 1998
THE WHO COLLECTION WHO 1985
THE WHO COLLECTION WHO 1988
WHO DO WE THINK WE ARE DEEP PURPLE 1973
WHO ELSE? – JEFF BECK 1999
WHO I AM BEVERLEY KNIGHT 2002
WHO IS JILL SCOTT JILL SCOTT 2000
WHO KILLED THE ZUTONS? – ZUTONS 2004
WHO LOVES YOU FOUR SEASONS 1976
WHO MADE WHO AC/DC 1986
WHO NEEDS GUITARS ANYWAY ALICE DEEJAY 2000
WHO PAYS THE FERRYMAN YANNIS MARKOPOULOS 1978
THE WHO SELL OUT WHO 1968
MY GENERATION WHO 1965
WHO WILL SAVE THE WORLD GROUNDHOGS 1972
WHOA NELLY NELLY FURTADO 2001
A WHOLE LOTTA SHAKY SHAKIN' STEVENS 1988
THE WHOLE STORY KATE BUSH 1986
THE WHOLE STORY – HIS GREATEST HITS CLIFF RICHARD 2000

WHOOPS! THERE GOES THE NEIGHBOURHOOD BLOW MONKEYS 1989

(WHO'S AFRAID OF) THE ART OF NOISE ART OF NOISE 1984

WHO'S BETTER, WHO'S BEST WHO 1988

WHO'S LAST WHO 1984

WHO'S NEXT WHO 1971

WHO'S THAT GIRL (OST) FILM SOUNDTRACK 1987

WHO'S ZOOMIN' WHO? – ARETHA FRANKLIN 1986

WHOSE SIDE ARE YOU ON MATT BIANCO 1984

WHY DO FOOLS FALL IN LOVE DIANA ROSS 1981

WHY THE LONG FACE BIG COUNTRY 1995

WICKED SINITTA 1989

WICKED GAME CHRIS ISAAK 1991

WICKED! – VARIOUS ARTISTS (EMI) 1992

WIDE ANGLE HYBRID 1999

WIDE AWAKE IN AMERICA U2 1985

WIDE AWAKE IN DREAMLAND PAT BENATAR 1988

WIDE OPEN SPACES DIXIE CHICKS 1999

THE WIDE WORLD OVER CHIEFTAINS 2002

WIGGLE IT 2 IN A ROOM 1991

WILD & WICKED SHANIA TWAIN 2000

WILD AND LONELY ASSOCIATES 1990

WILD CAT TYGERS OF PAN TANG 1980

WILD CHILD UNTOUCHABLES 1985

WILD DOGS RODS 1982

WILD FRONTIER GARY MOORE 1987

THE WILD HEART STEVIE NICKS 1983

WILD HONEY BEACH BOYS 1968

WILD HORSES WILD HORSES 1980

WILD LIFE MOTT THE HOOPLE 1971

THE WILD LIFE SLAUGHTER 1992

WILD MOOD SWINGS CURE 1996

THE WILD ONE VARIOUS ARTISTS (EMI) 1990

WILD ONE – THE VERY BEST OF THIN LIZZY THIN LIZZY 1996

WILD PLANET B-52'S 1980

THE WILD THE WILLING AND THE INNOCENT UFO 1981

WILD THINGS RUN FAST JONI MITCHELL 1982

WILD WOOD PAUL WELLER 1993

WILD! – ERASURE 1989

THE WILD, THE INNOCENT AND THE E. STREET SHUFFLE BRUCE SPRINGSTEEN 1985

WILDER TEARDROP EXPLODES 1981

WILDEST DREAMS TINA TURNER 1996

WILDFLOWERS TOM PETTY & HEARTBREAKERS 1994

THE WILDHEARTS MUST BE DESTROYED WILDHEARTS 2003

WILL DOWNING WILL DOWNING 1988

WILLENNIUM WILL SMITH 1999

WILLIAM BLOKE BILLY BRAGG 1996

WILLY AND THE POOR BOYS CREEDENCE CLEARWATER REVIVAL 1970

WILSON PHILLIPS WILSON PHILLIPS 1990

WIMOWEH KARL DENVER 1961

THE WIND WARREN ZEVON 2003

WIND AND WUTHERING GENESIS 1977

THE WIND DOWN ZONE VARIOUS ARTISTS (ELEVATE) 1993

WIND OF CHANGE – CLASSIC ROCK LONDON SYMPHONY ORCHESTRA & THE ROYAL CHORAL SOCIETY 1992

WIND SONG JOHN DENVER 1975

WINDJAMMER II WINDJAMMER 1984

WINDOW IN THE JUNGLE 10 CC 1983

WINDSONG RANDY CRAWFORD 1982

WINELIGHT GROVER WASHINGTON JR. 1981

A WING AND A PRAYER GERRY RAFFERTY 1993

WINGS AT THE SPEED OF SOUND WINGS 1976

WINGS GREATEST HITS WINGS 1978

WINGS OF A DOVE ANTHONY WAY 1997

WINGS OF HEAVEN MAGNUM 1988

WINGS OF JOY CRANES 1991

WINGS OF LOVE VARIOUS ARTISTS (A&M) 1991

WINGS OVER AMERICA WINGS 1977

WINGS WILDLIFE WINGS 1971

WINGSPAN – HITS AND HISTORY PAUL McCARTNEY 2001

WINNER IN YOU PATTI LABELLE 1986

WINNERS BROTHERS JOHNSON 1981

WINNER'S CIRCLE VARIOUS ARTISTS (EXPANSION) 1993

WINNING DAYS VINES 2004

WIPEOUT – 20 INSTRUMENTAL GREATS VARIOUS ARTISTS (IMPRESSION) 1984

WIPEOUT 2097: THE SOUNDTRACK VARIOUS ARTISTS (VIRGIN) 1996

WIRED JEFF BECK 1976

WIRED VARIOUS ARTISTS (POLYGRAM) 1997

WIRED FOR CLUBS (CLUB TRACKS VOLUME 1) VARIOUS ARTISTS (MERCURY) 1983

WIRED FOR SOUND CLIFF RICHARD 1981

WIRED TO THE MOON CHRIS REA 1984

WISEBLOOD CORROSION OF CONFORMITY 1996

WISH CURE 1992

WISH YOU WERE HERE PINK FLOYD 1975

WISHBONE ASH WISHBONE ASH 1971

WISHBONE FOUR WISHBONE ASH 1973

WISHFUL THINKING PROPAGANDA 1985

WISHING MARTINE MCCUTCHEON 2000

WITH A SONG IN MY HEART JOSE CARRERAS 1993

WITH LOVE DES O'CONNOR 1970

WITH LOVE BRENDAN SHINE 1984

WITH LOVE MICHAEL CRAWFORD 1989

... WITH LOVE RICHARD CLAYDERMAN 1999

WITH LOVING FEELING TONY CHRISTIE 1973

WITH THE BEATLES BEATLES 1963

WITH YOU IN MIND CHARLIE LANDSBOROUGH 1996

WITHOUT A SOUND DINOSAUR JR 1994

WITHOUT RESERVATIONS SIMON DUPREE & THE BIG SOUND 1967

WITHOUT THE AID OF A SAFETY NET (LIVE) BIG COUNTRY 1994

WITHOUT YOU I'M NOTHING PLACEBO 1998

WITHOUT YOUR LOVE DIONNE WARWICK 1985

WITNESS HALO JAMES 1990

WIZZARD BREW WIZZARD 1973

WOLF HUGH CORNWELL 1988

WOMAN VARIOUS ARTISTS (POLYGRAM) 1998

WOMAN 2 VARIOUS ARTISTS (UNIVERSAL) 1999

WOMAN 2 WOMAN TWO VARIOUS ARTISTS (POLYGRAM) 1994

WOMAN 3 VARIOUS ARTISTS (UNIVERSAL) 2000

A WOMAN AND A MAN BELINDA CARLISLE 1996

WOMAN IN ME LOUISE 1997

THE WOMAN IN ME SHANIA TWAIN 2000

WOMAN IN RED (OST) STEVIE WONDER & FEATURING DIONNE WARWICK 1984

WOMAN TO WOMAN VARIOUS ARTISTS (POLYGRAM) 1993

A WOMAN'S TOUCH VARIOUS ARTISTS (UNIVERSAL) 2002

WOMBLING SONGS WOMBLES 1974

WOMEN AND CAPTAIN FIRST CAPTAIN SENSIBLE 1982

WOMEN AND CHILDREN FIRST VAN HALEN 1980

WOMEN HOLD UP HALF THE SKY RUBY TURNER 1986

WOMEN IN UNIFORM/TWILIGHT ZONE IRON MAIDEN 1990

WONDER NO. 8 HONEYZ 1998

WONDERFUL ADAM ANT 1995

WONDERFUL MADNESS 1999

THE WONDERFUL AND FRIGHTENING WORLD OF... – FALL 1984

WONDERFUL LIFE BLACK 1987

WONDERFUL LIFE (OST) CLIFF RICHARD & THE SHADOWS 1964

WONDERFUL WORLD VARIOUS ARTISTS (DINO) 1994

A WONDERFUL WORLD TONY BENNETT & K.D. LANG 2003

WONDERLAND ERASURE 1986

WONDERLAND CHARLATANS 2001

WONDERWORLD URIAH HEEP 1974

THE WONDROUS WORLD OF SONNY AND CHER SONNY & CHER 1966

WOODEN FOOT COPS ON THE HIGHWAY WOODENTOPS 1988

WOODFACE CROWDED HOUSE 1991

WOODSTOCK JIMI HENDRIX 1994

WOODSTOCK (OST) FILM SOUNDTRACK 1970

THE WORD VARIOUS ARTISTS (ZOMBA) 1987

WORD GETS AROUND STEREOPHONICS 1997

WORD OF MOUF LUDACRIS 2002

WORD OF MOUTH TONI BASIL 1982

WORD OF MOUTH MIKE & THE MECHANICS 1991

WORD SALAD FISCHER-Z 1979

A WORD TO THE WISE GUY MIGHTY WAH! 1984

WORD UP CAMEO 1986

THE WORD VOLUME 2 VARIOUS ARTISTS (JIVE) 1988

WORDS F.R. DAVID 1983

WORDS TONY RICH PROJECT 1996

WORDS AND MUSIC BENNY HILL 1971

WORDS AND MUSIC BILLY CONNOLLY 1975

WORDS AND MUSIC HANK MARVIN 1982

WORDS OF LOVE BUDDY HOLLY & THE CRICKETS 1993

WORK 1989–2002 ORBITAL 2002

WORK PARTY GRANDMASTER MELLE MEL & THE FURIOUS FIVE 1984

WORK THAT BODY JACKIE GENOVA 1983

WORK, LOVELIFE, MISCELLANEOUS DAVID DEVANT & HIS SPIRIT WIFE 1997

WORKERS PLAYTIME BILLY BRAGG 1988

WORKIN' OVERTIME DIANA ROSS 1989

WORKING NIGHTS WORKING WEEK 1985

WORKING WITH FIRE AND STEEL – POSSIBLE POP SONGS VOLUME 2 CHINA CRISIS 1983

WORKINGMAN'S DEAD GRATEFUL DEAD 1970

WORKS EMERSON, LAKE & PALMER 1977

THE WORKS QUEEN 1984

THE WORKS OF RICE AND LLOYD WEBBER LONDON SYMPHONY ORCHESTRA 1994

WORKS VOLUME 2 EMERSON, LAKE & PALMER 1977

WORLD D:REAM 1995

THE WORLD BEATERS SING THE WORLD BEATERS ENGLAND FOOTBALL WORLD CUP SQUAD 1970 1970

WORLD CLIQUE DEEE-LITE 1990

WORLD COMING DOWN TYPE O NEGATIVE 1999

WORLD DANCE – THE DRUM + BASS EXPERIENCE VARIOUS ARTISTS (FIRM) 1997

WORLD DEMISE OBITUARY 1994

WORLD GONE WRONG BOB DYLAN 1993

WORLD IN MOTION JACKSON BROWNE 1989

WORLD IN UNION UNION 1991

WORLD IN UNION – ANTHEMS VARIOUS ARTISTS (POLYGRAM) 1995

WORLD IN UNION 2003 VARIOUS ARTISTS (DECCA) 2003

THE WORLD IS FULL OF MARRIED MEN (OST) FILM SOUNDTRACK 1979

WORLD MACHINE LEVEL 42 1985

WORLD MOODS VARIOUS ARTISTS (VIRGIN) 1998

THE WORLD NEEDS A HERO MEGADETH 2001

THE WORLD OF BLUES POWER VARIOUS ARTISTS (DECCA) 1969

THE WORLD OF BRASS BANDS VARIOUS ARTISTS (DECCA) 1969

THE WORLD OF CHARLIE KUNZ CHARLIE KUNZ 1969

THE WORLD OF CHRISTMAS CHOIR OF KING'S COLLEGE, CAMBRIDGE 1971

WORLD OF HIS OWN JOOLS HOLLAND 1990

THE WORLD OF HITS VOLUME 2 VARIOUS ARTISTS (DECCA) 1969

THE WORLD OF JOHNNY CASH JOHNNY CASH 1970

THE WORLD OF JOSEF LOCKE TODAY JOSEF LOCKE 1969

THE WORLD OF KENNETH MCKELLAR KENNETH MCKELLAR 1969

THE WORLD OF MANTOVANI MANTOVANI & HIS ORCHESTRA 1969

THE WORLD OF MANTOVANI VOLUME 2 MANTOVANI & HIS ORCHESTRA 1969

WORLD OF MORRISSEY MORRISSEY 1995

THE WORLD OF OLIVER ORIGINAL LONDON STAGE CAST SOUNDTRACK 1969

A WORLD OF OUR OWN SEEKERS 1965

WORLD OF OUR OWN WESTLIFE 2001

THE WORLD OF PHASE 4 STEREO VARIOUS ARTISTS (DECCA) 1969

THE WORLD OF PROGRESSIVE MUSIC (WOWIE ZOWIE) VARIOUS ARTISTS (DECCA) 1969

WORLD OF THE BACHELORS BACHELORS 1969
WORLD OF THE BACHELORS VOLUME 2 BACHELORS 1969
THE WORLD OF VAL DOONICAN VAL DOONICAN 1969
THE WORLD OF YOUR 100 BEST TUNES VARIOUS ARTISTS (DECCA) 1971
THE WORLD OF YOUR 100 BEST TUNES VOLUME 10 VARIOUS ARTISTS (DECCA) 1975
THE WORLD OF YOUR 100 BEST TUNES VOLUME 2 VARIOUS ARTISTS (DECCA) 1971
WORLD OUTSIDE PSYCHEDELIC FURS 1991
WORLD POWER SNAP! 1990
WORLD RADIO LEO SAYER 1982
WORLD SERVICE SPEAR OF DESTINY 1985
WORLD SHUT YOUR MOUTH JULIAN COPE 1984
WORLD WIDE EVERYTHING BUT THE GIRL 1991
WORLD WIDE LIVE SCORPIONS 1985
A WORLD WITHOUT DAVE CARTER – THE UNSTOPPABLE SEX MACHINE 1997
THE WORLD WITHOUT END MIGHTY LEMON DROPS 1988
WORLD WITHOUT TEARS LUCINDA WILLIAMS 2003
THE WORLD WON'T LISTEN SMITHS 1987
WORLD WRESTLING FEDERATION – THE MUSIC – VOLUME 4 JAMES A JOHNSTON 1999
WORLD WRESTLING FEDERATION – THE MUSIC – VOLUME 5 JAMES A JOHNSTON 2001
WORLDES BLYSSE MEDIAEVAL BAEBES 1998
THE WORLDS OF FOSTER AND ALLEN FOSTER & ALLEN 1988
THE WORLD'S WORST RECORD SHOW VARIOUS ARTISTS (YUK) 1979
WORLDWIDE 50 GOLD AWARD HITS VOLUME 1 – A TOUCH OF GOLD ELVIS PRESLEY 1970
WORRY BOMB CARTER – THE UNSTOPPABLE SEX MACHINE 1995
THE WORST ALBUM IN THE WORLD EVER... EVER! – SHIREHORSES 1997
WOULD YA LIKE MORE SCRATCHIN' – MALCOLM MCLAREN & THE WORLD FAMOUS SUPREME TEAM SHOW 1984
WOULD YOU BELIEVE HOLLIES 1966
WOULDN'T YOU LIKE IT BAY CITY ROLLERS 1975
WOW WHAT A PARTY VARIOUS ARTISTS (K-TEL) 1987
WOW! – BANANARAMA 1987
WOW! – LET THE MUSIC LIFT YOU UP VARIOUS ARTISTS (ARCADE) 1994
WOWEE ZOWEE PAVEMENT 1995
WOYAYA OSIBISA 1972
WRAP YOUR ARMS AROUND ME AGNETHA FALTSKOG 1983
WRECKIN' CREW METEORS 1983
WRECKING BALL EMMYLOU HARRIS 1995
WRECKLESS ERIC WRECKLESS ERIC 1978
WRESTLEMANIA – THE ALBUM WWF SUPERSTARS 1993
THE WRITING ON THE WALL BUCKS FIZZ 1986
THE WRITING'S ON THE WALL DESTINY'S CHILD 1999
WRITTEN IN RED STRANGLERS 1997
WU-TANG FOREVER WU-TANG CLAN 1997
WWE ORIGINALS VARIOUS ARTISTS (COLUMBIA) 2004
WWF AGGRESSION VARIOUS ARTISTS (PRIORITY) 2000
WWF – FORCEABLE ENTRY VARIOUS ARTISTS (COLUMBIA) 2002
X INXS 1990
X BELOVED 1996
X DEF LEPPARD 2002
THE X FACTOR IRON MAIDEN 1995
THE X LIST VARIOUS ARTISTS (VIRGIN) 2003
XANADU (OST) OLIVIA NEWTON-JOHN/ELECTRIC LIGHT ORCHESTRA 1980
THE XENON CODEX HAWKWIND 1988
XL – 1 PETE SHELLEY 1983
XL RECORDINGS – THE SECOND CHAPTER VARIOUS ARTISTS (XL RECORDINGS) 1991
XPANDER (EP) SASHA 1999
X-TRA NAKED SHABBA RANKS 1993
XXV SHADOWS 1983
XXX HIP HOP VARIOUS ARTISTS (UNIVERSAL) 2003
YANG FISH 1995

YANKEE HOTEL FOXTROT WILCO 2002
YARDBIRDS YARDBIRDS 1966
YEAH WANNADIES 2000
YEAH YEAH YEAH YEAH/OUR TROUBLED YOUTH BIKINI KILL/HUGGY BEAR 1993
YEAR OF THE CAT AL STEWART 1977
YEAR OF THE HORSE NEIL YOUNG & CRAZY HORSE 1997
YELLOW MOON DON WILLIAMS 1983
YELLOW SUBMARINE BEATLES 1969
YELLOW SUBMARINE SONGTRACK (OST) BEATLES 1999
YEMEN CUTTA CONNECTION BLACK STAR LINER 1996
YENTL (OST) BARBRA STREISAND 1983
THE YES ALBUM YES 1971
... YES PLEASE! – HAPPY MONDAYS 1992
YESSHOWS YES 1981
YESSONGS YES 1973
YESTERDAY ONCE MORE CARPENTERS 1984
YESTERDAY WENT TOO SOON FEEDER 1999
YESTERDAYS YES 1975
YESTERDAY'S DREAMS FOUR TOPS 1969
YESTERDAY'S MEMORIES JAMES LAST 1971
YESTERDAY'S MEMORIES DANIEL O'DONNELL 2002
YIELD PEARL JAM 1998
YIN FISH 1995
YOSHIMI BATTLES THE PINK ROBOTS FLAMING LIPS 2002
YOU AND ME BOTH YAZOO 1983
YOU ARE BEAUTIFUL STYLISTICS 1975
YOU ARE THE QUARRY MORRISSEY 2004
YOU ARE WHAT YOU IS FRANK ZAPPA 1981
YOU BOYZ MAKE BIG NOIZE SLADE 1987
YOU BREAK MY HEART IN 17 PLACES TRACEY ULLMAN 1983
YOU CAN ALL JOIN IN VARIOUS ARTISTS (ISLAND) 1969
YOU CAN DANCE MADONNA 1987
YOU CAN'T ARGUE WITH A SICK MIND JOE WALSH 1976
YOU CAN'T HIDE YOUR LOVE FOREVER ORANGE JUICE 1982
YOU CAN'T STOP ROCK 'N' ROLL TWISTED SISTER 1983
YOU CAUGHT ME OUT TRACEY ULLMAN 1984
YOU COULD HAVE BEEN WITH ME SHEENA EASTON 1981
YOU DON'T BRING ME FLOWERS NEIL DIAMOND 1979
YOU GOTTA GO THERE TO COME BACK STEREOPHONICS 2003
YOU GOTTA SAY YES TO ANOTHER EXCESS YELLO 1983
YOU GOTTA SIN TO GET SAVED MARIA MCKEE 1993
YOU KNOW IT'S ME BARBARA DICKSON 1981
YOU LIGHT UP MY LIFE JOHNNY MATHIS 1978
YOU MAKE ME FEEL LIKE SINGING A SONG MAX BYGRAVES 1974
YOU MIGHT BE SURPRISED ROY AYERS 1985
YOU MUST REMEMBER THIS... – VARIOUS ARTISTS (HAPPY DAYS) 1995
YOU NEVER CAN TELL CHUCK BERRY 1964
YOU SCARE ME TO DEATH MARC BOLAN 1981
YOU TAKE MY HEART AWAY SHIRLEY BASSEY 1977
YOU WANT IT, YOU GOT IT BRYAN ADAMS 1985
YOU WIN AGAIN VAN MORRISON/LINDA GAIL LEWIS 2000
YOU, ME & US MARTINE MCCUTCHEON 1999
YOU, ME AND ME MTUME 1984
YOU? ME? US? – RICHARD THOMPSON 1996
YOU'LL LOVE TO HATE THIS RICHARD BLACKWOOD 2000
YOU'LL NEVER KNOW RODNEY FRANKLIN 1980
YOU'LL NEVER WALK ALONE ELVIS PRESLEY 1971
YOU'LL NEVER WALK ALONE VARIOUS ARTISTS (V2) 1997
YOUNG AMERICANS DAVID BOWIE 1975
THE YOUNG AND THE HOPELESS GOOD CHARLOTTE 2003
YOUNG GIFTED & BLACK VARIOUS ARTISTS (TROJAN) 2002
YOUNG GODS LITTLE ANGELS 1991
YOUNG GUNS GO FOR IT VARIOUS ARTISTS (VIRGIN) 2000
YOUNG HEARTS RUN FREE CANDI STATON 1976
THE YOUNG ONES (OST) CLIFF RICHARD & THE SHADOWS 1961
YOUNG LUST – THE ANTHOLOGY AEROSMITH 2001
YOUNG TEAM MOGWAI 1997
YOUNG WARM AND WONDERFUL GENE PITNEY 1967
YOUNGER THAN YESTERDAY BYRDS 1967
YOUR ARSENAL MORRISSEY 1992

YOUR FAVOURITE HYMNS IAN TRACEY WITH THE LIVERPOOL CATHEDRALS' CHOIRS 1992
YOUR FILTHY LITTLE MOUTH DAVID LEE ROTH 1994
YOUR NEW FAVOURITE BAND HIVES 2002
YOUR SECRET LOVE LUTHER VANDROSS 1996
YOUR WOMAN SUNSHINE ANDERSON 2001
YOU'RE GONNA GET IT TOM PETTY & HEARTBREAKERS 1978
YOU'RE MY BEST THING DON WILLIAMS 1978
YOU'RE NEVER ALONE WITH A SCHIZOPHRENIC IAN HUNTER 1979
YOU'RE THE INSPIRATION – 16 ROMANTIC LOVE SONGS VARIOUS ARTISTS (COLUMBIA) 1991
YOU'RE THE ONE PAUL SIMON 2000
YOU'RE UNDER ARREST MILES DAVIS 1985
YOURS SINCERELY HARRY SECOMBE 1991
YOURS SINCERELY PASADENAS 1992
YOURSELF OR SOMEONE LIKE YOU MATCHBOX 20 1998
YOUTH AND YOUNG MANHOOD KINGS OF LEON 2003
THE YOUTH OF TODAY MUSICAL YOUTH 1982
YOUTHANASIA/HIDDEN TREASURE MEGADETH 1995
YOUTHQUAKE DEAD OR ALIVE 1985
YOU'VE COME A LONG WAY, BABY FATBOY SLIM 1998
YOU'VE GOT A FRIEND BARBARA WINDSOR 1999
YOU'VE GOT A FRIEND – THE BEST OF JAMES TAYLOR 2003
YOU'VE GOT THE POWER THIRD WORLD 1982
YOU'VE GOT TO LAUGH VARIOUS ARTISTS (TOWERBELL) 1986
ZAGORA LOOSE ENDS 1986
ZAPPA IN NEW YORK FRANK ZAPPA 1978
ZARAGON JOHN MILES 1978
ZAZU ROSIE VELA 1987
ZEBOP! – SANTANA 1981
ZEITGEIST LEVELLERS 1995
ZENYATTA MONDATTA POLICE 1980
ZERO SHE FLIES AL STEWART 1970
ZIGGY STARDUST – THE MOTION PICTURE DAVID BOWIE 1983
ZINC ALLOY AND THE HIDDEN RIDERS OF TOMORROW MARC BOLAN & T. REX 1974
ZINGALAMDUNI ARRESTED DEVELOPMENT 1994
ZIP STYLE METHOD JOHN COOPER CLARKE 1982
ZONES HAWKWIND 1983
ZOOLOOK JEAN-MICHEL JARRE 1984
ZOOM ELECTRIC LIGHT ORCHESTRA 2001
ZOOROPA U2 1993
ZOOT ZOOT MONEY & THE BIG ROLL BAND 1966
ZUCCHERO ZUCCHERO 1991
ZUMA NEIL YOUNG 1975

# ACKNOWLEDGEMENTS

During the course of researching and writing this book, I had access to a vast number of newspapers, magazines, books and on-line sources, and would like to acknowledge the following as being of particular assistance during the creation of this work:

**MAGAZINES:**
Billboard
Blues & Soul
Cashbox
Melody Maker
Music Week
NME
Record Collector
Record Mirror
Record World
Rolling Stone
Sounds

**BOOKS:**
The A-Z Of Record Labels (Sanctuary)
Omnibus Complete Book of the British Charts (various editions)
The Books of Golden Discs (Barrie & Jenkins)
Encyclopedia of Albums (Dempsey Parr)
Encyclopedia of Popular Music (Penguin)
Encyclopedia of Popular Music (Virgin)
Encyclopedia of Rock Obituaries (Omnibus)
Guinness British Hit Albums (various editions)
History of Rock partwork (Orbis)
Music Master (RED)
New Book of Rock Lists (Sidgwick & Jackson)
Record Research Top Pop Albums (various editions)
Rock Stars Encyclopedia (Dorling Kindersley)
Who's Who In Soul Music (Weidenfeld)

Factual information was supplied by the BPI (Kaylee Coxall), the IFPI (Nicola Craven), IPC (Nicola Parker) and the RIAA (John Henkel).

There were many websites that proved invaluable, too many to list all of them, but I would like to thank the following people for entering into email correspondence and enabling me to fill more than a few gaps:

Steve Ager, Andy Arthurs, Jan Benkmann, Andrea Britton, Brother Brown, Matt Cadman, Gary Dayborn, Gareth Deakin, Arne Eilers, James Endeacott, John Farrer, Karina Flatt, Nigel Gatherer, Billy Griffin, John Holman, Sten Holmberg, Denise Leigh, Marcella McAdam, Helena Noewens, Darryl Payne, Danielle Piffner, Anna Randles, Mark Robinson, Ciro Romano, Sophie Sasimowicz, Shel Talmy, Xavier Vanderkemp, Jan Voermans, Alan Watson, Mick Webster, Chris Wyles, everyhit.com, Pooterland Webmaster and Webmaster Clairerichards.net.

I would also like to thank the staff of Essential Works (John Conway, Katie Cowan, Mal Peachey, Mani Ramaswamy and Kate Ward), HarperCollins (Myles Archibald, Christina Hicks and Jane Hollyman) and the Pickwick Group (Andy Bonell, Mike Diplock, Amanda Grote, Ray Hartley, Mark Lawton, Helen Owen, Dom Rampello, Philip Ridout, Jim Scott, Adam Solomon, Carl Wade and especially Alan Eley and Sam Mamy, who read through an early manuscript, and two previous members of staff in Katie Dimmock and Nicki Forrestero, who I inadvertently omitted from the singles book when their efforts fully warranted a special mention – sorry!).

Thanks also to those who offered encouragement along the way: Paul Gambaccini, Phil Robinson, Jon Ward and Joel Whitburn. Also, to John Deacon, Bob Lewis and Kim Bayley, who removed some of the obstacles.

Finally, a word of gratitude to my family (Caroline, Jo and Steven) who thought the completion of the singles book would mean they got their dining room table back – they were wrong!!